D1189371

HUMAN ANATOMY & PHYSIOLOGY

HUMAN ANATOMY

Eldra Pearl Solomon, Ph.D.

Center for Research in Behavioral Medicine and Health Psychology
University of South Florida

Richard R. Schmidt, Ph.D.

Daniel Baugh Institute of Anatomy
Jefferson Medical College
Thomas Jefferson University

Peter James Adragna, Ph.D.

Aurora University

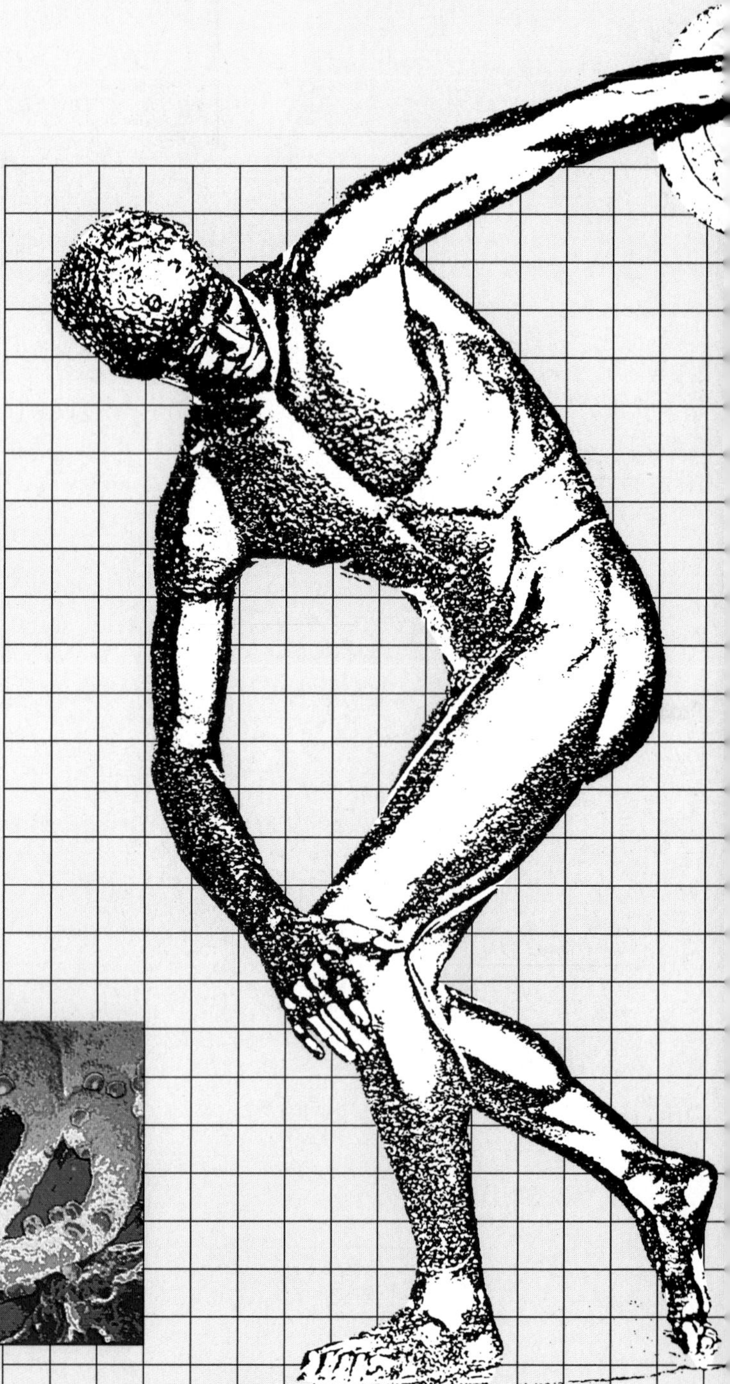

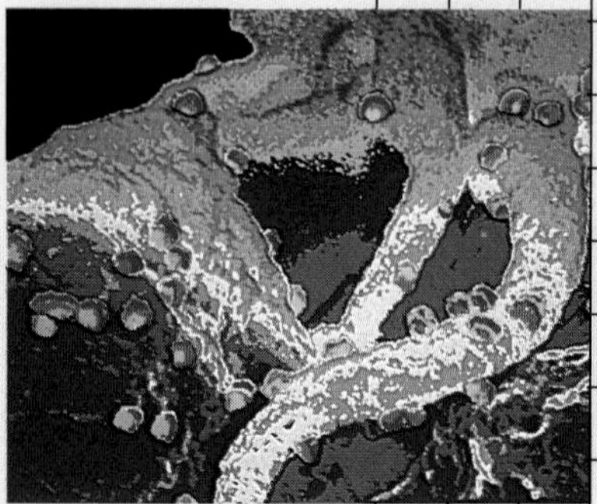

Saunders College Publishing

Philadelphia
Ft. Worth
Chicago
San Francisco
Montreal
Toronto
London
Sydney
Tokyo

& PHYSIOLOGY

SECOND EDITION

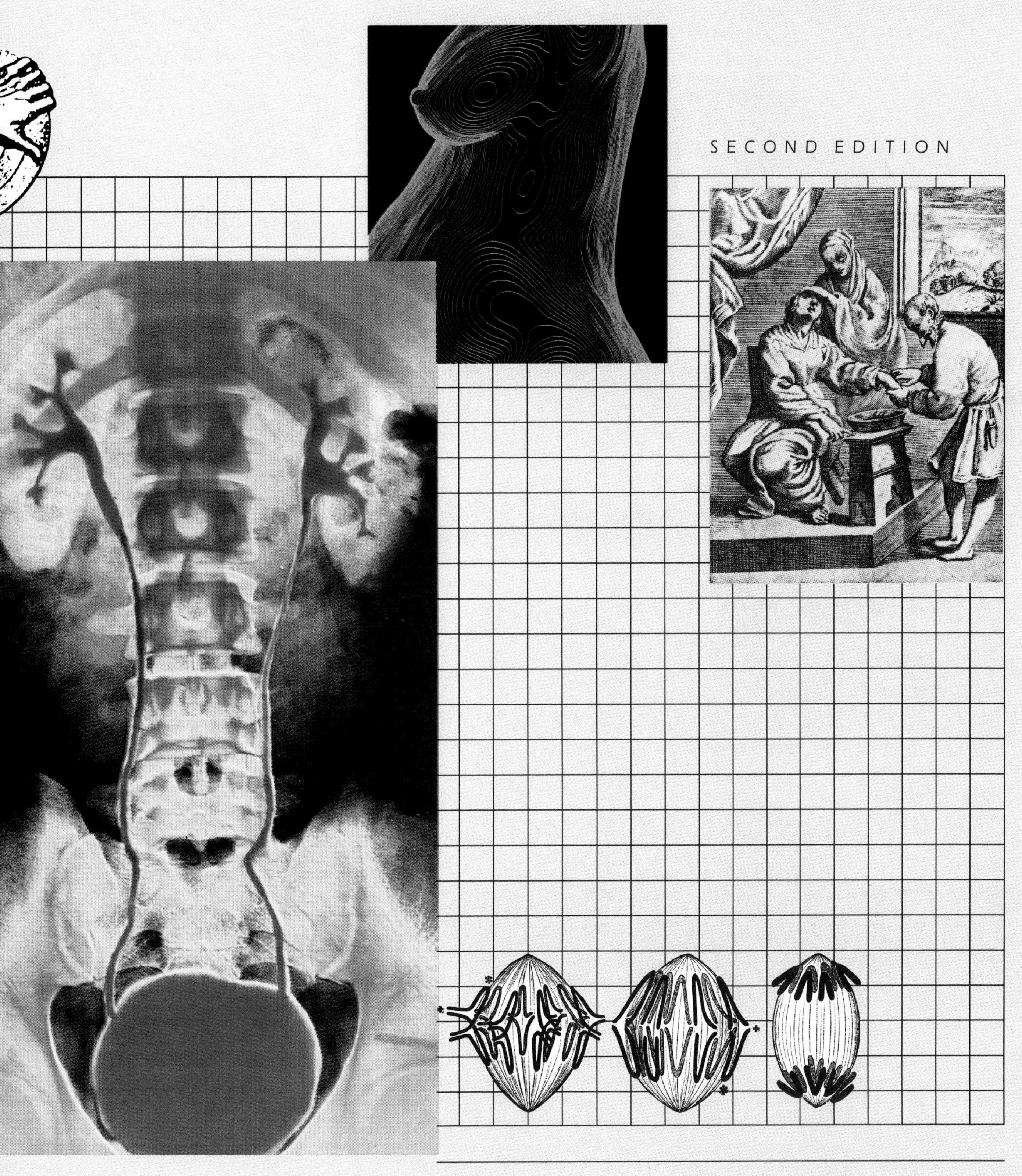

Text Typeface: Palatino
Compositor: York Graphic Services
Acquisitions Editor: Julie Levin Alexander
Developmental Editor: Ray Tschoepe, Gabrielle Goodman, Valerie Kish
Managing Editor: Carol Field
Project Editor: Maureen Iannuzzi
Copy Editor: Teresa L. Danielsen
Manager of Art and Design: Carol Bleistine
Art and Design Coordinator: Doris Bruey
Text Designer: Tracy Baldwin
Cover Designer: Lawrence R. Didona
Text Artwork: J & R Studio, Inc.
Layout Artist: Dorothy Chattin
Director of EDP: Tim Frelick
Production Manager: Charlene Squibb

Cover Credit: *Ballet dancer*: Custom Medical Stock Photo; *Model of neuron*: Photo Researchers, Inc.; Adult human head: Photo Researchers, Inc.

Printed in the United States of America

HUMAN ANATOMY AND PHYSIOLOGY, Second Edition

ISBN: 0-03-011914-6

Library of Congress Catalog Card Number: 89-043396

0123 032 987654321

For Amy
with admiration for who you are and with thanks for your help in writing this book

Eldra Solomon

For Dulcie, Ryan, Robert, Garret, Allison, Zachary, Chloë, Simona, Susan, and the man from Carouge

Richard Schmidt

For my loving parents, Peter J. Adragna, Sr. and Mary M. Adragna

Peter Adragna, Jr.

PREFACE

Human Anatomy and Physiology, second edition presents the human body as a marvel of biological engineering. A principal goal in preparing this book has been to share our sense of awe and excitement about the body's elegant design and function.

Audience

Human Anatomy and Physiology, second edition is designed for use in an introductory course in anatomy and physiology. The book is tailored to meet the needs of students in allied health, medical, and biology programs. Student populations served by this book include those studying for careers in nursing, medical assistance, physical therapy, radiology, nuclear medicine, radiation therapy, sonography, medical laboratory technology, dental hygiene, medical records, physical education, and mental health. This book can also be used successfully for premedical and predental students, and biological sciences majors, as well as many liberal arts students who elect to take a course in anatomy and physiology because of personal interest.

Philosophy and approach

Human Anatomy and Physiology, second edition portrays the human body as a living, functioning, homeostatic organism. We use a systems approach and emphasize how organs and body systems work together to carry on such complex functions as taking a step, running, or responding to stress. As we describe each of the body's many parts, we relate that part to its role in the organism and to its interaction with other structures.

From our own teaching experience we have found that students learn most effectively and most enjoyably when they can relate what they are learning to familiar issues, problems, and experiences. Thus, we relate material in the text to examples within the student's frame of reference. For example, when we describe melanin and pigment cells, we refer to their role in suntan and sunburn. When we discuss immunology, we apply the concepts to viral infections, immunization, and allergies.

Clinical material has been introduced where appropriate throughout the text. Most students enrolled in anatomy and physiology courses are curious about disease processes and other aspects of clinical physiology. Not only is this type of application of tremendous interest to them, but normal body functions are further illuminated when contrasted with the consequences of disruptions of the body's homeostasis. For example, the function of ADH becomes clearer when diabetes insipidus is explained, and the actions of insulin are better understood when the homeostatic imbalances that occur in diabetes mellitus are described.

Conceptual Approach

Emphasis has been placed on important concepts rather than on specific facts. Many anatomy and physiology textbooks present countless facts, leaving the student with scattered bits of unrelated information. All of the basic facts about the body and how it works are here in *Human Anatomy and Physiology,* but we have integrated them so that the student learns how these details fit together to produce the living, functioning organism.

Three ways the authors develop the conceptual approach are:

(1) Key concepts are presented at the beginning of each chapter.
(2) Headings and subheadings within each chapter are written in the form of conceptual statements.
(3) Beginning with Chapter 1, which presents an overview of several basic concepts, each chapter emphasizes the important concepts associated with the particular system being presented.

"Window on the Human Body" and "Window on the Animal Cell"

Two newly developed sets of acetate overlays, one of the human body, the other of the cell, are included in this text. Accurately rendered, state of the art drawings present progressively deeper views of the body and its systems, and of cell structure in a dynamic fashion. These two series of overlays will help students learn and remember the structures of the cell and parts of the body—and at the same time will make learning fun and exciting.

Use of sequence summaries

Sequence summaries within the text itself are used to simplify and summarize sequences of action presented in paragraph form. For example, paragraphs describing a sequence of blood flow are followed by a sequence summary that recaps the sequence of flow. The sequence summary extracts the core concept of the material discussed in preceding paragraphs.

Learning aids

In addition to the interesting, conversational reading style, the numerous learning aids that have been the hallmark of *Human Anatomy and Physiology* have been expanded and refined.

1. **Chapter outlines** at the beginning of each chapter provide the student with an overview of the material covered.
2. **Learning objectives** tell the student how to demonstrate mastery of the material covered in the chapter.
3. **Key concepts** summarize the main principles presented in the chapter.
4. **Concept-statement headings** introduce each section, informing students of the key ideas that will be discussed.
5. Numerous **tables,** many of them illustrated, summarize and organize material presented in the text.
6. Carefully rendered **illustrations,** over half of them new in this edition, support concepts covered in the text.
7. **Focus boxes,** such as those on AIDS (Chapter 23), and on crack cocaine and alcohol abuse (Chapter 15), spark student interest and present applications of the concepts discussed.
8. **Chapter summaries** in outline form at the end of each chapter provide a quick review of the material presented.
9. **Post Tests** following each chapter provide an opportunity to evaluate students' mastery of the material presented in the chapter; **answers** are provided at the end of each chapter.
10. **Review questions** focus on important concepts and applications.

11. **New terms** are boldfaced, permitting easy identification as well as adding emphasis, and phonetic pronunciations are given in parentheses for new terms.
12. A new, separate **glossary** is provided, facilitating rapid location of terms and definitions.
13. The **sequence summaries** described above are a valuable learning tool new to this edition.

Organization

Part I Organization of the human body

Chapter 1 provides an introduction to the human body, establishing an emphasis on homeostasis (homeodynamics) as a fundamental concept in physiology and a cohesive theme for this book. Chapter 2 provides the tools of chemistry needed to understand human physiology. In Chapter 3 the cell is described as the basic biological component of the body. The "Window on the Animal Cell" overlay series is an exciting addition to this edition. Chapter 4 describes tissues and includes illustrated tables of epithelial, connective, and muscle tissues. A section is included on neoplasms. The importance of the integumentary system to the integrity of the body is discussed in Chapter 5, which also includes sections on burns, inflammation, and repair of wounds.

Part II Support and movement

This section has been expanded, rewritten, and reorganized. Chapter 6 describes skeletal tissue. Skeletal remodeling, fractures and healing, bone disease, and hormones that affect the skeleton are among the topics presented. The chapter on the skeletal system in the preceding edition has been divided into two new chapters focusing on the axial (Chapter 7) and appendicular (Chapter 8) divisions, and these topics are covered in greater depth. Chapter 9 is a new chapter containing expanded coverage of joints.

Chapter 10 describes muscle tissue and Chapter 11 discusses the muscular system. Color photographs of superficial muscles of living human models are paired with newly created, highly realistic diagrams of both superficial and deep musculature.

Part III Regulation of body activities

This unit has been reorganized, expanded, and coverage increased from five to seven chapters. Chapter 12 describes neurons and their interaction with emphasis on transmission of impulses and integration. Chapter 13 focuses on the central nervous system and Chapter 14 on the peripheral nervous system. Chapter 15 is a new chapter integrating what has been learned in the preceding three chapters to explain neural function. A section on the effects of drugs on the nervous system includes focus boxes on alcohol abuse and crack cocaine. Chapter 16 describes the autonomic division of the nervous system. In the preceding edition the autonomic division was appended to the discussion of the somatic division of the peripheral nervous system. Here this important division is given the attention it deserves by making it the focus of an entire chapter. In Chapter 17 the sense receptors and organs are described in more detail than in the previous edition.

Chapter 18 emphasizes the role of the endocrine system in maintaining homeostasis. Discussion of the consequences of endocrine malfunction reinforces the concepts of normal endocrine physiology.

Part IV The circulatory system: internal transport and defense

Chapter 19 focuses on blood and its components. Chapter 20, on the heart, has been rewritten and contains more physiology than in the preceding edition. Chapter 21 describes the circulation, and Chapter 22 discusses the lymphatic system. Chapter 23, on immunity, has been carefully updated and a Focus on AIDS has been added.

Part V Obtaining oxygen, nutrients, and maintaining bodily fluids

Chapter 24, describing the respiratory system, has been entirely rewritten, and new art has been added. Several focus boxes of interest to the student (on smoking and air pollution, CPR, cough and sneeze reflexes, respiratory disorders) are included. Chapter 25 describes food processing by the digestive system, and Chapter 26 focuses on nutrition, metabolism, and thermoregulation.

Chapter 27 focuses on the urinary system with emphasis on the homeostatic function of the kidneys. Numerous sequence summaries simplify and recap the series of physiologic events presented. In Chapter 28, fluid and electrolyte balance are addressed, synthesizing concepts presented in association with several other systems. Focus boxes address fluid imbalance, electrolyte imbalance, and acid-base imbalance, emphasizing the clinical consequences of homeostatic imbalance.

Part VI Perpetuation of the human species

Chapter 29 discusses human reproduction, and Chapter 30 describes development. In Chapter 31 some basic concepts of inheritance are presented. Chapter 32, on exercise physiology, is a new chapter that applies concepts learned about several different systems to a topic of interest to most students.

Supplements

To further facilitate learning and teaching, a supplement package has been carefully designed for the student and instructor. For the student there is the **Student Resource Manual, HyperCard Tutorial, Laboratory Manual, Dictionary of Medical Terminology for Health Professionals, Body Art** and **Coloring Atlas of Human Anatomy.** For the instructor there is the **Instructor's Resource Manual, Lecture Outlines on Disk, Computerized Test Bank, Biosource Software, overhead transparencies,** and two **videotapes** from the television series **NOVA.**

Student Resource Manual

Contains the *chapter objectives, key concepts, outlines,* and *exercises* designed to enhance the student's understanding of anatomical relationships and complex physiological interactions.

HyperCard Tutorial

An anatomy tutorial based in the Macintosh Hypercard format.

Laboratory Manual

A fully illustrated, comprehensive guide to experiments and demonstrations that instructors can integrate into their course.

Dictionary of Medical Terminology for Health Professionals

Authored by Brian Smith and Bentley E. Smith

Body-Art

100 select pieces of art are reproduced from the text in black outline. Students may use Body-Art for note-taking, labeling, or coloring.

Coloring Atlas of Human Anatomy

Authored by Edwin Chin Jr. and Marvin M. Shrewsbury. This coloring atlas is designed to aid the anatomy student by clearly illustrating the anatomical structures to be learned. Coloring is an effective way to make the learning process more enjoyable.

Instructor's Resource Manual

This is the complete guide to course preparation. It includes the *chapter overview, learning objectives, key concepts, chapter outlines, key terms,* and suggestions for lecture outlines. In addition, it includes recommendations for integrating Body-Art™ overhead transparencies, videos, and software aids.

Lecture Outline on Disk

This is a formatted lecture outline that the instructor can use to facilitate lecture preparation.

Test Bank

This booklet contains 2500 test questions in various formats. In addition to this booklet, the test bank is also available as ExaMaster™ software for the Apple Macintosh® and the IBM PC®.

Software Tutorial Programs

Available through Biosource Software and Queue Intellectual Software for Apple II computers.

Overhead Transparency Acetates

225 full-color illustrations from the text, with legends. In addition to this, 100 full-color cadaver transparencies are available.

NOVA Videotapes

Students get a rare glimpse into complex human body systems through two cadaver dissections.

Acknowledgments

The authors have received a great deal of support and valuable input from family, friends, editors, students, and colleagues. We are grateful to our families and friends for their understanding, support, and encouragement as we struggled through many revisions and deadlines. We especially thank Amy Solomon, who helped write several chapters, Mical Solomon for his willingness to share his computer expertise, Belicia Efros for her help with reference material, Kathleen M. Heide for critically reading selected portions of the manuscript and for her encouragement, Janet Inlow for her valuable assistance, Dr. Anthony Farole of Jefferson Medical College for helpful consultation regarding the clinical aspects of the temporomandibular joint, and Dr. Edwin Masters of the Daniel Baugh Institute of Anatomy, Jefferson Medical College, for his professional expertise in generating human dissections from which several of the book's photographs were prepared.

We appreciate the support of our Publisher Elizabeth Widdicombe and our Acquisition Editor Julie Levin Alexander. Julie replaced Ed Murphy, who had expertly launched the project. Julie quickly assessed the complexities of the project and supported us as we made our way through the maze of development and production.

Our Developmental Editor Ray Tschoepe worked along with us on a daily basis and made a unique contribution by sharing his artistic talents to reconceptualize and draw much of the art. Gabrielle Goodman provided valuable input on the text and coordinated many aspects of the project. Valerie Kish served as a developmental reviewer and helped us sort through and make decisions about sometimes conflicting suggestions from numerous reviewers.

We thank our Project Editor Maureen Iannuzzi, who guided the project through the process of production. We appreciate the work of Art Director Carol Bleistine, who coordinated the art program and design. All of these dedicated professionals and many others at Saunders provided the skill and attention needed to produce *Human Anatomy and Physiology.* We thank them for their help and support throughout this project.

Our colleagues and students have provided valuable input by sharing their responses to the last edition of *Human Anatomy and Physiology* with us. We thank them and ask again for their comments and suggestions as they use this new edition. We can be reached through our editors at Saunders College Publishing.

Reviewers

We thank the many professors and researchers who have read the manuscript during various stages of its preparation and provided us with valuable suggestions for improving it. Their input has contributed greatly to our final product. They are:

Merlyn Anderberg, *Spokane Falls Community College*
Joe Anders, *North Harris Community College*
Jack Cote, *College of Lake County*
Carol Crowder, *North Harris Community College*
George Daston, *Montclair State College*
Blaine Ferrell, *Western Kentucky University*
Myron Fougeron, *Kearney State College*
Janet Gehres, *Albright College*
David Hammerman, *Long Island University*
Ann Harmer, *Orange Coast College*
Harold Heidtke, *Andrews University*
John Hertner, *Kearney State College*
Larry Hibbert, *Ricks College*
Melanie Hoag, *Drexel University*
Elvis Holt, *Indiana-Purdue at Ft. Wayne*
Thomas Hubbard, *Community College of Baltimore*
David Huey, *Louisiana State University at Alexandria*
Emron Jensen, *Weber State College*
Jerry Justus, *Arizona State University*
Janie Languirand, *Mississippi Gulf Coast Community College*
Bonnie Lustigman, *Montclair State College*
Wayne Mason, *Western Kentucky University*
Irwin Mickelberg, *Augsburg College*
Paul Miller, *Norwalk Community College*
Mohammed Mulkana, *Mississippi Gulf Coast Community College*
Stephen Person, *Lake Superior State College*
Dennis Rich, *Mattatuck Community College*
Geri Seitchik, *La Salle University*
Timothy Shaw, *Bethel College*
J.A. Shillicock, *Montclair State College*
Milton Stetson, *University of Delaware*
Cecelia Thomas, *Hinds Community College*
Robert Zaccaria, *Lycoming College*

CONTENTS OVERVIEW

CONTENTS

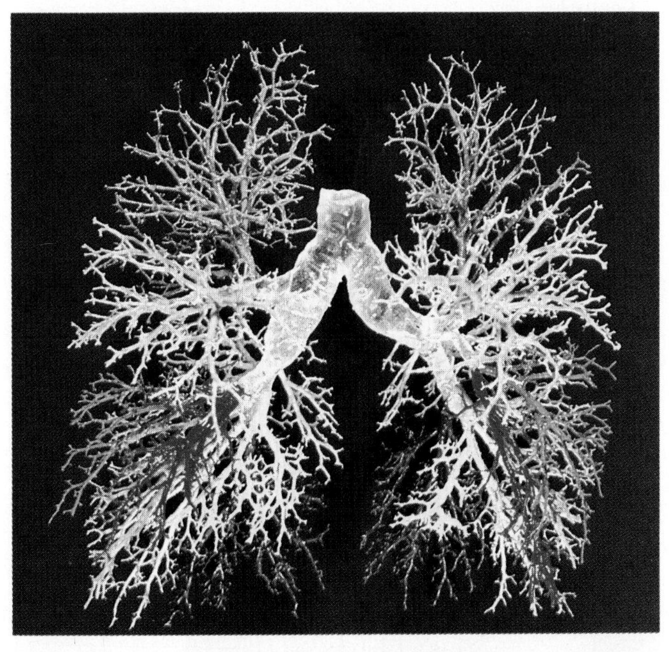

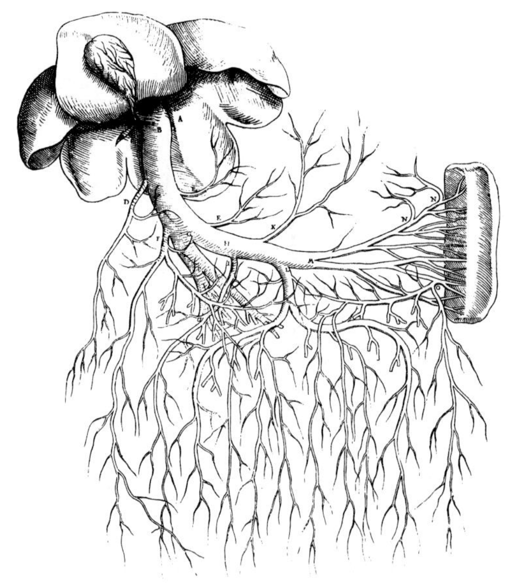

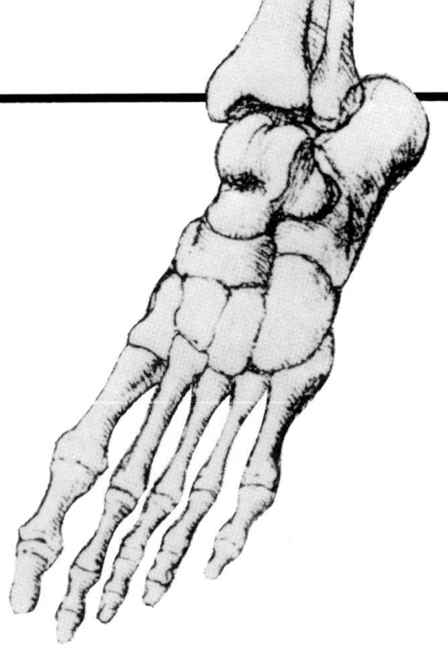

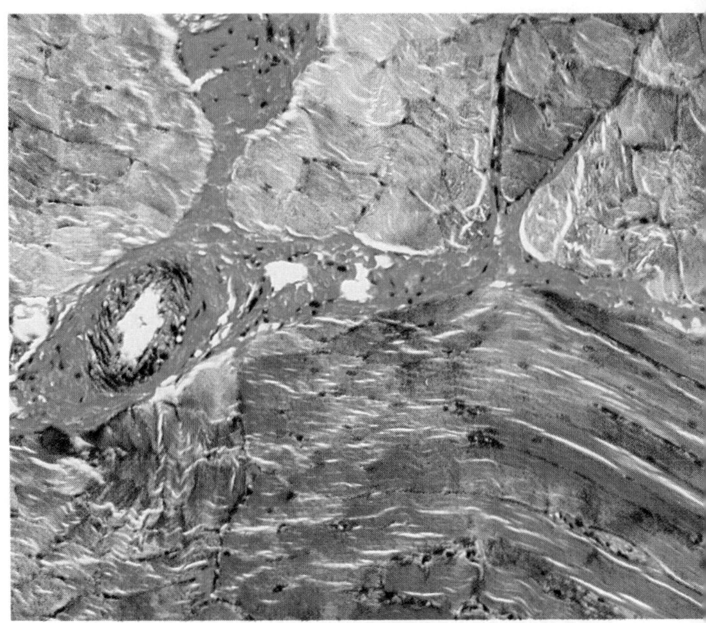

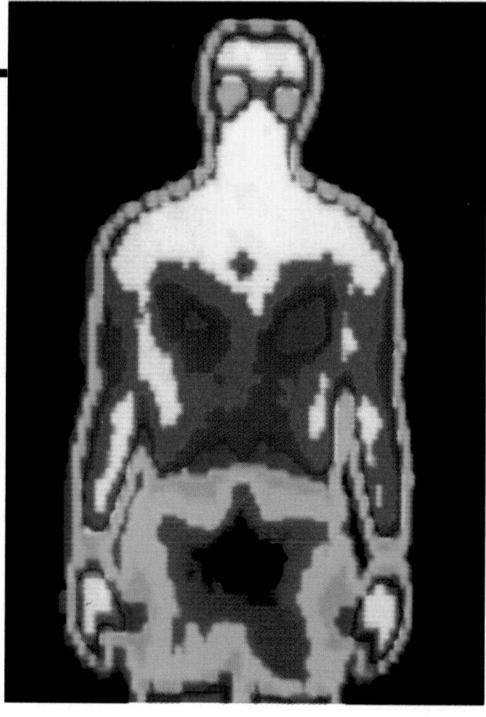

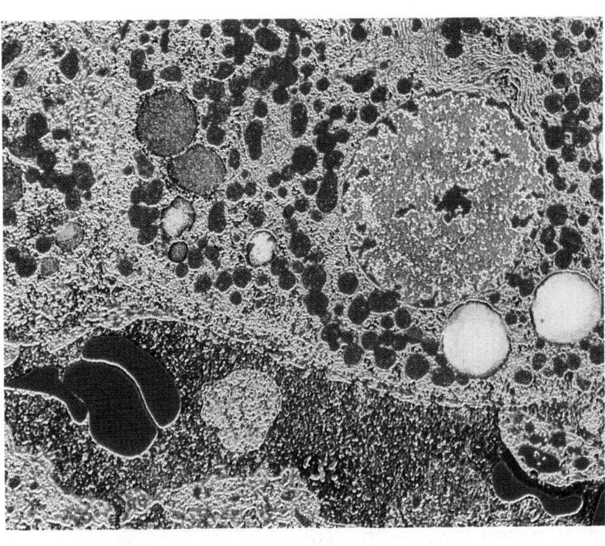

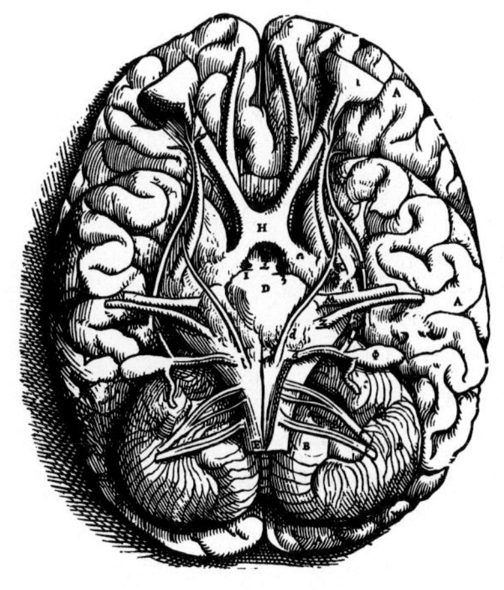

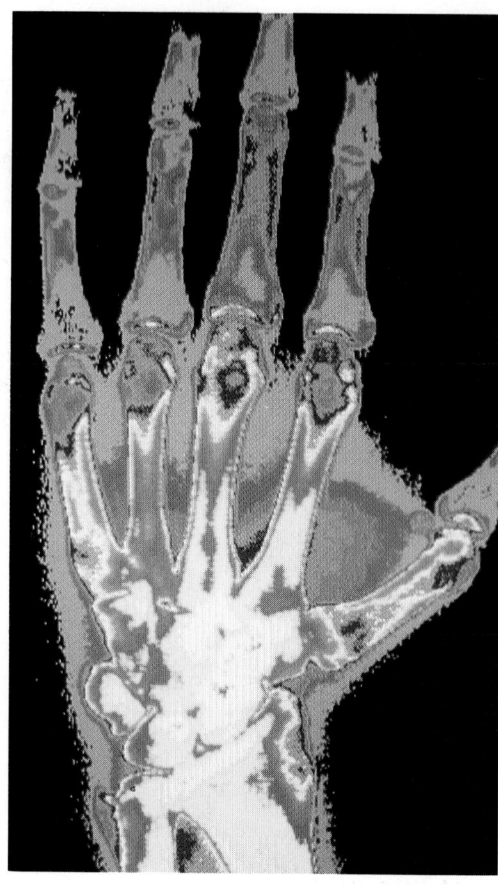

14
THE PERIPHERAL NERVOUS SYSTEM: SOMATIC SYSTEM 474

15
PERCEPTION OF SENSATION, MOTOR CONTROL, AND INFORMATION PROCESSING 498

16
THE PERIPHERAL NERVOUS SYSTEM: AUTONOMIC SYSTEM 526

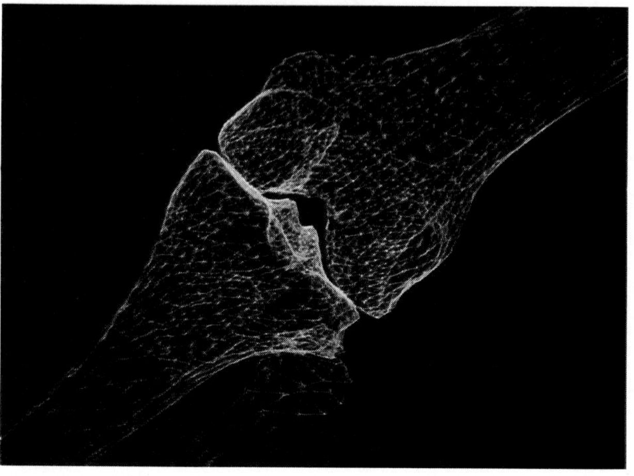

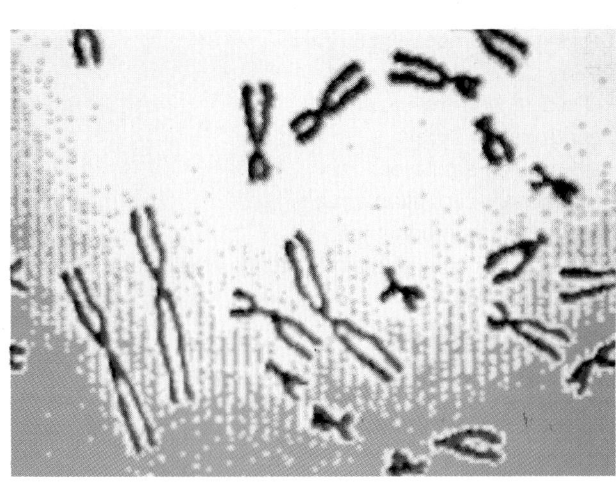

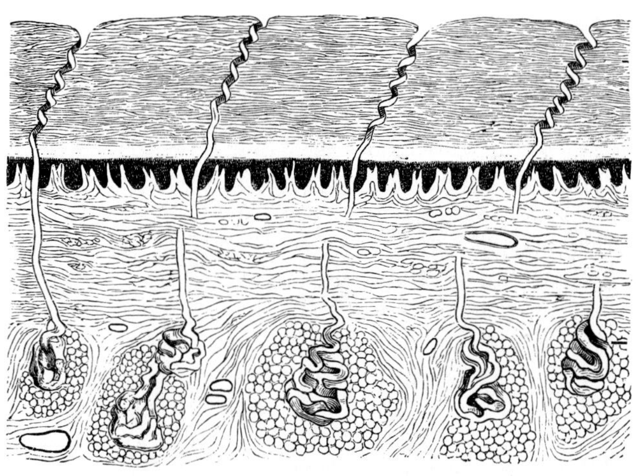

IV

THE CIRCULATORY SYSTEM: INTERNAL TRANSPORT AND DEFENSE 638

19

20

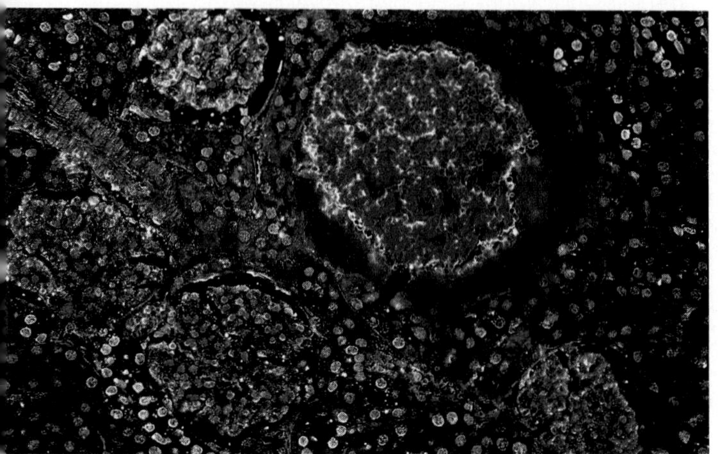

21

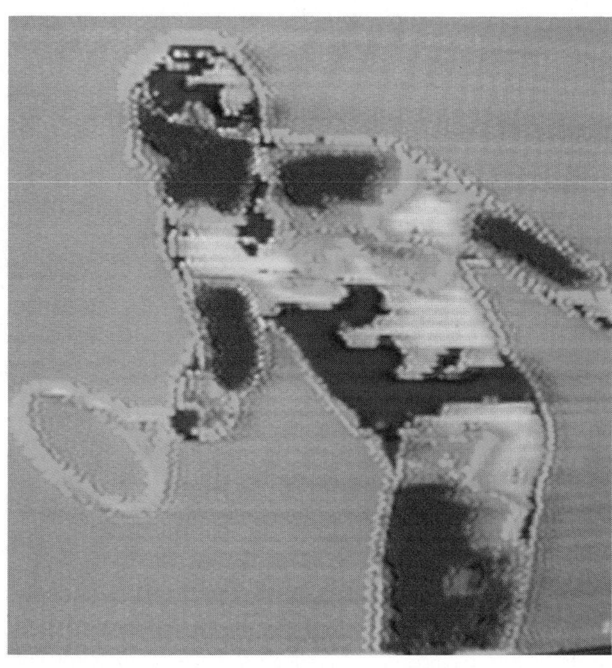

25

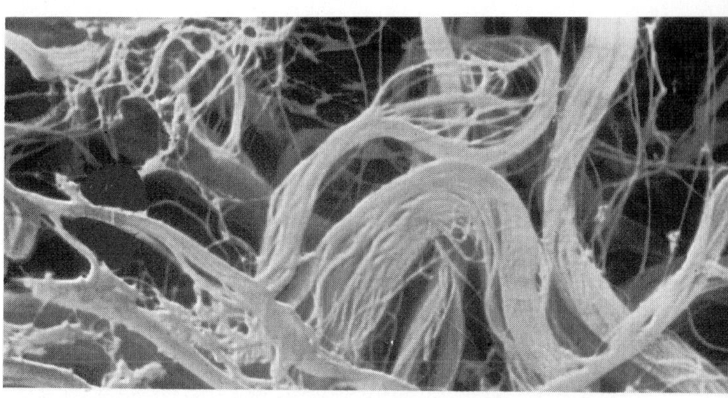

26

27
THE URINARY SYSTEM 950

28
FLUID, ELECTROLYTE, AND ACID-BASE BALANCE 984

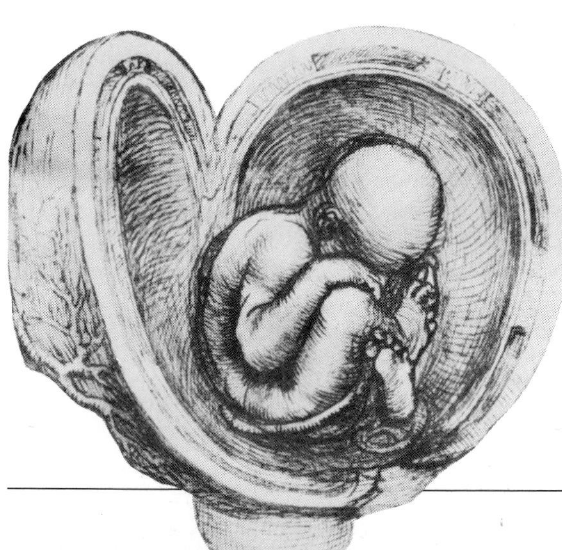

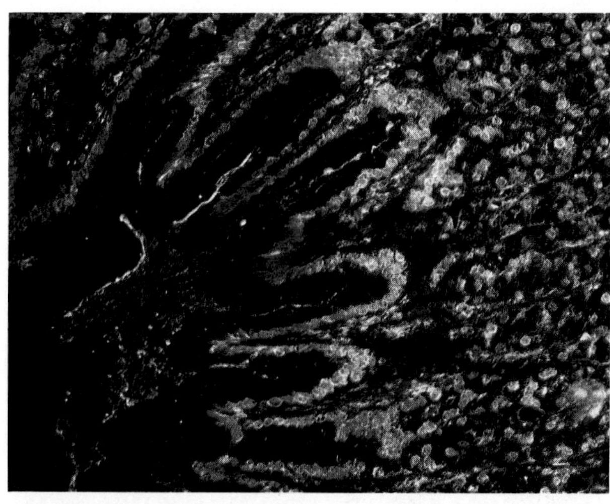

VI
PERPETUATION OF THE HUMAN SPECIES 1002

29
REPRODUCTION 1004

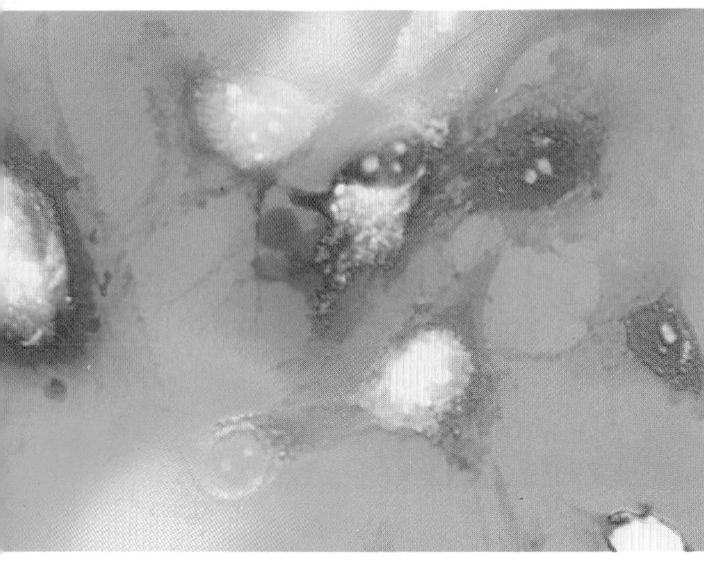

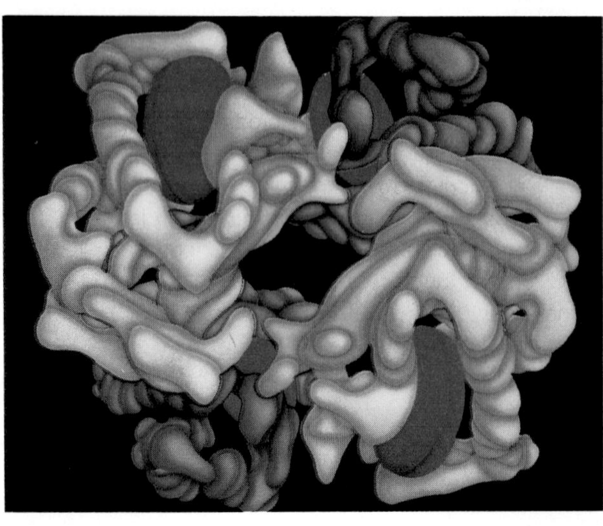

32
FUNDAMENTALS OF EXERCISE PHYSIOLOGY 1108

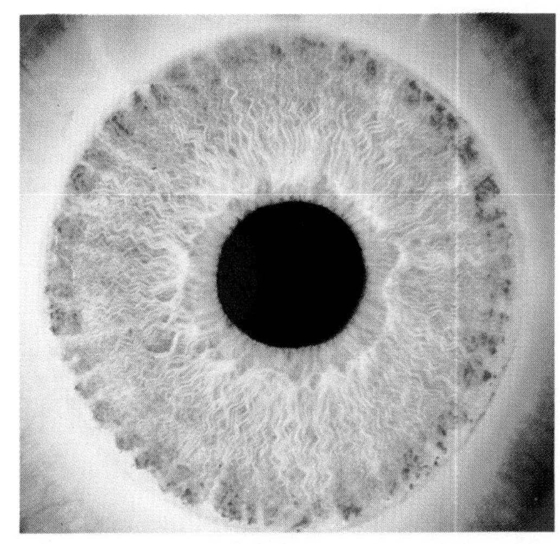

HUMAN ANATOMY & PHYSIOLOGY

ORGANIZATION OF THE BODY

The human body is much more than the sum of its parts. We will begin our study of human anatomy and physiology with an introduction to the human body as it really is—an integrated, functioning organism. After this introduction we will begin to study the body's parts, and this detailed consideration will occupy the greater part of this book. The body consists of thousands of components, most of them moving parts that function with mechanical and chemical subtlety, working together to perform countless specialized tasks with marvelous precision.

In studying so many details it is all too easy to lose sight of the forest because of the trees. We must understand the construction and function of each part, but we must also keep in mind how these parts are organized to form a living, breathing, thinking, and feeling human organism.

In Chapter 1 we will study the body as a whole—its systems, regions, and some of its basic physiological mechanisms. Here we will become acquainted with the levels of organization of the world within. The chemical level of organization will be discussed in Chapter 2, and many of the compounds that make up the body will be described. In Chapter 3 we will study the cell, the basic building block of the body, and its parts. How cells organize to form tissues will be the subject of Chapter 4. Finally, in Chapter 5, we will end this unit with the study of a body system, the integumentary system, which consists of the skin and its associated structures.

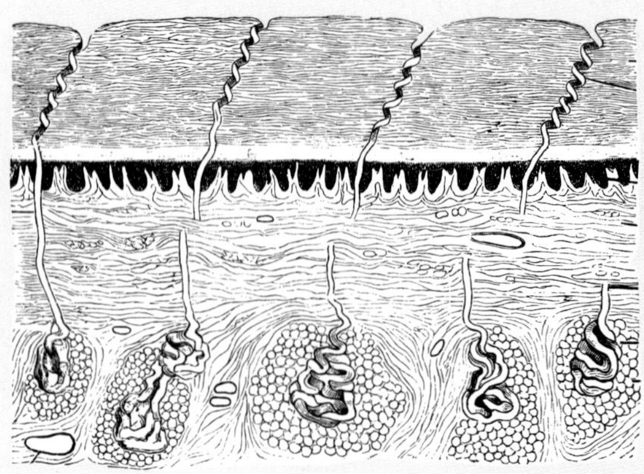

I

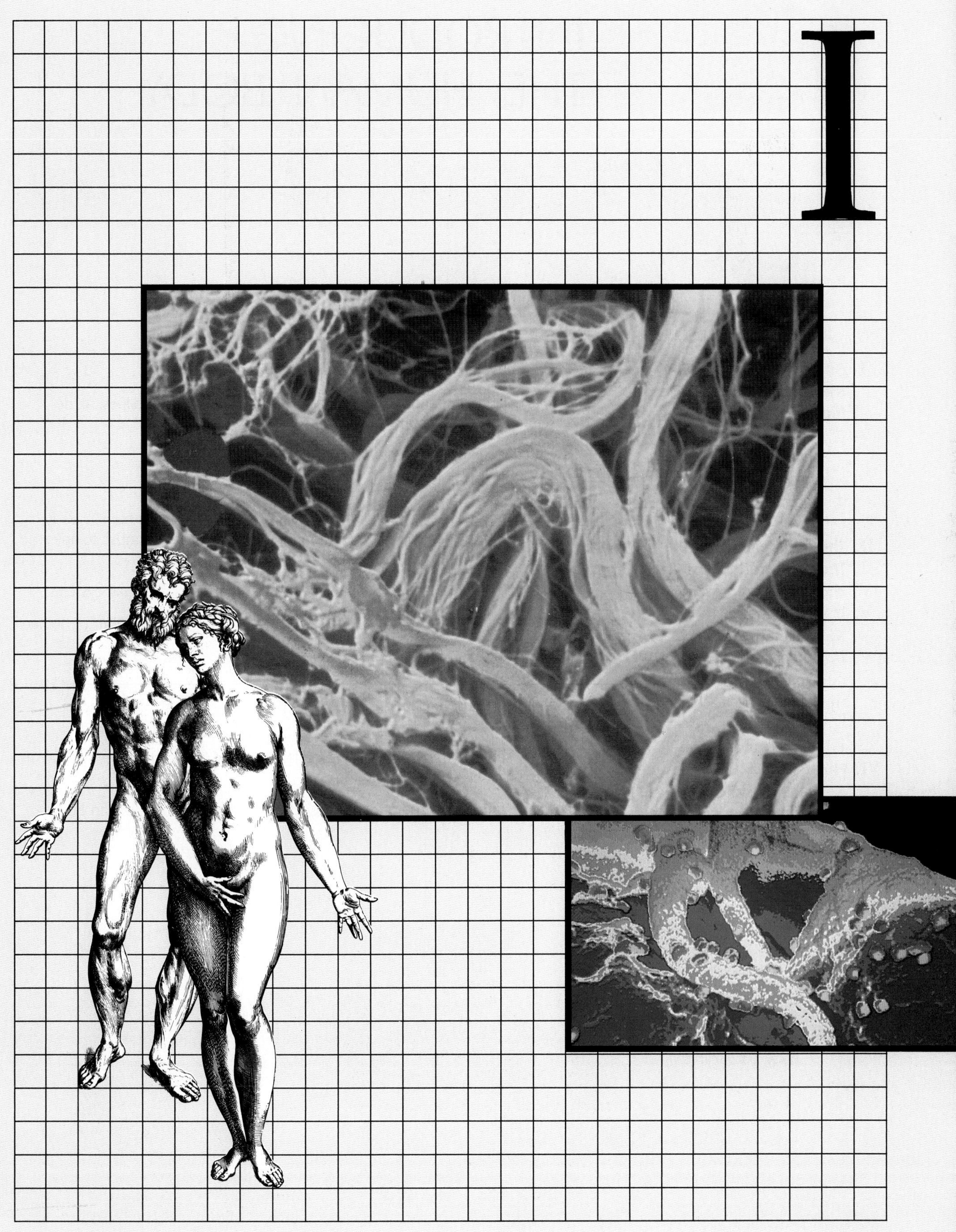

INTRODUCING THE HUMAN BODY

CHAPTER OUTLINE

LEARNING OBJECTIVES

After you have studied this chapter you should be able to:

1 Define anatomy and physiology and identify their subdisciplines, as described in this chapter.

2 Describe six requirements of life.

3 Describe six characteristics shared by living organisms.

4 List in sequence the levels of biological organization in the human body, starting with the simplest (the atom) and ending with the most complex (the organism).

5 Describe the homeostatic capabilities of the ten principal organ systems.

6 Define homeostasis and justify it as a basic functional mechanism of human physiology, giving examples.

7 Describe the anatomical position of the human body.

8 Define and use properly the principal orientational terms employed in human anatomy.

9 Draw sagittal, transverse, and frontal sections of body structures such as blood vessels or the brain.

10 Define and locate the principal regions and cavities of the human body.

(Fisher/Custom Medical Stock Photo.)

1

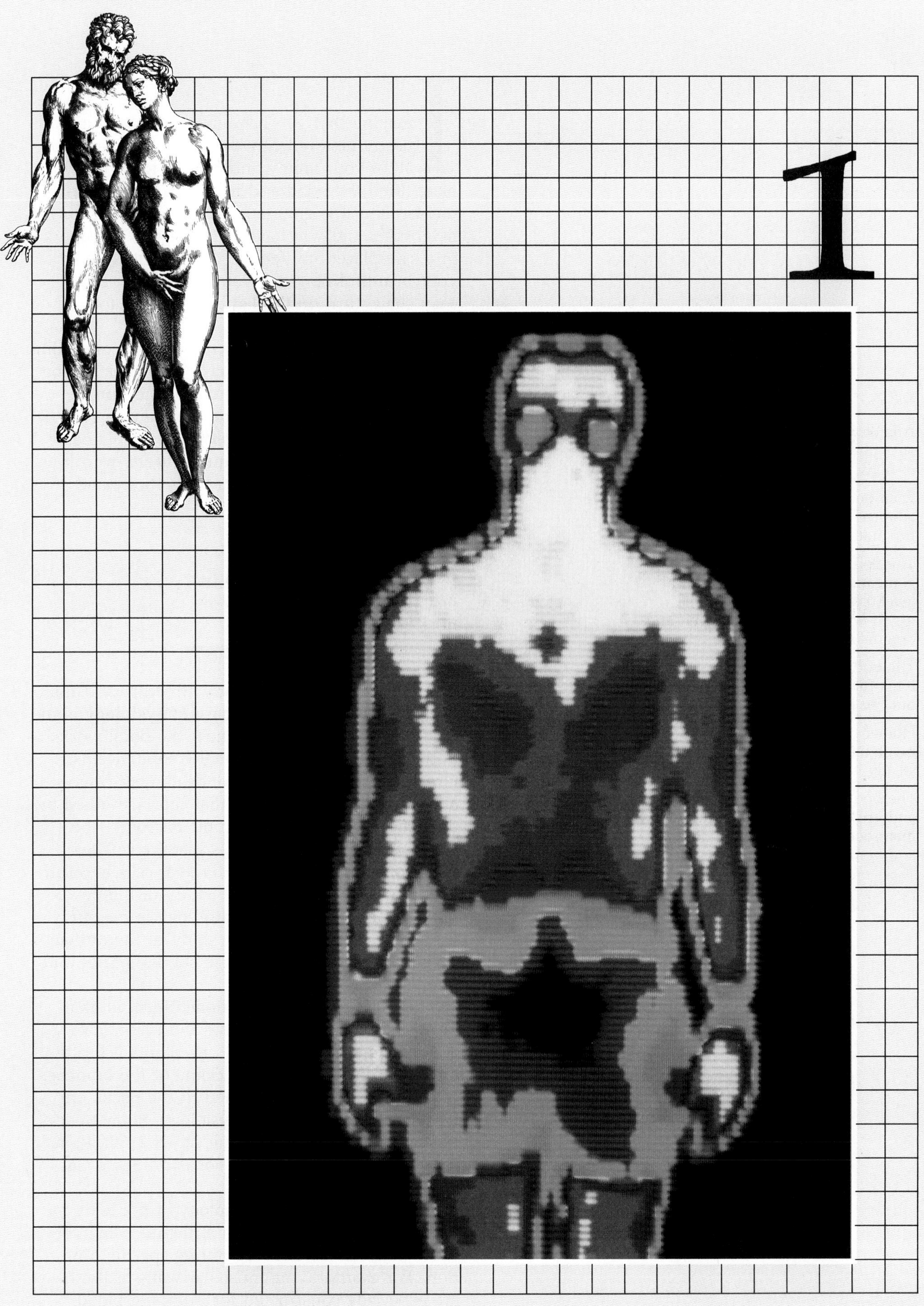

KEY CONCEPTS

Anatomy is the study of body structure; physiology is the study of body function.

Each body structure is exquisitely adapted for carrying out its specific functions.

The body has several levels of organization including the chemical level, cellular level, tissue level, organ level, body system level, and organismic level.

The body consists of ten main systems that operate together to carry out life processes.

Homeostasis is the body's automatic tendency to maintain a steady state.

The body may be divided into axial and appendicular regions; the two main body cavities are the dorsal and ventral cavities.

Imagine that you have just purchased a flashy new red convertible. You have taken all of your family and friends for rides, you have lifted the hood and made knowing comments about the engine for the benefit of your neighbors, and you have filed the official papers in a safe place. Still feeling really excited about your beautiful new car, you settle down in an easy chair, turn on the light, and begin to read the owner's manual.

You may or may not own a car, but one thing is certain: you do have a body. This book can be considered an owner's manual for the human body. Although this machine may have a remarkably good performance record, it is irreplaceable at any price and has no manufacturer's warranty. It seems only sensible to study the body and learn how it works.

Anatomy and physiology are the studies of structure and function

Anatomy is the study of body structure and the relationships among body parts. **Physiology** is the study of body function, or how the body works. Both are broad fields with many subdivisions. **Gross anatomy,** for example, deals with organs and structures of the body that can be studied by dissection, whereas microscopic anatomy, the study of tissues, is known as **histology.** The study of the structure of individual cells is called **cytology. Embryology** is the study of the development of the organism. **Pathology** is the study of disease processes. In our study of the human body we shall deal with these subdisciplines and many others.

Medical science is an applied form of anatomy and physiology that uses the findings of anatomists and physiologists to maintain health and treat disease (Fig. 1-1). Some of the branches of medical science are defined in the Focus on Applying Anatomy and Physiology: Some Specialties in Medical Science. Some career applications are briefly described in the Focus on Some Careers in the Health Sciences.

The anatomy and physiology of the body are intricately interrelated. Each structure is marvelously adapted for carrying out its specific function. For example, the muscular walls of the heart are especially constructed for pumping blood

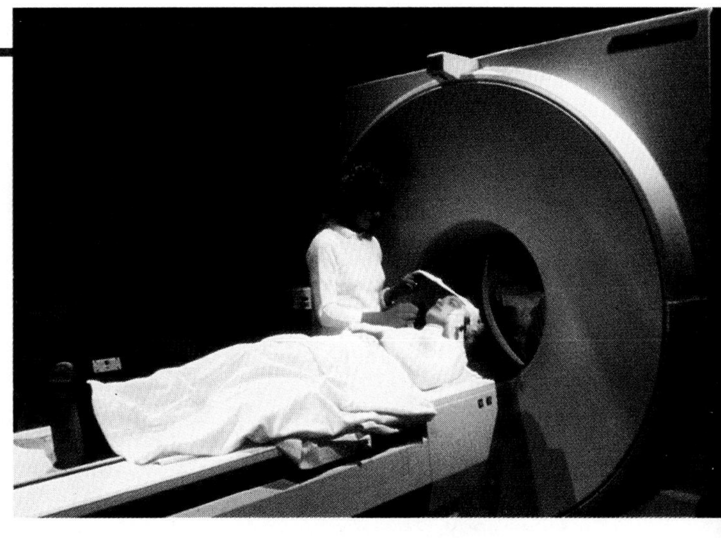

FIGURE 1-1

Medical science is an applied form of anatomy and physiology. During the past few decades knowledge of anatomy and physiology gained through research has contributed to the development of improved and more sophisticated methods of diagnosing and treating disease. Here a patient is being prepared for computerized tomography (CT) scanning. This is a process in which x-ray equipment is combined with a computer and cathode-ray tube to produce images of cross sections through the body. The image may be viewed on a television screen called the physician's console as shown in the illustration. For further information on CT scanning read Focus on Visualizing Body Parts Clinically. (Custom Medical Stock Photo.)

FOCUS ON . . . Applying anatomy and physiology: some specialties in medical science

Name of Specialization	Area of Concern
Allergy	Diagnosis and treatment of allergic conditions
Anesthesiology	Administration of drugs that produce a loss of sensation; such drugs are administered during surgical procedures
Cardiology	The heart and its diseases
Dermatology	Skin disorders
Endocrinology	Glands that release hormones, and hormone disorders
Epidemiology	The occurrence, distribution, and control of disease
Gastroenterology	Stomach and intestine and their disorders
Geriatrics	Health problems of elderly persons
Gynecology	The female reproductive system and its disorders
Hematology	Blood and blood disorders
Immunology	Mechanisms by which the body resists disease
Nephrology	Kidney disorders
Neurology	The nervous system and its disorders
Nuclear medicine	Use of radioisotopes in diagnosis and therapy
Obstetrics	Pregnancy and childbirth
Oncology	Tumors and cancer
Ophthalmology	The eyes and eye disorders
Orthopedics	Disorders and injuries of bone, joints, and muscles
Otorhinolaryngology	Ear, nose, and throat diseases
Pathology	Diagnosis of disease based on changes in cells and tissues
Pediatrics	Children's diseases
Pharmacology	Drugs and their actions and uses in treatment of disease
Podiatry	Foot ailments
Proctology	Diseases of the colon, anus, and rectum
Radiology	Radioactive substances, x-rays, and other ionizing radiations in the diagnosis and treatment of disease
Toxicology	Poisons
Urology	Disorders of the urinary tract and of the male reproductive organs

FOCUS ON . . . Some careers in the health sciences

Nursing	Registered nurses (RN) provide services that promote, maintain, and restore health. Licensed practical nurses (LPN) assist physicians and registered nurses in the examination and care of patients.
Radiologic technology	Radiologic technologists assist physicians with diagnostic radiologic procedures, including routine x-ray, computerized tomography (CT), magnetic resonance imaging (MRI), and angiographic procedures (visualizing blood vessels).
Radiation therapy technology	Radiation therapy technologists assist physicians with the management, control, and care of patients receiving radiation therapy treatment.
Nuclear medicine technology	Nuclear medicine technologists assist in the preparation and examination of patients when radioactive substances are used, such as in nuclear scanning.
Emergency medical technology	Emergency medical technicians with ambulance training perform basic life support measures at the scene of accidents. Paramedics are further trained in advanced life support.
Human services technology	Human services technicians serve as paraprofessionals in community agencies dealing in human services/mental health. Under professional supervision they perform such services as counseling and case management.
Medical technology	A medical technologist is skilled in the technical aspects of clinical laboratory procedures.
Occupational therapy	Occupational therapists work with patients debilitated by accidents, stroke, or other diseases. The therapist's job is to teach patients how to manage everyday tasks within their physical limitations.
Physical therapy	Physical therapists work with patients debilitated by accidents, stroke, or other diseases. They teach patients exercises to maintain muscle tone and strengthen muscles.
Physician assistant (PA)	A physician assistant performs certain of a physician's duties and serves as assistant to a primary care physician or as a surgeon's assistant. For example, a PA can perform a physical examination and routine therapeutic procedures such as injections or wound suturing.
Respiratory therapy	The respiratory therapist administers treatments for respiratory tract disorders as prescribed by the patient's physician.

from its hollow chambers. The blood is forced into large blood vessels with elastic walls that permit the vessels to expand as they fill with blood and then snap back to normal size. Between the chambers of the heart, flaplike valves prevent the blood from flowing backward. As you proceed with your study of the human body, look for relationships between the structure and function of the body parts you are studying. Remember that the size, shape, and structure of each part are related to the job it must perform.

An appropriate environment is necessary for life to exist

There are several requirements for life to exist and thrive. From their surroundings humans must be able to obtain or maintain the following:

1. **Water.** Water is not only essential to life, it is part of life (Fig. 1-2). The human body consists of about 60% water by weight. Most of the chemical activities essential to human life take place in a watery medium. Each day we lose water in urine, feces, sweat, and exhaled air. This fluid loss must be replaced by drinking liquids and eating foods containing water.

2. **Food.** Our food consists mainly of plants or animals that have eaten plants. (Even if we eat rattlesnake meat, the snake fed on mice that lived mainly on plant products such as seeds.) The food we consume is broken down into chemical substances needed by each of the body cells (microscopic building blocks of the body). These substances are used either as raw materials to make new chemical substances and body parts or as fuel molecules that cells break down in order to obtain energy.

3. **Oxygen.** Oxygen is a gas that makes up about 21% of our atmosphere. Like most living cells, those of the human body require a continuous oxygen supply in order to oxidize (break down) fuel molecules and obtain their energy. When deprived of this vital gas, most cells quickly deplete their available energy and die within a few minutes.

4. **Appropriate environmental temperature.** We could not survive upon a dark, frozen planet like Pluto, which has an average temperature of −184°C (−300°F), or upon a burning hot planet like Venus, which has an average temperature of 427°C (800°F). Even within Earth's more suitable temperature extremes, −88°C (−130°F) to 58°C (136°F), the body must sometimes work hard to maintain its own internal temperature.

5. **Suitable environmental pressure.** Seldom do we think of our need for suitable pressure, but we live at the bottom of an ocean of air that exerts a considerable pressure (compressing action) upon our bodies. This atmospheric pressure is important for normal breathing and for proper gas exchange in the lungs.

When we venture down into the ocean depths, the increased pressure can drive excess nitrogen gas into the blood and tissues, causing **nitrogen narcosis**—a condition resembling alcoholic intoxication that may lead to irrational, life-threatening behavior. Emerging from the sea can also be dangerous, for the sudden bubbling of nitrogen out of the tissues can cause damage and lead to decompression sickness, known commonly as "the bends."

Mountain climbers and pilots, on the other hand, must deal with decreased air pressure. Above 23,000 feet pilots must wear oxygen masks or have pressurized cabins to prevent loss of consciousness due to inadequate oxygenation. Astronauts venturing into outer space must wear pressurized suits because the absence of pressure would otherwise cause their blood to boil and their bodies to explode.

6. **Protection from harmful radiation.** If you have ever experienced a sunburn, you know that some of the sun's rays can be harmful. The thin ozone layer at the upper portion of our atmosphere filters out much of this harmful ultraviolet radiation. An increase in the amount of ultraviolet radiation reaching the earth's surface would cause an increase in mutations and skin cancer. Chlorofluorocarbon (Freon-type) refrigerants and spray-can propellants as well as nitrogen oxides released into the atmosphere by industrial processes and high-altitude jets hasten the breakdown of ozone. Recent evidence suggests that the rate of skin cancer is already increasing as the ozone layer has begun to diminish and more harmful radiation is penetrating the atmosphere.

FIGURE 1-2

Planet Earth seen from Apollo II, about 98,000 nautical miles away. Life on Earth depends on the liquid water that covers most of our planet. (NASA/Custom Medical Stock Photo.)

Living things have characteristics that distinguish them from nonliving things

Like all living things, human beings move, carry on self-regulated metabolism, respond to changes within the body and in the external environment, grow, reproduce, and adapt to long-term environmental changes. Let us consider each of these characteristics in turn.

1. **Movement.** A living organism must be able to move food into its body, distribute it to all parts of the body, and eject wastes. In the human body, the digestive tract moves food along; the heart pumps blood, which transports materials to and from all body regions; and many other involuntary forms of movement take place continually. Like most animals, we also have the ability to

make complex voluntary movements. As a result, we are able to play a concerto on the piano, return a tennis ball, or run from danger.

2. **Metabolism and homeostasis.** All the chemical processes that take place within the body are collectively referred to as **metabolism.** Two phases of metabolism are catabolism and anabolism. **Catabolism,** the breaking-down phase of metabolism, provides the energy needed to carry on life processes. Catabolic reactions convert the energy in food to forms that can be used by the body. For example, energy provided by catabolism is required for transmission of nerve impulses and for muscle contraction. **Anabolism,** the building, or synthetic, phase of metabolism, uses energy to produce the chemical substances and parts needed for growth and repair of the body and for maintaining all of the body systems.

Three interdependent aspects of metabolism are nutrition, synthesis of new materials, and cellular respiration (Fig. 1-3). **Nutrition** is the process of nourishing the body—that is, of supplying all cells of the body with nutrients (needed food substances). Food that is eaten must be broken down by digestion into small molecules that can be absorbed into the blood and then delivered to the cells. Some of these nutrients are then used as the ingredients for manufacturing new substances and body parts. The anabolic manufacturing process, called **synthesis,** requires the input of energy. Energy needed by cells is liberated from food molecules by a complex series of catabolic chemical reactions referred to as **cellular respiration.** Oxygen is required for cellular respiration. During this process nutrients used as fuel are slowly broken down, and the energy released is packaged within a special energy-holding molecule called **ATP (adenosine triphosphate).**

Metabolic activities occur continuously in every living cell and must be carefully regulated

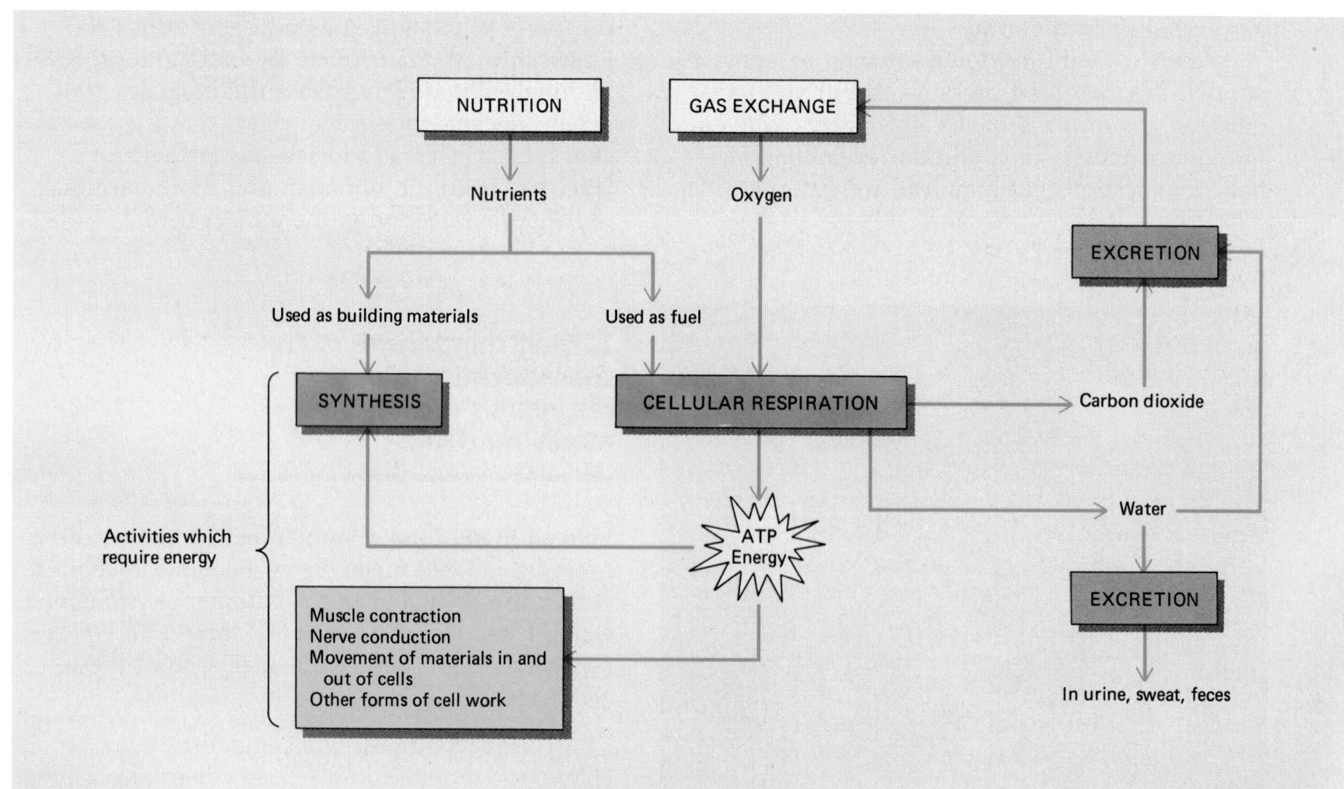

FIGURE 1-3

Interaction of metabolic activities. Some of the nutrients provided by proper nutrition are used to synthesize new substances and cell parts, while others are used as fuel for cellular respiration, a process that captures energy stored in food. The energy is needed for synthesis and for other cellular activities. Cellular respiration also requires oxygen, which is provided by the process of gas exchange. Wastes from the cells such as carbon dioxide and water must be excreted from the body. These interdependent processes are part of the body's metabolism.

to maintain a constant internal environment, or steady state, for the body. The organism must "know" when to manufacture what, or when more nutrients or energy are required. On the other hand, it must not produce too much of any substance. When enough of a product has been made, the manufacturing mechanisms must be turned off. The body is not equipped with a control panel filled with shiny buttons and levers, but it does possess sophisticated and precise control mechanisms. These mechanisms are self-regulating, and they work to maintain the internal steady state of the body within narrow limits.

The automatic tendency to maintain a relatively constant internal environment is called **homeostasis,** or **homeodynamics.** The mechanisms designed to maintain the steady state are **homeostatic mechanisms,** or **homeodynamic mechanisms.** The concept of homeostasis is so central to an understanding of physiology that we will examine it in more detail in a later section of this chapter and throughout the book.

3. **Responsiveness.** Living things respond to stimuli (changes that can cause a response) in the external environment and within the body itself. When danger threatens, you run or fight. When a change in the steady state of the body signals that you are hungry, you find food and eat.

4. **Growth and development.** Instances of growth are apparent in the nonliving world, such as a snowball enlarging as it rolls downhill. However, this type of size increase occurs by adding on materials to the outside. Living things grow by taking in raw materials such as food from the environment and using them to synthesize new living cells and tissues.

Growth is only one aspect of development. Cells must also specialize to perform specific functions, a process known as **cellular differentiation.** From the undifferentiated fertilized egg, more than 100 distinct types of cells develop in the human body. The structure of each of these cell types is adapted to perform a specific function or group of functions. For example, as a muscle cell differentiates, it assumes an elongated shape and produces the proteins that enable the cell to contract. As a red blood cell differentiates, it produces large quantities of hemoglobin, enabling the cell to carry out its task of oxygen transport.

5. **Reproduction.** One of the unique features of living organisms is their ability to produce offspring. We perpetuate ourselves by producing a new generation.

6. **Adaptation.** Articles manufactured by human beings are usually designed according to their intended use. Among vehicles, for instance, a truck has much greater cargo capacity than a family car but probably could carry fewer passengers. A bus could carry more passengers than the car. The distinctive design features of each of these machines fit them for their intended use.

In a somewhat analogous fashion, living things have features that fit them for their environment and their lifestyles. These features are known as **adaptations,** and all organisms, including human beings, have them. The thumb, which makes possible the manipulative grasp of the human hand, is a human adaptation, as is the upright, two-legged stance that allows us to use our hands for purposes other than locomotion. In addition, humans have a highly developed brain and larynx, which make symbolic language possible; a specialized placement of the eyes, which is necessary for exact depth perception; and much more.

Over the course of many generations, a species[1] may adapt to changes in the environment. This ability to stay in tune with new environmental conditions helps ensure the survival of the species.

The human body is precisely organized

One of the most striking features of life is its exquisite organization. The human body is not a shapeless heap. It is composed of many specialized parts, different in both form and function. The functions of these parts are elaborately coordinated to maintain the dynamic state called life. Just as an automobile mechanic must know how each part of an engine works to understand how the engine functions, we too must learn how the parts of the human body work before we can understand how the body functions as an integrated unit.

As in all complex organisms, there are several levels of structural organization in the human body (Fig. 1-4). The simplest is the **chemical level** consisting of atoms and molecules. **Atoms** are the

[1] A species is a population of organisms that interbreed in their natural environment to produce fertile offspring. Cows and horses are separate species.

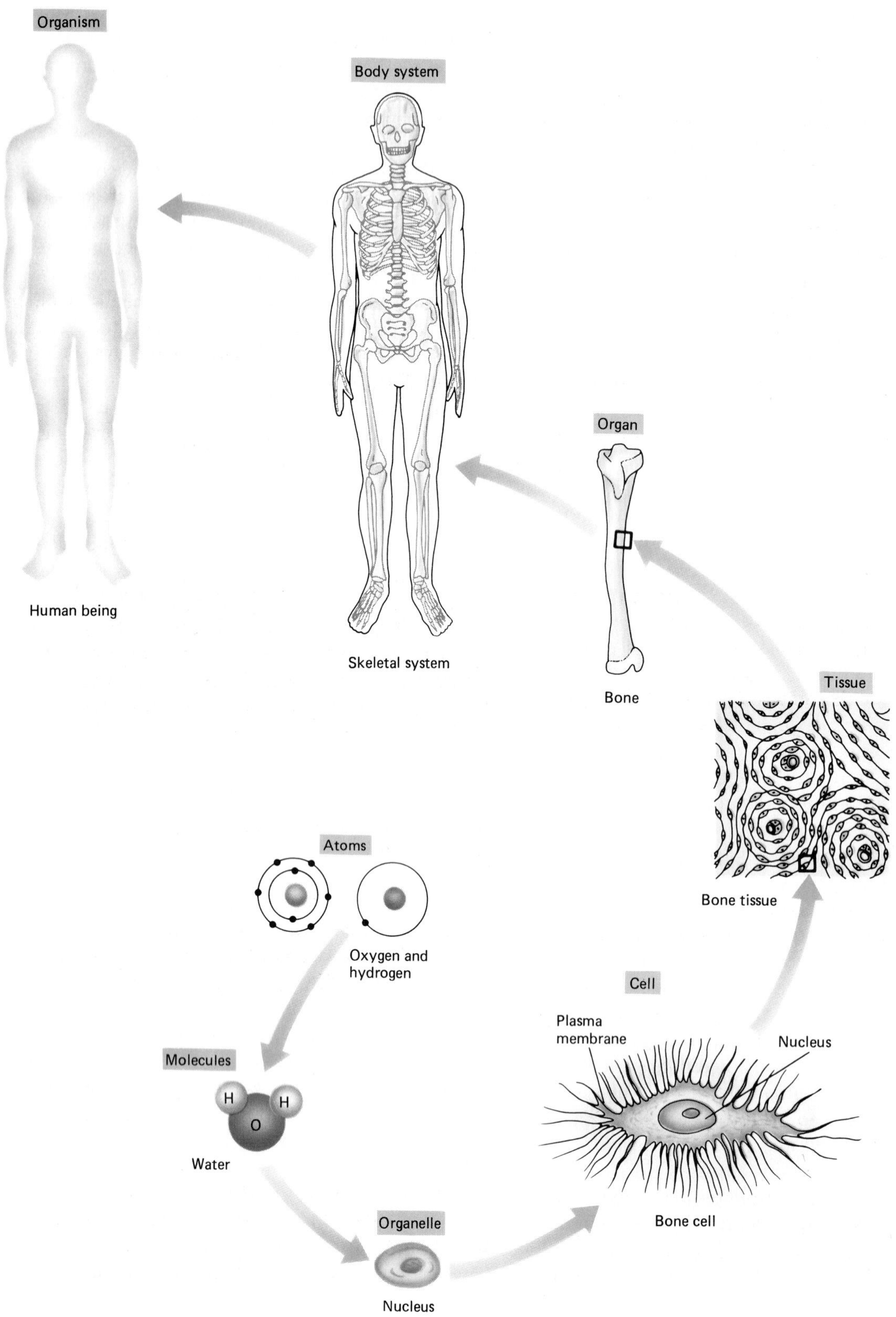

FIGURE 1-4

Levels of structural organization in the human body. Note the hierarchy from simple to complex.

basic units of all matter. An atom is the smallest amount of a chemical element (pure chemical substance such as iron, carbon, or calcium) that retains the characteristic properties of that element. Atoms can combine chemically to form **molecules.** For example, two atoms of hydrogen combine with one atom of oxygen to produce a molecule of water.

In our hierarchy of organization, the next most complex level is the **cellular level.** In living organisms atoms and molecules associate in specific ways to form cells. Cells are the basic building blocks of the body. They are the smallest units of living material capable of carrying on all the activities necessary for life. The human body is composed of about 75 trillion cells of more than 100 distinct types, such as blood cells, nerve cells, and muscle cells.

Although cells vary in size and shape according to their function, most are so small that they are visible only with a microscope. Each cell consists of specialized cell parts called **organelles.** One organelle, the **plasma membrane,** surrounds the cell and regulates substances entering or leaving it. Another, the **nucleus,** serves as the information and control center. Several other kinds of organelles scattered throughout the cell perform specific functions such as manufacturing needed substances or breaking down fuel molecules to provide energy.

In complex organisms like human beings, cells associate to form tissues. A **tissue** is a group of closely associated cells specialized to perform a particular function or group of functions. The four main types of tissue in the body are **muscle tissue, nervous tissue, connective tissue,** and **epithelial tissue.**

Various types of tissue may be organized into functional structures called **organs,** such as the brain, stomach, or heart. The heart consists mainly of a type of muscle tissue called cardiac muscle, but it is covered by epithelial tissue and also contains connective and nervous tissue.

A coordinated group of tissues and organs makes up a **body system,** or **organ system.** The circulatory system is an example of such an organ system. It consists of the heart, blood vessels, blood, lymph structures, and several other organs. We can identify ten different body systems. Working together with far greater precision and complexity than the most complicated machine designed by human beings, the body systems make up the complex living **organism**—that is, you yourself.

The body systems work together to maintain homeostasis

Just as an automobile has an electrical system, an engine, a transmission system, an air-conditioning system, and still others, so too the human body is composed of systems that work together to keep the body functioning. A body system consists of a group of organs and tissues that cooperate to perform specific functions. Table 1-1 summarizes and Figure 1-5 illustrates the systems of the human body.

The integumentary system provides a protective covering

The **integumentary system** consists of the *skin* and its *glands, nails,* and *hair.* Its job is to protect the body from injury, infection, and fluid loss. The sweat glands and blood vessels of the integumentary system help maintain a constant body temperature. Sensory receptors within the skin help keep the body in touch with the external environment.

Skeletal and muscular systems function in support and movement

The *skeletal* and *muscular* systems function together as a single mechanical system to permit effective body movement. Bones act as levers that transmit mechanical forces generated by muscle contractions.

The **skeletal system** consists of *bones, cartilage, ligaments,* and associated structures. In addition to its function in body movement, this system acts to support and protect the body. Without a skeletal system the body might resemble a giant jellyfish—a soft, spineless mass of tissues and organs. Other important jobs performed by the skeletal system include calcium and phosphorus storage and manufacture of blood cells.

The **muscular system** includes the large, *skeletal muscles* that enable us to move about at will and to breathe. *Cardiac muscle,* which makes up most of the heart, works involuntarily to pump blood. Many organs are equipped with *smooth muscles* that also function involuntarily. For example, smooth muscles in the walls of blood vessels help to maintain blood pressure, and those in the walls of the digestive tract help to mix the contents of the digestive system and move them along.

Nervous and endocrine systems regulate life processes

The nervous and endocrine systems continuously monitor body activities and adjust them appropriately in order to maintain a steady state. These systems determine what kinds of responses we make to changes in the body or in the external environment.

Sensory receptors and organs are components of the **nervous system** that keep us informed of changes in the world around us and of fluctuations in the body's steady state. The *nerves* serve as communication lines, transmitting messages from the sensory receptors to the *brain* and *spinal cord,* the main control centers of the body. These messages are evaluated and decisions are made within the brain and spinal cord. Then the decisions are transmitted over other nerves to the appropriate muscles or glands, which carry out the actual response.

TABLE 1-1

The body systems

System	Components	Functions	Homeostatic ability
Integumentary	Skin, hair, nails, sweat glands	Covers and protects body	Sweat glands help control body temperature; as barrier, skin helps maintain steady state
Skeletal	Bones, cartilage, ligaments	Supports body, protects; muscles attach to bones; provides calcium storage; blood cell formation	Helps maintain constant calcium level in blood
Muscular	Skeletal muscle, cardiac muscle, smooth muscle	Moves parts of skeleton, locomotion; pumps blood; aids movement of internal materials	Ensures such vital functions as nutrition through body movements; smooth muscle maintains blood pressure; cardiac muscle circulates the blood
Nervous	Nerves and sense organs, brain and spinal cord	Receives stimuli from external and internal environment, conducts impulses, integrates activities of other systems	Principal regulatory system
Endocrine	Pituitary, adrenal, thyroid, and other ductless glands	Regulates body chemistry and many body functions	Regulates metabolic activities and blood levels of various substances
Circulatory	Heart, blood vessels, blood; lymph and lymph structures	Transports materials from one part of body to another; defends body against disease	Transports oxygen, nutrients, hormones; removes wastes; maintains water and ionic balance of tissues
Respiratory	Lungs and air passageways	Exchanges gases between blood and external environment	Maintains adequate blood oxygen content; eliminates carbon dioxide
Digestive	Mouth, esophagus, stomach, intestines, liver, pancreas	Ingests and digests foods, absorbs them into blood	Maintains adequate supplies of fuel molecules and building materials
Urinary	Kidney, bladder, and associated ducts	Excretes metabolic wastes; removes substances present in excess from blood	Regulates blood chemistry in conjunction with endocrine system
Reproductive	Testes, ovaries, and associated structures	Reproduction; provides for continuation of species	Passes on genetic endowment of individual; maintains secondary sex characteristics

The **endocrine system** consists of glands without ducts known as endocrine glands. These glands secrete **hormones,** chemical messengers that help regulate the activities of other tissues and organs. Hormones are transported by the blood to other regions of the body, where target tissues bearing specific hormone receptors are affected by them. There the chemical messengers may trigger a particular response. The principal endocrine glands are illustrated in Figure 1-5.

The *hypothalamus* of the brain is the link between the nervous and endocrine systems. The hypothalamus regulates the *pituitary gland.* Sometimes referred to as the master gland, the pituitary gland releases growth hormone as well as hormones that regulate other endocrine glands.

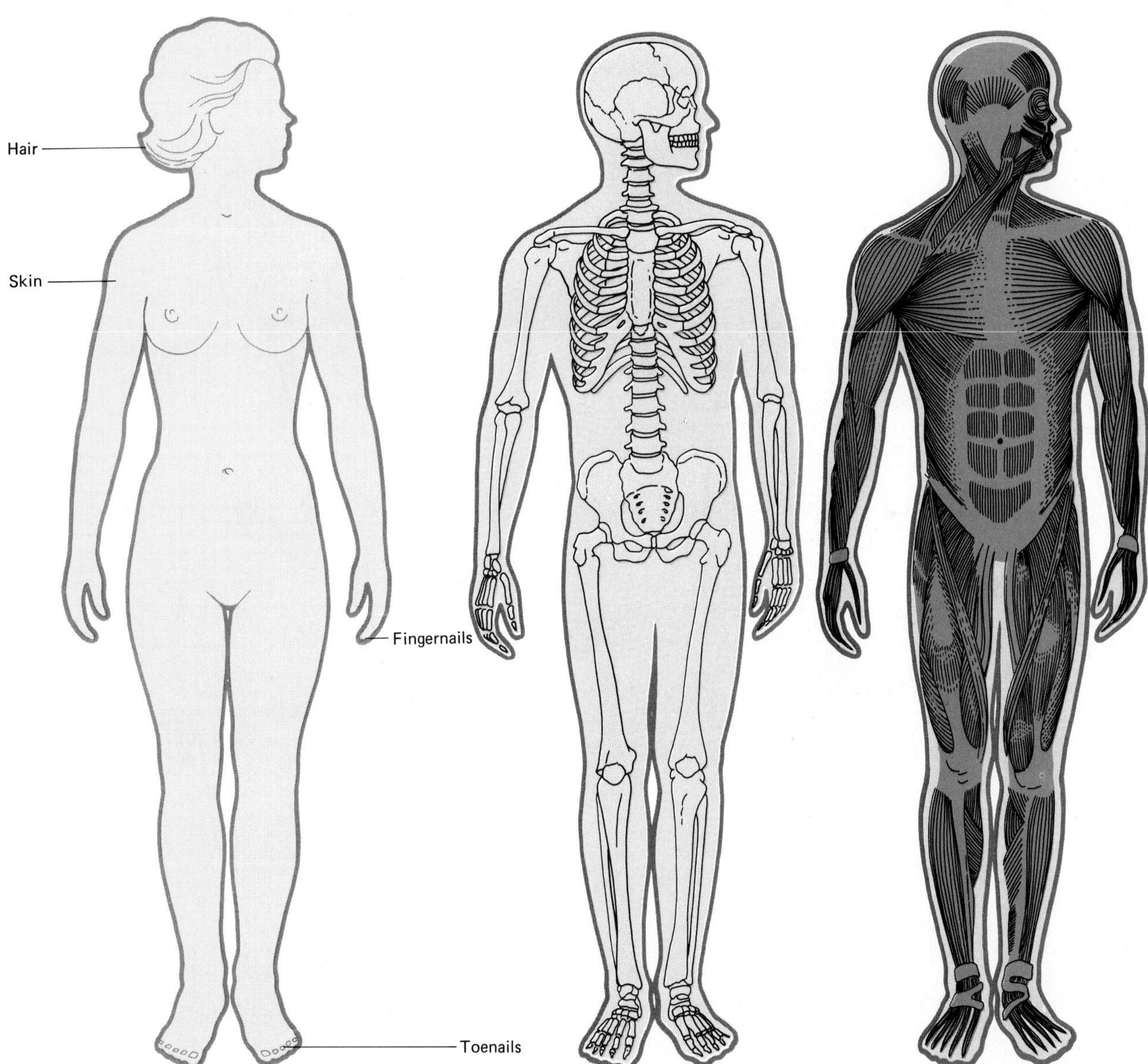

FIGURE 1-5

The principal systems of the human body.

(1) **The integumentary system.** This system consists of the skin and the structures derived from it. The integumentary system protects the body, helps regulate body temperature, and receives stimuli such as pressure, pain, and temperature.

(2) **The skeletal system.** Consisting of bones and cartilage, this system helps to support and protect the body.

(3) **The muscular system.** This system consists of the large skeletal muscles that enable us to move, as well as the cardiac muscle of the heart and the smooth muscle of the internal organs.

The *adrenal glands* release hormones that help us respond quickly to emergencies, and other hormones that regulate salt and fluid balance. Hormones from the *thyroid gland* regulate the rate of metabolism, while parathyroid hormone from the *parathyroid glands* helps regulate calcium metabolism. Among the other endocrine glands are the *islets of Langerhans* in the pancreas, which regulate the blood-sugar level, and the *gonads*—ovaries and testes—which secrete reproductive hormones.

Several systems run the machinery of the body

The cells of each tissue and organ require a continuous supply of nutrients and oxygen and a means of disposing of wastes. Body systems adapted to handle these needs are the circulatory system, respiratory system, digestive system, and urinary system.

As the transportation system of the body, the **circulatory system** delivers absorbed nutrients and oxygen to all the cells of the body and carries

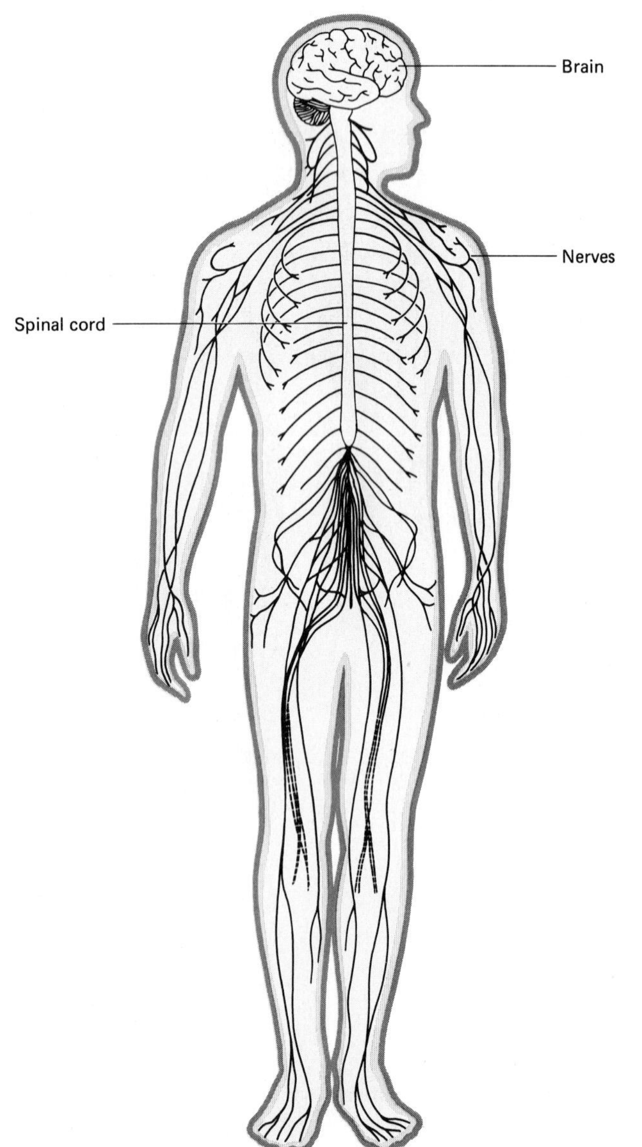

(4) **The nervous system.** The brain, spinal cord, sense organs, and nerves make up this system. The nervous system is the principal regulatory system.

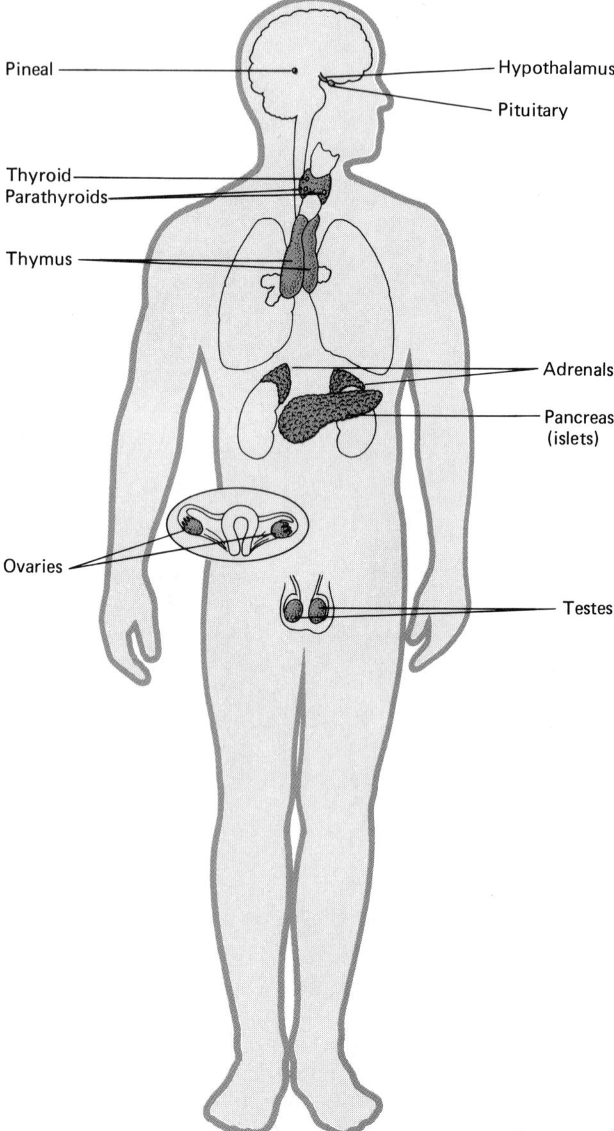

(5) **The endocrine system.** This system consists of the ductless glands that release hormones. It works with the nervous system in regulating metabolic activities.

waste from the cells to the organs that dispose of it. Hormones are also transported by the circulatory system. Included as part of the circulatory system are the *cardiovascular system,* which circulates the blood, and the *lymphatic system,* which is the body's principal defense system.

The **cardiovascular system** consists of the *heart,* the *blood,* and the *blood vessels.* From the heart, blood flows through arteries to the various organs of the body. Arteries branch into smaller and smaller vessels until the blood flows through the tiny, thin-walled capillaries. Here actual exchange of materials between the blood and cells takes place. Then blood is returned to the heart through the veins.

As blood flows through the capillaries some of its liquid component, called plasma, is forced out into the tissues through the leaky walls of these tiny blood vessels. Once it leaves the blood this fluid is known as *interstitial fluid* or *tissue fluid*. It keeps the cells moist and serves as the medium in which needed materials are delivered to the cells. As excess interstitial fluid accumu-

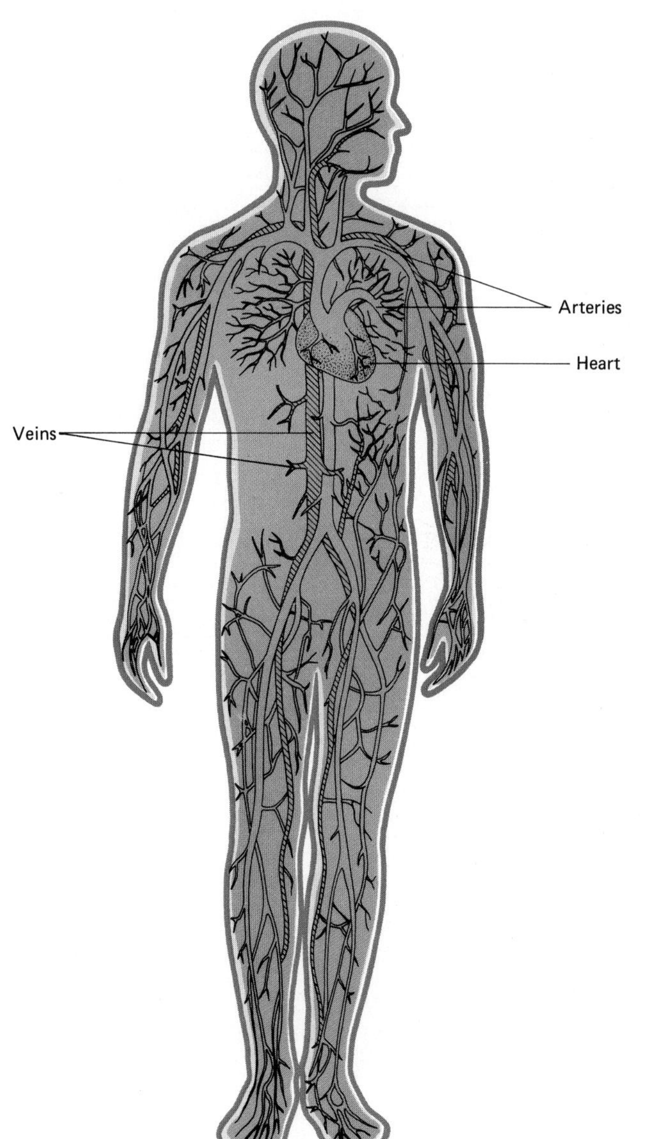

(6a) **The cardiovascular system** is a subsystem of the circulatory system. It serves as the transportation system of the body.

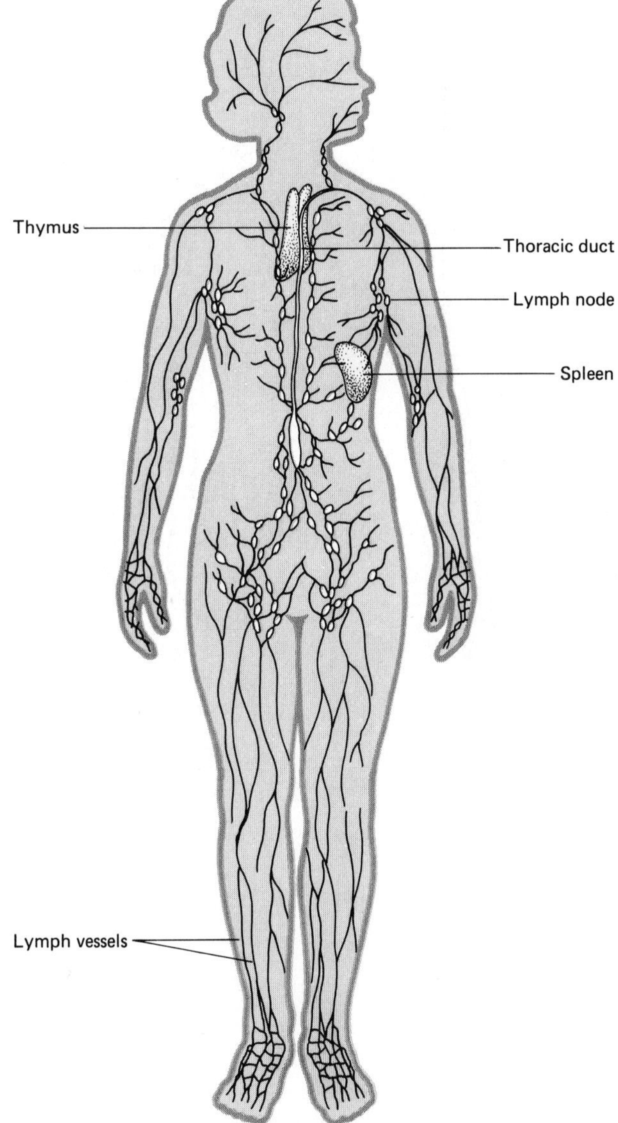

(6b) **The lymphatic system** is a subsystem of the circulatory system. This system returns excess tissue fluid to the blood and defends the body against disease.

lates it passes into the vessels of the **lymphatic system** and becomes the *lymph.* As it flows through the lymphatic system, lymph is filtered within *lymph nodes.* Lymph nodes produce cells needed for the body's defense against invading microorganisms. Eventually lymph is returned to the blood through two small ducts that lead into veins in the shoulder region.

In order to carry out the reactions of cellular respiration, cells require oxygen as well as fuel molecules. Oxygen is delivered to the blood by the **respiratory system,** which also removes carbon dioxide (a metabolic waste product) from the body. Organs of the respiratory system include the *air passageways* and the *lungs.*

Our food is digested by the **digestive system** which consists of the *digestive tract* and *accessory glands.* Food taken in through the mouth passes in sequence through the *pharynx* (back of the throat), *esophagus, stomach, small intestine,* and (if not absorbed into the circulatory system) the *large intestine.* The accessory glands—*salivary glands,*

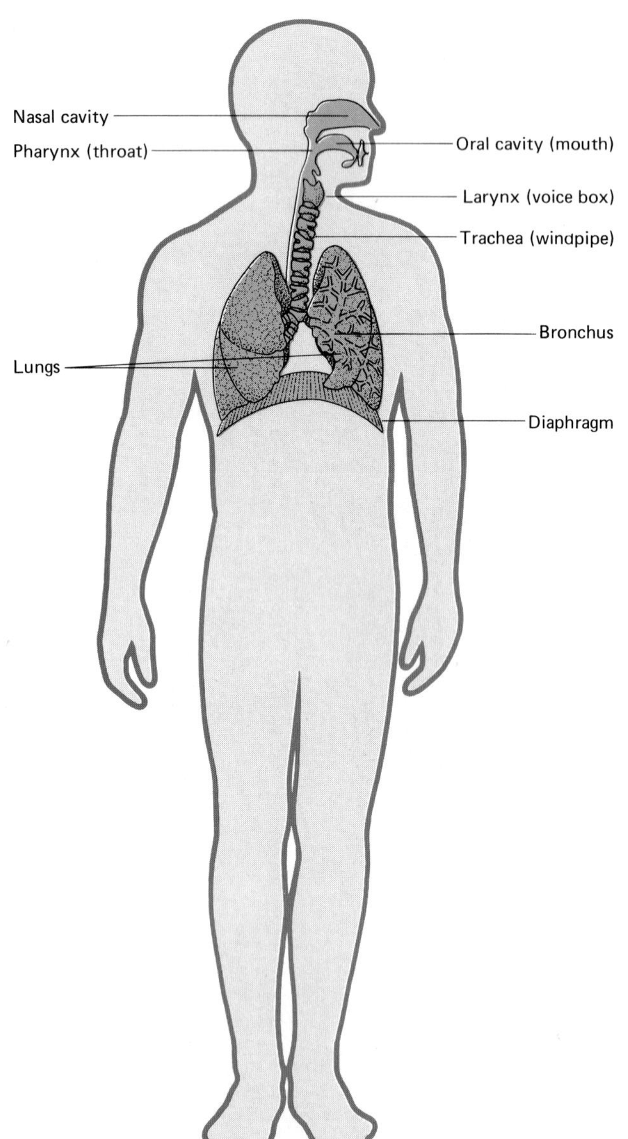

(7) **The respiratory system.** Consisting of the lungs and air passageways, this system supplies oxygen to the blood and eliminates carbon dioxide.

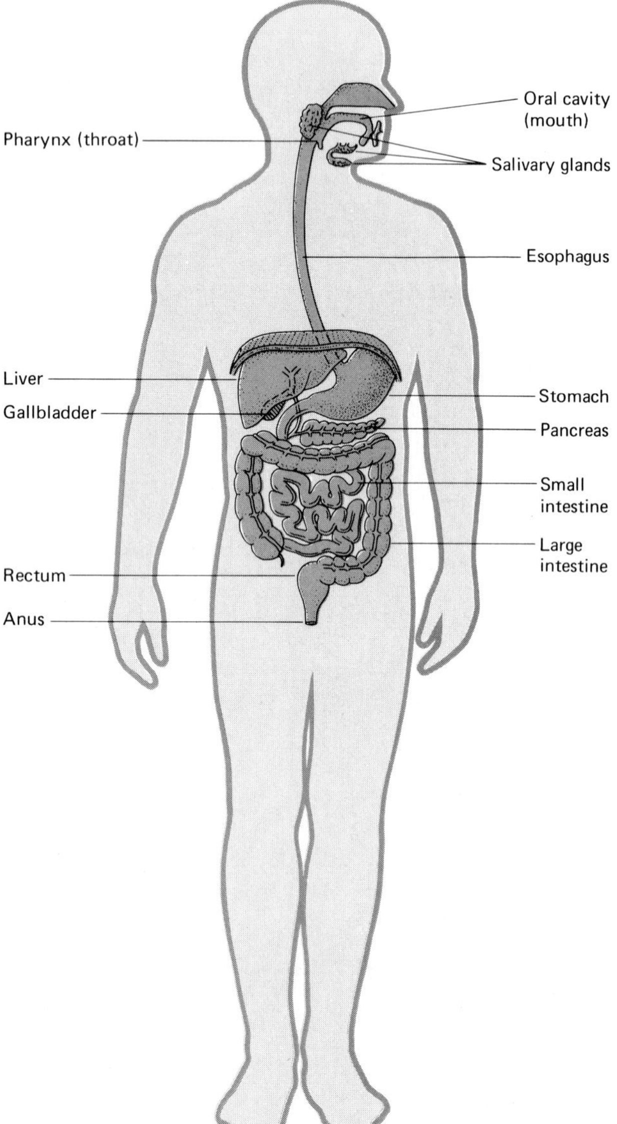

(8) **The digestive system.** The digestive tract and accessory organs mechanically and chemically break down food and eliminate wastes.

liver, and *pancreas*—secrete digestive juices containing *enzymes* that chemically break down food molecules. As food passes through the digestive tract it is mechanically and chemically broken down into smaller components that can be absorbed into the blood. Undigested and unabsorbed food materials pass out of the digestive tract through the anus as feces.

Metabolic waste disposal is mainly the job of the **urinary system.** The *kidneys* produce urine and are extremely important in maintaining the steady state of the blood and tissues. With the help of certain hormones, the kidneys maintain fluid and salt balance. They accomplish this by disposing of excess substances while carefully retaining materials that are in short supply. In addition to the kidneys, the urinary system consists of the *ureters,* which transport urine to the *urinary bladder* for storage, and the *urethra,* which delivers urine from the body.

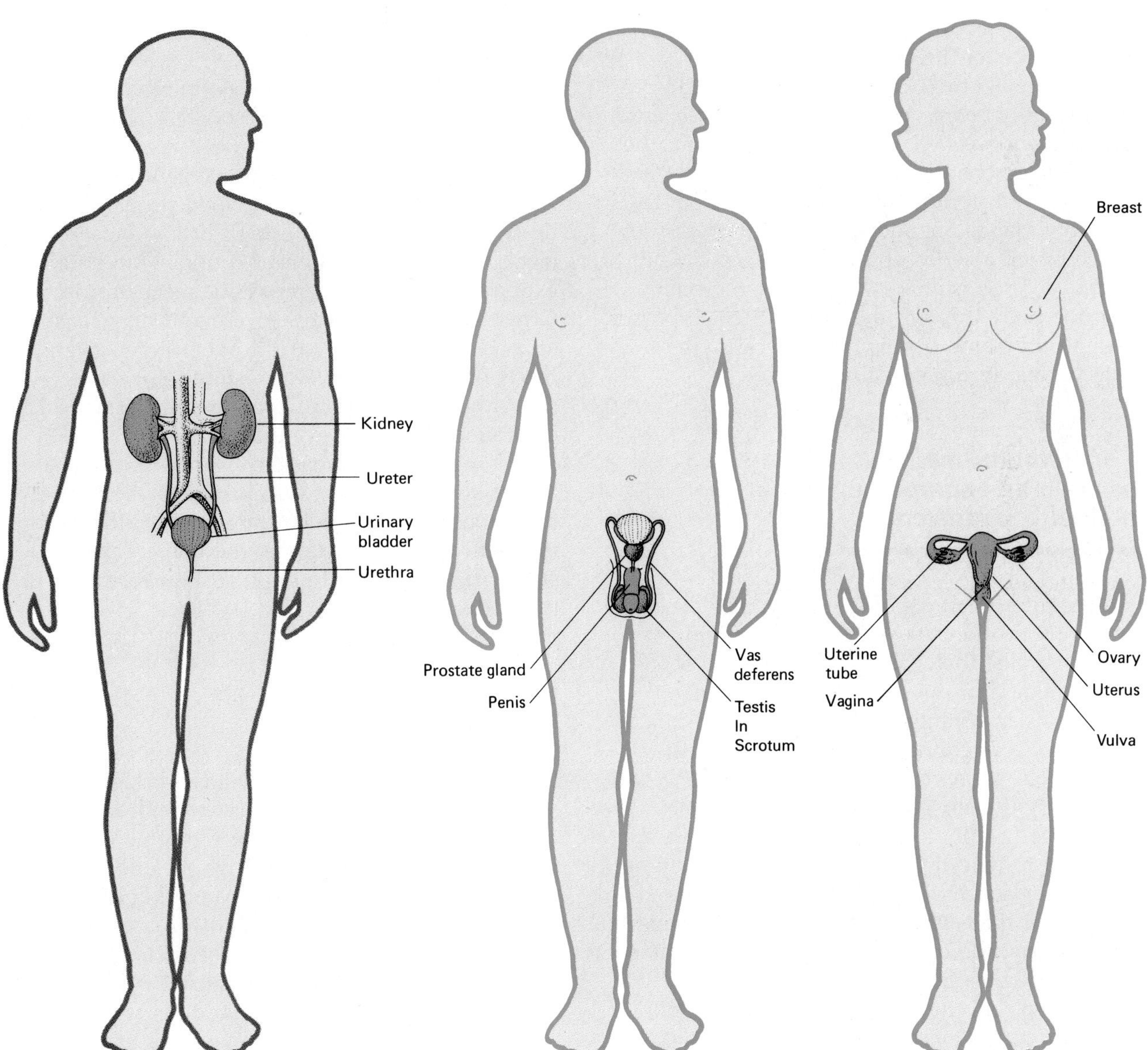

(9) **Urinary system.** The kidneys remove wastes and excess materials from the blood and produce urine. This system helps regulate blood chemistry.

(10) **Male and female reproductive systems.** Each reproductive system consists of gonads and associated structures. The reproductive system is responsible for maintaining the sexual characteristics as well as perpetuating the species.

The reproductive system perpetuates the species

The **reproductive system** provides for the production of gametes (sperm and eggs), fertilization of an egg (ovum), and incubation of the developing offspring. Organs of the female reproductive system include the *ovaries, uterine tubes, uterus, vagina, vulva,* and *breasts.* The ovaries (female gonads or reproductive glands) produce ova and release the female hormones estrogen and progesterone. Each month an ovum passes into a uterine tube, where it may be fertilized. If fertilized, the ovum is moved to the uterus, where the developing organism is incubated. The vagina receives the penis during sexual intercourse and serves as part of the birth canal.

In the male the reproductive system consists of the *testes, scrotum, penis, ducts that convey sperm,* and *accessory glands.* Located in the scrotum, the testes (male gonads) produce sperm and the male hormone testosterone. Fluid secretions from the accessory glands are added to the sperm as they pass through a series of ducts on their way out of the body. The resulting semen is then ejected from the body through the urethra, which passes through the penis, and is deposited into the female vagina during sexual intercourse.

Homeostatic mechanisms maintain an appropriate internal environment

In an adult human about 75 trillion cells are organized to form the tissues, organs, and body systems. "Strange that a harp of a thousand strings should remain in tune so long," remarked Sir William Osler, a nineteenth century physician. It still seems strange today that, complex as the human body is, remarkably little goes wrong with it. You might even say that it lasts a lifetime!

The body's fine performance record is due in large part to its exquisite control mechanisms for maintaining a constant, appropriate internal environment. If the cells of the body are to survive and function, the composition of the fluids that bathe them must be carefully maintained. An appropriate concentration of nutrients, oxygen and other gases, electrically charged particles called ions, and various other chemicals must be available at all times. In addition, internal temperature and pressure must be maintained within narrow limits.

As already defined, the term **homeostasis,** or **homeodynamics,** refers to the body's automatic tendency to maintain its steady state within narrow limits. First coined by the physiologist Walter Cannon, the term homeostasis is derived from the Greek words *homoios,* meaning "same," and *stasis,* "standing." Actually, the internal environment never really stays the same; it fluctuates within narrow limits. Thus, a dynamic equilibrium is maintained. For this reason, some biologists prefer the term homeodynamics.

The internal environment is carefully regulated by the interaction of many homeostatic mechanisms. All the body systems participate in these regulatory mechanisms, but most of them are ultimately controlled by the nervous and endocrine systems.

Stressors are changes in the internal or external environment that disturb homeostasis. Examples of external stressors are heat, cold, noise, abnormal pressure, or lack of oxygen. Internal stressors include changes in blood pressure, pH, or salt concentration, and high or low blood-sugar levels. Many stressors occur routinely and are expertly handled by homeostatic mechanisms. Other stressors are more severe and may cause serious disruption, or stress. When homeostatic mechanisms are unable to restore the steady state, the stress may lead to a malfunction, which can cause disease or even death.

Homeostasis is a basic concept in physiology. As we study the body systems we shall discuss numerous ways in which the systems interact to maintain the steady state of the body. Table 1-1 summarizes some of the homeostatic functions of the body systems.

Homeostatic mechanisms are feedback systems

How do homeostatic mechanisms work? Because somewhat similar mechanisms are built into some of our machines, an explanation of how one of these works will perhaps aid you in understanding homeostasis in the body. Many houses are equipped with a thermostat and furnace. When the temperature in the house begins to exceed the temperature at which the thermostat is set, the thermostat senses the change and shuts off the furnace (Fig. 1-6*a*). When the temperature falls too low, the thermostat turns the furnace on again. Although there is some fluctuation, the temperature of the house is maintained within comfortable limits. This is accomplished without

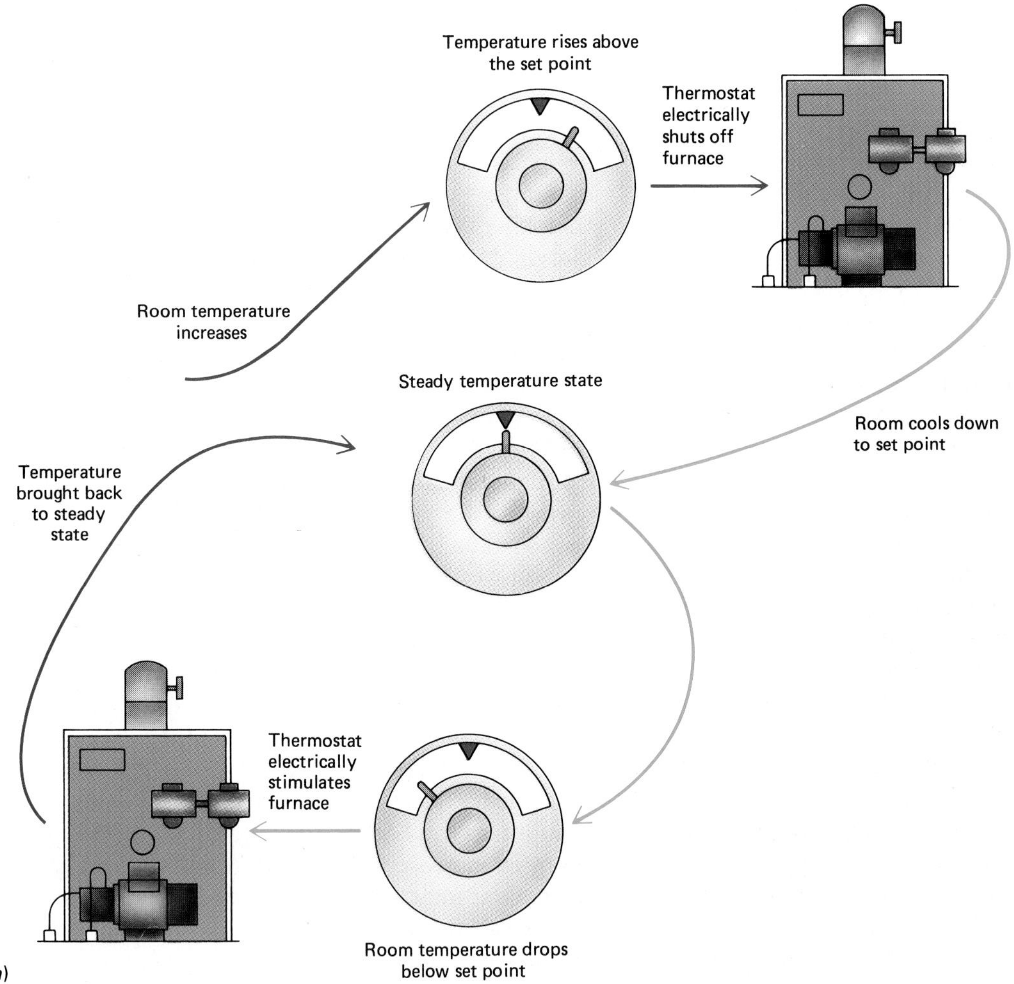

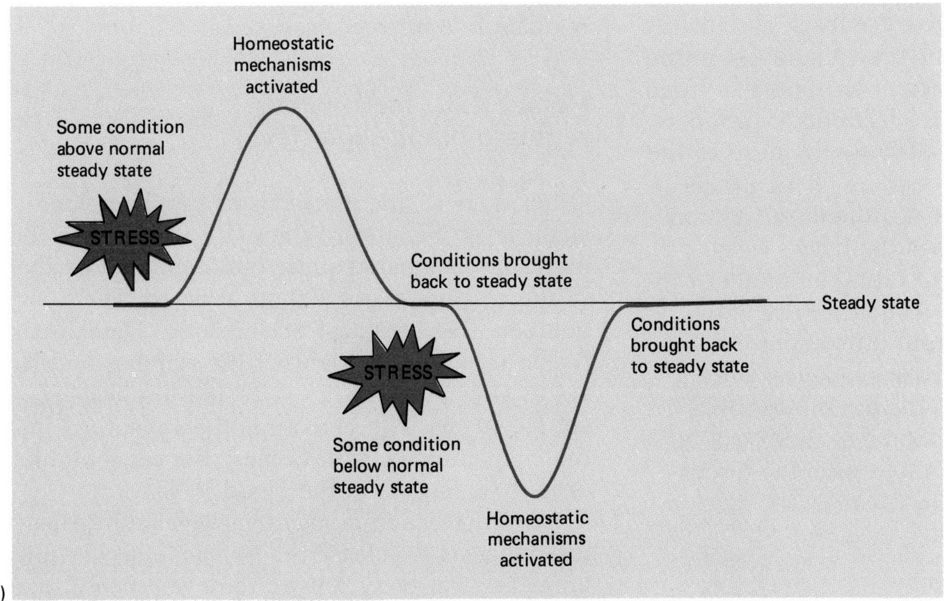

FIGURE 1-6

Homeostasis: the process of maintaining steady states. *(a)* The home furnace and thermostat illustrate the concept of negative feedback in maintaining a steady state. When the temperature rises, the thermostat is triggered to turn off the furnace. When the room temperature drops below the set level, the thermostat electrically stimulates the furnace to turn on. *(b)* Stressful stimuli, called stressors, disrupt homeostasis. In the body, any deviation from the steady state is regarded as a stress. Stress activates an appropriate homeostatic mechanism that brings conditions back toward the steady state.

any need to watch a thermometer and without any complicated apparatus for sensing such variables as outside temperature, sunlight intensity, wind velocity and direction, relative humidity, and the like.

The thermostat-furnace system, like many homeostatic mechanisms in the body, is a **feedback system.** In the body these systems are sometimes called **biofeedback systems.** Such a system consists of a cycle of events in which information about a change (in this case a change in temperature) is fed back into the system so that the regulator (the thermostat) can control the process (temperature regulation). When too much heat is generated, the increased temperature serves as input, triggering the thermostat to shut off the furnace. In this way the output can be changed to bring the temperature back to the desired steady state.

In this type of feedback system, the response counteracts the inappropriate change, thus restoring the steady state. This is a **negative feedback system,** because the response of the regulator is opposite (negative) to the output. Most homeostatic mechanisms in the body are negative feedback systems (Fig. 1-6*b*). When some condition varies too far from the steady state (either too high or too low), a control system using negative feedback brings the condition back to the steady state.

There are a few **positive feedback** systems in the body. In these systems the variation from the steady state sets off a series of changes that intensify the changes. A positive feedback cycle operates in the delivery of a baby. As the head of the baby pushes against the opening of the uterus (cervix), a reflex action causes the uterus to contract. The contraction forces the baby's head against the cervix again, resulting in another contraction, and the positive feedback cycle is repeated again and again until the baby is delivered. Many positive feedback sequences are vicious cycles that lead to disruption of steady states and even to death. Some of these will be discussed in later chapters (e.g., see the discussion of circulatory shock in Chapter 21).

Homeostatic mechanisms maintain body temperature

Human body temperature is maintained at about 37°C (98.6°F) by negative feedback mechanisms that operate somewhat like those in the home thermostat system (Fig. 1-7). When the temperature rises above normal, the change is sensed by a special "thermostat" in the hypothalamus of the brain. This temperature-regulating center sends messages by way of nerves to the sweat glands in the skin. When stimulated in this way, the sweat glands increase their secretion of perspiration. Evaporation requires heat, so as perspiration evaporates from the body surface, heat is lost from the body.

At the same time the sweat glands are being stimulated, messages are sent to the capillaries in the skin, causing them to dilate. More blood thus circulates in the skin, carrying heat to the body surface. Heat radiates from the surface. These homeostatic mechanisms help return body temperature to normal. When body temperature decreases below normal, homeostatic responses are reversed.

Should body temperature fall too low, messages from the brain cause us to shiver. The muscle contractions involved in shivering generate heat that helps raise the body temperature. Capillaries in the skin constrict so that less heat is brought to the body surface, and hormonal changes increase heat production by all body tissues. One may also help adjust body temperature by deliberate, adaptive behavior—for example, by moving into a warm location or putting on a sweater. When body temperature returns to normal, the changes are again reversed. Temperature regulation is further discussed in Chapter 26.

Homeostatic mechanisms regulate blood-sugar level

Other homeostatic mechanisms regulate blood-sugar level (Fig. 1-8). When you wake up in the morning your blood-sugar (glucose) level is about 90 mg of glucose per 100 ml of blood. Perhaps you eat a big breakfast that includes Danish pastry or a doughnut. Many of the starches and sugars in your breakfast are digested to glucose (a simple sugar). The glucose is then absorbed into the circulatory system, causing the concentration of glucose (sugar) in the blood to rise.

An increase in blood-sugar level stimulates the pancreas to release the hormone *insulin*. Insulin causes the body cells to remove glucose from the blood and stimulates the liver and muscle cells to store glucose (as glycogen). As a result, the glucose level in the blood decreases and returns to the normal fasting level of 90 mg/100 ml.

After several hours, when the glucose level of the blood begins to fall below the normal level, the pancreas releases the hormone *glucagon*. This hormone raises the blood-sugar level by stimulating the liver cells to slowly convert glycogen to glucose and thereby release their stored glucose. In this way, insulin and glucagon act in see-saw fashion to maintain a constant level—a steady state—of glucose in the blood.

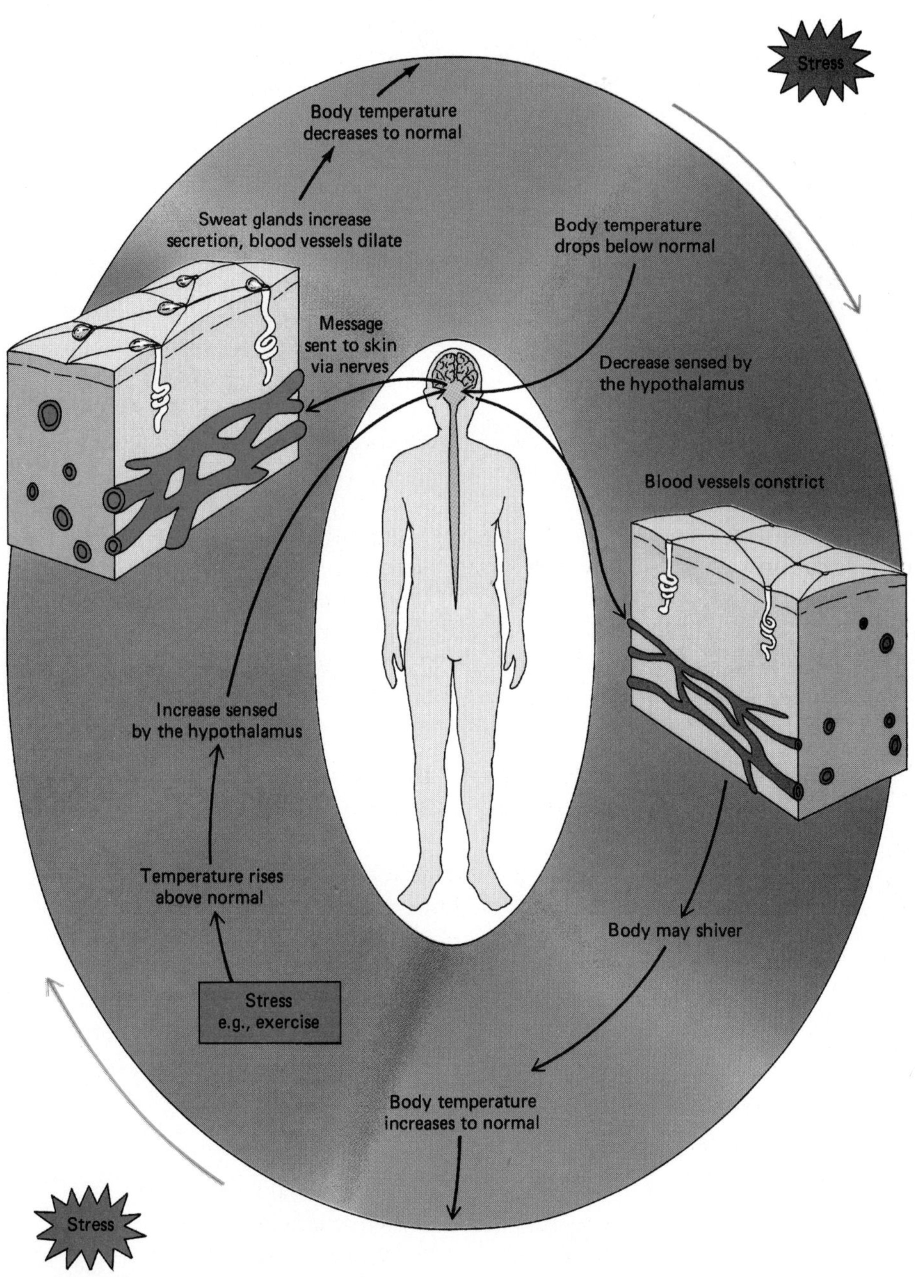

FIGURE 1-7

How body temperature is regulated by negative feedback mechanisms. An increase in body temperature above the normal range is a signal that activates homeostatic mechanisms that bring body temperature back to normal. Increased circulation of blood in the skin and increased sweating are mechanisms that help the body get rid of excess heat. When body temperature falls below the normal range, blood vessels in the skin constrict so that less body heat is carried to the skin. Shivering, in which muscle contractions generate heat, may also occur.

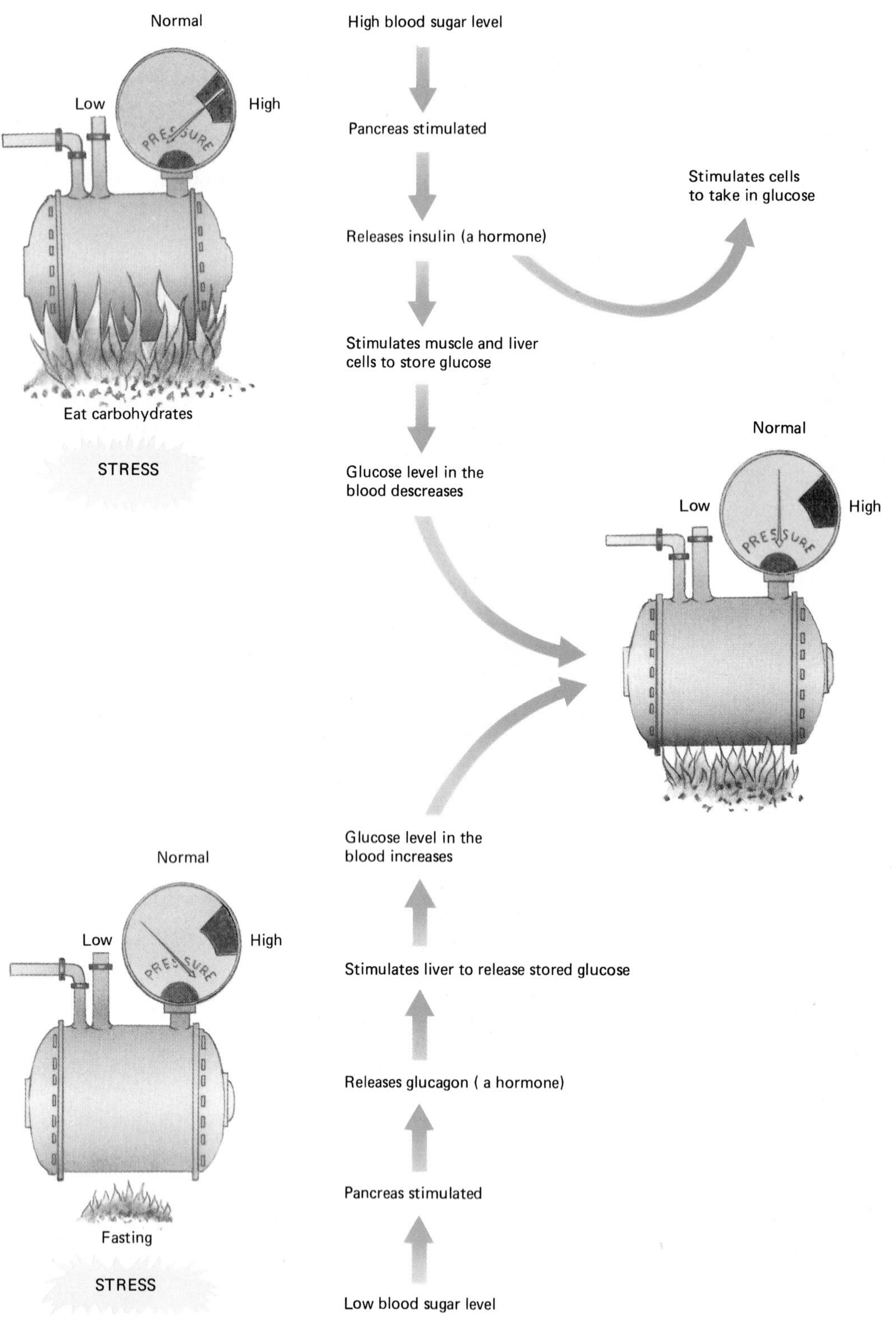

FIGURE 1-8

Homeostatic mechanisms regulate blood-sugar level. When the blood-sugar level rises above the steady state, the pancreas releases the hormone insulin, which stimulates glucose uptake by cells, causing the blood-sugar level to fall. When the level decreases below the steady state, the pancreas releases another hormone, glucagon, which causes the glucose level to rise.

The body has a definite plan

If you were to attempt to describe the human body, one of the first things you might say is that it consists of right and left halves that are mirror images; that is, it exhibits **bilateral symmetry.** Two important features that characterize us as vertebrates are the **cranium,** or brain case, and the backbone, or **vertebral column.** Humans are also mammals and so have hair, mammary (milk) glands, and four limbs, each with five digits bearing nails.

Anatomical directions are useful in identifying structures

In order to identify the structures of the body it is helpful to learn some basic terms and directions. Directional terms in human anatomy are relative, somewhat like directional terms in geography. Thus one could say that New York City is north of Baltimore but south of Bangor, Maine, or that Chicago is west of New York City but east of Portland, Oregon. Bear this in mind as you learn the anatomical directional terms. These terms are applied to the body when it is in the **anatomical position,** which means that the body is standing erect, eyes looking forward, arms at the sides of the body, and palms and toes directed forward (Fig. 1-9).

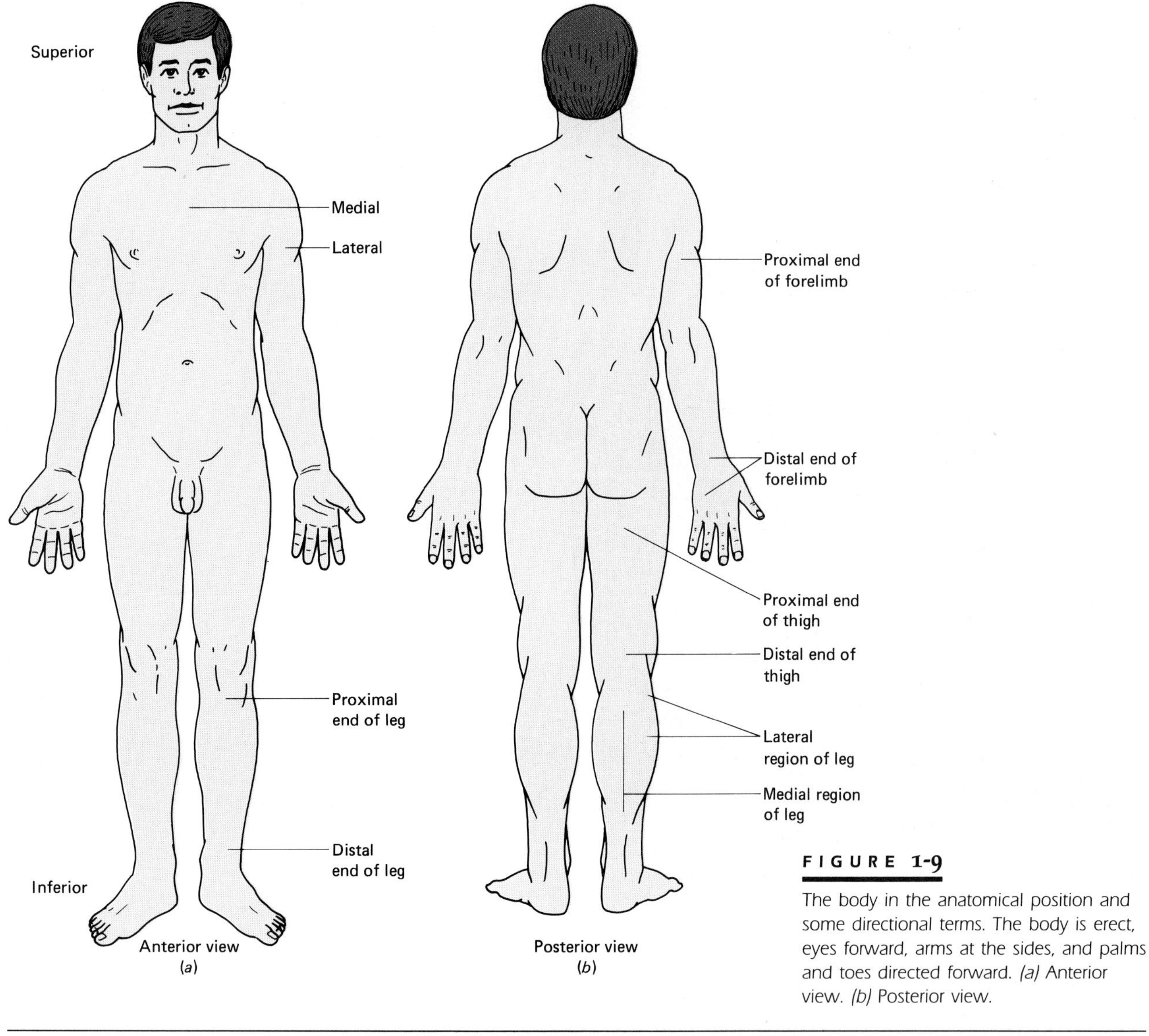

FIGURE 1-9

The body in the anatomical position and some directional terms. The body is erect, eyes forward, arms at the sides, and palms and toes directed forward. *(a)* Anterior view. *(b)* Posterior view.

1. **Superior (cephalic, craniad,** or **rostral).** Toward the head or upper part of a structure. The "North Pole" of the human body is the top of the head, its superior point (Fig. 1-9). Thus the heart is superior to the stomach because it is closer to the head.

2. **Inferior (caudad).** Have you ever wondered what the most inferior part of the body is? Anatomically, it is the soles of the feet. Inferior, far from indicating a value judgment, means located below, or toward the feet. The stomach is inferior to the heart. Inferior also refers to the lower surface of a structure. In human anatomy, the term caudad (toward the tail) is sometimes used instead of the word inferior.

3. **Anterior (ventral).** The front surface of the body. In a biped (two-legged animal) anterior is also ventral. Ventral refers to the belly-side of the organism. The stomach is anterior to the backbone. In a quadruped, these terms are used differently.

4. **Posterior (dorsal).** The rear (behind) surface of the body. Posterior and dorsal are the same in a biped. Dorsal always refers to the backside. The vertebral column is posterior to the stomach.

5. **Medial.** Closer to the midline of the body. The body axis is an imaginary line extending through the midline of the body. This main superior-inferior axis extends from the center of the top of the head to the groin. The navel is medial to the hip bone.

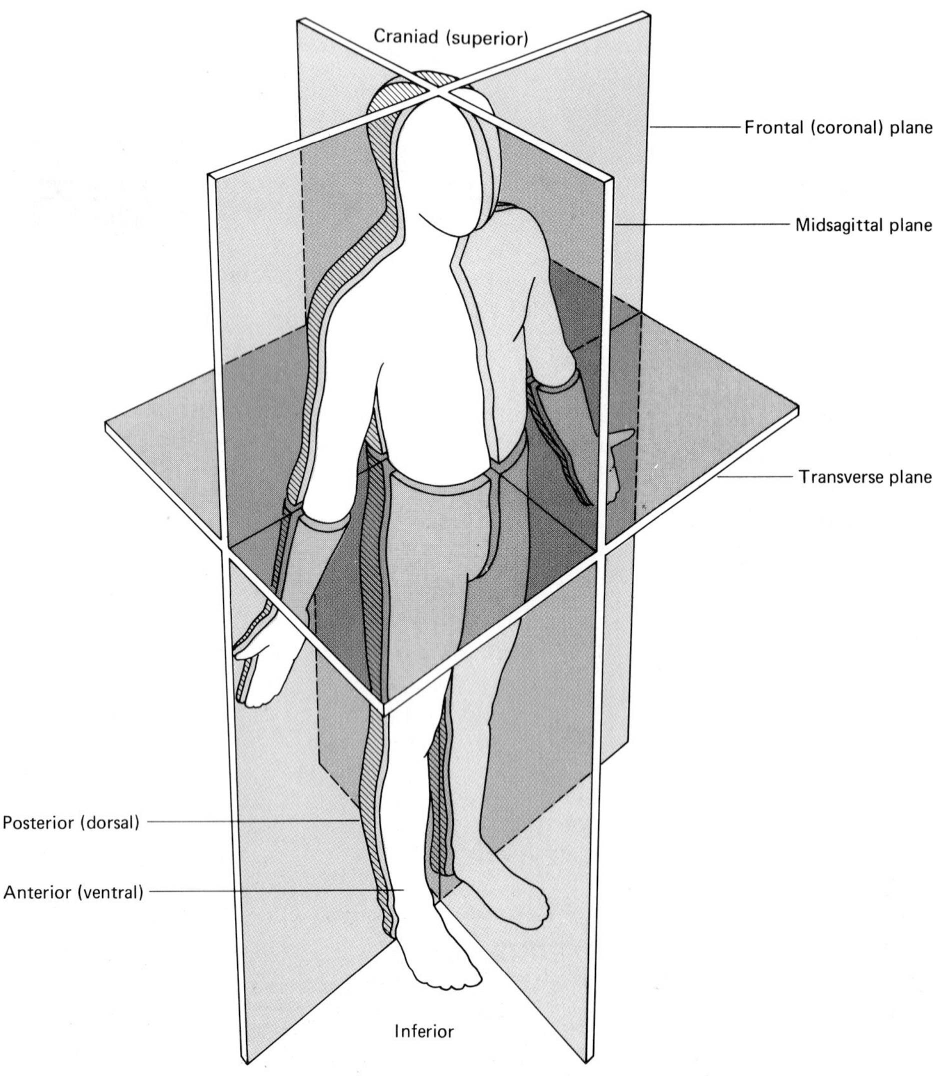

FIGURE 1-10

Planes of section. The body or its parts may be cut in sagittal, transverse, or frontal sections.

6. **Lateral.** Toward one side of the body. Thus the hip bone is lateral to the navel.

7. **Proximal.** Closer to the body midline or point of attachment to the trunk. This term is used especially in locating limb structures. Thus the wrist is proximal to the fingers.

8. **Distal.** Farther from the midline or point of attachment to the trunk. The fingers are distal to the wrist.

9. **Superficial.** Structures located toward the surface of the body. Blood vessels in the skin are superficial to those lying within the muscle.

10. **Deep.** Structures located farther inward (away from the body surface). Blood vessels in the muscle are deep to those in the skin.

11. **Parietal.** Pertaining to structures that form the wall of a body cavity; for example, the parietal peritoneum lines the abdominal cavity.

12. **Visceral.** Pertaining to an internal organ; for example, the visceral peritoneum forms the outer layer of the intestinal wall.

13. **Ipsilateral.** Located on the same side of the body. The right arm and right leg are ipsilateral.

14. **Contralateral.** Located on the opposite side of the body. The right arm and left leg are contralateral.

The body has three main planes

In studying anatomy as well as in clinical practice it is often helpful to show internal structures by cutting the body into sections, or slices. Such cuts are made along body planes, imaginary, flat surfaces that divide the body into specific parts (Fig. 1-10).

1. **Sagittal.** A sagittal plane divides the body into right and left parts. A **midsagittal** (or median) plane passes through the body axis and divides the body into two (almost) mirror-image halves.

2. **Transverse (horizontal** or **cross).** A plane at right angles to the body axis. It divides the body into superior and inferior parts.

3. **Frontal (coronal).** A plane that lies at right angles to a sagittal plane and divides the body into anterior and posterior parts.

In many diagnostic procedures bits of tissues or organs are removed from the body and sliced (sectioned) so that they can be examined by a pathologist for signs of disease. Many of the illustrations in this book include blood vessels or other structures that have been cut in various planes. Figure 1-11 illustrates a transverse (cross) section, an oblique section (a slice made at an angle) of a blood vessel, and a longitudinal (lengthwise) section.

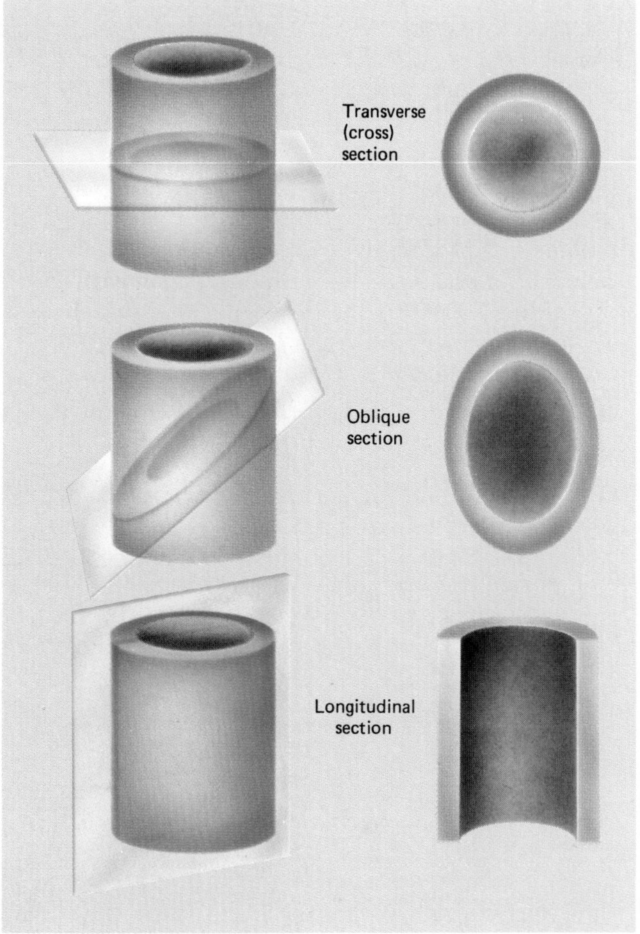

FIGURE 1-11

Sections through blood vessels. A body part such as a blood vessel may be cut in transverse, oblique, and longitudinal sections. Some organs, such as the brain, may also be cut in sagittal sections.

Specific body regions can be identified

The body may be subdivided into an **axial** portion, consisting of head, neck, and trunk, and an **appendicular** portion, consisting of the limbs. The trunk, or **torso,** consists of the thorax, abdomen, and pelvis (Fig. 1-12).

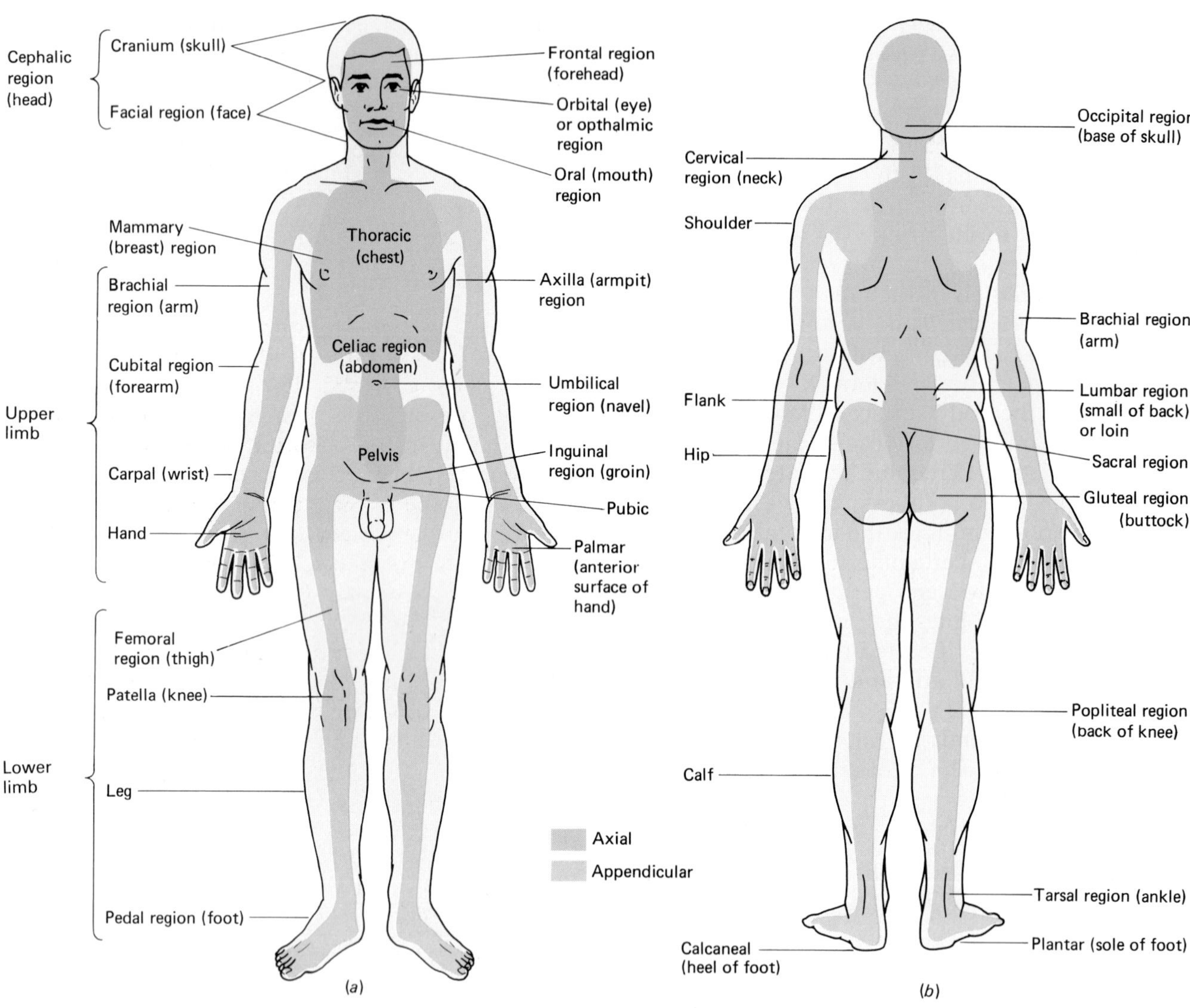

FIGURE 1-12

Some specific regions of the body. *(a)* Anterior view. *(b)* Posterior view.

Some of the terms used to indicate specific body regions or structures follow.

Region	Part of the body referred to
Abdominal	Portion of trunk below the diaphragm
Arm	Technically, the part of the upper limb between the shoulder and the elbow, as distinguished from the forearm. (Popularly, the term arm refers to the entire upper limb.)
Axillary	Armpit area
Brachial	Arm
Buccal	Inner surfaces of the cheeks
Calcaneal	Heel of foot
Carpal	Wrist
Celiac	Abdomen
Cephalic	Head
Cervical	Neck region
Costal	Ribs
Cranial	Skull
Cubital	Elbow or forearm
Cutaneous	Skin
Femoral	Thigh, the part of the lower limb between the hip and the knee
Forearm	Upper limb between the elbow and the wrist
Frontal	Forehead
Gluteal	Buttock
Groin	Depressed region between the abdomen and the thigh

Inguinal	Groin
Leg	Lower limb, especially the part from the knee to the foot
Lumbar	Loin, the region of the lower back and side, between the lowest rib and the pelvis
Mammary	Breasts
Occipital	Back of the head
Ophthalmic	Eyes
Oral	Mouth
Orbital	Bony cavity containing the eyeball
Palmar	Palm
Patellar	Knee
Pectoral	Chest
Pedal	Foot
Pelvic	Pelvis, the bony ring that girdles the lower portion of the trunk
Perineal	Region from the anus to the pubic arch; includes the region of the external reproductive structures
Plantar	Sole of the foot
Popliteal	Area behind the knee
Sacral	Base of spine
Tarsal	Ankle
Thoracic	Chest, the part of the trunk below the neck and above the diaphragm
Umbilical	Navel, depressed scar marking the site of entry of the umbilical cord in the fetus

There are two main body cavities

The body is a hollow structure. The spaces within the body, called **body cavities,** contain the internal organs, or **viscera.** The two principal body cavities are the *dorsal cavity* and the *ventral cavity* (Fig. 1-13). The bony **dorsal cavity,** located near the dorsal (posterior) body surface, may be subdivided into the **cranial cavity,** which holds the brain, and the **vertebral,** or **spinal, canal,** which contains the spinal cord. The **ventral cavity,** located near the ventral (anterior) body surface, is subdivided in turn into the **thoracic,** or chest, cavity and the **abdominopelvic cavity.**

Thoracic and abdominopelvic cavities are separated by a broad muscle, the **diaphragm,** which

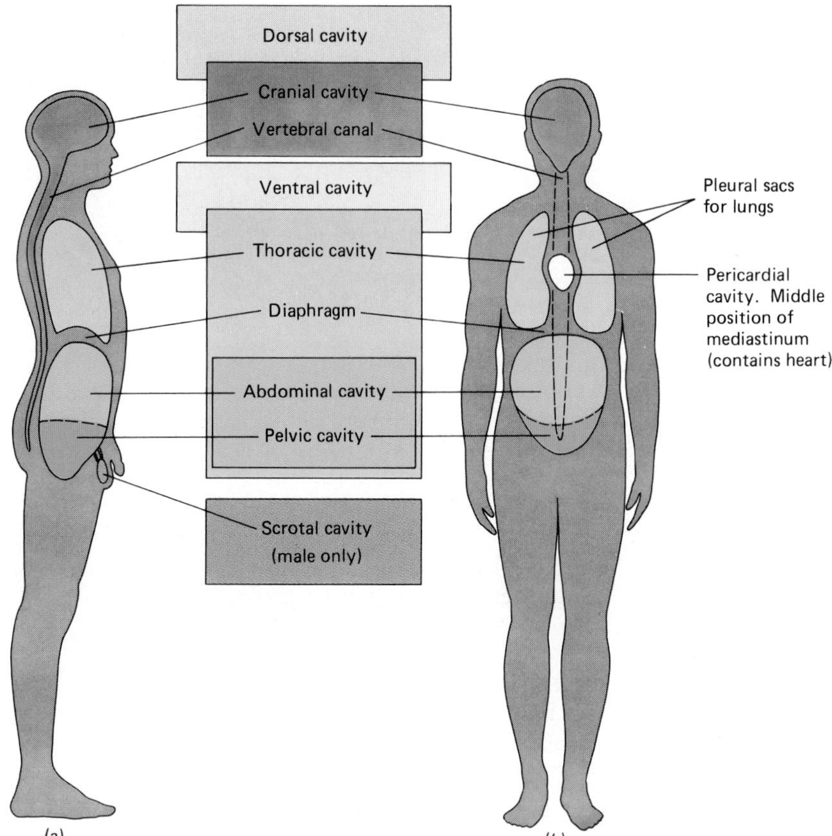

FIGURE 1-13

Principal cavities of the human body. *(a)* Lateral view of the body showing dorsal and ventral cavities and some of their subdivisions. *(b)* Anterior view, showing subdivisions of the ventral cavity. *(Figure continued on p. 28.)*

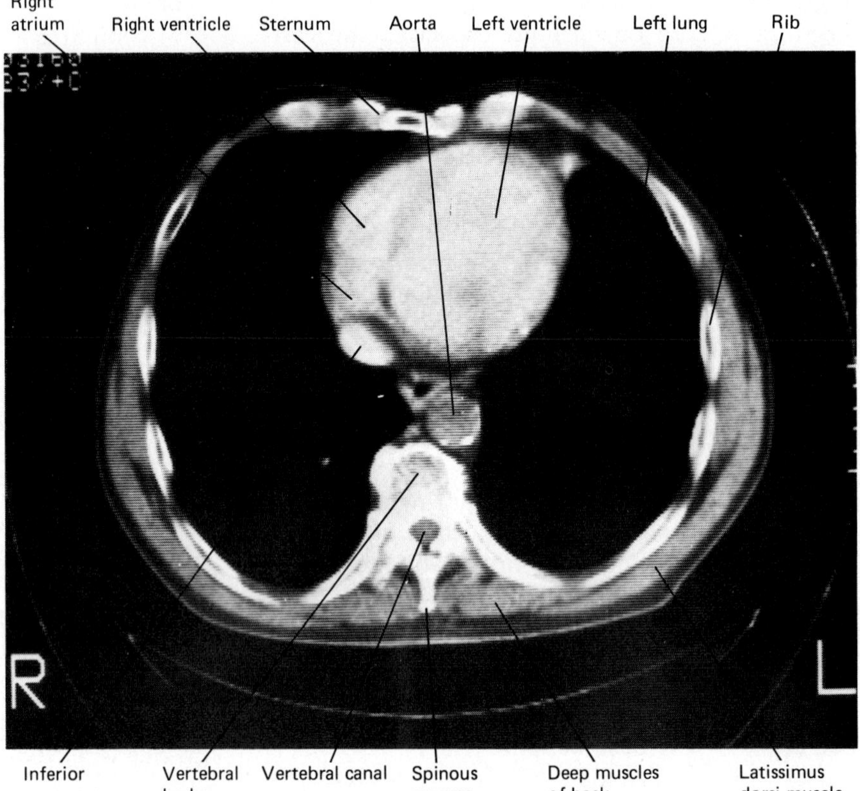

(c)

(c) and *(d)* Cross section and matching schematic drawing of the mediastinum, the region between the right and left pleural cavities. It is divided into superior, posterior, anterior, and middle regions. The superior mediastinum, containing large blood vessels, is the region above the pericardial sac, which holds the heart. The posterior mediastinum lies behind the heart and serves as a corridor through which pass the esophagus, trachea, and many large blood and lymphatic vessels. The anterior mediastinum lies between the sternum (breastbone) and the heart; it contains the thymus gland. The heart and the roots of great arteries and veins are located in the middle mediastinum.

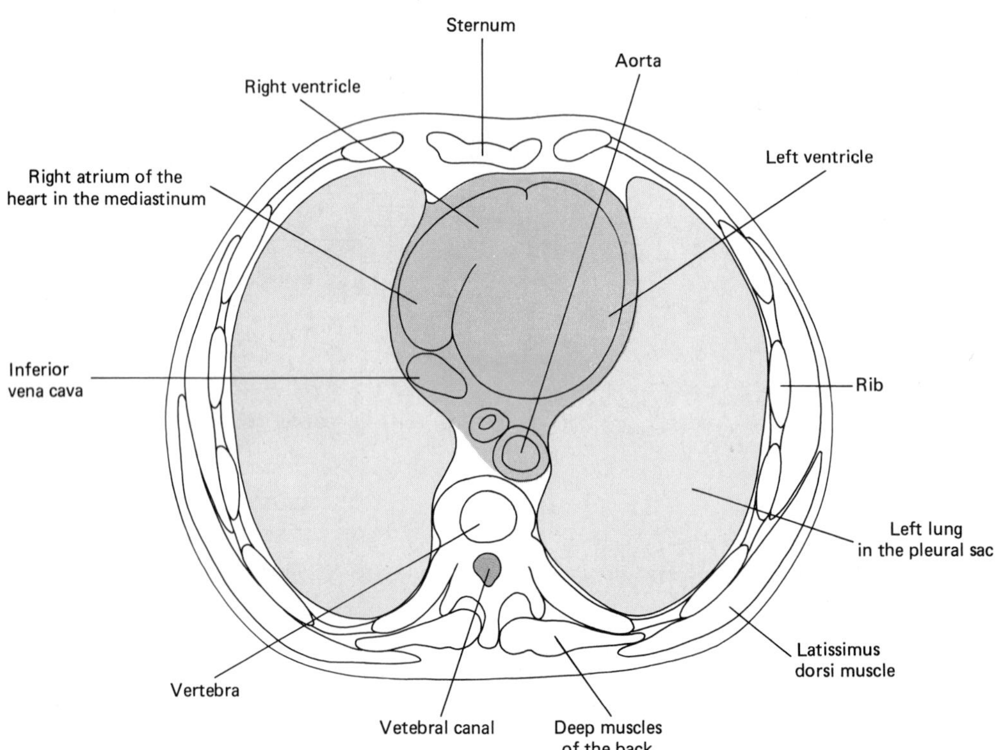

(d)

forms the floor of the thoracic cavity. Divisions of the thoracic cavity are the **pleural sacs,** each containing a lung, and the **mediastinum** between them. Within the mediastinum lies the heart, thymus gland, and parts of the esophagus and trachea. The heart is surrounded by yet another cavity, the **pericardial cavity.**

The upper portion of the abdominopelvic cavity is the **abdominal cavity,** which contains the stomach, small intestine, much of the large intestine, liver, gallbladder, pancreas, spleen, kidneys, and ureters. Although not separated by any kind of wall, the lower portion of the abdominopelvic cavity is the **pelvic cavity,** which holds the urinary bladder, part of the large intestine, and in the female, the reproductive organs. In males, the pelvic cavity has a small outpocket called the scrotal cavity, which contains the testes.

In addition to the two major body cavities and their subdivisions, several small cavities are located within the head. Among these are the oral cavity, containing the teeth and tongue; the nasal cavity within the nose; and the orbital cavities, containing the eyes.

To simplify the task of identifying internal organs or locating pain, health professionals divide the abdominopelvic cavity into four quadrants: right upper or superior, right lower or inferior, left lower or inferior, and left upper or superior (Fig. 1-14). These quadrants are established by a midsagittal and a transverse plane that pass through the umbilicus. Another system divides the abdominopelvic cavity into nine regions using two transverse and two sagittal planes. These nine regions of the abdomen are indicated in Figure 1-15.

It is important to integrate body structure and view the body as a whole

In this chapter you have been introduced to the body systems and their homeostatic functions. You have examined the principal regions and cavities of the body and have learned to follow anatomical directions and visualize body planes and

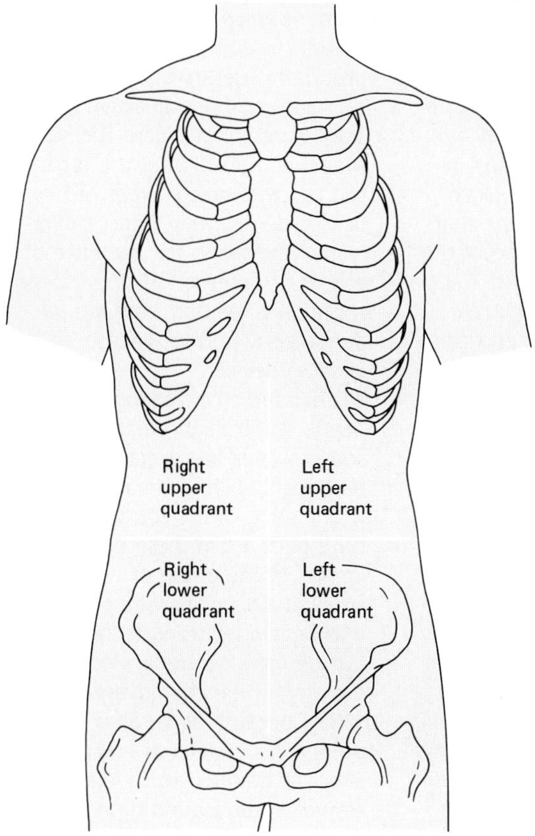

FIGURE 1-14

The abdominopelvic cavity can be divided into four quadrants by drawing imaginary transverse and sagittal lines through the umbilicus (navel).

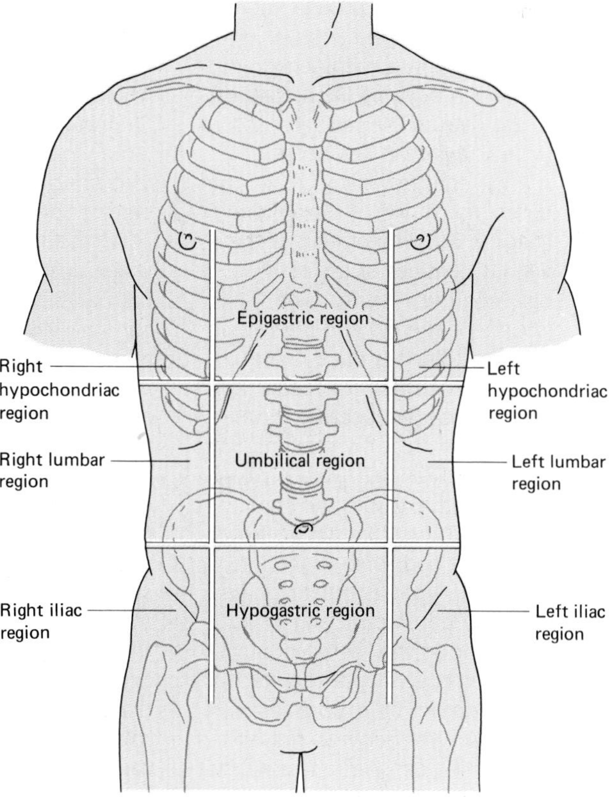

FIGURE 1-15

The abdominopelvic cavity can be divided into nine regions using two transverse and two sagittal planes. These regions can be used clinically to locate internal organs.

sections. Now you can begin to put all of this information together and apply all of these bits of knowledge to the body as a whole.

In the Window on the Human Body, View 1, all the parts have been put back together so that you can study them in relation to one another and to the body as an integrated, functioning organism. In View 2 some of the more superficial anterior structures have been removed so that you can see the structures that lie beneath them. Anterior structures have been progressively re-

FOCUS ON . . . Visualizing body parts clinically

A variety of techniques for visualizing body parts are currently available to help the physician in diagnosing disorders. With the development of these procedures career opportunities in the fields of radiology and nuclear medicine have greatly expanded. Some of the diagnostic techniques now being used are described below.

Conventional x-ray techniques X-rays are directed through a body part to an imaging device such as radiographic film or a television monitor. When film is used it is exposed, producing an image called an x-ray or, more properly, a roentgenogram (**rent**-gen-o-gram). Dense tissues in the path of the radiation absorb more x-rays than less dense tissues, so that fewer rays reach the photographic film. Thus, an x-ray image is a representation of the various densities of tissues lying between the x-ray machine (source of energy) and the film. In the body, bone is more dense than other tissues; it appears light on the x-ray film because it has absorbed more x-ray photons. Soft tissues such as the heart, cartilage, or connective tissues are less dense and therefore absorb fewer x-rays. Fat and some of the internal organs such as the lungs are relatively translucent, and so appear dark on the roentgenogram. Because conventional x-ray techniques do not by themselves differentiate well between tissues with similar densities, more sophisticated techniques have been developed.

Use of radiopaque dyes When two body structures have similar densities, a contrast medium may be used to visualize a structure by x-rays. The contrast medium may be a gas or a heavy metallic salt such as barium sulfate. Such a medium may be ingested as a suspension, as in the procedure for visualizing the upper digestive tract (upper GI series). Other types of contrast media may be injected intravenously, as in artery visualization (arteriogram) or kidney visualization (pyelogram). Sometimes a radiopaque dye is given in tablet form, as for example in the procedure for visualizing the gallbladder (cholecystogram).

Fluoroscopy In fluoroscopy internal body structures are examined using an x-ray machine that permits continuous viewing of the patient's internal structures. The image of the organ is projected onto a television screen, and organs are viewed in functional motion.

Isotopic tests Radioactive tracers are radioactive materials that can be introduced into the body and then traced to determine their pathway through the body or to evaluate the functioning of some organ that may take up the substance or excrete it. A radioactive tracer may be a natural substrate that has been labeled with a radioactive atom. For example, iodine, a natural substance used by the thyroid gland to make its hormones, can be introduced in radioactive form (^{131}I) to measure the function of the thyroid gland. The gland is viewed by obtaining an image from the radiation that is emitted from the patient's body. A tracer may also be a substance that is not normally present but will accumulate in a specific organ or region of the body. The amount that accumulates can be measured with a radiation detector. If the substance is being transported in the blood or excreted, samples of blood, urine, or feces can be taken at specific intervals and measured for radioactive content.

Nuclear scanning Scanning is a procedure used to visualize the distribution of a radioactive substance within an organ. The size, shape, and position of the organ can be determined. Areas of high or low density may provide information indicating the presence of cancer or other lesions. Again, the radiation is emitted from the patient's body and viewed on an imaging device.

Ultrasound Ultrasonographic pulses of ultrahigh frequency sound waves are directed at some body part, such as a valve in the heart. Some of the sound waves echo back. From these echoes, images of the organ can be constructed. This diagnostic procedure was developed using techniques first designed for radar and sonar. Ultrasound has the advantage of safety, because as far as is known there is no harmful or cumulative effect as there is with radiation. However, ultrasound has limited use because bones do not ade-

moved in Views 2 through 5, so that you can study the relationship of the deeper organs. View 6 is a dorsal view.

A different perspective is provided in Figure 1-16. These transverse sections through the head, mediastinum, and abdomen give you the opportunity to study the relationships between anterior and posterior structures within each of these body regions. Various clinical techniques for visualizing body parts are described in the Focus on Visualizing Body Parts Clinically.

quately reflect sound waves for images.

Thermography Thermography is used to evaluate the temperature of various tissues. Heat (infrared radiation) from the body strikes a mirror and is reflected onto the lens of a special camera. The camera converts heat into electrical energy. More heat emitted by the body causes more electricity to be produced by the camera, and the varying current changes the intensity of an imaging picture tube. This variation in the amount of light given from the tube is recorded on film. Thermograms are used to diagnose cancer. Malignant tumors often give off more heat than normal tissue or even nonmalignant growths. This technique is considered safe, but its use is limited owing to lack of imaging detail.

CT scanning Computed tomography (CT) combines x-ray equipment with a computer and cathode-ray tube to produce images of cross sections through the head or trunk. The x-ray source is rotated around the patient, and the x-ray detector on the other side of the patient rotates synchronously. Variations in the absorption of the radiation by the tissues are recorded, and a computer reconstructs an image in the form of an axial cross section. The image may be viewed on a television screen or photographed, or the computer may store it on discs. Photographs of CT scans are shown in Figure 1-16.

Positron-Emission Tomography (PET) This technique combines isotopic techniques with CT scanning. A radioactive tracer is administered to the patient. Then the radiation emitted is detected by fluorescent tubes positioned in a circle around the patient's body. The imaging information from the tubes is reconstructed by a computer in a manner similar to that of the CT scanner. However, CT scans provide views of tissue structure, while PET images provide a measure of cellular activity. For example, during a PET evaluation, radioactive glucose is injected into the patient's circulation. The patient's head is then placed into the PET apparatus. There, the radiation is detected and signals are sent to the computer. The signals are then put together to form an image. The radioactive glucose concentrates in the areas of the brain that are metabolically most active. These areas are visible on the image as bright spots.

Dynamic Spatial Reconstructor (DSR) This technique uses many x-ray tubes that revolve around the patient and rapidly produce large, three-dimensional images in any plane so that all aspects of an organ can be viewed. DSR permits the interior of an organ to be visualized.

Magnetic Resonance Imaging (MRI). Also called Nuclear Magnetic Resonance (NMR) This technique is used to diagnose intracranial and spinal lesions such as swelling of the brain; it is also helpful in diagnosing cardiovascular and soft-tissue abnormalities such as blood clots and tumors. The image shows structural and biochemical details in any plane. MRI uses nonionizing radiation, which is less damaging to body tissues than conventional x-rays. It "sees" right through bone and provides information about soft tissues.

MRI permits imaging of soft tissues by using the magnetic properties of atoms. This technique measures the density and energy loss of the nuclei of a specific element. The patient is placed in a chamber within a large, strong magnet. The magnetic field causes the protons in the atoms of hydrogen and certain other elements in the body to align. Short bursts of radio waves are released, which causes the protons to wobble. The frequencies of the wobbling motion and the radio waves eventually correspond. At that point resonance occurs. The radio signal is stopped. The protons then realign with the magnetic field. As this process occurs, they emit radio waves that provide information to a computer. The computer constructs images of organs by plotting the distribution of the hydrogen nuclei. The images can be displayed in color on a monitor. These images can provide information about metabolic activity in the tissue being viewed.

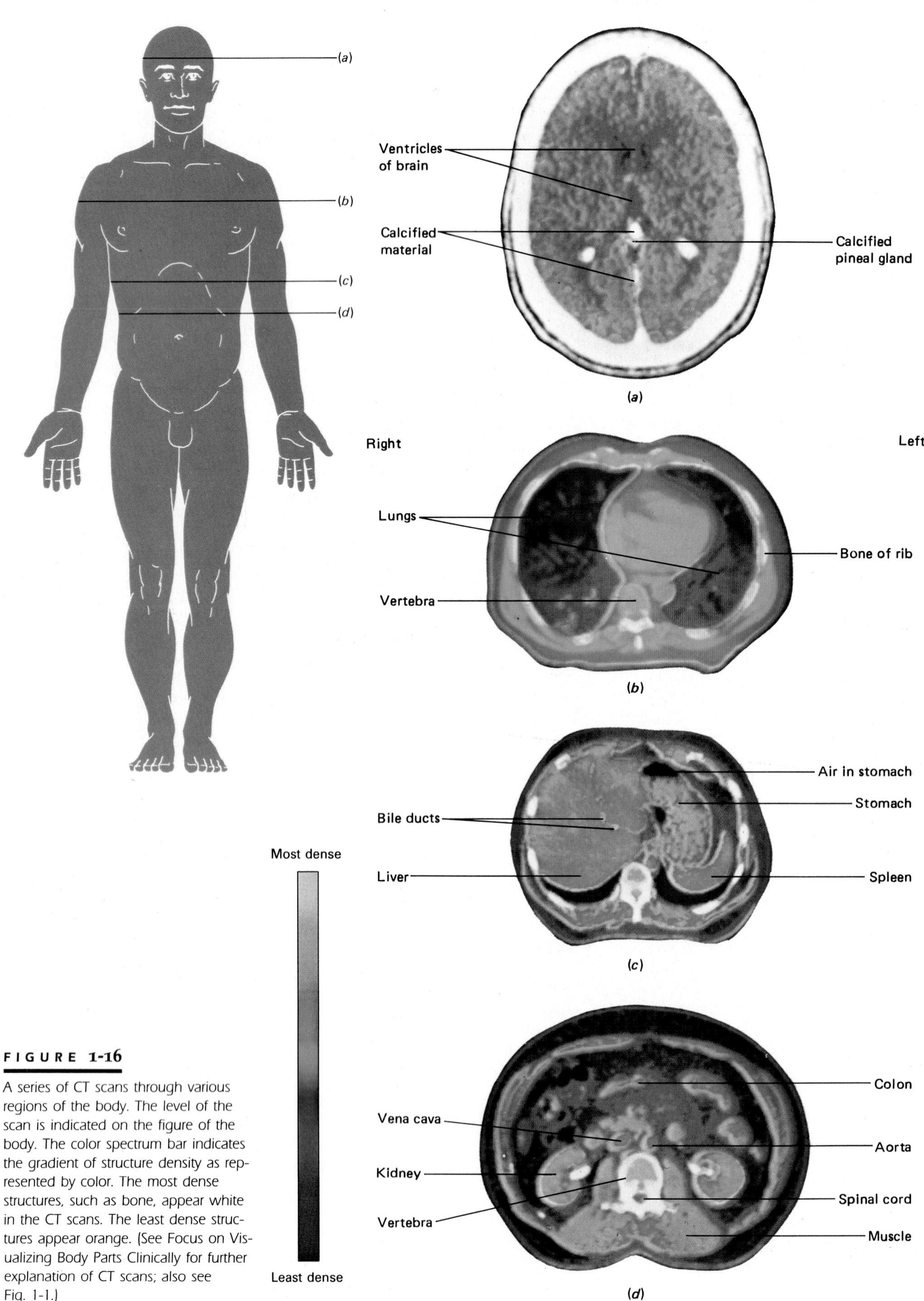

FIGURE 1-16

A series of CT scans through various regions of the body. The level of the scan is indicated on the figure of the body. The color spectrum bar indicates the gradient of structure density as represented by color. The most dense structures, such as bone, appear white in the CT scans. The least dense structures appear orange. (See Focus on Visualizing Body Parts Clinically for further explanation of CT scans; also see Fig. 1-1.)

WINDOW ON THE HUMAN BODY

Using Windows

"Windows" affords you a unique tour of human anatomy. The spatial relationships of each organ or organ system are revealed as you peel away successive "views."

Use the index inside to locate an anatomical structure which you have studied. Then locate the view(s) on which it is pictured. After you have located it by number, study its relationship to the surrounding structures and systems. Using this overlay design, you will find that the "window" not only reveals the coronal relationships of these organs, but also their position in transverse section, so that you can study them from superior to inferior *as well as* from anterior to posterior. These "views" afford you the opportunity to visualize the human body as an integrated functioning organism.

View	No.	Anatomic Structure
7	88	Acromion of the scapula
5,6	63	Adrenal (suprarenal) gland, Right
6	78	Anterior superior iliac spine
4,5,6	41	Aortic arch
5	56	Apex of the heart
4,5	49	Appendix
		Artery
6	69	Celiac trunk
4,6	48a.	Femoral
6	68	Left common carotid
5,6	61	Left common iliac
6	73	Left external iliac
6	72	Left internal iliac
6	67	Left subclavian
5	55	Pulmonary trunk
6	85	Right common carotid
6	84a.	Right subclavian
5,6	60a.	Superior mesenteric
3	32	Ascending colon
5	65	Atrium, Right
4	50	Caecum
6	69	Celiac trunk
6	83	Clavicle
3	32	Colon, ascending
3,5	29	Colon, descending
7	89	Coracoid of the scapula
3	36	Costocartilages
3,5	29	Descending colon
4,5,6	43	Diaphragm
4	51	Duodenum
6	76	Epididymis
5,6	57	Esophagus
3	23	Falciform ligament
7	95	Femur
3,4	33	Gall bladder
3	28	Greater omentum
7	94	Greater trochanter of the femur
7	90	Head of the humerus
3,4	21	Heart in the pericardial sac
4	52	Hepatic flexure
4	54	Horizontal fissure
7	90	Humeral head
6	78	Ilium, Anterior superior spine
6,7	79	Iliac crest
7	100	Inferior angle of the scapula
5,6	64	Inferior vena cava
4,6,7	45	Inguinal ligament
5	59	Kidney, Left
4	38	Larynx
7	101	Lateral border of the scapula
4	42	Left oblique fissure
4	34,24	Liver
3	24	Liver, Left lobe
3	34	Liver, Right lobe
3,4,5	19	Lung, Left
3,4	35	Lung Right
7	98	Lumbar vertebrae
		Muscle
2	14	Adductor longus
2,6	6	Biceps brachii
2,4	4	Deltoid
2	7	External abdominal oblique
7	97	Gluteus medius
		Muscle
2	11	Gracilis
6	71	Iliacus
2	8	Iliopsoas
2	1	Inferior belly of omohyoid
6	82	Intercostal
7	92	Latissimus dorsi
2	15	Pectineus
2	5	Pectoralis major
6	70	Psoas major
2	12	Rectus femoris
2,4	10	Sartorius
2	16	Serratus anterior
2	2	Sternocleidomastoid
2,4	9	Tensor fasciae latae
2	3	Trapezius
2	13	Vastus lateralis
3	17	Manubrium
		Nerve
7	93	Femoral
7	91	Intercostal
7	96	Obturator foramen
5	58	Pancreas
6	75	Penis
5	55	Pulmonary trunk
7	99	Ribs (11th and 12th)
4	53	Right oblique fissure
7	88	Scapula, Acromion
7	89	Scapula, Coracoid
7	100	Scapula, Inferior angle
7	101	Scapula, Lateral border
4	47	Scrotum
3,5	30	Sigmoid colon
3,4	31	Small intestine, Coils
3,5	25	Spleen
4	44	Splenic fissure
3	18	Sternal angle
3	37	Sternoclavicular joint
	20	Sternum, body
3,4	26	Stomach
5,6	66	Superior vena cava
5,6	63	Suprarenal (adrenal) gland, Right
6	77	Testis
4	39	Thyroid gland
4	40	Trachea
3,4	27	Transverse colon
5,6	62	Ureter, Right
3,4,5,6	46	Urinary bladder
6	74	Vas deferens
		Vein
4	48v.	Femoral
6	81	Hepatic
5,6	64	Inferior vena cava
6	80	Right renal
6	84v.	Right subclavian
5	60v.	Superior mesenteric
5,6	66	Superior vena cava
7	86	Vertebra, Seventh cervical
7	87	Vertebra, First thoracic
3	22	Xiphoid process

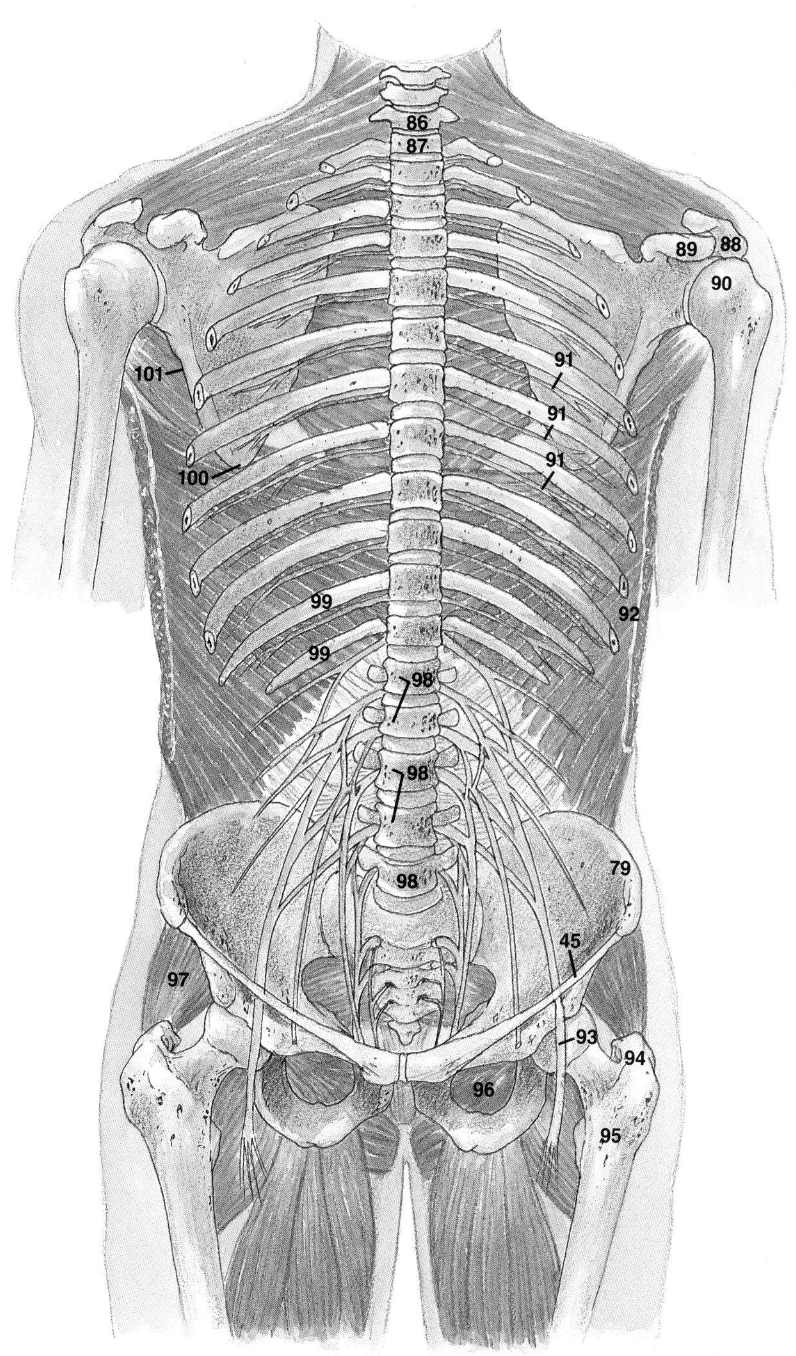

View #7

86 Seventh cervical vertebra
87 First thoracic vertrebra
88 Acromion of the scapula
89 Coracoid of the scapula
90 Head of the humerus
91 Intercostal nerves
92 Latissimus dorsi muscle
79 Iliac crest
45 Inguinal ligament
93 Femoral nerve
94 Greater trochanter of the femur
95 Femur
96 Obturator foramen
97 Gluteus medius muscle
98 Lumbar vertebrae
99 Ribs (11th and 12th)
100 Inferior angle of the scapula
101 Lateral border of the scapula

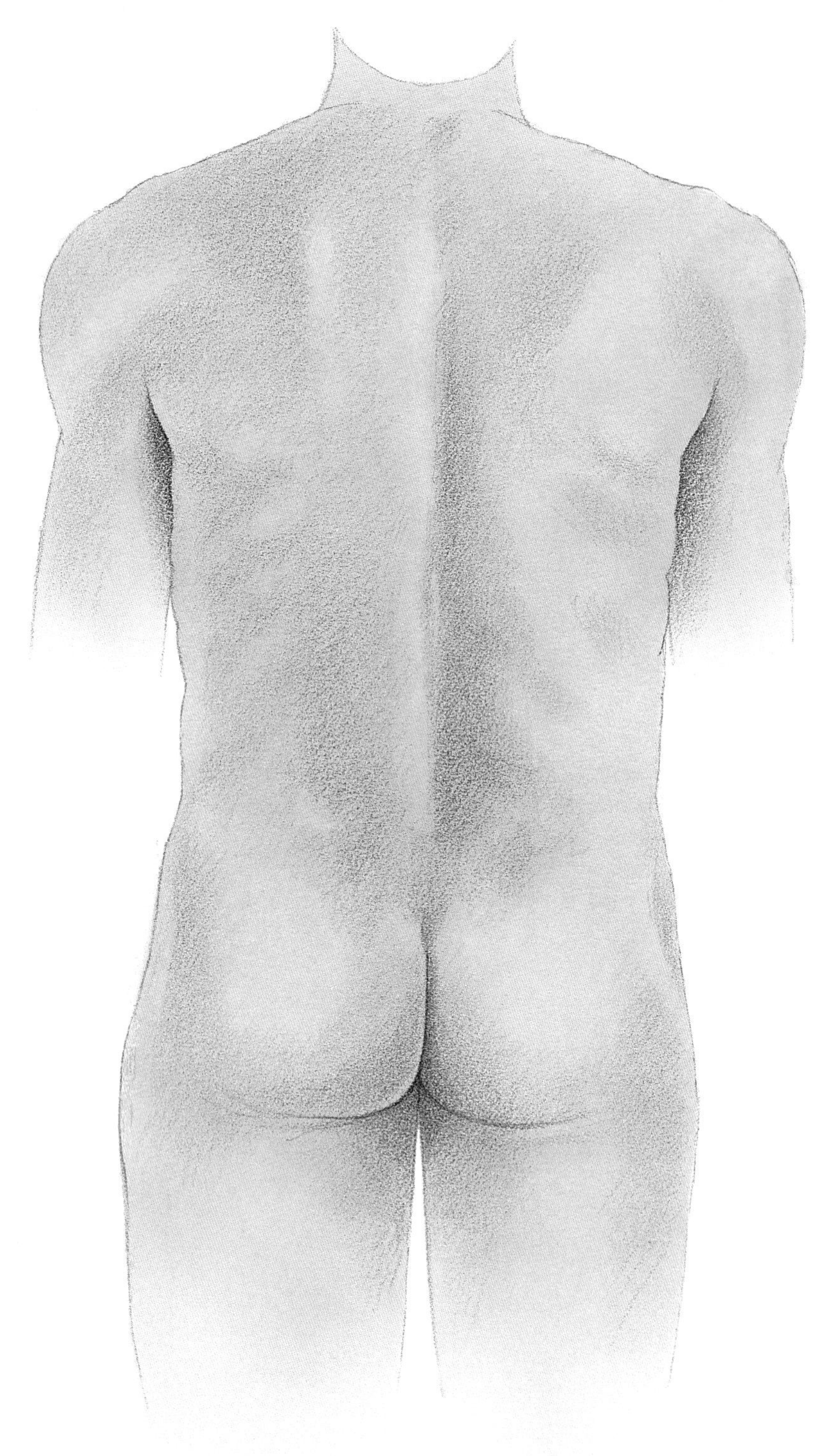

Posterior View

Summary

I. Anatomy is the science of body structure; physiology is the study of function, or how the body works.

II. For a living organism to survive, its environment must provide food, water, oxygen, appropriate temperature and pressure, and an atmosphere that provides protection from harmful solar radiation.

III. All living organisms grow, carry on metabolism, regulate themselves in order to preserve homeostasis, move, respond to changes in the external or internal environment, adapt to long-term environmental changes, and reproduce.

IV. We can identify several levels of organization within the human body.
   A. The simplest level of organization is the chemical level consisting of atoms and molecules.
   B. Atoms and molecules associate to form cellular organelles and cells.
   C. Cells associate to form tissues.
   D. Tissues may be organized to form organs such as the brain or heart.
   E. Certain tissues and organs may function together to make up a body system.
   F. Ten body systems work together to make up the human organism.

V. The body can be divided into ten different body systems that operate to maintain its integrity.
   A. The integumentary system provides a protective covering for the body and helps regulate body temperature.
   B. The skeletal and muscular systems work together as a mechanical system to permit effective movement.
   C. The nervous and endocrine systems regulate the activities of the body.
   D. The digestive system breaks down food so that nutrients can be absorbed into the blood.
   E. The respiratory system delivers oxygen to the blood and removes carbon dioxide from the body.
   F. The circulatory system transports nutrients and oxygen to all body cells and carries wastes from the cells to the excretory organs. The cardiovascular and lymphatic systems are part of the circulatory system.
   G. Waste disposal and regulation of blood composition is the function of the urinary system.
   H. The reproductive system of the male produces and delivers sperm; the reproductive system of the female produces ova and incubates the developing offspring. Both systems release hormones that establish and maintain sexuality.

VI. Homeostasis, also called homeodynamics, is the body's automatic tendency to maintain a constant internal environment, or steady state. In general, homeostasis is maintained by negative feedback mechanisms.

VII. Anatomical directional terms are applied to the body when it is in the anatomical position. In this position the body is standing erect, eyes looking forward, arms at the sides, and palms and toes directed forward. The principal directional terms are:

Term	Orientation
Superior (cephalic)	Upward; toward the head
Inferior	Downward; toward the feet
Anterior (ventral)	Belly surface; toward the front of the body
Posterior (dorsal)	Back surface; toward the back of the body
Medial	Toward the midline
Lateral	Toward the side
Proximal	Toward the midline or point of attachment to the trunk
Distal	Away from the midline or point of attachment to the trunk
Superficial	Toward the body surface
Deep	Within the body

VIII. The body or its organs may be cut along planes to produce different types of sections.
   A. A sagittal section divides the body into right and left parts.
   B. A transverse (or cross) section divides the body into superior and inferior parts.
   C. A frontal (or coronal) section divides the body into anterior and posterior parts.

IX. The body may be divided into axial and appendicular regions.
   A. The axial portion consists of head, neck, and trunk.
   B. The appendicular portion consists of the limbs.
   C. Terms such as abdominal, pectoral, and lumbar are used to refer to specific body regions or structures.

X. Two principal body cavities are the dorsal cavity and the ventral cavity.
   A. The dorsal cavity includes the cranial cavity and the vertebral canal.
   B. The ventral cavity is principally subdivided into the thoracic and abdominopelvic cavities.

Post-test

1. The science of body structure is called ____________; the study of body function is called ____________.
2. The chemical processes that take place in the body are collectively referred to as its ____________.
3. The complex series of chemical reactions that liberate energy from food molecules is called ____________.
4. The automatic tendency of the body to maintain a constant internal environment is called ____________.
5. Atoms combine chemically to form ____________.
6. The basic building blocks of the body are called ____________.
7. Various types of tissues may be organized to form ____________.
8. Chemical messengers released by endocrine glands are called ____________.

Matching

	Column A	Column B
____	9. The body's principal regulatory system	a. endocrine system
____	10. Includes the skin	b. integumentary system
____	11. Functions to support and protect the body	c. circulatory system
____	12. Transportation system	d. nervous system
____	13. Maintains adequate blood oxygen content	e. respiratory system
____	14. Its organs are the ductless glands that release hormones	f. skeletal system

	Column A	Column B
____	15. Heart in relation to lung	a. superficial
____	16. Wrist in relation to elbow	b. medial
____	17. Knee in relation to ankle	c. lateral
____	18. Skin in relation to muscle	d. deep
____	19. Stomach in relation to backbone	e. proximal
		f. distal
		g. anterior
		h. posterior

20. A cut that divides the body into right and left parts is a ____________ section.
21. A cut at right angles to the body axis is a ____________ section.
22. The head, neck, and trunk make up the ____________ portion of the body, while the limbs make up the ____________ portion.
23. The internal organs within the body cavities are referred to as ____________.

Matching

Select the most appropriate answers from the choices given.

____	24. head	a. cervical
____	25. skull	b. cephalic
____	26. cutaneous	c. cranial
____	27. pectoral	d. skin
____	28. neck	e. chest
____	29. armpit	f. axillary

30. Thoracic and abdominopelvic cavities are separated by the ____________.
31. Label the diagram opposite.

Review questions

1. Describe the position of each of the following using anatomic terms: (a) navel, (b) ear, (c) great toe, (d) elbow, (e) backbone.
2. Define homeostasis and give an example. Tell how your example is regulated by negative feedback mechanisms.
3. Describe six characteristics of a living organism.
4. List in sequence the levels of organization within the human organism, from atom to organism.
5. How does each body system function to maintain homeostasis?
6. Describe the anatomical position.
7. Identify the body cavities given in this chapter and give an organ or structure found in each.
8. Define each of the following: (a) cephalic, (b) cervical, (c) cranial, (d) abdominal, (e) sagittal, (f) proximal, (g) distal, (h) bilateral symmetry.
9. What is a roentgenogram? A CT scan?

Post-test answers

1. anatomy; physiology **2.** metabolism **3.** cellular respiration **4.** homeostasis **5.** molecules **6.** cells **7.** organs **8.** hormones **9.** d **10.** b **11.** f **12.** c **13.** e **14.** a **15.** b **16.** f **17.** e **18.** a **19.** g **20.** sagittal **21.** transverse (or cross) **22.** axial; appendicular **23.** viscera **24.** b **25.** c **26.** d **27.** e **28.** a **29.** f **30.** diaphragm **31.** See Fig. 1-12*a*.

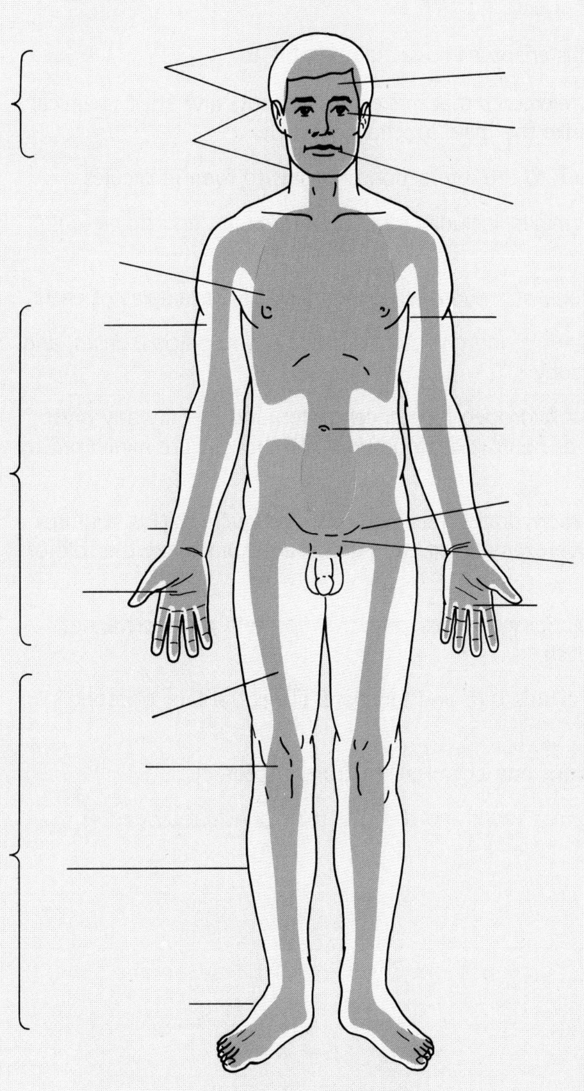

THE CHEMISTRY OF LIFE

CHAPTER OUTLINE

- I. **The composition of matter**
- II. **Atoms: the basic units of matter**
  - A. Structure of the atom
  - B. Protons
  - C. Neutrons and isotopes
    - □ Focus on radioisotopes
  - D. Electrons
- III. **Molecules and compounds**
  - A. Formulas
  - B. Chemical equations
  - C. Valence electrons
- IV. **Chemical bonds**
  - A. Ionic bonds
  - B. Covalent bonds
  - C. Hydrogen bonds
  - D. Chemical reactions
- V. **Inorganic compounds**
  - A. Water
  - B. Acids and bases
  - C. Salts
  - D. Buffers
- VI. **Organic compounds**
  - A. Carbon atom
  - B. Carbohydrates
    - 1. Monosaccharides
    - 2. Disaccharides and polysaccharides
  - C. Lipids
    - 1. Neutral fats
    - 2. Phospholipids
    - 3. Steroids
  - D. Nucleic acids
  - E. Proteins
    - 1. Amino acid subunits
    - 2. Levels of organization
- VII. **Enzymes**
  - A. How enzymes work
  - B. Cofactors
  - C. Regulation of enzyme activity
  - D. Optimum conditions
  - E. Enzyme inhibition

LEARNING OBJECTIVES

After you have studied this chapter you should be able to:

1 Identify the principal elements that make up the body, give their chemical symbols, and summarize the main functions of each.

2 Relate atomic structure to the interaction of atoms to form molecules.

3 Interpret chemical formulas, including structural formulas, and simple equations.

4 Contrast ionic, covalent, and hydrogen bonds, and give examples of each.

5 Describe the main types of inorganic compounds—water, acids, bases, and salts—found in the body.

6 Define pH in terms of hydrogen ion concentration and identify any given pH as acid, alkaline, or neutral; describe how pH changes are minimized by buffers.

7 Chemically define carbohydrates, fats, proteins, and nucleic acids, and identify their subunits; give examples of each group and summarize the role of each in the body.

8 Distinguish among monosaccharides, disaccharides, and polysaccharides, giving examples of each.

9 Compare the chemical structure and functions of neutral fats, phospholipids, and steroids.

10 Summarize the functions and chemical structure of proteins.

11 Summarize how enzymes work and describe their principal properties.

Francis Leroy, Biocosmos/Science Photo Library.

2

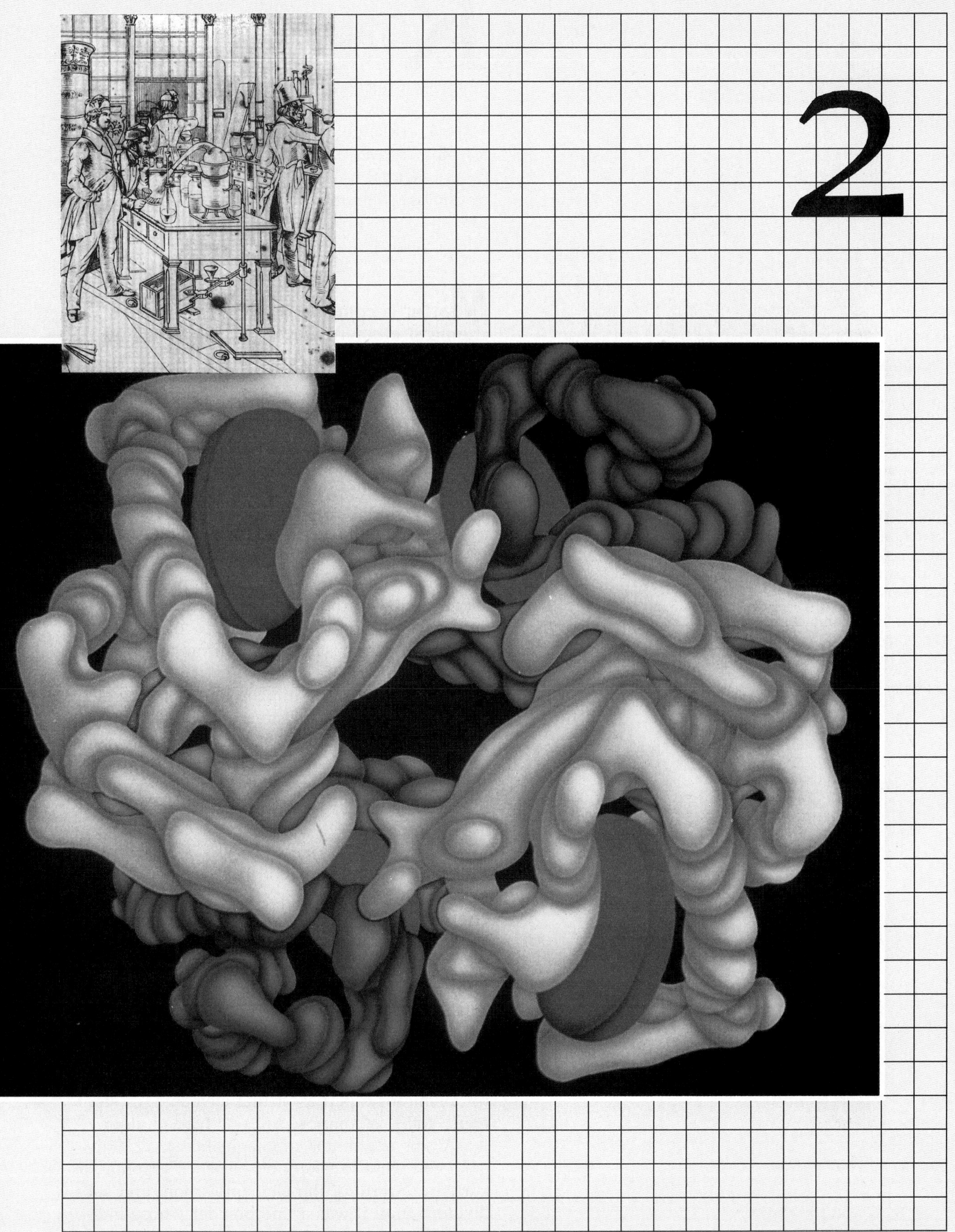

Reduced to its simplest components, the body is an array of atoms and molecules. Life depends upon the precise interaction of these chemical units. Just as learning to count is necessary for mastering arithmetic and a knowledge of the alphabet is required in learning to read, so a knowledge of basic chemistry is essential to an understanding of human physiology. The branch of chemistry that relates directly to life processes is called **biochemistry** (life chemistry).

KEY CONCEPTS

The atoms of a molecule or compound are held together by forces of attraction between them known as chemical bonds.

Inorganic compounds important in living things are water, mineral salts, acids, and bases.

Organic compounds are the main structural components of cells, serve as sources of energy, and are important components of metabolic reactions.

Important organic compounds in the body include carbohydrates, lipids, nucleic acids, and proteins.

Matter is composed of chemical elements

All matter, living and nonliving alike, is composed of **chemical elements,** pure substances that cannot be broken down into simpler substances by chemical reactions. Gold, calcium, and oxygen are examples. Can you think of others? There are about 105 different kinds of elements. Of these, 92 occur naturally in the universe; the others have been produced in the laboratory. About 98% of a cell's content by weight is composed of only six elements—carbon, hydrogen, oxygen, nitrogen, calcium, and phosphorus. About 14 other elements are consistently present in cells, but in small quantities.

Instead of writing out the name of each element, chemists use a system of abbreviations called **chemical symbols.** For example, the chemical symbol for carbon is C, and for oxygen, O. Table 2-1 lists the chemical symbols for some of the elements that make up the human body.

Atoms are the basic units of matter that participate in chemical reactions

Imagine dividing a bit of gold into smaller and smaller pieces. Eventually the smallest possible particle would be obtained, and this particle would be an atom of gold. An **atom** is the smallest unit of an element that retains the characteristic chemical properties of that element. An **element,** then, is composed of one type of atom.

Atoms are almost unimaginably small. Suppose you were to take a bit of pencil graphite, a fairly pure form of the element carbon, and subdivide it until it was a fine powder whose individual grains were visible only under the most powerful microscope. Each minute grain would still consist of hundreds of thousands of carbon atoms. Indeed, thousands of carbon particles would not weigh enough to register on the most sensitive chemical balance. Atoms range in size from 0.00000001 (10^{-8}) cm to 0.00000005 (5×10^{-8}) cm. If atoms were lined up end to end, it would take more than 100 million of them to measure an inch!

The atom consists of a nucleus and electrons

The term atom was coined by Democritus, a Greek scientist, who believed that all things, even the human soul, were composed of these tiny particles. (He thought the atoms of the soul were the noblest of them all.) Atoms, he said, could not be divided themselves, but in various combinations they made up all things. Though it was

TABLE 2-1

Elements that make up the human body

Name	Chemical symbol	Approximate composition by mass (%)	Importance or function
Oxygen	O	65	Required for cellular respiration; present in most organic compounds; component of water
Carbon	C	18	Backbone of organic molecules; can form four bonds with other atoms
Hydrogen	H	10	Present in most organic compounds; component of water
Nitrogen	N	3	Component of all proteins and nucleic acids
Calcium	Ca	1.5	Structural component of bones and teeth; important in muscle contraction, conduction of nerve impulses, and blood clotting
Phosphorus	P	1	Component of nucleic acids; structural component of bone; important in energy transfer
Potassium	K	0.4	Principal positive ion (cation) within cells; important in nerve function; affects muscle contraction
Sulfur	S	0.3	Component of most proteins
Sodium	Na	0.2	Principal positive ion in interstitial (tissue) fluid; important in fluid balance; essential for conduction of nerve impulses
Magnesium	Mg	0.1	Needed in blood and other body tissues
Chlorine	Cl	0.1	Principal negative ion (anion) of interstitial fluid; important in fluid balance; component of sodium chloride
Iron	Fe	Trace amount	Component of hemoglobin and myoglobin; component of certain enzymes
Iodine	I	Trace amount	Component of thyroid hormones

Other elements found in very small amounts in the body include manganese (Mn), copper (Cu), zinc (Zn), cobalt (Co), fluorine (F), molybdenum (Mo), selenium (Se), and a few others. They are called trace elements.

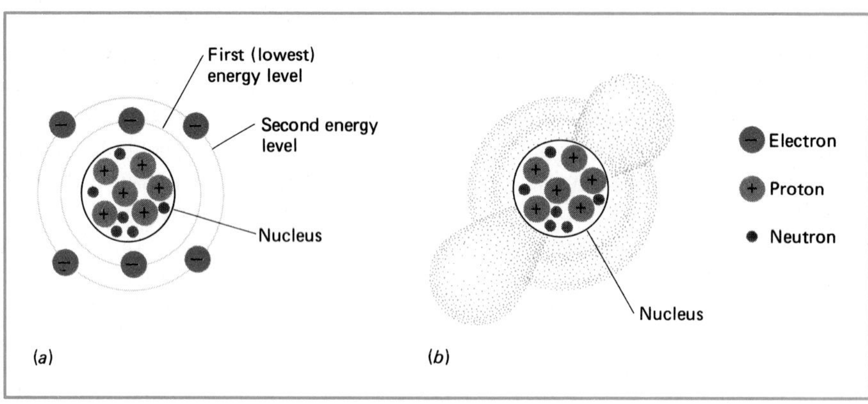

FIGURE 2-1

Two ways of representing an atom. (*a*) Bohr model of a carbon atom. Although the Bohr model is not an accurate way to depict electron configuration, it is commonly used because of its simplicity and convenience. (*b*) An electron cloud. Dots represent the probability of the electron's being in that particular location at any given moment.

not quite original with him, Democritus, who was born about 460 B.C., is nevertheless said to be the father of the atomic theory. Although much recycled by the earth's ecological processes, some atoms of Democritus may well reside in you.

If we were to cut apart an atom, we would see that it is a hollow structure composed mainly of empty space. In its center there is an **atomic nucleus** surrounded by a number of negatively charged particles called **electrons.** The nucleus contains most of the atomic mass. Within the nucleus are **protons,** positively charged particles, and **neutrons,** which have no electrical charge. Neutrons and protons together are referred to as *nucleons*.

In 1913 the Danish physicist Niels Bohr introduced a planetary model of atomic structure in which the electrons move about the nucleus in specific **electron shells** or **energy levels** (Fig. 2-1a). Today chemists use more sophisticated models in which electrons are located in clusters, or orbitals, within each energy level. Because electrons continuously move about, an atom can be depicted as a nucleus surrounded by an electron cloud (Fig. 2-1b). The density of areas within the cloud represents the probability of an electron being in a particular location at any given moment.

Protons determine the atomic number of an atom

How can we tell one element from another? Each type of atom has a characteristic number of protons in its nucleus known as its **atomic number.** For example, an atom of the element hydrogen always has one proton in its nucleus, so its atomic number is 1. A carbon atom contains six protons in its nucleus, and its atomic number is 6. An atom's **atomic weight** is defined by the total number of neutrons and protons in the atom. The common form of carbon has six protons and six neutrons on its nucleus; its atomic weight is 12.

Isotopes differ in number of neutrons

Ordinarily, the number of neutrons is also constant for any type of atom. However, in a very small percentage of certain atoms, the number of neutrons may be different. For example, there are no neutrons in the nucleus of an ordinary hydrogen atom, but among every 5000 or so ordinary hydrogen atoms, there is one that has one neutron in its nucleus. An even smaller proportion of hydrogen atoms contains two neutrons. Such atoms of an element with different numbers of neutrons are called **isotopes.**

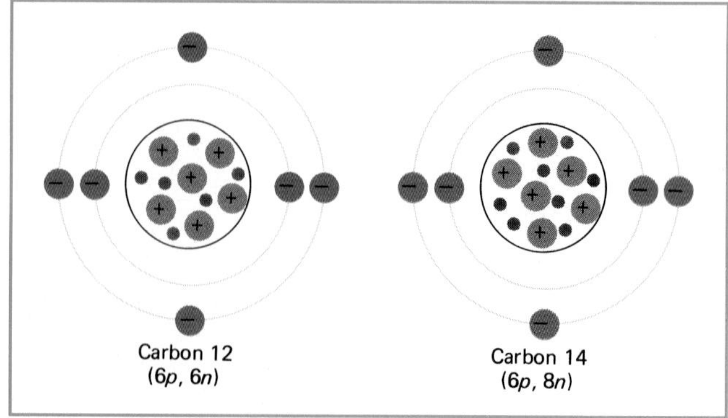

FIGURE 2-2

Isotopes of carbon. Carbon-12 is the more common isotope of carbon. Its nucleus contains six protons and six neutrons, so its atomic mass (weight) is 12. Carbon-14 is a rare radioactive isotope of carbon. Because it contains eight neutrons in its nucleus rather than six, its atomic mass is 14. Both types of carbon have six protons, so both are atomic number 6.

Some isotopes are stable; others, called **radioisotopes** or radionuclides, break down and release high-energy radiation as they decay. Two isotopes of carbon are shown in Figure 2-2. Carbon-12, the more common isotope of carbon, has six neutrons. Carbon-14, a radioisotope, has eight neutrons in its nucleus. Carbon-14 is often used in research to trace the fate of carbon atoms in metabolic processes. Use of radioisotopes in medicine is discussed in the Focus on Radioisotopes.

Electrons are located in energy levels outside the nucleus

Electrons are negatively charged particles that whirl around the atomic nucleus. In an isolated atom, there are the same number of electrons as there are protons. Thus, though opposite in sign, the charges of electrons and protons are equal, and the atom is electrically neutral. A hydrogen atom consists of one proton and one electron. A carbon atom consists of six protons and six electrons, as well as six neutrons.

Electrons do not actually circle the nucleus in specific orbits but rather whirl around the nucleus, sometimes close to it, sometimes farther away. Although the Bohr model does not portray this constant motion, this model is used here because it is helpful for understanding the fundamentals of atomic structure and chemical bonding. Figure 2-3 uses Bohr models to illustrate the structures of several biologically important atoms.

Most atoms have more than one electron shell, and each shell holds a characteristic maximum number of electrons. For the first shell the maximum is two, for the second it is eight, for the third 18. For example, an atom of oxygen, which has eight electrons, has two electrons in the first shell and six in the second (Fig. 2-3c). Electrons are held in their specific shells by the force of their attraction for the positive protons in the nucleus, balanced against the centrifugal force that tends to pull them away from the nucleus.

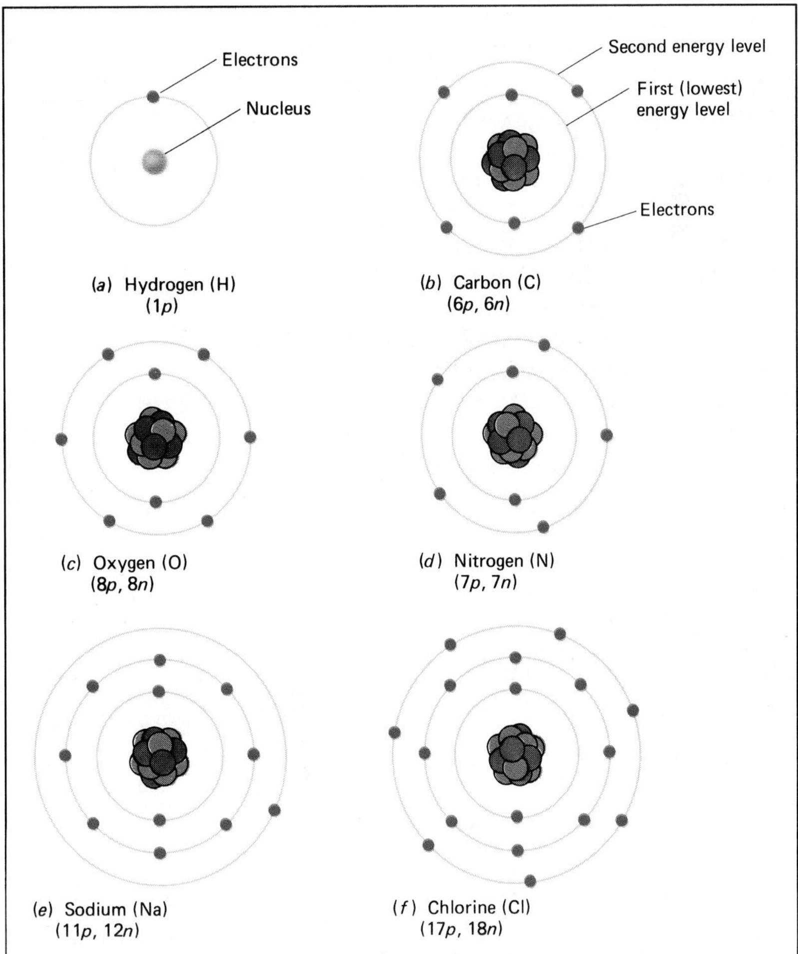

FIGURE 2-3

Bohr models of some biologically important atoms. *(a)* Hydrogen, *(b)* carbon, *(c)* oxygen, *(d)* nitrogen, *(e)* sodium, *(f)* chlorine. Each circle represents an energy level, or electron shell. Electrons are represented by dots on the circles; *p*, proton; *n*, neutron.

FOCUS ON . . . Radioisotopes

Radioisotopes are useful in research and in medicine for both diagnosis and treatment of diseases. Despite the difference in the number of neutrons, the body treats all isotopes of a given element in a similar way. In one test for thyroid function, radioactive iodine is injected intravenously. The rate of iodine uptake by the thyroid gland is then measured with a radiation counter placed over the patient's neck.

Radioactive atoms can be used to "tag" molecules because they are easily detected even in very low concentrations. For example, a drug can be tagged so that its fate in the body can be traced. The active component in marijuana (tetrahydrocannabinol or THC) has been labeled and administered intravenously. By measuring the amount of radioactivity in the blood and urine at successive intervals, it was determined that this compound remains in the body for several weeks.

Because radiation can interfere with cell division, radioisotopes have been used in the treatment of cancer (a disease characterized by uncontrolled cell division). Radioisotopes are also used to measure the rate of red blood cell production and many other aspects of body function. (For other clinical uses of radioisotopes see Focus on Visualizing Body Parts Clinically [Chapter 1].)

Atoms form molecules and compounds

Two or more atoms may combine chemically to form a **molecule.** When two atoms of oxygen combine chemically, a molecule of oxygen is formed. Different kinds of atoms can combine to form chemical compounds. A **compound** is composed of at least two different types of chemically combined atoms. Water is a chemical compound consisting of one atom of oxygen combined with two atoms of hydrogen.

Formulas are used to describe molecules

A **chemical formula** is a shorthand method for describing the chemical composition of a molecule. Chemical symbols are used to indicate the types of atoms in the molecule, and subscript numbers are used to indicate the number of each type of atom present. The chemical formula for molecular oxygen, O_2, tells us that this molecule consists of two atoms of oxygen. In the same way, the chemical formula for water, H_2O, tells us that each molecule of water consists of two atoms of hydrogen and one atom of oxygen. (Note that when a single atom of one type is present, it is not necessary to write 1; for example, one does not write H_2O_1.)

A **structural formula** shows not only the types and numbers of atoms in a molecule but also their arrangement. In any specific type of molecule the atoms are always arranged in the same way. From the chemical formula for water, H_2O, a novice could only guess whether the atoms were arranged H—H—O or H—O—H. The structural formula, H—O—H, settles the matter, indicating that the two hydrogen atoms are attached to the oxygen atom. In the case of water this arrangement is the only one chemically possible. But there are other substances that consist of the same atoms yet have different chemical properties owing to alternative arrangements. Such substances are known as **structural isomers.** The sugars glucose, fructose, and galactose are examples (Fig. 2-13).

Chemical equations describe chemical reactions

In a chemical equation the **reactants** (that is, the substances that participate in the reaction) are usually written on the left side of the equation and the **products** (the substances formed by the reaction) are usually written on the right side. The arrow, meaning "yields," indicates the direction in which the reaction tends to proceed. Sometimes the reaction will go backward as well as forward, and a balance or **equilibrium** may be established in which a certain amount of the product continuously breaks up to form the reactants again.

A number preceding a chemical symbol or formula indicates the number of atoms or molecules reacting. Thus 2 Na means two atoms of sodium and 2 NaCl means two molecules of sodium chloride. The absence of a number indicates that only one atom or molecule is present.

Valence electrons determine the chemical properties of an element

The electrons in the outer shell of an atom are its **valence electrons.** The number of valence electrons determines the types of chemical associations that an atom is able to make. The object of the game is to gain stability. The atom achieves its most stable state by filling its outermost shell with the maximum number of electrons. Eight is a stable number for the outermost shell of many atoms. (Hydrogen and helium are exceptions; they each require only two electrons because they have a single shell.)

A few gases, including helium, argon, and neon, naturally possess a stable number of electrons in their outer shell. Because of this stability, these gases do not normally participate in chemical reactions and are known as **inert gases.** Only atoms whose outermost shell is not filled are capable of entering into chemical combinations with other atoms. Atoms tend to accept, donate, or share electrons with other atoms until they reach a stabilized state.

The number of electrons that an atom can accept, share, or donate is designated by a number from 0 to 7. This valence number is preceded by a plus or minus sign, which indicates whether the atom will donate or accept electrons. For example, hydrogen's valence number is +1, indicating that it can donate or share one electron. After donating the electron (which, you recall, has a negative charge), the atom is left with a proton. With one more proton than electron its charge is +1. Chlorine's valence number of −1 tells us that a chlorine atom can accept one electron. (It will then have one more electron than proton.) With a valence of −2, oxygen can accept or share two electrons.

Ordinarily, if an atom has more than four electrons in its unstable outer shell it behaves as an **electron acceptor,** taking electrons from other atoms to complete its outer shell. An atom with fewer than four electrons in its outer shell generally behaves as an **electron donor,** giving away the electrons in its unstable outer shell. **Metals,** such as iron, copper, calcium, and sodium, most frequently act as electron donors. **Nonmetals,** such as oxygen and chlorine, tend to behave as electron acceptors. By knowing the number of valence electrons, chemists can predict how atoms will react with one another.

Chemical bonds hold atoms together

The atoms of a molecule are held together by forces of attraction called **chemical bonds.** Each bond represents a certain amount of potential chemical energy. Bond energy is the energy necessary to break a bond. In a drawing of a structural formula, the lines represent the chemical bonds between the atoms.

Two main types of chemical bonds are ionic and covalent bonds. Another type that is particularly important in biochemistry is the hydrogen bond.

Ionic bonds hold oppositely charged atoms together

When an atom gains or loses electrons, it becomes electrically charged and is called an **ion.** Positively charged ions, such as Na^+, are called **cations.** Negatively charged ions, such as Cl^-, are called **anions.** An ionic bond is formed when one atom donates an electron to another. Each atom becomes charged as a result of this exchange, and because of these charges the atoms are attracted to one another.

An **ionic compound** is a substance consisting of anions and cations that are bonded together by their opposite charges. The bonds between these ions are **ionic bonds.** Common table salt, sodium chloride (NaCl), is an ionically bonded compound. Studying its formation will help in understanding how such compounds are formed (Fig. 2-4).

Sodium in its pure, chemically uncombined form is a silvery metal so soft that one can easily cut it with a knife, and so strongly reactive chemically that when it is immersed in water it reacts violently, catching fire and often exploding, showering the vicinity with droplets of molten, burning sodium metal. Chlorine is, if anything, an even less congenial substance. A dense, yellow-green gas, it was used as a poison gas in

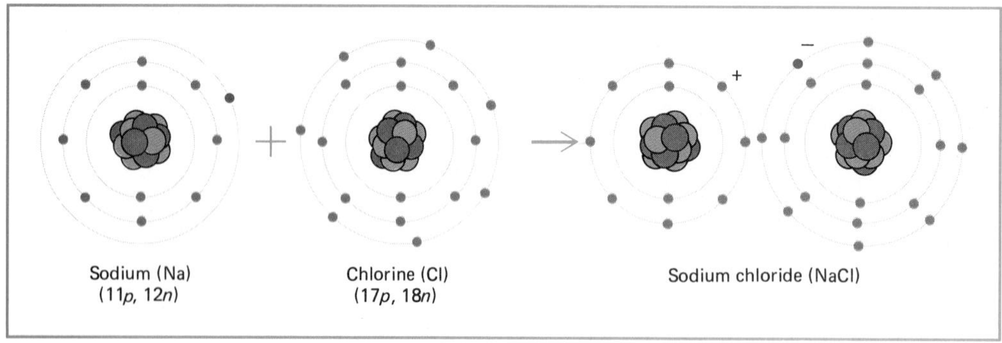

FIGURE 2-4

Formation of an ionic compound. Sodium donates its single valence electron to chlorine, which has seven electrons in its outer energy level. With this additional electron, chlorine completes its outer energy level. The two atoms are now electrically charged ions. They are attracted to one another by their unlike electrical charges, forming the ionic compound sodium chloride. The force of attraction holding these ions together is called an ionic bond.

World War I and today is used in minute quantities to kill bacteria in water and sewage. Yet when combined with each other, these two potent chemicals, sodium and chlorine, form common, innocuous table salt. How is this possible?

With 11 protons in its nucleus, the sodium atom also has 11 electrons, two in the first shell, eight in the second, and one left over in the third. Like other atoms with fewer than four electrons in the outermost shell, sodium seeks stability by ridding itself of its outermost electron.

Chlorine, on the other hand, has a nucleus with 17 protons, and thus also possesses 17 electrons. The first two shells account for ten, leaving seven in the outermost. If an atom has more than four electrons in that shell, it will tend to gain more electrons until it has a total of eight. With seven outermost electrons the chlorine atom has a vacancy for one more.

With one element ready to give and the other to gain, sodium and chlorine form a natural partnership and, given an opportunity, will exchange an electron. If placed together, a violent reaction occurs. The experimenter will find at the bottom of the reaction container a fine powder of solid table salt—just the thing for sprinkling on popcorn. Unlike the violently reactive parent substances, the salt is relatively unreactive. The reason is that now the outermost shells of the atoms of both participating elements each have a total of eight electrons. They are effectively stable.

But what has happened to these atoms electrically? The sodium now has one more proton than electrons and has become a positively charged ion. On the other hand, the chlorine now has one more electron than protons and is a negatively charged chloride ion. These charges are what attract the two ions to one another and what, in fact, constitute their ionic bond.

$$\underset{\text{2 Sodium atoms}}{2\,\mathrm{Na}} + \underset{\text{1 Chlorine molecule}}{\mathrm{Cl_2}} \longrightarrow \underset{\text{2 Sodium chloride molecules}}{2\,\mathrm{NaCl}}$$

Three kinds of compounds that contain ionic bonds are simple acids, bases (alkaline substances), and salts. When these compounds are dissolved in water, their ions tend to dissociate (separate) and increase in mobility. Here are some examples.

$$\underset{\text{Calcium chloride}}{\mathrm{CaCl_2}} \longrightarrow \underset{\text{Calcium ion}}{\mathrm{Ca^{2+}}} + \underset{\text{Chloride ion}}{2\mathrm{Cl^-}}$$

$$\underset{\text{Sodium sulfate}}{\mathrm{Na_2SO_4}} \longrightarrow \underset{\text{Sodium ion}}{2\,\mathrm{Na^+}} + \underset{\text{Sulfate ion}}{\mathrm{SO_4^{2-}}}$$

In the last equation the sulfate ion is an example of a complex ion. Instead of a single charged ion it consists of a group of atoms that are bonded to one another. Several biologically important ions are listed in Table 2-2.

Electrons are shared in covalent bonds

We have seen that ionic bonds are established by electron exchange. In **covalent bonds,** electrons are neither gained nor lost. Instead, atoms share electrons. Very strong, stable bonds are formed in this way.

Because an atom of hydrogen has only one electron in its single shell, it is not stable. (Recall

TABLE 2-2

Some biologically important ions		
Name	**Formula**	**Charge**
Sodium	Na^+	1 +
Potassium	K^+	1 +
Hydrogen	H^+	1 +
Magnesium	Mg^{2+}	2 +
Calcium	Ca^{2+}	2 +
Iron	Fe^{2+} or Fe^{3+}	2 + [iron(II)] or 3 + [iron(III)]
Ammonium	NH_4^+	1 +
Chloride	Cl^-	1 −
Iodide	I^-	1 −
Carbonate	CO_3^{2-}	2 −
Bicarbonate	HCO_3^-	1 −
Phosphate	PO_4^{3-}	3 −
Acetate	CH_3COO^-	1 −
Sulfate	SO_4^{2-}	2 −
Hydroxide	OH^-	1 −
Nitrate	NO_3^-	1 −
Nitrite	NO_2^-	1 −

that the first shell holds a maximum of two electrons.) When two hydrogen atoms share their electrons chemically they each achieve chemical stability (Fig. 2-5a). These two electrons revolve about the nuclei of both hydrogen atoms of the molecule.

Two oxygen atoms also achieve stability by forming covalent bonds with one another. Each oxygen atom has six electrons in its outer shell. To become stable, two oxygen atoms share two pairs of electrons, forming molecular oxygen. When two pairs of electrons are shared in this manner, the covalent bond is referred to as a **double bond** (Fig. 2-5b). When three pairs of electrons are shared, the covalent bond is called a triple bond.

When oxygen combines with two atoms of hydrogen to form water, one pair of electrons is shared between the oxygen and each hydrogen atom. Oxygen thus achieves stability with eight electrons in its outer shell, while each hydrogen atom also becomes stable by filling its single electron shell (Fig. 2-5c).

In hydrogen and oxygen as in many covalent compounds, electrons are equally shared. In other covalent bonds, electrons are closer to one atom than another. For example, in water, electrons tend to stay closer to the nucleus of the oxygen atom than to the hydrogen nuclei (Figure 2-5c). This type of bond is a **polar covalent bond,** one in which electrons are more strongly attracted to one atom than another.

Hydrogen bonds form and break with relative ease

When hydrogen is combined with oxygen (or with another electronegative atom), it has a partial positive charge because its electron is positioned closer to the oxygen atom. A **hydrogen bond** is a very weak chemical bond formed between an already bonded hydrogen atom and a negatively charged atom such as oxygen or nitrogen (Fig. 2-6). Both the hydrogen and the negatively charged atom are already bonded to other atoms. The atoms involved may be in two parts of the same molecule or in two different molecules.

Hydrogen bonds help determine the three-dimensional structure of large molecules such as proteins and DNA. Although hydrogen bonds are relatively weak individually, so many of them occur in large molecules that together they provide great strength and help stabilize molecules.

Hydrogen (H) (1*p*) + Hydrogen (H) (1*p*) → Molecular hydrogen (H_2) or H-H

(*a*)

Oxygen (O) (8*p*, 8*n*) + Oxygen (O) (8*p*, 8*n*) → Molecular oxygen (O_2) (double bond is formed) or O=O

(*b*)

Hydrogen (H) (1*p*) + Oxygen (O) (8*p*, 8*n*) + Hydrogen (H) (1*p*) → Water molecule (H_2O) or H-O-H

Oxygen part

Partial negative charge at oxygen end of molecule

Hydrogen parts

Partial positive charge at hydrogen end of molecule

(*c*)

FIGURE 2-5

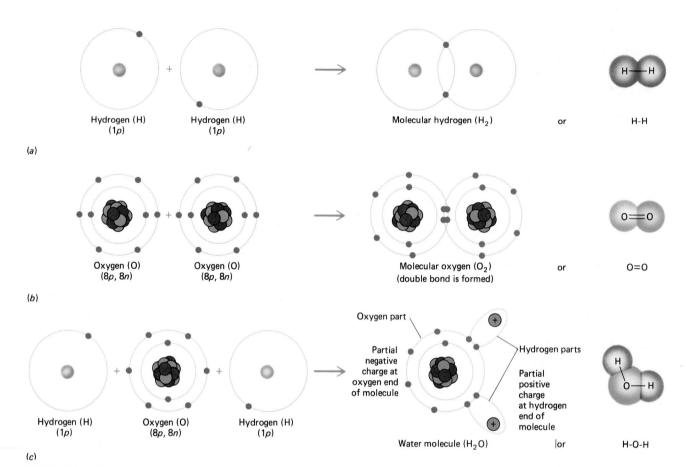

Formation of covalent compounds. (*a*) Two hydrogen atoms achieve stability by sharing electrons, thereby forming a molecule of hydrogen. The structural formula shown on the right is a simpler way of representing molecular hydrogen. The straight line between the hydrogen atoms represents a single covalent bond. (*b*) Two oxygen atoms share two pairs of electrons to form molecular oxygen. Note the double bond. (*c*) When two hydrogen atoms share electrons with an oxygen atom, the result is a molecule of water. Note that the electrons tend to stay closer to the nucleus of the oxygen atom than to the hydrogen nuclei. This results in a partial negative charge on the oxygen portion of the molecule, and a partial positive charge at the hydrogen end. Although the water molecule as a whole is electrically neutral, it is a polar covalent compound.

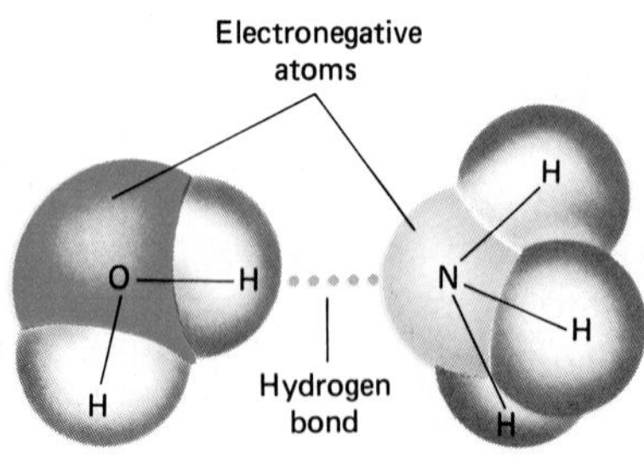

FIGURE 2-6

A hydrogen bond. The nitrogen atom of an ammonia molecule (NH_3) is joined to a hydrogen atom of a water molecule (H_2O) by a hydrogen bond. In a hydrogen bond, a hydrogen atom linked to an electronegative atom by a covalent bond is shared with another electronegative atom by a weak electrical attraction.

Chemical reactions involve the synthesis or breaking of bonds

Energy plays an important part in chemical reactions. This specific type of energy is referred to as **chemical energy.** In order to form a chemical bond, energy must be added. When a bond is broken, energy is released. There are many types of reactions that occur in living cells. Chemical reactions are illustrated by chemical equations.

In a **synthesis reaction** two or more ions, atoms, or molecules bond together to form a new molecule. This type of reaction is necessary for the building processes of the body such as manufacture of new cell parts, bone development, or hair and nail growth. Synthesis reactions are anabolic reactions because they involve the building of new molecules from smaller ones. An example of a synthesis reaction is the combining of the simple sugars glucose and fructose to form the larger sugar sucrose (table sugar). Note that an enzyme, a type of catalyst, is required to regulate this reaction.

$$\text{Glucose} + \text{Fructose} \xrightarrow{\text{Enzyme}} \text{Sucrose} + \text{Water}$$

In the synthesis of many organic compounds, water is produced from hydrogen and oxygen split off from the reactants. (In the past this type of reaction has been referred to as a dehydration synthesis. However, this term is no longer preferred because the process is often more complex than might be inferred by the single reaction shown here.)

Decomposition reactions involve the breaking of bonds of a large molecule to get smaller molecules, ions, or atoms. The process of breaking down food employs decomposition reactions. Since breaking bonds releases energy, one can see why eating a good breakfast is so important. Decomposition reactions are catabolic reactions. An example of a decomposition reaction is the breakdown of sucrose during digestion to glucose and fructose.

$$\text{Sucrose} + \text{Water} \xrightarrow{\text{Enzyme}} \text{Glucose} + \text{Fructose}$$

Note that water is needed for the breakdown of sucrose; this type of reaction is referred to as a *hydrolysis reaction.*

When both synthesis and decomposition are reciprocally involved, the reaction is an **exchange reaction.** Some reactions are **reversible reactions** in which case the product may revert to the reactants. Reversible reactions may be indicated by double arrows. The longer arrow indicates that the reaction tends to proceed to the right.

$$N_2 + 3\,H_2 \rightleftarrows 2\,NH_3$$

Many inorganic compounds are essential to living organisms

Chemical compounds can be divided into two broad groups—*inorganic* and *organic.* **Inorganic compounds** are relatively simple substances whose atoms are generally linked by ionic bonds. Organic compounds are usually large and complex and always contain carbon. Their atoms are linked mainly by covalent bonds (although in complex molecules other types of bonds are also present). Both types of compounds are integral components of the body.

Among the important groups of inorganic compounds are water, simple acids, bases, and salts. These substances are required in appropriate amounts for water balance, acid-base balance, and many cell activities such as transmission of nerve impulses and muscle contraction.

Water is an essential ingredient of life

Water accounts for about 60% of the body weight of an adult. It is important both inside cells and between cells and plays a vital role in moving materials within cells and from one place in the body to another. Blood plasma, which is 90% water, transports nutrients, hormones, and other substances throughout the body and carries wastes from the cells to the organs of excretion. Wastes are carried from the body in urine and sweat, both of which are more than 95% water.

Because water dissolves more substances better than anything else, it is considered the most important biological *solvent.* The molecular motion of dissolved substances permits them to contact and interact with one another. As a result, almost all chemical reactions that are essential to life take place in a watery medium. In many reactions that occur in the body, water is a reactant or product.

Water has the ability to absorb considerable heat without rapidly changing its own temperature. When heat is released as a result of muscle activity, for example, the blood can absorb the excess heat and bring it to the body surface. From there, heat radiates away from the body (this process creates the flushed look that occurs after violent exertion). When we sweat, heat is also carried away from the body as the perspiration evaporates. Vaporization (change in state from liquid to gas) of water requires energy, and in evaporation of sweat that energy comes from body heat. We get rid of about 25% of body heat by water evaporation from the skin and lungs. Thus, water helps to maintain the constant temperature of the body.

In water the electrons of the two hydrogen atoms tend to stay closer to the nucleus of the oxygen atom than to the nuclei of the hydrogen atoms. This occurs because the larger size of the positively charged oxygen nucleus tends to attract

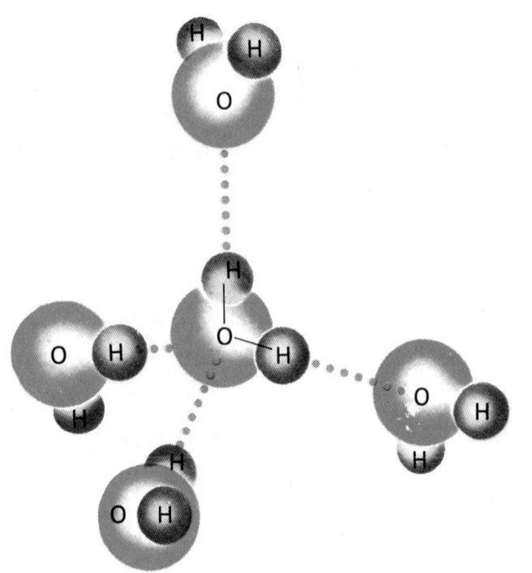

FIGURE 2-7

Hydrogen bonding of water molecules. Each water molecule tends to form hydrogen bonds with four neighboring water molecules. The hydrogen bonds are indicated by dotted lines. The covalent bonds between the hydrogen and oxygen atoms are represented by solid lines.

the hydrogen electrons more strongly than can either of the smaller hydrogen nuclei. As a result, the oxygen end of the molecule has a relative negative charge compared with the hydrogen ends. Chemists use the term *dipole* to refer to molecules such as water that have opposite charges at two ends of the molecule. Because of these charges, adjacent water molecules tend to form hydrogen bonds with one another. The positively charged hydrogen ends of one water molecule are electrically linked to the negatively charged portions of two other water molecules. In water, each molecule tends to form hydrogen bonds with four adjacent water molecules (Fig. 2-7).

Hydrogen bonding of water molecules accounts for many of the properties of water. For example, it explains why water is resistant to changes in temperature. The temperature of a substance rises as its molecules move more quickly. Because water molecules are linked by hydrogen bonds, increased molecular movement is difficult, and so is temperature increase. Of course, if enough energy is supplied in the form of heat, these hydrogen bonds can be broken and evaporation will occur. As already discussed, evaporation has a cooling effect and is important in temperature regulation in many organisms.

The polarity of water molecules allows water to be a strong solvent. Its electrical charges exert a force upon compounds immersed in it, thus causing bits of the substance to separate and dissolve. For example, when a lump of salt (or sugar) is placed in water, molecules are slowly pulled away from the lump to form new associations with the water molecules themselves (Fig. 2-8).

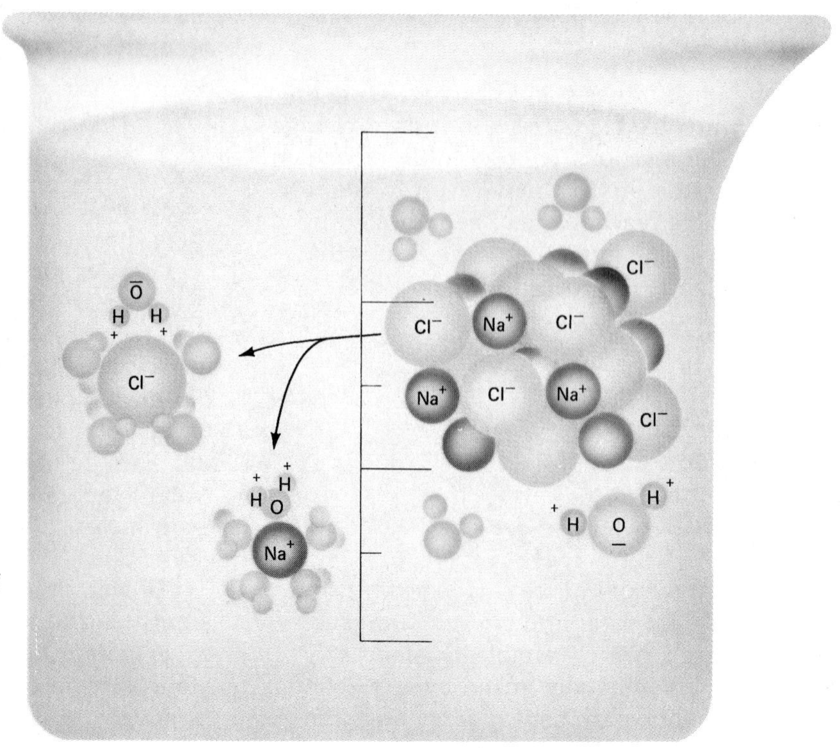

FIGURE 2-8

The crystal lattice of a salt like NaCl is held together by the strong ionic bonds between the Na^+ and Cl^- ions, and considerable energy is required to pull the ions apart. When NaCl is added to water, the negative ends of the water molecules are attracted to the positive sodium ions and tend to pull them away from the chlorine ions. At the same time, the positive ends of the water molecule are attracted to the negative chlorine ions, separating them from the sodium ions. When dissolved, each of the sodium and chlorine atoms is surrounded by water molecules electrically attracted to it.

Another important characteristic of water molecules is their slight tendency to *ionize*—that is, to dissociate into hydrogen ions (H^+) and hydroxide ions (OH^-). In pure water a very small number of water molecules form ions in this way, forming an equal number of hydrogen and hydroxide ions.

$$\underset{\text{Water}}{HOH} \rightleftarrows \underset{\text{Hydrogen ion}}{H^+} + \underset{\text{Hydroxide ion}}{OH^-}$$

The arrows indicate that the reaction proceeds in both directions. New ions are produced at the same rate that some of the old ones recombine to form water once again. An equilibrium, or balance, is established in which the concentration of both types of ions remains constant. In water the ionization equilibrium leans greatly toward the left, so that at any one time very little of the water is actually ionized. In fact, out of every 550 million or so water molecules only one will be ionized at any given time.

Acids and bases are measured by pH

An **acid** is a compound that dissociates in solution to produce hydrogen ions and some type of anion. Acids are often referred to as proton donors. They have a characteristic sour or tart taste and often have a sharp odor. Perhaps the most familiar acid in the body is the hydrochloric acid (HCl) of the stomach. Another acid that plays an important role in body chemistry is carbonic acid (H_2CO_3).

The strength of an acid depends upon the degree to which it dissociates in water. HCl is a very strong acid because most of its molecules dissociate, producing hydrogen and chloride ions.

$$\underset{\text{Hydrochloric acid}}{HCl} \longrightarrow \underset{\text{Hydrogen ion}}{H^+} + \underset{\text{Chloride ion}}{Cl^-}$$

Carbonic acid, on the other hand, is a weak acid because it dissociates very little. This compound is well tolerated in the body and even occurs normally in the blood.

$$\underset{\text{Carbonic acid}}{H_2CO_3} \longrightarrow \underset{\text{Hydrogen ion}}{H^+} + \underset{\text{Bicarbonate ion}}{HCO_3^-}$$

A **base,** or alkali, is a compound that dissociates in solution to form hydroxide ions (OH^-) and whatever cation the molecule yields. Bases characteristically taste bitter and feel slippery. Some compounds with basic properties, however, do not contain hydroxide ions. For this reason, a base is better defined as a proton acceptor. Sodium hydroxide (NaOH) is an example of a common base.

$$\underset{\text{Sodium hydroxide}}{NaOH} \longrightarrow \underset{\text{Sodium ion}}{Na^+} + \underset{\text{Hydroxide ion}}{OH^-}$$

How can the acidity or alkalinity of a solution be determined? Although acids taste sour and bases are bitter, tasting is not a recommended method! Instead, solutions may be tested with litmus paper, an acid-base indicator found in basic chemistry sets. Litmus paper turns red when dipped in an acidic solution and blue when dipped into a basic solution.

A still more sophisticated method for determining acidity or alkalinity involves the use of a pH meter. This is an instrument that measures **pH,** the relative acidity or alkalinity of a solution, on a scale that ranges from 0 to 14. Seven is neutral (Fig. 2-9). The pH of pure water is 7. The

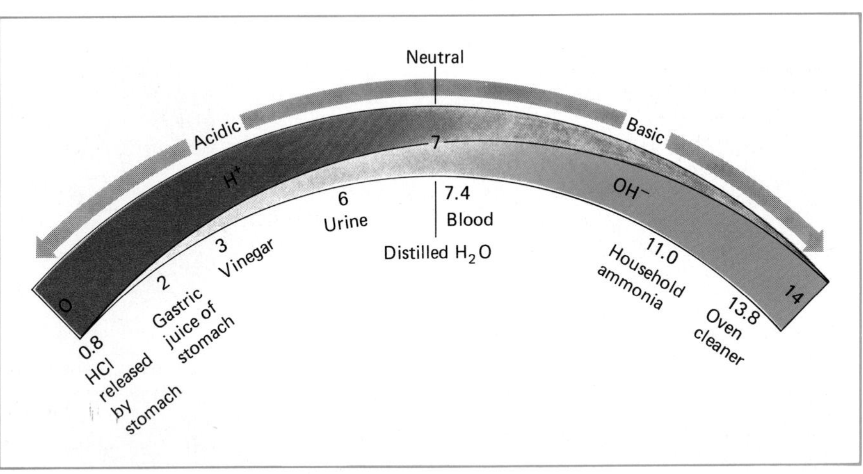

FIGURE 2-9

The pH scale. A solution with a pH of 7 is neutral because the concentrations of H^+ and OH^- are equal. The lower the pH below 7, the more H^+ ions are present, and the more acidic the solution is. As the pH increases above 7, the concentration of H^+ ions decreases and the concentration of OH^- increases, making the solution more alkaline (basic).

higher the number above 7, the greater the alkalinity. A pH of less than 7 indicates an acidic solution.

The pH of a solution is defined as the negative logarithm of the hydrogen ion concentration [log $(1/[H^+])$]. The more acidic a solution is, the more hydrogen ions are present in the solution and consequently, the lower the pH will be. Thus a pH of 4 is much more acidic than a pH of 6. Because a logarithmic scale is used for pH measurement (which we will not discuss in detail), actual acidity increases much faster than the numerical change in pH might seem to indicate. A pH of 5, for example, is ten times as acidic as a pH of 6—that is, it represents a tenfold increase in hydrogen ion concentration. A pH of 4 represents another tenfold increase. Thus a pH of 4 is 100 times more acidic than a pH of 6.

Acids and bases neutralize each other and form salts

Inorganic salts are a source of many important mineral ions such as sodium, chlorine, calcium, and magnesium. Such ions are essential for fluid balance, acid-base balance, nerve and muscle function, blood clotting, bone formation, and many other aspects of body function.

A **salt** is a compound that ionizes to yield a positive ion other than H^+ and a negative ion other than OH^-. A salt is produced when a strong acid and a strong base react with one another.

$$\underset{\text{Hydrochloric acid}}{HCl} + \underset{\text{Sodium hydroxide}}{NaOH} \longrightarrow \underset{\text{Sodium chloride}}{NaCl} + \underset{\text{Water}}{H_2O}$$

The salt dissociates and its ions are important in a variety of metabolic activities.

Compounds that dissociate to form ions in water are called **electrolytes** because, as charged particles, they can conduct an electric current. In the body, electrolytes are important in many vital processes, such as conduction of nerve impulses and muscle contraction (Fig. 2-10). Different electrolytes dissociate to different degrees because some have stronger bonds than others. Substances that are covalently bonded, such as sugars and proteins, do not readily dissociate and are referred to as nonelectrolytes.

Buffers maintain pH

Many homeostatic mechanisms work to maintain appropriate pH levels. What is appropriate varies somewhat from one location in the body to another. For example, the pH within the stomach is highly acidic (about 2), whereas the pH of blood is about 7.4. Generally, the pH for a given tissue such as blood must be maintained within very narrow limits. Should the blood become too acidic, coma and death may result. A process known as *buffering* helps to maintain appropriate pH levels (Fig. 2-11).

A **buffer** consists of a weak acid plus a salt of that acid. One of the most common buffering systems, and one that is important in human blood and tissues, involves the salt sodium bicarbonate ($NaHCO_3$) and carbonic acid (H_2CO_3). Bicarbonate ions are formed in the body as follows:

$$\underset{\text{Carbon dioxide}}{CO_2} + \underset{\text{Water}}{H_2O} \rightleftarrows \underset{\text{Carbonic acid}}{H_2CO_3} \rightleftarrows \underset{\text{Hydrogen ion}}{H^+} + \underset{\text{Bicarbonate ion}}{HCO_3^-}$$

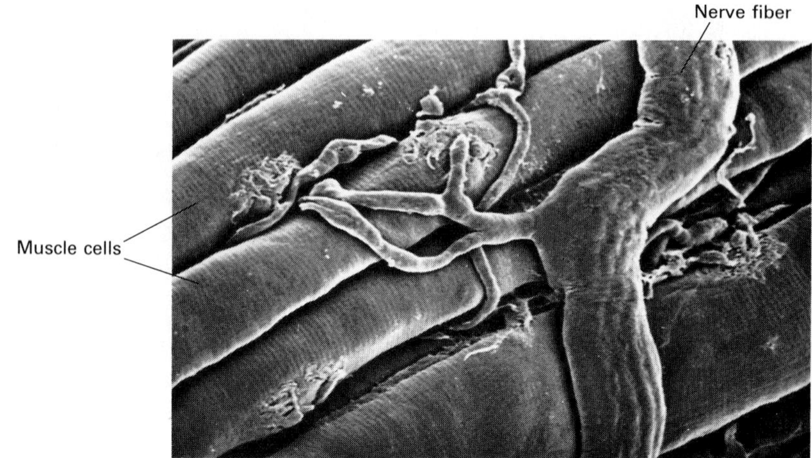

FIGURE 2-10

Sodium, potassium, and chlorine ions are among the ions essential in the conduction of a nerve impulse. This scanning electron micrograph shows a nerve fiber communicating with several muscle cells (approximately ×900). The nerve fiber transmits impulses to the muscle cells, stimulating them to contract. The muscle cells are rich in calcium ions, which are essential for muscle contraction. (From Desaki, J.: "Vascular Autonomic Plexuses and Skeletal Neuromuscular Junctions: A Scanning Electron Microscopic Study," *Biomedical Research Supplement,* 139–143, 1981.)

The bicarbonate ions may then combine with sodium to form the salt sodium bicarbonate.

$$\underset{}{HCO_3^-} + Na^+ \rightleftharpoons \underset{\text{Sodium bicarbonate}}{NaHCO_3}$$

As indicated by the arrows, the reaction is readily reversible.

When excess hydrogen ions are present in blood or other body fluids, bicarbonate ions combine with them to form carbonic acid, a weak acid.

$$Na^+ + HCO_3^- + H^+ + Cl^- \rightleftharpoons H_2CO_3 + NaCl$$

In this way a strong acid (one that dissociates to a great extent) is converted to a weak acid (one that dissociates very little) and a salt.

Buffers also work to reduce pH when excessive numbers of hydroxide ions are present. A buffer may release hydrogen ions, which combine with the hydroxide ions to form water.

$$\underset{\substack{\text{Sodium}\\\text{hydroxide}\\\text{(a strong base)}}}{NaOH} + H_2CO_3 \longrightarrow \underset{\substack{\text{Sodium}\\\text{bicarbonate}}}{NaHCO_3} + H_2O$$

In this reaction, hydroxide ions from sodium hydroxide combine with hydrogen from carbonic acid, forming water.

FIGURE 2-11

Buffering is used clinically as a remedy for excess stomach acid. The bubbles are carbon dioxide from the reaction between an acid (citric acid) and the bicarbonate ion (HCO_3^-) from sodium bicarbonate.

Organic compounds are the main structural components of the body

Organic compounds are large, complex compounds containing carbon. Hydrogen is also a component of organic compounds. In living systems, many organic compounds also contain oxygen, nitrogen, phosphorus, and sulfur. Organic compounds are the main structural components of the body and the energy source for all life processes. Organic compounds are participants in thousands of metabolic reactions, and some serve as enzymes that regulate chemical reactions. In all organic compounds the chain of atoms that makes up the principal axis of the molecule consists of carbon atoms. In a way, the chemistry of the carbon atom is the chemistry of life itself.

The versatility of the carbon atom permits the formation of the large complex molecules essential to life

Carbon has the most versatile combining properties of any type of atom and forms very strong covalent bonds. With four electrons in its outer shell, a carbon atom can form four bonds with other atoms. For example, a carbon atom can combine with four hydrogen atoms as in methane

```
    H
    |
H—C—H
    |
    H
```

or it can combine with a variety of atoms,

```
H   H
 \ /
  N  H
  |  |
H—C—C—H
  |  |
  H  H
```

Sometimes carbon forms a **double bond** in which two pairs of electrons are shared either with another carbon atom or with some other type of atom.

```
H       H        H  O
 \     /         |  ‖
  C=C         H—C—C—OH
 /     \         |
H       H        H
```

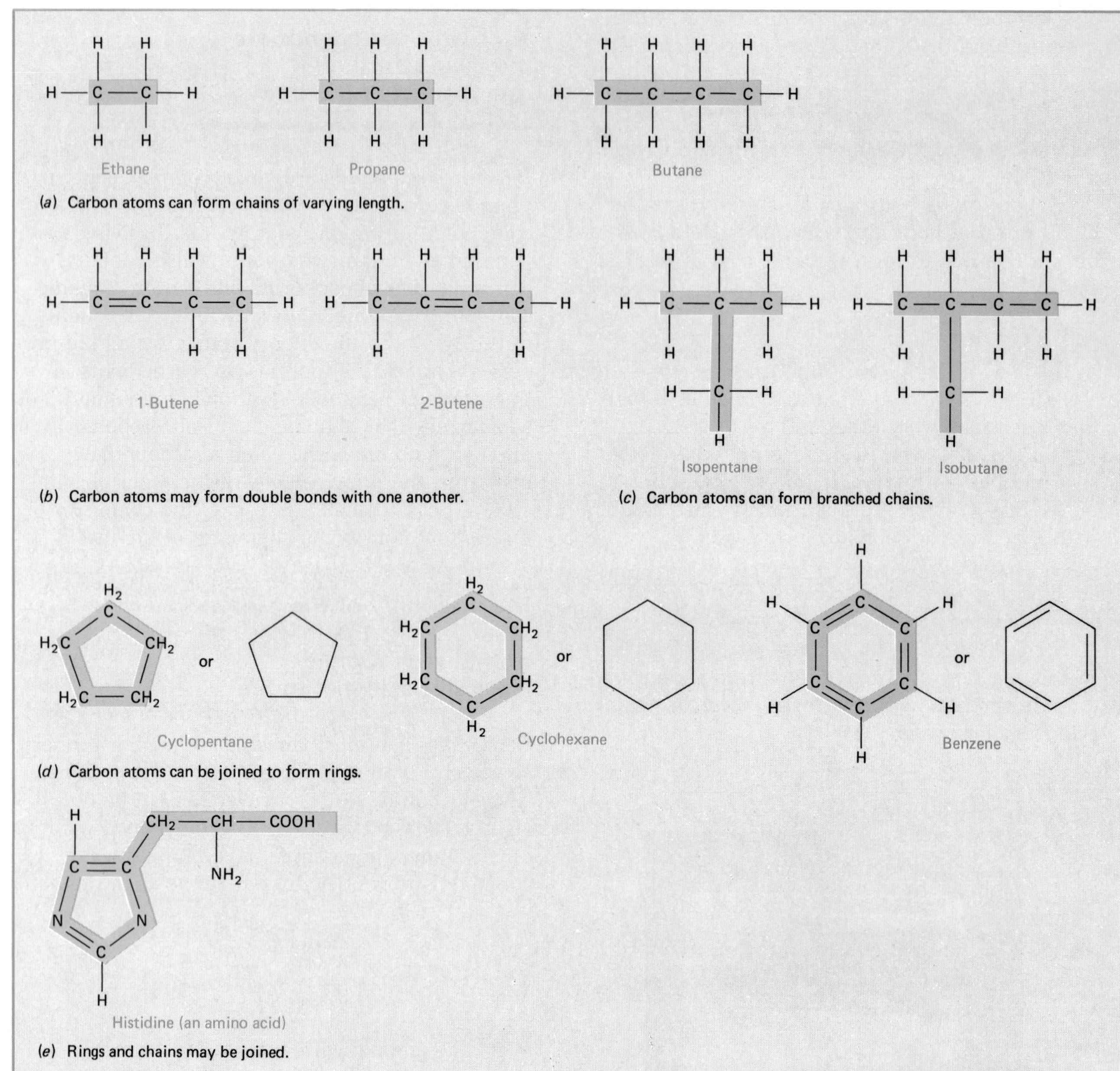

FIGURE 2-12

Some simple organic compounds. These structural formulas illustrate common variations in the architecture of organic molecules. Note that each carbon atom forms four covalent bonds.

When doubly bonded to another atom, carbon can combine with only two additional atoms. The total number of bonds formed is always four.

Carbon atoms can join to form long, chainlike molecules called **polymers,** which are large molecules made up of many similar units. Sometimes carbon atoms form ringlike molecules, as in some of the carbohydrates that we shall discuss below. Some common variations in the structure of organic compounds are illustrated in Figure 2-12.

The hydrocarbon backbone of an organic compound does not interact readily with other carbons. However, one or more of the hydrogen atoms bonded to the carbon skeleton can be replaced with other groups of atoms. These groups of atoms, referred to as **functional groups,** readily form associations such as ionic and hydrogen bonds with other molecules. In this way functional groups help determine the types of chemical reactions that take place.

Each class of organic compound is characterized by one or more specific functional groups. For example, as illustrated in Table 2-3, alcohols

TABLE 2-3

Some biologically important functional groups

Functional group	Structural formula	Class of compounds characterized by group	Example	Description
Hydroxyl	R—OH	Alcohols	H—C(H)(H)—C(H)(H)—OH Ethanol (the alcohol contained in beverages)	Polar because electronegative oxygen attracts covalent electrons
Amino	R—NH_2	Amines	R—C(NH_2)—C(=O)—OH Amino acid	Ionic; amino group acts as base
Carboxyl	R—C(=O)—OH	Carboxylic acids (organic acids)	R—C(NH_2)—C(=O)—OH Amino acid	Ionic; the H can dissociate as an H^+ ion
Ester	R—C(=O)—O—R	Esters	H—C(H)(H)—C(=O)—O—C(H)(H)—H Methyl acetate	Related to carboxyl group, but has hydrocarbon group in place of the OH hydrogen; polar
Carbonyl	R—C(=O)—H	Aldehydes	H—C(=O)—H Formaldehyde	Carbonyl carbon bonded to at least one H atom; polar
	R—C(=O)—R	Ketones	H—C(H)(H)—C(=O)—C(H)(H)—H Acetone	Carbonyl group bonded to two other carbons; polar
Methyl	R—CH_3	Component of many organic compounds	H—C(H)(H)—OH Methanol (wood alcohol)	Nonpolar
Phosphate	R—O—P(=O)(OH)—OH	Organic phosphates	R—O—P(=O)(OH)—OH Phosphate ester (as found in ATP)	Dissociated form of phosphoric acid; the phosphate ion is covalently bonded by one of its oxygen atoms to one of the carbons; ionic
Sulfhydryl	R—SH	Thiols	CH_2(SH)—CH(NH_2)—C(=O)—OH Cysteine	Helps stabilize internal structure of proteins

contain functional groups called hydroxyl groups (—OH). Note that the symbol R is used to represent the remainder of the molecule of which the functional group is a part. Most biological compounds have two or more different functional groups.

An important property of functional groups found in biological molecules is their solubility in water. Positively and negatively charged functional groups are water-soluble because they associate strongly with the polar water molecules.

Four important classes of organic compounds are *carbohydrates, lipids, nucleic acids,* and *proteins.* Table 2-4 summarizes some information about these compounds. Let us examine their structures and functions.

TABLE 2-4

Some of the biologically important groups of organic compounds

Class of compound	Description	Component elements	How to recognize	Principal functions
Carbohydrates	Carbohydrates have approximately as many oxygen atoms as carbon atoms and twice as many hydrogens as carbons (when allowance is made for water loss when sugar units are linked)	C, H, O	Count the carbons, hydrogens, and oxygens	Cellular fuel; energy storage; components of other compounds, e.g., nucleic acids
	1. Monosaccharides, the simple sugars $(CH_2O)_n$. For the most part, these are six-carbon (hexose) molecules like glucose whose backbones may be shown as straight lines but are actually arranged in ring formations. Glucose and fructose are examples. Ribose is a pentose (five-carbon) monosaccharide		Look for the ring shapes: ⬡ hexose ⬠ or pentose	
	2. Disaccharide (two sugars) e.g., sucrose, maltose, lactose		Two sugar units	
	3. Polysaccharide (many units) e.g., starch, glycogen, cellulose		Many sugar subunits	
Lipids	1. Neutral fats. Combination of glycerol with one to three fatty acids. One fatty acid—monoacylglycerol; two fatty acids—diacylglycerol; three fatty acids—	C, H, O	Look for glycerol at one end of molecule: H, H—C—OH, H—C—OH, H—C—OH, H	Energy storage; thermal insulation; support of organs

Carbohydrates are important fuel molecules

Starches, sugars, and cellulose are examples of **carbohydrates.** Composed of carbon, hydrogen, and oxygen, carbohydrates are important fuel molecules. Because each carbohydrate molecule has twice as many hydrogen atoms as oxygen atoms, the same ratio (2:1) found in water, early chemists thought that carbohydrates were combinations of water and carbon, that is, hydrates (water) of carbon. The name has stuck, though of course we no longer think of carbohydrates in such simple terms. Based on molecular size, carbohydrates may be classified as *monosaccharides, disaccharides,* or *polysaccharides.*

(Continued)

Class of compound	Description	Component elements	How to recognize	Principal functions
	fatty acids contain double carbon-to-carbon linkages (C═C), they are unsaturated; otherwise they are saturated			
	2. Phospholipids. Glycerol attached to one or two fatty acids and to an organic base that contains phosphorus	C, H, O, P, N	Look for glycerol and side chain containing phosphorus and nitrogen.	Components of cell membranes
	3. Steroids. Complex molecules containing carbon atoms arranged in four interlocking rings (three rings contain six carbon atoms each and the fourth ring contains five)		Look for four interlocking rings	Some are hormones; other biologically important steroids are cholesterol, bile salts, and vitamin D
Proteins	One or more polypeptides (chains of amino acids) coiled or folded in characteristic shapes	C, H, O, N, usually S	Look for amino acid units joined by C—N bonds	Structural components; serve as enzymes; muscle proteins
Nucleic acids	Backbone composed of alternating pentose and phosphate groups, from which nitrogenous bases protrude. Occurs as a double (DNA) or single (RNA) strand. DNA contains deoxyribose, guanine, cytosine, adenine, and thymine. RNA contains ribose, guanine, cytosine, adenine, and uracil	C, H, O, N, P	Look for a pentose-phosphate backbone. DNA forms a characteristic double helix	Storage, transmission, and expression of genetic information

MONOSACCHARIDES CONTAIN FROM THREE TO SEVEN CARBON ATOMS

Monosaccharides (one sugar), or simple sugars, contain from three to seven carbon atoms. *Ribose* and *deoxyribose* (containing one less oxygen atom) are common *pentoses,* monosaccharides that contain five carbons. These sugars are components of the nucleic acids (DNA, RNA, and related compounds). *Glucose, fructose, galactose,* and other sugars that consist of six carbons are called *hexoses* (Figure 2-13).

Glucose, the most common monosaccharide in living organisms, has the chemical formula $C_6H_{12}O_6$. Fructose (fruit sugar) and galactose have the same chemical formula as glucose, but because their atoms are arranged differently their chemical properties are distinct. Glucose, fructose, and galactose are isomers.

The "stick" formulas in Figure 2-13 give a clear but somewhat unrealistic picture of monosaccharide structures. In living cells the molecules are actually bent into ring configurations. The ring structures of glucose and fructose are shown in Figure 2-14. (Corresponding carbon atoms have been numbered.)

DISACCHARIDES AND POLYSACCHARIDES ARE COMPOSED OF MONOSACCHARIDE UNITS

Two monosaccharides may combine chemically to form a **disaccharide.** The two monosaccharide units are joined by a type of covalent bond called

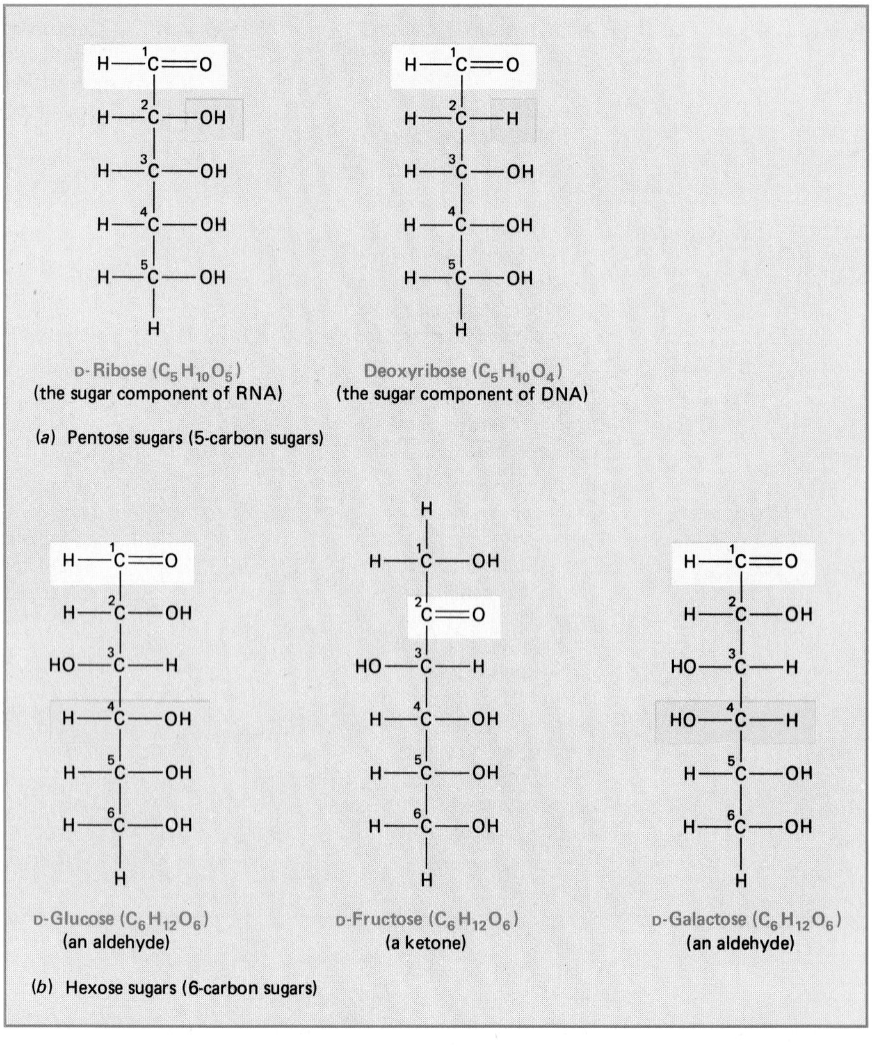

D-Ribose ($C_5H_{10}O_5$)
(the sugar component of RNA)

Deoxyribose ($C_5H_{10}O_4$)
(the sugar component of DNA)

(*a*) Pentose sugars (5-carbon sugars)

D-Glucose ($C_6H_{12}O_6$)
(an aldehyde)

D-Fructose ($C_6H_{12}O_6$)
(a ketone)

D-Galactose ($C_6H_{12}O_6$)
(an aldehyde)

(*b*) Hexose sugars (6-carbon sugars)

FIGURE 2-13

Structural formulas of some important monosaccharides (simple sugars). The monosaccharides are represented here as straight chains, called stick formulas. Although it is convenient to show monosaccharides in this form, they are more accurately depicted as ring structures (Fig. 2-14). Note that glucose, fructose, and galactose are isomers—they have the same chemical formula, $C_6H_{12}O_6$, but their atoms are arranged differently.

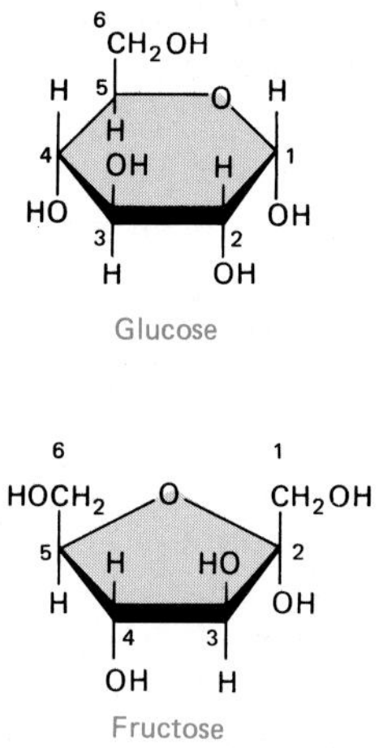

FIGURE 2-14

Two monosaccharides, glucose and fructose, drawn to represent their ring structures. At each angle in the ring is a carbon atom; its presence is understood by convention. Each number on the ring or on an attached group corresponds to the numbered carbons in the stick diagrams of glucose and fructose shown in Figure 2-13. The thick, tapered bonds in the lower portion of each ring indicate that the molecule is a three-dimensional structure. The thickest portion of the bond is interpreted as being the part of the molecule nearest the viewer.

a **glycosidic linkage,** which generally forms between carbon 1 of one molecule and carbon 4 of the other molecule. When two glucose molecules combine chemically, they form *maltose* (the sugar in malt). A molecule of glucose chemically combined with a molecule of fructose forms sucrose, the sugar we use to sweeten our foods. Each of these reactions is regulated by an enzyme.

$$\underset{\text{Glucose}}{C_6H_{12}O_6} + \underset{\text{Fructose}}{C_6H_{12}O_6} \xrightarrow{\text{Enzyme}} \underset{\text{Sucrose}}{C_{12}H_{22}O_{11}} + \underset{\text{Water}}{H_2O}$$

Structural formulas for compounds in this reaction are shown in Figure 2-15. The bond formed between glucose and fructose can be broken to produce glucose and fructose again.

$$\underset{\text{Sucrose}}{C_{12}H_{22}O_{11}} + \underset{\text{Water}}{H_2O} \xrightarrow{\text{Enzyme}} \underset{\text{Glucose}}{C_6H_{12}O_6} + \underset{\text{Fructose}}{C_6H_{12}O_6}$$

This is the reaction that occurs during digestion of sucrose (Fig. 2-15). Because water is added during the breakdown of sucrose, this is referred to as a *hydrolysis reaction.*

More than two monosaccharides may combine chemically to form longer carbohydrate chains. A chain of a few units is called an *oligosaccharide.* Most carbohydrates are **polysaccharides** (many

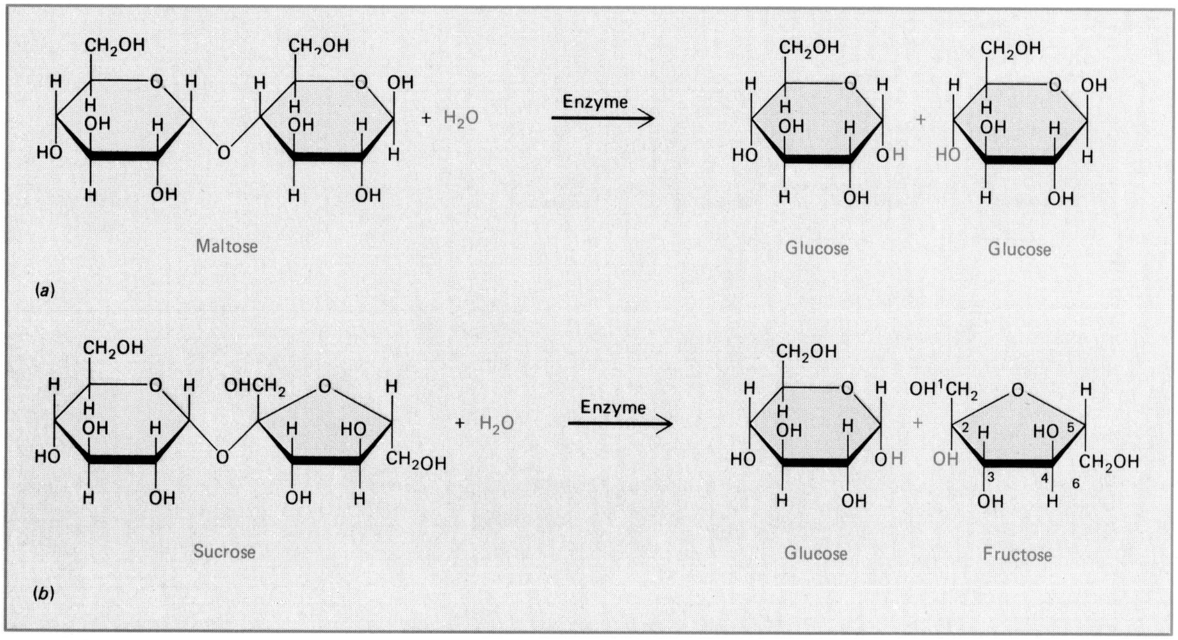

FIGURE 2-15

A disaccharide can be split, yielding two monosaccharide units. (*a*) Maltose may be broken down (as it is during digestion) to form two molecules of glucose. This is a hydrolysis reaction that requires the addition of water. (*b*) Sucrose can be broken down, yielding a molecule of glucose and a molecule of fructose. This is also a hydrolysis reaction.

sugars), long chains consisting of repeating units of a simple sugar.

Glycogen (animal starch) from meat and dairy products and **starch** from plants are important sources of carbohydrate in our diet. During digestion these polysaccharides are broken down into glucose molecules. After they are absorbed from the small intestine into the circulatory system, they are transported to the liver and muscles. In these organs, glucose molecules can be stored as glycogen for future use. Large numbers of glucose molecules are chemically linked to produce glycogen (Fig. 2-16). Later, as needed, glucose is split off from the glycogen and released into the blood for use by the cells.

Plant cells store carbohydrates not as glycogen but as plant starch. This polysaccharide consists of repeating units of maltose. **Cellulose,** the polysaccharide responsible for the rigidity of the plant cell wall, is the most plentiful organic compound on earth. Although we do not possess the enzymes needed to digest it, cellulose serves as bulk within the intestine, mechanically stimulating the elimination of undigested food.

Lipids are important in fuel storage, cell membranes, and hormones

Lipids are fatlike substances that are soluble in organic solvents such as alcohols. Like carbohydrates, they are composed of carbon, hydrogen, and oxygen; however, in proportion they contain much less oxygen per molecule. Some types of lipids that are especially important in the body are neutral fats, phospholipids, steroids, prostaglandins, and waxes. Of the waxes we will say only that ear wax is an example. Prostaglandins have wide effects on body chemistry. These fatty acid-like compounds are discussed in Chapter 18.

NEUTRAL FATS STORE LARGE AMOUNTS OF ENERGY

Neutral fats yield the most fuel energy by weight of any food substance. They provide more than twice as much energy as either proteins or carbohydrates. However, the body does not use fats as efficiently as carbohydrates so a large amount of

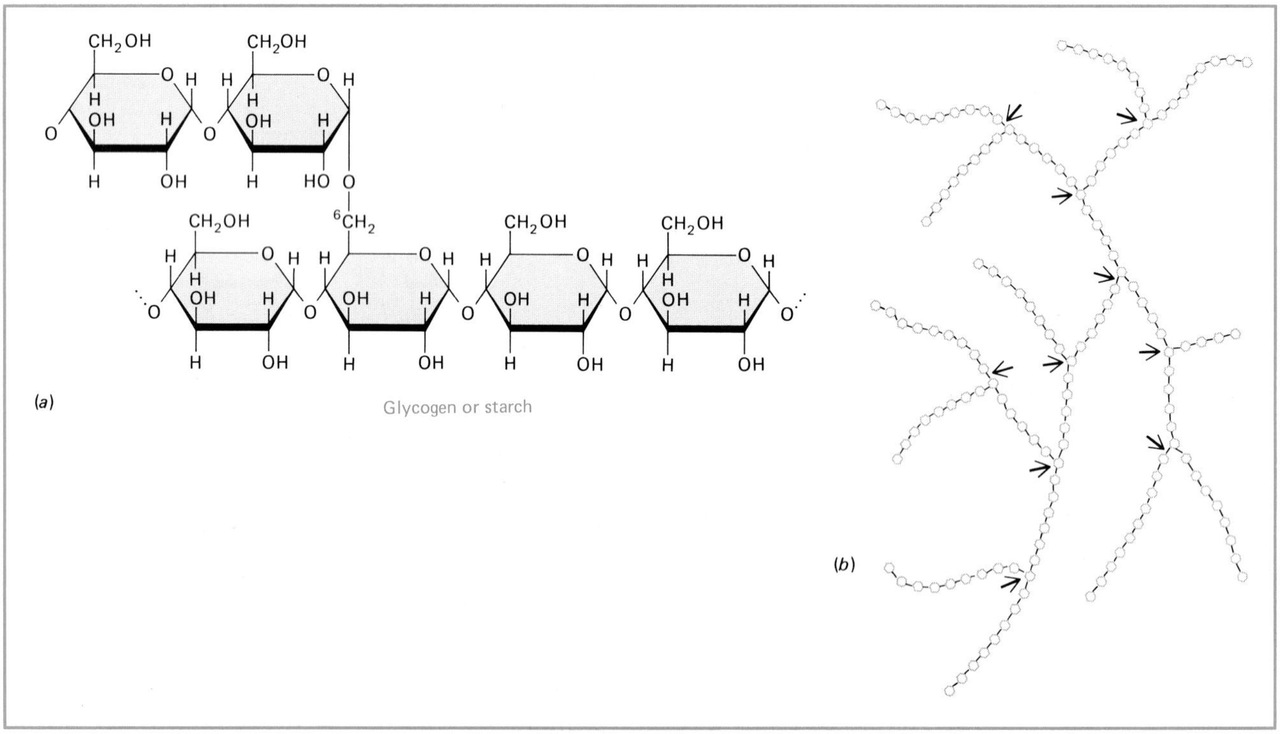

(a) Glycogen or starch

(b)

FIGURE 2-16

Molecular structure of glycogen or starch. *(a)* These molecules are branched polysaccharides composed of glucose molecules joined by glycosidic bonds. At the branch points there are bonds between carbon 6 of a glycogen in the straight chain and carbon 1 of the glucose in the branching chain. Glycogen is more highly branched than starch. *(b)* Diagrammatic representation of starch or glucose. The arrows represent the branch points.

the fat goes unused. Fat molecules are stored mainly in the cells of adipose (fat) tissue.

A neutral fat consists of two components, glycerol and one or more fatty acids. **Glycerol** is a three-carbon alcohol that contains three hydroxyl (—OH) groups (Fig. 2-17). A **fatty acid** is a straight chain of carbon atoms in which most of the carbons are attached to hydrogen atoms. A characteristic group known as a **carboxyl group** (—COOH) is found at one end. About 30 different kinds of fatty acids are commonly found in animal lipids. One fatty acid differs from another

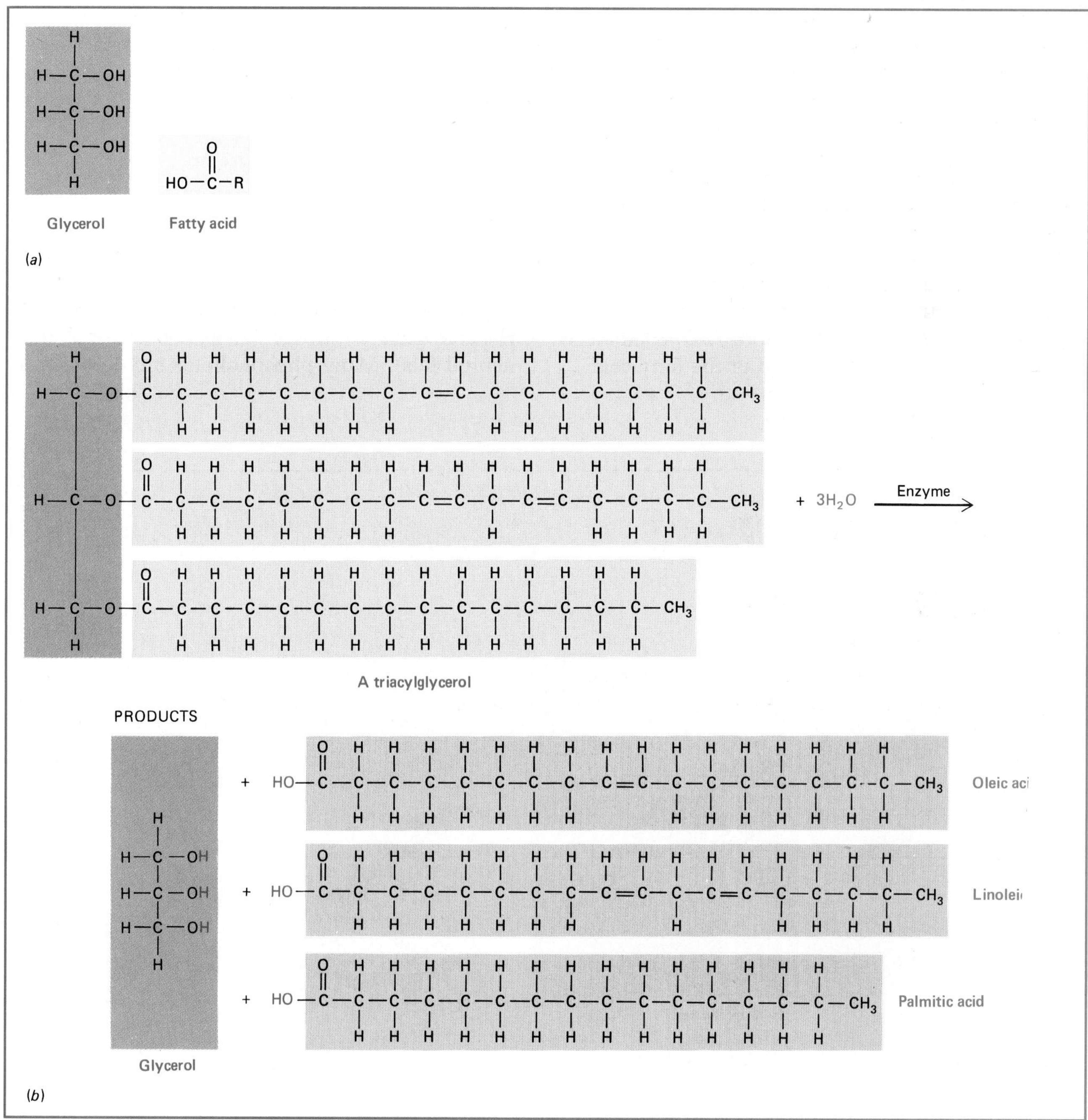

FIGURE 2-17

Neutral fats. (*a*) Structure of glycerol and of a fatty acid. The carboxyl (—COOH) group is present in all fatty acids. The R represents the remainder of the molecule, which varies with each type of fatty acid. (*b*) Hydrolysis of a triglyceride (triacylglycerol) yields glycerol plus three fatty acids.

in the number and arrangement of carbon and hydrogen atoms in its chain. At least two fatty acids (linoleic and arachidonic acids) are *essential* nutrients, which must be included in the diet.

Saturated fatty acids contain the maximum number of hydrogen atoms chemically possible, while **unsaturated fatty acids** contain carbon atoms that are doubly bonded to one another rather than fully saturated with hydrogens. Saturated fats are generally solid at room temperature and are major contributors to coronary heart disease. These fats are found mainly in meat and dairy products. Fats containing unsaturated fatty acids are oils, and most of them are liquid at room temperature. Foods derived from plants contain mainly unsaturated fatty acids. Coconut and palm are exceptions that contain mainly saturated fatty acids.

When a glycerol molecule combines chemically with one fatty acid, a *monoglyceride* (also called monoacylglycerol) is formed. To combine with glycerol the carboxyl end of the fatty acid attaches to one of the hydroxyl groups. During this reaction water is split off. Conversely, during digestion, glycerides may be hydrolyzed to produce fatty acids and glycerol. Two fatty acids linked to a glycerol constitute a *diglyceride* (diacylglycerol).

Three fatty acids attached to a glycerol is a **triglyceride** (triacylglycerol). The triglyceride shown in Figure 2-17 contains two unsaturated fatty acids and one saturated fatty acid. A triglyceride containing three unsaturated fatty acids is referred to as a *polyunsaturated fat*.

PHOSPHOLIPIDS ARE IMPORTANT COMPONENTS OF CELL MEMBRANES

A **phospholipid** consists of a glycerol molecule attached to one or two fatty acids and also attached to an organic base that contains phosphorus and usually nitrogen (elements absent in the neutral fats). Many phospholipids are derivatives

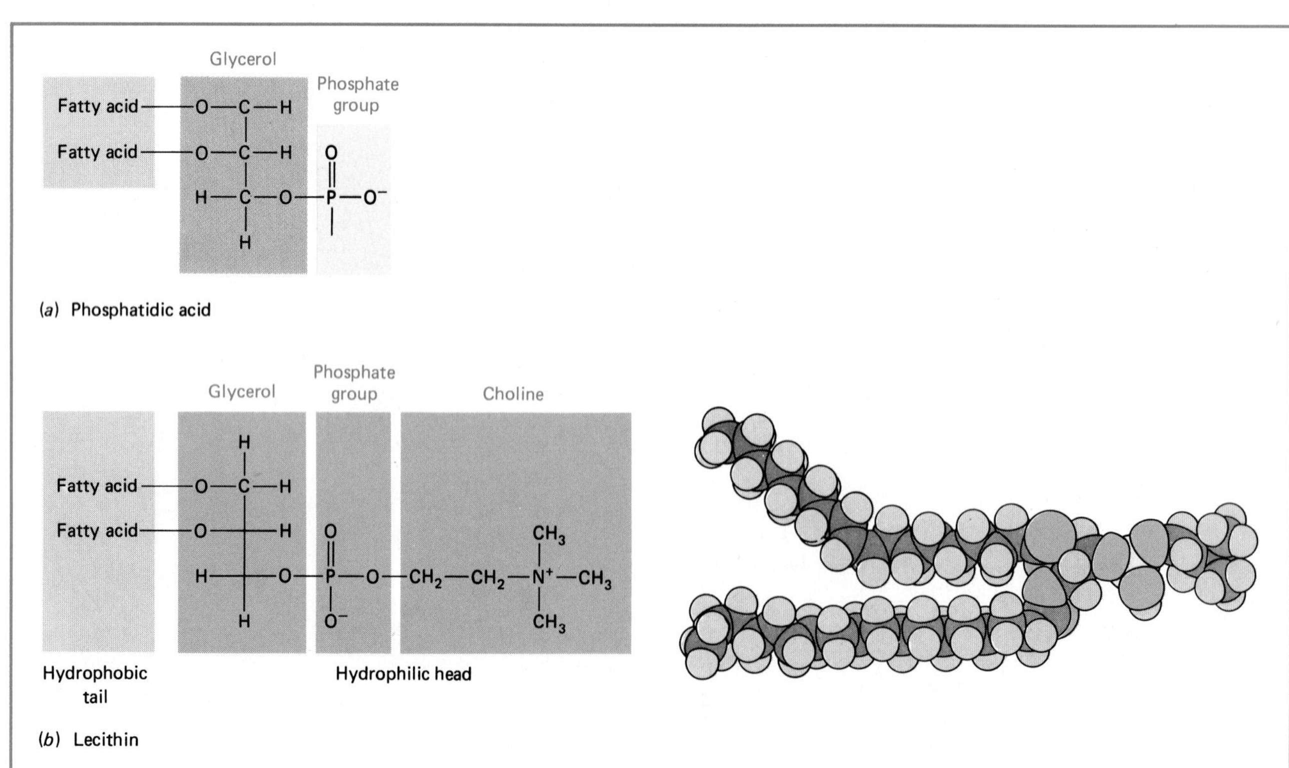

FIGURE 2-18

Phospholipids. *(a)* Many phospholipids are derivatives of phosphatidic acid, a compound consisting of glycerol chemically combined with two fatty acids and a phosphate group. *(b)* Lecithin is a phospholipid found in cell membranes. It forms when phosphatidic acid combines with the compound choline. The structural formula for lecithin is shown here along with a space-filling model.

of *phosphatidic acid* which consists of glycerol chemically combined with two fatty acids and a phosphate group (Fig. 2-18).

The two ends of the phospholipid molecule differ physically as well as chemically. Because the base end is charged and so tends to be attracted to water, it is said to be **hydrophilic** ("water-loving"). The fatty acid end is repelled by water and is therefore **hydrophobic** ("water-hating").

The polarity of phospholipid molecules causes them to take up a certain configuration in the presence of water, with their hydrophobic tails together and their hydrophilic heads facing outward toward the surrounding water. These molecules form a double layer of phospholipid, a **lipid bilayer.** Electron microscopy has revealed that the cell's outer boundary, the plasma membrane, is just such a lipid bilayer (Fig. 2-19). This thin and very elastic membrane enables the cell to move, carry out its life activities, and maintain its internal integrity. Lecithin, a phospholipid found in cell membranes, is shown in Figure 2-18.

The lipid bilayer of the plasma membrane appears to be in the liquid state, with lumps of protein, probably single molecules or aggregates of a few molecules each, in it. The proteins are embedded in the membrane.

CHOLESTEROL AND CERTAIN HORMONES ARE STEROIDS

Steroids are a group of organic compounds that have a structure quite different from that of other lipids. Their carbon atoms are arranged in four interlocking rings. (Three rings contain six carbon atoms each, and the fourth ring contains five.) Characteristic side chains of carbon atoms extend from these rings. The length and structure of these side chains distinguish one type of steroid from another (Fig. 2-20).

Among the steroids of biological importance are vitamin D, bile salts, cholesterol, and certain hormones. Bile salts mechanically break down fats in the intestine, preparing them for enzymatic digestion. **Cholesterol** is a steroid characteristic of animal but not of plant tissues. This compound is the most abundant steroid in the human body. Cholesterol is a component of plasma membranes and serves as a precursor (raw material) of other

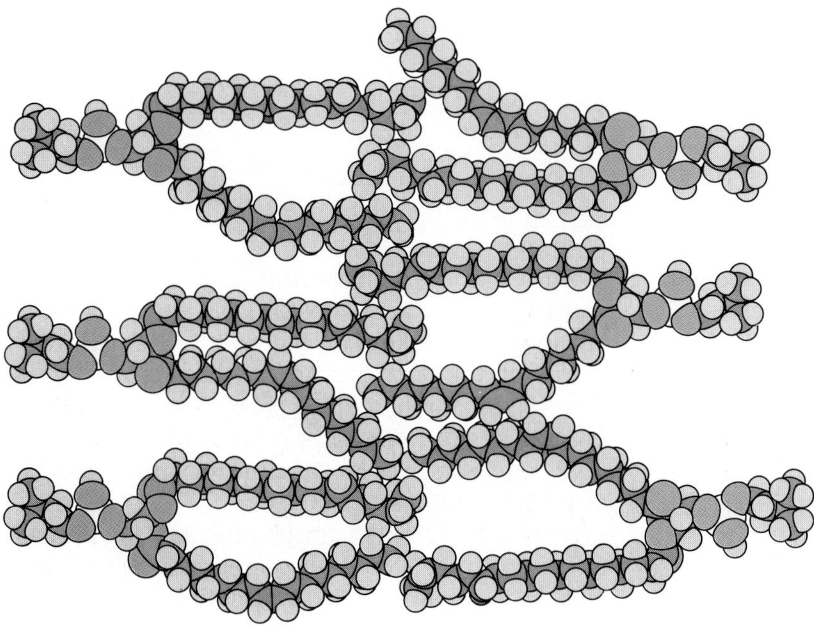

(*a*)

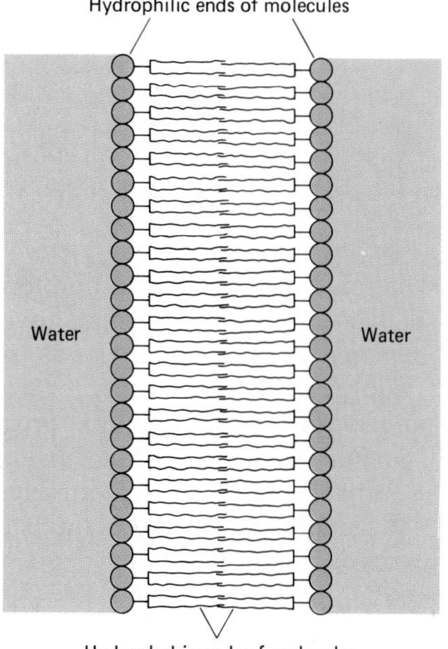

(*b*)

FIGURE 2-19

In the presence of water, lipid molecules orient themselves with their hydrophilic water-soluble heads facing outward toward the surrounding water. The hydrophobic tails extend in the opposite direction. (*a*) Space-filling model of complex lipids in a bilayer. Two layers of phospholipid molecules are present with their hydrophobic tails meeting in the middle. (*b*) A lipid bilayer such as this is found in cell membranes.

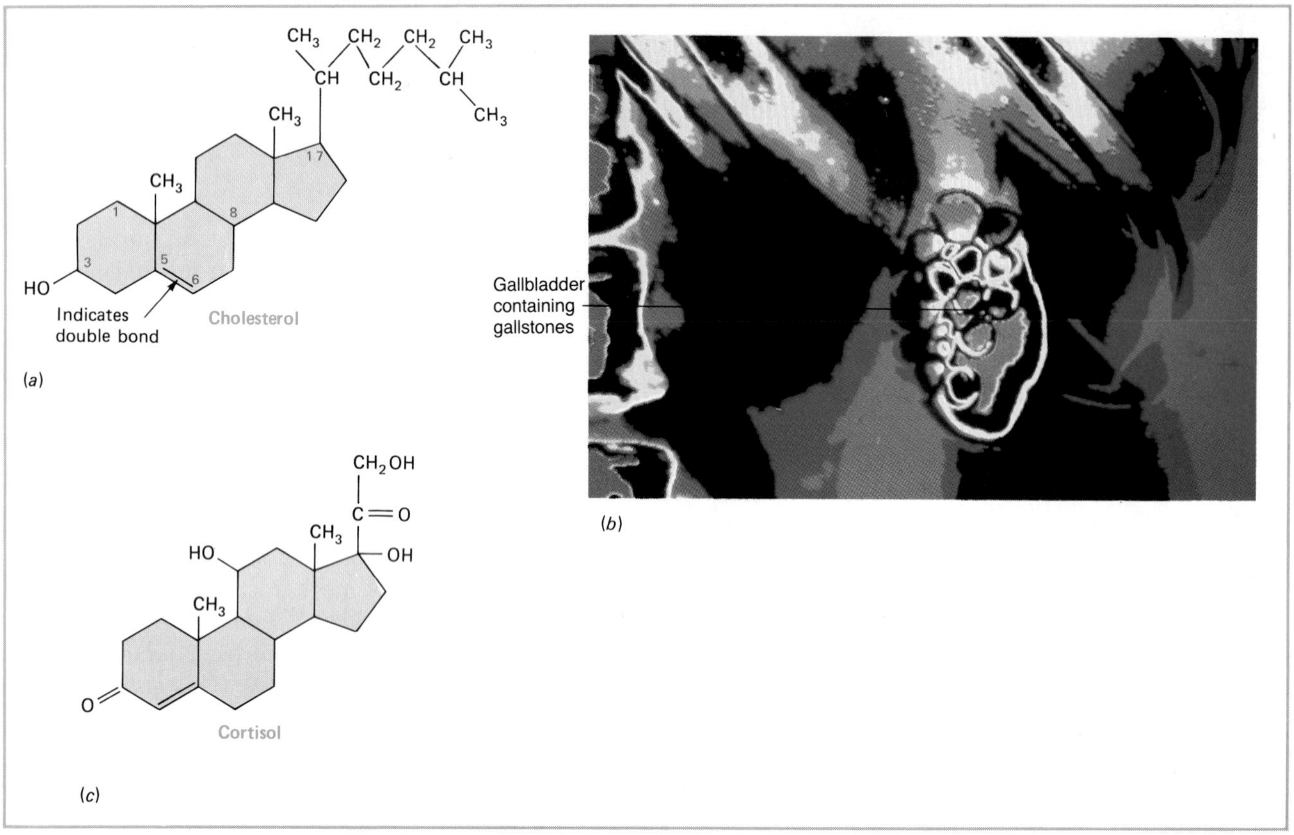

FIGURE 2-20

Steroids. All steroids have the basic skeleton of four interlocking rings of carbon atoms. Note that a carbon atom is present at each point in each ring. Each of the first three rings contains six carbon atoms, and the fourth ring contains five. For simplicity, hydrogen atoms have not been drawn within the ring structures. (*a*) Cholesterol, the most abundant steroid in the body, is used to make other steroids. (*b*) Gallstones, such as those present in the gallbladder shown here, form from cholesterol. (*c*) Cortisol is a steroid hormone secreted by the adrenal cortex, an endocrine gland.

steroids such as steroid hormones. Both male and female reproductive glands (ovaries and testes), as well as the adrenal glands, produce steroid hormones. Progesterone, for example, is a female reproductive hormone that prepares the body for pregnancy and then helps maintain pregnancy. Cortisol, the principal hormone secreted by the adrenal cortex, is important in helping the body cope with stress.

Nucleic acids store information

Perhaps no other chemical compounds are under as much intensive investigation as the **nucleic acids.** These substances store the information that governs the structure and function of the organism and its components. The two main varieties of nucleic acid are **deoxyribonucleic acid (DNA)** and **ribonucleic acid (RNA).** DNA contains the "recipes" for making all the types of protein required by the organism and constitutes the **genes** themselves, the hereditary material of the cell. Three types of RNA—*messenger RNA, transfer RNA,* and *ribosomal RNA*—function in the process of protein synthesis.

The nucleic acids consist of carbon, hydrogen, oxygen, nitrogen, and phosphorus, arranged in molecular subunits called **nucleotides.** In turn, the nucleotide has three components: (1) a *five-carbon sugar,* either ribose (in RNA) or deoxyribose (in DNA); (2) *phosphoric acid;* and (3) a *nitrogenous base* that may be either a double-ringed **purine** or a single-ringed **pyrimidine** (Fig. 2-21). The nucleotides in DNA contain the purines **adenine**

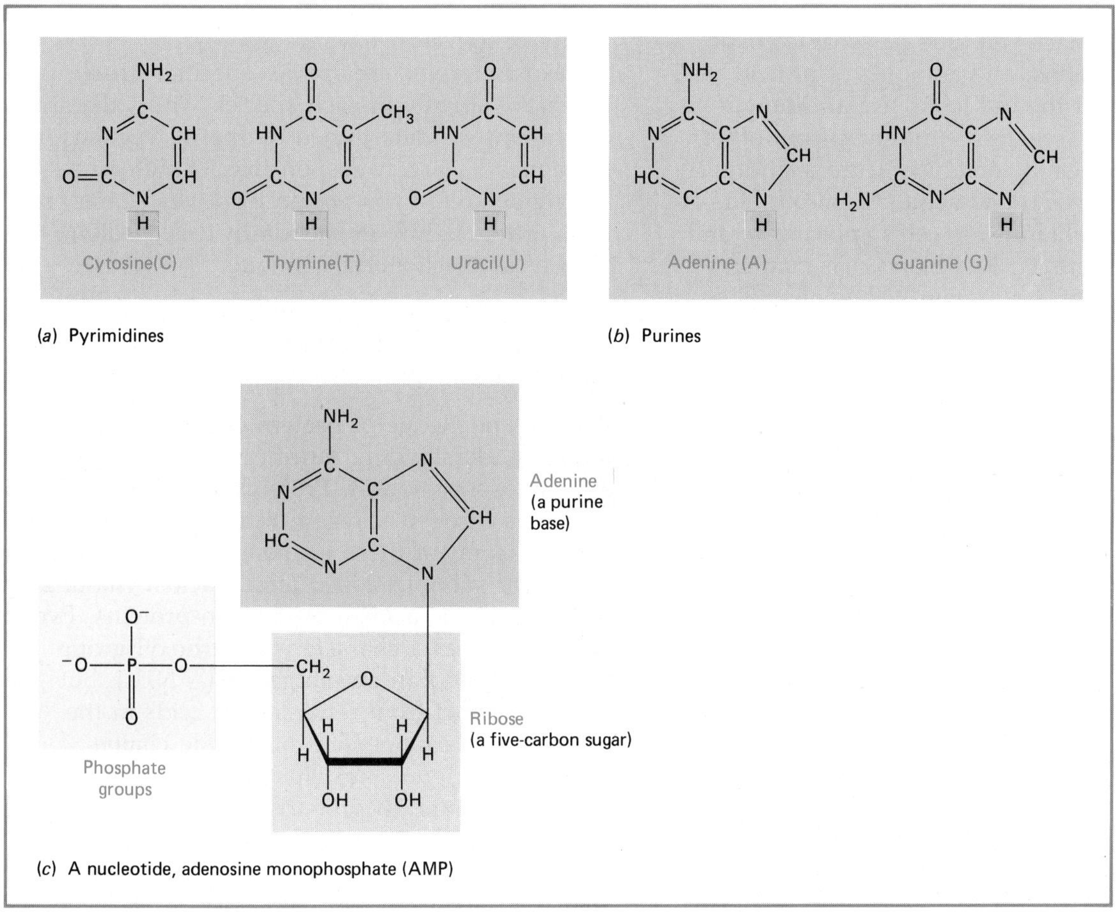

(a) Pyrimidines

(b) Purines

(c) A nucleotide, adenosine monophosphate (AMP)

FIGURE 2-21

A nucleic acid consists of subunits called nucleotides. Each nucleotide consists of (1) a nitrogenous base, which may be either a purine or a pyrimidine, (2) a five-carbon sugar, either ribose (in RNA) or deoxyribose (in DNA), and (3) a phosphate group. (*a*) The three major pyrimidine bases found in nucleotides. (*b*) The two major purine bases found in nucleotides. (*c*) A nucleotide, adenosine monophosphate (AMP).

(A) and **guanine (G)** and the pyrimidines **cytosine (C)** and **thymine (T).** The nucleotides in RNA contain the purines adenine and guanine and the pyrimidines cytosine and **uracil (U).**

Both DNA and RNA consist of long chains of nucleotides. Information is coded in the unique sequence of the four kinds of nucleotides present in the chain (Fig. 2-22). DNA is composed of two nucleotide chains wound around each other in a *double helix*. RNA is generally found as a single nucleotide chain.

Adenosine triphosphate (ATP) is a nucleotide that stores energy and serves as the energy currency of the cell. ATP is composed of adenine, ribose, and three phosphate groups. The two phosphates at the end of the molecule are joined to the nucleotide by energy-rich bonds. Energy is required to make these bonds and when they are broken energy is released. ATP will be discussed in Chapter 26.

Proteins function as building blocks and enzymes

Proteins are among the main structural components of cells and tissues. They are responsible for growth and repair, as well as maintenance of the body. Some proteins serve as enzymes, catalysts that regulate the thousands of different chemical reactions that take place in a living system. Others serve as hormones, antibodies, or compounds that transport substances.

The protein constituents of a cell are the clue to its lifestyle. Each cell type has characteristic types, distributions, and amounts of protein that determine what the cell looks like and how it functions. A muscle cell is different from other cell types because it contains a large quantity of the proteins myosin and actin. These proteins are mainly responsible for the cell's appearance and its ability to contract. Red blood cells contain large amounts of the protein hemoglobin. This red pigment combines with oxygen and is responsible for the color of the red blood cell and its ability to transport oxygen.

Most proteins are species-specific—that is, they vary slightly in each species. Thus, the array of proteins (as determined by the instructions in the genes) is largely responsible for differences among species. Even within a species, some proteins differ slightly in each individual, making each of us biochemically unique.

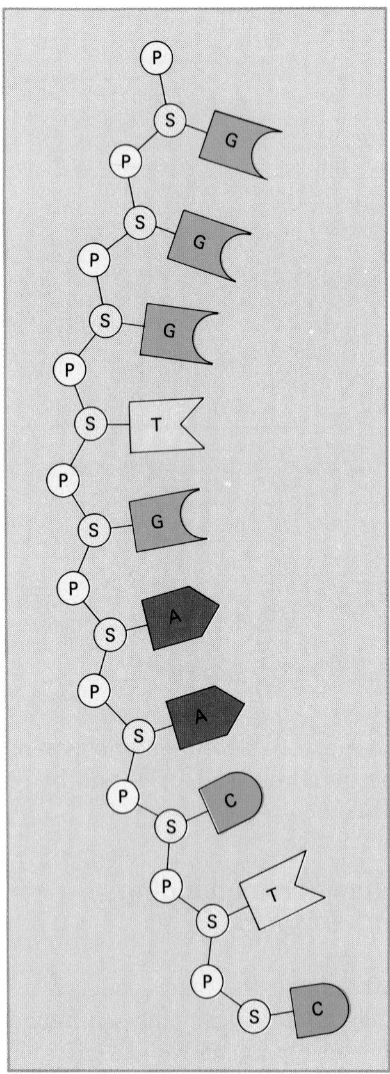

FIGURE 2-22

Schematic diagram of part of a nucleic acid molecule, DNA. Information is coded in the sequence of bases. P, phosphate; S, sugar; G, guanine; C, cytosine; A, adenine; T, thymine.

PROTEINS CONSIST OF AMINO ACID SUBUNITS

A basic knowledge of protein chemistry is essential for understanding nutrition, as well as other aspects of metabolism. Proteins are composed of carbon, hydrogen, oxygen, nitrogen, and usually sulfur. Atoms of these elements are arranged in molecular subunits called **amino acids.** About 20 different amino acids are found in proteins. Every amino acid has a characteristic **carboxyl group** (—COOH) and an **amino group** (—NH_2), but each is distinct from other amino acids in the number and arrangement of its side chains (R groups). Figure 2-23 illustrates the amino acids commonly found in proteins. In this illustration the amino acids are grouped by the properties of their side chains. Amino acids with nonpolar side chains are hydrophobic. Those with polar side chains are hydrophilic.

Amino acids combine chemically with each other by bonding the carboxyl group of one molecule to the amino group of another. The covalent bond linking two amino acids is called a **peptide bond.** When two amino acids combine, a **dipeptide** is formed (Fig. 2-24); a longer chain of amino acids is a **polypeptide.**

A protein consists of one or more long polypeptides, each containing from about 50 to as many as 2500 amino acids. The polypeptides making up a protein are twisted or folded, forming a macromolecule with a three-dimensional shape. This shape, or *conformation,* determines the function of the protein. For example, the unique shape of an enzyme permits it to "recognize" and act on the particular substance it regulates.

In *fibrous proteins* the polypeptide chains are arranged in long sheets. In *globular proteins* the polypeptide chains are tightly folded into a compact spherical shape. Most enzymes are globular proteins.

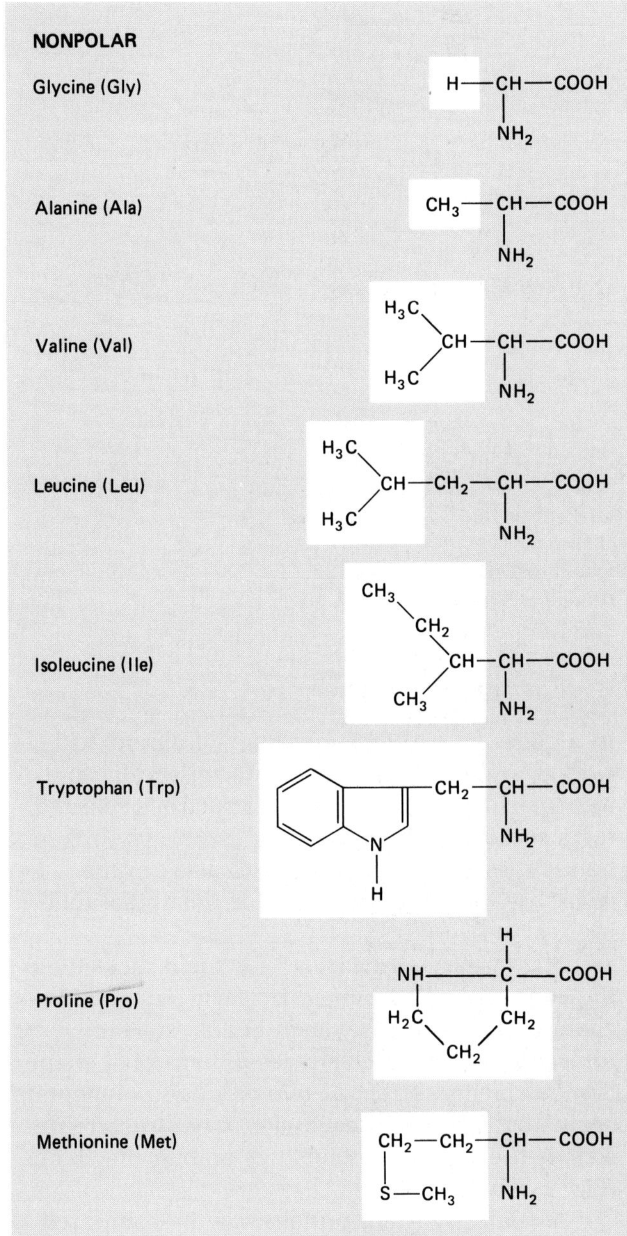

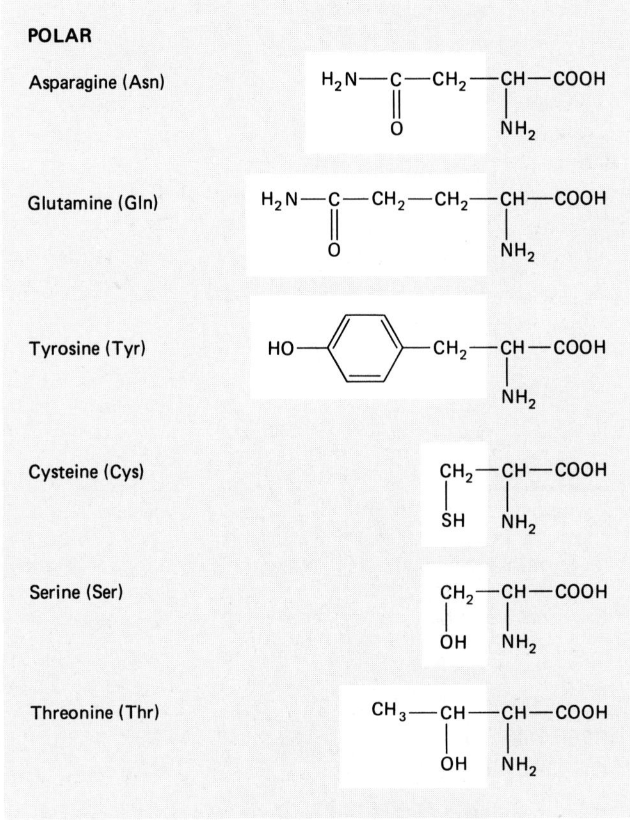

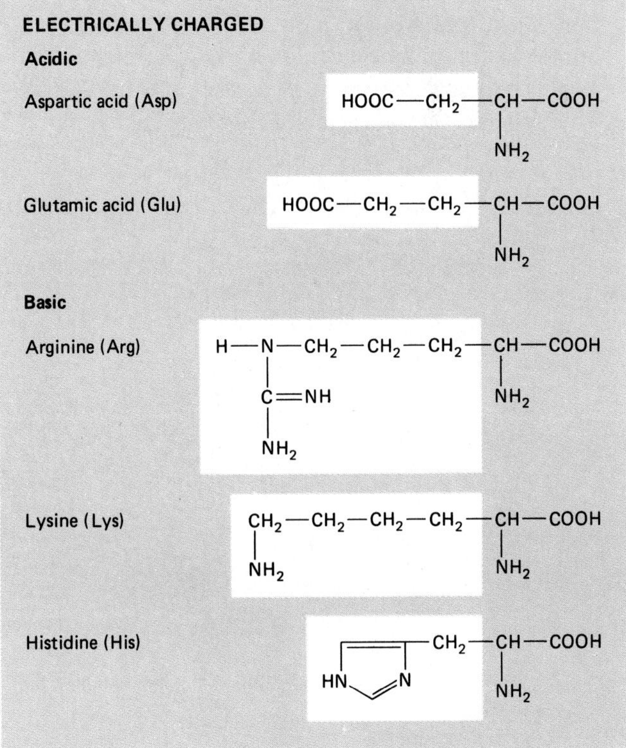

FIGURE 2-23

The amino acids commonly found in proteins. The amino acids are grouped here according to the properties of their side chains (R groups). The three-letter symbols are the conventional abbreviations for the amino acids.

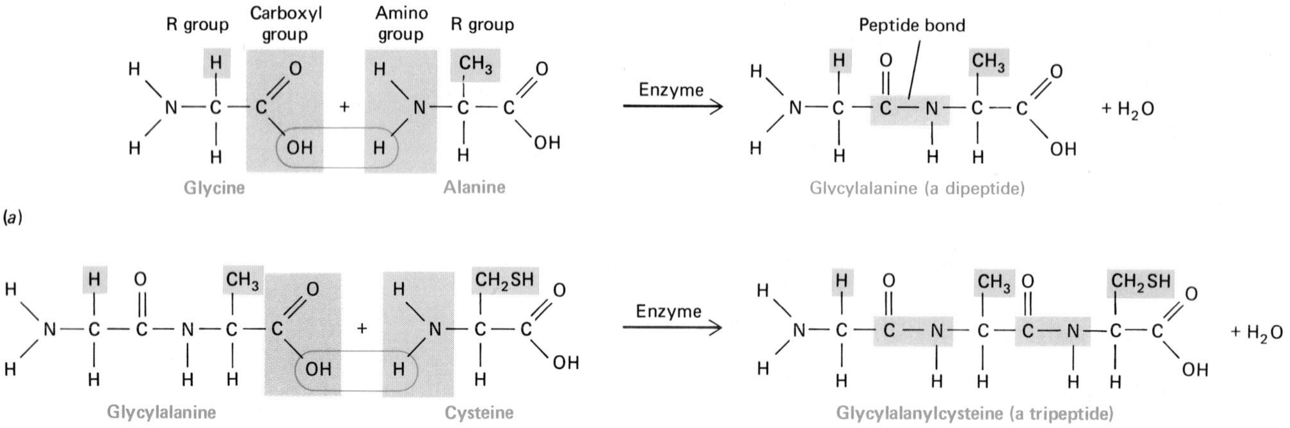

R group
Carboxyl group
Amino group
R group
Glycine + Alanine —Enzyme→ Glvcylalanine (a dipeptide) + H_2O
Peptide bond

(a)

Glycylalanine + Cysteine —Enzyme→ Glycylalanylcysteine (a tripeptide) + H_2O

(b)

FIGURE 2-24

Formation of peptide chains. (*a*) Formation of a dipeptide. Two amino acids combine chemically to form a dipeptide. Water is produced as a by-product during this reaction. (*b*) A third amino acid is added to the dipeptide to form a chain of three amino acids (a tripeptide or small polypeptide). The bond between two amino acids is a peptide bond. Additional amino acids can be added to form long polypeptide chains.

PROTEINS HAVE FOUR LEVELS OF ORGANIZATION

Four levels of organization can be distinguished in the protein molecule—primary, secondary, tertiary, and quaternary (Fig. 2-25). The sequence of amino acids in the peptide chain(s) is referred to as the **primary structure** of a protein (Fig. 2-26a). The specific sequence is specified by instructions in a gene. Due to the properties of amino acid side groups, polypeptides characteristically fold into specific coiled or pleated structures referred to as **secondary structure** (Fig. 2-26b). Hydrogen bonds that form between amino acids in the chain are largely responsible for this initial folding.

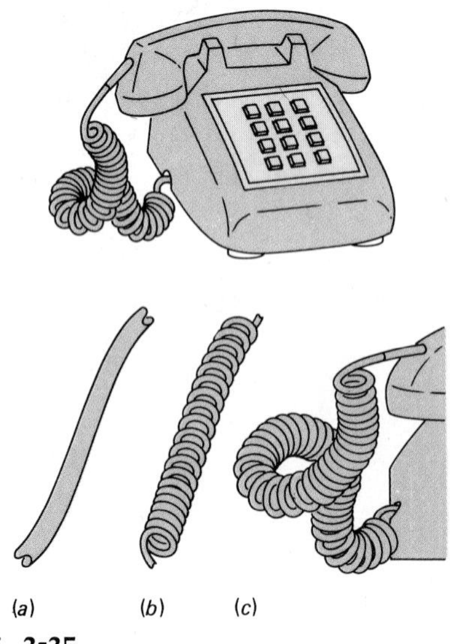

(a) (b) (c)

FIGURE 2-25

Protein structure. The telephone cord provides a familiar example for illustrating (*a*) primary, (*b*) secondary, and (*c*) tertiary structure.

The **tertiary structure** of a protein molecule is the overall shape assumed by each polypeptide chain (Fig. 2-27a). The chain bends, coils, or folds, forming a specific three-dimensional shape. Some proteins consist of two or more polypeptide chains bonded together; **quaternary structure** describes the spatial relationships among the chains (Fig. 2-27b).

A relatively small protein may be composed of 500 or 600 amino acids. Hemoglobin consists of 574 amino acids arranged in four polypeptide chains. Its chemical formula is $C_{3032}H_{4816}O_{872}N_{780}S_8Fe_4$. Most proteins are much larger. A few small proteins, such as the hormone insulin, have been made synthetically in the laboratory (Fig. 2-26a).

It should be clear that the various proteins differ from one another with respect to the number, types, and arrangement of amino acids that they contain. The 20 amino acids found in biological proteins may be thought of as letters of a protein alphabet. Each protein is a word made up of certain types, numbers, and arrangements of amino acid letters. Thus, not all kinds of amino acids must be present in any particular protein.

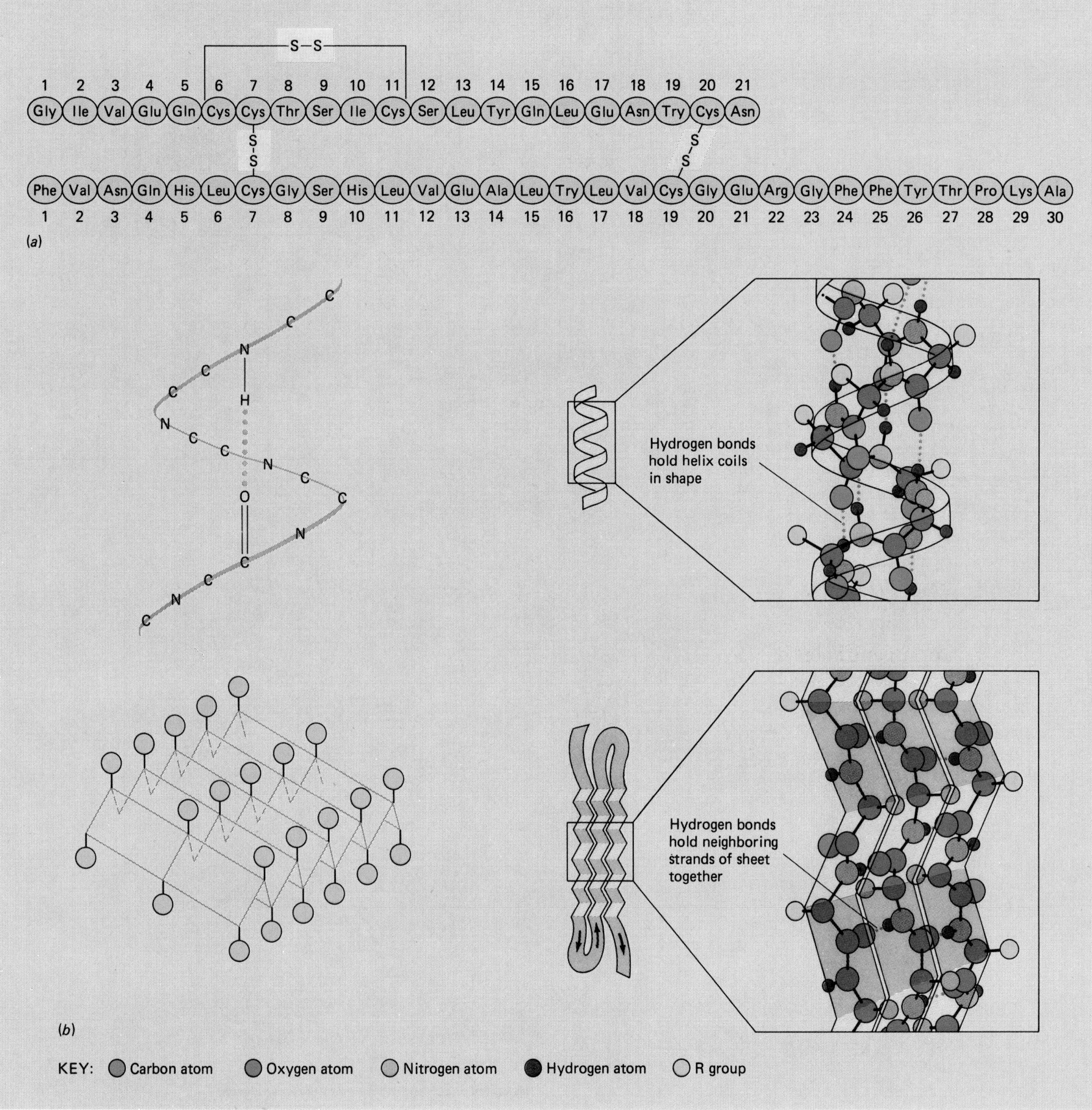

FIGURE 2-26

Primary and secondary structure of a protein. (*a*) The primary structure of the two polypeptide chains that make up the protein insulin. The primary structure is the linear sequence of amino acids. Each oval in the diagram represents an amino acid. The letters inside the ovals are symbols for the names of the amino acids. Insulin is a very small protein. (*b*) The secondary structure of proteins is commonly an alpha helix. The folds in the helix are held together mainly by hydrogen bonds between oxygen and hydrogen atoms. In some proteins, such as the silk protein fibroin, the backbone of the polypeptide chain is stretched out into a zigzag structure.

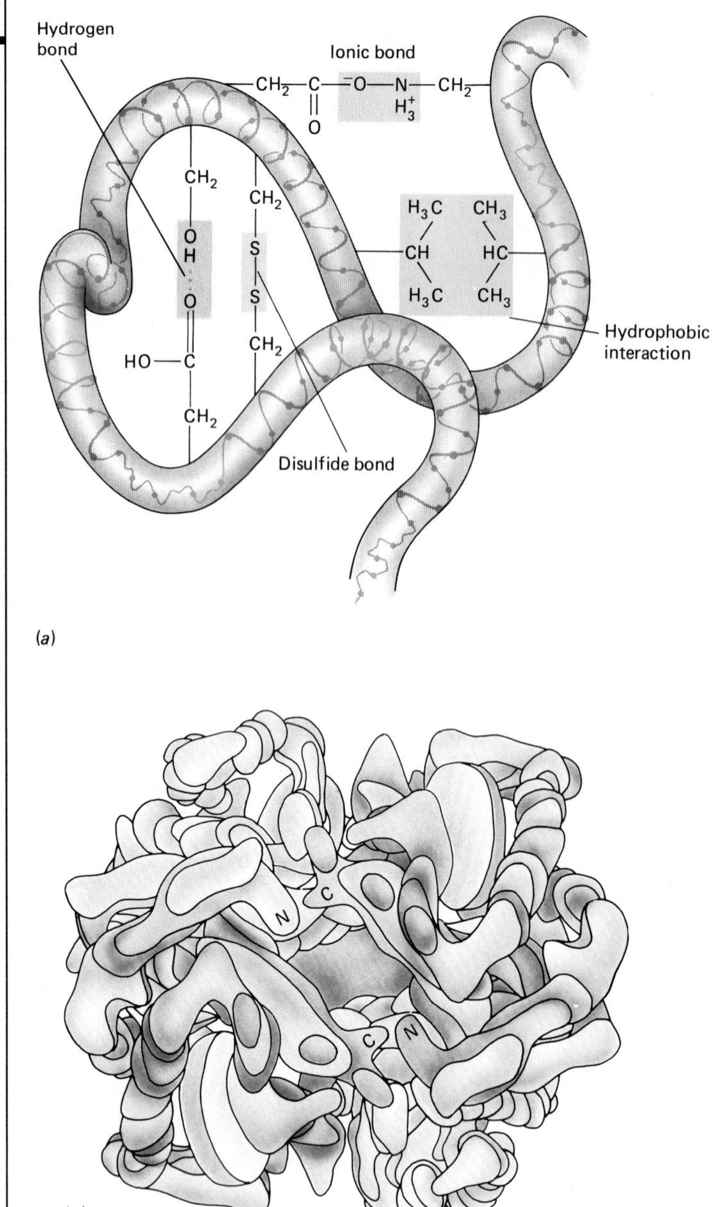

FIGURE 2-27

Tertiary and quaternary protein structure. (*a*) The tertiary structure results from the coiling and folding of the alpha helix (or other secondary structure) into an overall globular or other shape. Hydrogen bonds, bonds between sulfur atoms, ionic attractions between R groups, and other attractions between atoms are among the forces that hold the parts of the molecule in the designated shape. (*b*) Proteins that consist of more than one polypeptide subunit assume a final quaternary shape. Hemoglobin, a globular-shaped protein containing four polypeptide subunits, is illustrated here. Its quaternary structure consists of the final shape in which the subunits combine. In hemoglobin each polypeptide encloses an iron-containing structure (shown as green discs). Also see chapter opening art.

Clinical highlight

In some cases the variance of just one amino acid in a protein chain can be crucial. In sickle-cell anemia (a hereditary disease that in the United States is most common among people of African ancestry) the protein hemoglobin of the red blood cells is defective. The abnormal protein alters the shape of the red blood cells from biconcave discs to crescents and makes them more fragile. Not only are the affected individuals anemic, but their deformed blood cells tend to clog their capillaries in recurrent, painful episodes. In sickle-cell hemoglobin one of the 574 amino acids in the sequence is the wrong one, rendering the entire molecule defective. (A minor amino acid defect does not always make this much difference. Many hemoglobin variants have been identified that produce no harmful side effects.)

Enzymes are chemical regulators

Thousands of different chemical reactions take place within the living cell. All these chemical processes must be precisely controlled and coordinated, because they interlock like a multitude of assembly processes on a modern production line. In the manufacture of an automobile, for example, it might not be possible to complete a car without some seemingly minor part such as a ball bearing or special bolt. Elaborate planning and scheduling are necessary to ensure that all parts are delivered to the workers by the time they are needed.

It is this concept of control that is emphasized here. Most cellular chemical reactions proceed by a series of steps, so that a given molecule may go through as many as 20 or 30 chemical transformations before it reaches some final state. Then the seemingly completed molecule may enter yet another chemical pathway and be totally transformed or perhaps consumed in the course of energy production. The changing needs of the cell require a system for flexible chemical control. The key elements of this control system are the remarkable enzymes.

Enzymes form temporary complexes with their substrates

Most body chemistry would not operate effectively without enzymes. **Enzymes** are organic catalysts that greatly increase the speed of chemical reactions without being consumed themselves. Some enzymes can increase the speed of certain reactions hundreds or thousands of times. Most enzymes are proteins but recent research has suggested that certain nucleic acids act as enzymes, as well.

Consider the enzyme carbonic anhydrase. Like most enzymes, its name has the distinctive **-ase** ending. Carbonic anhydrase is found in several tissues and types of cells, especially the kidney and red blood cells. This enzyme promotes and speeds up the formation of carbonic acid from carbon dioxide (a normal waste product of cellular life processes) in this way:

$$\underset{\text{Carbon dioxide}}{CO_2} + \underset{\text{Water}}{H_2O} \xrightarrow{\text{Carbonic anhydrase}} \underset{\text{Carbonic acid}}{H_2CO_3}$$

Carbonic acid would be able to form without the enzyme, but its rate of formation would be uselessly slow. The enzyme is necessary for the reaction to proceed to a biologically significant extent. In this case, water and carbon dioxide would be called substrates. **Substrates** are the chemicals upon which the enzyme operates. Carbonic acid is the product.

Enzymes form temporary chemical complexes with their substrates. These **enzyme-substrate complexes** then break up, releasing the product and regenerating the original enzyme for reuse.

Enzyme + Substrate 1 + Substrate 2 ⟶ Enzyme-substrate complex

Enzyme-substrate complex ⟶ Enzyme + Product(s)

Notice that the enzyme itself is not permanently altered or consumed by the reaction.

Why does the enzyme-substrate complex break up into chemical products that are different from those that participated in its formation? As you can see in Figure 2-28, each enzyme molecule

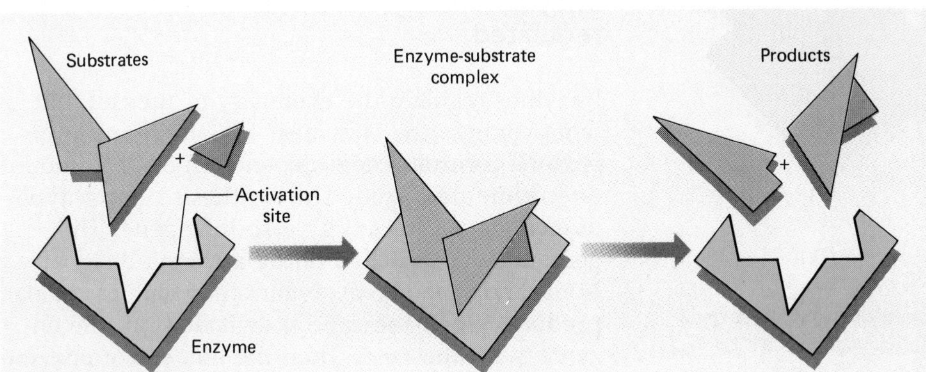

FIGURE 2-28

Lock-and-key mechanism for enzyme action. The substrates fit the active sites of the enzyme molecule much as keys fit locks. However, in this model the lock acts on the key rather than the other way around. Note that when the products separate from the enzyme, the enzyme is free to catalyze production of additional products. The enzyme is not permanently changed by the reaction. In recent years the lock-and-key concept of enzyme action has undergone some modification, as shown in Figure 2-29.

has one or more regions called **active sites,** which have been shown in a few enzymes to be actual indentations in the enzyme molecule. These active sites are located close to one another on the enzyme's molecular surface, so that during the course of a reaction, substrate molecules occupying these sites are temporarily brought close together and react with one another. The new chemical compound thus formed has little affinity for the enzyme and is released from it.

An enzyme will not make complexes with just any substrate. In fact enzymes are highly specific. According to the **lock-and-key model** of enzyme action, an enzyme can be thought of as a molecular lock into which only specifically shaped molecular keys—the reactants, or substrate—can fit.

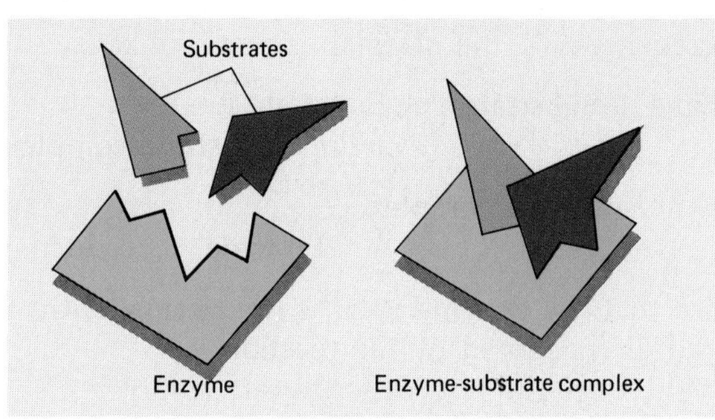

(a)

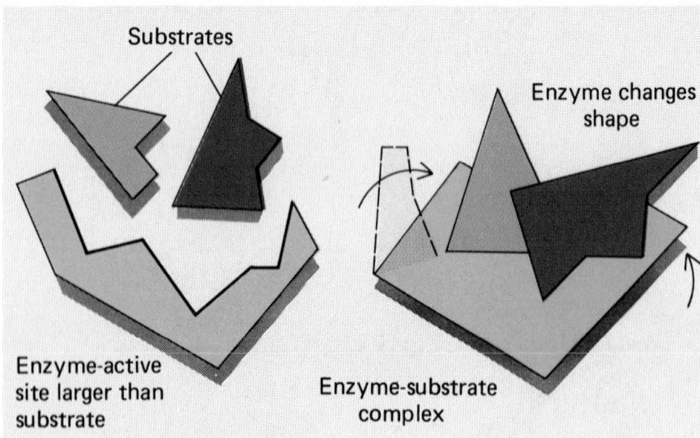

(b)

FIGURE 2-29

Comparison of models of enzyme action. (a) The lock-and-key model. (b) The induced-fit model. Chemical reactions are favored when substrate molecules get close enough to one another to react, when they are presented to each other in the right orientation, and when their existing chemical bonds are strained. Enzymes often do all three of these things. The straining of the substrate's bonds is accomplished by the apparent fact that most active sites are a bit bigger than the size of their substrate molecules. Accordingly, when a fit is forced upon them, the active site exerts a kind of pull on the substrate, helping to pull it apart. To be sure, the fit of the enzyme and substrate must not be too poor, or they will have no affinity for one another.

Unlike a lock and key, however, the shape of the enzyme does not seem to be exactly complementary to that of the substrates. According to the **induced-fit model** of enzyme action, when the substrate combines with the enzyme, it may induce a change in the shape of the enzyme molecule (Fig. 2-29). This is possible because the active sites of an enzyme are not rigid. The change in shape results in an optimum fit for the substrate-enzyme interaction and can put strain on the substrate. This stress may help bonds break, thus promoting the reaction.

Many enzymes require cofactors

Many enzymes require a smaller, nonprotein molecule, called a **cofactor,** in order to operate. A cofactor usually acts as an acceptor or donor of atoms that are removed from or contributed to the substrate. The cofactor of some enzymes is a metal ion. Most of the trace elements—elements like iron, copper, zinc, and manganese, which are required in very small amounts—function as cofactors.

An organic, nonpolypeptide compound that serves as a cofactor is called a **coenzyme** (Fig. 2-30). Most vitamins are coenzymes or serve as raw materials from which coenzymes are synthesized. This is apparently why most vitamins are necessary for health. Vitamin deficiency leads to physiological imbalances and may result ultimately in death.

Enzyme activity is carefully regulated

Enzymes regulate the chemistry of the cell, but what controls the enzymes? One mechanism of enzyme control simply depends upon the amount of enzyme produced. The synthesis of each type of enzyme is directed by a specific gene. The gene may be switched on by a chemical signal from a hormone or by some other type of cellular product. When the gene is switched on, the enzyme is synthesized. Then the amount of enzyme present influences the rate of the reaction. Up to a maximum value the rate of an enzyme-dependent reaction increases as the concentration of the enzyme increases.

The product of one enzymatic reaction may control the activity of another enzyme, especially in a sequence of enzymatic reactions. For example, in the following system,

$$A \xrightarrow{\text{Enzyme 1}} B \xrightarrow{\text{Enzyme 2}} C \xrightarrow{\text{Enzyme 3}} D \xrightarrow{\text{Enzyme 4}} E$$

each step is catalyzed by a different enzyme. The final product, E, may inhibit the activity of Enzyme 1. When the concentration of E is low, the sequence of reactions proceeds rapidly. However, as the concentration of E increases, it serves as a signal for Enzyme 1 to slow down and eventually stop functioning. Inhibition of Enzyme 1 stops this entire sequence of reactions. Note that in this type of enzyme regulation the formation of a product inhibits an earlier reaction in the sequence. Recall from Chapter 1 that this is a negative feedback control mechanism.

Another method of enzymatic control, *conformational regulation,* depends upon the activation of enzyme molecules that have been manufactured and are present already in an inactive form in the cytoplasm. In the inactive form the active sites of the enzyme are inappropriately shaped to fit the substrates. The configuration must be altered before the enzyme can function. Among the factors that influence protein configuration are acidity and alkalinity and the concentration of certain salts.

Some enzymes, called **allosteric enzymes,** have a receptor site, called an **allosteric site,** on some region other than the active site. A **regulator** substance can bind to the allosteric site and inhibit the enzyme. When the enzyme is needed, another compound may remove the regulator, activating the enzyme.

Enzymes work best under optimum conditions

Enzymes generally work best under certain narrowly defined optimum conditions. These include appropriate temperature, pH, and salt concentration. For example, if an enzyme has an optimum temperature, its activity slows as the temperature decreases, and increases as the temperature increases above the optimum up to a certain point. If the temperature gets too high, however, the enzyme will be denatured, or altered in shape, by the heat. A denatured protein is one in which the secondary and higher level structures have been changed. (When egg white is cooked, it changes in consistency as the protein is denatured. This change is irreversible.)

Similarly, each enzyme has an optimum pH. Pepsin, the protein-digesting enzyme of the stomach, works best under very acidic conditions, but the starch-digesting enzyme (amylase) in pancreatic juice functions best in an alkaline medium.

Enzymes may be inhibited

Enzymes may be rendered less effective or even nonfunctional by certain chemical agents called **inhibitors.** Enzyme inhibition may be *reversible* or *irreversible.* Reversible inhibitors can be competitive or noncompetitive.

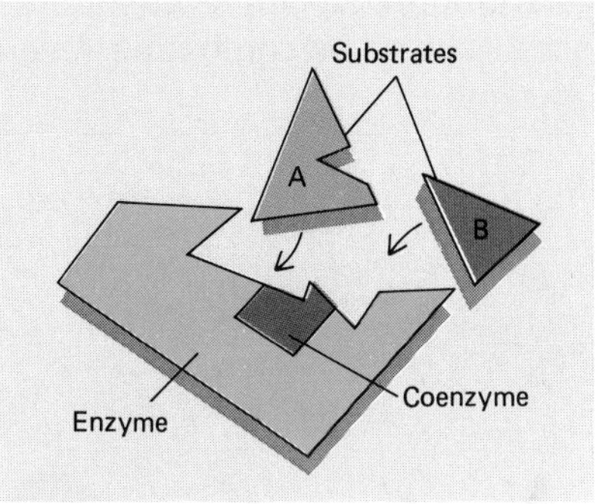

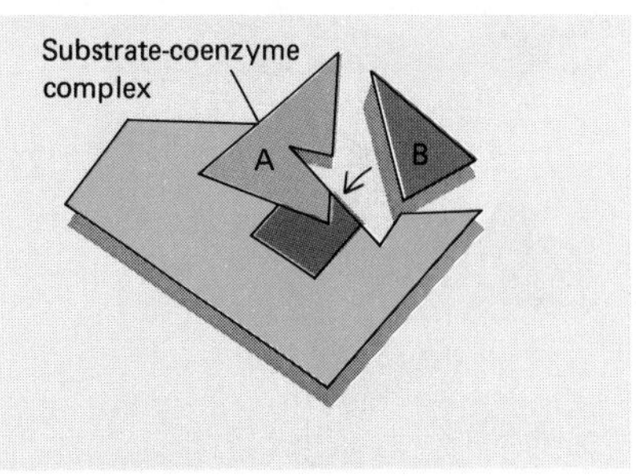

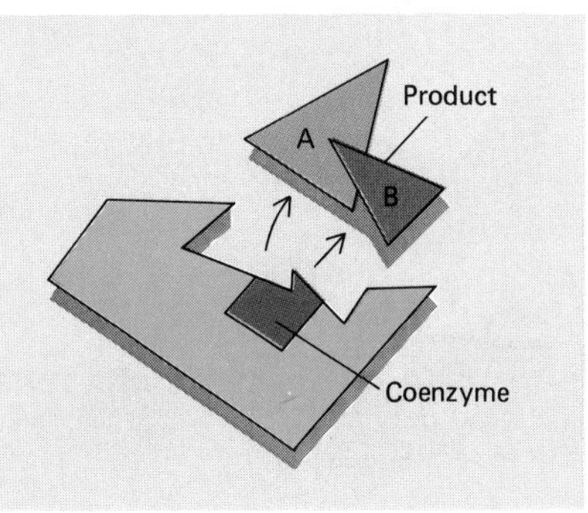

FIGURE 2-30

Coenzyme action. Some enzymes require a coenzyme to facilitate the attachment of the substrate to the enzyme's active sites. First one substrate combines with the coenzyme to form a coenzyme-substrate complex. Then the complex combines with the second substrate, forming a new complex that yields the products and releases the coenzyme.

In **competitive inhibition** the inhibitor competes with the substrate for the active site of the enzyme. The inhibitor is similar chemically to the substrate of the enzyme, yet not similar enough to substitute for the normal substrate or to act as the normal substrate ordinarily would. When an inhibitor attaches to the active site of the enzyme, the normal substrate cannot combine with the active site. The inhibitor occupies the active site only temporarily and does not damage the enzyme irreversibly (Fig. 2-31).

In **noncompetitive inhibition** the inhibitor binds with the enzyme at a site other than the active site. Such an inhibitor renders the enzyme inactive by altering its shape. Many metabolic substances are noncompetitive inhibitors that regulate enzyme activity by combining reversibly with the enzyme.

Irreversible inhibitors combine with a functional group of an enzyme and permanently inactivate or destroy the enzyme. A number of insecticides and other poisons are enzyme inhibitors. Penicillin is a drug that acts as an irreversible inhibitor. This antibiotic and its chemical relatives inhibit a bacterial enzyme, transpeptidase, that is responsible for establishing some of the vital chemical linkages in the material of which the bacterial cell wall is composed. Unable to produce new cell walls, susceptible bacteria are prevented from multiplying effectively, as shown in Figure 2-32. Since human body cells do not possess cell walls and do not employ this enzyme, penicillin is harmless to humans, except for the occasional allergic reaction.

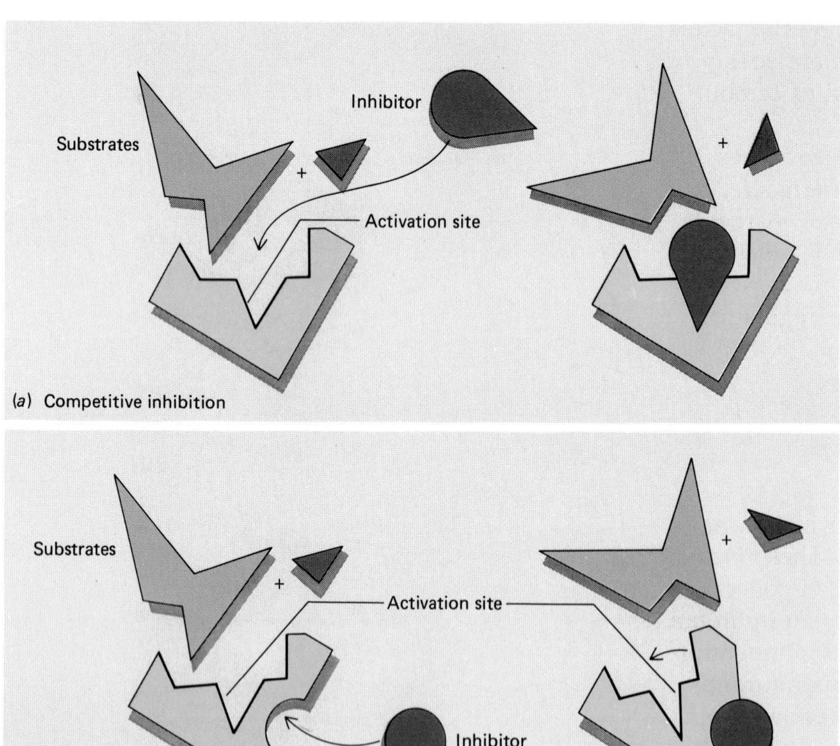

FIGURE 2-31

Competitive and noncompetitive inhibition. (*a*) In competitive inhibition the inhibitor competes with the normal substrate for the active site of the enzyme. A competitive inhibitor occupies the active site only temporarily. (*b*) In noncompetitive inhibition, the inhibitor binds with the enzyme at a site other than the active site, altering the shape of the enzyme and so inactivating it. Noncompetitive inhibition may be reversible.

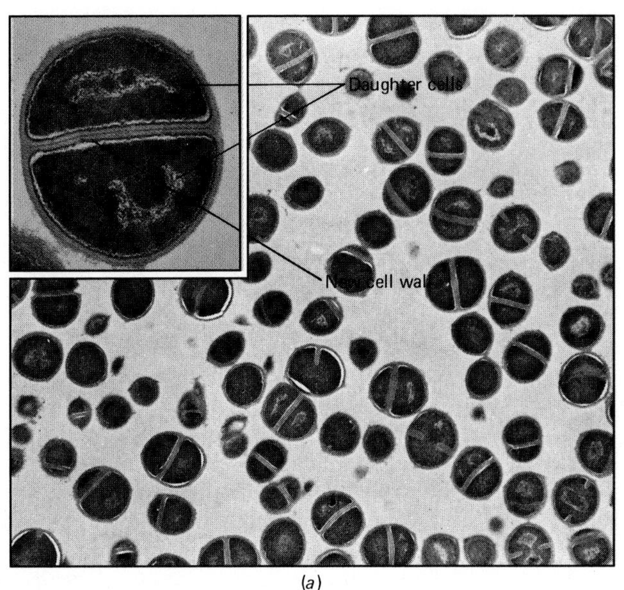

(a)

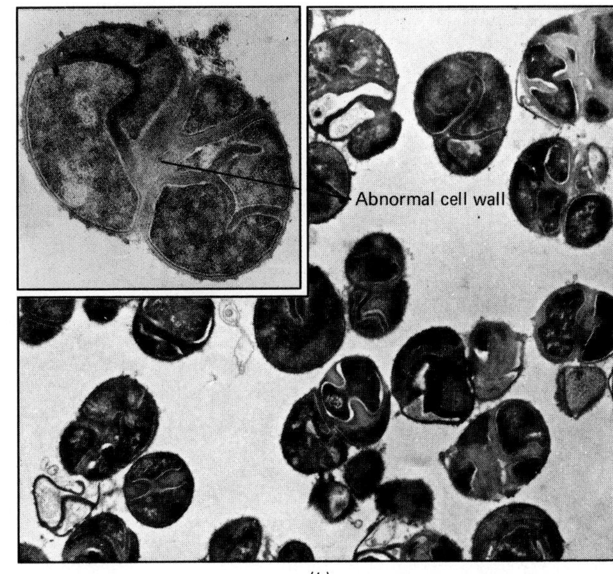

(b)

FIGURE 2-32

Antibiotic damage to bacterial cell walls. Penicillin is an irreversible enzyme inhibitor. (*a*) Normal bacteria. Insert shows the new cell wall laid down between daughter cells of a dividing bacterium. (*b*) Penicillin has damaged these bacterial cell walls. The inserts are magnified approximately ×54,000. (Courtesy of Victor Lorian and Barbara Atkinson, with permission of the *Journal of Clinical Pathology*.)

Summary

I. The atom is the smallest unit of a chemical element that retains the characteristic properties of that element.
  A. Examples: A carbon atom is the smallest unit of carbon. A calcium atom is the smallest possible unit of calcium.
  B. An atom consists of subatomic particles including electrons, protons, and neutrons.

II. A molecule consists of two or more atoms chemically bonded together.
  A. The composition of a molecule may be described by a chemical formula, such as H_2O, or by a structural formula, such as H—O—H.
  B. The electrons in the outer shell of an atom are its valence electrons. They are the electrons that an atom can donate, accept, or share.

III. The atoms of a molecule are held together by forces of attraction between them called chemical bonds.
  A. An ionic bond is formed when one atom donates an electron to another, each atom thereby becoming charged and attracted to the other because of these electrical charges.
  B. Covalent bonds are very strong chemical bonds formed by electron sharing.
  C. Hydrogen bonds are very weak chemical bonds formed between hydrogen atoms and negative atoms. For example, molecules of water form hydrogen bonds with one another.

IV. Inorganic compounds are simple substances such as water, salts, and certain acids and bases.
  A. Water is an essential component of living things; water is an important solvent and functions to transport materials from one location in the body to another. Water also helps maintain a constant body temperature.
  B. Acids dissociate to form hydrogen ions; bases usually dissociate to form hydroxide ions. The stronger an acid, the lower its pH. The stronger a base, the higher its pH.
  C. A salt is a compound that contains a positive ion other than H^+ and a negative ion other than OH^-.
  D. Buffering, which requires a weak acid plus a salt of that acid, helps to maintain appropriate pH.

V. Organic compounds are complex molecules that contain carbon; they are the main structural components of cells, serve as an energy source for cells, and some are enzymes that regulate chemical reactions.
  A. Carbohydrates include the sugars and starches; they consist of carbon, hydrogen, and oxygen.
    1. Monosaccharides are simple sugars such as glucose.
    2. Monosaccharides combine with one another to form disaccharides and polysaccharides.
    3. Disaccharides and polysaccharides may be split apart by a hydrolysis reaction, in which water is added.
    4. Most carbohydrates are polysaccharides; these are long chains consisting of repeating units of a simple sugar. Glycogen and cellulose are examples.
  B. Like carbohydrates, lipids are composed of carbon, hydrogen, and oxygen, but in proportion they contain much less oxygen.
    1. The body stores fuel in the form of neutral fats. A fat consists of glycerol combined with one to three fatty acids.
      a. Three types of neutral fats are monoglycerides, diglycerides, and triglycerides.
      b. Fatty acids, and therefore fats, can be saturated or unsaturated.
    2. Phospholipids are components of cell membranes. A phospholipid consists of a glycerol molecule combined with one or two fatty acids and also is attached to an organic base that contains phosphorus.
    3. Cholesterol, bile salts, and certain hormones are important steroids. A steroid consists of four interlocking rings from which characteristic side chains extend.
  C. DNA and RNA are nucleic acids; they store information that governs the structure and function of the organism. Nucleic acids are composed of carbon, hydrogen, oxygen, nitrogen, and phosphorus; these atoms are arranged in molecular subunits called nucleotides.
  D. Proteins are composed of molecular subunits called amino acids, which in turn are composed of carbon, hydrogen, oxygen, nitrogen, and often sulfur.
    1. Proteins are important structural components of cells and tissues, and some are enzymes.
    2. One protein differs from another in the number, types, and arrangement of amino acids.
    3. A protein has primary, secondary, and tertiary structure. If the protein consists of two or more polypeptide chains, it also has quatenary structure.

VI. Enzymes are organic catalysts that regulate chemical reactions.
  A. Enzymes act by bringing substrates into close contact so that they can easily react with one another.
  B. A cell can regulate enzyme activity by controlling the amount of enzyme produced or by regulating conditions that influence the configuration of the enzyme.
  C. Enzymes work best at a specific temperature and pH.
  D. In competitive inhibition the enzyme is temporarily rendered ineffective; in noncompetitive inhibition the enzyme is irreversibly damaged.

Post-test

1. Negatively charged particles that whirl about the atomic nucleus are called ______________.
2. The chemical formula for a compound containing one atom of calcium and two atoms of chlorine should be written as ______________.
3. A(n) ______________ bond is formed when one atom donates an electron to another.
4. Positively charged ions such as Na^+ are called ______________.
5. The products are written on the ______________ side of an equation.
6. Covalent bonds are formed when atoms share ______________.
7. A(n) ______________ is a compound that dissociates in solution to produce ______________ and some type of anion.
8. A solution with a pH of 9 would be ______________; one with a pH of 6 would be ______________.
9. A buffer consists of a weak ______________ and a salt of that ______________.
10. Buffers function to maintain appropriate ______________.
11. Organic compounds are large, complex compounds that contain______________.

Matching

Select the most appropriate answer choice from column B.

	Column A	Column B
____	12. Simple sugar	a. protein
____	13. Glycogen is an example	b. monosaccharide
____	14. Cholesterol is an example	c. steroid
____	15. DNA is an example	d. nucleic acid
____	16. Consists of glycerol and fatty acids	e. polysaccharide
____	17. May serve as an enzyme	f. neutral fat

18. Proteins are composed of subunits called ______________.
19. The substance upon which an enzyme acts is called the ______________.
20. In ______________ an inhibitor occupies the active site of an enzyme temporarily.

Review questions

1. Explain in words what the following chemical formulas mean: (a) H_2O, (b) $C_6H_{12}O_6$, (c) H_2CO_3.
2. Write a structural formula for (a) water, (b) carbon dioxide.
3. Define (a) atom, (b) molecule, (c) valence electrons, (d) pH.
4. Explain how an ionic bond forms and give a specific example.
5. How does a covalent bond differ from an ionic bond? Give an example of a compound formed with covalent bonds.
6. What can you say about each of the following solutions in terms of acidity or alkalinity? (a) solution with a pH of 7, (b) solution with a pH of 2.
7. Write a chemical equation describing the ionization of (a) water, (b) carbonic acid, (c) sodium chloride.
8. Why are buffers important in living systems? How do they work?
9. How do organic compounds differ from inorganic compounds?
10. Compare (a) monosaccharides, (b) disaccharides, and (c) polysaccharides.
11. Distinguish between (a) saturated and unsaturated fats, (b) monoglyceride and triglyceride.
12. Why are each of the following biologically important: (a) steroids, (b) phospholipids, (c) polysaccharides, (d) nucleic acids, (e) amino acids?
13. To which class of organic compounds do each of the following belong: (a) glucose, (b) DNA, (c) cellulose, (d) enzymes, (e) steroids?
14. Draw a structural formula of a simple amino acid and identify the carboxyl and amino groups.
15. There are thousands of different kinds of proteins. How does one protein differ chemically from another?
16. Describe how enzymes work. What is a coenzyme?
17. Identify three factors that influence enzymatic activity.
18. Compare competitive and noncompetitive enzyme inhibition.

Post-test answers

1. electrons 2. $CaCl_2$ 3. ionic 4. cations
5. right 6. electrons 7. acid; hydrogen ions
8. alkaline (basic); acidic 9. acid; acid 10. pH
11. carbon 12. b 13. e 14. c 15. d
16. f 17. a 18. amino acids 19. substrate
20. competitive inhibition

THE CELL: BUILDING BLOCK OF THE BODY

CHAPTER OUTLINE

- I. **The cell**
  - □ Focus on cell size
  - □ Focus on how cells are studied
  - A. Plasma membrane
  - B. Endoplasmic reticulum
  - C. Golgi complex
  - D. Lysosomes
  - E. Peroxisomes
  - F. Mitochondria
  - G. Cytoskeleton
  - H. Centrioles
  - I. Cilia and flagella
  - J. Nucleus
- II. **Movement through the plasma membrane**
  - A. Diffusion
    - 1. Dialysis
    - 2. Facilitated diffusion
  - B. Osmosis
  - C. Filtration
  - D. Active transport
  - E. Exocytosis and endocytosis
- III. **The cell cycle**
  - A. Interphase
  - B. Mitosis
    - 1. Prophase
    - 2. Metaphase
    - 3. Anaphase
    - 4. Telophase
  - C. Cytokinesis
  - D. Why is mitosis important?
  - E. Maintaining efficient cell size.
  - F. Factors affecting the cell cycle

LEARNING OBJECTIVES

After you have studied this chapter you should be able to:

1 Justify considering the cell the basic unit of life.

2 Characterize cells with respect to size range, shape, and general features.

3 Describe, locate, and list the functions of the principal organelles and be able to label them on a diagram or photomicrograph.

4 Describe the structure of the plasma membrane and list its functions.

5 Distinguish between smooth and rough endoplasmic reticulum and describe how ribosomes can be functionally connected with the endoplasmic reticulum.

6 Explain how the Golgi complex packages secretions and manufactures lysosomes.

7 Describe specific functions of lysosomes and explain what happens when they become leaky.

8 Justify calling mitochondria the power plants of the cell.

9 Relate microtubules to centrioles, cilia, and flagella.

10 Describe the structure and functions of the nucleus and its contents.

11 Summarize how materials pass through plasma membranes, distinguishing between passive and active processes.

12 Given concentrations and membrane characteristics, predict the direction of diffusion of solutes and solvents across differentially permeable membranes.

13 Solve simple problems involving osmosis; for example, predict whether cells will swell or shrink under various osmotic conditions.

14 Describe mechanisms by which cells actively move materials into their cytoplasm; for example, active transport, phagocytosis, and pinocytosis.

15 Describe the stages of a cell's life cycle.

16 Describe the process of mitosis and summarize its significance with respect to maintaining a constant chromosome number.

HTLV-III AIDS virus infecting T-4 lymphocyte. (CDC/RG/Peter Arnold, Inc.)

3

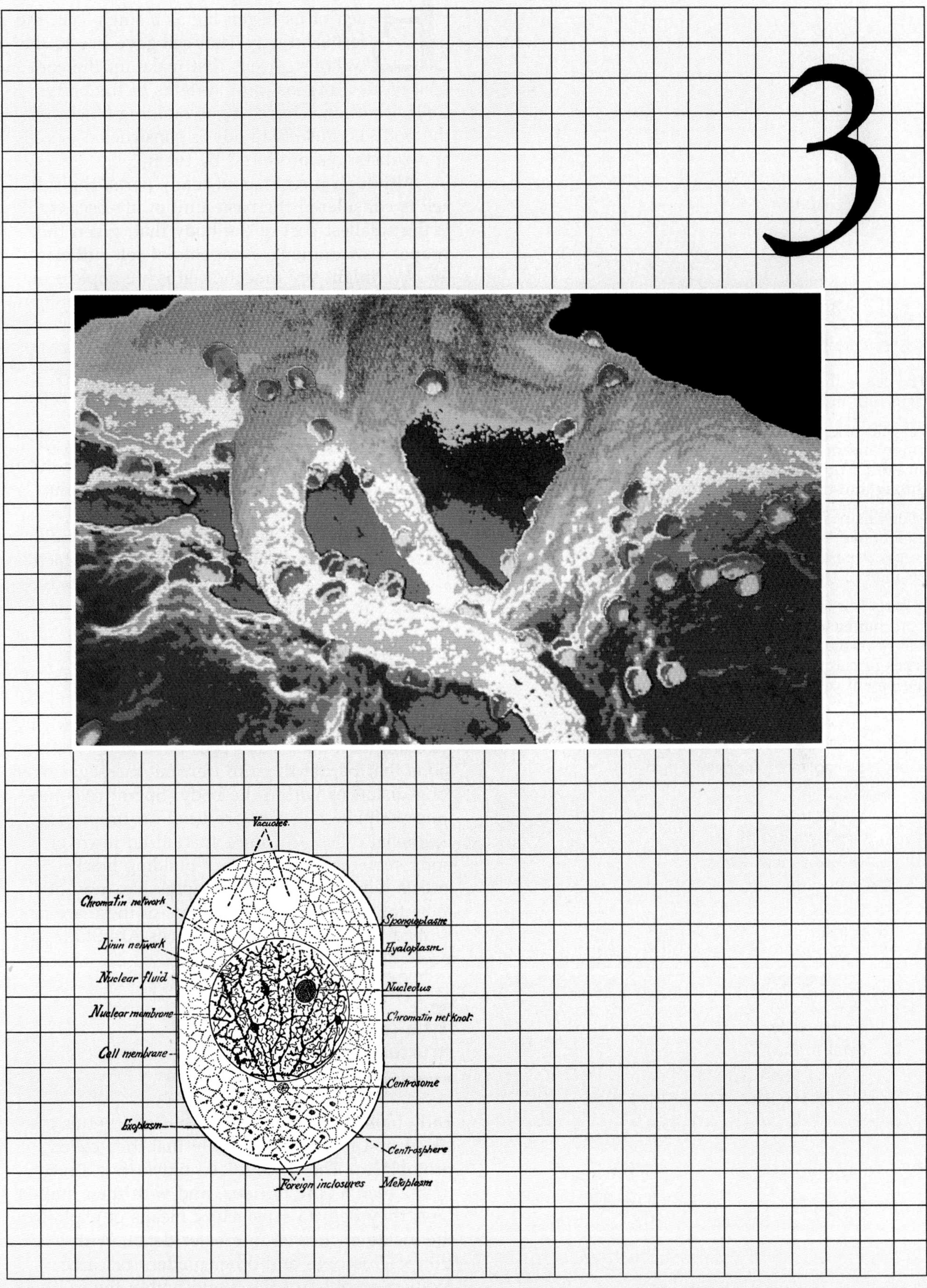
Vacuoles.
Chromatin network
Spongioplasm
Linin network
Hyaloplasm
Nuclear fluid
Nucleolus
Nuclear membrane
Chromatin net knot.
Cell membrane
Centrosome
Exoplasm
Centrosphere
Foreign inclosures
Metaplasm

KEY CONCEPTS

The cell is the smallest self-sufficient unit in the body.

All cells are surrounded by a membrane and most contain a nucleus and other organelles scattered throughout the cytoplasm.

Materials pass through the plasma membrane via a variety of processes depending on size and composition of the material.

Mitosis is a form of nuclear division that ensures that each new cell will have the identical number and types of chromosomes present in the parent cell.

Each of us began life as a single cell, the fertilized egg. That cell gave rise to the trillions of cells that make up the complex tissues, organs, and systems of the body. Cells are often referred to as building blocks of the body because the body is constructed of cells and substances produced by them.

Although it consists of many parts, the **cell** itself is considered the basic unit of life because it is the smallest part of the body that, given the proper environment, is capable of self-sufficient life. We might say that the cell is a complete metabolic unit, because it has all the basic equipment and chemical know-how needed for its own maintenance and growth. If their environmental needs are met, cells can be kept alive in laboratory bottles for many years. No cell part is capable of such survival.

Most cells are microscopic in size. A "typical" cell is about 10 micrometers (about 1/2500 inch) in diameter (see Focus on Cell Size). This means that if you could line up about 2500 typical cells end to end, the resulting cellular parade would measure only 1 inch. Even the egg cells, which are among the largest cells in the human body, are only about as large as a period on this page.

The size as well as the shape of a cell is related to the specific functions it must perform (Fig. 3-1). For instance, the neutrophil, a type of white blood cell, can change its shape as it flows along through the tissues of the body, destroying invading bacteria. Nerve cells have long extensions that permit them to transmit messages over long distances within the body. Sperm cells have long whiplike tails that are used for propulsion. Epithelial cells, which are specialized to cover body surfaces, look like tiny building blocks. Scientists have developed an impressive array of tools for studying the cell. Some of these are described in the Focus on How Cells Are Studied, pages 88–89.

The cell is a microcosm of structure and activity

Early biologists thought that the cell interior consisted of a homogeneous jelly that they called protoplasm. They recognized only a few structures, such as the nucleus, and with their limited tools they had no satisfactory means of exploring the inside of the cell in greater detail. With electron microscopes and other modern research tools, perception of the world within the cell has been vastly expanded. Scientists have found inside the cell a fabulously dynamic and complex world of ceaseless activity and bewildering chemical transformations. We are beginning to gain an understanding of what is really going on inside the cells of the body.

Today, the word protoplasm is no longer used. The jelly-like material outside the nucleus is referred to as **cytoplasm** (**sigh**-toe-*plazm*), and the corresponding jelly-like material within the nucleus is called the nucleoplasm (**new**-klee-oh-*plazm*) or karyoplasm. Scattered throughout the cell are tiny structures called **organelles** (little organs) that perform jobs within the cell just as organs do in the larger body.

Cytoplasm consists mainly of water (up to 90%) containing amino acids, simple sugars, and other substances used to manufacture larger molecules. Also present are thousands of different kinds of enzymes and molecules used in cellular metabolism, as well as ions that maintain an appropriate biochemical environment.

Most of the organelles within the cell are enclosed by membranes. These membrane-bound organelles effectively partition the cytoplasm into different compartments. The membrane acts as a barrier, making it possible for the chemical contents of the organelle to be different from the chemical environment in the general cytoplasm or in other organelles. These differences in organelle content allow metabolic processes to occur in an orderly, efficient manner.

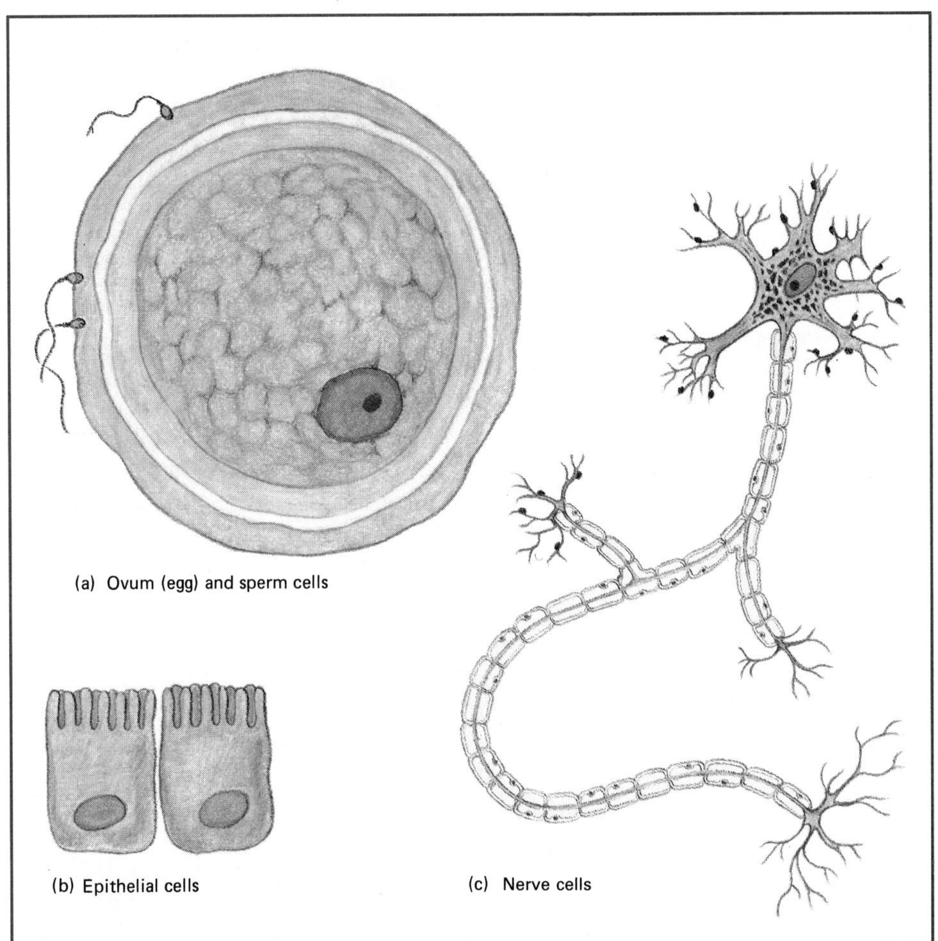

FIGURE 3-1

The size and shape of cells are related to their functions. *(a)* An ovum (egg cell) and sperm cells. Ova are among the largest cells; sperm are comparatively tiny. Note the long tail (flagellum) used by the sperm in locomotion. By whipping its flagellum, the sperm can move toward the egg. *(b)* Epithelial cells join to form tissues that cover body surfaces or line body cavities. *(c)* Among the most highly specialized cells, the nerve cell may live for more than a hundred years without dividing. Its long extensions are adaptations for transmitting neural messages from one part of the organism to another.

FOCUS ON . . . Cell size

Most cells are microscopic. The average cell in the human body ranges from 10 to 30 micrometers in diameter. Red blood cells are about 7 micrometers in diameter. The largest cell in the human body is the ovum, or egg cell. It is about the size of a period on this page. The longest cells are neurons, the nerve cells. Neurons have long cytoplasmic extensions that can measure a meter in length. Even though they are long, these cells are still microscopic.

The smallest cells are those of mycoplasma and other bacteria. Viruses are not considered cells because they cannot carry on life processes outside of a living host cell. Cell nuclei range in size from about 3 to 10 micrometers in diameter. Mitochondria are about the same size as bacteria.

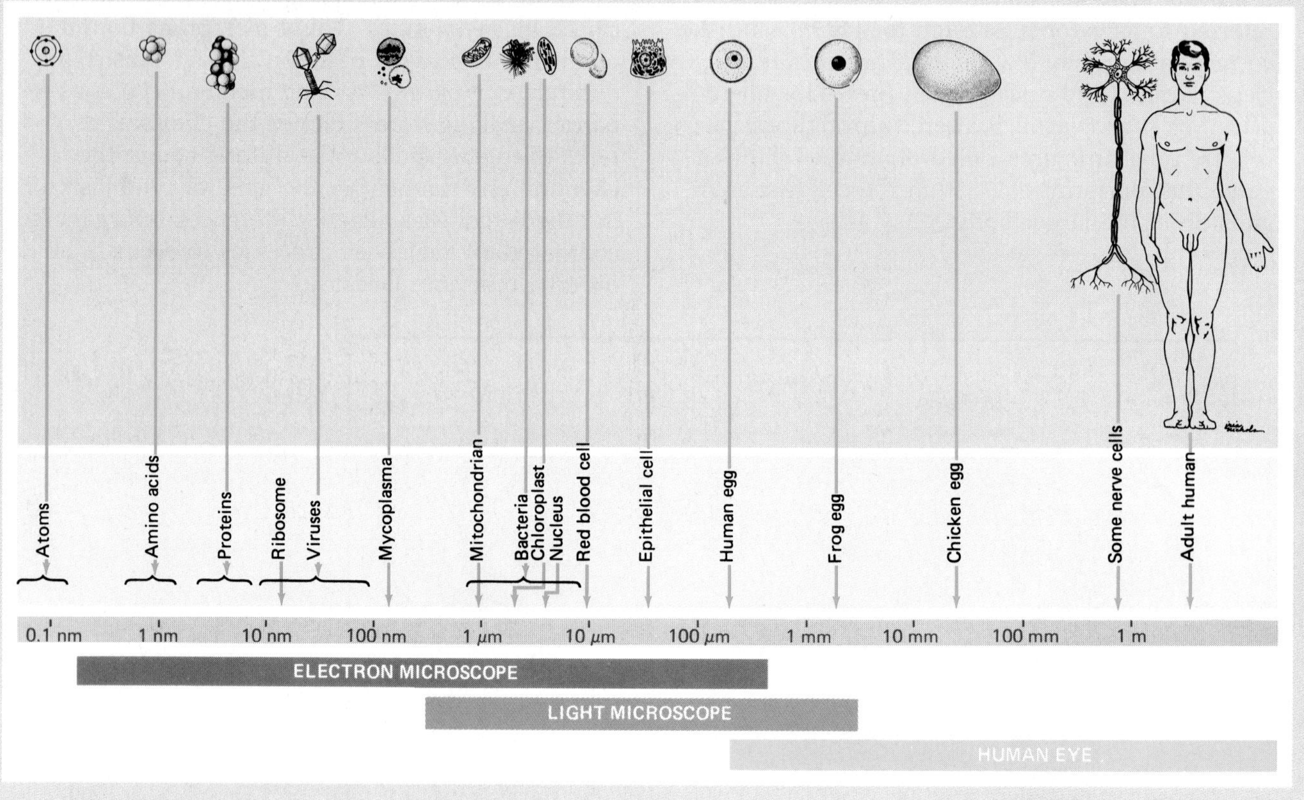

The characteristics of the various cellular organelles are summarized in Table 3-1. You may find this table useful as an introduction and later as a checklist for review. Many of the organelles are shown in Figure 3-2 and the Window on the Animal Cell.

The plasma membrane functions in structure, regulation, and communication

The **cell membrane,** or **plasma membrane,** is the delicate, limiting membrane that surrounds every cell. It is so thin, about 6 to 10 nanometers,[1] that it can be seen only with the electron microscope (Fig. 3-3).

The plasma membrane:

1. Encloses the contents of the cell. The plasma membrane prevents the materials within the cell from spilling out and mixing with substances in the extracellular environment. It helps the cell to maintain its shape and protects the inner contents from mechanical injury.
2. Regulates molecular "traffic" passing into and out of the cell. If the plasma membrane were completely permeable, materials would pass freely into and out of the cell. The cell contents would reflect the chemical composition of the surrounding tissue fluid, with disastrous results. Fortunately, the plasma membrane is selectively permeable. This means that the membrane can allow certain materials

[1] A nanometer (nm) is equal to one-billionth of a meter (10^{-9} m).

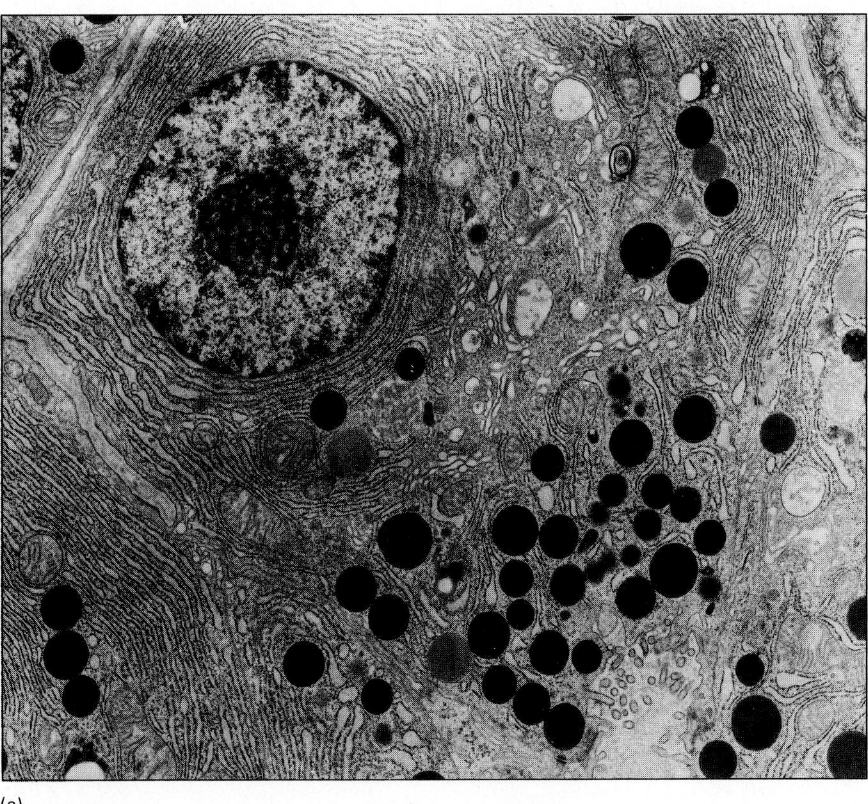

(a)

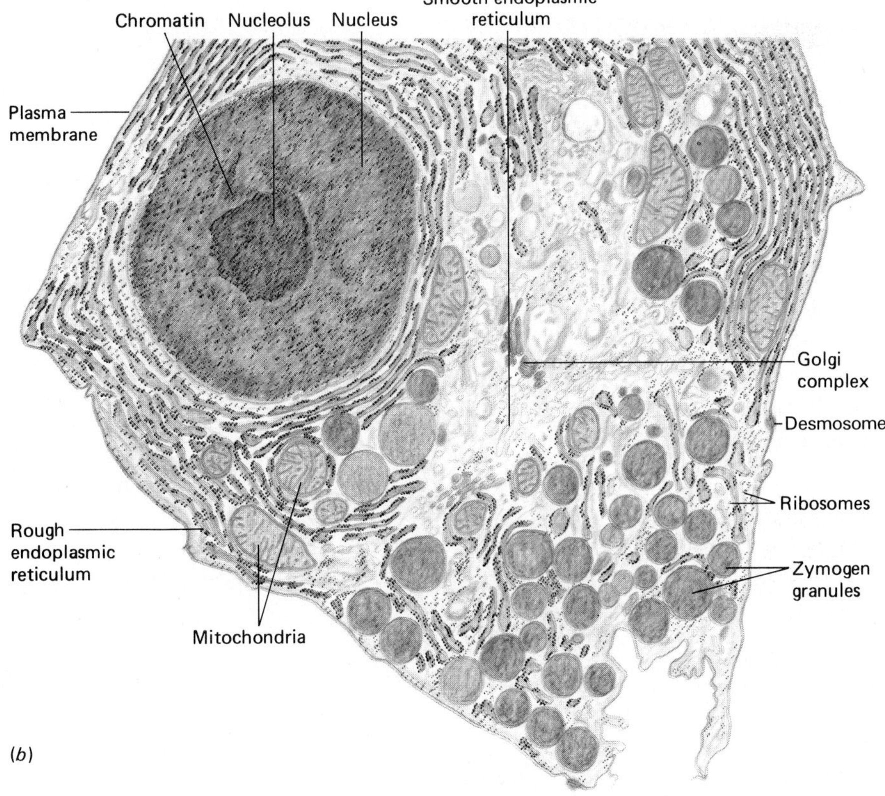

(b)

FIGURE 3-2

The structure of a human pancreas cell. *(a)* Electron micrograph of a human pancreas cell, magnified ×16,000. Most of the structures of a typical cell are present here; however, like most of the cells of a complex, multicellular animal, this cell has certain features that permit it to carry out a specialized function. The larger, circular dark bodies within the cell are zymogen granules containing inactive enzymes. Released from their storage cells and activated, these enzymes facilitate reactions such as the breaking down of peptide bonds during the digestion of proteins. (Courtesy of Dr. Susumu Ito, Harvard Medical School.) *(b)* A drawing based on the electron micrograph, emphasizing the important structures of the cell. Desmosomes are structures that help maintain adhesion between cells.

TABLE 3-1

Cell structures and their functions		
Structure	**Description**	**Function**
The membrane system of the cell		
Plasma membrane (cell membrane)	Membrane boundary of living cell	Encloses the cell; regulates movement of materials in and out of cell; communicates with other cells
Endoplasmic reticulum (ER)	Network of internal membranes extending through cytoplasm	Synthetic site of membrane lipids and many membrane proteins; origin of intracellular transport vesicles carrying proteins to be secreted
Smooth	Lacks ribosomes on outer surface	Lipid biosynthesis; drug detoxification
Rough	Ribosomes stud outer surface	Manufacture of many proteins destined for secretion or for incorporation into membranes
Ribosomes	Granules composed of RNA and protein; some attached to ER, some free in cytoplasm	Synthesize polypeptides
Golgi complex	Stacks of flattened membrane sacs	Modifies proteins, packages secreted proteins, sorts other proteins to vacuoles and other organelles
Lysosomes	Membranous sacs	Contain enzymes that break down ingested materials, secretions, wastes
Vacuoles	Membranous sacs	Transport and store ingested materials, wastes, water
Peroxisomes	Membranous sacs containing a variety of enzymes	Sites of many diverse metabolic reactions
Energy-transducing organelle		
Mitochondria	Sacs consisting of two membranes; inner membrane is folded to form cristae	Site of most reactions of cellular respiration; transformation of energy originating from glucose or lipids into ATP
The cytoskeleton		
Microtubules	Hollow tubes made of subunits of tubulin protein	Provide structural support; have role in cell and organelle movement and cell division; components of cilia, flagella, centrioles
Microfilaments	Solid, rodlike structures consisting of actin protein	Provide structural support; play role in cell and organelle movement and cell division
Centrioles	Pair of hollow cylinders located near center of cell; each centriole consists of nine microtubule triplets (9×3 structure)	Mitotic spindle forms between centrioles during cell division; may anchor and organize microtubule formation in animal cells
Cilia	Relatively short projections extending from surface of cell; covered by plasma membrane; made of two central and nine peripheral microtubules ($9 + 2$ structure)	Movement of materials on surface of some tissues
Flagella	Long projections made of two central and nine peripheral microtubules ($9 + 2$ structure); extend from surface of cell; are covered by plasma membrane	Cellular locomotion by sperm cells
The cell nucleus		
Nucleus	Large structure surrounded by double membrane; contains nucleolus and chromosomes	Control center of cell
Nucleolus	Granular body within nucleus; consists of RNA and protein	Site of ribosomal RNA synthesis; ribosome subunit assembly
Chromosomes	Composed of a complex of DNA and protein known as chromatin; visible as rodlike structures when the cell divides	Contain genes (units of hereditary information that govern structure and activity of cell)

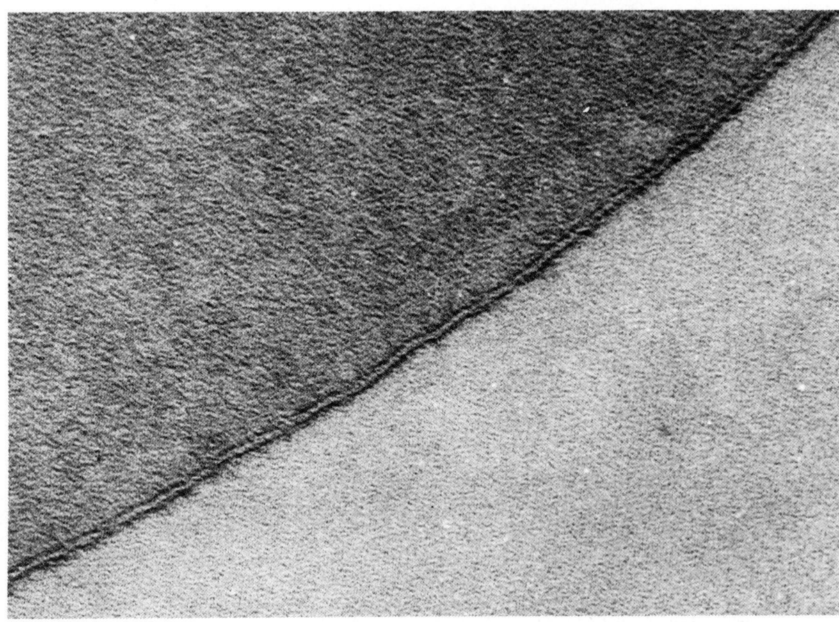

(a)

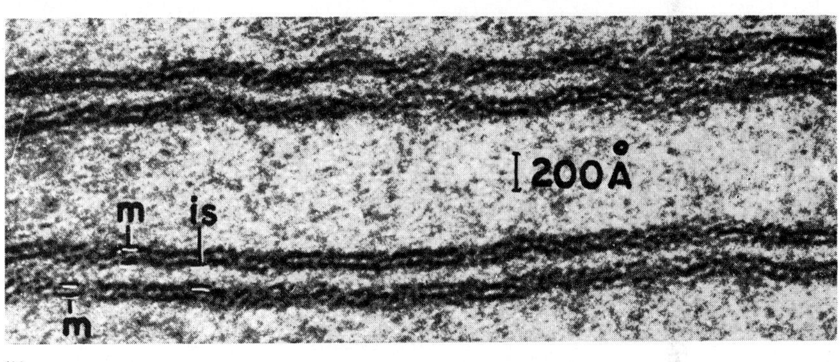

(b)

FIGURE 3-3

The plasma membrane. *(a)* The plasma membrane is the interface between the cell and its environment. (Omikron/Photo Researchers, Inc.) *(b)* Electron micrograph (approximately ×240,000) of a portion of a plasma membrane. The dark lines represent the hydrophilic heads of the lipids; the light zone represents the hydrophobic tails. m, membrane; is, intracellular space. The black line is a size marker indicating 200 Angstrom units or 20 micrometers.

to enter the cell while preventing the entry of others. The membrane also regulates the exit of materials so that waste products or secretions can leave the cell at appropriate times. Several ways in which the plasma membrane regulates passage of materials will be discussed later in this chapter.

3. Communicates with other cells and organs. The plasma membrane is equipped with certain proteins on its surface that permit other cells to recognize it. Based on such recognition, some cells adhere to one another to form tissues.

Cell surfaces are also equipped with receptor proteins, which receive chemical messages from endocrine glands or other types of cells. Messenger molecules combine with receptor proteins in much the same way that enzymes combine with their substrates. Such a message stimulates the cell to respond in a certain way. Thus, by receiving messages, the plasma membrane helps to control activities within the cell.

Recall from Chapter 2 that the plasma membrane consists of a rather fluid lipid bilayer in which are embedded a variety of proteins distributed in a mosaic pattern. This concept of the plasma membrane is illustrated in Figure 3-4. Known as the **fluid mosaic model,** it is currently the most widely accepted model of membrane structure.

The lipids of the plasma membrane present a barrier to the passage of materials. The proteins permit selective transport of water-soluble substances. Proteins that are water-soluble and are thought to be weakly bound to the surface of the membrane are known as **peripheral proteins.** Those that penetrate into the hydrophobic regions of the lipid bilayer are called **integral proteins.** Some of the integral proteins pass all the way through the membrane so that parts of the proteins protrude from each surface. Some integral proteins are organized to form tiny channels through which small water-soluble molecules enter and exit.

The endoplasmic reticulum may be associated with ribosomes

The **endoplasmic reticulum (ER)** (*en*-doe-**plas**-mik reh-**tik**-yoo-lum) is a system of parallel membranes that extends throughout the cytoplasm of many cells (Fig. 3-5). The cavities formed by the sheets of ER membrane are called cisternae (singlular, cisterna; a Latin word meaning reservoir). In electron micrographs the ER may appear to be discontinuous because the photograph shows a thin slice through the cell. In fact the ER is continuous in three dimensions.

Somewhat like a complex tunnel system, the ER provides passages through which materials can be transported from one part of the cell to another. By dividing the cytoplasm into compartments (much as walls divide a building into rooms), the ER helps to separate cell contents and activities. The ER membranes and their cisternae contain many types of enzymes that catalyze a variety of chemical reactions. Cisternae may also serve as temporary storage areas for certain substances.

Two types of ER can be distinguished, smooth and rough. **Rough ER (RER)** has a granular appearance that results from the presence of organelles called **ribosomes** (**rye**-bow-sowms) along its outer walls. Ribosomes consist of RNA and protein, and function as factories where proteins are assembled. Not all ribosomes are attached to the rough ER. Some float freely in the

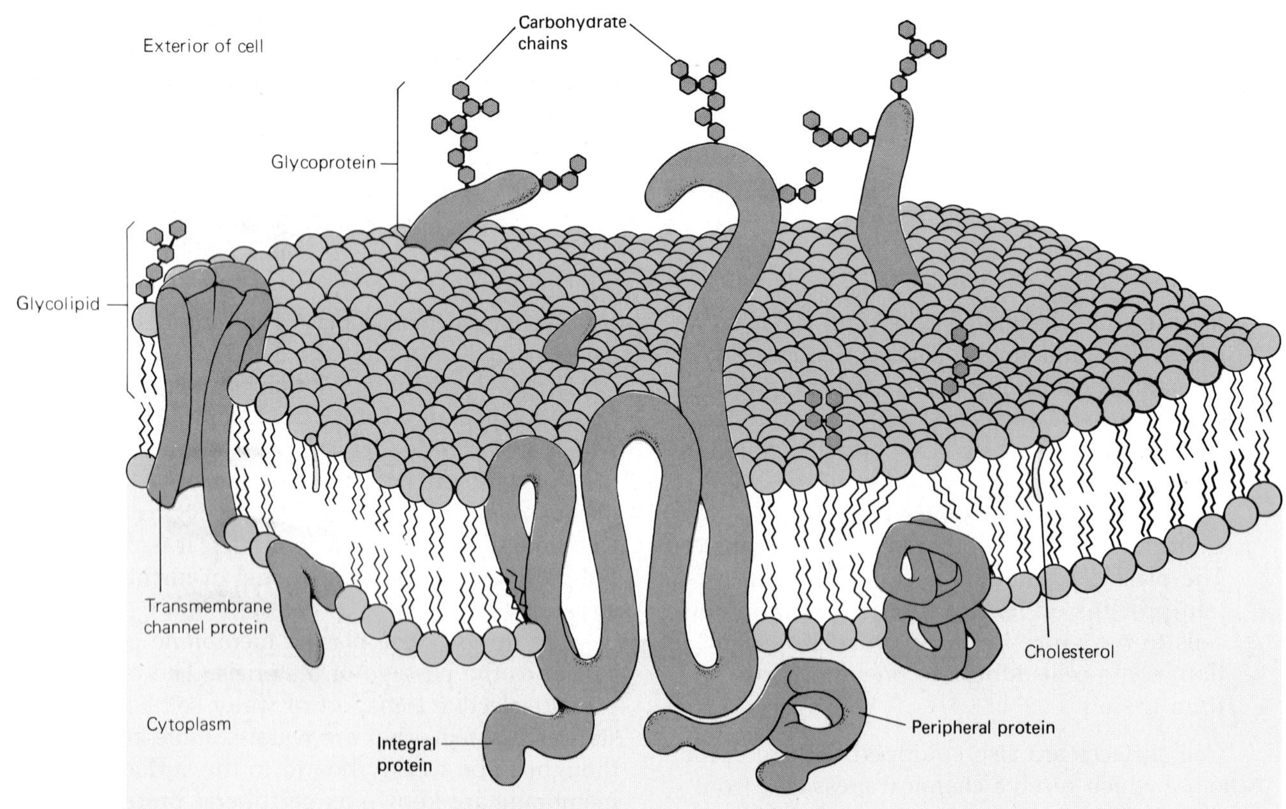

FIGURE 3-4

The fluid mosaic model of membrane structure. A representation of the plasma membrane, illustrating the various structures of some of the membrane proteins found in human cells.

cytoplasm and are thought to be involved in the manufacture of proteins for use within the cell. Rough ER is especially extensive in cells that manufacture proteins for export from the cell, such as those that secrete digestive enzymes.

Smooth ER (SER), so-called because it lacks ribosomes, is the main site of fatty acid and phospholipid metabolism. Smooth ER also produces steroids in certain cells. In muscle cells it is involved in calcium storage and affects muscle contraction.

Clinical highlight

Smooth ER is important in breaking down drugs and other chemicals such as carcinogens (cancer-causing compounds). The liver is a major detoxification center for the body and so contains extensive smooth ER. When an experimental animal is injected with the barbiturate phenobarbital, the amount of smooth ER in the liver cells increases. Also, enzymes known to break down phenobarbital increase in concentration within the smooth ER membranes when this drug is administered over a period of time.

Rough and smooth ER are continuous with one another. The two types are interconvertible, and the cell can change rough ER into smooth ER (or vice versa) according to its needs.

The Golgi complex processes, sorts, and delivers proteins

Looking somewhat like stacks of pancakes, the **Golgi complex (goal**-jee) is composed of layers of platelike membranes. In many types of cells, the Golgi complex is located at one side of the nucleus (Fig. 3-6). In others there may be several Golgi complexes consisting of separate stacks of membranes dispersed throughout the cell.

The Golgi complex functions principally as a protein processing and packaging plant. This organelle is most highly developed in cells that are specialized for secretion. As protein is manufactured along the rough ER, it is wrapped in a bit of ER membrane, forming a tiny vesicle. These vesicles are transported to the Golgi complex, with which they fuse to form new Golgi complex membranes. Within the Golgi complex the protein is modified in various ways. Often some carbohydrate component is added to the protein to form a glycoprotein (a protein with complex polysaccharides attached to a number of amino acids).

Some proteins follow a path through the Golgi complex that directs them to a particular location in the cell; secretory proteins follow a different route that directs them to the plasma mem-

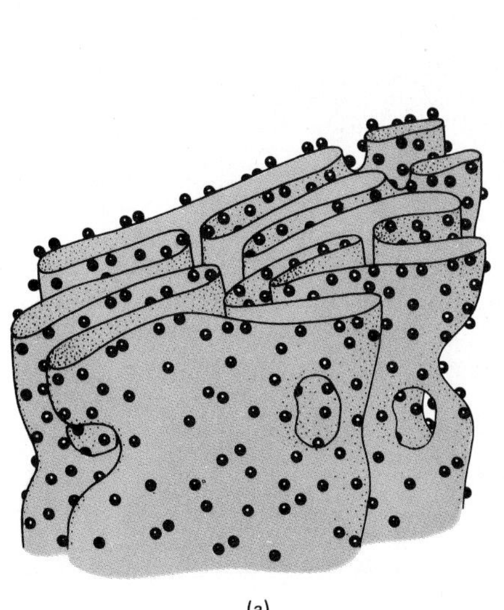

(a)

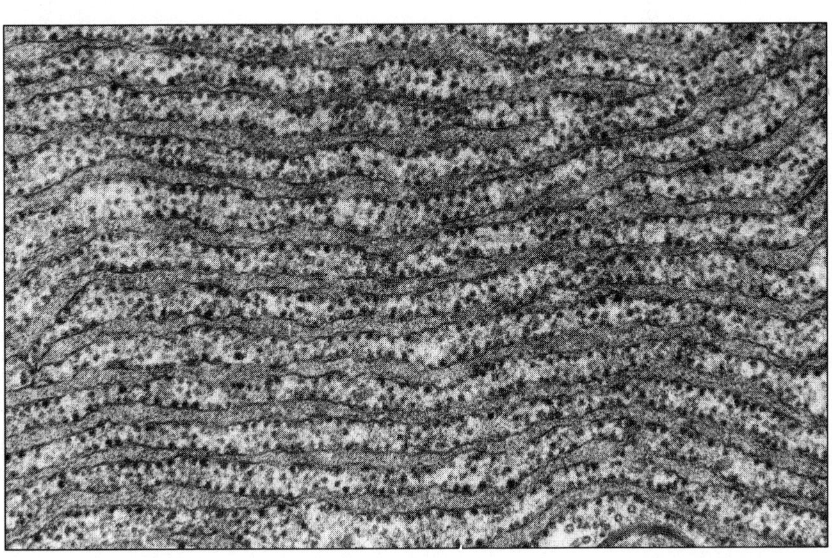

(b)

FIGURE 3-5

Rough endoplasmic reticulum. *(a)* Diagram of rough ER. *(b)* Electron micrograph of the rough ER from a secretory cell of the sea anemone *Metridium*. This form of ER consists of parallel arrays of broad flat sacs or cisternae. The outer surface of their limiting membranes is studded with ribosomes (approximately ×70,000). (Courtesy of Dr. E. Anderson.)

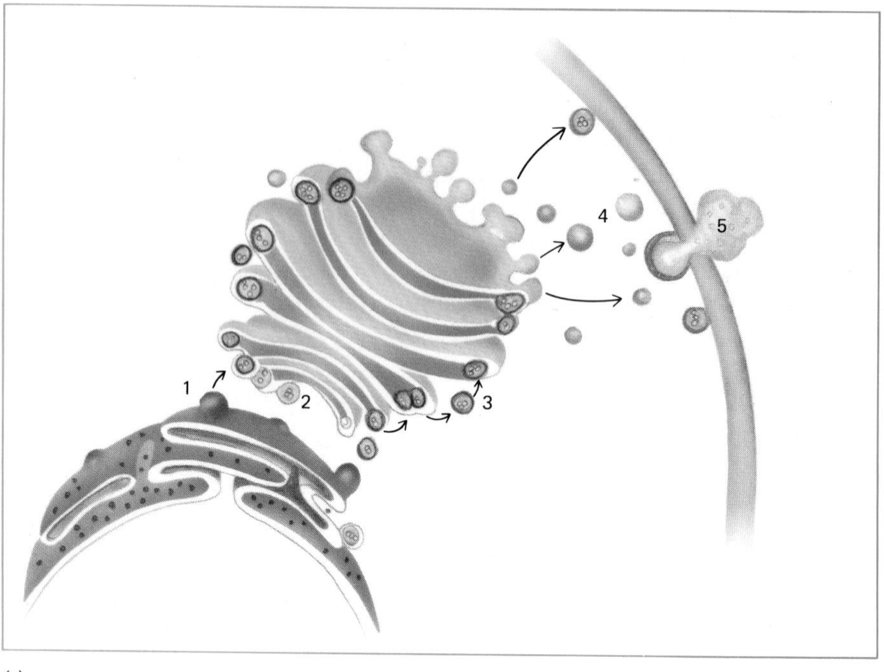

(a)

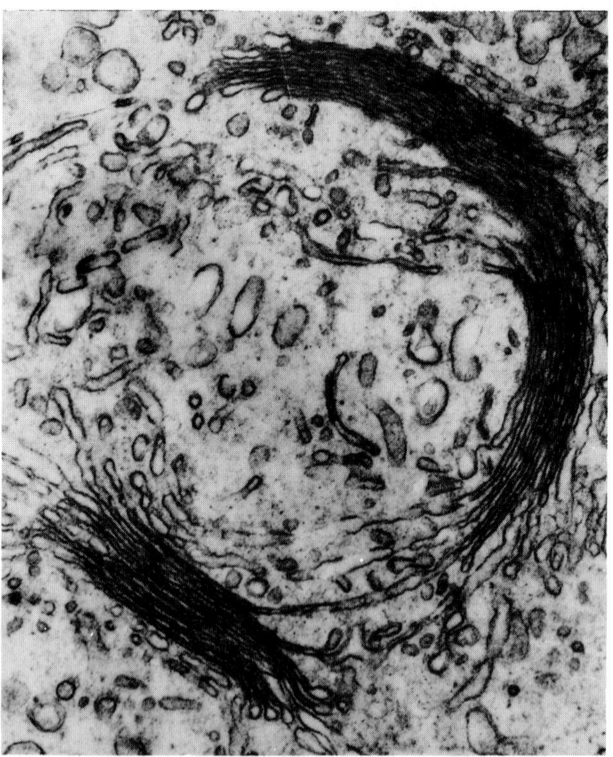

(b)

FIGURE 3-6

The Golgi complex. This drawing shows the Golgi complex during a secretory cycle of a goblet cell. The tiny mucus droplets join to form larger drops, which are then released from the cell. (1) Proteins (or lipids) formed in the ER are released from the ER. (2) These macromolecules enter the outer face of the Golgi complex. (3) As they pass through the Golgi in a series of vesicles, these molecules are modified. (4) They leave the inner face of the Golgi complex in secretory vesicles. (5) The vesicles fuse with the plasma membrane and the secretion is released from the cell. *(b)* Electron micrograph of a section through the Golgi complex from a sperm cell of a ram. (Don Fawcett, Photo Researchers, Inc.)

brane. The secretion may be packaged within a vesicle made from the Golgi complex membrane. Such **secretory vesicles** (called secretory granules when the secretion within them is dense) are released from the Golgi complex. These vesicles may fuse with the plasma membrane and release their contents outside the cell. Cells lining the digestive tract package and release digestive enzymes in this manner, and goblet cells in the lining of the digestive tract produce and secrete mucus in this way. In an actively secreting cell such as a goblet cell, the Golgi complex may completely renew its membranes every 30 minutes!

Not all cells secrete proteins, but even in nonsecreting cells the Golgi complex performs the important function of packaging intracellular digestive enzymes in the form of lysosomes.

Lysosomes contain digestive enzymes

Intracellular digestive enzymes are needed to break down foreign material taken into the cell and also to break down worn-out cell parts. These enzymes are manufactured along the rough endoplasmic reticulum and then transported to the Golgi complex. There the enzymes are identified and sorted to the lysosomes by unique carbohydrate signals that have been attached to the proteins. The enzymes are packaged, that is, wrapped in a bit of Golgi complex membrane, and then pinched off and separated from the Golgi complex. Each little bag or vesicle of digestive enzymes is a **lysosome** (**lye**-sow-sowm). The lysosomes are then dispersed throughout the cytoplasm (Fig. 3-7).

Lysosomes are used to break down foreign matter that has been ingested by the cell. When a white blood cell ingests bacteria or when some other phagocytic (scavenger) cell ingests debris, this foreign matter is surrounded by a vesicle consisting of part of the cell's plasma membrane. One or more of the cell's lysosomes then fuses with the vesicle containing the foreign matter (see Fig. 3-21). The lysosome pours its powerful digestive enzymes into the vesicle, destroying the material within it.

When a cell dies, lysosomes release their enzymes into the cytoplasm, where they break down the cell itself. This "self-destruct" system accounts for the rapid deterioration of many cells following death.

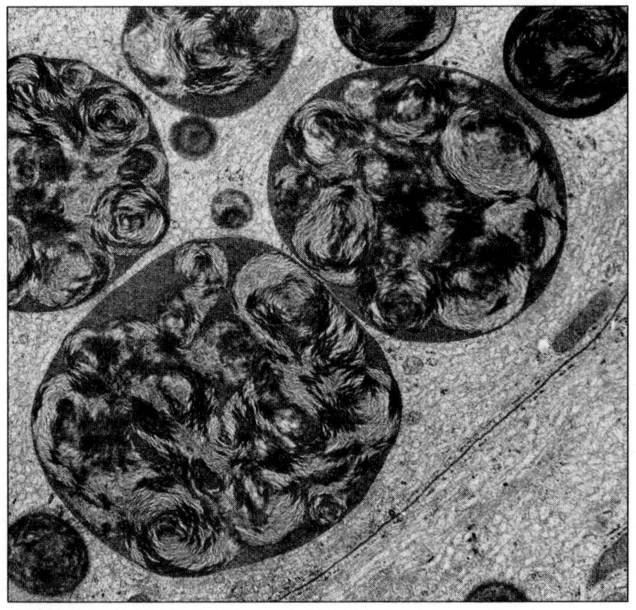

(*a*)

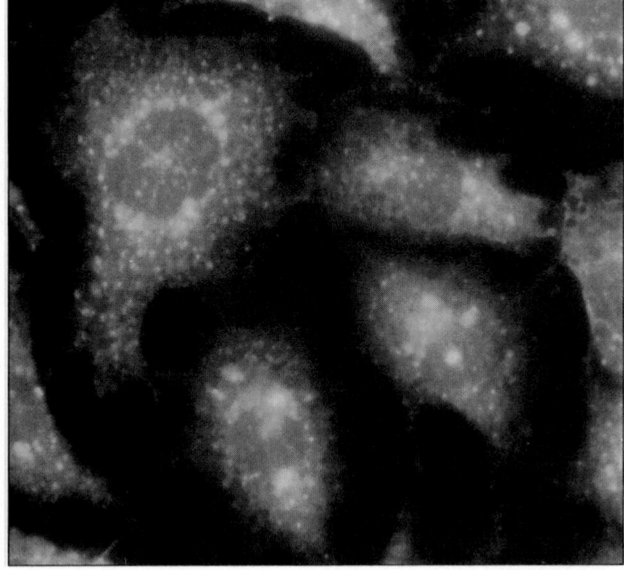

(*b*)

FIGURE 3-7

Lysosomes. *(a)* Electron micrograph showing different stages of lysosome formation. Primary lysosomes bud off from the Golgi complex. After a lysosome encounters material to be digested it is known as a secondary lysosome. The secondary lysosomes shown here contain various materials being digested. (Don Fawcett, Photo Researchers Inc.) *(b)* Distribution of lysosomes in cells. (Courtesy of Dr. Paul Gallup.)

FOCUS ON . . . How cells are studied

One of the most important tools for the study of cell structure is the microscope. In fact, cells were first described by Robert Hooke in 1665 when he examined a piece of cork using a microscope he had made himself. Hooke did not actually see cells in the cork; rather, he saw the walls of dead cork cells. Not until much later was it realized that the interior of the cell was an important part of the structure.

Refined versions of the *light microscope,* which use visible light for illumination, along with the development of certain organic chemicals that specifically stain different structures in the cell, enabled biologists to discover by the early twentieth century that cells contain a number of different internal structures called **organelles** (literally, "little organs"). We now know that each type of organelle in a cell performs specific functions required for the cell's existence. The development of biological stains was essential for those discoveries, since the interior of most cells is transparent in the light microscope. Most of the methods used to prepare and stain cells for observation, however, also killed the cells in the process. More recently, sophisticated types of light microscopes have been developed that use interfering waves of light to enhance the internal structures of cells. With *phase contrast* and *Nomarski differential interference* microscopes, it is now possible to observe some of the internal structures of unstained living cells. One of the most striking things that can be observed with these microscopes is that living cells contain numerous internal structures that are constantly moving and changing in shape and location.

Cells and their components are so small that ordinary light microscopes can distinguish only the gross details of many cell parts. In most cases all that can be seen clearly is the outline of a structure and its ability to be stained by certain dyes and not by others. Not until the development of the **electron microscope (EM),** which came into wide use in the 1950s, were researchers able to study the fine details, or **ultrastructure,** of cells.

Two features of a microscope determine how clearly you can view a small object. The **magnification** of the instrument is the ratio of the size of the image seen with the microscope to the actual size of the object. The best light microscopes usually magnify an object no more than 1000 times, whereas the electron microscope can magnify it 250,000 times or more. The other, even more important, feature of a microscope is its **resolving power.** Resolving power is the ability to see fine detail and is defined as the minimum distance between two points at which they can both be distinguished separately rather than being seen as a single blurred point. Resolving power depends on the quality of the lenses and the *wavelength* of the illuminating light; the shorter the wavelength,

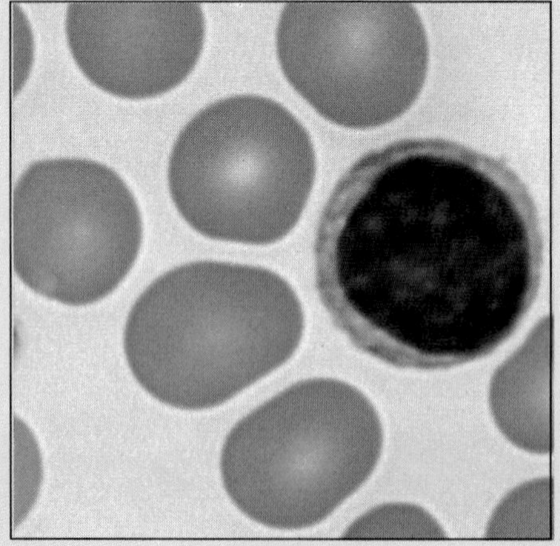

(*a*)

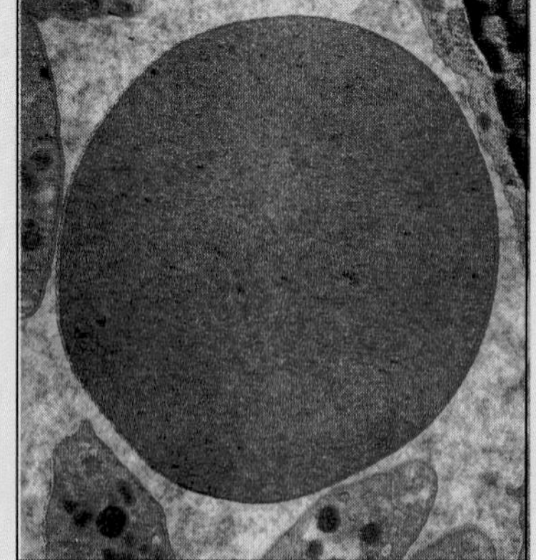

(*b*)

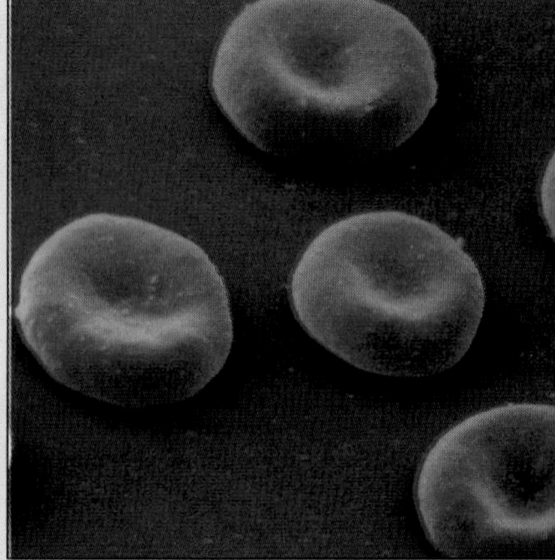

(*c*)

Comparison of a photograph taken with a modern light microscope and two taken with an electron microscope. (*a*) Light microscope of red blood cell (approximately ×500). (*b*) Transmission electron microscope of red blood cell. (David M. Phillips/Visuals Unlimited.) (*c*) False-color scanning electron micrograph of red blood cells (×10,500). (Stanley Flegler/Visuals Unlimited.)

the greater the resolution. The visible light used by light microscopes has wavelengths ranging from 400 to 700 nanometers (nm); this limits the resolution (resolving power) of the light microscope to details no smaller than the diameter of a small bacterial cell.

Whereas the best light microscopes have about 500 times more resolving power than the human eye, the electron microscope has a resolving power 10,000 times greater than the eye (see figure). This is because electrons have very short wavelengths, on the order of about 0.1 to 0.2 nm. Although this implies that the limit of resolution in the electron microscope comes close to that of the diameter of a water molecule, such resolution is difficult to achieve with biological material. It can be approached, however, when isolated molecules such as proteins or DNA are examined.

The image formed by the electron microscope cannot be seen directly. The electron beam itself consists of the charged electrons, which are focused by electromagnets in much the same way that images are focused by glass lenses in a light microscope. For **transmission electron microscopy (TEM)** one prepares an extraordinarily *thin section* of the specimen by embedding the cells or tissue in plastic, cutting the plastic with a glass or diamond knife, and then placing the preparation on a small metal grid. The electron beam passes through the specimen and then falls on a photographic plate or a fluorescent screen. When you look at electron microscope photographs in this chapter (and elsewhere), keep in mind that they represent only a thin cross section of a cell. In order to reconstruct how something inside the cell looks in three dimensions, it is necessary to study many consecutive cross-sectional views (called serial sections) through the object.

In another type of electron microscope, the **scanning electron microscope (SEM),** the electron beam does not pass through the specimen. Instead, the specimen is coated with a thin gold film. When the electron beam strikes various points on the surface of the specimen, secondary electrons are emitted whose intensity varies with the contour of the surface. The recorded emission patterns of the secondary electrons give a three-dimensional picture of the surface of the specimen. This special kind of micrograph provides information about the shape and external features of the specimen that cannot be obtained with the transmission electron microscope.

The electron microscope is a powerful tool for studying cell structure, its primary benefit lying in its ability to provide views of the different parts of cells under different conditions. To determine the *function* of cell parts, it was necessary to develop other approaches. Researchers had to be able to purify different parts of cells so that physical and chemical methods could be used to determine what they do. There are a number of methods for purifying cell organelles that involve **cell fractionation** procedures. Generally, cells are broken apart as gently as possible and then the mixture is subjected to centrifugal force by spinning in a device called a **centrifuge.** The greater the number of rpm's (revolutions per minute), the greater the force. This permits various cell components to be separated on the basis of their different densities. Today, cell biologists often use a combination of experimental approaches to understand the function of cellular structures.

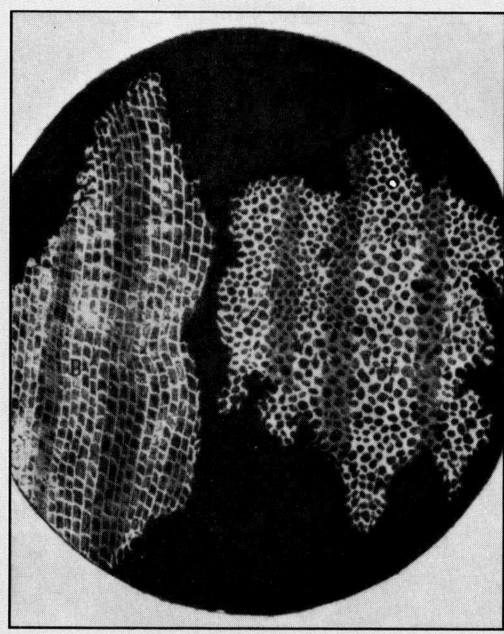

A drawing by Robert Hooke of the microscopic structure of a thin slice of cork. Hooke was the first to describe cells, basing his observations on the cell walls of these dead cork cells. Hooke used the term *cell* because the tissue reminded him of the small rooms that monks lived in during that period. (From the book *Micrographica*, published in 1665, in which Hooke described many of the objects that he had viewed using the compound microscope he had constructed.)

During development of the embryo some cells must die as structures are sculptured out of formless cellular masses. For example, in the early embryo the hand develops first as a solid stump. As the individual fingers are fashioned, the cells forming the tissue between them must die. The destruction of these cells is carried out very selectively and with great precision by lysosomal enzymes. The process of bone reformation utilizes lysosomal enzymes to dissolve old bone. Vitamin A appears to be associated with lysosome activation. When excess amounts of vitamin A are added to bone tissue, bone is removed.

Some forms of tissue damage and some aspects of the aging process may be related to leaky lysosomes. Rheumatoid arthritis is thought to result in part from damage done to cartilage cells in the joints by enzymes that have been released from lysosomes. Cortisone-type drugs, which are used as anti-inflammatory agents, stabilize lysosome membranes so that leakage of damaging enzymes is reduced.

Peroxisomes are organelles similar in structure to lysosomes

Peroxisomes (peh-**roks**-ih-sowms) are membrane-bound organelles that contain a variety of enzymes that promote an array of metabolic reactions. During some of these reactions, such as in the breakdown of fats, hydrogen peroxide (H_2O_2) is produced. Hydrogen peroxide, the active ingredient in most bleaches, is toxic to the cell. Peroxisomes contain the enzyme catalase that splits hydrogen peroxide, rendering it harmless. Although present in most cells, peroxisomes are most prevalent in liver and kidney cells.

Sufficient catalase must be present in the cell to destroy hydrogen peroxide promptly after it is formed. Catalase breaks down the H_2O_2 into water and oxygen in the following reaction:

$$2\ H_2O_2 \longrightarrow 2\ H_2O + O_2$$

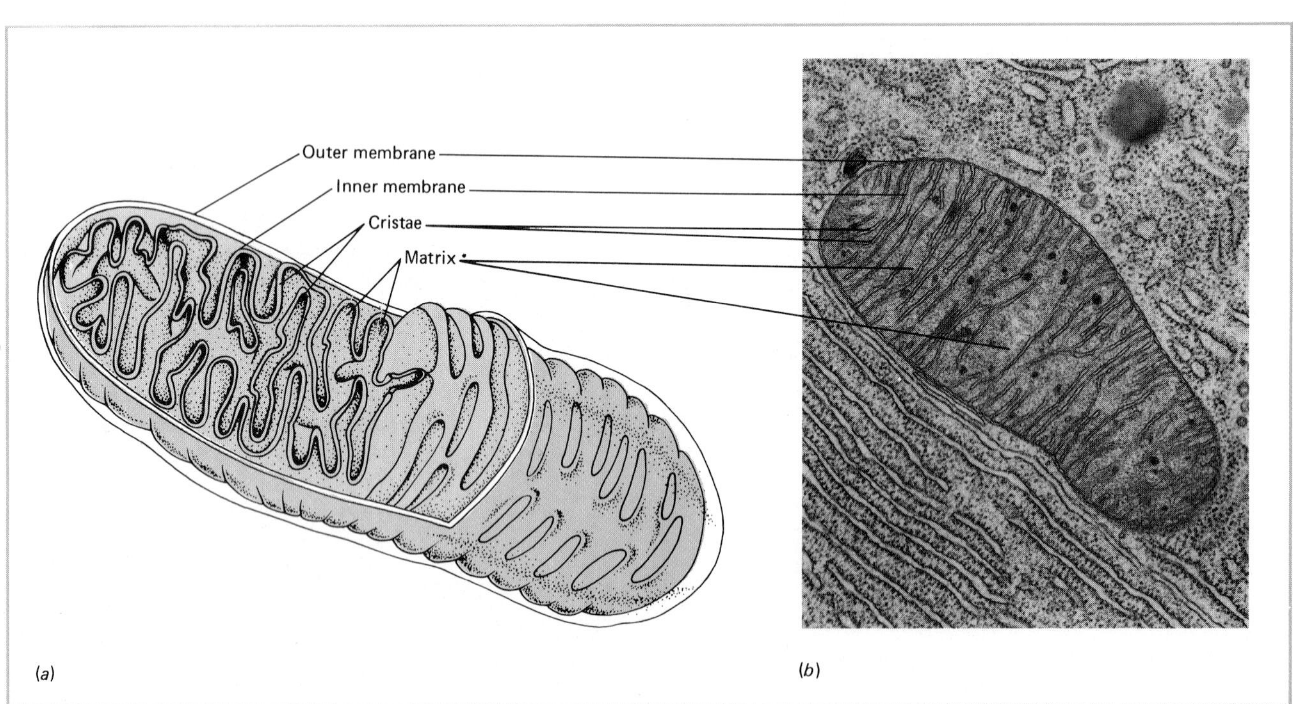

FIGURE 3-8

The mitochondrion. *(a)* Diagram of a mitochondrion cut open to show the cristae. *(b)* Electron micrograph of a typical mitochondrion from the pancreas of a bat showing the cristae and matrix. Note the extensive rough endoplasmic reticulum at the lower left (approximately ×80,000). (Courtesy of Keith R. Porter.)

The mitochondria are the powerhouses of the cell

Cells contain tiny power plants called **mitochondria** (*my*-tow-**kon**-dree-uh) in which most of the reactions of cellular respiration take place. Recall that during cellular respiration fuel molecules are broken down and some of their chemical energy is stored within the energy-rich bonds of ATP. The energy from ATP can then be used by the cell as needed. Because of its high energy expenditure, a liver cell may contain more than 1000 mitochondria, and a muscle cell even more.

Although their size and shape may vary somewhat, a typical mitochondrion is sausage-shaped and may measure up to 0.8 micrometers in length, making it one of the largest organelles (Fig. 3-8). When viewed in the living cell, mitochondria appear to be in continuous motion.

Each mitochondrion consists of a sac composed of two membranes. The outer membrane encloses the mitochondrial contents. The compartment between the two membranes is the **intermembrane space.** Numerous folds of the inner membrane, called **cristae** (**kris**-tee), project into the central compartment, or **matrix,** of the mitochondrion. Just as shelves increase the storage surface of a closet, the cristae increase the available membrane surface within the mitochondrion. Some of the enzymes needed for cellular respiration are arranged along the cristae. Other enzymes are dissolved in the contents of the matrix.

Each mitochondrion has a small amount of DNA, enough to specify about 15 proteins. It also contains ribosomes. Indeed, mitochondria manufacture some of their own proteins and are able to reproduce themselves.

The cytoskeleton is the internal structure of the cytoplasm

Microtubules, microfilaments, and intermediate filaments are three different types of structures that make up the **cytoskeleton,** the internal skeletal framework of the cell. This framework is a flexible scaffolding that can be rapidly assembled or disassembled by the cell. These skeletal components are thought to maintain the shape of the cell, to move materials within the cell, and to aid in movement of the cell itself. This scaffolding is held together by even smaller filaments that make up the **microtrabecular lattice** (*my*-krow-trah-**bek**-u-lar). The lattice extends throughout the cell (Fig. 3-9).

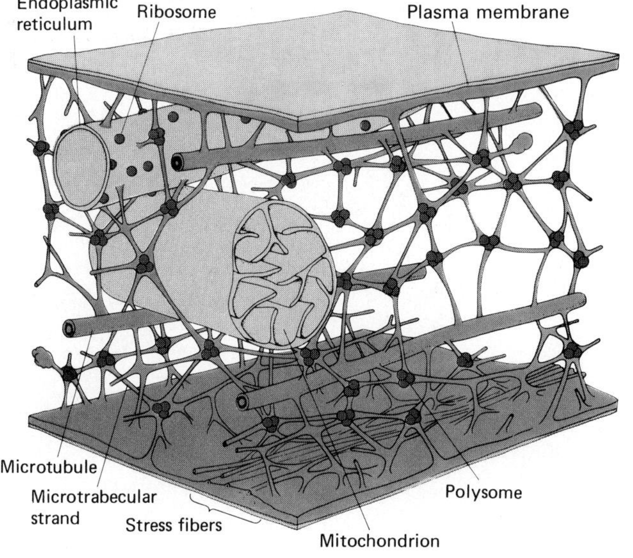

(a)

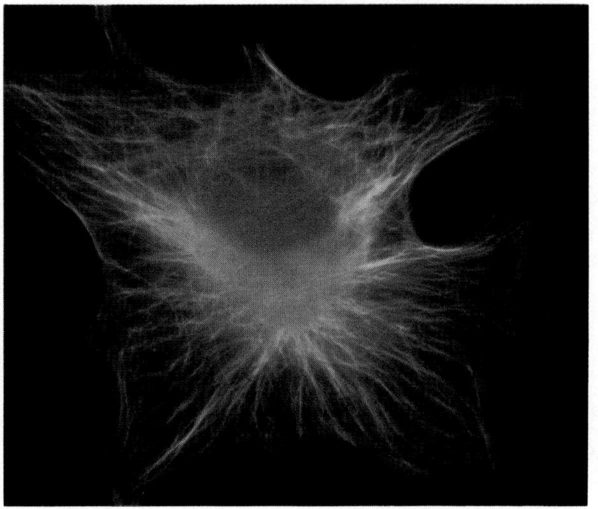

(b)

FIGURE 3-9

Elements of the cytoskeleton. *(a)* Model of the microtrabecular lattice drawn about 200,000 times its actual size. The lattice is traversed by microtubules that appear to be attached to the trabeculae of the lattice. *(b)* Micrograph showing a fibroblast cell. Microfilaments are stained in red; microtubules are stained green. (M. Schliwa/Visuals Unlimited.)

Microfilaments are tiny rodlike filaments with contractile properties. Some microfilaments contain a protein called **actin,** while others contain a protein called **myosin.** These microfilaments are essential for the contraction of muscle but are also present in nonmuscle cells. Microfilaments function in supporting cell structure and assisting in cellular movement.

Microtubules are slightly larger, cylindrical structures. They are spirally arranged hollow rods whose walls are composed mainly of alternating subunits of two kinds of **tubulin** protein. These proteins automatically associate with one another to produce microtubules whenever they are present and when the chemical conditions within the cell are appropriate. It has been proposed that microtubules form conducting tracks along which substances may travel throughout the cytoplasm. Although they are often found scattered singly or in clusters in the cytoplasm, microtubules also organize to form larger cellular structures such as centrioles, cilia, flagella, and the spindle that forms during mitosis.

Intermediate filaments appear to function in supporting the structure of the cell but they are still under investigation. They are very stable, tough fibers made of polypeptides. Intermediate filaments may exist in bundled form or as individual filaments. Their structure varies depending on cell type.

Centrioles function in cell reproduction

Each cell possesses two tiny **centrioles** (**sen**-tree-oles), organelles that function in cell division and appear to play a role in microtubule assembly. Each centriole is a hollow cylinder composed of nine sets of three microtubules (Fig. 3-10). Centrioles are located within a dense area of cytoplasm, the **centrosome** (**sen**-trow-*sowm*), which is usually near the nucleus.

Cilia and flagella are used in locomotion

Cilia (**sil**-ee-uh), tiny hairlike organelles projecting from the surfaces of many types of cells, help to move materials that are outside the cell. The cells lining the respiratory passages, for example, are equipped with cilia, which ceaselessly beat to propel a layer of mucus containing trapped dirt particles and other debris away from the lungs. Cilia beat from 10 to 40 times per second, and their movement is coordinated so that thousands of cilia work together to move the fluid along.

Flagella (flah-**jel**-ah), which aid in locomotion, are much longer than cilia but have the same basic structure. Flagella in human sperm cells serve as whiplike tails that are used to propel the sperm.

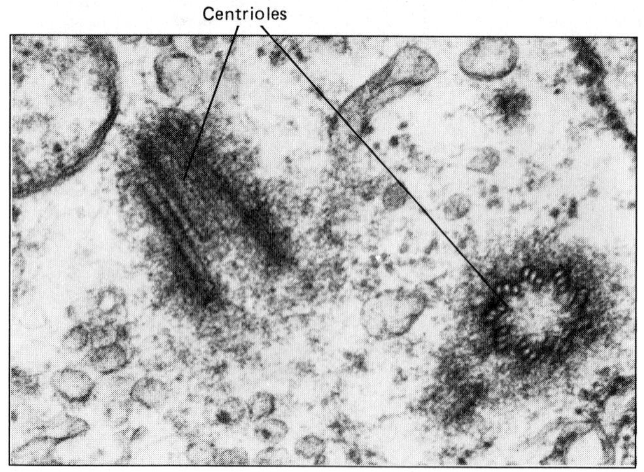

(*a*)

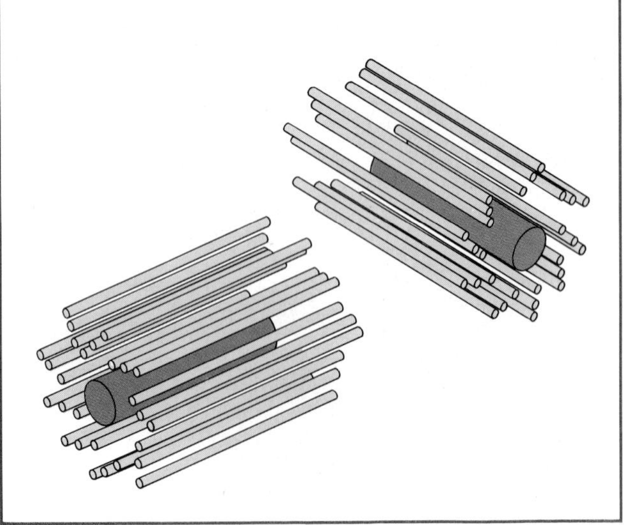

(*b*)

FIGURE 3-10

Centrioles. *(a)* Electron micrograph of a pair of centrioles from monkey endothelial cells. Note that one centriole has been cut longitudinally and one transversely. (B. F. King, School of Medicine, University of California, Davis/BPS.) *(b)* A line drawing of the centrioles.

Each cilium or flagellum consists of a slender, cylindrical stalk covered by an extension of the plasma membrane. The core of the stalk contains a group of microtubules (Fig. 3-11). The arrangement of these microtubules is characteristic and occurs in all cilia and flagella (except bacterial flagella). There are nine pairs of outer microtubules, each pair resembling a figure eight in cross section. The pairs are connected to one another by *dynein* proteins that extend like arms (Fig. 3-11). In the center of a cilium or flagellum there are two single microtubules. The **9 + 2 arrangement** of microtubules is characteristic of cilia and flagella found in humans and other animals.

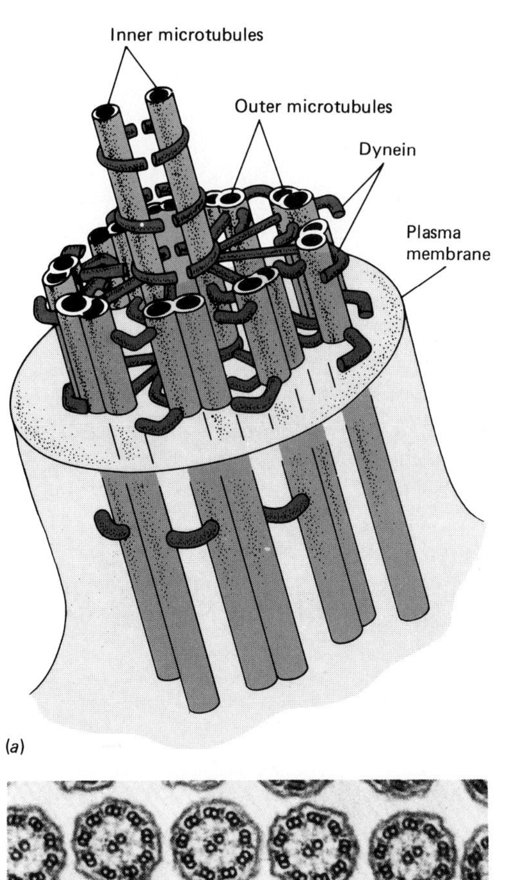

(*a*)

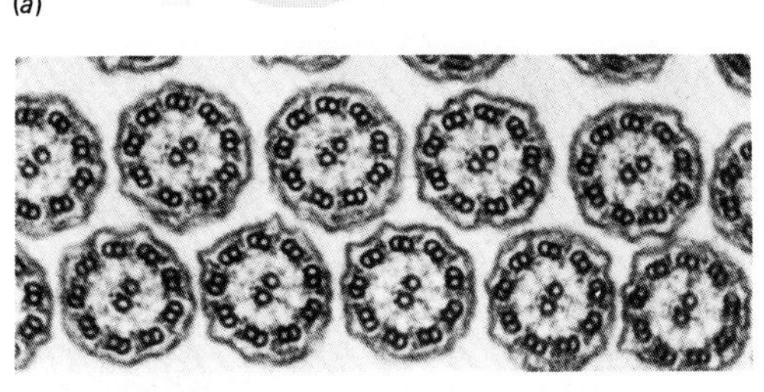

(*b*)

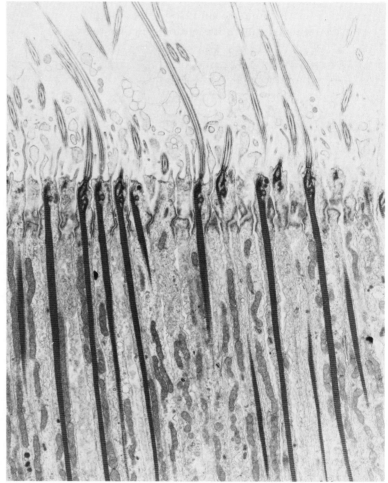

(*c*)

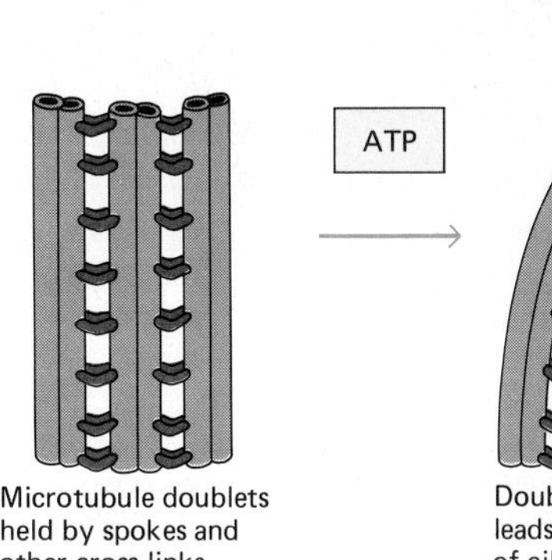

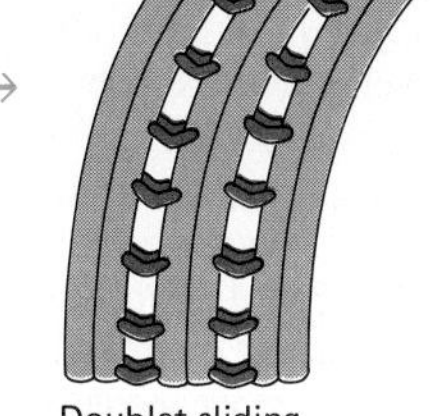

(*d*)

FIGURE 3-11

Cilia. *(a)* Structure of a cilium. Each cilium contains 10 pairs of microtubules in a 9 (pairs) + 2 arrangement. The arms shown in the figure are force-generating proteins that use energy from ATP to bend the cilia by "walking" up and down the neighboring pair of microtubules. *(b)* Electron micrograph of cross sections through cilia showing the 9 + 2 arrangement of microtubules. (Omikron, Photo Researchers, Inc.) *(c)* Electron micrograph of the bases of the cilia that cover the gills of the primitive chordate *Amphioxus.* Notice the striated rootlets that penetrate deep into the cell, and the long wormlike mitochondria arranged along them. Presumably the mitochondria provide the energy for the ciliary contraction (approximately ×12,000). (Dr. M. C. Holley.) *(d)* The dynein arms move the microtubules by forming and breaking cross bridges on the adjacent microtubules so that one tubule "walks" down its neighbor.

The base of the cilium or flagellum consists of a structure called the **basal body,** which is constructed exactly like a centriole. The basal body appears to be the organizing structure for new cilia and flagella.

Cilia and flagella move either the cell itself or adjacent fluid with an action similar to that of the arm of a human swimmer. This motion is achieved by a sliding action of the outer tubules. The dynein proteins use the energy stored in ATP in such a way that the protein arms on one pair of tubules are able to "walk" along the adjacent pair of tubules, causing the entire structure to bend back and forth. Thus, the microtubules on one side of a cilium or a flagellum extend farther toward the tip than those on the other side, resulting in a beating motion. The function of the central tubules is not entirely understood but may be related to the control of movement of the entire organelle.

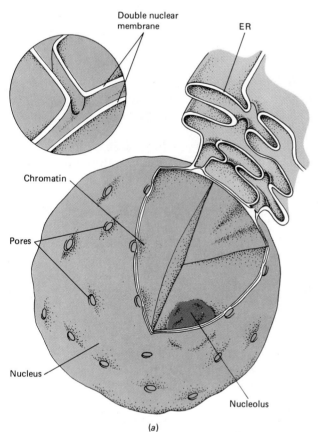

Double nuclear membrane
ER
Chromatin
Pores
Nucleus
Nucleolus

(a)

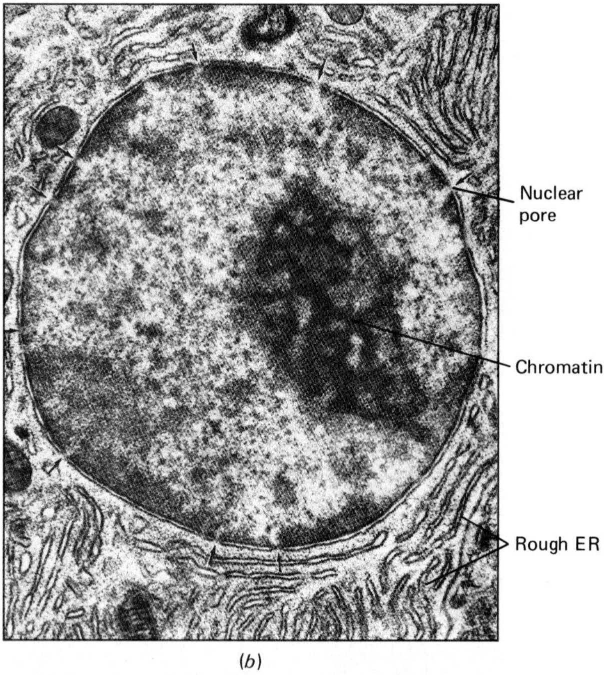

(b)

(c)

FIGURE 3-12

The cell nucleus. *(a)* A portion of the nucleus has been cut away to show the interior and the continuity of the outer nuclear membrane with the ER. *(b)* Electron micrograph showing the nucleus of a pancreatic acinar cell. Note the two membranes that form the nuclear envelope. Arrows indicate nuclear pores (approximately ×40,000). (Don Fawcett.) *(c)* Scanning electron micrograph of the surface of the nuclear membrane (approximately ×60,000). The outermost of the two nuclear membranes is shown above, but it has been partly broken to expose part of the inner membrane, shown below. (Courtesy of Dr. Daniel Branton, University of California, Berkeley.)

The nucleus contains the genetic information of the cell

The **nucleus** (**new**-klee-us) is a large, spherical organelle that serves as the library and control center of the cell (Fig. 3-12). Most cells have only one nucleus, but some (e.g., skeletal muscle cells) are multinucleated. The nucleus is enclosed by a double membrane, the **nuclear membrane** or **nuclear envelope.** This envelope is interrupted by many rather large pores that selectively permit passage of materials in and out of the nucleus.

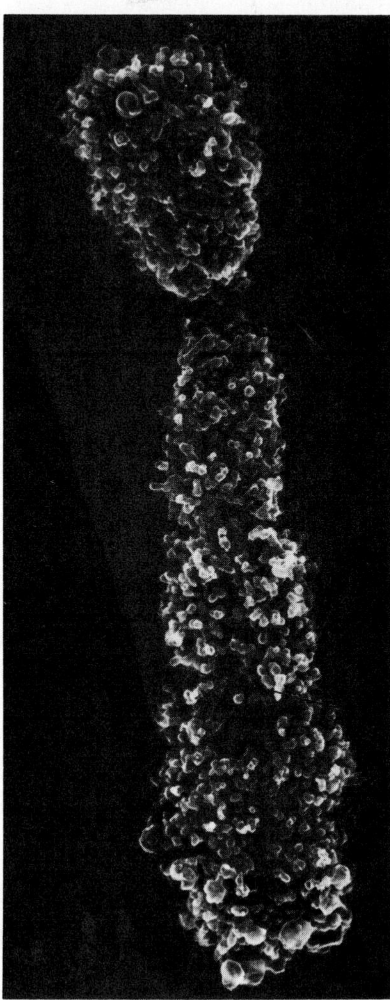

FIGURE 3-13

Scanning electron micrograph of a chromosome from a hamster cell. Just prior to division, the loose threads of DNA that make up the chromosomes shrivel into the knotted coils you see here (magnification ×15,000). (Courtesy of Drs. Susanne M. Gollin and Wayne Wray, Kleber Cytogenetics Laboratory, Department of Medicine, Baylor College, and Biology Department, The Johns Hopkins School of Medicine.)

The **nucleoplasm** (**new**-klee-oh-*plazm*), also called karyoplasm, inside the nucleus is thicker and less fluid than the cytoplasm. In a cell that is not in the process of division, loosely coiled, fibrous material called **chromatin** (**krow**-mah-tin) can be seen as a darkly staining granular material scattered throughout the nucleoplasm. Chromatin consists of DNA, together with a class of proteins called histones, and a small amount of RNA. The DNA is wound around a core of histone proteins. You may recall that DNA is the material in which the genetic information of the cell is stored—that is, the DNA makes up the genes. Chemically coded within the DNA are the instructions for producing all the proteins needed by the cell. Proteins, in turn, determine what the cell will look like and what functions it will perform.

When a cell prepares to divide, the chromatin fibers become more tightly coiled and condense to form discrete rod-shaped bodies, the **chromosomes** (Fig. 3-13). Each chromosome contains several hundred genes arranged in a specific linear order; the genes are composed of DNA. The chromosomes may be thought of as a chemical cookbook for the cell, and each gene as a recipe for a specific protein.

The **nucleolus** (new-**klee**-oh-lus) (little nucleus) is a specialized region within the nucleus. One or more of these rounded bodies may be present, but they are most prominent in cells that are actively synthesizing protein. The nucleolus is not walled off from the rest of the nucleus by a membrane. The nucleolus is a factory where the RNA components of ribosomes are assembled and some protein components are added as well. Ribosomes may also be stored in the nucleolus temporarily.

Materials move through the plasma membrane by both passive and active processes

Because it permits the passage of certain types of molecules while restricting the movement of others, the plasma membrane is described as **selectively permeable.** Responding to varying environmental conditions or cellular needs, the plasma membrane may present a barrier to a particular substance at one time and then actively promote its passage at another. By regulating chemical traffic in this way, the cell controls its own composition. The distribution of ions and molecules inside the cell can be very different from that outside the cell.

Materials move passively by physical processes such as diffusion, osmosis, and filtration, or they can be moved actively by physiological processes such as active transport, phagocytosis, or pinocytosis (Table 3-2). Such active physiological processes require the expenditure of energy by the cell.

Diffusion is a passive process

If we were to open a bottle of ammonia and place it on a front-row desk in a closed classroom, within a few moments students in the second row would begin to smell ammonia. Some time later the acrid odor would be evident in every part of the room. How does this happen? Molecules move out of the bottle and distribute themselves throughout the room. This is an example

TABLE 3-2

Mechanisms for moving materials through cell membranes

Process	How it works	Energy source	Example
Physical process			
Diffusion	Net movement of molecules (or ions) from region of greater concentration to region of lower concentration	Random molecular motion	Movement of oxygen in tissue fluid
Dialysis	Passage of small solute molecules through a selectively permeable membrane	Random molecular motion	Kidney dialysis
Facilitated diffusion	Carrier protein in plasma membrane accelerates movement of relatively large molecules from region of higher to region of lower concentration	Random molecular motion	Movement of glucose into cells
Osmosis	Water molecules diffuse from region of higher to region of lower concentration through differentially permeable membrane	Random molecular motion	Water enters red blood cell placed in distilled water
Physiological process			
Active transport	Protein molecules in plasma membrane transport ions or molecules through membrane; movement may be against concentration gradient (i.e., from region of lower to region of higher concentration)	Cellular energy	Pumping of sodium out of cell against concentration gradient
Endocytosis			
Phagocytosis	Plasma membrane encircles particle and brings it into cell by forming vacuole around it	Cellular energy	White blood cells ingest bacteria
Pinocytosis	Plasma membrane takes in fluid droplets by forming vesicles around them	Cellular energy	Cell takes in needed solute dissolved in tissue fluid
Exocytosis	Plasma membrane ejects materials; vesicle filled with material fuses with plasma membrane	Cellular energy	Secretion of mucus
Receptor-mediated endocytosis	A specific receptor-protein on the plasma membrane recognizes and binds with a large molecule (ligand). The receptor-ligand complex is transported into the cell	Cellular energy	Cell takes in large molecules such as proteins

of **diffusion,** the net movement of molecules or ions from a region of high concentration to one of lower concentration due to random molecular motion.

Diffusion occurs as a result of the continuous motion of the molecules of fluids (liquids and gases). When one molecule collides with another it may bounce off and move in another direction. Millions of such collisions may take place each second. Even though this molecular motion is random, it accounts for the thorough mixing of molecules that occurs in fluids. Thus in our example, the ammonia molecules distribute themselves thoroughly among the other molecules in the air of the classroom. Probability favors the movement of molecules from regions where they are more concentrated to regions where they are less concentrated (Fig. 3-14). Eventually the molecules are evenly distributed. We can say that diffusion involves a net movement of particles down a **concentration gradient,** a change in concentration of a substance from one region to another.

The rate of diffusion is a function of the size and shape of the molecules, their electrical charges, and the temperature. Lighter molecules move faster than heavy ones. As the temperature rises, the thermal energy increases, and the molecules move faster. Thus, the rate of diffusion increases.

Diffusion is an important process in living systems. For example, nutrients diffuse throughout the cytoplasm of a cell. Diffusion can also occur across membranes. Gases and many nutrients move into and out of cells by diffusion.

DIALYSIS SEPARATES SMALL PARTICLES FROM LARGE PARTICLES

Small molecules in a liquid can be separated from larger ones by **dialysis** (die-**al**-ih-sis). This process depends upon the passage of small solute molecules through a selectively permeable membrane (Fig. 3-15). The pores of this type of membrane will not permit passage of larger molecules. Although dialysis does not normally occur in the body, it is clinically important.

Clinical highlight

You may know something about kidney dialysis. In this process the blood of a patient with a kidney disorder passes through a long, coiled tube immersed in a tank filled with solution (see Chapter 27). Pores in the tubing permit small molecules in the blood (such as the waste product urea) to dialyze out of the blood and into the surrounding solution, which is eventually discarded. Larger molecules (e.g., proteins) cannot pass through the pores and remain in the blood. By regulating the concentration of various substances in the tank solution, the passage of even small molecules can be controlled selectively. For example, by placing in the tank solution a concentration of sodium that is equal to the desired concentration of sodium in the blood, the appropriate sodium concentration of the blood can be maintained, thus helping to compensate for the poorly functioning kidneys.

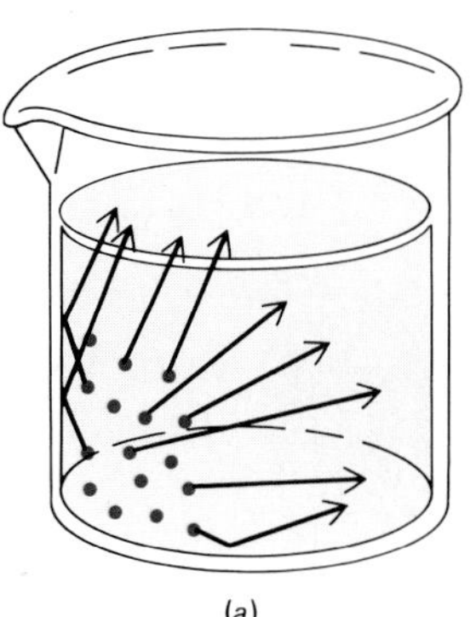
(*a*)

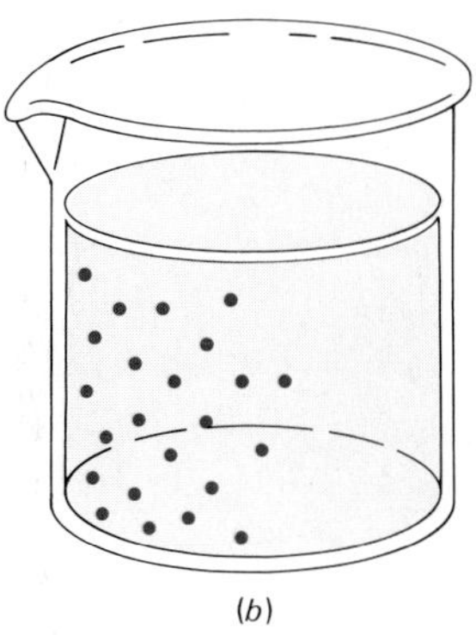
(*b*)

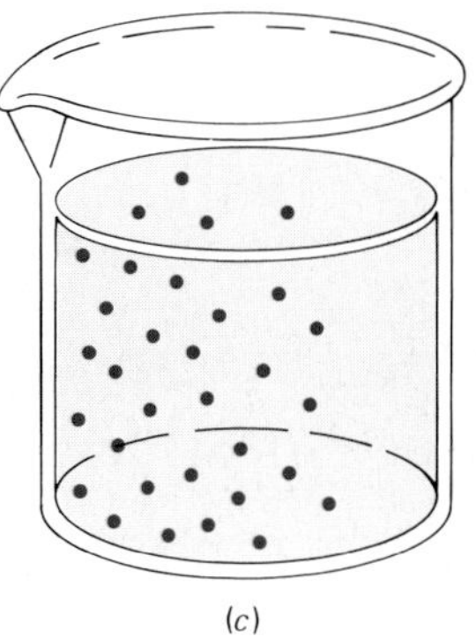
(*c*)

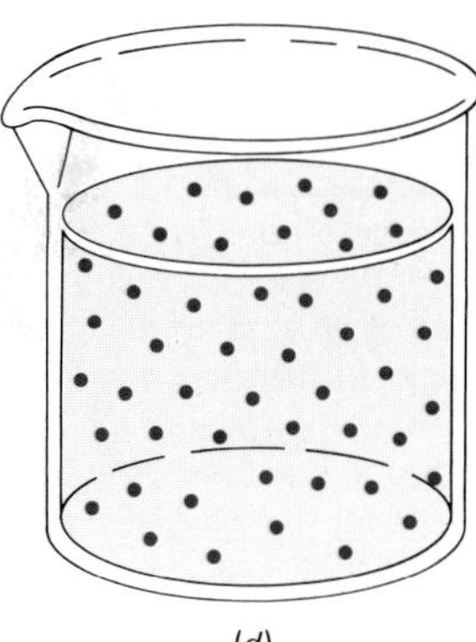
(*d*)

FIGURE 3-14

The process of diffusion. When a small lump of sugar is dropped into a beaker of water, its molecules dissolve *(a)* and begin to diffuse (*b* and *c*). Over a long period of time, diffusion results in an even distribution of sugar molecules throughout the water *(d)*.

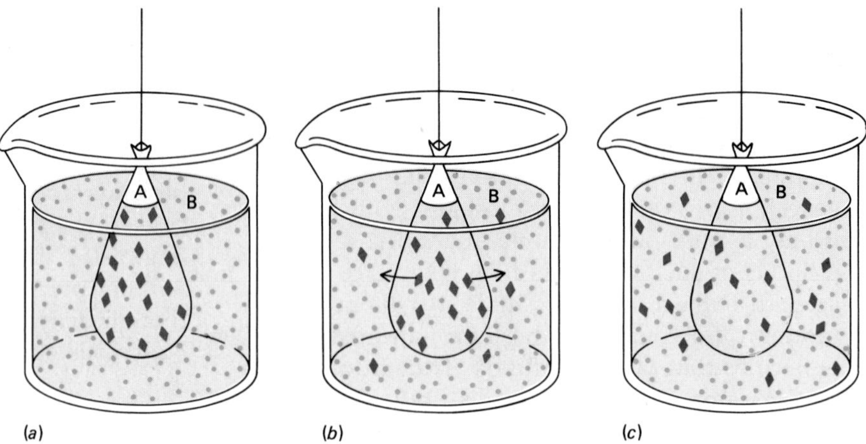

FIGURE 3-15

Dialysis. *(a)* A cellophane bag filled with a sugar solution is immersed in a beaker of water. The cellophane acts as a selectively permeable membrane, permitting passage of the sugar and water molecules, but preventing passage of larger molecules. *(b)* The arrows indicate the net movement of sugar molecules through the membrane and into the water of the beaker. *(c)* Eventually the sugar becomes distributed equally between the two compartments. Although sugar molecules continue to diffuse back and forth, the net movement is zero. The same is true for the water molecules. Blue dots represent water molecules; red diamonds represent sugar molecules.

FACILITATED DIFFUSION REQUIRES A CARRIER PROTEIN

Most cells in the body depend upon a continuous supply of glucose as an energy source. However, glucose is a relatively large, polar molecule that cannot easily diffuse through the lipid regions of the plasma membrane. A mechanism called **facilitated diffusion** ensures its passage. An integral protein (permease) in the plasma membrane temporarily combines with the glucose (or other solute) molecule and accelerates its movement through the membrane (Fig. 3-16). This carrier protein works somewhat like an enzyme in that it is not changed by the reaction. After the solute molecule has been transported, the protein is free to bind with another solute molecule.

The carrier molecule can transfer solute equally well either into the cell or out of it. The direction of transport depends upon the relative concentration of the solute. Movement proceeds from the region of greater concentration to the region of lower concentration. Facilitated diffusion is not dependent on energy input by the cell.

Facilitated diffusion is also important in the movement of other substances such as amino acids through plasma membranes. The carrier protein is specific for each substance being transported. For example, each different sugar has a different carrier protein.

Osmosis is the movement of water molecules through a selectively permeable membrane

Osmosis is a special kind of diffusion in which molecules of water pass through a selectively permeable membrane, moving from the region where the water molecules are more concentrated to where they are less concentrated. Most solute

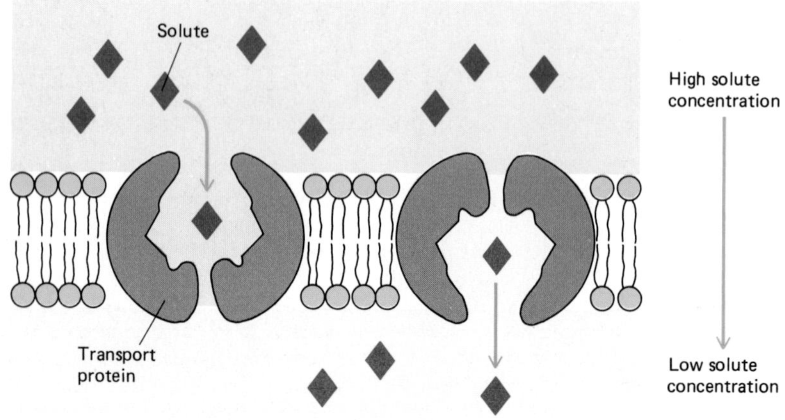

FIGURE 3-16

A model for the facilitated diffusion of glucose. The transport protein is capable of binding glucose on the outside of the cell and then changing its shape so that a channel is opened to the inside of the cell. When the glucose molecule is released on the inside, the protein reverts to its original shape and is ready to bind to the next molecule.

molecules cannot diffuse freely through the selectively permeable plasma membrane, but water (solvent) molecules can pass freely through it.

When living cells are placed in a solution that has a solute (and therefore a water) concentration equal to that in the cells, water molecules move in and out of the cells at the same rate. The net movement of water molecules is, therefore, zero (Fig. 3-17). A solution such as this, which is the same strength as the solute concentration of the cells, is said to be **isotonic** to the cells. When placed in an isotonic solution, the volume of cells stays the same as when the cells are surrounded by body fluids.

Cells may find themselves in a solution that is of greater or lesser solute concentration than the solute concentration within the cytoplasm. If the solution is of greater solute concentration, it is said to be **hypertonic** (above strength) to that of the cell; if it is of lesser solute concentration, it is **hypotonic** (under strength) compared with the cell. (See Table 3-3.)

Suppose that we place some living cells in distilled water that contains 100% water (solvent) molecules. If the total number of solute molecules in the cells amounted to 1% of the total molecules present, then water molecules would account for only 99% of the total. Like solute molecules, water molecules tend to move from a region where they are more concentrated to a region where they are less concentrated. Thus water molecules from the hypotonic solution will diffuse inward across the plasma membrane. Remember that solutes have a tendency to diffuse in the opposite direction, but the plasma membrane prevents them from "leaking out" to any great extent. Instead, they may be thought of as being trapped within the cell and exerting an **osmotic**

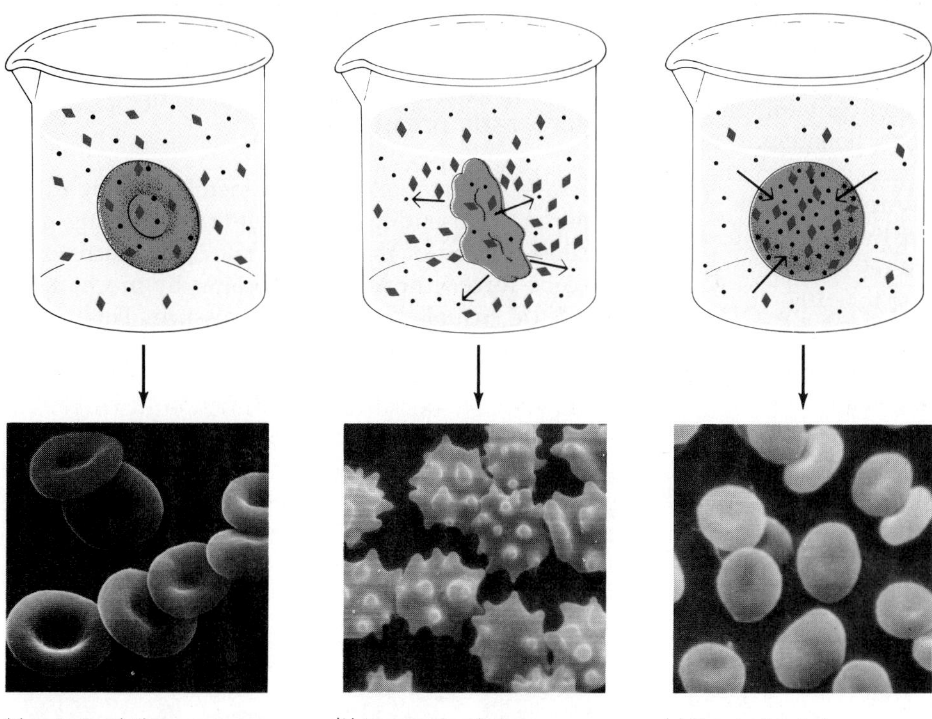

(*a*) Isotonic solution (*b*) Hypertonic solution (*c*) Hypotonic solution

FIGURE 3-17

Osmosis and the living cell. *(a)* A cell is placed in an isotonic solution. Because the concentration of solutes (and thus water molecules) is the same in the solution as in the cell, the net movement of water molecules is zero. *(b)* A cell is placed in a hypertonic solution. This solution has a greater solute concentration (thus a lower water concentration) than the cell and therefore exerts an osmotic pressure on the cell. This results in a net movement of water molecules out of the cell, causing the cell to dehydrate, shrink, and perhaps die. *(c)* A cell is placed in a hypotonic solution. The solution has a lower solute (and thus a greater water) concentration than the cell. The cell contents thus exert an osmotic pressure on the solution, drawing water molecules inward. There is a net diffusion of water molecules into the cell, causing the cell to swell and perhaps even to burst. (Micrographs of human red blood cells courtesy of Dr. R. F. Baker, University of Southern California Medical School.)

TABLE 3-3

How osmosis works

Solute concentration in solution A	Solute concentration in solution B	Tonicity	Solute diffusion	Solvent diffusion
Greater	Less	A hypertonic to B B hypotonic to A	A to B	B to A
Less	Greater	B hypertonic to A A hypotonic to B	B to A	A to B
Equal	Equal	Isotonic	Equal	Equal

pressure (a kind of pulling force) upon the less concentrated solution on the other side of the membrane. So much water may enter the cell that it swells and bursts.

On the other hand, when cells are placed in a hypertonic solution, water tends to diffuse out of them. The cells may become dehydrated, shrink, and die. Can you explain this in terms of the relative concentrations of water molecules in the two solutions? Remember, a solution containing more solute molecules contains proportionately fewer water molecules, so that the water and solute concentrations are reciprocally related. Note also that the terms hypertonic and hypotonic are relative to each other. A 5% solution is hypertonic to a 2% solution but is hypotonic to a 10% solution.

Physiological activities and homeostasis depend upon appropriate osmotic balance. With the help of certain hormones, the kidneys regulate the excretion of salts and water in the urine. Even when you eat an entire package of potato chips, the kidneys ensure that the salt concentration of your blood remains within normal limits. (How this is accomplished will be discussed in Chapter 27.)

Filtration involves hydrostatic pressure

Passage of materials through membranes by diffusion or osmosis depends upon the unceasing molecular motion of those materials. Substances may also be forced through membranes by mechanical pressure, usually hydrostatic pressure. This process is called **filtration.** Blood pressure forces

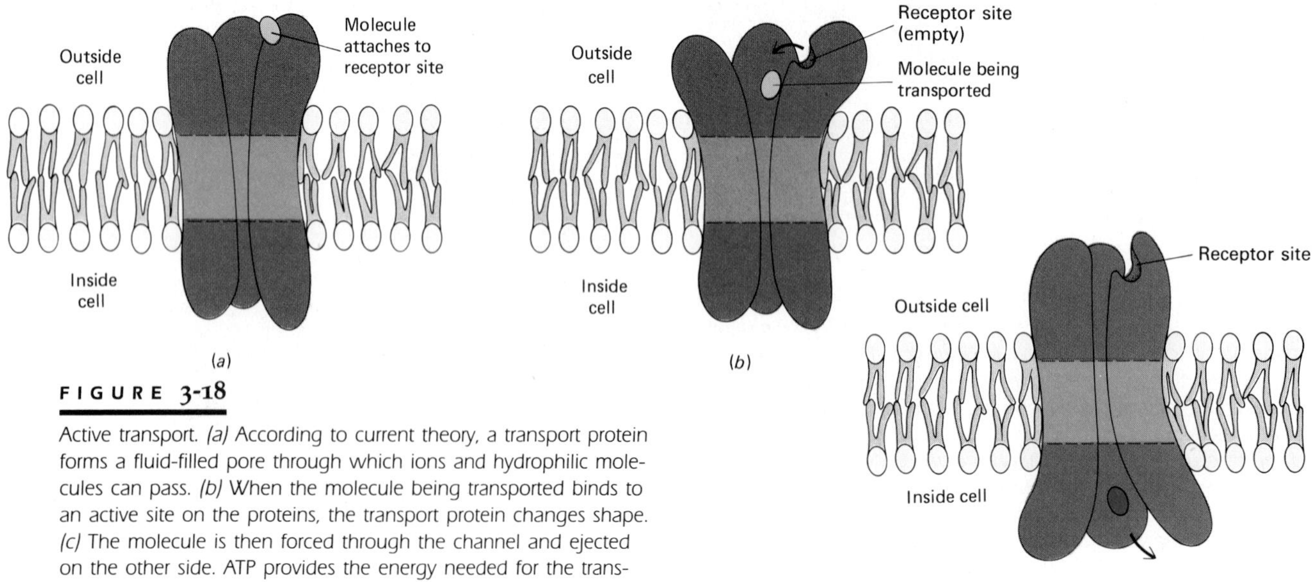

FIGURE 3-18

Active transport. *(a)* According to current theory, a transport protein forms a fluid-filled pore through which ions and hydrophilic molecules can pass. *(b)* When the molecule being transported binds to an active site on the proteins, the transport protein changes shape. *(c)* The molecule is then forced through the channel and ejected on the other side. ATP provides the energy needed for the transport.

some of the liquid part (plasma) of the blood through the capillary wall in this way, forming tissue fluid. Movement of the plasma is from a region of greater pressure to a region of lesser pressure. Filtration is also the first step in urine production. In the kidneys, hydrostatic pressure forces plasma and small ions and molecules out through the thin walls of certain specialized capillaries. The fluid passes into structures called Bowman's capsules and then into the kidney tubules.

Active transport requires energy

The chemical composition of the cytoplasm is not identical to that outside the cell. For example, the concentration of sodium outside the cell is about 10 times greater than inside, and the potassium concentration is about 35 times greater inside the cell than outside. Such differences are essential to the well-being of the cell. Yet, given the opportunity to do so, diffusion would quickly eliminate these differences in solute concentration. Thus the cell must counteract the effects of diffusion.

The cell maintains appropriate concentrations of some substances by **active transport.** In this process the cell moves materials from a region of low concentration to a region of higher concentration. Working "uphill" against a concentration gradient requires energy. The cell uses the energy of ATP to drive active transport. Expenditure of energy in active transport is an example of how cells must work just to remain alive.

Substances are actively transported through the membrane by protein molecules that act as pumps. These cellular pumps are integral proteins that extend through the plasma membrane. The proteins form channels that extend through the membrane (Fig. 3-18). The ion or molecule being transported combines with the protein within the channel. A conformational change takes place in the protein that results in the ion being squeezed through the pore and then released.

One of the best-studied active transport mechanisms is the **sodium-potasium pump,** which pumps sodium ions out of the cell and at the same time pumps potassium ions into the cell (Fig. 3-19). There are an estimated 200 to 300 sodium pumps per cell. Each time three sodium ions are pumped out, two potassium ions are pumped into the cell. Unlike facilitated diffusion, active transport pumps a substance in only one direction—against its tendency to diffuse. Thus sodium is always pumped out of the cell, and potassium is always transported into the cell.

There are other types of active transport mechanisms. For example, in some cells sugar molecules are phosphorylated (i.e., phosphorus is added to them) as they pass through the cell membrane. After the phosphorus is added, the sugar cannot diffuse out through the plasma membrane. In this form of active transport, energy is needed to attach phosphate to the sugar.

Exocytosis and endocytosis are used to transport large materials into or out of the cell

Large materials such as particles of food, or even whole cells, must sometimes be moved into or out of a cell. This type of transport is a form of

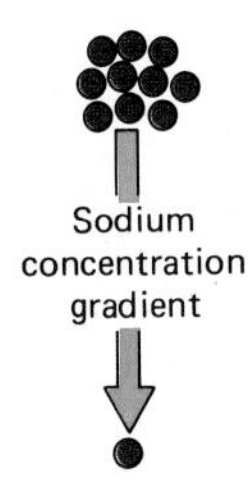

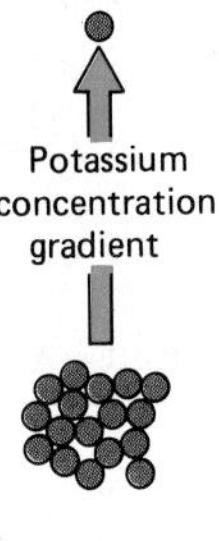

FIGURE 3-19

The sodium-potassium pump is an active transport system powered by ATP. Each molecule of ATP used results in the transport of three sodium ions out of the cell and two potassium ions into the cell.

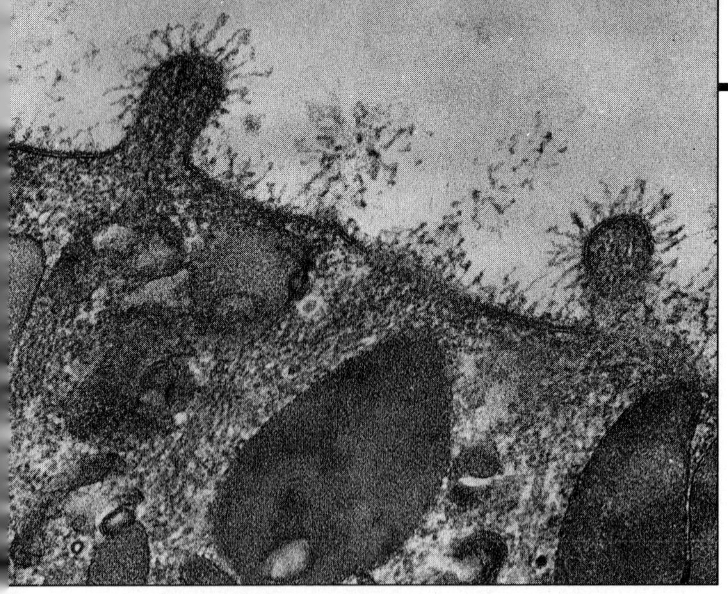

FIGURE 3-20

Exocytosis. A high-magnification electron micrograph of the upper surface of a secreting cell (approximately ×125,000). Secretion granules can be seen in the cytoplasm approaching the plasma membrane. The filaments projecting diffusely from the cell surface are of unknown significance but may be proteins. (J. F. Gennaro, Photo Researchers, Inc.)

cellular work and requires that the cell expend energy. In **exocytosis** (*ex*-oh-sigh-**tow**-sis), a cell ejects waste products or secretions (Fig. 3-20). The substance to be ejected is enclosed in a vesicle. The membrane of the vesicle fuses with the plasma membrane, and the contents of the vesicle are released to the outside. In this process, the membrane of the secretory vesicle is incorporated into the plasma membrane.

Large substances are taken into the cell by **endocytosis** (*en*-doe-sigh-**tow**-sis). In this process, materials outside the cell are enclosed within special vesicles made from folds of the plasma membrane. Three types of endocytosis are phagocytosis, pinocytosis, and receptor-mediated endocytosis.

In **phagocytosis** (*fag*-oh-sigh-**tow**-sis), which literally means "cell eating," the cell ingests large

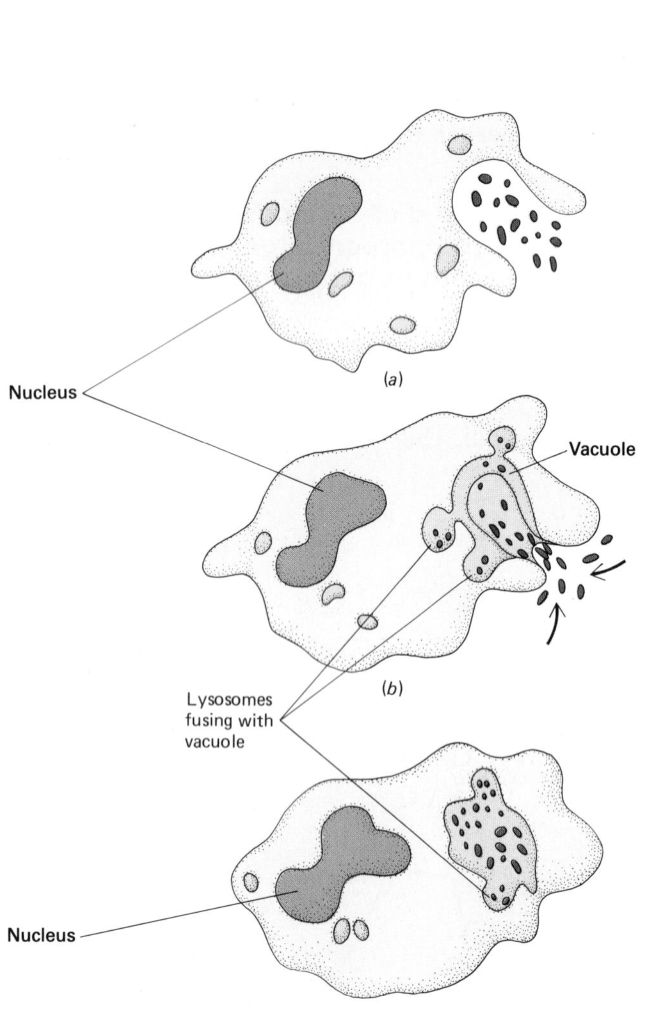

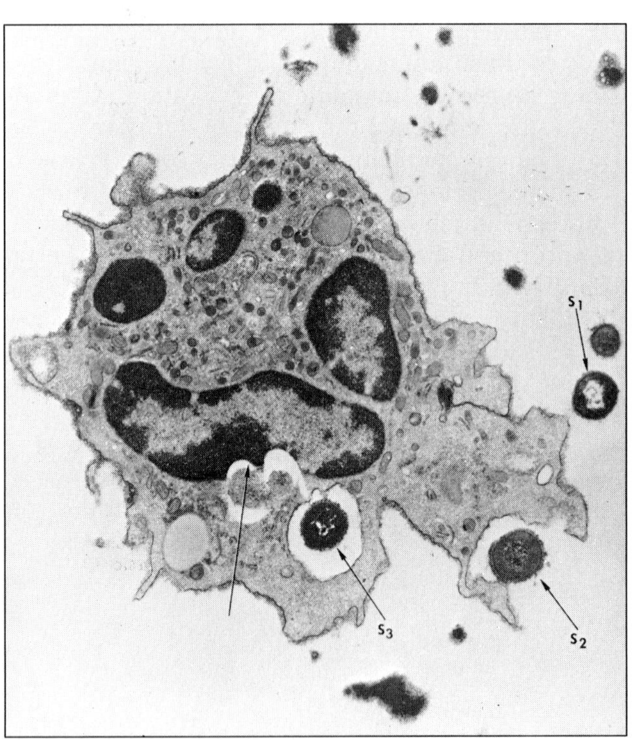

FIGURE 3-21

Phagocytosis. *(a)* In phagocytosis the cell ingests large solid particles, such as bacteria. Folds of the plasma membrane surround the particle to be ingested, forming a small vacuole around it. *(b)* This vacuole then pinches off inside the cell. *(c)* Lysosomes may fuse with the vacuole and pour their potent digestive enzymes onto the digested material. *(d)* A white blood cell in the presence of *S. pyogenes* (approximately ×23,000). One bacterium (S_1) is free, one bacterium (S_2) is being phagocytized, and a third bacterium (S_3) has been phagocytized and is seen within a vacuole (phagosome). Note that near the vacuole (see arrow) the white blood cell's own nucleus has been partly digested. (J. G Hadley, Battelle/BPS.)

solid particles, such as bacteria or cell debris. A small part of the plasma membrane encircles the particle to be ingested, forming a small bag of membrane like a tiny plastic sandwich bag around it (Fig. 3-21). This tiny vesicle then pinches off from the plasma membrane and may float freely through the cytoplasm. Certain white blood cells ingest invading bacteria or debris in this way. As mentioned earlier, lysosomes then fuse with such vesicles and pour their powerful enzymes onto the foreign material to digest it.

Cells not only eat, they also drink. Cell drinking is called **pinocytosis** (Fig. 3-22). Actually, the result appears to be intake of dissolved materials including protein and other macromolecules. In this process, tiny droplets of fluid adhere to the plasma membrane. The membrane then folds inward, forming a pinocytotic vesicle that surrounds the fluid. The vesicle then pinches off from the plasma membrane. The contents of pinocytotic vesicles are slowly transferred into the cytoplasm, and the vesicles themselves seem to become smaller and smaller until they disappear.

In **receptor-mediated endocytosis** specific proteins or particles combine with receptor proteins embedded in the plasma membrane. The molecule bound with the receptor is referred to as a **ligand.** The receptor-ligand complex then migrates into a coated pit. The coated pit is a region on the cytoplasmic surface of the membrane coated with whisker-like structures. During endocytosis coated pits are converted to coated vesicles (Fig. 3-23). The coating on a vesicle consists of proteins, which form a basket-like structure around it. Within seconds after the vesicles are released into the cytoplasm the coating is removed from them. The vesicles then fuse with other similar vesicles, forming endosomes. In these larger vesicles, the material being transported is free inside and no longer attached to the membrane receptors. The receptor proteins are separated from the ingested particles, and the proteins are returned to the plasma membrane for reuse. The vesicle containing the ingested particles may then fuse with lysosomes which digest the particles. Some component may then be released into the cytoplasm for use by the cell.

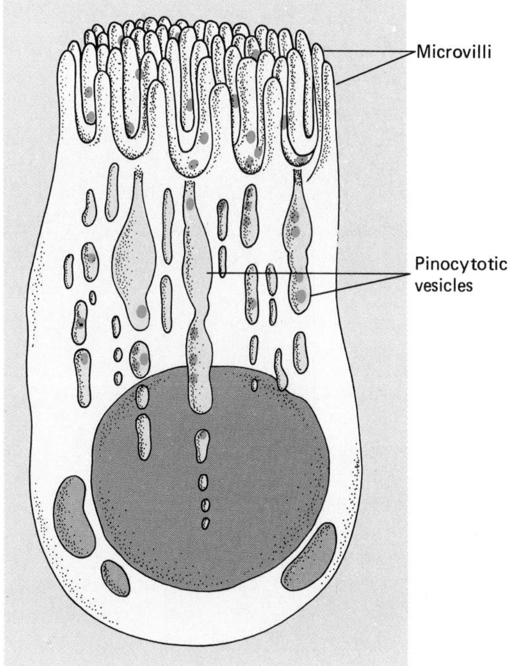

FIGURE 3-22

In pinocytosis tiny droplets of fluid are trapped by folds of the plasma membrane, which then pinch off into the cytoplasm as little vesicles of fluid. The content of these vesicles is slowly transferred to the cytoplasm across their membrane linings.

The cell cycle extends from one division to the next

In cells that are capable of dividing, the **cell cycle** is the period from the beginning of one cell division to the beginning of the next division. The length of the cell cycle varies in different cell types. Certain types of cells in the body divide almost continuously and so have very short life cycles. Several million blood cells are produced in the body every second from undifferentiated cells in the bone marrow. Certain cells in the skin and in the intestinal lining also divide continuously, replacing cells that wear off. The life cycle of these actively dividing cells is only a few hours.

Other cells never divide at all after birth. The life cycle of the highly specialized muscle and nerve cells may last a lifetime. These cells are ordinarily unable to replace themselves. As they wear out by aging or are destroyed by disease, we are left with fewer and fewer.

Cell division involves two main processes, *mitosis,* or nuclear division, and *cytokinesis,* or division of the cytoplasm. By convention, the cell cycle is divided into five major phases—interphase and the four phases of mitosis (Fig. 3-24). These phases are characterized by changes in the nuclear material of the cell. The phases are not distinct from one another but blend almost imperceptibly, one into the next.

Interphase occurs between cell divisions

The cell spends most of its life in **interphase** (meaning between phases), the period between mitoses. During interphase the cell actively synthesizes new materials and grows. Before mitosis actually begins, the chromatin and centrioles must be duplicated.

Interphase may be divided into three subphases (Fig. 3-24). The first gap phase (G_1) follows cell division. This is a period of rapid growth, and RNA, protein, and other materials are synthesized at this time. During the next subphase, the synthesis phase (S), raw materials in the cell are used to manufacture an exact duplicate of the cell's DNA. Components needed to produce chromosomes are synthesized, and the centrioles are duplicated. During the second gap phase (G_2), the RNA and protein needed to produce structures required for mitosis are synthesized.

Mitosis is nuclear division

Before the cytoplasm of a cell divides to form two cells, the cell undergoes nuclear division, or **mitosis** (my-**tow**-sis). In mitosis the chromosomes are precisely duplicated, and a complete set is distributed to each end of the parent cell. When the cytoplasm of the parent cell divides, forming two cells, each new cell contains the identical number

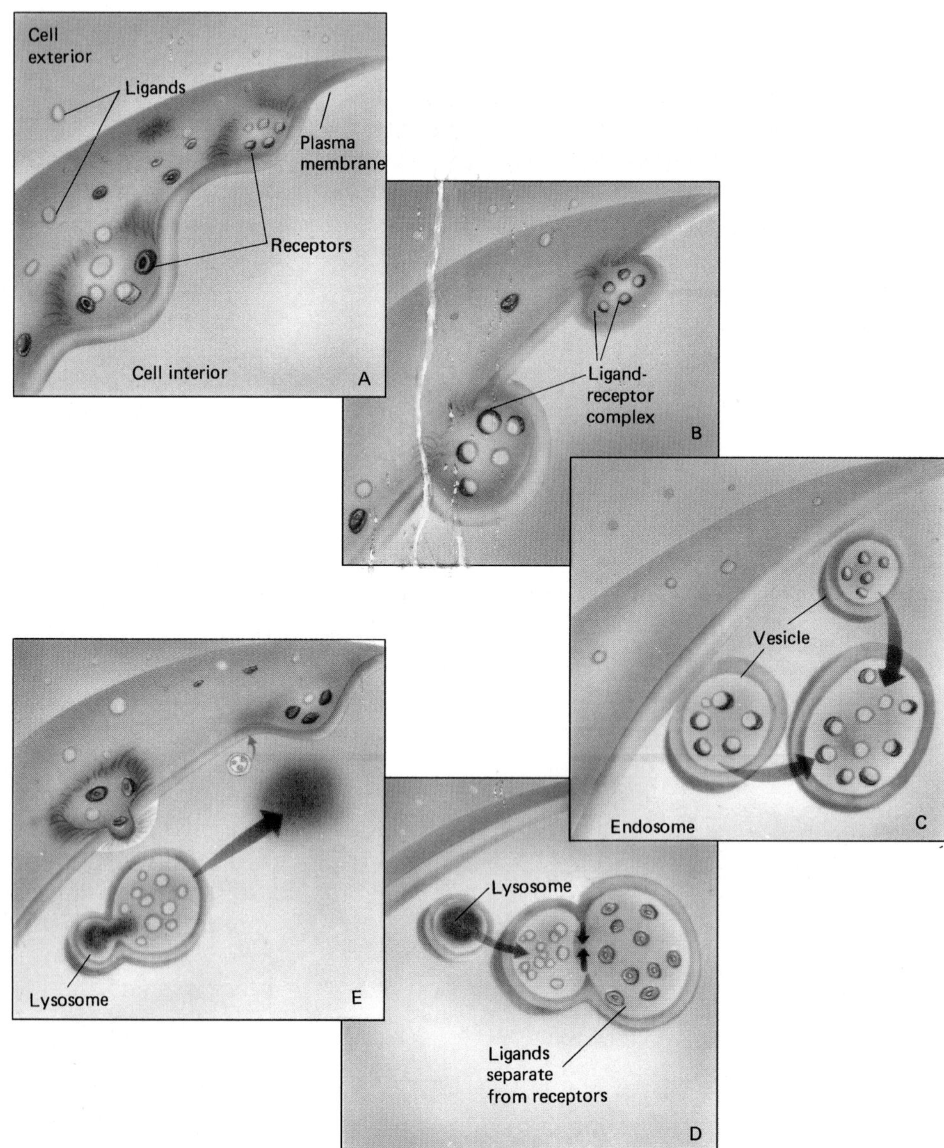

FIGURE 3-23

Receptor-mediated endocytosis. *(a)* Ligands (proteins or other large molecules) combine with specific receptors on the plasma membrane. *(b)* After the ligand-receptor complex is formed, the membrane invaginates and forms a vesicle around the ligands. *(c)* Vesicles move into the cytoplasm and combine with other vesicles, forming endosomes. *(d)* The ligands separate from the receptors. *(e)* The receptors are returned to the plasma membrane and recycled. Lysosomes fuse with the vesicle containing the ingested ligands and digest the ligands. Components may be released into the cytoplasm.

and types of chromosomes present in the parent cell (Fig. 3-25).

Let us consider the origin of the organism. When a fertilized egg divides, forming two cells, each of the new cells receives a complete copy of all its genetic information. After hundreds of divisions every cell in the body (with the exception of the sex cells) contains a complete set of the original chromosomes contributed by the sperm and egg. Sex cells (sperm and eggs) undergo a special process called **meiosis,** which halves their number of chromosomes. (This will be discussed in Chapter 29.)

PROPHASE IS THE FIRST PHASE OF MITOSIS

During **prophase,** the first stage of mitosis, the chromatin coils tightly, forming structures that are visible as dark X-shaped bodies under the light microscope. These are the **chromosomes.** At this time each chromosome consists of a pair of identical **sister chromatids.** Each chromatid contains a constricted region called the **centromere.** Sister chromatids are tightly associated in the vicinity of their centromeres. During interphase the amount of chromatin that must condense to make a chromosome may be an entire centimeter in length. It must contract hundreds of times to fit into the compact, microscopically visible mitotic chromosome.

Other dramatic events take place during prophase. The nucleolus becomes disorganized and the nuclear envelope dissolves. Each pair of centrioles begins to migrate toward an opposite end, or pole, of the cell. Microtubules form and some appear to radiate out from the centrioles. Cell fibers form and organize into the **mitotic spindle,** a structure consisting mainly of microtubules. Toward the end of prophase, the centromere of each chromatid becomes attached to some of the spindle microtubules (Figure 3-25). The chromatids then become aligned along the equator of the cell.

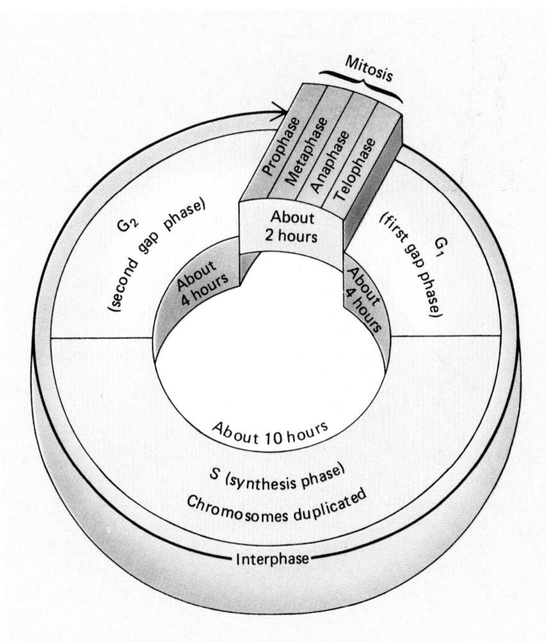

FIGURE 3-24

Phases in the life cycle of a cell. Time relations are illustrative only; actual times vary with the cell type.

DURING METAPHASE THE CHROMOSOMES ARE LINED UP ALONG THE EQUATOR

Metaphase is the phase of mitosis during which the chromosomes are aligned along the equator of the cell. Centromeres of sister chromatids are attached by spindle microtubules to opposite poles of the cell.

Each chromatid is now completely condensed and appears quite thick and discrete. In fact, chromosomes can be seen more clearly in metaphase than at any other stage. They are sometimes photographed in this stage and studied clinically to determine whether chromosome abnormalities exist.

CHROMATIDS SEPARATE DURING ANAPHASE

During **anaphase** the chromatids of each chromosome separate and start to move away from one another. Once separated, each chromatid is considered an individual chromosome. The microtubules of the spindle begin to pull one set of chromosomes to one pole of the spindle and the other set to the opposite pole.

TELOPHASE IS THE FINAL PHASE OF MITOSIS

With the arrival of a complete set of chromosomes at each pole of the cell, **telophase** begins. The chromatin of each chromosome now begins to uncoil and disperse. The spindle disappears, the nucleolus reorganizes, and a nuclear envelope

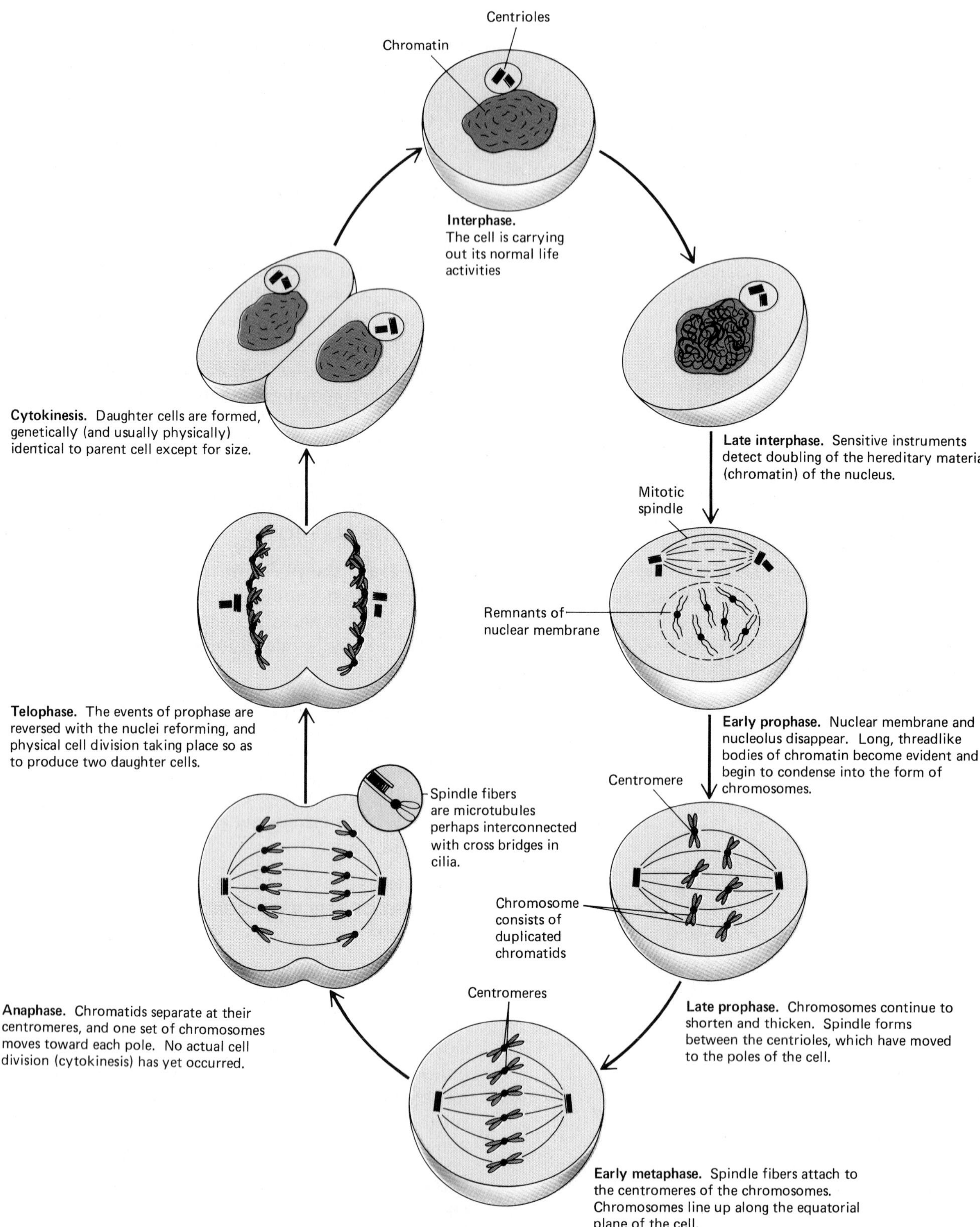

FIGURE 3-25

The cell cycle. Individual phases in the cycle are explained in labels within the figure. The drawings are of a generalized cell with six chromosomes (diploid number).

forms around each set of chromosomes. Cytokinesis usually takes place during this stage.

Cytokinesis is the division of the cytoplasm to form two cells

Cytokinesis (*sigh*-tow-kye-**nee**-sis) generally takes place during telophase. Microfilaments containing the contractile protein actin bring about a constriction of the cell around its equator. This **cleavage furrow** constricts the cell more and more until it has completely divided the cell in two. Cell division is complete by the end of telophase. Each new cell now enters the G_1 period of interphase, thus beginning a new cell cycle.

Mitosis ensures that each cell will be genetically identical

Recall that all the genetic information for the production of proteins is coded within the DNA and contained within the chromosomes. Mitosis ensures that the genetic information will be precisely duplicated and distributed to each new cell. No genetic information is lost and no new information is added. Each of the two new cells has the potential to function exactly like the parent cell.

Cells divide to maintain efficient size

Why do cells divide? Every cell in your body can be traced back to the fertilized egg that was produced by the union of your parents' egg and sperm cells. You may have wondered why we are composed of trillions of cells. Why trillions rather than thousands or hundreds, or just one or two? What determines the size of a cell and what prevents cells from growing indefinitely?

Probably the main reason that cells do not get very big is that it would be inefficient for them to do so. As a cell increases in size, its volume increases at a greater rate than its surface area (Fig. 3-26). (The surface of a sphere increases in proportion to the square of its radius, while the volume increases as the cube of its radius.) Thus when a cell reaches a critical size its plasma membrane (that is, its surface) can no longer provide sufficient oxygen and nutrients for all regions within the cell. Wastes produced within the cell must move longer distances before they can exit through the plasma membrane.

Another factor that limits cell size is the amount of cytoplasm that a nucleus can control. Very large cells generally have more than one nucleus. An organism with many small cells rather than one large one has other advantages. Cells can specialize to perform different functions, so that labor is divided among different groups of cells. By assigning different tasks to each group of cells, an organism can be highly proficient at performing a wide variety of activities.

The factors just identified limit the maximum size of a unicellular organism such as an amoeba or bacterium. If larger organisms are to exist, it is necessary for them to be multicellular. In humans, as in all organisms, when a cell reaches a size that approaches the limits of efficiency, the cell divides to form two cells. Although each new cell is half the size of the parent cell, the relative surface area of both the plasma membrane and the nuclear membrane is greatly increased in proportion to the cell volume.

Many factors affect the cell cycle

Under optimal conditions of nutrition, temperature, and pH, the length of the cell cycle appears to be constant for each type of cell. Under less favorable conditions, the cell cycle may be slowed. Studies suggest that the length of the cell cycle for each type of cell is the time required for the cell to carry out some precise program that has been built into it. The program has two aspects: one involves replication of the genetic ma-

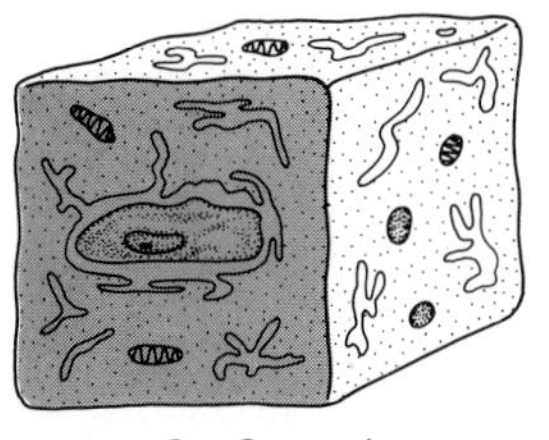

One 2-cm cube

(*a*)

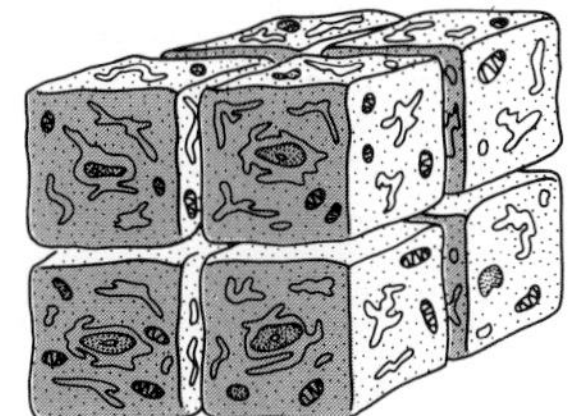

Eight 1-cm cubes

(*b*)

FIGURE 3-26

Eight small cells have a much greater surface (plasma membrane) area in relation to their total volume than one large cell. This concept might be easier to grasp if you imagine that each of these cells is a potato. The amount of mashed potatoes you could prepare from eight small potatoes would be the same as from one large one, but which would you rather peel?

terial (the chromosomes) and the other involves growth of the cell by the synthesis of various components.

Growth factors are small proteins that control the cell cycle. Each type of growth factor stimulates a specific type of cell. For example, a nerve growth factor stimulates nerve cells to produce substances that control the onset of the S phase. Some growth factors circulate in the blood, whereas others diffuse from adjacent cells.

Chalones (**kal**-owns) are substances that inhibit mitosis by countering the action of growth factors. Like growth factors, chalones are very specific, generally affecting only one type of tissue. For example, skin cells produce chalone that inhibits mitosis in neighboring skin cells. When skin cells are damaged, they are thought to synthesize less chalone. This decrease releases cells in the region of the wound from the inhibition. Cells in the wounded area divide until they have produced enough cells to heal the wound. Then, the new cells produce sufficient chalone to inhibit further mitoses.

Antibiotics such as streptomycin and the tetracyclines prevent cell division indirectly by inhibiting protein syntheis in bacterial cells; this prolongs the G_1 phase of the cell cycle. Some drugs used in chemotherapy, a form of cancer treatment, block enzymes involved in DNA synthesis and cell division. Because cancer cells divide much more rapidly than most normal body cells, they are most affected by these drugs. Unfortunately, any rapidly dividing cell in the body such as bone marrow cells that give rise to blood cells and cells lining the intestine are also affected by drugs used in chemotherapy.

Summary

I. The cell is considered the basic unit of life because it is the smallest self-sufficient unit in the body; the body consists of cells and their products.
   A. Most cells are microscopic, but their size and shape vary according to their function.
   B. The microscope has been one of the biologist's most important tools for studying the internal structure of the cell.

II. All cells are bounded by a plasma membrane and most have a nucleus and other types of organelles dispersed within their cytoplasm.
   A. The plasma membrane protects the cell and regulates the passage of materials into and out of the cell.
   B. The endoplasmic reticulum (ER) is a system of internal membranes that plays a role in the transport and storage of materials within the cell.
      1. The smooth ER lacks ribosomes; it produces steroids in certain types of cells.
      2. The rough ER is studded along its outer walls with ribosomes, tiny organelles that manufacture proteins.
   C. The Golgi complex is a membranous organelle that concentrates some kinds of secretions, adds carbohydrate components to some proteins, and packages secretions for export from the cell. The Golgi complex also produces lysosomes.
   D. Lysosomes function in intracellular digestion and form the self-destruct system of the cell.
   E. Peroxisomes are associated with hydrogen peroxide metabolism.
   F. Mitochondria, the power plants of the cell, are the sites of most of the reactions of cellular respiration, which yields energy for the cell.
   G. Hollow microtubules, rodlike microfilaments, and intermediate filaments make up the cytoskeleton.
   H. Centrioles, cilia, and flagella are composed of microtubules.
      1. Centrioles play a role in mitosis.
      2. Cilia function in the movement of materials located outside the cell, for example, in the movement of a stream of mucus along the respiratory passages.
      3. Flagella are important in the movement of sperm cells.
   I. The nucleus is the control center of the cell.
      1. DNA, which makes up the genes, is found within the chromatin material in the nucleoplasm.
      2. The nucleolus, an organelle located within the nucleus, functions in the assembly of ribosomes.

III. Materials move through the plasma membrane passively by physical processes such as diffusion, osmosis, and filtration, or they can be actively transported by physiological processes such as active transport, phagocytosis, and pinocytosis. Passive processes do not require the expenditure of energy on the part of the cell; active processes do.
   A. Diffusion is the movement of molecules or ions from one region to another due to their random molecular motion. Due to probability, the net movement of molecules in diffusion is from a region of greater concentration to a region of lower concentration.
      1. In dialysis, small molecules can be separated from larger ones in a liquid by diffusion. The small molecules can pass through membrane pores that are too small to permit passage of larger molecules.
      2. In facilitated diffusion, certain types of molecules pass through the membrane by temporarily combining with certain proteins within the membrane. Movement is always from the region of greater concentration to the region of lower concentration.
   B. Osmosis is a special kind of diffusion in which molecules of water diffuse through a selectively permeable membrane, resulting in a net movement from a region where the water molecules are more concentrated to where they are less concentrated.
   C. In filtration, substances are forced through a membrane by hydrostatic pressure.
   D. In active transport, cells expend energy to transport materials across membranes contrary to their tendencies to diffuse.
   E. In phagocytosis, the cell ingests large solid particles by enclosing them in a vesicle pinched off from the plasma membrane.
   F. In pinocytosis, tiny droplets of fluid containing solute are trapped by folds in the plasma membrane and enclosed in vesicles.

IV. The cell cycle extends from one cell division to the next. A cell reproduces itself by undergoing mitosis and then dividing to form two new cells.
   A. The stages in the life cycle of a cell include the following:
      1. Interphase—chromatin is duplicated in preparation for mitosis. During this stage the cell is not undergoing mitosis.
      2. Prophase—first stage of mitosis; chromatids become short and thick; nuclear membrane and nucleolus become disorganized; centrioles begin to move apart; spindle begins to form.

3. Metaphase—chromosomes are lined up along the equator of the cell; spindle has formed.
4. Anaphase—identical chromatids separate at their centromeres and move to opposite poles of the cell.
5. Telophase—complete set of chromosomes is now at each pole of the cell; cytokinesis generally occurs; nuclear membrane and nucleolus reorganize; chromosomes elongate; spindle becomes disorganized so that it is no longer visible.

B. The plasma membrane-to-cell volume ratio is important in limiting cell size.

Post-test

Matching

Select the most appropriate answer from Column B for each question in Column A. The same answer may be used as many times as appropriate or not at all.

	Column A	Column B
____	1. Regulates passage of materials into cell	a. ribosomes
____	2. Network of internal membranes that extends throughout cytoplasm	b. endoplasmic reticulum (ER)
____	3. Site of cellular respiration	c. mitochondria
____	4. Membranous sacs containing digestive enzymes	d. microtubules
____	5. Chromosomes located here	e. nucleus
____	6. Components of cilia	f. lysosomes
____	7. Packages proteins	g. Golgi complex
____	8. Granules that manufacture protein	h. flagellum
		i. plasma membrane

9. Folds of the inner membrane of a mitochondrion are called ______________.
10. If a cell is placed in a hypertonic solution the net passage of water molecules will be from the ______________ to the ______________.
11. A cell engulfs a bacterium; this is an example of ______________.
12. Active transport requires the expenditure of ______________ by the cell.
13. In pinocytosis the plasma membrane takes in ______________.
14. The chromosomes line up on the equator of the cell during the stage of mitosis called ______________.
15. Actual division of the cytoplasm to form two cells is called ______________.
16. The chromatin material duplicates itself during ______________.
17. Lysosomes are produced by the ______________ ______________.
18. The plasma membrane consists of a fluid ______________ bilayer in which are embedded molecules of ______________.
19. Ribosomes are distributed over the outer surfaces of the ______________ ______________.
20. Tiny hairlike structures that project from the surfaces of some cells and function in movement of materials outside the cell are called ______________.
21. Label the diagram of the cell.

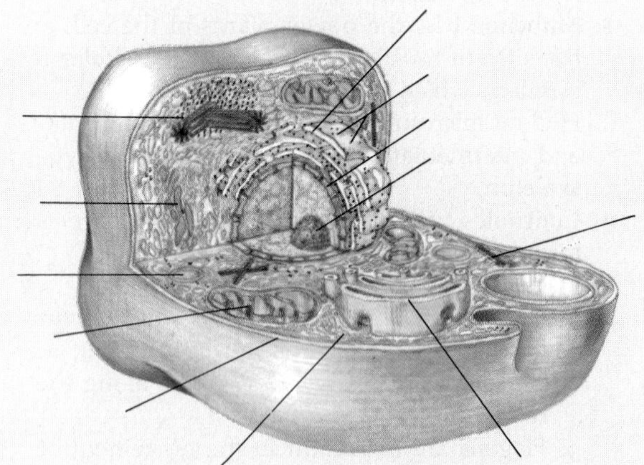

Review questions

1. What are the functions of the plasma membrane? Describe its structure.
2. What is the function of the smooth endoplasmic reticulum? the rough ER?
3. Trace the fate of a protein secretion from its synthesis to its expulsion from the cell.
4. Draw a diagram of a cell and label at least eight organelles. Give the function of each organelle you labeled.
5. Explain why the nucleus is considered the control center of the cell.
6. Describe how each of the following mechanisms works and give an example of each: (a) diffusion, (b) dialysis, (c) facilitated diffusion, (d) osmosis, (e) filtration, (f) active transport, (g) exocytosis, (h) phagocytosis, (i) pinocytosis, (j) receptor-mediated endocytosis.
7. If red blood cells are accidentally placed in a hypotonic solution, what happens to them? What would happen if red blood cells were placed in a hypertonic solution? An isotonic solution?
8. What is the significance of mitosis? What is cytokinesis?
9. Trace the stages in the life cycle of a cell and briefly explain what happens during each stage.

Post-test answers

1. i 2. b 3. c 4. f 5. e 6. d 7. g 8. a 9. cristae 10. cell; solution 11. phagocytosis 12. energy 13. droplets of fluid containing solute 14. metaphase 15. cytokinesis 16. interphase (synthesis phase of interphase) 17. Golgi complex 18. lipid; protein 19. rough endoplasmic reticulum 20. cilia 21. See Figure 3-2 or the Window on the Animal Cell.

TISSUES: THE FABRIC OF THE BODY

CHAPTER OUTLINE

- I. **Functions of epithelial tissue**
  - A. Covering and lining epithelium
    - 1. Shapes of epithelial cells
    - 2. Arrangements of epithelial cells
    - 3. Types of covering and lining epithelium
      - a. Simple squamous epithelium
      - b. Simple cuboidal epithelium
      - c. Simple columnar epithelium
      - d. Stratified squamous epithelium
      - e. Pseudostratified columnar epithelium
      - f. Transitional epithelium
  - B. Glandular epithelium
- II. **Connective tissue**
  - A. Specialized cells
  - B. Fibers
  - C. Connective tissue proper
    - 1. Loose connective tissue
    - 2. Dense connective tissue
    - 3. Elastic connective tissue
    - 4. Reticular connective tissue
  - D. Adipose tissue
  - E. Cartilage
  - F. Bone
  - G. Blood, lymph, and tissues that produce blood cells
- III. **Muscle tissue**
  - A. Skeletal muscle
  - B. Cardiac muscle
  - C. Smooth muscle
- IV. **Nervous tissue**
- V. **Membranes**
  - A. Mucous membranes
  - B. Serous membranes
- VI. **Neoplasms: Abnormal growths of tissue**
  - A. Certain mutations lead to cancer
  - B. Cancer cells are invasive
  - C. Early diagnosis increases survival

LEARNING OBJECTIVES

After you have studied this chapter you should be able to:

1 Define the term tissue and describe the four principal types of tissue in the body.

2 Relate the functions of epithelial tissue to its structure.

3 Contrast the three main shapes of epithelial cells and tell how epithelial cells may be arranged in a tissue.

4 Describe the main types of covering epithelium and locate each in the body.

5 Compare the various types of exocrine glands.

6 List the main types of connective tissue and describe their functions.

7 Compare the types of fibers found in connective tissues and describe the main types of connective tissue cells.

8 Compare loose and dense connective tissue proper.

9 Describe the maturation of a fat cell and the appearance of fat tissue under a microscope.

10 Compare the structure of cartilage and bone.

11 Compare the three types of muscle tissue and their functions.

12 Summarize the function of nervous tissue and distinguish between neurons and glial cells.

13 Distinguish between benign and malignant neoplasms and between cancer tissue and normal tissue.

14 Describe the apparent causes and cellular basis of cancer.

Conjunctive tissue collagen fibers, retinal layer (×500). (CNRI/Phototake.)

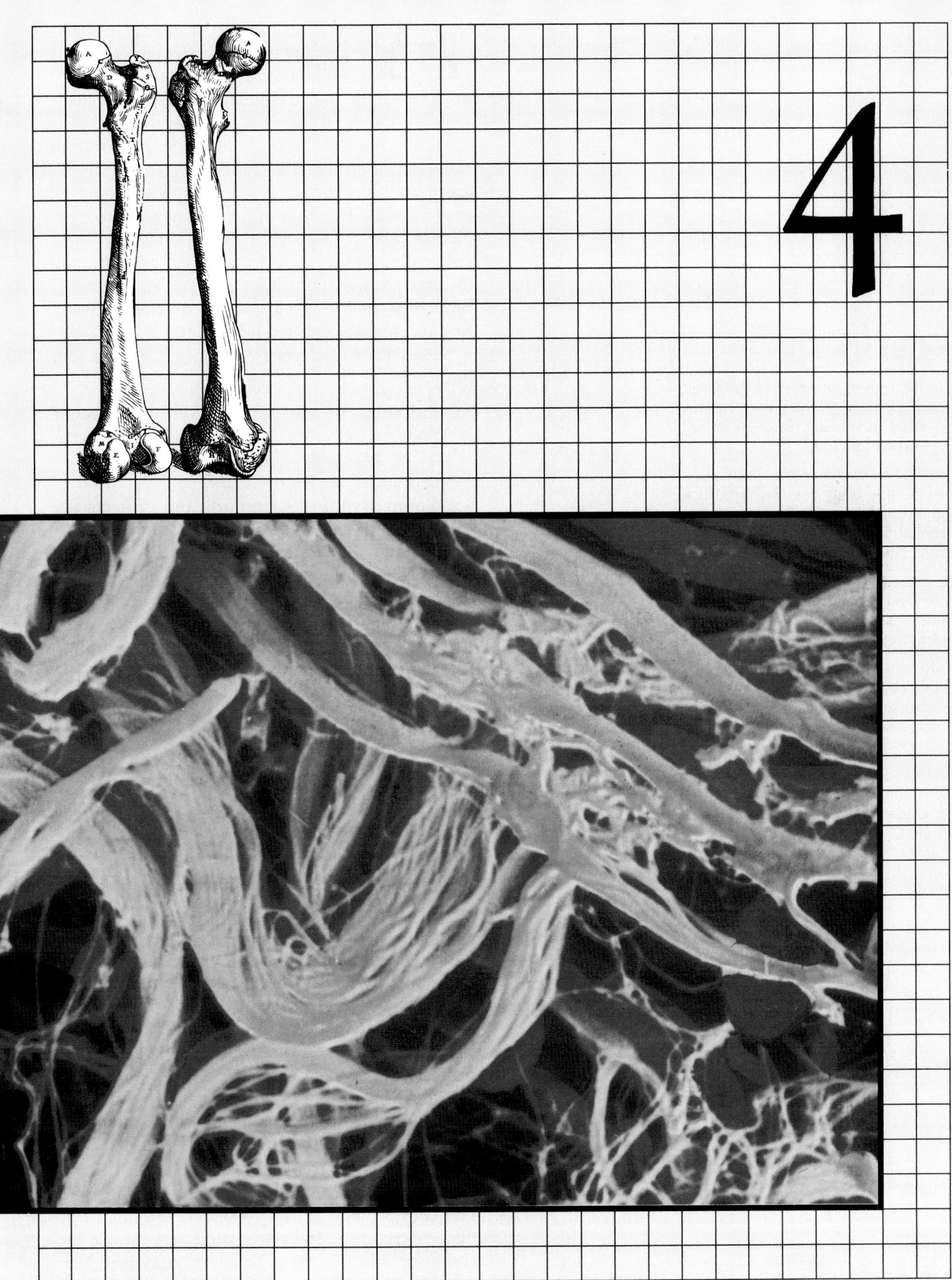
4

KEY CONCEPTS

A tissue is a group of closely associated cells that work together to perform a specific function or group of functions.

Epithelial tissues cover body surfaces, line body cavities, and form glands; among the functions of epithelial tissue are protection, absorption, and secretion.

Connective tissue holds parts of the body together, supports the body, and protects underlying structures.

Muscle tissue is composed of cells specialized to contract; three types of muscle tissue are skeletal, cardiac, and smooth muscle.

Nervous tissue is specialized to receive stimuli, transmit information, and control the actions of muscle and glands.

A **tissue** is a group of closely associated cells that work together to carry out a specific function or group of functions. Each type of tissue is composed of cells with a characteristic size, shape, and arrangement. The cells of a tissue produce the important nonliving materials that lie between the cells and are part of the tissue. If the body were composed only of cells, it would appear somewhat like a blob of jelly. The nonliving components of the tissue, called intercellular substances, give the body its strength and help it to maintain its shape. The branch of anatomy that focuses on the study of tissues is **histology** (his-**tol**-o-gee).

Four principal types of tissues make up the body.

1. **Epithelial tissue** (*ep*-ih-**theel**-ee-al) protects the body by covering all of its free surfaces and lining its cavities. Some epithelial tissue is specialized to form glands.
2. **Connective tissue** supports and protects the organs of the body; it connects and holds parts of the body together.
3. **Muscle tissue** is specialized for moving the body and its parts.
4. **Nervous tissue** receives and transmits messages so that the various parts of the body can communicate with one another.

Epithelial tissue covers body surfaces, lines body cavities, and forms glands

Epithelial tissue, also called **epithelium** (*ep*-ih-**theel**-ee-um), serves several important functions.

1. **Protection.** The main job of epithelial tissue is protection. Epithelial tissue covers the body and lines all the body cavities, thus providing a protective shield for the underlying tissues. For example, the outer layer of the skin is composed of epithelial tissue that protects the body from mechanical injury, from excessive water loss, and from invading microorganisms.

2. **Absorption.** In some parts of the body, epithelium absorbs, or takes in, certain materials. Epithelium lining the digestive tract is responsible for absorbing molecules of digested food.

3. **Secretion.** In some epithelial tissues, certain cells are specialized to secrete specific products. Secretion is the production and release of some substance such as sweat or enzymes. Mu-

cous cells in the lining of the intestine secrete mucus, a slippery, protective substance. When large amounts of specialized secretions are needed, epithelium is arranged into special structures called glands.

4. **Excretion.** Epithelial cells lining the kidney tubules *excrete* certain materials. (Excretion is the process of ridding the body of metabolic waste products.)

5. **Surface transport.** In the respiratory passageways, epithelium protects underlying tissues, secretes fluid and mucus that keep the lining moist, and transports mucus containing trapped particles. Such epithelial cells are equipped with cilia that beat in a coordinated manner so that a thin sheet of mucus containing trapped dirt particles is continuously moved away from the lungs.

6. **Sensory functions.** The taste buds in the mouth and olfactory (smelling) structures in the nose consist of epithelium specialized to receive sensory information.

Epithelial tissue consists of cells that fit tightly together. Very little intercellular substance is present. Adjacent cells are held together by structures called *cell junctions.* One type of junction is the **desmosome** (**des**-muh-sohm), a thickened region of the plasma membranes of two adjacent cells. *Spot desmosomes* are disc-shaped points of contact between two cells where the cells seem to be riveted together. The desmosome consists of proteins and thin filaments that bind the cells together. A *belt desmosome* forms a band of cell-to-cell adhesion that extends around each cell and attaches it to adjacent cells.

One surface of epithelial tissue is free and in contact with either fluid or air, whereas the other surface is supported by underlying connective tissue. The epithelial tissue is attached to the connective tissue beneath it by a thin extracellular layer, the **basement membrane.** There are generally two components of the basement membrane—a basal lamina and a reticular lamina. The **basal lamina** consists of a collagen and glycoprotein material secreted by the epithelial cells. The **reticular lamina** consists of reticular fibers (tiny connective tissue fibers to be discussed in a later section) and glycoproteins secreted by the underlying connective tissue.

Nerve cells may occasionally be found between the cells of epithelial tissue, but blood vessels are not present. Epithelial tissue is avascular (without blood vessels). Epithelial cells are dependent upon the connective tissue beneath for their blood supply. Nutrients and oxygen diffuse from the blood vessels within the connective tissue to nourish the epithelial cells. The epithelial covering of the skin does not usually permit the blood to show through. However, when one blushes or becomes sunburned, the blood vessels within the connective tissue expand, and the skin then appears pink.

Epithelial tissue may be classified as (1) covering and lining epithelium and (2) glandular epithelium.

Epithelium is specialized to cover and line body surfaces

Epithelial tissue that covers body surfaces consists of tight-fitting cells that are firmly attached to one another, forming sheets of cells, or **membranes.** The free surface of the outer cells of an epithelial membrane may have specialized structures such as cilia or microvilli (microscopic, finger-like projections of the plasma membrane).

Many epithelial membranes are subjected to continuous wear and tear. As outer cells are sloughed off, they must be replaced by new ones from below. Some epithelial tissues have a rapid rate of mitosis so that new cells are continuously produced to take the place of those lost (Fig. 4-1). Epithelial tissue may be classified according to the shape of its cells or by the arrangement of the cells into layers.

EPITHELIAL CELLS HAVE THREE MAIN SHAPES

We can identify three main shapes of epithelial cells. As you study the following sections, notice the relationship between the structure and organization of each type of epithelial tissue and its function.

1. **Squamous** (**skway**-mus) **cells** are thin and flattened.

2. **Cuboidal cells** appear as small cubes when the tissue is viewed in cross section. Actually, each cell has a complex shape, usually that of an eight-sided polyhedron.

3. **Columnar cells** look like tiny columns or cylinders when viewed from the side. The nucleus may be seen toward the base of each cell. In cross section, or looking down at their top surface, these cells appear hexagonal in shape.

EPITHELIUM MAY BE SIMPLE, STRATIFIED, OR PSEUDOSTRATIFIED

Epithelial tissue may be **simple,** that is, composed of one layer of cells, or **stratified,** in which cells are arranged in two or more layers. Simple epithelium is usually present in areas where materials must diffuse through the tissue or in which substances are secreted, excreted, or absorbed. Stratified epithelial tissue is located in regions where protection is a primary function.

A third arrangement is **pseudostratified epithelium,** so called because its cells falsely appear to be layered. Close inspection shows that there is actually only one layer of cells. All these cells

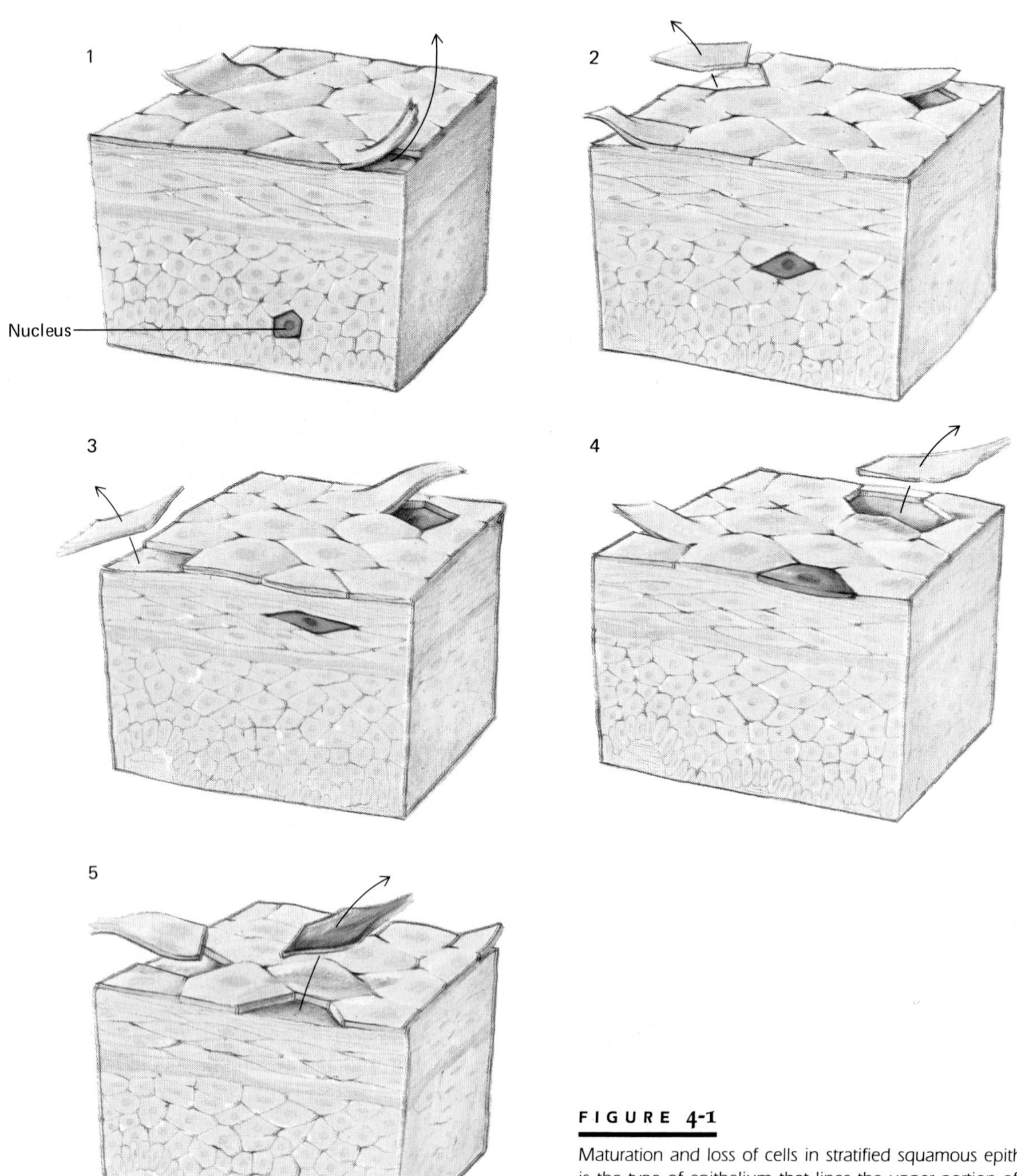

FIGURE 4-1

Maturation and loss of cells in stratified squamous epithelium. This is the type of epithelium that lines the upper portion of the digestive tract. Follow the colored cell from its origin in (1) to its loss in (5). As the dead outer cells are continuously worn away, they must be replaced by younger cells beneath.

rest on a basement membrane, but not every cell is tall enough to reach the free surface of the tissue. This may give the false impression that there are two or more cell layers. Some of the respiratory passageways are lined with pseudostratified epithelium equipped with cilia. The cilia help keep foreign matter out of the lungs.

THERE ARE SEVERAL TYPES OF COVERING AND LINING EPITHELIUM

Based on combinations of layers and cell shape, we can identify several types of epithelial tissue. The types of epithelial tissue and their locations in the body are summarized in Table 4-1. In strat-

TABLE 4-1

Epithelial tissues

Tissue name	Main locations	Functions	Description and comments
Simple squamous epithelium	Air sacs of lungs, kidney glomerulus, outer surface of eardrum, lining of blood vessels (endothelium), lining of body cavities (mesothelium)	Passage of materials where little or no protection is needed	Like all epithelium, provided with a basement membrane secreted by the cells. The cells are flat (often so flat that the cytoplasm cannot be discerned) and arranged as a single layer. Simplest of all epithelial tissues
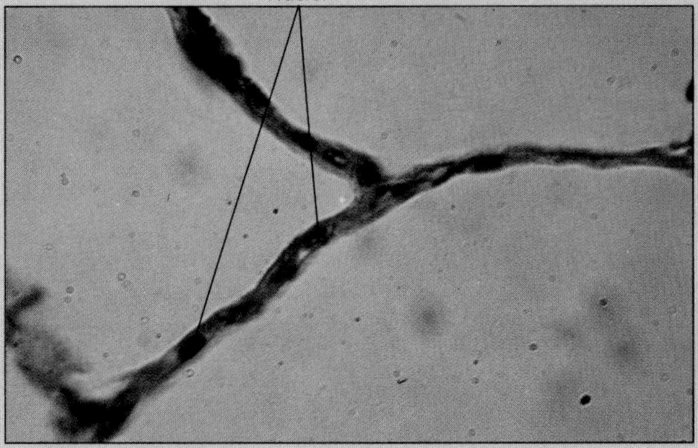 Nuclei (Approximately ×350)			
Simple cuboidal epithelium	Kidney tubules, gland ducts, thyroid follicles	Secretion and absorption	A single layer of cells that appears box-shaped in tissue sections, sometimes with microvilli for absorption
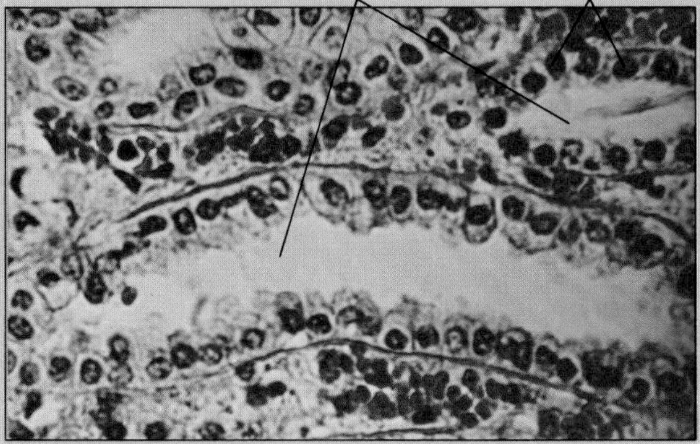 Lumen of tubule; Nuclei of cuboidal epithelial cells (Approximately ×450)			

(table continued on p. 118)

TABLE 4-1

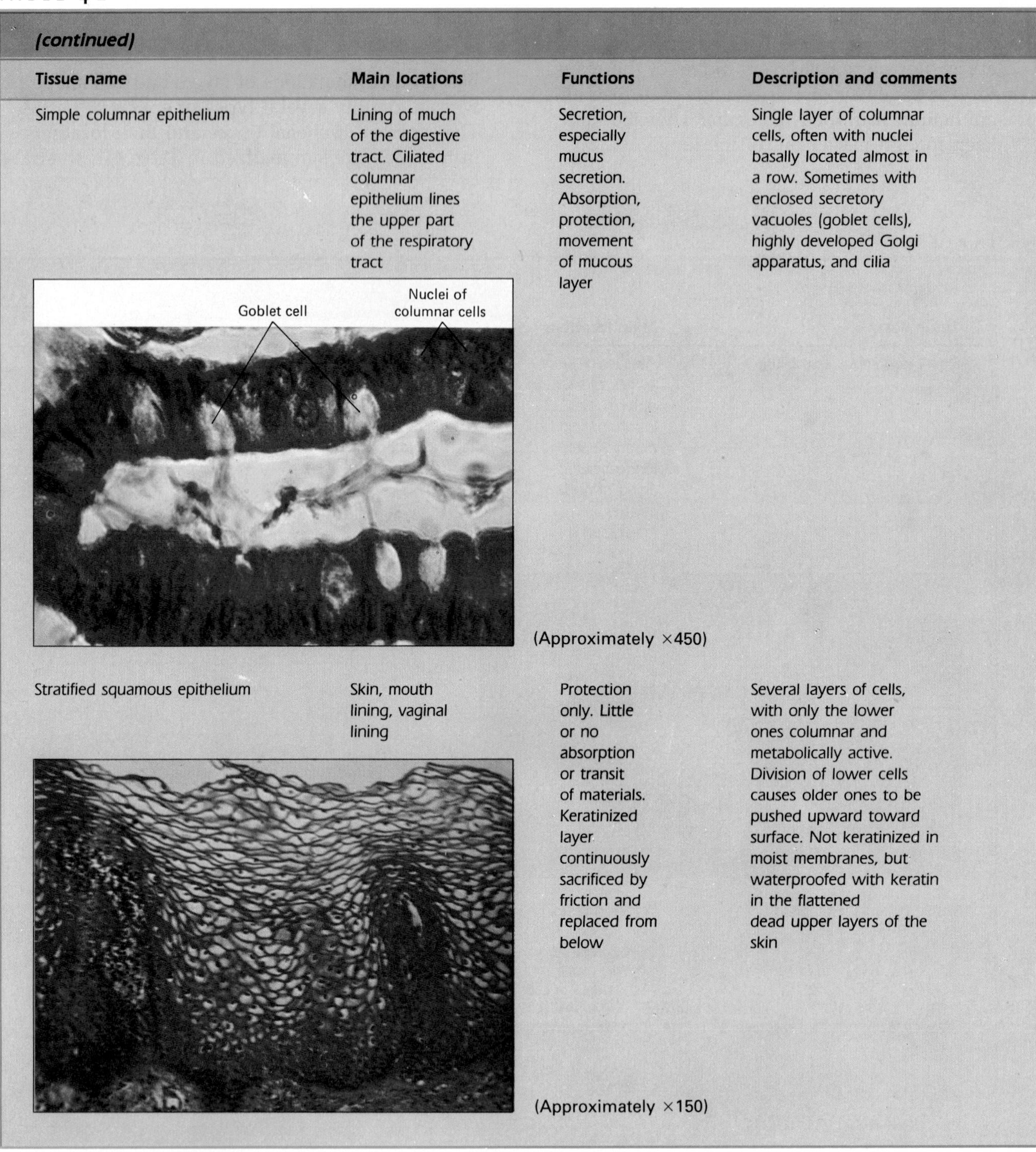

(continued)

Tissue name	Main locations	Functions	Description and comments
Simple columnar epithelium	Lining of much of the digestive tract. Ciliated columnar epithelium lines the upper part of the respiratory tract	Secretion, especially mucus secretion. Absorption, protection, movement of mucous layer	Single layer of columnar cells, often with nuclei basally located almost in a row. Sometimes with enclosed secretory vacuoles (goblet cells), highly developed Golgi apparatus, and cilia
		(Approximately ×450)	
Stratified squamous epithelium	Skin, mouth lining, vaginal lining	Protection only. Little or no absorption or transit of materials. Keratinized layer continuously sacrificed by friction and replaced from below	Several layers of cells, with only the lower ones columnar and metabolically active. Division of lower cells causes older ones to be pushed upward toward surface. Not keratinized in moist membranes, but waterproofed with keratin in the flattened dead upper layers of the skin
		(Approximately ×150)	

ified epithelium the shape of the cells at the free surface determines the name of the tissue. Thus in stratified squamous epithelium the outer cells are squamous in shape, but deeper in the membrane the cells may be more cuboidal or even columnar.

Simple squamous epithelium

With its thin, flattened cells, simple squamous epithelium permits efficient transfer of materials. The nucleus of each cell is thicker than the cell itself and causes the plasma membrane to bulge

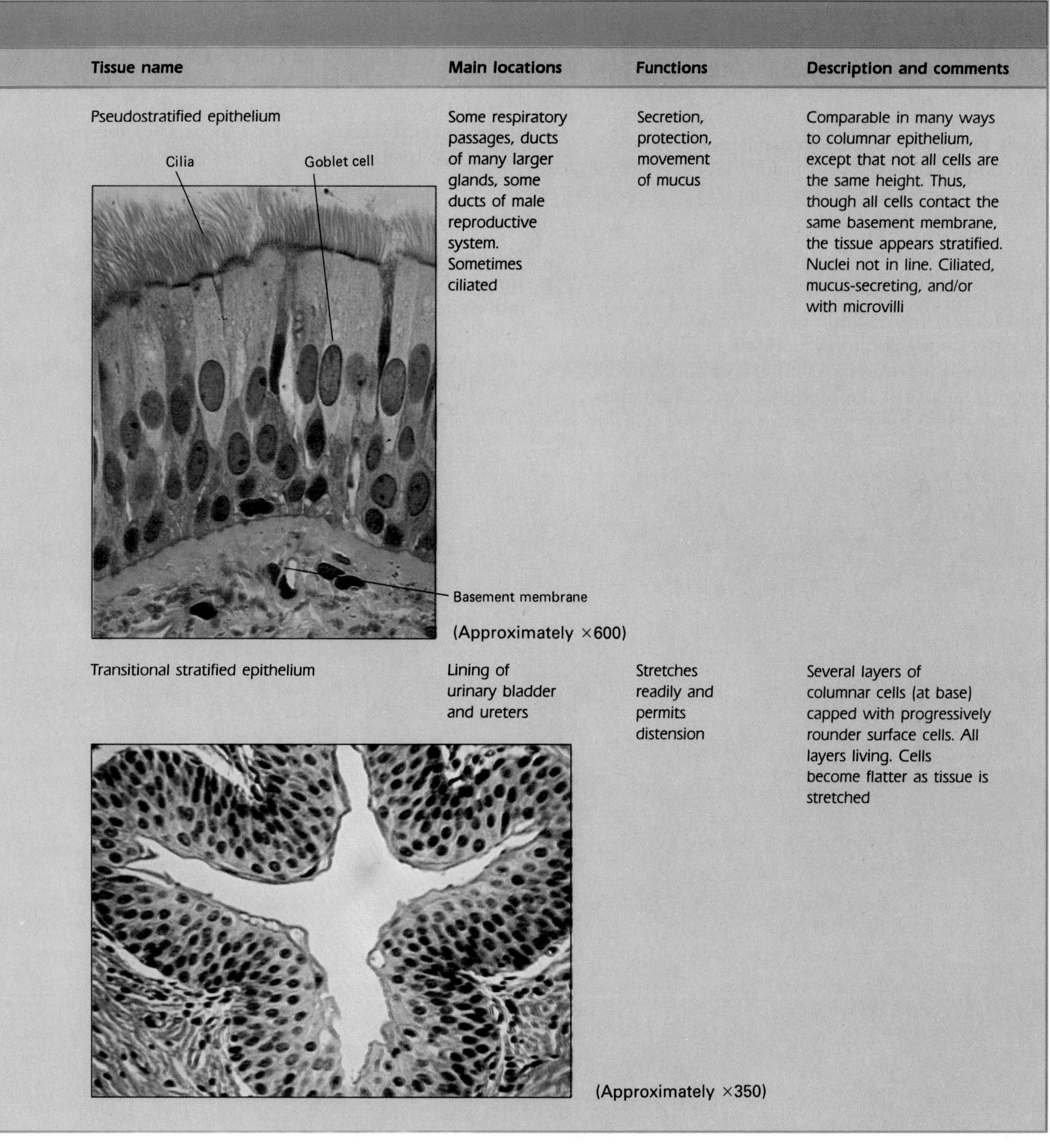

Tissue name	Main locations	Functions	Description and comments
Pseudostratified epithelium (Approximately ×600)	Some respiratory passages, ducts of many larger glands, some ducts of male reproductive system. Sometimes ciliated	Secretion, protection, movement of mucus	Comparable in many ways to columnar epithelium, except that not all cells are the same height. Thus, though all cells contact the same basement membrane, the tissue appears stratified. Nuclei not in line. Ciliated, mucus-secreting, and/or with microvilli
Transitional stratified epithelium (Approximately ×350)	Lining of urinary bladder and ureters	Stretches readily and permits distension	Several layers of columnar cells (at base) capped with progressively rounder surface cells. All layers living. Cells become flatter as tissue is stretched

outward. In some sections the nuclei are far more visible than the rest of the cell. Air sacs in the lungs are composed of this thin tissue, enabling oxygen and carbon dioxide to diffuse freely in and out of the lung. The inner walls of blood and lymph vessels are lined with a smooth, low-friction layer of simple squamous epithelium called **endothelium.** The lining of the body cavities consists of simple squamous epithelium called **mesothelium.**

Simple cuboidal epithelium

Specialized for secretion and absorption, simple cuboidal epithelial tissue is found in the kidney tubules as well as in certain glands and ducts of glands. Simple cuboidal epithelium consists of a single layer of cube-shaped cells. Their free surfaces may be equipped with microvilli which function in absorption of fluid. Cells specialized for secretion have a well developed Golgi complex and secretory vesicles.

Simple columnar epithelium

In addition to providing protection for underlying tissues, simple columnar epithelium may also be specialized for secretion and absorption. This tissue lines most of the digestive tract. Columnar cells that line the intestine are equipped with microvilli and they absorb molecules of digested food. Specialized cells within this tissue, called **goblet cells,** produce and secrete large amounts of mucus (see Fig. 4-2 and Table 4-2). As they fill with mucus, goblet cells bulge, assuming a flask or goblet shape. Simple columnar epithelium, characterized by cilia, is found in parts of the reproductive tract.

Stratified squamous epithelium

Because it is several cell layers thick, stratified squamous epithelium is well suited to protect underlying tissues. Cells of the outer rows are squamous, but those deeper down may be cuboidal or even columnar. This type of epithelium lines the mouth, the upper portion of the digestive system, the vagina, and the anal canal. As a

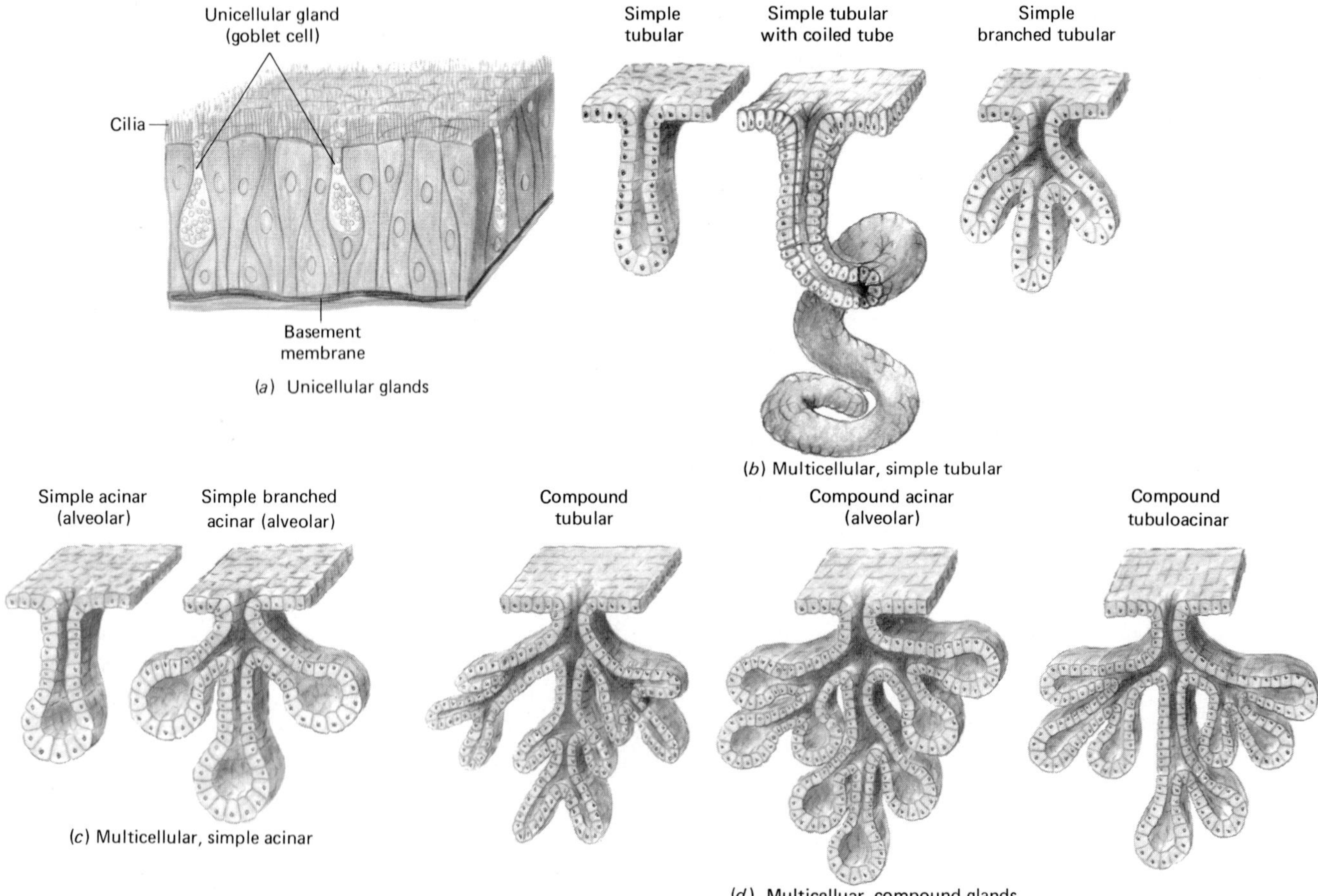

FIGURE 4-2

Types of exocrine glands. (*a*) A goblet cell is a unicellular gland that secretes mucus. (*b*) Simple tubular glands are multicellular. The simple tube may be coiled or branched. (*c*) Simple acinar (alveolar) glands. In acinar glands, the secretory units are rounded in shape. (*d*) Compound glands.

result of wear and tear, the outer cells of these membranes continuously wear away and must be replaced by cells from beneath. Cells in the deeper layers continuously undergo mitosis and divide. As they mature, these new cells eventually replace those at the outer surface (Fig. 4-1).

Stratified squamous epithelium also makes up the outer layer (epidermis) of the skin. As the outer layers of these cells die, they form a hardened layer of **keratin,** a tough, fibrous, waterproofing protein.

Pseudostratified columnar epithelium

As already described, pseudostratified columnar epithelium consists of a single layer of cells, some tall, some short. The nuclei of the shorter cells form a row closer to the bottom of the tissue than do the nuclei of the longer cells. In cross section this gives the impression of two or more rows of nuclei, and thus two or more rows of cells. In the pseudostratified columnar epithelium of the respiratory passageways, the longer cells are either ciliated or are goblet cells that secrete mucus. It is thought that the shorter cells may lengthen and take the place of the longer cells as these are worn away.

Transitional epithelium

Transitional epithelium is similar to stratified squamous epithelium, but it has the ability to stretch, a characteristic that makes it well suited to line the urinary bladder. When unstretched, the cells on the inner surface are round. As the bladder fills with urine, these cells become more flattened and somewhat squamous in shape. In this way the bladder stretches to accommodate a large volume of urine.

Glandular epithelium is specialized for secretion

A **gland** consists of one or more epithelial cells that produce and discharge a particular product. Two main types of glands are endocrine and exocrine glands. **Endocrine glands** lack ducts (tubes through which the secretion can pass) and release their products, called **hormones,** into the surrounding tissue fluid. The hormone usually diffuses into the blood, which transports it to its destination. The thyroid and adrenal glands are examples of endocrine glands. These and other endocrine glands will be discussed in Chapter 18.

Exocrine glands, in contrast, consist of (1) the groups of specialized epithelial cells or secretory units that produce the secretion and (2) the ducts, also made of epithelial cells, which conduct the secretion to some body surface (Fig. 4-2). For example, sweat passes from sweat glands through ducts to the surface of the skin, and salivary gland ducts conduct saliva into the mouth.

Exocrine glands may be *unicellular* (composed of one cell) like goblet cells, but most are *multicellular.* A multicellular gland may be simple, with only one unbranched duct, or compound. An example of a simple gland is the sweat gland, which has a single unbranched duct. The secretory unit of a sweat gland is a coiled tubule. In a compound gland the duct branches to conduct the secretion from many parts of the gland. The liver and pancreas are examples of large compound glands.

If the epithelial cells of the secretory unit of a gland are arranged like a tube, the gland is known as a *tubular gland.* In a *coiled tubular gland,* the secretory unit is a coiled tube. A *branched tubular gland* has a secretory unit that is both tubular and branched.

If the secretory units are round, the gland is an **acinar gland** (**as**-ih-nar), and the secretory units are referred to as acini ("berries"). These glands are also referred to as alveolar (little hollow sac) glands.

In a **compound gland,** one with a branched duct, the secretory units can be tubular, acinar, or a combination of both types. The pancreas and the parotid salivary gland contain tubular and acinar secretory units and are appropriately referred to as *tubuloacinar glands.* The types of exocrine glands based on type of secretory unit and degree of branching of the duct are summarized in Table 4-2.

There are still other ways to classify exocrine glands. **Mucous glands** release mucus; **serous glands** secrete a clear, watery substance; and **mixed glands** release both.

Glands release their secretions in different ways. Most glands are **merocrine glands,** which release their secretions without loss of cytoplasm or damage to their cells. The salivary glands and the pancreas are merocrine glands. In a **holocrine gland,** cells accumulate the secretion, then die and become part of the secretion. The dead cell is replaced by a new cell. Sebaceous (oil) glands in

TABLE 4-2

Types of Exocrine Glands

Type	Description	Examples
Unicellular	Composed of one cell; secretes the glycoprotein mucin, which combines with water to form mucus	Goblet cell is only example in human
Multicellular	Composed of many cells	
Simple	Has one, unbranched duct	
Tubular	The secretory unit is a straight tube that opens onto the epithelial surface; no duct is present	Intestinal glands
Coiled tubular	Secretory unit is a coiled tubule; an unbranched duct conveys the secretion to the surface	Sweat glands
Branched tubular	Secretory unit is tubular and branched; duct may be absent	Gastric glands, uterine glands
Branched acinar (alveolar)	Secretory unit is shaped like a sac and several acini are arranged along a duct	Sebaceous (oil) glands in skin
Compound	Duct branches	
Tubular	Secretory unit is tubular	Liver, testes
Acinar	Secretory unit is saclike	Salivary glands (submandibular and sublingual)
Tubuloacinar	Secretory unit is both tubular and saclike	Pancreas, parotid salivary glands

the skin are holocrine glands. In an **apocrine gland,** the secretion accumulates at the outer (apical) region of the cell. The droplets of secretion are surrounded by the plasma membrane and then pinched off from the cell and ejected. The mammary gland is an example of an apocrine gland.

Connective tissue joins body structures

Connective tissue is the most abundant and widespread tissue in the body. Its main function is to join together the other tissues of the body. Connective tissues also support the body and its structures and protect underlying organs. In addition, almost every organ in the body has a supporting framework of connective tissue, called **stroma.** The epithelial components of the organ, called the **parenchyma** (pah-**renk**-ih-muh), are supported and cushioned by the stroma.

There are many kinds of connective tissues and many systems for classifying them. Some of the main types of connective tissue are (1) connective tissue proper, (2) adipose tissue, (3) cartilage, (4) bone, and (5) blood, lymph, and tissues that produce blood cells (see Table 4-3). These tissues vary widely in the details of their structure and in the functions they perform.

Unlike the closely fitting cells of epithelial tissues, the cells of connective tissue are usually separated by large amounts of **intercellular substance.** The nonliving intercellular substance is produced by living cells. It consists of threadlike, microscopic fibers scattered throughout an amorphous (without definite form) **matrix.** The matrix is usually a viscous, semifluid gel composed of polysaccharide and protein complexes and tissue fluid. (In blood the matrix consists mainly of water and does not have fibers.)

Connective tissue contains specialized cells

Several different kinds of cells are found in connective tissue. Some, like bone cells, are characteristic of one particular type of connective tissue. Other kinds of cells are found in several different tissue types. The cells described in this section are found in connective tissue proper, especially a variety called loose connective tissue. However, many of these cell types are found in other varieties of connective tissue as well.

Connective tissues develop from an embryonic tissue called **mesenchyme** (**mez**-en-kime) (Fig. 4-3), and mesenchyme cells are the ancestors of most connective tissue cells. A population of mesenchyme cells is thought to persist in adult connective tissues. These undifferentiated (unspecialized) cells can give rise to other cell types. Mesenchyme cells are frequently found along the outer walls of capillaries. Some of these cells have long branching extensions of their cytoplasm that wrap around the capillary; these cells are called *pericytes.*

Fibroblasts are cells that produce both the fibers of connective tissue and the protein and carbohydrate complexes of the matrix. Once released from the fibroblasts, specific protein components arrange themselves to form the characteristic fibers.

Microscopic study of connective tissue prepared with standard stains reveals fibroblasts, which can be identified by their somewhat irregular shape (Fig. 4-4). The cytoplasm appears to extend outward in the form of processes. A young, active fibroblast has an elongated nucleus with lightly-staining chromatin, and often a prominent nucleolus.

Fibroblasts are especially active in developing tissue and in healing wounds. As tissues mature, the numbers of fibroblasts decrease and they become less active. Inactive fibroblasts are called **fibrocytes.** The cytoplasm of a fibrocyte stains so lightly that when viewed through the light microscope it may not be visible at all. These cells must usually be identified by their flattened, oval nuclei.

Another cell type common in connective tissue is the **macrophage,** or scavenger cell. Macro-

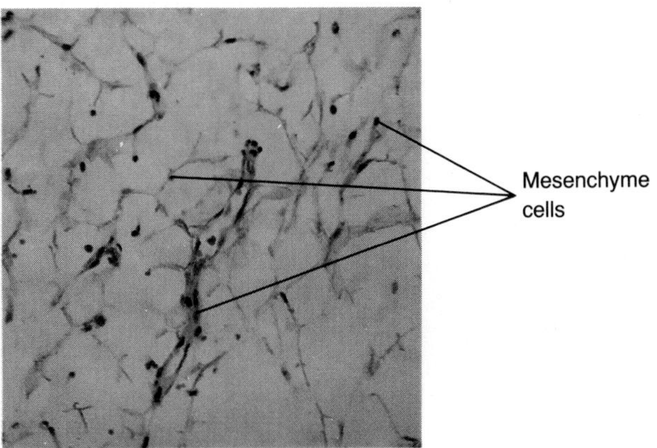

FIGURE 4-3

Mesenchyme. This embryonic tissue gives rise to the various types of connective tissue. Mesenchyme cells are the ancestors of most connective tissue cells (approximately ×75).

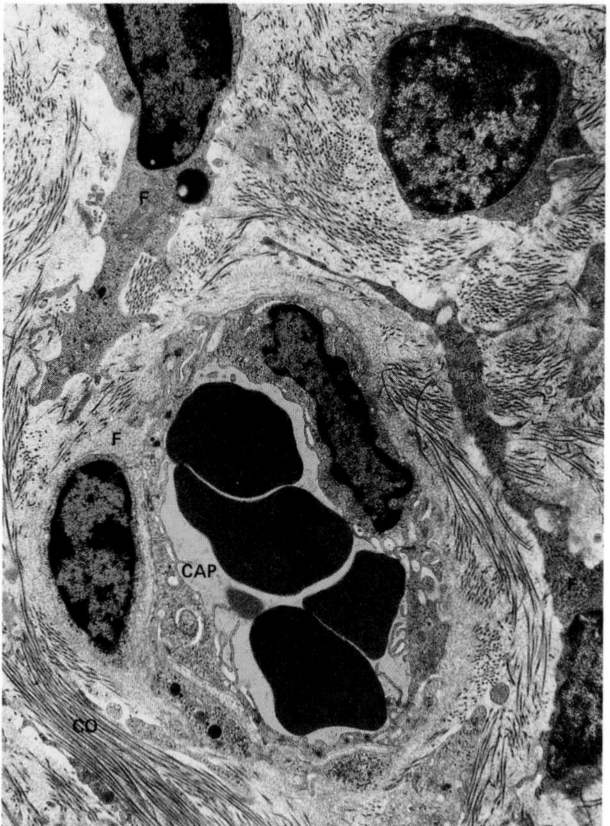

FIGURE 4-4

Electron micrograph showing several fibroblasts in connective tissue. A capillary with coagulated blood is shown. Note the collagen fibers. (F, fibroblasts; N, nucleus; CAP, capillary; RBC, red blood cell; CO, collagen) (Approximately ×13,650) (Courtesy of Dr. Lyle C. Dearden)

phages clean up cellular debris and phagocytize foreign matter, including bacteria. They also secrete a variety of substances such as antiviral agents.

Macrophages develop in the connective tissues from certain blood cells called *monocytes*. Young macrophages are oval, and the nucleus, which looks like an indented oval, may be found toward one end of the cell. Traditionally, two types of macrophages have been recognized: *fixed macrophages,* or *histiocytes,* which remain stationary in a tissue, and *wandering macrophages,* which move freely through the connective tissues. Recently, investigators have discovered that when stimulated, fixed macrophages can become migrating macrophages and move to the site of infection or injury.

In some organs macrophages are given special names. For example, in the liver they are called *Kupffer cells.* All the macrophages and related cells with phagocytic abilities are sometimes referred to collectively as the **reticuloendothelial system.** This system includes the specialized endothelium lining the sinusoids (special blood vessels) of the spleen and bone marrow. Some histologists prefer the term *mononuclear phagocyte system,* which includes all of the specialized phagocytic cells and their precursors, but excludes some cell types (e.g., endothelial cells) included in the reticuloendothelial system.

Mast cells are large cells filled with distinctive granules. They are often observed along small blood vessels. Mast cells contain several important substances, including *heparin,* an anticoagulant; *serotonin,* which causes contraction of smooth muscle; and *histamine,* a chemical that causes blood vessels to enlarge (dilate). The role of mast cells in allergic reactions will be discussed in Chapter 23.

Other cells that reside in ordinary connective tissue include adipose (fat) cells, white blood cells, and plasma cells. The latter produce antibodies (proteins that help defend the body against disease-causing organisms).

Connective tissue has collagen, reticular, and elastic fibers

The three types of connective tissue fibers are collagen fibers, reticular fibers, and elastic fibers. **Collagen fibers,** the most numerous, are referred to as white fibers because when they are present in great numbers the tissue containing them appears white (Fig. 4-5). These fibers are composed of the protein collagen, the most abundant protein in the body.

Collagen is a very tough substance, and collagen fibers give great strength to structures in which they occur. (In fact, meat is tough because of its collagen content. When collagen is boiled in water, however, it becomes hydrated and turns into gelatin.) The tensile strength of these flexible fibers has been compared to that of steel. Collagen fibers are wavy and highly resistant to stretching, and their structure allows the tissue to be stretched without actually stretching the fibers. **Tendons,** structures that attach muscles to bone, and **ligaments,** structures that join bones, consist mainly of collagen fibers.

Reticular fibers are very fine, branched fibers. Many tissues and organs are supported by a delicate internal network of reticular fibers. (The word reticular comes from a Latin word meaning net.) Like collagen fibers, reticular fibers are composed of collagen and some glycoprotein.

Elastic fibers, or yellow fibers, stretch easily and then, like a rubber band, snap back to their normal length when the stress is removed. These fibers are an important component of structures that must stretch. For example, elastic fibers in the walls of the air sacs in the lungs enable these sacs to stretch as they fill with air and then snap back to force air out of the lungs during expiration. In large arteries elastic fibers permit the blood vessel to stretch as it fills with blood. Elastic fibers are composed mainly of a protein called elastin.

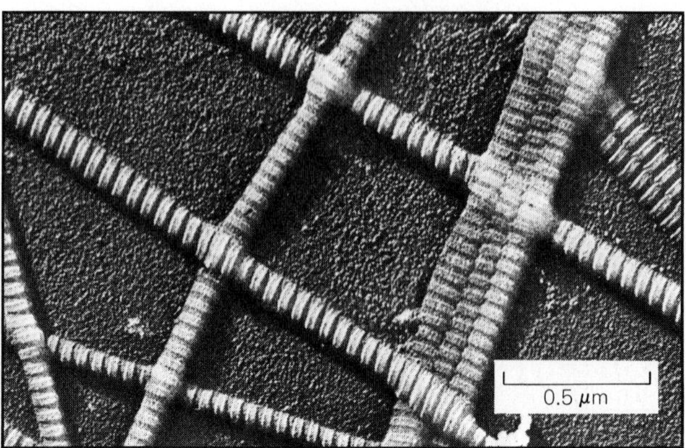

FIGURE 4-5

Collagen fibers (approximately ×50,000). Each fiber is made up of thousands of triple helices. (Jerome Gross.)

Connective tissue proper connects body structures

The main function of connective tissue proper is to connect body structures. Types of connective tissue proper include loose connective tissue, dense connective tissue, elastic connective tissue, and reticular connective tissue (Table 4-3).

LOOSE CONNECTIVE TISSUE IS WIDELY DISTRIBUTED

Loose connective tissue, also called areolar tissue, consists of fibers strewn in all directions throughout a semifluid matrix (Fig. 4-6). Fibroblasts and macrophages are the most numerous cells present, but many other types of connective tissue cells are also scattered throughout.

Loose connective tissue is the most widely distributed connective tissue in the body. It is found as a thin filling between body parts and serves as a reservoir for water and salts. Nerves, blood vessels, and muscles are wrapped in this tissue. Together with adipose tissue, loose connective tissue forms the subcutaneous (below the skin) layer, the layer that attaches the skin to the tissues and organs beneath.

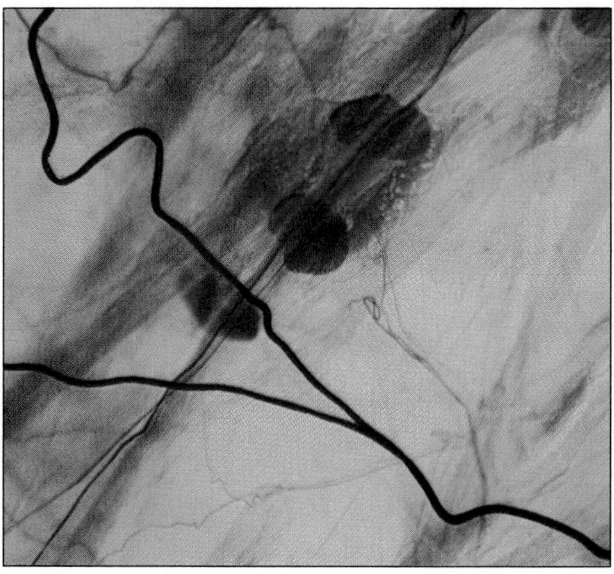

FIGURE 4-6

Loose connective tissue. Note that the collagen is stained pink and the elastic fibers black. Fibroblasts are also visible in this photomicrograph (approximately ×1000). (Ed Reschke/Peter Arnold, Inc.)

DENSE CONNECTIVE TISSUE CAN BE IRREGULAR OR REGULAR

Dense connective tissue consists almost entirely of intercellular substance. Fewer cells are present than in loose connective tissue, and these lie embedded within the intercellular substance. Collagen fibers predominate. Dense connective tissue is very strong, though somewhat less flexible than loose connective tissue.

In *irregular dense connective tissue,* the collagen fibers are arranged in bundles distributed in all directions through the tissue. This type of tissue is found in the lower layer (dermis) of the skin where it permits considerable flexibility.

In *regular dense connective tissue,* the collagen bundles are arranged in a definite pattern. This arrangement makes the tissue greatly resistant to stress. Tendons consist of regular dense connective tissue.

ELASTIC CONNECTIVE TISSUE PROVIDES STRENGTH AND ELASTICITY

Elastic connective tissue consists of bundles of parallel elastic fibers that give the tissue a yellow color. Small amounts of loose connective tissue are found between the bundles, and flattened fibroblasts are present between the elastic fibers. As its name implies, when elastic connective tissue is stretched, it snaps back into shape.

Elastic connective tissue provides strength as well as elasticity. It is found in certain ligaments, such as those between the vertebrae; in certain large arteries that stretch when filled with blood; in the heart; and in the respiratory passageways.

RETICULAR CONNECTIVE TISSUE PROVIDES SUPPORT

Reticular connective tissue is composed mainly of interlacing reticular fibers. It forms a stroma (framework) that supports many organs, including the liver, lymph nodes, spleen, and bone marrow.

Adipose tissue is an energy reservoir

In an average person, **adipose (fat) tissue** accounts for about 10% of the total body weight. Its main function is to store fat and release it when fuel is needed for cellular work. Adipose tissue

(text continued on p. 129)

TABLE 4-3

Connective tissues

Tissue name	Main locations	Functions	Description and comments
Loose (areolar) connective tissue 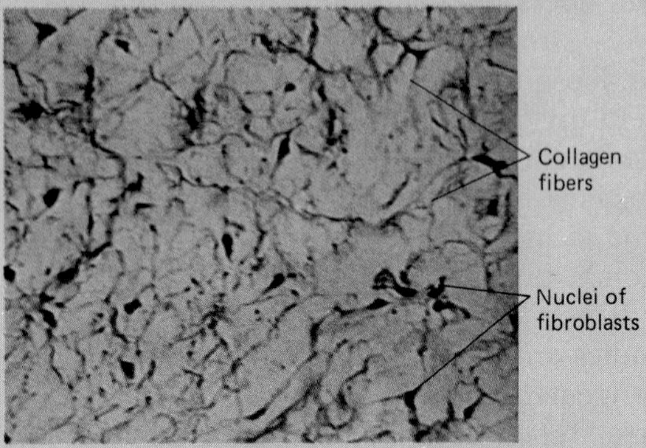 (Approximately ×200)	Every place where support must be combined with elasticity; e.g., subcutaneous layer of skin	Support	Elastic and inelastic fibers produced by fibroblast cells embedded in a semifluid matrix and mixed with a miscellaneous group of other cells
Dense connective tissue 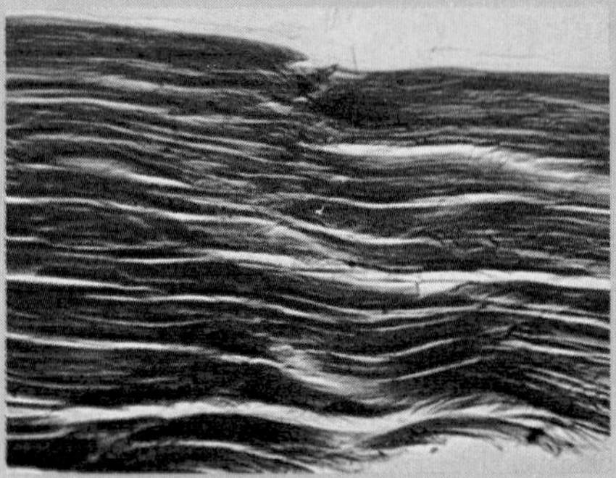 (Approximately ×200)	Tendons, strong attachments between organs; dermis of skin	Support; transmission of mechanical forces	Bundles of interwoven collagen fibers interdigitated with rows of fibroblast cells
Elastic connective tissue 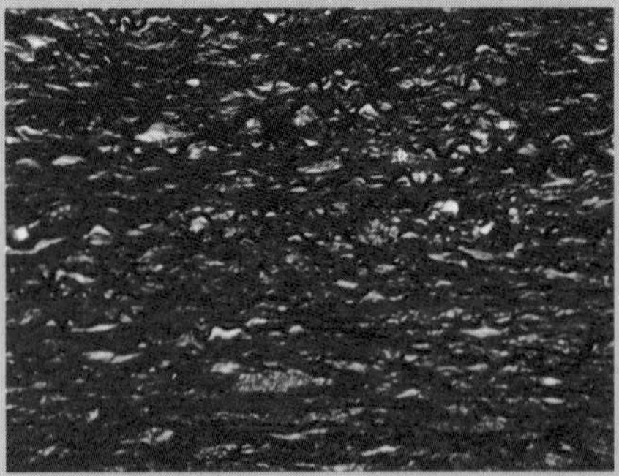 (Approximately ×300)	Structures that must both expand and return to their original size, such as lung tissue, large arteries	Confers elasticity	Branching elastic fibers interspersed with fibroblasts

Tissue name	Main locations	Functions	Description and comments
Reticular connective tissue  (Approximately ×500)	Framework of liver, lymph nodes, spleen, thymus	Support	Consists of interlacing reticular fibers (From Bloom, William and Don W. Fawcett. *A Textbook of Histology,* 10th ed. W. B. Saunders, Philadelphia, 1975.)
Adipose connective tissue 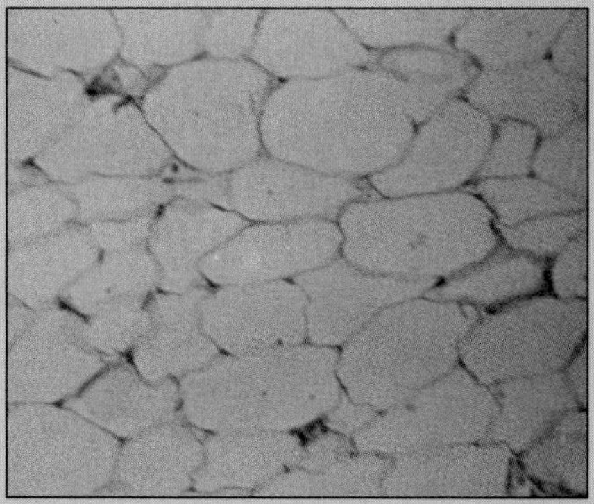 (Approximately ×150)	Subcutaneous layer; pads around certain internal organs	Food storage, insulation, support of such organs as breasts, kidneys	Fat cells are asteroidal at first; fat droplets accumulate until typical ring-shaped cells are produced
Hyaline cartilage 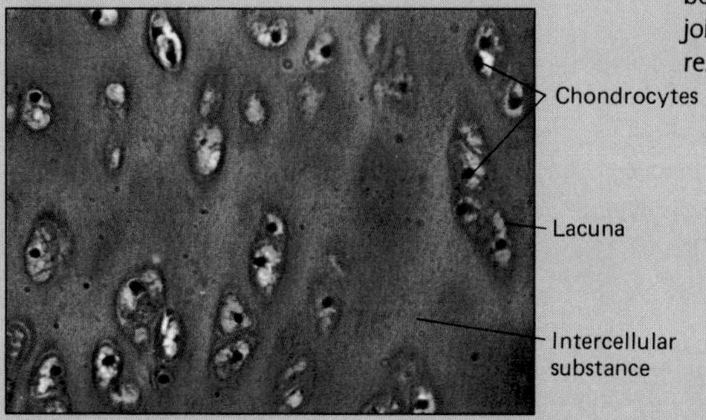 Chondrocytes Lacuna Intercellular substance (Approximately ×300)	Forms ends of bones; synovial joint surfaces; respiratory tubes	Flexible support and the reduction of friction in bearing surfaces	No visible fibers. The cells (chondrocytes) are separated from one another by the gristly intercellular substance and occupy little spaces in it

(*table continued on p. 128*)

TABLE 4-3

(continued)

Tissue name	Main locations	Functions	Description and comments
Fibrocartilage 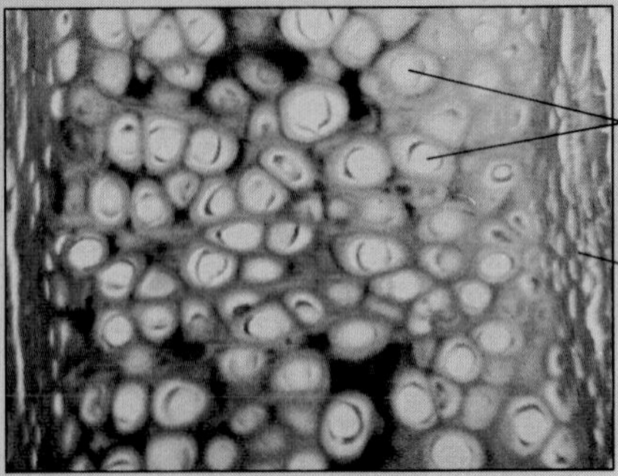 Chondrocytes Collagen bundles (Approximately ×300)	Symphysis pubis of pelvis; intervertebral discs	Support, connection, and shock absorption	Like hyaline cartilage, but with white collagen fibers embedded in the matrix
Elastic cartilage 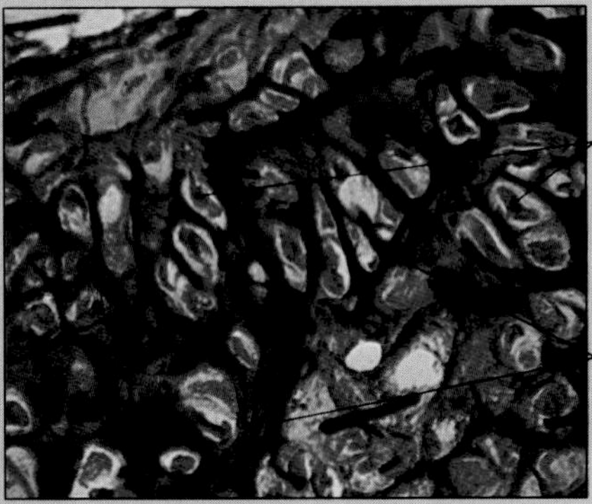 Chondrocytes Bundles of elastic fibers (Approximately ×300)	External ear, epiglottis, and parts of the respiratory system	Support where flexibility is also important	Like hyaline cartilage, but with elastic fibers embedded in the matrix
Bone  Lacunae Haversian canal Matrix (Approximately ×150)	Bones of skeleton	Support, protection of internal organs, calcium reservoir; skeletal muscles attach to bones	Osteocytes located in lacunae. In compact bone, lacunae arranged in concentric circles about haversian canals
Blood 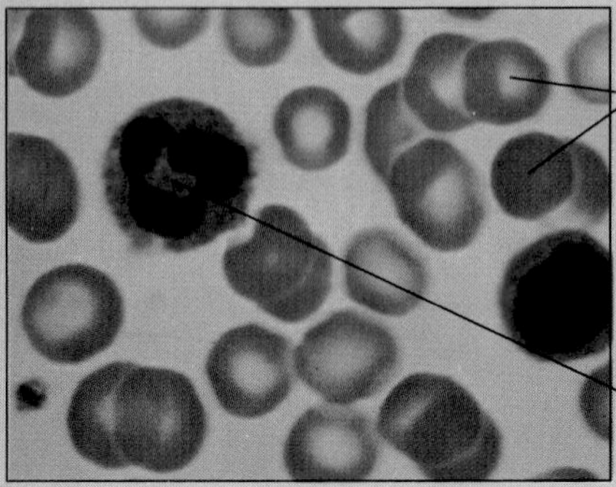 Red blood cells White blood cell (Approximately ×1100)	Within heart and blood vessels of circulatory system	Transports oxygen, nutrients, wastes, and other materials	Consists of cells dispersed in a fluid intercellular substance

also helps to shape the body, forming pads that act as shock absorbers as well as contributing aesthetic qualities. Adipose tissue provides insulation. Because fat is a poor heat conductor, it helps prevent loss of body heat through the skin.

About half the cells of adipose tissue are the *fat cells*, or *adipocytes*, themselves. They are organized into groups called *lobules*. Loose connective tissue between the lobules supports the cells and permits passage of blood vessels and nerves into the tissue.

An immature fat cell is somewhat star-shaped. As fat droplets accumulate within the cytoplasm, the cell assumes a more rounded appearance (Fig. 4-7). Fat droplets eventually merge with one another until finally a single large drop of fat is present. This large drop occupies most of the volume of the mature fat-storing cell. The cytoplasm and its organelles are pushed to the cell edges, where a bulge is typically created by the nucleus. A cross section of such a fat cell looks like a ring with a single stone and is sometimes called a signet ring cell. (Cytoplasm forms the ring, and the nucleus, the stone.)

When you study a section of adipose tissue through a microscope, it may remind you of chicken wire. The "wire" is represented by the rings of cytoplasm, and the large spaces indicate where fat drops existed before they were dissolved by chemicals used to prepare the tissue. The empty spaces may cause the cells to collapse, resulting in a wrinkled appearance.

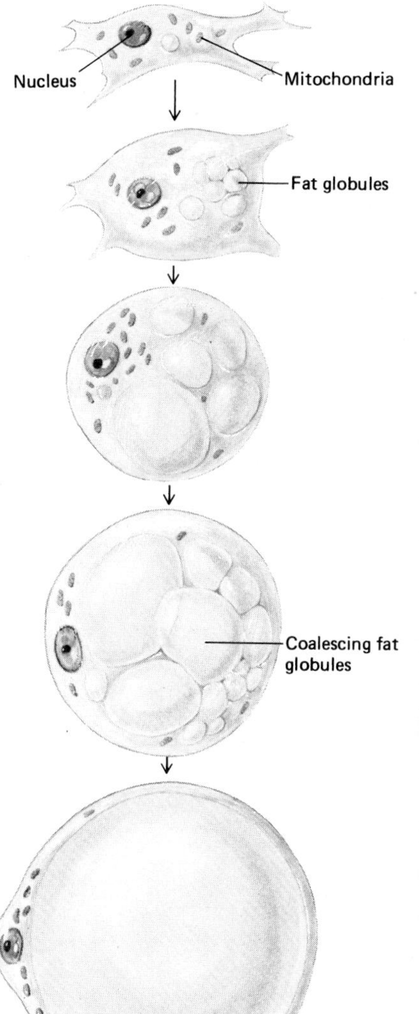

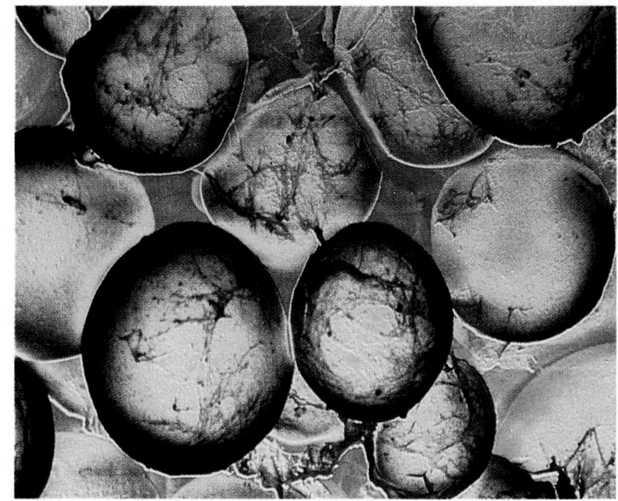

(b)

FIGURE 4-7

Storage of fat in a fat cell. (a) As more and more fat droplets accumulate in the cytoplasm, they coalesce, forming a very large globule of fat. Such a globule may occupy most of the cell, pushing the cytoplasm and organelles to the periphery. (b) Scanning electron micrograph of fat cells laden with fat (approximately ×100). (CNRI/Phototake.)

Cartilage provides support

Cartilage is a hard, strong connective tissue that provides support for some soft tissues and forms a sliding area for joints so that bones can move easily. During fetal (before birth) development, cartilage forms much of the skeleton. Most of this cartilage is gradually replaced by bone. In a mature individual, cartilage is found mainly at the ends of the bones and in the joints. It also occurs in the nose, ears, in the rings in the wall of the trachea (windpipe), in association with ribs and vertebrae, and in a few other places.

Cartilage cells, called **chondrocytes** (**kon**-drow-sites), secrete a tough intercellular substance around themselves consisting of fibers and a firm gel. Eventually the cells come to reside within tiny cavities called **lacunae** (lah-**koo**-nee) (Fig. 4-8), which are separated from one another by the intercellular substance. Cartilage tissue lacks nerves, lymph vessels, and blood vessels. Chondrocytes are nourished by diffusion of nutrients from capillaries outside the cartilage. In order to reach the chondrocytes, nutrients must diffuse through the intercellular substance. Cartilage tissue is usually surrounded by a dense connective tissue membrane called the **perichondrium** (*per*-ih-**kon**-dree-um; peri, around + chondr, cartilage).

Three types of cartilage are hyaline, fibrocartilage, and elastic cartilage. **Hyaline cartilage** (**hy**-ah-lin), the most common type, forms the ends of bones at joints and makes up the anterior ends of the ribs (the costal cartilages). It also occurs in the nose and in rings in the walls of the respiratory tract.

In the body, this tissue has a translucent blue-white appearance. In fact, its name is derived from its smooth, glasslike quality (from the Greek word *hyalinos*, meaning glass). Although there is a great deal of collagen within the matrix of hyaline cartilage, fibers are usually not visible in microscopic preparations.

Fibrocartilage is a shock-absorbing tissue found in structures subject to great stress, such as the discs between the vertebrae and the knee joint. Its characteristics are intermediate between those of hyaline cartilage and dense connective tissue. Fibrocartilage may be recognized by the great number of collagen fibers visible in its ma-

Cartilage

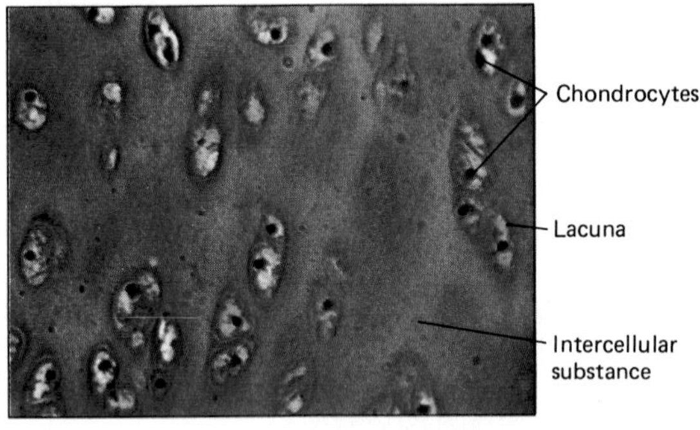

(a)

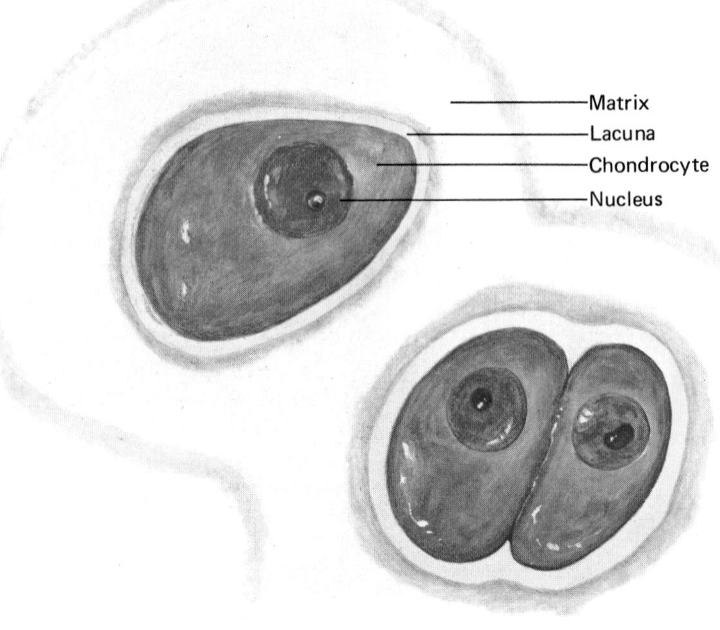

(b)

FIGURE 4-8

Cartilage. (*a*) A photomicrograph of cartilage tissue (approximately ×100). (*b*) Cartilage cells, called chondrocytes, become trapped in small spaces called lacunae. The rubbery matrix contains collagen fibers.

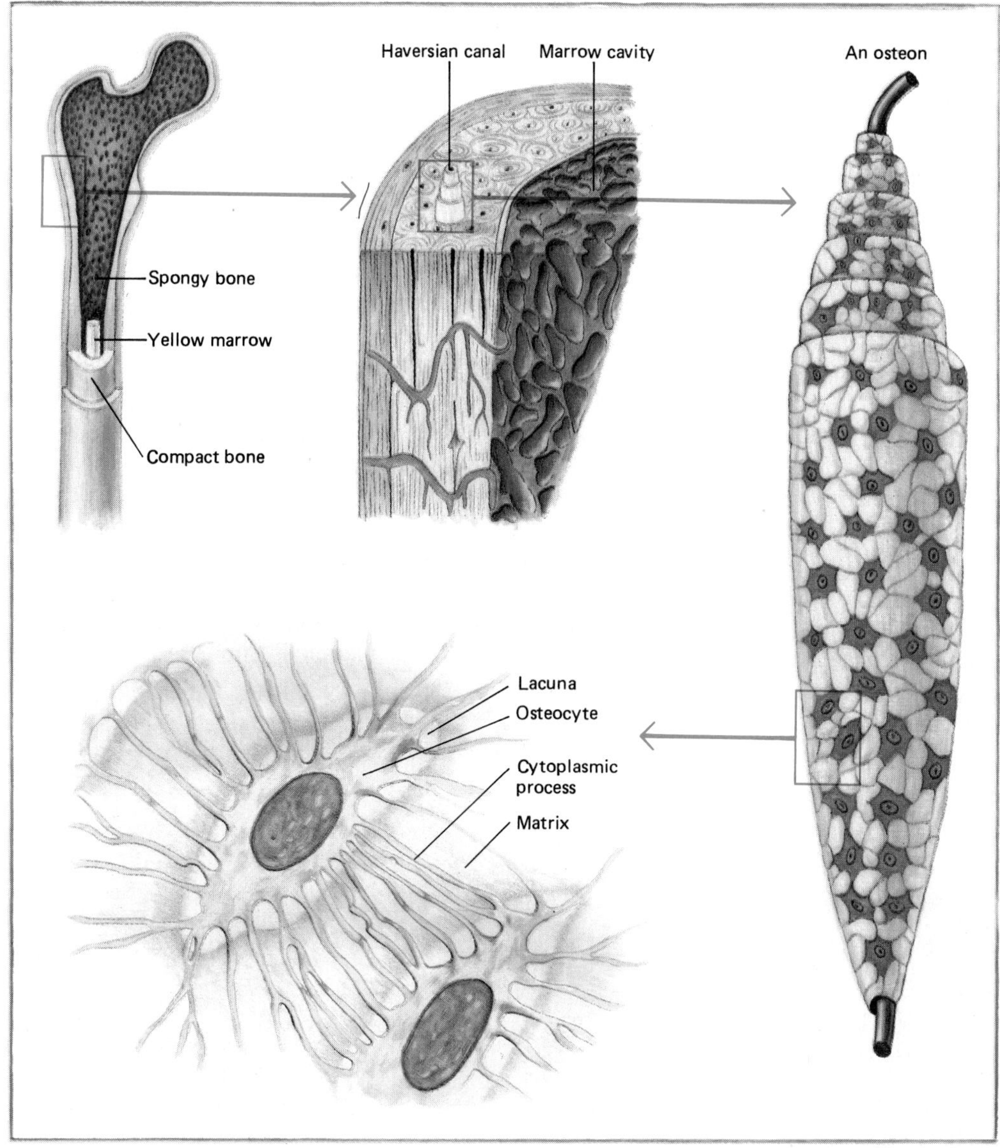

FIGURE 4-9

Compact bone is made up of units called osteons. Blood vessels and nerves run through the haversian canal within each osteon. In bone the matrix is rigid and hard. Osteocytes become trapped within lacunae but communicate with one another by way of cytoplasmic processes that extend through tiny canals called canaliculi.

trix. The amorphous matrix is limited to the outer edges of the lacunae in which the chondrocytes reside. No perichondrium is present.

Elastic cartilage is found in the external ear and in parts of the respiratory system. It is similar to hyaline cartilage, but its chondrocytes produce elastic fibers as well as collagen fibers.

Bone is the main supporting tissue of the body

Bone, or osseous tissue, is the supporting tissue of the mature skeleton. An extremely rigid tissue, bone supports the body, protects internal organs, and serves as an important storage reservoir of calcium and phosphorus. The intercellular substance of bone contains a great deal of collagen. Mineral salts, mainly calcium phosphate and calcium carbonate, are laid down over the collagen fibers, adding to their hardness. Bone cells, called **osteocytes** (**os**-tee-oh-*sites*), are located in lacunae (Fig. 4-9).

In compact bone the lacunae are arranged in concentric circles around central channels called **haversian canals** (hah-**ver**-shun). Blood vessels and nerves run through these canals. A system of tiny tubes, called **canaliculi** (*kahn*-ah-**lik**-u-lie), perforates the intercellular substance and link the lacunae with one another. The canaliculi serve as channels through which nutrients and waste materials are exchanged.

Bones are covered by a tough connective tissue membrane, the **periosteum** (*per*-ee-**os**-tee-um; peri, around + oste, bone), which functions both in the growth of bone and in the attachment of muscle tendons to it. Bone and cartilage will be discussed in more detail in Chapter 6.

Blood, lymph, and tissues that produce blood cells are also connective tissues

You may be surprised that blood and lymph are considered connective tissues. Like all connective tissues, they consist of specialized cells dispersed in an intercellular substance. **Blood** and **lymph** are circulating tissues that bring various parts of the body into communication.

Blood consists of *red blood cells* (erythrocytes), *white blood cells* (leukocytes), and *platelets* dispersed in a straw-colored liquid called *plasma*. The plasma consists mainly of water plus several types of proteins, nutrients, respiratory gases, hormones, and ions. Red blood cells transport oxygen from the lungs to all of the cells of the body, and carbon dioxide from the cells to the lungs. White blood cells defend the body against foreign agents including microorganisms that cause disease. Platelets function in blood clotting.

Blood cells are produced in another kind of connective tissue, the **red bone marrow.** This tissue, rich in reticular fibers, is found within certain bones. Blood and lymph will be discussed in greater detail in Chapters 19 and 22, respectively.

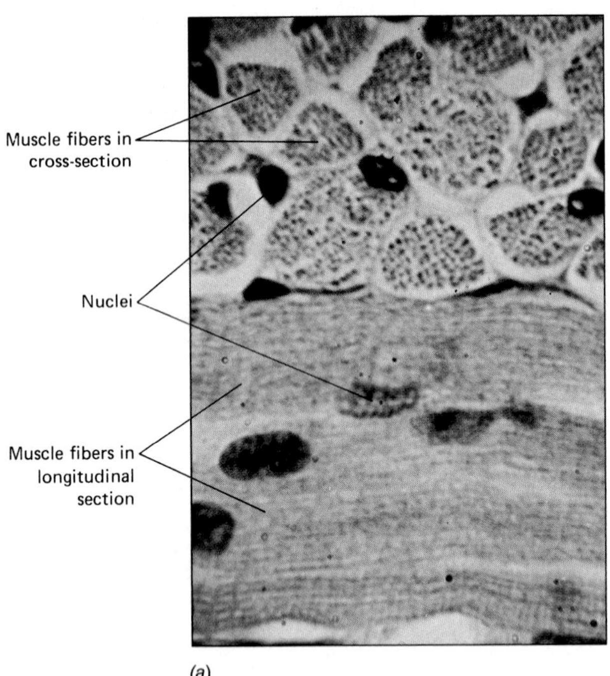

(a)

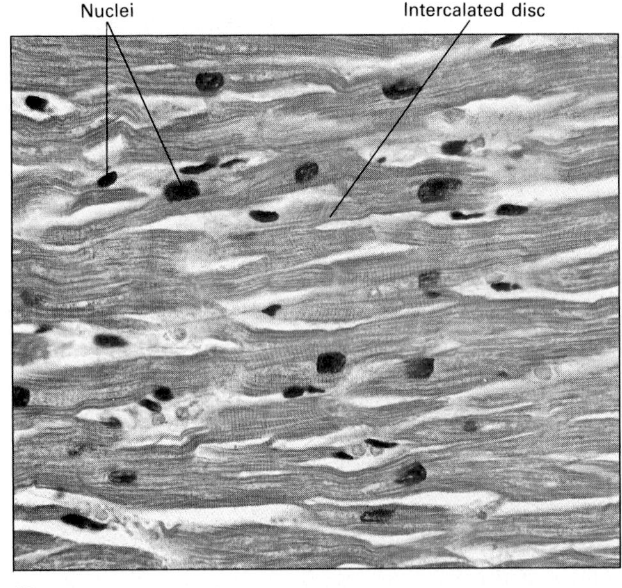

(b)

Nuclei

(c)

FIGURE 4-10

Muscle tissue. *(a)* Skeletal muscle is striated, voluntary muscle (approximately ×1000). *(b)* Cardiac muscle tissue is striated, has branched fibers, and is involuntary. The special junctions between cardiac muscle cells are called intercalated discs. (Al Lammé/Phototake.) *(c)* Smooth muscle tissue lacks striations and is involuntary (approximately ×450).

Muscle tissue is specialized to contract

Muscle tissue is composed of cells specialized to contract, or shorten. When muscle cells contract they become shorter and thicker, causing body parts attached to them to move. Because they are long and narrow, muscle cells are referred to as **fibers.** Muscle fibers are usually arranged in bundles or layers surrounded by connective tissue. Three types of muscle tissue are *skeletal muscle, cardiac muscle,* and *smooth muscle* (Fig. 4-10; Table 4-4).

Skeletal muscle is under voluntary control

When we think of muscles we normally think of the voluntary muscles that enable us to walk, run, or move the body in some other way. Such movements are the job of the **skeletal muscles,** which are attached to the bones. Not all movement caused by skeletal muscle contraction is voluntary. Some such movement occurs without conscious decision. For example, we do not have to direct the diaphragm and chest muscles to contract each time we breathe.

Skeletal muscle cells have a striped, or striated, appearance (Fig. 4-10a). Each muscle fiber has several nuclei located just under the plasma membrane. Skeletal muscle fibers contract when stimulated by nerves.

Cardiac muscle is involuntary

As you might guess from its name, **cardiac muscle** is found in the heart. Like skeletal muscle, it is striated. The fibers of cardiac muscle are joined end to end, and branch and rejoin to form complex networks (Fig. 4-10b). Generally, only one nucleus is found in each cell. The nuclei are positioned more toward the interior of the cell than is the case in skeletal muscle. A characteristic feature of cardiac muscle is the presence of structures called **intercalated discs** (in-**ter**-kah-lay-ted), which mark the junctions between adjoining fibers.

The heart does not have to be instructed to contract every second or so; cardiac muscle con-

TABLE 4-4

Types of muscle tissues

	Skeletal	Smooth	Cardiac
Location	Attached to skeleton	Walls of stomach, intestines, etc.	Walls of heart
Type of control	Voluntary	Involuntary	Involuntary
Shape of fibers	Elongated, cylindrical, blunt ends	Elongated, spindle-shaped, pointed ends	Elongated, cylindrical fibers that branch and fuse
Striations	Present	Absent	Present
Number of nuclei per fiber	Many	One	One
Speed of contraction	Most rapid	Slowest	Intermediate
Ability to remain contracted	Least	Greatest	Intermediate

(*a*) Skeletal muscle fibers

(*b*) Smooth muscle fibers

(*c*) Cardiac muscle fibers

traction is normally involuntary. Automatic, rhythmic contraction of cardiac muscle fibers continues even when they are isolated from the body.

Smooth muscle is located in internal organs

Smooth muscle is found in the walls of many internal organs. Action of this tissue moves food through the digestive tract, changes the diameter of the blood vessels, opens and closes passageways, and performs whatever other internal structural movements are necessary. As is true of cardiac muscle, smooth muscle contraction is involuntary.

Smooth muscle fibers are spindle-shaped and have only one nucleus per cell. The nucleus is elongated and can usually be seen near the center of the cell. Smooth muscle is so named because its fibers lack striations (Fig. 4-10c).

Nervous tissue controls muscles and glands

Nervous tissue (Fig. 4-11) is specialized to receive stimuli, to transmit information, and to control the action of muscles and glands. Though the bulk of nervous tissue is located within the brain and spinal cord, bundles of nerve fibers—the nerves—are dispatched to all parts of the body to pick up information from the sensory receptors and to return information in the form of neural impulses (messages) from the brain and spinal cord.

Nervous tissue consists of **nerve cells called neurons** and supporting cells called **glial cells** (or neuroglia). Neurons are specialized to receive and transmit impulses. A typical neuron consists of a *cell body* that contains the nucleus and most of the cytoplasm and two types of cytoplasmic extensions. *Dendrites* are highly branched extensions of the cell body that receive nerve impulses and transmit them to the cell body. The *axon* is a single, long extension of the cell body that transmits impulses away from the cell body.

Glial cells are smaller than neurons but more numerous. They support nervous tissue, line cavities in the brain and spinal cord, and carry on phagocytosis. They may have a number of other functions. Some connective tissue, including blood vessels, is found within nervous tissue. In Chapter 10 we will discuss nervous tissue in more detail.

Membranes cover or line body surfaces

Membranes are sheets of tissue that cover or line body surfaces. An **epithelial membrane** consists of epithelial tissue and a layer of underlying connective tissue. The main types of epithelial membranes are mucous membranes, serous mem-

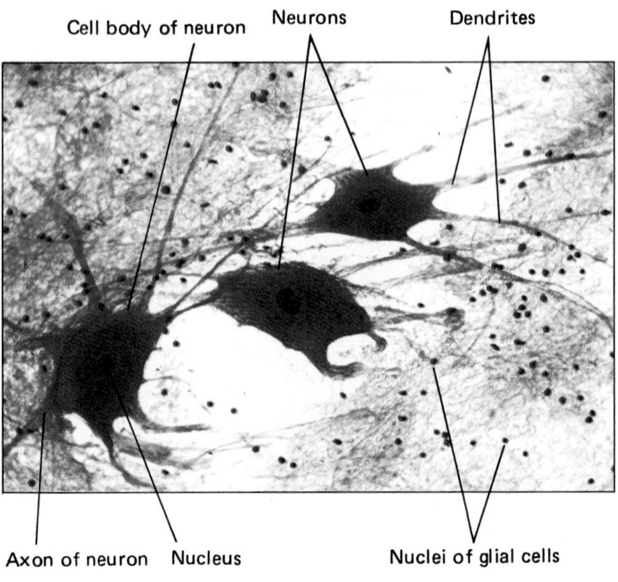

FIGURE 4-11

Nervous tissue consists of neurons and glial cells (approximately ×500). (Ed Reschke.)

branes, and the skin, which is a cutaneous membrane. The skin will be the focus of the next chapter. Another type of membrane, the synovial membrane, lines the joint cavities. A synovial membrane does not contain epithelium and consists of connective tissue. The synovial membrane will be described in Chapter 9.

Mucous membranes line body cavities that open to the outside of the body

A **mucous membrane,** or **mucosa,** lines a body cavity that opens to the outside of the body. The epithelial layer secretes mucus, which lubricates the tissue and prevents drying out. Mucous membranes line the digestive, respiratory, urinary, and reproductive tracts. The type of epithelial tissue in different mucous membranes varies. For example, the mucous membrane of the intestine contains simple columnar epithelium whereas the mucous membrane of the esophagus contains stratified squamous epithelium. In some respiratory passageways, the mucous membrane contains pseudostratified epithelium equipped with cilia.

The connective tissue layer of a mucous membrane is a lamina propria that connects the epithelium to the underlying tissue. This connective tissue contains the blood vessels that bring oxygen and nutrients to the epithelium and remove waste.

Serous membranes line cavities that contain fluid

A **serous membrane,** or **serosa,** lines a body cavity that does not open to the outside of the body. The cavity contains fluid secreted by the serous membrane. A serous membrane consists of a thin layer of loose connective tissue covered by a layer of simple squamous epithelium called mesothelium.

A serous membrane folds, forming a double-walled sheet of tissue. The portion of the membrane attached to the wall of the cavity is the **parietal membrane,** whereas the part of the membrane that covers the organs inside the cavity is the **visceral membrane.** Thus, the serous membrane lining the thoracic cavity is the parietal pleura, while the portion of that membrane covering the lungs is the visceral pleura. Similarly the serous membrane, or pericardium, lining the pericardial cavity around the heart, consists of an outer parietal pericardium and an inner visceral pericardium that forms the outer layer of the heart. The serous membrane lining the abdominal cavity is the parietal peritoneum; the portion of the peritoneum that covers the abdominal and some pelvic organs is the visceral peritoneum.

Neoplasms: abnormal growths of tissue

A **neoplasm** (**nee**-oh-plazm; new growth), or **tumor,** is an abnormal growth of tissue. The study of neoplasms is called **oncology** (ong-**kol**-o-jee), and physicians who specialize in abnormal growths are **oncologists.** A neoplasm may be **benign** ("kind") or **malignant** ("wicked").

A benign tumor tends to grow slowly, and its cells stay together and do not spread to other parts of the body. Because benign tumors form discrete masses, often surrounded by connective tissue capsules, they can usually be removed surgically. Unless a benign neoplasm develops in a place where it interferes with the function of a vital organ, it is not lethal.

A malignant neoplasm, or **cancer,** usually grows much more rapidly than a benign tumor. Neoplasms that develop from connective tissues or muscle are referred to as *sarcomas,* and those that originate in epithelial tissue are called *carcinomas.* Unlike the cells of benign tumors, cancer cells do not retain the typical structural features of the cells from which they originate.

Certain mutations lead to cancer

Cancer is thought to be triggered by mutation of genes that control growth and cell division. A **mutation** is a permanent chemical change in the gene. Most cancer cells have one or more mutated genes, referred to as **oncogenes.** Oncogenes arise from normal genes, called *proto-oncogenes,* that are involved in the regulation of growth and development. Certain oncogenes have been found to stimulate abnormal release of growth factors. Others appear to stimulate continuous production of proteins normally found only in the nuclei of cells that are about to undergo mitosis. Some cancers may be triggered by the absence of a gene, rather than by the presence of oncogenes.

If indeed many cancers are triggered by mutations, what causes the mutations? Many mutations are the result of chance errors that occur during the replication of DNA. However, about 80% of cancer cases can be traced to environmental factors. The probability of mutations is greatly increased by a number of environmental factors, including the following:

1. *Ionizing radiation* such as x-rays and gamma rays. Survivors of Hiroshima and Nagasaki have a higher incidence of leukemia than persons not exposed to radiation. Patients who have been treated clinically with gamma rays for conditions such as acne have an increased incidence of cancer. Ultraviolet light from exposure to the sun has been identified as an important cause of skin cancer.
2. *Certain chemicals or irritants* referred to as **carcinogens** (cancer-causing agents) such as asbestos from insulation, benzene, and a host of other industrial pollutants. Carcinogens in cigarette smoke are responsible for about one-fourth of all cancer deaths.
3. *Viruses* have been shown to cause cancer in experimental animals and may be linked to certain human cancers. Viruses have been linked to cervical cancer, Kaposi's sarcoma, and Burkett's lymphoma. A family of related viruses has been linked with a type of lymphoma and leukemia.

Why some persons are more susceptible to cancer than others remains a mystery. In some families there is a hereditary tendency that increases the risk of certain types of cancer, but heredity accounts for only a small number of cancer cases even in high-risk families. Cancer cells apparently arise frequently in all of us, but in most persons the immune system (the system that provides protection from disease organisms and foreign invaders) is capable of destroying them. According to this theory, cancer is a failure of the immune system (See Focus on Immunosurveillance in Chapter 23).

Different persons are known to have varying levels of tolerance to carcinogens. Certain personality factors and styles of coping with stressful life events have been hypothetically linked with higher risk for cancer. For example, studies suggest that individuals who deny and repress anger, and who respond to negative life events with chronic hopelessness and depression, are at higher risk for developing cancer.

Cancer cells are invasive

When a cancer cell multiplies, all the cells derived from it bear the identical defect. When the mutation interferes with the control mechanisms of these cells, they begin to behave abnormally. Two basic defects in behavior that characterize most cancer cells are wild and rapid multiplication and abnormal relations with neighboring cells. Normal cells respect one another's boundaries and form tissues in an orderly, organized manner. In contrast, cancer cells are less adhesive to one another than normal cells and tend to wander through the tissues. They grow helter-skelter upon one another and infiltrate normal tissues (Fig. 4-12). Apparently they are no longer able to receive or respond to signals from surrounding cells; communication is lacking.

Studies indicate that many neoplasms grow to only a few millimeters in diameter and then enter a dormant stage, which may last for months or even years. At some point, cells of the neoplasm release a chemical substance that stimulates nearby blood vessels to develop new capillaries that grow out toward the neoplasm and infiltrate it. Once a blood supply is ensured, the neoplasm grows rapidly and soon becomes life-threatening.

Death from cancer is almost always caused by **metastasis** (meh-**tas**-tah-sis), which is a migration of cancer cells via blood or lymph channels to distant parts of the body. Once there, they multiply, forming new malignant neoplasms, which compete with normal cells for nutrients and may interfere with the function of the tissues being invaded. Cancer often spreads so rapidly and extensively that surgeons are unable to locate all the malignant masses.

Early diagnosis increases survival

Cancer is the second highest cause of death in the United States, and despite recent advances in its treatment, there is no miracle cure on the horizon. Although the prognosis is better in some types of cancer, overall fewer than 50% of cancer patients survive 5 years from the time their cancer is first diagnosed. Currently the key to survival is early diagnosis and treatment with a combination of surgery, radiation therapy, drugs that suppress mitosis (chemotherapy), and immunotherapy, which stimulates the body's defenses.

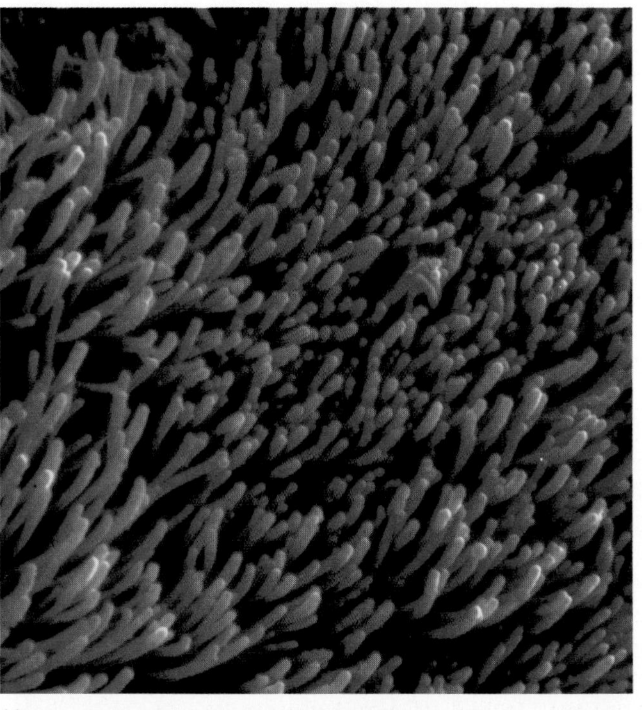

(a)

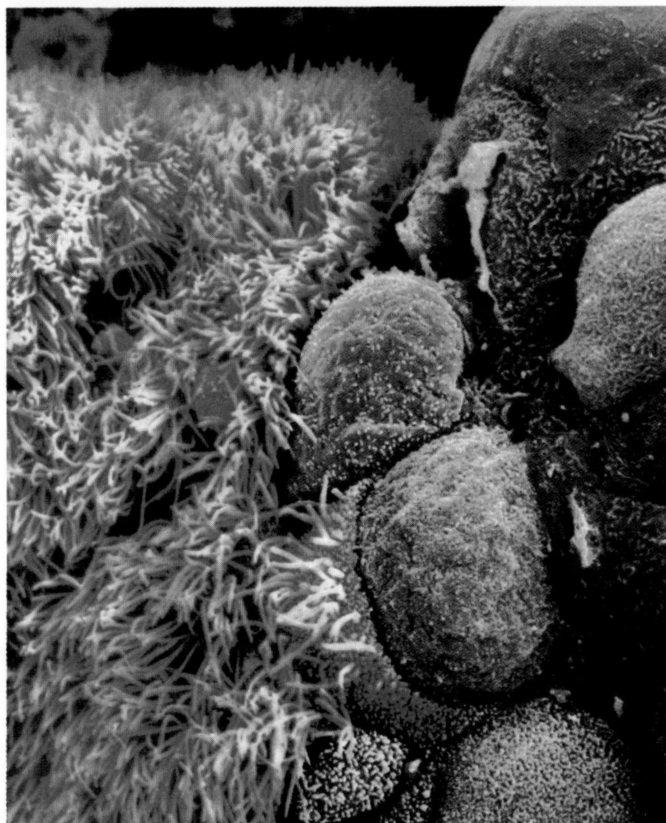

(b)

FIGURE 4-12

Cancer cells multiply rapidly and invade normal tissues, interfering with normal function. (*a*) A healthy bronchial passageway is lined with ciliated cells. The cilia, magnified here about 4000 times, sweep dust and other foreign particles away from the lungs (×4000). (*b*) Cancer cells (shown in green) invade the bronchial wall and crowd out normal cells lining the bronchial tube (×3000). (© Bochringer Ingelheim International GmbH.)

Surgical removal of the tumor and adjacent tissue is most successful when the tumor is small and the cancer has not metastasized. In radiation therapy ionizing radiation is used to destroy cancer cells by inhibiting their ability to multiply. Radiation affects rapidly dividing tissue most, so cancer cells are most susceptible. However, normal body tissues that proliferate rapidly, such as the lining of the digestive tract or bone marrow cells that give rise to blood cells, may also be affected. Chemotherapy is most commonly used when the cancer has metastasized. Most antineoplastic drugs interfere with cell division and damage normal body cells as well as cancer cells.

Cancer is difficult to treat successfully because it is not a single disease. Cancer is an entire family of closely related diseases—there are more than 100 distinct varieties—with different causes. Each type of cancer may have slightly different characteristics, and progression of the disease may vary. Conquering cancer depends on a greater understanding of basic control mechanisms and communication systems of cells.

Summary

I. A tissue is a group of closely associated cells that work together to perform a specific function or group of functions. Four main types of tissue are epithelial, connective, muscle, and nervous tissue.

II. Epithelial tissue covers the body surfaces and lines its cavities; some epithelial tissue is specialized to form glands.
   - A. The functions of epithelial tissue include protection, absorption, secretion, excretion, surface transport, and reception of sensory information.
   - B. Epithelial cells may be squamous, cuboidal, or columnar in shape.
   - C. Epithelial tissue may be simple, stratified, or pseudostratified.
   - D. Epithelial tissue that covers or lines body surfaces consists of epithelial membranes, sheets of cells that are firmly attached to one another.
      1. Simple squamous epithelium consists of a single layer of thin, flattened cells through which materials may easily pass.
      2. Simple cuboidal epithelium consists of a single layer of cube-shaped cells.
      3. Simple columnar epithelium consists of a single layer of elongated cells whose nuclei are located near the base of each cell. It is specialized for protection, absorption, and secretion.
      4. Stratified squamous epithelium consists of several layers of epithelial cells; the surface layer consists of squamous cells. It is specialized to protect underlying tissues.
      5. Pseudostratified columnar epithelium appears stratified because the cells are different lengths and their nuclei are located at different levels within the cells, giving the impression of two layers of cells.
      6. Transitional epithelium, found in the urinary bladder, has the ability to stretch.
   - E. A gland consists of one or more epithelial cells specialized to produce and discharge a particular product.
      1. Endocrine glands secrete hormones into the surrounding tissue fluid; these glands lack ducts.
      2. Exocrine glands, which may be unicellular or multicellular, release their secretions into ducts.

III. Connective tissue joins other tissues of the body together, supports the body, and protects underlying organs.
   - A. Some main types of connective tissue are connective tissue proper, adipose tissue, cartilage, bone, blood, lymph, and tissues that produce blood cells.
   - B. Cells of connective tissue are usually separated by large amounts of intercellular substance.
   - C. Mesenchyme cells are undifferentiated cells that give rise to many types of connective tissue cells. Fibroblasts are cells that produce the fibers and the protein and carbohydrate complexes of the matrix. Macrophages are scavenger cells. Mast cells contain histamine, heparin, and serotonin.
   - D. Collagen fibers, reticular fibers, and elastic fibers are characteristic of connective tissue.
   - E. Connective tissue proper connects the body structures and may be loose, dense, elastic, or reticular.
      1. Loose connective tissue (areolar) is the most widely distributed connective tissue in the body; it is found as a filling between body parts and in the subcutaneous layer.
      2. Dense connective tissue consists mainly of collagen fibers and is very strong. It may be irregular (in dermis of skin) or regular (tendons).
      3. Elastic connective tissue consists mainly of bundles of parallel elastic fibers that snap back into place when stretched. This tissue is located in the heart, walls of large arteries, and in the respiratory passageways.
      4. Reticular connective tissue consists mainly of reticular fibers; it forms a supporting network for some organs.
   - F. Adipose tissue stores fat and releases it when fuel is needed by the body cells.
   - G. Cartilage is a hard, strong connective tissue that forms the outer parts of bones at joints and gives support to some soft tissues.
      1. Three types of cartilage are hyaline, fibrocartilage, and elastic cartilage.
      2. Hyaline cartilage, the most common type, forms the ends of bones at joints and is the major support of the nose and the fetal skeleton.
      3. Fibrocartilage has characteristics between those of hyaline cartilage and dense connective tissue.
      4. Elastic cartilage is similar to hyaline cartilage but has elastic fibers as well as collagen fibers.
   - H. Bone is the rigid supporting tissue of the mature skeleton.
      1. Osteocytes are located in lacunae and surrounded by intercellular substance consisting of mineral salts laid down over collagen fibers.

2. In compact bone, the lacunae are arranged in concentric circles around central tubes called haversian canals.

I. Other connective tissues include blood, lymph, and the tissues that produce blood cells.

IV. Muscle tissue is composed of cells specialized to contract.
   A. Skeletal muscle is striated and is under voluntary control.
   B. Cardiac muscle is striated and is controlled by involuntary neural messages from the brain.
   C. Smooth muscle, also involuntary, is responsible for movement of food through the digestive tract, changing the diameter of blood vessels, and other forms of movement within body organs.

V. Nervous tissue is specialized to receive stimuli, to transmit information, and to control the action of muscles and glands.

VI. Neoplasms are a result of abnormal tissue growth and may be benign or malignant.
   A. Cancer is triggered by a mutation in the genes that code for cell growth and division.
   B. Cancer cells are characterized by wild multiplication and metastasis to other locations.
   C. Malignant tumors are more likely to be successfully removed if they are caught before the cancer has metastasized.

Post-test

Matching

Select the most appropriate answer from Column B. The same answer may be used more than once or not at all.

Column A	Column B
____ 1. Covers body surfaces	a. muscle tissue
____ 2. Supports organs of the body	b. epithelial tissue
____ 3. Transmits messages to various parts of the body	c. connective tissue
____ 4. Specialized for moving body parts	d. nervous tissue
____ 5. Forms glands	
____ 6. Fibroblasts are found in this tissue	
____ 7. Bone is an example	

Column A	Column B
____ 8. Makes up the outer layer (epidermis) of skin	a. simple squamous epithelium
____ 9. Lines intestines	b. stratified squamous epithelium
____ 10. Makes up air sacs of lungs	c. simple cuboidal epithelium
____ 11. Most widely distributed connective tissue in body; fills space between many body parts	d. simple columnar epithelium
____ 12. Stores fat and releases it when fuel is needed	e. adipose tissue
____ 13. Contains chondrocytes	f. loose connective tissue
____ 14. Contains haversian systems (osteons)	g. bone
____ 15. Contracts only when stimulated by nerves	h. cartilage
	i. cardiac muscle
	j. skeletal muscle

16. Glands that secrete a clear, watery substance are called ______________ glands.
17. Glands that lack ducts are called ______________ glands.
18. The intercellular substance of connective tissue usually consists of threadlike microscopic ______________ scattered through an amorphous ______________.
19. The three main types of fibers found in connective tissue are ______________ ______________ ______________.
20. Undifferentiated cells found in connective tissue and thought to give rise to other cell types are ______________ ______________.

Review questions

1. Define the term tissue. List the four basic types of tissue found in the body and give their general functions.
2. Contrast epithelium with connective tissue.
3. Contrast simple, stratified, and pseudostratified epithelium.

4. Draw a diagram of each of the following types of epithelium, briefly describe and locate them in the body, and give the functions of each. (a) simple squamous, (b) simple cuboidal, (c) simple columnar, (d) stratified squamous, (e) pseudostratified, (f) transitional.
5. Define the term gland, and contrast endocrine and exocrine glands.
6. Compare simple and compound exocrine glands and give an example of each.
7. Describe the microscopic appearance of the following connective tissues, give the functions of each, and locate them in the body. (a) loose connective tissue, (b) dense connective tissue, (c) adipose tissue, (d) cartilage, (e) bone.
8. Briefly compare the three types of muscle tissue with respect to structure, function, and location.
9. Contrast a benign neoplasm with a malignant one. In what ways do cancer cells differ from normal cells?

Post-test answers

1. b 2. c 3. d 4. a 5. b 6. c 7. c
8. b 9. d 10. a 11. f 12. e 13. h
14. g 15. j 16. serous 17. endocrine
18. fibers; matrix 19. collagen, elastic, reticular
20. mesenchyme cells

THE INTEGUMENTARY SYSTEM

CHAPTER OUTLINE

- **I. Functions of the skin**
- **II. Layers of the skin**
  - A. Epidermis
  - B. Dermis
- **III. Specialized structures**
  - A. Hair
  - B. Epidermal glands
    - 1. Sebaceous glands
    - 2. Sweat glands
    - 3. Ceruminous glands
  - C. Nails
- **IV. Skin color**
- **V. Skin in stress**
  - A. Repair of wounds
    - □ Focus on skin disorders
  - B. Burns
  - C. Skin cancer

LEARNING OBJECTIVES

After you have studied this chapter you should be able to:

1 Identify the structures that make up the integumentary system.

2 Relate each function of the integumentary system to the structure of the system, and explain how each function helps maintain homeostasis.

3 Draw and label a diagram of the skin including the strata of the epidermis.

4 Trace a basal cell through the epidermal strata, describing its differentiation and eventual fate.

5 Contrast the structure and functions of the epidermis, dermis, and subcutaneous layer.

6 Describe the origin and structure of hair and explain its growth.

7 Describe the origin of sebaceous glands and describe the secretion of sebum.

8 Describe the homeostatic action of sweat glands in maintaining normal body temperature.

9 Locate apocrine sweat glands and give their functions.

10 Describe the structure of a nail.

11 Describe the process of pigmentation and explain how the skin responds homeostatically to excessive exposure to sunlight.

12 Describe the process of inflammation and its characteristic symptoms, and explain why it is a homeostatic mechanism.

13 Describe the process of wound healing.

14 Distinguish between first-, second-, and third-degree burns, and tell how each is treated.

15 Relate exposure to ultraviolet light to skin cancer and identify three types of skin cancer.

Scanning electron micrograph of hair follicle and sebaceous (oil) gland. Basal cells are present at top (× 10). (CNRI/Phototake.)

5

KEY CONCEPTS

The integumentary system consists of the skin and its hair, nails, and glands.

The integumentary system protects the body, helps prevent dehydration, helps maintain body temperature, and helps excrete excess water and wastes.

The skin consists of two main layers: epidermis and dermis.

The cells of the epidermis proliferate continuously, mature, and then die as they move toward the surface of the skin; as they are sloughed off, they are replaced.

The skin with its glands, hair, nails, and other structures makes up the **integumentary system** (in-*teg*-yoo-**men**-tah-ree), the body's tough outer protective covering (Fig. 5-1). This is the body system with which you are most intimately acquainted, perhaps because it is at least partly exposed to view. Perhaps for this reason a good deal of attention is lavished upon the skin. It is scrubbed, creamed, and coated with cosmetics; its hair is cut, shaved, curled, and otherwise fashioned; and its nails are manicured.

The skin is also important in communication. You may touch, kiss, squeeze, stroke, or hit it. Involuntary changes in the skin reflect emotional states. For example, you may blush with embarrassment, blanch with fear or rage, redden with exertion, or sweat excessively when anxious. In addition, the appearance, coloration, temperature, and feel of the skin are important indicators of general health and of many disease states. The branch of medicine that focuses on the diagnosis and treatment of skin disorders is **dermatology.**

The skin functions as a protective barrier

The skin is the outer boundary of the body—the part in direct contact with the external environment. It is subjected to continuous wear and tear, to drying, to cold and heat, to toxic substances, and often to cuts, bruises, scrapes, and wounds. One of the largest organs—almost 6 square meters (20 or so square feet)—the skin helps to preserve the balanced internal environment. The skin presents a barrier to ultraviolet light and to foreign substances that might otherwise enter the body. It also presents a barrier to water and other substances within the body that might otherwise leak out. We can summarize the numerous functions of the skin as follows:

1. **Protection.** Skin serves as a protective barrier against mechanical injury and penetration of many kinds of harmful chemicals. Anyone who has suffered a bout with poison ivy knows, however, that some substances do manage to get through the skin. Absorption through the skin of some chemicals (e.g., phenol) can cause damage to internal organs, and absorption of biocides such as Parathion can result in lethal poisoning. However, all in all the skin does a remarkable job

of keeping most foreign materials out of the body.

2. **Defense.** The skin is the body's first line of defense against disease organisms. Though many types of bacteria make their home on the body's surface, healthy skin prevents their entrance into the interior.

3. **Prevention of dehydration.** The cells of the body are immersed in an internal sea, a carefully regulated, dilute salt solution essential to life. Yet, as terrestrial creatures, humans move about in the relatively dry environment of air. The skin prevents excessive loss of moisture so that the cells do not dry out. We can even swim in salt water that is hypertonic to body tissues without shrinking. Acting also to keep materials out, this relatively waterproof integument makes it possible to swim for hours in fresh water without becoming waterlogged.

FIGURE 5-1

Scanning electron micrograph of the surface of the skin (approximately ×250). (Courtesy of Dr. Karen A. Holbrook.)

4. **Maintenance of body temperature.** Humans are almost naked organisms. Their lack of an insulating fur coat is compensated for by a complex temperature-regulating system. Extensive capillary networks and sweat glands in the skin are an important part of that system.

5. **Excretion of wastes.** Sweat glands also excrete excess water and some wastes from the body.

6. **Reception of stimuli.** Located within the skin are sensory structures for receiving stimuli of touch, pressure, heat, cold, and pain. These receptors relay important information about the environment to the central nervous system.

7. **Vitamin D synthesis.** Skin is the site of vitamin D synthesis. When skin is exposed to the ultraviolet rays of the sun, a cholesterol compound in the skin is converted to vitamin D.

The skin consists of epidermis and dermis

Skin consists of two main layers: an outer **epidermis** (*ep*-ih-**dur**-mis) and an inner **dermis** (**dur**-mis). The epidermis is a thin epithelial membrane. Dermis, a thicker layer, consists of connective tissue. A deep extension of the dermis, the **subcutaneous layer** (*sub*-kew-**tay**-nee-us), anchors the skin to the underlying tissues (Fig. 5-2).

The epidermis continuously replaces itself

Epidermis is composed of stratified squamous epithelium. Cells continuously proliferate from its deepest region, then mature as they are pushed toward the outer surface by newer cells beneath. Eventually they die and slough off. Over most parts of the body the epidermis is only about as thick as a page of this book, yet it consists of four or five sublayers, or **strata** (**stray**-tah).

Several types of cells can be distinguished in the epidermis. Most numerous are the **keratinocytes** (keh-**rat**-ih-no-*sites*) which synthesize **keratin.** An insoluble protein, keratin imparts strength and waterproofing to the epidermis and thus is essential to the protective functions of the skin. A second type of cell in the epidermis is the **melanocyte** (**mel**-ah-no-*site*), or pigment cell. Melanocytes produce the pigment **melanin.** Another epidermal cell type, the *Langerhans cell*, is a type of macrophage produced in bone marrow. Langerhans cells migrate to the epidermis where they participate in immune responses. Exposure to ultraviolet light impairs the function of these cells.

The strata of the epidermis, from deepest to most superficial, are described below (Fig. 5-2).

1. **Stratum basale.** The deepest portion of the epidermis is the stratum basale (ba-**say**-lee). This sublayer is also called the *stratum germinativum* or *malpighian layer.* Stratum basale consists of a single layer of cuboidal or low columnar epithelial cells resting on the basal lamina and underlying dermis. Adjacent epithelial cells are attached by desmosomes. Stratum basale is the reproductive layer of the epidermis; the basal cells constantly divide by mitosis, providing a continuous supply of new cells to replace those lost from the upper strata.

2. **Stratum spinosum.** Some of the cells proliferated in the basal layer are pushed upward to form the stratum spinosum, also called the *prickle cell layer.* This layer consists of about ten rows of cells that fit closely together and are connected by desmosomes. When skin tissue is fixed for microscopic examination, the cells of this layer shrink slightly, causing the desmosomes to protrude visibly. This gives the cells a prickly or spiny appearance, from which they get their name. As prickle cells mature, they lose their ability to divide.

3. **Stratum granulosum.** Moving outward toward the skin surface, prickle cells gradually flatten and become part of the stratum granulosum. The cells of this layer contain granules filled with **keratohyalin** (*ker*-ah-tow-**hi**-a-lin), a chemical precursor to keratin.

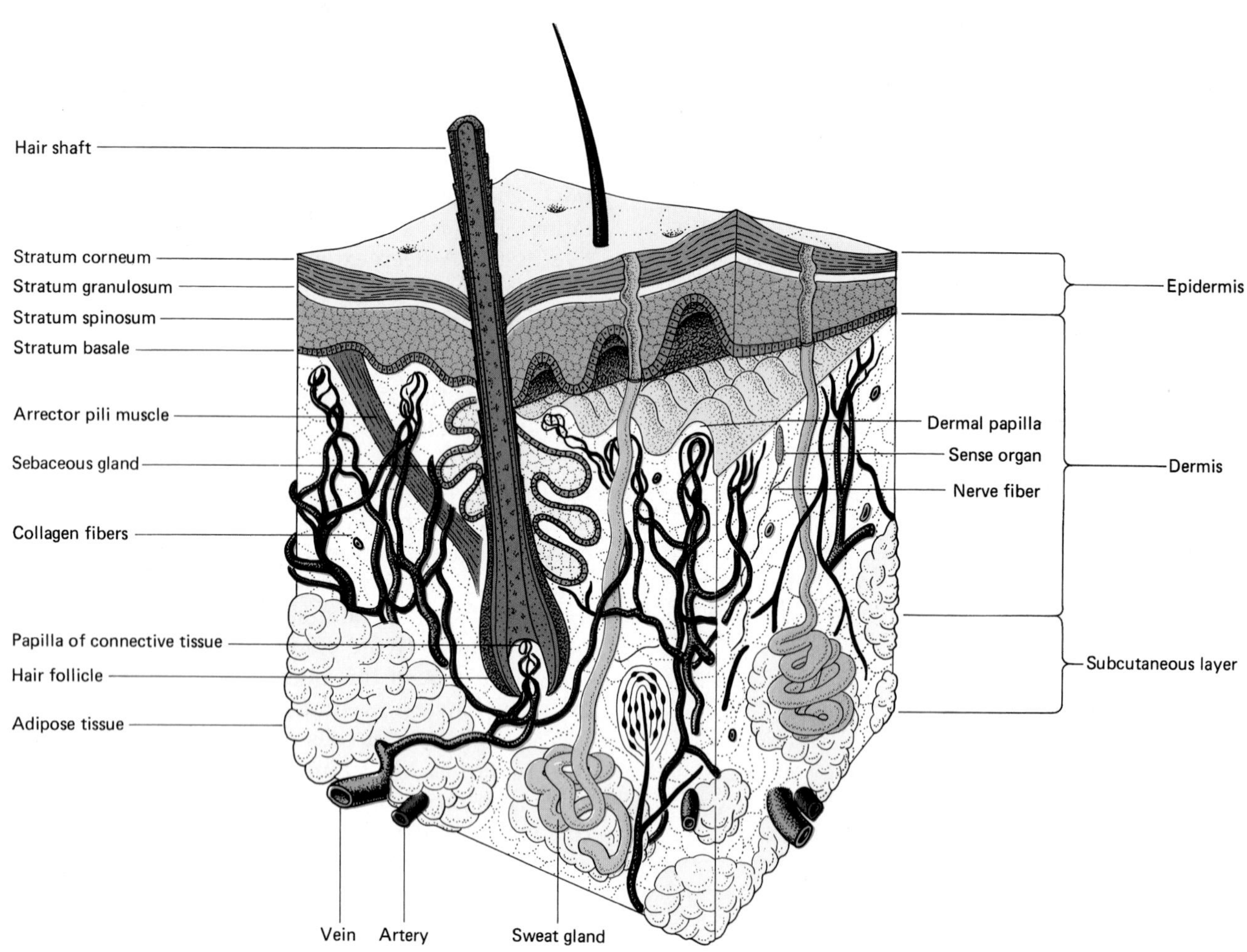

FIGURE 5-2

Microscopic structure of the skin. The epidermis is raised at one end to show the dermal papillae.

4. **Stratum lucidum.** This layer is present only in the thick skin of the palms and soles and is often difficult to see. When visible it appears as a wavy, thin line just above the stratum granulosum.

5. **Stratum corneum.** As cells continue to be pushed toward the outer surface, they move into the outer horny layer of skin, the stratum corneum. The nuclei and other organelles are destroyed by lysosomal enzymes, and the cells die. Stratum corneum consists of about 20 layers of dead cells in various stages of disintegration. Each cell becomes a tiny sac of keratin, the tough waterproofing protein of the epidermis. As they are pushed outward, these cells resemble dead scales. They are closely packed together and serve as a waterproof protective covering for the body.

It takes about 2 weeks for a basal cell to be pushed up into the stratum corneum, then another 2 weeks for the remains of that cell to slough off. Thousands of dead cells slough off the skin surface each day, only to be replaced by new ones from the deeper layers of the epidermis.

The dermis consists of connective tissue

The dermis is the thick layer of skin beneath the epidermis (Fig. 5-2). Its average thickness is 1 to 2 millimeters but is more than 3 millimeters thick on the soles and palms. The dermis is thinner in females than in males. Blood vessels and nerves, which are generally absent in epidermal tissue, are found throughout the dermis. Specialized skin structures such as hair follicles and glands are formed from cells of stratum basale but push down into the dermis and are located there. Cells of the dermis as well as the deeper layers of the epidermis are bathed by tissue fluid.

The upper portion of the dermis, the **papillary layer** (**pap**-il-*lar*-ee), consists of loose connective tissue containing collagen and elastic fibers. The papillary layer has many small finger-like projections called **papillae** (pah-**pil**-ee), which project into the epidermal tissue. Extensive networks of capillaries in the papillae deliver oxygen and nutrients to the cells of the epidermis and also function in temperature regulation.

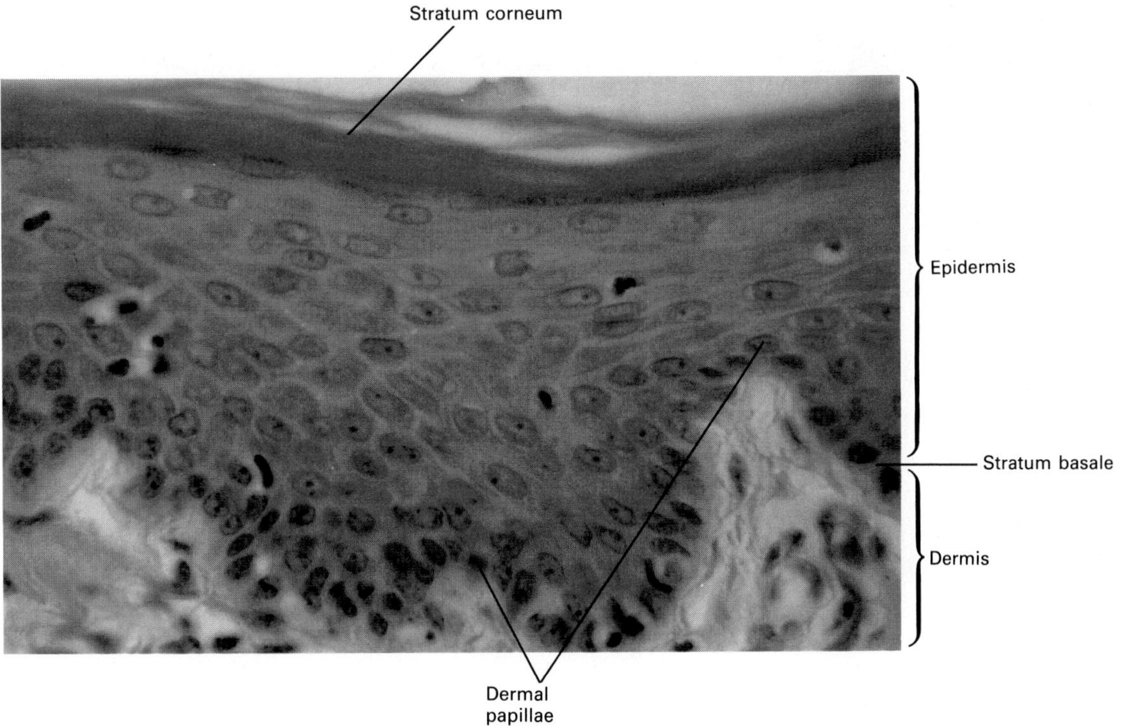

FIGURE 5-3

Photomicrograph of skin. Epidermis and papillary layer of dermis. Note the scalelike cells of the stratum corneum sloughing off the surface of the skin. (David Phillips/Visuals Unlimited.)

Patterns of ridges and grooves visible on the skin of the soles and palms, including the fingertips, reflect the arrangement of the dermal papillae beneath. Unique to each individual, these patterns provide the fingerprints so useful to law enforcement officials. The epidermal ridges are friction ridges that enable us to hold onto objects we grasp.

The region of the dermis below the papillary layer is called the **reticular layer** (reh-**tik**-u-lar). The reticular layer consists of irregular dense connective tissue composed mainly of collagen and elastic fibers. This layer gets its name from the reticular (netlike) arrangement of the interlacing collagen fibers. Collagen is largely responsible for the mechanical strength of the skin. Together collagen and elastic fibers permit the skin to stretch and then resume its original shape again.

The subcutaneous layer, or **superficial fascia,** is a deep extension of the dermis. This layer consists of loose connective tissue, usually including adipose tissue. The subcutaneous layer attaches the skin to underlying tissues, but because of its loose construction, the skin may be moved about over the muscle and bone beneath.

This thick fatty layer helps to protect underlying organs from mechanical shock and also insulates the body, thus conserving heat. Fat stored within the adipose tissue can be mobilized and utilized for energy when adequate food is not available. Distribution of fat in the subcutaneous layer is largely responsible for the characteristic body contours of the female as compared with the male.

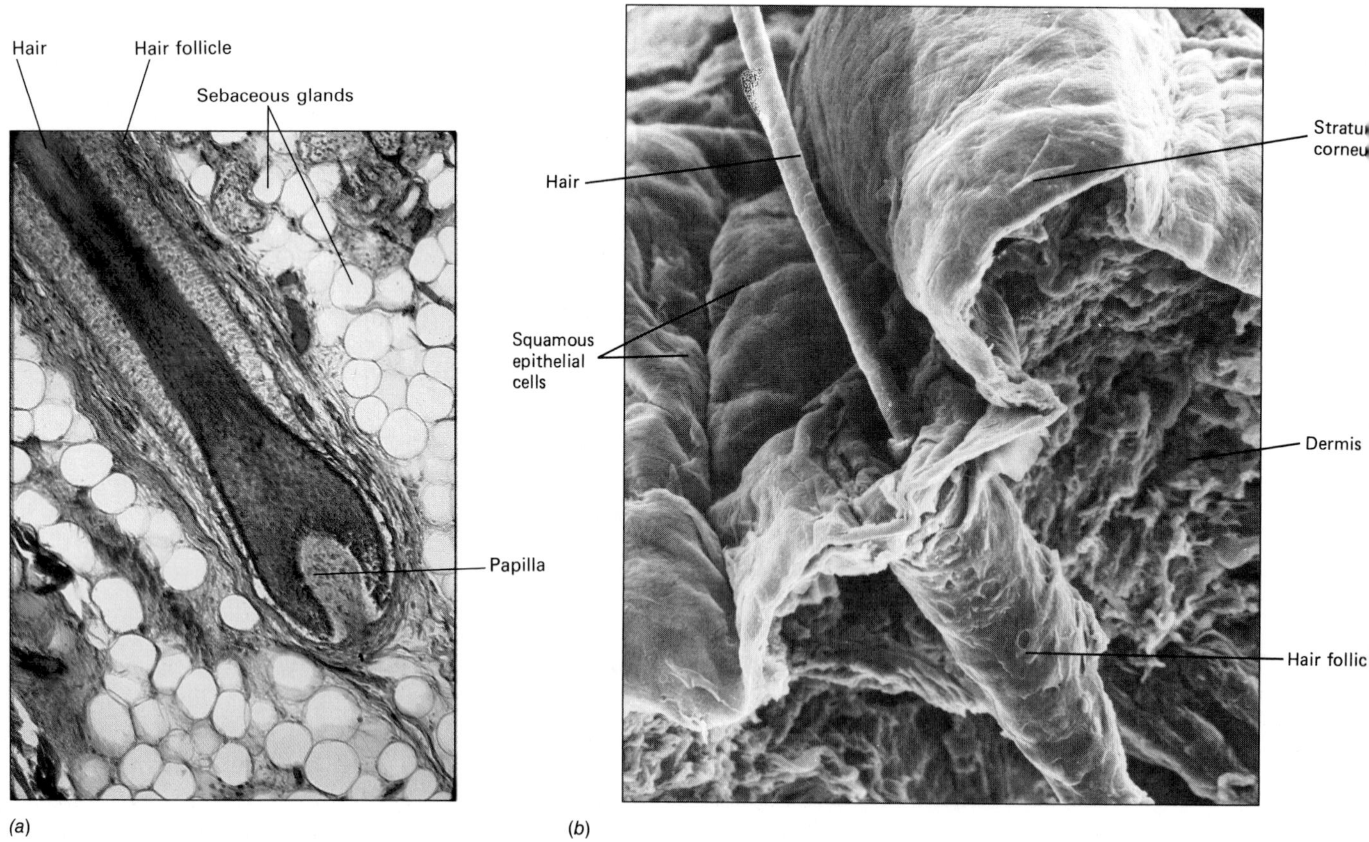

FIGURE 5-4

(a) Photomicrograph of hair (approximately ×150). Note persistent nuclei in hair cells.
(b) Scanning electron micrograph of human skin showing hair follicle (approximately ×250).
(Courtesy of Dr. Karen A. Holbrook.)

Specialized structures of the skin include hair, glands, and nails

During embryonic development, thousands of small groups of epidermal cells from the stratum basale push down into the dermis. They multiply and differentiate to form hair follicles and glands. Hair and nails have protective functions.

The main function of hair is protection

Hair protects the head from injury and from the sun. On other parts of the body, hair also serves a protective function. For example, the eyelashes protect the eyes from foreign matter. Hair also plays a role in sexual attraction. It is found on all skin surfaces except the palms and soles. On the less hairy parts of the body the fine, short, downy hairs are hardly noticeable.

The part of the hair that we see is the **shaft;** the portion below the skin surface is the **root** (Figs. 5-1 and 5-4). The root together with its epithelial and connective tissue coverings is called the **hair follicle.** At the bottom of the follicle is a **papilla** (a little mound) of connective tissue containing capillaries that deliver nourishment to the cells of the follicle.

Just above the papilla is a group of epithelial cells, derived from the stratum basale, which multiplies, giving rise to the cells of the hair. Each hair consists of cells that proliferate, manufacture keratin as they move outward, and then die. The shaft of the hair consists of dead cells and their products. That is why hair can be cut without any sensation of pain. As long as the follicle remains intact, new hair will continue to grow. If the follicle is destroyed, as by electrolysis, no new hair can form. New hair follicles are not formed after birth.

Hair grows in cycles. Each hair follicle goes through a growing phase, followed by a resting phase. After that, a new hair begins to grow in the same follicle, pushing the old one out. In humans the phases are not synchronized, so that there is always some hair growing while some follicles rest. Normally about 90% of scalp hair is in the growth phase. Up to 90 hairs may be shed each day, but since the scalp has about 100,000, they are hardly missed. Besides, the ones shed are rapidly replaced. Scalp hair grows about 1 inch every 2 to 3 months. How long a particular hair grows depends upon the length of time it spends in its growth phase. This varies somewhat among individuals. Cutting or shaving hair has no effect on its growth.

Because keratin can be stretched, hair can be elongated, especially when wet. Chemical bonds that help hold the protein bundles in the hair together can be broken by the reducing agents (agents that add electrons) used in permanent waves. Hair can then be curled as desired and the chemical bonds established in new positions by applying oxidizing agents (agents that remove electrons). Some persons have the genes for producing hair that curls naturally. Hair color, also determined genetically, depends upon the amount and distribution of pigment.

Tiny bundles of smooth muscle are associated with hair follicles. These **arrector pili** muscles contract in response to cold or fear, making the hairs stand up straight. Skin around the hair shaft is pulled up into "gooseflesh."

Epidermal glands are found in the dermis

Like hair follicles, sebaceous glands and sweat glands develop from epidermal cells that move down into the dermis (Fig. 5-5).

SEBACEOUS GLANDS ARE ATTACHED TO HAIR FOLLICLES

Sebaceous glands (see-**bay**-shus), sometimes called "oil glands," are generally attached to hair follicles. They are connected to the hair follicles by little ducts through which they release their secretion (Fig. 5-6). These glands are largest and most numerous on the face and scalp but are found all over the body except in the palms, soles, and dorsal surfaces of the feet. In a few regions—lips, tip of the penis, labia minora of the external female genitals, and a few others—the sebaceous glands are not associated with hairs and their ducts open directly onto the surface of the skin.

Sebaceous glands are holocrine glands, which means that the cells themselves become part of the secretion. Sebaceous gland cells proliferate, and then some die as they move outward. The dead cells break down, becoming **sebum** (**see**-bum), an oily mixture of cholesterol, fats, and other substances. Sebum functions to oil the hair, lubricate the surface of the skin, and form an oily film that retards water loss from the body surface. Sebum inhibits the growth of certain bacteria and may have antifungal properties.

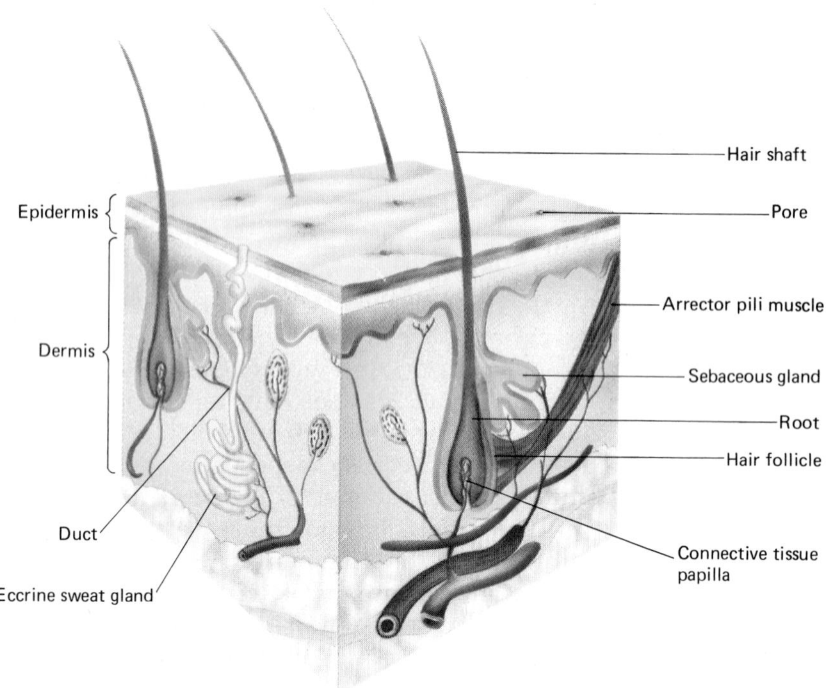

FIGURE 5-5

Glands of the skin. An eccrine sweat gland is a simple, tubular exocrine gland with a coiled duct. A sebaceous gland is a simple, branched acinar (alveolar) gland that releases its secretion into a hair follicle. The sebaceous gland is a holocrine gland.

During childhood, sebaceous glands are relatively inactive. At puberty they are activated by increased secretion of the hormone testosterone in both males and females. This stepped-up activity sometimes leads to the lesions (abnormal changes) characteristic of acne, a condition very common during puberty.

Sometimes sebum accumulates in the duct of the sebaceous gland and hair follicle and obstructs it, forming a comedo (blackhead or whitehead). In a blackhead, or open *comedo,* sebum and dead cells containing the dark pigment melanin block the duct. The black color is due to the melanin rather than to dirt. It is thought that blackheads evolve from whiteheads (closed comedos) in which the keratin is less compact and the duct narrower.

Should the duct of the sebaceous gland rupture, allowing sebum, keratin, and perhaps bacteria to spill into the dermis, the skin becomes inflamed. The red *papules* (pimples) and *pustules* (lesions containing pus) characteristic of acne are formed in this way. Squeezing these lesions (as many persons do) causes an increase in the inflammation and may lead to scarring.

SWEAT GLANDS HELP REGULATE BODY TEMPERATURE

About 3 million sweat glands (also called sudoriferous glands) in the skin help regulate body temperature. In the process they excrete excess water and small amounts of nitrogen wastes. Sweat glands are most numerous on the forehead, soles, and on the palms (about 3000 per square inch), where they provide moisture that strengthens grip. There are two types of sweat glands based on structure and location: *eccrine sweat glands* and *apocrine sweat glands.*

Each **eccrine sweat gland** is a tiny coiled tube in the dermis or subcutaneous tissue, with a duct that extends up through the skin and opens onto the surface (Figs. 5-2 and 5-5). Water and solutes from the interstitial fluid pass into the sweat gland, partly by diffusion and partly by active transport. Sodium chloride (salt) is then returned to the interstitial fluid by the cells lining the sweat gland duct, a process known as reabsorption. Sweat, or perspiration, consists mainly of water, some salts, and a trace of the nitrogenous waste products urea and uric acid. When profuse sweating occurs, the rate of salt reabsorption cannot keep up with the large amounts of sweat excreted, so that proportionately more salt is lost in the sweat. This is why people engaged in strenuous physical exercise must replace salts to maintain homeostasis.

Within the body, heat is generated by metabolic activities and by muscular movements. Because heat is required for evaporation, the body becomes cooler as sweat evaporates from the skin. About 1 quart of water is excreted in sweat each day. Normally, though, perspiration is not noticed. Only when it is produced more quickly than it can evaporate does it accumulate on the skin and cause annoyance. This is most apt to happen on a humid day when the air already contains a great deal of water vapor.

Apocrine sweat glands are found in association with hairs and concentrated in a few specific areas of the body such as the armpits and genital areas. These glands discharge into hair follicles.

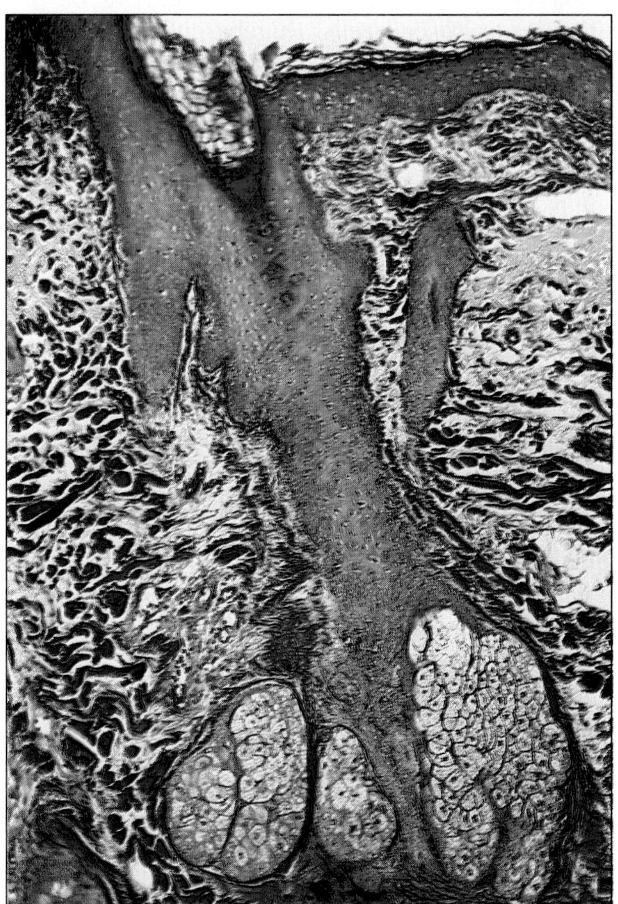

FIGURE 5-6

Photomicrograph of sebaceous glands (light-staining areas) at base of hair in human scalp. Hair follicle (slanting red-staining structure) and epidermis (horizontal red-staining area) are visible. Also note blood vessels in the dermis (approximately ×25). (Ed Reschke.)

Their secretion is thick, sticky, and initially odorless. However, certain bacteria that inhabit the skin surface begin to decompose this secretion, causing it to become odorous. Deodorants kill these bacteria and replace the odor with a more perfumed scent; antiperspirants reduce moisture, thereby inhibiting the growth of bacteria. Emotional stress or sexual stimulation promotes secretion of these glands. Apocrine glands begin to function at puberty. These glands are more numerous in other mammals and their main function appears to be production of a distinctive body odor or scent.

Both eccrine and apocrine sweat glands are merocrine glands; they release their secretions without loss of cytoplasm or damage to their cells. The name apocrine sweat glands was coined when histologists thought that some of the apical cytoplasm was lost in the process of secretion. However, investigators now think that the cell fragments seen in the lumen of the gland in histological preparations are artifacts of the process of preparing the tissue.

CERUMINOUS GLANDS ARE LOCATED IN THE EAR CANAL

Ceruminous glands (seh-**roo**-mih-nus) are modified sweat glands found in the external auditory meatus (ear canal). These coiled tubular glands are located in the submucosa. Their ducts open either directly onto the surface of the ear canal or into sebaceous ducts. The secretion of the ceruminous glands together with secretion from the sebaceous glands is **cerumen,** or wax. Cerumen provides a sticky barrier to foreign agents entering the ear canal.

Nails consist mainly of keratin

Nails are horny plates that cover the dorsal surfaces of the terminal ends of the fingers and toes. Nails are a modification of the horny epidermal cells and consist mainly of a closely compressed, tough keratin. The **nail bed** is the visible region beneath the body of the nail. The nail bed lacks a stratum corneum (Fig. 5-7). The proximal edge of the nail plate is the **root** of the nail.

Nails are somewhat transparent and they appear pink because blood in the underlying capillaries shows through. Near the root there is a whitish crescent-shaped region called the **lunula.**

The **cuticle** (or eponychium) is a narrow region of epidermis that spreads onto the free surface of the nail plate.

The epithelium beneath the lunula is called the **nail matrix.** This region is responsible for nail growth. Superficial cells of the nail matrix are continuously converted into nail substance. Growth is continuous at a rate of about 0.1 millimeter per day. Though continuously being worn down at their distal ends, nails are also deliberately trimmed. Lost nails are regenerated, but the process requires several months.

Melanin helps determine skin color

Three factors determine skin color. When the pigment hemoglobin in the red blood cells combines with oxygen, forming oxyhemoglobin, it has a bright red color. Oxyhemoglobin in the underlying blood vessels gives skin a reddish color. A second component of skin color is the pigment **carotene** (**kar**-oh-teen) which is ingested in fruits, vegetables, and egg yolk. Carotene, which is converted to vitamin A in the skin, imparts a yellow shade to skin. Finally, the protein **melanin** (**mel**-uh-nin) is produced by pigment cells, called *melanocytes.* Depending on the amount present, melanin contributes a brown to black color to the skin.

Skin color is inherited. In dark-skinned individuals the melanocytes are more active and produce more and larger granules of melanin. A combination of melanin and carotene is responsible for the yellowish skin color of Asiatic individuals. An *albino* is a person of any race who has inherited the inability to produce the pigment melanin.

The melanocytes are located in the stratum basale of the epidermis and in the connective tissue of the dermis. Melanocytes synthesize melanin from the amino acid tyrosine. An enzyme called tyrosinase catalyzes the reaction. Derived from embryonic nerve tissue, melanocytes have long cytoplasmic projections similar to the dendrites of nerve cells (Fig. 5-8). They use these projections to transfer pigment granules to other epidermal cells. Cells that receive pigment carry it with them as they move into the stratum corneum, thereby imparting a characteristic coloration to the skin. Melanocytes present in the lowest layer of hair follicle cells pass pigment granules on to hair cells, thereby giving color to hair as well as to skin. Melanocyte-stimulating hormone (MSH), produced by the anterior pituitary gland, stimulates melanin synthesis and dispersion of melanocytes throughout the epidermis.

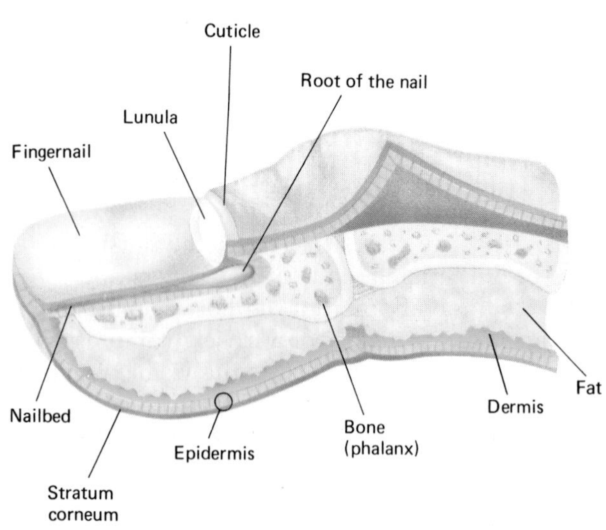

FIGURE 5-7

Nails form from keratinized epithelial cells produced in the lunula region of the nail.

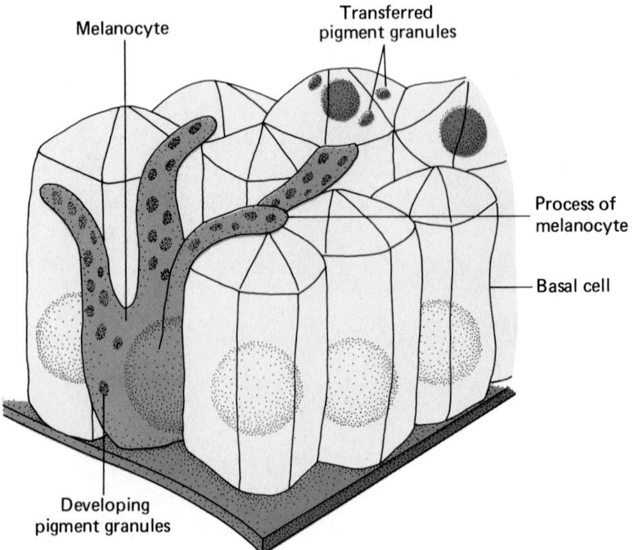

FIGURE 5-8

A melanocyte containing pigment granules. These granules are apparently released from the tips of the long cytoplasmic processes and enter surrounding epidermal cells.

Melanin is an important protective screen against the sun because it absorbs harmful ultraviolet rays. Exposure to the sun stimulates an increase in the amount of melanin produced and causes the skin to become darker. The suntan is a protective response to exposure to ultraviolet rays. Melanin may be distributed unevenly, especially in light-skinned individuals, resulting in freckling.

Exposure to sun can be harmful. When the melanin is not able to absorb all the ultraviolet rays the skin becomes inflamed, or sunburned. The tan so prized by sun worshippers is actually a sign that the skin has been exposed to too much ultraviolet radiation. Excessive exposure to sun over a period of years, especially in fair-skinned individuals, eventually results in wrinkling of the skin and sometimes in skin cancer. Because dark-skinned people have more melanin, they suffer less sunburn, wrinkling, and skin cancer.

The skin is subject to many types of stress

As the outermost part of the body, the skin is subject to cuts, scratches, bruises, burns, poisons, bacterial invasion, and other insults (See Focus on Skin Disorders). When injured, the skin has an amazing ability to repair itself. The skin also reflects inner turmoil. It flushes, pales, sweats, and bristles with the emotions; it scales, weeps, cracks, and swells with allergies. Pale skin may indicate anemia, yellowish skin may signal liver malfunction, and blue skin may indicate circulatory or respiratory disorder. Skin is also subject to several types of cancer.

FOCUS ON . . . Skin disorders

Abscess: a cavity formed in disintegrating tissue in which pus collects

Callus: a slightly thickened area of stratum corneum (the horny layer of the epidermis) that develops in response to constant friction or pressure

Carbuncle: a painful cluster of boils in the deep dermis and subcutaneous tissue; a type of infection with abscesses that discharge pus to the skin surface

Corn: similar to a callus, but the thickened tissue is more separated and distinct from surrounding tissue; caused by friction and pressure

Cyst: a thick-walled sac that contains fluid or semisolid material

Decubitus ulcer: a bedsore; a pressure sore that develops in patients confined to bed for long periods of time, especially when they are unable to change position frequently

Dermatitis: inflammation of the skin

Furuncle: a boil; a localized infection (usually caused by staphylococcal bacteria) that develops into an abscess that drains to the skin surface

Impetigo: an acute bacterial infection of the skin characterized by lesions that rupture and develop distinct yellow crusts

Miliaria: heat rash; prickly heat; acute inflammation of the skin associated with blocked sweat gland ducts

Nevus: a lesion (disruption of normal tissue structure) containing melanocytes (pigment cells); a mole

Nodule: a solid mass larger than 1 cm that is formed from groups of cells or cell products within the dermis or subcutaneous tissue

Papule: a small, elevated solid lesion formed from cells, cell products, or accumulated fluid in the dermis or epidermis; usually smaller than 0.5 cm; a pimple

Pediculosis: a skin disease caused by infestation of blood-sucking lice

Phthirus: a species of louse that infects the pubic area and is most often spread by sexual contact (pubic lice are commonly referred to as "crabs")

Pruritus: itching of the skin when there is no visible lesion; may be due to irritation of a sensory nerve

Psoriasis: a genetically determined skin disease in which papules and plaques form, especially on the elbows and knees

Pustule: a small elevation (vesicle) of the skin containing pus

Scabies: a condition caused by infestation with itch mites, characterized by severe itching

Shingles: a viral disease characterized by painful blisters along certain nerve pathways; more formally called herpes zoster

Wart: an epidermal growth induced by infection by a specific virus

The skin repairs wounds

A **wound** is any bodily injury caused by physical means that disrupts the normal continuity of structures. When the skin (or any other tissue) is injured, it reacts homeostatically by attempting to protect itself against harmful agents and by repairing the wound. Mechanisms are activated that destroy invading bacteria, dilute harmful chemicals, dispose of dead or injured cells, and even wall off the injured area. These reactions, collectively referred to as **inflammation,** are characterized by *redness, swelling, heat,* and *pain.* Inflammation, the most basic pathological response, helps protect the tissue from further injury and sets up the conditions that promote repair.

Suppose that you have just cut your finger. It bleeds, but not for long because the blood clots

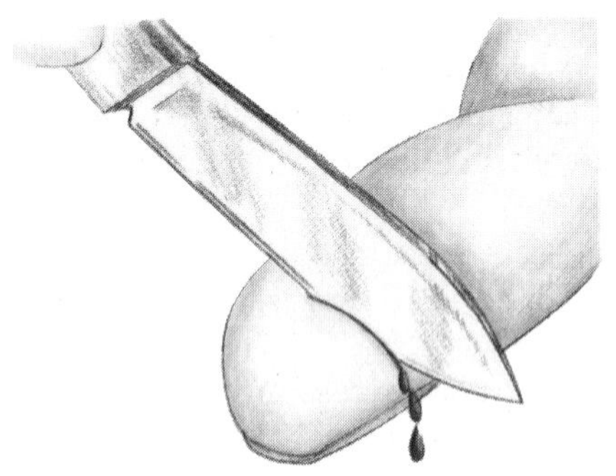

A typical cut or wound heals by a definite series of events.

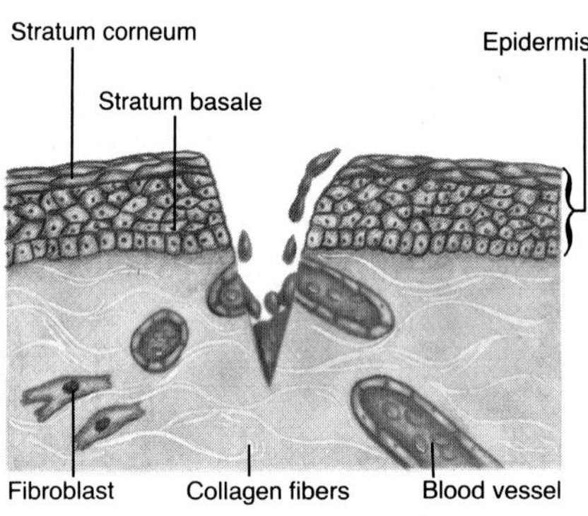

(1)

When injury occurs blood vessels may be severed, resulting in bleeding. Within seconds blood begins to clot.

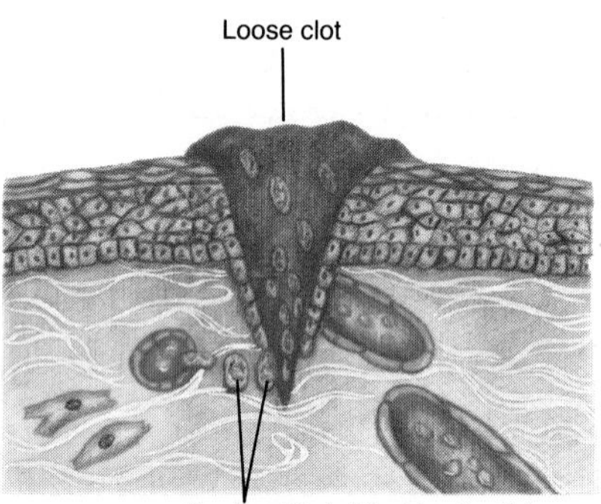

(2)

Several hours later blood has formed a loose clot. Large numbers of neutrophils (white blood cells) migrate into clot and nearby tissue, attracted by chemicals released by cells and bacteria in wounded area. Nearby blood vessels dilate. Epidermal cells have begun to divide and to migrate down over surface of injured tissue.

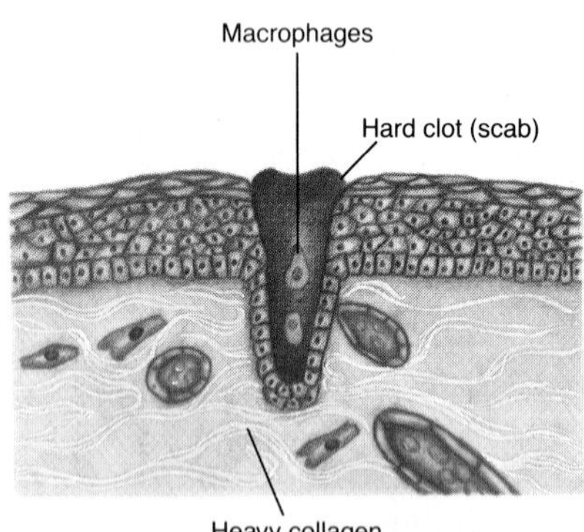

(3)

Within two days epidermal cells have covered injured tissue, or have covered area adjacent to them. Fibroblasts have migrated into area and begin producing collagen fibers necessary to reinforce repair. Macrophages (large janitor cells) have moved into area to clean up debris and bacteria. Developing collagen begins to force floor of wound upward. Clot hardens, forming scab.

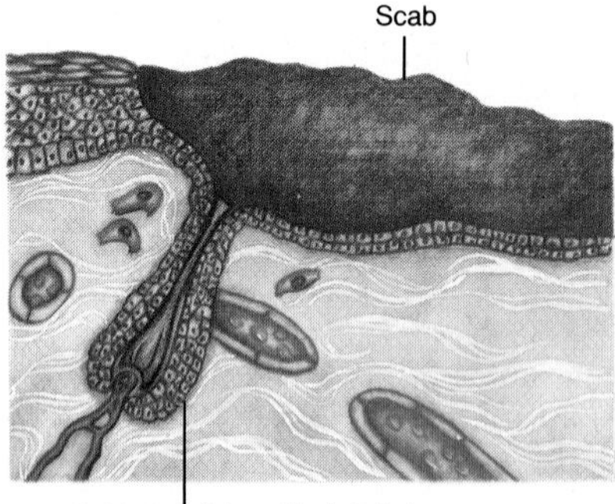

(3a)

If wound is broad and shallow, healing may differ slightly in that epithelial cells derived from linings of hair follicles and sweat glands may spread over injured area much more quickly than adjacent surface cells could do by themselves.

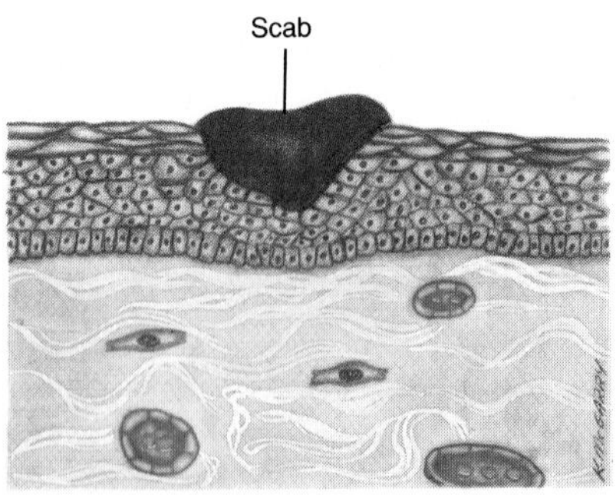

(4)

About a week after wound has occurred the scab has hardened and contracted, pulling walls of injury together. Epidermal cells have multiplied beneath it and thickening mass of collagen fibers has made wound shallower. Scab sloughs off but repair is not quite complete. Further production of dermis and thickening of epidermis must continue for some time before maximum strength is restored.

FIGURE 5-9

Repair of a wound.

(Fig. 5-9). Chemicals such as histamines are released by cells in the injured area, causing the blood vessels to dilate (increase in diameter) and become more permeable. As a result, large amounts of fluid may leave the blood and enter the injured area, causing swelling (edema). The excess fluid exerts pressure on nerves and other tissues, resulting in pain. Yet the fluid helps dilute harmful substances that may be present and delivers large quantities of oxygen and nutrients needed in the repair process. Because of the unusually large amount of blood in the area, the skin may feel warm and appear red. Clots form in the interstitial fluid, slowing the spread of bacteria and toxic materials. This mechanism serves to wall off the injured area.

A chemical produced by injured tissue is thought to trigger the release of large numbers of white blood cells from storage areas in the bone marrow. White blood cells pass out of the blood vessels and phagocytize bacteria, dead cells, and other foreign material. When bacterial infection is present, **pus,** a creamy fluid containing dead white blood cells and bacteria, may be produced.

If the wound damages blood vessels, blood leaks out and a clot forms. Soon after it forms, the blood clot contracts and begins to dehydrate, forming a scab, a temporary covering that seals the defect in the skin.

A decrease in chalones occurs due to the injury, leading to increased cell division in the wound area. Basal cells in the epidermis multiply rapidly, and epithelial cells from the sides of the wound migrate beneath the scab, eventually meeting and covering the wound. When the epithelial cells come into contact with other epithelial cells, their lateral migration is inhibited. Once the wound has been patched, the epithelial cells proliferate to form the strata of the epidermis, that is to resurface the wounded area. As the number of cells increases, so does the chalone level, resulting in slowing of cell division. Cell division stops when the damaged tissue has been repaired. This is a good example of a feedback mechanism that helps maintain homeostasis.

By the time the scab finally falls off, new epidermis is fully formed beneath. Fibroblasts from the subcutaneous layer and dermis multiply and produce collagen, which accumulates slowly and eventually fills in the wound beneath the epidermis.

If the wound is sufficiently severe, *granulation tissue* develops as an early step in the healing process. This is a very vascular, temporary connective tissue, highly resistant to infection. Large numbers of capillary loops impart a granular appearance to this tissue. Gradually, granulation tissue is replaced by *scar tissue.* The difference between scar tissue and normal dermis is that in scar tissue the collagen is more dense, its fibers are arranged somewhat differently, and it contains fewer cells and blood vessels. Scar tissue may lack hair, sweat glands, and sensory receptors.

Formation of scar tissue is a process of collagen synthesis and collagen breakdown that continues for many months and even years after a wound appears to have healed. During this time the scar tissue is remodeled—that is, the collagen fibers are rearranged so as to impart maximum strength to the tissue.

Sometimes an imbalance occurs between collagen production and breakdown, resulting in formation of abnormal types of scars. *Hypertrophic scars* are those that contain excess amounts of collagen but still conform to the original size and shape of the wound; *keloids* are large bulging scars that may extend far beyond the bounds of the wound.

Though most internal organs in humans are able to repair themselves when wounded, they do not do a very good job of regenerating their specialized functional tissues. Usually functional tissue is replaced by connective tissue scarring, so that the organ may not perform its duties as effectively as before the injury.

Burns can be life threatening

Burns are thermal injuries that may result from direct heat, certain chemicals, electricity, or radiation. Excessive heat denatures (coagulates) cell proteins, leading to injury or death of the cells. Of the 2 million people burned in the United States each year, about 100,000 are hospitalized and about 12,000 die as a result of their wounds.

Least serious are first-degree burns, such as sunburn, in which the epidermis remains intact. Blood vessels in the dermis dilate, causing mild inflammation, with redness and slight swelling. **First-degree burns** are sensitive to the touch and may be moist. The skin usually heals within a few days without scarring. First-degree burns require no special treatment, but pain may be relieved by immersing the burned area in cold water.

Second-degree burns (also called partial-thickness burns), may be superficial or deep dermal burns. In superficial second-degree burns, the epidermis and superficial dermis are damaged. Excessive fluid between dermis and epidermis may accumulate in blisters. Such burns usually heal in 2 to 3 weeks by proliferation of epithelial cells from hair follicles and other dermal appendages. In deep second-degree burns, many dermal appendages are destroyed. As a result there is less capacity for regeneration of tissue and greater probability of scarring. After initial treatment with cold water, second-degree burns are treated by soaking in salt water.

In **third-degree** (or full-thickness) **burns,** portions of the epidermis, dermis, and subcutaneous tissue are destroyed. Nerve endings in the area may be destroyed, so the victim feels little or no pain. The skin surface may appear white, bright red, or it may be black, charred, and leathery. Sometimes skin with third-degree burns has a normal appearance.

Without its protective shield the body is in grave danger, and the entire organism reacts profoundly to the crisis. Because the burned skin is unable to retain body fluids, large amounts of fluid may leave the body, resulting in shock. If this fluid (with its salts and protein) is not quickly replaced, the individual may die. Another serious threat is infection, because disease organisms can readily gain access to the exposed tissues. Third-degree burns require immediate skilled medical treatment, including intravenous replacement of lost fluids and electrolytes, treatment with antibiotics, and skin transplants (necessary in full-thickness burns because tissues are not able to repair themselves). If third-degree burns are extensive, the patient often dies despite heroic efforts to prolong life.

Risk of death following extensive burns is roughly proportional to the percentage of body surface that has been damaged. When more than 20% of the body has been burned the injury may well be lethal, but of course the depth of the injury affects the prognosis. Figure 5-10 illustrates the Lund and Browder method used clinically to estimate the percentage of the body surface area (BSA) affected by burns.

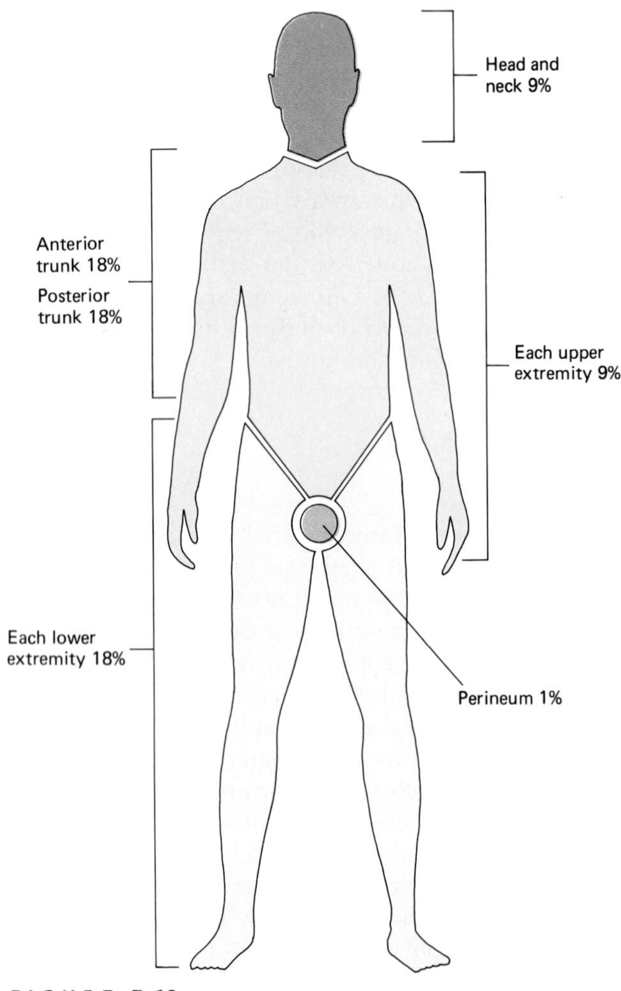

FIGURE 5-10

The Lund and Browder method is used clinically for estimating the extent of burns. When more than 20% of the body has been burned, the injury is often fatal.

Most skin cancer can be prevented

Skin cancer is most frequently caused by excessive, chronic exposure to the ultraviolet radiation of sunlight. Other causes are exposure to arsenic compounds, x-rays, and radioactive materials such as radium. Most forms of skin cancer progress relatively slowly; with skilled treatment there is a high cure rate.

The most common type of skin cancer is **basal cell carcinoma,** in which cells in the basal layer of the epidermis are altered and then malfunction (Fig. 5-11). They no longer honor the boundary between epidermis and dermis. As they migrate into the dermis and subcutaneous tissues they erode normal tissue, causing erosive ulcers. Malignant basal cells appear to have lost their ability to form keratin and to mature normally. Because metastasis is uncommon in this type of cancer, when the disease is diagnosed early there is a good chance for a cure.

A second type of skin cancer, **squamous cell carcinoma,** begins in the prickle cells of the stratum spinosum (but may also develop in other parts of the body where squamous epithelium occurs). In this type of cancer the cells continue to form keratin and to differentiate. Most frequently, squamous cell carcinomas occur on parts of the body that are exposed to the sun. If the condition is untreated, metastasis may occur.

The incidence of **malignant melanoma** is rapidly increasing. Exposure to ultraviolet light is the main cause of this cancer. Some forms of this disease spread rapidly and may cause death within a few months after diagnosis. Other forms are less virulent and have high cure rates. About half of malignant melanomas arise from melanocytes (pigment cells) in normal skin, while the rest develop from pigmented moles (nevi). Survival depends upon early diagnosis and treatment.

Most skin cancer can probably be prevented by protecting the body from sunlight and other forms of ultraviolet radiation. Tanning machines that use artificial light to induce tanning subject the body to ultraviolet rays and are therefore potentially harmful. Those who choose to expose themselves to sunlight can protect their skin by limiting the time they are in the sun and by applying sunscreens containing ingredients such as para-aminobenzoic acid (PABA).

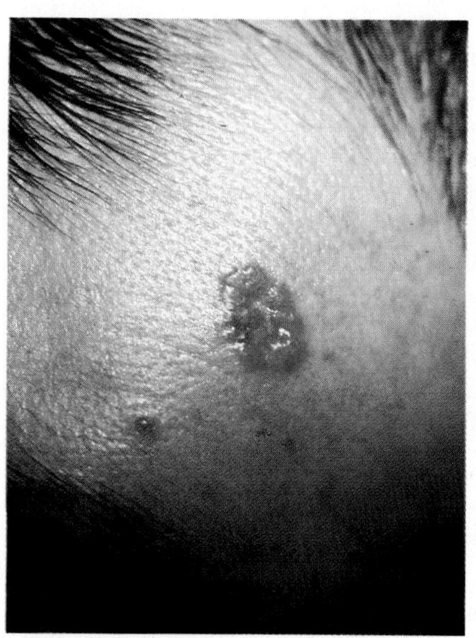

(*a*)

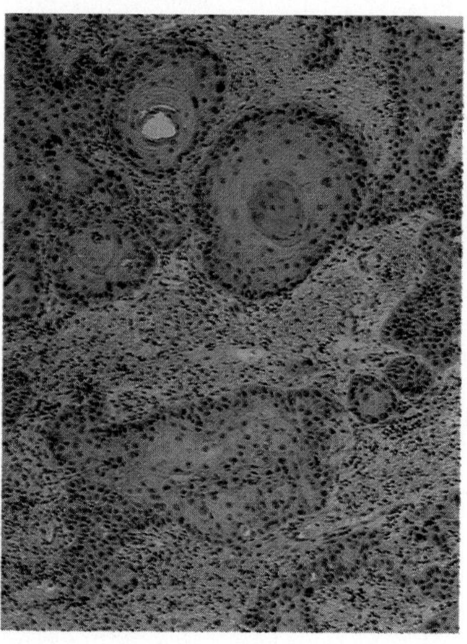

(*b*)

FIGURE 5-11

Skin cancer. (*a*) Photograph of a basal cell carcinoma on a patient's head. (Ken Green/Visuals Unlimited.) (*b*) Photomicrograph of squamous cell carcinoma (approximately ×150). Compare with normal skin in Fig. 5-3. (John D. Cunningham/Visuals Unlimited.)

Summary

I. The integumentary system consists of the skin and its hair, nails, and glands.

II. The integumentary system functions to:
   - A. Protect against mechanical and chemical injury.
   - B. Protect against invasion by disease.
   - C. Prevent dehydration.
   - D. Help maintain constant body temperature.
   - E. Excrete wastes.
   - F. Help inform the central nervous system of changes in the external environment by means of sensory receptors within the skin.
   - G. Produce vitamin D.

III. As a basal cell moves outward through the layers of the epidermis it becomes first prickle-shaped, then flattened, as it differentiates and produces keratin. Eventually it becomes filled with keratin, then dies, becoming scalelike, and finally is sloughed off the skin surface.

IV. The dermis consists of connective tissue containing large amounts of collagen. It gives substance to the skin, holds the blood vessels that bring nourishment to the epidermal cells, and contains sensory receptors and epidermal structures such as hair follicles and glands.

V. The subcutaneous layer consists of connective tissue, including fat. This tissue cushions underlying structures against mechanical injury, connects skin with tissues beneath, and stores energy in the form of fat.

VI. Hair follicles and sebaceous glands arise from epidermal cells that push down into the dermis during early development.

VII. Sweat glands release onto the skin surface a dilute salt water, which evaporates, cooling the body. These glands play an important role in maintaining normal body temperature.

VIII. Melanocytes in the basal layer produce pigment granules and pass them on to other epidermal cells, including those that form hair. Melanin absorbs ultraviolet rays from the sun, preventing damage to dermis and blood vessels.

IX. Inflammation is a reaction by the tissues aimed at protecting them from further injury or irritation. Symptoms are redness, swelling, heat, and pain.

X. In first-degree burns there is mild inflammation but the epidermis remains intact; in second-degree burns epidermal cells die and inflammation and blistering occur; in third-degree burns the damage may extend into the subcutaneous tissue, exposing the victim to fluid loss and infection.

XI. Skin cancer can be caused by excessive exposure to ultraviolet radiation from the sun, arsenic compounds, x-rays, and radioactive materials.

Post-test

1. The skin with its glands, hair, nails, and other structures makes up the ____________ system.
2. The two main layers of the skin are the outer ____________ and the inner ____________.
3. The deepest stratum of the epidermis is the ____________ ____________.
4. Cells of the stratum granulosum contain many ____________.
5. The tough waterproofing protein of the epidermis is ____________.
6. The outermost stratum of the epidermis is stratum ____________.
7. The ____________ ____________ beneath the dermis consists of loose connective tissue.
8. The root of a hair together with its coverings is called a ____________ ____________.
9. Contraction of the arrector pili muscles makes the ____________ stand on end.
10. ____________ glands are attached to each hair follicle by ducts; they secrete an oily substance called ____________.
11. Sweat consists mainly of ____________ with some ____________ and a trace of urea.
12. Nails consist mainly of tough, compressed ____________.
13. Pigment granules are produced by ____________ located in the ____________ ____________ of the epidermis.
14. The body's basic response to injury is ____________.
15. The symptoms of inflammation are ____________, ____________, ____________, and ____________.
16. The least serious burns are ____________ degree burns.
17. The main cause of malignant melanoma is exposure to ____________.
18. The most common type of skin cancer is ____________ ____________ ____________.

19. Label the diagram.

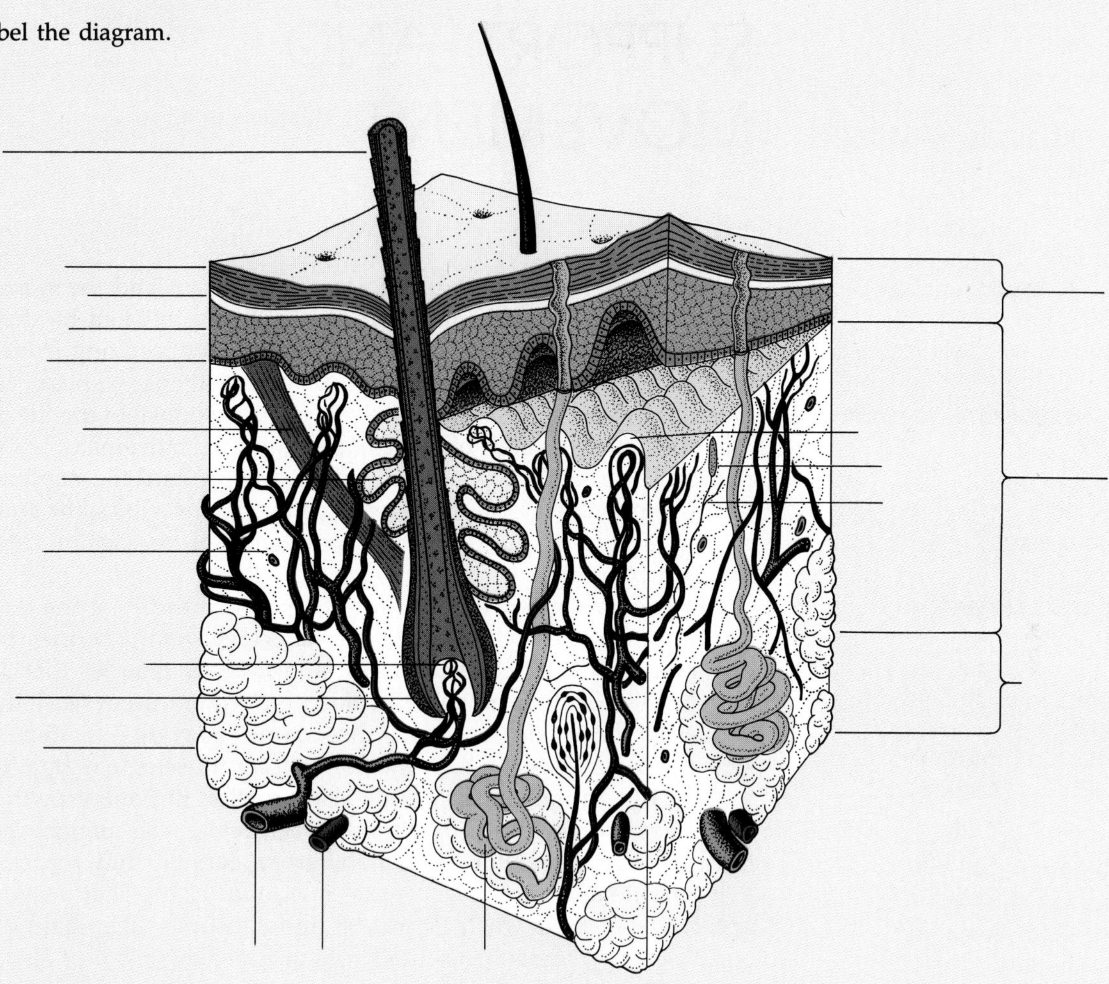

Review questions

1. In what ways does the skin help preserve homeostasis?
2. Compare the structure of the epidermis with that of the dermis.
3. Which cells of the epidermis actively divide? Which differentiate?
4. What are the functions of the dermis? The subcutaneous layer?
5. What is the function of the sebaceous glands? What happens when they malfunction?
6. How do sweat glands help regulate body temperature?
7. Why is melanin important? How does it get into the skin cells?
8. What are the principal characteristics of inflammation?
9. Suppose you step on a nail. How does the body respond to the injury? Describe the healing process.
10. Why must burns of different degrees be treated differently? Explain.
11. What is the most common type of skin cancer? What is the most common cause of skin cancer?

Post-test answers

1. integumentary **2.** epidermis; dermis **3.** stratum basale **4.** granules **5.** keratin **6.** corneum **7.** subcutaneous layer **8.** hair follicle **9.** hairs **10.** Sebaceous; sebum **11.** water; salts **12.** keratin **13.** melanocytes; stratum basale **14.** inflammation **15.** redness, pain, heat, swelling **16.** first **17.** ultraviolet light **18.** basal cell carcinoma. **19.** See Figure 5-2.

SUPPORT AND MOVEMENT

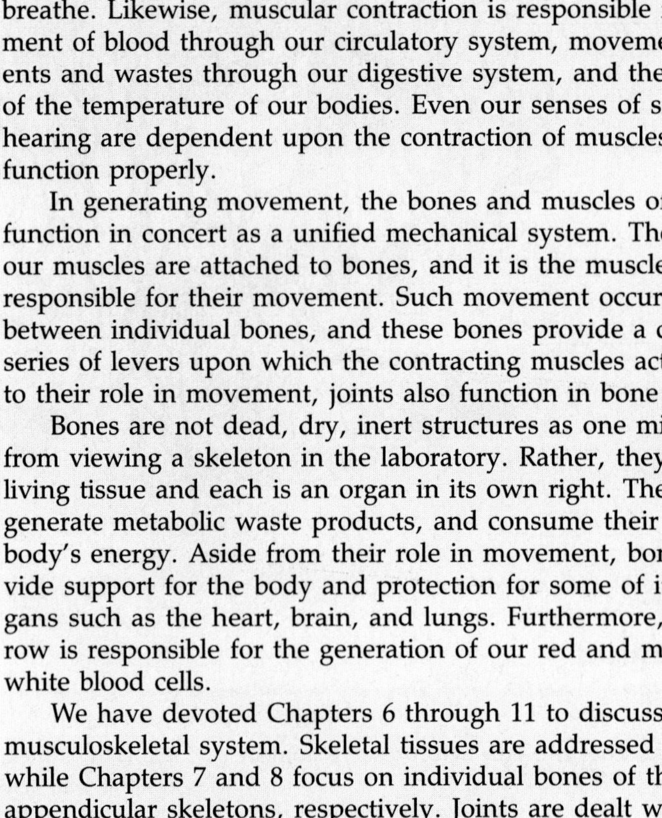

Many of our physiological processes and the expression of nearly all of our thoughts are initiated by the generation of movement. Movement resulting from contraction of our muscles enables us to write, eat, play, speak, and breathe. Likewise, muscular contraction is responsible for the movement of blood through our circulatory system, movement of nutrients and wastes through our digestive system, and the regulation of the temperature of our bodies. Even our senses of sight and hearing are dependent upon the contraction of muscles in order to function properly.

In generating movement, the bones and muscles of the body function in concert as a unified mechanical system. The majority of our muscles are attached to bones, and it is the muscles that are responsible for their movement. Such movement occurs at joints between individual bones, and these bones provide a continuous series of levers upon which the contracting muscles act. In addition to their role in movement, joints also function in bone growth.

Bones are not dead, dry, inert structures as one might expect from viewing a skeleton in the laboratory. Rather, they represent living tissue and each is an organ in its own right. They respire, generate metabolic waste products, and consume their share of the body's energy. Aside from their role in movement, bones also provide support for the body and protection for some of its vital organs such as the heart, brain, and lungs. Furthermore, bone marrow is responsible for the generation of our red and many of our white blood cells.

We have devoted Chapters 6 through 11 to discussion of the musculoskeletal system. Skeletal tissues are addressed in Chapter 6 while Chapters 7 and 8 focus on individual bones of the axial and appendicular skeletons, respectively. Joints are dealt with in Chapter 9. Muscle tissue is covered in Chapter 10, and individual muscles of the muscular system are addressed in Chapter 11.

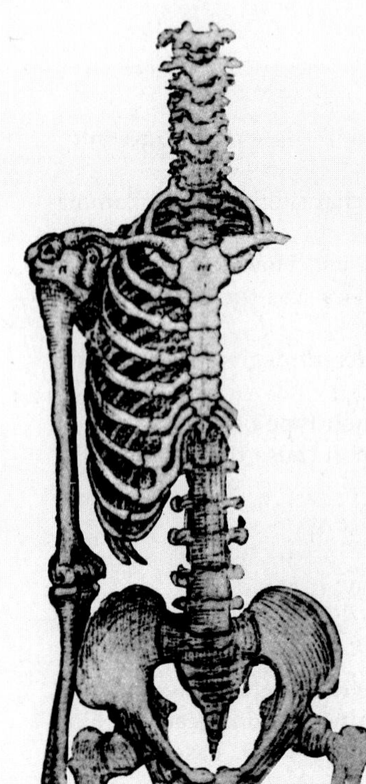

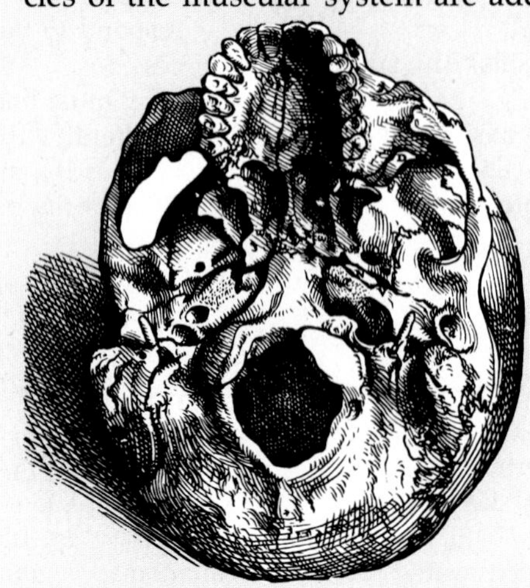

II

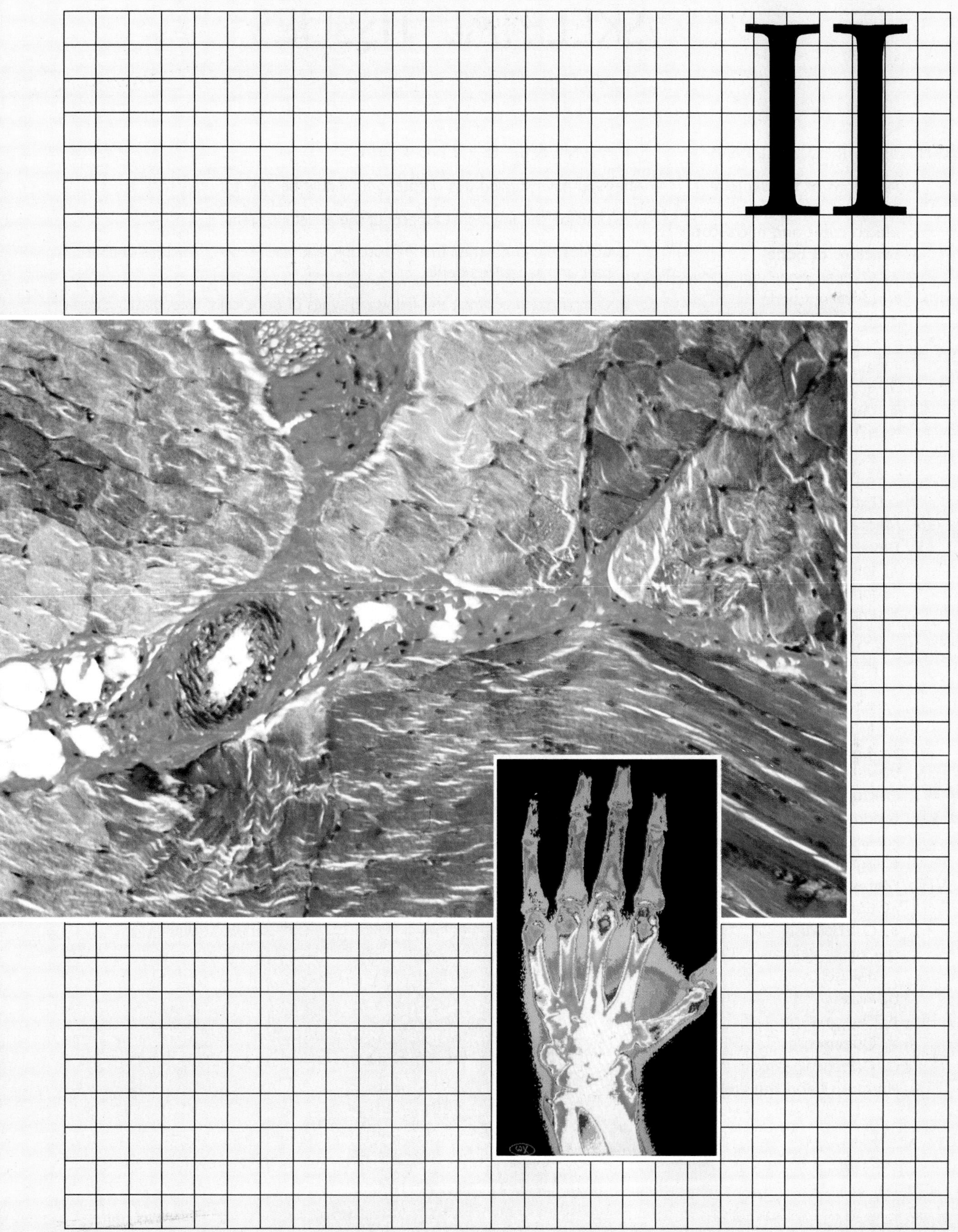

SKELETAL TISSUES

CHAPTER OUTLINE

I. **Functions of the skeletal system**

II. **Macroscopic and microscopic structure of bone**
- A. Compact bone and cancellous bone
  - 1. Epiphyseal plate and metaphysis
  - 2. Periosteum
  - 3. Endosteum
- B. Osteoprogenitor cells
  - 1. Osteoblasts
  - 2. Osteocytes
  - 3. Osteoclasts
- C. Extracellular matrix of bone

III. **Mechanism of calcification**

IV. **Development of bone**
- A. Intramembranous bone formation
- B. Endochondral bone formation
  - 1. Zone of resting or reserve cartilage
  - 2. Zone of proliferation
  - 3. Zone of maturation
  - 4. Zone of calcification

V. **Woven and lamellar bone**

VI. **Fractures and healing**

VII. **Tendons and ligaments**
- A. Tendons
- B. Ligaments

VIII. **Diseases of bone**
- A. Osteogenesis imperfecta
- B. Osteoporosis
- C. Osteitis deformans (Paget's disease)
- D. Rickets
- E. Osteomalacia
- F. Osteomyelitis
- G. Osteogenic sarcoma

IX. **Hormones and the skeleton**

LEARNING OBJECTIVES

After you have studied this chapter you should be able to:

1 Describe the functional aspects of the skeletal system.

2 Compare and contrast the macroscopic and microscopic structure of compact and cancellous bone.

3 Compare and contrast the following types of bone cells: osteoblasts, osteocytes, and osteoclasts.

4 Describe the extracellular matrix of bone.

5 Describe the mechanism of calcification.

6 Compare and contrast intramembranous and endochondral bone formation.

7 Describe the following: (a) zone of resting, or reserve, cartilage, (b) zone of proliferation, (c) zone of maturation, (d) zone of calcification.

8 Compare and contrast woven and lamellar bone.

9 Describe the different types of bone fractures and discuss the healing process.

10 Describe the structure and function of tendons and ligaments.

11 Describe how frictional stress is reduced at points where tendons act across two bones or adjacent tendons.

12 Describe the following diseases of bone: (a) osteogenesis imperfecta, (b) osteoporosis, (c) osteitis deformans (Paget's disease), (d) rickets, (e) osteomalacia, (f) osteomyelitis, (g) osteogenic sarcoma.

13 Compare and contrast the effects of various hormones upon the skeletal system.

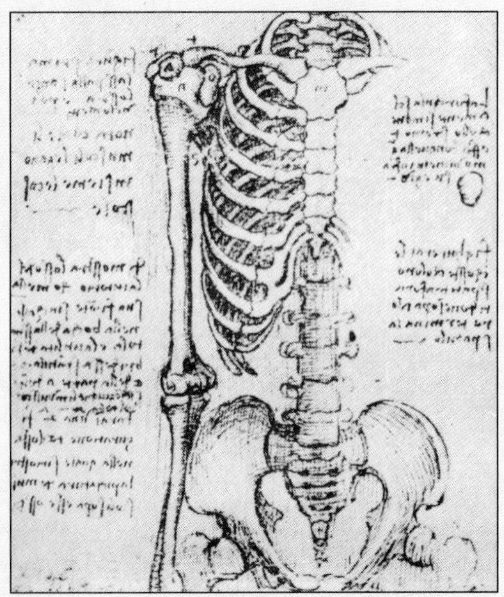

Bone in human thigh (×250). (Manfred Kage/Peter Arnold, Inc.)

6

KEY CONCEPTS

Two basic histological types of bone are compact bone and cancellous bone.

The periosteum and endosteum both possess osteogenic potential.

Extracellular matrix of bone composed of inorganic salts and an organic matrix rich in collagen and ground substance.

Bone is formed either by endochondral or intramembranous ossification.

As long bones grow in length, new chondrocytes arise on the epiphyseal side of the epiphyseal plate; cartilage on the diaphyseal side is replaced by bone.

Enlargement of bones by means of coordinated removal and deposition of bone permits growth without excessive increases in weight.

Fracture healing typically involves the formation of a procallus, a fibrocartilaginous callus, and an osseous callus.

Tendons serve to attach muscle to bone whereas ligaments attach bone to bone.

As you begin your study of the skeletal system, it is essential that you take a moment to consider one of the most basic tenets of biology; that is, the relationship that exists between structure and function. By virtue of its complex developmental and organizational aspects, all of which reflect its functional capacities, the skeletal system represents one of the most structurally and functionally diverse systems of the human body.

In Chapter 4 we discussed the various types and characteristics of connective tissue in general. The skeletal system is composed primarily of connective tissue—not only bone and cartilage, but tendons and ligaments as well. All of these anatomical features contribute to the structural and functional aspects of the skeletal system as we know it. The skeletal system plays a functional role in the following: (1) support, (2) protection, (3) movement, (4) mineral storage, and (5) hematopoiesis.

Functions of the skeletal system include support and protection

One of the obvious functions of the skeletal system is that of **support.** Mere observation of the articulated skeleton in the laboratory setting permits you to arrive at this conclusion. The ribs, together with the sternum and thoracic vertebrae, support the thoracic, or chest, wall, much as the beams and buttresses of a cathedral support its ceiling. As you view the articulated skeleton and in your own mind imagine where various internal organs are located, it is also apparent that **protection** is another important function of the skeletal system. The bones of the skull enclose and protect the brain, and the spinal cord resides comfortably within an osseous canal formed by the sequential placement of the vertebrae that constitute the vertebral column. The organs, blood vessels, and nerves of the pelvic region, in addition to certain portions of the digestive system, are protected by the bony pelvis.

The **transmission of forces** generated by muscular contraction is another specific role of the skeletal system and thus it is intimately involved with the production of movement. The skeletal and muscular systems are arranged to provide a functional system of forces and levers that permits movement of individual body parts as well as movement of the body as a whole. Vital biological activities such as breathing also depend upon this close functional association between the bones and muscles of the body.

One function of the skeletal system which might not be immediately apparent to you is that of **hematopoiesis,** the formation of blood cells. The marrow cavity of certain bones provides a unique microenvironment for the generation and maturation of the body's numerous types of blood cells. Even less obvious is the role that bone plays in the **storage and release of minerals** such as calcium and phosphorus. Bone serves as a warehouse for both of these vital substances. The endocrine system (as seen later in this chapter as well as in Chapter 18) works closely with the skeletal system in order to maintain the necessary balance between input and output to assure a proper concentration of these substances in the extracellular environment.

The macroscopic and microscopic architecture of bone is distinctly characteristic

Bone, like the other connective tissues, is composed of cells, fibers, and an extracellular matrix of bone, which is calcified and therefore very hard.

One can distinguish between compact and cancellous bone with the naked eye

There are two basic histological types of bone which are easily distinguishable with the naked eye: compact bone and cancellous (spongy) bone. A longitudinal or transverse section of a long bone such as the humerus or femur provides a good example for making this distinction (Fig. 6-1). The **diaphysis** (di-**af**-ih-sis), or shaft, of such a long bone appears as a cylinder with a thick wall composed of **compact bone.** This type of bone has the appearance of a solid mass; however, it too has a unique microscopic structure. The inner portion of the wall of the cylindrical diaphysis lines the narrow cavity and is occupied by **cancellous,** or **spongy, bone.**

Cancellous bone is a lattice network of branching bone spicules termed **trabeculae** (trah-**bek**-yoo-lee) which are so arranged as to form a complex system of interconnecting spaces. The ends, or **epiphyses** (e-**pif**-ih-sees), of a long bone also consist largely of cancellous bone covered with a thin layer of compact bone. A thin layer of hyaline cartilage, the **articular cartilage,** overlies the compact bone of the epiphyses.

THE DIAPHYSIS AND METAPHYSIS ARE SEPARATED BY THE EPIPHYSEAL PLATE IN GROWING INDIVIDUALS

The epiphyses of typical long bones arise from ossification centers that are distinct from that of the diaphysis. The epiphyseal plate, or disc, separates the epiphysis from the diaphysis in growing long bones and is composed of cartilage (Figs. 6-1 and 6-2). The region where the **epiphyseal plate** blends with the diaphysis is called the **metaphysis** (meh-**taf**-ih-sis) and is typically characterized by the presence of columns of cancellous bone.

THE PERIOSTEUM EXHIBITS OSTEOGENIC POTENTIAL

For the most part, bones are covered on their external surfaces by a layer of specialized connective tissue known as the **periosteum** (per-ee-**os**-tee-um) (Fig. 6-1). It is the periosteum to which tendons and ligaments make their attachment on bone. The periosteum has osteogenic (bone forming) potential and is a necessary structure for nutrition, growth of bone, and repair of injured bone.

Those areas on the epiphyses that are covered by articular cartilage do not possess a periosteal covering. Furthermore, a periosteum is not present on sesamoid bones (those formed within the substance of a tendon) such as the patella (knee cap).

The periosteum typically consists of two layers, an outer **fibrous periosteum** and an inner **osteogenic layer** (*os*-tee-o-**jen**-ick). Its microscopic appearance is dependent upon its functional status. During the period of bone growth the inner layer contains many cells known as **osteoblasts.** When growth has ceased, these same cells change their morphology so that they have a more fibroblast-like appearance. When bone is injured, however, they again assume osteoblast morphology and enter into the formation of new bone.

Blood vessels and elastic fibers are present in the osteogenic layer of the periosteum. The fibrous periosteum contains fewer cells than the osteogenic layer. The fibrous periosteum is traversed by numerous blood vessels, nerves, and lymphatics as these structures make their way into the underlying bone. Dense bundles of collagenous fibers, called **Sharpey's fibers,** course inward from the periosteum and penetrate the outer regions of compact bone. These fibers firmly anchor the periosteum to the underlying bone.

ENDOSTEUM ALSO POSSESSES OSTEOGENIC POTENTIAL

The **endosteum** (end-**oss**-tee-um) is a thin cellular layer, usually composed of a single layer of cells, which lines the cavities of haversian canals as well as the marrow cavities of cancellous bone. It has reduced amounts of intercellular matrix and connective tissue fibers compared to the periosteum. However, it does have the capacity to form new bone; that is, it has osteogenic potential.

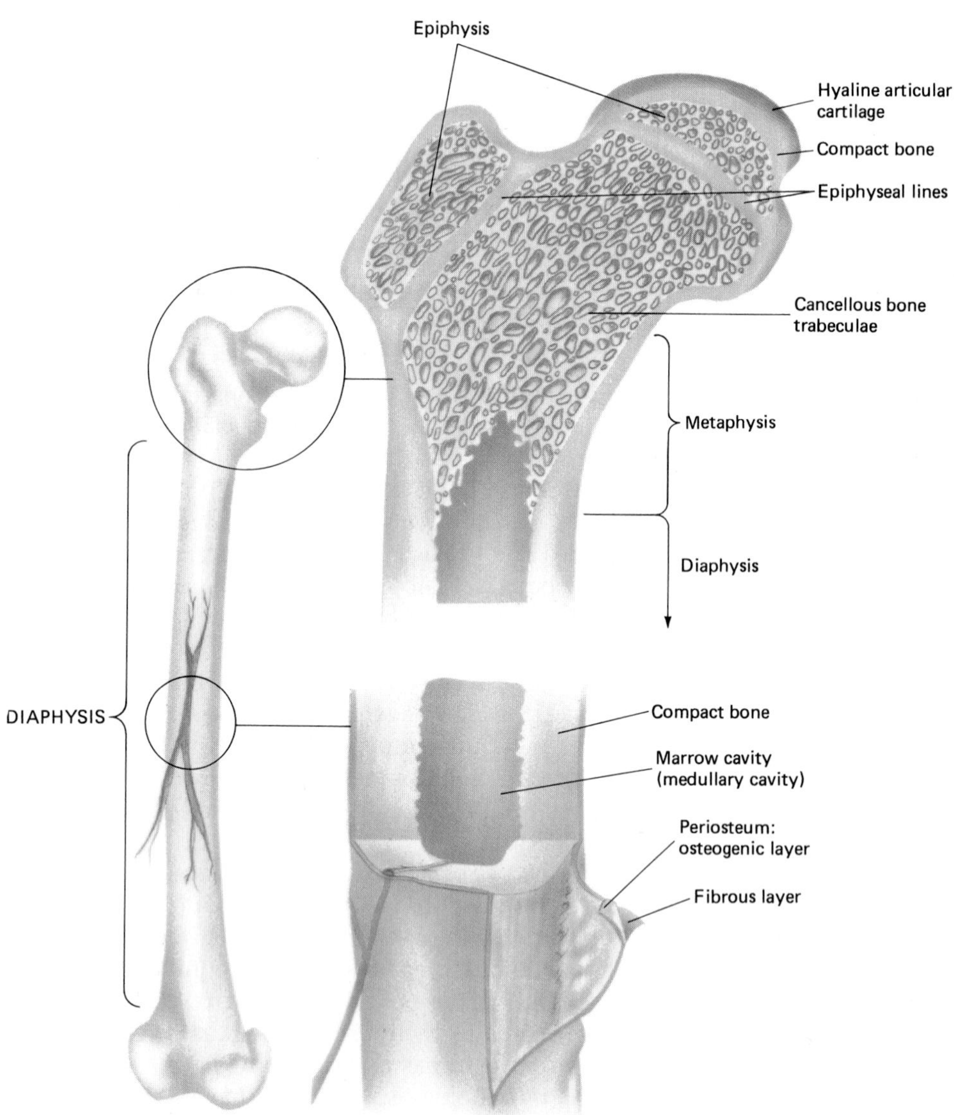

FIGURE 6-1

Structural components of the femur. In the detailed view of the epiphysis and metaphysis, notice the epiphyseal line, hyaline cartilage, and distribution of compact and cancellous bone. The epiphysis and diaphysis are united at the metaphysis. In the detailed view of the diaphysis, notice the compact bone, marrow cavity, and periosteum.

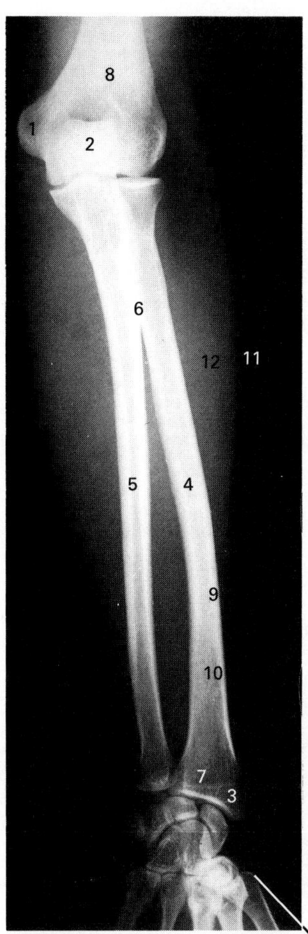

FIGURE 6-2

Radiograph (x-ray) of the bones of the right forearm in a position of supination (palm-up). Examine the following features: (1) medial condyle of humerus; (2) head of ulna; (3) styloid process of radius; (4) radius; (5) ulna; (6) radial tuberosity; (7) epiphyseal line of the distal radius; (8) humerus; (9) compact bone; (10) cancellous (spongy) bone; (11) skin and subcutaneous tissue; (12) muscle.

Osteoprogenitor cells give rise to the characteristic cells of bone

The **osteoprogenitor cells** impart an osteogenic potential to the endosteum and inner layer of the periosteum. As the osteoprogenitor cells differentiate they become osteoblasts, which have the ability to form the matrix of bone. Osteoprogenitor cells exhibit marked activity during the period of active bone growth. Although they are relatively inactive once growth has ceased, they are activated again during fracture repair and internal remodeling of adult bone. It is not clear whether these same osteoprogenitor cells also have the potential to give rise to additional cell types, for example, fibroblasts, adipocytes (fat cells), or hematopoietic (blood-forming) cells.

OSTEOBLASTS ARE THE BONE–FORMING CELLS

The osteoblasts are located on the surfaces of developing or growing bone and are the cells that play a prominent role in the generation of bone matrix. The primary mission of osteoblasts is the production of collagen and ultimately bone. During periods of active growth, they possess an abundant endoplasmic reticulum, characteristic for cells undergoing active protein synthesis, and their cytoplasm is extremely basophilic.

OSTEOCYTES RESIDE WITHIN THE LACUNAE OF ESTABLISHED BONE

As bone grows and osteoblasts deposit collagen and ground substance (organic matrix of bone prior to calcification) around themselves, they become entrapped within spaces termed **lacunae** (lah-**koo**-nee). Calcification of the matrix occurs and the cells within the lacunae are then referred to as **osteocytes.** However, osteocytes are not totally isolated cells. Each is in contact with nearby osteocytes through elongated cellular processes located within minute canals termed **canaliculi** (*kan*-ah-**lik**-yoo-lie).

Osteocytes are also metabolically active cells. Recent experimental data suggests that the osteocytes play an important role in the regulation of blood calcium levels. This is achieved through the action of *parathyroid hormone* on the osteocytes which causes them to release calcium from bone by means of a process termed *osteocytic osteolysis.*

OSTEOCLASTS ARE THE PRINCIPAL CELLS INVOLVED IN BONE RESORPTION

The **osteoclasts** are very large, multinucleated cells that function in the **resorption** (removal) of bone (Fig. 6-3). Although their precise origin has long been a topic of controversy, it is currently accepted that osteoclasts arise from the fusion of white blood cells. Osteoclast formation with subsequent bone resorption is stimulated when parathyroid hormone levels in the blood remain elevated for a long period of time.

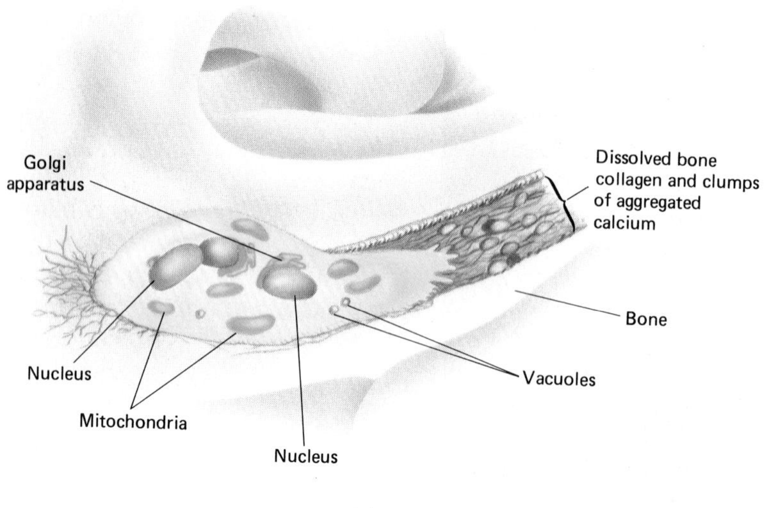

(a)

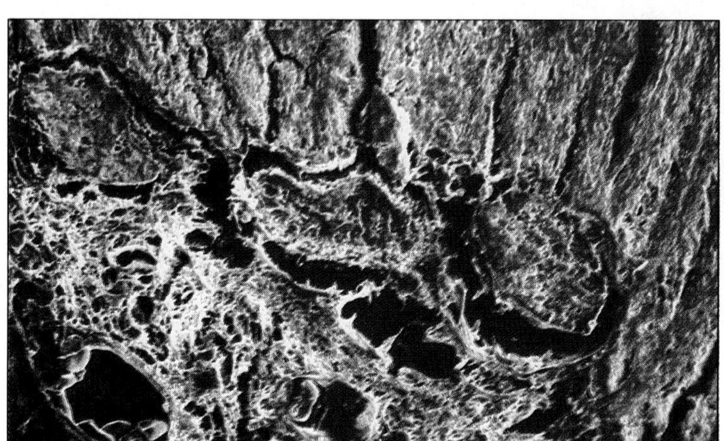

(b)

FIGURE 6-3

The human osteoclast. (a) Schematic representation of a human osteoclast active during bone resorption. Notice that the multinucleated osteoclast leaves behind it a trail of dissolved bone and collagen. (b) Scanning electronmicrograph (×500) of a human osteoclast (Dr. Daniel Grande/Peter Arnold, Inc.)

The extracellular matrix of bone consists of inorganic salts and an organic matrix

The extracellular matrix of bone is composed of inorganic salts and an organic matrix referred to as **osteoid.** Inorganic salts constitute approximately 50% of the dry weight of bone and are largely responsible for giving bone its property of hardness. Calcium phosphate, in the form of *hydroxyapatite crystals,* is regularly distributed along collagen fibers within the extracellular matrix. Bone matrix also contains substantial quantities of carbonate and citrate ions together with significant amounts of sodium, magnesium, and potassium.

In geographical regions where drinking water has been treated with fluoride, it is common to find hydroxyl groups in the hydroxyapatite crystals replaced by fluoride ions. Calcium ions may be replaced by those of radon, lead, or strontium when these ions find their way into the body. The radioactive isotopes of calcium and phosphorus substitute for their respective stable forms within hydroxyapatite crystals of bone and have proven to be valuable tools for scientists in their investigations of normal and abnormal bone physiology. On the other hand, there are certain isotopes that have an affinity for localizing in bone, for example strontium-90, which can have very harmful effects on bone as well as on the hematopoietic cells of the marrow. Cancer of bone, *osteogenic sarcoma,* may develop when radioactive isotopes are present in bone at high enough doses and for long periods of time.

Ground substance and *collagen* (Fig. 6-4) make up the organic matrix of bone and together represent approximately 50% of the dry weight of bone. Macromolecules known as *glycosaminoglycans* (*gly*-ko-**sam**-ean-o-gly-kans) are present within the ground substance of bone and cartilage. The matrix of bone, however, contains far fewer amounts of these compounds than does that of cartilage. Those glycosaminoglycans, which have been shown to exist within the extracellular matrix of bone, include hyaluronic acid, chondroitin sulfate, and keratin sulfate. Although the exact function of these macromolecules within the ground substance is not known, some investigators think they may play a role in regulating the deposition of calcium salts.

Collagen is by far the major constituent of the organic matrix; in the adult it represents approximately 90 to 95% of the organic matrix. Although several specific types of collagen are found in the human body, the type located in the matrix of bone is largely Type I collagen. Collagen fibers are composed of three intertwined strands of protein linked together lengthwise, with each strand being longer than any osteoblast. How is it then that osteoblasts are able to produce them? The answer is that collagen fibers are not formed within the cell. Rather, the osteoblasts synthesize a soluble protein, **tropocollagen** (*tro*-po-**kol**-ah-jen), which when exported from the cell becomes collagen and forms fibers spontaneously.

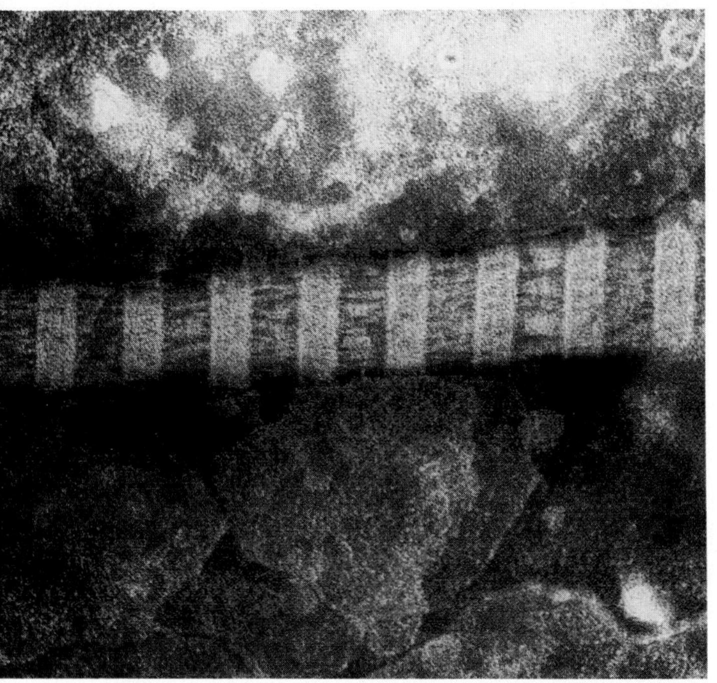

FIGURE 6-4

Collagen fibril (approximately × 135,000). (Michael C. Webb/Visuals Unlimited)

Collagen is primarily responsible for imparting to bone the properties of toughness and great tensile strength. Two simple experiments will demonstrate the existence and importance of collagen in bone. First, take a small bone, such as the wishbone of a chicken, and soak it in vinegar or lemon juice for a few days. This will dissolve much of the calcium from the bone, leaving only the collagen. As a result the bone will become so soft and elastic that it may actually be tied in a knot. On the other hand, if a bone is baked in a pottery kiln long enough to destroy all of the organic components, it will lose all of its toughness and elasticity. It becomes so brittle that a mere touch will result in its disintegration.

Hydroxyapatite crystals form during the calcification of bone matrix

The precise manner by which calcium is deposited within the organic matrix of bone is not completely understood. Experimental evidence suggests that collagen, either acting alone or in conjunction with glycosaminoglycans, plays a significant role in calcium deposition. Collagen appears to possess numerous active sites throughout its molecular structure that catalyze the precipitation of calcium and phosphate from surrounding tissue fluids. The salts that are initially deposited are converted to the hydroxyapatite crystalline form at a later time.

Results of numerous *in vitro* (in an artificial environment) studies have shown that collagen from other body tissues is also capable of precipitating calcium salts from tissue fluids. Furthermore, evidence also supports the suggestion that osteoblasts may synthesize and secrete a substance capable of neutralizing a putative inhibitor of hydroxyapatite formation. This would seem to fit with the fact that calcium salts are not ordinarily precipitated by collagen in regions of the body other than bone. However, pathological states do arise where this does occur, for example, the deposition of calcium salts within the walls of arteries in a condition known as arteriosclerosis.

Bone develops either through intramembranous or endochondral ossification

The formation of bone is called *osteogenesis* (*os*-tee-oh-**jen**-ih-sis) or **ossification** (*os*-ih-fi-**ka**-shun). Two developmental sequences by which bone may be formed are **intramembranous** (*in*-trah-**mem**-brah-nus) and **endochondral** (*en*-do-**kon**-dral) **bone formation.** Both types of bone formation involve the replacement of existing connective tissue by bone itself. In the case of endochondral bone formation, the bone replaces an existing *cartilage* model. A primitive *connective tissue* precedes bone development during intramembranous bone formation. Many of the bones of the skull are partly or wholly the result of intramembranous formation, whereas the long bones such as the humerus and femur are entirely of endochondral origin.

Intramembranous bone formation occurs within embryonic connective tissue (mesenchyme)

Bones that develop by this method include the flat bones of the skull, portions of the clavicle (collarbone), and parts of the lower jaw, or mandible. We refer to those bones of the body that develop by intramembranous formation as **membrane** (tabular) **bones.** Focus your attention at this time on Figure 6-5 which depicts the development of intramembranous bone.

One of the earliest events one may observe in this type of bone formation is a condensation (closely packed cells) of the embryonic connective tissue, or **mesenchyme** (**mez**-en-kime), which soon becomes extensively infiltrated with an abundant vascular supply. A gel-like extracellular matrix containing randomly distributed collagen fibrils surrounds these mesenchymal cells. The cells themselves assume a stellate (star-like) shape and remain in contact with one another through their long, slender processes.

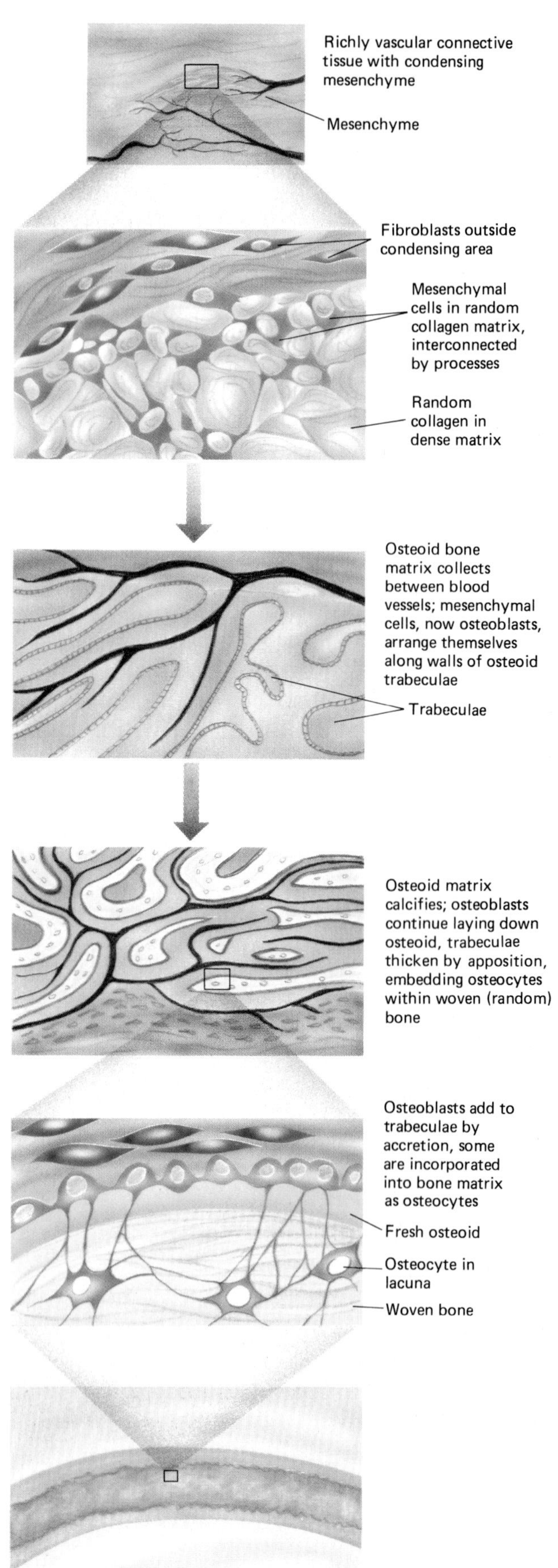
Richly vascular connective tissue with condensing mesenchyme
Mesenchyme
Fibroblasts outside condensing area
Mesenchymal cells in random collagen matrix, interconnected by processes
Random collagen in dense matrix
Osteoid bone matrix collects between blood vessels; mesenchymal cells, now osteoblasts, arrange themselves along walls of osteoid trabeculae
Trabeculae
Osteoid matrix calcifies; osteoblasts continue laying down osteoid, trabeculae thicken by apposition, embedding osteocytes within woven (random) bone
Osteoblasts add to trabeculae by accretion, some are incorporated into bone matrix as osteocytes
Fresh osteoid
Osteocyte in lacuna
Woven bone

FIGURE 6-5

Intramembranous bone formation. This type of bone formation is typical for the flat bones of the skull. The sequence illustrated incorporates events beginning with condensation of the mesenchyme and extending through the establishment of woven bone and matrix calcification.

Subsequently a dense eosinophilic material (stains red with certain dyes) appears in the existing extracellular matrix. This material forms the earliest trabeculae of membrane bone. Nearby cells develop a basophilic (stains blue with certain dyes) appearance, undergo enlargement (hypertrophy), and take up new positions along these trabeculae. The cells that do this are then termed osteoblasts and will form the bone matrix itself.

As the osteoblasts synthesize and secrete *osteoid* into their surrounding microenvironment, the trabeculae become larger. Both collagen and proteoglycans are found in this newly produced osteoid of the enlarging trabeculae. Because the collagen fibrils are characteristically arranged in a random pattern within this matrix, we refer to this stage of intramembranous bone formation as **woven bone.** This early form of intramembranous, or membrane, bone typically contains numerous large channels that contain blood vessels.

Very soon after the initial osteoid is laid down by the osteoblasts it becomes impregnated with calcium phosphate. All newly synthesized osteoid then becomes calcified shortly after it is deposited in the matrix. Figure 6-6 is a photomicrograph of intramembranous bone at this stage of development. Note that between the calcified portion of the trabecula and the osteoblasts there exists only a narrow region of newly deposited, uncalcified osteoid. As these processes of osteoid deposition and calcification continue, some osteoblasts near the surface of the trabeculae become entrapped within the new osteoid. When this occurs the cells are known as osteocytes.

Although they are isolated within lacunae of the calcifying matrix, the osteocytes remain in contact with the osteoblasts on the surface of the trabeculae through long cellular extensions which are located in minute channels called canaliculi. Such contact is necessary in order for osteocytes to obtain required nutrients and rid themselves of metabolic waste products because by virtue of their position within the lacunae they are somewhat removed from the nearest blood supply. As the osteoblasts are lost during the formation of osteocytes, new osteoblasts continuously arise through division and differentiation of osteoprogenitors among the surrounding primitive mesenchymal cell population.

Certain regions of the developing intramembranous bone undergo changes as the process continues, forming compact bone. The trabeculae continue to expand and encroach upon the spaces occupied by the nearby blood vessels. The collagen fibrils within the bone matrix are still randomly arranged, but less so than in the woven bone. Ultimately the bone takes on an irregularly concentric appearance and resembles **lamellar bone** (lah-**mel**-are; mature) (Fig. 6-7). In true lamellar bone the collagen is arranged in distinct concentric rings called **lamellae** (lah-**mel**-ee). However, because its collagen fibrils are still randomly arranged, it cannot be designated as lamellar bone per se.

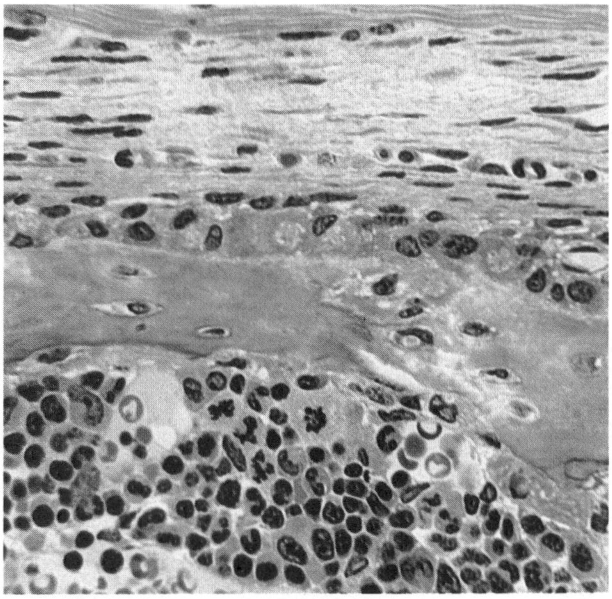

FIGURE 6-6

Photomicrograph of intramembranous bone formation (×100). (R. Calentine/Visuals Unlimited.)

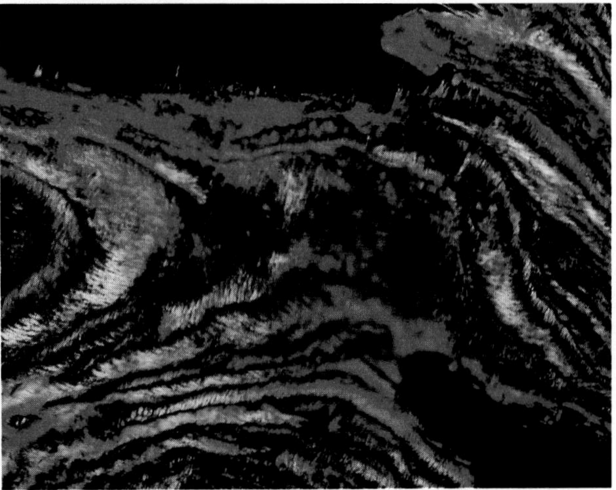

FIGURE 6-7

Photomicrograph of lamellar bone (×200). (Dr. Michael Klein/Peter Arnold, Inc.)

Woven bone persists in some regions and gives rise to *spongy bone.* In these areas the trabeculae no longer continue to enlarge and the adjacent vascular tissue gives rise to hematopoietic elements. As development of the membrane bone ceases, the cells of the surrounding primitive connective tissue condense to become the periosteum (Fig. 6-8). The osteoblasts located on the surface of the trabeculae form the endosteum. Cells of the endosteum take on an appearance similar to that of fibroblasts although they have the potential to resume bone formation at a later time if it becomes necessary.

Endochondral bone formation occurs within a pre-existing cartilaginous model of the future bone

The majority of the bones of the human body are the result of **endochondral ossification.** Because this process involves the replacement of a cartilaginous model of the future bone by bone itself, it is also known as intracartilaginous bone formation.

Figure 6-9 portrays the formation of a typical long bone (e.g., humerus or femur). During the embryonic period of development, the mesenchyme cells in the region of the future bone proliferate and become tightly packed, forming a rough outline of the bone to be formed. Next, these mesenchyme cells continue to differentiate into chondrocytes and secrete cellular products into the extracellular matrix. Finally, a recognizable model (composed of hyaline cartilage) of the prospective bone is established. The cells located at the edges of the model give rise to the *perichondrium.* Certain cells of the perichondrium differentiate into fibroblasts while others retain characteristics of the primitive mesenchyme.

Growth in length of the cartilage model occurs mainly at its ends and soon the chondrocytes in the midportion become greatly enlarged (hypertrophied). Calcification of the intercellular substance in this region begins as the enlarged chondrocytes secrete enzymes such as phosphatase. The cartilage model also increases in width. This is accomplished through **appositional growth,** in which new cartilage is produced on the sides of the model by proliferation and differentiation of cells within the surrounding perichondrium.

As development continues, the perichondrium is invaded by capillaries. With the onset of capillary invasion, some cells of the perichondrium differentiate into osteoblasts and osteocytes and a thin layer of bone is established around the midportion of the cartilage model (Fig. 6-9). The connective tissue cells that reside on the surface of this thin layer of bone are now termed the *periosteum.* The innermost cells of the periosteum retain

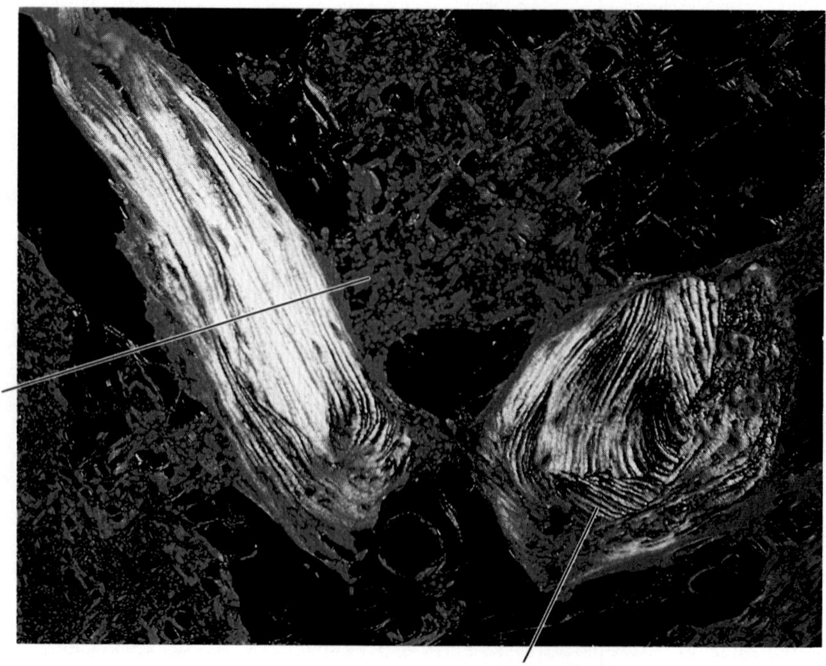

FIGURE 6-8

Photomicrograph of woven and lamellar bone (× 100). (Dr. Michael Klein/Peter Arnold, Inc.)

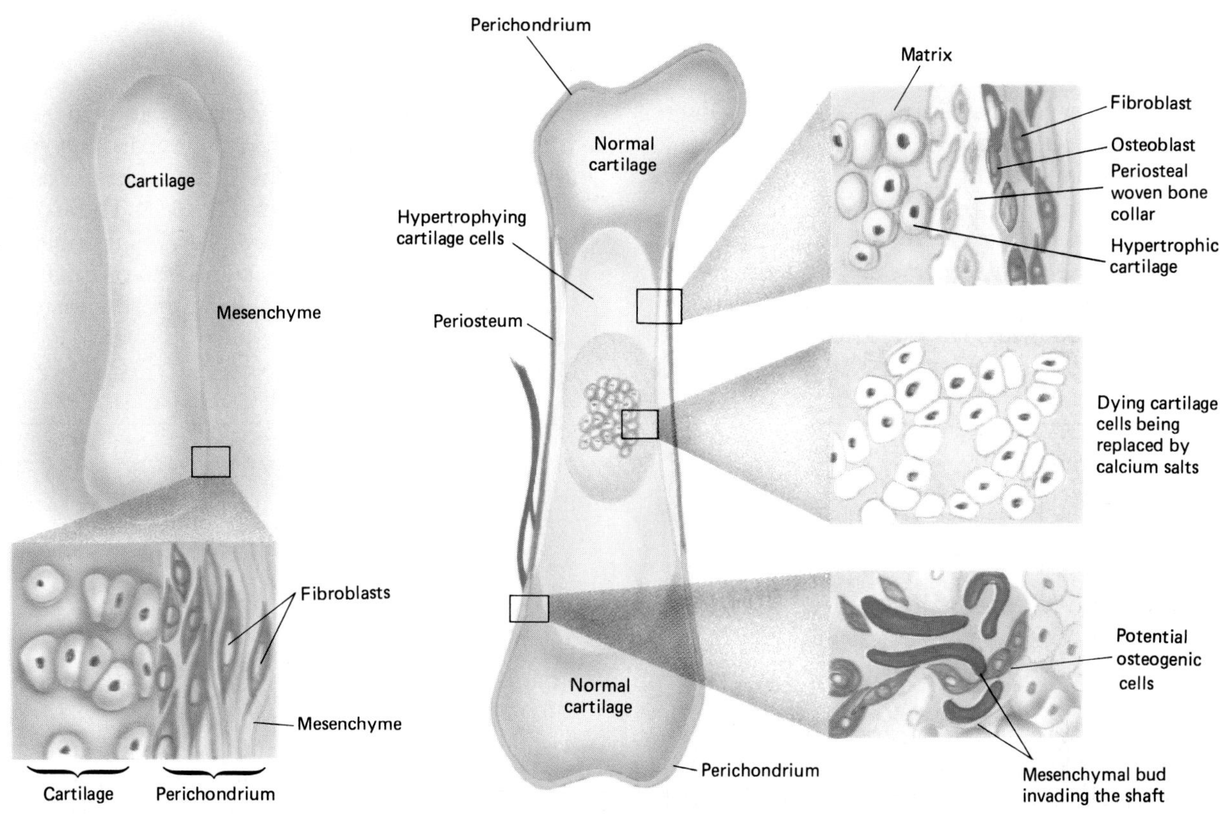

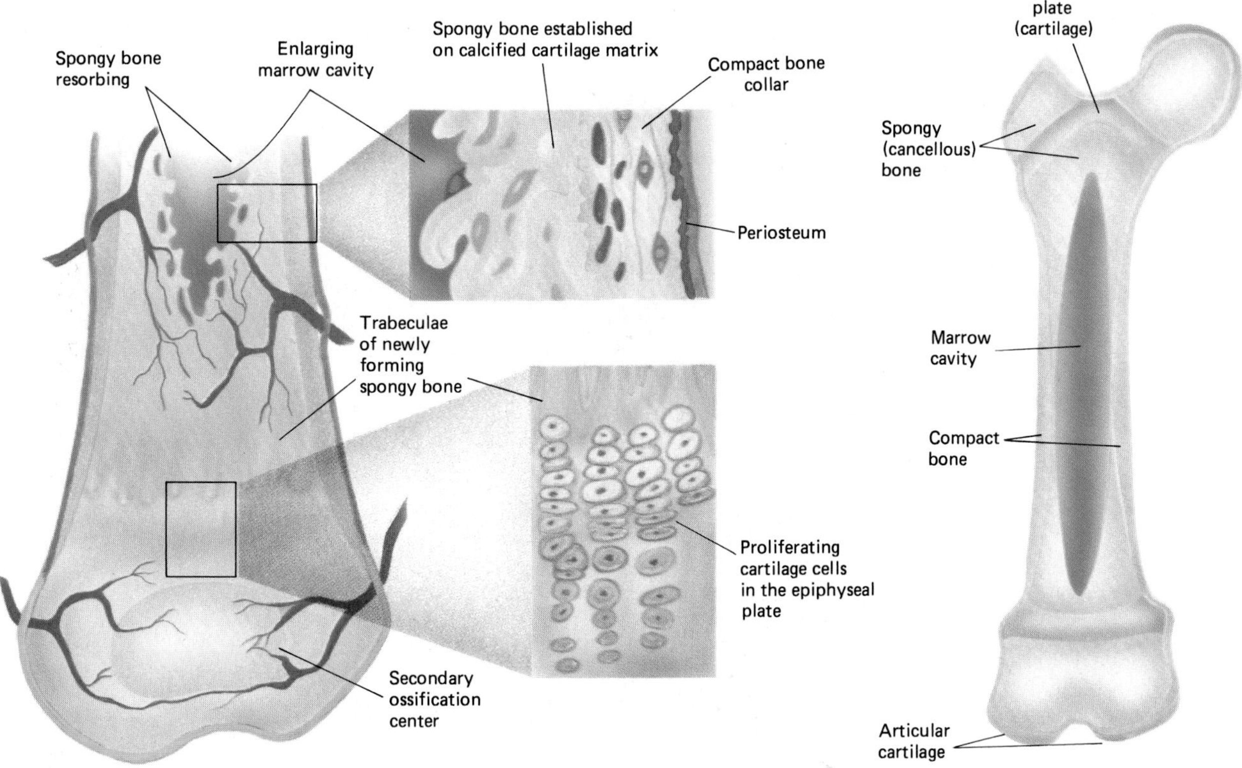

FIGURE 6-9

Endochondral bone formation. Schematic representation of the events occurring during formation of the femur. Notice that this type of bone formation involves the replacement of a cartilaginous model of the future bone by bone itself.

their capacity to give rise to chondrocytes even into adulthood. This is evidenced by the formation of cartilage during the repair of a fracture (see Fig. 6-10).

With time the calcified cartilage in the midportion of the model begins to break down and disintegrate. Subsequently this region is also invaded by blood vessels, osteoblasts, and osteocytes, all of which make their way into the area of degenerating calcified cartilage from the surrounding periosteum. When this occurs, a *center of ossification* is established (Fig. 6-9). The osteocytes then produce a bone intercellular substance which is deposited on the remnants of calcified cartilage. Bone that is laid down in this manner is termed *cancellous bone.*

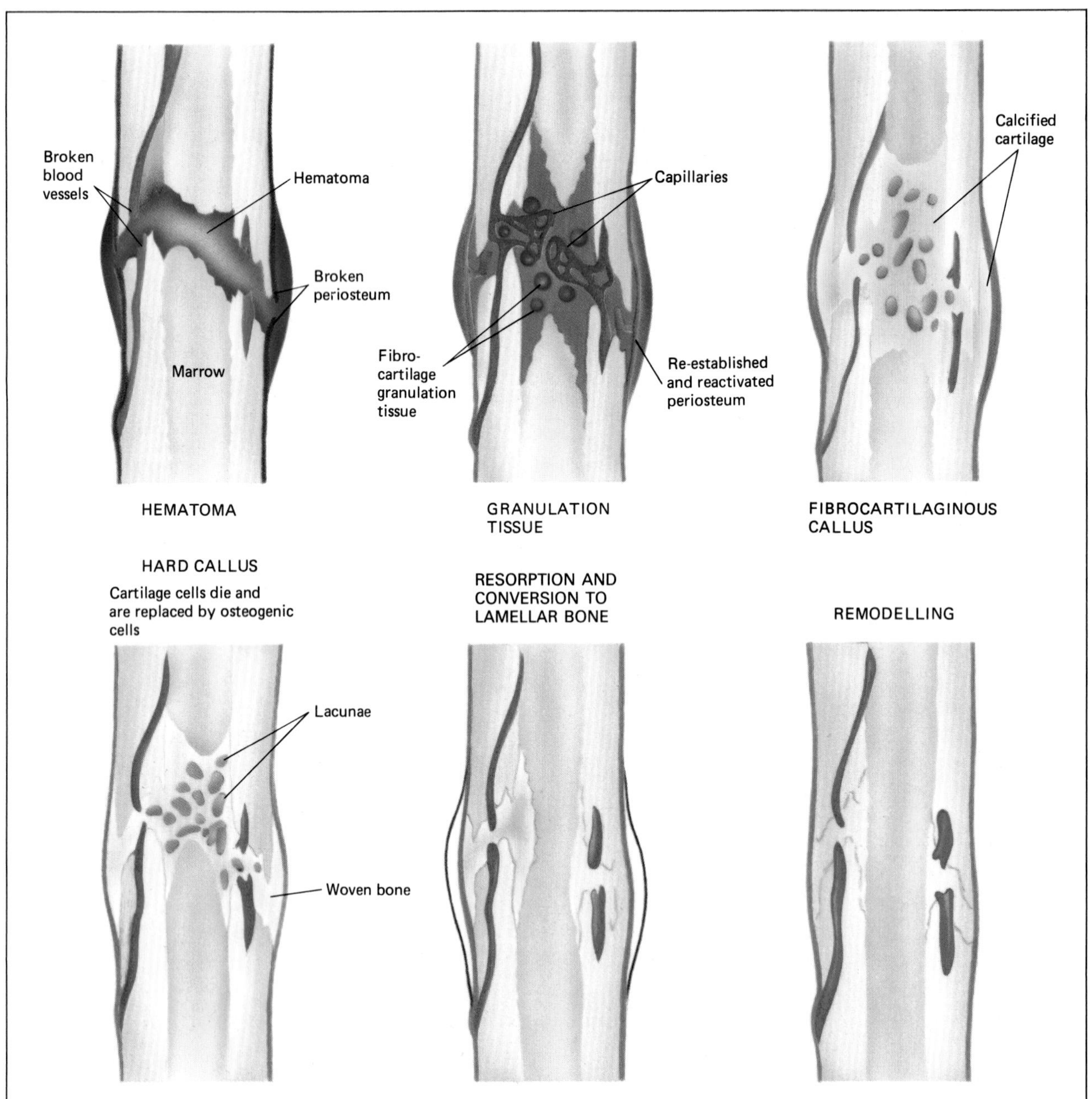

FIGURE 6-10

Fracture healing. Schematic representation of major events occurring during the healing of a fracture. Notice the formation of the granulation tissue, fibrocartilaginous callus, and the osseous (hard) callus. The osseous callus, once formed, typically undergoes a significant degree of remodeling.

As the cartilage model continues to grow in length at its ends by **interstitial growth** (without removal of the pre-existing bone), the center of ossification also expands lengthwise in both directions. The cartilage adjacent to the advancing bone breaks down and is replaced by cancellous bone. In this manner the shaft, or diaphysis, of the long bone is formed. The central region of cancellous bone within the diaphysis is resorbed eventually, and the marrow cavity is thus established (Fig. 6-9). As bone growth continues, the bone that lines the marrow cavity is constantly removed while osteocytes derived from the surrounding periosteum deposit new bone on the external surface. Thus, the bone becomes larger in diameter through this process of **appositional growth;** as the marrow cavity enlarges, new bone is added to the surface of the diaphysis.

Secondary centers of ossification develop in the ends or epiphyses of the larger long bones while the *primary center* originates in the diaphysis. The processes responsible for the formation of these epiphyseal centers of ossification are essentially the same as those occurring in the diaphysis.

Only a thin layer of hyaline cartilage, termed **articular cartilage,** remains on the surface of the epiphysis when ossification is complete. There is a transverse layer of cartilage that persists between the bone of the diaphysis and that of the epiphysis. This cartilaginous layer is known as the **epiphyseal plate** and is very important for the future growth in length of the long bone after birth (Fig. 6-11). Epiphyseal plates are not replaced by bone (a process termed epiphyseal closure) until the bones have attained their final length.

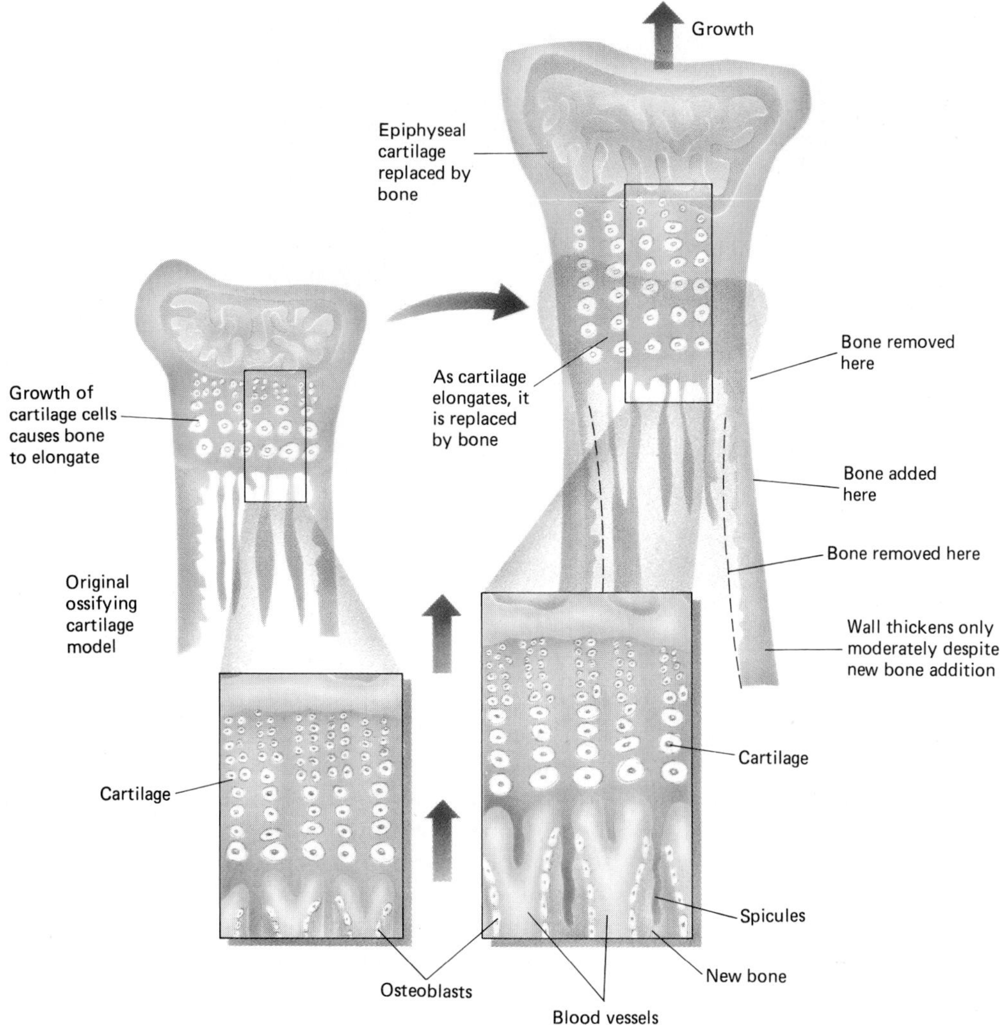

FIGURE 6-11

Schematic representation of bone remodeling that is associated with bone growth.

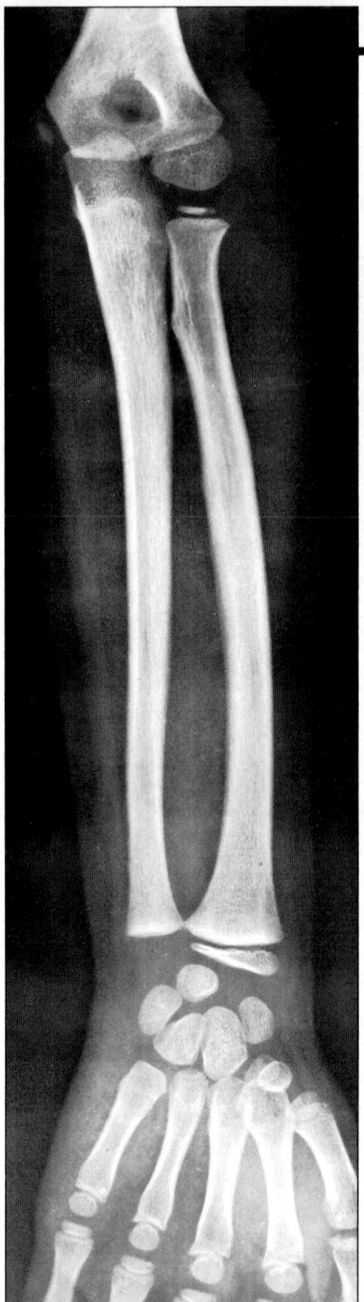

(a)

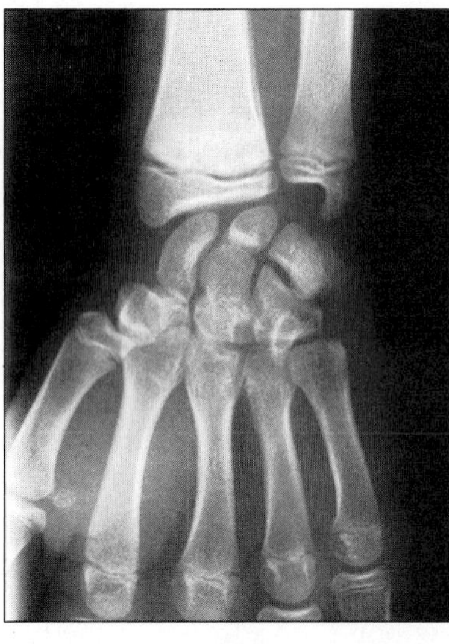

(b)

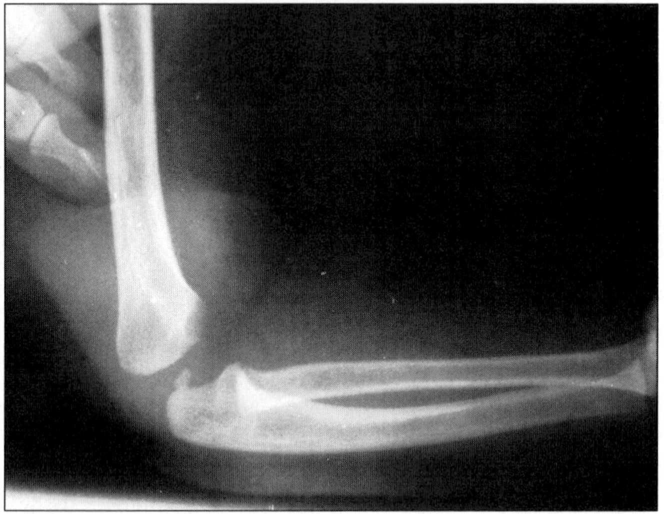

(c)

FIGURE 6-12

Radiographs (x-rays) of immature long bones of the forearm illustrating epiphyseal plates. Compare the degree of bone development and the extent of epiphyseal closure in (*a*) and (*b*). Notice that the film shown in (*b*) is from an older individual than that in (*a*). Bones of the left forearm and elbow of a 3-year-old boy are shown in (*c*). Notice the great amount of apparent space between these bones at the elbow. This space is actually occupied by cartilage that does not show up in such a film because it is radiotransparent. A tiny epiphysis, belonging to the proximal portion of the ulna, is just discernible in the region of the elbow joint.

Clinical highlight

The precise age at which epiphyseal closure occurs varies for different long bones. Generally closure occurs earlier in females (18 years) than in males (21 years). Furthermore, in certain long bones the plate at one epiphysis is replaced by bone earlier than that at the other end. In immature long bones, epiphyseal plates are easily discernible on roentgenograms such as those represented in Figure 6-12. Since the epiphyseal plates are so vitally important to growth in length of the long bones, it is understandable that injury to this region might significantly alter normal bone growth in the affected individual.

Microscopic examination reveals that epiphyseal plates are composed of four distinct regions, or *zones*, of cells (Fig. 6-13). Proceeding from the epiphyseal end to the diaphyseal end these are the (a) **zone of resting,** or **reserve cartilage;** (b) **zone of proliferation;** (c) **zone of maturation;** and (d) **zone of calcification.** As the long bone grows in length, new chondrocytes arise through continuous mitotic divisions on the epiphyseal side of the cartilaginous plate; cartilage on the diaphyseal side is replaced by bone. The characteristic features of each of the four zones of the epiphyseal plate are described in the following sections.

THE ZONE OF RESTING, OR RESERVE, CARTILAGE CONSISTS LARGELY OF HYALINE CARTILAGE

The irregularly spaced chondrocytes of this zone are situated directly adjacent to the bone of the epiphysis. The primary purpose of the *resting zone* of cartilage is to firmly attach the cartilaginous plate to the epiphyseal bone. Blood vessels located at the interface of the resting zone and the epiphyseal bone supply nutrients to the more distantly located chondrocytes of the epiphyseal plate by the process of diffusion. Chondrocytes of the resting zone do not contribute to the growth in length of the bone.

CHONDROCYTES DIVIDE AND ARE STACKED IN LONG COLUMNS IN THE ZONE OF PROLIFERATION

Chondrocytes of this region are characteristically stacked on top of one another in a series of columns (Fig. 6-13). These cartilage cells undergo substantial proliferation, and significant numbers of mitotic figures may be observed within this zone. Cells needed to replace those chondrocytes that *hypertrophy* (enlarge) and die in the zone of maturation are generated in this *zone of proliferation.* The zone of proliferation is partially responsible for the expansion in length of the epiphyseal plate.

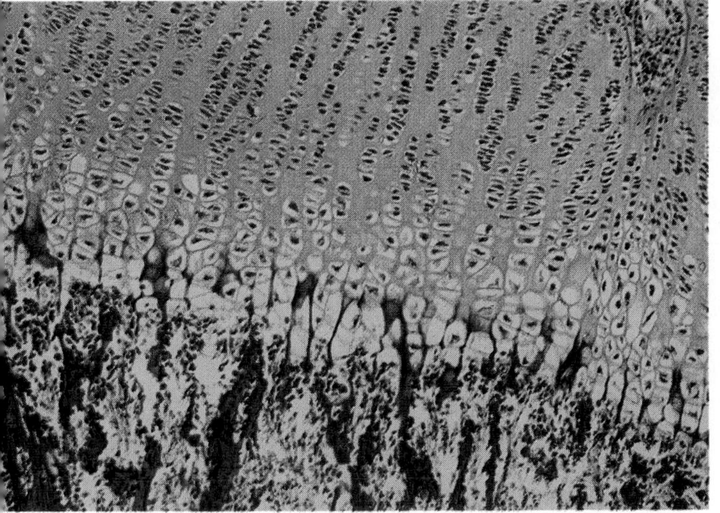

FIGURE 6-13

Developing endochondral bone. Photomicrograph illustrating the microscopic appearance of the epiphyseal plate region (× 100). How many of the cell regions or zones mentioned in your text can you identify. (Bruce Iverson/Visuals Unlimited.)

CHONDROCYTES HYPERTROPHY WITHIN THE ZONE OF MATURATION

The chondrocytes in this next region are also arranged in characteristic columns; however, they are much larger than those cells of the preceding zone (Fig. 6-13). Hypertrophy of the chondrocytes in this zone also contributes to lengthwise growth of the epiphyseal plate. The youngest cells of this *zone of maturation* are those located closest to the zone of proliferation; the older, more mature cells are situated more towards the diaphysis. The ultimate fate of the chondrocytes in the zone of maturation is cell death. As the most mature chondrocytes begin to secrete phosphatase enzymes, the surrounding extracellular matrix material undergoes calcification and the chondrocytes subsequently die.

CHONDROCYTES DIE AND THE CARTILAGE MATRIX ACQUIRES HYDROXYAPATITE CRYSTALS IN THE ZONE OF CALCIFICATION

The functional significance of the *zone of calcification* is similar to that of the resting zone described earlier, that is, attachment. It serves to unite the epiphyseal plate firmly with the adjacent diaphyseal bone (Fig. 6-13). Because calcification of the cartilage matrix has effectively cut off the supply of essential nutrients, this region is composed primarily of dead or dying cells. Capillaries, osteoclasts, and osteoblasts from the diaphyseal region make their way into the zone of calcification. Osteoclasts begin to remove the disintegrating calcified cartilage, and osteoblasts subsequently lay down new bone on the calcified spicules that remain. The formation of bone in this region of the epiphyseal plate is very active and serves to strengthen the attachment between bone and cartilage at this junction.

It should be clear from the foregoing discussion that the shaft or diaphysis of a long bone can grow in length only by the process of *appositional growth.* Lengthening of the diaphysis is not possible by *interstitial growth* in which there is no removal of pre-existing matrix. Furthermore, as new bone is added to the region adjacent to the zone of calcification, bone removal (resorption) takes place at the boundary of the marrow cavity. These two processes occur at similar rates so that the region where new bone is being deposited remains approximately the same thickness throughout the period of bone growth. Likewise, the thickness of the epiphyseal plate also remains relatively constant throughout this same period.

Lamellar bone is synonymous with mature bone whereas woven bone is of a primary or immature nature

The bone that is initially produced during intramembranous and endochondral ossification is referred to as *woven bone*. Collagen fibers of woven bone run in a multitude of directions and lack the highly ordered and parallel configuration characteristic of *lamellar bone* which ultimately replaces it. Woven bone is totally unsuitable for the stresses and strains encountered by the adult skeleton.

Clinical highlight

This can be seen easily in patients with **osteitis deformans (Paget's disease),** a condition of unknown origin that converts mature tissue of the adult skeleton back into woven bone. This process leads to endless deformities, primarily related to excessive distortion in response to stress. This causes bone weakness and painful joint destruction.

Woven bone, as you have seen, does not provide the strength and support properties so characteristic of the bones comprising the adult skeleton. However, this does not mean that it serves little purpose or is of small consequence to us. On the contrary, the existence of woven bone provides the essential framework or foundation on which grain-oriented lamellar bone will subsequently be laid down during the process of bone remodeling. This has been illustrated in Figure 6-14.

Although the precise mechanisms by which bone cells determine how bone is to be remodeled and in which direction the grain is to run are unknown, current studies provide some insight into the processes involved. Investigators have known for some time that electrical fields develop in the apatite crystals and collagenous fibers of a bone when the bone is subjected to a simple physical stress, for example, bending. The resultant electrical forces may then serve as specific cues or guidelines for the osteoblasts as they lay down new bone in a precise orientation as well as for osteoclasts participating in bone resorption.

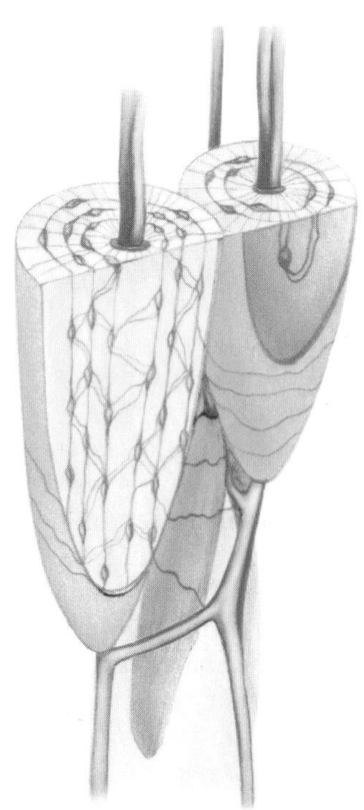

(a)

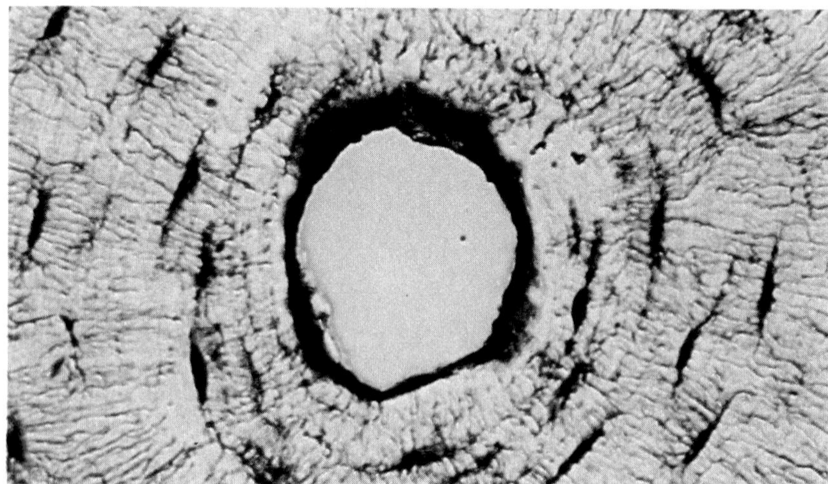

(b)

FIGURE 6-14

(*a*) Structure of an osteon. Successive layers of osteoblasts become wrapped around a blood vessel, with the "grain" of the bone layers directed at angles to one another. Such a perfect osteon is seldom if ever found in actual bone because osteons need to be packaged tightly and because constant remodeling and replacement continues in all bone throughout life. (*b*) Photomicrograph of lacunae and canaliculi (×400). The large number of canaliculi permit the movement of materials from one osteocyte to another with relative ease. (Bruce Iverson/Visuals Unlimited.)

Clinical highlight

The generation of weak electrical current (millivolt range) via electrodes implanted in bone has likewise been shown to speed up the processes of bone repair and remodeling. Dental researchers are currently investigating the possible use of weak electrical fields to facilitate the repositioning of teeth: a task ordinarily accomplished through the wearing of braces for lengthy periods of time in many instances.

Although the remodeling of bone is most prominent during the period of active growth, we know that it is basically a continuous event. The physical stresses imposed by mere body weight and muscular forces may be essential elements to this process.

As woven bone is formed it is almost immediately removed by osteoclasts and replaced with *lamellar bone*. This new bone is typically deposited in concentric rings around a centrally located blood vessel (Fig. 6-15). Furthermore, strength and stability are imparted to the lamellar bone as it is laid down because collagen fibers in adjacent rings are arranged at definite angles to one another. The osteoblasts that are trapped in lacunae at the interface of adjacent rings become osteocytes and remain in direct contact with their neighbors via tiny cellular processes located in canaliculi (Fig. 6-15). The central blood vessel together with its surrounding concentric rings of bone (varying from four to twenty in number) and osteocytes is known as an **osteon** or **haversian system.** Their overall configuration appears spindle-shaped. Several such osteons are illustrated in Figure 6-14.

The canaliculi not only serve to interconnect the osteocytes of a particular osteon, but also reach the cavity where central vessels are located. The central blood vessels of one osteon also connect with those of neighboring systems via branches lying within passages known as **Volkmann's canals.** Because the central vessels communicate with vessels on the surface of the bone as well as with those in the marrow spaces, a magnificent transport system is established. Nutrients can be delivered to and waste products removed from the osteocytes of each haversian system.

The most distinct and highly ordered osteons are typically found in the outer compact layers

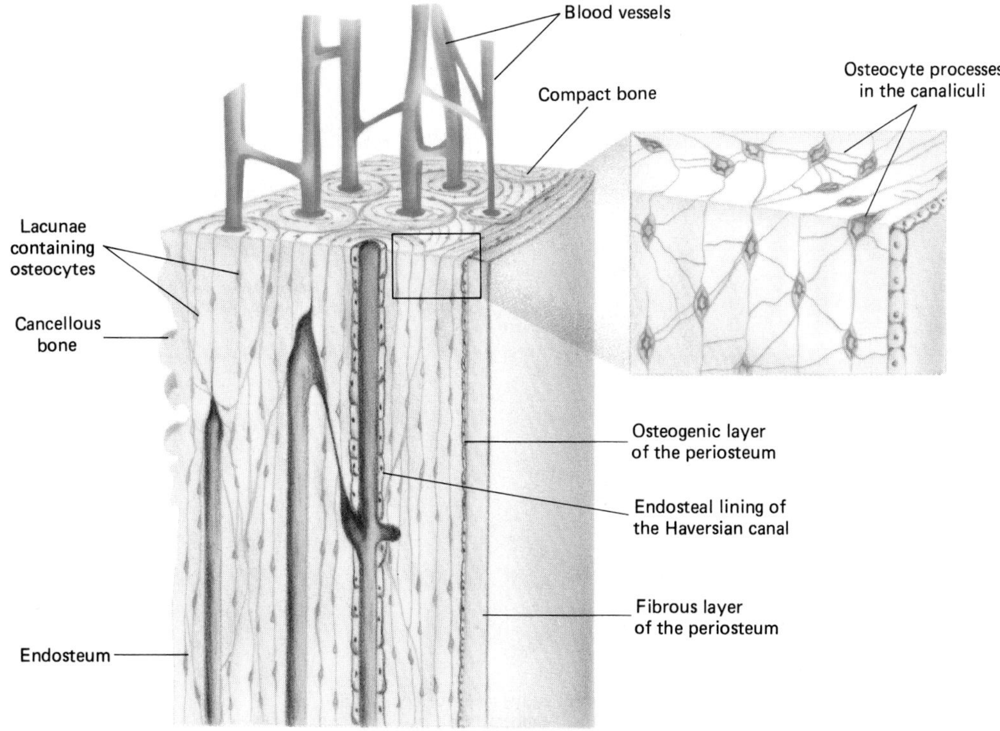

FIGURE 6-15

Three-dimensional schematic illustrating the cross-sectional and longitudinal appearance of the various components that enter into the formation of compact cortical bone.

near the external surface of bones. This is termed **cortical bone** and is usually represented as a thin shell-like layer. Interspersed among these well-differentiated osteons are the remnants of earlier osteons which have been incompletely removed as a result of bone remodeling. These vary considerably in size, have irregular shapes, and constitute what are collectively known as the **interstitial lamellae.**

Cancellous bone, which we discussed earlier, has a spongier consistency compared to cortical bone and is located in the central portion of most bones. Interspersed among its spicules are minute blood-filled cavities known as **cancellae.** Since the spicules are thin and small, blood within the cancellae easily nourishes the nearby osteocytes—an arrangement that takes the place of the haversian architecture described previously.

Bone may grow without actually forming distinct osteons, but this type of lamellar bone is constructed in a manner similar to osteon development. All bone begins as woven bone; however, most of it will eventually become lamellar bone.

Many bones continue to grow even after the onset of sexual maturity. Membranous bones grow via the action of their periosteum, and as bone is removed from their inner cavities, new bone is laid down near the surface. This coordinated removal and deposition of bone permits the marrow cavity to enlarge in concert with the addition of new bone externally. Thus, the bone enlarges in size, but without an excessive increase in weight.

Furthermore, as bone grows it changes not only in size but also in shape. These changes necessitate a continuous and extensive remodeling, with older haversian systems being replaced with new ones (Fig. 6-16). Thus, perfect spindle-shaped osteons as depicted in Figure 6-14 are

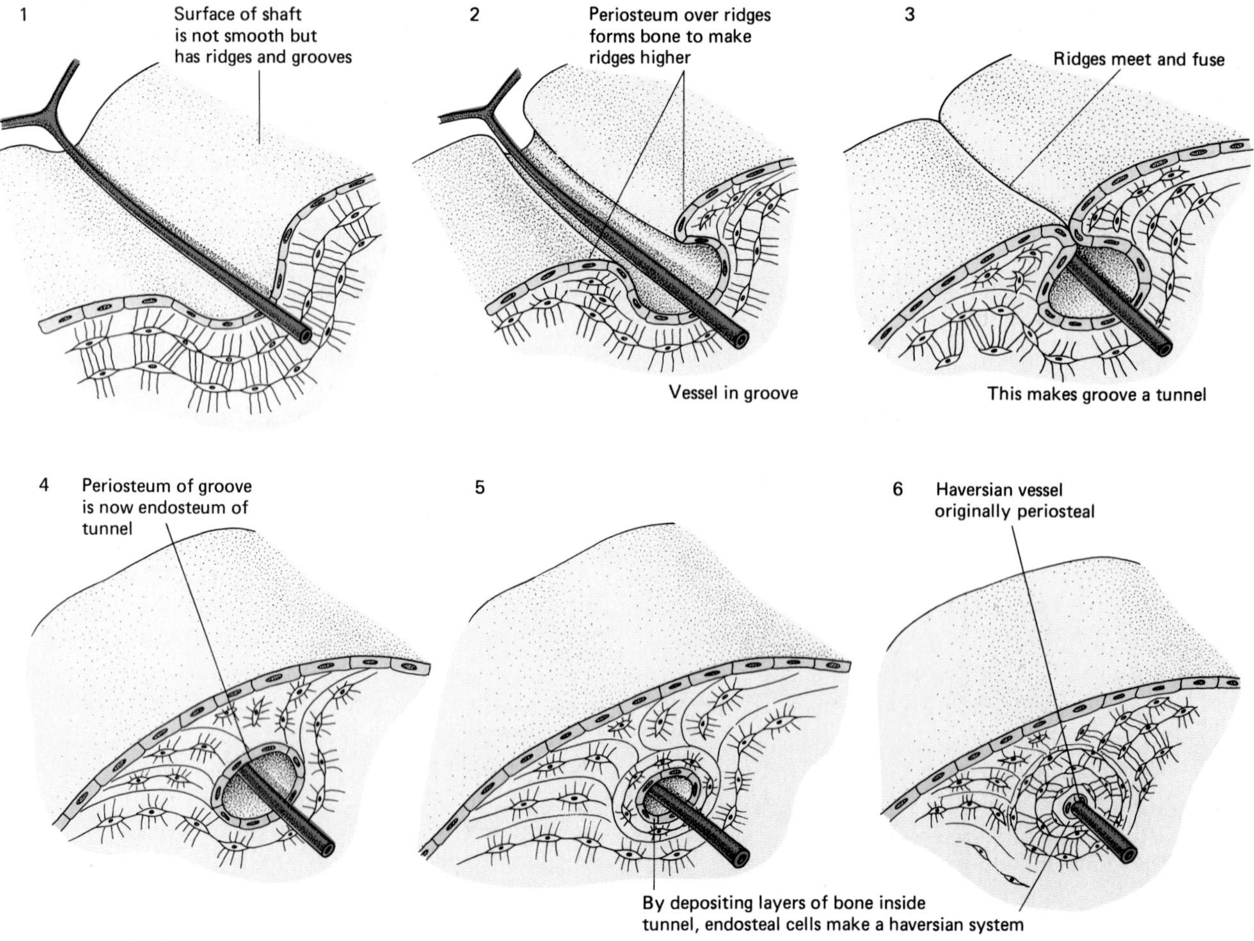

FIGURE 6-16

One type of haversian remodeling of bone, produced when osteoclasts excavate a groove on the surface of the bone.

rarely seen in actual bone specimens. The older haversian systems become eroded to varying degrees to accommodate the new, and portions of them remain behind as the interstitial lamellae described earlier. The density and grain pattern of bone must be continuously reoriented to keep pace with changing stresses accompanying alterations in an individual's habits and lifestyle. Hence, even adult bone undergoes remodeling. For example, excessive marching may spontaneously fracture foot bones of military recruits unless the remodeling events can keep up with the new stresses that have been suddenly imposed. Clinically, similar fractures have likewise been observed in joggers and ballet dancers. During the course of an individual's lifetime, it is estimated that the mature haversian systems are replaced approximately ten times.

Healing of fractures involves an orderly sequence of events leading to restoration of the original bone structure

Bones are by no means indestructible and, as we are aware, they sometimes break (Fig. 6-17). Clinically a broken bone is termed a **fracture** and, depending on its extent and nature, it is typically classified as one of the following types. A bone that is broken completely through has a **complete fracture.** If the break extends through only a portion of the bone, it is termed an **incomplete** or **green stick fracture.** When the skin overlying the break remains intact, the break is classified as a **closed** or **simple fracture.** A **compound fracture,** on the other hand, is one in which the broken bone pierces the surrounding tissue and becomes exposed on the surface of the skin. In certain instances a bone may actually become fragmented or splintered and such a break is termed a **comminuted fracture.** If the fracture occurs in an already diseased bone, it is termed a **pathologic fracture.**

Ordinarily most fractures heal readily if proper treatment is provided. The primary requirement for the healing of a fracture is that the broken ends of the bone make contact with one another. That is, the fracture must be **reduced.** However, any one of several concomitant problems may arise which also need consideration. For example, infection or impairment of the local blood supply may occur, either one of which complicates the healing process.

Suppose that you have a simple closed fracture located near the middle of your humerus. What is the important sequence of events in the healing process that will lead to the repair of your fracture? Although the healing process is a continuous one, it is typically arranged into three stages for descriptive purposes.

First is the conversion of the blood clot (hematoma) to a soft tissue callus, termed the **procallus,** at the fracture site. This begins immediately following the occurrence of the fracture and is usually completed within 48 hours. A loose meshwork of fibrin is first laid down. Next, the local destruction of red blood cells provides a stimulus for an inflammatory reaction which is characterized by swelling (edema), increased blood flow, and infiltration of white blood cells. Soon the macrophages and fibroblasts arrive and initiate their activities. The former phagocytize the red cell debris while the latter begin the repair process by laying down connective tissue. Thus, the procallus is established at the fracture site and initially serves to bind the fracture together.

The second stage in the healing process is represented by the conversion of the rather weak procallus to a more stable configuration, the **fibrocartilaginous callus.** Fibroblasts continue to lay down a fibrous connective tissue network, and newly formed chondroblasts begin their formation of cartilaginous spicules throughout the callus. These events take place during the third and fourth days following the injury.

By the end of the first week, one is able to observe aggregates of newly formed bone and cartilage throughout the entire callus. The osteoblasts and chondroblasts most likely originate from the periosteum and endosteum of the fracture site. The inflammatory response subsides over the next few days and additional bone is laid down within the callus. Eventually the entire fibrocartilaginous callus is replaced by bone and is termed the **osseous callus.** Reaching maximum size within two or three weeks, it has a spindle-shaped configuration in that it is ordinarily wider in diameter than the original bone and extends for some distance on either side of the fracture site (Fig. 6-18). Even as the osseous callous is being established it is undergoing some degree of remodeling. This process continues and with time only the eye of the trained forensic pathologist will be able to detect if the original bone had been fractured.

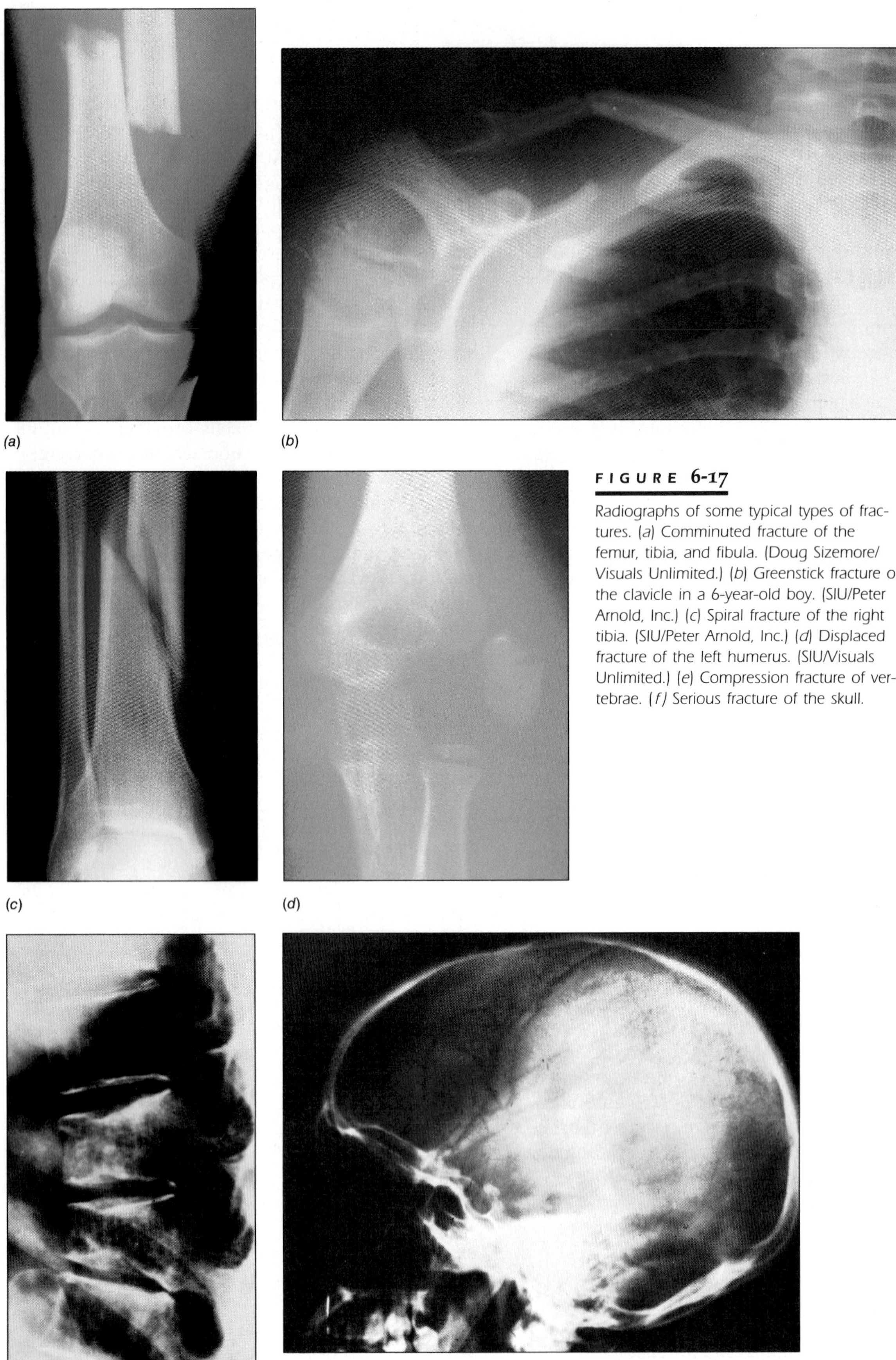

FIGURE 6-17

Radiographs of some typical types of fractures. (*a*) Comminuted fracture of the femur, tibia, and fibula. (Doug Sizemore/Visuals Unlimited.) (*b*) Greenstick fracture of the clavicle in a 6-year-old boy. (SIU/Peter Arnold, Inc.) (*c*) Spiral fracture of the right tibia. (SIU/Peter Arnold, Inc.) (*d*) Displaced fracture of the left humerus. (SIU/Visuals Unlimited.) (*e*) Compression fracture of vertebrae. (*f*) Serious fracture of the skull.

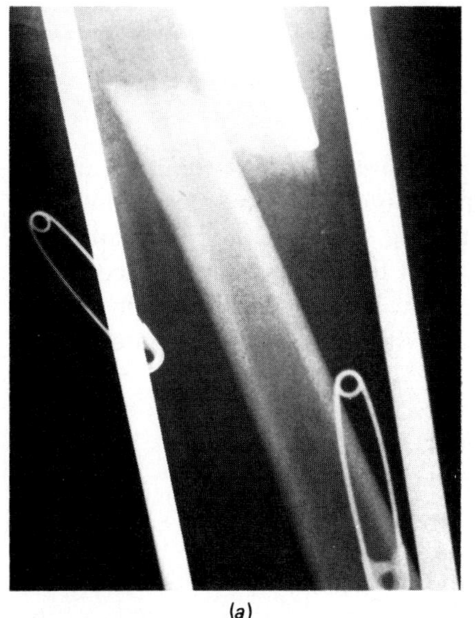

(a)

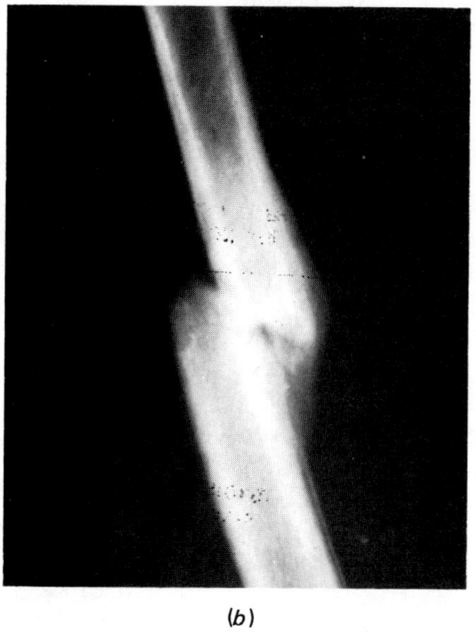

(b)

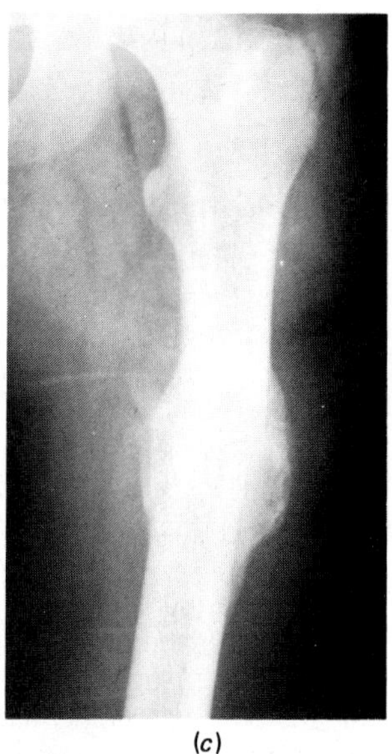

(c)

FIGURE 6-18

(a) A recently broken femur. The odd collection of shadows and safety pins results from the temporary splint that was applied to the injured limb. (b) Healing, showing the formation of a callus. Healing and union do not necessarily depend upon bringing the fractured edges exactly together. (c) Fracture showing a fully developed callus splinting the broken ends of the femur together.

Clinical highlight

Until recently bone could not be induced to unite with other materials, which made replacement of missing bone difficult. Replacement bone grafts obtained from expendable regions of the skeleton were often tried, but were not always practical. Today several new synthetic polymers have been developed and demonstrate significant promise as replacements for lost segments of bone. Because these new materials contain certain ceramics that appear to offer cues for bone remodeling similar to those of bone itself, osteoblasts attach newly formed bone to the synthetic material much as they would to natural bone adjacent to the original fracture site.

Tendons and ligaments link structures

Tendons and ligaments are both composed of dense regular connective tissue. As such, they are well suited for uniting various structures of the body.

Tendons attach muscle to other structures

Tendons are composed of dense regular connective tissue and contain a large number of parallel collagen bundles. These collagen bundles comprising the tendon are responsible for its shiny, white appearance. Tendons function in the attachment of muscle to other structures, typically to bone. The collagen fibers of a tendon blend with muscle fibers at one end and with the fibrous periosteum covering the bone at the other. Certain tendon fibers may actually be attached to the substance of the bone itself or to cartilage. Those fibers attaching the tendon to bone are similar to those that serve to anchor the periosteum, that is, Sharpey's fibers (Fig. 6-19). As bones grow and develop, it becomes necessary for the points of attachment of tendons to move. Just how this is accomplished is not yet well understood.

Tendons vary markedly in their shape and thickness. Some are cordlike whereas others are broad and flat and are termed **aponeuroses** (*ap*-oh-new-**row**-sees). The prolonged action of tendons across two bones or over adjacent tendons can result in frictional stress and possible damage to the tendon. Protection in such instances is afforded by the presence of a **bursa** (**burr**-suh) or **tendon sheath.** When a tendon sheath is present, it is located superficial to the outermost covering of the tendon itself, the **peritendineum** (pear-ee-**ten**-din-ee-um). The space between the two is frequently connected to the cavity of the adjacent joint and is lubricated with a thin layer of fluid. In certain cases, cartilage may actually develop within a tendon *(sesamoid bone)* at a point subject to pronounced frictional stress.

Clinical highlight

Because the parallel arrangement of the collagen bundles of tendons imparts such powerful resistance to severe stress, it is not uncommon for the bony attachment of the tendon to tear away from the bone rather than for the tendon to break. Once damaged, however, tendons, ligaments, and cartilage all heal quite slowly due to their rather sparse vascular supply. In aging athletes and dancers the great heel, or Achilles, tendon is often ruptured by forces that would easily be tolerated by younger individuals. In addition to arthritic problems involving tendons, overenthusiastic joggers not uncommonly develop a traumatic inflammation called **tendonitis** of this and other tendons. They may also develop inflammatory changes referred to as **bursitis** accompanied by calcium deposits in bursae of the feet.

Ligaments bind bones together

Ligaments serve to bind two bones or bony parts together (Fig. 6-20). They are composed of collagen bundles, together with varying amounts of elastic fibers. As in the case of tendons, the connective tissue fibers of ligaments typically run in the same direction, that is, parallel to one another. This imparts considerable strength to ligaments and therefore they permit little stretching. Exceptions to this include the ligaments (*ligamentum flava* of the vertebral column) composed primarily of elastic fibers. Such ligaments stretch upon pulling, contract upon relaxation, and therefore tend to remain more or less taut.

Some ligaments associated with synovial joints actually constitute portions of the fibrous wall of the joint capsule. The collateral ligaments of the knee joint represent a prime example of this arrangement (Fig. 6-21). Although ligaments vary considerably in their gross appearance, they function primarily in limiting the range of motion of the joints with which they are associated.

Bone is subject to numerous disease processes

Consider for a moment just how vastly complex bone is as a living tissue. Recall the variety of its differentiated cell types, its crystalline components, fibrous elements and arrangements, as well as the hematopoietic cells within its marrow. Given the degree of its biological complexity, it is not surprising that bone is the target of many and varied diseases. As one might suspect, bone may also be involved secondarily in several disease states. We will limit our discussion to a few principal and primary diseases of bone.

Osteogenesis imperfecta is an inherited disorder of collagen maturation and aggregation

Osteogenesis imperfecta is a relatively uncommon congenital disorder resulting from abnormal connective tissue synthesis. Clinically the disease is characterized by (a) thin, poorly formed bones; (b) multiple fractures; (c) loose joints; (d) stunting;

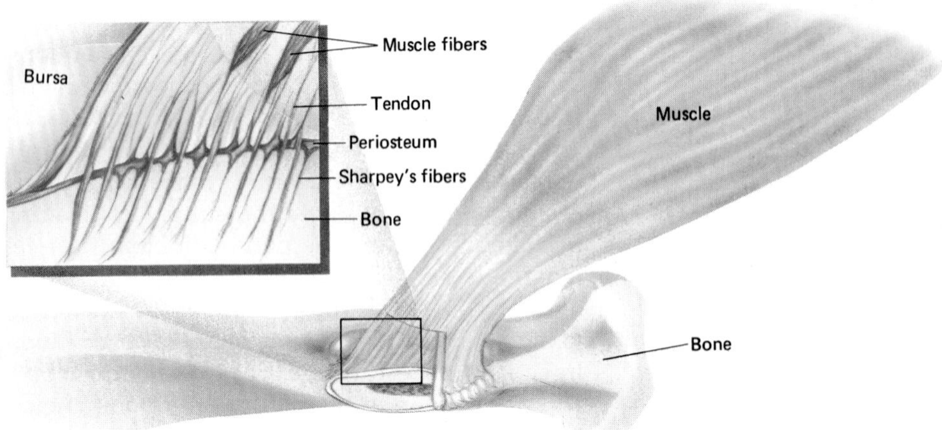

FIGURE 6-19

Attachment of tendon to bone. The tendon is a specialized connective tissue structure that typically transmits muscular pull to bone.

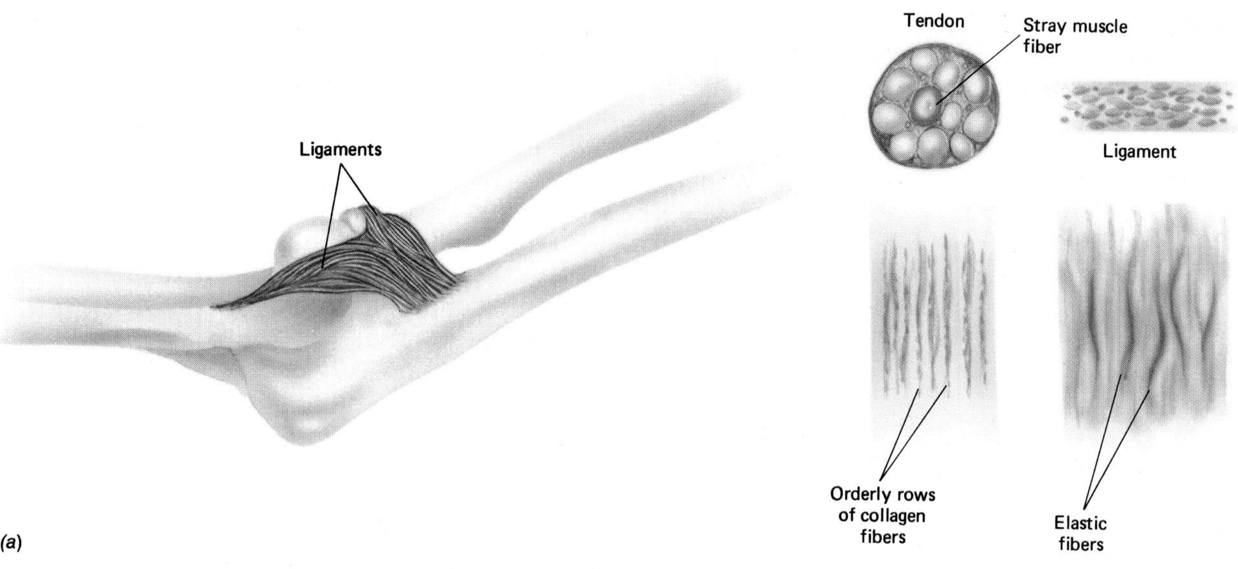

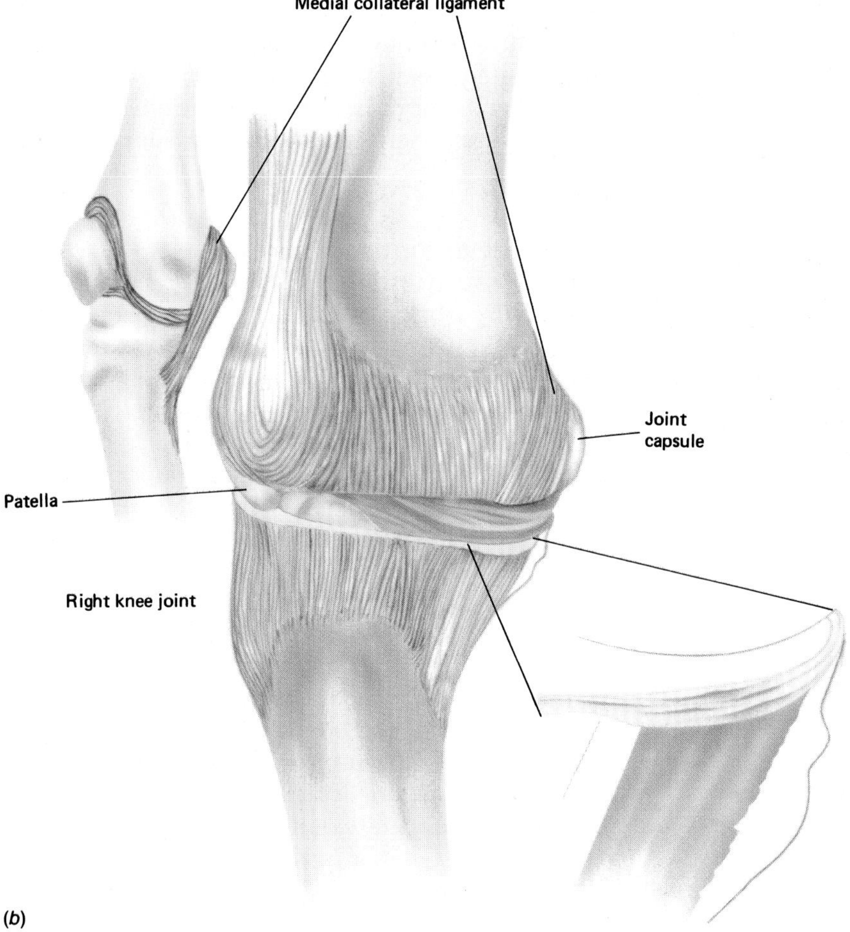

FIGURE 6-20

(*a*) Two ligaments of the elbow joint are the radial collateral ligament and annular ligament of the radius. Notice also certain structural differences between a tendon and ligament. (*b*) Medial (tibial) collateral ligament of the right knee joint. This ligament actually constitutes a thickened portion of the fibrous capsule of the knee joint. Compare this schematic with the radiograph of the knee joint in Fig. 6-21.

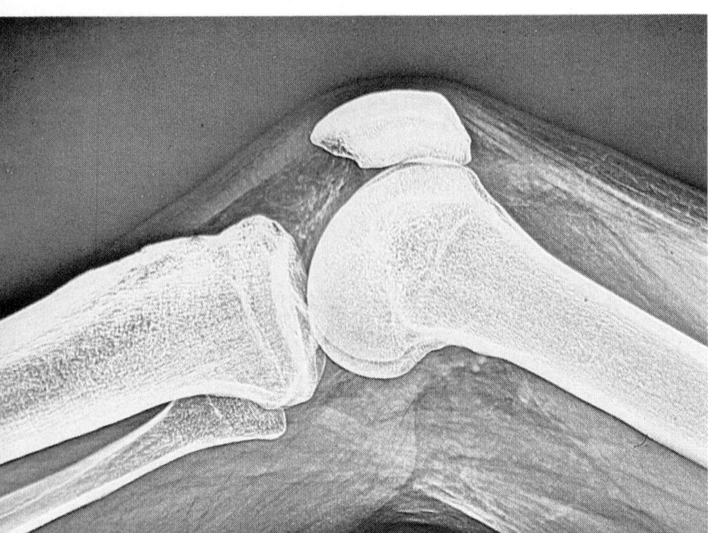

FIGURE 6-21

Radiograph (x-ray) of the knee. Compare this with the schematic illustrated in Fig. 6-20 (*b*). (CNRI/Phototake.)

(e) discoloration of the teeth; (f) scoliosis (*sko*-lee-**oh**-sis); (g) deafness; and (h) sclerae (white outer protective covering of eyeball) that have a bluish tint. Cortical bone is exceedingly thin, and cancellous trabeculae tend to be small and much reduced in number. Lack of normal amounts of bone matrix gives the appearance of osteocytes being crowded tightly together.

Individuals with osteogenesis imperfecta live for varying periods of time depending upon the severity of their affliction, but generally not much beyond the onset of puberty. In those with less severe forms of the disease, fractures may not become apparent until the child becomes more physically active.

The absence of a normal quantity of bone is known as osteoporosis

Osteoporosis, simply stated, is a disease characterized by a severe reduction in bone mass. It cannot be detected by routine radiographic analysis until approximately 30% loss of the bone mass has occurred. Therefore it may go clinically undetected for several years. Bone obtained from osteoporotic patients has a mineral composition similar to normal bone and is adequately mineralized.

The disease is an almost inevitable occurrence with advancing age and affects females more frequently than males. Although the entire skeleton is affected, the vertebral column and pelvis are most frequently and severely involved. Cortical bone is reduced in thickness, cancellous trabeculae are reduced in number, and the marrow cavities significantly enlarged. The end result is a net loss of bone mass. In all bones affected there is a predisposition to the development of fractures (pathologic fractures).

Many hypotheses have been put forth as to the cause of osteoporosis; however, to date no single cause has withstood the test of rigorous clinical assessment. Included among these are certain endocrine malfunctions (hyperparathyroidism, hypothyroidism, and hyperadrenocorticism), vitamin C deficiency, malignant diseases of bone, reduction in ovarian steroids, and prolonged bed rest. Thus, perhaps what has been viewed for so long as a single disease is in reality several disease states each having its own unique cause but all ultimately resulting in an overall loss of bone mass. Treatment of osteoporosis includes exercise, calcium supplements, and estrogen administration.

In osteitis deformans bones become structurally and chemically abnormal

Osteitis deformans or Paget's disease is a disease of unknown etiology (cause) and is rarely seen in individuals under the age of 40 years. Males acquire the disease with twice the frequency of females. Osteitis deformans is characterized by greatly exaggerated bone remodeling processes, that is, increased bone destruction accompanied by increased bone deposition. The net result is that normal bone is replaced by a less rigid and inadequately mineralized osteoid tissue together with a significant amount of fibrotic material. Although enlarged, the bones are soft and porous and unable to withstand ordinary amounts of pressure. Characteristic deformities may result. Typically these include enlargement of the skull together with bowing of the femurs and tibias. This disease may involve the entire skeleton or remain localized to an individual bone. Furthermore, patients with osteitis deformans are prime candidates for the development of osteogenic sarcoma.

Vitamin D deficiency in growing children may lead to rickets

Children with vitamin D deficiency are unable to absorb calcium and phosphate from the digestive tract, and may develop **rickets.** Blood levels of phosphate are greatly reduced in patients with rickets. However, calcium levels tend to be only slightly depressed because the increased activity of the parathyroid glands results in enhanced bone resorption.

Although the increased bone resorption protects the individual from developing **hypocalcemia** (low level of calcium in the blood), the bones become progressively weaker with time. Osteoblasts lay down increased amounts of osteoid tissue which fails to become calcified due to the lack of adequate calcium and phosphate ions. Should the condition persist to the point where the bones become depleted of calcium, blood levels of calcium may drop rapidly and the individual may develop tetanic respiratory spasm leading to death. Treatment of rickets includes a diet rich in calcium and phosphate together with vitamin D supplementation.

Osteomalacia, in its literal sense, means a "softening" of bone

Osteomalacia is typically described as the adult form of rickets, although rarely does it result from a dietary deficiency of calcium or vitamin D. However, if an individual is unable to absorb fat from the diet, vitamin D deficiency may develop because it is one of the fat-soluble vitamins. The inability to absorb fat (termed steatorrhea) results in vitamin D, calcium, and phosphate being passed along with the feces. Although older individuals do not require the same amount of calcium as do children with actively growing bones, a prolonged deficiency of this ion frequently leads to severely weakened bones.

Individuals with severe and prolonged kidney damage may develop a form of osteomalacia known as renal rickets. This occurs when the kidneys are no longer able to process vitamin D to its active metabolite. In *congenital hypophosphatemia* (low level of phosphate in the blood at birth), osteomalacia may also develop because there is markedly reduced phosphate reabsorption from the renal tubules. This form of the disease is termed vitamin D–resistant rickets and must be treated with phosphate compounds rather than vitamin D and calcium.

Bacterial or fungal infections of bone may lead to osteomyelitis

Serious bacterial or fungal infections of bone may occur. An infection involving bone marrow as well as bone itself is termed **osteomyelitis.** These usually begin as acute infections and if inappropriately treated may become chronic in nature. However, this is rarely the case today due to the number and wide availability of antibiotics and antifungal agents.

Osteosarcoma is the most common and malignant form of bone sarcoma

This disease is the second most common malignancy of bone in young individuals. Incidence of the tumor peaks at approximately 20 years of age; when seen in the older population it is usually associated with osteitis deformans (Paget's disease) as mentioned previously. The tumors arise beneath the periosteum, elevate it as they grow, and ultimately penetrate the cortical bone as well. Patients suffer from pain, swelling, and tenderness over the affected regions. **Osteogenic sarcoma** proceeds rapidly and the prognosis for affected individuals is very poor.

Growth and maintenance of skeletal tissue are influenced by several hormones

Several of the endocrine glands secrete hormones that have either direct or indirect effects upon the growth or maintenance of the human skeleton. Although these will be discussed in more depth in Chapter 18, it is appropriate to mention them briefly at this time. **Growth hormone** is secreted by the anterior pituitary gland and indirectly promotes the growth of cartilage and bone. It does so by stimulating the liver to produce low molecular weight proteins known as **somatomedins.** Researchers have characterized at least four different somatomedins and all appear to exhibit similar effects on bone and cartilage. One mechanism by which they affect growth of skeletal tissue is through their regulation of collagen and chondroitin sulfate deposition.

The steroid sex hormones, for example, testosterone and estrogens, have a marked influence on bone growth and are present in both sexes. **Testosterone,** which is secreted by specific cells of the testes and adrenal cortex, strongly promotes bone growth and is largely responsible for the growth spurt that occurs at puberty in the male and female. This hormone markedly stimulates protein synthesis and results in an increased production of bone matrix. Enhanced matrix production leads subsequently to an increased deposition of calcium salts. Thus, testosterone functions to increase the size as well as the strength of bones. Prolonged secretion of **estrogen,** as well as testosterone, promotes the closure of the epiphyseal plates of long bones and thereby terminates any further lengthening of such bones. Estrogen is much more potent in this regard than is testosterone and for this reason growth in the female typically ends at an earlier age than in the male.

Surgical removal of the thyroid gland (thyroidectomy) led to the discovery of the importance of the parathyroid glands to skeletal tissue. These four small glands are closely attached to the posterior aspect of the thyroid gland and were removed along with the thyroid before the development of more precise surgical techniques. The parathyroid glands were found to be responsible for the production of **parathyroid hormone.** This hormone causes the absorption of calcium and phosphate from existing bone.

Prolonged secretion of parathyroid hormone stimulates osteoclastic activity and leads ultimately to the resorption of bone itself. Parathyroid hormone also functions to maintain a proper level of calcium in the blood through the absorption of calcium from bone as well as inhibiting its excretion by the kidneys. Should the level of calcium in the blood and extracellular fluid fall significantly, nerve and muscle fibers respond with increased excitability. Such a state often leads to spasms and frequently to convulsions.

If the blood levels of calcium and phosphate are significantly elevated, the secretion of parathyroid hormone ceases and **calcitonin,** a thyroid hormone, is released. The effects of calcitonin in reducing the level of blood calcium stem primarily from its ability to inhibit the activity of osteoclasts while promoting osteoblastic activity.

Another important function of parathyroid hormone is its role in converting vitamin D to its active metabolite, 1,25-dihydroxycholecalciferol. This metabolite of vitamin D has extremely potent effects on calcium absorption from the intestinal tract as well as upon the deposition and reabsorption of bone.

Summary

I. The skeletal system provides support and protection, transmits muscular forces, produces blood cells, and stores calcium and phosphate.

II. The two basic types of bone are compact and cancellous (spongy) bone.
   - A. The diaphysis, or shaft, of a long bone is formed of compact bone.
   - B. The epiphyses, or ends, of long bones are formed largely of cancellous bone.

III. Specialized connective tissue coverings called the periosteum and endosteum line the external and internal surfaces of bone, respectively.
   - A. The outer layer of the periosteum is fibrous. The inner layer of the periosteum is called the osteogenic (bone-forming) layer. Sharpey's fibers, composed of collagen, anchor the periosteum to the underlying bone.
   - B. The endosteum, which lines haversian canals and the marrow cavity, also exhibits osteogenic potential.

IV. Osteoprogenitor cells, osteoblasts, osteocytes, and osteoclasts represent the four types of bone cells.
   - A. Osteoprogenitor cells differentiate and give rise to osteoblasts.
   - B. The osteoblasts produce collagen and the organic matrix of bone, which are laid down prior to its calcification.
   - C. Osteocytes are osteoblasts that have become trapped within the lacunae of calcifying bone.
   - D. Osteoclasts are large, multinucleated cells that function in the resorption of bone.

V. The extracellular matrix of bone is composed of inorganic salts and an organic matrix called osteoid.
   - A. The inorganic salts impart the characteristic hardness to bone and constitute approximately 50% of its dry weight. Calcium phosphate exists largely in the form of hydroxyapatite crystals within the matrix of bone.
   - B. The organic matrix of bone consists primarily of Type I collagen and glycosaminoglycans. Osteoblasts secrete a soluble protein called tropocollagen which forms collagen fibers in the matrix.

VI. Hydroxyapatite crystals form during the calcification of the matrix of bone. This process is influenced by the presence of collagen and/or glycosaminoglycans.

VII. Bone arises from either intramembranous or endochondral bone formation. Both processes involve the replacement of existing connective tissue by bone itself.
   - A. During intramembranous bone formation, embryonic mesenchyme condenses and membrane bone is laid down. The osteoid of the membrane bone is later impregnated with calcium phosphate and undergoes calcification. Woven bone gives rise to compact bone in certain regions and persists as cancellous, or spongy, bone in others. Lamellar bone is synonymous with mature bone, whereas woven bone is of a primary or immature nature.
   - B. Most bones in the body arise as a result of endochondral bone formation. This process involves the replacement of a cartilaginous model of the future bone by bone itself.

VIII. The epiphyseal plates are important for the growth in length of long bones. These plates are composed of four distinct zones or regions of cells: the zone of resting or reserve cartilage; zone of proliferation; zone of maturation; zone of calcification. The diaphysis of a long bone may grow in length only by the process of appositional growth.

IX. Once formed, bone undergoes a continuous process of remodeling.

X. Osteocytes remain in contact with one another through cellular processes located within microscopic canals called canaliculi. As lamellar bone is formed, bone is deposited in concentric rings around a central blood vessel. This vessel, together with its surrounding rings of bone and osteocytes, is called an osteon or haversian system. The osteons are roughly spindle-shaped, and their blood vessels are in contact with those of neighboring systems via passages called Volkmann's canals.

XI. A broken bone is called a fracture. Depending on its extent and nature, fractures may be classified as complete, incomplete, closed, compound, comminuted, or pathologic. Reduction of a fracture involves bringing the ends of the broken bone into contact with one another. A procallus, fibrocartilaginous callus, and an osseous callus form during fracture healing.

XII. Tendons serve to attach muscles to other structures while ligaments unite bone with bone.

XIII. Bone is subject to numerous disease processes. Some principal and primary diseases of bone include osteogenesis imperfecta, osteoporosis, osteitis deformans (Paget's disease), rickets, osteomalacia, osteomyelitis, and osteosarcoma.

XIV. Several hormones have either direct or indirect effects upon the growth and maintenance of skeletal tissue. Included among these are growth hormone, testosterone, estrogen, parathyroid hormone, and calcitonin.

Post-test

1. The primary functions of the skeletal system are _____________ and _____________.
2. Bones are covered on their external surface by a layer of specialized connective tissue known as the _____________.
3. Dense collagenous fibers that serve to anchor the periosteum to the underlying bone are termed _____________ fibers.
4. Microscopic channels interconnecting lacunae are termed _____________.
5. The extracellular matrix of bone is composed primarily of _____________ and _____________.
6. Each epiphyseal plate is composed of the following regions:
   (a)
   (b)
   (c)
   (d)
7. The shaft or _____________ of a long bone can grow in length only by the process of _____________ growth, while its width increases by a process termed _____________ growth.
8. The central blood vessel together with its concentric rings of bone and osteocytes is termed an _____________ or _____________.
9. Six different types of bone fractures are _____________, _____________, _____________, _____________, _____________, and _____________.
10. Inflammation of a tendon is termed _____________.
11. Although ligaments vary markedly in their gross appearance, their primary function is to limit the range of _____________ of the joints with which they are associated.
12. List and describe seven important diseases of bone:
    (a)
    (b)
    (c)
    (d)
    (e)
    (f)
    (g)
13. Vitamin D is converted to its active metabolite by _____________ _____________.

Review questions

1. Describe the functional aspects of the skeletal system.
2. Describe how bone, tendons, and ligaments are functionally related to one another.
3. Compare and contrast intramembranous and endochondral bone formation.
4. Describe the difference between woven and lamellar bone. Describe how woven bone is converted into lamellar bone.
5. Define an osteon or haversian system. What is its functional significance?
6. Describe the mechanism by which bones grow in length as well as in diameter.
7. Describe the process by which a bone fracture is healed.
8. Describe the actions of calcitonin and parathyroid hormone upon the skeletal system.
9. How is it that osteocytes, embedded within lacunae, receive their necessary nutrients and eliminate their metabolic waste products?
10. Describe the structure and function of Volkmann's canals.
11. Describe osteitis deformans (Paget's disease).
12. Describe the process of bone remodeling.
13. Compare and contrast the functions of osteoblasts, osteocytes, and osteoclasts.

Post-test answers

1. support, protection **2.** periosteum **3.** Sharpey's **4.** canaliculi **5.** inorganic salts; osteoid **6.** (a) zone of resting or reserve cartilage (b) zone of proliferation (c) zone of maturation (d) zone of calcification **7.** diaphysis; appositional; interstitial **8.** osteon; haversian system

9. complete, green stick, simple or closed, compound, comminuted, pathologic **10.** tendonitis **11.** motion **12.** (a) osteogenesis imperfecta (b) osteoporosis (c) osteitis deformans (Paget's disease) (d) rickets (e) osteomalacia (f) osteomyelitis (g) osteogenic sarcoma **13.** parathyroid hormone

THE AXIAL SKELETON

CHAPTER OUTLINE

I. **Functions of the skeletal system**
II. **Shapes of typical bones**
III. **Features of bones**
IV. **Divisions of the human skeleton**
V. **The skull**
  A. General features of the skull
    1. Sutures of the skull
    2. Cranial fossae
  B. Bones of the cranium
    1. Frontal bone
    2. Occipital bone
    3. Sphenoid bone
    4. Ethmoid bone
    5. Parietal bones
    6. Temporal bones
  C. Bones of the facial skeleton
    1. Mandible
    2. Maxillae
    3. Nasal bones
    4. Vomer
    5. Lacrimal bones
    6. Inferior nasal conchae
    7. Palatine bones
    8. Zygomatic bones
VI. **The hyoid bone**
VII. **The vertebral column**
  A. Basic structure of a typical vertebra
  B. Characteristics of individual vertebrae
    1. Atlas
    2. Axis
    3. Inferior cervical vertebrae
    4. Thoracic vertebrae
    5. Lumbar vertebrae
    6. Sacrum
    7. Coccyx
VIII. **The thoracic skeleton**
  A. Sternum
  B. Ribs
    1. Features of a typical rib
    2. Ribs with special features

LEARNING OBJECTIVES

After you have studied this chapter you should be able to:

1 Relate the functions of the skeletal system.

2 Describe the general classification of bones according to their shape.

3 Compare and contrast the general features of bones.

4 Compare and contrast the axial and appendicular divisions of the skeleton.

5 Describe the sutures and fontanelles of the skull.

6 Describe the anterior, middle, and posterior cranial fossae.

7 List and discuss the important features of the bones of the cranium.

8 List and discuss the important features of the bones of the facial skeleton.

9 Describe the hyoid bone.

10 Describe the general arrangement of the vertebrae in forming the vertebral column.

11 Describe the primary and secondary curves of the vertebral column.

12 Describe the basic structure of a typical vertebra.

13 Discuss and compare the structural characteristics of vertebrae located in specific regions of the vertebral column.

14 Describe the thoracic skeleton.

15 Describe the sternum.

16 Describe the features of a typical rib.

17 Describe those ribs that possess special features.

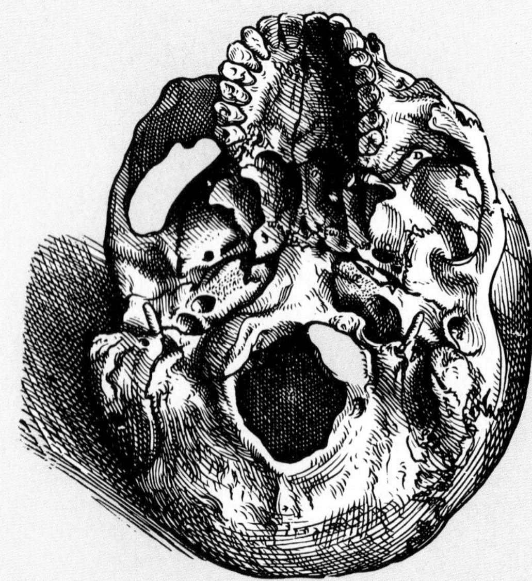

(*top*) False color sagittal scan of the cervical spine region. (*bottom*) False color coronal scan of the abdominopelvic region. (CNRI/Science Photo Library/Photo Researchers, Inc.)

7

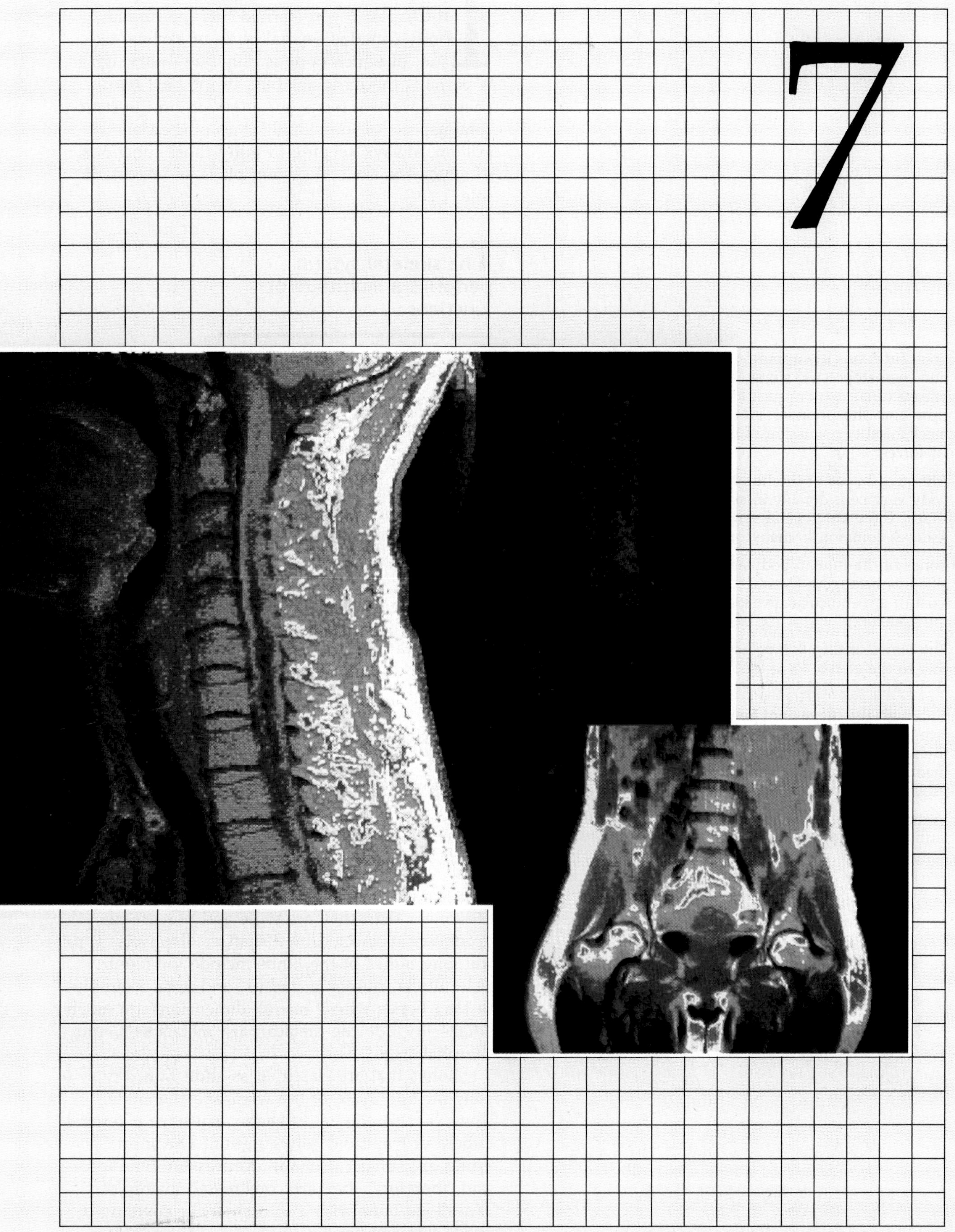

KEY CONCEPTS

Bone functions in support, protection, hematopoiesis, storage and release of substances such as calcium and phosphorus, and in the mechanical transmission of muscular forces.

Although bones of the human body vary considerably in size and shape, there are general surface features common to many of them.

Bones of the human body are classified as belonging to either the axial or appendicular division of the skeleton.

The bones of the skull belong either to the cranial or to the facial skeleton.

Although the movement between two adjacent vertebrae is not great, the summation of all such movements along the vertebral column provides considerable flexibility.

Vertebrae share certain basic similarities and also display regionally distinct features.

In Chapter 6 you learned that the human body contains several types of skeletal tissue, of which bone is only one—although it is perhaps the most obvious. In the next two chapters we will focus our attention on the structural aspects of individual bones of the skeletal system, always keeping in mind those functions in which the skeletal system plays an important role.

The skeletal system performs a multitude of functions

Five specific functions of the bone were provided in Chapter 6. As you continue with the study of the individual bones of the skeletal system, it is important to keep these functions in mind. The close interaction between the muscular and skeletal systems provides the basis for bodily movements. The roles of the skeletal system in support and protection are especially evident. Although very important, its role in mineral storage and release and in blood cell formation might be less obvious to some of us. Thus, the skeletal system is a dynamic system that provides several important and varied services for our everyday existence.

Bones of the skeleton have a variety of shapes

The bones that comprise the human skeleton can be classified as belonging to one of four basic types: long bones, short bones, flat bones, and irregular bones. The **long bones** of the skeleton are longer than they are wide and possess two epiphyses connected by a shaft or diaphysis. Typical long bones of the limbs include the femur, tibia, fibula, humerus, radius, and ulna. Examples of long bones whose overall dimensions are much smaller include the metacarpals, metatarsals, and the phalanges.

Bones that are classified as **short bones** typically include those of the wrist and the ankle. They vary somewhat in shape, but have a general cuboid or trapezoid configuration. The short bones are subject primarily to pressure-type forces and, therefore, they are constructed mainly of cancellous bone with a thin shell-like covering of hard, compact bone.

Included among the bones classified as being **flat** are the bones of the cranium. Their structure is such that a layer of cancellous bone is typically sandwiched between an inner and outer layer of compact bone. The layer of cancellous bone is called the **diploë,** and the layers of compact bone are termed the *inner table* and the *outer table.* Other examples of flat bones include the sternum, scapula, and ribs.

Any bone that cannot be easily placed into one of the three previous categories is designated an **irregular bone.** Examples of irregular bones, which typically possess very complex shapes, include certain bones of the facial skeleton as well as bones of the vertebral column.

Sesamoid bones and wormian bones are two other bone types present in the human body, but they do not fall into any of the four groups just discussed. **Sesamoid bones** develop within the substance of a tendon, especially in those regions where significant pressure occurs. The patella (knee cap), located within the tendon of the quadriceps muscle group, is a sesamoid bone. **Wormian,** or *sutural bones,* represent small islands of bone that are located within the joints between certain cranial bones. These are inconstant in number from one person to another.

Bones of the skeleton have features in common

We have seen that the bones of the human skeleton vary considerably in their size and shape. Although the morphology (structure) of their surfaces also is subject to great variation, there are certain surface features that are common to many bones. In general these surface features, also called *surface markings,* have a similar structure-function relationship in various bones.

Articular (ar-**tik**-yoo-lar) **surfaces** of bones represent those areas where one bone forms a joint with another. Such surfaces may be quite small and are then called **facets** (**fa**-sets). Facets may also serve to attach tendons and ligaments to bones. If the articular surface is shaped like a knuckle it is referred to as a **condyle** (**kon**-dial). The term **trochlea** (**trok**-lee-a) is applied to such a surface when it is grooved as in a pulley.

Bones also present a number of elevations and depressions on their surface. **Fossa** is the term used to describe a depression on the surface of a bone. If the depression is elongated, it is called a **groove** or **sulcus** (**sul**-kus). Grooves and sulci may contain tendons or blood vessels. An opening on the surface of a bone is termed a **foramen** and may serve to transmit nerves, blood vessels, or ligaments. A **meatus** represents a tubelike passageway coursing through the substance of a bone. Openings of a cleftlike nature that are located between adjacent bones are termed **fissures.**

A large, distinct projection on the surface of a bone is called a **process.** If such a process is elongated and pointed, it is termed a **spine,** and if shaped like a hook it is called a **hamulus** or **cornu.** Projections that are well localized and rounded in appearance are referred to as **tuberosities** or **tubercles;** the latter generally refers to the smaller form. Tendons and ligaments usually are attached to these structures. The femur has two rather large rounded projections near its proximal end called the **greater** and **lesser trochanters** (troe-**kan**-ters). When a small projection occurs adjacent to a condyle, it is termed an **epicondyle** (*ep*-ee-**kon**-dial) and generally permits the attachment of ligaments for that particular joint. The proximal expanded end of many long bones (e.g., the femur, tibia, and humerus) is called the **head.**

Some bones possess elongated elevations of bone that are known as **crests** or **lines.** These crests or lines also serve for the attachment of tendons, ligaments, and other connective tissue structures. On the other hand, some bones possess relatively large areas that are quite smooth and are simply pitted by numerous tiny foramina. Such surfaces usually represent areas where muscle fibers are attached directly to the surface of the bone, and the foramina transmit blood vessels supplying this region.

Bones of the skeleton belong to either the axial or appendicular division

The bones of the human skeleton are typically classified as belonging either to the **axial** or to the **appendicular division** (*a*-pen-**dick**-you-lar). There are 80 bones that make up the axial division of the skeleton and they are all situated around the central axis of the body. These include the bones of the skull (22) and vertebral column (26), the auditory ossicles (6), the hyoid bone (1), ribs (24), and the sternum (1). This method of classification is not merely for didactic reasons. It has a phylogenetic meaning as well because the axial skeleton is representative of the primary skeleton of the earlier vertebrates.

The appendicular division of the skeleton consists of 126 bones. These are the bones of the upper limb and lower limb and those responsible for connecting the limbs with the axial division, that is, the pelvic girdle and shoulder girdle. The individual bones of the axial and appendicular divisions and their number are summarized for you in Table 7-1.

Before proceeding with more detailed descriptions of various individual bones, take a few moments to identify the bones that make up these divisions of the skeleton. Do this while referring to Figures 7-1 and 7-2. Keep in mind that neither the hyoid bone nor the auditory ossicles appear in these figures.

The facial skeleton and cranium comprise the skull

The human skull is a complex structure and in part its architectural design may reflect the complexity of the functions for which it is responsible. The skull is involved in just about everything we do in our day-to-day routine. It plays a role in our speech, hearing, vision, balance, breathing, and feeding. Moreover, the skull houses and protects the most elaborate portion of our central nervous system, the brain.

Although the human skull consists of 22 individual bones, these are typically grouped into two sets: bones of the **cranium** (those that enclose the brain) and bones of the **facial skeleton.** There are eight bones that make up the cranium; two of these are paired while four are individual. The bones that constitute the cranium are the: *frontal* (1), *occipital* (1), *sphenoid* (1), *ethmoid* (1), *parietal* (2), and *temporal* (2). The facial skeleton is made up of 14 bones; twelve are paired and two are individual. Bones of the facial skeleton include the: *maxilla* (2), *zygomatic* (2), *nasal* (2), *lacrimal* (2), *palatine* (2), *inferior nasal concha* (2), *vomer* (1), and *mandible* (1). Take a few minutes now and identify these bones while referring to Figures 7-3 through 7-8. See also Table 7-2, Foramina of the Skull.

(*text continued on p. 202*)

TABLE 7-1

Bones of the human skeletal system
Axial division of skeleton (total of 80 bones)
Skull (Total of 22 Bones)
Cranium (Total of 8 bones)
Frontal bone (1)
Occipital bone (1)
Sphenoid bone (1)
Ethmoid bone (1)
Parietal bone (2)
Temporal bone (2)*
Face (Total of 14 bones)
Mandible (1)
Maxilla (2)
Nasal bone (2)
Vomer (1)
Lacrimal bone (2)
Inferior nasal concha (2)
Palatine bone (2)
Zygomatic bone (2)
Hyoid bone (1)
Vertebral Column (Total of 26 Bones)
Cervical vertebra (7)
Thoracic vertebra (12)
Lumbar vertebra (5)
Sacrum (1; through fusion of 5)
Coccyx (1; through fusion of 4)
Thorax (Total of 25 Bones)
Sternum (1)
Ribs (24)
Appendicular skeleton (total of 126 bones)
Pectoral (Shoulder) Girdles (Total of 4 Bones)
Clavicle (2)
Scapula (2)
Upper Limbs (Total of 60 Bones)
Humerus (2)
Radius (2)
Ulna (2)
Carpals (16)
Metacarpals (10)
Phalanges (28)
Pelvic (Hip) Girdle (Total of 2)
Coxal bone (Hip or Innominate) (2)
Each from the fusion of three, i.e., ilium, ischium, and pubis
Lower Limbs (Total of 60 Bones)
Femur (2)
Patella (2)
Tibia (2)
Fibula (2)
Tarsals (14)
Metatarsals (10)
Phalanges (28)
Total number of bones in entire skeleton = 206

*Each temporal bone contains three tiny bones that play an important role in the hearing mechanism. These bones are called the auditory ossicles and are known as the malleus, incus, and stapes. Because they are associated with the sense of hearing, they are discussed in more detail in Chapter 17.

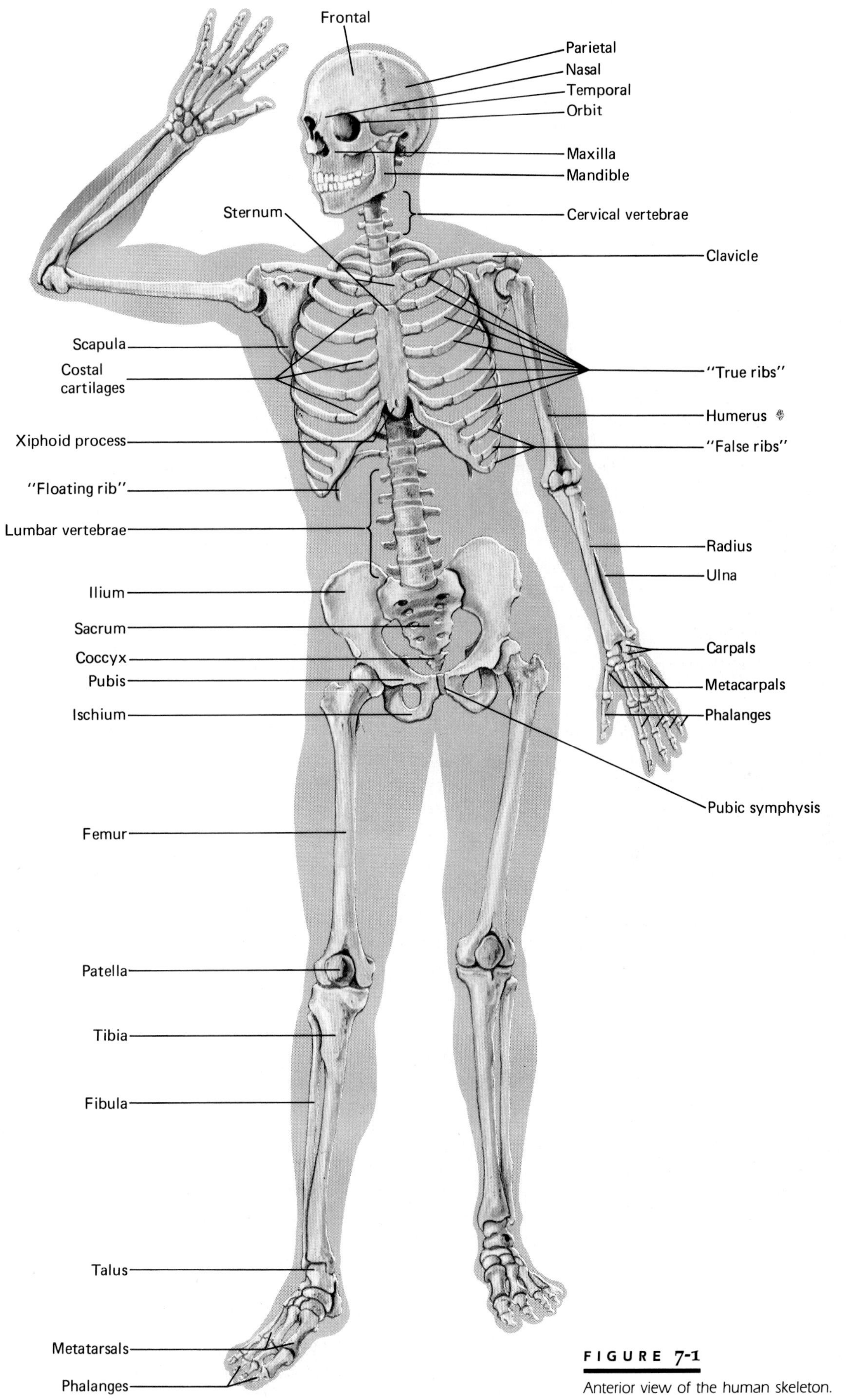

FIGURE 7-1
Anterior view of the human skeleton.

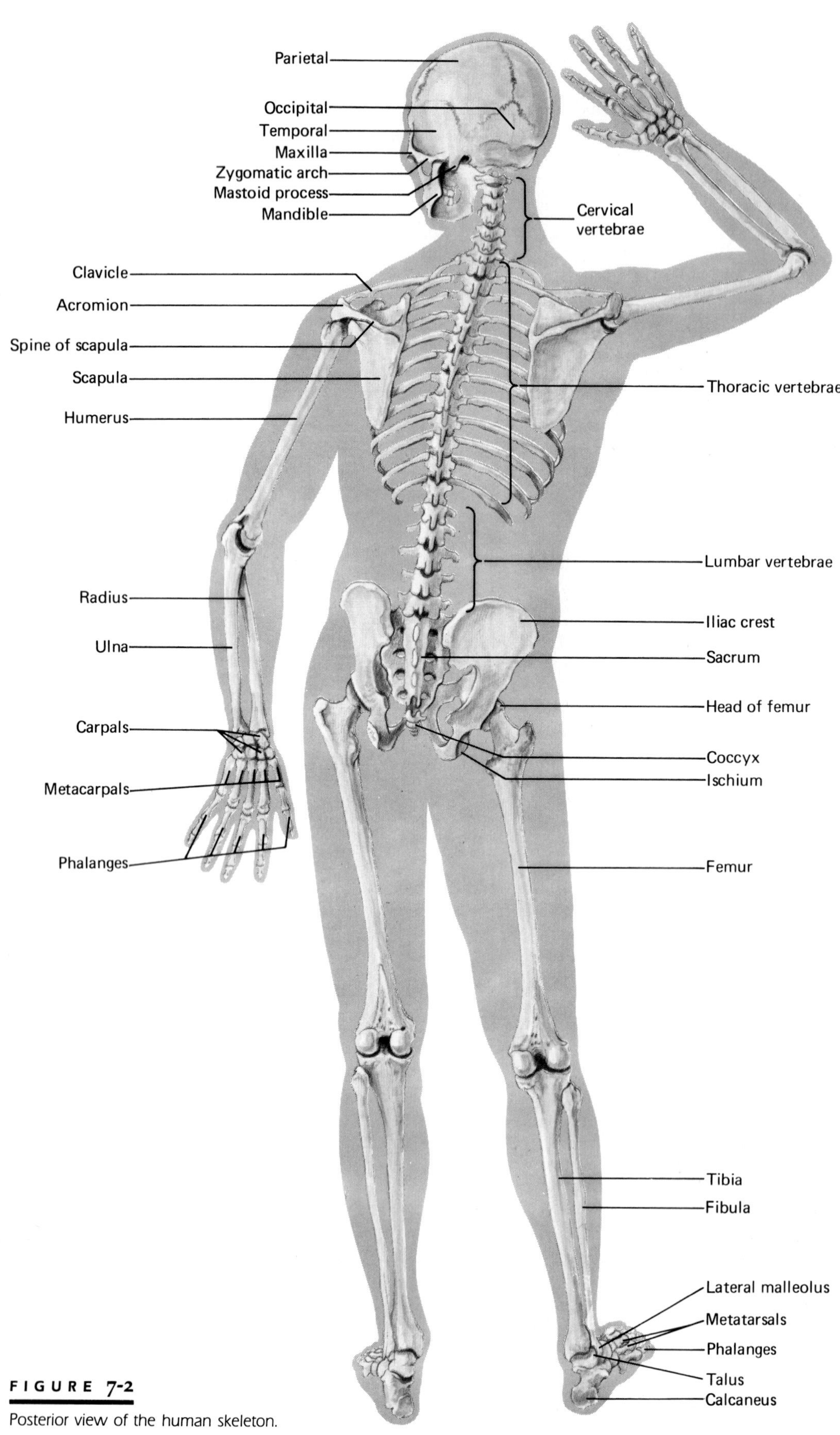

FIGURE 7-2

Posterior view of the human skeleton.

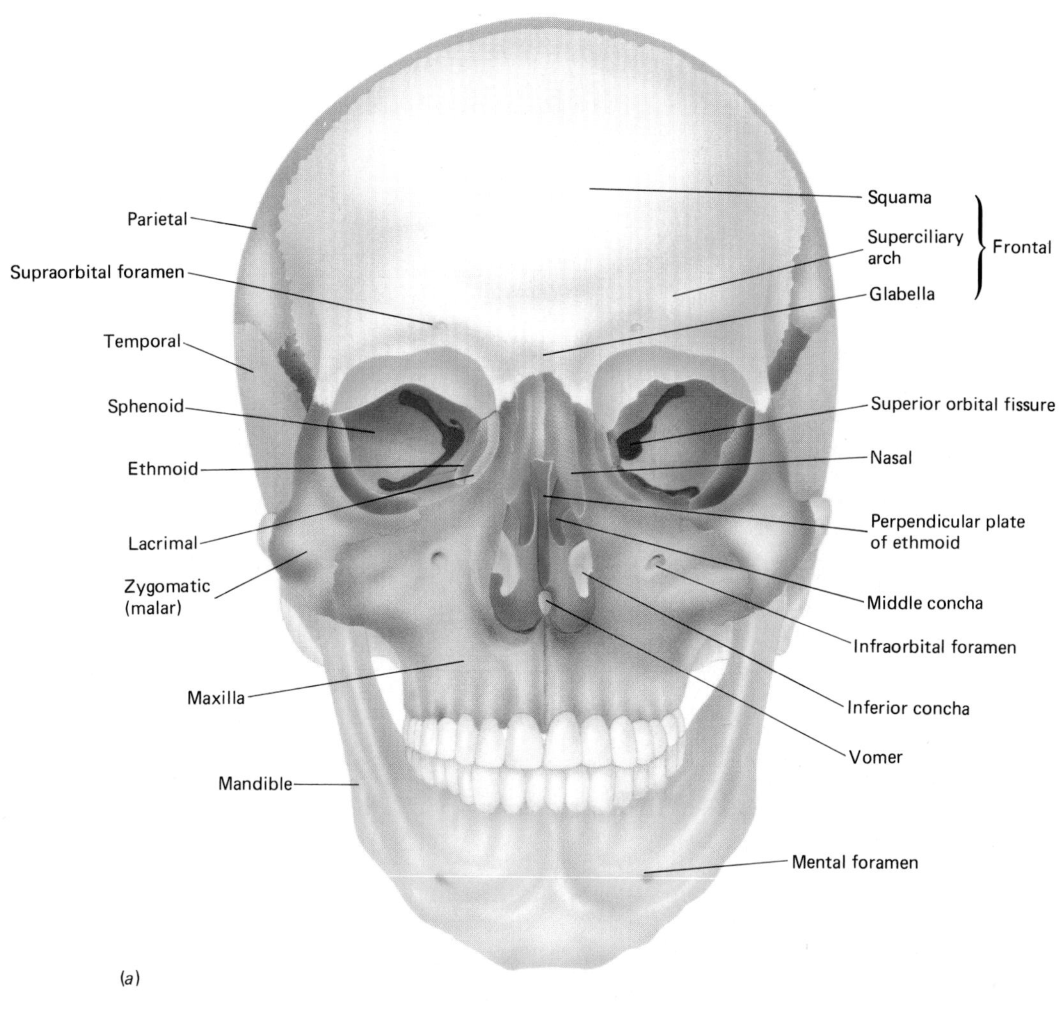

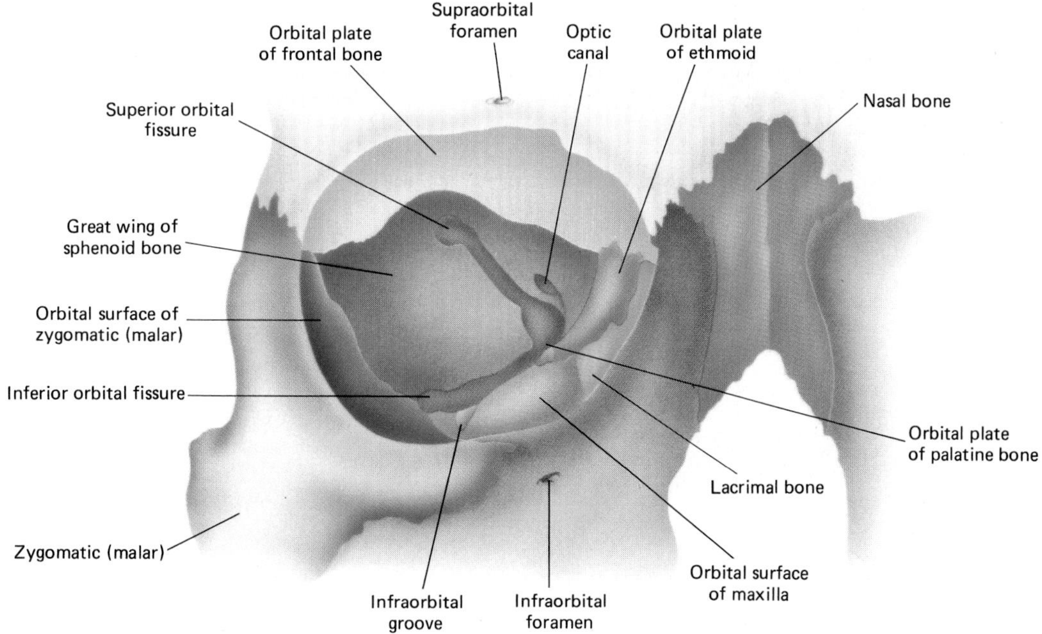

FIGURE 7-3

(a) Anterior view of the human skull. *(b)* Detailed view of the bones contributing to the formation of the right orbital cavity.

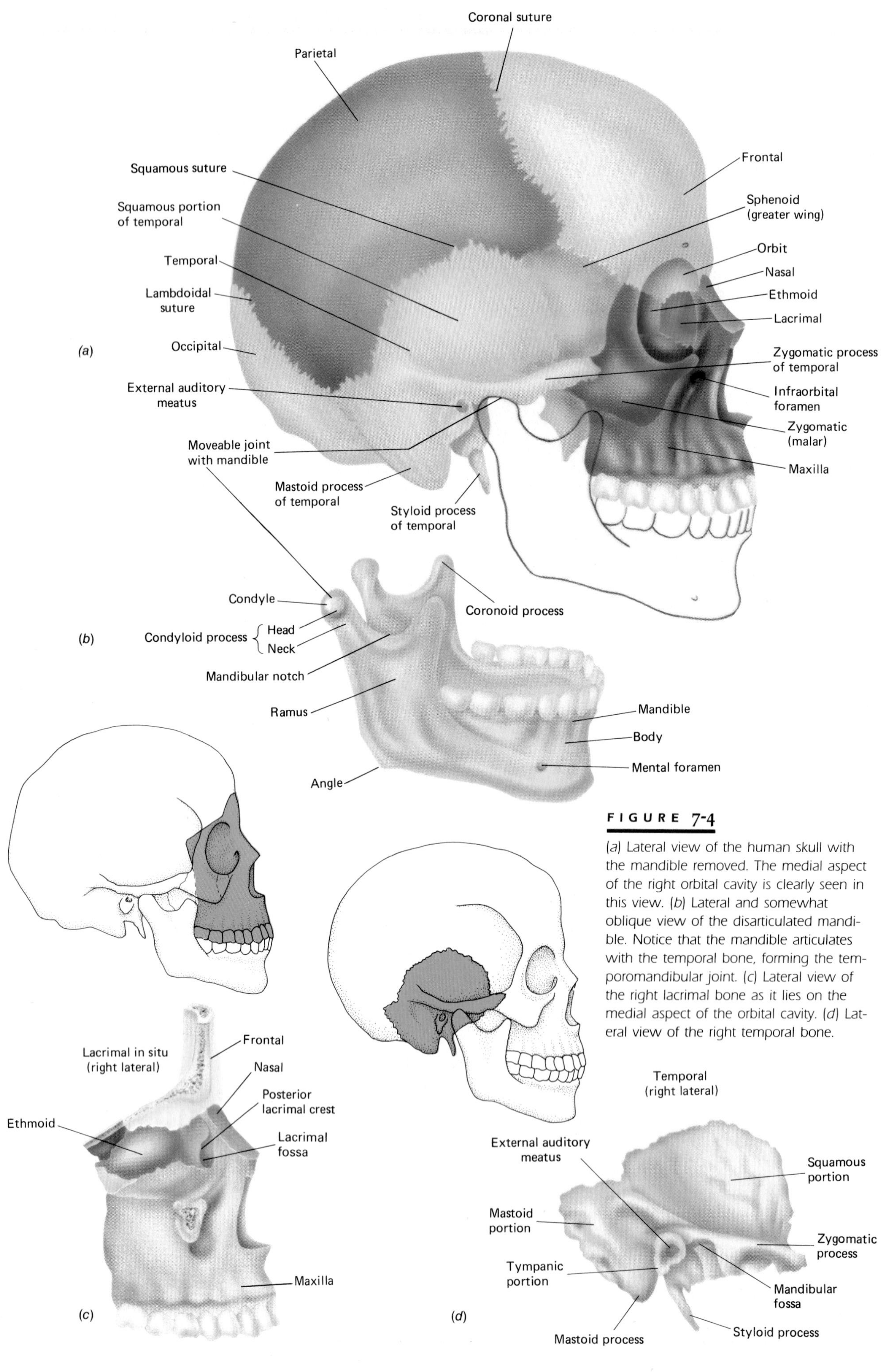

FIGURE 7-4

(*a*) Lateral view of the human skull with the mandible removed. The medial aspect of the right orbital cavity is clearly seen in this view. (*b*) Lateral and somewhat oblique view of the disarticulated mandible. Notice that the mandible articulates with the temporal bone, forming the temporomandibular joint. (*c*) Lateral view of the right lacrimal bone as it lies on the medial aspect of the orbital cavity. (*d*) Lateral view of the right temporal bone.

Sagittal section

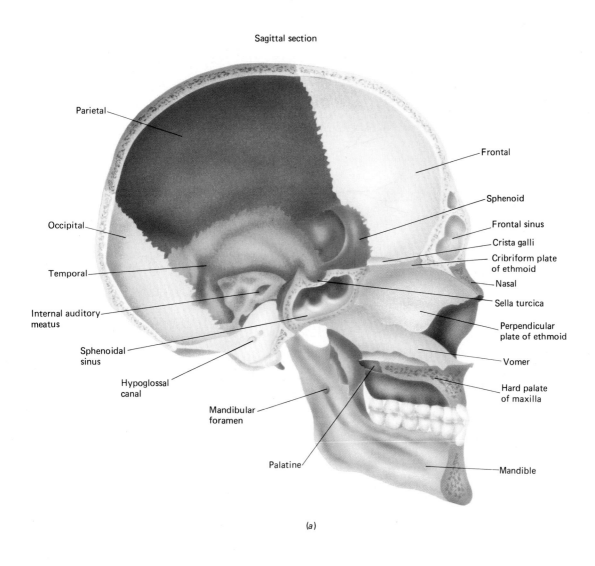

Parietal
Frontal
Sphenoid
Occipital
Frontal sinus
Crista galli
Cribriform plate of ethmoid
Temporal
Nasal
Sella turcica
Internal auditory meatus
Perpendicular plate of ethmoid
Sphenoidal sinus
Vomer
Hypoglossal canal
Hard palate of maxilla
Mandibular foramen
Palatine
Mandible

(a)

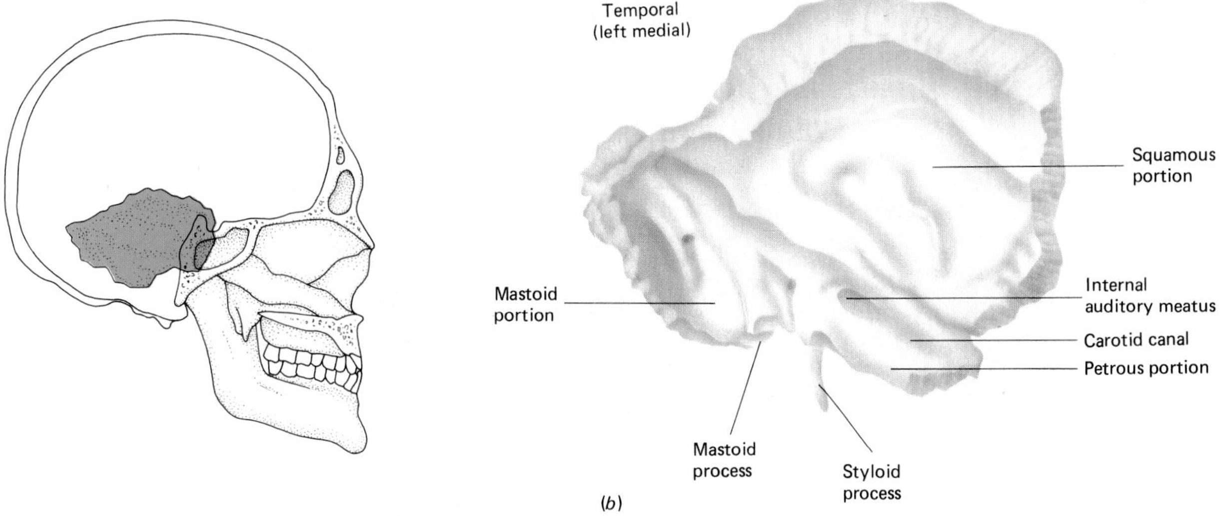

FIGURE 7-5

(a) The internal aspect of the bones of the human skull as seen in sagittal section. (b) Medial aspect of the left temporal bone.

(Fig. 7-5 continued on next page)

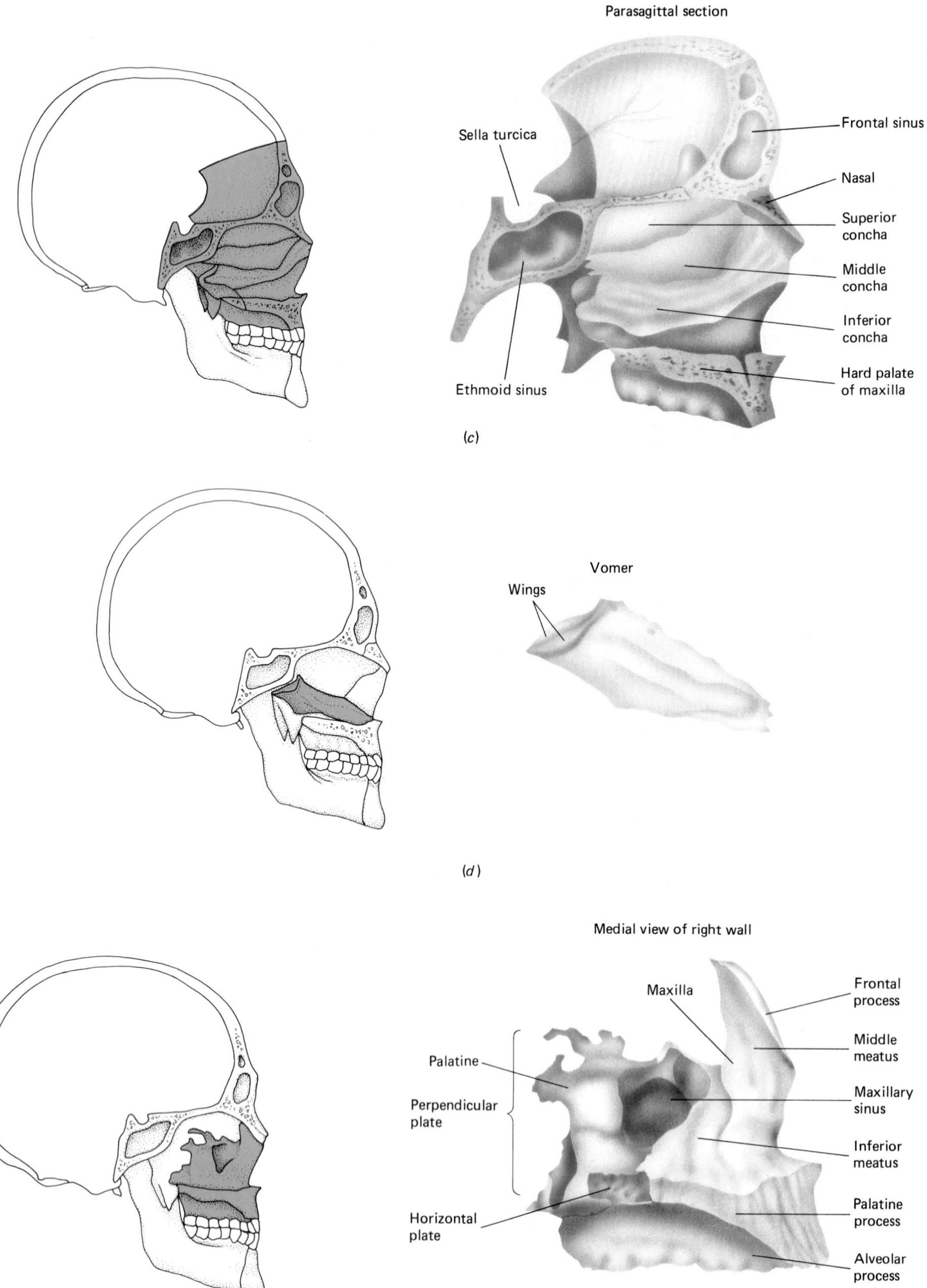

(*c*) Lateral aspect of left nasal cavity. Notice the superior and middle conchae, which belong to the ethmoid bone. The inferior concha is a separate bone. (*d*) Right lateral aspect of the vomer. (*e*) Medial aspect of the left maxilla and palatine bones.

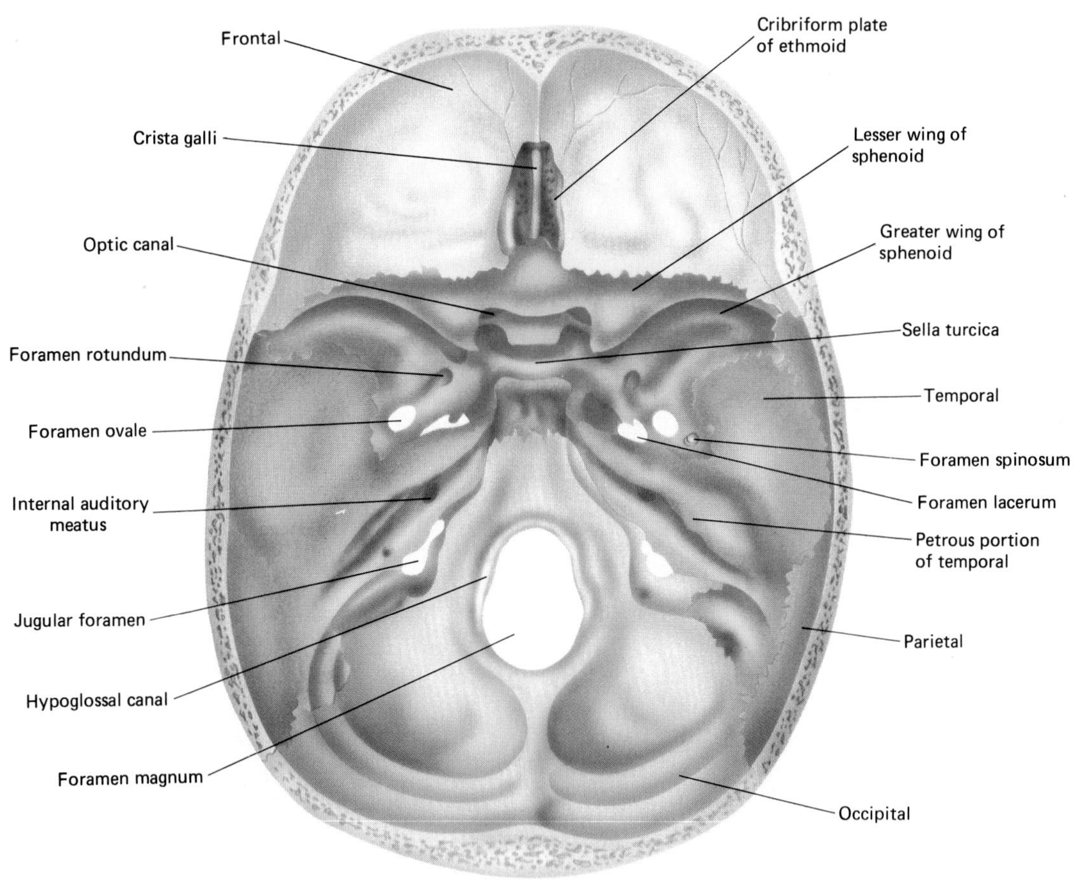

Superior view of cranial floor

(a)

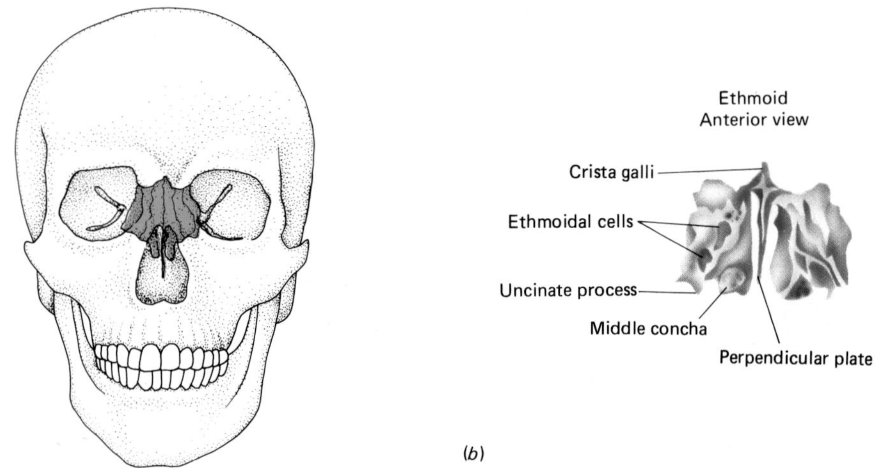

(b)

FIGURE 7-6

(a) Internal aspect of the base of the human skull. Notice that the ethmoid bone will be removed and examined separately. (b) Anterior view of ethmoid bone.

(*Fig. 7-6 continued on next page*)

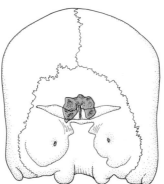

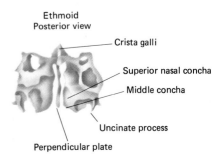

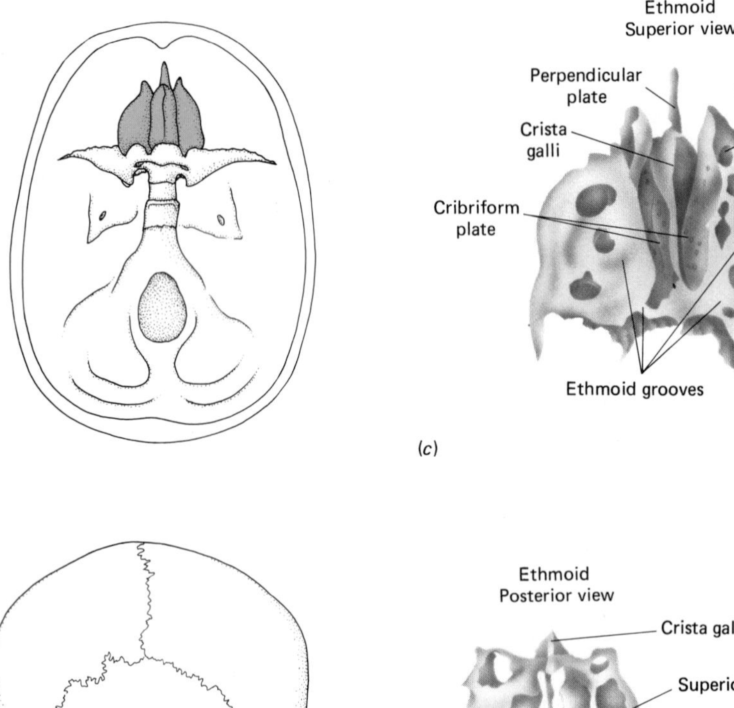

(c) Superior view of ethmoid bone; compare with part (a) of this figure. (d) Posterior view of ethmoid bone.

General features of the skull include the sutures and cranial fossae

You have already seen that some of the bones of the skull are paired whereas others are unpaired. Most of the bones of the skull are united by immovable joints called **sutures**. The only bone of the skull that is freely movable is the mandible. It is connected to the rest of the skull by a synovial joint called the temporomandibular joint.

The periosteal covering on the external surface of the skull is termed the **pericranium** (*per*-i-**krane**-ee-um); the covering that lines its inner surface is the **endocranium.** Furthermore, the endocranium is formed from a portion of the meninges (specifically the dura mater), the connective tissue coverings that surround the brain and spinal cord.

MANY BONES OF THE SKULL ARE UNITED BY SUTURES

A **suture** represents a special type of fibrous joint in which the participating bones are closely opposed to one another. Ordinarily the sutures of the skull become obliterated as the individual ages. However, the time of closure is not always a reliable indicator of a person's age. Furthermore, there are certain disease states, for example, hydrocephalus and cretinism, in which closure of the sutures is considerably delayed. Major sutures of the skull (Fig. 7-9, p. 204) include:

sagittal suture—between the two parietal bones
coronal suture—between the two parietal bones and frontal bone
lambdoid suture—between the two parietal bones and occipital bone
squamosal suture—between the parietal bone and temporal bone

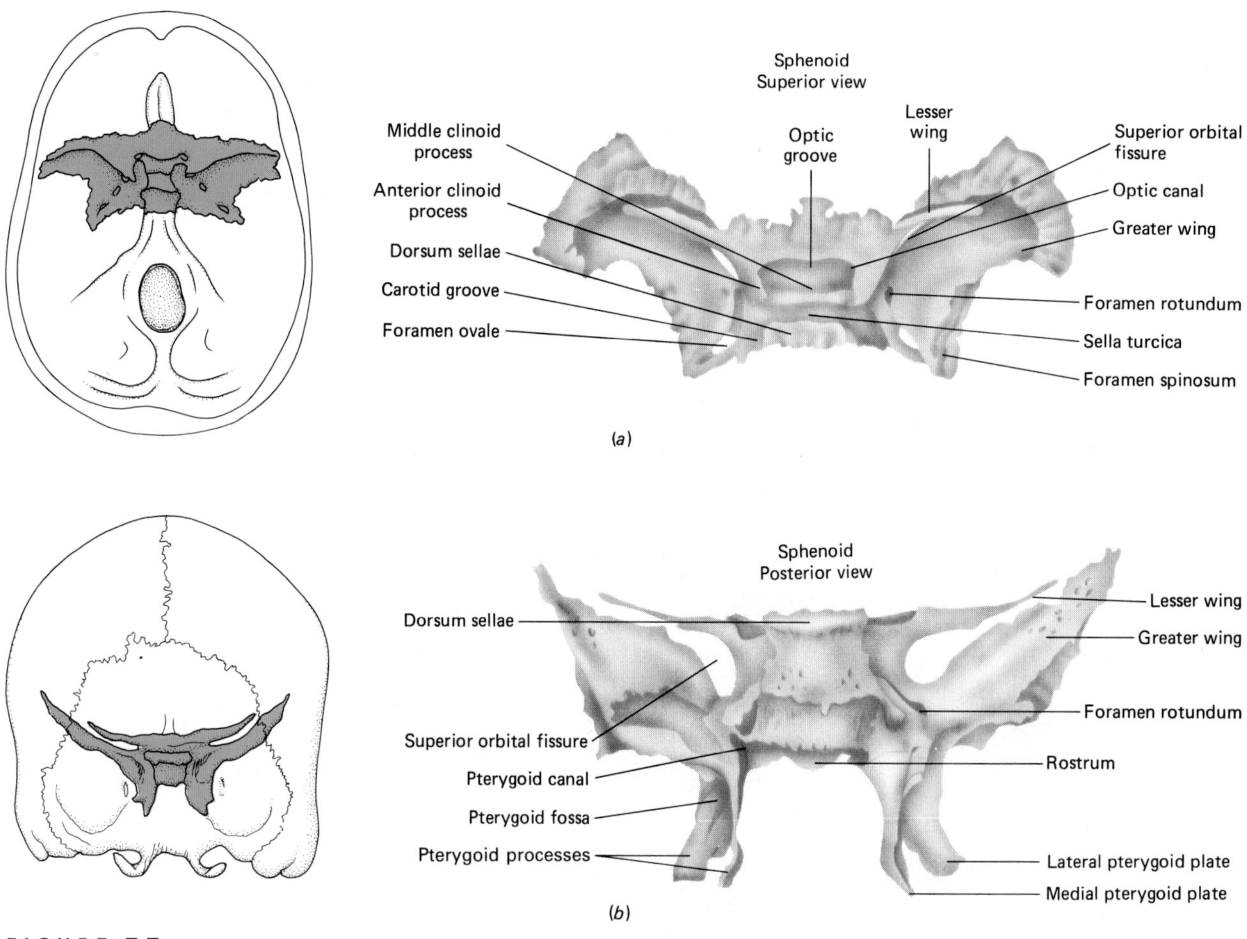

FIGURE 7-7

Two views of the sphenoid bone. *(a)* Superior view; compare with Figure 7-6*(a)*. *(b)* Posterior view of sphenoid bone; compare with Figure 7-3 *(a* and *b)*.

The point at which the coronal suture intersects with the sagittal suture is called the **bregma** (Fig. 7-9). In the fetus and infant it represents the site of a membranous area termed the **anterior fontanelle.** This is one of the newborn's several "soft spots" and represents an incompletely ossified region of the skull. Ordinarily these are replaced by bone sometime before 2 years of age. The **posterior fontanelle** is located at the junction of the sagittal suture with the lambdoid suture. This is called the **lambda,** and closes at approximately 2 months of age. Other fontanelles of much smaller size are also present for relatively short periods of time after birth.

The highest point on the skull is called the **vertex** and lies on the sagittal suture a short distance behind the bregma. There is a median projection on the external surface of the occipital bone midway between the foramen magnum and the lambda. This bump, which can be easily palpated in most individuals, is termed the **external occipital protuberance** or **inion.**

THREE CRANIAL FOSSAE LIE WITHIN THE CRANIAL CAVITY

Focus now on Figure 7-6 and notice that the internal surface of the base of the skull is shown with the calvaria removed. The *calvaria* is a domelike portion of the skull including parts of the frontal, parietal, and occipital bones that is removed at autopsy or during dissection. The figure demonstrates the fact that this inner aspect of the skull is divided naturally into three distinct regions. These are the anterior, middle, and posterior cranial fossae.

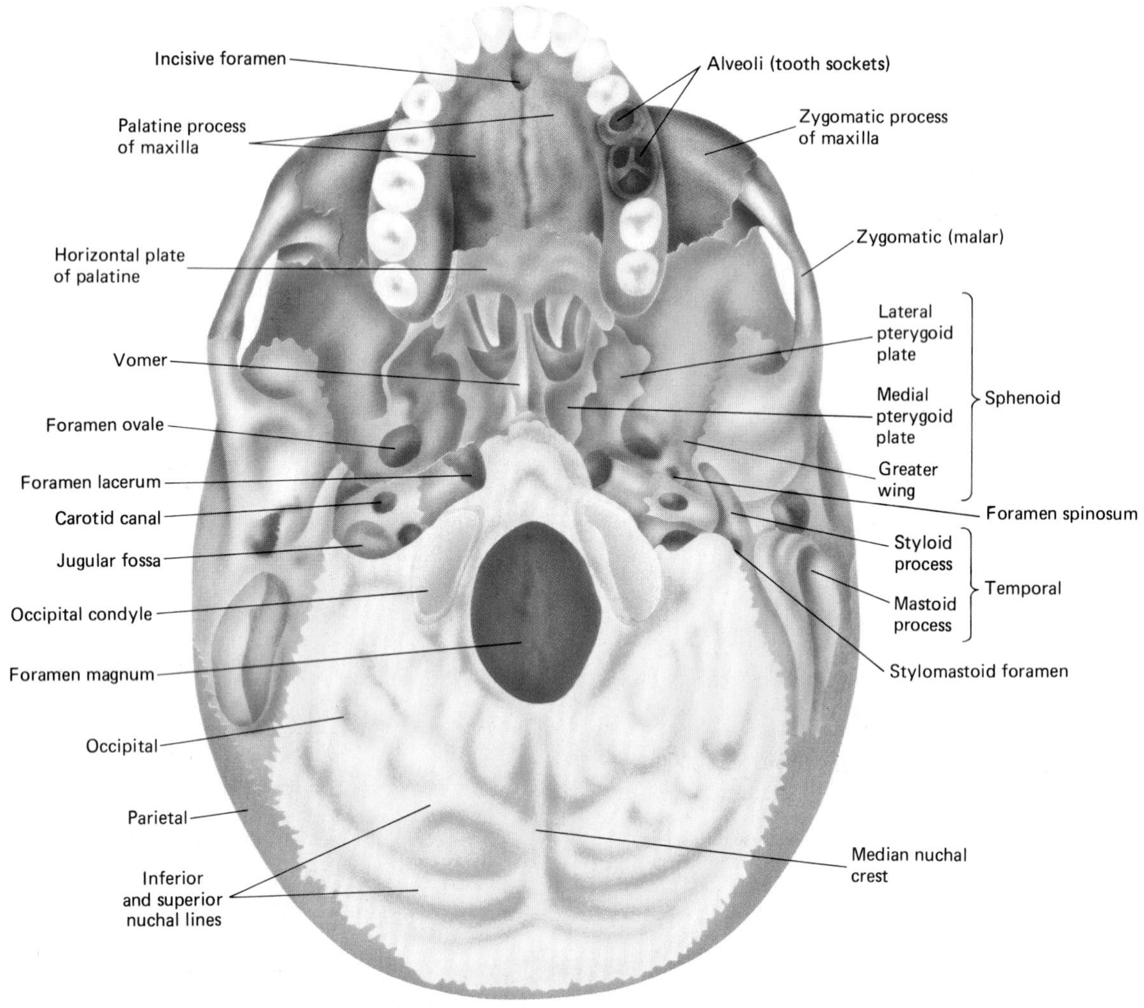

FIGURE 7-8

Inferior surface of the base of the human skull. Notice the occipital condyles that form articulations with the first cervical vertebra. The brain and spinal cord are continuous through the large foramen magnum in the occipital bone.

(1) **Anterior cranial fossa.** This fossa is bounded by the frontal bone in front and on the sides. The floor of this fossa is formed by the orbital plates of the frontal bone, the cribriform plate of the ethmoid bone, the lesser wings, and part of the body of the sphenoid bone.

(2) **Middle cranial fossa.** This fossa lies behind and below the anterior cranial fossa. The smaller central portion of this fossa is formed by the body of the sphenoid bone. The lateral aspect of the fossa on each side is formed by the greater wing of the sphenoid, the temporal bone, and the parietal bone. The temporal lobes of the cerebral hemispheres are housed within the middle cranial fossa.

(3) **Posterior cranial fossa.** Located behind and below the middle fossa, this represents the largest and deepest of all the cranial fossae. The occipital bone as well as the mastoid and petrous portions of the temporal bones contribute to its formation. A major distinguishing feature in the floor of this fossa is the foramen magnum, a large opening through which the brainstem above becomes continuous with the spinal cord below. The cerebellum, pons, and medulla oblongata of the brain are housed within the posterior cranial fossa.

TABLE 7-2

Foramina of the skull

Opening	Location	Structures transmitted
Hypoglossal canal	Superior to occipital condyles	Hypoglossal nerve (CN XII)
Carotid canal	Petrous portion of temporal bone	Internal carotid artery; sympathetic plexuses
Nasolacrimal canal	Within lacrimal bone	Lacrimal duct
Optic canal	Between body and roots of lesser wing of sphenoid bone	Optic nerve (CN II); ophthalmic artery
Pterygoid canal	Anterior to foramen lacerum in middle cranial fossa	Nerve of pterygoid canal
Superior orbital fissure	Between greater and lesser wings of sphenoid bone	Oculomotor nerve (CN III); trochlear nerve (CN IV); abducens nerve (CN VI); ophthalmic division of trigeminal nerve (CN V); ophthalmic veins
Inferior orbital fissure	Bordered by the greater wing of sphenoid, maxilla, and palatine bones	Maxillary division of trigeminal nerve (CN V); zygomatic nerve; infraorbital artery
Foramen magnum	Occipital bone	Medulla oblongata; meninges; spinal portion of accessory nerve (CN XI); vertebral arteries; anterior and posterior spinal arteries; subarachnoid space; sympathetic plexuses
Foramen lacerum	Bordered by petrous portion of temporal, sphenoid, and occipital bones	Branch of ascending pharyngeal artery
Jugular foramen	Between occipital and temporal bones posterior to the carotid canal	Internal jugular vein; glossopharyngeal nerve (CN IX); vagus nerve (CN X); accessory nerve (CN XI)
Infraorbital foramen	Below inferior orbital margin in maxilla	Infraorbital nerve and artery
Mandibular foramen	Medial aspect of mandibular ramus	Inferior alveolar nerve, artery, and vein
Mental foramen	Anterolateral aspect of mandible inferior to second premolar tooth	Mental nerve, artery, and vein
Cribriform plate	Posterolateral to crista galli of ethmoid bone	Olfactory nerve (CN I)
Foramen ovale	Greater wing of sphenoid bone posterior to foramen rotundum in middle cranial fossa	Mandibular division of trigeminal nerve (CN V)
Foramen rotundum	Posteromedial to superior orbital fissure in middle cranial fossa	Maxillary division of trigeminal nerve (CN V)
Foramen spinosum	Posterolateral to foramen ovale in middle cranial fossa	Middle meningeal artery and vein; meningeal branch of trigeminal nerve (CN V)
Stylomastoid foramen	Between styloid and mastoid processes of temporal bone on inferior aspect of skull	Facial nerve (CN VII)
Supraorbital foramen (may be present as a notch only)	Superior margin of orbit	Supraorbital nerve and artery
Greater palatine foramen	Posterolateral aspect of hard palate	Greater palatine nerve, artery, and vein
Lesser palatine foramen	Posterolateral aspect of hard palate	Lesser palatine nerve, artery, and vein
Incisive foramen	In midline of hard palate just posterior to central incisor teeth	Nasopalatine nerve; branches of greater palatine arteries and veins
Internal acoustic meatus	Posterior aspect of petrous portion of temporal bone	Facial nerve (CN VII); vestibulocochlear nerve (CN VIII)
Zygomaticofacial foramen	Lateral aspect of zygomatic bone	Zygomaticofacial nerve, artery, and vein
Anterior and posterior ethmoidal foramina	Junction of medial wall and roof of orbit	Anterior and posterior ethmoidal nerves, arteries, and veins

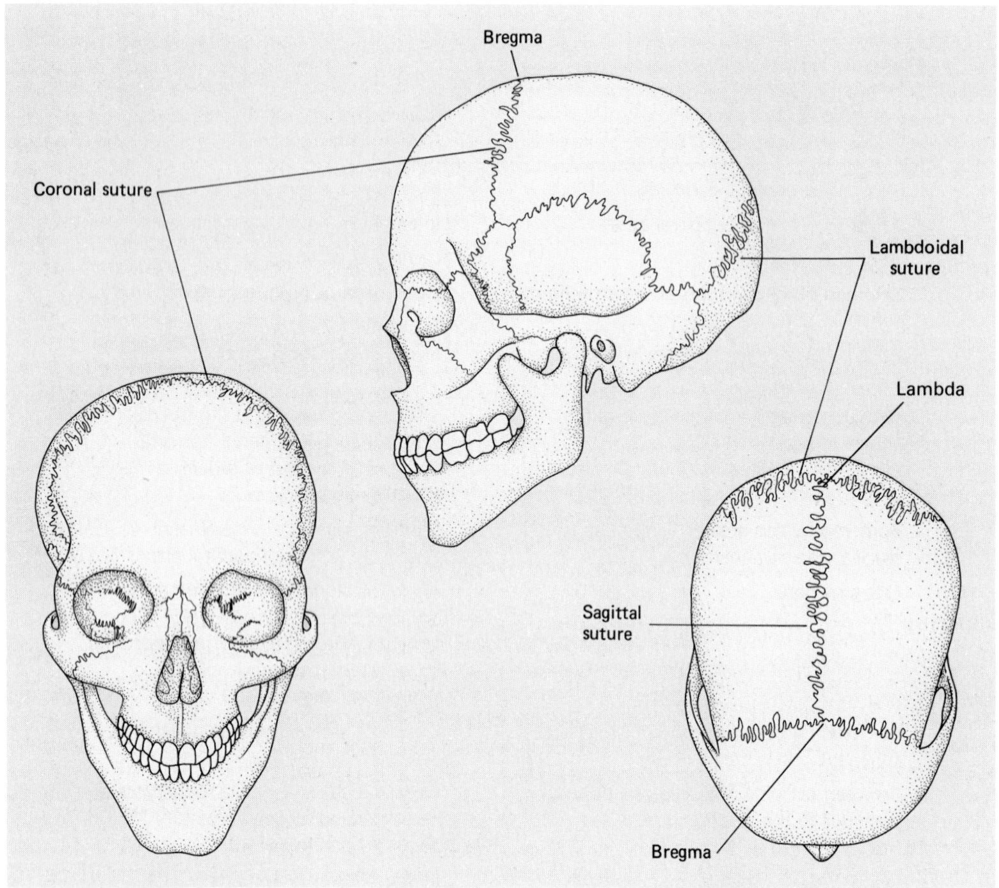

FIGURE 7-9

Major sutures of the human skull as seen in anterior, left lateral, and superior views.

The cranium is composed of eight individual bones

The cranium represents those bones of the skull that house the brain. Eight bones make up the cranium. These are as follows: (1) frontal bone, (2) parietal bones, (2) temporal bones, (1) occipital bone; (1) ethmoid bone, and (1) sphenoid bone.

THE FRONTAL BONE FORMS A PORTION OF THE ORBIT AND THE FOREHEAD

As you begin your examination of the individual bones of the skull you should keep in mind that the frontal bone (Figs. 7-3, 7-4, and 7-6) develops through the fusion of two separate bones. The two halves of this bone are originally separated during fetal and newborn life by a suture that usually disappears between 5½ and 6 years of age. It is termed a *metopic suture* and usually presents no problem to the individual concerned should it persist beyond this time. The frontal bone is a thick structure consisting of cancellous bone situated between two layers of compact bone. The portion that contributes to the formation of the orbit and anterior cranial fossa, however, is composed primarily of compact bone.

Your first impression may be that the frontal bone contributes primarily to the formation of the forehead. If you examine the frontal bone more closely, however, you will find that it has a horizontal portion that participates in the formation of the roof of the orbit as well as the anterior cranial fossa. The *superciliary arches* are the two raised portions on each side of the frontal bone that unite in the midline immediately above the *nasal spine* in a smooth elevation termed the *glabella.* The nasal portion of the frontal bone articulates with the two nasal bones, the maxillae, the lacrimal bones, and the ethmoid bone.

Directly below the superciliary arches we find the *supraorbital margins* of the frontal bone. These form the upper margins of the orbital opening. At the junction of the medial one-third with the lateral two-thirds of this margin you will find the **supraorbital notch** or **foramen,** which serves for the passage of the supraorbital vessels and nerve. The lateral extension of the supraorbital margin terminates as the *zygomatic process* of the frontal bone and enters into articulation with the frontal process of the zygomatic bone.

Within the substance of the frontal bone and lateral to the nasal spine we find the cavities of the **frontal sinuses** (Fig. 7-5), which will be discussed further in Chapter 24. These sinuses lie between the lamellae of the frontal bone and are seldom symmetrical in appearance. They tend to be larger in males and usually reach their maximum size after puberty. As the individual ages, bone may be absorbed from the inner surfaces of the sinuses, thereby leading to their expansion.

Interestingly, the frontal bone develops through the process of intramembranous ossification from two separate centers. These are located directly above the superciliary arches. Although the frontal bone appears as a single structure in the adult, the two halves are separated by the *metopic* or *frontal suture* in the fetus and newborn.

THE POSTERIOR PORTION OF THE SKULL IS FORMED LARGELY BY THE OCCIPITAL BONE

The occipital bone is a large bone (Figs. 7-4 through 7-6 and 7-8) that forms much of the base of the cranium. It possesses a large oval-shaped opening called the **foramen magnum** (Figs. 7-6 and 7-8) through which the vertebral canal communicates with the cranial cavity. It is through this opening that the medulla oblongata with its accompanying meninges, the vertebral arteries, and the spinal portion of the eleventh cranial nerve (spinal accessory nerve; CN XI) pass. It consists of *squamous, basilar,* and *lateral portions* (Fig. 7-6). The occipital bone consists primarily of two compact lamellae (thin leaves or plates of bone) separated by a layer of cancellous bone. A portion of the bone is formed through the process of intramembranous ossification and the remainder is developed via endochondral ossification.

The **external occipital protuberance** is located on the external aspect of the squamous portion midway between the foramen magnum and the most superior portion of the bone. Extending between the external occipital protuberance and the foramen magnum is an elevated region of bone termed the *external occipital crest.* The *superior* and *inferior nuchal lines* extend laterally from this crest and serve for the attachment of various muscles.

The internal aspect of the occipital bone is divided into four rather distinct regions by ridges of bone that unite at the **internal occipital protuberance** (Fig. 7-6). The upper two regions or depressions serve to accommodate the occipital lobes of the cerebrum, whereas the lower two house the posterior poles of the cerebellum on each side. Above the internal occipital protuberance, the **falx cerebri** (fold of dura separating the two cerebral hemispheres), enclosing the superior sagittal sinus, attaches to the midline crest of bone; below is the attachment for the **falx cerebelli** (fold of dura projecting between the two halves of the cerebellum), which houses the occipital sinus. Attachments for the **transverse sinuses,** represented by the **tentorium cerebelli** (fold of dura between the cerebellum and the occipital lobes of the cerebrum), are located on the ridge of bone extending laterally from the internal occipital protuberance. The region where these sinuses meet in the midline near the internal occipital protuberance is termed the *confluence of the sinuses.*

On the inferior aspect of the occipital bone are the **occipital condyles,** which serve for articulation with the atlas, or first cervical vertebra. The occipital bone also articulates with the two parietal bones, the sphenoid bone, and the two temporal bones (Figs. 7-4 through 7-6). In addition to the foramen magnum, there is a **hypoglossal canal** located laterally on each side of the former opening. Each canal transmits the twelfth cranial (hypoglossal; CN XII) nerve as well as a meningeal branch of the ascending pharyngeal artery.

THE SPHENOID BONE HAS CHARACTERISTIC GREATER AND LESSER WINGS

This bone is typically described as representing a bird with outstretched wings. It consists of a main body from which are suspended two pair of wings, the greater and lesser wings (Figs. 7-5 through 7-8). Furthermore, the **pterygoid processes** (**ter**-i-goid) extend downward from the junction of the greater wings with the body of the sphenoid. Each pterygoid process is composed of a medial and lateral pterygoid plate. These are separated posteriorly from one another by a depression or hollow called the **pterygoid fossa** (Fig. 7-7*b*).

The **greater wings** extend upward and laterally from the body of the sphenoid. The outer surface of each has a convex shape and, as can be seen in Figure 7-4, articulates with the temporal, parietal, frontal, zygomatic, and maxillary bones. The concave upper surfaces of these two wings support portions of the temporal lobes of the brain and help to form part of the middle cranial fossa (Fig. 7-6*a*). Each of the greater wings has an orbital surface that contributes to formation of the posterolateral wall of the orbital cavity (Fig. 7-3*b*).

The **lesser wings** are significantly smaller than the greater wings. They project in a lateral direction from the body of the sphenoid and lie above the level of the greater wings. In the interval between the lesser and greater wings, there is a triangular opening called the **superior orbital fissure** that connects the middle cranial fossa with the orbit in front (Fig. 7-3*b*). Two bony struts attach each of the lesser wings to the sphenoid body. The opening between each pair of these struts is termed the **optic canal.**

The **body,** or central portion, of the sphenoid bone is situated between the occipital bone posteriorly and the ethmoid bone anteriorly. Laterally the body of the sphenoid articulates with the temporal bone on each side. This portion of the sphenoid bone contains two of the **paranasal sinuses** (air cavities of bones which communicate with the nasal cavity proper), which are separated from one another by a bony partition. On the superior aspect of the sphenoid body there is a depression or hollow termed the **sella turcica** (**ter**-si-kuh), or "Turkish saddle," which serves to accommodate the pituitary gland. Focus your attention on the lateral radiograph of the skull (Fig. 7-10) and locate the sella turcica. The posterior boundary of the sella turcica is called the **dorsum sellae** and from it the body of the sphenoid slopes gently downward toward the occipital bone, forming a region known as the *clivus* (**klive**-us). The clivus serves to support the upper portion of the pons.

The sphenoid bone presents a number of important paired openings, or foramina, some of which have been mentioned earlier. If one is available, examine a disarticulated sphenoid bone. Openings, or foramina, to be observed include the **foramen ovale, foramen rotundum, foramen spinosum, pterygoid canal, optic canal,** and the **superior orbital fissure.** The sphenoid (greater wing) together with portions of the temporal and occipital bones form an additional foramen called the **foramen lacerum** (Fig. 7-8). Refer to Table 7-2 which lists the specific structures passing through these openings.

THE MEDIAL WALL OF THE ORBIT IS FORMED IN PART BY THE ETHMOID BONE

The **ethmoid bone** is a small bone with a cuboid shape and consisting of four basic parts (Fig. 7-6*b*, *c*, and *d*). These are the **cribriform** (**krib**-ri-form) **plate,** the **perpendicular plate,** and the two *labyrinths.* The cribriform plate is located on the upper surface of the ethmoid, and the labyrinths project laterally from the midline on each side. The perpendicular plate of the ethmoid is attached above to the horizontally placed cribriform plate and lies in the interval between the two labyrinths.

The cribriform plate of the ethmoid bone forms part of the anterior cranial fossa (Fig. 7-6*a*).

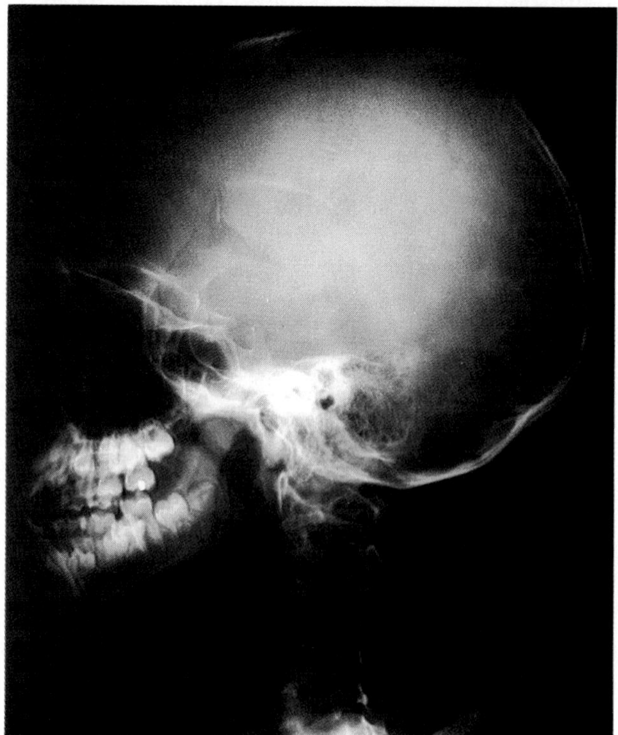

FIGURE 7-10

Lateral radiograph (x-ray) of the human skull. The pituitary gland lies within the sella turcica, or "Turkish saddle," of the sphenoid bone. (SIU/Peter Arnold, Inc.)

This plate is perforated by numerous openings (olfactory foramina) that serve to transmit the first cranial nerves (olfactory nerves, CN I). A distinct bony projection, termed the **crista galli,** is directed upward from the cribriform plate in the midline. The crista galli serves for the attachment of the falx cerebri. Below, the cribriform plate forms a portion of the upper part of the nasal cavity.

The perpendicular plate of the ethmoid is perhaps a little more difficult to visualize than is the cribriform plate, especially on the articulated skull. However, close examination will show that the perpendicular plate helps to form part of the nasal septum by articulating with another bone called the vomer. Some of the septal cartilage of the nose is likewise attached to the perpendicular plate.

Extending laterally and then downward from the cribriform plate on each side of the ethmoid are the two labyrinths. These bony masses contain numerous air cells that constitute the ethmoidal group of paranasal sinuses. The medial and lateral walls of each labyrinth are covered by a thin layer of bone. The lateral surface of each labyrinth forms a portion of the medial wall of the orbital cavity as can be seen in Figures 7-3 and 7-4*a*. The medial surface of each labyrinth, on the other hand, helps to form part of the lateral wall of the nasal cavity on its respective side (Fig. 7-5*c*). This surface of each labyrinth also is marked by two curved projections of very thin bone called the **superior** and **middle nasal conchae** (**kong**-kee) (Fig. 7-5*c*). The presence of the conchae permits inhaled air to be effectively filtered and circulated prior to its passage through more distal regions of the respiratory passages. Between these two conchae lies an elongated and narrow fissure termed the **middle meatus** of the nasal cavity (Fig. 7-5*c*).

THE PAIRED PARIETAL BONES FORM A LARGE PORTION OF THE SIDE AND TOP OF THE SKULL

The two **parietal bones** (Fig. 7-4*a*) form the major portion of the roof and lateral surfaces of the cranium. The external surface of each parietal bone is smooth, convex, and marked by the presence of two curved lines called the *superior* and *inferior temporal lines.* The temporal lines represent the attachment of origin for one of the muscles of mastication, the *temporalis muscle.*

The internal surface of each parietal bone is concave and presents numerous markings. Some of these markings appear as small branching channels that house blood vessels supplying the outermost covering of the brain, the dura mater. Impressions are also present on this surface representing sites that house various convolutions (cerebral gyri) of the brain.

Each parietal bone articulates in front with the frontal bone to form the coronal suture (Fig. 7-4*a*). The sagittal suture is formed by the articulation of the two parietal bones in the midline on the superior aspect of the cranium (Fig. 7-9). A large venous channel, called the *superior sagittal sinus,* is attached to the inner surface of each parietal bone directly beneath the superior sagittal suture. The lambdoidal suture is located along the line of articulation between the parietal bones and the occipital bone posteriorly. The lower border of the parietal bones also articulates with the greater wing of the sphenoid and the temporal bone. The joint between the temporal bone and the parietal bone is called the *squamosal suture* (Fig. 7-4).

THE TEMPORAL BONES CONTAIN THE ORGANS OF HEARING AND EQUILIBRIUM

The **temporal bones** help to form part of the sides as well as the base of the skull (compare Figs. 7-4 and 7-8). Furthermore, each contributes to the formation of the middle and posterior cranial fossa (Fig. 7-6). Each temporal bone consists of four characteristic parts. These are the (1) *squamous portion,* (2) *petrous portion,* (3) *mastoid portion,* and (4) *styloid process.*

The external surface of the squamous portion appears as a shell-like expansion of bone that gives attachment to the temporalis muscle. It is smooth and convex and may present a groove for one of the temporal arteries. An elongated bony projection, the **zygomatic process,** can be seen to extend forward from the lower border of the squamous part of the temporal bone. This process articulates in front with the temporal process of the zygomatic bone, thus forming the **zygomatic arch.**

Below the zygomatic process and just in front of the **external acoustic (auditory) meatus** (ear canal) is a depression called the *mandibular fossa.* Immediately anterior to this fossa is a rounded projection known as the *articular tubercle.* Movements of the mandible, such as those that occur during eating and speaking, take place between the condylar process of the mandible and the aforementioned fossa and tubercle. We refer to this specific joint as the **temporomandibular (TM) joint**. Near the base of the zygomatic process and directly behind the mandibular fossa lies the external acoustic meatus, which leads to the middle ear cavity. The inner limit of the meatus is ordinarily closed by the tympanic membrane (eardrum).

In Figure 7-5*b* the petrous portion of the temporal bone is shown viewed from above as it lies in the base of the skull. Notice that the petrous part is a thick, wedgelike projection of the temporal bone situated between the sphenoid bone in front and the occipital bone behind. Another important feature that can be observed in this figure is that the anterior part of the petrous portion helps to form the middle cranial fossa. Its posterior part contributes to the formation of the posterior cranial fossa.

The internal ear is situated within the substance of the petrous part of the temporal bone. The opening of the **internal acoustic meatus** can also be observed in Figures 7-5 and 7-6*a* and it is through this opening that the facial nerve (CN VII) and vestibulocochlear nerve (CN VIII) are transmitted. The **carotid canal** is also located within the petrous part of the temporal bone (Fig. 7-8). It is through this canal that the internal carotid artery passes to supply structures within the skull. Another opening located just posterior to the carotid canal, the **jugular foramen,** is formed in part by the petrous portion of the temporal bone in addition to part of the adjacent occipital bone. Structures that pass through this opening include the glossopharyngeal nerve (CN IX), vagus nerve (CN X), accessory nerve (CN XI), and the internal jugular vein.

Inferior and posterior to the external acoustic meatus you can find the mastoid portion of the temporal bone. Its posterior surface is often perforated by an opening, the *mastoid foramen*. Through this passes a small emissary vein connecting with the sigmoid sinus and a minute branch of the occipital artery. A distinct conical process, the **mastoid process,** projects downward behind the external acoustic meatus. Several muscles of the neck and back attach to the mastoid process, as we will see in a later chapter. Within the substance of the mastoid portion are located several *mastoid air cells,* although their precise number is variable. They are lined by mucous membrane and form a network of interconnecting chambers that eventually communicate with the *middle ear cavity* (*tympanic cavity*). Certain air cells are separated from the contents of the posterior cranial fossa by only a very thin partition of bone.

The **styloid process** is a pointed, slender projection that extends downward and forward from the lower surface of the temporal bone (Fig. 7-4). Several muscles and ligaments are attached to this process. Focus your attention on Figure 7-8 and notice that between the styloid process medially and the mastoid process laterally there is an opening called the **stylomastoid foramen.** It is through this opening that the stylomastoid artery and the facial nerve (CN VII) pass.

Clinical highlight

The facial nerve, as it exits the stylomastoid foramen, is subject to injury during childbirth if the physician uses forceps. This arises from the fact that the mastoid process is poorly developed at this time and the nerve is therefore relatively unprotected on its lateral aspect.

The facial skeleton is composed of fourteen bones

Most of the facial skeleton is formed by the upper and lower jaws. Additional bones contributing to the facial skeleton include the palatine, nasal, zygomatic, vomer, and inferior nasal conchae.

THE MANDIBLE FORMS THE LOWER JAW

The **mandible** (Figs. 7-3 through 7-5), or lower jaw, is by far the largest bone of the facial skeleton. It has a **body** and two **rami** that project upward from its angles on each side. The body is horseshoe-shaped and contains the teeth of the lower jaw in its **alveolar process.** Notice (Fig. 7-4) that atop each ramus there are two projections of bone separated by a wide notch (*mandibular notch*). The more anterior one is called the **coronoid process** and the posterior one is termed the **head** or **condylar process**. The constricted portion of bone immediately below the head is called the **neck** of the mandible.

The mandible develops through the fusion of two fetal bones during intrauterine life. Evidence for this may sometimes be seen on its anterior surface where a small ridge of bone is located in the midline between the two central incisor teeth. This ridge represents the site of a former joint called the *mental symphysis.* An opening called the **mental foramen** is located on each side of the body directly below the second premolar tooth. The mental nerve and blood vessels emerge from the mandible through this opening.

The medial surface of the mandible has a number of characteristic features. A prominent tonguelike projection of bone, called the *lingula,* is located on the inner surface of each ramus. Immediately adjacent to the lingula is an opening termed the **mandibular foramen.** The inferior alveolar nerve and vessels pass through the mandibular foramen to enter the mandibular canal, which lies within the body of the mandible. Dentists frequently use the lingula as a landmark in locating the mandibular foramen for the proper placement of a needle for the injection of anesthetics.

THE MAXILLAE HOLD THE UPPER TEETH AND FORM A LARGE PORTION OF THE HARD PALATE

The two maxillae (Figs. 7-3 and 7-4) fuse during development to form the entire upper jaw. They also contribute to the formation of the roof of the mouth, the floor of the orbital cavity, and the floor and lateral walls of the nasal cavities. In addition to a **body,** each maxilla has four characteristic processes: (1) **alveolar,** (2) **palatine,** (3) **frontal,** and (4) **zygomatic.**

The body of the maxilla is roughly pyramidal in shape and contains within its substance a large cavity called the *maxillary sinus.* The maxillary sinuses are connected with the nasal cavity and together they represent another pair of the paranasal sinuses. The maxillary sinuses vary in size between skulls and from one side to the other in the same skull.

Clinical highlight

The fact that the walls of the maxillary sinus are very thin predisposes the individual to a number of important clinical problems. For example, a "blow-out" fracture of the orbit may result in the displacement of bony fragments into the maxillary sinus below (Figs. 7-3 and 7-5*e*). On the other hand, a tumor growing within the maxillary sinus may displace the eyeball upward, grow into the nasal or oral cavity, or extend itself forward onto the cheek.

The *alveolar process* of each maxilla houses the teeth of the upper jaw. The horizontally placed *palatine processes* are ordinarily fused in the midline to form the anterior three-fourths of the hard palate or roof of the mouth. The *frontal process* of each maxilla is directed upward and is in contact with the frontal, nasal, and lacrimal bones. The *zygomatic process* is a large projection having the shape of a truncated pyramid. It articulates with the zygomatic bone.

Just below each orbit (the bony cavity in which the eyeball is housed) there is an opening in the body of the maxilla that is called the **infraorbital foramen** (Fig. 7-3). This foramen transmits the infraorbital artery and nerve. It is continuous posteriorly with the infraorbital canal and infraorbital groove. The *palatine process* of each maxilla meets its counterpart on the opposite bone in the midline and forms the major portion of the hard palate (posterior portion of roof of mouth) whose oral surface is concave. Failure of such fusion to occur during development of the individual results in a congenital defect known as **cleft palate.**

Once the palatine processes of the two maxillae fuse, they give rise to a midline depression called the *incisive fossa.* This depression is located on the hard palate (formed by parts of the maxillary and palatine bones) immediately behind the lateral incisor teeth and contains openings for the *incisive canals,* which transmit the greater palatine artery and the nasopalatine nerves to the roof of the mouth. Where the two palatine processes meet in the midline anteriorly, there exists a sharp projection termed the *anterior nasal spine* (Fig. 7-4).

Near the posterior portion of the orbit between the greater wing of the sphenoid bone and the maxilla, there exists an opening called the *inferior orbital fissure* (Fig. 7-3). This fissure is essentially continuous with another opening known as the *superior orbital fissure,* which lies between the greater and lesser wings of the sphenoid bone. The infraorbital fissure transmits the maxillary division of the trigeminal nerve (CN V), the zygomatic nerve, and the infraorbital artery and nerve.

THE PAIRED NASAL BONES FORM THE BRIDGE OF THE NOSE

The **nasal bones** are paired and, together with the frontal processes of the maxillae, form the bridge (upper part of the external nose) of the nose (Figs. 7-3 and 7-4). The remainder of the nose is formed primarily of cartilage. In addition to the nasal bone of the opposite side, each nasal bone articulates with the frontal, maxillary, and ethmoid bones.

THE UNPAIRED VOMER CONTRIBUTES TO PART OF THE NASAL SEPTUM

The **vomer** is thin and flat and forms the posteroinferior portion of the nasal septum (wall) (Fig. 7-5). The nasopalatine nerves and vessels are housed in a groove located along its sides. The inferior border of the vomer articulates with the maxillae and the palatine bones, and its anterior border articulates with the ethmoid and the nasal septal cartilage. Since the vomer is responsible for forming a major portion of the primary septum between the nasal cavities, if it is deviated to one side or the other, the resulting nasal cavities will be of unequal size.

THE LACRIMAL BONES FORM PART OF THE ORBIT

The **lacrimal bones** are the smallest bones of the facial skeleton and form part of the medial wall of the orbit (Figs. 7-3 and 7-4). The anterior border of each lacrimal bone forms the *lacrimal fossa* with the frontal process of the maxilla on the same side. This fossa serves to house the lacrimal sac (structure that collects the tears), which empties into the nasal cavity through the nasolacrimal canal.

THE INFERIOR NASAL CONCHAE LIE WITHIN THE NASAL CAVITY

The **inferior nasal conchae** (**konk**-kee) are situated on the lateral walls of the nasal cavities. They project into the nasal cavities below the level of the superior and middle conchae of the ethmoid bone. The lateral surface of each of these bones forms the inferior meatus of the nose and serves to promote effective circulation and filtration of inhaled air prior to its passage to the lungs.

THE PALATINE BONES FORM THE POSTERIOR PORTION OF THE HARD PALATE

The **palatine bones** are paired bones of the facial skeleton and their horizontal plates form the posterior portion of the roof of the mouth, or *hard palate* (Figs. 7-4, 7-5, and 7-8). Furthermore, the palatine bones contribute to the formation of the floor and lateral wall of the nasal cavity as well as the floor of the orbital cavity. The maxillary surface of the perpendicular plate forms a passageway with the maxilla called the **greater palatine canal,** which transmits the greater palatine vessels and nerve. Additional openings, the **lesser palatine foramina,** are located behind the former openings and serve to transmit the lesser palatine nerves and arteries.

THE ZYGOMATIC BONES FORM THE PROMINENCE OF THE CHEEK

The **zygomatic (malar) bones** form the prominence of the cheek as well as part of the floor and lateral wall of each orbital cavity. The frontal processes of the zygomatic bones articulate with the frontal bone and the greater wing of the sphenoid. The *temporal process,* together with the zygomatic process of the temporal bone, forms the **zygomatic arch.** On the lateral surface of each zygomatic bone there is an opening that transmits the zygomaticofacial vessels and nerve. This opening is called the **zygomaticofacial foramen.**

The hyoid bone does not form an articulation with another bone

The **hyoid bone** is different from all other bones of the skeleton in that it does not articulate with another bone. It is a U-shaped bone (Fig. 7-11) and is suspended from the styloid processes of the temporal bones by the stylohyoid ligaments. It has a body and two *greater* and *lesser horns,* or *cornua.* The hyoid bone can be palpated in the region of the neck between the larynx and the mandible.

The vertebral column houses the spinal cord and is composed of individual vertebrae

The individual bones of the vertebral column are called the **vertebrae.** Together they form a strong bony column that has several important functions. In addition to supporting the head, the vertebral column houses and protects the spinal cord. Some of the vertebrae articulate with the ribs, and many of the back muscles are attached

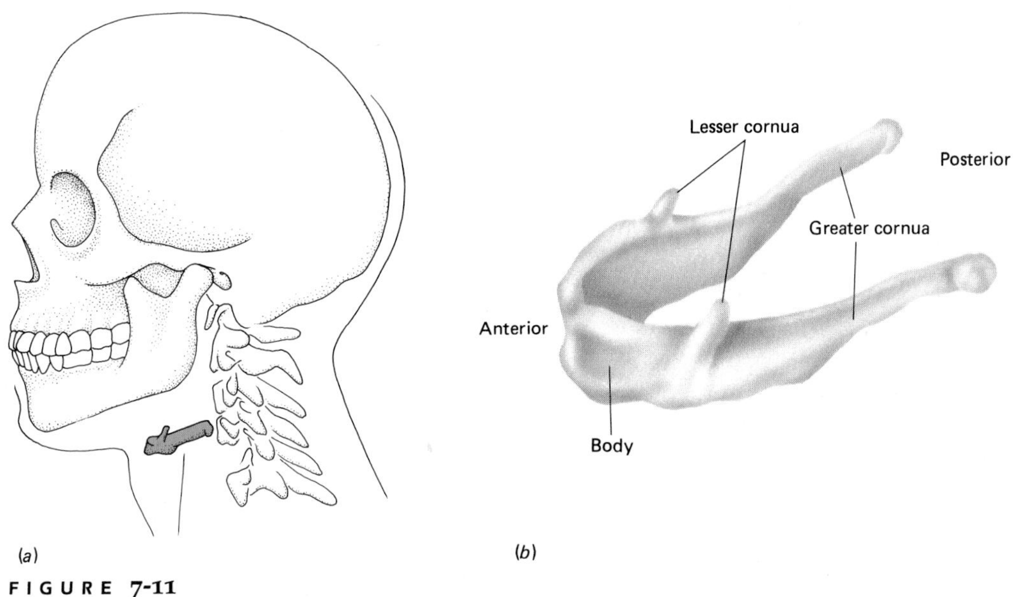

FIGURE 7-11

The hyoid bone does not articulate with another bone. Here it is seen in a lateral and somewhat oblique view.

to the vertebral column as well. Movement of the vertebral column occurs anteriorly, posteriorly, and laterally. Although the movement between any two adjacent vertebrae is not very great, the summation of all such movements between all the vertebrae gives the vertebral column considerable flexibility. This can be easily appreciated by watching the performance of a championship gymnast.

As you begin your examination of the vertebral column, notice that in the adult it is typically composed of 33 individual vertebrae (Fig. 7-12). (The individual sacral and coccygeal vertebrae fuse during development to form two separate bones, the sacrum and coccyx.) The vertebral column is typically divided into five distinct regions each with a specific number of vertebrae. Starting at the base of the skull and progressing inferiorly they are: *7 cervical vertebrae* located in the neck, *12 thoracic vertebrae* located along the posterior wall of the thorax, *5 lumbar vertebrae* in the region of the lower back, *5 sacral vertebrae* that have fused into a single bone called the *sacrum,* and typically *4 coccygeal* vertebrae that have also fused to form a single entity called the *coccyx.* Spend a few moments at this time to examine each of these regions in Figure 7-12.

Notice at this time that the vertebral column, when viewed from its lateral aspect, does not lie in a straight line. Rather, it is characterized by the presence of four distinct curves. The cervical and lumbar curves are concave in the posterior direction whereas the thoracic and sacral curves are convex in the posterior direction. During fetal development the vertebral column has only a single curve and this is convex in the posterior direction.

Two postnatal events are primarily responsible for development of the cervical and lumbar curves. The cervical curve develops as the child learns to hold his or her head in the upright position. The lumbar curve develops as a result of the child's learning to stand and walk. These two curves are also called *secondary curves* as they develop subsequent to the occurrence of these childhood milestones. The thoracic and sacral curves are termed *primary curves* because they basically resemble the single curvature of the developing fetal vertebral column.

Intervertebral foramina are openings located between adjacent vertebrae (Figs. 7-12 through 7-14). It is through these foramina that the spinal nerves pass to be distributed to various parts of the body. Individual vertebrae, beginning with the axis and ending with the sacrum, are separated from one another by fibrocartilaginous discs known as the **intervertebral discs.** Each disc is composed principally of a tissue similar to fibrous cartilage surrounded by a tough connective tissue capsule. The cartilage of the disc differentiates into two concentrically arranged parts—a tough, outer layer called the *annulus fibrosus,* and a softer, almost semiliquid core, termed the *nucleus pulposus.*

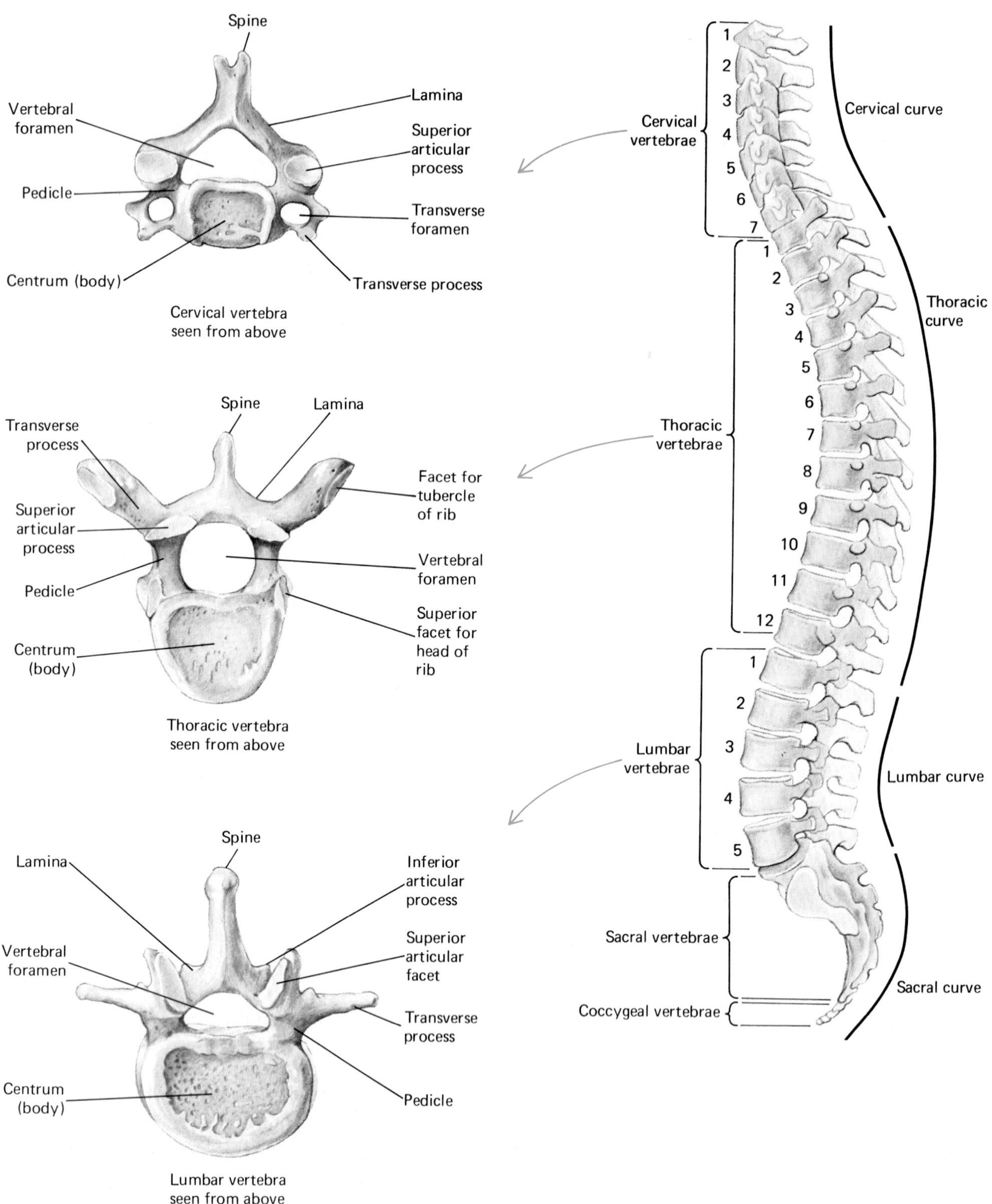

FIGURE 7-12

The vertebral column, the vertebrae, and the sacrum and coccyx together with superior views of individual cervical, thoracic, and lumbar vertebrae.

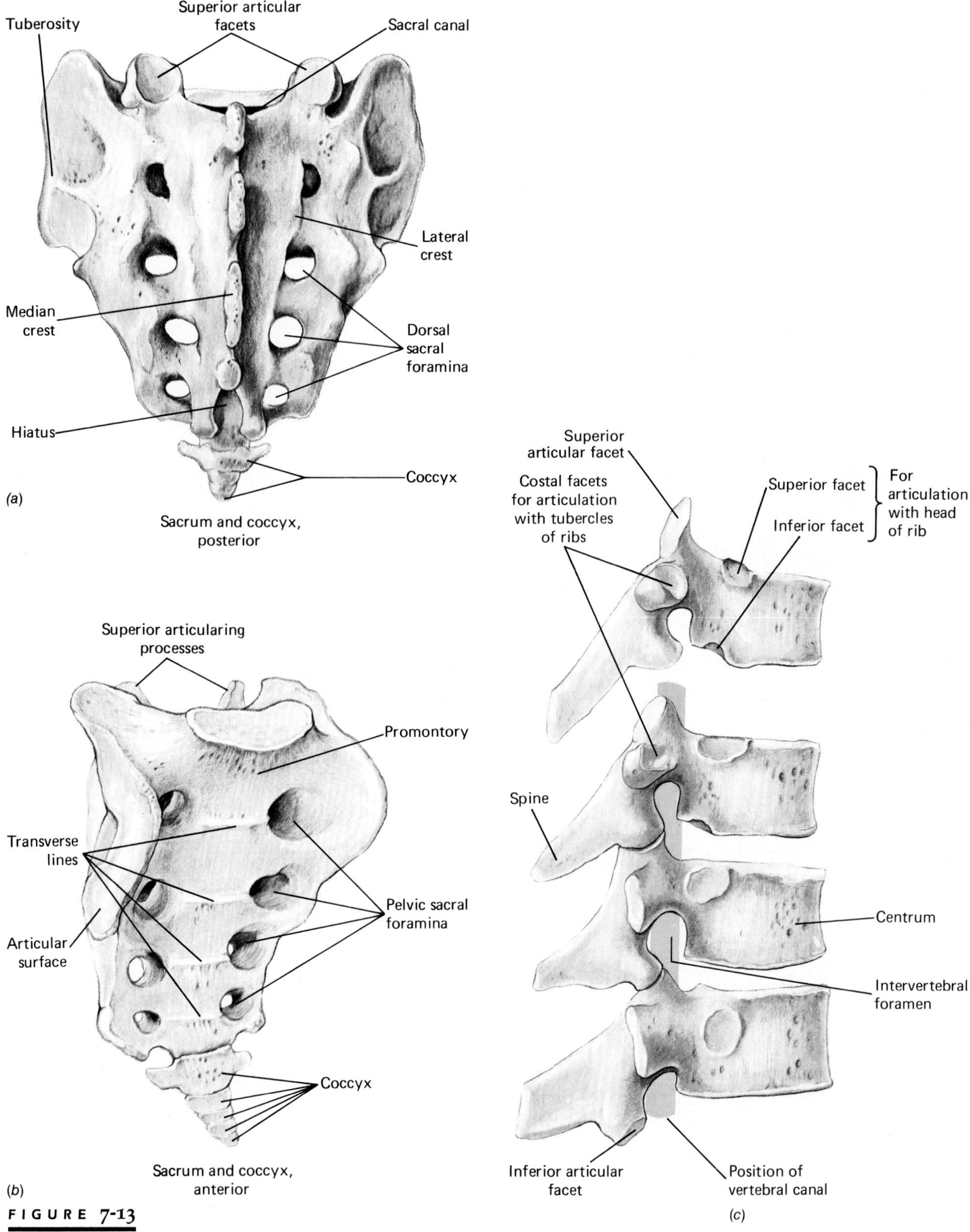

FIGURE 7-13

(*a*) Posterior (dorsal) aspect of the sacrum and coccyx. (*b*) Anterior (ventral) and somewhat oblique view of the sacrum and coccyx. (*c*) Lateral view of several vertebrae, illustrating the manner in which they articulate.

The intervertebral discs are responsible for bearing gravitational pressures and other major forms of stress that are transmitted through the vertebral column. In essence they behave somewhat like cushions that separate the bodies of adjacent vertebrae. Since they must absorb the full force of gravity and all manner of shocks, they are subject to a great deal of wear and tear.

Clinical highlight

Sometimes a rupture of the connective tissue capsule (annulus fibrosus) occurs. In severe cases the herniated (ruptured) disc may move in a posterolateral direction and thereby impinge upon the root of a spinal nerve. This has been illustrated for you in Figure 7-14. Pressure on the spinal nerve root can lead to excruciating pain and even paralysis. Surgical removal of the bulging disc is carried out to correct such a condition.

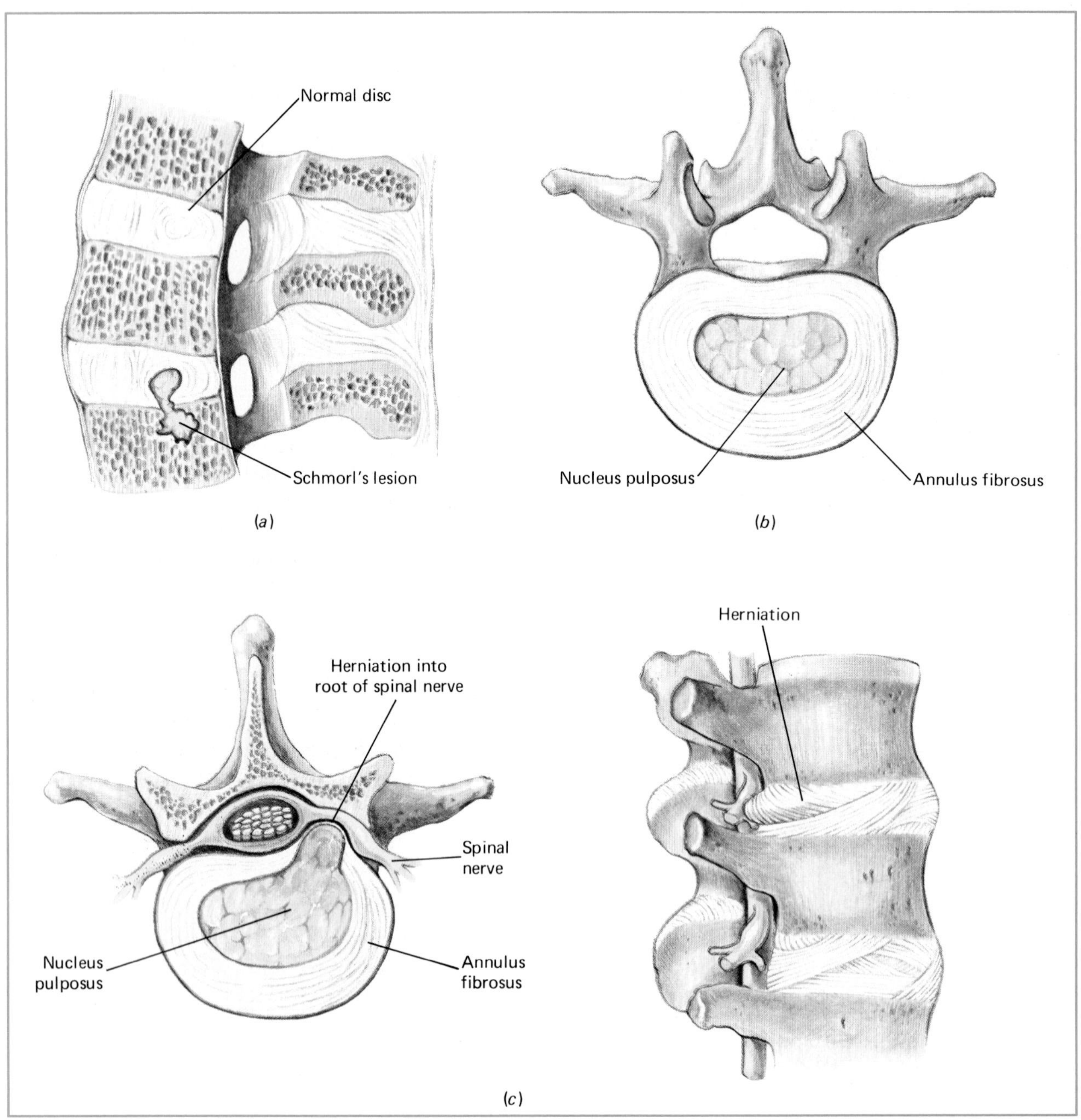

FIGURE 7-14

(a) Sagittal section through the vertebral column, illustrating a normal disc and a usually harmless Schmorl's lesion of a disc. (b) Superior aspect of a normal intervertebral disc. (c) Illustrates how a herniated disc may exert pressure upon the root of a spinal nerve.

Many vertebrae have common features and are considered as typical vertebrae

The cervical, thoracic, lumbar, sacral, and coccygeal vertebrae show considerable regional variation with regard to their shape, size, and unique characteristics. However, all vertebrae, regardless of their placement within the vertebral column, have certain basic similarities.

The basic structure of a typical vertebra (Fig. 7-12) consists of two portions. The anterior part is the **body,** or **centrum.** Posteriorly, a **neural arch** encloses an opening called the **vertebral foramen.** In the fully articulated vertebral column the **vertebral canal,** which contains the spinal cord, is formed by adjacent vertebral foramina.

The body is generally cylindrical in shape and has a roughened appearance on its superior and inferior surfaces where it articulates with the intervertebral discs. Its anterior, posterior, and lateral surfaces are marked by the presence of tiny openings through which small arteries and veins pass.

Two projections extend posteriorly from the vertebral body. These are short, thick processes known as the **pedicles** (**ped**-ih-kills) (Fig. 7-12). Above and below, each pedicle is slightly notched. When the vertebrae articulate with one another, these adjacently placed notches contribute to the formation of the intervertebral foramina. The pedicles unite with the **laminae** (**lam**-in-ee), which are situated even more posteriorly, and in doing so they effectively complete the neural arch (Fig. 7-12).

A marked projection extends posteriorly and inferiorly from where the laminae meet in the midline. This is the **spinous process.** Extending laterally from the junction of each pedicle and lamina there is a **transverse process.** In addition to these projections there are four others of which you should take note. There are two **superior articular processes** that serve for articulation with the vertebra immediately above, and the two **inferior articular processes** permit the vertebra to articulate with the one immediately below. The superior and inferior articular processes form mobile joints between adjacent vertebrae.

Certain vertebrae possess highly specialized features

Some vertebrae exhibit very distinguishing characteristics. These unique features are discussed in detail below.

THE ATLAS IS THE FIRST CERVICAL VERTEBRA

The mythical Atlas held the world on his shoulders. So, too, the **atlas,** or first cervical vertebra (C1), supports the globe of the skull on two elongated articular facets. Perhaps the most unusual of the cervical vertebrae, the atlas (Fig. 7-15) has no spinous process. Instead it bears a **posterior tubercle** located on the **posterior arch.** Moreover, there is no body, or centrum, but on each side there is a mass of lateral bone bearing on its superior surface the synovial joint facets that accept the occipital condyles of the skull above. These are the *superior articular facets.* On the under surface, the *inferior articular facets* form another pair of synovial joints with superior facets of the axis vertebrae below.

The **anterior arch** of the atlas has a tiny projection that extends forward and is called the *anterior tubercle.* The posterior surface of the anterior arch also has a small synovial facet that articulates with the **dens,** or **odontoid process,** of the axis vertebrae below. A ligament completes the socket into which this process of the axis fits. Two transverse foramina for the passage of the vertebral arteries and veins are situated laterally on each side of the vertebral canal. The massive *transverse processes* of the atlas can be palpated in the neck just below the level of the mastoid processes of the skull, especially when the neck is rotated to the side. Try to palpate these structures on yourself.

THE BODY OF THE ATLAS IS FUSED WITH THE AXIS

Although Atlas was thought to uphold the world in antiquity, today we know that it rotates in space on its axis. The second cervical vertebra (C2), or **axis** (Figs. 7-15 and 7-16), provides a similar service for the skull, which rotates, along with the atlas, around the dens of the axis vertebra. This process, the pivot of the head, extends upward from the body of the axis. There is no equivalent process on the inferior surface, that being occupied by a typical centrum and intervertebral disc articulation.

Like the atlas, and indeed all cervical vertebrae, the axis possesses a transverse foramen on either side. Numerous muscles and ligaments attach upon the laminae and spinous process of the axis vertebra. In fact the spinous process of the axis vertebra is distinctly divided (bifid) for the attachment of the *ligamentum nuchae,* a strong ligament that aids in keeping the neck erect.

THE LOWER FIVE CERVICAL VERTEBRAE ARE UNIFORM IN THEIR BASIC STRUCTURE

The remaining **cervical vertebrae** (C3–C7) each possess two *superior* and two *inferior articular facets,* a large *centrum* (body), and *transverse foramina* (Figs. 7-12 and 7-16). Notice that these transverse foramina are unique to the cervical vertebrae and can be used as a landmark for their identification. The seventh cervical vertebra (C7) has a characteristically long spinous process. Thus, it is termed the vertebra prominens; it serves for the attachment of the lower end of the ligamentum nuchae. The *vertebra prominens* can usually be palpated at the base of the neck in the midline. Try this on yourself or a partner. The cervical spinous processes serve in general for the attachment of the ligamentum nuchae as well as for neck and back muscles involved in movement of the neck. Spinous processes of the third, fourth, and fifth cervical vertebrae are more notably bifid (exhibiting a cleft) than that of the second.

THE TWELVE THORACIC VERTEBRAE ARTICULATE WITH THE RIBS

The twelve **thoracic vertebrae** (T1–T12; Figs. 7-12, 7-13, and 7-16) tend to be larger and stronger than the cervical vertebrae above. They have characteristic **facets** or **demifacets** (half-facets) on their bodies for articulation with the heads of the ribs. The body of the first thoracic vertebrae has one complete facet (superior) and one demifacet (inferior) whereas that of the second thoracic vertebra has two demifacets (one above and one below). The head of the first rib articulates with the complete facet on T1, and that of the second rib forms a joint with the inferior demifacet of T1 and the superior demifacet of T2. The third through the eighth thoracic vertebrae each have demifacets arranged like that of T2. The ninth thoracic vertebra (T9) has only a single demifacet

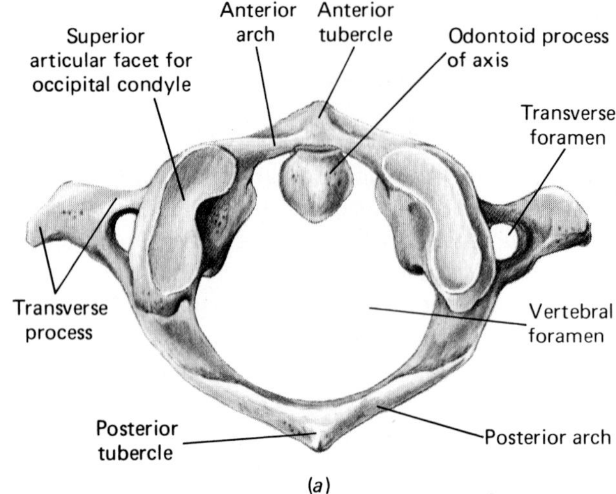

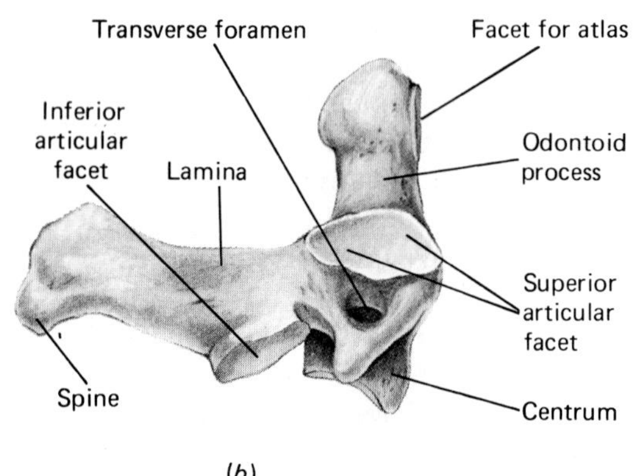

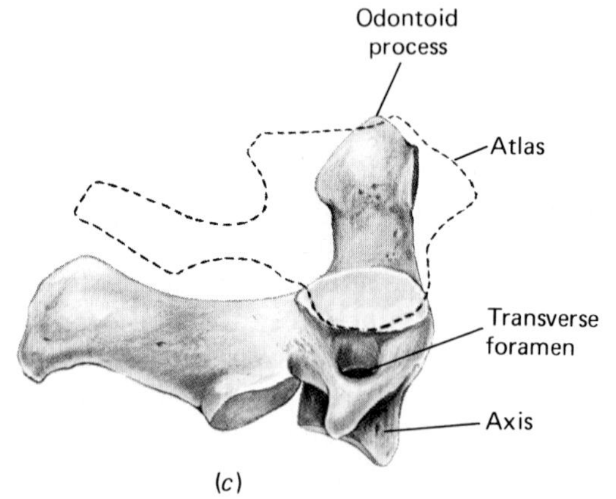

FIGURE 7-15

(*a*) Superior aspect of the atlas, or first cervical vertebra. (*b*) Lateral aspect of the axis, or second cervical vertebra. (*c*) Manner in which the atlas and axis articulate.

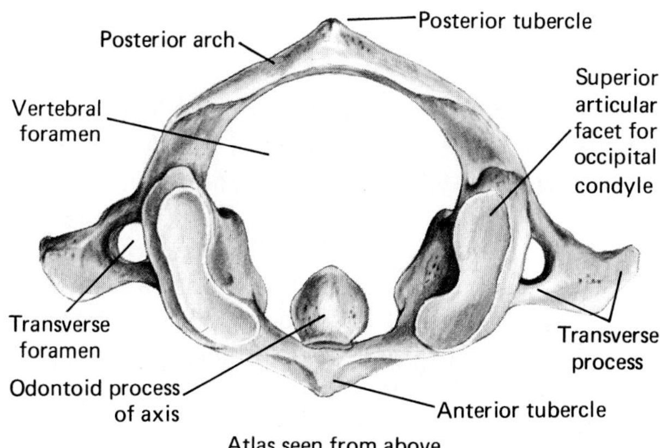

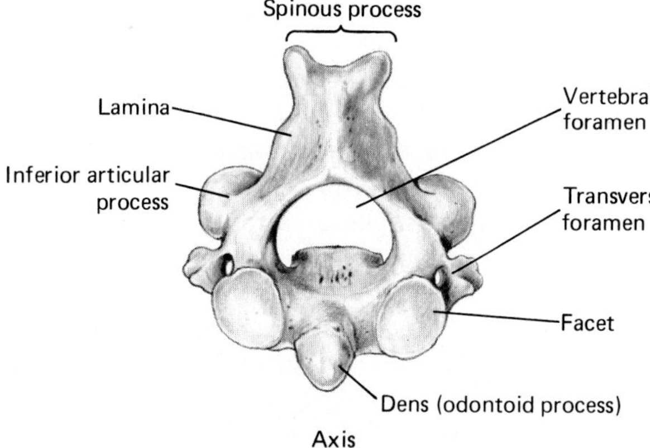

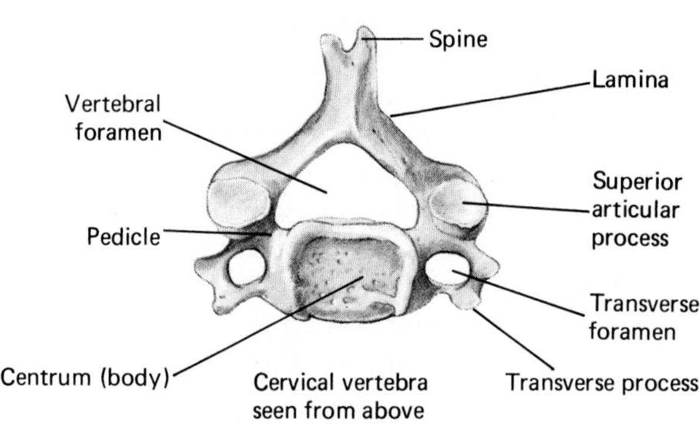

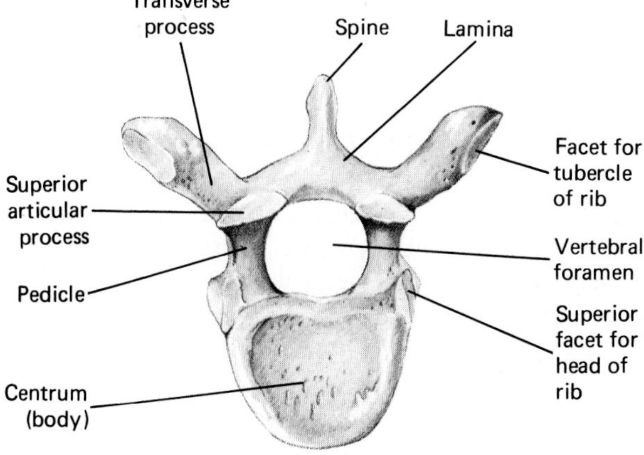

FIGURE 7-16

Superior aspect of the atlas, axis, lower cervical vertebra, and thoracic vertebra.

on each side for articulation with the head of the ninth rib. The remaining thoracic vertebrae (T10–T12) each possess a complete facet on each side of their bodies for articulation with the head of the rib.

In addition to the facets and demifacets just discussed, the first ten thoracic vertebrae (T1–T10) each have a facet on their transverse processes that forms a synovial joint with the tubercle of the rib to which it corresponds numerically; that is, the tubercle of the seventh rib articulates with the facet on the transverse process of T7. The spinous processes of the thoracic vertebrae are directed posteriorly and inferiorly. The spinous process of the first (T1) appears more like a cervical vertebra and that of the last (T12) looks more like a lumbar vertebra.

THE BODIES OF LUMBAR VERTEBRAE INCREASE IN SIZE PROGRESSIVELY FROM SUPERIOR TO INFERIOR

Because they support a major part of the weight of the body, the **lumbar vertebrae** (Figs. 7-12 and 7-17) are very large, with heavy bodies. Moreover, the lumbar region of the vertebral column is responsible for much of the flexibility of the trunk. There are five lumbar vertebrae (L1–L5) and none of them have facets like the thoracic vertebrae have for articulation with the ribs. The bodies of the lumbar vertebrae are generally wider from side to side then they are in an anterior-to-posterior direction.

The vertebral foramen tends to be larger than that of the thoracic vertebrae and has a characteristic triangular shape to it. The thick spinous processes are nearly horizontal in position and have a quadrangular shape. It is to these spinous processes as well as the transverse processes of the lumbar vertebrae that the great muscles of the back attach. The superior articular facets for the vertebra above face medially; the inferior pair are directed laterally for articulation with the vertebrae below.

Clinical highlight

The twisting, shearing forces to which the lumbar part of the vertebral column is subjected are severe. In the kind of strenuous activity that involves radical movements, intervertebral pressures can exceed several hundred pounds per square inch, at least momentarily. The combination of force and violent movement is probably responsible for the vast array of lower back problems to which we are susceptible, especially those involving injured intervertebral discs.

FIVE INDIVIDUAL SACRAL VERTEBRAE FUSE TO FORM THE SACRUM

So named because in some ancient cultures it was considered sacred to the gods, the **sacrum** (Figs. 7-13 and 7-17) is the sole connection between the vertebral column and the great bones of the pelvic girdle. Forces generated by the lower limbs and the trunk converge upon this strong, triangular-shaped bone. It consists of five fused vertebrae. These vertebrae can be separated in a child's skeleton because the cartilaginous growing surfaces are not yet ossified. The lines of fusion may be observed on the concave anterior surface of the adult sacrum, and indeed, the intervertebral discs remain unossified in many instances even into middle age.

The base of the sacrum is the superior portion and possesses articular facets for the fifth lumbar vertebra. On the pelvic (anterior) surface there is a ridge of bone projecting forward from what was the upper body of the first sacral vertebrae. This is called the *sacral promontory*. In the female the sacral promontory may be palpated through the vagina (per vaginum) and serves as a landmark to the obstetrician in making various obstetrical measurements important for the delivery of the child at birth.

The pelvic surface has four pairs of openings termed the *pelvic (anterior) sacral foramina,* which communicate with the *sacral canal* within the substance of the sacrum. The posterior (dorsal) surface of the sacrum likewise has four pairs of *posterior (dorsal) sacral foramina* which also interconnect with the sacral canal. These foramina serve for the passage of numerous nerves and blood vessels.

On the convex posterior surface are the median and lateral *sacral crests,* which represent the fusion of the sacral spinous and transverse processes, respectively. The apex of the sacrum is directed inferiorly and has an articular surface for the coccyx. Formed by the vertebral foramina of the fused sacral vertebrae, the sacral canal is roughly triangular in shape. Its superior opening lies between the two superior articular facets. Its inferior opening is called the *sacral hiatus.* It is through the sacral hiatus that the filum terminale emerges (the inferior extension of the innermost covering of the spinal cord) and passes downward to attach to the coccyx.

The *sacral cornua* are situated at the sides of the hiatus and represent the inferior articular processes of the last sacral vertebra. Ligaments connect the cornua of the sacrum with those of the coccyx. The upper portion of the lateral surface of the sacrum possesses a large auricular surface through which the sacrum articulates with the ilium. The joint thus formed is known as the **sacroiliac joint.**

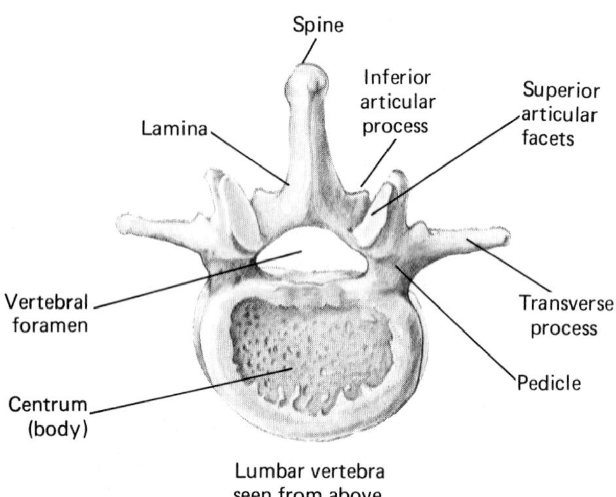

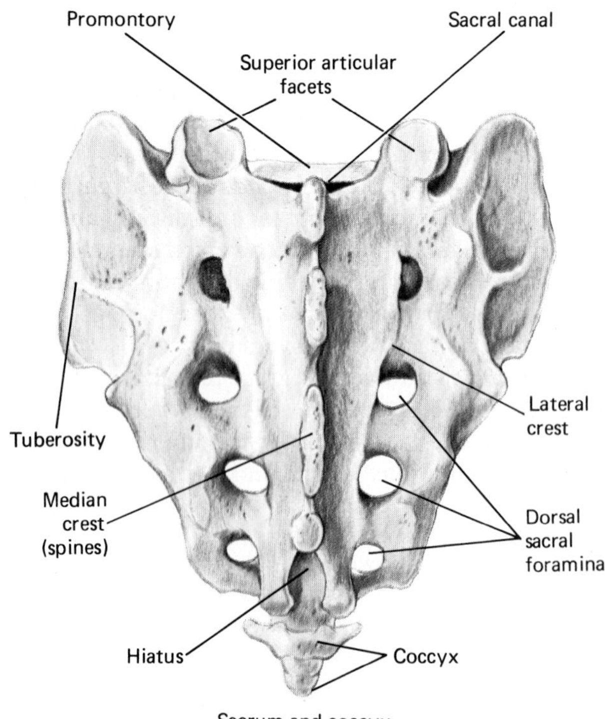

FIGURE 7-17

Superior aspect of a lumbar vertebra and the dorsal (posterior) aspect of the sacrum and coccyx.

THE COCCYX REPRESENTS THE MOST INFERIOR PORTION OF THE VERTEBRAL COLUMN

The **coccyx** (Figs. 7-13 and 7-17) has a triangular shape and usually consists of four fused vertebrae. Like the sacrum, its base is directed superiorly and its apex inferiorly. Though it is small, it is by no means an unimportant bone, serving as the origin of several pelvic and hip muscles (including the gluteus maximus, the coccygeus, the levator ani, and the sphincter ani). Thus, a fractured coccyx is no trivial misfortune. On its dorsal surface we find the *coccygeal cornua,* which are united by ligaments with the sacral cornua above. The coccygeal cornua and the rudimentary transverse process on each side of its base are remnants of the first coccygeal vertebrae.

The skeleton of the thorax is composed of the ribs, sternum, and thoracic vertebrae

That portion of the trunk that we call the **thorax** or chest contains several skeletal components. These are as follows: the *sternum,* the *costal cartilages, twelve pairs of ribs,* and the bodies of the *thoracic vertebrae.* Together these elements constitute what is known as the rib or **thoracic cage.** The thoracic cage is narrower above than below and is compressed in an anterior-posterior direction. It houses such vital organs as the heart and lungs as well as offering protection to certain abdominal structures like the liver and spleen. Its superior opening is termed the *thoracic inlet,* and its inferior opening, covered over by the muscular diaphragm, is called the *thoracic outlet.* Identify the components of the thoracic cage in Figures 7-18 and 7-19.

The sternum articulates with several ribs and with the upper limb

The **sternum** (Fig. 7-18) consists of three distinct portions which are, from superior to inferior, (1) the **manubrium,** (2) the **body,** and (3) the **xiphoid** (**ziff**-oid) **process.** The body of the sternum originally developed from four separate segments; however, the only indication of this in the adult may be the presence of three transverse ridges on its anterior surface. The sternum is longer in males than in females, averaging approximately 17 centimeters in length in adult males.

Clinical highlight

In certain individuals the sternum may be greatly depressed or sunken below the level of the chest wall. Such a condition is termed *funnel chest* and often times does not present any significant problems for the person concerned. This bone is frequently used for obtaining bone marrow samples for laboratory studies due to its easy accessibility and the thinness of its outer layer of compact bone.

The manubrium of the sternum is roughly triangular in shape. Its superior border is markedly concave and forms what we call the *jugular* or *suprasternal notch.* Lateral to the suprasternal notch on each side is an articular facet for the clavicle, below which is located another facet for the costal cartilage of the first rib. The costal cartilage of the second rib articulates with the manubrium and the body of the sternum where they unite. In fact where they join, they form a distinct angle that is used as a guide by physicians for determining the precise location of the second rib and subsequently specific intercostal spaces. This easily identifiable anatomical landmark is termed the **sternal angle.**

The body of the sternum is located between the manubrium and the xiphoid process. It represents the longest part of the sternum and is generally broader below than above. The anterior surface, as mentioned before, frequently has three transverse ridges that signify its development from four separate elements. The costal cartilages of the second through the seventh ribs articulate along the lateral margin on each side of the sternal body.

The xiphoid process is the smallest portion of the sternum and exhibits considerable individual variation in terms of size and shape. The costal cartilage of the seventh rib articulates with the upper part of the xiphoid process. Although the xiphoid process is cartilaginous in the younger person, it is frequently ossified in the adult. Several muscles attach to the xiphoid process including fibers of the rectus abdominis and the diaphragm.

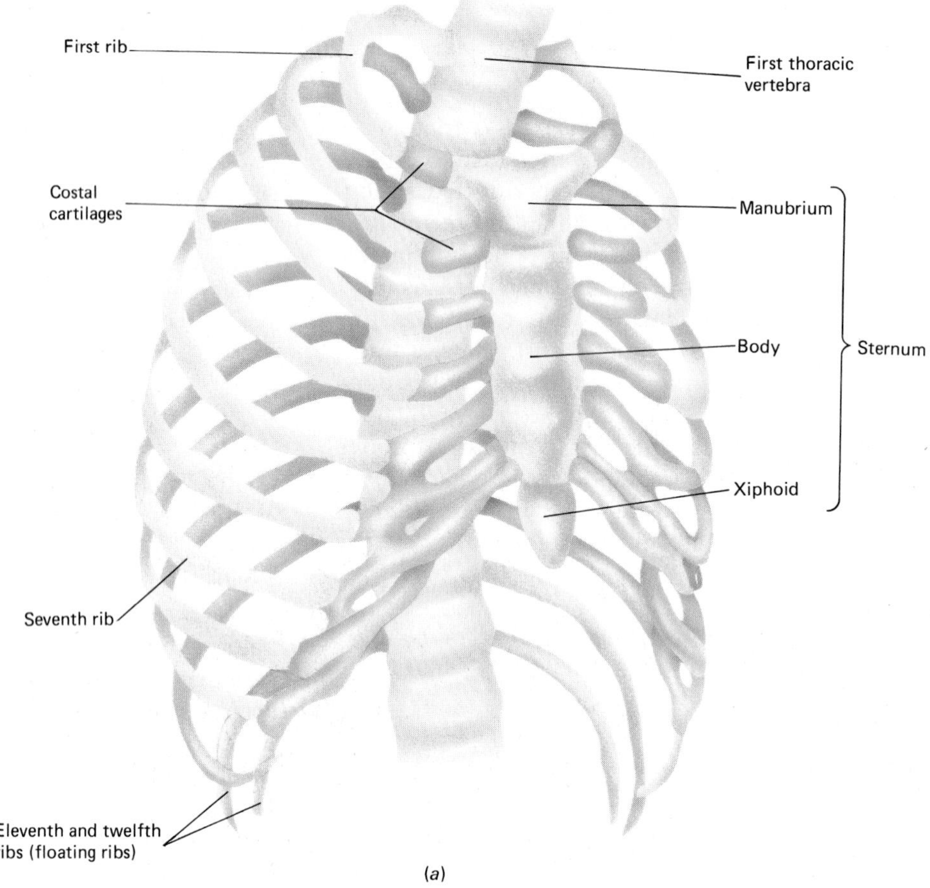

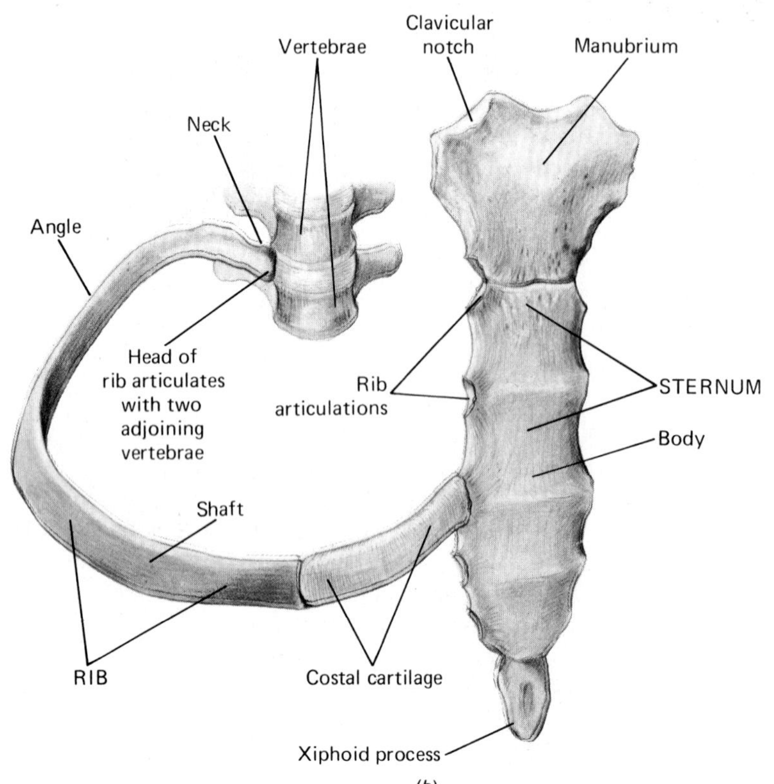

FIGURE 7-18

(a) Anterolateral view of the structures comprising the thoracic cage. These include the ribs, sternum, thoracic vertebrae, and costal cartilages through which the ribs attach to the sternum. *(b)* Articulations of a rib with the vertebral column and with the sternum. Notice the costal cartilage that intervenes between the rib and the sternum.

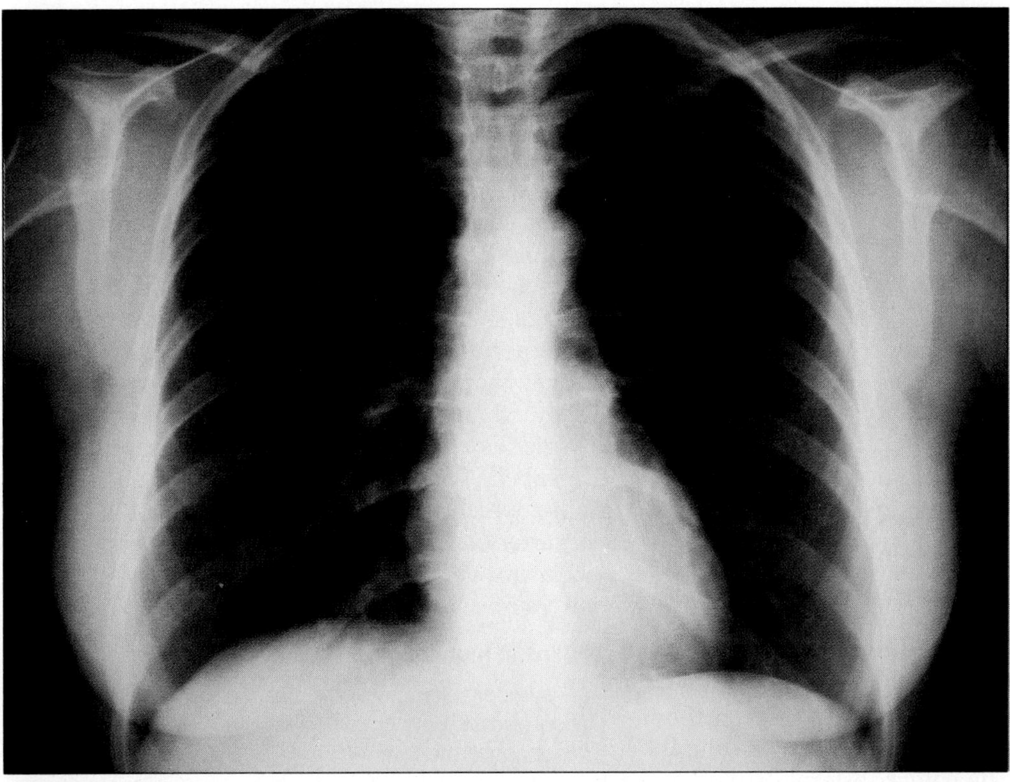

FIGURE 7-19

Anteroposterior radiograph (x-ray) of the thorax. Compare with Figure 7-18. How many components of the thoracic cage are you able to identify? (PhotoEdit.)

Twelve pairs of ribs contribute to the thoracic skeleton

Twelve pairs of elongated, C-shaped, flattened bones called **ribs** (Fig. 7-18) extend downward and forward from the thoracic vertebrae behind. The first seven pairs of ribs are connected directly to the sternum by their **costal cartilages.** These ribs are called the **true ribs** or vertebrosternal ribs; the remaining ribs are termed the **false ribs.** Three pairs of false ribs, the eighth, ninth, and tenth, all articulate through their costal cartilages with the cartilage of the rib above and are therefore also known as the vertebrochondral ribs. The anterior ends of the eleventh and twelfth ribs are free and are therefore designated as the **floating** or **vertebral ribs.** The ribs become progessively longer from the first to the seventh and then progressively shorter from the eighth to the twelfth. The interval between adjacent ribs is called an *intercostal space* and, as you will see in a later chapter, this space contains the intercostal muscles, nerves, and vessels.

THE TYPICAL RIBS EXHIBIT SEVERAL COMMON FEATURES

Since the third through the ninth pair of ribs have several distinguishing features in common, they are often referred to as typical ribs (Fig. 7-20). Each of these ribs has three basic parts, a *head, neck,* and *shaft.* The **head** of the rib has two articular facets which form synovial joints with the vertebral bodies. The lower facet articulates with the vertebral body which corresponds in number to the rib; the upper facet on the head of the rib articulates with the vertebral body immediately above. For example, the fifth rib articulates with both the fourth and fifth thoracic vertebrae.

Directly lateral from the head of the rib is a projection on the surface called the **tubercle.** The tubercle has an **articular facet** and a **nonarticular facet** on its surface. The articular facet forms a synovial joint with a facet on the transverse process of the vertebra of the same number as the rib. Located between the head and the tubercle is a constricted part of the rib known as the **neck.**

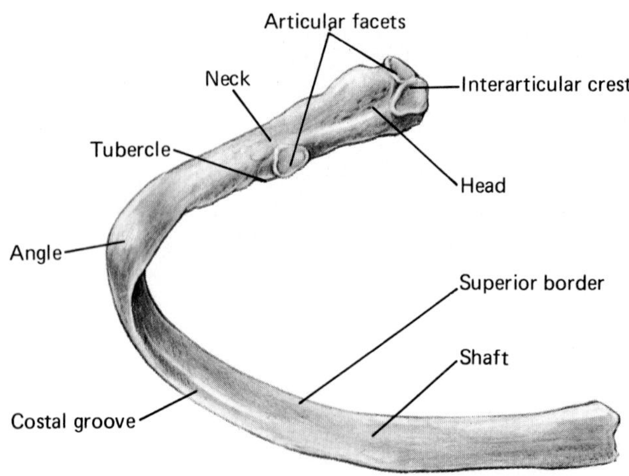

FIGURE 7-20

Posteroinferior aspect of a typical rib. Notice the articular facets for articulation with the vertebral column.

The **shaft** of the rib is the portion that extends posterolaterally and then anteriorly from the region of the tubercle. The point at which the shaft turns to become directed anteriorly is called the **angle** of the rib. The convex external surface of the shaft is also directed upward as well as laterally. An elongated furrow, called the *costal groove,* is located on the internal surface of the shaft along its inferior border. This groove houses the posterior intercostal vessels and the intercostal nerve.

Clinical highlight

A physician can insert a needle into the space between two ribs in order to aspirate fluid from the pleural cavity. The needle is placed close to the upper border of the rib below in order to avoid injury to the nerve and blood vessels lying in or near the costal groove of the rib above.

FIVE PAIRS OF RIBS HAVE VERY SPECIAL FEATURES

The **first rib** helps to form the superior opening (thoracic inlet) of the thoracic skeleton as we mentioned earlier. This rib (Fig. 7-21) is ordinarily the shortest of all the ribs and has superior and inferior surfaces. Its head has a single articular facet for the first thoracic vertebra and at its anterior end the first rib articulates, through its costal cartilage, with the manubrium of the sternum. The superior surface of the first rib has two grooves that are separated from each other medially by a bony projection called the *scalene tubercle* to which is attached the scalenus anterior muscle. The subclavian artery lies in the more posterior groove which is termed the groove for the subclavian artery. Anterior to the scalene tubercle the subclavian vein lies in the groove for the subclavian vein.

Clinical highlight

It is important to note that the apex, or uppermost portion of each lung, together with its pleural covering, rises above the level of the first rib. Therefore, this portion of the lungs is susceptible to puncture wounds that pass just above the level of the clavicle near its medial end.

The **second rib,** like the first, is very curved. Its head has two articular facets, one each for the first and second thoracic vertebrae. Near the midpoint of its shaft, the second rib has a bony tu-

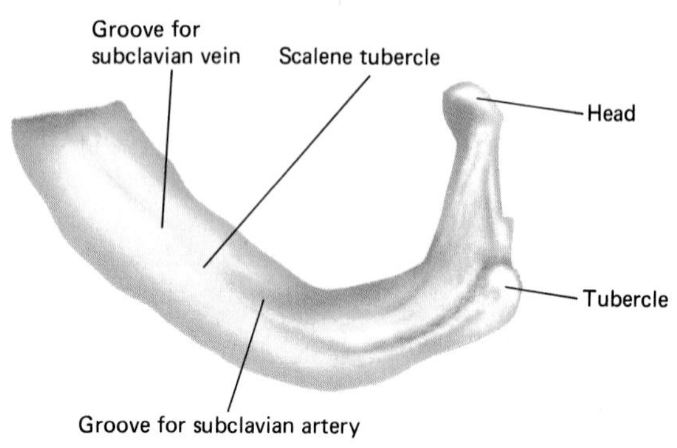

FIGURE 7-21

Superior aspect of the left first rib. Notice the grooves for the subclavian artery and vein.

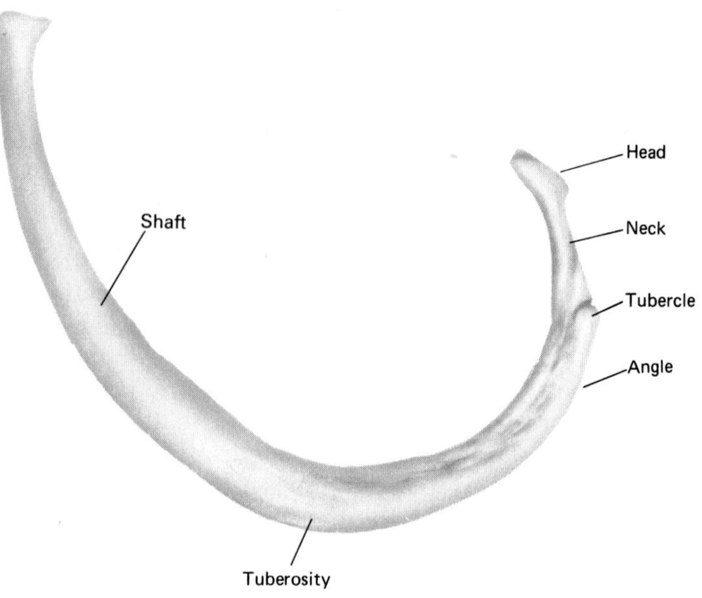

FIGURE 7-22

Superior aspect of the left second rib. Notice the tuberosity for a portion of the serratus anterior muscle.

berosity to which is attached a portion of the serratus anterior muscle (Fig. 7-22).

The **tenth, eleventh,** and **twelfth ribs** usually possess a single articular facet on their heads and these form synovial joints with the vertebrae of the corresponding number. The features that have been previously described as being characteristic of typical ribs are either poorly marked or absent from the eleventh and twelfth ribs. The anterior ends of the last two ribs generally have a very pointed shape to them (Fig. 7-18a).

Clinical highlight

The twelfth rib is located posterior to the kidney on each side of the body. Its precise length, which is variable, is an important consideration for the surgeon when exposing the kidney from a posterior approach.

Summary

I. The skeleton plays important roles in the following functions:
- A. Support for soft tissues and organs
- B. Protection of organs
- C. Formation of blood (hematopoiesis)
- D. Storage and release of calcium and phosphorus
- E. Transmission of muscular forces

II. Bones are classified according to their shape as being (a) long bones, (b) short bones, (c) flat bones, or (d) irregular bones. Two other important types of bone are sesamoid bones and wormian bones. Wormian bones are located within the sutures between certain bones of the skull; sesamoid bones are formed within the substance of tendons.

III. Bones of the skeleton have certain surface features in common that, in general, have specific structure-function relationships. Included among these are:
- A. Articular surfaces, which may be classified as a (1) facet, (2) condyle, or (3) trochlea.
- B. Depressions, which may be termed (1) fossae, (2) grooves, or (3) sulci.
- C. Openings called (1) foramina or (2) fissures. The latter occur between adjacent bones.
- D. A meatus or tubelike passageway within the substance of a bone.
- E. Processes, referred to as (1) tubercles, (2) tuberosities, (3) trochanters, (4) spines, (5) hamuli, or (6) cornua.
- F. Elevations known as (1) crests or (2) lines.

IV. The human skeleton is typically divided into the axial and the appendicular skeleton.
- A. The axial skeleton consists of the skull, hyoid bone, vertebral column, ribs, sternum, and auditory ossicles.
- B. The appendicular skeleton consists of the bones of the pelvic and shoulder girdles as well as the bones of the upper and lower limbs.

V. The skull articulates with the atlas.
- A. Twenty-two bones make up the skull, which is composed of the cranium and facial skeleton.
- B. Immovable joints between the bones of the skull are called sutures. Sutures of importance include the (1) sagittal suture, (2) squamosal suture, (3) coronal suture, and (4) lambdoidal suture.
- C. The anterior and posterior fontanelles represent membrane-filled spaces or "soft spots" between the cranial bones of the fetus or infant.
- D. There are eight bones that constitute the cranial skeleton. These are as follows: frontal (1), parietal (2), temporal (2), occipital (1), sphenoid (1), and ethmoid (1).
- E. Fourteen bones comprise the facial skeleton. These are the: nasal (2), mandible (1), zygomatic (2), palatine (2), vomer (1), inferior nasal conchae (2), maxillae (2), and lacrimal (2).
- F. Certain bones of the skull contain paranasal sinuses that communicate with the nasal cavity. These bones are the: (a) maxillae, (b) ethmoid, (c) sphenoid, and (d) frontal.

VI. The only bone of the skeleton that does not articulate with another bone is the hyoid. It is U-shaped and serves for the attachment of various ligaments and muscles.

VII. The vertebral column consists of a series of individual as well as fused vertebrae.
- A. There are 7 cervical vertebrae, 12 thoracic vertebrae, 5 lumbar vertebrae, 1 sacrum, and 1 coccyx. The last two are formed through the fusion of several individual vertebrae. Intervertebral discs form cushions between the individual vertebral bodies.
- B. The vertebral column has two primary curves and two secondary curves. The former are designated as the thoracic and sacral curves whereas the latter are represented by the cervical and lumbar curves.
- C. Although the vertebrae possess several common characteristics, there are certain vertebrae that have special or unique features. These features may be utilized in determining whether or not a vertebra belongs to the cervical, thoracic, or lumbar region of the vertebral column.

VIII. The thoracic skeleton is composed of the (1) sternum, (2) costal cartilages, (3) ribs, and (4) thoracic vertebrae. The thoracic skeleton affords protection to the lungs, heart, great vessels, and some upper abdominal organs.

Post-test

1. List the five main functions of the skeletal system.
   (a) ______________
   (b) ______________
   (c) ______________
   (d) ______________
   (e) ______________
2. Bones of the body may be classified according to their shape as being: (a) ______________, (b) ______________, (c) ______________, or (d) ______________.
3. An articular surface, if it is rather small in size, is called a ______________. If it is large and shaped like a knuckle it is known as a ______________. When an articular surface is grooved as in a pulley it is called a ______________.
4. When a depression on the surface of a bone is elongated it is known as a ______________ or ______________.
5. A cleftlike opening formed between adjacent bones is called a ______________.
6. A surface process of bone, when shaped like a hook, is known as a ______________ or ______________. If the process is simply elongated and pointed, it is referred to as a ______________.
7. The human skeleton can be divided into two basic parts, the ______________ skeleton and the ______________ skeleton. The ______________ skeleton contains the greater number of bones.
8. The periosteal covering on the external surface of the skull is the ______________ while that which lines the inner surface is the ______________.
9. The bregma is located at the intersection of the ______________ suture with the ______________ suture, whereas the lambda is situated at the intersection of the ______________ suture and the ______________ suture.
10. The bregma and lambda represent the sites of the anterior and posterior ______________, respectively.
11. The inner aspect of the base of the skull is divided naturally into the anterior, middle, and posterior cranial ______________.
12. Label all of the following on the accompanying figure:
    (a) Internal acoustic (auditory) meatus
    (b) Jugular foramen
    (c) Foramen magnum
    (d) Foramen ovale
    (e) Foramen rotundum
    (f) Crista galli
    (g) Optic canal
    (h) Occipital bone
    (i) Frontal bone
    (j) Cribriform plate
    (k) Sphenoid bone: (greater wings and lesser wings)
    (l) Sella turcica
    (m) Foramen spinosum
    (n) Temporal bone

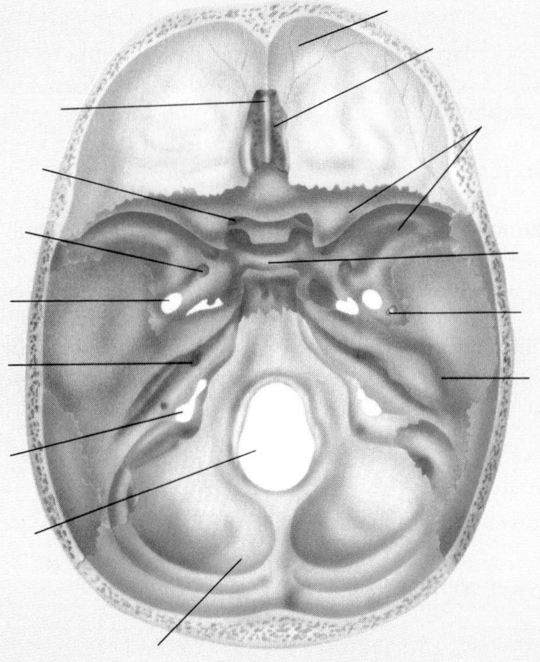

13. The two bones that contribute to the formation of the zygomatic arch are the ______________ and the ______________ bones.
14. The occipital ______________ articulate with the atlas, or first cervical vertebra.
15. The part of the sphenoid bone that houses the pituitary gland is called the ______________.
16. Branches of the olfactory nerves pass through the openings in the ______________ plate of the ______________ bone.
17. The characteristic parts of the temporal bone are the ______________, ______________, ______________ portions and the ______________process.
18. The carotid canal is located within the ______________ portion of the temporal bone.
19. Air cells are located in the ______________ portion of the temporal bone.
20. The ______________ ______________ nerve and vessels pass through the mandibular foramen to enter the ______________ canal within the mandible.
21. The major portion of the hard palate is formed by the ______________ processes of the ______________ bones.
22. The only bone of the axial skeleton that does not articulate with another bone is the ______________ bone.
23. Bones of the skull that contain cavities making up the four groups of paranasal sinuses are the ______________, ______________, ______________, and ______________ bones.
24. The two secondary curves of the vertebral column are the ______________ curve and the ______________ curve.
25. The opening formed by the neural arch and the body of a vertebra is called the ______________. The transverse process of a vertebra arises from the point of junction of the ______________ with the ______________.
26. The individual vertebrae may be classified as belonging to either the ______________, ______________, or ______________ region. The ______________ and ______________ represent bones of the vertebral column that have resulted through the fusion of several individual vertebrae.
27. The seventh cervical vertebra is often called the ______________ ______________.
28. There are ______________ cervical vertebrae, ______________ thoracic vertebrae, ______________ lumbar vertebrae, one ______________, and one ______________ constituting the vertebral column.
29. There are ______________ pairs of true ribs and ______________ pairs of false ribs. The last two pairs of false ribs are also known as ______________ ribs.
30. The ______________, ______________, and ______________ are the three portions of the sternum.
31. The first rib has two grooves on its upper surface; one is for the ______________ artery and the other for the ______________ vein.

Review questions

1. Describe what is meant by a wormian bone. Where are they generally located in the body?
2. Describe what is meant by a sesamoid bone and give an example.
3. Compare and contrast a fossa, foramen, and meatus.
4. Describe what is meant by the following terms: (a) tuberosity, (b) tubercle, (c) epicondyle.
5. List some everyday functions with which the skull is associated.
6. Distinguish between the cranium and the calvaria.
7. Describe the following: (a) sagittal suture, (b) coronal suture, (c) lambdoid suture, and (d) squamosal suture.
8. List all the bones of the cranial skeleton.
9. List all the bones of the facial skeleton.
10. List the structures that pass through the jugular foramen.
11. Describe the structures passing through the stylomastoid foramen.
12. Describe the two basic parts of an intervertebral disc and discuss the function of the disc.
13. Why are the cervical and lumbar curves of the vertebral column designated as secondary rather than primary curves?
14. Describe how the individual vertebrae are arranged so that a vertebral canal is formed to house the spinal cord.
15. Describe the articulations of the ribs with individual vertebral bodies and their transverse processes. Be specific in your description.
16. Describe the sacrum and the coccyx. Prepare your own diagrams in order to facilitate your description.
17. Compare and contrast the thoracic inlet and the thoracic outlet.
18. Describe a typical rib and then discuss the arrangement of the ribs as they contribute to the thoracic skeleton.

Post-test answers

1. (a) support, (b) protection, (c) hematopoiesis, (d) mineral storage and release, (e) transmission of muscular forces **2.** (a) long, (b) short, (c) flat, (d) irregular **3.** facet; condyle; trochlea **4.** groove, sulcus **5.** fissure **6.** hamulus, cornu; spine **7.** appendicular, axial; appendicular **8.** pericranium; endocranium **9.** coronal; sagittal; sagittal, lambdoid **10.** fontanelles **11.** fossae **12.** See Figure 7-6*a*. **13.** zygomatic, temporal **14.** condyles **15.** sella turcica **16.** cribriform; ethmoid **17.** squamous, petrous, mastoid; styloid **18.** petrous **19.** mastoid **20.** inferior alveolar; mandibular **21.** palatine; maxillary **22.** hyoid **23.** ethmoid, sphenoid, frontal, maxillary **24.** cervical, lumbar **25.** vertebral foramen; pedicle, lamina **26.** cervical, thoracic, lumbar; sacrum, coccyx **27.** vertebra prominens **28.** seven; twelve; five; sacrum, coccyx **29.** seven; five; floating **30.** manubrium, body, xiphoid process **31.** subclavian, subclavian

THE APPENDICULAR SKELETON

CHAPTER OUTLINE

I. **Bones of the pectoral (shoulder) girdle**
   A. Scapula
   B. Clavicle
II. **Bones of the upper limb**
   A. Humerus
   B. Radius
   C. Ulna
   D. Bones of the hand
      1. Carpal, or wrist, bones
      2. Metacarpals, or bones of the palm
      3. Phalanges
III. **Bones of the pelvic (hip) girdle**
   A. Ilium
   B. Ischium
   C. Pubis
IV. **Pelvis**
V. **Bones of the lower limb**
   A. Femur
   B. Patella, or kneecap
   C. Tibia
   D. Fibula
   E. Bones of the foot
      1. Tarsal, or ankle, bones
      2. Metatarsals or bones of the feet
      3. Phalanges

LEARNING OBJECTIVES

After you have studied this chapter you should be able to:

1 Describe the bones of the pectoral girdle.

2 Compare and contrast the bones of the upper limb and the lower limb.

3 Describe the bones that comprise the pelvic girdle.

4 Describe the articulations responsible for uniting the appendicular skeleton with the axial skeleton.

5 Describe the characteristic features of the bones comprising the appendicular skeleton.

6 Compare and contrast the pelvic inlet and pelvic outlet.

7 Compare and contrast the true pelvis and false pelvis.

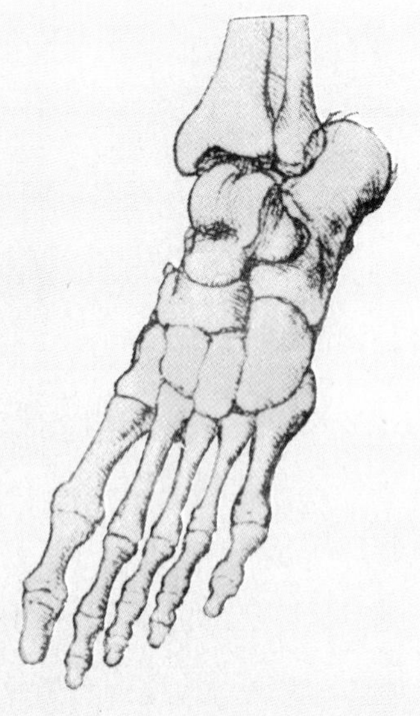

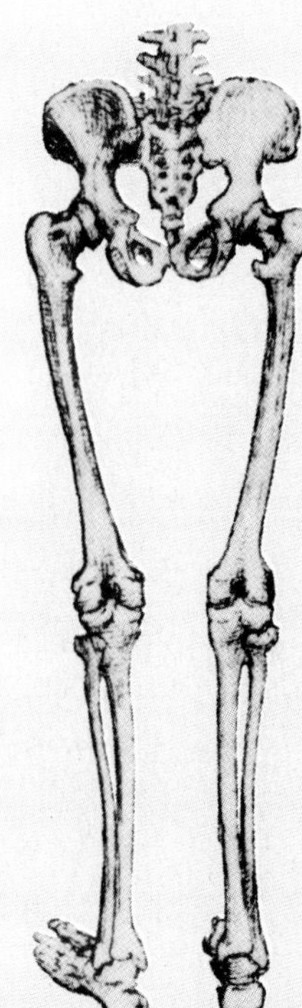

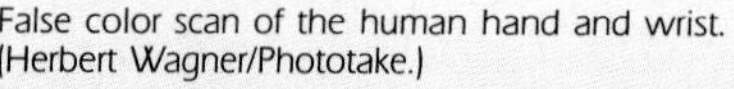

False color scan of the human hand and wrist. (Herbert Wagner/Phototake.)

8

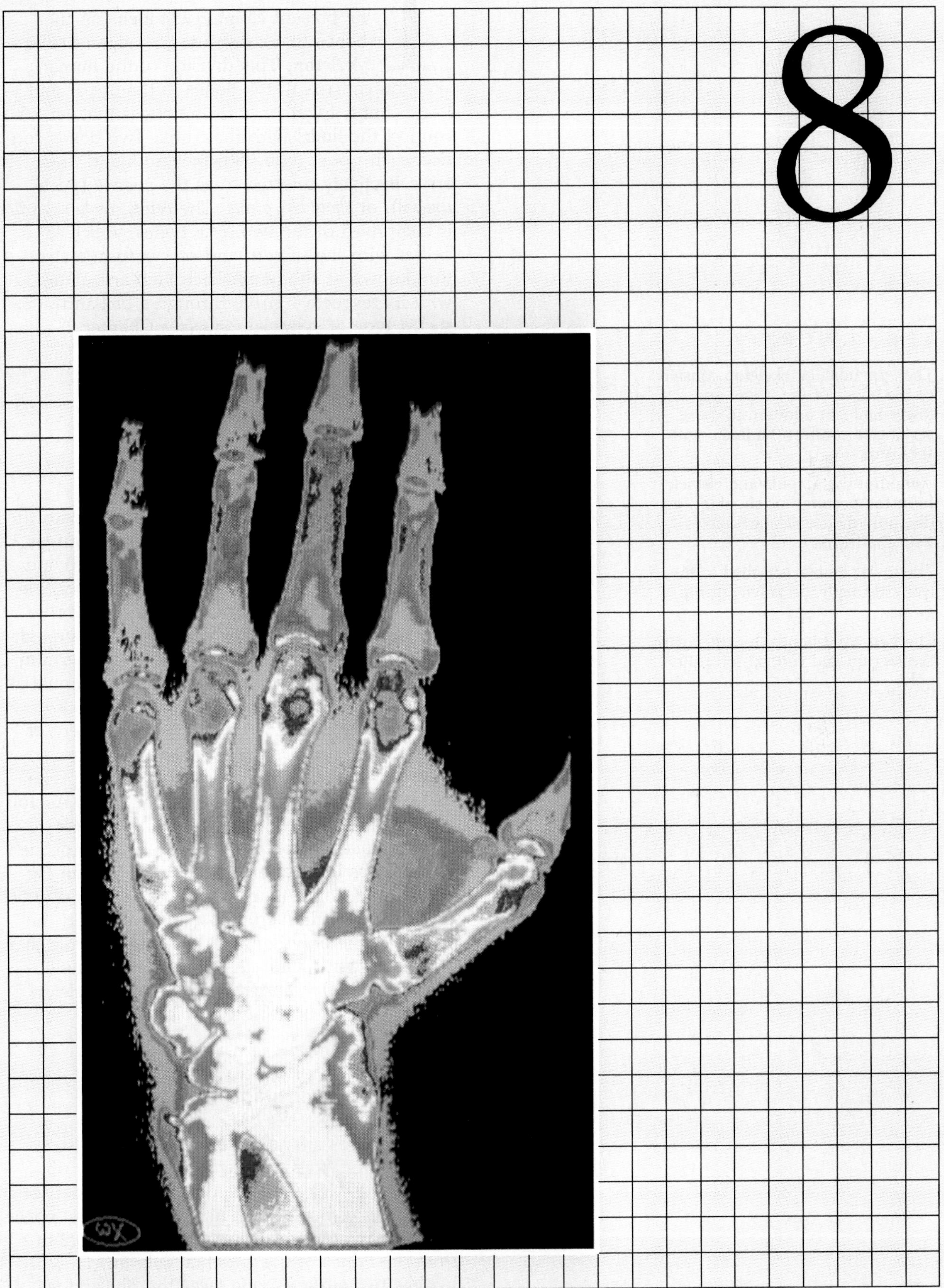

KEY CONCEPTS

The appendicular skeleton consists of the bones of the upper and lower limbs in addition to those serving to connect the limbs with the trunk.

Although the scapula and clavicle form the pectoral, or shoulder, girdle, only the clavicle articulates with the trunk.

The lower limb is attached to the trunk through the pelvic, or hip, girdle.

The two coxal bones, together with the sacrum and coccyx, form the pelvis.

The present chapter will focus on the bones that constitute the **appendicular skeleton.** This division of the human skeleton consists of the bones of the upper and lower limbs, together with the bones that serve to connect the limbs with the trunk. Two bones connect each upper limb with the trunk and these are collectively referred to as the *pectoral* (**peck**-toe-ral), or *shoulder, girdle.* The *pelvic,* or *hip, girdle* is comprised of the two *coxal* bones, which together with the sacrum and coccyx form a structure known as the *pelvis.* Each limb articulates with its respective girdle through a ball-and-socket type of synovial joint (see Chapter 9).

The scapula and clavicle comprise bones of the pectoral (shoulder) girdle

The bones of each upper limb are united with the axial skeleton through the **pectoral,** or **shoulder, girdles.** Two bones, the **clavicle** (**klav**-i-kul) and **scapula** (**skap**-you-la), make up each pectoral girdle and are depicted for you in Figure 8-1. The more anterior, or ventral, bone in the pectoral girdle is the clavicle. It articulates with the sternum at the *sternoclavicular* joint and with the scapula at the *acromioclavicular* joint (a-*kro*-me-o-kla-**vick**-you-lar). The dorsal, or posterior, component of the pectoral girdle is the scapula. It articulates with the clavicle as well as with the most proximal bone of the upper limb, the humerus. As you will see in Chapter 9, the shoulder joints are freely mobile and permit extensive motion of the upper limbs in a variety of planes. Focus on Figure 8-1 and notice that the pectoral girdles do not articulate with the vertebral column. Rather, the clavicle is the only bone of the pectoral girdle that articulates with the axial skeleton. Thus, the entire upper limb is united with the axial skeleton via a single joint, the *sternoclavicular joint.*

The scapula is also known as the "shoulder blade"

The **scapula** is a large, flattened, triangular bone that lies on the posterolateral aspect of the rib cage (Fig. 8-2). In this position it overlies the second through the seventh ribs and its medial border is located approximately 5 centimeters (2 in.) from the bones of the vertebral column. The scapula has two surfaces; one faces the ribs and is known as the *costal surface*, and the other is directed posteriorly and is termed the *dorsal surface*. The costal surface (Fig. 8-2) has a slight concavity to it, known as the **subscapular fossa** (sub-**skap**-you-lar). The dorsal surface is divided into two regions by the **spine** of the scapula (Fig. 8-3). The area above, or superior to, the spine is termed the **supraspinous fossa** (*soo*-pra-**spy**-nus); that which lies below, or inferior to, the spine is called the **infraspinous fossa.** These last two fossae communicate with each other laterally through the *spinoglenoid notch* (*spy*-no-**glen**-oid). All three fossae serve for the attachment of various shoulder muscles.

Each scapula presents three borders and two angles. The thin medial border of the scapula lies in close proximity to the vertebral column and is therefore referred to as the **vertebral border.** Its **lateral,** or **axillary, border** is considerably thicker and lies closer to the upper limb. The **superior border** of the scapula is merely the uppermost edge of the triangular bone. It is thin and sharp and is characterized by the presence of a small notch called the *suprascapular notch,* which is located near its lateral aspect. The **inferior angle** is located at the point where the axillary and vertebral borders meet, and the **superior angle** lies at the point of junction of the axillary border with the superior border.

Examine Figure 8-2 and notice that at the lateral aspect of the superior border there is an anterior projection arising from the scapula termed the **coracoid process** (**kor**-uh-koid). The short head of the biceps brachii muscle and the coracobrachialis muscle (both muscles of the arm) attach to this process. If you let your arm hang freely by your side, you can palpate the coracoid process through your skin just below the lateral third of the clavicle.

The lateral aspect of the spine of the scapula is expanded to form a projection known as the **acromion** (a-**kro**-me-on) (Fig. 8-2). You can easily palpate this process by first locating the spine of the scapula and then following it laterally to the point where it becomes expanded. The acromion articulates with the lateral border of the clavicle at the *acromioclavicular joint*.

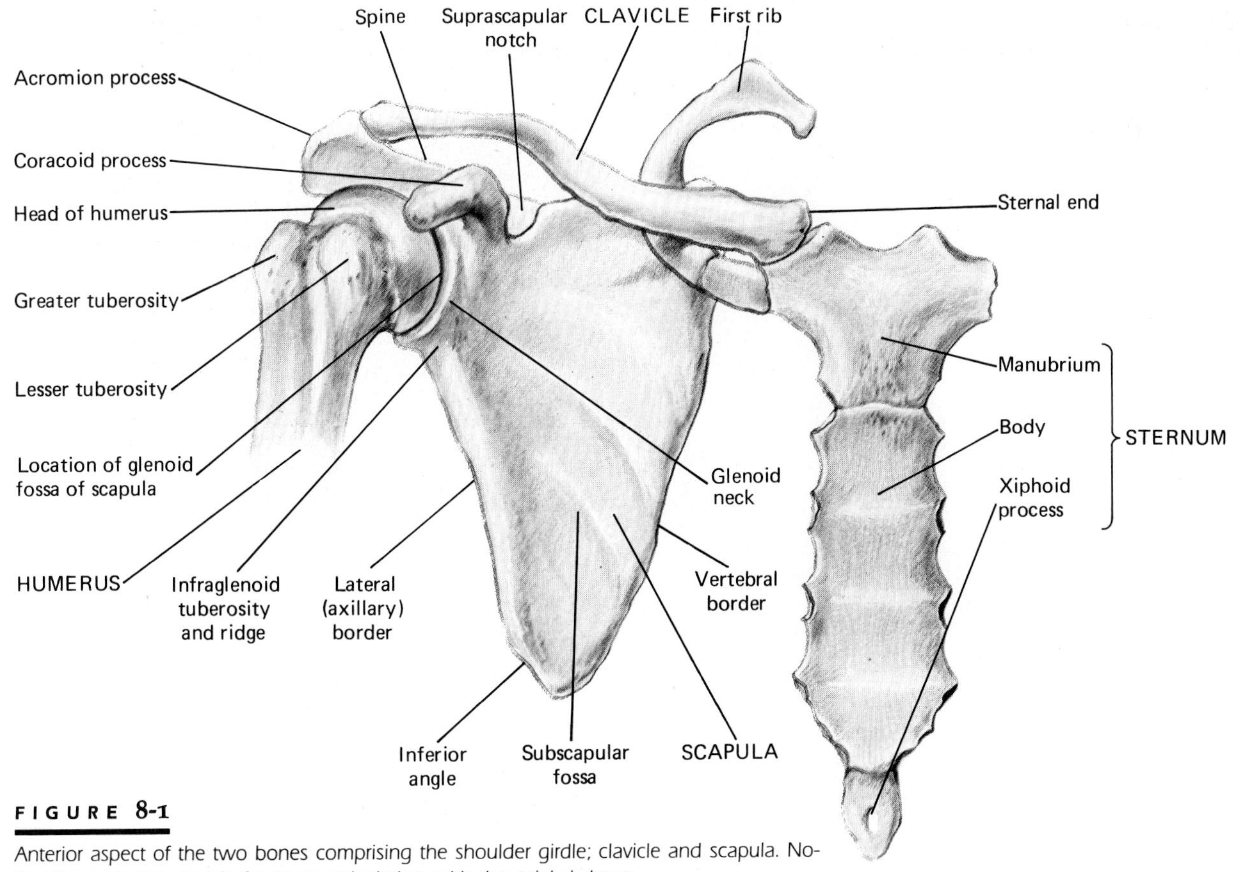

FIGURE 8-1

Anterior aspect of the two bones comprising the shoulder girdle; clavicle and scapula. Notice that only the clavicle forms an articulation with the axial skeleton.

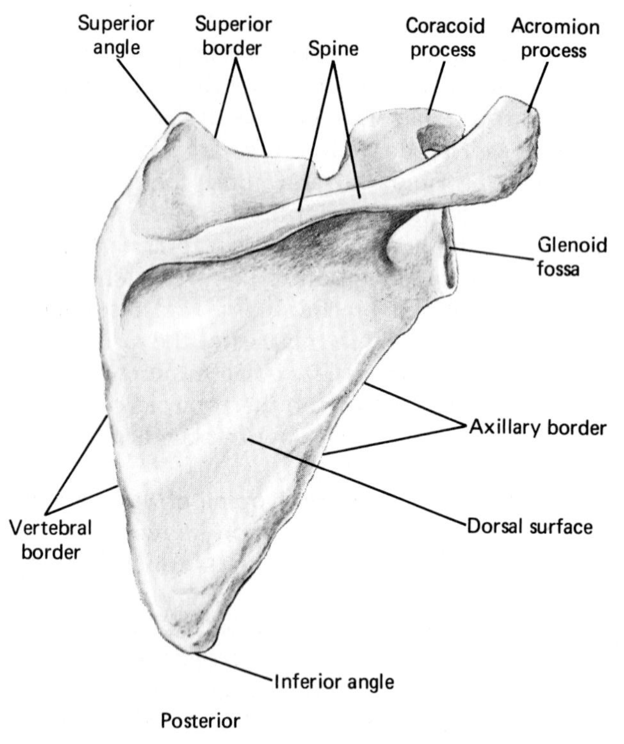

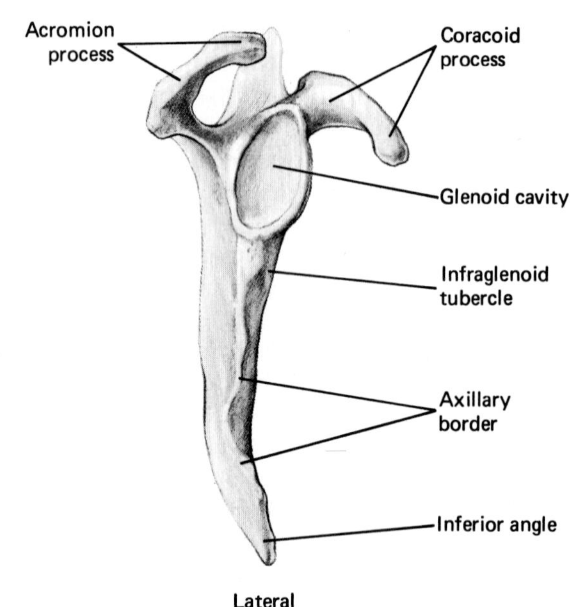

(a)

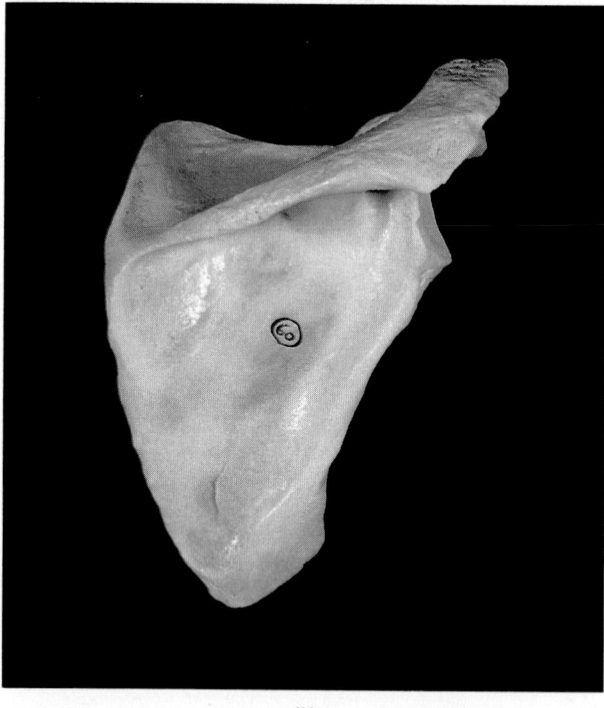

(b)

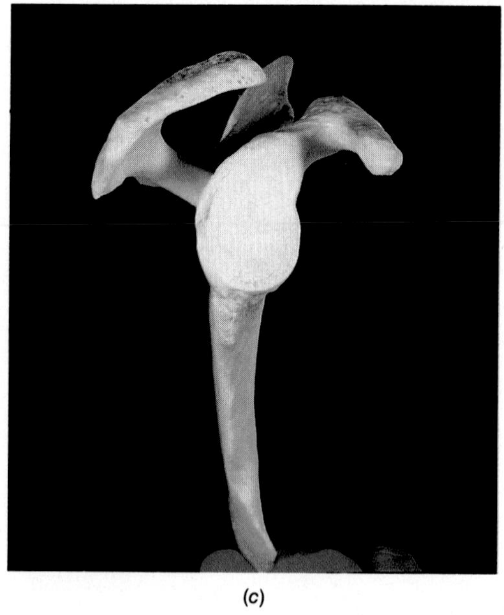

(c)

FIGURE 8-2

The (*a*) posterior and lateral aspects of the right scapula. The scapula is one of the two bones of the shoulder girdle. (*b*) Photograph of posterior aspect of scapula. Can you determine whether this is a right or left scapula? (R. Wehr/Custom Medical Stock). (*c*) Photograph of lateral aspect of scapula. (R. Wehr/Custom Medical Stock.)

A large concavity known as the **glenoid cavity** is situated at the superior angle of the scapula. Examine this cavity in Figure 8-2*c*, which is a lateral view of the right scapula, and note that it lies anterior and inferior to the acromion. In the living subject there is a rim of cartilage attached to the circumference of the glenoid cavity and this is called the *glenoid labrum*. The head of the humerus articulates with the scapula at the glenoid cavity and thus forms the shoulder joint.

The clavicle, or "collarbone," forms the single articulation between the trunk and upper limb

The **clavicle,** also known as the *collarbone,* extends almost horizontally between the manubrium of the sternum medially and the acromion laterally and is the first bone in the body to undergo ossification. Try palpating the clavicle on another subject, or on yourself, and note that you can do this easily throughout its entire length. It is through the clavicle that forces of the entire upper limb are transmitted to the axial skeleton. The precise positioning of the clavicle permits the upper limb to move free and clear of the trunk as in the swinging of the arms while strolling through the park or running a 100-meter sprint. The clavicle has a distinctly curved shape with the middle two-thirds being convex in the anterior direction. The lateral one-third is concave in the anterior direction.

The lateral end of the clavicle is flattened and is called the *acromial* end (Fig. 8-3). It is this end that articulates with the scapula at the acromioclavicular joint. The medial, or *sternal, end* of the clavicle has a rounded appearance and serves to articulate with the manubrium of the sternum *(sternoclavicular joint)* as well as with the costal cartilage of the first rib (Fig. 8-3). Figure 8-1 illustrates that the sternal end projects above the level of the jugular notch of the manubrium and may therefore be palpated in this location without difficulty.

There is a small projection located on the inferior surface of the clavicle near its acromial end. This is called the *conoid tubercle* and to it is attached a portion of the *coracoclavicular ligament* (Fig. 8-3*b*). On the inferior surface near its sternal end the clavicle presents a small roughened area that provides attachment for the *costoclavicular ligament*.

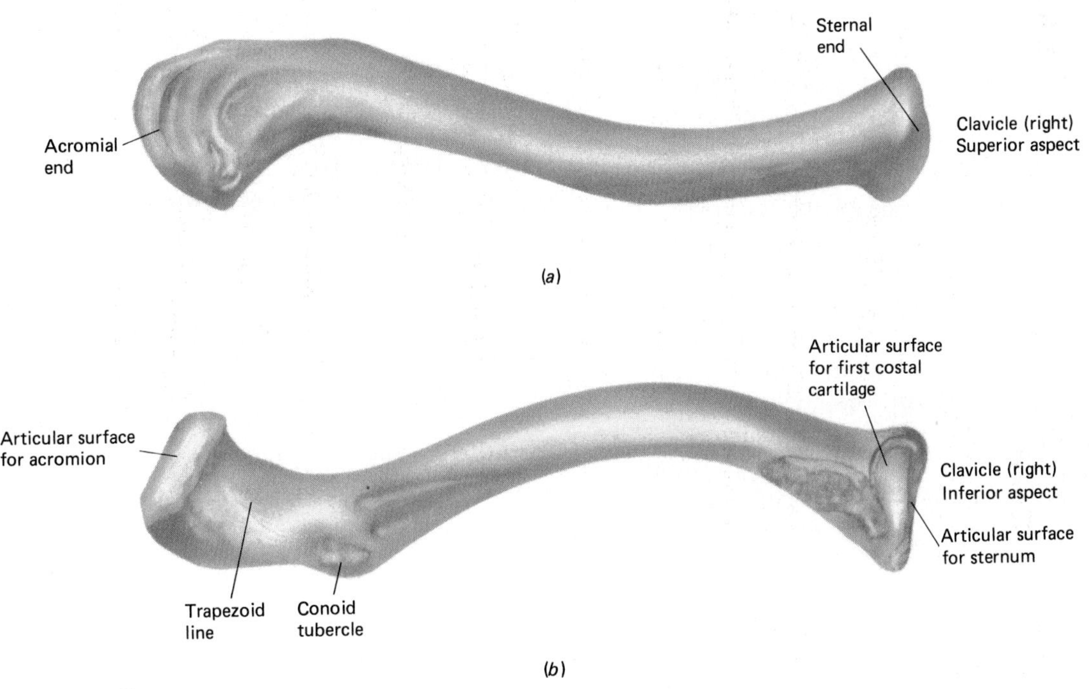

FIGURE 8-3

The (*a*) superior aspect and (*b*) inferior aspect of the right clavicle. The clavicle is one of the two bones comprising the shoulder girdle.

Clinical highlight

When one falls on his or her shoulder directly or attempts to break a fall with an outstretched upper limb, the clavicle is prone to fracture because it is primarily responsible for transmission of forces from the upper limb to the axial skeleton. Fractures of the clavicle most frequently occur at the junction of the middle two-thirds with the lateral one-third; that is its weakest point. The lateral end of the fractured clavicle is usually depressed since it is drawn downward by the weight of the upper limb, whereas the medial fragment of the clavicle is usually elevated to a certain extent. **Greenstick fractures** (Chapter 6) of the clavicle are particularly common in children. Large blood vessels and portions of the brachial nerve plexus may be subject to injury in severe fractures of the clavicle when bone fragments are driven in a posterior direction.

There is a congenital malformation that occurs in the human population in which the clavicle is totally or partially absent. This abnormality of the clavicle is usually accompanied by delayed ossification of certain bones of the skull. This combination of defects involving the clavicle and the skull is called the **cleidocranial** (*kly*-doe-**kra**-knee-al) **dysostosis** (*dis*-oss-**toe**-sis).

Bones of the upper limb include those of the arm, forearm, wrist, and hand

Each upper limb contains 30 bones and these are as follows: humerus (1), radius (1), ulna (1), carpals (8), metacarpals (5), phalanges (14). These bones are located within distinct regions of the upper limb: arm (humerus), forearm (radius and ulna), wrist (carpal bones), palm (metacarpals), and digits (phalanges). It is important to understand this division of the upper limb into these respective regions. When we refer to the arm, we mean that portion of the upper limb located between the shoulder joint and the elbow joint. "Arm" simply does not mean the entire upper limb. We will now discuss the individual bones of the upper limb beginning with the most proximal bone, the humerus, and progressing distally to the phalanges of the thumb and fingers.

The humerus is the single bone of the arm

The **humerus** (**hew**-mur-us) is the only bone of the arm and it articulates proximally with the scapula at the glenoid cavity and distally with the two bones of the forearm, the radius and the ulna. Notice in Figure 8-4 the anterior and posterior views of the right humerus.

The proximal portion of the humerus is characterized by a large, rounded **head** that is directed upward and medially. Circumscribing the margin of the head is a constriction called the **anatomical neck.** Two additional projections at this end of the humerus, the **greater** and **lesser tubercles,** lie lateral and anterior to the head, respectively (Fig. 8-4). Important muscles of the shoulder are attached to the greater and lesser tubercles. The elongated depression located between these two tubercles is termed the **intertubercular sulcus** or **bicipital groove** because it houses the tendon of the long head of the biceps brachii muscle (see Chapter 11). The region where the proximal end of the humerus becomes tapered to blend with the shaft is known as the **surgical neck.** Fractures occurring in this region may result in damage to the axillary nerve and to branches of the axillary artery, all of which pass close to this portion of the bone.

The proximal portion of the shaft has a cylindrical shape; its more distal aspect has more of a flattened and triangular appearance. Unless you apply firm pressure it is difficult to palpate the shaft of the humerus because it is thoroughly covered by several large muscles of the arm. The middle one-third of the posterior surface is characterized by a groove that houses the radial nerve, and fractures of the shaft at this level may compromise this structure. This groove is called the **sulcus for the radial nerve.** The most prominent feature of the shaft, the **deltoid tuberosity,** is located near its midportion along the anterolateral surface. This elevated, roughened area (Fig. 8-4) serves for the attachment of the deltoid muscle.

The distal end of the humerus is much wider in its transverse plane than it is in its anteroposterior plane (Fig. 8-4). As a whole it has a condylar appearance and possesses both articular and nonarticular surfaces. Projecting medially there is a roughened surface called the **medial epicondyle** (epi-**kon**-dial), which you can easily palpate through your skin in this region.

Clinical highlight

The ulnar nerve lies in close proximity to the posterior surface of the medial epicondyle and may sustain injury when the latter is fractured. This projection is often called the "crazy," or "funny," bone by the layman because bumping of its posterior surface may exert such pressure on the ulnar nerve as to produce a tingling or numbing sensation throughout the forearm and hand.

The **lateral epicondyle** lies opposite its medial counterpart and may be palpated with equivalent ease. In fact if you are to extend the forearm at the elbow joint, a lateral depression will appear on your skin posterior to the joint. The lateral epicondyle may be palpated by placing your index finger in this depression. Both of these epicondyles serve as attachments for superficial muscles of the forearm.

The articular surface of the distal end of the humerus is divided into lateral and medial portions. Notice (Figs. 8-4 and 8-5) that the more lateral surface has a spherelike appearance and is called the **capitulum** (ka-**pit**-you-lum). The capitulum articulates with the head of the radius. The pulley-like surface located more medially is known as the **trochlea** and articulates with the trochlear notch of the ulna. On the posterior sur-

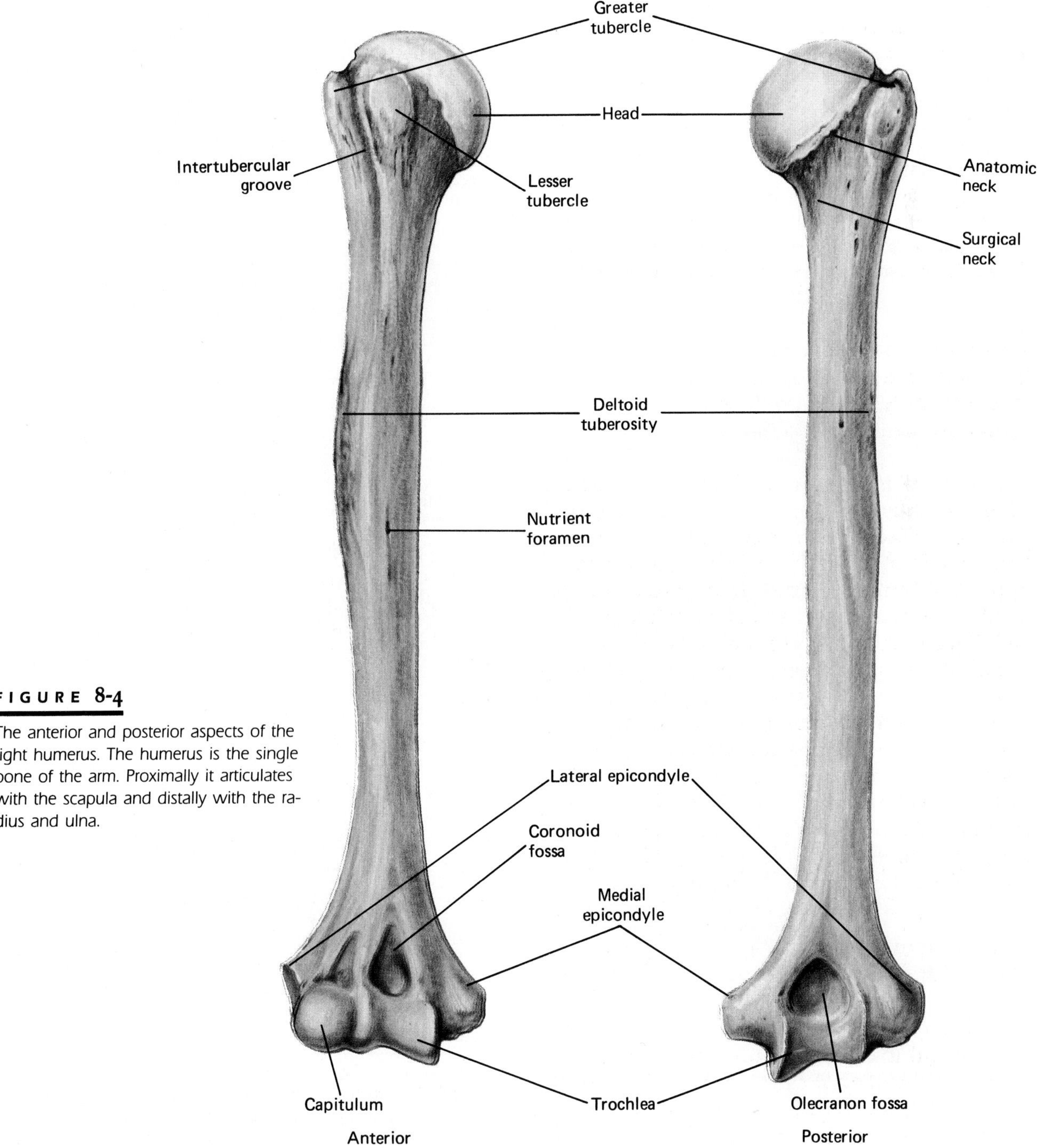

FIGURE 8-4

The anterior and posterior aspects of the right humerus. The humerus is the single bone of the arm. Proximally it articulates with the scapula and distally with the radius and ulna.

face of the humerus, between the two epicondyles and directly above the trochlea, you will find a rather deep depression called the **olecranon fossa** (oh-le-**krah**-non). When the forearm is extended at the elbow this fossa receives the olecranon process of the ulna. On the anterior surface and also directly above the trochlea another depression is present, the **coronoid fossa.** The coronoid fossa accepts the coronoid process of the ulna during flexion of the forearm at the elbow joint.

In the anatomical position the radius is the more lateral of the two forearm bones

The more lateral of the two bones of the forearm is called the **radius** (Figs. 8-5 and 8-6). At its proximal end you will find the disc-shaped articular surface of the **head,** which articulates with the capitulum of the humerus and with the radial notch on the ulna. The constricted portion of the radius that lies immediately below the head is called the **neck.** The **radial tuberosity** is a roughened projection that is situated just inferior to the medial part of the neck and serves for attachment of the tendon of the biceps brachii muscle.

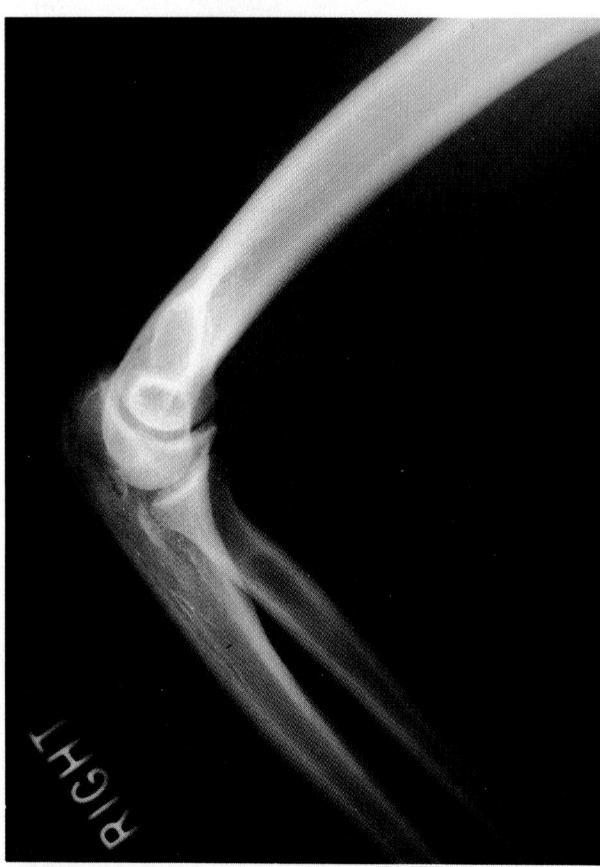

FIGURE 8-5

Radiograph of the bones comprising the elbow joint.

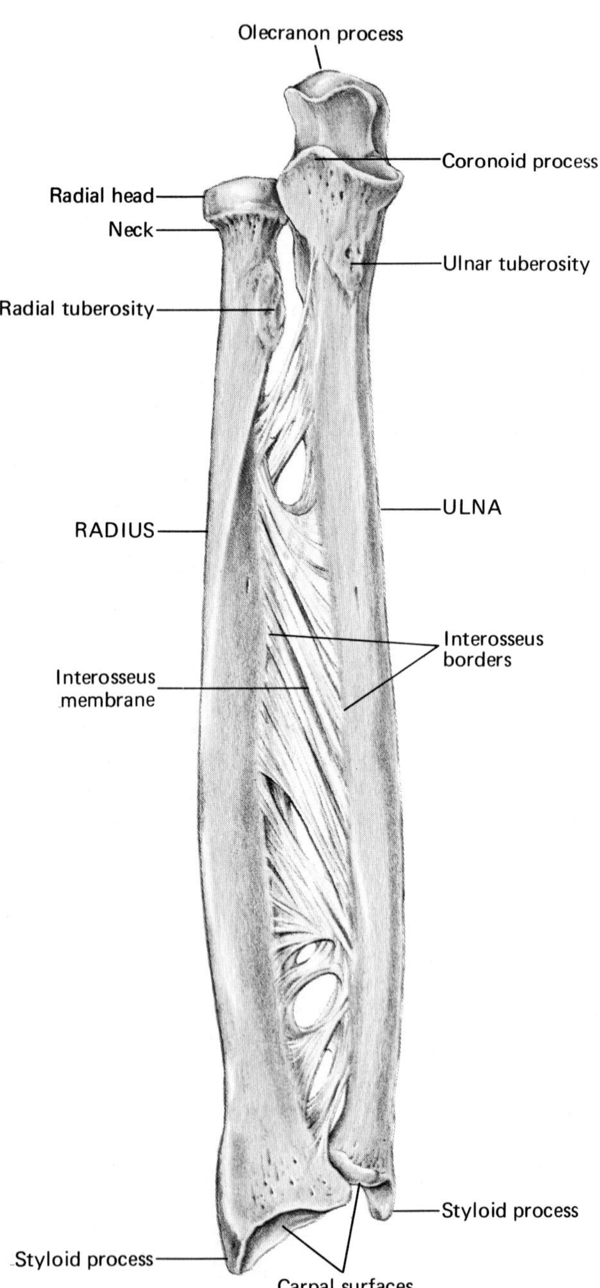

FIGURE 8-6

Anterior aspect of the bones of the right forearm. Notice that the radius and ulna are interconnected by the presence of an interosseous membrane. This is a very broad, thin, tough ligament that serves to unite the two bones of the forearm.

The distal end of the radius is greatly expanded and is characterized by a distinct projection on its lateral aspect called the **styloid process.** This process may be palpated at the lateral side of the wrist without much difficulty. Medially there is a shallow depression known as the **ulnar notch** that receives the head of the ulna. The large articular surface at the distal end of the radius participates in the formation of the wrist joint through articulation with two of the carpal bones, the scaphoid and lunate bones.

The ulna is medial to the radius in the anatomical position

The medial bone of the forearm in the anatomical position is the **ulna** (Figs. 8-5 and 8-6). When the forearm is pronated (palm directed posteriorly) the radius crosses anterior to the ulna; however, in the supinated (palm directed anteriorly) position the two bones of the forearm lie roughly parallel to each other. The distal end of the ulna possesses a rounded process called the **head;** the proximal end has the form of a large, expanded hook. The shaft of the ulna is cylindrical in its distal quarter and triangular in its proximal three-quarters.

The **olecranon process** and the **coronoid process** are both located on the proximal end of the ulna (Fig. 8-6). The olecranon process lies most superior and is received by the olecranon fossa of the humerus during extension of the forearm at the elbow. Fibers of the triceps brachii muscle attach to the olecranon process. Below and anterior to the olecranon process you will find the coronoid process which, during flexion of the forearm, is received by the coronoid fossa on the anterior surface of the humerus (Figs. 8-5 and 8-6). Some fibers of the brachialis muscle attach to the coronoid process.

Between the olecranon and coronoid processes lies an articular surface known as the **trochlear** (**trok**-lee-ar), or **semilunar, notch** (Figs. 8-5 and 8-6), which serves to articulate with the trochlea of the humerus. The lateral aspect of the coronoid process possesses a small concave articular surface for the head of the radius and is called the **radial notch.** A roughened region of bone just below and lateral to the coronoid process also serves for the attachment of some fibers of the brachialis muscle and is called the **ulnar tuberosity** (Fig. 8-6).

The **styloid process** is a small, distinct projection that lies on the posteromedial aspect of the head (Fig. 8-6). It is possible for you to palpate the styloid process of the ulna through the skin on the posterior and medial aspect of your wrist when the forearm is supinated. The styloid process of the ulna lies at a slightly higher level than the styloid process of the radius. The tendon of the extensor carpi ulnaris muscle lies in a groove between the head and the styloid process on the posterior surface of the bone. The **head** of the ulna also possesses a small convex articular surface for the **ulnar notch** on the distal end of the radius. The bones of the wrist are separated from the distal end of the ulna by an articular disc.

Carpals, metacarpals, and phalanges comprise the bones of the hand

The remaining portion of the upper limb is called the hand and its bones are distributed between three distinct regions: (1) bones of the wrist, or **carpal bones;** (2) bones of the palm, or **metacarpals;** and (3) bones of the digits, or the **phalanges** (fa-**lan**-jeez). Twenty-seven bones constitute the skeletal framework of each hand.

EIGHT CARPAL BONES COMPRISE THE SKELETON OF THE WRIST

The wrist is composed of eight **carpal bones.** The anterior (palmar) and posterior (dorsal) surfaces of the carpal bones are depicted in Figure 8-7. Notice how the eight carpal bones are arranged in two rows (proximal and distal) of four bones each. Proceeding from lateral to medial side, the four bones of the proximal row are the: **scaphoid, lunate, triquetral,** and the **pisiform.** The carpals in the distal row are from lateral to medial the: **trapezium, trapezoid, capitate,** and the **hamate.**

The carpal bones of the proximal row form articulations with the distal end of the radius and with the articular disc of the distal radioulnar joint. This row of carpals is arranged such that it has a convex shape to it that is directed toward the bones of the forearm (Figs. 8-7 and 8-8). Furthermore, the dorsal aspect of all the carpals has a slight convexity to it, whereas the palmar surface is deeply concave.

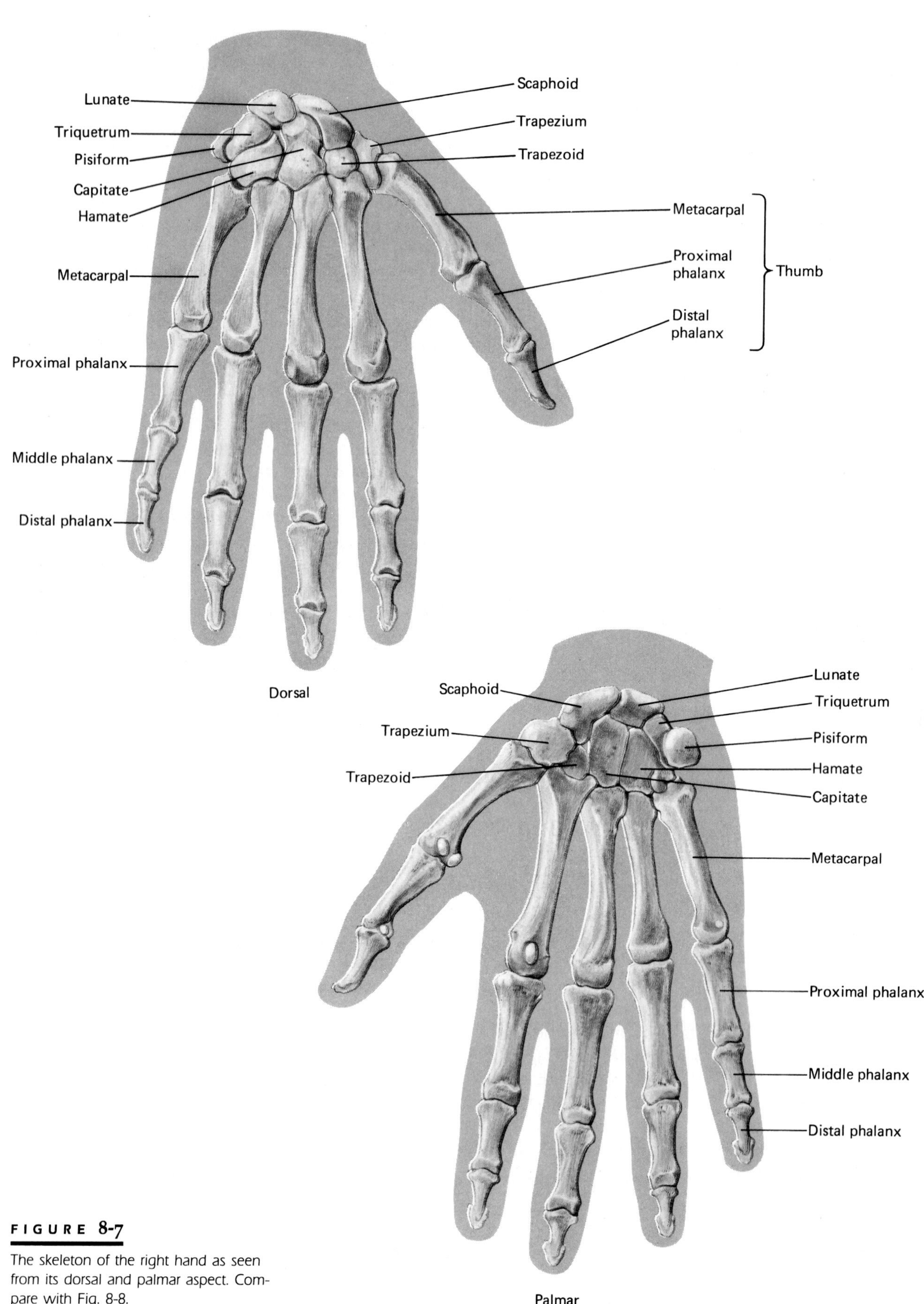

FIGURE 8-7

The skeleton of the right hand as seen from its dorsal and palmar aspect. Compare with Fig. 8-8.

Clinical highlight

The most commonly fractured carpal bone is, without a doubt, the scaphoid, which is the most lateral bone of the proximal row (Figs. 8-7 and 8-8). The fact that most fractures of the scaphoid occur perpendicular to the long axis of the bone presents a special problem to the physician because the proximal portion of the bone in many individuals has a rather poor blood supply. If this is the case, the two fragments may fail to unite during the healing process due to the inadequate blood supply of the proximal fragment.

EACH DIGIT HAS ITS OWN METACARPAL BONE

There are five **metacarpals,** or bones of the palm. These are depicted in Figures 8-7 and 8-8. They are referred to as metacarpal I through V beginning laterally with the metacarpal of the thumb. Each metacarpal has a cylindrical **shaft** that is expanded proximally to form the **base** and distally to form the **head.**

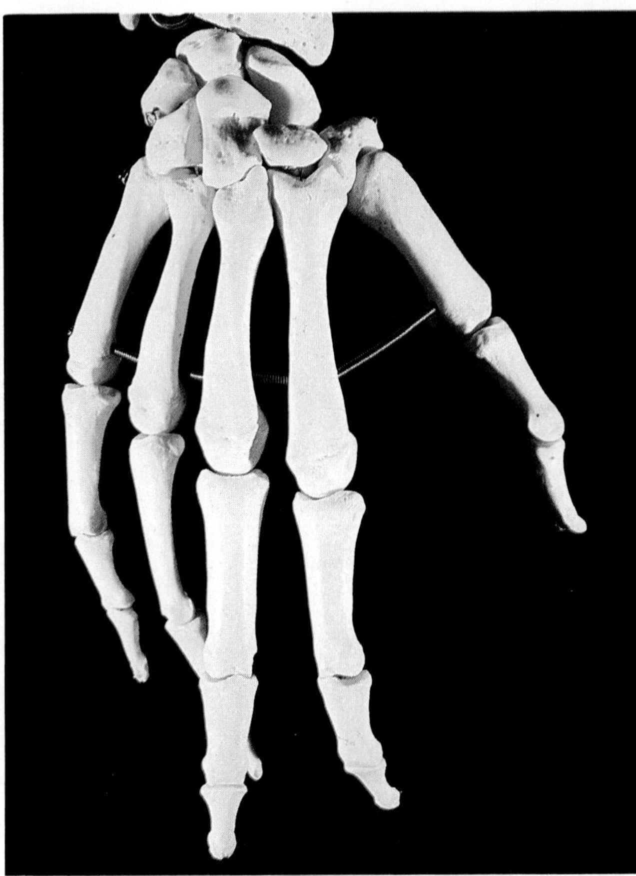

FIGURE 8-8

Photograph of bones of the right hand. Compare with Fig. 8-7. (Manfred Kage/Peter Arnold, Inc.)

The "knuckles" are formed by the heads of the metacarpals and can best be appreciated when you make a fist with your hand. The head of each metacarpal articulates with one of the phalanges located in the proximal row of each digit (Figs. 8-7 and 8-8). The base of metacarpal I articulates with the trapezium, whereas that of metacarpal II forms joints with the trapezoid, capitate, trapezium, and metacarpal III. The capitate and metacarpals II and IV all articulate with the base of metacarpal III. The base of metacarpal IV articulates with the capitate, hamate, metacarpal III, and metacarpal V. The base of metacarpal V articulates with the hamate and metacarpal IV.

EACH DIGIT HAS THREE PHALANGES, WITH THE EXCEPTION OF THE FIRST (THUMB), WHICH HAS ONLY TWO

There are a total of 14 **phalanges** in each hand and these are distributed between the five digits (Figs. 8-7 and 8-8). The first digit, or thumb, has two phalanges; the remaining four digits have three phalanges each. In lay terminology the second digit is called the index finger, the third the middle finger, the fourth the ring finger, and the fifth, or little finger, is often called the pinky. Although smaller than the metacarpals, the phalanges each have a proximal **base,** a **shaft,** and a distally located **head** (Fig. 8-7). In the thumb there is a proximal and a distal **phalanx,** whereas in the other digits there is an additional intermediate phalanx. The phalanges serve for the attachment of several muscles and ligaments.

Two hip (coxal) bones and the sacrum constitute the pelvic (hip) girdle

Figure 8-9 depicts the bones of the **pelvic (hip) girdle.** Notice that the pelvic girdle is composed of two bones called the **coxal** (**kox**-sal), or **innominate, bones.** The two coxal bones **(os coxae)** constitute the right and left halves of the pelvis and are united posteriorly by the sacrum at the **sacroiliac joints** and in front by the **pubic symphysis** (**sim**-fuh-sis).

Focus on Figure 8-10*a*. This is a lateral view of the right coxal, or innominate, bone. Each coxal bone is derived from the fusion of three individual bones during development and their lines of fusion have been indicated for you (the dashed lines). In fact the three individual bones can be quite easily distinguished from one another in a radiograph of a newborn. The most superior and largest of the three, the **ilium,** is seated directly atop the remaining two bones. The most posterior is the **ischium,** and the anterior one is the **pubis.**

A rather deep concavity, known as the **acetabulum** (a-si-**tab**-you-lum), is located on the lateral surface of each coxal bone; this depression represents the region of fusion between the ilium, ischium, and the pubis. As shown in Figures 8-10 and 8-11, the acetabulum consists of a central depression called the **acetabular fossa** and a more peripheral area termed the **lunate surface.** The lunate surface is interrupted in its inferior aspect by a notch called the **acetabular notch.** The head of the femur articulates with the lunate surface in forming the hip joint; the acetabular fossa represents a nonarticular surface (Fig. 8-11). The acetabular fossa is occupied by a ligament that connects the head of the femur with the coxal bone (Fig. 8-12). The contribution of the ilium, ischium, and pubis to the acetabulum is two-fifths, two-fifths, and one-fifth, respectively. For reasons of clarity in our discussion of the adult coxal bones we will address the ilium, ischium, and pubis as if they remained as individual entities.

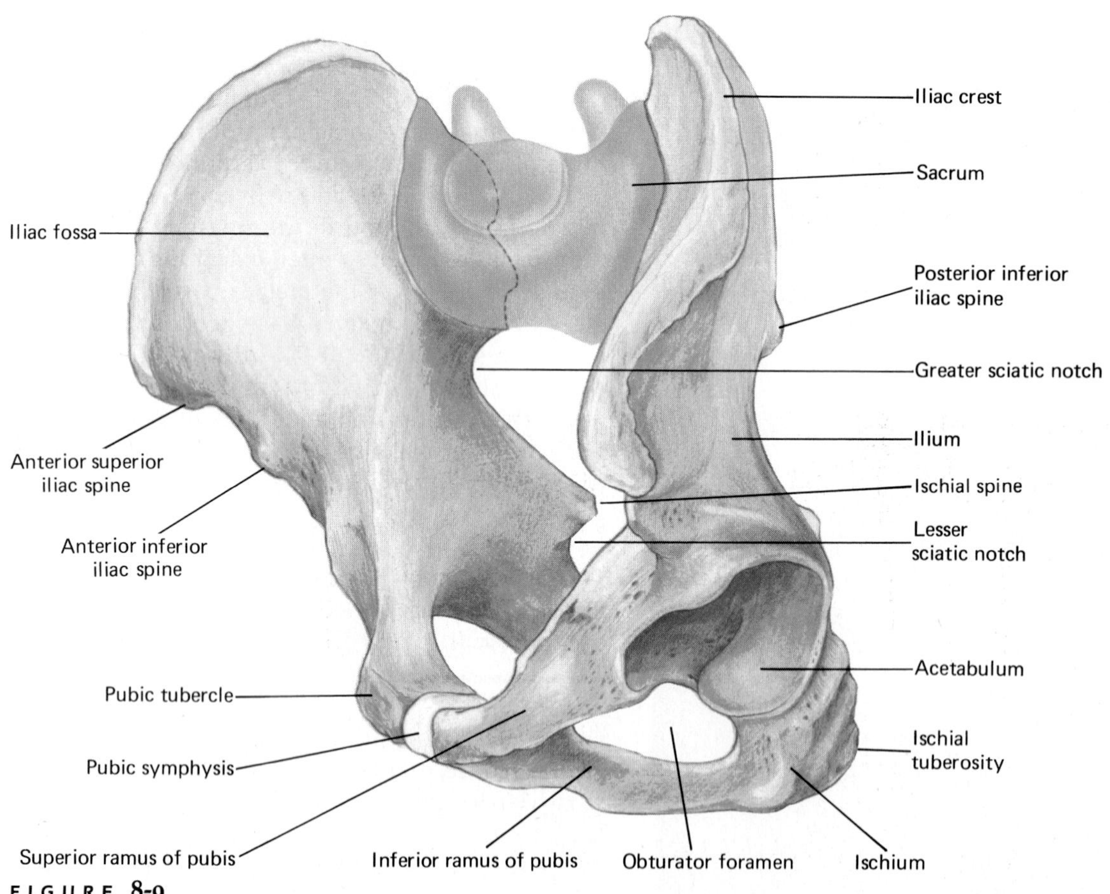

FIGURE 8-9

The two coxal (hip) bones articulate with the sacrum posteriorly through the sacroiliac joints. Anteriorly they articulate through the pubic symphysis. Neither of these joints is freely movable, but the latter does loosen considerably in preparation for childbirth in the female. The total structure, that is the coxal (hip) bones together with the sacrum, is called the pelvic girdle. The coxal (hip) bones are considered as being part of the appendicular skeleton.

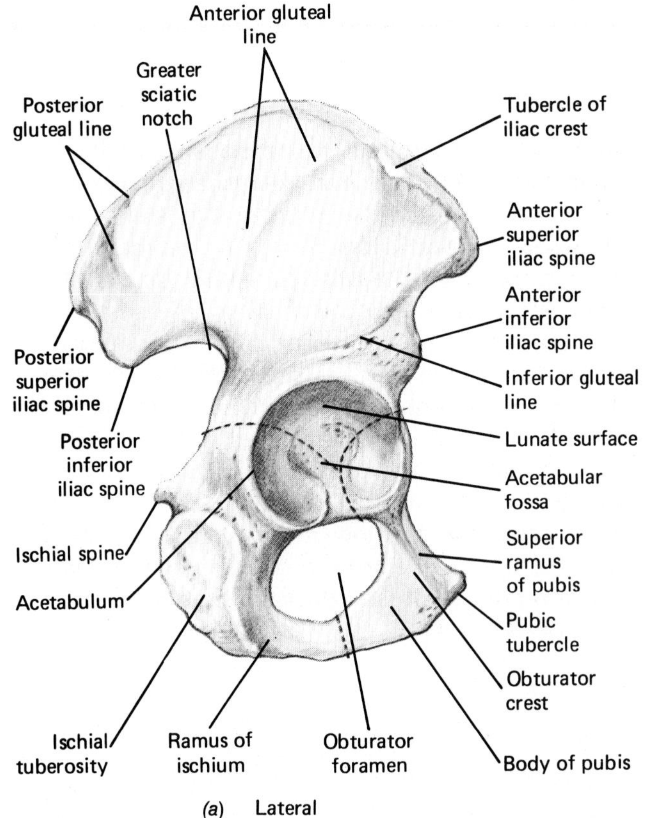

(*a*) Lateral

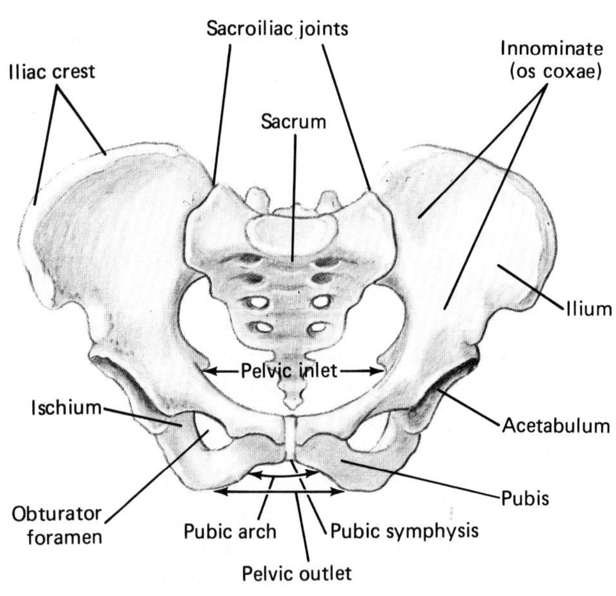

(*b*) Female pelvis, anterior

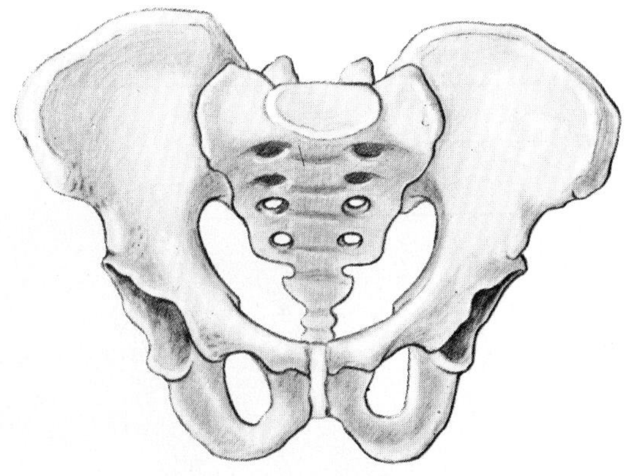

(*c*) Male pelvis, anterior

FIGURE 8-10

(*a*) Lateral aspect of right coxal (hip) bone. In the adult, the ilium, ischium and pubis are fused with one another and should be considered as a single coxal (hip) bone. (*b*) Anterior aspect of female pelvic girdle. (*c*) Anterior aspect of male pelvic girdle. In many instances, but not all, the male pubis is narrower than the female, and in the male the subpubic angle also tends to be more acute. Some pelves, however, are difficult to classify by sex.

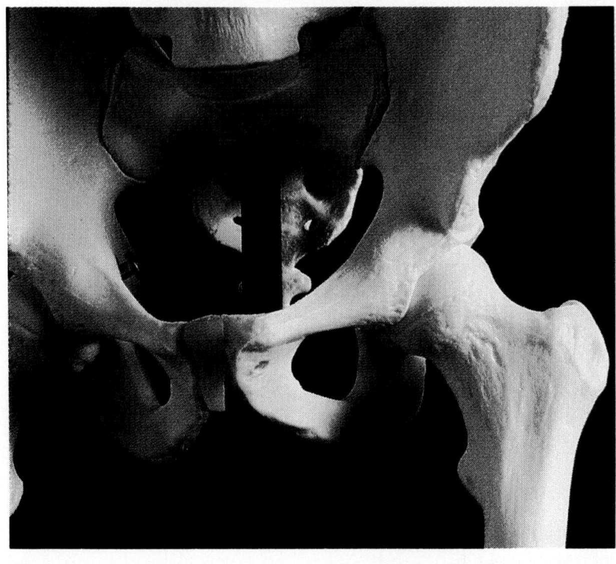

(*a*)

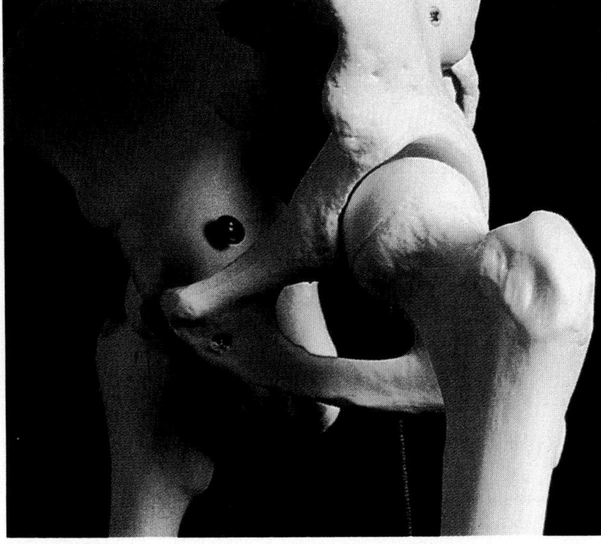

(*b*)

FIGURE 8-11

The adult human pelvic girdle as seen in (*a*) anterior and (*b*) anterolateral views. (SIU/Visuals Unlimited.)

The ilium lies superior to the ischium and pubis

The ilium is the most superior and the largest of the three bones that have undergone fusion to form the adult coxal bone. As we proceed with our description it will be helpful if you refer to Figures 8-9 and 8-10 for orientation. The superior border of the ilium has an S-shaped curve to it and extends from the **posterior superior iliac spine** behind to the **anterior superior iliac spine** in front. A shallow concavity separates the posterior superior iliac spine from the **posterior inferior iliac spine.** Similarly, the **anterior inferior iliac spine** is situated almost immediately below the anterior superior iliac spine. These spines serve for the attachment of various muscles, ligaments, and other connective tissue structures.

Located on the iliac crest, just posterior to the anterior superior iliac spine, is a prominent bony projection called the **tubercle of the iliac crest** (Fig. 8-10). The deep concavity on the posterior border of the ilium, anterior and inferior to the posterior inferior iliac spine, is called the **greater sciatic notch** (sigh-**at**-ic). Ordinarily, this notch is converted to an opening termed the **greater sciatic foramen** by the presence of ligamentous fibers.

The greater portion of the ilium is expanded to form a winglike area termed the **ala.** Its lateral surface (Fig. 8-10) is convex and has three promi-

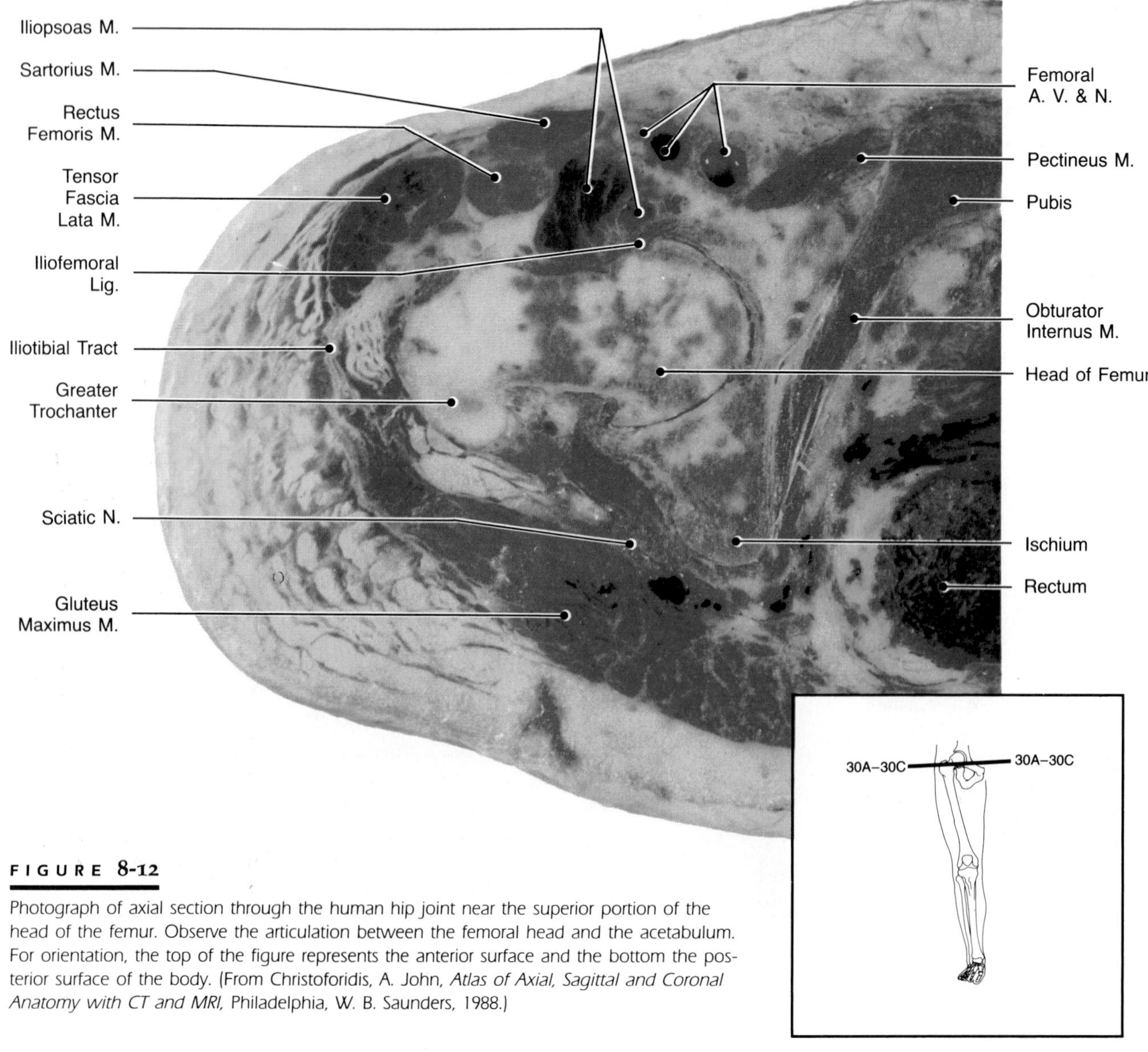

FIGURE 8-12

Photograph of axial section through the human hip joint near the superior portion of the head of the femur. Observe the articulation between the femoral head and the acetabulum. For orientation, the top of the figure represents the anterior surface and the bottom the posterior surface of the body. (From Christoforidis, A. John, *Atlas of Axial, Sagittal and Coronal Anatomy with CT and MRI,* Philadelphia, W. B. Saunders, 1988.)

nent ridges known as the **inferior gluteal** (**glue**-tee-al), **anterior gluteal,** and the **posterior gluteal lines.** Muscles of the buttock, or gluteal muscles, attach to these lines as well as to the surfaces that intervene between them. Note (Fig. 8-9) that the medial surface of the upper expanded portion of the ilium is concave and forms a deep depression that we call the **iliac fossa.** Posteriorly on this surface of the ilium there is an articular surface for the sacrum, and the resulting articulation is called the **sacroiliac joint.**

The ischium has a tuberosity upon which we rest our weight when sitting

This portion of the coxal bone lies inferior to the ilium and posterior to the pubis (Fig. 8-10). It consists of a **body** and an anterior projection called the **ramus of the ischium.** The body has fused with the ilium and pubis in the region of the acetabulum. The ramus of the ischium unites in front with the pubis and thus completes a large opening located immediately below the acetabulum that is known as the **obturator foramen** (**ob**-tur-*a*-tor). The boundaries of this opening are formed solely by the ischium and the pubis. This foramen is, for the most part, largely covered over by muscle fibers and a dense connective-tissue membrane.

The ischium presents three additional prominent features. All of these are situated along the posterior border of the bone and, from above to below, these are the: (1) **ischial spine,** (2) **lesser sciatic notch,** and (3) **ischial tuberosity.** The ischial spine can be palpated per vaginum (through the vaginal wall). It represents an important landmark to the physician not only for determining specific pelvic measurements but also for the proper positioning of a needle for delivery of anesthesia to the pudendal nerve during childbirth. In Figures 8-9 and 8-10 notice the position of the lesser sciatic notch immediately inferior to the ischial spine. As with the greater sciatic notch, the lesser notch is also converted to a foramen, the **lesser sciatic foramen,** by the presence of ligamentous fibers. The very large bony projection located just below the lesser sciatic notch is called the **ischial tuberosity.** It is important to point out that when we are in the sitting position, a large portion of our upper body weight is supported by the ischial tuberosities of the two coxal bones.

The two pubic bones articulate in the midline at the pubic symphysis

The pubis consists of a **body, superior ramus,** and an **inferior ramus** (Figs. 8-9 and 8-10). It represents the most anteroinferior aspect of the coxal bone and participates in the formation of the acetabulum as well as the obturator foramen. The pubis is united to its fellow on the opposite side by a fibrocartilaginous joint called the **pubic symphysis** (Fig. 8-9). Below the pubic symphysis the inferior rami of the two pubic bones form an angle known as the **subpubic angle,** or the **pubic arch.** The pubic arch (Fig. 8-10*b* and *c*) is commonly more acute in males (less than 90°) than in females (greater than 90°).

The pelvis is divided into true (greater) and false (lesser) pelves

The **pelvis** is the anatomical unit formed by the two coxal bones, the sacrum, and the coccyx (Fig. 8-10). Therefore the pelvis is composed of two bones (coxal) belonging to the appendicular skeleton and two bones (sacrum and coccyx) that form part of the axial skeleton. The pelvis is typically divided into two regions that are separated by an oblique imaginary plane. This plane passes through the **sacral promontory** and the **linea terminalis** on both sides and in front. The features that comprise the linea terminalis on each side are the (1) arcuate line of the ilium, (2) pectineal line of the pubis, and (3) crest of the pubis. The term applied to the opening represented by the boundaries of this imaginary plane is the **superior pelvic aperture,** or **pelvic inlet.** That portion of the pelvis situated above the plane of the superior pelvic aperture is called the **greater,** or **false, pelvis** and is formed largely by the expanded iliac fossae laterally and the upper part of the sacrum posteriorly. The constricted portion of the pelvis that lies below the plane of the superior pelvic aperture is called the **lesser,** or **true, pelvis.** The **inferior pelvic aperture,** or **pelvic outlet,** is represented by the inferior boundary of the lesser pelvis and is not nearly as regular in form as that of the superior pelvic aperture.

The greater and lesser pelves are continuous and certain organs in this region may be common to both. Furthermore, the greater pelvis houses some structures typically described as belonging to the abdominal cavity, for example, coils of the small intestine. One of the functions of the pelvis is to provide protection for the organs situated in this region. The anterior wall of the greater pelvis is somewhat deficient in its bony construction. Thus, the organs located here receive their protection from the muscles constituting the anterior abdominal wall. The overall dimensions of the greater pelvis are much larger than those of the lesser pelvis. Therefore, in the female, those of the lesser pelvis are of significant importance to the obstetrician during childbirth since it is through the inferior pelvic aperture (pelvic outlet) that the newborn must ultimately pass.

Bones of the lower limb include those of the thigh, knee, leg, ankle, and foot

Each lower limb has the same number of bones as each upper limb—60. The lower limb is divided into a number of specific regions. The thigh extends from the hip joint to the knee and contains a single bone known as the femur. The region located between the knee joint and the ankle is termed the leg and includes two bones, the tibia and fibula. The remaining bones constitute the ankle and the foot. Refer now to Figures 7-1 and 7-2 and observe the anterior and posterior views of the bones of each lower limb.

The femur forms the skeleton of the thigh

The single bone of the thigh is called the **femur** and represents, without a doubt, the heaviest and longest bone of the body (Figs. 8-13 and 8-12). The proximal and distal ends of the femur are marked by numerous prominent features that are discussed below. Intervening between the proximal and distal ends of the bone is its lengthy **shaft,** which is marked posteriorly by a prominent ridge of bone known as the **linea aspera** (Fig. 8-13), which serves for the attachment of various muscles and is continued distally as the **supracondylar ridges.** Because the femur is extensively covered with muscles it is not easily palpable, with the exception of portions of its proximal and distal ends near the hip and knee joints, respectively.

The large spherical projection located at the proximal end of the femur is called the **head** and, as mentioned earlier, this structure articulates with the coxal bone at the acetabulum. A small depression, or pit, is situated on the head and is called the **fovea capitis** (**foe**-vee-a). It represents the site for attachment of a ligament that, at its opposite end, is attached to the acetabular fossa. The constricted portion of bone that unites the head with the shaft is known as the **neck** of the femur and forms an angle **(angle of inclination)** with the shaft (Fig. 8-13). The arterial supply to the head of the femur may become compromised when the neck of the femur is fractured.

Notice that lateral and superior to the neck, there is a large bony prominence termed the **greater trochanter** (tro-**kan**-ter); a smaller projection located below the level of the neck in a more posteromedial position is called the **lesser trochanter.** Both of these prominences represent sites for the attachment of various muscles. The ridge of bone on the anterior surface of the femur and connecting the greater and lesser trochanters is referred to as the **intertrochanteric line** (*in*-ter-tro-**kan**-ter-ik). On the posterior surface, the **intertrochanteric crest** is represented by a ridge of bone coursing between the two trochanters.

The distal end of the femur is constructed in such a fashion as to permit its articulation with the tibia. The expanded portions of the distal femur responsible for this articulation are the **lateral** and **medial condyles** (Figs. 8-13 and 8-14). The smaller prominences, one located above each condyle, are known as the **lateral** and **medial epicondyles** (Fig. 8-13). Anteriorly the articular surface of each condyle merges with its fellow of the opposite side so as to provide a separate articular surface for the kneecap or **patella** (puh-**tell**-a). This surface is called the **patellar surface** (Figs. 8-13 and 8-14) of the femur. A rather deep depression exists between the two condyles posteriorly and is termed the **intercondylar fossa** (Figs. 8-13 and 8-14).

The patella, or kneecap, is a sesamoid bone

The **patella,** or kneecap, is a sesamoid bone that develops within the tendon of the quadriceps femoris muscle. It has a triangular shape and is located on the anterior aspect of the knee joint (Figs. 8-14 and 8-16). The **base** of the patella is broad and is directed superiorly while its **apex** is pointed and is directed inferiorly. That portion of the quadriceps femoris tendon that lies inferior to the apex of the patella and is attached to the tibia is known as the **ligamentum patellae,** or **patellar ligament.**

The posterior surface of the patella is divided into two articular surfaces by a bony ridge. The lateral articular surface is the larger of the two and serves for articulation with the lateral condyle of the femur. The medial articular surface is smaller and receives the medial condyle of the femur. The patella is easily palpable and can be moved from side to side when the tendon of the quadriceps femoris is relaxed. Try this by sitting on the floor with your leg extended at the knee. Relax the quadriceps femoris muscle and grasp the patella between your thumb and index finger and gently move it from side to side. Some upward and downward movement may also be possible in this position but not nearly to the extent that you can move it medially and laterally.

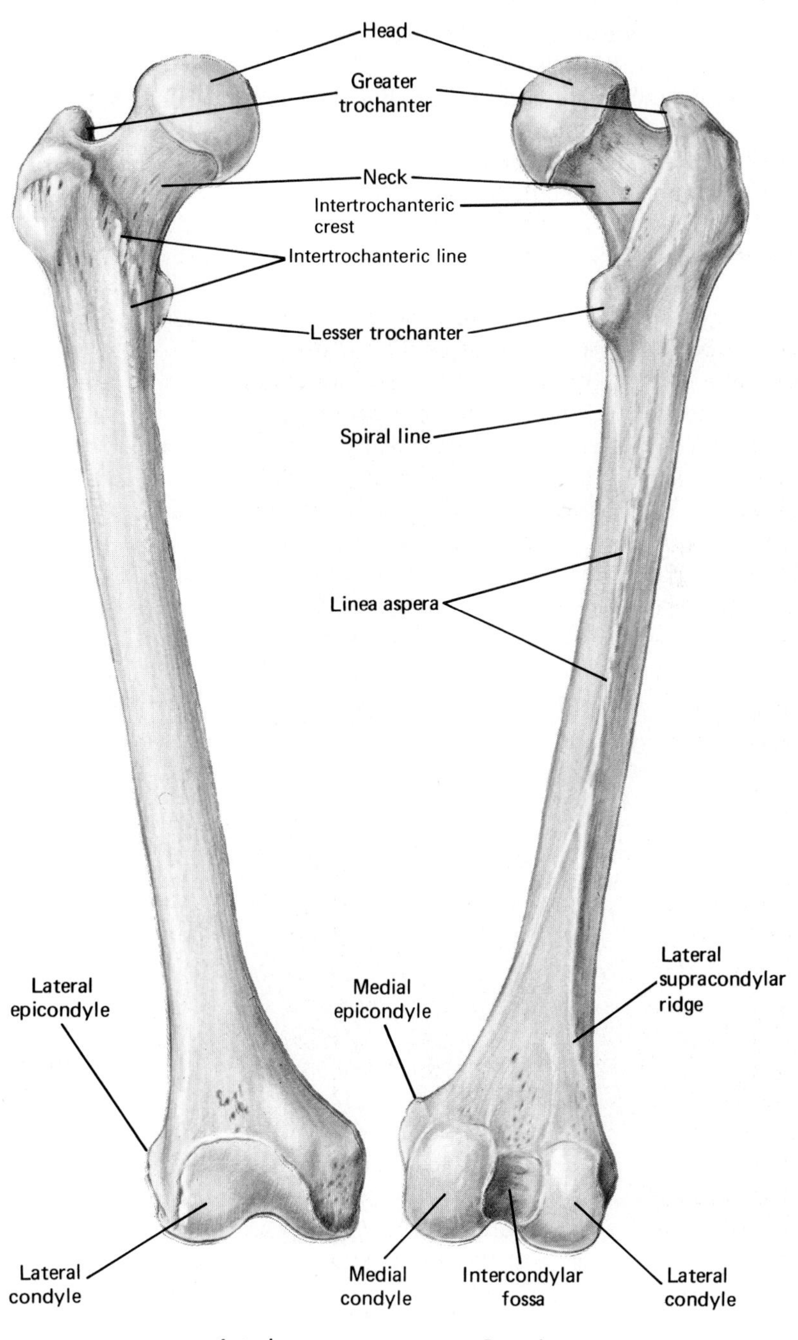

FIGURE 8-13

Anterior and posterior aspects of the right femur. The femur articulates proximally with the acetabulum of the coxal (hip) bone and distally with the patella (knee cap) and tibia.

The tibia is the more medial of the two bones of the leg

The **tibia,** also known as the shinbone, is the more medially located bone of the leg (Fig. 8-15). Of all the bones in the body, only the femur is longer and heavier. The fact that the tibia may be palpated throughout its entire length on its anterior surface is, in part, responsible for the numerous bruises you probably have experienced over the years after being bumped or kicked in the "shins." The tibia, being the larger of the two leg bones, is entirely responsible for transmitting the weight from the femur to the ankle and foot when in the standing position. It has a shaft, proximal end, and distal end. Proximally the tibia articulates with the femur and the proximal end of the fibula. Distally it articulates with the talus of the ankle and the distal end of the fibula.

The proximal end is expanded to form a **lateral** and **medial condyle.** The superior aspect of each condyle is smooth and serves for articulation with the respective condyle of the femur. The lower, posterior portion of the lateral tibial condyle presents an articular facet for the proximal end of the fibula. A prominent bony projection, the **tibial tuberosity,** is located on the anterior surface of the tibia in the midline just below the

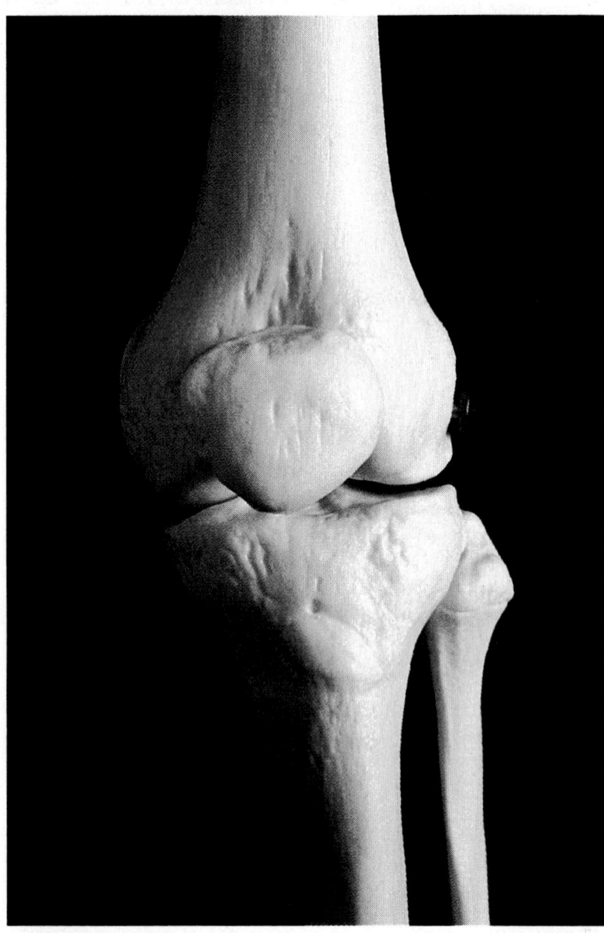

FIGURE 8-14

Photograph of anterior aspect of the bones of the human knee joint.

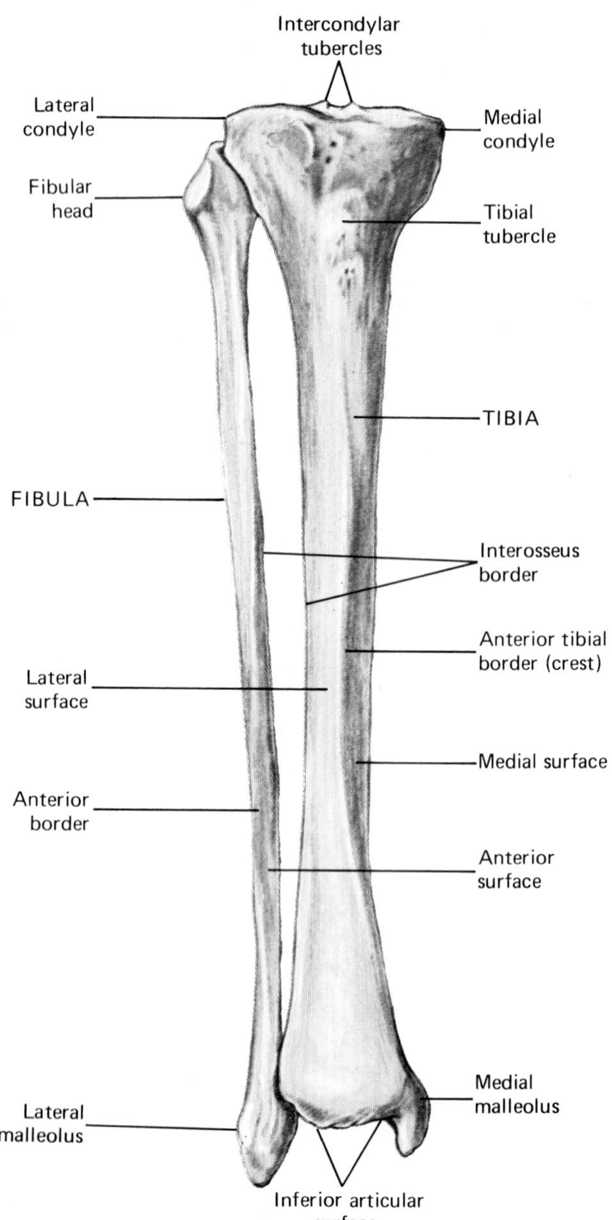

FIGURE 8-15

Anterior aspect of the right tibia and fibula, bones of the leg. Notice that the smaller fibula is located lateral to the larger tibia.

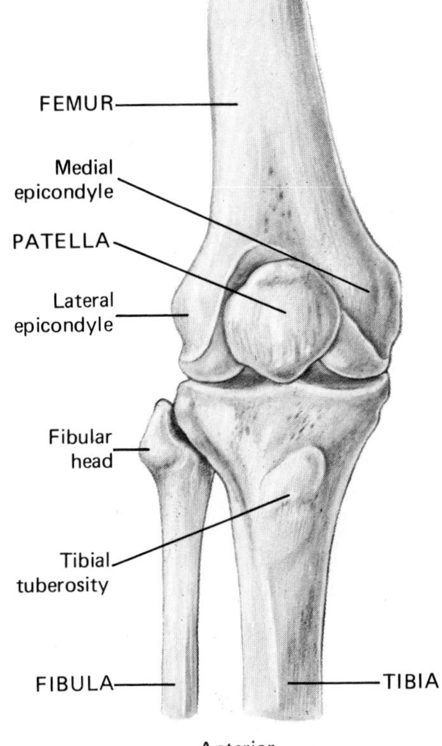

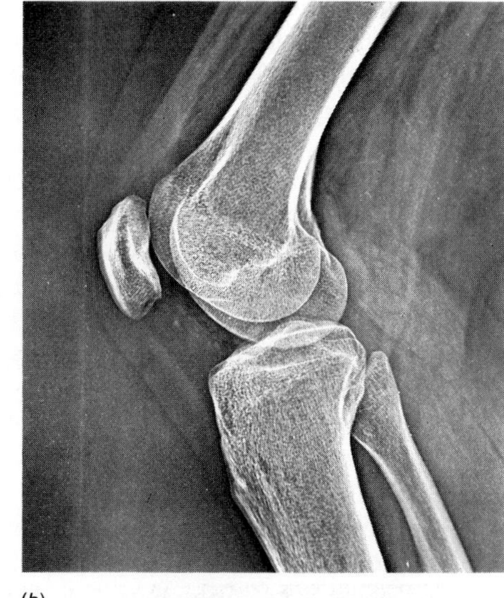

FIGURE 8-16

(*a*) Anterior aspect of the right knee joint. (*b*) Lateral radiograph (x-ray) of the knee joint. Note the position of the patella (knee cap), that is embedded in the tendon of the quadriceps femoris muscle located on the anterior aspect of the thigh. This tendon is attached to the tibia of the leg, and when the muscle contracts, its tendon pulls on the tibia and extends (straightens) the leg at the knee. The patella facilitates the movement of the tendon across the angle formed by the knee joint when the leg is flexed.

(*a*) (*b*)

two condyles (Figs. 8-15 and 8-16). The patellar ligament attaches to this tuberosity.

The medial aspect of the distal end of the tibia is expanded to form the **medial malleolus** (mal-**lee**-oh-lus) whereas its lateral surface has a small articular facet, the **fibular notch,** for the distal end of the fibula (Figs. 8-15 and 8-17). The medial malleolus forms a prominent projection on the medial aspect of the ankle that you can easily palpate. On the posterior surface of the distal end of the tibia there is a distinct groove, the **malleolar groove,** in which lie the tendons of the tibialis posterior and flexor digitorum longus muscles. The inferior articular surface of the distal tibia, including that of the medial malleolus, serves for articulation with the body and the medial aspect of the talus, respectively (Fig. 8-17).

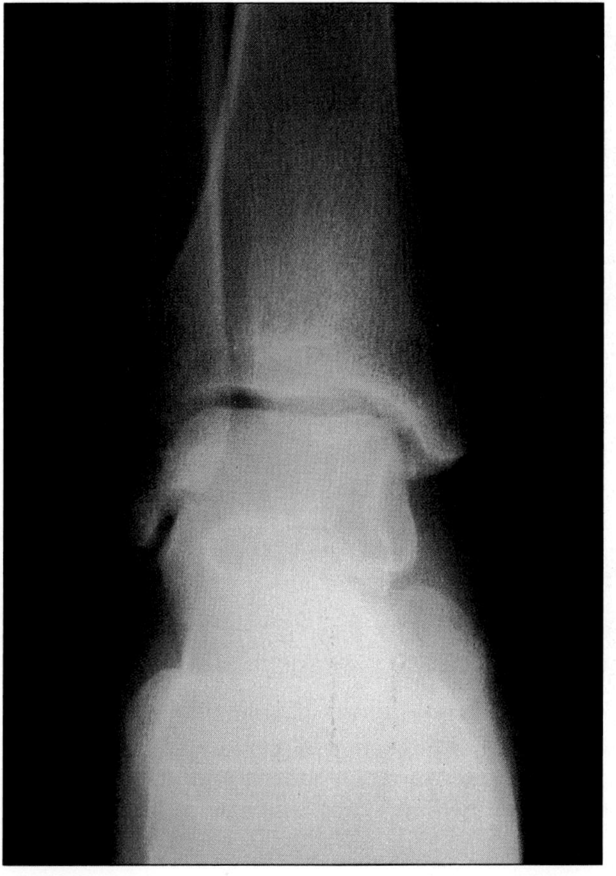

FIGURE 8-17

Radiograph of the bones participating in formation of the ankle joint. Are you able to determine whether this is a left or right ankle joint? Notice the position of the medial and lateral malleoli. Also, the only bone of the foot which enters into the formation of the ankle joint is the talus.

The smaller and more lateral of the two leg bones is the fibula

The more lateral of the two leg bones is called the **fibula** and it is considerably thinner and lighter than the tibia (Fig. 8-15). It has a shaft and proximal and distal ends. The proximal end, which is somewhat enlarged, is termed the **head** and it articulates with the lateral condyle of the tibia. The **neck** of the fibula is situated immediately below the head where the bone becomes constricted and the shaft begins. It is here that the common peroneal nerve winds around the lateral aspect of the fibula. You may be able to palpate this nerve while exerting rather firm pressure to this region of the fibula. The shaft of the fibula is heavily invested by muscle and cannot be easily palpated.

The distal end of the fibula is expanded to form the **lateral malleolus.** This projection lies approximately 1 centimeter lower than the medial malleolus (Figs. 8-15 and 8-17) and is also easily palpable. The inner aspect of the lateral malleolus has an articular surface for the lateral surface of the talus. Thus, the talus is situated between the lateral and medial malleoli. The distal end of the fibula also possesses an articular facet for the fibular notch of the tibia.

Tarsals, metatarsals, and phalanges constitute the skeleton of the foot

The remaining bones of the lower limb constitute the bones of the foot. These are 26 in number and, like those of the hand, are arranged in three distinct regions. These are as follows: (1) the ankle, or **tarsal** bones; (2) the metatarsals; and the (3) phalanges. The **dorsal** aspect of the foot is that which you see when you look down at your feet while standing; the **plantar** surface is represented by the sole. These terms are of importance in the description of various movements of the foot, for example, dorsiflexion and plantar flexion.

ONLY THE TALUS ARTICULATES WITH THE BONES OF THE LEG

The seven **tarsal** bones, or tarsus, are the: (a) **talus,** (b) **calcaneus** (kal-**kane**-ee-us), (c) **cuboid,** (d) **navicular** (na-**vick**-you-lar), and (e) **medial** (1st), **intermediate** (2nd), and **lateral** (3rd) **cuneiform** (que-**knee**-i-form) **bones.** Of all the tarsal bones, only the talus (ankle bone) articulates with the bones of the leg, that is the tibia and fibula. The tarsal bones are similar to the carpal bones of the wrist, but tend to be both larger and stronger because of their role in supporting and distributing the weight of the body. Congenital anomalies of the tarsal bones are not uncommon and these may be directly related to a variety of foot disorders.

The tarsal bones (Figs. 8-18 and 8-19) are arranged in proximal and distal rows like the carpal bones of the wrist; however, medially there is an additional bone placed between the two rows. The bones of the proximal row are the talus (medially) and the calcaneus (laterally). Those of the distal row are, from lateral to medial, the cuboid, lateral cuneiform, intermediate cuneiform, and medial cuneiform. On the medial aspect of the foot the bone that is interposed between the proximal and distal rows is called the navicular. Notice (Figs. 8-18 and 8-19) that the navicular lies between the talus behind and the three cuneiform bones in front.

EACH DIGIT OF THE FOOT HAS A SINGLE METATARSAL

Each foot has five **metatarsals** and these are situated between the tarsal bones behind and the phalanges in front. The metatarsals are numbered I through V starting with the most medial and proceeding to the most lateral (Fig. 8-18). As with the metacarpals of the hand, each metatarsal possesses a **base,** a **shaft,** and a **head.** The base is the most proximal portion; the shaft intervenes between this and the head, which is the most distal aspect.

Metatarsal I is the shortest and thickest of all metatarsals. Its base articulates with the medial cuneiform. The longest of the metatarsals is metatarsal II whose base articulates with all three cuneiform bones and the third metatarsal. The base of metatarsal III articulates with the lateral cuneiform and metatarsals II and IV. Metatarsal IV is shorter and thinner than metatarsal III and its base articulates with the base of metatarsals III and V as well as the cuboid. The base of the fifth metatarsal possesses a prominent projection on its lateral aspect called the **tuberosity of the fifth metatarsal** (Figs. 8-18 and 8-19). This tuberosity can be palpated easily through the skin on the

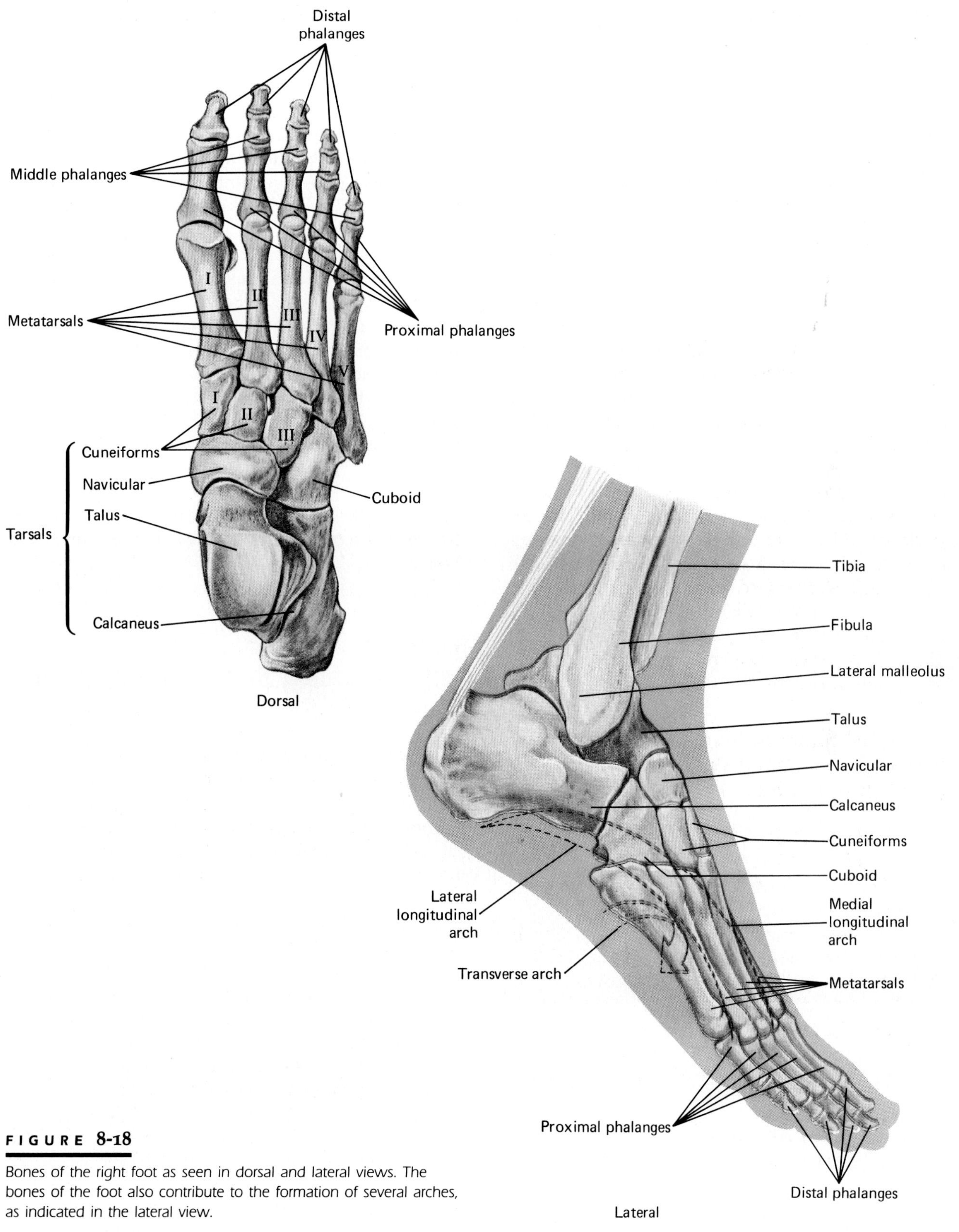

FIGURE 8-18

Bones of the right foot as seen in dorsal and lateral views. The bones of the foot also contribute to the formation of several arches, as indicated in the lateral view.

lateral aspect of your foot approximately half the distance between your heel and the tip of your little toe. The base of metatarsal V articulates with two bones, the cuboid and the base of metatarsal IV.

EACH DIGIT OF THE FOOT HAS THREE PHALANGES, EXCEPTING THE FIRST, WHICH HAS ONLY TWO

As in the fingers, there are 14 phalanges in each foot. The great toe possesses two and the remaining toes each have three (Figs. 8-18 and 8-19). In general they tend to be shorter and stouter than the phalanges of the fingers. Each phalanx has a **base,** a **shaft,** and a **head** (Fig. 8-18). Again the base is proximal, the head distal, and the shaft intervenes between the two extremities.

The proximal phalanges all articulate through their bases with the head of their respective metatarsals (metatarsophalangeal joints). In the great toe the head of the proximal phalanx simply articulates with the base of the remaining phalanx (distal interphalangeal joint). In the other digits the proximal row articulates with the bases of the intermediate phalanges (intermediate interphalangeal joints). The heads of the four intermediate phalanges articulate with the bases of their respective distal phalanges (distal interphalangeal joints). These articulations are depicted in Figure 8-18.

Notice (Fig. 8-18) that the bones of each foot are arranged in such a fashion as to produce three distinct arches. The **transverse arch** is formed by the navicular, the three cuneiform bones, the cuboid, and metatarsals I through V. The remaining two arches are called the **medial**

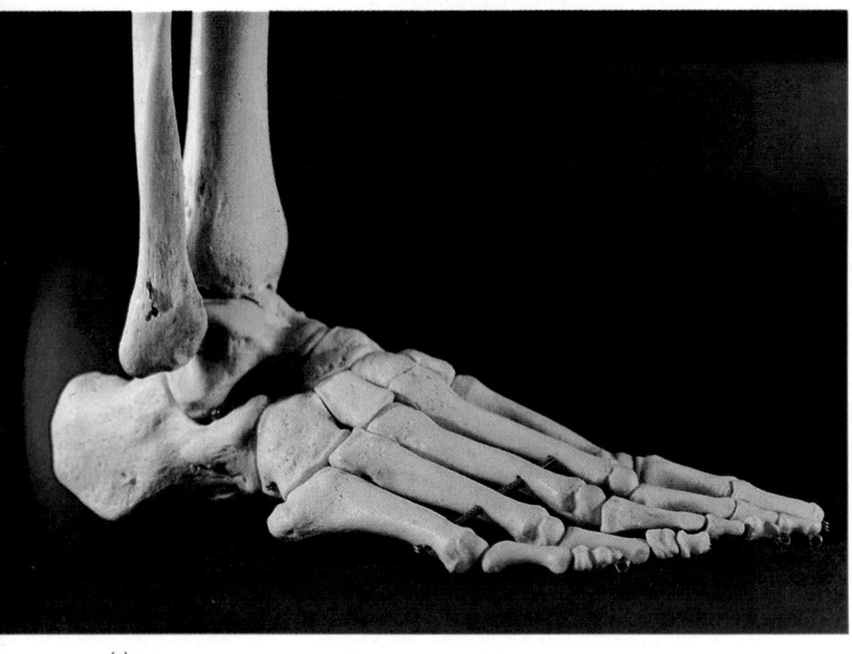

(a)

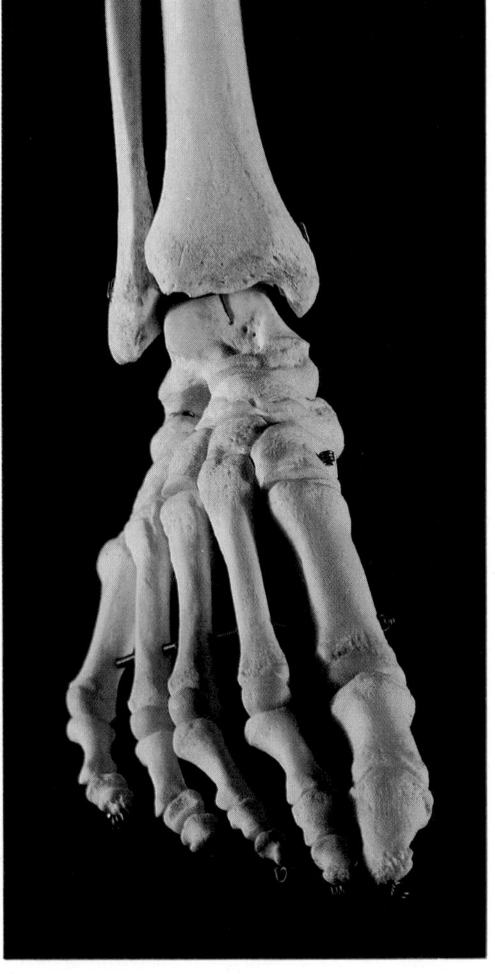

(b)

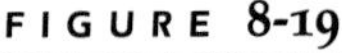

FIGURE 8-19

Photographs of the (*a*) lateral and (*b*) dorsal (anterior) aspects of the foot. (Manfred Kage/Peter Arnold, Inc.) Are you able to determine whether this is a left or right foot? Compare with Fig. 8-18.

and **lateral longitudinal arches.** The medial longitudinal arch is comprised of the talus, calcaneus, navicular, three cuneiform bones, and metatarsals I, II, and III. The calcaneus, cuboid, and metatarsals IV and V are responsible for formation of the lateral longitudinal arch. Of the two longitudinal arches, the medial one is certainly the most prominent (Fig. 8-18). These arches are by no means fixed: that is, they give as the weight of the body is transmitted to the ground and resume their original configuration as the weight is removed.

Summary

I. The appendicular skeleton consists of the bones of the upper and lower limbs, together with those that serve to unite them with the trunk.

II. Bones that constitute the pectoral girdle are the clavicle and the scapula. The former articulates with the sternum at the sternoclavicular joint and with the scapula at the acromioclavicular joint.

III. Bones that constitute the skeleton of the upper limb are: (a) humerus, (b) radius, (c) ulna, (d) 8 carpals, (e) 5 metacarpals, and (f) 14 phalanges. These are distributed throughout distinct anatomical regions of the upper limb known as the (a) arm, (b) forearm, (c) wrist, (d) palm, and (e) digits.

IV. The pelvic girdle is composed of two coxal, or innominate, bones. Each of these is derived from the fusion of three separate bones designated as the (a) ilium, (b) ischium, and (c) pubis.

V. The skeleton of the pelvis is formed by the two coxal bones together with the sacrum and coccyx. (a) It is characterized by the presence of a pelvic inlet and pelvic outlet. (b) The region located superior to the pelvic inlet is termed the false, or greater, pelvis whereas that inferior to the inlet is known as the true, or lesser, pelvis.

VI. Bones that constitute the skeleton of the lower limb are: (a) femur, (b) patella, (c) tibia, (d) fibula, (e) 7 tarsals, (f) 5 metatarsals, and (g) 14 phalanges. These are distributed throughout distinct anatomical regions of the lower limb known as the (a) thigh, (b) knee, (c) leg, (d) ankle, and (e) foot.

Post-test

1. The clavicle and the scapula constitute the __________ girdle.
2. The only articulation between the upper limb and the axial skeleton occurs at the __________ joint.
3. The point at which the axillary and vertebral borders of the scapula meet is termed the __________ __________.
4. The clavicle articulates with the __________ at the acromioclavicular joint.
5. __________ dysostosis is a combination of congenital malformations involving the clavicle as well as the skull.
6. The bones constituting the skeleton of the upper limb are the: (a) __________, (b) __________, (c) __________, (d) 8 __________, (e) 5 __________, and (f) 14 __________.
7. The axillary artery may be damaged when there is a fracture involving the __________ neck of the humerus.
8. The ulnar nerve lies immediately posterior to the __________ epicondyle of the humerus.
9. The __________ is an articular surface located between the olecranon and the coronoid processes of the ulna.
10. The proximal row of carpals, from lateral to medial, consists of the __________, __________, __________, and __________. Those of the distal row, also from lateral to medial, are the __________, __________, __________, and __________.
11. Knuckles are formed by the __________ of the underlying metacarpal bones.
12. Another term for coxal bone is the __________ bone.
13. The __________ girdle is composed of the two coxal bones. However, each coxal bone results from the fusion of three separate bones called the __________, __________, and __________.
14. Anteriorly, the two coxal bones are united via a fibrocartilaginous joint known as the __________ __________.
15. The greater and lesser pelves are demarcated from each other by an imaginary plane that passes through the __________ __________.
16. The bones of the leg are termed the __________ and __________.
17. There are seven __________ bones in each foot.
18. __________ is the proper term we apply to the bone designated by laymen as the "shinbone."
19. Although there are __________ tarsal bones in each foot, only the __________ articulates with the tibia and fibula of the leg.
20. The __________ toe is also termed the first digit of the foot.

Review questions

1. Compare and contrast the bones that constitute the pectoral and pelvic girdles.
2. Describe the articulations of the clavicle and its importance in transmitting forces from the upper limb to the axial skeleton. Also address the fact that bone fragments of a fractured clavicle are of clinical significance especially if they are driven posteriorly.
3. Describe fractures of the following in view of important structures located in the immediate vicinity: (a) middle one-third of the humerus, (b) medial epicondyle of the humerus, (c) surgical neck of the humerus, (d) neck of the fibula.
4. Describe how the digits of the hand are numbered and provide the layman's term for each.
5. Which of the carpal bones is most frequently fractured and why are such fractures of such importance?
6. Compare and contrast the greater and lesser pelves.
7. Describe the anatomical features of the femur and list all of the bones with which it articulates.
8. Describe the anatomical features of the tibia and fibula.
9. Describe the transverse and longitudinal arches of the foot.

Post-test answers

1. pectoral **2.** sternoclavicular **3.** inferior angle **4.** scapula **5.** Cleidocranial **6.** (a) humerus (b) radius (c) ulna (d) carpals (e) metacarpals (f) phalanges **7.** surgical **8.** medial **9.** trochlea **10.** scaphoid; lunate; triquetral; pisiform; trapezium; trapezoid; capitate; hamate **11.** heads **12.** hip **13.** pelvic; ilium, ischium, pubis **14.** pubic symphysis **15.** pelvic inlet **16.** tibia, fibula **17.** tarsal **18.** Tibia **19.** seven; talus **20.** great

JOINTS

CHAPTER OUTLINE

- **I. Functions of joints**
- **II. Classification of joints**
  - A. Functional approach
  - B. Structural approach
    - 1. Fibrous joints
      - a. Sutures
      - b. Gomphosis
      - c. Syndesmosis
    - 2. Cartilaginous joints
      - a. Symphysis
      - b. Synchondroses
    - 3. Synovial joints
- **III. Classification of synovial joints**
  - a. Plane, or gliding, joints
  - b. Ginglymus, or hinge, joints
  - c. Trochoid, or pivot, joints
  - d. Condylar joints
  - e. Ellipsoid joints
  - f. Saddle joints
  - g. Spheroid, or ball-and-socket, joints
- **IV. Movements at synovial joints**
  - □ Focus on body movements
  - A. Flexion
  - B. Extension
  - C. Abduction
  - D. Adduction
  - E. Pronation and supination
  - F. Inversion and eversion
  - G. Dorsiflexion and plantar-flexion
  - H. Protraction and retraction
  - I. Rotation
  - J. Circumduction
  - K. Opposition
  - L. Limitations to joint movement
- **V. Innervation of joints**
- **VI. Levers**
  - A. First-class levers
  - B. Second-class levers
  - C. Third-class levers
- **VII. Joint disorders**
  - A. Arthritis
    - 1. Infectious arthritis
    - 2. Gouty arthritis
    - 3. Osteoarthritis
    - 4. Rheumatoid arthritis
  - B. Tennis elbow and other miseries
  - □ Focus on three joints

LEARNING OBJECTIVES

After you have studied this chapter you should be able to:

1 Describe the functional classification of joints.

2 Describe the classification of joints as to the three basic types: fibrous joints, cartilaginous joints, and synovial joints.

3 Describe the various components of a synovial joint.

4 Describe and give examples of the subtypes of fibrous, cartilaginous, and synovial joints.

5 Define uniaxial, biaxial, and multiaxial movement at joints.

6 Compare and contrast the various types of movements that are permitted at synovial joints.

7 Describe the innervation of joints.

8 Compare first-, second-, and third-class levers and provide examples of each type.

9 Describe the various types of joint disorders.

10 Describe in depth the examples of selected joints including their classification, structural components, and movements.

11 Describe those factors that ordinarily limit movement of a synovial joint.

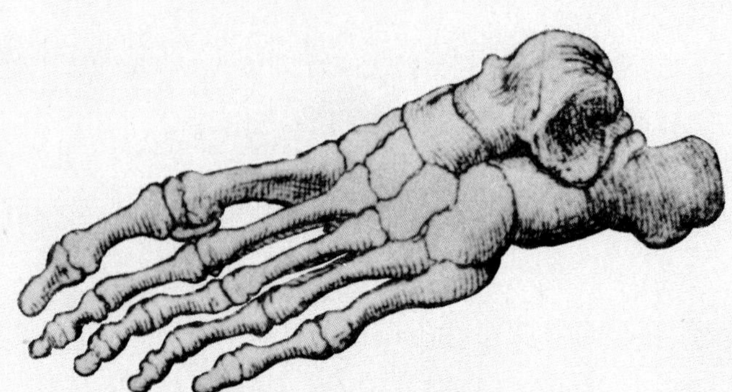

(*right*) Computer-generated image of a knee joint. (Evans and Sutherland/PhotoEdit.)

9

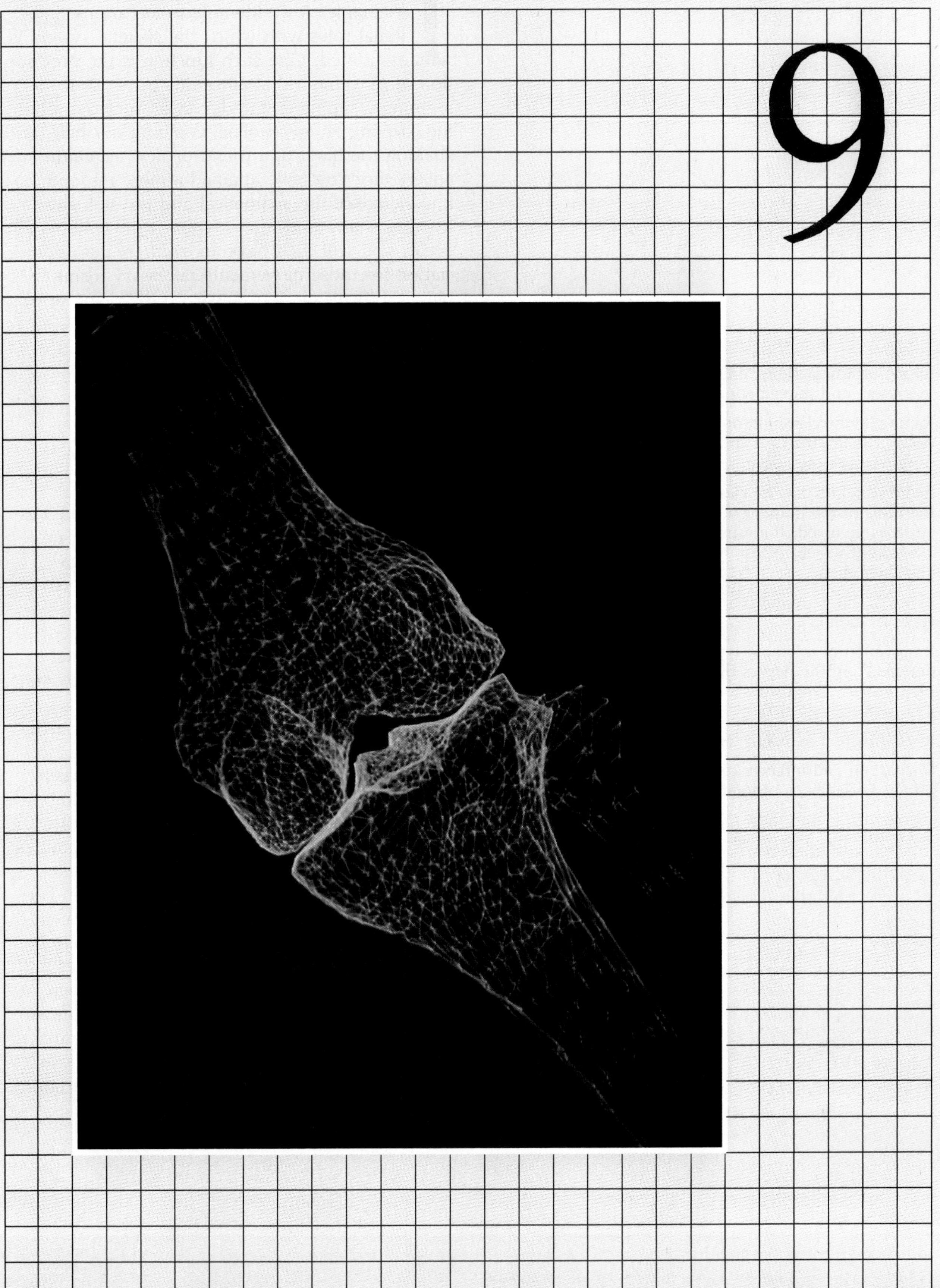

KEY CONCEPTS

Joints, or articulations, are involved in growth and movement.

Joints may be classified on the basis of their structure and degree of movement they permit.

Synovial joints may be classified on the basis of the number of articular surfaces involved, the number of axes about which motion occurs, and their shape.

Synovial joints permit four basic types of motion.

Innervation of a joint is typically derived from the nerves that supply muscles responsible for moving it.

Joints function as fulcra for levers.

Dislocation and inflammation are primary disabilities of joints.

In Chapter 6 we identified the various functional roles with which the skeletal system is associated. One such function is the production of movement that allows us to perform the seemingly simple day-to-day tasks such as walking, driving an automobile, combing our hair, or shaking the hand of a friend or new acquaintance. Once you have attained a more in-depth knowledge of the anatomical and physiological features that permit these types of movements to occur, you will then have an even greater appreciation for those movements necessary for us to play a difficult piece of music on the piano or to excel as a gymnast.

Growth and movement are the primary functions of joints

Although the individual bones of the skeletal system are typically quite rigid in nature, they provide sites for attachment of muscles and ligaments. In doing so they provide a continuous series of levers upon which contracting muscles act to bring about a great variety of movements. This arrangement of intervening rigid skeletal structures that permits varying degrees of twisting, angular movement, and displacement is made possible by the presence of **joints,** or **articulations** (ar-**tik**-yoo-*lay*-shuns). A joint, or articulation, is defined as the site of contact between bones or between cartilage and bone. It is important for you to realize that, although we have emphasized *movement* in the introductory remarks to this chapter, the function of all joints is not necessarily associated with that specific role. For example, joints between certain bones of the craniofacial skeleton permit the developing brain to grow and expand within its osseous confines until such developmental processes have been brought to completion. In fact, *growth,* not movement, is the primary function applied to temporary zones of cartilage that are found interposed between the epiphyses and diaphyses of certain bones.

Joints may be classified on either a functional or structural basis

Typically joints may be classified by two different methods. One is related to their functional role whereas the other is based on their structural configuration. You will soon come to appreciate the considerable degree of overlap that exists between these two approaches.

Joints permit movement and growth

As already discussed, certain joints are present in order for growth to occur. Growth may apply to the bone itself or to another structure such as the brain that is encased within developing bones. Other joints are present in order for varying degrees of movement to occur. Thus, we can further classify such joints based on the relative degree of movement they allow. According to the functional classification, there are three types of joints. The joints we consider to be immovable are designated as **synarthroses** (*sin*-are-**throw**-sees). Joints that permit a slight amount of movement are termed **amphiarthroses** (*am*-fee-are-**throw**-sees), and those we consider as freely movable are known as **diarthroses** (*die*-are-**throw**-sees). As we proceed with the classification based on joint structure, keep in mind these three classes of joints and the degree of movement they permit. This should help to strengthen your understanding of the structure-function relationships applicable to the study of joints.

Three types of joints are defined on the basis of structural configuration

The classification of joints based on their structural configuration is rather straightforward. However, it is most appropriate at this time to define a few terms that should facilitate the development of your knowledge with regard to this classification scheme.

Ligaments are strong, tensile, connective tissue cords, or bands, that serve the function of uniting bones. Ligaments are quite often intimately associated with joints, and they lend varying degrees of stability to them. Ligaments differ in their connective tissue composition throughout the body. Certain joints have ligaments associated with them that are composed of very dense bundles of collagenous fibers while in others the connective tissue component consists largely of elastic fibers. The latter can be stretched somewhat without tearing and return to their original length once the tension is terminated. Those ligaments that are composed primarily of collagenous fibers, on the other hand, are considered to be almost unstretchable.

Bursae (**ber**-say) are closed fibrous sacs that are filled with a small volume of viscous fluid. The internal lining of a bursa consists of a thin membranous layer of tissue similar to that which lines certain joint cavities. Bursae are frequently located near joints where tendons are subject to frictional forces brought about by adjacent tendons, bones, or ligaments. By virtue of their structure and their location near joints, bursae serve to lessen these frictional forces as movement ensues. The *prepatellar bursa* (Fig. 9-1) serves to illustrate another aspect of bursa function, the cushioning of forces that develop between the bones of a joint and the overlying skin. Here, the bursa is located in a position between the skin and the underlying bone. Although we have defined a bursa as being a closed sac, there are instances in which a bursa communicates with the cavity of a joint. The shoulder joint (Fig. 9-2) and knee joint (Fig. 9-1) are examples of joints in which bursae communicate directly with the joint cavities.

Clinical highlight

When inflammation of a bursa occurs the condition is termed **bursitis** (ber-**sigh**-tis). Although the precise cause of bursitis is unknown, it is thought that trauma, even in the form of excessive exercise, is a significant contributing factor. Joints at which bursitis is most frequently encountered include the shoulder, knee, and the elbow. Bursitis can be extremely painful and its treatment in early stages commonly incorporates supportive measures and local injections of cortisone or other similar steroidal compounds. Surgical excision is usually reserved for the more advanced stages of bursitis when calcification of bursal tissues occurs.

Synovial tendon sheaths (si-**no**-vee-uhl) are bursal sacs that surround certain tendons. The tendon pushes into the sac so that eventually the

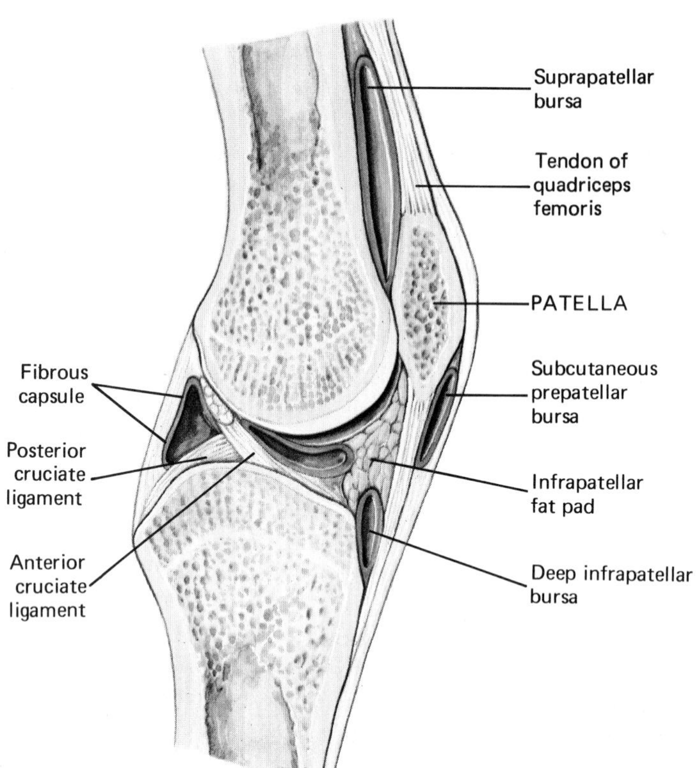

FIGURE 9-1

Sagittal view of the knee joint. Notice the patella (knee cap) embedded within the tendon of the quadriceps femoris muscle. Portions of the anterior and posterior cruciate ligaments are also shown. These represent examples of ligaments that have an intracapsular location.

entire circumference of the tendon is surrounded by a bursa, now known as a synovial tendon sheath. The functional significance of these sheaths is to reduce frictional forces that occur between the tendons and adjacent structures. Examples of synovial tendon sheaths are those associated with the long flexor tendons of the forearm muscles as they course through the wrist and enter the hand (Fig. 9-3).

Clinical highlight

Inflammation of synovial tendon sheaths is termed **tenosynovitis** (ten-oh-sin-oh-**vie**-tis). Individuals afflicted with such a condition experience great pain as movement ensues and frequently become disabled because of the severe pain. Trauma as well as direct bacterial invasion may lead to the development of tenosynovitis.

Classification of joints based on their structural configuration permits us to identify three basic types. Thus, joints are considered as being either of the **fibrous, cartilaginous,** or **synovial** type. Only synovial joints are characterized by the presence of a *joint cavity.* Fibrous and cartilaginous joints lack a joint cavity and as such the participating bones are united by fibrous tissue and cartilage, respectively. The following is a more in-depth discussion of each one of these three types of joints.

FIBROUS JOINTS LACK A JOINT CAVITY

Fibrous joints (Fig. 9-4) permit little or no movement. Thus they are either synarthroses or amphiarthroses. As mentioned earlier, fibrous joints do not have a joint cavity and the participating bones are bound rigidly together by fibrous connective tissue. The three specific types of fibrous joints are (1) **sutures** (**soo**-churs), (2) **gomphoses** (gom-**foe**-sees), and (3) **syndesmoses** (sin-dez-**moe**-sees).

Sutures are a type of fibrous joint

This type of fibrous joint is restricted to bones of the skull (Fig. 9-4). Here the participating bones are bound tightly together by a thin, intervening layer of fibrous connective tissue that we term the *sutural ligament.* With advancing age this sutural ligament within certain sutures is transformed into bone. Such transformation is a slow process and results in the formation of a *synostosis* (sin-oss-**toe**-sis), that is, the complete conversion of fibrous connective tissue within the suture to bone.

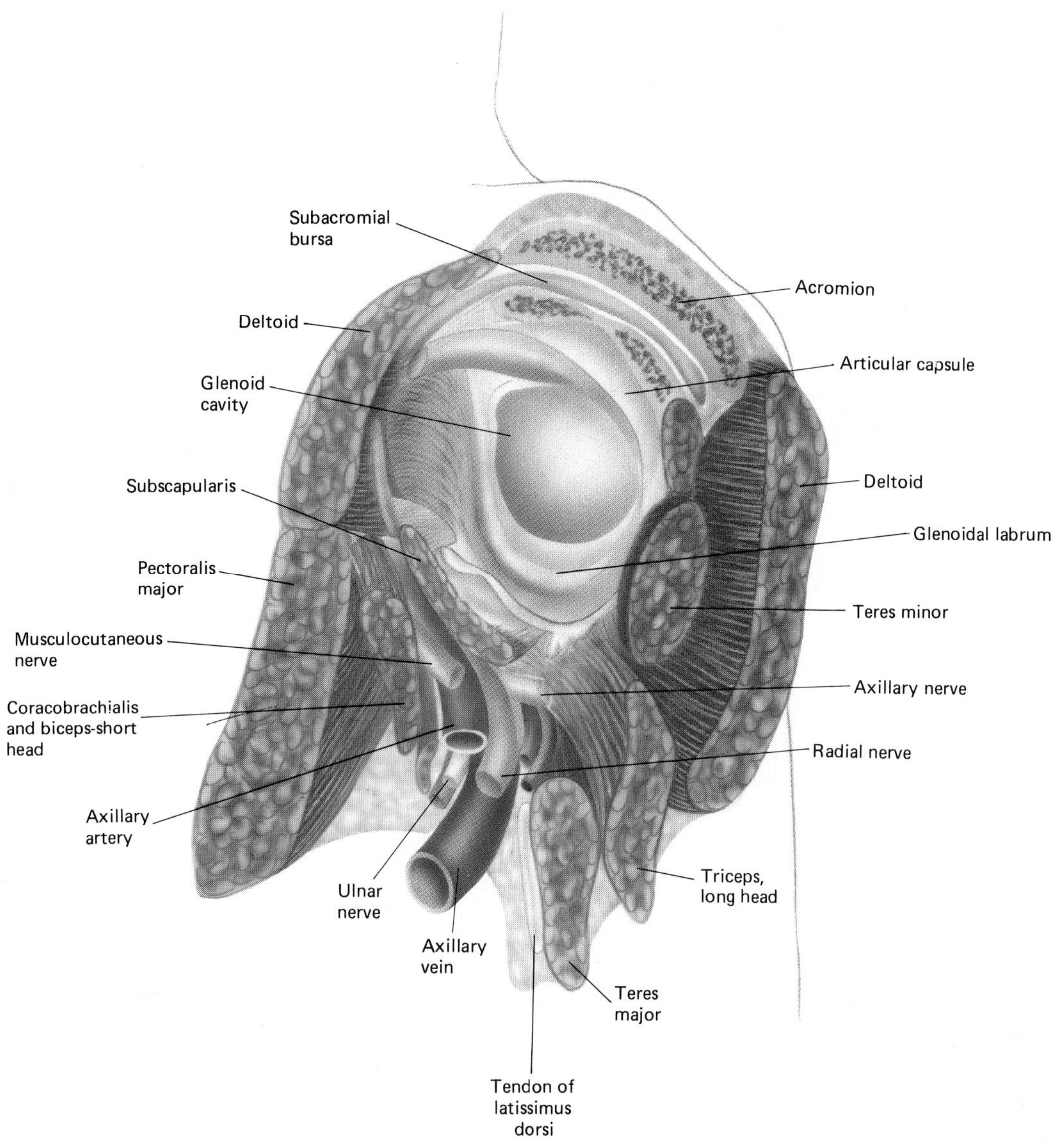

FIGURE 9-2

Oblique view of the left shoulder joint. The humerus has been removed in order to expose the internal features of the joint.

Examination of a disarticulated skull (Fig. 9-5) illustrates the fact that some sutures possess sawlike (serrated) processes and others are characterized by the presence of toothlike (denticulate) projections. The margins of still others are beveled in a reciprocal manner so that the participating bones overlap one another at their site of contact. Consideration of these various marginal characteristics of the bones, together with the presence of the sutural ligament, makes more clear the immovable nature of such joints and their classification as synarthroses.

A gomphosis is a peg-and-socket type joint

The teeth are fixed in the maxilla (upper jaw) and mandible (lower jaw) by a specialized form of fibrous joint known as a **gomphosis** (Fig. 9-6, p. 265). This is a synarthrosis and is essentially a peg-and-socket type of joint. The "peg" is represented by the root(s) of the tooth and the "socket" by the bony cavity in which the tooth resides. The root of the tooth is coated with a thin cement layer into which are anchored collagenous fibers of the *periodontal ligament*. The oppo-

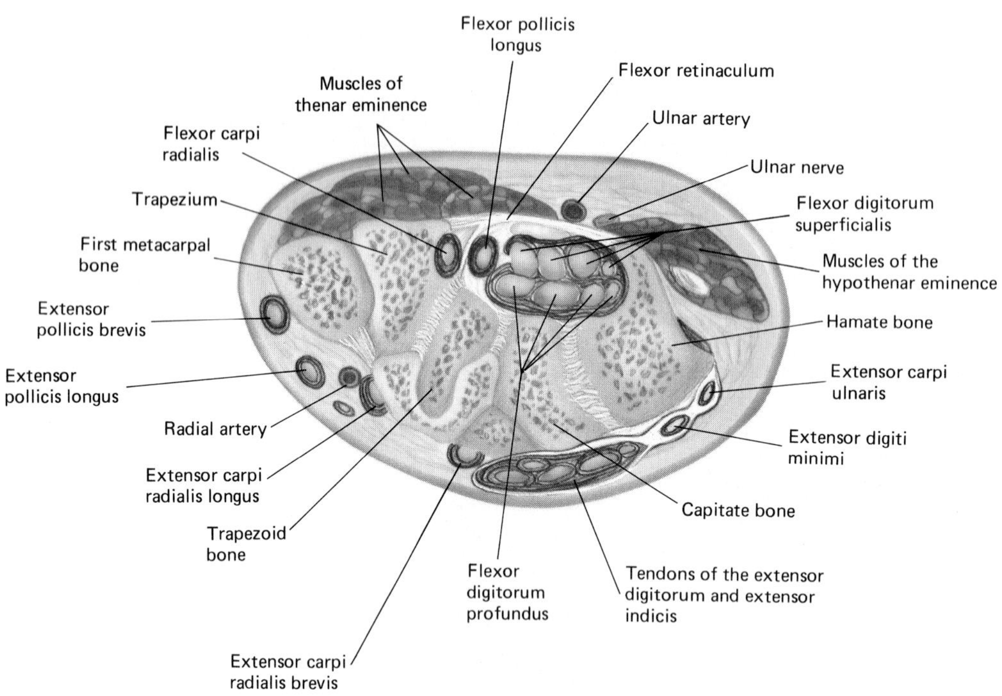

FIGURE 9-3

The right wrist as seen in transverse section. For orientation, remember that you are viewing the distal surface of the section, that is, the surface near the finger tips. Notice the tendons as they lie surrounded by their synovial sheaths.

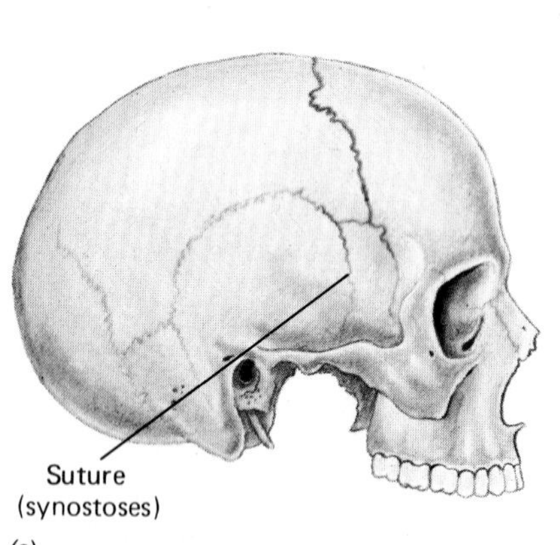

(a)

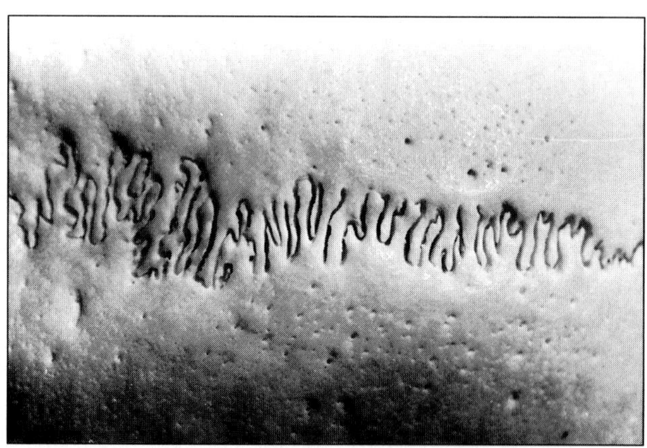

(b)

FIGURE 9-4

A suture is one type of fibrous joint. (a) The sutures of the skull are examples of fibrous joints. (b) Photograph of suture occurring between two bones of the skull. This type of joint lacks a joint cavity; the bones are united by fibrous connective tissue called the sutural ligament.

Articulates with opposite parietal bone
Frontal angle
Occipital angle
Sphenoid angle
Mastoid angle

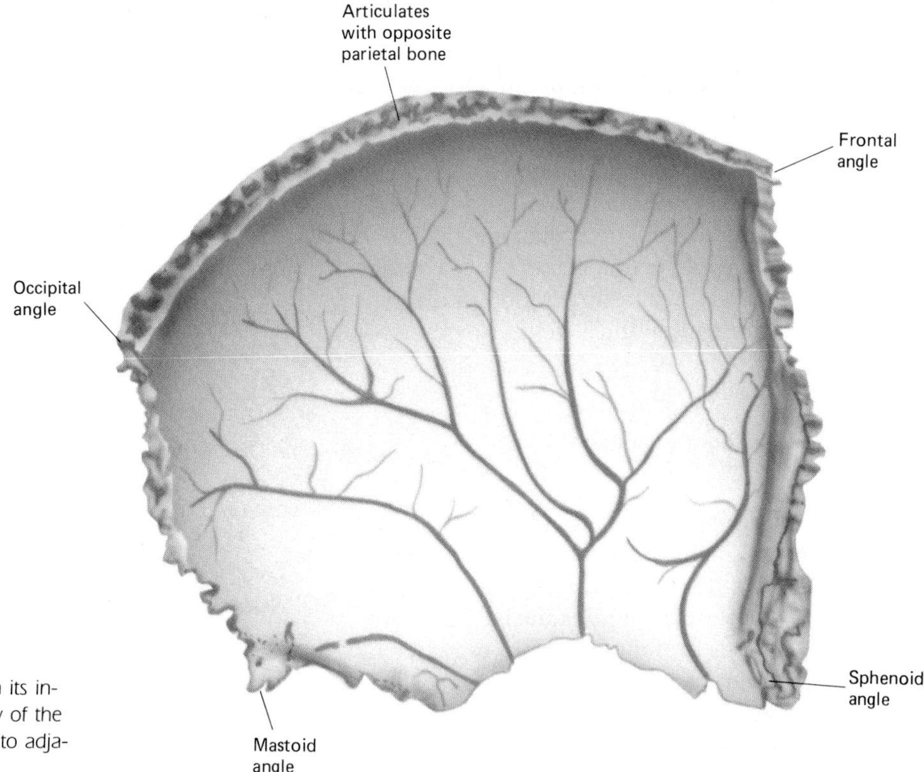

FIGURE 9-5

The left parietal bone as seen from its internal aspect. Notice the irregularity of the edges of the bone that are united to adjacent bones through sutures.

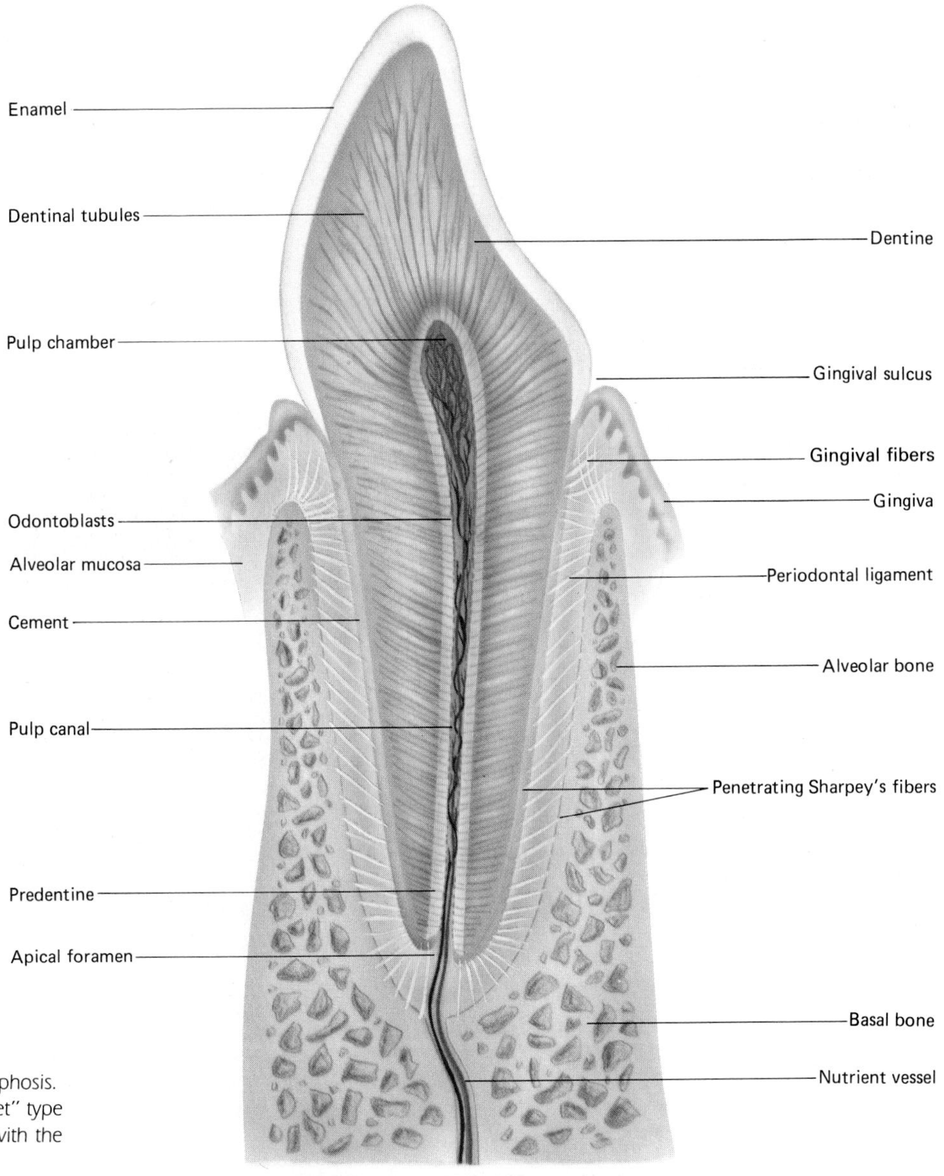

Enamel
Dentinal tubules
Dentine
Pulp chamber
Gingival sulcus
Gingival fibers
Gingiva
Odontoblasts
Alveolar mucosa
Periodontal ligament
Cement
Alveolar bone
Pulp canal
Penetrating Sharpey's fibers
Predentine
Apical foramen
Basal bone
Nutrient vessel

FIGURE 9-6

One type of fibrous joint, the gomphosis. This is essentially a "peg-and-socket" type joint. The teeth form gomphoses with the maxillae and mandible.

site ends of these fibers are attached to the alveolar bone and thus form a rigid suspension for the individual tooth. Collagenous fibers that constitute the periodontal ligament extend from the neck of the tooth to the apical region of the root (Fig. 9-6).

Syndesmoses are slightly movable fibrous joints

This type of fibrous joint is slightly movable and as such is functionally classified as an amphiarthrosis. The distal tibiofibular joint (Fig. 9-7) is the best example of a **syndesmosis.** Here the participating bones are bound firmly together by a layer of intervening fibrous tissue termed the **interosseous ligament** (in-ter-**os**-ee-us). Structurally the syndesmosis is similar to a suture; however, in the former there is generally a greater quantity of fibrous tissue present and the participating bones are not configured to fit together as tightly as they are in the latter type of joint.

BONES OF CARTILAGINOUS JOINTS ARE UNITED BY CARTILAGE

Cartilaginous (kar-ti-**laj**-in-us) joints represent the second basic type of articulation in the structural classification scheme. Like the fibrous joint, the cartilaginous joint also lacks a joint cavity. In the cartilaginous joint, however, the participating bones are held firmly together by intervening cartilage. Functionally, these joints resemble fibrous joints in that they permit little if any movement. Two types of cartilaginous joints are **symphyses** (**sim**-fih-sees) and **synchondroses** (sin-kon-**dro**-sees).

The pubic symphysis and joints between vertebrae are cartilaginous joints

A good example of a **symphysis** is the joint between the bodies of the two pubic bones, known as the *pubic symphysis* (Fig. 9-8). In this joint the adjacent surfaces of the two pubic bones are

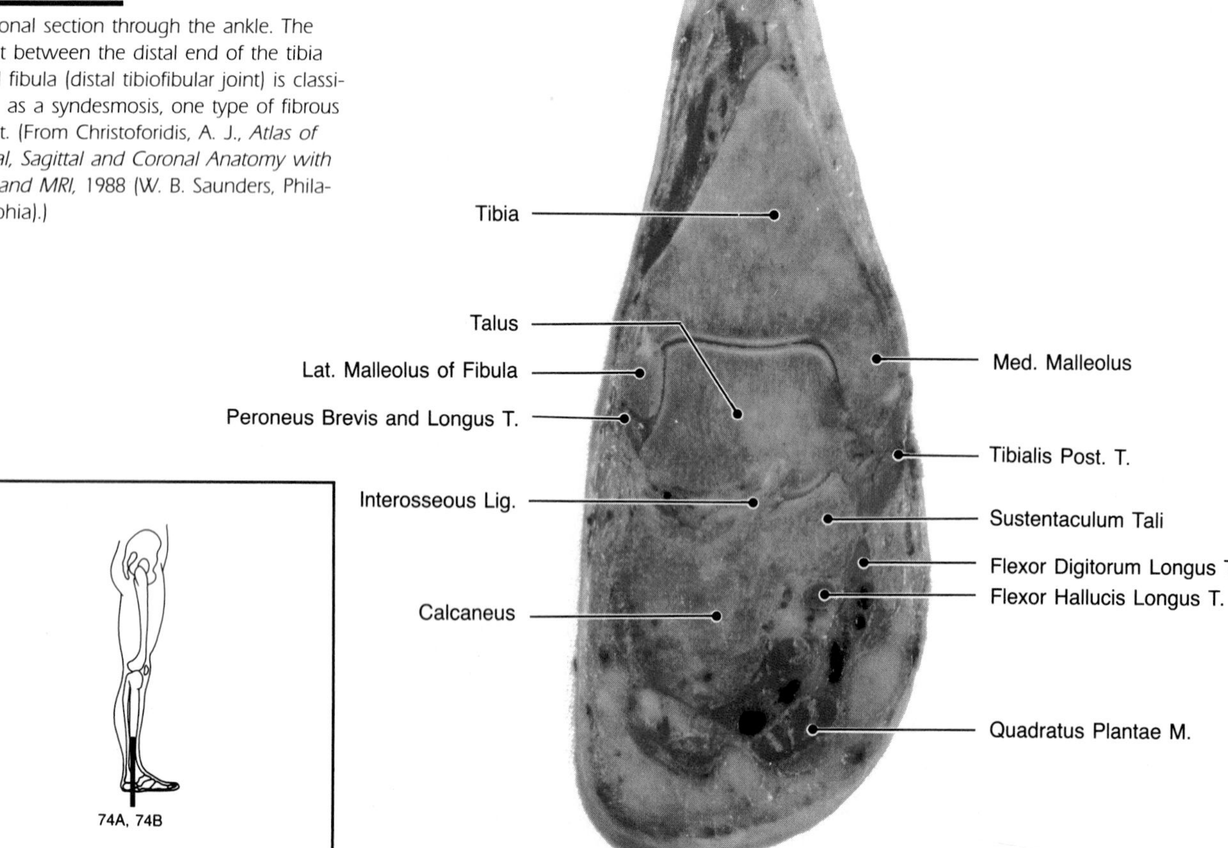

FIGURE 9-7

Coronal section through the ankle. The joint between the distal end of the tibia and fibula (distal tibiofibular joint) is classified as a syndesmosis, one type of fibrous joint. (From Christoforidis, A. J., *Atlas of Axial, Sagittal and Coronal Anatomy with CT and MRI*, 1988 (W. B. Saunders, Philadelphia).)

bound together by an *interpubic disc* consisting of fibrocartilage. Additional stability for the pubic symphysis is provided above by the *superior pubic ligament* and inferiorly by the *arcuate pubic ligament.* This joint is an amphiarthrosis because some displacement does occur in the female, particularly during the process of parturition (act or process of giving birth).

The joint that exists between the bodies of two adjacent vertebrae (Fig. 9-9) represents another example of a symphysis. Here the two vertebral bodies are separated from each other by the *intervertebral disc,* a portion of which is composed of fibrocartilage. The thickness of the intervertebral disc is not uniform from one joint to another along the vertebral column. The joints between the bodies of adjacent vertebrae are given added stability by the presence of two ligaments: the *anterior longitudinal ligament,* which is located on the anterior surface of the vertebral bodies, and the *posterior longitudinal ligament,* which is situated within the vertebral canal along the posterior surface of the vertebral bodies. Fibers from both ligaments are also attached to the intervertebral discs. The degree of movement that occurs between any two adjacent vertebral bodies is quite small; however, the summation of such individual motions imparts a relatively broad range of motion to the vertebral column as an intact unit.

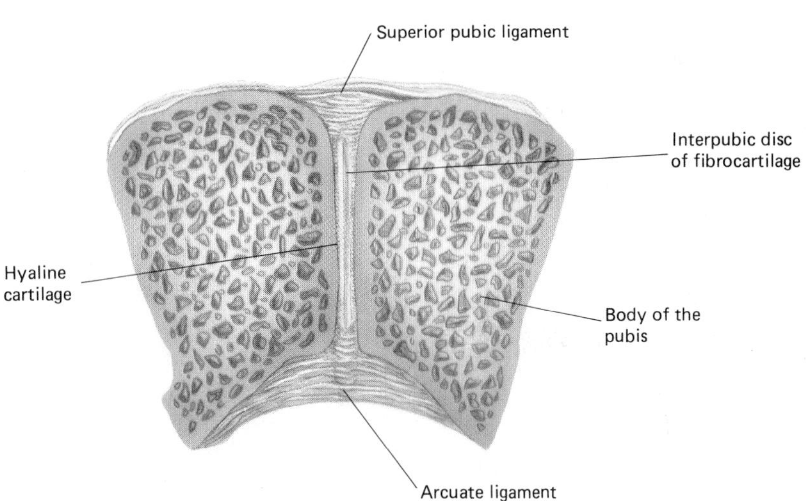

FIGURE 9-8

The pubic symphysis represents a type (symphysis) of cartilaginous joint. The interpubic disc is composed of fibrocartilage.

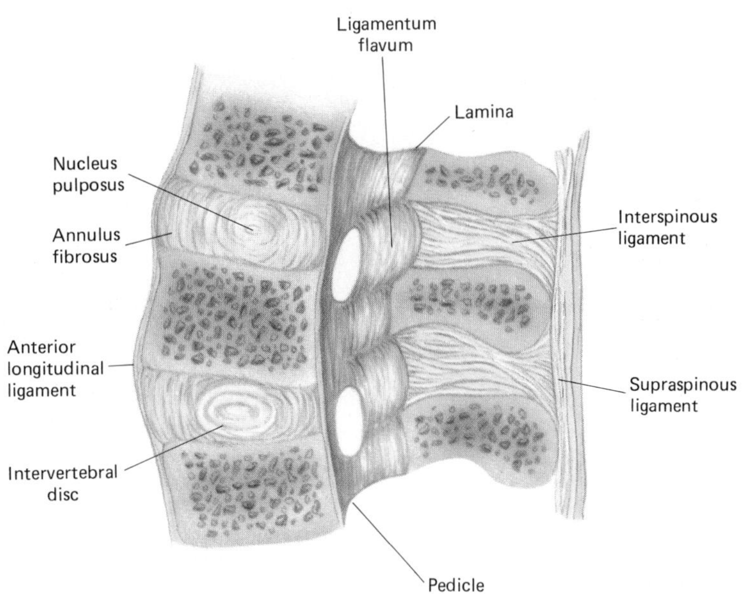

FIGURE 9-9

The joint between the bodies of adjacent vertebrae is an example of a symphysis. A portion of the intervertebral disc consists of fibrocartilage.

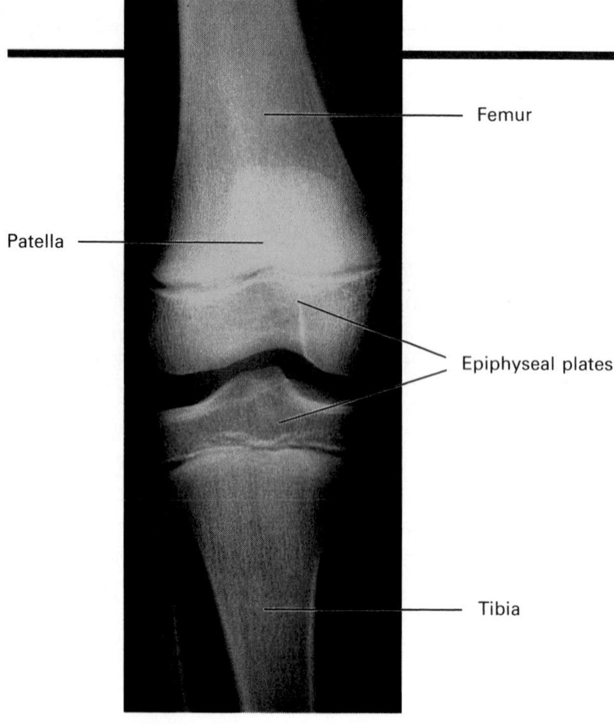

FIGURE 9-10

Synchondroses are cartilaginous joints involved in growth. In this radiograph of the knee, notice the epiphyseal catilaginous plates (seen as empty spaces) located between the epiphyses and diaphyses of the growing bones. (Phototake.)

Synchondroses are joints of a temporary nature

Hyaline cartilage is the connecting material in the type of cartilaginous articulation known as a **synchondrosis.** This type of cartilaginous joint is most clearly exemplified by the epiphyseal cartilaginous plate located between the epiphysis and diaphysis of a growing bone (Fig. 9-10). The synchondrosis is not a permanent type of joint and from a functional point of view, it is considered as being immovable. Thus, it is also classified as a synarthrosis. If you contrast radiographic films of a young person with those of an elderly individual (Fig. 9-11*a* and *b*), you will notice that these cartilaginous plates are gradually replaced by bone as growth ceases. As mentioned earlier, this gradual process involving replacement of intervening fibrous tissue or cartilage with bone results in the formation of a synostosis.

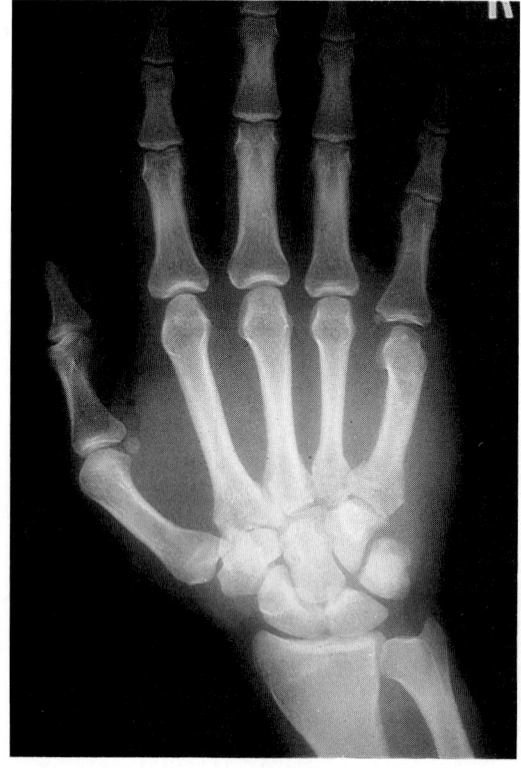

(*a*)

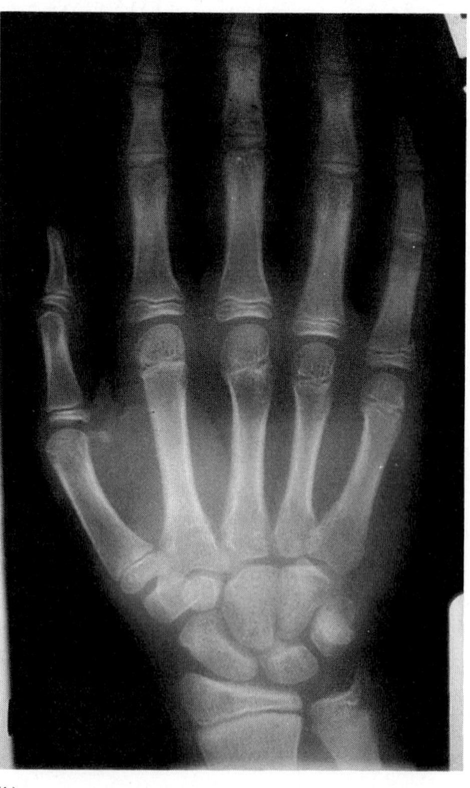

(*b*)

FIGURE 9-11

(*a*) Radiograph (x-ray) of an adult hand. Compare this with (*b*), which is a radiograph of a child's hand. Notice the presence of the epiphyseal plates in the child. These cartilaginous joints are called synchondroses and are eventually replaced by bone. (PhotoEdit.)

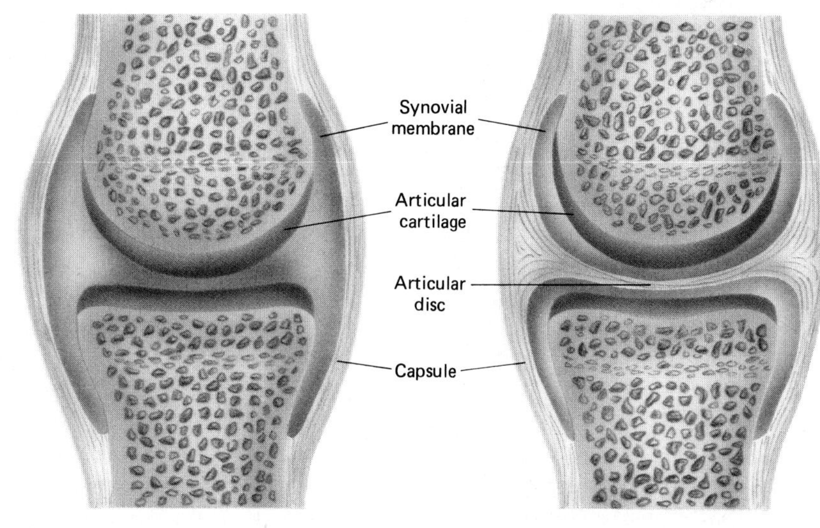

FIGURE 9-12

Schematic representations of the components of a synovial joint. *(a)* Section through a simple synovial joint. *(b)* Section through a synovial joint that contains an articular disc.

SYNOVIAL JOINTS ARE FREELY MOVABLE

The anatomical and physiological characteristics of **synovial joints** are quite different from those of the two preceding types you have encountered, that is, fibrous and cartilaginous. The participating bones of a synovial joint are bound together by a **fibrous capsule** (Fig. 9-12). In addition to the fibrous capsule, we often find ligaments associated with synovial joints. These ligaments may be located outside (Fig. 9-13) of the fibrous capsule or may in fact be found within the same (Fig. 9-13). A space, the **synovial cavity** (Fig. 9-12), surrounds the portions of the bones entering into the formation of this type of joint, and the opposing surfaces are usually covered with a thin layer of hyaline cartilage. This thin covering of cartilage is known as the **articular cartilage** (ar-**tik**-yoo-lar).

In the temporomandibular joint (Fig. 9-14), however, fibrous connective tissue containing small groups of chondrocytes substitutes for hyaline cartilage on the surfaces of the participating bones. The articular cartilage of synovial joints does not serve to bind the bones together as in a syndesmosis, but acts as a friction-reducing interface between the two opposing bony surfaces. The thickness of the articular cartilage varies depending upon location as well as on the age of the individual. For example, as a person ages the articular cartilage tends to become more brittle, thinner, and less cellular. Articular cartilage lacks blood vessels and nerves and its nutrition is believed to be derived in part from the synovial fluid as well as the blood vessels of the marrow spaces.

The fibrous capsule usually surrounds the synovial joint completely. The connective tissue fibers of the capsule impart both strength and flexibility to the joint through their interlacing as well as parallel arrangement. Thus, depending on

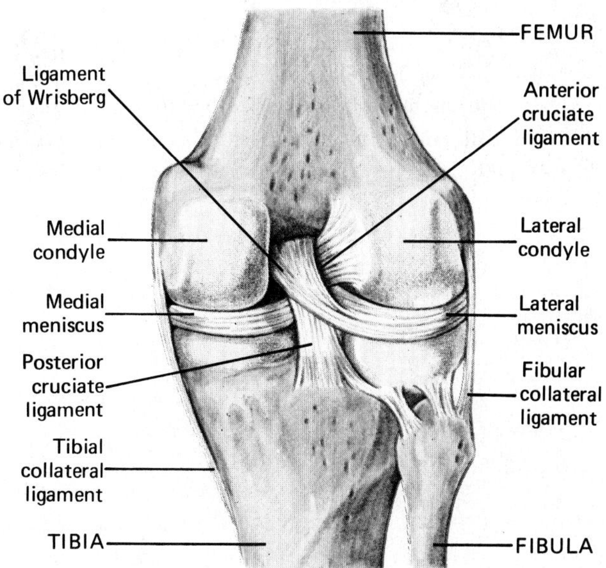

FIGURE 9-13

Posterior view of the knee joint illustrating portions of the anterior and posterior cruciate ligaments. These are ligaments located in an intracapsular position. Notice that the fibular collateral ligament lies in an extracapsular position. Are you able to discern whether this is a right or left knee?

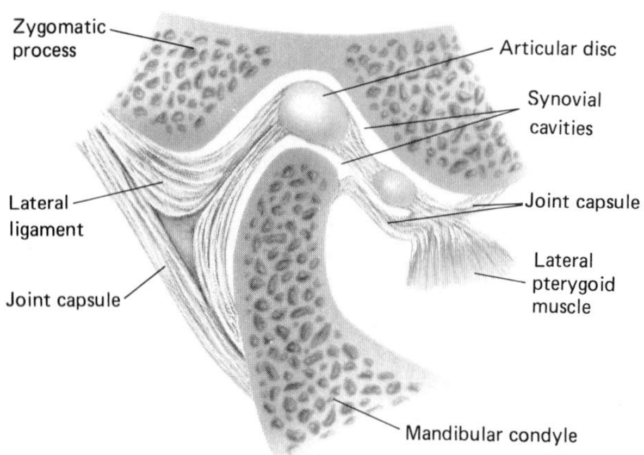

FIGURE 9-14

Section through the temporomandibular joint. Notice that the joint is divided into upper and lower synovial cavities by the presence of the articular disc. Each cavity is lined by a synovial membrane.

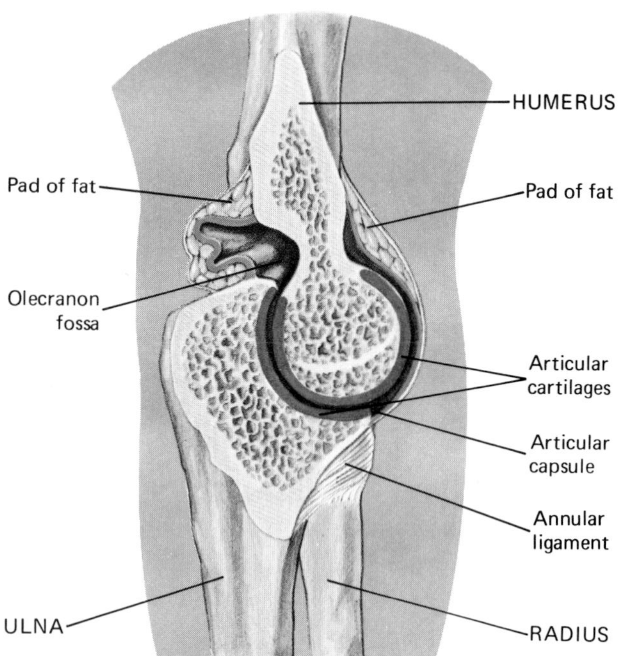

FIGURE 9-15

Sagittal section through the elbow joint. Notice the sac-like extension of the synovial cavity posterior to the olecranon fossa. Although not shown in this figure, the synovial cavity frequently extends onto the surface of the radius after passing beneath the annular ligament.

the specific type of synovial joint, a variable range of motion is permitted while dislocation is resisted by the tensile strength of the capsule. Fibers of the capsule are attached to the periosteum of the participating bones near the boundaries of the articular cartilages. Their precise attachment, however, varies considerably from one synovial joint to another. Blood vessels and nerves also penetrate the fibers of the capsule to reach the joint. Depending on the specific joint, saclike extensions of the synovial membrane may also penetrate the fibrous capsule for varying distances (Fig. 9-15).

Ligaments associated with synovial joints are constructed and arranged so as to limit abnormal or excessive motion of the bones concerned. They are flexible enough to permit the normal range of motion at the joint but strong enough to resist the extremes of such movement, for example, hyperextension of the knee joint. Ligaments of the joint are represented by localized bundles of connective tissue fibers oriented parallel to one another. These specific types of ligaments are generally named according to their location or with respect to their attachment.

Some synovial joints possess *accessory ligaments.* Accessory ligaments are distinct structures and are not mere thickenings of the fibrous capsule. Furthermore, the accessory ligaments may be located in an intracapsular (anterior and posterior cruciate ligaments of the knee; Fig. 9-16) as well as an extracapsular (fibular collateral ligament of the knee; Fig. 9-13) position. Finally, in many instances the fibrous capsule of the synovial joint is reinforced by the presence or expansions of adjacent tendons. An example is the oblique popliteal ligament (Fig. 9-17) of the knee joint, which is a fibrous expansion of the tendon of the semimembranosus muscle.

A thin membranous layer of tissue called the **synovial membrane** lines all of the nonarticular aspects of a synovial joint, including synovial tendon sheaths and bursae that may communicate with the joint cavity (Fig. 9-15). The synovial membrane produces the **synovial fluid,** which has nutritive as well as friction-reducing properties. This membrane lines the inner aspect of the fibrous capsule and is closely applied to the nonarticular surfaces of bones within the joint. It also envelops any ligaments or tendons that happen to be located in an intracapsular position. The synovial membrane, however, is not present on the articular cartilages. In certain synovial joints accumulations of adipose tissue occur within the synovial membrane and these are termed *articular fat pads* (Fig. 9-15). These are thought to increase the surface area of the synovial membrane, thereby facilitating the distribution of synovial fluid throughout the joint cavity.

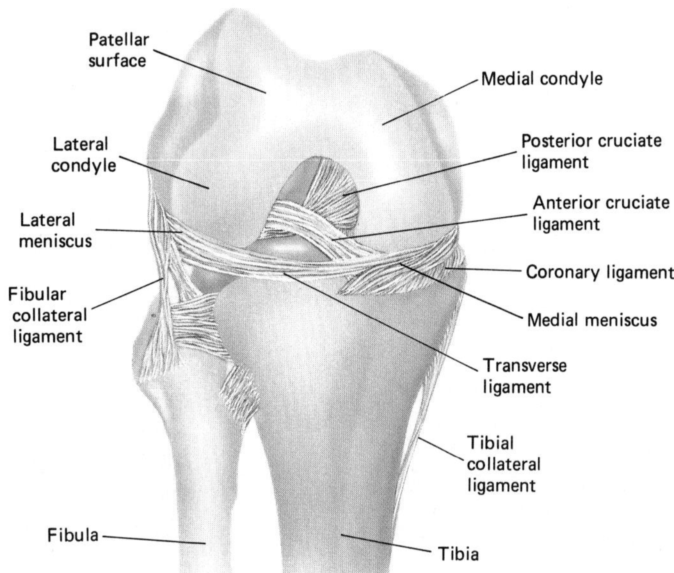

FIGURE 9-16

Anterior aspect of the knee joint with the patella (knee cap) removed. Notice portions of two intracapsular ligaments, the anterior and posterior cruciate ligaments. The fibular collateral ligament is located in an extracapsular position. Are you able to discern whether this is a right or left knee?

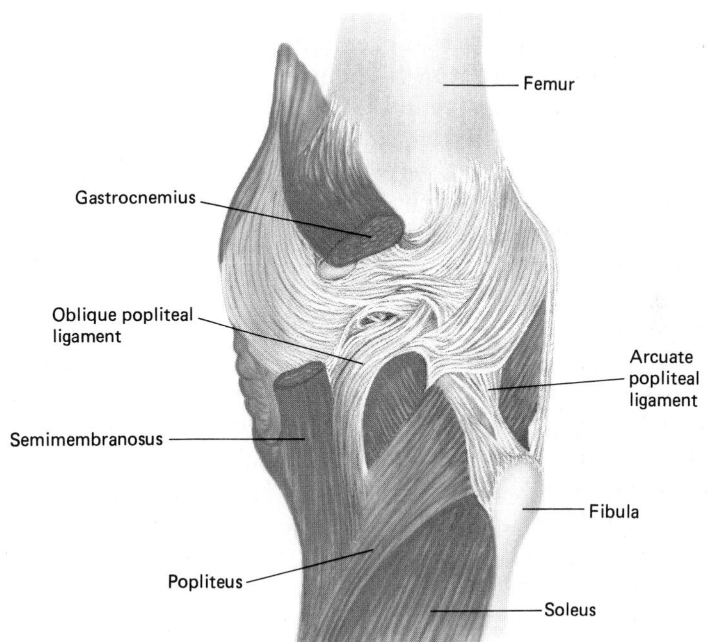

FIGURE 9-17

Posterior aspect of the right knee illustrating the oblique popliteal ligament. This structure is actually the fibrous expansion of the tendon of the semimembranous muscle.

Synovial fluid is a generally viscous fluid that has a clear or pale yellow tint to it. It contains a number of cell types and its volume is variable from joint to joint, although even from the knee joint it is possible to remove only about 500 microliters of fluid under normal conditions. Cell types ordinarily found in the synovial fluid include macrophages, free synovial cells, and various white blood cells, e.g., lymphocytes and polymorphonuclear leukocytes.

Synovial fluid is derived from plasma and contains significant amounts of a mucopolysaccharide, hyaluronic acid. It is thought that the viscosity or plasticity of synovial fluid stems mainly from the presence of the hyaluronic acid. Viscosity of the fluid ordinarily decreases with increasing movement of the joint. The hyaluronic acid found in synovial fluid is currently believed to be produced and elaborated by specific cell types of the synovial membrane known as A

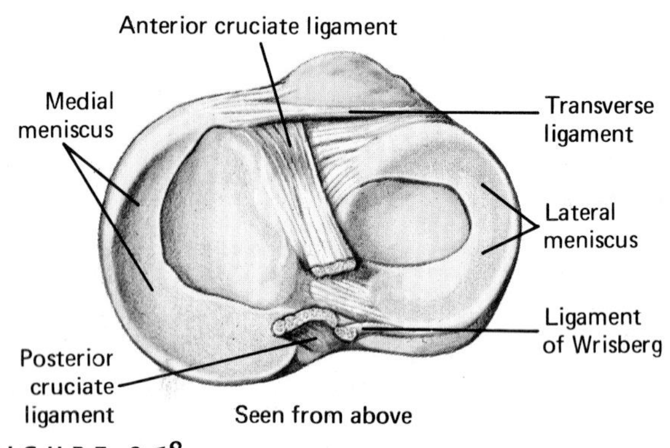

FIGURE 9-18

Superior aspect of the menisci of the right knee joint. Notice also the attachments of the anterior and posterior cruciate ligaments.

cells. The A cells also possess considerable phagocytic activity and are in part responsible for removal of debris and infectious organisms that may accumulate within the joint.

An additional structure found in certain types of synovial joints is called a **meniscus** (meh-**nis**-kus), or **articular disc** (Figs. 9-18 and 9-19). Menisci consist predominantly of fibrocartilage and are found where the articular surfaces of the participating bones lack congruity (coincident throughout). Thus, they add to the stability of the joint. They also may divide a joint cavity into two completely separate compartments, each with its own synovial membrane. At their peripheral boundaries they may be attached to the fibrous capsule of the joint. Although the precise functional role of menisci is not known, several functions other than stability have been proposed. These include facilitation of the spread of synovial fluid, protective action for the peripheral margins of articular cartilages, and shock absorption. It is probable that the articular discs contribute to several of these functions.

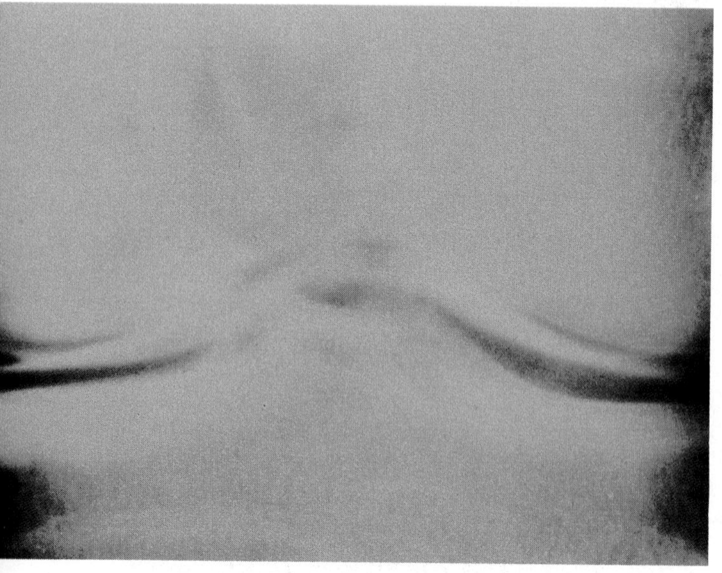

FIGURE 9-19

Radiograph (x-ray) of the human knee illustrating the presence of a torn medial meniscus. (SIU and Visuals Unlimited).

Synovial joints are frequently classified by their shape

Several methods, all with varying degrees of complexity, have been employed in the classification of synovial joints. Synovial joints may be described as being *simple, compound,* or *complex.* A simple synovial joint has only two articulating surfaces. An example is the distal interphalangeal joint (Fig. 9-11*a*). In a compound synovial joint there are more than two articulating surfaces. An example of a compound type is the elbow joint (Fig. 9-15). Here the distal extremity of the humerus articulates with the radius and the ulna. In addition, within the same fibrous articular capsule, the radius and ulna articulate with one another. If an articular disc, or meniscus, is present within the joint (Figs. 9-18 and 9-19), the joint is designated as the complex type.

Motion about one, two, or three perpendicular axes is also employed as a means for classifying synovial joints. Hence, a joint with movement about a single axis is called *uniaxial.* One that permits independent movement about two perpendicular axes is termed *biaxial.* Finally, when three axes of movement are involved together with all possible intermediate movements as in the shoulder joint, we classify the joint as the *multiaxial* type.

The shape of the different synovial joints, however, has been the most widely used criterion for the basis of their classification. Synovial joints are subdivided into seven different types. Some of these are quite distinct from each other, whereas others may represent variations of one type or another.

Flat articular surfaces characterize plane, or gliding, joints

In the **plane,** or **gliding,** type of synovial joint the participating bones possess rather flat surfaces for the purpose of articulation. This type of joint is biaxial, in that movement is ordinarily permitted about two axes, that is, slight gliding motions in a single plane but at right angles to each other. The intermetatarsal joints represent plane joints as do certain of the intercarpal and intertarsal joints (Figs. 9-11*a*). Movement in other directions is resisted by the presence of short, taut ligaments, as well as the close proximity of adjacent bones.

Ginglymus, or hinge, joints are typically uniaxial

This type of synovial joint is uniaxial. Motion permitted is usually that of flexion and extension within a single plane. In this type of joint, collateral ligaments usually provide additional stability. Typical examples of the **ginglymus** (**gin**-gli-mus), or **hinge,** joint include the humeroulnar aspect of the elbow joint, the interphalangeal joints, and the talocrural (tah-low-**kroo**-ruhl), or ankle, joint (Fig. 9-15).

Rotation typically occurs at trochoid, or pivot, joints

As you move your head from side to side or alternately pronate and supinate your palms, you will have utilized synovial joints of the **trochoid** (**trow**-koid), or **pivot,** type. These joints are uniaxial in that they permit movement, in this case rotation, about a single axis. The joint is characterized by a "pivotal" component and a "ringlike" component. The *dens,* a projection of the axis vertebra, represents the pivot aspect of the atlantoaxial joint (Fig. 9-20), and the ringlike aspect is formed by the anterior body of the atlas and its transverse ligament.

The proximal radioulnar articulation of the elbow joint is also classified as a trochoid, or pivot, joint. Here, the head of the radius is permitted to rotate within the ringlike structure formed by the *annular ligament* and the radial notch on the ulna (Fig. 9-15). If you examine these two joints just mentioned you will find that in one instance (radioulnar joint) the pivot rotates

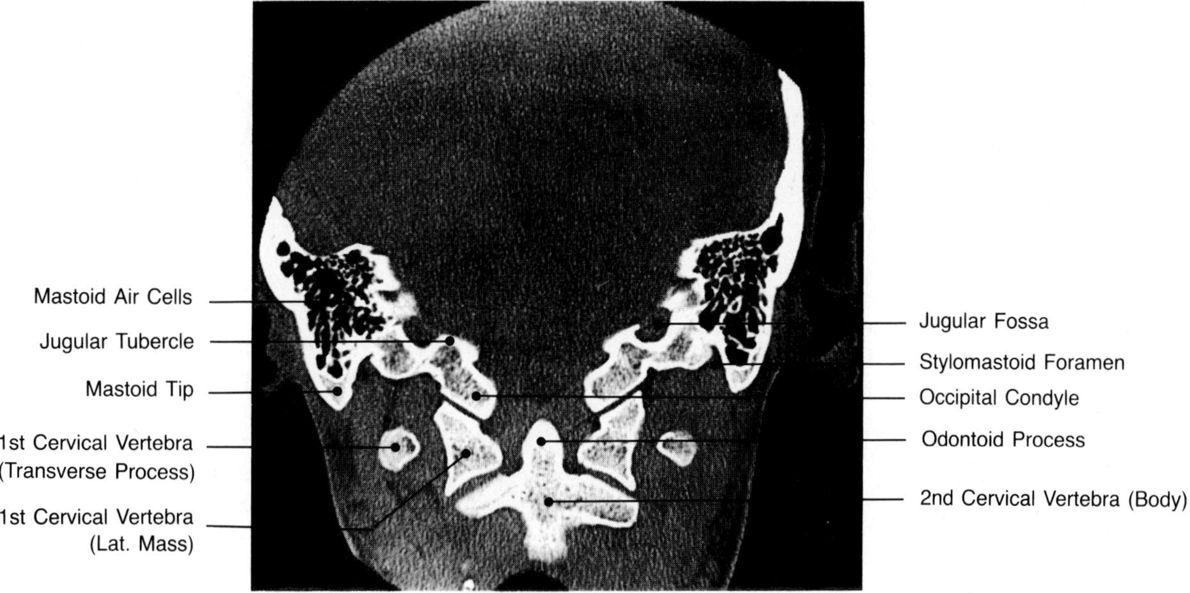

FIGURE 9-20

Scan illustrating a coronal section through the base of the skull. Notice the articulations between the occipital bone and the atlas, and between the atlas and axis. The odontoid (dens) process of the axis forms the pivotal portion of the atlantoaxial joint. (From Christoforidis, A. J., *Atlas of Axial, Sagittal and Coronal Anatomy with CT and MRI,* W. B. Saunders, Philadelphia, 1988.)

with the ring and in the other (atlantoaxial joint) the ring rotates around the pivot.

Condylar joints permit biaxial movement

Condylar joints (**kon**-di-lar) are for the most part biaxial with regard to movements they permit. Although there is usually a primary plane of motion consisting of flexion and extension, there is ordinarily some degree of rotation that is also permissible in a plane set at ninety degrees to the former. The movement between the femoral condyles and the tibia at the knee is representative of the condylar type of synovial joint, as is the temporomandibular joint (Fig. 9-14).

Ellipsoid joints permit movement about two axes set at right angles to one another

Ellipsoid joints (ee-**lip**-soyd) are biaxial and characterized by the articulation of an oval, convex surface of one bone with the concave depression in another. The radiocarpal joint (Fig. 9-11*a*) at the wrist and the metacarpophalangeal joints are all examples of the ellipsoid type. Movements that are permitted include flexion-extension and abduction-adduction, that is, motion along two axes set at right angles to each other. Any movement along a third axis, for example, rotation, is resisted not only by adjacent ligaments but by the shapes of the articulating bones themselves.

A saddle joint permits opposition of the thumb

The **saddle joint** is also biaxial and is most frequently discussed in terms of the carpometacarpal joint of the thumb (Fig. 9-11*a*). Examination of the saddle joint reveals that it is a mere variation of the ellipsoid type, although it generally permits greater flexibility in movement than does the latter. In the carpometacarpal joint of the thumb the fibrous capsule is quite thick, but also loose, and therefore facilitates movement here. There are three accessory ligaments associated with this joint between the trapezium and metacarpal of the thumb. The primary movement permitted at the carpometacarpal joint of the thumb is one of back-and-forth and side-to-side. However, there exists an ever-so-slight amount of dependent rotation that goes along with the combined primary movements. Since this rotation cannot occur independently of the other movements, the joint remains classified as biaxial. The primary movements together with the slight rotation do make it possible, though, for opposition of the thumb to take place.

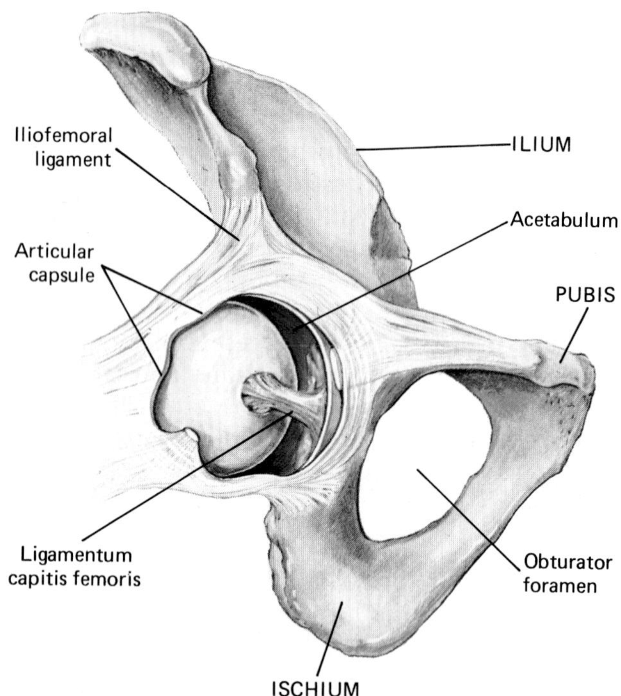

FIGURE 9-21

The fibrous capsule of the right hip joint has been opened to expose some of its internal features. The ligamentum capitis femoris is also called the ligamentum teres femoris or the round ligament of the femoral head.

Spheroid joints permit the widest range of motion

The hip joint (Fig. 9-21) and the shoulder joint (Fig. 9-22) are examples of the **spheroid,** or **ball-and-socket, type** of synovial joint. Each of these involves the large rounded head of one bone and a concavity or cuplike depression on another. In the hip joint, for example, the head of the femur fits into a cuplike cavity in the hipbone called the *acetabulum* (Fig. 9-21). Spheroid joints are multiaxial; that is, they permit movement along three separate axes. Movements are those of flexion-extension, abduction-adduction, and rotation.

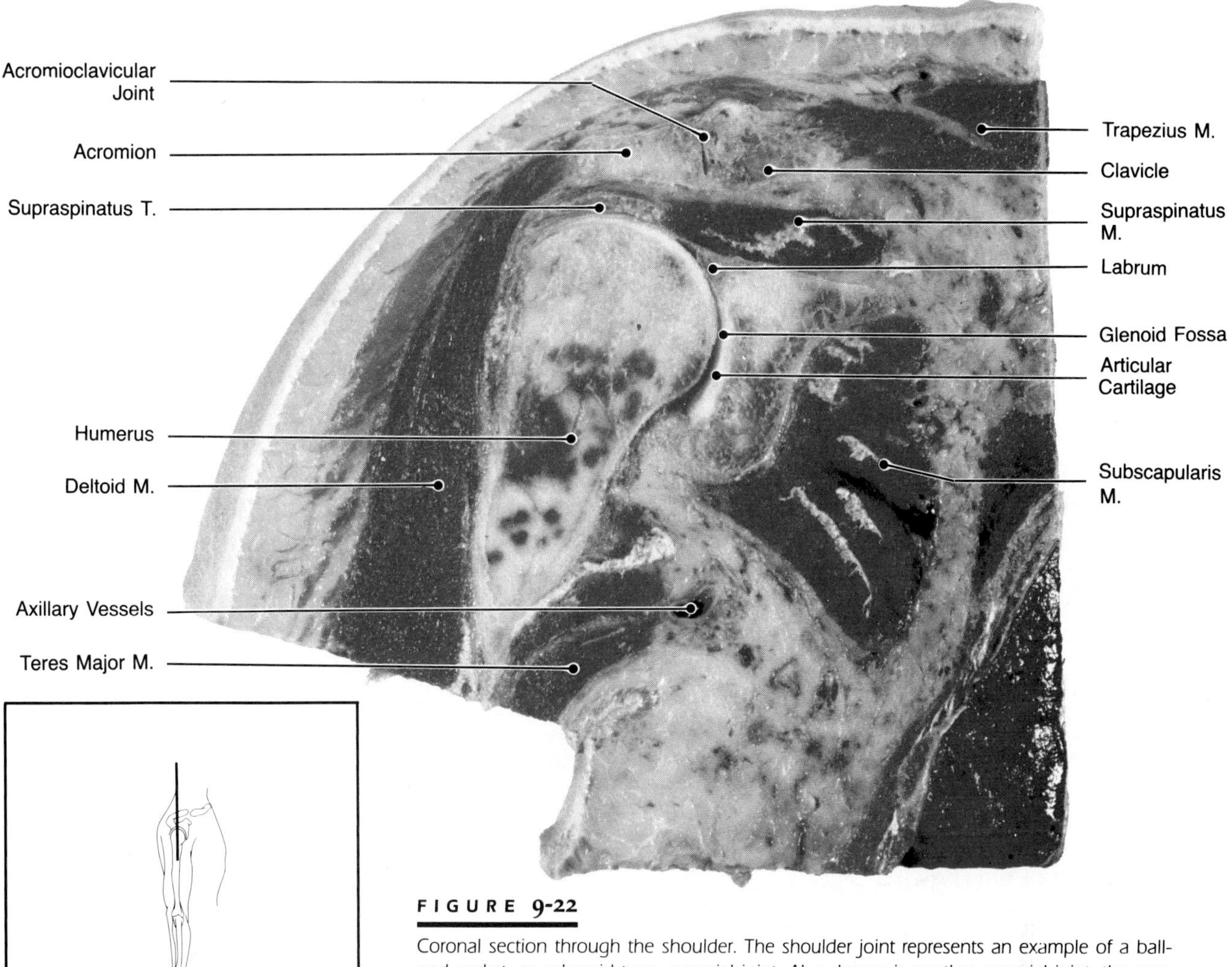

FIGURE 9-22

Coronal section through the shoulder. The shoulder joint represents an example of a ball-and-socket, or spheroid type, synovial joint. Also shown is another synovial joint, the acromioclavicular joint. The latter is of the plane, or gliding, type. (From Christoforidis, A. J., *Atlas of Axial, Sagittal and Coronal Anatomy with CT and MRI,* 1988 (W. B. Saunders, Philadelphia).)

Four types of motion are produced at synovial joints

We generally consider the movements permitted by synovial joints as being of four basic types. These are: *gliding, angular, circumduction,* and *rotation.* Thus far you have reviewed the specific types of joints that allow these kinds of movement. It should be evident by now that these four basic motions are frequently combined to produce an infinite variety of bodily movements. These are illustrated for you in Focus on Body Movement and will be described further below.

Flexion is an angular movement

Flexion is an angular movement that results in the reduction of the angle between the adjoining bones. If you try to touch the tip of your shoulder with your index finger you will have flexed your forearm at the elbow joint. When you squat to pick up an item you've dropped on the floor your knees will flex while doing so.

Extension is essentially the opposite of flexion

Extension is also an angular movement and is basically the opposite of flexion; that is, it is a movement that increases the angle between adjoining bones. When you bend your head forward as in prayer your neck is flexed, and as it is raised to the upright position extension occurs. If you continue to move a joint past its normal limit of extension then *hyperextension* occurs. Hyperextension of the elbow, knee, and cervical spine (as in "whiplash" injury) is a common cause of joint trauma.

Abduction represents motion away from the median plane

This type of angular movement is typically described as that which occurs in a direction away from the median plane of the body. Standing erect and lifting your right lower limb off the floor in a lateral direction is an example of **abduction** at the hip joint. Abduction also occurs with respect to the digits; however, the plane of reference for the movement is different. In the case of the fingers, the midline of the middle digit serves as the reference point and abduction is movement away from this point. Abduction of the toes is carried out with the midline of the second toe representing the point of reference for the movement.

Angular motion toward the median plane is called adduction

Adduction is the opposite of abduction. In this instance the direction of movement is toward the median plane of the body. With respect to the lower limb in the example cited above for abduction, this would simply mean the return of the limb to the anatomical position such that the foot

FOCUS ON . . . Body movements

Circumduction: A combination of movements that makes a body part describe a circle.

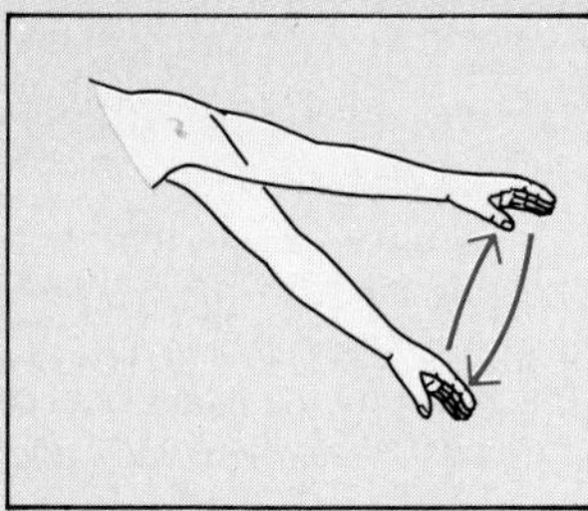

Rotation: The pivoting of a body part around its axis, as in shaking the head. No rotation of any body part is complete (i.e., 360 degrees).

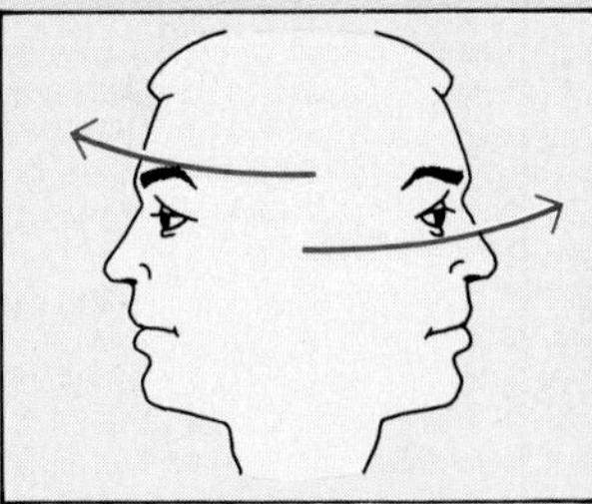

Pronation: A movement of the forearm that in the extended position brings the palm of the hand to a downward position. Applies only to the forearm.

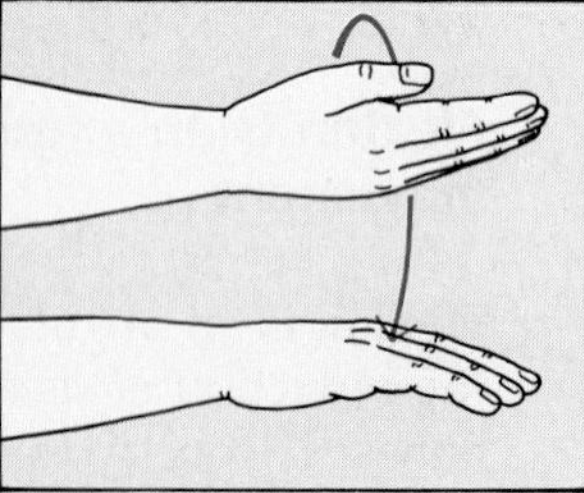

Supination: The opposite of pronation. When the forearm is in the extended position, this movement brings the palm of the hand upward.

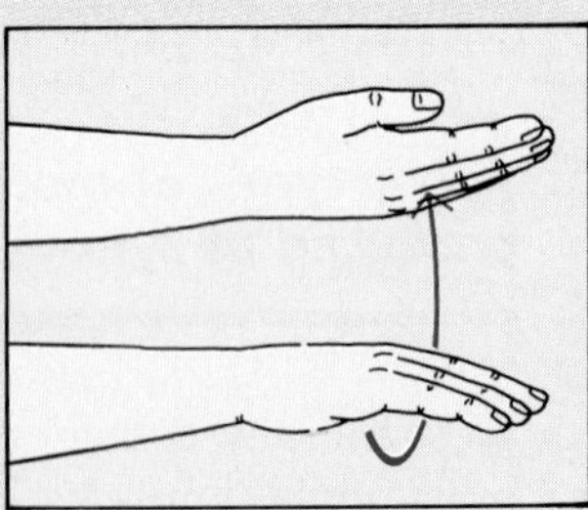

Flexion: The bending of a joint; usually a movement that reduces the angle that two movably articulated bones make with each other. When one crouches, the knees are flexed.

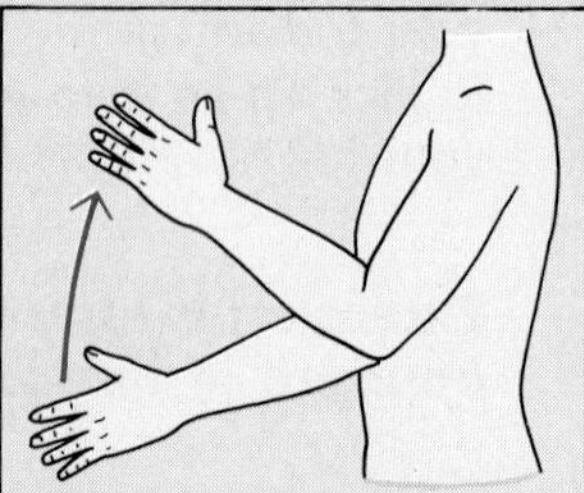

Extension: The opposite of flexion, it increases the angle between two movably articulated bones, usually to a 180-degree maximum. If the angle of extension exceeds 180 degrees (as is possible when throwing back the head), this action is termed hyperextension.

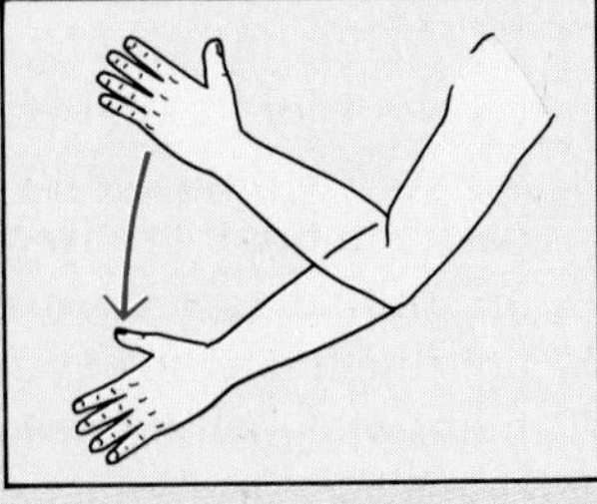

would again rest upon the floor. Likewise, the point of reference for adduction of the digits is the same as for abduction.

Pronation and supination are movements of the forearm and hand

In the anatomical position the palms of the hands are directed forward or anteriorly. **Pronation** of the forearm occurs when you turn the palms so that they face posteriorly. Turning the palms of the hands so that they again are directed anteriorly involves **supination** of the forearm. When the forearm is flexed at the elbow, pronation and supination involves turning of the palms of the hands so that they face downward and upward, respectively.

Inversion and eversion refer to movements of the foot

Commonly these types of movement are ascribed to the ankle joint; however, strictly speaking this is not the case. The two joints that permit the movements of **inversion** and **eversion** of the foot to occur are the (a) *subtalar joint* and the (b) *talocalcaneonavicular joint.* During inversion the medial border of the foot is elevated so that the sole (plantar aspect) of the foot is directed medially. Tension developing in the peroneal muscles, located on the lateral side of the leg, is a chief factor in limiting this movement. Eversion involves elevation of the lateral border of the foot such that the sole of the foot is directed laterally. This movement is limited in part by tension in the tibialis anterior and tibialis posterior muscles. Eversion has a much more restricted range of motion than does inversion.

Inversion: An ankle movement that turns the sole of the foot medially. Applies only to the foot.

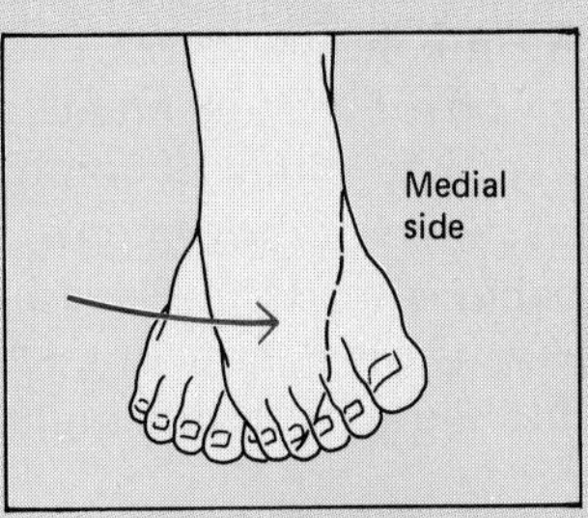

Eversion: The opposite of inversion. It turns the sole of the foot laterally.

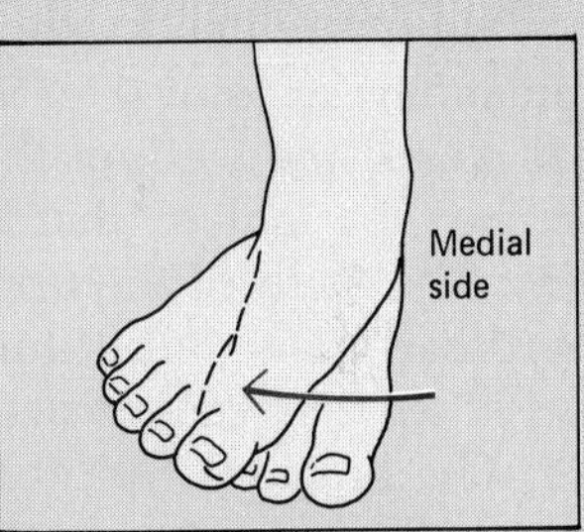

Protraction: The protrusion of some body part, e.g., the lower jaw.

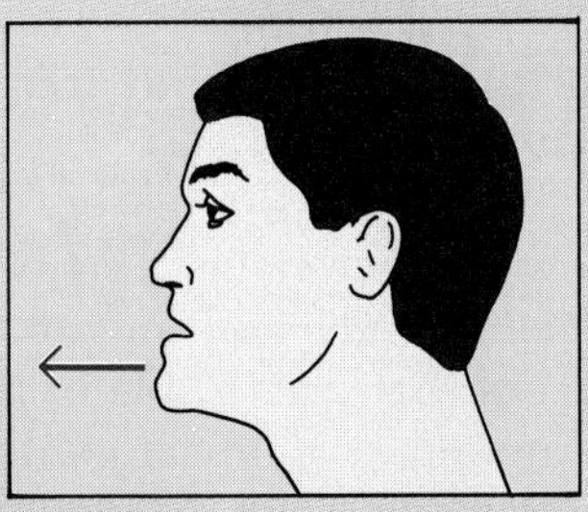

Retraction: The opposite of protraction.

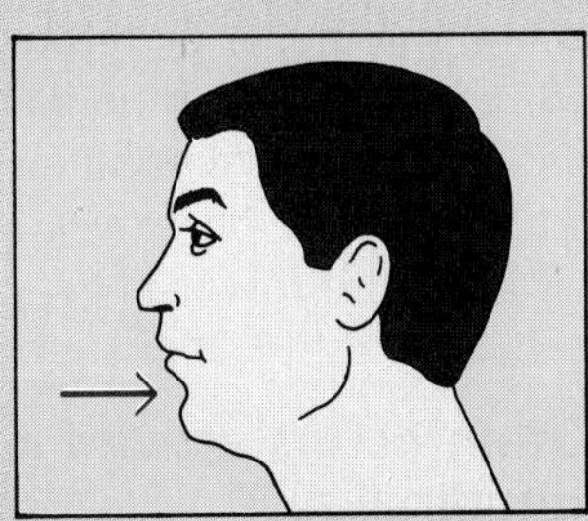

Abduction: A movement of a bone or limb away from the median plane of the body. Abduction in the hands and feet is the movement of a digit away from the central axis of the limb. One abducts the fingers by spreading them apart.

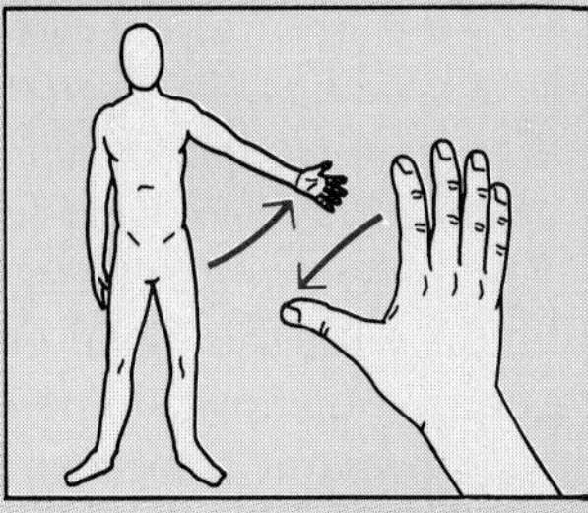

Adduction: The opposite of abduction, involving approach to the median plane of the body or, in the case of the limbs, to the central axis of a limb.

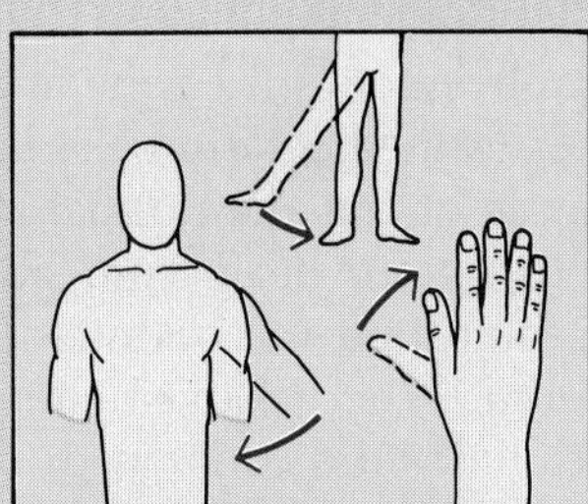

Dorsiflexion and plantar-flexion are movements of the ankle joint

Dorsiflexion and **plantar-flexion** are movements unique to the *ankle* or *talocrural joint.* During dorsiflexion the angle between the dorsum of the foot and the anterior surface of the leg is reduced. Dorsiflexion is limited by tension in the Achilles tendon (tendo calcaneus) as well as by various ligaments. Rupture of the Achilles tendon may result when dorsiflexion occurs abruptly or when the movement is carried past the range of motion of the joint. The opposite movement, plantar-flexion, increases this angle as the heel is raised and the toes are pointed downward. Plantar-flexion is limited by tension in muscles of the anterior compartment of the leg in addition to the presence of several ligaments.

The temporomandibular joint exhibits protraction and retraction

The classical example of these types of movements is represented by the mandible at the temporomandibular joint (Fig. 9-14). When the lower jaw is closed the teeth of the mandible and maxilla come into contact, that is, the position of *occlusion.* The teeth of the upper and lower jaws are not ordinarily in contact during the position of rest. Rather they remain separated from one another. The process of protruding or thrusting your mandible forward is termed **protraction.** The reverse movement, or **retraction,** involves the drawing of the mandible backward to the position of rest. Other movements associated with the mandible include *depression* (opening) and *elevation* (closing) of the lower jaw.

Rotation occurs around a longitudinal axis

The movement of a bone around its longitudinal axis is termed **rotation.** Earlier we provided the example of the atlantoaxial joint (Fig. 9-20). As you turn your head from side to side the atlas rotates around the odontoid process of the axis vertebra. Where movements of the upper and lower limbs are concerned, rotation can occur in either the lateral or medial direction. For example, turning of the anterior surface of the thigh laterally is defined as lateral (external) rotation whereas turning it so that it faces medially is called medial (internal) rotation.

Circumduction is a combination of individual movements

Circumduction represents a composite of the individual movements of flexion, extension, abduction, adduction, and rotation. It is best exemplified by moving your outstretched arm in a circle. In doing so your outstretched limb circumscribes an imaginary cone in the air. The apex of the cone is represented by the joint between the scapula and humeral head, while the base is traced out by your hand.

Only the thumb may be opposed

The type of movement called **opposition** is unique to the thumb. You can easily demonstrate opposition by grasping a small object between your thumb and index finger. This form of movement involves rotation in addition to adduction. Each of these movements of the thumb is produced by a different combination of muscles. The total range of movements of which the thumb is capable is made possible by the interaction of several muscles contracting simultaneously, as in twiddling (circumducting) the thumbs, for example.

Various factors limit joint movement

Now that we have described for you the various types of body movements, let us discuss those factors that play a role in limiting the movement permitted at synovial joints. Briefly, the four features responsible for limiting movement at a synovial joint are: (a) *the shapes of the bones involved in the articulation,* (b) *the tension of the associated ligaments,* (c) *apposition of soft tissue structures upon movement at the joint, and* (d) *muscle tension.*

The olecranon process of the ulna and its articulation with the distal end of the humerus is an example of how shape of the bones involved helps to prevent hyperextension of the elbow joint. Fracture of the olecranon process may occur during rapid and forced hyperextension at the elbow joint. Full tension is not achieved in the ligaments associated with the knee joint until the leg is extended at the knee. Their tension is reduced during flexion of the leg at the knee when the articular surfaces of the tibia and femur do not require the same degree of contact as they do during extension.

Restricted movement that is brought about by the opposing surfaces of soft tissue parts is evident as you flex your leg at the knee. Note that the surface of your calf is brought into contact with the posterior aspect of your thigh. A similar situation occurs between the forearm and arm as one flexes the forearm at the elbow joint.

That muscle tension is likewise involved in the restriction of movements at joints is evidenced by the following example. Stand erect and attempt to flex your thigh at the hip joint with your knee in the flexed position. You will notice that this is easily accomplished and you can actually bring the anterior surface of your thigh into direct contact with your anterior body wall. On the other hand, attempt to flex your thigh at the hip joint with your leg extended at the knee. Unless you are in superb physical condition (preferably an All-Pro punter) you will encounter a fair amount of difficulty since tension in the posterior muscle of the thigh (hamstrings) tends to restrict this movement. All of these factors are of considerable importance for a comprehensive understanding of joint movements.

Joints are innervated by nerves supplying muscles responsible for their movement

A rather obvious consideration, but one that is often neglected, is the manner in which joints are innervated. In order to develop a thorough understanding of normal joint function, a knowledge of joint innervation is essential. Such knowledge will also strengthen your appreciation for the pathways concerning the development of pain subsequent to joint inflammatory disorders and traumatic injury.

The general principle involved here is that the nerves that supply a movable joint are derived from the same nerves that innervate the muscles responsible for movement at that joint. This makes sense in that this type of organization lends itself to the establishment of neuronal reflex pathways that play an important role not only in the production of active movement at the joint, but in the maintenance of posture as well. Nerves that innervate the fibrous capsule of a joint are usually distributed to rather defined regions of the capsule. However, experience tells us that there is a considerable degree of overlap in such distribution between adjacent nerves.

Free nerve endings are abundant at the peripheral margins of the joint capsule and at the sites of ligament attachment. Such endings are believed to be responsible for the transmission of impulses associated with pain. These pain fibers usually end in the smooth muscle of blood vessel walls. Other types of nerve endings found within the joint capsule include Ruffini end organs, pacinian corpuscles, and those that resemble Golgi tendon organs (see Chapter 17; Sense Organs).

The manner in which the synovial membrane is innervated differs considerably from that of the fibrous capsule and, for all practical purposes, it is generally considered as being rather insensitive to pain. With the exception of relatively few free nerve endings the synovial membrane lacks the other specialized end organs mentioned above in regard to the joint capsule. Free nerve endings that are present in the synovial membrane, however, are also associated with the smooth muscle of the local blood vessels.

Most bones function as levers

There would be no reason to have movable joints at all except for the fact that the joints permit movement by acting as fulcra for levers. Most bones act as levers and the action they bring about is in a large way dependent upon the nature of their joints and the way the muscles that move them are attached. A joint therefore represents a fixed point or **fulcrum** about which the lever will be permitted to move. The bone(s) that moves at the joint will have two forces acting upon it. One **force** is generated by the contraction of muscle necessary to move the joint in a predetermined plane. The other force is simply one of **resistance** to such ensuing movement. Positioning of the fulcrum, resistance, and force necessary to overcome the resistance form the basis for the classification of levers. Focus on Figure 9-23 and notice that three basic types of levers are illustrated by examples taken from the human body.

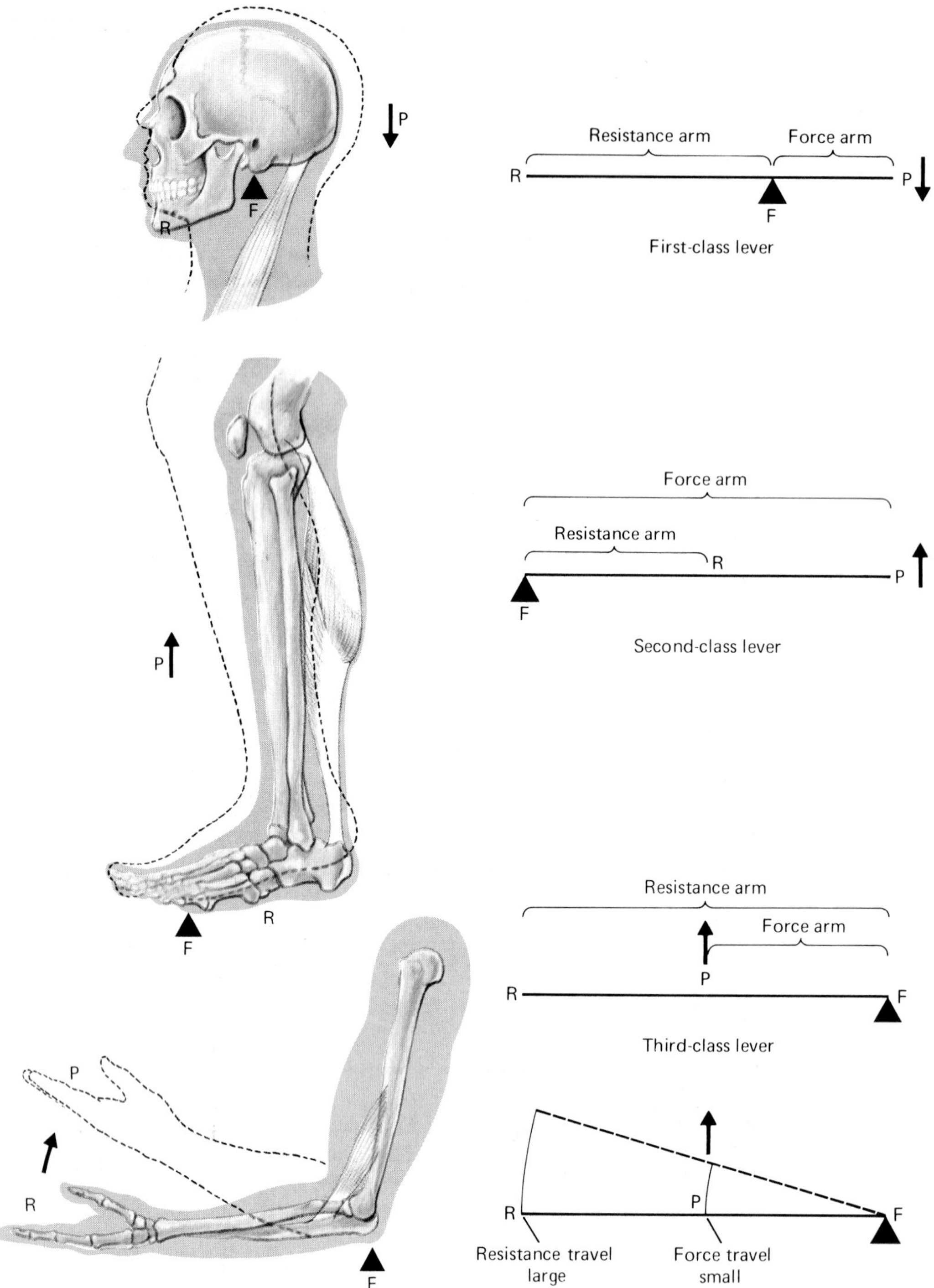

FIGURE 9-23

Classes of levers. The majority of joints in the human body represent levers of the third-class category. In this instance, the mechanical advantage is sacrificed in favor of greater distance of movement.

First-class levers have the fulcrum placed between the resistance and the force

The fulcrum of a **first-class lever** is located between the resistance and the force generated to overcome the resistance. An example of a first-class lever is the contraction of neck muscles used to raise the head from the bowed to the upright position. In this instance the fulcrum is represented by the atlanto-occipital joint and the resistance by the weight of the bowed head.

Second-class levers have resistance between the fulcrum and the force

In a **second-class lever** the resistance is located between the fulcrum and the force generated to overcome the resistance. You can demonstrate a second-class lever by raising up on your toes. The metatarsal-phalangeal joints (especially that of the great toe) provide the fulcrum for this lever. The weight of the erect body is directed downward to a point just in front of the ankle joint and therefore represents the resistance to be overcome. Contraction of the gastrocnemius (calf) muscles provides the force needed to move the weight of the body at the fulcrum. Other examples of second-class levers in the human body are rare.

The force is located between the fulcrum and resistance in third-class levers

This type of lever is the most common form represented in the body. In the **third-class lever** we find the resistance at one end of the lever and the fulcrum at the other end. The force generated to overcome the resistance is located between that resistance and the fulcrum. Contraction of the iliopsoas (iliacus and psoas major muscles) muscle to produce flexion of the thigh at the hip joint is a good example. Here the weight of the thigh constitutes the resistance while the hip joint represents the fulcrum. The force of the contracting iliopsoas muscle lies between these two and as it overcomes the resistance it draws the anterior thigh toward the ventral body wall in flexion.

In general the arrangement of third-class levers in the body sacrifices force for distance traveled; that is, the resistance can usually be moved through a considerable range. However, it requires a much greater force to move the resistance. The biceps brachii muscle can contract only a few inches, yet the forearm and hand travel over a much greater distance. In the lower limb the muscles of the thigh insert relatively close to the fulcrum represented by the knee joint and as such they must be powerful indeed to generate any substantial force with regard to the foot and leg. The mechanical arrangement of the entire lower limb permits us to take long steps, but its reverse mechanical advantage requires powerful muscles of the thigh and hip regions. The femur serves as an attachment for muscles responsible for moving the leg at the knee. Additionally the femur is a site for attachment of muscles of the pelvic region that move the lower limb as a whole or flex the trunk at the hip when the lower limb is fixed.

It has been said that the human body is built for speed rather than for power. The reverse mechanical advantage of the lower limbs permits us to run relatively fast. This property is enhanced by the angles of attachment of most of the leg and thigh muscles, which are usually of an oblique nature. This particular arrangement permits a relatively small change in length to produce a major movement of the bones and therefore of the limb as a whole. Obviously, an organism should be able to cover more ground at a faster rate if its strides are longer.

Dislocation and inflammation represent the major forms of joint disorders

The major disabilities to which joints are subject are **dislocation** and **inflammation.** Dislocations may involve several types of damage, depending on the kind and direction of the destructive mechanical force to which the joint has been subjected. Displacement of a bone from its joint can be accompanied by injury to ligaments, tendons, and the fibrous joint capsule. In general, dislocations are most easily treated when damage to these structures has been minimal. Effective dislocation repair, even in the presence of some ligament damage, can be achieved by immobilizing the injured joint in a cast.

Because the epiphyses of long bones participate in the synovial joints of those bones, the soft cartilaginous epiphyses of children make them particularly vulnerable to epiphyseal fractures. Furthermore, their relatively soft, elastic ligaments also predispose them to joint dislocation. A parent who is eager to reach the top of a set of stairs with a young child will often exert a strong pull on the child's arm and literally lift him by this single, outstretched limb. Such an action can be quite painful for the child, and the elbow will frequently dislocate.

Inflammatory involvement of a joint is known as **arthritis.** Different forms of arthritis exist and their classification is dependent upon several criteria. These include: (1) precise cause of the inflammation, (2) the specific joint(s) involved, and

(3) whether the onset of the inflammation is of an *acute* or *chronic* nature.

ARTHRITIS MAY RESULT FROM INFECTION

Although any joint may be involved in **infectious arthritis,** certain ones are affected more often than others. The joints that are commonly involved include the knee, hip, ankle, elbow, wrist, and shoulder. This form of arthritis usually results from the direct invasion of the joint by an infectious organism. This invasion may be the direct result of trauma or the joint may be seeded via the blood by organisms arising from localized infection elsewhere in the body.

Early in the course of the disease, the synovial membrane becomes edematous (swollen due to excess fluid) and the synovial fluid takes on a cloudy appearance with some neutrophils (a type of white blood cell) being present in an aspirated sample. As the condition worsens the synovial membrane becomes progressively more inflamed and the synovial fluid is transformed into a thickened, characteristic puslike material. If not attended to promptly, the inflammatory process may extend to the articular cartilage of the joint. Failure to recognize and treat this form of arthritis can ultimately lead to destruction of the joint surfaces, severe scarring, and calcification within the joint. Mobility of the affected joint could be severely restricted if these processes are permitted to occur.

BIOCHEMICAL ABNORMALITIES MAY LEAD TO JOINT INFLAMMATION

Gout is a systemic disorder of *uric acid metabolism*. It may occur naturally or as the result of treatment with certain pharmaceutical agents. One characteristic feature of gout is the acute and chronic involvement of the joints. The chronic form of gout is characterized by the deposition of uric acid crystals on the articular surfaces of joints and by the formation of **tophi** (**toe**-fye) in the fibrous capsule and other connective tissue structures near the joint. A tophus consists of a core of uric acid crystals surrounded by cells typical of an inflammatory response. Tophi may also be found in the valves of the heart, the ear lobes, and the kidneys.

Clinical highlight

If the disease is left untreated, the tophi associated with the articular cartilage may expand, coalesce, and eventually erode the entire articular surface. Treatment of gout can frequently be carried out with dietary management alone which minimizes the intake of purines (precursors of uric acid). In other instances drugs may be required that mobilize deposits of tophi, abort acute attacks of arthritis, or inhibit the synthesis of uric acid.

THE MOST COMMON FORM OF JOINT INFLAMMATORY DISEASE IS OSTEOARTHRITIS

This disorder has a long and insidious pathogenesis. Although **osteoarthritis** is the most common form of arthritis (affecting more than 40 million people in the United States alone), to date there is no known cure or method for completely arresting the disease. In actuality it is a degenerative disease and not one characterized by inflammation. In osteoarthritis the articular cartilage deteriorates and becomes eroded, and new bone in the form of "spurs" is formed at its periphery. Initially small fissures and fractures occur in the articular cartilage. This is followed by exposure of the underlying bone. Cartilaginous projections then develop along the margins of the degenerating articular cartilage and these eventually undergo ossification. Some of these may break off and, together with small pieces of degenerating cartilage, lie free within the synovial cavity. They are then known as "joint mice."

Clinical highlight

Aging, together with its cumulative stress and trauma, seems to be the most significant contributing factor to the development of osteoarthritis. In the aged individual, there is apparently a reduced amount of chondroitin sulfate present within the matrix of articular cartilage. Some investigators suspect that this may somehow be involved with the pathogenesis of the disease. The precise contribution of this paucity of chondroitin sulfate to the disease process and whether the reduction is the result of decreased synthesis or increased degradation are not known at the present time.

AUTOIMMUNITY IS MOST LIKELY THE BASIS FOR RHEUMATOID ARTHRITIS

Rheumatoid arthritis is a chronic, generalized inflammation of many body tissues that affects the joints in particular. Although its precise cause is unknown, there exists a substantial amount of data that suggest that the disease has an immunological basis, that is, one of autoimmunity. It is closely related to *systemic lupus erythematosus (SLE),* another connective tissue disease that has an immunological basis.

Rheumatoid arthritis typically, but not exclusively, involves small joints of the periphery. It is usually bilaterally symmetrical, that is, affecting the same joints on both sides of the body to a greater or lesser degree. Initially rheumatoid arthritis involves an inflammation of the synovial membrane, which becomes edematous and contains numerous lymphocytes and plasma cells. An antibody known as *rheumatoid factor (RF)* can also be detected in the serum in greater than 85% of all persons with this disease. Its serum titer appears to be related to the severity of the disorder. Immune complexes have also been detected within cells of the synovial membrane.

As the synovial membrane becomes more inflamed with progression of the disease, it eventually is replaced by a mass of highly vascularized tissue containing many lymphocytes and plasma cells; it is then termed a **pannus.** Later, regions of cell death along with the deposition of fibrinoid material occur in the pannus. The articular cartilage then begins to undergo erosion due to mechanical and inflammatory influences attributable to the pannus. Movement of the joint ruptures vessels in the highly vascularized pannus, leading to the extravasation of blood in the synovial cavity and the formation of a fibrin clot. Exposed ends of the underlying bone are then united by the laying down of fibrous tissue, which subsequently undergoes calcification. Thus, the joint often becomes totally immovable, or *ankylosed* (ang-kill-**lowzed**), since the participating bones have essentially undergone fusion.

Rheumatoid arthritis may occur at any age, often without warning. It may disappear inexplicably, and may or may not recur. The prospects for recovery are generally brighter if the onset occurs during childhood rather than in middle or old age. The symptoms of this disease can often be controlled to some degree by steroid or other anti-inflammatory medication, or even sometimes by dietary management. Neither of these methods or any other known treatment will completely arrest or reverse the disease process itself.

The incurability of rheumatoid arthritis is not easy to accept if one is afflicted with such a relentlessly progressing, crippling form of disease. It is depressing to reflect on the financial impoverishment, unnecessary further loss of health, and embitterment suffered by those who understandably grasp at any hope for a cure, however remote. To further complicate the issue, rheumatoid arthritis is such a whimsical disease that spontaneous remission of symptoms may easily be attributed to the activities of some spurious healer.

Additional joint miseries include sprains and inflammation of tendon sheaths

Although tendons are not really considered parts of a joint, at least as a rule, ligaments are. These are subject to a variety of disorders, paramount among which are probably **sprains.** A sprain usually is the result of forcing a joint beyond its normal range of motion or in an inappropriate direction without actual dislocation. Almost every one of us has experienced a sprain of the talotibial joint of the ankle region. Structures damaged as a result of a sprain may include muscles, tendons, ligaments, blood vessels, and nerves. The initial reaction is considerable swelling, which represents a kind of natural splinting process. Within weeks, or sometimes months, the swelling, pain, and weakness decline as the ruptured ligaments are repaired and the joint tightens up again. Repeated sprains can weaken the ligaments of a joint capsule, and corrective surgery may be necessary to prevent recurrent dislocation.

Tendons can also be stretched or torn, as can the connective tissue harness (fascia) of the muscle itself. This type of injury is far less serious than a sprain and confusingly enough it is termed a **strain.** Severe muscle strains, particularly those involving muscle bulging through rents in the muscle sheath, can require surgery, but many such injuries eventually recover without clinical treatment.

Tendon sheaths and joint capsule extensions are also prone to inflammatory disorders, which can progress to a permanent and painful deposition of calcium salts on the tendon. "Tennis elbow," for example, often originates as a strain of the lateral forearm muscles near their attachment to the epicondyles of the humerus. A frequent cause of this type of injury is the violent pronation and supination of the hand, as often occurs in playing tennis. The inflammation can then spread to adjacent bursae. The condition may be alleviated by wrapping the muscle origins with a snug band, injections of steroids at the site of injury, topical application of the anti-inflammatory drug dimethylsulfoxide (DMSO), and, if need be, surgical intervention.

FOCUS ON . . . Three joints

The ankle (talocrural) joint

The **talocrural,** or **ankle, joint** is typically described as being of the uniaxial variety. You should keep in mind, however, that studies have revealed that the basic motions permitted, that is, dorsiflexion and plantar-flexion of the foot, are really the end product of several more complex movements. Notice (Fig. *a*) that the bones that participate in the talocrural joint are the (a) distal end of the tibia and its malleolus, (b) malleolus of the fibula, and (c) body of the talus.

The articular surfaces are covered with hyaline cartilage, and the bones, together with the *inferior transverse tibiofibular ligament,* represent a mortise-like arrangement (a groove or slot into which another piece fits) that holds the body of the talus tightly. This is especially true during dorsiflexion because the talus is wider anteriorly than it is posteriorly.

The capsule of the talocrural joint is strengthened on its medial aspect by the *deltoid ligament* (Fig. *b*). Three ligaments are present on the lateral aspect of the joint. These are the (1) *anterior talofibular ligament,* (2) *posterior talofibular ligament,* and (3) *calcaneofibular ligament.* Collectively, these are known as the *lateral ligament* (Fig. *c*). The medial and lateral ligaments permit dorsi- and plantar-flexion while restricting anteroposterior movement of the talus. The axis of movement lies immediately distal to the two malleoli. The lateral ligament is not as strong as the deltoid ligament and is more frequently injured (sprained) when the talocrural joint is suddenly twisted inward as a result of running or walking on uneven terrain. Examine the radiograph and MRI scan (Figs. *d* and *e*) of the talocrural joint.

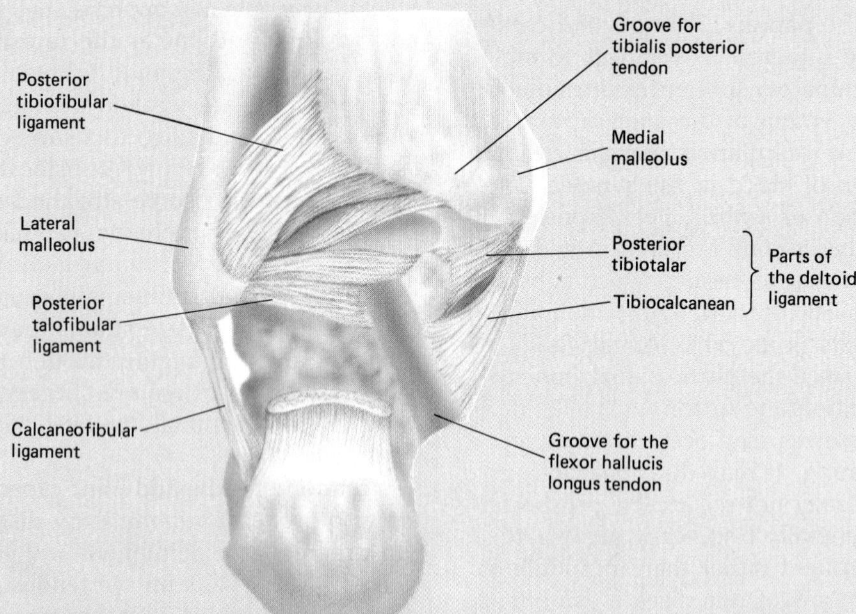

(*a*) Posterior aspect of the talocrural (ankle) joint illustrating the relationships between the bones and ligaments. Are you able to discern whether this is a left or right talocrural joint? Compare with Fig. 9-7.

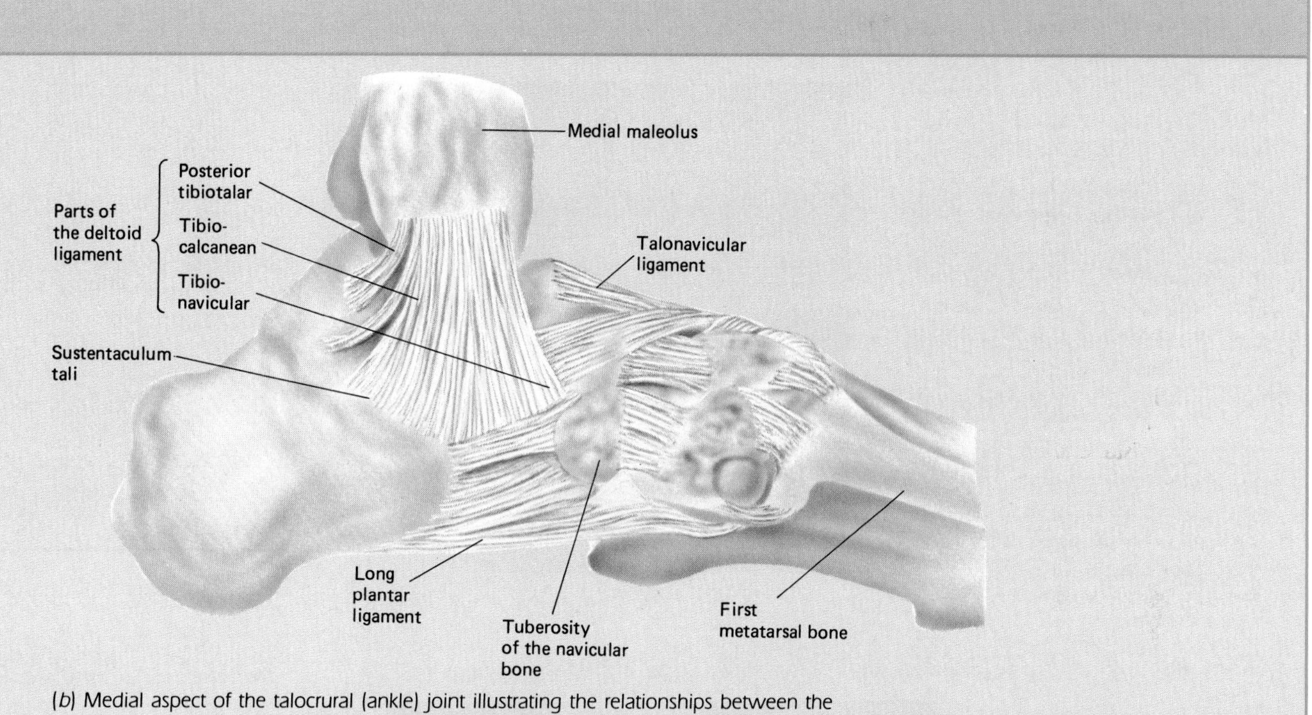

(*b*) Medial aspect of the talocrural (ankle) joint illustrating the relationships between the bones and ligaments. Notice the three portions of the large deltoid ligament.

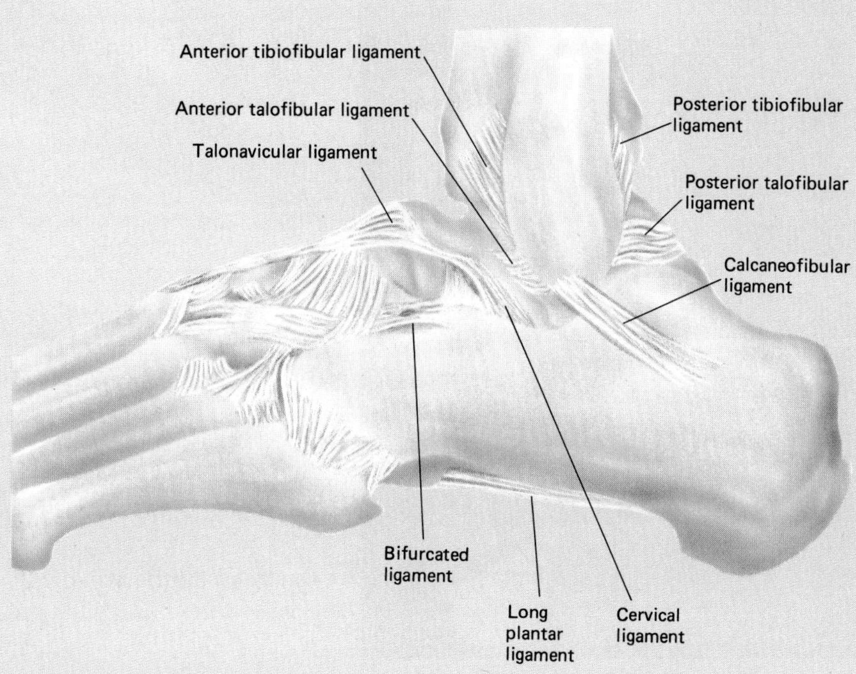

(*c*) Lateral aspect of the talocrural (ankle) joint illustrating the relationships between the bones and ligaments.

(box continued on next page)

FOCUS ON . . . Three Joints *(continued)*

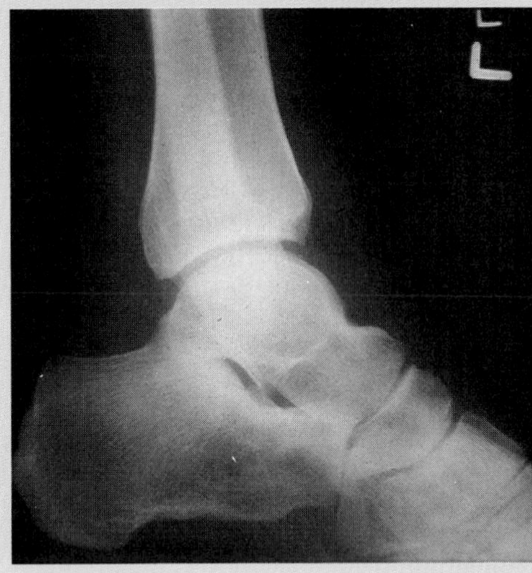

Radiograph of the talocrural (ankle) joint. Can you identify the bones illustrated in this view? (PhotoEdit.)

74A, 74B

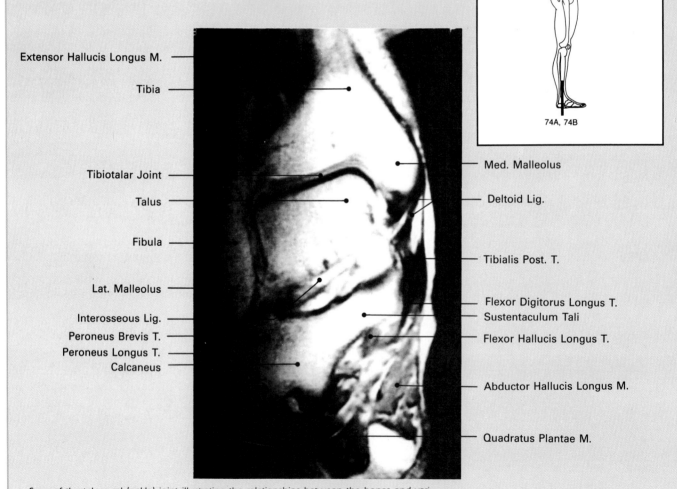

Extensor Hallucis Longus M.
Tibia
Tibiotalar Joint
Talus
Fibula
Lat. Malleolus
Interosseous Lig.
Peroneus Brevis T.
Peroneus Longus T.
Calcaneus
Med. Malleolus
Deltoid Lig.
Tibialis Post. T.
Flexor Digitorus Longus T.
Sustentaculum Tali
Flexor Hallucis Longus T.
Abductor Hallucis Longus M.
Quadratus Plantae M.

Scan of the talocrural (ankle) joint illustrating the relationships between the bones and various soft tissue structures. (Christoforidis, A. J., *Atlas of Axial, Sagittal and Coronal Anatomy with CT and MRI,* 1988 (W. B. Saunders, Philadelphia).)

The hip (coxal) joint

The **hip (coxal)** joint is a synovial joint of the spheroid (ball-and-socket) variety (Fig. *f*). It is formed by the **femoral head** and the **acetabulum** of the coxal bone. The joint is strong and stable and is surrounded by several powerful muscles. The capsule of the joint extends from the coxal bone to the femur and some of its fibers are thickened so as to form three distinct ligaments. These are the (1) *iliofemoral ligament,* (2) *pubofemoral ligament,* and (3) *ischiofemoral ligament* (Figs. *f* and *g*). The iliofemoral ligament is Y-shaped and is the strongest of the three. The deeper fibers of the ischiofemoral ligament are circularly arranged around the joint and are called the *zona orbicularis* (Fig. *h*).

The acetabulum is deepened by the presence of a fibrocartilaginous lip known as the *acetabular labrum* (Fig. *i*). The acetabulum does not form a complete ring due to the presence of the *acetabular notch.* This notch is bridged by the *transverse acetabular ligament* (Fig. *i*). The head of the femur is attached to the margin of the acetabulum and to the transverse acetabular ligament by an additional ligament called the *ligamentum teres (round) of the femur* (Fig. *i*).

The hip joint is well constructed for movement, support, and the transmission of weight. Movements of the thigh at the hip joint include (1) flexion, (2) extension, (3) abduction, (4) adduction, (5) circumduction, and (6) rotation. The trunk also moves upon the hip joint, for example, when a person is performing sit-ups. Examine the radiograph (Fig. *j*) of the hip joint.

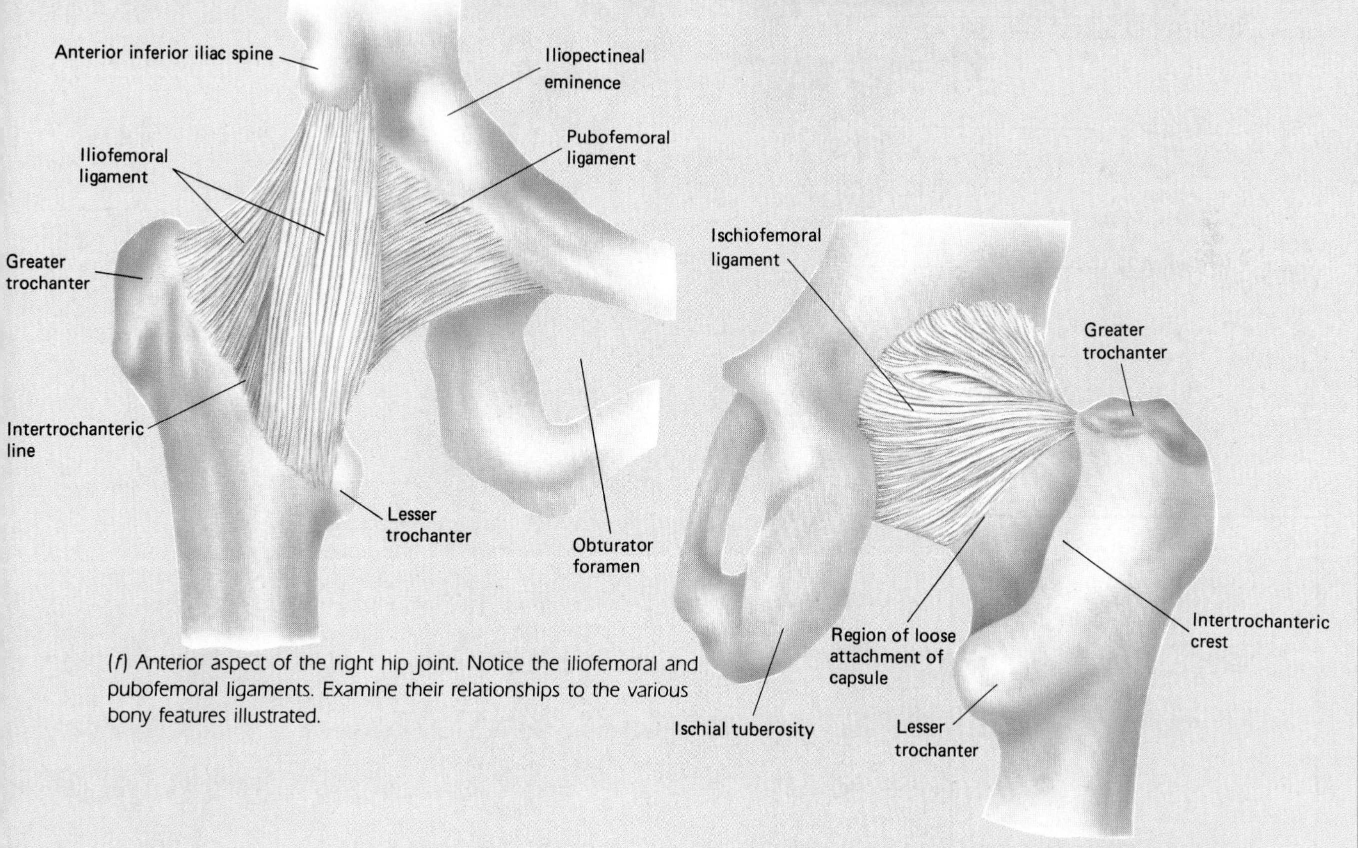

(*f*) Anterior aspect of the right hip joint. Notice the iliofemoral and pubofemoral ligaments. Examine their relationships to the various bony features illustrated.

(*g*) Posterior aspect of the right hip joint. Notice the ischiofemoral ligament that covers most of the posterior aspect of the joint. Also examine the bony features associated with this view of the hip joint.

(*box continued on next page*)

FOCUS ON . . . Three joints (*continued*)

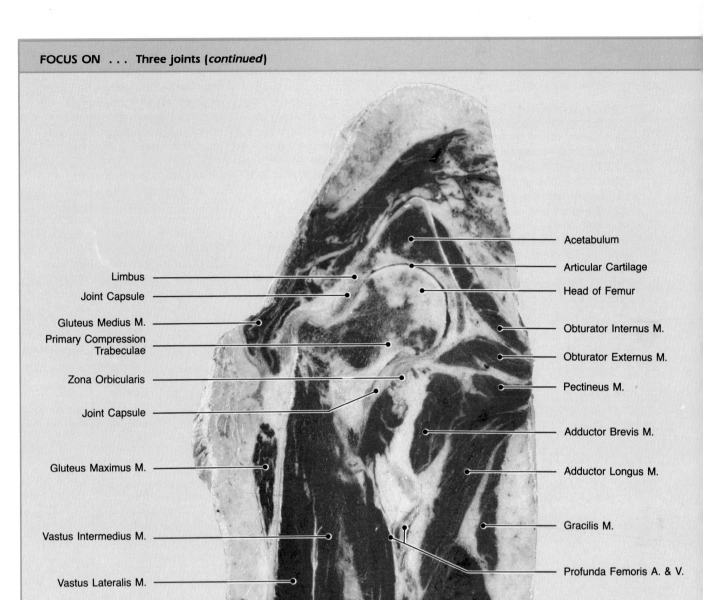

Acetabulum
Limbus
Articular Cartilage
Joint Capsule
Head of Femur
Gluteus Medius M.
Obturator Internus M.
Primary Compression Trabeculae
Obturator Externus M.
Zona Orbicularis
Pectineus M.
Joint Capsule
Adductor Brevis M.
Gluteus Maximus M.
Adductor Longus M.
Gracilis M.
Vastus Intermedius M.
Profunda Femoris A. & V.
Vastus Lateralis M.
Adductor Magnus M.
Fascia Lata
Vastus Medialis M.

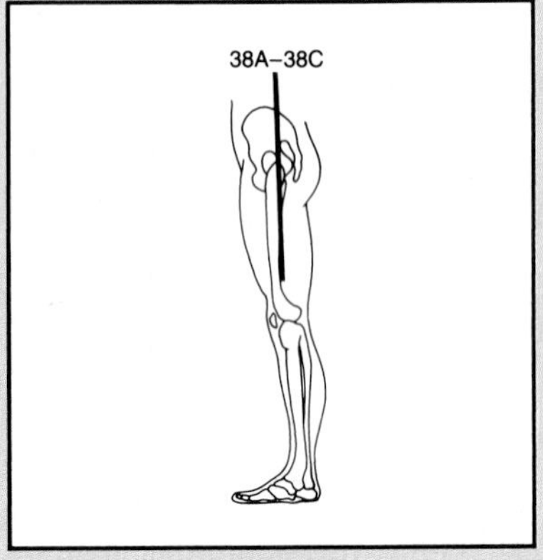

Coronal section through the hip joint. Notice the placement of the femoral head within the acetabulum. Also examine the relationship of various soft tissue structures to the hip joint. (From Christoforidis, A. J., *Atlas of Axial, Sagittal and Coronal Anatomy with CT and MRI*, 1988 (W. B. Saunders, Philadelphia).)

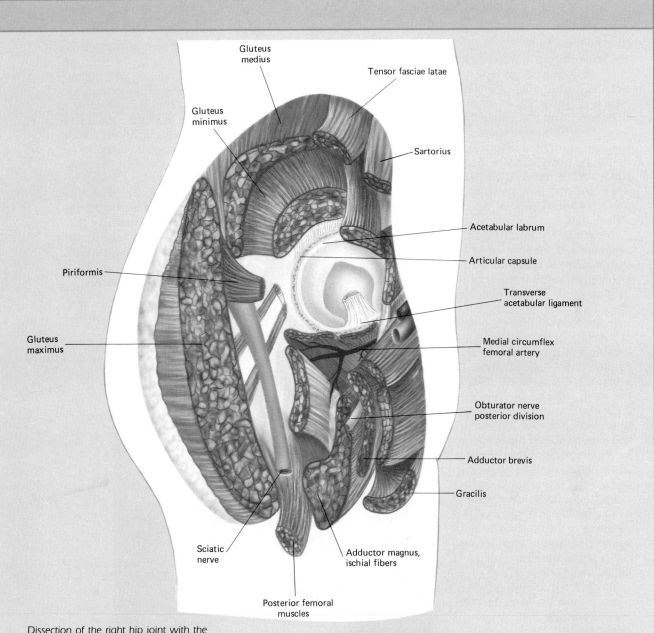

Gluteus medius
Tensor fasciae latae
Gluteus minimus
Sartorius
Acetabular labrum
Articular capsule
Piriformis
Transverse acetabular ligament
Gluteus maximus
Medial circumflex femoral artery
Obturator nerve posterior division
Adductor brevis
Gracilis
Sciatic nerve
Adductor magnus, ischial fibers
Posterior femoral muscles

Dissection of the right hip joint with the femur removed. Examine the relationships of the various soft tissue structure to the hip joint. Most of these provide additional stability to the joint.

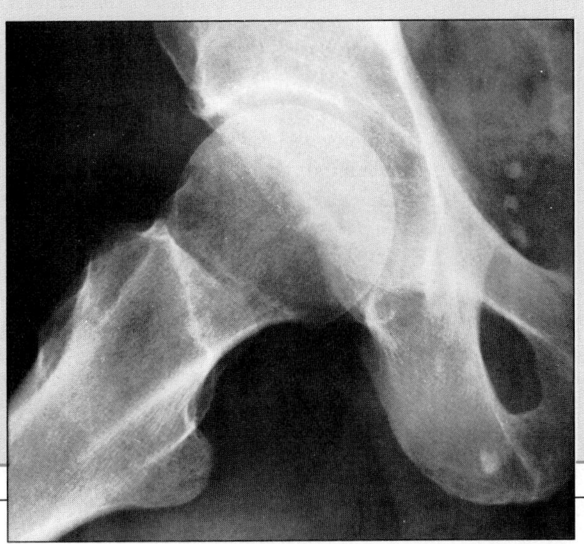

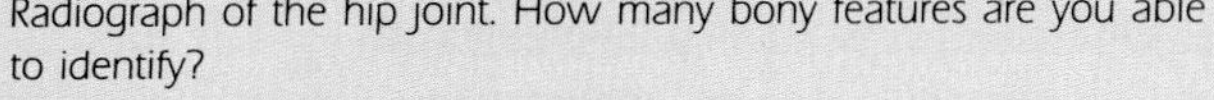

Radiograph of the hip joint. How many bony features are you able to identify?

(continued)

The knee joint

The **knee joint** is a synovial joint of the condylar type and represents the largest joint in the body (Figs. 9-17 and 9-1). Surfaces of three bones form this articulation. These are the (1) medial and lateral condyles of the **femur,** (2) medial and lateral condyles of the **tibia,** and (3) **patella.** The capsule of the knee joint is typically thin and interconnects the femur, tibia, and patella.

The *medial* and *lateral menisci (semilunar cartilages)* are wedge-shaped pieces of fibrocartilage that are attached to the condyles of the tibia (Fig. 9-18). They serve to deepen the condyles of the tibia for articulation with the condyles of the femur above and are connected anteriorly by the *transverse ligament* (Fig. 9-18). The medial meniscus is C-shaped and the lateral one is more circular. Because the former is anchored to the *tibial collateral ligament* it is less mobile and more frequently ruptured during injuries resulting from twisting of the flexed knee. The *fibular collateral ligament* is situated on the lateral aspect of the knee joint and is more cordlike in appearance compared to the tibial collateral ligament. Unlike the latter, the fibular collateral ligament is not attached to a meniscus.

Within the joint itself there are two additional ligaments, the *anterior* and *posterior cruciate ligaments* (Fig. 9-1). These interconnect the femur and tibia and are named according to their attachments on the tibia. Notice that these two ligaments are crossed and somewhat resemble the letter X when viewed from either their anterior or posterior aspect (Fig. 9-16). The cruciate ligaments most likely function in limiting rotational movements of the knee joint. Furthermore, the anterior cruciate ligament limits posterior slipping of the femur on the tibia, and the posterior cruciate ligament limits the opposite movement.

The capsule of the knee joint is strengthened posteriorly by a fibrous expansion derived from the tendon of the semimembranosus muscle (Fig. 9-17). This expansion is called the *oblique popliteal ligament* and courses superolaterally across the back of the joint. The joint capsule is strengthened anteriorly by the *patellar ligament* and on its sides by fibrous extensions from the vastus medialis and lateralis muscles, the *medial* and *lateral retinacula* of the patella.

Movements of the knee joint are very complex and combine hinge motion with those of gliding, rolling, and rotation. The articular surfaces of the joint are more congruent and the joint is most stable at the end of extension.

Football players are subject to several types of knee injuries, the most common of which is called the "unhappy triad." This injury typically results when the flexed knee is struck from its lateral aspect as, for example, when a running back plants his foot to negotiate a change in direction. The structures torn in this particular injury are the (a) tibial collateral ligament, (b) medial meniscus, and (c) anterior cruciate ligament.

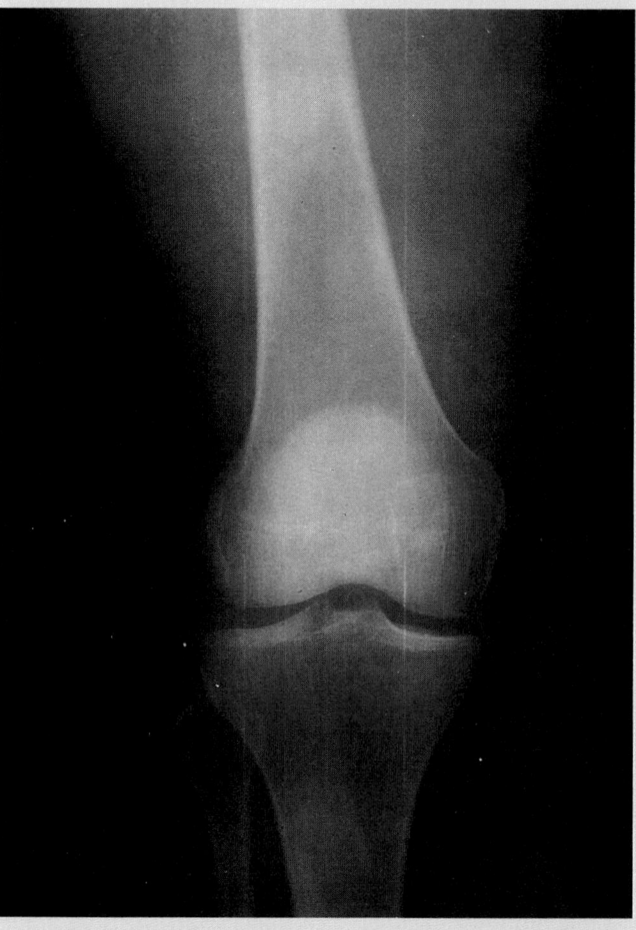

(*k*) Anteroposterior radiograph (x-ray) of the knee. (PhotoEdit.)

Summary

I. Any connection between bones is a joint, or articulation.

II. Functional criteria can be used to classify joints as:

A. Synarthroses—essentially an immovable joint in which the participating bones are united by fibrous connective tissue.

B. Amphiarthroses—joints that permit a slight degree of movement; participating bones are united by fibrous connective tissue.

C. Diarthroses—joints that are freely movable.

III. Joints may also be classified according to their structure:

A. Fibrous—essentially immovable (synarthrotic) with the exception of the syndesmoses. These joints lack a joint cavity, and the participating bones are united by fibrous tissue. Different types of fibrous joints include:

1. Sutures
2. Gomphoses
3. Syndesmoses

B. Cartilaginous—This type of joint also lacks a joint cavity, and the participating bones are connected by cartilage. Functionally they permit little if any movement and are classified as:

1. Symphyses
2. Synchondroses

C. Synovial—These joints are freely movable (diarthrotic). However, there are several factors to consider with regard to limitation of normal joint movement. Structurally they possess a joint cavity, articular surfaces composed of hyaline cartilage, and a synovial membrane that lines the fibrous joint capsule and that produces synovial fluid. These joints also have accessory ligaments and may contain an articular disc(s). Depending upon the number of articular surfaces involved and whether an articular disc is present, synovial joints may be described as being simple, compound, or complex. Typically, synovial joints are classified as being:

1. Plane, or gliding
2. Ginglymus, or hinge
3. Trochoid, or pivot
4. Condylar
5. Ellipsoid
6. Saddle
7. Spheroid, or ball-and-socket

IV. The types of movements permitted at the various synovial joints include:

A. Flexion-extension
B. Abduction-adduction
C. Pronation-supination
D. Inversion-eversion
E. Dorsiflexion-plantar-flexion
F. Protraction-retraction
G. Rotation
H. Circumduction
I. Opposition

V. Joints receive their innervation from nerves that also supply the muscles responsible for movement at the joint. The fibrous capsule and the synovial membrane differ with respect to the specific types of nerve endings they contain.

VI. Joints act as fulcra for levers and thus permit movement to occur. Joints of the human body may be described as representing either first-, second-, or third-class levers. Most of the joints we possess are of the third-class variety.

VII. Joint disorders discussed include:

A. Dislocations

B. Sprains—joint injury due to forcing the structure beyond its normal range of motion or in an inappropriate direction without dislocation; muscles, tendons, ligaments, blood vessels, and nerves associated with the joint may be injured.

C. Arthritis—inflammatory disease of joints; there are several types of arthritis.

VIII. Features of the ankle, knee, and hip joints emphasized include the following: (a) their detailed anatomical structure, (b) methods used for their clinical evaluation, (c) movements permitted, and (d) relevant clinical applications.

Post-test

1. The diarthrodial, or ______________, joints are the most freely movable of all. These consist of a connective tissue ______________ and possess articular surfaces composed of ______________ cartilage. Within the joint cavity there occurs ______________ fluid, which serves as a lubricant. This fluid is produced by cells of the ______________ membrane.

2. The types of nerve endings that are found associated with joints include: ______________ ______________ ______________, ______________ ______________ ______________, ______________, and ______________ ______________ ______________.
3. ______________ is a degenerative, noninflammatory disease of joints that usually spares the synovial membrane.
4. The talocrural joint is the current anatomical term for the ______________ joint.
5. Dorsiflexion and plantar-flexion are the principal movements permitted at the ______________ joint. The movements permitted at the talocalcaneo and the talocalcaneonavicular joints are known as ______________ and ______________.
6. Most of the movable joints of the human body can be functionally classified as ______________-class levers.
7. The articulation between a tooth and the jaw is an example of a specialized type of fibrous joint known as a ______________.
8. The joints that exist between the bodies of adjacent vertebrae represent a specialized form of the cartilaginous joints known as ______________.
9. A ginglymus joint is one form of a ______________ joint.
10. The presence of tophi is a characteristic feature of a disease known as ______________. A pannus, on the other hand, is associated with an inflammatory disease of joints called ______________ arthritis.
11. Movement of the index finger away from a reference line passing through the longitudinal axis of the middle finger is known as ______________.
12. The carpometacarpal joint of the thumb represents a specialized form of synovial joint called a ______________ joint.
13. The cruciate ligaments of the knee are an example of ______________-capsular ligaments.
14. Flexion, extension, abduction, and adduction are all examples of ______________ movements.
15. The articular discs associated with the knee joint are also called ______________.

Review questions

1. Describe what is meant by a bursa. List the factors that might be responsible for the occurrence of the condition known as bursitis.
2. Describe four features that under normal circumstances tend to restrict movements at a joint.
3. Compare and contrast a sprain and a strain.
4. Describe the following movements: flexion, abduction, circumduction, inversion, dorsiflexion, and rotation. Please give an example of a joint where each is permitted.
5. Describe the innervation of movable joints. Why is the innervation of movable joints important?
6. Describe what is meant by accessory ligaments. Give an example of one that is located in an intracapsular position. Give an example of one that has an extracapsular location.
7. Demonstrate the following movements: pronation, supination, protraction, retraction, plantar-flexion, and eversion.
8. Describe what is meant by a dislocation.
9. Describe and illustrate in a simple diagram the components of a synovial joint.
10. Compare and contrast the manner in which the bones of fibrous, cartilaginous, and synovial joints are bound together.
11. Describe all of the subtypes of synovial joints and give at least one example of each from the human body.
12. Describe what is meant by the term arthritis. Elaborate on the forms of arthritis presented for you in the present chapter.
13. What is a meniscus? Give an example of a joint that has two menisci present.
14. Describe the composition, origin, and functional roles of synovial fluid.
15. Describe a synovial tendon sheath. What is its function? What is meant by the term tenosynovitis?
16. Describe the subtypes of fibrous and cartilaginous joints. Give examples of each from the human body.
17. Compare and contrast a pannus and a tophus.
18. Describe a synostosis and give an example from the human body.
19. Explain why certain joints are said to exist for the purpose of permitting growth.
20. Explain how the terms uniaxial, biaxial, and multiaxial apply to a discussion of joint movement.
21. Explain the differences in the planes of reference for the movements of abduction and adduction as applied to the digits and to the upper and lower limbs as a whole.

Post-test answers

1. synovial; capsule; hyaline; synovial; synovial
2. free nerve endings, Ruffini end organs, pacinian corpuscles, Golgi tendon organs
3. osteoarthritis
4. ankle
5. talocrural (ankle); inversion, eversion
6. third
7. gomphosis
8. symphyses
9. uniaxial
10. gout; rheumatoid
11. abduction
12. saddle
13. intra
14. angular
15. menisci

MUSCLE TISSUE

CHAPTER OUTLINE

LEARNING OBJECTIVES

After you have studied this chapter you should be able to:

1 Describe the gross and microscopic structure of skeletal muscle.

2 Describe the mechanisms of synaptic transmission, depolarization, and calcium release as they relate to the control of muscle contraction.

3 Describe the molecular aspects of skeletal muscle contraction.

4 Describe the processes by which the energy requirements for skeletal muscle contraction are typically met.

5 Compare and contrast isometric and isotonic exercise.

6 Describe several physiological aspects of muscle contraction as they relate to sports activities.

7 Compare and contrast the structure and action of smooth muscle and skeletal muscle.

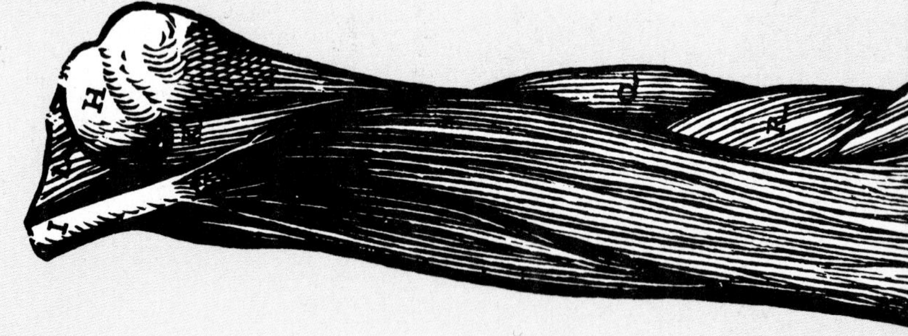

Skeletal muscle. (Biophoto Associates/Science Source/Photo Researchers, Inc.)

10

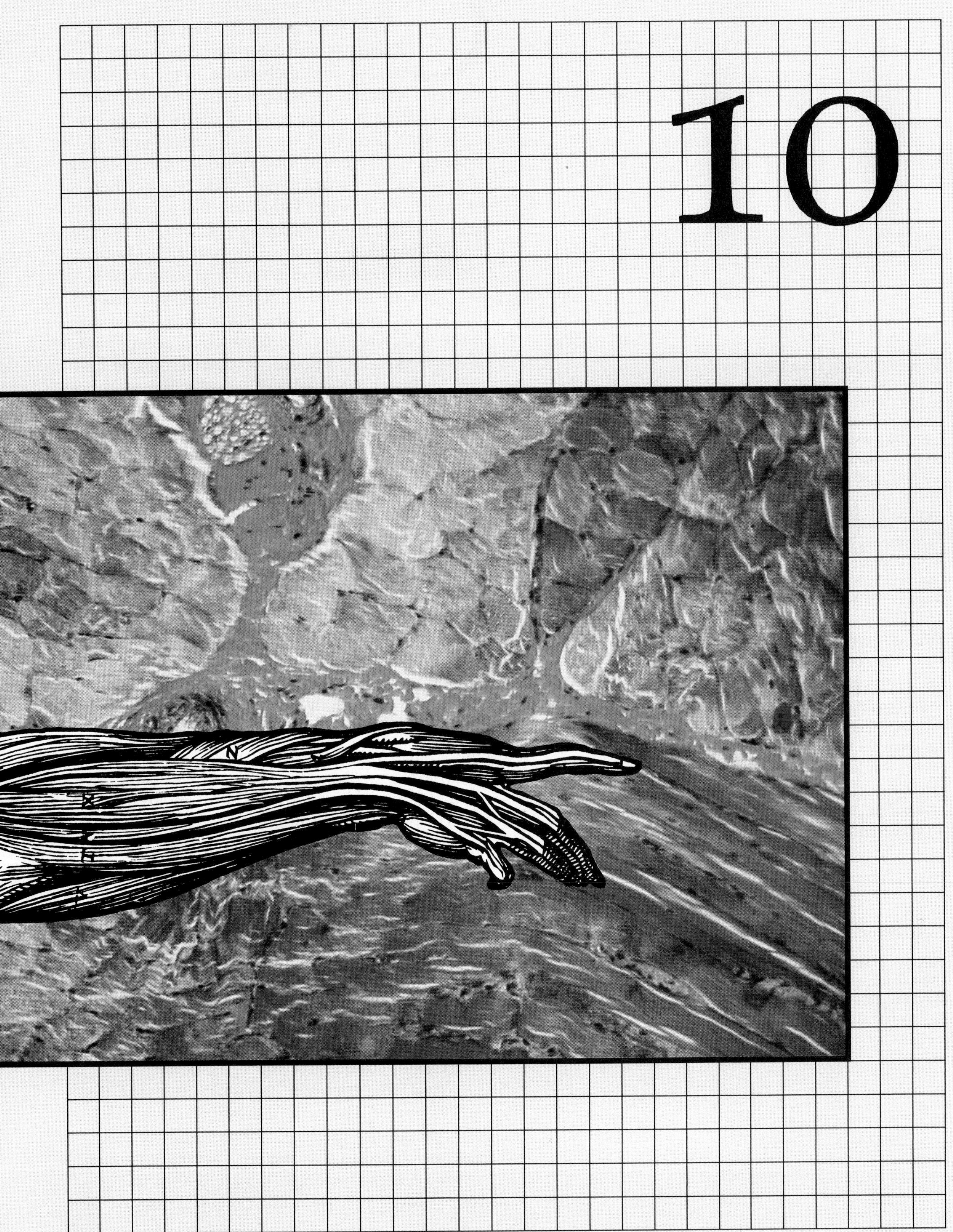

KEY CONCEPTS

Skeletal muscle fibers are enveloped and anchored to connective tissue. Since most skeletal muscle fibers do not extend the entire length of a given muscle, it is the connective tissue that is responsible for the mechanical transmission of forces generated by the contracting muscle fibers.

Sarcomeres are capable of independent contraction, and when they contract simultaneously they produce contraction of the muscle fiber as a whole.

Skeletal muscle fibers normally contract only when a sufficient stimulus is applied by a nerve ending.

The informational signal required for contraction results from electrical changes along the plasma membrane of a muscle fiber.

Neuronal control of most human skeletal muscle is characterized by an all-or-none phenomenon.

Muscle fibers utilize ATP as an immediate source of energy for the contractile process. Creatine phosphate acts as a means of storing chemical energy.

Smooth muscle fibers, although they contract more slowly than do skeletal muscle fibers, are better suited for sustained contraction.

Consider for a moment the various forms of movement your body produces on a daily basis. Some are rather obvious: walking, chewing a piece of gum, rising from a sitting position, playing the piano, or typing at your computer keyboard. Other forms of movement, like breathing, the continuous beating of your heart, constriction of your pupils when encountering a bright light, and the passage of food through your digestive tract, are not as obvious. Although the types of movement and our conscious perception of them vary considerably, each movement is brought about by specialized cells termed **muscle fibers.** These specialized cells of the body are typically classified as components of either **skeletal, smooth,** or **cardiac** muscle tissue. In this chapter we will consider the morphologic and functional aspects of skeletal and smooth muscle; those of cardiac muscle will be addressed in Chapter 20.

Each voluntary muscle is an organ in its own right

The biceps brachii muscle will serve as an example of a typical skeletal muscle. It is the major muscle mass of the arm and is illustrated in the next chapter (Fig. 11-4). The biceps brachii has two points of origin located on the scapula; hence the term biceps, which means "two heads" in Latin. The dual origin gives rise to a single, spindle-shaped bulge, or **belly,** which inserts upon the tuberosity of the radius, a bone of the forearm. If you grasp the edge of your desk and rhythmically tense the biceps brachii muscle of that arm, you may be able to visualize its insertion all the way to the radius. Its origin, however, will be much more difficult to demonstrate and use of a skeleton will prove helpful. The biceps brachii receives its blood supply via branches from a single artery that enter the muscle near its center. This arrangement is advantageous in that the vessel is not subjected to excessive stretching or kinking when the muscle moves during the processes of contraction and relaxation.

Focus your attention on Figure 10-1. The first part (*a*) of this schematic represents a cross section through the thigh and depicts the various muscles located in this region. Part (*b*) illustrates a cross section of a single muscle within this group. Notice that each muscle is surrounded by

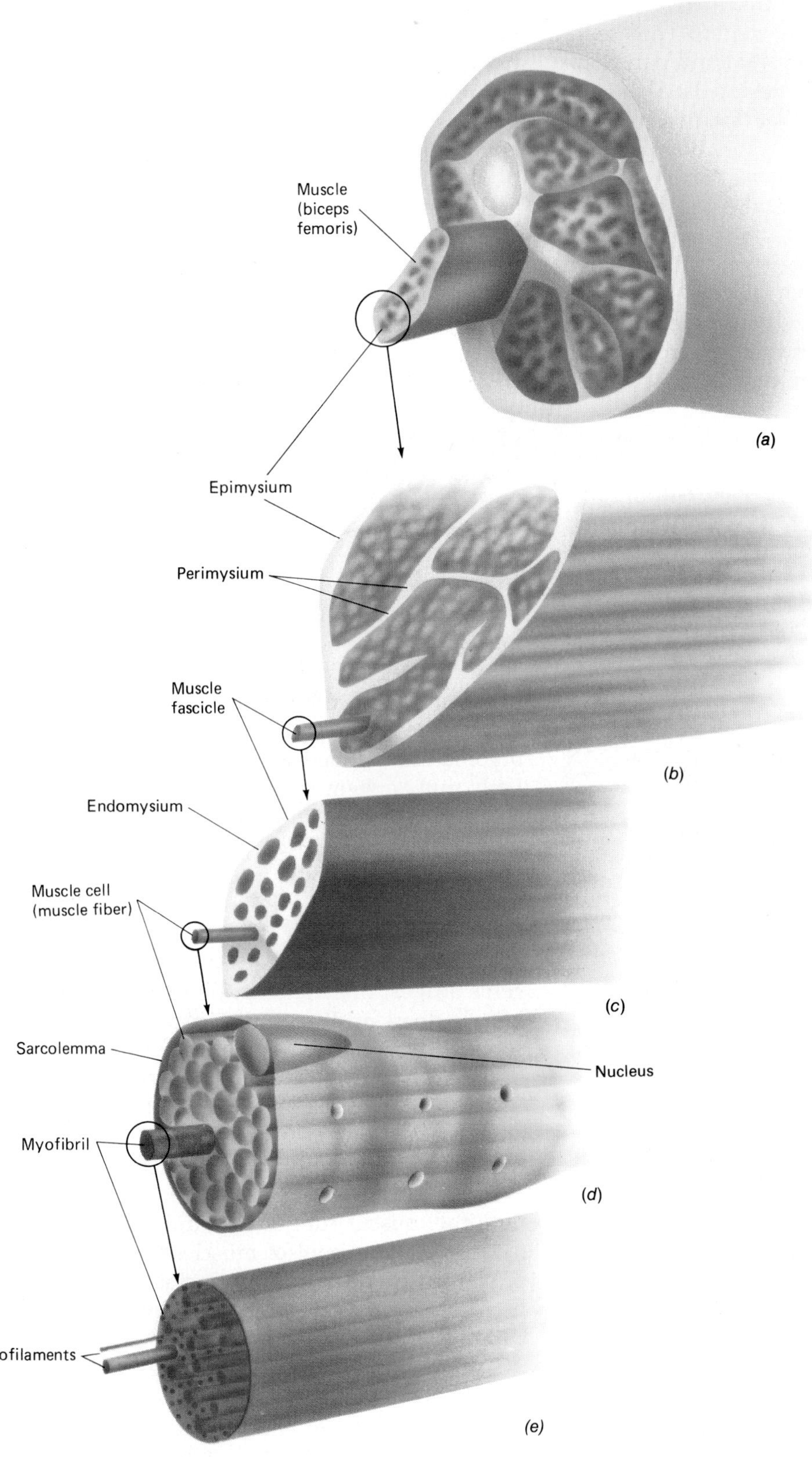

FIGURE 10-1

Cross section of the thigh dissected into smaller and smaller parts *(a)* Section through the entire thigh. *(b)* A single muscle. *(c)* and *(d)* Microscopic views of the muscle. *(e)* Arrangement of the contractile filaments.

an external, dense, connective tissue envelope called the **epimysium** (*ep*-i-**miz**-ee-um). Thin septa extend inward from the epimysium and partition the muscle into bundles of muscle cells. These connective tissue septa are called the **perimysium** (*per*-i-**miz**-ee-um), and the individual bundles of muscle cells are known as **fascicles** (**fas**-ih-kuls) (Fig. 10-1*b* and *c*). Furthermore, the perimysium gives rise to connective tissue wrappings that in turn surround individual muscle cells, that is, the **endomysium** (*end*-o-**miz**-ee-um) (Fig. 10-1*c* and 10-2). It is important to realize that the epimysium, perimysium, and endomysium represent true connective tissue and are directly continuous with one another. Each is composed of fibroblasts, blood vessels, lymphatics, and varying amounts of collagen and elastic fibers.

As the muscle cells contract, they pull upon the connective tissue in which they are wrapped. Collagen fibers of the endomysium are anchored to attachment points located in the plasma membrane of the muscle cells and in turn are attached to the ends of contractile fibrils within those cells. Because tendons are actually extensions of the epimysium, contraction will ultimately exert a pull on the tendons that subsequently will move the bones to which they are attached. In most instances the individual muscle cells do not extend the entire length of a given muscle. Therefore it is the connective tissue that is responsible for the mechanical transmission of forces generated by the contracting muscle cells.

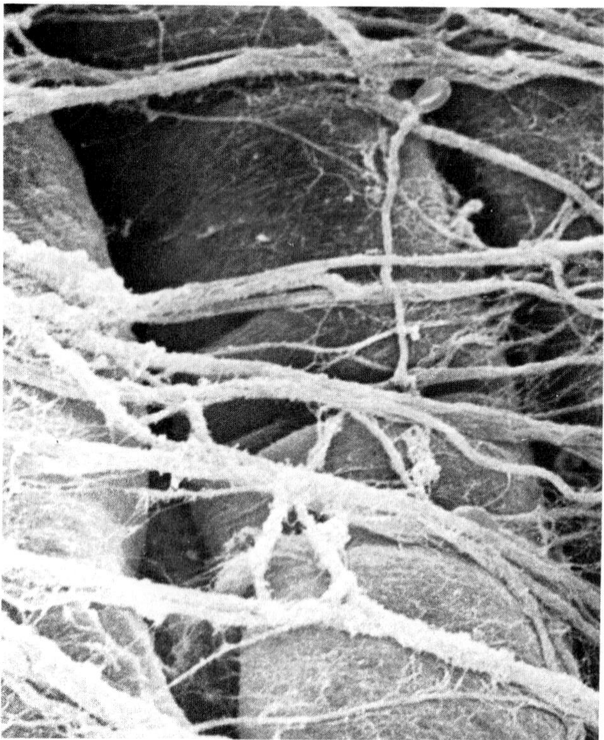

FIGURE 10-2

Scanning electron micrograph showing the tiny collagen fibers of the endomysium that bind skeletal muscle cells together (×1200). (From Borg, Thomas K., and Caulfield, James B.: Morphology of connective tissue in skeletal muscle. Tissue and Cell, vol. 12, pp. 197–207, 1980. © 1980 Longman Group, Ltd.)

Skeletal muscle cells are highly specialized for the contractile process

Skeletal muscle cells, or **muscle fibers,** are multinucleated and vary markedly in length. Some muscles of our bodies contain muscle fibers up to 30 centimeters in length. The diameter of muscle fibers ranges from 10 to 100 microns.

Muscle develops in the embryo from the embryonic tissue called **mesoderm** (**mes**-oh-derm). Early muscle stem cells termed *myoblasts* possess a single nucleus and undergo fusion with other muscle stem cells. Thus, the resulting muscle fiber contains more than one nucleus. As illustrated in Figure 10-3, the nuclei of skeletal muscle fibers are located near the cell periphery adjacent to the plasma membrane. Characteristic transverse stripes, or **striations,** develop in skeletal muscle fibers as differentiation proceeds, and soon the cells become some of the most striking in the body.

Once the muscle fibers have obtained their adult nerve and connective tissue relationships, they cease to multiply. With further growth and exercise individual fibers enlarge (hypertrophy) until the musculature of the adult is formed. In fact, the enlargement of muscles as a result of prolonged exercise is due principally to the hypertrophy of existing muscle fibers, not to the addition of new ones.

As the individual ages, the inevitable loss of muscle fibers is not balanced by an increase in cell proliferation, as might be the case, for example, in liver tissue. Aged muscle is often dramatically atrophied, with much of the original muscle having been replaced by connective tissue. Repair of actual muscle injury, however, often is accompanied by the differentiation of new muscle cells from undifferentiated precursor cells called **satellite cells** (Fig. 10-4). These cells are located among the fibers of practically all mature muscles.

Some organelles of muscle fibers have names that differ from similar structures in other cells. The plasma membrane of a muscle fiber is termed the **sarcolemma** (*sar*-ko-**lem**-a), and the cytoplasm (excluding the myofibrils) is called the **sarcoplasm** (**sar**-ko-plazm). Furthermore, the smooth endo-

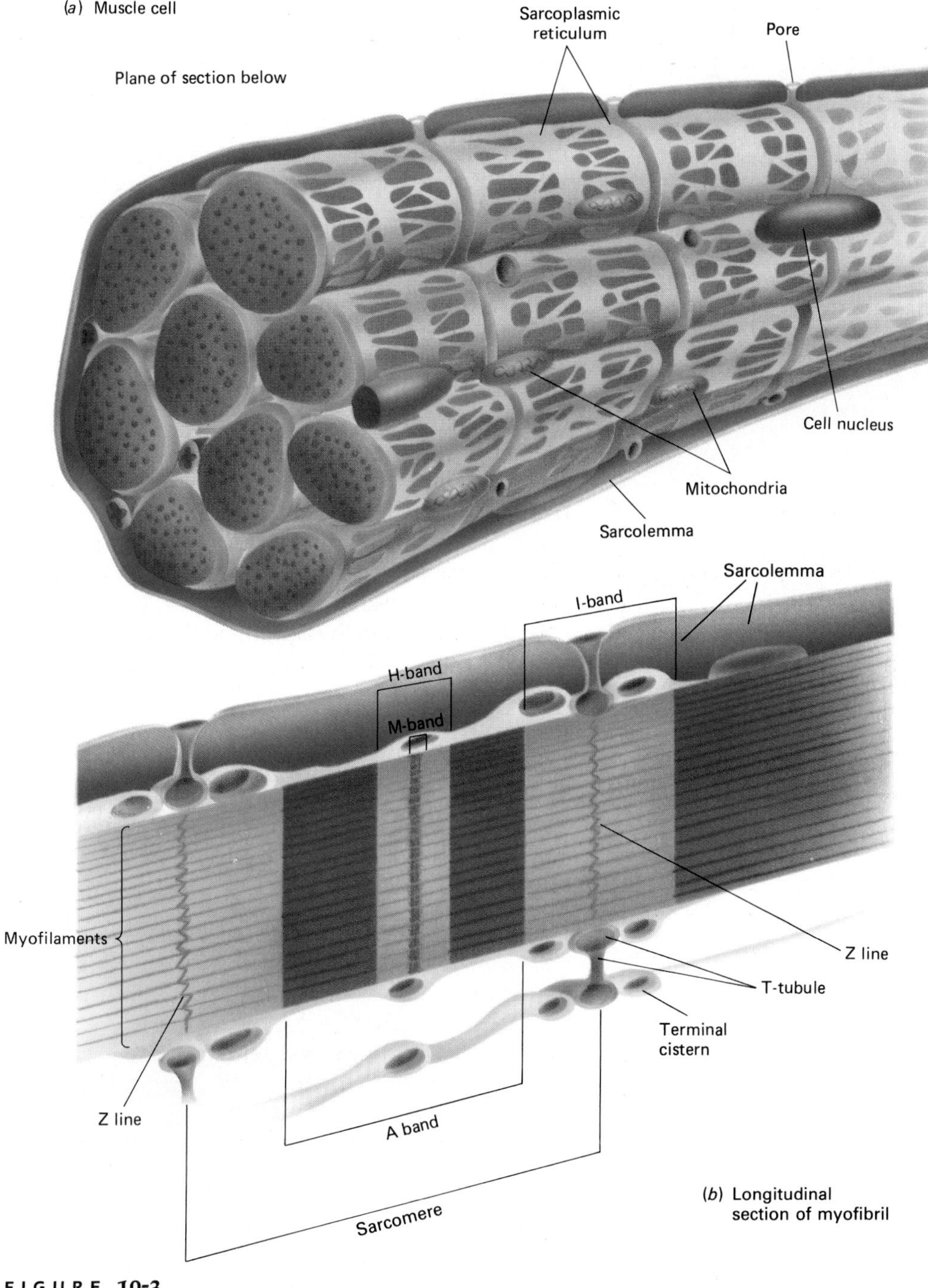

FIGURE 10-3

The structure of a skeletal muscle cell. Notice the eccentric placement of the nuclei, just under the sarcolemma.

plasmic reticulum of muscle fibers is known as the **sarcoplasmic reticulum** (*sar*-ko-**plaz**-mik re-**tik**-yoo-lum). The sarcoplasmic reticulum is composed of many membrane-lined **sarcotubules** which form an intricate network around individual myofibrils. Another characteristic feature of muscle fibers is the presence of **transverse,** or **T, tubules.** These represent invaginations of the sarcolemma and as such open onto the surface of the fiber externally and penetrate deep into the interior of the muscle fiber in the other direction. All of these structures are illustrated in Figure 10-3.

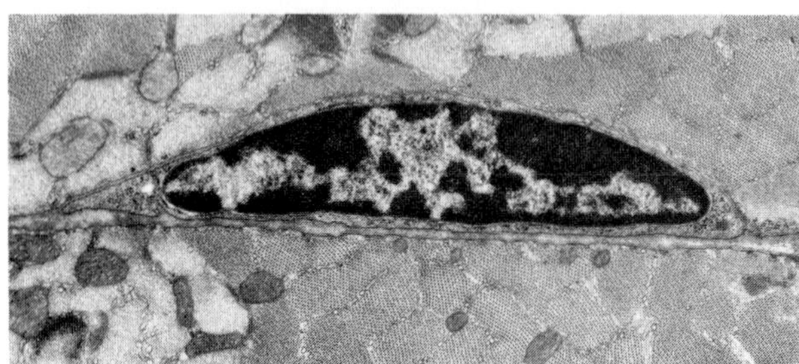

(a)

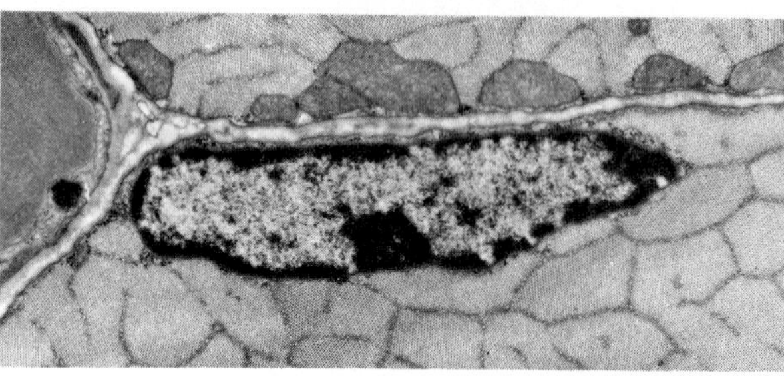

(b)

FIGURE 10-4

(a) Satellite cell from skeletal muscle (×19,450) and *(b)* Nucleus of skeletal muscle cell (×15,900). (From Snow, M. H.: "A quantitative ultrastructural analysis of satellite cells in denervated fast and slow muscles of the mouse." *Anat. Rec.*, 207:593–604, 1984, Alan R. Liss, Inc.)

Notice also that a muscle fiber is almost completely filled with cylindrical structures called **myofibrils** (my-oh-**fye**-brils) which have diameters of 1 to 2 microns (Fig. 10-3). These myofibrils contain individual **myofilaments** (*my*-oh-**fil**-uh-munts) which are responsible for the contraction of the myofibrils and therefore of the muscle fiber as a whole. Some myofilaments have a diameter of approximately 6 nanometers and are termed **thin filaments;** others have diameters approaching 15 nanometers. The latter are known as **thick filaments.** Thin filaments are composed primarily of a protein called **actin** (*ack*-tin) and thick filaments are made up mostly of the protein **myosin** (*my*-o-sin).

The manner in which the thin and thick myofilaments are arranged within the muscle fiber give the cell its characteristically striated, or banded, appearance (Figs. 10-5 and 10-6). The two types of filaments are positioned longitudinally within the cell such that they overlap one another as illustrated in Figure 10-6. It is important to realize that the length of the various

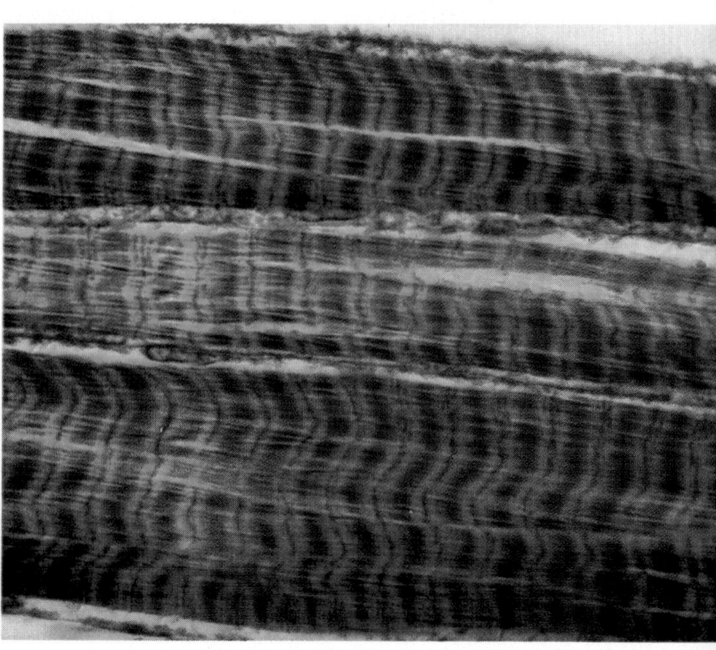

FIGURE 10-5

Photomicrograph of skeletal muscle cells (approximately ×400). (David M. Phillips/Visuals Unlimited.)

bands changes with the degree of contraction of the muscle fiber. The repeating functional unit of each muscle fiber is termed a **sarcomere** (**sar**-ko-meer) and is defined as the region located between two adjacent **Z lines** (Fig. 10-6). The Z lines are formed as a result of a complex interweaving of myofilaments. Individual sarcomeres are capable of independent contraction, and when many of them contract simultaneously they produce contraction of the muscle fiber as a whole.

The **I bands** are located at both ends of the sarcomere, immediately adjacent to the Z line, and are composed of thin myofilaments only (Fig. 10-6). Hence, they appear light when viewed with the light microscope. The central portion of the muscle fiber is occupied by a much darker region termed the **A band** and consists of overlapping thin and thick myofilaments. Within the A band is a lighter area made up exclusively of thick filaments and designated as the **H band** (Fig. 10-6). Close examination of the H band reveals a much more dense region near its center called the **M band** which may represent fine connections between adjacent thick filaments.

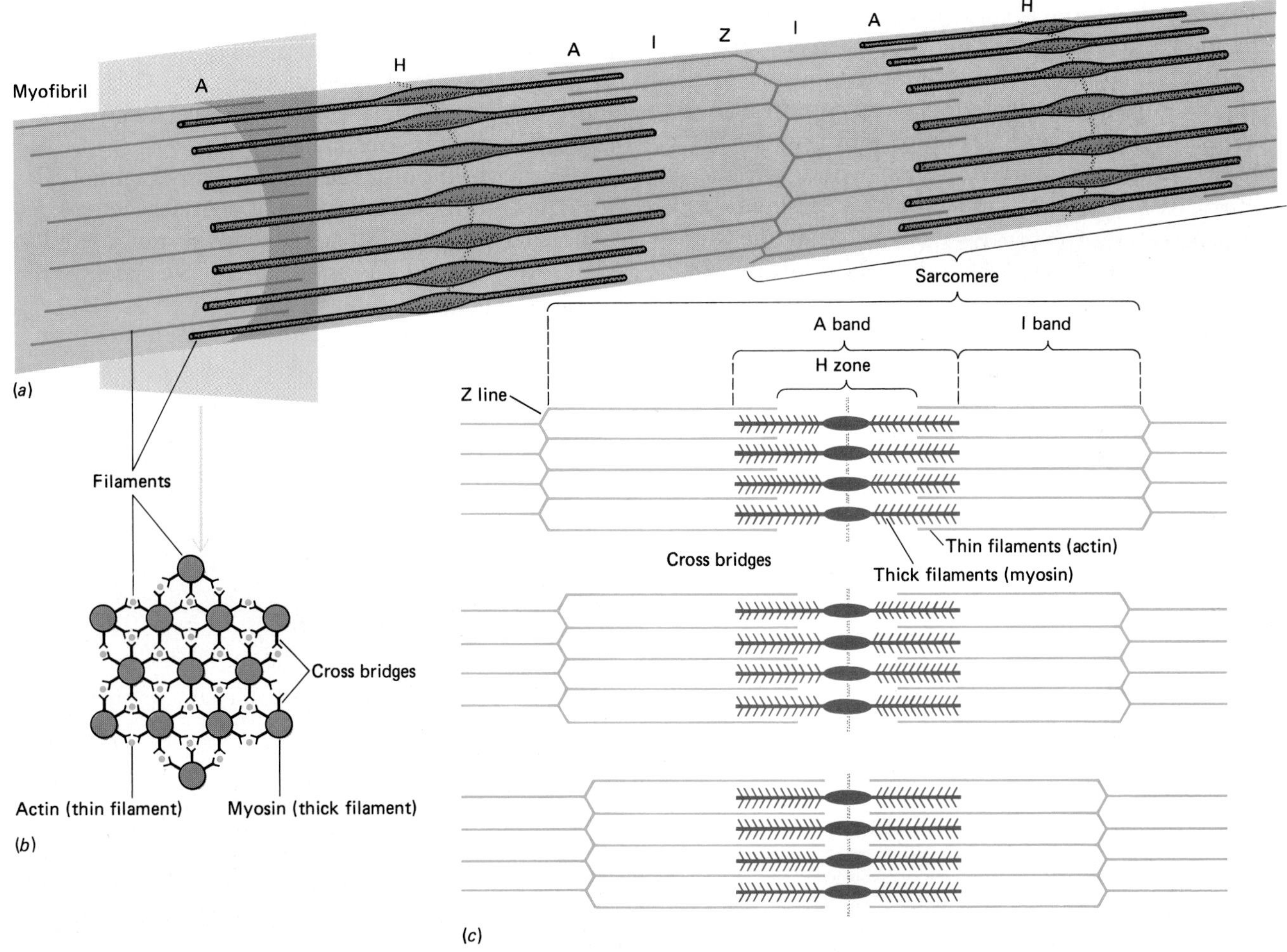

FIGURE 10-6

(a) A myofibril stripped of the accompanying membranes. The Z lines mark the ends of the sarcomeres. *(b)* Cross section of myofibril shown in *a*. *(c)* Filaments slide past each other during contraction. Notice that the thick filaments run the width of the A band; thin filaments run through the I band and overlap the thick filaments within the A band. The H band, which lies in the center of the A, is an area of thick filaments only. In the top drawing of *(c)* the myofibril is relaxed. In the middle drawing, the filaments have slid toward each other, increasing the amount of overlap and shortening the sarcomere. At bottom, maximum contraction has occurred; the sarcomere has shortened considerably.

Skeletal muscle ordinarily contracts following stimulation from a nerve ending

Skeletal muscle is under voluntary, or conscious, control. If it were to contract spontaneously, our muscles would jitter uncontrollably rather than contracting in a useful manner to produce desired movements. Therefore, skeletal muscle fibers normally contract only when a sufficient stimulus is applied by a nerve ending.

Typically a motor nerve (a nerve that innervates muscle) divides into several branches before it terminates, and each branch is distributed to an individual muscle fiber. Thus, a nerve impulse passing along a neuron will result in the simultaneous contraction of all the muscle fibers that particular nerve cell innervates. A group of muscle fibers that all receive their innervation from a single neuron is called a **motor unit** (Fig. 10-7). Motor units vary markedly in size and may involve two to several thousand muscle fibers. Moreover, an individual muscle such as the biceps brachii may contain hundreds or thousands of individual motor units. Later you will see that the strength of muscular contraction is dependent upon the actual number of motor units activated simultaneously.

The functional junction of a neuron and muscle fiber is called the **myoneural junction** (*my*-oh-**new**-ral), **neuromuscular junction,** or **motor end plate** (Fig. 10-8). Skeletal muscle fibers may have one to several such junctions distributed along their length. However, the membranes of the neuron and muscle fiber do not fuse or even make direct contact at these junctions. Rather, they remain separated by a microscopic space known as the **myoneural cleft,** or **neuromuscular junction** (Fig. 10-8). The terminal portions of the nerve cell that participate in the myoneural junction contain numerous mitochondria in addition to large quantities of small, membranous vesicles. These vesicles represent the storage houses for **acetylcholine** (*as*-uh-teel-**ko**-leen), and each vesicle may contain as many as 10,000 molecules of this neurotransmitter substance.

A nerve impulse reaching the myoneural junction induces the release of acetylcholine. This substance rapidly diffuses across the myoneural cleft, and upon reaching acetylcholine receptors

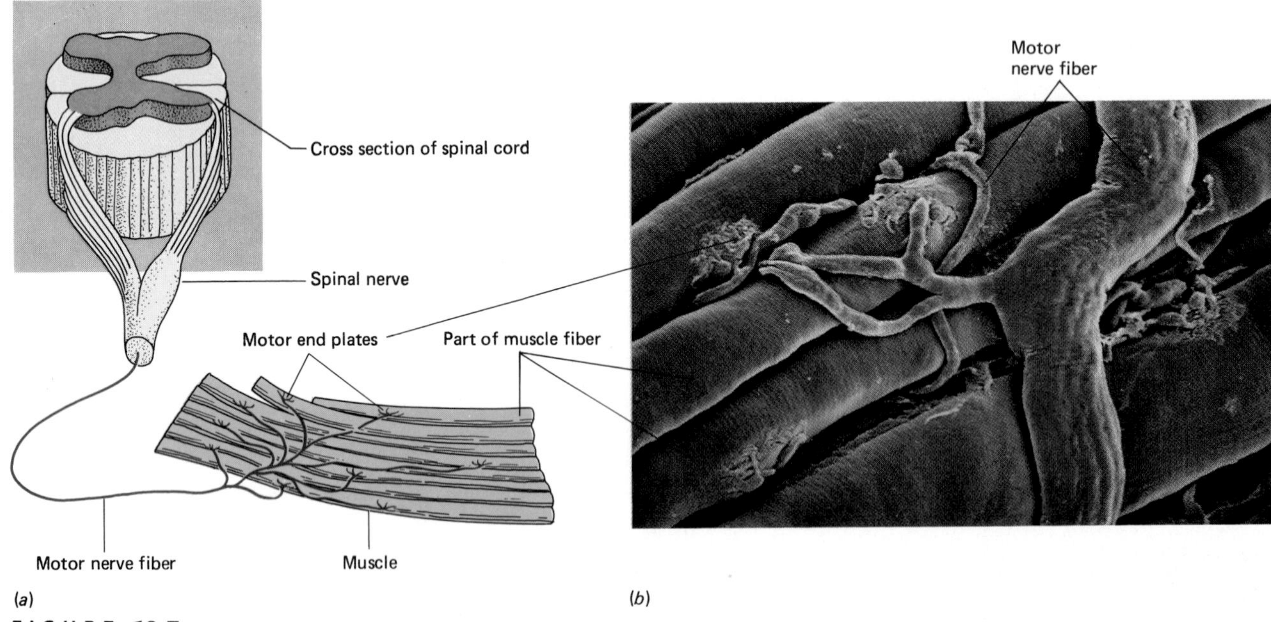

FIGURE 10-7

(a) Motor unit. A typical motor unit includes many more muscle fibers than appear here. Motor units average about 150 muscle fibers each, but some units have less than a dozen fibers while others have several hundred. *(b)* Photomicrograph of some of the cells in a motor unit. Notice how the large neuron branches send subdivisions to each cell in the motor unit (×100). (Ed Reschki/Peter Arnold.)

present on the muscle fiber membrane, causes a temporary electrical **depolarization** of its membrane (Fig. 10-8). (Depolarization is discussed in more detail in Focus on Depolarization and in Chapter 12.) The depolarization travels rapidly along the surface of the muscle fiber membrane in a wavelike manner. Almost as soon as acetylcholine initiates the process of depolarization, the neurotransmitter substance is enzymatically destroyed by an enzyme called **acetylcholinesterase** (*as*-uh-teel-*ko*-li-**nes**-tur-ace). This destruction prevents the muscle fiber from undergoing continuous depolarization.

Clinical highlight

Myasthenia gravis (MG) is an autoimmune disease affecting mostly females in the 25- to 45-year age group. In this disease antibodies are generated toward the acetylcholine receptors present on the muscle fiber membrane in the myoneural junction. The antibodies compete with acetylcholine for the existing receptor sites and with time the muscles become progressively weaker. In fact the muscles may be unable to contract at all. Ordinarily there may be as many as 25 to 40 million acetylcholine receptors in any given myoneural junction. However, in MG only 10 to 30% of these may be available for acetylcholine binding. Facial and neck muscles are typically involved at the onset of the disease, and limb musculature is usually affected later on.

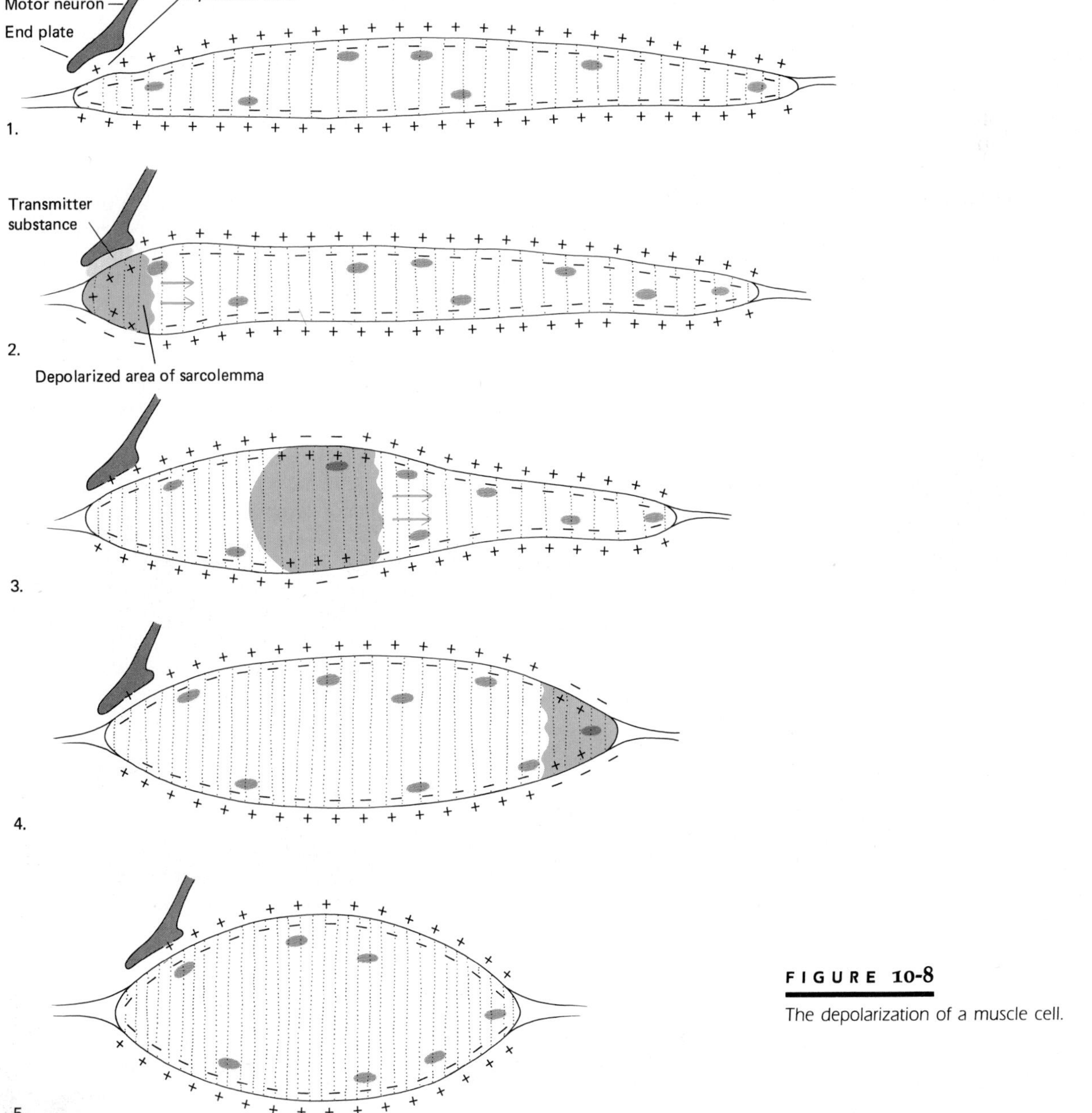

FIGURE 10-8

The depolarization of a muscle cell.

Clinically, treatment of MG has had several approaches. These include (a) steroids to reduce antibody levels; (b) anticholinesterase drugs, which inhibit and/or prolong the enzymatic destruction of acetylcholine and thereby increase its availability to receptors; (c) removal of the thymus, or *thymectomy*; and (d) drugs that suppress the immune system and thus decrease antibody synthesis.

In order for contraction to occur, the wave of depolarization needs to be conveyed to the contractile elements within the muscle fiber. What is the mechanism by which this is achieved? Recall for a moment that the T tubules are actually invaginations of the sarcolemma that project far into the interior of the cell and come to lie in close proximity to components of the sarcoplasmic reticulum (Fig. 10-3). This arrangement permits the wave of depolarization to make its way to the interior of the cell where the contractile elements await. As the depolarization spreads along the T tubule system it causes the release of calcium ions contained within vesicles of the sarcoplasmic reticulum. Calcium diffuses throughout the sarcoplasm and fiber contraction is initiated. Once contraction has taken place, the vesicles reabsorb

FOCUS ON . . . Depolarization

Depolarization is the term applied to the electrical changes responsible for transmitting information along the plasma membrane. This process occurs in all types of muscle, in nerve cells, and perhaps in all tissue. In the case of muscle cells, it transmits the signal for contraction from the myoneural junction to all parts of the muscle, however long that fiber may be.

Although depolarization will be addressed in more detail in Chapter 12, it is useful here to summarize it as follows: When resting, the interior and exterior of the sarcolemma bear different electrical charges, with the exterior being positively charged and the interior being negatively charged.

The contrasting charges are accounted for by differing concentrations of specific ions on the two sides of the sarcolemma. For example, there is considerably more potassium inside the cell than outside, and there is much more sodium outside the cell than inside. These ionic differences are maintained by special proteins in the sarcolemma that actively pump ions in or out of the cell. The resulting charge differential between the interior and exterior of a resting cell sarcolemma is termed the **resting potential.**

When the motor nerve releases its transmitter substance (acetylcholine in the case of skeletal muscle fibers), this substance then diffuses through the microscopic myoneural cleft. A change in membrane permeability occurs when the neurotransmitter substance reaches the sarcolemma. This results in a charge reversal between the interior and exterior of the plasma membrane, so that temporarily the outside becomes negatively charged and the inside becomes positively charged. This charge disturbance is known as depolarization.

If the muscle fiber is small, the entire sarcolemma may become depolarized at one time, but it is more typical for a **wave** of depolarization to sweep over the fiber, followed immediately by restoration of the resting potential. Thus, at any one time only a moving zone of the sarcolemma is actually depolarized (Fig. 10-8). As we discussed in the main text, the depolarization of the muscle fiber plasma membrane is not confined to the sarcolemma, but passes inward on the membrane of the T tubules, where it causes calcium to be released from the sarcoplasmic reticulum and initiates contraction.

Depolarization, at least in skeletal muscle fibers, begins at the acetylcholine receptors. These receptors are plasma membrane protein complexes. They bridge the plasma membrane and possess receptor sites that accept any acetylcholine molecules that diffuse across the 200-angstrom unit myoneural cleft.[1] Once the acetylcholine is bound to the receptor complex, the protein of the receptor undergoes a conformational change causing a channel to open within it.

Sodium and potassium, normally maintained in very different concentrations on the two sides of the sarcolemma by the sodium pump (and possibly by a separate potassium pump), now rush through this channel by diffusion. This massive ionic shift triggers the initial depolarization of the sarcolemma, which immediately becomes self-sustaining and is propagated down the length of the muscle fiber.

Focus on the remarkable scanning electron micrographs taken by Yasuo Uehara, Junzo Desaki, and Takashi Fujiwara of the Ehime University School of Medicine in Japan.[2] Notice a number of neuromuscular junctions (*a*), one of which has been stripped away (*b*) to disclose the features of the muscle-side of the neuromuscular junction. It is evident that the sarcolemma of this region is elaborately sculptured to form a multitude of microscopic ridges and valleys. The acetylcholine receptors are situated at the crests of these ridges (×2000 and ×5700 for *a* and *b*, respectively).

[1] An angstrom unit (Å) equals 10^{-8} cm.
[2] From Junzo Desaki and Yasuo Uehara: "The overall morphology of neuromuscular junctions as revealed by scanning electron microscopy." Journal of Neurocytology 10:101–110, 1981.

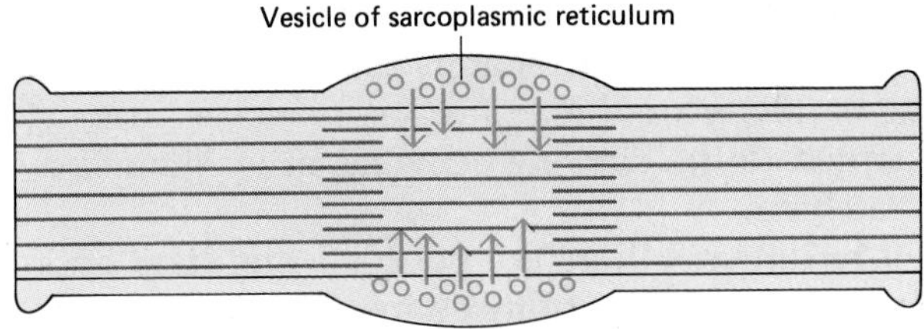

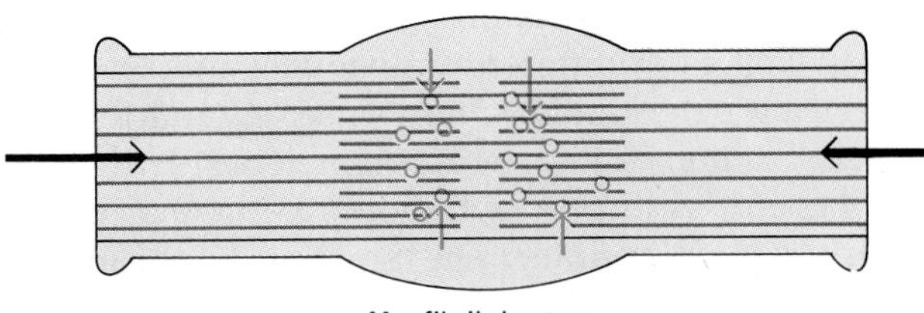

Calcium actively reabsorbed into vesicles; myofibril relaxes

FIGURE 10-9

When calcium is released from the sarcoplasmic reticulum, myofibril contracts; when calcium is reabsorbed by the sarcoplasmic reticulum, myofibril relaxes.

calcium by means of an active-transport mechanism, and the muscle fiber is readied for the next stimulus (Fig. 10-9).

In almost all human skeletal muscle, the neuronal control processes result in an **all-or-none** phenomenon—either the muscle fiber contracts or it does not. A single depolarization will typically produce an individual **simple twitch** lasting but a fraction of a second. With the possible exception of the eyeblink, we all realize that whole muscles ordinarily do not respond in an all-or-none manner. Certainly none of us exerts an equivalent amount of force to write a letter as to move a refrigerator. How is it then that continuous action, strength gradation, and delicacy of control are made possible?

Two principal mechanisms are involved. (1) Every muscle contains many motor units. The strength of a muscular contraction is dependent upon the number of such units that are activated simultaneously. Muscles that require very delicate control, such as those governing eye movement, contain many more motor units, each composed of significantly fewer cells than those whose action need less precision, such as muscles of the back. (2) In order for a neuron to produce a sustained contraction as opposed to a simple twitch, it merely needs to stimulate a muscle fiber several times in quick succession. In doing so the individual contractions will actually fuse into one smoothly sustained event known as a **tetanic contraction** (Fig. 10-10). This will not only last much longer but will be several times stronger than a simple twitch.

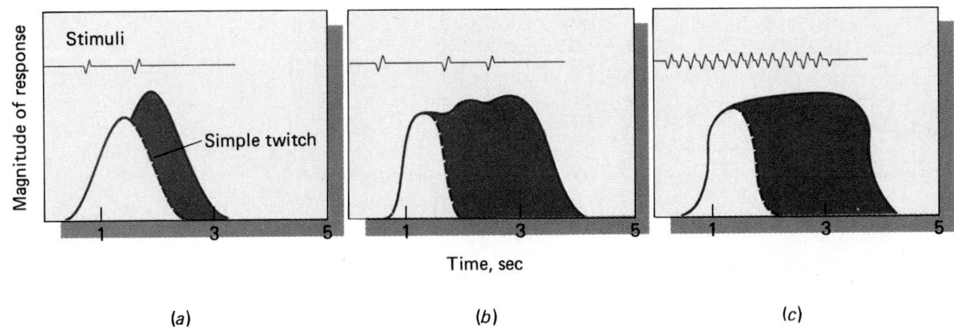

FIGURE 10-10

Tetany in skeletal muscle. *(a)* The length of time a muscle contracts can be considerably prolonged by repetitive stimuli that are close in time. Notice how in this instance two stimuli produce not two simple twitches but a much longer-lasting response. *(b)* Several stimuli close together cause an even longer-lasting response. *(c)* High frequency stimulation causes a single, smoothly sustained contraction called tetanus.

All vertebrates possess two distinct types of skeletal muscle fibers that contract at different rates. These are termed **fast-twitch** and **slow-twitch** muscle fibers, although intermediate types also exist. In many birds entire muscles are almost exclusively composed of one fiber type, with the "dark meat" consisting chiefly of slow-twitch and the "white meat" of fast-twitch fibers. Table 10-1 compares the characteristics of the two fiber types, and these are summarized as follows: Fast-twitch fibers are most suitably adapted to high-intensity exercise, which, while it is sustained, is largely anaerobic (not requiring oxygen) in nature, as will be presently explained. Longer term, more fully aerobic (requiring oxygen) types of exercise are best served with slow-twitch fibers. Thus, in a chicken or other bird that rarely flies, the wing muscles of the breast are composed of fast-twitch white fibers for the sake of quick escape from predators. Slow-twitch fibers of the darkly colored leg muscles, however, are adapted to the daylong activities of walking and scratching.

In humans there are no white and dark muscles corresponding to those in birds. Microscopic examination of human skeletal muscle, however, reveals fast-twitch and slow-twitch as well as intermediate type fibers (Fig. 10-11). These fiber types vary in their proportions in different muscles as well as in different individuals and are genetically determined. One whose leg and thigh muscles contain a high proportion of fast-twitch fibers could, with proper training, become a remarkably good sprinter. On the other hand, marathon activities would better suit the athlete possessing a greater proportion of slow-twitch fibers.

TABLE 10-1

Some characteristics of slow-twitch and fast-twitch muscle cells

Characteristic	Slow Twitch	Fast Twitch
Fatigability	Low	High
Contraction time	Long	Short
Relaxation time	Long	Short
Creatine phosphate content*	Low	High
Enzymes of anaerobic respiratory pathways	Low	High
Enzymes of aerobic respiratory pathways	High	Low
Capillary density	High	Low
Mitochondria content	High	Low
Glycogen content	No significant difference	
Fat content	High	Low
Myoglobin content	High†	Low
Myosin ATPase activity‡	High	Low
Activity during high-intensity (sprintlike) exercise	Low	High
Activity during long-term sustained (marathon-like) exercise	High	Low

*Creatine phosphate is an energy storage chemical found in muscle cells from which energy for contraction can be obtained for a time without respiration.

†Muscles with high slow-twitch fiber content appear dark principally because of their myoglobin content.

‡Muscles operate by the energy of ATP as liberated by the contractile protein myosin. The ability of myosin to liberate energy from ATP and to employ it in contraction is known as myosin ATPase activity.

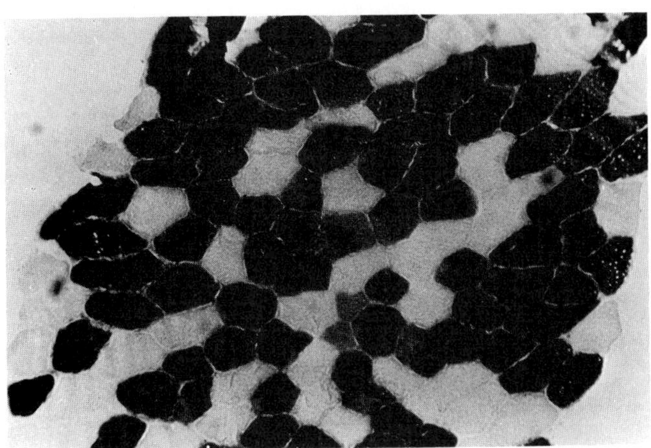

FIGURE 10-11

Transverse section of several muscle fibers showing the localization of succinic dehydrogenase activity, which reflects the location of mitochondria. Small (red) fibers are rich in mitochondria, especially along the periphery; (white) fibers have a low mitochondrial content. (From Fox, Edward L., and Matthews, Donald K.: The Physiological Basis of Physical Education and Athletics. Philadelphia, Saunders College Publishing, 1981.)

Clinical highlight

Many substances can interfere with muscle control. For example, anticholinesterase pesticides and nerve gases can lead to tetanic contraction by preventing the enzymatic destruction of acetylcholine by acetylcholinesterase. Curare (kur-**ar**-ee), used by South American Indians to poison arrowheads and kill fish, interferes with acetylcholine receptors that normally bind this neurotransmitter substance. Such interference prevents contraction and leads to suffocation because the fish is no longer able to force water past its gills. Curare is also capable of killing humans as a result of respiratory paralysis, but it and related drugs are typically used in much smaller doses as muscle relaxants to facilitate various surgical procedures. The toxin produced by botulinus bacteria, one of the most poisonous substances known to humankind, acts at the myoneural junction by blocking the release of acetylcholine from nerve endings.

Energy for muscular contraction is derived from ATP

Muscle fibers, like all cells, utilize **adenosine triphosphate (ATP)** as a source of energy. ATP has no equivalent in any commonly manufactured device, but it provides the necessary energy for all life processes, for example, muscular contraction. Muscle fibers derive energy from ATP much in the same way an automobile engine derives energy from burning gasoline, and similarly, these fibers convert the stored energy from this fuel into mechanical motion. Like other cells, muscle fibers also resemble an automobile in utilizing oxygen much of the time and, by an indirect process, combining this oxygen with the fuel. This produces water, carbon dioxide, and heat as end products, while liberating partially usable energy. However, an important difference in this analogy lies in the manner in which energy is transferred from the burning of the fuel to the mechanical parts.

ATP consists of an organic body plus a tail composed of three phosphate groups. The structural formula for ATP is illustrated in Figure 10-12. The last two phosphate groups are attached to the remainder of the molecule by *high-energy chemical bonds (pyrophosphate bonds),* which are readily formed and readily broken. Phosphate is easily added to the body of the molecule and easily detached. The addition of phosphate requires energy whereas its detachment liberates energy.

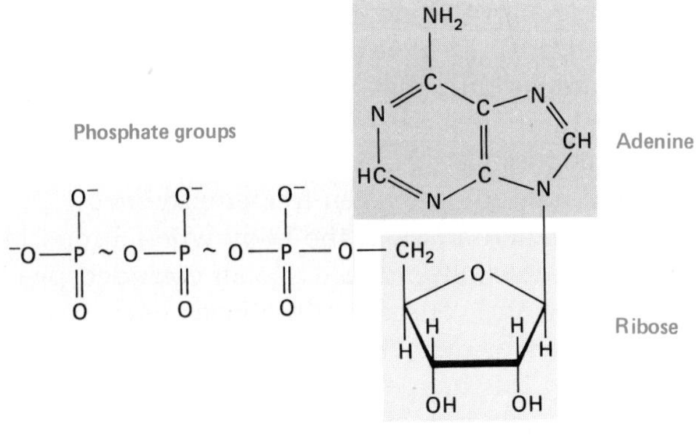

Phosphate groups

Adenine

Ribose

FIGURE 10-12

The structure of ATP, a nucleotide that has energy-rich bonds joining the two terminal phosphate groups to the nucleotide.

Since muscle fibers must frequently expend large amounts of energy on relatively short notice, the energy must be stored in a readily available form. However, ATP is not employed by muscle fibers for long-term storage. In this instance the energy of ATP is stored by transferring its terminal phosphate group, together with much of the energy contained in its chemical bond, to another compound, **creatine** (**kree**-uh-tin), thus forming **creatine phosphate (CP).** The molecule of ATP that has lost its terminal phosphate group is now called **adenosine diphosphate (ADP).** Upon demand, CP transfers its energy back to ADP by means of an enzyme called *creatine phosphokinase (CPK)*, forming ATP, which is then able to provide the needed energy for muscular contraction.

Creatine phosphate resembles somewhat a storage battery where energy from ATP is stored temporarily, to be reconverted into ATP when necessary. It is believed that this rather roundabout system of energy transfer and storage renders the muscle fiber somewhat more resistant to oxygen deprivation than would be the case if ATP alone were utilized. Equally important is the fact that CP is used for storage of energy for muscular contraction only. Therefore other cellular processes cannot compete directly with contraction for its energy stores. Evidence also supports the notion that CP can be used as an energy source through cleavage of its own phosphate group.

Resting muscle fibers, on the other hand, derive most of their energy requirements from the breakdown of **fatty acids,** with a small contribution from the breakdown of **glycogen.** Fatty acids are broken down to a compound called **acetate** by a group of enzymes located within the mitochondria. This process is termed **beta oxidation.** The acetate then enters the *citric acid* (Krebs) *cycle* where the resulting energy is transferred to ATP (see Chapter 26).

During active work, muscle fibers rely primarily upon *glucose* as their energy source. These reactions are **aerobic;** that is, they are dependent completely upon the presence of oxygen. However, it is possible for a muscle fiber to contract for some time in an oxygen-free environment. Such a situation arises in the body when a muscle fiber exerts itself strenuously for an extended period of time and consequently utilizes more oxygen than can be delivered by the blood per unit time. When this happens, the muscle fiber meets some of its energy requirements by oxygen-free, or **anaerobic,** metabolism. This part of the pathway, however, is markedly less efficient than the aerobic mechanism, in that it requires up to 18 times as much fuel to produce an equivalent amount of ATP. Since the anaerobic pathway is so inefficient, muscle fibers possess large emergency stores of glycogen (a polysaccharide carbohydrate). During strenuous exercise the glycogen is rapidly converted to **lactic acid.** The lactic acid that accumulates in the muscles and body as a result of this anaerobic process leads to the sensation of fatigue and in certain instances to cramping and pain in skeletal muscles.

Lactic acid is also transported to the liver and to other muscles where it is broken down aerobically. Because this process requires oxygen, a runner who has just finished a 100-meter dash will pant and puff afterwards for some time. It is much as if the athlete has incurred an **oxygen debt** that now must be repaid. Energy released by the breakdown of some of the lactic acid is utilized in turn to metabolize the remaining lactic acid back into glucose. The metabolic events just described are summarized for you in Figure 10-13 and are discussed further in Chapter 26.

Many muscles appear red because they possess a red pigment called **myoglobin** (*my*-oh-**glow**-bin). Myoglobin is similar to *hemoglobin* (*hee*-muh-**glow**-bin) and may in fact be mistaken for the latter during laboratory procedures designed to test for the presence of blood in the urine or feces. Myoglobin can be liberated from muscle fibers damaged by crushing injuries or unaccustomed exercise, such as sometimes occurs in military training. Occasionally, large quantities of liberated myoglobin may seriously damage the kidneys.

The functions of myoglobin in the muscle fiber are twofold. (1) It serves as an intermediary responsible for the transfer of oxygen from hemoglobin of erythrocytes (e-**rith**-row-sites; red blood cells) to the aerobic metabolic processes of the muscle fiber. As will be discussed in more detail in Chapter 24, hemoglobin of the blood is subject to a chemical influence termed the **Bohr effect.** In brief, this phenomenon reflects the effect of pH on the oxygen-carrying capacity of hemoglobin. For example, when pH levels fall, oxygen is released from the blood. Thus, an actively contracting muscle that is producing lactic acid and/or carbon dioxide is likely to lower the pH of the blood circulating through it, and this will result in the release of oxygen, which the laboring muscles require. Although it is chemically similar to hemoglobin, myoglobin does not experience the Bohr effect; that is, its oxygen uptake is not affected by alterations in pH levels. Consequently, the myoglobin of active muscle fibers has a higher oxygen-binding capacity than the hemoglobin of the blood passing through it, so that the oxygen given off by the hemoglobin is readily absorbed by the muscle fiber. (2) Myoglobin is also believed to possess a modest oxygen-storing capacity that is of use to the muscle during intermittent but strong contraction. Blood flow in the vessels supplying a muscle may be compromised during strenuous contraction. If the contraction is not too prolonged, the muscle cell may subsist for a short time on the oxygen bound to the myoglobin and need not rely immediately upon anaerobic respiration.

FIGURE 10-13

The mechanism of oxygen debt.

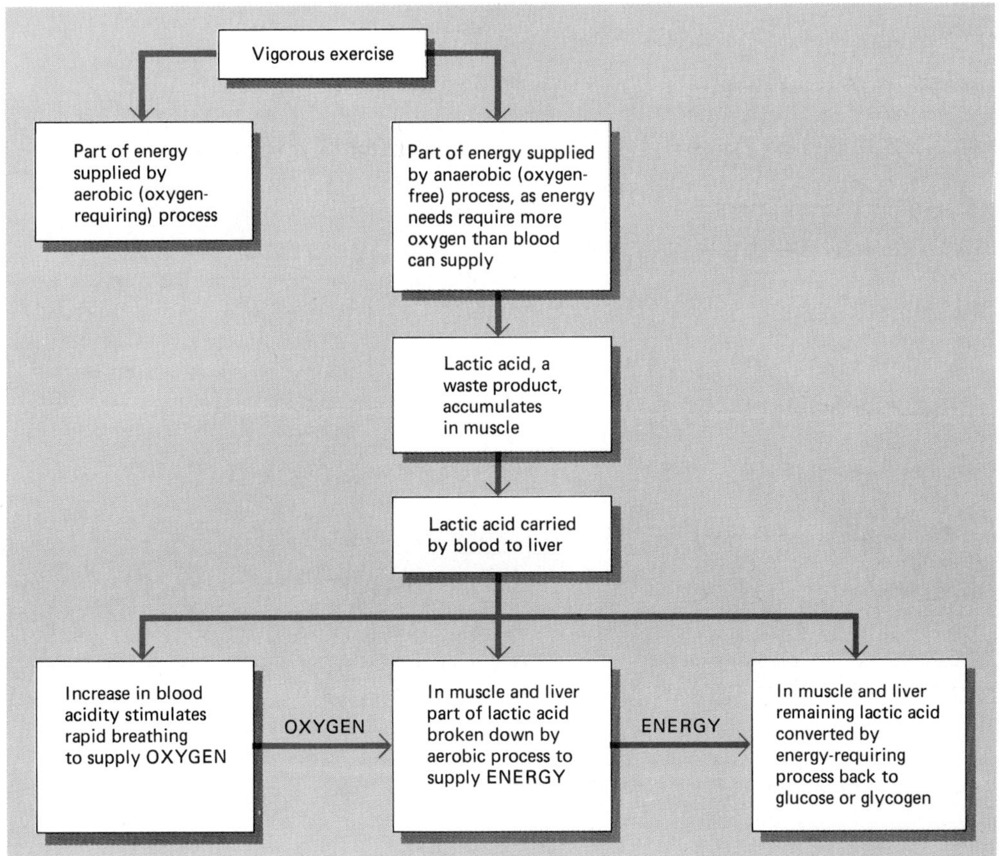

Muscle cells transform chemical energy into mechanical motion

Thus far we have focused on the structural components of the muscle fiber and on the mechanisms by which energy is obtained to make these parts function. Now let's discuss how that energy is transformed from its original chemical form to the mechanical form in which it appears when one takes a step, rides a bicycle, or plays a piano. Although some aspects of the explanation are still unproven, muscular activity is believed to occur at the molecular level in the following manner.

Muscle contraction occurs by a mechanism called the **sliding filament process.** What causes the thin actin filaments to slide inward among the thick myosin filaments? The process is very complex and incorporates chemical and mechanical forces together with the formation of **cross bridges** between myosin and actin filaments. As you have seen, the depolarization of the muscle fiber plasma membrane and T tubule system leads to the release of large quantities of calcium ions from the sarcoplasmic reticulum. This release of calcium initiates the active forces between the various contractile filaments, and the process of contraction begins. Furthermore, energy in the form of ATP is required to complete the contraction process.

Each **myosin molecule** is made up of six polypeptide chains which are intertwined to form a double helix. One end of each myosin molecule is folded into two globular structures called the **heads,** and the remainder of the molecule is termed its **tail.** The complete myosin molecule has a molecular weight of nearly 480,000. Moreover, each **myosin filament** is composed of approximately 200 separate myosin molecules. The heads of individual myosin molecules extend away from the body of the myosin filament; they are positioned on flexible, armlike appendages (Fig. 10-14). Together, the heads and armlike appendages form the cross bridges mentioned previously. An important feature of the myosin head is that it has the ability to break down ATP in the presence of calcium and use the liberated energy for the contraction process.

The other component of the sliding filament process is the actin filament (Fig. 10-14). Actin filaments are attached strongly by their bases to the Z bands, and their free ends protrude into the adjacent sarcomeres. Actually this filament is composed of three separate elements, *actin, tropomyosin* (*troe*-poe-**my**-o-sin), and *troponin* (**troe**-poe-nin). Each actin filament consists of a double-stranded *F-actin molecule,* which is formed by the interaction of two *G-actin molecules.* One molecule of ADP is attached to each G-actin molecule and these are believed to represent the **active sites** on actin filaments that interact with myosin cross bridges during contraction. Furthermore, two **tropomyosin** molecules are intertwined with each actin filament and in the resting state are thought to mask the active sites on the filament, thereby preventing interaction with myosin cross bridges (Fig. 10-14). The final component of the actin filament is a complex of three globular proteins known as **troponin.** This complex not only serves to bind the tropomyosin to the actin, but has a definite affinity for binding calcium ions.

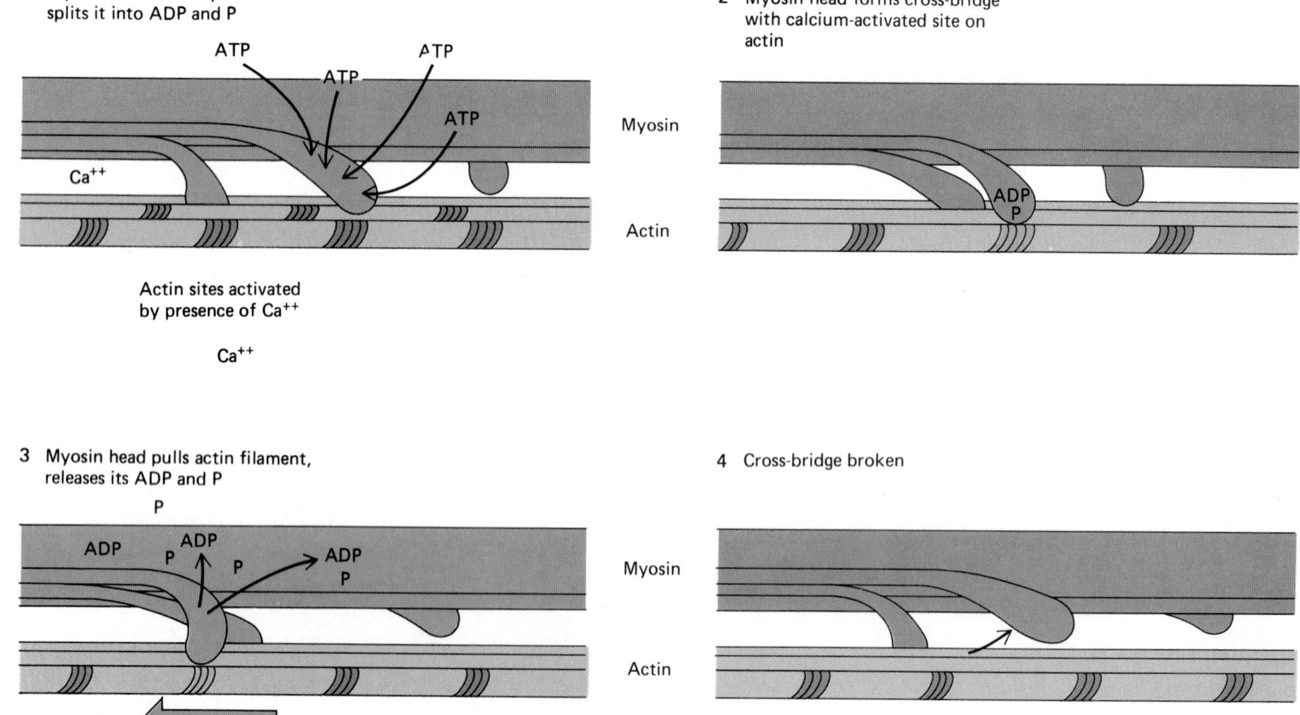
1 Myosin head takes up ATP splits it into ADP and P
ATP
ATP
ATP
ATP
Ca^{++}
Actin sites activated by presence of Ca^{++}
Ca^{++}
Myosin
Actin
2 Myosin head forms cross-bridge with calcium-activated site on actin
ADP
P
3 Myosin head pulls actin filament, releases its ADP and P
P
ADP
ADP
P
P
ADP
P
Myosin
Actin
4 Cross-bridge broken

FIGURE 10-14

How the cross bridges are believed to move the thin and thick filaments past each other in muscle contraction.

Once calcium ions are released from the sarcoplasmic reticulum, many are bound to the troponin complex. This is believed to cause a conformational change in the troponin complex, allowing the tropomyosin to move deeper into the space between the intertwined G-actin molecules. In doing so the active sites on the actin are "unmasked," so interaction with myosin cross bridges may proceed (Fig. 10-14). ATP is bound to the head of the cross bridge and energy is released as it is cleaved to form ADP. Myosin heads immediately attach to the active sites, which brings about another conformational change, this time in the cross bridge. This change appears to result in a bending of the cross bridge such that the actin filament is pulled along in a direction corresponding to the bend. The two strands are pulled past one another for a distance of approximately 143 angstrom units (an angstrom unit is equal to 10^{-8} centimeters). Once this occurs the ADP is released from the head so that another ATP molecule may attach. The myosin head then detaches from the active site, returns to its normal position, and combines with another site located further down the actin filament and the process repeats itself. These events are schematically represented for you in Figure 10-14.

Consider the molecular events involved in this contraction mechanism in this way: First, if you substitute the word "leg" for cross bridge, the entire process resembles a footstep, and all the cross bridges working together resemble the leg action of a centipede. Second, if this view of contraction is correct, each step requires the consumption of the usable energy of one or perhaps two molecules of ATP per step. That is, at the conclusion of the process the ATP yields ADP and phosphate. These are put back together using the energy of metabolism as discussed previously, and the energy stored within the new ATP molecule is made available for other processes. With thousands of cross bridges in a single muscle fiber, and as many sites of attachment, a single, simple twitch must conceivably employ astronomical numbers of ATP molecules. The physiological aspects of muscle contraction are illustrated in Fig. 10-15.

Clinical highlight

When a person dies, the ATP of muscles breaks down and is not replenished. Hence, the binding of cross bridges to actin filaments forms connections that cannot be released, and a stiffening of the muscles develops. This stiffness is called **rigor mortis.** Incidentally, rigor mortis does not produce active contraction of muscle fibers, rather it produces stiffness only. With time the entire contractile apparatus disintegrates and the muscles become pliable once again.

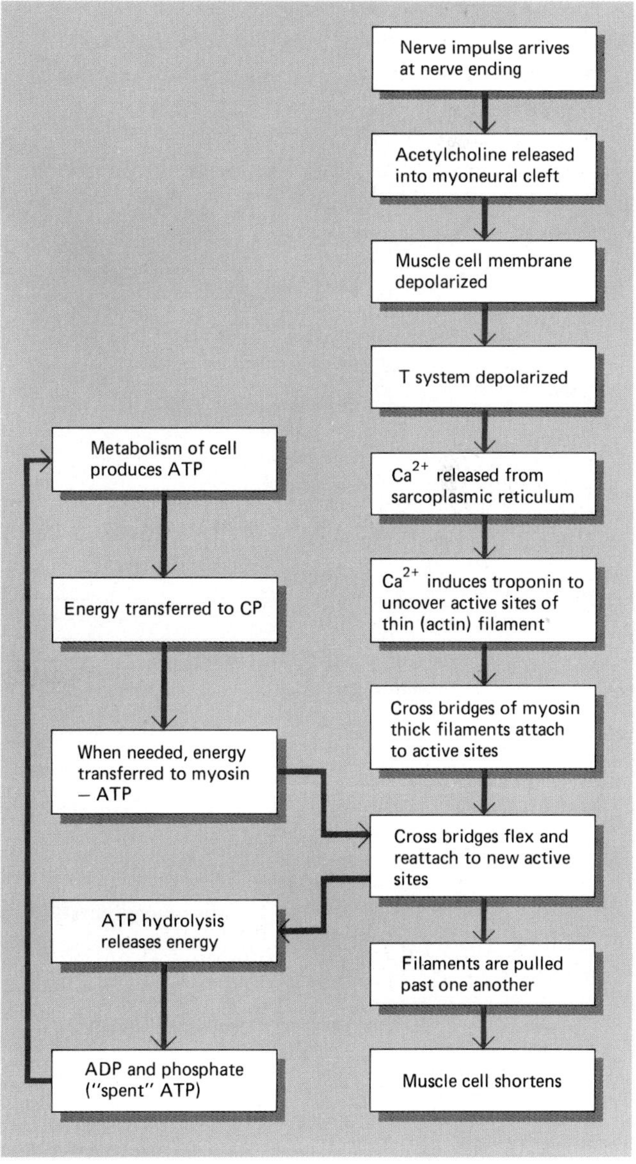

FIGURE 10-15

Summary of the major events of muscle contraction.

Isometric contraction is responsible for the existence of muscle tone

Muscle fibers increase in size, or hypertrophy, as a result of exercise. This leads to enlargement and strengthening of the muscle being exercised. If the exercise involves movement, as in weight lifting, it is said to be **isotonic** (*eye*-so-**ton**-ik), for although the muscle shortens during this form of exercise, its tension does not increase significantly. **Isometric** exercise (*eye*-so-**met**-rik), on the other hand, occurs when contraction does not actually lead to shortening of the muscle, but its tension is increased markedly. This occurs when pushing against an immovable object or by opposing antagonistic muscles. Isotonic and two forms of isometric exercise are illustrated for you in Figure 10-16. See also Focus on Isometric and Isotonic Exercise.

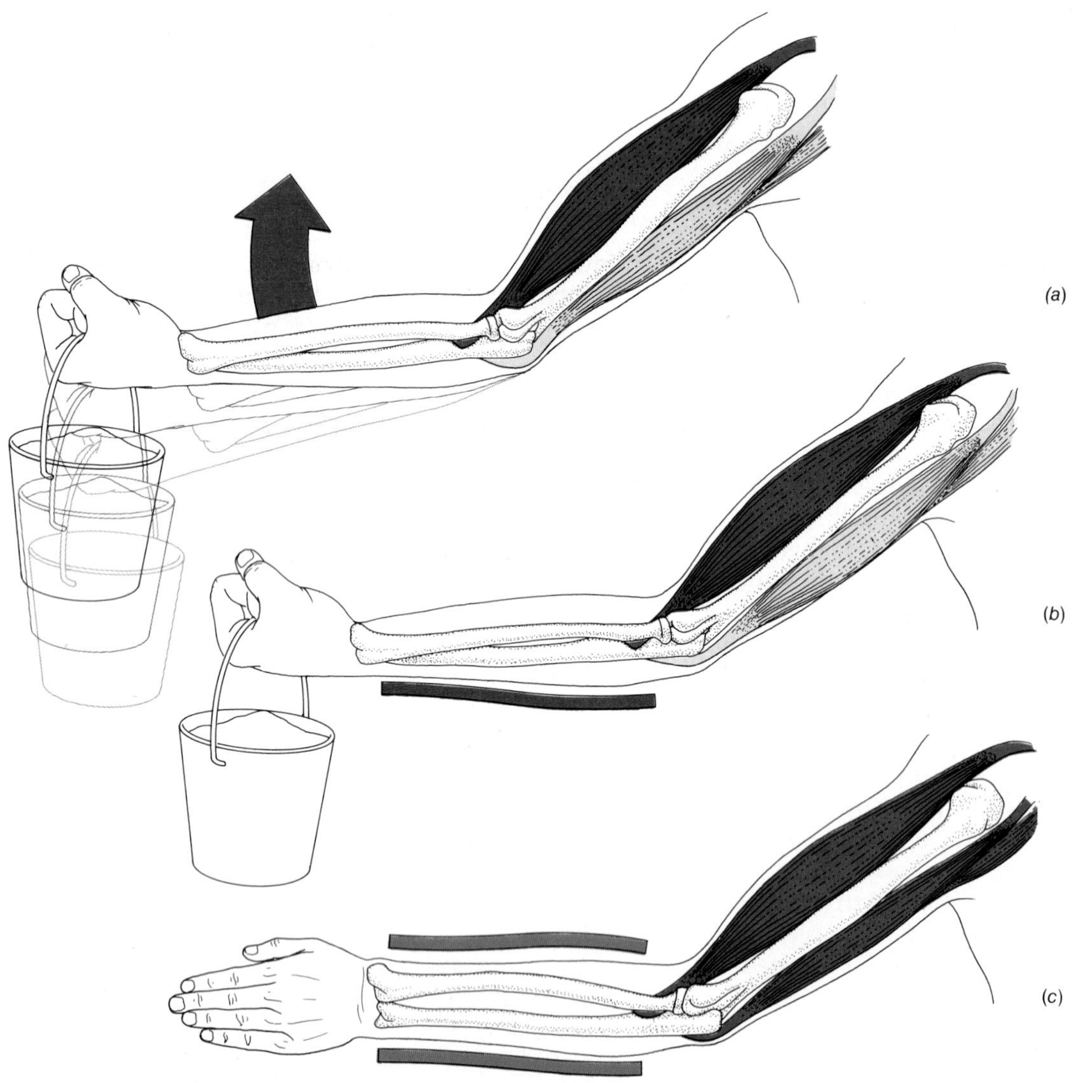

FIGURE 10-16

(a) Isotonic exercise. The force of muscle contraction is greater than the opposing force of the weight. The muscle shortens, pulling the forearm toward it. *(b)* and *(c)* Two varieties of isometric exercise. The force of muscle contraction is met by an equal opposing force, so that the muscle cannot shorten and no movement occurs. Tension within the muscle is great.

Isometric muscle contractions have more importance than merely their role in an exercise protocol. **Muscle tone** is a state of continuous muscle contraction that falls into the isometric category. This type of contraction is responsible for helping the abdominal wall muscles keep the underlying viscera in place and the postural muscles keeping us upright. Finally, isometric contraction permits muscles that do not actually move a body part in a particular action to guide its motion. As you will see in Chapter 11, such muscles are of particular significance in functioning of the hip and shoulder joints.

A condition representing the opposite of muscle hypertrophy is muscle **atrophy** (**a**-troe-fee). This process occurs when a muscle or group of muscles is no longer used or when a muscle is employed only for very weak contractions. The muscles become wasted under these conditions. Such disuse atrophy is likely to take place when the upper or lower limb is placed in a cast for the purpose of mending a fractured bone. It has been estimated that such disuse atrophy, even if it lasts for as little as a month, may reduce the original muscle mass by as much as 50%.

Clinical highlight

Another cause of muscle atrophy is denervation as sometimes results from traumatic injury. Once the nerve supply to a muscle is lost, atrophy sets in immediately. A person may regain full function of a denervated muscle if reinnervation occurs during the first few (2 to 4) months following the injury. Failure of the muscle to become reinnervated within this time frame usually leads to the complete degeneration of muscle fibers and their gradual replacement by adipose (fat) and fibrotic tissue.

Muscle strength, power, and endurance are considerations in sports

In the sports arena, muscles play the primary role in all athletic events. The strength, power, and endurance of the muscles are the significant considerations here. Muscle **strength** is directly related to muscle size; that is, contractile force is proportional to the cross-sectional area of the muscle. An athlete whose muscles are hypertrophied as a result of prolonged training will also possess substantially more muscle strength.

Muscle **power** is defined as the amount of work achieved by a muscle over a specific time interval. Factors influencing muscle power include not only the strength of the muscle, but its **velocity of contraction** and its **rate of contraction** as well. Simply stated, this quality permits the athlete to produce a great degree of power for a relatively short period of time, for example, in a 100-meter dash. This capability is markedly reduced in longer events such as the marathon. However,

FOCUS ON . . . Isometric and isotonic exercise

Few forms of exercise can be classified as purely isometric or isotonic; however, most approach one or the other of these types. In recent times isometric exercises have become increasingly popular, in part because they require little in the way of equipment and can often be performed at odd times and locations during the day without the need of a gymnasium. Moreover, isometric exercises cause muscles to hypertrophy to a greater extent than do isotonic exercises. Unfortunately, while isometric exercise may efficiently increase the size and strength of muscles, it does little for cardiovascular fitness.

Isotonic exercise, on the other hand, appears to increase the vascularity of skeletal and cardiac muscle such that the muscles and heart develop increased numbers of capillaries, probably metabolize lactic acid more readily, and become more resistant to fatigue. This is especially true if the exercise activity selected is active, such as running, jogging, or even walking, rather than static, such as weight lifting. Of course there is no reason—if one has the time and energy—not to take up both weight lifting and jogging. Furthermore, the exercise machines currently marketed have an advantage in that they provide changing degrees of resistance over the entire range of a muscle's action. This feature tends to improve not only muscular size and strength, but cardiovascular fitness as well.

athletic performance should not decline appreciably under such circumstances because the efficiency with which power is converted to performance tends to be lower during events of relatively short, rapid activity.

Finally there is the consideration of muscular **endurance.** Nutrition is a major factor here. Endurance is influenced greatly by the quantities of glycogen stored in the muscles at the initiation of a particular athletic event. A diet rich in carbohydrates is most desirable because this permits the athlete to store much greater quantities of glycogen compared to mixed or high-fat diets.

The amount of ATP present in the muscles of athletes is sufficient to permit rigorous muscular activity for only a few seconds. Therefore, the breakdown of creatine phosphate becomes important for the liberation of stored energy to form new ATP. This occurs very rapidly and, together with the energy stored in existing ATP, this energy provides the athlete with maximal activity for a short duration. An additional source of ATP derives from the anaerobic breakdown of glycogen to glucose and subsequent conversion of glucose to pyruvic acid. This conversion results in the release of energy in the form of ATP. Pyruvic acid may enter the oxidative pathway for more ATP generation if sufficient oxygen is available. However, if oxygen is lacking, the pyruvic acid is converted to lactic acid anaerobically.

The generation of ATP through the anaerobic conversion of glucose to lactic acid occurs nearly twice as rapidly as ATP formed by means of aerobic events in mitochondria; it therefore provides the athlete with substantial quantities of energy for a moderate period of time. During longer periods of physical activity, fatty acids, amino acids, and glucose are metabolized aerobically, and the energy that is released is in turn utilized to generate additional ATP. Thus, it is evident that existing ATP and creatine phosphate provide energy to the performing athlete for a very short interval, whereas the aerobic metabolism of fatty acids, glucose, and amino acids serves this purpose during prolonged activity. The anaerobic conversion of glucose to lactic acid functions in an intermediate manner in this regard.

The oxygen debt must be repaid following strenuous exercise

Another important consideration that needs to be addressed in regard to muscular activity during athletic events is that of **recovery;** that is, how fast can the various energy systems be restored? The energy system utilizing existing ATP and creatine phosphate for muscle contraction is capable of total recovery in approximately 4 to 5 minutes following strenuous activity. Lactic acid is responsible for the fatigue associated with rigorous exercise and therefore imposes a limitation as to its usefulness as an energy source. Thus, recovery of this system to a state where it once again provides a source of energy is dependent upon the rate at which the athlete can eliminate or metabolize lactic acid from the body—a process that requires about an hour once the physical activity has ceased. Finally, the recovery of the aerobic system of energy production may take as long as 24 to 48 hours, and even longer in those individuals not on a high-carbohydrate diet.

When an athlete undertakes a strenuous training program, muscle hypertrophy occurs mainly as a result of the increase in diameter of already existing muscle fibers. There are also internal changes that accompany this hypertrophy. For example, the number of myofibrils and mitochondria tends to increase in proportion to the degree of hypertrophy. The amount of creatine phosphate and ATP may likewise increase as much as 20 to 40%. Additionally, glycogen and fat stores within the enlarged muscle fiber are increased as are the enzymes necessary for aerobic metabolism.

Smooth muscle cells differ structurally and functionally from skeletal muscle cells

Smooth muscle is widely distributed throughout the body. Regions where it is found include: (a) the wall of the digestive tract; (b) ducts of various glands; (c) walls of veins, arteries, and lymphatic trunks; (d) skin; and (e) the iris and ciliary body of the eye.

Smooth muscle cells, unlike skeletal muscle, have a single nucleus (mononucleate) which is centrally located. Smooth muscle cells are typically long and spindle-shaped and do not possess distinct boundaries as seen with skeletal muscle fibers. Although they have the same contractile elements as do skeletal muscle, they do not possess sarcomeres. Thus, smooth muscle cells do not exhibit characteristic striations except when special stains are employed (Fig. 10-17). Recent evidence suggests that the sarcoplasm of smooth muscle cells contains relatively more actin than that of skeletal muscle fibers. Furthermore, smooth muscle cells vary markedly in their length depending upon their location.

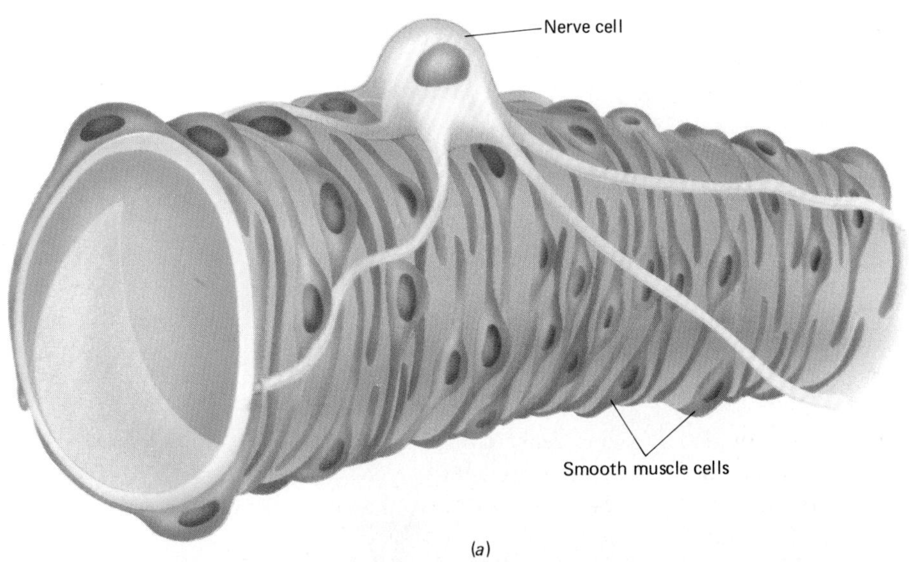

(a)

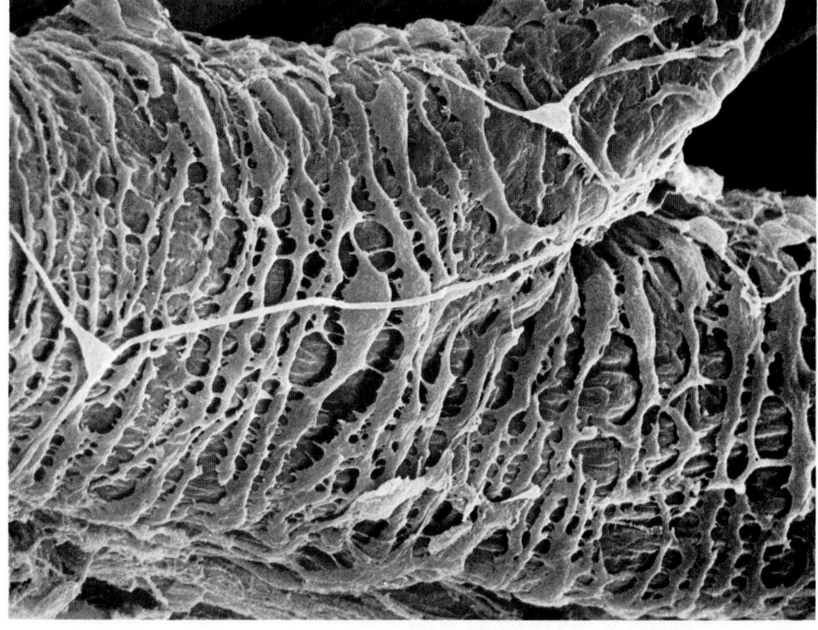

(b)

FIGURE 10-17

(a) Smooth muscle cells. A single nerve cell may innervate several smooth muscle cells in passing, yet many smooth muscle cells have no direct nervous connections at all. *(b)* Scanning electron micrograph of the autonomic innervation of the smooth muscle cells of a small vein. The thin white fibers are autonomic nerve axons, and the triangular bodies where these branch are Schwann cells. The neurons are arranged to stimulate large numbers of smooth muscle cells (arranged in rings around the vein) at the same time (×900). (From Desaki, Junzo: "Vascular autonomic plexuses and skeletal neuromuscular functions: A scanning electron microscopic study." Biomedical Research Supplement 139–143, 1981.)

Smooth muscle cells tend to be closely packed and in specific areas the intercellular space is greatly narrowed such that the adjacent plasma membranes are separated only by a microscopic space. These specialized junctions are believed to represent regions of low electrical resistance and are termed **gap junctions** or **nexuses** (Fig. 10-18). Experimental evidence suggests that excitatory impulses may be able to pass directly from one smooth muscle cell to another by means of such junctions, without necessarily involving nerves. Thus, a wave of contraction can pass through a

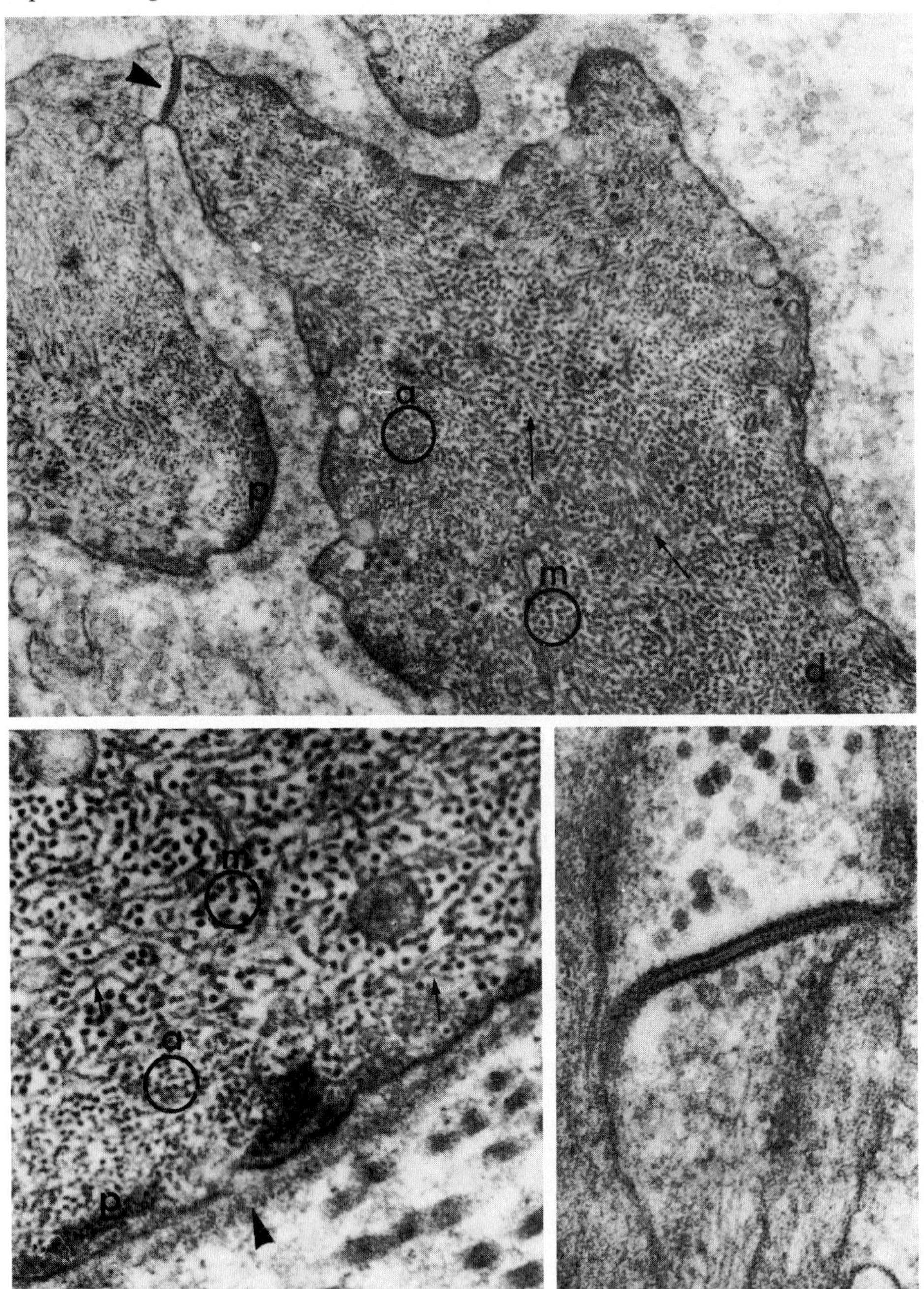

FIGURE 10-18

Electron micrographs of smooth muscle (musculus trachealis). *Top,* Transverse section showing a nexus *(arrowhead)* and cytoplasmic filaments of three sizes: thick (myosin, *m*) myofilaments, thin (actin, *a*) myofilaments, and intermediate (×44,000). *Bottom left,* A higher magnification to show filament types (×180,000). *Bottom right,* A nexus or gap junction between two smooth muscle cell processes, above and below (×68,000). (From Leeson, Thomas S., and Leeson, C. Roland: Histology, 4th ed. Philadelphia, W. B. Saunders Co., 1981.)

layer of some types of smooth muscle all by itself. An exception to this is the existence of **multiunit smooth muscle**. In this instance each smooth muscle cell has its own innervation, and impulses do not pass from cell to cell.

Smooth muscle is innervated, however, quite differently than is skeletal muscle. A nerve fiber may run across many smooth muscle cells, often lying in a groove in their external surface. At each muscle cell there exists a swelling in the neuron in which the neurotransmitter substance is stored; thus, each swelling represents the location of a myoneuronal contact (Fig. 10-17). As with skeletal muscle, smooth muscle may respond to acetylcholine, but it may also respond to other neurotransmitter molecules, such as *norepinephrine,* and certain hormones circulating in the blood. As you will see in Chapters 13 and 18, the differing responses of smooth muscle tissues to these neurotransmitter molecules are very important.

Although smooth muscle contracts at a slower rate than other types of muscle, it is able to sustain this contraction for relatively long periods of time without utilizing a significant amount of energy. Smooth muscle rarely respires anaerobically; perhaps it cannot. Recent evidence indicates that smooth muscle utilizes a kind of functional rigor mortis in which ATP is depleted normally during contraction to such an extent that the cross bridges become semipermanently attached to the active sites. This results in the formation of "latch bridges" which are released only when additional ATP is provided. This latch-bridge contraction requires no energy to continue once it has been established.

Unlike skeletal muscle, stretching of smooth muscle fibers in itself initiates contraction. This feature is of particular physiological significance in terms of hollow viscera whose contents need to be moved along or evacuated, for example, the urinary bladder and digestive tract. Furthermore, smooth muscle is capable of two general types of contraction, that is, **rhythmic contraction** and **tonic contraction**. The precise mechanism by which these occur, however, is not yet fully understood.

The fact that smooth muscle has a great ability to squeeze and shorten makes it ideally suited for such functions as moving material through the gastrointestinal tract and regulating the diameter of blood vessels. However, because it responds slowly to stimuli, it is not satisfactorily suited for running, jumping, or flying. Thus very few active animals employ smooth muscle for the purpose of locomotion.

Contraction is not restricted to muscle cells

Although muscle tissue is specialized for the production of movement, a number of other cell types share this property. This should not be surprising as movement is one of life's most basic qualities. Scientific experiments have provided evidence for the existence of myosin in certain embryonic cells, that undergo migration in order to form the basic structure of the developing embryo. Myosin is found in fibroblasts, which contract during wound healing, thereby helping to pull the severed tissues together.

Mobile leukocytes that crawl through body tissues seeking foreign organisms or substances to devour also contain myosin. This molecule occurs in all dividing cells, because **cytokinesis** (*sigh*-to-kin-**ee**-sis), physical cell division, is dependent upon the contraction of a ring of cytoplasm that produces a growing furrow between the separating daughter cells. A heavy concentration of myosin is located beneath this furrow. Actin is difficult to demonstrate in cells, but because myosin has no known role except interaction with actin, it is not unreasonable to assume that almost all cellular movement (excepting that which occurs by means of cilia or flagella) occurs by a mechanism fundamentally similar to that found in muscle cells.

Summary

I. Externally a muscle is surrounded by a connective tissue wrapping called the epimysium. The epimysium is continuous with projections of connective tissue, the perimysium, which in turn envelop bundles of muscle fibers known as fascicles. The perimysium continues further into the muscle's interior and gives rise to the endomysium, which surrounds individual muscle fibers.

A. Skeletal muscle cells are long, multinucleated, and subdivided into sarcomeres. Each sarcomere is a contractile unit containing thick (myosin) and thin (actin) filaments which, by pulling themselves past one another via cross bridges, produce contraction.

B. The molecular events involved with muscle contraction are powered by ATP associated with the heads of cross bridges located between the actin and myosin filaments. Once the existing ATP is utilized, it is immediately replaced via the breakdown of another high-energy compound called creatine phosphate.

II. Acetylcholine is released into the myoneural cleft when a nerve impulse reaches the motor end plate. When the acetylcholine binds to receptors on the plasma membrane of the muscle fiber, it initiates depolarization of the muscle plasma membrane. The enzyme acetylcholinesterase then rapidly destroys acetylcholine.

A. The area of depolarization travels down the muscle fiber plasma membrane in a wavelike manner and enters the T tubule system. Once inside the cell, the depolarization causes vesicles of the sarcoplasmic reticulum to release their stores of calcium ions.

B. The calcium ions stimulate muscle contraction by unmasking the active sites of the actin filaments; when the ions are reabsorbed, muscle relaxation is permitted.

III. Muscle tissue is distinctive metabolically in its use of creatine phosphate, myoglobin, and anaerobic respiration.

A. Creatine phosphate acts as a means of storing chemical energy.

B. Myoglobin is a respiratory pigment that transfers oxygen to the contracting muscle fiber. It also serves to store oxygen for use during active contraction.

C. Anaerobic respiration occurs when the muscle must exercise beyond the capacity of the circulatory system to deliver oxygen to it. The end product in this instance is lactic acid, which is subsequently metabolized in muscles and the liver. Some oxygen is required for this last process and for the replenishment of ATP and creatine phosphate; the oxygen requirement under these circumstances is called the oxygen debt.

IV. Smooth muscle consists of mononucleated cells that are very closely attached to one another. Smooth muscle contracts slower than skeletal muscle, but it is better suited for sustained contraction.

Post-Test

1. Skeletal muscles are typically attached to a ______________.
2. The connective tissue envelope that surrounds (a) the entire muscle, (b) its fascicles, and (c) individual muscle fibers is divided into the ______________, ______________, and ______________, respectively.
3. Please label the accompanying diagram appropriately.
4. The inward extension of the muscle fiber plasma membrane forms a series of microscopic tunnels known as the ______________. Depolarization spreads within the cell by this pathway, resulting in the release of ______________ by vesicles of the ______________ ______________. This release in turn initiates the process of muscular contraction.
5. All the skeletal muscle fibers in a ______________ ______________ are innervated by the same neuron, and therefore all tend to contract simultaneously. When the neuron is depolarized, ______________ is released from vesicles in its end plate and this transmitter then diffuses into the ______________ ______________. Once released, this substance is rapidly destroyed by the enzyme ______________.
6. A single stimulus, if it exceeds the threshold of minimum excitation required by a muscle, will produce a ______________ ______________. (a) A series of such stimuli, if close enough together, will produce ______________ ______________, a laboratory curiosity in which contractions become progressively stronger. (b) If the stimuli are even closer together, a smooth, sustained contraction called ______________ will occur; this is the manner in which our muscles habitually operate.
7. A single muscle functional unit is called a ______________, and it contains two types of myofilaments. The thick filaments are composed of

_______________ and the thin ones _______________. Cross bridges from the thick filaments attach to _______________ _______________ on the thin filaments.

8. Cross bridges are attracted to successive points of anchorage along the actin filament using a steplike motion to pull on the filament. The cross bridges require _______________ to release their previous hold and to bend in preparation for the next step.
9. The principal function of creatine phosphate is to serve as an _______________ storehouse.
10. Myoglobin is believed to function in the storage and transfer of _______________ within the muscle fiber. Should the muscle have to respire _______________, the waste product generated will be _______________ _______________.
11. Smooth muscle is usually not under _______________ control, although it may be influenced consciously. It lacks the characteristic _______________ of skeletal muscle. Moreover, smooth muscle can be made to contract by simple _______________ of its fibers.

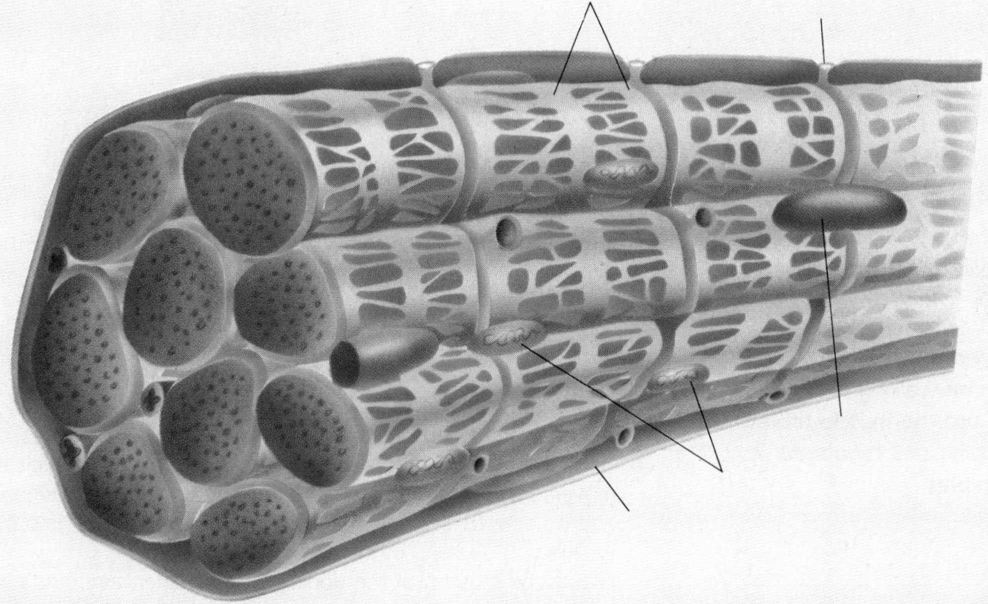

Review questions

1. Describe the gross and microscopic structure of a typical muscle.
2. Describe in detail the sliding filament mechanism of muscle contraction.
3. Describe the metabolic pathways by which muscle derives the energy it requires for contraction.
4. Describe what is meant by tetanic contraction.
5. What are the roles of tropomyosin and troponin in muscle contraction?
6. Describe the molecular features of actin and myosin.
7. Describe the disease known as myasthenia gravis.
8. Describe the following: (a) muscle tone, (b) isometric exercise, (c) isotonic exercise, (d) oxygen debt.
9. Compare and contrast muscle strength, power, and endurance.
10. Describe the metabolic considerations pertinent to muscle contraction while participating in rigorous sports activities.
11. Compare and contrast smooth and skeletal muscle with regard to their structure and function.
12. Describe the neuronal control of muscle contraction.

Post-test answers

1. bone 2. epimysium; perimysium; endomysium 3. Compare with Fig. 10-3 4. T tubules; calcium; sarcoplasmic reticulum 5. motor unit; acetylcholine; myoneural cleft; acetylcholinesterase 6. simple twitch; wave summation; tetany 7. sarcomere; myosin; actin; active sites 8. ATP 9. energy 10. oxygen; anaerobically; lactic acid 11. voluntary; striations; stretching

THE MUSCULAR SYSTEM

CHAPTER OUTLINE

I. **Musculoskeletal dynamics**
II. **Muscle shapes and functions**
- □ Focus on the temporomandibular joint
- □ Focus on grips of the hand
- □ Focus on arm muscles grouped by function
- □ Focus on walking

III. **How to use the muscle tables**
IV. **Index to muscles tabulated**
V. **Muscle tables**

LEARNING OBJECTIVES

After you have studied this chapter you should be able to:

1 Give a functional interpretation of the various muscle shapes (i.e., relate the shapes of the muscles to the way in which they function in the human body).

2 Summarize the regional and wholebody interactions of muscles, joints, and bones in particular physical activities as specified by your instructor. For example:
   a. Group muscles of the lower limb (thigh and leg) into functional categories—flexors, extensors, adductors, abductors, and rotators.
   b. List agonists (using the names of supplied muscles) in typical lower limb movements such as standing erect from a squatting position and kicking, and be able to describe the action of involved lower limb muscles in walking.
   c. Group the muscles of the upper limb (shoulder, arm, and hand) into functional categories—flexors, extensors, and so on.
   d. Arrange the trunk muscles into functional groups.
   e. List agonist muscles in such representative motions of the head and neck as nodding, shaking, and chewing, and describe joint action in each case.
   f. Describe the typical function of representative intrinsic and extrinsic muscles of the thumb.

3 Commit to memory the names, origins, actions, and typical functions of the tabulated muscles (and be able to give them in response to an appropriate stimulus).

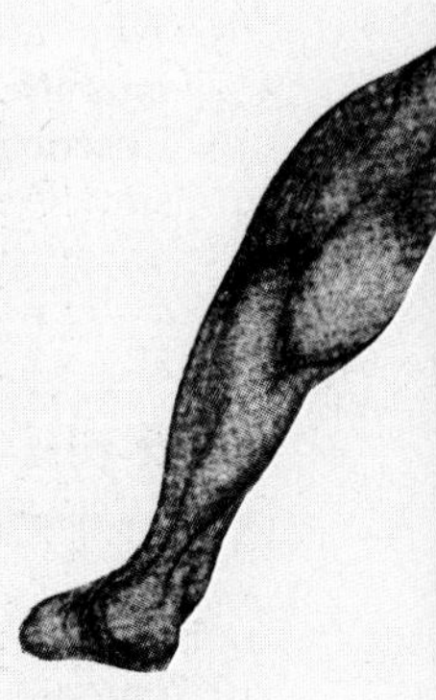

False-color thermogram of a performing ballet artist. (Montrosel/Custom Medical Stock Photo.)

11

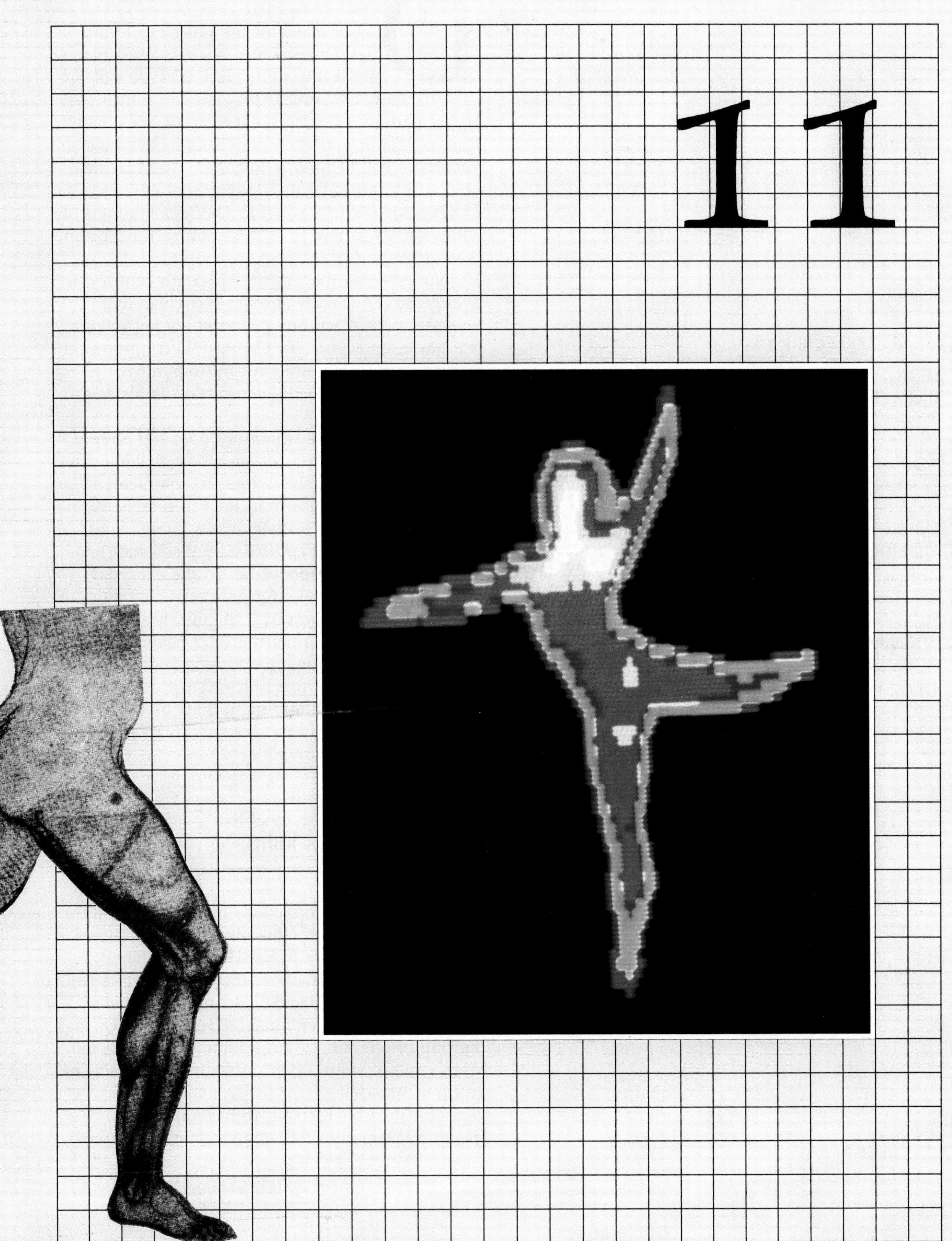

KEY CONCEPTS

Muscles oppose, or antagonize, one another such that movement produced by one can always be reversed by another.

Muscles can stabilize the skeleton by contracting to produce important supporting functions.

Muscles are organs, and their only operation is that of contraction.

Contracting muscles always pull; they never push.

The mechanical pull of a muscle is transmitted by means of an organic cable—the tendon.

Synergistic muscles act in concert with muscles called prime movers.

"Do not make all the muscles of your figures apparent, because even if they are in the right place they do not show prominently unless the limbs in which they are located are exerting great force or are greatly strained . . . if you do otherwise you will have imitated a bag of nuts rather than a human figure." With these words in what is now called the CODEX MADRID, Leonardo DaVinci exhorted his fellow artists to pay close attention to function in their rendering of the human body.

No less now than in the sixteenth century, it is imperative for each of us to recognize that muscles work. Each one of our everyday actions is a muscular action. Sir Charles Sherrington said it succinctly: " . . . all man can do is move things, and his muscular contraction is his sole means thereto."

Dissection in the laboratory does not simply reveal a muscle with a certain shape that the student hopes to recognize when the instructor points to it; still less is it an item in a table of origins and insertions. Rather, it is a living, functional motor, one of approximately 600 such motors that enable our bodies to do the everyday things we so often take for granted—climbing, drawing, walking, running, singing, breathing, and eating. It is essential that you never be satisfied with simply knowing anything less than how a muscle works and precisely what it does, or you, too, will view the human body as being little more than a bag of nuts.

Muscles function in movement, support, and in the stabilization of joints

Muscles undergo contraction, but if muscles were not attached to bones, this physiological process would be of little use to us. Hence, as they shorten during contraction, they pull upon bones to which they are attached. Because not one of them pushes, muscles must be arranged such that the pull of one muscle on a bone is counteracted by the pull of some other, antagonistic, muscle or group of muscles.

Most muscles are said to have an **origin,** or less movable point of attachment, and an **inser-**

tion, or more movable point of attachment. Without both of these anchorages, muscles would be unable to move bones. The arrangement of the bones of the skeleton makes it possible for muscles to oppose, or **antagonize,** one another, so that movement produced by one can always be reversed by another. Antagonism also limits and controls motions, especially when groups of muscles function collectively. Otherwise many common movements would go too far, as when a baby, attempting to feed himself, splashes cereal all over his face.

The normal adult nervous system provides very precise control for muscle groups. Such control enables one to aim a golf ball for a hole in one, send a bowling ball exactly into a cluster of pins to produce a strike, and carve a miniature statuette. These tasks could never be accomplished without muscular antagonism in addition to muscular movement.

Muscles can also stabilize the skeleton by contracting to produce important supporting functions. All muscles, but especially the abdominal muscles, are almost always in some degree of contraction. This **tone,** as it is called, permits them to assist in holding the abdominal viscera in position. Fibers of one of these muscle layers run at an angle to the fibers of the adjacent layer, much as the grain of a plywood layer runs at right angles to the grain of the adjoining layer. Such a physical arrangement compresses and holds in the underlying viscera. Should these muscles *atrophy* (wasting away or diminution in size) or lose their tone as a result of a sedentary living style, the viscera press upon them and protrude. The more stretched the abdominal muscles become, the more tone they lose. Regular abdominal exercises prevent such a dismal loss of one's figure.

Many muscles, particularly those related to the pelvic and shoulder girdles, function primarily in fixation and stabilization of adjacent joints that otherwise would be too loose for effective control. Such muscles are called **synergists.** Synergists act in concert with muscles called the **prime movers,** which are directly responsible for a specific movement. In the absence of this fixating and stabilizing function of muscles many joints could not be kept together, and many important movements would not be able to be performed.

Muscles vary in shape and size, and share a common operation—that of contraction

Muscle tissue comprises at least 40% of the weight of the average individual, and bone comprises roughly another 20%. Thus, the combined contribution of the musculoskeletal system to our body weight is on the order of 60%. Clearly, we are mostly muscle and bone. Of course, the exact proportion contributed by the musculoskeletal system varies regionally within the body, with little else in the limbs and much more in the trunk. The limbs account for a large proportion of the body weight—approximately 41% all together. If you consider that much of the trunk musculature is functionally part of the limbs, it is easy to appreciate how important walking and manipulation must be to the body, for great resources are devoted to them. Not that muscles are restricted to these activities.

Consider the trunk muscles that are used in breathing, the neck muscles that turn the head, the muscles that move the eyes, or the nearly microscopic muscles of the high-fidelity system of the middle ear. Each has a unique function and location, and it is the function and location that determine the multitude of origins, insertions, actions, and shapes of our muscles.

It is worth repeating that however great the variety of muscles may be, there is only one muscle operation—**contraction.** No muscle can do more than shorten. Muscles function to pull parts of the body closer together or, by mechanical arrangements of pulleys and levers, to pull them farther apart. In each instance *muscles pull; they never push.*

It might seem that the most mechanically efficient shape for a muscle would be one in which all the muscle fibers could pull together, directly in line with the desired motion. Thus, they might all be anchored to some relatively immovable origin and might run in a broad sheet of parallel fibers to a more movable insertion. However, because a muscle can contract only about 45% at the most (and typically much less), such a sheet of muscle fibers could produce substantial movement only if it were very long as well as broad. These considerations restrict the occurrence of sheetlike muscles to locations such as the area

(text continued on p. 329)

FOCUS ON . . . The temporomandibular joint

The mandible is slung from the skull between the masseter and the medial pterygoid muscles (Fig. 11-1), which are so powerful that the weight of the body can easily be suspended from the clenched jaws. By asymmetric contraction these muscles move the jaw not only up and down but also from side to side. They are aided in their action by the temporal muscles.

The same muscles on the contralateral side oppose them in the sense that their pull tends to pull the jaw to the opposite side. The collective action of the internal pterygoid and masseter muscles is opposed by the lateral pterygoid and digastric, which are positioned to open the mouth. (The jaw depressors are far weaker than their antagonists.) The jaw may be protruded, which is a responsibility of the lateral pterygoid plus the anterior portion of the temporalis. It may also be retracted, which involves all jaw muscles (except the temporalis) and, perhaps, the digastric and other muscles.

The complex motions of chewing are made possible by the remarkable mobility of the **temporomandibular joint** (TMJ), the joint of the body that most easily permits motion in four directions. This mobility results from its loose ligamentous connections, which suspend it from the upper jaw, plus its construction as a compound joint with *two* synovial cavities. The condyle of the mandible rests upon a fibrocartilaginous disc called the **meniscus.** The meniscus is interposed between the condyle itself and the upper jaw. It divides the joint capsule into two compartments.

When the mouth is opened wide the condyle slips out of the

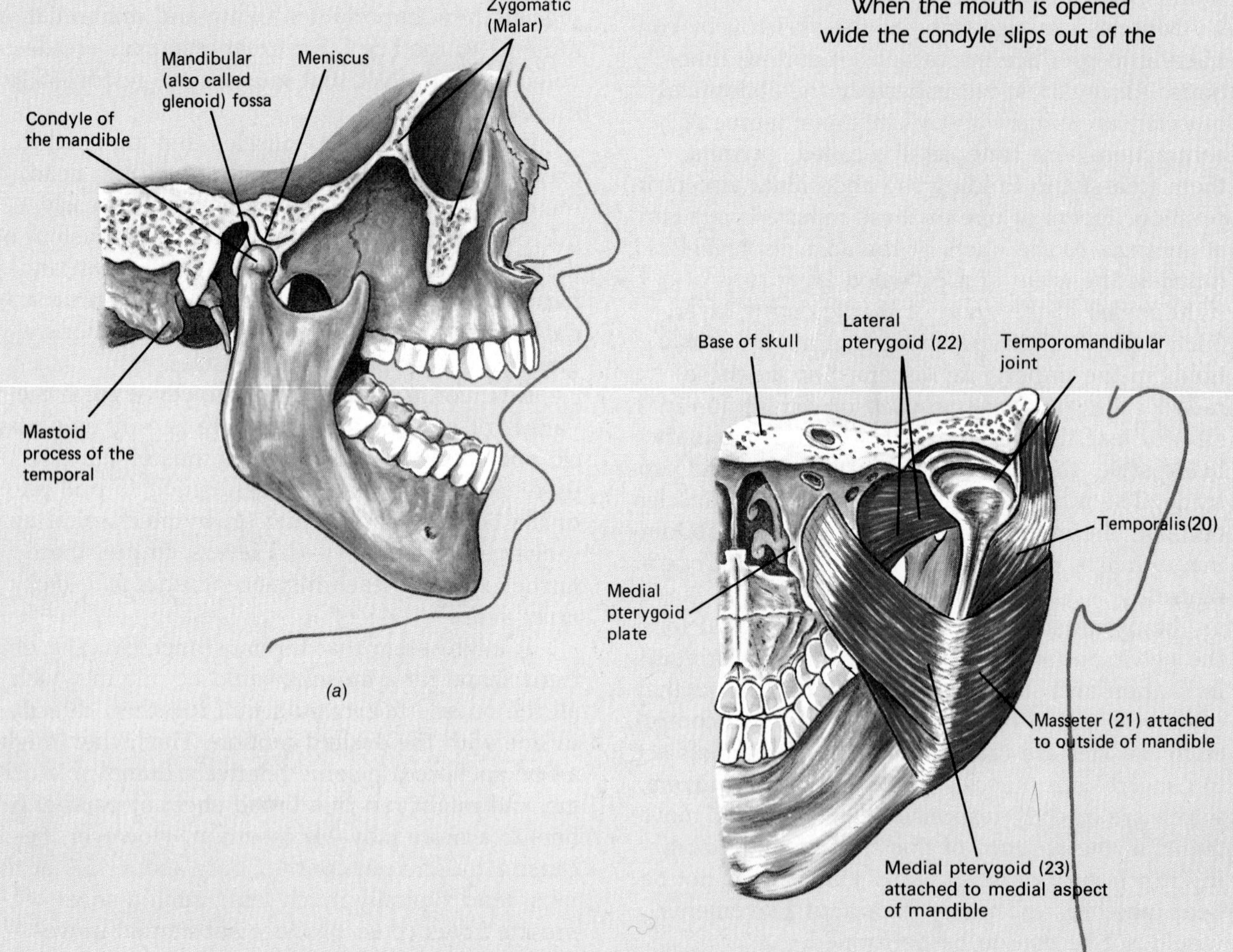

glenoid fossa and rides over the articular tubercle of the temporal bone; that is, it travels forward in a kind of functional dislocation (somewhat similar to the motion that occurs when an adjustable pair of pliers is opened very widely). This allows the mouth to open much more widely than if the condyle were to remain in the glenoid fossa. (The wall of the glenoid fossa is so weak that it probably could not function in heavy mastication anyway.) One may think of the glenoid fossa as the home of the condyle, from which it departs to do its work.

As the mouth opens, a special connection of the external pterygoid muscle pulls the meniscus forward so that it remains between both bony articular surfaces in all positions. A glance at the diagrams will show how mismatched these surfaces are. The meniscus fills in these mismatched irregularities.

Lateral movement of the jaw, so important in chewing, depends upon the ability of the remarkable TMJ to dislocate functionally on one side of the jaw while the condyle on the other side of the jaw remains more or less in the glenoid fossa.

Changes in chewing habits, produced perhaps by disease or by dental work, will alter and adapt the surfaces of the TMJ over a period of time to the changed functional stresses of chewing. Unfortunately, extreme stress of disease such as arthritis will sometimes set up strains that exceed the range of tolerance even of the TMJ, leading to functional disorders of chewing called the **TMJ syndrome.**

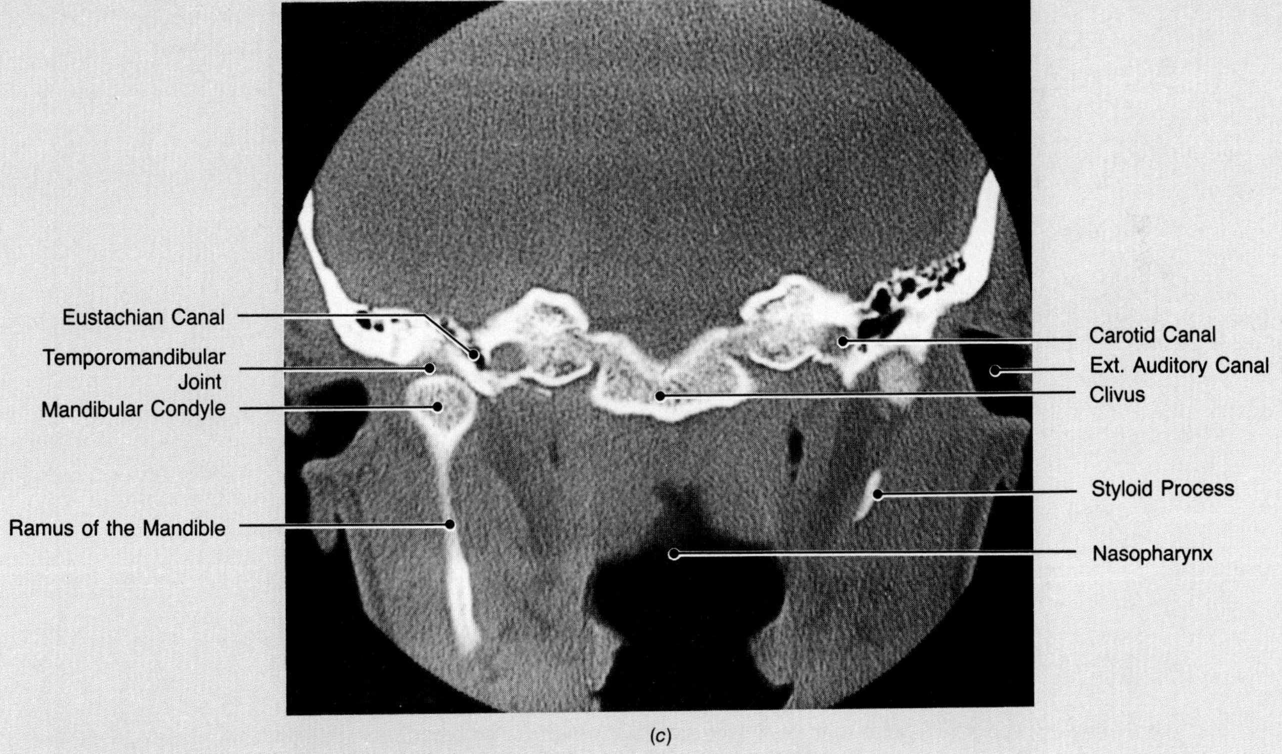

FIGURE 11-1

The temporomandibular joint and the muscles of mastication. (*a*) Lateral view with muscles removed. (*b*) Posterior view including muscles of mastication. (*c*) CT (computer tomography) scan of the temporomandibular joint. (From Christoforidis, A. John, *Atlas of Axial, Sagittal, and Coronal Anatomy,* Philadelphia, W.B. Saunders, 1988.)

FOCUS ON . . . Grips of the hand*

Prehension Patterns	***Description***
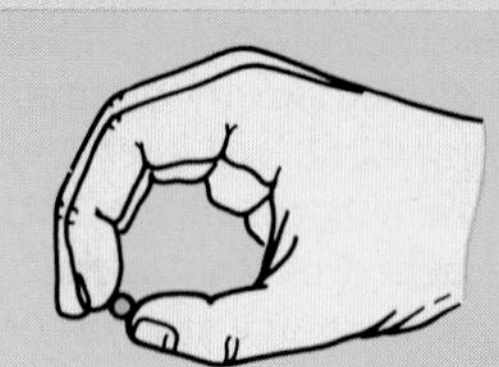	***Fingertip Prehension*** This grip is used for picking up tiny items. It involves primarily the thumb and index finger. It is not a very stable type of pinch but requires the most coordination.
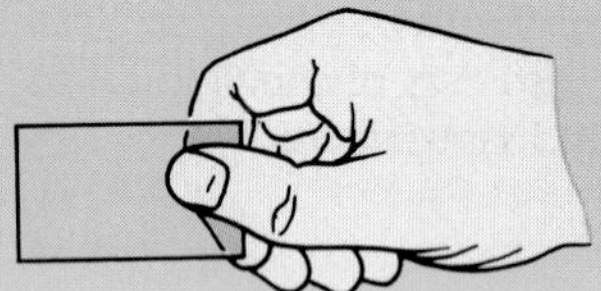	***Lateral Prehension*** In this case the thumb is *adducted* and *flexed* against the lateral surface of the index finger. The first dorsal interosseous muscle stabilizes the index finger. This grip is used to turn a key, hold a plate or a hand of cards, or wind a watch. A larger surface area is involved; thus the grip is more stable than fingertip prehension but produces less of an opening between digits, so smaller objects can be held with lateral prehension. The grip usually involves a stronger pinch, with larger interosseii and other muscles coming into play.
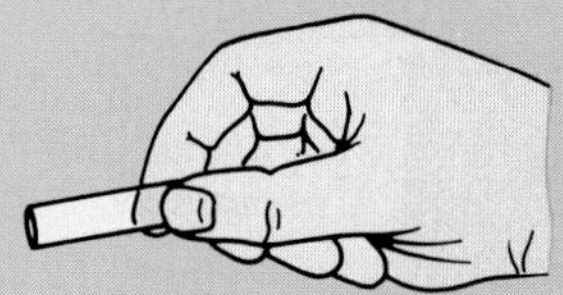	***Palmar Prehension*** This is the most versatile pinch, the one used most often for picking up and holding objects. The pads of the index and middle fingers and thumb are used for pinching. This stable pinch can begin with a very wide opening, making it possible to pick up large objects.
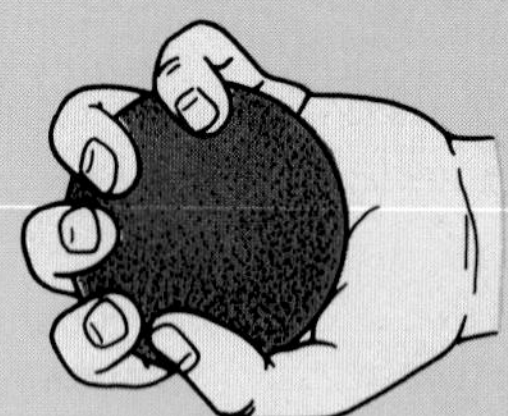	***Spherical Grasp*** This grip is used when holding anything round.
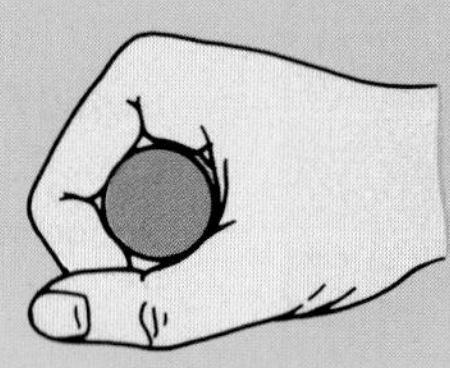	***Cylindrical Grasp*** This is the crudest type of prehension. It is a stable grasp because the whole width of the palm gives stability. It requires wrist extension with flexion of the fingers and thumb and is used when grasping a cup, telephone, or stair rail.
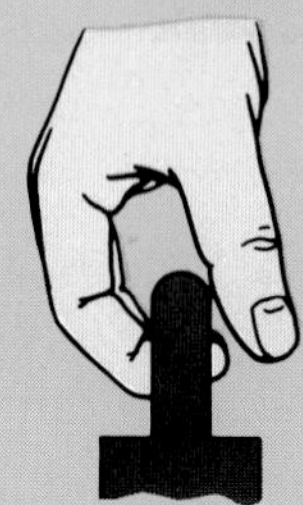	***Hook Grasp*** This grip does not require the use of the thumb but does require that the fingers be able to flex completely. It is used when carrying a suitcase or a bucket of water, or when hanging onto a cliff.

*Courtesy of Mrs. Susan Shortridge

FOCUS ON . . . Arm muscles grouped by function

It is not practical to attempt a summary of arm motions in the space available. This box, which is set up in tabular form, is provided as a convenient means of learning the actions of the main arm and shoulder muscles, which in combination produce the motions of the hand and arm as a whole. Not all the muscles listed are of equal importance. The prime movers are shown in boldface type. Can you identify each tabulated muscle in the diagrams and associate it with its function? See Figure 11-2.

Joint	Flexors	Extensors	Abductors	Adductors	Rotators, fixators
Wrist	**flexor carpi radialis** **palmaris longus** **flexor carpi ulnaris** long flexors of the hand	**extensor carpi radialis longus** **extensor carpi radialis brevis** **extensor carpi ulnaris** long extensors of the hand	**flexor carpi radialis** **extensor carpi radialis longus** extensor carpi radialis brevis extrinsic muscles of the thumb	**flexor carpi ulnaris** **extensor carpi ulnaris**	
Elbow	**biceps brachii** **brachioradialis** flexor carpi radialis longus **pronator teres** flexor carpi radialis palmaris longus flexor digitorum superficialis flexor carpi ulnaris **brachialis**	**triceps** extensor carpi radialis brevis extensor digitorum extensor carpi ulnaris supinator **anconeus**			Medial rotators (pronators): **pronator teres** **pronator quadratus** palmaris longus flexor carpi radialis brachioradialis Supinators: biceps brachii **supinator** extensor carpi radialis longus brachioradialis
Shoulder	**biceps brachii** **coracobrachialis** **pectoralis major** deltoid (upper portion)	**infraspinatus** **latissimus dorsi** **teres major** **long head of triceps** **posterior part of the deltoid** **sternal portion of pectoralis major**	**Middle part of deltoid** **supraspinatus** biceps (long head)	**pectoralis major** **latissimus dorsi** **teres major** **subscapularis** **coracobrachialis** triceps (long head)	Medial rotators: **subscapularis** **latissimus dorsi** **teres major** **pectoralis major** **anterior part of deltoid** Lateral rotators: **infraspinatus** **teres minor** **posterior part of deltoid**

Use this table in conjunction with the appropriate Tables beginning with 11-2.

Note: The shoulder joint is especially subject to downward dislocation; upon stress such dislocation will actually occur if there is any laxity in the action of the four muscles of the rotator cuff (the supraspinatus, infraspinatus, teres minor, and subscapularis). Together they roughly encircle the head of the humerus and, by hugging it close to the obliquely inclined glenoid fossa of the scapula, prevent it from slipping downward. The deltoid also assists in this task.

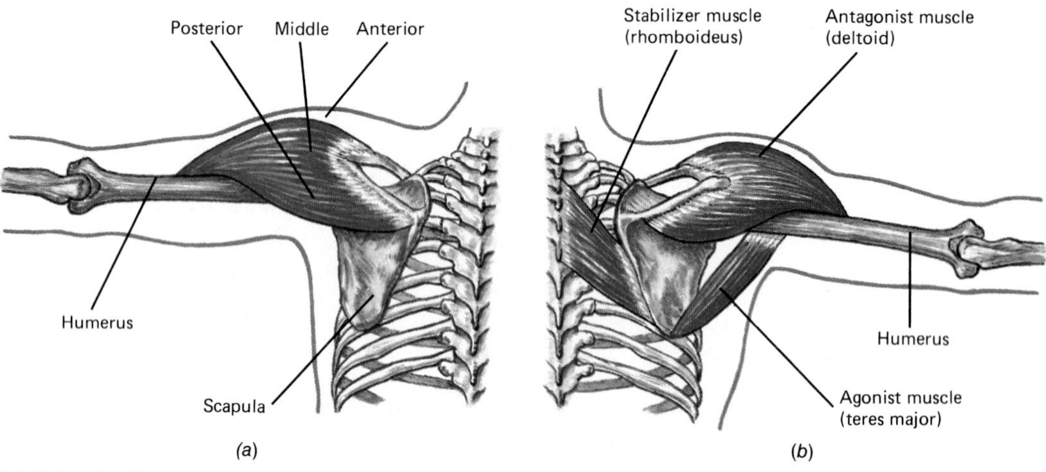

FIGURE 11-2

(*a*) How the three parts of the deltoid muscles interact to cause abduction of the shoulder. The anterior and posterior portions neutralize one another's nonabductive actions. (*b*) The teamwork of three arm adductors. The rhomboideus majors holds the scapula in place as the teres major acts.

FOCUS ON . . . Walking

An extremely large number of potential motions is available to the thigh. The ball-and-socket construction of the hip joint makes this range of motion possible. However, even though the joint of which the femoral head is a part has many ligaments, the design of this joint would cause immediate loss of balance the moment precise muscular control of leg motion lapsed.

The movement that the lower limb actually undergoes (in contrast to the vast range of possible movements) results not only from the action of the main muscles contributing to the power of the movement **(agonists)** but also from that of many **synergist** muscles that modify the direction and mode of action of the agonists. The synergists do not shorten greatly but supply a tension that prevents the lower limb from wobbling in an inappropriate direction.

The greatest of the thigh muscles are the flexors and extensors of the leg (Table 11-7), both of which are of extreme importance in walking. The flexors are located in the posterior "compartment" of the thigh, the extensors in the anterior "compartment." The big anterior extensor muscle mass is known as the **quadriceps femoris.** The quadriceps actually consists of four muscles, all inserting on the tibia via the patellar tendon. This tendon passes over the front of the knee and contains an embedded bone, the **patella,** or kneecap, which is faced with hyaline cartilage posteriorly and participates in the complex knee joint.

Since the quadriceps is a compound muscle with four origins, or heads, its name, which means "four heads" in Latin, is appropriate. The four quadriceps muscles are the **rectus femoris,** which originates on the ilium; the **vastus lateralis,** which originates on the linea aspera of the femur; the **vastus medialis** and the **vastus intermedius,** which also originate on the femur. The rectus femoris and vastus lateralis are frequently employed as sites for the intramuscular self-administration of injected drugs, particularly insulin.

The **hamstring** group of muscles is the flexor equivalent of the quadriceps. The name arose from the tendons of this muscle mass, by means of which the entire thigh of a hog used to be hung to cure in a smokehouse. The hamstrings consist of the **biceps femoris,** the **semimembranosus,** and the **semitendinosus,** inserting via their tendons on opposite sides of the posterior aspect of the leg and producing thereby the hollow of the knee. Because the knee joint is almost exclusively a hinge joint, there is little call for the potential ability of the thigh muscles to rotate the leg. This is only possible when the leg is

FOCUS ON . . . Walking (*continued*)

flexed, as in skiing, in some swimming strokes, and in dancing the Russian Zhazitska.

As in the case of the forearm, the leg contains more muscles than does the limb segment proximal to it, which is the thigh. But where the flexors of the fingers are collectively very powerful in the forearm, the flexors of the toes in the leg are not notable. This reflects the difference in the function of the two appendages, since the arm is rarely used for locomotion in human beings, and the leg is rarely used for pronation. The big leg muscles are the gastrocnemius and the soleus, which give the foot its big pushoff in walking. Because the dorsiflexion of the foot that follows a step is not usually performed against resistance, the antagonistic muscles such as the tibialis anterior are much smaller. But small as it is, the tibialis anterior is by far the largest of the dorsiflexors of the foot (Table 11-8).

Note that most of the great muscles of the thigh are two-joint muscles that extend across both the hip joint and the knee joint. This fact tends to complicate their action so that under many circumstances these two-joint muscles have the opposite effect on the two parts of the leg. Thus, in walking, the quadriceps femoris both extends the leg and flexes the thigh at the hip joint. Such multiple actions represent a saving of energy, since, although the motions are opposites, they produce a single action using the different leg segments. It has been calculated that if all of our leg muscles were one-joint muscles rather than two-joint muscles (as is the case), it would take 33% more energy to walk.

In walking, the human body recurrently teeters on the edge of disaster, continually falling forward, pivoting on the fixed foot, then catching the body with the other leg and foot just before the body becomes dangerously overbalanced.

The heel hits the ground first, then the ball of the foot. The gastrocnemius and soleus muscles then contract, lifting the heel and with it the entire body. Next, the peroneus muscles act to transfer the body weight to the ball of the foot. The lateral off-center push thus generated is balanced by the abduction and flexing of the little toe. Finally, a battery of big-toe flexors causes that structure to give the foot its final push off the ground. Meanwhile the lower limb has been extended at the knee and hip joints by appropriate muscle action.

Once the foot is off the ground, the leg must flex and swing forward like a pendulum. At the same time the gluteus minimus and medius contract, causing the pelvis to tilt medially, bringing the center of gravity of the body directly over the leg that is anchored to the ground. This pulls the lifted leg even farther up. Simultaneously (probably by action of the gluteus maximus, at least in *rapid* walking), the pelvis pivots around the hip joint of the fixed leg, helping to swing the free leg forward still farther.

These motions are assisted by trunk muscles often called the lateral flexors of the spine. The leg then extends, the pelvis tilts over it, the center of gravity of the body shifts, and as the heel contacts the ground, another step begins.

This by no means ends the story. The human gait consists of at least six separate and complicated component motions that would take many pages to describe, even to the small extent that they are understood. The human lower limb is actually less easily able to stand than to walk; it is designed for motion. Our joints do not lock when we stand. Whatever stability we have in standing is due to intermittent or continuous isometric contraction of virtually all the lower limb muscles. Even so, there is some tendency to fall in one direction or the other.

As soon as the various position-sensitive sense receptors report an incipient tilt to the central nervous system, an immediate adjustment is automatically made by the contraction of counterbalancing muscles. A soldier standing at rigid attention teeters through a series of arcs that can be measured by sensitive instruments, although they may not be readily visible to a sergeant's eye.

between the ribs (intercostal spaces), where movement is necessarily limited, or the abdomen, where the traits of muscular sheets are actually an advantage.

Most muscles, however, have a shape in which their fibers converge rather than lie parallel to one another, so that each fiber exerts force upon some central tendon, somewhat as an entire team might be able to pull upon a single rope in a tug of war. In this manner great force can be exerted upon a tendon, which in turn transmits this pull to whatever bone it may be inserted into. Such a convergent arrangement of muscle fibers tends to produce **fusiform** muscle shapes (if they are round) or **pennate** ones (if they are flat) (Fig. 11-3).

Focus your attention on Figures 11-4 through 11-7. These will serve to illustrate that limb muscles generally do not lie directly over the parts of the body that they move. They typically insert near a joint, so that most of the muscle mass lies proximal to whatever part it acts upon. Moreover, the origin of a muscle tends to be broader than its insertion. In general, limbs are broader proximally and tend to taper gradually down to ankle or wrist. The broadest origins occur on such massive structures as the pelvis or scapula, with many insertions being quite remote from the body of the muscle. Thus, their pull is transmitted over several inches by means of an organic cable—the *tendon*.

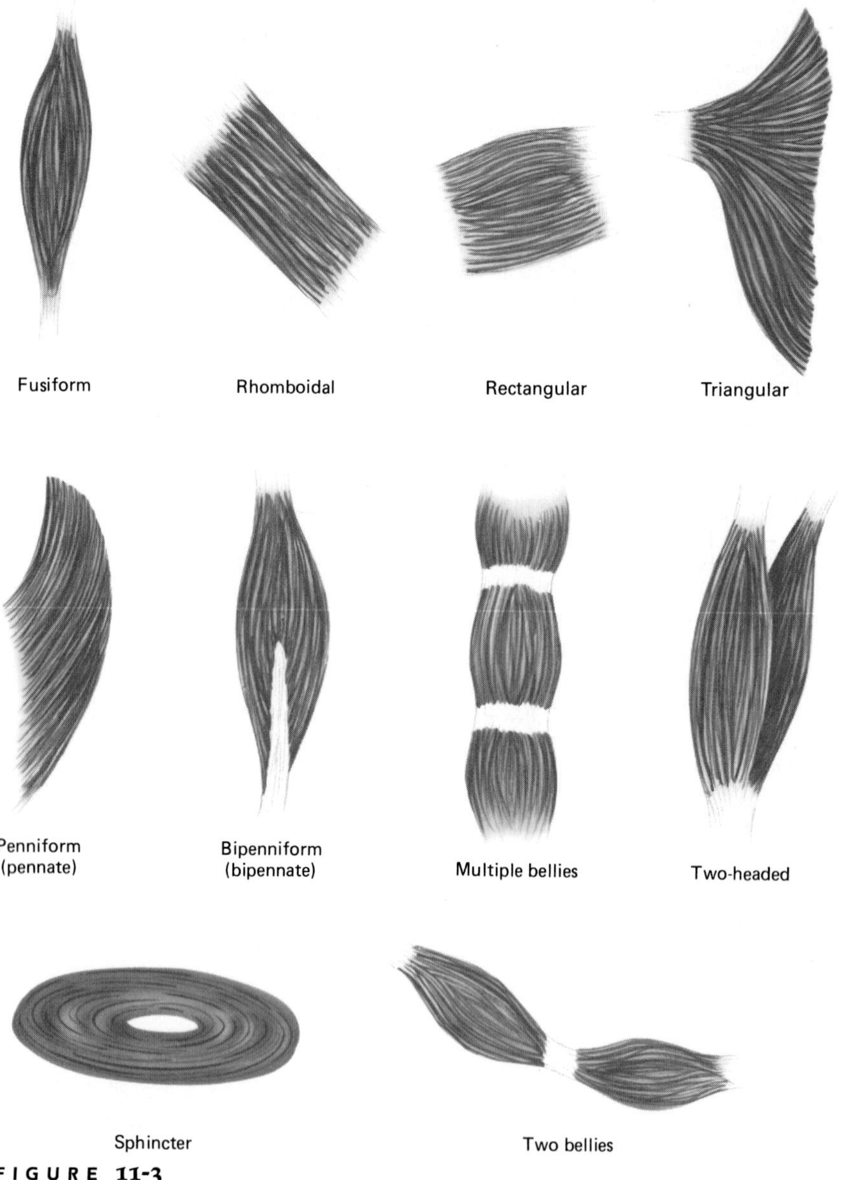

FIGURE 11-3

Muscle shapes.

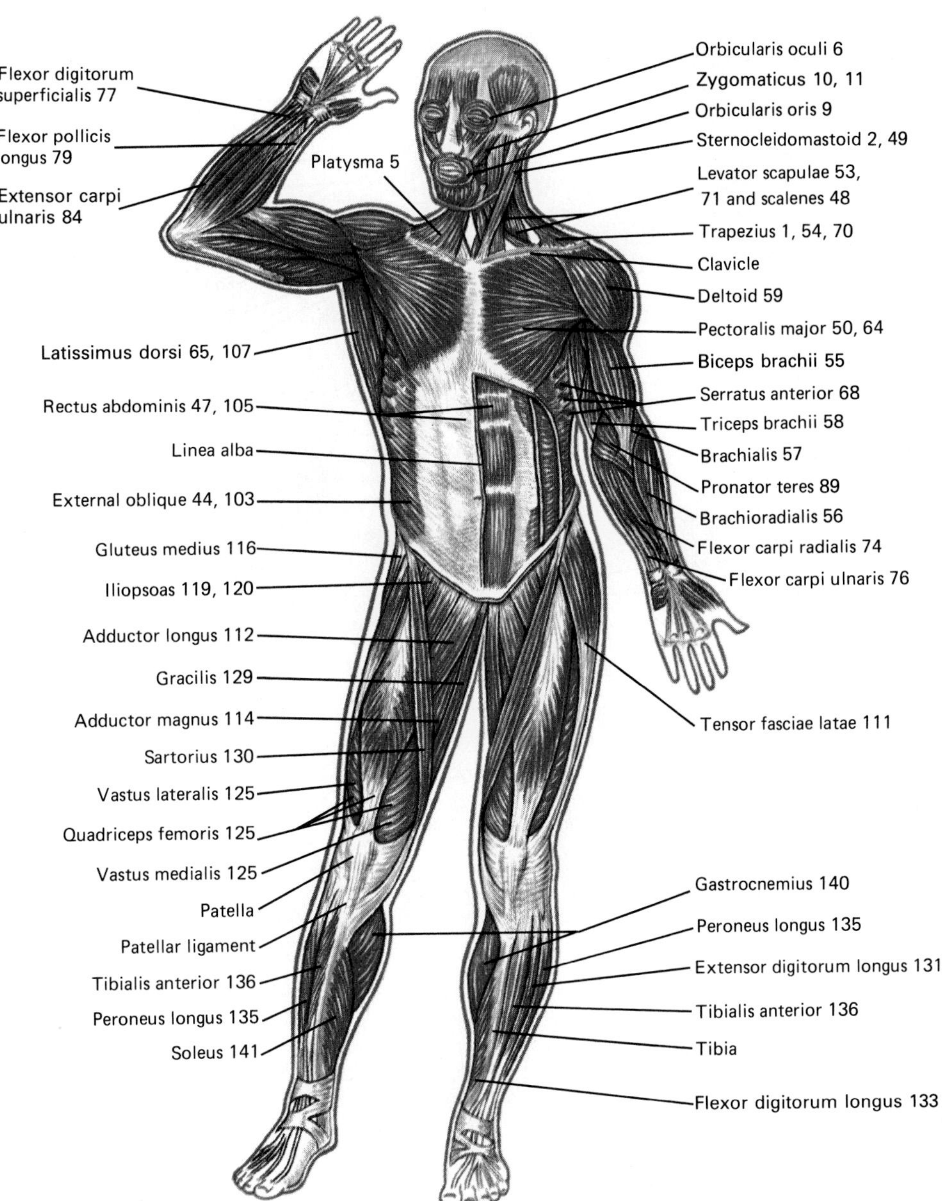

Flexor digitorum superficialis 77
Flexor pollicis longus 79
Extensor carpi ulnaris 84
Platysma 5
Latissimus dorsi 65, 107
Rectus abdominis 47, 105
Linea alba
External oblique 44, 103
Gluteus medius 116
Iliopsoas 119, 120
Adductor longus 112
Gracilis 129
Adductor magnus 114
Sartorius 130
Vastus lateralis 125
Quadriceps femoris 125
Vastus medialis 125
Patella
Patellar ligament
Tibialis anterior 136
Peroneus longus 135
Soleus 141
Orbicularis oculi 6
Zygomaticus 10, 11
Orbicularis oris 9
Sternocleidomastoid 2, 49
Levator scapulae 53, 71 and scalenes 48
Trapezius 1, 54, 70
Clavicle
Deltoid 59
Pectoralis major 50, 64
Biceps brachii 55
Serratus anterior 68
Triceps brachii 58
Brachialis 57
Pronator teres 89
Brachioradialis 56
Flexor carpi radialis 74
Flexor carpi ulnaris 76
Tensor fasciae latae 111
Gastrocnemius 140
Peroneus longus 135
Extensor digitorum longus 131
Tibialis anterior 136
Tibia
Flexor digitorum longus 133

FIGURE 11-4

Anterior superficial muscles.

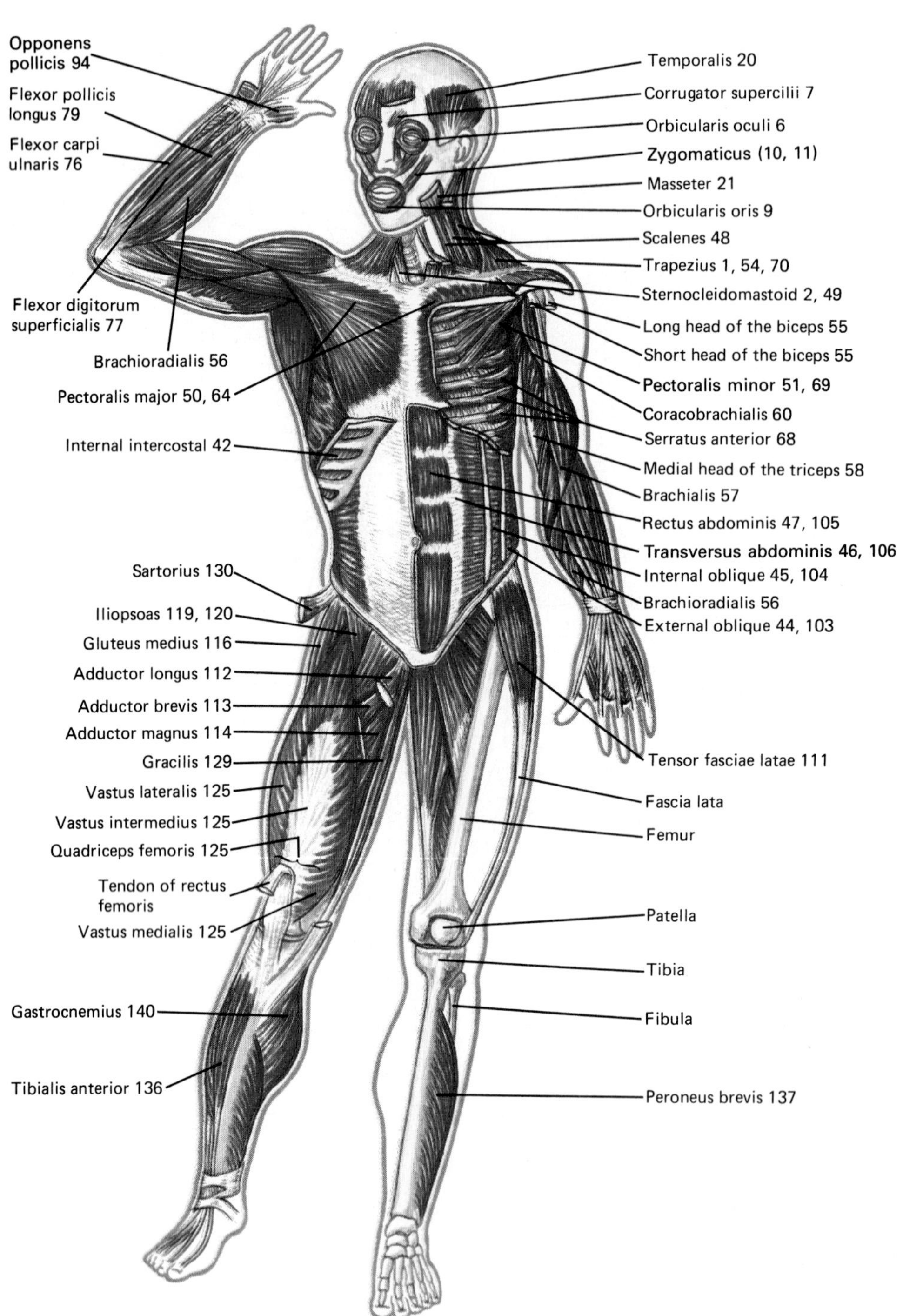
Opponens pollicis 94
Flexor pollicis longus 79
Flexor carpi ulnaris 76
Flexor digitorum superficialis 77
Brachioradialis 56
Pectoralis major 50, 64
Internal intercostal 42
Sartorius 130
Iliopsoas 119, 120
Gluteus medius 116
Adductor longus 112
Adductor brevis 113
Adductor magnus 114
Gracilis 129
Vastus lateralis 125
Vastus intermedius 125
Quadriceps femoris 125
Tendon of rectus femoris
Vastus medialis 125
Gastrocnemius 140
Tibialis anterior 136
Temporalis 20
Corrugator supercilii 7
Orbicularis oculi 6
Zygomaticus (10, 11)
Masseter 21
Orbicularis oris 9
Scalenes 48
Trapezius 1, 54, 70
Sternocleidomastoid 2, 49
Long head of the biceps 55
Short head of the biceps 55
Pectoralis minor 51, 69
Coracobrachialis 60
Serratus anterior 68
Medial head of the triceps 58
Brachialis 57
Rectus abdominis 47, 105
Transversus abdominis 46, 106
Internal oblique 45, 104
Brachioradialis 56
External oblique 44, 103
Tensor fasciae latae 111
Fascia lata
Femur
Patella
Tibia
Fibula
Peroneus brevis 137

FIGURE 11-5

Anterior deep muscles.

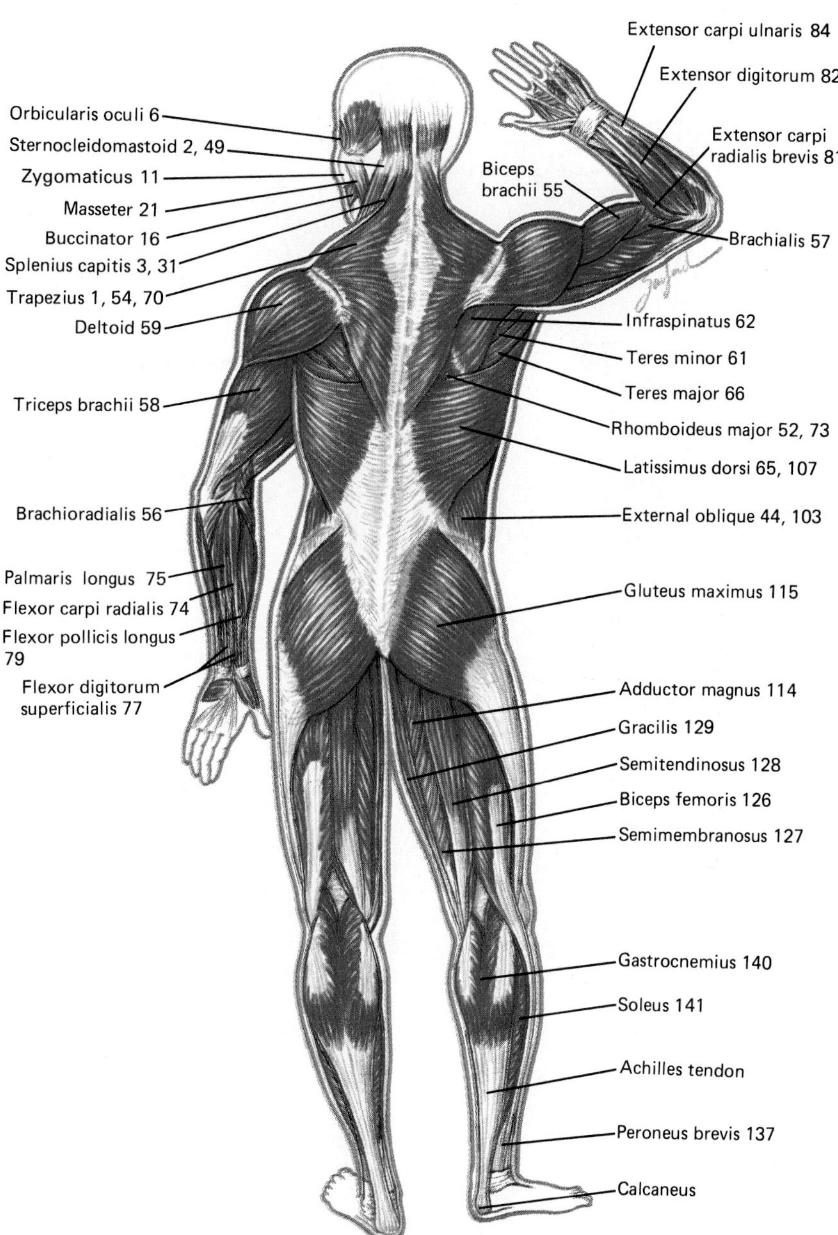
Extensor carpi ulnaris 84
Extensor digitorum 82
Extensor carpi radialis brevis 81
Biceps brachii 55
Brachialis 57
Orbicularis oculi 6
Sternocleidomastoid 2, 49
Zygomaticus 11
Masseter 21
Buccinator 16
Splenius capitis 3, 31
Trapezius 1, 54, 70
Deltoid 59
Infraspinatus 62
Teres minor 61
Teres major 66
Triceps brachii 58
Rhomboideus major 52, 73
Latissimus dorsi 65, 107
Brachioradialis 56
External oblique 44, 103
Palmaris longus 75
Flexor carpi radialis 74
Flexor pollicis longus 79
Gluteus maximus 115
Flexor digitorum superficialis 77
Adductor magnus 114
Gracilis 129
Semitendinosus 128
Biceps femoris 126
Semimembranosus 127
Gastrocnemius 140
Soleus 141
Achilles tendon
Peroneus brevis 137
Calcaneus

FIGURE 11-6

Posterior superficial muscles.

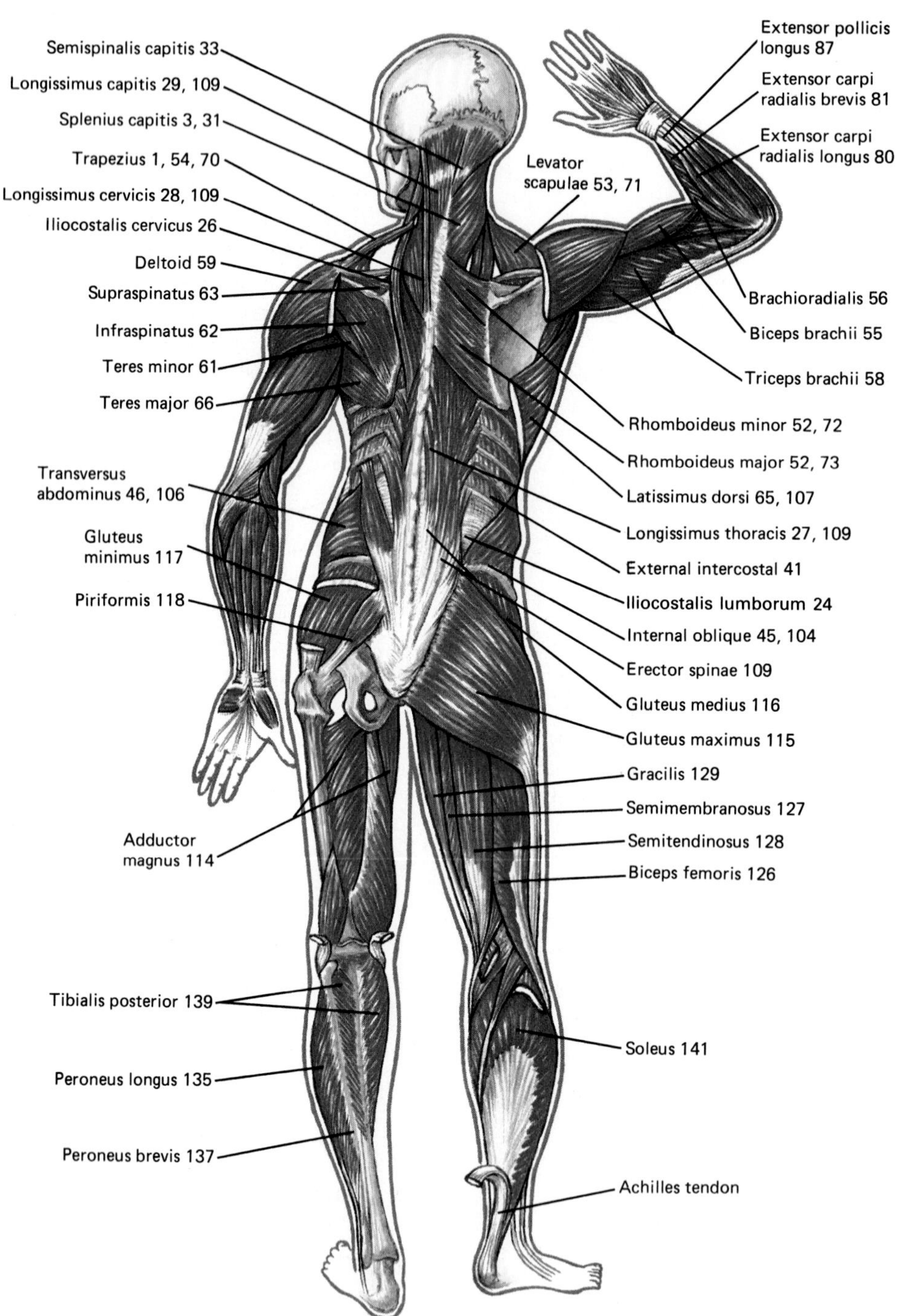
Semispinalis capitis 33
Longissimus capitis 29, 109
Splenius capitis 3, 31
Trapezius 1, 54, 70
Longissimus cervicis 28, 109
Iliocostalis cervicus 26
Deltoid 59
Supraspinatus 63
Infraspinatus 62
Teres minor 61
Teres major 66
Transversus abdominus 46, 106
Gluteus minimus 117
Piriformis 118
Adductor magnus 114
Tibialis posterior 139
Peroneus longus 135
Peroneus brevis 137
Levator scapulae 53, 71
Extensor pollicis longus 87
Extensor carpi radialis brevis 81
Extensor carpi radialis longus 80
Brachioradialis 56
Biceps brachii 55
Triceps brachii 58
Rhomboideus minor 52, 72
Rhomboideus major 52, 73
Latissimus dorsi 65, 107
Longissimus thoracis 27, 109
External intercostal 41
Iliocostalis lumborum 24
Internal oblique 45, 104
Erector spinae 109
Gluteus medius 116
Gluteus maximus 115
Gracilis 129
Semimembranosus 127
Semitendinosus 128
Biceps femoris 126
Soleus 141
Achilles tendon

FIGURE 11-7

Posterior deep muscles.

Use of the muscle tables facilitates a functional understanding of the musculoskeletal system

Ultimately, the usefulness of this chapter will be determined by how well you are able to apply your knowledge practically, or clinically. Simply learning lists of muscle names, though necessary, is only a partial means to that end. Without an understanding of function, the major task of learning these muscles will seem much like memorizing the pages of a telephone directory. Neither the authors nor your instructors believe in memorization for its own sake. You will, however, be asked for the amount of memorization appropriate for your course, so that one may better understand the healthy and diseased operation of the human body. Never be satisfied to answer the question, "What is its name?" without also being able to answer, "What does it do?" In other words, attempt to gain a meaningful understanding of the musculoskeletal system from a functional point of view.

To help you with this task, the body has been divided into regions, each receiving separate consideration. Many, but by no means all, of the important muscles are summarized in a table provided for each region. Also, for ready reference **an alphabetic index of all tabulated muscles is provided at the beginning of the table section.** It is quite possible that not all of these muscles will be addressed in the course you are taking. Your instructor may use this index as a checklist to indicate just which muscles you are required to study.

In the following tables, the muscles are arranged into functional, anatomical groups. For example, the muscles moving the foot are located mainly in the leg. To study a muscle, then, you need to know roughly where it is located; if in doubt, consult one of the major figures. Suppose you are interested in the tibialis posterior muscle. The muscle index designates it number 139. Leafing through the muscle tables you will see that Table 11-8 covers muscles 131 through 153. Because the muscle number is 139, look for the muscle whose name is preceded by 139 in boldface type. (Occasionally a muscle belongs to more than one functional group and is listed in more than one table. In such instances the muscle will have more than one number.)

Because the action of a muscle depends chiefly on how it is attached to the bones, in many cases we have arranged the muscles according to their insertion, since that is the more movable attachment. What they move depends upon that attachment, and whether that information is useful to you will depend on how well you know the bones. To continue using muscle 139 as our example, it is clear from the cross-head in Table 11-8 that the tibialis posterior inserts upon the medial cuneiform bone (one of the tarsals) of the foot. The table indicates that this, although it is its major insertion, is not the only one.

The muscle origins are listed, as are the actions. Formal action, however, is not always quite the same as the actual function of the muscle in the body. Notice that the comments section sometimes gives a function that is not an action in the usual sense. The comments section may also indicate whether the muscle is deep or superficial—information that is of considerable importance in the dissecting room. Remember also that because the human body is bilaterally symmetrical, most muscles listed represent one of a pair of such muscles.

The innervation is typically given in two ways: first, by the name of the chief nerve supplying the muscle, and second, by an abbreviated reference to the appropriate cranial or spinal nerve roots. This knowledge is required in some courses and is of great practical and clinical importance, for example, in back injuries, which may involve the spinal cord or its nerve roots. One could infer spinal nerve damage by tabulating the muscles that are affected. Paralysis of the flexor muscles of the knee might possibly indicate damage to the fifth lumbar and first sacral spinal nerves. Paralysis of the elbow flexors (such as the biceps muscle) may indicate damage to the fifth and sixth cervical nerves. (In most instances, the study of muscle innervation may be postponed until the nervous system has been studied.)

Finally, notice that these tables do not include some of the smaller muscles whose functions are associated with sense organs, such as the stapedius muscle of the middle ear or the extrinsic muscles of the eye. We have reserved discussion of these muscles for inclusion in the chapter devoted to the sense organs, Chapter 17.

Index to muscles tabulated*

NOTE: Numbers refer to muscle numbers, NOT pages.

*Muscle tabulation is as follows:
1–23, Table 11-1
24–54, Table 11-2
55–73, Table 11-3
74–102, Table 11-4
103–110, Table 11-5
111–124, Table 11-6
125–130, Table 11-7
131–153, Table 11-8
154–159, Table 11-9
160–162, Table 11-10
163–168, Table 11-11
169–177, Table 11-12

TABLE 11-1

Muscles of the head and neck, functionally grouped

Neck muscles

1 Trapezius (paired)*

Origin:	Occipital bone, ligamentum nuchae, seventh cervical (C7) and spinous processes of all twelve thoracic vertebrae (T1–T12)
Insertion:	Three parts: (1) lateral third of clavicle, (2) acromion process and middle of spine of scapula, and (3) root of spine of scapula
Action:	Retracts scapula (toward spine); rotates scapula superiorly; together with other muscles attached to the scapula, it helps to control the position of that bone during movement of the upper limb; elevates the point of the shoulder; extends and bends neck laterally when shoulder is fixed
Innervation:	Accessory nerve (CN XI); Cervical plexus (ventral rami of C3–C4; these cervical fibers are proprioceptive only)
Comments:	The two muscles are located superficially and together they resemble a trapezium

2 Sternocleidomastoid (paired)

Origin:	Two origins: (1) anterior aspect of the manubrium of the sternum and (2) medial third of the clavicle
Insertion:	Occipital bone and the mastoid process of the temporal bone
Action:	One contracting alone tilts head toward shoulder on that side and turns face toward side on which the muscle is not contracting; acting together they flex the cervical spine and elevate the sternum
Innervation:	Accessory nerve (CN XI); cervical plexus (ventral rami of C2 and C3; these cervical fibers are proprioceptive only)
Comments:	Forms a prominent landmark as it courses obliquely across the neck; its anterior border and sternal attachment are easily palpated when the head is turned to the opposite side; *torticollis,* or wry neck, is a condition in which one of these muscles exists in a contracted state producing a twisting of the neck and an unnatural position of the head

3 Splenius capitis (paired)

Origin:	Ligamentum nuchae, spinous processes of seventh cervical (C7) and upper three or four thoracic vertebrae (T1–T4)
Insertion:	Occipital bone and the mastoid process of the temporal bone
Action:	Extend neck and draw head posteriorly when both act together; acting alone it rotates the head toward the side of the contracting muscle
Innervation:	Cervical plexus (dorsal rami of C2 and C3)
Comments:	Muscles located deep to the trapezius and the rhomboids; inserted deep to the sternocleidomastoid on the mastoid process

4 Longissimus capitis (paired)

Origin:	Transverse processes of upper four or five thoracic vertebrae (T1–T5) and articular processes of lower three or four cervical vertebrae (C4–C7)
Insertion:	Mastoid process of the temporal bone
Action:	Extends and rotates the head
Innervation:	Cervical plexus (dorsal rami of C1–C3)
Comments:	Together with the longissimus thoracis and longissimus cervicis they form the intermediate division of the erector spinae muscles

5 Platysma (paired)

Origin:	Fascia covering the pectoralis major and deltoid muscles
Insertion:	Inferior border of mandible; skin and superficial fascia of lower face; blending with fibers of muscles associated with angle and lower part of mouth
Action:	Anterior fibers assist in depressing mandible; pull lower lip and angle of mouth inferiorly; widens mouth in cases where inspiration is sudden and deep
Innervation:	Facial nerve (CN VII)
Comments:	Varies markedly in its extent; may be absent unilaterally or bilaterally

Muscles of the head and neck, functionally grouped (*continued*)

Facial Muscles†

6 Orbicularis oculi (paired)

Origin:	Frontal bone, maxilla, and lacrimal bone
Insertion:	Skin and subcutaneous tissue of eyelids and area surrounding the orbit
Action:	Close the eyelids either reflexively or voluntarily
Innervation:	Facial nerve (CN VII)
Comments:	Form the sphincter muscles of the eyelids; are very thin and complex in their circular arrangement; may assist in drawing tear fluid into the lacrimal sac by helping to dilate the latter; please consult a major anatomical text‡ for a more detailed description

7 Corrugator supercilii (paired)

Origin:	Frontal bone just above medial margin of orbit
Insertion:	Skin of forehead above medial part of the superior orbital margin
Action:	Involved in frowning; draws medial portion of the eyebrow inferiorly and toward midline producing vertically arranged wrinkles of skin overlying forehead
Innervation:	Facial nerve (CN VII)
Comments:	A small muscle with a pyramidal shape; located deep to orbicularis oculi and the frontal belly of the epicranius muscle

8 Epicranius, or Occipitofrontalis

General:	This muscle consists of two occipital bellies and two frontal bellies interconnected by a tough aponeurosis termed the *galea aponeurotica* that covers the superior and lateral portions of the skull. The aponeurosis is attached to the pericranium by loose connective tissue, thereby giving the former some degree of movement. Since the aponeurosis is also firmly anchored to the skin of the scalp, it carries the latter with it as it moves

Occipital belly (paired)

Origin:	Superior nuchal line of occipital bone and mastoid process of temporal bone
Insertion:	Galea aponeurotica
Action:	Draws the skin of the scalp backwards
Innervation:	Facial nerve (CN VII)
Comments:	Represents the posterior portion of the epicranius muscle

Frontal belly (paired)

Origin:	Galea aponeurotica
Insertion:	Skin and subcutaneous tissue overlying the superior margin of the orbit; blend with fibers of corrugator supercilii and orbicularis oculi
Action:	Elevate eyebrows and draw skin of forehead upward; may also act to draw the skin of forehead downward
Innervation:	Facial nerve (CN VII)
Comments:	Represents the anterior portion of the epicranius muscle

9 Orbicularis oris

Origin:	Indirectly from maxilla and mandible by means of the buccinator, zygomaticus major, and zygomaticus minor; some fibers also arise from the skin and subcutaneous tissue adjacent to the lips and mouth
Insertion:	Skin and subcutaneous tissue surrounding the lips and mouth
Action:	Closes and protrudes lips while compressing them against the teeth
Innervation:	Facial nerve (CN VII)
Comments:	Thin and complexly arranged sphincter muscle with fibers coursing in many different directions and forming several strata; together with other muscles of the lips, it serves an important role in mastication and articulation

(*table continued on next page*)

Muscles of the head and neck, functionally grouped (*continued*)

Facial Muscles†

10 Zygomaticus major (paired)

Origin:	Zygomatic (malar) bone
Insertion:	Some fibers blend with those of the orbicularis oris, others attach to skin and subcutaneous tissue at the angles of the mouth
Action:	Draws the angles of the mouth superiorly and laterally as in laughing and smiling
Innervation:	Facial nerve (CN VII)

11 Zygomaticus minor (paired)

Origin:	Zygomatic (malar) bone
Insertion:	Blends with muscle fibers that form the mass of the upper lip
Action:	Elevates upper lip
Innervation:	Facial nerve (CN VII)
Comments:	Contracting together with the levator labii superioris, it serves to deepen the furrow between the upper lip and the side of the nose

12 Levator labii superioris (paired)

Origin:	Maxilla and zygomatic (malar) bone
Insertion:	Blend with additional muscle fibers making up the mass of the upper lip
Action:	Elevates and everts the upper lip
Innervation:	Facial nerve (CN VII)
Comments:	Contracting together with the zygomaticus minor serves to deepen the furrow between the upper lip and the side of the nose

13 Depressor labii inferioris (paired)

Origin:	Mandible
Insertion:	Skin and subcutaneous tissue of lower lip; also blends with fibers of orbicularis oris
Action:	Draws lower lip inferiorly and laterally
Innervation:	Facial nerve (CN VII)
Comments:	At its origin its fibers blend with those of the platysma

14 Mentalis (paired)

Origin:	Mandible
Insertion:	Skin and subcutaneous tissues overlying chin
Action:	Elevates and protrudes the lower lip; wrinkles the skin overlying the chin when sipping through a straw or expressing doubt
Innervation:	Facial nerve (CN VII)

15 Risorius (paired)

Origin:	Fascia that invests the parotid gland
Insertion:	Skin and subcutaneous tissue at the angle of the mouth
Action:	Retracts (draws laterally) the angle of the mouth
Innervation:	Facial nerve (CN VII)

16 Buccinator (paired)

Origin:	Maxilla and mandible; also from a fibrous connection extending between the pterygoid hamulus of the sphenoid bone and the mandible—the pterygomandibular raphe
Insertion:	Blend with fibers of the orbicularis oris

Muscles of the head and neck, functionally grouped *(continued)*	
Facial Muscles†	
Action:	Compress cheeks against the teeth during mastication and sucking; assist in expelling air from the mouth as when one inflates a balloon
Innervation:	Facial nerve (CN VII)
Comments:	Muscle is pierced by the parotid duct as it courses from parotid gland to oral cavity
17 Levator labii superioris alaquae nasi (paired)	
Origin:	Maxilla
Insertion:	Medial slip attaches to alar cartilage of nose and to skin overlying it; lateral slip blends with fibers of orbicularis oris and levator labii superioris in upper lip
Action:	Medial slip dilates the nostril, and lateral slip elevates and everts upper lip
Innervation:	Facial nerve (CN VII)
18 Depressor anguli oris (paired)	
Origin:	Mandible
Insertion:	Blends with fibers of orbicularis oris and risorious at angle of mouth
Action:	Draws angle of mouth inferiorly and laterally during opening
Innervation:	Facial nerve (CN VII)
Comments:	At its origin its fibers blend with those of the platysma
Lower jaw muscles	
19 Digastric (paired)	
Origin:	Mastoid process of temporal bone
Insertion:	Mandible; hyoid
Action:	Depresses mandible; can elevate hyoid
Innervation:	Facial nerve (CN VII) innervates posterior belly; mandibular branch of trigeminal nerve (CN V) innervates anterior belly
Comments:	Uniquely shaped muscle in that two bellies are united by an intermediate tendon that perforates the stylohyoid muscle; also attached to the hyoid by means of a connective tissue loop; the differential innervation results from the separate embryonic derivation of the two bellies
20 Temporalis (paired)	
Origin:	Temporal fossa
Insertion:	Coronoid process and anterior border of the mandibular ramus
Action:	Elevates mandible, thereby closing mouth and approximating the teeth; protrudes mandible
Innervation:	Trigeminal nerve (CN V, mandibular division)
Comments:	In the relaxed state the muscle is difficult to palpate; when contracted, however, the border of its attachment to the temporal fossa is easily detected
21 Masseter (paired)	
Origin:	Maxilla; zygomatic arch
Insertion:	Lateral aspect and angle of mandible; coronoid process of mandible
Action:	Elevates mandible, thereby occluding the teeth; plays minor role in protraction and retraction of the mandible
Innervation:	Trigeminal nerve (CN V, mandibular division)
Comments:	Easily palpated when contracted during clenching of the teeth; parotid gland overlies its posterior margin

(table continued on next page)

Muscles of the head and neck, functionally grouped (*continued*)	
Lower jaw muscles	
22 Lateral pterygoid (paired)	
Origin:	Dual origin: (1) greater wing of sphenoid and (2) lateral aspect of lateral pterygoid plate of sphenoid
Insertion:	Neck of mandible; capsule and articular disc of temporomandibular (TM) joint
Action:	Pulls condylar process and articular disc of TM joint forward, thereby assisting in opening the mouth; functions in side-to-side movements of mandible; protracts mandible
Innervation:	Trigeminal nerve (CN V, mandibular division)
Comments:	That portion of the muscle that attaches to the articular disc of the TM joint was originally connected to the malleus, one of the three small bones of the middle ear. This connection is lost during later embryonic life
23 Medial pterygoid (paired)	
Origin:	Medial aspect of lateral pterygoid plate of sphenoid; pyramidal process of palatine bone; maxilla
Insertion:	Medial aspect of ramus and angle of mandible
Action:	Protrudes and assists in elevating mandible; functions in side-to-side movements of mandible
Innervation:	Trigeminal nerve (CN V, mandibular division)
Comments:	A portion of the parotid gland lies on its lateral surface

*A paired muscle is simply one of a pair. Thus, there are actually two trapezius muscles, one on each side of the neck.

†Note that all muscles involved in facial expression receive their innervation through the facial nerve (CN VII); all muscles that function in mastication are innervated by branches of the trigeminal nerve (CN V). Some muscles inserting inferiorly on the hyoid bone and pharyngeal cartilages are described in Table 11-2.

‡Such as Gray's Anatomy, Philadelphia, PA, W. B. Saunders Co., 1980.

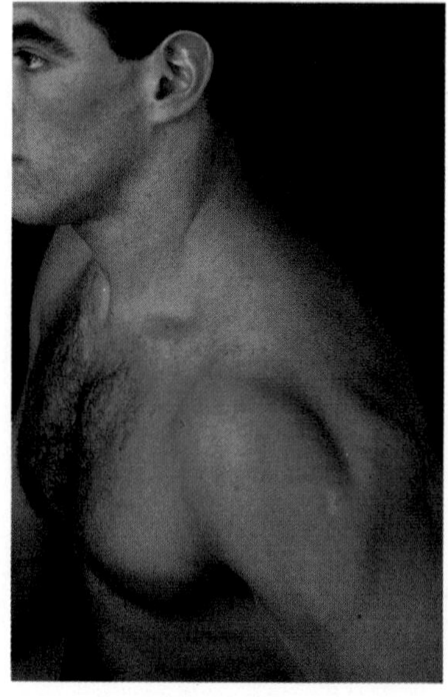

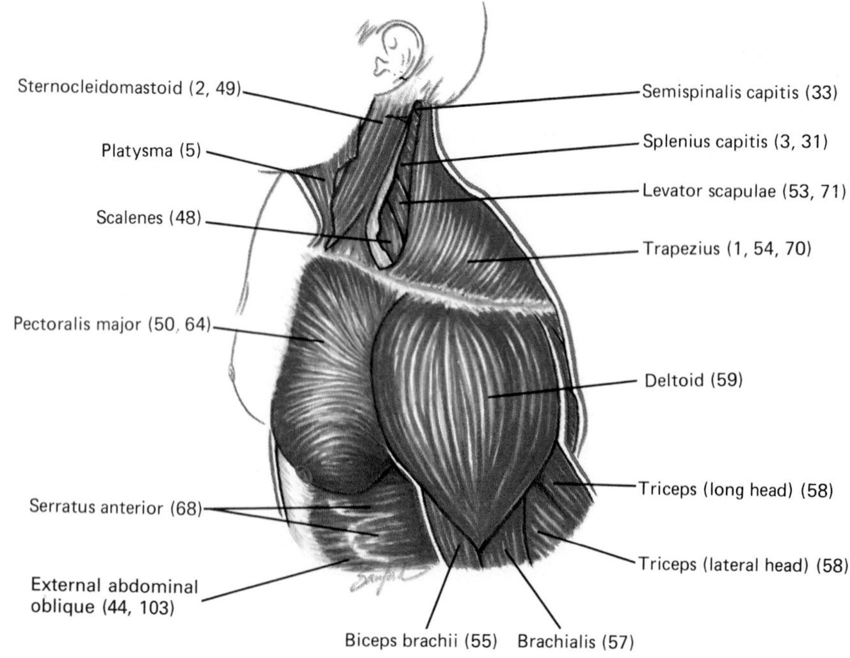

Shoulder and lateral aspect of neck.

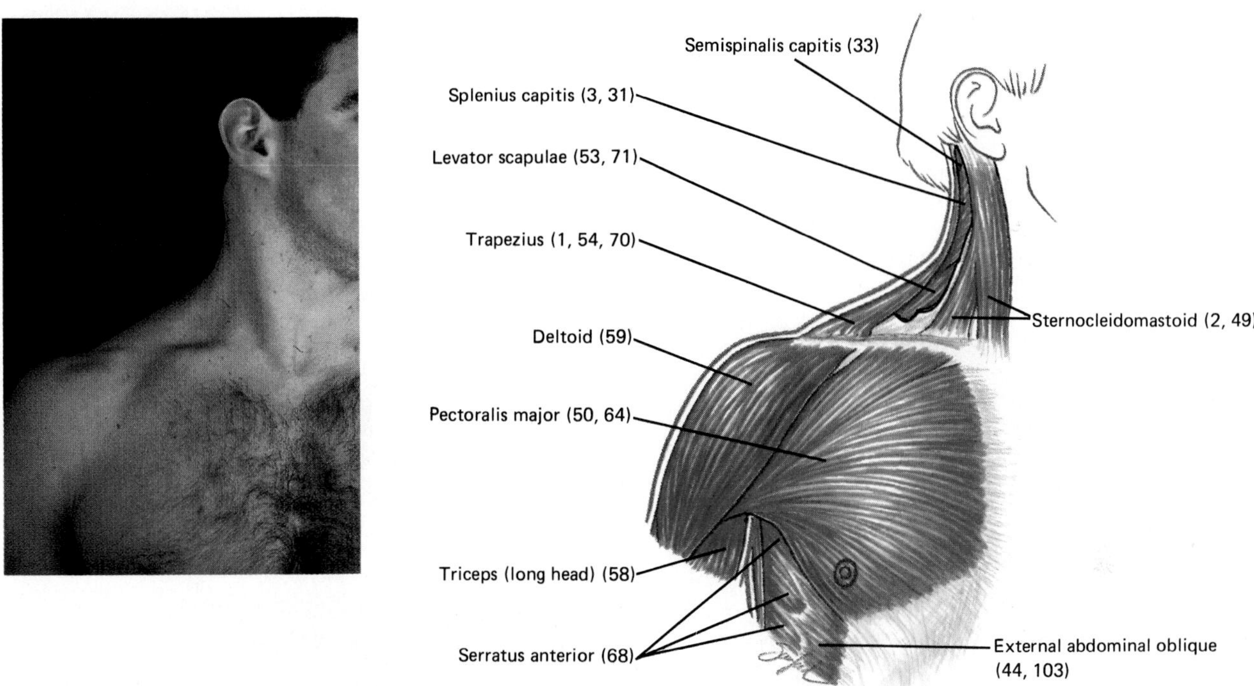

Anterolateral aspect of neck; superficial pectoral and shoulder region.

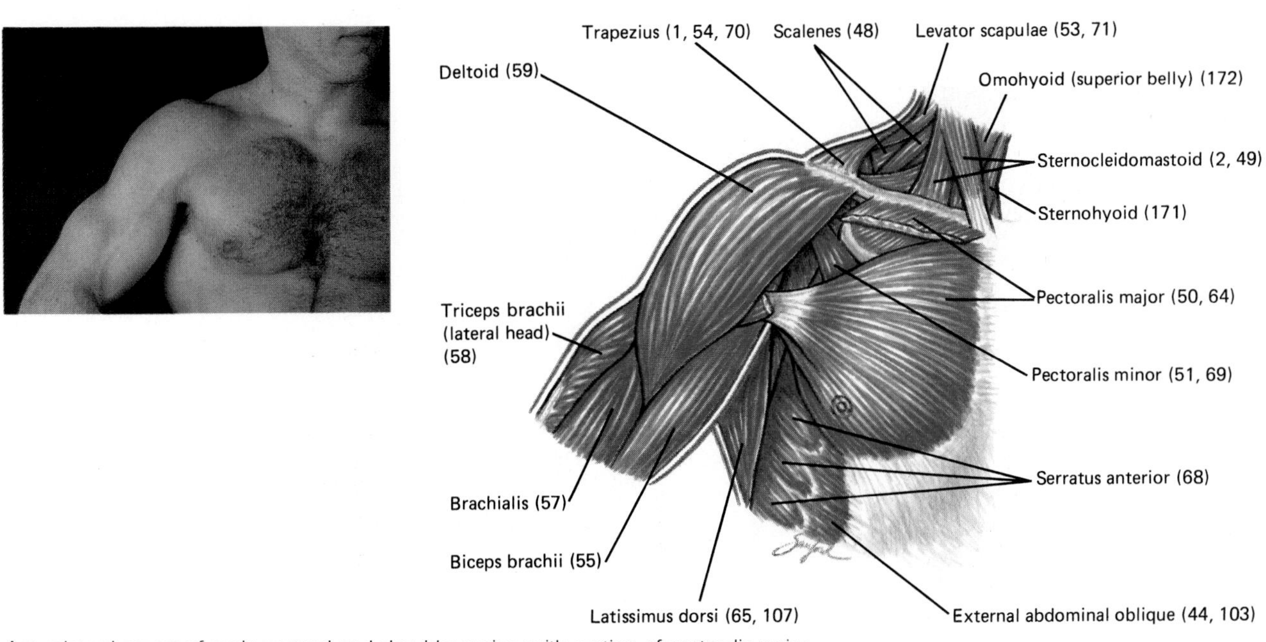

Anterolateral aspect of neck; pectoral and shoulder region with portion of pectoralis major removed.

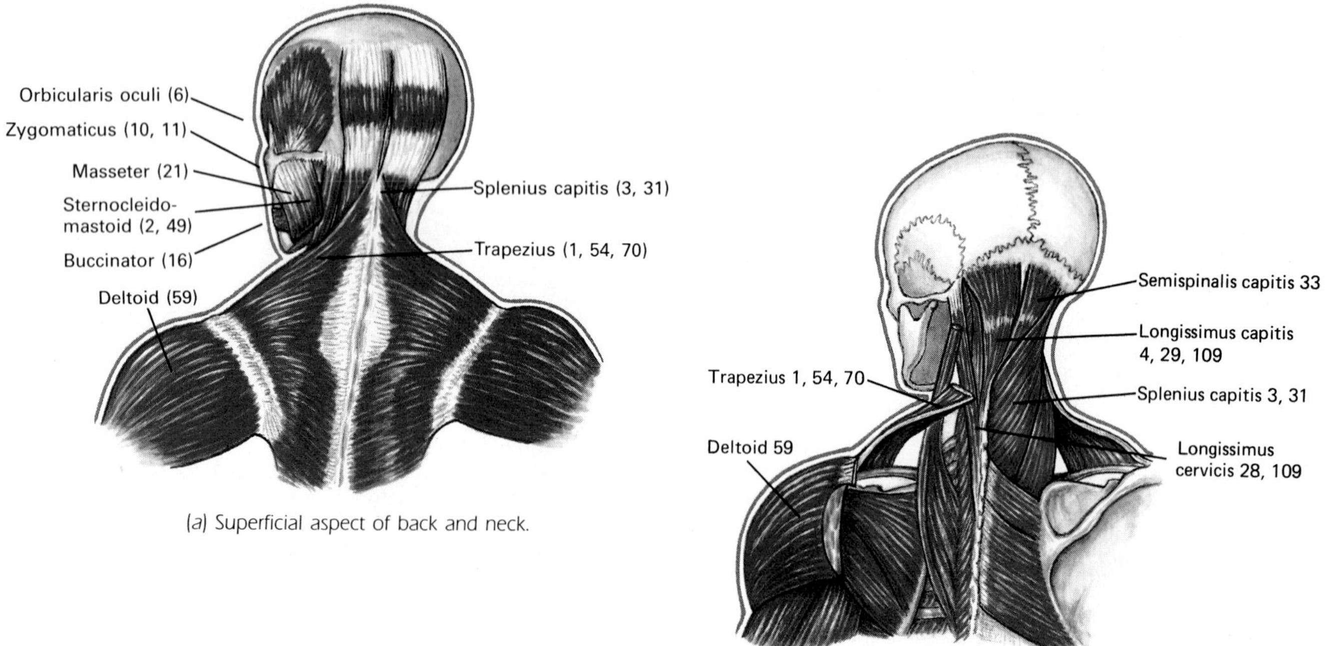

(a) Superficial aspect of back and neck.

(b) Deep aspect of back and neck.

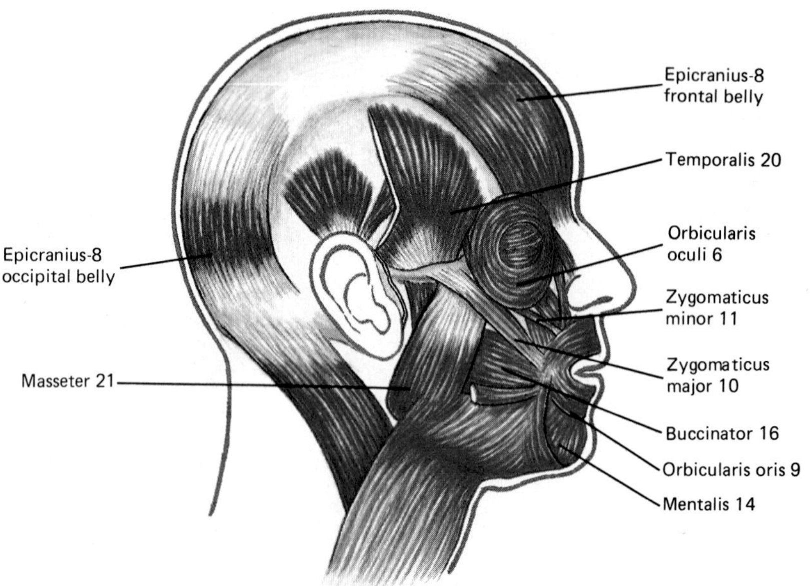

(c) Lateral aspect of head and neck.

TABLE 11-2

Trunk muscles	
NOTE: This table summarizes the principal intrinsic trunk muscles, whether respiratory or not. Emphasis, however, is upon respiration. Respiratory muscles are starred (*), and those used only in forced respiration are marked with a (†). For respiratory muscles, inspiration or expiration is indicated in each instance. (See also Table 11-5.)	
I Erector spinae group (sacrospinalis)	
24 Iliocostalis lumborum	
Origin:	Iliac crest
Insertion:	Lower six or seven ribs
25 Iliocostalis thoracis	
Origin:	Lower six ribs
Insertion:	Upper six ribs and transverse process of seventh cervical vertebra
26 Iliocostalis cervicis	
Origin:	Third through sixth rib
Insertion:	Transverse processes of fourth, fifth, and sixth cervical vertebrae
27 Longissimus thoracis	
Origin:	Ilium and lumbar vertebrae
Insertion:	Transverse processes of all thoracic vertebrae; ribs 2–12
28 Longissimus cervicis	
Origin:	Upper six thoracic vertebrae
Insertion:	Transverse processes of second through seventh cervical vertebrae
29 Longissimus capitis	
Origin:	Transverse processes of upper four cervical vertebrae
Insertion:	Mastoid process of temporal bone
30 Spinalis	
Origin:	Spinous processes of upper lumbar and lower thoracic vertebrae
Insertion:	Spinous processes of upper thoracic vertebrae
Comments:	May be subdivided into three groups: (a) spinalis thoracis, (b) spinalis cervicis, and (c) spinalis capitis
Action:	All muscles of the erector spinae group extend the vertebral column when contracting bilaterally; when contracting unilaterally, they produce lateral flexion of vertebral column, as in belly dancing; longissimus capitis extends cervical spine and turns face to same side; Principal extensors of vertebral column; lie in groove along vertebral column between spinous and transverse processes
Innervation:	Dorsal rami of spinal nerves
II Splenius group	
31 Splenius capitis	
Origin:	Lower half of ligamentum nuchae; spinous processes of upper six thoracic and last cervical vertebrae
Insertion:	Occipital bone and mastoid process of temporal bone
Action:	Flex neck laterally and rotate face to same side if contracting unilaterally; extend head on neck if contracting bilaterally
Innervation:	Dorsal rami of middle cervical spinal nerves
Comments:	Relatively large muscle situated on back of neck

(*table continued on next page*)

Trunk muscles (*continued*)	
II Splenius group	
32 Splenius cervicis	
Origin:	Same as for splenius capitis (see above)
Insertion:	Transverse processes of the upper two to four cervical vertebrae
Action:	Flex neck laterally if contracting unilaterally; extend cervical spine when contracting bilaterally
Innervation:	Dorsal rami of lower cervical nerves
Comments:	Assists splenius cervicis in its actions
III Semispinalis group	
33 Semispinalis capitis	
Origin:	Transverse processes of upper six thoracic vertebrae and articular processes of lower three or four cervical vertebrae
Insertion:	Near nuchal line of occipital bone
Action:	Acting unilaterally it flexes neck laterally; acting bilaterally, extends neck; also extends head on neck and turns face toward opposite side
Innervation:	Dorsal rami of spinal nerves
Comments:	Largest muscle occupying posterior aspect of the neck; all components of the semispinalis group tend to function as a unit rather than as individual muscles
34 Semispinalis cervicis	
Origin:	Transverse processes of upper six thoracic vertebrae
Insertion:	Spinous processes of second through fifth cervical vertebrae
Action:	Flexes vertebral column laterally and rotates vertebrae toward opposite side during unilateral contraction; extends cervical region of column during bilateral contraction
Innervation:	Dorsal rami of spinal nerves
Comments:	Located deep to erector spinae
35 Semispinalis thoracis	
Origin:	Transverse processes of lower six thoracic vertebrae
Insertion:	Spinous processes of seventh cervical and upper four thoracic vertebrae
Action:	Flexes vertebral column laterally and rotates vertebrae toward opposite side during unilateral contraction; extends thoracic region of column when contracting bilaterally
Innervation:	Dorsal rami of spinal nerves
Comments:	Located deep to erector spinae
IV Suboccipital group	
36 Rectus capitis posterior major	
Origin:	Spine of axis
Insertion:	Occipital bone beneath lateral aspect of inferior nuchal line
Action:	Extends head and rotates face toward same side
Innervation:	Dorsal ramus of first cervical nerve (C1, suboccipital nerve)
Comments:	Begins as a small round tendon and broadens as it nears its insertion; forms superomedial boundary of suboccipital triangle, which is of clinical significance because it contains the vertebral artery; if blood flow in the artery is reduced due to atherosclerotic lesions, excessive turning of the head may further impede flow such that dizziness results due to impaired vascular flow to brain stem

Trunk muscles (*continued*)	
IV Suboccipital group	
37 Rectus capitis posterior minor	
Origin:	Posterior tubercle of atlas
Insertion:	Medial aspect of inferior nuchal line of occipital bone
Action:	Extends head
Innervation:	Dorsal ramus of first cervical nerve (C1, suboccipital nerve)
Comments:	Inserts medial to rectus capitis posterior major
38 Obliquus capitis superior	
Origin:	Transverse process of atlas
Insertion:	Occipital bone between superior and inferior nuchal lines
Action:	Extends head and bends it laterally toward the same side
Innervation:	Dorsal ramus of first cervical nerve (C1, suboccipital nerve)
Comments:	Forms superolateral border of suboccipital triangle
39 Obliquus capitis inferior	
Origin:	Spine and lamina of axis
Insertion:	Transverse process of atlas
Action:	Rotates face toward same side
Innervation:	Dorsal ramus of first cervical nerve (C1, suboccipital nerve)
Comments:	Forms inferolateral border of suboccipital triangle; larger of two obliquus muscles
40 Quadratus lumborum† (See Table 11-5)	
Anterior trunk muscles	
41 External intercostals*	
Origin:	Inferior border of rib above intercostal space
Insertion:	Superior border of rib below intercostal space
Action:	Enlarges lateral and anteroposterior dimensions of thorax by elevating ribs
Innervation:	Intercostal nerves (T1–T11)
Comments:	Most superficial muscle of intercostal space; function during inspiration
42 Internal intercostals*	
Origin:	Superior border of rib below intercostal space
Insertion:	Inferior border of rib above intercostal space
Action:	Costal fibers reduce lateral and anteroposterior dimensions of thorax by bringing adjacent ribs together; interchondral fibers elevate ribs and thus enlarge these dimensions
Innervation:	Intercostal nerves (T1–T11)
Comments:	Costal fibers function in exhalation; interchondral fibers function during inspiration
43 Diaphragm	
Origin: Insertion:	Fibers attached to posterior aspect of xiphoid process, internal surfaces of lower six ribs and bodies of upper three lumbar vertebrae
Action:	Increases volume of thoracic cavity
Innervation:	Phrenic nerve (C3–C5)
Comments:	Central tendon is subject to herniation where esophagus passes through it (hiatus hernia). Recent evidence suggests that a portion of the diaphragm may also function during expiration; it is the principal muscle of inspiration

(*table continued on next page*)

Trunk muscles (*continued*)

Anterior trunk muscles

44 External abdominal oblique†

(Assists in forced expiration) (See Table 11-5)

45 Internal abdominal oblique†

(Assists in forced expiration) (See Table 11-5)

46 Transversus abdominis†

(Assists in forced expiration) (See Table 11-5)

47 Rectus abdominis†

(Assists in forced expiration) (See Table 11-5)

48 Scalenes† (1) Anterior (2) Medius (3) Posterior

Origin:	(1) Transverse processes of third through sixth cervical vertebrae (2) Transverse processes of axis and lower five cervical vertebrae (3) Transverse processes of fourth, fifth, and sixth cervical vertebrae
Insertion:	(1) Scalene tubercle and ridge on upper surface of first rib (2) Upper surface of first rib (3) Lateral surface of second rib
Action:	Elevate ribs and flex vertebral column
Innervation:	(1) Ventral rami of cervical spinal nerves (C4–C6) (2) Ventral rami of cervical spinal nerves (C3–C8) (3) Ventral rami of cervical spinal nerves (C6–C8)
Comments:	The scalene muscles, and in particular the medius, function during quiet inspiration as well as in forced inspiration.

49 Sternocleidomastoid†

(Assists only in forced expiration) (See Table 11-1)

50 Pectoralis major†

In order for the humerothoracic and scapulohumeral muscles to have a respiratory function, it is necessary for the arms to be fixed—the humerus becomes the less movable origin and the thorax becomes the more mobile insertion (functional reversal of origin and insertion); certain of these muscles have controversial roles in respiratory movements and are so indicated by the symbol (?). Pectoralis major functions only during forced inspiration (See Table 11-3).

51 Pectoralis minor†

(Forced inspiration) (?) (See Table 11-3)

52 Rhomboideus† (1) Major (2) Minor

(Forced inspiration) (?) (See Table 11-3)

53 Levator scapulae†

(Forced inspiration) (See Table 11-3)

54 Trapezius†

(Forced inspiration) (See Table 11-2)

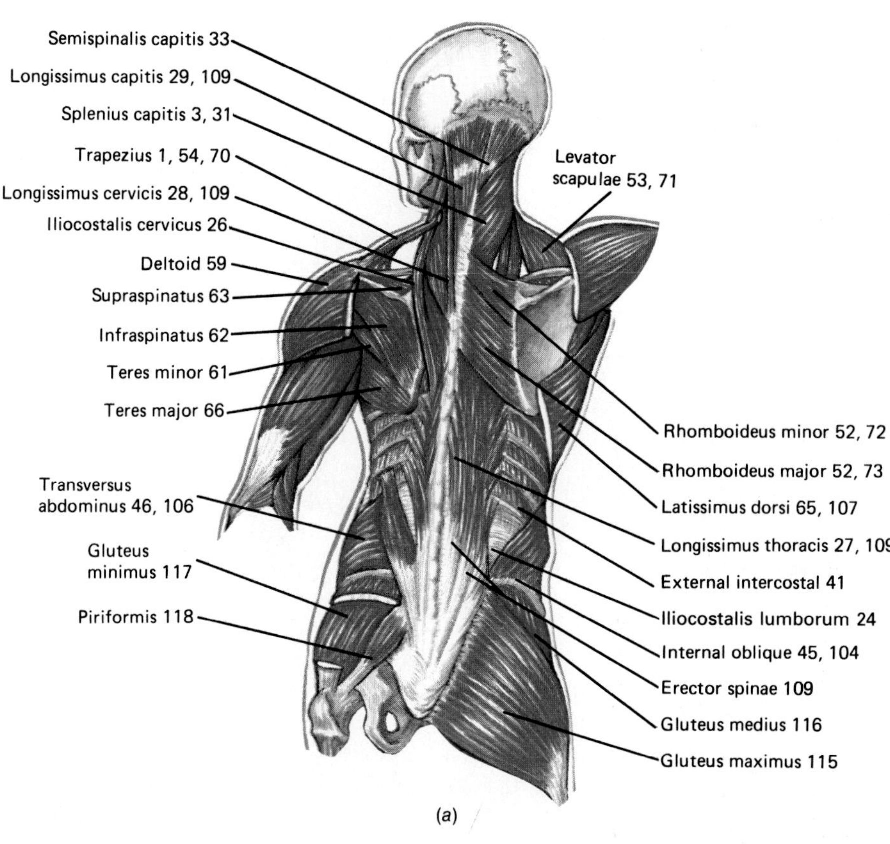

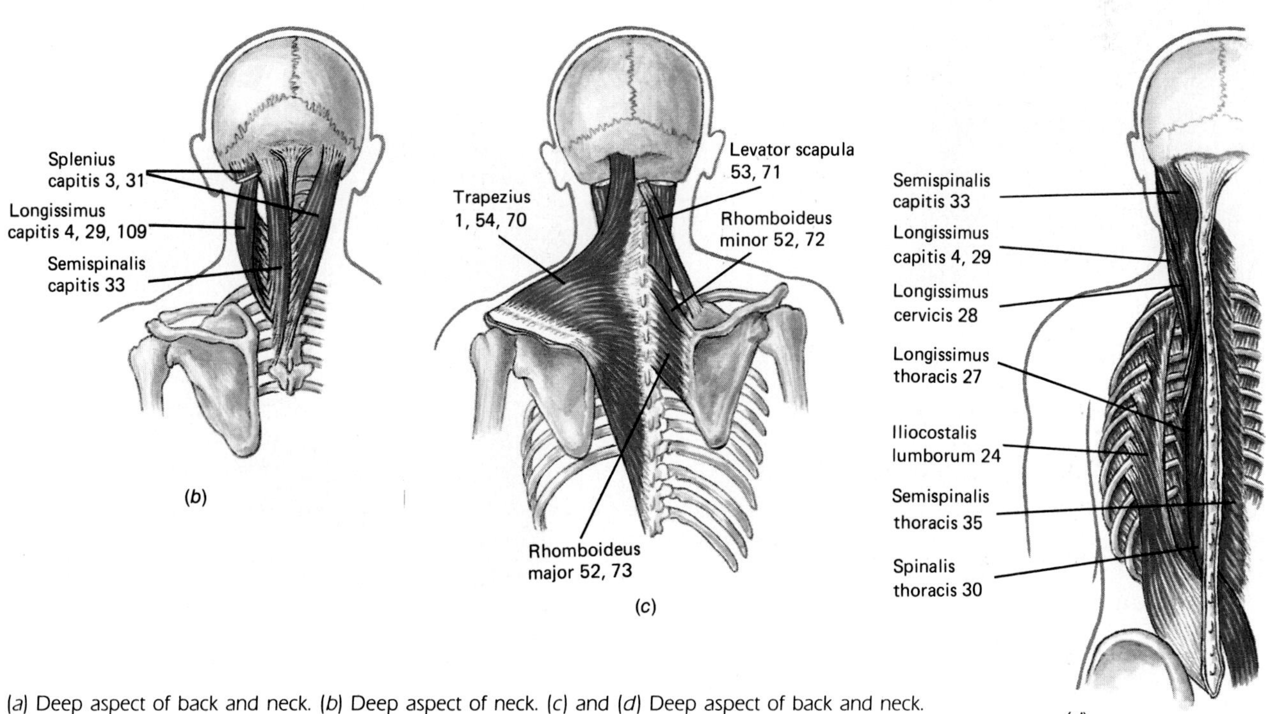

(*a*) Deep aspect of back and neck. (*b*) Deep aspect of neck. (*c*) and (*d*) Deep aspect of back and neck.

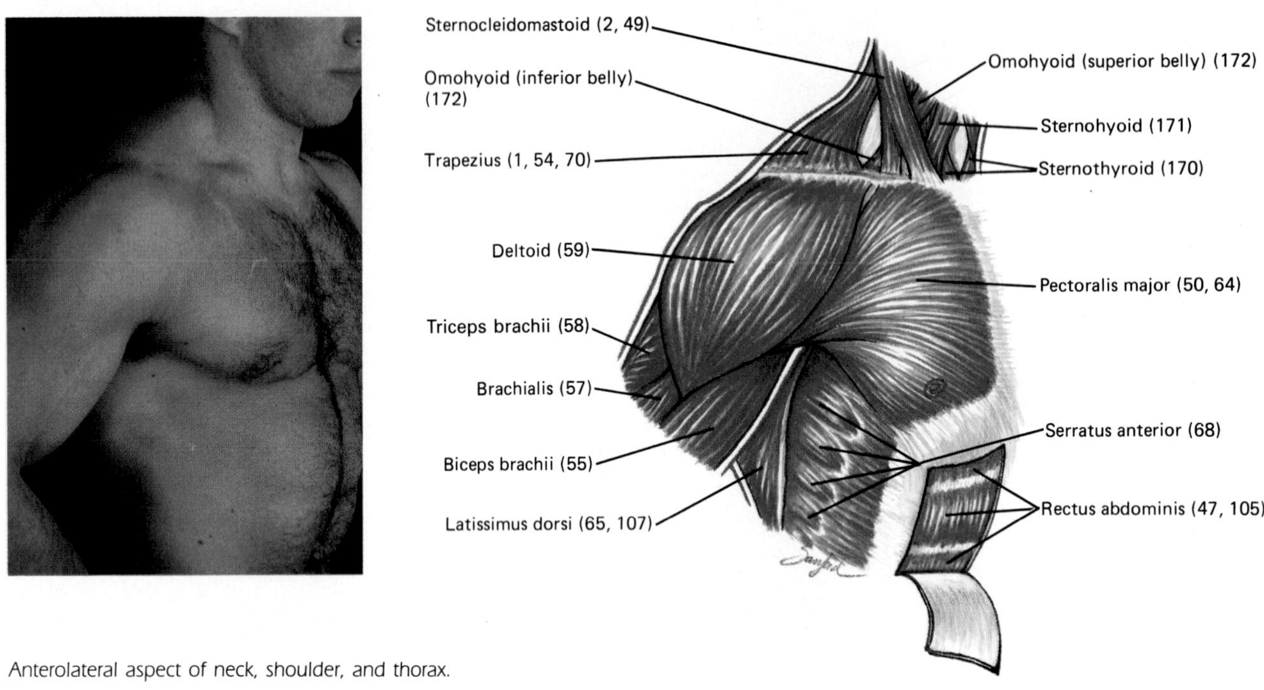

Anterolateral aspect of neck, shoulder, and thorax.

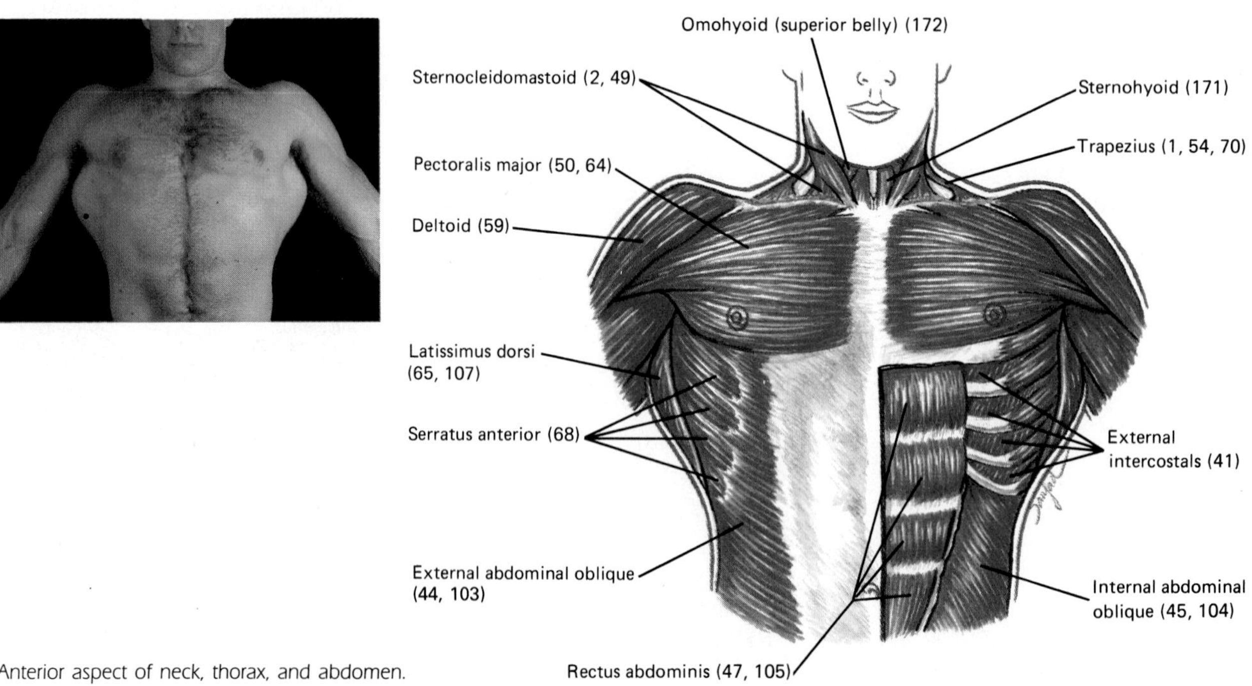

Anterior aspect of neck, thorax, and abdomen.

TABLE 11-3

Muscles of the arm and shoulder	
Muscles inserting upon the radius	
55 Biceps brachii	
Origin:	Dual: (a) long head from tubercle of scapula and (b) short head from coracoid process of scapula
Action:	Flexes forearm at elbow and supinates forearm
Innervation:	Musculocutaneous nerve (C5 and C6)
Comments:	Inserts upon tuberosity of radius; a powerful supinator when forearm is flexed as when using a screwdriver
56 Brachioradialis	
Origin:	Lateral supracondylar ridge of humerus
Action:	Flexes forearm at elbow
Innervation:	Radial nerve (C5–C7)
Comments:	Distal end of radius immediately proximal to styloid process; most superficial muscle on lateral aspect of forearm
Muscle inserting upon the ulna	
57 Brachialis	
Origin:	Lower half of anterior aspect of humerus
Action:	Flexes forearm at elbow
Innervation:	Musculocutaneous nerve (C5 and C6)
Comments:	Inserts upon coronoid process and tuberosity of ulna; primary flexor of forearm; lies deep to biceps brachii
Muscles inserting upon the humerus	
58 Triceps brachii	
Origin:	Three heads of origin: (a) long head from infraglenoid tubercle of scapula, (b) lateral head from posterior aspect of humerus superior to radial groove, (c) medial head from posterior aspect of humerus below radial groove
Action:	Extends forearm at elbow
Innervation:	Radial nerve (C6–C8)
Comments:	Inserts upon olecranon process of ulna; principal extensor of forearm; assists in extension and adduction of arm at shoulder
59 Deltoid	
Origin:	Lateral third of clavicle; spine and acromion process of scapula
Action:	(a) Anterior fibers flex and medially rotate humerus, (b) middle fibers represent principal abductor of humerus, (c) posterior fibers extend and laterally rotate humerus
Innervation:	Axillary nerve (C5 and C6)
Comments:	Inserts upon deltoid tuberosity of humerus; thick, powerful muscle overlying shoulder joint; has a triangular shape
60 Coracobrachialis	
Origin:	Coracoid process of scapula
Action:	Flexes arm at shoulder
Innervation:	Musculocutaneous nerve (C5–C7)
Comments:	Inserts on middle third of medial aspect of humerus; is pierced by musculocutaneous nerve

(*table continued on next page*)

Muscles of the arm and shoulder (*continued*)	
Muscles inserting upon the humerus	
61 Teres minor	
Origin:	Lateral border of scapula
Action:	Laterally rotates humerus at shoulder; assists in stabilizing shoulder joint
Innervation:	Axillary nerve (C5 and C6)
Comments:	Its tendon, together with those of supraspinatus, infraspinatus, and subscapularis, forms the "rotator cuff" of the shoulder; inserts upon the greater tubercle of the humerus
62 Infraspinatus	
Origin:	Infraspinous fossa of scapula
Action:	Laterally rotates humerus at shoulder; assists in stabilizing shoulder joint
Innervation:	Suprascapular nerve (C5 and C6)
Comments:	Tendon forms part of "rotator cuff"; inserts upon greater tubercle of the humerus
63 Supraspinatus	
Origin:	Supraspinous fossa of scapula
Action:	Abducts humerus at shoulder; assists in stabilizing shoulder joint
Innervation:	Suprascapular nerve (C4–C6)
Comments:	Tendon forms part of "rotator cuff"; inserts upon greater tubercle of the humerus; in injuries of the "rotator cuff" this tendon is the one most frequently torn
64 Pectoralis major	
Origin:	Dual: (1) clavicular head from anterior aspect of clavicle; (2) sternal head from anterolateral aspect of sternum
Action:	Adducts and medially rotates the humerus
Innervation:	Medial pectoral nerve (C8–T1)
Comments:	Inserts via a folded tendon into greater tubercle of humerus; functions in forced respiration (see Table 11-2)
65 Latissimus dorsi	
(See Table 11-5)	
66 Teres major	
Origin:	Dorsal aspect of inferior angle of scapula
Action:	Adducts and medially rotates humerus; assists in extending the flexed arm and stabilizes shoulder joint during abduction
Innervation:	Lower subscapular nerve (C6 and C7)
Comments:	Inserts on medial border of intertubercular groove of the humerus
67 Subscapularis	
Origin:	Subscapular fossa of scapula
Action:	Medially rotates humerus; assists in stabilizing shoulder joint
Innervation:	Upper and lower subscapular nerves (C5–C7)
Comments:	Thick, triangular-shaped muscle whose tendon forms part of "rotator cuff"; inserts upon lesser tubercle of the humerus

Muscles of the arm and shoulder (*continued*)	
Muscles inserting upon the costal (anterior) aspect of the scapula	
68 Serratus anterior	
Origin:	External surfaces of upper eight ribs
Action:	Protracts and fixes scapula against chest wall; assists in raising glenoid cavity upward when arm is lifted above the head
Innervation:	Long thoracic nerve (C5–C7)
Comments:	Inserts upon anterior aspect of medial border of scapula; its lower fibers of origin interdigitate with those of external abdominal oblique; paralysis of long thoracic nerve results in a "winged scapula" (medial border stands out) when patient pushes against an immovable object
69 Pectoralis minor	
Origin:	Superior border of the third, fourth, and fifth ribs
Insertion:	Coracoid process of the scapula
Action:	Pulls scapula inferiorly and anteriorly; when the scapula is fixed, as in forced respiration, it serves to elevate the ribs (forced inhalation) (?); assists in rotation of scapula leading to depression of the point of the shoulder
Innervation:	C6–C8
Comments:	A thin triangular muscle located deep to the pectoralis major muscle (see Table 11-2)
Muscles inserting upon dorsal (posterior) surface of the scapula	
70 Trapezius	
(See Table 11-2)	
71 Levator scapulae	
Origin:	Transverse processes of the first through the fourth cervical vertebrae
Insertion:	Medial (vertebral) border of the scapula between the superior angle and the medial end of the spine of the scapula
Action:	Elevates the scapula; fixes the neck during forced inspiration
Innervation:	Cervical plexus (C3–C5)
Comments:	The vertebral attachments of this muscle are subject to considerable variation (see Table 11-2)
72 Rhomboideus minor	
Origin:	Ligamentum nuchae; spinous process of the seventh cervical and first thoracic vertebrae
Insertion:	Medial end of the spine of the scapula
Action:	Draws scapula superomedially; fixes the head and neck during respiration
Innervation:	Dorsal scapular nerve (C4 and C5)
Comments:	Lies superior to the rhomboideus major and is usually separated from it by a small interval (see Table 11-2)
73 Rhomboideus major	
Origin:	Spinous processes of the second through the fifth thoracic vertebrae; also from the ligaments connecting the spinous processes (supraspinous ligaments)
Insertion:	Medial border of the scapula inferior to the fibers of rhomboideus minor
Action:	Draws scapula superomedially; fixes the head and neck during respiration
Innervation:	Dorsal scapular nerve (C4 and C5)
Comments:	Lies inferior to the rhomboideus minor muscle from which it is typically separated by a small interval

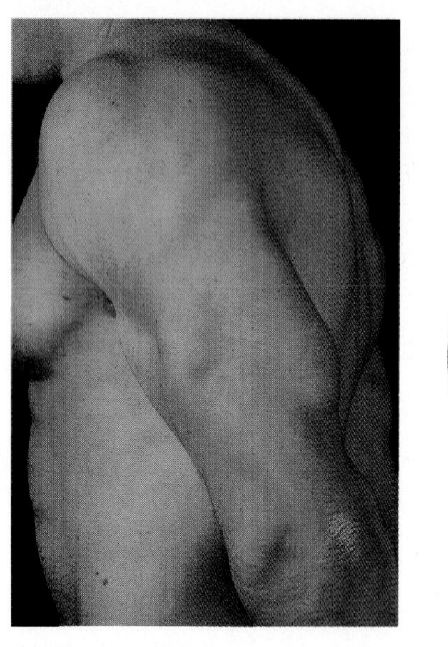

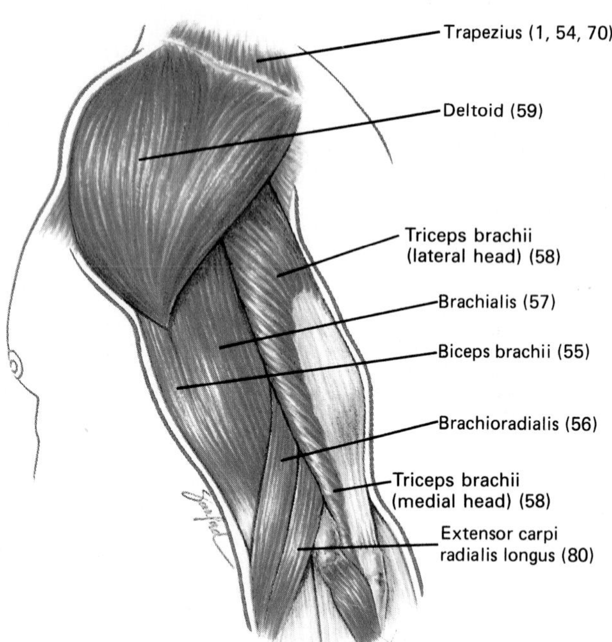

Lateral aspect of left shoulder and arm.

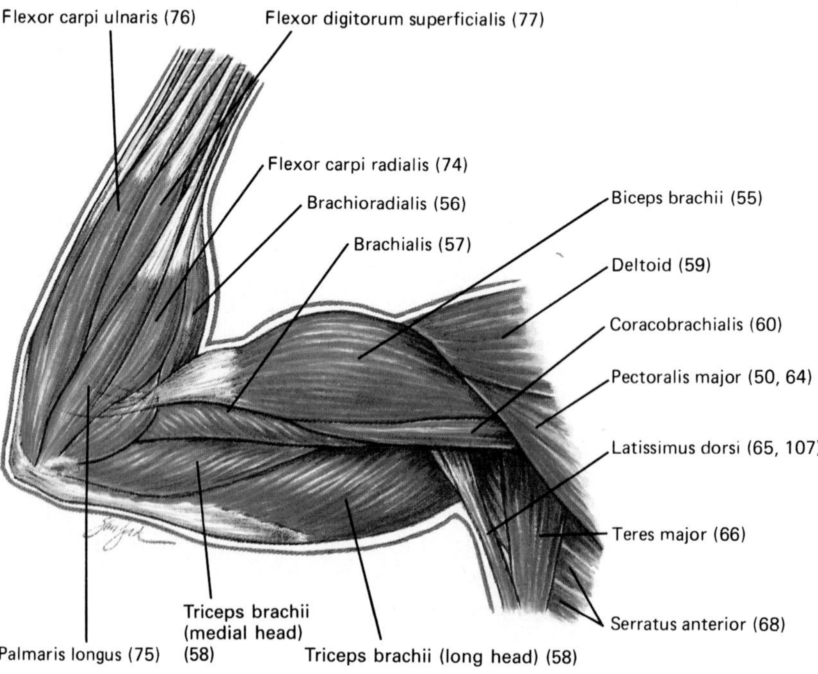

Medial aspect of arm and forearm.

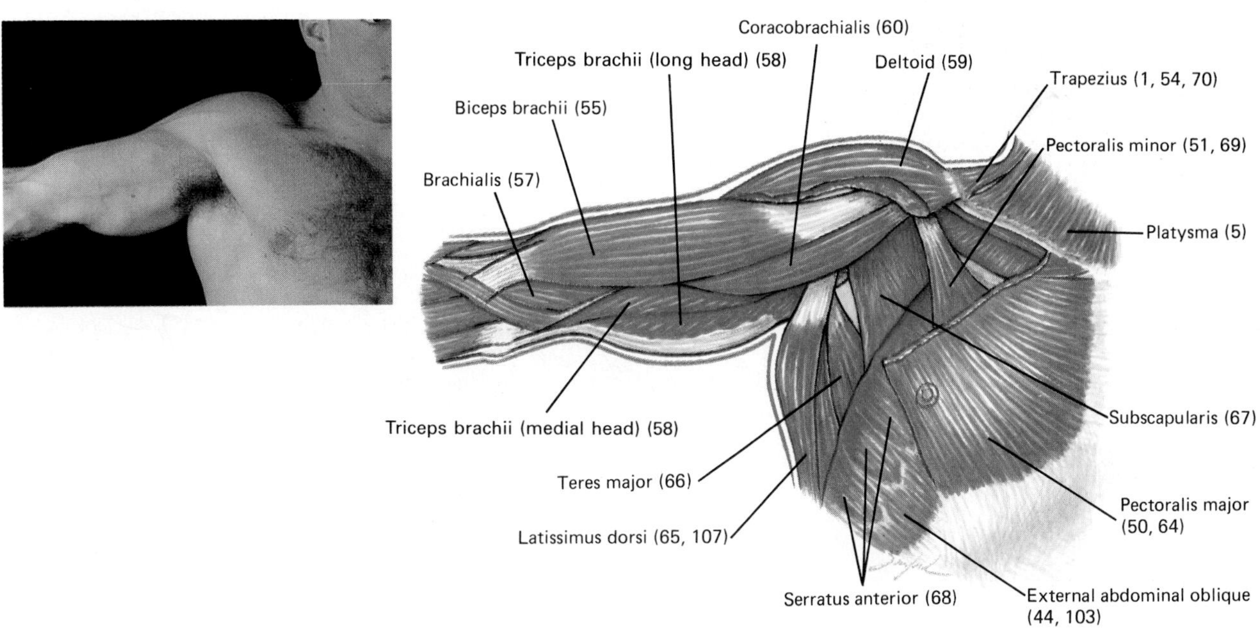
Coracobrachialis (60)
Triceps brachii (long head) (58)
Deltoid (59)
Trapezius (1, 54, 70)
Biceps brachii (55)
Pectoralis minor (51, 69)
Brachialis (57)
Platysma (5)
Subscapularis (67)
Triceps brachii (medial head) (58)
Teres major (66)
Pectoralis major (50, 64)
Latissimus dorsi (65, 107)
Serratus anterior (68)
External abdominal oblique (44, 103)

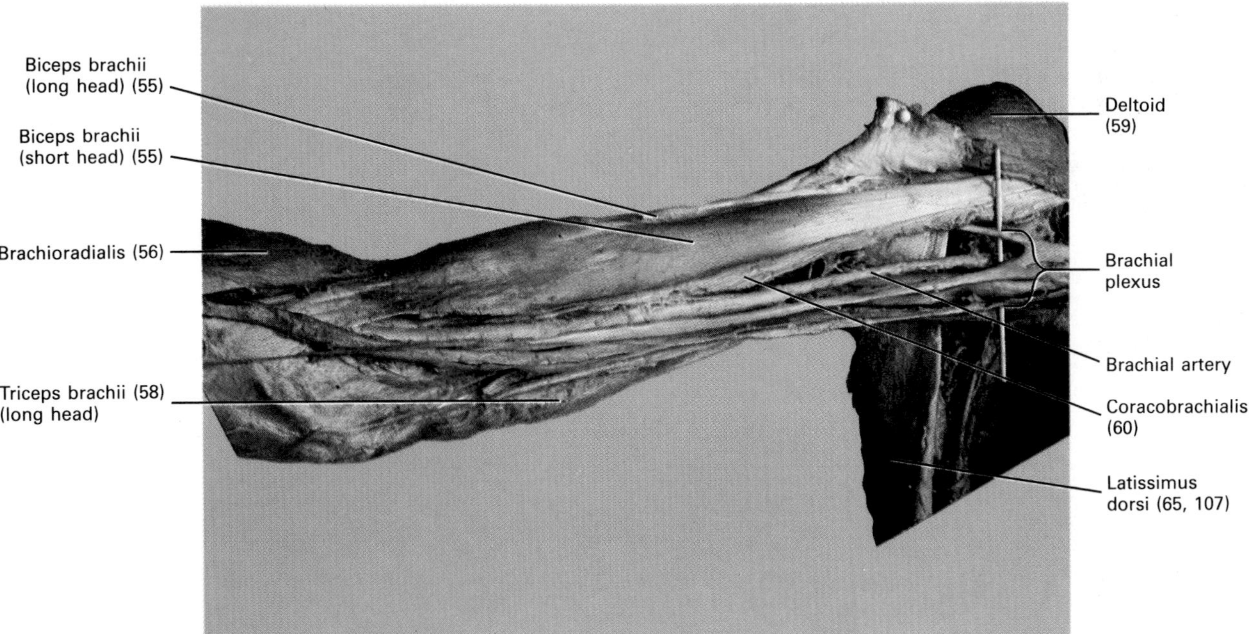
Biceps brachii (long head) (55)
Biceps brachii (short head) (55)
Deltoid (59)
Brachioradialis (56)
Brachial plexus
Brachial artery
Triceps brachii (58) (long head)
Coracobrachialis (60)
Latissimus dorsi (65, 107)

Pectoral region and anteromedial aspect of arm.

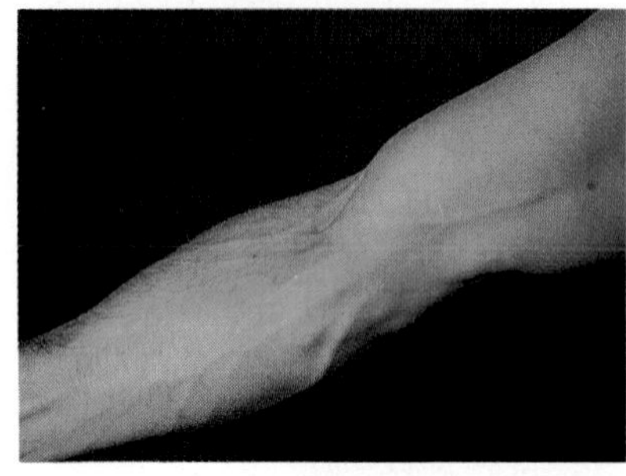

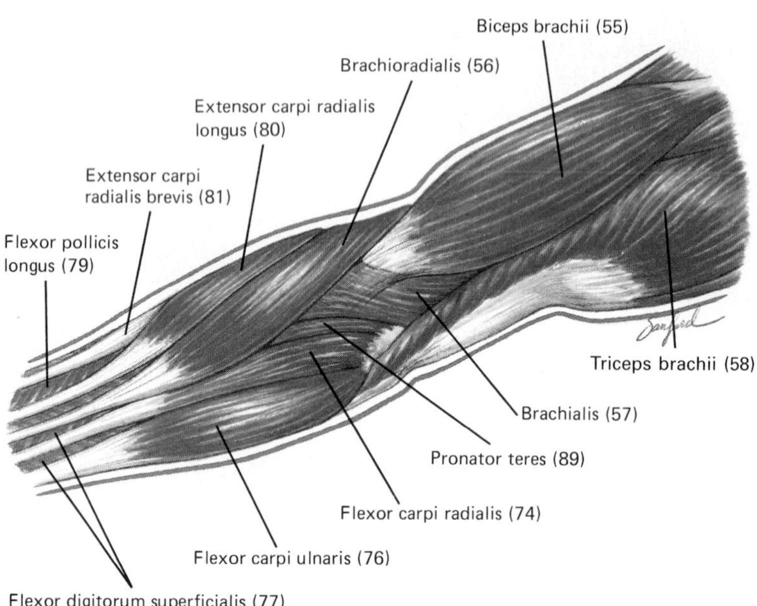
Biceps brachii (55)
Brachioradialis (56)
Extensor carpi radialis longus (80)
Extensor carpi radialis brevis (81)
Flexor pollicis longus (79)
Triceps brachii (58)
Brachialis (57)
Pronator teres (89)
Flexor carpi radialis (74)
Flexor carpi ulnaris (76)
Flexor digitorum superficialis (77)

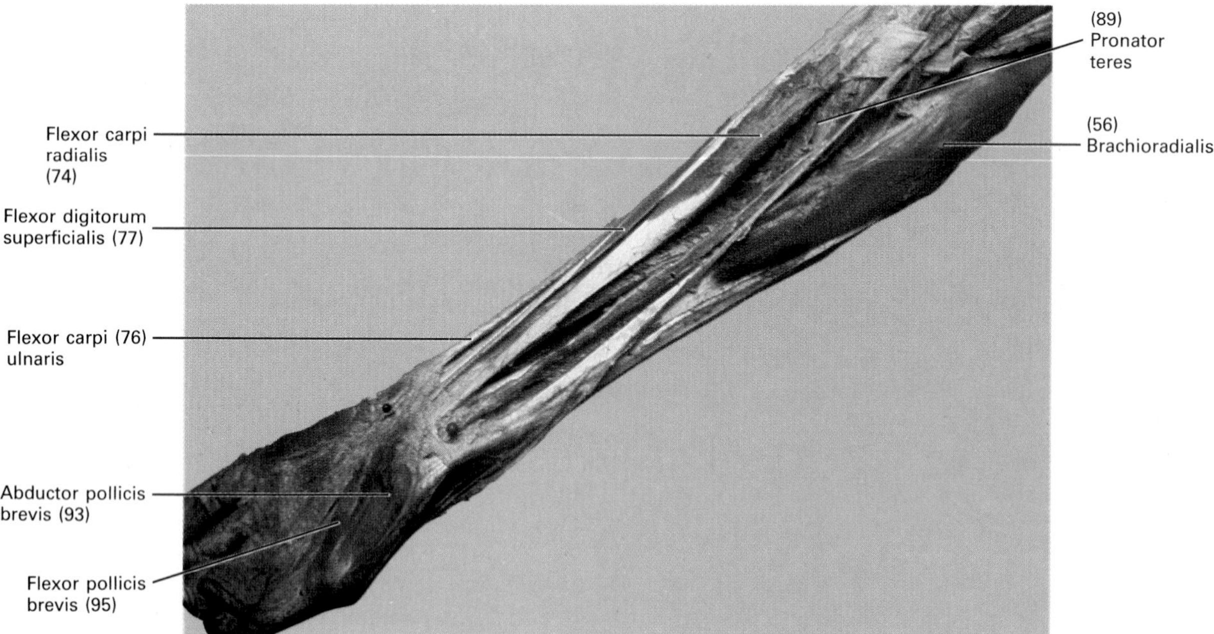
(89) Pronator teres
(56) Brachioradialis
Flexor carpi radialis (74)
Flexor digitorum superficialis (77)
Flexor carpi (76) ulnaris
Abductor pollicis brevis (93)
Flexor pollicis brevis (95)

Anterior aspect of arm and forearm.

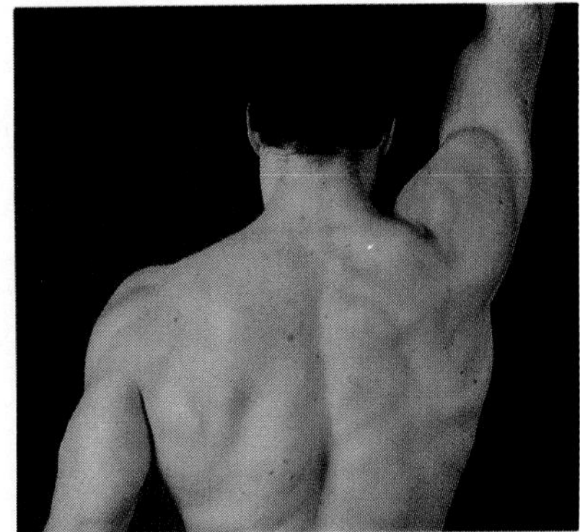

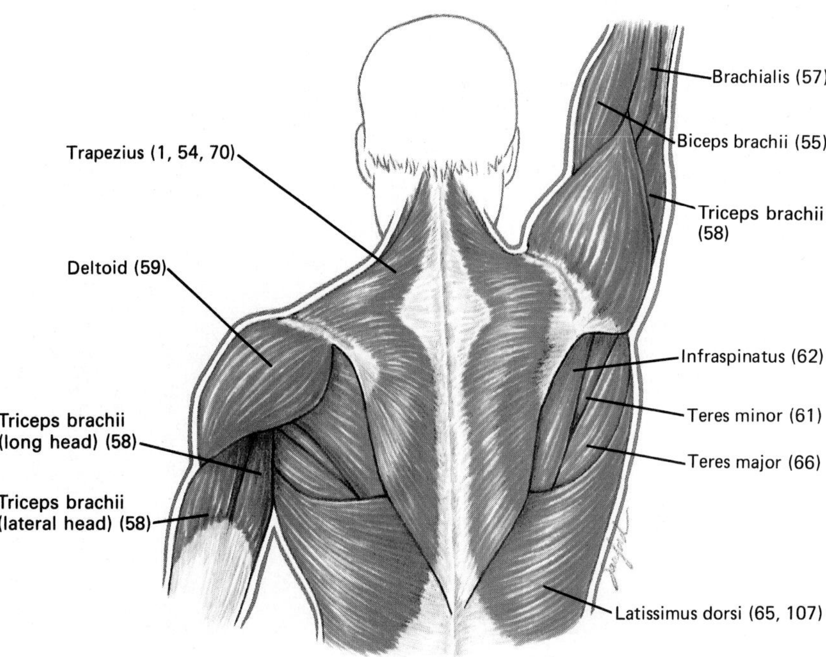

Posterior aspect of shoulder and back.

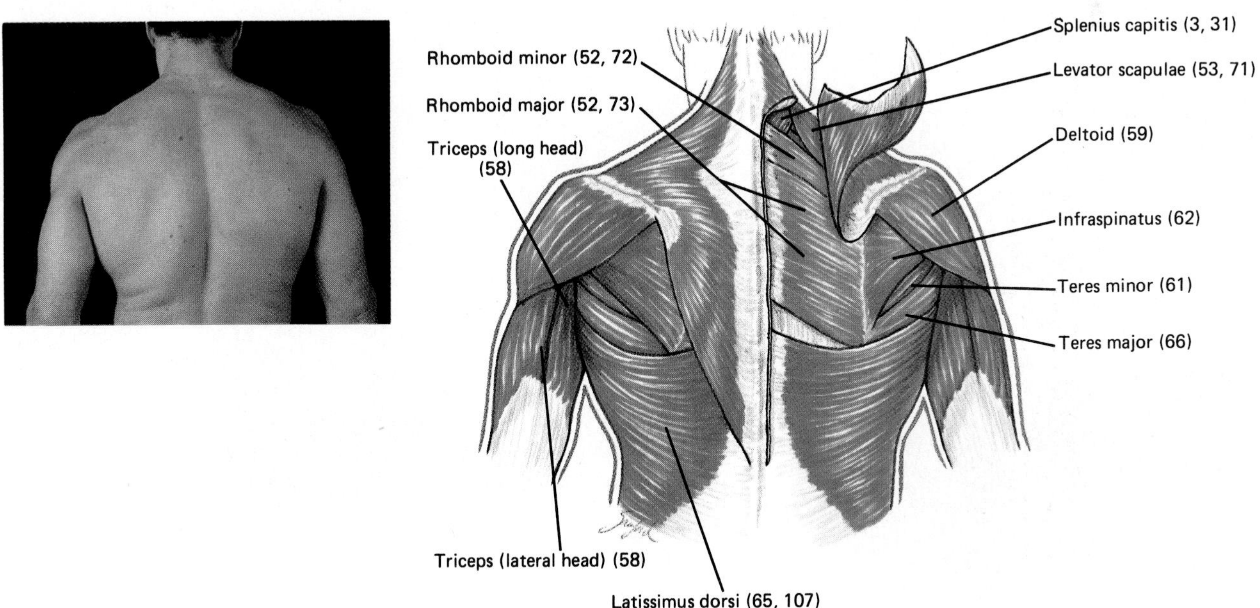

Posterior aspect of shoulder and back with trapezius reflected.

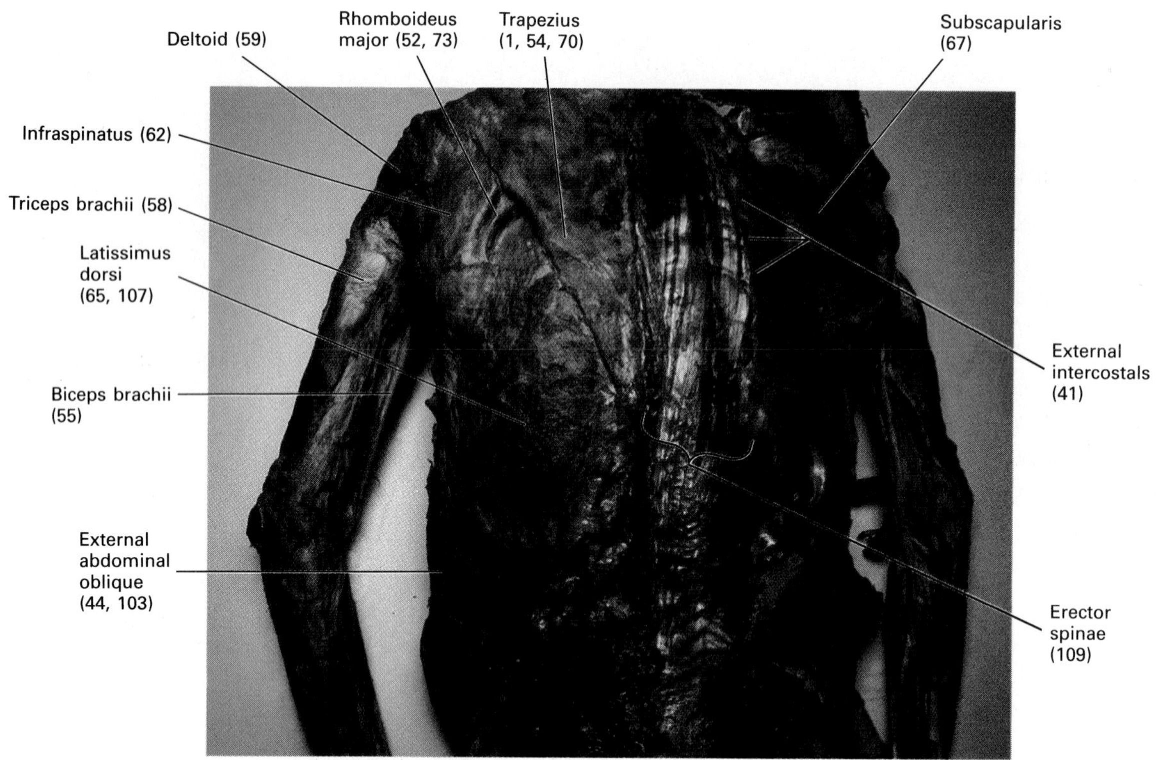

Posterior aspect of shoulder and back (*continued*)

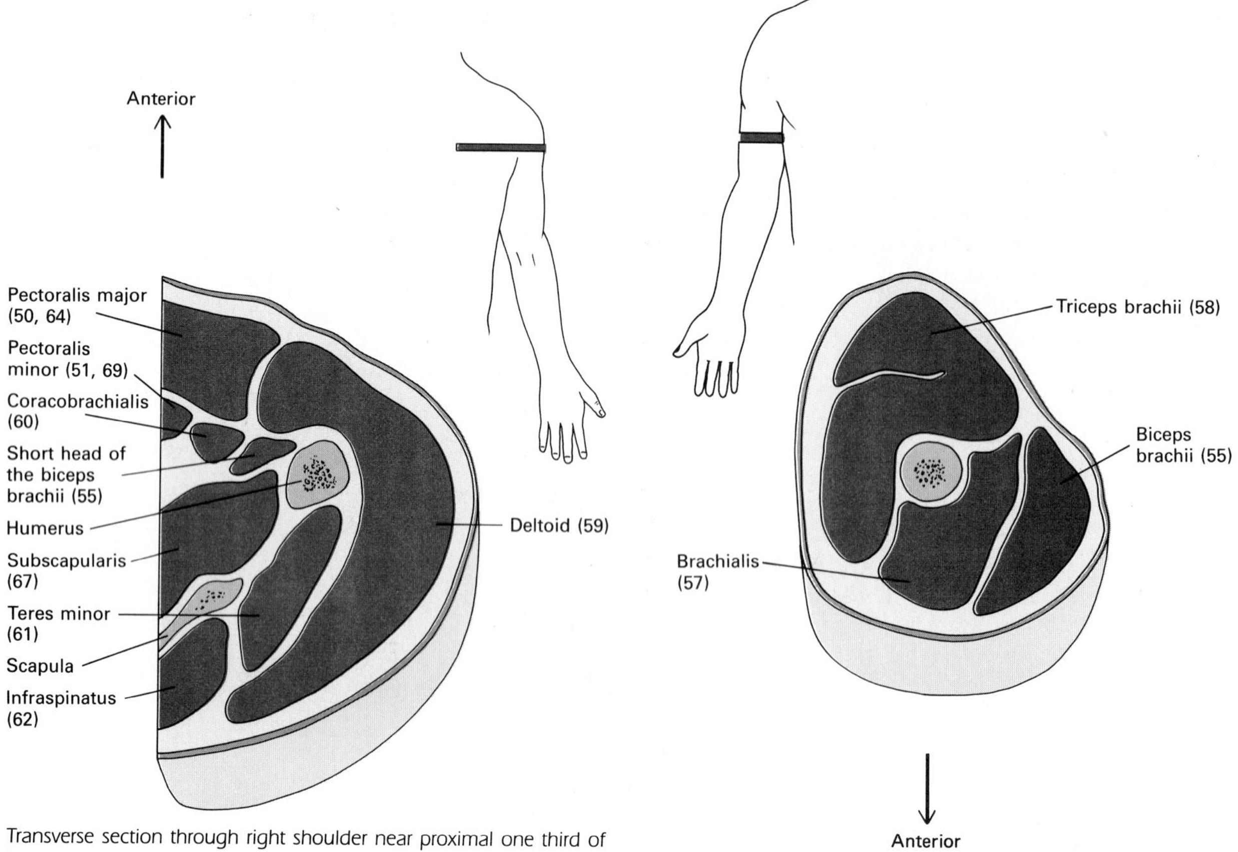

Transverse section through right shoulder near proximal one third of humerus.

Transverse section through arm at level of midhumerus.

TABLE 11-4

Muscles of forearm and hand

Flexor muscles located superficially in the forearm

74 Flexor carpi radialis

Origin:	Medial epicondyle of humerus
Insertion:	Base of second metacarpal
Action:	Abducts hand and flexes hand at wrist
Innervation:	Median nerve (C6 and C7)
Comments:	Its cordlike tendon is easily palpable at the wrist and serves as a landmark for locating the radial artery, which lies just lateral to it

75 Palmaris longus

Origin:	Medial epicondyle of humerus
Insertion:	Palmar aponeurosis
Action:	Flexes hand at wrist
Innervation:	Median nerve (C7 and C8)
Comments:	Is absent in approximately 20% of all individuals; when present, its tendon is easily palpable at wrist and serves as a landmark for locating the median nerve, which lies just lateral to it

76 Flexor carpi ulnaris

Origin:	Dual origin: (a) medial epicondyle of humerus and (b) olecranon process and posterior border of ulna
Insertion:	Pisiform bone; hamate bone; base of fifth metacarpal bone
Action:	Adducts and flexes hand at wrist
Innervation:	Ulnar nerve (C7 and C8)
Comments:	Ulnar nerve and artery lie lateral to its tendon at the wrist; most medial of the superficial flexor muscles in forearm

77 Flexor digitorum superficialis

Origin:	Dual origin: (a) medial epicondyle of humerus and coronoid process of ulna and (b) upper portion of anterior aspect of radius
Insertion:	Anterior aspect of bodies of middle phalanges of second through fifth digits
Action:	Flexes proximal interphalangeal joints of medial four digits; flexes metacarpophalangeal joints of medial four digits; flexes hand at wrist
Innervation:	Median nerve (C7, C8, and T1)
Comments:	Largest of superficial muscles in forearm

Flexor muscles located deep in the forearm

78 Flexor digitorum profundus

Origin:	Upper three-fourths of anterior and medial aspect of ulna; interosseous membrane between ulna and radius
Insertion:	Bases of distal phalanges of second through fifth digits
Action:	Flexes distal interphalangeal joints of medial four digits; assists in flexing proximal interphalangeal joints and metacarpophalangeal joints of medial four digits, as well as the hand at the wrist
Innervation:	Dual: (a) medial portion associated with the fourth and fifth digits through the ulnar nerve (C8 and T1); (b) lateral portion associated with the second and third digits through median nerve (C8 and T1)
Comments:	Only muscle capable of flexing the distal phalanges of the second through fifth digits

(table continued on next page)

Muscles of forearm and hand (*continued*)

Flexor muscles located deep in the forearm

79 Flexor pollicis longus

Origin:	Anterior aspect of radius and interosseous membrane between radius and ulna
Insertion:	Anterior aspect of base of distal phalanx of thumb
Action:	Flexes interphalangeal joints and metacarpophalangeal joints of thumb; assists in flexion of hand at wrist
Innervation:	Anterior interosseous branch of median nerve (C8 and T1)
Comments:	Situated lateral to flexor digitorum profundus

Extensor muscles located superficially in the forearm

80 Extensor carpi radialis longus

Origin:	Supracondylar ridge of the humerus
Insertion:	Posterior aspect of base of second metacarpal bone
Action:	Extends and abducts hand at wrist
Innervation:	Radial nerve (C6 and C7)
Comments:	Is partially hidden by the overlying brachioradialis muscle

81 Extensor carpi radialis brevis

Origin:	Dual: (a) lateral epicondyle of the humerus and (b) radial collateral ligament of elbow joint
Insertion:	Posterior aspect of base of third metacarpal bone
Action:	Extends and abducts hand at wrist
Innervation:	Deep branch of radial nerve (C7 and C8)
Comments:	Assists extensor carpi radialis longus in fixing wrist during flexion of fingers

82 Extensor digitorum

Origin:	Lateral epicondyle of the humerus
Insertion:	Lateral and dorsal surfaces of distal phalanges of medial four digits
Action:	Extends digits at interphalangeal and metacarpophalangeal joints; extends hand at wrist
Innervation:	Posterior interosseous branch of radial nerve (C7 and C8)
Comments:	Principal extensor muscle of the fingers

83 Extensor digiti minimi

Origin:	Lateral epicondyle of the humerus
Insertion:	Lateral and dorsal surfaces of distal phalanges of fifth digit
Action:	Extends fifth digit at metacarpophalangeal and interphalangeal joints
Innervation:	Posterior interosseous branch of radial nerve (C7 and C8)
Comments:	Its action permits individual extension of the fifth digit

84 Extensor carpi ulnaris

Origin:	Dual: (a) lateral epicondyle of humerus and (b) posterior aspect of ulna
Insertion:	Base of fifth metacarpal bone
Action:	Extends and adducts hand at wrist together with the extensor carpi radialis and flexor carpi radialis, respectively
Innervation:	Posterior interosseous branch of radial nerve (C7 and C8)
Comments:	A long thin muscle whose tendon lies in groove between the head and styloid process of ulna

Muscles of forearm and hand (*continued*)

Extensor muscles located deep in the forearm

85 Abductor pollicis longus

Origin:	Posterior aspect of radius and ulna and interosseous membrane between radius and ulna
Insertion:	Base of first metacarpal bone
Action:	Abducts and extends thumb at carpometacarpal joint
Innervation:	Posterior interosseous branch of radial nerve (C7 and C8)
Comments:	Its tendon, together with that of extensor pollicis brevis, forms the anterior boundary of the "anatomical snuff box"; pulse of radial artery can be felt on the floor of the "snuff box"

86 Extensor pollicis brevis

Origin:	Posterior aspect of radius and interosseous membrane between radius and ulna
Insertion:	Base of proximal phalanx of thumb
Action:	Extends thumb at carpometacarpal and metacarpophalangeal joints
Innervation:	Posterior interosseous branch of radial nerve (C7 and C8)
Comments:	Its tendon, together with that of abductor pollicis longus, forms the anterior boundary of the "anatomical snuff box"; pulse of the radial artery can be felt on the floor of the "snuff box"

87 Extensor pollicis longus

Origin:	Middle third of posterior aspect of the ulna and interosseous membrane between the radius and ulna
Insertion:	Base of distal phalanx of thumb
Action:	Extends metacarpophalangeal and interphalangeal joints of thumb; also assists in abducting and laterally rotating the extended thumb
Innervation:	Posterior interosseous branch of radial nerve (C7 and C8)
Comments:	Its tendon forms the posterior boundary of the "anatomical snuff box"; pulse of radial artery can be felt on floor of the "snuff box"

88 Extensor indicis

Origin:	Distal third of posterior aspect of ulna and interosseous membrane between radius and ulna
Insertion:	Distal phalanx of second digit
Action:	Extends second digit independently at the metacarpophalangeal joint; assists in extension of hand at wrist
Innervation:	Posterior interosseous branch of radial nerve (C7 and C8)
Comments:	Common insertion with extensor digitorum; lies medial to extensor pollicis longus

Muscles that rotate the hand and forearm

89 Pronator teres

Origin:	Dual: (a) medial epicondyle of humerus and (b) coronoid process of ulna
Insertion:	Middle portion of lateral aspect of radius
Action:	Pronates forearm and flexes forearm at elbow
Innervation:	Median nerve (C6 and C7)
Comments:	A fusiform muscle that assists pronator quadratus

90 Pronator quadratus

Origin:	Distal fourth of anterior aspect of the ulna
Insertion:	Distal fourth of anterior aspect of the radius
Action:	Pronates forearm; assisted by pronator teres
Innervation:	Anterior interosseous branch of median nerve (C8 and T1)
Comments:	Quadrangular-shaped muscle and most deeply situated muscle on anterior aspect of forearm

(*table continued on next page*)

Muscles of forearm and hand (*continued*)

Muscles that rotate the hand and forearm

91 Supinator

Origin:	Lateral epicondyle of humerus; crest of ulna; radial collateral ligament of elbow joint
Insertion:	Proximal third of the radius (lateral, posterior, and anterior aspects)
Action:	Supinates forearm
Innervation:	Deep branch of radial nerve (C5 and C6)
Comments:	Assisted by biceps brachii during forced supination; functions alone during unopposed supination

Intrinsic muscles of the hand*

92 Adductor pollicis

Origin:	Dual: (a) oblique head from bases of second and third metacarpal bones, capitate, and nearby carpal bones and (b) transverse head from third metacarpal bone
Insertion:	Base of proximal phalanx of the thumb
Action:	Adducts thumb
Innervation:	Deep branch of ulnar nerve (C8 and T1)
Comments:	Fan-shaped muscle that brings thumb toward the palm and provides power for the grasping movement

Muscles of thenar eminence

93 Abductor pollicis brevis

Origin:	Scaphoid; trapezium; flexor retinaculum
Insertion:	Base of proximal phalanx of the thumb
Action:	Abducts thumb
Innervation:	Recurrent branch of median nerve (C8 and T1)
Comments:	Assists opponens pollicis in initial stages of opposition

94 Opponens pollicis

Origin:	Trapezium and flexor retinaculum
Insertion:	Anterior and lateral aspect of first metacarpal bone
Action:	Opposes thumb
Innervation:	Recurrent branch of median nerve (C8 and T1)
Comments:	Opposition of thumb is a complex movement involving several muscles; section of the median nerve at the wrist (as may occur during wrist slashing) results in an inability to oppose the thumb

95 Flexor pollicis brevis

Origin:	Trapezium and flexor retinaculum
Insertion:	Base of proximal phalanx of the thumb
Action:	Flexes thumb at carpometacarpal and metacarpophalangeal joints
Innervation:	Recurrent branch of median nerve (C8 and T1)
Comments:	Assists in opposition of thumb

Muscles of hypothenar eminence

96 Abductor digiti minimi

Origin:	Pisiform bone
Insertion:	Base of proximal phalanx of fifth digit
Action:	Abducts fifth digit
Innervation:	Deep branch of ulnar nerve (C8 and T1)
Comments:	Assists in flexion of metacarpophalangeal joint of fifth digit

Muscles of forearm and hand (*continued*)

Muscles of hypothenar eminence

97 Flexor digiti minimi brevis

Origin:	Hamate bone and flexor retinaculum
Insertion:	Base of proximal phalanx of fifth digit
Action:	Flexes fifth digit at metacarpophalangeal joint
Innervation:	Deep branch of ulnar nerve (C8 and T1)
Comments:	Situated lateral to abductor digiti minimi

98 Opponens digiti minimi

Origin:	Hamate bone and flexor retinaculum
Insertion:	Medial aspect of fifth metacarpal bone
Action:	Brings fifth metacarpal anteriorly and laterally, thereby bringing fifth digit into opposition with thumb
Innervation:	Deep branch of ulnar nerve (C8 and T1)
Comments:	Situated deep to the abductor and flexor muscles of the fifth digit; deepens hollow in palm of hand

99 Palmaris brevis

Origin:	Flexor retinaculum and palmar aponeurosis
Insertion:	Skin on medial aspect of palm
Action:	Deepens hollow and wrinkles skin on medial aspect of palm
Innervation:	Superficial branch of ulnar nerve (C8 and T1)
Comments:	Situated within fascia overlying hypothenar eminence

Lumbrical muscles

100 Lumbricals (four)

Origin:	Tendons of flexor digitorum profundus
Insertion:	Distal phalanges of second through fifth digits
Action:	Flex digits at metacarpophalangeal joints
Innervation:	Dual: (a) second and third lumbricals through the median nerve (C8 and T1) and (b) fourth and fifth lumbricals through the ulnar nerve (C8 and T1)
Comments:	Assist in extending digits at interphalangeal joints due to their insertion into the extensor expansions

Interossei muscles

101 Dorsal interossei (four)

Origin:	Each from between two metacarpal bones, for example, the first is between the first and second metacarpals
Insertion:	Proximal phalanges and extensor expansion of the second through fifth digits
Action:	Abduct fingers
Innervation:	Deep branch of ulnar nerve (C8 and T1)
Comments:	Abduction occurs with reference to the axial plane passing through the midline of the third digit

102 Palmar interossei (four)

Origin:	Anterior aspect of the first, second, fourth, and fifth metacarpal bones
Insertion:	Base of proximal phalanges and extensor expansions of first, second, fourth and fifth digits
Action:	Adducts digits
Innervation:	Deep branch of ulnar nerve (C8 and T1)
Comments:	Adduction occurs with reference to the axial plane passing through the midline of the third digit

*Intrinsic muscles of the hand are conveniently grouped as follows: (a) three muscles of *thenar eminence,* (b) four muscles of *hypothenar eminence,* (c) adductor pollicis, (d) four lumbricals, (e) four dorsal interossei, and (f) four palmar interossei. The thenar and hypothenar eminences are the prominent bulges located on the lateral and medial sides of the palm, respectively. They are produced by the underlying short muscles of the thumb (thenar) and little finger (hypothenar).

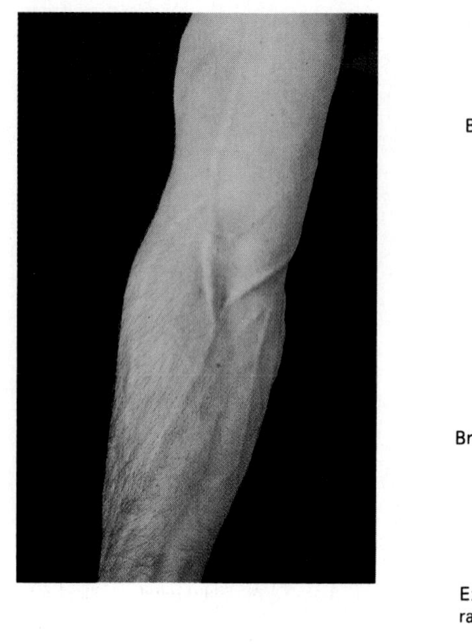

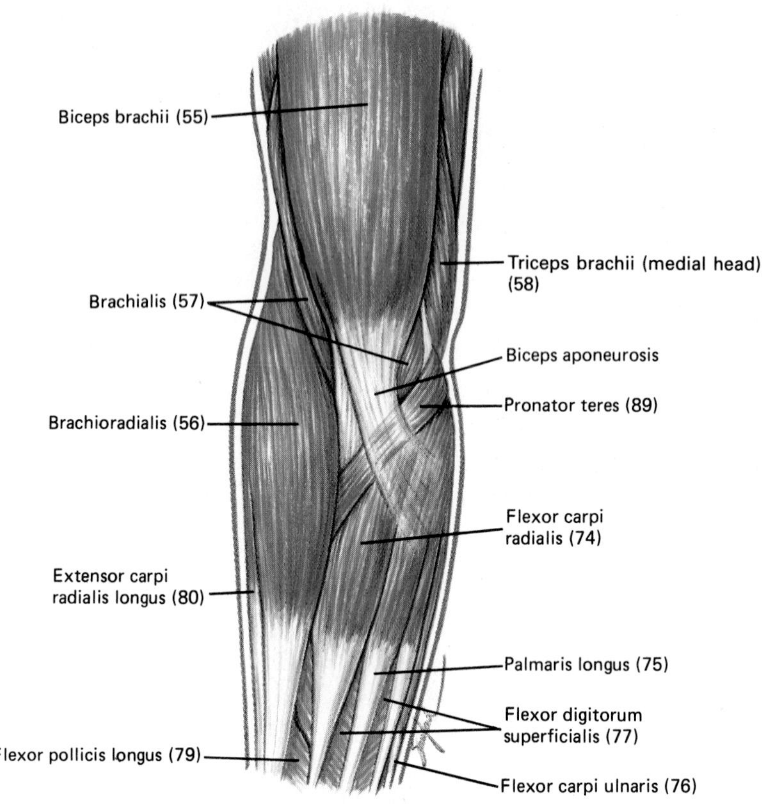

Anterior aspect of arm and forearm.

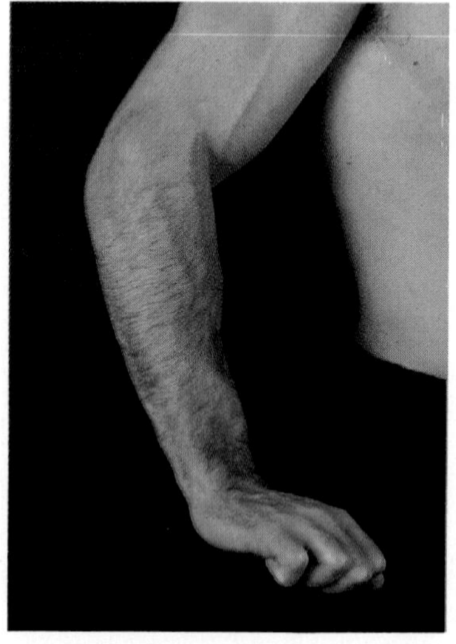

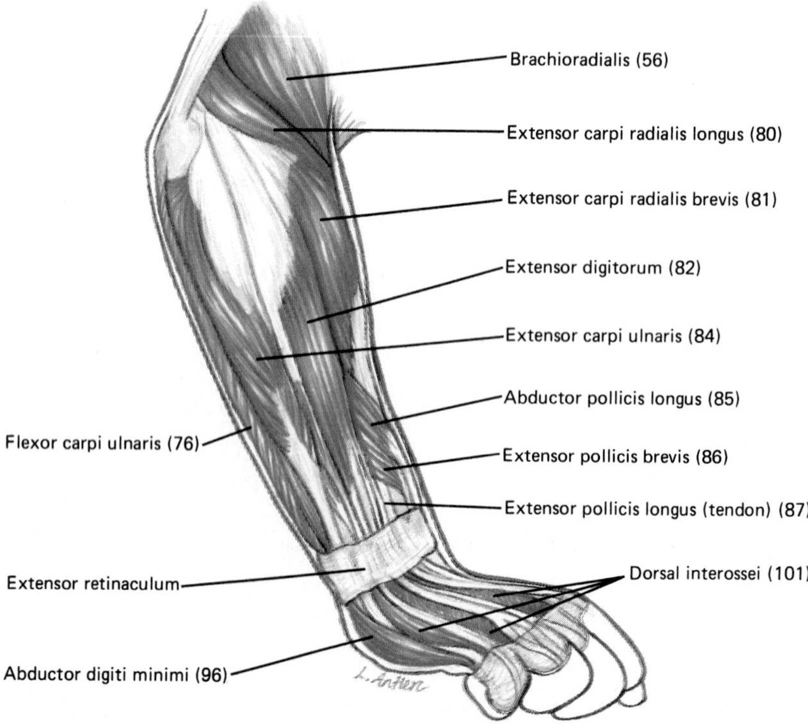

Lateral aspect of forearm and hand.

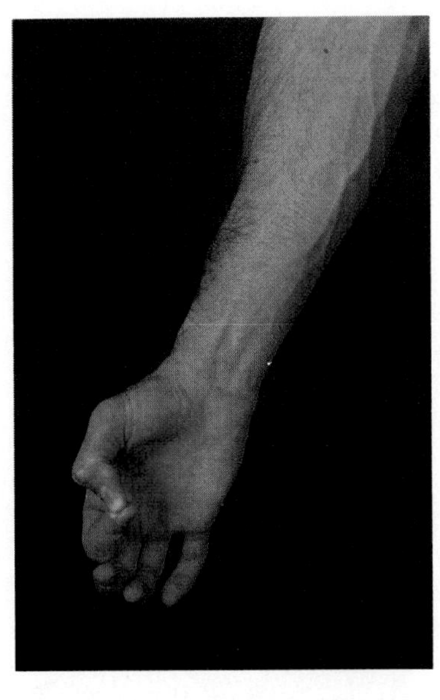

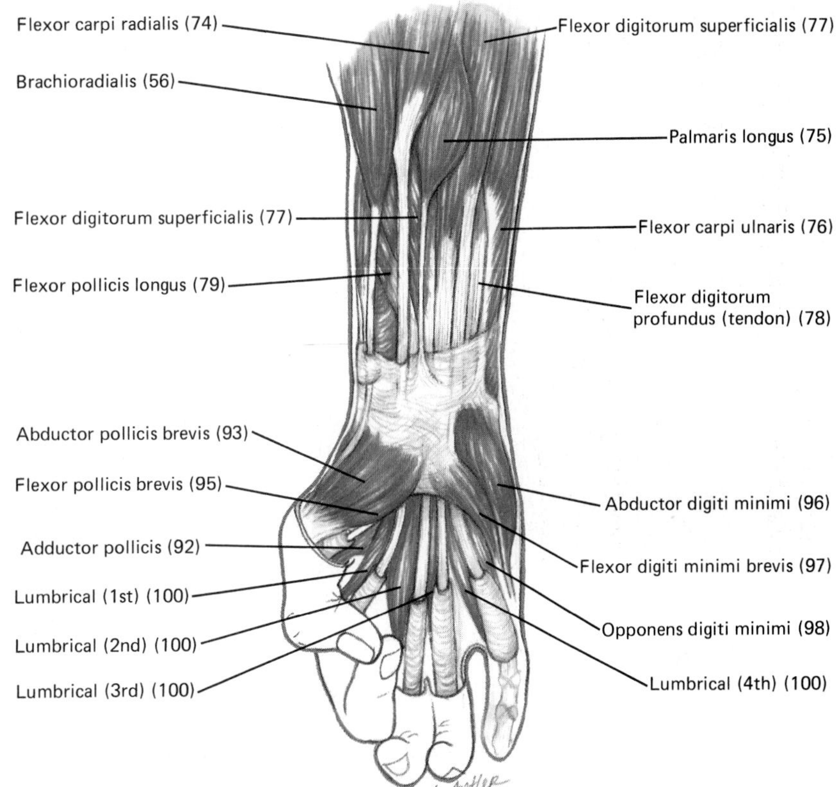
Flexor carpi radialis (74)
Flexor digitorum superficialis (77)
Brachioradialis (56)
Palmaris longus (75)
Flexor digitorum superficialis (77)
Flexor carpi ulnaris (76)
Flexor pollicis longus (79)
Flexor digitorum profundus (tendon) (78)
Abductor pollicis brevis (93)
Flexor pollicis brevis (95)
Abductor digiti minimi (96)
Adductor pollicis (92)
Flexor digiti minimi brevis (97)
Lumbrical (1st) (100)
Opponens digiti minimi (98)
Lumbrical (2nd) (100)
Lumbrical (3rd) (100)
Lumbrical (4th) (100)
L. Antler

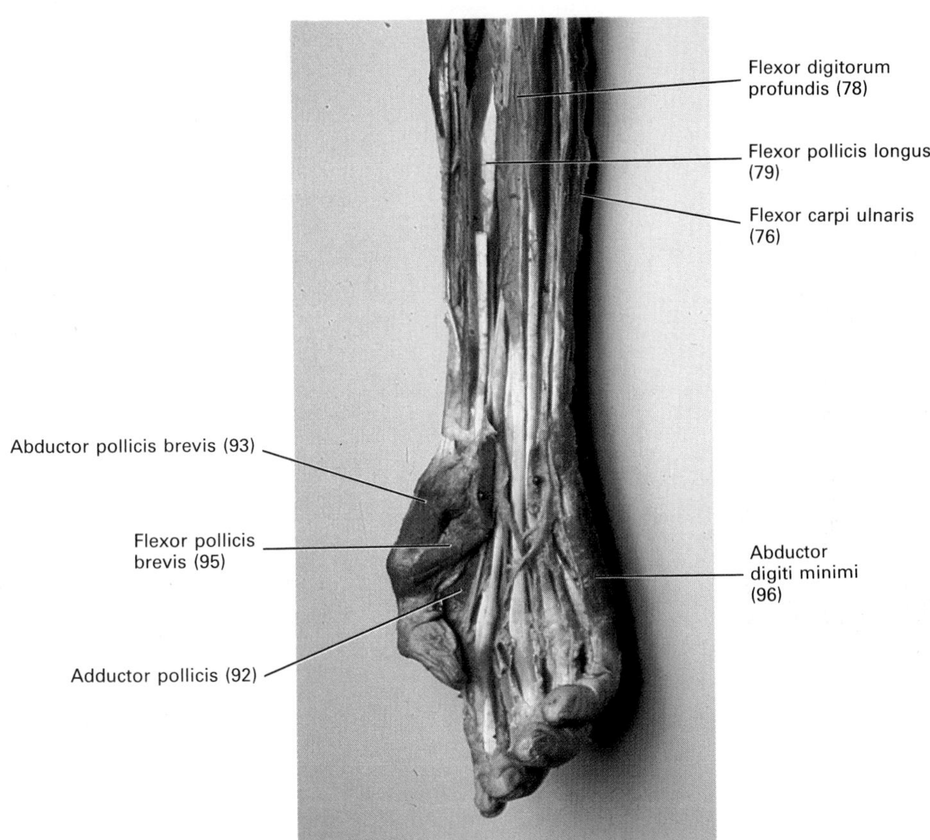
Flexor digitorum profundis (78)
Flexor pollicis longus (79)
Flexor carpi ulnaris (76)
Abductor pollicis brevis (93)
Flexor pollicis brevis (95)
Abductor digiti minimi (96)
Adductor pollicis (92)

Anterior aspect of forearm and hand.

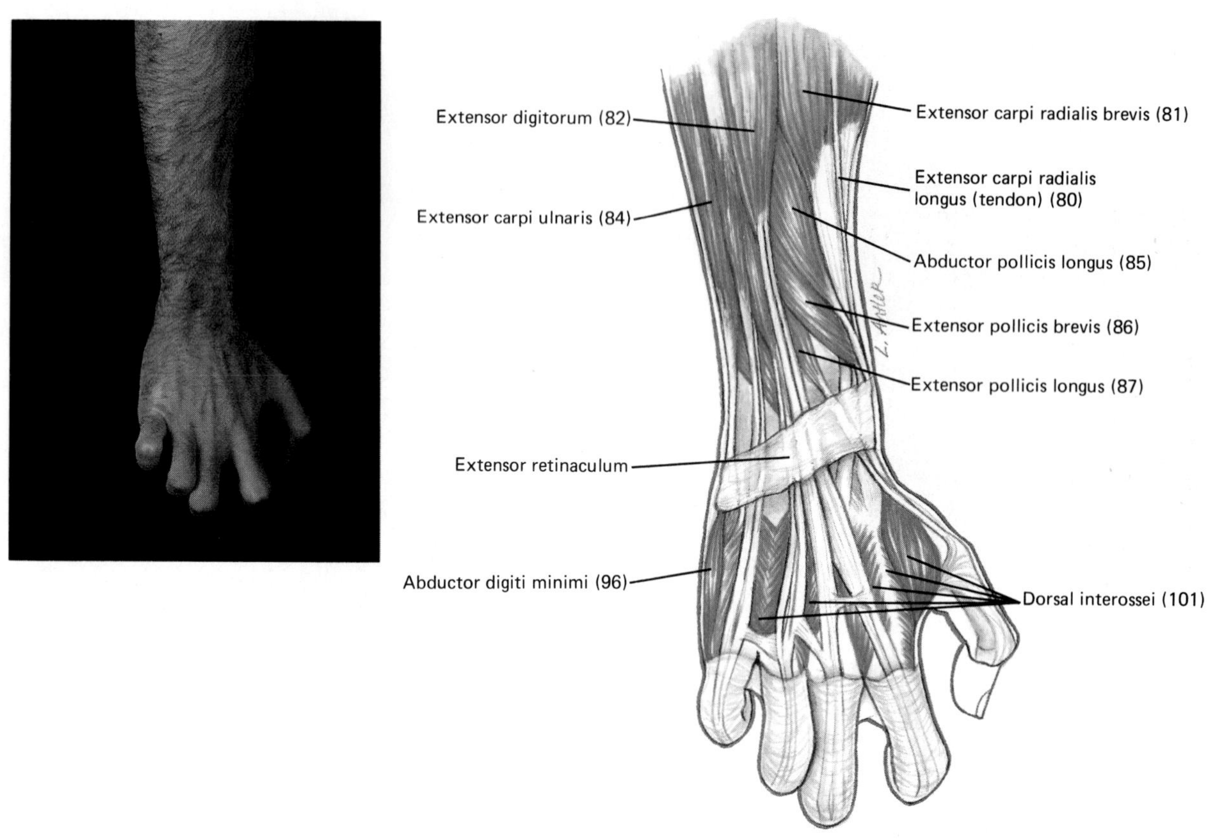
Extensor digitorum (82)
Extensor carpi ulnaris (84)
Extensor retinaculum
Abductor digiti minimi (96)
Extensor carpi radialis brevis (81)
Extensor carpi radialis longus (tendon) (80)
Abductor pollicis longus (85)
Extensor pollicis brevis (86)
Extensor pollicis longus (87)
Dorsal interossei (101)

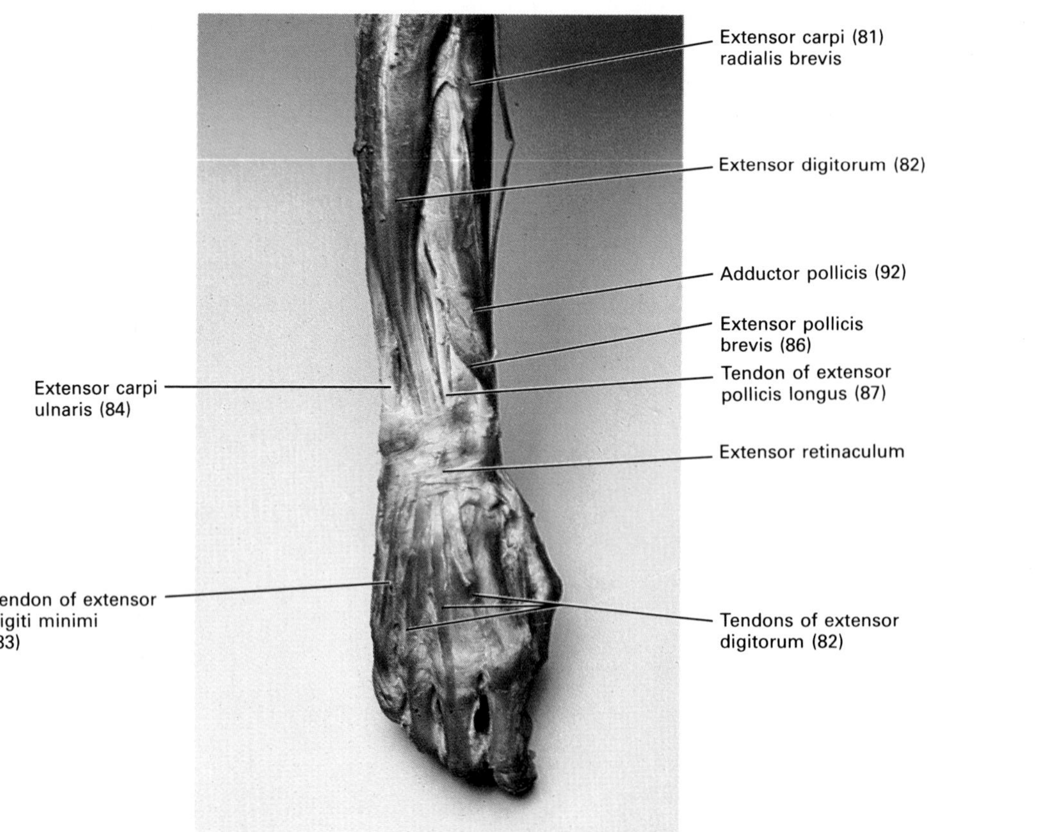
Extensor carpi (81) radialis brevis
Extensor digitorum (82)
Adductor pollicis (92)
Extensor pollicis brevis (86)
Tendon of extensor pollicis longus (87)
Extensor retinaculum
Tendons of extensor digitorum (82)
Extensor carpi ulnaris (84)
Tendon of extensor digiti minimi (83)

Posterior aspect of forearm and hand.

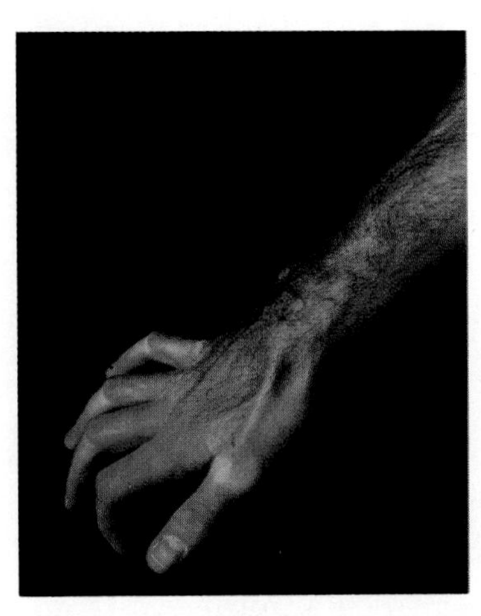

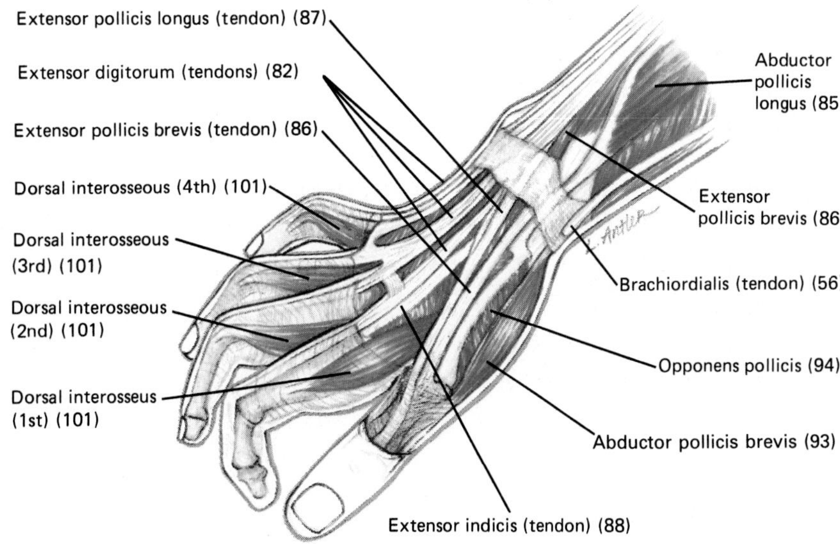

Posteromedial aspect of forearm and hand.

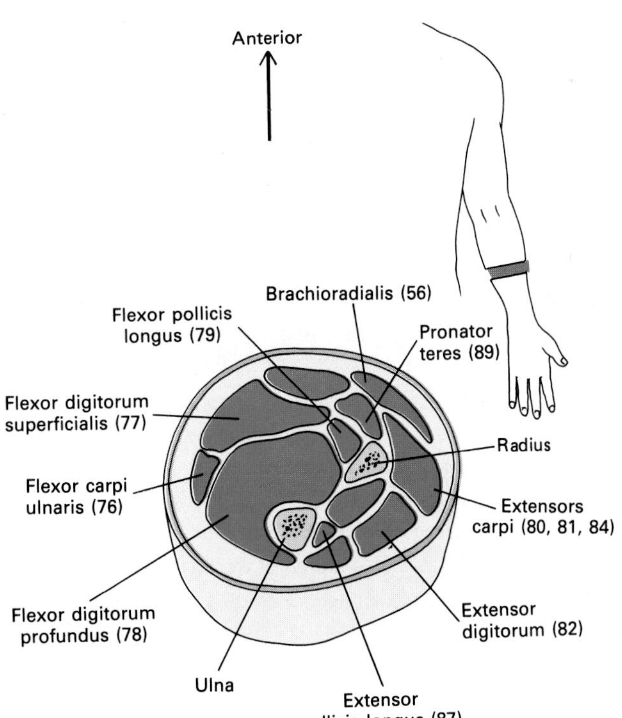

Transverse section through midforearm.

TABLE 11-5

Trunk muscles with pelvic attachment*	
103 External abdominal oblique†	
Origin:	Lower eight ribs
Insertion:	Iliac crest and linea alba through a broad aponeurosis
Action:	Flexes and laterally rotates trunk when pelvis is fixed; increases intra-abdominal pressure and thus assists in the passing of feces, voiding of urine, exhalation, and childbirth
Innervation:	Ventral rami of T8–T12; subcostal nerve; iliohypogastric nerve
Comments:	The lowermost border of its aponeurosis forms what is termed the inguinal ligament, which spans the interval between anterior superior iliac spine and the pubic tubercle; assists in maintaining abdominal viscera in position
104 Internal abdominal oblique†	
Origin:	Iliac crest; inguinal ligament and thoracolumbar fascia
Insertion:	Lower three or four ribs; linea alba via a broad aponeurosis; some fibers also attach to the pubic bone
Action:	Flexes and laterally rotates trunk when pelvis is fixed; increases intra-abdominal pressure and thus assists external oblique in actions described above; helps maintain position of abdominal viscera
Innervation:	Ventral rami of T8–T12; subcostal nerve; iliohypogastric nerve; ilioinguinal nerve
Comments:	Its uppermost fibers are continuous with the internal intercostal muscles
105 Rectus abdominis†	
Origin:	Pubic bone and symphysis pubis
Insertion:	Xiphoid process of sternum; costal cartilages of the fifth through seventh ribs
Action:	Flexes trunk when pelvis is fixed; draws pelvis anteriorly when trunk is fixed
Innervation:	Ventral rami of T8–T12; subcostal nerve
Comments:	Long straplike muscle of anterior abdominal wall; separated from its partner on opposite side by the linea alba; its fibers are interrupted by three *tendinous intersections;* enclosed by aponeuroses of two oblique muscles and transversus abdominis in a structure termed the *rectus sheath*
106 Transversus abdominis†	
Origin:	Iliac crest; inguinal ligament; thoracolumbar fascia; costal cartilages of lower six ribs
Insertion:	Linea alba through a broad aponeurosis; pubic bone
Action:	Assist in maintaining position of abdominal viscera; increase intra-abdominal pressure
Innervation:	Ventral rami of T8–T12; subcostal nerve; iliohypogastric nerve; ilioinguinal nerve
Comments:	Lies deep to the internal oblique muscle
107 Latissimus dorsi‡	
Origin:	Iliac crest; lower three or four ribs; thoracolumbar fascia; spines of lower six thoracic vertebrae
Insertion:	Humerus (intertubercular sulcus)
Action:	Adducts, extends, and medially rotates humerus; assists in pulling trunk superiorly and anteriorly when arms are fixed above the head as in doing a "chin-up" (functional reversal of origin and insertion)
Innervation:	Thoracodorsal nerve (C6–C8), a branch of the brachial plexus
Comments:	Flat, large, triangular muscle located superficially on the back; typically very well developed in swimmers and gymnasts

TABLE 11-5

Trunk muscles with pelvic attachment* ***(continued)***	
108 Quadratus lumborum‡	
Origin:	Iliac crest
Insertion:	Twelfth rib; transverse processes of first four lumbar vertebrae; sometimes to transverse process of twelfth thoracic vertebra
Action:	Laterally flexes lumbar spine when pelvis is fixed; extends lumbar spine; fixes the twelfth rib; assists in inspiration by helping to fix the position of the diaphragm
Innervation:	Ventral rami of T12, L1–L4
Comments:	Quadrangular muscle located on posterior abdominal wall
109 Erector spinae (sacrospinalis)‡	
Fibers of the sacrospinalis, or erector spinae, diverge in the upper lumbar region to form three muscular columns. These are designated (from lateral to medial) as the (a) iliocostalis, (b) longissimus, and (c) spinalis. (See Table 11-2 for more complete description.)	
110 Psoas minor‡	
Origin:	Body of twelfth thoracic and first lumbar vertebrae; intervertebral disc between T12 and L1
Insertion:	Pubic bone; iliopubic eminence; iliac fascia
Action:	Weak flexor of trunk when pelvis is fixed
Innervation:	Branch of L1
Comments:	May be absent in as many as 35 to 45% of all individuals

*Muscles with pelvic attachments are typically arranged into three groups: (a) those inserting upon the femur (see Table 11-6), (b) muscles of the trunk, and (c) the muscles of the pelvic floor (see Table 11-9).

†Abdominal muscles

‡Back muscles

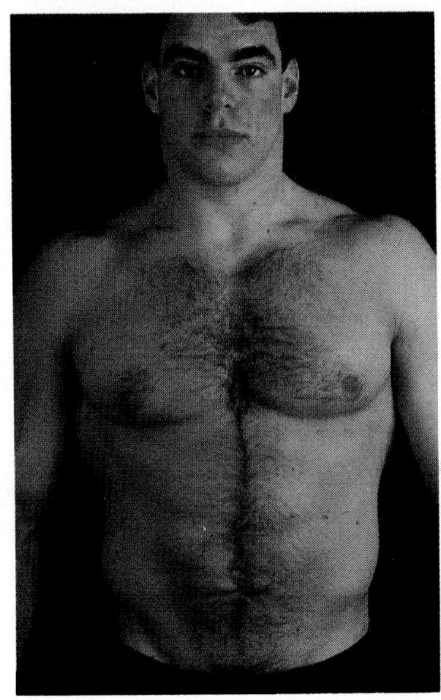

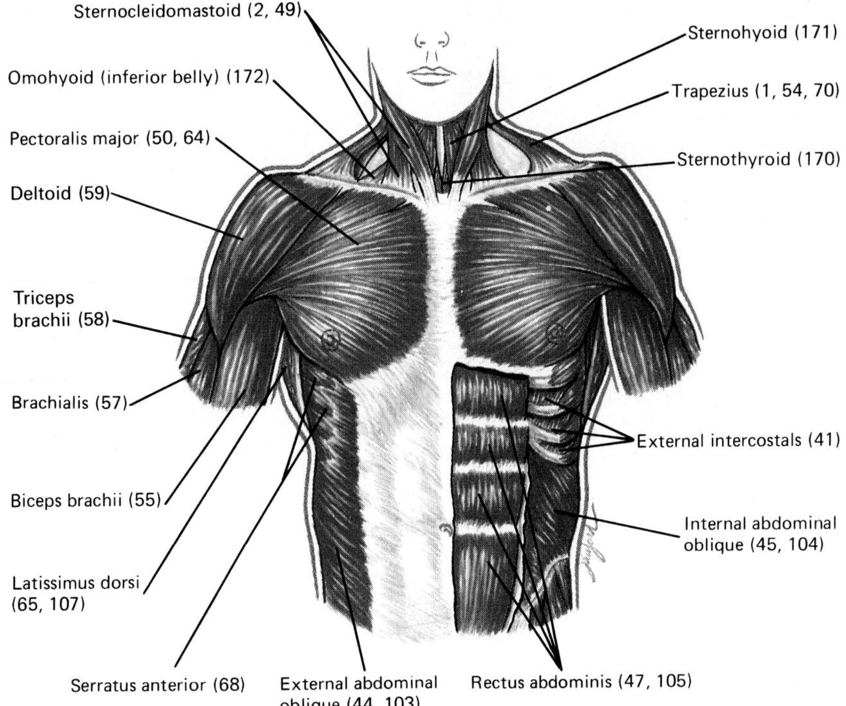

Anterior aspect of neck, thorax, and abdomen.

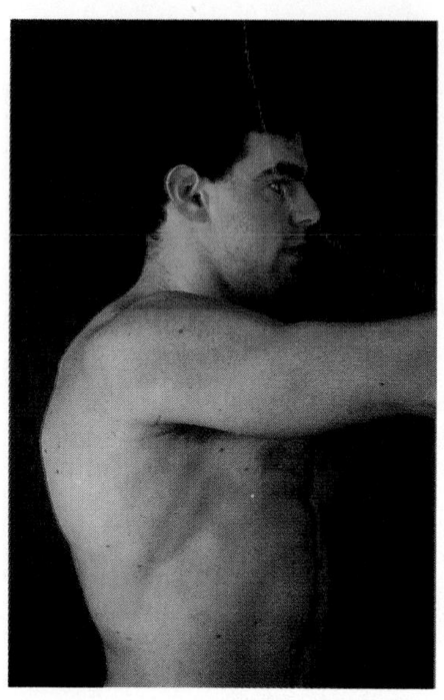

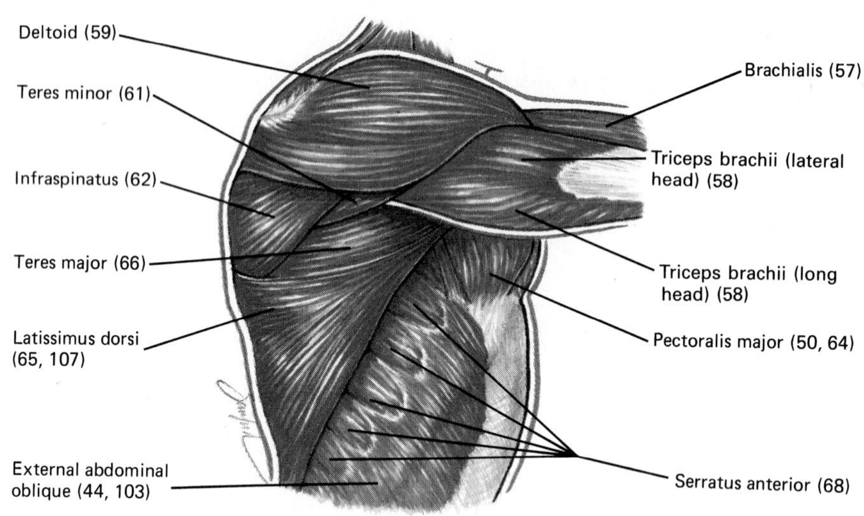

Lateral aspect of shoulder and thorax.

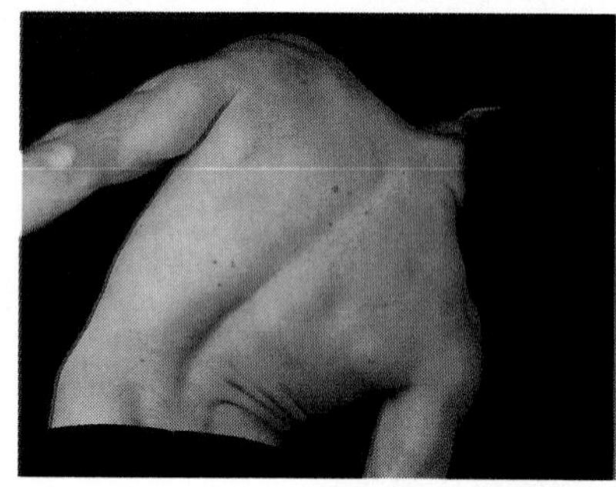

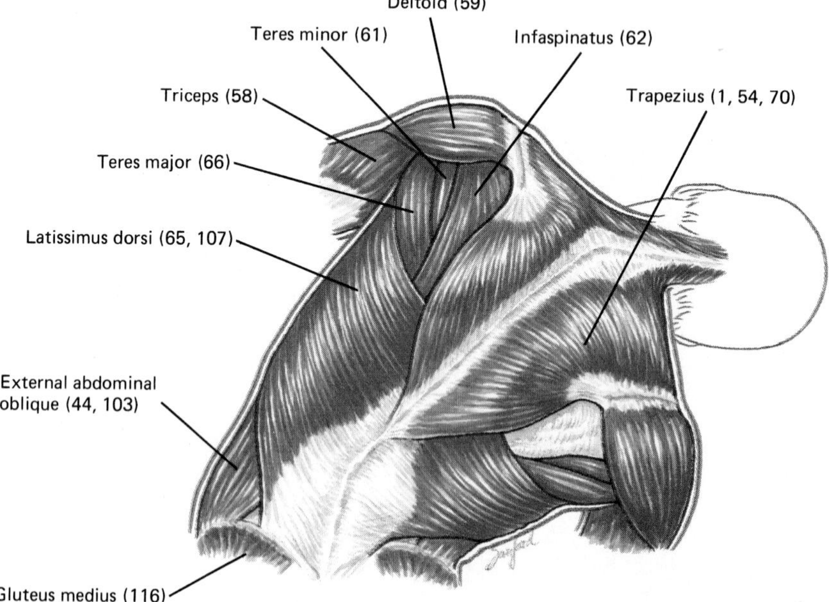

Posterior aspect of superficial back.

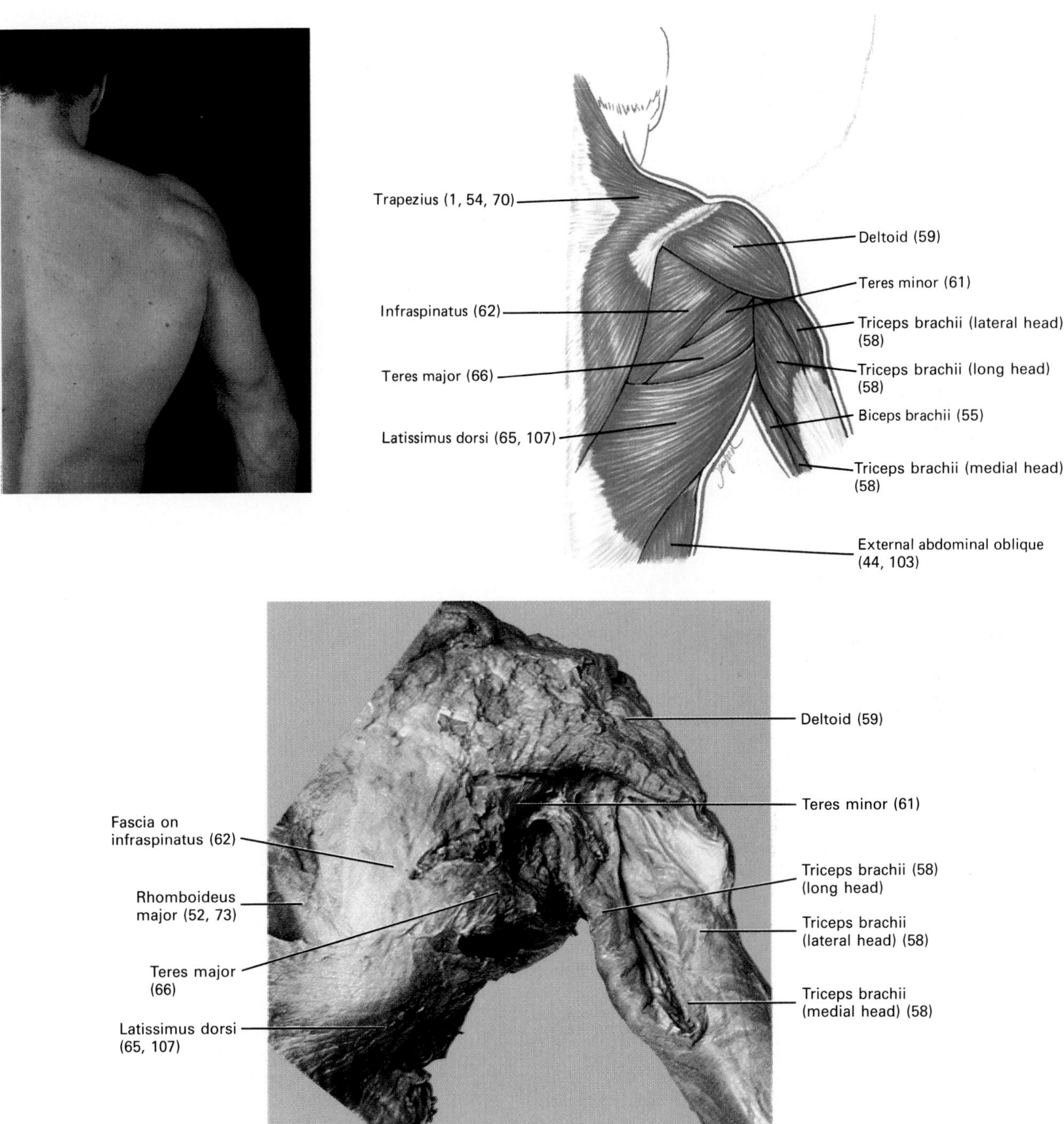
Trapezius (1, 54, 70)
Deltoid (59)
Teres minor (61)
Infraspinatus (62)
Triceps brachii (lateral head) (58)
Teres major (66)
Triceps brachii (long head) (58)
Biceps brachii (55)
Latissimus dorsi (65, 107)
Triceps brachii (medial head) (58)
External abdominal oblique (44, 103)
Deltoid (59)
Teres minor (61)
Fascia on infraspinatus (62)
Triceps brachii (58) (long head)
Rhomboideus major (52, 73)
Triceps brachii (lateral head) (58)
Teres major (66)
Triceps brachii (medial head) (58)
Latissimus dorsi (65, 107)

Posterior aspect of superficial back.

TABLE 11-6

Pelvic muscles of the thigh (*continued*)	
All muscles in this table insert on the femur	
111 Tensor fasciae latae	
Origin:	Anterior aspect of iliac crest
Action:	Flexes and medially rotates thigh; when acting through its attachment to the iliotibial tract, it extends and laterally rotates leg at knee
Innervation:	Superior gluteal nerve (L4 and L5)
Comments:	Inserts into iliotibial tract, which is a strong band of fascia coursing along lateral aspect of thigh; the tract inserts on the lateral condyle of the tibia
112 Adductor longus	
Origin:	Symphysis pubis of pelvis
Action:	Adducts and medially rotates thigh; assists in the early stage of flexion of thigh at hip
Innervation:	Obturator nerve (L2–L4)
Comments:	Most anterior of the three adductors; inserts on the medial third of linea aspera (superficial)
113 Adductor brevis	
Origin:	Body and inferior ramus of pubis
Action:	Adducts and medially rotates thigh; assists in the early stage of flexion of thigh at hip
Innervation:	Obturator nerve (L2–L4)
Comments:	Located between the adductor longus and magnus; inserts on upper third of linea aspera (deep)
114 Adductor magnus	
Origin:	Inferior pubic ramus, ramus of ischium, and ischial tuberosity
Action:	Upper fibers adduct, flex, and medially rotate the thigh; lower fibers assist the hamstring muscles in extension of thigh at hip
Innervation:	Upper fibers by obturator nerve (L2–L4); lower fibers by tibial division of sciatic nerve (L2–L4)
Comments:	Most posterior of the three adductors; inserts along entire length of femur; femoral artery and femoral vein pass through an opening in its tendinous insertion near lower portion of the femur
115 Gluteus maximus	
Origin:	Ilium, sacrum, and coccyx; also from sacrotuberous ligament and aponeuroses of erector spinae muscles
Action:	The primary extensor of thigh; extends and laterally rotates thigh; stabilizes the knee joint; upper fibers assist in abduction of thigh
Innervation:	Inferior gluteal nerve (L5, S1 and S2)
Comments:	Fibers insert upon iliotibial tract and the gluteal tuberosity; little used in slow walking, but important in climbing and fast walking; not active while standing still; favored site for intramuscular injections, which must be given in the upper-outer quadrant of the muscle to avoid injury to underlying nerves and vessels; largest and most powerful muscle in body (superficial)
116 Gluteus medius	
Origin:	Lateral aspect of ilium between iliac crest and posterior gluteal line above and anterior gluteal line below; also from deep fascia covering its anterior portion
Action:	Abducts and medially rotates thigh; together with gluteus minimus it plays an important role in stabilizing the trunk in the upright position when the opposite foot leaves the ground as in walking or running
Innervation:	Superior gluteal nerve (L4 and L5, S1)
Comments:	Inserts on external aspect of greater trochanter; paralysis of gluteus medius and minimus leads to a positive *Trendelenburg sign,* that is, the pelvis tilts on the unsupported side when the patient attempts to stand on the affected limb; these patients lean their trunk toward the side of the affected limb when walking in an attempt to compensate for the tilting of the pelvis on the opposite side

TABLE 11-6

Pelvic muscles of the thigh (*continued*)	
All muscles in this table insert on the femur	
117 Gluteus minimus	
Origin:	Outer aspect of ilium between anterior and posterior gluteal lines as well as from margin of greater sciatic notch
Action:	Abducts and medially rotates thigh; functions with gluteus medius in stabilizing trunk in upright position when opposite foot leaves ground as in walking or running
Innervation:	Superior gluteal nerve (L4 and L5, S1)
Comments:	See gluteus medius above
118 Piriformis	
Origin:	By means of three digitations from ventral aspect of sacral vertebrae and from capsule of the sacroiliac joint
Action:	Laterally rotates the extended thigh and abducts the flexed thigh
Innervation:	L5, S1 and S2
Comments:	Located partly within pelvis and partly posterior to the hip joint; leaves pelvis through greater sciatic foramen; inserts upon greater trochanter of femur; muscle is frequently pierced by the common peroneal nerve
119 Iliacus	
Origin:	Upper two-thirds of iliac fossa; portion of iliac crest; superolateral aspect of sacrum
Action:	Bends trunk and pelvis forward as in raising from a lying to a sitting position; flexes thigh upon pelvis and laterally rotates thigh
Innervation:	Femoral nerve (L2 and L3)
Comments:	Majority of its fibers blend with lateral aspect of psoas major tendon and insert upon lesser trochanter of femur; additional fibers insert inferior to lesser trochanter of femur
120 Psoas major	
Origin:	Transverse processes and bodies of lumbar vertebrae; body of twelfth thoracic vertebra; intervertebral discs interposed between the adjacent vertebrae
Action:	Flexes thigh upon pelvis; laterally rotates thigh; bends trunk and pelvis anteriorly when acting with iliacus
Innervation:	Ventral rami of L1–L3
Comments:	Inserts upon lesser trochanter of femur together with most fibers of iliacus; together with iliacus is commonly considered as single muscle, the *iliopsoas;* infections involving lower thoracic and lumbar vertebrae may spread into thigh via the fascia covering the psoas major; 60% of all bodies possess a very small psoas minor muscle that lies anterior to psoas major; the former, when present, is a weak flexor of the trunk
121 Quadratus femoris	
Origin:	Upper, external portion of ischial tuberosity
Action:	Laterally rotates thigh; weak adductor of thigh
Innervation:	L5 and S1
Comments:	A flat, quadrangular muscle that lies in a horizontal plane; inserted upon upper portion of trochanteric crest of femur; lies posterior to hip joint and neck of femur
122 Obturator externus	
Origin:	Ischiopubic rami and most of the outer aspect of the obturator membrane covering the obturator foramen
Action:	Laterally rotates and adducts thigh; helps to stabilize femur
Innervation:	Obturator nerve (L2–L4)
Comments:	A flat, triangular-shaped muscle that assists quadratus femoris

(table continued on next page)

TABLE 11-6

Pelvic muscles of the thigh (*continued*)	
All muscles in this table insert on the femur	
123 Obturator internus	
Origin:	Within pelvis from ischiopubic rami and from pelvic surface of obturator membrane covering obturator foramen
Action:	Laterally rotates extended thigh; abducts the flexed thigh
Innervation:	L5 and S1
Comments:	Fibers pass out of pelvis through the lesser sciatic foramen and insert upon the greater trochanter of the femur; its tendon also receives fibers from the two very small gemelli muscles, superior and inferior, which assist obturator internus in its actions
124 Pectineus	
Origin:	Pubis
Action:	Adducts thigh and flexes thigh on pelvis
Innervation:	Femoral nerve (L2–L4)
Comments:	A flat, quadrangular muscle; may be bilaminar in which case it typically has a dual innervation, that is, femoral and obturator nerves

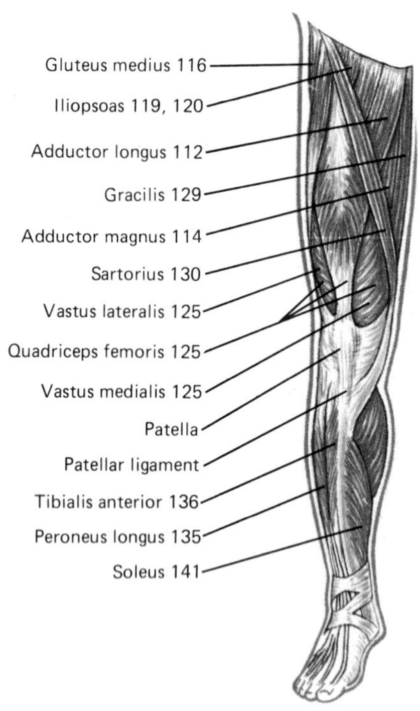

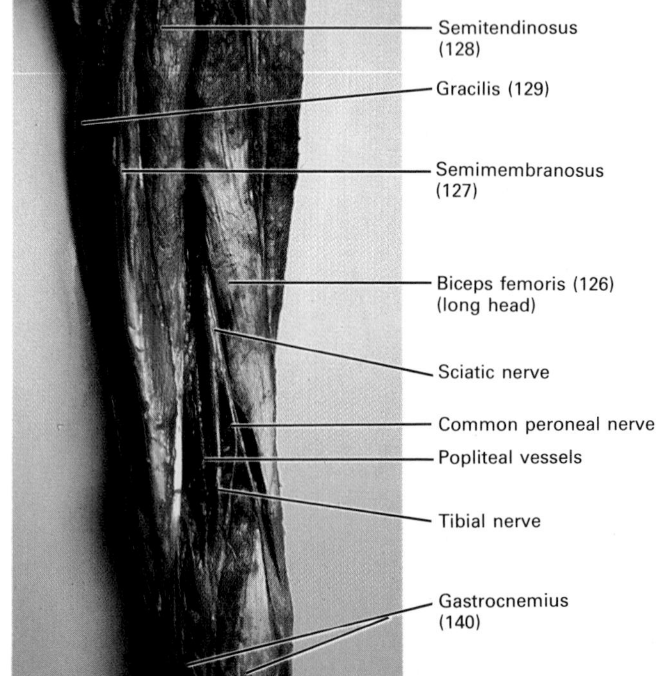

(*a*) Anterior aspect of thigh and leg.
(*b*) Gluteal region and posterior aspect of thigh and leg.

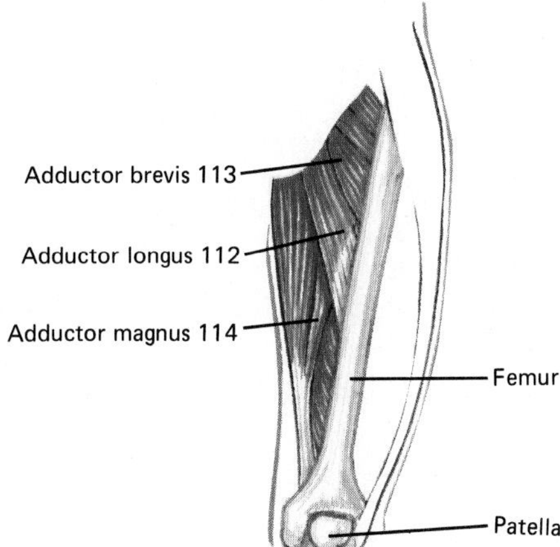

Adductors of the thigh.

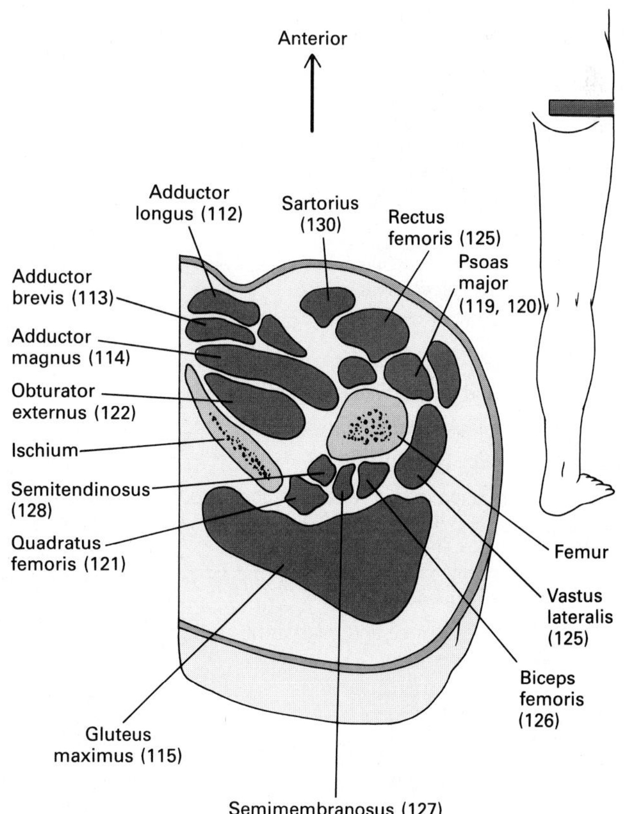

Transverse section through proximal one third of thigh.

TABLE 11-7

Major intrinsic muscles of the thigh	
125 Quadriceps femoris	
General:	Large superficial muscle covering nearly all of the anterolateral aspect of the thigh; typically described as consisting of four parts: (a) *rectus femoris,* (b) *vastus lateralis,* (c) *vastus medialis,* and (d) *vastus intermedius*
Origin:	Rectus femoris arises from ilium and the three vasti from shaft of femur
Action:	All four parts extend the leg at the knee; rectus femoris also flexes thigh
Innervation:	Femoral nerve (L2–L4)
Comments:	Tendinous fibers of all four parts unite to form a single tendon attaching to the base and sides of the patella; the patella is actually a sesamoid bone within the quadriceps tendon; fibers extending beyond the patella and attaching to the tubercle of the tibia are collectively termed the *ligamentum patellae*
126 Biceps femoris	
Origin:	Dual origin: (1) long head from ischial tuberosity, (2) short head from linea aspera of femur
Action:	Extends thigh at hip and flexes leg at knee; laterally rotates leg when knee is partially flexed; laterally rotates thigh when hip is extended
Innervation:	Long head via tibial division and short head via common peroneal division of sciatic nerve (L5, S1 and S2)
Comments:	Insertion is largely on the head of the fibula with some fibers also attaching to the lateral condyle of the tibia; short head may be absent; tendon formed by fibers of the long and short heads is known as the ''lateral hamstring'' tendon
127 Semimembranosus	
Origin:	Ischial tuberosity
Action:	Extends, adducts, and medially rotates thigh; medially rotates leg when knee is partially flexed; flexes leg at knee
Innervation:	Tibial division of sciatic nerve (L5, S1 and S2)
Comments:	Fibers insert upon medial condyle of tibia; tendons of semimembranosus and semitendinosus (see below) are collectively termed the ''medial hamstring'' tendons
128 Semitendinosus	
Origin:	Ischial tuberosity
Action:	Flexes leg at knee and extends thigh; medially rotates leg when knee is partially flexed; medially rotates thigh when hip is extended
Innervation:	Tibial division of sciatic nerve (L5, S1 and S2)
Comments:	Insertion on medial aspect of tibia near that of sartorius and gracilis; its long cylindrical tendon lies on the surface of semimembranosus
129 Gracilis	
Origin:	Body and inferior ramus of pubis as well as from a portion of the ischial ramus
Action:	Flexes and medially rotates the leg; adducts thigh
Innervation:	Obturator nerve (L2–L4)
Comments:	Inserts upon medial surface of tibia below condyle; most superficial of the adductor group of muscles
130 Sartorius	
Origin:	Anterior superior iliac spine
Action:	Flexes leg at knee and thigh at hip, especially when both movements are conducted together; abducts and laterally rotates thigh
Innervation:	Femoral nerve (L2–L4)
Comments:	Insertion upon medial aspect of tibia near that of gracilis and semitendinosus; longest muscle in body; used to be especially well developed in tailors (sartorii) due to their cross-legged squat while sewing; very prominent straplike muscle that passes diagonally across anterior surface of thigh

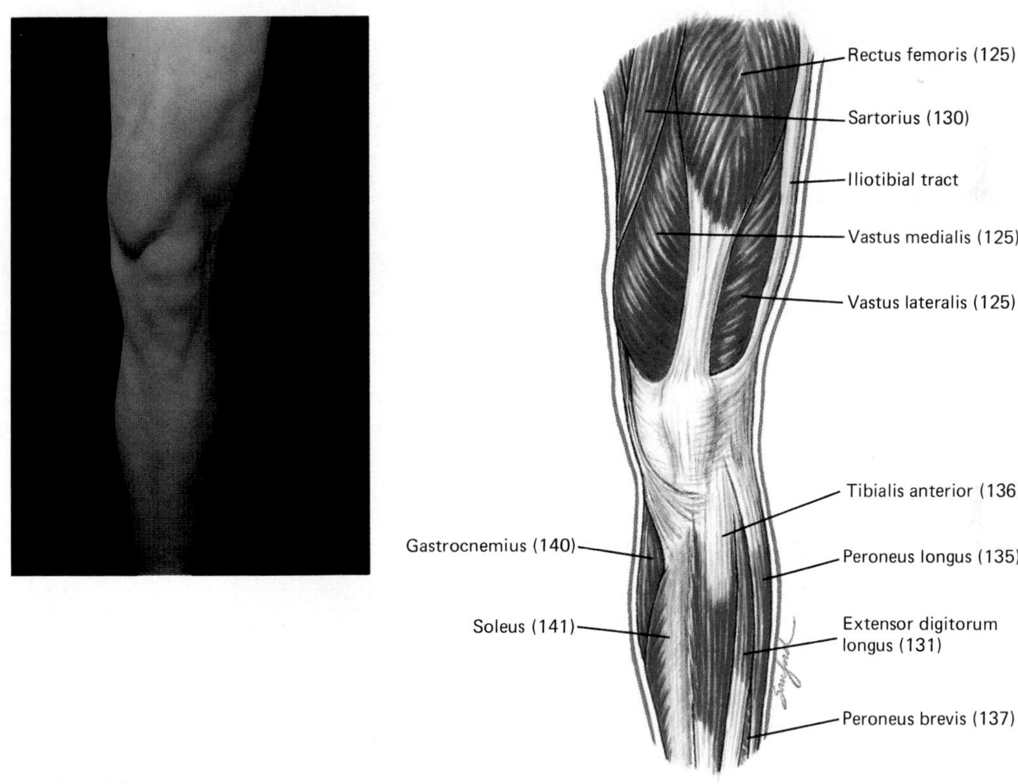
Rectus femoris (125)
Sartorius (130)
Iliotibial tract
Vastus medialis (125)
Vastus lateralis (125)
Tibialis anterior (136)
Gastrocnemius (140)
Peroneus longus (135)
Soleus (141)
Extensor digitorum longus (131)
Peroneus brevis (137)

Anterior thigh and leg.

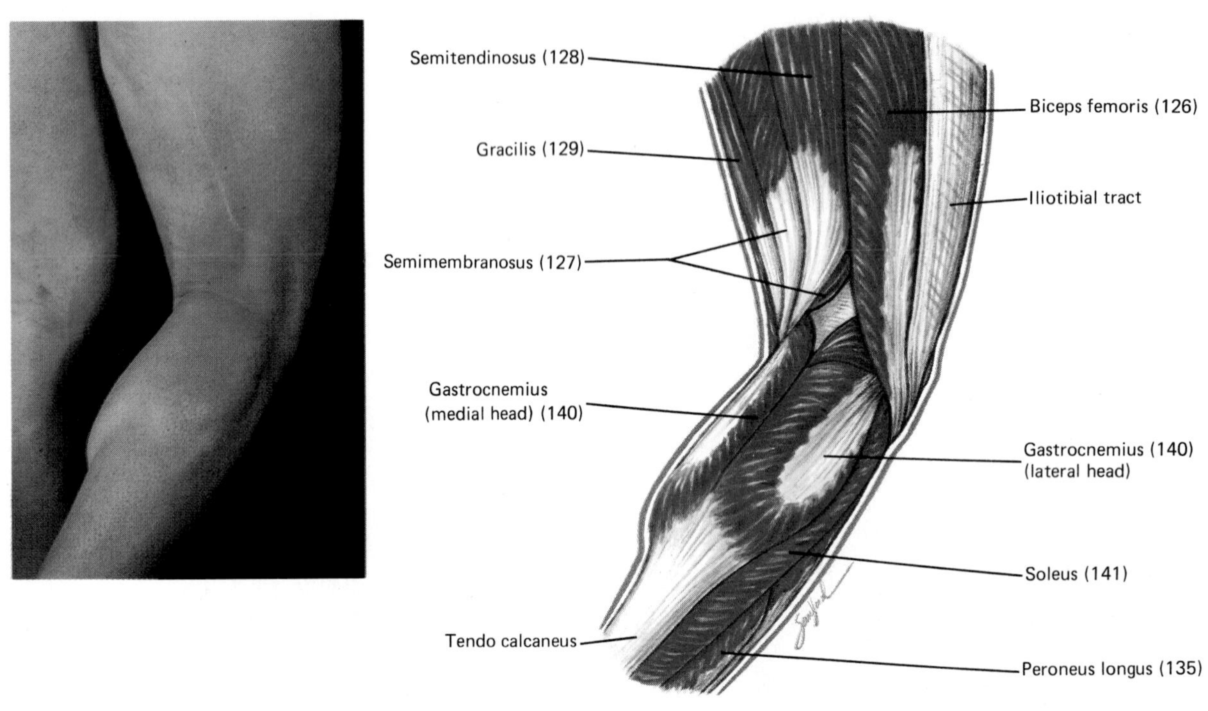
Semitendinosus (128)
Gracilis (129)
Semimembranosus (127)
Gastrocnemius (medial head) (140)
Tendo calcaneus
Biceps femoris (126)
Iliotibial tract
Gastrocnemius (140) (lateral head)
Soleus (141)
Peroneus longus (135)

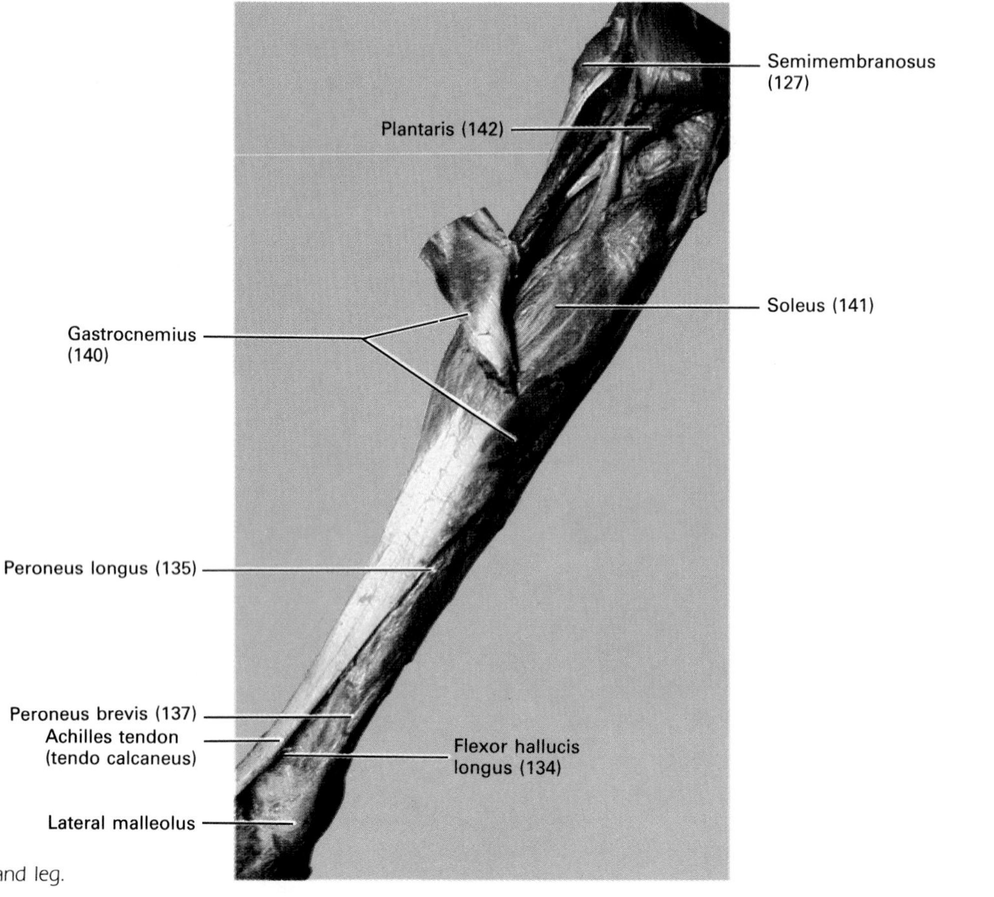
Semimembranosus (127)
Plantaris (142)
Soleus (141)
Gastrocnemius (140)
Peroneus longus (135)
Peroneus brevis (137)
Achilles tendon (tendo calcaneus)
Flexor hallucis longus (134)
Lateral malleolus

Posterolateral thigh and leg.

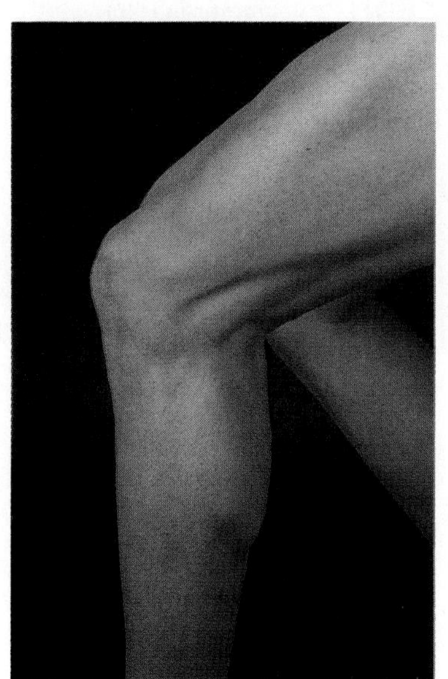

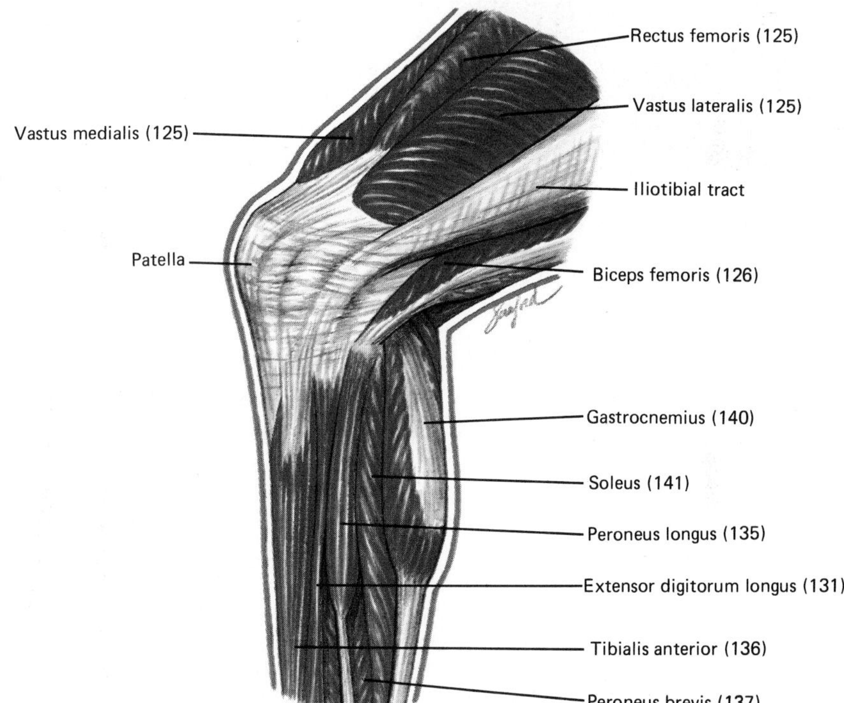

Anterolateral thigh and leg.

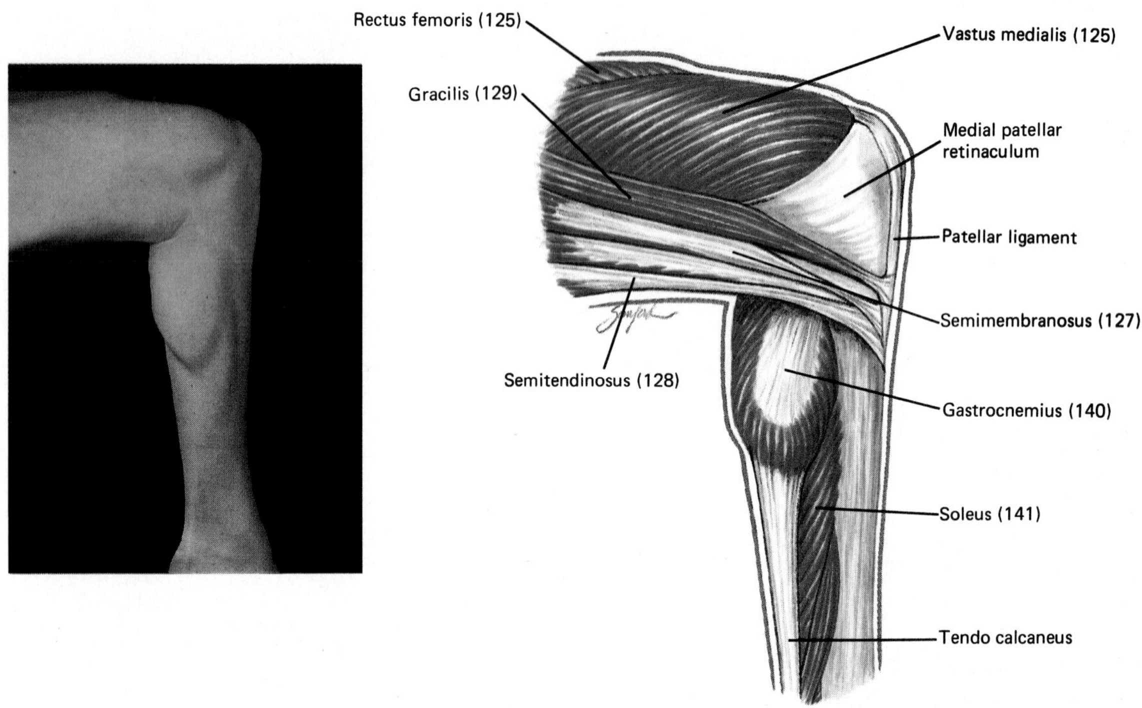

Medial thigh and leg.

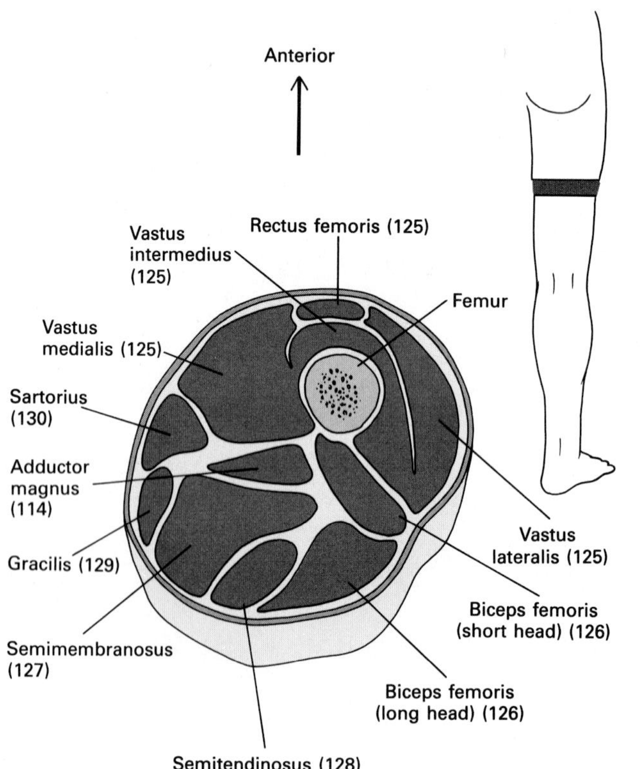

Transverse section through midthigh.

TABLE 11-8

Major muscles of the leg and foot	
Muscles inserting on the distal phalanges of the foot	
131 Extensor digitorum longus	
Origin:	Lateral condyle of tibia; upper three-fourths of fibula; upper portion of interosseous membrane between tibia and fibula
Action:	Extends second through fifth toes; together with tibialis anterior it dorsiflexes the foot
Innervation:	Deep peroneal branch of common peroneal nerve (L4, L5, and S1)
Comments:	Tendon divides into four slips on dorsum of foot that pass to the lateral four toes
132 Extensor hallucis longus	
Origin:	Middle portion of medial aspect of tibia; interosseous membrane between tibia and fibula
Action:	Extends great toe and dorsiflexes the foot
Innervation:	Deep peroneal branch of common peroneal nerve (L4, L5, and S1)
Comments:	Inserts upon distal phalanx of great toe; its fibers of origin may be fused with those of extensor digitorum longus
133 Flexor digitorum longus	
Origin:	Posteromedial aspect of tibia
Action:	Flexes lateral four toes and plantar-flexes foot
Innervation:	Tibial nerve (S2 and S3)
Comments:	A deep muscle whose tendon passes posterior to the medial malleolus
134 Flexor hallucis longus	
Origin:	Inferior portion of posterior aspect of fibula; inferior aspect of interosseous membrane between tibia and fibula
Action:	Flexes great toe and plantar-flexes foot
Innervation:	Tibial nerve (S2 and S3)
Comments:	A deep muscle that inserts upon distal phalanx of great toe
Muscles inserting upon the first metatarsal of the foot	
135 Peroneus longus	
Origin:	Head and upper two-thirds of fibula with additional fibers from lateral condyle of tibia
Action:	Plantar-flexes and everts foot
Innervation:	Superficial peroneal branch of common peroneal nerve (L5, S1, and S2)
Comments:	Together with peroneus brevis maintains concavity of sole of foot during walking; shifts weight to ball of foot in walking; some of its fibers also insert upon medial cuneiform bone
136 Tibialis anterior	
Origin:	Upper two-thirds of lateral aspect of tibia and interosseous membrane between tibia and fibula
Action:	Dorsiflexes and inverts foot; helps support longitudinal arch on sole of foot during walking and running
Innervation:	Deep peroneal branch of common peroneal nerve (L4, L5, and S1)
Comments:	A superficial muscle that is inactive during standing; functions in recovery stroke of stepping

(*table continued on next page*)

Major muscles of the leg and foot (*continued*)

Muscles inserting on the fifth metatarsal bone of the foot

137 Peroneus brevis

Origin:	Lower two-thirds of lateral aspect of fibula
Action:	Everts and plantar-flexes foot; plays role in limiting inversion of foot
Innervation:	Superficial peroneal branch of common peroneal nerve (L5, S1, and S2)
Comments:	Functions in balancing leg on foot

138 Peroneus tertius

Origin:	Lower third of medial aspect of fibula
Action:	Dorsiflexes foot when acting as part of extensor digitorum longus; assists in eversion of foot
Innervation:	Deep peroneal branch of common peroneal nerve (L5 and S1)
Comments:	Typically described as being part of extensor digitorum longus; its tendon is often considered as the fifth tendon of the latter

Muscle inserting on the medial cuneiform bone (a tarsal) of foot

139 Tibialis posterior

Origin:	Posterior aspect of tibia and fibula; posterior surface of interosseous membrane between tibia and fibula
Action:	Powerful invertor of foot; assists in plantar-flexion of foot; helps support longitudinal arch on sole of foot
Innervation:	Tibial nerve (L4 and L5)
Comments:	Tendon passes posterior to medial malleolus and then divides for insertion upon medial cuneiform and several other tarsal and metatarsal bones; helps distribute weight of body to metatarsal heads during walking

Muscles inserting on calcaneus (a tarsal) of foot

140 Gastrocnemius

Origin:	Dual origin: (1) medial condyle and posterior surface of femur and (2) lateral condyle of femur; additional fibers arise from capsule of knee joint
Action:	Plantar-flexes foot; flexes knee
Innervation:	Tibial nerve (S1 and S2)
Comments:	Acts upon two joints, knee and ankle; inserts upon calcaneus together with soleus as a common tendon called the *Achilles tendon* (tendo calcaneus); lies superficial to soleus on posterior surface of leg; forms the belly of the "calf"; together with the soleus it forms the *triceps surae*

141 Soleus

Origin:	Head and upper fourth of posterior aspect of fibula; middle third and soleal line of tibia
Action:	Plantar-flexes foot; helps to steady leg on foot during standing
Innervation:	Tibial nerve (S1 and S2)
Comments:	Together with the gastrocnemius it forms a muscular mass called the *triceps surae,* which shares a common tendon of insertion, the *Achilles tendon*

142 Plantaris

Origin:	Lateral condyle of femur
Action:	Weakly assists gastrocnemius in its actions
Innervation:	Tibial nerve (S1 and S2)
Comments:	Rudimentary muscle in human; its short, cylindrical belly gives rise to a long, narrow, flat tendon that joins the *Achilles tendon;* its tendon is often mistaken for a nerve by beginning students in the dissecting room, hence the term "freshman's nerve"

Major muscles of the leg and foot (*continued*)

Intrinsic muscles of the foot*

143 Extensor digitorum brevis

Origin:	Superior aspect of calcaneus
Action:	Assists extensor digitorum longus in extending the middle three toes; extends only the proximal phalanx of great toe
Innervation:	Deep peroneal branch of common peroneal nerve (S1 and S2)
Comments:	Only muscle intrinsic to dorsal surface of foot; its medial portion gives rise to tendon inserting on proximal phalanx of great toe and is sometimes designated as the extensor hallucis brevis; the remaining three tendons blend with those of the extensor digitorum longus and are distributed to the second through fourth toes

144 Abductor hallucis

Origin:	Calcaneus, plantar aponeurosis, and flexor retinaculum
Action:	Abducts and flexes great toe
Innervation:	Medial plantar nerve (S2 and S3)
Comments:	Inserts on base of proximal phalanx of great toe

145 Flexor digitorum brevis

Origin:	Calcaneus and plantar aponeurosis
Action:	Flexes lateral four toes
Innervation:	Medial plantar nerve (S2 and S3)
Comments:	Each of its four tendons is perforated by a tendon of the flexor digitorum longus before inserting upon the middle phalanx of the lateral four toes

146 Abductor digiti minimi

Origin:	Calcaneus and plantar aponeurosis
Action:	Flexes and abducts fifth (little) toe
Innervation:	Lateral plantar nerve (S2 and S3)
Comments:	Stronger flexor than abductor

147 Flexor digitorum accessorius (quadratus plantae)

Origin:	Calcaneus and long plantar ligament
Action:	Counteracts medial pull of flexor digitorum longus tendon and flexes distal phalanges of lateral four toes
Innervation:	Lateral plantar nerve (S2 and S3)
Comments:	Tendon joins that of the flexor digitorum longus

148 Lumbricals (four)

Origin:	Arise from the four tendons of flexor digitorum longus; the first arises from medial aspect of most medial tendon of flexor digitorum longus; the second through the fourth arise from two adjacent tendons of the long flexor
Action:	Flex lateral four toes at joint between metatarsal and proximal phalanx; assist in extension of the interphalangeal joints of lateral four toes
Innervation:	(First lumbrical) medial plantar nerve (S2 and S3); (second through fourth lumbricals) lateral plantar nerve (S2 and S3)
Comments:	Insert upon proximal phalanx of lateral four toes; some fibers blend with extensor tendons on dorsum of foot

(*table continued on next page*)

Major muscles of the leg and foot (*continued*)

Intrinsic muscles of the foot*

149 Flexor hallucis brevis

Origin:	Cuboid and lateral cuneiform
Action:	Flexes great toe
Innervation:	Medial plantar nerve (S2 and S3)
Comments:	Some fibers originate from tendon of tibialis posterior muscle; inserts upon proximal phalanx of great toe

150 Adductor hallucis

Origin:	Dual: (1) oblique head from second through fourth metatarsal bones and tendon of peroneus longus; (2) transverse head from ligaments connecting metatarsals and proximal phalanges of third through fifth toes
Action:	Adducts great toe
Innervation:	Lateral plantar nerve (S2 and S3)
Comments:	Both heads insert upon lateral sesamoid bone and proximal phalanx of great toe

151 Flexor digiti minimi brevis

Origin:	Base of fifth metatarsal and tendon of peroneus longus
Action:	Flexes fifth toe
Innervation:	Lateral plantar nerve (S2 and S3)
Comments:	Inserts upon base of proximal phalanx of fifth toe

152 Dorsal interossei (four)

Origin:	Numbered first through fourth in medial to lateral direction; first arises from metatarsals of great and second toes; second through fourth arise from metatarsals of second and third, third and fourth, and fourth and fifth toes, respectively
Action:	Abduct the second through fourth toes; note that the reference axis for abduction is the midline of the second toe
Innervation:	Lateral plantar nerve (S2 and S3)
Comments:	First inserts upon medial aspect of phalanges of second toe; remaining three insert upon lateral aspect of phalanges of second through fourth toes

153 Plantar interossei (three)

Origin:	Numbered first through third in medial to lateral direction and arise from base of third, fourth, and fifth metatarsals, respectively
Action:	Adduct the third through fifth toes toward the second toe; note that the reference axis for adduction is the midline of the second toe
Innervation:	Lateral plantar nerve (S2 and S3)
Comments:	First, second, and third insert upon proximal phalanges of third, fourth, and fifth toes, respectively

*The muscles of the foot are typically described as being arranged in four layers. The first layer is the most superficial and contains the abductor hallucis, flexor digitorum brevis, and abductor digiti minimi. Proceeding inward, the second layer is made up of the flexor accessorius (quadratus plantae) and four lumbricals. The third layer contains the flexor hallucis brevis, adductor hallucis, and flexor digiti minimi brevis. The fourth and deepest layer is composed of the four dorsal and three plantar interossei.

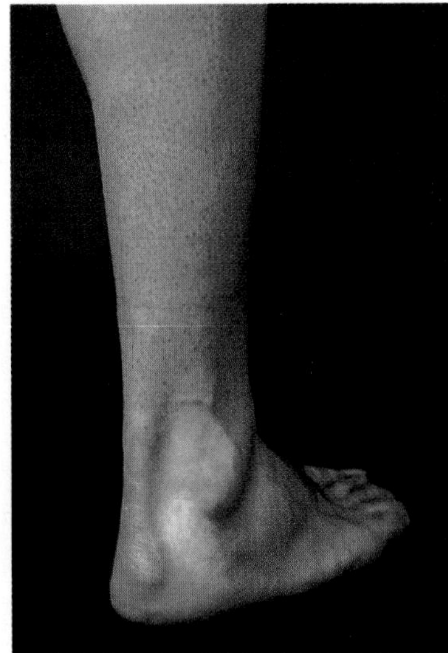

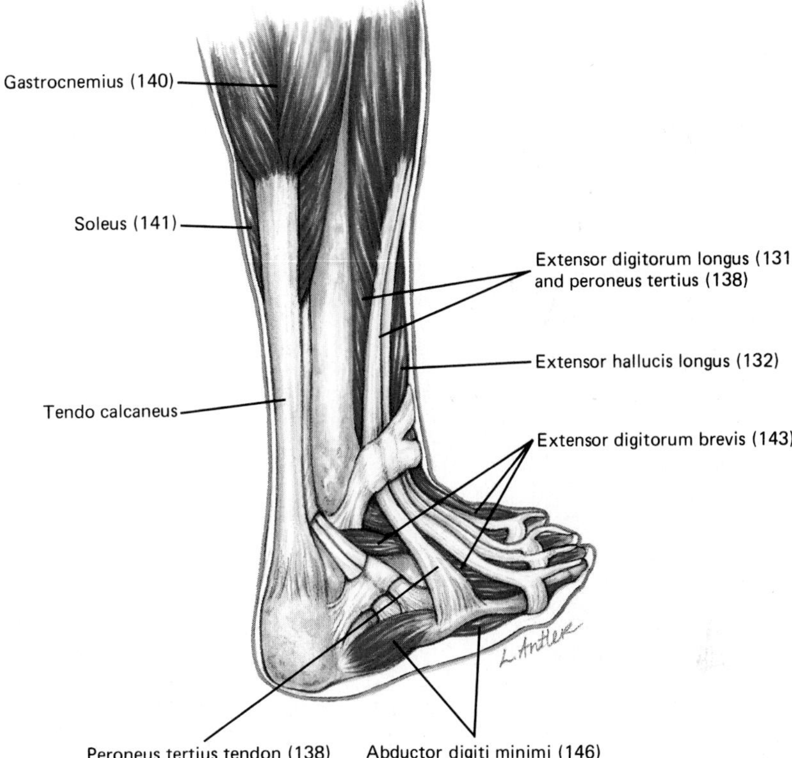

Posterolateral aspect of leg and foot.

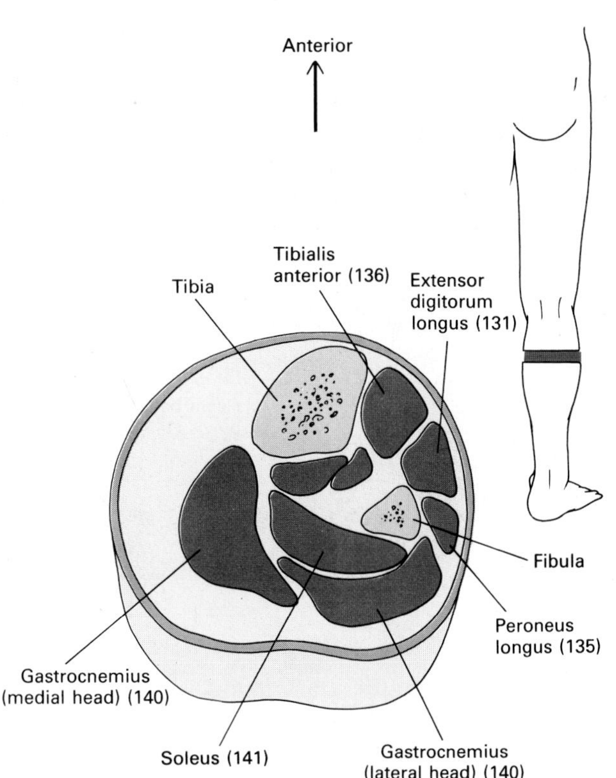

Transverse section through proximal one third of leg.

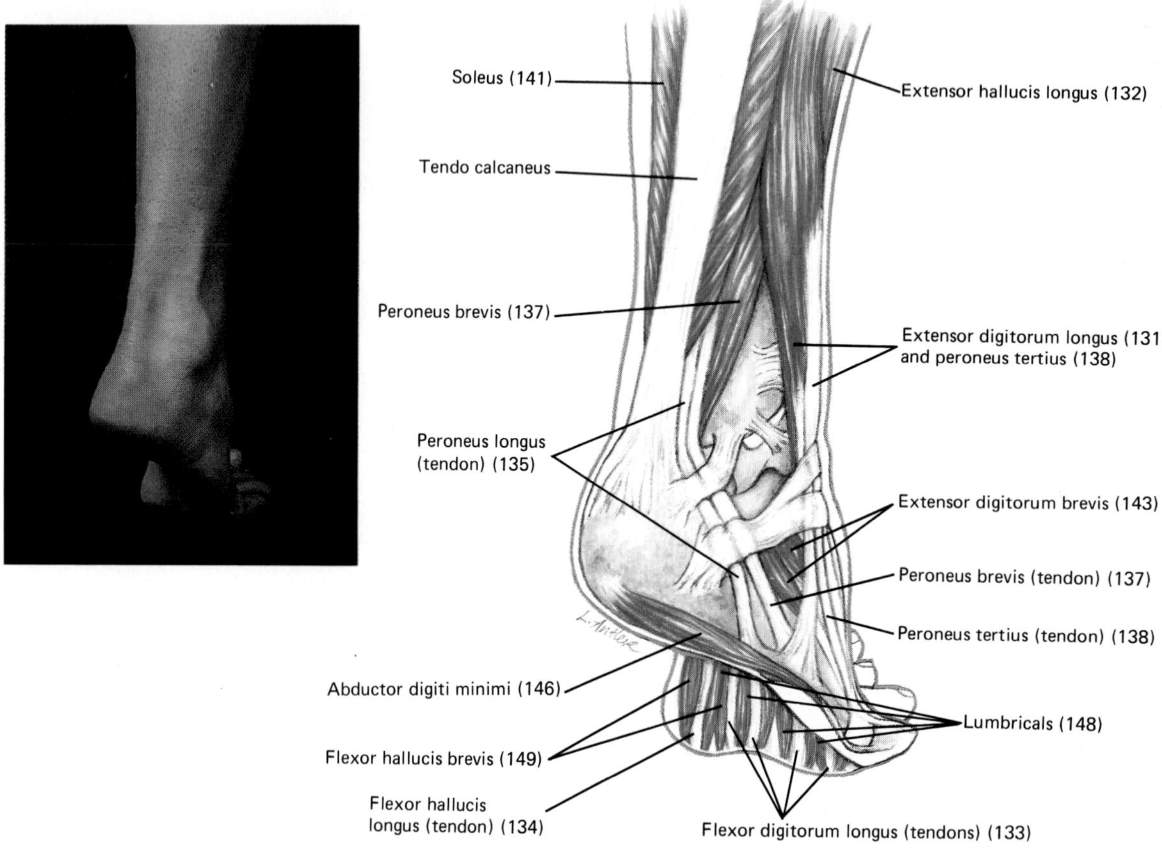

Soleus (141)
Extensor hallucis longus (132)
Tendo calcaneus
Peroneus brevis (137)
Extensor digitorum longus (131) and peroneus tertius (138)
Peroneus longus (tendon) (135)
Extensor digitorum brevis (143)
Peroneus brevis (tendon) (137)
Peroneus tertius (tendon) (138)
Abductor digiti minimi (146)
Lumbricals (148)
Flexor hallucis brevis (149)
Flexor hallucis longus (tendon) (134)
Flexor digitorum longus (tendons) (133)

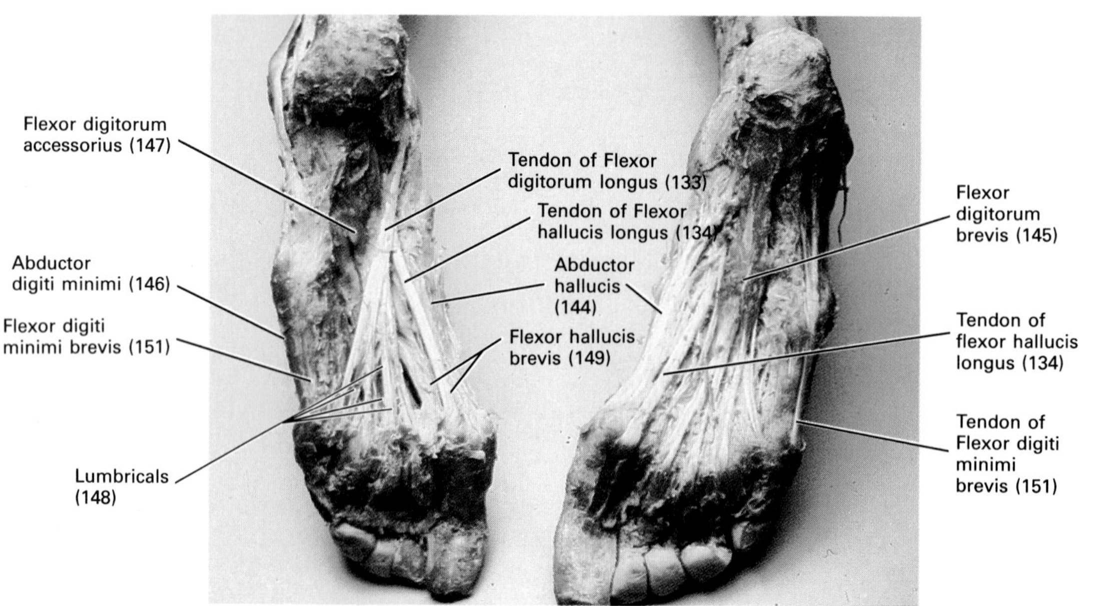

Flexor digitorum accessorius (147)
Tendon of Flexor digitorum longus (133)
Tendon of Flexor hallucis longus (134)
Flexor digitorum brevis (145)
Abductor digiti minimi (146)
Abductor hallucis (144)
Flexor digiti minimi brevis (151)
Flexor hallucis brevis (149)
Tendon of flexor hallucis longus (134)
Tendon of Flexor digiti minimi brevis (151)
Lumbricals (148)

Posterolateral leg and foot with plantar aspect of foot exposed.

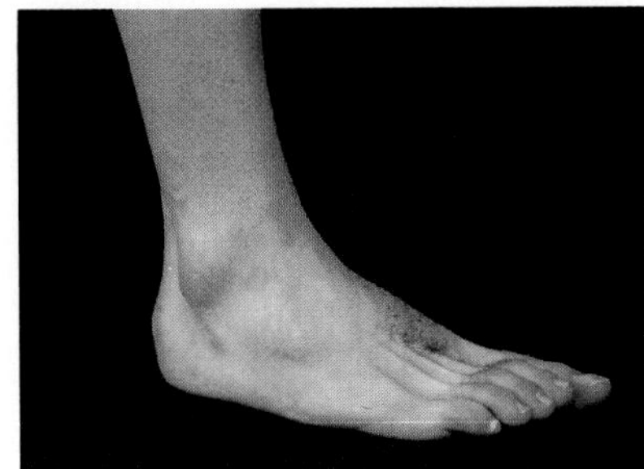

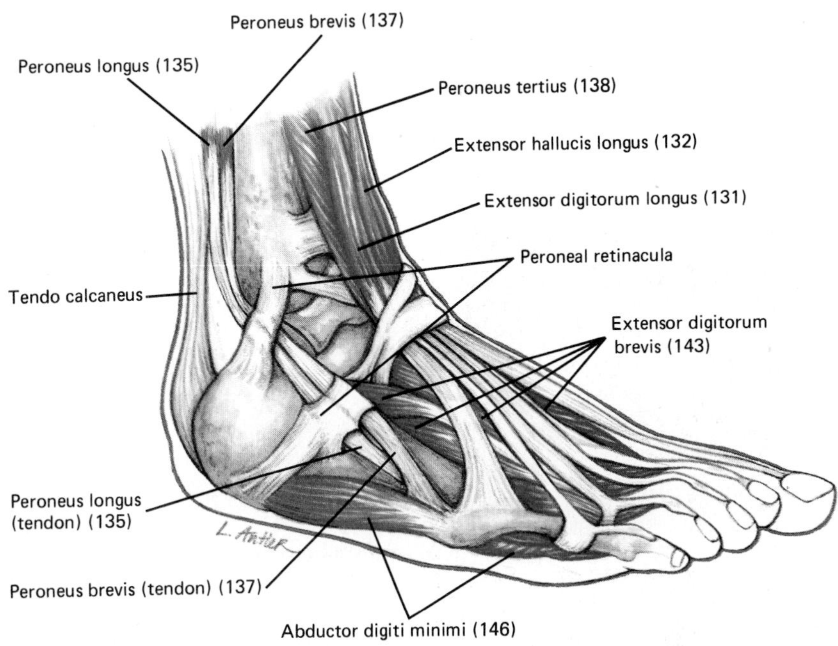
Peroneus brevis (137)
Peroneus longus (135)
Peroneus tertius (138)
Extensor hallucis longus (132)
Extensor digitorum longus (131)
Peroneal retinacula
Tendo calcaneus
Extensor digitorum brevis (143)
Peroneus longus (tendon) (135)
L. Antler
Peroneus brevis (tendon) (137)
Abductor digiti minimi (146)

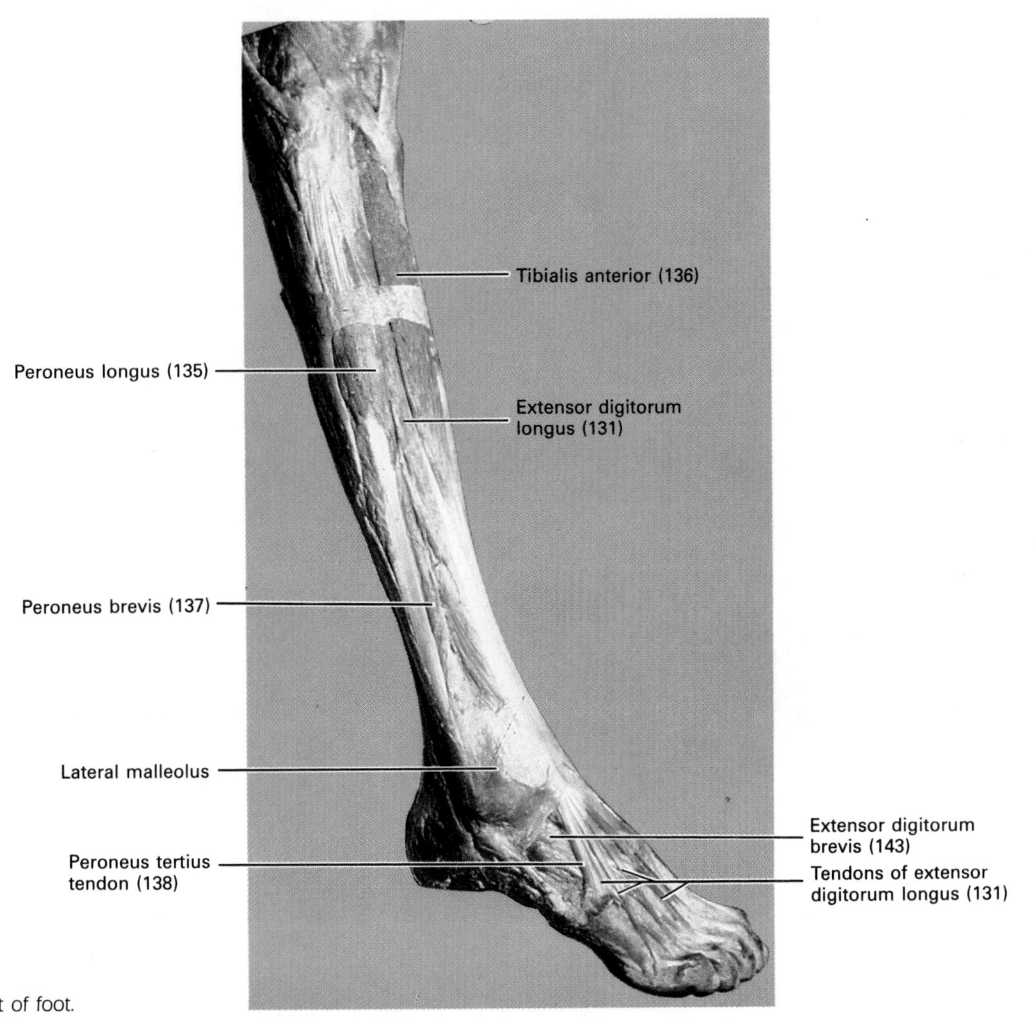
Tibialis anterior (136)
Peroneus longus (135)
Extensor digitorum longus (131)
Peroneus brevis (137)
Lateral malleolus
Extensor digitorum brevis (143)
Peroneus tertius tendon (138)
Tendons of extensor digitorum longus (131)

Anterolateral aspect of foot.

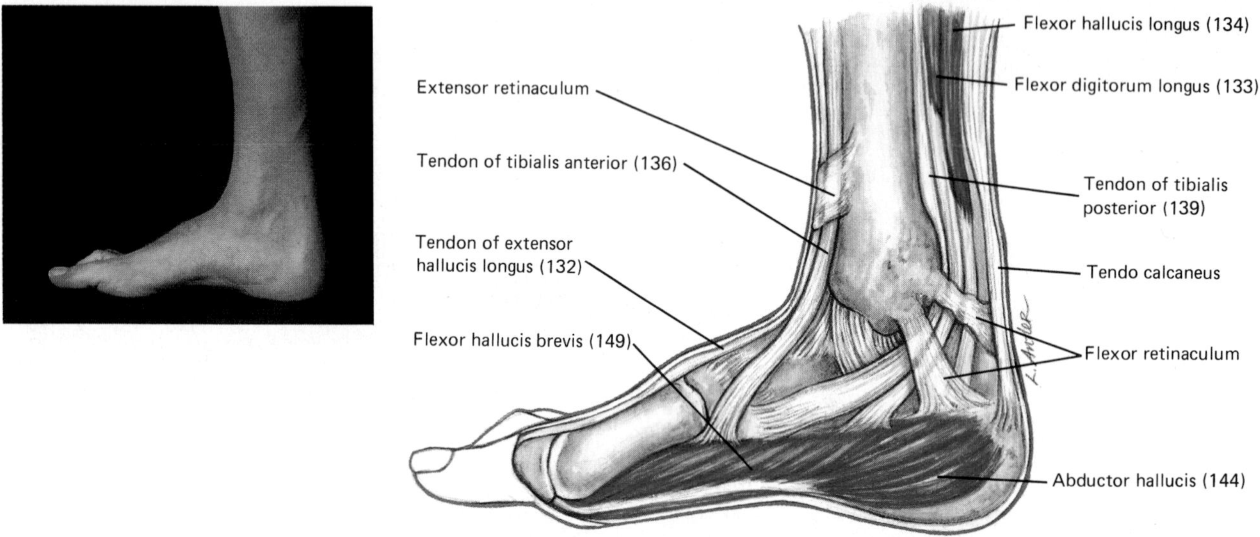
Flexor hallucis longus (134)
Flexor digitorum longus (133)
Extensor retinaculum
Tendon of tibialis anterior (136)
Tendon of tibialis posterior (139)
Tendon of extensor hallucis longus (132)
Tendo calcaneus
Flexor hallucis brevis (149)
Flexor retinaculum
Abductor hallucis (144)

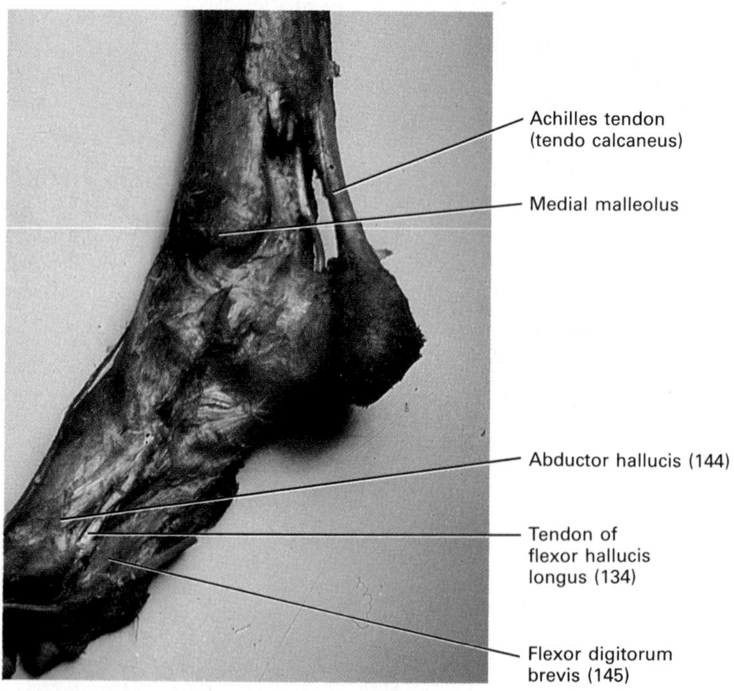
Achilles tendon (tendo calcaneus)
Medial malleolus
Abductor hallucis (144)
Tendon of flexor hallucis longus (134)
Flexor digitorum brevis (145)

Medial aspect of foot.

TABLE 11-9

Muscles of the pelvic floor* and perineum†

154 Ischiocavernosus

Origin:	Tuberosity of ischium; rami of ischium and pubis
Insertion:	Corpus cavernosa of penis in the male; clitoris in the female
Action:	Assists in maintaining erection of clitoris in the female and penis in the male
Innervation:	Pudendal nerve (perineal branch, S2–S4)
Comments:	Superficial; covers crura of penis and clitoris

155 Bulbocavernosus

Origin:	Central tendon of perineum (perineal body)
Insertion:	Perineal membrane (inferior fascia of the urogenital diaphragm‡) in male and female; corpus spongiosum of penis and dorsum of penis in male; root and dorsum of clitoris and pubic arch in the female
Action:	MALE: Assists erection of penis; helps propel seminal fluid through urethra and expel final drops of urine when voiding. FEMALE: Assists erection of clitoris
Innervation:	Pudendal nerve (perineal branch, S2–S4)
Comments:	Superficial; covers penile bulb in male and the vestibular bulbs in the female; note that each vestibular bulb is a homologue of half of the bulb of the penis

156 Superficial transversus perineus

Origin:	Tuberosity of ischium
Insertion:	Central tendon of perineum (perineal body)
Action:	Assists in stabilization of the central tendon of the perineum (perineal body)
Innervation:	Pudendal nerve (perineal branch, S2–S4)
Comments:	Assists in expelling urine in both male and female as well as semen in the male; the deep transversus perineus is not shown in the accompanying diagrams because it is located within the urogenital diaphragm, that is, deep to the perineal membrane (inferior fascia of urogenital diaphragm)

157 Levator ani

Origin:	Dual origin: (1) pubococcygeus portion from the pubis and (2) iliococcygeus portion from the ischial spine
Insertion:	(1) Fibers of pubococcygeus portion attach to the urethra, anal canal, central tendon of the perineum, and the coccyx; (2) fibers of the iliococcygeus portion attach to the coccyx
Action:	Together, both portions assist in supporting the pelvic viscera (organs) and elevating the pelvic floor a short distance; pull anus anteriorly and constrict it slightly
Innervation:	Sacral nerves (S3 and S4) and pudendal nerve (perineal branch, S2–S4)
Comments:	The *puborectalis* is also part of the levator ani, but is not shown in the accompanying diagrams because it is more deeply placed. The levator ani form the major part of the funnel-shaped pelvic floor. Compare the frontal (coronal) sections with the perineal views to fully appreciate this muscle's arrangement. The *coccygeus* muscle (hidden by the overlying gluteus maximus) helps to close off, or complete, the posterior portion of the pelvic floor

158 Sphincter urethrae

Origin:	Transverse perineal ligament (anterior border of the urogenital diaphragm) and fascia enclosing the pudendal vessels
Insertion:	In the male its fibers form a circular ring around the urethra before attaching to the central tendon of the perineum; in the female the fibers course posteriorly on each of the urethra and attach to the anterior wall of the vagina
Action:	Constrict urethra in both sexes and assist in expelling the final drops of urine; in the male it also assists in the ejaculation of seminal fluid from the urethra
Innervation:	Pudendal nerve (perineal branch, S2–S4)
Comments:	In both sexes the sphincter urethrae have a stratified arrangement, that is, they are composed of deep and superficial fibers. This muscle is also located within the urogenital diaphragm

(table continued on next page)

Muscles of the pelvic floor* and perineum† (*continued*)	
159 Sphincter ani externus	
Origin:	Anococcygeal ligament and coccyx by means of the anococcygeal raphe
Insertion:	Some fibers attach to the central tendon of the perineum, others blend with those of the puborectalis and superficial transversus perinei
Action:	Constricts anal canal and keeps anus closed
Innervation:	Pudendal nerve (inferior rectal branch, S2 and S3) and perineal branch of S4
Comments:	Sphincter is continuous with the circular layer of muscle that surrounds the rectum above; the sphincter ani externus is under voluntary control, whereas the sphincter ani internus functions in an involuntary manner; during defecation both sphincters are relaxed and the lower portion of the anal canal is opened

*The floor of the pelvis is funnel-shaped and is formed almost entirely by the levator ani with a small contribution posteriorly from the coccygeus muscles. You might say that the floor prevents the pelvic viscera (organs) from falling out through the pelvic outlet.

†The diamond-shaped anatomical region termed the *perineum* is limited anteriorly by the pubic symphysis, laterally by the ischial tuberosities, and posteriorly by the coccyx. It lies between the medial aspect of the thighs and the buttocks at the most inferior region of the trunk. Typically it is subdivided, by an imaginary line passing between the two ischial tuberosities, into an anterior *urogenital triangle* and a posterior *anal triangle.* The former contains portions of the external genitalia whereas the anal canal and anus lie in the latter. Lateral to the anus is a potential space located between the urogenital diaphragm anteriorly and the gluteus maximus posteriorly. It is completely occupied by adipose and dense connective tissue strands. On each side this region is termed the *ischiorectal fossa* and lies between the pelvic floor above and the skin below.

‡The *urogenital diaphragm* lies within the urogenital triangle and is formed by the deep transversus perinei and sphincter urethrae muscles in addition to a layer of superior and inferior fasciae. It encloses portions of the urogenital ducts and gives additional strength to that portion of the pelvic floor situated above it.

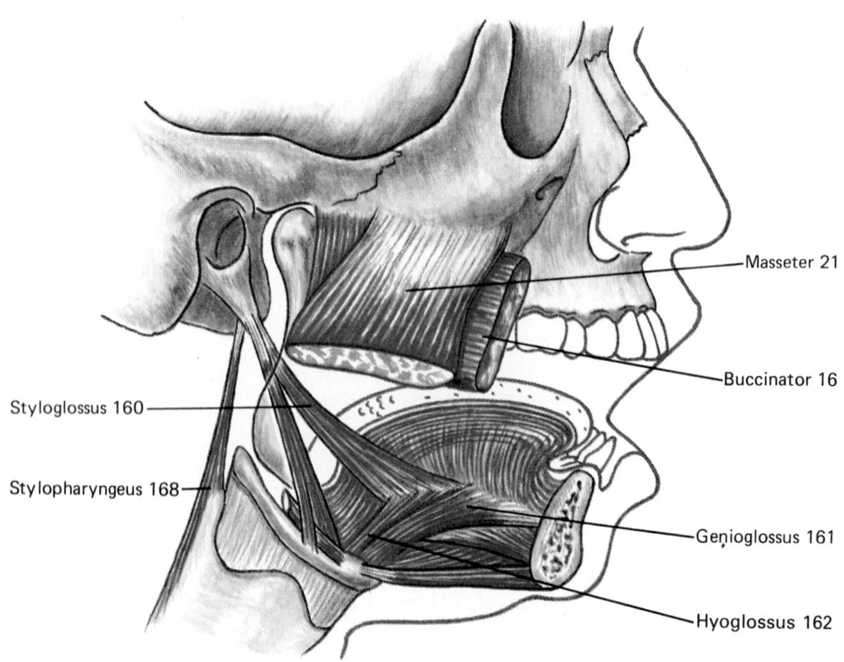

Muscles that move the tongue.

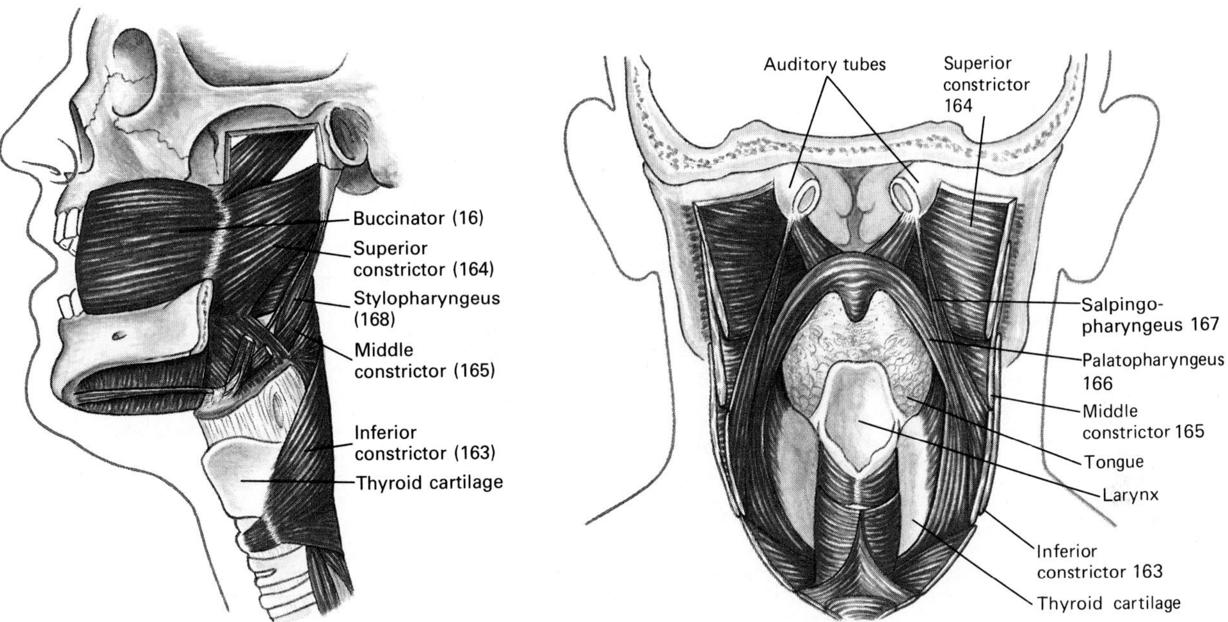

Muscles of the pharynx.

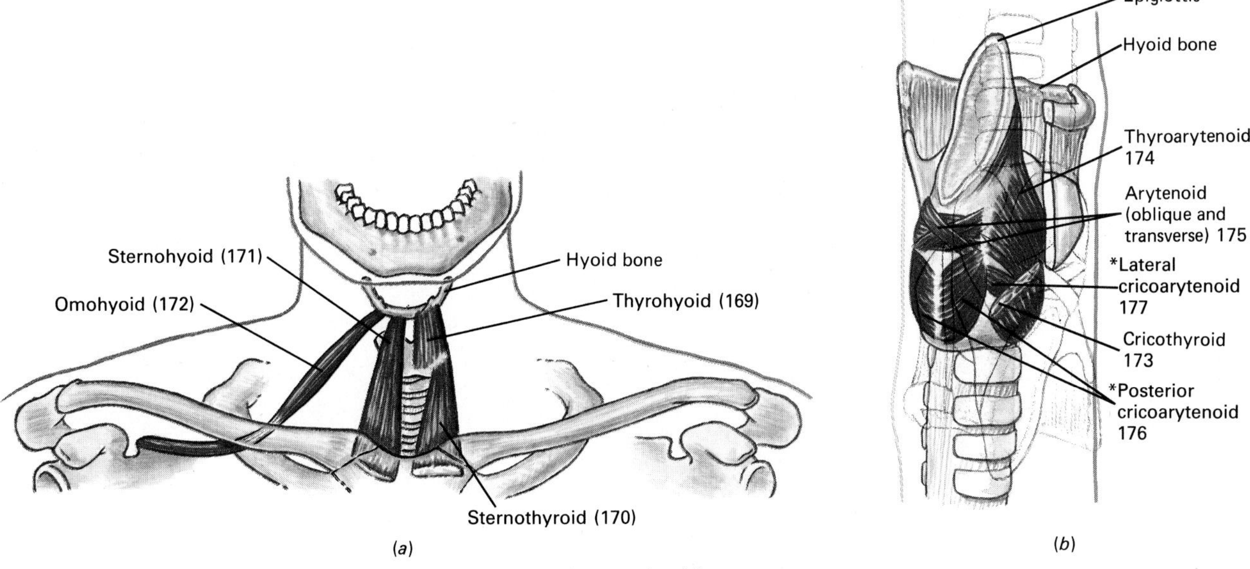

Muscles of the larynx *Cricoarytenoid muscles are not listed in the muscle tables.

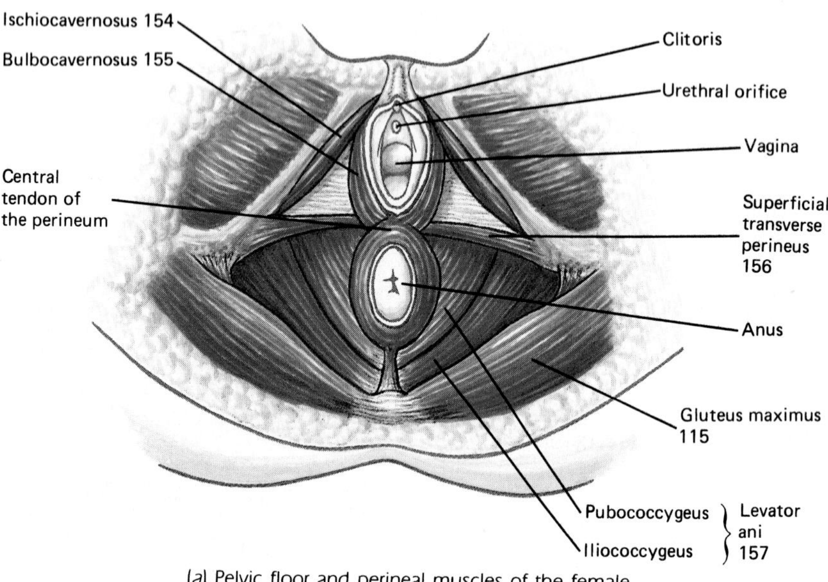

(a) Pelvic floor and perineal muscles of the female.

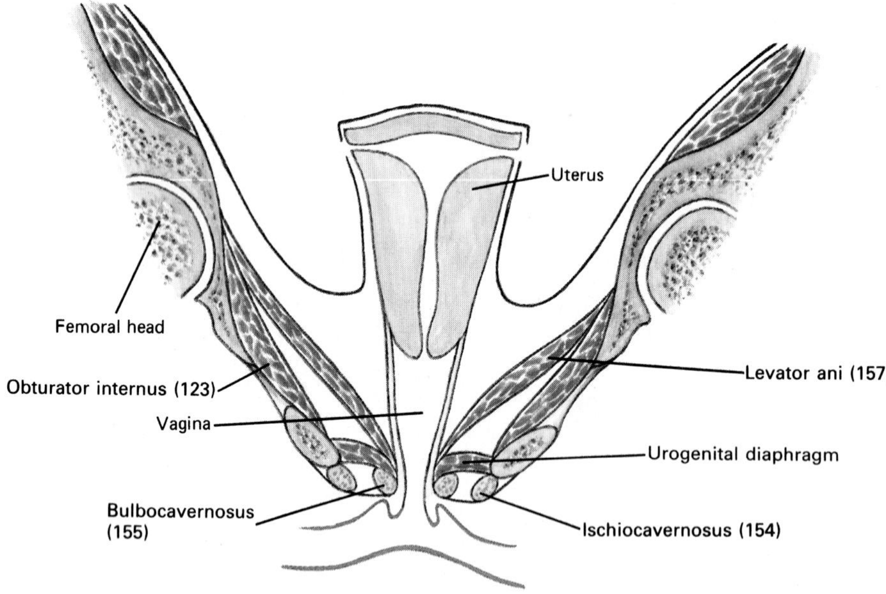

(b) Female pelvis in frontal (coronal) section.

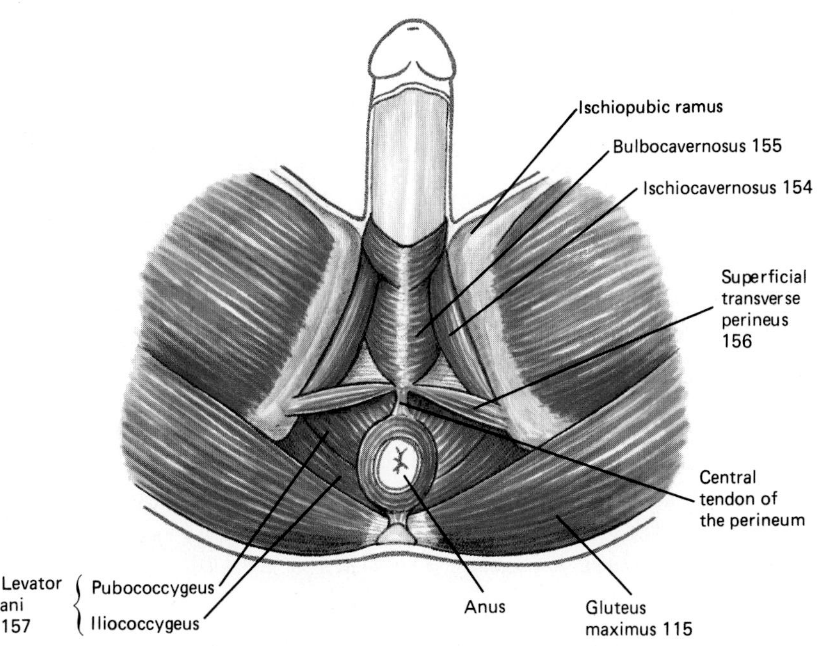

(c) Pelvic floor and perineal muscles of the male.

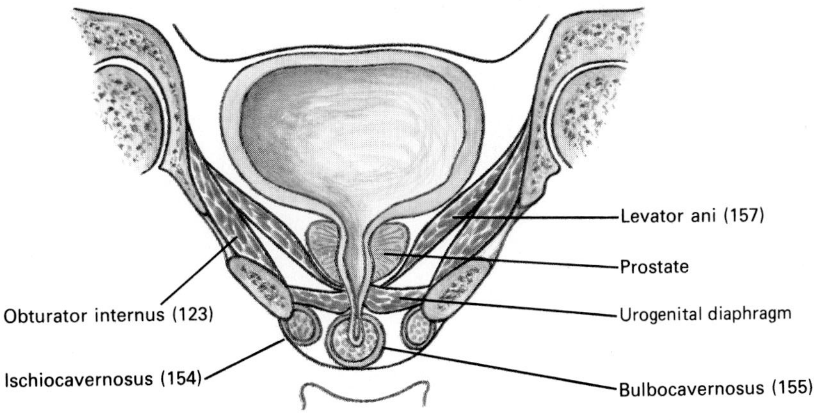

(d) Male pelvis in frontal (coronal) section.

TABLE 11-10

Tongue muscles*	
These muscles provide movement of the tongue	
160 Styloglossus	
Origin:	Styloid process of temporal bone and stylomandibular ligament
Insertion:	Side and inferior aspect of tongue
Action:	Retracts tongue (moves it backward); elevates tongue
Innervation:	Hypoglossal nerve (CN XII)
161 Genioglossus	
Origin:	Mandible
Insertion:	Inferior aspect of tongue and body of hyoid bone
Action:	Protracts tongue (moves it forward); depresses tongue
Innervation:	Hypoglossal nerve (CN XII)
Comments:	Its attachment to the mandible helps prevent the tongue from moving posteriorly and obstructing respiration; the tongue may be kept forward by pulling the mandible forward
162 Hyoglossus	
Origin:	Hyoid bone (body)
Insertion:	Side and inferior aspect of tongue
Action:	Draws down the sides of the tongue; depresses tongue
Innervation:	Hypoglossal nerve (CN XII)

*These muscles together with the palatoglossus (not shown) are called the *extrinsic* muscles of the tongue. The *intrinsic* muscles of the tongue are contained within the substance of the tongue itself and are arranged in several planes: (a) transverse, (b) vertical, (c) superior longitudinal, and (d) inferior longitudinal. All muscles of the tongue receive their innervation via the hypoglossal nerve (CN XII) with the exception of the palatoglossus (accessory nerve; CN XI). The position of the tongue is dependent upon the extrinsic muscles whereas its form is dependent on both extrinsic and intrinsic groups.

TABLE 11-11

Muscles of the pharynx*

163 Inferior constrictor†

Origin:	Larynx (cricoid and thyroid cartilages)
Insertion:	Fibrous raphe in midline of posterior pharynx
Action:	Helps move food into esophagus by constriction of the inferior pharynx
Innervation:	Pharyngeal plexus
Comments:	Thickest of the three constrictors; its most inferior fibers are continuous with the circular muscle fibers of the esophagus

164 Superior constrictor

Origin:	Sphenoid (pterygoid process), mandible, and pterygomandibular raphe
Insertion:	Fibrous raphe in midline of posterior pharynx
Action:	Helps move food into the esophagus by constriction of the superior pharynx
Innervation:	Pharyngeal plexus
Comments:	Thinnest of the three constrictors

165 Middle constrictor

Origin:	Hyoid (greater and lesser cornua); stylohyoid ligament
Insertion:	Fibrous raphe in midline of posterior pharynx
Action:	Helps move food into the esophagus by constriction of the middle portion of the pharynx
Innervation:	Pharyngeal plexus
Comments:	Overlaps fibers of the superior constrictor above; its lowest fibers are overlapped by those of the inferior constrictor below

166 Palatopharyngeus

Origin:	Soft palate
Insertion:	Posterior border of thyroid cartilage and the side of the pharynx
Action:	Assists in closing the nasopharynx during the process of swallowing; elevates pharynx and larynx
Innervation:	Pharyngeal plexus
Comments:	Forms the palatopharyngeal arch

167 Salpingopharyngeus

Origin:	Eustachian (auditory) tube
Insertion:	Fibers blend with those of the palatopharyngeus to reach posterior border of the thyroid cartilage
Action:	Opens the auditory tube and also elevates pharynx and larynx during the process of swallowing
Innervation:	Pharyngeal plexus

168 Stylopharyngeus

Origin:	Styloid process of temporal bone
Insertion:	Some fibers blend with the constrictors; others insert with palatopharyngeus into posterior border of thyroid cartilage
Action:	Assists in dilation and elevation of the pharynx during swallowing and speech
Innervation:	Glossopharyngeal nerve (CN IX)
Comments:	Long and slender muscle that passes between the superior and middle constrictors

*The *pharynx* is a region located between the oral and nasal cavities and the esophagus. It is a musculofibrous tube and is typically subdivided into three regions, *nasopharynx, oropharynx,* and *laryngopharynx.*

†The constrictor muscles of the pharynx are arranged like a series of three nested funnels. In swallowing, the superior constrictor delivers a bolus to the middle constrictor, which in turn places it in the territory of the inferior constrictor. The latter ultimately squeezes it into the esophagus. The pharyngeal plexus contains fibers from the vagus nerve, glossopharyngeal nerve, and the sympathetic trunk.

TABLE 11-12

Muscles of the larynx*

169 Thyrohyoid

Origin:	Larynx (thyroid cartilage)
Insertion:	Greater cornu and body of hyoid
Action:	Elevation of thyroid cartilage and depression of hyoid bone
Innervation:	C1 and C2 and descending branch hypoglossal nerve (CN XII)
Comments:	May be considered as superior extension of the sternothyroid muscle

170 Sternothyroid

Origin:	Sternum (manubrium)
Insertion:	Thyroid cartilage
Action:	Depression of the thyroid cartilage
Innervation:	C1–C3
Comments:	Located deep to the sternohyoid muscle

171 Sternohyoid

Origin:	Sternum (manubrium) and clavicle
Insertion:	Body of hyoid bone
Action:	Depression of the hyoid bone
Innervation:	C1–C3
Comments:	Parallel, but superficial, to the sternothyroid

172 Omohyoid

Origin:	Scapula and superior transverse ligament
Insertion:	Body of hyoid bone
Action:	Depression of the hyoid bone
Innervation:	C1–C3
Comments:	Has two bellies separated by an intermediate tendon; a band of deep cervical fascia attaches the intermediate tendon to the clavicle and first rib

173 Cricothyroid

Origin:	Larynx (cricoid cartilage)
Insertion:	Lamina and inferior cornua of thyroid cartilage
Action:	Elongate and tense the vocal cords
Innervation:	Vagus nerve (CN X, its external laryngeal branch)

Muscles of the larynx* (*continued*)

174 Thyroarytenoid

Origin:	Thyroid cartilage and cricothyroid ligament
Insertion:	Arytenoid cartilage
Action:	Shortens and relaxes vocal ligaments; also approximates the vocal folds
Innervation:	Vagus nerve (CN X, its recurrent laryngeal branch)

175 Arytenoid (oblique and transverse)

Origin:	Arytenoid cartilage
Insertion:	Both the oblique and transverse arytenoid muscles insert on the opposite arytenoid cartilage
Action:	Moves arytenoid cartilages together and closes the glottis (transverse arytenoid); approximates the arytenoid cartilages and epiglottis (oblique arytenoids)
Innervation:	Vagus nerve (CN X, its recurrent laryngeal branch)
Comments:	Transverse arytenoid is a single muscle that interconnects the two arytenoid cartilages; the oblique arytenoids cross each other as their fibers pass from the arytenoid cartilage on one side to that on the opposite side (some fibers continue upward to the epiglottis and are called the aryepiglotticus muscle on each side)

176 Posterior cricoarytenoid

Origin:	Cricoid cartilage
Insertion:	Arytenoid cartilage
Action:	Opens the glottis
Innervation:	Vagus nerve (CN X, its recurrent laryngeal branch)

177 Lateral cricoarytenoid

Origin:	Cricoid cartilage
Insertion:	Arytenoid cartilage
Action:	Closes the glottis
Innervation:	Vagus nerve (CN X, its recurrent laryngeal branch)

*Together, the thyrohyoid, sternothyroid, sternohyoid, and omohyoid muscles are designated as the *extrinsic* muscles of the larynx. See Table 11-11 for muscles of the pharynx that attach to and move the larynx as well. The *intrinsic* muscles of the larynx consist of the cricothyroid, thyroarytenoid, arytenoids, and the posterior and lateral cricoarytenoids.

Post-test

Because of the tremendous variation in the degree of detail in which this material is taught, please have all the objectives of your instructor clearly in mind before beginning to study. Many instructors provide a checklist of muscles to be studied. The muscle index of this chapter is convenient for this purpose. The post-test that follows will be appropriate for many courses, but obviously not for all. Please keep in mind that your instructor may require knowledge not covered on this practice exercise.

1. Label the accompanying diagram.
2. Muscles that act with a prime mover and help to stabilize a joint during its movement are called ________________.
3. Two muscles that plantar-flex the foot during walking are the ________________ and the ________________.
4. Muscles that flex the leg at the knee joint are located on the ________________ side of the thigh. Most of them cross ________________ joints between their origin and insertion.
5. A wasting away or diminution of muscle size is called ________________.

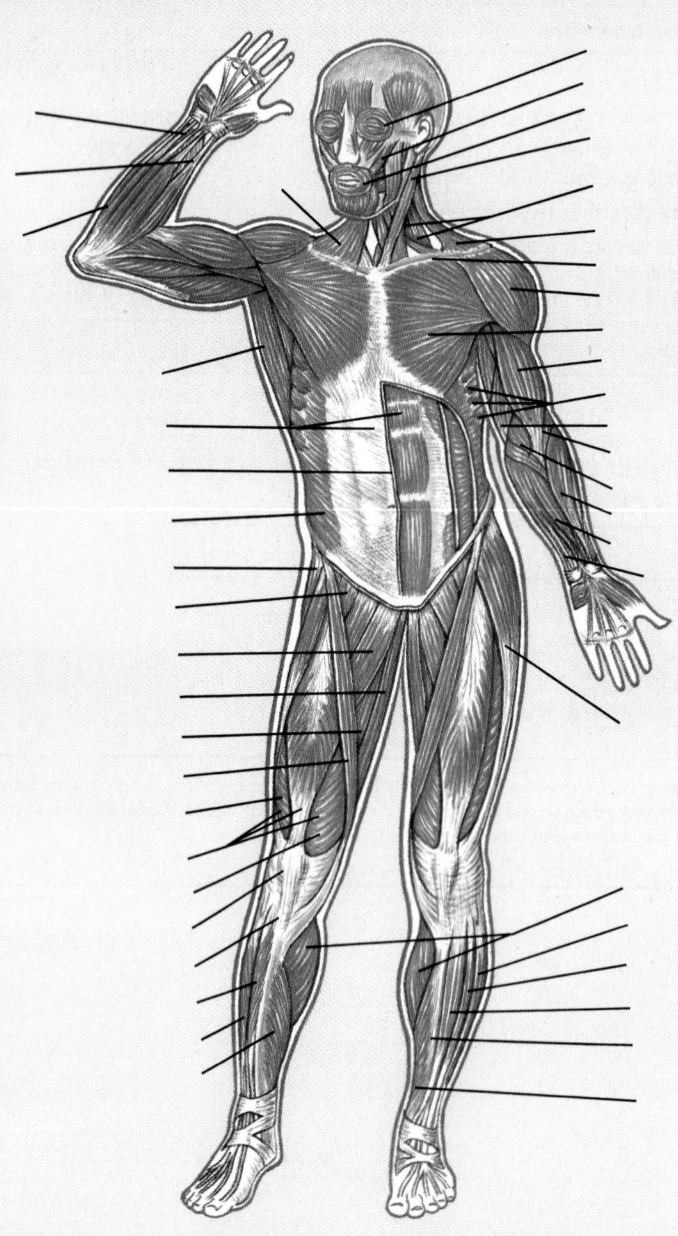

6. In the hand there are ______ lumbricals and ______ interossei muscles.
7. The opponens pollicis is an ______ muscle of the hand, whereas the flexor digitorum is an ______ muscle of the hand.
8. ______ ______ is the crudest type of prehension.

Review questions

1. Construct a table similar to Box 11-1 for muscles of the thigh, leg, and foot.
2. Describe muscles that are active in shaking the head from side to side. In nodding of the head.
3. List the intrinsic muscles of the foot.
4. How do the power and precision grips of the hand differ? Describe the differences in muscle action that account for them.
5. Which muscles are active in:
   a. Biting an apple?
   b. Opening the mouth as when a physician examines your pharynx?
   c. Chewing gum? (List from the start of one chewing cycle to the start of the next.)
6. Describe the arm and shoulder muscles that are active in raising a barbell to waist level by flexing the arm at the elbow. In lowering it gradually again.
7. Why is the main mass of a muscle not usually located over the part that it moves?
8. Describe the main agonists (prime movers) and antagonists active in:
   a. The leg while bicycling.
   b. The shoulder, arm, and forearm while doing push-up exercises.
   c. The shoulder, arm, and forearm while doing chin-up exercises.
   d. The thigh while walking up a flight of stairs.

Post-test answers

1. See Figure 11-4. 2. synergists
3. gastrocnemius, soleus 4. posterior (dorsal); two
5. atrophy 6. four; eight 7. intrinsic; extrinsic
8. Cylindrical grasp

REGULATION OF BODY ACTIVITIES

Think of the countless activities taking place in your body at this very moment. Your heart is beating at an appropriate rate and with appropriate force. You are breathing rhythmically. Your kidneys are filtering your blood and removing wastes from it. Thousands of chemical reactions are regulating the concentrations of nutrients, ions, and gases in your blood and in your cells, ensuring a continuous supply of raw materials and fuel molecules for the billions of cells in your body.

You are not even aware of most of these complex activities. You may even have difficulty in comprehending them when you read about them. Yet these processes are continuously and precisely regulated by control mechanisms within the body so that homeostasis is maintained. The two great regulatory systems in the body are the nervous system and the endocrine system.

The nervous system is responsible for making the rapid adjustments necessary to maintain homeostasis. It responds to changes in the environment, both external and internal, by signaling muscles to contract and glands to secrete their products appropriately. The endocrine system, which works comparatively slowly, regulates the metabolic activities of the body.

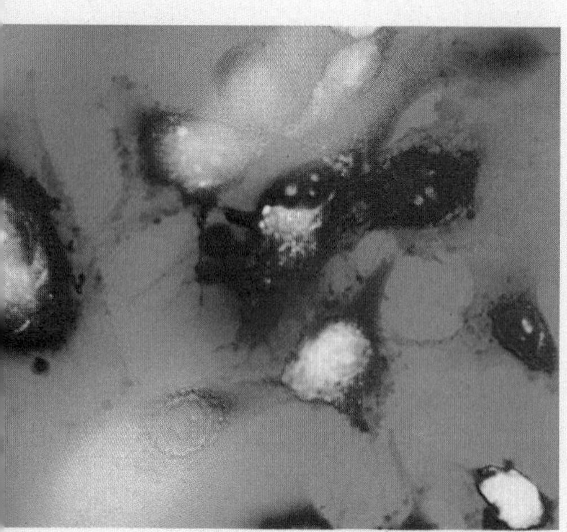

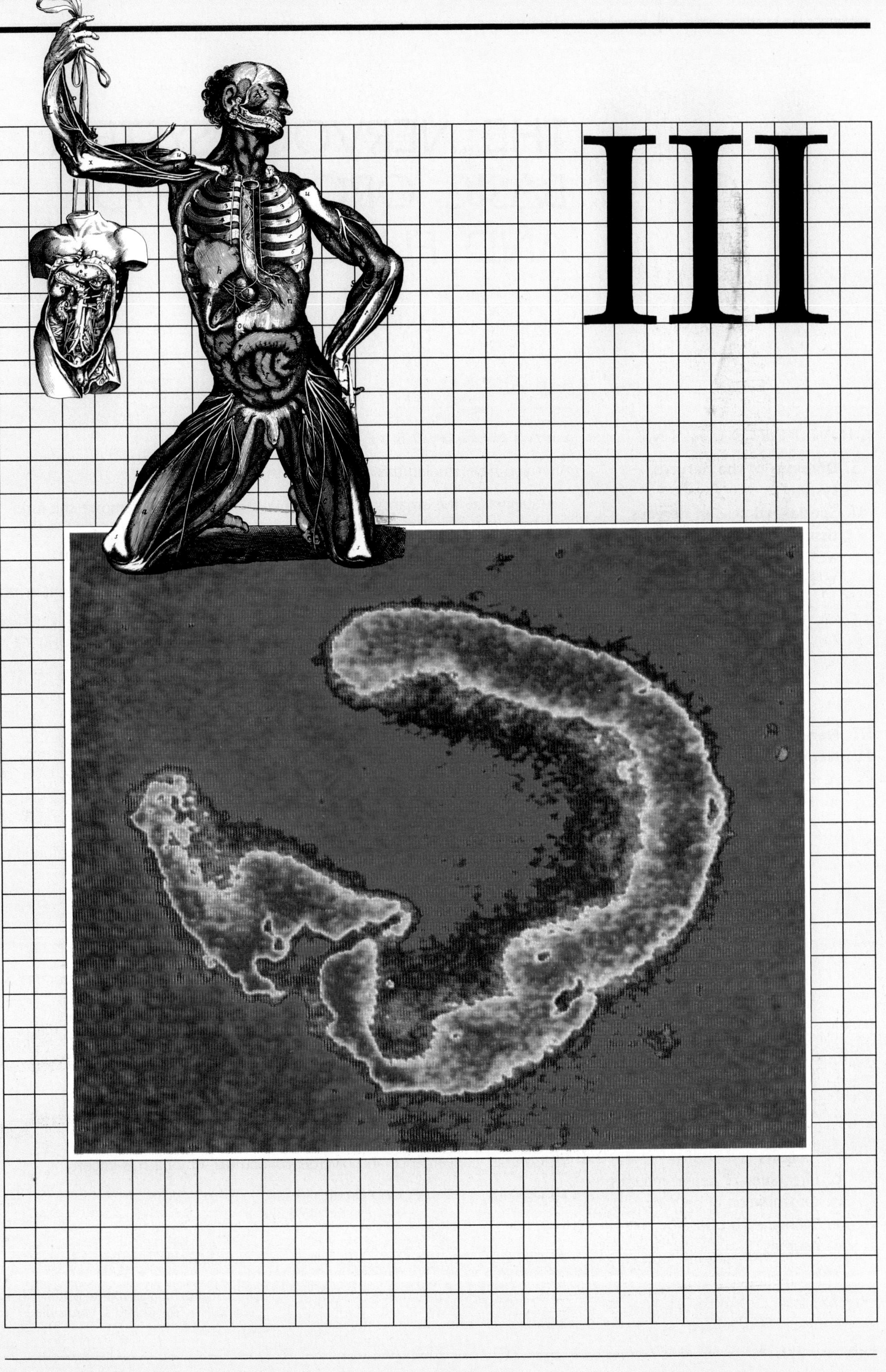

III

THE NERVOUS SYSTEM: BASIC ORGANIZATION AND FUNCTION

CHAPTER OUTLINE

- I. **Divisions of the nervous system**
- II. **Specialized cells of nervous tissue**
  - A. Glial cells
  - B. Neurons
    - 1. Nucleus
    - 2. Dendrites
    - 3. Axon
      - a. Myelin sheath
      - b. Cellular sheath
    - 4. Classification of neurons
- III. **Nerves and ganglia**
- IV. **Neural function**
  - A. Reception
  - B. Transmission
    - 1. Transmission along neurons
      - a. Resting potential
      - b. Action potential
      - c. Saltatory conduction
      - d. All-or-none law
      - e. Certain substances affect excitability
    - 2. Transmission between neurons
      - a. Signals may be excitatory or inhibitory
      - b. Graded potential
      - c. Neurotransmitters
    - 3. Classification of nerve fibers
  - C. Integration of neural impulses
  - D. Organization of neurons
  - E. Spontaneous discharge of neurons

LEARNING OBJECTIVES

After you have studied this chapter you should be able to:

1 Summarize the organization of the nervous system, and compare the functions of the central and peripheral nervous systems.

2 Compare the functions of the different types of glial cells.

3 Draw a typical neuron, label its parts, and give the functions of each, including myelin and cellular sheaths.

4 Describe the process of nerve regeneration.

5 Compare the functions of afferent, efferent, and association neurons.

6 Distinguish between nerve and tract; ganglion and nucleus.

7 Briefly describe the four basic processes on which all neural responses depend—reception, transmission, integration, and response.

8 Describe the general action of receptors.

9 Explain the ionic basis of resting membrane potential.

10 Relate the propagation of an action potential to changes in ion distribution.

11 Indicate two factors that affect intensity of sensation.

12 Compare continuous with saltatory conduction.

13 Contrast the effects of too much and too little calcium on neural function.

14 Trace the events that take place in synaptic transmission. (Draw diagrams to support your description.)

15 Identify the neurotransmitters described in the chapter, and identify mechanisms for inactivating neurotransmitters.

16 Identify factors that affect speed of transmission.

17 Describe how a postsynaptic neuron integrates incoming stimuli and "decides" whether to fire.

18 Contrast convergence and divergence, and tell why each is important.

19 Describe a reverberating circuit.

Light micrograph of human nerve cells in culture optical stain (×160). (VU/SIU © Visuals Unlimited.)

12

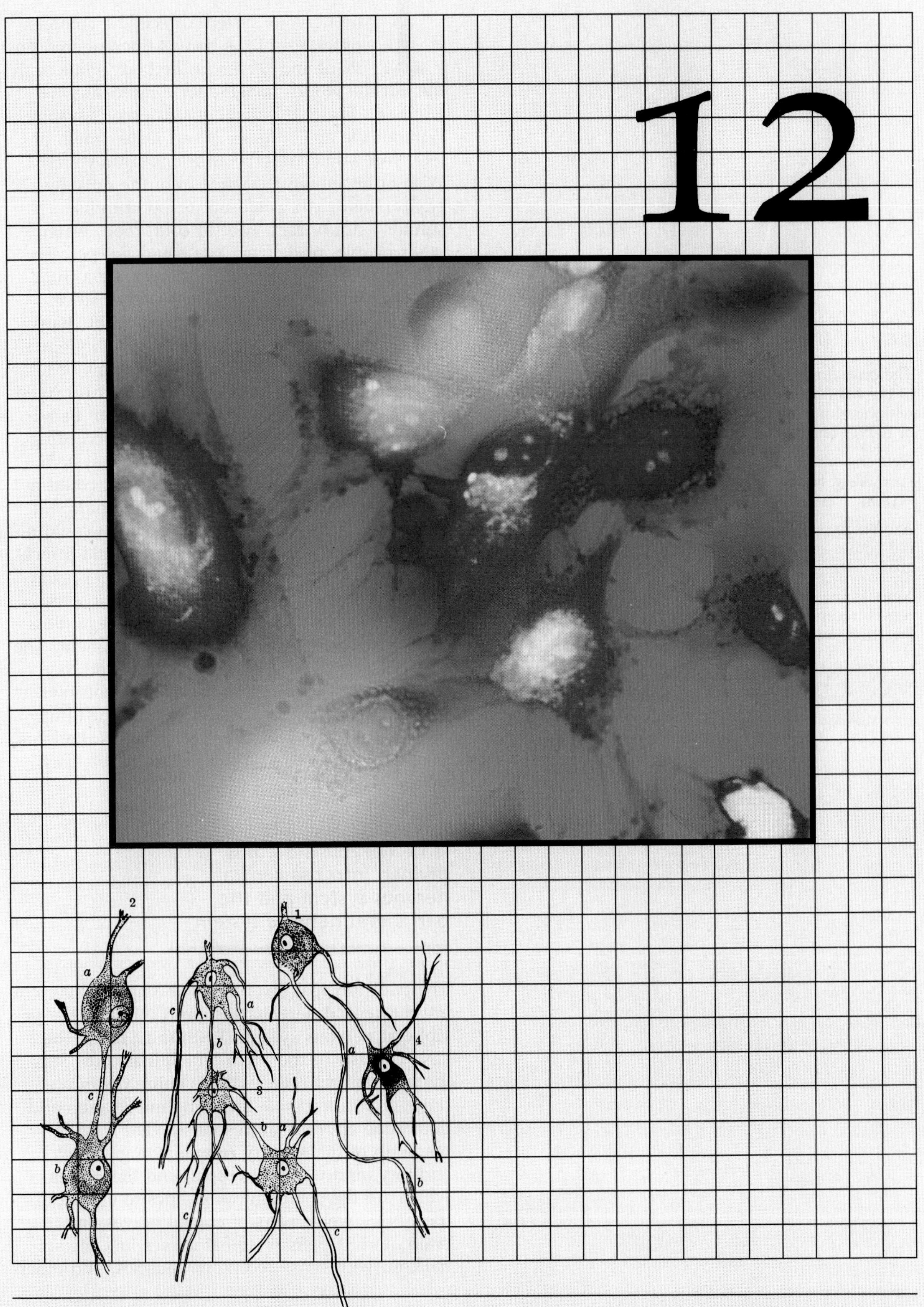

KEY CONCEPTS

The central nervous system consists of the brain and spinal cord; the peripheral nervous system consists of nerves and sensory receptors.

Neurons and glial cells perform specialized functions in the nervous system.

Axons are organized into nerves; cell bodies are organized into ganglia.

Neural function includes four processes: reception, transmission, integration, and response.

The nervous system directs the complex processes of the body's internal environment and serves as the body's link with the outside world. Imagine for a moment what it would be like to exist without a nervous system. Without the ability to see, hear, taste, smell, or feel, you would truly be an island unto yourself. With no incoming messages from the outside environment, you could not respond to its stimuli—sun or rain, heat or cold, food, water, other people, or danger. You could not perceive that you were about to be run down by a truck or that your hand was resting on a hot stove.

And what of the world within? What chaos would reign if each organ system acted independently without reference to other systems or to the body's overall needs! Body temperature could not be regulated, urine volume could not be adjusted, blood could not be distributed according to changing needs. Even the endocrine system, the body's second great control system, could not function properly. Groups of muscles could not contract in an orchestrated manner. You could no more think or express emotion than could a rock!

Fortunately, everyone has a nervous system that, together with the endocrine system, acts continuously to maintain homeostasis regardless of most changes in the external environment. The nervous system enables us to survive and to thrive. It is not surprising that the nervous system is by far the most complex both structurally and functionally of all the body systems. Perhaps for this reason it is also the system that is least understood.

The nervous system is divided into the central nervous system and the peripheral nervous system

The two principal divisions of the nervous system are the **central nervous system (CNS)** and the **peripheral nervous system (PNS)** (Fig. 12-1). The CNS consists of the **brain** and **spinal cord.** Serving as a control center for the entire organism, these organs integrate incoming information and determine appropriate responses. The PNS is made up of the **sensory receptors** (e.g., touch, auditory, and visual receptors) and the **nerves,** which are the communication lines to and from the CNS. Twelve pairs of cranial nerves link the brain, and 31 pairs of spinal nerves link the spinal cord with sense receptors, muscles, and other parts of the body. The peripheral nerves continually inform the CNS of changing conditions and then transmit its "decisions" to appropriate muscles and glands that bring about the adjustments needed to preserve homeostasis.

For convenience the PNS may be subdivided into somatic and autonomic divisions. Many receptors and nerves concerned with changes in the external environment are **somatic;** many that regulate the internal environment are **autonomic.**

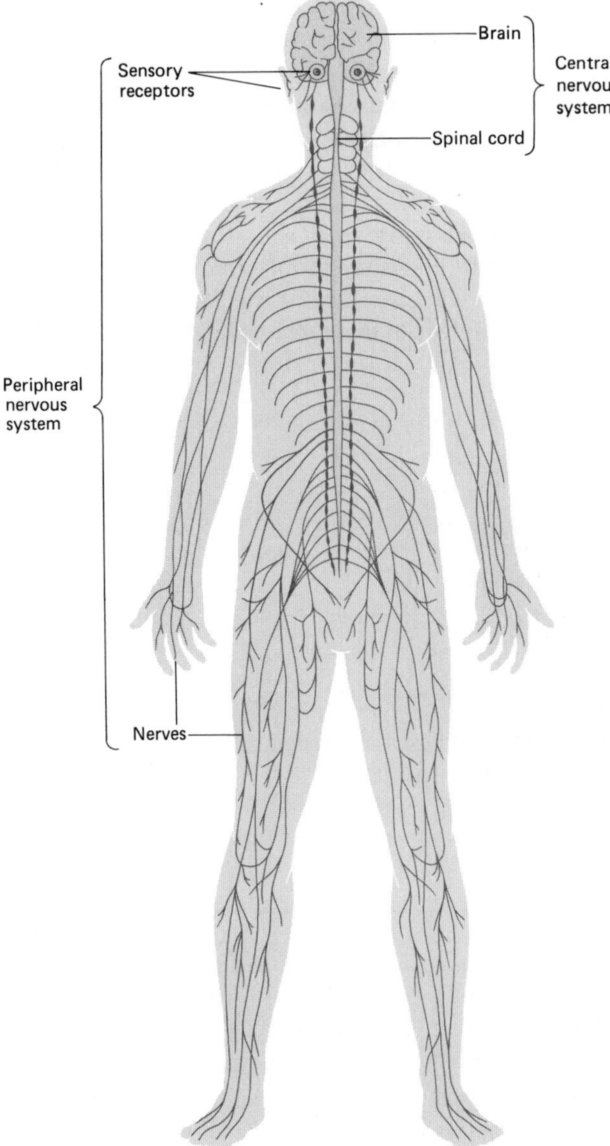

FIGURE 12-1

The nervous system has two main divisions, the central nervous system and the peripheral nervous system. The central nervous system consists of the brain and spinal cord. The peripheral nervous system consists of the sensory receptors and the nerves that link the central nervous system with all the parts of the body.

Both systems have **afferent nerves (sensory)** that transmit messages from receptors to the CNS, and **efferent nerves (motor)** that transmit information back from the CNS to the structures that must respond.[1]

In the autonomic system there are two kinds of efferent nerves—sympathetic and parasympathetic nerves (see Table 12-1). In general, the **sympathetic nerves** operate to stimulate organs and to mobilize energy, especially in response to stress. The **parasympathetic nerves** influence organs to conserve and restore energy, particularly when one is engaged in quiet, calm activities such as studying anatomy and physiology. Many organs are innervated by both types of nerves, which act upon the organ in an antagonistic way. For example, the heart rate is slowed by impulses from its parasympathetic nerves and quickened by messages from its sympathetic nerves.

Neurons and glial cells are specialized cells of nervous tissue

Cell types unique to the nervous tissue are **neurons** and **glial cells.** Neurons are specialized to receive and transmit information; glial cells provide structural support for the neurons.

Glial cells support and protect the neurons

In other tissues, for example, bone, the functional cells are supported by connective tissue and the tough intercellular substances are secreted by connective tissue cells. Within the nervous system, support and protection are provided by specialized cells called **glial cells** (Fig. 12-2). Collectively, these cells are referred to as the **neuroglia** (literally, nerve glue) because they seem to "glue" the neurons together. Unlike many types of connective tissue cells, glial cells do not secrete a tough matrix, so the tissue of the CNS is firm, but soft.

Clinical highlight

From a clinical standpoint these cells are of great interest because they give rise to most of the tumors that develop in the CNS. Glial cells are believed to be responsible for 40 to 45% of intracranial tumors.

[1] In the classification used here, afferent pathways are included as part of the autonomic system.

There are about ten times as many glial cells as neurons in the body. The following types of glial cells have been identified within the CNS:

1. **Oligodendrocytes.** The oligodendrocytes (*ol*-ih-go-**den**-drow-sites) wrap their plasma membranes around neurons, forming sheaths about them. These sheaths, composed of a fatty material called **myelin** (**my**-eh-lin), will be described shortly.

2. **Astrocytes.** The cytoplasm of an astrocyte extends into numerous elongated processes, giving the cell a star-shaped appearance. Some astrocyte processes are in direct contact with capillaries, and in fact, the capillaries within the CNS are almost completely surrounded by astrocyte processes. In this way, astrocytes help form the blood-brain barrier, which prevents or slows the entrance of unwanted substances from the blood into brain tissue. The role of astrocytes in providing structural support is well established. These cells also help seal off damaged tissue and form scar tissue following injury.

3. **Ependymal cells.** Ependymal (eh-**pen**-dih-mal) cells line the cavities (ventricles) of the brain and the central canal of the spinal cord.

4. **Microglia.** Sometimes called brain macrophages, microglia (mi-**krog**-lee-ah) are small cells scattered throughout the tissue of the brain and spinal cord. Microglia become active in response to inflammation or injury. At such times they become mobile and protect the nervous system by phagocytizing invading microorganisms and cleaning up cellular debris.

Schwann cells are found in nervous tissue outside of the CNS. Sometimes classified as glial cells, these cells wrap neurons of the PNS in myelin sheaths and form cellular sheaths around them.

Neurons are highly specialized to receive and transmit information

The neuron is the structural and functional unit of the nervous system. It is distinguished from all other cells by its long cytoplasmic extensions. Let us examine the structure of the most common variety, a **multipolar neuron** (Fig. 12-3). The

TABLE 12-1

Divisions of the nervous system		
Central nervous system (CNS)		
Brain	*Spinal cord*	
Peripheral nervous system (PNS)		
Somatic system	*Autonomic system*	
(1) Receptors		
(2) Afferent nerves		
Transmit (sensory) information from receptors to CNS	Transmit information from receptors in organs to CNS	
(3) Efferent nerves		
Transmit (motor) information from CNS to skeletal muscles	Transmit information from CNS to glands and involuntary muscles in organs	
	Sympathetic nerves	*Parasympathetic nerves*
	Generally stimulate activity that results in mobilization of energy (e.g., speed heartbeat)	Stimulate activity that results in energy conservation or restoration (e.g., slow heartbeat)

multipolar neuron consists of a prominent cell body that has numerous cytoplasmic extensions called *dendrites* at one end and a single, long cytoplasmic extension, the *axon,* at its opposite end.

THE CELL BODY CONTAINS THE NUCLEUS

Although the **cell body** (also called **soma,** or **perikaryon**) contains less than one-tenth of the cell's total volume, it houses the nucleus and many other organelles including mitochondria, Golgi complexes, and lysosomes. Most of the materials needed by the neuron are synthesized in the cell body. A characteristic feature of the cell body is the presence of **Nissl substance** (chromatophilic substance), which consists of deeply staining regions, clumps of rough endoplasmic reticulum, and free ribosomes. Nissl substance functions in protein synthesis.

Microtubules, microfilaments, and neurofilaments, the main components of the neuron cytoskeleton, are distributed throughout the cytoplasm. This cytoskeleton helps maintain the shape of the neuron, and also helps transport materials and organelles down the axon. Microtubules are oriented along the length of the axon. They are thought to form tracks along which organelles are transported.

Microfilaments, like the thin filaments of muscle cells, are composed of actin. These filaments are found just under the plasma membrane and are anchored to the membrane by proteins, principally a protein called *fodrin.* Microfilaments continuously form and dissociate.

Neurofilaments, similar to intermediate filaments found in other cell types, are the main support system of the neuron. Bundles of neuro-

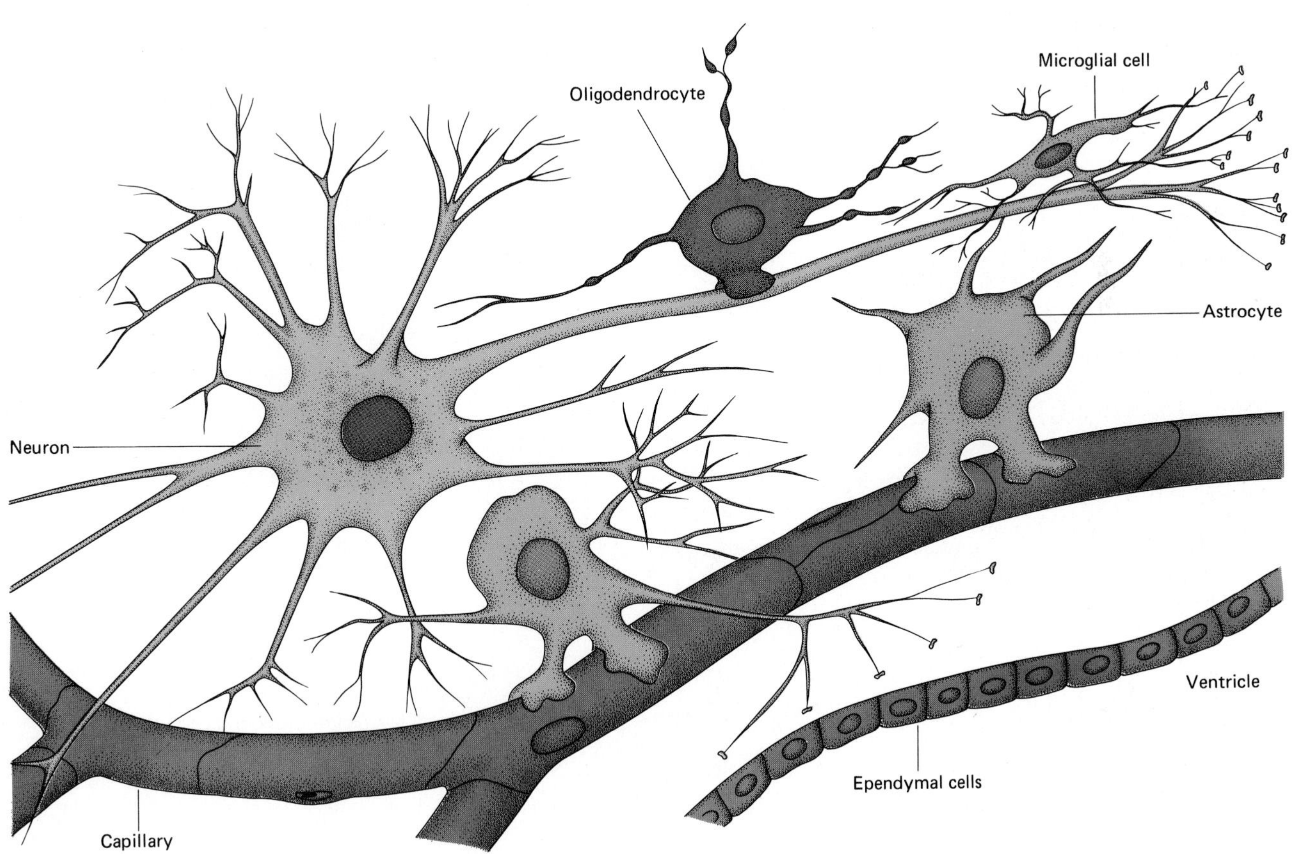

FIGURE 12-2

Glial cells. Oligodendrocytes form sheaths around neurons in the CNS. Two astrocytes are shown extending their processes to the surface of a capillary. Microglial cells phagocytize invading microorganisms and clean up cellular debris. Ependymal cells line the cavities of the brain and spinal cord.

filaments, called *neurofibrils,* are visible with the light microscope when nervous tissue is prepared using silver impregnation methods. In Alzheimer's disease and certain other degenerative brain diseases, the neurofilaments form lesions known as neurofibrillary tangles.

DENDRITES TRANSMIT IMPULSES TOWARD THE CELL BODY

Dendrites are highly branched extensions of the cytoplasm that project from the cell body. Dendrites are specialized to receive neural impulses and conduct them toward the cell body. Their surfaces are dotted with thousands of tiny **dendritic spines** where they form junctions with other neurons. The cytoplasm within the dendrites contains the same types of organelles found in the cell body.

THE AXON TRANSMITS IMPULSES AWAY FROM THE CELL BODY

The **axon** arises from a thickened area of the cell body, the **axon hillock.** It transmits neural messages from the cell body toward another neuron or toward a muscle or gland. The axon contains mitochondria and neurofilaments, but the absence of Nissl bodies renders the axon incapable of protein synthesis. The **axoplasm** (its cytoplasm) is enveloped by a plasma membrane known as the **axolemma.**

Although microscopic in diameter, an axon may extend several feet in length. For example, neurons that exit from the lower portion of the spinal cord and innervate the foot may be almost a meter (more than 3 ft) long in a tall person. Probably because it is so long, an axon is often referred to as a **nerve fiber.** Perhaps the relative dimensions of neuron parts can be better appreci-

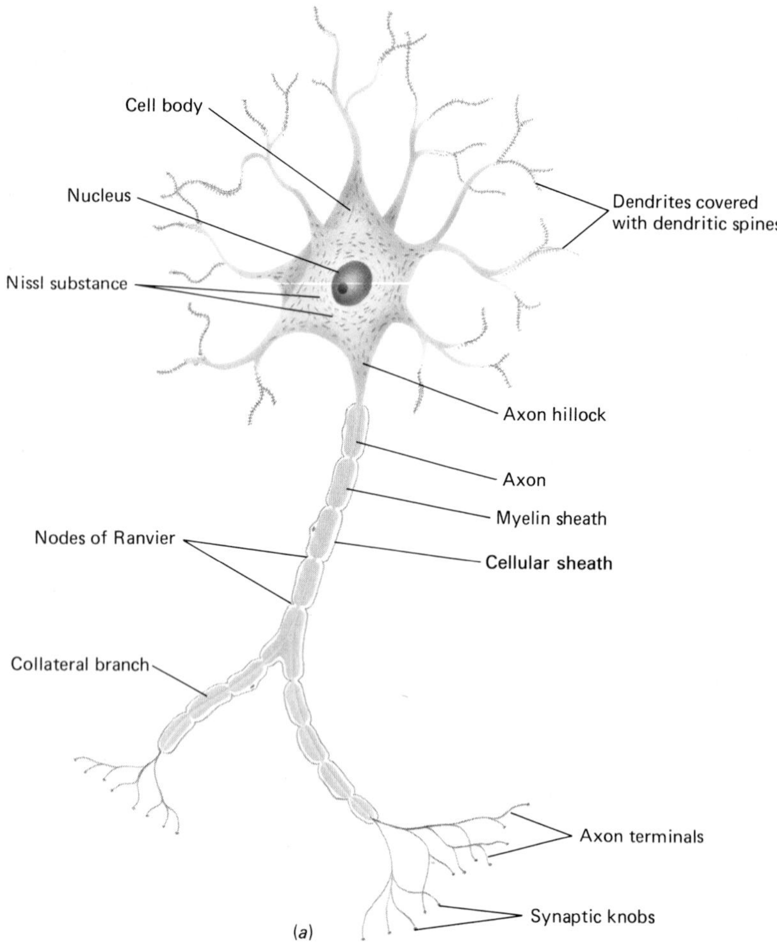

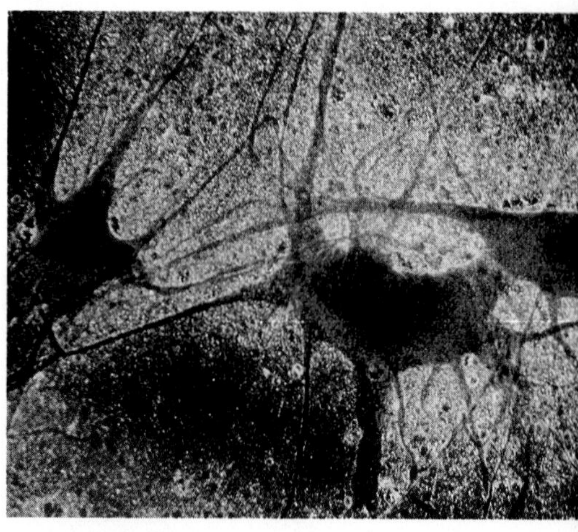

(*b*)

FIGURE 12-3

Structure of a multipolar neuron. (*a*) The multipolar neuron consists of a cell body, dendrites, and an axon. The axon of this neuron is myelinated; the myelin sheath is shown, as well as the cellular sheath. Cellular sheaths are found only around axons of peripheral neurons. (*b*) Photomicrograph of nervous tissue showing two multipolar neurons. (VU/CBS © Visuals Unlimited.)

ated with the following analogy. If the cell body were the size of a tennis ball, its axon might extend up to 1.6 kilometers (1 mi) in length but measure only 1.3 centimeters (0.5 in.) in diameter; its dendrites would branch to fill a large living room.

Along its course an axon can give off branches known as **collaterals.** At its distal end the axon divides extensively into thousands of thin branches called **axon terminals** (or telodendria). These branches are studded with tiny enlargements called **synaptic knobs** (or terminal buttons). Synaptic knobs release chemical compounds called **neurotransmitters** that transmit impulses from one neuron to another.

Proteins and organelles are synthesized in the cell body and must be transported down the axon. These materials are used for maintenance and growth of the neuron and for regeneration of peripheral nerve fibers. Two mechanisms are responsible for intracellular transport, **axoplasmic flow** and **axonal transport.**

Axoplasmic flow slowly transports new axoplasm and proteins from the cell body toward the synaptic knobs at a speed of about 1 millimeter (0.04 in.) per day. The new axoplasm travels by protoplasmic streaming and is used for regenerating axons and renewing axoplasm where needed.

Axonal transport, faster than axoplasmic flow, transports materials at a rate of about 400 millimeters per day. Axonal transport can be either away from the cell body or toward it. This type of transport is thought to involve microtubules that form stationary tracks along which organelles are moved. This movement requires ATP and calcium. The materials transported include membranous organelles and substances that form the axolemma and the synaptic knobs. Used organelles are transported back to the cell body where they are recycled or broken down. Growth factors, taken up at the axon terminal, are transported back to the cell body where they stimulate protein synthesis.

Axons of many neurons of the PNS are covered by two sheaths—an inner **myelin sheath** and an outer **cellular sheath,** or **neurilemma.** Both sheaths are produced by Schwann cells.

The myelin sheath provides insulation

Myelin is a white, lipid-rich substance that makes up the plasma membrane of the Schwann cell. This fatty material is an excellent electrical insulator that speeds the conduction of nerve impulses. To produce the myelin sheath, the Schwann cell winds its plasma membrane about the axon several times (Figs. 12-4 and 12-5). Between successive Schwann cells, gaps called **nodes of Ranvier** occur in the myelin sheath. At these points, which are from 50 to 1500 micrometers (μm) apart, the axon is not insulated with myelin.

Almost all axons more than 2 micrometers in diameter are myelinated—that is, they possess myelin sheaths. Those of smaller diameter are generally unmyelinated. In the CNS, myelin sheaths are formed by oligodendrocytes rather than by Schwann cells. Myelin is responsible for

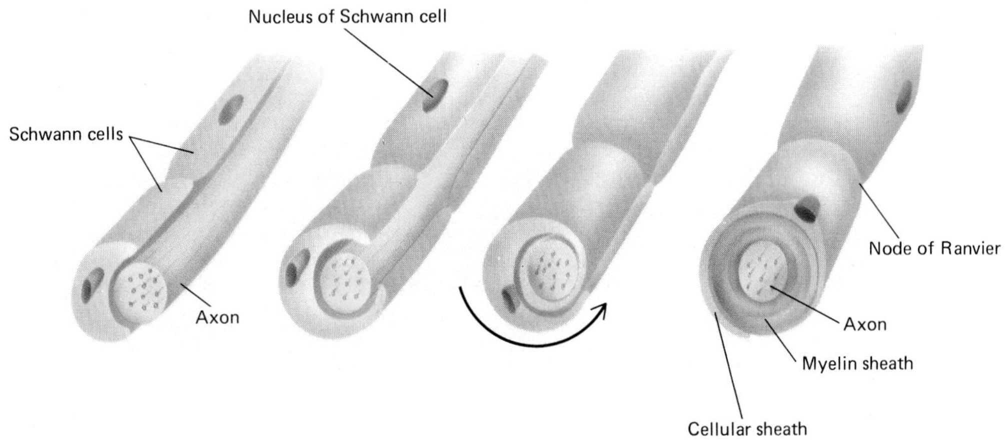

FIGURE 12-4

Formation of the myelin sheath around the axon of a peripheral neuron. A Schwann cell wraps its cell membrane around the axon many times to form the insulating myelin sheath. The rest of the Schwann cell remains outside the myelin sheath, forming the cellular sheath.

the white color of the *white matter* of the brain and spinal cord and of myelinated peripheral nerves.

Clinical highlight

Multiple sclerosis (MS) is a neurological disease that affects some 300,000 persons in the United States alone. In this disease patches of myelin deteriorate at irregular intervals along neurons in the CNS. The myelin and oligodendrocytes are replaced by astrocytes, which form a hard matrix around the neurons. As the affected axons lose their myelin sheaths, conduction of impulses is slowed. Victims of this disease suffer from symptoms of impaired neural function including loss of coordination, difficulty in seeing, tremor, and partial or complete paralysis of parts of the body. The cause of multiple sclerosis remains a medical mystery, but there is some evidence that a measles-like virus may be responsible in genetically susceptible individuals. Macrophages and white blood cells invade the CNS, and as they destroy the virus they may also destroy the myelin sheaths. Another hypothesis is that the MS patient produces antibodies that destroy myelin.

The myelin sheath is destroyed as a result of some other diseases (e.g., Guillain-Barré syndrome) and upon exposure to certain toxic substances. The germicide hexachlorophene was used in many hospitals and as an ingredient in some widely marketed deodorant soaps until it was shown that hexachlorophene can pass through the skin and make its way through the circulation to the brain, where it destroys myelin. Exposure to lead or organic tin compounds can cause permanent defects in myelinization of neurons in children.

The cellular sheath guides regenerating axons

Cellular sheaths (neurilemmas) are found only around peripheral nerve cells. They are formed from the bulk of the Schwann cells that remain along the axon outside the myelin sheath. The cellular sheath is important in the regeneration of injured neurons. When neurons are severed, the part of the axon distal to the cut is separated from its cell body, the source of needed materials. As a result, it degenerates. However, its Schwann cells remain and proliferate by mitosis, filling the gap between the cut ends (Fig. 12-6). After several weeks tiny sprouts emerge from the cut end of the axon and enter the empty cord of Schwann cells. This cellular sheath acts as a tunnel, guiding the growth of the new axon sprouts. Growth is slow, about 4 millimeters (0.2 in.) per day at best. Eventually, though, the growing tip does reach the muscle (or other appropriate structure) and functional contact is made. Extra axon sprouts that may have entered the cellular sheath eventually degenerate. Should the axon sprout grow through a neighboring cellular sheath that ends in the wrong place, the sprout usually degenerates.

For many years it was thought that regeneration could not occur in the CNS because neurons there lack cellular sheaths. Now it is known that neurons in the CNS do attempt to regenerate but

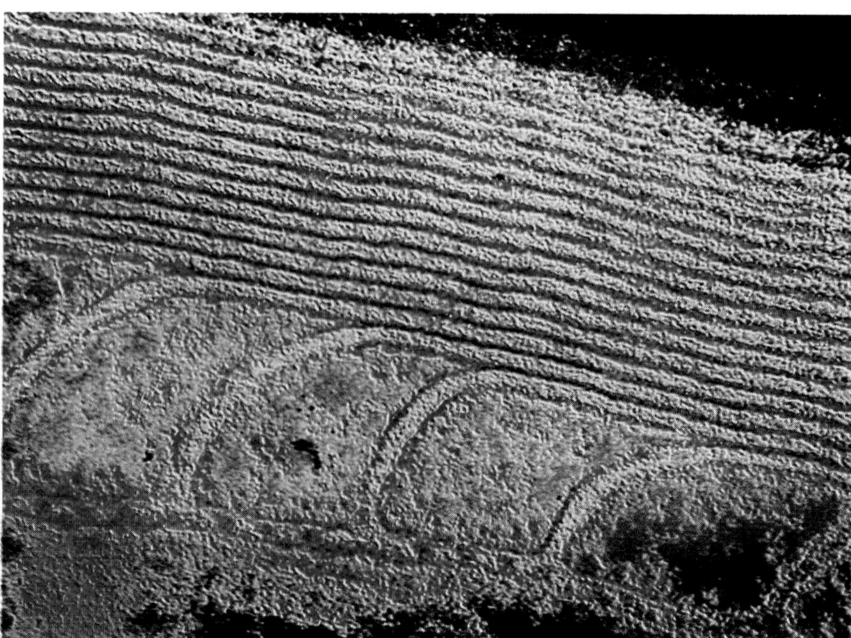

FIGURE 12-5

False-color transmission electron micrograph showing the myelin sheath surrounding the human auditory nerve. In longitudinal section, concentric layers of the myelin sheath appear as orange bands at top of image (approximately ×88,000). (Photo Researchers, Inc.)

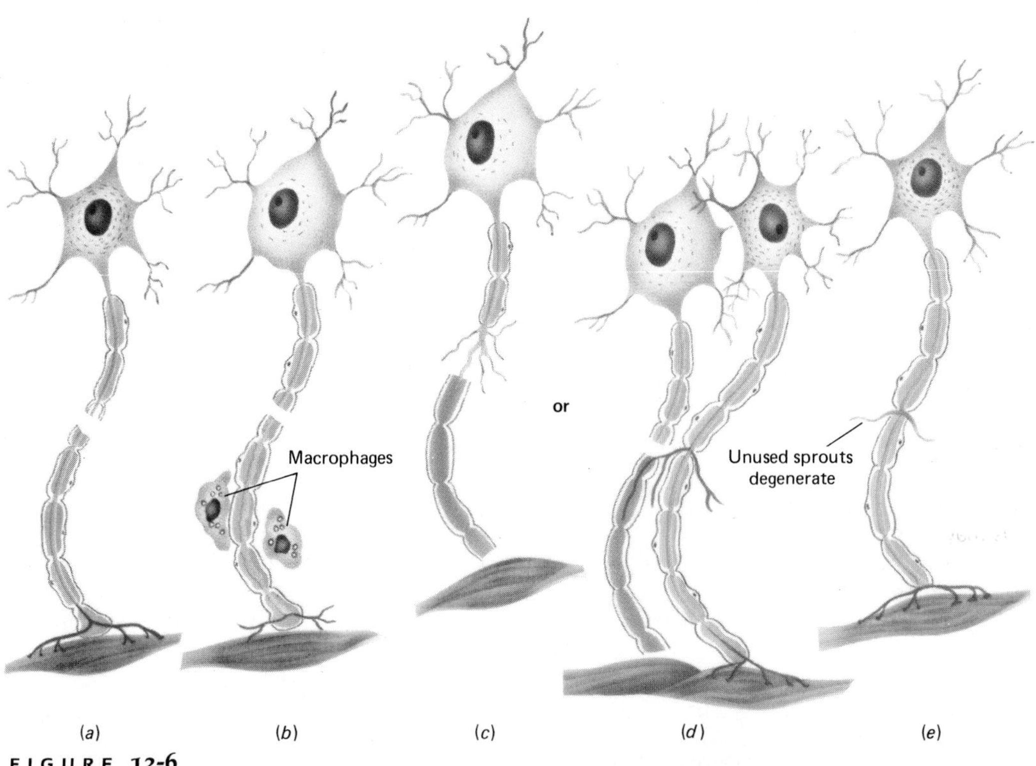

FIGURE 12-6

Regeneration of an injured neuron. (*a*) Neuron is severed. (*b*) Now separated from its nucleus, the part of the axon distal to the injury degenerates. Its myelin sheath also degenerates, and macrophages phagocytize the debris. The cell body enlarges and the Nissl substance breaks down, a sign of increased protein synthesis. (*c*) The tip of the severed axon begins to sprout, and one or more sprouts may find their way into the distal cellular sheath, which has remained intact. The sprout grows slowly and becomes myelinated. (*d*) Sometimes an adjacent undamaged neuron may send a collateral sprout into the cellular sheath of the damaged neuron. (*e*) Eventually the neuron may regenerate completely, so that function is restored. Unused sprouts degenerate.

their growth is prevented by scar tissue formed at the site of injury by glial cells.

Nerve regeneration also occurs when collateral branches of uninjured adjacent axons sprout and enter a cord of Schwann cells. This type of regeneration apparently occurs in both the PNS and CNS. Since mature neurons are ordinarily not capable of mitosis, cell bodies must be intact in order for regeneration to take place.

NEURONS MAY BE CLASSIFIED BY STRUCTURE OR FUNCTION

The neuron just described is a **multipolar neuron,** one that has many short dendrites and a single long axon. Motor neurons and also many of the neurons within the CNS are of this type. Some neurons, called **bipolar** neurons, have only one dendrite and one axon (Fig. 12-7). These are found in the retina of the eye, in the inner ear, and in olfactory nerves. Still other neurons are **unipolar,** with only a single fiber that functions as both axon and dendrite. Unipolar neurons begin as bipolar neurons in the embryo, but during development the axon and dendrite fuse into one process. Most sensory neurons are unipolar. The distal portion of the fiber that extends from the sensory receptor to the cell body may be considered a dendrite because it conducts information to the cell body. However, because of its length and because it conducts information like an axon, some anatomists prefer to call it an axon. The proximal portion of the fiber that conducts information from the cell body to the CNS is an axon.

Neurons are also classified according to function. Already mentioned are afferent (sensory) neurons that transmit information from receptors to the CNS, and efferent (motor) neurons that relay messages from the CNS to the muscles and

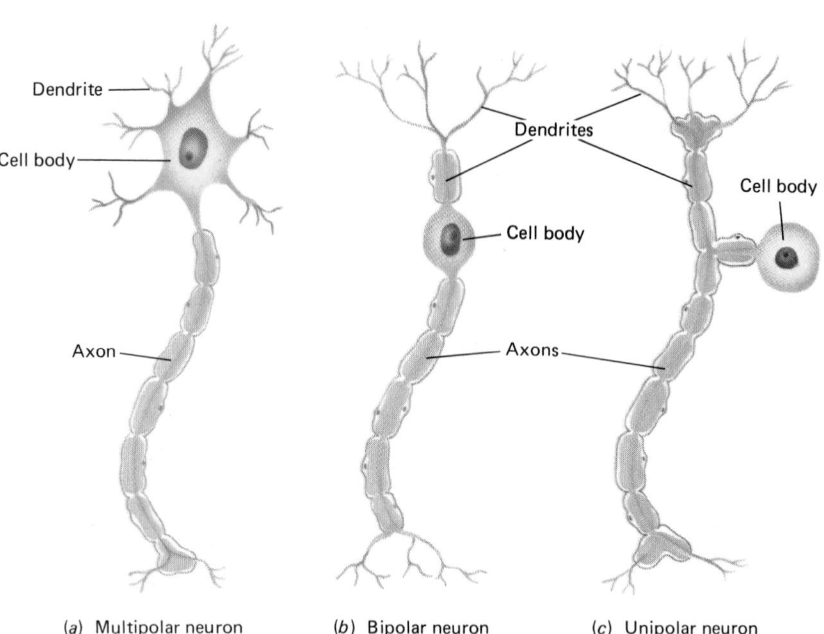

FIGURE 12-7

Types of neurons classified according to the number of processes. (*a*) A multipolar neuron. This type of neuron has many short dendrites and one long axon. Motor neurons are of this type. (*b*) A bipolar neuron. A bipolar neuron has one axon and one dendrite. This type of neuron is found in the retina of the eye, in the olfactory nerve, and in the nerves coming from the inner ear. (*c*) A unipolar neuron has a short process that divides into two long processes. The distal process may be called either a dendrite or an axon. Because it functions like a dendrite we refer to it as a dendrite. Sensory neurons are unipolar.

glands that carry out the response. Linking sensory and motor neurons are a third group of neurons, the **association neurons,** or **interneurons,** which lie within the CNS. Association neurons receive information from sensory neurons and send neural messages to the effectors via appropriate motor neurons.

Nerves are bundles of axons and ganglia are groups of cell bodies

A **nerve** usually consists of several bundles of axons called **fascicles** (**fas**-ih-kuls) (Fig. 12-8). Each individual axon is surrounded by its own connective tissue sheath, the **endoneurium** (*en*-doe-**nyoo**-ree-um) and in turn each fascicle is wrapped in its own sheath called a **perineurium** (*per*-ih-**nyoo**-ree-um). Fibrous connective tissue, the **epineurium** (*ep*-ih-**nyoo**-ree-um), surrounds the nerve and holds the fascicles together. A nerve may be compared to a telephone cable. The axons are like the individual wires, and the myelin, cellular, and connective tissue sheaths are like the insulation.

Since nerves consist of bundles of axons, you might wonder where the cell bodies attached to those axons are located. These are generally grouped together in a mass known as a **ganglion.** Many ganglia are located just outside the spinal cord. Within the CNS, the terminology is somewhat different. Collections of cell bodies are generally referred to as **nuclei,** or **centers,** rather than ganglia, and bundles of axons are known as **tracts** instead of nerves.

Neural function includes reception, transmission, integration, and response

Imagine that you are driving down the street and the traffic light on the corner ahead turns red. Automatically you step on the brake and bring your vehicle to a smooth stop. Each day you make hundreds of such responses without even thinking about them. What steps are involved in even so simple a response?

First, you must receive the information that the traffic light has turned red, a process called **reception** (Fig. 12-9). In this example the information that the light is red is received by visual receptors in the eyes. But it is not enough just to see red. This information must be delivered by sensory neurons to the CNS, the process of **transmission,** or conduction. In the CNS the information provided by the sensory neurons is interpreted as a "red light" and an appropriate response is determined; this process is known as **integration.** Appropriate motor neurons transmit

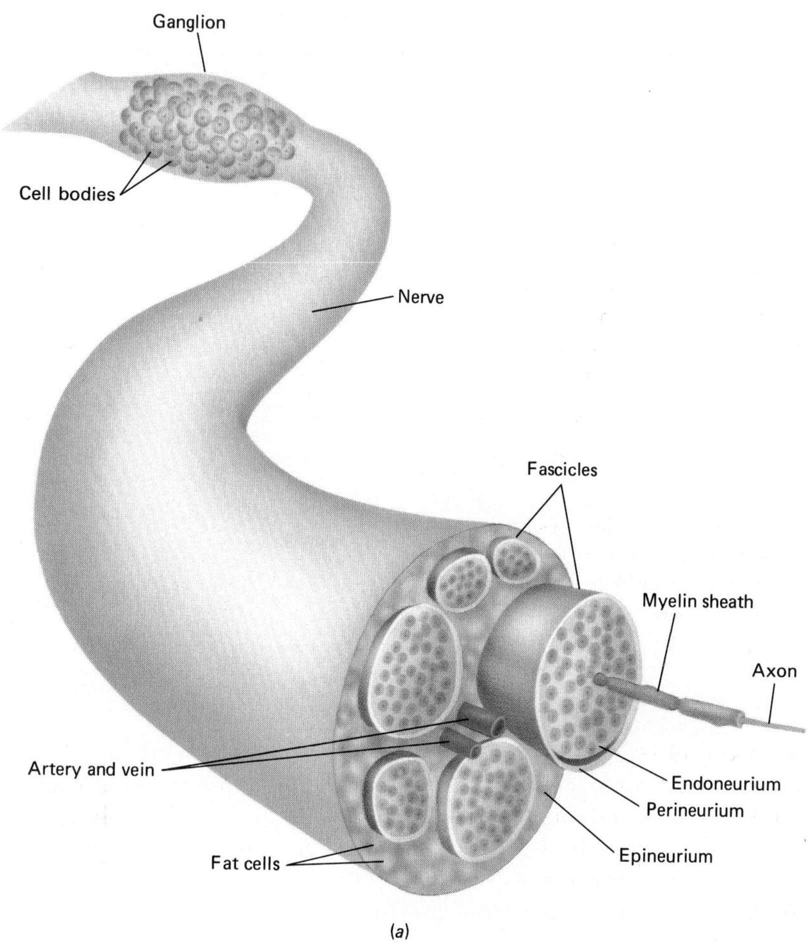

(b)

FIGURE 12-8

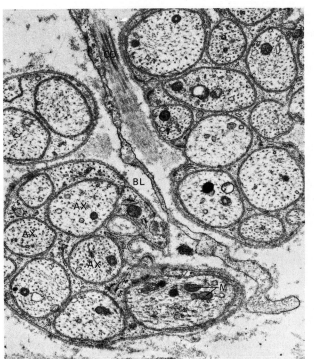

(*a*) Structure of a nerve and a ganglion. A nerve consists of bundles of axons held together by connective tissue. The cell bodies belonging to these axons are grouped together in a ganglion. (*b*) Electron micrograph showing cross section through a portion of the sciatic nerve. The axons shown here are unmyelinated (approximately ×30,000). AX, axon; M, mitochondria; CO, collagen fibers; BL, basal lamina. (Courtesy of Dr. Lyle C. Dearden)

the message to the selected muscles, directing them to lift the foot from the gas pedal and press down on the brake, the actual **response,** or **effect.** Muscles and glands are the body's chief **effectors.** Every neural response depends upon these four processes: reception, transmission, integration, and actual response.

From the example just given, it should be clear that neural messages travel over sequences of neurons. Sensory neurons transmitted the information from the visual receptors to association neurons within the CNS. Then a message was relayed to appropriate motor neurons, which transmitted it to the muscles involved in effecting the response. The neurons of the nervous system are organized into millions of such sequences, called **neural circuits.** Neurons are arranged so that the axon of one neuron in the circuit forms

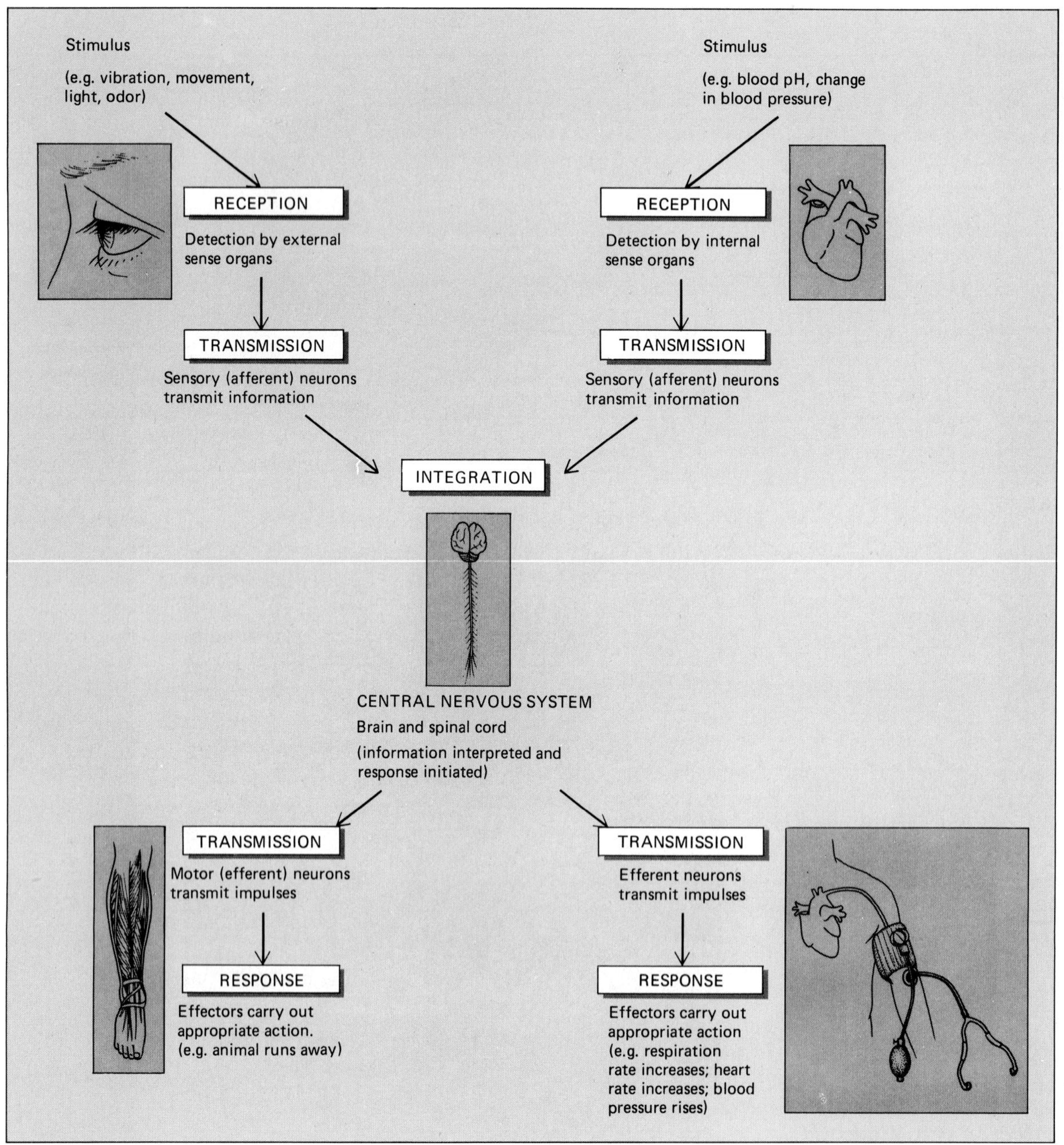

FIGURE 12-9

Flow of information through the nervous system.

junctions with the dendrites and cell bodies of the next neuron in the circuit. A junction between two neurons or between a neuron and an effector is called a **synapse** (**sin**-aps).

The simplest example of a neural response in human beings is the **reflex action,** a predictable, automatic response to a specific stimulus. Most of the internal mechanisms of the body are regulated by reflex actions. For example, a change in body temperature acts as a stimulus, causing the temperature-regulating center of the brain stem to mobilize homeostatic mechanisms that act to bring body temperature back to normal. Reflex action will be discussed in Chapter 13.

Stimuli are received and converted into neural impulses during reception

The most familiar receptors are the complex sense organs in the head—eyes, ears, nose (olfactory epithelium), and taste buds. In addition, thousands of tiny sensory receptors in the skin enable you to feel pressure, light touch, warmth, cold, and pain. Less familiar are the receptors located in muscles and tendons, the **muscle spindles** and **Golgi tendon organs,** which are sensitive to changes in muscle length and tension. Their continuous reports to the CNS are responsible for maintaining muscle tone and for ensuring that movements will be smooth and coordinated. Still other types of receptors located deep within the body keep the brain apprised of changes in the internal environment.

Receptors are specialized to react to specific changes in their environment. They convert various forms of energy (e.g., sound or light) into neural impulses. Normally each type of receptor reacts to only one kind of stimulus. Receptors in the eye are not stimulated by sound waves, nor are touch receptors in the skin sensitive to light. Once stimulated, though, each type of receptor sends the same neural message. The CNS "reads" what the message says by "knowing" which neuron delivered it and to which specific point in the CNS it is delivered. For example, if an electrical stimulus is applied to a neuron that normally transmits messages telling the brain that a cold receptor has been stimulated, the person will perceive the feeling of cold in the area served by that neuron. Sense receptors are discussed in greater detail in Chapter 17.

Transmission is the journey of the message through the nervous system

Once a receptor has been stimulated, the message must be transmitted to the CNS and then back to appropriate effectors. Information must be conducted through a sequence of neurons. How is a neural message transmitted along an individual neuron? And how is it conducted from one neuron to the next in the sequence?

TRANSMISSION OCCURS ALONG NEURONS

Once a neuron has been stimulated sufficiently, it transmits a neural impulse along the entire length of its axon. This transmission is an electrochemical process that depends upon changes in ion distribution.

The resting potential is the difference in electric charge across the plasma membrane

In a **resting neuron,** one that is not transmitting an impulse, the inner surface of the plasma membrane is negatively charged compared with the interstitial fluid surrounding it (Fig. 12-10). The resting neuron is said to be *electrically polarized;* that is, the inside of the membrane and the extracellular fluid outside are oppositely charged. When electrical charges are separated in this way, they have the potential of doing work should they be permitted to come together. The difference in potential between the two sides of the membrane is referred to as the **resting potential,** or simply, the **membrane potential.** The resting potential may be thought of as an imbalance in electric charge across the plasma membrane.

The resting potential may be expressed in units called millivolts. (A millivolt equals one-thousandth of a volt and is a unit for measuring electrical potential.) The resting potential of a neuron amounts to about 70 millivolts (mV). By convention this is expressed as -70 millivolts because the inner surface of the plasma membrane is negatively charged relative to the interstitial fluid. The potential can be measured by placing one electrode, insulated except at the tip, inside the cell and a second electrode on the outside surface. The two electrodes are connected with an

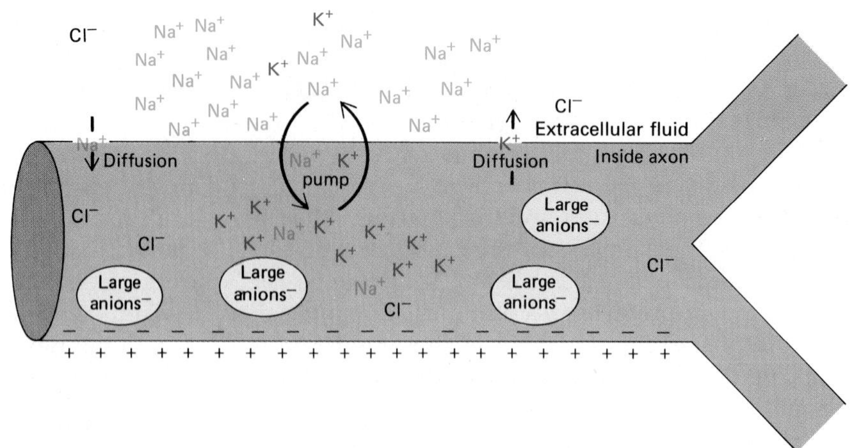

FIGURE 12-10

Segment of an axon of a resting (nonconducting) neuron. Sodium-potassium pumps in the cell membrane actively pump sodium out of the cell and potassium in. Sodium is unable to diffuse back to any extent, but potassium does diffuse out along its concentration gradient. Negatively charged proteins and other large anions are present in the cell. Because of the unequal distribution of ions, the inside of the axon is negatively charged compared with the extracellular fluid.

instrument such as a galvanometer, which measures current by electromagnetic action (Fig. 12-11). If both electrodes are placed on the outside surface of the neuron, no potential difference between them is registered; all points on the outside of the membrane are at the same potential. The neuron can be thought of as a biological battery. If its plasma membrane, which is only about one-millionth of a centimeter thick, were 1 centimeter thick, the membrane potential would amount to an impressive 70,000 volts!

How does the resting potential develop? It is a direct result of a slight excess of positive ions outside the plasma membrane and a slight excess of negative ions inside the membrane. The distribution of ions inside neurons and in the extracellular fluid surrounding them is similar to that of most other cells in the body. The K^+ concentration is about 30 times greater inside a resting neuron than outside the cell. The Na^+ concentration is about 14 times greater outside than inside the neuron.

This ionic imbalance is brought about by several factors. The neuron plasma membrane has very efficient sodium-potassium pumps that actively transport sodium out of the cell and potassium ions into the cell. Because the pumps work against a concentration gradient and an electrochemical gradient, ATP is required. For every three sodium ions pumped out of the cell, two potassium ions are pumped into the cell. Thus more positive ions are pumped out than in. A pump that transports unequal quantities of ions that affect the membrane potential is referred to as **electrogenic.**

Ions also cross the membrane by diffusing through membrane proteins that form ion-specific channels. Ions move through them from an area of higher to an area of lower concentration (Fig. 12-12). However, the ease with which an ion passes through an ion channel varies for each type of ion. Sodium ions move through sodium channels much less easily than potassium ions pass through potassium channels. In fact, in the resting neuron the membrane is up to 100 times more permeable to potassium than to sodium. Consequently, sodium ions pumped out of the neuron cannot easily pass back into the cell, but potassium ions pumped into the neuron are able to diffuse out.

Potassium ions leak out through the membrane along their concentration gradient until the positive charge outside the membrane reaches a level that repels the outflow of more positively charged potassium ions. A steady state is reached when the potassium outflow equals the inward flow of sodium ions. At this point a potential difference of about −70 millivolts has developed across the membrane, establishing the resting potential.

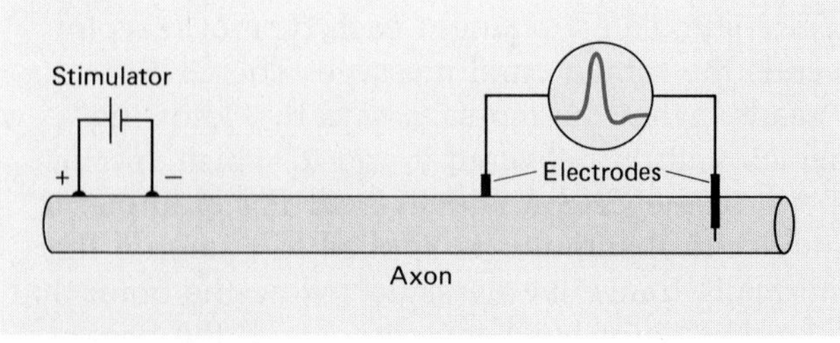

FIGURE 12-11

The electrical potential across the membrane can be measured by placing one electrode inside the axon and another on the outside surface. The electrodes are connected with a galvanometer. The change in potential that occurs as a neural impulse is transmitted is shown.

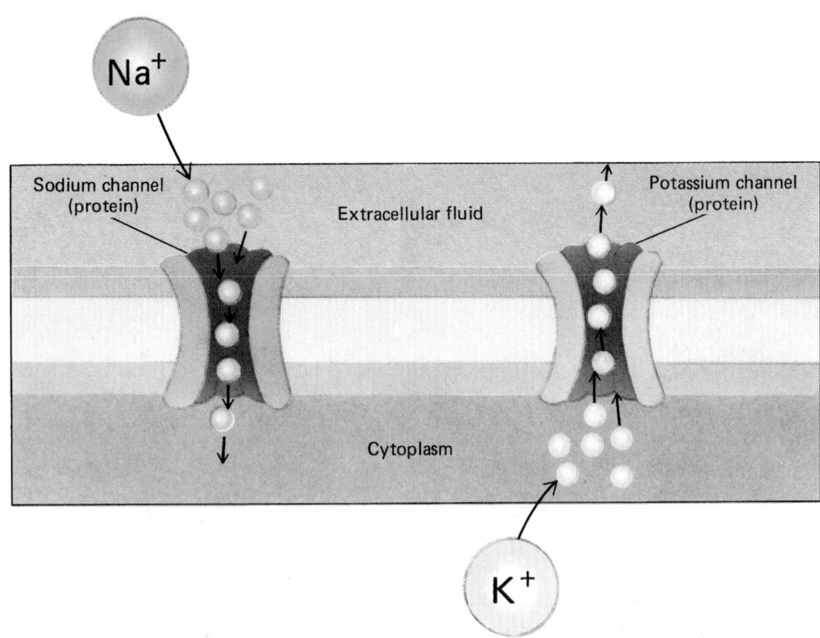

FIGURE 12-12

Proteins in the plasma membrane form ion-specific channels. Ions move through these channels down their concentration gradient from a region of higher to a region of lower concentration.

Contributing to the overall ionic situation are large numbers of negatively charged proteins and organic phosphates within the neuron that are too large to diffuse out. Some of the potassium ions within the cell help to neutralize these negative charges, but there are not enough potassium ions to neutralize them all. The plasma membrane is permeable to negatively charged chloride ions, but because of the positively charged ions that accumulate outside the membrane, chloride ions are attracted to the outside and tend to accumulate there.

The resting potential is due mainly to the presence of large protein anions inside the cell and to the outward diffusion of potassium ions along their concentration gradient. However, the conditions for this diffusion must first be set by the action of the sodium-potassium pumps. It is important to understand that the active transport of ions by these pumps is a form of cellular work and therefore requires energy.

The nerve impulse is an action potential

Neurons are highly excitable cells. They have the ability to respond to stimuli and to convert stimuli into neural impulses. An electrical, chemical, or mechanical stimulus may alter the resting potential by increasing the permeability of the membrane to sodium. If the neuron membrane is only slightly stimulated, only a local disturbance may occur in the membrane. However, if the stimulus is sufficiently strong, it may result in an **action potential**—that is, the propagation of a **neural impulse.**

In addition to the sodium-potassium pumps and passive ion channels already discussed, the plasma membrane of the axon and cell body contains specific **voltage-activated ion channels.** These channels are sensitive to voltage across the membrane (Fig. 12-13). When the voltage reaches a certain critical point, the **threshold level,** gates open, allowing the passage of specific ions through these channels.

The membrane of the neuron can **depolarize** up to about 15 millivolts, that is, to a resting potential of about −55 mV, without actually initiating an impulse. However, when the extent of depolarization is greater than −55 millivolts, the threshold level is reached. At that point the voltage-activated sodium ion channels open and Na^+ flows into the cell. Sodium ions pass into the cell until a second set of gates closes the channels. These inactivating gates close after a certain amount of time; they are dependent on time rather than voltage.

When the threshold level is reached, K^+-sensitive channels also open. These channels open more slowly and stay open until they sense a particular voltage, that of the membrane potential.

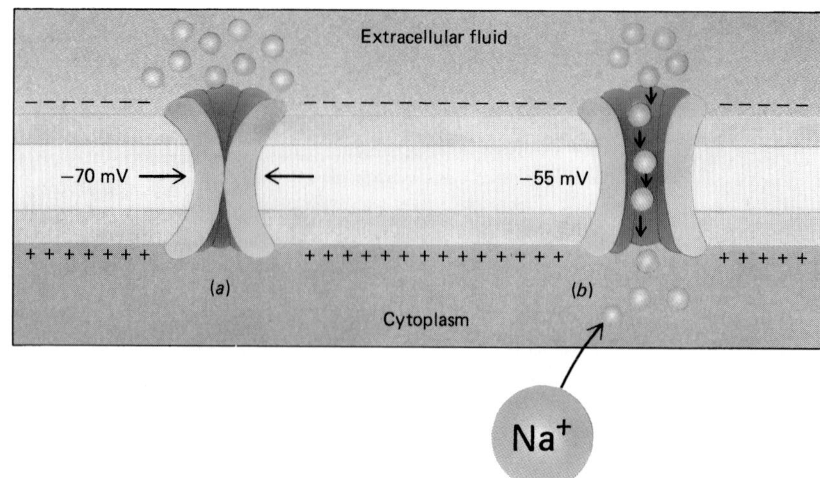

FIGURE 12-13

Voltage-activated ion channels are present in the plasma membrane of the axon and cell body. (*a*) In the resting state, the voltage-activated Na^+ channel is closed. (*b*) When the voltage reaches threshold level, the voltage-activated gate opens, allowing Na^+ to flow into the cell. After a certain amount of time elapses, inactivating gates close the channels.

An almost explosive action occurs as the action potential is produced. The neuron membrane quickly reaches zero potential and even overshoots to about +35 millivolts so that there is a momentary reversal in polarity. The sharp rise and fall of the action potential are collectively referred to as a **spike.** Figure 12-14 illustrates an action potential that has been recorded by placing one electrode inside an axon and one just outside.

The action potential is an electrical current of sufficient strength to induce collapse of the resting potential in the adjacent area of the membrane. The area of depolarization then spreads like a chain reaction down the length of the axon. Thus, a neural impulse is transmitted as a **wave of depolarization** that travels down the neuron. The impulse moves along the axon at a constant velocity (and amplitude) for each type of neuron.

Conduction of a neural impulse is somewhat analogous to burning a trail of gunpowder. Once the gunpowder is ignited at one end, the flame moves steadily along from one end of the trail to the other by igniting the powder particles ahead of it. Of course there is no way of restoring the gunpowder to its original condition after it has burned, but the nerve cell does restore itself!

By the time the action potential moves a few millimeters down the axon, the membrane over which it has just passed begins to **repolarize** (Figs. 12-15 and 12-16). The sodium gates close so that the membrane again becomes impermeable to sodium. Potassium gates in the membrane open at this time, allowing potassium to leak out at the point of stimulation. This leakage of potassium ions returns the interior of the membrane to its relative negative state, repolarizing the membrane. This entire mechanism—depolarization and then repolarization—can take place in less than 1 millisecond.

Even though repolarization takes place very quickly, the redistribution of sodium and potassium to normal resting conditions requires a bit more time. Resting conditions are reestablished when the sodium-potassium pump actively transports excess sodium out of the cell. It should be clear that as the wave of depolarization moves

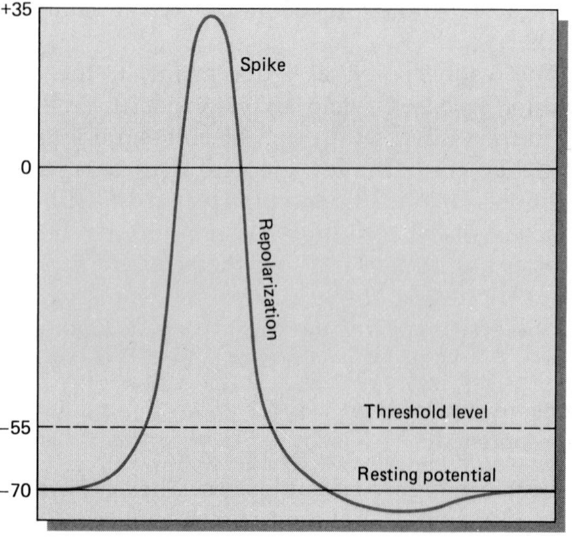

FIGURE 12-14

A graph showing the various stages of an action potential. When the axon depolarizes to about −55 mV, an action potential is generated.

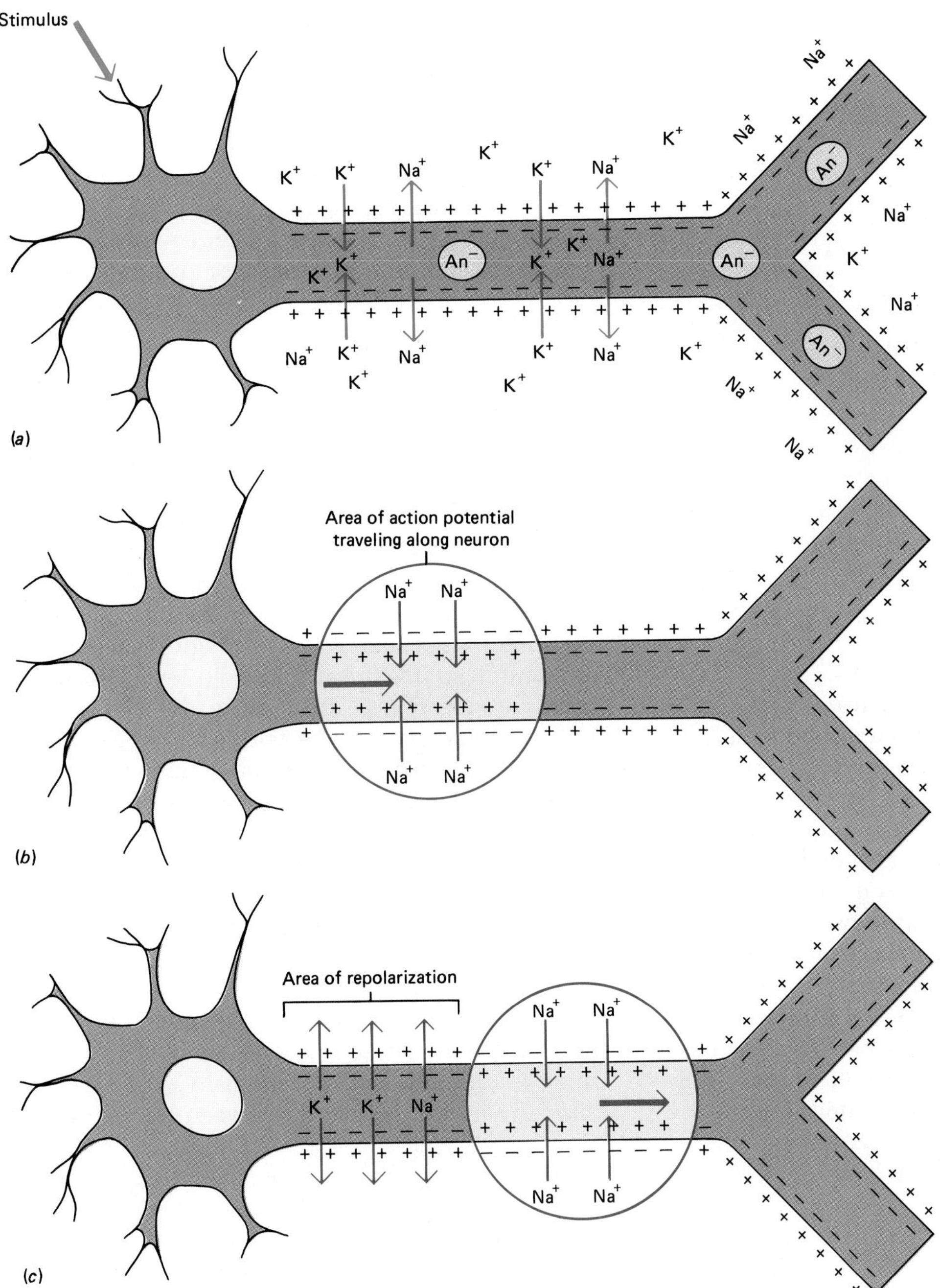

FIGURE 12-15

Transmission of an impulse along an axon. (*a*) The dendrites (or cell body) of a neuron are stimulated sufficiently to depolarize the membrane to firing level. The axon in (*a*) is shown still in the resting state. (*b*) and (*c*) An impulse is conducted as a wave of depolarization that travels down the axon. At the region of depolarization, Na^+ flows into the cell. As the impulse passes along from one region to another, polarity is quickly reestablished. Potassium ions flow outward until the resting potential is restored. Sodium is slowly pumped back out of the axon so that resting conditions are reestablished.

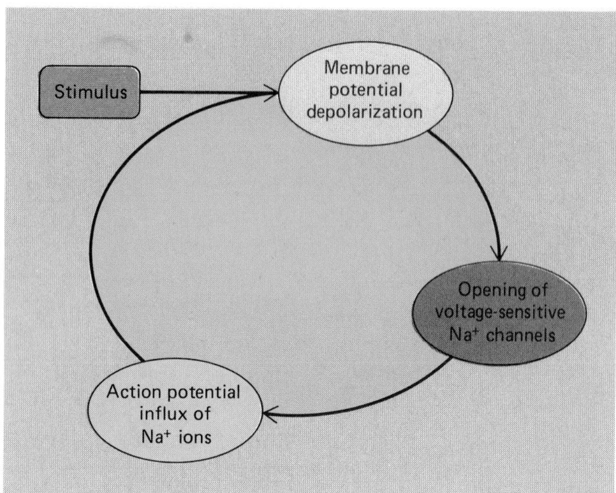

FIGURE 12-16

After conducting an action potential, the neuron has the ability to repolarize and reestablish resting conditions.

down the membrane of the neuron, the normal polarized state is quickly reestablished behind it. We might imagine the action potential as a ring-shaped zone of negative charge traveling along the axon from one end to the other.

During the millisecond or so that it is depolarized, the axon membrane is in an **absolute refractory period** when it cannot transmit another action potential no matter how great a stimulus is applied. Then, for a few additional milliseconds, while the resting condition is being reestablished, the axon can transmit impulses only when they are more intense than is normally required. This time is the **relative refractory period.** Even with the limits imposed by their refractory periods, most neurons can transmit several hundred impulses per second.

Saltatory conduction is rapid

The smooth, progressive impulse transmission just described is characteristic of unmyelinated neurons and called **continuous conduction.** Conduction in myelinated axons depends upon a similar pattern of current flow. However, in myelinated neurons the myelin acts as an effective insulator around the axon except at the nodes of Ranvier, where the axon membrane makes direct contact with the surrounding interstitial fluid. In these neurons depolarization jumps along the axon from one node of Ranvier to the next (Fig. 12-17). The ion activity at the active node serves to depolarize the next node along the axon. Known as **saltatory conduction,** this type of impulse transmission is faster than the step-by-step continuous conduction type. A myelinated axon can conduct an impulse up to 50 times faster than the fastest unmyelinated axon.

Saltatory conduction has another advantage over continuous conduction—it requires less energy. Only the nodes depolarize, so fewer sodium and potassium ions are displaced due to leakage. As a result, the cell does not have to work as hard to reestablish resting conditions each time an impulse is conducted.

The neuron obeys an all-or-none law

Any stimulus too weak to depolarize the neuron to threshold level will not fire the neuron. It merely sets up a local response that fades and dies within a few millimeters from the point of stimulus. A stimulus strong enough to depolarize the neuron to its critical threshold level will result in the propagation of an impulse along the axon. The threshold level varies with each type of neuron and with the experimental conditions. For example, receptor neurons have lower thresholds to certain stimuli than other types of neurons. A stimulus stronger than necessary to fire a particular neuron results only in the propagation of an identical action potential. The neuron either propagates an action potential or it does not. There is no variation in the strength of a single impulse. Thus the neuron obeys an **all-or-none-law.**

But how can this be? Sensations, after all, do come in different levels of intensity. We have no difficulty in distinguishing between the pain of a severe toothache and that of a minor cut on the hand. This apparent inconsistency is explained by the fact that intensity of sensation depends upon the number of neurons stimulated and upon their frequency of discharge. Suppose you burn your hand. The larger the area burned, the more pain receptors will be stimulated and the more neurons will be depolarized. Also, the stronger the stimulus, the greater the number of action potentials per unit of time that each neuron will transmit.

Certain substances affect excitability

Any substance that increases the permeability of the plasma membrane to sodium causes the neuron to become more excitable than normal. Other substances decrease the permeability of the membrane to sodium, making the neuron less excitable. Calcium balance is also essential to normal neural function. When insufficient numbers of calcium ions are present, the sodium gates apparently do not close completely between action potentials, allowing sodium to leak into the cell. This lowers the resting potential, bringing the neuron closer to firing. The neuron thus fires more easily and sometimes even spontaneously. As a result, the muscle innervated by the neuron may go into spasm. This condition is called **low-calcium tetany.** On the other hand, when calcium ions are too numerous, neurons are less excitable and more difficult to fire.

Clinical highlight

Many narcotics and anesthetics block conduction of nerve impulses. Local anesthetics such as procaine and cocaine are thought to decrease the permeability of the neuron to sodium. Excitability may be so reduced that the neuron cannot propagate an impulse through the anesthetized region.

DDT and other chlorinated hydrocarbon biocides interfere with the action of the sodium pump. When nerves are poisoned by these substances, they are unable to transmit impulses. Although the human nervous system can be damaged by these poisons, fortunately insects are even more sensitive to them.

SYNAPTIC TRANSMISSION OCCURS BETWEEN NEURONS

Recall that a synapse is the junction between two neurons or between a neuron and effector. There are two types of neuroeffector junctions. The junction between a neuron and a glandular cell is known as a **neuroglandular junction.** The junction between a neuron and a muscle cell is called a **neuromuscular junction, myoneural junction,** or **motor end plate.**

A neuron that terminates at a specific synapse is referred to as a **presynaptic neuron;** a neuron that begins at the synapse is known as the **postsynaptic neuron.** Note that these terms are relative to a specific synapse. A postsynaptic neuron with respect to one synapse may be presynaptic to the next synapse in the sequence.

Based on how presynaptic and postsynaptic neurons communicate, two types of synapses have been identified: **electrical synapses** and **chemical synapses.** In electrical synapses, the presynaptic and postsynaptic neurons occur very close together (within 2 nanometers of one another) and form connections called **gap junctions.** The two cells are connected by a protein channel called a *connexon.* Such synaptic junctions allow the passage of ions from one cell to another. Thus, an impulse can be **electrically** transmitted from the presynaptic neuron to the postsynaptic neuron.

Electrical synapses are found between axons and cell body, axons and dendrites, dendrites and dendrites, and between two cell bodies. Such synapses permit rapid communication between cells. They also help synchronize the activity of many adjacent cells.

Most synapses in the body are thought to be chemical synapses in which the pre- and postsynaptic cells are separated by a relatively wide (20 nanometers or so) space, the **synaptic cleft.** Because depolarization is a property of the plasma membrane, when an impulse reaches the end of the axon it is unable to jump the gap. An entirely different mechanism—a chemical mechanism—is needed to conduct the "message" across the synaptic cleft to the postsynaptic neuron.

When an impulse reaches the synaptic knobs at the end of a presynaptic axon, it stimulates the release of a chemical **neurotransmitter,** also called **transmitter substance,** into the synaptic cleft. This chemical messenger swiftly diffuses across the

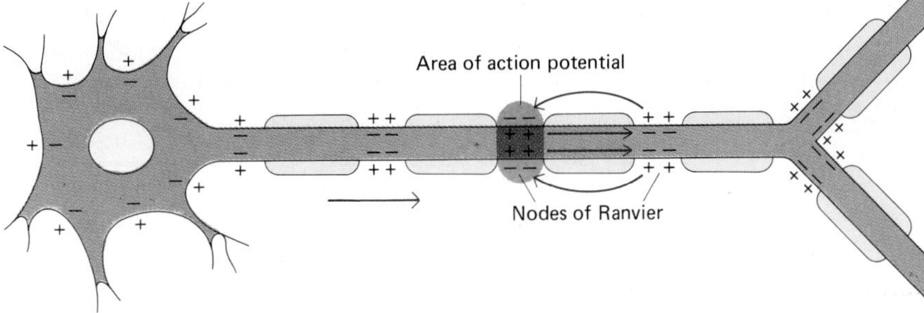

FIGURE 12-17

Saltatory conduction. In a myelinated axon the impulse leaps along from one node of Ranvier to the next. (Nodes of Ranvier are not drawn to scale.)

tiny gap and affects the permeability of the postsynaptic membrane (Fig. 12-18). If sufficient neurotransmitter is present, the postsynaptic membrane may be depolarized to the point of setting off an action potential.

The synaptic knobs continuously synthesize neurotransmitter. Mitochondria in the synaptic knobs provide the ATP required for this synthesis (Figs. 12-19 and 12-20). Needed enzymes are produced in the cell body and are transported down the axon to the synaptic knobs. After it is produced, the neurotransmitter is stored in small membrane-bound sacs, **synaptic vesicles,** within the cytoplasm of the synaptic knobs.

Each time an action potential reaches the synaptic knob, the resulting change in membrane potential activates voltage-sensitive calcium channels. Calcium ions from the surrounding tissue fluid then pass into the axon terminal. The Ca^{2+} induces several hundred synaptic vesicles to fuse with the presynaptic membrane and release their contents into the synaptic cleft by the process of exocytosis (Fig. 12-20 and the electron micrograph on the first page of this chapter).

Each synaptic vesicle releases a fixed (quantum) number of neurotransmitter molecules. For example, each vesicle containing the neurotransmitter acetylcholine releases about 10,000 molecules.

Neurotransmitter then diffuses across the synaptic cleft and combines with specific **receptors** on the dendrites or cell bodies of postsynaptic neurons. These receptors are proteins that form **chemically activated ion channels.** When the neu-

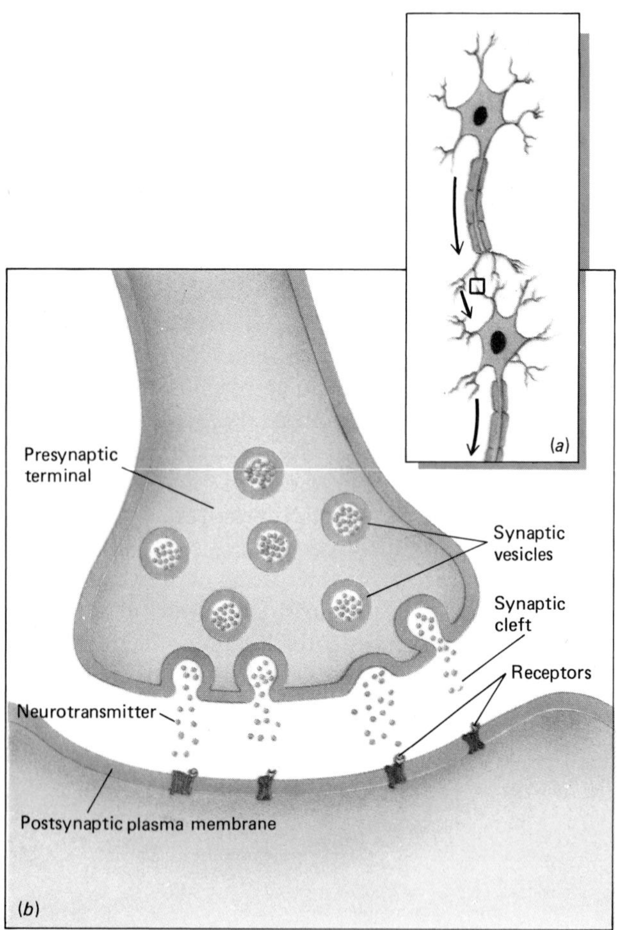

FIGURE 12-18

Transmission of an impulse between two neurons or from a neuron to an effector. *(a)* Most neurons are separated by a relatively wide space, the synaptic cleft. Such junctions are called chemical synapses. The action potential is unable to jump across the synaptic cleft between the two neurons. *(b)* The problem is solved by the release of neurotransmitter from vesicles within the synaptic knobs of the axon. The neurotransmitter diffuses across the synaptic cleft and may trigger an impulse in the postsynaptic neuron.

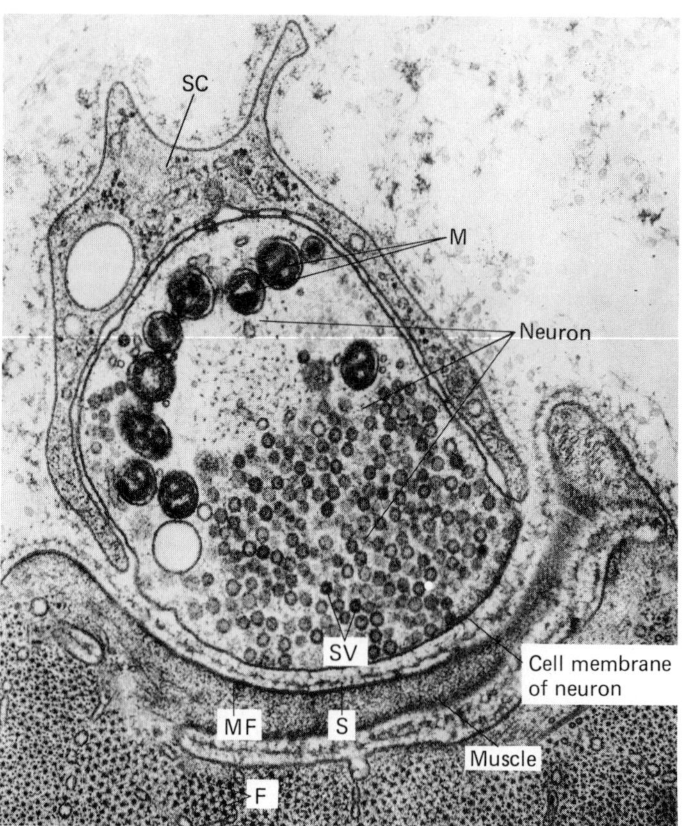

FIGURE 12-19

Electron micrograph of a synaptic knob filled with synaptic vesicles containing neurotransmitter. This is a motor neuron synapsing with a muscle fiber. Note the abundance of mitochondria in the synaptic knob. What is their importance here? (approximately ×20,000). SC, Schwann cell; M, mitochondria; SV, synaptic vesicles; S, synaptic cleft; MF, membrane of muscle fiber; F, filaments of muscle. (Courtesy of Dr. John Heuser)

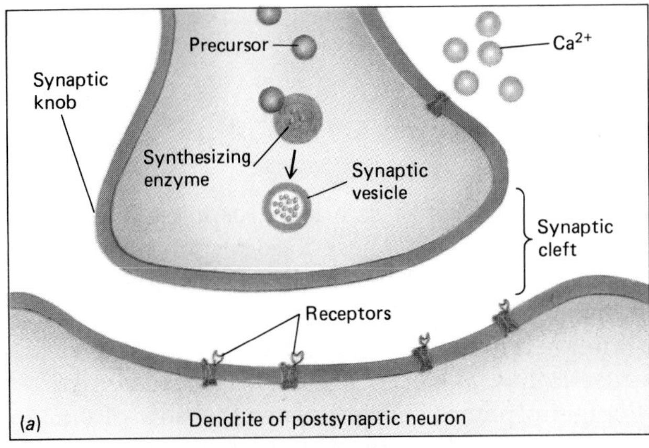

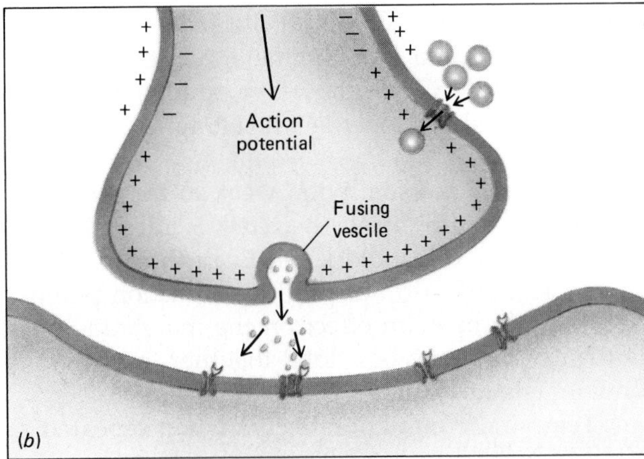

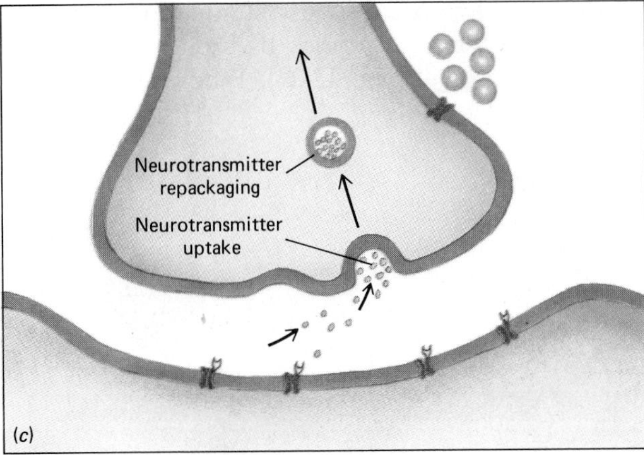

FIGURE 12-20

In the synaptic knobs, neurotransmitter molecules are synthesized and packaged in synaptic vesicles (*a*). (*b*) When an action potential reaches the synaptic knob, voltage-sensitive calcium channels open allowing Ca^{2+} to pass into the synaptic knob. The Ca^{2+} induces synaptic vesicles to fuse with the presynaptic membrane and release their contents into the synaptic cleft. Neurotransmitter diffuses across the synaptic cleft and combines with specific receptors on the postsynaptic membrane. (*c*) Uncombined neurotransmitter move back into the synaptic knob by a re-uptake mechanism.

rotransmitter binds with the receptor, the channel opens, permitting the passage of specific ions through the membrane (Fig. 12-21). The resulting redistribution of ions affects the electrical potential of the membrane, either depolarizing or hyperpolarizing it. If sufficiently intense, such a local depolarization can set off a propagated action potential.

If repolarization is to occur quickly, any excess neurotransmitter in the synaptic cleft must be removed. Some neurotransmitters are inactivated by enzymes. Others are taken back into the presynaptic axon terminal by a pumping mechanism.

Signals may be excitatory or inhibitory

When a neurotransmitter combines with a receptor on the surface of a postsynaptic neuron, the effect can be either to bring the neuron closer to firing or to take it farther away from firing. If the effect is to partially depolarize the membrane, the neuron is brought closer to firing, and the change

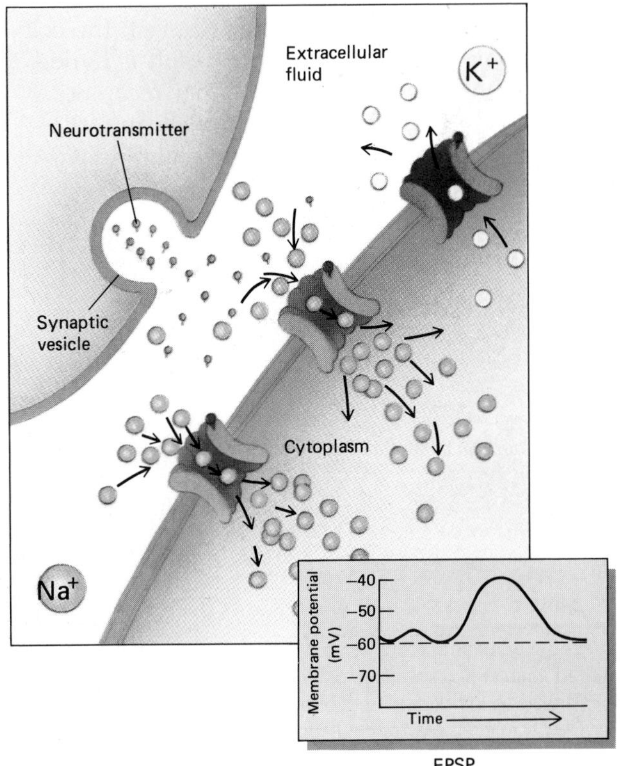

FIGURE 12-21

When a neurotransmitter binds to a receptor, an EPSP may be initiated. In the mechanism shown, a chemically activated sodium channel opens allowing sodium to flow into the cell.

in potential is called an **excitatory postsynaptic potential,** or **EPSP.**

Several mechanisms may bring about excitatory transmission. We have already discussed chemically activated channels that open when neurotransmitters bind to neurotransmitter receptors on the plasma membrane of the postsynaptic neuron. The resulting influx of sodium ions depolarizes the neuron (Fig. 12-21). When the neurotransmitter serotonin combines with its receptor, K^+ channels close. This mechanism involves the enzyme **adenylate cyclase.** The activation of the receptor results in activation of adenylate cyclase in the postsynaptic membrane. Adenylate cyclase then converts ATP to **cyclic AMP (cAMP).** Cyclic AMP then activates a protein kinase. This enzyme phosphorylates a protein that closes the K^+ channels. The result is depolarization.

Some neurotransmitter-receptor combinations *hyperpolarize* the postsynaptic membrane; that is, they raise its membrane potential. This, of course, takes the neuron farther away from the firing level, so a potential change in this direction is called an **inhibitory postsynaptic potential,** or **IPSP.** As with EPSPs, there are several ways that an IPSP can be produced. When the neurotransmitter binds to the receptor, K^+ channels may open (Fig. 12-22*a*). As K^+ leaves the cell, the cell becomes more negative, and the result is hyperpolarization of the membrane. Other receptors that produce IPSPs permit Cl^- to flow into the cell (Fig. 12-22*b*). This increased membrane permeability to Cl^- also hyperpolarizes the membrane.

Graded potentials vary in magnitude

Each EPSP and IPSP is a local response in the neuron membrane. These local responses are referred to as **graded potentials** because they vary in magnitude depending on the strength of the stimulus applied. Local changes in potential can cause a flow of electric current. The greater the change in potential, the greater the flow of current. Such a local current flow can function as a signal only over a very short distance, because it fades out within a few millimeters of its point of origin. As we will see, however, graded potentials can be added together, resulting in action potentials.

One EPSP is usually too weak to trigger an action potential by itself. Its effect is subliminal, that is, below threshold level. Even though subthreshold EPSPs do not produce an action potential, they do have an effect on the membrane potential. EPSPs may be added together, a process known as **summation.**

Temporal summation occurs when repeated stimuli cause new EPSPs to develop before previous EPSPs have decayed. By summation of several EPSPs, the neuron may be brought to the critical firing level (Fig. 12-23). When several syn-

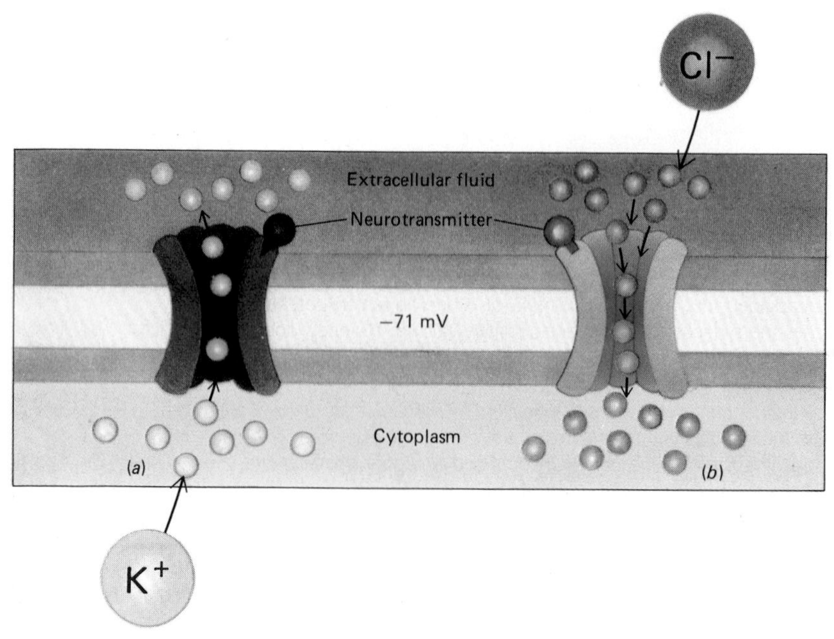

FIGURE 12-22

When a neurotransmitter binds to a receptor, an inhibitory postsynaptic potential (IPSP) may be initiated. (*a*) Chemically activated K^+ channels may open, permitting K^+ to pass out of the cell. This leads to hyperpolarization of the membrane. (*b*) Chloride channels may open permitting Cl^- to pass into the cell. The increased negative charge inside the cell hyperpolarizes the membrane.

aptic knobs release neurotransmitter simultaneously, the postsynaptic neuron will be stimulated at several places at the same time. This effect, called **spatial summation,** can also bring the postsynaptic neuron to the threshold level.

Even with summation, the postsynaptic neuron may not be depolarized sufficiently to conduct an impulse. However, the neuron is said to be **facilitated,** meaning that its membrane is nearer the threshold for firing than it would normally be in the resting state. Further stimulation of the neuron can more easily bring the neuron to the firing level. Facilitation is discussed further in a later section and is illustrated in Figure 12-26.

Many types of neurotransmitters are known

More than 60 different substances are now known or suspected of being neurotransmitters, and a number of neuropeptides have been identified that modulate the effect of neurotransmitters. Low molecular weight neurotransmitters are synthesized in the presynaptic axon terminals. Needed enzymes are produced in the cell body and delivered by axonal transport to the terminals. Neurotransmitters that are neuropeptides are synthesized in the cell body and transported to the axon terminals.

Many types of neurons secrete two or even three different types of neurotransmitters. Moreover, a postsynaptic neuron may have receptors for more than one type of neurotransmitter. Indeed, some of its receptors may be excitatory and some inhibitory.

Two neurotransmitters that have been studied extensively are acetylcholine and norepinephrine (NE). In Chapter 10 we discussed how **acetylcholine** is released from motor neurons that innervate skeletal muscle, and how this neurotransmitter diffuses across the neuromuscular junction to trigger muscle contraction. Acetylcholine is also released by some neurons in the autonomic system and by some neurons in the brain. Cells that release this neurotransmitter are referred to as **cholinergic neurons.**

Acetylcholine has an excitatory effect on skeletal muscle, increasing the permeability of the muscle fiber membrane to sodium by opening the sodium channels. The influx of sodium depolarizes the membrane, generating an action potential and leading to contraction. In cardiac muscle, acetylcholine has an inhibitory effect, resulting in a decrease in heart rate. Whether a neurotransmitter excites or inhibits is apparently a property of the postsynaptic receptors with which it combines. After acetylcholine is released by a presynaptic neuron and combines with receptors on the postsynaptic neuron, excess acetylcholine must be removed. This is accomplished by the enzyme cholinesterase, which breaks it down into its chemical components choline and acetate.

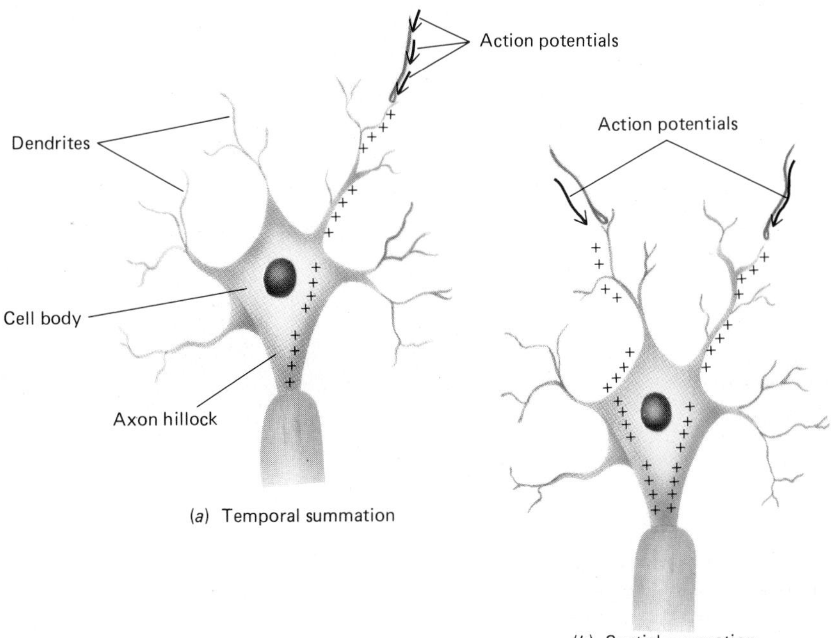

FIGURE 12-23

Summation of EPSPs. (*a*) Temporal summation. (*b*) Spatial summation.

Norepinephrine (*nor*-ep-ih-**nef**-rin) is released by sympathetic neurons and by many neurons in the brain and spinal cord. Neurons that release norepinephrine are called **adrenergic neurons** (*ad*-ren-**er**-jik). Norepinephrine and the neurotransmitters **epinephrine** and **dopamine** (**doe**-pah-mean) belong to a class of compounds called **catecholamines** (kat-eh-**kol**-ah-mean), or **biogenic amines.** After release, most of the excess catecholamines are reabsorbed into the vesicles in the synaptic knobs. Some are degraded by the enzymes catechol-O-methyltransferase and **monoamine oxidase (MAO).** MAO is also thought to help regulate the concentration of catecholamines in the synaptic knobs. Catecholamines affect mood, and many drugs that modify mood do so by altering the levels of these substances in the brain (Table 15-1).

Other neurotransmitters are listed in Table 12-2. They include *serotonin, glutamate, gamma aminobutyric acid* (GABA) (**gam**-ma am-*ee*-no-byoo-**teer**-ik), *glycine,* and the *endorphins.* GABA is an

TABLE 12-2

Some neurotransmitters

Substance	Origin	Comments
Acetylcholine	Neuromuscular (nerve–muscle) junctions; preganglionic autonomic endings;* postganglionic parasympathetic nerve endings; parts of brain	Inactivated by cholinesterase
Norepinephrine	Postganglionic sympathetic endings; reticular activating system; areas of cerebral cortex, cerebellum, and spinal cord	Reabsorbed by vesicles in synaptic knob; inactivated by MAO (monoamine oxidase); norepinephrine level in the brain affects mood
Dopamine	Limbic system; cerebral cortex; basal ganglia; hypothalamus	Thought to affect motor function; may be involved in pathogenesis of schizophrenia;† amount reduced in Parkinson's disease
Serotonin (5-HT, 5-hydroxytryptamine)	Limbic system; hypothalamus, cerebellum; spinal cord	May play a role in sleep; LSD antagonizes serotonin; thought to be inhibitory
Epinephrine	Hypothalamus; thalamus; spinal cord	Identical to the hormone released by the adrenal glands
GABA (γ-aminobutyric acid)	Spinal cord; cerebral cortex; Purkinje cells in cerebellum	Acts as inhibitor in brain and spinal cord; may play role in pain perception
Glutamate	Cerebral cortex; brain stem	Potent excitatory neurotransmitter; excess glutamate is transported into glial cells where it is converted to glutamine. The glutamine is then transported back into the presynaptic terminal where it is recycled
Glycine	Released by neurons mediating inhibition in spinal cord	Acts as an inhibitor
Endorphins	CNS and pituitary gland	Neuropeptides that have morphine-like properties and suppress pain; may help regulate cell growth; linked to learning and memory; synthesized in the cell body
Enkephalins	Brain and gastrointestinal tract	Neuropeptides thought to inhibit pain impulses by inhibiting release of substance P (see below); bind to same receptors in brain as morphine; synthesized in the cell body
Substance P	Brain and spinal cord; sensory nerves; intestine	Transmits pain impulses from pain receptors into CNS

*These and other structures listed in this table are discussed in Chapters 13 and 16.

†Studies suggest that the brains of schizophrenics have more dopamine receptors than those of nonschizophrenics.

inhibitory neurotransmitter in the brain and spinal cord. Glycine is thought to be an inhibitor in the spinal cord. It is released by some association neurons in the spinal cord that are known to be exclusively inhibitory.

NERVE FIBERS MAY BE CLASSIFIED IN TERMS OF SPEED OF CONDUCTION

In the laboratory it can be demonstrated that an impulse can move in both directions within a single axon. However, in the body, an impulse generally stops when it reaches the dendrites because there is no neurotransmitter there to conduct it across the synapse. This limitation imposed by neurotransmitter makes neural transmission *unidirectional* at the synapse. Thus, neural pathways function as one-way streets, with the usual direction of transmission from the axon of the presynaptic neuron across the synapse to the dendrite or cell body of the postsynaptic neuron.

Compared with the speed of an electrical current or the speed of light, a nerve impulse travels rather slowly. The speed of a nerve impulse varies from about 0.5 meter per second to more than 120 meters (400 ft) per second. What factors affect speed of transmission? In general, the greater the diameter of an axon, the greater its speed of conduction. The largest neurons seem also to be the most heavily myelinated, and the more myelin it has, the faster a neuron transmits impulses. In myelinated neurons, the length between successive nodes of Ranvier is also important. The farther apart the nodes, the faster the axon conducts.

Nerve fibers may be classified into three main groups on the basis of fiber diameter and velocity of transmission. **Type A fibers** are myelinated and have the greatest diameter. They conduct impulses with the greatest velocity (up to about 120 meters per second). Type A fibers include those that transmit impulses from touch, pressure, pain, temperature, and other receptors in the skin, and from receptors in skeletal muscles to the CNS. Type A fibers are also found in motor nerves that transmit impulses from the CNS to the skeletal muscles. Thus, both sensory and motor nerves that are part of withdrawal reflex pathways (e.g., withdrawing one's hand or foot from a painful stimulus) consist of rapidly conducting type A fibers.

Type B fibers are medium-sized, myelinated neurons that conduct impulses much more slowly (3 to 15 meters per second) than type A fibers. Type B fibers are found in the autonomic nervous system, where they conduct impulses from the CNS to relay centers called ganglia. Within the ganglia, type B fibers synapse with **type C fibers,** which conduct impulses to the smooth muscle of the viscera and to glands. Other type C fibers are unmyelinated sensory neurons (including some concerned with pain) of the peripheral nerves. Type C fibers are the smallest and slowest nerve fibers. They are unmyelinated and are apparently incapable of saltatory conduction. Their conduction velocity is only about 0.5 to 2 meters per second.

When considering speed of conduction through a sequence of neurons, the number of synapses must be taken into account, because each time an impulse is conducted from one neuron to another there is a slight synaptic delay (about 0.5 millisecond). This delay is due to the time required for the release of neurotransmitter, its diffusion, and its binding to postsynaptic membrane receptors.

Neural impulses must be integrated

Neural integration is the process of sorting and interpreting incoming signals and determining an appropriate response. Each neuron synapses with hundreds of other neurons. Indeed, as much as 40% of a postsynaptic neuron's dendritic surface and cell body may be covered by synaptic knobs of presynaptic neurons (Fig. 12-24). It is the job of the dendrites and cell body of every neuron to integrate the hundreds of messages that continually bombard them.

EPSPs and IPSPs are continually occurring in postsynaptic neurons. Neurotransmitter received as inhibitory sets up IPSPs that cancel the effects of some of the EPSPs. The postsynaptic cell body and dendrites continually tabulate such molecular transactions. When sufficient excitatory neurotransmitter predominates, the neuron is brought to threshold level, and an action potential is generated.

It is important to remember that each EPSP or IPSP does not initiate an all-or-none response. Rather, each is a *local response* (i.e., it does not travel like an action potential) that may be added to or subtracted from other EPSPs and IPSPs.

After the neuron membrane has completed its chemical tabulations, the neuron may be inhibited, facilitated, or brought to threshold level. If sufficient EPSPs have been received to bring the neuron to threshold level, an all-or-none action potential is initiated and travels down the axon. This mechanism provides for integration of hundreds of "messages" (EPSPs and IPSPs) before an impulse is actually transmitted along the axon of a postsynaptic neuron. Such an arrangement permits the neuron and the entire nervous system a far greater range of response than would be the case if every EPSP generated an action potential.

Where does neural integration take place? Every neuron acts as a tiny integrator, sorting through (on a molecular level) the hundreds and thousands of bits of information continually released upon it. Since more than 90% of the neurons in the body are located in the CNS, most neural integration takes place there, within the brain and spinal cord. These neurons are responsible for making most of the "decisions." In the next chapter these organs will be examined in some detail.

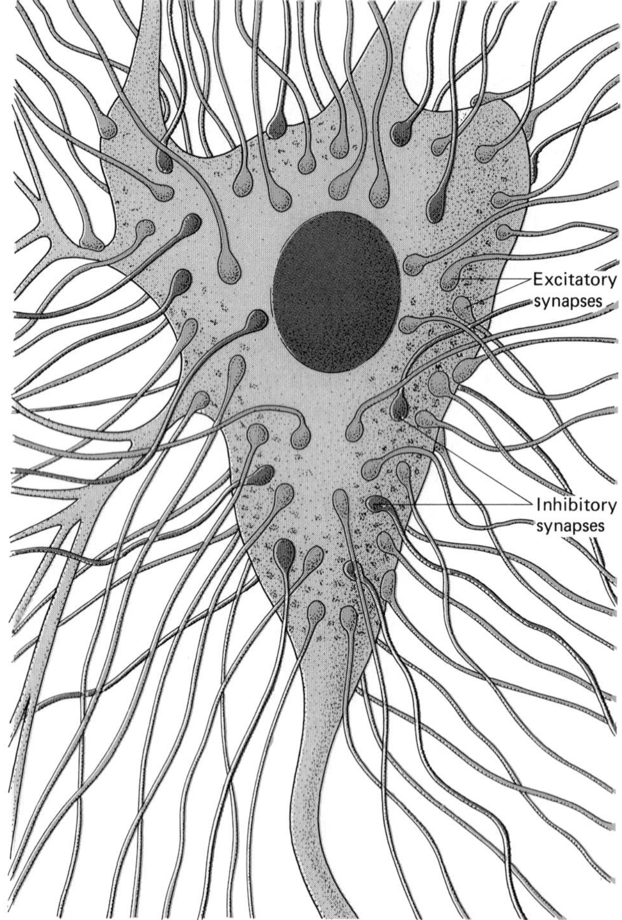

FIGURE 12-24

As much as 40% of the cell body and dendritic surface of a postsynaptic neuron may be covered by synaptic knobs of presynaptic neurons. The dendrites may be thought of as extensions of the neuron that increase its surface area for reception and integration of neural information.

Neurons are organized into circuits

The CNS contains millions of neurons, but it is not just a tangled mass of nerve cells. Its neurons are organized into separate **neuronal pools,** or networks, and within each pool the neurons are arranged in specific pathways, or **circuits.** Although each pool has some special features, the neural circuits in all of the pools share many organizational features. For example, convergence and divergence are probably characteristic of all neural circuits.

Convergence means that a single neuron is controlled by signals coming together from two or more presynaptic neurons (Fig. 12-25*a*). An association neuron in the spinal cord, for instance, may receive converging information from sensory neurons entering the cord, from neurons bringing information from various parts of the brain, and from neurons coming from different levels of the spinal cord. Information from all these sources is integrated before a neural message (action potential) can be sent and an appropriate motor neuron stimulated. Convergence is an important mechanism by which the CNS can integrate the information that impinges on it from various sources.

Divergence refers to the arrangement in which a single presynaptic fiber stimulates many postsynaptic neurons (Fig. 12-25*b*). Each presynaptic neuron may branch and synapse with up to 25,000 or more different postsynaptic neurons. For example, a single neuron transmitting an impulse from the motor area of the brain may synapse with hundreds of association neurons in the spinal cord, and each of these in turn may diverge, so that hundreds of muscle fibers may be stimulated.

Figure 12-26 illustrates the mechanism of **facilitation** introduced earlier in this chapter. Neither neuron A nor neuron B can by itself fire neurons 2 or 3. However, stimulation by either A or B does depolarize the neuron somewhat. This

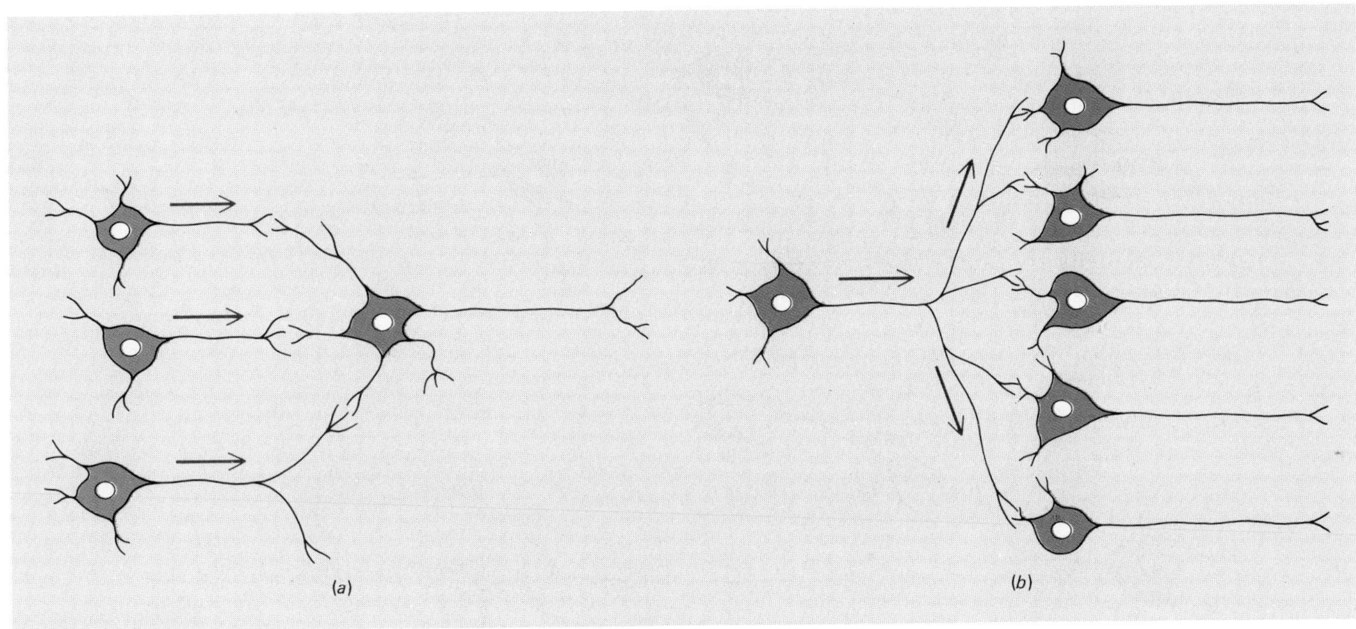

FIGURE 12-25

(*a*) Convergence of neural input. Several presynaptic neurons synapse with one postsynaptic neuron. This organization in a neural circuit permits one neuron to receive signals from many sources. (*b*) Divergence of neural output. A single presynaptic neuron synapses with several postsynaptic neurons. This organization allows one neuron to communicate with many others.

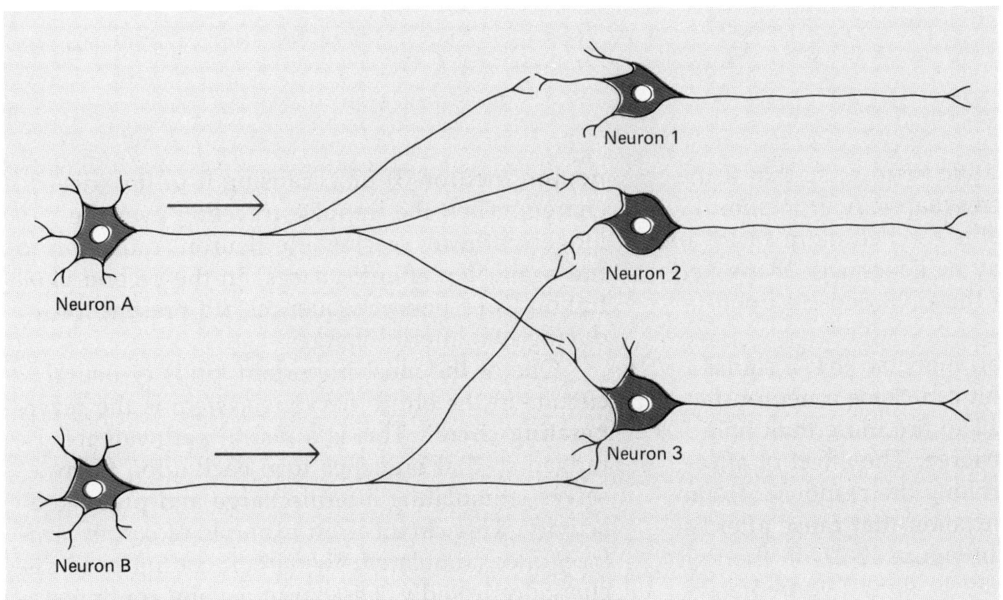

FIGURE 12-26

Facilitation. Neither neuron A nor neuron B can by itself fire neurons 2 or 3. However, stimulation by either A or B does depolarize the neuron toward threshold level (if the stimulation is excitatory). This facilitates the postsynaptic neuron so that if the other presynaptic neuron stimulates it, threshold level may be reached and an action potential generated.

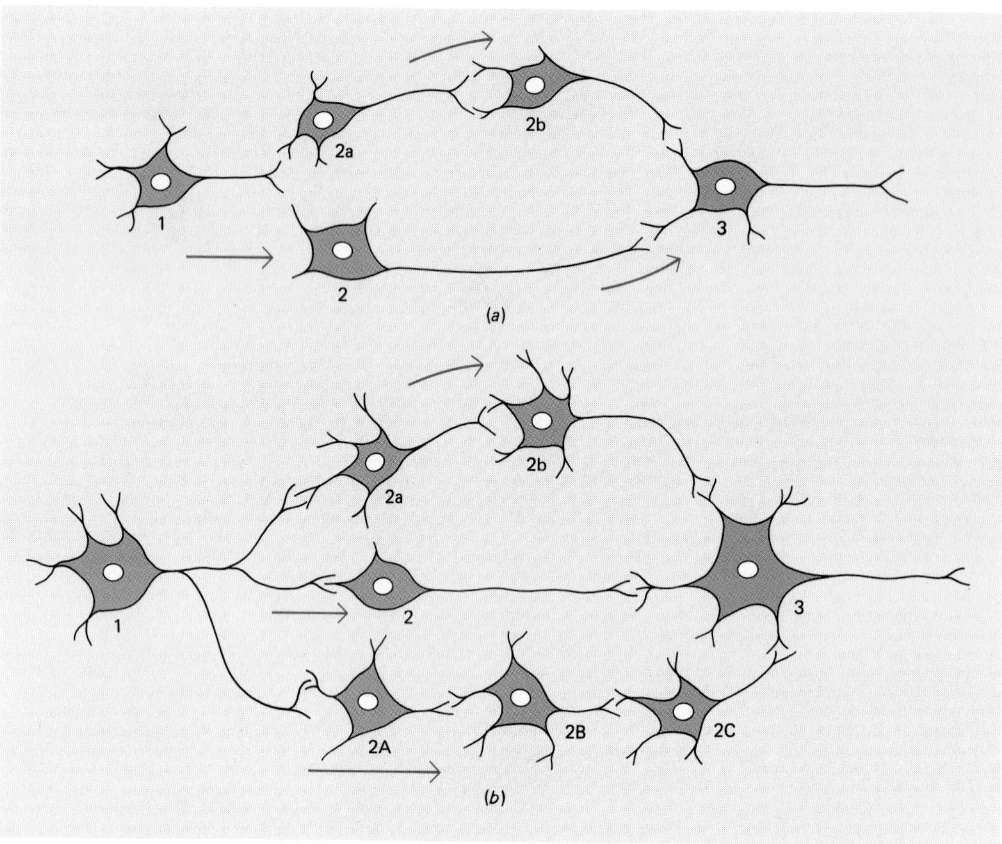

FIGURE 12-27

Afterdischarge. (a) The first neuron in the sequence activates two neural pathways. An impulse traveling through neuron 2 reaches neuron 3 first, because it crosses fewer synapses. The impulse traveling over neurons 2a and 2b reaches neuron 3 afterward, causing it to fire a second time. (b) A more complex neural circuit in which two afterdischarges occur. (Why? Explain in terms of the number of neurons in each pathway.)

facilitates the postsynaptic neuron, so that if the other (or any other) presynaptic neuron stimulates it, threshold level is reached more easily and an action potential may be generated. Many neural interactions within the CNS depend upon facilitation.

Neurons may be arranged so that a signal entering a neural circuit can cause a neuron farther along in the circuit to fire more than once. This is called **afterdischarge.** The effect of afterdischarge can be to prolong the response. Examples of neuronal organization that cause afterdischarge are illustrated in Figure 12-27. In the first example an impulse travels along two pathways to the same neuron, and both pathways lead to the same response. The impulse traveling over the pathway with fewer synapses reaches the neuron (neuron 3) first, causing it to fire (discharge). Then the impulse traveling over the longer pathway reaches the neuron, causing it to fire again, the afterdischarge. In the second illustration three neural sequences are present, producing two afterdischarges.

One of the most important kinds of neural circuits in the entire nervous system is the **reverberating circuit.** This is a neural pathway arranged so that branches turn back upon themselves, stimulating afterdischarge and prolonged activity. This circuit is an example of *positive feedback;* once stimulated, the circuit continues to discharge repeatedly. Discharge usually continues until the synapses involved become fatigued (due

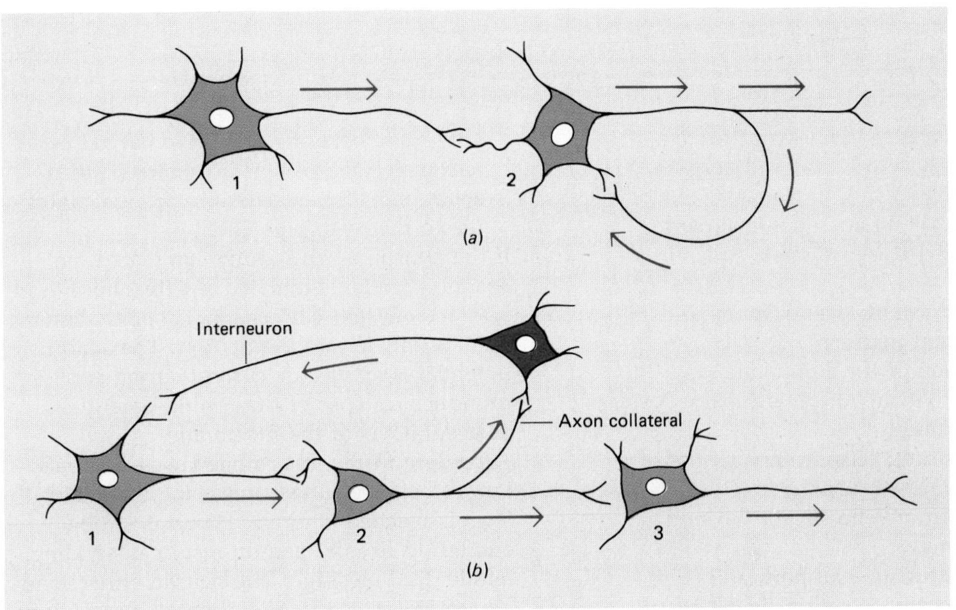

FIGURE 12-28

Reverberating circuits. (*a*) A simple reverberating circuit in which an axon collateral of the second neuron turns back upon its own dendrites so that the neuron continues to stimulate itself. (*b*) In this neural circuit an axon collateral of the second neuron synapses with an interneuron. The interneuron synapses with the first neuron in the sequence. New impulses are thus triggered again and again in the first neuron, causing reverberation. See text for explanation of factors that can bring a halt to this reverberation.

to depletion of neurotransmitter) or until they are stopped by some sort of inhibition.

Two examples of reverberating circuits are shown in Figure 12-28. In the first, a collateral of the postsynaptic neuron feeds back upon its own dendrites to restimulate itself. In the second example an axon collateral of the second neuron in the chain synapses upon an interneuron. The interneuron, in turn, synapses with the first neuron in the sequence, triggering a new impulse.

Much more complex varieties of reverberating circuits have been postulated. They are thought to be important in rhythmic breathing, in maintaining wakefulness, and perhaps in short-term memory.

Neurons may discharge spontaneously

During life, activity never ceases within the nervous system. Continuous input from sensory receptors accounts for much of this activity but probably not all. Some physiologists think that there may be active pacemakers within the nervous system that function like the pacemaker of the heart. Pacemaker neurons might periodically discharge spontaneously, setting up reverberating circuits. This would account for action potentials and rhythmic discharges otherwise unexplained.

Summary

I. The two principal divisions of the nervous system are the central nervous system (CNS) and peripheral nervous system (PNS).
   A. The CNS consists of the brain and spinal cord.
   B. The PNS may be divided into somatic and autonomic systems.
      1. Each of these subsystems has receptors and afferent and efferent neurons.
      2. The efferent portion of the autonomic system is divided into sympathetic and parasympathetic systems.

II. Glial cells are the supporting cells of nervous tissue.
   A. Oligodendrocytes form myelin sheaths around axons of CNS neurons.
   B. Astrocytes provide structural support, and ependymal cells line cavities within the CNS.
   C. Microglial cells are phagocytic.
   D. Schwann cells, found only in the PNS, form myelin sheaths around some axons.

III. Neurons transmit messages.
   A. The main structures of a neuron are the cell body, the axon, and the dendrites.
   B. Synaptic knobs at the ends of axons release neurotransmitter.
   C. Axons of the neurons in the PNS may be covered by both a cellular sheath and a myelin sheath.
      1. The cellular sheath functions in regeneration of injured neurons.
      2. The myelin sheath serves as insulation.
      3. Both sheaths are produced by Schwann cells.

IV. Every response involves a sequence of several steps.
   A. Reception—a stimulus must be received by the receptors.
   B. Transmission—the information contained in the stimulus must be transmitted to the CNS.
   C. Integration—information must be sorted and interpreted so that an appropriate response can be determined.
   D. Transmission—a message must be delivered from the CNS to the appropriate effectors.
   E. Actual response—the effector contracts (or secretes), producing the actual response to the stimulus.

V. Transmission of neural messages along a neuron is an electrochemical process.
   A. When a neuron is not conducting an impulse, it has a resting potential.
      1. This resting potential is brought about mainly by the outward diffusion of potassium along its concentration gradient.
      2. Large numbers of negatively charged protein molecules within the axon and the action of sodium-potassium pumps contribute to the resting potential.
   B. If the neuron is sufficiently stimulated, an action potential is initiated. At threshold level voltage-activated Na^+ channels open, allowing Na^+ to diffuse into the neuron. The action potential is an electric current strong enough to induce collapse of the resting potential in adjacent areas of the membrane.
   C. According to the all-or-none law, an impulse cannot be transmitted unless the threshold level is reached, and any stimulus strong enough to fire the neuron results in sending an identical message. The neuron either sends a message or it does not; there is no variation in the intensity of a single impulse.

VI. Transmission of an impulse from one neuron to another across a synapse generally depends upon the release of neurotransmitter.
   A. Presynaptic neurons release neurotransmitter from their synaptic knobs.
   B. Molecules of neurotransmitter combine with receptors on the postsynaptic neurons, resulting in EPSPs and IPSPs.
   C. Acetylcholine, norepinephrine, dopamine, and serotonin are examples of neurotransmitters.
   D. After it is released into the synaptic cleft, excess neurotransmitter may be inactivated by enzymatic action or reabsorbed into the synaptic vesicles.

VII. The surface of a postsynaptic neuron is continually exposed to EPSPs and IPSPs and responds by tabulating them, the process of neural integration. When sufficient EPSPs are present to depolarize the membrane, an impulse is transmitted.

VIII. Within the neuronal pools of the CNS, neurons are arranged in circuits. Many circuits have organizational features in common.
   A. Convergence and divergence provide the opportunity for complex neural interactions at synapses, including facilitation and reverberation.
   B. In a reverberating circuit several pathways are interconnected by interneurons that act to initiate new sets of impulses. This permits the neurons to continue to discharge (reverberate) even after the original message has run its course.

Post-test

1. The CNS consists of the ______________ and the ______________ ______________.
2. Sense receptors and nerves belong to the ______________ nervous system.
3. Sensory nerves are also called ______________ nerves.
4. The supporting cells of nervous tissue are called ______________ cells.
5. Cells that are specialized to transmit impulses are called ______________.
6. The nucleus of a nerve cell is located within the ______________ ______________.
7. The process of a neuron specialized to transmit impulses away from the cell body is the ______________.
8. Synaptic knobs release ______________.
9. Because it is very long, an axon is often called a ______________ ______________.
10. A mass of cell bodies outside the CNS is termed a ______________; within the CNS it is called a ______________.
11. The first step in any type of neural action is ______________ of a stimulus.
12. The junction between two neurons is called a ______________.
13. Two types of effectors are ______________ and ______________.
14. Any stimulus that increases the permeability of the neuron to sodium may result in transmission of a(n) ______________, also called an ______________.
15. After an impulse has passed a particular point on the axon, that portion of the axon enters a brief ______________ ______________.
16. Cholinergic neurons release ______________ as a neurotransmitter.
17. The process of adding together EPSPs is known as ______________.
18. Adrenergic neurons release ______________.
19. Sodium is actively transported out of the resting neuron by a mechanism called the ______________ ______________.
20. Insufficient calcium (lowers or raises?) ______________ the resting potential, bringing the neuron (closer to, farther from?) ______________ firing.

Review questions

1. What are some differences between neurons within the CNS and those of the PNS? Between their supporting cells?
2. Suppose you sever a nerve in your finger. Describe how it might regenerate. Draw a diagram to illustrate your description.
3. What are voltage-activated channels? How do they work?
4. Give examples of reception, conduction, integration, and response.
5. Name the body's chief effectors.
6. Describe the transmission of an impulse along an unmyelinated axon. A myelinated axon.
7. How does the nervous system signal intense pain as opposed to minor pain?
8. How is neural function affected by the presence of too many calcium ions? Too few?
9. Contrast continuous with saltatory conduction.
10. How are neural messages generally conducted from one neuron to another?
11. What factors affect speed of neural transmission?
12. Suppose that a postsynaptic neuron receives both excitatory and inhibitory impulses simultaneously. How does it "decide" whether to fire?
13. Why is convergence important? Divergence?
14. What is a reverberating circuit?

Post-test answers

1. brain, spinal cord **2.** PNS (peripheral nervous system) **3.** afferent **4.** glial **5.** neurons **6.** cell body **7.** axon **8.** neurotransmitter substance **9.** nerve fiber **10.** ganglion; nucleus **11.** reception **12.** synapse **13.** muscles, glands **14.** (neural) impulse, action potential **15.** refractory period **16.** acetylcholine **17.** summation **18.** norepinephrine **19.** sodium pump **20.** lowers, closer to

THE CENTRAL NERVOUS SYSTEM

CHAPTER OUTLINE

LEARNING OBJECTIVES

After you have studied this chapter you should be able to:

1 Describe the structures that protect the brain and spinal cord.

2 Trace the formation and circulation of the cerebrospinal fluid.

3 Label on a diagram the principal divisions of the brain and the other brain structures discussed in this chapter.

4 Describe the structure and functions of the medulla.

5 Describe the structure and functions of the pons and midbrain.

6 Describe the structure and functions of the thalamus and hypothalamus.

7 Describe the structure and functions of the cerebellum.

8 Describe the structure and functions of the cerebrum.

9 Identify the lobes of the cerebrum and name the principal areas and functions associated with each lobe.

10 Identify the basal ganglia and describe their functions.

11 Contrast the functions of the cerebral hemispheres.

12 Describe the actions of the limbic system and identify its structures.

13 Relate four main types of brain wave patterns with the kind of activity they reflect.

14 Cite the actions of the reticular activating system.

15 Describe the structure of the spinal cord or label its structures on a diagram.

16 Describe two functions of the spinal cord; compare and contrast the functions of the ascending and descending tracts.

17 Compare a stretch reflex with a flexor (withdrawal) reflex.

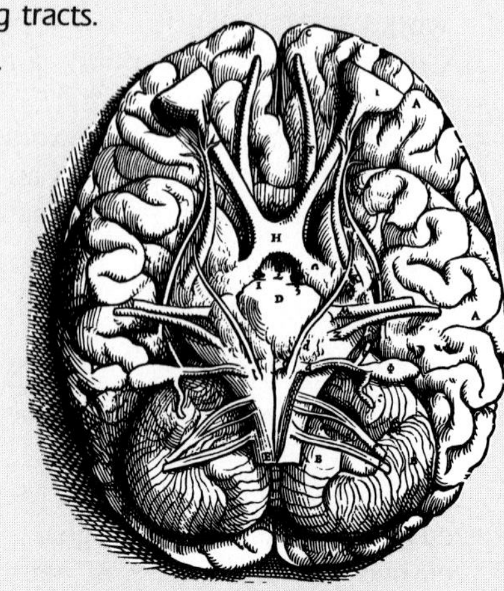

Pseudocolor CAT scan. (Custom Medical Stock Photo.)

13

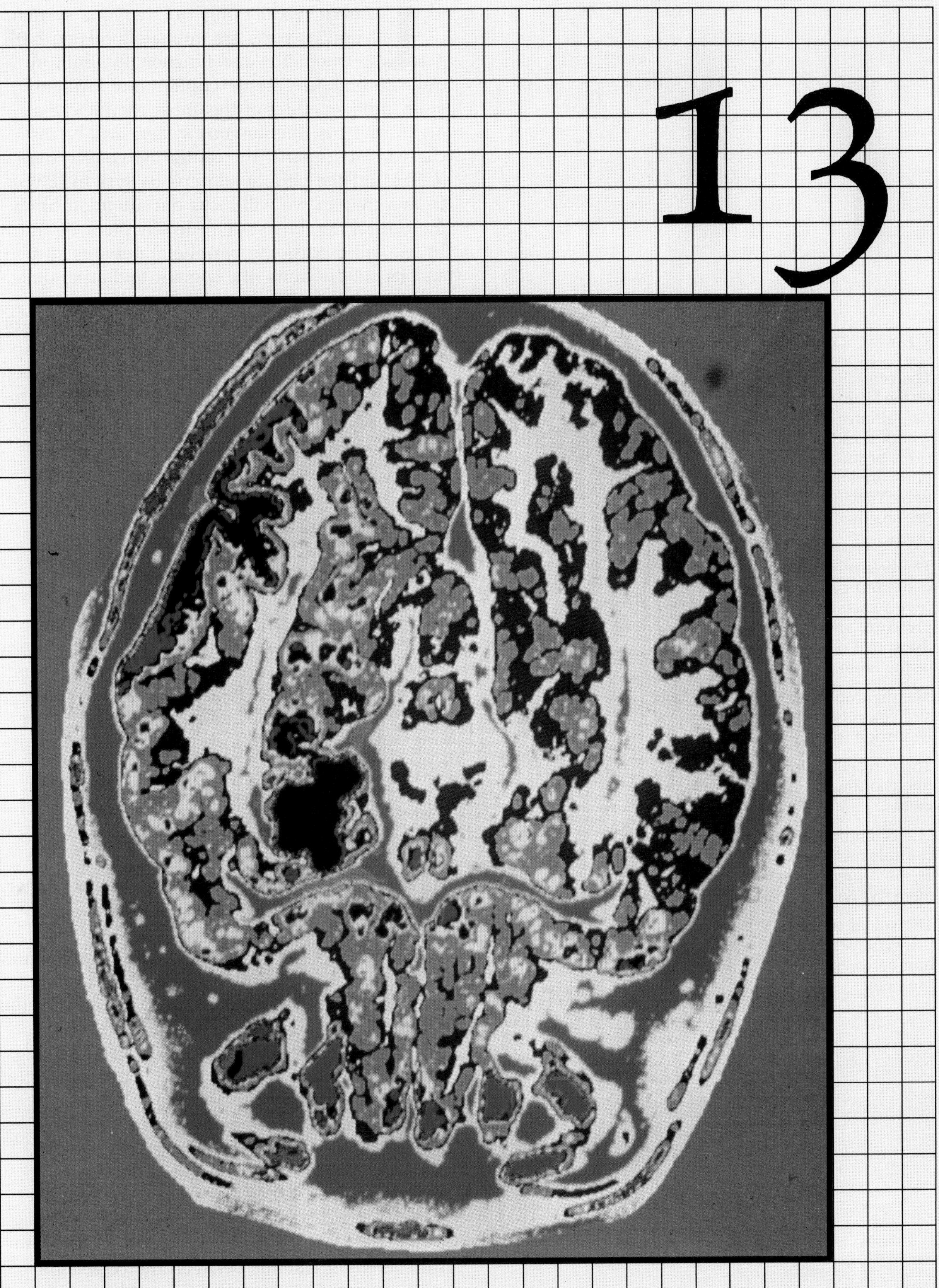

KEY CONCEPTS

The central nervous system consists of the brain and spinal cord; most neural integration takes place within these organs. The main divisions of the brain are the medulla, pons, midbrain, diencephalon (which includes thalamus and hypothalamus), cerebellum, and cerebrum.

The brainstem (medulla, pons, and midbrain) controls basic life processes such as heart rate, blood pressure, and breathing and links the spinal cord with various parts of the brain.

The diencephalon is a relay center and controls autonomic and many endocrine functions.

The cerebellum is responsible for fine coordination of muscle movements.

The cerebrum interprets sensation, controls motor activities, and serves as the center of intellect, reason, memory, and consciousness.

The spinal cord controls many reflex actions and transmits information between peripheral nerves and the brain.

There is really only one nervous system, and its parts are intimately related both structurally and functionally. Still, in order to organize the description and facilitate your understanding of this most complex of all organ systems, the nervous system will be discussed in two parts: the central nervous system (CNS) and the peripheral nervous system (PNS). In this chapter we will focus our attention upon the central nervous system. In Chapters 14 and 16 we will discuss the peripheral nervous system and its subdivisions, the somatic and autonomic systems.

The central nervous system, the main control system of the body, consists of the brain and spinal cord. Information from the external and internal environment is transmitted from receptors to the CNS for integration before action can be taken. Nerve impulses that activate the muscles and glands originate in the CNS.

The CNS is carefully protected

The soft, fragile brain and spinal cord are the most carefully protected organs in the body. Both are encased in bone and covered by three layers of connective tissue—the **meninges** (meh-**ninj**-ees; singular, *meninx*). Brain and spinal cord are also bathed in a cushioning fluid, the **cerebrospinal fluid.**

The meninges are connective tissue coverings

The outermost of the meninges is the dura mater, the middle meninx is the arachnoid, and the innermost is the pia mater (Fig. 13-1). The **dura mater** is a thick, tough membrane. In the cranium it also serves as an internal periosteum to the skull bones. In some regions the two layers of the dura mater are separated by large blood vessels called sinuses. These vessels drain blood leaving the brain and deliver it to the jugular veins in the neck (Fig. 13-2).

The dura mater forms four partitions, or septa, that subdivide the cranium into compartments. The largest of these partitions is the **falx cerebri,** which dips down between the cerebral hemispheres (Fig. 13-2). The falx cerebri attaches to the crista galli of the ethmoid bone. The **tentorium cerebelli** extends between the cerebellum and the posterior portion of the cerebrum.

In the region of the spinal cord, the **epidural space** lies between the bone and dura mater. A potential space, the **subdural space,** separates the dura mater from the arachnoid in both cranial and spinal cord regions.

The **arachnoid** is a thin, delicate membrane. Projections from the arachnoid extend like the threads of a web to the pia mater. Between the arachnoid and the pia mater is the **subarachnoid space,** which contains cerebrospinal fluid. This shock-absorbing fluid will be discussed in the next section. The **pia mater** is a very thin, vascular membrane that adheres closely to the brain and spinal cord, following each curve or indentation of tissue.

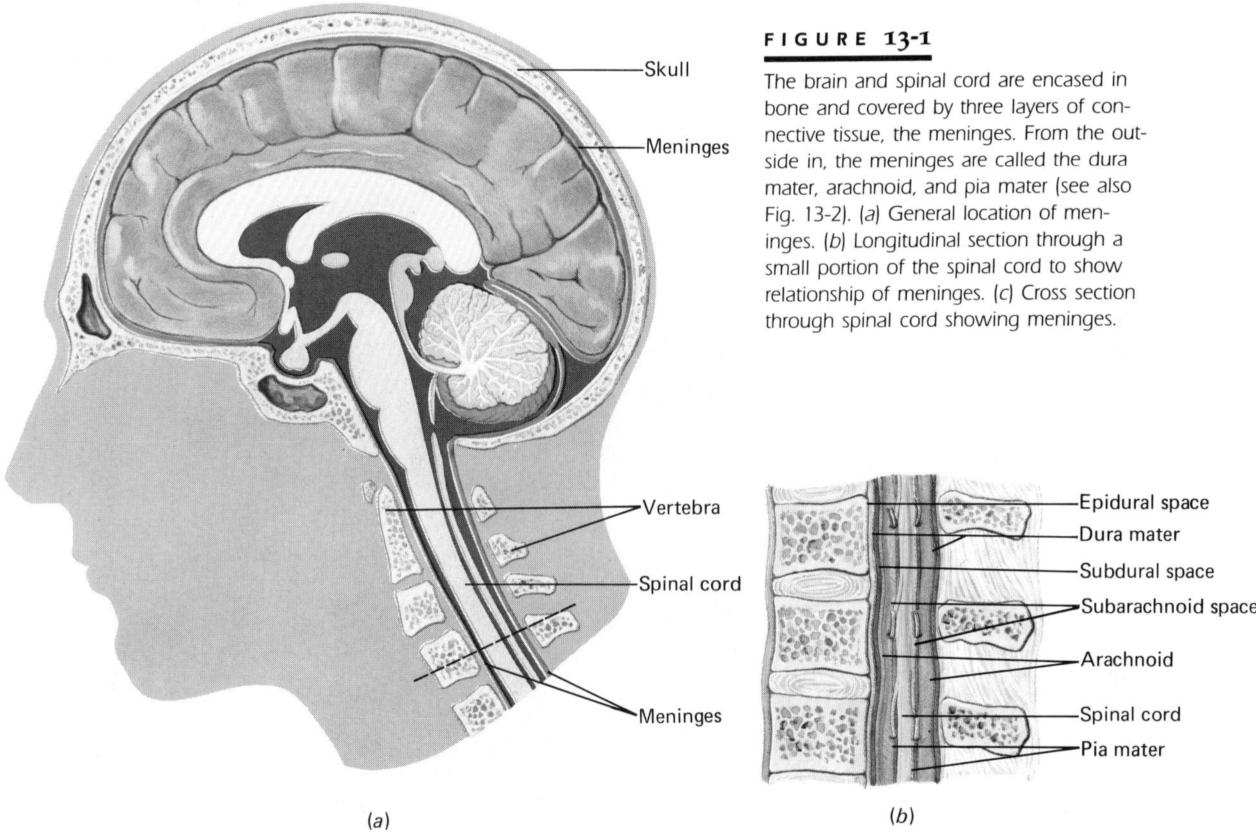

FIGURE 13-1

The brain and spinal cord are encased in bone and covered by three layers of connective tissue, the meninges. From the outside in, the meninges are called the dura mater, arachnoid, and pia mater (see also Fig. 13-2). (*a*) General location of meninges. (*b*) Longitudinal section through a small portion of the spinal cord to show relationship of meninges. (*c*) Cross section through spinal cord showing meninges.

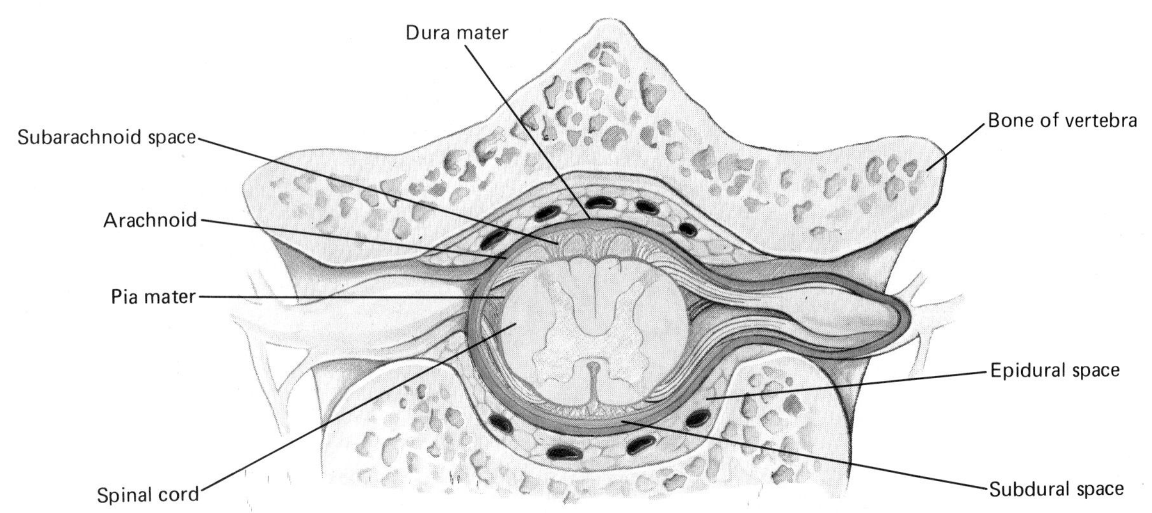

Clinical highlight

Meningitis is an inflammation of the meninges. It is usually due to infection by bacteria or viruses. Fever, headache, and stiff neck are common symptoms of meningitis. Before the era of antibiotics, bacterial meningitis was almost always fatal. Now more than 90% of patients survive when the disease is diagnosed and treated in its early stages. Only a few survivors are left with permanent damage such as cranial nerve damage, recurrent convulsions, and mental retardation.

Viral meningitis is usually a self-limited disease from which the patient recovers fully. However, some viruses that cause meningitis can spread, causing inflammation of the brain itself. This more serious illness is **encephalitis.** The mortality from encephalitis depends partly upon the particular virus causing the infection and may be as high as 50%.

The cerebrospinal fluid cushions the CNS

In addition to its blood supply, the CNS is served by another watery medium, the cerebrospinal fluid (CSF). About 135 milliliters of this clear, colorless fluid fills the ventricles (the cavities within the brain) and the subarachnoid spaces around the brain and spinal cord (Fig. 13-3). Although the CSF is 99% water, it contains glucose, proteins, urea, and salts. Most of the CSF is produced by networks of capillaries, the **choroid plexuses,** which project from the pia mater into the ventricles.

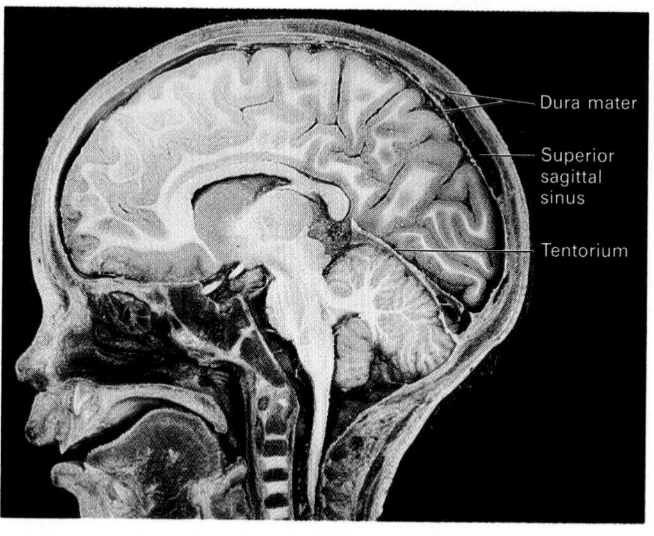

(a)

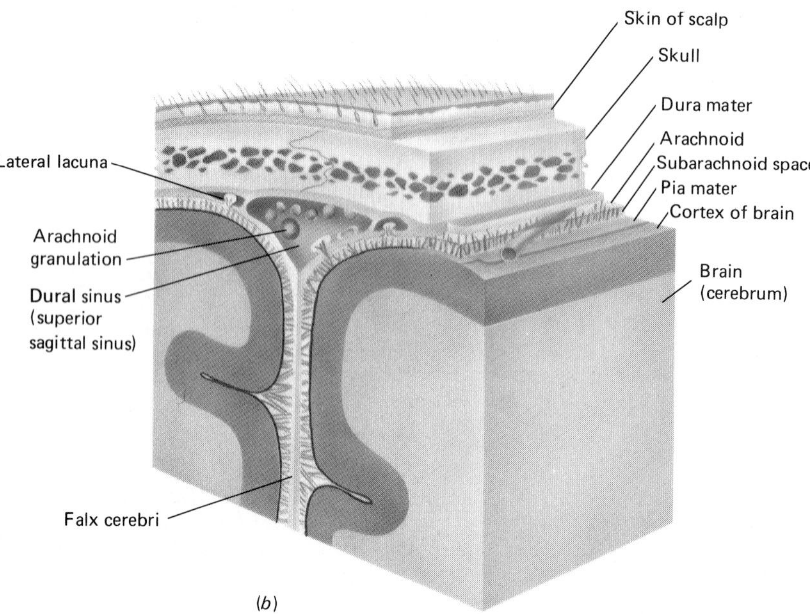

(b)

FIGURE 13-2

The protective coverings of the brain. *(a)* Hemisected human head, divided in the sagittal plane. Much more than the brain is visible in this photograph. The falx cerebri separating the two halves of the cerebrum, and the cut edge of the tentorium between the cerebrum and cerebellum are shown. (© CNRI/Phototake, Inc.) *(b)* Frontal section through the superior part of the brain. Note the large sinus shown between two layers of the dura mater. Blood leaving the brain flows into such sinuses and then circulates to the large jugular veins in the neck. The falx cerebri, the partition between the cerebral hemispheres, is shown.

After it is produced, the CSF circulates inferiorly through the ventricles. More fluid is added from the choroid plexus in each ventricle. From the fourth ventricle the CSF passes through small apertures into the subarachnoid space. Some of it moves downward to fill the subarachnoid space around the spinal cord, while the rest moves upward around the brain. Finally it is reabsorbed into the blood through structures called **arachnoid granulations.** These structures project from the arachnoid layer into large blood sinuses within the dura mater. Normally, the rates of CSF production and reabsorption are balanced.

A major function of the CSF is to cushion the brain and spinal cord. The brain actually floats in the CSF. The CSF provides vital protection against mechanical injury. Fluids cannot be compressed very much and so they dissipate mechanical forces. When the head is jolted, the CSF absorbs the shock, preventing the brain and spinal

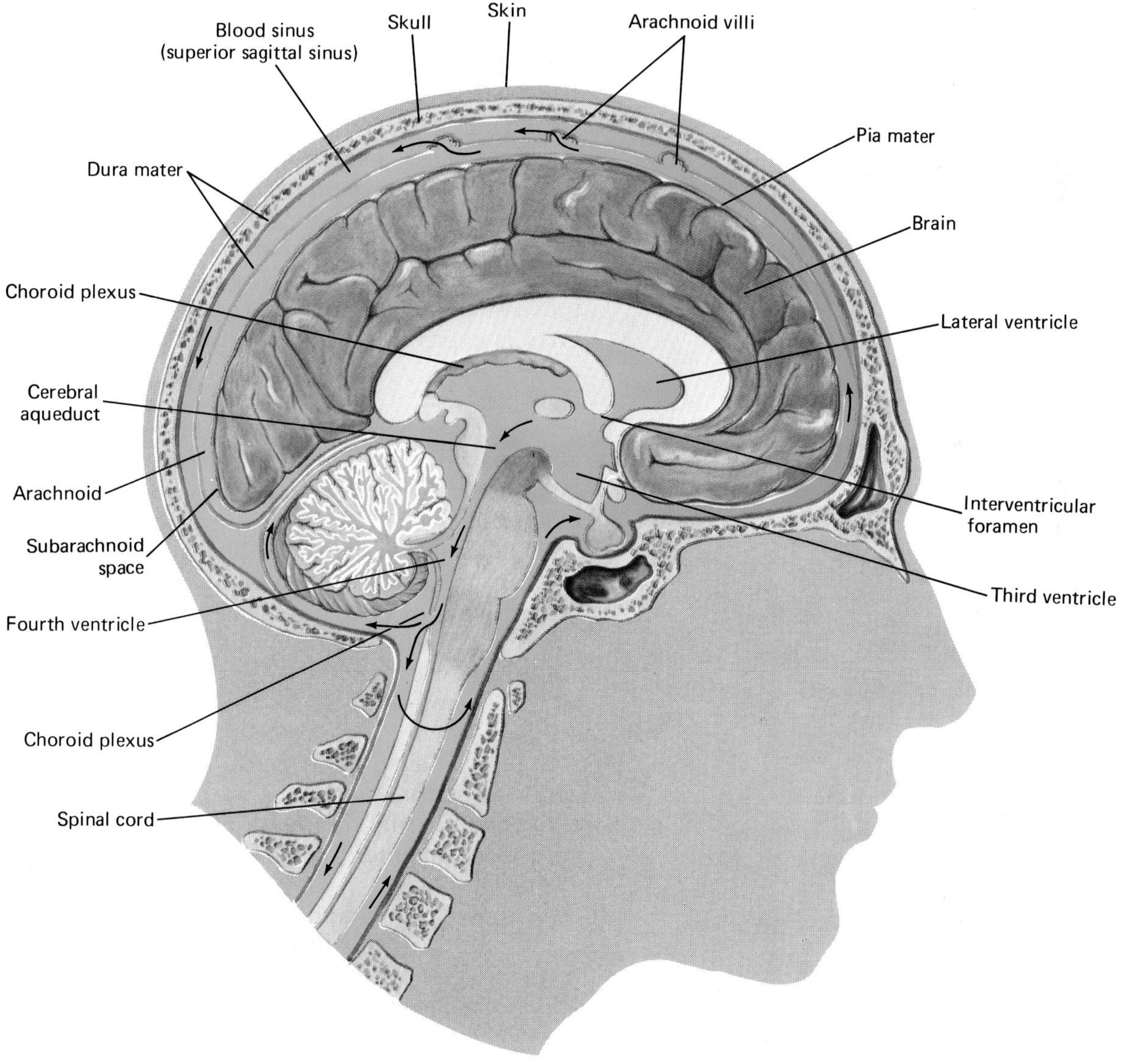

FIGURE 13-3

Circulation of the cerebrospinal fluid in the brain and spinal cord. A midsagittal section of the brain is shown. Cerebrospinal fluid is produced by the choroid plexuses in the walls of the ventricles. The fluid circulates through the ventricles and subarachnoid space. It is continuously produced and continuously reabsorbed into the blood of the dural sinuses through the arachnoid granulations.

cord from bumping against the bony walls that surround them. Head injuries can result in concussion or contusion of the brain. (See Focus on the CNS in Stress.) CSF also dissolves and transports substances filtered from the blood and serves as a medium for the exchange of nutrients and waste products between the blood and the brain.

Clinical highlight

A normal volume of CSF is essential to normal nervous system function. Blockage of CSF flow or abnormally rapid production can result in hydrocephalus, which means literally "water in the head." As CSF accumulates, the resulting pressure can cause enlargement of the skull in children and, eventually, brain damage; in severe cases, mental retardation may result. Hydrocephalus occasionally occurs in adults but is most common as a birth defect in infants and children.

When CSF is removed for diagnostic purposes, the patient is kept lying down for several hours until the normal volume can be replaced by the choroid plexuses. Should the patient attempt to sit up or turn his head from side to side while the CSF volume is still depleted, the brain is jolted, and intense pain or headache may result.

The human brain is a highly complex organ

Not even the most intricate computer begins to rival the complexity of the human brain. A soft, wrinkled mass of tissue weighing about 1.4 kilograms (3 lb), the human brain is the most complex organ known. Each of its 25 billion neurons is functionally connected to as many as 1000 others, and there may be as many as 10^{14} synapses. No wonder that scientists have barely begun to unravel the tangled neural circuits that govern human physiology and behavior.

What we do know is that at any moment millions of messages are flashing through the brain. They bring information to the brain about the state of the body and transmit "decisions" back to the organs maintaining an appropriate heart rate, blood pressure, respiration rate, temperature, muscle tone, and blood chemistry. At the same time the brain receives and responds to hundreds of messages from the outer environment—a ringing telephone, the aroma of a steak dinner, the sounds of traffic, the printed words on this page.

The brain is dependent on its blood supply

Brain cells require a continuous supply of oxygen and glucose. Although the brain accounts for only about 2% of the body weight, it receives about 20% of the blood pumped by the heart each minute, and consumes about 20% of the oxygen used by the body at rest.

Blood is delivered to the brain by four arteries—two internal carotid arteries and two vertebral arteries. These arteries give rise to branches that form an arterial circuit (circle of Willis). This circuit helps ensure that the brain cells will continue to receive an adequate blood supply even if one of the arteries serving the brain becomes impaired in some way. The circulation of the brain will be discussed in more detail in Chapter 21.

The brain is so dependent upon its blood supply that when deprived of it, consciousness may be lost very quickly, and irreversible damage may occur within a few minutes. In fact, the most common cause of brain damage is a stroke (cerebrovascular accident), in which a portion of the brain is deprived of its blood supply (often because a blood vessel has been blocked by a blood clot).

Needed substances such as glucose, amino acids, oxygen, and certain ions pass easily into brain tissue from the blood circulating within brain capillaries. However, the passage of many other substances is impeded by a protective mechanism called the **blood-brain barrier.** This barrier slows or prevents certain materials from entering brain tissues. Some substances, for example, the waste products urea and creatinine and the hormone insulin, pass into the brain tissue very slowly. Some proteins as well as arsenic and gold are almost completely blocked out. The antibiotic erythromycin passes easily through the blood brain barrier, but most antibiotics, including penicillin, can enter the brain only to a limited extent.

Electron micrograph studies show that the brain capillaries are structurally different from capillaries elsewhere in the body. The epithelial cells that make up brain capillaries are continuous and they are joined with tight intercellular junctions. These cells appear to form a complete wall. There is also a substantial basement membrane surrounding the capillaries. Large numbers of astrocytes surround brain capillaries and extensions of these glial cells form a covering around the capillaries.

FOCUS ON . . . The CNS in stress	
Amnesia	Lack or loss of memory, especially inability to recall past experiences
Alzheimer's disease	Also called presenile dementia; a degenerative disorder characterized by loss of cells from the cerebral cortex and areas of the limbic system and loss of memory for recent events (retrograde amnesia); occurs in late middle and old age
Aphasia	A loss of language function in which comprehension or expression of words is impaired as a result of injury to the language areas in the cerebral cortex
Apraxia	Impaired ability to carry out purposeful learned motor acts (e.g., getting dressed) despite the physical ability and willingness to perform them; apparently caused by a lesion in the neural pathways that retain memory of learned patterns of movement
Ataxia	Partial or complete loss of ability to coordinate voluntary movements; there are many causes, including cerebellar damage
Cerebral palsy	Term applied to a number of motor disorders resulting from CNS damage at birth and characterized by an impairment of voluntary movement
Cerebrovascular accident (CVA)	Commonly called stroke. The commonest cause of neurological disability in Western countries; ischemic (deficiency of blood due to a blocked blood vessel) or hemorrhagic injury to the brain resulting from vascular disorder; may result from thrombosis (presence of a blood clot), embolism (blocking of an artery by a clot carried to the area by the blood current), or hemorrhage
Coma	A state of unconsciousness from which the patient cannot be aroused even by powerful stimulation; unarousable unresponsiveness
Concussion of the brain	Loss of consciousness owing to a blow to the head with possible temporary impairment of higher mental functions (e.g., retrograde amnesia). Many of the effects of concussion are due to edema in brain
Contusion of the brain	A bruise of the brain with loss of consciousness resulting from direct trauma to the head; often associated with skull fracture. Considered a more severe injury than concussion
Convulsion	A violent involuntary contraction or series of contractions of the skeletal muscles
Dementia	A general term for mental deterioration
Encephalitis	Inflammation of the brain; the term is often restricted to indicate inflammation of viral origin. (Inflammation caused by bacterial invasion is called cerebritis.)
Glioma	A neoplasm of the brain or spinal cord; it is a tumor of the glial cells
Hemiplegia	Paralysis of one side of the body
Huntington's chorea	A hereditary disease beginning in adulthood and characterized by mental deterioration and rapid, jerky involuntary movements; now usually called Huntington's disease
Narcolepsy	A disorder of unknown cause in which the patient may fall asleep frequently and at inappropriate times
Poliomyelitis	An acute viral infection that may involve the CNS, causing lesions that result in paralysis of various muscle groups. In the United States the number of cases was 21,000 per year before the introduction of polio vaccine in 1955. That number has dramatically decreased since.
Stroke	See cerebrovascular accident, above

The brain and spinal cord develop from the neural tube

The nervous system is one of the first systems to differentiate and function in the early embryo. All neurons must be manufactured before birth. To accomplish this feat it has been estimated that an average of 45,000 neurons per minute must be produced by mitosis and must differentiate during the months of prenatal life.[1] Indeed, much of the genetic information is concerned with directing the brain's construction.

The nervous system begins to develop during the third week of embryonic development with the formation of the **neural plate,** a region of flattened tissue. The neural plate grows and folds, forming the **neural tube.** In the early embryo the brain and spinal cord differentiate from the neural tube. The cephalic (superior) portion of the tube expands and differentiates into the structures of the brain while the inferior section of the tube develops into the spinal cord. The brain and spinal cord remain continuous and their central cavities communicate. Early development of the nervous system is discussed and illustrated in Chapter 30.

As the brain begins to develop, three enlargements develop in the cephalic portion of the neural tube. These three primary vesicles are the (1) **prosencephalon,** or **forebrain,** (2) **mesencephalon,** or **midbrain,** and (3) **rhombencephalon,** or **hindbrain.** As development continues, these vesicles grow and the brain region bends (flexes), subdividing to form five secondary vesicles. The prosencephalon subdivides to form the **telencephalon** and **diencephalon** (Fig. 13-4; Table 13-1). The telencephalon then gives rise to the cerebrum, and the diencephalon to the thalamus and hypothalamus. The mesencephalon forms the midbrain. The rhombencephalon subdivides to form the **metencephalon** and **myelencephalon.** The metencephalon gives rise to the cerebellum and pons, and the myelencephalon develops into the medulla.

The most posterior part of the brain, the medulla, is continuous with the spinal cord. Its cavity, the **fourth ventricle,** communicates inferiorly with the **central canal** of the spinal cord. Superiorly, the fourth ventricle communicates with the

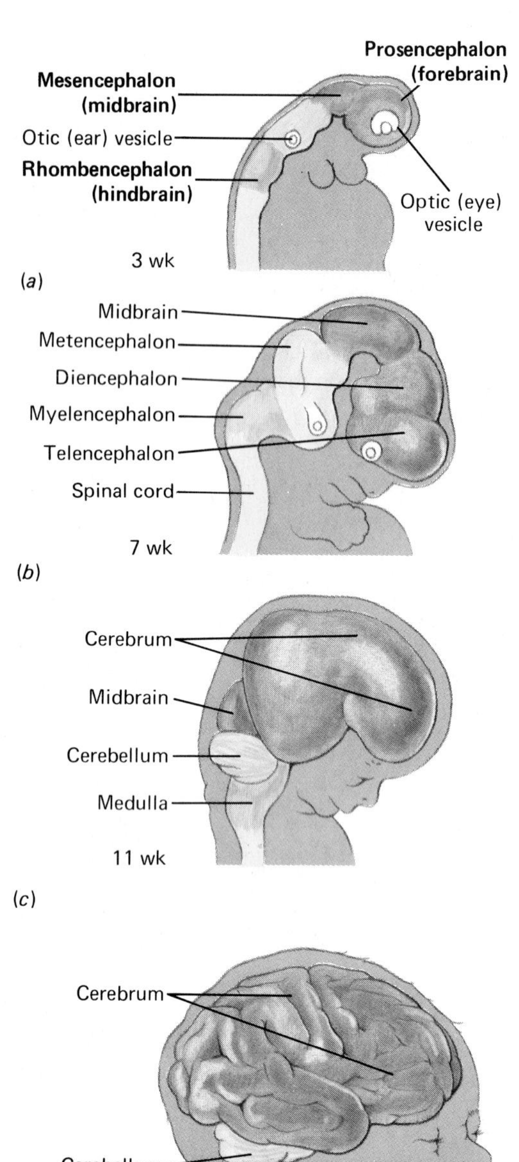

FIGURE 13-4

Development of the central nervous system. *(a)* At 3 weeks of development the primary vesicles—forebrain, midbrain, and hindbrain—are evident. *(b)* By 7 weeks the brain has flexed and the five secondary vesicles can be identified. *(c)* By 11 weeks of development, the cerebrum has grown back over the diencephalon and midbrain. *(d)* Newborn. The cerebrum has grown back over much of the brain and has folded to form convolutions. The thalamus, hypothalamus, and pons are labeled in the midsagittal section shown in Figure 13-7.

[1] Noback, Charles R., and Demarest, Robert J.: The Human Nervous System, 2nd ed. New York, McGraw-Hill Book Company, 1975.

TABLE 13-1

Divisions of the brain		
Division	**Description**	**Functions**
Medulla	Most inferior portion of the brainstem; continuous with spinal cord. Its white matter consists of nerve tracts passing between the spinal cord and various parts of the brain. Its gray matter consists of nuclei. The anterior portion consists mainly of the pyramids. Contains part of the reticular formation, the olives, and nuclei of cranial nerves IX through XII.* Its cavity is the fourth ventricle.	Contains vital centers (within its reticular formation) that regulate heartbeat, respiration, and blood pressure. Contains reflex centers that control swallowing, coughing, sneezing, and vomiting. Relays messages to other parts of the brain.
Pons	Consists mainly of nerve tracts passing between the medulla and other parts of the brain. Forms a bulge on the anterior surface of the brainstem. Contains respiratory centers and nuclei of cranial nerves V through VIII.	Serves as a link connecting various parts of the brain. Helps regulate respiration. By virtue of its cranial nerve nuclei, helps regulate chewing, facial expression, and certain eye movements.
Midbrain	Just superior to the pons. Cavity is the cerebral aqueduct. Anteriorly, consists of cerebral peduncles (which in turn are made up of crus cerebri, substantia nigra, and tegmentum). Posteriorly, tectum consists of corpora quadrigemina. Within midbrain are nuclei of cranial nerves III and IV and the red nucleus.	Superior colliculi mediate visual reflexes; inferior colliculi mediate auditory reflexes. Cranial nerves III and IV control certain eye movements. Red nucleus integrates messages concerning muscle tone and posture.
Diencephalon	Consists of two parts:	
Thalamus	Located on each side of the third ventricle. Consists of two masses of gray matter partly covered by white matter and contains many important nuclei, e.g., the geniculate nuclei.	Main relay center conducting information between spinal cord and cerebrum. Incoming messages are sorted and partially interpreted within the thalamic nuclei before being relayed to the appropriate centers in the cerebrum.
Hypothalamus	Forms ventral floor of third ventricle. Contains many nuclei. Optic chiasma mark the crossing of the optic nerves. The mamillary bodies are concerned with olfactory messages and certain feeding reflexes. The infundibulum connects the pituitary gland to the hypothalamus.	Contains centers for control of body temperature, appetite, and water balance. Regulates pituitary gland and links nervous and endocrine systems. Helps control autonomic system. Involved in some emotional and sexual responses.
Cerebellum	Second largest part of brain. Consists of two lateral cerebellar hemispheres connected by the vermis and is superior to the fourth ventricle.	Responsible for smooth, coordinated movement. Maintains posture and muscle tone, and helps maintain equilibrium.
Cerebrum	Largest, most prominent part of the brain. The longitudinal fissure divides the cerebrum into right and left hemispheres, each containing a lateral ventricle. Each hemisphere is divided into six lobes: frontal, parietal, occipital, temporal, limbic, and central lobe.	Center of intellect, memory, language, and consciousness. Receives and interprets sensory information from all sense receptors. Controls motor functions.
Cerebral cortex	Convoluted, outer layer of gray matter covering the cerebrum. Functionally divided into:	
	(1) Motor areas	Control voluntary movement and certain types of involuntary movement.
	(2) Sensory areas	Receive incoming sensory information from eyes, ears, touch, and pressure receptors, and other sense receptors. Sensory association areas interpret incoming sensory information.
	(3) Association areas	Responsible for thought, learning, language, judgment, and personality; store memories. Connect sensory and motor areas.
White matter	Consists of association fibers, which connect neurons within the same hemisphere; commissure fibers, which interconnect the two hemispheres (e.g., corpus callosum and fornix); and projection fibers, which are part of ascending and descending tracts. Basal ganglia are located within the white matter.	Links various areas of the brain.

*Cranial nerves are discussed in more detail in Table 14-1.

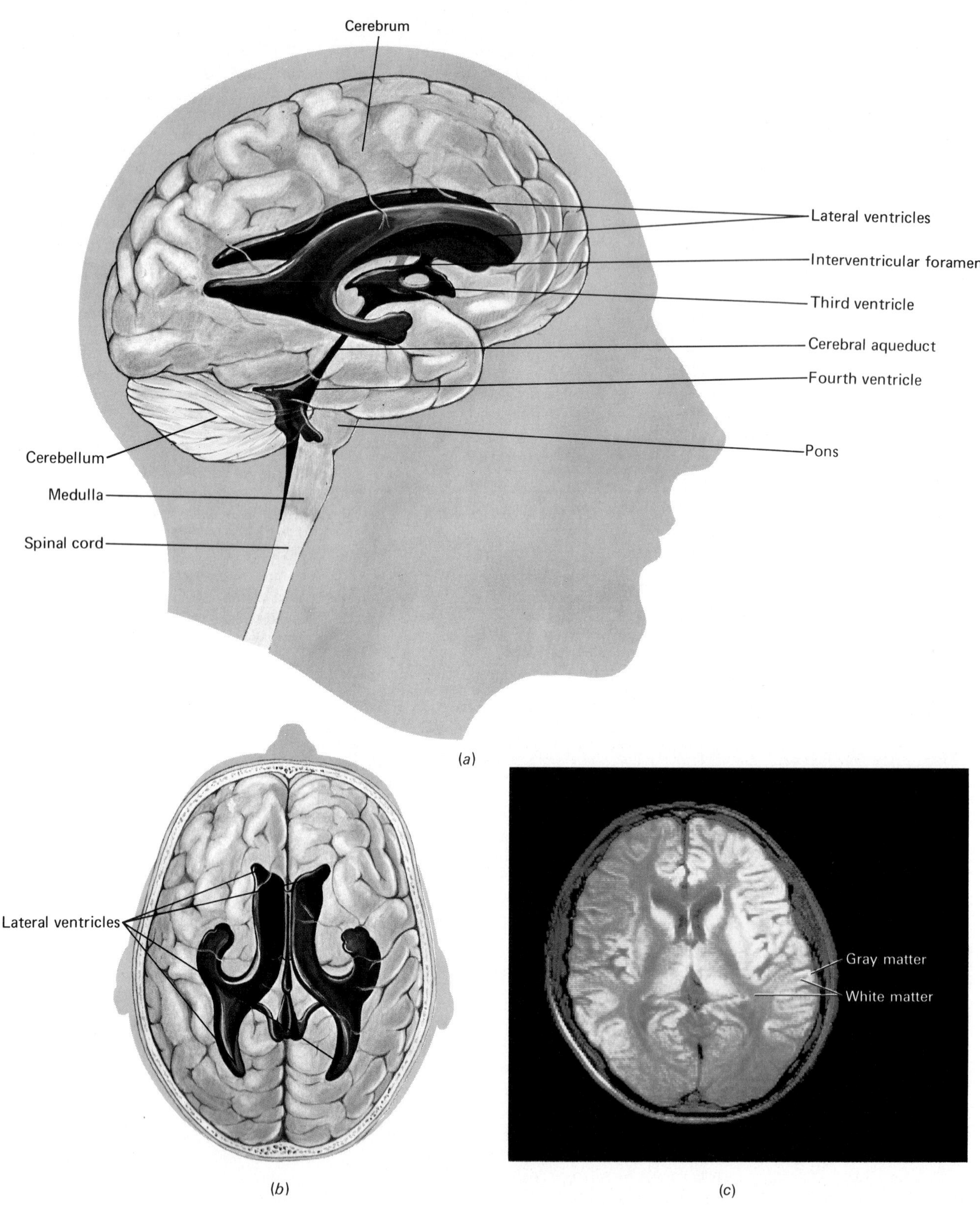

FIGURE 13-5

The ventricles of the brain. (*a*) Lateral view. (*b*) Superior view. (*c*) CT scan showing lateral ventricles. (CNRI/Science Photo Library/Photo Researchers, Inc.)

cerebral aqueduct, a channel that runs through the midbrain (Fig. 13-5). The cerebral aqueduct connects the fourth ventricle with the **third ventricle,** a cavity within the diencephalon. Finally, the interventricular foramina connect the third ventricle with each **lateral ventricle,** also called the **first** and **second ventricles.** The lateral ventricles are located within the cerebrum.

The main divisions of the brain are the medulla, pons, midbrain, diencephalon (which includes the thalamus and hypothalamus), cerebellum, and cerebrum (Figs. 13-6 through 13-10 and Table 13-1). The medulla, pons, and midbrain make up the **brainstem,** the elongated portion of the brain that looks like a stalk for the cerebrum.

The medulla contains vital centers

More formally known as the **medulla oblongata** (meh-**dul**-ah *ob*-long-**gah**-tuh), the medulla is the most inferior portion of the brainstem. Caudally, it is continuous with the spinal cord. Its cavity, the fourth ventricle (Figs. 13-5 and 13-7), is continuous with the central canal of the spinal cord. About 2.5 centimeters (1 in.) long, the medulla consists of white matter and gray matter, somewhat like the spinal cord below. The white matter consists mainly of nerve tracts passing between the spinal cord and the various portions of the brain. Because of its position, all nerve tracts passing between the spinal cord and the upper divisions of the brain must pass through the medulla. The *gray matter* of the medulla consists mainly of various nuclei (groups of cell bodies).

The anterior (ventral) surface of the medulla consists mainly of two prominent bulges of white matter known as the **pyramids** (Figs. 13-9 and 13-10). The pyramids contain descending fibers (axons that transmit impulses down the cord) of the **pyramidal tracts,** bundles of axons that pass from the cerebrum (cerebral cortex) to the spinal cord. Just superior to the junction of the medulla with the spinal cord, about 80% of the pyramidal fibers cross, or *decussate,* forming what is called the *decussation of the pyramids.* The pyramidal (lateral and anterior corticospinal) tracts are the major voluntary motor pathways through which nerve fibers from the cerebrum pass through the

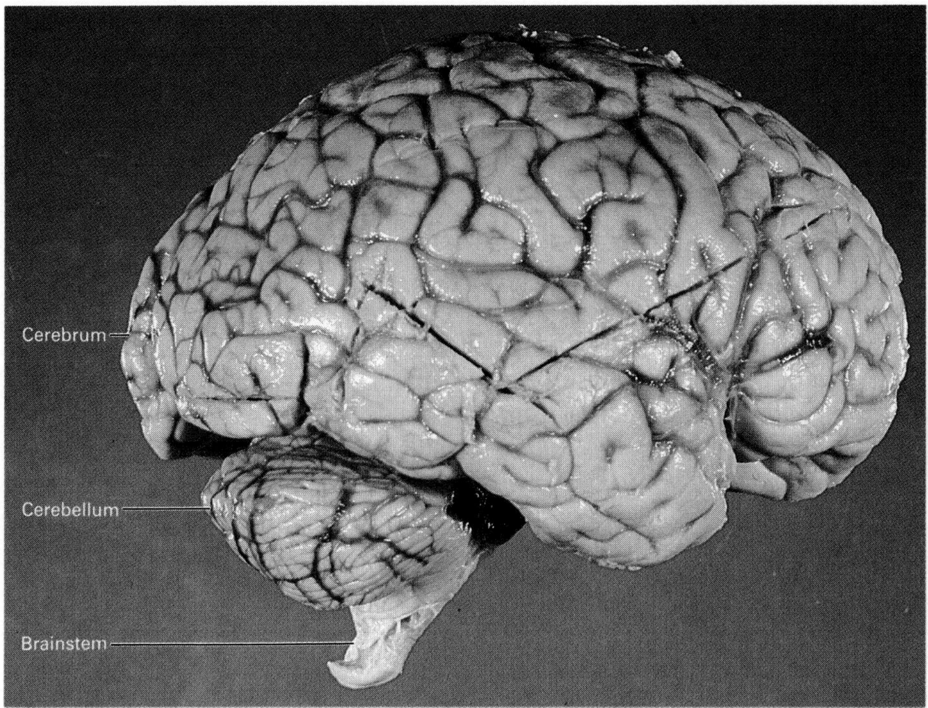

FIGURE 13-6

Photograph of the brain. Lateral view. Note that the cerebrum covers the diencephalon and part of the brainstem. (University of Southern California/PhotoEdit.)

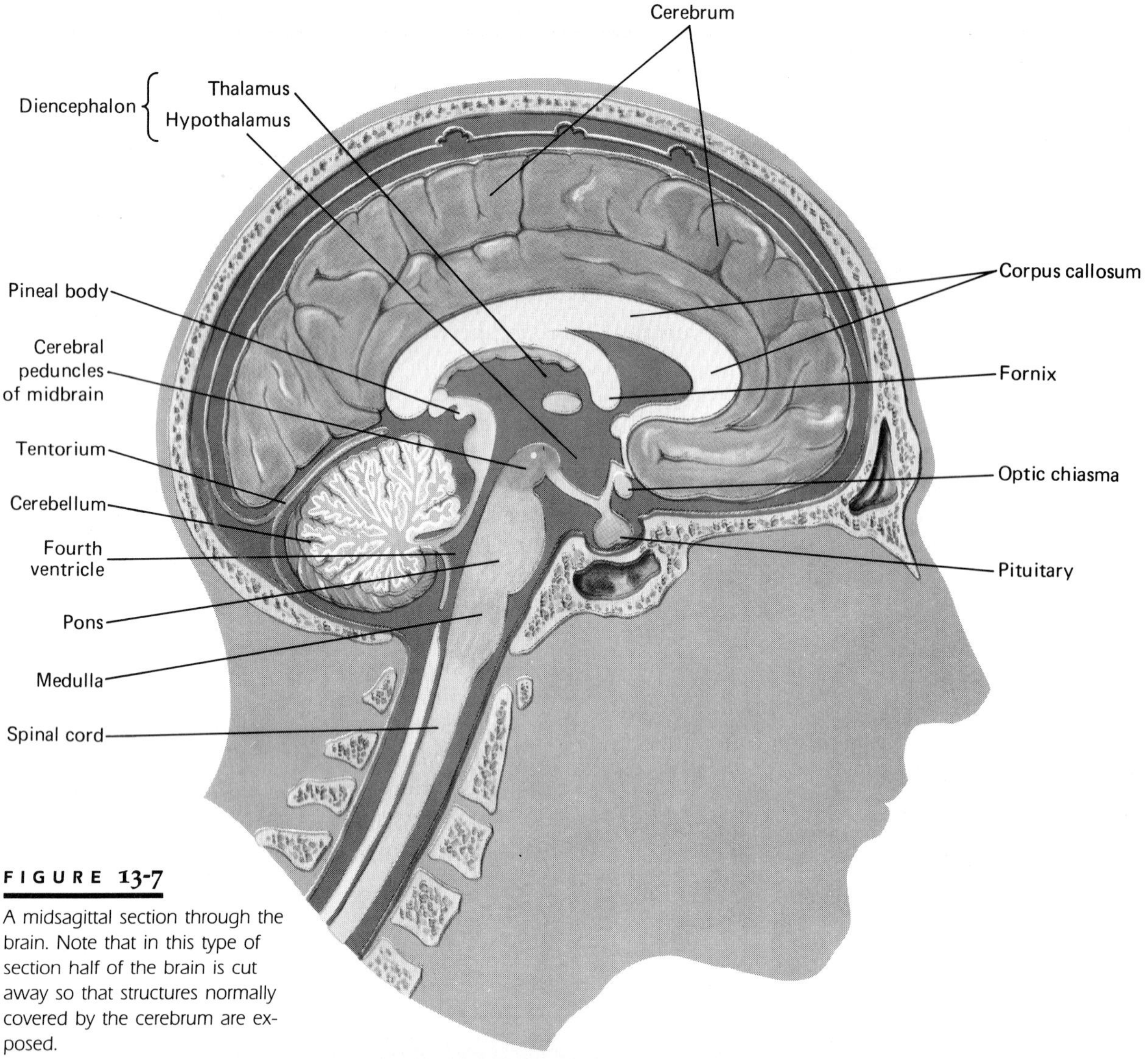

Cerebrum

Diencephalon { Thalamus, Hypothalamus

Pineal body

Cerebral peduncles of midbrain

Tentorium

Cerebellum

Fourth ventricle

Pons

Medulla

Spinal cord

Corpus callosum

Fornix

Optic chiasma

Pituitary

FIGURE 13-7

A midsagittal section through the brain. Note that in this type of section half of the brain is cut away so that structures normally covered by the cerebrum are exposed.

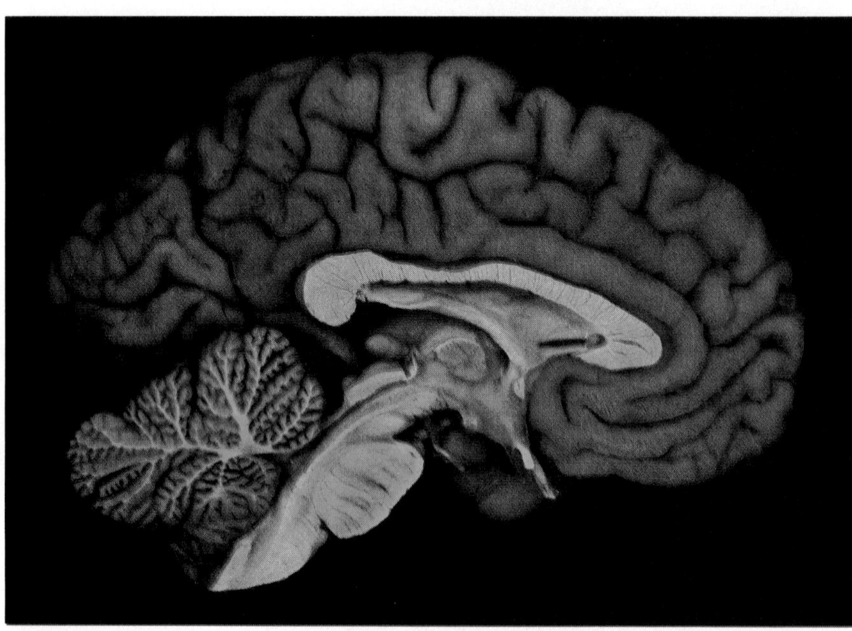

FIGURE 13-8

Photograph of the brain. Midsagittal view. Using Fig. 13-7 and the text as a guide, identify the structures shown in this figure. (Dr. Colin Chumbley/Science Photo Library/Photo Researchers, Inc.)

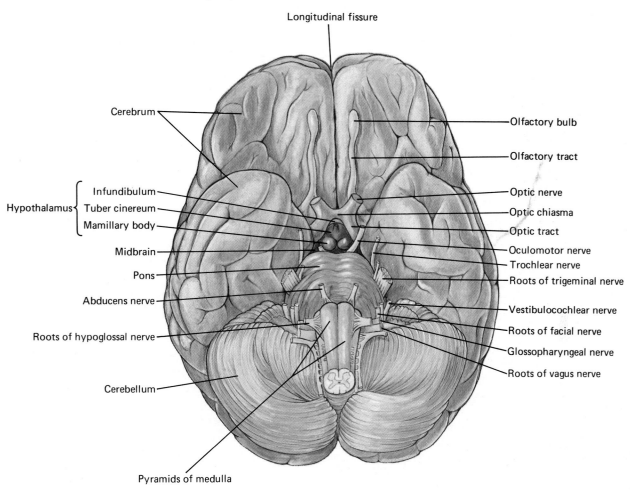

FIGURE 13-9

Basal (inferior) aspect of the brain. The cranial nerves will be discussed in greater detail in Chapter 14.

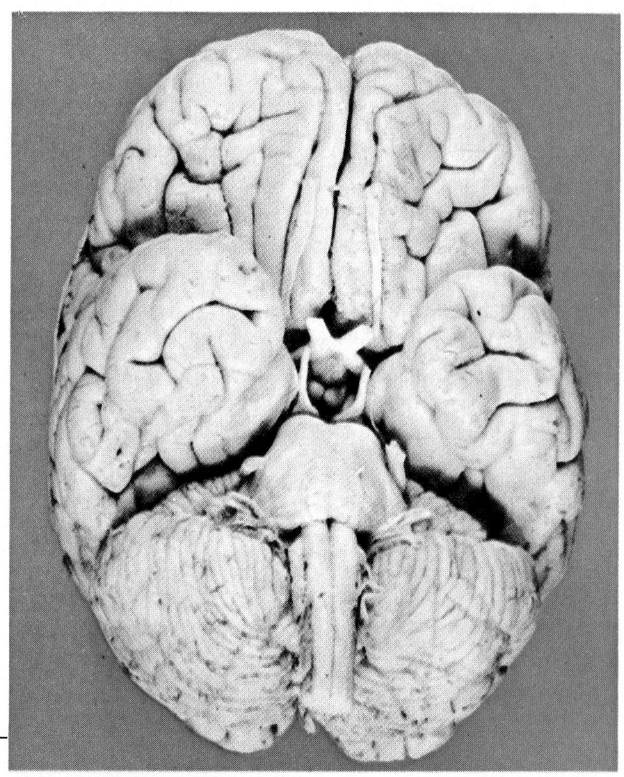

FIGURE 13-10

Photograph of the basal (inferior) aspect of the brain. Using Fig. 13-9 as a guide, identify as many structures as you can. (Dissection by Dr. E. L. Rees. From Williams and Warwick (eds.): Gray's Anatomy, 36th ed. Philadelphia, W. B. Saunders Company, 1980) brain and down the spinal cord. Decussation within the pyramids rearranges the nerve fibers so that the right side of the brain controls the movement of the left side of the body, and vice versa.

The posterior (dorsal) region of the medulla consists in part of the upward continuation of two pairs of ascending spinal tracts: the **fasciculi gracilis** and the **fasciculi cuneatus.** (These tracts convey information regarding touch, pressure, and body position.) Most of the fibers of the fasciculi gracilis end within the prominent **nucleus gracilis** in the posterior portion of the medulla. There these fibers synapse with neurons that convey the information to other areas of the brain. Similarly, fibers of the fasciculi cuneatus synapse with neurons in the **nucleus cuneatus,** also located within the posterior portion of the medulla.

The **olive** is a flattened oval mass on each upper lateral surface of the medulla. It is composed of the *inferior olivary nucleus* and two *accessory olivary nuclei.* These nuclei are made up of neuron cell bodies that send axons to the cerebellum through the *inferior cerebellar peduncles.* (A peduncle is simply a thick bundle of nerve fibers.)

A vast complex of intermingled gray and white matter known as the **reticular formation** extends from the spinal cord through the medulla and upward through the brainstem and thalamus. The reticular formation is important in keeping the cerebrum conscious and alert. Within the reticular formation of the medulla are several vital reflex centers.

The medulla contains discrete nuclei that serve as **vital centers.** They include the **cardiac centers** that control heart rate, the **vasomotor centers** that control blood pressure by regulating the diameter of the blood vessels, and **respiratory centers** that initiate and regulate breathing. Because the medulla contains these vital centers, a blow to the back of the head that damages the medulla may be fatal. Centers for other reflex actions such as vomiting, sneezing, coughing, and swallowing are also found within the medulla.

Twelve pairs of **cranial nerves** emerge from the brain and transmit information between the brain and sensory receptors in muscles and visceral organs. Four cranial nerves, designated cranial nerves IX through XII, originate within the medulla, and their nuclei are located there (see Table 14-1). *Cranial nerve IX,* the *glossopharyngeal,* relays information regarding taste, salivation, and swallowing. *Cranial nerve X,* the *vagus,* conveys information to and from many thoracic and abdominal organs. *Cranial nerve XI,* the *spinal accessory,* delivers messages governing movement of the head and shoulders. (Part of this nerve originates in the upper portion of the spinal cord.) *Cranial nerve XII,* the *hypoglossal,* delivers messages from the medulla to the tongue muscles. *Cranial nerve VIII,* the *vestibulocochlear,* is synaptically connected to nuclei located in both the medulla and pons. This is a sensory nerve that delivers messages regarding hearing and equilibrium.

The pons is a bridge to other parts of the brain

More formally known as the **pons varolii** (va-**row**-lee-i), the pons forms a bulge on the anterior (ventral) surface of the brainstem. The pons is just superior to the medulla with which it is continuous; its posterior surface is hidden by the cerebellum. The word pons means bridge, and indeed the pons serves as a link connecting various parts of the brain. In fact, the pons consists mainly of nerve fibers passing between the medulla and other parts of the brain. Some fibers run transversely, passing laterally to the *middle cerebellar peduncles,* which consist of fibers that pass from the pons to the cerebellum.

The pons contains centers that help regulate respiration. Centers for the reflexes mediated by cranial nerves V through VII are also located within the pons. *Cranial nerve V,* the *trigeminal,* conveys impulses regarding sensation in the face and head and helps control chewing movements. *Cranial nerve VI,* the *abducens,* helps direct eye movements. *Cranial nerve VII,* the *facial,* is responsible for facial expression and conveys impulses regarding taste. The pons also receives information from *cranial nerve VIII,* the *vestibulocochlear,* regarding equilibrium.

The midbrain contains centers for visual and auditory reflexes

The **midbrain,** or *mesencephalon,* extends from the pons to the diencephalon. Only about 2 centimeters in length, it is the shortest portion of the brainstem. Its cavity, the *cerebral aqueduct,* connects the third and fourth ventricles (Fig. 13-5).

Anteriorly (ventrally), the midbrain consists of the right and left **cerebral peduncles,** large bundles of neurons connecting the cerebrum with lower portions of the brain and with the spinal cord. Each cerebral peduncle has several component parts. The **crus cerebri** is made up of several descending tracts. The **substantia nigra** is an area of deeply pigmented neurons thought to be involved in motor function (Fig. 13-11). Fibers that project from this area are rich in the neurotransmitter dopamine and are involved in Parkinson's disease (to be discussed in a later chapter).

Another component of the cerebral peduncle is the dorsal **tegmental** portion, which contains part of the reticular formation, ascending pathways, and several important nuclei. The nuclei of *cranial nerves III*, the *oculomotor*, and *IV*, the *trochlear*, regulate eye movement. Another important nucleus within the reticular formation is the **red nucleus,** an oval mass of neurons with a pinkish color. Neurons conveying impulses regarding muscle tone and posture from the cerebellum and motor areas of the cerebrum synapse within the red nucleus. This information is then transmitted via the *rubrospinal tract* (an extrapyramidal pathway) to various regions of the spinal cord.

The roof of the midbrain, called the **tectum,** lies posterior to the cerebral aqueduct. It consists of four rounded bodies, the **corpora quadrigemina.** Larger and darker in color, the paired superior bodies are called the **superior colliculi;** they serve as visual reflex centers for head and eyeball movements in response to certain types of visual and other stimuli. The paired **inferior colliculi** are relay centers for auditory information that is sent into the auditory regions of the cerebrum.

In many vertebrates the midbrain is the largest region of the brain, but in humans most of its functions have been assumed by the cerebrum. Still, many reflex actions are integrated there, including pupillary constriction in response to light, turning the head to hear a sound better (in dogs and some other animals the ears are turned to funnel the sound), and righting reflexes. Righting reflexes help people maintain a normal standing position and hold their heads upright. (In a cat they help the animal land on its feet when it falls or is dropped.)

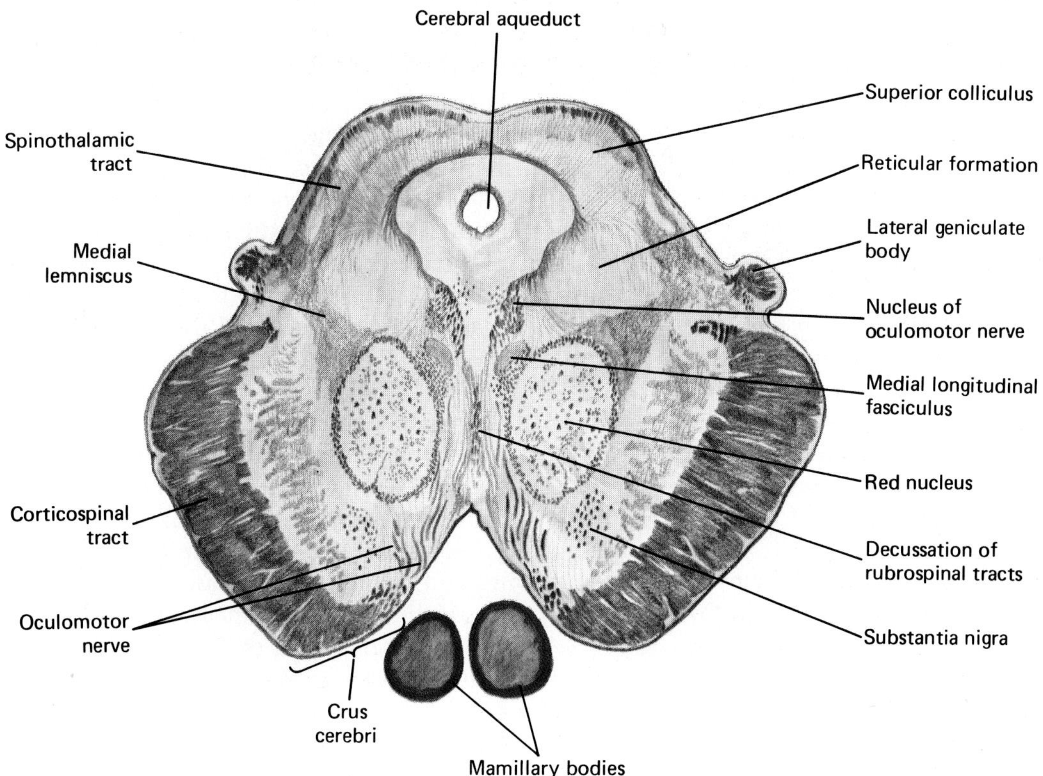

FIGURE 13-11

Cross section through brain showing some of the structures of the midbrain. (In this section, the mamillary bodies of the hypothalamus are visible.)

The diencephalon includes the thalamus and hypothalamus

The **diencephalon** is the part of the brain between the cerebrum and the midbrain. Its cavity is the *third ventricle* (Fig. 13-5). Among its important structures are the thalamus, hypothalamus, and pineal body.

The **pineal body,** or *epiphysis,* projects from the roof of the third ventricle and emerges from the depression between the superior colliculi. The philosopher Descartes thought that the pineal gland was the seat of the soul, and even today its function is the focus of much debate. It is now known to be an endocrine gland, and its functions will be discussed further in Chapter 18.

Before puberty the pineal gland begins to decrease in size, and small bits of calcium carbonate and other minerals appear in its tissue. This is important clinically, for the mineral makes the pineal gland visible on x-rays of the skull, and displacement from its normal position is evidence of a possible brain tumor.

THE THALAMUS IS AN IMPORTANT RELAY CENTER

The **thalamus** consists of two oval masses of gray matter partially covered by a thin layer of white matter. One mass is located on each side of the third ventricle, and each is about 3 centimeters long.

The thalamus is a major relay center. Nuclei in the thalamus serve as relay stations for all sensory information, except smell, to the cerebrum. Afferent neurons coming from all the sense receptors (except the olfactory epithelium of the nose) synapse within these nuclei. Neural messages arriving from these afferent neurons are sent on into the cerebrum. Other nuclei relay information about ongoing movement to motor areas in the cerebrum. Many neurons in descending motor pathways also synapse within nuclei of the thalamus.

The **medial geniculate nuclei** receive messages from the auditory receptors of the ears by way of the inferior colliculi. These messages are then relayed into the cerebrum. The **lateral geniculate nuclei** receive visual information from the eyes and relay impulses into appropriate areas of the cerebrum. **Ventral nuclei** relay information regarding taste and other sensations. The **ventral lateral nuclei** receive motor information from the cerebellum and relay the information into the cerebrum. The **ventral anterior nuclei** also relay motor information.

The thalamus also interprets many types of sensory information. We become vaguely aware of sensory input when impulses reach the thalamus. If sensory areas of the cerebrum are destroyed, the person can still be conscious of pain, temperature, crude touch, and pressure. The thalamus also helps one associate feelings of pleasantness or unpleasantness with sensory impulses. Movements involved with expressing emotions such as rage or fear are also influenced by this portion of the brain, as well as by the hypothalamus.

THE HYPOTHALAMUS HELPS MAINTAIN HOMEOSTASIS

The **hypothalamus** forms the floor and part of the lateral walls of the third ventricle (Figs. 13-7 and 13-16*b*). It lies inferior to the thalamus. Many nuclei are located within the hypothalamus. Some of these are distinct, but others are diffuse and difficult to distinguish from the surrounding tissue. Afferent and efferent neurons connect these centers with all other parts of the central nervous system.

Some well-defined structures usually considered part of the hypothalamus are the optic chiasma, tuber cinereum, infundibulum, and mamillary bodies. The **optic chiasma** is located in the floor of the hypothalamus. This prominent X-shaped structure is formed by the crossing of part of each optic nerve. Just caudal to the optic chiasma is the **tuber cinereum,** a convex mass of gray matter. From the midline of the tuber cinereum, a stalk of tissue called the **infundibulum** extends downward, connecting the pituitary gland to the hypothalamus. Thus, the pituitary gland is suspended inferiorly from the floor of the hypothalamus. The **mamillary bodies** are small paired masses that mark the caudal limit of the anterior surface of the hypothalamus. The mamillary bodies activate feeding reflexes such as swallowing and licking the lips, and may also be involved in relaying olfactory messages.

A small but mighty part of the brain, the hypothalamus helps regulate an impressive number of mechanisms essential to maintaining homeostasis. Here are some of its functions:

1. The hypothalamus is the most important relay station and output pathway between

the cerebral cortex and the lower autonomic centers. It is sometimes called the control center of the autonomic system. For example, stimulation of anterior and medial areas in the hypothalamus results in a decrease in heart rate. (Through what area of the brainstem would neurons effecting such a change have to act?) In this role the hypothalamus serves as an important link between "mind" (cerebrum) and "body" (physiological mechanisms). Persons who learn to control consciously certain physiological activities that normally proceed automatically are probably exercising control by way of the hypothalamic pathways. More will be said about the autonomic regulatory functions of the hypothalamus in Chapter 16.

2. The hypothalamus is the link between the nervous and endocrine systems. Wedded both anatomically and physiologically to the pituitary gland, the hypothalamus produces several releasing hormones that regulate the secretion of specific hormones from the anterior pituitary. In addition, cells of the **supraoptic nuclei** within the hypothalamus manufacture antidiuretic hormone (ADH), which helps regulate the volume of plasma (and of urine). Cells of the **paraventricular nuclei** produce the hormone oxytocin, important in uterine contraction during childbirth and in release of milk from the breast. Both these hormones are sent to the posterior pituitary gland for storage and eventual release into the blood, as will be described in Chapter 18.

3. The hypothalamus helps maintain fluid balance. ADH produced by its cells regulates the volume of water excreted by the kidneys. In addition, a **thirst center** in the hypothalamus contains cells sensitive to the concentration of electrolytes in the blood. When electrolytes become too concentrated, the sensation of thirst is felt.

4. Body temperature is regulated by the hypothalamus. When body temperature rises, messages from the **temperature regulating center** in the hypothalamus cause blood vessels in the skin to dilate and sweat glands to step up their rate of excretion. These homeostatic mechanisms cool the body, bringing its temperature back to normal. Should body temperature fall below normal, the hypothalamus sends messages causing blood vessels in the skin to constrict and muscles to shiver. These mechanisms conserve body heat and increase heat production.

5. As will be discussed in Chapter 25, the appetite and satiety centers within the hypothalamus regulate food intake.

6. The hypothalamus influences sexual behavior and the affective (emotional) aspects of sensory input. Centers here help us decide whether something is pleasant or painful.

The cerebellum is responsible for fine coordination of movement

The second largest part of the brain, the cerebellum consists of two lateral masses called **hemispheres** and a medial connecting portion, the **vermis** (Fig. 13-12). The two hemispheres are partially separated by a fold of the dura mater, the **falx cerebelli.** The outer layer of the cerebellum, called the **cerebellar cortex,** consists of gray matter; beneath it, the organ is composed mainly of white matter.

The cerebellum is divided into regions called **lobes** that are separated from one another by grooves called **fissures.** The cerebellar cortex is pushed up into numerous long parallel folds called **folia.** When the cerebellum is cut, its inside surface has a treelike appearance and is referred to as the **arbor vitae** (tree of life). About 30 million large neurons called **Purkinje cells** are found in the cerebellar cortex. These cells integrate information regarding motor activity so that the cerebellum can keep us informed about the position of the body. Their axons, which are the only output from the cerebellar cortex, carry impulses to the nuclei of the cerebellum for relay into the brainstem.

Three pairs of peduncles, the superior, middle, and inferior, connect the cerebellum with other parts of the brain. The **inferior cerebellar peduncle** transmits information about ongoing movement from the spinal cord to the cerebellar cortex. The **middle cerebellar peduncle** delivers information from the pons to the cerebellar cortex. This information originates in sensory receptors including the eyes, as well as in motor areas of the cerebrum. The **superior cerebellar peduncle** is the main *output* pathway from the cerebellum. Its neurons transmit information to the thalamus and brainstem (and then it is relayed to other parts of the CNS). One of the most important output pathways of the cerebellum is to the red nucleus in the midbrain, which relays information from the cerebellum to the spinal cord.

The cerebellum is responsible for fine coordination of muscle movements. We can identify three main functions:

1. The cerebellum helps make muscular movements smooth instead of jerky and steady rather than trembling. When the cerebellum is damaged, movements essential in running, walking, writing, talking, and many other activities become uncoordinated.
2. The cerebellum helps maintain muscle tone, and thus posture.
3. Impulses from the vestibular apparatus (organ of balance) in the inner ear are continuously delivered to the **flocculonodular lobe** of the cerebellum (Fig. 13-12), which uses that information to help maintain equilibrium and posture.

The cerebellum ensures that movements generated elsewhere in the CNS are carried out smoothly and effectively. Using feedback control mechanisms, the cerebellum compares intention (instructions for movement transmitted by the cerebrum) with actual performance and compensates for errors. As the cerebellum receives output information from receptors in muscles, tendons, and joints, it compares that information with input from the cerebrum. The cerebellum produces an "error" signal, modifying the input from the cerebrum. In this way the message to the muscles is refined and the muscles respond smoothly and accurately. Because no mechanism for storing information is present, the continuous input from muscles, tendons, inner ear, and other parts of the brain must be immediately interpreted and acted upon.

The cerebellum also functions in the actual generation of movements. The lateral regions of the cerebellar cortex appear to be involved in the generation of rapid, ballistic movements. Unlike slow movements, these may not be monitored by feedback control. Instead, the cerebellum preprograms the duration of fast movements. The Purkinje cells fire before the movement begins. Additional research is needed to clarify cerebellar function.

Clinical highlight

When the cerebellum is damaged, movement is impaired on the same side of the body as the damage. Muscles do not become paralyzed, but movements become **ataxic,** meaning uncoordinated. Ataxia results from errors in the direction, range, and rate of movement. A staggering, "drunken" gait is characteristic, speech may be slurred, and the patient, in attempting to touch an object, overshoots first to one side and then to the other (intention tremor). In one clinical diagnostic test for cerebellar damage, the patient is asked to place a finger on his or her own nose. A patient with cerebellar damage will miss the mark and may miss several times before finding the target. The motion is inaccurate because an appropriate "error" signal is not produced. Chronic alcoholism results in degeneration of Purkinje cells resulting in an ataxic gait.

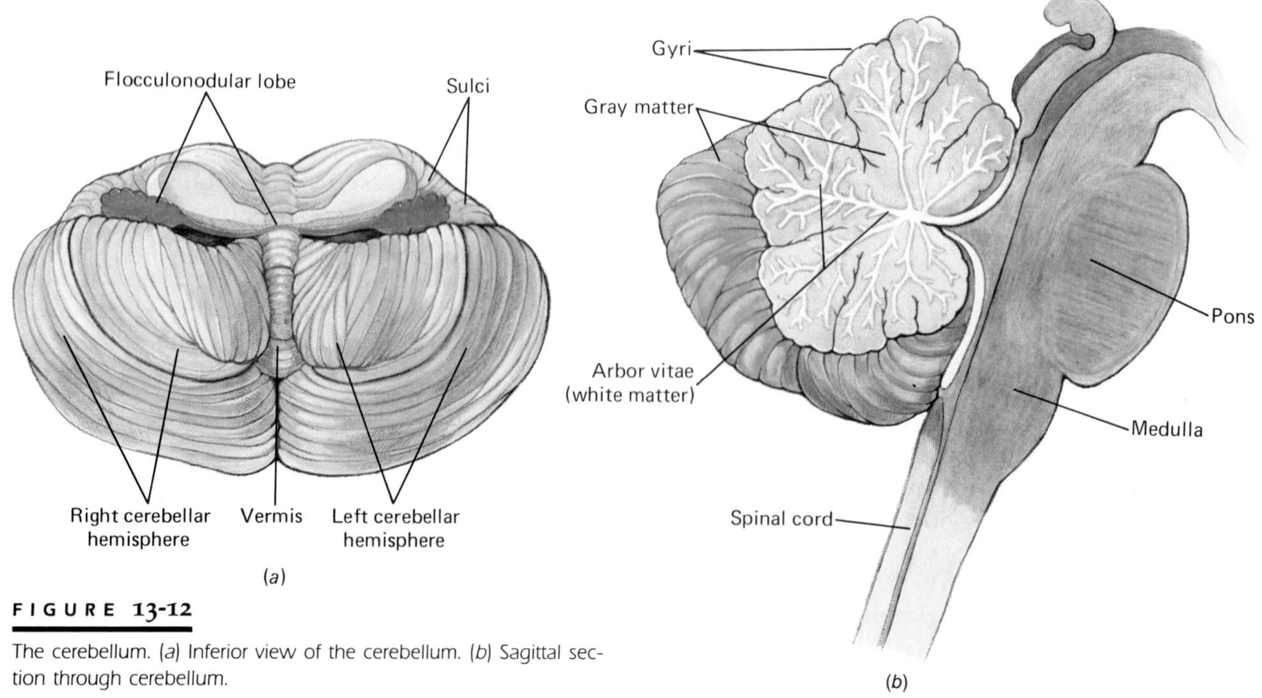

FIGURE 13-12

The cerebellum. (*a*) Inferior view of the cerebellum. (*b*) Sagittal section through cerebellum.

The cerebrum is the largest, most prominent part of the brain

More than 12 billion neurons and 50 billion glial cells are found within the **cerebrum,** the largest and most prominent part of the human brain. The cerebrum controls motor activities, interprets sensation, and serves as the center of intellect, memory, language, and consciousness.

THE CEREBRUM IS DIVIDED INTO HEMISPHERES AND LOBES

The thin (2- to 5-millimeters) outer layer of the cerebrum consists of gray matter and is called the **cerebral cortex.** Beneath it lies white matter containing nuclei (which are composed of gray matter). The two cavities within the cerebrum are known as the *lateral ventricles.*

In the embryo the cerebrum grows rapidly, enlarging out of proportion to the rest of the brain. It grows backward over the brainstem and also folds upon itself, forming **convolutions,** or **gyri** (**jie**-rie; singular, gyrus). Grooves, called **sulci** when shallow and **fissures** when deep, separate the gyri from one another. Patterns of gyri and sulci are apparently unique to each individual and even vary between the two hemispheres of the same brain. So convoluted is the human brain that about two-thirds of the cerebral cortex lies along the walls of the fissures and sulci.

The cerebrum is partially divided into right and left halves, the right and left **cerebral hemispheres,** by a deep groove called the **longitudinal fissure** (Fig. 13-13). A sickle-shaped extension of the dura mater called the **falx cerebri** extends into this fissure. The cerebrum is separated from the cerebellum by the **transverse fissure** (Fig. 13-14).

Fissures and sulci divide each hemisphere into six **lobes:** *frontal, parietal, occipital, temporal* (named after the bones that protect them), *central* (*insula*) and *limbic.* The first five of these lobes are

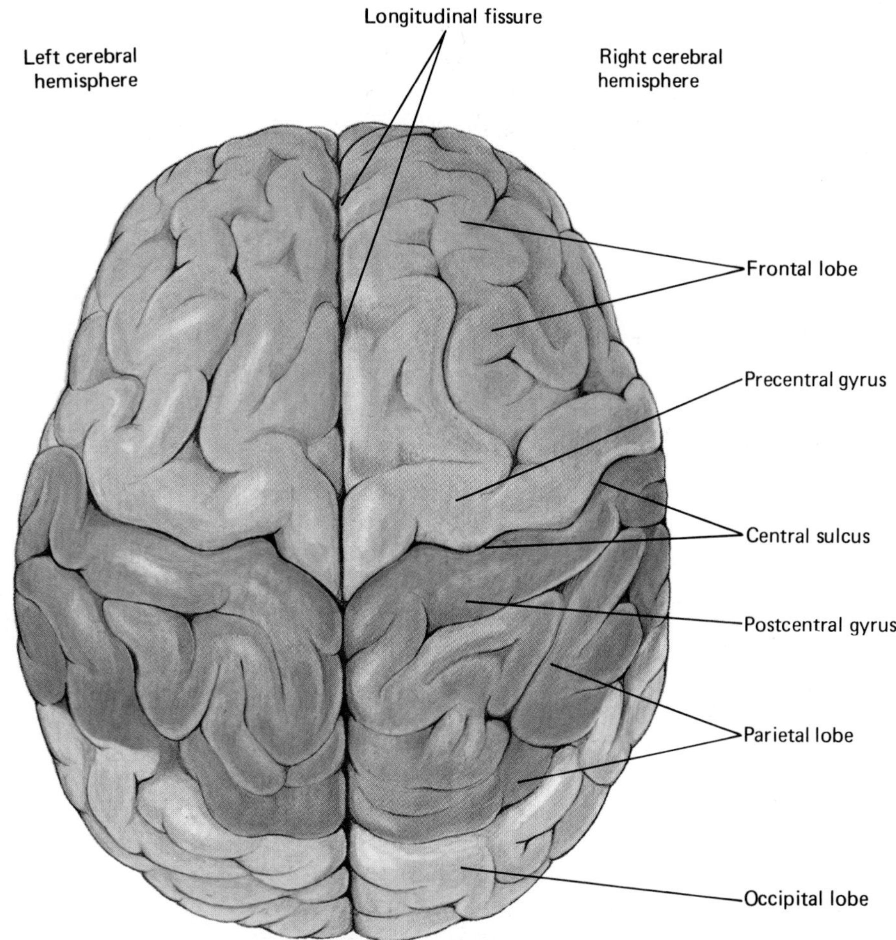

FIGURE 13-13

Superior view of the cerebrum.

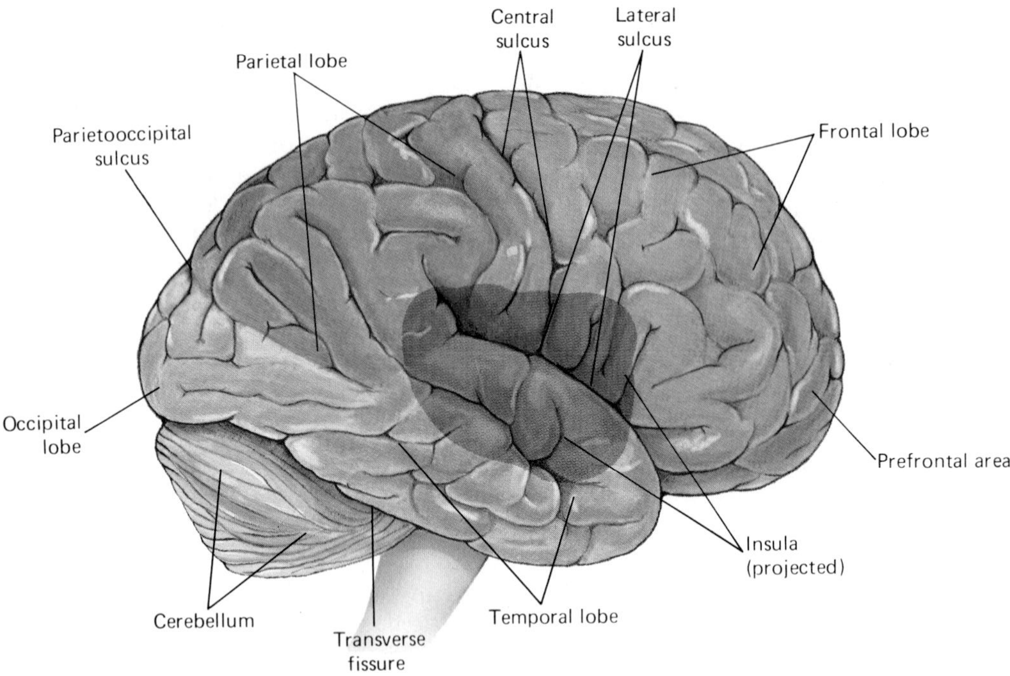

FIGURE 13-14

Lateral view of the cerebrum, showing lobes. Part of the brain has been made transparent so that the underlying insula can be seen.

shown in Figures 13-13 and 13-14. Each frontal lobe is separated from a parietal lobe by a **central sulcus** and from a temporal lobe by a **lateral sulcus.** Each parietal lobe is separated from an occipital lobe by a **parieto-occipital sulcus.** Hidden from surface view, the central lobe is located deep within the cerebrum. The limbic lobe is the ring of cortex and associated structures that surrounds the ventricles of the cerebrum (Fig. 13-15).

MOST OF THE CEREBRAL CORTEX IS NEOCORTEX

Two types of cortex can be distinguished histologically within the cerebrum—old and new. From an evolutionary standpoint, the "old cortex," or paleocortex, is viewed as the original cortex because it is found in all vertebrates (animals with a vertebral column). In human beings the old cortex is concerned with interpreting odors and with neural mechanisms associated with emotional behavior.

All the rest of the human cortex (about 90%) is referred to as the **neocortex** because anatomists believe that it evolved more recently. In fact, the neocortex is found only in mammals and is best developed in humans. It is composed of six layers of nerve cell bodies, which can be distinguished histologically. Five main types of neurons are present. Most common are the **pyramidal cells,** so named because they have a characteristic pyramid shape and extensive, branching dendrites. Their axons give off one or more collaterals, which may turn back toward the dendrites or synapse with other types of neurons projecting in other directions. The main axons of the pyramidal cells project into the white matter of the cerebrum.

WHITE MATTER OF THE CEREBRUM SERVES THREE FUNCTIONS

The white matter of the cerebrum is composed of myelinated fibers of neurons organized to carry out three functions:

1. **Association fibers** transmit impulses between neurons within the same hemisphere.
2. **Commissure fibers** connect an area of one cerebral hemisphere with the corresponding area of the other hemisphere.
3. **Projection fibers** are part of descending pathways leaving the cortex and going to other

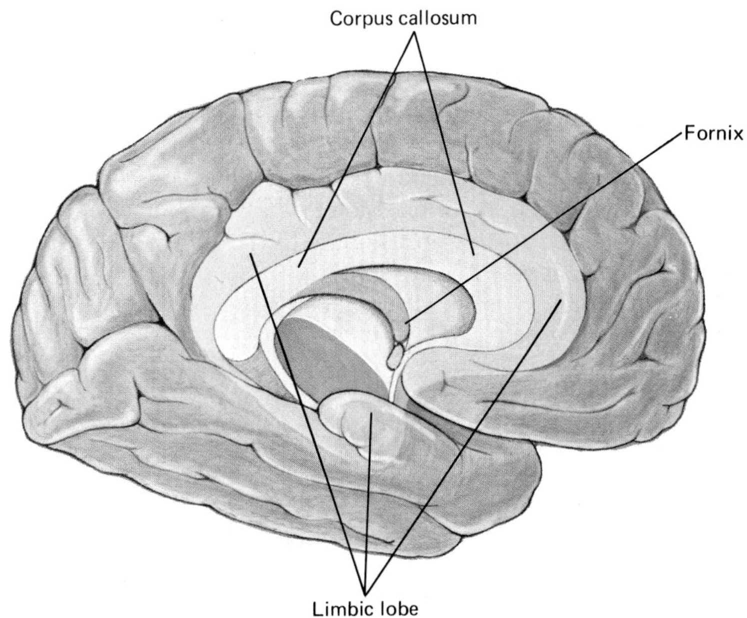

FIGURE 13-15

Medial view of the left cerebral hemisphere showing the structures that make up the limbic lobe.

parts of the brain or spinal cord or of ascending pathways coming from the other parts of the brain.

The largest commissure, the **corpus callosum,** connects most of the neocortex of the two hemispheres (Fig. 13-7). The commissure of the **fornix** connects the old cortex with the thalamus. The **anterior commissure** connects those neocortical areas not joined by fibers of the corpus callosum as well as parts of the old cortex with the neocortex.

THE BASAL GANGLIA FUNCTION IN MOTOR CONTROL

Deep within the white matter of the cerebrum lie the **basal ganglia** (also called cerebral nuclei), paired groups of nuclei of gray matter. The basal ganglia play an important role in movement. Two of the most prominent basal ganglia are the **caudate nucleus** and the **lentiform nucleus** (Fig. 13-16). Each lentiform nucleus consists of two parts, the **putamen** and the **globus pallidus.** The putamen and caudate nucleus are collectively referred to as the **corpus striatum.**

Just how the basal ganglia function is not clearly understood. In birds, reptiles, and other vertebrates in which the motor cortex is absent or very rudimentary, the basal ganglia are large and appear to function like the human motor cortex. In humans the basal ganglia are thought to be involved in planning and programming movement. Complex neural circuits link them with the cerebral cortex, providing opportunities for information feedback. Apparently, the ganglia use the sensory information fed to them from various sensory pathways to help the association areas of the cortex make appropriate decisions for responding to sensory input. The basal ganglia are responsible for many of the subconscious movements of the body.

THE CEREBRUM HAS SENSORY, MOTOR, AND ASSOCIATION FUNCTIONS

Human beings are distinguishable from other organisms by the intricate development of the cerebral cortex. The neural basis of those human qualities that we cherish so highly—abilities to reason, communicate by language, make intellectual and moral judgments, create poetry and art, invent computers and artificial hearts—resides within this soft gray mass of tissue.

For convenience we may divide the multitude of functions performed by the cerebrum into three categories:

1. **Sensory functions.** The cerebrum receives information from the eyes, ears, taste and olfactory receptors, and sense receptors in the skin, muscles, and other organs. It then interprets these messages so that we "know" what we are seeing, hearing, tasting, smelling, or feeling. These functions are carried out by certain areas of

the cerebrum known as sensory areas. Sensory function will be discussed in more detail in Chapters 15 and 17.

2. **Motor functions.** The cerebrum is responsible for all voluntary movement and for some involuntary movement. Motor function resides in the motor areas of the cerebral cortex. Motor function will be discussed further in Chapter 15.

3. **Association functions.** Association is a term used to describe all of the intellectual activities of the cerebral cortex. These include learning and reasoning, memory storage and recall, language abilities, and even consciousness. Association areas also link sensory with motor areas.

You might wonder which part of the cerebrum is responsible for each function. Determining which bit of brain tissue does what is no easy task. How simple it would be if we could assign

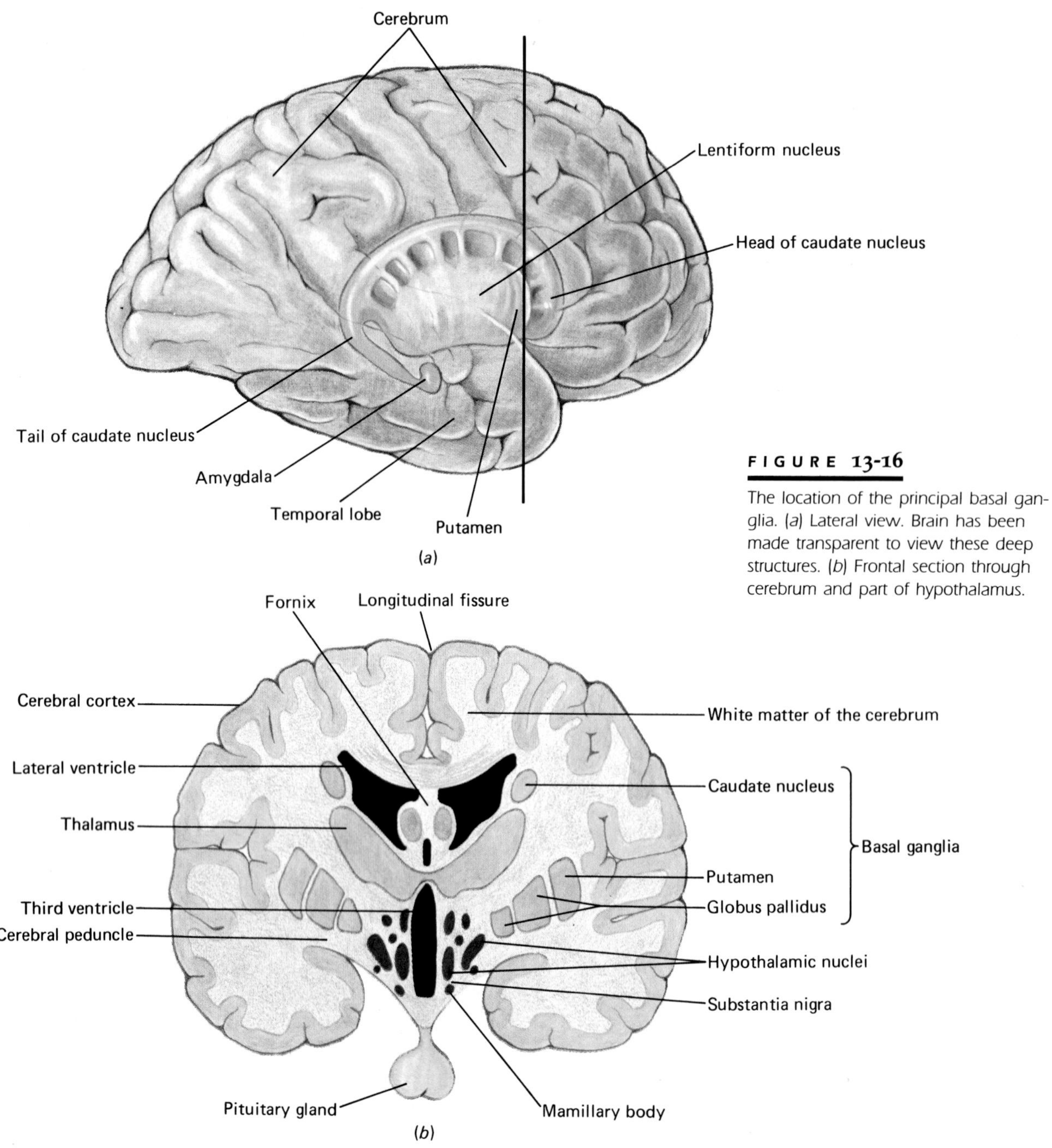

FIGURE 13-16

The location of the principal basal ganglia. (*a*) Lateral view. Brain has been made transparent to view these deep structures. (*b*) Frontal section through cerebrum and part of hypothalamus.

a specific function to each gyrus or lobe! However, although some areas of the cerebrum do specialize in specific sensory or motor functions, many different parts of the brain are involved in performing each task.

How have investigators localized certain functions? One way is by operating on experimental animals and creating lesions in various specific areas of the brain. By carefully observing how the lesion affects behavior after the animal has recovered from the surgery, scientists have learned much about the function of these areas. Sometimes parts of the brain are ablated (i.e., removed) in order to study the effects of loss of a particular area.

Humans who have suffered brain damage because of an accident or disease or as a result of surgery performed to remove tumors have also contributed to our knowledge of brain function. Much has also been learned by electrically stimulating specific areas of the brain of consenting patients undergoing brain surgery. Because the brain has no pain or other sensory receptors, surgeons need use only a local anesthetic to cut through the overlying skull structures. The patient can be kept fully conscious while surgeons and physiologists directly stimulate various areas of the brain. Together patient and investigator can analyze the response. For example, when a specific motor area is stimulated, the patient may flex his or her big toe, or when a specific association area is stimulated, the patient may report hearing the lullaby sung some 40 years earlier while being rocked to sleep.

On the basis of these and other types of studies (especially histological study), investigators have attempted to draw maps of the brain, indicating which area is most responsible for each function. **Brodmann's classification,** one of the most widely used, is shown in Figure 13-17.

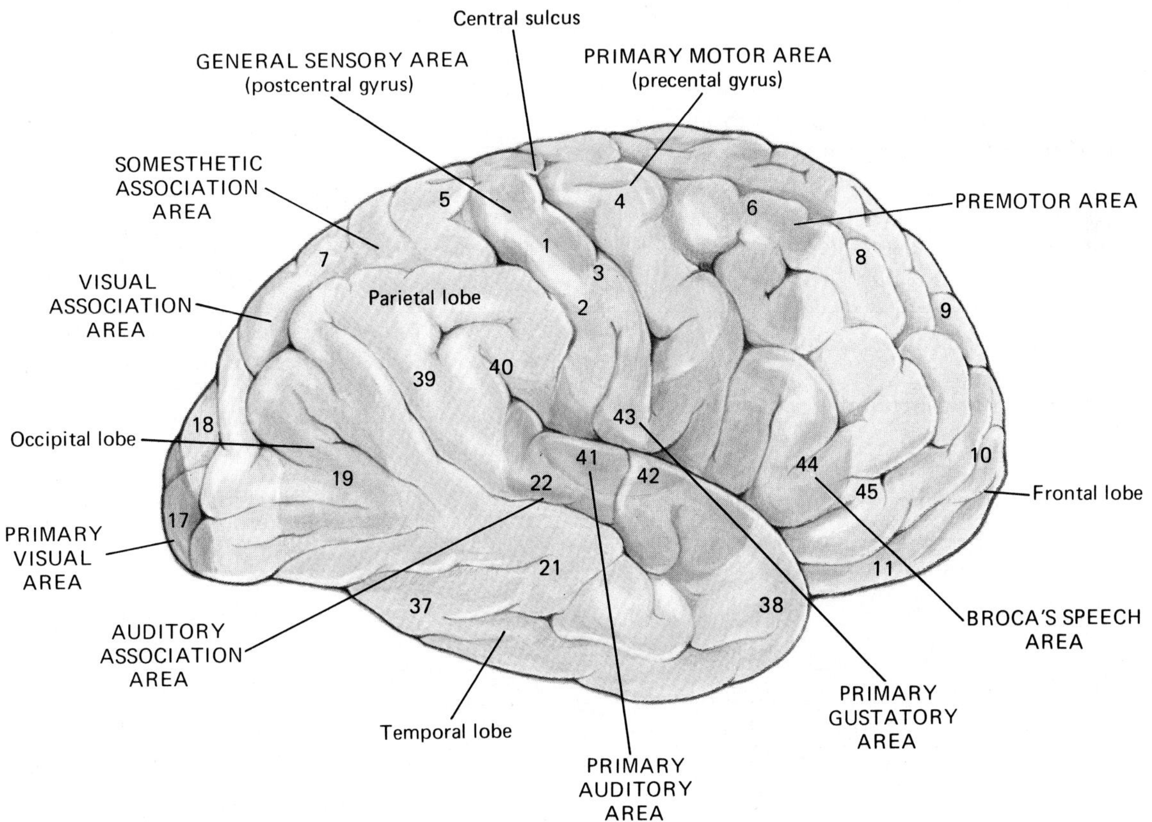

FIGURE 13-17

Map of the lateral surface of the cerebral cortex showing some of the functional areas and some of the areas of Brodmann. Areas 4, 6, and 8 are motor areas. Areas 1, 2, 3, 17, 41, 42, and 43 are primary sensory areas. Areas 9, 10, 11, 18, 19, 22, 37, 39, and 40 are association areas.

LOBES OF THE CEREBRUM SPECIALIZE IN SPECIFIC FUNCTIONS

As already described, each cerebral hemisphere is divided into six lobes. The anterior portion of each **frontal lobe** is an association area known as the **prefrontal area.**

Clinical highlight

For many years prefrontal lobotomies were in vogue as a treatment for some forms of mental illness and for relief of intractable pain. In this procedure the neural connections between the prefrontal area and the rest of the brain were cut, and the prefrontal area was removed. Today, the surgical procedure has been modified and usually consists of severing the tracts connecting the prefrontal and frontal lobes with the thalamus. It is now performed mainly in patients suffering from severe chronic pain. Although such patients still feel the pain, they no longer seem to mind it. Instead, they experience a false feeling of euphoria (well-being). Persons who have been subjected to prefrontal lobotomy are less emotional and less excitable but suffer characteristic personality changes. They tend to be tactless and do not seem to care as much about personal appearance or social mores.

Just anterior to the central fissure lies the **precentral gyrus** of the frontal lobe. Because voluntary movements of skeletal muscles are controlled from this area (area 4 according to Brodmann's classification), it is known as the **motor cortex,** or **primary motor area.** Just anterior to the precentral gyrus is the **premotor** area, also called the *motor association area,* which plays a part in motor function. One part of the premotor area, known as **Broca's speech area,** is concerned with directing the formation of words.

The **parietal lobe** has a **primary sensory area,** the **postcentral gyrus** (areas 1, 2, and 3 in Brodmann's classification), which receives information from the sensory receptors in the skin and joints. This information is relayed to the parietal lobe by way of the thalamus. Important **sensory association areas,** also located within the parietal lobe, integrate information received by the primary sensory area, and also receive and integrate information about visual, auditory, and taste sensations from other areas of the cortex and thalamus. Through this integration process, persons become aware of themselves in relation to their environment. They are able to interpret characteristics of objects that they feel with their hands and to comprehend spoken and written language.

Home of the **visual cortex,** the **occipital lobe** receives information from the thalamus about what we see and integrates the information in order to formulate an appropriate response. The area that receives the visual information is known as the **primary visual area;** the portion that integrates the information is the **visual association area.**

The **temporal lobe** contains both neocortex and old cortex. Its neocortex is concerned with reception and integration of auditory messages. Part of the temporal lobe is concerned with emotion, personality, memory and behavior as a result of its connections with limbic and frontal lobes.

The **limbic lobe** is thought to be a link between emotional and cognitive (thought) mechanisms. This lobe is an important part of the limbic system, which is named for it and will be discussed in a later section.

Neural pathways of the **central lobe** (insula) are not understood. This lobe is thought to be involved in both autonomic and somatic activities.

ONE HEMISPHERE IS GENERALLY DOMINANT FOR SPEECH AND MOTOR FUNCTIONS

How many left-handed persons do you know? Probably not very many, for 90% of us are right-handed. The remaining 10% are left-handed or ambidextrous. In right-handed persons the left cerebral hemisphere is more highly developed for the motor functions related to handedness. In about 95% of adults (regardless of handedness) the left hemisphere is dominant for language abilities, including the ability to speak, read, learn mathematics, and perform all other intellectual functions associated with language. The speech area in the dominant hemisphere is typically larger than in the nondominant hemisphere. This size difference is apparent by the thirty-first week of fetal development.

Until recently the left cerebral hemisphere was thought to be dominant in all respects in most persons. Now research indicates that the two hemispheres actually complement one another, and that the right hemisphere specializes in its own specific functions. Apparently the right hemisphere specializes in spatiotemporal matters. It is important in recognizing faces, identifying objects on the basis of shape, and appreciating and recognizing music and form. Some have suggested that creative abilities reside here.

How does cerebral specialization come about? According to current theory, the left temporal lobe (especially Wernicke's area) is usually larger than the right at birth. For this reason the child uses the left side of the brain more than the right, and that side becomes better developed for language activities.

Sometimes the presence of a tumor necessitates the surgical removal of the left hemisphere. When such surgery is performed in very young children, the right hemisphere learns to take over the language functions. After about age 13, however, a person has great difficulty in training the right hemisphere.

Clinical highlight

Lesions in the dominant adult hemisphere cause **aphasias,** impairments in reception, manipulation, or expression of words. For example, a lesion in the left temporal or parietal lobe may result in *fluent aphasia,* in which the patient can speak but is unable to place key words correctly in sentences. Current research aimed at seeking techniques for best teaching the right hemisphere to take over the functions of the left has important implications for stroke patients. (In such patients a cerebral vascular accident has cut off the blood supply to some area of the brain, damaging the tissue.)

Under normal circumstances sensory input and probably memories are transferred by way of the corpus callosum from one hemisphere into the other so that they are stored in both. If one hemisphere is destroyed or damaged, at least some of the information is retained by the other.

Some very interesting experiments have been performed on "split-brain animals," in which all connecting neurons between the two cerebral hemispheres have been severed and the optic chiasma has been cut in the midsagittal plane. When such an animal is taught to respond to a visual stimulus using only one eye (by covering the other), it does not recognize the stimulus with the other eye. The information has been processed in only one side of the brain.

The limbic system is an action system

The **limbic system** is an action system of the brain that plays a role in emotional responses, autonomic responses, subconscious motor and sensory drives, sexual behavior, biological rhythms, and motivation, including feelings of pleasure and punishment. Certain structures of the cerebrum and diencephalon make up the limbic system (Fig. 13-18). They include (1) the **limbic lobe,** which consists of **two gyri of the cerebral hemisphere** (the cingulate gyrus and hippocampal gyrus); (2) the **hippocampus** (*hip*-o-**kam**-pus; an area of old cortex in the cerebrum); (3) the **amygdala** (ah-**mig**-dah-lah; a complex of nuclei within the cerebrum, near the optic tract); (4) the **olfactory nerves, bulb,** and **tract;** (5) **areas of the thalamus;** (6) **areas of the hypothalamus** (including the mamillary bodies); and (7) the **fornix.**

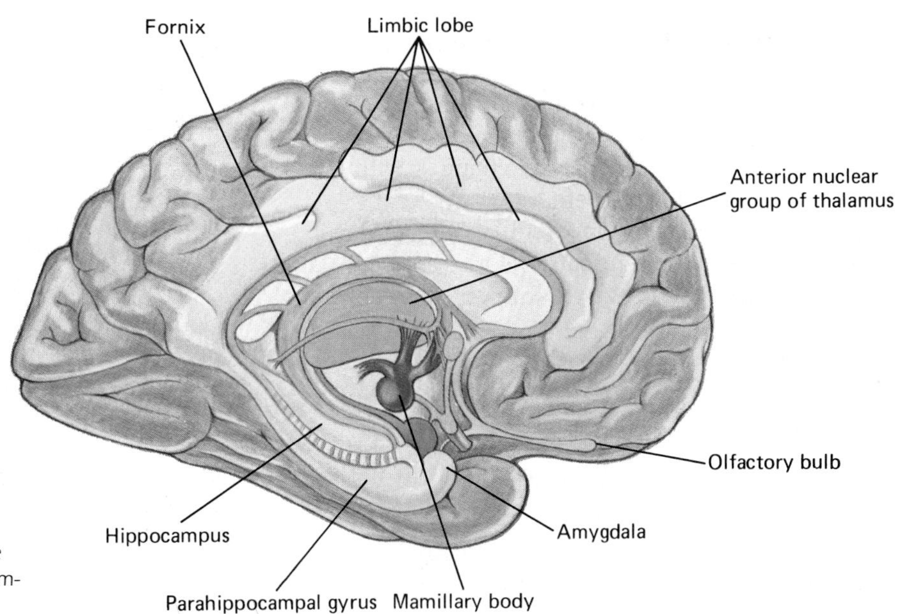

FIGURE 13-18

The limbic system. Structures labeled are generally considered to be part of the limbic system.

The limbic system affects the emotional aspects of behavior. Stimulation of certain areas of the limbic system in an experimental animal results in fear and punishment responses. Stimulation of other areas of the limbic system increases the general activity level of the animal and may cause fighting behavior and extreme rage.

When an electrode is implanted in the so-called reward center of the limbic system, a rat will press a lever that stimulates this area thousands of times per hour. Stimulation of this area is apparently so rewarding that an animal will forego food and drink and may continue to press the lever until it drops from exhaustion.

In a similar type of experiment, an electrode can be implanted in the "punishment" center of the limbic system so that the animal receives continuous stimulation. Only when it presses a lever is the current turned off. The animal quickly learns to press the lever to avoid stimulation of the punishment center. If such stimulation is continued for 24 hours or so, the animal becomes severely ill and may even die. The reward and punishment centers are thought to be very important in influencing motivation and behavior.

The brain continuously exhibits electrical activity

Continuous electrical activity within the brain can be measured by placing electrodes on the surface of the scalp and recording differences in electrical potentials. Patterns of activity called brain waves can be traced, producing a record called an **electroencephalogram (EEG)** (Fig. 13-19).

Brain waves are evoked primarily from the cerebral cortex, but some result from input from pathways projected through the thalamus. The rhythms arise from synchronized cyclic activity of groups of neurons. One's EEG is as unique as one's fingerprints, but the EEG changes with the state of consciousness or emotion.

Often brain waves are irregular, but under some conditions distinct patterns can be recorded. Four main kinds of wave rhythms have been distinguished:

1. The **alpha-wave** rhythm, a slow-frequency,[1] synchronized wave pattern, is evoked when a person is relaxed and resting with eyes closed. This rhythm is most prominent in the occipital region.

2. **Beta** rhythm is characteristic of states of heightened mental activity, such as information processing or problem solving. The beta-wave pattern is a fast-frequency rhythm most prominent in the frontal and parietal regions and is referred to as a desynchronized pattern.

3. **Delta** waves are slow, large waves associated with normal sleep.

4. **Theta** waves occur primarily in the parietal and temporal regions in children but are also evoked in some adults when they are under emotional stress, especially frustration or disappointment.

Clinical highlight

The EEG is a valuable clinical tool used to help localize brain tumors and diagnose many neurological disorders. In epilepsy, brain neurons discharge in an uncontrolled and excessive manner. The EEG is sometimes helpful in localizing lesions in the brain that are responsible for the discharge in one type of epilepsy known as focal epilepsy. Characteristic EEG patterns are also apparent during epileptic seizures, attacks characterized by convulsions and lack of responsiveness.

In the recent past a person with no pulse or heartbeat was considered dead. Now, however, new methods of resuscitation often bring life to those who would have been considered dead by older definitions. Respirators and other such devices can maintain vital functions even when a patient cannot carry on life processes on his or her own. For these reasons the criterion for con-

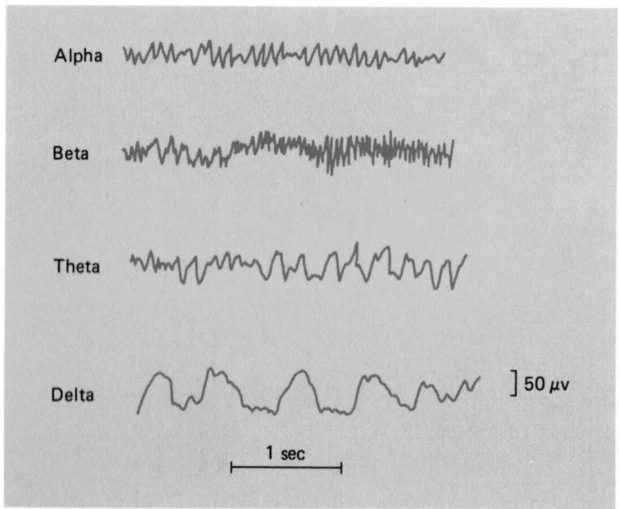

FIGURE 13-19

Different types of brain wave rhythms.

[1] Frequency refers to the number of waves generated per second.

sidering a patient dead has changed and now revolves about the presence of brain waves. When electrical activity in the brain ceases and cannot be detected over a period of several hours, a patient may be pronounced dead.

Can one learn to control brain waves? Some investigators believe that those who tend to be anxious and exhibit beta waves for no good reason might be taught to induce the relaxed alpha state. Subjects have had some success in controlling their brain-wave patterns by the use of EEG machines that permit them to see and listen to their brain waves. With such continuous feedback they are able to condition themselves to produce alpha waves. Perhaps some day persons with psychosomatic disorders may be taught to relax in this way and will no longer need tranquilizers and other drugs. Many persons have invested in their own biofeedback machines and are attempting to condition themselves to relax. Others approach the same end by various means of meditation. Studies have indicated that meditation produces an altered metabolic state. Metabolic rate, blood pressure, and heart rate decrease, and alpha waves become dominant. Experienced meditators have been found to lapse into sleep for about 40% of the time they were in meditation.

The reticular activating system maintains consciousness

Sometimes called the arousal system, the **reticular activating system (RAS)** is a complex polysynaptic pathway in the brainstem and thalamic reticular formation (Fig. 13-20). It receives messages from neurons in the spinal cord and from many other parts of the nervous system and communicates with the cerebral cortex by complex circuits. The RAS is ultimately responsible for maintaining consciousness, and the extent of its activity determines the state of alertness. When the RAS bombards the cerebral cortex with stimuli, you feel alert and are able to focus your attention on specific thoughts. When its activity slows, you begin to feel sleepy. Sometimes when you are listening to a boring lecture, the RAS becomes habituated to the monotonous repetition of the professor's voice. As its signals become progressively weaker, the cerebrum may lapse into sleep.

When you feel sleepy but are trying to stay awake, it helps to move about. This is because the motor cortex sends messages back to the RAS, stimulating impulses in it that in turn are relayed back to the cerebral cortex. Most of you have had the misfortune of tossing and turning at night when you could not seem to get an upsetting experience or upcoming exciting event out of your mind. Association areas of the cerebral cortex also send neural messages back into the RAS, which again return to the cerebrum to keep you awake. And surely you have had the experience of being jolted from a sound sleep by a ringing clock. This so-called arousal reaction occurs when the RAS receives sensory input (in this case from the auditory tracts) and funnels the message to the cerebral cortex.

Within the RAS, neural messages may be inhibited, enhanced, or modified in other ways. By altering sensory input, the RAS has an important effect on the way in which one reacts to various stimuli. The RAS causes activity in the entire brain and even the spinal cord. When the lower portion of the RAS is stimulated electrically, activity is heightened throughout the nervous system for as long as half a minute. Should the RAS be severely damaged, the unfortunate victim may pass into a deep, permanent coma.

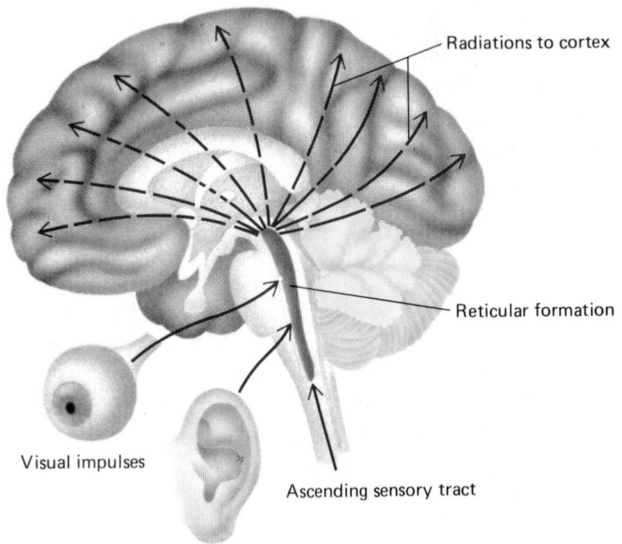

FIGURE 13-20

The reticular activating system. The mesencephalic headquarters of the reticular formation receives input from a variety of sensory pathways.

The spinal cord conveys information to and from the brain

The spinal cord is the elongated, roughly cylindrical portion of the CNS that occupies the vertebral canal of the vertebral column. It is the inferior extension of the brain (see chapter opening photograph). The spinal cord has two main functions: (1) it controls many reflex activities of the body and (2) it transmits information back and forth from peripheral nerves to the brain via its ascending and descending tracts.

The structure of the spinal cord varies at different levels

A slightly flattened hollow cylinder, the spinal cord emerges from the base of the brain at the level of the foramen magnum of the occipital bone and extends caudally to the level of the second lumbar vertebra (Fig. 13-21). The average length of the spinal cord is about 45 centimeters (17 in.), although this varies somewhat with the length of the trunk, and its diameter is about that of a finger. Generally, the spinal cord tapers from its cranial to its caudal end. However, it has two bulges, the **cervical** and **lumbar enlargements.** The large spinal nerves that supply the upper and lower limbs emerge from these regions.

At its caudal end the spinal cord narrows to a sharp tip called the **conus medullaris** (**ko**-nus med-yoo-**lar**-is). From the end of the conus an extension of the pia mater known as the **filum terminale** (**fi**-lum ter-mih-**nal**-ee) continues to the very end of the vertebral column, where it attaches to the coccyx (Fig. 13-22). Although the dura and arachnoid layers do not extend so far caudally, they also extend below the level of the cord. The subarachnoid space extends to the level of the second sacral vertebra.

Thirty-one pairs of **spinal nerves** exit from successive levels of the cord. Nerves from the lower region of the cord pass caudally to below the level of the conus medullaris before they leave the vertebral canal. Because of their resemblance to a horse's tail they are aptly known as the **cauda equina** (**kaw**-dah ee-**kwi**-nah) (Fig. 13-23).

Clinical highlight

The anatomy of the caudal end of the spinal cord is of clinical importance because a hollow needle can be inserted into the subarachnoid space between the neural arches of the third and fourth lumbar vertebrae. Known as a **spinal tap** or **lumbar puncture,** this procedure can be used to safely withdraw small amounts of cerebrospinal fluid without damaging the cord itself. Analysis of this fluid can be helpful in diagnosing certain CNS disorders. For example, the cerebrospinal fluid can be examined for gross appearance, pressure, glucose and protein content, the number and types of blood cells present, and the presence of bacteria, viruses, or fungi. The presence of certain types of proteins can help confirm a diagnosis of multiple sclerosis. Certain types of meningitis can be diagnosed by techniques that measure the concentration of bacterial proteins in the CSF. Samples of CSF can also be cultured to determine what kinds of bacteria, viruses, or fungi are present. Blood in the CSF may provide a clue in the diagnosis of cerebral hemorrhage. When indicated, lumbar puncture is often followed by CT scanning, which is now considered a more dependable method for diagnosing cerebral hemorrhage, brain tumors, and certain other conditions that affect the CSF.

When some CSF is removed and replaced with air, x-ray films can be made of the cavities within the brain and, indirectly, structures that lie between the ventricles and the meninges can be visualized. Such x-rays are called pneumoencephalograms. The position of the patient's head can be manipulated to change the distribution of the air so that a particular area can be viewed. Hydrocephalus and tumors that displace or deform the ventricles can be revealed by this technique.

Injection of an anesthetic into the subarachnoid space blocks neural transmission from sensory neurons. This type of anesthesia is commonly called a "spinal" or, if administered very low in the subarachnoid space, a "saddle block." Injection of a local anesthetic into the epidural space is called epidural anesthesia, or sometimes caudal block. Epidural anesthesia is commonly administered to women during childbirth.

Several longitudinal fissures divide the spinal cord into regions. In the midanterior line is the deepest groove, the **anterior** (ventral)[1] **median fissure.** Opposite on the posterior (dorsal) surface is the more shallow **posterior** (dorsal) **fissure.** Lateral grooves are less well defined. A cross section through the spinal cord reveals a small central

[1]The terms anterior and ventral, and posterior and dorsal are used interchangeably in human nervous system anatomy. For the sake of consistency we will use anterior and posterior in this discussion with an occasional reference to ventral and dorsal as a reminder that these terms are commonly used.

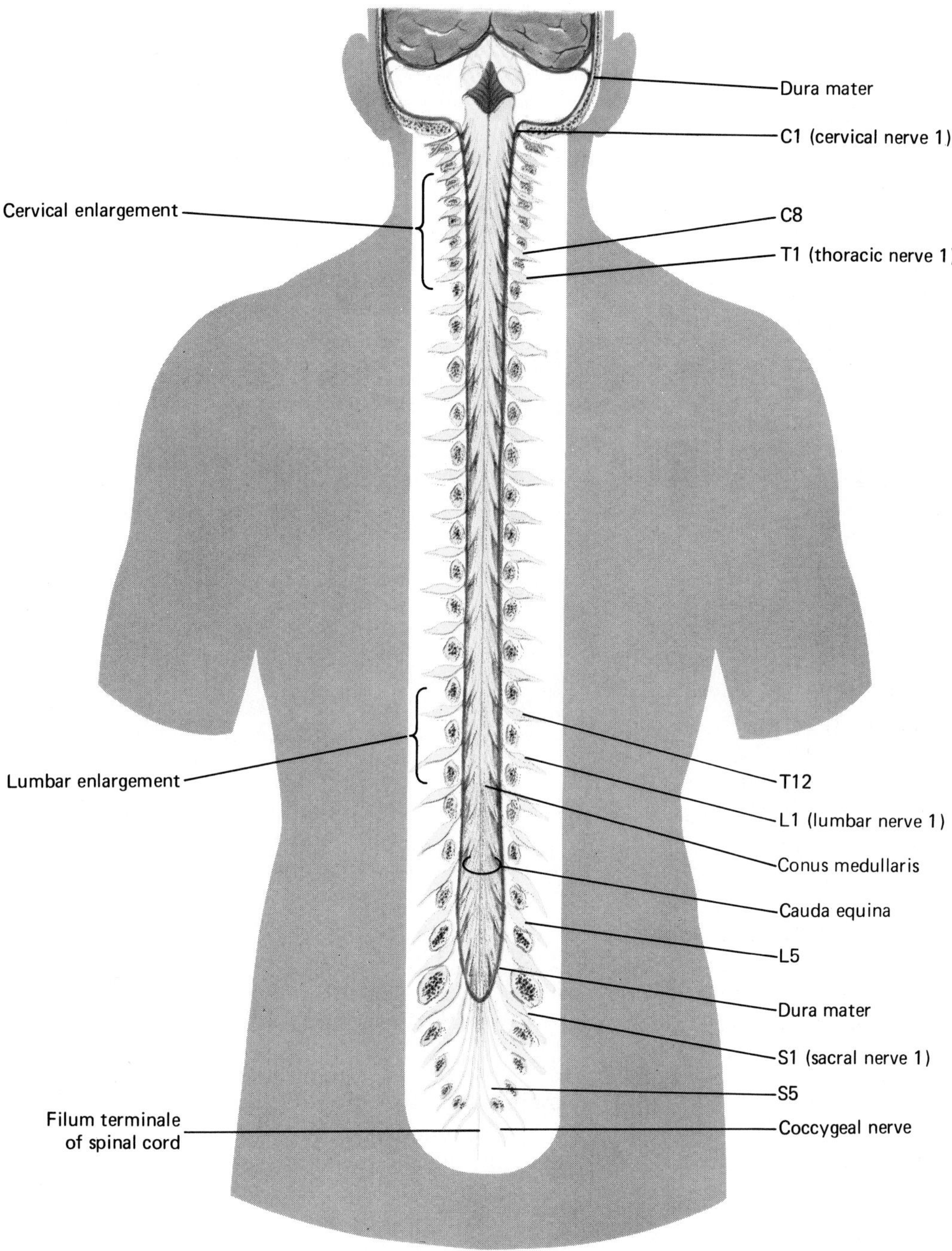

FIGURE 13-21

Posterior view of the spinal cord. Roots of the spinal nerves are shown. Spinal nerves are named for the general region of the vertebral column from which they originate, and they are numbered in sequence.

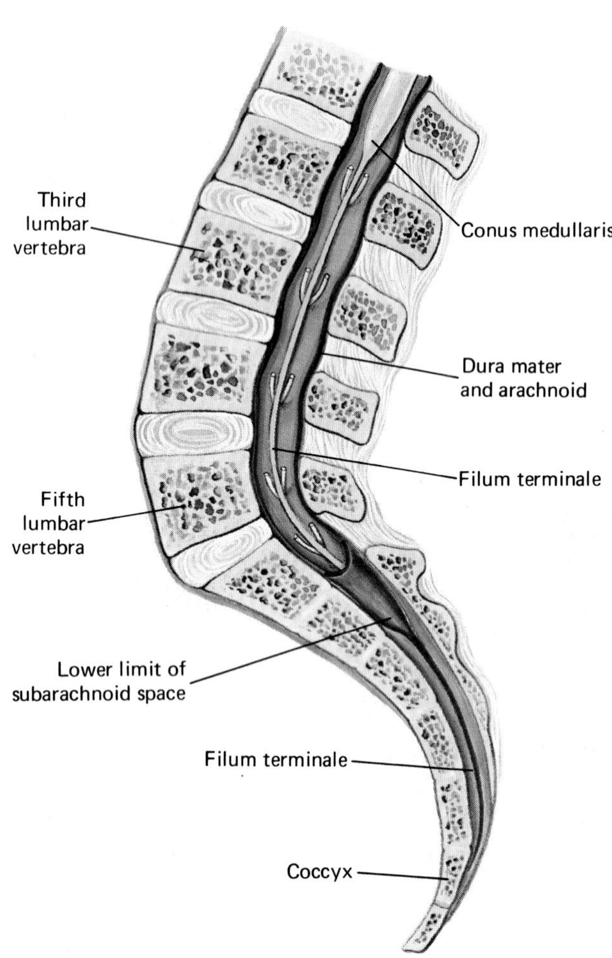

FIGURE 13-22

Median sagittal section of the lumbosacral portion of the vertebral column showing the conus medullaris and filum terminale. The subarachnoid space has been exposed inferiorly to the level of the first sacral vertebra to show the filum terminale.

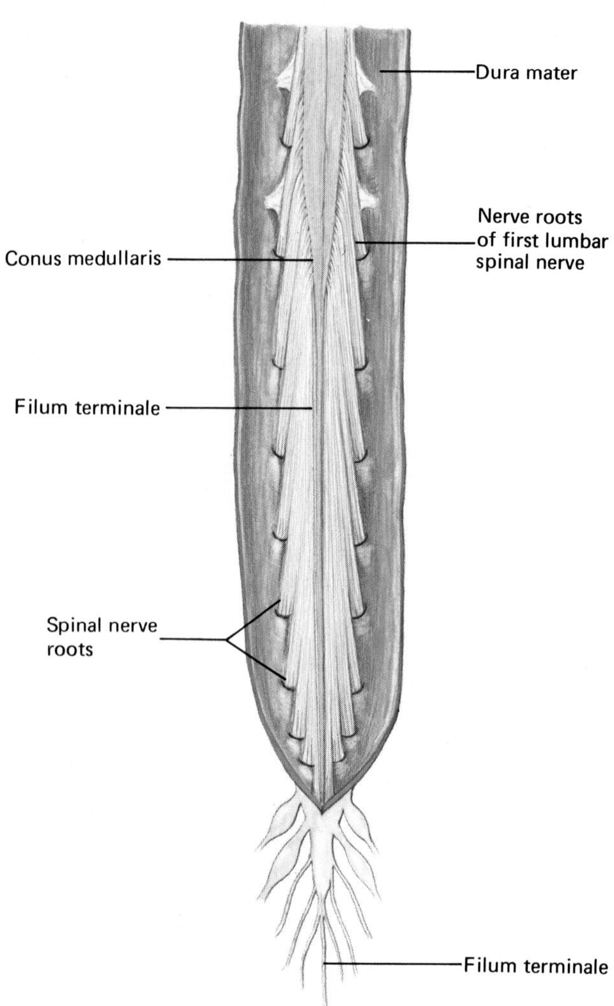

FIGURE 13-23

Posterior view of the inferior end of the spinal cord showing the cauda equina. The dura and arachnoid have been partially removed.

canal surrounded by an area of gray matter shaped somewhat like the letter H (Figs. 13-24 and 13-25). Outside the gray matter the cord is composed of white matter.

The gray matter of the spinal cord is divided into columns

The gray matter consists of large masses of cell bodies, dendrites of association and efferent neurons, and unmyelinated axons. Such axons are oriented at right angles to the long axis of the cord. Gray matter is also rich in blood vessels and glial cells. The gray matter is subdivided into sections called **columns,** or **horns.** The right and left halves of the H-shaped area of gray matter are connected by a bar of gray matter called the **gray commissure.** The anterior (ventral) portions of the H are the **anterior columns;** the posterior (dorsal) segments are the **posterior columns.** From the second thoracic to the first lumbar segment of the cord, small lateral gray columns project from the intermediate portion of the H.

The white matter consists of spinal tracts

The white matter of the spinal cord consists of myelinated axons arranged into bundles, called **tracts** or **pathways,** that pass up and down from the brain. In each half of the cord the white matter is arranged into three columns, or **funiculi** (fuh-**nik**-u-lie): anterior, posterior, and lateral fu-

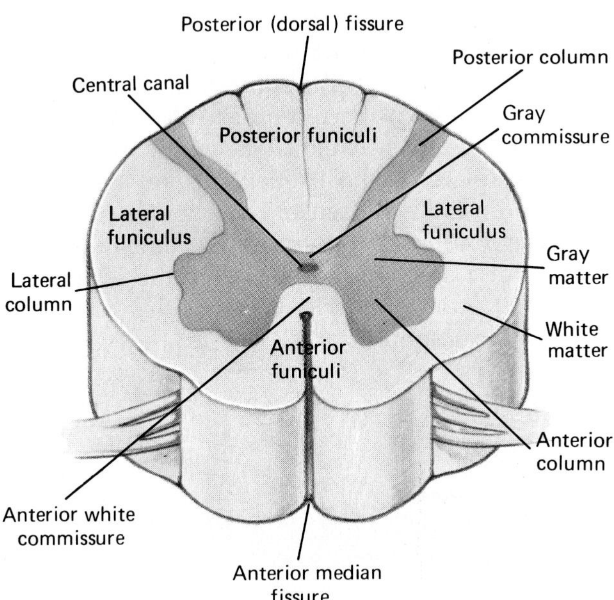

FIGURE 13-24

Cross section through the spinal cord.

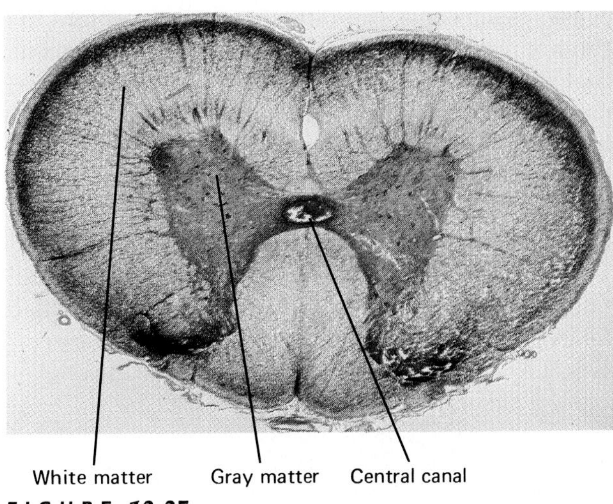

FIGURE 13-25

Photomicrograph of a cross section through the spinal cord (approximately ×10). (M. I. Walker/Photo Researchers, Inc.)

niculi. In turn, each funiculus is subdivided into tracts, called **fasciculi** (fah-**sik**-yoo-lie). Long **ascending tracts** carry sensory impulses upward to the brain; **descending tracts** conduct impulses (the "decisions") from the brain back down the cord toward the efferent neurons.

For example, the **spinothalamic tracts,** which are part of the anterior and lateral funiculi on each side of the cord, consist of the axons of neurons that receive pain and temperature information from sensory neurons reporting from the skin. The *lateral* spinothalamic tract axons convey this information to the brain. The **lateral** and **anterior corticospinal** (also referred to as the pyramidal) **tracts** are descending tracts that convey voluntary motor impulses from the brain (cerebrum) to spinal nerves at various levels in the cord.

All of the axons within a single ascending or descending tract transmit the same type of information. For example, the lateral spinothalamic tract transmits pain and temperature information to the brain, whereas the **spinocerebellar tracts** convey messages from kinesthetic receptors (those concerned with position of limbs and trunk) in muscles and tendons to the brain. The principal ascending and descending tracts are described in Table 13-2 and illustrated in Figure 13-26.

The spinal cord controls many reflex actions

The **reflex arc** is a simple neural pathway linking receptor, CNS, and effector. A reflex action is a predictable, automatic response to a specific stimulus. Many internal mechanisms are regulated by reflex actions. For example, a change in blood

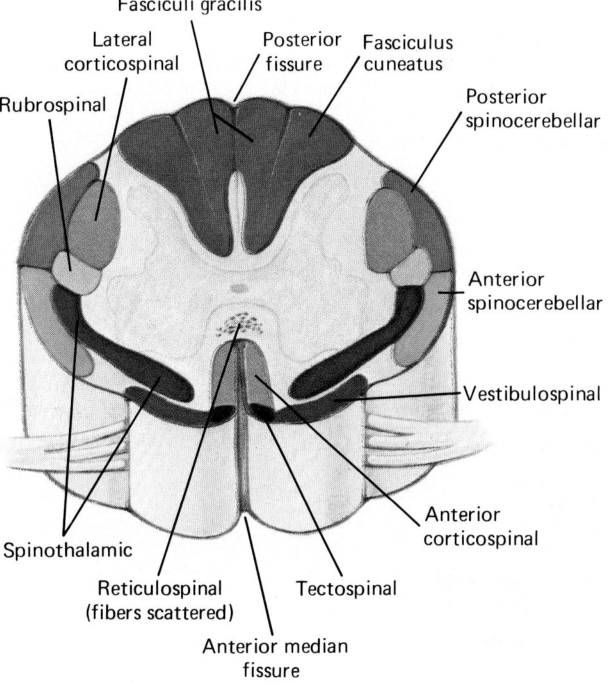

FIGURE 13-26

Cross section of spinal cord showing positions of some major ascending and descending tracts. The ascending tracts are shown in color. Descending tracts are shown in gray.

pressure acts as a stimulus that causes centers in the brainstem to activate homeostatic mechanisms that bring blood pressure back to normal. Many responses to external stimuli, such as withdrawing from painful stimuli, are also reflex actions. For example, when you accidentally place your hand on a hot pot, you jerk it back before you even become consciously aware of the situation.

Even the simplest reflex action involves reception, transmission, integration, and response. The following components are present in all reflex arcs.

1. A receptor, a dendrite or sensory structure, that receives the stimulus.
2. A sensory (afferent) neuron that transmits the impulses from the receptor to the CNS.
3. A reflex center in the CNS, where integration takes place. In most reflex arcs, an association neuron links the sensory and motor neurons.
4. A motor (efferent) neuron that transmits an impulse away from the CNS to the effector.
5. An effector, a muscle or gland, that carries out the response.

TABLE 13-2

Some important ascending and descending tracts of the spinal cord

Name of tract	Location	Origin	Termination	Function
Ascending tracts				
Spinothalamic* (also called anterolateral)	Anterior and lateral funiculi	Posterior gray columns; fibers cross to opposite side of cord	Mainly in thalamus; message relayed to cerebral cortex. As fibers pass through brainstem, numerous collaterals are given off to the reticular activating system	Conveys information regarding touch, temperature, and pain
Fasciculus cuneatus and fasciculus gracilis (medial lemniscal pathway)	Posterior funiculi	Axons of afferent neurons that enter posterior (dorsal) columns and ascend on same side of cord	Nucleus cuneatus and nucleus gracilis in medulla; messages are relayed to nucleus in thalamus and then to cerebral cortex. The second-order neurons in the pathway cross, so that the message is relayed to the opposite side of the cerebral cortex	Conveys information from skin, joints, and muscle tendons regarding touch, pressure, vibration, position of body, and movement of joints. Fasciculus cuneatus conveys information from the upper portion of the body; fasciculus gracilis from the lower portion of the body. The longest neurons in the body are those in the fasciculus gracilis; they extend from the foot to the medulla
Posterior spinocerebellar	Posterior region of lateral funiculi	Posterior gray columns; fibers do not cross to opposite side of cord	Cerebellum	Conveys information about subconscious proprioception (appreciation of body position, balance, and direction of movement). The very large myelinated fibers of this tract are among the fastest conducting fibers in the body
Anterior spinocerebellar	Anterior region of lateral funiculi	Posterior gray columns; some fibers cross to opposite side of cord, but some do not cross	Cerebellum	Conveys information about movement and position of entire limbs

A **spinal reflex** is carried out by the spinal cord and does not require participation by the brain. That some reflex arcs do not require the functioning of the brain can be shown by a demonstration frequently carried out in college physiology labs. A piece of acid-soaked paper is applied to the back of a frog whose brain has been destroyed. The frog reacts by moving its leg to flick off the paper. No matter how many times the paper is applied, the frog performs the same response. A frog with a functioning brain will try a different response after two or three applications. The brainless frog's response demonstrates that reflex actions are automatic and may occur without brain functioning. (See Focus on Some Clinically Important Reflexes.)

Some reflex actions (e.g., the pupillary reflex of the eye) do involve parts of the brain. However, these are the so-called lower parts, functionally similar to the spinal cord, and have nothing to do with conscious thought. Sometimes, though, reflex actions are subject to conscious inhibition or facilitation (promotion). An example is the reflex that voids the urinary bladder when

TABLE 13-2

(continued)

Name of tract	Location	Origin	Termination	Function
Descending tracts				
Pyramidal tracts				
Lateral corticospinal	Lateral funiculi	Cerebral cortex; fibers cross in medulla	Anterior gray column where the fibers synapse with spinal nerves	Convey impulses directing precise, skilled voluntary movement. These impulses are conveyed from one side of the cerebral cortex to the opposite side of the spinal cord (from there they are conveyed by spinal nerves that terminate in skeletal muscles)
Anterior corticospinal	Anterior funiculi	Cerebral cortex	Fibers cross in spinal cord just before synapsing in anterior gray column of cord	
Extrapyramidal tracts				
Rubrospinal	Lateral funiculi	Red nucleus of midbrain; fibers cross immediately	Anterior gray column	Conveys impulses concerning muscle tone and posture to spinal nerves that innervate skeletal muscles
Reticulospinal	Anterior funiculi	Reticular formation of brainstem; most fibers do not cross, but a few cross to the other side	Anterior gray column of cord; synapse with motor neurons	Conveys impulses that regulate motor activities related to posture and muscle tone
Vestibulospinal	Anterior funiculi	Vestibular nuclei of medulla; fibers do not cross	Anterior gray column of cord	Conveys impulses that influence muscle tone and help maintain posture and equilibrium
Tectospinal	Anterior funiculi	Midbrain (superior colliculi); fibers cross to opposite side of brain	Anterior gray column of cord in cervical region	Thought to convey impulses controlling reflex postural movements of head, neck, and upper limbs in response to visual stimuli

*Some textbooks separate the spinothalamic tracts into anterior and lateral tracts, but recent studies show that there is no physiological basis for doing so.

it fills with urine. In babies urination occurs by reflex whenever the bladder becomes full, but in early childhood we learn to facilitate the reflex by consciously stimulating it before the bladder pressure reaches the critical level. We also learn to inhibit the reflex consciously should the bladder become full at an inconvenient time or place. Another example would be a mother's conscious inhibition of a withdrawal reflex if it meant dropping a hot pot of soup upon her child at play on the floor.

THE STRETCH REFLEX IS MONOSYNAPTIC

The **stretch reflex** is the simplest type of reflex, requiring a chain of only two sets of neurons (Fig. 13-27). Because this reflex involves only one group of synapses (between sensory and motor neurons), it is known as a **monosynaptic reflex.** An example is the simple knee jerk, or **patellar reflex.** When the tendon of the relaxed quadriceps femoris muscle (the muscle that extends the knee joint) is tapped suddenly, the muscle is stretched, and specialized receptors called **muscle spindles** send impulses through sensory neurons to the spinal cord. (Muscle spindles are discussed in Chapter 17.) There, sensory neurons synapse with motor neurons, which transmit impulses to motor units of the quadriceps femoris, stimulating it to contract. The leg quickly extends or kicks out.

In order for the leg to extend, antagonistic muscles that cause the leg to flex must be inhibited. This inhibition is accomplished by activating inhibitory interneurons in the anterior column of the spinal cord. The stimulation of one muscle and simultaneous inhibition of antagonistic muscles is called **reciprocal inhibition** (or reciprocal innervation).

The patellar reflex consists of (1) a muscle spindle that receives the stimulus; (2) a sensory

FOCUS ON . . . Some clinically important reflexes

Reflex	Stimulus	Response	Clinical use
Babinski sign	Stroking lateral aspect of sole of foot	Before 1½ years of age, results in extension of big toe, abduction of other four toes. After 1½ years, plantar reflex is normally displayed. The plantar reflex is marked by curling under (flexion) of all toes and slight flexion of anterior part of foot	Exhibition of positive Babinski sign after 1½ years indicates a lesion usually in the upper portion of the corticospinal tract
Patellar (knee jerk)	Tapping the patellar ligament	Extension of the leg	Absence of patellar reflex indicates damaged afferent or efferent nerves to the muscle or reflex centers in the second, third, or fourth lumbar segments of the spinal cord; reflex is not observable in people with neurosyphilis or chronic diabetes
Achilles (ankle jerk)	Tapping the calcaneal (Achilles) tendon	Extension of the foot	Absence of Achilles reflex indicates damage to the nerve cells in the lumbosacral segment of the spinal cord or damaged nerves that supply the posterior leg muscles; not observable in people with neurosyphilis, chronic diabetes, alcoholism, and subarachnoid hemorrhages
Abdominal	Stroking the lateral portion of the abdomen	Abdominal muscle contraction	Absence of reflex may be due to lesions in the corticospinal system or in the peripheral nerves, lesions in the reflex centers of the thoracic section of the spinal cord, or multiple sclerosis
Pupil	Bright light	Pupil of eye constricts (decreases in diameter)	Anoxia (lack of oxygen) and anticholinergic agents cause the pupils to be fixed and bilaterally wide; pinpoint pupils with little reactivity to light are seen in lesions of the pons and in opiate overdose

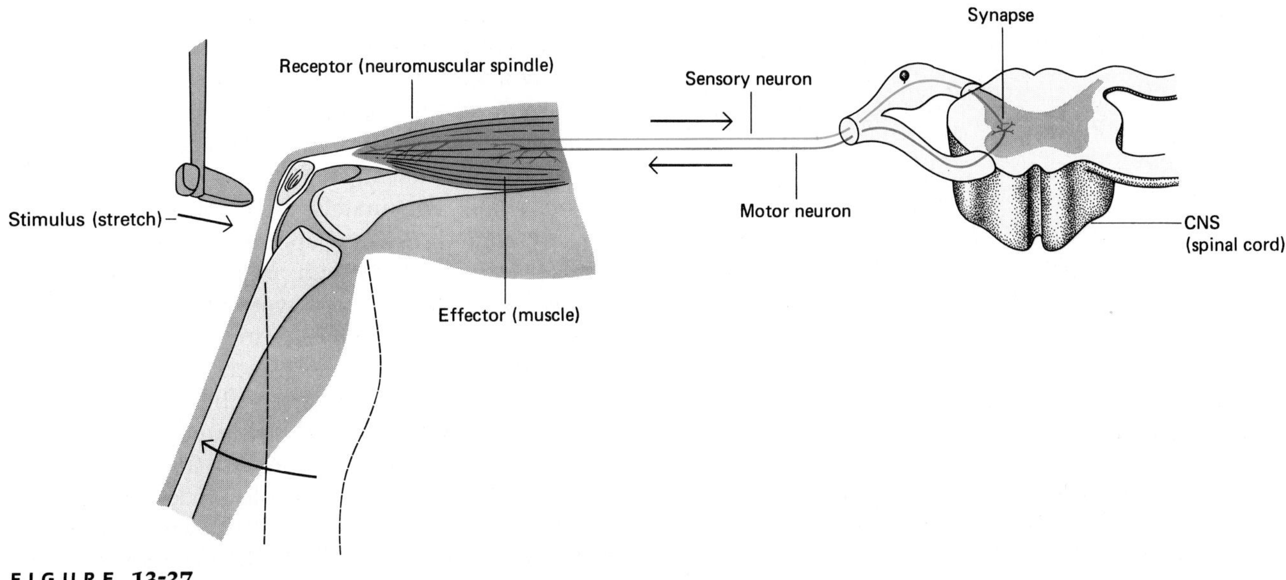

FIGURE 13-27

The patellar reflex is a monosynaptic reflex because a chain of only two neurons (one synapse) is necessary. A sensory neuron transmits the message to the spinal cord, and a motor neuron (shown in color) transmits an impulse back to the appropriate muscle.

neuron that transmits impulses to the spinal cord; (3) the CNS, where integration takes place (in this case at the synapses between sensory and motor neurons); (4) a motor neuron that transmits the "decision" to the effector; and (5) a muscle that serves as the effector. The patellar reflex is used clinically to diagnose nerve damage. If the reflex response is exaggerated, it may reflect damaged spinal tracts. If the response is unpronounced, it may indicate damaged reflex centers in the spinal cord or damaged peripheral nerves. (See Focus on Spinal Cord Injuries.)

FOCUS ON . . . Spinal cord injuries

An estimated 150,000 Americans suffer from spinal cord injury, and about 8000 new cases occur each year. Many victims are young males injured during sports activities such as diving or skiing, in automobile accidents, or by gunshots. Most of the damage occurs at the time of the accident, but further injury can result when a person with spinal cord damage is moved, unless care is taken to keep the body in alignment.

When the cord is injured, there is often destruction of gray matter, and bleeding may occur. Spinal shock occurs immediately following the injury. All sensation is lost below the level of the injury, reflex activity (including autonomic reflexes) ceases, and flaccid paralysis occurs. In flaccid paralysis there is a complete loss of muscle tone in the affected muscles. Spinal shock is thought to occur when normal neural activity in the cord ceases. Apparently the brain discharges messages that are continuously transmitted down through the cord, and spinal cord function depends upon this background of neural impulses. Spinal shock is usually temporary, lasting in humans for up to several weeks. When reflex function does return, there is often a lasting hyperexcitability of cord functions that results in muscle spasms.

The extent and location of spinal cord damage, of course, determine the type and seriousness of injury. When complete or substantial transection (severing) of the spinal cord occurs above the fifth cervical segment, respiratory paralysis may result, causing immediate death. Slightly less extensive damage to the cord above the fifth cervical segment may result in **quadriplegia.** In a quadriplegic, both upper and lower limbs are paralyzed. (Paralysis is a complete loss of muscle control.) Damage to the cord at the thoracic-lumbar region usually results in **paraplegia,** paralysis of the lower limbs.

THE FLEXOR REFLEX IS POLYSYNAPTIC

Flexor reflexes, also called withdrawal reflexes, are **polysynaptic,** requiring participation of three sets of neurons: sensory, association, and motor (Fig. 13-28). Flexor receptors involve stimulation of receptors in the skin. They permit a part of the body to be reflexly withdrawn when it is painfully stimulated. Obviously then, withdrawal reflexes are protective, helping to maintain the integrity of the body.

Suppose you accidentally rest your hand on a hot stove. Almost instantly, and before you become consciously aware of the pain, you jerk your hand away. Pain receptors (dendrites of sensory neurons) have sent messages through sensory neurons to the spinal cord. There each neuron synapses with an association neuron. Integration takes place, and impulses are sent via appropriate motor neurons to flexor muscles in the arm and hand instructing them to contract, jerking the hand away from the harmful stimulus. At the same time that the flexor muscles contract, the antagonistic extensor muscles are inhibited.

Within 0.5 second after a stimulus initiates a withdrawal reflex in one limb, the opposite limb begins to extend. This is known as the **crossed extensor reflex;** it helps the body keep its balance. The crossed extensor reflex results from contraction of muscles in the opposite limb. By involving more neurons, more complex responses are possible.

Suppose, for example, you step on a nail. If your only response were to jerk your foot from the sharp object, you might meet an even more perilous fate. Fortunately, your arms and hands quickly extend outward and your leg muscles tighten to ensure that you are able to balance safely on one foot. If you were to attempt to count the muscles necessary to effect this response, the number might reach almost 100. Each muscle is in turn composed of thousands of muscle bundles, each signaled by a neuron. Think, then, of all the neurons, and just the right ones at that, activated by the simple prick of that nail.

Not only does the body withdraw by reflex from a painful stimulus, but the brain must be informed of the situation. The spinal cord sends messages through its ascending tracts to let the conscious areas of the brain know what has happened (e.g., that you have stepped on a nail or burned your hand). You become aware of the pain and can make decisions about first-aid measures. Messages directing voluntary movement are then sent from the brain via the descending tracts to the appropriate motor nerves. None of this is part of the reflex action, however.

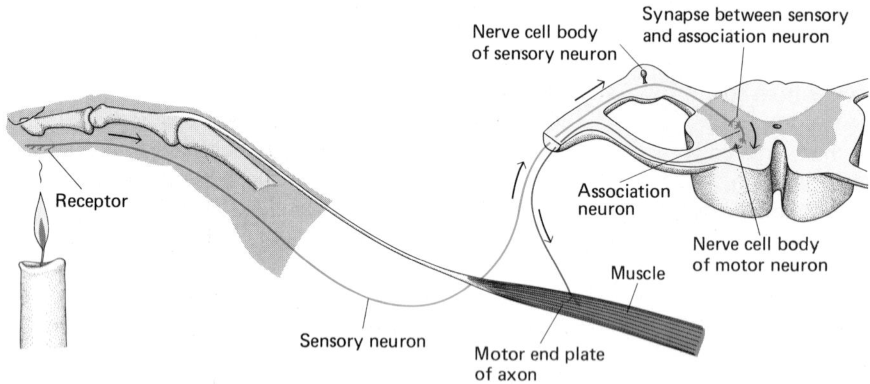

FIGURE 13-28

A withdrawal reflex is polysynaptic. The one shown here involves a chain of three neurons. A sensory neuron transmits the message from the receptor to the CNS, where it synapses with an association neuron. Then an appropriate motor neuron (shown in color) transmits an impulse to the muscles that move the hand away from the flame (the response).

Summary

I. The brain and spinal cord are protected by bone, cerebrospinal fluid, and three connective tissue coverings called meninges—the dura mater, arachnoid, and pia mater.

II. The main divisions of the brain are the medulla, pons, midbrain, diencephalon (including thalamus and hypothalamus), cerebellum, and cerebrum.

III. The medulla is the inferior portion of the brainstem. It contains many structures that perform a variety of functions.
   A. The medulla contains all nerve tracts passing from the spinal cord to any part of the brain and those tracts descending from the brain to the spinal cord.
   B. The medulla contains vital centers that control respiration, heart rate, and blood pressure.
   C. The medulla contains centers that control reflex actions such as swallowing, vomiting, sneezing, and coughing.
   D. The medulla contains nuclei of cranial nerves IX through XII.

IV. The pons serves as a bridge connecting various parts of the brain.
   A. It consists of nerve tracts passing through it.
   B. It helps to regulate respiration.
   C. The pons serves as a center for reflexes mediated by cranial nerves V through VIII.

V. The midbrain is the shortest part of the brainstem.
   A. Ventrally the midbrain consists of the cerebral peduncles.
   B. It contains the nuclei of cranial nerves III and IV.
   C. Its tectum (roof) consists of the corpora quadrigemina.
      1. The superior colliculi are visual reflex centers.
      2. The inferior colliculi are auditory reflex centers.

VI. The thalamus, part of the diencephalon, is a major relay station for impulses going to and from the cerebrum. It contains many nuclei.
   A. The medial geniculate nuclei are relay centers for auditory messages.
   B. The lateral geniculate nuclei are relay centers for visual messages.
   C. When sensory impulses reach the thalamus, one becomes vaguely aware of them.

VII. The hypothalamus, which is part of the diencephalon, forms the floor of the third ventricle. Its many functions include the following:
   A. Serving as a link between the nervous and endocrine systems.
   B. Serving as a link between the cerebrum and the lower autonomic centers.
   C. Helping regulate temperature.
   D. Helping maintain water balance.
   E. Influencing emotional and sexual behavior.
   F. Regulating satiety and appetite.

VIII. The cerebellum consists of two hemispheres connected by the vermis. Its functions include:
   A. Making muscular movements smooth and coordinated.
   B. Maintaining posture.
   C. Maintaining equilibrium.

IX. The cerebrum is divided into right and left hemispheres by the longitudinal fissure.
   A. The cerebral cortex consists of gyri separated by sulci or fissures.
   B. The white matter of the cerebrum contains the basal ganglia.
   C. Each hemisphere is divided into lobes.
      1. The frontal lobes contain the motor cortex and the premotor area, which includes Broca's speech area.
      2. The parietal lobes receive sensory information and integrate it.
      3. The occipital lobes receive and interpret visual information.
      4. The temporal lobes receive and interpret auditory information and are also involved in emotion, personality, behavior, and memory storage.
      5. The limbic lobes are concerned with olfaction and with emotional behavior.
   D. The functions of the cerebrum may be divided into three groups: sensory, motor, and association.
   E. In most persons the left cerebral hemisphere is specialized for language as well as for handedness; the right hemisphere is specialized for recognition of faces, shapes, and perhaps recognition of melodies and other artistic endeavors.

X. The limbic system functions in emotional responses, autonomic responses, motivation, sexual behavior, and biological rhythms.

XI. The RAS sends impulses into the cerebrum, helping to maintain consciousness. When the pace of these impulses slows, one may become sleepy.

XII. The spinal cord is continuous with the medulla and extends to the level of the second lumbar vertebra.
   A. Below the conus medullaris, the filum terminale and cauda equina extend caudally.
   B. In cross section the spinal cord reveals a central canal surrounded by gray matter and an outer portion of white matter.

1. Each half of the white matter is arranged into anterior, posterior, and lateral funiculi.
2. Each funiculus is divided into tracts called fasciculi.

c. The spinal cord functions as a reflex control center and transmits information back and forth between the brain and the peripheral nerves.

1. In a reflex pathway, a stimulus results in a predictable, automatic response.
2. Stretch reflexes are monsynaptic; the patellar reflex is an example.
3. Flexor reflexes (withdrawal reflexes) are polysynaptic; an association neuron is interposed between sensory and motor neurons.

Post-test

1. The tough outer meninx protecting the brain and spinal cord is the ____________ ____________.
2. The subarachnoid space contains the ____________.
3. The cavities within the brain are called ____________.
4. The medulla, pons, and midbrain make up the ____________.

Match

____ 5. Vital centers found here
____ 6. Contains the corpora quadrigemina
____ 7. Helps maintain posture and equilibrium
____ 8. Controls voluntary movement
____ 9. Link between nervous and endocrine systems
____ 10. Contains nuclei of cranial nerves V through VIII
____ 11. Contains geniculate nuclei

a. cerebrum
b. cerebellum
c. midbrain
d. medulla
e. pons
f. hypothalamus
g. thalamus

Match

____ 12. Contains Broca's speech area
____ 13. Contains auditory areas
____ 14. Contains visual areas
____ 15. Concerned with olfaction

a. occipital lobes
b. frontal lobes
c. temporal lobes
d. limbic lobes
e. parietal lobes

16. In most persons the ____________ cerebral hemisphere is dominant for speech.
17. The ____________ functions to maintain consciousness.
18. The ____________ wave pattern is evoked when a person is resting with eyes closed.
19. The conus medullaris is the caudal tip of the ____________ ____________.
20. Nerves for the lower region of the spinal cord that extend caudally below the conus before leaving the vertebral canal make up the ____________ ____________.
21. The white matter of the cord consists of ____________ and ____________ tracts.
22. The corticospinal tracts are also known as the ____________ tracts.
23. Three types of neurons in a withdrawal reflex are ____________, ____________, and ____________ neurons.
24. The ____________ reflex is the simplest type of reflex; an example is the ____________ reflex.
25. Label the diagram.

Review questions

1. List and describe the structures that protect the brain and spinal cord.
2. Trace the development of the CNS from the embryonic neural tube.
3. How does the crossing of the pyramidal fibers affect neural function?
4. How do the right and left cerebral hemispheres communicate?
5. Identify the part of the brain most closely associated with each of the following functions:
   a. Regulation of body temperature
   b. Regulation of heart rate
   c. Reflex center for pupil constriction
   d. Link between nervous and endocrine systems
   e. Interpretation of language
   f. Maintenance of posture

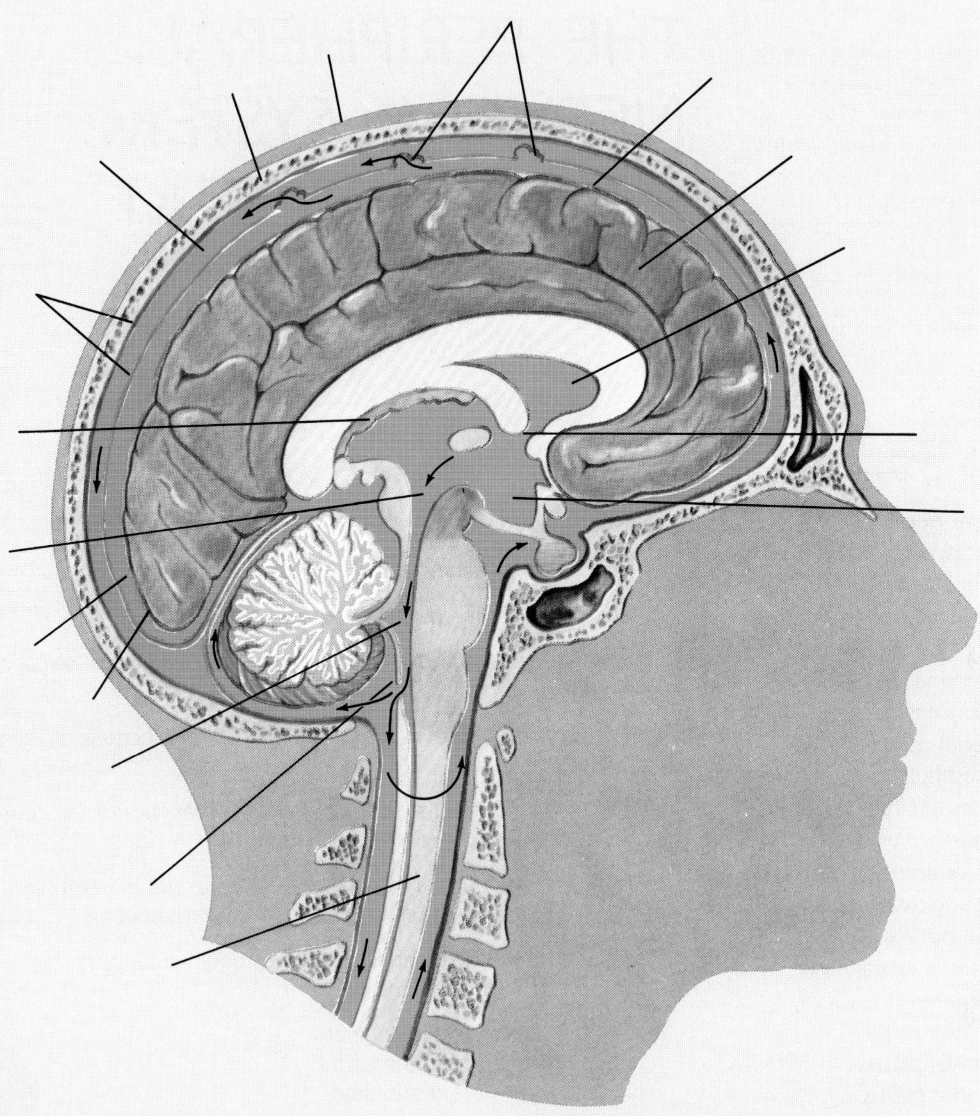

6. How have scientists pinpointed functions of various parts of the cerebrum?
7. What is the pyramidal system? Describe its functions.
8. In which part of the cerebrum would you find (a) the basal ganglia, (b) Broca's speech area, (c) primary motor area, (d) primary visual area, (e) central sulcus?
9. What functions does the left cerebral hemisphere specialize in in most persons? The right?
10. How are EEGs used clinically?
11. What is the RAS? What does it do?
12. Draw and label a cross section through the spinal cord.
13. Imagine that you have just burned your finger with a match. Describe the events that occur. Draw a diagram of the polysynaptic reflex pathway, label its parts, and relate the diagram to your description.

Post-test answers

1. dura mater **2.** CSF (cerebrospinal fluid) **3.** ventricles **4.** brainstem **5.** d **6.** c **7.** b **8.** a **9.** f **10.** e **11.** g **12.** b **13.** c **14.** a **15.** d **16.** left **17.** RAS (reticular activating system) **18.** alpha **19.** spinal cord **20.** cauda equina **21.** ascending, descending **22.** pyramidal **23.** afferent (sensory), association, efferent (motor) **24.** stretch; patellar **25.** See Fig. 13-3.

THE PERIPHERAL NERVOUS SYSTEM: SOMATIC SYSTEM

CHAPTER OUTLINE

I. The cranial nerves
- A. I. Olfactory nerves
- B. II. Optic nerves
- C. III. Oculomotor nerves
- D. IV. Trochlear nerves
- E. V. Trigeminal nerves
- F. VI. Abducens nerves
- G. VII. Facial nerves
- H. VIII. Vestibulocochlear nerves
- I. IX. Glossopharyngeal nerves
- J. X. Vagus nerves
- K. XI. Spinal accessory nerves
- L. XII. Hypoglossal nerves

II. The spinal nerves
- A. Branches of spinal nerve
- B. Ventral rami
  1. Cervical plexus
  2. Brachial plexus
  3. Lumbar plexus
  4. Sacral plexus
  5. Coccygeal plexus
- C. Thoracic nerves

III. Segmental innervation
- □ Focus on the PNS in stress

LEARNING OBJECTIVES

After you have studied this chapter you should be able to:

1 List the cranial nerves and give the functions of each.

2 Relate spinal nerve names to their locations.

3 Describe (label on a diagram) the structure of a typical spinal nerve, including roots and rami.

4 Cite the name, spinal nerve components, and functions of the principal plexuses.

5 Identify the principal superficial and deep branches of the cervical plexus and describe their general distribution.

6 Describe the sequence of nerve structures in the brachial plexus and identify its principal peripheral nerves and their distribution.

7 Identify the principal peripheral nerves originating in the lumbar plexus and describe their distributions.

8 Identify the principal peripheral nerves emerging from the sacral plexus and cite the distribution of each.

9 Describe the distribution of the intercostal nerves.

10 Describe the segmental innervation of the body, defining the terms dermatome and myotome and summarizing the clinical significance of segmental innervation.

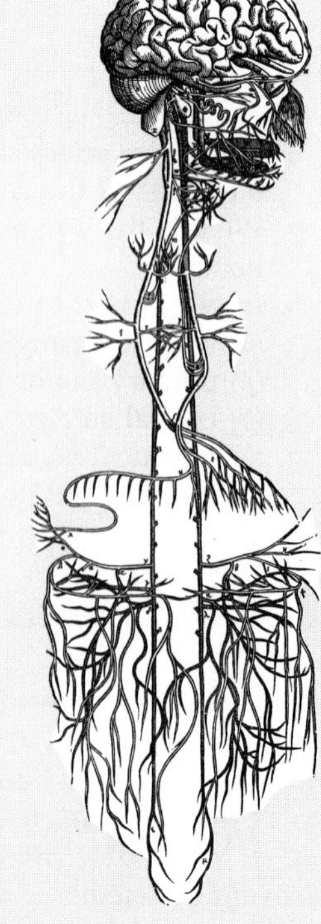

(top) Photomicrograph of neuromuscular junction. (John D. Cunningham/Visuals Unlimited.) *(bottom)* Scanning electron micrograph of human bone marrow showing efferent neurons with dendrites. The tissue has been impregnated with silver. (Manfred Kage.)

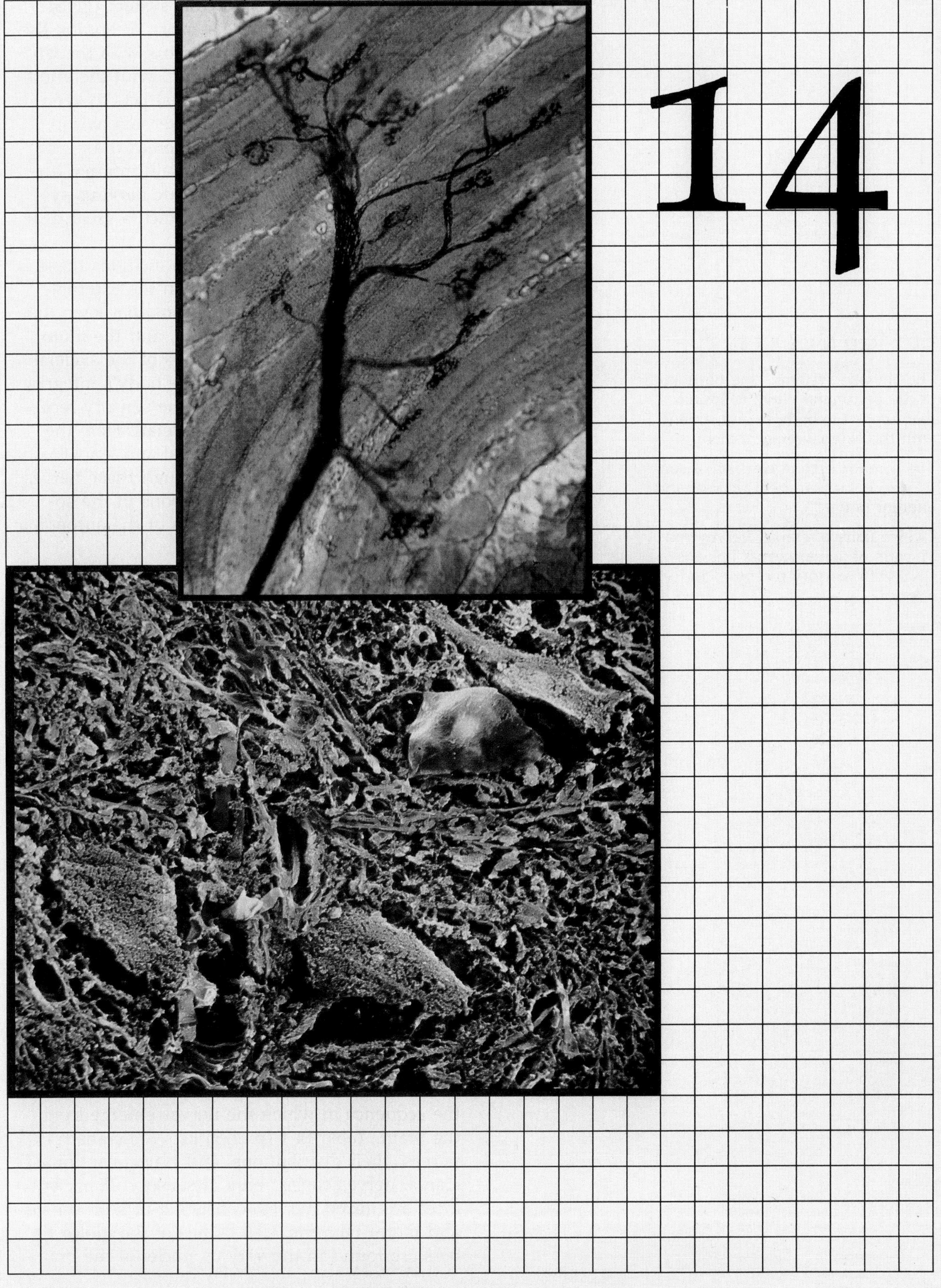

14

KEY CONCEPTS

The somatic system is the portion of the peripheral nervous system that keeps the body in adjustment with the external environment.

The somatic system consists of sensory receptors, afferent nerves, and efferent nerves.

Twelve pairs of cranial nerves and 31 pairs of spinal nerves link the CNS with sensory receptors and effectors.

The **peripheral nervous system (PNS)** comprises all the sensory receptors, the nerves that link receptors with the CNS, and the nerves that link the CNS with the effectors. That portion of the PNS that acts to keep the body in balance with the external environment is the **somatic system,** whereas the nerves and receptors designed to maintain internal homeostasis make up the **autonomic nervous system.** These systems are not distinct; a great deal of overlap occurs.

The somatic nervous system includes those receptors that react to changes in the external environment, the sensory neurons that keep the CNS informed of those changes, and the motor neurons that adjust the positions of the skeletal muscles in order to maintain the body's integrity and well-being. In Chapter 17 the sensory receptors will be discussed in some detail. Here the communication lines—the cranial and spinal nerves—will be described. Through these nerves run the sensory and motor neurons of the somatic system as well as neurons of the autonomic system.

The cranial nerves link the brain with many receptors and with muscles and glands

Twelve pairs of nerves emerge from the brain itself. Of these, ten pairs emerge from various parts of the brainstem, one pair from the cerebrum, and one from the thalamus (Fig. 14-1, p. 478). These cranial nerves transmit information to the brain from the special sensory receptors regarding the senses of smell, sight, hearing, and taste, and from general sensory receptors, especially in the head region. They also bring orders from the CNS to the voluntary muscles that control movements of the eyes, face, mouth, tongue, pharynx, and larynx and provide communication between the CNS and many internal organs.

Cranial nerves are designated by roman numerals as well as by name. The numbers indicate the sequence in which the nerves emerge from the brain. Table 14-1 (p. 479) lists the cranial nerves, their distributions, and functions. Some cranial nerves consist only of sensory fibers, but most are mixed nerves, consisting of both sensory and motor neurons. Cell bodies of the motor fibers are found in the various nuclei of the brainstem, whereas most cell bodies of the sensory fibers are located in ganglia outside the brain.

I. The olfactory nerves transmit information regarding smell

The **olfactory nerves** are sensory nerves that transmit information about smell from the olfactory mucosa in the upper part of the nasal passages. These nerves consist of bipolar neurons with unmyelinated axons. The axons pass through tiny openings in the cribriform plate of the ethmoid bone and terminate in the olfactory bulbs, extensions of the cerebrum that lie just above the cribriform plate. (The olfactory bulbs are part of the limbic system.) Within the olfactory bulbs the neurons synapse with olfactory neurons that make up the olfactory tract. Neurons of the olfactory tract project to the olfactory area of the cerebrum (within the temporal lobe) and to the amygdala (a group of nuclei within the temporal lobe). The olfactory system is the only sensory system that passes directly to the cerebral cortex without synapsing within the thalamus. Olfaction is discussed in Chapter 17.

II. The optic nerves transmit information regarding vision

Like the olfactory nerves, the **optic nerves** are entirely sensory. They convey impulses from the visual receptors, the rods and cones of the retina of each eye. The myelinated axons of the bipolar neurons that make up the optic nerves enter the skull through the optic foramina. Parts of the two optic nerves cross on the anterior surface of the hypothalamus, forming the **optic chiasma.** Within the optic chiasma, neurons from the medial portion of each retina cross to the opposite side; those from the lateral portion remain on the same side.

Neurons pass caudally from the chiasma, forming the optic tracts. Most neurons of the optic tracts end in the lateral geniculate nuclei of the thalamus. There they synapse before sending impulses into the visual areas of the occipital lobes. Some of the neurons of the optic tracts project to the superior colliculi of the midbrain. These send messages to cranial nerves (oculomotor, trochlear, and abducens) that control eye movement. Through these reflex pathways, light stimulates many types of motor responses.

III. The oculomotor nerves innervate muscles of the eye

Although the **oculomotor nerves** (*ok*-u-low-**mow**-tor) are mixed nerves, conveying both sensory and motor information, they are mainly motor nerves. The neurons of the oculomotor nerves originate within nuclei in the anterior portion of the midbrain. Each oculomotor nerve passes from the skull through the superior orbital fissure in the orbit. Its neurons innervate some of the extrinsic muscles that move the eyeball, muscles that move the upper eyelid, and certain smooth muscles of the eye.

The axons that innervate smooth muscle cells in the eyeball pass through the *ciliary ganglion.* These axons control the sphincter muscle of the iris, a structure that constricts, narrowing the pupil, in response to light. Some of these fibers control the ciliary muscle that accommodates (adjusts) the lens of the eye for close vision. Sensory neurons of the oculomotor nerves convey information from muscle spindles within the eyeball muscles to the midbrain.

IV. The trochlear nerves innervate extrinsic eye muscles

The **trochlear nerves** (**trok**-lee-ar) are also mixed nerves and are mainly motor. Their nuclei lie within the midbrain just caudal to the nuclei of the oculomotor nerves. These are the only cranial nerves that emerge from the dorsal surface of the brainstem. After exiting from the skull through the superior orbital fissures, the trochlear nerves innervate the superior oblique muscles of the eyeballs. Thus, these nerves help control movement of the eyeballs. Sensory neurons of the trochlear nerves transmit information from muscle spindles (sensory receptors) in the superior oblique muscles to the midbrain.

V. The trigeminal nerves have three main branches

The largest of the cranial nerves, the **trigeminal nerves** (tri-**jem**-ih-nal) are mixed nerves. As its name implies, each trigeminal nerve has three main branches—**ophthalmic, maxillary,** and **mandibular** (Fig. 14-2). The cell bodies of most of the sensory neurons of the trigeminal nerve are

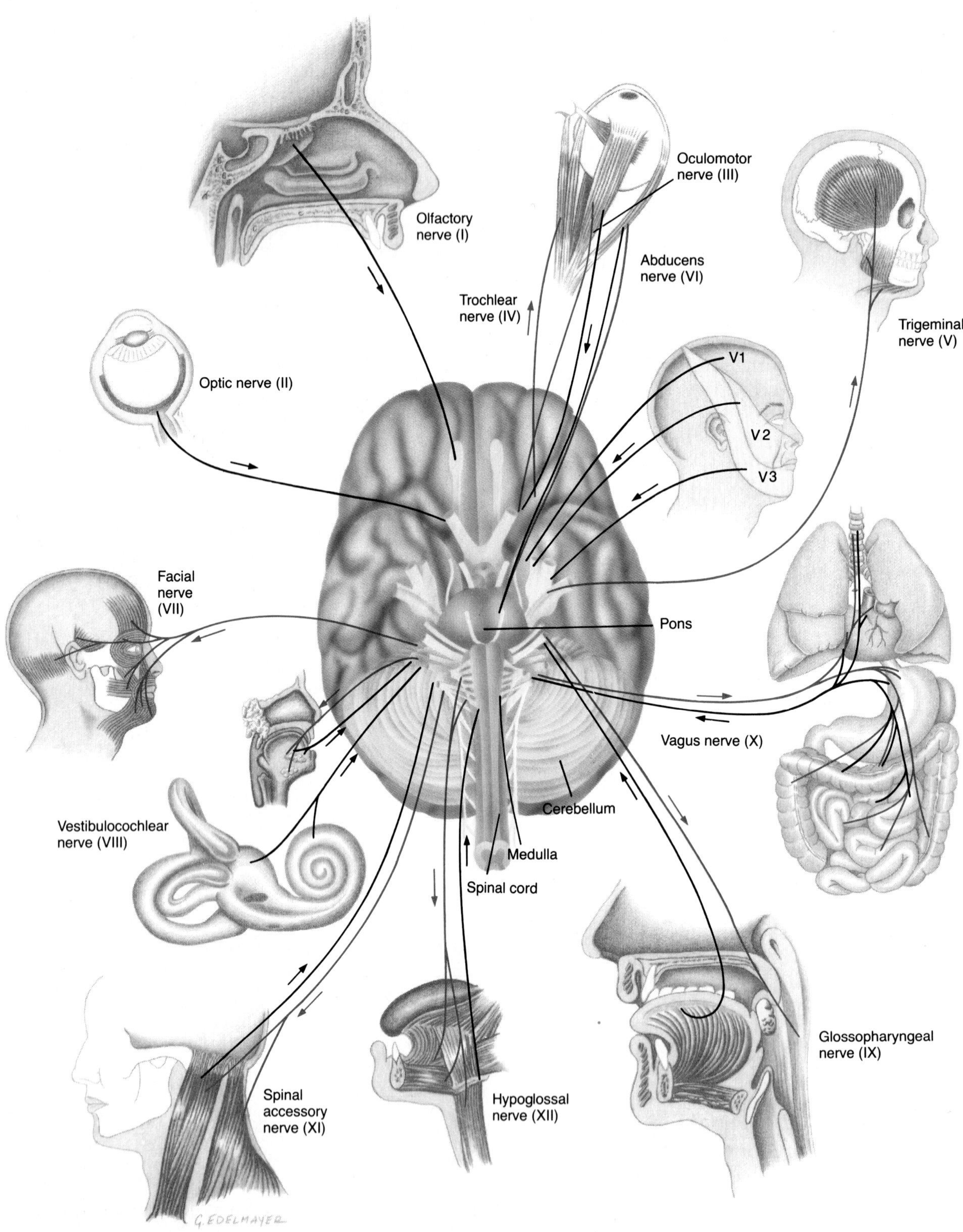

FIGURE 14-1

Basal surface of the brain showing emergence of the cranial nerves. Black indicates sensory; color indicates motor fibers.

TABLE 14-1

The cranial nerves		
Name	**Function**	**Distribution**
I. Olfactory	Sensory: smell	Transmit messages from the olfactory mucosa to olfactory bulbs
II. Optic	Sensory: vision	Transmit messages from the retina of the eye to the thalamus and midbrain, where they synapse with neurons that convey messages to the visual areas of the occipital lobes
III. Oculomotor	Mixed, but mainly motor: movement of eyeball and eyelid; regulation of pupil size; accommodation of lens for near vision	Midbrain to eye muscles (superior rectus, medial rectus, inferior rectus, inferior oblique)
	Sensory: messages regarding condition of innervated muscles	Convey messages from eye muscles to the brain
IV. Trochlear	Mixed, but mainly motor: movement of eyeball	Midbrain to superior oblique eye muscle
	Sensory: messages regarding condition of innervated muscles	Superior oblique muscle to midbrain
V. Trigeminal	Mixed. Sensory: sensations of head and face	Face and scalp to pons
	Motor: chewing	Pons to muscles of mastication
Ophthalmic branch	Sensory	Conveys messages from upper eyelid, surface of eye, tear glands, part of nose, scalp, and forehead
Maxillary branch	Sensory	Conveys messages from upper teeth, upper gum, upper lip, palate, and skin of face
Mandibular branch	Sensory	Conveys messages from lower teeth, lower gum, lower lip, skin of jaw, and part of scalp
	Motor	Pons to muscles of mastication
VI. Abducens	Mixed, but mainly motor: eye movement	Pons to lateral rectus muscle of the eye
	Sensory: messages regarding condition of lateral rectus	Lateral rectus muscle to pons
VII. Facial	Mixed. Sensory: taste	Taste buds on tongue to medulla
	Motor: facial expression, secretion of saliva and tears	Pons–medulla junction to muscles of the face and scalp, and to salivary and tear glands
VIII. Vestibulocochlear	Sensory: hearing and equilibrium	Cochlea and semicircular canals of inner ear to pons–medulla junction
Vestibular branch	Sensory: equilibrium	Organs of equilibrium of inner ear to vestibular nuclei
Cochlear (auditory) branch	Sensory: hearing	Organ of hearing in cochlea of inner ear to medulla, then to inferior colliculi of midbrain
IX. Glossopharyngeal	Mixed. Sensory: taste	Taste buds in tongue to medulla; receptors in carotid arteries to medulla
	Motor: swallowing, saliva secretion	Medulla to muscles of pharynx; medulla to parotid salivary gland
X. Vagus	Mixed. Sensory: sensation from larynx, trachea, heart, and other thoracic and abdominal organs	Various organs to medulla
	Motor: movement of various organs, e.g., heart	Medulla to muscles of the pharynx, larynx, thoracic and abdominal viscera
XI. Spinal accessory	Mixed, but mainly motor: movement of shoulders and head	Medulla and spinal cord to muscles of the shoulder and neck; and to muscles of the pharynx and larynx
	Sensory: messages regarding condition of innervated neck and shoulder muscles	Muscle spindles of shoulder and neck muscles to spinal cord
XII. Hypoglossal	Mixed, but mainly motor: tongue movement	Medulla to tongue muscles
	Sensory: messages regarding condition of tongue	Muscle spindles in tongue to medulla

within the **trigeminal ganglion** located in a fossa on the inner surface of the petrous region of the temporal bone. The ophthalmic branch conveys sensory information from the upper eyelid, surface of the eye, lacrimal (tear) glands, side of the nose, upper region of the nasal cavity, forehead, and anterior portion of the scalp. This branch enters the skull through the superior orbital fissure.

The maxillary branch transmits sensory information from the upper teeth, gum, and lip, from the skin of the face, and from the palate. This branch enters the skull through the foramen rotundum. The sensory neurons of the mandibular branch transmit information from the lower teeth, gum, and lip, from the skin of the jaw, and from the temporal area of the scalp. The mandibular branch enters the skull through the foramen ovale.

After passing through the trigeminal ganglia, sensory messages are transmitted to the pons. All the motor neurons of the trigeminal nerve originate in the motor nucleus of the fifth nerve within the pons. They emerge from the pons along with sensory fibers of the trigeminal. Then they bypass the trigeminal ganglion and pass into the mandibular branch. These motor neurons provide the sole innervation of the muscles of mastication. Sensory neurons from the muscles of mastication are also part of the trigeminal nerve.

Clinical highlights

Irritation of the trigeminal nerve, called **trigeminal neuralgia,** or tic douloureux, can cause excruciating pain over the distribution of the nerve. Its cause is not known. The condition is sometimes relieved by surgery in which the trigeminal nerve is cut proximal to the trigeminal ganglion.

VI. The abducens nerves innervate extrinsic eye muscles

The **abducens nerves** (ab-**do**-senz) are mixed but mainly motor cranial nerves that emerge from a nucleus within the pons. Motor neurons from each abducens nerve leave the skull through the superior orbital fissure and innervate the lateral rectus muscle, one of the extrinsic eyeball muscles. Sensory neurons transmit impulses from the lateral rectus muscle to the pons.

VII. The facial nerves control facial expression

The **facial nerves** are mixed nerves that emerge from the brainstem at the level of the pons. Their sensory neurons gather information from the taste receptors on the anterior two-thirds of the tongue; their cell bodies lie within the geniculate

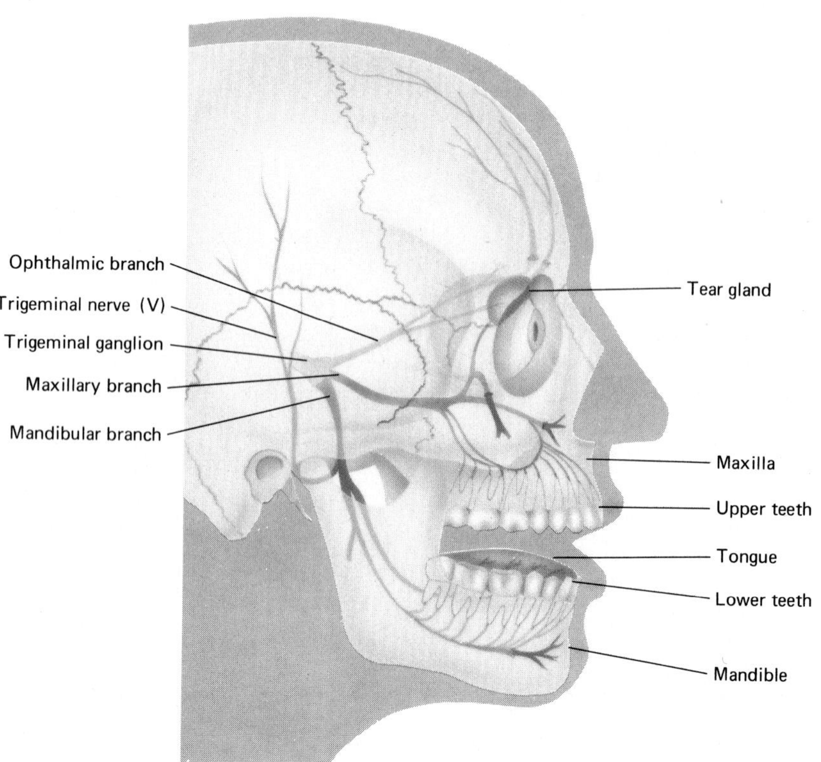

FIGURE 14-2

The trigeminal nerve, cranial nerve V, is a mixed nerve with three branches that supply the face and head.

ganglia. Motor neurons of the facial nerve control the muscles of facial expression and supply the lacrimal glands and certain salivary glands (submaxillary and sublingual). The cell bodies of these motor neurons lie within nuclei located in the pons.

Clinical highlight

Bell's palsy is a common disorder of the facial nerve in which pain and facial weakness or paralysis may develop. Although its cause is unknown, it is thought to involve swelling of the facial nerve due to immune or viral disease. Complete spontaneous recovery usually occurs after several months.

VIII. The vestibulocochlear nerves transmit information regarding hearing and equilibrium

The **vestibulocochlear nerves** (ves-*tib*-u-low-**kok**-lee-ar) are sensory cranial nerves. As its name implies, each nerve consists of two branches, the cochlear and the vestibular. The *cochlear,* also called the auditory, *branch* transmits auditory information from the ear. Impulses from the organ of hearing (organ of Corti) in the cochlea of the inner ear are transmitted to the cochlear nuclei within the medulla and then to the inferior colliculi. From here information is transmitted to the medial geniculate nuclei of the thalamus and then to the auditory areas within the temporal lobes. Buzzing or ringing in the ears (tinnitus) is a common symptom of damage to the cochlear nerves.

The *vestibular branch* conveys information about equilibrium and orientation of the head in space. Impulses are transmitted from the organs of equilibrium (semicircular canals, saccule, and utricle) of the inner ears to the vestibular nuclei in the medulla. From here, messages are dispatched to the cerebellum and spinal cord. Many complex linkages connect these nerves with the reticular formation, other cranial nerves, and other parts of the brain.

IX. The glossopharyngeal nerves function in taste and swallowing

The **glossopharyngeal nerves** (*glos*-oh-fah-**rin**-jee-al) are mixed nerves that emerge from the medulla and exit from the skull through the jugular foramina. Sensory neurons of each glossopharyngeal nerve transmit impulses from the taste receptors on the posterior one-third of the tongue. Other sensory neurons of this nerve convey touch, pain, and temperature sensations from the tongue, tonsils, and eustachian tubes. Still others bring information about blood pressure from sensory receptors within certain blood vessels (the carotid arteries).

Motor neurons of the glossopharyngeal nerve convey messages to the parotid salivary glands. Other motor neurons innervate the stylopharyngeus muscle, which raises the pharynx during swallowing and speech.

X. The vagus nerves innervate many internal organs

The **vagus nerves** (**vay**-gus) are mixed nerves that emerge from the medulla and pass through the jugular foramina. They pass downward through the neck and branch to innervate many structures within the thorax and abdomen. Sensory neurons of the vagus transmit information from many organs including the pharynx, larynx, trachea, esophagus, heart, and abdominal viscera. These messages are conveyed to the medulla and pons. Motor neurons of the vagus nerves innervate almost all of the thoracic and abdominal organs.

XI. The spinal accessory nerves innervate neck and shoulder muscles

The **spinal accessory** (or simply accessory) **nerves** are mixed nerves that are primarily motor. Each spinal accessory nerve emerges from both the brainstem and the spinal cord. The cranial portion of the nerve originates in the medulla, passes through the jugular foramen, and innervates voluntary muscles of the pharynx, larynx, and palate involved in swallowing.

The spinal portion of the nerve emerges from the first five segments of the cervical region of the cord. Its axons join, enter the foramen magnum, and after joining the cranial portion, exit from the skull through the jugular foramen. These neurons convey impulses to the trapezius and sternocleidomastoid muscles that help move the head. Sensory neurons of this nerve receive information from the same muscles innervated by the motor fibers and deliver them to the spinal cord via ganglia in the upper cervical region.

XII. The hypoglossal nerves innervate the tongue

Although they are mixed nerves, the **hypoglossal nerves** (*hy*-po-**glos**-al) are mainly motor. They emerge from the medulla, leave the skull through the hypoglossal canals, and supply the muscles of the tongue. Sensory neurons of the hypoglossal nerves convey impulses regarding position from muscle-spindle receptors within the tongue.

The spinal nerves link the spinal cord with various structures

Thirty-one pairs of **spinal nerves** emerge from the spinal cord. They are all mixed nerves, transmitting sensory information to the cord through their afferent neurons and motor information from the central nervous system to the various parts of the body through their efferent neurons.

Spinal nerves are named for the general region of the vertebral column from which they originate and are numbered in sequence. There are eight pairs of cervical spinal nerves, numbered C1 to C8; 12 pairs of thoracic spinal nerves, numbered T1 to T12; five pairs of lumbar spinal nerves, numbered L1 to L5; five pairs of sacral spinal nerves, numbered S1 to S5; and one pair of coccygeal spinal nerves (Fig. 14-5). The first cervical nerve exits from the vertebral canal between the occipital bone and the atlas. The other spinal nerves exit from the vertebral column through intervertebral foramina. For example, the fourth cervical nerve passes through the intervertebral foramen between the third and fourth cervical vertebrae.

Each spinal nerve has two points of attachment with the cord. The **dorsal** (posterior) **root** consists of sensory (afferent) fibers that transmit information from the sensory receptors to the spinal cord (Fig. 14-3). Just before the dorsal root joins with the cord, it is marked by a swelling: the **spinal ganglion,** also called the **dorsal root ganglion.** This ganglion consists of the cell bodies of the sensory neurons. The **ventral** (anterior) **root** consists of motor (efferent) fibers leaving the cord. Cell bodies of the motor neurons are located within the gray matter of the cord. Dorsal and ventral roots unite at the intervertebral foramen to form the spinal nerve (Fig. 14-3).

Each spinal nerve divides into four branches

Just after a spinal nerve emerges from the vertebral column, it divides into several branches called **rami** (**ray**-my): dorsal ramus, ventral ramus, meningeal ramus, and rami communicantes (Fig. 14-4). The **dorsal** (posterior) **ramus** of each nerve consists of fibers that supply the muscles and skin of the posterior portion of the body in that region. The dorsal ramus branches, giving rise to various nerves. The **ventral** (anterior) **ramus** consists mainly of fibers that innervate the anterior and lateral body trunk in that area as well as the limbs. Be careful not to confuse the dorsal and ventral rami with the dorsal and ventral roots.

Small **meningeal** branches innervate the meninges and blood vessels of the spinal cord and the vertebrae. Fourth branches, the **rami communicantes,** will be described in conjunction with the sympathetic division of the autonomic system.

Most ventral rami form plexuses

Except for the branches of nerves T2 to T11, the ventral rami of the spinal nerves do not pass directly to the body structures they innervate. Instead, the ventral rami of several spinal nerves form networks called **plexuses.** The main plexuses are the cervical plexus, the brachial plexus, the lumbar plexus, and the sacral plexus. These are illustrated in Figure 14-5, listed in Table 14-2, and described in the following sections. Also see the muscle tables in Chapter 11.

Each plexus is a tangled network of fibers from all of the spinal nerves involved. Within a plexus the fibers of a spinal nerve may separate and then regroup with fibers that originated in other nerves. Thus, nerves emerging from a plexus consist of neurons that originated in several different spinal nerves. Peripheral nerves that emerge from a plexus may be named for the region of the body that they innervate. Each of these peripheral nerves may give rise to smaller nerve branches.

THE CERVICAL PLEXUS IS LOCATED IN THE NECK

Formed by the ventral rami of the upper four cervical nerves and contributions from C5, the **cervical plexus** lies deep within the neck. The nerves

Dorsal gray horn
Dorsal white columns
POSTERIOR
Lateral white column
Ventral gray horn
Ventral white column
Lateral gray horn
Dorsal root filaments
Dorsal root
Dorsal root ganglion
Spinal pia mater
Subarachnoid space
Spinal arachnoid
Ventral root
Spinal nerve
Ventral root filaments
Spinal dura mater
ANTERIOR

FIGURE 14-3

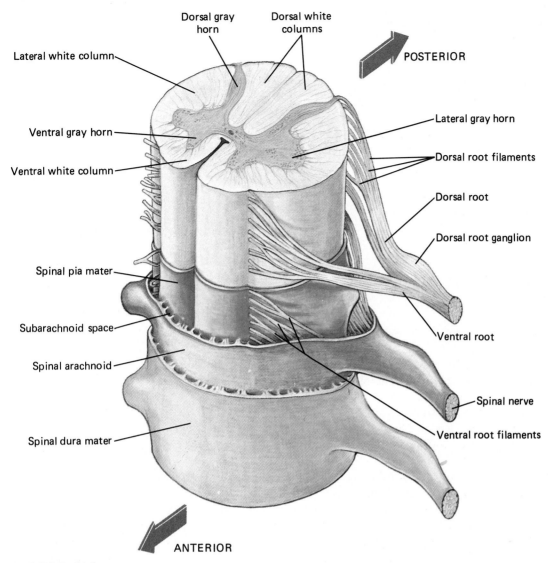

Dorsal (posterior) and ventral (anterior) roots merge to form a spinal nerve. (See also photograph at beginning of chapter.) Black indicates sensory; color indicates motor fibers.

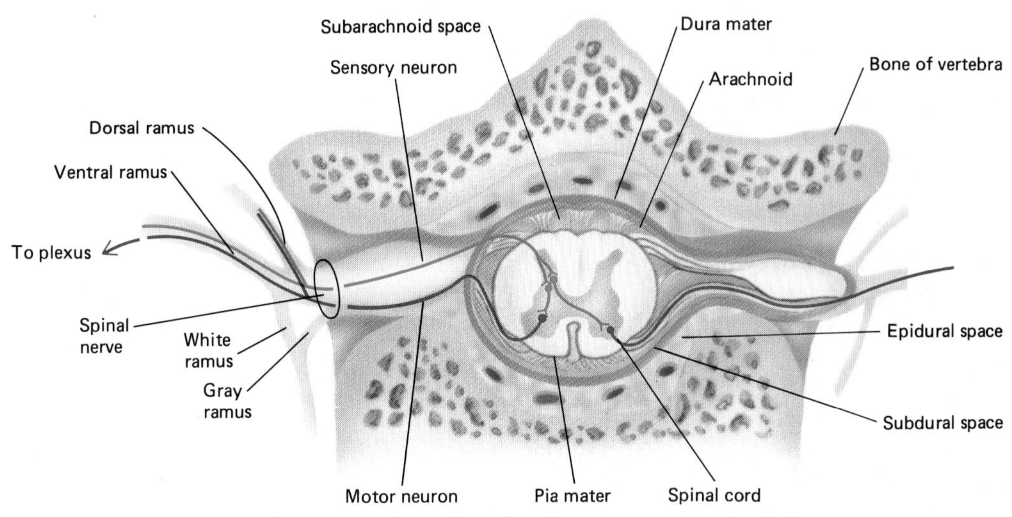

FIGURE 14-4

Branches of a spinal nerve.

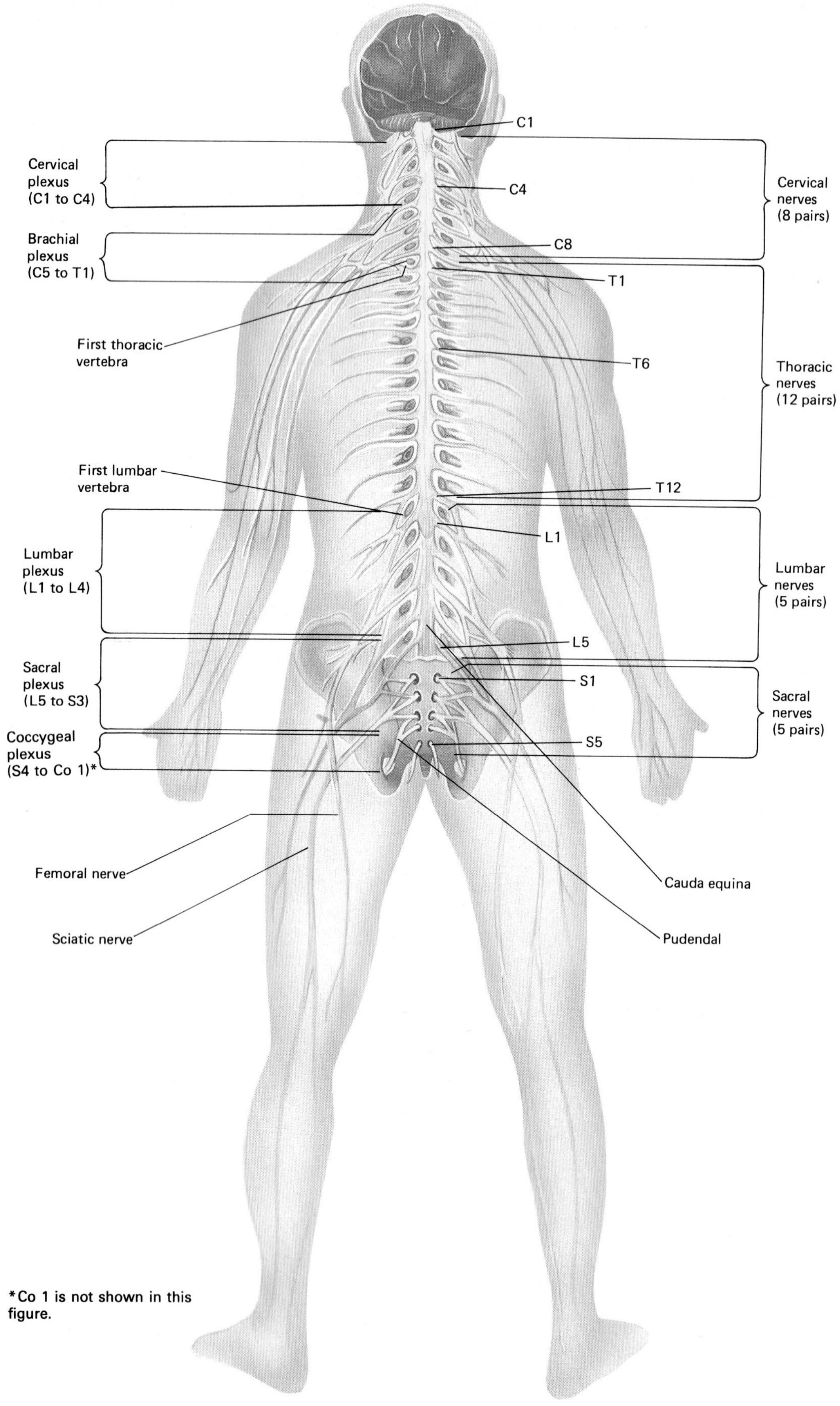

FIGURE 14-5

The spinal nerves and some of their major branches and plexuses.

that arise from this plexus innervate muscles of the neck and areas of skin on the head, neck, and chest. The branches of the cervical plexus can be divided into two groups—superficial and deep (Table 14-3). The superficial branches supply the skin, whereas the deep branches are mainly distributed to the muscles.

Branches from the cervical plexus also communicate with cranial nerves X, the vagus, and XII, the hypoglossal. The principal nerves that emerge from the cervical plexus are listed in Table 14-2 and the plexus is illustrated in Figure 14-6.

TABLE 14-2

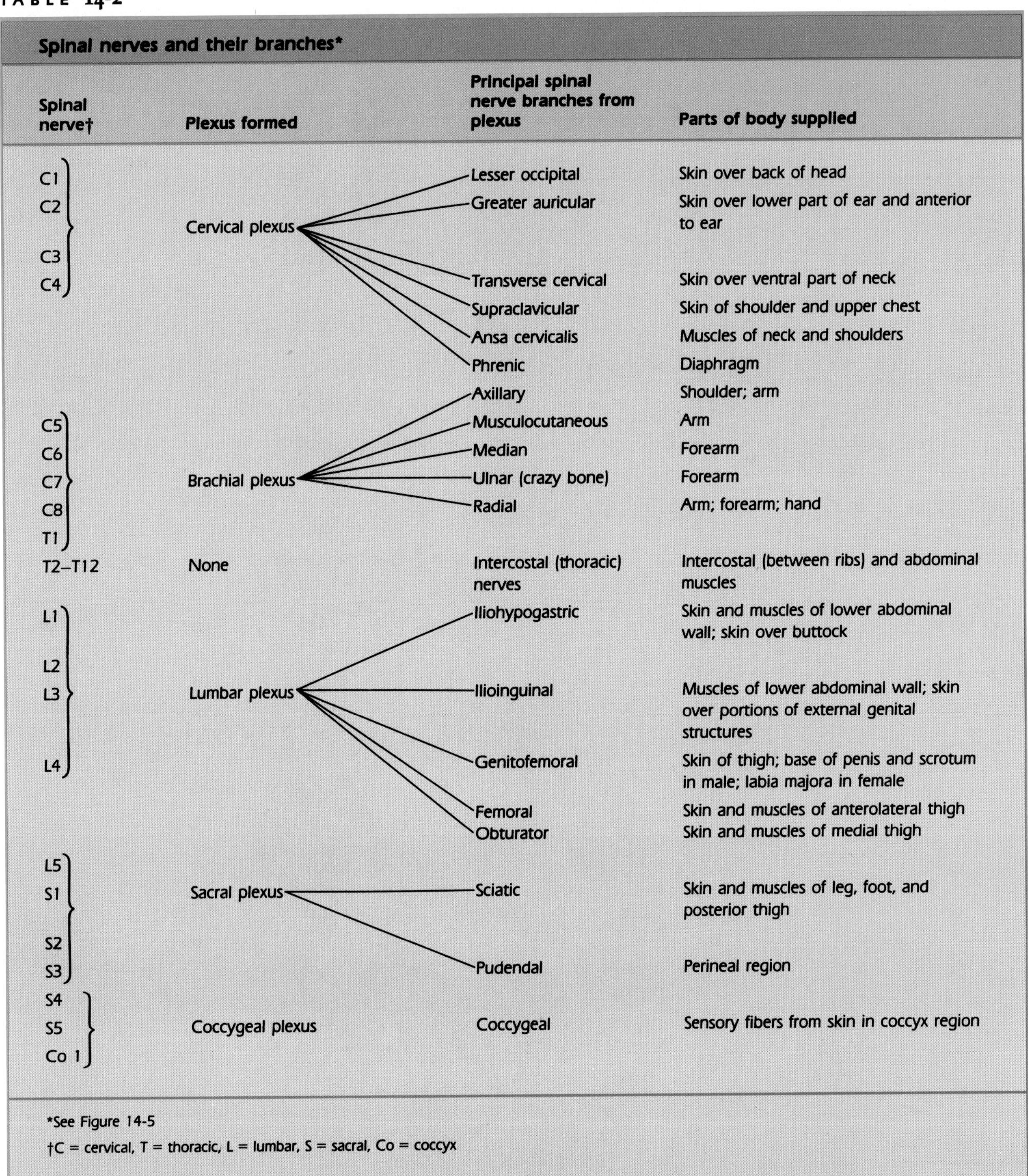

Spinal nerves and their branches*

Spinal nerve†	Plexus formed	Principal spinal nerve branches from plexus	Parts of body supplied
C1–C4	Cervical plexus	Lesser occipital	Skin over back of head
		Greater auricular	Skin over lower part of ear and anterior to ear
		Transverse cervical	Skin over ventral part of neck
		Supraclavicular	Skin of shoulder and upper chest
		Ansa cervicalis	Muscles of neck and shoulders
		Phrenic	Diaphragm
C5–C8, T1	Brachial plexus	Axillary	Shoulder; arm
		Musculocutaneous	Arm
		Median	Forearm
		Ulnar (crazy bone)	Forearm
		Radial	Arm; forearm; hand
T2–T12	None	Intercostal (thoracic) nerves	Intercostal (between ribs) and abdominal muscles
L1–L4	Lumbar plexus	Iliohypogastric	Skin and muscles of lower abdominal wall; skin over buttock
		Ilioinguinal	Muscles of lower abdominal wall; skin over portions of external genital structures
		Genitofemoral	Skin of thigh; base of penis and scrotum in male; labia majora in female
		Femoral	Skin and muscles of anterolateral thigh
		Obturator	Skin and muscles of medial thigh
L5, S1–S3	Sacral plexus	Sciatic	Skin and muscles of leg, foot, and posterior thigh
		Pudendal	Perineal region
S4, S5, Co 1	Coccygeal plexus	Coccygeal	Sensory fibers from skin in coccyx region

*See Figure 14-5

†C = cervical, T = thoracic, L = lumbar, S = sacral, Co = coccyx

TABLE 14-3

The cervical plexus		
Peripheral nerves	**Spinal nerves**	**Distribution**
Superficial branches (supply skin)		
Lesser occipital	C2	Skin over back of head
Greater auricular	C2, C3	Skin over lower part of ear and skin of face over parotid gland
Transverse cervical	C2, C3	Skin over anterior aspect of neck
Supraclavicular	C3, C4	Skin of shoulder and upper chest
Deep branches (mainly motor)		
Ansa cervicalis	C1–C4	Muscles of neck
Phrenic	C3–C5	Diaphragm

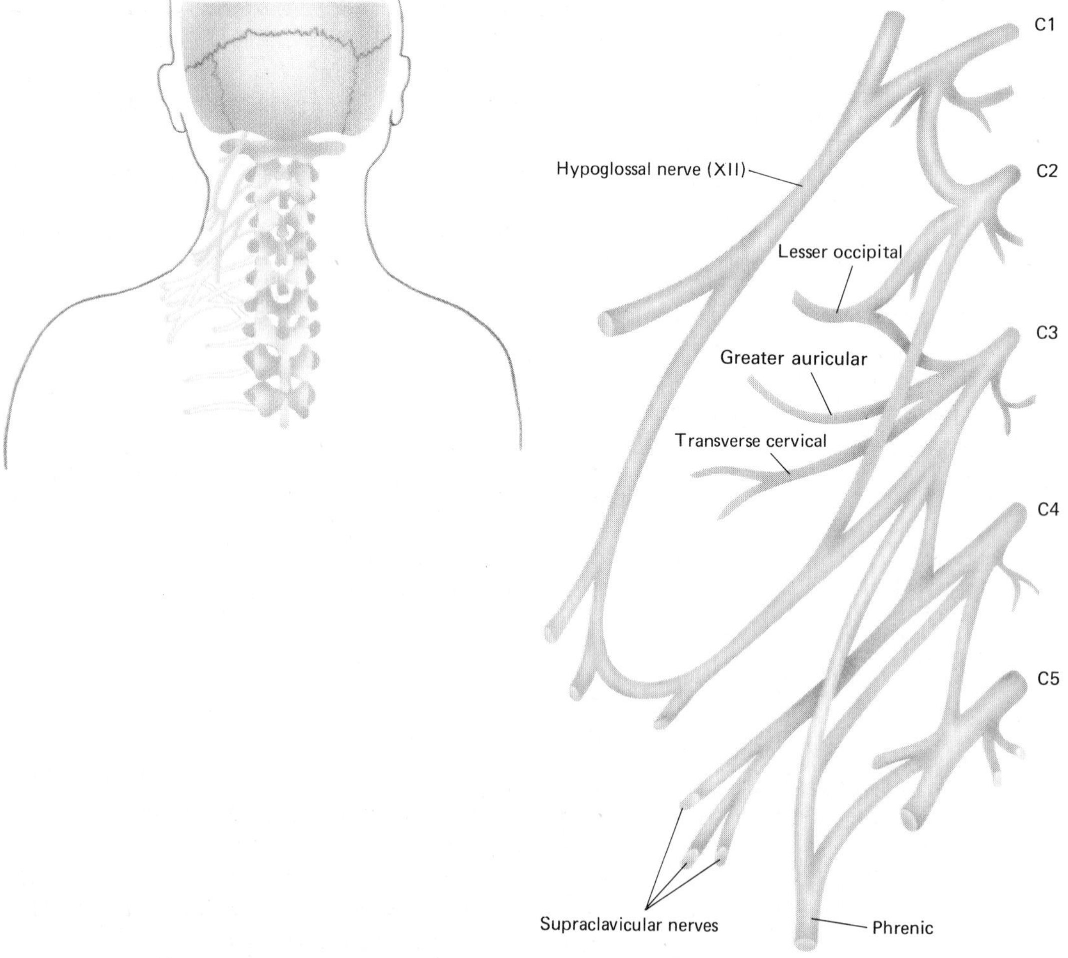

FIGURE 14-6

The cervical plexus. The ventral rami are numbered.

The **phrenic nerves,** deep branches of the cervical plexus, are the motor nerve supply to the diaphragm. Each phrenic nerve arises mainly from neurons of the fourth cervical nerve but also receives fibers from the third and fifth cervical nerves. Because contractions of the diaphragm are essential to breathing, damage to these nerves or to the spinal cord above their origin results in paralysis of the diaphragm and death from asphyxiation (lack of oxygen).

THE BRACHIAL PLEXUS IS LOCATED IN THE LOWER NECK

The **brachial plexus** is formed by the ventral rami of C5 to C8 and T1, with contributions from C4 and T2. On each side, the plexus extends downward and laterally from the lower cervical region toward the axilla (armpit). The nerves that emerge from the brachial plexus innervate the upper limb and some muscles of the neck and shoulder.

The roots of the brachial plexus are the ventral rami of the spinal nerves indicated above. These roots join to form three **nerve trunks** (Fig. 14-7). The roots of C5 and C6 join to form the *upper trunk* of the plexus. Nerve C7 becomes the *middle trunk.* Nerves C8 and T1 unite to form the *lower trunk* of the plexus. In the region of the clavicle, each of these trunks splits into an *anterior* and *posterior division.* The divisions then unite to form cords. The anterior divisions of the upper and middle trunks join to form the *lateral cord* of the plexus. The anterior division of the lower trunk continues as the *medial cord.* The posterior divisions of all three trunks unite to form the *posterior cord.* Peripheral nerves arise from the cords. In summary, then, the sequence of nerve structures in the brachial plexus is:

roots → trunks → divisions → cords → peripheral nerves

The principal peripheral nerves that emerge from the brachial plexus are listed in Table 14-4 and illustrated in Figures 14-7 and 14-8 (p. 490).

Clinical highlight

Disorders of the brachial plexus may cause a mixed sensory and motor disorder of the upper limb on that side. During birth, the brachial plexus is sometimes injured when the physician exerts too much pull on the infant's head before its shoulders have emerged from the birth canal. As a result, the newborn may suffer from impaired sensory and motor function in the affected limb and sometimes retarded growth of the limb.

THE LUMBAR PLEXUS LIES WITHIN THE PSOAS MAJOR MUSCLE

The **lumbar plexus** is formed by the ventral rami of spinal nerves L1 to L4, with a contribution from T12. Like the brachial plexus, the lumbar plexus consists of roots and an anterior and posterior division. This plexus lies anterior to the transverse processes of the lumbar vertebrae within the posterior portion of the psoas major muscle.

Nerves that emerge from the lumbar plexus serve the skin and muscles of the lower abdominal wall, the thigh, and external genital structures (Table 14-5). The largest of these nerves is the **femoral,** which supplies the skin and anterior muscles of the thigh (Fig. 14-9, p. 491).

THE SACRAL PLEXUS IS LOCATED IN THE WALL OF THE PELVIC CAVITY

The **sacral plexus** is formed by the ventral rami of part of L4, of L5, of S1 to S3, and part of S4. It lies on the posterior wall of the pelvic cavity posterior to the intestine. It includes roots and an anterior and posterior division.

Nerves that emerge from this plexus innervate the lower limbs, buttocks, and perineal region (Table 14-6, p. 494). The **sciatic nerve,** which is the main branch of the sacral plexus, is the largest nerve in the body. It supplies all of the muscles of the leg and foot, as well as the posterior muscles of the thigh.

Clinical highlight

Pain radiating down the leg along the distribution of the sciatic nerve or its branches is known as **sciatica** (sy-**at**-ih-kah). Such pain is most commonly a result of compression of the nerve root from a ruptured (herniated) intervertebral disc. Sciatica often accompanies low back pain and may be related to degenerative joint disease in the lumbosacral area.

THE COCCYGEAL PLEXUS GIVES RISE TO THE COCCYGEAL NERVE

The **coccygeal plexus** (kok-**sij**-ee-al) is formed by a branch of the ventral ramus of the fourth sacral nerve and by the rami of the fifth sacral and coccygeal nerves. It gives rise to the small coccygeal nerve, which consists of sensory fibers from the skin in the region of the coccyx.

TABLE 14-4

The brachial plexus		
Peripheral nerves	**Spinal nerves**	**Distribution**
Emerging from roots		
Dorsal scapular	C5	Levator scapulae, rhomboideus major, rhomboideus minor muscles
Long thoracic	C5–C7	Serratus anterior muscle
Emerging from trunks		
Nerve to subclavius	C5, C6	Subclavius muscle
Suprascapular	C5, C6	Supraspinatus and infraspinatus muscles
Emerging from lateral cords		
Lateral pectoral	C5–C7	Pectoralis major muscle
Musculocutaneous	C5–C7	Biceps brachii, coracobrachialis muscles, greater part of brachialis muscle
Median (lateral head)	C5–C7	(See distribution of median nerve below)
Emerging from posterior cords		
Upper subscapular	C5, C6	Subscapularis muscle
Thoracodorsal	C6–C8	Latissimus dorsi muscle
Lower subscapular	C5, C6	Subscapularis and teres major muscles
Axillary	C5, C6	Skin of shoulders and upper arm; deltoid and teres minor muscles
Radial	C5–C8, T1	Skin of arm, forearm, and hand; extensor muscles of arm and forearm
Emerging from medial cords		
Medial pectoral	C8, T1	Pectoralis major and pectoralis minor muscles
Medial cutaneous of forearm	C8, T1	Skin of forearm
Medial cutaneous of arm	C8, T1	Skin of lower third of arm
Ulnar	C8, T1	Skin of medial third of hand; flexor carpi ulnaris and flexor digitorum profundus muscles
Median (medial head)	C8, T1	Median and lateral heads of median nerve form median nerve; innervate skin of lateral two-thirds of hand; flexor muscles of arm and several intrinsic muscles of hand

TABLE 14-5

The lumbar plexus		
Peripheral nerves	**Spinal nerves**	**Distribution**
Iliohypogastric	L1	Skin and muscles of lower back, hip, and lower abdominal wall
Ilioinguinal	L1	Skin of upper medial thigh and external genitals; muscles of lower abdominal wall
Genitofemoral	L1, L2	Skin of anterior thigh, external genitals
Lateral cutaneous	L2, L3	Skin of lateral thigh
Femoral	L2–L4	Skin of anterolateral thigh, leg, and foot; flexor muscles of thigh; extensor muscles of leg
Obturator	L2–L4	Skin of medial thigh; adductor muscles of leg

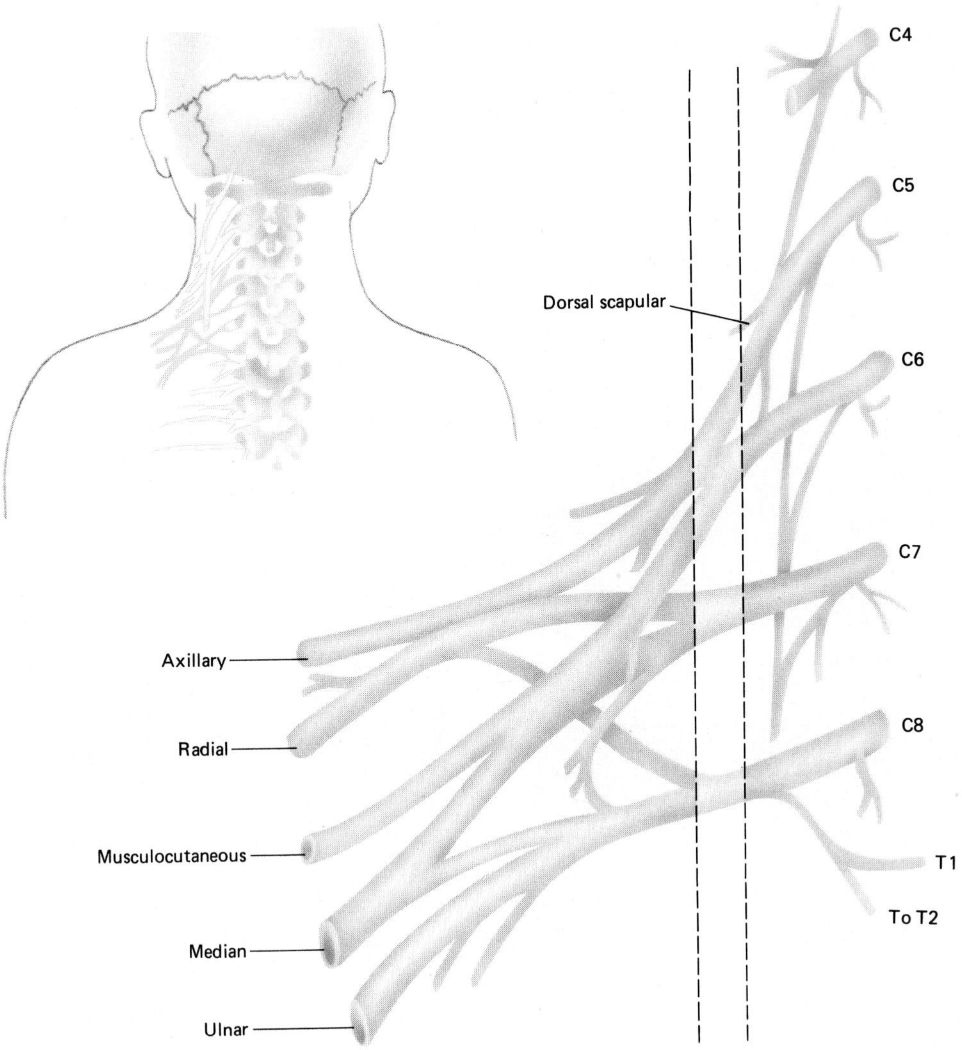

FIGURE 14-7

The brachial plexus. The ventral rami of these cervical and thoracic spinal nerves are labeled. The posterior divisions of the trunks and their branches are in color.

Thoracic nerves are intercostal nerves

The first 11 thoracic spinal nerves are the **intercostal nerves.** The ventral ramus of T1 divides into two branches. The larger branch becomes part of the brachial plexus, but the smaller branch is the first intercostal nerve. Spinal nerves T2 to T11 do not contribute to any plexus. They are distributed directly to structures in the thoracic and abdominal walls. Among the structures they innervate are the intercostal muscles, abdominal muscles, and the skin of the anterior and lateral chest wall and abdomen. The dorsal rami of the thoracic nerve supply the deep muscles of the back and the skin in the dorsal region of the thorax.

The body has segmental innervation

The entire body surface below the neck is innervated by the spinal nerves. The area of skin supplied by any one spinal nerve through both of its rami is called a **segment,** or **dermatome** (dermah-tome). Each dermatome is named for the

(text continued on p. 492)

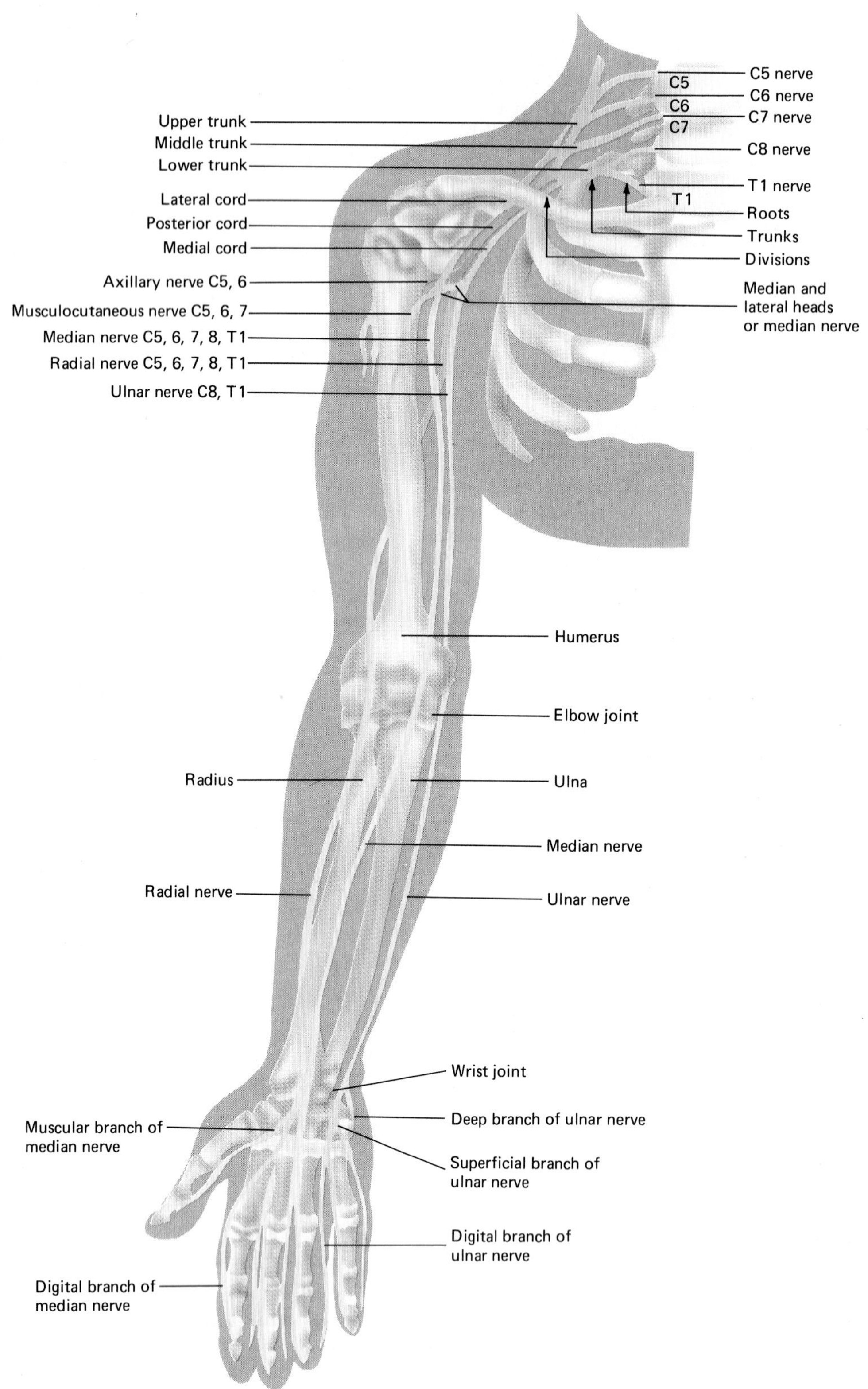

FIGURE 14-8

Nerves of the upper limb.

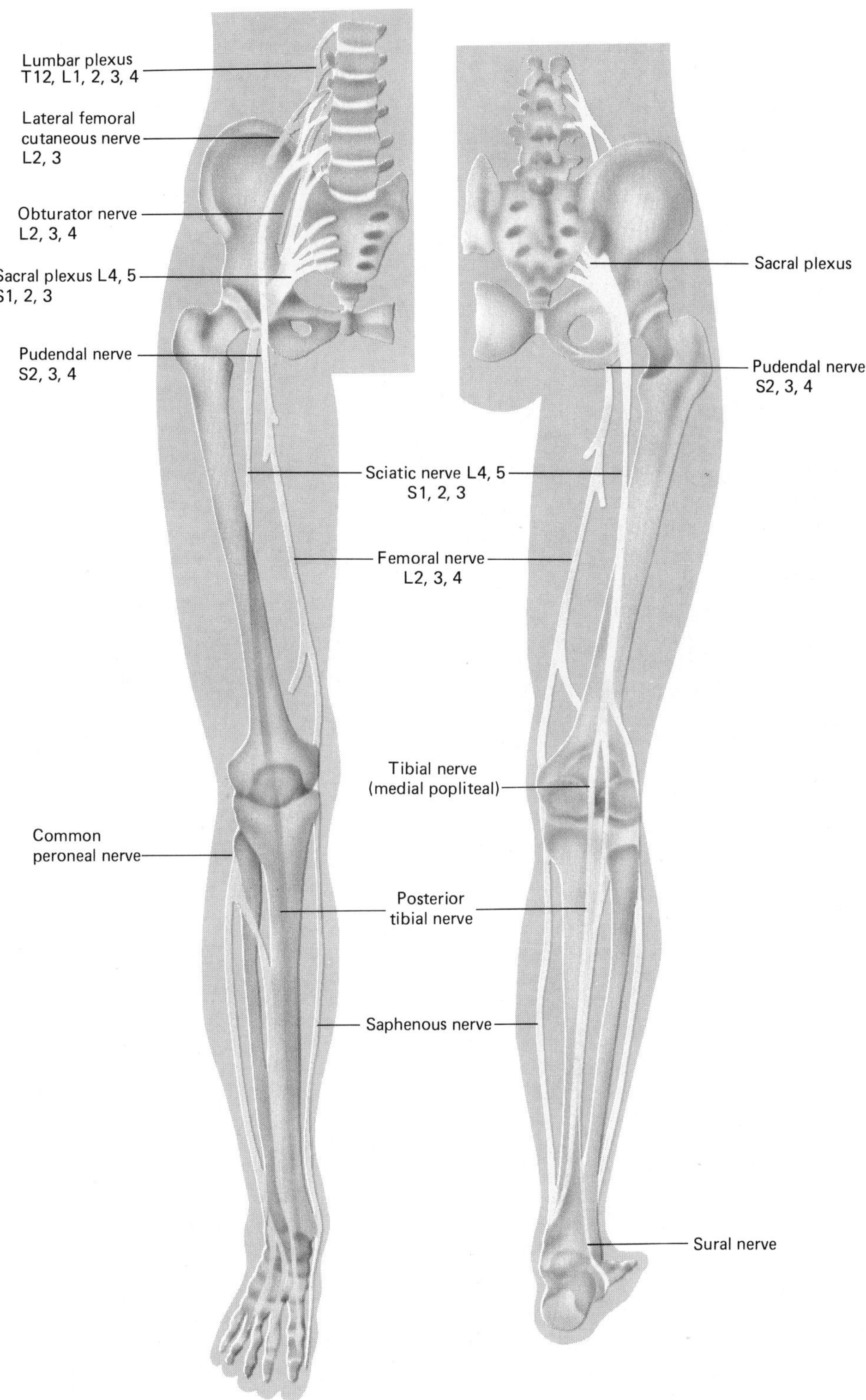

FIGURE 14-9

Nerves of the lower limb.

principal spinal nerve that serves it. Most of the skin of the face and scalp is supplied by branches of the trigeminal nerve, cranial nerve V.

Fortunately, there is an overlap of innervation. If a single spinal nerve is injured, the dermatome will still be supplied by nerves that serve segments on either side of it. As a result there is little loss of sensation. Figure 14-10 illustrates the dermatomes on the anterior body surface. Muscles are also segmentally innervated; muscle segments are termed **myotomes.**

Clinical highlight

Knowledge of the segmental innervation of the body is useful clinically, since this information can help determine which nerve has been damaged. When there is loss of sensation in a particular dermatome, a physician can identify which spinal nerve or which region of the spinal cord is damaged. For example, if the skin of the upper thigh is stimulated and the patient does not perceive sensation, the physician will have reason to think that the L2 nerve is not functioning. When movement is affected, the physician can similarly trace the malfunction to a specific spinal nerve. Conversely, if the level of the lesion is known, one can predict which areas of the body and which functions will be affected.

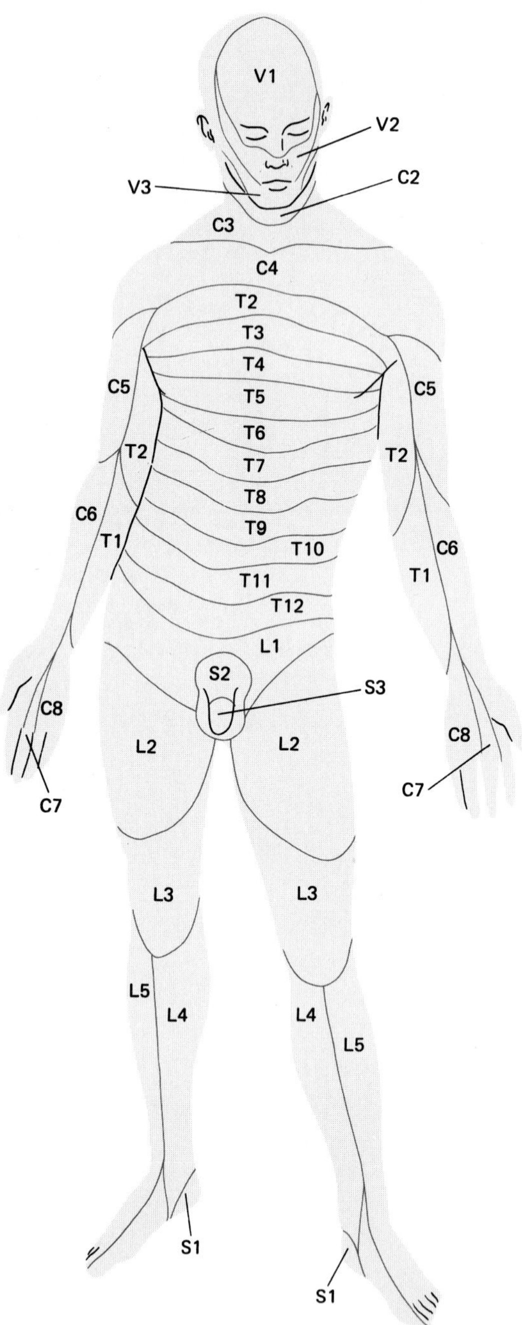

FIGURE 14-10

Distribution of spinal nerves and branches of the trigeminal nerve to segments of the body surface. Each segment is named for the principal spinal nerve that serves it: C, cervical segments; T, thoracic segments; L, lumbar segments; S, sacral segments; V, trigeminal segments. (Anatomists do not entirely agree on the designation of specific segments. This is due in part to the extensive overlap of neurons that supply them.)

FOCUS ON . . . The PNS in stress

Guillain-Barré syndrome	An acute progressive disease of the PNS characterized by muscular weakness and some distal sensory loss; usually begins after an infection. Thought to involve an immunological attack on the patient's peripheral nerves. Life-threatening respiratory paralysis sometimes also occurs.
Neuralgia	Spasms of pain that extend along the dermatomes of one or more nerves.
Neuritis	A disorder of the PNS involving pain and tenderness over involved nerves; paralysis, wasting, and loss of reflexes may occur.
Peripheral neuritis	Also called peripheral neuropathy; a general term indicating functional disturbances or pathological changes in the PNS.
Polyneuritis	Neuritis that involves many nerves simultaneously.
Sciatica	Refers to pain anywhere along the course of the sciatic nerve; may be caused by displacement of an intervertebral disc, which causes pain to radiate from the back into the buttocks and into the lower limb along the posterior or lateral aspect of the sciatic nerve.
Shingles	An acute infection of the nervous system caused by a virus called herpes zoster (the same virus that causes chickenpox). The virus infects the cell bodies in the spinal ganglia. Symptoms include localized pain along the distribution of the nerves and in the cutaneous areas (dermatomes) supplied by the peripheral sensory nerves arising in the affected ganglia. Skin blisters occur over the affected area.

TABLE 14-6

The sacral plexus

Peripheral nerves	Spinal nerves	Distribution
Superior gluteal	L4, L5, S1	Gluteus minimus, gluteus medius, and tensor fasciae latae muscles
Inferior gluteal	L5–S2	Gluteus maximus muscle
Nerve to piriformis	S1, S2	Piriformis muscle
Nerve to quadratus femoris and superior gemellus	L5, S1, S2	Quadratus femoris and superior gemellus muscles
Nerve to obturator internus and inferior gemellus	L4, L5, S1	Obturator internus and inferior gemellus muscles
Posterior femoral cutaneous	S1–S3	Skin of leg and posterior thigh, gluteal region, and perineum
Perforating cutaneous	S2, S3	Skin over buttock
Sciatic	L4–S3	Divides into tibial and common peroneal nerves; sends branches to hamstring muscles and adductor magnus muscle
Tibial	L4–S3	Gives rise to several branches including the sural, medial plantar, and lateral plantar; supplies the knee joint; gastrocnemius, plantaris, soleus, popliteus muscles; skin of leg and foot; muscles of foot
Common peroneal	L4–S2	Divides into a (1) superficial peroneal that innervates the peroneus longus and peroneus brevis muscles and skin of leg and foot; and (2) deep peroneal that innervates tibialis anterior, extensor hallucis longus, peroneus tertius, and extensor digitorum brevis muscles and skin over great and second toes
Pudendal	S2–S4	Skin of genital structures; skin and muscles of perineum

Summary

I. The somatic system is the part of the PNS that keeps the body in adjustment with the external environment. It consists of sensory receptors and nerves.

II. Twelve pairs of cranial nerves link the brain with many sensory receptors and effectors. Table 14-1 summarizes the cranial nerves.

III. Thirty-one pairs of spinal nerves link the spinal cord with sensory receptors and effectors. Table 14-2 summarizes the spinal nerves.

A. Each spinal nerve has a dorsal root consisting of sensory fibers and a ventral root consisting of motor fibers. Within the intervertebral foramen, the roots unite to form a spinal nerve.

B. Each spinal nerve divides to form four branches. The dorsal ramus supplies the skin and muscles of the dorsal part of the body; the ventral ramus supplies the ventral and lateral body trunk; meningeal branches supply meninges and blood vessels of the spinal cord and vertebrae; rami communicantes consist of sympathetic fibers.

C. The ventral rami of several spinal nerves may join to form a plexus. The principal plexuses are the cervical, brachial, lumbar, and sacral. The principal peripheral nerves emerging from each plexus are summarized in Tables 14-3 through 14-6.

D. The area of skin supplied by a spinal nerve is a dermatome; the area of muscle innervated by a spinal nerve is a myotome.

Post-test

1. The part of the PNS that keeps the body in adjustment with the external environment is the ______________ system.
2. The second cranial nerve is the ______________ nerve; the tenth cranial nerve is the ______________ nerve.
3. The cranial nerve that innervates the muscles of facial expression is cranial nerve (number) ______________, the ______________ nerve.
4. Axons of the ______________ nerves pass through the cribriform plate and terminate in the ______________.
5. The three main branches of the trigeminal nerve are the ______________, ______________, and ______________.
6. The vestibulocochlear nerve transmits sensory information from the ______________ and from the ______________.
7. There are ______________ pairs of cervical spinal nerves and ______________ pairs of thoracic spinal nerves.
8. The dorsal root of a spinal nerve consists of ______________.
9. The ventral ramus of a spinal nerve supplies the ______________.
10. The ventral rami of several spinal nerves may interconnect to form a ______________.
11. The ______________ plexus is formed by the ventral rami of C5 to C8 and T1.
12. The phrenic nerves are deep branches of the ______________ plexus; they innervate the ______________.
13. In the brachial plexus the ventral rami join to form three nerve ______________; each of these structures then splits into an anterior and posterior ______________.
14. The largest nerve emerging from the lumbar plexus is the ______________.
15. The main branch of the sacral plexus is the ______________ nerve.
16. The first 11 thoracic nerves are the ______________ nerves.
17. The segment of skin supplied by a spinal nerve is called a ______________.

Review questions

1. What are the main components of the peripheral nervous system?
2. List the cranial nerves and their principal functions.
3. Locate the origin of the (a) second cervical nerve and (b) the first thoracic nerve.
4. What is the function of the dorsal ramus of each spinal nerve? The ventral ramus?
5. Give the origin and distribution of each of the following: (a) phrenic nerve, (b) trigeminal nerve, (c) femoral nerve, (d) sciatic nerve.
6. What is the clinical significance of the segmental innervation of the body?
7. Label the diagram.

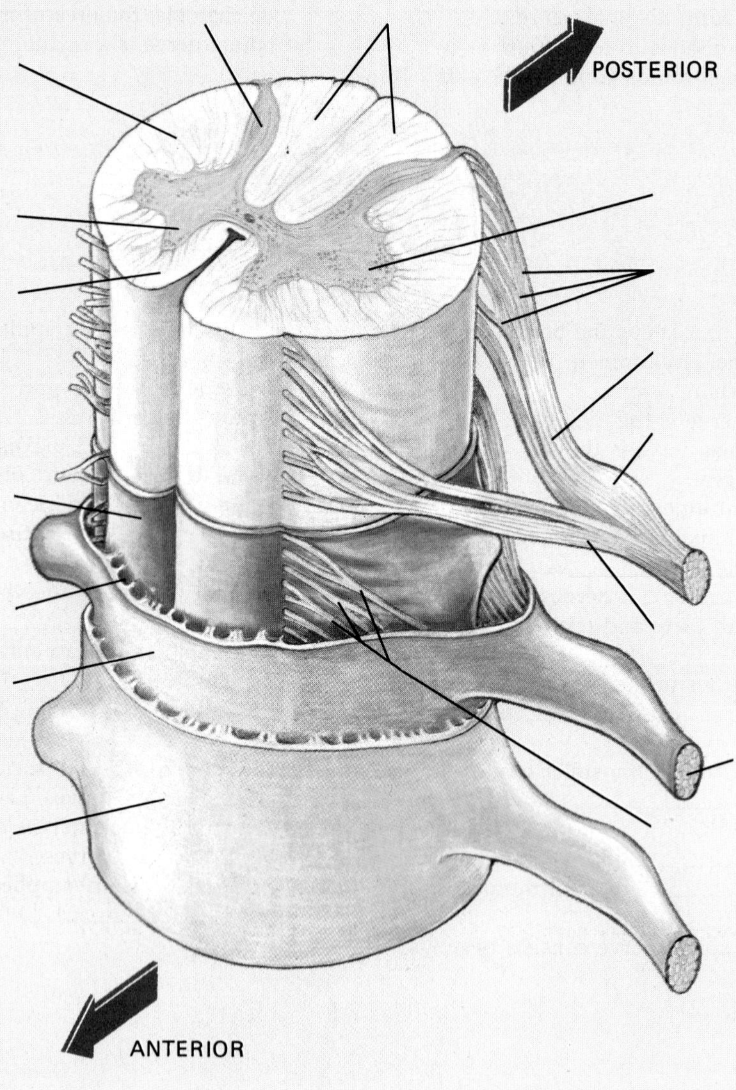

Post-test answers

1. somatic 2. optic; vagus 3. VII; facial 4. olfactory; olfactory bulb 5. ophthalmic, maxillary, mandibular 6. ear (organ of Corti in the cochlea), organs of equilibrium 7. 8; 12 8. sensory (afferent) fibers 9. ventral and lateral body wall 10. plexus 11. brachial 12. cervical; diaphragm 13. trunks; division 14. femoral 15. sciatic 16. intercostal nerves 17. dermatome

PERCEPTION OF SENSATION, MOTOR CONTROL, AND INFORMATION PROCESSING

CHAPTER OUTLINE

- **I. Perception of sensation**
  - A. Touch perception
  - B. Pain perception
  - C. Visual perception
  - D. Sound perception
- **II. Integration of movement**
  - A. Motor system organization
  - B. Motor cortex
  - C. Premotor and supplemental areas
  - D. Voluntary movement
    - □ Focus on dopamine and motor function
  - E. Maintaining posture
- **III. Learning and memory**
  - A. Types of learning
  - B. Information processing
  - C. Memory storage
  - D. Formation of memory circuits
- **IV. The effects of environmental experience**
- **V. Stages of sleep**
- **VI. Effect of drugs on the nervous system**
  - □ Focus on alcohol abuse
  - □ Focus on crack cocaine

LEARNING OBJECTIVES

After you have studied this chapter you should be able to:

1 Compare the serial and parallel organization of the sensory systems.

2 Trace the pathway of a neural message regarding touch.

3 Trace the pathway of a neural message regarding pain.

4 Describe how pain can be inhibited or facilitated.

5 Define referred pain and explain its anatomic basis.

6 Trace the pathway taken by a visual message.

7 Trace the pathway taken by an auditory message.

8 Compare the serial and parallel organization of the motor system.

9 In general terms compare the sensory homunculus with the motor homunculus.

10 Identify structures involved in motor function; trace the sequence of events that occur in making a voluntary movement.

11 Summarize how the body maintains posture.

12 Compare associative with nonassociative learning and describe subtypes of learning under each of these categories.

13 Compare sensory memory, short-term memory, and long-term memory and explain how they interact.

14 Summarize what is known about the physiological (neuronal) basis of information storage.

15 Identify structures that are essential for information storage.

16 Cite experimental evidence linking environmental stimuli with demonstrable changes in the brain and with learning and motor abilities.

17 Compare REM with non-REM sleep.

18 Describe the actions and effects of various drugs on nervous system function.

(Douglas B. Nelson/Peter Arnald, Inc.)

15

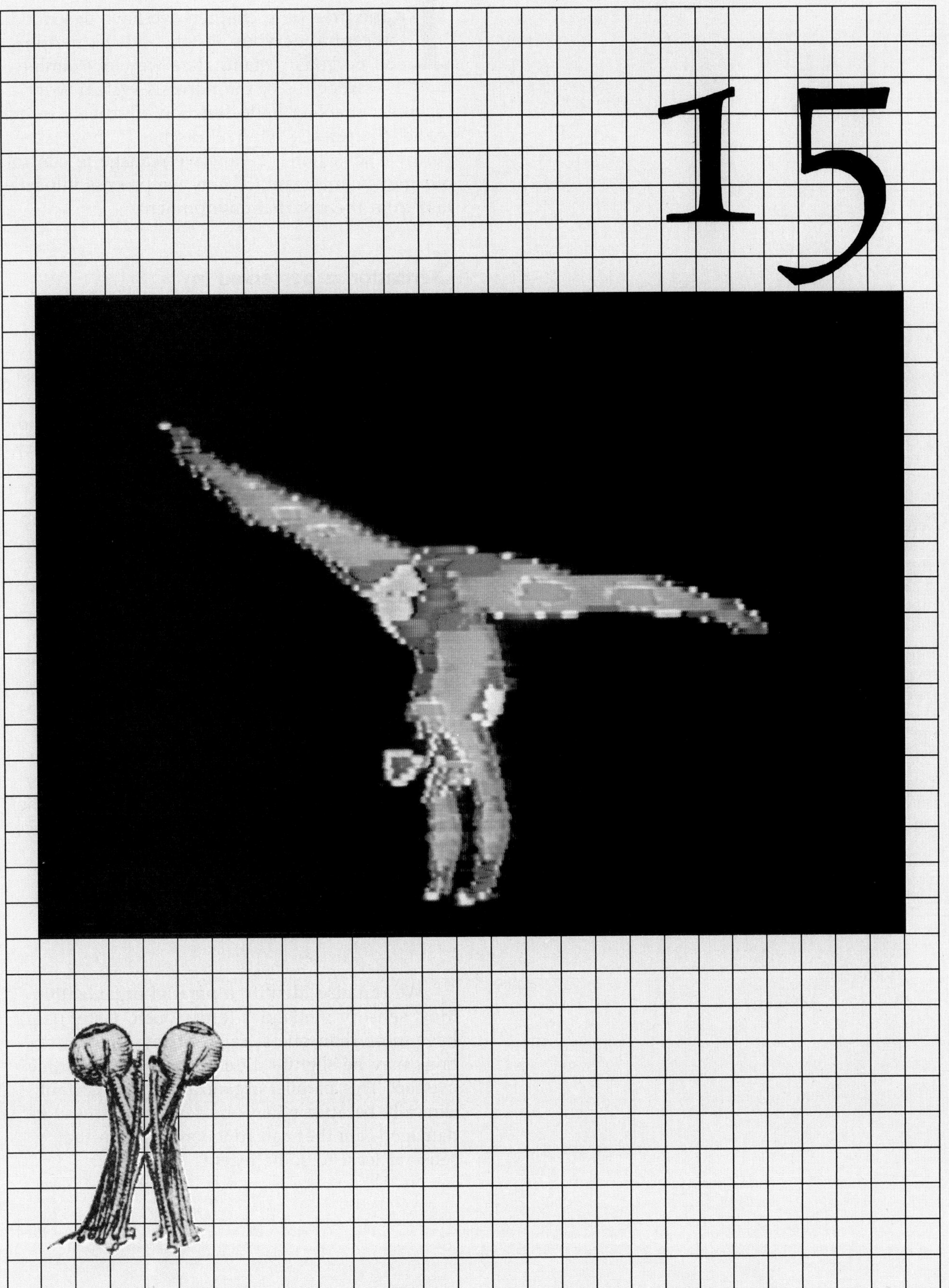

In the preceding chapters we have described the central nervous system and the peripheral nervous system. Here we will examine how the structures of the nervous system work together, enabling us to function effectively in our world. Specifically, we will discuss (1) how we perceive sensation, (2) how we manage to control our movements, and (3) how we process information from the external environment.

KEY CONCEPTS

Perception of sensation takes place in the brain.

Sensory-motor integration takes place in the brain; voluntary motor impulses are transmitted via the pyramidal pathway; involuntary motor impulses are transmitted via the extrapyramidal tracts.

Information processing involves focusing attention, moving information from sensory memory to short-term memory, and then moving information to long-term memory for storage.

Two main phases of sleep are non-REM and REM. Dreams occur during REM sleep.

Sensation is perceived in the brain

In order to maintain homeostasis, the body must continuously adjust to changes in its environment. The first step in the process is for the body to sense what is going on. Thousands of sensory receptors on the body surface assist in this task. These receptors receive stimuli regarding touch, pressure, temperature, and pain. How the receptors work will be the subject of Chapter 17. Here we will focus on how we become aware of sensory stimuli. **Perception** is the conscious awareness of a sensory stimulus (Fig. 15-1). What neural pathways do sensory impulses take to the brain? How do we become aware of what we are feeling, seeing, hearing, smelling, or tasting?

Sensory systems are organized in both series and parallel. In its **serial organization** we can identify a *hierarchy* of structures that transmit information from receptors at the body surface (or in internal organs) to the CNS and then to higher and higher levels of the CNS. A typical sequence might be:

Receptor ⟶ sensory neuron ⟶ ascending tract in spinal cord ⟶ medulla ⟶ thalamus ⟶ sensory areas in cerebral cortex

We can also identify a **parallel organization.** Most sensory modalities (e.g., touch, taste, pain) have more than one serial pathway. Their functions may be slightly different but there is some overlap. This parallel organization is important clinically because when one sensory pathway is damaged, another can function to retain that sense at least to some extent.

Touch perception occurs in the parietal lobe

Imagine that you have just touched your cat. From the sensory receptors in the skin, information is transmitted via sensory neurons to the spinal cord. These neurons pass upward as part of ascending tracts in the spinal cord. The ascending tracts that convey impulses from touch receptors are the *fasciculus gracilis* and *fasciculus cuneatus* in the posterior funiculus (posterior column).

Impulses are transmitted through a sequence of three neurons in this sensory pathway. The **first-order neuron** transmits the message from the receptor to the *nucleus gracilis* in the medulla (Fig. 15-2). There the first-order neuron synapses with a **second-order neuron** on the same side of the body. The cell body of the second-order neuron is located in the nucleus gracilis or nucleus cuneatus. The second-order neuron *crosses* to the opposite side of the medulla and then enters the *medial lemniscal pathway,* which passes upward to the thalamus. The second-order neuron synapses with a **third-order neuron** within a nucleus in the *thalamus.*

When impulses reach the thalamus, you begin to become vaguely aware of the furry sensation. From the thalamus, messages are conveyed by the third-order neuron to the *primary sensory areas* in the postcentral gyrus of the parietal lobe. Nearby *sensory association areas* (Brodmann areas 5 and 7) in the parietal lobe help to integrate the information. Only then do you become fully aware that you have touched something furry.

Receptor ⟶ first-order neuron ⟶ nucleus gracilis ⟶ second-order neuron $\xrightarrow{\text{crosses}}$ enters medial lemniscal pathway ⟶ nucleus in thalamus ⟶ third-order neuron ⟶ sensory areas in parietal lobe

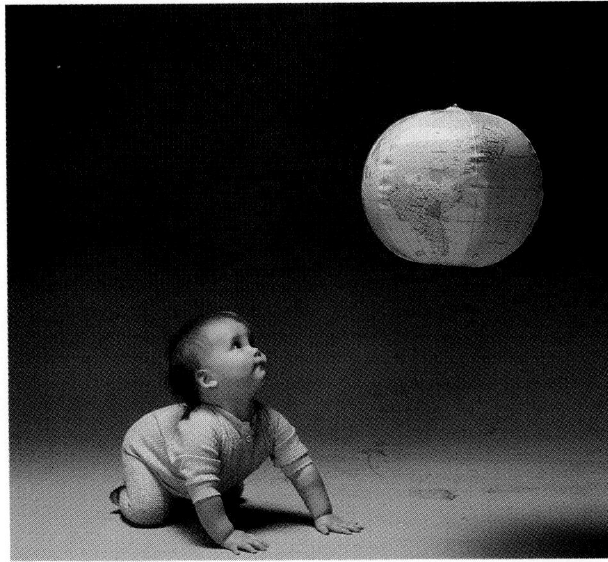

FIGURE 15-1

Our powers of sensation and perception allow us to interact with the world around us. (Eric Kroll/Taurus Photos, NYC.)

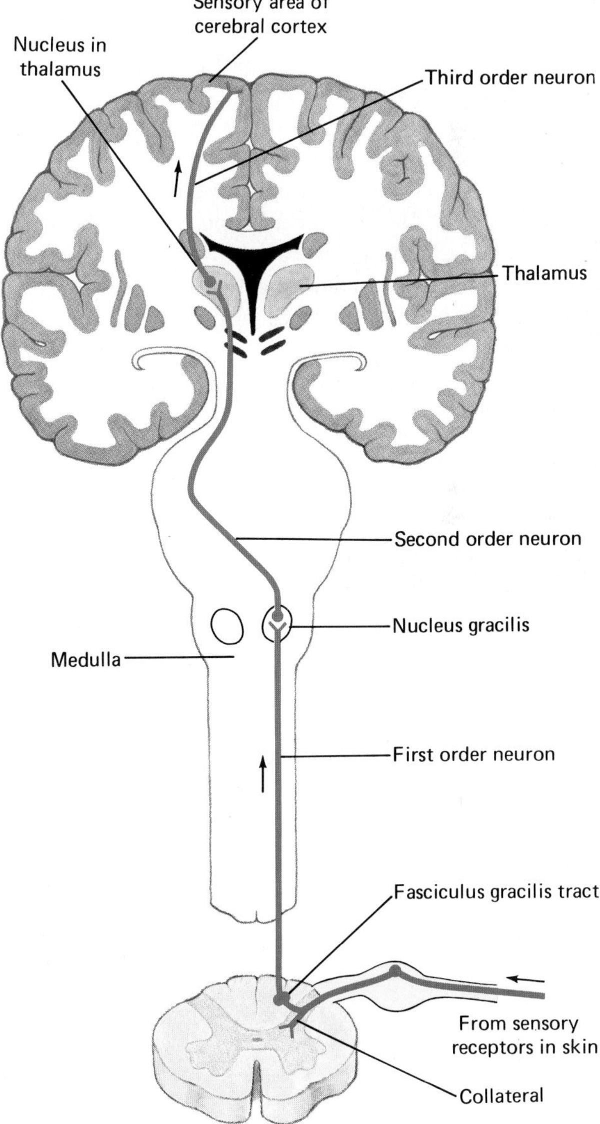

FIGURE 15-2

Sensory pathway for transmission of neural information from touch or pressure receptors in the skin via fasciculus gracilis (the medial lemniscal pathway) to the brain.

Figure 15-3 illustrates a cross section through the postcentral gyrus showing which area of cortex receives sensory input from each body part. Each side of the brain receives sensory information from the *opposite* side of the body. This bizarre figure, called a **sensory homunculus,** shows what you might look like if your body were proportioned according to the amount of cerebral cortex devoted to sensory input from each body part. The lips, face, and thumb (all richly endowed with sensory receptors) have the most sensory cortex to receive their neural messages. The skin of the trunk has few sensory receptors and little sensory cortex devoted to its input. This representation is actually well suited for survival. After all, it is much more important to continually evaluate sensory input from those parts of the body most closely in contact with the environment than from areas such as the body trunk that may experience nothing more significant than an occasional tickle.

The sensory cortex is organized so that all of the neurons sensitive to one type of sensation are grouped together in vertical columns. For example, each neuron within a vertical column might be activated by the touch receptors of the upper lip.

Pain perception takes place in the parietal lobe

Pain is a protective mechanism that signals us to react to remove the source of the discomfort. Dendrites of certain sensory neurons distributed throughout the body surface act as pain receptors. The brain has no pain receptors, and visceral organs have few. When stimulated, the first-order neurons send messages to the spinal cord. Within the cord the first-order neuron synapses with an association neuron that relays the message to at least one more association neuron. The message is transmitted to a second-order neuron that crosses to the opposite side of the spinal cord. Then the second-order neuron becomes part of the *spinothalamic tract,* which passes upward through the brain stem to the *thalamus* (Fig. 15-4), where awareness of pain begins. The second-order neuron synapses within the ventral posterolateral nucleus in the thalamus.

From the thalamus, messages are transmitted by a third-order neuron through the internal capsule to the *primary sensory* and *sensory association areas* in the parietal lobe. At that time the individual becomes fully aware of the pain and can analyze the situation. How intense is the pain? How threatening is the situation? What can be done

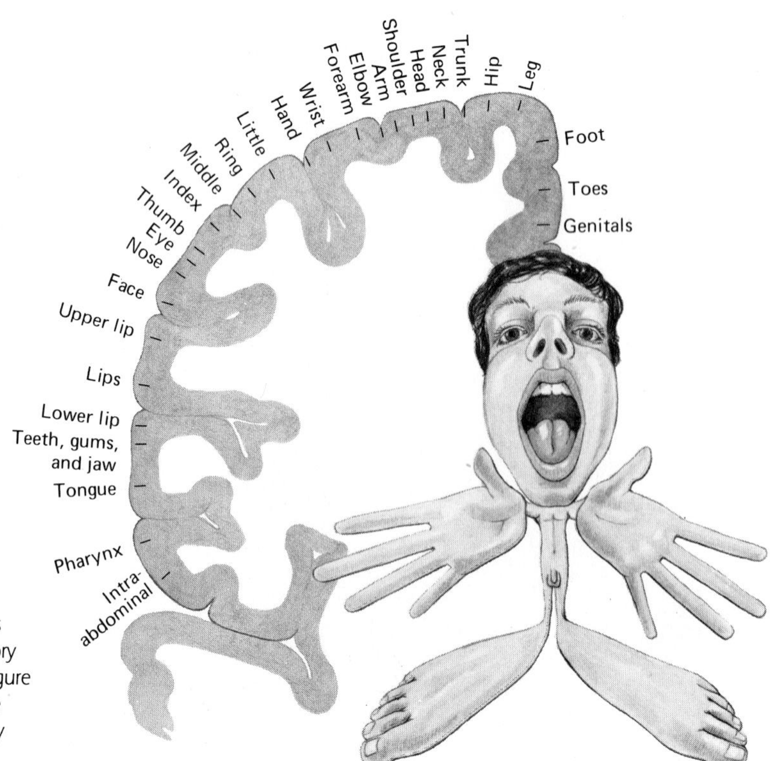

FIGURE 15-3

A cross section through the postcentral gyrus showing which area of cortex receives sensory input from each body part. The grotesque figure shown here is proportioned according to the amount of cerebral cortex devoted to sensory input from each body part.

about it? From the thalamus, messages are also sent to the *limbic system*, where the affective (emotional) aspects of the discomfort can be evaluated. When certain areas, referred to as punishment areas, within the limbic system are stimulated, avoidance behavior is initiated.

Pain receptors ⟶ first-order neuron ⟶ association neurons (in cord) ⟶ second-order neuron $\xrightarrow{\text{crosses}}$ becomes part of spinothalamic tract ⟶ ventral posterolateral nucleus in thalamus ⟶ third-order neuron ⟶ sensory areas in parietal lobe

The physiology of pain is not completely understood. Neurons that transmit pain impulses into the spinal cord and brain release the neurotransmitter **substance P.** Pain can be inhibited or facilitated at many levels. Opiates, such as morphine, are *analgesic drugs* (drugs that relieve pain). They work by blocking the release of substance P. The body has its own pain control system. Morphine-like peptides, the endorphins and enkephalins, are produced by the brain, pituitary gland, and by interneurons in the spinal cord. Like the opiate drugs, these peptides inhibit the

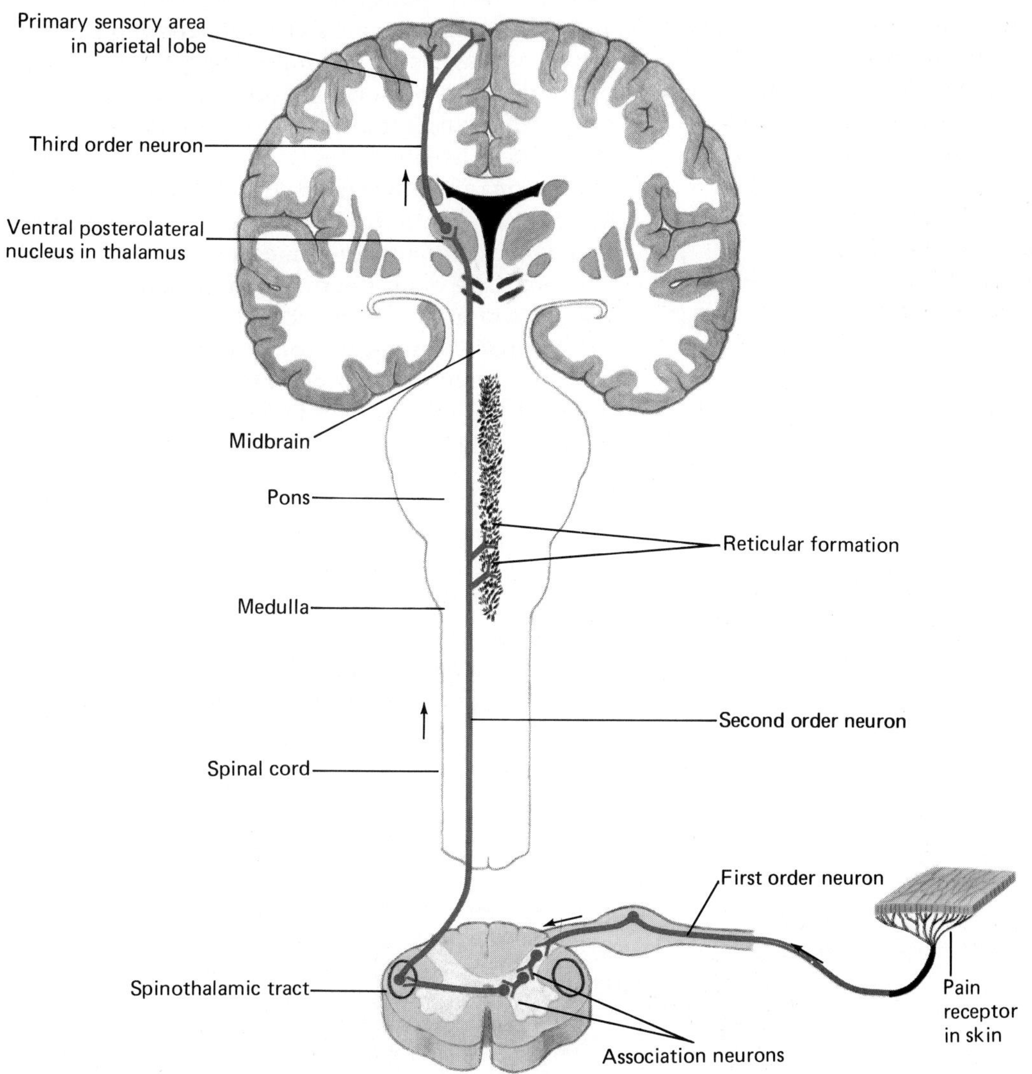

FIGURE 15-4

Sensory pathway for transmission of neural information from pain receptors. The first-order neurons are sensory neurons that synapse with neurons of the spinothalamic pathway within the spinal cord. The second-order neurons cross to the opposite side of the spinal cord and then pass upward through the brainstem to a nucleus within the thalamus. There they synapse, and the third-order neurons transmit impulses to the primary sensory areas in the parietal lobe.

release of substance P from pain-transmitting neurons. The neurotransmitter GABA is also thought to inhibit release of substance P in some parts of the brain.

Inhibitory interneurons in the spinal cord are thought to be the key neurons that modify pain sensation. These neurons receive input from higher centers of the brain as well as from sensory neurons from the body's surface. You may have had the experience of relieving pain by rubbing your skin around an injured area. Stimulation of large numbers of touch receptors inhibits pain signals, apparently by stimulating the inhibitory neurons in the spinal cord.

That the input from higher brain centers influences pain perception is demonstrated by the fact that the situation we are in affects pain perception. For example, a professional fighter may virtually ignore a long series of well-delivered blows. He may not experience pain until the fight is over. Similarly, seriously wounded soldiers have reported feeling little pain because to them the injury represented a ticket home.

The intensity of pain depends partly upon how one has learned to deal with pain. Fear and anxiety tend to intensify pain. Thus, having a cavity filled can be a far more painful experience for those who experience terror at the sound of the dentist's drill.

A child with a bruised knee may heighten the feeling of pain emotionally. How adults respond to a child's pain is important. When parents devote a great deal of attention to the pain experienced by a hurt child, the child learns to magnify the discomfort to increase the reward. (Recall the rat pressing the bar.) Diverting the child's attention from the discomfort, on the other hand, tends to minimize pain perception.

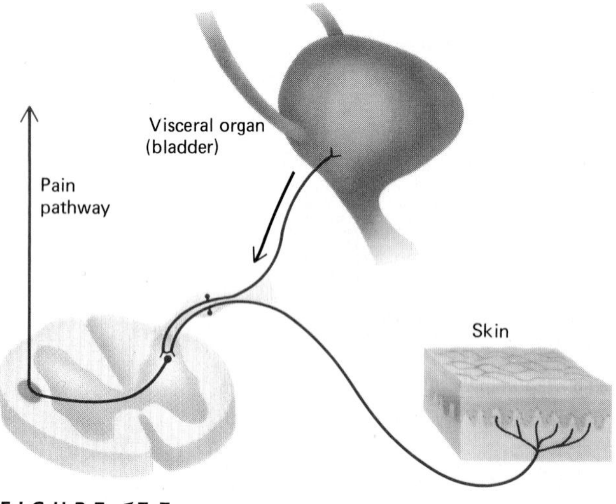

FIGURE 15-5

In a referred-pain pathway, nerve fibers from the body surface and from an internal organ converge on the same neurons in the pain pathway.

Most visceral organs are poorly supplied with pain receptors, which explains why pain from visceral structures is often difficult to locate. In fact, the pain is often *referred* to a superficial area that may be some distance away from the organ involved. The area to which the pain is referred generally receives its innervation from the same level of the spinal cord as does the visceral organ involved. Nerve fibers from the body surface and from an internal organ converge on the same neurons in the pain pathway (Fig. 15-5).

A headache is sometimes **referred pain** from the blood vessels or meninges beneath the surface of the skull. A person with angina who feels cardiac pain in his left arm is experiencing referred pain. The pain originates in the heart as a result of ischemia (insufficient oxygen), but it is felt in the arm. Neurons from both the heart and the arm converge upon the same neurons in the spinal cord. The brain interprets the incoming message as coming from the body surface because somatic pain is far more common than visceral pain; the brain acts on the basis of its past experience. When visceral pain is felt both at the site of the distress and as referred pain, it may seem to spread, or *radiate,* from the organ to the superficial area.

Sometimes when a limb is amputated, the patient feels **phantom pain,** that is, pain from the missing limb. This is because when stimulated, the severed nerve reports impulses to the CNS, which "remembers" the nerve only in conjunction with its original site of innervation, the missing limb.

Clinical highlight

Through the ages humans have developed methods for relieving pain. **Acupuncture** is one of the oldest techniques still in use. For thousands of years acupuncture has been used to relieve pain, but how it works has remained a mystery. Some neurobiologists think that endorphins may explain its mechanism of action. There is now some evidence that acupuncture needles stimulate nerves deep within the muscles, which in turn stimulate the pituitary gland and parts of the brain to release endorphins. The endorphins may inhibit neurons in the brain that normally fire in response to pain.

A much more recent clinical method for relieving pain is transcutaneous electrical nerve stimulation. In this procedure a battery-powered device called a TENS (transcutaneous electric nerve stimulator) unit is used.

Electrodes attached to the skin over a painful area stimulate the skin producing a mild tingling or massaging sensation. The stimulation may interrupt pain impulses being transmitted to the spinal cord or may increase endorphin production. Stimulation of the area may also increase circulation which facilitates healing.

In a few patients, electrodes have been implanted in appropriate areas of the brain so that the patient can stimulate his brain at will. This procedure is thought to relieve pain by stimulating the release of endorphins.

Visual perception occurs in the occipital lobe

The **optic nerves** convey visual messages from the retina of each eye to the **lateral geniculate nuclei** of the thalamus. In the pathway to the thalamus, the optic nerves partially cross, forming the **optic chiasma** (ki-**az**-mah) on the anterior surface of the hypothalamus. As they continue from the optic chiasma, the optic nerves are referred to as the **optic tracts** (Fig. 15-6). Messages from the two eyes are thought to be integrated within the geniculate nuclei so that a single visual picture is formed.

From the geniculate nuclei, messages are transmitted to the *primary visual area* in the occipital lobe (Fig. 15-7). Visual neurons also project to other areas of the brain. For example, from the optic tracts neurons project to the hypothalamus (perhaps for regulating circadian, or daily, rhythms) and neurons project to the superior colliculus for control of certain eye movements.

The *primary visual area* (Brodmann area 17) is also called the *striate area* because it has a striated appearance. The primary visual area is not capable of fully interpreting what is being seen. Messages must be sent to the *visual association areas* (18 and 19) in the occipital lobes for additional processing. Visual signals may then be transmitted to areas (20 and 21) in the posterior portion of the temporal lobe. In these areas, complex visual patterns such as printed words are interpreted.

When the primary visual area in the occipital lobe is stimulated, bright colors, flashes of light, or even simple shapes like lines or stars may be seen. More complex interpretations, such as those of letters or words, are thought to be made in the temporal association areas. Destruction of the primary visual areas in both hemispheres results in total blindness. Lesions in the visual association areas may result in visual agnosia, the inability to recognize familiar objects.

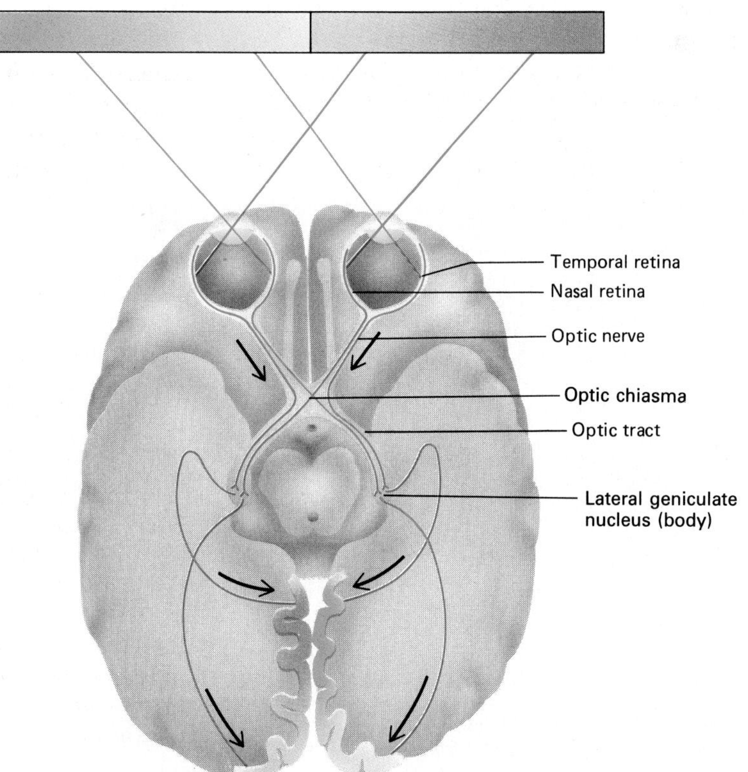

FIGURE 15-6

Visual pathway.

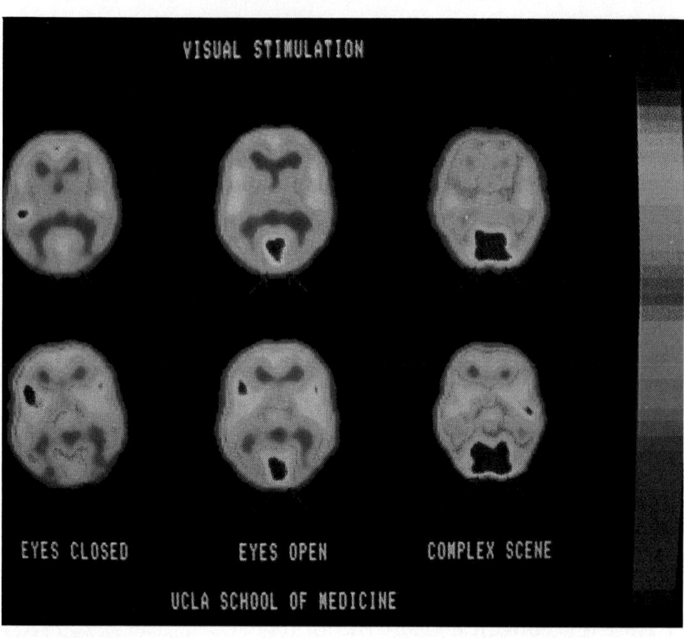

FIGURE 15-7

Positron computed tomography (PCT) scans of the brain comparing three levels of visual stimulation. PCT scans reflect the brain's use of glucose to fuel its activity. A volunteer was injected with a minute dose of a radioactive chemical that binds to glucose molecules in the blood. The glucose tends to concentrate in parts of the brain where there is increased activity. It is detected by its emission of radioactivity in the form of subatomic particles called positrons. The signals that result are processed by a computer giving maps that show which parts of the brain respond to different stimuli. (Dr. M. Phelps and Dr. J. Mazziotta et al./Neurology/Science Photo Library/Photo Researchers, Inc.)

Sound is perceived in the temporal lobe

Neurons of the **cochlear branch** of the *vestibulocochlear nerve* terminate in the cochlear nuclei in the brainstem. From there impulses are transmitted to the **inferior colliculus,** and then on to the **medial geniculate nuclei** in the thalamus. Neurons from the thalamus project to the **primary auditory areas** in the temporal lobes (Fig. 15-8).

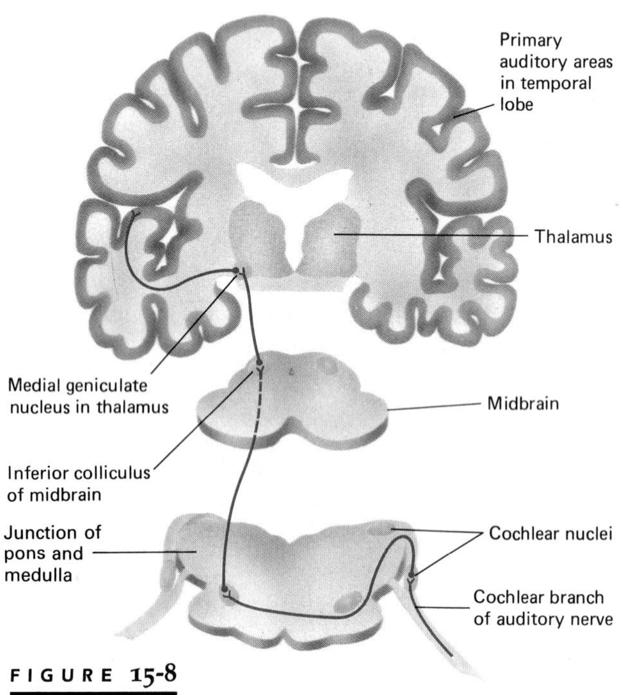

FIGURE 15-8

Auditory pathway.

The primary auditory area enables a person to hear ambiguous sounds but not specific words or melodies. For these interpretative feats the cooperation of adjacent **auditory association areas** is necessary. Loss of both primary auditory areas may result in deafness. If only the auditory association areas are damaged, a person may hear sounds but be unable to understand the spoken word.

Movement is integrated at many levels of the CNS

The CNS is continuously informed about conditions in the internal and external environment by the sensory system of receptors and sensory nerves. Responses to this information depend on the **motor system,** which converts the incoming signals to appropriate action. The motor system consists of the areas of the CNS and the PNS that control movement.

We have already discussed many structures that play a part in controlling and executing movement. Among them are the motor areas of the cerebral cortex, basal ganglia, cerebellum, descending spinal tracts, and motor nerves. Here we will attempt to integrate some of this information to give some idea of just how movement is controlled. Recall that muscles and glands are the body's effectors because they effect (carry out) changes in response to sensory input. The efferent (motor) neurons have been referred to as the **"final common pathway"** of the motor system because they are the target of all motor processing. When the motor system and effectors work smoothly together, the range of responses possible extends from simple reflex actions such as the knee jerk to complex voluntary feats such as playing tennis or playing the violin.

The motor system has both serial and parallel organization

Simple, automatic motor actions such as reflexes are organized at the level of the spinal cord or brain stem. Progressively more complex motor activities are organized at successively higher levels of the CNS. Thus, the motor system has a serial (or hierarchical) organization (Fig. 15-9). The spinal cord is at the lowest end of the series of motor control structures. Next in the *series* is the brainstem, which integrates motor commands descending from higher levels. The brainstem also processes input ascending from the sensory receptors and special senses. Third in the motor system series of structures is the motor cortex (Brodmann area 4), and finally, the premotor areas (area 6). In this arrangement, the highest motor structures in the series affect the levels below. Thus, the premotor area transmits information to the motor cortex. The motor cortex sends information to the brainstem and the brainstem transmits to the spinal cord.

Each level of the series receives sensory input so that commands from higher centers can be modified along the way. Another feature of the motor system is that higher centers can control the information transmitted to them; they can accept or inhibit sensory input. In addition to the four levels in the hierarchy, the cerebellum and basal ganglia are structures that help regulate motor activity. In fact these structures may actually plan and coordinate complex motor activities.

The motor system also has a *parallel organization*. Each component can independently affect the motor neurons. For example, information from both the motor cortex and brainstem can affect the motor neurons at the same time. Commands from higher levels of the motor system can inhibit or facilitate reflex activity.

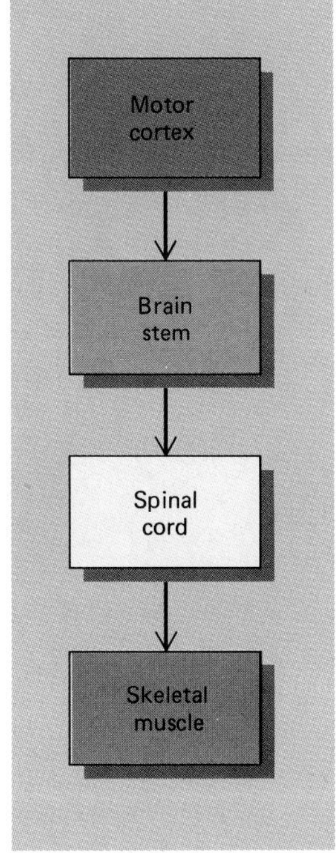

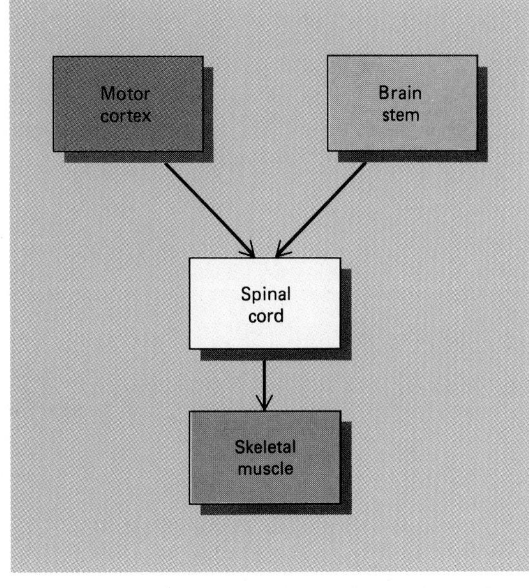

FIGURE 15-9

Serial and parallel organization of the motor system. *(a)* In its serial organization, the highest motor structures in the series affect the levels below. *(b)* In its parallel organization, each component can independently affect the motor neurons.

The motor cortex has been mapped

Electrical stimulation of primary motor areas (precentral gyrus) in the cerebral cortex results in the movement of specific muscles. By studying the responses to electrical stimulation of successive regions of the primary motor area, investigators have developed a map showing which tiny bit of tissue controls specific muscles or small groups of muscles. Most of the primary motor area lies in the precentral gyrus.

Neurons at the top of the precentral gyrus control movements of the feet; those at the bottom control facial muscles. Muscle groups that engage in the most skilled and precise movements—muscles of the hands and muscles responsible for facial expression—are represented by the greatest amount of cortical area. Thus, many more neurons are devoted to controlling movements of the hands and face than of the trunk. To illustrate this point, a **motor homunculus** is presented in Figure 15-10. The parts of this figure are roughly proportional in size to the amount of cortical tissue devoted to their regulation.

Premotor and supplemental areas program movement

Motivation to satisfy hunger, thirst, or sexual needs probably originates in subcortical areas of the brain such as the hypothalamus. These subcortical areas are thought to transmit information to the premotor and supplemental cortex (Brodmann areas 6 and 8). These cortical areas program the movements necessary to satisfy the need.

The **premotor area,** also called the *motor association area,* lies just rostral to the primary motor area (precentral gyrus) (Fig. 15-11). Stimulation of this area produces motor responses similar to many produced when the primary motor area is stimulated, probably because these areas are neurally connected. Stimulation of certain parts of the premotor area produces orientational movements. These movements, thought to be motor responses to engagement of attention, include turning the head or twisting the trunk around in order to see or hear better. Such movements are different from any evoked by stimulation of the primary motor area. The premotor area is also thought to

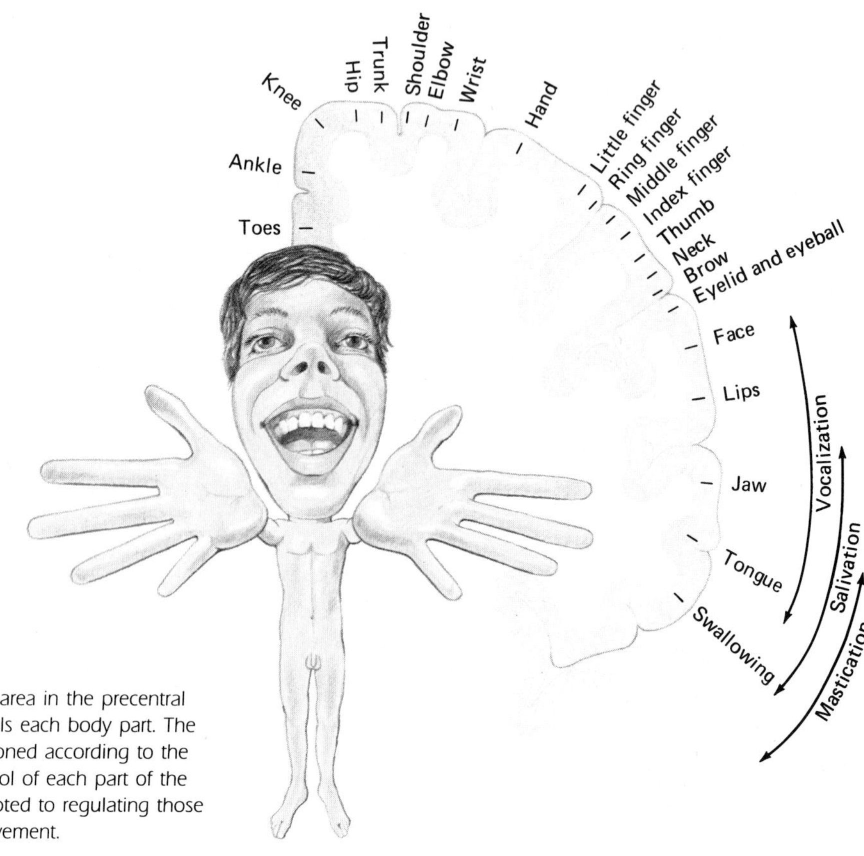

FIGURE 15-10

A cross section through the primary motor area in the precentral gyrus showing which area of cortex controls each body part. The motor homunculus shown here is proportioned according to the amount of cerebral cortex devoted to control of each part of the body. Note that more cortical tissue is devoted to regulating those body parts capable of skilled, complex movement.

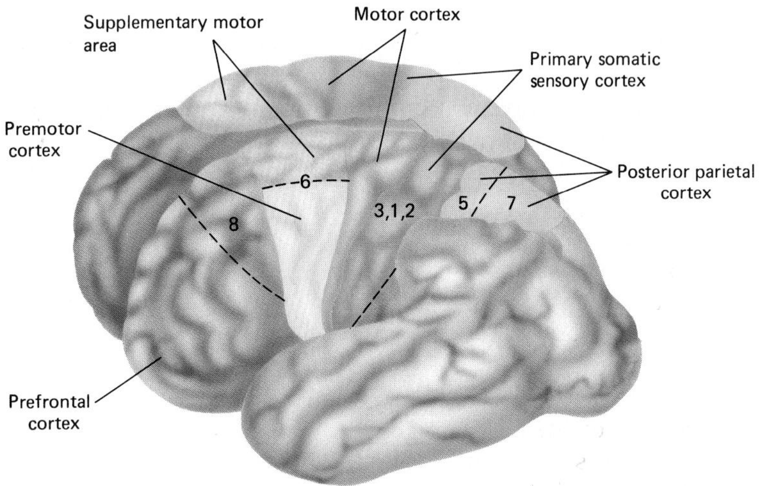

FIGURE 15-11

Areas of the cerebral cortex involved in motor control.

be responsible for other involuntary movements and for movements concerned with maintaining posture. The **supplemental area** helps maintain posture and sends input to the motor cortex important in controlling limb muscles. There is evidence that the premotor and supplemental areas control coordinated movements involving the simultaneous contraction of many muscles.

Voluntary movement must be planned

What is the sequence of events that takes place when you perform a voluntary movement? Making a movement requires a plan of action, and complex interaction of series and parallel processes is required. The actual decision to make the movement is probably made in association areas in the cerebral cortex. The posterior parietal cortex receives visual and somatic sensory information and transmits messages to the premotor and supplemental areas. Decisions to move are influenced by the continuous sensory input reaching the cortex from the sense receptors (Fig. 15-12).

The reticular formation in the brainstem and thalamus also receives continuous input from the sense receptors as well as messages from the association areas of the cortex. Responding to this input, the reticular formation sends messages that eventually reach the motor cortex and influence motor activity.

Once a decision has been made, messages are transmitted into the *pyramidal pathway* (the corticospinal tracts). This pathway is concerned with the performance of fine, skilled, learned movements. Many collaterals extend from neurons of the pyramidal pathway even before they leave the brain. These collaterals inform the *basal ganglia, cerebellum*, and parts of the brainstem of the intended movement (see Focus on Dopamine and Motor Function, p. 512). In response, these structures send messages back into the motor areas, adjusting and smoothing out the movement so that it is precise. Figure 15-12 is a simplified diagram illustrating some of the structures involved in controlling voluntary movement.

As discussed earlier, the basal ganglia and cerebellum are also thought to generate certain types of movement patterns. The cerebellum initiates rapid movements and the basal ganglia may initiate slow, steady movements. Their signals are routed to the motor areas of the cortex where they are adjusted in terms of continuing input from sense receptors.

After a decision to make a movement has been made and the movement has been refined, messages are transmitted from the brain to the appropriate motor neurons. Neurons of the pyramidal tract descend from the motor cortex to the medulla (Fig. 15-13). Within the pyramids of the medulla, about 80% of the pyramidal-tract fibers cross to the opposite side of the body to form the *lateral corticospinal tracts* that proceed down through the cord. The rest of the pyramidal fibers descend as the *anterior corticospinal tracts*, crossing just before they end. The pyramidal tract is the only pathway that passes directly, that is, without synapsing, from the cerebral cortex to the spinal cord. Within the cord, about 10% of the pyramidal axons synapse directly with motor neurons; the others synapse with association neurons in the cord, which in turn make contact with motor neurons.

Clinical highlight

Damage to pyramidal-tract fibers results in *paresis* (weakness or slight paralysis) of the affected muscles. Spasticity occurs, a condition in which there is an abnormal increase in muscle tone. A characteristic "clasp-knife" response occurs when an affected part is passively moved. In this response, the affected part shows a gradual increase in resistance and then a sudden relaxation.

Maintaining posture is an involuntary motor action

Posture, the position of the body, depends upon automatic muscle activity that counters the pull of gravity. When you are standing, the vestibular nuclei and certain other nuclei in the reticular formation transmit continuous messages into the spinal cord via the **extrapyramidal tracts.** Recall that the extrapyramidal pathway consists of all nonpyramidal neurons that transmit motor signals to the spinal cord (review Table 13-2). These tracts are mainly concerned with gross movements and posture.

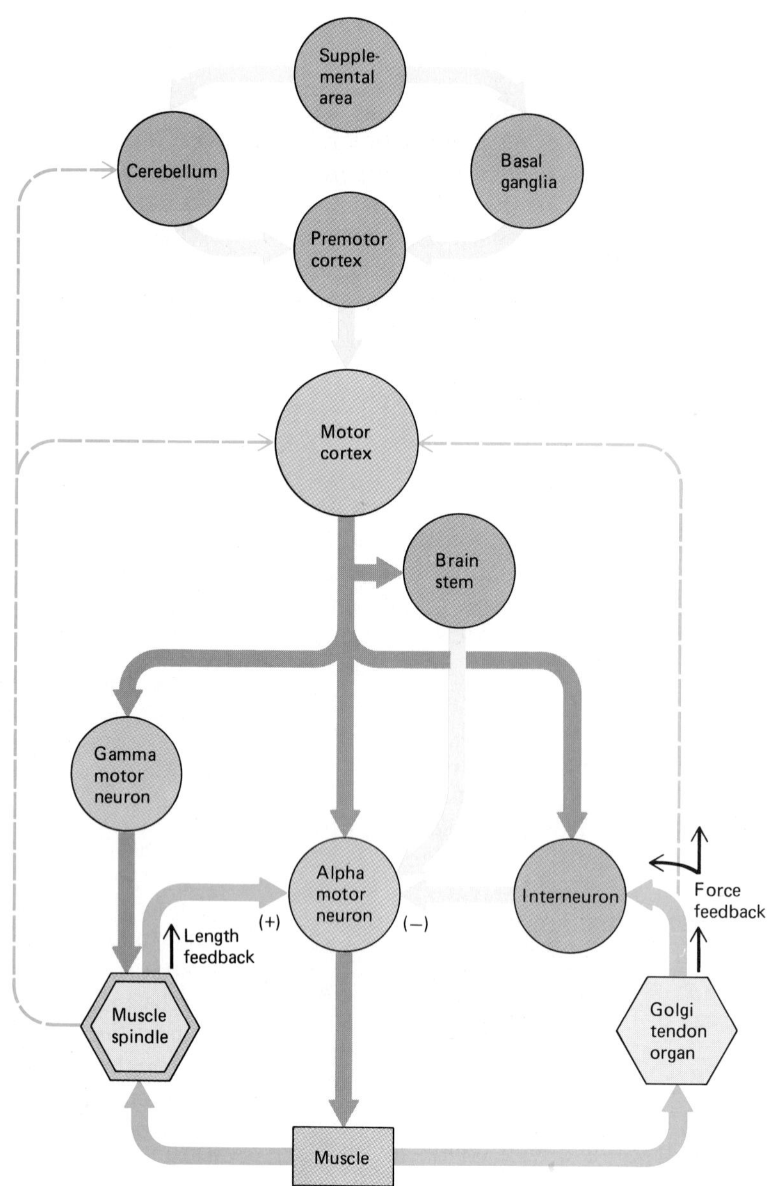

FIGURE 15-12

Control of voluntary movement. Many neurons are involved in making a decision to move and then in the actual execution of a voluntary movement. Some of the pathways are shown in this very simplified diagram.

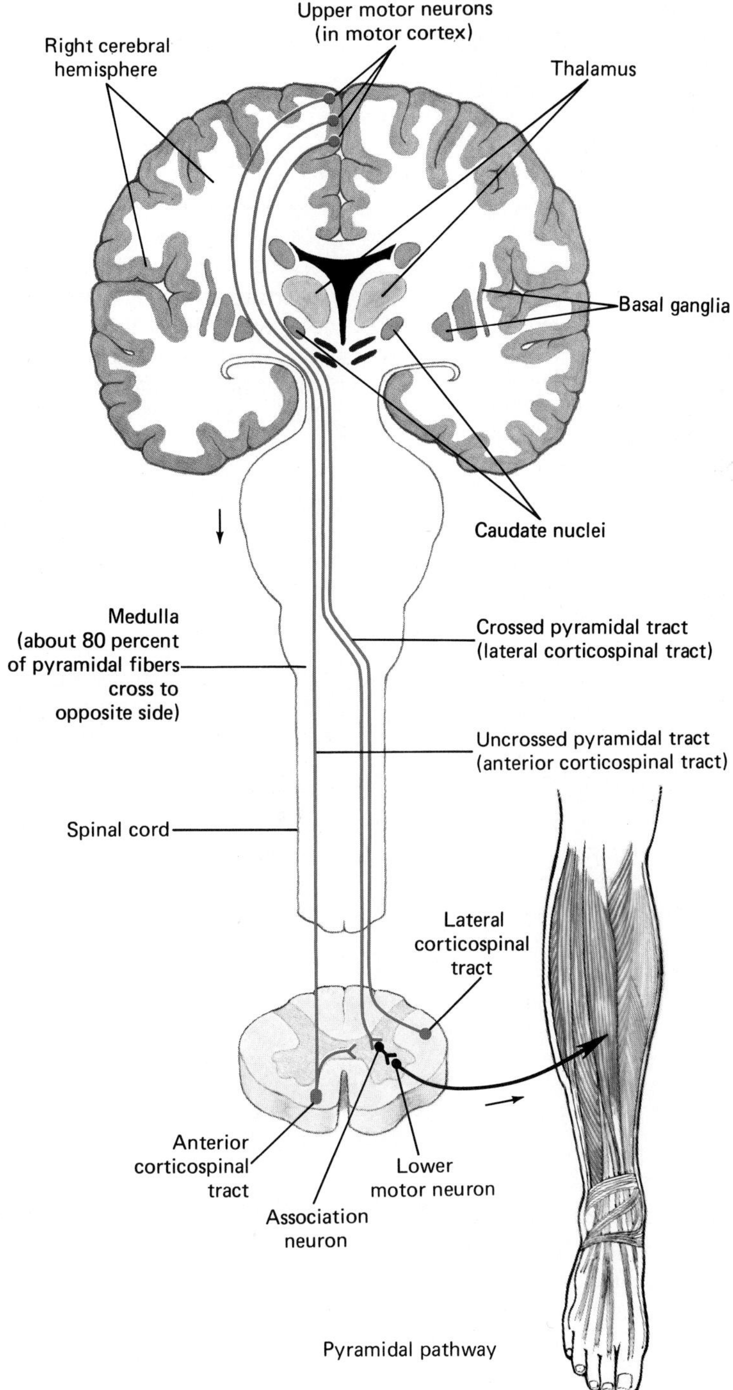

FIGURE 15-13

The pyramidal pathway. This pathway is concerned with the execution of skilled and learned movements. Neurons of the pyramidal pathway (corticospinal tracts) are the only neurons that pass directly from the cerebral cortex to the spinal cord without synapsing.

FOCUS ON . . . Dopamine and motor function

The neurotransmitter dopamine is important in motor function. An interesting series of unrelated events led to the discovery of dopamine's action. During the mid-1950s the drug reserpine became popular as a major tranquilizer used to treat psychiatric patients. Then, in 1959, investigators noticed that some patients taking reserpine developed extrapyramidal symptoms such as muscle rigidity and tremor. These symptoms were very similar to those seen in patients with Parkinson's disease, a disorder in which movement is difficult and shaky. Victims of Parkinson's suffer from tremor (especially when they are not attempting to move) and slowness of speech, and they have a shuffling gait.

These observations led to studies showing that the drug reserpine greatly reduces the amount of dopamine within the caudate nucleus and putamen (two of the basal ganglia). Investigators then discovered that patients with Parkinson's disease have decreased numbers of neurons that produce dopamine and a decrease in dopamine in their basal ganglia.

When attempts to administer dopamine to these patients were not successful, it was discovered that dopamine cannot cross the blood-brain barrier. However, a substance known as L-dopa, from which dopamine is synthesized in the body, does penetrate the blood-brain barrier and enter the brain. L-dopa relieves the symptoms of Parkinson's disease in about two-thirds of patients. About 1 million persons in the United States alone are victims of Parkinson's disease.

Dopamine is an inhibitory neurotransmitter released by neurons that extend from the substantia nigra (in the midbrain) to the basal ganglia. These neurons make up the nigrostriatal tract. Dopamine apparently inhibits neurons that secrete the excitatory neurotransmitter acetylcholine. When the substantia nigra deteriorates (as happens in Parkinson's disease), the neurons of the nigrostriatal tract no longer secrete dopamine in the caudate nucleus and putamen. Without the normal inhibitory effect of the dopamine, the acetylcholine pathways become overactive. Normal function of the basal ganglia depends on a balance between excitatory and inhibitory neurotransmitters. Without this balance, the basal ganglia cannot function appropriately and overactivity of certain neurons occurs, resulting in the motor symptoms of Parkinson's disease.

Even in healthy persons, the aging process causes changes in motor abilities. Body movements and even reflexes slow, and movement becomes more difficult. Studies suggest that these changes may be related to dopamine depletion, and treatment with L-dopa may be helpful.

Too much dopamine can cause symptoms of schizophrenia. In fact, persons suffering from schizophrenia may have an abnormally large number of dopamine receptors in their brains, resulting in too much dopamine activity.

The messages transmitted down the extrapyramidal tracts instruct the extensor muscles to stiffen the limbs (Fig. 15-14). Such muscle action opposes gravity and permits the limbs to support the body so that you do not fall over. The degree of contraction depends upon the organs and structures involved in maintaining equilibrium. The *vestibular apparatus* in the inner ear is one of the sense organs that receives information regarding equilibrium and sends messages to the *vestibular nuclei* in the brainstem. (The inner ear will be discussed in Chapter 17.)

Within the CNS, the cerebrum, cerebellum, basal ganglia, many parts of the brainstem, and the spinal cord are all involved in the complex extrapyramidal regulation of body balance. Neurons of the extrapyramidal tract even receive information via collaterals from neurons of the pyramidal tract. Maintenance of posture provides a stable background against which intricate voluntary movements can take place.

Clinical highlight

Damage to the extrapyramidal system results in involuntary movements such as tremors as well as impairment of voluntary movement such as very slow response or even spastic paralysis. In spastic paralysis voluntary control of movement is lost, but the reflex pathway remains intact so that, when stretched, the muscle can still contract by reflex.

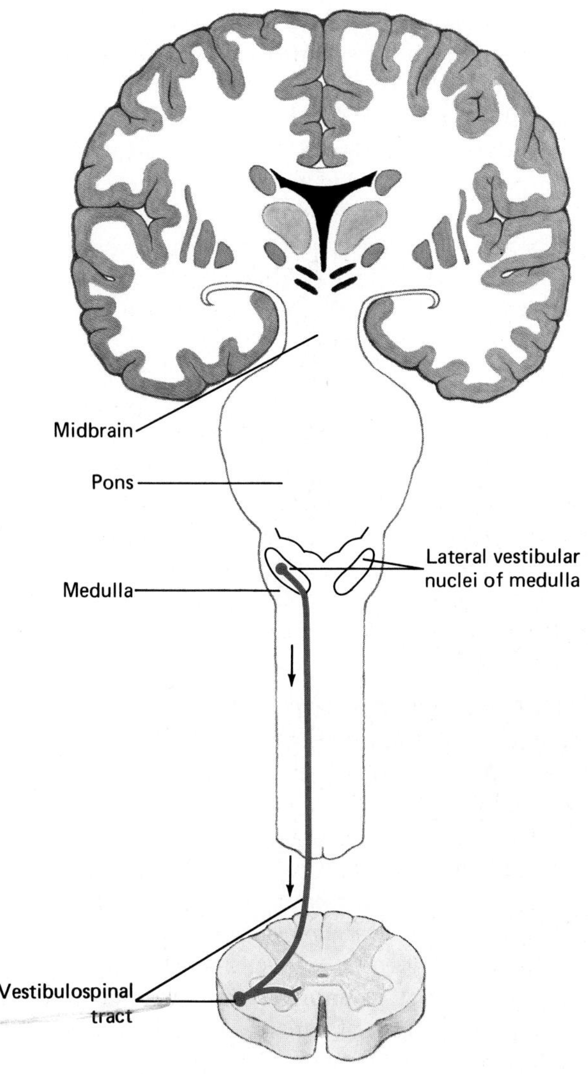

FIGURE 15-14

An extrapyramidal pathway. The vestibulospinal pathway shown here conveys impulses concerning maintenance of posture and equilibrium. (What type of information is conveyed to the vestibular nuclei? From where? How are impulses conveyed from the spinal cord to the muscles?)

Learning and memory depend on information processing systems

Survival and success depend to a large extent on learning and remembering. Each of us has learned to eat, drink, walk, talk, write, read, and take care of our personal needs. The 50,000 or so words that you have learned to use and to manipulate in sentences and paragraphs are important tools for making your way in the world. **Learning** may be defined as a change in behavior due to experience. Learning involves the acquisition of knowledge about the world. Learned responses can be shaped to conform to changes that we experience in our environment. **Memory** is the storage, or retention, of that knowledge and the ability to recall it. Mechanisms by which the brain learns and remembers have been the subject of extensive research, but the brain does not easily yield its secrets, and these activities are still poorly understood.

In order to learn, we must (1) focus attention on specific stimuli, whether they are the words on a printed page or an angry wasp buzzing overhead; (2) compare incoming sensory information with stimuli previously encountered; and (3) store information in long-term memory.

There are two main types of learning

Learning can be nonassociative or associative. In some forms of **nonassociative learning** we adapt to a single type of stimulus in order to enhance our survival. Types of nonassociative learning include habituation, sensitization, imprinting, and insight learning. In **habituation** we tune out a constant or repeated stimulus (and this decrease in response to the stimulus is not due to sensory adaptation). We may respond to the background noise of traffic outside our window for a time, but soon we habituate to it. Our response to the stimulus changes as a result of experience. Habituation can be adaptive because it eliminates unnecessary responses to a stimulus, conserving time and energy for more important behaviors (Fig. 15-15).

In **sensitization** there is an increased probability that we will respond to a stimulus. For example, after being bitten by a dog, we might respond fearfully to dogs for a time. **Imprinting** occurs only during specific critical periods. Some investigators have suggested that children learn languages more easily than adults because they are in a critical period for language acquisition. **Insight learning** is the intuitive (insightful) solution to a problem that one has not attempted to solve before. Insight learning involves an "aha experience" in which we suddenly recognize the relationships of factors in the situation and "see" the solution. Insight learning allows us to solve problems we have never before encountered.

In **associative learning** we change our behavior due to an association we make between two stimuli. Two types of associative learning are classical conditioning and operant conditioning. In 1927, the Russian physiologist Pavlov performed a **classical conditioning** experiment in which he taught dogs to salivate in response to a bell. Normally when food (the unconditioned stimulus) is presented to dogs, they salivate (the unconditioned response). For a period of several days Pavlov rang a bell just before he fed the dogs. The animals learned to associate the bell (the conditioned stimulus) with food (the unconditioned stimulus). Whenever they heard the bell, even when no food was present, the dogs began to salivate. (Salivation to the bell was a conditional response.) A functional pathway had developed between the auditory pathways and the autonomic centers controlling salivation. Although the part of the brain necessary for interpreting the sensory input (the sound of the bell) was essential, the new pathway was probably established at subcortical levels.

In **operant conditioning** (also called instrumental conditioning) the subject learns to perform a task (operate on the environment) in order to obtain a reward or to avoid punishment. By this method pigeons have learned how to press bars or perform dances in order to receive food, rats have learned how to perform many feats in order to obtain food or avoid electric shock, children learn to behave in appropriate ways, and people have learned how to control certain autonomic activities (Fig. 15-16).

In these types of learning, as well as in more sophisticated learning, motivation is a key factor. When we are rewarded for doing something, we tend to repeat the behavior because the reward is reinforcing. When a type of behavior causes unpleasant consequences (punishment), we try to avoid that behavior in the future. Some investigators think that all learning is based on reward or avoidance of punishment. A child learns the multiplication tables in order to win the approval of his or her teacher and parents (and perhaps peers as well). Sometimes the reward is not immediate. As we mature, most of us learn to wait patiently for a reward that may not occur for a long period of time. This is called delayed gratification. For example, a college student may work very hard for several years before receiving a diploma.

Information processing involves three levels of memory

Just how the brain stores information and retrieves the memory on command has been the subject of much speculation. According to current theory there are three levels of memory—sensory memory, short-term memory, and long-term memory. **Sensory memory** is the persistence for a brief period of time of sensory experience. Sen-

FIGURE 15-15

In the type of learning known as habituation, an animal's unlearned response to constant or repeated stimulation wanes as a result of experience. These pigeons have habituated to the presence of humans and so remain unperturbed by human intrusion. (Janet Goldwater.)

sory memory has a high capacity for information, but that information is lost within about 1 second. Attention is an important component of sensory memory. At any moment we are bombarded with thousands of bits of sensory information. Those bits of information that we focus our attention on, are registered in sensory memory. While information is in sensory memory, pattern recognition, the process of identifying the stimuli, can begin.

In order for a sensory memory to be identified or recognized, we must relate it to past experience or past knowledge, and this requires further processing. As pattern recognition and encoding occur, we become aware of stimuli. **Short-term memory** is the information we are aware of at the moment. The capacity of short-term memory is very small; it can hold only about seven chunks of information. A chunk corresponds to some unit such as a word, syllable, or number.

FIGURE 15-16

Operant conditioning. To study operant conditioning, an animal is placed in a chamber that contains a button which, when pressed, releases food into the chamber. At first, the animal presses the button accidentally. Very quickly, the animal makes an association between pushing the button and receiving food (a reward). (Animals Animals © 1988 G. I. Bernard.)

Short-term memory involves recalling information for a few seconds or minutes. Usually when you look up a phone number, you remember it only long enough to dial. Should you need the same number the next day, you would have to look it up again. Keeping information in short-term memory requires *rehearsal.* In order to remember a phone number long enough to dial it, you repeat it over and over. Redirecting your attention to other stimuli interferes with remembering the information already present, resulting in forgetting. Short-term memory is necessary for comprehending speech.

One theory of short-term memory suggests that it is based on reverberating circuits. A memory circuit may continue to reverberate for several minutes until it fatigues or until new signals are received that interfere with the old.

Once we have processed information into **long-term memory,** we no longer have to focus attention on it in order to remember. When information is selected for long-term storage, the brain is thought to rehearse the material and then store it in association with similar memories. Long-term memory has an unlimited capacity, and storage may be permanent.

Retrieval of information stored in long-term memory is of considerable interest—especially to students. Some researchers believe that once information is deposited in long-term memory it remains within the brain permanently. The trick is how to find where you filed it away when you need it. When you seem to forget something, the problem may be that you have not effectively searched for the memory. Information retrieval can be improved by careful, effortful storage. One way to improve information retrieval is to form strong associations between items when they are being stored.

Sensory memory, short-term memory, and long-term memory are all part of the information processing system. Sensory memory can be viewed as a component of short-term memory, and short-term memory can be thought of as an activated component of long-term memory (Fig. 15-17). Information can be transferred back and forth from one component to another. For example, information from long-term memory can be retrieved and temporarily transferred to short-term memory. At that time we are focused on the activated information.

Memory storage involves changes in synaptic function

What physiological changes take place during memory storage? Studies of animal learning have uncovered cellular mechanisms that may also operate in human learning. In at least some types of learning, physical or chemical changes take place in the synaptic knobs or postsynaptic neurons that permanently facilitate or inhibit the transmission of impulses within a newly established circuit. In some cases specific neurons may become more sensitive to neurotransmitter. Each time a memory is stored, a new neural pathway is facilitated or inhibited. Such an altered circuit is known as a **memory trace** or memory engram.

In habituation (learned decrease in response to a repeated stimulus), there is a decrease in synaptic transmission. The decrease results from the inactivation of calcium channels in the presynaptic terminal (Fig. 15-18). The decrease in calcium ion flow into the presynaptic neuron results in decreased release of neurotransmitter.

In sensitization, an increase in response to a stimulus, the cellular mechanism responsible is presynaptic facilitation. At least one mechanism underlying classical conditioning is similar. Pairing the unconditioned stimulus and the conditioned stimulus activates cellular activities that enhance the excitability of the postsynaptic neuron.

Other theories of memory storage have been proposed. Some investigators think that either RNA or proteins may serve as memory molecules. A more recent theory suggests that it is not the location of neurons or the establishment of specific pathways that matter, but the rhythm at which neurons fire. According to this view, each time something new is learned, cells in many parts of the brain learn a new rhythm of firing. This theory has an advantage of not requiring the localization of memory in the brain, something that no one has been able to demonstrate.

ENVIRONMENT

SENSORY MEMORY → Information lost within about 1 second

Focus of attention

Large capacity

SHORT-TERM MEMORY → Information lost within about 20 seconds

Limited capacity

Rehearse information

LONG-TERM MEMORY

Large capacity

Information is encoded

FIGURE 15-17

A simplified representation of the human information processing system. Sensory memory is represented as an activated component of short-term memory. Short-term memory is depicted as an activated component of long-term memory.

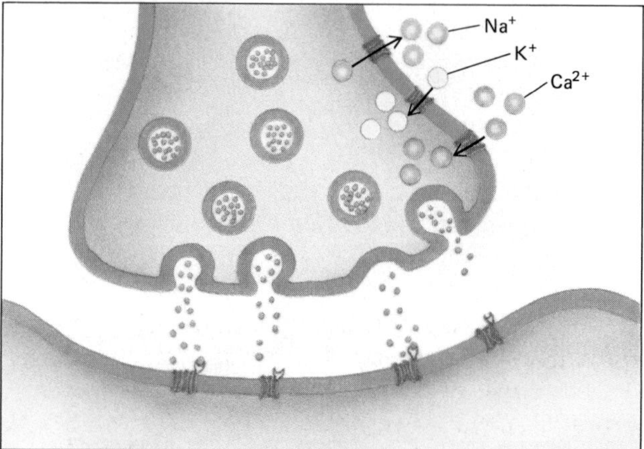

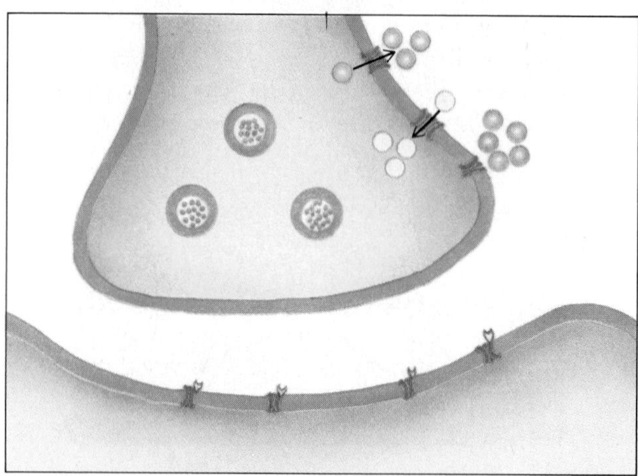

FIGURE 15-18

The biochemical basis of habituation. At the cellular level, habituation can be explained by a decrease in synaptic transmission. *(a)* This decrease is thought to result from a decrease in the inward passage of Ca^{2+} ions. *(b)* When Ca^{2+} channels close, neurotransmitter (T) is not released.

Memory circuits are formed throughout the brain

Researchers have spent years working with the brains of experimental animals without finding specific regions where information is stored. Some forms of learning can take place in association areas within lower brain regions, for example, the thalamus. Even very simple animals (e.g., worms) that completely lack a cerebral cortex are capable of some types of learning.

When large areas of cerebral cortex are destroyed, information is lost somewhat in proportion to the extent of lost tissue. However, no specific area can be labeled the "memory bank." Apparently, memory circuits form throughout the cerebral cortex and also involve many other areas of the brain. Both sensory and motor pathways may be involved.

The association areas of the cerebral cortex, the hippocampal gyri and amygdala of the limbic system, and the thalamus are some of the structures involved in learning and remembering. The association areas concerned with interpretation of visual, auditory, and other general sensory information all meet in the **general interpretative area.** This area lies in the posterior portion of the superior temporal lobe and in the anterior portion of the angular gyrus (at the posterior end of the lateral fissure where the parietal, temporal, and occipital lobes all come together). The general interpretative area is thought to play a very important role in cerebration (thinking) because impulses from all of the sensory areas are received and integrated there. The temporal portion of the general interpretative area is called **Wernicke's area.** This area is an important center for language function because the ability to recognize and interpret words resides here.

Clinical highlight

Damage to the general interpretative area may prevent understanding of what one hears or reads, even though one may still be able to read the words. This person may be able to recognize words but unable to arrange them into a coherent thought. Speech may be well articulated and grammatically correct, but it lacks meaning. This condition is known as *fluent aphasia.*

Neurons within the association areas form highly complex pathways. Axons of the pyramidal cells give off collaterals that feed back by way of association neurons to the dendrites of the pyramidal cells from which they came. This lays the anatomical groundwork for complicated reverberation. Collaterals also synapse with other neurons, and some synapse with inhibitory neurons that feed back to the original cell. This provides for negative feedback inhibition.

Several minutes are required for a memory to become consolidated within the long-term memory bank. Should a person suffer a brain concussion or undergo electroshock therapy, for example, memory of what transpired immediately prior to the incident may be completely lost. This is known as *retrograde amnesia.*

The limbic system is important in storing information. When the hippocampal gyri (of the limbic system) are removed, a person can recall information stored in the past but loses the ability to convert new short-term memories into long-term ones. That is, the person is no longer able to store new information and so can form no new memories.

Experience affects the brain

Studies show that environmental experience may cause physical as well as chemical changes in brain structure. When rats are provided with a stimulating environment and given the opportunity to learn, they exhibit an increase in the size of neuronal cell bodies and in the nuclei of brain neurons. They develop a great number of glial cells and show increased concentration of synaptic contacts. Some investigators have reported that the cerebral cortex actually becomes thicker and heavier. Characteristic biochemical changes also take place. Other experiments have indicated that animals reared in a complex environment may be able to process and remember information more quickly than animals not provided with such advantages. Rats provided with basic necessities, but deprived of stimulation and/or social interaction, do not exhibit these changes.

Early environmental stimulation can also enhance the development of motor areas in the brain. Experiments on young rats have shown that when the animals are encouraged to exercise, their brains become slightly heavier than those of controls. Characteristic changes occur within the cerebellum, including the development of larger dendrites and more numerous dendritic spines. On the basis of this research, investigators have suggested that physical stimulation may help a young child to develop his or her physical potential.

During early life there are apparently certain critical or sensitive periods of nervous system development that are influenced by environmental stimuli. For example, when the eyes of young mice first open, large numbers of dendritic spines form on neurons in the visual cortex. When the animals are kept in the dark and deprived of visual stimuli, fewer dendritic spines form. If the mice are exposed to light later in life, some new dendritic spines form but never the number that develop in a mouse reared in a normal environment.

Such studies linking the development of the brain with environmental experience support the concept that early stimulation is extremely important for the neural, motor, and intellectual development of children. Hence the rapidly expanding educational toy market and widespread acceptance of early education programs. It is also possible that continuing environmental stimulation is needed to maintain the status of the cerebral cortex in later life.

Several stages of sleep can be identified

A 21-year-old person has spent about 7 years and 4 months of her life sleeping. Just what is sleep, and why do we spend so much time doing it? We can define sleep as a state of unconsciousness during which the cerebrum rests and from which a person can be aroused by external stimuli. When signals from the RAS slow down so that the cerebral cortex is deprived of activating input, a person lapses into sleep. Although we tend to be alert in the presence of attention-holding stimuli, there is a limit beyond which sleep is inevitable.

Two main phases of sleep are recognized: **REM (rapid-eye-movement) sleep** and **non-REM sleep.** Non-REM sleep is also referred to as slow-wave sleep. Based on changes in the electrical activity of the brain, four stages of non-REM sleep can be identified. A person passes from stage 1 through stage 4 about three to five times

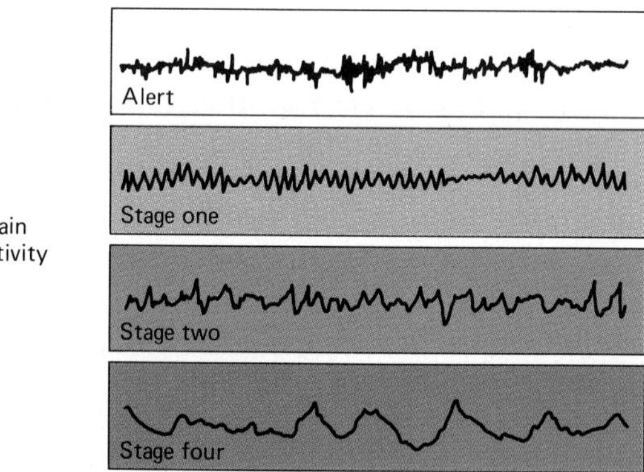

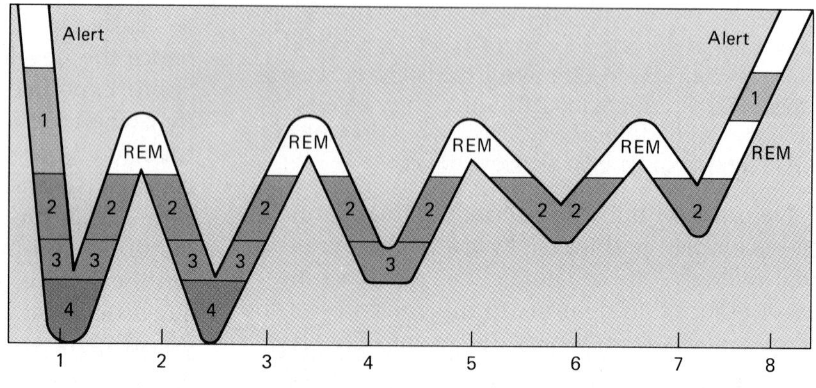

FIGURE 15-19

(a) The electrical activity of the brain during various stages of sleep can be shown on EEGs. (b) During the night, a person goes through three to five cycles. Each cycle includes a sequence of sleep stages.

each night. Stage 1 has the lowest amplitude and highest frequency of electrical activity; stage 4 has the highest amplitude and lowest frequency (Fig. 15-19).

During the first 45 minutes of sleep, the progression from stage 1 to stage 4 occurs. Although the skeletal muscles are relaxed, the sleeper may move about to find a comfortable position. Heart rate and blood pressure decrease during stage 4.

During the next 45 minutes of sleep, the electrical activity of the brain returns to stage 1. In stage 1 of this sleep cycle, the sleeper goes into REM sleep. During REM sleep, which accounts for about 25% of total sleep time, the skeletal muscles are inhibited from moving. However, the eyes move rapidly about beneath the closed but fluttering lids. Heart rate and blood pressure increase during REM sleep. Brain waves change to a desynchronized pattern of beta waves, similar to those that occur during wakefulness. Investigators claim that everyone dreams during REM sleep, although some individuals do not recall their nocturnal adventures. Dreams may occur when norepinephrine is released within the reticular activating system (RAS) during REM sleep, generating impulses that are fed into the cerebral cortex. Three to five REM episodes occur each night.

The hypothalamus and brainstem are responsible for the *sleep-wake cycle*. The **suprachiasmatic nucleus** (above the optic chiasma) in the hypothalamus is considered the body's biological clock. This nucleus receives input from the retina regarding light and dark. In turn, the suprachiasmatic nucleus is thought to send input to the **preoptic area** nearby. Electrical stimulation of the preoptic area results in non-REM sleep.

Sleep can also be induced by injecting the neurotransmitter serotonin into the preoptic nucleus. A group of neurons, known as the **raphe** (**ray**-fee) **nuclei,** located in the midline of the medulla is viewed as a major sleep-inducing area. This area may generate REM sleep. Neurons from the raphe nuclei are thought to release serotonin in the preoptic nucleus. Serotonin may inhibit signals passing through the RAS, thus inducing sleep. Descending fibers from the raphe nuclei may be responsible for inhibiting motor neurons. This prevents motor activity planned and programmed during dreaming from being carried out.

When you were a baby, you may have been rocked to sleep in a rocking chair. Or you may recall falling asleep to the swaying of a moving automobile. Such motions rhythmically stimulate receptors in the organs of balance within the inner ear; these act upon the sleep centers. Low-frequency stimulation of these centers is thought to activate them, inducing sleep.

Mental activity continues during sleep, and many fine discriminations are made within the RAS. The woman who manages to sleep through the rumbling of passing traffic or the loud noise of a jet flying overhead leaps quickly to her feet at the sound of her infant's cry. And the smell of smoke or sound of a burglar's activity arouses most individuals from the soundest sleep.

Why human beings must sleep at all is an unanswered question. When a person stays awake for unusually long periods, he or she becomes fatigued and irritable and does not perform even routine tasks well. Perhaps certain waste products of metabolism build up within the nervous system during periods of wakefulness, and sleep gives the nervous system the opportunity of catching up in disposing of them. Individuals deprived of sleep for several days become disoriented and may eventually exhibit psychotic symptoms.

REM sleep also appears to be essential, for when subjects are permitted to sleep during non-REM time but are awakened each time they enter the REM stage, they become anxious and irritable. After the experiment, when they are allowed to sleep normally again, they go through a rebound period during which they spend more sleep time than usual in the REM stage. Several weeks may be required before normal sleep patterns are reestablished.

Clinical highlight

Difficulty in sleeping or disturbed sleep patterns are referred to as **insomnia.** This condition is commonly associated with anxiety or depression. Insomnia can be treated with psychotherapy aimed at reducing the anxiety. Relaxation techniques are often helpful.

Narcolepsy is an inherited disorder in which the patient frequently and suddenly lapses into REM sleep, often at inappropriate times. In this condition, there is some defect in the mechanism for inhibiting REM sleep.

Many drugs affect nervous system function

About 25% of all prescribed drugs are taken to alter psychological conditions, and almost all the drugs commonly abused regulate mood. Many of these drugs act by altering the levels of neurotransmitters within the brain. In particular, levels

FOCUS ON . . . Alcohol abuse

Alcohol abuse is responsible for more than 100,000 deaths each year and costs our society more than $100 billion annually. According to pollster Louis Harris, there are 28 million alcoholics in the U.S., and about one in three homes include someone with a serious drinking problem. Alcohol abuse is not limited to adults. About 4.6 million adolescents, or nearly one of every three high school students, experience negative consequences from alcohol use, including difficulty with parents, poor performance at school, and breaking the law. In 1986 alcohol was still the drug most widely abused by youth in the United States.

Alcohol abuse results in physiological, psychological, and social impairment for the abuser and also has serious negative consequences for family, friends, and society.

Alcohol abuse has been linked to:

More than 50% of all traffic fatalities
More than 50% of violent crimes
More than 50% of suicides
More than 60% of cases of child abuse and spouse abuse
The birth of 15,000 babies annually with serious birth defects because their mothers drank alcohol excessively during pregnancy
Increased risk of breast cancer. Recent studies suggest that as little as three drinks per week increase the risk of breast cancer by 50%.
Greater risk of liver disease and brain impairment. (Clinical effects are seen in women having consumed only about half as much alcohol as men.)

Alcohol accumulates in the blood because absorption occurs more rapidly than oxidation and excretion. Alcohol causes depression of the CNS. Effects of various blood alcohol levels are: 50 mg/dL causes sedation; 50–150 mg/dL results in loss of coordination; 150–200 mg/dL produces intoxication; 300–400 mg/dL may result in unconsciousness. Blood levels more than 500 mg/dL may be fatal. Alcohol is oxidized to carbon dioxide and water. About 10% is excreted unchanged in expired air, urine, and sweat. Blood alcohol levels are usually estimated from the amount present in expired air.

Alcohol commonly causes cirrhosis of the liver, peripheral nerve degeneration, brain damage, and cardiac damage accompanied by arrhythmias. Gastritis and damage to the pancreas are also common.

Tolerance in those who drink excessive amounts of alcohol occurs because cells of the CNS adapt to the presence of the drug. Physical dependence develops along with tolerance, and withdrawal may result in serious physiological derangements that can lead to death.

According to one study, children see more than 100,000 beer commercials on television before they are legally old enough to drink. Congress is currently discussing legislation that would force the alcoholic beverage industry to place labels on its products warning that alcohol can cause mental retardation and other birth defects and that it impairs the ability to drive or operate machinery. However, there is strong opposition from the alcohol industry which spends $2 billion annually on advertising.

Treatment for alcohol problems involves various forms of psychotherapy, including behavioral modification. The group support offered by Alcoholics Anonymous (AA) has proved effective for many struggling with alcohol abuse.

(Frank Siteman/Taurus Photos.)

FOCUS ON . . . Crack cocaine

The majority of persons now seeking treatment for drug abuse are crack cocaine addicts. Cocaine use by teenagers alone has increased about 400% during the past ten years, involving an estimated 2 million youngsters. Crack is a very concentrated and extremely powerful form of cocaine—5 to 10 times as addictive as other forms of cocaine. This drug is produced in illegal makeshift labs by converting powdered cocaine into small "rocks," which are up to 80% pure cocaine. Crack is smoked in pipes or in tobacco or marijuana cigarettes.

Use of crack results in an intense, brief high beginning in 4 to 6 seconds and lasting for 5 to 7 minutes. Physiologically, crack stimulates a massive release of catecholamine neurotransmitters (norepinephrine and dopamine) in the brain and is thought to block reuptake. Excitation of the sympathetic nervous system occurs and users report feelings of self-confidence, power, and euphoria. As the neurotransmitters are depleted, the high is followed by a "crash," a period of deep depression. The abuser experiences an intense craving for another crack "hit" in order to get more stimulation.

Some abusers spend days smoking crack without stopping to eat or sleep. Although a vial of rocks can be obtained for about $20, many abusers develop habits that cost hundreds of dollars a week. Supporting an expensive drug habit leads many abusers to prostitution, drug dealing, and other forms of crime.

Cocaine addicts report problems with memory, fatigue, depression, insomnia, paranoia, loss of sexual drive, violent behavior, and attempts at suicide. Crack can cause respiratory problems, brain seizures, cardiac arrest, and elevation of blood pressure leading to stroke. Many users have suffered fatal reactions to impurities in the drug or have died as a result of accidents related to drug use.

Smoking crack cocaine stimulates a massive release of catecholamines in the brain. Thousands of individuals have become so addicted to crack cocaine that they have sacrificed their savings, homes, cars, jobs, and families in order to support their habit. (Lawrence Migdale/Photo Researchers, Inc.)

of norepinephrine, serotonin, and dopamine are thought to influence affective (emotional) behavior. For example, when excessive amounts of norepinephrine are released in the RAS, we feel stimulated and energetic, whereas low concentrations of this neurotransmitter reduce anxiety. Table 15-1 lists several commonly used and abused drugs and gives their effects.

Habitual use of almost all mood drugs may result in **psychological dependence,** in which the user becomes emotionally dependent upon the drug. When deprived of it, the user craves the feeling of euphoria (well-being) that the drug induces. Some drugs induce **tolerance** when they are taken continuously for several weeks. This means that an increasingly larger amount is required in order to obtain the desired effect. Tolerance often occurs because the liver cells are stimulated to produce larger quantities of the enzymes that metabolize and inactivate the drug.

Use of some drugs (such as heroin) also results in **physical dependence** (addiction), in which tolerance develops and other physiological changes take place. See Focus on Alcohol Abuse and Focus on Crack Cocaine. When the drug is withheld, the addict suffers physical illness and characteristic withdrawal symptoms.

TABLE 15-1

Effects of some commonly used drugs

Name of drug	Effect on mood	Actions in body	Dangers associated with abuse
Barbiturates (e.g., Nembutal, Seconal)	Sedative-hypnotic;* "downers"	Inhibit impulse conduction in RAS: depress CNS, skeletal muscle, and heart; depress respiration; lower blood pressure; cause decrease in REM sleep	Tolerance, physical dependence, death from overdose, especially in combination with alcohol
Methaqualone (e.g., Quaalude, Sopor)	Hypnotic	Depresses CNS; depresses certain polysynaptic spinal reflexes	Tolerance, physical dependence, convulsions, death
Meprobamate (e.g., Equanil, Miltown; "minor tranquilizers")	Antianxiety drug;† induces calmness	Decreases REM sleep; relaxes skeletal muscle; depresses CNS	Tolerance, physical dependence; coma and death from overdose
Valium, Librium ("mild tranquilizers")	Reduce anxiety	May reduce rate of impulse firing in limbic system; relax skeletal muscle	Minor EEG abnormalities with chronic use; very large doses cause physical dependence
Phenothiazines (chlorpromazine; "major tranquilizers")	Antipsychotic; highly effective in controlling symptoms of psychotic patients	Affect levels of catecholamines in brain (block dopamine receptors, inhibit uptake of norepinephrine, dopamine, and serotonin); depress neurons in RAS and basal ganglia	Prolonged intake may result in Parkinson-like symptoms
Antidepressant drugs (e.g., Elavil)	Elevate mood; relieve depression	Block uptake of norepinephrine, so more is available to stimulate nervous system	Central and peripheral neurological disturbances; incoordination; interference with normal cardiovascular function
Alcohol	Euphoria; relaxation; release of inhibitions	Depresses CNS; impairs vision, coordination, judgment; lengthens reaction time	Physical dependence; damage to pancreas; liver cirrhosis; possible brain damage
Narcotic analgesics (e.g., morphine, heroin)	Euphoria; reduction of pain	Depress CNS; depress reflexes; constrict pupils; impair coordination; block release of substance P from pain-transmitting neurons	Tolerance; physical dependence; convulsions; death from overdose

*Sedatives reduce anxiety; hypnotics induce sleep.

†Antianxiety drugs reduce anxiety but are less likely to cause drowsiness than the more potent sedative-hypnotics.

TABLE 15-1

(continued)

Name of drug	Effect on mood	Actions in body	Dangers associated with abuse
Cocaine	Euphoria; excitation followed by depression	CNS stimulation followed by depression; autonomic stimulation; dilates pupils; local anesthesia; inhibits reuptake of norepinephrine	Mental impairment; convulsions; hallucinations; unconsciousness; death from overdose
Amphetamines (e.g., Dexedrine)	Euphoria; stimulant; hyperactivity; "uppers," "pep pills"	Stimulate release of dopamine and norepinephrine; block reuptake of norepinephrine and dopamine into neurons; inhibit monoamine oxidase (MAO); enhance flow of impulses in RAS: increase heart rate; raise blood pressure; dilate pupils	Tolerance; possible physical dependence; hallucinations; death from overdose
Caffeine	Increases mental alertness; decreases fatigue and drowsiness	Acts on cerebral cortex; relaxes smooth muscle; stimulates cardiac and skeletal muscle; increases urine volume (diuretic effect)	Very large doses stimulate centers in the medulla (may slow the heart); toxic doses may cause convulsions
Nicotine	Psychological effect of lessening tension	Stimulates sympathetic nervous system; combines with receptors in postsynaptic neurons of autonomic system; effect similar to that of acetylcholine, but large amounts result in blocking transmission; stimulates synthesis of lipid in arterial wall	Tolerance; physical dependence; stimulates development of atherosclerosis
LSD (lysergic acid diethylamide)	Overexcitation; sensory distortions; hallucinations	Alters levels of transmitters in brain (may inhibit serotonin and increase norepinephrine); potent CNS stimulator; dilates pupils sometimes unequally; increases heart rate; raises blood pressure	Irrational behavior
Marijuana	Euphoria	Impairs coordination; impairs depth perception and alters sense of timing; inflames eyes; causes peripheral vasodilation; exact mode of action unknown	In large doses, sensory distortions, hallucinations; evidence of lowered sperm counts and testosterone (male hormone) levels

Summary

I. Sensation is perceived in the brain.
   A. Sensory systems are organized in both series and parallel.
   B. In a typical sensory pathway transmitting information regarding touch, a first-order neuron conveys information from the receptor to the nucleus gracilis in the medulla. A second-order neuron crosses to the opposite side of the brain, enters the medial lemniscal pathway, and then transmits the information to the thalamus. A third-order neuron transmits information to the primary sensory areas in the parietal lobe. Neurons connect the primary sensory areas with sensory association areas.
   C. The parts of the body that have the greatest density of sensory receptors are represented by the greatest proportion of the sensory cortex.
   D. Pain is a protective mechanism that can be facilitated or inhibited at many levels.
      1. Neurons that transmit pain impulses release substance P.
      2. Endorphins and enkephalins are released from the CNS and pituitary gland and inhibit release of substance P.
      3. Pain from internal organs is often referred to a superficial area.
   E. Visual messages are transmitted along the following pathway:

      Optic nerves → optic chiasma → optic tracts → lateral geniculate nucleus → primary visual area in occipital lobe → visual association areas

   F. Auditory messages are transmitted along the following pathway:

      Cochlear nerves → cochlear nucleus in brainstem → inferior colliculi → medial geniculate nuclei in thalamus → primary auditory areas in temporal lobes → auditory association areas

II. The motor system consists of the areas of the CNS and PNS that control movement.
   A. The motor system has both serial and parallel organization.
   B. Muscle groups that carry out the most precise, skilled movements are represented by the greatest area in the motor cortex.
   C. After a decision to make a voluntary movement has been made in the association areas of the cerebral cortex, motor messages are transmitted into the pyramidal pathway. These messages are refined via collaterals from pyramidal neurons that go to the basal ganglia, cerebellum, and parts of the brainstem.
      1. Neurons of the pyramidal tract descend from the motor cortex between the basal ganglia to the medulla.
      2. About 80% of the pyramidal-tract fibers cross within the pyramids of the medulla before descending through the cord.

III. Learning is a change in behavior that results from experience; memory is the storage of knowledge and the ability to retrieve it.
   A. Types of nonassociative learning include habituation, sensitization, imprinting, and insight learning.
   B. Two types of associative learning are classical conditioning and operant conditioning.
   C. Information is transferred from sensory memory to short-term memory, and then to long-term memory; information can be transferred from one component to another.
   D. Memory storage involves inhibition or facilitation of impulses as a result of changes in synaptic function.
   E. Memories appear to be stored throughout the association areas of the cerebrum.

IV. The physical structure and chemistry of the brain can be altered by environmental experience.

V. Two main phases of sleep are REM and non-REM sleep.
   A. There are four stages of non-REM, or slow-wave, sleep.
   B. During REM sleep, skeletal muscles are inhibited, rapid eye movements occur, and the sleeper dreams.
   C. The hypothalamus and brainstem are responsible for the sleep-wake cycle.

VI. Some of the types of drugs that affect the nervous system are amphetamines, barbiturates, meprobamate, phenothiazines, antidepressants, narcotic analgesics, and alcohol.

Post-test

1. The conscious awareness of a sensory stimulus is known as ______________.
2. First-order neurons transmitting information regarding touch end in the ______________ gracilis of the ______________.
3. One becomes vaguely aware of sensation when impulses reach the ______________.
4. Pain from a visceral organ is often ______________ to a superficial area.
5. Neurons transmitting pain information release the neurotransmitter ______________.

6. The primary visual area is located in the ______________ lobe.
7. The final common pathway of the motor system is the ______________ ______________.
8. The ______________ ______________ is at the lowest end of the series of motor control structures.
9. A decision to make a voluntary movement is transmitted via the ______________ pathway.
10. The ability to store and recall information is called ______________.
11. In the type of learning known as ______________ we tune out repeated stimuli.
12. In ______________ conditioning the subject learns to behave in a certain way in order to obtain a reward.
13. Information is transferred from sensory memory to ______________ memory and then into ______________ memory.
14. The general interpretative area is thought to play a key role in ______________.
15. Persons with Parkinson's disease have too little ______________ in their basal ganglia.
16. In ______________ a larger amount of a drug is needed in order to get the desired effect.
17. Dreams occur during ______________ sleep.
18. The raphe nucleus is thought to induce ______________.
19. Label the diagram.

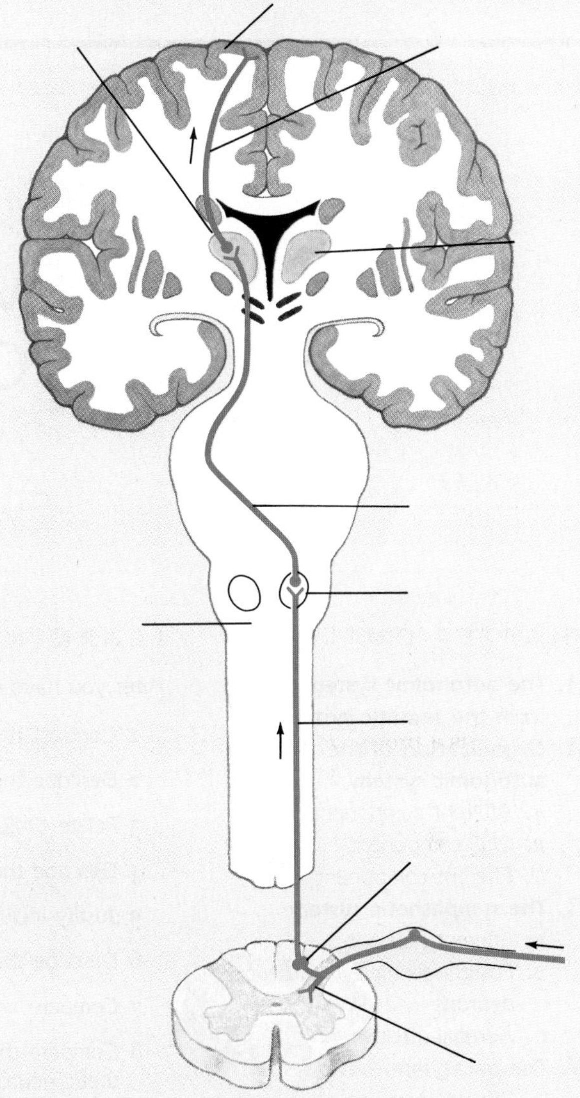

Review questions

1. What are the advantages of having parallel as well as serial organization in the sensory and motor systems?
2. Why does a patient experience cardiac pain in his or her left arm? Explain.
3. What happens when the primary visual areas are destroyed?
4. What are some similarities between the sensory homunculus and the motor homunculus?
5. Contrast habituation with sensitization.
6. Compare nonassociative with associative learning.
7. Summarize how information is processed through the three levels of memory.
8. With what functions are each of the following structures associated? (a) Wernicke's area, (b) hippocampal gyri, (c) medial geniculate nucleus, (d) superior colliculus, (e) spinothalamic tract, (f) medial lemniscal pathway, (g) basal ganglia, (h) sensory association areas.
9. Justify providing a baby with an enriched environment.
10. Compare REM with non-REM sleep. Why do you think sleep is necessary?
11. What are the effects on the nervous system of (a) amphetamines, (b) barbiturates, (c) phenothiazines, (d) alcohol?

Post-test answers

1. perception 2. nucleus; medulla 3. thalamus 4. referred 5. substance P 6. occipital 7. efferent (motor) neuron 8. spinal cord 9. pyramidal 10. memory 11. habituation 12. operant 13. short-term; long-term 14. thinking (language) 15. dopamine 16. tolerance 17. REM 18. sleep

THE PERIPHERAL NERVOUS SYSTEM: AUTONOMIC SYSTEM

CHAPTER OUTLINE

I. The autonomic system differs from the somatic system

II. Organization of the autonomic system

- A. Afferent component
- B. CNS component
- C. Efferent component

III. The sympathetic system

- A. Efferent neurons
- B. Postganglionic sympathetic neurons
- C. Adrenal medulla

IV. The parasympathetic system

- A. Efferent neurons
- B. The parasympathetic system is cholinergic

V. Types of receptors

- □ Focus on pharmacology of the autonomic system

VI. The effects of sympathetic and parasympathetic inputs

LEARNING OBJECTIVES

After you have studied this chapter you should be able to:

1 Contrast the somatic and autonomic systems.

2 Describe the components of a reflex pathway in the autonomic system.

3 Relate CNS structures to autonomic function.

4 Describe the efferent pathway of the sympathetic system.

5 Justify including the adrenal medulla as part of the sympathetic system.

6 Describe the efferent pathway of the parasympathetic system.

7 Compare and contrast the sympathetic with the parasympathetic system.

8 Compare the neurotransmitters released by sympathetic and parasympathetic neurons (both preganglionic and postganglionic).

9 Describe cholinergic and adrenergic receptors on target cells.

10 List several organs innervated by the sympathetic system and several organs innervated by the parasympathetic system, and give the effects of such stimulation; cite examples of organs innervated by both systems.

The iris is innervated by both sympathetic nerves (causing it to dilate in the absence of light) and parasympathetic nerves (causing it to constrict in response to bright light, as shown here). (Ralph C. Eagle M.D./Science Source/Photo Researchers, Inc.)

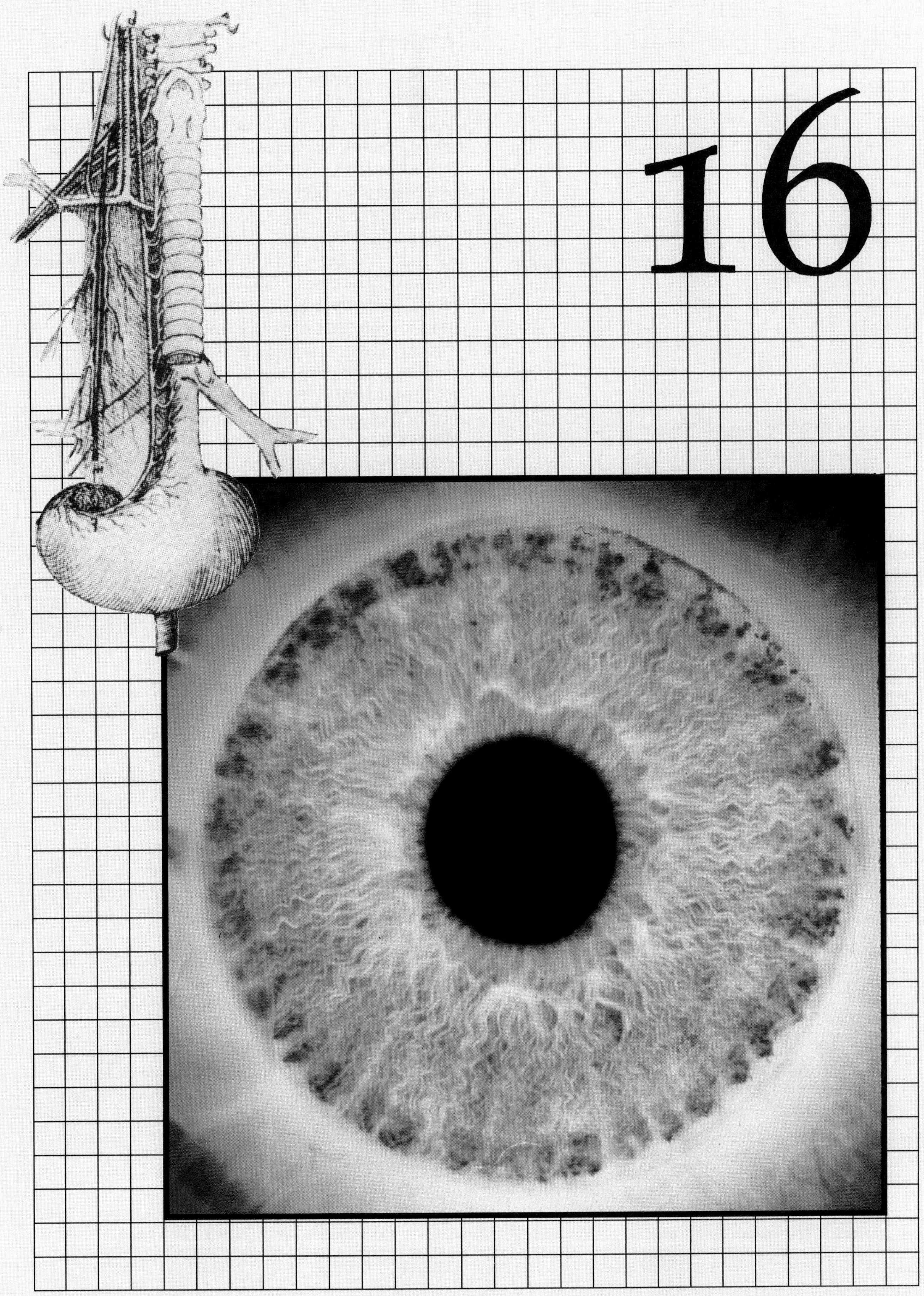

16

KEY CONCEPTS

The autonomic nervous system (ANS) maintains the internal environment and coordinates life processes essential to survival.

The ANS is organized into reflex pathways; included are receptors, afferent nerves, CNS, and efferent nerves. The effectors are smooth muscle, cardiac muscle, and glands.

The efferent portion of the ANS is subdivided into sympathetic and parasympathetic components; an autonomic efferent pathway always consists of two neurons.

The sympathetic system dominates during stressful times, activating processes that mobilize energy, whereas the parasympathetic system is most active during periods of relaxation, acting to restore energy.

The autonomic nervous system (ANS) maintains a steady state within the internal environment. As external and internal conditions change, this system helps maintain a constant body temperature, appropriate blood pressure and heart rate, and the salt concentration of the blood. When the level of nutrients in the blood falls, it senses the body's need for food and activates food-seeking behavior and digestive processes. Similarly, the ANS senses when the body begins to dehydrate and activates mechanisms that conserve and replenish fluids. The ANS also functions in waste disposal, sexual response, and response to stressors. Thus the ANS coordinates life processes essential to survival. This system works automatically and generally without direct voluntary control (though voluntary input can influence this system). Its effectors are smooth and cardiac muscle and glands.

The autonomic system differs from the somatic system

While the somatic portion of the nervous system operates to preserve the integrity of the organism with reference to the external environment, the ANS regulates the internal environment (Table 16-1). The somatic system controls skeletal muscle, whereas the ANS controls smooth muscle, cardiac muscle, and glands. In the somatic system, the efferent pathway consists of a single motor neuron. In the ANS, two neurons link the CNS with the effector. Ganglia are present in the efferent component of the ANS, but not in the somatic system. The somatic system uses the neurotransmitter acetylcholine exclusively, whereas the ANS has two main neurotransmitters—acetylcholine and norepinephrine. Injury to a nerve in the somatic system may lead to paralysis and atrophy of muscles. In the ANS an effector can remain functional following nerve damage. However, its function can no longer be regulated to meet the changing needs of the body.

TABLE 16-1

Comparison of efferent components of somatic and autonomic nervous systems

Characteristic	Somatic system	Autonomic system
Structures innervated (effectors)	Skeletal (voluntary) muscle	Smooth (involuntary) muscle, cardiac muscle, glands
General role	Adjustments to external environment	Adjustments within internal environment (homeostasis)
Number of neurons from CNS to effector	One	Two
Ganglia outside CNS	None	Chain ganglia, collateral ganglia, or terminal ganglia (near effector)
Neurotransmitter	Acetylcholine	Acetylcholine; norepinephrine by sympathetic postganglionic neurons
Effect of nerve destruction on effector	Paralysis and atrophy	Effector remains functional but is not able to respond to changing needs of body

The ANS is organized into reflex pathways

Like the somatic system, the ANS is functionally organized into **reflex pathways** (Fig. 16-1). Receptors within the viscera (internal organs) relay information via afferent nerves to the CNS. There the information is integrated at various levels, and the decisions are transmitted along efferent nerves to the appropriate muscles or glands.

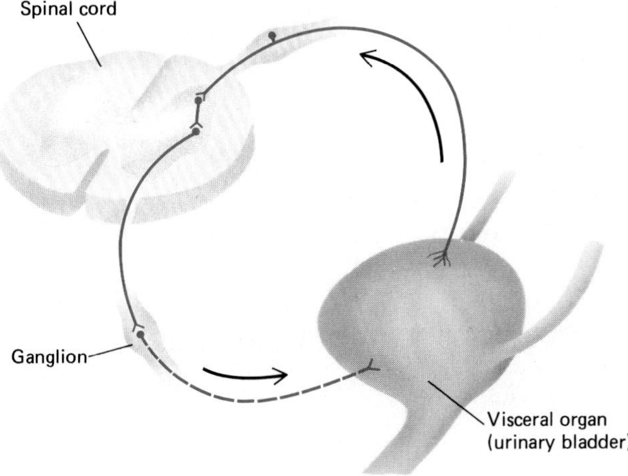

FIGURE 16-1

An autonomic reflex. An afferent neuron delivers impulses to the CNS where the information is integrated. Then, a series of two efferent neurons transmits impulses to the effector.

Traditionally the afferent nerves were not included as part of the autonomic system. Along with many neurobiologists we have broadened the classification of the autonomic system to include the afferent nerves because functionally they are an important component of the system.

The afferent component transmits sensory information

Sensory information from the viscera is transmitted to the CNS by **afferent neurons** located in somatic nerves and in visceral nerves and plexuses. Afferent neurons that terminate within the spinal cord have their cell bodies in the spinal ganglia. Those within cranial nerves have their cell bodies in the ganglia associated with each specific cranial nerve.

Afferent neurons carry information about visceral activities such as peristalsis; visceral sensations, such as pain or fullness; and messages regarding blood pressure, respiration, and heartbeat. These afferent neurons are thought to synapse with association neurons within the CNS. This same sensory input may affect both somatic and autonomic output.

The CNS regulates autonomic activities

At one time physiologists believed that the autonomic system was independent of the CNS, that is, autonomous. We now know that this is not true and that there is a CNS component of the

ANS. The CNS components that regulate the autonomic system include the **spinal cord, brainstem,** and **hypothalamus.** Although the hypothalamus is considered the main subcortical center for autonomic regulation, centers within the brainstem (especially the medulla) and spinal cord are also very important. In addition, areas of the **cerebral cortex,** particularly parts of the limbic system, can influence autonomic responses by sending messages to other parts of the CNS. Autonomic responses may also be influenced by the **cerebellum,** but this mechanism is not yet understood.

Many life processes depend upon visceral reflexes. Recall that somatic reflex activity is integrated within the CNS. Similarly, in visceral reflexes neural impulses are integrated in the CNS. Sensory messages from a receptor in an organ are delivered to the CNS, where they are integrated. Appropriate sympathetic or parasympathetic messages are then transmitted to the organ to regulate its activities.

An example of an autonomic reflex integrated in the spinal cord is the contraction of the full urinary bladder (Fig. 16-1). As the bladder fills with urine, stretch receptors in the bladder wall are stimulated. These receptors send signals via pelvic nerves to the sacral segments of the spinal cord. Impulses from the spinal cord are sent to the bladder wall through parasympathetic nerves, stimulating muscles in its wall to contract.

Many visceral functions are mediated through centers in the brainstem. Reflexes that regulate heart rate, blood pressure, respiration, and vomiting are integrated within the medulla. These centers project their "decisions" by way of neurons that run through the reticulospinal tracts to the appropriate autonomic nerves that emerge from the spinal cord. The pons contains respiratory centers in addition to those within the medulla.

The mechanisms by which the hypothalamus influences autonomic centers in the brainstem and spinal cord are not known. However, stimulation of various areas of the hypothalamus can increase or decrease arterial blood pressure, rate of heartbeat, activity in the digestive tract, and many other visceral functions. In addition, the hypothalamus influences the autonomic system by affecting emotion. The cerebrum and hypothalamus apparently exert strong influences over autonomic response to stress. When these higher centers experience stress, they stimulate the sympathetic system. Consequences of severe or prolonged stress are discussed in Chapter 18.

Normally, the autonomic system functions quite automatically. One does not consciously direct the rate of the heartbeat. Nor are people generally aware of their blood-sugar level or of the diameters of their blood vessels. Yet persons who practice **yoga** (a Hindu system of physical and mental exercises aimed at developing physical and spiritual health by achieving relaxation of body and mind) have known for centuries that it is possible to gain conscious control over autonomic activities. **Transcendental meditation (TM)** is another system for achieving a higher state of consciousness through relaxation techniques.

Research on persons practicing relaxation techniques such as TM indicates that changes occur in physiological activity. Metabolic rate, heart rate, and blood pressure decrease. Alpha waves, which are characteristic of a relaxed yet awake state, increase. By learning to induce a relaxation response subjects can modify the way in which stressful events affect the sympathetic nervous system. Studies suggest that the relaxation response decreases the body's response to norepinephrine.

In recent years some sophisticated **biofeedback** techniques have been developed to help people learn how to relax and control certain visceral activities (Fig. 16-2). Biofeedback provides a

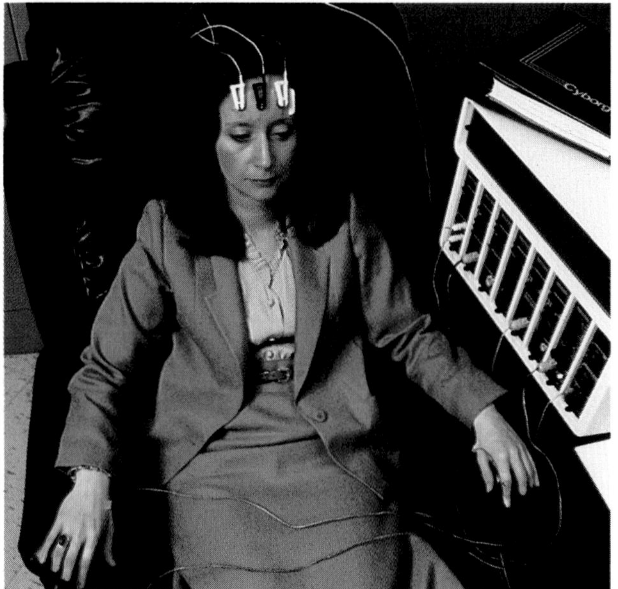

FIGURE 16-2

Individuals undergoing dental or medical procedures, or who experience chronic pain, can be taught to control pain through biofeedback. By monitoring her own heart rate and muscle tension, this woman is learning to relax and consciously control pain. (Robert Goldstein/Science Source/Photo Researchers, Inc.)

person with visual or auditory evidence concerning the status of an autonomic body function. For example, a tone may be sounded when blood pressure is lowered. Using such techniques, subjects have learned to control autonomic activities such as brain-wave pattern, blood pressure, heart rate, and blood-sugar level. Subjects have learned to prevent or reduce the pain of headaches, to decrease muscle tension, and even to modify abnormal heart rhythm. Biofeedback has also been successful in helping to rehabilitate patients who have suffered strokes and in teaching women how to relax during childbirth. These feats depend upon operant conditioning of the autonomic nervous system.

The efferent component includes sympathetic and parasympathetic divisions

The **efferent** portion of the autonomic system is subdivided into sympathetic and parasympathetic systems. Many organs are innervated by both (Fig. 16-3). Although both sympathetic and parasympathetic systems function continuously, the **sympathetic system** dominates during stressful times, whereas the **parasympathetic system** is most active during periods of emotional calm and physical rest (Table 16-2). Thus the sympathetic system dominates when you are rushing to class or taking a test, and the parasympathetic system

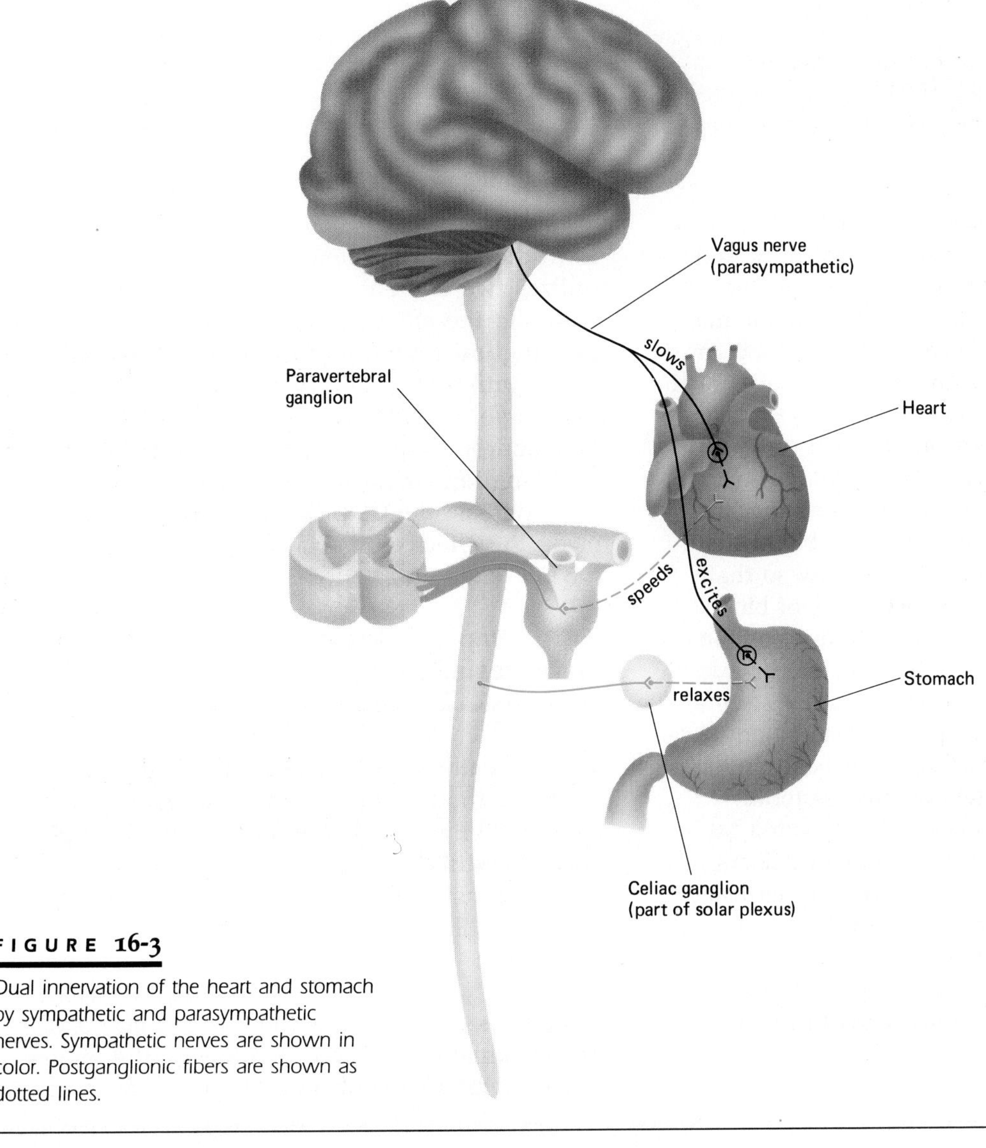

FIGURE 16-3

Dual innervation of the heart and stomach by sympathetic and parasympathetic nerves. Sympathetic nerves are shown in color. Postganglionic fibers are shown as dotted lines.

TABLE 16-2

Comparison of sympathetic with parasympathetic system

Characteristic	Sympathetic system	Parasympathetic system
General effect	Prepares body to cope with stressful situations	Restores body to resting state after stressful situation; actively maintains normal configuration of body functions
Extent of effect	Widespread throughout body	Localized
Neurotransmitter released at synapse with effector	Norepinephrine (usually)	Acetylcholine
Duration of effect	Lasting	Brief
Outflow from CNS	Thoracolumbar levels of spinal cord	Craniosacral levels (from brain and spinal cord)
Location of ganglia	Chain and collateral ganglia	Terminal ganglia
Number of postganglionic fibers with which each preganglionic fiber synapses	Many	Few

is in control after you have finished a relaxing dinner and are sitting down in front of the television set. However, there may sometimes be a stress-induced increase in parasympathetic messages to the stomach. Such overstimulation causes excessive secretion of acidic digestive juices in the stomach and may lead to peptic ulcers.

The sympathetic system is associated with mobilizing energy during stress situations. Its nerves increase blood pressure, speed the rate and force of the heartbeat, increase blood-sugar concentration, and reroute blood flow so that skeletal muscles receive the amounts of blood necessary to support their maximum effort. In contrast, the parasympathetic system works in the opposite way, acting to conserve and restore energy (Table 16-3). Its nerves decrease blood pressure, decrease the rate of the heartbeat, and stimulate the digestive system to process food.

Although many organs are innervated by both sympathetic and parasympathetic fibers, each organ tends to be dominated primarily by one or the other system rather than served equally by both. The two systems function together smoothly to orchestrate the numerous complex activities continuously taking place within the body.

Instead of utilizing a single efferent neuron, as in the somatic system, the autonomic system utilizes two efferent neurons between the spinal cord and the effector. The first neuron, called the **preganglionic neuron,** has a cell body and dendrites within the CNS. Its axon, part of a peripheral nerve, ends by synapsing with a postganglionic neuron. The dendrites and cell body of the **postganglionic neuron** are located within a ganglion outside the CNS. Its axon terminates near or on the effector organ.

The sympathetic system mobilizes energy

The sympathetic system gears the body for action. Although the sympathetic system operates continually, its effects are most dramatic during very stressful situations.

Neurons of the sympathetic system emerge from the spinal cord through the ventral roots of the thoracic and two upper lumbar spinal nerves. Based on this origin, the sympathetic system is sometimes referred to as the *thorccolumbar outflow* of the spinal cord. The cell bodies of the preganglionic sympathetic fibers that emerge from the

TABLE 16-3

Autonomic effects on various effectors

Effector	Receptor	Sympathetic action	Parasympathetic action
Heart	β	Increases rate and strength of contraction	Decreases rate; no direct effect on strength of contraction
Bronchial tubes	β	Dilation	Constriction
Blood vessels			
Arterioles	α, β	Generally constricts	No known effect for most
Veins	α, β	Constricts and dilates	No known function
Skeletal muscle		Increased strength	No effect
Adipose tissue	β	Stimulates release of fatty acids	No known effect
Iris of eye	α	Dilation of pupil	Constriction of pupil
Sweat glands	α	Stimulates	Slight stimulation
Lacrimal (tear) glands	—	No effect	Stimulates secretion
Salivary glands	α	Thick, viscous secretion	Profuse, watery secretion
Gastric glands	—	Inhibits	Stimulates
Adrenal medulla	—	Stimulates secretion of epinephrine and norepinephrine	No known effect
Intestine	α, β	Inhibits motility	Stimulates motility and secretion
Liver	β	Stimulates glycogen breakdown	Slight glycogen synthesis
Gallbladder and bile ducts	—	Relaxation	Contraction
Pancreas	α, β	Inhibits enzyme and insulin secretion; promotes glucagon secretion	Stimulates secretion of enzymes and insulin
Urinary bladder	α, β	Contraction of internal sphincter	Relaxation of internal sphincter
Sex organs	α	Vasoconstriction resulting in ejaculation in male	Vasodilation and erection in both sexes

spinal cord are located in the interomedial lateral nuclei of the spinal cord.

Efferent neurons pass through the white rami communicantes

Efferent neurons pass through the branch of each spinal nerve known as the white ramus. Together, the white rami are referred to as the **white rami communicantes** (koe-*myoo*-neh-**kan**-teez; sing., communicans). These branches appear white because the preganglionic sympathetic neurons are myelinated.

After passing through the white rami communicantes, these neurons pass into the ganglia of the *paravertebral sympathetic ganglion chain.* Each of these paired chains is a series of 22 ganglia located along the length of the vertebral column (Fig. 16-4). Most of the preganglionic neurons end within the ganglia and synapse there with postganglionic efferent neurons.

Axons of some of the postganglionic neurons leave the ganglion as various sympathetic nerves. Some postganglionic fibers form autonomic plexuses around major blood vessels. Sympathetic nerves innervate blood vessels and organs in the head, neck, and thoracic region.

Axons of some postganglionic neurons reenter the spinal nerves by way of the **gray rami communicantes.** This branch appears gray because the postganglionic fibers are not myelinated. These postganglionic fibers travel with the other fibers of the spinal nerve and eventually branch off, forming a visceral nerve that innervates smooth muscle and sweat glands (Fig. 16-5).

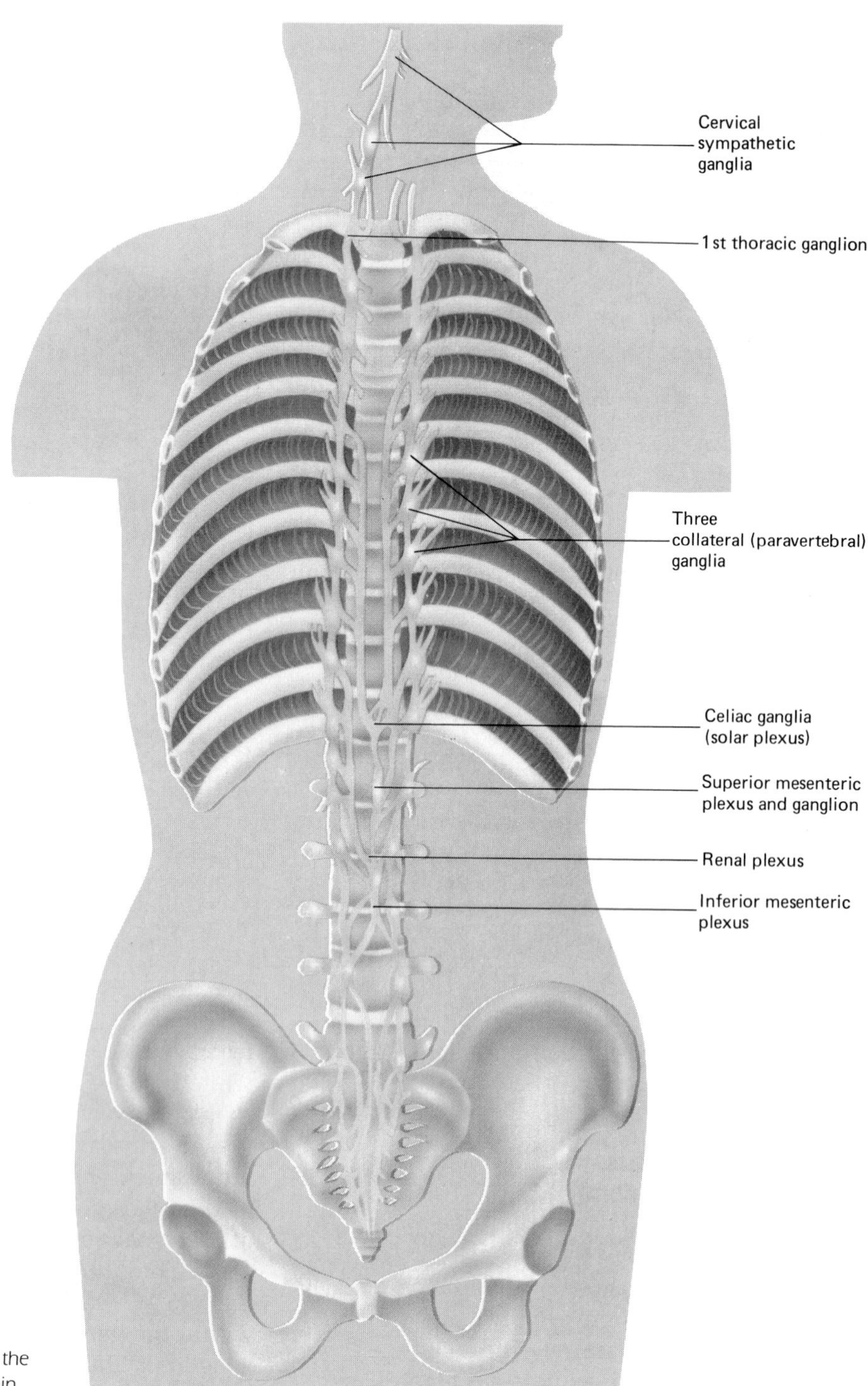

FIGURE 16-4

The sympathetic nervous system. Note the paravertebral sympathetic ganglion chain.

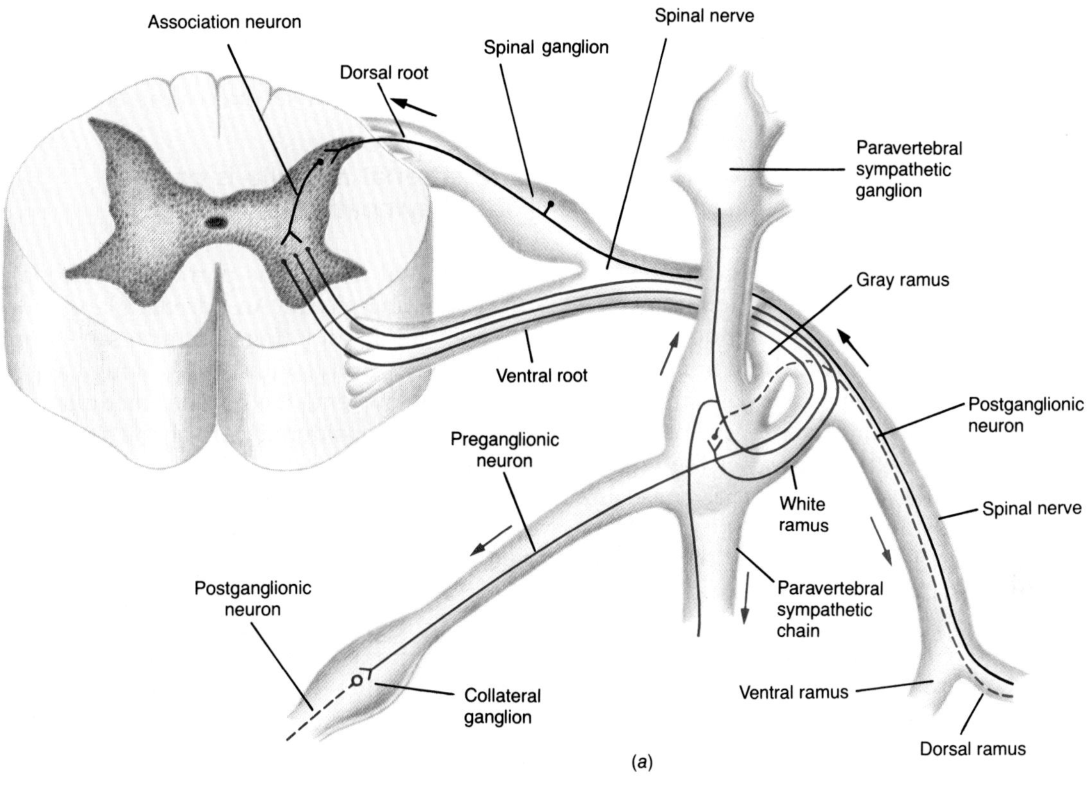

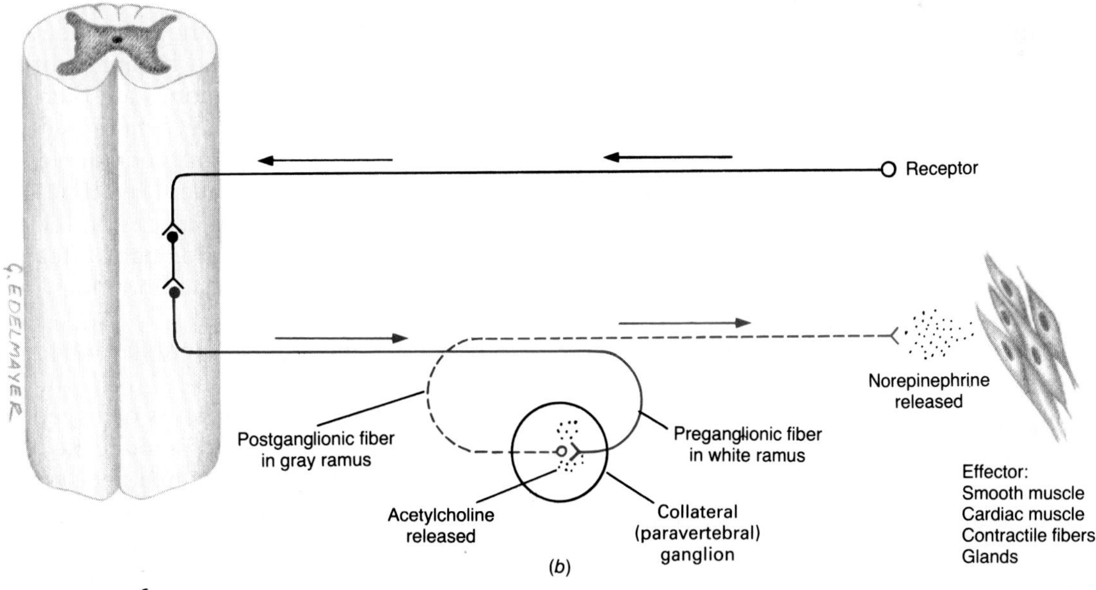

FIGURE 16-5

Functional relationships of the sympathetic nervous system. (*a*) A reflex pathway of the sympathetic nervous system. (*b*) Diagrammatic representation of the sympathetic reflex pathway. Dark line represents afferent component, solid colored line represents preganglionic efferent component, and dotted colored line represents postganglionic efferent component in both parts of the figure.

Preganglionic sympathetic neuron ⟶ through white ramus communicans ⟶ ganglion of paravertebral sympathetic chain ⟶ synapses with postganglionic sympathetic neuron ⟶ some axons pass through a gray ramus communicans ⟶ re-enters a spinal nerve ⟶ visceral nerve ⟶ innervates smooth muscle or gland

Some preganglionic neurons do not end in the ganglia of the paravertebral chain but instead pass on to ganglia located in the abdomen close to the aorta and its major branches. Such preganglionic neurons are called **splanchnic nerves.** The ganglia in which they synapse are collectively known as **collateral ganglia,** or **prevertebral ganglia,** and are individually named after the blood vessels with which they are associated. For example, the celiac ganglia and the nerves associated with them surround the beginning of the celiac artery. Preganglionic fibers that end in collateral ganglia have their origin in the lower six thoracic and first two lumbar levels of the spinal cord. Postganglionic neurons from the collateral ganglia innervate smooth muscles and glands of the abdominal and pelvic viscera and their blood vessels. These include organs of the digestive, urinary, and reproductive systems.

Association neurons within the ganglia extend the potential range of response. There are more postganglionic neurons than preganglionic neurons. Consequently, each preganglionic neuron synapses with several (perhaps 30 or more) postganglionic neurons (an example of divergence). As a result, sympathetic effects tend to be quite widespread rather than precise, usually involving many organs simultaneously. To complicate the pathways further, each postganglionic neuron may receive input from many different preganglionic neurons, an instance of convergence.

Postganglionic sympathetic neurons are adrenergic

Preganglionic sympathetic neurons secrete the neurotransmitter acetylcholine, that is, they are cholinergic fibers. Most sympathetic postganglionic neurons release norepinephrine as the neurotransmitter at the effector synapse, that is, they are adrenergic. However, those that innervate sweat glands generally release acetylcholine.

Just how the autonomic fibers terminate upon effectors is not clear. No end plates comparable to those in skeletal muscle have been identified in smooth muscle, cardiac muscle, or glands. It is thought that the neurotransmitter simply diffuses from the axons to several of the effector cells.

The adrenal medulla is part of the sympathetic system

The adrenal medulla is part of the adrenal gland, an endocrine gland. An adrenal gland is located above each kidney (Fig. 1-5; also see Window on the Human Body, View 6). Although part of the endocrine system, the adrenal medulla is also sometimes considered part of the sympathetic system.

The adrenal medulla is innervated by preganglionic sympathetic fibers that pass from the spinal cord through the chain ganglia and through visceral nerves. The preganglionic fibers end on cells in the adrenal medulla that secrete epinephrine and norepinephrine directly into the blood. These special cells are somewhat like neurons and may be thought of as taking the place of postganglionic sympathetic neurons. In fact, they have the same embryonic origin as postganglionic sympathetic neurons.

Stimulation of the sympathetic nerves to the adrenal medulla results in the release of large amounts of epinephrine and norepinephrine into the circulation. These hormones are then carried to all the tissues of the body, where they reinforce the action of the sympathetic nerves. Interestingly, their effects last about ten times longer than those caused by norepinephrine released by sympathetic nerves. This prolonged effect results from the slow removal of the hormones from the circulation.

In a way, the adrenal medulla provides a safety mechanism that is useful if the direct sympathetic pathway to an organ is damaged or destroyed. On the other hand, should the adrenal medulla be damaged, the sympathetic system in some measure compensates for its loss. When an experimental animal is deprived of its sympathetic nervous system and adrenal medulla, it is able to survive if kept in a calm, nonthreatening environment. The animal's metabolic rate is low; it is very sensitive to cold; and it is unable to respond physiologically to stress. Although not absolutely essential to life, the sympathetic system helps the body to maintain homeostasis and to adjust to the continuous physical and emotional stresses of life.

The parasympathetic system conserves and restores energy

The parasympathetic system regulates the body's involuntary, restorative processes such as digestion. This system is dominant when the body is nonthreatened and relaxed. Its activities result in conserving and storing energy.

Neurons of the parasympathetic system emerge from the brainstem as part of cranial nerves III, VII, IX, and X (vagus) and from the sacral region of the spinal cord as part of the second, third, and fourth sacral spinal nerves. About 75% of all parasympathetic fibers are in the vagus nerves (Fig. 16-6). Because of their origin from the brain and sacral region of the cord, the parasympathetic nerves are sometimes referred to as the *craniosacral outflow*.

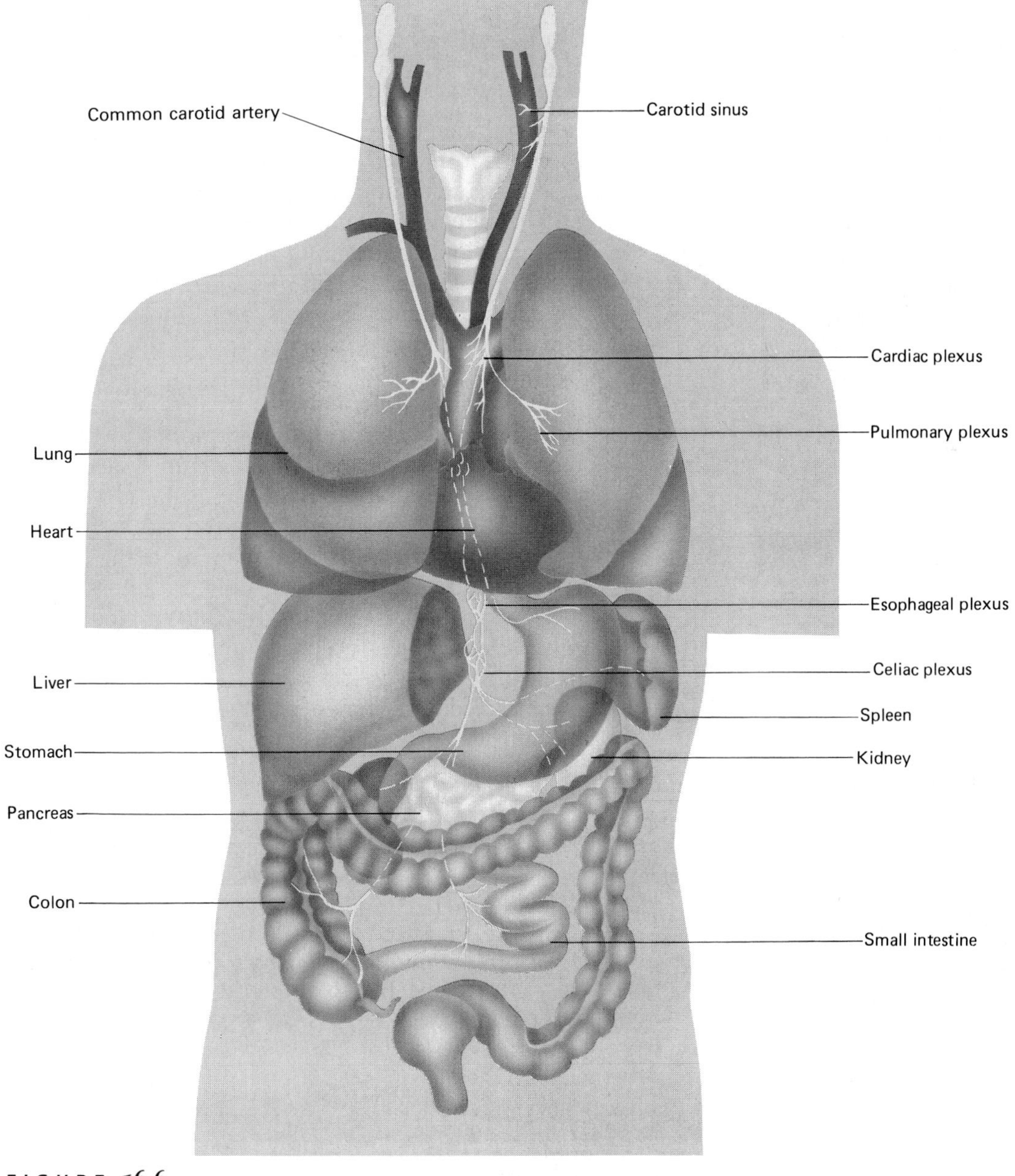

FIGURE 16-6

Distribution of the vagus nerve (CNX).

Efferent neurons synapse in terminal ganglia

Preganglionic parasympathetic fibers have long axons, some myelinated and some unmyelinated. These fibers synapse with postganglionic neurons in terminal ganglia located near or within the walls of the organs that they innervate.

> Preganglionic parasympathetic neuron ⟶ synapses in terminal ganglion ⟶ postganglionic parasympathetic neuron ⟶ visceral neuron ⟶ innervates smooth muscle of viscera

Neurons from the cranial region innervate the eyes, other structures of the head, and thoracic and abdominal viscera. Branches of the vagus innervate the heart, lungs, liver, pancreas, esophagus, stomach, small intestine, and proximal portion of the large intestine (Fig. 16-6). The sacral parasympathetic fibers form the pelvic nerves (also called nervi erigentes). They innervate the distal portion of the large intestine, urinary system, and reproductive system, including the erectile tissues. The parasympathetic nerves do not innervate the blood vessels or sweat glands.

Unlike the sympathetic preganglionic neurons, those of the parasympathetic system synapse with only a few postganglionic neurons. For this reason, the effects of the parasympathetic system are more precise and localized.

The parasympathetic system is cholinergic

In the parasympathetic system, both preganglionic and postganglionic fibers release the neurotransmitter acetylcholine. For this reason the parasympathetic system is known as a cholinergic system, and its postganglionic fibers are referred to as cholinergic fibers. After it is released, excess acetylcholine is rapidly deactivated by cholinesterase. As a result, parasympathetic effects are brief compared with sympathetic effects.

Target cells have various types of receptors

The neurotransmitters released by postganglionic neurons of the autonomic system combine with receptors in the plasma membranes of the effector cells. These receptors are usually proteins. When the neurotransmitter combines with the receptor some change is thought to be triggered within the plasma membrane. Either an enzyme is activated or the permeability of the membrane to some ion or other substance changes. Such changes apparently activate the response within the effector organ.

Acetylcholine activates two types of cholinergic receptors, muscarinic receptors and nicotinic receptors (Fig. 16-7). **Muscarinic receptors** were so named because they are activated by muscarine, a poison found in toadstools. Nicotine, a poisonous drug obtained from tobacco,[1] activates the **nicotinic receptors** but not the muscarinic. (Many of the effects of tobacco use on the body can be explained by the effects of nicotine on the autonomic system.)

Muscarinic receptors are present in all effector cells stimulated by postganglionic parasympathetic neurons and also in those stimulated by postganglionic sympathetic neurons that release acetylcholine. Nicotinic receptors are found on the postganglionic neurons of both sympathetic and parasympathetic systems. They are also present in the plasma membranes of skeletal muscle fibers and the hormone-producing cells of the adrenal medulla.

Norepinephrine activates two main types of adrenergic receptors, **alpha receptors** and **beta receptors.** Epinephrine activates both types of receptors equally. Norepinephrine has a more pronounced effect upon the alpha receptors. Stimulation of these receptors may have different results. For example, stimulation of alpha receptors causes vasoconstriction (narrowing) of blood vessels, whereas beta-receptor stimulation causes dilation of blood vessels. Stimulation of either alpha or beta receptors, however, causes relaxation of the intestine.

Clinical highlight

An understanding of the different types of receptors is important clinically because certain drugs are used to stimulate or to block certain types of receptors. For example, the bronchial constriction that occurs in asthma can be countered by stimulation of beta receptors of the bronchial smooth muscle using such drugs as theophylline or caffeine. **Beta-blockers** are drugs that block the action of epinephrine at beta receptors on effector cells. These drugs are used to treat angina, hypertension, and arrhythmias of the heart. Focus on Pharmacology of the Autonomic System gives a brief summary of some of the effects of drugs on these receptors.

[1] Nicotine is used as an insecticide in agriculture and to kill external parasites in veterinary medicine.

FOCUS ON . . . Pharmacology of the autonomic system

Drug	Mode of action	Clinical uses
Sympathomimetic drugs		
Also called adrenergic drugs. These stimulate physiological responses similar to those produced by the sympathetic adrenergic nerves and mimic the action of norepinephrine.		
Epinephrine	Acts directly on both alpha and beta receptors	Used in asthma and other allergic diseases; stimulates relaxation of constricted respiratory passageways and reduction of swelling
Isoproterenol	Acts directly on beta receptors	Drug of choice in cardiac resuscitation
Phenylephrine (Neo-synephrine)	Acts directly on alpha receptors; constricts small blood vessels in lining of nose, thus relieving nasal congestion	Used as a decongestant
Ephedrine	Causes release of norepinephrine from synaptic vesicles	Ephedrine and epinephrine were the original adrenergic drugs; many of the drugs currently in use for treating asthma and other allergic disorders, and used to stimulate the heart, are derivatives of ephedrine
Amphetamine	Causes accumulation of norepinephrine in synaptic clefts	No longer in widespread clinical use; sometimes used to treat narcolepsy and hyperkinetic symptoms in children
Adrenergic blocking drugs		
Reserpine	Blocks synthesis and storage of norepinephrine	Used in management of some types of hypertension (high blood pressure); used in some psychotic patients unable to tolerate phenothiazines
Propranolol (e.g., Inderal)	Blocks beta receptors	Used to relieve pain in angina (a heart disease discussed in Chapter 20); by decreasing sympathetic stimulation it reduces heart rate and strength of contractions; useful in controlling some tremors and preventing migraine headaches
Cholinomimetic drugs		
Also called parasympathomimetic drugs. These drugs stimulate physiological responses similar to those produced by acetylcholine or activation of the parasympathetic system. Acetylcholine activates **muscarinic** and **nicotinic receptors.**		
Pilocarpine	Acts directly on the muscarinic receptors	Used in ophthalmology to constrict iris of the eye
Cholinergic blocking drugs		
Also called anticholinergic drugs.		
Atropine	Blocks action of acetylcholine on muscarinic receptors of cholinergic effector cells	Used to prepare patients for surgical anesthesia; inhibits salivary, nasal, and bronchial secretions that might block respiratory passages; used in treatment of poisoning with anticholinesterase agents, e.g., nerve gases or organophosphate pesticides
Scopolamine	Blocks action of acetylcholine on muscarinic receptors of cholinergic effector cells	In low oral doses used as a remedy for motion sickness; in obstetrics, used to promote drowsiness with amnesia (twilight sleep) during labor

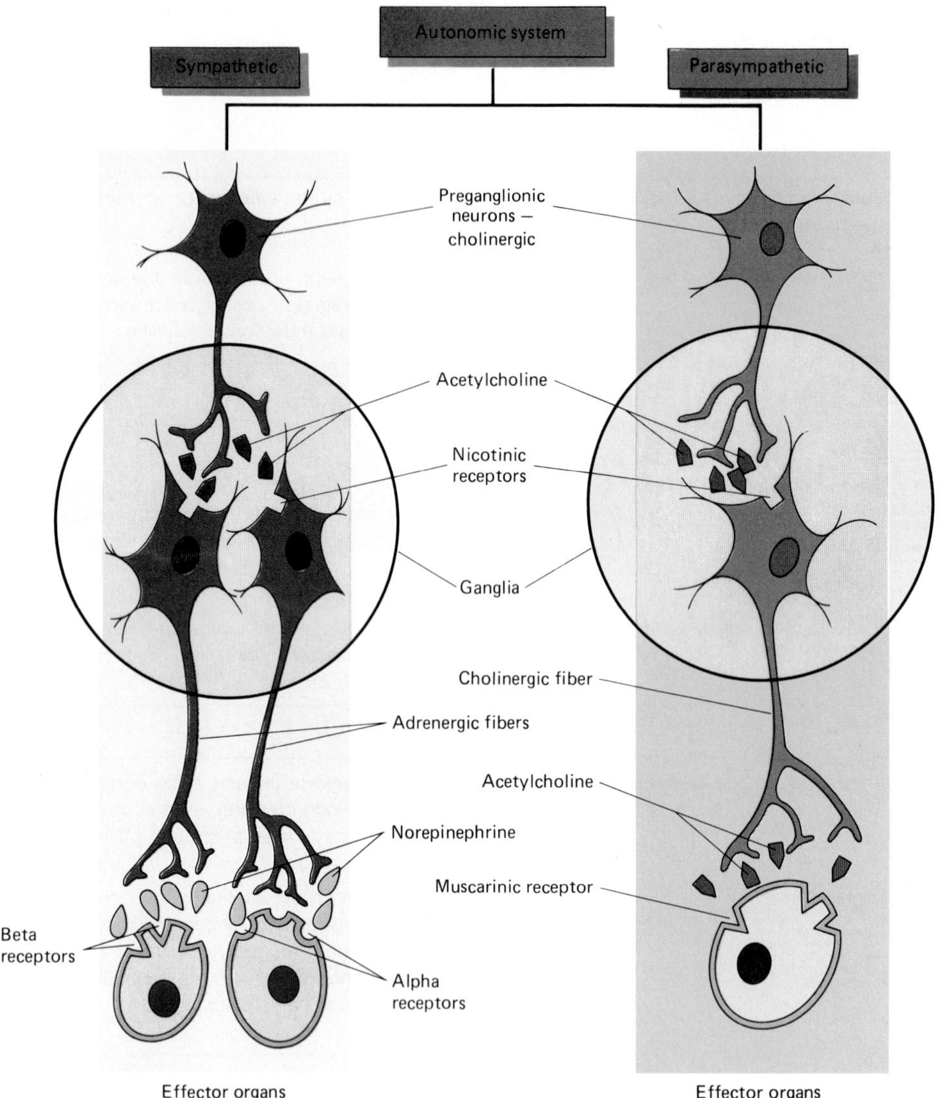

FIGURE 16-7

Plasma membrane receptors of effector cells of the autonomic system.

Sympathetic and parasympathetic inputs to an organ have opposite effects

Some organs are innervated by both sympathetic and parasympathetic nerves and may be stimulated by one type of nerve and inhibited by the other. For example, sympathetic nerves increase both the rate and force of contraction of the heart, increasing its effectiveness as a pump. Parasympathetic (vagus) nerves cause the opposite effects, decreasing the heart's pumping effectiveness and allowing it some measure of rest (Fig. 16-8).

The digestive system is mainly under parasympathetic control. Parasympathetic stimulation increases peristalsis (waves of muscle contraction) so that food is moved along more quickly. Sympathetic stimulation is not necessary for the normal function of the digestive system, but strong sympathetic stimulation does inhibit the movement of food through the digestive tract. Table 16-3 summarizes some autonomic effects on various organs.

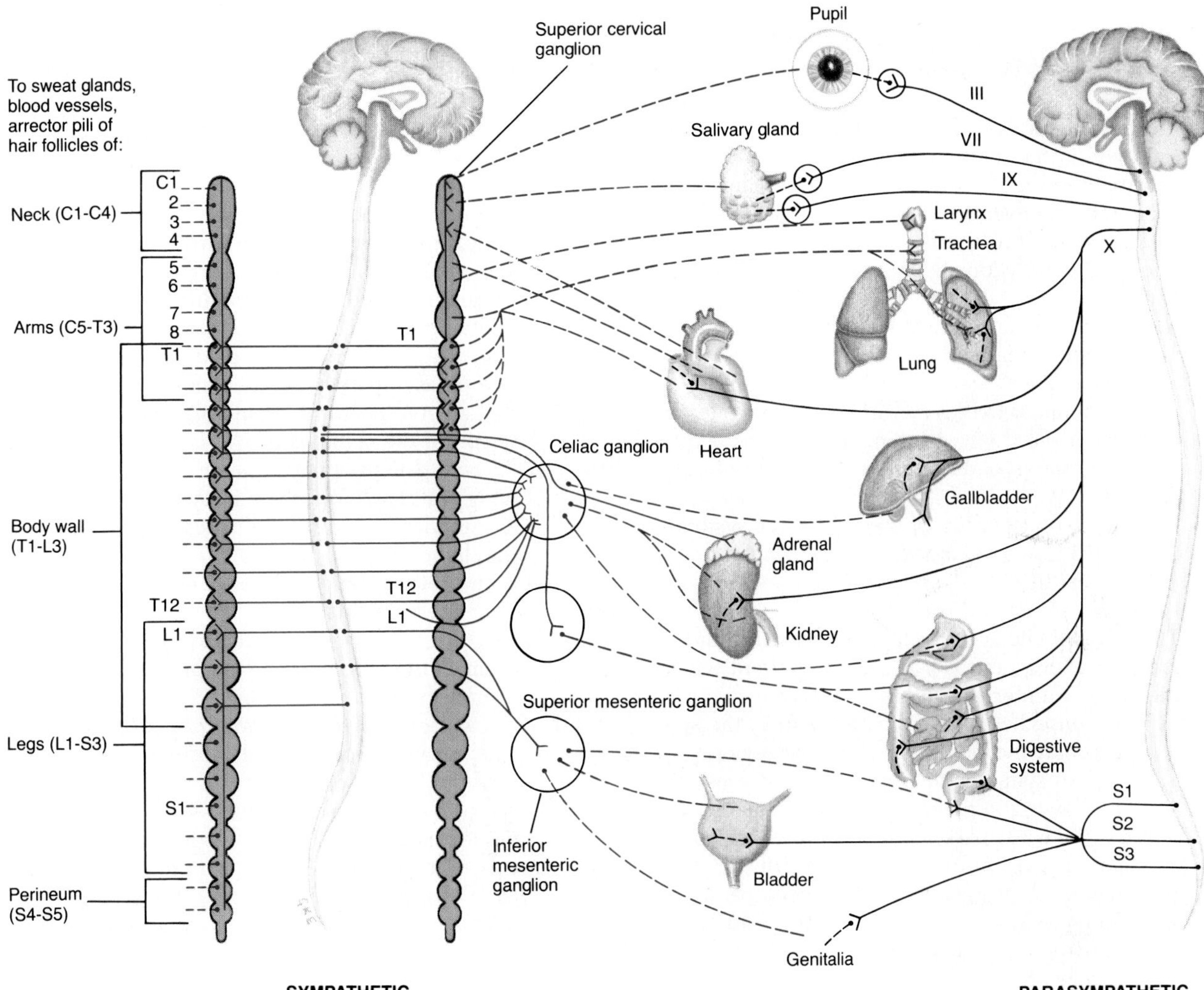

FIGURE 16-8

Sympathetic and parasympathetic nervous systems. For clarity, peripheral and visceral nerves of the sympathetic system are shown on separate sides of the cord. Complex as it appears, this diagram has been greatly simplified. (Colored lines represent sympathetic nerves, black lines represent parasympathetic nerves, and dotted lines represent postganglionic nerves.) See Table 16-3 for specific action of the nerves.

Summary

I. The autonomic system works to maintain a steady state within the internal environment, whereas the somatic portion of the PNS helps the organism cope with the external environment. (See Table 16-1 for other differences.)

II. The ANS is functionally organized into reflex pathways.
   A. Afferent fibers of the autonomic system run through cranial and spinal nerves along with somatic fibers.
   B. Autonomic activities are influenced by many parts of the CNS, including areas of the cerebral cortex, the hypothalamus, brainstem, and spinal cord.
   C. The efferent portion of the autonomic system is divided into sympathetic and parasympathetic systems; their neurons also are components of certain spinal and cranial nerves.

III. The sympathetic system regulates activities that mobilize energy and is especially important when the body is under stress.
   A. The sympathetic system emerges from the spinal cord at the thoracic and lumbar regions.
   B. A typical sympathetic pathway might consist of the following: a preganglionic fiber emerges from the cord, passes through the white ramus communicans, and ends in a sympathetic chain ganglion. A postganglionic fiber then passes through a gray ramus communicans and reenters a spinal nerve. Eventually this fiber branches off, forming a visceral nerve that innervates smooth muscle or sweat glands.
   C. Preganglionic fibers release acetylcholine; most sympathetic postganglionic neurons release norepinephrine.
   D. The adrenal medulla is sometimes considered part of the sympathetic system because it is stimulated by sympathetic nerves and releases epinephrine and norepinephrine.

IV. The parasympathetic system acts to restore energy and is dominant during periods of relaxation.
   A. The parasympathetic system consists of nerves that emerge from the brain and from the sacral region of the spinal cord.
   B. Parasympathetic preganglionic fibers synapse with postganglionic fibers in terminal ganglia located near or within the walls of the organs they innervate.
   C. Both preganglionic and postganglionic fibers release acetylcholine.

V. The type of receptor on the postsynaptic neuron determines the type of response produced by the neurotransmitter.
   A. Acetylcholine activates two types of cholinergic receptors—muscarinic and nicotinic.
   B. Norepinephrine and epinephrine activate two types of adrenergic receptors—alpha and beta.

VI. Some organs are innervated by both sympathetic and parasympathetic nerves; for example, the heart is stimulated by sympathetic nerves and its pumping effectiveness is decreased by parasympathetic (vagus) nerves.

Post-test

1. The portion of the PNS that functions to maintain a steady state within the internal environment is the ______________ system.
2. The ANS controls ______________ muscle, ______________ muscle, and ______________.
3. The main subcortical center for autonomic regulation is the ______________.
4. The paravertebral ganglion chain consists of cell bodies of ______________ neurons.
5. Efferent neurons of the sympathetic system pass out of the spinal cord through the branch of each spinal nerve known as the ______________ ramus.
6. Sympathetic ganglia located close to the aorta and its main branches are ______________ ganglia.
7. Preganglionic sympathetic and parasympathetic neurons secrete the neurotransmitter ______________.
8. Most postganglionic sympathetic neurons release ______________.
9. The adrenal medulla releases ______________ and ______________.
10. Parasympathetic preganglionic fibers synapse in ______________ ganglia.
11. The rate and force of contraction of the heart are increased by its ______________ nerves.
12. The digestive system is stimulated by ______________ nerves.
13. Label the drawing.

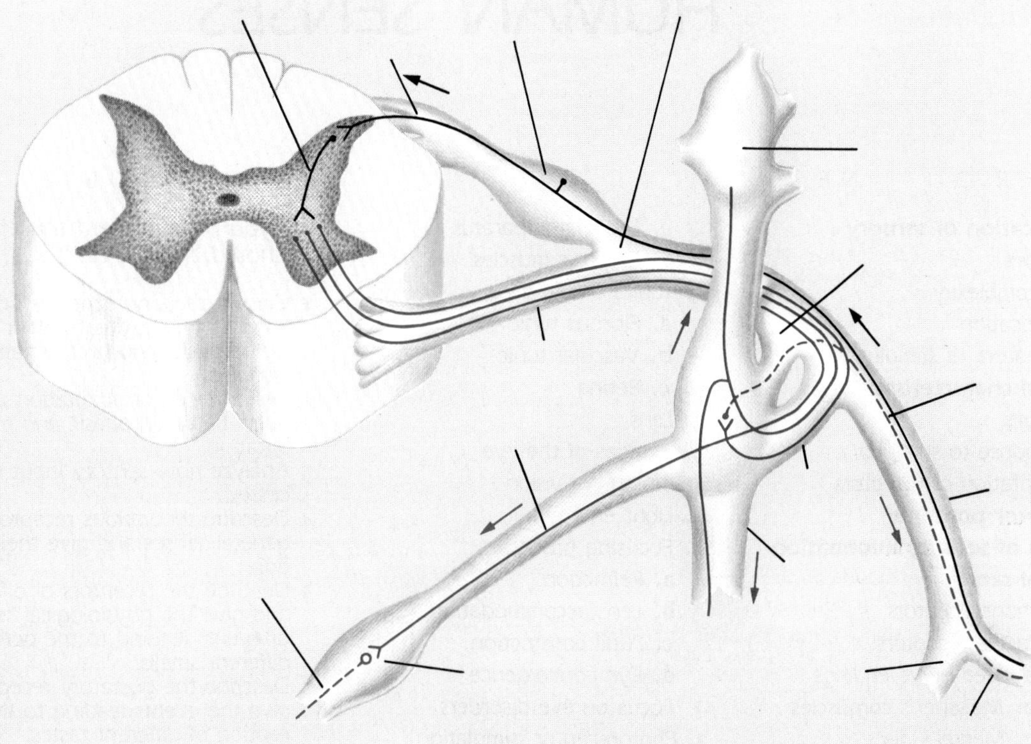

Review questions

1. Contrast the somatic and autonomic nervous systems.
2. Trace a neural impulse through a reflex pathway of the sympathetic system.
3. Identify the cell bodies found in each of the following: (a) paravertebral chain ganglion, (b) collateral ganglion, (c) terminal ganglion.
4. Identify the neurotransmitter released by (a) preganglionic autonomic fibers, (b) postganglionic sympathetic neurons, (c) postganglionic parasympathetic neurons.
5. How does the adrenal medulla function to enhance sympathetic response?
6. What types of receptors are activated by acetylcholine? by norepinephrine? How might it be clinically important to know about the various types of receptors (e.g., muscarinic, alpha, and beta of the autonomic system) and their effectors?
7. Contrast sympathomimetic with adrenergic blocking drugs.
8. Give several examples of how the sympathetic and parasympathetic systems work together to maintain homeostasis.
9. Explain why the autonomic system is somewhat misnamed.

Post-test answers

1. autonomic 2. smooth, cardiac; glands 3. hypothalamus 4. sympathetic 5. white 6. collateral 7. acetylcholine 8. norepinephrine 9. epinephrine, norepinephrine 10. terminal 11. sympathetic 12. parasympathetic 13. See Figure 16-5*a*.

HUMAN SENSES

CHAPTER OUTLINE

- **I. Classification of sensory receptors**
  - A. By complexity
  - B. By location
  - C. By nature of stimulus
- **II. General characteristics of receptors**
  - A. Response to stimulus
  - B. Adaptation of receptors
- **III. Generator potential**
- **IV. Coding of sensory information**
- **V. General senses**
  - A. Mechanoreceptors
    - 1. Tactile receptors
      - a. Free nerve endings
      - b. Meissner's corpuscles
      - c. Merkel's discs
      - d. Root hair plexuses
      - e. Ruffini's end-organs
      - f. Krause's end-bulbs
      - g. Pacinian corpuscles
    - 2. Proprioceptors
      - a. Muscle spindle
      - b. Golgi tendon organ
      - c. Joint kinesthetic receptors
  - B. Thermoreceptors
  - C. Nociceptors
- **VI. Special senses**
  - A. Olfaction
    - 1. Chemoreception
    - 2. Stereochemical theory
  - B. Taste reception
    - 1. Primary taste sensations
    - 2. Contributing receptors
  - C. Anatomy of vision
    - 1. Accessory structures of the eye
      - a. Orbital cavities
      - b. Eyebrows
      - c. Eyelids and eyelashes
      - d. Conjunctiva
      - e. Lacrimal apparatus
      - f. Extrinsic muscles
    - 2. Tunics of the eye
      - a. Fibrous tunic
      - b. Vascular tunic
      - c. Retina
    - 3. Lens
    - 4. Cavities of the eye
  - D. Physiology of vision
    - 1. Light energy
    - 2. Focusing processes
      - a. Refraction
      - b. Lens accommodation
      - c. Pupil constriction
      - d. Eye convergence
    - □ Focus on eye disorders
    - 3. Photoreceptor stimulation
      - a. Visual pigments
      - b. Stimulation of rods
      - c. Stimulation of cones
    - 4. Light and dark adaptation
    - 5. Neural pathway of vision
  - E. Anatomy of the ear
    - 1. Outer ear
    - 2. Middle ear
    - 3. Inner ear
      - a. Labyrinths
      - b. Vestibule
      - c. Semicircular canals
      - d. Cochlea
  - F. Physiology of hearing
    - 1. Sound waves
    - 2. Outer and middle ear
    - 3. Cochlea
    - 4. Pitch transmission
    - 5. Loudness transmission
  - G. Physiology of equilibrium
    - 1. Static equilibrium
    - 2. Dynamic equilibrium
    - □ Focus on ear disorders
  - H. Embryology of the eye
  - I. Embryology of the ear

LEARNING OBJECTIVES

After you have studied this chapter you should be able to:

1. Classify sensory receptors on the basis of complexity, by their location in the body, and by the nature of the stimulus.
2. Define receptor adaptation and distinguish between phasic and tonic adaptation.
3. Analyze how sensory input is processed.
4. Describe the various receptors of the general senses and give their function.
5. Describe the receptors of olfaction and give the physiological sequence of events leading to the perception of different smells.
6. Describe the gustatory receptors and give the events leading to the perception of different tastes.
7. Describe the accessory structures of the eye and compare their functions.
8. Trace the transmission of light through the eye.
9. List the extrinsic muscles of the eye and their functions.
10. Compare the structure and function of the tunics of the eyeball.
11. Explain the focusing of an image on the retina of the eye and the causes and corrections for those images not normally focused on the retina.
12. Compare the properties of the photoreceptors of the eye.
13. List the physiological sequence of events in the transduction of light by the photoreceptors.
14. Describe the neural route leading to visual perception.
15. Describe the structure and function of the outer, middle, and inner ear.
16. List the sequence of events in the transmission of sound waves through the ear to the organ of Corti.
17. Explain the role of the oval and round windows in the transmission of pressure waves.
18. Analyze the differences in processing the amplitude and the frequency of sound waves.
19. Describe the structures of the inner ear involved with static and dynamic equilibrium.
20. Identify the effects of sensory information on static equilibrium.
21. Contrast the abnormalities of static and dynamic equilibrium.
22. Describe the embryology of the eye and ear.

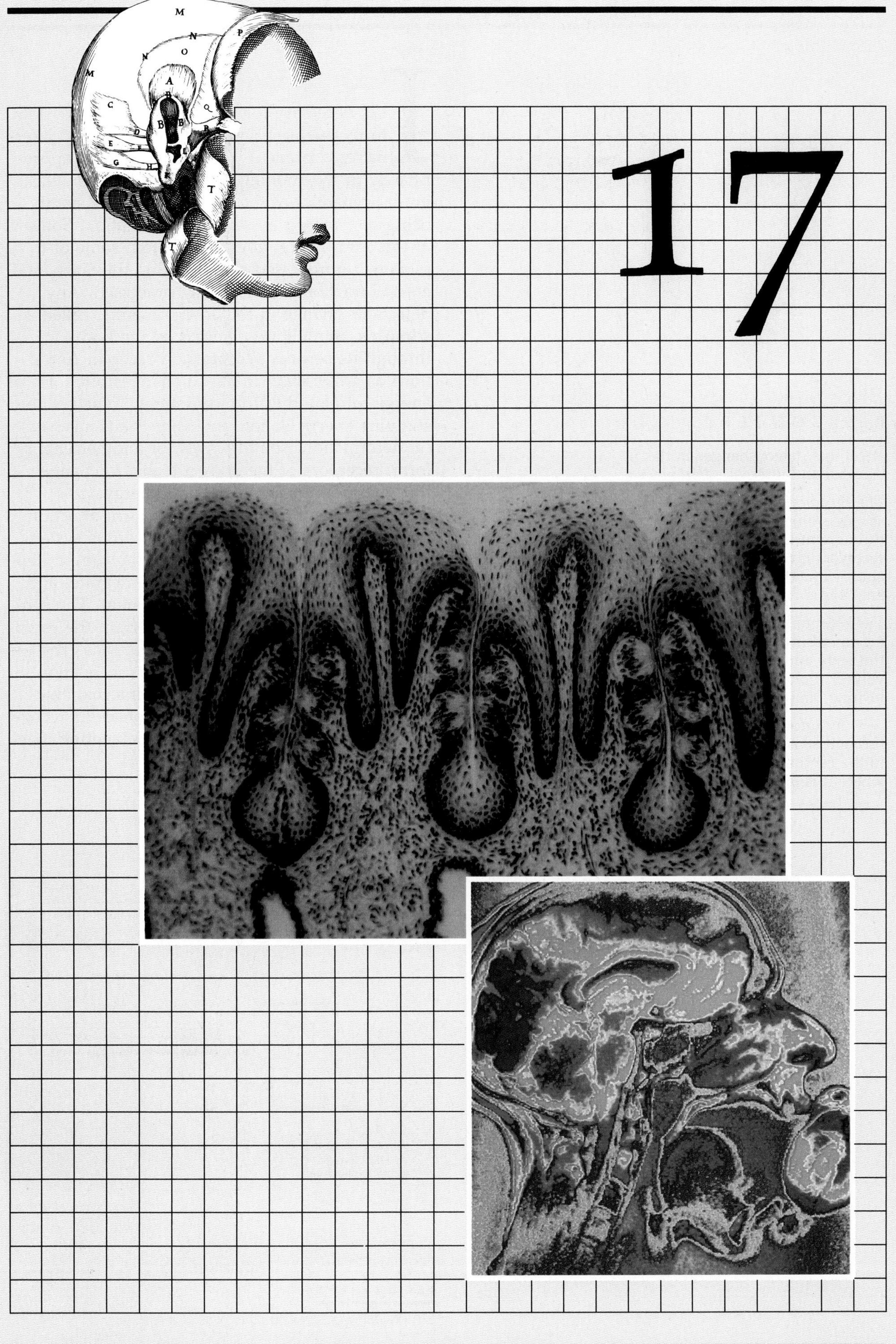
17

KEY CONCEPTS

Receptors detect changes in the external and internal environments.

The receptors for the general senses are widely dispersed throughout the body and include receptors involved in touch, pressure, vibration, stretch, pain, heat, and cold.

The receptors for the special senses are found in very localized areas of the body and include receptors involved in olfaction, taste, vision, hearing, and equilibrium.

Sensory information travels through sensory (afferent) neurons to the central nervous system where it is integrated.

It is necessary for the central nervous system to receive input about the external and internal environment in order to respond appropriately in maintaining the well-being and homeodynamics of the body. We are constantly being bombarded by sensory information. Some of this information goes undetected, some of it remains unprocessed after entering the body, and a small fraction is consciously processed. Any detectable change in the environment is called a **stimulus.** Stimuli are detected by the body through its **sensory receptors.** A receptor functions as a *transducer* in that it changes one form of energy into another form of energy. Whether the stimulus energy is light intensity, heat, mechanical deformation, sound waves, or another energy form, receptors of the body are able to change this energy into electrochemical energy.

Electrochemical energy in the form of action potentials is the language of the nervous system. It is only in this energy form that the central nervous system can receive, process, integrate, and respond to changes in the environment. The central nervous system receives input from the receptors by way of sensory (afferent) neurons. The state of awareness a person exhibits in relation to the conditions of the external and internal environment is called **sensation.** The conscious recognition of sensory stimuli is called **perception.** See Figure 17-1.

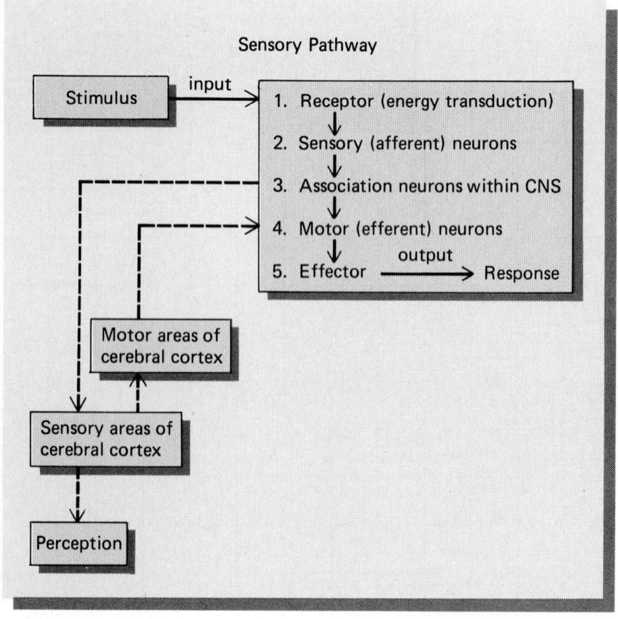

FIGURE 17-1

Sensory pathway showing other parts of a reflex arc.

TABLE 17-1

Receptors of the general senses

Structure	Classification: By complexity	By location	By nature of stimulus	Major specific stimulus	Major location	Adaptation
Free nerve endings (dendrites)	Simple	Exteroceptors, enteroceptors	Mechanoreceptors (maybe thermoreceptors), nociceptors	Pressure Pain (chemicals, mechanical damage, temperature extremes)	Epidermis, dermis, connective tissues, cornea, mucosae, glands, most tissues	Tonic
Merkel's discs	Simple	Exteroceptors	Mechanoreceptors	Light pressure (touch)	Epidermis; lips, fingertips	Tonic
Root hair plexuses	Simple	Exteroceptors	Mechanoreceptors	Deflection	Dermis (hair follicles); hairy parts of body	Phasic
Meissner's corpuscles	Simple	Exteroceptors	Mechanoreceptors	Light pressure, touch discrimination, low-frequency vibration	Dermis; fingertips, lips, eyelids, external genitalia, nipples	Phasic
Pacinian corpuscles	Simple	Exteroceptors, enteroceptors	Mechanoreceptors	Deep pressure, stretch, high-frequency vibration	Subcutaneous tissue and in deeper tissues including viscera and mesenteries; fingers, soles of feet, external genitalia, nipples	Phasic
Ruffini's end-organs	Simple	Exteroceptors	Mechanoreceptors (possibly thermoreceptors for warmth)	Crude touch, deep pressure (warmth)	Deep in dermis and joint capsules; conjunctiva, lips, oral cavity	Tonic
Krause's end-bulbs	Simple	Exteroceptors	Mechanoreceptors, (possibly thermoreceptors for cold)	Light pressure (cold)	Skin, muscles, tendons, mouth, genitals	—
Muscle spindles	Simple	Proprioceptors	Mechanoreceptors	Stretch	Skeletal muscles	Tonic
Golgi tendon organs	Simple	Proprioceptors	Mechanoreceptors	Stretch	Skeletal muscles	Tonic
Joint kinesthetic receptors	Simple	Proprioceptors	Mechanoreceptors	Stretch	Joint capsules	Tonic

Sensory receptors are classified by complexity, location, and the nature of the stimulus

Sensory receptors come in a variety of shapes and sizes. They may be located on the surface of the body or within deep structures. Different receptors usually respond to different stimuli. Classification schemes for sensory receptors focus on their complexity, location, and the nature of the stimulus.

Receptors are classified by complexity

Sensory receptors are classified by the complexity of their make-up as being either **simple** or **complex** (Tables 17-1 and 17-2). Simple receptors furnish input associated with the **general senses,** including touch, pressure, vibration, stretch, pain, heat, and cold. The general senses monitor sensory input from multiple locations throughout the body instead of from one or a few sites; therefore, the simple receptors are very widespread. Simple receptors may be dendrites of sensory neurons or nerve endings covered by a capsule of connective tissue (encapsulated).

The **special senses** are made up of complex receptors responding to specific stimuli at very localized sites in the body. These receptors and their associated structures are referred to as *sense organs.* The special senses are complex both in their construction and in their neuronal pathways. The special senses include those of olfaction, taste, vision, hearing, and equilibrium.

Receptors are classified by their location in the body

By location, receptors are classified as being exteroceptors, enteroceptors, or proprioceptors (see Tables 17-1 and 17-2). **Exteroceptors** (*eks*-ter-oh-**sep**-tors) are located near the surface of the body and respond to various stimuli of the external environment. Exteroceptors include those of touch, pressure, pain, temperature, taste, olfaction, hearing, and vision.

Enteroceptors (*en*-ter-o-**sep**-tors) are also called **visceroceptors** (*vis*-er-oh-**sep**-tors). Enteroceptors detect stimuli originating from within the body. They are located mainly in the visceral organs and the blood vessels and respond to internal pain, pressure, stretch, and chemical changes. Their input to the central nervous system via sensory neurons is usually monitored unconsciously, but upon integration they may lead to a variety of feelings such as discomfort, thirst, and hunger.

The **proprioceptors** (*pro*-pree-oh-**sep**-tors) are those receptors that detect changes in the condition of the skeletal muscles, tendons, and joints. They also include the equilibrium receptors of the inner ear. Even though they are internal, they are more restricted in their location than are the enteroceptors. Proprioceptors provide the central nervous system with information concerning movement, equilibrium, and body position.

Senses may also be classified as somatic or visceral based on the location of their receptors in the body. **Somatic senses** have their receptors associated within the body wall and include receptors of the skin (cutaneous) and the proprioceptors of the muscles, tendons, and joints. **Visceral senses** include those in which the receptors are located within visceral organs.

Receptors are classified by the nature of the stimulus

Receptors are classified by the nature of the stimulus detected as mechanoreceptors, chemoreceptors, photoreceptors, thermoreceptors, and nociceptors (see Tables 17-1 and 17-2).

Mechanoreceptors detect touch, pressure, vibrations, tickle, and itch. The cutaneous receptors of touch and pressure are examples of mechanoreceptors, as are the proprioceptors and the inner ear receptors. The stretch receptors of the gastro-

TABLE 17-2

Receptors of the special senses

		Classification					
Sense organ	Specific receptors	By complexity	By location	By nature of stimulus	Major specific stimulus	Major location	Adaptation
Olfactory membrane	Olfactory cell	Complex	Exteroceptors	Chemoreceptors	Chemicals in solution	Superior nasal cavity	Phasic
Taste bud	Gustatory cell	Complex	Exteroceptors	Chemoreceptors	Chemicals in solution	Dorsum of tongue, pharynx	Phasic
Eye	Rods and cones	Complex	Exteroceptors	Photoreceptors	Light intensity	Eye	Tonic
Ear							
Cochlea	Organs of Corti (hair cells)	Complex	Exteroceptors	Mechanoreceptors	Deflection (vibration)	Inner ear	Tonic
Vestibular apparatus	Maculae and cristae (hair cells)	Complex	Proprioceptors	Mechanoreceptors	Deflection	Inner ear	Phasic

intestinal (GI) tract, lungs, blood vessels, and urinary bladder are also classified as mechanoreceptors.

Chemoreceptors detect dissolved chemicals. Chemoreception includes olfaction, taste, and the detection of chemical levels in the body fluids. The concentrations of water, oxygen, carbon dioxide, and glucose in the body fluids are being constantly monitored by chemoreceptors.

Photoreceptors respond to changes in electromagnetic (photo) energy in the environment. Photoreceptors are located within the retina of the eye. **Thermoreceptors** detect changes in temperature over time.

Some physiologists classify pain receptors as **nociceptors.** Nociceptors can respond to chemical changes, mechanical damage, and temperature extremes.

Receptors have some general characteristics

Receptors exhibit certain shared characteristics such as specificity, adaptation, graded responses, and modes of intensity coding.

Most receptors respond best to a particular stimulus

Although they can respond to a variety of energy forms, receptors generally respond to one type of stimulus more readily than to another. This occurs because the receiving sites of the receptor are more specific to a certain type of stimulus. For instance, chemicals cause olfactory receptors to become activated whereas light energy causes activation of photoreceptors of the eyes. Additionally, a particular receptor has a lower threshold, or minimal excitability, to a particular form of stimulus energy. Any other form of energy will normally not be detected by the receptor because of a higher threshold for that stimulus. The stimulus that meets the lowest threshold for exciting the particular receptor is called the **adequate stimulus.** The receptor, therefore, usually detects its adequate stimulus. The adequate stimulus for the photoreceptors of the retina is light energy; the adequate stimulus for taste and olfaction is chemicals in solution.

Receptors are also specific in that they normally produce the same sensation even if they respond to a different type of energy. A poke to the closed eye will cause light flashes even though the stimulus is mechanical.

The sensation received by the activation of a particular type of receptor is called a sense **modality.** Besides vision, olfaction, hearing, taste, and touch, other sense modalities include pressure, pain, equilibrium, body position, warmth, cold, stretch, and chemoreception in body fluids.

Sensory (afferent) neurons take the information from the receptor to the central nervous system. The dendrites of a single sensory neuron may conduct input from a number of receptors. A **sensory unit** is a single sensory neuron and all the receptors it receives input from. The area of the body leading to the activation of the sensory neuron is called its *receptive field.* The sensory neuron, or pathway, taking a particular type of sensory information to the brain is also specific in that it only conveys information about one particular sense.

Most conscious sensation is relayed to the sensory areas of the cerebral cortex. This area of the cortex integrates the information and interprets it as coming from the appropriate sensory area. The projection of the sensory input to the correct receptor is important in eliciting the proper response. If an irritating substance is placed in the mouth, the cortex must project the stimulation as coming from the mouth in order to remove it.

Receptors decrease sensitivity after continued stimulation

Most receptors decrease their sensitivity to a particular stimulus if it is continued for a prolonged period of time. This decreased sensitivity to the stimulus is called **adaptation.** The rate at which this desensitivity occurs varies with the type of receptor. Some receptors adapt very quickly and are called **phasic receptors.** These receptors are important in monitoring changes in stimulation. Examples of phasic receptors include those of touch, pressure, and olfaction. Other receptors adapt less quickly, or not at all, to a sustained stimulus. These receptors are called **tonic receptors.** Tonic receptors are important in monitoring the homeodynamics of the body. They include nociceptors, chemoreceptors in the blood vessels, and proprioceptors involved in body position (Fig. 17-2).

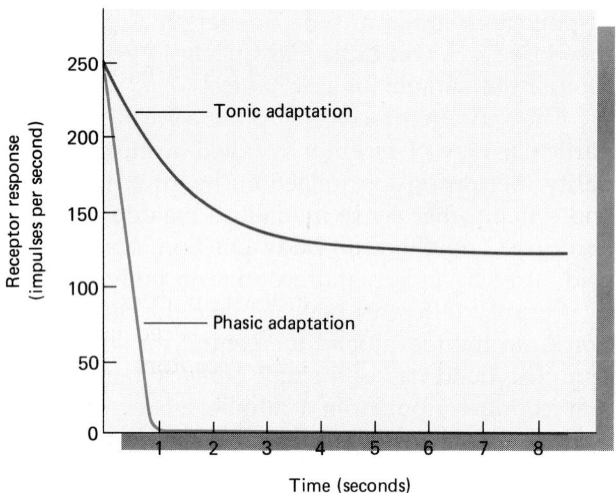

FIGURE 17-2

Receptor responses to stimulation showing phasic (blue) and tonic (red) adaptation.

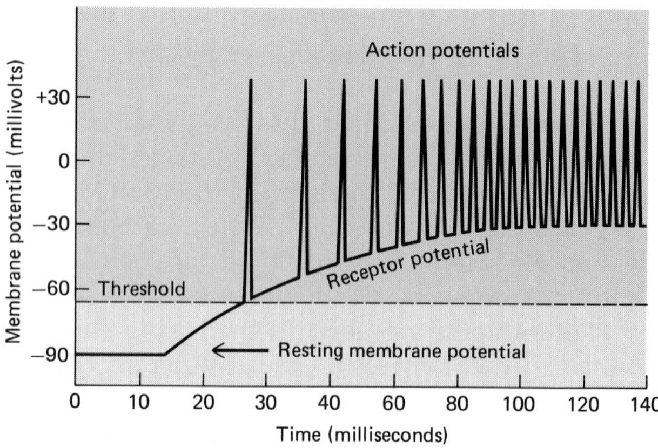

FIGURE 17-3

Comparison of generator potentials of receptor to action potentials of sensory neuron.

The receptor produces a generator potential in response to the stimulus

The detection of the stimulus by a receptor causes a depolarization in the plasma membrane of the receptor, which is called a **generator,** or **receptor, potential.** This generator potential is an electrochemical response to the stimulus energy as it is being absorbed into the receptor. It is believed that the stimulus increases the permeability of the receptor membrane to small ions. Because sodium ions (Na^+) are in higher concentration outside the receptor, Na^+ moves into the receptor, resulting in the depolarization. Potassium ions (K^+) move out of the receptor but to a lesser extent than Na^+ moves in. The net movement of more Na^+ in than K^+ out results in a depolarization, the generator potential. This mechanism is similar to the generation of an excitatory postsynaptic potential (EPSP). The magnitude of a generator potential is proportional to the intensity of the stimulus. This type of reaction to a stimulus is called a *graded response*. Increasing the intensity of the stimulus increases the response (the magnitude of the generator potential). Once the generator potential reaches the threshold potential of the sensory neuron, the sensory neuron fires an action potential (Fig. 17-3).

The sensory neurons carry sensory information via action potentials toward the central nervous system. Most of the sensory input from somatic areas reaches the spinal cord through the dorsal roots of spinal nerves. The part of a sensory neuron within a spinal nerve is the peripheral branch. It is similar to the dendrite of the neuron. The peripheral branch leads to the cell body, located within a dorsal root ganglion. The central branch, the axon-like part of the neuron, courses through the gray matter of the spinal cord.

Stimulus strength is coded for by the frequency of action potentials

The generator potential of the receptor is a local, graded response. The action potential of the sensory neuron follows the all-or-none law. Therefore, the generator potential increases in magnitude with increasing stimulus strength, but the action potential of a single sensory neuron has a constant magnitude no matter how large the generator potential that initiates it. If all sensory information is conveyed to the central nervous system by action potentials of a constant magnitude, then how can a person perceive the intensity of a stimulus?

Although increases in the magnitude of a generator potential do not change the magnitude of the action potential of the sensory neuron, increases in generator potentials can increase the frequency of the action potentials. Thus, coding of stimulus strength is determined by the frequency of the action potentials of sensory neurons (Fig. 17-3). This relationship can be expressed in the word equation:

↑ Stimulus strength ⟶ ↑ magnitude of generator potential ⟶ ↑ frequency of action potentials

A generator potential does have an upper limit of magnitude, which also puts an upper limit on the frequency of action potentials generated by a single receptor. As the strength of a stimulus increases, the area it affects usually increases. In this way, more receptors and extensions of peripheral branches of the same sensory neuron may be activated. This can increase the frequency of action potentials in the sensory neuron.

↑ Stimulus strength ⟶ ↑ number of receptors activated ⟶ ↑ action potentials propagated in branches ⟶ ↑ frequency of action potentials in main sensory neuron

As the stimulus strength continues to increase, the receptive fields of other sensory neurons are usually affected. The additional sensory input from more receptive fields of other sensory neurons, or *recruitment,* is interpreted in the brain as an increase in stimulus intensity.

↑ Stimulus strength ⟶ ↑ number of sensory units activated ⟶ ↑ sensory input to brain

In summary, information about the strength of a stimulus is transmitted to the brain by: (1) variations in the frequency of action potentials generated by a single receptor and (2) variations in the number of receptors activated by the stimulus.

The general senses are widespread throughout the body

The general senses include mechanoreceptors, thermoreceptors, and nociceptors.

Mechanoreceptors include tactile and positional receptors

The **mechanoreceptors** include the tactile receptors (touch, pressure, vibration, tickle, and itch) and the positional receptors, which include the proprioceptors and stretch receptors. Tactile receptors, along with most thermoreceptors and nociceptors, are often referred to as **cutaneous receptors** because they are associated with the skin. They are unevenly distributed over the body, with some areas (lips, fingers) having high concentrations and other areas (buttocks) having far less.

TACTILE RECEPTORS ARE FREE OR ENCAPSULATED DENDRITES

The tactile receptors are at least six in number and may be either free or encapsulated nerve dendrites. Some of the tactile receptors are located in the skin or just beneath the skin and include free nerve endings, Meissner's corpuscles, Merkel's discs, root hair plexuses, and Krause's end-bulbs. Others may also be located within deeper tissues, such as Ruffini's end-organs and Pacinian corpuscles (Fig. 17-4).

Free nerve endings

The **free nerve endings** are simple and superficial receptors. They are found throughout the skin and other tissues. The cornea of the eye contains no other type of nerve ending. These receptors detect touch, pressure, and pain. Some recent physiological research has reported the existence of free nerve endings that are very sensitive to tickle and itch. These receptors are mainly located in the superficial layers of the skin and when activated usually activate the scratch reflex.

Meissner's corpuscles

The **Meissner's corpuscles** (**mice**-nerz) are fine-touch receptors. They are encapsulated nerve endings associated with the nonhairy areas of the skin. They are found in high concentrations in the lips, fingertips, and other areas of the body having high two-point discrimination sensitivity. A *two-point discrimination,* detected by using a two-point touch threshold test, is the ability to detect that two points of an area are being simultaneously touched instead of one (Fig. 17-5). Different areas of the body have higher two-point discriminations than others. The tongue is able to detect two points separated by only 1.5 millimeters. Other areas with very high two-point discriminations are the lips, fingertips, palms, toes, nipples, glans penis, and clitoris. See Table 17-3 for a comparison of some two-point thresholds of the various parts of the body. Meissner's corpuscles are phasic in their adaptation. Their adaptation occurs within a fraction of a second.

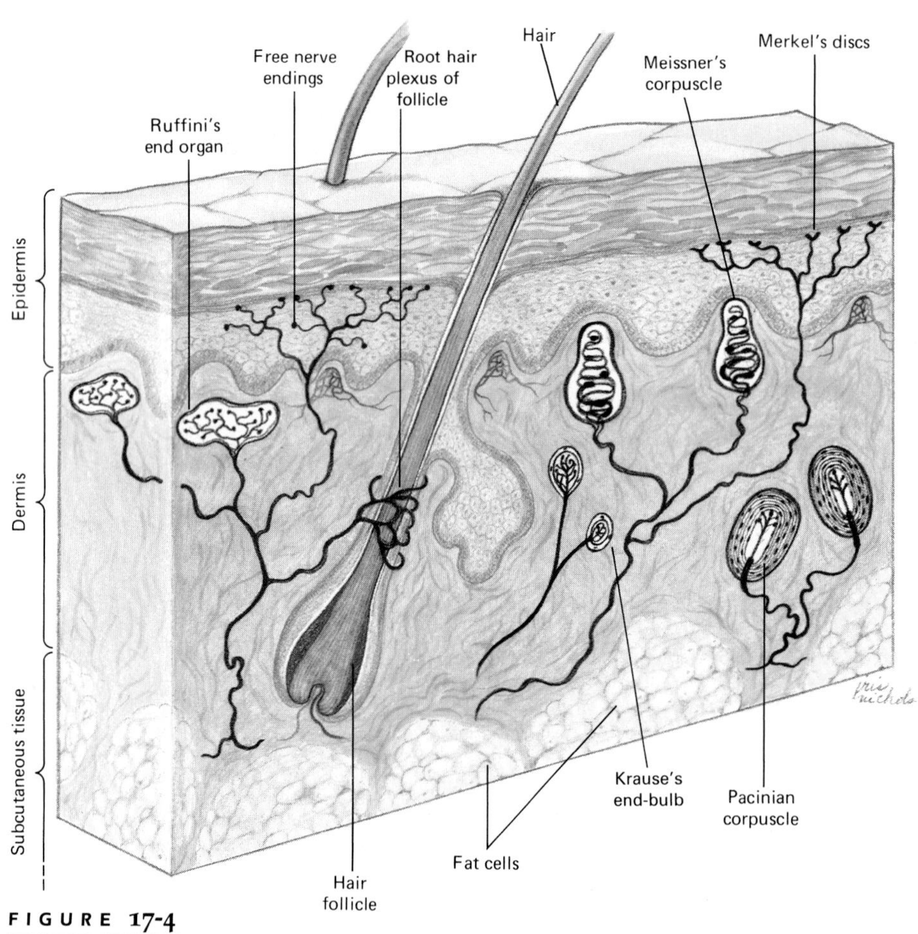

FIGURE 17-4

Cutaneous receptors.

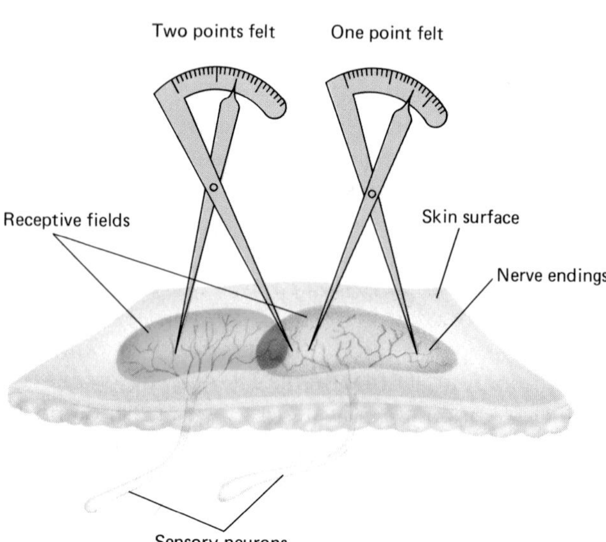

FIGURE 17-5

Two-point touch threshold test. When only one receptive field is stimulated, only one point is felt. When each point touches a different receptive field, then two points are felt.

TABLE 17-3

The two-point touch threshold for different regions of the body

Body region	Two-point touch threshold (mm)
First finger	2
Thumb	3
Big toe	10
Palm of hand	13
Forehead	18
Sole of foot	22
Abdomen	36
Back	42
Thigh	46
Upper arm	47
Calf	48

Source: From Weinstein, S. and D. R. Kenshalo (editors), The Skin Senses, 1968. (Courtesy of Charles C. Thomas, Publisher, Springfield, Illinois.)

Merkel's discs

Merkel's discs (**Mer**-kelz) are actually one type of an expanded-tip tactile receptor, having disc-shaped dendritic extensions. They detect light touch and pressure. They are also highly concentrated in nonhairy areas such as the lips and the fingertips. The Merkel's discs are tonic in adaptation and they provide a steady-state awareness of pressure against the skin.

Root hair plexuses

Dendrites of specialized free nerve endings coil around the follicles of hairs. As the hairs move, they stimulate these dendrites. The **root hair plexuses** are fine-touch receptors responding to slight movements of the hairs of the body. These receptors are phasic in their adaptation and therefore function in the detection of movement and initial contact of an object with the body.

Ruffini's end-organs

Ruffini's end-organs (roo-**fe**-neez), crude- (blunt-) touch and pressure receptors, are encapsulated nerve endings. These are found in the deep layers of the skin and in deep tissues. They are also located in joint capsules and function in the detection of joint motion. These receptors are tonic adaptors providing sensory input from heavy pressure and joint angulations.

Krause's end-bulbs

Krause's end-bulbs are also thought to be mechanoreceptors, possibly modified Meissner's corpuscles. They are located closer to the periphery than Ruffini's end-organs. They are most concentrated in the dermis, lips, mouth, and conjunctiva of the eye. Historically, both Ruffini's end-organs and Krause's end-bulbs have been considered to be thermoreceptors; Ruffini's end-organs as warmth receptors and Krause's end-bulbs as cold receptors. However, current investigators suggest that Ruffini's end-organs and Krause's end-bulbs are actually mechanoreceptors. Thermoreceptors are thought to be free nerve endings.

Pacinian corpuscles

The **Pacinian corpuscles** are large, encapsulated, onion-shaped receptors. They consist of a dendrite surrounded by concentric layers of connective tissue. Pacinian corpuscles respond to heavy pressure and vibrations. The pacinian corpuscles are located deep within the skin and in deeper tissues including fascia in the body. They are abundant near the joints and skeletal muscles, the palms and soles, the external genitalia, the breasts, and the GI tract. They tend to be phasic adaptors responding to rapid movements and vibrations.

PROPRIOCEPTORS GIVE RISE TO THE KINESTHETIC SENSE

Proprioceptors are mechanoreceptors located within skeletal muscles, tendons, joints, and the inner ear. Proprioceptors send sensory information to the brain allowing us to know the location of one body part in relation to another, the degree of joint flexibility, the degree of muscle contraction and tendon stress, and head and body position in movement. This provides us with a conscious awareness of body position and movement known as the **kinesthetic sense** (*kin*-es-**thet**-ik).

The kinesthetic sense has a predictive nature in that as the brain receives input from the proprioceptors, it can predict the position of the body part in the next few seconds and correct other structures in order to maintain balance. Much of the sensory input from the proprioceptors is unconscious and functions in maintaining muscle coordination. The three major types of proprioceptors found associated with skeletal muscle, tendons, and joints are: the *muscle spindle,* the *Golgi tendon organ,* and the *joint kinesthetic receptor.*

Muscle spindles

Muscle spindles are located within skeletal muscle, running parallel to the skeletal muscle fibers (Fig. 17-6). Muscle spindles are made up of several modified muscle fibers, the **intrafusal fibers,** that are surrounded by a connective tissue sheath. At the center of the muscle fibers, the cell is nonstriated and has a concentration of nuclei. The nuclei can exist within a central bunch (nuclear bag fibers) or as a central chain (nuclear chain fibers). The intrafusal fibers are centrally innervated by type Ia nerve fibers. The branches of the type Ia fibers, the primary fibers, end as *annulospiral endings*. Branches of type II fibers are called secondary fibers and their endings are referred to as *flower spray endings*. The skeletal muscle fibers surrounding the muscle spindles are referred to as **extrafusal fibers.**

As a muscle stretches, the muscle spindles are also stretched and stimulate the sensory neurons which send action potentials to the spinal cord. The frequency of the action potentials increases with increased stretching. From the spinal cord, the sensory input is conveyed to the brain which is kept informed about muscle length and tension. Motor stimulation is also reflexly activated in the spinal cord, causing the same muscle to contract, shorten, and bring muscle tension back to normal. This is the **stretch reflex.**

↑ Muscle stretching ⟶ ↑ muscle spindle stimulation ⟶ ↑ sensory neuron input ⟶ spinal cord integration ⟶ ↑ motor neuron output ⟶ ↑ muscle contraction ⟶ ↓ muscle stretching

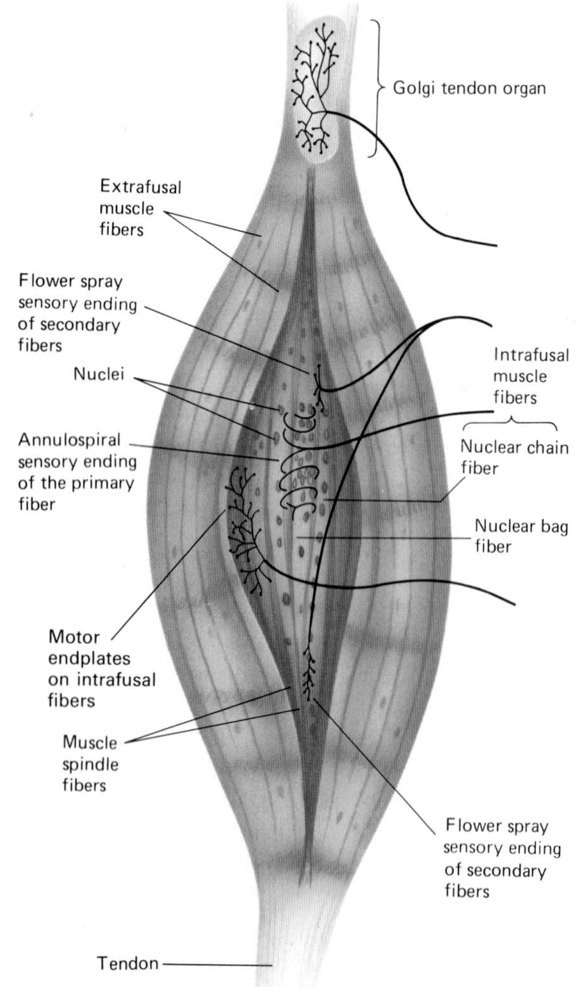

FIGURE 17-6

Proprioceptors. Muscle spindle (showing intrafusal muscle fibers and innervations) and Golgi tendon organ.

Golgi tendon organs

The **Golgi tendon organs** are located in the tendons near the muscle insertion (Fig. 17-6). The Golgi tendon organ consists of tendon fibers surrounded by dendrites of sensory neurons. These fibers and dendrites are encapsulated by connective tissue. When the tendons become stretched, the Golgi tendon organs are stimulated and send sensory information to the central nervous system. The CNS reflexly responds by motor output to the muscle, inhibiting contraction. This reduces the tension of the tendon and protects against overextension and damage to the tendon and muscle. Besides affording protection to the tendon and muscle, the Golgi tendon organs are important in maintaining posture.

↑ Muscle and tendon tension ⟶ ↑ Golgi tendon organ stimulation ⟶ ↑ sensory input ⟶ spinal cord integration ⟶ ↓ motor output ⟶ ↓ muscle contraction ⟶ ↓ muscle and tendon tension

Joint kinesthetic receptors

The **joint kinesthetic receptors** are encapsulated receptors of several types. Those resembling Ruffini's end-organs are located in the joint capsules and respond to pressure. Small Pacinian corpuscles surrounding the capsules react to acceleration and deceleration. Other receptors in ligaments act like Golgi tendon organs and inhibit muscle contraction when the joint is strained.

Thermoreceptors are sensitive to temperature changes

The **thermoreceptors,** believed to be naked nerve endings, are sensitive to changes in temperature. They are widely distributed throughout the body and are particularly concentrated in the areas of the lips, mouth, and anus. Most areas of the body contain three to ten times the number of cold receptors than warmth receptors. People are able to perceive variations in temperature extending from freezing cold to burning hot. The extremes (below 10°C and above 45°C) involve pain receptors. Cold, cool, neutral, warm, and hot involve the thermoreceptors. Cold receptors are most active between 10°C and 20°C. The warmth receptors are most active between 25°C and 45°C. See Figure 17-7. Thermoreceptors adapt quickly to changes in temperatures and also respond to steady thermal states.

Nociceptors are pain receptors

The sensation of pain is a protective mechanism that makes the brain aware of tissue injury and damage. (Refer to Chapter 15.) Typical pain receptors are the dendrites of free nerve endings. **Nociceptors,** or **pain receptors,** are located in most tissues of the body and are nonspecific in that they respond to many different types of stimuli. These receptors are very sensitive to chemicals released by distressed cells and by the excessive stimulation of other types of receptors. For instance, temperatures up to 45°C stimulate warmth receptors, but beyond this temperature pain receptors are stimulated to give the sensation of burning (Fig. 17-7). Nociceptors are tonic and adapt very slowly if at all. This is important in that the perception of pain urges the person to stop the activity causing pain or to seek medical intervention to prevent serious tissue damage.

Pain is usually classified by its origins: somatic or visceral. **Somatic pain** originates from the skin (superficial somatic pain) or from the muscles, tendons, joints, and fascia (deep somatic pain). **Visceral pain** has its origins in the visceral organs of the body.

As discussed in Chapter 15, visceral pain may be perceived as coming from an area superficial to the actual pain site or even a superficial area distant from the site of pain. This sensation of pain is called referred pain. The point of the body to which the pain is referred and the actual site of the pain have nerve supplies from similar areas of the spinal cord. Common areas of referred pain are demonstrated in Figure 17-8.

The special senses are localized to one or a few areas of the body

The special senses function in smell, taste, vision, hearing, and equilibrium.

The receptors for smell (olfaction) are located in the nasal cavity

The chemoreceptors for the sense of olfaction are called **olfactory cells.** They are actually bipolar neurons. There are about 100 million of these olfactory cells in the **olfactory membrane.** The olfactory membrane is a modified section of the nasal mucous membrane. It is located in the superior part of the nasal cavity near its association with the cribriform plate of the ethmoid bone (Fig. 17-9*a*).

The end of the olfactory cell adjacent to the nasal cavity is the dendritic end. Each olfactory cell dendrite terminates in a swelling called the **olfactory vesicle** which contains several cilia. These cilia are called **olfactory hairs.** The other end of the olfactory cell is its axon. Associated with the olfactory cells are **olfactory (Bowman's) glands, supporting (sustentacular) cells,** and

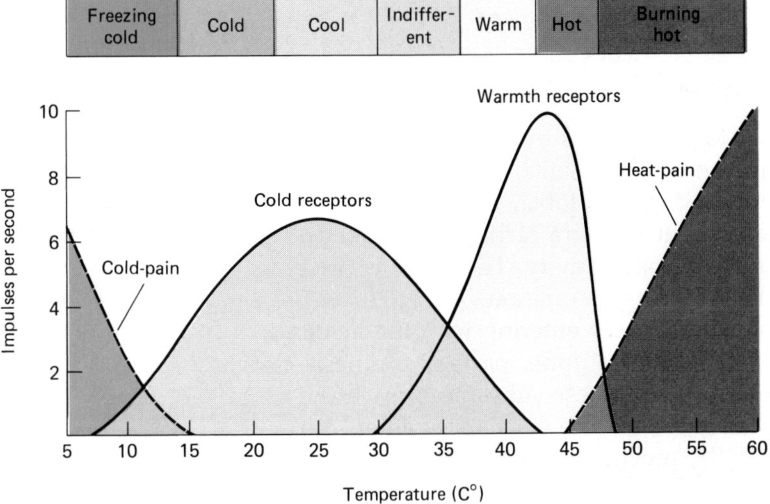

FIGURE 17-7

Temperature ranges for cold receptors, warmth receptors, and pain receptors. (The responses of these fibers are drawn from original data collected in separate experiments by Zotterman, Hensel, and Kenshalo.)

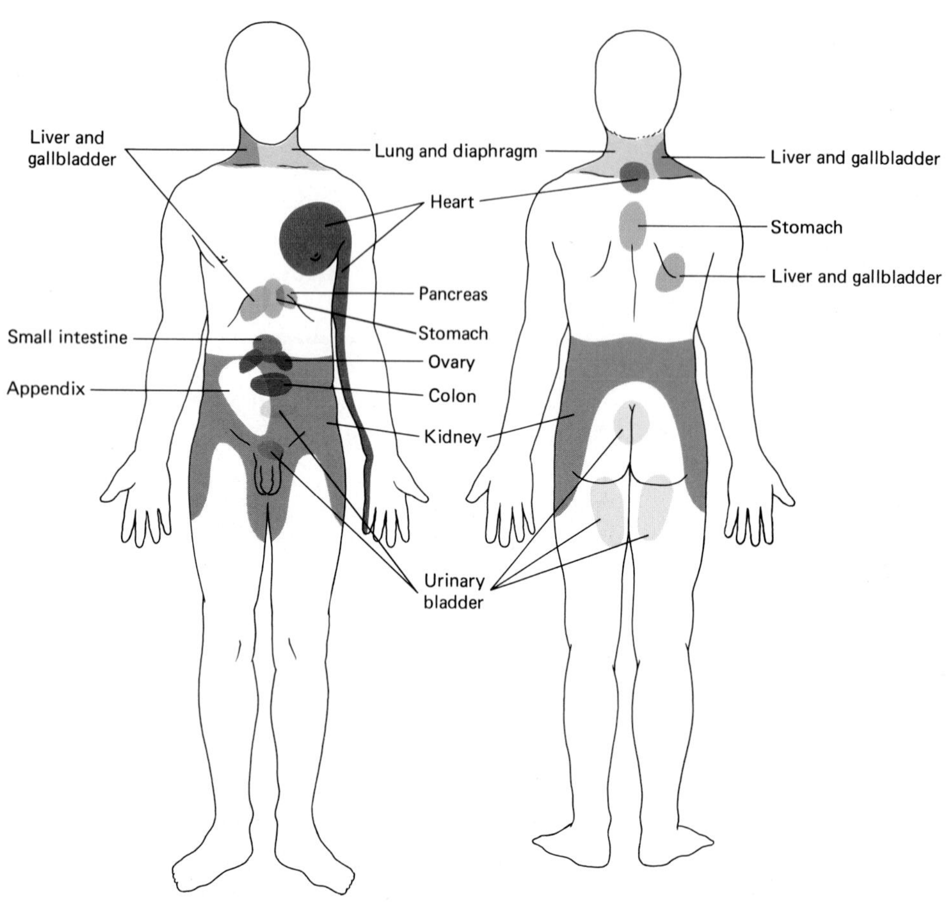

FIGURE 17-8

Referred pain areas of the body. The colored areas depict cutaneous areas to which visceral pain is referred.

basal cells (Fig. 17-9*b,c*). The olfactory glands secrete mucus that keeps the olfactory membrane moist, serving to dissolve many odoriferous substances. The mucus is constantly replaced, allowing for the sensation of new odors.

OLFACTION INVOLVES CHEMORECEPTION

In order to be detected by the olfactory cells, a substance must be volatile, somewhat dissolvable in water, and lipid-soluble. Odors can be distinguished only if they are carried by the air and enter into the nasal cavity. The sense of smell is more keen during inspiration.

Some substances entering with the inspired air do not reach the upper parts of the nasal cavity. Sniffing helps these substances reach the olfactory membrane. The substances enter into solution in the mucus in order to come in contact with the olfactory hairs. They must also be lipid-soluble because the olfactory hairs are composed primarily of lipid material. The sensitivity of the olfactory hairs is very great and very small amounts of substances can be detected.

When chemicals contact the olfactory hairs, they combine with specific protein receptors of the membrane of the olfactory hair. This union causes a change in the permeability of the olfactory hair membrane, causing a depolarization. A generator potential develops that initiates nerve action potentials along the axon of the olfactory cell.

Odoriferous substance in upper nasal cavity ⟶ combination with receptor protein on olfactory hair ⟶ depolarization ⟶ generator potential of olfactory cell ⟶ action potential in olfactory axon

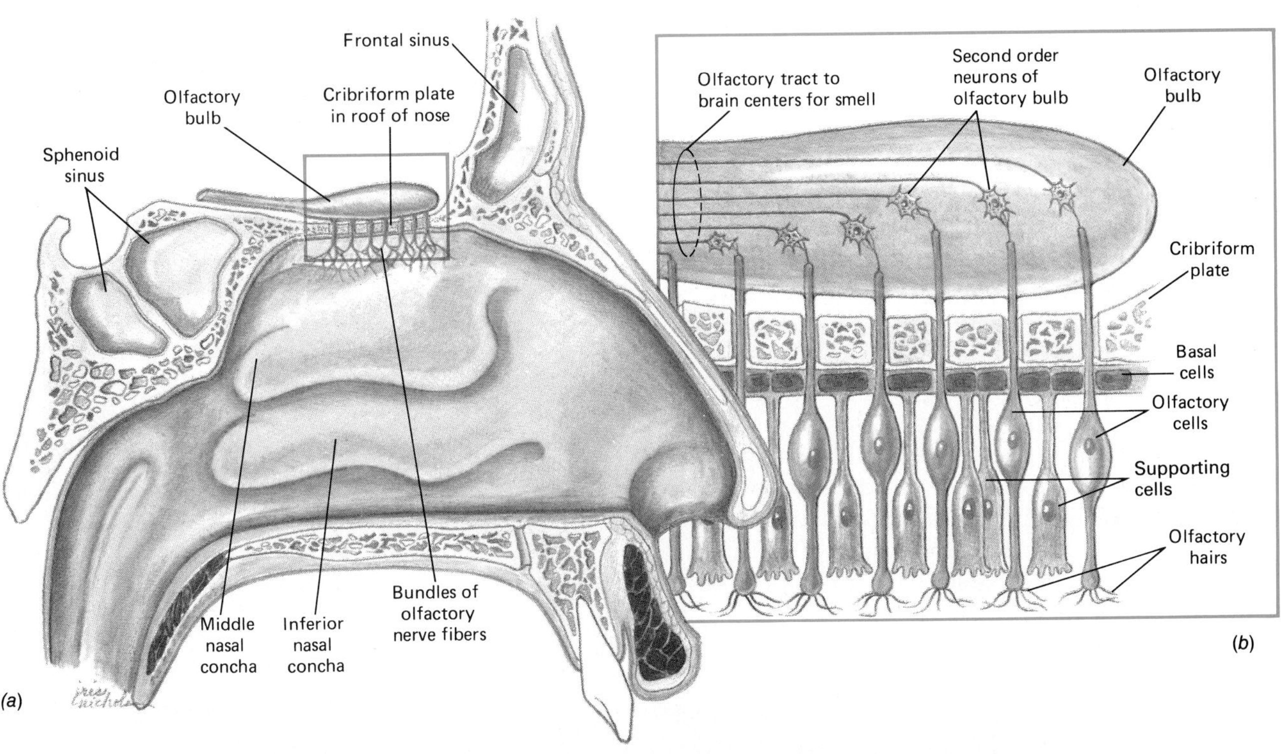

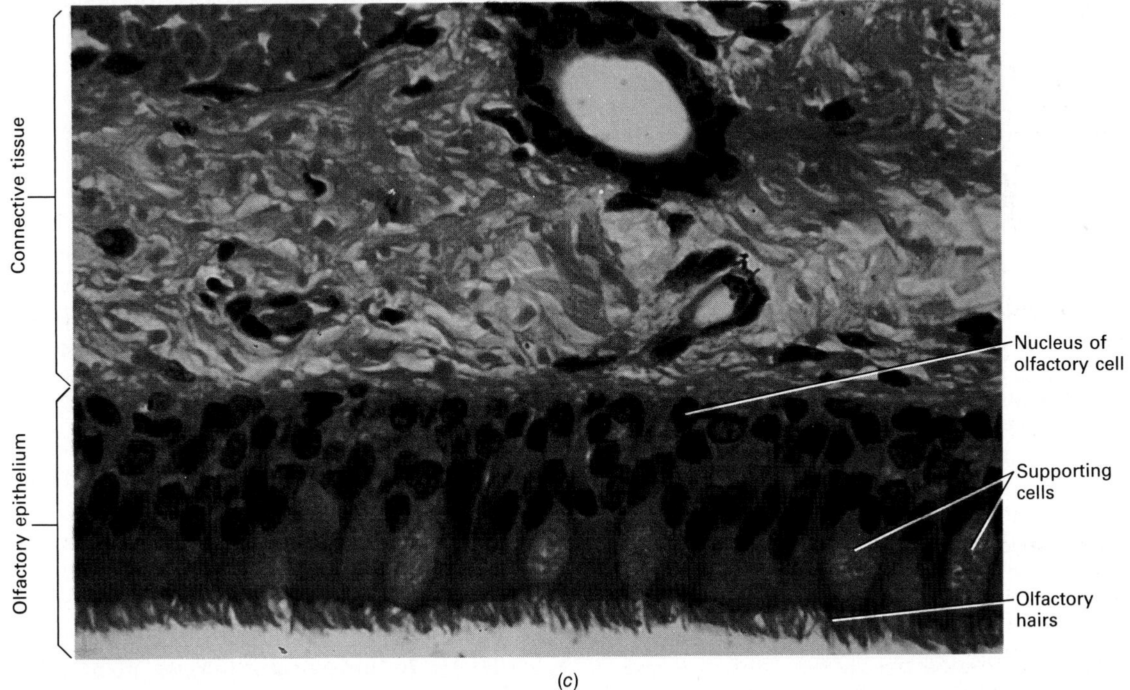

FIGURE 17-9

Olfactory receptors. (*a*) Location of olfactory receptors in nasal cavity. (*b*) Magnification of olfactory receptors. (*c*) Photomicrograph of olfactory receptors (×300).

THE STEREOCHEMICAL THEORY OF OLFACTION EXPLAINS DISCRIMINATION OF THOUSANDS OF ODORS

There may exist as many as 50 specific protein receptors on the olfactory hairs. Each of these receptors of the olfactory hairs reacts with a particular type of substance based on its chemical configuration. Furthermore, the specific receptors are believed to react optimally with a particular substance but also to be stimulated to a lesser extent by a wide variety of substances. The greater the number of receptors reacting with a particular type of substance, the greater will be the generator potential. It is believed that different olfactory hairs contain differing types and amounts of receptors. This **stereochemical theory of olfaction** provides a system capable of discriminating between thousands of different odors.

There has been much research done on the classification of primary olfactory sensations. One attempt identifies seven primary classes of odors: *camphoraceous, musky, floral, pepperminty, ethereal, pungent,* and *putrid*. However, recent investigations suggest there may be more than 50 primary smells.

Olfactory cells have very low thresholds. Hence, only trace amounts of a substance need to be present to be detected. Each olfactory receptor can adapt about 50% in the first second after detection of a stimulus. The adaptation of the olfactory cells is not fast enough, however, to account for the complete insensitivity to some smells after only one minute of exposure to them. One possible explanation for the quick adaptation to smell is through an inhibitory effect of the central nervous system on the olfactory bulbs. After stimulation by a particular odor, the central nervous system may send inhibitory impulses to the olfactory bulbs to block transmission of impulses back to the brain.

Clinical highlight

Zinc deficiency causes a loss of sensitivity to the chemical senses. It is known that zinc is a growth factor for taste buds and probably has a similar role for the olfactory cells. **Anosmias** (an-**oz**-me-uz), olfactory disorders occurring due to an absence of the sense of smell, are caused mainly by a zinc deficiency but other common causes include head injuries, nasal cavity inflammation, and aging.

The generator potentials of the olfactory cells are transformed into nerve impulses of the olfactory axons. The olfactory axons merge to form the **olfactory nerves (CN I).** The olfactory nerves pass through the pores of the cribriform plate and terminate in the **olfactory bulbs** (Fig. 17-9*b*). The olfactory bulbs are located at the inferior surface of the frontal lobes of the cerebrum.

The synapses at the olfactory bulbs include the axons of the olfactory nerves and dendrites of neurons of the olfactory bulbs. The axons of these neurons become the **olfactory tracts** which course posteriorly to the primary olfactory areas of the cerebral cortex. Olfaction is the only sense that is conducted directly to the brain without synapsing first in the thalamus. Once in the cerebral cortex, the impulses are integrated and interpreted as the sense of smell.

Olfactory cells ⟶ olfactory nerves ⟶ olfactory bulbs ⟶ olfactory tracts ⟶ cerebral cortex

Taste (gustation) receptors are located within the taste buds

The sense of taste is located in the taste buds, which are located primarily within the papillae (small elevations) of the dorsum of the tongue. Some taste buds are also located on the roof of the mouth and the pharynx. Adults have about 10,000 taste buds. Children have more.

The **taste buds** contain about 40 modified epithelial cells. Some of these cells are the **gustatory (taste) cells,** and others are supporting cells and basal cells. The gustatory cells (**gus**-ta-*toe*-re) have a possible lifespan of up to ten days and are constantly being replaced by new sensory cells derived from the division of the basal cells. The outer tips of the gustatory cells are arranged around a small **taste pore.** Each taste cell has several **gustatory hairs** extending into the taste pore. It is postulated that special receptors are located on the gustatory hairs that serve in the reception for taste. Intimately associated with the gustatory cells are networks of taste nerve fibers. See Figure 17-10*a*,*b*.

The taste buds of the tongue are located on three of the four types of **papillae** (pa-**pil**-ee). Roughly half of the taste buds are found associated with the *circumvallate papillae* (*ser*-kum-**val**-ate) of the posterior of the tongue (Fig. 17-10*c*). Other taste buds are on the *fungiform* (**fun**-ji-form) *papillae* located on the front two-thirds of the tongue. A moderate number of taste buds are located on the *foliate papillae* of the lateral surfaces of the tongue. The *filiform papillae* do not ordinarily contain taste buds.

SWEET, SALTY, SOUR, AND BITTER ARE THE PRIMARY TASTE SENSATIONS

There are four primary sensations of taste: *sweet, salty, sour,* and *bitter* (Fig. 17-10c). Each of these primary taste sensations is the result of a different sensitivity and response to various chemical groups by gustatory cells at different areas of the tongue. According to the **stereochemical theory of gustation,** each cell is believed to be sensitive to the four primary taste sensations and also to show a specificity to one or two of them. This gives each cell a taste profile demonstrating response patterns to the primary senses. Sweet and salty tastes are detected primarily at the tip of the tongue. Sour is detected mainly at the sides of

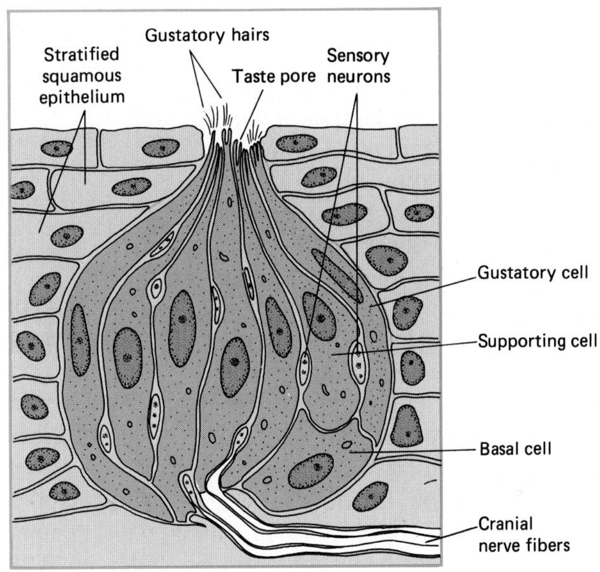

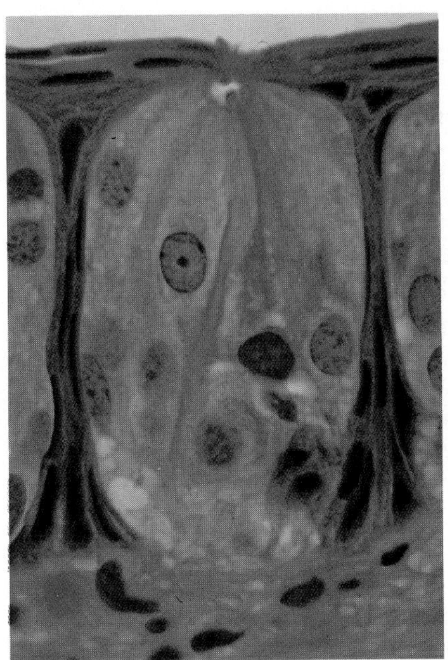

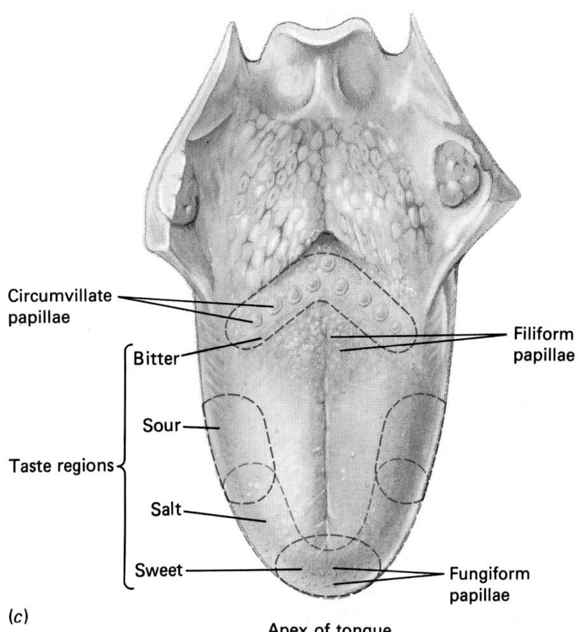

FIGURE 17-10

Taste buds and taste zones. (*a*) Structure of a taste bud. (*b*) Photomicrograph of a taste bud. (*c*) Location of taste zones on the tongue.

the tongue, bitter taste at the circumvallate papillae of the posterior tongue.

A sour taste usually results from sensing acids, with the intensity of the taste proportional to the H^+ ion concentration. A salty taste is detected from the sensing of ionized salts. Sweetness is caused by several groups of chemcials including sugars, aldehydes, alcohols, glycols, ketones, esters, and amino acids. A bitter taste is usually detected by sensing long-chain organic compounds containing nitrogen and to sensing alkaloids.

In order to be detected by the gustatory cells, substances must be dissolved in the saliva of the oral cavity. The substance combines with a receptor of the gustatory hair, changing the permeability of its membrane and causing a depolarization. This depolarization gives rise to a generator potential. The magnitude of the generator potential is proportional to the concentration of the stimulating substance. Saliva is important in removing substances from the vicinity of the gustatory hairs, allowing the generation of new taste sensations.

Taste adaptation occurs quickly. Sometimes a person is unable to taste the same substance within a minute of continuous stimulation. The central nervous system has been postulated as the site of progressive adaptation to taste. Higher brain centers are also responsible for determining taste preference. This explains why previous experience plays an important role in the selection of certain foods.

The sensory neurons affiliated with the gustatory cells initiate action potentials in response to the generator potentials. These sensory impulses travel within three cranial nerves to the medulla. The **facial nerve** (CN VII) carries taste impulses from the anterior two-thirds of the tongue. The **glossopharyngeal nerve** (CN IX) takes the impulses from the posterior third of the tongue. The **vagus nerve** (CN X) carries afferent taste fibers originating in the pharynx. From the medulla, the impulses pass through the thalamus and terminate at the lower tip of the postcentral gyrus of the parietal cortex.

TASTE SENSATIONS ALSO INVOLVE OTHER RECEPTORS

Although the sense of taste is due mainly to the stimulation of the gustatory cells, other receptors may play a role in modifying the total taste sensation. Tactile receptors, thermoreceptors, and pain receptors in the mouth provide input as to the texture, temperature, and irritation of certain foods.

Olfaction is also very important in taste perception. Both taste and smell are detected by chemoreceptors and they tend to complement one another. A severe cold may completely mask the taste of many foods due to mucous membrane inflammation and increased mucus blockage of receptor sites. Food odors can stimulate the olfactory cells thousands of times more strongly than their chemical action on gustatory cells. In fact, about 80% of what we perceive as taste is actually smell!

Clinical highlight

Nerve damage to the sensory nerves carrying information on taste can alter taste. For example, damage to the glossopharyngeal nerves (CN IX) decreases the ability to detect a bitter taste. The glossopharyngeal nerves carry sensory input from the posterior third of the tongue where most bitter detection lies.

The anatomy of the eyes includes many structures

The eyes are complex sense organs that are supported externally by several structures. Internally, the eyes contain many parts, all working together to process sensory information for vision.

ACCESSORY STRUCTURES PROTECT AND SUPPORT THE EYES

The eyes are protected and supported by a number of accessory structures including the orbital cavities, eyebrows, eyelids, eyelashes, conjunctiva, lacrimal apparatus, and the extrinsic muscles of the eye (Fig. 17-11*a*,*b*).

Orbital cavities

The eyes are located within the eye **orbits.** The orbital cavities of the eyes are made up of sections of seven bones: frontal, sphenoid, ethmoid, lacrimal, zygomatic, maxilla, and palatine (see Chapter 7). These bones of the orbits support and protect the eyes.

Eyebrows

The **eyebrows** are located superior to the eyes and superficial to the superciliary ridges of the frontal bones. They contain coarse, short hairs running transversely and they also contain sebaceous glands that secrete oil. The eyebrows protect the eyes by shading them and by stopping perspiration and objects from contacting them from above.

Eyelids and eyelashes

The **eyelids,** or **palpebrae** (**pal**-peh-bree), extend from the superior and inferior edges of the orbits. The space between the upper and lower eyelids is the **palpebral fissure.** The eyelids meet at the medial and lateral angles of the orbit called the **canthi.** The medial canthus contains a reddish elevation called the **caruncle** (**kar**-ung-kul) which is the remnant of a third eyelid. The caruncle possesses sebaceous and sudoriferous (sweat) glands that secrete a white substance that sometimes accumulates at the medial canthus.

Each eyelid consists of a fold of skin with layers of connective tissue, a tarsal plate, tarsal glands, skeletal muscle, and part of the conjunc-

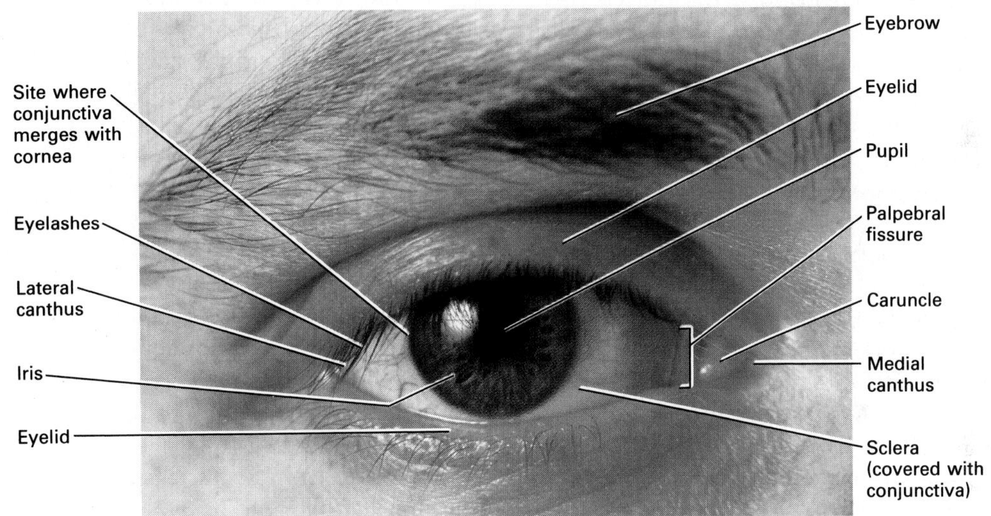

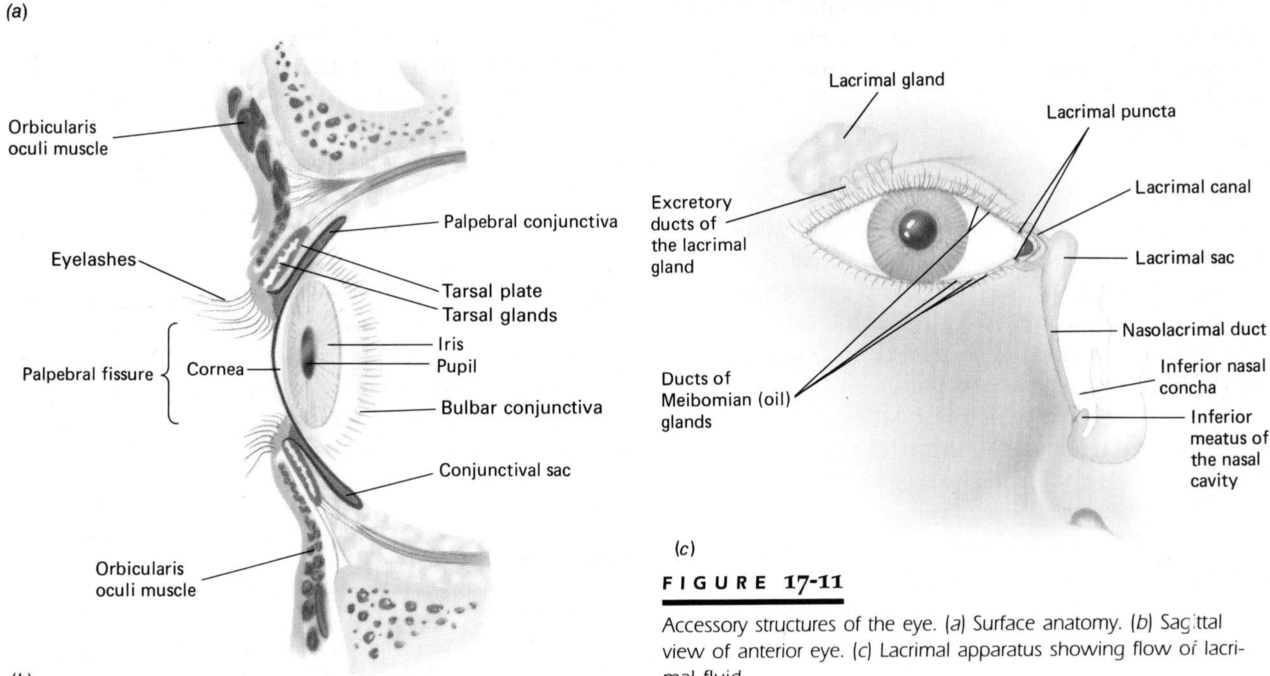

FIGURE 17-11

Accessory structures of the eye. (*a*) Surface anatomy. (*b*) Sagittal view of anterior eye. (*c*) Lacrimal apparatus showing flow of lacrimal fluid.

tiva. The **tarsal plate** is made up of tough connective tissue sheets and provides the structural support of the eyelid. It supports modified sebaceous glands called **tarsal,** or **meibomian glands** (my-**bow**-me-an). The ducts of the tarsal glands open onto the edges of the eyelids. The oil that is secreted by the tarsal glands helps to keep the cornea moist and lubricates the eyelids, keeping them from sticking together. An infection of the tarsal glands results in the formation of a cyst on the eyelid called a *chalazion* (kuh-**lay**-zee-un). Large sebaceous glands called **ciliary glands,** or **glands of Zeis,** are associated with the follicles of the eyelashes near the edges of the eyelids. Between the follicles are modified sweat glands. A *sty* is an infection of a ciliary gland.

The tarsal plate also supports the muscles associated with the eyelid. The **orbicularis oculi** muscle encircles the eye and its contraction closes the eyelid. The upper eyelid contains the **levator palpebrae superioris** muscle, which contracts to raise the upper eyelid and accounts for the upper eyelid being more mobile than the lower one. A reflex blinking of the eyelids occurs every 3 to 7 seconds. This functions to prevent the desiccation (drying out) of the exposed eye by spreading secretions over it and to keep this area free of dust and other foreign materials.

The **eyelashes** form a row of curved short hairs projecting from the free borders of the eyelids. The eyelashes of the upper eyelid are longer than those of the lower eyelid. The eyelashes protect the eyes from airborne objects. They are innervated by nerve endings called *root hair plexuses,* which are stimulated by anything touching the eyelashes and which cause a reflex blinking to occur.

Conjunctiva

The **conjunctiva** (*kon*-junk-**tie**-vuh) is a mucous membrane covering the inner surface of each eyelid and the anterior surface of the eye. Mucus secreted by the conjunctiva helps to keep the eye lubricated and moist. The part of the conjunctiva lining the inner surface of the eyelids is the **palpebral conjunctiva** which is relatively thick. The thinner **bulbar (ocular) conjunctiva** lines the anterior surface of the eye. The angles formed at the junctions of the palpebral and bulbar conjunctiva form the **superior** and **inferior conjunctival sacs.** These conjunctival sacs protect the eye by preventing objects from entering the deep unexposed areas of the external eye. Medication to the eye is often administered to the conjunctival sacs.

Clinical highlight

Conjunctivitis is an inflammation of the conjunctiva resulting in reddened eyes. **Pinkeye** is a highly contagious form of conjunctivitis caused by bacteria and viruses. If the conjunctiva becomes dry and scaly, it may be indicative of vitamin A deficiency. Vitamin A deficiency causes a marked decrease in mucus secretion.

Lacrimal apparatus

The **lacrimal apparatus** is made up of the lacrimal glands, lacrimal ducts, lacrimal canals, lacrimal sacs, and nasolacrimal ducts (Fig. 17-11*c*). The **lacrimal glands** are located at the superior lateral part of the orbital cavities. The lacrimal glands are compound tubuloacinar glands that secrete a dilute saline solution called **lacrimal secretion,** or **tears.** The tears are carried through a series of 6 to 12 excretory **lacrimal ducts** to the palpebral conjunctiva of the upper eyelid.

The tears contain mucus, antibodies, and lysozyme. Tear secretion averages about 1 milliliter per day. The mucus helps to lubricate and keep the exposed surface of the eye moist and clean. The reflex blinking of the eyelids spreads the tears over the eye and helps to maintain a moist film over it. The antibodies and lysozyme protect the eye from bacterial infection.

Much of the tears secreted evaporate. Excess tears accumulate at the medial canthus and are continually drained from the eye through two small pores, the **puncta lacrimalia,** located in the lacrimal papilla of each eyelid. The puncta lacrimalia open into the two **lacrimal canals** which take the tears into a **lacrimal sac.** The lacrimal sac fills the lacrimal fossa of the lacrimal bone. From the lacrimal sac, the tears pass into the **nasolacrimal duct,** which empties into the nasal cavity at the inferior meatus.

Excess tears ⟶ medial canthus ⟶ puncta lacrimalia ⟶ lacrimal canals ⟶ lacrimal sac ⟶ nasolacrimal duct ⟶ nasal cavity

Clinical highlight

Tear secretion increases when irritants or foreign objects make contact with the eye. Emotional states can also stimulate parasympathetic stimulation of the lacrimal glands and increase secretion. This is what happens during crying. The excess tears drain into the nasal cavity, explaining why a person who cries also experiences sniffles. Also, when the intranasal openings of the nasolacrimal ducts are blocked, as experienced during a cold or allergic reaction, the tears accumulate at the medial canthus and the eyes water.

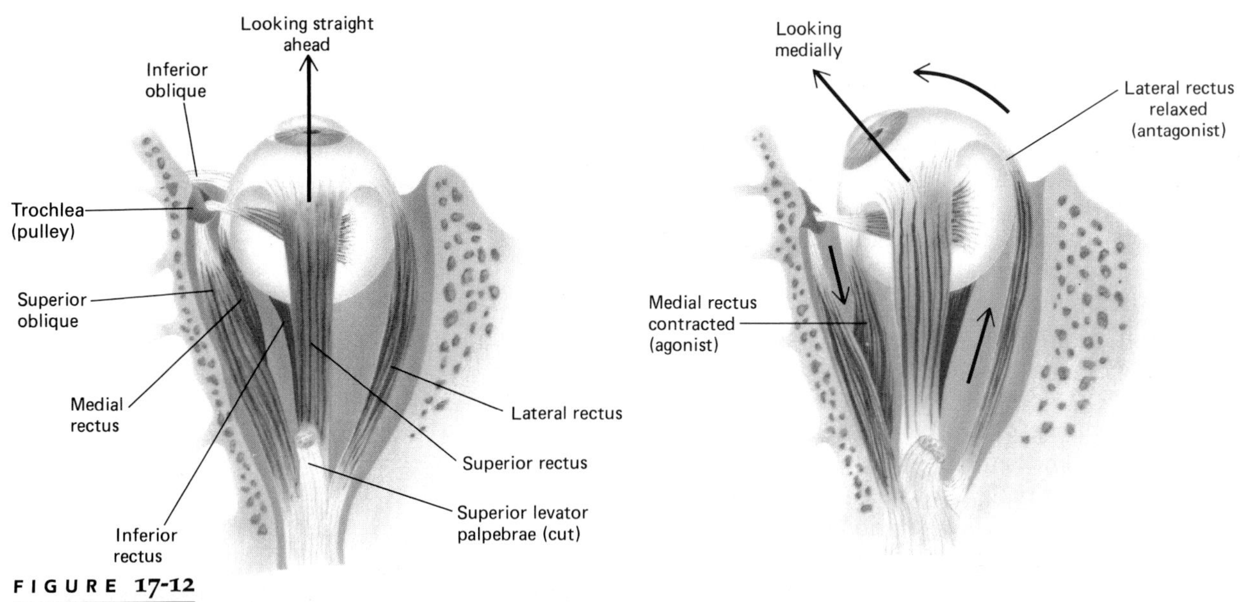

FIGURE 17-12

Superior views of the right eye. Contraction of the medial rectus muscle moves the eyeball in the direction of the nose. If the medial rectus were to relax and its antagonist, the lateral rectus, to contract, the eye would look in a lateral direction.

Extrinsic muscles

The **extrinsic muscles** of the eye are those muscles that originate from outside the eye and function in eye support and movement. These muscles also allow us to fix a gaze on stationary or moving objects and coordinate both eye movements so that they function together. They are probably the most precisely controlled of all the skeletal muscles. The extrinsic eye muscles act very rapidly and their motor units are very small, containing only 8 to 12 muscle fibers. They also have numerous muscle spindles.

There are six extrinsic eye muscles: superior rectus, inferior rectus, lateral rectus, medial rectus, superior oblique, and inferior oblique (Fig. 17-12 and Table 17-4). The rectus muscles all originate from a fibrotendinous ring, the annular ring, of the posterior orbit. Their insertions are directly on the fibrous coat of the eye surface. The **superior rectus** muscle rolls the eye upward and it is controlled by the oculomotor nerve (CN III). The **inferior rectus** rolls the eye downward. It is controlled by the oculomotor nerve (CN III). The **lateral rectus** moves the eye to the lateral

TABLE 17-4

The extrinsic muscles of the eye

Extrinsic eye muscle	Cranial nerve Innervation	Action on eye
Superior rectus	Oculomotor (CN III)	Elevates and rolls eye upward
Inferior rectus	Oculomotor (CN III)	Depresses and rolls eye downward
Medial rectus	Oculomotor (CN III)	Moves eye medially
Lateral rectus	Abducens (CN VI)	Moves eye laterally
Superior oblique	Trochlear (CN IV)	Depresses and moves eye laterally (this action is made possible only by the trochlea)
Inferior oblique	Oculomotor (CN III)	Elevates and moves eye laterally

side and is controlled by the abducens nerve (CN VI). The **medial rectus,** which is controlled by the oculomotor nerve (CN III), moves the eye to the medial side.

The **superior oblique** muscle also originates at the annular ring and proceeds along the medial surface of the orbit. Its tendon passes through a cartilaginous loop called the *trochlea.* The trochlea acts as a pulley. Upon leaving the trochlea, the tendon makes a right-angle turn and inserts on the superior surface of the eye (Fig. 17-12). When the superior oblique muscle contracts, the eye rolls downward and laterally. It is controlled by the trochlear nerve (CN IV). The **inferior oblique** muscle has its origin at the anterior and medial aspect of the orbit, from which it runs laterally and diagonally to its insertion on the inferior surface of the eye. Contraction of the inferior oblique muscle rotates the eye upward and laterally. The inferior oblique is controlled by the oculomotor nerve (CN III).

THE EYE CONTAINS THREE LAYERS CALLED TUNICS

The eye is spherical in shape and possesses three layers, or coats: the outer fibrous tunic, the middle vascular tunic, and the inner retinal tunic (Table 17-5).

Fibrous tunic

The **fibrous tunic** is the outer coat of the eyeball. It is made up of an anterior and posterior portion. The anterior portion of the fibrous tunic is the cornea; the posterior portion is the sclera (Fig. 17-13). The **cornea** (**kor**-nee-a) is transparent and has a greater curvature than the sclera. This is important in refracting light and focusing the light in the eye. Its outer surface is covered by an epithelial layer that is continuous with the bulbar conjunctiva. The connective tissue of the cornea is regularly arranged and does not contain a blood supply. Therefore, it does not have the immune mechanisms present elsewhere in the body and is not rejected if transplanted. The cornea does have a rich nerve supply, with most of the nerve endings serving as nociceptors. Stimuli to the cornea reflexly cause blinking and increased secretion by the lacrimal glands.

The **sclera** (**skle**-rah) is made up of dense fibrous connective tissue and forms the posterior five-sixths of the fibrous tunic. It is white in color and opaque. The sclera protects the inner parts of the eye and provides a tough surface on the eyeball for muscle insertion. It serves to maintain the shape of the eye. At its posterior margin, it is continuous with the dura mater of the brain and is pierced by the optic nerve.

Vascular tunic

The **vascular tunic,** or **uvea** (**yoo**-vee-a), is the layer of the eye containing most of the blood vessels supplying the eye. It is made up of three parts: the choroid, the ciliary body, and the iris

TABLE 17-5

Summary of structures of the eye

Structure	Function
Fibrous tunic	
Cornea	Refracts light; important in focusing
Sclera	Maintains shape of eye and protects eye; also serves in muscle attachment
Vascular tunic	
Iris	Controls amount of light transmitted to retina
Ciliary body	Changes shape of lens (accommodation) and secretes aqueous humor
Choroid	Absorbs light, and its blood vessels supply eye tunics
Retina	
Pigmented layer	Absorbs light and stores vitamin A
Nervous layer	Receives light and transduces it to action potentials
Lens	Refracts light; important in accommodation
Anterior cavity	Maintains shape of eye and refracts light through its aqueous humor
Posterior cavity	Maintains shape of eye and refracts light through its vitreous humor
Fluids	
Aqueous humor	Fills anterior cavity, helping to maintain shape of eye; refracts light; maintains intraocular pressure
Vitreous humor	Fills posterior cavity and maintains intraocular pressure, which lends shape to eye and keeps retina firmly pressed against choroid; refracts light

(Fig. 17-13). The **choroid** (**ko**-royd) is highly vascular and pigmented. The blood vessels supply the eye tunics. Its brown pigments serve to absorb light. The anterior part of the choroid becomes the **ciliary body** (**sil**-ee-air-ee). The ciliary body consists of smooth muscle, the **ciliary muscles,** which changes the shape of the lens and thereby helps in focusing. It also contains **ciliary processes,** which produce the **aqueous humor** that fills the anterior cavity of the eye. The ciliary body is attached to the lens by a circular **suspensory ligament** (Fig. 17-14*a*).

The most anterior part of the vascular tunic consists of the **iris,** which is continuous with the ciliary body posteriorly. It is suspended between the cornea and the lens. The iris, which has a flat doughnut structure, contains circular and radial smooth muscle. The center hole of the iris is the **pupil,** through which light passes into the eye. The circular muscles contract in response to bright light and when viewing nearby objects. This makes the pupil constrict. In dim light or when viewing far away objects, the radial muscles of the iris contract and the pupil dilates. These muscles are controlled by autonomic nerves. Sympathetic stimulation causes a contraction of the radial muscles and the pupils dilate. This may be the reaction to an interesting sight or an excited emotional frame of mind. The pupils constrict when the circular muscles contract due to parasympathetic stimulation (Fig. 17-14*b*). This may occur if someone or something is boring to us. If you want to know whether you are appealing to another person, look into their eyes. Are their pupils dilating or constricting? Our eyes may not only be a window to the outside, but a mirror to the inside as well!

The color of the eyes is due to the amount of pigment in the iris. The only pigment of the iris is brown in color. When the concentration of this pigment is high, the eyes appear black or brown in color. When the concentration of the pigment is low, the color of the eyes are green, blue, or gray.

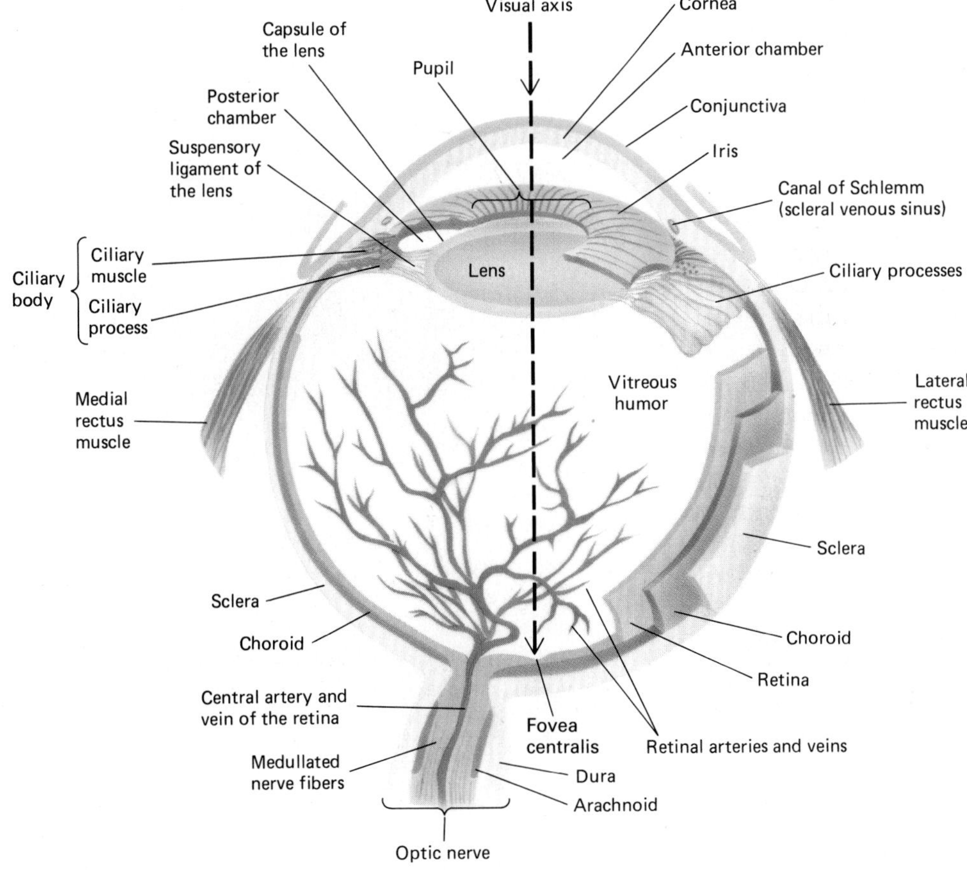

FIGURE 17-13

Structure of the eye (transverse section).

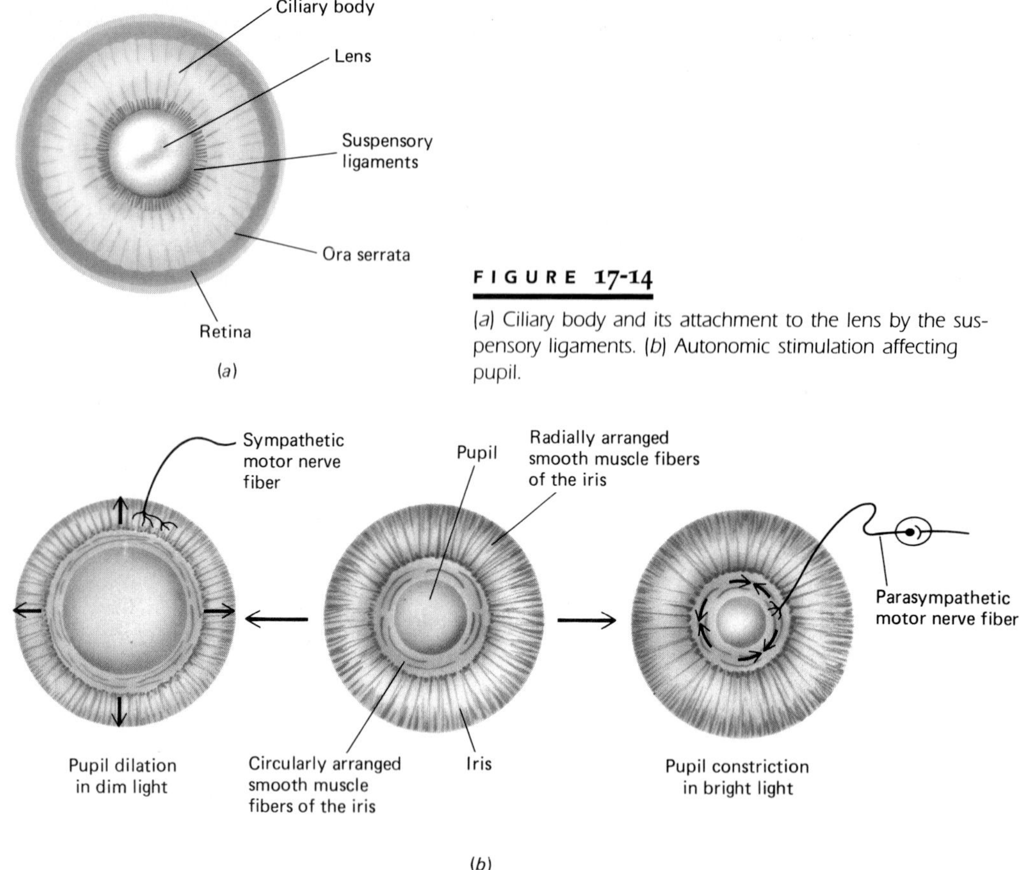

FIGURE 17-14

(a) Ciliary body and its attachment to the lens by the suspensory ligaments. (b) Autonomic stimulation affecting pupil.

Retina

The innermost layer of the eyeball is the **retinal tunic** or **retina.** The retina contains two layers: an outer pigmented layer and an inner nervous layer. The **pigmented layer** is a thin, nonvisual layer adhering to the choroid. It runs from the posterior end of the eyeball anteriorly to the back of the ciliary body and the iris. It absorbs light and stores vitamin A. The **nervous layer** is a thicker, transparent layer that extends anteriorly to the edge of the ciliary body where it ends in a jagged border called the **ora serrata** (**oh**-rah ser-**ray**-tah). The nervous layer is made up of three zones of neurons: an outer zone of photoreceptor neurons, a middle zone of bipolar neurons, and an inner zone of ganglion neurons (Fig. 17-15).

The outer zone of the nervous layer contains the millions of **photoreceptors.** The actual photoreceptors, the rods and the cones, are the modified dendrites of the photoreceptor neurons. See Table 17-6 for a summary. The **rods** are more numerous and more widespread than the cones. There are more than 100 million rods in each eye and they are concentrated in the peripheral parts of the retina. The rods are stimulated by low light intensities and serve in black-and-white vision in dim light. They also are stimulated by shapes and movement. Color vision comes from the stimulation of the **cones** to bright light. They are less sensitive to illumination than are the rods and

TABLE 17-6

Comparison of photoreceptors

Characteristic	Rod	Cone
Photopigments	1 (rhodopsin)	3 (blue-sensitive pigment, green-sensitive pigment, red-sensitive pigment)
Acuity	Low	High
Threshold (illumination)	Low	High
Type of vision	Black-white	Color
Most concentrated location	Peripheral	Central (fovea centralis)
Shape of outer segment	Cylindrical	Conical
Wavelength peak sensitivity	505 nm	Blue cones—445 nm Green cones—535 nm Red cones—570 nm
Estimated total number	20 million	7 million

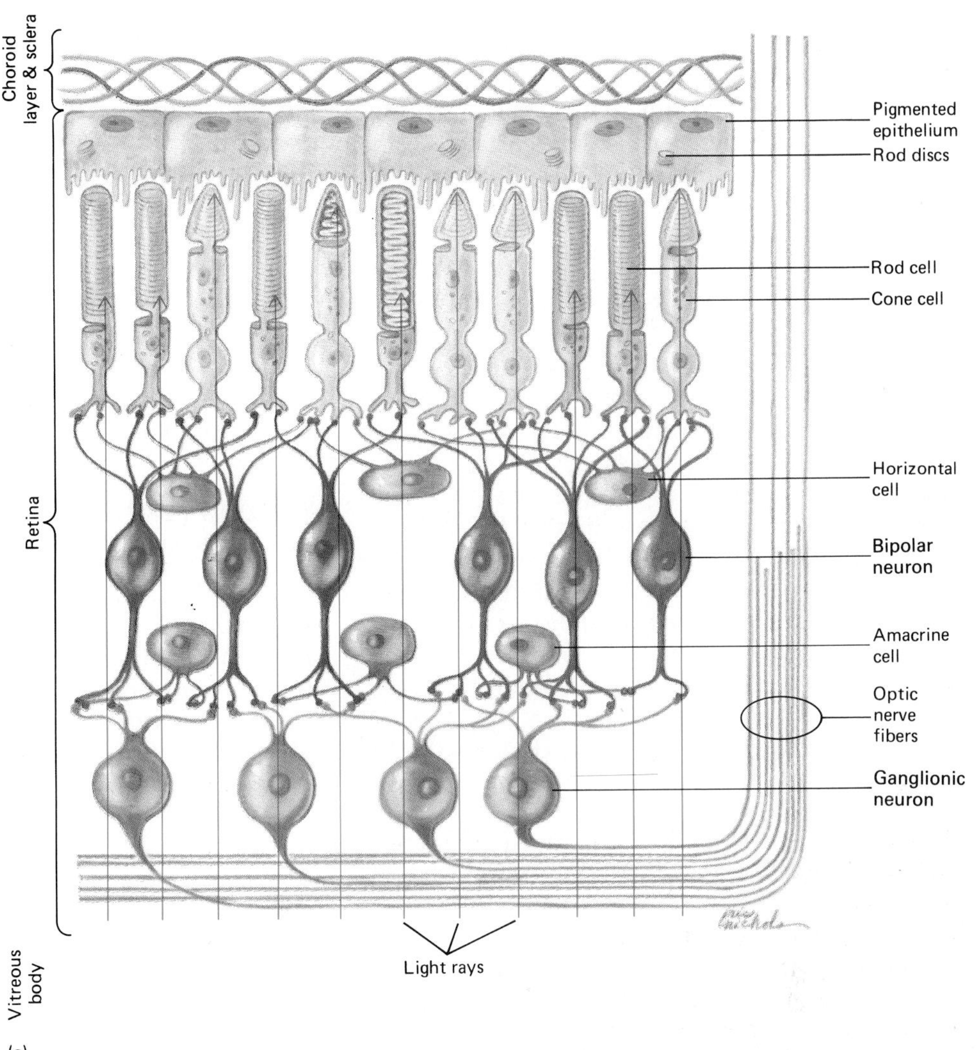

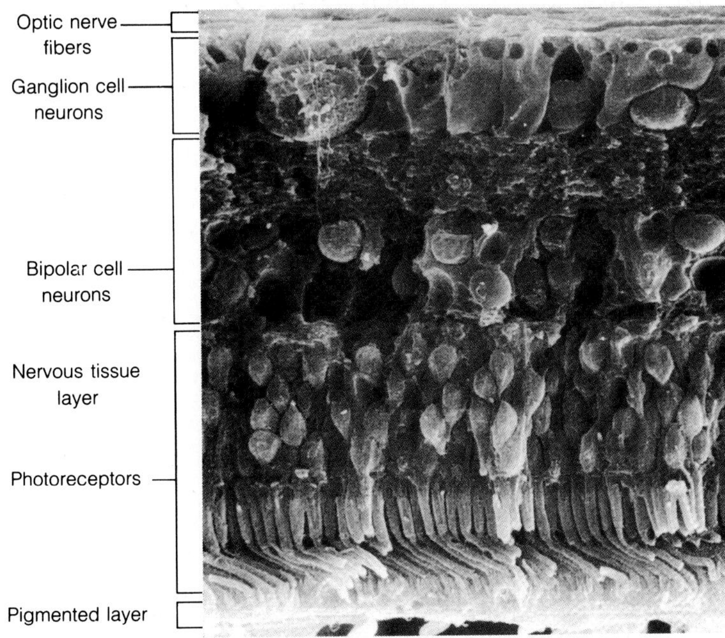

FIGURE 17-15

(*a*) Diagram of retina. (*b*) Retinal layers (scanning electron micrography, ×1246). (From *Tissues and Organs: A Text-Atlas of Scanning Electron Microscopy* by Richard G. Kessel and Randy H. Kardon, © 1979 W. H. Freeman and Co.)

require a greater light intensity to be stimulated. Cones also have high acuity (the ability to distinguish between two points), whereas the rods have low acuity. There are about 7 million cones in each eye and they are most concentrated in the depression near the posterior center of the retina called the **fovea centralis.** This is the area of sharpest vision. No rods are found in the fovea centralis. Surrounding the fovea centralis, the yellowish **macula lutea** (**mak**-yoo-la **loo**-te-a) is another area rich in cones. The macula lutea is also referred to as the *yellow spot* (Fig. 17-16).

Both the rods and the cones have dendrites with an inner segment and an outer segment connected by a thin stalk possessing a cilium. The **outer segment** of the rods is more elongated and cylindrical than the shorter and more tapered outer segment of the cones. The **inner segment** of the rods joins to the cell body via a thin dendrite, whereas the inner segment of the cones is adjacent to and continuous with its cell body. **Photosensitive pigments** of the photoreceptors are contained in discs of the outer segments.

The middle zone of the retina contains the **bipolar neurons.** These neurons receive stimulation from their synapses with the photoreceptors. Branches from several rods typically synapse with a single bipolar neuron. The bipolar neuron receives input from only a few cones. The greater convergence of rod input allows for more summation in the bipolar neurons, which enables them to respond to lower light intensities. This same convergence lowers acuity. Only one cone synapses with a single bipolar neuron within the fovea centralis. This provides for high acuity and very sharp visual imaging.

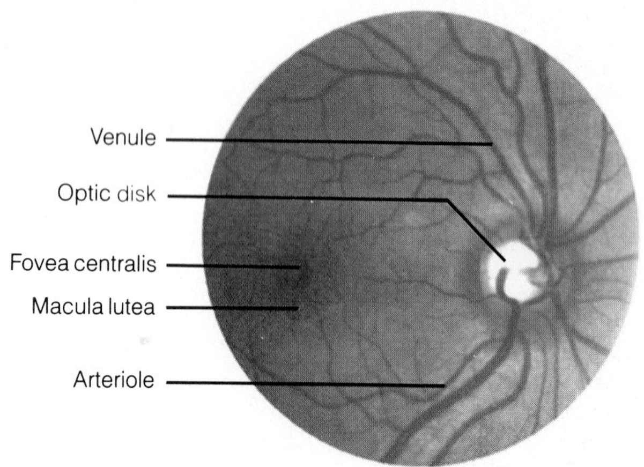

FIGURE 17-16

Retina showing fovea centralis, macula lutea, and optic disc.

The bipolar neurons synapse with the **ganglion neurons** of the inner zone of the retina. Several bipolar neurons synapse on one ganglion neuron. The axons of the ganglion neurons turn outward at the area of the optic disc and join to form the **optic nerve** (CN II).

Medial to the fovea centralis is the **optic disc.** The optic disc marks the location from which the optic nerve (CN II) leaves the eye. There are no photoreceptors in the optic disc and therefore it is also known as the **blind spot** (Fig. 17-17). Passing through the optic disc and the center of the optic nerve are the *central artery* and the *central vein,* which supply blood to the retina.

THE LENS FUNCTIONS IN FOCUSING AND DISTANCE ADJUSTMENTS

Posterior to the pupil and the iris and medial to the ciliary body is the **lens.** Consisting of concentric layers of protein, the lens is a clear biconvex structure that is held in position by the suspensory ligament. It is flexible and can change shape in response to the contraction of the ciliary muscles of the ciliary body. Changes in the shape of the lens change the visual focus. This change of visual focus is called **accommodation.** When close objects are viewed the lens thickens, which provides for more bending (refraction) of the light rays and better focusing of the image on the retina. The viewing of distant objects flattens the lens. Even though the cornea provides for a greater focusing of the light rays, the lens is important in fine focusing and in distance adjustments.

Close object viewed ⟶ ↑ lens thickening ⟶ ↑ light refraction ⟶ better focusing on retina

Distant object viewed ⟶ ↑ lens flattening ⟶ ↓ light refraction ⟶ better focusing on retina

FIGURE 17-17

We are ordinarily unaware of the blind spot in our vision produced by the optic disc. To demonstrate its existence, cover the left eye while focusing the right eye on the cross. Then move the page back and forth until the image of the dot seems to disappear. When this happens, the image of the dot has fallen on the optic disc.

THE CAVITIES OF THE EYE ARE FLUID-FILLED

The lens and the iris divide the interior of the eye into two cavities: a small anterior cavity and a large posterior cavity (Fig. 17-13). The **anterior cavity** is subdivided into two chambers: the anterior chamber and the posterior chamber. The **anterior chamber** is located between the cornea and the iris. The **posterior chamber** of the anterior cavity is found between the iris and the suspensory ligaments and the lens (Fig. 17-13). Both chambers of the anterior cavity are filled with a clear fluid called the **aqueous humor.** Aqueous humor is secreted into the posterior chamber by the choroid plexuses within the ciliary processes. The rate of secretion is about 5 to 6 milliliters per day. The aqueous humor passes through the pupil into the anterior chamber. It supplies nutrients and oxygen to the lens and the cornea which do not have blood supplies. By its constant production, it also maintains an **intraocular pressure** of about 20 mmHg within the anterior cavity. This pressure is important in maintaining the shape of the eyeball. The aqueous humor is drained from the anterior chamber through the **canal of Schlemm,** or the **venous sinus,** and into the bloodstream (Fig. 17-13).

> Aqueous humor secretion by choroid plexus of ciliary process ⟶ through pupil ⟶ anterior chamber ⟶ canal of Schlemm ⟶ bloodstream

The large **posterior cavity** is located between the lens and the retina. A clear, jelly-like fluid, the **vitreous humor** (vit-ree-us), fills the posterior cavity. The vitreous humor is formed in embryonic development and is not subject to the dynamic replacement seen with the aqueous humor. Functions of the vitreous humor include the maintenance of intraocular pressure and the transmission of light onto the retina. The intraocular pressure of the posterior cavity helps to maintain the shape of the eyeball and keeps the nervous layer of the retina pressed firmly against the pigmented layer of the retina.

Clinical highlight

Glaucoma is an eye disease in which an increased intraocular pressure causes damage to the retina and the optic nerve. The cause of the increased pressure is a build up of the aqueous humor, which presses the lens inward. Glaucoma is the second most common cause of blindness. It is often treated by drugs that inhibit the secretion of aqueous humor or enhance its outflow, or by surgery that promotes its drainage.

The eyes function in vision

Vision is the culmination of several processes involving the focusing and reception of light rays and the transmission of sensory information to the occipital lobe for integration and interpretation.

LIGHT ENERGY IS DETECTED BY PHOTORECEPTORS

Of the entire electromagnetic radiation spectrum, the only energy wavelengths detected by human photoreceptors are from 400 to 700 nanometers (Fig. 17-18). This visible light spectrum ranges

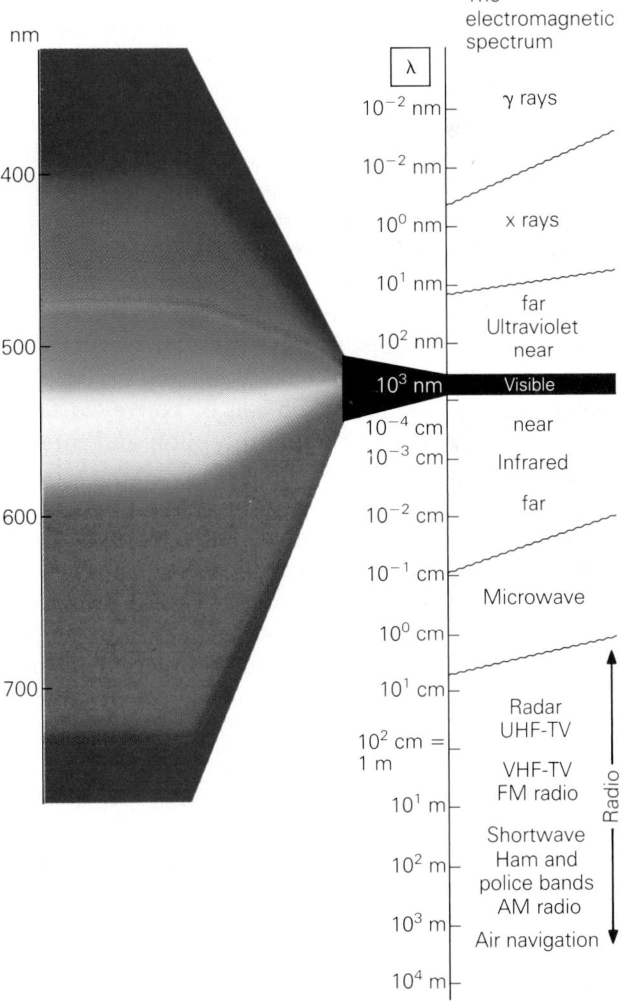

FIGURE 17-18

Electromagnetic spectrum showing a magnification of the visible light range (1 Å = 10^{-10} m; 1 nm = 10^{-9} m). (Adapted from Rhoades, R., and Pflanzer, R., *Human Physiology,* 1989 (Saunders College Pub., Philadelphia).)

from the shortest wavelengths of violet to the longest wavelengths of red. The color of an object results from the reflection of the wavelengths of that color. Objects appearing white reflect all wavelengths of light. Black objects absorb all wavelengths of light. Light energy travels in waves of packets, or photons, at a speed of 186,000 miles per second.

FOCUSING PROCESSES INCLUDE REFRACTION, ACCOMMODATION, PUPILLARY CONSTRICTION, AND EYE CONVERGENCE

In order for an image to be focused on the retina, light rays must be transmitted and refracted through several media. Light rays passing through the cornea pass through the aqueous humor of the anterior chamber, the pupil, and the posterior chamber to the lens. From the lens, the light rays are transmitted through the vitreous humor of the posterior cavity to the retina. With the passage of light rays through the eye, the refraction of the light, accommodation of the lens, constriction of the pupil, and the convergence of the eyes serve to focus an image on the retina. Once the image is focused, the photoreceptors can initiate the transduction of the light energy into the electrochemical energy of the nervous system and the information can be conveyed to the cerebral cortex for visual reception and integration.

Images are focused onto the retina in an inverted form, or upside down. Reflected light from the right side of an object is focused on the left side of the retina and vice versa. Hence the images on the retina are the mirror images of the viewed objects. We do not see an inverted, mirror image because the brain learns to automatically interpret the visual image as the exact object being viewed.

Refraction

Each of the four different media of the eye (cornea, aqueous humor, lens, vitreous humor) has a different optical density. Each, therefore, will bend the light rays entering it to a different degree. This bending of light rays upon entering a medium of different density is called **refraction.** Most refraction takes place as light rays from the air enter the more dense and convex structure of the cornea. It is estimated that about 80% of the light refraction for vision occurs at the air-cornea interface. Less refraction takes place upon the cornea-aqueous humor interface. The aqueous humor-lens interface and the lens-vitreous humor interface provide additional refraction that can be altered by changing the shape of the lens (Fig. 17-19*a*). This provides a fine adjustment necessary for focusing the image sharply on the retina.

When an object is more than 6 meters (20 ft) away from the eyes, the reflected light rays travel almost parallel to one another. These rays are focused upon the fovea centralis of the retina mainly by the cornea and a "relaxed," flattened lens. No change in the shape of the lens is necessary to refract the light any more. The distance from an object to the eye that results in focusing on the fovea centralis without accommodation is called the **far point of vision.** For normal eyes, the far point of vision is 6 meters and beyond. Closer objects reflect light in such a way that the light rays are more divergent. In this case, additional refraction is needed to focus the image on the retina. Without the additional refraction, the image focuses behind the retina. The additional refraction of the light rays is accomplished by changing the shape of the lens (Fig. 17-19*b*,*c*).

Lens accommodation

If objects closer than 6 meters away are to be focused onto the retina, the lens must thicken to increase the refraction of the incoming light rays. This accommodation of the lens is under the control of parasympathetic nerves to the ciliary muscles of the ciliary body. When the parasympathetic neurons stimulate the ciliary muscles to contract, they pull the ciliary body forward and inward. This narrows the ring of the ciliary body and decreases the tension on the suspensory ligaments attached to the lens. The lens takes on a more spherical shape with a greater curvature. This results in an increased refraction of the incoming light rays so that the image is directed to the retina. The visual cortex also sends impulses to the ciliary muscles to cause further accommodation.

There does exist a limit to which the lens can accommodate. Objects any closer than 10 centimeters to the eye cannot be sharply focused by a young adult. This distance of 10 centimeters is called the **near point of vision** and it increases with age. At 40 years of age it is about 20 centimeters, and at 60 years it is about 80 centimeters.

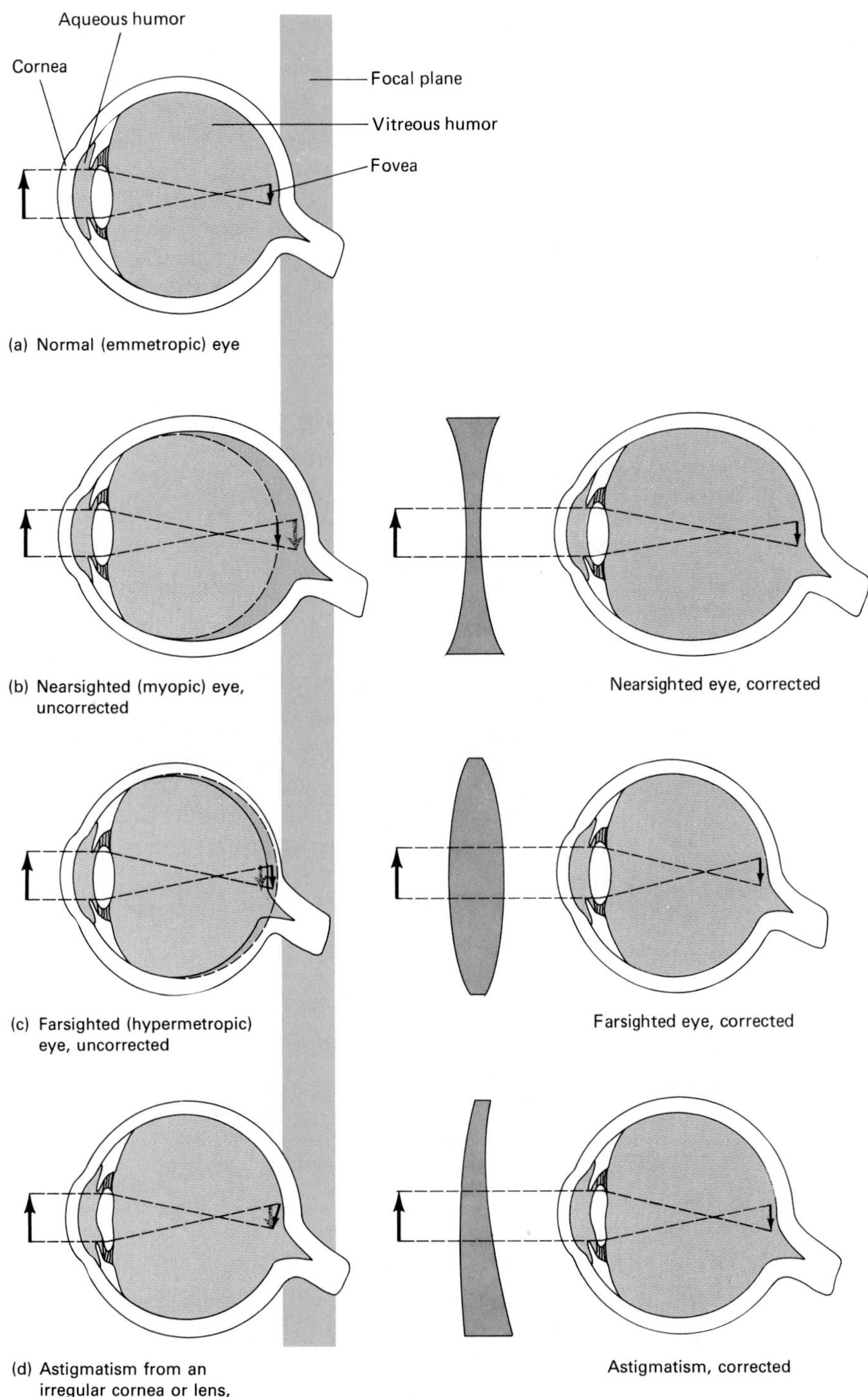

FIGURE 17-19

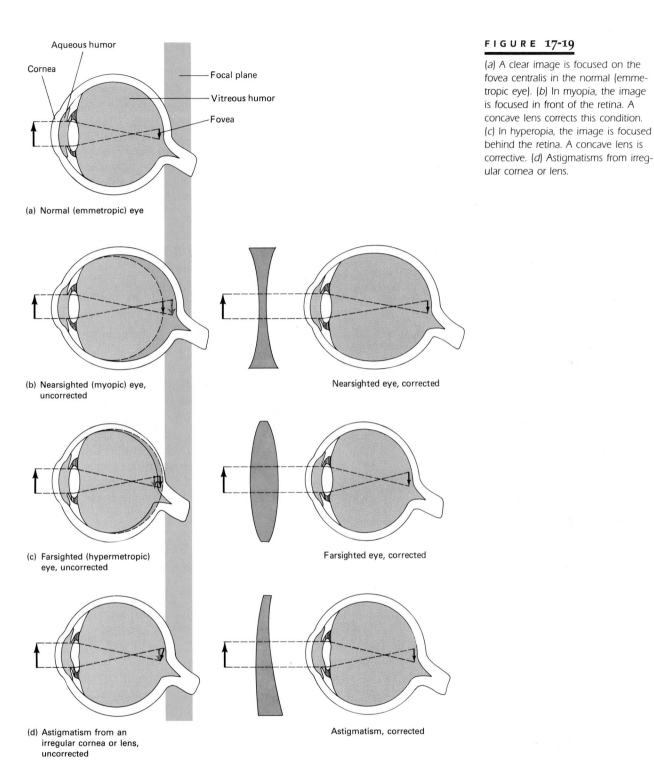

(*a*) A clear image is focused on the fovea centralis in the normal (emmetropic eye). (*b*) In myopia, the image is focused in front of the retina. A concave lens corrects this condition. (*c*) In hyperopia, the image is focused behind the retina. A concave lens is corrective. (*d*) Astigmatisms from irregular cornea or lens.

Pupil constriction

When viewing close objects, there is also a stimulation of the circular muscles of the iris by the parasympathetic nerves, causing them to contract and constrict the pupil. This prevents the divergent light rays from entering the peripheral areas of the lens, which would not undergo sufficient refraction and would cause a blurred image.

Hence the entering light rays are directed to the fovea centralis. Another function of constriction of the pupil is to protect the retina from intense light stimulation.

Clinical highlight

The ability to focus an object on the retina is dependent upon the degree of accommodation of the lens and the shape of the eyeball. Those of us who can focus an image on the retina from an object 6 meters (20 ft) away have normal, or **emmetropic,** vision (Fig. 17-19*a*). If the lens is thick and accommodation is too great or if the eyeball is too long, then the image of distant objects is focused in front of the retina instead of on it. This condition is called **myopia** (my-**oh**-pe-uh). In this case, the person sees near objects fine but distant objects are blurred. These people are *nearsighted,* or *myopic,* and need a concave lens to correct the focusing of distant objects (Fig. 17-19*b*).

If lens accommodation is too weak due to a thin lens or if the eyeball is too short, the image of near objects is focused behind the retina. This person has **hyperopia (hypermetropia)** or *farsightedness.* Vision of distant objects is fine but close objects are blurred. To correct the hyperopic condition, convex lenses are used to permit greater convergence of the light rays (Fig. 17-19*c*).

Astigmatisms result from irregular curvatures of the cornea or lens. Vision is blurred or distorted because the light rays end up being focused at two different points on the retina (Fig. 17-19*d*).

Corrective glasses can adjust light refraction and improve vision. *Contact lenses* may also be used to correct focusing problems. The contact lens fits on the surface of the cornea atop a layer of tears. The outer surface is the corrective surface and the inner surface is ground to fit the curvatures of the cornea.

Eye convergence

Humans use **single binocular vision** in viewing an object. In other words, both eyes focus on the same object. The light rays that enter the eyes are focused onto corresponding points of the two retinas (Fig. 17-20). The viewing of nearby objects requires the eyes to rotate medially in order for the light rays to hit the same points of the two retinas. This medial movement of the eyes by extrinsic muscles to facilitate the alignment of both of the eyes to the object being viewed is called **convergence.** The medial rectus muscles are particularly important in convergence. The closer the object being viewed, the greater the degree of convergence needed to maintain single binocular vision. Viewing objects close to the tip of the nose causes so much convergence of the eyes that the person appears "cross-eyed." See Focus on Eye Disorders.

Clinical highlight

Double vision, **diplopia** (dih-**plo**-pe-uh), results when the contraction of the extrinsic muscles is not coordinated. The eyes focus on different areas of the visual field and two images are seen. Another condition resulting from uncoordinated extrinsic eye muscles is **strabismus** (stra-**biz**-mus). In this condition, the eyes do not move in unison. Strabismus is commonly called "crossed eyes."

PHOTORECEPTORS OF THE RODS AND CONES CONTAIN LIGHT-SENSITIVE PIGMENTS

Visual pigments

The photoreceptors are made up of light-sensitive pigments containing a chromophore (light-absorbing) molecule attached to a protein. The chromophore of all visual pigments is **retinal;** the type of protein in the pigment is an **opsin.** Retinal is also called *retinene* or *retinaldehyde.* It is a derivative of vitamin A. Retinal is a common component of the four types of visual pigments, one in the rods (rhodopsin) and three types in the cones. The distinct nature of the four visual pigments lies with differing opsins. Each opsin determines the particular light wavelengths that each visual pigment will respond to.

Retinal can exist in two varying chemical configurations, or isomers. *All-trans retinal* is a chemi-

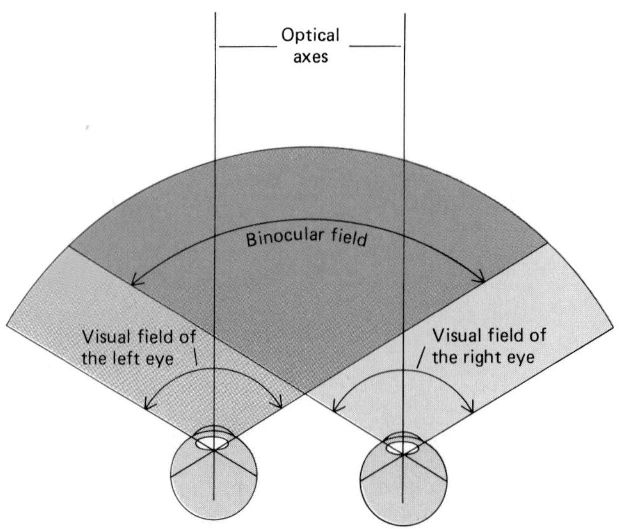

FIGURE 17-20

Visual fields of both eyes. Binocular vision results from the overlap of the visual fields of both eyes.

FOCUS ON . . . Eye disorders

Achromatopia (a = lack of; chromat = color; ops = eye). Achromatopia is an abnormal visual perception of colors.

Ametropia (ametro = disproportionate; ops = eye). Ametropia is a condition in which parallel light rays do not come to a focus on the retina.

Anopsia (an = lack of; opsia = vision). Anopsia is the suppression of vision in one eye.

Blepharitis (blepharo = eyelid; itis = inflammation of). Blepharitis is an inflammation of the edges of the eyelid.

Cataract Cataract is an opacity of the lens. There is a degradation of the lens protein and a movement of water into the lens. Cataracts may develop from head injuries, exposure to intense heat, and exposure to ultraviolet light and other forms of radiation. The majority of cases, however, are associated with the aging process. Cataract is the most common disorder causing blindness.

Keratitis (kerato = cornea; itis = inflammation of). Keratitis is an inflammation or infection of the cornea. It may be viral or bacterial in origin or may result from corneal burns due to chemicals or ultraviolet light.

Keratoiritis (kerato = cornea; ir = iris; itis = inflammation of). Keratoiritis is an inflammation of the cornea and iris.

Nystagmus Nystagmus is a constant involuntary rhythmic oscillation of the eye. It may be horizontal, vertical, or rotatory.

Presbyopia (presby = old; ops = eye). Presbyopia is a condition in which the lens loses its elasticity and the eyes cannot focus close objects. This condition usually accompanies aging.

Ptosis Ptosis is a paralytic falling or drooping of the upper eyelid.

Retinal detachment Separation of the retinal layers, retinal detachment, may result in permanent blindness. The separation can be caused by head injuries. If the retina is torn, vitreous humor may leak between the retinal layers. The person experiences impaired vision, complaining of dark blotches or light flashes. Early detection can lead to correction by surgery or laser treatment.

Senile macular degeneration (SMD) Senile macular degeneration is a condition in which there is a proliferation of blood vessels over the macula lutea. Distorted vision or blindness results.

Trachoma Trachoma is a chronic contagious form of conjunctivitis caused by a virus.

cally stable, straight molecule; *11-cis retinal* is an unstable, curved isomer of the molecule. 11-*cis* retinal is able to combine with an opsin, but the all-*trans* form is unable to attach to an opsin.

Stimulation of the rods

The visual pigment of the rods is **rhodopsin** (visual purple). Rhodopsin consists of retinal and the opsin **scotopsin.** When there is no light present, the retinal is in the 11-*cis* form and is combined with the scotopsin, forming rhodopsin. Without light or when the eyes are closed, rhodopsin molecules can become very concentrated in the rods.

When stimulated by light, the 11-*cis* retinal undergoes a conformational change to all-*trans* retinal. This causes it to break away from the scotopsin in progressive stages (bathorhodopsin to lumirhodopsin to metarhodopsin I to metarhodopsin II to pararhodopsin). The all-*trans* retinal is converted back to the 11-*cis* form, which combines with the scotopsin to regenerate rhodopsin (Fig. 17-21).

The intermediate metarhodopsin II is a photoexcited form of rhodopsin that activates the protein *transducin,* which in turn activates a phosphodiesterase that converts cyclic guanosine monophosphate (cGMP) to 5′-GMP. This decreases the amount of cGMP in the cytoplasm of the rods, which closes Na^+ channels. A hyperpolarization of the rod results. This hyperpolarization is the generator potential of the rods. Hence, light causes the rods to hyperpolarize and dark causes them to depolarize.

Metarhodopsin II $\longrightarrow$ transducin activation $\longrightarrow$ phosphodiesterase stimulation $\longrightarrow$ $\downarrow$ cyclic GMP $\longrightarrow$ Na^+ channels close $\longrightarrow$ hyperpolarization $\longrightarrow$ generator potential

Clinical highlight

Nyctalopia(**nik**-tuh-**low**-pe-uh), **night blindness,** occurs whenever there is a disruption of rod function. Vision is very poor in dim light. Vitamin A deficiency is the major cause and, if prolonged, can lead to rod degeneration.

Stimulation of cones

The chemical events in the excitation of cones are similar to those in rods except that there are three different types of cones and each is sensitive to a different wavelength of light. The three types of cones each possess a different visual pigment. The visual pigments of the cones are less sensitive to light than is rhodopsin and it takes a greater light intensity to activate them. The opsins of the cones are called **photopsins.** Each photopsin is sensitive to a different range of wavelengths. Red cones, which make up 74% of the total cones, are the most sensitive to wavelengths around 570 nanometers. The brain interprets this wavelength as the color red. Green cones (10%) are highly sensitive to wavelengths near 535 nanometers. Wavelengths close to 445 nanometers activate the blue cones (16%). See Figure 17-22.

The cones are used in color vision but a person is able to see many more colors than red, green, and blue. This is because color perception is a combination of simultaneous and differential inputs from the three cone types. Yellow is perceived when wavelengths of about 580 nanometers enter the eye. At this wavelength, red cones

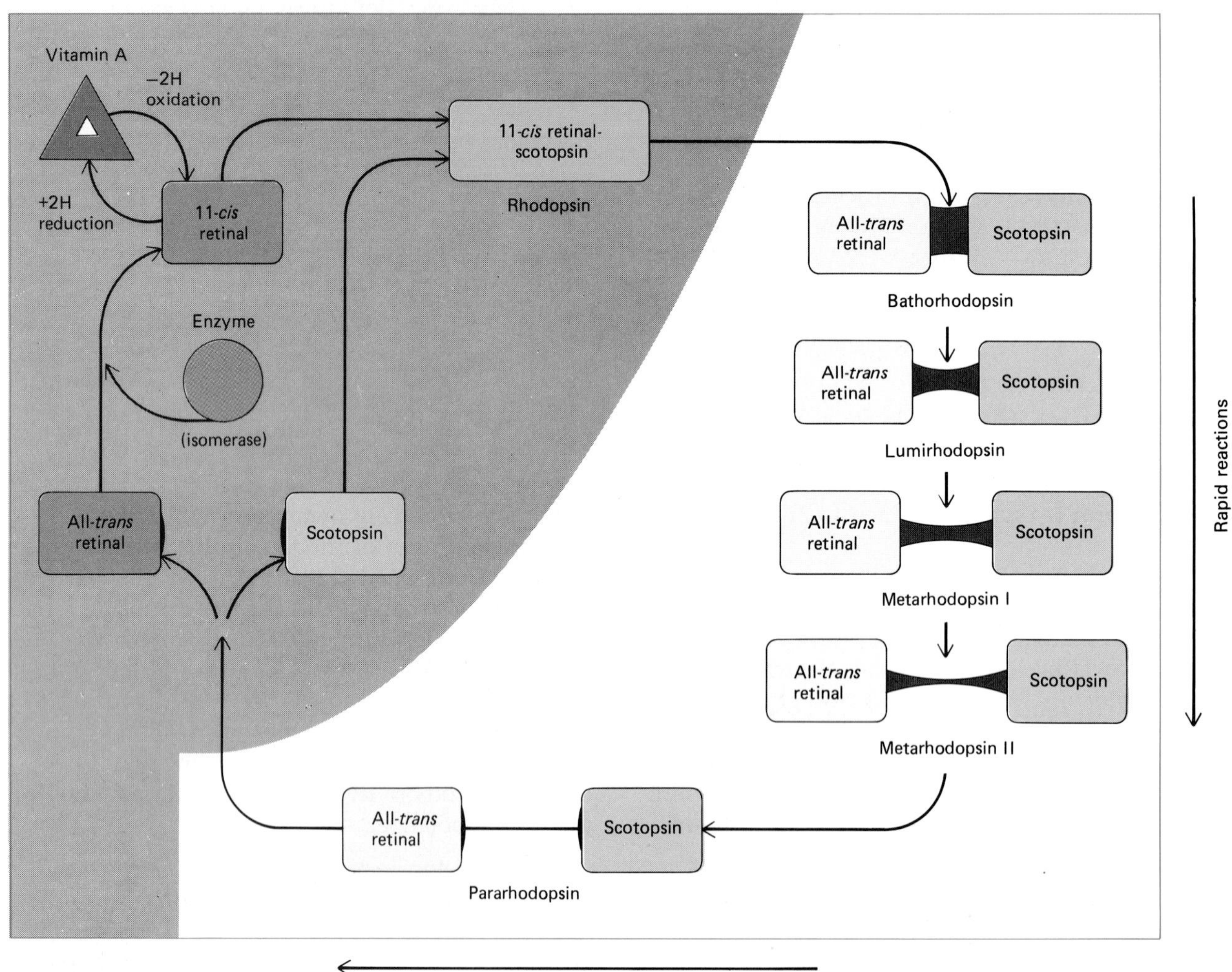

FIGURE 17-21

Chemical changes in rhodopsin leading to the transduction of light energy.

are activated and green cones are also activated to a lesser extent. The blue cones do not respond at this wavelength. Increasing the wavelength above 580 nanometers makes the color more orange. White is perceived when all the cones are equally stimulated; black is perceived when none of the cones are stimulated.

Clinical highlight

If a cone type is missing, the person is unable to distinguish some colors as distinct from others. This is genetically based and affects males (sex-linked) much more than females. The person is said to be **color-blind.** The most common form of color blindness is *red-green color blindness.* Cones most sensitive to red or green light are deficient or absent and the person is unable to distinguish between these colors, seeing red and green as the same color. People usually learn to compensate by using visual cues and by judging the intensity of the color.

LIGHT AND DARK ADAPTATION IMPROVE VISION IN BRIGHT AND DIM LIGHT

If a person enters a brightly lit room from a dimly lit room, the light seems extremely bright and glaring. Vision is poor but improves as the intensity of light most of the photoreceptors respond to (visual threshold) rises and the eyes adapt. This is known as **light adaptation** and it usually takes about 5 minutes. The presence of bright light causes the breakdown of the visual pigments of the rods and the cones into retinal and opsin.

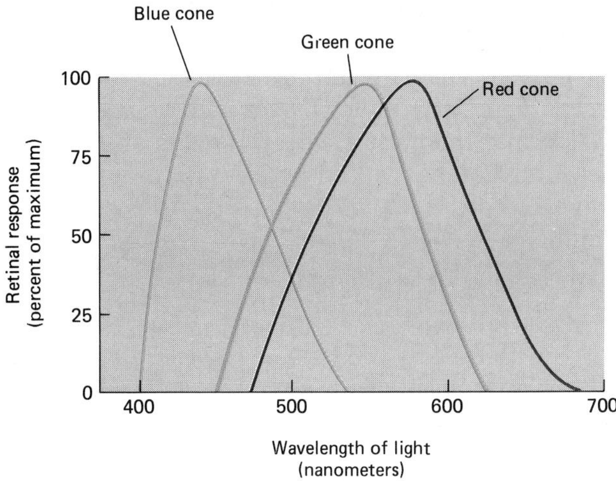

FIGURE 17-22

Wavelength sensitivities of the three types of cones.

The retinal is converted to vitamin A. Prolonged exposure to bright light decreases the concentration of visual pigments in the rods and cones. The result is a reduced sensitivity of the eye to light. A greater intensity of light is needed to maintain effective vision.

If a person is exposed to bright light for a long time and then enters a dark room, the person initially sees nothing but blackness. This occurs because most of the rhodopsin has been broken down in the bright light and the cones are inactive in the dim light. With time, the rhodopsin molecules re-form and their concentration increases. This causes the sensitivity of the retina to increase and the visual threshold to decrease. Vision improves slowly over a period of 20 minutes or longer. This phenomenon is called **dark adaptation.** When a person is exposed to darkness for a prolonged time, more and more of the visual pigments form from the retinal and the opsins. There is an increase in the amount of vitamin A that is converted to retinal, which leads to more visual pigments being produced. The greater concentrations of visual pigments increase the sensitivity of the eyes to light.

Light and dark adaptation are also facilitated by the constriction and dilation of the pupil and by the adaptation of the neurons of the visual pathway. With light adaptation there is a concurrent constriction of the pupil and an inhibition of rod functioning by neural interconnections. Dark adaptation shows a pupillary dilation and a decline in neural input within seconds after the initial burst of activity.

THE NEURAL PATHWAY OF VISION LEADS TO THE OCCIPITAL LOBE

Generator potentials formed in the dendrites of the rods and the cones pass through the cell bodies and into their axons. At the synapse with the bipolar neurons, neurotransmitters cause an excitation of the bipolar neurons. The bipolar neurons carry excitatory signals to the ganglion neurons.

The nervous layer of the retina contains two types of cells that help to transmit information laterally, the horizontal cells and the amacrine cells (Fig. 17-15). The **horizontal cells** provide a lateral inhibition to adjacent areas that are not as strongly activated. If the bipolar neurons are hyperpolarized or not conveying signals, the horizontal cells serve to excite bipolar cells of adjacent peripheral fields. Therefore, the input from the peripheral areas is antagonistic to the central area and serves to increase the perceptual contrasts of the visual field. These cells also help in color differentiation. **Amacrine cells** synapse with ganglion cells and provide input on changes in the intensity of illumination on the retina.

When the bipolar neurons stimulate the ganglion neurons, the ganglion neurons propagate action potentials that are conducted down their axons. The axons of the ganglion cells converge to form the **optic nerve** (CN II) which leaves the posterior part of the eye at the optic disc. These axons pass through the **optic chiasma** which is the point at which some of the axons cross over to the opposite side. Axons from the medial aspect of each eye cross over; axons from the lateral aspect of each eye do not cross over. Upon passing through the optic chiasma, the axons enter into the **optic tracts.** Each optic tract contains axons from the lateral aspect of the ipsilateral eye and axons from the medial aspect of the contralateral eye. Therefore, each optic tract contains information from the same half of the visual field. The right optic tract conveys information on the left half of the visual field; the left optic tract conveys information on the right half of the visual field.

The optic tracts end at the **lateral geniculate nuclei** of the thalamus. Here the ganglion neuron axons synapse with thalamic neurons whose axons pass to the **visual areas of the occipital lobes** of the cerebrum (see Fig. 15-6, p. 505). The visual area of the right occipital lobe interprets information from the left half of an object and the visual area of the left occipital lobe interprets information from the right half of an object.

Photoreceptor ⟶ bipolar neuron ⟶ ganglion neuron ⟶ optic nerve (CN II) ⟶ optic chiasma ⟶ optic tract ⟶ lateral geniculate nucleus ⟶ visual cortex of occipital lobe

The ear consists of an outer, middle, and inner part

The ear contains the receptors for hearing and those for equilibrium. The ear is made up of three major parts: the outer ear, the middle ear, and the inner ear. The **outer ear** and the **middle ear** function only in hearing. The **inner ear** functions in both hearing and equilibrium.

THE OUTER EAR CONDUCTS SOUND WAVES INTERNALLY

The **outer ear,** or **external ear,** is specially constructed to receive the sound waves and conduct them internally. The funnel-shaped part of the outer ear is the auricle, or *pinna*. The outer ear also consists of the external auditory canal and the tympanic membrane (Fig. 17-23).

The **auricle** is a prominent flap of elastic cartilage that is covered by a thick skin and attached to the side of the head. It is attached to the head by muscles and ligaments. The **helix** is the rim of the auricle. The **lobule** is the inferior part of the auricle that contains connective tissue but lacks cartilage. Sound waves are collected by the auricle and directed to the external auditory canal.

The **external auditory canal** is an S-shaped tube about an inch in length extending from the auricle to the tympanic membrane. It courses through the external auditory meatus of the temporal bone. The canal is lined by cartilage and covered by skin. Fine hairs and sebaceous glands are found at its outer end. The inner skin contains modified sweat glands, the **ceruminous glands** (se-**roo**-mi-nus), which secrete a yellow-brown substance called **cerumen.** Cerumen is commonly called earwax. The hairs and cerumen help in trapping foreign particles and keeping them away from the tympanic membrane. The cerumen also keeps the tympanic membrane pliable and waterproof. The external auditory canal acts as a resonating chamber for sound waves in the range of human speech.

Commonly called the eardrum, the **tympanic membrane** (tim-**pan**-ik) separates the outer ear from the middle ear. The tympanic membrane is a thin, double-layered membrane of epithelium and connective tissue. Its outer surface is covered by skin and its inner surface is lined by a mucous membrane. The eardrum has a diameter of about 1 centimeter. It is cone-shaped with its apex projecting into the middle ear. Vibrations of the tympanic membrane, caused by incoming sound waves, transmit energy to the structures of the middle ear.

Clinical highlight

A rupturing of the tympanic membrane may result from head trauma, foreign objects, or infections. Blood and cerebrospinal fluid may leak through a ruptured tympanic membrane if a skull fracture occurs.

THE MIDDLE EAR CONTAINS THE EAR OSSICLES

The **middle ear,** or **tympanic cavity,** is an air-filled chamber found within the temporal bone. The middle ear is lined with a mucous membrane that is continuous with the mucous membrane of the pharynx. The external boundary of the middle ear is the tympanic membrane, and the internal boundary is a bony plate containing two membrane-covered openings—a superior *oval window* and an inferior *round window.*

The wall of the middle ear contains two openings—a posterior one leading into the mastoid sinus and an anterior one leading into the eustachian tube. The **tympanic antrum** is the chamber connecting the posterior wall of the middle ear to the mastoid air cells of the mastoid process of the temporal bone. The **eustachian (auditory) tube** connects the middle ear to the nasopharynx. Its function is to equilibrate the air pressures on either side of the tympanic membrane. This serves to prevent a rupturing of the eardrum by sudden changes in atmospheric or internal pressure.

When atmospheric pressure decreases, as when a person ascends to high altitudes, the pressure in the middle ear is greater than that of the atmosphere and the tympanic membrane bows outward. This can result in discomfort and pain. It also interferes with hearing. Yawning, chewing, swallowing, or blowing the nose cause the eustachian tube to open and the pressure in the middle ear decreases and equalizes with the atmospheric pressure.

↓ Atmospheric pressure ⟶ ↑ middle ear pressure ⟶ tympanic membrane bows outward ⟶ ↑ discomfort ⟶ yawn, swallow, etc. ⟶ open eustachian tube ⟶ ↓ middle ear pressure

Clinical highlight

The continuity of the mucous membrane of the middle ear, mastoid sinus, eustachian tube, and pharynx can allow a respiratory or throat infection to spread into the middle ear, **otitis media.** The infection may even move into the mastoid sinus, causing **mastoiditis** which could spread to the meninges of the brain.

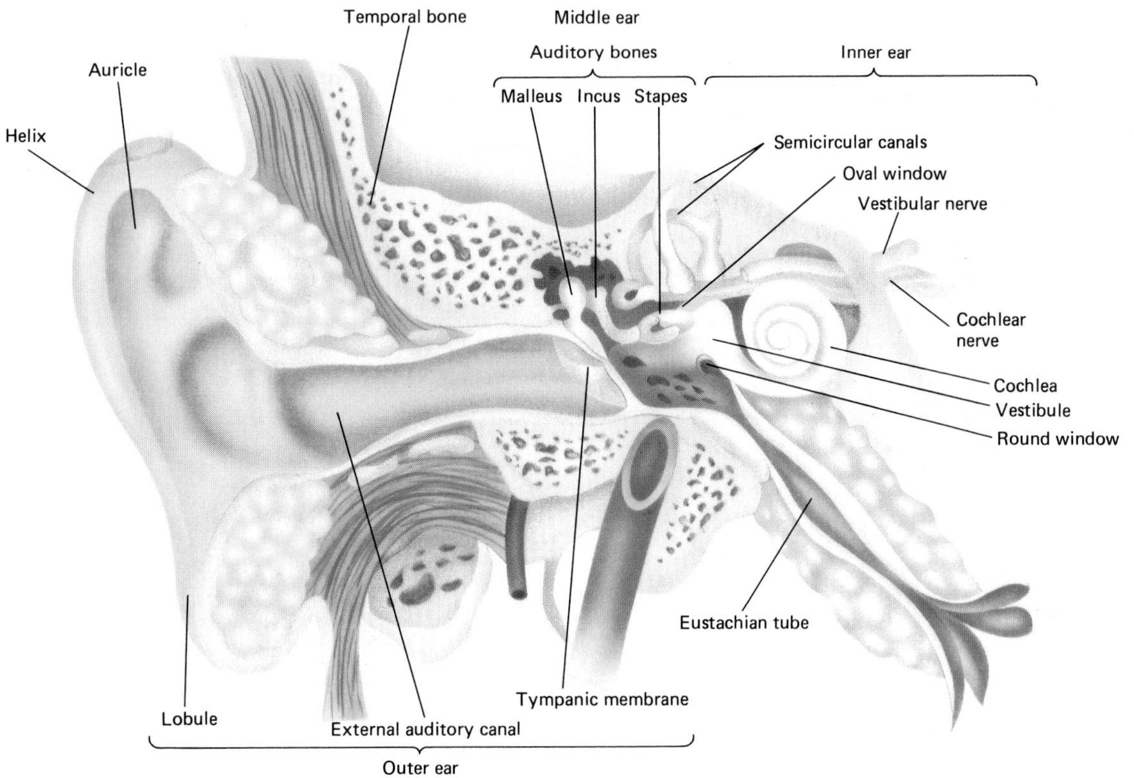

FIGURE 17-23

Anatomy of the outer, middle, and inner ear.

A series of three tiny bones extends across the middle ear from the tympanic membrane to the oval window. These bones are attached to the wall of the middle ear by ligaments. The three bones are collectively called the **ear ossicles** and are individually named according to their shape (Fig. 17-24). The outermost ossicle is the **malleus** (hammer) which has its "handle" attached to the inner surface of the tympanic membrane. The intermediate ossicle is the **incus** (anvil) which articulates with the other ossicles by synovial joints. The innermost ossicle is the **stapes** (stirrup). The footplate of the stapes rests upon the **oval window** (fenestra vestibuli). The ossicles transmit the vibrations of the tympanic membrane to the oval window, which will stimulate the inner ear. The ossicles magnify the force of the vibrations by acting as levers.

Two small skeletal muscles are associated with the middle ear: the tensor tympani and the stapedius muscle (Fig. 17-24). These muscles contract when stimulated through the **tympanic reflex.** The *tensor tympani* muscle pulls the malleus medially. This action increases the tension on the eardrum and decreases the magnitude of the vibrations transmitted to the oval window. This protects the inner ear from injury due to loud noises. The *stapedius* muscle is the smallest skeletal muscle of the body. It is attached to the stapes and pulls it posteriorly. This reduces the magnitude of the vibrations transmitted to the oval window and, like the tensor tympani, it serves in protection from loud noises.

THE INNER EAR CONTAINS TWO LABYRINTHS, THE VESTIBULE, SEMICIRCULAR CANALS, AND THE COCHLEA

Labyrinths

The **inner ear,** or **labyrinth** (**lab**-i-rinth), consists of a complex series of chambers and canals that contain the organs involved in hearing and equilibrium. It is structurally divided into two major sections: a *membranous labyrinth* and a *bony labyrinth* (Fig. 17-25). The **membranous labyrinth** is located within the **bony labyrinth.** It is covered by epithelium and filled with a fluid called **endolymph.**

The bony labyrinth is also referred to as the **osseous,** or **perilymphatic, labyrinth.** It consists of a series of bony chambers and canals within the petrous portion of the temporal bone. These spaces are surrounded by a thin sheath. The fluid **perilymph** fills the spaces of the bony labyrinth. There are three separate compartments of the bony labyrinth based on their shape: the vestibule, semicircular canals, and cochlea.

Vestibule

The **vestibule** occupies a central position within the bony labyrinth. It separates the semicircular canals from the cochlea. The membranous labyrinth within the vestibule contains two sacs connected by a duct. These sacs are the **utricle** and the **saccule,** and their adjoining duct is the **endolymphatic duct.** These sacs contain special areas, the **maculae,** which possess sensitive hair cells that function in static equilibrium.

Semicircular canals

The three **semicircular canals** occupy the lateral part of the bony labyrinth. They extend from the vestibule at approximately right angles to each other. There is an **anterior, lateral,** and **posterior canal.** Each canal contains an inner extension of the membranous labyrinth called the **anterior, lateral,** and **posterior semicircular ducts.** The semicircular ducts have a small swelling, the **ampulla**

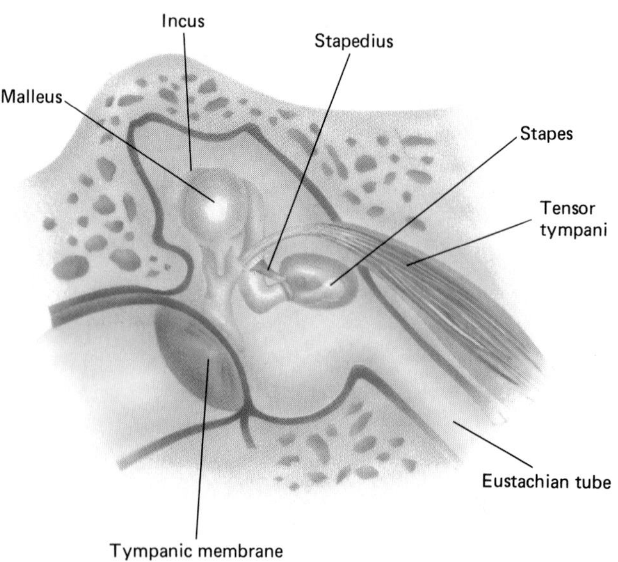

FIGURE 17-24

Auditory muscles to the middle ear (medial view).

(am-**pool**-la), at their bases with the utricle. These ampullae contain **ampullary crests** which are ridges possessing groups of sensitive hair cells called **cristae** (**kris**-tay). The hairs of the hair cells are embedded in a gelatinous substance called the **cupula** (**kyewp**-yoo-la). The cristae function in dynamic equilibrium.

The vestibule (utricle and saccule) and the semicircular ducts with their ampullae make up the principal organ of equilibrium, the **vestibular apparatus** (Fig. 17-25).

Cochlea

The **cochlea** (**kok**-le-a) is a snail-shaped subdivision of the bony labyrinth within the temporal bone. Extending from the vestibule, it makes 2½ turns around a central bony core called the **modiolus** (moe-**dee**-oh-lus) (Fig. 17-26*a*). A bony shelf, the spiral lamina, projects from the modiolus into the lumen of the cochlea. From the spiral lamina, the **vestibular** and **basilar membranes** cross the cochlea, dividing it into three longitudinal chambers. The chamber between these membranes is called the **cochlear duct,** or **scala media.** The cochlear duct is the membranous labyrinth of the cochlea and is filled with endolymph. The endolymph is believed to be secreted by a highly vascularized mucosa of the lateral wall of the cochlear duct, the **stria vascularis** (Fig. 17-26*b*). The chamber formed above the vestibular membrane is the **scala vestibuli,** and the chamber formed below the basilar membrane is the **scala tympani.** The scala vestibuli and the scala tympani are filled with perilymph. The lateral end of the scala vestibuli communicates with the oval window. It extends the length of the cochlea and is continuous with the scala tympani at the cochlear apex which is called the **helicotrema** (*hel*-i-ko-**tree**-ma). The scala tympani continues laterally to end at the round window.

Within the cochlear duct are found the **organs of Corti,** or **spiral organs** (Fig. 17-26*c*). The organs of Corti are the organs of hearing. They are located on the basilar membrane. The organs of Corti contain sensory hair cells and supporting cells running along the entire length of the cochlea. The hair cells exist as a single row of inner hair cells and several rows of outer hair cells (Fig. 17-27). Hairs from these cells extend into the endolymph and contact the **tectorial membrane.** The tectorial membrane is a flexible gelatinous flap that extends from the spiral lamina and projects over the organs of Corti. The basal ends of the

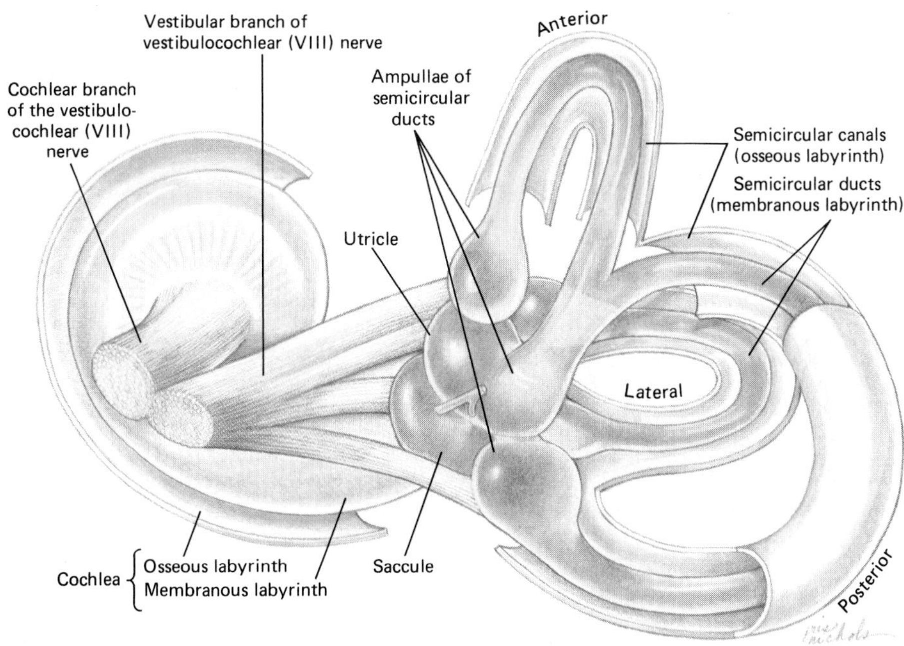

FIGURE 17-25

Posterior view of labyrinths of the inner ear. Outer white color shows the bony labyrinth. Inner orange color depicts the membranous labyrinth.

hair cells within the basilar membrane are in contact with dendrites of the **cochlear nerve.**

For a summary of the structures of the outer and middle ear, see Table 17-7.

Physiology of hearing involves the inner ear

Hearing encompasses the detection of loudness and pitch. These mechanisms involve sensory receptors and their precise location within the inner ear.

SOUND TRAVELS IN WAVES

Sound is produced by moving objects displacing air molecules. The alternating compressions and decompressions of the air ripple out from the source as waves. The sound waves most keenly detected by human ears are between 1000 and 4000 cycles per second, or hertz (Hz). The entire audible range extends from 20 to 20,000 hertz.

The distance between the peaks and valleys of a sound wave is called its **amplitude.** Amplitude is experienced as loudness and is measured in units called decibels (dB). The distance between adjacent wave peaks is the **wavelength.** The number of wavelengths occurring per unit

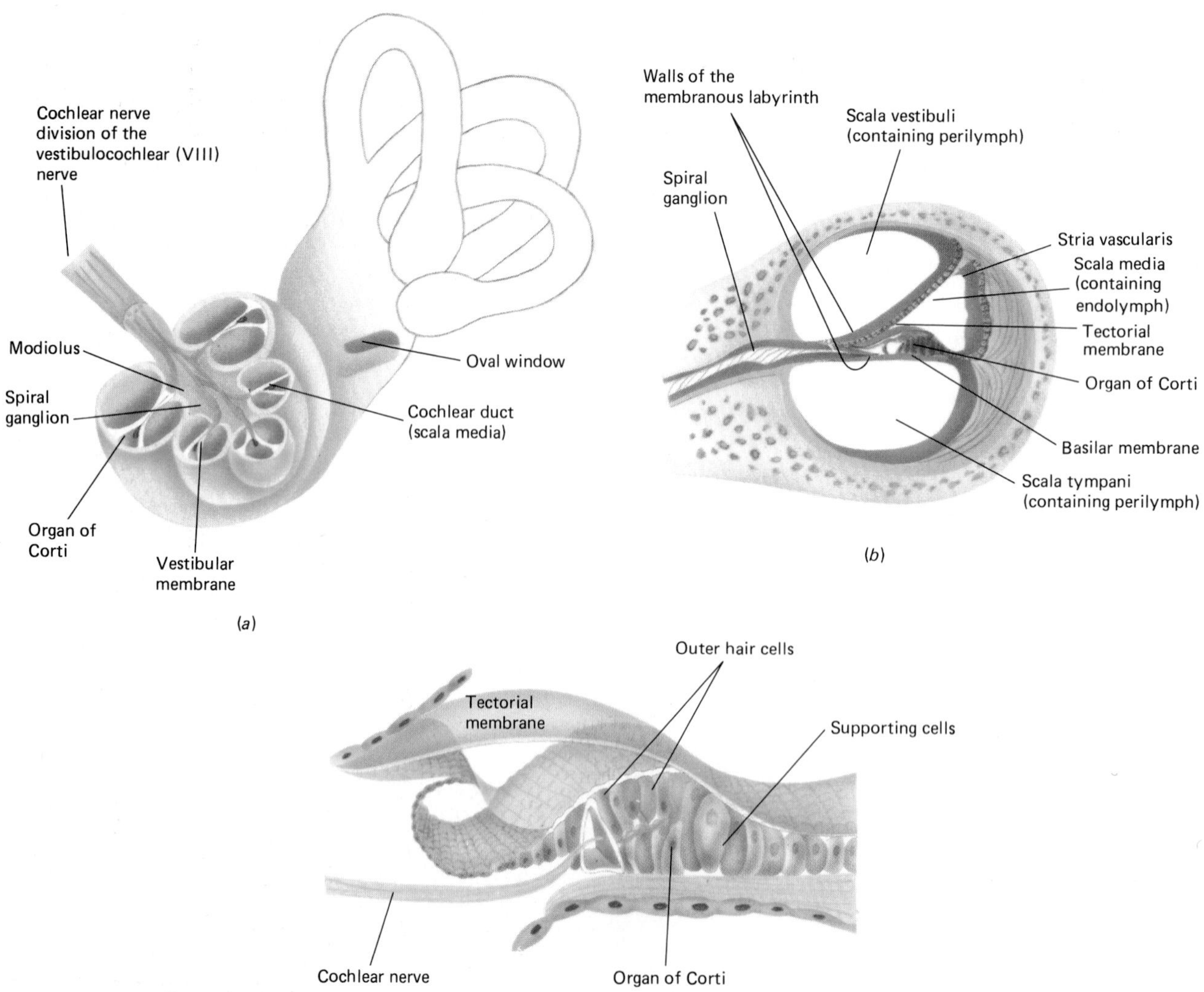

FIGURE 17-26

Anatomy of the cochlea. (*a*) Cross section of coiled cochlea. (*b*) Enlargement showing chambers. (*c*) Organ of Corti.

TABLE 17-7

Summary of structures of the outer and middle ear	
Structure	**Function**
Outer ear	
Auricle	Collects and directs sound waves
External auditory canal	Conducts sound waves to tympanic membrane
Tympanic membrane	Vibrates in response to sound waves, and transmits vibrations to middle ear
Middle ear	
Ear ossicles (malleus, incus, stapes)	Transmit sound waves (as vibrations) to oval window
Eustachian tube	Equalizes pressure on both sides of tympanic membrane
Tensor tympani and stapedius muscles	Protect inner ear by reducing the magnitude of middle ear vibrations from loud noises

time is the **frequency.** The frequency of sound waves is experienced as pitch. The greater the frequency, the higher the pitch. Sounds of different qualities have variations within their vibrations. These are called **overtones** (Fig. 17-28).

THE FUNCTION OF THE OUTER AND MIDDLE EAR IS TO TRANSMIT SOUND WAVES

The initial step in the perception of sound is the entrance of sound waves into the external auditory canal. The auricle of the ear collects and directs sound waves into the canal. The external auditory canal transmits the sound waves internally. When the sound waves reach the end of the canal, they push against the tympanic membrane and cause it to alternately bow inward and outward. This vibration of the eardrum is proportional to the force and frequency of the sound waves. The greater the force of the sound waves, the greater the degree of deflection of the eardrum. The degree of deflection determines loudness. High-frequency sounds cause the tympanic membrane to vibrate faster; those of low fre-

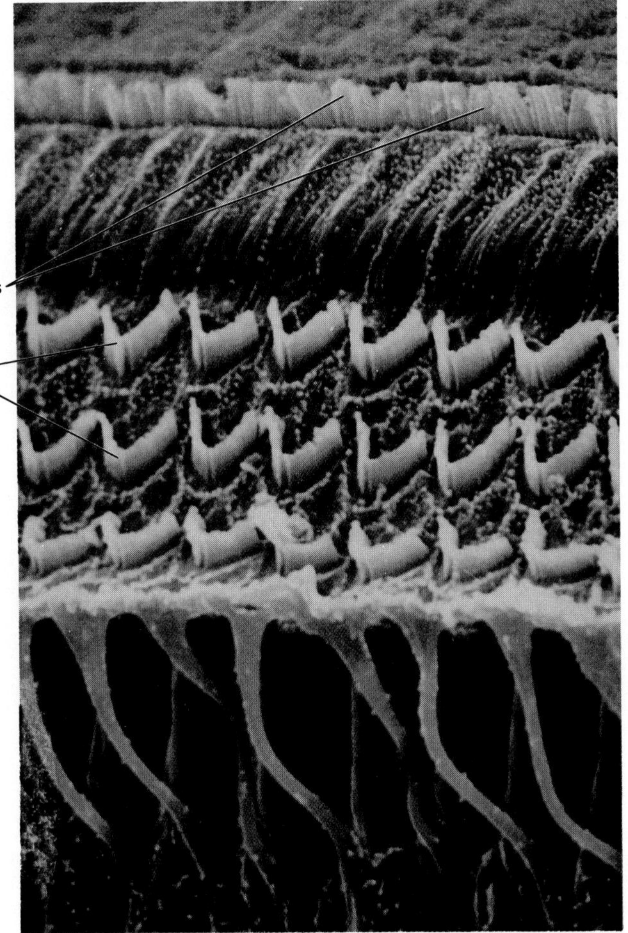

FIGURE 17-27

The inner and outer hair cells of the organ of Corti (scanning electron micrograph, ×2420).

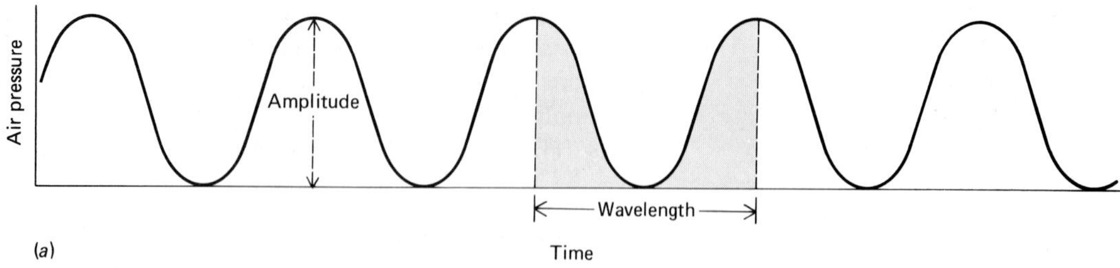

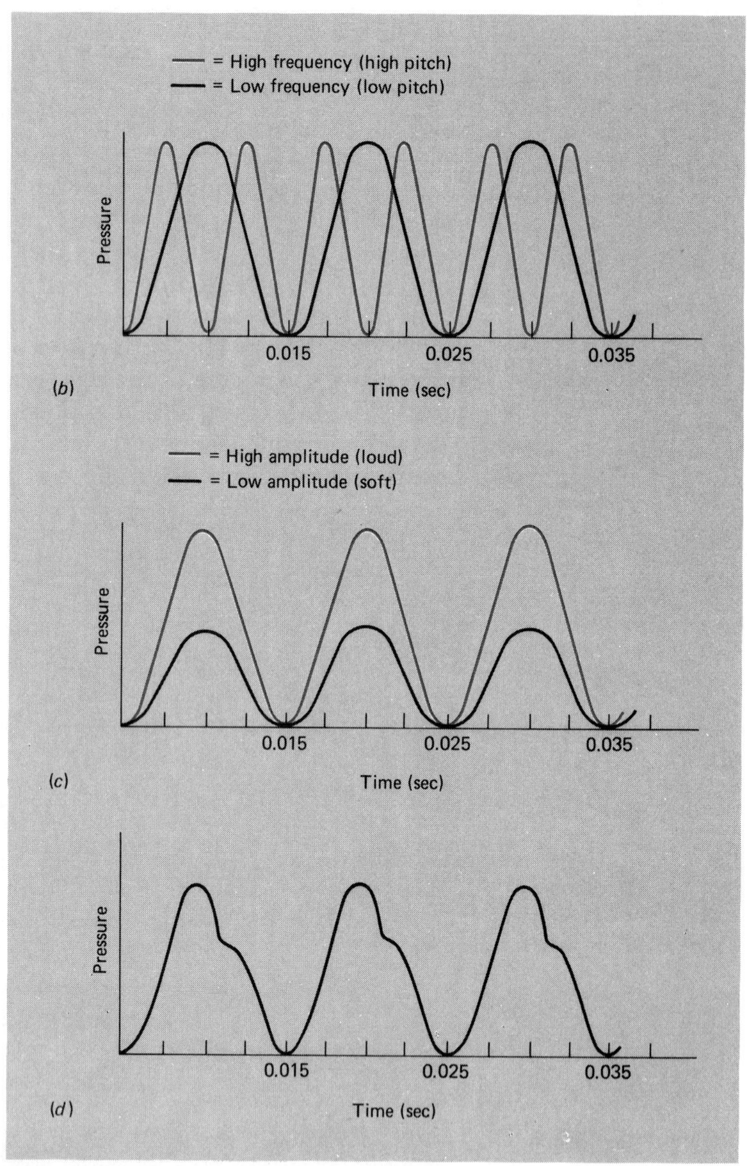

FIGURE 17-28

(*a*) Sound waves showing amplitude and wavelength. (*b*) Frequency. The red wave has a shorter wavelength and therefore produces more wavelengths in 0.035 seconds than the black one does. The number of wavelengths per second is called the frequency, which the hearing apparatus interprets as pitch. (*c*) Amplitude. The red wave has a greater amplitude (height) and therefore sounds louder. (*d*) Overtones. Most sound waves are not the perfectly symmetric curves seen in (*a*), (*b*), and (*c*). Instead, most waves have bumps and dips, which are responsible for the difference in quality between sounds such as the human voice and a clarinet sounding the same note.

quency result in slower vibrations. The frequency of vibration determines pitch.

The vibrations of the eardrum cause the malleus to vibrate. These vibrations are passed on to the incus and stapes. The stapes rocks back and forth and, in doing so, causes the oval window to bow in and out. The transmission of sound waves from the larger tympanic membrane to the much smaller oval window results in a 22-fold increase in the force transmitted per unit area.

Sound waves at auricle ⟶ external auditory canal ⟶ tympanic membrane ⟶ malleus-incus-stapes ⟶ oval window

THE COCHLEA CONTAINS THE RECEPTORS FOR HEARING

The vibration of the oval window causes a vibration in the perilymph of the scala vestibuli. The resulting waves of the perilymph travel down the length of the scala vestibuli and are transmitted into the scala tympani. The pressure exerted by these waves also causes the vestibular membrane to bow inward and then outward. This pressure is dissipated into the endolymph of the cochlear duct, which forces the basilar membrane to alternately bulge into the scala tympani and then into the cochlear duct. The vibration of the basilar membrane stimulates the organs of Corti by forcing the hairs of the hair cells to push and pull against the tectorial membrane.

Oval window vibration ⟶ pressure waves in scala vestibuli ⟶ transmission to cochlear duct ⟶ vibration of basilar membrane ⟶ hair cells of organ of Corti stimulated

When the hairs of the hair cells are moved, they open ion channels in the hair plasma membranes; potassium (K^+) ions rapidly move in, causing a depolarization. This depolarization results in a generator potential, which in turn opens calcium (Ca^{2+}) channels at the bases of the hair cells, causing Ca^{2+} to move in. The Ca^{2+} binds vesicles at these bases to the membrane, causing a release of neurotransmitter, which stimulates sensory neurons to fire action potentials.

Pressure waves transmitted to the scala tympani are dissipated by the round window. The bowing of the round window into the middle ear cavity helps to eliminate reverberations of the waves, and echoing effects are dampened.

PITCH TRANSMISSION OCCURS ALONG THE BASILAR MEMBRANE

The basilar membrane exhibits different degrees of flexibility, or resonance. Its proximal end (the end closer to the oval window) is stiffer than the distal end. High-frequency sounds cause the proximal end of the basilar membrane to vibrate more than other parts. Low-frequency sounds cause the distal end of the basilar membrane to vibrate more. Therefore, sounds of various frequency are sorted out along the length of the basilar membrane. The greater the vibration of the basilar membrane, the greater the stimulation of the sensory hair cells of the organs of Corti in that area of the membrane. Sensory neurons take action potentials to the brain, which spatially sorts out the stimulated receptor areas, thus differentiating various pitches (Fig. 17-29).

High pitch ⟶ maximal displacement at proximal end of basilar membrane
Low pitch ⟶ maximal displacement at distal end of basilar membrane

LOUDNESS TRANSMISSION INVOLVES THE FREQUENCY OF ACTION POTENTIALS

The greater the sound wave intensity, the greater the magnitude of the vibrations of the tympanic membrane, the ossicles, the oval window, and the basilar membrane. For any particular pitch, the greater the vibrations of the basilar membrane means that more hair cells will be stimulated. This produces generator potentials of greater magnitude, which result in a higher frequency of action potentials in the sensory neurons going to the brain. The loudness of a sound of a particular pitch is coded by the frequency of action potentials transmitted from a specific area of the basilar membrane to the brain. Prolonged exposure to high-intensity noises can cause damage to the hair cells of the organs of Corti and result in hearing impairment.

↑ Sound intensity ⟶ ↑magnitude of vibrations of tympanic membrane, ossicles, oval window, and basilar membrane ⟶ ↑ stimulation of hair cells ⟶ ↑ generator potential ⟶ ↑ frequency of action potentials in cochlear neurons

The vestibular apparatus functions in equilibrium

Sensory receptors within the vestibular apparatus of the inner ear function in static and dynamic equilibrium.

THE MACULAE FUNCTION IN STATIC EQUILIBRIUM

Static equilibrium is the orientation of the body relative to the ground. This gravitational balance involves posture and the positioning of the head and body. The utricle and the saccule of the vestibule function in static equilibrium.

Both of these structures contain areas of specialized cells, the **maculae** (Fig. 17-30). The maculae contain hair cells and supporting cells. Each hair cell has numerous microvilli called *stereocilia* and a cilium called a *kinocilium.* It is believed that the supporting cells produce a gelatinous substance, the **otolithic membrane,** which contains small particles of calcium carbonate called **otoliths.** The presence of the otoliths makes the gelatinous substance heavier than the endolymph and, along with gravity, a force is continuously

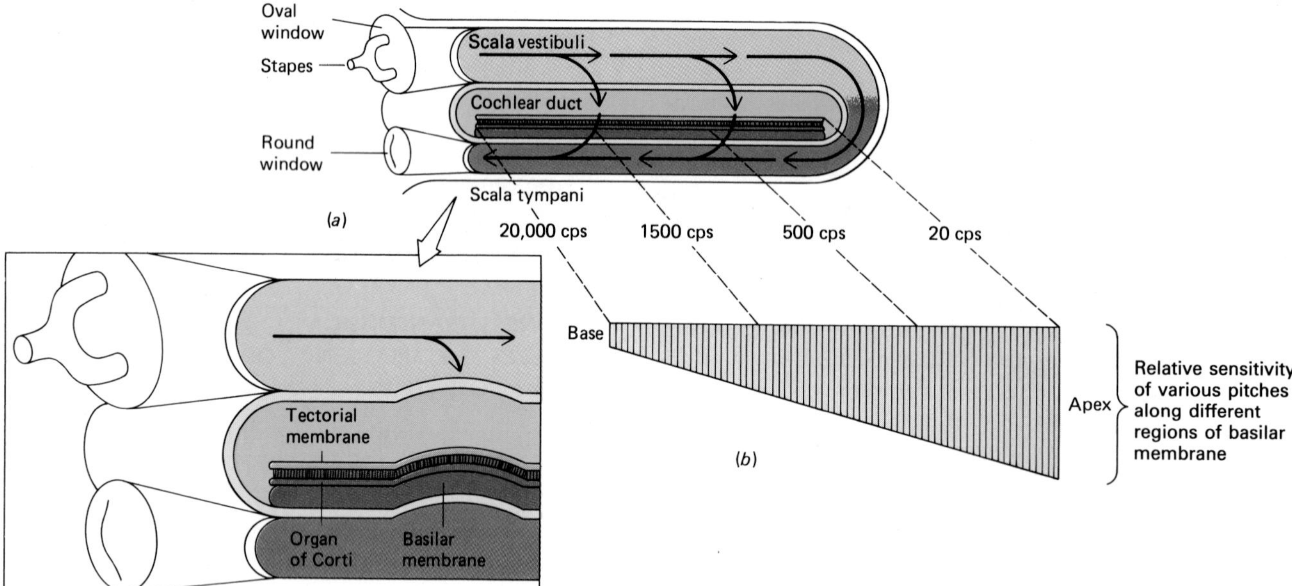

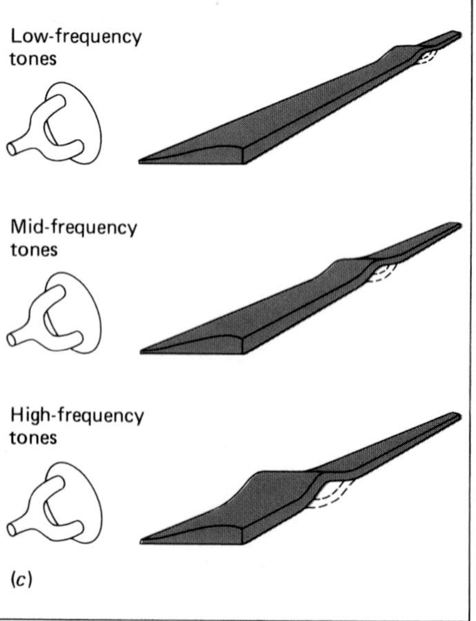

FIGURE 17-29

(a) Diagram of uncoiled cochlea showing transmission of pressure waves. (b) The basilar membrane showing relative lengths of basilar fibers. (c) Maximum displacements of basilar membrane to different sound wave frequencies (pitch). (Adapted from Rhoades, R., and Pflanzer, R., *Human Physiology,* 1989 (Saunders College Pub., Philadelphia).)

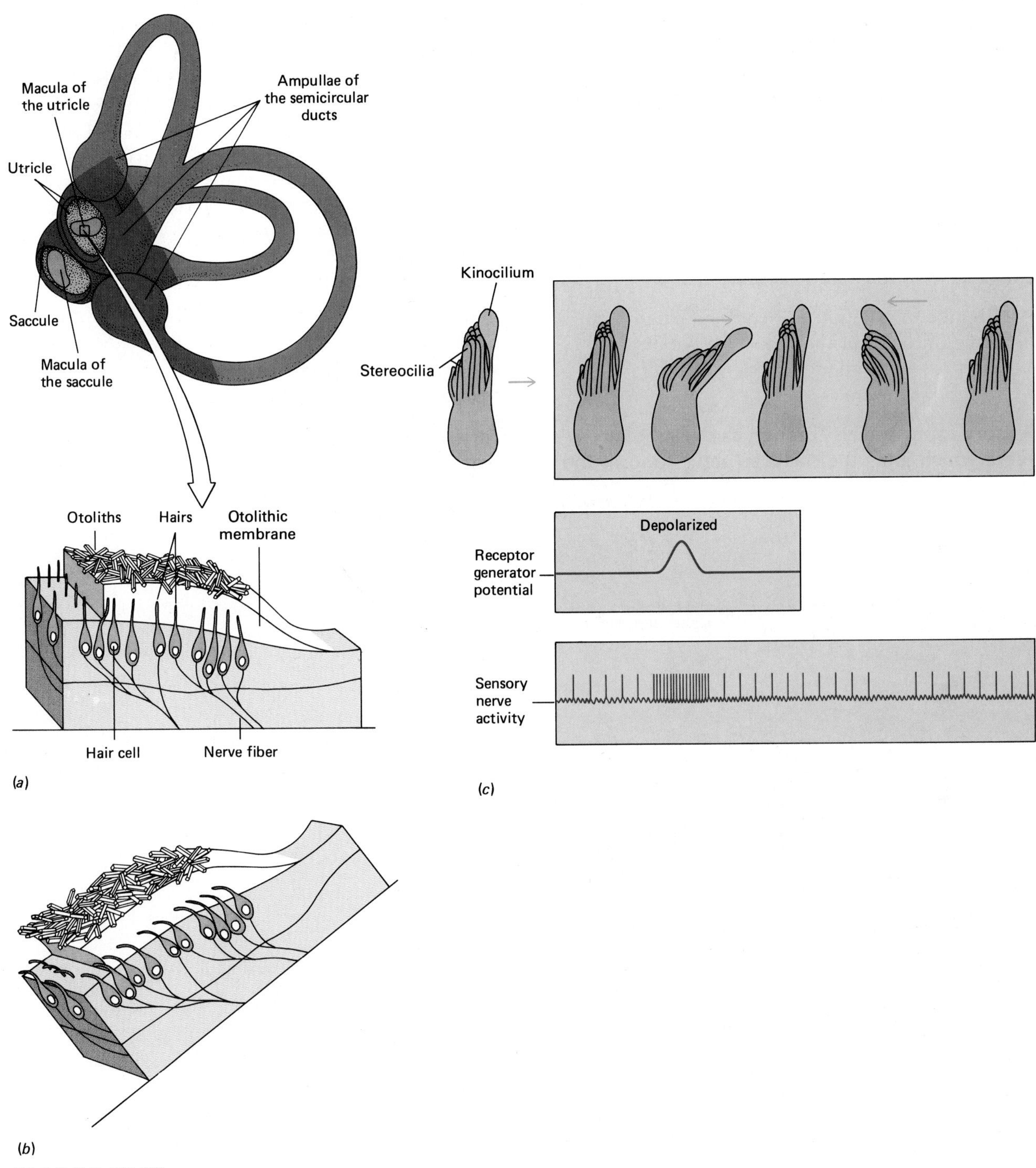

FIGURE 17-30

Structures of static equilibrium. (*a*) Anatomy of macula. (*b*) The effect of gravity on macula when head is not in an upright position. (*c*) Bending of hair cells when otolithic membrane is displaced (arrows), showing the resultant frequency of action potentials in vestibular nerve.

exerted upon the hair cells. Any change in the position of the head causes a change in the direction of the force exerted on the hairs. This results in a bending of the hairs in a particular direction, which stimulates dendrites of vestibular neurons. Different head positions cause different displacements of the hairs, which cause different sensory inputs to the brain. If the head is tilted to the right, there is a greater sensory input to the brain from the right utricle and saccule and less input from the left utricle and saccule.

> Change in position of head ⟶ change in force on hairs of maculae ⟶ bending of hairs ⟶ stimulation of dendrites of vestibular neurons

Sensory input travels through the **vestibular nerve** which joins the cochlear nerve to form the **vestibulocochlear nerve** (CN VIII). These nerves convey sensory information on static equilibrium to the vestibular nuclei of the medulla. Information is also sent to the nuclei of the cranial nerves controlling eye movements (CN III, IV, VI) and to the spinal accessory nerve (CN XI), which helps to control head and neck movements. The cerebellum also receives constant input from the utricles and saccules. This permits the cerebellum to adjust motor output from the cerebral cortex and thereby coordinate muscle control over static equilibrium.

THE CRISTAE FUNCTION IN DYNAMIC EQUILIBRIUM

The ampullae of the semicircular ducts contain receptors for dynamic equilibrium (Fig. 17-31*a*).

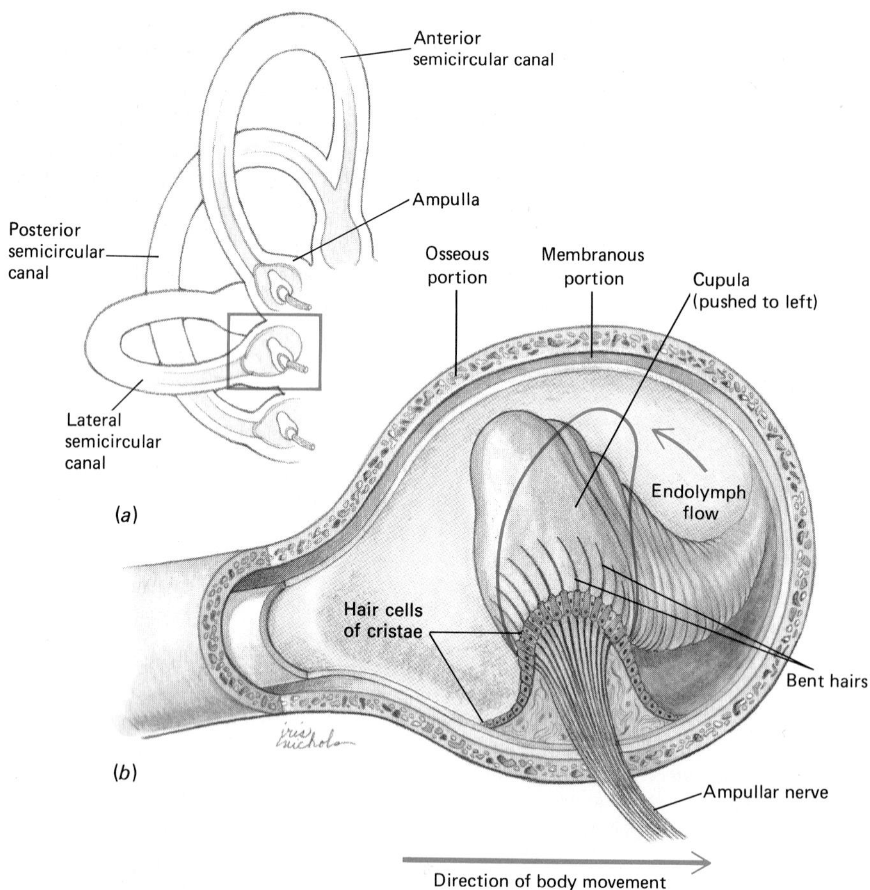

FIGURE 17-31

Structures of dynamic equilibrium. (*a*) Cristae positioned in ampullae. (*b*) Diagram of enlarged crista.

Within each ampulla is a **crista** containing sensitive hair cells that become excited by rotational (angular) deceleration and acceleration of the head. The crista also contains supporting cells. Hairs of the hair cells are suspended in a gelatinous cap called the **cupula** (Fig. 17-31*b*). The cupula has a higher density than the surrounding endolymph.

Because the semicircular canals project in three different directions at right angles to each other (frontal, sagittal, and transverse), their ampullae can detect movement in three-dimensional space.

Angular movement causes the endolymph in the semicircular ducts to move in a direction opposite the rotation. The inertia of the endolymph causes it to lag behind the movement of the body and this causes a displacement of the cupula and the hairs of the hair cells. This bending of the hairs produces a depolarization of the hair cells. The resulting generator potential initiates action potentials in sensory neurons located at the bases of the hair cells. The axons of these neurons travel in the vestibular nerve. The brain interprets the sensory input as a head movement opposite to that of the bending of the hairs. This is the exact direction of the actual angular movement.

Change in angular motion ⟶ movement of endolymph in semicircular duct in direction opposite motion ⟶ displacement of cupula ⟶ bending of hairs of crista ⟶ depolarization of hair cells ⟶ generator potential ⟶ action potential in sensory neuron of vestibular neuron ⟶ brain interprets input opposite to that of bending of hairs

If the rotation or movement should continue at a constant velocity for a time, the endolymph movement ceases as it catches up to the speed of the body and stimulation also ceases. This explains why one is unable to detect movement traveling at speeds of a constant velocity or why a blindfolded person who is spun at a constant velocity is unable to tell if he or she is even moving.

For a summary of the structures and functions of the inner ear see Table 17-8. See also Focus on Ear Disorders.

Embryology of the eye

The primitive eyes originate as lateral outpocketings of the brain. The diencephalon of the embryonic brain forms two lateral **optic vesicles** by the fourth week of development (Fig. 17-32). As the vesicles develop, their distal ends invaginate to form the double-layered **optic cups.** The inner layer of the optic cup becomes the nervous layer of the retina; the outer layer becomes the pigmented layer of the retina. The proximal ends of the optic vesicles elongate and develop into the **optic stalks** which become incorporated into the future optic nerves. A groove on the underside of each optic cup and optic stalk called the **optic fissure** provides a pathway for nerves and blood vessels supplying the inner eyeball. This fissure closes prior to birth and encompasses the optic nerves and blood vessels.

TABLE 17-8

Summary of structures of the inner ear

Structure	Receptor site	Receptor (accessory structures)	Function	Sensory innervation
Cochlea	Organ of Corti	Hair cells (tectorial membrane, basilar membrane)	Hearing	Cochlear nerve
Vestibular apparatus				
Utricle	Macula	Hair cells	Static equilibrium	Vestibular nerve
Saccule	Macula	Hair cells (otolithic membrane, otoliths)	Static equilibrium	Vestibular nerve
Semicircular ducts	Crista	Hair cells (cupula)	Dynamic equilibrium	Vestibular nerve

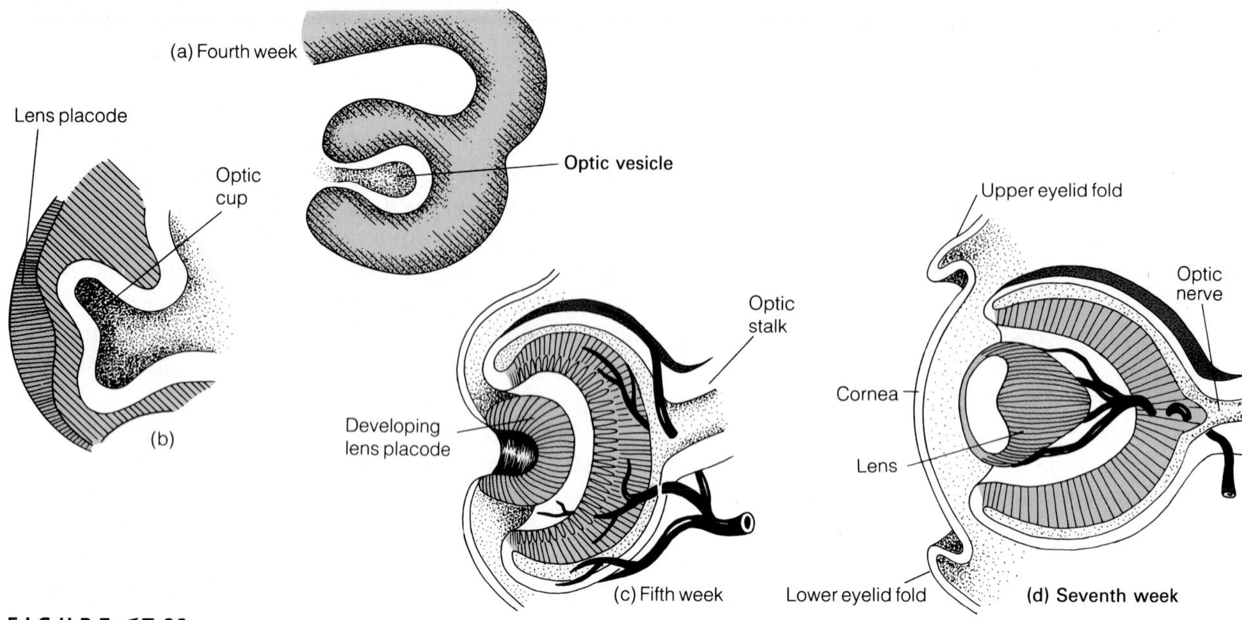

FIGURE 17-32

Embryology of the eye.

FOCUS ON . . . Ear disorders

Deafness Deafness is an impairment of hearing. In *conduction deafness,* the cause lies in the conduction of sound waves through the outer and middle ear. Some of the possible causes include impacted cerumen (wax), a ruptured eardrum, a serious middle ear infection, or otosclerosis. *Sensorineural deafness* involves damage to the inner ear or the cochlear nerve. Exposure to high-intensity noise is one cause of sensorineural deafness. With aging, there is a thickening of the eardrum, a decrease in the number of sensory hair cells, and otosclerosis, which may all contribute to hearing loss.

Eustachitis (eustach = eustachian tube; itis = inflammation of). Eustachitis is an inflammation of the eustachian tube.

Labyrinthitis (labyrinth = labyrinth; itis = inflammation of). Labyrinthitis is an inflammation of the labyrinth of the inner ear.

Meniere's syndrome Meniere's syndrome is a disorder of the inner ear thought to be caused by a dilation of the membranous labyrinth. It usually involves only one ear. Symptoms include tinnitus (see below), hearing loss, headache, and vertigo.

Motion sickness Motion sickness is an equilibrium disorder that results from an exaggerated stimulation of the vestibular apparatus by movement. Symptoms include increased salivation, yawning, profuse sweating, pallor, and hyperventilation followed by nausea and vomiting.

Myringitis (myringa = eardrum; itis = inflammation of). Myringitis is an inflammation of the tympanic membrane. It is also referred to as tympanitis.

Otalgia (oto = ear; algia = pain). Otalgia is pain in the ear, or earache.

Otitis (oto = ear; itis = inflammation of). Otitis is an inflammation of the ear.

Otitis media (oto = ear; itis = inflammation of; media = middle). Otitis media is an acute infection and inflammation of the middle ear. Pathogens commonly enter through the eustachian tube. Inflammation obstructs the eustachian tube and earache develops. The heightened pressure in the middle ear cavity may cause a rupturing of the eardrum.

Otosclerosis (oto = ear; sclerosis = hardening). Otosclerosis is a condition in which there is formation of spongy bone around the oval window. Often the stapes becomes fixed to the oval window. This decreases the transmission of vibrations and can lead to conduction deafness.

Presbycusis (presby = old; akousis = hearing). Presbycusis is the impairment of hearing brought about by old age.

Tinnitus Tinnitus is a ringing or buzzing in the ears.

Vertigo Vertigo is a dizziness or a sensation of rotation of one's self or of one's surroundings. It may originate in the ear (*peripheral vertigo*), with a disorder of the central nervous system (*central vertigo*), or have a psychological basis (*psychogenic vertigo*).

As the optic vesicles enlarge, the surface ectoderm adjacent to the optic cups thickens to become **lens placodes** (**plak**-odes). These develop into **lens vesicles** by the fifth week and become surrounded by the optic cups. The lens vesicles eventually separate from the surface ectoderm to become the lenses. The cornea develops from a thin layer of mesoderm growing between the lens vesicles and the eyelid folds.

The fibrous and vascular tunics of the eye develop from mesenchyme (mesodermal) cells that aggregate outside of the optic cups. This mesenchyme also gives rise to the muscles and connective tissue of the eye.

Embryology of the ear

The ear develops from all three germ layers, with the inner ear developing first. Between the third and fourth weeks of embryonic development, a lateral thickening on each side develops on the surface ectoderm near the rhombencephalon (hindbrain). This thickening is called the **otic** (**oh**-tik) **placode** (Fig. 17-33). The otic placode invaginates to become the **otic pit.** With further development, the edges of the otic pit join and lose their connection with the surface ectoderm. The resulting closed sac is called the **otic vesicle.** The otic vesicle becomes the structures of the membranous labyrinth. Surrounding mesoderm becomes the bony labyrinth. Fibers from the vestibulocochlear nerve (CN VIII) grow toward the otic vesicle and innervate it.

As the inner ear structures are forming, lateral pouches of the endoderm of the pharynx arise. These outpocketings are the **pharyngeal pouches.** The first pharyngeal pouch develops into the middle ear cavity and eustachian tube. The ear ossicles develop from the cartilage of this pouch and the second one.

Surface ectoderm gives rise to most of the outer ear. An indentation of the surface ectoderm, called the **branchial groove,** develops into the external auditory canal. The auricle of the outer ear is derived from a series of swellings of the tissue surrounding the canal. The outer layer of the tympanic membrane develops from ectodermal cells of the branchial groove.

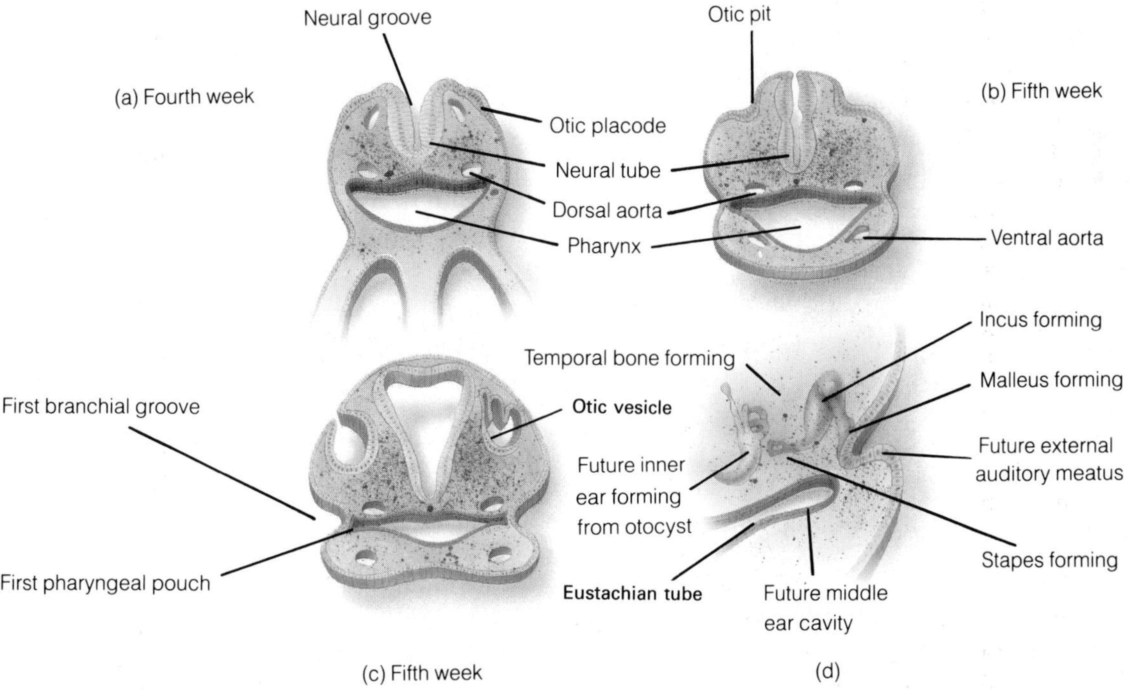

FIGURE 17-33

Embryology of the ear.

Summary

I. Sensory input about the external and internal environments is conveyed to the central nervous system.
   A. Stimuli are detectable changes in the environment.
   B. Receptors change, or transduce, the stimulus energy into electrochemical energy.
   C. Sensory (afferent) neurons take sensory input to the central nervous system. The conscious recognition of sensory stimuli is called perception.

II. The classification of sensory receptors is by receptor complexity, the location of the receptor in the body, and the nature of the stimulus.
   A. Classified by complexity, sensory receptors are either simple or complex. The general senses of the body are simple receptors. The special senses of the body are complex receptors.
   B. Classified by their location in the body, sensory receptors are exteroceptors (on surface of body), enteroceptors (within the body, especially in viscera), and proprioceptors (in skeletal muscle, tendons, and joints).
   C. By the nature of the stimulus, receptors are classified as mechanoreceptors, chemoreceptors, photoreceptors, thermoreceptors, and nociceptors.
   D. A decreased sensitivity to a stimulus over time is called adaptation. Receptors that adapt very quickly are called phasic receptors. Receptors that adapt slowly or not at all are called tonic receptors.
   E. The depolarization of a receptor upon stimulation is called a generator, or receptor, potential.
   F. Sensory information is coded by the frequency of the action potentials in sensory neurons and the number of receptors activated by the stimulus.

III. The general senses consist of mechanoreceptors (tactile receptors and proprioceptors), thermoreceptors, and nociceptors.
   A. The tactile receptors (touch, pressure, vibration, tickle, and itch) are mechanoreceptors. Tactile receptors include free nerve endings, Meissner's corpuscles, Merkel's discs, root hair plexuses, Ruffini's end-organs, Krause's end-bulbs, and pacinian corpuscles.
   B. Proprioceptors are mechanoreceptors located within the skeletal muscles (muscle spindles), tendons (Golgi tendon organs), joints (joint kinesthetic receptors), and the inner ear.
   C. Thermoreceptors respond to changes in temperature. Cold receptors are most sensitive to changes in temperature in the 10°C-to-20°C range. Warmth receptors respond best to changes in the 25°C-to-45°C range.
   D. Nociceptors, or pain receptors, are nonspecific and respond to many different types of stimuli. Somatic pain originates from the skin and muscles. Visceral pain originates in the visceral organs of the body.

IV. Olfactory receptors respond to chemicals.
   A. The olfactory receptors are located in the olfactory membrane of the superior nasal cavity.
   B. The sensory pathway for olfaction includes the olfactory nerves (CN I), olfactory bulbs, olfactory tracts, and the primary olfactory areas of the cerebral cortex.

V. The sense of taste is located in the taste buds.
   A. The gustatory cells of the taste buds are the taste receptors.
   B. The four primary sensations of taste are sweet, salty, sour, and bitter.
   C. Gustatory sensory input travels through the facial (CN VII), glossopharyngeal (CN IX), and vagus (CN X) nerves.
   D. About 80% of what we perceive as taste is actually smell.

VI. The photoreceptors are the rods and cones of the retina of the eye.
   A. The accessory structures of the eye include the orbits, eyebrows, eyelids and eyelashes, conjunctiva, lacrimal apparatus, and extrinsic muscles of the eye.
   B. The tunics of the eye are the outer fibrous tunic (cornea, sclera), the middle vascular tunic (choroid, ciliary body, iris), and the inner retinal tunic (pigmented layer, nervous layer).
   C. The outer zone of the nervous layer of the retina contains the rods and cones. Rods are stimulated by low light intensities and serve in black-and-white vision in dim light. Cones respond to bright light and serve in color vision. Cones are most concentrated in the fovea centralis.
   D. Sensory input from the photoreceptors travels through bipolar neurons and ganglion neurons. The axons of ganglion neurons travel through the optic nerves (CN II).
   E. There is an anterior and posterior cavity in each eye. The anterior cavity contains an anterior and posterior chamber filled with aqueous humor. The posterior cavity is filled with vitreous humor.
   F. Focusing of light rays on the retina involves refraction of the light, lens accommodation, pupil constriction, and eye convergence.
   G. The photoreceptors are made up of photopigments. Photopigments contain a chromophore, retinal, attached to an opsin. There are four types of photoreceptive cells: rods, blue cones, green cones, and red cones.

H. From the optic nerves, visual sensory input travels through the optic chiasma, optic tracts, lateral geniculate nuclei of the thalamus, and the visual areas of the occipital cortex.

VII. The receptors for hearing and equilibrium are located in the inner ears.

A. The ears are made up of the outer ear (auricle, external auditory canal, tympanic membrane), middle ear (ossicles), and inner ear (bony and membranous labyrinths).

B. Sound receptors are found in the organs of Corti along the basilar membrane of the cochlea of the inner ear.

C. Static equilibrium is detected by hair cells in the maculae of the utricles and saccules. Dynamic equilibrium is detected by hair cells in the cristae of the ampulla of the semicircular ducts.

D. Sensory input of hearing travels in the cochlear nerve, and input about equilibrium travels in the vestibular nerve. These nerves join to form the vestibulocochlear nerve (CN VIII).

Post-test

Match (multiple answers may be appropriate.)

____	1. Muscle spindles	a. chemoreceptor
____	2. Cristae	b. nociceptor
____	3. Rods	c. mechanoreceptor
____	4. Ruffini's end-organs	d. photoreceptor
____	5. Free nerve endings	e. thermoreceptor
____	6. Meissner's corpuscles	
____	7. Golgi tendon organs	
____	8. Gustatory cells	
____	9. Maculae	
____	10. Organs of Corti	
____	11. Cones	
____	12. Root hair plexuses	
____	13. Pacinian corpuscles	
____	14. Olfactory cells	

____ 15. Receptors responding to stimuli from the external environment are classified as: (a) proprioceptors, (b) enteroceptors, (c) exteroceptors.

____ 16. Vibrations of the stapes are transmitted to the: (a) round window, (b) oval window, (c) tympanic membrane, (d) auricle.

____ 17. The middle ear communicates with the nasopharynx through the: (a) eustachian tube, (b) scala tympani, (c) external auditory canal, (d) membranous labyrinth.

____ 18. The choroid is part of which layer of the eye: (a) pigmented layer of retina, (b) vascular layer, (c) fibrous layer, (d) nervous layer of retina.

____ 19. An example of a tonic receptor is an: (a) olfactory cell, (b) pain receptor, (c) pacinian corpuscle, (d) Meissner's corpuscle.

____ 20. Which one of the following receptors is activated by a hyperpolarization? (a) Merkel's disc, (b) gustatory cell, (c) pacinian corpuscle, (d) rods.

____ 21. Sensory input about equilibrium travels through which cranial nerve? (a) I, (b) VIII, (c) IX, (d) II, (e) X.

____ 22. Nearsightedness is referred to as: (a) myopia, (b) emmetropia, (c) astigmatism, (d) hyperopia.

____ 23. Which extrinsic eye muscle causes the eye to turn toward the nose? (a) superior oblique, (b) medial rectus, (c) lateral rectus, (d) inferior rectus.

____ 24. In the embryo, the double-layered optic cup becomes the: (a) retina, (b) iris, (c) cornea, (d) lens.

____ 25. The membranous labyrinth of the ear develops from the: (a) otic vesicles, (b) pharyngeal pouch, (c) branchial groove, (d) vestibulocochlear nerve.

Review questions

1. Compare the innervations and functions of the radial and circular smooth muscles of the iris and how they affect the size of the pupil.
2. Define "referred pain" and give examples.
3. How are different pitches and sound intensities detected by the hair cells of the inner ear?
4. Why does sniffing odors improve taste?
5. How can one discern many different colors when there are only red cones, green cones, and blue cones?
6. Trace sensory input from photoreceptors to the primary visual area of the occipital cortex.

7. Describe the differences in the reception of static and dynamic equilibrium.
8. Explain why a person is unable to see upon entering a dim room from a brightly lit one.
9. Describe abnormalities resulting from problems with the extrinsic muscles of the eyes.
10. Compare differences in phasic and tonic receptors, giving examples.
11. Explain how a generator potential differs from an action potential.
12. Give the physiological sequence of events necessary for a Golgi tendon organ to bring about a decrease in tendon tension.
13. Trace the flow of excess tears from the lacrimal glands to the nasal cavity.
14. Explain how the rods and the cones actually transduce light energy.
15. Give the physiological sequence of events in the transmission and transduction of sound waves from the auricle of the outer ear to the organs of Corti in the inner ear.
16. Label the numbered structures on the following diagrams. (See Figs. 17-13 and 17-24.)

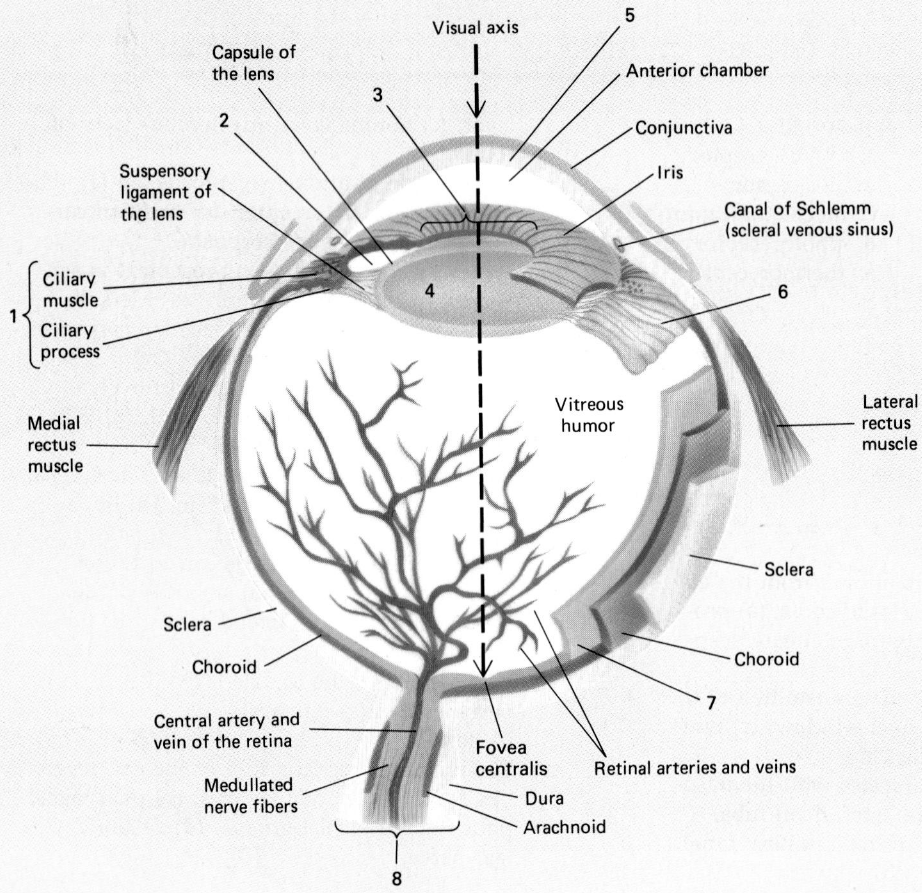

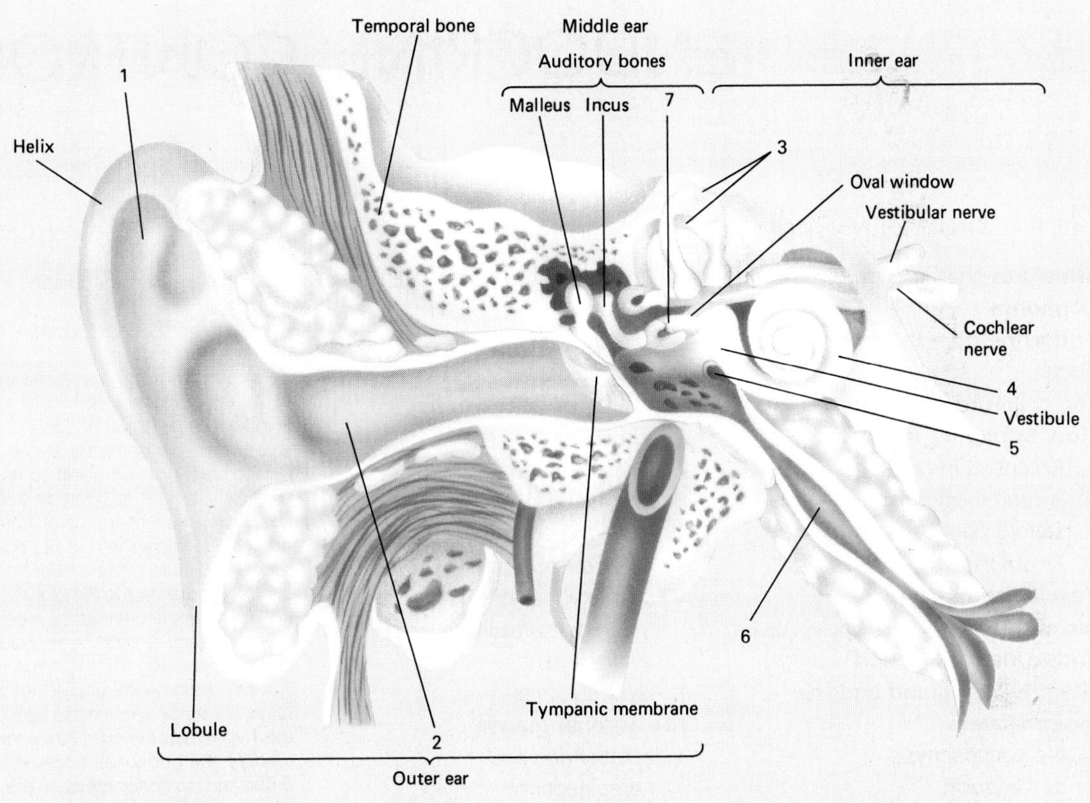

Post-test answers

1. c **2.** c **3.** d **4.** c (e) **5.** b, e **6.** c
7. c **8.** a **9.** c **10.** c **11.** d **12.** c
13. c **14.** a **15.** c **16.** b **17.** a **18.** b
19. b **20.** d **21.** b **22.** a **23.** b **24.** a
25. a

ENDOCRINE CONTROL

CHAPTER OUTLINE

- I. **Structures that secrete hormones**
- II. **Endocrine glands have no ducts**
- III. **The chemistry of hormones**
- IV. **How hormones work**
  - A. Receptors in target cells
  - B. Second messengers
  - C. Steroid hormones
  - D. Prostaglandins
- V. **Regulation of hormone secretion**
- VI. **Endocrine malfunction**
- VII. **The pituitary gland and the hypothalamus**
  - A. Neurohypophysis
    - 1. Oxytocin
    - 2. Antidiuretic hormone
  - B. Adenohypophysis
    - 1. Regulation by the hypothalamus
    - 2. Growth hormone
      - a. Regulation of growth hormone
      - b. Disturbances in growth
    - 3. Prolactin (lactogenic hormone)
    - 4. Tropic hormones
- VIII. **The thyroid gland**
  - A. Production of thyroid hormones
  - B. Functions of thyroid hormones
  - C. Regulation of thyroid hormone secretion
- IX. **Parathyroid glands**
  - A. Function of parathyroid hormones
  - B. Regulation of PTH secretion
  - C. Calcitonin
  - D. Disorders of calcium metabolism
- X. **The islets of Langerhans**
  - A. Insulin
  - B. Glucagon
  - C. Regulation of insulin and glucagon secretion
  - D. Diabetes mellitus
    - 1. Metabolic effects of diabetes mellitus
    - 2. Treatment
  - E. Hypoglycemia
- XI. **The adrenal glands**
  - A. Epinephrine and norepinephrine
    - 1. Fight-or-flight response
    - 2. Secretion of epinephrine and norepinephrine
  - B. Adrenal cortex
    - 1. Sex hormones
    - 2. Mineralocorticoids
    - 3. Regulation of aldosterone secretion
    - 4. Glucocorticoids
      - a. Clinical uses
      - b. Regulation of glucocorticoid secretion
    - 5. Malfunctions of adrenocortical secretion
- XII. **The effects of stress on homeostasis**
- XIII. **The pineal gland**
- XIV. **Other hormones**

LEARNING OBJECTIVES

After you have studied this chapter you should be able to:

1 Distinguish between endocrine and exocrine glands.
2 Define the term hormone and describe the functions of hormones.
3 Identify the principal endocrine glands and locate them anatomically in the body.
4 Relate an endocrine gland to its target tissues with regard to function and location.
5 Describe the mechanisms of hormone action, including the role of second messengers such as cyclic AMP.
6 Describe how endocrine glands are regulated by negative-feedback mechanisms; relate to each specific hormone discussed.
7 Justify describing the hypothalamus as the link between neural and endocrine systems. (Describe the mechanisms by which the hypothalamus exerts its control.)
8 Identify the hormones released by the anterior and posterior lobes of the pituitary, give their origin, and describe their actions.
9 Describe the actions of growth hormone on growth and metabolism, and describe the consequences of hyposecretion and hypersecretion.
10 Identify the hormones secreted by the thyroid gland and summarize their physiological actions.
11 Describe the feedback control mechanisms by which thyroid hormone secretion is regulated (be able to draw a diagram to illustrate the mechanisms), and describe the consequences of hyposecretion and hypersecretion.
12 Summarize the interrelationships of parathyroid hormone, vitamin D, and calcitonin in regulating calcium levels in the blood and interstitial fluid.
13 Contrast the actions of insulin and glucagon.
14 Relate the physiological bases of diabetes mellitus and hypoglycemia to their metabolic and clinical symptoms.
15 Describe the role of the adrenal medulla in the body's physiological responses to stress, specifying the actions of the adrenal hormones epinephrine and norepinephrine.
16 Describe the actions of mineralocorticoids and glucocorticoids, summarize how their secretion is regulated, and give the effects of malfunction.

Hormone receptors in the hippocampus of an infant. (Wolf/Explorer/Photo Researchers, Inc.)

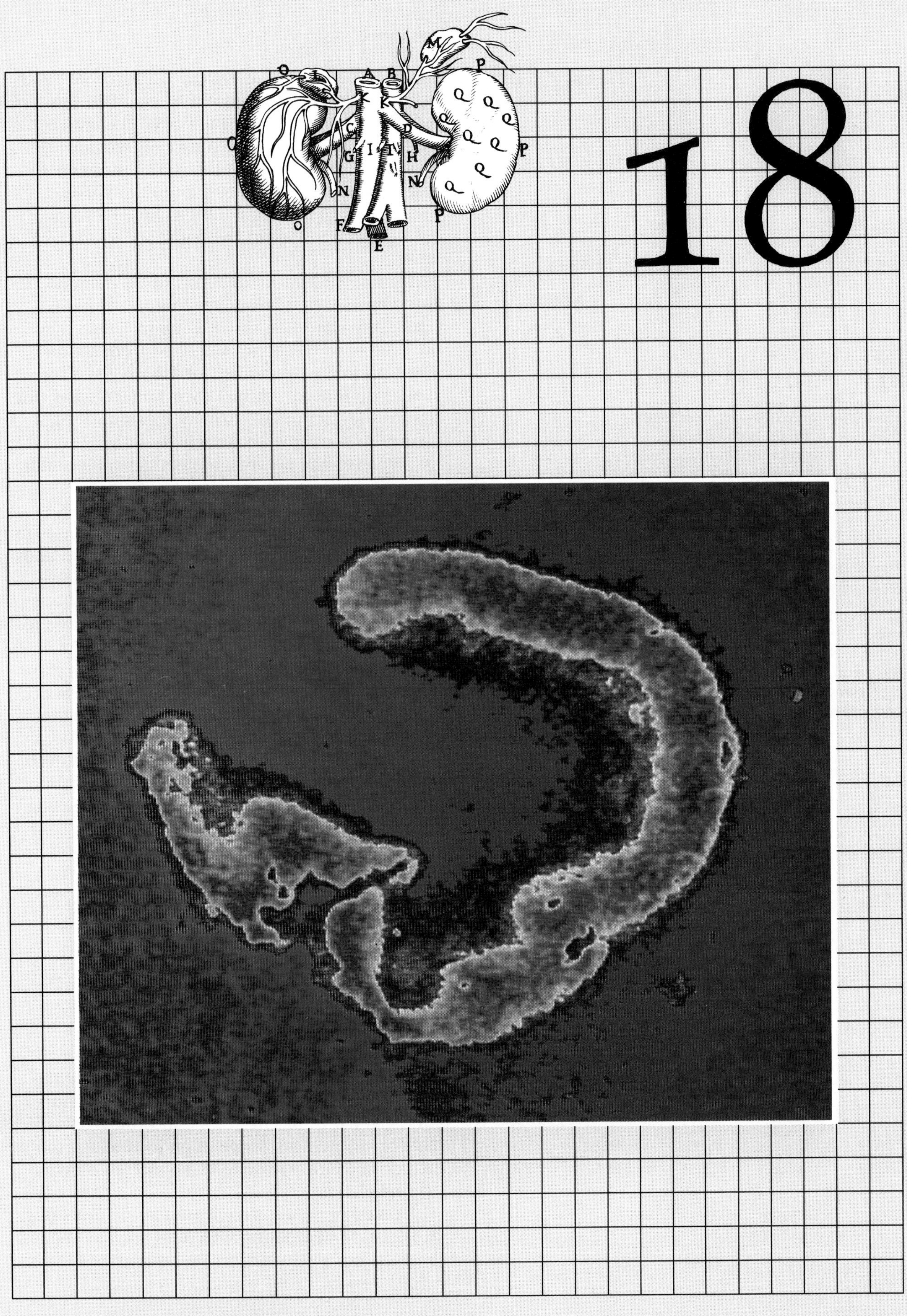
18

KEY CONCEPTS

Hormones are chemical messengers that help regulate homeostasis, growth, and reproduction and help the body cope with stress.

Many hormones are produced by endocrine glands and transported to their target tissues by the blood.

Hormone secretion is regulated by feedback control mechanisms.

The hypothalamus is the link between nervous and endocrine systems; the hypothalamus regulates the pituitary gland, and the pituitary gland regulates several other endocrine glands.

The endocrine system works closely with the nervous system to maintain the steady state of the body. The endocrine system helps regulate such diverse activities as growth, reproduction, utilization of nutrients by cells, the adjustment of salt and fluid balance, and metabolic rate. In addition, the endocrine system is important in the body's adaptation to stress.

Endocrine control depends upon chemical messengers called **hormones** that have specific regulatory effects on the cells upon which they act. The term hormone is derived from a Greek word meaning "to arouse" or "to excite." Hormones do indeed "excite" their **target tissues** (the tissues they act upon), usually by stimulating a change in some metabolic activity.

Whereas the nervous system generally sends its messages over short distances, hormones released by the endocrine system can have widespread effects throughout the body. Responses to nervous system stimulation tend to be rapid and brief. In contrast, responses to hormones may require several hours or even longer and effects may be long lasting. Sometimes the target tissue may be very specific, as in the case of the male hormone testosterone, which causes hair to grow on the face but not on the scalp. In other cases the entire body can be the target. For example, the thyroid hormones stimulate metabolic rate in most cells. Many hormones have multiple effects.

The study of endocrine function and malfunction, known as **endocrinology,** is a very exciting field of biological research.

Hormones are secreted by glands and neurons

Hormones are secreted by (1) endocrine glands, (2) neurons, and (3) other types of cells.

Hormones secreted by **endocrine glands** (glands without ducts) were the first hormones identified, and traditionally, hormones were defined as chemical messengers secreted by endocrine glands. In recent years endocrinologists have broadened the scope of endocrinology to include chemical messengers not secreted by endocrine glands.

Some hormones are released by neurons (Fig. 18-1). These **neurohormones** (**new**-row-*hor*-mones)

ow-se-
ıss two
r mus.
l mes-
se
mo y
wh. wth
facto n-
ples.

Endocrine glands have no ducts

The principal endocrine glands are illustrated in Figure 18-2 and described in Table 18-1. Recall (Chapter 4) that we can distinguish between endocrine glands and exocrine glands. Exocrine glands such as sweat glands have ducts into which they release their products. The ducts gen-

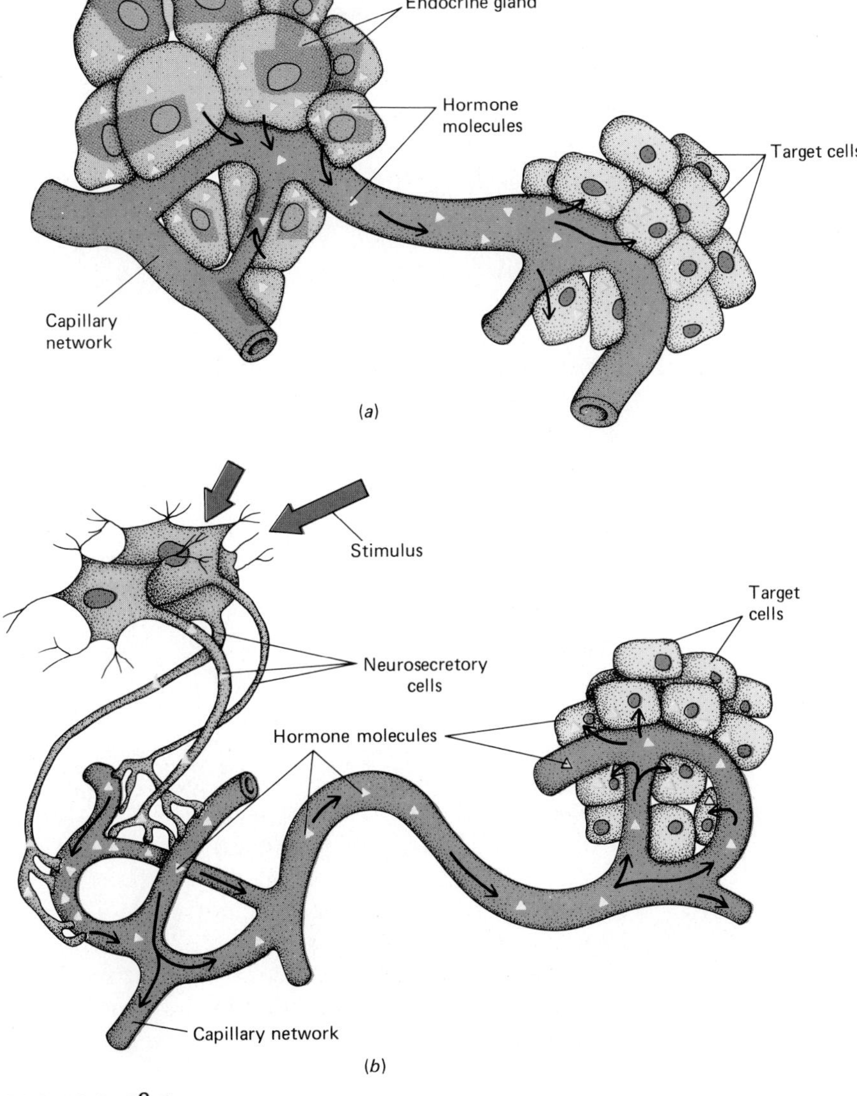

FIGURE 18-1

Hormones are secreted by the cells of endocrine glands, (*a*). Some hormones are secreted by neurosecretory cells, (*b*). Hormones are generally transported by the blood and are taken up by target cells.

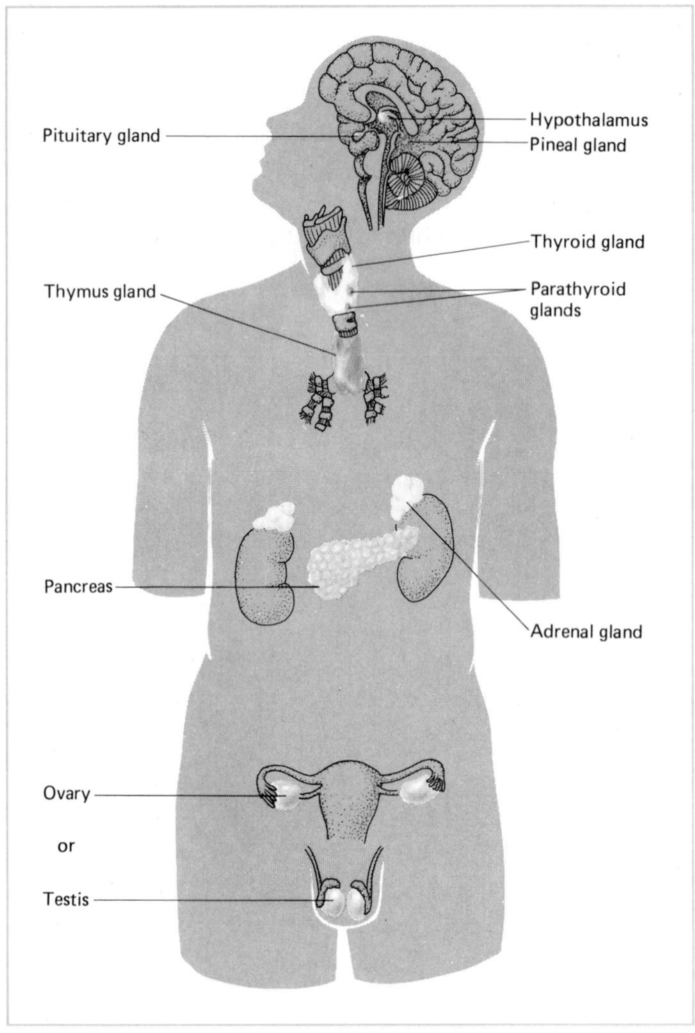

FIGURE 18-2

Location of the principal endocrine glands. Gonads of both female (ovaries) and male (testes) are shown.

TABLE 18-1

Some endocrine glands and their hormones*		
Endocrine gland and hormone	**Target tissue**	**Principal actions**
Hypothalamus Releasing and release-inhibiting hormones	Anterior lobe of pituitary	Stimulates or inhibits secretion of specific hormones
Hypothalamus (production) *Posterior lobe of pituitary* (storage and release)		
Oxytocin	Uterus Mammary glands	Stimulates contraction Stimulates ejection of milk into ducts
Antidiuretic hormone (vasopressin)	Kidneys (collecting ducts)	Stimulates reabsorption of water; conserves water

TABLE 18-1 (*continued*)

Endocrine gland and hormone	Target tissue	Principal actions
Anterior lobe of pituitary		
Growth hormone	General	Stimulates growth by promoting protein synthesis
Prolactin	Mammary glands	Stimulates milk production
Thyroid-stimulating hormone	Thyroid gland	Stimulates secretion of thyroid hormones; stimulates increase in size of thyroid gland
Adrenocorticotropic hormone	Adrenal cortex	Stimulates secretion of adrenal cortical hormones
Gonadotropic hormones (follicle-stimulating hormone, FSH; luteinizing hormone, LH)	Gonads	Stimulate gonad function and growth
Thyroid gland		
Thyroxine (T_4) and triiodothyronine (T_3)	General	Stimulate metabolic rate; essential to normal growth and development
Calcitonin	Bone	Lowers blood-calcium level by inhibiting bone breakdown by osteoclasts
Parathyroid glands		
Parathyroid hormone	Bone, kidneys, digestive tract	Increases blood-calcium level by stimulating bone breakdown; stimulates calcium reabsorption by kidneys; activates vitamin D
Islets of Langerhans of pancreas		
Insulin	General	Lowers glucose concentration in the blood by facilitating glucose uptake and utilization by cells; stimulates glycogenesis; stimulates fat storage and protein synthesis
Glucagon	Liver, adipose tissue	Raises glucose concentration in the blood by stimulating glycogenolysis and gluconeogenesis; mobilizes fat
Adrenal medulla		
Epinephrine and norepinephrine	Muscle, cardiac muscle, blood vessels, liver, adipose tissue	Help body cope with stress; increase heart rate, blood pressure, metabolic rate; reroute blood; mobilize fat; raise blood-sugar level
Adrenal cortex		
Mineralocorticoids (aldosterone)	Kidney tubules	Maintain sodium and phosphate balance
Glucocorticoids (cortisol)	General	Help body adapt to long-term stress; raise blood-glucose level; mobilize fat
Pineal gland		
Melatonin	Gonads, pigment cells, other tissues(?)	Influences reproductive processes in hamsters and other animals; pigmentation in some vertebrates; may control biorhythms in some animals; may help control onset of puberty in humans
Ovary†		
Estrogens (Estradiol)	General; uterus	Develop and maintain sex characteristics in female; stimulate growth of uterine lining
Progesterone	Uterus; breast	Stimulates development of uterine lining
Testis‡		
Testosterone	General; reproductive structures	Develops and maintains sex characteristics of males; promotes spermatogenesis; responsible for adolescent growth spurt
Inhibin	Anterior lobe of pituitary	Inhibits FSH release

*The ovaries and testes and their hormones are discussed in Chapter 29. The digestive hormones are described in Chapter 25.

†For more detailed description see Table 29-2.

‡For more detailed description see Table 29-1.

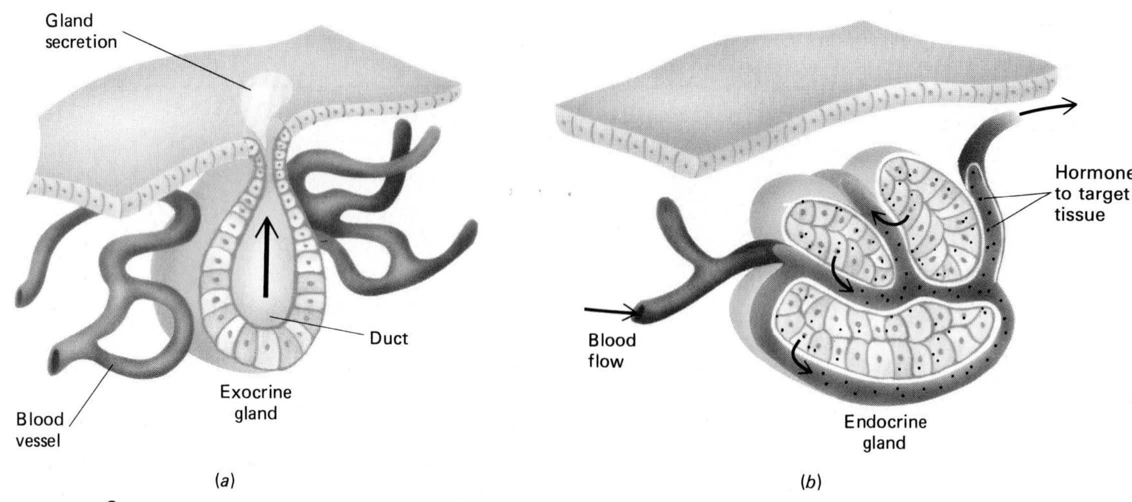

FIGURE 18-3

Comparison of *(a)* exocrine with *(b)* endocrine gland. The secretion of an exocrine gland passes into a duct which conveys it to its final destination. For example, sweat passes through the duct of a sweat gland to reach the surface of the skin. The hormone of an endocrine gland is released into the interstitial fluid and may diffuse into the blood, which transports it throughout the body.

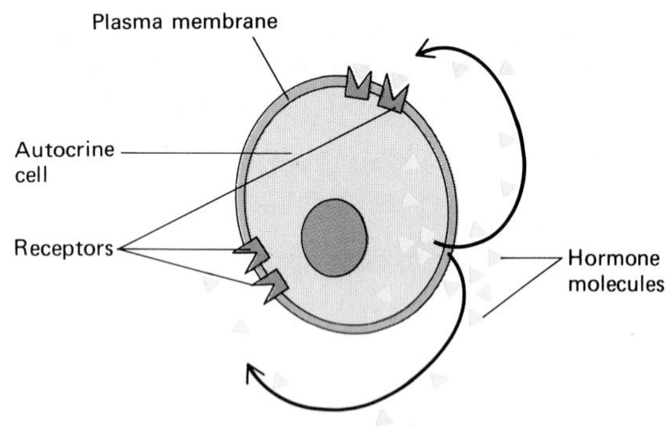

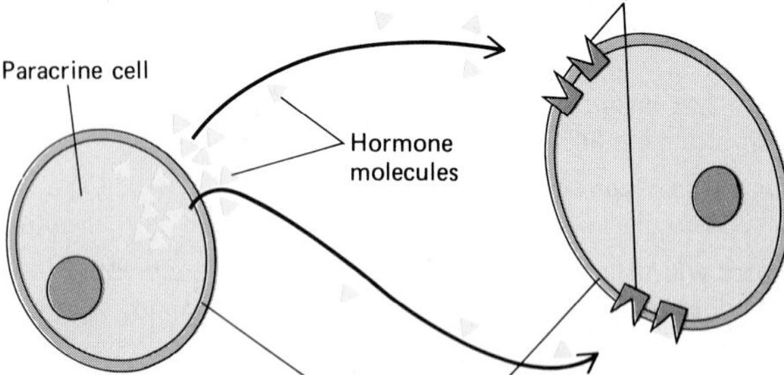

FIGURE 18-4

Comparison of autocrine *(a)* and paracrine *(b)* regulation.

erally deliver the secretion to an external or internal body surface. An endocrine gland does not have a duct through which to release its secretion (Fig. 18-3). Instead it simply releases its hormone into the surrounding interstitial fluid. The hormone may then diffuse into a capillary and be transported by the blood to its **target tissue,** where it will exert its influence. However, not all hormones are transported by the bloodstream.

In **paracrine** regulation, the target cell is close to the cell releasing the hormone. The secreted hormone diffuses to the neighboring target tissue. These hormones are appropriately referred to as local mediators. The target tissue may be another endocrine gland, or it may be an entirely different type of tissue, such as bone or liver (Fig. 18-4). In **autocrine** regulation, hormones act upon the very cell from which they were secreted.

Many types of chemicals serve as hormones

Although hormones are chemically diverse, they generally belong to one of three different chemical groups: (1) steroids, (2) amino acid derivatives, and (3) peptides or proteins. A fourth group, made up of the prostaglandins, are derived from fatty acids.

Steroid hormones are derived from cholesterol and secreted by the sex glands and by the adrenal cortex (Fig. 18-5). Progesterone, one of the female sex hormones, is used in both males and females to produce several other steroid hormones including those secreted by the adrenal cortex (Fig. 18-6).

Chemically the simplest hormones are those derived from the amino acid tyrosine; they are referred to as **amines.** Examples of hormones that are amines are the thyroid hormones produced by the thyroid gland and epinephrine and norepinephrine produced by the medulla of the adrenal gland (Fig. 18-7).

Oxytocin and antidiuretic hormone, produced by neurosecretory cells in the hypothalamus, are short **peptides** composed of nine amino acids. Seven of the amino acids are identical in the two hormones, but the actions of these hormones are quite different.

The hormones glucagon, secretin, adrenocorticotropic hormone (ACTH), and calcitonin are somewhat longer peptides with about 30 amino acids in the chain. Insulin, secreted by the islets of Langerhans in the pancreas, is a protein consisting of two peptide chains joined by disulfide bonds (Fig. 2-26a, p. 67).

Hormones act on target cells

Most endocrine glands secrete small amounts of their hormones continuously. Thus, at any moment 30 to 40 different hormones may be present in the blood. Many of them are there in minute amounts, some in concentrations as low as one-millionth of a milligram per milliliter. Steroid hormones and some peptide hormones are transported bound to proteins in the blood called plasma proteins. Large peptides and protein hormones are soluble in the blood and are carried free in the blood plasma.

Hormones diffuse into the interstitial tissues and are taken up by target tissues. Several different hormones might be involved in regulating the metabolic activities of a single target tissue. Often hormones have *synergistic* effects; that is, the presence of one enhances the effect of the other.

Hormones are also taken up by the liver, which inactivates some hormones, and the kidneys, which excrete them. Clinically, the rate of secretion of a specific hormone can be estimated indirectly by analyzing the rate of its excretion in the urine.

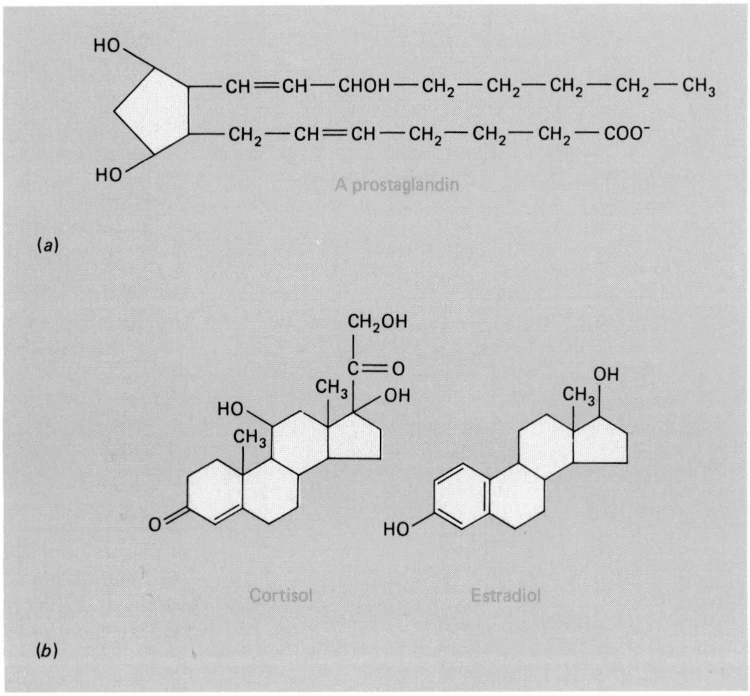

FIGURE 18-5

Hormones derived from fatty acids and steroids. *(a)* Prostaglandins are derived from fatty acids. *(b)* Cortisol and estradiol, steroid hormones secreted by the adrenal cortex.

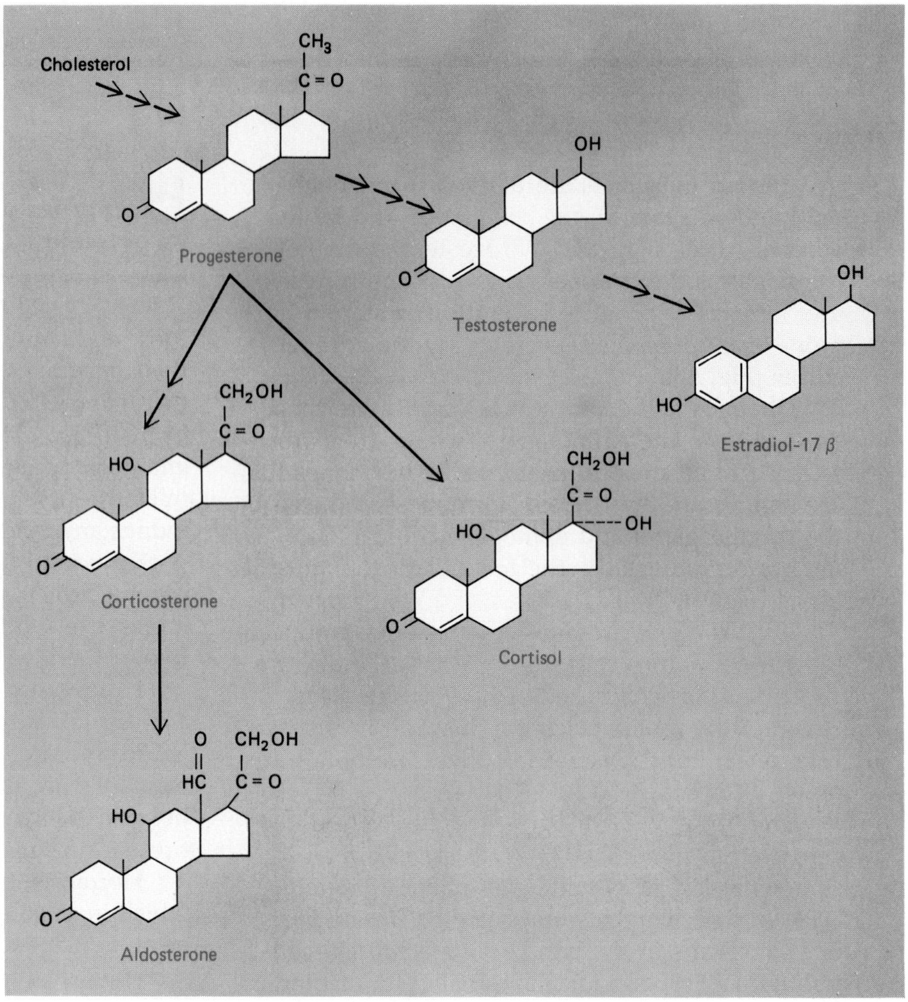

Cholesterol

Progesterone

Testosterone

Estradiol-17 β

Corticosterone

Cortisol

Aldosterone

FIGURE 18-6

The sequence of reactions by which progesterone, a female sex hormone, is used to synthesize testosterone (the principal male hormone), estradiol (a principal female hormone), and hormones secreted by the adrenal cortex (the glucocorticoids corticosterone and cortisol, and the mineralocorticoid aldosterone). Progesterone is synthesized from cholesterol. Multiple arrows indicate that intermediate steps are involved that have been omitted from the diagram. Note that the methyl (CH_3) groups attached to each line extending upward have been omitted.

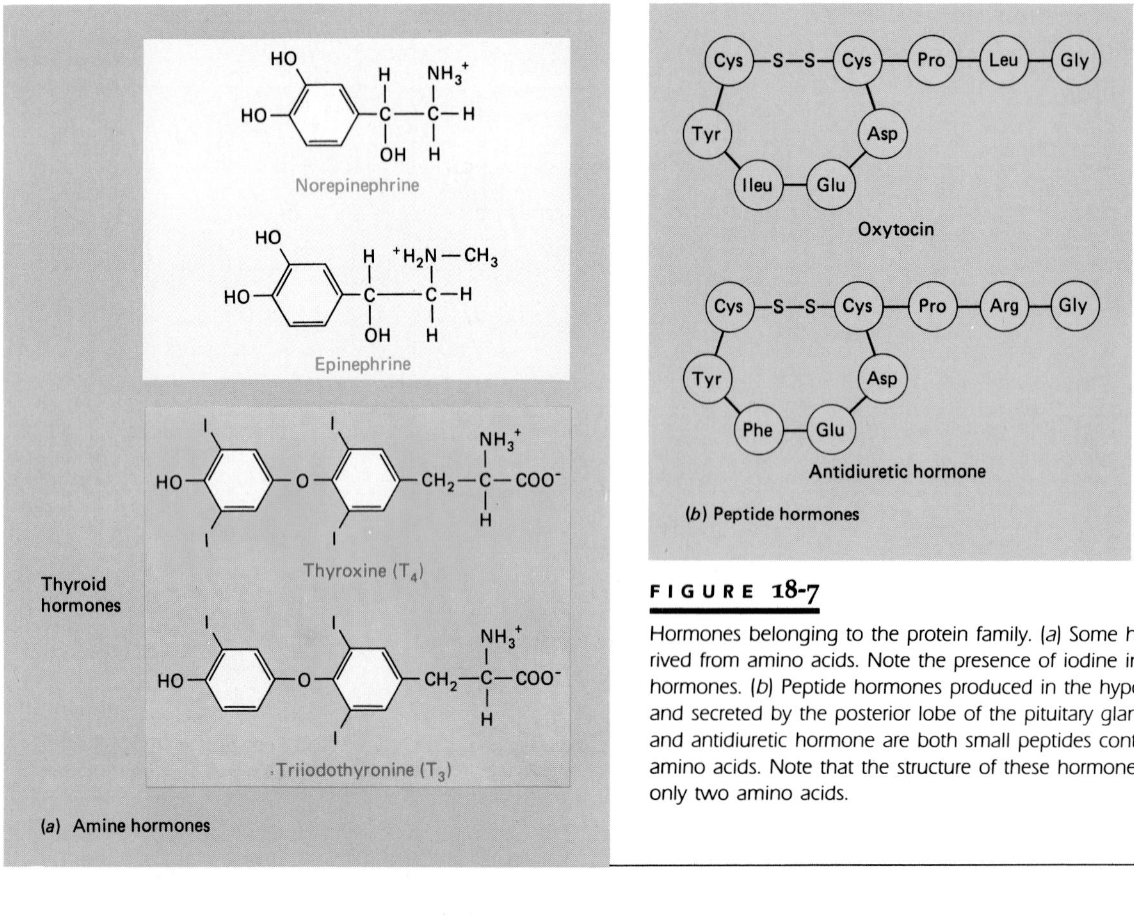

Norepinephrine

Epinephrine

Thyroid hormones

Thyroxine (T_4)

Triiodothyronine (T_3)

(*a*) Amine hormones

Oxytocin

Antidiuretic hormone

(*b*) Peptide hormones

FIGURE 18-7

Hormones belonging to the protein family. (*a*) Some hormones derived from amino acids. Note the presence of iodine in the thyroid hormones. (*b*) Peptide hormones produced in the hypothalamus and secreted by the posterior lobe of the pituitary gland. Oxytocin and antidiuretic hormone are both small peptides containing nine amino acids. Note that the structure of these hormones differs by only two amino acids.

Hormones combine with receptors in target cells

A hormone may pass through many tissues seemingly "unnoticed" until it reaches its target tissue. How does the target tissue "recognize" its hormone? Specialized receptor proteins on or in the target cell bind the hormone. This is a highly specific process. The receptor site is like a lock, and the hormones are like different keys. Only the hormone that fits the lock can influence the metabolic machinery of the cell.

A hormone generally does not directly affect the activity of the cell it regulates. When the hormone combines with the receptor, a series of reactions is activated. Because the hormone turns on the system, it is referred to as the **first messenger.** How does the hormone influence the activity of the cell?

Many hormones act through second messengers

Peptide hormones combine with receptors on the plasma membrane of the target cell. Then a hormonal message is relayed to the appropriate site within the cell by a **second messenger** (Fig. 18-8).

In the 1960s Earl Sutherland identified **cyclic AMP** (adenosine monophosphate; cAMP) as a hormone intermediary, and it is the second messenger that has been most extensively studied. When the hormone combines with its receptor protein on the extracellular face of the plasma membrane, a membrane-bound enzyme, **adenylate cyclase,** is activated. Adenylate cyclase, however, is located on the cytoplasmic side of the plasma membrane. How then does this activation occur?

A third protein, known as **G protein,** is also located on the cytoplasmic side of the plasma membrane and acts as a shuttle for communication between the receptor and adenylate cyclase (Fig. 18-9). Two types of G protein exist. One type, G_s, stimulates adenylate cyclase, and the other, G_i, inhibits it. When the system is inactive, G protein binds to **guanosine diphosphate,** or **GDP,** which is similar to the hydrolyzed form of ATP, ADP.

Most hormones bind to a stimulatory receptor, resulting in activation of adenylate cyclase. After the receptor-hormone complex is formed, GDP falls off of the G protein and the G protein binds to **guanosine triphosphate (GTP).** GTP, like ATP, stores energy in the form of high-energy phosphate bonds. The acquisition of GTP produces a conformational change in the G protein that enables the G protein to bind with, and thereby activate, adenylate cyclase.

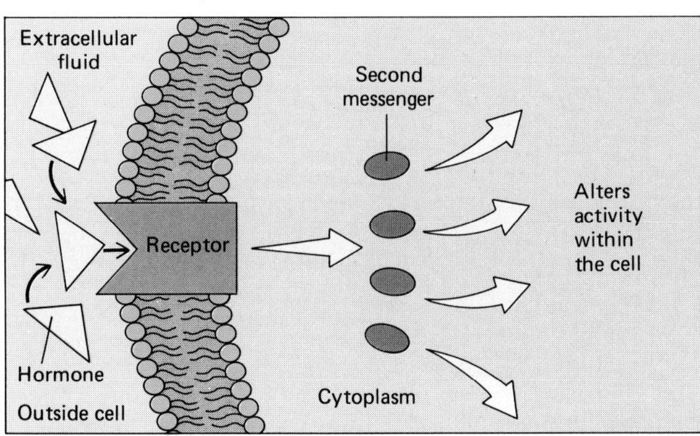

FIGURE 18-8

Peptide hormones combine with receptors on the plasma membrane of a target cell. The hormonal message is relayed by a second messenger.

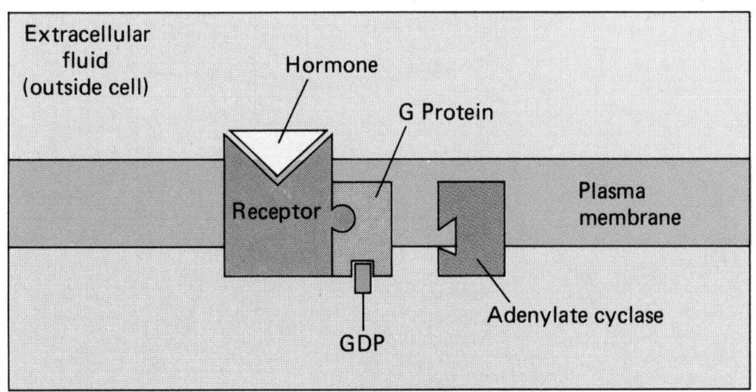

(*a*) Cytoplasm

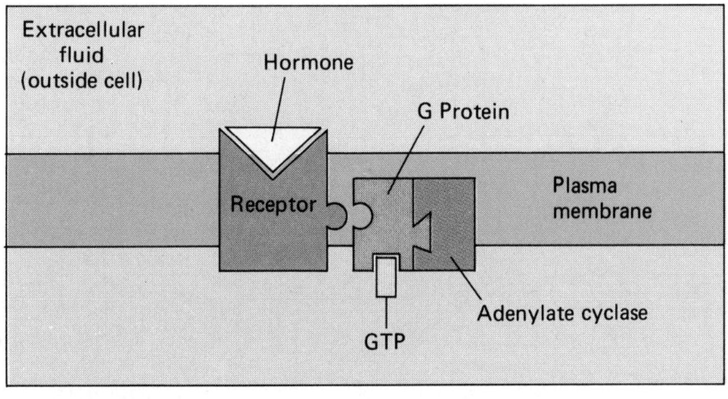

(*b*) Cytoplasm

FIGURE 18-9

Role of the G protein. (*a*) A hormone binds to a receptor on the plasma membrane. The hormone-receptor complex binds to a G protein. (*b*) GDP on the G protein is replaced by GTP. G protein undergoes a conformational change (change in shape) allowing it to bind with adenylate cyclase. The adenylate cyclase is activated and catalyzes the conversion of ATP to cAMP.

Once activated, adenylate cyclase catalyzes the conversion of the chemical compound adenosine triphosphate (ATP) to cyclic AMP (Fig. 18-10). The cyclic AMP then activates one or more enzymes known as **protein kinases.** Each type of protein kinase catalyzes the phosphorylation of (addition of a phosphate group to) a specific protein. The phosphorylation of the protein causes it to trigger the chain of reactions that leads to the specified metabolic effect. Any increase in cyclic AMP is temporary; it is rapidly inactivated by enzymes known as phosphodiesterases that convert it to AMP.

Protein kinases are enzymes that inhibit or activate other enzymes. Also, each different protein kinase acts on a different type of enzyme. There are different types in each kind of target cell and even within different organelles of the same target cell. As a result, protein kinases are able to produce a wide variety of responses. For example, activation of one type of protein kinase may have a metabolic effect on the cell, whereas another protein kinase may affect membrane permeability, and a third may activate genes (Fig. 18-11).

Another important second messenger is the calcium ion. As certain hormones bind to their receptors on the plasma membrane, calcium channels open, resulting in an influx of extracellular calcium. Cyclic AMP can also increase the cellular concentration of calcium by releasing calcium stored in the smooth ER. Once the calcium concentration in the cell is increased, calcium ions bind to the protein **calmodulin** (kal-**mod**-u-lin). The calcium-calmodulin complex can then activate certain enzymes. Some cellular processes regulated by this complex include membrane phosphorylation, neurotransmitter release, and microtubule disassembly.

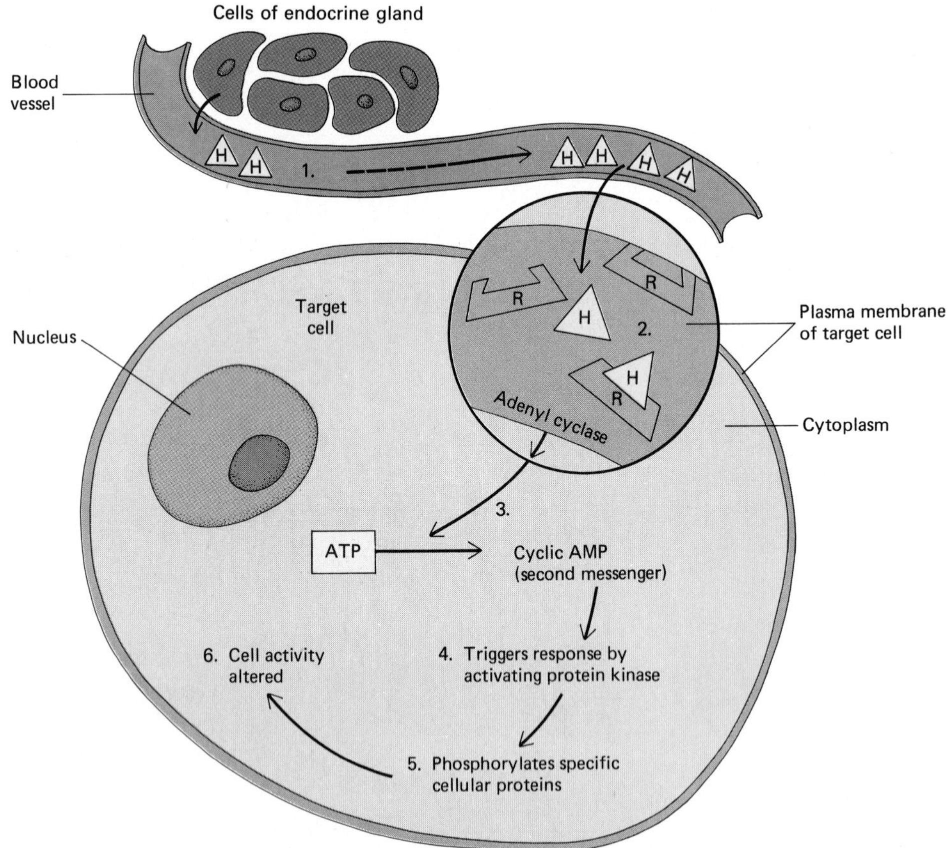

FIGURE 18-10

Overview of the second messenger mechanism of hormone action. After they are (1) secreted by an endocrine gland and transported by the blood to a target cell, peptide hormones (2) combine with receptors in the plasma membrane of a target cell. (3) The hormone-receptor combination activates an enzyme, adenylate cyclase, located on the inner surface of the membrane. The adenylate cyclase catalyzes the conversion of ATP to cyclic AMP, a second messenger. (4) Cyclic AMP then activates a protein kinase which (5) phosphorylates a specific protein. (6) The activity of the cell is altered.

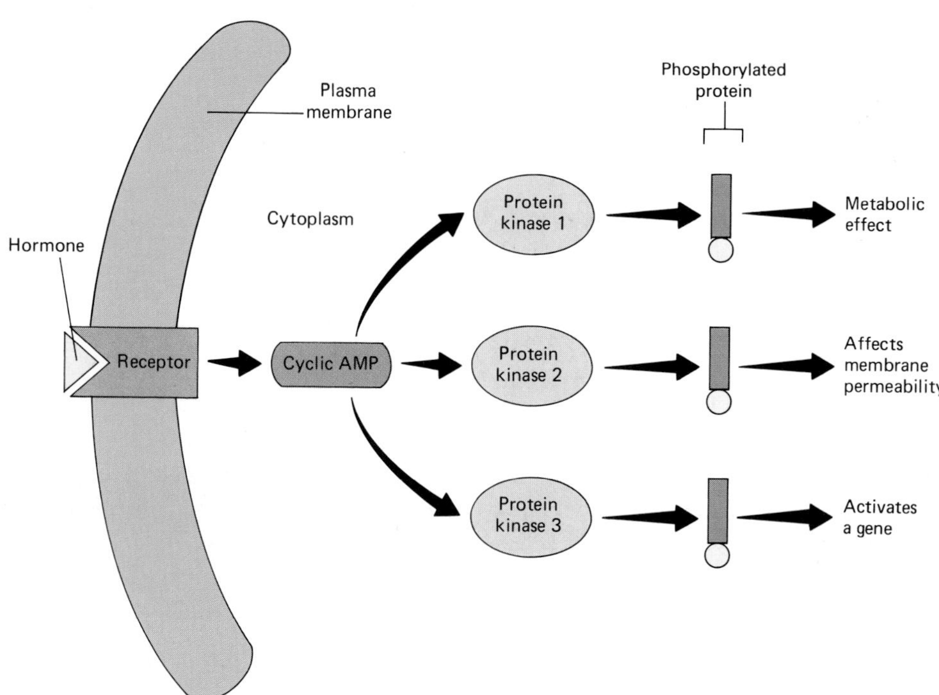

FIGURE 18-11

When a hormone binds to a receptor on the cell surface and increases the amount of cyclic AMP in the cell, protein kinases are activated. Protein kinases phosphorylate proteins leading to a variety of effects.

Steroid hormones activate genes

Steroid hormones and thyroid hormones are relatively small, lipid-soluble molecules that pass easily through the plasma membrane of a target cell, through the cytoplasm, and into the nucleus (Fig. 18-12). Specific protein receptors in the nucleus combine with the hormone to form a hormone-receptor complex. Until recently, receptors for steroid hormones were thought to be present in the cytoplasm of target cells. However, investigators now think that the receptors are either on the nuclear envelope or within the nucleus.

The receptors are mobile, soluble proteins that combine with a specific hormone. The hormone-receptor complex then interacts with specific acceptor sites on the DNA. This interaction activates appropriate genes and leads to the synthesis of needed proteins. These proteins may stimulate changes in cell activities.

Prostaglandins are local chemical mediators

Prostaglandins (*pros*-tah-**glan**-dins) are a group of closely related lipids (fatty acids, each with a 5-carbon ring in its structure) synthesized and released by many different tissues in the body.

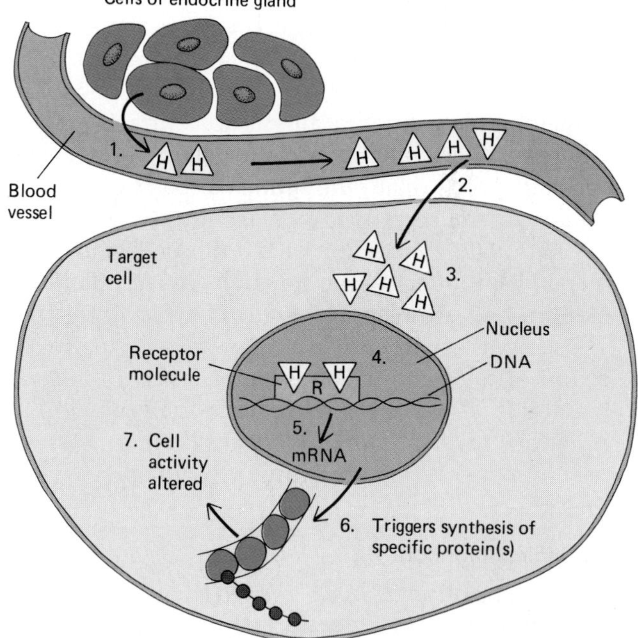

FIGURE 18-12

Activation of genes by steroid hormones. (1) Steroid hormones are secreted by an endocrine gland and transported to a target cell. (2) Steroid hormones are small, lipid-soluble molecules that pass freely through the plasma membrane. (3) The hormone passes through the cytoplasm to the nucleus. (4) Inside the nucleus, the hormone combines with a receptor. Then, the steroid hormone-receptor complex combines with a protein associated with the DNA. (5) This activates specific genes, leading to the mRNA transcription and (6) synthesis of specific proteins. The proteins cause the response recognized as the hormone's action (7).

These include the prostate gland (where they were first identified), lungs, liver, and digestive tract. Although present in very small quantities, prostaglandins exert a wide range of physiological, hormone-like actions on many tissues and body processes. They are often referred to as **local hormones** because they act on cells in their immediate vicinity.

Prostaglandins interact with other hormones to regulate various metabolic activities. Prostaglandins mimic many of the actions of cyclic AMP. Depending upon the specific tissue type, they stimulate or inhibit formation of cyclic AMP. In this way, prostaglandins can modulate cellular response to hormones that use cyclic AMP as a second messenger.

Prostaglandins are classified in several groups designated as PGA through PGI on the basis of their chemical structure. A subscript number is used to identify the number of double bonds in their side chains; thus, PGE_1, for example, has one double bond, whereas PGF_2 has two double bonds.

Various prostaglandins have different actions on different tissues. Members of the A and E groups tend to reduce blood pressure; those of the F group raise it. Some prostaglandins cause capillary constriction; others dilate capillaries. Some stimulate smooth muscle to contract, whereas others cause muscle to relax. Various prostaglandins dilate the bronchial passageways, inhibit gastric secretion, increase intestinal motility, stimulate contraction of the uterus, regulate metabolism, affect nerve function, cause inflammation, and are responsible for blood clotting. Those synthesized in the temperature-regulating center of the hypothalamus cause fever. In fact, the ability of aspirin and acetaminophen (Tylenol) to reduce fever and decrease pain (long a mystery) depends upon inhibiting prostaglandin synthesis.

Clinical highlight

Because prostaglandins are involved in the regulation of so many metabolic processes, they have great potential for a variety of clinical uses. At present prostaglandins are used clinically to induce labor in pregnant women, to induce abortion, and to promote healing of ulcers in the stomach and duodenum. Their use as a birth-control drug is being investigated. Some investigators think that these substances may someday be used to treat such illnesses as asthma, arthritis, kidney disease, certain cardiovascular disorders, nasal congestion, and even cancer.

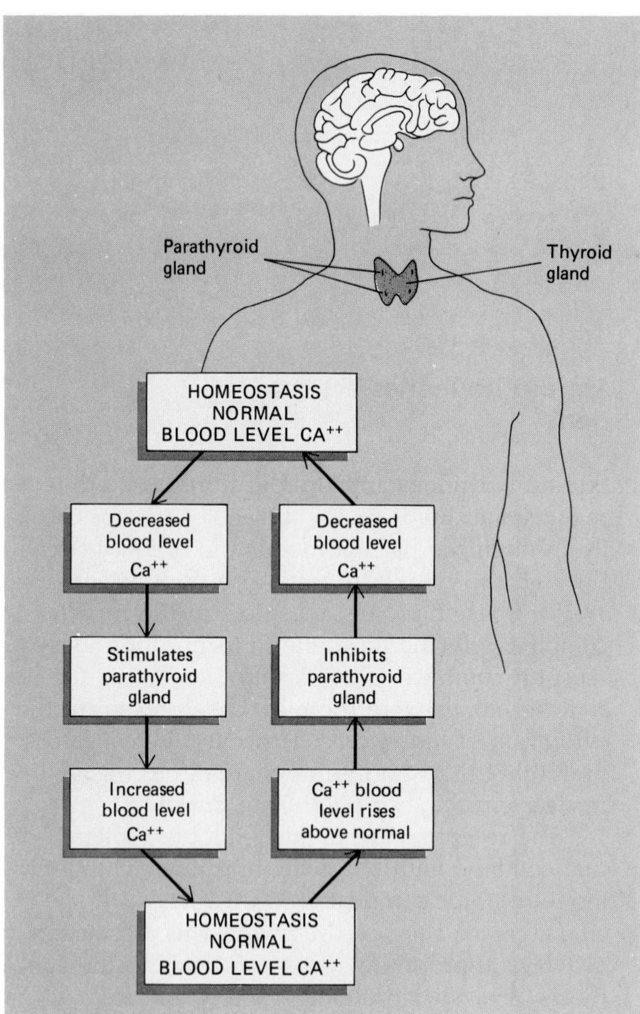

FIGURE 18-13

Regulation of hormone secretion by negative feedback. When the calcium level in the blood falls below normal, the parathyroid glands are stimulated to release more parathyroid hormone. This hormone acts to increase the calcium level in the blood, thus restoring homeostasis. Should the calcium level exceed normal, the parathyroid glands are inhibited and slow their release of hormone. This diagram has been simplified. Calcitonin, a hormone secreted by the thyroid gland, works antagonistically to parathyroid hormone and is important in lowering blood calcium concentration.

Hormone secretion is regulated by feedback control

How does an endocrine gland "know" how much hormone to release at any given moment? Hormone secretion is self-regulated by feedback control mechanisms. Information regarding the hormone level or its effect is fed back to the gland, which then responds in a homeostatic manner. The parathyroid glands of the neck, which help regulate calcium level in the blood, provide a good example of *negative feedback.*

Parathyroid hormone helps regulate the calcium concentration in the blood. Even a slight decrease in calcium concentration is sensed by the parathyroid glands. They respond by increasing their secretion of parathyroid hormone (Fig. 18-13). Parathyroid hormone stimulates release of calcium from bones and increases reabsorption of calcium by the kidney tubules. These actions increase the calcium concentration in the blood and tissues.

When calcium concentration rises above normal limits, the parathyroid glands are inhibited and diminish their output of hormone. Note that both responses are negative feedback mechanisms, because in both cases the effects are opposite (negative) to the stimulus.

Negative feedback forms the basis of most hormone regulation. As you will see, variations of this theme abound, many involving the hypothalamus and pituitary gland. A few examples of *positive feedback* regulation are known, including the system that regulates release of oxytocin from the pituitary gland. In positive feedback, the output increases the hormone secretion, rather than turning it off.

Many clinical syndromes are a result of endocrine malfunction

In a system as complex as the endocrine system there are many opportunities for things to go wrong. When a disorder or disease process affects an endocrine gland, the rate of secretion often becomes abnormal. In **hyposecretion** the gland decreases its hormone output. This condition deprives target cells of needed stimulation. In **hypersecretion** a gland increases its output to abnormal levels. This condition overstimulates target cells, causing imbalance in the opposite direction.

In some endocrine disorders an appropriate amount of hormone may be secreted but target cells may not be able to take it up and utilize it. There may be insufficient numbers of receptor proteins, or the receptor proteins may not function properly. Any of these abnormalities leads to predictable metabolic malfunctions with accompanying clinical syndromes (Table 18-2). Some of

TABLE 18-2

Consequences of endocrine malfunction

Hormone	Hyposecretion	Hypersecretion
Growth hormone	Pituitary dwarf	Gigantism if malfunction occurs in childhood; acromegaly in adult
Thyroid hormones	Cretinism (in children); myxedema, a condition of pronounced adult hypothyroidism (BMR is reduced by about 40%; patient feels tired all of the time and may be mentally slow); goiter, enlargement of the thyroid gland (see figure)	Hyperthyroidism; increased metabolic rate, nervousness, irritability
Parathyroid hormone	Spontaneous discharge of nerves; spasms; tetany; death	Weak, brittle bones; kidney stones
Insulin	Diabetes mellitus	Hypoglycemia
Adrenocortical hormones	Addison's disease (body cannot synthesize sufficient glucose by gluconeogenesis; patient is unable to cope with stress; sodium loss in urine may lead to shock)	Cushing's disease (edema gives face a full-moon appearance; fat is deposited about trunk; blood-glucose level rises; immune responses are depressed)

these will be described as the specific endocrine glands are discussed.

Two major endocrine glands in the brain are the pituitary gland and the hypothalamus

Endocrine activity is controlled directly or indirectly by the hypothalamus, which links the nervous and endocrine systems. In response to input from other areas of the brain and from hormones in the blood, neurons of the hypothalamus secrete several releasing and inhibiting hormones. These hormones act on specific cells in the pituitary regulating production and secretion of several pituitary hormones. The hypothalamus also produces two hormones—oxytocin and antidiuretic hormone—which are stored in the pituitary gland.

The **pituitary gland,** also called the **hypophysis** (hi-**pof**-ih-sis), is a remarkable organ the size of a pea and weighing only about 0.5 grams (0.02 oz). Connected to the hypothalamus by a stalk of neural tissue called the **infundibulum** (in-fun-**dib**-u-lum), or pituitary stalk, the pituitary gland lies in a bony cavity, the sella turcica, of the sphenoid bone. Sometimes called the master gland of the body, the pituitary secretes at least nine distinct hormones. These hormones control the activities of several other endocrine glands and influence a wide range of physiological processes (Fig. 18-14).

The pituitary gland consists of two main lobes, the anterior and posterior lobes. These lobes are different in embryological origin, function, and structure. In the embryo the anterior lobe develops from tissue that forms the roof of

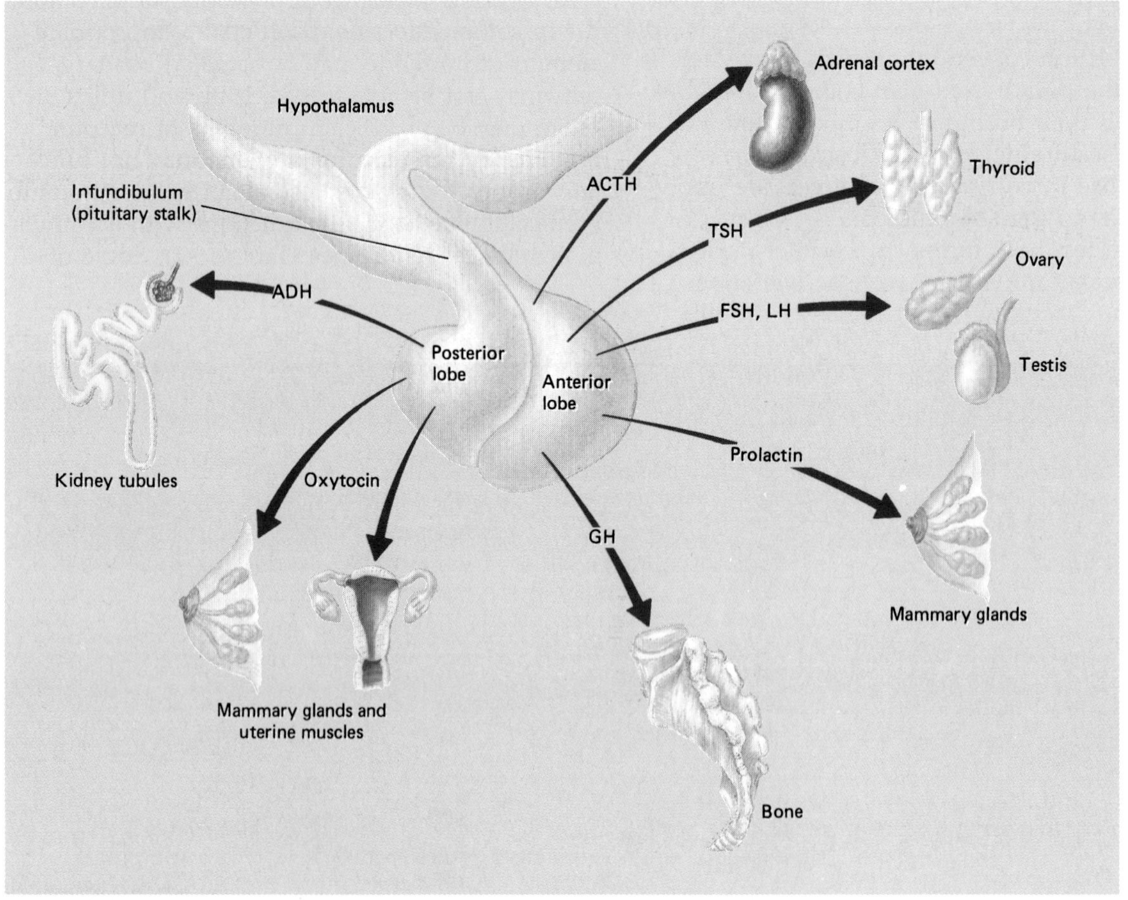

FIGURE 18-14

The pituitary gland is suspended from the hypothalamus by the infundibulum. Shown here are hormones released by the pituitary gland and the target tissues they act upon.

the mouth; the posterior lobe forms from an outpocketing of the developing hypothalamus. Both lobes are connected to the hypothalamus.

Some vertebrates have an intermediate lobe, which secretes two hormones called melanocyte-stimulating hormones (MSH). These hormones regulate skin pigmentation. In humans, the intermediate lobe, called the pars intermedia, is poorly developed, and its function, if any, remains unclear. Humans do manufacture MSH, but it is secreted by the anterior lobe.

The neurohypophysis releases two hormones

The **posterior lobe** of the pituitary gland, or **neurohypophysis** (*new*-row-hi-**pof**-ih-sis), is an extension of the hypothalamus, from which it develops. The neurohypophysis consists mainly of cells known as **pituicytes** (pih-**too**-ih-sites) which are similar to glial cells in the nervous system. Pituicytes do not secrete hormones. They provide support for axon terminals that extend from **neurosecretory** cells located in the hypothalamus. These neurosecretory cells produce the hormones *oxytocin* and *antidiuretic hormone.*

More specifically, oxytocin is produced by the cells of the paraventricular nuclei. Antidiuretic hormone is produced by the cells in the supraoptic nuclei. These polypeptide hormones are produced in the cell bodies of neurons. They are enclosed within little vesicles and moved by axonal transport down the axons of the neurosecretory cells. These axons extend through the infundibulum into the posterior lobe (Fig. 18-15). Hormones accumulate in the axon endings until the neuron is stimulated, whereupon the hormones are released and pass into surrounding capillaries.

OXYTOCIN HELPS PREPARE THE BODY FOR CHILDBIRTH

Oxytocin (*ox*-see-**tow**-sin) is a peptide hormone (Fig. 18-7) that stimulates contraction of smooth muscle in the wall of the uterus. Oxytocin also stimulates contractile cells around mammary ducts, thus promoting release of milk from the breast. Toward the end of pregnancy, oxytocin levels rise, stimulating the strong contractions of the uterus needed to expel the baby. Oxytocin is sometimes administered clinically (under the name Pitocin) to initiate or speed labor. It may also be administered immediately after childbirth to control hemorrhage and recover uterine tone.

When an infant sucks at its mother's breast, sensory neurons are stimulated. These neurons signal the hypothalamus to release oxytocin. The hormone stimulates contraction of cells surrounding the milk glands so that milk is let down into the ducts, from which it can be sucked. Because the oxytocin also stimulates the uterus to contract, breast feeding promotes rapid recovery of the uterus to nonpregnant size after childbirth. Males have about the same amount of oxytocin circulating in their blood as females, but its function in them is unknown.

ANTIDIURETIC HORMONE REGULATES FLUID BALANCE

Antidiuretic hormone (ADH), also called **vasopressin** (*vas*-oh-**pres**-in), regulates fluid balance in the body and indirectly helps control blood pressure. ADH helps the body conserve water by increasing water reabsorption from the collecting ducts in the kidney (see Chapter 27). This peptide hormone increases the amount of cyclic AMP in cells of the collecting ducts, which increases permeability to water. The result is a decrease in urine output and an increase in extracellular fluid.

ADH secretion is regulated by the volume and osmotic pressure of the blood. An increase in osmotic pressure is detected by sensitive receptors located in the hypothalamus called **osmoreceptors** (*oz*-mow-re-**sep**-tors). Once stimulated, the osmoreceptors trigger ADH synthesis from the neurosecretory cells of the hypothalamus. The hormone is transported to the neurohypophysis and released into the bloodstream whereby it travels to the kidneys. More water is reabsorbed and the blood is diluted. Conversely, when the blood becomes too diluted, osmoreceptors send signals to reduce ADH secretion.

When the blood volume falls below normal, blood pressure also falls, allowing stretch receptors in the wall of the heart to relax. A signal is sent to the hypothalamus to release more ADH. As a consequence, water is retained and blood volume increases. Receptors in certain arteries also report to the hypothalamus regarding blood pressure. When blood pressure rises, these mechanisms act to inhibit ADH secretion, thus permitting greater water excretion. Blood volume and pressure decrease.

Clinical highlight

Other factors are known to affect ADH secretion. Nicotine, barbiturates, anxiety, trauma, acetylcholine, and some anesthetics increase ADH secretion. You might have wondered why alcohol consumption increases urine output. Alcohol inhibits ADH secretion, increasing urine output and causing the feeling of thirst.

Damage to the ADH-producing cells of the hypothalamus (which sometimes occurs as a consequence of a tumor) may result in ADH deficiency. This leads to the condition called **diabetes insipidus,** in which urine volume cannot be regulated effectively. Enormous quantities of urine, up to 30 liters per day, may be excreted. Of course this fluid loss must be replaced or serious dehydration would rapidly develop. Diabetes insipidus may be treated in a number of ways including injection of ADH or use of an ADH nasal spray. Diabetes insipidus can also occur when the kidneys become insensitive to the action of ADH.

Another way that ADH raises blood pressure is by constricting arterioles. Following blood loss (and accompanying decrease in blood pressure), ADH secretion increases dramatically; this is a homeostatic mechanism for restoring blood pressure. ADH is often referred to as vasopressin because of its effect on blood pressure.

The adenohypophysis secretes six different hormones

The **anterior lobe** of the pituitary gland, or **adenohypophysis** (*ad*-eh-no-hi-**pof**-ih-sis), secretes six hormones, including growth hormone, prolactin, and several tropic hormones. The anterior lobe

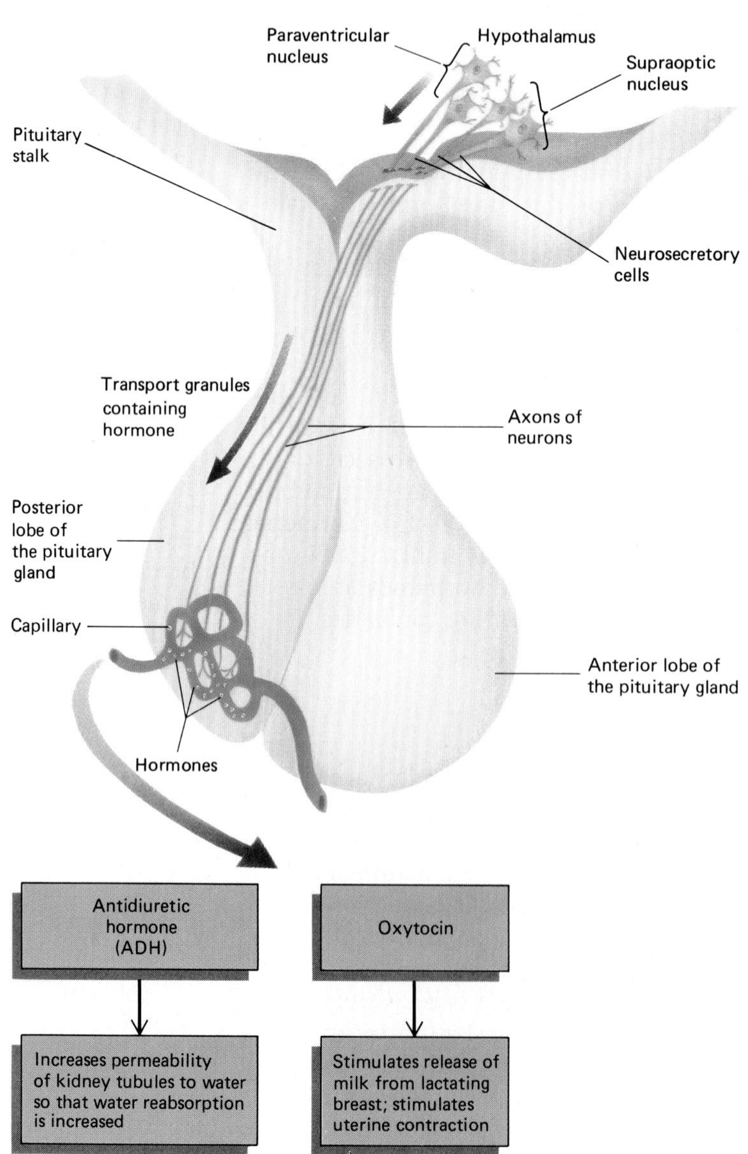

FIGURE 18-15

The hormones released by the posterior lobe of the pituitary gland are actually manufactured in cells of the hypothalamus. The axons of these neurons extend down into the posterior lobe of the pituitary. The hormones are packaged in granules that flow through these axons and are stored in their ends. The hormone is released into the interstitial fluid as needed and then transported by the blood.

also secretes a peptide called β-lipotropin, the precursor of endorphins and enkephalins (the morphine-like substances produced by the body that function in pain perception; see Chapter 15).

THE SECRETION OF HORMONES FROM THE ADENOHYPOPHYSIS IS CONTROLLED BY THE HYPOTHALAMUS

Each of the anterior pituitary hormones is regulated in some way by a **releasing hormone** (also called releasing factor) and in some cases also by an **inhibiting hormone** (inhibiting factor) produced in the hypothalamus (Table 18-3). At appropriate times these neurohormones are released by the hypothalamus. They diffuse into capillaries and circulate with the blood through portal veins to the anterior lobe. (A portal vein does not deliver blood to a larger vein or directly to the heart but connects two sets of capillaries.) This vital system of blood vessels connecting the hypothalamus with the anterior pituitary is called the **hypothalamopituitary portal system.** Within the anterior lobe of the pituitary, the portal veins divide into a second set of capillaries from which the hormone can diffuse into the tissue of the anterior pituitary gland (Fig. 18-16).

Sometimes we speak loosely of the pituitary gland being stimulated or inhibited, but it should be understood that certain receptors within the hypothalamus are generally affected first. They in turn control the pituitary.

At this point you may well wonder: if the hypothalamus controls the pituitary (which in turn controls many other glands and activities of the body), what controls the hypothalamus? As will soon become clear, the hypothalamus responds to feedback from both hormones and the nervous system.

GROWTH HORMONE STIMULATES SKELETAL GROWTH

Almost everyone is fascinated by the process of growth. Small children measure themselves periodically against their parents, eagerly awaiting that time when they too will be "big." Whether one will be tall or short depends upon many factors, including genes, diet, hormonal balance, and even emotional nurturance.

Growth hormone (GH) (also called **somatotropin** [*sow*-mah-toe-**tro**-pin]) stimulates body growth mainly by increasing uptake of amino acids by the cells and by stimulating protein synthesis. Because it prompts cells to build proteins, growth hormone is referred to as an anabolic hormone.

The effects of GH on growth of the skeleton are indirect (Fig. 18-17). The hormone stimulates the liver to produce peptides called **somatomedins** (*so*-mah-toe-**me**-dins). These growth factors (1) promote the linear growth of the skeleton by stimulating growth of cartilage in the epiphyseal plates and (2) stimulate general tissue growth and increase in size of organs; this results from stimulation of protein synthesis and other anabolic processes.

Growth hormone also affects fat and carbohydrate metabolism. It promotes mobilization of fat from adipose tissues, raising the level of free fatty acids in the blood. In this protein-sparing operation, fatty acids become available for cells to use

TABLE 18-3

Hormones involved in regulating anterior pituitary secretion

Hormone	Primary effect on anterior pituitary*
Corticotropin-releasing hormone (CRH)	Stimulates ACTH secretion
Thyrotropin-releasing hormone (TRH)	Stimulates TSH secretion
Gonadotropin-releasing hormone (GnRH)	Stimulates LH and FSH secretion
Growth-hormone-inhibiting hormone (GHIH) (Somatostatin)	Inhibits GH secretion
Growth-hormone-releasing hormone (GHRH)	Stimulates GH secretion
Prolactin-releasing hormone (PRH)	Stimulates prolactin secretion
Prolactin-inhibiting hormone (PIH)	Inhibits prolactin secretion

*Several of the releasing hormones influence the secretion of more than one anterior pituitary hormone. For simplicity, only the primary effects of the releasing hormones are presented here.

as fuel. How does this help to promote growth? Fat mobilization by GH is also important during fasting or when a person is under prolonged stress, situations in which the blood-sugar level is low. Can you explain why?

Human growth hormone has several actions that result, directly or indirectly, in raising the blood-sugar level. It inhibits glucose uptake and utilization by the cells. Because the glucose that does enter cells cannot be utilized as fuel, it is stored as glycogen. As a result, cells become laden with glycogen. Liver cells convert some of the glycogen to glucose and release it into the blood. The blood-glucose level rises, causing **hyperglycemia** (literally, high blood-glucose). Too much growth hormone over a long period of time

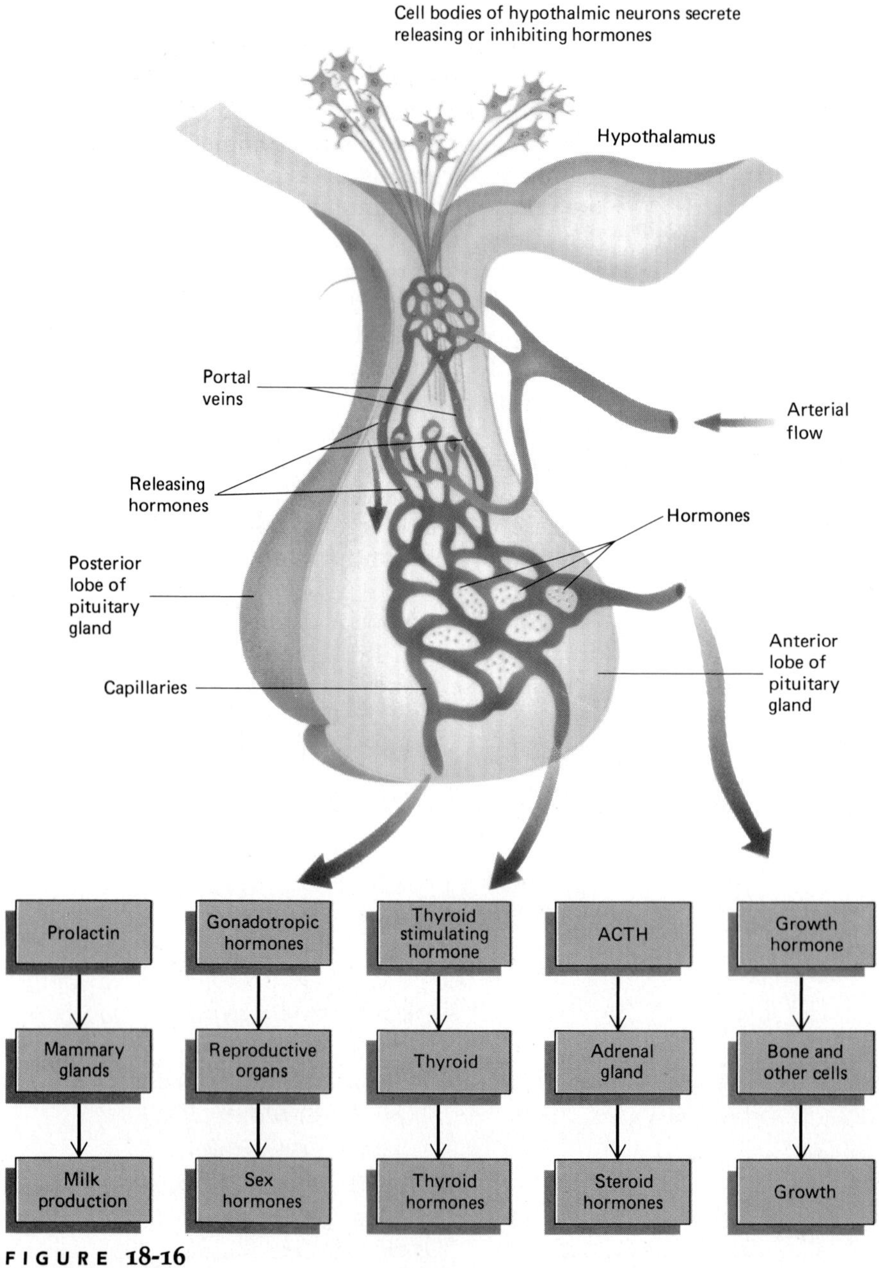

FIGURE 18-16

The hypothalamus secretes several specific releasing and inhibiting hormones, which reach the anterior lobe of the pituitary gland by way of portal veins. Each releasing hormone stimulates the synthesis of a particular hormone by the cells of the anterior lobe.

can result in a type of diabetes mellitus (pituitary-induced). (Diabetes mellitus will be discussed in a later section in this chapter.) This is referred to as the **diabetogenic effect** (*di*-ah-*bet*-o-**jen**-ik) of growth hormone. These effects may result from the stimulation by growth hormone of the pancreatic hormone glucagon.

Growth hormone secretion is regulated by the hypothalamus

Growth hormone is secreted in adults as well as in growing children. This hormone is secreted in pulses throughout the day. Secretion of growth hormone is regulated by both a **growth-hormone-releasing hormone (GHRH)** and **growth-hormone-inhibiting hormone (GHIH)** (also called **somatostatin** [*so*-mah-toe-**stat**-in]) released by the hypothalamus. A high level of growth hormone in the blood signals the hypothalamus to secrete the inhibiting hormone, and the pituitary release of growth hormone slows (Fig. 18-18). A low level of growth hormone in the blood stimulates the hypothalamus to secrete the releasing hormone, so that the pituitary gland is stimulated and releases more growth hormone. Many other factors influence secretion, including the nutritional status of the body and stress. Growth hormone secretion is increased by **hypoglycemia** (*hy*-pow-gly-**see**-me-ah; low blood-sugar level) and by a decrease in amino acid concentration in the blood. Growth hormone secretion is inhibited by hyperglycemia, suggesting that a diet very high in carbohydrates might inhibit growth. Physical and emotional stress also stimulate GH secretion.

Remember your parents telling you to get plenty of sleep, eat properly, and exercise in order to grow? These age-old notions are supported by recent studies. Secretion of growth hormone does increase during exercise, probably be-

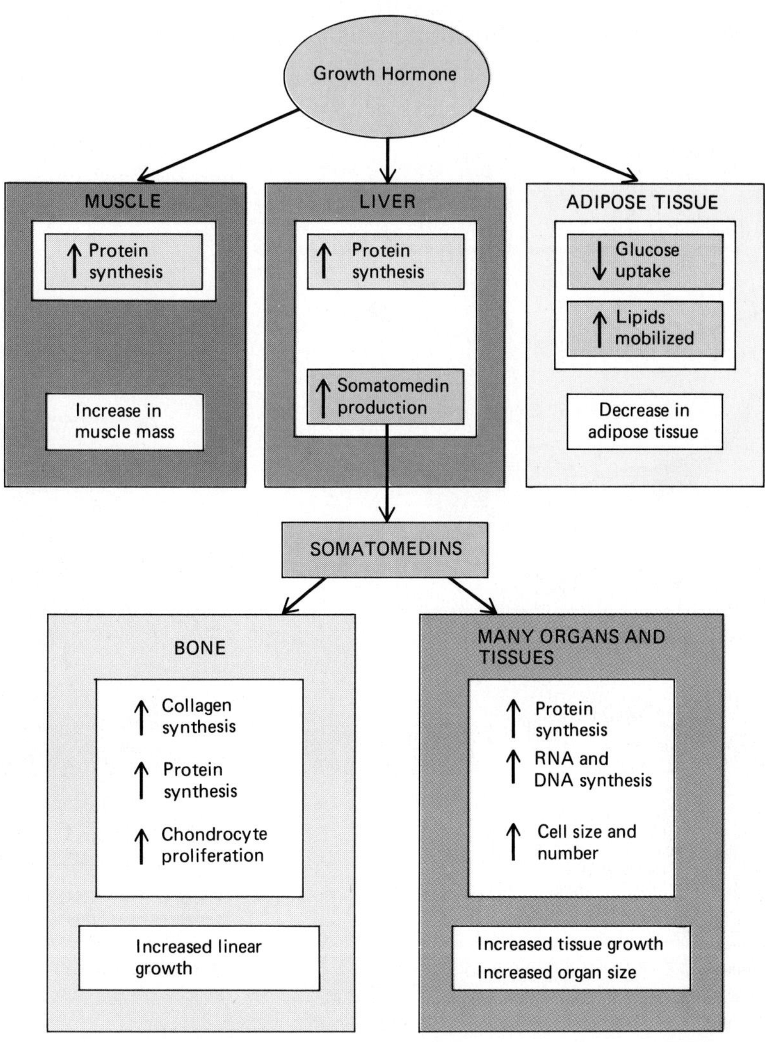

FIGURE 18-17

Growth hormone has direct effects on muscle, liver, and adipose tissue. GH has indirect effects on bone and many other tissues that result from somatomedin production.

cause rapid metabolism by muscle cells lowers the blood-sugar level. GH is also secreted in a series of pulses 2 to 4 hours after a meal. And growth hormone secretion also occurs about 1 hour after the onset of deep sleep.

Emotional support is also necessary for proper growth. Growth may be retarded in children who are deprived of cuddling, playing, and other forms of nurture, even when their physical needs (food and shelter) are amply met. In extreme cases, childhood stress can produce actual dwarfism (psychosocial dwarfism). Some emotionally deprived children exhibit abnormal sleep patterns, which may be the basis for decreased secretion of growth hormone.

Other hormones also influence growth. Thyroid hormones appear to be necessary for normal growth-hormone secretion and function. Sex hormones must be present for the adolescent growth spurt to occur. However, the presence of sex hormones eventually cause the growth centers within the long bones to ossify, fusing the epiphyses to the diaphyses, so that further increase in height is impossible even when growth hormone is present.

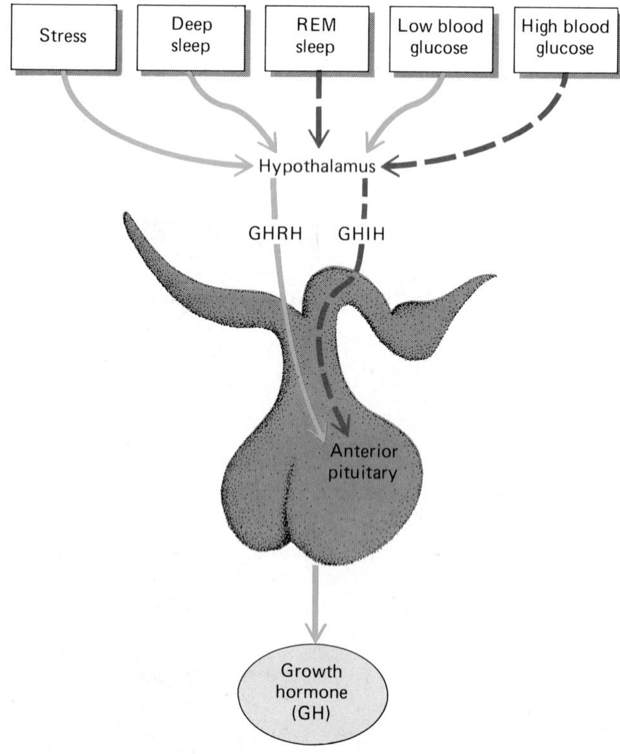

FIGURE 18-18

Regulation of growth hormone secretion.

Inappropriate amounts of growth hormone secretion result in abnormal growth

Have you ever wondered why circus midgets failed to grow normally? They are probably **pituitary dwarfs,** that is, individuals whose pituitary gland did not produce sufficient growth hormone during childhood. Though miniature, a pituitary dwarf has normal intelligence and is usually well proportioned. If the growth centers in the long bones are still open when this condition is initially diagnosed, it can be treated clinically by injection with growth hormone, which can now be synthesized commercially.

Can you think of other mechanisms that might fail and result in growth problems? How about the regulating hormones from the hypothalamus? Or suppose growth hormone is secreted normally but somatomedin is not released from the liver? A recent study showed that in a tribe of African pygmy, normal amounts of growth hormone are secreted, but due to a genetic defect, insufficient amounts of one of the somatomedins are produced. Other forms of dwarfism result from lack of responsiveness of target tissues.

Circus giants and other abnormally tall individuals develop when the anterior pituitary secretes excessive amounts of growth hormone dur-

FIGURE 18-19

The world's tallest woman, Sandy Allen, with her family. Ms. Allen's growth is due to an excess of growth hormone. She is 2.22 meters (7 ft, 7 1/4 in.) tall.

ing childhood. This condition is referred to as **gigantism** (ji-**gan**-tizm). See Figure 18-19.

If hypersecretion of growth hormone (or somatomedin) occurs during adulthood, the individual cannot grow taller. However, a condition known as **acromegaly** (*ak*-row-**meg**-ah-lee; large extremities) results in which the bones, especially those in the hands, feet, and face, increase in diameter (Fig. 18-20). Connective tissue also thickens, and body organs may increase in size. An early sign of this disorder may be the need for a wider shoe, or fingers so thickened that rings no longer fit. Another symptom of acromegaly is increase in the diameter of the mandible, causing the lower jaw to protrude.

PROLACTIN (LACTOGENIC HORMONE) FUNCTIONS IN THE SECRETION OF MILK DURING LACTATION

During lactation (milk production), **prolactin** (pro-**lak**-tin) stimulates the cells of the mammary glands to produce milk. (Recall that oxytocin stimulates *release* of milk from the breasts.) The hypothalamus regulates prolactin secretion with a prolactin-releasing hormone and a prolactin-inhibiting hormone. When the infant sucks at the breast, a reflex to the hypothalamus is initiated. The reflex suppresses secretion of prolactin-inhibiting hormone from the hypothalamus, allowing the pituitary to secrete prolactin. As long as the infant continues to suckle, milk production continues, even for years. Once the mother stops nursing the baby, however, milk production ceases within a few days. Prolactin-releasing hormone appears to stimulate prolactin secretion after inhibition has occurred for a long period of time. The function of prolactin in males is not known.

TROPIC HORMONES STIMULATE OTHER ENDOCRINE GLANDS

The anterior lobe of the pituitary gland secretes four **tropic hormones,** that is, hormones that stimulate the activity of other endocrine glands. The tropic hormones are: *thyroid-stimulating hormone (TSH),* which acts on the thyroid gland; *adrenocorticotropin (ACTH),* which acts on the adrenal cortex; and the *gonadotropins, follicle-stimulating hormone (FSH)* and *luteinizing hormone (LH),* which control the activities of the gonads (sex glands). Thyroid-stimulating hormone and ACTH will be discussed in association with their target glands. The gonadotropins will be taken up in Chapter 29 in conjunction with the discussion of reproduction.

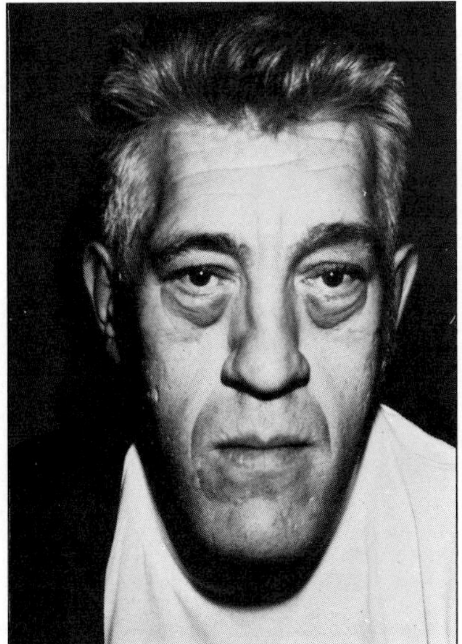

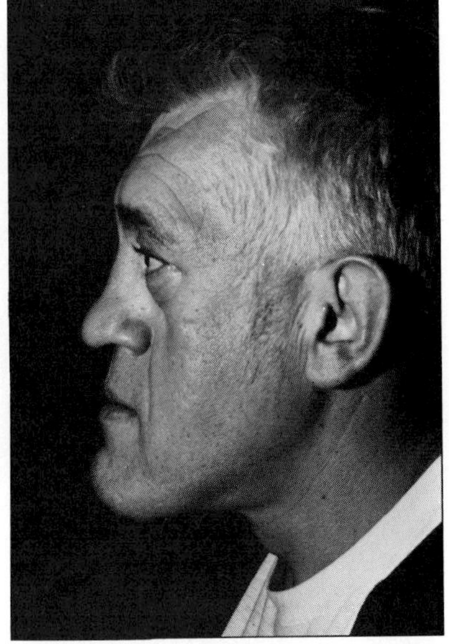

FIGURE 18-20

Patient with acromegaly. Note enlarged nose and ears and prominent jaw and cheekbones. (From Cecil, Textbook of Medicine, 15th ed. Beeson, McDermott, and Wyngaarden (Eds.), Philadelphia, W. B. Saunders, 1979; Courtesy of Dr. Gordon Williams.)

The thyroid gland is located in the neck

Shaped somewhat like a shield, the **thyroid** (**thy**-roid) **gland** is located in the neck, anterior to the trachea and just inferior to the larynx (Fig. 18-21). Its two lobes of dark red glandular tissue are connected by a bridge of tissue, the thyroid isthmus, which overlies the second and third rings of tracheal cartilage. Each lobe is about 5 centimeters long.

Internally the gland cells of the thyroid are arranged into millions of saclike follicles (Fig. 18-22). Each follicle consists of a single layer of cuboidal epithelial cells surrounding a lumen (space) filled with a protein substance referred to as **colloid.** The thyroid gland secretes two thyroid hormones and a hormone called calcitonin (which will be discussed in conjunction with the parathyroid glands).

Thyroid hormones require iodide for production

The two hormones usually referred to as the **thyroid hormones** are **triiodothyronine,** or **T3** (because it has three iodine atoms), and **thyroxine,** or **T4** (because it has four iodine atoms). Thyroxine is the principal hormone. These hormones are synthesized from the amino acid tyrosine and from iodine.

Cells of the thyroid follicles synthesize a protein called **thyroglobulin.** Thyroglobulin is then secreted into the colloid for storage (Fig. 18-23). Using an iodine-trapping mechanism referred to as the "iodide pump," thyroid cells efficiently remove iodide (the ionic form of iodine) from the blood. The iodide is passed on into the colloid where it is converted to iodine. The iodine then combines with tyrosine within the thyroglobulin, forming T3 and T4. Several weeks' supply of T3 and T4 can be stored in the colloid.

As thyroid hormones are needed by the body cells, the cells of the thyroid follicles ingest colloid by pinocytosis. Then, with the help of lyso-

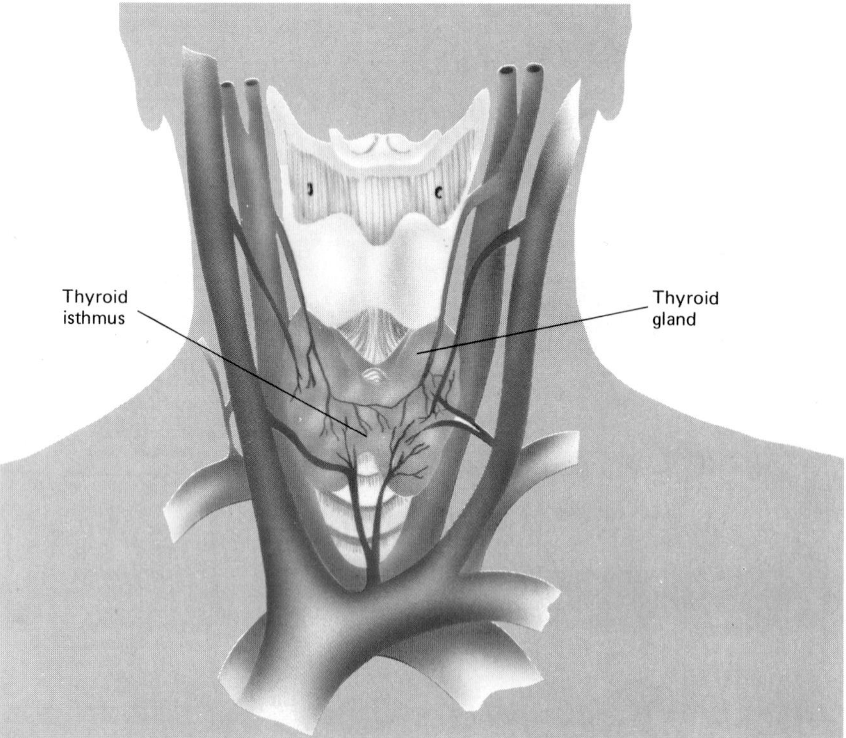

FIGURE 18-21

The thyroid gland is located in the neck, anterior to the trachea and just inferior to the larynx. It consists of two lobes of dark red glandular tissue connected by a bridge of tissue, the thyroid isthmus.

somal enzymes, the T3 and T4 are split from the thyroglobulin and enter the blood. Most of it is transported bound to plasma protein.

The protein-bound iodine, or PBI, is an index of the amount of circulating thyroid hormones and is still sometimes measured clinically for just that purpose. (A normal PBI level would be about 6 micrograms per 100 milliliters of plasma.) This clinical test has been largely replaced by techniques that measure the amounts of circulating T3 and T4 specifically.

Thyroid hormones function in metabolism and growth

The thyroid hormones have widespread effects in the body. Their two principal actions are to stimulate metabolic rate and to promote growth. Let us examine these effects and three additional ones.

1. The thyroid hormones stimulate the rate of metabolism in almost all body tissues. (Brain tissue and lymph nodes are among the exceptions.) These hormones are thought to increase the rate of cellular respiration probably by increasing the efficiency with which the mitochondria produce ATP. Fuel is "burned" more quickly so oxygen consumption increases, as does heat production. This is known as the **calorigenic effect** of the thyroid hormones.

2. Thyroid hormones are essential to normal growth and development. They promote protein synthesis and enhance the effect of growth hormone.

3. Thyroid hormones affect many aspects of carbohydrate metabolism. They increase the rate of carbohydrate absorption from the digestive tract and promote rapid uptake of glucose by the cells.

4. Thyroid hormones promote lipid metabolism. For example, they stimulate mobilization of fat from the adipose tissues and stimulate the oxidation of fatty acids by the cells. They also lower the concentration of circulating cholesterol, triglycerides, and phospholipids.

5. Thyroid hormones speed up actions of the nervous system. The result is increased blood pressure, stronger heartbeat, increased gastrointestinal motility (often resulting in diarrhea), and anxiety.

Thyroid hormones accomplish these diverse actions by acting on DNA. This action results in the synthesis of specific enzymes and other proteins.

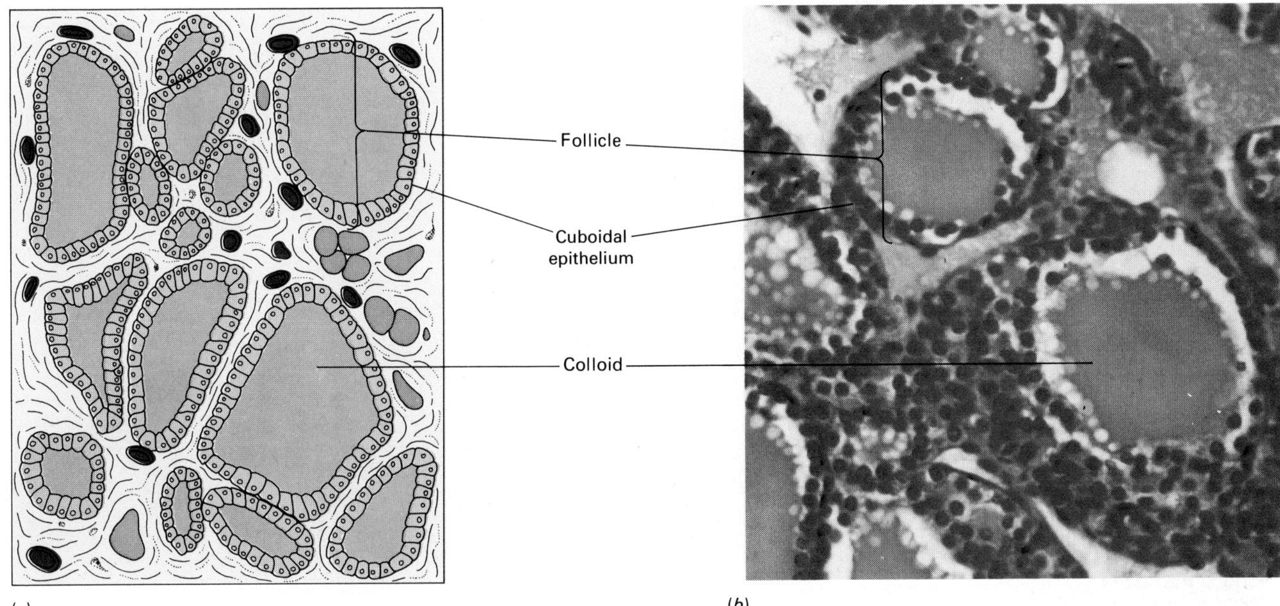

FIGURE 18-22

Thyroid tissue. (*a*) Internally the gland cells of the thyroid are arranged into millions of sac-like follicles. Each follicle consists of a single layer of cuboidal cells surrounding a lumen filled with colloid. (*b*) Photomicrograph of thyroid tissue (approximately ×425). (*b*, Bruce Iverson/Visuals Unlimited.)

The secretion of thyroid hormone is regulated by a feedback system

The regulation of thyroid hormone secretion depends mainly upon a feedback system between the anterior lobe of the pituitary (adenohypophysis) and the thyroid gland (Fig. 18-24). The anterior lobe secretes **thyroid-stimulating hormone (TSH),** which acts by way of cyclic AMP to increase iodine uptake, promote synthesis and secretion of thyroid hormones, and increase the size of the gland itself. When the normal concentration of thyroid hormones in the blood falls, the anterior pituitary secretes more thyroid-stimulating hormone. When the level of thyroid hormones in the blood rises above normal, the anterior pituitary is inhibited and slows its release of thyroid-stimulating hormone.

↓ Thyroid hormones ⟶ anterior pituitary ⟶ ↑ TSH ⟶ thyroid ⟶ ↑ thyroid hormones

↑ Thyroid hormones - - → anterior pituitary ⟶ ↓ TSH ⟶ thyroid ⟶ ↓ thyroid hormones

Too much thyroid hormone in the blood may also affect the hypothalamus, inhibiting secretion of TSH-releasing hormone. However, the hypo-

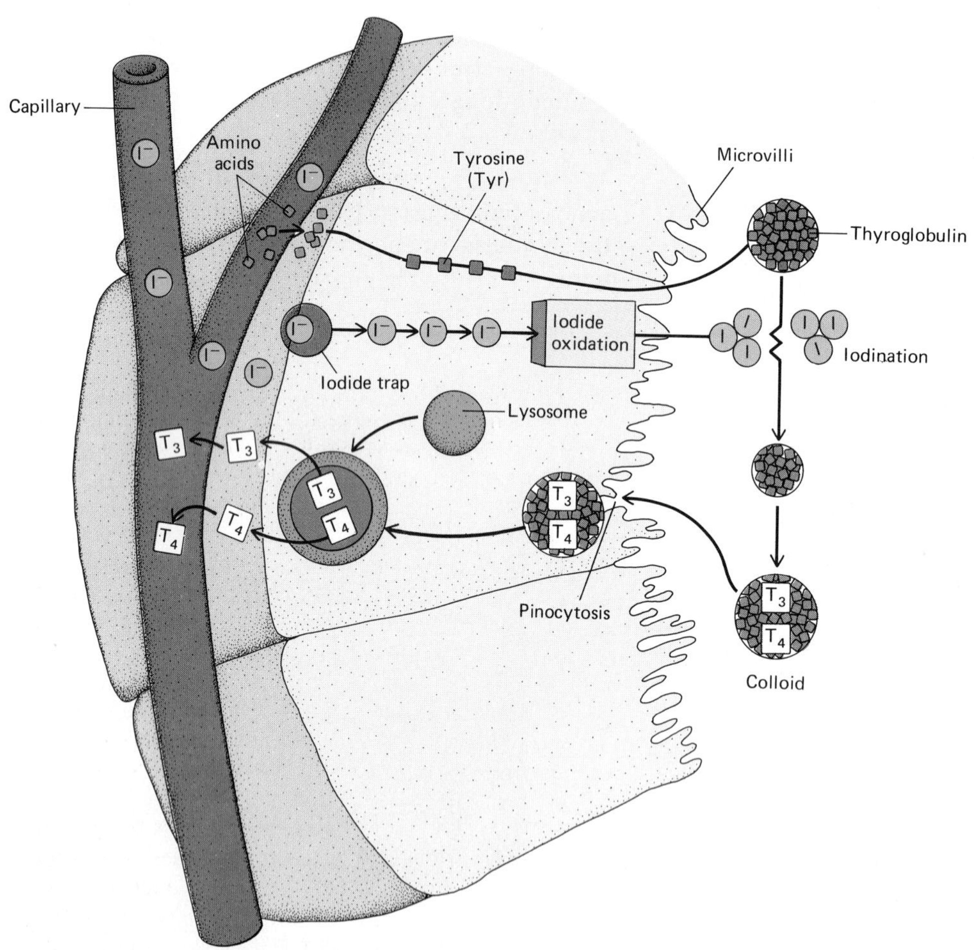

FIGURE 18-23

Physiology of the thyroid gland. Cells of the thyroid gland actively transport iodine into their cytoplasm and also synthesize thyroglobulin. The amino acid tyrosine combines with the thyroglobulin, and in the colloid, iodine is added. Both T4 and T3 are synthesized in this way. As more hormone is needed, follicle cells ingest colloid by pinocytosis. With the help of lysosomal enzymes, the hormone is released from the thyroglobulin and diffuses into the blood. It is transported in chemical combination with a protein in the blood plasma.

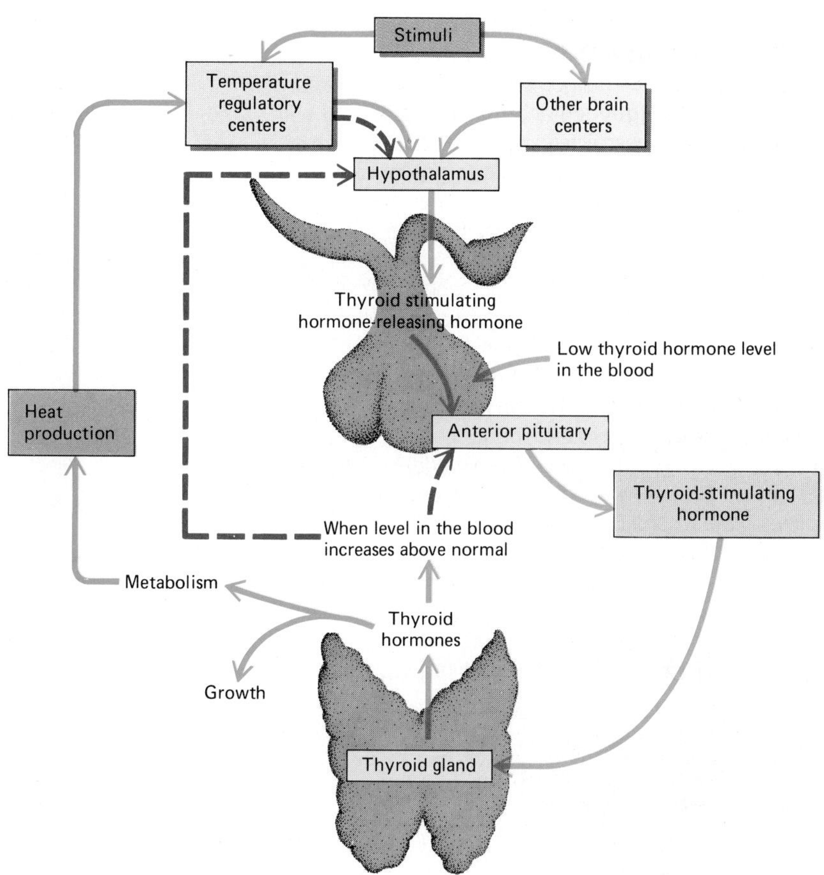

FIGURE 18-24

Regulation of thyroid hormone secretion. Green arrows indicate stimulation; red arrows indicate inhibition.

thalamus is thought to exert its regulatory effects primarily in certain stressful situations, such as extreme weather change. In human infants, exposure to very cold weather stimulates the hypothalamus to increase secretion of TSH-releasing hormone, thereby raising body temperature through increased metabolic heat production. Extreme anxiety and emotional excitement may also play a role in hypothalamic control of thyroid secretion. However, these emotional states cause a decrease in TSH secretion, perhaps because metabolic rate is increased by the stimulation of the sympathetic nervous system.

Clinical highlight

Extreme **hypothyroidism** (*hi*-pow-**thy**-roi-dizm) during infancy and childhood results in low metabolic rate and retarded mental and physical development, a condition called **cretinism** (**kree**-tin-ism). (A cretin is very different from a pituitary dwarf.) When diagnosed and treated early enough, cretinism can be prevented.

An adult who feels like sleeping all the time, who is devoid of energy, and who is mentally slow or even confused may also be suffering from hypothyroidism. When there is almost no thyroid function, the basal metabolic rate (BMR) is reduced by about 40% and the patient develops the condition called **myxedema** (*mik*-se-**dee**-muh). In myxedema, a general edema develops and cholesterol levels rise, leading to atherosclerosis. Hypothyroidism, like cretinism, can be treated by using thyroid pills to replace the missing hormones.

Hyperthyroidism does not cause abnormal growth but does increase metabolic rate by 60% or even more. This increase in metabolism results in swift utilization of nutrients, causing the individual to be hungry and to increase food intake. But this is not sufficient to meet the demands of the rapidly metabolizing cells, so these patients often lose weight. They also tend to be anxious, irritable, and emotionally unstable. In some forms of hyperthyroidism the thyroid gland and eyes are very prominent.

A common form of hyperthyroidism is **Graves' disease,** in which the thyroid gland increases in both size and activity. These increases are due to a group of abnormal antibodies (proteins normally produced to defend the body against bacteria and other foreign invaders) that the body produces against the thyroid-stimulating hormone receptors in the thyroid cells. When these antibodies bind with the receptors, they activate them just as though TSH were present. This results in long-acting stimulation of the thyroid gland, and may cause enlargement of the thyroid gland (goiter). Graves' disease can be treated with drugs or by surgery, or sometimes by injecting large amounts of radioactive iodine, which destroys some of the thyroid tissue.

Any abnormal enlargement of the thyroid gland is termed a **goiter** (**goy**-ter) and may be associated with either hypo- or hypersecretion (Fig. 18-25). One cause is Graves' disease; another is **endemic goiter** caused by dietary iodine deficiency. Without iodine the gland cannot make thyroid hormones, so their concentration in the blood decreases. In compensation, the anterior pituitary secretes large amounts of TSH, and the thyroid gland enlarges, sometimes to gigantic proportions. Because the problem is lack of iodine, enlargement of the gland cannot increase production of the hormones, for the needed ingredient is still missing. Thanks to iodized salt, such simple goiter is no longer common in the United States. In other parts of the world, however, an estimated 200 million persons still suffer from this easily preventable disorder.

Substances that inhibit iodine uptake or effectiveness are called **goitrogens.** Vegetables of the turnip family contain goitrogens. If eaten raw and in excessive quantities, these vegetables may produce goiter. Cooking the vegetable inactivates the goitrogens.

FIGURE 18-25

Goiter resulting from iodine deficiency. (John Paul Kay/Peter Arnold, Inc.)

Parathyroid glands are located near the thyroid

The **parathyroid glands** (*par*-uh-**thy**-royd) are embedded in the connective tissue that surrounds the posterior surfaces of the lateral lobes of the thyroid gland (Fig. 18-26). Usually there are four glands, but the number may vary from two to ten. Each parathyroid gland is a yellowish-brown structure about 0.5 centimeter in diameter. These glands are very vascular and in the adult contain two main types of cells, *chief cells* and *oxyphil cells.* The chief cells secrete **parathyroid hormone (PTH),** a small protein that regulates the calcium level of the blood and interstitial fluid. It is suspected that the oxyphil cells function in producing reserve quantities of PTH.

Parathyroid hormones regulate the concentration of calcium ions in the blood

Appropriate concentrations of calcium are essential for normal nerve and muscle function, bone metabolism, plasma-membrane permeability, and blood clotting. Parathyroid hormone acts by way of cyclic AMP to increase calcium levels. Its target tissues are the kidney tubules, bone, and, indirectly, the intestine (Fig. 18-27). Its actions include the following:

1. PTH stimulates release of calcium from the bones. About 99% of the body's calcium is found in the bones, but as you may recall from Chapter 6, bone is an active tissue. It is continuously being broken down and remodeled. And there is a constant exchange of calcium between the bone and the blood. PTH acts to increase the numbers and activities of the osteoclasts so that more bone tissue is broken down and more calcium is released into the blood.
2. PTH stimulates calcium reabsorption by the kidney tubules, raising the blood-calcium level while preventing loss by excretion.
3. PTH activates vitamin D, which then increases the amount of calcium absorbed from the intestine. Vitamin D also acts independently of PTH to stimulate calcium release from bone.
4. PTH also affects phosphate homeostasis. When bone is broken down, phosphate is released into the blood. PTH acts to increase phosphate excretion in the urine, thus lowering the level of phosphate in the blood.
5. PTH increases the rate of absorption of calcium, magnesium, and phosphate from the gastrointestinal tract into the blood.

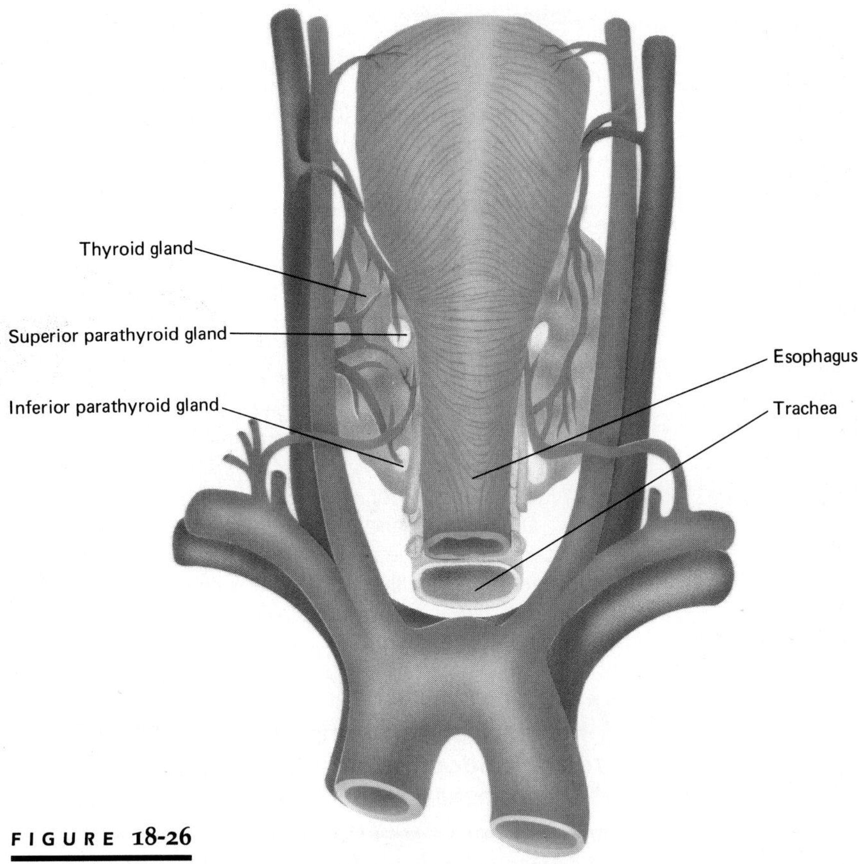

FIGURE 18-26

The parathyroid glands are embedded in the connective tissue that surrounds the posterior surfaces of the lateral lobes of the thyroid gland. There are usually four glands. This is a posterior view of the esophagus, thyroid gland, and parathyroid glands.

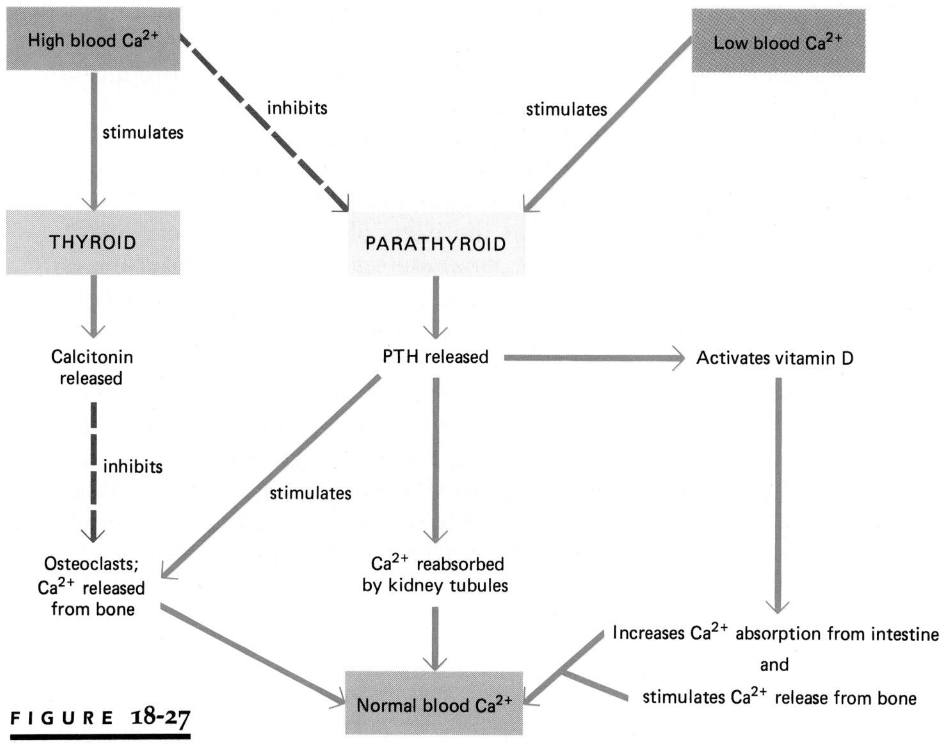

FIGURE 18-27

Regulation of calcium metabolism. Broken lines indicate inhibition.

PTH secretion is regulated by calcium concentration

The bones act very effectively to remove excess calcium from the blood. However, when the bones have become saturated with calcium salts, the resulting rise in calcium level in the interstitial fluid directly affects the parathyroid glands, decreasing their output of PTH. Conversely, when the level of calcium in the blood and interstitial fluid falls even slightly, parathyroid hormone secretion increases. Regulation of PTH secretion is thus directly dependent upon the level of calcium in the blood and interstitial fluid (Figs. 18-13 and 18-27).

↑ Calcium ⟶ parathyroid glands ⟶ ↓PTH
↓ Calcium ⟶ parathyroid glands ⟶ ↑ PTH

Calcitonin works antagonistically to parathyroid hormone

When calcium levels become excessive (about 20% above normal), **calcitonin** (*kal*-sih-**toe**-nin) is released from the thyroid gland and quickly acts to inhibit removal of calcium from bone. Calcitonin operates mainly as a short-term but very rapid mechanism for regulating calcium level.

Insufficient or excess quantities of PTH may result in disorders of calcium metabolism

Insufficient secretion of PTH results in inactivity of the osteoclasts in bone and a consequent fall in calcium level in blood and interstitial fluid. Nerve fibers become more and more excitable and may discharge spontaneously, causing muscles to twitch and to go into spasms or even tetany. Spasm of the muscles of the larynx interferes with respiration and may lead to death. The normal blood-calcium level is about 10 milligrams per 100 milliliters; when the level falls about 40%, to about 6 milligrams per 100 milliliters, tetany occurs. A level of about 4 milligrams per 100 milliliters can be fatal.

Clinical highlight

The symptoms of **hypoparathyroidism** can be relieved by injection of calcium or parathyroid hormone. Clinically the condition is usually treated with large quantities of vitamin D. Can you explain why this treatment is effective?

Hyperparathyroidism is often caused by small benign tumors called **adenomas,** which cause overproduction of parathyroid hormone. So much calcium may be removed from the bones that they are weakened and may be easily fractured. The kidneys attempt to excrete the excess calcium mobilized from the bones. So much calcium may be present in the urine that crystals of calcium precipitate and aggregate to form kidney stones. In severe cases the heart may be affected by the high calcium levels, and calcium deposits may form in various soft tissues of the body.

During pregnancy the fetus removes large amounts of calcium from the mother's blood in order to manufacture bone. If sufficient calcium is not provided by the mother's diet, parathyroid secretion rises, causing decalcification of her bones.

The islets of Langerhans are the endocrine portion of the pancreas

Usually thought of as a digestive organ, the pancreas is an elongated gland that lies in the abdomen posterior to the stomach and partially surrounded by a loop of the small intestine (Fig. 18-28). The pancreas has both exocrine and endocrine components. Its exocrine cells produce digestive enzymes and bicarbonates; This aspect of its function will be discussed in Chapter 25. Here we will discuss its endocrine function.

More than a million small clusters of cells known as the **islets of Langerhans** (**eye**-lits of **lahng**-er-hanz) are scattered throughout the pancreas (Fig. 18-29). Several distinct varieties of cells may be identified within each islet. About 70% of the islet cells are **beta** (β) **cells** that produce the hormone insulin. **Alpha** (or α) **cells** secrete the hormone glucagon. The **delta** (or δ) **cells** produce somatostatins, also called growth-hormone-inhibiting hormones (GHIH), the same growth-inhibiting hormone released by the hypothalamus. Secretion of somatostatin is stimulated by several factors including increased glucagon and blood-glucose levels. Somatostatin inhibits insulin secretion.

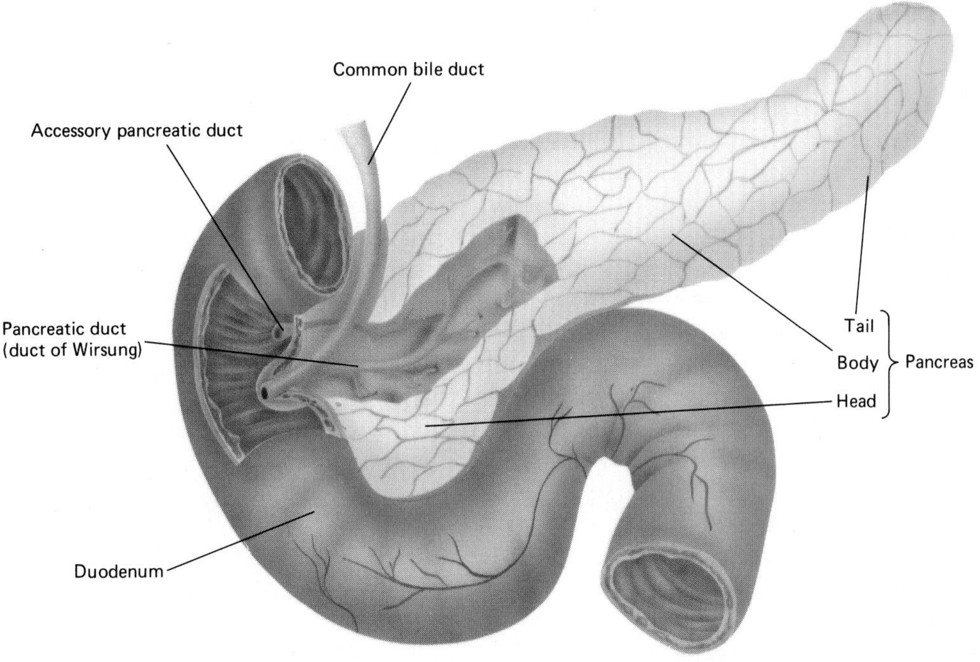

FIGURE 18-28

The pancreas lies in the abdomen posterior to the stomach and partially surrounded by a loop of small intestine. It is both an exocrine and an endocrine gland.

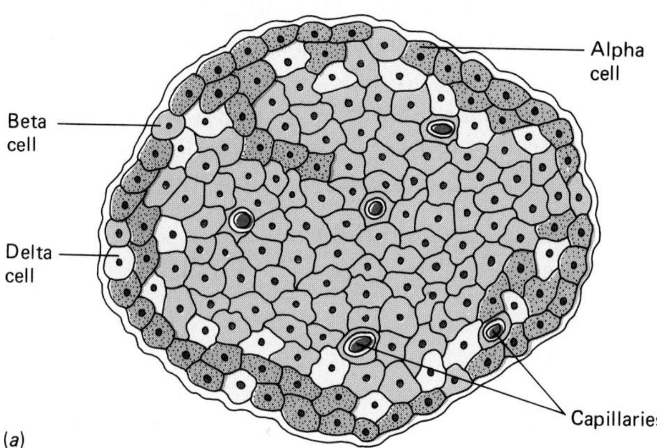

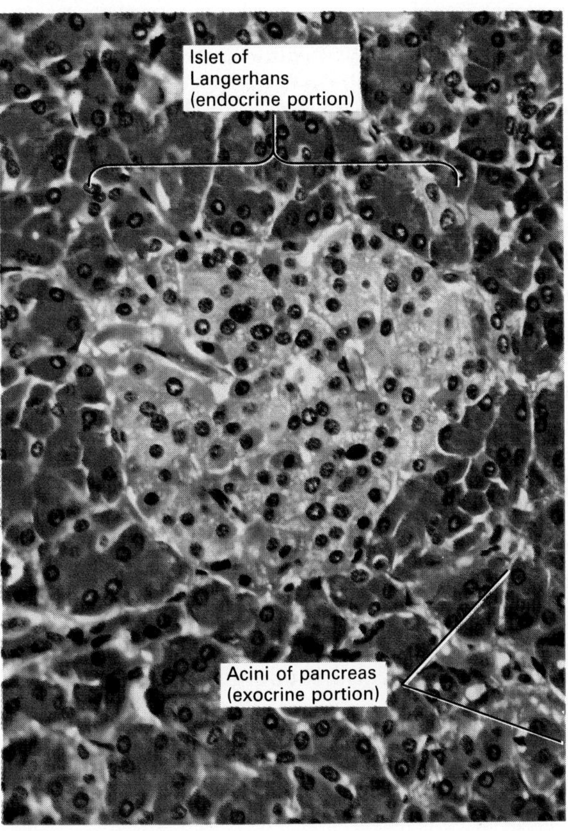

FIGURE 18-29

Microscopic view of endocrine tissue of pancreas. (*a*) Diagram of an islet of Langerhans within the pancreas. (*b*) Photomicrograph of an islet (×100). (Ed Reschke.)

Insulin regulates the level of glucose in the blood

Insulin is a protein hormone that exerts widespread influence on metabolism. It stimulates the storage of glucose, amino acids, and fatty acids and promotes the entry of potassium into cells. Its principal action is to facilitate transport of glucose into most cells, especially muscle and fat cells. By stimulating cells to take up glucose from the blood, insulin lowers the blood-glucose level.

In the presence of insulin, excess glucose taken up by muscle cells is stored as glycogen, and excess glucose in fat cells is converted to fat and stored. Liver cells are very permeable to glucose and do not need the help of insulin to take it up. However, insulin acts to increase the amount of an enzyme (glucokinase) in liver cells. This enzyme phosphorylates (adds phosphate to) glucose so that it cannot diffuse out of the liver; thus insulin acts to trap glucose inside liver cells. The hormone also stimulates glycogen formation and storage in the liver. When the liver cells are filled to capacity with glycogen, any additional glucose is converted to fat in the liver and then sent to the adipose tissues for storage.

Insulin affects protein metabolism by increasing active transport of amino acids into cells and by stimulating protein synthesis. Normal insulin levels are essential for normal growth.

Glucagon acts antagonistically to insulin

Glucagon (**gloo**-kuh-gon), also a protein, stimulates the mobilization of glucose, fatty acids, and amino acids from storage depots into the blood. Glucagon's principal action is to raise the blood-sugar level. It does this by stimulating liver cells to convert glycogen to glucose, a process called **glycogenolysis** (*gly*-ko-jeh-**nol**-ih-sis), and by stimulating the liver cells to make glucose from noncarbohydrates, a process called **gluconeogenesis** (*gloo*-ko-*nee*-oh-**jen**-eh-sis). Glucagon also promotes release of fat stores from adipose tissue, thereby raising fatty acid levels in the blood and providing nutrients for gluconeogenesis. Note that all these actions are opposite to those of insulin. Glucagon is also thought to be secreted by certain cells in the wall of the stomach and duodenum.

Insulin and glucagon are regulated by blood-sugar level

Secretion of insulin and glucagon is directly controlled by the blood-sugar level (Fig. 18-30). After a meal, when the blood-glucose level rises as a result of intestinal absorption, the beta cells are stimulated to increase insulin secretion. Then, as the cells remove glucose from the blood, decreasing its concentration, insulin secretion decreases accordingly. Insulin release is also stimulated by an increase in amino acid level or an increase in the concentration of certain substances known as ketone bodies in the blood.

$\uparrow$ Glucose concentration $\longrightarrow$ β cells $\longrightarrow$ $\uparrow$ insulin $\longrightarrow$

$\downarrow$ glucose concentration $\longrightarrow$ β cells $\longrightarrow$ $\downarrow$ insulin

When one has not eaten for several hours, the blood-sugar level begins to fall. When it falls from its normal fasting level of about 90 milligrams per 100 milliliters to about 70 milligrams per 100 milliliters, the alpha cells of the islets secrete large amounts of glucagon. Glucose is mobilized from the liver stores, and the blood-sugar level returns to normal. The alpha cells actually react to the glucose concentration with their own cytoplasm, which reflects the blood-sugar level. When the blood-sugar level is high, there is normally a high level of glucose within the alpha cells, and glucagon secretion is inhibited.

$\downarrow$Glucose concentration $\longrightarrow$ α cells $\longrightarrow$ $\uparrow$ glucagon $\longrightarrow$ glucose concentration$\uparrow$

$\uparrow$ Glucose concentration $\longrightarrow$ α cells $\longrightarrow$ $\downarrow$ glucagon

It should be clear that insulin and glucagon work together but in opposite ways to keep the blood-sugar level within normal limits. When glucose level rises, insulin release brings it back to normal; when it falls, glucagon acts to raise it again. The insulin-glucagon system is a powerful, fast-acting mechanism for keeping the blood-sugar level normal. Can you think of reasons why it is important to maintain a constant blood-sugar level? Perhaps the most important one is that brain cells are completely dependent upon a continuous supply of glucose because they are normally unable to utilize any other nutrient as fuel. As you will see, several other hormones affect the blood-sugar level.

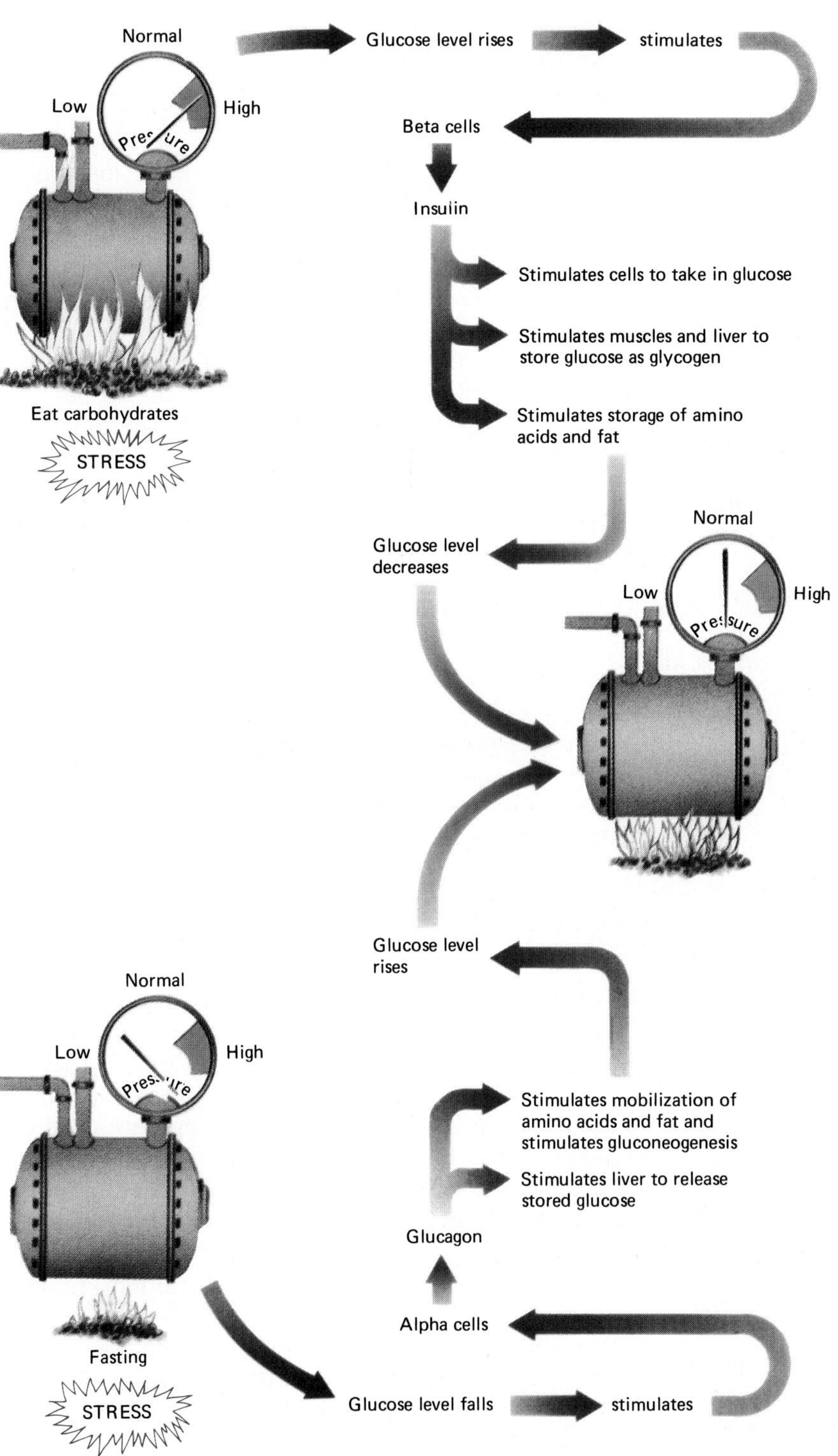

FIGURE 18-30

Regulation of blood-sugar level by insulin and glucagon.

Diabetes mellitus is a disorder associated with insulin production

The principal disorder associated with pancreatic hormones is **diabetes mellitus** (die-uh-**bee**-teez **mel**-ih-tus). Although many of the symptoms of diabetes can be controlled, the long-term complications of this disorder reduce life expectancy by as much as one-third. Compared with nondiabetics, diabetics have a rate of blindness 25 times greater, of kidney disease 17 times greater, of gangrene 17 times greater, and of heart disease twice as great. There are an estimated 10 million diabetics in the United States alone, and almost 40,000 persons die annually as a result of this disorder, making it the third most common cause of death.

Diabetes should be considered a group of diseases rather than a single disorder. Although there is an inherited tendency to this disorder, it is thought that certain environmental factors trigger its actual development. Two distinct clinical varieties of diabetes mellitus have been identified, type I and type II.

Insulin-dependent diabetes, referred to as **type I diabetes,** usually develops before age 20. This disorder is marked by a dramatic decrease in the number of beta cells (sometimes to less than 10% the normal number) in the pancreas. This loss of beta cells results in insulin deficiency. Type I diabetes is clinically treated with insulin injections to relieve the carbohydrate imbalance that results. The disease is believed to be an autoimmune condition in which the body develops antibodies to the beta cells in the pancreas. The antibodies destroy the tissue.

More than 90% of all cases are non-insulin-dependent diabetes, or **type II.** This type develops gradually, usually in overweight persons over age 40. In many cases of type II diabetes, sufficient insulin is released by the islets of Langerhans. The problem is that the target cells are not able to take up the insulin and use it. One current suggestion is that as one becomes obese, one increases food intake substantially. This leads to excessive secretion of insulin, and, through a negative-feedback mechanism, the number of insulin receptors on the target cells is decreased. With fewer receptors, the cells are not effective in taking up the insulin from the blood and using it.

THERE ARE THREE MAJOR METABOLIC EFFECTS OF DIABETES MELLITUS

Similar metabolic disturbances occur in all cases of diabetes mellitus. Three major metabolic effects of diabetes are: (1) decreased utilization of glucose, (2) increased fat mobilization, and (3) increased protein utilization.

1. **Decreased utilization of glucose.** In diabetics, cells dependent upon insulin can take in only about 25% of the glucose they require for fuel. Glucose remains in the blood, and the blood-glucose level rises **(hyperglycemia).** The blood-sugar load is further increased by the liver, which cannot effectively trap glucose or store glycogen without insulin. Instead of the normal fasting level of about 90 milligrams per 100 milliliters, the diabetic may have from 300 to more than 1000 milligrams per 100 milliliters.

Whereas glucose does not appear in the urine of nondiabetics, the blood-glucose concentration is so high in the diabetic that sugar spills out into the urine **(glycosuria).** Although not completely reliable, a simple test for glucose in the urine is useful in screening for diabetes and for evaluating control of glucose metabolism in known diabetics. Despite the large quantities of glucose present in the blood of diabetics, the cells cannot utilize it and must turn to other sources of fuel.

2. **Increased fat mobilization.** Fortunately the absence of insulin promotes mobilization of fat stores, so that the blood-fatty acid level rises, providing nutrients for cellular respiration. But unfortunately the blood-lipid level may reach five times the normal level, leading to development of atherosclerosis. And also unfortunately, the increased fat metabolism by the cells increases formation of **ketone bodies** (acetone and other breakdown products of fat metabolism). Ketone bodies build up in the blood, a condition known as **ketosis.** Ketone bodies can interfere with normal pH balance by releasing hydrogen ions. The pH can become too low, causing **acidosis.** If sufficiently marked, acidosis can lead to coma and death.

When the ketone level rises in the blood, ketones appear in the urine and provide another useful clinical indication of diabetes. When ketones are excreted in the urine, they take sodium with them, and the resulting sodium depletion contributes further to acidosis and its fatal consequences.

3. **Increased protein utilization.** Lack of insulin also causes protein wasting. Normally, pro-

teins are constantly being broken down and built up. Without insulin to stimulate protein synthesis, the balance is disturbed and there is a shift in the direction of protein breakdown. Amino acids are taken to the liver and converted to glucose, further compounding the excess glucose problem. The untreated diabetic becomes thin and emaciated, despite (usually) a voracious appetite.

When sugar and ketones are excreted by the kidneys, they take water with them because of increased urinary osmotic pressure. **Polyuria** (*pol*-ee-**yoo**-ree-uh), or increased urine volume, results, causing dehydration. Constant thirst **(polydipsia)** is another clinical symptom of diabetes.

DIABETES CAN BE EFFECTIVELY TREATED

Clinical highlight

Type II diabetes (non-insulin dependent) is generally a mild disorder and can be treated by maintaining an appropriate body weight and by carefully managing the diet. In more serious cases, tolbutamide and related drugs may be taken orally to stimulate the islets to produce insulin. However, it has been shown that these drugs have undesirable side effects such as heart disease, and there has been a shift away from their use.

In type I diabetes (insulin dependent) daily injections of insulin are used to regulate carbohydrate metabolism. Insulin is a protein so it cannot be taken orally because it would be digested by enzymes in the digestive tract.

Hypoglycemia may be a warning sign of diabetes

Hypoglycemia (low blood-sugar level) is sometimes seen in people who later develop diabetes. It may be an overreaction by the islets to glucose challenge. Too much insulin is secreted in response to carbohydrate ingestion. About 3 hours after a meal the blood-sugar level falls below normal, making the individual feel very drowsy. If this reaction is severe enough, the patient may become uncoordinated or even unconscious.

Clinical highlight

Serious hypoglycemia may develop if diabetics inject themselves with too much insulin or if too much is secreted by the islets because of a tumor. The blood-sugar level may fall drastically, depriving the brain cells of their needed supply of fuel. *Insulin shock* may result, a condition in which the patient may appear to be drunk or may become unconscious, suffer convulsions or brain damage, or even die.

The adrenal glands secrete hormones that function in metabolism and stress

The paired **adrenal glands** (a-**dree**-nul) are small yellow masses of tissue that lie in contact with the superior surface of the kidneys (Fig. 18-31). Each gland consists of a central portion, the **adrenal medulla,** and a larger outer section, the **adrenal cortex** (Fig. 18-32). Although wedded anatomically, the adrenal medulla and cortex develop from different types of tissue in the embryo and function as distinct glands. Both secrete hormones that help to regulate metabolism, and both help the body to deal effectively with stress.

The adrenal medulla synthesizes epinephrine and norepinephrine

The adrenal medulla develops from neural tissue and, as discussed in Chapter 16, is sometimes considered part of the sympathetic nervous system. Some physiologists regard the adrenal medulla as a modified sympathetic ganglion because its secretion is controlled by sympathetic preganglionic fibers. The secretory cells, called **chromaffin cells,** are somewhat like neurons and may be thought of as sympathetic postganglionic neurons.

Two types of chromaffin cells can be distinguished. Epinephrine is secreted by the larger cells that contain less dense granules, whereas norepinephrine is secreted in lesser quantities by smaller cells with vesicles containing denser granules.

EPINEPHRINE AND NOREPINEPHRINE PLAY AN INTEGRAL ROLE IN THE FIGHT–OR–FLIGHT RESPONSE

The adrenal medulla secretes the catecholamines epinephrine (adrenaline) and norepinephrine (noradrenaline) (Fig. 18-7). Norepinephrine is the same substance secreted as a neurotransmitter by sympathetic neurons and by some neurons in the central nervous system. Its effects are identical to those of the neurotransmitter but last about ten times longer because the hormone is removed from the blood more slowly than it is removed from synapses. About 80% of the hormone output of the adrenal medulla is epinephrine. Epinephrine and norepinephrine are sympathomimetic (*sim*-pah-thow-mi-**met**-ik), which means that they promote actions that mimic those produced by the sympathetic nervous system.

Appropriately referred to as the emergency gland of the body, the adrenal medulla prepares us physiologically to cope with threatening situations. If a monster were suddenly to appear before you, hormone secretion from this gland would initiate an alarm reaction enabling you to think quickly, then fight harder or run much faster than normally. Metabolic rate could increase as much as 100%.

The adrenal medullary hormones cause blood to be rerouted in favor of those organs essential for emergency action. Blood vessels to the skin and most internal organs are constricted, while those to the brain, muscles, and heart are dilated. Constriction of the blood vessels to the skin has the added advantage of decreasing blood loss from superficial wounds. (It also explains the sudden paling that comes with fear or rage.) Strength of contraction of skeletal muscles increases.

Under the influence of the adrenal medullary hormones, the heart beats faster and contracts with greater strength. Thresholds in the reticular activating system (RAS) of the brain are lowered, increasing alertness.

Virtually all of the airways enlarge so that one breathes more effectively. In fact, epinephrine and related drugs are used clinically to relieve nasal congestion and asthma.

Both glucose and fatty acid levels in the blood rise, assuring needed fuel for extra energy. These hormones raise fatty acid levels in the blood by mobilizing fat stores from adipose tissue. They raise the blood-sugar level by increasing the

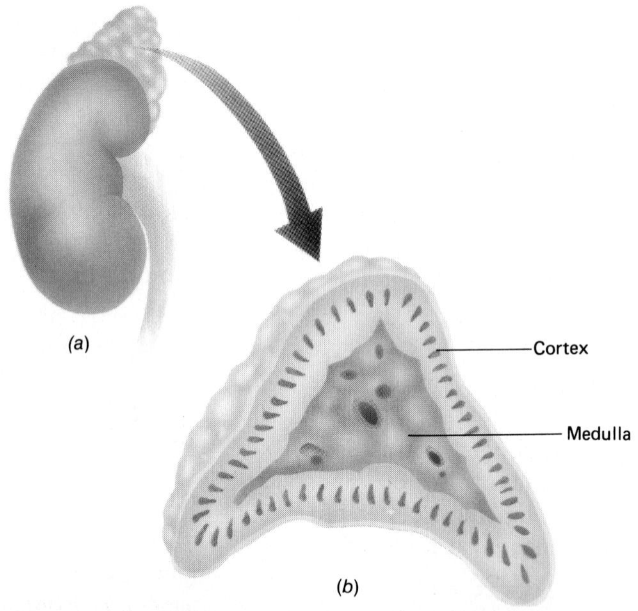

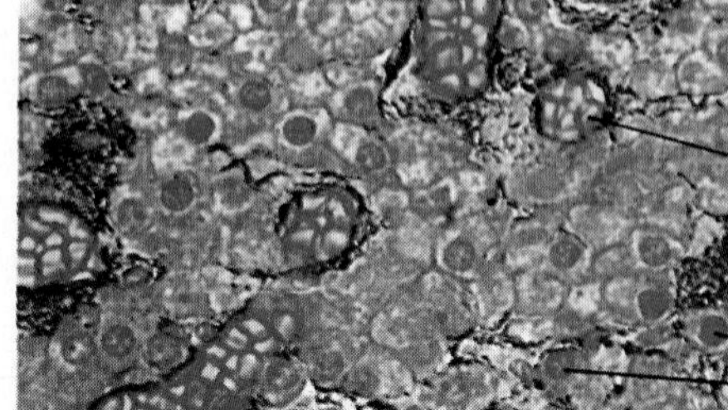

FIGURE 18-31

Adrenal glands. (*a*) The paired adrenal glands are small yellow masses of tissue that lie in contact with the superior surface of the kidneys. (*b*) The adrenal gland consists of a central medulla and an outer cortex. (*c*) Photomicrograph of the cellular organization of the adrenal medulla (×348). (© Phototake.)

amount of glucose absorbed from the intestine, stimulating glycogenolysis, and promoting conversion of muscle glycogen to lactic acid.

Many of the effects of epinephrine and norepinephrine are similar, but their effects on the cardiovascular system are somewhat different. Norepinephrine constricts the blood vessels and increases blood pressure. Epinephrine increases blood pressure by increasing cardiac output (the volume of blood pumped each minute).

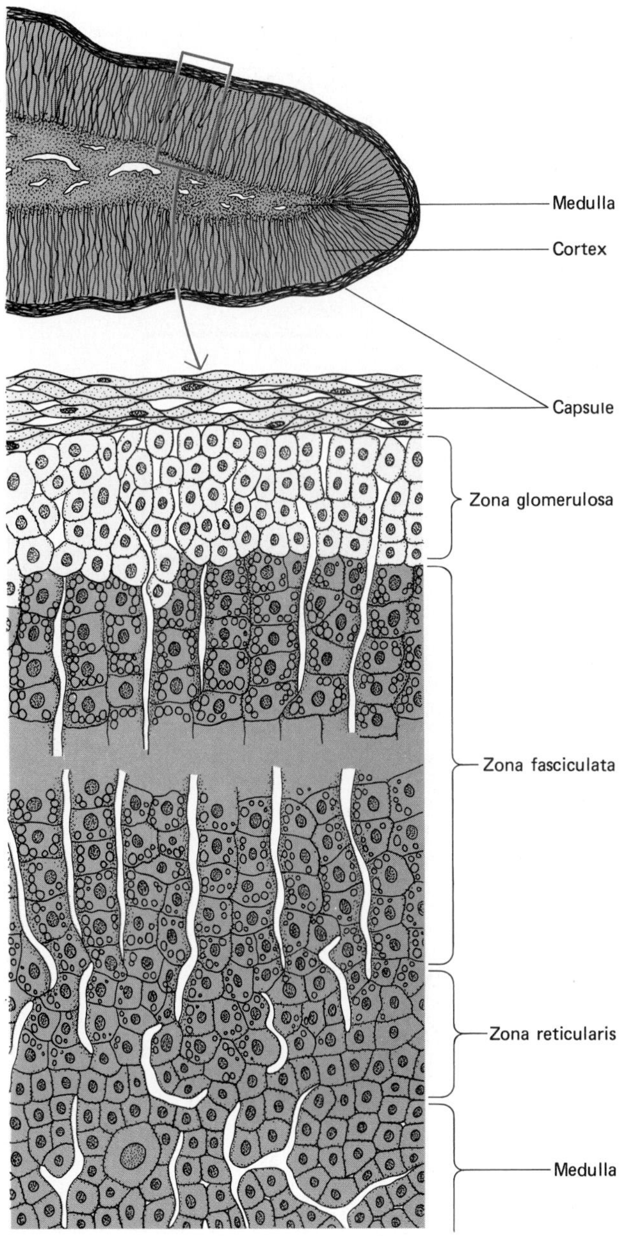

FIGURE 18-32

Section through human adrenal gland.

ACETYLCHOLINE TRIGGERS SECRETION OF EPINEPHRINE AND NOREPINEPHRINE

Under normal conditions both epinephrine and norepinephrine are secreted continuously in small amounts. Their secretion is under nervous control. When anxiety is aroused, neural messages are sent through sympathetic nerves to the adrenal medulla. Acetylcholine released by preganglionic neurons triggers release of the hormones.

> Anxiety ⟶ hypothalamus ⟶ sympathetic nerves ⟶ ↑ acetylcholine
> ⟶ adrenal medulla ⟶
> ↑ epinephrine and norepinephrine

(In Chapter 16, we discussed a similar effect: when sympathetic preganglionic neurons release acetylcholine, postganglionic neurons may be depolarized and they release norepinephrine.)

The adrenal cortex secretes steroid hormones

The **adrenal cortex** is divided into three zones (Fig. 18-32). The outer region just under the capsule is the **zona glomerulosa;** its cells produce hormones known as **mineralocorticoids** (*min*-er-al-o-**kor**-tih-koids). The middle region of the cortex, the **zona fasciculata,** produces mainly the **glucocorticoids** (*gloo*-ko-**kor**-tih-koids). Cells of the inner **zona reticularis** produce sex hormones, mainly male sex hormones, or **androgens.**

All the hormones of the adrenal cortex are steroids synthesized from cholesterol. From 30 to 50 different steroids have been identified in the adrenal cortex, but most of these are intermediate chemicals produced during the synthesis of the principal hormones. Some of the intermediates behave like hormones, but they are not as potent, and normally they are not released.

SEX HORMONES ARE RELEASED BY THE ADRENAL CORTEX

Very small amounts of both androgens (hormones that have masculinizing effects) and **estrogens** (hormones that have feminizing effects) are secreted by the adrenal cortex in both sexes. In males, the amounts of these hormones released are so small that they have little physiological effect. However, in females, most of the androgens are produced by the adrenal glands. These male hormones may play some part in stimulating the adolescent growth spurt in females and in the development of female pubic and axillary hair. Under certain irregular conditions (tumor or congenital enzyme deficiency), androgens may be secreted in large enough quantities to cause abnormalities. Large amounts of androgens secreted in the female, for example, cause masculinization, including growth of facial and body hair, small breasts, and enlarged clitoris (an external female genital structure homologous to the penis).

MINERALOCORTICOIDS REGULATE WATER AND ELECTROLYTE BALANCE

Aldosterone (al-**dos**-ter-own) is the principal mineralocorticoid. Its main function is to maintain homeostasis of sodium and potassium ions. It does this mainly by stimulating the kidneys to conserve sodium and to excrete potassium. Aldosterone also acts upon sweat glands, salivary glands, and the digestive tract, stimulating retention of sodium and loss of potassium.

When the adrenal glands do not function properly and the level of aldosterone in the blood becomes too low, an increased amount of sodium is excreted in the urine. Water leaves the body with the sodium. This reduces the volume of fluid in the body, especially the blood volume, and may result in a dangerous reduction in blood pressure. The role of aldosterone in maintaining fluid balance will be discussed in more detail in Chapter 27.

ALDOSTERONE SECRETION IS REGULATED BY CHANGES IN THE BLOOD AND INTERSTITIAL FLUID

Secretion of aldosterone depends upon at least four factors (Fig. 18-33). An increase in potassium-ion concentration of the interstitial fluid

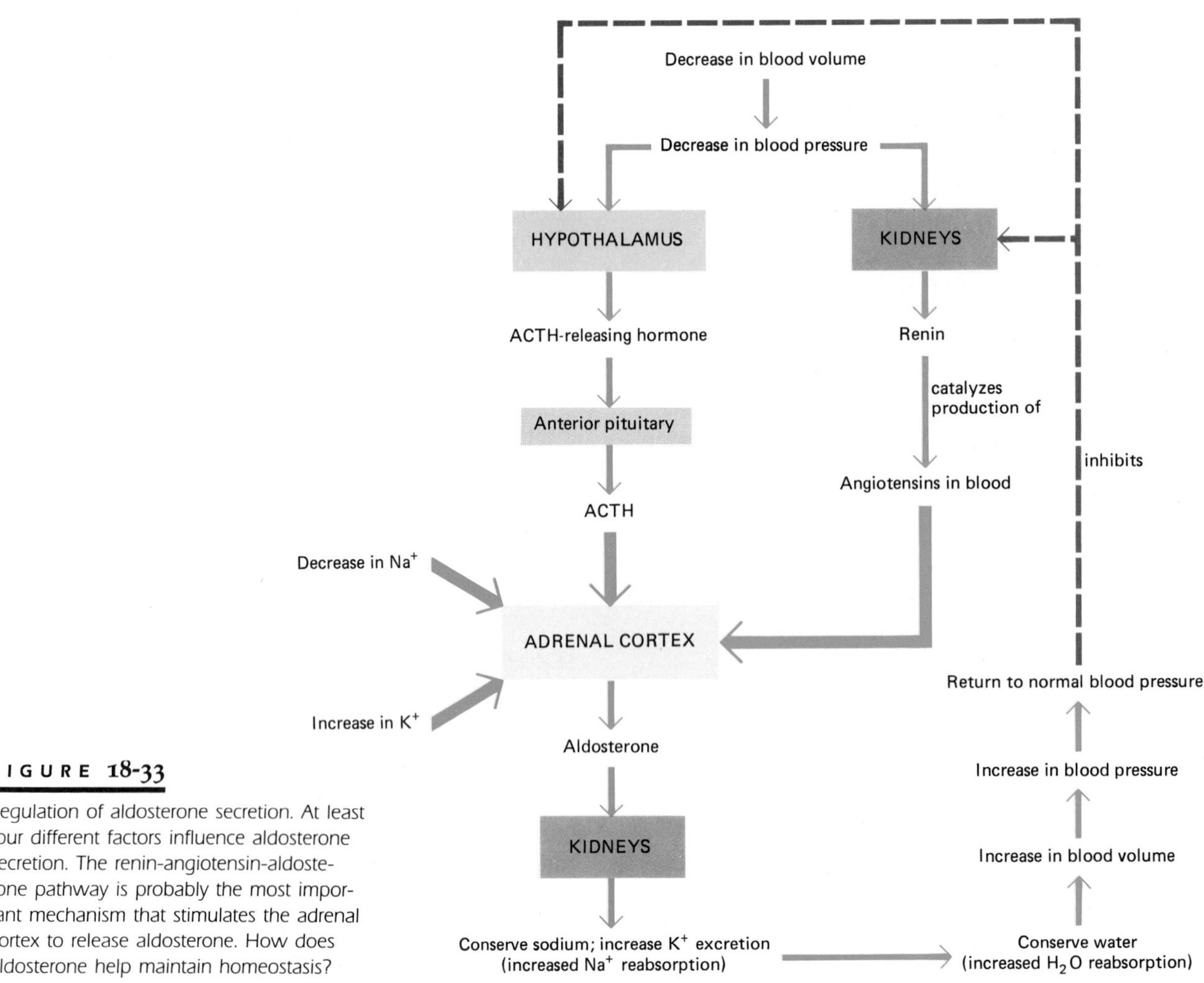

FIGURE 18-33

Regulation of aldosterone secretion. At least four different factors influence aldosterone secretion. The renin-angiotensin-aldosterone pathway is probably the most important mechanism that stimulates the adrenal cortex to release aldosterone. How does aldosterone help maintain homeostasis?

stimulates aldosterone secretion, as does a decrease in sodium concentration. The hormone ACTH from the anterior pituitary may also have a stimulating effect. Perhaps the most important mechanism, though, is the renin-angiotensin-aldosterone pathway.

The **renin-angiotensin-aldosterone pathway** is activated when the pressure of blood flowing through the kidneys decreases below normal. The kidneys release **renin,** which leads to the activation of **angiotensin** hormones in the blood. These hormones stimulate aldosterone secretion. As a result, more sodium is conserved by the kidneys, causing more water to be retained. With additional fluid intake, blood volume and pressure return to normal, and then aldosterone secretion decreases. (The renin-angiotensin-aldosterone pathway is discussed in more detail in Chapter 27.)

GLUCOCORTICOIDS FUNCTION IN RESPONSE TO STRESS

Cortisol (also called **hydrocortisone**) accounts for about 95% of the glucocorticoid activity of the adrenal cortex. *Corticosterone* and *cortisone* are glucocorticoids of minor importance. The principal action of cortisol (and other glucocorticoids) is to promote gluconeogenesis in the liver.

Cortisol helps to provide the nutrients for gluconeogenesis by stimulating the transport of amino acids into liver cells while at the same time inhibiting amino acid transport into other types of cells. Cortisol also promotes mobilization of fat from adipose tissue, thereby providing fatty acids that can be used as fuel molecules in cellular respiration. The hormone exerts a mild inhibitory effect on glucose utilization by many body cells.

All these actions contribute to formation of large amounts of glucose and glycogen in the liver and also tend to raise glucose levels in the blood. In the presence of excess amounts of cortisol, the blood-sugar level may be as much as 50% or more above normal, inducing a state of adrenal diabetes.

The metabolic effects of cortisol assure adequate fuel supplies to the cells when the body is under stress. Thus, the adrenal cortex provides an important backup system for the adrenal medulla. The physiology of stress will be discussed in further detail later in this chapter.

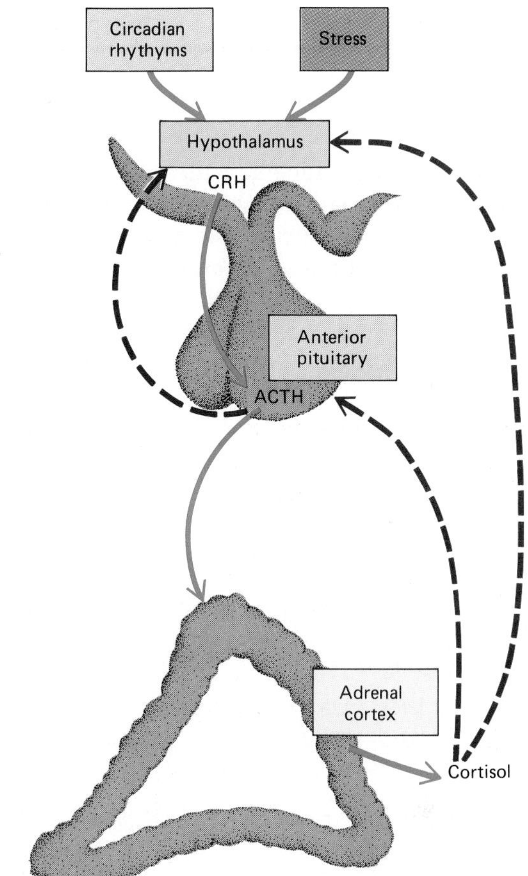

FIGURE 18-34

Regulation of glucocorticoid secretion.

GLUCOCORTICOIDS ARE USED CLINICALLY

Clinical highlight

Glucocorticoids are used clinically to reduce inflammation in allergic reactions, infections, arthritis, acute glomerulonephritis (a kidney disorder), and certain types of cancer. The administered hormone helps to stabilize lysosome membranes so that they do not destroy tissues with their potent enzymes. Glucocorticoids also reduce inflammation by decreasing the permeability of capillary membranes, thereby reducing swelling. They also reduce the effects of histamine and inhibit formation of **bradykinins,** substances that cause dilation of blood vessels.

When used in large amounts over long periods of time, glucocorticoids can cause serious side effects. They decrease the number of lymphocytes in the body and can cause atrophy of lymph tissue, reducing the patient's ability to fight infections. Other side effects include ulcers, hypertension, diabetes mellitus, and atherosclerosis.

GLUCOCORTICOID SECRETION IS REGULATED BY ACTH FROM THE PITUITARY

ACTH secretion is controlled by a corticotropin-releasing hormone from the hypothalamus (Fig. 18-34). Almost any type of stress is reported to the hypothalamus, which activates the system so that ACTH is released from the anterior lobe of the pituitary. This results in the rapid release of large amounts of cortisol. When the body is not under stress, high levels of cortisol in the blood inhibit both the hypothalamus and the pituitary.

Stress ⟶ hypothalamus ⟶ corticotropin-releasing hormone ⟶ anterior pituitary ⟶ ACTH ⟶ adrenal cortex ⟶ cortisol

MALFUNCTIONS OF ADRENOCORTICAL SECRETION RESULT IN CLINICAL DISORDERS

Clinical highlight

Abnormally large amounts of glucocorticoids, whether due to disease or clinical administration, result in the condition called **Cushing's syndrome** (Fig. 18-35). Fat is mobilized from the lower part of the body and deposited about the trunk. Edema gives the patient's face a full-moon appearance. The blood-sugar level rises, causing adrenal diabetes. If this condition persists for several months, the beta cells in the pancreas may "burn out" from working to secrete sufficient insulin to lower the blood-sugar level. This can result in permanent diabetes mellitus. Reduction in protein synthesis causes weakness and decreases immune responses, so that the patient often dies of infection.

Destruction of the adrenal cortex and the resulting decrease in aldosterone and cortisol secretion cause **Addison's disease.** Reduction in cortisol prevents the body from regulating blood-sugar levels because it cannot synthesize enough glucose by gluconeogenesis. The patient also loses the ability to cope with stress; if cortisol levels are significantly depressed, even the stress of mild infections can cause death. In severe cases, lack of aldosterone results in tremendous loss of sodium in the urine, depleting the interstitial fluid. Plasma volume falls, and the patient usually dies of shock within a few days if untreated. In persons with Addison's disease, secretion of melanocyte-stimulating hormone by the pituitary is increased, causing marked pigmentation of the skin and mucous membranes.

Stress threatens homeostasis

Good health and survival depend upon the maintenance of homeostasis. Certain stimuli called **stressors** that disrupt the steady state of the body must therefore be dealt with swiftly and effectively. Stressors, whether in the form of infection, disease, arguments, or even the anxiety of taking a test for which one is not fully prepared, may threaten homeostasis, putting the body in a state of **stress.** The brain sends messages activating the sympathetic nervous system and the adrenal glands. Epinephrine and norepinephrine are released, and the body prepares for fight or flight or, more simply, to cope with the problems at hand. The hypothalamus also signals the anterior pituitary hormonally to secrete ACTH, which increases cortisol secretion, thereby adjusting metabolism to meet the increased demands of the stressful situation.

Some stressors are short-lived. We react to the situation and quickly resolve it. In doing so, we eliminate the threat to homeostasis. Other stressors may last for days, weeks, or even years. A chronic disease, or an unhappy marriage or job

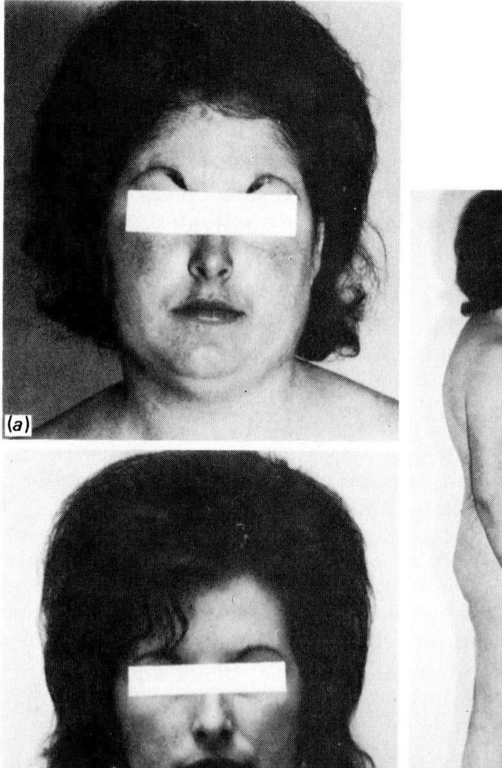

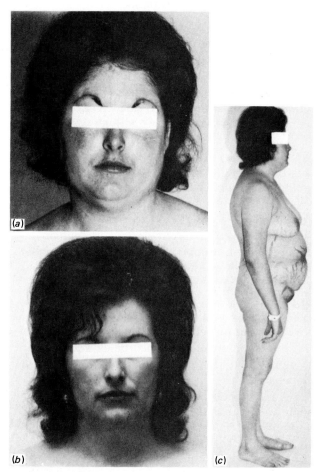

FIGURE 18-35

A patient with Cushing's syndrome (*a*) and (*c*) before treatment, and (*b*) 1 year after treatment (removal of an adrenal adenoma). (From Beeson, et al.: Cecil Textbook of Medicine, 15th ed., Philadelphia, W. B. Saunders, 1979, p. 2153)

situation are examples of long-term stress. General anxiety and tension are examples of nonspecific stressors.

Physiologist Hans Selye introduced the term **general adaptation syndrome (GAS)** to describe the body's response to stress. He divides the syndrome into three phases. The first is the *alarm reaction,* in which the sympathetic system and adrenal medulla prepare the body for fight or flight. The heart beats faster, pulse and blood pressure rise, blood is rerouted, metabolic rate increases, and all the other physiological changes take place that facilitate coping with an emergency situation.

If stress continues over a long period, a second stage, the *resistance reaction,* is initiated. During this stage, blood pressure remains abnormally high and metabolism is geared to help the body resist the effects of the stressor, whether fighting infection or dealing with an emotional problem. Protein breakdown is characteristic of the resistance stage (Fig. 18-36). Levels of many hormones, including cortisol, aldosterone, thyroxine, and growth hormone, are elevated.

The final phase of the GAS is the *stage of exhaustion,* in which the body appears unable to utilize available cortical hormones and may succumb permanently to the stressor. It should be noted that Selye's explanations are somewhat controversial and are not accepted by all physiologists.

It has been suggested that in our fast-paced society, fraught as it is with stressors, many persons remain in the resistance stage of the GAS almost continuously. Selye has suggested that such chronic stress is harmful because of the side effects of long-term elevated levels of cortisol.

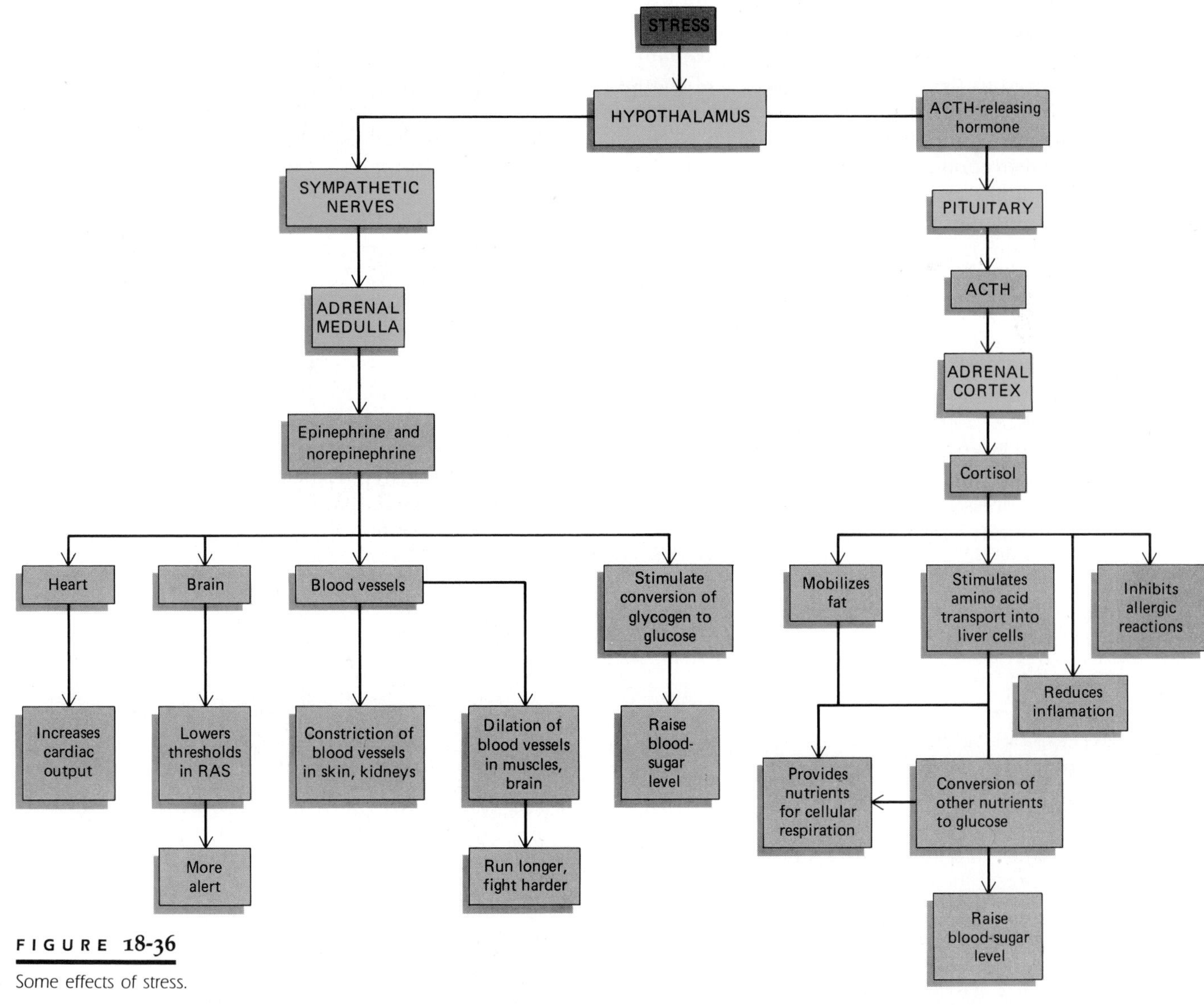

FIGURE 18-36

Some effects of stress.

While glucocorticoids are helpful in reducing inflammation, they can also interfere with normal immune responses, so that infection spreads. Chronic high blood pressure may contribute to heart disease, and increased levels of fat in the blood may promote atherosclerosis. When experimental animals are injected with large amounts of glucocorticoids, such disease states are induced, and similar effects are seen when large doses are administered clinically to patients. Among the diseases linked to excessive amounts of adrenocortical hormones are ulcers, high blood pressure, atherosclerosis, and arthritis.

The pineal gland secretes melatonin

The **pineal gland** (**pin**-ee-al) projects from the roof of the third ventricle of the brain. Secretion of its hormone, **melatonin,** follows a circadian (daily) rhythm tied to daily and seasonal changes in light. Melatonin appears to control physiological responses to light cycles (the biological clock) in some vertebrates. For example, it influences the size of sex glands in the hamster, pigmentation in some vertebrates, and activity in some birds. In humans its function has long been a mystery, but there is now evidence that exposure to light results in suppression of melatonin secretion. The plasma concentration of melatonin is high in the dark and very low in the light. When normal humans are given large doses of melatonin, they become less alert and sleepy. Melatonin may be important in promoting sleep. Researchers are looking for a link between a certain type of depression (seasonal affective disorder) and melatonin concentration.

Melatonin may help control the onset of puberty (period of sexual maturation) in the male. This idea is based upon research that found an abrupt decrease in melatonin concentration during early puberty, suggesting that melatonin may inhibit sexual maturation. Of course the question remains, what causes the drop in melatonin level?

Another hormone secreted by the pineal gland, **adrenoglomerulotropin** (ah-*dree*-noe-glo-*mer*-u-loe-**troe**-pin), is believed to play a role in the secretion of aldosterone from the adrenal cortex. Norepinephrine, serotonin, and histamine are examples of other substances found in the pineal gland.

Several other organs of the body secrete hormones

The kidneys secrete **renal erythropoietin factor (REF)** (ee-*rith*-row-**poy**-eh-tin), which will be discussed in Chapter 27. The hormone **thymosin** (**thy**-mow-sin), released by the thymus gland, functions in the immune system and will be discussed in Chapter 23. Several hormones released by the digestive tract will be discussed in Chapter 25. **Secretin** (seh-**kree**-tin), released by the duodenum (the first part of the small intestine), was the very first hormone to be described. Its function was demonstrated in 1902 by the physiologists Bayliss and Starling.

A hormone known as **atrial natriuretic factor (ANF)** is released by stretched cardiac muscle fibers in response to increased blood volume. ANF acts upon the renin-angiotensin system, the kidneys, and the hypothalamus to reduce blood pressure. Many other hormones have been identified; some will be discussed with the organs that secrete them.

Summary

I. The endocrine system regulates homeostasis of many metabolic processes; it consists of endocrine glands and tissues that release hormones.

- A. Endocrine glands are ductless glands that secrete hormones into the interstitial fluid.
- B. Hormones are chemical messengers secreted by endocrine glands and some other tissues that are transported to target tissues by the blood and that stimulate the target tissue to change some metabolic activity.

II. Several mechanisms of hormone action are known.

- A. Many nonsteroid hormones bind to receptors on the plasma membrane of target cells. This activates a second messenger, such as cyclic AMP, which triggers the chain of events leading to the actual response.
- B. Steroid hormones enter target cells and combine with receptors within the nucleus. The steroid-receptor complex activates specific genes.

III. Endocrine glands are self-regulated by systems of negative feedback controls.

IV. The hypothalamus is the link between the nervous and endocrine systems.

- A. Cells of the hypothalamus secrete several types of releasing and inhibiting hormones that regulate the secretion of hormones by the anterior pituitary gland. For example, release of growth-hormone-releasing hormone from the hypothalamus stimulates the anterior pituitary gland to secrete growth hormone.
- B. Cells of the hypothalamus also produce the hormones oxytocin and antidiuretic hormone (ADH).

V. The posterior pituitary gland releases the hormones oxytocin and ADH.

- A. Oxytocin stimulates the uterus to contract and stimulates release of milk from the lactating breast.
- B. ADH acts on the kidney ducts to promote reabsorption of water (i.e., water conservation).

VI. The anterior pituitary gland releases growth hormone, prolactin, and several tropic hormones.

- A. Growth hormone promotes growth by promoting protein synthesis. It acts on long bones via intermediary substances called somatomedins.
  1. Hyposecretion of growth hormone during childhood stunts growth.
  2. Hypersecretion causes gigantism; hypersecretion during adulthood may result in acromegaly.
- B. Prolactin stimulates milk production in the lactating breast.
- C. The tropic hormones include thyroid-stimulating hormone (TSH), ACTH, and the gonadotropic hormones.

VII. The thyroid hormones T3 and T4 stimulate the rate of metabolism.

- A. A rise in thyroid hormone level in the blood inhibits secretion of thyroid-stimulating hormone by the pituitary; a decrease stimulates TSH secretion.
- B. Extreme hypothyroidism in childhood may result in cretinism; hypothyroidism in an adult leads to myxedema.

VIII. The parathyroid glands secrete parathyroid hormone (PTH), which increases calcium levels in the blood and interstitial fluid.

- A. PTH stimulates release of calcium from bones, stimulates calcium conservation by the kidneys, and helps activate vitamin D.
- B. An increase in calcium level inhibits parathyroid hormone secretion; a decrease in calcium level stimulates secretion.

IX. The islets of Langerhans secrete insulin and glucagon, hormones that regulate the glucose level in the blood.

- A. Insulin lowers the blood-sugar level by stimulating uptake and storage of glucose by the cells.
- B. Glucagon raises the blood-sugar level by stimulating glycogenolysis and gluconeogenesis.

X. The adrenal glands consist of the adrenal medulla and the adrenal cortex; both release hormones that help the body cope with stress.

- A. The adrenal medulla releases epinephrine and norepinephrine, which increase heart rate, metabolic rate, and strength of muscle contraction, and which reroute the blood to organs that need more blood in times of stress.
- B. The adrenal cortex releases cortisol, which promotes gluconeogenesis in the liver, thereby raising the blood-sugar level; this hormone provides backup to the adrenal medullary hormones.
- C. The adrenal cortex also releases aldosterone, which helps maintain sodium and potassium balance.

XI. In response to stress the adrenal medulla initiates an alarm reaction that prepares the body physiologically to cope; secretion of cortisol by the adrenal cortex ensures a steady supply of needed nutrients for the rapidly metabolizing cells.

Post-test

1. Endocrine glands lack ______________ and release ______________.
2. A hormone may be defined as a ______________ ______________.
3. A second messenger important in the mechanism of action of many hormones is ______________.
4. The ______________ serves as the link between nervous and endocrine systems.
5. The hormone ______________ stimulates contraction of the uterus.
6. The hormone ______________ stimulates milk production in the lactating breast.
7. Growth hormone is produced by the ______________ ______________.
8. Oxytocin is produced by the ______________.
9. Oxytocin is stored and released by the ______________ ______________ when needed.
10. Hypersecretion of growth hormone during childhood may result in ______________.
11. The action of the thyroid hormones is to ______________.
12. In addition to the thyroid hormones, the thyroid gland produces a hormone called ______________, which acts to ______________ ______________.
13. A hormone that raises the level of sodium in the blood is ______________.
14. Blood-sugar level is lowered by the hormone ______________.
15. Glucagon acts to ______________ blood-sugar level.
16. The adrenal medulla releases ______________ and ______________.
17. In diabetes mellitus cells must turn to ______________ and ______________ for fuel.
18. Cushing's disease may result from too much ______________.
19. Cretinism may result from ______________.
20. Beta cells in the islets of Langerhans produce ______________.
21. Label the diagram.

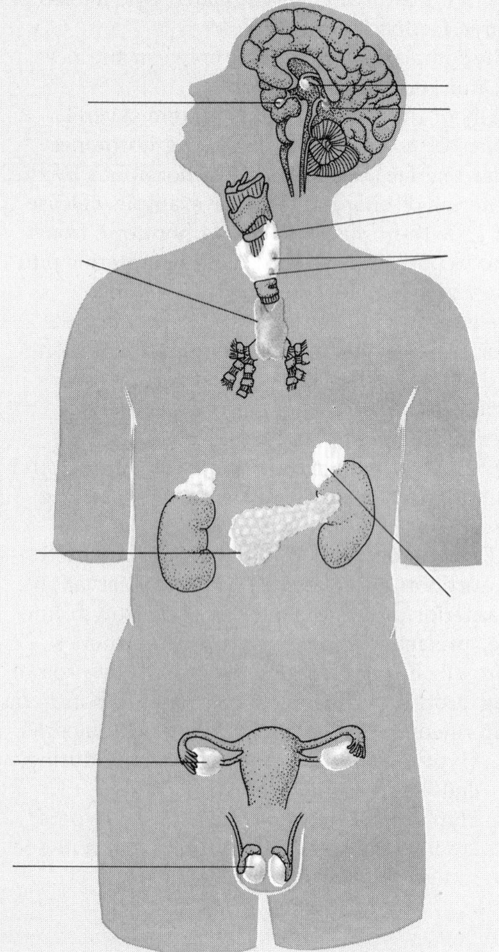

Review questions

1. Compare the mechanism of action of steroid hormones with that of protein-type hormones.
2. List the hormones released by the anterior lobe of the pituitary gland and give their actions.
3. What are the physiological actions of parathyroid hormone?
4. How are the parathyroid glands regulated?
5. Draw a diagram to illustrate how the thyroid gland is regulated by negative feedback mechanisms.
6. What is cyclic AMP? What are prostaglandins?
7. Describe the disorders associated with impaired growth-hormone secretion.
8. What are the symptoms associated with impaired calcium metabolism?
9. How do adrenal glands help the body adjust to stress?
10. How is the blood-sugar level regulated? Describe the role of each of the hormones that influence blood-sugar level.
11. What physiological disturbances are associated with diabetes mellitus?
12. Identify three types of hormones secreted by the adrenal cortex and give the action of each type.

Post-test answers

1. ducts; hormones **2.** chemical messenger that stimulates a change in some metabolic activity **3.** cyclic AMP **4.** hypothalamus **5.** oxytocin **6.** prolactin **7.** anterior pituitary **8.** hypothalamus **9.** posterior pituitary **10.** gigantism **11.** stimulate rate of metabolism **12.** calcitonin; lower calcium level in the blood **13.** aldosterone **14.** insulin **15.** increase (raise) **16.** epinephrine, norepinephrine **17.** fatty acids, protein **18.** cortisol (glucocorticoids) **19.** hyposecretion of thyroid hormones during early childhood **20.** insulin **21.** See Figure 18-2.

THE CIRCULATORY SYSTEM: INTERNAL TRANSPORT AND DEFENSE

As the transportation system of the body, the circulatory system links all the organ systems. It delivers nutrients, oxygen, and hormones to the cells and transports cellular wastes from the cells to the excretory organs. The circulatory system also plays a key role in defending the body against disease.

The circulatory system consists of two subsystems—the cardiovascular system and the lymphatic system.

1. In the cardiovascular (CV) system the heart pumps blood through a vast, continuous network of blood vessels (arteries, capillaries, and veins).
2. As blood flows through the microscopic, thin-walled capillaries, materials are exchanged between the blood and the interstitial fluid bathing the tissues of the body.
3. The lymphatic system collects excess interstitial fluid and returns it to the blood, and it defends the body against disease by producing cells (lymphocytes) that recognize invading microorganisms (viruses, bacteria, fungi) as well as altered body cells (cancer cells).

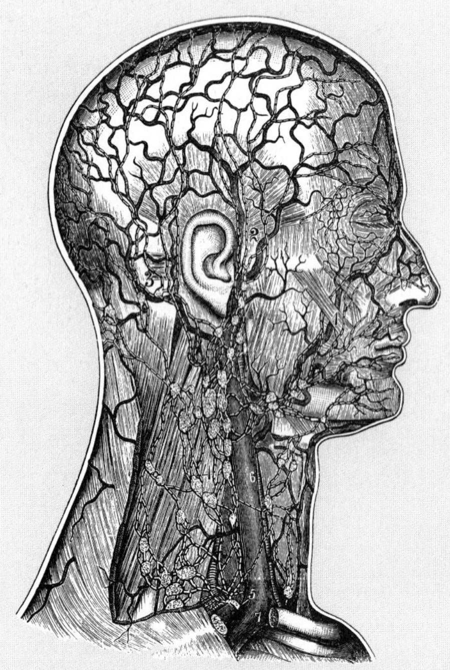

IV

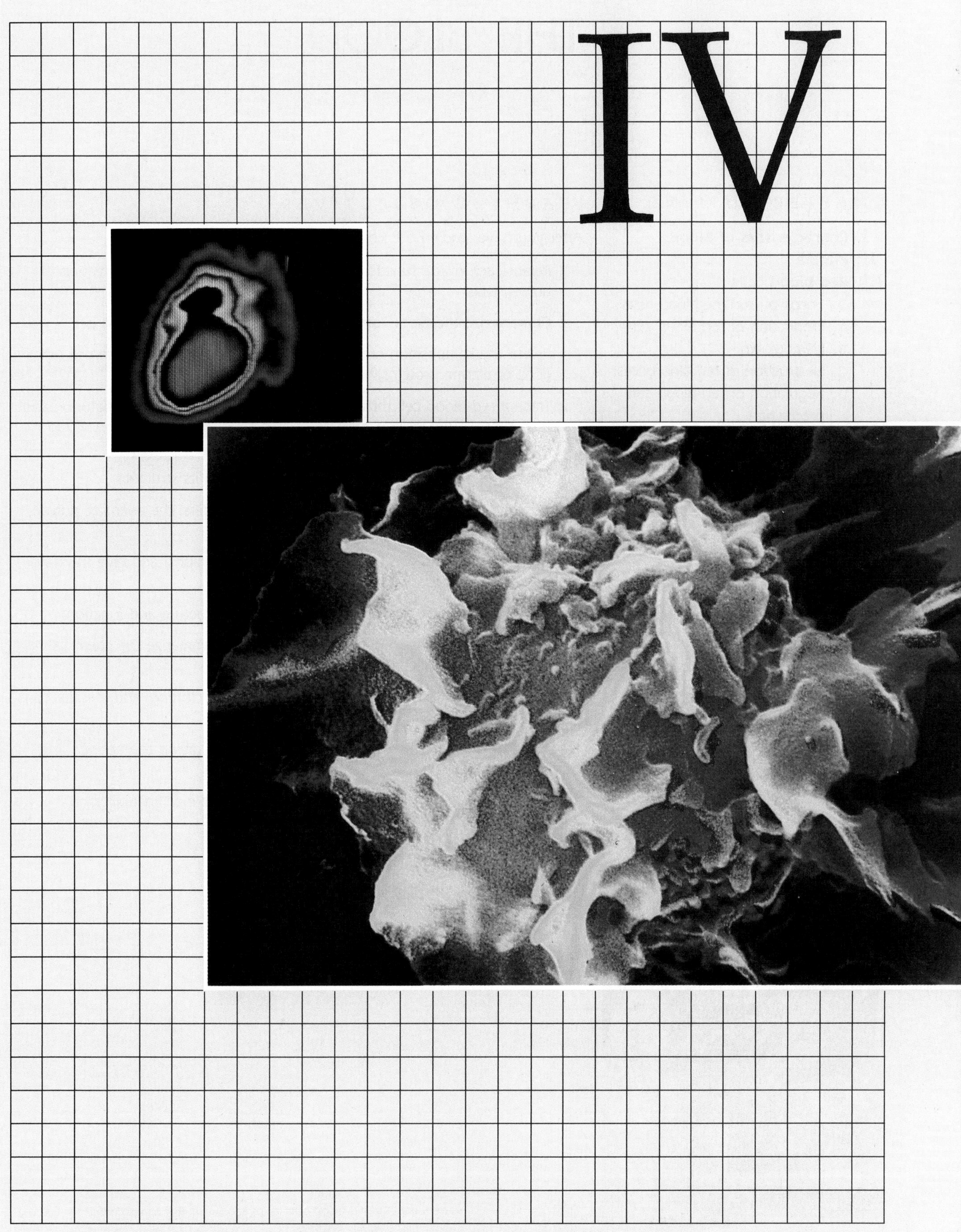

THE BLOOD

CHAPTER OUTLINE

LEARNING OBJECTIVES

After you have studied this chapter you should be able to:

1 Relate each of the functions of the circulatory system to preservation of homeostasis.

2 Characterize the blood, describing its volume, composition, and pH.

3 Relate the composition of blood plasma to its functions (include the functions of plasma proteins).

4 Trace a red blood cell through its life cycle from stem cell to maturity, and then destruction; include the role of erythropoietin in regulation of red blood cell production.

5 Relate the function of a mature red blood cell to its structure.

6 Describe the following common blood cell disorders: the anemias, polycythemia, and leukemia.

7 Describe (or identify in diagrams or photomicrographs) and give the functions of the types of white blood cells.

8 Trace the origin of a platelet, and describe its structure and function.

9 Describe the formation of a platelet plug, and summarize the chemical events of blood clotting.

10 Identify factors that prevent inappropriate blood clotting, and identify conditions that contribute to inappropriate clotting.

11 Compare the ABO and Rh blood group systems, giving the antigen and antibody associated with each blood group.

12 Describe the problems that can result from blood incompatibility.

(*top*) Scanning electron micrograph of red blood cells (color enhanced). (Bill Longscore/Science Source.) (*bottom*) Blood clot. (David Phillips/Visuals Unlimited.)

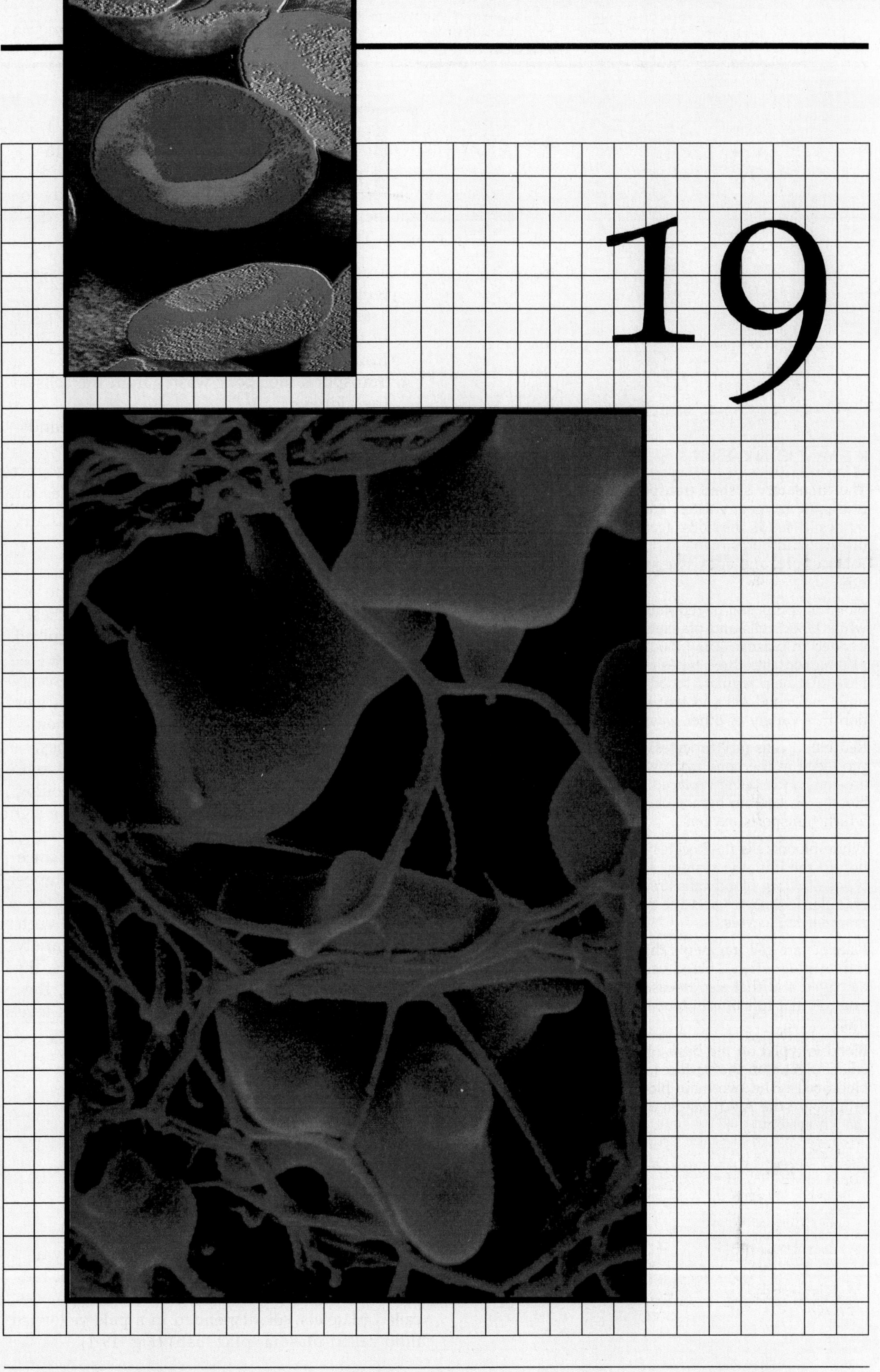

19

KEY CONCEPTS

The circulatory system transports nutrients, oxygen, wastes, and hormones; defends the body against disease; and helps regulate fluid balance, pH, and body temperature.

Blood is composed of red and white blood cells and platelets suspended in plasma. The blood plasma contains three types of proteins that help regulate blood volume and blood pH and that function in a variety of other ways.

Red blood cells (erythrocytes) are produced in the bone marrow and are constantly being replaced. Red blood cells contain hemoglobin which transports oxygen.

White blood cells (leukocytes) function in the immune system. Two types of white blood cells are the granular leukocytes and the nongranular leukocytes.

Platelets are cell fragments that form a plug when a blood vessel is damaged and that also release compounds that function in blood clotting.

Blood is typed on the basis of specific antigens on the surfaces of red blood cells. The two main blood groups are the ABO system and the Rh system.

The circulatory system contributes to homeostasis by transporting needed materials from one part of the body to another and by protecting the body against disease. The circulatory system:

1. Transports nutrients from the digestive system to all cells of the body.
2. Transports oxygen from the lungs to all cells of the body, and transports carbon dioxide from the cells to the lungs.
3. Transports metabolic wastes from the cells to the kidneys.
4. Transports hormones from endocrine glands and neurosecretory cells to target tissues.
5. Protects the body against disease by recognizing and attacking foreign macromolecules (antigens) that enter the body.
6. Helps regulate body temperature.
7. Helps regulate fluid and salt balance.

Substances are transported in the fluid tissue of the circulatory system, the **blood.** From earliest time the vital nature of this fluid was recognized. When blood left the body, life departed also. Through the ages the blood has retained a somewhat mystical quality. Even today, although we know it is really the genes that link the generations, we speak of blood-brothers, blood lines, and blood being thicker than water. In peak emotional states, we even speak of our blood boiling, or of sweating blood. Some even faint at the sight of it!

Blood is of prime importance clinically, since samples of it are easily obtained, and its composition reveals a great deal about the state of the body. Millions of blood tests are performed each day to determine such information as the variety and condition of blood cells present, the pH, the blood volume, the concentration of glucose, the concentration of hemoglobin, and the blood levels of lipids, proteins, and salts.

Blood is a viscous fluid composed of cells and platelets suspended in plasma

The thick red fluid that oozes from the body when a blood vessel has been cut is actually a complex connective tissue. Blood consists of red blood cells, white blood cells, and cell fragments called platelets, all suspended in a pale yellowish fluid called **plasma** (**plaz**-mah) (Fig. 19-1).

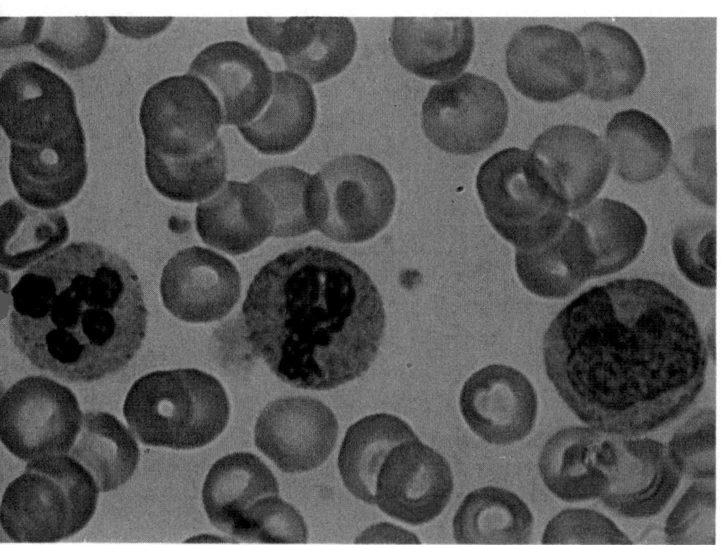

FIGURE 19-1

Blood consists of red blood cells, white blood cells, and cell fragments called platelets suspended in a fluid called plasma. (Fred Hossler/Visuals Unlimited.)

The continuous motion of blood in the body keeps the blood cells suspended throughout the plasma. When blood is drawn from the body and prevented from clotting, however, the blood cells gradually sink to the bottom, leaving the straw-colored plasma above them (Fig. 19-2). In the laboratory this settling process can be accelerated by using a centrifuge that spins blood-filled glass tubes at high speed, hurling the cells to the bottom of each tube. Red blood cells then make up the bottom layer, about 45% of the total blood volume. A thin grayish layer consisting of white blood cells and platelets forms just above the red cells. This layer is called the **buffy coat.**

The percentage of red blood cells present in the total blood volume can be read directly off a specially calibrated tube. This percentage is known as the **hematocrit** (he-**mat**-o-krit). Determination of the hematocrit is one of the routine clinical blood tests, further described in Focus on Routine Blood Tests.

Normal circulating blood volume is about 8% of body weight. In a man weighing about 70 kilograms (154 lb), blood volume should be about 5.6

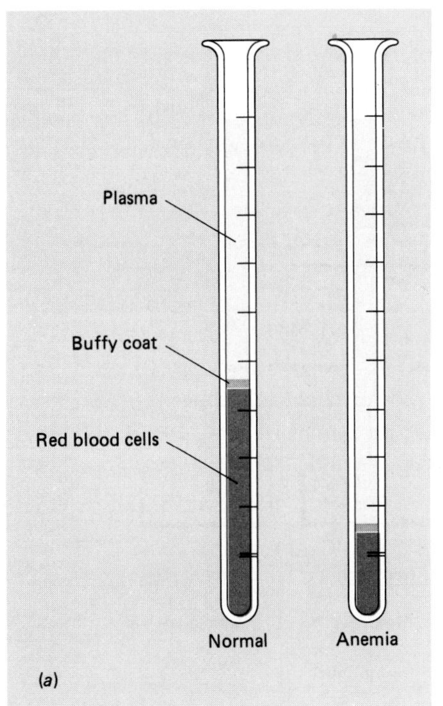

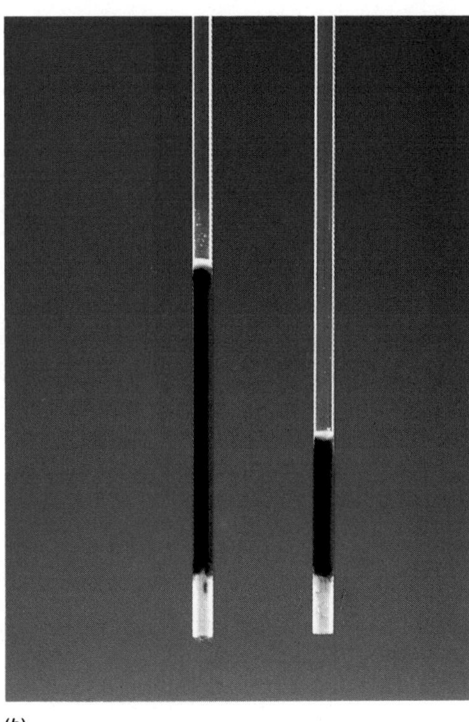

(b)

FIGURE 19-2

Hematocrits. (a) Diagram of the components of hematocrits in the normal and in the anemic individual. (b) Photograph of hematocrits in the normal (left) and anemic (right) individual. (James Hayden/Phototake NYC.)

liters (about 6 qt). The normal pH of blood is slightly alkaline, ranging between 7.35 and 7.45.

Viscosity refers to the measure of a liquid's resistance to flow. A liquid that pours slowly, such as molasses, has a higher viscosity than milk, for example. The hematocrit indicates the viscosity of the blood, because the greater the percentage of cells, the more friction (cells rubbing together), and thus the greater the viscosity. When the hematocrit is normal, the viscosity of blood is about three times that of water, which has a viscosity of 1.0. This indicates that, because blood flows less easily than water, about three times more pressure is needed to force whole blood through a tube than to force an equal volume of water through the same tube.

Let us now consider the plasma and cellular components of the blood in more detail (Fig. 19-3).

The plasma contains albumins, globulins, and fibrinogen

Plasma contains almost 92% water, about 7% protein, about 1% salts (such as Na^+, K^+, Ca^{2+}, Cl^-, and HCO_3^-), and varying amounts of materials being transported, including dissolved gases, nutrients, metabolic wastes, and hormones (see Table 19-1). When the proteins involved in clotting have been removed, the remaining liquid is called **serum.**

Plasma proteins may be divided into three groups, or fractions: the **albumins, globulins,** and **fibrinogen** (fye-**brin**-o-jin). Because of their tendency to become ionized (due to their carboxyl and amino groups), plasma proteins help to maintain the appropriate pH of the blood. In fact, plasma proteins are responsible for about 15% of the buffering capacity of the blood.

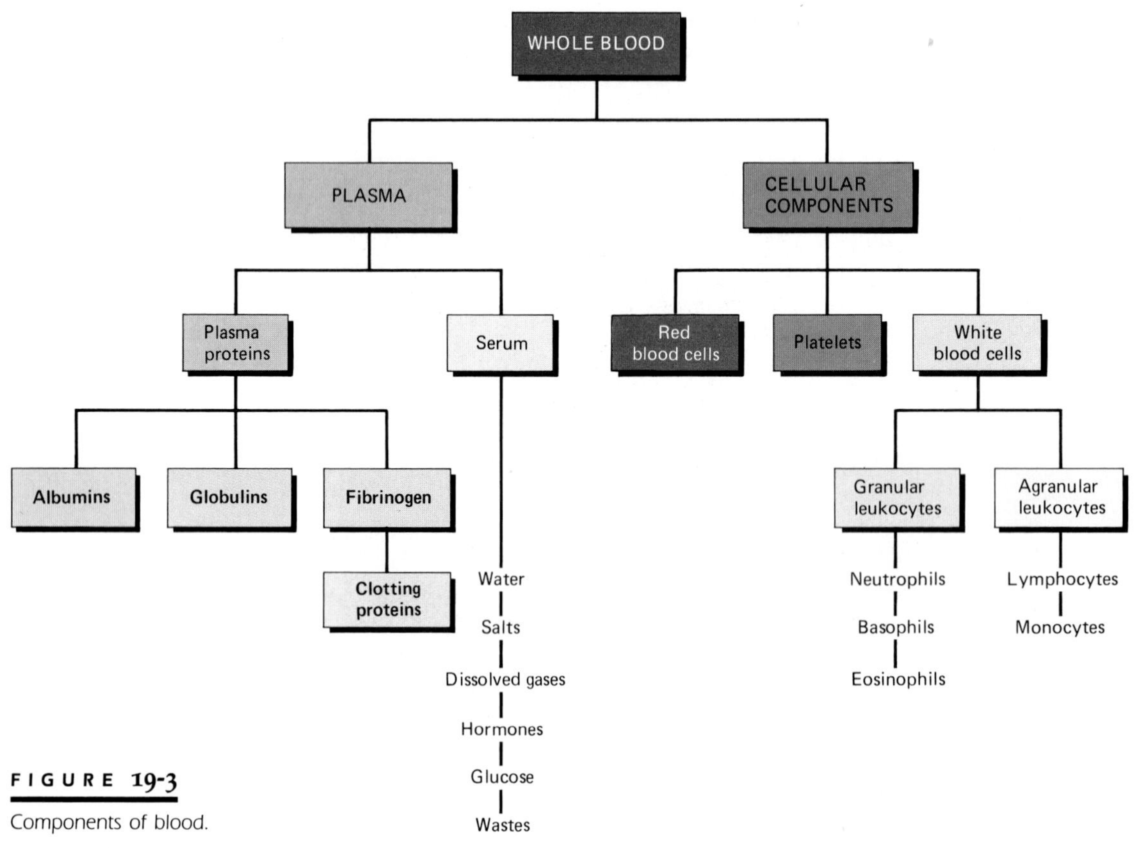

FIGURE 19-3

Components of blood.

Albumins, which account for about 55% of the plasma proteins, are more concentrated in the plasma than in the interstitial fluid. This high concentration contributes to the blood's viscosity. Albumins transport materials such as pigments, hormones (such as thyroid hormones), and certain drugs.

Plasma proteins, especially albumins and globulins, are important in maintaining blood volume. As blood flows through the capillaries, some of the plasma seeps through the capillary walls and passes into the tissues. However, because large protein molecules have difficulty passing through the capillary walls, most of the plasma proteins remain in the blood. There they exert an osmotic force called **colloid osmotic pressure,** which helps pull water and dissolved salts back into the blood. As discussed in Chapter 3, osmotic pressure is developed when two solutions containing different concentrations of solute are separated by a membrane more permeable to the solvent than to the solute. A hypertonic solution is one of high osmotic pressure, while a hypotonic solution has a low osmotic pressure. Thus, water tends to pass from regions of low osmotic pressure (i.e., low solute concentration but high water concentration) to adjacent regions of high osmotic pressure (i.e., high solute concentration but low water concentration).

Globulins account for about 38% of the plasma proteins. One group of the globulins, the **gamma globulins,** serves as **antibodies,** substances that provide immunity against disease. Alpha and beta globulins transport lipids, hormones, vitamins, iron, and other substances.

Fibrinogen, which comprises about 7% of the plasma proteins, and several other plasma proteins are involved in the clotting process. With the exception of the gamma globulins, the plasma proteins are manufactured in the liver.

TABLE 19-1

Some components of plasma

Component	Normal range	Description
Water	92% of plasma	
Total protein	6–8 g/100 ml	
Albumins	4–5 g/100 ml	Help maintain osmotic pressure; contribute to viscosity; transport substances
Globulins	2–3 g/100 ml	Gamma globulins are antibodies; alpha and beta globulins transport lipids, hormones, and other substances
Fibrinogen	0.3 g/100 ml	Important in clotting
Glucose	70–100 mg/100 ml*	Nutrient in transport
Urea nitrogen (BUN)	8–25 mg/100 ml	Measurement of urea wastes in transport
Nonprotein nitrogen	25–40 mg/100 ml	Nitrogen from urea and other nitrogen wastes and also from amino acids
Total lipids	450–1000 mg/100 ml	
Cholesterol	150–220 mg/100 ml	
Neutral fat	80–240 mg/100 ml	
Calcium	8.5–10.5 mg/100 ml	
Chloride	355–380 mg/100 ml	
Iron	0.04–0.21 mg/100 ml	
Potassium	12–20 mg/100 ml	
Sodium	310–350 mg/100 ml	

*Also expressed as mg % or mg/dl (deciliter).

Red blood cells are biconcave discs that transport oxygen

Red blood cells (RBCs), or **erythrocytes** (ee-**rith**-row-sites), are the most numerous and one of the most specialized cell types in the body. They are adapted exclusively for producing and packaging **hemoglobin,** which in turn functions to transport oxygen. An adult male has about 3×10^{13} (30 trillion) red blood cells circulating in his blood, or about 5.4 million per cubic millimeter (mm^3). A female has slightly fewer—about 4.8 million per cubic millimeter. Each red blood cell is about 7.5 micrometers in diameter and its maximum thickness is about 2.6 micrometers. About 3000 red blood cells lined up end to end would span only about 1 inch!

A mature red blood cell is a tiny, flexible, biconcave disc. (Biconcave means thinner in the center than around the edge.) The concavity of the disc is apparent on scanning electron micrographs. When viewed under an ordinary light microscope the center portion of the red blood cell appears relatively clear because the cytoplasm is thinnest there. The mature red blood cell lacks a nucleus as well as other organelles (Fig. 19-4).

When a red blood cell passes through the blood vessels it must often squeeze through very narrow capillaries, some as narrow as 3 micrometers. The necessary flexibility is provided by a framework of protein (especially a type called spectrin) that gives the red blood cell its shape and ability to bend. Red cells tend to aggregate like stacks of coins. Such rolls of red blood cells, referred to as **rouleaux** (roo-**low**), form and then dissociate repeatedly.

FOCUS ON . . . Routine blood tests

Test	Description
Complete blood count (CBC)	Consists of four separate tests: (1) measurement of hemoglobin, (2) hematocrit, (3) white blood cell count and differential (percentage of each white cell type), (4) examination of red blood cells and platelets. (Sometimes a red blood cell count is also made.)
Hemoglobin	Hemoglobin and hematocrit tests are used to check for anemia and polycythemia and to follow the progress of an anemic patient. Normal adult value: 12 to 15 g/100 ml for women; 14 to 17 g/100 ml for men. Whole blood is treated chemically so that the hemoglobin forms a stable pigment (cyanmethemoglobin); then the optical density of the solution is measured in a photometer. (Optical density is directly proportional to concentration of hemoglobin.)
Hematocrit	Hematocrit is an indication of percentage of red cells per unit of blood volume. Normal adult values: 36 to 46% for women; 42 to 54% for men. Blood is centrifuged. Then the volume of red cells is read off a scale on the tube; expressed as percentage of whole blood volume.
White blood cell count (WBC)	Used in diagnosis of bacterial infection and in certain diseases such as leukemia. Used to monitor the effects of radiation or drug therapy that may depress WBC to dangerous levels. Whole blood is mixed with a weak acid solution for the purpose of diluting the blood and hemolyzing the red cells. The diluted blood is placed in a counting chamber (hemocytometer: a microscope slide with a well and a grid marking off tiny squares) and the white cells are counted. Then the number per cubic millimeter can be calculated.
Red blood cell count (RBC)	May be counted manually as in WBC, or an electronic cell counter may be used.
Differential cell count	Used to determine the relative number of each type of white cell in the blood. The differential cell count can be made by analysis of a stained blood smear.
Platelet count	Used in diagnosis of bleeding disorders and in evaluating effects of chemotherapy or radiation therapy on platelet production. Blood is diluted and stained; then platelets are counted in a counting chamber.
Prothrombin time (PT)	Used when clotting disorder is suspected and when monitoring response to oral anticoagulant therapy. Plasma is isolated from drawn blood. Calcium is added to plasma in the presence of tissue thromboplastin. Time elapsed between Ca^{2+} addition and clot formation is prothrombin time (normal plasma clotting time is about 11 seconds).

In intravenous therapy, the fluids infused through a vein must be isotonic with the blood. When placed in a *hypertonic* solution, red blood cells shrink, owing to loss of water. Due to this shrinkage their plasma membranes are thrown into folds, and they are said to be **crenated** (**kree**-nate-ed). In *hypotonic* solution red cells absorb water, become enlarged, and assume a spherical shape. The plasma membrane also may rupture, allowing the hemoglobin to leak out. The plasma membranes of ruptured red blood cells appear as colorless ghosts. This destruction of red blood cells with the release of hemoglobin is called **hemolysis** (he-**mol**-ih-sis). Certain chemicals, such as those found in snake venom, may also cause hemolysis.

About 23% of the carbon dioxide in the blood is transported in combination with hemoglobin, but most of it is carried in the plasma as bicarbonate ions. Red blood cells contain an enzyme, carbonic anhydrase, that converts carbon dioxide and water to bicarbonate, thereby facilitating transport of this gas to the lungs. This matter will be discussed in greater detail in Chapter 24.

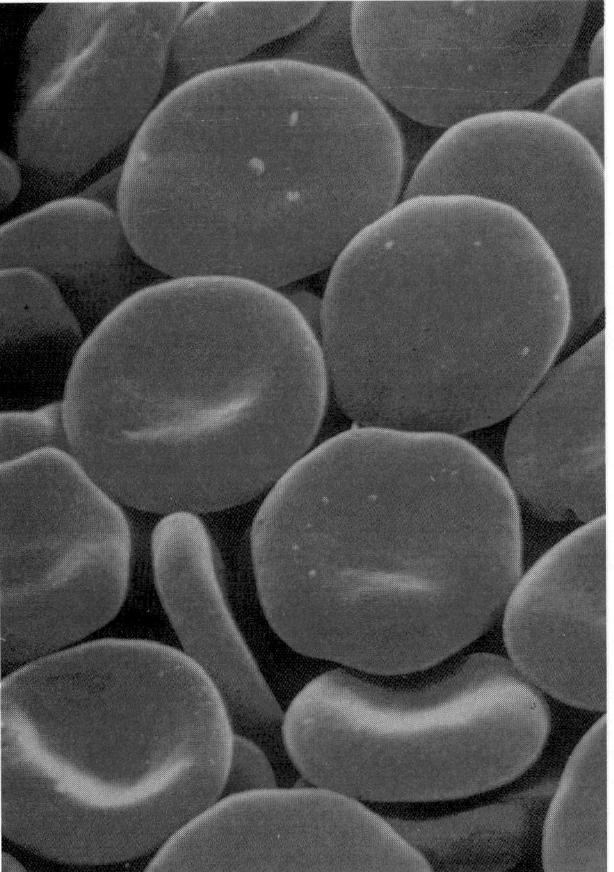

FIGURE 19-4

Scanning electron micrograph of red blood cells (approximately ×11,000). (David M. Phillips/Visuals Unlimited.)

Red blood cells must be continuously manufactured

Every second about 2.4 million red blood cells must be manufactured to replace a similar number that wear out and are destroyed. In adults, **erythropoiesis** (ee-*rith*-row-poy-**ee**-sis), or red blood cell manufacture, takes place in the red bone marrow of the vertebrae, ribs, sternum, skull, and proximal epiphyses of the long bones. In children, red blood cells are produced in the marrow of almost all bones, and before birth they are manufactured in the liver, spleen, and lymph nodes as well.

In the bone marrow there are **stem cells,** also called colony-forming units, or **hemocytoblasts,** which multiply to give rise to several types of committed stem cells. That is, each is committed to give rise to just one kind of blood cell and will produce only that specific type of blood cell (Fig. 19-5). One type of committed stem cell, the **proerythroblast** (*pro*-ee-**rith**-row-blast) (also known as a **rubriblast**),[1] undergoes a number of mitotic divisions, giving rise to **basophilic erythroblasts**[2] **(prorubricytes).** The basophilic erythroblast then multiplies by mitosis to produce **polychromatophilic erythroblasts** (*pol*-ee-krow-*mat*-oh-**fil**-ik) **(rubricytes).** These cells have sufficient hemoglobin to exhibit pink staining areas within the cytoplasm. They also have nuclei and all the organelles needed to synthesize large amounts of hemoglobin. As hemoglobin accumulates in the cytoplasm, the nucleus gradually becomes smaller (almost as though to accommodate a large quantity of hemoglobin).

Each polychromatophilic erythroblast divides to produce **normoblasts** (**nor**-mow-blasts) **(metarubricytes).** The nucleus of a normoblast becomes

[1] There are several systems for naming developing blood cells. Technical terms given in parentheses are those recommended by the International Committee on Nomenclature.

[2] The term basophilic refers to the fact that this cell stains readily with basic dyes. This is due to large numbers of ribosomes in the cell that manufacture hemoglobin. The cytoplasm of these basophilic cells stains blue.

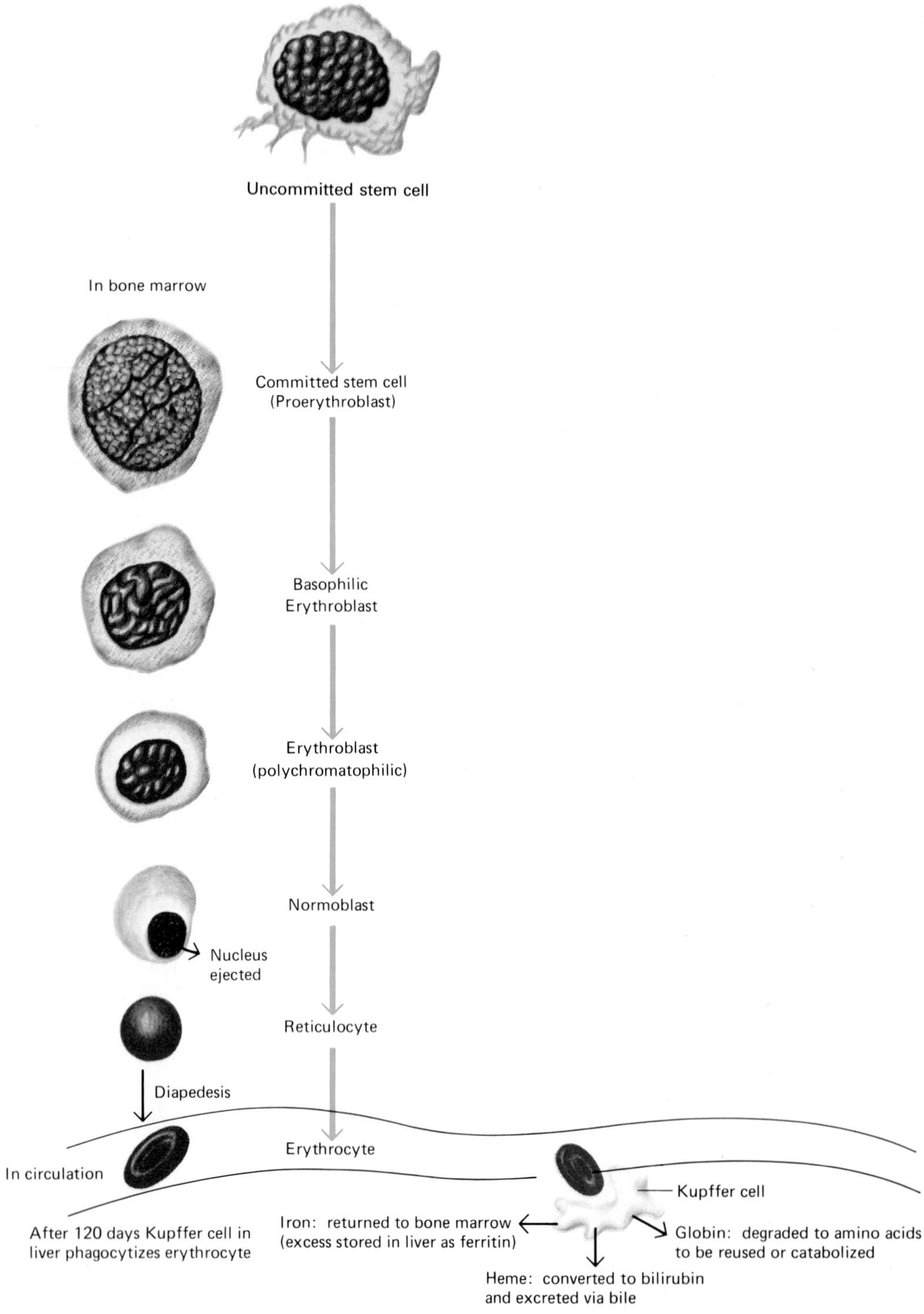

FIGURE 19-5

Life cycle of a red blood cell. Under the influence of erythropoietin, stem cells in the bone marrow give rise to proerythroblasts. The proerythroblasts multiply to produce basophilic erythroblasts. These in turn give rise to polychromatophilic erythroblasts containing large amounts of hemoglobin. These cells multiply to produce normoblasts, which eject their nuclei and become reticulocytes. Reticulocytes enter the circulation and become mature erythrocytes. After about 120 days the red blood cell is phagocytized by macrophages in the liver or spleen and its components are recycled or excreted.

smaller and darker and is then expelled from the cell (Fig. 19-6). Ejected nuclei are phagocytized by macrophages in the bone marrow.

Once the nucleus is expelled, the cell is known as a **reticulocyte** (re-**tik**-you-low-*site*). During the next day or so, the reticulocyte produces additional hemoglobin and ejects its remaining organelles. Reticulocytes squeeze through the intact walls of capillaries within the bone marrow, a process called *diapedesis* (*dye*-ah-peh-**dee**-sis), to enter the circulation. During the first day or two in the circulation, the reticulocyte completes its differentiation, becoming a mature red blood cell, or erythrocyte. Three to five days are required for a stem cell to give rise to a fully differentiated mature erythrocyte.

Oxygen binds to hemoglobin in the red blood cells

The oxygen-binding red pigment hemoglobin gives red blood cells as well as whole blood their red color. **Hemoglobin** is a protein made of four subunits, each consisting of a polypeptide chain (the globin portion of the molecule) attached to a **heme** group, the part of the molecule containing iron. Two of the polypeptide subunits are known as **alpha chains,** and each of these consists of 141 amino acids. The other two polypeptides are the **beta chains,** each containing 146 amino acids. Hemoglobin synthesis requires amino acids, specific enzymes, and certain vitamins and minerals, including iron and copper. Each hemoglobin molecule can combine with four molecules of oxygen, binding one oxygen molecule to each of its iron atoms.

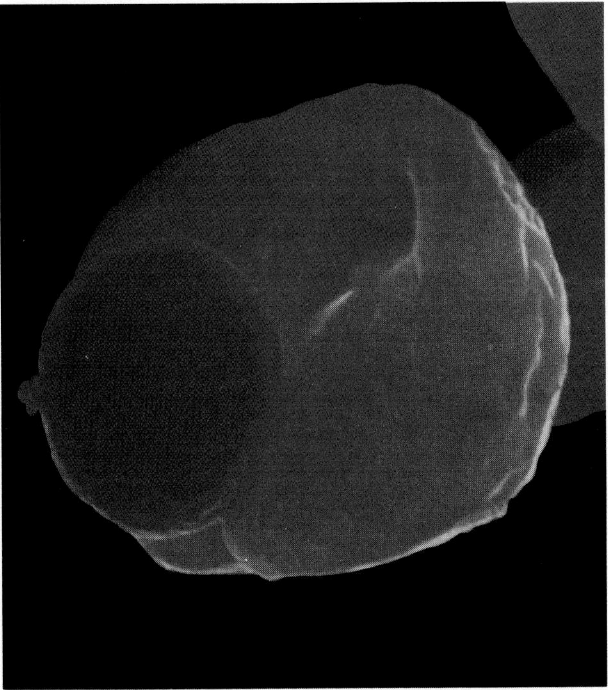

FIGURE 19-6

Red blood cell expelling its nucleus. (Lennart Nilsson/Boehringer Ingelheim International GmbH, from *The Incredible Machine,* p. 122)

As blood circulates through the lungs, oxygen diffuses into the blood and into the red blood cells, where it combines weakly with hemoglobin to form **oxyhemoglobin.**

$$\text{Hemoglobin} + \text{oxygen} \longrightarrow \text{oxyhemoglobin}$$

When blood circulates through the brain or some other tissue where cells are low in oxygen, the reverse reaction occurs.

$$\text{Oxyhemoglobin} \longrightarrow \text{oxygen} + \text{hemoglobin}$$

The oxygen then diffuses out of the capillaries and into the cells. (These reactions will be discussed in greater detail in Chapter 24.)

All blood is red, but the shade varies somewhat. Oxyhemoglobin is bright red and is responsible for the color of blood as it flows through arteries, which contain oxygen-rich arterial blood. Hemoglobin not combined with oxygen, referred to as *reduced hemoglobin,* is darker in color and is responsible for the bluish appearance of veins.

In order to function properly, hemoglobin must be maintained in its reduced, or ferrous (Fe^{2+}), state. Small amounts are converted to the oxidized, or ferric (Fe^{3+}), state, but enzymes in the erythrocytes act continually to reconvert it. In its ferric form, hemoglobin, referred to as **methemoglobin** (met-**he**-mow-*glow*-bin), is incapable of transporting oxygen. When blood is exposed to certain drugs or other oxidizing agents, large amounts of methemoglobin may be produced. Because it is dark in color, methemoglobin imparts a bluish color to the skin (**cyanosis**) when present in large amounts.

A small amount of carbon dioxide is transported in combination with hemoglobin. Carbon dioxide combines with a different portion of the hemoglobin molecule than oxygen does, allowing hemoglobin to transport both oxygen and carbon dioxide simultaneously.

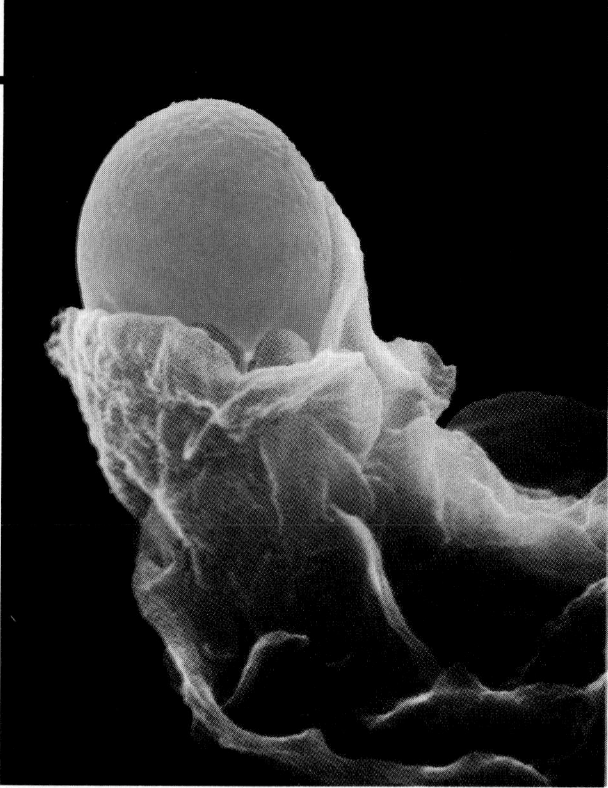

FIGURE 19-7

A macrophage phagocytizing a worn-out red blood cell. (Lennart Nilsson/Boehringer Ingelheim International, from *The Incredible Machine,* p. 123.)

Clinical highlight

Carbon monoxide (CO) is a poisonous gas that combines with hemoglobin over 200 times more readily than does oxygen. What is more, carbon monoxide forms a strong chemical bond at the same sites on the hemoglobin molecule that normally bind oxygen. Carbon monoxide combined with hemoglobin is called **carboxyhemoglobin.** This compound has a half-life of about 3 hours, meaning that even after 3 hours of breathing pure air, half of the carboxyhemoglobin remains.

There is a concentration of about 0.5% carboxyhemoglobin in normal blood. Cigarette smokers average ten times this amount—about 5%, ranging all the way to 16%, depending on the amount of inspiration and other factors. Thus, a smoker has about 4.5% less oxygen circulating in his blood than a nonsmoker. A carboxyhemoglobin level of greater than 5% is also associated with an increased incidence of atherosclerosis ("hardening of the arteries"), a progressive disorder in which arteries become clogged with fatty plaque.

The destruction of red blood cells releases iron into the blood

The average circulating life span of a red blood cell is about 120 days. Without a nucleus and other organelles, a red blood cell is unable to synthesize proteins. When their enzymes break down, they cannot be replaced. As red blood cells age, changes occur in their plasma membranes that enable macrophages to identify them. Old or damaged cells are phagocytized in the liver, spleen, or bone marrow by macrophages that are closely associated with blood vessels in these organs (Fig. 19-7).

After a macrophage has ingested a red blood cell, lysosomal enzymes break down its hemoglobin and its components are recycled. Peptides are degraded to individual amino acids and reused by cells for protein synthesis. Iron is released into the blood, where it is bound to a globulin plasma protein called **transferrin** (trans-**fare**-in). The iron is transported to the bone marrow, where it is recycled. Excess iron may be stored in the liver as **ferritin.** The rest of the heme portion of the hemoglobin is broken down into **biliverdin** (*bil*-ih-**ver**-din), a greenish pigment. Then, biliverdin is reduced to the bile pigment **bilirubin** (bil-ih-**roo**-bin) and transported to the liver for excretion from the body in the bile.

Red blood cell production is regulated by erythropoietin

Although millions of red blood cells are destroyed every minute, equal numbers are produced, so that the total number of circulating red cells remains constant. A hormone called **erythropoietin** (ee-*rith*-row-**poy**-eh-tin) regulates erythropoiesis (Fig. 19-8). Erythropoietin is secreted mainly by the kidneys, but is also manufactured in the liver. This hormone circulates in the blood and upon reaching the bone marrow, stimulates committed stem cells to differentiate. Erythropoietin also shortens the time required for red blood cells to mature.

Secretion of erythropoietin is regulated by feedback mechanisms. Secretion is inhibited by an abnormal increase in the number of circulating red blood cells. It is stimulated by a decrease in oxygen in arterial blood and by deficiency of hemoglobin. Thus, loss of blood or cardiovascular malfunction that results in reduced amounts of oxygen to the cells causes stepped-up erythropoietin production and more rapid manufacture of red cells. Regulation of red blood cell production by erythropoietin is thus a homeostatic mechanism for maintaining normal numbers of erythrocytes and an adequate oxygen supply for the cells.

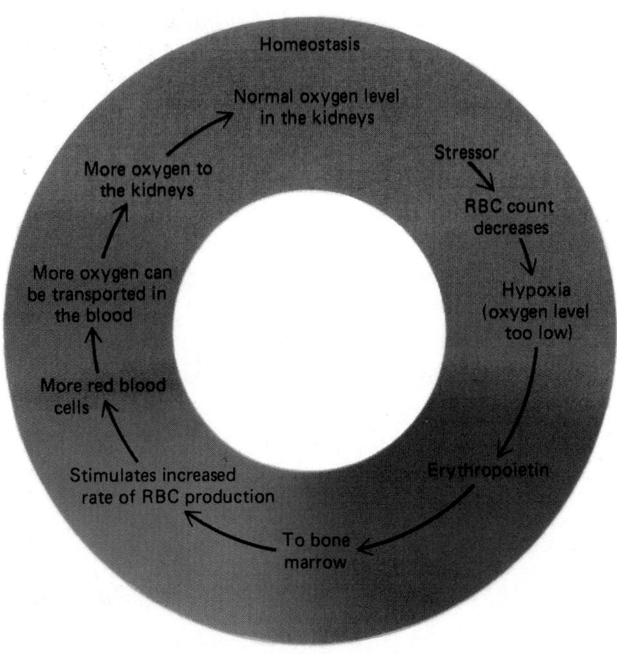

FIGURE 19-8

Regulation of red blood cell production. A low level of oxygen in the kidneys stimulates the release of erythropoietin, the hormone that stimulates erythropoiesis.

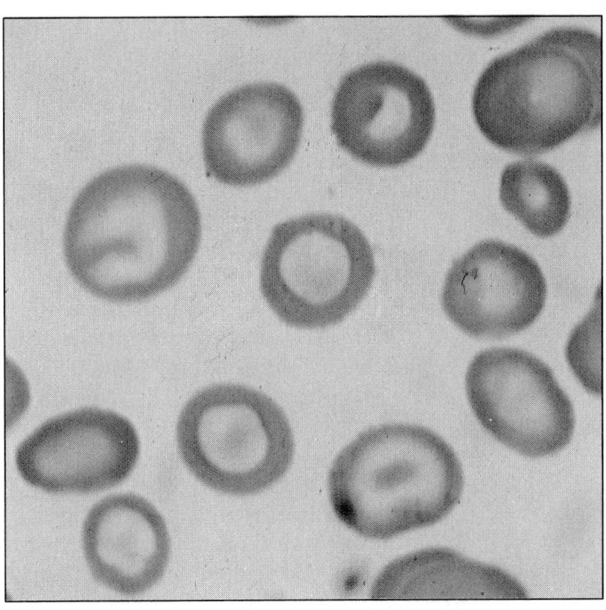

FIGURE 19-9

Red blood cells from an individual with acute anemia. Note that the cells are hypochromic (due to lack of hemoglobin) and microcytic (approximately X1000). (Martin M. Rotker/Taurus Photos.)

Anemia results in reduced oxygen transport

A deficiency of hemoglobin, usually accompanied by a reduction in the number of red blood cells, is termed **anemia** (a-**nee**-me-ah). With decreased amounts of hemoglobin, oxygen transport is reduced and the demand of the cells for oxygen is not met. Clinical symptoms reflect the problem. Patients complain of feeling excessively tired and devoid of energy. They may appear pale and exhibit nail deformities, and when exerting themselves even slightly, may become short of breath.

Can you think of conditions that might cause anemia? Three general causes are (1) loss of blood, (2) decreased production of red blood cells, and (3) increased rate of red blood cell destruction (the **hemolytic anemias**). When blood is lost by hemorrhage, the entire blood volume is decreased. If the victim survives, the plasma level will be restored (without treatment) in 2 to 3 days, but several weeks may be required to manufacture sufficient red cells to bring their numbers back to normal.

Clinical highlight

Two causes of decreased red blood cell production are nutritional deficiency (nutritional anemia) and failure of the bone marrow to function normally (aplastic anemia). Iron deficiency in the diet is the most common cause of anemia. The body cannot synthesize hemoglobin without iron. It would be like trying to make a chocolate cake without chocolate; an essential ingredient would be missing. In **iron-deficiency anemia** the red blood cells are **hypochromic** (pale) and tend to be microcytic, or smaller than normal (Fig. 19-9). Their numbers may be reduced to 3 million per cubic millimeter or even less.

In **pernicious anemia** there is a deficiency of vitamin B_{12} or of **intrinsic factor,** a glycoprotein secreted by the stomach and essential for vitamin B_{12} absorption in the small intestine. Vitamin B_{12} and intrinsic factor together form **erythrocyte maturation factor,** which is necessary for red blood cells to mature normally. When vitamin B_{12} is inadequately present in the diet, or when there is a genetic lack of intrinsic factor, red blood cells do not mature normally. Large numbers of immature cells pass into the circulation. These large, immature red cells are said to be **hyperchromic** because they are filled with great quantities of hemoglobin, as can be readily seen by viewing them under a microscope. These cells also have fragile membranes that rupture easily, leaving the patient deficient in oxygen-carrying capacity. Pernicious anemia is treated with large amounts of vitamin B_{12} and folic acid (both B-complex vitamins).

Another type of anemia in which red cells are simply not manufactured is **aplastic anemia,** which may be caused by excessive exposure to ionizing radiation. This is one of the reasons why diagnostic x-rays are now taken less frequently and with greater care than in former years when the damaging effects of x-rays were unknown. Drugs used in cancer therapy, as well as some other drugs (including certain antibiotics) and some chemical poisons, may also cause aplastic anemia.

There are many varieties of hemolytic anemia. One common type is **sickle-cell anemia,** caused by a mutation in the gene containing the "recipe" for making hemoglobin. In the altered gene, one incorrect amino acid has been substituted in the sequence of 146 amino acids in each beta chain of the hemoglobin molecule. Referred to as **hemoglobin S,** this abnormal hemoglobin forms intermolecular cross-links, forming long crystals when exposed to low concentrations of oxygen. The crystals elongate and deform the cell so that it assumes a sickle or other bizarre shape (Fig. 19-10). Damage to the plasma membrane by the crystals makes the cells so fragile that they rupture and are destroyed in great numbers.

This mutation is found principally in persons of African descent. In those with only one mutant gene for this disorder about 30% of the hemoglobin is of the S variety. They are said to have the sickle-cell trait but not the disease, because their cells do not sickle under ordinary conditions. Persons with two abnormal genes (one from each parent) do exhibit symptoms of the disease. In Africa, malaria was for centuries a major cause of death. Those with the sickle-cell trait are afforded some protection against the malaria parasite that lives in the blood. Thus, the spread of this mutant gene is thought to have conferred a selective advantage (individuals with this gene were more likely to survive and reproduce).

Thalassemia is an inherited disease in which there is a decrease in the synthesis of one or more hemoglobin polypeptide chains. (One common type of thalassemia is known as Cooley's anemia.) This disorder is found mainly in persons of Mediterranean, African, and Southeast Asian ancestry. Thalassemia can result in severe anemia, and is usually treated with blood transfusions.

Polycythemia is characterized by production of excessive numbers of red blood cells

Primary polycythemia (polycythemia vera) is a serious disorder in which there is increased production of red blood cells, neutrophils, and platelets. An increased hematocrit is indicative of this disorder. The increased blood volume and viscosity lead to impaired circulation. Clinical symptoms include headaches, weakness, and visual disturbances.

Secondary polycythemia may develop as a homeostatic compensation when insufficient oxygen is reaching the tissues. For example, when an individual moves to a region with a very high altitude, the decreased atmospheric pressure and lower oxygen concentration make it more difficult for hemoglobin to become saturated with oxygen. The body compensates by manufacturing abnor-

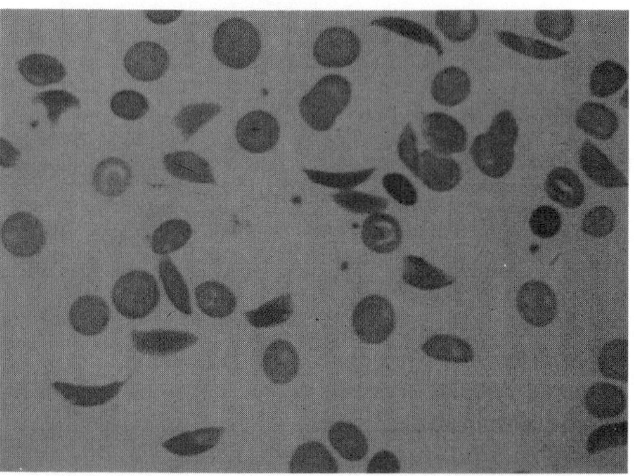

(a)

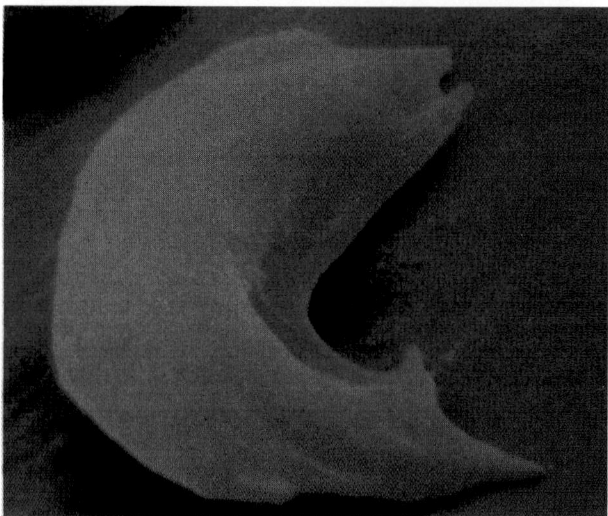

(b)

FIGURE 19-10

Sickle-cell anemia. (*a*) Blood from a patient with sickle-cell anemia. Note the abnormal shape of some of the red blood cells (approximately X125). (*b*) Scanning electron micrograph of a single sickled red blood cell. (*a*, SIU/Visuals Unlimited; *b*, Stanley Flegler/Visuals Unlimited.)

mally large numbers of red blood cells. Polycythemia also develops sometimes to compensate for the poor oxygenation typical of chronic lung disease. The decreased oxygen that results from cigarette smoking may cause reversible polycythemia.

White blood cells defend the body from disease

White blood cells, or **leukocytes** (**loo**-koe-sites) defend the body against disease-causing agents. Unlike red blood cells, white blood cells have nuclei (Figs. 19-11 and 19-12). White blood cells develop from stem cells in the red bone marrow (Fig. 19-13), although some types complete their maturation elsewhere in the body. Like red blood cells, the white blood cells enter the circulation by diapedesis. Time spent in the circulation varies from a few hours for some types of leukocytes to months or even years for other types.

While red blood cells do their work within the blood, many white blood cells leave the circulation by diapedesis and perform their duties in various body tissues. They move about like amebas, flowing along by pushing their plasma membrane into extensions called pseudopods and then flowing into the pseudopod region. As they wander through the body, the white blood cells phagocytize dead cells, bacteria, and other foreign matter.

White blood cells are outnumbered by red blood cells almost 700 to 1 (Table 19-2). Normally, an adult has about 7000 white blood cells per cubic millimeter of blood. White blood cells may be classified in two groups, the granular leukocytes and the nongranular leukocytes. Granular leukocytes include the neutrophils, basophils, and eosinophils. Nongranular leukocytes are lymphocytes and monocytes.

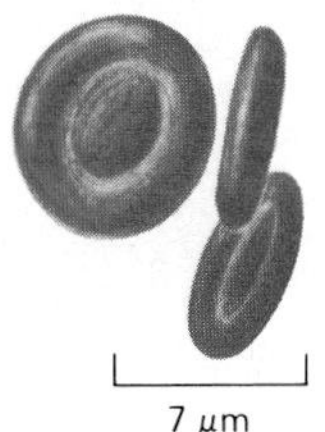

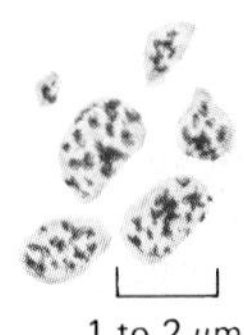

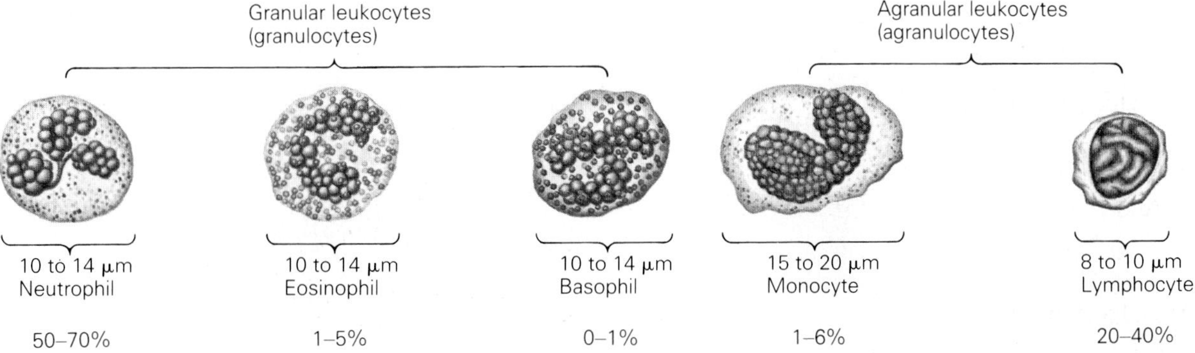

FIGURE 19-11

Principal varieties of blood cells in the circulating blood.

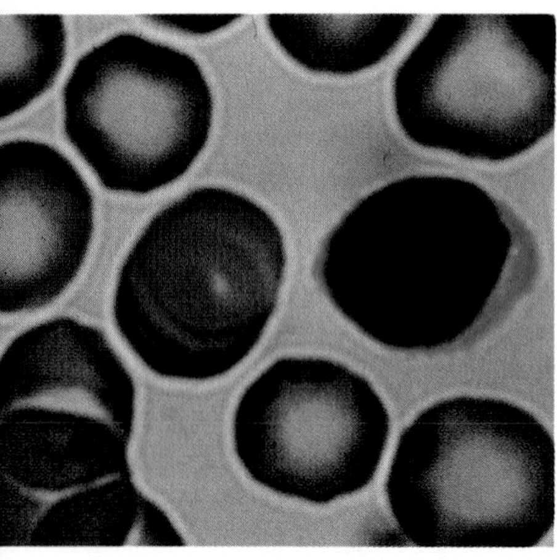
(a)

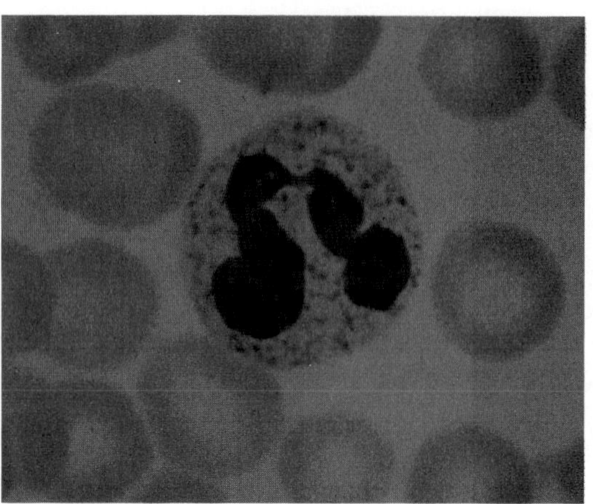
(b)

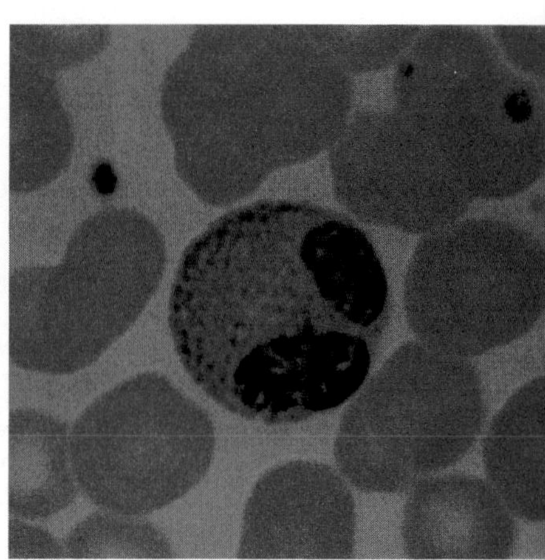
(c)

FIGURE 19-12

Photomicrographs of circulating blood cells. (*a*) A lymphocyte surrounded by red blood cells. (*b*) A neutrophil. Note the lobed nucleus. (*c*) An eosinophil. (*a*, Biophoto Associates/Science Source/Photo Researchers, Inc.; *b*, John D. Cunningham/Visuals Unlimited; *c*, Cabisco/Visuals Unlimited.)

TABLE 19-2

Cellular components of blood

Component	Normal range	Function	Pathology
Red blood cells	Male: 5.4 million/mm^3 (±0.8) Female: 4.8 million/mm^3 (±0.6)	Oxygen transport; carbon dioxide transport	Too few: anemia Too many: polycythemia
Platelets (Thrombocytes)	130,000–370,000/mm^3	Essential for clotting	Clotting malfunctions; bleeding; easy bruising
White blood cells (WBC) (total)	5000–10,000/mm^3		
Neutrophils	About 60% of WBC	Phagocytosis	Too many: may be due to bacterial infection, inflammation, leukemia (myelogenous)
Eosinophils	1–3% of WBC	Some role in allergic response	Too many: may result from allergic reaction, parasitic infection
Basophils	1% of WBC	May play role in prevention of clotting in body	
Lymphocytes	25–35% of WBC	Produce antibodies; destroy foreign cells	Atypical lymphocytes present in infectious mononucleosis; too many may be due to leukemia (lymphocytic), certain viral infections
Monocytes	6% of WBC	Differentiate in tissues to form macrophages	May increase in monocytic leukemia, tuberculosis, fungal infections

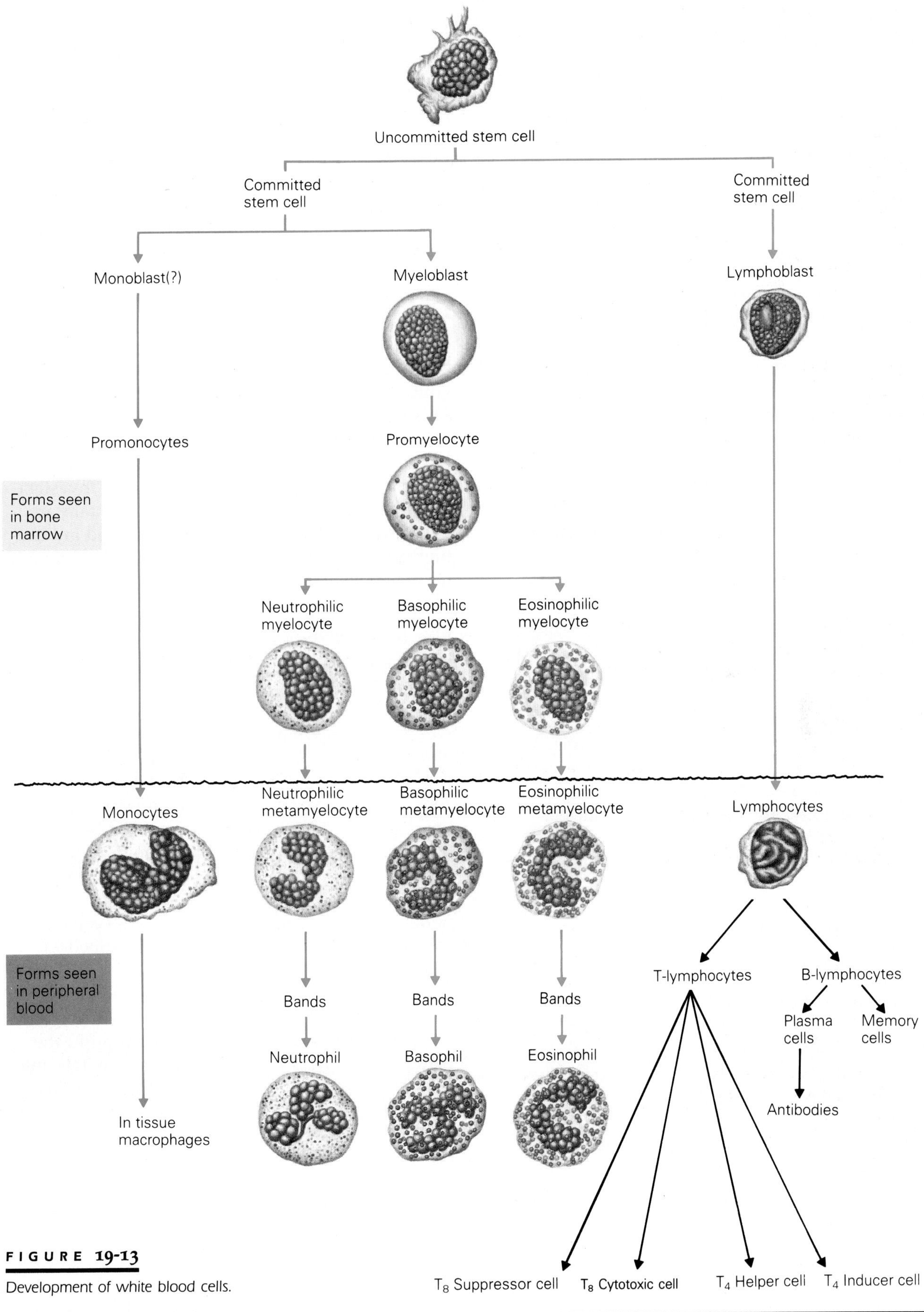

FIGURE 19-13

Development of white blood cells.

Granular leukocytes have distinctive granules in their cytoplasm

The granules in **granular leukocytes** contain potent enzymes that destroy ingested bacteria. Most of these granules are lysosomes. Three types of granular leukocytes are distinguished on the basis of the staining properties of their granules. The staining properties reflect genuine and important differences in the granules and in the functions of the cells themselves.

Neutrophils (**noo**-troe-fils) have neutral staining properties. When blood cells are stained in the standard way, the granules of a neutrophil give its cytoplasm a lavender color. The nucleus of a neutrophil generally has two to five lobes that may be connected to one another by very thin strands. Because the shape of the nucleus may vary, neutrophils are often referred to as **polymorphs,** or **polymorphonuclear leukocytes.**

Neutrophils account for about 60% of all leukocytes. Normally, neutrophils complete their development in the bone marrow (Fig. 19-13) before entering the circulation. In certain disease states, however, large numbers of immature neutrophils may be released into the blood. The maturity of a neutrophil can be determined by the shape of its nucleus. In a very immature neutrophil the nucleus looks like an indented oval. As the neutrophil matures, this indentation deepens so that the nucleus has a horseshoe shape. At this stage the cell may be referred to as a **band,** or **stab,** neutrophil. Because most neutrophils are not released into the blood until the nucleus is segmented into two or more lobes, only 1 to 2% of circulating neutrophils normally are band neutrophils.

Once the neutrophils enter the blood, they remain in the circulation for only about 10 hours. After that time, the neutrophils leave through a capillary wall and enter the connective tissues. There they seek out, ingest, and destroy bacteria. Because they are so adept at this job, neutrophils are a very important defense mechanism against disease. After a day or two in the tissues, many neutrophils enter the digestive tract or urinary tract and are swept from the body with wastes. Others die and are phagocytized by macrophages. More than 100 billion neutrophils must be manufactured each day to replace those that leave the circulation and die.

Eosinophils (ee-oh-**sin**-oh-fils) have granules that stain bright red with the acid dye eosin. These granules are slightly larger and more numerous than those seen in neutrophils. Eosinophils, which account for only 1 to 3% of the circulating leukocytes, help control allergic reactions. For example, they release enzymes that inactivate **histamine,** a chemical released during allergic reactions. The relative number of eosinophils in the blood increases during allergic reactions and also in some parasitic infections such as tapeworm or hookworm infection.

Basophils (**bay**-so-fils) account for less than 1% of the circulating leukocytes. When stained with basic dyes their large granules stain deep blue. Basophils are thought to be involved in both allergic and inflammatory reactions. These cells contain large amounts of histamine, which may be released in injured tissue in order to increase inflammation. Because they also contain heparin, an anticlotting chemical, some investigators think that basophils may help maintain an appropriate balance between clotting and anticlotting processes. Basophils may also play a role in fat metabolism.

Nongranular leukocytes lack specific granules in their cytoplasm

Nongranular leukocytes include the lymphocytes and monocytes. **Lymphocytes** (**lim**-foe-sites) account for about 30% of all circulating leukocytes. As seen in stained preparations, a lymphocyte has a large purple nucleus surrounded by a thin light blue ring of cytoplasm. Although they are produced from stem cells in the bone marrow, lymphocytes continue to proliferate in the lymph nodes, thymus, and spleen. Their life cycle and role in immune responses will be described in Chapter 23.

Monocytes, the largest of the white blood cells, stain less intensely. They comprise about 6% of white blood cells. After circulating in the blood for about 24 hours, monocytes migrate into the connective tissues. There, they develop into **macrophages.** These scavenger cells have a tremendous capacity for phagocytizing bacteria, dead cells, and other matter littering the tissues.

An abnormal white blood cell count may signify infection

Measuring the number of white blood cells is one of the most useful services of the clinical laboratory. A white blood cell count elevated above 10,000 per cubic millimeter, a condition called **leukocytosis** (*loo*-koe-cy-**toe**-sis), may indicate the presence of bacterial infection. Most commonly neutrophils are responsible for the increase in the number of white blood cells. However, in allergic responses or parasitic infestations, the number of eosinophils may be greatly increased. The proportional representation of each kind of blood cell is reported in the **differential blood cell count.**

Viral infections can cause depressed white cell counts, a condition called **leukopenia** (*loo*-koe-**pee**-nee-ah), which is usually indicative of a decreased number of circulating neutrophils. Rheumatoid arthritis, cirrhosis of the liver, and certain other disorders may also be accompanied by leukopenia. Exposure to radiation and certain drugs, including those used in cancer chemotherapy, may also severely depress white cell production.

Because bacterial infections tend to increase the white cell count, whereas viral infections tend to decrease the white cell count, physicians often consider the results of blood tests before prescribing antibiotics. Such drugs (e.g., penicillin and streptomycin) are effective against bacteria but do not affect viruses.

Leukemia is characterized by overpopulation of white blood cells

Leukemia is a form of cancer in which any one of the kinds of white blood cells proliferates wildly within the bone marrow. Their sheer numbers crowd out developing red blood cells and platelets, leading to anemia and impaired blood clotting. Although there may be a dramatic rise in the white blood cell count, many of the white cells are immature or abnormal and are unable to protect the body against disease. Thus, death in leukemia patients often results from bacterial infection.

Clinical highlight

Leukemia may be **chronic,** in which case the patient may live for several years. In **acute** leukemia the majority of white cells in the blood are immature forms and the disease proceeds rapidly, leading to death in days or weeks. Although leukemia can occur at any age, the chronic variety is more common in adults, and the acute form is usually found in children. Acute lymphocytic leukemia (ALL) is the most common form of childhood leukemia.

A virus has been linked to leukemia in mice, cats, and some other animals, but attempts to establish a viral cause in humans have not been successful. Exposure to environmental factors such as radiation (especially during childhood) and certain chemicals (especially benzene) have been linked to leukemia. An increase in certain forms of leukemia was suffered by the irradiated populations of Hiroshima and Nagasaki following World War II. Although no actual cure for leukemia has been found, radiation treatment and therapy with antimitotic drugs (drugs that inhibit cell proliferation) can induce partial or complete remissions lasting for months or years in some patients.

Platelets function in hemostasis

Platelets, also called **thrombocytes** (**throm**-bow-cites), are not complete cells. They are tiny fragments of membrane-enclosed cytoplasm that are pinched off from **megakaryocytes** (meg-ah-**kar**-ee-oh-sites), giant cells in the bone marrow (Fig. 19-14). Each megakaryocyte can give rise to several thousand platelets. Because platelets have no nucleus, their life span is brief—less than 10 days in the circulation. Platelets number about 300,000 per cubic millimeter of circulating blood.

Platelets function in two ways to stop bleeding, a process referred to as **hemostasis** (*he*-mow-**stay**-sis). They physically plug breaks in blood vessel walls, and they release chemicals that promote clotting.

Platelets form a temporary plug

Within 2 seconds after a blood vessel is cut, the wall of the vessel contracts in a vascular spasm so that the flow of blood through the injured vessel is slowed. When platelets come in contact with collagen fibers exposed in the wall of the damaged blood vessel, they become sticky and adhere to the collagen fibers (Fig. 19-15). These platelets release adenosine diphosphate (ADP), which attracts other platelets. As new platelets arrive on the scene, they also release ADP, so that still more platelets join in patching the hole in the vessel wall. Platelets also release a type of prostaglandin that activates platelets. Some investigators think that small tears occur frequently in the walls of small blood vessels but are undetected because they are immediately patched with platelet plugs.

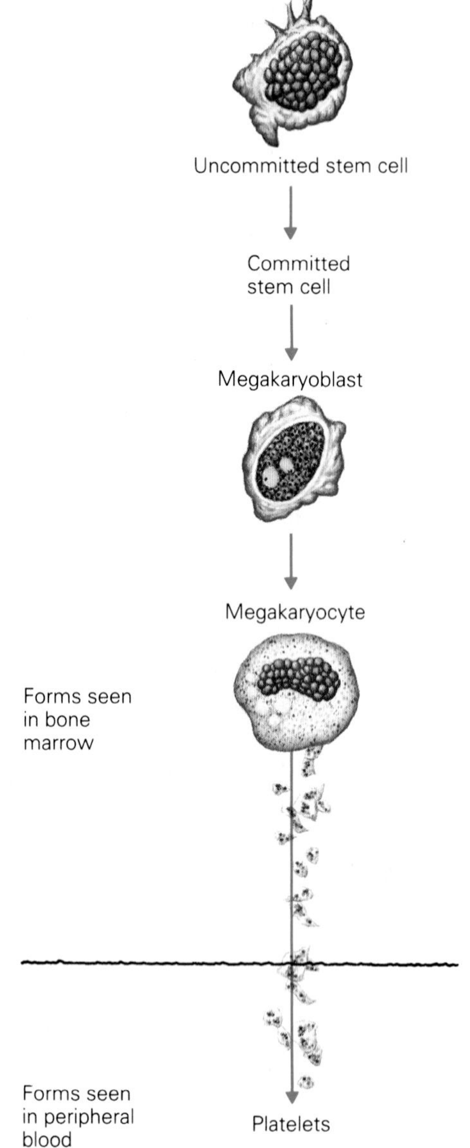

FIGURE 19-14

Development of platelets.

Clinical highlight

Aspirin has been shown to inhibit platelet aggregation by inhibiting the formation of prostaglandins. Aspirin is now used to reduce inappropriate clotting within blood vessels; such clotting can lead to strokes and heart attacks.

Coagulation results in a more permanent blood clot

A more permanent blood clot begins to form within 20 seconds of a serious injury, or within 2 minutes of a minor wound. The process of blood clotting, called **coagulation,** leads to the formation of a blood clot, a gel consisting of insoluble fibers and trapped blood cells and platelets. More than 30 different substances that affect clotting have been found in the blood. Chemicals involved in clotting are called **clotting factors,** or **coagulation factors** (Table 19-3).

Although the process of blood clotting is complex, we can view it as a sequence of three main steps (Fig. 19-16):

1. In response to damaged tissue, a series of reactions (involving clotting factors) takes place, resulting in formation of a complex of substances called **prothrombin activator.**

2. The prothrombin activator catalyzes the conversion of a plasma globulin called **prothrombin** to its active form, **thrombin.** Calcium ions must be present for this reaction to take place. Prothrombin is manufactured in the liver with the help of vitamin K.

3. The thrombin acts as an enzyme to convert the plasma protein fibrinogen to **fibrin,** an insoluble fibrous protein that polymerizes, forming long fibrin threads that form the webbing of the clot.

$$\text{Prothrombin} \xrightarrow{\text{prothrombin activator, } Ca^{2+}} \text{thrombin}$$

$$\text{Fibrinogen} \xrightarrow{\text{thrombin}} \text{loose fibrin}$$

$$\xrightarrow{\text{factor XIII, } Ca^{2+}} \text{dense fibrin}$$

The fibrin threads trap blood cells, platelets, and plasma, which help to strengthen the clot (Fig. 19-16). The plasma, in which the fibrin is suspended, gels so that the developing clot consists of a gel laced by fibrin webbing and containing blood cells. Within a few minutes after clot formation the clot begins to contract and squeezes out serum, that is, plasma containing neither fibrinogen nor clotting factors. As the clot contracts, the ends of the damaged blood vessel are

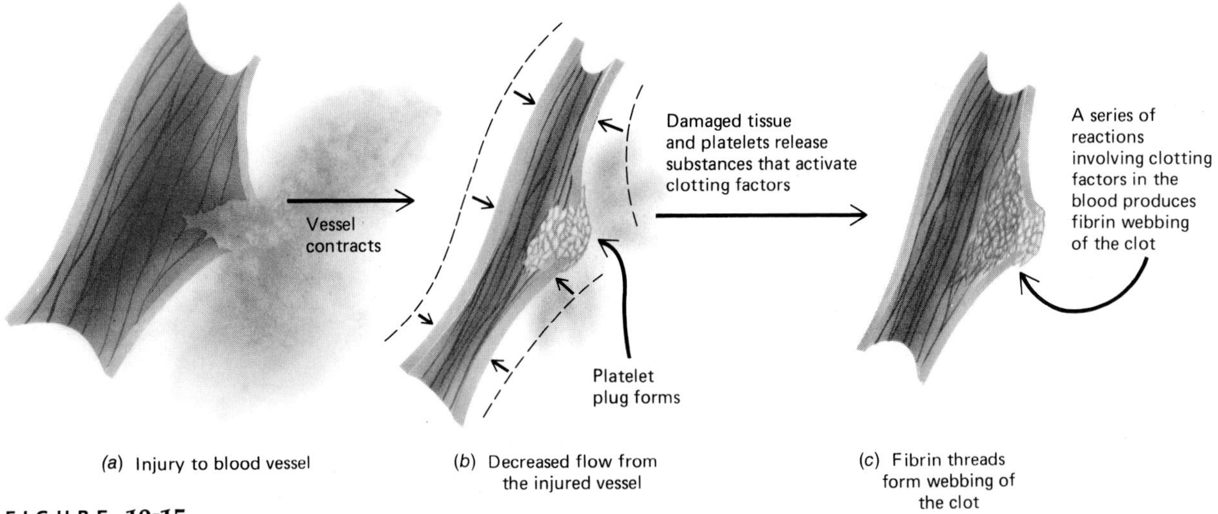
Vessel
contracts
Damaged tissue
and platelets release
substances that activate
clotting factors
Platelet
plug forms
A series of
reactions
involving clotting
factors in the
blood produces
fibrin webbing
of the clot
(a) Injury to blood vessel
(b) Decreased flow from
the injured vessel
(c) Fibrin threads
form webbing of
the clot

FIGURE 19-15

Overview of hemostasis.

pulled closer together, and the clot itself becomes smaller and harder. Calcium ions and clotting factor XIII are required for the conversion of loose fibrin to dense fibrin.

The reactions leading to formation of prothrombin activator can follow either of two pathways, the intrinsic pathway or the extrinsic pathway (Fig. 19-17).

TABLE 19-3

Clotting factors in the blood	
Factor I	Fibrinogen
Factor II	Prothrombin
Factor III	Tissue thromboplastin
Factor IV	Calcium
Factor V	Proaccelerin; labile factor
Factor VII*	Stable factor
Factor VIII	Antihemophilic factor
Factor IX	Plasma thromboplastin component; Christmas factor; antihemophilic factor B
Factor X	Stuart-Prower factor
Factor XI	Antihemophilic factor C
Factor XII	Hageman factor
Factor XIII	Fibrin-stabilizing factor
PL	Platelet phospholipids

*Factor VI has been dropped because it was found not to be an independent factor

THE INTRINSIC PATHWAY IS ACTIVATED WHEN THE BLOOD ITSELF IS INJURED

In the **intrinsic pathway,** formation of prothrombin activator is initiated by a clotting factor present in the blood itself, that is intrinsic to the blood. When blood comes into contact with collagen fibers exposed when the blood vessel wall is injured, inactive clotting factor XII is converted to active clotting factor XII. Simultaneously, damaged platelets release phospholipids. Active factor XII triggers a cascade of complex reactions involving several clotting factors. Active factor XII activates factor XI, and active factor XI activates factor IX. Together activated factors IX and VIII activate factor X. Platelet phospholipids and calcium ions are essential for factor X activation. Activated factor X, factor V, platelet phospholipids, and calcium ions together make up the complex called prothrombin activator. As noted earlier, prothrombin is converted to thrombin by this complex.

Clinical highlight

In persons with **hemophilia** ("bleeder's disease"), one of the clotting factors is absent due to a genetic mutation. About 83% of hemophiliacs have classic hemophilia, in which factor VIII, also known as antihemophilic factor, is absent. Transfusion of the appropriate purified clotting factor (or of normal fresh plasma) into a hemophiliac relieves the tendency to bleed for a few days. Persons with severe hemophilia generally die in early life.

THE EXTRINSIC PATHWAY IS ACTIVATED WHEN A BLOOD VESSEL WALL OR TISSUES OUTSIDE THE BLOOD VESSELS ARE DAMAGED

In the **extrinsic pathway,** the formation of prothrombin activator is triggered by substances released by damaged blood vessels or damaged tissues outside the circulatory system. These substances are released by tissues *outside,* or extrinsic to, the blood itself. Damaged tissues release a complex of several substances referred to as **tissue thromboplastin** (Fig. 19-17). This complex consists of phospholipids and a proteolytic (protein-destroying) enzyme.

Tissue thromboplastin activates factor VII. Then the tissue thromboplastin and activated factor VII activate factors IX and X. Activated factor X complexes with phospholipids (released as part of the tissue thromboplastin) Ca^{2+}, and also with factor V, forming prothrombin activator. The remaining reactions are the same as in the intrinsic pathway.

Note that in both pathways the sequence of reactions leads to the formation of fibrin. In both intrinsic and extrinsic pathways (except for the first two steps in the intrinsic pathway), calcium ions are necessary for every reaction.

Some blood clotting is harmful

Although blood clotting is a vital homeostatic mechanism, it is obviously important that the

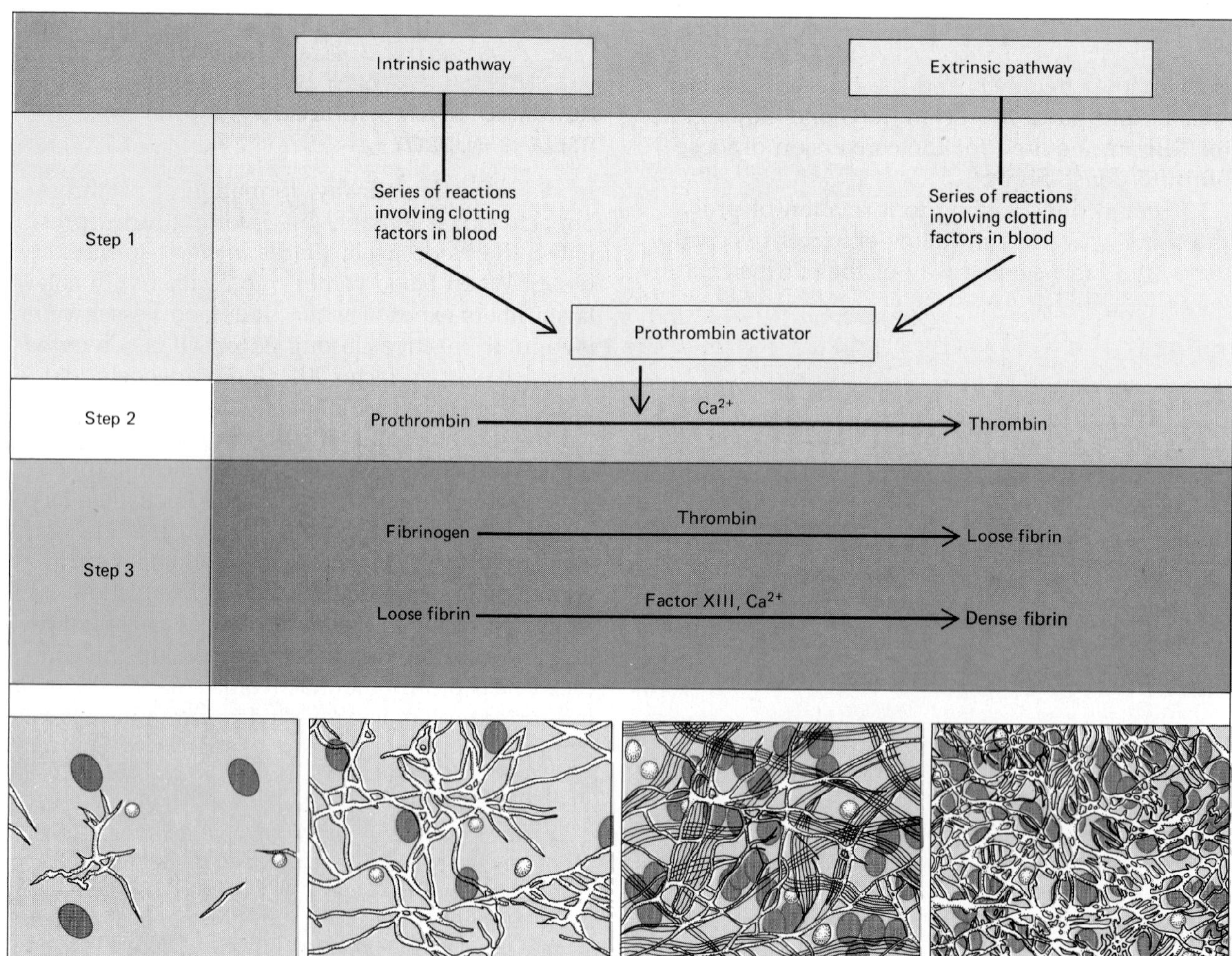

FIGURE 19-16

Three main steps of the blood clotting process. In the final step fibrinogen is converted to fibrin. Then fibrin polymerizes to form long threads that form the webbing of the clot. Blood cells, platelets, and plasma become trapped among the fibrin threads and help to strengthen the clot. (Also see photograph on first page of this chapter.)

process not occur inappropriately. Whether blood coagulates depends on several mechanisms. Clotting itself involves a positive feedback cycle. Once formed, thrombin activates many of the other blood clotting factors in addition to fibrin. Its actions result in production of more prothombin activator which then increases production of more thrombin. This creates what could become a vicious cycle resulting in extension of the clot to dangerous proportions. Fortunately, normal blood flow carries clotting factors away so that within moments after the initial tissue damage, the concentration of clotting factors is too low for the clotting process to continue.

Clots do not usually form in intact blood vessels because the endothelial lining is very smooth and so does not permit activation of the intrinsic clotting pathway. In addition, the blood vessel lining is coated with a layer of negatively charged proteins that repel the platelets and clotting factors. When injured, however, the lining becomes rough and loses its negative charge. Platelets are attracted to the roughened blood vessel lining, where they may be damaged. Platelet phospholipids are then released, clotting factors are activated, and clots may form within the blood vessel.

The lining of arteries becomes roughened in the disease atherosclerosis (discussed in Chapter 21). Platelets may be damaged on the fatty plaques containing calcium that form in the arterial wall. Clotting that occurs in an unbroken blood vessel is referred to as **thrombosis.** A clot that forms within a blood vessel is called a **thrombus.** A thrombus may become so large that the flow of blood through the vessel is impeded.

Clots that form along the inner surface of blood vessels sometimes break away and move through the circulation to other parts of the body. Such a detached clot is called an **embolus.** Emboli tend to become trapped within small blood vessels in the lungs and may lead to death by interfering with pulmonary circulation. Some people are more prone to embolism than others, perhaps because one or more of the clotting factors are present in excessive amounts.

Inappropriate clotting may occur when blood flow is sluggish, a condition referred to as **stasis.**

Intrinsic pathway
Damaged tissue (blood)
activates
Factor XII (Hageman factor)
activates
Factor XI
activates
Factor IX
Platelet phospholipids
Factor VIII
Ca^{2+}
activates
Factor X → Activated Factor X

Extrinsic pathway
Damaged tissue
releases
Tissue thromboplastin
activates
Factor VII
Ca^{2+}
activates
Factor IX → Activated Factor X

Activated Factor X
Factor V
Platelet phospholipids
Ca^{2+}
Prothrombin activator

Prothrombin —(Prothrombin activator, Ca^{2+})→ Thrombin
Fibrinogen —(Thrombin)→ Loose fibrin
Loose fibrin —(Factor XIII, Ca^{2+})→ Dense fibrin

(a)

(b)

FIGURE 19-17

Blood clotting. (*a*) Intrinsic and extrinsic pathways are shown. Clotting factors are numbered by order of discovery rather than by sequence of reactions. (*b*) False-color-scanning electron micrograph of red blood cells enmeshed in fibrin. (*b*, Di-Tony Brain/Science Photo Library/Photo Researchers, Inc.)

When a person stands or sits in one position for a long period of time, blood tends to pool in the veins. Stasis permits activated clotting factors to accumulate and interact.

Anticoagulants in the blood help prevent abnormal clotting. Normally, there is a homeostatic balance between the substances that promote clotting and the anticoagulants in the blood. The anticoagulants predominate, so the blood does not clot. One of the most important anticoagulants in the blood is **antithrombin III.** This enzyme binds to thrombin and inactivates it.

Plasmin is an enzyme activated by a combination of thrombin, activated factor XII, and lysosomal enzymes from damaged tissues. Plasmin slowly dissolves fibrin and functions also in normal clotting, slowly breaking down clots as healing occurs.

Heparin is another powerful anticoagulant. Released by basophils and mast cells (a type of cell found in connective tissues), heparin inactivates several clotting factors and inhibits the production of thrombin.

Clinical highlight

Heparin is used extensively in treating certain cardiovascular diseases. A number of other anticoagulant drugs also are used clinically to inhibit undesirable clotting. One of these, dicumarol, acts by keeping the liver from using vitamin K that is needed to produce prothrombin and several other clotting factors. Anticoagulants are used clinically to prevent new clots from forming, but they do pose the risk of excessive bleeding should the patient become injured.

When blood is withdrawn clinically and placed in a glass vessel, contact with the glass vessel initiates clotting. When it is desirable to maintain the blood in a liquid state, anticoagulants such as oxalate or citrate are added. These deionize, sequester, or precipitate calcium ions in the blood so that clotting reactions (which require calcium) cannot proceed.

Successful blood transfusions depend on blood groups

In the seventeenth century the blood of lambs was transfused into human beings in the hope of restoring purity and youth. Later attempts at transfusing blood from one human into another were hardly more successful and occasionally were disastrous. Not until Landsteiner discovered the ABO blood groups early in this century did the practice of blood transfusion develop into a successful science.

Today it is known that the blood of the donor must be carefully matched with the blood of the recipient. If the blood is not compatible, a **transfusion reaction** will occur. This is a serious allergic reaction in which antibodies in the recipient's blood attack the foreign red blood cells in the transfused blood, causing them to **agglutinate** (clump) (Fig. 19-18). Hemolysis of the red blood cells occurs, and free hemoglobin is liberated into the plasma. In severe reactions intravascular clotting and kidney damage may result.

Agglutination occurs because red blood cells have certain proteins called **antigens,** or **agglutinogens,** on their surfaces, which are different in persons with different blood types. Certain **antibodies,** also called **agglutinins,** are present in the blood plasma. These recognize foreign agglutinogens and attack them, causing agglutination.

Although many kinds of agglutinogens are associated with red blood cells, the most important from the viewpoint of transfusion therapy are those of the ABO and Rh systems. By taking these into account, whole blood or individual blood components can be successfully transfused into patients in need.

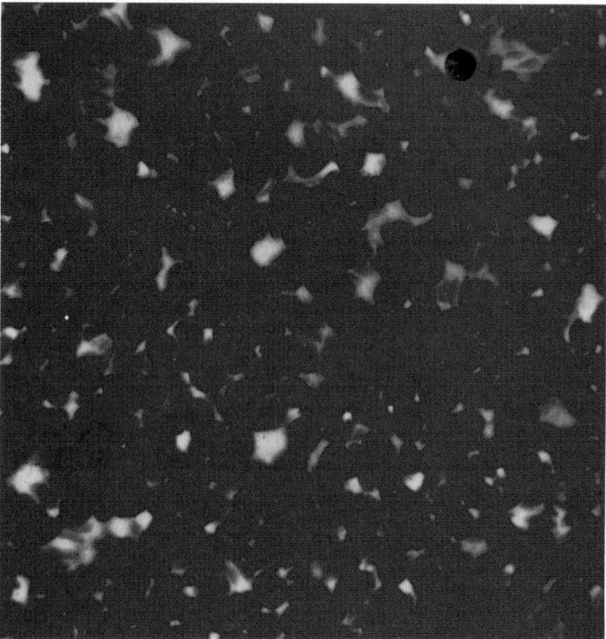

FIGURE 19-18

Mismatched blood transfusions can be fatal. For example, if a person with type B blood receives a transfusion of type A blood, antibodies in her type B blood recognize the type A blood as foreign. These antibodies, called agglutinins, can cause the type A blood cells to clump. (David M. Phillips/Visuals Unlimited.)

Clinical highlight

Whole blood is used to restore an adequate volume of circulating blood after hemorrhage or during surgery. Plasma is sometimes used to expand blood volume or to supply needed clotting factors. Packed red cells are given to patients suffering from severe anemia or to patients whose blood is otherwise deficient in oxygen-carrying capacity. Even preparations of white blood cells or platelets can be transfused when the need is clinically indicated.

The ABO system consists of antigens A and B

Humans have either type A, B, AB, or O blood. Those with type A blood have type A antigen, also called type A agglutinogen, on the surface of their red blood cells. They also have antibodies known as anti-B agglutinins, which circulate in the plasma and act against type B agglutinogens. In a transfusion, if such an individual is accidentally given type B blood, his or her antibodies will combine with the type B antigens on the surfaces of the donated red blood cells, causing them to agglutinate and producing hemolysis. This can be fatal, especially if the mistake should ever be repeated.

Those with type B blood have red cells coated with type B antigen and have type A antibody. Those with type AB have both types of antigen and neither type of antibody. And those with type O blood have neither A nor B antigens, but they do have antibodies against both A and B (see Table 19-4). Type O persons are sometimes referred to as universal donors because they have neither A nor B antigens. Theoretically, they can donate blood to persons of A, B, AB, or O type. Those with type AB blood are universal recipients, because they lack A and B antibodies and therefore do not react badly to any ABO blood type.

In actual practice, blood is carefully matched, and each patient receives blood only of his or her own type. Blood typing is routinely carried out by mixing a sample of a person's blood with serum containing different types of antibodies to determine if agglutination occurs. Perhaps you have tried this in the laboratory (Fig. 19-19).

The Rh system is based on the presence of Rh agglutinogens

Named in honor of the rhesus monkeys in which it was originally worked out, the **Rh system** consists of at least eight different kinds of Rh antigens, each referred to as an Rh factor. By far the most important is antigen D. Most persons of western European descent are Rh positive, which means that they have antigen D on the surfaces of their red blood cells (as well as the antigens of the ABO system appropriate to their blood type). The 15% or so of persons of western European descent who are Rh negative have no antigen D and will produce antibodies against that antigen when exposed to Rh-positive blood.

Unlike the antibodies of the ABO system, antibody D does not occur in the blood of Rh-negative persons unless they have been exposed to the D antigen. Once antibodies to Rh-positive blood have been produced, they remain in the blood. Should Rh-positive blood be transfused again, even years later, a severe reaction is likely to take place.

TABLE 19-4

ABO blood types*

			Frequency in U.S. population (%)		
Blood type	**Antigen on RBC (agglutinogen)**	**Antibodies in plasma (agglutinin)**	Western European descent	African descent	Genotypes (see Chapter 31)
O	—	Anti-A, anti-B	43	50	OO
A	A	Anti-B	45	29	AO or AA
B	B	Anti-A	8	17	BO or BB
AB	A, B	—	4	4	AB

*This table and the discussion of the ABO system have been simplified somewhat. Actually, some type A individuals have two type A agglutinogens and are designated type A_1, while those with only one agglutinogen are termed type A_2.

Clinical highlight

Although several kinds of maternal-fetal blood type incompatibilities are known, Rh incompatibility is probably the most common. Rh incompatibility can cause serious problems when an Rh-negative woman and an Rh-positive man produce an Rh-positive baby. At the time of birth a small amount of the baby's blood may mix with the mother's, stimulating her body to produce antibodies against the Rh-positive blood. If she should carry an Rh-positive child in a subsequent pregnancy,[3] her antibodies can cross the placenta (the organ of exchange between mother and developing baby) and cause hemolysis of the baby's red cells (Fig. 19-20). Breakdown products of the hemoglobin released into the circulation damage many organs, including the brain. This type of hemolytic disease is known as **erythroblastosis fetalis.**

When Rh-incompatibility problems are suspected, blood can now be exchanged in utero, that is, while the child is still within the mother's uterus. Rh-negative women are now treated during pregnancy, immediately after the birth of each Rh-positive child, or at the termination of pregnancy by miscarriage or abortion with an anti-Rh preparation containing Rh-immune globulin. These passively acquired antibodies prevent an active immune response to the red blood cells, perhaps by clearing the Rh-positive cells from the mother's blood very quickly. This action minimizes the chance of sensitizing her own lymphocytes to make anti-Rh-positive antibodies that could harm her next baby. The inheritance of the ABO and Rh blood group systems is discussed in Chapter 31.

[3] Rh incompatibility often develops quite slowly over a period of several pregnancies.

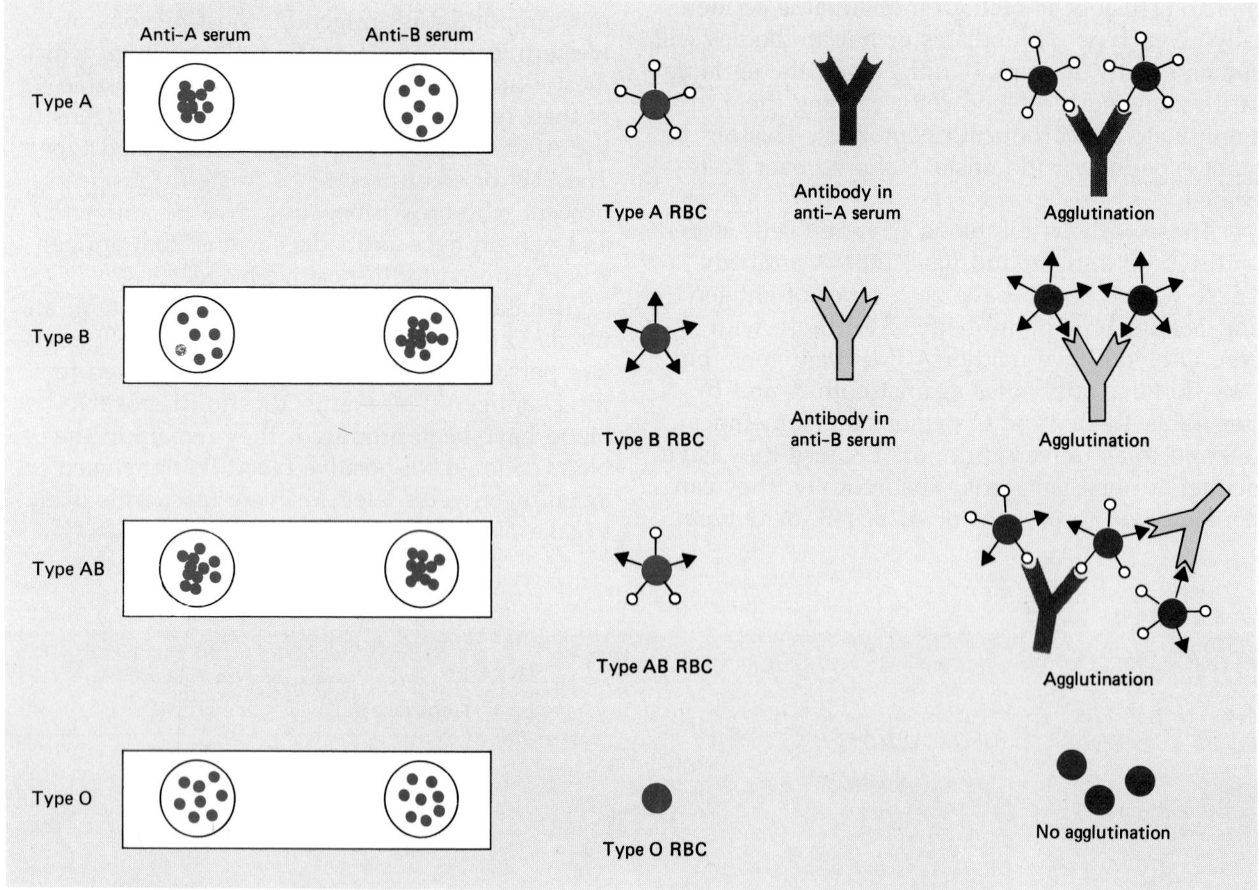

FIGURE 19-19

Typing blood. Each blood type has a different combination of antigen (agglutinogen) and antibody (agglutinin). In typing blood, serum containing antibody to type A blood is placed on a slide, and serum containing antibody to type B is placed in a separate area of the slide. A drop of blood is mixed with each type of serum. If the blood contains A antigen, it will agglutinate with the anti-A serum. If the blood contains B antigen, it will agglutinate with the anti-B serum.

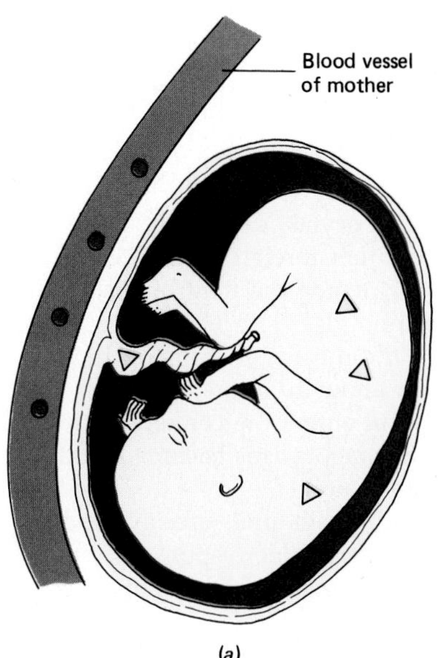

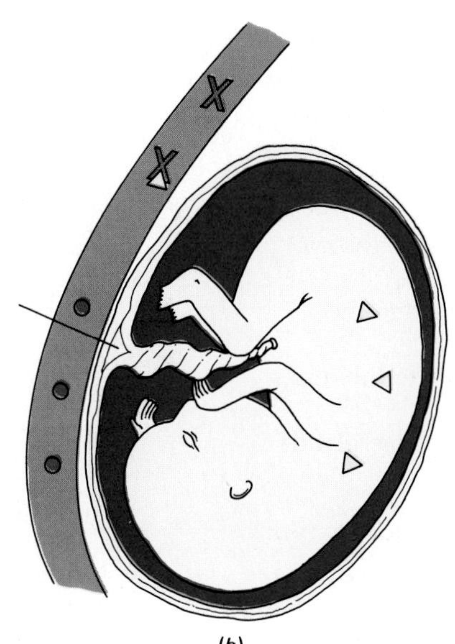

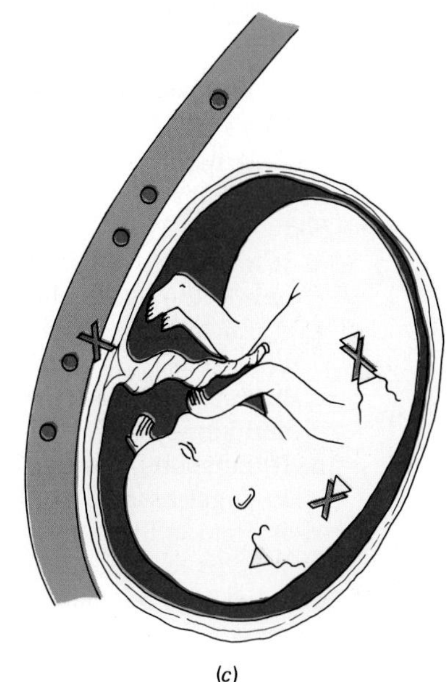

FIGURE 19-20

Rh incompatibility can cause serious problems when an Rh-negative woman and an Rh-positive man produce Rh-positive offspring. *(a)* Some Rh^+ red blood cells leak across the placenta from the fetus into the mother's blood. *(b)* The woman produces D antibodies in response to the D antigen on the Rh^+ RBCs. *(c)* Some of the D antibodies cross the placenta and enter the blood of the fetus, causing hemolysis. The fetus may develop erythroblastosis fetalis.

Summary

I. The circulatory system may perform more vital functions than any other single system in the body.
   A. It transports nutrients from the digestive system to the body cells.
   B. It transports oxygen from the lungs to the body cells.
   C. It transports wastes from the cells to the lungs and kidneys.
   D. It transports hormones from endocrine glands to target tissues.
   E. It protects the body against disease.
   F. It helps to regulate body temperature.
   G. It helps to regulate fluid and salt balance.

II. Blood is a connective tissue consisting of red blood cells, white blood cells, and platelets suspended in plasma.

III. Blood plasma consists of about 92% water, about 7% plasma proteins, salts, nutrients, oxygen and other gases, hormones, and wastes.
   A. The three fractions of plasma proteins are albumins, globulins, and fibrinogen.
   B. Plasma proteins exert colloid osmotic pressure and thereby help maintain blood volume. They also regulate blood pH.
   C. Gamma globulins serve as antibodies; other globulins and albumins transport substances; and fibrinogen enables blood to clot.

IV. Red blood cells, or erythrocytes, are the most numerous cells in the body.
   A. Red blood cells are produced in the bone marrow, and their rate of production is regulated by erythropoietin.
   B. A mature red blood cell is a tiny, biconcave disc that transports hemoglobin.
   C. Worn-out red blood cells are removed from the circulation by macrophages in the liver, spleen, and bone marrow.
   D. A deficiency of hemoglobin (usually accompanied by a deficient number of red blood cells) is called anemia. Anemia may result from loss of blood, decreased rate of red blood cell production, or increased rate of red blood cell destruction.

V. White blood cells, or leukocytes, defend the body against pathogens and other foreign substances.
   A. Granular leukocytes include the neutrophils, basophils, and eosinophils.
      1. Neutrophils are the most numerous of the leukocytes. After about 10 hours in the blood, a neutrophil enters the connective tissues, where it phagocytizes bacteria, dead cells, and foreign matter.
      2. Both basophils and eosinophils are involved in inflammatory and allergic responses.
   B. Nongranular leukocytes include the lymphocytes and monocytes.
      1. Lymphocytes play an important role in immune responses.
      2. Monocytes migrate into the connective tissues and become macrophages.

VI. Platelets are cell fragments formed from megakaryocytes in the bone marrow.
   A. Platelets patch tears in blood vessel walls by aggregating and forming a platelet plug.
   B. Platelets release chemicals that promote blood clotting.

VII. In transfusion therapy blood types must be carefully matched to prevent transfusion reaction.
   A. People with type A blood have type A antigen and type B antibodies and therefore must not be given type B or AB blood.
   B. People with type B blood have type B antigen and type A antibodies and must not be given type A or AB blood.
   C. People with type AB blood have both types of antigens, and those with type O blood have neither type of antigen but both types of antibodies.
   D. People with Rh-positive blood have antigen D on the surfaces of their red blood cells, as well as antigens of the appropriate ABO type. Rh-negative individuals may produce antibody D when exposed to antigen D.

Post-test

1. The function of red blood cells is to transport ________________.
2. Colloid osmotic pressure is a force exerted by the plasma ________________.
3. Gamma globulins serve as ________________.
4. Fibrinogen functions in blood ________________ ________________.
5. Destruction of red blood cells with the release of hemoglobin is termed ________________.
6. Red blood cells are produced in the ________________ ________________.
7. Oxygen is transported in chemical association with the protein ________________.

8. A deficiency of hemoglobin is called ______.
9. Excessive exposure to ionizing radiation may cause ______ anemia.
10. If you were to move to a high altitude, your ______ ______ count would go up significantly.
11. The most numerous type of leukocyte in the circulation is the ______.
12. White blood cells develop from stem cells in the ______ ______.
13. After monocytes enter the tissues, they differentiate to form ______.
14. Leukocytosis refers to an elevation of the ______ ______ count.
15. Megakaryocytes give rise to ______.
16. Fibrinogen is converted to ______ in the presence of a catalyst called ______.
17. Prothrombin is a globulin manufactured in the ______.
18. A clot formed within a blood vessel is a ______.
19. People with type B blood have ______ antigens on the surfaces of their red blood cells and ______ antibodies (agglutinins) in their plasma.
20. Erythroblastosis fetalis may occur when there is ______ incompatibility. This may occur when a woman with ______ type blood produces a baby with ______ type blood.

Review questions

1. List several functions of the circulatory system and identify which specific structures carry out each job.
2. What are the functions of the plasma proteins as a group? Of globulins specifically?
3. How is red blood cell production regulated?
4. In what ways are mature red blood cells specifically adapted to their function?
5. List in sequence the major events in the life cycle of a red blood cell and tell where each takes place.
6. Give three general causes of anemia. Give specific causes of (a) aplastic anemia, (b) sickle-cell anemia.
7. What are the functions of (a) neutrophils, (b) basophils, (c) monocytes?
8. What physiological disturbances are caused by leukemia?
9. Starting with prothrombin activator, describe the final reactions in the formation of a blood clot.
10. Contrast the extrinsic and intrinsic pathways of blood clotting.
11. What is the role of plasmin? Why is vitamin K important?
12. Imagine that a patient with type AB blood is accidentally given type A blood in a transfusion. What, if any, ill effects might occur? What if a patient with type O blood were given type A blood?
13. Describe the physiological cause of the disease erythroblastosis fetalis.

Post-test answers

1. oxygen 2. proteins 3. antibodies 4. clotting 5. hemolysis 6. red bone marrow 7. hemoglobin 8. anemia 9. aplastic 10. red blood cell 11. neutrophil 12. red bone marrow 13. macrophages 14. white blood cell 15. platelets 16. fibrin; thrombin 17. liver 18. thrombus 19. type B; type A 20. Rh; Rh negative; Rh positive.

THE HEART

CHAPTER OUTLINE

- **I. Anatomy of the heart**
  - A. Covering of the heart
    - □ Focus on diseases of the pericardium
  - B. Wall of the heart
  - C. Chambers of the heart
    - □ Focus on congenital defects of the septa
  - D. Valves
    - □ Focus on diseases of the valves of the heart
  - E. Coronary arteries and veins
    - □ Focus on ischemic heart disease
- **II. Cardiac physiology**
  - A. Conduction system
  - B. Cardiac muscle
  - C. Cardiac cycle
  - D. Heart sounds
    - □ Focus on cardiac surface anatomy
  - E. Cardiac output
    - □ Focus on abnormal heart sounds
  - F. Regulation of stroke volume
  - G. Regulation of heart rate
    1. Neural control
    2. Hormonal influences
    3. Effects of temperature
    4. Effects of ions
    5. Effects of sex and age
  - H. Other conditions that affect cardiac output
  - I. The electrocardiogram
  - J. Disturbances in cardiac rate and rhythm

LEARNING OBJECTIVES

After you have studied this chapter you should be able to:

1 Describe the location of the heart within the mediastinum.

2 Describe the structural features of the pericardium.

3 Describe the structural features of the endocardium, myocardium, and epicardium.

4 Describe the coronary arteries and their distribution to the heart.

5 Identify the chambers of the heart and compare their structure.

6 Locate the atrioventricular and semilunar valves, compare their structure, and describe how they function.

7 Describe the consequences of common valvular deformities.

8 Trace the path of an action potential through the conduction system of the heart.

9 Compare and contrast cardiac muscle with skeletal muscle.

10 Describe the events of the cardiac cycle. Define systole and diastole.

11 Describe the circulation of the heart itself.

12 Describe the pressure changes that occur during the cardiac cycle.

13 Correlate normal heart sounds with the events of the cardiac cycle.

14 Define cardiac output and identify the factors that determine it.

15 Explain neural regulation of heart rate, and describe the influences of other factors (e.g., ion effects and body temperature) on heart rate.

16 Relate Starling's law of the heart to cardiac output.

17 Identify factors that affect stroke volume.

18 Correlate the principal waves of an ECG with the events of the cardiac cycle. Describe the common arrhythmias and other disorders that can be diagnosed with the help of an ECG.

Nuclear scan of heart. (© 1985 SIU/Peter Arnold, Inc.)

20

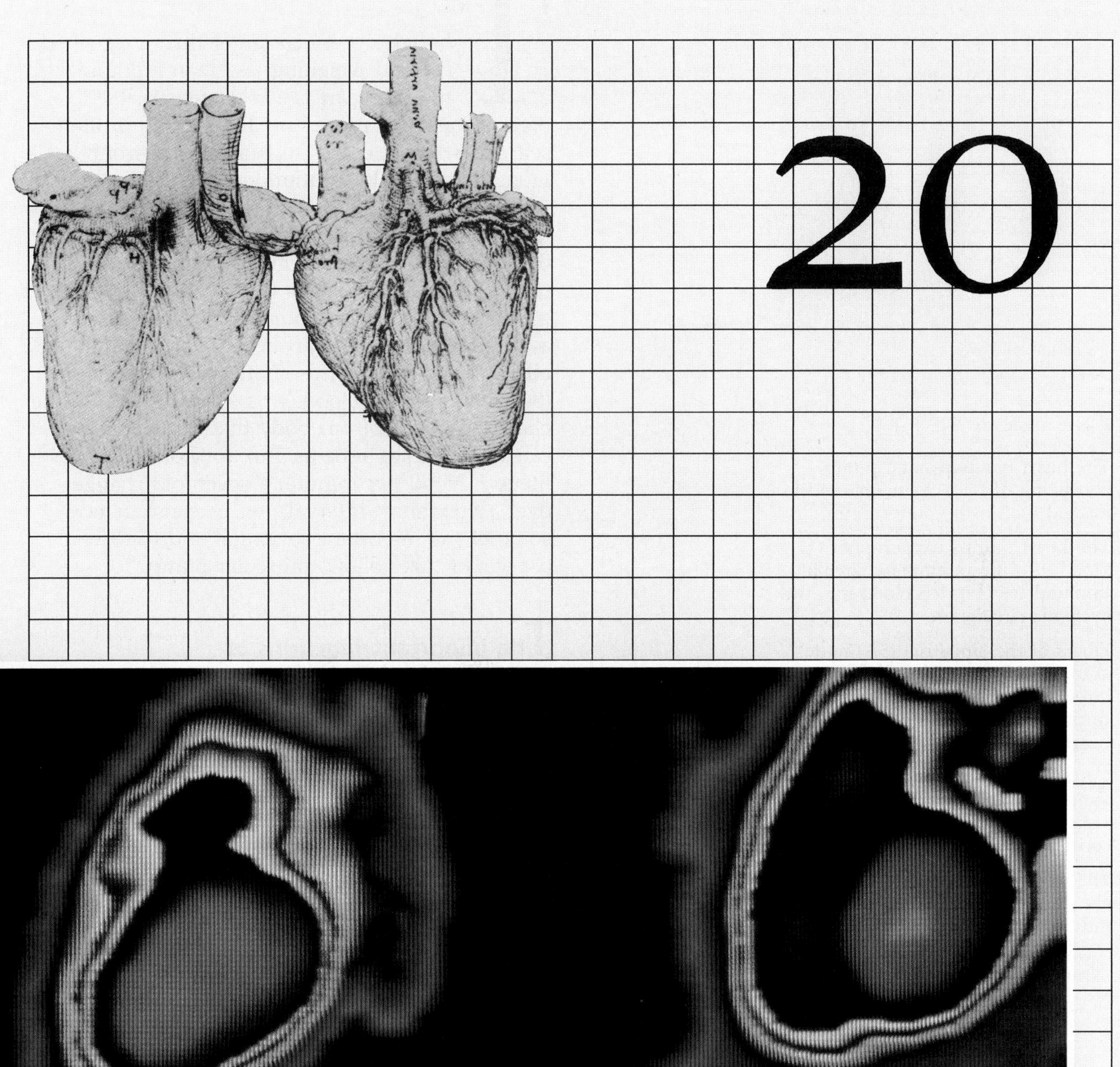

KEY CONCEPTS

The heart is a two-sided pump, consisting of four chambers, and is located within the pericardium.

The heart pumps oxygen-poor blood into the pulmonary circulation and oxygen-rich blood into the systemic circulation.

Fibers of the sinoatrial (SA) node automatically generate rhythmic impulses, which then spread throughout the remainder of the heart's conduction system.

Cardiac function is influenced by venous return, the autonomic nervous system, hormones, and the concentrations of various ions.

The electrocardiogram (ECG) is clinically the single most useful indicator of cardiac function.

Though not much larger than a clenched fist and weighing less than a pound, the human heart is a most remarkable organ. The heart represents the rhythm of life itself and when it ceases to beat, death is only moments away. Its continuous and rhythmic beating ensures circulation of the blood throughout the entire body. This in turn leads to the delivery of oxygen, nutrients, hormones and other regulatory molecules to, as well as the removal of waste products from, each of our organs. During an average lifetime the heart beats approximately 2.5 billion times and pumps about 300 million liters (80 million gal) of blood. It is so responsive to the changing needs of our body that cardiac output can vary from as little as 5 to a maximum of 35 liters of blood per minute, a sevenfold change, over a very short interval. Let us consider now some of the important structural and functional aspects of this hollow, muscular pump.

The important functions of the heart are reflected in its anatomy

Figure 20-1 serves to illustrate the position of the heart as it lies in the **mediastinum** (mee-dee-as-**tie**-num), the region between the two lungs that holds several organs. The heart rests on the muscular diaphragm and is attached via its covering to this muscular partition that separates the chest and abdominal cavities. The heart is a four-chambered, hollow, muscular organ that has a conical shape. Approximately two-thirds of its mass lies to the left of the body's midline. It measures about 12 centimeters in length, 9 centimeters in width at its broadest part, and 6 centimeters in thickness. The base of the heart is directed posterosuperiorly and from it emerge two of the great vessels, the aorta and the pulmonary trunk; the superior vena cava and inferior vena cava enter its right side (Figs. 20-1 and 20-2). Opposite the base is the apex of the heart which is made up largely of the tip of the left ventricle. It is directed anteroinferiorly and to the left and is located about 8 centimeters from the body's midline in the fifth intercostal space, that is, between the fifth rib above and the sixth below (Fig. 20-1). Although its exact position varies somewhat from individual to individual and with respiratory movements, the apex beat may be palpated or

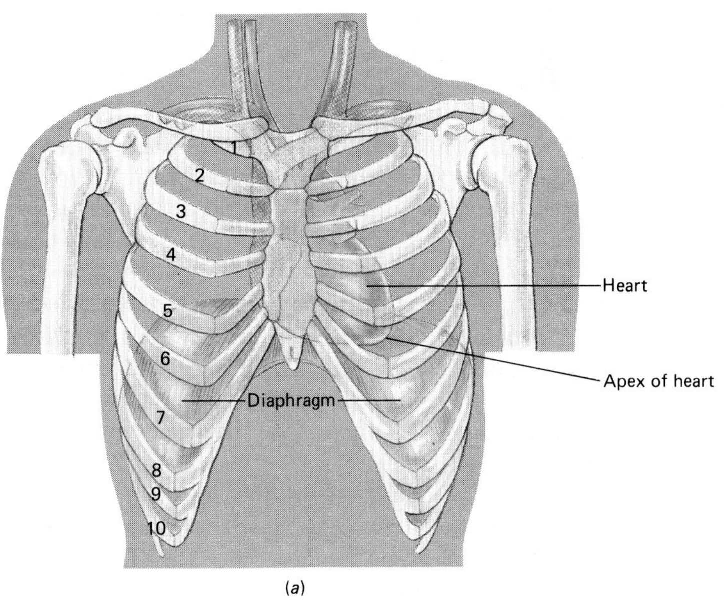

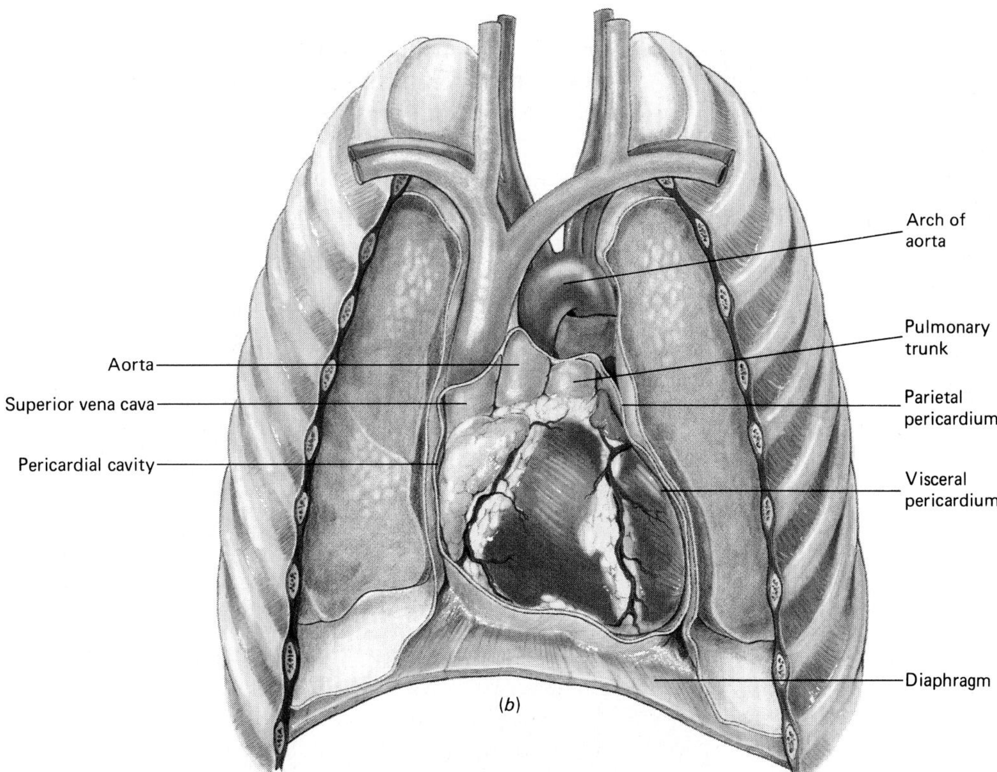

FIGURE 20-1

The heart is positioned within the mediastinum between the lungs. (*a*) Position of the heart within the mediastinum. (*b*) The heart and the roots of the great vessels as shown with a portion of the pericardium removed.

heard best in this location. Try to feel the apex beat on yourself or a partner by pressing your finger tips over the left fifth intercostal space. Often the pulsations of the apex beat may be observed visually.

The pericardium is a loose-fitting sac that houses the heart

Within the mediastinum, the heart and origins of the great blood vessels are enclosed in a loose-fitting sac termed the **pericardium** (*per*-i-**kar**-de-um) (Fig. 20-1). This protective sac is composed of two layers separated by a potential space called the **pericardial cavity** (*per*-i-**kar**-de-al). The outer layer is termed the **parietal pericardium,** and the inner layer is called the **visceral pericardium.** During embryonic development the heart invaginates the pericardial sac much like pushing a clenched fist into a large balloon. As shown in Figure 20-3, this results in the formation of a double-walled sac that surrounds the heart and the origins of great vessels entering and leaving the heart.

The parietal pericardium consists of an *outer layer of thick, fibrous connective tissue* and an *inner serous layer*. The serous layer, consisting largely of mesothelium together with a small amount of connective tissue, forms a simple squamous epithelium and secretes a small amount of fluid (Fig. 20-4). The fibrous layer of the parietal pericardium is attached to the diaphragm and fuses with the outer wall of the great blood vessels entering and leaving the heart. Thus, the parietal pericardium forms a strong protective sac for the heart and serves also to anchor it within the mediastinum.

The serous layer of the parietal pericardium is reflected around the origins of the great vessels and then onto the heart itself as the outer layer of the visceral pericardium. The inner layer of the visceral pericardium consists of a thin layer of connective tissue. Together, the two layers of the visceral pericardium constitute the outer layer of

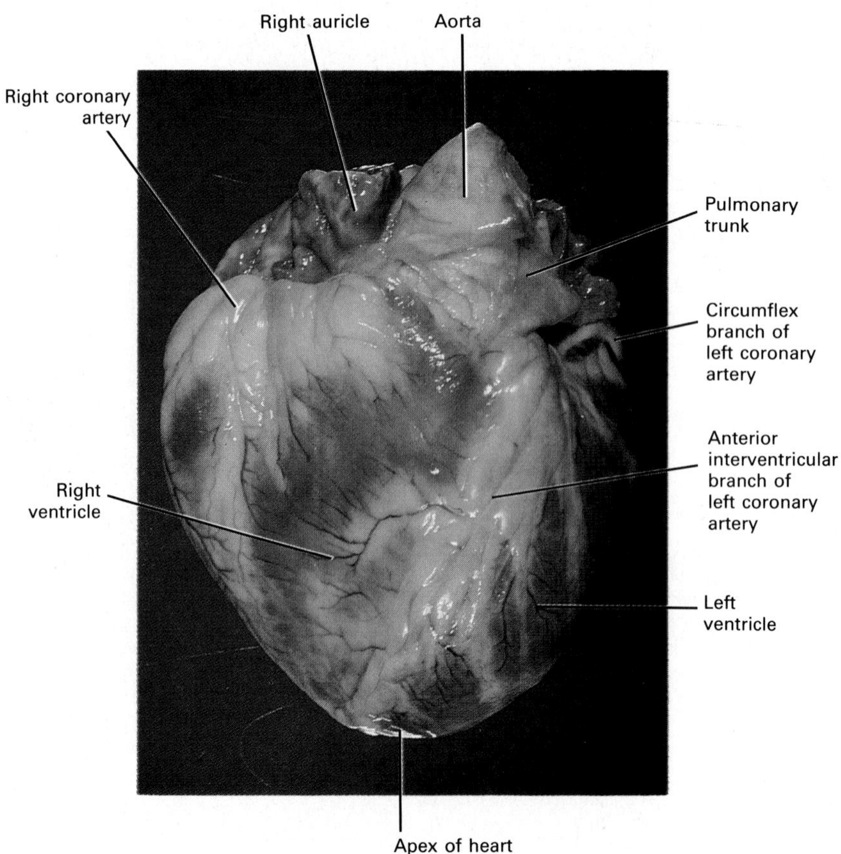

FIGURE 20-2

Anterior surface of the human heart. Notice the amount of fat deposited along the course of the right and left coronary arteries.

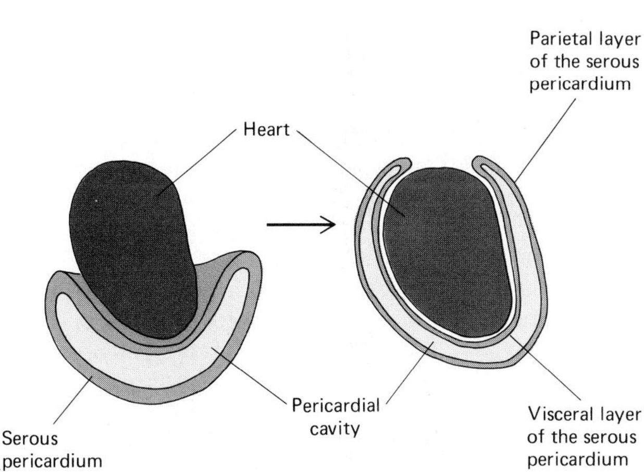

FIGURE 20-3

Relationship of the pericardial cavity and two portions of serous pericardium to the heart.

the heart wall, or **epicardium** (*ep*-i-**kar**-de-um). See Figure 20-4.

The pericardial cavity (Fig. 20-4) is simply a potential space as are the other great serous cavities, the peritoneal cavity and pleural cavities. Here, the mesothelial linings of the visceral and parietal pericardium lie in close approximation, separated only by a thin layer of lubricating fluid. The total volume of pericardial fluid normally present is approximately 25 to 35 milliliters. This fluid moistens the opposing surfaces and facilitates movement of the heart within the pericardial sac as the former contracts and relaxes.

The wall of the heart consists of three layers

During embryogenesis the heart develops from the fusion of a pair of simple blood vessels. Thus you might expect that its wall is structured somewhat similarly to the wall of a large blood vessel. Indeed, the wall of the heart consists of three dis-

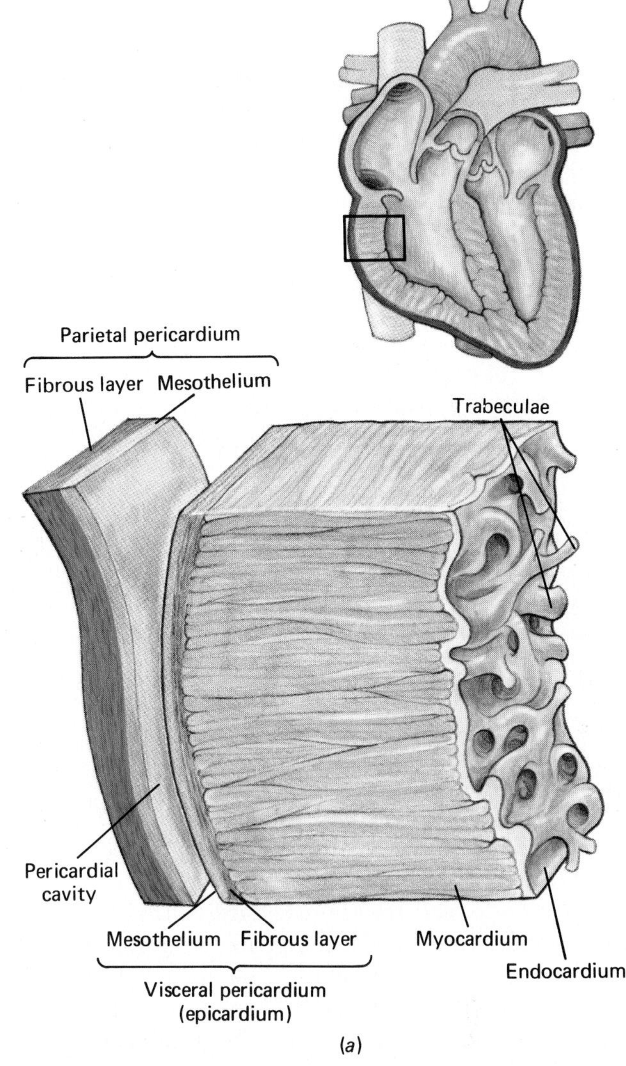

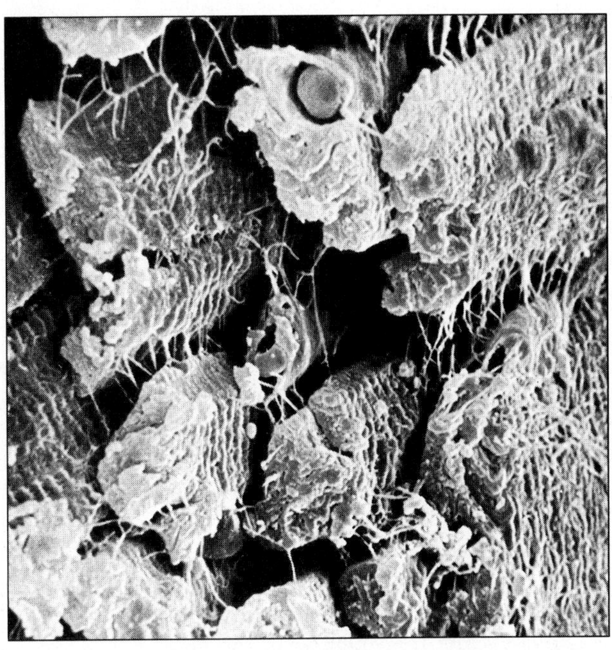

FIGURE 20-4

(*a*) The pericardium and the layers of the heart wall. (*b*) The collagen framework of the heart (approximately X5550). (Courtesy of J. B. Caulfield and T. K. Boro.)

FOCUS ON . . . Diseases of the pericardium

The typical forms diseases of the pericardium may assume include pericardial (1) *inflammation*, (2) *effusion*, and (3) *constriction*. Inflammation of the pericardium is termed **pericarditis** (*per*-i-kar-**die**-tis) and is by far the most common form of pericardial disease. Pericarditis may occur subsequent to some viral or bacterial infections or it may accompany certain connective tissue disorders such as systemic lupus erythematosus. Additional causes include trauma, myocardial infarction, allergic and hypersensitivity disorders, exposure to certain chemical agents, neoplastic disease, and congenital abnormalities of the pericardium.

Pericardial effusion represents the accumulation of fluid within the pericardial cavity in amounts exceeding that normally present. In certain instances the fluid may be the consequence of an inflammatory process, whereas in other cases it may be blood itself. If continued effusion is left unchecked, the end result is a typically fatal condition called **cardiac tamponade** (**tam**-po-nod), in which normal cardiac filling and cardiac output are severely impaired.

Pericardial constriction may occur subsequent to pericarditis and pericardial effusion. Adhesions may develop within the pericardial cavity, and the serous pericardium itself may become fibrous and thickened. It may also become calcified in some instances. The end result is obstruction or constriction of the heart chambers or the openings of the great veins entering the right atrium. If the constrictive process is left unchecked, tissue death or **necrosis** (ne-**krow**-sis) of the myocardium may also develop.

tinct layers, and these are, from the inside out, the (1) endocardium, (2) myocardium, and (3) epicardium.

The **endocardium** (en-doe-**kard**-ee-um) is composed of an endothelial lining that rests upon a connective tissue foundation. The endothelium lines the interior of the entire heart, including the valves, and is continuous with the inner lining of the great blood vessels that enter and leave the heart (Fig. 20-4).

The **myocardium** (my-oh-**kard**-ee-um) constitutes the greatest mass of the heart wall (Fig. 20-4). It is a thick layer of cardiac muscle whose individual cells are intricately branched and interwoven to form a complex network whose rhythmical contraction is responsible for the pumping of the blood. There are regional differences in the thickness of the myocardium. For example, the myocardium of the left ventricle is nearly three times as thick as that of the right. This permits the left ventricle to pump blood against the much greater resistance offered by the blood vessels that channel blood to all the regions of the body.

As discussed earlier, the outer layer of the heart wall is called the **epicardium** (ep-ee-**kard**-ee-um) and is the same as the visceral pericardium (Fig. 20-4). The connective tissue upon which its mesothelium rests is continuous with the *endomysium* (connective tissue sheaths) of the underlying cardiac muscle cells. This layer of connective tissue may contain considerable amounts of fat, particularly along the blood vessels located on the surface of the heart.

The wall of the heart is richly supplied with blood vessels, nerves, and lymphatic vessels. Within the heart wall, abundant collagen fibers form a framework for attachment of cardiac muscle and the valves (Fig. 20-4*b*). This so-called "skeleton" of the heart also divides the heart into right and left halves and separates the atria and ventricles. This separation is evident on the surface of the heart and is marked by the presence of a groove called the **coronary sulcus.** Within the coronary sulcus lie some of the arteries that supply the heart wall as well as some of the veins that serve to return blood from the heart wall to the right atrium.

Two atria and two ventricles constitute the chambers of the heart

The heart consists of four chambers: **right atrium, right ventricle, left atrium,** and **left ventricle.** Various aspects of their internal and external surfaces are presented in Figures 20-5 through 20-7. The **atria** (Fig. 20-6) are chambers that receive blood from the veins and function as reservoirs between contractions of the heart. The **ventricles** (Fig. 20-6) are responsible for pumping the blood

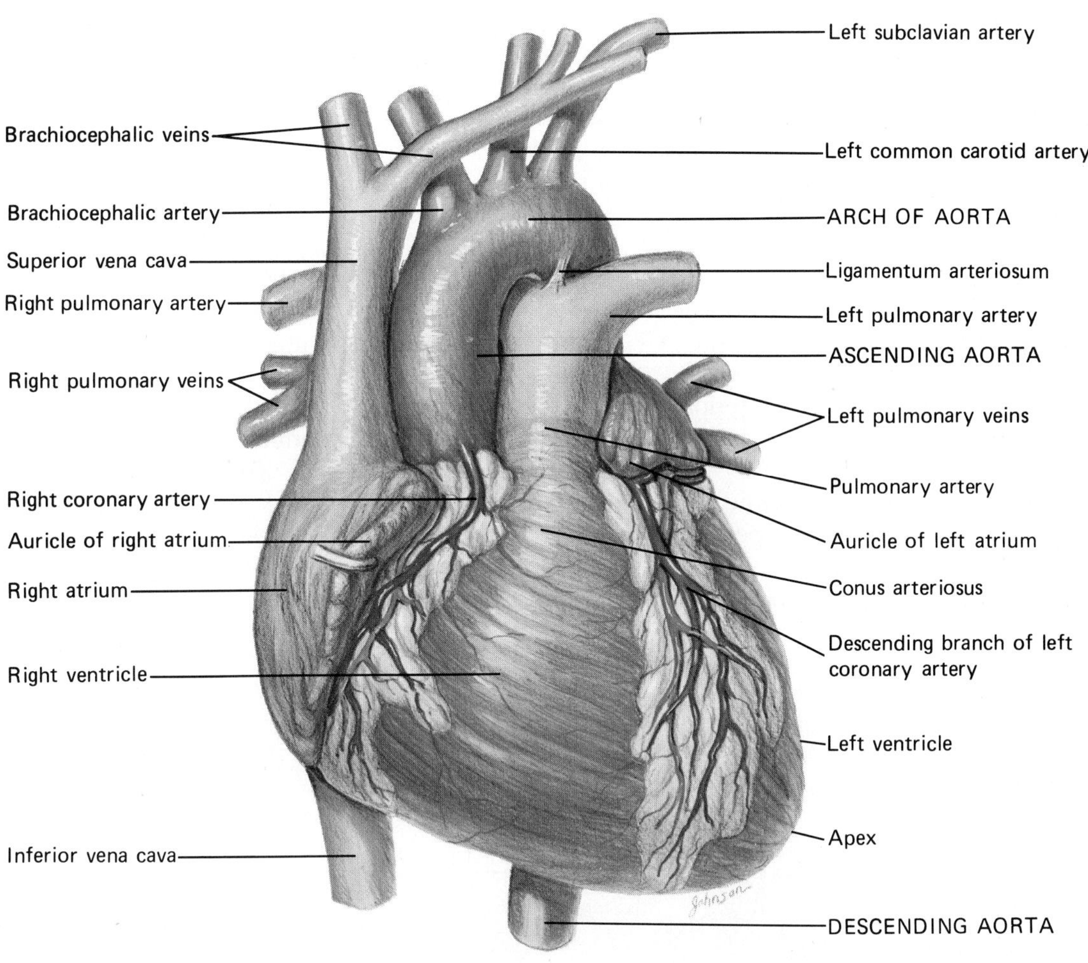

FIGURE 20-5

Anterior aspect of the heart and the great vessels. (From Guyton, Arthur C., *Textbook of Medical Physiology,* Philadelphia, W. B. Saunders, 1986.)

into the great arteries (aorta and pulmonary trunk) leaving the heart.

Consider the heart as a double, or two-sided, pump. The right atrium of the heart receives **deoxygenated (oxygen-poor) blood,** that is blood somewhat depleted of its oxygen supply, returning from the body's tissues. The right ventricle then pumps this blood into the **pulmonary circulation** (vascular network of the lungs) via the pulmonary trunk. The **pulmonary arteries** (Fig. 20-6) convey the deoxygenated blood to the lungs, where gases are exchanged. The newly oxygenated (oxygen-rich) blood is returned to the left atrium by the four **pulmonary veins** (Figs. 20-5 through 20-7). Next, the left ventricle pumps the blood, via the aorta, into the **systemic circulation,** the network of vessels that serves all the body's tissues. In summary, the pattern of blood flow is as follows:

Right atrium ⟶ right ventricle ⟶ pulmonary circulation ⟶ left atrium ⟶ left ventricle ⟶ systemic circulation

Interposed between the right and left sides of the heart are walls, or **septa** (**sep**-tuh) (Fig. 20-6). The wall situated between the two atria is called the **interatrial septum** (in-ter-a-**tree**-uhl) (Fig. 20-6); that between the ventricles is termed the **interventricular septum** (*in*-ter-ven-**trik**-u-lar) (Fig. 20-8, p. 678). In the interior of the right atrium there is a characteristic depression on the wall of the interatrial septum. This is called the **fossa ovalis** (**o**-val-us) and represents the location of a previous opening, the **foramen ovale** (o-**val**-ee), which existed in the fetal heart (Figs. 20-6 and 20-9). Prior to birth this opening permitted blood to be shunted directly from the right atrium into the left atrium, diverting blood from the fetus's nonfunctioning lungs. (See Focus on Congenital Defects of the Septa.)

Focus your attention on Figure 20-5 and notice that the right and left atria have earlike extensions, or **auricles** (aw-**rik**-uhls), that project anteriorly. In fact when viewing the anterior surface of the heart, the auricle is about all you can see of the left atrium. The auricles serve to increase the volume of their respective atria. The interior of each atrium is characteristically smooth except for that of the auricle which is roughened by the presence of small, projecting, muscular bundles called the **musculi pectinati** (mus-**que**-lie peck-**tin**-ah-tee).

The walls of the atria are much thinner than those of the ventricles. This is most likely explained by the fact that their job is to pump blood into their respective ventricles, which requires markedly less force than pumping blood into the systemic or pulmonary circulation. For example, the left ventricle, having by far the thickest wall, must create sufficient pressure to force blood into the **aorta** (the largest artery in the body) and on through the thousands of miles of blood vessels that constitute the systemic circulation.

The right atrium receives blood returning from all parts of the systemic circulation and is slightly larger than the left. This blood reaches the right atrium via two large veins, the superior and inferior vena cavae. The **superior vena cava** opens into the upper posterior region of the right

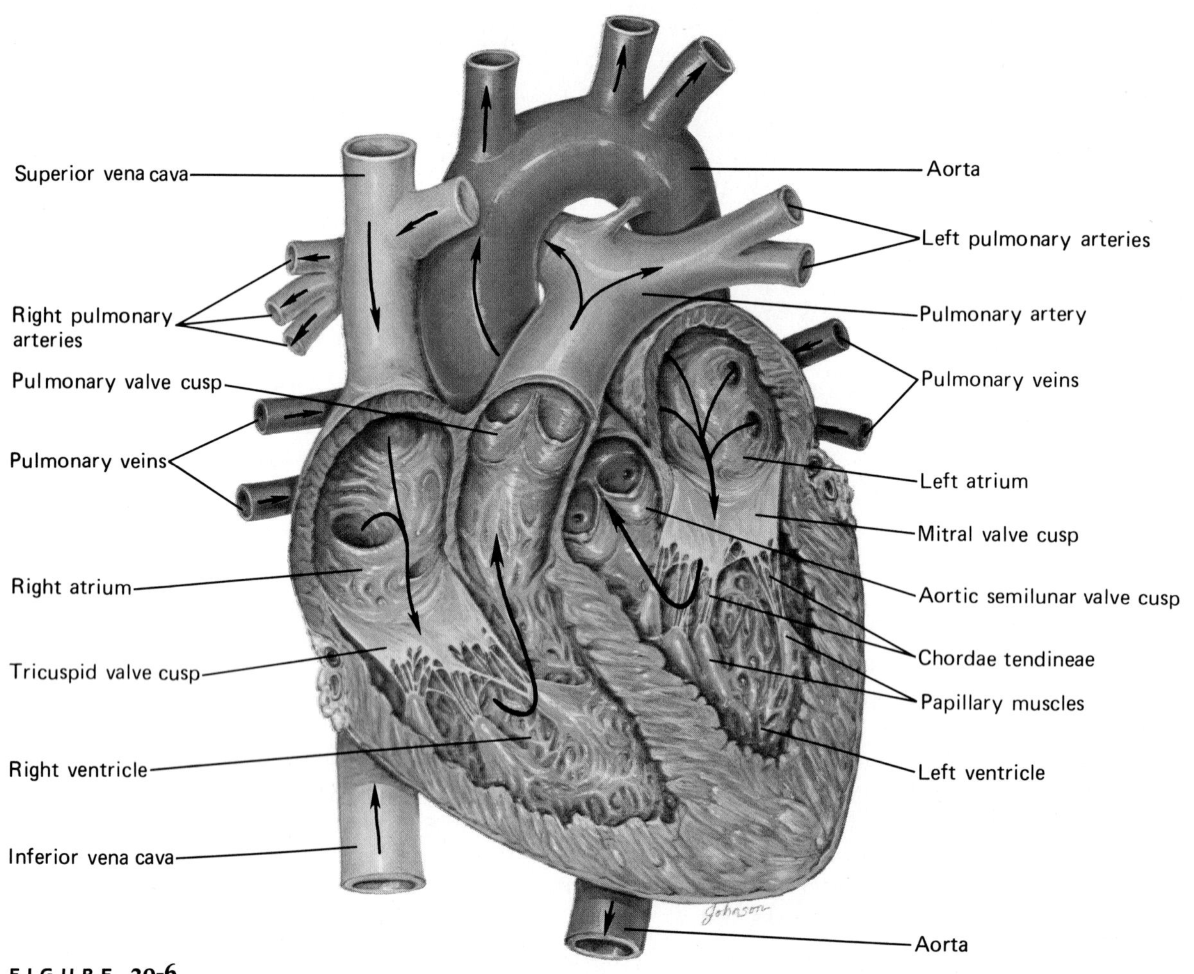

FIGURE 20-6

Coronal section through the heart and great vessels. (From Guyton, Arthur C., *Textbook of Medical Physiology*, Philadelphia, W. B. Saunders, 1986.)

FOCUS ON . . . Congenital defects of the septa

Congenital malformations of the heart typically include openings in the interatrial or the interventricular septa. Clinically these are termed **atrial septal defects (ASD)** or **ventricular septal defects (VSD),** respectively.

By far the most common ASD is the result of a patent foramen ovale, the failure of the fetal opening between the two atria to close at birth. In some individuals a very small opening may persist throughout life without resulting in clinical symptoms. Abnormal embryonic development of the interatrial wall may result in the occurrence of much larger openings. Rarely, the interatrial septum may be completely absent, a condition which is clinically termed a **common atrium**.

The most frequently occurring congenital defect involving the heart is VSD and is typically associated with the upper or membranous portion of the interventricular septum. Single or multiple septal defects also occur in the muscular portion of the ventricular septum although these are less common. Multiple VSD in the muscular portion give rise to a condition known as the "Swiss cheese" form of VSD. Some VSD are diagnosed at birth, but others may go undetected for 4 or 5 years after birth. Overall, VSD occur in approximately 10 of every 10,000 live births. There are recorded cases in which there is complete absence of the interventricular septum. Clinically this condition is termed **cor triloculare biatriatum,** a three-chambered heart.

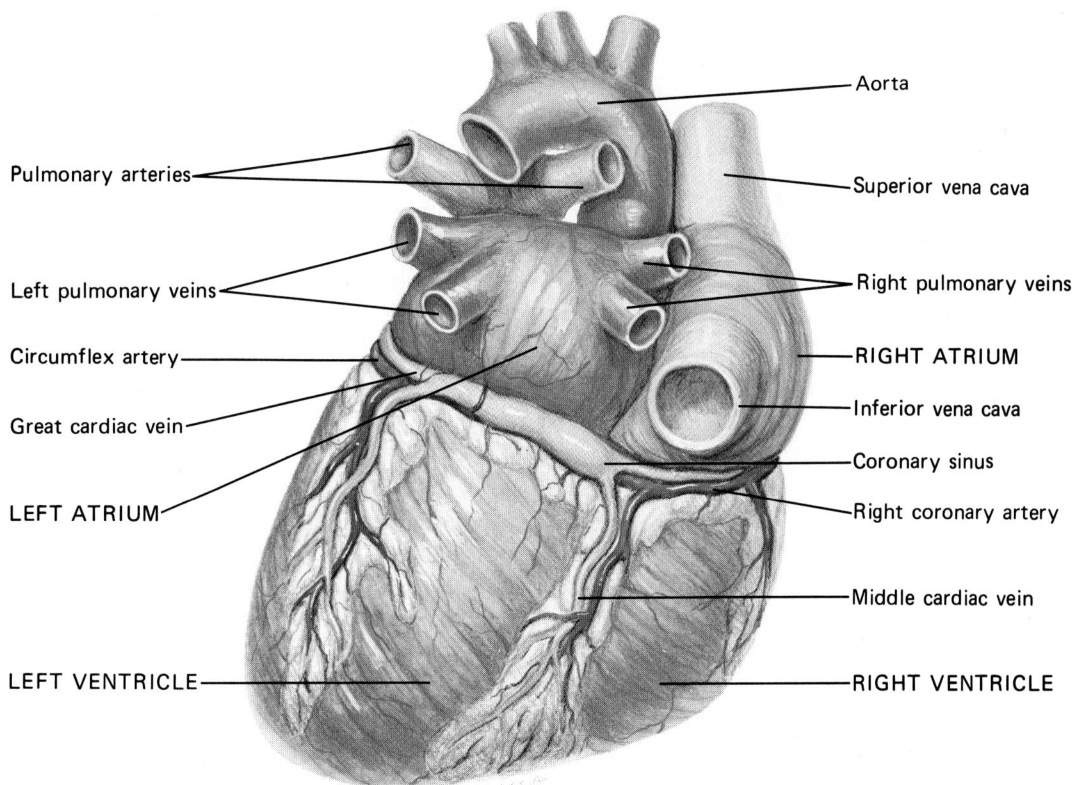

FIGURE 20-7

Posterior aspect of the heart and great vessels. (Guyton, Arthur C., *Textbook of Medical Physiology*, Philadelphia, W. B. Saunders, 1986.)

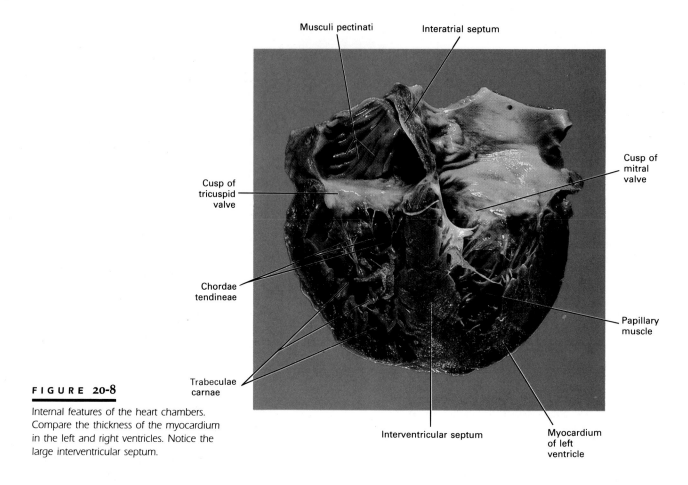

Musculi pectinati
Interatrial septum
Cusp of tricuspid valve
Cusp of mitral valve
Chordae tendineae
Papillary muscle
Trabeculae carnae
Interventricular septum
Myocardium of left ventricle

FIGURE 20-8

Internal features of the heart chambers. Compare the thickness of the myocardium in the left and right ventricles. Notice the large interventricular septum.

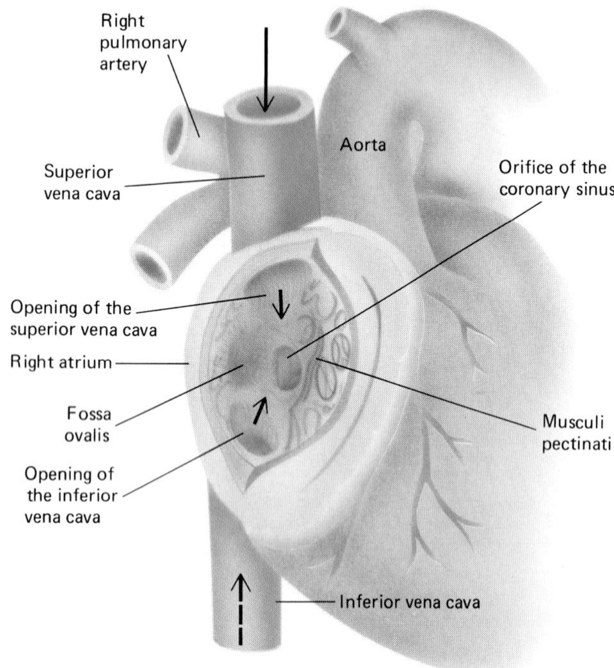

FIGURE 20-9

Schematic representation of the interior of the right atrium. Note the position of the fossa ovalis and the opening for the coronary sinus.

atrium, and the **inferior vena cava** enters the floor of the atrium near the interatrial septum (Figs. 20-5 and 20-6). The **coronary sinus,** which returns blood from the heart wall itself and lies within the coronary sulcus, empties its contents into the right atrium as well (Figs. 20-7 and 20-9). Although most of the blood of the heart wall is returned to the right atrium via the coronary sinus, there are additional microscopic veins *(venae cordis minimae)* present that empty into all four chambers of the heart as well.

The left atrium is located for the most part on the posterior surface of the heart (Fig. 20-7). It extends to the right posterior to the pulmonary trunk and origin of the aorta. It receives oxygenated blood from the lungs via the four pulmonary veins that open into its interior, two on each side of the midline of its upper posterior wall.

The right ventricle (Fig. 20-6) pumps blood into the **pulmonary trunk,** the large common stem of the right and left **pulmonary arteries.** The opening of the pulmonary trunk is guarded by the **pulmonic** (pulmonary) **valve**, which prevents the backflow of blood when the ventricle relaxes

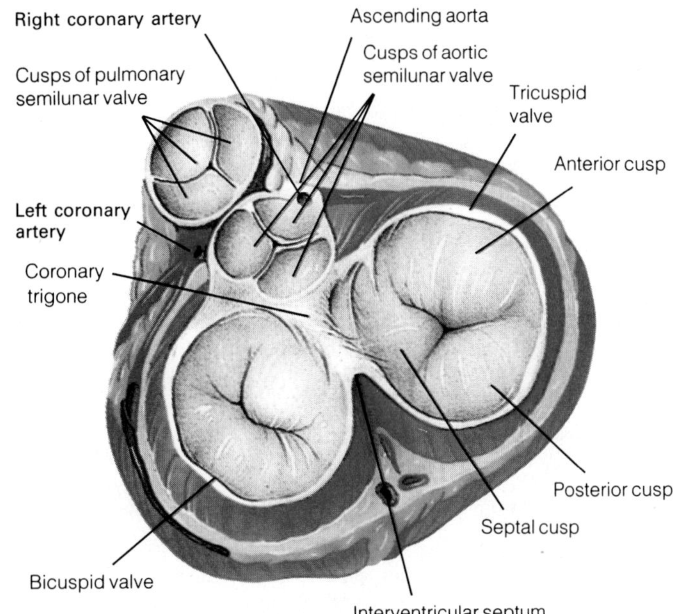

FIGURE 20-10

Superior aspect of the heart illustrating the aortic and pulmonic valves, the tricuspid and bicuspid valves.

(Fig. 20-10). The left ventricle forms the **apex** of the heart and is directed inferiorly and to the left (Fig. 20-5). When the left ventricle contracts, blood is pumped into the aorta and from there into the systemic circulation. The opening of the aorta is guarded by the **aortic valve** (Fig. 20-10) and prevents backflow of blood during relaxation of the left ventricle.

The interior of both ventricles is characterized by the presence of irregularly arranged columns of muscle called the **trabeculae carnae** (trah-**bek**-u-lee **kar**-nay) (Fig. 20-11). These are more nu-

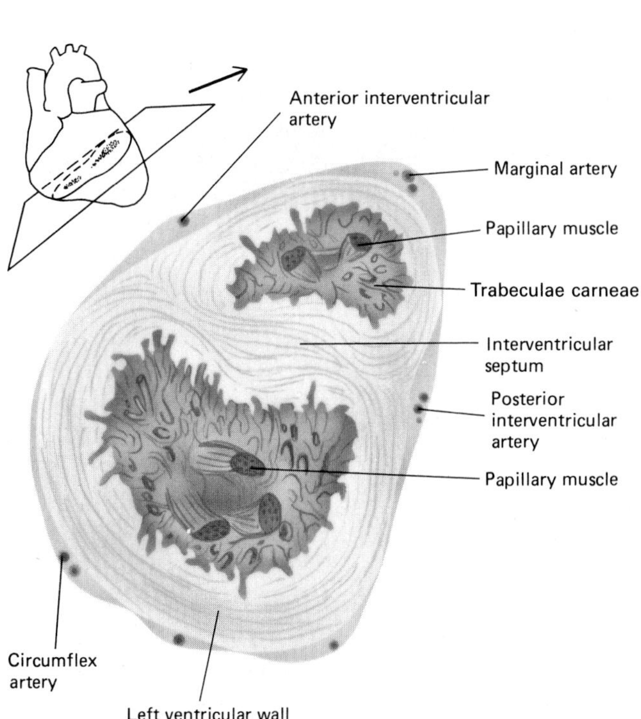

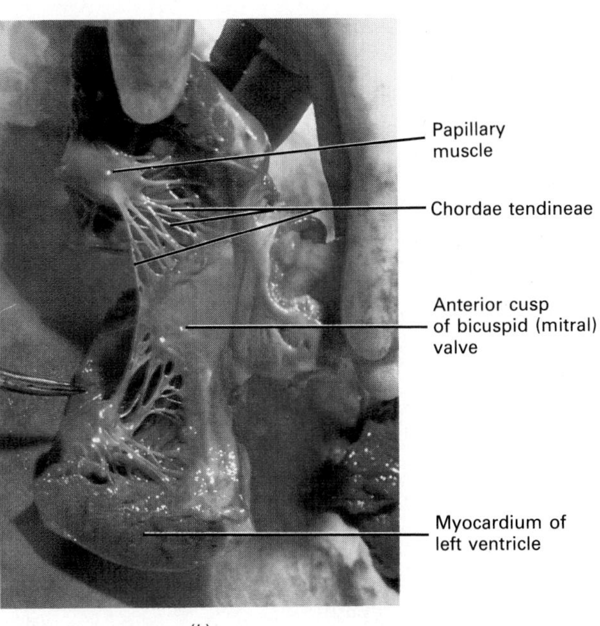

FIGURE 20-11

Structure of the right and left ventricles. (*a*) Cross-section through the apical portions of the left and right ventricles. (*b*) Anterior cusp of the bicuspid (mitral) valve. Notice the attachment of the cusp to the papillary muscle by the chordaetendineae. (John Watney/Photo Researchers, Inc.)

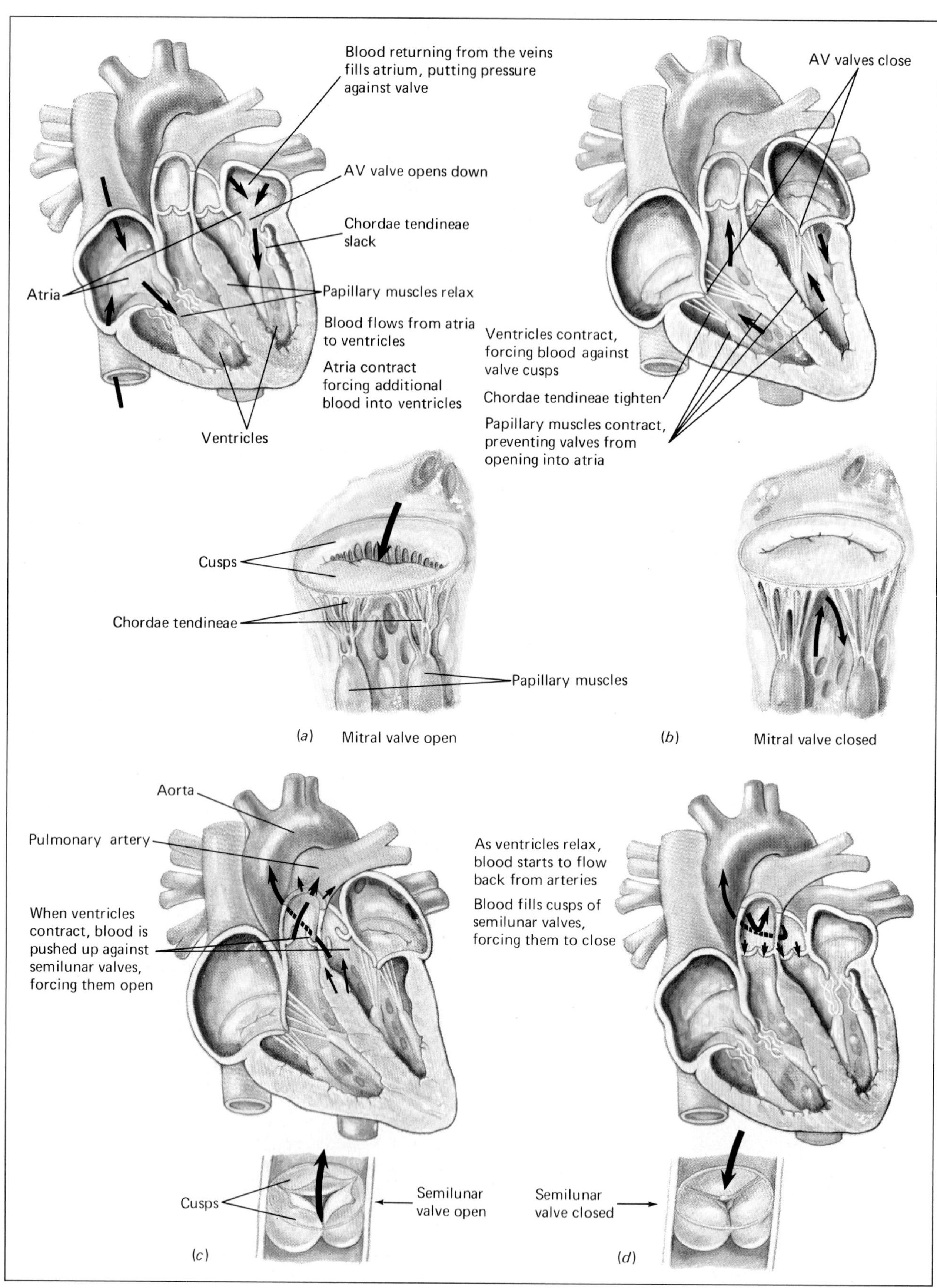
Blood returning from the veins fills atrium, putting pressure against valve
AV valve opens down
Chordae tendineae slack
Atria
Papillary muscles relax
Blood flows from atria to ventricles
Atria contract forcing additional blood into ventricles
Ventricles
AV valves close
Ventricles contract, forcing blood against valve cusps
Chordae tendineae tighten
Papillary muscles contract, preventing valves from opening into atria
Cusps
Chordae tendineae
Papillary muscles
(a) Mitral valve open
(b) Mitral valve closed
Aorta
Pulmonary artery
When ventricles contract, blood is pushed up against semilunar valves, forcing them open
As ventricles relax, blood starts to flow back from arteries
Blood fills cusps of semilunar valves, forcing them to close
Cusps
Semilunar valve open
Semilunar valve closed
(c)
(d)

FIGURE 20-12

The functioning of the valves of the heart during the directional flow of blood through the heart.

merous in the left than in the right ventricle. Also present in the ventricles are the **papillary muscles** (Fig. 20-11). These protruding muscular pillars are connected to thin, white, fibrous connective tissue cords, the **chordae tendineae** (**kor**-dee ten-**din**-ee-ay; "heart strings"), which in turn attach to the leaflets of their respective atrioventricular valves (Fig. 20-11).

Cardiac valves serve to direct blood through the heart

Once blood has been pumped from either atrium into the corresponding ventricle, pressure in the ventricle becomes greater than in the atrium. As the atrium relaxes, blood must be prevented from flowing back into it. This is accomplished by the presence of the right and left **atrioventricular** (*a*-tre-o-ven-**trik**-u-lar) or **AV valves,** which guard the orifice between each atrium and ventricle (Figs. 20-6 and 20-11).

Each of the atrioventricular valves consists of flaps, or **cusps,** of fibrous tissue that project from the heart wall (cardiac skeleton) into the opening between the atrium and ventricle. These cusps are covered with a layer of endothelium that is continuous with the endothelial lining (endocardium) of the heart. The right AV valve has three cusps, *anterior, posterior,* and *septal,* and is therefore called the **tricuspid valve** (tri-**kus**-pid) (Fig. 20-10). The left AV valve possesses only two cusps, the *anterior* and *posterior,* and is termed the **bicuspid** (bi-**kus**-pid), or **mitral, valve** (Fig. 20-10).

As the atria are filled with blood, the cusps of the AV valves are forced open and the blood flows into the corresponding ventricle (Fig. 20-12). Then, as the ventricles contract, blood is forced back against the valve cusps, pushing them up toward the atria and approximating them with each other so as to seal off the atrioventricular opening. The cusps are prevented from everting into the atria during ventricular contraction by contraction of the papillary muscles. Therefore it might be helpful to consider the cusps of the AV valves as swinging doors that swing in only one direction. (See Focus on Diseases of the Valves of the Heart.)

The exits of the ventricles, that is, the aortic and pulmonary openings, are guarded by the **aortic** and **pulmonic valves,** respectively (Fig. 20-12). The aortic valve is situated in the left ventricle and the pulmonic valve in the right ventricle. Each of these valves consists of three cusps which have the shape of a half moon. Hence, they are also termed the **semilunar valves** (Fig. 20-12). The

FOCUS ON . . . Diseases of the valves of the heart

Disease processes involving the AV valves, aortic valve, and pulmonic valve have two basic effects: they result in either narrowed (stenotic) or leaky (insufficient) valves. Most cases of valvular heart disease are due to congenital abnormalities or result from inflammation accompanying diseases such as rheumatic fever or syphillis. In the case of rheumatic fever, the mitral and aortic valves are most frequently affected.

Thickening of the mitral valve results in narrowing of the orifice of the mitral valve, or what is termed **mitral stenosis.** This impedes the flow of blood from the left atrium into the left ventricle. As a result, the pressure in the left atrium is increased due to its incomplete emptying, and cardiac output is reduced because there is inadequate filling of the left ventricle. Mitral stenosis also results in characteristically abnormal heart sounds due to turbulence of blood flowing from atrium to ventricle and to the opening and closing of the narrowed valve.

Valvular insufficiency occurs when a valve cusp is shortened or by some other mechanism prevented from closing completely. When this happens, blood is permitted to regurgitate into the preceding chamber. In the case of **mitral valve insufficiency,** blood flows backward into the left atrium when the left ventricular pressure exceeds that of the left atrium. As a result left atrial pressure increases and cardiac output declines. The increase in left atrial pressure may also increase the pressure in the pulmonary circulation and allow pulmonary edema to develop.

When the left ventricle fills, it must also accommodate the regurgitated blood in addition to the volume it would ordinarily handle. This leads to a ventricular overload and may result in a dilation and hypertrophy of the left ventricle. Sometimes it is possible for the physician to surgically remove a diseased valve and replace it with an artificial valve.

free border of each cusp is directed upward into the lumen of its respective vessel.

The heart has its own system of vessels

The heart itself is supplied with blood delivered by the two **coronary arteries** and their branches (Fig. 20-13). The **right coronary artery** takes its origin from the aorta just distal to the aortic valve and appears on the surface of the heart between the pulmonary trunk and the auricle of the right atrium. Major branches of the right coronary artery include its *marginal branch, posterior interventricular branch,* and *AV nodal branch.* The right coronary artery is distributed to the right atrium, right ventricle, and variable portions of the left atrium and left ventricle (Fig. 20-14).

The **left coronary artery** also arises from the base or ascending portion of the aorta. It is at first located between the pulmonary trunk and auricle of the left atrium. Major branches of the left coronary artery include its *anterior interventricular branch* and its *circumflex branch.* Thus, the left coronary artery supplies both ventricles, the interventricular septum and the left atrium (Fig. 20-14). See Focus on Ischemic Heart Disease.

Most of the blood supplied by the coronary arteries is returned to the right atrium by way of the **coronary sinus** (Figs. 20-6, 20-7, and 20-9). Tributaries of the coronary sinus include the *great cardiac vein, middle cardiac vein,* and *small cardiac vein* (Fig. 20-15). As mentioned earlier, numerous microscopic veins, the venae cordis minimae, open directly into the heart chambers.

FOCUS ON . . . Ischemic heart disease

Thirty to forty percent of all deaths in the United States each year are due to **ischemic heart disease** resulting from coronary artery insufficiency. In cases where there is acute coronary artery occlusion, death is sudden. On the other hand, ischemic disease may be a chronic condition in which the heart pumping process is continuously weakened over an extended period of days, weeks, or even years.

The formation of **atherosclerotic plaques** within the walls of the coronary arteries is the most common cause of ischemic heart disease. In atherosclerosis large quantities of cholesterol become deposited beneath the intima of the vessel wall. Subsequent to the deposit of cholesterol, the regions undergo fibrosis and frequently become calcified. The diameter of the vessel's lumen becomes progressively reduced and blood flow is impeded.

Certain individuals are known to be genetically predisposed to the development of atherosclerosis. In certain instances this condition is related to an inherited **familial hypercholesterolemia** (*hi*-per-ko-*les*-ter-ol-**ee**-me-ah), in which the excess cholesterol occurs typically in the form of **low-density lipoprotein (LDL).** This is thought to be the result of too few receptors for the low-density lipoproteins in many cells throughout the body. Others who ingest large quantities of cholesterol and additional fats also put themselves at risk for developing atherosclerotic lesions.

As mentioned above, death from ischemic heart disease may occur suddenly as a result of acute coronary artery occlusion. This is typically seen in individuals having existing atherosclerotic lesions. One cause of acute coronary artery occlusion is the development of a **thrombus,** or blood clot, at the site of the atherosclerotic lesion. As the clot enlarges, it simply occludes the vessel at that point. Should the thrombus become detached from the vessel wall, it is termed an **embolus,** and is typically carried to a more distal location, blocking the vessel at that site.

Another potential cause of acute coronary artery occlusion are focal spasms of these vessels. Many clinicians believe that such spasms may result from nervous reflexes as well as from irritation of the vessel by the margins of atherosclerotic lesions.

There are several risk factors that accentuate the development and progression of atherosclerosis and subsequently increase the occurence of coronary heart disease. These include: (1) *high serum lipid levels* and *high dietary fat intake,* (2) *cigarette smoking,* (3) *hypertension,* and (4) *obesity.* Scientific evidence supports the notion that dietary lipid intake and elevated serum lipid levels are predominantly responsible for predisposing the individual to the risk of atherosclerosis.

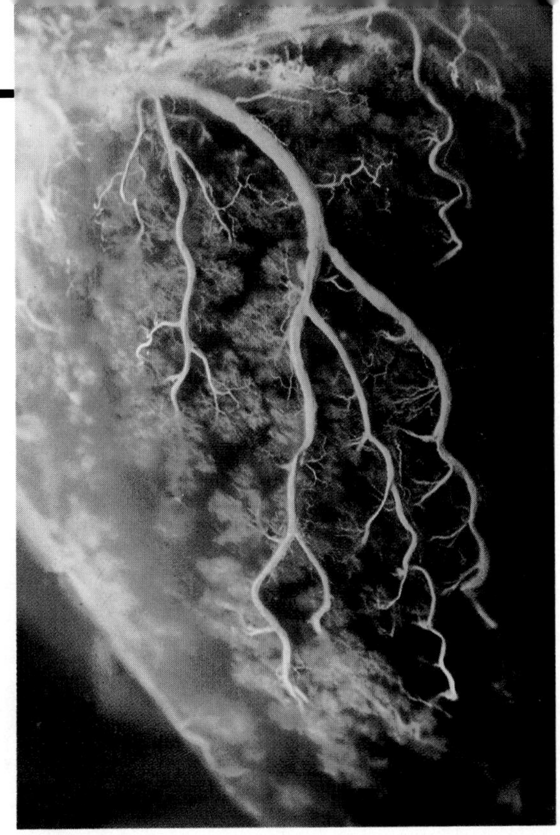

FIGURE 20-13

Photograph of the coronary vascular tree supplying the heart. (Science Photo Library/ Photo Researchers, Inc.)

FIGURE 20-14

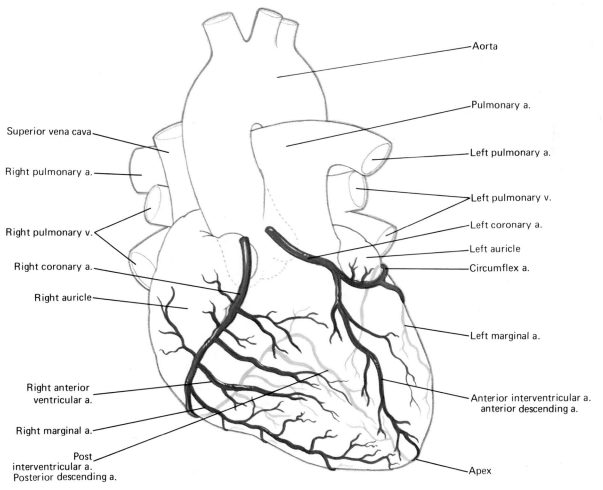

The principal arteries that serve the heart.

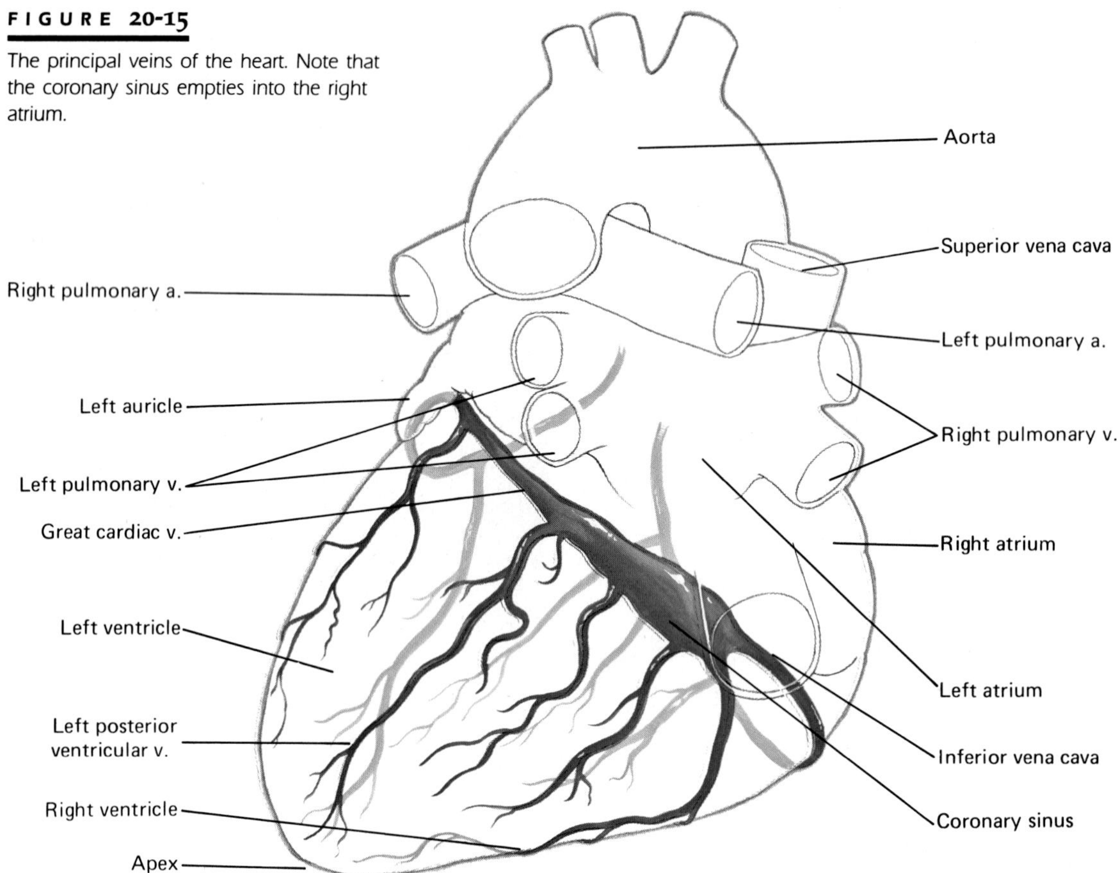

FIGURE 20-15

The principal veins of the heart. Note that the coronary sinus empties into the right atrium.

Cardiac function is dynamic and subject to several control mechanisms

When surgically removed from the body, the heart will continue to beat for several hours provided it is perfused with the appropriate nutrients and salts. This is possible because the heart possesses its own specialized conduction system and can beat independently even after being separated from its nerve supply. Thus, the extrinsic (arising external to the heart) nerve supply serves to modulate the intrinsic (inherent to the heart itself) beating established by the heart.

The heart's conduction system is composed of specialized cardiac muscle

There are four basic components to the heart's conduction system: (1) sinoatrial node, (2) internodal fiber bundles, (3) atrioventricular node, and (4) atrioventricular bundle. Each is composed of a specialized type of cardiac muscle and is illustrated schematically in Figure 20-16. The **sinoatrial (SA) node** is a small mass of specialized cardiac muscle situated in the superior aspect of the right atrium. It lies along the anterolateral margin of this chamber between the orifice of the superior vena cava and the auricle. The specialized cardiac muscle of the SA node is characterized by the property of automatic self-excitation and it initiates each beat of the heart. Therefore, the SA node is often referred to as the **pacemaker** of the heart.

Since the fibers of the SA node fuse with the surrounding atrial muscle fibers, the action potential generated in the nodal tissue spreads throughout both atria at a rate of approximately 0.3 meter per second and produces atrial contraction. Interspersed among the atrial muscle fibers are several **internodal fiber bundles** which conduct the action potential to the **atrioventricular (AV) node** with a greater velocity (approximately 1.0 meter per second) than ordinary atrial muscle. The AV node is located in the right atrium near the lower part of the interatrial septum. Here there is a short delay (approximately 0.1 second) in transmission of the impulse to the ventricles.

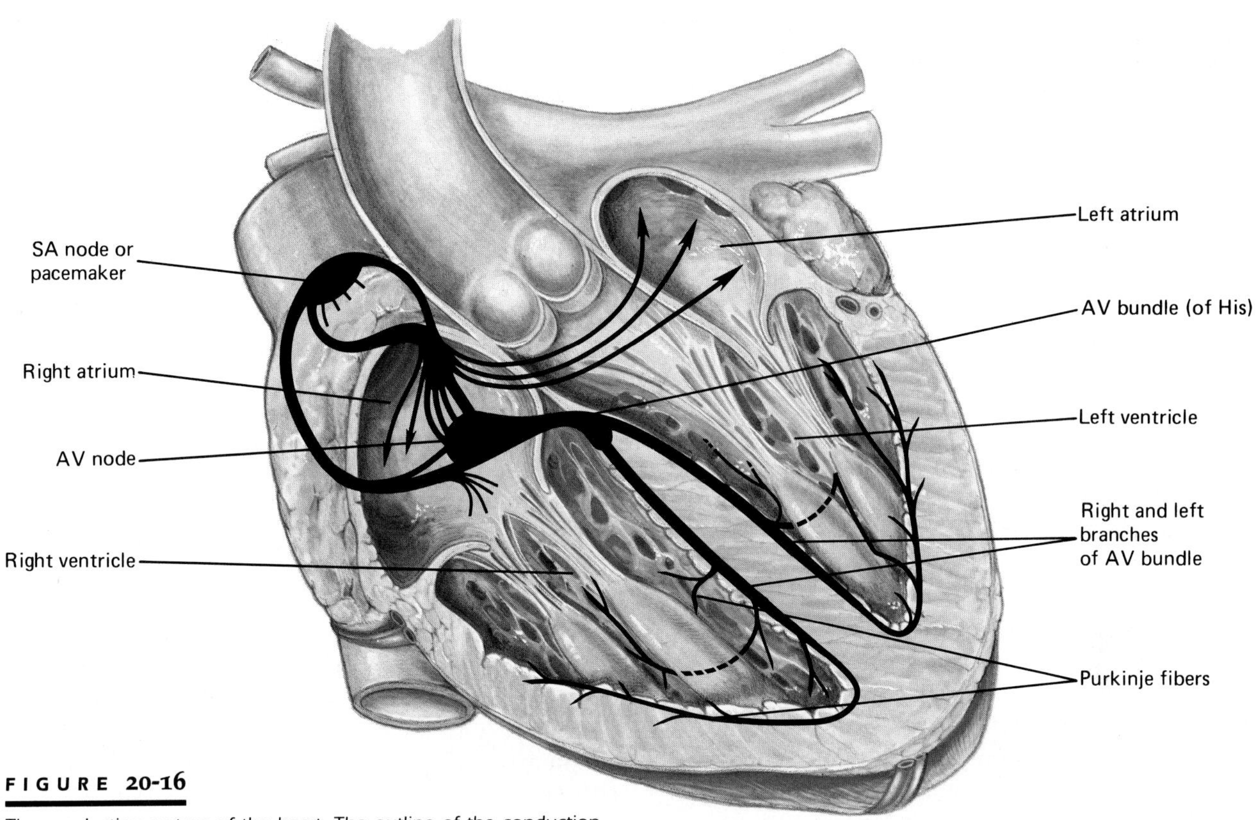

FIGURE 20-16

The conduction system of the heart. The outline of the conduction system has been superimposed on the heart so that the view is very diagrammatic (e.g., the SA node is actually in the posterior wall of the right atrium).

This is important because it permits the atria to complete their contraction and empty their blood into the ventricles before the ventricles contract. The delay occurs within the fibers of the AV node itself as well as in special junctional fibers that connect the node with ordinary atrial fibers.

Once the action potential leaves the AV node, it enters specialized muscle fibers called **Purkinje fibers.** These are grouped into a mass termed the **atrioventricular (AV) bundle,** or the **bundle of His** (Fig. 20-16). The Purkinje fibers are very large and conduct the action potential at about six times the velocity of ordinary cardiac muscle (i.e., 1.5 to 4.0 meters per second). Thus the Purkinje fibers permit a very rapid and simultaneous distribution of the impulse throughout the muscular walls of both ventricles (Fig 20-17).

As the AV bundle leaves the AV node, it descends in the interventricular septum for a short distance and then divides into two large branches, the **right** and **left bundle branches.** Each of these descends along its respective side of the interventricular septum immediately beneath the endocardium and divides into smaller and smaller branches. Terminal Purkinje fibers extend beneath the endocardium and penetrate approximately one-third of the distance into the myocardium. Their endings terminate upon ordinary cardiac muscle within the ventricles, and the impulse proceeds through the ventricular muscle at about 0.3 to 0.5 meters per second. This results

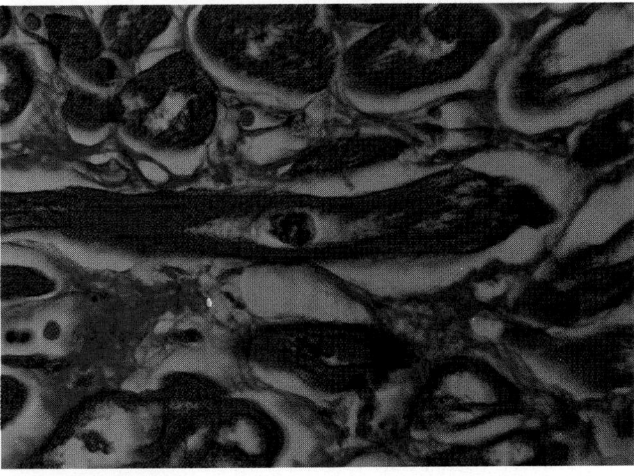

FIGURE 20-17

Photomicrograph of human Purkinje fibers. (Cabisco/Visuals Unlimited.)

in a contraction of the ventricles that proceeds upward from the apex of the heart toward its base. The pathway taken by each action potential generated by the SA node is:

SA node ⟶ atrial muscle ⟶ internodal fibers ⟶ AV node ⟶ AV bundle ⟶ right and left bundle branches ⟶ ventricular muscle

Cardiac muscle differs from skeletal muscle in several ways

Cardiac muscle and skeletal muscle have some features in common. Like skeletal muscle, cardiac muscle is striated, has dark Z lines (Fig. 20-18*b*), and possesses myofibrils that contain actin and myosin filaments. During systole these filaments slide over one another in much the same manner as in skeletal muscle contraction.

On the other hand, cardiac muscle has several unique properties. You have already seen that it is capable of intrinsic contraction (contraction without being triggered by a nerve impulse). This is a characteristic of all cardiac muscle and does not apply solely to specialized fibers of the SA node. If the SA node is destroyed, the heart will continue to pulsate, though at a much reduced rate due to the cells of the AV node. Skeletal muscle, however, contracts only when stimulated via a nerve impulse. Since it would not be desirable for skeletal muscle to contract spontaneously and rhythmically, the advantages of this arrangement should be obvious!

When you view cardiac muscle with a microscope a particularly striking feature becomes apparent—the muscle cells exhibit a characteristic branching pattern. Notice in Figure 20-18*a* that the parallel muscle cells are interconnected by diverging branches. Furthermore, one or sometimes two nuclei are present within each cell and are more centrally located than the nuclei of skeletal muscle cells.

Another unique feature of cardiac muscle is the presence of dense bands called **intercalated discs** (in-**ter**-kah-lay-ted) that separate individual cells from one another at their ends (Fig. 20-18*b*). These discs represent specialized cell junctions between cardiac muscle cells—junctions that offer very little resistance to the passage of an action potential from one cell to the next. The resistance here is so low that ions move freely through this permeable junction and thus permit the entire atrial or ventricular muscle mass to function as one giant cell. For this reason cardiac muscle is frequently referred to as a *functional syncytium* (sin-**sih**-shee-um), a single functional unit.

The **fibrous skeleton** of the heart separates the atrial syncytium from the ventricular syncytium; therefore an impulse from the former must pass through the AV node before triggering the latter. The connective tissue network of the fibrous skeleton lies within the septa between the atria and ventricles. It is important in that it pro-

(*a*)

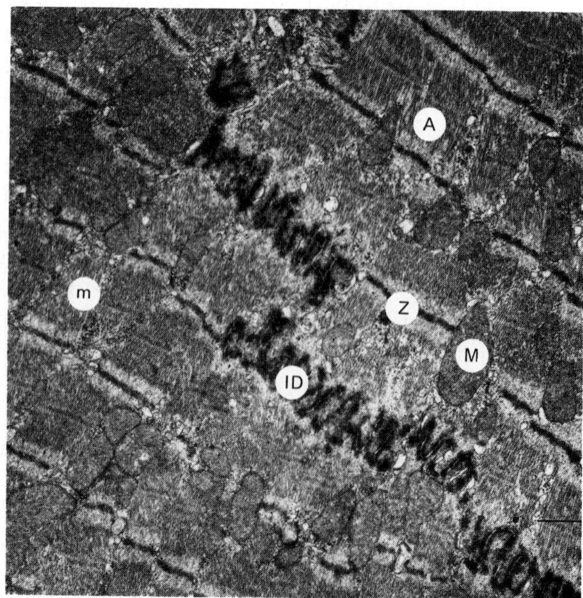

(*b*)

FIGURE 20-18

Cardiac muscle. (*a*) Photomicrograph of cardiac muscle as observed with the light microscope. (*b*) Electron micrograph of cardiac muscle. A, a band; Z, z line; M, mitochondrion; ID, intercalated disc. (*a*, John D. Cunningham/Visuals Unlimited; *b*, courtesy of Lyle C. Dearden.)

vides for attachment of cardiac muscle and lends support to the AV valves.

Because cardiac muscle functions as a syncytium, stimulation of an individual muscle cell results in the contraction of all the muscle cells. This is an application of the all-or-none principle. Although the principle applies only to individual cells in skeletal muscle, if the stimulus in cardiac muscle is great enough to initiate contraction of a single cell, the entire muscular syncytium will undergo contraction.

As an action potential travels along cardiac muscle, it is thought to pass along the T tubules within the cells, causing release of calcium ions from the sarcoplasmic reticulum. In skeletal muscle cells there are two T tubule systems per sarcomere, whereas in cardiac muscle there is only one. Although the T tubule system of cardiac muscle is larger, it takes somewhat longer for calcium ions to diffuse into the central portion of the sarcomere. Furthermore, as the action potential spreads along the plasma membrane of cardiac muscle, a markedly decreased permeability to potassium ions occurs. This leads to a decreased outflow of potassium ions from the cell, extending the plateau of the action potential and prolonging the period required for repolarization. Thus, cardiac muscle contracts at a slower rate than does skeletal muscle.

Once the calcium ions reach the myofibrils, they initiate reactions responsible for causing the actin and myosin filaments to slide over one another—the actual contractile process. Within approximately 500 milliseconds (ms) the action potential is over, the calcium ions have been returned to the sarcoplasmic reticulum, and the muscle relaxes.

The cardiac cycle consists of contraction and relaxation phases

The spontaneous generation of an action potential within the SA node initiates a sequence of events known as the **cardiac cycle.** Each cardiac cycle lasts approximately 0.8 second and spans the interval from the end of one heart contraction to the end of the subsequent heart contraction. Ordinarily this occurs about 72 times each minute. The cardiac cycle has two basic components: (1) a contraction phase during which blood is ejected from the heart and (2) a relaxation phase during which the chambers of the heart are filled with blood. The contractile phase is called **systole** (**sis**-tuh-lee) and the relaxation phase is termed **diastole** (dye-**ass**-tuh-lee).

The spontaneous generation of an action potential within the SA nodal tissue represents the start of the cardiac cycle. This electrical impulse spreads throughout the atrial muscle and leads to contraction of the two atria. As the atria contract, the AV valves remain open and additional blood is forced into the ventricles from the veins. A large amount of blood has already passed from the atria to the ventricles prior to atrial contraction. The aortic and pulmonary (pulmonic) semilunar valves remain closed (Fig. 20-12).

After the ventricles have filled (mostly by blood returning from the large veins) and the atria have contracted, the AV valves close as the ventricles begin their contraction. Ventricular contraction forces blood through the semilunar valves into the aorta and pulmonary trunk (Fig. 20-12). Next, as the ventricles begin to relax, the aortic and pulmonic semilunar valves close, the AV valves open, and blood flows into the ventricles to begin another cycle. While the atria are in systole, the ventricles are relaxed (in diastole). The atria relax during ventricular systole and remain in this phase even during a portion of ventricular diastole.

Focus your attention on Figure 20-19, which depicts the changes in pressure and blood volume during the cardiac cycle. Blood (like any other fluid) tends to flow from a region of high pressure to one of lower pressure. Therefore, as each chamber of the heart fills with blood, the pressure increases within it. The blood moves out of the chamber, that is, when the various one-way valves guarding those chambers permit it to do so. For example, intra-atrial pressure increases as blood from the veins enters them, and this pressure increases further during atrial systole. As the ventricles contract, the blood is forced in a retrograde fashion against the AV valves, which causes them to bulge inward slightly toward the atria and which also elevates atrial pressure. In doing so, the AV valves are effectively closed and blood is prevented from regurgitating back into the atria. Near the end of ventricular systole the AV valves are still closed and since the atria are in the process of filling, this too contributes to a rise in intra-atrial pressure.

Even before the atria enter systole, the ventricles are filled with blood to approximately 70% of their capacity. When the atria do finally contract, additional blood enters the ventricles and elevates the intraventricular pressure. As the ventricles contract, blood is forced backward, closing the

AV valves, and a sharp rise in ventricular pressure occurs.

Although the ventricles exist as closed chambers for a brief moment, the pressure within them soon exceeds that in the aorta and pulmonary trunk. When this happens the aortic and pulmonic semilunar valves are forced open under pressure and blood rushes out of the ventricles and is driven into these large vessels. Accompanying the opening of the semilunar valves is a rapid decline in intraventricular pressure that continues until the pressure within the ventricles becomes less than that of the atria. When this pressure differential is reached, blood within the atria pushes the AV valves open and begins to fill the ventricles once again.

Normal heart sounds result from proper closure of cardiac valves

With the aid of a stethoscope you can hear the characteristic sounds of the normal heartbeat, typically described as a **"lub-dub."** These sounds are produced by the closure of the heart valves. The **first heart sound** or "lub" results from closure of

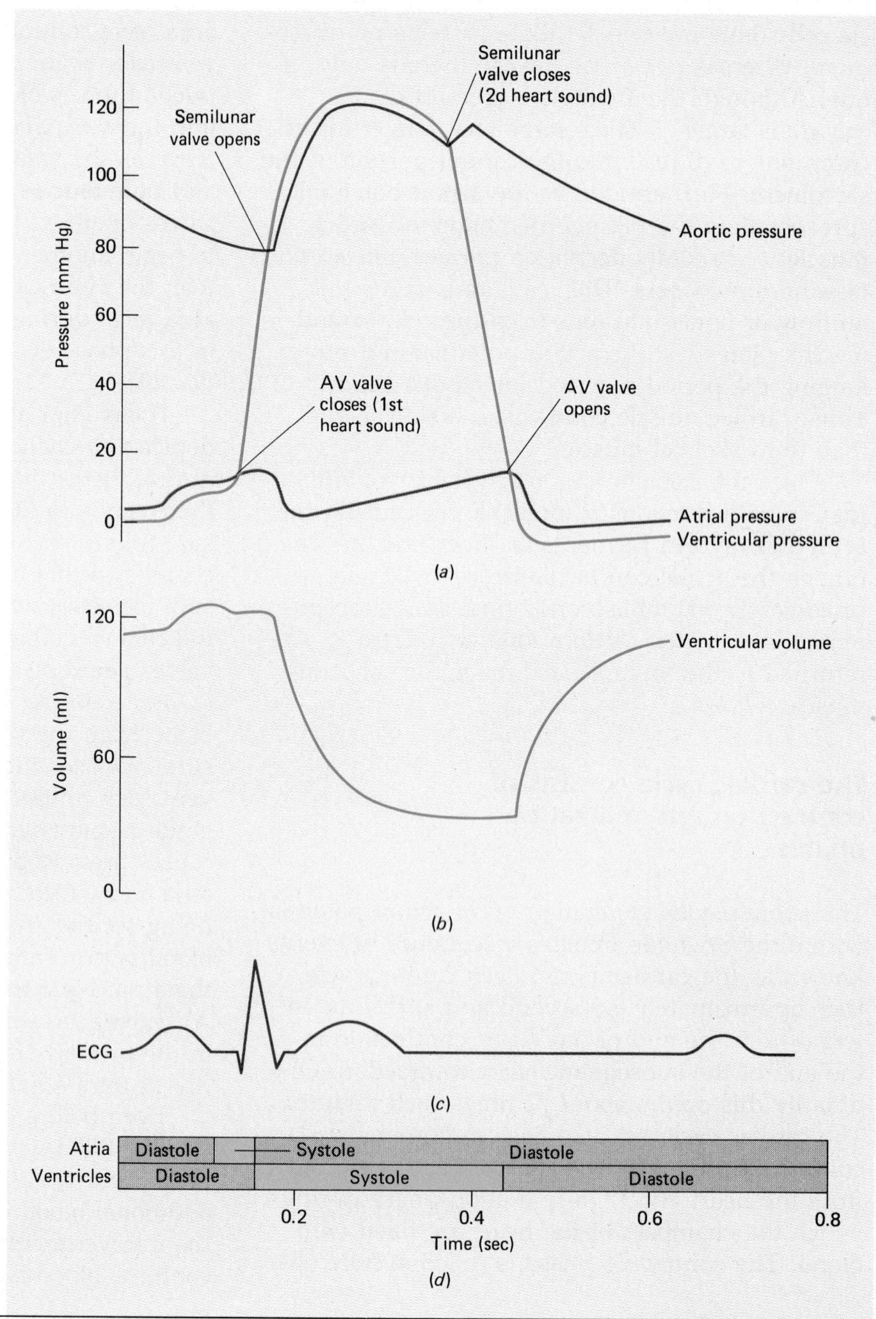

FIGURE 20-19

The cardiac cycle. (*a*) Pressure changes that occur in the left atrium, left ventricle, and aorta during a cardiac cycle. Notice the events that are responsible for the heart sounds. (*b*) Changes in the volume of blood in the left ventricle during the cardiac cycle. (*c*) A normal ECG in relation to the cardiac cycle. (*d*) Systole and diastole of the atria and ventricles related to time.

the tricuspid and mitral valves. It is a rather low-pitched and a relatively long sound which, as indicated in Figure 20-19, represents the beginning of ventricular systole.

The **second heart sound,** or "dub," marks the beginning of ventricular diastole. It is produced by closure of the aortic and pulmonary (pulmonic) semilunar valves when the intraventricular pressure begins to fall. This "dub" sound is typically heard as a sharp snap because the semilunar valves tend to close much more rapidly than the AV valves. Because diastole occupies more time than systole, a brief pause occurs after the second heart sound when the heart is beating at a normal rate. Therefore, the pattern that one hears is one of: "lub-dub" pause, "lub-dub" pause, and so on.

Sometimes, especially in young normal individuals, a **third heart sound** can be heard. This sound is produced by the very rapid influx of blood into the partially filled ventricle. It is typically very faint and as such difficult to hear except by the more seasoned health professional. See Focus on Abnormal Heart Sounds.

Cardiac output is a function of stroke volume and heart rate

Let us concentrate now on the work that is performed by the beating heart. The volume of blood pumped by one ventricle during one beat is called the **stroke volume.** Because cardiac work performance is typically related to a fixed time interval (i.e., one minute), one may calculate the **cardiac output** by simply multiplying the stroke volume by the number of times the ventricles beat per minute. Thus, the *cardiac output represents that volume of blood pumped by one ventricle in one minute.* For example, in a resting adult the heart might beat 72 times per minute and pump about 70 ml of blood with each ventricular contraction. This being the case,

$$\begin{aligned}\text{Cardiac output} &= \text{stroke volume} \times \text{heart rate (number of ventricular contractions/min)}\\ &= 70 \text{ ml/stroke} \times 72 \text{ strokes/min}\\ &= 5040 \text{ ml/min } (5.04 \text{ liters/min})\end{aligned}$$

FOCUS ON . . . Cardiac surface anatomy

It is important to know clinically where the structures of the heart lie beneath the body surface. In an average adult male, the apex of the heart is located a little below and medial to the left nipple, about 9 cm from the midline. The heartbeat (apex beat) can be seen and felt at the apex. The sternocostal surface of the heart can be projected on to the anterior chest wall, forming an irregular quadrangular area there.

The lower border of the heart extends from the apex to the right sixth costal cartilage; it corresponds to the lower margin of the right ventricle. The right border extends upward from the level of the sixth costal cartilage to the level of the upper border of the third costal cartilage. The left border may be represented by a line drawn from the apex upward and medially to the lower border of the second costal cartilage. The upper limits of the atria may be roughly represented by a line that joins the upper ends of the right and left borders.

The positions of the cardiac valves are shown in the figure. However, the best sites for listening to the valve sounds clinically are not directly over each valve; they are indicated by the positions of the letters A, P, T, and M (aortic, pulmonary, tricuspid, and mitral).

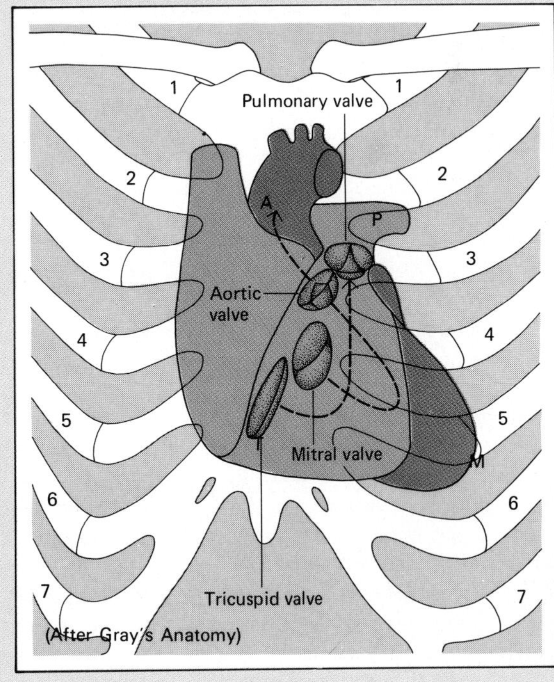

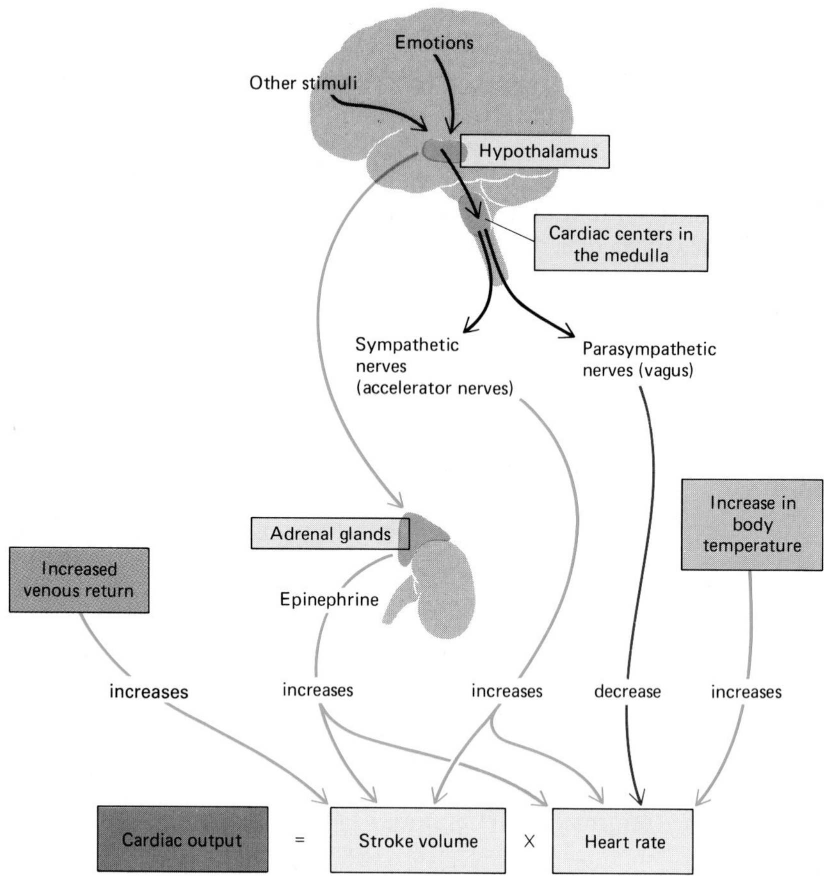

FIGURE 20-20

Some factors that influence cardiac output.

Although the cardiac output for the resting adult heart is ordinarily on the order of 5 to 6 liters per minute, during strenuous exercise the heart may increase its output four or five times. Simple multiplication demonstrates that under such conditions the heart may pump as much as 20 to 30 liters of blood per minute. Even more amazingly, the heart of a well-trained athlete can increase its output up to seven times.

The *maximum percentage that the cardiac output can be increased above normal* is defined as the **cardiac reserve.** Therefore, if during exercise the out-

FOCUS ON . . . Abnormal heart sounds

Abnormal heart sounds occur quite commonly, and certain ones provide the physician with valuable diagnostic information. One type, the **heart murmur,** is the result of turbulent blood flow. If this turbulence is of sufficient magnitude, it will generate vibrations that result in the production of sound waves. Even in a normal heart, during very strenuous exercise, a murmur may be heard. This is simply due to turbulence resulting from very rapidly flowing blood under such conditions. More typically, though, a murmur is indicative of valvular disease. When a valve does not close properly it permits a retrograde (backward) flow of blood. The ensuing turbulence leads to the production of a characteristic hissing sound.

Murmurs also occur when a valve becomes narrowed and its surface roughened. An example of such a disorder is **aortic valvular stenosis** (narrowing of the aortic semilunar valve), which impedes the flow of blood from the left ventricle into the aorta. Thus, during left ventricular systole, a tiny stream of blood is forced through a much narrowed opening but at a tremendous rate. The resulting turbulence within the lumen of the aorta sets up intense vibration and leads to a loud murmur.

It should be clear from the preceeding examples that significant information may be obtained about certain cardiac disorders by pinpointing the specific location of a murmur and observing its time of occurrence during the course of the cardiac cycle. (See Focus on Diseases of the Valves of the Heart.)

put can increase to a maximum of five times normal, the cardiac reserve is 400%. From the previous equation and from Figure 20-20, it should be clear that cardiac output varies as a function of either stroke volume or heart rate. Let us examine just how these two important variables are regulated.

Stroke volume is regulated largely by the volume of venous return and by the autonomic nervous system

Stroke volume, or the volume of blood pumped by one ventricle during one contraction, has a direct effect upon cardiac output. Although the ventricles do not eject all of their blood when they contract, the more forcefully they contract, the greater the volume of blood ejected. Moreover, the volume of blood returned to the heart via the great veins varies from time to time. Thus, *stroke volume is regulated mainly by venous return and by sympathetic stimulation.*

The volume of blood delivered to the heart by the great veins, the **venous return,** together with subsequent stretching of the cardiac muscle, is perhaps the most important determinant of cardiac output. *The greater the volume of blood returned to the heart via the veins, the greater the volume of blood pumped by the heart.* This relationship, known as **Starling's law of the heart,** permits the heart to pump all of the blood returned to it within physiological limits. As additional quantities of blood fill the chambers of the heart, cardiac muscle cells are stretched to a greater extent and subsequently contract with a greater force. Thus, increased quantities of blood are pumped into the arteries. Increasing the stroke volume in this manner can raise the normal output of 5 liters per min to a maximum output of approximately 14 liters per minute.

When the venous return is even greater, the heart is able to keep pace with the excessive volume only through **sympathetic stimulation,** leading to an increased heart rate and force of contraction. The release of norepinephrine by sympathetic nerve fibers not only increases heart rate but also increases the force of cardiac muscle contraction. This increased force of contraction is distinct from that which is brought about by an increased blood volume, as mentioned previously. *Epinephrine* (*ep*-i-**nef**-rin), a hormone released by the adrenal medulla, has a similar effect on cardiac muscle (see Chapter 18). Thus, when the force of contraction increases, the stroke volume increases, and this in turn leads to an increase in cardiac output.

Regulation of heart rate is influenced by several factors

You learned previously that the heart is capable of beating independently of its bodily control systems. However, in order to adapt its rate to the changing needs of the body, it is subject to the most careful regulation by the nervous system. Additional factors such as hormones, fluctuations in body temperature, and concentrations of various ions also influence heart rate.

THE AUTONOMIC NERVOUS SYSTEM IS RESPONSIBLE FOR NEURONAL CONTROL OF HEART RATE

The heart is innervated by both components of the autonomic nervous system. Parasympathetic fibers decrease heart rate, whereas sympathetic fibers increase heart rate. **Parasympathetic innervation** originates in the *cardiac inhibitory center* in the medulla and is conveyed to the heart by way of the vagus nerves (CN X). Both the SA and AV nodes are richly supplied with vagal fibers. There is a minor distribution of vagal fibers to muscle of the atria and ventricles. When these parasympathetic fibers are stimulated they release *acetylcholine,* which slows the heart rate. Normally, the parasympathetic innervation represents the dominant neural influence on the heart.

Maximal stimulation of vagal fibers can actually lead to a complete cessation of ventricular contraction. This can result from either a block in impulse transmission through the AV junctional fibers or complete inhibition of rhythmic signal generation by the SA node. Even with continued parasympathetic stimulation, the ventricles will begin to beat (10 to 40 beats per minute) after a short interval (typically 5 to 10 seconds). This phenomenon is called **ventricular escape** and is the result of new rhythmic impulses being generated in an abnormal site, for example, the AV bundle.

The heart receives its **sympathetic innervation** from nerves originating in the medulla *(cardiac accelerating center)* and upper thoracic spinal cord. These reach the myocardium via several nerves sometimes referred to as the **accelerator nerves.** Sympathetic fibers innervate SA and AV nodal tissue as well as cardiac muscle cells themselves. When stimulated, the sympathetic fibers release *norepinephrine,* which leads not only to an increase in heart rate, but to an increase in the strength of ventricular and atrial contraction as well. The heart rate may nearly triple, and the strength of contraction may nearly double, under the influence of maximal sympathetic stimulation.

Various parts of the circulatory system relay messages (e.g., regarding blood pressure) to the cardiac centers, which respond by sending messages to the heart via the vagus nerves. In this manner the cardiac centers are responsible for maintaining a balance between the inhibitory effects of the parasympathetic nerves and the stimulatory effects of the sympathetic nerves. When the parasympathetic messages decrease, the sympathetic nerves are able to function in an unopposed manner and thereby increase the heart rate. For example, severance of vagal nerve fibers results in an increased heart rate.

HEART RATE IS INFLUENCED BY VARIOUS HORMONES

Under conditions of stress, *epinephrine* and *norepinephrine* are released from the tissues of the adrenal medulla into the general circulation. Each of these hormones produces an increase in heart rate. Thyroid hormones, *thyroxine* and *triiodothyronine,* also accelerate the heart rate and this is most likely due to a direct effect of these substances on the heart. The strength of heart contraction is also modulated by thyroid hormones. In slight excess they increase the strength of contraction, whereas in marked excess they actually reduce the strength of contraction.

BODY TEMPERATURE AFFECTS HEART RATE

Elevation of the body temperature markedly increases the heart rate. This most probably results from an increased permeability of cardiac muscle-cell plasma membranes to the passage of various ions, thereby causing an accelerated generation of rhythmic action potentials. During fever, for example, it is not uncommon for the individual to experience a heart rate in excess of 100 beats per minute. *Lowering of the body temperature,* or **hypothermia,** is accompanied by a reduction in heart rate. This latter observation is taken advantage of clinically, for example, when the patient's temperature is deliberately lowered during heart surgery.

FLUCTUATIONS IN ION CONCENTRATIONS ALSO INFLUENCE HEART RATE

The effects of calcium, potassium, and sodium on action potentials and membrane potentials were addressed previously in Chapter 12. Furthermore, the importance of calcium ions in the contraction of skeletal muscle has been discussed in Chapter 10, and their role in cardiac muscle contraction was indicated earlier in the present chapter. It should be apparent then that the concentrations of these particular ions within the extracellular environment may have a significant influence on cardiac function. Ordinarily the concentrations of these ions are kept within appropriate limits and thus do not affect the heart adversely. However, in instances where their concentration becomes excessive or deficient, cardiac function may be seriously affected.

An excess of potassium ions in the extracellular environment markedly reduces the heart rate as well as the strength of contraction. On the other hand, spastic contraction of the heart results from the presence of excess calcium ions. This typically results from the direct effects of calcium ions upon the contractile process of cardiac muscle. A marked reduction in the calcium ion concentration has effects similar to those observed with high potassium levels.

Excessive levels of sodium ions result in depression of cardiac function, which is thought to stem from their competition with calcium ions at some critical site during the contractile process. At the other extreme, a deficiency of sodium ions in the extracellular environment leads to the development of a potentially lethal condition called **cardiac fibrillation** (fih-bril-**lay**-shun). In this situation, the cardiac muscle contracts at an extremely high rate and in an uncoordinated fashion such that little or no blood is actually pumped by the heart.

SEX AND AGE ARE IMPORTANT CONSIDERATIONS WITH REGARD TO HEART RATE

The heart rate is also influenced by the sex and the age of an individual. In adult females the heart rate is typically 70 to 80 beats per minute. In adult males it is somewhat slower, approximately 70 beats per minute. The infant heart beats about 120 times per minute, and that of a child about 77 times per minute. Although the adult heart beats approximately 72 times per minute, its rate does slow somewhat with advancing age.

Additional factors also affect cardiac output

The heart of a trained athlete will actually undergo enlargement (up to 50% in extreme cases) and increase its pumping efficiency. Even under resting conditions, such a heart is capable of pumping more than 20 liters of blood per minute without the assistance of sympathetic stimulation. Thus, the heart (and pulse) rate of the trained athlete at rest is frequently less than 50 beats per minute. Moreover, in the athlete this resting heart rate increases less during exercise than in the untrained individual.

Conditions sometimes develop in which the volume of venous return to the heart is markedly reduced (e.g., during hemorrhage), and cardiac output is significantly decreased. A diseased heart is simply not able to pump all of the blood delivered to it—a condition called **cardiac failure.** Furthermore, since the right and left halves of the heart really represent two distinct and separate pumps, either may fail independently of the other. Any condition that impairs the ability of the heart to pump blood can lead to the onset of cardiac failure. Cardiac valvular disease, congenital malformations of the heart, reduced coronary blood flow, and hypertension are but a few of the causes of cardiac failure.

The normal electrocardiogram consists of a P wave, QRS complex, and a T wave

The waves of depolarization that spread through the heart during each cardiac cycle generate electrical currents, which in turn spread through the interstitial fluid and onto the body's surface. Recording electrodes, placed on the surface of the body on opposite sides of the heart, are used to detect such electrical potentials. These signals are then transmitted to an **electrocardiograph,** which amplifies and records the electrical activity. The record that results from this procedure is termed an **electrocardiogram (ECG,** or **EKG).** If desired, the output of the electrocardiograph may also be tape recorded. Oscilloscopes, rather than ink-writing electrocardiographs, are often used in operating rooms and in intensive-care facilities to continuously monitor heart function by displaying a moving beam of electrons on a screen. The pattern of the electron beam reflects the difference in electrical potential between the electrodes (electrocardiographic leads) located on various parts of the body.

Calibration lines are present on all electrocardiograms (Fig. 20-21). Those placed horizontally are utilized for voltage determination. Typically these are arranged such that 1 millivolt is equivalent to a deflection of 10 small divisions in either the upward (positive) or downward (negative) direction. The voltages obtained during a normal electrocardiogram are dependent upon the placement of the recording electrodes (leads) on the body's surface. Vertically placed lines on the electrocardiogram are used for time calibration. Typically, one inch in the horizontal direction is equivalent to 1 second. Each inch is divided into five segments representing 0.2 second. These smaller units are further subdivided into units representing 0.04 seconds each. The elements of voltage and time are important components for the proper interpretation of the electrocardiogram.

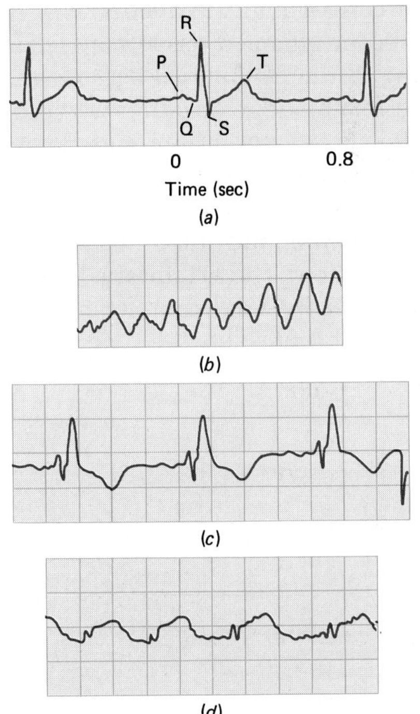

FIGURE 20-21

Electrocardiograms. (*a*) Normal. (*b*) Ventricular fibrillation. (*c*) Right bundle branch block. (*d*) Myocardial infarction. Some of the cardiac muscle has been damaged during a "heart attack." Notice the marked ST interval.

The normal electrocardiogram (Fig. 20-21*a*) consists of three basic features, a **P wave,** a **QRS complex,** and a **T wave.** It is not uncommon for the QRS complex to be seen as three separate waves. The electrical currents produced as the atrial muscle cells depolarize prior to contraction lead to the generation of the **P wave.** This is followed by the **QRS complex** and results from currents generated as the ventricles depolarize prior to their contraction. Hence, both the *P wave and the QRS complex represent depolarization waves.* Subsequent to ventricular contraction, the ventricles repolarize, and the electrical currents that are produced generate the **T wave.** Therefore, the *T wave is one of repolarization* and typically occurs 0.25 to 0.35 second following ventricular depolarization.

As indicated above, the shapes of the different waves and the time intervals between them are crucial in the proper evaluation of the electrocardiogram. The interval between the beginning of the P wave and the beginning of the QRS complex is designated by the **PQ interval.** Repolarization of the atria is also masked by the QRS complex. Since the Q wave is often absent, it is also termed the **PR interval** and represents the duration of time (normally about 0.16 second) between the onset of atrial contraction and the onset of ventricular contraction. In patients with heart disease, scarred or inflamed tissue may lead to a lengthening of the PR interval because more time is required for the depolarization wave to spread through the atrial myocardium and the AV node.

The time required for the generation of the QRS complex is termed the **QRS duration** and represents the amount of time needed for ventricular depolarization. The **QT interval** extends from the beginning of the QRS complex to the end of the T wave and represents the time required for ventricular contraction and repolarization. Typically, the normal QT interval lasts for approximately 0.35 second. The **ST interval** represents the time required for the ventricles to repolarize and extends from the S wave to the termination of the T wave.

Clinically, the electrocardiogram is probably the single most useful indicator of cardiac function. All parameters of heart function tend to be reflected in the electrocardiogram. Any alteration in the transmission of impulses through the heart can result in abnormal electrical currents in tissues adjacent to the heart. Such abnormal electrical currents will be reflected in altered shapes of waves appearing on the electrocardiogram.

Disturbances occur in heart rate and rhythm

In the general population, individuals with normal hearts may have either very rapid or very slow heart rates. However, in many instances such extremes may be indicative of very serious cardiac disorders. **Tachycardia** (from *tachy,* fast, and *cardia,* heart; *tak*-e-**kar**-de-ah) refers to a fast heart rate, typically designated as more than 100 beats per minute. Figure 20-22*a* illustrates what an electrocardiogram obtained from an individual with tachycardia would look like. Tachycardia may result from fever, stimulation of cardiac sympathetic nerves, certain hormones or drugs, or may be caused by weakening of the heart muscle itself. When the myocardium is unable to pump blood effectively, homeostatic reflexes are activated that subsequently increase the heart rate.

The term **bradycardia** (from *brady,* meaning slow; *brad*-e-**kar**-de-ah) is usually employed to designate a heart rate of less than 60 beats per

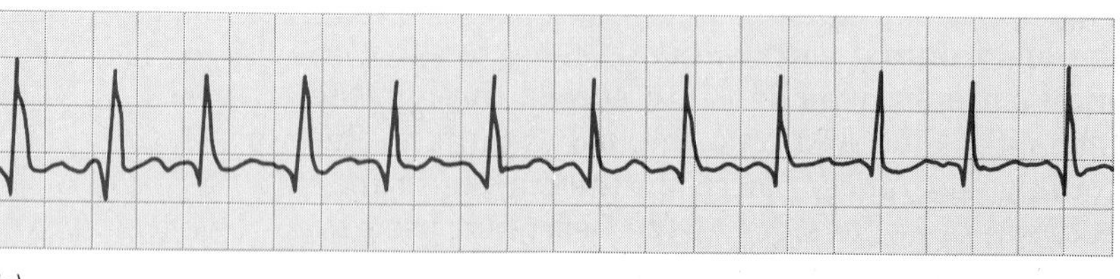

(*a*)

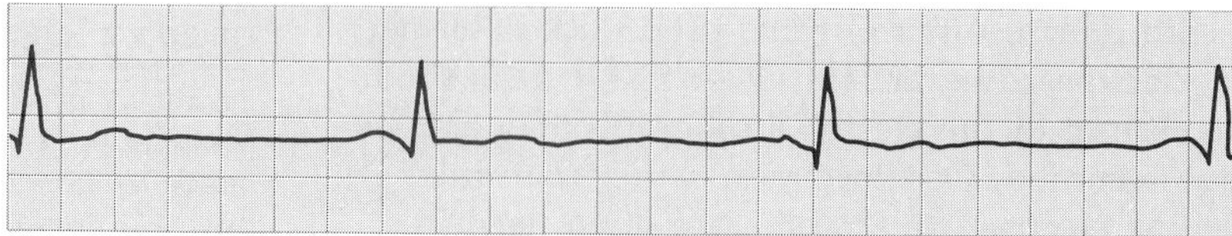

(*b*)

FIGURE 20-22

Electrocardiograms illustrating (*a*) tachycardia and (*b*) bradycardia.

minute and is a condition common to athletes. Remember that the heart of an athlete generally pumps a greater stroke volume output per beat than that of the nonathlete. However, bradycardia may also result from decreased body temperature, certain drugs, or via stimulation of the heart by its parasympathetic nerve fibers (vagus nerve; CN X). Bradycardia may occur in patients with atherosclerotic lesions of the carotid sinus region of the carotid artery. (The carotid sinus will be discussed in Chapter 21.) A person with bradycardia would have an electrocardiogram similar to that illustrated in Figure 20-22*b*.

Arrhythmia (ah-**rith**-me-ah) is the term applied to any alteration in the normal rhythm of the heart beat. In the condition known as **atrial flutter** the atria may contract as much as 300 times per minute, that is, contracting two or three times for each ventricular contraction. Even though the atria beat at an excessively high rate, the waves of contraction occur in a synchronous manner. This particular arrhythmia is frequently due to dilation of the atria as a result of cardiac valvular disease.

The heart also beats very rapidly in a condition termed **fibrillation.** However, in this instance the waves of contraction are asynchronous. Numerous small waves of depolarization may spread in all directions throughout the myocardium so that the heart is unable to contract as a whole, with the result that blood cannot be pumped. A patient with **atrial fibrillation** may tolerate the condition for many years since venous pressure continues to force blood into the ventricles. Although the effectiveness of the heart may be reduced to approximately 30%, this level of cardiac function is still compatible with life.

Ventricular fibrillation, on the other hand, is a life-threatening condition because no blood is pumped into the arteries (Fig. 20-21*b*). Approximately one out of every four persons dies in ventricular fibrillation. There are several causes of this condition, including electrical shock, inadequate oxygen supply to the myocardium, heart attacks, trauma, and the effects of certain drugs. A heart in ventricular fibrillation is unable to restore its normal rhythm by itself.

Clinical highlight

The heart can be **defibrillated** by applying a brief but strong electrical current to the chest wall. This stimulates depolarization of all the cardiac muscle fibers simultaneously, so that all contractions momentarily cease. If the SA node then begins to function, normal cardiac rhythm may be reestablished.

When the transmission of an action potential becomes delayed or blocked at some point in the conduction system, a condition known as **heart block** ensues. **Sinoatrial block** (*si*-no-**a**-tre-al) is a rare condition in which the impulse generated in the SA node is prevented from entering the atrial muscle. The ventricles may acquire a new rhythm, usually from the AV node, and continue to beat, although at a slower pace.

Conditions that decrease or completely block the transmission of an impulse through the atrioventricular bundle of His result in what is termed **atrioventricular heart block.** If transmission is not completely interrupted, the condition is known as **incomplete heart block.** Several conditions may either block or lead to a significant delay in the rate of conduction through the AV bundle and these include: (1) lack of adequate blood supply (ischemia) to AV nodal fibers, which may be the result of coronary artery insufficiency; (2) presence of scar tissue, which may lead to compression of the AV bundle; (3) inflammatory processes involving the AV bundle or the AV node; (4) excessive stimulation of vagus nerve (CN X) fibers. Two forms of heart block, first-degree and second-degree, are of the incomplete type.

Ordinarily, the time interval between the initiation of the P wave and the initiation of the QRS complex is approximately 0.16 second. This interval (PR interval) may vary somewhat with the heart rate. However, if it exceeds 0.20 second in an individual with a normal heart rate, the person is considered to have **first-degree heart block.**

Second-degree heart block is a condition in which some atrial impulses reach the ventricles while others do not. This typically occurs when the PR interval is between 0.25 and 0.45 second. As a result the atria may beat two or three times before the ventricles do. This type of heart block yields a characteristic ECG pattern wherein QRS complexes may be "dropped" following some of the P waves (Figure 20-23*a*). If every other QRS complex is dropped, the heart is said to have a 2:1 rhythm with regard to atrial beats and ventricular beats, respectively. It is not uncommon for individuals with second-degree heart block to develop 3:2 or even 3:1 rhythms. Lastly, should a block occur within one of the Purkinje bundles (**right** or **left bundle branch block**), the ventricles may not contract synchronously (Fig. 20-21*c*). In this instance an impulse may spread through one ventricle more rapidly than through the other. The resulting ECG pattern would exhibit an abnormally long QRS complex (Fig. 20-21*c*).

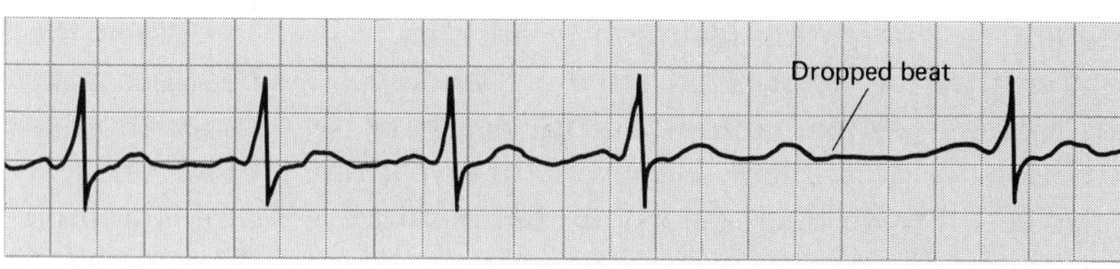

(a)

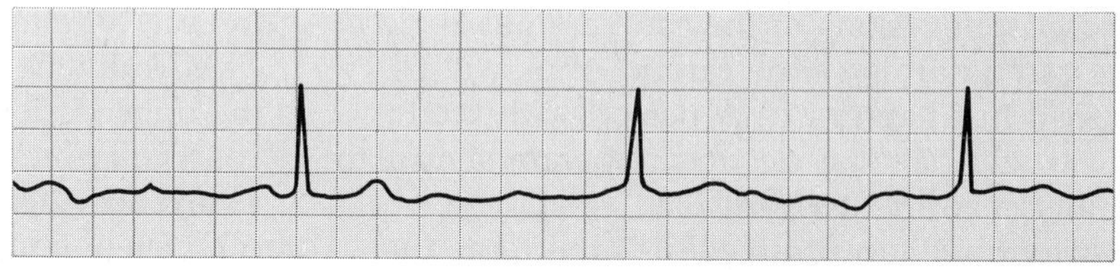

(b)

FIGURE 20-23

Electrocardiograms illustrating (*a*) second degree heart block and (*b*) complete heart block.

Should the conditions leading to delayed conduction in the AV node or AV bundle become very severe, a total block of impulses traveling from the atria to the ventricles may occur. This is considered as **complete AV heart block,** or **third-degree heart block** (Fig. 20-23*b*). The atria continue to beat at their normal rate or even at an accelerated rate (sometimes as high as 100 times per minute). The ventricles also beat, but much slower than normal (typically about 40 beats per minute). In this form of heart block the ventricles beat independent of the atria and utilize impulses generated by the AV node as their pacemaker. They have, in a sense, escaped from their normal atrial control.

Clinical highlight

Some individuals exhibit a special form of third-degree heart block in which the total block occurs periodically. In such cases the ventricles stop beating for approximately three to five seconds, the brain is deprived of blood, and the person typically faints. Subsequently, as a result of ventricular "escape," blood flow to the brain resumes and the individual recovers from the faint. Patients who suffer from periodic fainting spells as a result of this form of heart block are said to exhibit the **Stokes-Adams syndrome.**

Clinical highlight

Artificial pacemakers are frequently implanted in individuals with severe heart-block syndromes. Such a procedure involves the implantation of the pacemaker beneath the skin and connection of its electrodes to the heart. The pacemaker serves as an external source of continuous, rhythmic impulses to drive the heart at a normal rate and with a normal rhythm.

Impulses may also arise in regions of the heart other than the SA node. These are considered as **ectopic foci** and they typically generate impulses at irregular times during the normal cardiac rhythm. Such foci have the potential of initiating premature or **ectopic beats.** As a result of the refractory period that follows the premature ectopic beat, the onset of the next normal beat is generally delayed. When the next beat does occur, it may be unusually strong and startling, giving rise to a pounding sensation within the chest. Although the premature ectopic beats are not serious in themselves, they may be indicative of underlying heart damage. Conditions that may lead to the production of ectopic foci include (1) development of calcified regions within the heart that press upon and irritate cardiac muscle fibers, (2) focal areas of ischemia, (3) stress, and (4) abnormal AV node stimulation resulting from the toxic effects of caffeine, nicotine, and certain drugs.

Summary

I. The heart is a hollow, muscular organ that lies within the mediastinum between the lungs. Its apex is directed downward and to the left, and its base is directed upward, posteriorly, and to the right.
   A. The heart is enclosed within a sac called the pericardium. The pericardium consists of parietal and visceral portions that are separated by the pericardial cavity.
   B. The bulk of the heart wall consists of the myocardium, or middle muscular layer. The endocardium is the innermost region of the heart wall and lines the chambers of the heart. It consists of an endothelial lining resting upon a thin layer of connective tissue. The outermost layer, or epicardium, is represented by the visceral pericardium, that is, the serous lining of the pericardial cavity that is reflected onto the heart and beginning of the great vessels.
   C. The heart has four chambers: right and left atria, which receive blood returning to the heart; and right and left ventricles, which pump blood out into the great arteries.
   D. The opening between each atrium and ventricle is guarded by an atrioventricular (AV) valve, which prevents regurgitation of blood into the atria.
      1. The AV valve between the right atrium and right ventricle is termed the tricuspid valve.
      2. The AV valve between the left atrium and left ventricle is termed the bicuspid, or mitral, valve.
   E. The semilunar valves (aortic and pulmonary) are located between each ventricle and the artery into which it pumps blood.
      1. The aortic valve is situated between the left ventricle and the ascending aorta.
      2. The pulmonary (pulmonic) valve is situated between the right ventricle and the pulmonary trunk.
   F. The heart muscle itself receives its blood supply from a pair of coronary arteries and is drained by accompanying cardiac veins.

II. The heart has its own conduction system and can beat independently of its nerve supply. However, elaborate mechanisms exist to regulate the heartbeat so that its rate and strength of contraction adjust to the changing needs of the body.
   A. Each heartbeat is initiated in the sinoatrial (SA) node. The action potential spreads through the atria, causing atrial contraction. One group of fibers conducts the action potential to the AV node. From here it spreads through the Purkinje fibers and ultimately reaches the ordinary fibers of the ventricles.
   B. The sequence of events that occurs during one complete heartbeat is termed a cardiac cycle.
      1. Each cardiac cycle begins with the generation of an action potential in the SA node that results in atrial systole.
      2. Additional blood is forced into the ventricles as the atria undergo contraction.
      3. Ventricular systole occurs next, forcing blood through the semilunar valves into the systemic and pulmonary circulations. Simultaneously, the atria have returned to diastole and are again filling with blood.
      4. As the ventricles enter diastole, the aortic and pulmonic valves close, while the tricuspid and mitral valves open once again.
   C. The first heart sound results from closure of the AV valves and is heard as a "lub" with the aid of a stethoscope. Closure of the semilunar valves produces the second heart sound and is heard as a "dub."
   D. Cardiac output is defined as the amount of blood pumped by one ventricle in a period of 1 minute. According to Starling's law of the heart, the more blood returned to the heart by the veins, the greater the volume of blood that will be pumped during the next ventricular systole.
   E. Cardiac output equals stroke volume multiplied by heart rate.
      1. Stroke volume depends upon venous return and sympathetic stimulation.
      2. Heart rate is regulated mainly by sympathetic and parasympathetic nerves but is influenced by hormones, body temperature, sex, age, and the concentration of certain ions such as calcium, potassium, and sodium.
   F. An electrocardiogram (ECG) begins with a P wave, representing the spread of an impulse throughout the atria just prior to atrial contraction. This is followed by a QRS complex, which indicates that the impulse has entered and is spreading throughout the ventricular walls prior to the onset of ventricular contraction. The T wave is seen next and represents ventricular repolarization.
   G. Common cardiac arrhythmias include flutter, fibrillation, ectopic beats, and various forms of heart block.
   H. Ischemic heart disease has several causes. Most often it is of a chronic nature, although it may occur acutely.

Post-test

1. The heart is located within the chest cavity in a region termed the ______.
2. The heart lies within a tough sac called the ______.
3. The major portion of the heart wall is made up of cardiac muscle and is termed the ______.
4. The partition that separates the ventricles from each other is termed the ______ ______.
5. The right AV valve is typically called the ______ valve, and the left AV valve is known as either the ______ or ______ valve.
6. The aortic and pulmonary (pulmonic) valves are also known as the ______ valves.
7. Cusps of the AV valves are anchored to papillary muscles by the ______ ______.
8. The ______ ______ is called the pacemaker of the heart.
9. Cardiac muscle fibers are separated from one another by specialized cellular junctions called ______ discs.
10. The action potential spreads from the AV node to the ventricles by specialized muscle fibers known as ______ fibers.
11. The right and left coronary arteries arise from the ______.
12. During the cardiac cycle the period of contraction is termed ______, and the period of relaxation is called ______.
13. The volume of blood pumped by one ventricle during one beat is the ______ ______.
14. The volume of blood pumped by one ventricle during one minute is the ______ ______.
15. Heart rate is slowed by ______ nerves and is increased by ______ nerves.
16. Norepinephrine increases both the heart rate and its ______ of contraction.
17. An ECG begins with a ______ wave, which represents the spread of an action potential over the ______.
18. The condition in which the heart beats greater than 100 times per minute is termed ______.
19. If the heart beats very rapidly in an uncoordinated manner, it is said to be in ______.
20. Label the following diagram.

Review questions

1. Compare and contrast the parietal and visceral pericardium.
2. Relate the structure of the heart wall to the heart's function.
3. Compare and contrast the structural and physiological differences between skeletal and cardiac muscle.
4. Describe the conduction system of the heart.
5. Describe the arterial supply and venous drainage of the heart itself.
6. Trace the blood flow through the heart chambers, describing the events of the cardiac cycle.
7. Describe stroke volume and cardiac output and relate both to Starling's law of the heart.
8. Describe the regulation of heart rate by sympathetic and parasympathetic innervation.
9. Compare and contrast the characteristic waves of a normal ECG.
10. Describe how each of the following influences cardiac output: (a) release of epinephrine during stress, (b) elevated body temperature, (c) athletic training.
11. Describe ischemic heart disease, including some of its causes.
12. Compare and contrast the effects of calcium, potassium, and sodium ions on heart function.
13. Compare and contrast the following: (a) first-degree heart block, (b) second-degree heart block, and (c) third-degree heart block.
14. Describe the potential causes of premature ectopic heartbeats.
15. Describe atrial flutter and atrial fibrillation.
16. Describe the physiological significance of intercalated discs.
17. Discuss the reason for cardiac muscle being referred to as a functional syncytium.
18. Draw a graphic representation of the cardiac cycle comparing atrial pressure, ventricular pressure, aortic pressure, and ventricular volume. Indicate where the semilunar and AV valves open and close.

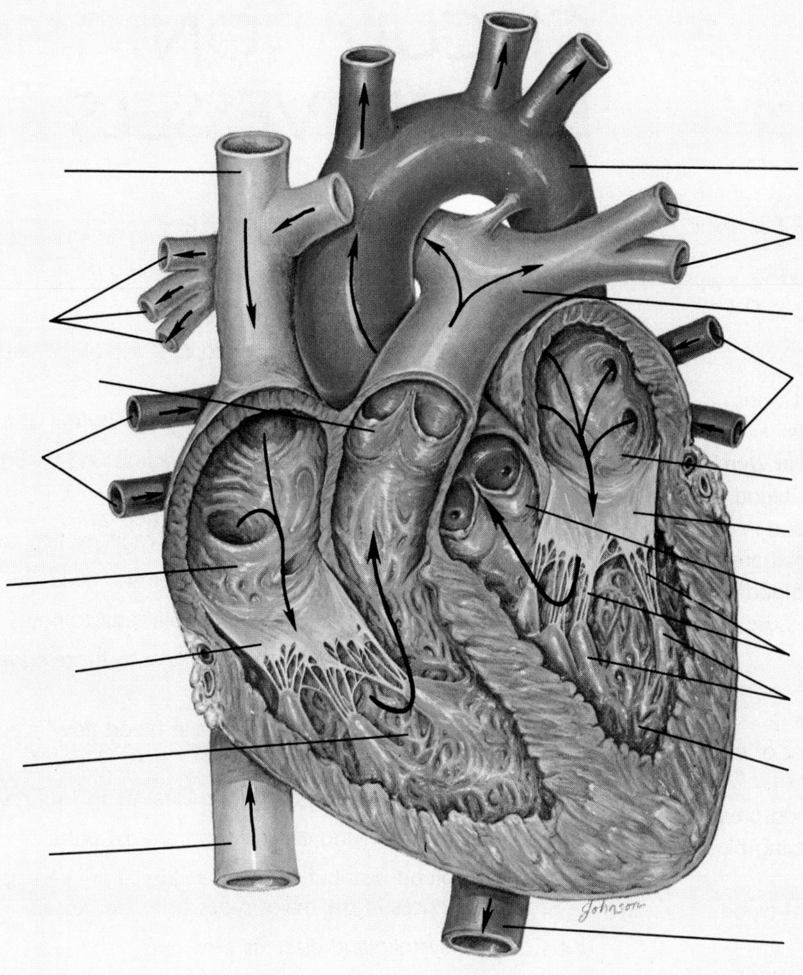

Post-test answers

1. mediastinum **2.** pericardium **3.** myocardium **4.** interventricular septum **5.** tricuspid; bicuspid, mitral **6.** semilunar **7.** chordae tendineae **8.** sinoatrial (SA) node **9.** intercalated **10.** Purkinje **11.** aorta (ascending) **12.** systole; diastole **13.** stroke volume **14.** cardiac output **15.** parasympathetic; sympathetic **16.** force **17.** P; atria **18.** tachycardia **19.** fibrillation **20.** See Figure 20-6.

CIRCULATION: THE BLOOD VESSELS

CHAPTER OUTLINE

I. Blood vessel types
- A. Blood vessel wall
- B. Arteries
- C. Capillaries
- D. Venules and veins
- E. Anastomoses

II. General vascular dynamics
- A. Principles of blood flow
- B. Blood distribution
- C. Cross-sectional area
- D. Velocity of blood
- E. Vascular pressure differences
- F. Pulse

III. Blood pressure
- A. Measurement of blood pressure
- B. Systemic blood pressures
- C. Factors affecting blood pressure
- D. Regulation of blood pressure

IV. Capillary exchanges
- A. Gases and nutrients
- B. Fluid movement

V. Venous return

VI. Pathways of circulation
- A. Pulmonary circulation
- B. Systemic circulation

VII. Tables and figures of major systemic arteries and veins
- A. Major systemic arteries
- B. Major systemic veins
- C. Cerebral circulation
- D. Hepatic portal system

VIII. Cardiovascular disease
- □ Focus on clinical terms related to the heart and circulation
- A. Hypertension
- B. Atherosclerosis
- C. Ischemic heart disease
- □ Focus on bypass surgery

IX. Aging of the cardiovascular system

X. Vascular system development

LEARNING OBJECTIVES

After you have studied this chapter you should be able to:

1 Define the artery, capillary, and vein.

2 Compare the anatomical dimensions of the blood vessels and compare the tunics of different blood vessels.

3 Differentiate between elastic arteries, distributing arteries, and arterioles.

4 Explain the significance of vasoconstriction and vasodilation.

5 Compare the two types of capillaries.

6 Relate the anatomical framework of a capillary bed to its function.

7 Explain the importance of valves in veins.

8 Compare the different types of vascular anastomoses.

9 Compare the relationship of blood flow to a pressure gradient and to resistance.

10 Discuss why the pressure gradient in blood flow is equal to the mean arterial pressure.

11 Discuss the major factors affecting total peripheral resistance.

12 Explain the underlying causes of an arterial pulse.

13 Contrast blood distribution, cross-sectional area, velocity of blood, and pressure differences in the major types of blood vessels.

14 Compare systolic and diastolic pressures.

15 Define pulse pressure and mean arterial pressure.

16 Explain how the factors affecting cardiac output and peripheral resistance can alter blood pressure.

17 Give the physiological sequence of events occurring upon stimulation of the vasomotor center of the medulla.

18 Give the physiological sequence of events for baroreceptor and chemoreceptor regulation of blood pressure.

19 Explain the intrinsic controls of blood vessels in regulating blood pressure.

20 Explain the exchange of gases and nutrients at the systemic capillaries.

21 Compare the hydrostatic pressures and osmotic pressures operating at the capillary, and relate them to fluid filtration and absorption.

22 Explain the various mechanisms for returning venous blood to the heart.

23 Compare the pulmonary circulation to the systemic circulation.

24 Give the physiological sequence of events operating in nonprogressive and progressive circulatory shock.

25 Trace blood flow through the major arteries and veins of the body.

26 Define the risk factors for and the development of atherosclerosis.

27 Differentiate between the types of hypertension and describe ischemic heart disease, angina pectoris, and myocardial infarction.

Circulatory pattern of the head obtained by means of radio-opaque contrast media. (Manfred Kage/Peter Arnold, Inc.)

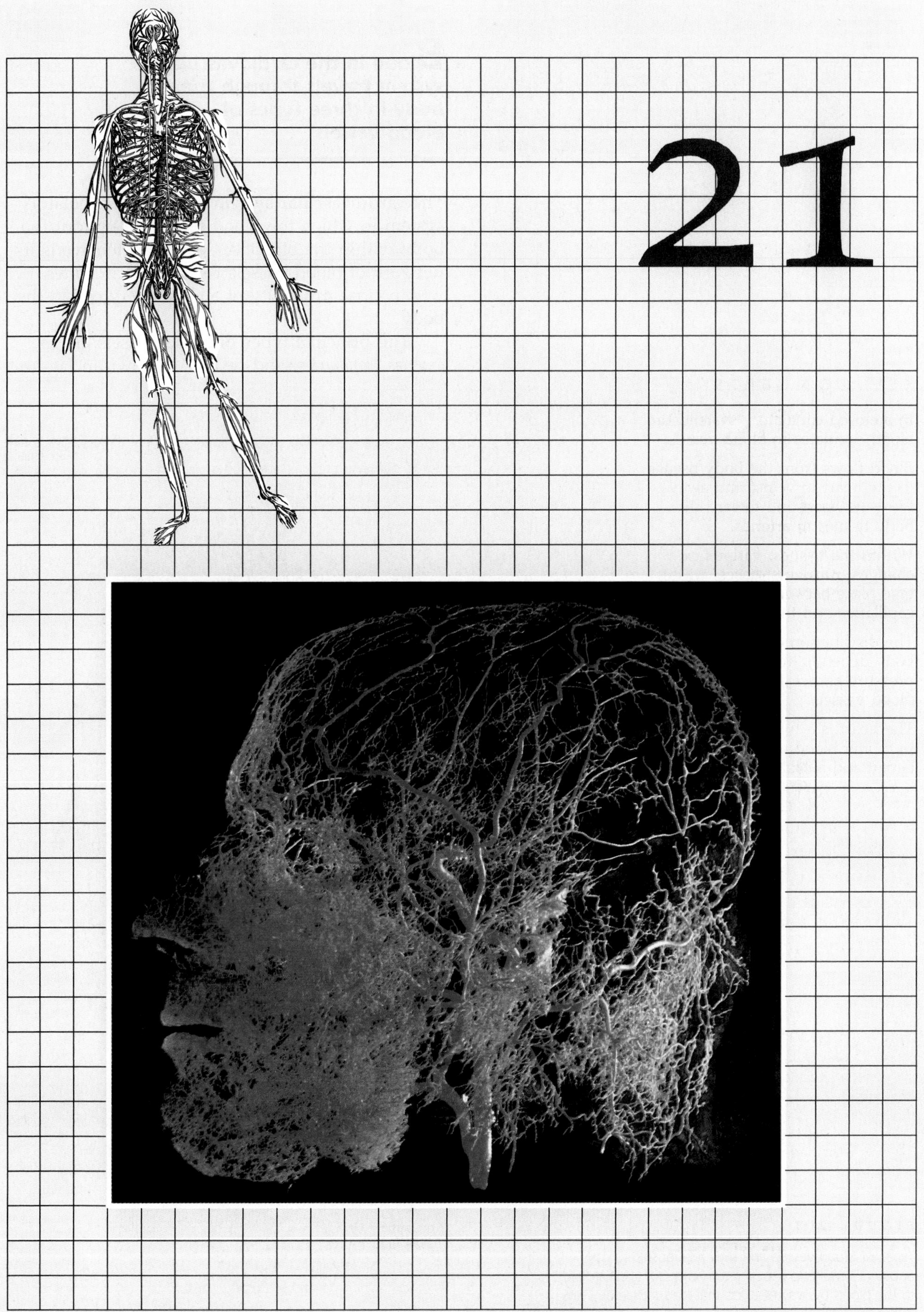

21

Blood in the cardiovascular system travels through the body in three types of blood vessels

The **cardiovascular system** is a closed circulatory system in which the blood flows throughout the body within the blood vessels. So extensive is its network of blood vessels that blood circulates within close proximity of almost every cell in the body.

The principal types of blood vessels are the *arteries, capillaries,* and *veins.* As shown in Figure

KEY CONCEPTS

In a closed circulatory system, the blood circulates in blood vessels.

Blood flows from the body tissues to the heart in veins, and away from the heart and toward the body tissues in arteries.

Within the tissues, various exchanges (nutrients, gases, wastes) take place between the blood in the capillaries and the tissue cells.

The distribution of blood in the body depends upon differences in pressure and resistance in the blood vessels.

The heart is a two-pump system pumping blood into a pulmonary circuit and a systemic circuit.

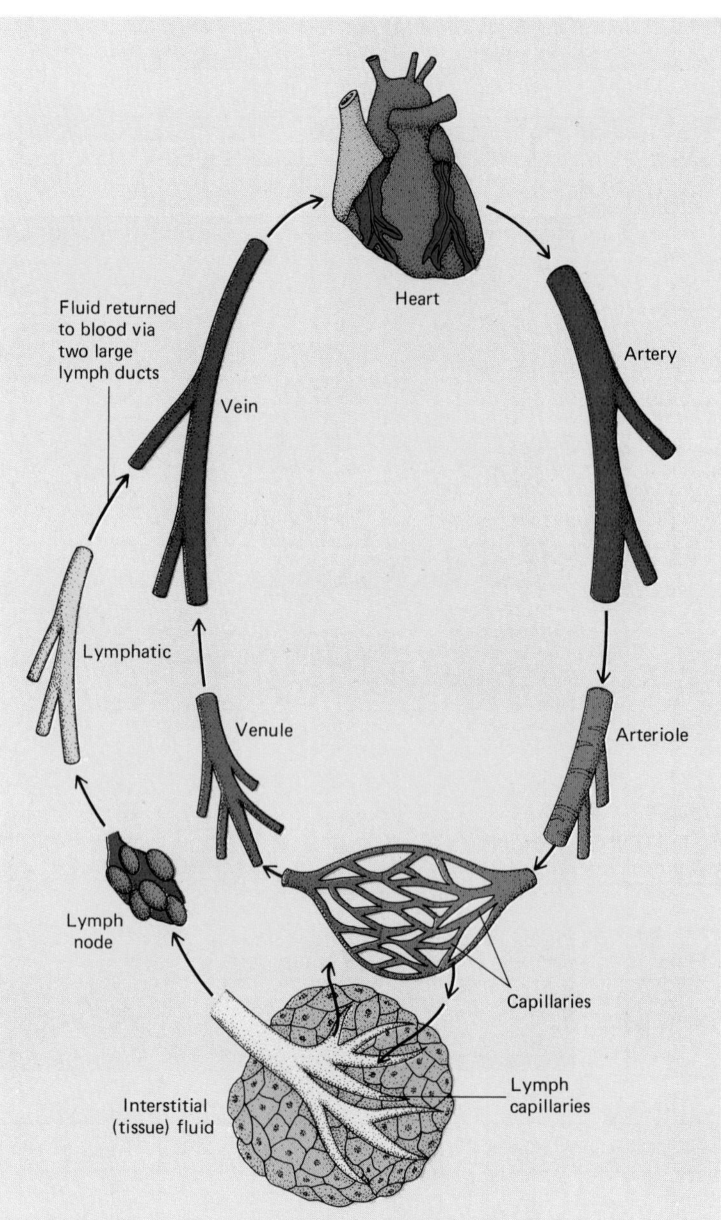

FIGURE 21-1

Types of blood vessels and their relationship to one another. Lymphatic vessels return excess interstitial fluid to the blood by way of ducts that lead into large veins in the shoulder region.

21-1, the heart delivers blood into the **arteries.** These vessels branch into smaller arteries and, eventually, into the **arterioles** (ar-**teer**-ee-olz), which distribute the blood to the various tissues and organs of the body. From the arterioles, blood flows through **capillaries,** in which various exchanges take place between the blood and the tissue cells. The capillaries form extensive networks within each tissue. Blood passes from the capillaries into **venules** (**ven**-yoolz) and then is conducted back toward the heart by larger and larger **veins.** The different types of blood vessels vary anatomically with respect to their length, diameter, thickness, and the composition of their walls (Table 21-1).

The blood vessel wall consists of tunics

The wall of an artery or a vein has three layers, or **tunics:** an internal tunica intima, a middle tunica media, and an external tunica adventitia (Fig. 21-2). The **tunica intima** (**too**-nih-kuh **in**-tih-muh), or **tunica interna,** consists of (1) a lining of endothelium (simple squamous epithelium) that is in contact with the blood in the **lumen** (space inside) of the vessel, and (2) an underlying thin layer of connective tissue rich in elastic fibers, called the **internal elastic membrane (basement membrane).** The tunica intima is an extension of the endocardial lining of the heart and is the only tunic that is present in all types of blood vessels.

Tunica media (**me**-dee-uh) consists of elastic connective tissue and circular smooth muscle cells. In large arteries the tunica media is the thickest layer and contains several layers of elastic fibers. The smooth muscle of the tunica media is innervated by sympathetic nerves of the autonomic nervous system.

Tunica adventitia (*ad*-ven-**tih**-shuh), or **tunica externa,** is a relatively thin layer in arteries but is the thickest layer in the walls of large veins. It consists mainly of elastic and collagen fibers. Nerves, lymphatic vessels, and even tiny blood vessels are found within the connective tissue of tunica adventitia. These tiny blood vessels are located in the walls of large arteries and veins and nourish the cells of the walls. Such vessels are called the **vasa vasorum** (**va**-suh va-**sor**-um), which means "vessels of the vessels."

TABLE 21-1

Types of blood vessels

Type of vessel	Function	Description
Artery	Conducts blood away from the heart	Wall has three layers: the tunica intima consists of an endothelial lining with some connective tissue beneath; the tunica media consists of smooth muscle and connective tissue, mainly elastic fibers; the tunica adventitia consists of connective tissue rich in elastic and collagen fibers
Arteriole	Small artery that conducts blood from larger artery to capillary. By constricting and dilating appropriately, an arteriole helps regulate blood pressure and the amount of blood distributed to a tissue	Wall has three layers as in larger arteries. Muscle of tunica media is well defined
Capillary	Exchange vessel. Its thin wall permits diffusion of oxygen, nutrients, wastes, and other materials between blood and interstitial fluid	Wall consists mainly of the endothelium of tunica intima
Sinusoid	Exchange vessels found in place of capillaries in some tissues, e.g., liver, spleen, and bone marrow	Endothelial lining may be roughened by the projection of macrophages reaching into the vessel between the endothelial cells. Lining may also have gaps
Venule	Conducts blood from capillary to a larger vein	Wall usually has three layers, but tunica intima and tunica media are very thin. Tunica adventitia is the thickest layer
Vein	Conducts blood back toward heart	Wall has three layers, with tunica adventitia the thickest. Many veins have valves that prevent backflow of blood

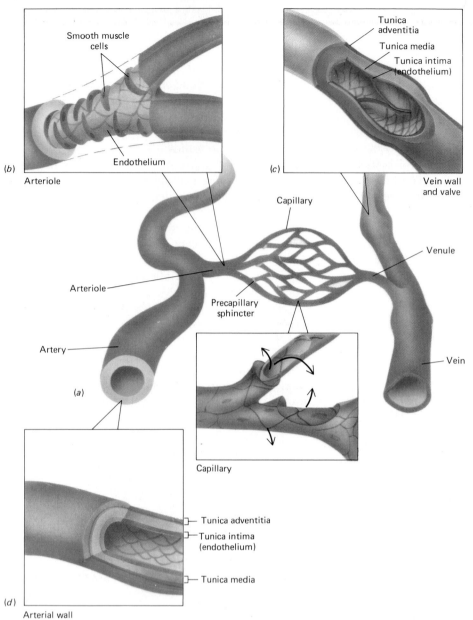

Smooth muscle cells

Endothelium

(b) Arteriole

Tunica adventitia

Tunica media

Tunica intima (endothelium)

(c) Vein wall and valve

Capillary

Venule

Arteriole

Precapillary sphincter

Artery

Vein

(a)

Capillary

Tunica adventitia

Tunica intima (endothelium)

Tunica media

(d) Arterial wall

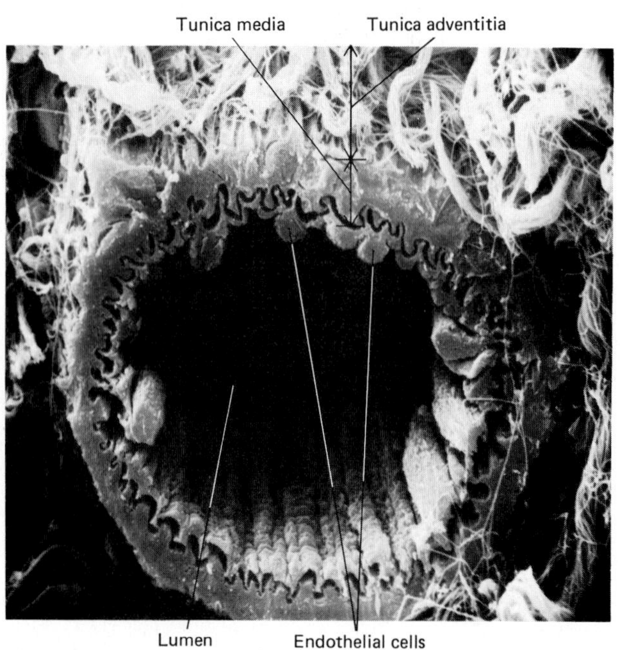

FIGURE 21-2

Structure of blood vessel walls. (a–d) Diagrams illustrating differences in wall tunics of the major blood vessels. (e) Scanning electron micrograph of an arteriole showing the three layers of its wall. The vessel shown here is magnified almost 4000 times. (From Kessel, R. G., and Karden, R. H.: *Tissues and Organs: A Text-Atlas of Scanning Electron Microscopy,* 1979.)

Arteries carry blood away from the heart

An **artery** is a thick-walled blood vessel carrying blood away from the heart and to the body tissues under relatively high pressure. All arteries in the adult except the pulmonary arteries carry oxygenated blood. The blood within the arteries is referred to as *arterial blood.* Based on size and function, there are three main kinds of arteries: elastic arteries, muscular arteries, and arterioles (Table 21-2).

ELASTIC ARTERIES ARE RICH IN ELASTIC FIBERS

The largest of the arteries are the **elastic arteries.** These arteries have diameters averaging about 2.5 centimeters (1 in.). Examples of elastic arteries include the aorta, the branches of the aortic arch, the common iliac arteries, and the pulmonary trunk. The tunica media of these arteries contains more elastic fibers and less smooth muscle. Their walls are relatively thin compared to the large diameters of their lumen. Their layers of elastic fibers allow them to stretch to receive the blood pumped into them by ventricular contraction.

During the relaxation of the ventricles, the elastic arteries recoil, maintaining a driving force of the blood as it flows into the smaller arteries. The distension and recoiling of the elastic arteries maintains a continuous pressure for uniform blood flow into the smaller arteries. Because they function in carrying the blood from the heart to the muscular arteries, they are also referred to as the *conducting arteries.*

MUSCULAR ARTERIES DISTRIBUTE THE BLOOD TO THE BODY ORGANS

The elastic arteries conduct the blood to the **muscular (distributing) arteries.** They have an average diameter of about 0.4 centimeter. These arteries distribute the blood to the various organs of the body. The distributing arteries are medium and small in diameter. Examples of distributing arteries include the axillary, brachial, intercostal, mesenteric, and femoral arteries. The tunica media of the distributing arteries contain more smooth muscle than elastic fibers. Hence they are less distensible and capable of a greater degree of extrinsic control by sympathetic nerves.

ARTERIOLES ARE IMPORTANT IN DETERMINING BLOOD PRESSURE AND BLOOD DISTRIBUTION

From the distributing arteries, blood flows into the smallest of the arteries, the **arterioles.** The diameter of an arteriole averages about 30 micrometers. The several hundred million arterioles carry the blood into the capillaries of the body tissues. The arterioles closest to the arteries have all three tunics, with the tunica media being com-

TABLE 21-2

Types of arteries

Type	Diameter (average)	Function	Composition	Examples
		blood by distending and recoiling; maintain uniform blood flow to smaller arteries	elastic fibers and less smooth muscle	
Muscular (distributing)	0.4 cm	Distribute blood to organs of body	Tunica media contains more smooth muscle and less elastic fibers	Axillary, brachial, femoral, intercostal arteries
Arterioles	30 μm	Regulate blood pressure and amount of blood distributed to each tissue by dilating and constricting	Arterial end: tunica media is composed mainly of smooth muscle Capillary end: tunica intima surrounded by a few scattered smooth muscle fibers	Each organ has extensive arteriolar branches

posed of mainly smooth muscle and a few elastic fibers. In the more distal arterioles, the endothelium of the tunica intima is surrounded by only a few scattered smooth muscle fibers (Figs. 21-2).

Arterioles are very important in regulating blood pressure and in determining the amounts of blood distributed to each tissue. This is possible through the innervation of sympathetic nerves to the smooth muscle of the tunica media. This innervation also occurs in other arteries and in veins. Impulses from these nerves stimulate the smooth muscle to contract, reducing the luminal diameter of the blood vessel. Such narrowing of the blood vessel is called **vasoconstriction.** When sympathetic input is inhibited, the smooth muscle fibers relax and the diameter of the vessel increases. This is called **vasodilation.**

Changes in blood vessel diameter are also under intrinsic controls brought about by local factors. Local factors such as changes in CO_2 and O_2 can cause intrinsic smooth muscle contraction or relaxation. These changes are proportional to the metabolic needs of the tissue served as well as the demands of the body as a whole. For example, arterioles may dilate in response to increased carbon dioxide or decreased oxygen within the specific tissue. During exercise, as skeletal muscle is rapidly metabolizing, arteriolar vasodilation results in a more-than-tenfold increase in blood flow to the skeletal muscle. Increased blood flow to a tissue in response to increased metabolic activity is called **active hyperemia.**

If all the blood vessels in the body underwent vasodilation, there would not be enough blood to fill them completely. Hence, if the arterioles to some organs undergo a vasodilation, the arterioles to other organs must vasoconstrict. Blood is distributed to the tissues according to their needs at any particular moment. Normally the liver, kidneys, brain, and skeletal muscle receive the highest percent of the total blood flow of the body (5.8 liters per minute). However, in cases of sudden stress requiring rapid action, more blood is quickly shunted to the skeletal muscles and also to the heart and skin. This is due to a vasodilation of the arterioles to these organs. At such times there is an arteriolar vasoconstriction in other organs, like the kidneys and the abdominal organs, resulting in a decreased blood flow to them. See Figure 21-3 for a comparison of blood flow distributions at rest and during strenuous exercise.

Capillaries are the sites of exchange

The microscopic **capillaries** have a wall only one cell layer thick consisting of endothelium of the tunica intima. Each individual capillary is only about 1 millimeter (0.04 in.) long with a luminal diameter averaging 0.01 millimeter. Many capillaries are so narrow that red blood cells must pass through them in single file (Fig. 21-4*a*).

Capillaries are the sites of various exchanges between the blood and the tissue cells. The endothelium of the capillary wall is very thin and semipermeable. Plasma and small solutes are able to pass through it but many large molecules are not. The respiratory gases (oxygen and carbon dioxide), nutrients, and metabolic wastes easily diffuse through the capillary wall. Refer to the section of capillary exchanges later in this chapter for a more detailed explanation.

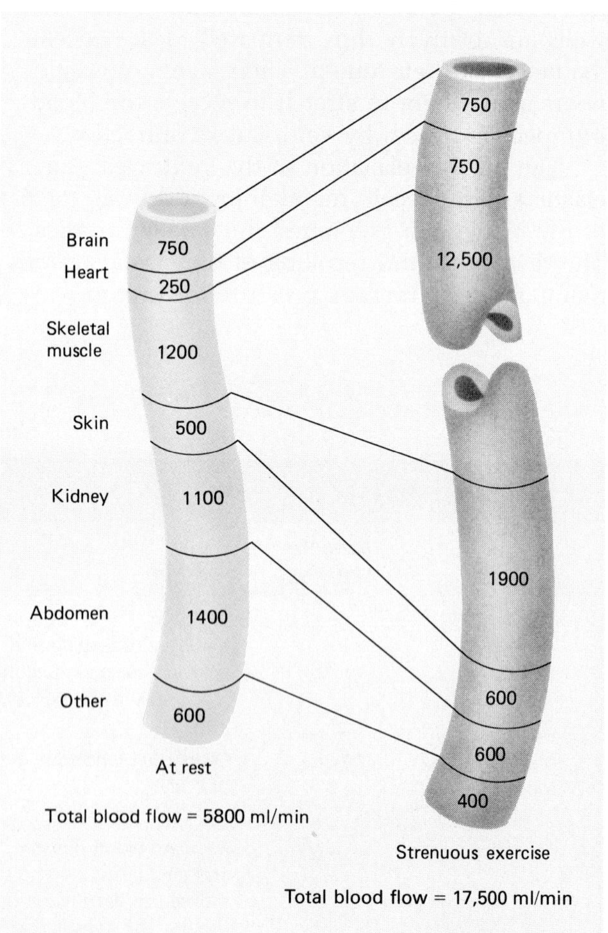

FIGURE 21-3

Distribution of blood flow to selected body organs at rest and during strenuous exercise.

The capillaries form complex networks so extensive that almost every cell of the body is within 50 micrometers of one. Indeed, if the more than 10 billion capillaries of the body could be placed end to end, they would span about 60,000 miles! These networks, or **capillary beds,** usually begin with an extension of the arteriole called the **metarteriole** (Fig. 21-5*a*). At the proximal end of the metarterioles, they are surrounded by scattered smooth muscle fibers forming **precapillary sphincters.** By contracting or relaxing, precapillary sphincters regulate blood flow into the capillaries. The distal end of the metarteriole, lacking smooth muscle fibers, is referred to as a **thoroughfare channel.** Blood flowing in these channels does not undergo any exchange.

True capillaries usually branch from arterioles or the proximal ends of metarterioles and drain into the distal ends of the same metarterioles (Fig. 21-5). Precapillary sphincters are present at the branching of the capillary groups from the metarteriole or arteriole. (No precapillary sphincters are found in the heart.) The true capillaries are the sites of exchanges between the blood and the tissue cells.

There are basically two different types of capillaries found in the body tissues: continuous capillaries and fenestrated capillaries. **Continuous capillaries** have endothelial linings that form tight junctions with adjacent cells and are uninterrupted, with the exception of very narrow intercellular pores (Fig. 21-4*b*). These capillaries are very common, located throughout muscle, adipose tissue, the lungs, and the central nervous system. In the brain, these pores are missing, and their absence provides a substantial part of the very restrictive blood-brain barrier.

The **fenestrated** (**fen**-e-stray-ted) **capillaries** have intercellular pores, or fenestrations, along their endothelial lining (Fig. 21-4*b*). These pores are 20 times wider than those of the continuous capillaries and are typically covered by a thin membrane, or diaphragm. The pores can change their permeability, or the degree to which they allow fluid and small solutes to pass through. Hence they permit extensive diffusion. Fenestrated capillaries are found associated with the mucosa of the villi of the small intestine, the ciliary processes of the eyes, and within endocrine glands. The glomerular capillaries in the kidneys

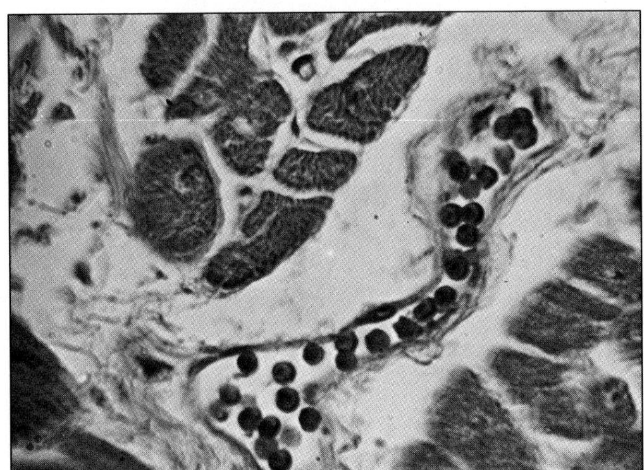

(*a*)

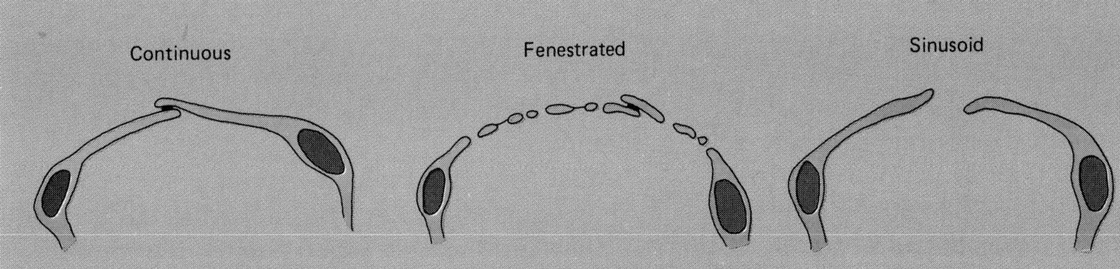

(*b*)

FIGURE 21-4

(*a*) Photomicrograph of a portion of a capillary network. Note that the red blood cells must pass through the capillary in almost single file. (*b*) Classification of capillaries based on the continuity of the endothelial layer: continuous, fenestrated, and sinusoid.

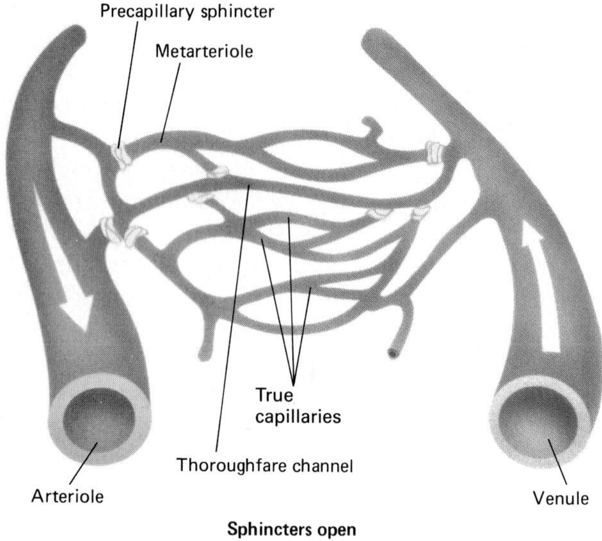

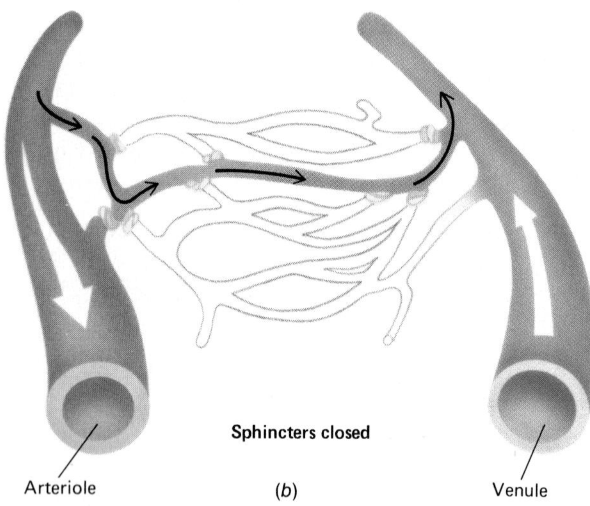

FIGURE 21-5

A capillary network. (*a*) Precapillary sphincters are open and blood flows through true capillaries. (*b*) Precapillary sphincters are closed and blood flows through thoroughfare channel.

are fenestrated capillaries with open pores lacking diaphragms (Table 21-3).

In the liver, lymphatic tissues, bone marrow, and some endocrine glands, arterioles and venules are connected by modified capillaries called **sinusoids.** The endothelial cells lining a sinusoid do not all come into contact with one another, leaving gaps in the wall (Fig. 21-4*b*). For this reason sinusoids are very leaky. Macrophages lie along the outer walls of sinusoids and extend their pseudopods into the vessels to remove worn-out blood cells, foreign matter, and cellular debris from the circulation.

TABLE 21-3

Permeability in terms of hydraulic conductivity of capillaries in various parts of the body*

Organ	Conductivity†	Type of endothelium
Brain (excluding circumventricular organs)	3	Continuous
Skin	100	Continuous
Skeletal muscle	250	Continuous
Lung	340	Continuous
Heart	860	Continuous
Gastrointestinal tract (intestinal mucosa)	13,000	Fenestrated
Glomerulus in kidney	15,000	Fenestrated

*Data courtesy of J. N. Diana.

†Units of conductivity are $cm^3 sec^{-1} dyne^{-1} \times 10^{-13}$.

Venules and veins carry blood toward the heart

Blood from the capillaries is collected by the **venules,** which drain into small veins. The parts of the venules arising from the capillaries have a tunica intima and a very thin tunica adventitia, and the parts draining into veins also contain scattered smooth muscle fibers forming a thin tunica media.

A **vein** is a thin-walled blood vessel carrying blood toward the heart under relatively low pressure. In the adult, all veins except for the pulmonary veins carry deoxygenated (oxygen-poor) blood. The blood within veins is referred to as *venous blood.* Veins contain the same three tunics as arteries with less smooth muscle in their thin tunica media. The tunica adventitia contains much collagen and elastic fibers and is the thickest layer of the vein wall. In general, veins have thinner walls than arteries and greater luminal diameters. The largest veins have bundles of longitudinally arranged smooth muscle fibers in their tunica adventitia.

Most veins larger than 2 millimeters in diameter have one-way valves positioned in such a way that they can conduct blood against the force of gravity. A vein valve usually consists of two cusps formed by inward extensions of the tunica intima (Fig. 21-6). These valves are arranged to

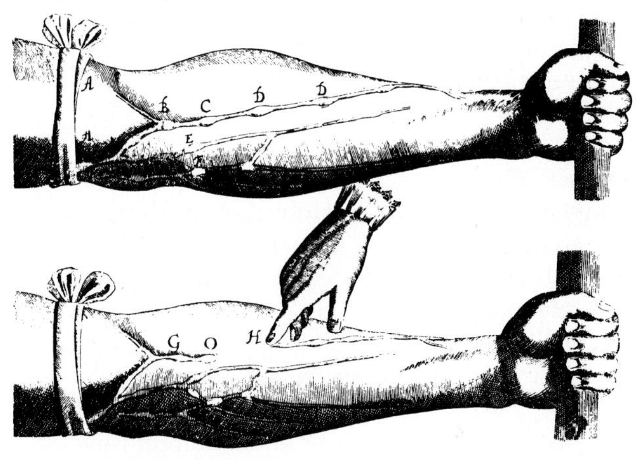

(a)

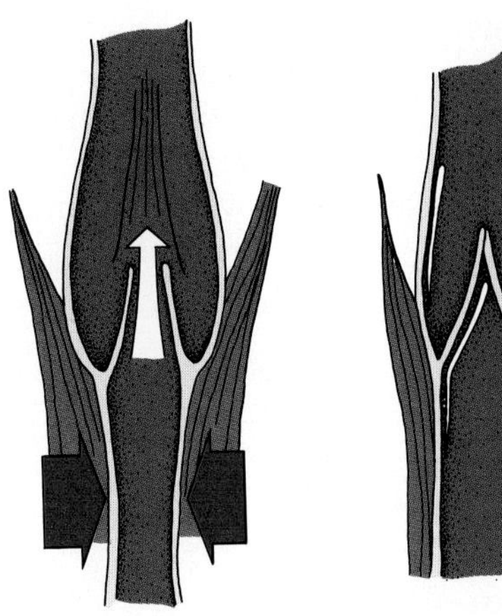

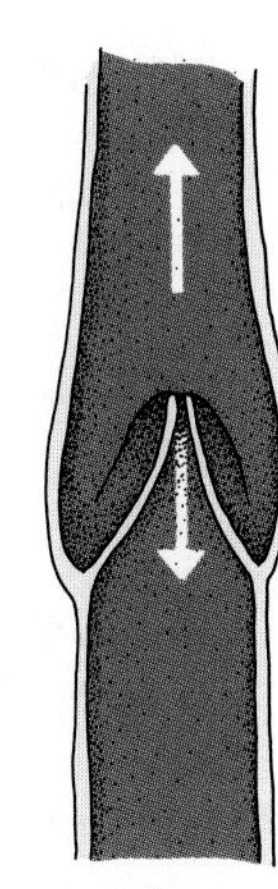

(b)

FIGURE 21-6

(*a*) The functioning of valves as shown in William Harvey's book in 1628. *A* is a tourniquet above the elbow preventing venous blood flow. Part 2 shows blood being milked from *G* to *H*. The valve at *O* stops proximal flow. (*b*) A valve in a vein usually consists of two cusps formed by inward extensions of the vein wall. Vein valves prevent backflow of blood.

permit blood to flow toward the heart, not backward in the opposite direction.

When one stands for a long period of time, blood accumulates in the veins of the legs. In persons engaged in occupations in which they must stand for long periods each day, such pooling of the blood can eventually stretch the veins. Then, because the cusps no longer meet, the competence of the valves is destroyed. This often leads to **varicose veins,** especially in those who have inherited weak vein walls and in obese individuals.

Clinical highlight

A varicose vein is wider than the usual vein, and is elongated and tortuous as well. Frequently the elastic tissue within the wall of such a vein deteriorates. Varicose veins occur mainly in the superficial veins of the legs because these veins are not well supported but must bear the weight of the blood within them. **Hemorrhoids** are varicosities of the veins in the anal region. They occur when venous pressure is constantly elevated, as in chronic constipation (due to straining) and during pregnancy (due to pressure of the enlarged uterus upon veins in the pelvic region).

In a few areas of the body there exist specialized veins, the **venous sinuses,** that have only a thin flattened endothelium and no smooth muscle. They are important drainage beds. Lacking the outer tunics, these venous sinuses are supported by surrounding tissue. The coronary sinus of the heart, the splenic sinuses, and the dural sinuses (intracranial sinuses) of the brain are examples.

Anastomoses provide alternate paths for blood flow

The distal ends of blood vessels supplying a body structure may be joined by a **collateral channel,** also called a **vascular anastomosis** (a-*nas*-to-**moe**-sis). Anastomoses permit blood to flow between the joined vessels. Such junctions may occur between arteries (arterial anastomoses), between veins at their origin (venous anastomoses), or between an arteriole and a venule (arteriovenous anastomoses). An anastomosis between an arteriole and a venule permits blood to bypass a capillary network.

An anastomosis provides an alternative channel of blood supply to a particular area. For example, anastomoses are commonly found around joints, where movement may temporarily impede blood flow through one channel. If an artery supplying a particular organ is slowly blocked by disease or is tied off during surgery, blood may flow through the alternate pathway provided by the anastomosis. Tissue damage and even gangrene can result if there is an occlusion to an artery lacking an anastomosis. These arteries are called *end-arteries*. Sometimes an entirely new capillary network develops from a collateral channel. This **collateral circulation** may be life-preserving in certain cardiovascular disease states where normal circulation to an area—for instance, part of the heart wall—is impeded.

Blood is unevenly distributed in the blood vessels because of vascular dynamics

Many factors influence the amount of blood distributed in the blood vessels. Blood flow is largely determined by pressure and resistance. Blood velocity depends upon the cross-sectional area of the vessels.

Blood flow involves pressure gradients and resistance

Blood flow is the volume of blood passing through a particular vessel in a specific period of time. At rest the total blood flow of the body is equal to the cardiac output, or about 5.8 liters per minute. Blood flow (F) is directly proportional to a pressure difference (ΔP) and inversely proportional to resistance (R). Therefore, $F = \Delta P/R$.

Pressure Blood flow is directly proportional to a pressure gradient, or the difference between the pressure at opposite ends of a vessel. The pressure within a vessel is the force per unit area exerted by the blood on the walls of the vessel. The pumping of the blood by the heart imparts this energy to the blood. Where F equals blood flow and ΔP equals a pressure gradient (expressed in mmHg), then the direct relationship between F and ΔP can be expressed as:

$$F \propto \Delta P$$

If the systemic circulation is considered as a single unit, then its blood pressure would be the difference between the aortic pressure and the late venae cavae pressure (near their entry into the right atrium). Because the aortic pressure is essentially similar to that in all the large systemic arteries, it is equivalent to the mean arterial pressure (90 to 100 mmHg). The blood pressure of the venae cavae just prior to their entrance into the right atrium is very close to zero. Therefore, the pressure difference in the entire systemic circulation is essentially the mean blood (arterial) pressure, or 90 to 100 mmHg.

Resistance Blood flow is inversely proportional to resistance. Resistance is mainly due to frictional forces that oppose blood movement through a vessel. These forces include the friction produced by the components of the blood encountering the vessel wall (vessel length and diameter are major factors) and the friction produced between the components bombarding each other (which relates to viscosity). Where F equals blood flow and R equals resistance, the inverse relationship between F and R is expressed as:

$$F \propto \frac{1}{R}$$

Vascular resistance is proportional to the viscosity of the blood. The more blood cells and proteins in the blood, the greater the viscosity and the greater the resistance. Vascular resistance is proportional to the length of the vessel. The longer the length, the greater the resistance to blood flow. Vascular resistance is inversely related to the fourth power of the radius of the vessel. Larger vessels offer much less resistance than smaller ones.

With v representing viscosity, l representing length, and r^4 being the radius of the vessel to the fourth power, the following formula defines R:

$$R \propto \frac{v(l)}{r^4}$$

Because most of the resistance in the systemic circulation is within the smaller vessels (arterioles, capillaries) far from the heart, the term *total peripheral resistance* is often used.

Because $F \propto 1/R$, by substituting the resistance factors, we get:

$$F \propto \frac{r^4}{v(l)}$$

The Poiseuille-Hagen equation combines the relationships of both pressure and resistance to flow and is given as:

$$F = \Pi \frac{\Delta P(r^4)}{8v(l)}$$

Note that changes in the radius of a vessel have a profound effect on blood flow. If the radius doubles, the blood flow increases 16-fold.

There are two major circuits of blood flow

Blood flows through a continuous network of blood vessels that forms a double circuit connecting (1) heart and lungs and (2) heart and all tissues. The left ventricle pumps blood into the **systemic circulation,** which brings oxygenated (oxygen-rich) blood to all the different tissues and organs. Blood returns to the right atrium of the heart somewhat deoxygenated but loaded with carbon dioxide wastes. It is pumped by the right ventricle into the **pulmonary circulation.** The pulmonary arteries carry blood to the lungs, where the respiratory gases are exchanged. Then pulmonary veins return the blood, rich in oxygen once more, to the left atrium. Blood then passes into the left ventricle and is pumped into the systemic circulation again, repeating the double cycle. This general pattern of circulation is shown in Figure 21-7. A more detailed view is shown in Figure 21-8.

The distribution of blood throughout the entire vascular system varies greatly between its components (Fig. 21-9). At rest, the pulmonary circulation contains about 9% of the blood at any point in time, the heart has 7%, and the systemic circulation holds the remaining 84%. Within the systemic circulation, the arteries contain about 15% of the blood, the capillaries contain only 5%, and the veins have 64%.

The large volume of blood within the systemic veins allows them to serve as **blood reservoirs.** A vasoconstriction of the veins by sympathetic stimulation permits a fast redistribution of this blood to areas of the body where it is needed. This occurs during skeletal muscle activity with the blood moving from the venous reservoirs into the muscles. Blood loss as occurs in hemorrhage also can be compensated for by a redistribution of the venous reservoirs through vasoconstriction.

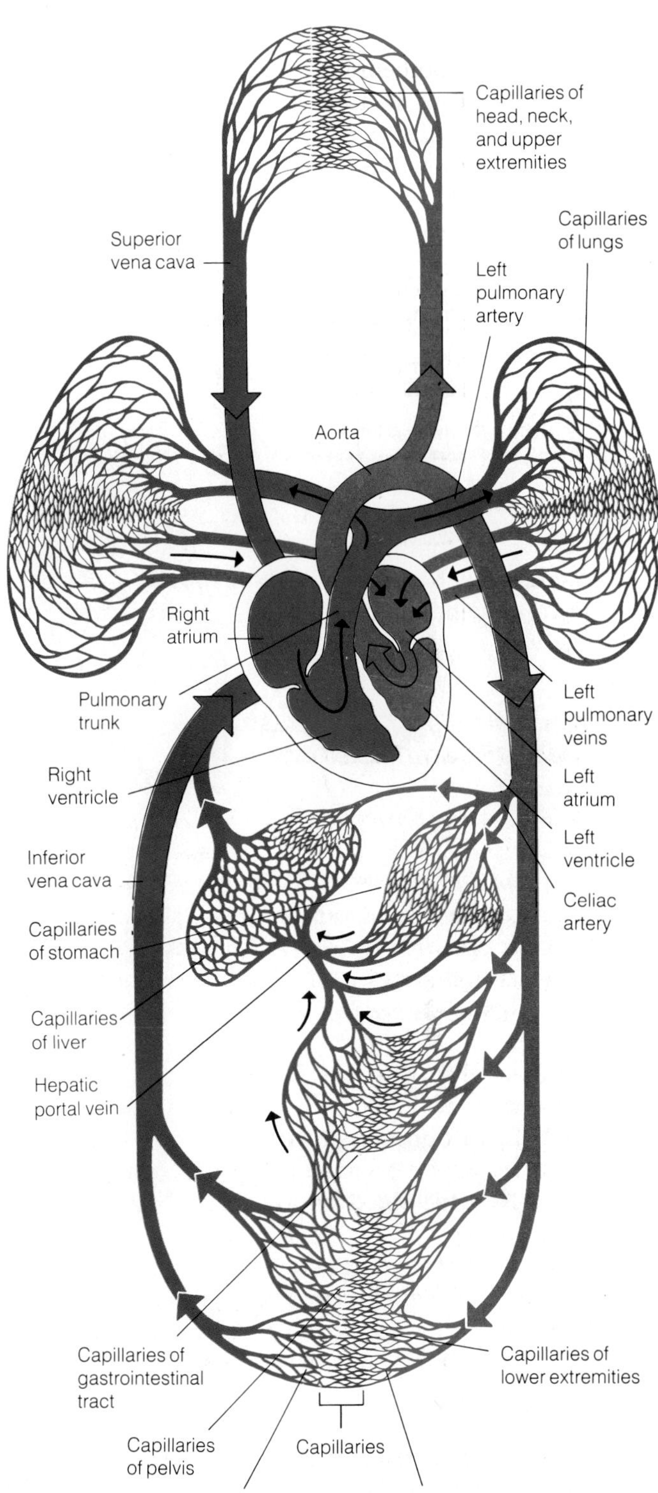

FIGURE 21-7

Circulation through the systemic and pulmonary circuits. Red represents oxygenated (oxygen-rich) blood. Blue represents deoxygenated (oxygen-poor) blood. Purple shows oxygen exchange at various tissue capillaries.

Cross-sectional area is the greatest in the capillaries

Each blood vessel type varies greatly in cross-sectional area, with the capillaries constituting the greatest percent of the total and having a cross-sectional area more than 600 times that of the

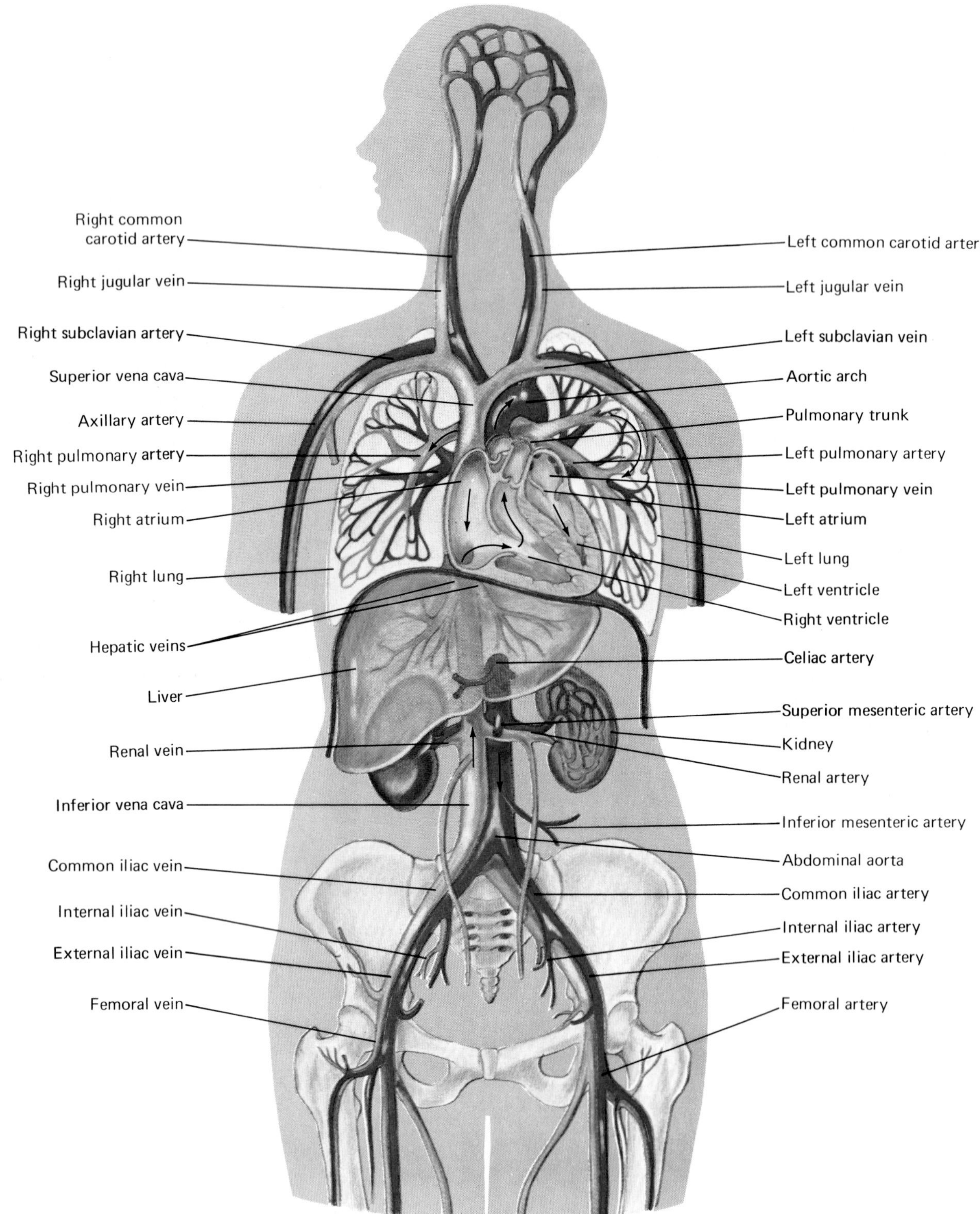

FIGURE 21-8

Circulation of blood through some of the principal arteries and veins. Blood vessels carrying oxygenated blood are red; those carrying deoxygenated blood are blue.

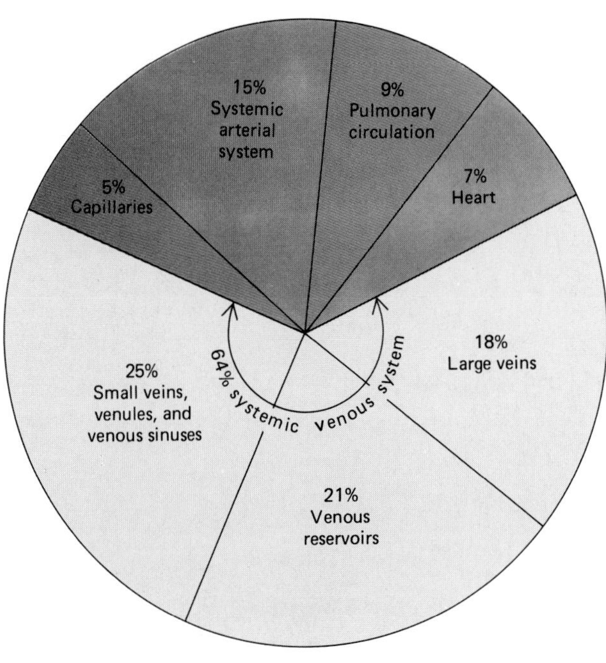

FIGURE 21-9

Blood distribution in the various vascular components expressed as a percentage of total blood volume.

aorta (Table 21-4 and Fig. 21-10*a*). Note that the venous vessels have a cross-sectional area four times that of corresponding arterial vessels. This shows that the venous vessels have a much greater storage capacity than their arterial counterparts.

Blood velocity is inversely proportional to cross-sectional area

Generally, the velocity of blood flow in any vascular component is inversely proportional to its cross-sectional area. The greater the cross-sectional area, the slower the blood flow in that area. Compare Figure 21-10*a* with 21-10*b*. Blood velocity is the greatest in the aorta (40 cm/sec) where the cross-sectional area is low. Velocity of blood flow is the lowest in the capillaries that have the greatest cross-sectional area. This slow blood flow provides sufficient time for the exchange of gases, nutrients, wastes, and other substances. As small venules combine to form larger and larger veins, the velocity of the venous blood increases with the decreasing cross-sectional area.

Blood pressure is highest in the arteries and lowest in the veins

Blood circulates throughout the blood vessels largely in response to a pressure difference between parts of the vascular system. The movement of blood is from a higher pressure to a lower pressure. Much of the pressure is dissipated as the blood travels within the arterioles. The average blood pressure in the aorta is about 100 mmHg compared to a mean capillary pressure

TABLE 21-4

The anatomy of blood vessels

Vessel	Lumen diameter	Wall thickness	Number*	Blood pressure (mm Hg)	Blood flow velocity (cm/sec)	Total cross-sectional area (cm^2)
Aorta (elastic)	3.2 cm	2 mm	1	100	33–40	8
Muscular arteries	0.4 cm	1 mm	100	100–40	5	20
Arterioles	30 μm	20 μm	10^8	40–30	2.5	700
Capillaries	8 μm	1 μm	10^{10}	30–18	0.5	5000
Venules	20 μm	2 μm	10^9	18–10	1	3000
Veins	0.5 cm	0.5 mm	100	10–5	3.5	20
Venae cavae	3 cm	1.5 mm	2	5–0	15	14

*Numbers of arterioles, capillaries, and venules are only approximations.
Data sources: John B. West, Best and Taylor's *Physiological Basis of Medical Practice,* 11th edition, Williams and Wilkins, Baltimore, MD (1985); J. W. Wood, *The Venous System,* in Scientific American, 218:86–99 (1968); Malcolm S. Gordon, *Animal Physiology: Principles and Adaptations,* 3d edition, Macmillan Publishing Co., Inc., New York, NY (1977)

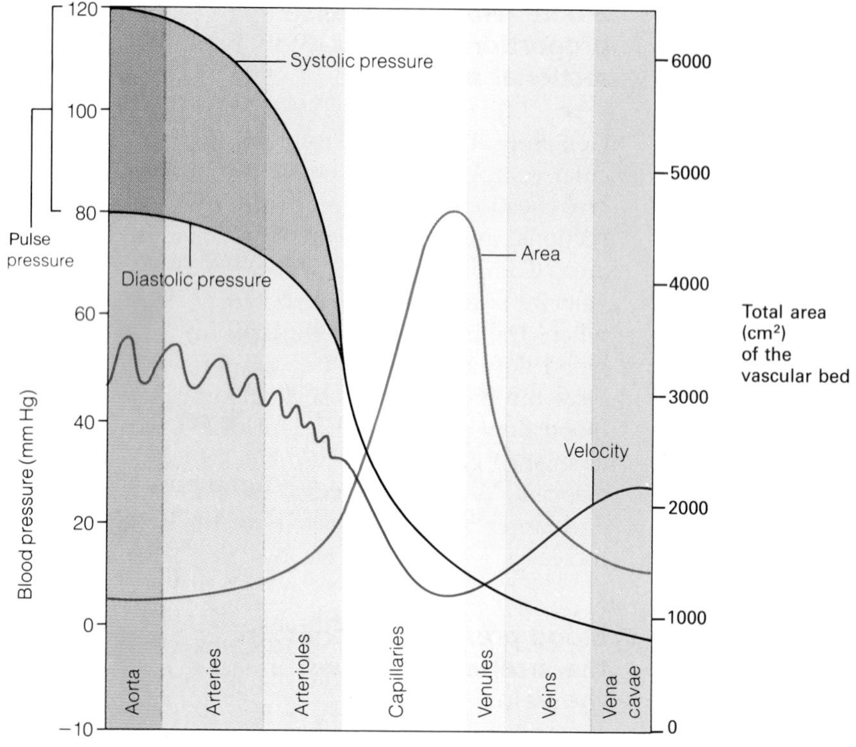

FIGURE 21-10

Relationship between total cross-sectional area, velocity of blood flow, and blood pressure in various blood vessels of the systemic circulation.

near 17 mmHg and a late venae cavae pressure close to 0 mmHg. See Figure 21-10*c* and Table 21-4.

Pulse is caused by an elastic expansion and recoil

Each time the left ventricle pumps blood into the aorta, the aortic wall stretches. This expansion moves down the aorta and its branches in a wave that is faster than the flow of the blood itself. As soon as the wave has passed, the elastic arterial wall snaps back to its normal size. This alternate expansion and recoil of an artery is the **arterial pulse.**

The ability of the large arteries to expand and then snap back to their original diameter is important in maintaining a continuous flow of blood. As the left ventricle forces a large volume of blood into the aorta during systole, the aorta expands to accommodate it. During diastole, as the walls of the aorta recoil to normal size, the blood is kept flowing into the capillaries. Were it not for this mechanism, blood would rush through the arteries and into the arterioles and capillaries in enormous gushes each time the ventricle contracted, and the delicate walls of the capillaries would soon be damaged.

When you place your finger over an artery near the skin surface, you can feel the pulse. The radial artery in the wrist is most frequently used to measure pulse, but the common carotid artery in the neck region or any other superficial artery that lies over a bone or other firm structure may be used (Fig. 21-11). These locations are sometimes referred to as **pressure points** because pressure applied here may stop arterial bleeding if the wound is distal to the pressure point. By the time the pulse wave has reached the capillaries it has been spent, so that capillaries have no pulse.

The number of pulsations counted per minute indicates the number of heartbeats per minute, because every time the heart contracts a pulse wave is initiated. Because it takes time for the pulse wave to pass from the ventricle to the artery, the pulse is felt just after ventricular contraction.

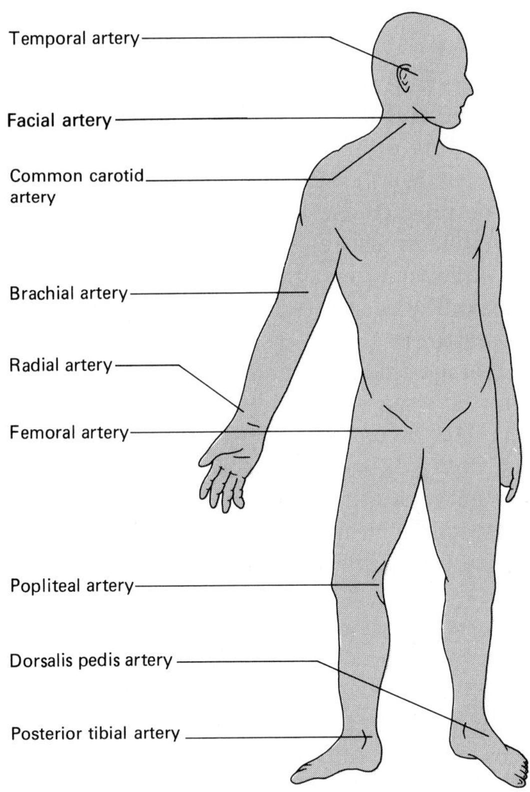

FIGURE 21-11

The pulse may be felt at any of the locations indicated in the diagram. These are all arteries that lie near the body surface over a bone or other firm structure.

Large veins near the heart also develop a pulse because of the contraction of the right atrium. The external jugular vein in the neck region is sometimes used to measure venous pulse.

Blood pressure is the force exerted by the blood on the vessels

Blood in a closed system exerts a force on the walls of the vessels. This is called blood pressure. Many factors contribute to blood pressure.

Blood pressure is measured with a sphygmomanometer

In arteries, blood pressure rises during systole and falls during diastole. A blood pressure reading is expressed as systolic pressure over diastolic pressure. For example, normal blood pressure for a young adult would be about 120/80. (The numbers refer to mmHg, millimeters of mercury.) Systolic pressure is represented by the numerator, diastolic pressure by the denominator. The systolic pressure may vary greatly with physical exertion and emotional stress.

Clinically, blood pressure is measured with a **sphygmomanometer** (*sfig*-mo-ma-**nom**-e-ter) and stethoscope. The sphygmomanometer consists of a manometer (a column of mercury calibrated in millimeters) connected by a rubber tube to an inflatable rubber cuff. An air pump with a valve is attached to the cuff.

To measure the pressure, the cuff is wrapped around a patient's arm over the brachial artery (Fig. 21-12). Air is pumped into the cuff until the air pressure is great enough to compress the artery so that no pulse is heard on the anterior surface of the elbow joint (using the stethoscope). Then the valve is opened slightly so that the pressure in the cuff begins to fall. Soon, a distinct sound is heard as blood spurts into the artery again. The pressure at that instant is read as the systolic pressure. The sound gets louder and then changes in quality, and finally becomes inaudible. These tapping sounds, the **sounds of Korotkoff** (ko-**rot**-kof), are the result of discontinuous turbulent blood flow and continue as long as the cuff pressure is higher than the diastolic pressure. Pressure at the instant the sound is no longer audible is read as the diastolic pressure. Table 21-5 shows normal values for blood pressure readings in healthy men and women.

Systemic blood pressure drives the blood into the tissues

When the left ventricle contracts during systole, blood is pumped into the aorta. However, only about one-third of the stroke volume actually leaves the arteries at this time. The extra volume of blood entering the aorta and elastic arteries causes them to distend. Systemic blood pressure in the arteries at the peak of ventricular ejection is at its highest level and is called the **systolic pressure.** An average systolic pressure in healthy adults at rest is 120 mmHg (Fig. 21-10). As the ventricles relax during diastole, the elastic arteries passively recoil, supplying the rest of the vascular system with a continuous flow of blood. The blood volume in the arteries is decreasing during

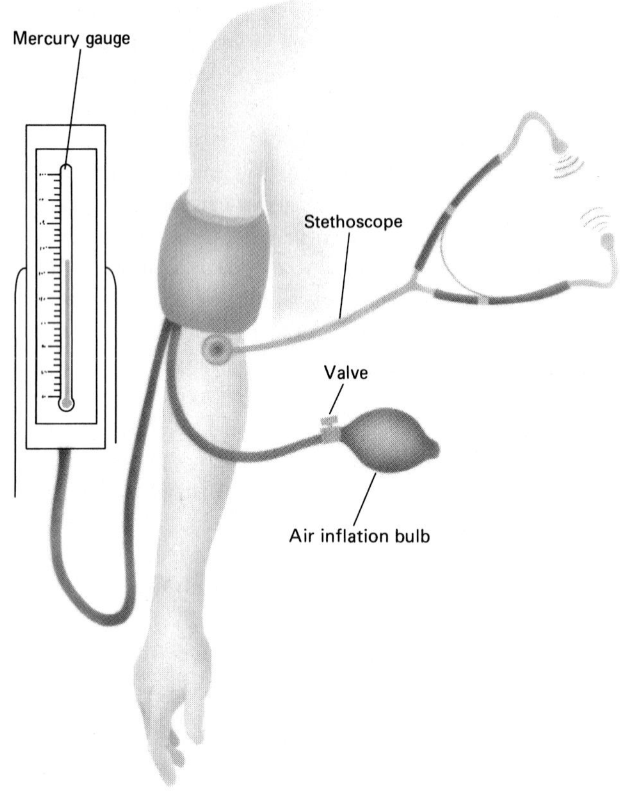

FIGURE 21-12

Measurement of blood pressure using a sphygmomanometer.

diastole and, with it, the blood pressure. The lowest pressure in the arteries, therefore, occurs during diastole and is called the **diastolic pressure.** At rest, the diastolic pressure of a healthy adult averages about 70 to 80 mmHg. Thus a normal blood pressure reading for a young adult might be 120/80.

Pulse pressure is due to the difference between systolic and diastolic pressures. For a blood pressure reading of 120/80, the pulse pressure is 40 mmHg. Factors that can raise the pulse pressure include an increase in stroke volume (increases systolic pressure), decreased heart rate (decreases diastolic pressure), and decreased arterial distensibility as in arteriosclerosis (increases systolic pressure).

The **average (mean) blood pressure** drives the blood into the tissues throughout the entire cardiac cycle. The mean arterial pressure is not an arithmetic half-way value, because the time period for diastole is much longer than the time taken in systole. The mean arterial pressure is given by the following formula:

$$\text{Mean arterial pressure} = \text{diastolic pressure} + 1/3 \text{ pulse pressure}$$

In a healthy person at rest, the mean arterial pressure is about 93 mmHg [80 mmHg + (1/3)40 mmHg].

Using the relationship developed earlier, $F = \Delta P/R$, and substituting cardiac output for F, mean blood pressure for ΔP, and peripheral resistance for R, and solving for blood pressure, the formula becomes:

$$\text{Blood pressure} = \text{cardiac output} \times \text{peripheral resistance}$$

TABLE 21-5

Mean systolic and diastolic blood pressures (with standard deviations) in healthy people

	Males		Females	
Age (years)	Systolic	Diastolic	Systolic	Diastolic
20–24	123 ± 13.7	76 ± 9.9	116 ± 11.8	72 ± 9.7
30–34	126 ± 13.6	79 ± 9.7	120 ± 14.0	75 ± 10.8
40–45	129 ± 15.1	81 ± 9.5	127 ± 17.1	80 ± 10.6
50–54	135 ± 19.2	83 ± 11.3	137 ± 21.3	84 ± 12.4
60–64	142 ± 21.1	85 ± 12.4	144 ± 22.3	85 ± 13.0
70–74	145 ± 26.3	82 ± 15.3	159 ± 25.8	85 ± 15.3
80–84	145 ± 25.6	82 ± 9.9	157 ± 28.0	83 ± 13.1

Factors affecting blood pressure include cardiac output, peripheral resistance, and blood volume

Any factor that alters cardiac output or peripheral resistance can cause blood pressure to change. An increase in cardiac output usually results in an elevated blood pressure, as does an increase in peripheral resistance (Fig. 21-13).

CARDIAC OUTPUT CHANGES WITH CHANGES IN HEART RATE AND STROKE VOLUME

Any factor changing the cardiac output can also change blood pressure. The major factors determining cardiac output are given in the formula:

$$\text{Cardiac output} = \text{heart rate} \times \text{stroke volume}$$

Increasing heart rate or stroke volume can increase blood pressure by increasing cardiac output. The major extrinsic factors increasing heart rate include increased sympathetic stimulation (and decreased parasympathetic stimulation), increased epinephrine and other hormones, and increased temperature. Some of the major factors contributing to an increased stroke volume include increased venous return to the heart, sympathetic stimulation, and increased epinephrine.

PERIPHERAL RESISTANCE IS DETERMINED MAINLY BY THE STATE OF THE ARTERIOLES

Increases in peripheral resistance increase blood pressure. Decreased resistance lowers blood pressure. At rest, the viscosity of the blood and the vessel lengths do not appreciably change but the

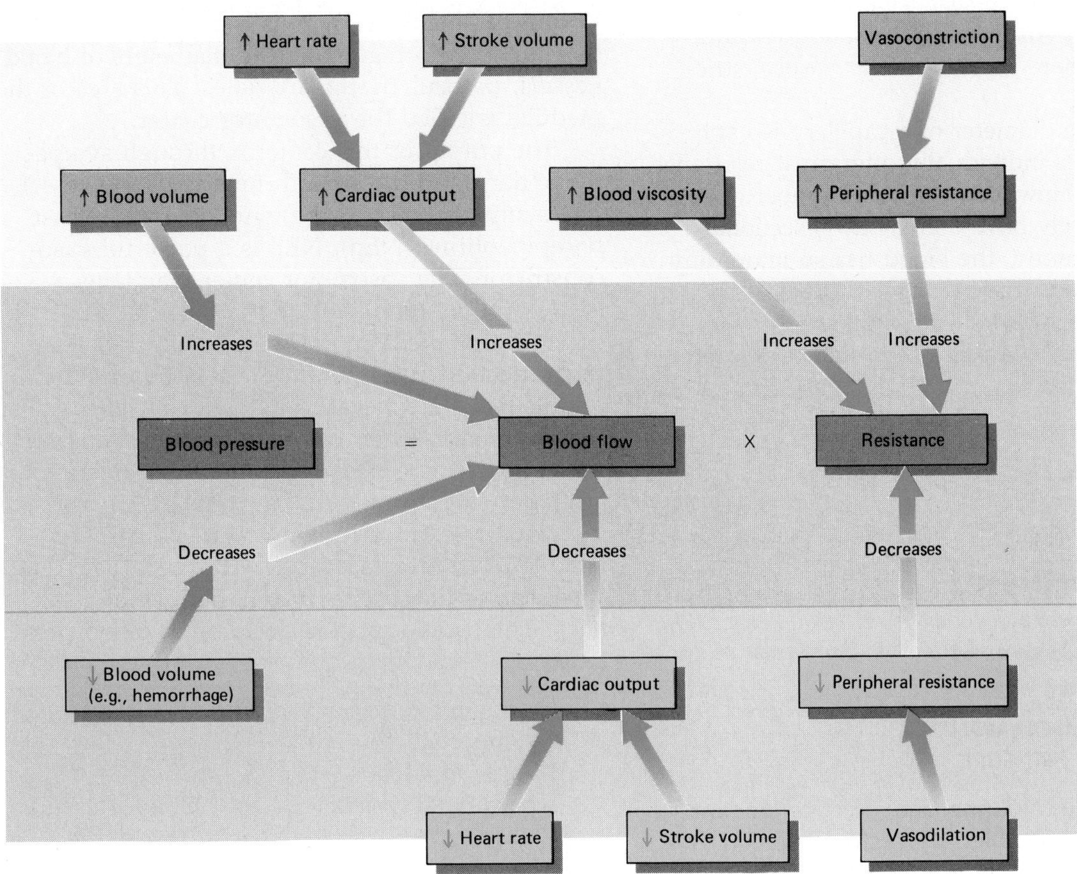

FIGURE 21-13

Some factors that influence blood pressure. Note that according to the equation, any factor that increases either blood flow or resistance increases blood pressure. Any factor that decreases either blood flow or resistance decreases blood pressure.

radius of some of the blood vessels can be increased or decreased by local (chemical) and extrinsic factors (sympathetic nerves and hormones). Because resistance is inversely proportional to the fourth power of the vessel radius, *a small change in the diameter of a blood vessel causes a big change in blood pressure.* For instance, if the radius doubled, the resistance would be reduced to one-sixteenth of its former value, and the flow would increase fully 16-fold.

Because arteries are large, their walls offer little resistance to blood flow. Arterioles, though, have a much smaller diameter and so offer a great deal of resistance to blood flow. This permits relatively high pressure to build up in the arteries supplying them. More important, because arterioles can dilate and constrict, they can alter the amount of resistance to blood flow and thereby influence the blood pressure and the rate of flow. In fact, the amount of blood pressure within the arterial system as a whole is regulated mainly by the degree of vasoconstriction or vasodilation of the arterioles. Arteriolar vasodilation decreases peripheral resistance and hence, lowers blood pressure. An increase in blood pressure results when there is an arteriolar vasoconstriction.

Because the diameter of a capillary is very small, capillaries individually offer great resistance to blood flow. However, the vast number of capillaries collectively have a great cross-sectional area. Put differently, the blood has so many tiny capillary channels through which to pass that the total resistance, when all the capillaries are considered together, is far less than that of the arterioles.

Clinical highlight

Blood viscosity normally does not affect blood pressure appreciably unless it changes dramatically. In a condition such as **polycythemia,** in which the number of red blood cells increases markedly, the blood viscosity also increases, causing a rise in resistance and a rise in blood pressure. In **anemia** or conditions of blood loss, blood viscosity decreases, causing a fall in blood pressure.

CHANGES IN BLOOD VOLUME AFFECT BLOOD PRESSURE

Changes in blood volume also affect cardiac output, which can alter blood pressure. If blood volume is reduced by hemorrhage or by chronic bleeding, the blood pressure drops. On the other hand, an increase in blood volume causes an increase in blood pressure. For example, a high dietary intake of salt causes retention of water. This, in turn, may result in an increase in blood volume and lead ultimately to an increase in blood pressure.

Regulation of blood pressure includes cardiovascular centers of the medulla, chemicals, and hormones

Extrinsic and intrinsic factors regulate blood pressure. The brain center that regulates much of the vascular dynamics is located in the medulla. Pressure-sensitive receptors and chemical-sensitive receptors monitor conditions within the blood vessels. Certain chemicals and hormones can alter the diameters of arterioles.

VASOMOTOR CENTER ACTIVATION CAUSES VASOCONSTRICTION

Within the medulla, there is a group of neurons that function in regulating the diameters of blood vessels, particularly the arterioles. This area of the medulla is called the **vasomotor center.**

The output of this center is through sympathetic nerves to the smooth muscle of the vessels. The sympathetic postganglionic neurons release norepinephrine (NEp). NEp is a powerful vasoconstrictor. The vasomotor center maintains a basal level of stimulation to the blood vessels which keeps their smooth muscle in a low state of contraction and, therefore, the arterioles are in a tonic low state of vasoconstriction. In this way, the vasomotor center can regulate peripheral resistance. By increasing sympathetic stimulation to arteriolar smooth muscle, vasoconstriction and increased resistance result. When sympathetic stimulation is decreased below the basal level, the vasodilation that occurs lowers peripheral resistance. This would cause a decrease in blood pressure.

Vasomotor center activation ⟶
↑ sympathetic output ⟶
↑ vasoconstriction ⟶
↑ peripheral resistance ⟶ ↑ blood pressure

Skeletal muscle receives a dual innervation of sympathetic nerves. While some of these sympathetic nerves release NEp, others release acetylcholine (ACh) which causes vasodilation. These sympathetic vasodilator nerves only innervate the vessels of skeletal muscle. They allow more blood to be shunted to skeletal muscle during periods of exercise or stress and are activated only at these times.

HIGHER BRAIN CENTERS CAN ALTER BLOOD PRESSURE

The **cerebral cortex** and the **hypothalamus** send input to the **medulla** and can alter blood pressure. Stress, emotions, changes in body temperature, and exercise can cause an increase in vasomotor activity through stimulation by these higher brain centers.

BARORECEPTORS RESPOND TO CHANGES IN BLOOD PRESSURE

Specialized nerve cells called **baroreceptors,** or **pressoreceptors,** are located in the walls of the large arteries in the thoracic and neck regions. They are most abundant in the walls of the aortic arch, in the carotid sinus (a small expansion in each internal carotid artery just superior to the point where it branches off from the common carotid), in the vena cavae, and in the right atrium. These baroreceptors are sensitive to changes in blood pressure. When an increase in blood pressure stretches their walls, they send impulses via sensory nerves to the cardiac centers in the medulla. Parasympathetic nerves are stimulated and cause the heart rate to slow, decreasing cardiac output and bringing the blood pressure back to normal. Sympathetic nerves are simultaneously inhibited, decreasing heart rate and cardiac contractile force (Fig. 21-14*a*).

↑ Blood pressure ⟶ ↑ baroreceptor activity ⟶ ↑ sensory input ⟶ cardiac centers of medulla ⟶ ↑ parasympathetic output ⟶ ↓ heart rate ⟶ ↓ cardiac output ⟶ ↓ blood pressure

Baroreceptors also send impulses to the vasomotor center in the medulla, inhibiting sympathetic nerves that supply arterioles and veins. The effect is to dilate the arterioles (and veins), lowering peripheral resistance and thereby decreasing blood pressure.

↑ Blood pressure ⟶ ↑ baroreceptor activity ⟶ ↑ sensory input ⟶ vasomotor center of medulla ⟶ ↓ sympathetic output ⟶ ↑ vasodilation ⟶ ↓ peripheral resistance ⟶ ↓ blood pressure

Any slight decrease in blood pressure, such as the change that occurs when you get up out of bed in the morning, causes the baroreceptors to decrease their steady rate of firing. As a result, sympathetic nerves send messages to the blood vessels, causing vasoconstriction. Blood pressure then increases. The cardiac centers in the medulla also slow their parasympathetic messages to the heart. This allows the sympathetic nerves to dominate so that the heart beats faster and blood pressure is increased. These neural reflexes act continuously to maintain a steady state of blood pressure. They ensure, for example, that you do not faint each time you get up from a prone position. So sensitive are the baroreceptors to changes in blood pressure that they even respond to each systole by sending more impulses, and to each diastole by decreasing their output.

Strong pressure exerted over the carotid sinuses in the neck can cause the baroreceptors there to fire so rapidly that arterial blood pressure may fall 20 mmHg or so in a normal person. In some older persons with narrowed arteries, a tight collar can exert pressure upon the carotid sinuses, causing fainting. Such pressure may even cause the heart to stop beating.

CHEMORECEPTORS ARE LOCATED IN THE CAROTID AND AORTIC BODIES

Another neural mechanism for bringing falling blood pressure back toward homeostasis involves chemoreceptors in certain arteries, including the carotid arteries and the aortic arch. These chemoreceptors consist of chemically sensitive cells clustered in tiny organs called **carotid** and **aortic bodies.**

When the arterial blood pressure falls below about 80 mmHg, the oxygen level in the blood may decrease because circulation is less effective. The carbon dioxide level and the concentration of hydrogen ions increase, however, because the slow flow of blood does not remove them effectively. The chemoreceptors respond to these chemical changes by sending messages by way of sensory nerves to the vasomotor center in the medulla of the brain. This reflex center responds by sending sympathetic neural messages to the blood vessels, stimulating them to constrict, thus increasing peripheral resistance and blood pressure (Fig. 21-14*b*).

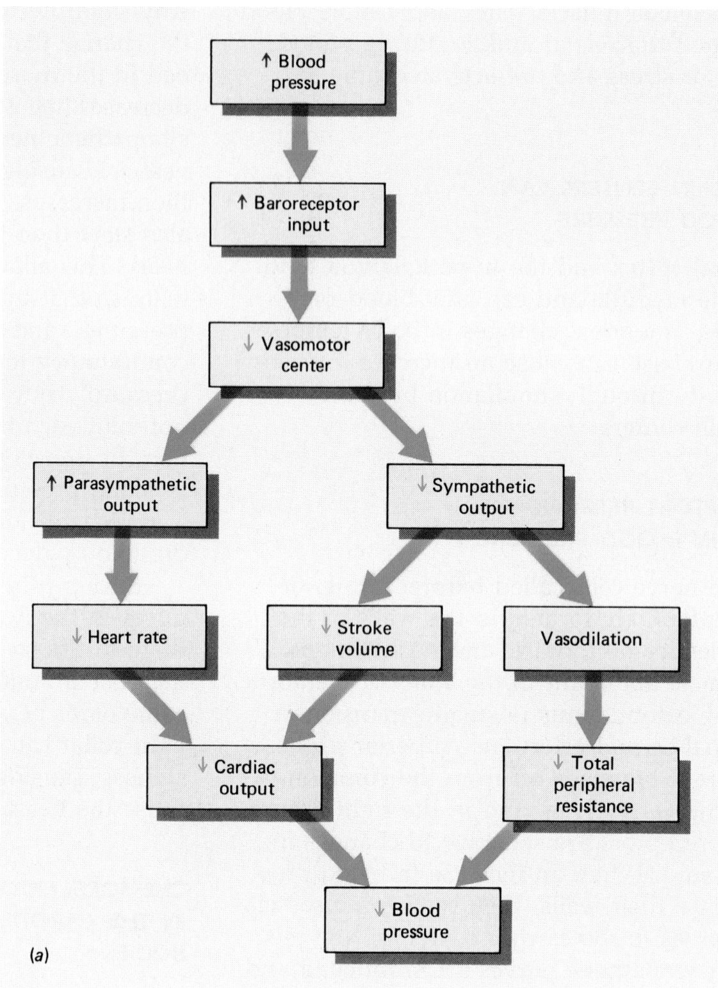

FIGURE 21-14(*a*)

Regulation of blood pressure by baroreceptors.

↓ Blood pressure ⟶ ↓ O_2 level, ↑ CO_2 level, and ↑ H^+ levels in blood ⟶ ↑ chemoreceptor activity ⟶ ↑ sensory input ⟶ ↑ vasomotor center in medulla ⟶ ↑ sympathetic output ⟶ ↑ vasoconstriction ⟶ ↑ peripheral resistance ⟶ ↑ blood pressure

VASODILATORS LOWER BLOOD PRESSURE

Kinins These vasodilator peptides are present in the blood and in various tissues. The action of kinins is similar to that of histamine. They cause a constriction in visceral smooth muscle but a vasodilation in the smooth muscle of the blood vessels. This vasodilation lowers peripheral resistance and lowers blood pressure. Within certain tissues, the local vasodilation they cause increases blood flow to that tissue. This is found during active secretion in sweat glands, salivary glands, and the exocrine parts of the pancreas.

↑ Kinin release ⟶ vasodilation ⟶ ↓ peripheral resistance ⟶ ↓ blood pressure

Atrial natriuretic peptide (ANP) ANP, which is secreted by the atria of the heart, causes a generalized vasodilation, which decreases peripheral resistance. ANP also antagonizes vasoconstrictor substances and reduces aldosterone release. It stimulates the kidneys to excrete sodium and water, which lowers blood volume and cardiac output. Both the decreased peripheral resistance and cardiac output cause a drop in blood pressure.

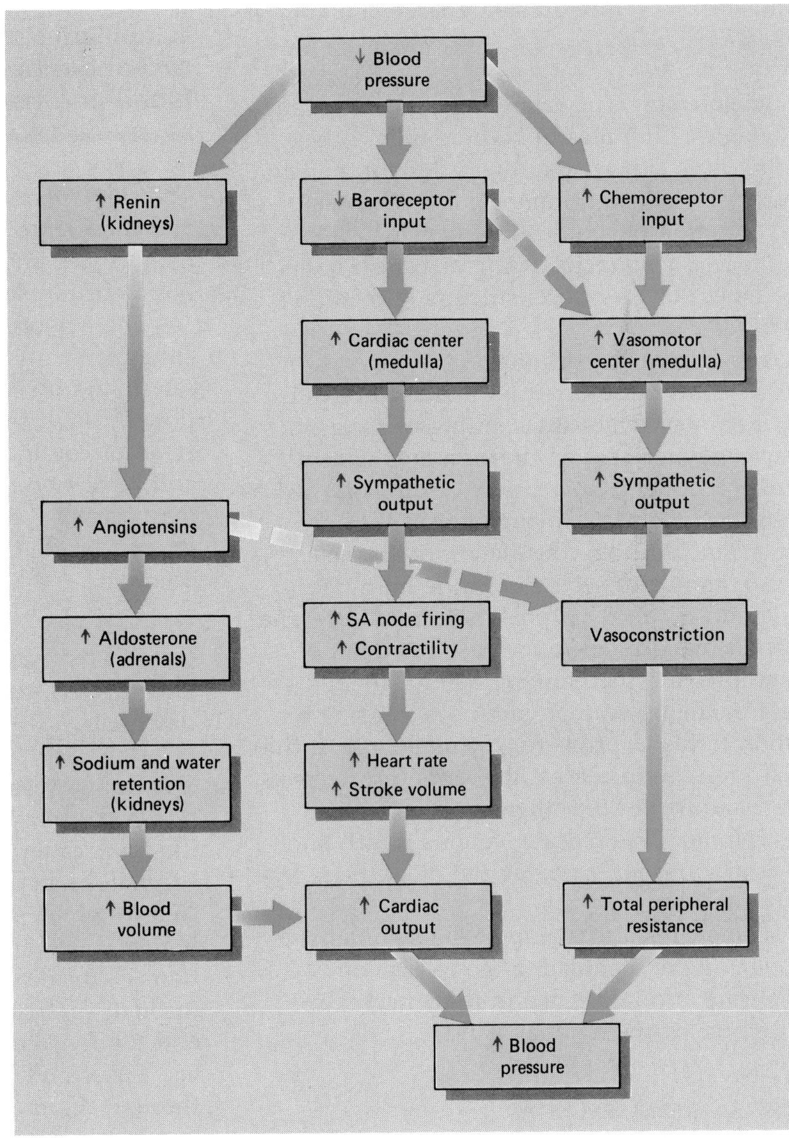

FIGURE 21-14(*b*)

Some regulatory mechanisms bringing a low blood pressure back to normal.

VASOCONSTRICTORS ELEVATE BLOOD PRESSURE

Epinephrine (Ep) and norepinephrine (NEp) These hormones are released into the blood by the adrenal medulla during stress. They work in conjunction with an enhanced sympathetic output. NEp has a generalized vasoconstrictor effect in the body. This increases peripheral resistance and elevates blood pressure. Epinephrine causes vasoconstriction except within the vessels of the skeletal muscle and liver. Epinephrine also increases heart rate, stroke volume, and cardiac output.

Antidiuretic hormone (ADH) ADH is produced in the hypothalamus and released by the posterior pituitary. With dramatic drops in blood volume, more ADH is released, which results in powerful vasoconstriction and an increase in water retention by the kidneys. Both measures help to elevate the blood pressure. Alcohol inhibits the release of ADH and, therefore, contributes to increased water excretion and a drop in blood pressure. Alcohol also depresses the vasomotor center of the medulla. This results in a vasodilation, especially to the periphery, as seen in a flushed skin upon imbibing large amounts of alcohol.

Renin-angiotensin The renin-angiotensin system takes about 20 minutes to become fully active. Although it is slower than the reflex controls and the adrenal medulla hormones, it has a much longer duration of action. Angiotensins are powerful vasoconstrictors. Angiotensin II is one of the most potent vasoconstrictors known (Fig. 21-14*b*).

When the blood pressure of the kidneys decreases, the kidneys release a substance called renin. Renin catalyzes the splitting of a plasma protein, angiotensinogen, to form angiotensin I. An enzyme located in a variety of capillary beds converts angiotensin I to angiotensin II. Angiotensin II causes constriction of arterioles and also stimulates secretion of the hormone aldosterone from the adrenal cortex. Aldosterone acts upon the kidneys to increase retention of sodium ions and therefore of water. The fluid content of the blood then increases, causing an elevation in blood pressure. Normally, when the arterial pressure increases, the kidneys excrete a greater volume of fluid, thereby reducing the blood volume. This reduces venous return and thus cardiac output, bringing the blood pressure back to normal.

Angiotensins also act upon the sympathetic nervous system, stimulating the release of epinephrine and norepinephrine by nerve endings and by the adrenal glands.

AUTOREGULATION SERVES AS AN INTRINSIC CONTROL OF BLOOD PRESSURE

Intrinsic, or local, **controls** exist in the vessels and tissues that can alter blood pressure. A higher blood pressure causes more fluid to move out of the capillaries and into the interstitium. This reduces blood volume and blood pressure. Active hyperemia also operates locally. Increasing the activity of an organ causes a decrease in O_2, and increases various metabolites such as CO_2, H^+, and K^+. These directly relax smooth muscle of arterioles, causing a vasodilation and an increased blood flow to that organ.

Capillaries serve in exchanges between the blood and tissue cells

The slow velocity of blood through the capillaries and their large cross-sectional area supply adequate space and time for exchanges to take place between the blood and the interstitial fluid.

The smooth muscles of the precapillary sphincters and of the metarterioles themselves intermittently contract and relax, causing blood flow through the capillaries to be interrupted instead of continuous. This intermittent contraction and relaxation is called **vasomotion.** Vasomotion may occur several times per minute. The tissue oxygen level is a primary factor in regulating vasomotion.

Gases and nutrients are exchanged mainly by diffusion

The capillary serves as the site of exchanges between the blood and the tissue cells. Interstitial fluid is located between the two. The exchange of respiratory gases and nutrients is mainly by diffusion in which substances pass from an area of higher concentration to one of lower concentration. Diffusion of water-soluble substances occurs through the junctions of continuous capillaries and the fenestrae (pores) of fenestrated capillaries. Gases and fat-soluble substances diffuse through the membrane of the capillary's endothelium. Oxygen and nutrients diffuse out of the capillary and, from the interstitial fluid, diffuse into the tissue cells. Carbon dioxide and other metabolic wastes move in the opposite direction. Endocytosis and exocytosis also move larger molecules through the capillary wall.

Fluid movement involves filtration and absorption

Water and small-solute exchanges are dependent upon opposing forces favoring either filtration of the fluid or its absorption. *Filtration* favors the diffusion of fluid out of the capillary and into the interstitium, whereas *absorption* favors diffusion from the interstitium into the capillary.

The forces operating in filtration-absorption dynamics are of two types: hydrostatic forces and osmotic forces. **Hydrostatic forces** develop as a result of the weight of water against a wall. **Osmotic forces** are the result of nonpermeable solutes (like proteins) drawing water to themselves. Through osmosis, water moves from a region of higher concentration of water to one of a lower concentration or in the direction of the higher concentration of nonpermeating solutes.

Hydrostatic forces The capillary blood pressure serves as the major hydrostatic force favoring filtration. This **capillary hydrostatic pressure** (CHP) is higher at the arteriolar end of the capillary (30 mmHg) than at the venular end (10 mmHg). This means that more fluid is filtered at the arteriolar end of the capillary. The interstitial fluid also has a hydrostatic pressure of its own. Because fluid is continuously being removed from the interstitium by the lymphatic system, the **interstitial fluid hydrostatic pressure** (IFHP) is a negative pressure of about −5 mmHg. Because the IFHP is negative, it favors filtration.

Osmotic forces The blood plasma contains a large amount of protein (mainly albumin and globulin) whereas the interstitial fluid usually has very little protein. This plasma protein contributes to a high osmotic pressure within the capillary. The **capillary osmotic pressure** (COP) averages about 28 mmHg and favors the absorption of fluid from the interstitium into the capillary. An **interstitial fluid osmotic pressure** (IFOP) of about 6 mmHg favors filtration of fluid out of the capillary.

Net forces The forces favoring filtration are the CHP, IFHP, and the IFOP. At the arteriolar end of the capillary, the total filtration force is 41 mmHg and the total absorption force is the COP (28 mmHg). See Figure 21-15.

Total filtration force (arteriolar end) = CHP (30 mmHg) + IFHP (5 mmHg) + IFOP (6 mmHg) = 41 mmHg

Total absorption force = COP = 28 mmHg

The net filtration (outward) force is the difference between these total opposing forces, or 13 mmHg.

Net filtration force (arteriolar end) = total filtration force (41 mmHg) − total absorption force (28 mmHg) = 13 mmHg

At the venular end of the capillary the CHP is 10 mmHg, the IFHP is 6 mmHg, and the IFOP is 5 mmHg. The total filtration force at the venular

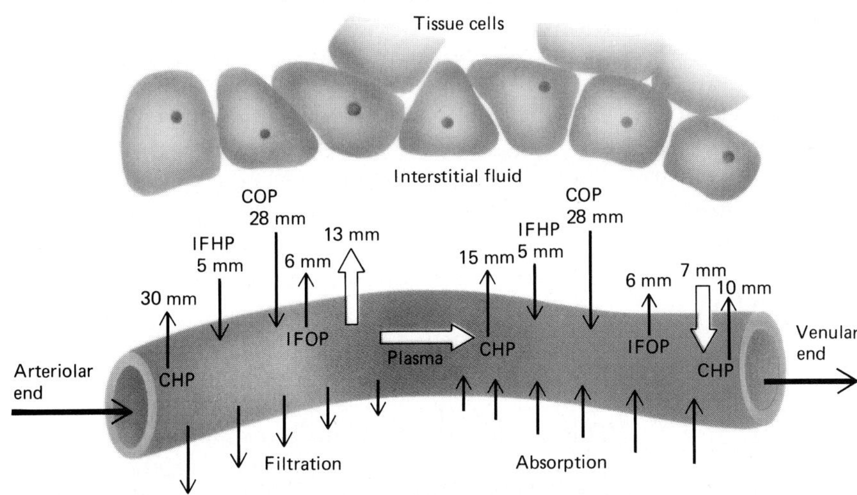

FIGURE 21-15

Capillary dynamics showing hydrostatic and osmotic forces moving fluid out of capillary (filtration) and into capillary (absorption).

end of the capillary is 21 mmHg and the total absorption force is the COP of 28 mmHg.

> Total filtration force (venular end) = CHP (10 mmHg) + IFHP (5 mmHg) + IFOP (6 mmHg) = 21 mmHg
>
> Total absorption force = COP = 28 mmHg

The net force at the venular end of the capillary is a net absorption force of 7 mmHg.

> Net absorption force (venular end) = total absorption force (28 mmHg) − total filtration force (21 mmHg) = 7 mmHg

Note that more filtration occurs at the arteriolar end of the capillary and more absorption takes place at its venular end. There is more fluid moving out of the capillary at the arteriolar end than moving in at the venular end. The net filtration rate for the entire body averages about 2 milliliters per minute. This fluid does not accumulate within the interstitial fluid because the lymphatic system carries it off to the venous drainage at the base of the neck.

There exists a near equilibrium between the fluid filtered out of the capillary and the fluid reabsorbed by the capillary along with the amount returned to the circulation by the lymphatics. This was first observed about 100 years ago by E. H. Starling, and it is referred to as **Starling's law of the capillaries.** If this equilibrium did not exist, plasma would be lost from the vessels and within 24 hours circulation would cease.

Another possible explanation for the movement of fluid at the capillary is based on vasomotion, especially opening and closing of the precapillary sphincters. When opened, the sphincters allow for a higher capillary hydrostatic pressure to move fluid out of the capillary. A closed precapillary sphincter causes the capillary hydrostatic pressure to fall and more fluid moves into the capillary.

Venous return occurs despite low venous blood pressure

The deoxygenated blood entering the venules is at a very low pressure (10 mmHg) and is flowing at a velocity of only 0.04 centimeters per second. As the venous blood enters larger and larger veins, its velocity increases but the venous pressure remains very low. The venous pressure in the veins of the limbs is only about 6 to 8 mmHg. The pressure of the right atrium is 0 mmHg.

Veins are very distensible and readily expand to accommodate more blood without appreciably increasing venous pressure. The venous return from below the heart also has to work against the force of gravity. Besides possessing **valves,** there are other mechanisms that facilitate venous return.

Skeletal muscle pump Many of the deep veins are located within skeletal muscle. When a muscle contracts and shortens, it compresses the veins within it. This compression serves to increase blood flow toward the heart. Valves prevent a backflow of the blood (Fig. 21-16).

> Skeletal muscle contraction ⟶ ↑ compression of deep veins ⟶ ↑ venous blood flow toward heart

Respiratory (thoracoabdominal) pump During the inspiration stage of breathing, the diaphragm bows downward as the thoracic volume increases. This causes an increase in intra-abdominal pressure and a decrease in intrathoracic pressure. The increase in intra-abdominal pressure compresses abdominal veins and increases the venous blood flow toward the heart. A decreased intrathoracic pressure facilitates the venous blood of the inferior vena cava of this area into the right atrium.

> Diaphragm bows down during inspiration ⟶ ↑ abdominal pressure ⟶ ↑ compression of veins ⟶ ↑ venous blood flow toward heart
>
> Diaphragm bows down during inspiration ⟶ ↑ thoracic volume ⟶ ↓ thoracic pressure ⟶ ↑ venous return into right atrium

Sympathetic nerves If venous pressure becomes too low, sympathetic nerves are reflexly stimulated and cause a vasoconstriction of veins. This vasoconstriction serves to increase venous blood pressure and venous return to the heart. Even though the vasoconstriction does increase peripheral resistance, veins have large diameters and hence the resistance generated is small.

> ↓ Venous pressure ⟶ ↑ vasomotor center activity ⟶↑ sympathetic output ⟶ venous vasoconstriction ⟶ ↑ venous blood pressure ⟶ ↑ venous return to heart

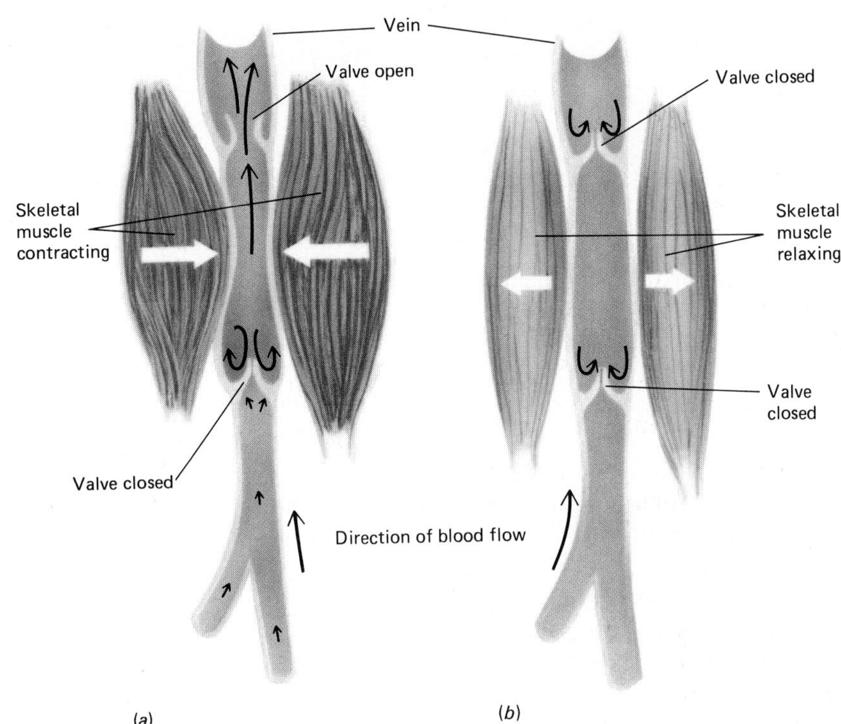

FIGURE 21-16

Skeletal muscle pump showing valve function. (*a*) Contracting skeletal muscle compresses vein and opens superior valve. (*b*) Relaxing skeletal muscle, showing the closing of valve to prevent a backflow of blood.

Clinical highlight

In **circulatory shock** blood pressure may fall so drastically that blood flow to the tissues is inadequate and tissue damage results. Shock can result from a number of conditions, including hemorrhage. In hemorrhage, blood loss results in decreased venous return and therefore reduced cardiac output. **Traumatic shock,** which is usually caused by physical injury, can occur without hemorrhage because of actual damage to the capillaries. Fluid is lost from the blood, and the person may "bleed to death" physiologically without actually losing a drop of blood. Venous return and cardiac output become too low to sustain life.

In fainting, peripheral blood vessels become dilated, so that blood pools in them and cardiac output falls. If a person who has fainted is kept in an upright position the shock may deepen, resulting in death. Luckily, when a person faints he generally falls into a horizontal position, which helps to restore normal cardiac output.

Shock may be **nonprogressive** (or compensated), in which case sympathetic reflexes and other mechanisms are able to compensate for the decreased blood volume. By vasoconstriction and increased fluid conservation, cardiac output can be increased sufficiently to maintain life (Fig. 21-17). In **progressive shock,** blood flow is so reduced that the compensatory mechanisms are not successful. A vicious cycle develops involving positive feedback, in which the heart weakens, brain activity decreases, and cardiac output progressively decreases. As shock continues to deepen, the heart, brain, blood vessels, and other organs become more damaged, further worsening the shock (Fig. 21-18).

Pathways of circulation include a pulmonary and a systemic circuit

As discussed in the previous chapter, the heart acts as a double-pump, driving blood into the pulmonary and the systemic circulation.

Pulmonary circulation carries blood to and from the lungs

Venous blood enters the pulmonary circuit via the pulmonary trunk as it leaves the right ventricle. This blood is high in CO_2 and low in O_2. The **pulmonary trunk** bifurcates into the **right** and **left pulmonary arteries,** taking the relatively deoxygenated blood to the right and left lungs, respectively. As each pulmonary artery enters the lungs, it branches into **lobar arteries.** Three lobar arteries serve the right lung and two supply the left lung. The lobar arteries branch extensively into arterioles and then into the **pulmonary capillaries** that are intimately associated with the alveoli (lung air sacs). CO_2 diffuses out of the pulmonary capillaries and into the alveoli. O_2 diffuses from the alveoli into the pulmonary capillaries.

(text continued on p. 728)

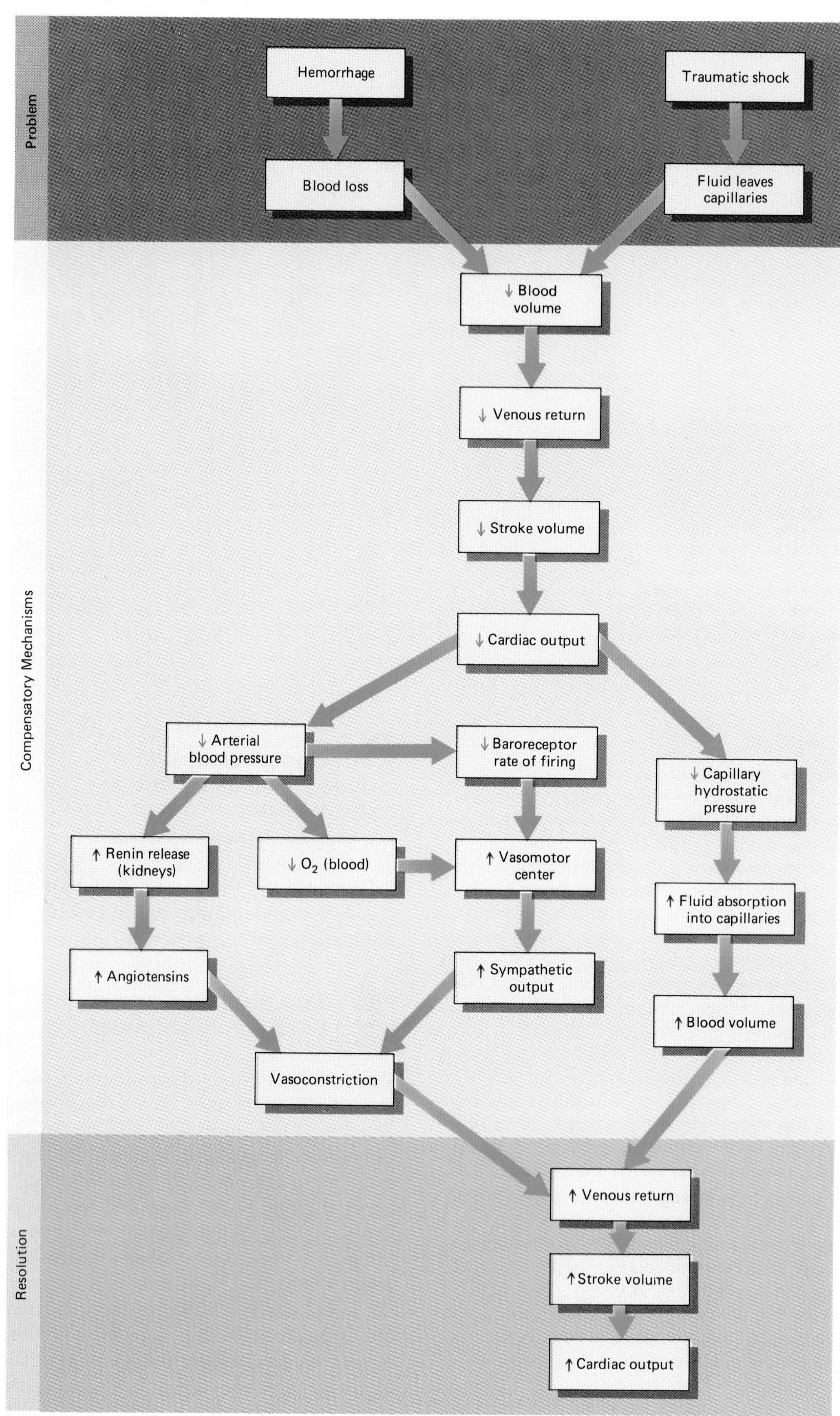

FIGURE 21-17

Homeostatic mechanisms that increase cardiac output in nonprogressive circulatory shock.

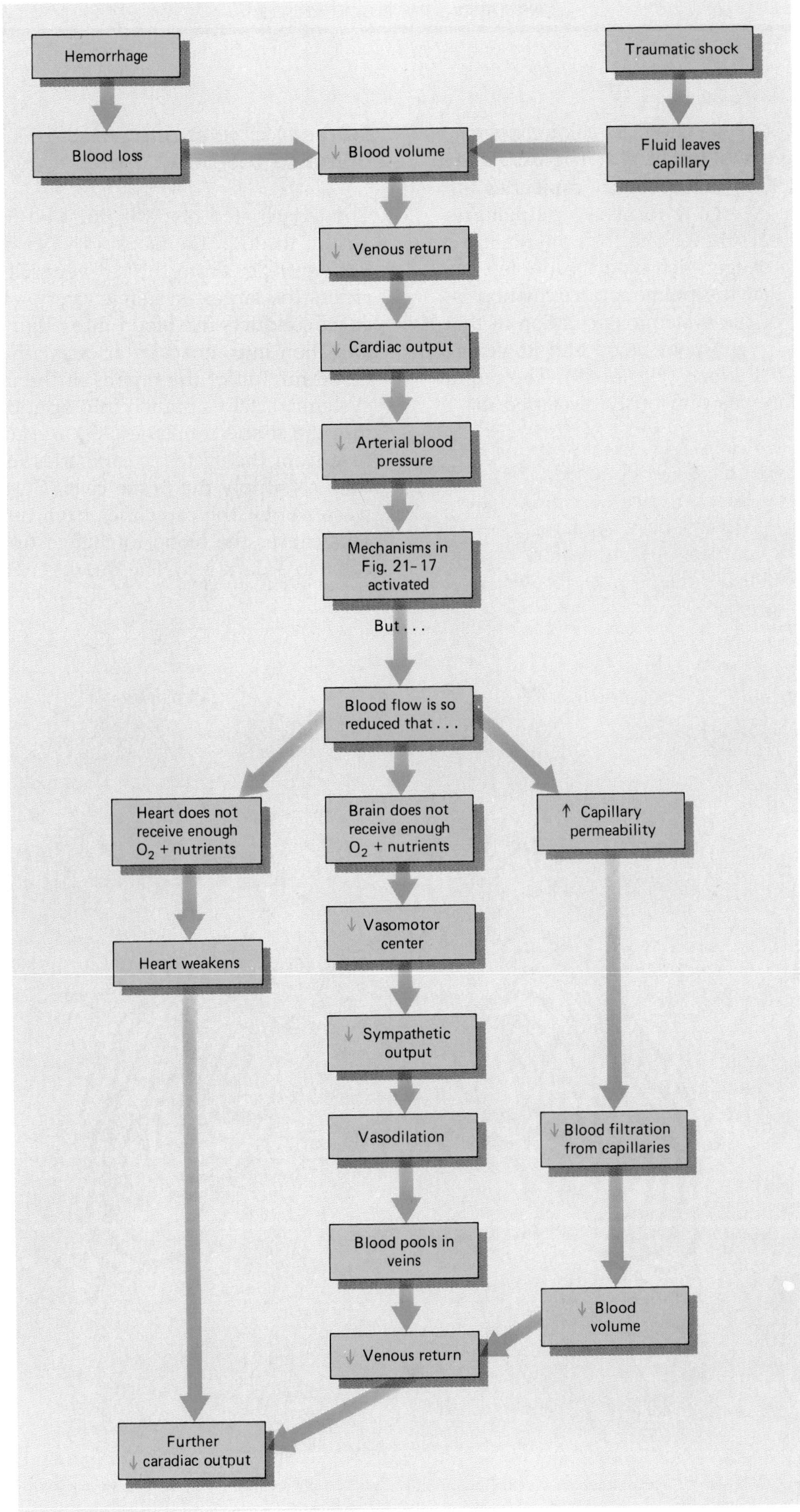

FIGURE 21-18

In progressive circulatory shock, positive feedback mechanisms develop and act to deepen the shock.

As the blood is oxygenated, its color changes from a dark red to a bright red. The oxygenated blood flows from the pulmonary capillaries into venules that converge to form two **pulmonary veins** leaving each lung. The four pulmonary veins take the oxygen-rich blood to the left atrium. Note that the pulmonary circulation is opposite that of the systemic circulation in that its arteries carry oxygen-poor blood and its veins carry oxygen-rich blood (Fig. 21-19). The pulmonary circulation was previously discussed in Chapter 20.

> Pulmonary trunk ⟶ pulmonary arteries ⟶ lobar arteries ⟶ pulmonary arterioles ⟶ pulmonary capillaries ⟶ pulmonary venules ⟶ pulmonary veins ⟶ left atrium

Systemic circulation carries blood to the body tissues

The oxygenated blood is pumped from the left atrium through the bicuspid valve and into the left ventricle. From the left ventricle, the blood enters the largest systemic artery—the **aorta.** The aorta conducts the blood into other elastic arteries and then into muscular arteries which take the blood into all of the organs of the body. Here the systemic arteries branch into arterioles and then into the tissue capillaries. O_2 and nutrients diffuse from the systemic capillaries into the interstitium to supply the tissue cells. CO_2 and metabolic wastes enter the capillaries from the tissue cells. This causes the blood to change from a bright red color to a dark red. The deoxygenated blood is

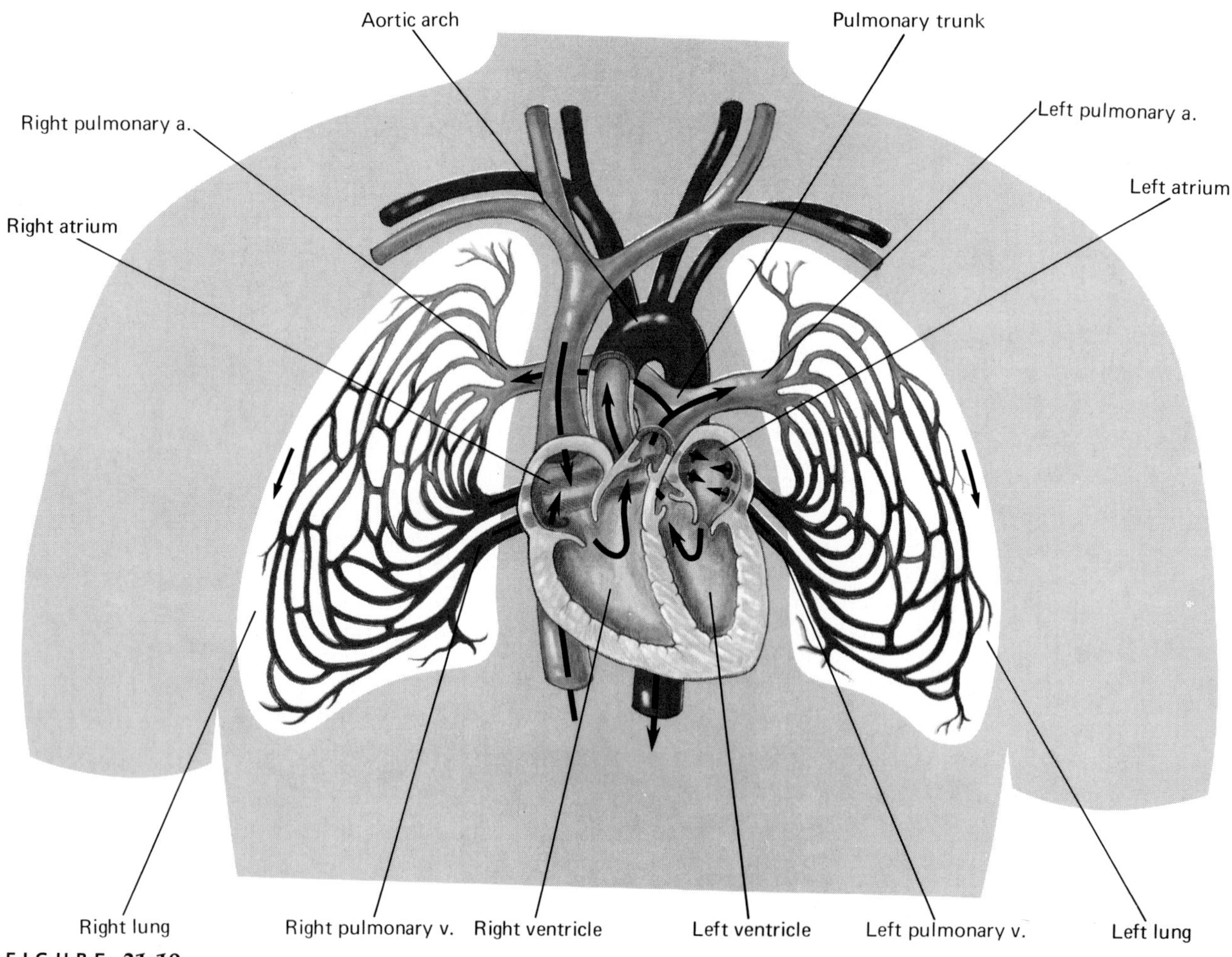

FIGURE 21-19

The pulmonary circulation. Pulmonary arteries are shown in blue because they carry deoxygenated blood; pulmonary veins are shown in red because they transport oxygenated blood.

drained from the capillaries into venules. Venules converge to form larger and larger veins until all the venous blood flows into two major veins—the **superior** and **inferior venae cavae.** From the venae cavae, the venous blood enters the right atrium and passes through the tricuspid valve into the right ventricle—ready to enter the pulmonary circuit.

Tables and figures illustrate the major systemic arteries and veins

The following tables and figures identify and describe the systemic circulation in more detail. Tables 21-6 to 21-12 and Figures 21-20 to 21-31 feature the major arteries of the systemic circulation. Tables 21-13 to 21-18 and Figures 21-32 to 21-37 feature the major veins of the systemic circulation. A summary of blood flow through the principal vessels and the heart is provided in Figure 21-41, p. 762.

Cerebral circulation supplies the brain

Four arteries, the two **internal carotid arteries** and the two **vertebral arteries** (branches of the subclavian arteries), supply the brain with blood (Figs. 21-20, 21-21, and 21-23). The vertebral arteries pass through the foramen magnum and join on the ventral surface of the brainstem to form the **basilar artery.** The basilar artery branches into the **right** and **left posterior cerebral arteries.** The internal carotid arteries enter the cranial cavity in the middle cranial fossa. Their terminal branches are the **anterior cerebral arteries** and the **middle cerebral arteries.** Small communicating arteries join the two anterior and the middle and posterior cerebral arteries, forming a circular anastomosis at the base of the brain. This anastomosis is known as the **circle of Willis.** Should one of the arteries serving the brain become blocked or impaired in some way, this interconnecting arterial circuit helps ensure that the brain cells will continue to receive an adequate blood supply through other vessels.

From the brain capillaries, blood drains into large **venous sinuses** located in folds of the dura mater. These empty into the **internal jugular veins** at either side of the neck, and blood flows into the **brachiocephalic veins.** The brachiocephalic veins drain into the **superior vena cava,** which takes the blood to the heart.

The hepatic portal system carries absorbed nutrients

As you have seen, blood generally flows from arteries to capillaries to veins. Blood normally flows through a series of veins directly to the heart. However, there are a few exceptional veins that carry blood to a second set of exchange vessels—either capillaries or sinusoids. Such veins are called **portal veins.** One such system of veins, the **hepatic portal system,** transports blood from the organs of the digestive system to the liver (Figs. 21-22 and 21-36).

Blood reaches the intestines through the **mesenteric arteries** and enters the capillaries in the intestinal villi (tiny projections of the intestinal wall through which food molecules are absorbed). Then blood rich in nutrients passes from these capillaries into the **superior mesenteric vein.** This vein empties into the **hepatic portal vein,** which conducts blood to the liver. There the hepatic portal vein gives rise to an extensive network of hepatic sinusoids, which provide the opportunity for liver cells to remove nutrients whose concentrations in the blood are above homeostatic levels. Eventually the hepatic portal sinusoids deliver blood to the **hepatic veins,** which leave the liver and empty into the inferior vena cava. Would you guess that the blood in the hepatic portal vein is rich in oxygen? Remember, it has already served the intestine. If the liver cells had to depend on whatever oxygen might be left in the blood coming from the hepatic portal vein, they probably could not survive very long. To solve this problem the liver is supplied with oxygenated blood by the **hepatic artery.** Its branches feed into the hepatic sinuses, where its blood mixes with the venous blood from the hepatic portal vein. All the blood is returned to the heart via the hepatic veins flowing into the inferior vena cava.

(*text continued on p. 754*)

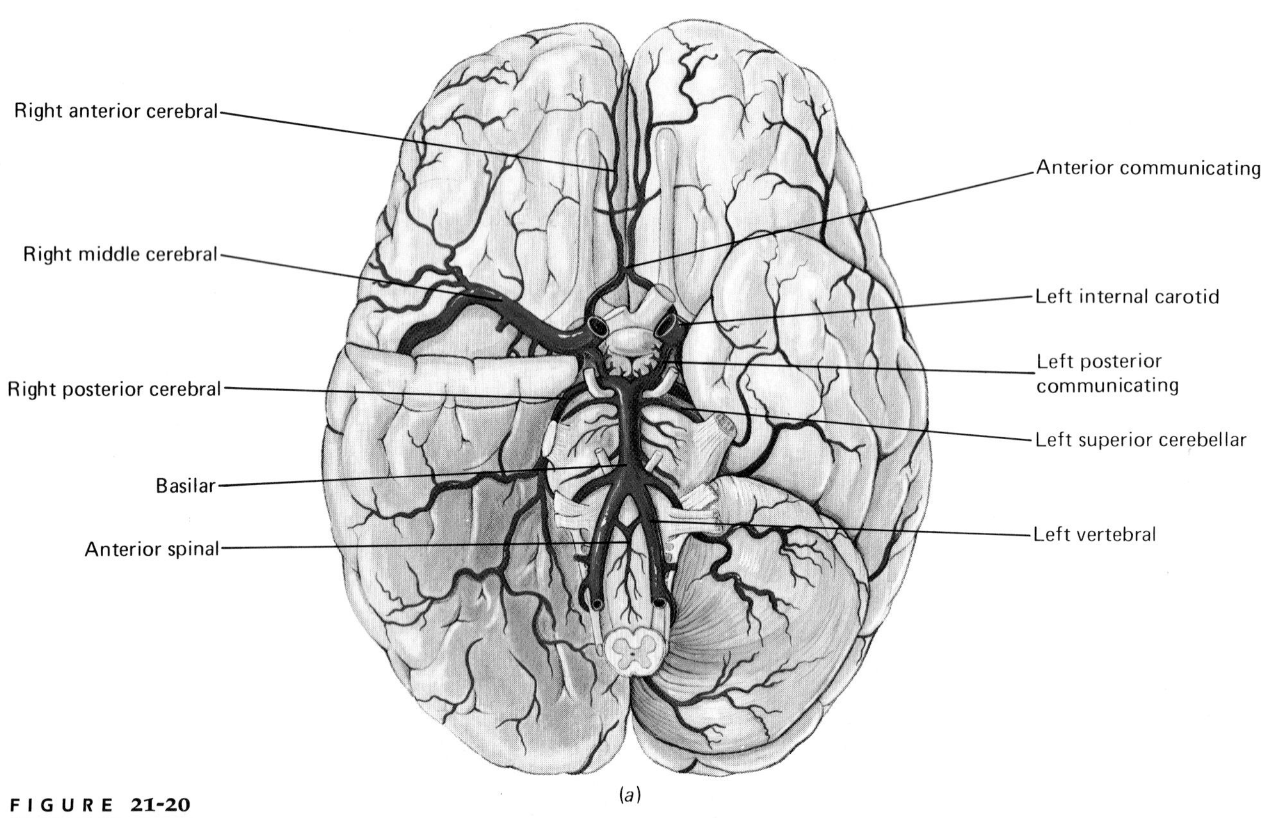

FIGURE 21-20

(a) Arterial circulation in the brain. Note the circle of Willis, which is made up of arterial anastomoses. It provides alternative circulatory pathways to ensure an adequate blood supply to the brain tissue.

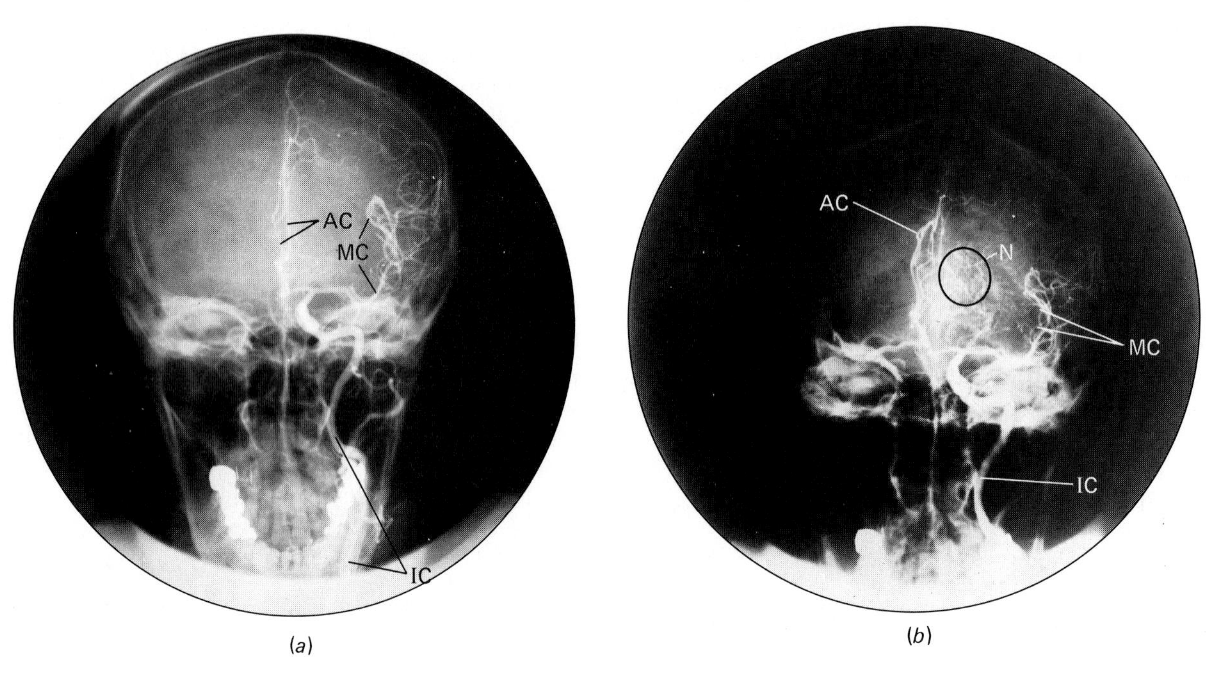

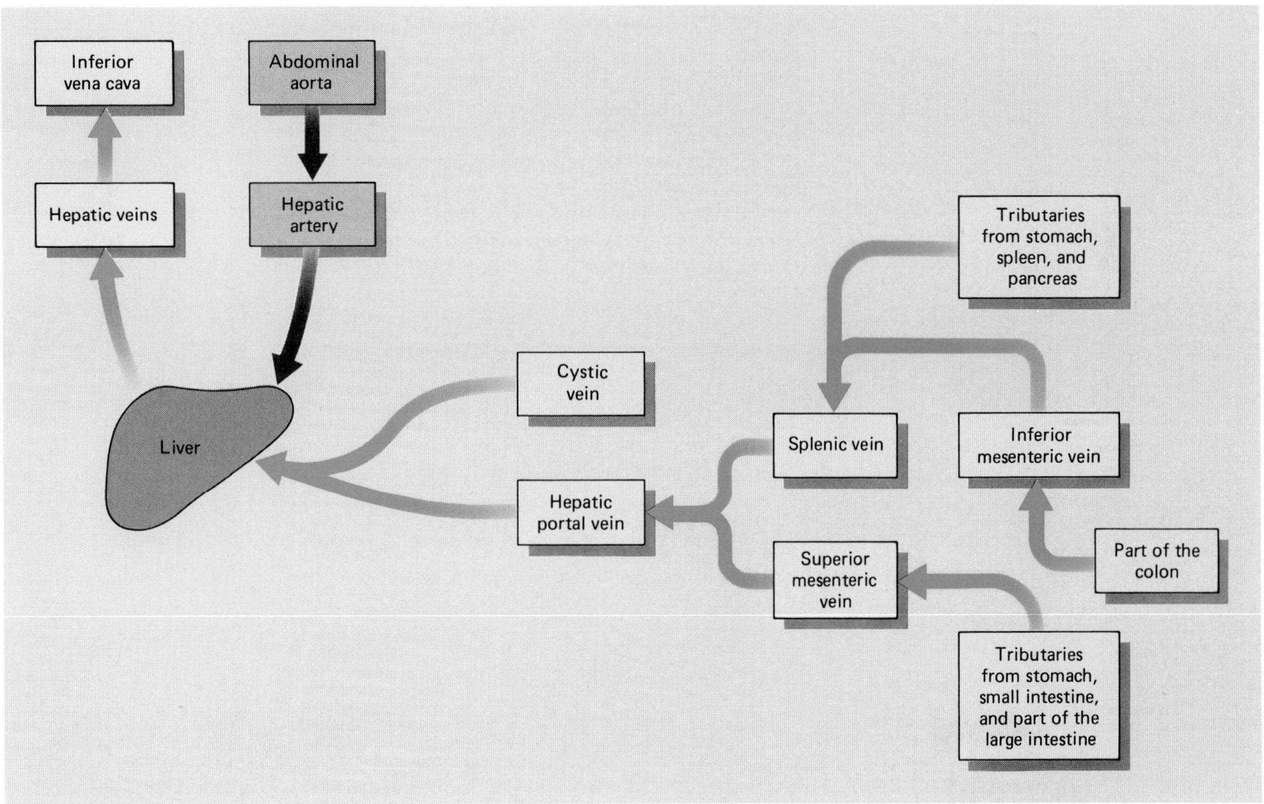

FIGURE 21-22

Flow chart pattern of blood flow through hepatic portal system.

◀ **FIGURE 21-21**

Two arteriograms of the brain from a patient with a glioblastoma (brain cancer). (*a*) This film was taken at the first symptoms of the disease and did not show any abnormality. The second x-ray (*b*) was one of a series of arteriograms taken 4 months later. The vascular area indicated represents the location of the neoplasm. Note that the anterior cerebral arteries have been displaced to the right by the neoplasm. AC, anterior cerebral arteries; N, neoplasm; MC, branches of middle cerebral artery; IC, internal carotid artery.

TABLE 21-6

Branches of the ascending aorta	**See Figures 20-14 and 20-15.**
Branch*	**Description and region supplied**
Right coronary artery (S)	Branches from the ascending aorta just superior to the aortic valve. Gives off marginal branch before it passes to the posterior surface of the heart. At the posterior interventricular groove the right coronary artery anastomoses with the left coronary artery. The right coronary artery supplies the right atrium. Its **marginal artery** supplies the right ventricle. Near its termination the right coronary gives off the **posterior interventricular artery** (posterior descending), which supplies both ventricles.
Left coronary artery (S)	Branches from the ascending aorta just superior to the aortic valve. Larger than the right coronary artery. Encircles the heart to the left and anastomoses with the right coronary artery at the posterior interventricular groove. Supplies branches to the left atrium and left ventricle, as well as the right ventricle. Main branches include the **anterior interventricular artery** (anterior descending), which descends in the anterior interventricular groove; the **left marginal artery;** and the **circumflex artery,** which serves the walls of the left ventricle and left atrium.

*In the following tables, blood vessels are in pairs (right and left) unless indicated as single (S).

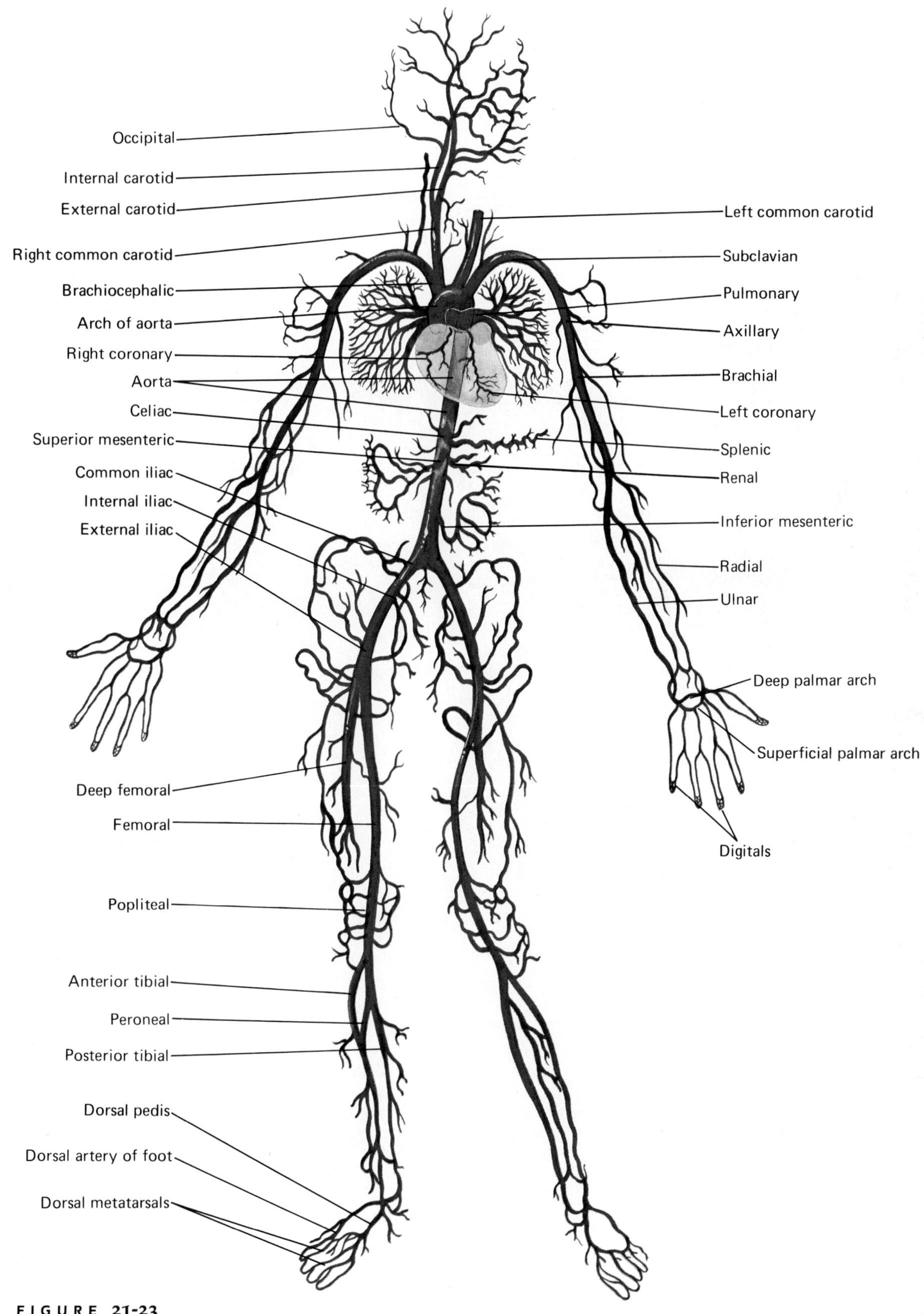

FIGURE 21-23

A detailed view of the principal arteries of the systemic circulation. The head is turned to the side and only the branches of the right common carotid are shown in the head region.

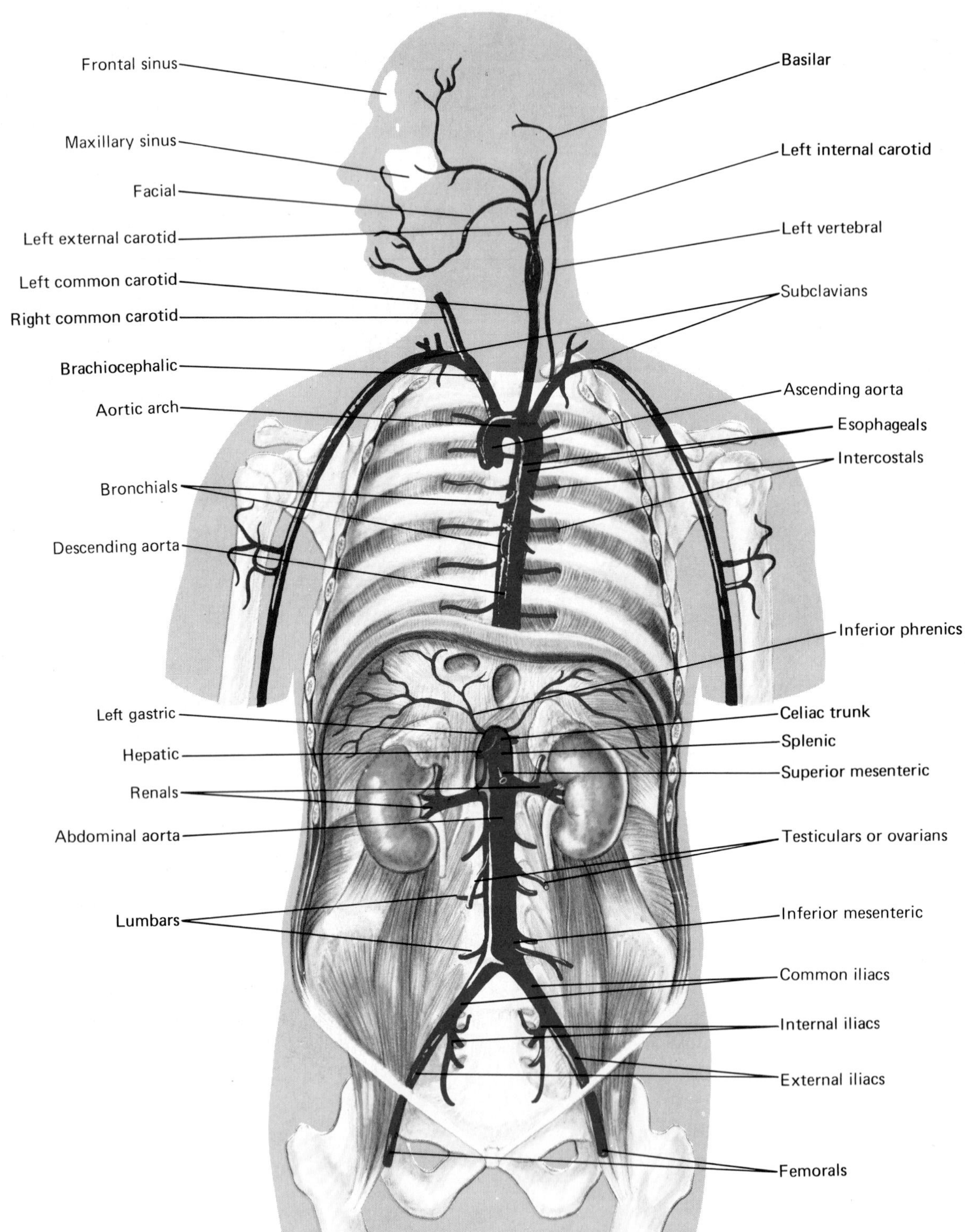
Frontal sinus
Maxillary sinus
Facial
Left external carotid
Left common carotid
Right common carotid
Brachiocephalic
Aortic arch
Bronchials
Descending aorta
Left gastric
Hepatic
Renals
Abdominal aorta
Lumbars
Basilar
Left internal carotid
Left vertebral
Subclavians
Ascending aorta
Esophageals
Intercostals
Inferior phrenics
Celiac trunk
Splenic
Superior mesenteric
Testiculars or ovarians
Inferior mesenteric
Common iliacs
Internal iliacs
External iliacs
Femorals

FIGURE 21-24

The aorta and its principal branches.

TABLE 21-7

The aorta and its principal branches

Division of aorta	Arterial branch	Region supplied
Ascending aorta	Coronary arteries	Wall of heart
Aortic arch	Brachiocephalic (innominate)	
	Right common carotid	Branches into external carotid (supplying neck and head) and internal carotid (supplying brain and head)
	Right subclavian	Sends branches to neck and right upper limb
	Left common carotid	Branches into external carotid (supplying neck and head) and internal carotid (supplying brain and head)
	Left subclavian	Sends branches to neck and left upper limb
Thoracic aorta	*Visceral Branches:*	
	Pericardial	Pericardium
	Bronchial	Bronchi of lungs
	Esophageal	Esophagus
	Parietal Branches:	
	Several pairs of posterior intercostal arteries	Intercostal and other chest muscles, and pleurae. Join with other arteries that serve chest wall and anterior abdominal wall
	Subcostal	Last pair of arteries to branch from thoracic aorta. Serve abdominal wall
	Superior phrenic	Posterior diaphragm
Abdominal aorta	*Visceral Branches:*	
	Celiac	Branches to supply the liver (common hepatic artery), stomach (left gastric artery), and spleen, pancreas, and stomach (splenic artery)
	Superior mesenteric	Small intestine; ascending colon and proximal two thirds of transverse colon; pancreas
	Suprarenal (middle)	Adrenal glands
	Renal	Kidneys; adrenal glands
	Ovarian (in female)	Ovaries
	Testicular (in male)	Testes
	Inferior mesenteric	Distal one third of transverse colon, descending colon, sigmoid colon, and rectum
	Common iliac	
	External	Lower limbs
	Internal	Branches supply gluteal muscles, urinary bladder, uterus, vagina
	Parietal Branches:	
	Inferior phrenic	Diaphragm (inferior surface); adrenal glands
	Lumbar	Spinal cord and lumbar region of back
	Middle sacral	Sacrum, coccyx, gluteus maximus, and rectum

TABLE 21-8

Branches of common carotid arteries	
Branches and sub-branches	**Region supplied**
Right common carotid (S)	The right and left common carotid arteries are the main arteries of the head and neck (Fig. 21-26). The right common carotid passes upward along the side of the trachea into the neck. (You can feel the carotid pulse by gently pressing your fingertips over this area.) At the upper level of the larynx, the common carotid divides into **external** and **internal carotid arteries.**
External carotid	Passes upward on the side of the head. Gives off branches that serve structures in neck, pharynx, face, ear, and skull.
Superior thyroid	Thyroid gland and larynx.
Lingual	Tongue and salivary glands beneath the tongue.
Facial	Pharynx and various parts of the face.
Occipital	Neck muscles, scalp, and meninges.
Posterior auricular	Ear and scalp.
Superficial temporal	The smaller terminal branch of the external carotid. Supplies the parotid gland and the masseter muscle and gives off branches that supply surface structures of the face and scalp.
Maxillary	The larger terminal branch of the external carotid. Its branches supply the upper and lower jaws, the teeth, muscles of mastication, nose, and dura mater of the brain.
Internal carotid	Formed from the common carotid artery. Passes upward along the pharynx and into the skull. Main blood supply to the brain. At its origin the internal carotid has a slight swelling, the **carotid sinus.** This area is supplied with nerve endings that make up a tiny sense receptor called a baroreceptor. It responds to changes in blood pressure. Near the carotid sinus is another sense receptor, the **carotid body,** that responds to a decrease in oxygen in the blood. Both of these sense receptors help to regulate blood pressure. Branches of the internal carotid artery include the ophthalmic artery, the posterior communicating artery, and its terminating branches, the anterior and middle cerebral arteries.
Ophthalmic	Branches from the internal carotid. Supplies the eyeball and structures within the orbit.
Posterior communicating	Branches from the internal carotid artery and forms part of the circle of Willis (Fig. 21-20). (See discussion in text in section on cerebral circulation.)
Anterior and middle cerebral	Terminal branches of the internal carotid. Supply the cerebrum.
Left common carotid (S)	Branches directly from the aortic arch. Corresponds to the right common carotid just described, and its branches correspond to those on the right side.

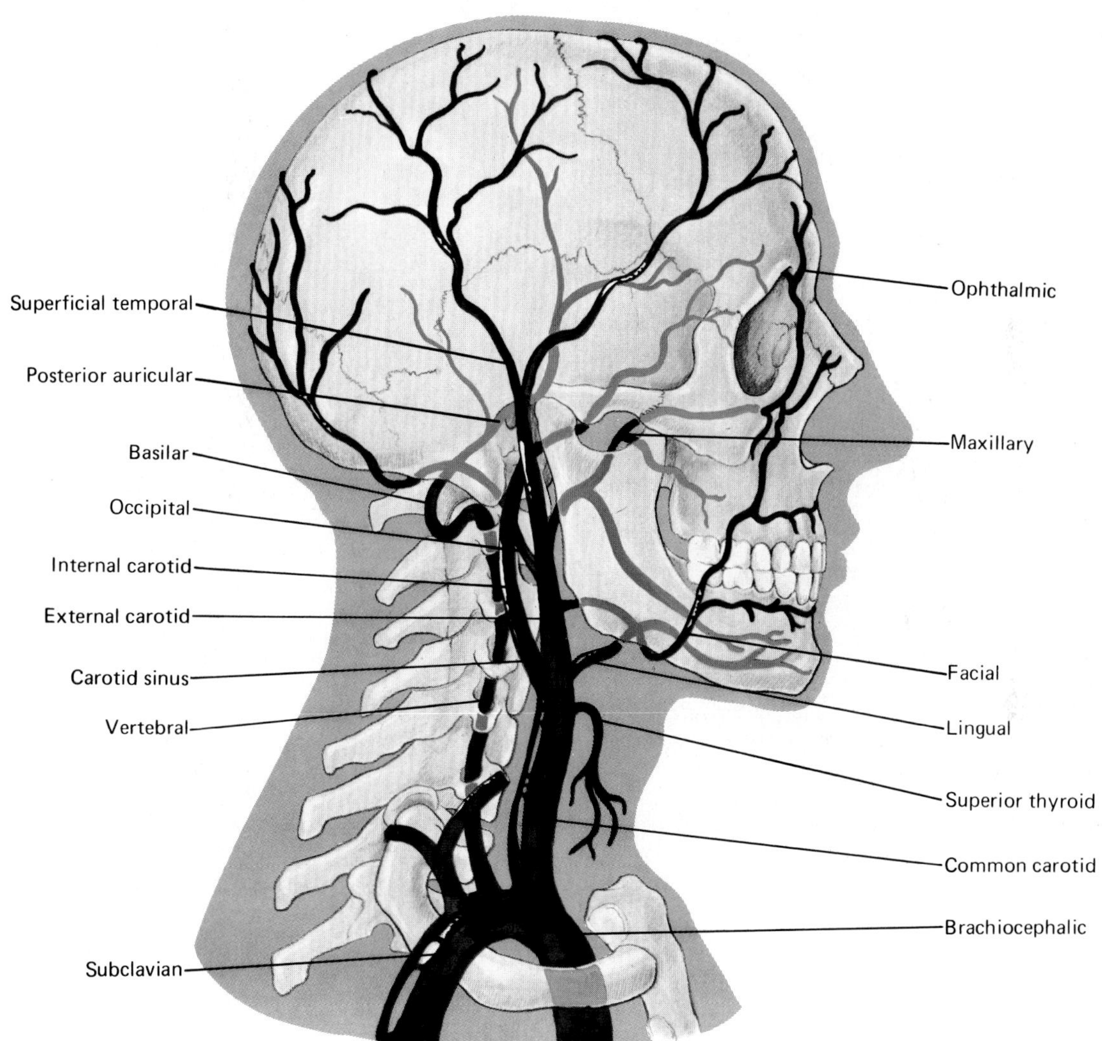

FIGURE 21-25

The principal arteries of the neck and head.

TABLE 21-9

Branches of the right subclavian artery	
Branches and sub-branches	**Region supplied**
Brachiocephalic (innominate) (S)	First and largest branch of the arch of aorta (Fig. 21-26*b*). It is 4–5 cm in length. Ascends through the mediastinum to a point near the junction of the right clavicle and sternum. There it branches to form the right subclavian artery and the right common carotid artery.
Right sublcavian (S)	Passes to right shoulder. Gives off several branches including (1) the vertebral artery, (2) the thyrocervical trunk, and (3) the internal thoracic (mammary) artery. At the lateral border of the first rib, the right subclavian becomes the right axillary artery.
Vertebral	Supplies the neck, part of the spinal cord, and the brain. It passes upward in the neck through the transverse foramina of the upper six cervical vertebrae and enters the skull via the foramen magnum. The right vertebral joins with the left vertebral to form the basilar artery at the base of the brain (Fig. 21-20).
Thyrocervical	Supplies the thyroid gland, trachea, larynx, and other tissues of the neck.
Internal thoracic (mammary)	Supplies the thymus, pectoral muscles, and mammary glands. Sometimes it is surgically repositioned to supply the heart muscle when the coronary arteries have been seriously blocked by atherosclerosis.
Axillary	Begins at the outer border of the first rib (Fig. 21-26*b*). At the lower border of the teres major muscle (i.e., as it passes into the arm), it becomes the brachial artery. Supplies pectoral muscles, shoulder muscles, shoulder joint
Brachial	As the axillary artery passes into the arm, it becomes the brachial artery. The brachial **artery** passes down through the arm. In the forearm, about 1 cm below the elbow joint, it divides to form the **radial** and **ulnar** arteries. The lateral radial and medial ulnar arteries supply the hand and fingers. In the palm region they anastomose to form the two palmar arches—the **superficial** and **deep palmar arches.** From these arches arise the **digital arteries,** which serve the thumb and fingers.

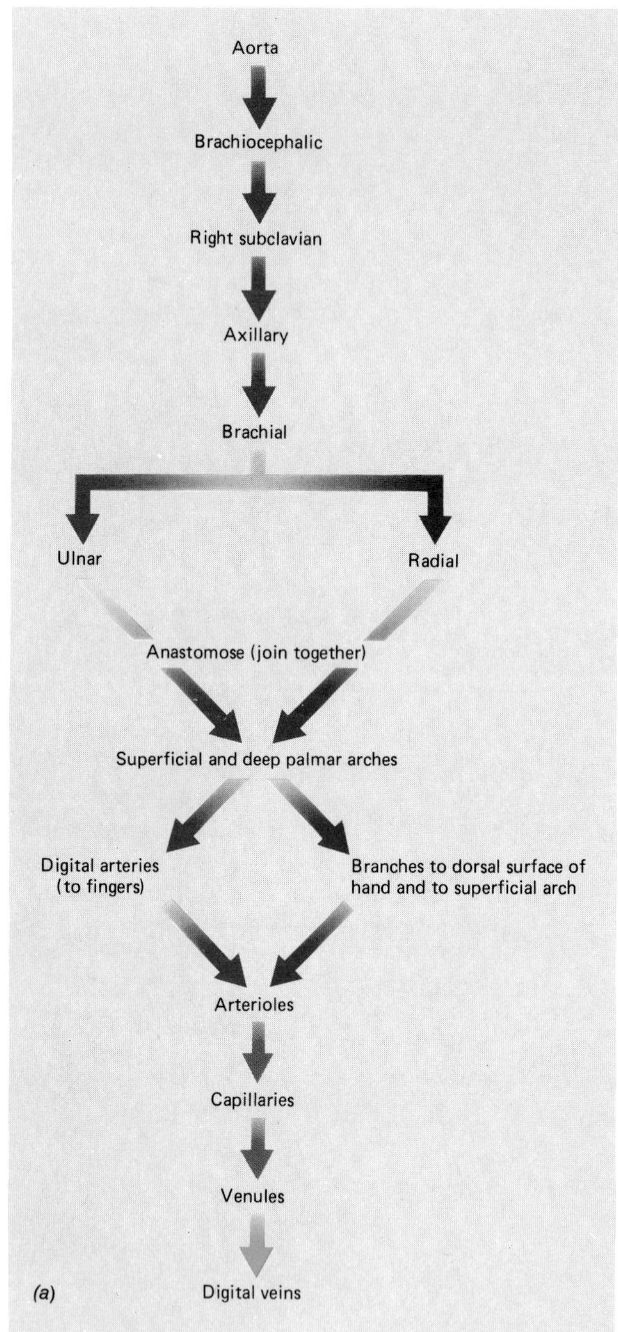

FIGURE 21-26

(*a*) Flow chart pattern of arterial circulation of upper limb.

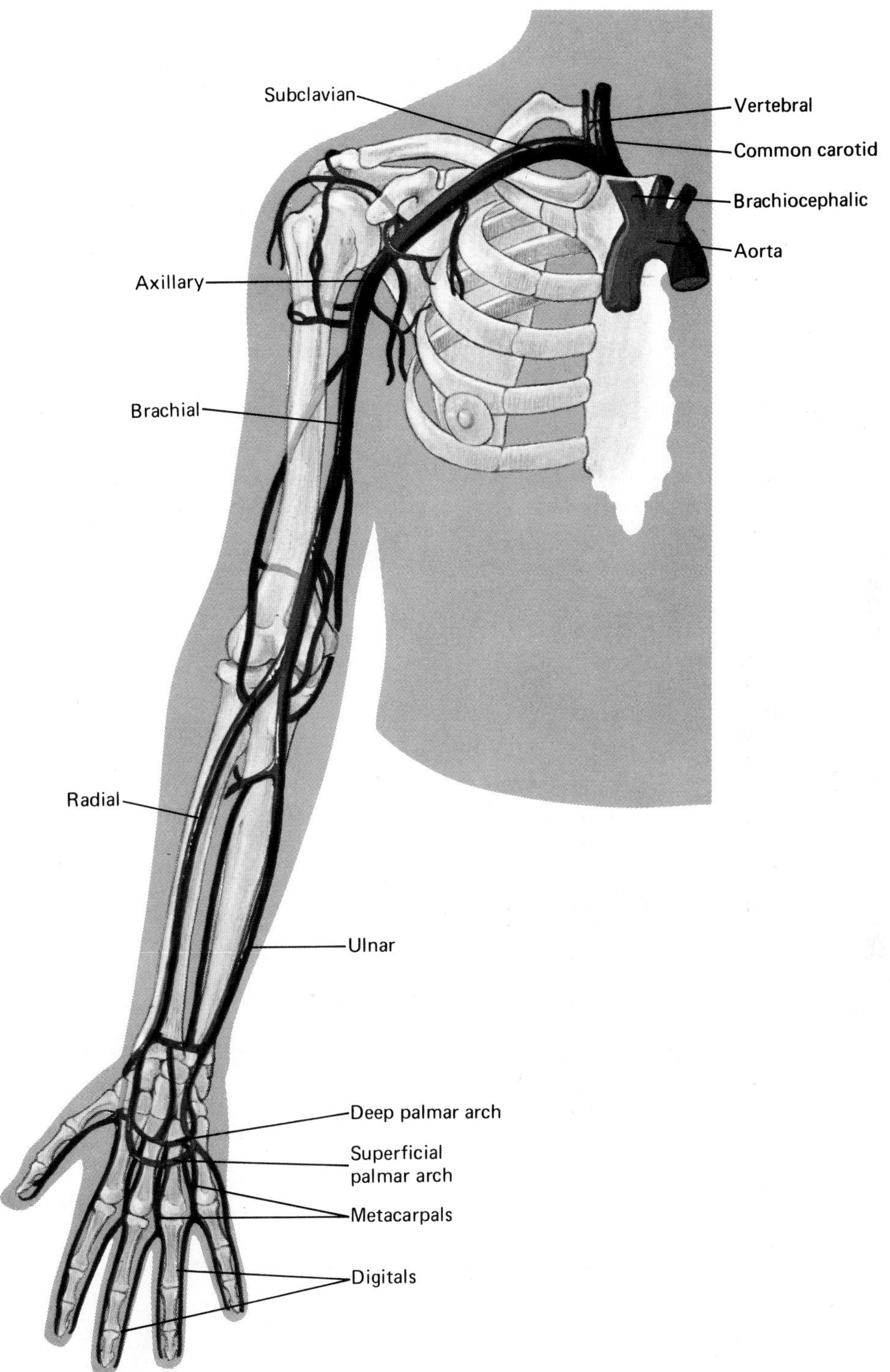

(*b*) Arterial circulation in the right upper limb.

TABLE 21-10

Branches of the thoracic aorta	
The thoracic aorta is the portion of the descending aorta that runs along the posterior mediastinum	
Branches	**Description and region supplied**
Visceral Branches	
Pericardial	A few small vessels that supply the pericardium
Bronchial	Vary in number, usually one right and two left; supply bronchial tubes (nonrespiratory tissues)
Esophageal	Four or five arteries; supply esophagus
Mediastinal	Numerous; supply lymph nodes and connective tissue of the mediastinum
Phrenic	Several small vessels that supply posterior diaphragm
Parietal branches	
Posterior intercostal	Usually nine pairs; supply intercostal muscles, deep muscles of back, vertebrae, and spinal cord
Subcostal	Last pair of arteries to branch from thoracic aorta; parallel with intercostal arteries; also the anterolateral abdominal wall

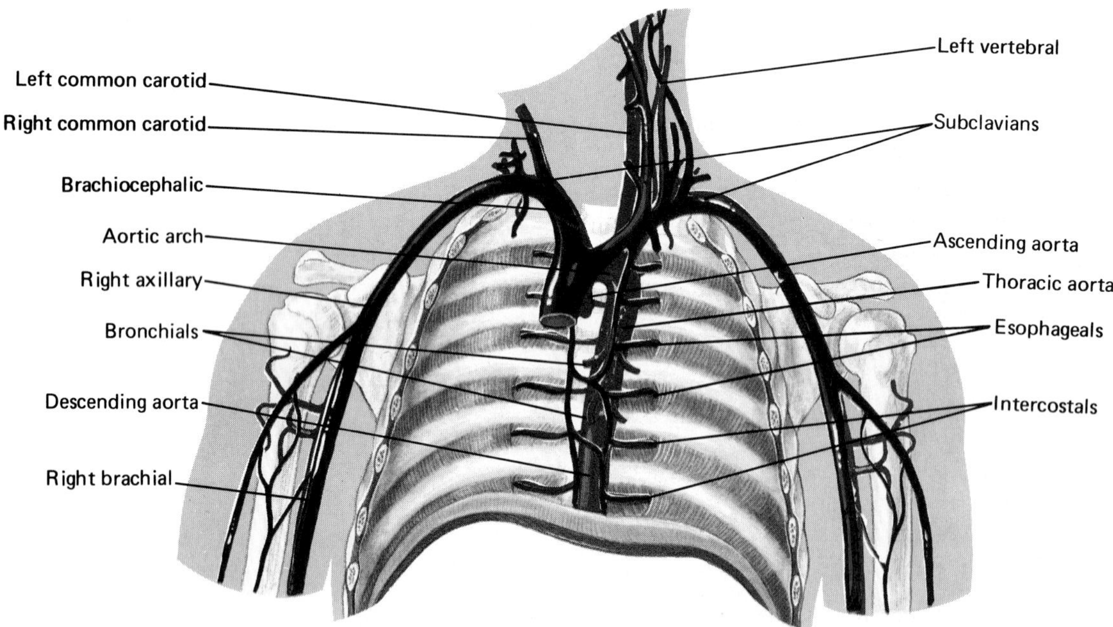

FIGURE 21-27

Arteries of thorax.

TABLE 21-11

Branches of the abdominal aorta	
The abdominal aorta is the portion of the descending aorta below the level of the diaphragm (see Fig. 21-28).	
Branches	**Region supplied**
Visceral branches	
Celiac (S)	Sometimes called celiac trunk (Figs. 21-28 and 21-29). First artery to branch from abdominal aorta. It has three branches: the common hepatic artery, left gastric artery, and splenic artery.
Left gastric (S)	Supplies stomach
Common hepatic (S)	Supplies liver and gallbladder; pancreas; duodenum
Splenic (S)	Largest branch of celiac; supplies spleen, pancreas, and stomach
Superior mesenteric (S)	Supplies small intestine, ascending colon and proximal two thirds of transverse colon; pancreas
Suprarenal (middle)	Supplies adrenal glands
Renal	Supplies kidneys; adrenal glands (inferior suprarenal arteries)
Testicular	In male only; extends into scrotum and supplies testes
Ovarian	In female only; supplies ovaries
Inferior mesenteric (S)	Distal one third of transverse colon, descending colon, sigmoid colon, and rectum
Parietal branches	
Inferior phrenic	Supplies inferior surface of diaphragm; adrenal glands (superior suprarenal arteries)
Lumbar	Usually four pairs; supplies muscles and skin of back and spinal cord
Middle sacral (S)	A small branch from the posterior of the aorta just before it branches to form the common iliac arteries. Descends in midline, ending in coccyx. Supplies sacrum, coccyx, and rectum

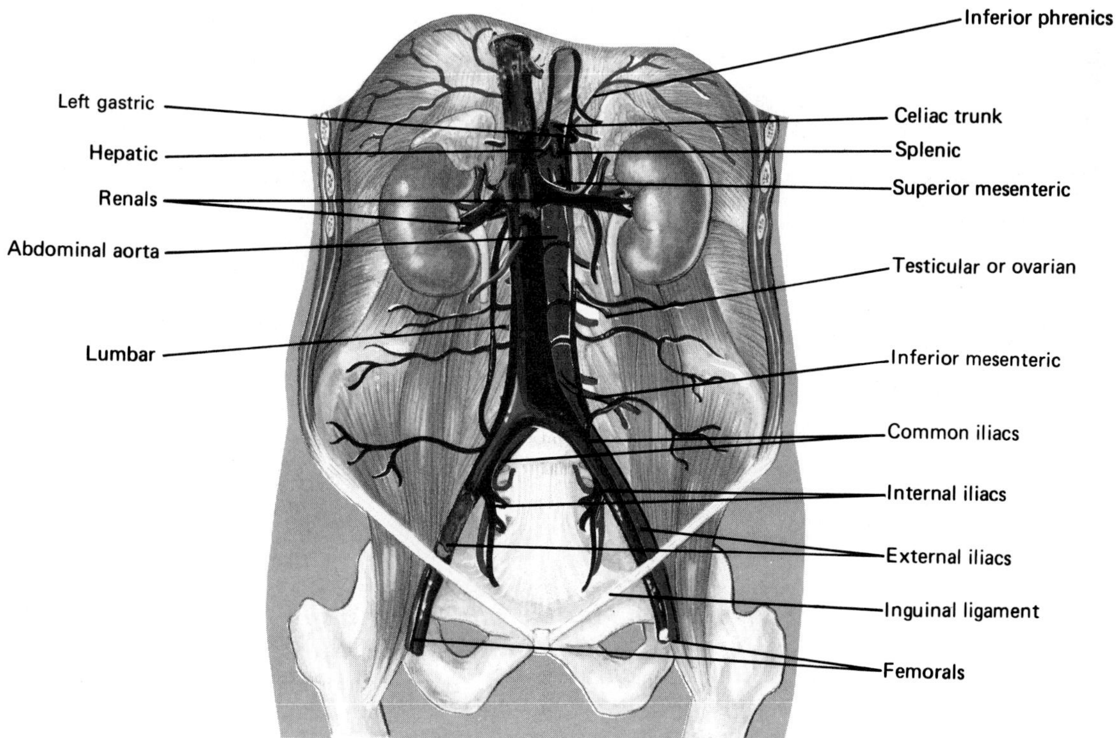

FIGURE 21-28

Abdominal aorta and principal branches in anterior view.

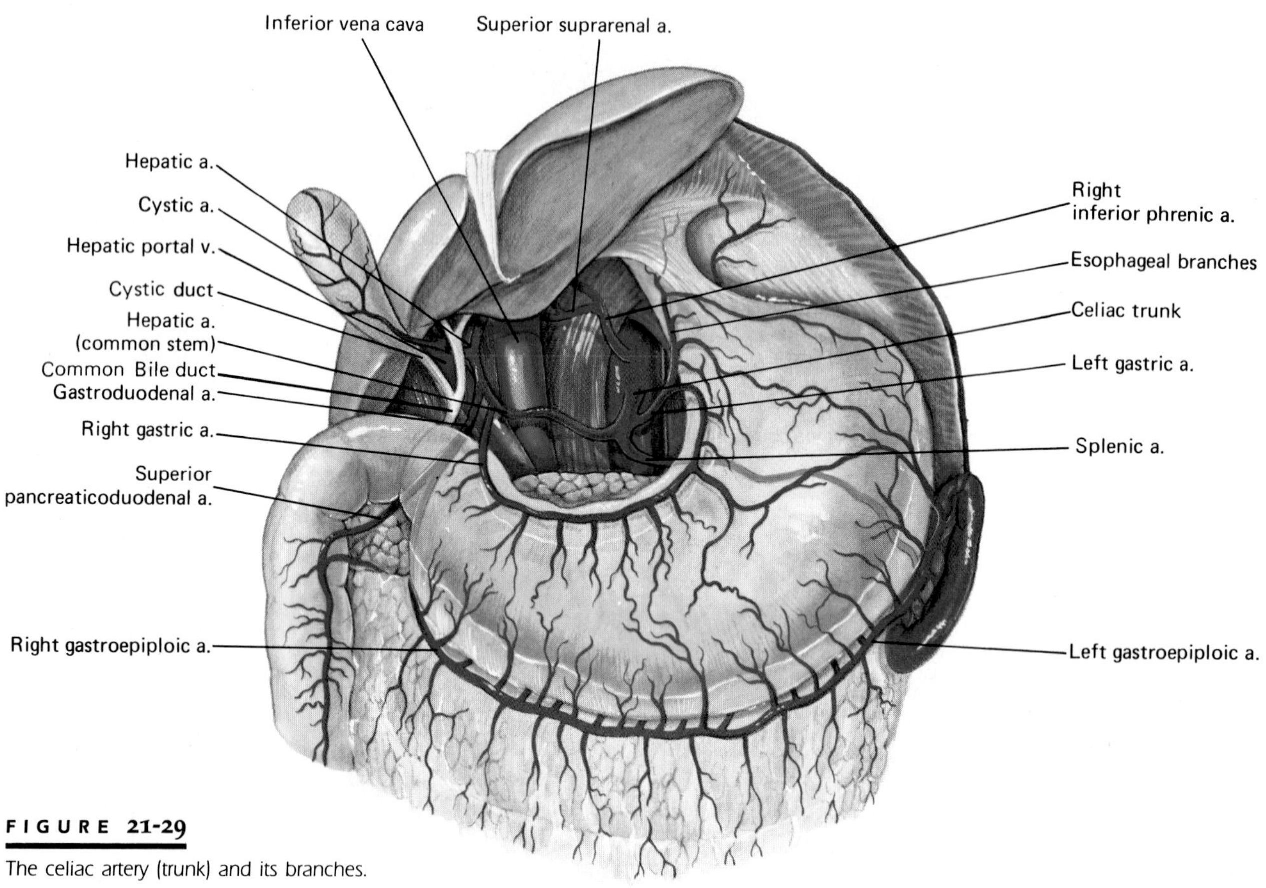

FIGURE 21-29

The celiac artery (trunk) and its branches.

TABLE 21-12

Arteries of the pelvis and lower limbs

Artery	Description and region supplied
Common iliac	The abdominal aorta divides at the level of the fourth lumbar vertebra to form the paired common iliac arteries. Between the fifth lumbar vertebra and the sacrum, each common iliac divides to form external and internal iliac arteries (Fig. 21-30)
Internal iliac	Gives rise to several branches. Supplies urinary bladder, rectum, prostate gland in male, uterus and vagina in female, gluteal and pelvic muscles
External iliac	Supplies blood to lower limbs. The external iliacs are larger than the internal iliacs. From its origin at the division of the common iliac artery, each external iliac descends into the thigh. It gives off branches at the level of the inguinal ligament and then becomes the femoral artery
Femoral	Chief artery of the lower limb. Femoral descends along posterior medial part of thigh. At the back of the knee, the femoral artery becomes the popliteal
Popliteal	Branches of the popliteal supply the knee joint and muscles of the leg. At the lower border of the popliteal fossa, the popliteal artery divides to form the anterior and posterior tibial arteries
Anterior tibial	Descends between the tibia and fibula. Gives branches to the skin and muscles of the leg. Continues on the dorsum of the foot as the **dorsalis pedis artery,** which supplies the foot and toes (Fig. 21-30)
Posterior tibial	Passes down the leg beneath the calf muscle. Some of its branches become part of the anastomoses of the knee and ankle. In the ankle region it divides into **medial** and **lateral plantar arteries,** which supply the foot and toes (Fig. 21-30)
Peroneal	Branches from posterior tibial. Supplies structures on medial side of the fibula and calcaneus. Sends branches that become part of the anastomosis of the ankle; also sends branches to the heel

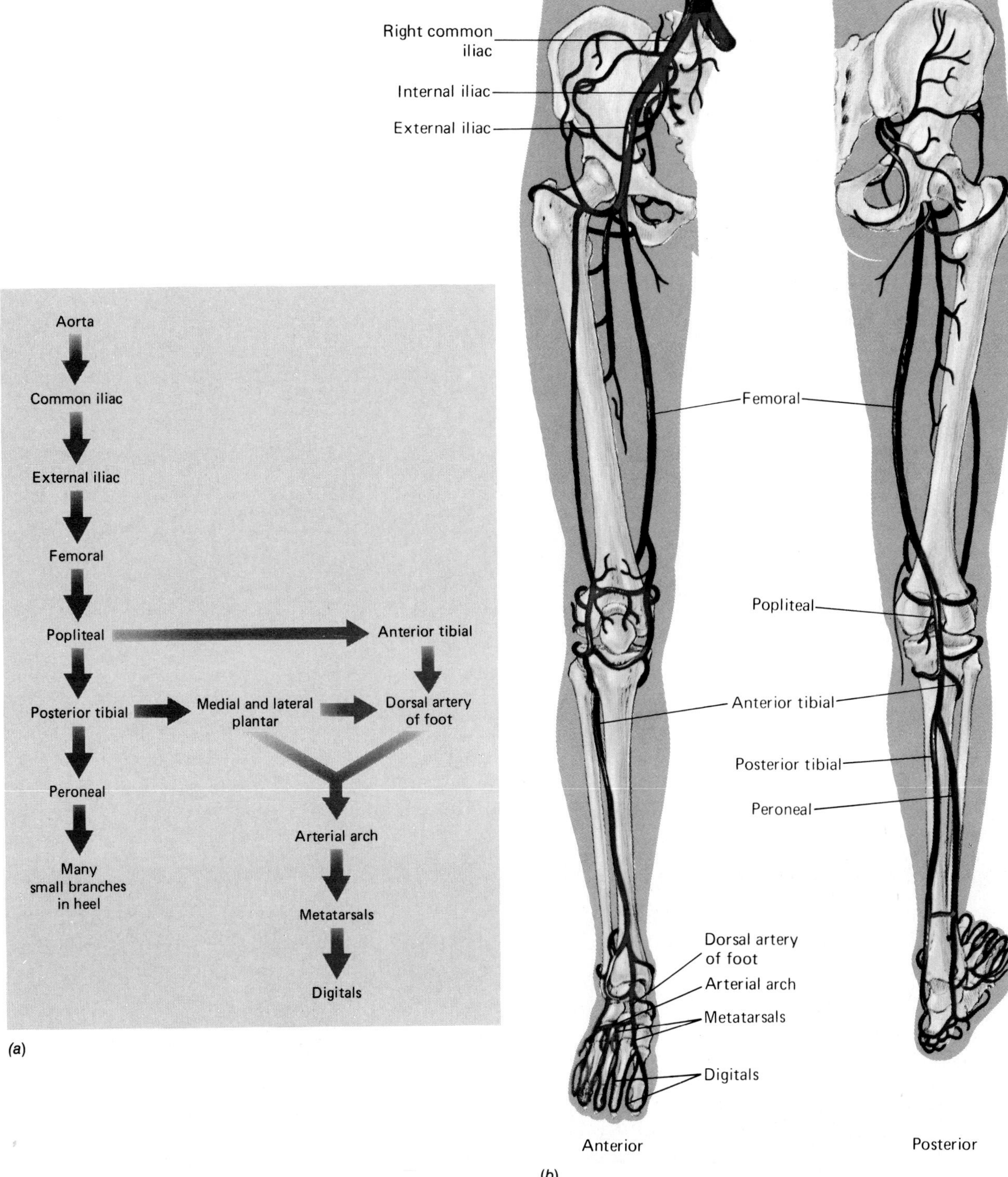

FIGURE 21-30

(*a*) Flow chart of arterial circulation in lower limb. (*b*) Arterial circulation in the right lower limb. The medial and lateral plantar arteries cannot be seen in these views.

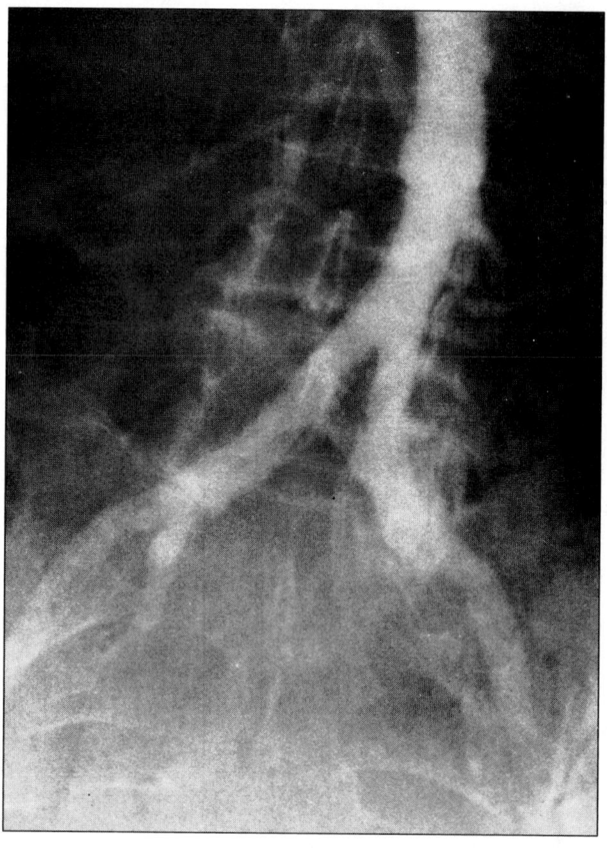

FIGURE 21-31

Arteriogram of the lower portion of the aorta, showing it branching into the common iliac arteries. (Courtesy of Jon N. Ehringer)

TABLE 21-13

Veins draining into the venae cavae

Vein	Formed from	Area(s) drained
Into superior vena cava:		
Internal jugular	Sinuses of dura mater	Brain, skull
External jugular	Veins of face	Muscles and skin of face and scalp
Subclavian	Axillary, cephalic, basilic and their tributaries, scapular, and thoracic veins	Upper limbs, chest, breast
Brachiocephalic (innominate)	Internal jugular, external jugular, and subclavian	Brain, face, neck, and upper limbs
Azygos	Lumbar and intercostal veins	Posterior aspect of thoracic and abdominal cavities
Into inferior vena cava:		
Hepatic	Sinusoids of liver	Liver
Renal	Veins of kidney	Kidney; left testis; left ovary
Right ovarian or testicular	Veins of right ovary or testis	Ovaries or testes
Common iliac	External iliac (extension of the femoral vein)	Lower limbs
	Internal iliac	Organs of pelvis and perineum

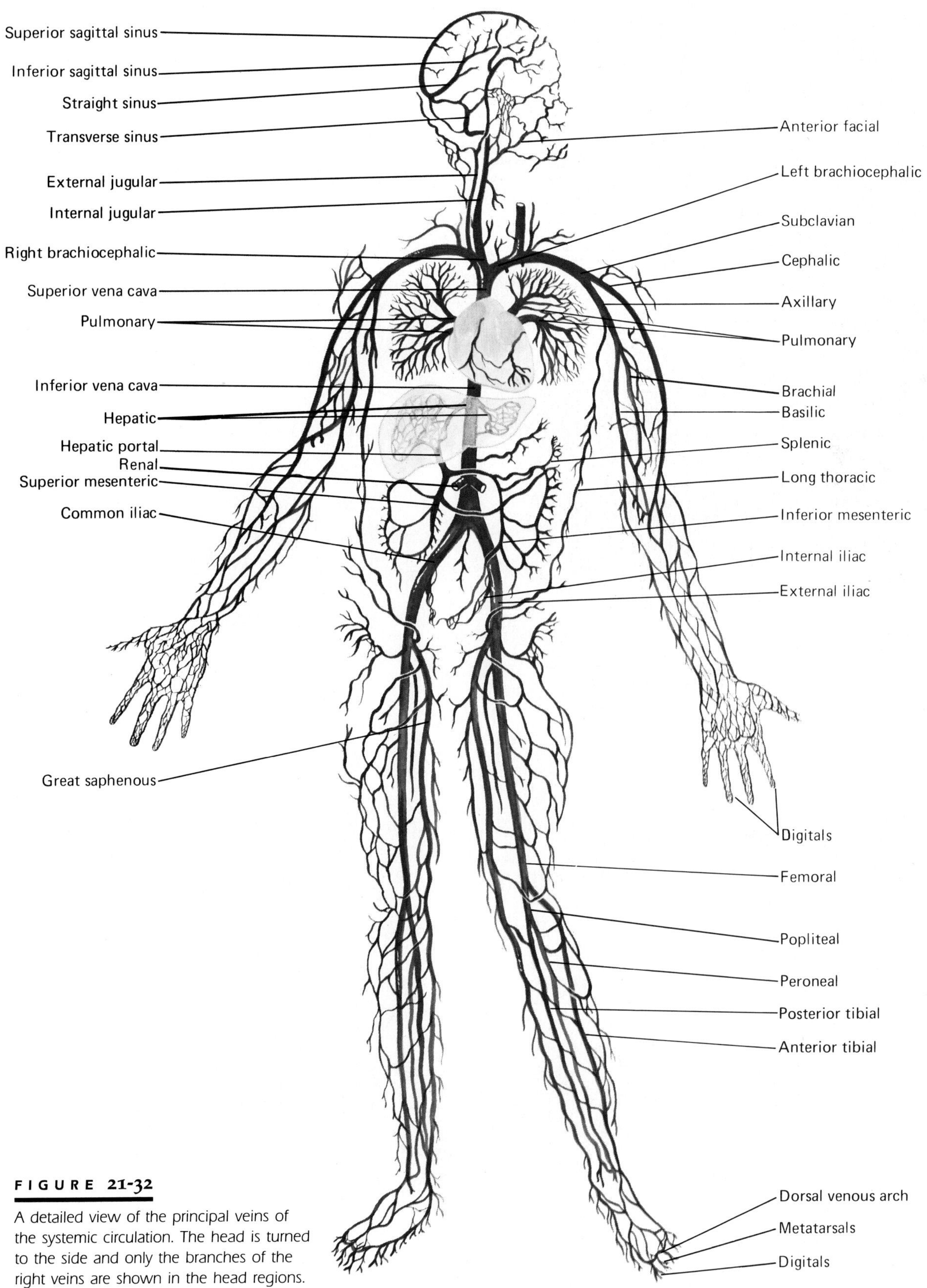

FIGURE 21-32

A detailed view of the principal veins of the systemic circulation. The head is turned to the side and only the branches of the right veins are shown in the head regions.

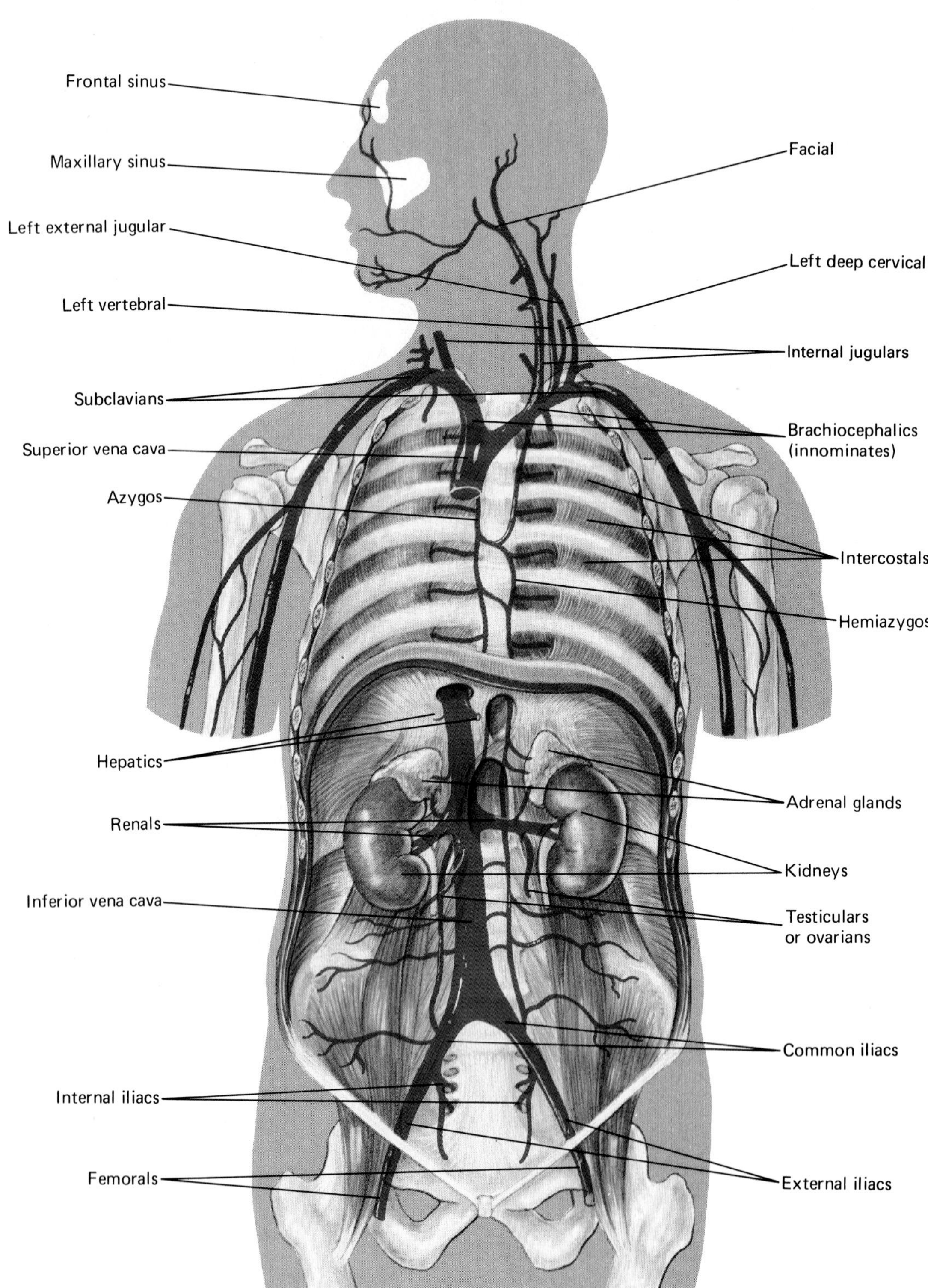

FIGURE 21-33

Principal veins entering the superior and inferior vena cava.

TABLE 21-14

Veins of the head and neck	
Vein	**Description and region drained**
External jugular	Receives blood from scalp and face veins. Begins at about the level of the parotid gland, then runs down the neck toward the middle of the clavicle. Empties into the subclavian vein at the base of the neck (Fig. 21-34)
Internal jugular	Receives blood from the brain, face, and neck. Begins at the base of the skull in the jugular foramen as a direct continuation of the **sigmoid sinus** (a sinus within the dura that drains blood from the brain). Each internal jugular runs down through the neck within the **carotid sheath** (a connective tissue sheath in which also run the common and internal carotids and the vagus nerve). Behind the sternal end of the clavicle, the internal jugular unites with the subclavian vein to form the brachiocephalic vein. The brachiocephalic empties into the superior vena cava

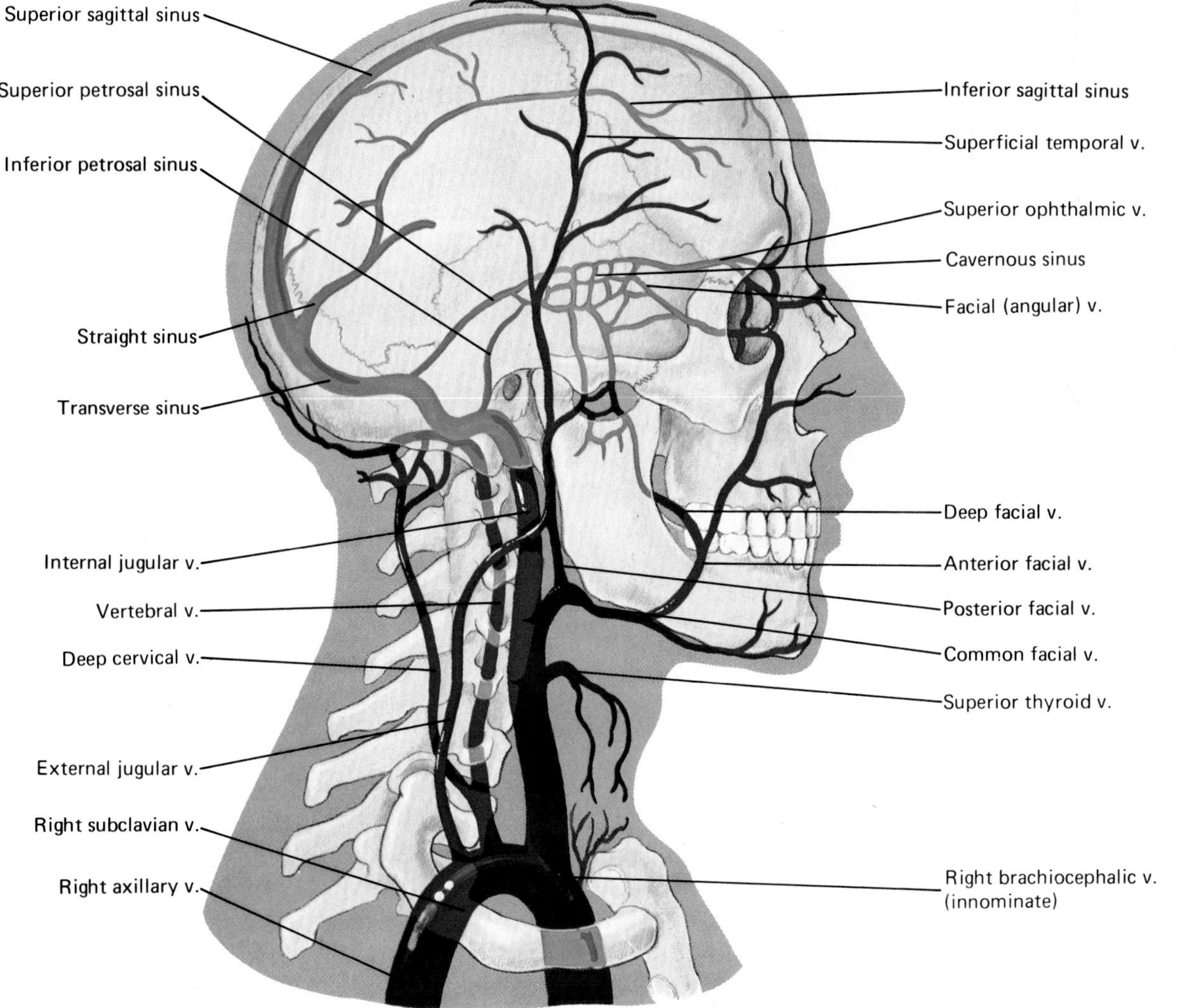

FIGURE 21-34

The principal veins of the head and neck.

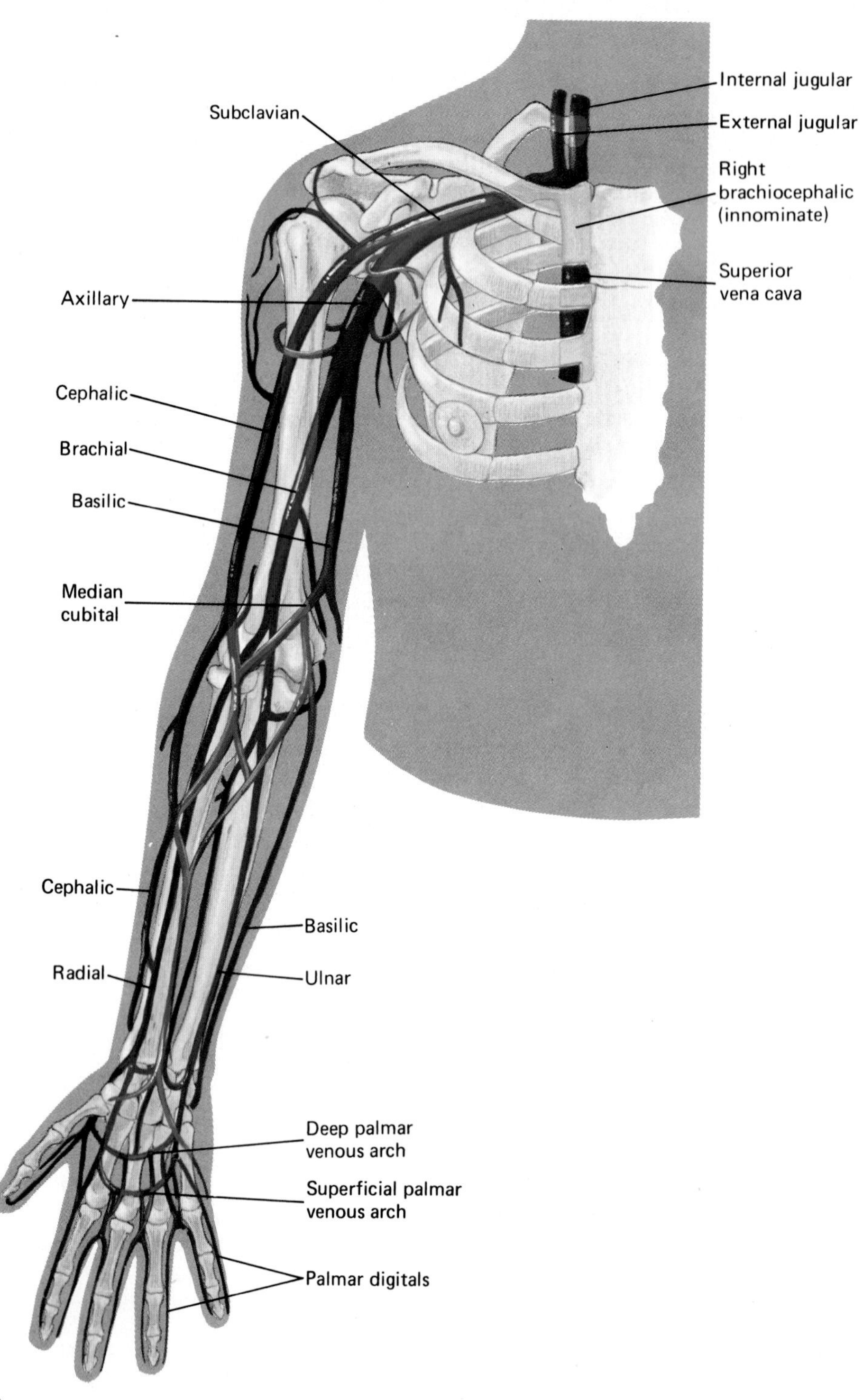

FIGURE 21-35

(a) Venous circulation in the right upper limb.

Veins of the upper limb and shoulder	
The veins of each upper limb can be divided into superficial veins and deep veins. The two sets anastomose with each other. Superficial veins are located just under the skin in the subcutaneous tissue. The deep veins accompany the arteries	
Vein	**Description and region drained**
Superficial veins	
Cephalic	Begins in dorsal arch of hand, then winds upward to anterior surface of forearm. Below elbow it gives off the **median cubital vein,** which joins the basilic. It ascends up the arm lateral to the biceps. In upper third of the arm it lies between the deltoid and the pectoralis major. It empties into the axillary vein just below the level of the clavicle (Fig. 21-35)
Basilic	Begins in the ulnar portion of the dorsal venous arch of hand. Ascends on posterior surface of the ulnar side of forearm, then turns forward to anterior surface below elbow. It is joined by the **median cubital vein,** the arm vein most often used for drawing blood samples, intravenous injections, and cardiac catherization. The basilic continues upward medial to the biceps. At the lower border of the teres major the basilic becomes the axillary vein
Deep veins	
Brachial (2P)	In each arm there is a brachial vein on each side of the brachial artery. It receives blood from the **radial** and **ulnar** veins, which in turn drain the **palmar arches.** Near the lower margin of the subscapularis they join the axillary vein
Axillary	Each axillary vein begins at the lower border of the teres major as the continuation of the basilic vein. At the outer border of the first rib it becomes the subclavian vein
Subclavian	Begins as the continuation of the axillary vein at the outer border of the first rib. At the medial border of the scalenus anterior it unites with the internal jugular vein to form the brachiocephalic vein

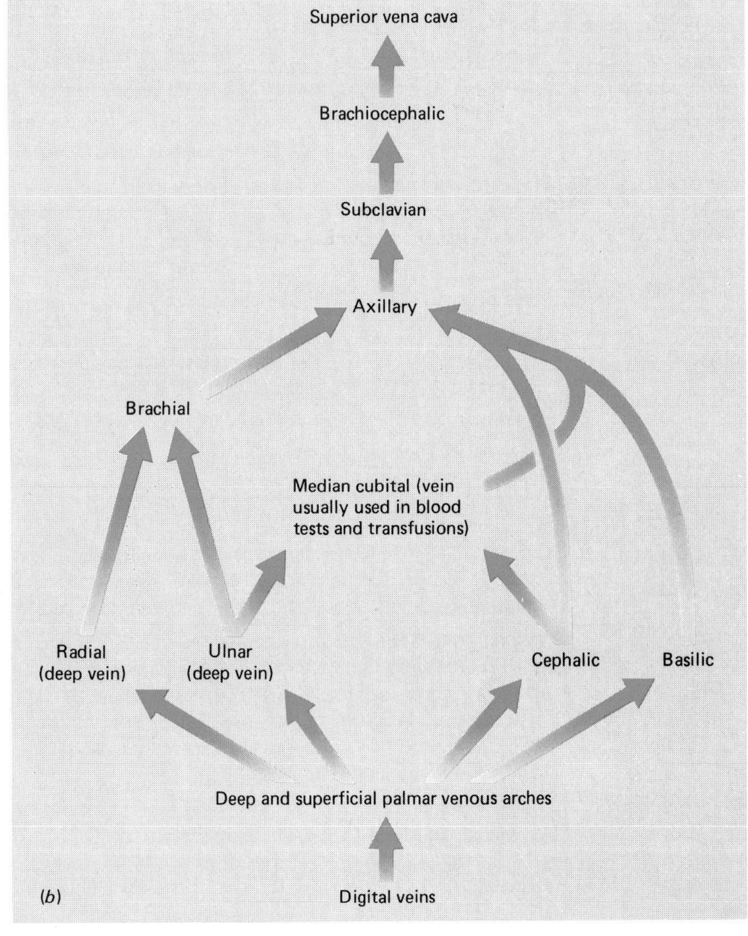

(*b*) Flow chart pattern of venous circulation of upper limb.

TABLE 21-16

Veins of the Thorax	
Vein	**Description and region drained**
Brachiocephalic (innominate)	Two large venous trunks in the lower part of the neck and upper part of the thorax. Each is formed by the union of the internal jugular vein and the subclavian vein. The two brachiocephalic veins unite to form the superior vena cava (Fig. 21-33)
Superior vena cava (S)	Drains blood from the upper portion of the body and delivers it to the right atrium. Formed by the junction of the brachiocephalic veins. The superior vena cava is about 7 cm long
Azygos (S)	The origin of the azygos vein varies. Sometimes it arises from the posterior surface of the inferior vena cava at about the level of the renal veins. It ascends upward into the mediastinum and empties into the superior vena cava. It drains the body wall, the bronchi and lungs, and many other parts of the body. The azygos vein represents an important bypass for blood returning to the heart from the lower part of the body. If the inferior vena cava is obstructed, blood may return to the heart by way of the azygos
Hemiazygos (S)	Starts on the left as the azygos does on the right. Ascends as high as the eighth thoracic vertebra and ends in the azygos vein. Its tributaries include the lower three posterior intercostal veins and the vein formed by the union of the ascending lumbar and subcostal veins of the left side (Fig. 21-33)

TABLE 21-17

Veins of the pelvis and abdomen	
Vein	**Description and region drained**
External iliac	Each external iliac vein is an upward continuation of a femoral vein. Begins behind the inguinal ligament and ends in front of the sacroiliac joint, where it joins with the internal iliac vein to become the common iliac vein (Fig. 21-37)
Internal iliac	Receives blood from veins that drain the pelvic body wall, buttock, rectum, bladder, and other pelvic structures. Joins with the external iliac to become the common iliac vein
Common iliac	Each is formed by the union of the external and internal iliac veins in front of the sacroiliac joint. They ascend to the right side of the fifth lumbar vertebra, where they join to form the inferior vena cava
Inferior vena cava (S)	Receives blood from all of the body below the diaphragm and delivers it to the right atrium of the heart. Formed by the junction of the common iliac veins anterior to the fifth lumbar vertebra. Ascends anterior to the vertebral column to the right of the aorta. Empties into the lower posterior region of the right atrium
Lumbar	Four on each side. They receive blood from vessels in the body wall. Each empties into the inferior vena cava or the azygos vein
Testicular	Drains testis and epididymis. The right testicular empties into the inferior vena cava just below the level of the renal veins. The left testicular empties into the left renal
Ovarian	Corresponds to testicular vein. Receives blood from ovary and uterus. Enlarges during pregnancy
Renal	Anterior to renal arteries. Receives blood from kidneys. Empties into inferior vena cava
Suprarenal	Drains adrenal glands. Right suprarenal empties into inferior vena cava. Left suprarenal empties into left renal
Hepatic	Receives blood from the liver. Begins at **sublobular veins,** which receive blood from **intralobular veins,** which in turn collect blood from liver sinusoids. The number of hepatic veins varies. They pass out from the posterior surface of the liver and empty immediately into the inferior vena cava
Hepatic portal (S)	Formed from the junction of the superior mesenteric vein and the **splenic vein** (at the level of the second lumbar vertebra). About 8 cm long. Receives blood from the splenic, superior mesenteric, **left gastric, right gastric,** and **cystic veins.** Note that the venous blood from most of the digestive system below the diaphragm drains into the hepatic portal system. The hepatic portal vein brings blood rich in nutrients from the intestine to the liver (see the section on the hepatic portal system in the text). In the liver the hepatic portal vein gives rise to an extensive network of sinusoids. (Fig. 21-36)
Superior mesenteric (S)	Collects blood from the small intestine and part of the large intestine. Behind the pancreas it joins the splenic vein to form the hepatic portal vein.
Inferior mesenteric (S)	Collects blood from the large intestine. Usually empties into the splenic vein

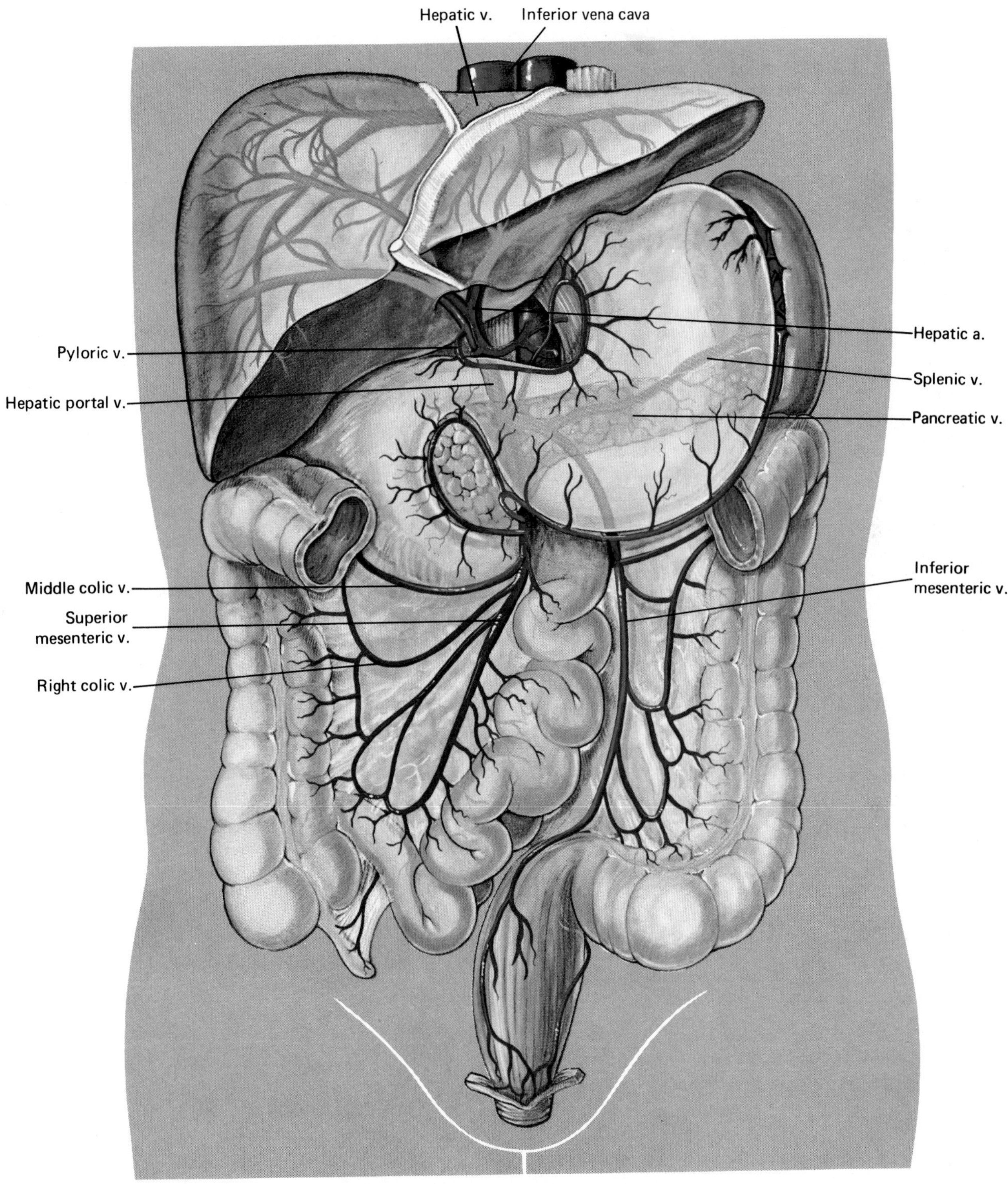

FIGURE 21-36

The hepatic portal system. Blood circulating through the hepatic portal vein has already passed through capillaries in the intestine and is partly depleted of its oxygen supply. Oxygenated blood is delivered to the liver by the hepatic arteries. Its branches deliver blood to the hepatic sinuses where the oxygenated blood mixes with the venous blood from the hepatic portal vein. Circulation within the liver tissue is illustrated in Figure 21-22.

TABLE 21-18

Veins of the lower limb

As in the upper limb, these veins can be divided into superficial and deep veins. The superficial veins are just under the skin in the subcutaneous tissue (superficial fascia); the deep veins accompany the arteries. Both sets of veins have numerous valves

Vein	Description and region drained
Superficial veins	
Great saphenous	Longest vein in body. Begins in foot where it receives blood from the toes and foot and ascends along the medial side of the leg and thigh. About 3 cm below the inguinal ligament (in groin) it empties into the femoral vein (Fig. 21-37)
Small saphenous	Begins in foot. Ascends along the middle of the back of the leg. A few cm above the knee joint it empties into the popliteal vein. It drains blood from the foot and back of the leg
Deep veins	
Posterior tibial	Begins behind the medial malleolus from the union of the **medial** and **lateral plantar veins.** Accompanies the posterior tibial artery, ascending deep within the muscles at the back of the leg. Receives blood from the calf muscles, the communicating vessels that join with the superficial leg veins, and the **peroneal veins** (which drain the foot). Unites with the anterior tibial just behind the knee to form the popliteal vein
Anterior tibial	Upward continuation of veins in foot. Ascends between the tibia and fibula, then joins with the posterior tibial vein behind the knee to form the popliteal vein
Popliteal	Formed by the union of the anterior and posterior tibial veins behind the knee. Receives blood from the small saphenous. Above the knee the popliteal vein continues upward as the femoral vein
Femoral	Accompanies femoral artery. Begins as the continuation of the popliteal vein above the knee. At the level of the inguinal ligament, it becomes the external iliac vein. Runs up the posterior thigh, draining blood from deep structures. In the groin region it receives blood from the great saphenous vein

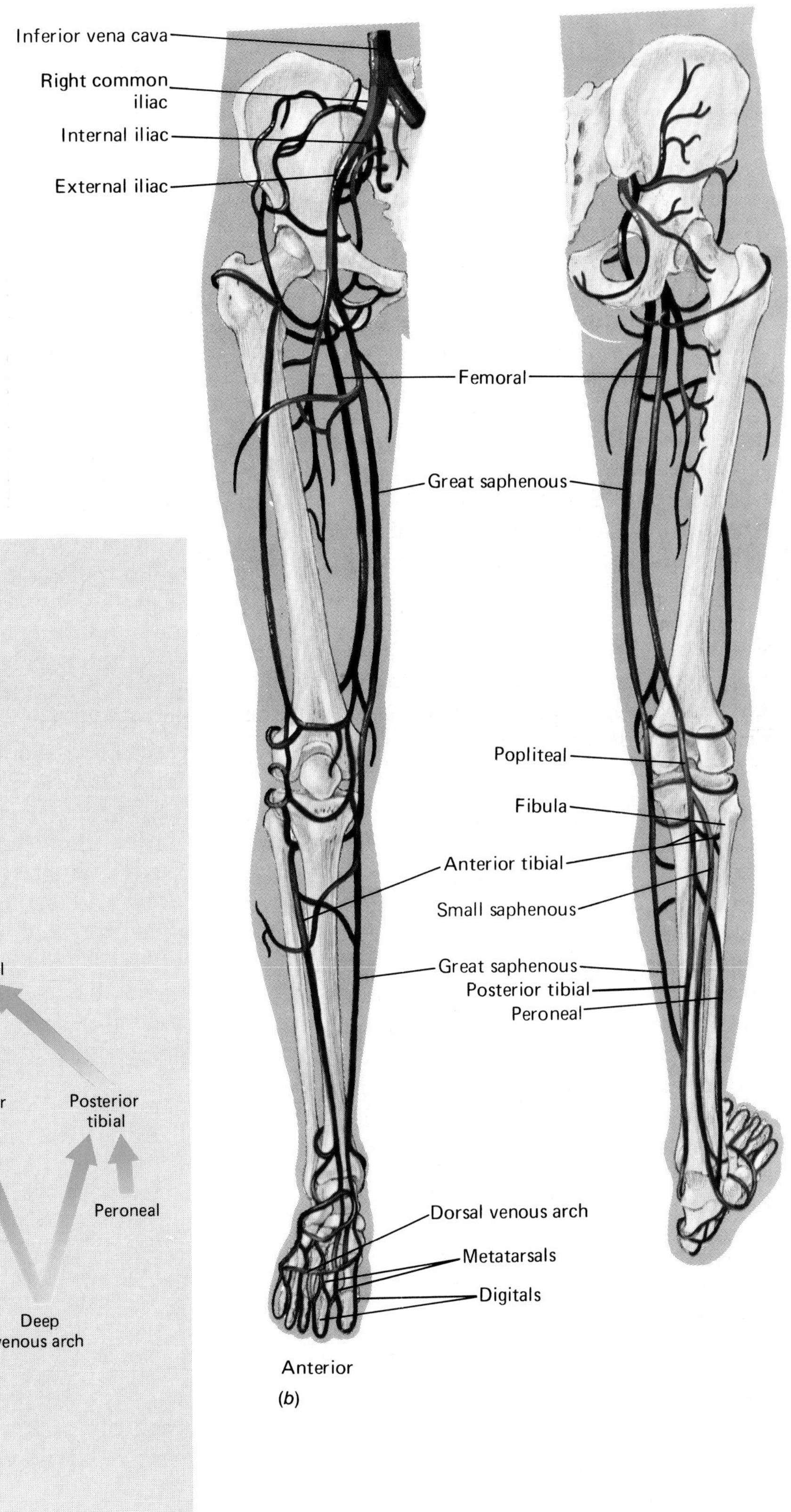

Inferior vena cava

Common iliac

External iliac

Femoral

Popliteal

Great saphenous

Small saphenous

Anterior tibial

Posterior tibial

Medial marginal

Lateral marginal

Peroneal

Dorsal venous arch

Deep venous arch

Metatarsal

(a) Digital

FIGURE 21-37

(a) Flow chart of venous circulation in lower limb. (b) Venous circulation in the right lower limb. The principal superficial veins are the great and small saphenous veins.

Cardiovascular disease is a killer

An estimated 63 million Americans (one in four) have some form of **cardiovascular disease,** and more than half of all deaths (about 1 million) in the United States each year are caused by this type of disease. Cardiovascular disease increased as a cause of death in the United States from about 14% in 1937 to about 55% in 1962, leading some to describe the problem as epidemic. However, during the past decade there has been a 25% decline in death rates from heart disease and a 40% decrease in stroke fatalities. This trend has not occurred in some other Western countries where the mortality rate from cardiovascular disease has continued to increase. The majority of patients with cardiovascular disease have hypertension, atherosclerosis, or ischemic heart disease. These diseases are interrelated and it is common for a patient to suffer from a combination of all three. See Focus on Clinical Terms Related to the Heart and Circulation.

Hypertension is high blood pressure

About one in every five persons in the United States has **hypertension** (high blood pressure). An elevated diastolic pressure is considered the most important indicator of hypertension. When the diastolic pressure consistently reads over 95 mmHg, the patient may be suffering from hypertension. Recent findings from the Framingham Heart Study suggest that a high systolic reading is also indicative of a higher risk of heart disease. The blood pressure for a person with hypertension is 160/95 mmHg or higher. Twenty-five million or more persons have borderline hypertension (blood pressure between 140/90 and 160/95). This disease is a major contributing factor in atherosclerosis, heart attacks, and strokes and can also cause renal (kidney) failure.

Clinical highlight

Hypertension is sometimes referred to as the "silent killer" because it does not usually cause symptoms until actual damage has occurred in the blood vessels. Lack of symptoms causes many persons to be unaware that they have hypertension and others not to take the condition seriously. Even when the condition has been diagnosed and medications prescribed, many patients neglect to follow through on treatment.

Cases of hypertension are classified as secondary or essential. **Secondary hypertension** occurs as a result of some other disorder, usually involving the kidneys. For example, when the arteries leading into the kidneys are narrowed by disease, the arterial pressure may seem low to the kidneys. They respond by secreting inappropriately large amounts of renin. Renin activates angiotensins, which are potent vasoconstrictors, and thus blood pressure rises. More than 85% of patients with high blood pressure have **essential hypertension.** By definition essential hypertension has no known cause, but it is now thought that this condition is a complex disorder that may result from disturbances of any of the control mechanisms that regulate blood pressure. These disturbances have been tentatively linked to a number of environmental factors acting in persons who are genetically predisposed to hypertension. Among the suspected environmental factors being studied are obesity and high dietary sodium (salt) intake.

Although the cause of essential hypertension is not fully understood, the abnormality in hypertension almost always appears to be increased vascular resistance, especially in the arterioles and small arteries. The heart must pump against this increased resistance, and so hypertension places a burden upon the heart. The left ventricle may increase in size and eventually deteriorate in function. Persons with hypertension that has gone untreated for years commonly die of congestive heart failure, cerebral vascular accident (often a small blood vessel breaks in the brain, resulting in hemorrhage), kidney failure, or myocardial infarction (heart attack).

Clinical highlight

Although there is no cure for hypertension, the disease can usually be controlled by medications that lower blood pressure, weight loss, and a restricted sodium intake. When sodium intake is reduced, the body retains less water. This reduces blood volume and thus lowers blood pressure. Diuretics, a group of drugs used to control blood pressure, also cause depletion of salt and water. Again, blood volume decreases, lowering blood pressure.

Atherosclerosis is the major form of arteriosclerosis

Arteriosclerosis is a general term used to describe a number of conditions in which the arteries thicken and lose their elasticity. Arteriosclerosis is also referred to as a hardening of the arteries. **Atherosclerosis** is the most common form of arte-

FOCUS ON . . . Clinical terms related to the heart and circulation

Aneurysm	A saclike outpocketing of the wall of an artery, vein, or, heart chamber caused by abnormal dilatation. Occurs as a consequence of damage to or weakening of the wall
Angina pectoris	Thoracic pain referred from the heart, which may cause a feeling of suffocation or impending death. Usually caused by lack of oxygen to the myocardium. Episodes may be triggered by excitement or physical exertion
Angiogram	An x-ray of blood vessels that have been filled with a contrast medium (a solution that permits the vessel to show clearly in an x-ray)
Arrhythmia	Abnormal heart rhythm
Arteriogram	An x-ray of an artery or group of arteries that have been injected with a contrast medium
Arteritis	Inflammation of an artery
Atherosclerosis	The most common form of arteriosclerosis. A progressive disease in which smooth muscle cells and fatty deposits accumulate, forming atheromatous plaques within the lining of arteries that impede the flow of blood
Bradycardia	Very slow heart rate; less than 60 beats per minute
Cardiac arrest	A condition in which the heart stops beating completely
Cardiac catheterization	Introduction of a small catheter (tube) through a blood vessel and into the heart; permits the sampling of blood, determination of pressure within the heart, or detection of cardiac disorders
Cardiac tamponade	Pathological compression of the heart caused by accumulation of fluid in the pericardial cavity
Congestive heart failure	Condition in which the heart is unable to pump sufficient blood during systole; may result in pulmonary edema
Defibrillator	An electronic apparatus used to stop fibrillation of the atria or ventricles by the application of brief electric shock to the heart either directly or through electrodes placed upon the chest wall
Embolism	The sudden blockage of an artery by a thrombus (clot) that has moved from its point of origin, or by foreign material that has flowed along with the blood
Hypercholesterolemia	Excess cholesterol in blood
Hypertension	High blood pressure in the arteries. A diastolic pressure consistently over 95 mmHg or a systolic pressure consistently over 160 mmHg is indicative of hypertension.
Hypotension	Low blood pressure in arteries; often associated with a dramatic drop in blood pressure as in circulatory shock
Ischemia	Deficiency of blood to a tissue or organ, usually due to functional constriction or obstruction of a blood vessel
Myocardial infarction (MI)	A condition in which prolonged ischemia results in death of a portion of the heart muscle and its eventual replacement with nonfunctional scar tissue. An MI is commonly referred to as a heart attack
Palpitation	Unusually rapid heartbeat
Phlebitis	Inflammation of a vein. The condition may be marked by thickening of the vein wall and by formation of a thrombus
Raynaud's disease	A vascular disease characterized by bilateral attacks of cyanosis and ischemia mainly of fingers and toes. Skin becomes pale and may burn. Symptoms are precipitated by cold or emotional stress. This condition occurs almost exclusively in females
Tachycardia	Very rapid heart rate; usually applied to a heart rate above 100 beats per minute
Thrombophlebitis	Inflammation of the veins accompanied by thrombus development
Thrombus	A clot formed within a blood vessel that may obstruct blood flow

riosclerosis and is the most common cause of death in the United States. Atherosclerosis involves the laying down of fatty deposits of plaque within the inner lining of the arteries. Although it can affect almost any artery, the disease most often develops in the aorta and the coronary and cerebral arteries. As a result, *myocardial infarction* and *cerebral vascular accidents* are two major consequences of atherosclerosis.

RISK FACTORS CAN ACCELERATE THE ATHEROSCLEROTIC PROCESS

Although there is apparently no single cause of atherosclerosis, several risk factors have been identified. These have been determined by studying large populations and evaluating the frequency with which certain factors correspond with development of the disease. Valuable information has been gathered in the Framingham Heart Study, a study of several thousand residents of Framingham, Massachusetts. During a period of more than 30 years, participants in this study have been examined periodically. Development of heart disease in these patients has been linked statistically with certain characteristics and chemical measurements. Among the most important risk factors are (1) elevated levels of cholesterol in the blood (hyperlipidemia), a condition that is often associated with diets rich in total calories, total fats, saturated fats, and cholesterol; (2) hypertension—the higher the blood pressure, the greater the risk (Fig. 21-38); (3) cigarette smoking—the risk of developing atherosclerosis is two to six times greater in smokers than in nonsmokers and is proportionate to the number of cigarettes smoked daily; (4) diabetes mellitus.

Age and gender are also considered risk factors. The risk of developing atherosclerosis and its complications increases with age. There is a 10- to 15-year lag in the development of atherosclerosis in women as compared with men until about 50 years of age. After that, the rates in both sexes are more similar. It has been suggested that female estrogen hormones offer some protection to women until after the menopause when the concentration of these hormones decreases.

Other suggested risk factors that are being studied include obesity, hereditary predisposition, lack of exercise, stress and behavior patterns, and dietary factors such as excessive intake of salt and refined sugar.

DEVELOPMENT OF ATHEROSCLEROSIS INVOLVES CHOLESTEROL

In atherosclerosis, fatty lesions called *atheromatous plaques* (*ath*-er-**owe**-ma-tus) develop over a period of many years within the tunica intima of the arterial wall. The earliest stage of the disease is thought to be damage to the endothelial cells. Smooth muscle cells from the tunica media then proliferate and migrate into the damaged areas of the intima. Lipids, especially cholesterol, from the blood accumulate within the mass of smooth muscle forming a fatty plaque. In 1987, the National Heart, Lung, and Blood Institute (NHLBI) recommended that all Americans 20 years of age or older have a cholesterol level test every 5 years. Levels should be below 200 milligrams per deciliter of blood. Levels above 240 are dangerously high, putting the person at high risk of heart disease. Fibroblasts may infiltrate the plaque, contributing a connective tissue component. Eventually, calcium is deposited in the plaque, decreasing the elasticity of the artery and making the arterial wall hard.

Currently the *response-to-injury theory* is the most widely accepted explanation of how atherosclerosis begins. According to this theory the endothelium lining the artery is injured by the force of the blood in hypertension, by certain toxins such as carbon monoxide (inhaled in large amounts by cigarette smokers), by antibodies that may build up in response to chemicals in ciga-

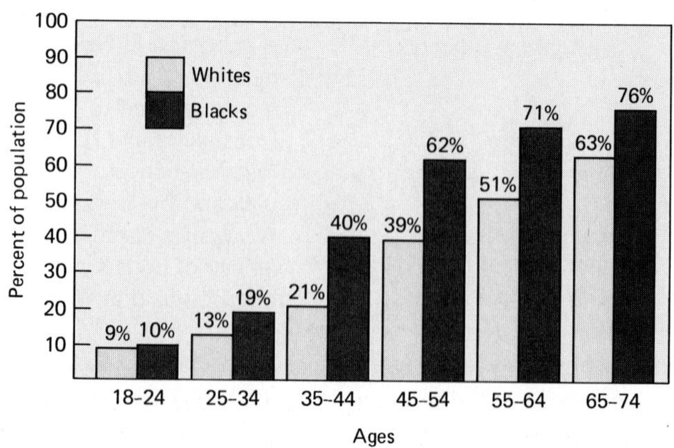

FIGURE 21-38

Occurrence of high blood pressure in the United States. (Data taken from the 1984 Joint National Committee on Detection, Evaluation, and Treatment of High Blood Pressure.)

rette smoke or other foreign substances, or perhaps by high blood concentrations of cholesterol. Whatever the cause of injury, once the endothelium is damaged, platelets aggregate and release a substance that stimulates smooth muscle cell proliferation. Smooth muscle cells from the tunica media migrate to the area of injury. At the same time the damaged endothelial lining permits entrance of cholesterol and other substances from the circulating blood.

Another theory explaining development of atherosclerosis is the *monoclonal theory.* Proponents of this theory suggest that atheromatous plaques are benign tumors, each formed from a single cell that has undergone mutation. Such mutations may be caused by exposure to radiation, viruses, certain metabolic substances in the blood such as cholesterol, or mutagenic chemicals, such as the aryl hydrocarbons of cigarette smoke. The mutation may even be inherited. It has been shown that aryl hydrocarbons are transported in the blood by the same low-density lipoproteins that transport cholesterol. The higher the concentration of lipoproteins in the blood, the more aryl hydrocarbons can be transported. Cholesterol itself can be converted in the body to a chemical mutagen (cholesterol epoxide), and the level of this chemical has been shown to be raised in persons with high blood-cholesterol levels.

Whichever theory is correct, once atheromatous plaques begin to form, the disease progresses over a period of many years. Affected arteries lose their ability to stretch as they fill with blood and become increasingly occluded (blocked) as the plaque enlarges (Fig. 21-39). Advanced lesions may ulcerate, bleed, or result in thrombus formation.

COMPLICATIONS OF ATHEROSCLEROSIS CAN BE DEADLY

As blood vessels become narrowed by the accumulation of atheromatous plaque, the amount of blood they are able to deliver decreases. Perhaps the most common complication of atherosclerosis is ischemic heart disease, which occurs when the coronary arteries become so clogged that the heart tissue is deprived of oxygen.

Another complication of atherosclerosis is arterial spasm, which sometimes occurs as a result of irritation due to the plaque. If one of the coronary arteries goes into spasm, flow of blood to the heart may be interrupted with serious consequences.

Sometimes atherosclerotic plaque so weakens the wall of an artery that the wall balloons outward, forming an **aneurysm** (**an**-u-rizm). The weakened wall may rupture, causing hemorrhage. This type of aneurysm occurs most frequently in the aorta where pressure is highest.

When atherosclerosis occurs in cerebral arteries, the blood supply to the brain may be diminished. Should an artery serving the brain be occluded by the plaque itself or by a thrombus or embolism (in this case an embolism is a thrombus that has moved from its point of origin), a portion of the brain may be completely deprived of oxygen and nutrients. Such **cerebrovascular accidents (CVA)** are commonly referred to as **strokes.**

Cardiac failure, the inability of the heart to maintain an adequate circulation, sometimes occurs as a complication of atherosclerosis. **Chronic (congestive) heart failure** may develop slowly as atherosclerotic disease progresses, reducing the effectiveness of the circulation. **Acute heart failure** may occur suddenly as a result of a heart attack precipitated by atherosclerosis.

TREATMENT INCLUDES DIET CHANGES

In advanced cases atherosclerosis may be treated with anticoagulants, drugs that lower lipid levels in the blood, bypass surgery, or even heart transplantation. A few studies suggest that progression of the disease may be slowed and some regression of lesions may take place when dietary intake of cholesterol is severely limited so that cholesterol levels in the blood drop to below 150 milligrams per 100 deciliters. However, further research is necessary to confirm these findings. Since there is no real cure for atherosclerosis, emphasis must be placed on prevention by reduction of the risk factors leading to the disease.

Ischemic heart disease results if the cardiac blood supply is inadequate

Ischemic heart disease is a broad term used to cover several clinical disorders that result from imbalance between the heart muscle's need for oxygen and the adequacy of the supply. The term ischemic (is-**kee**-mic) refers to the inadequae

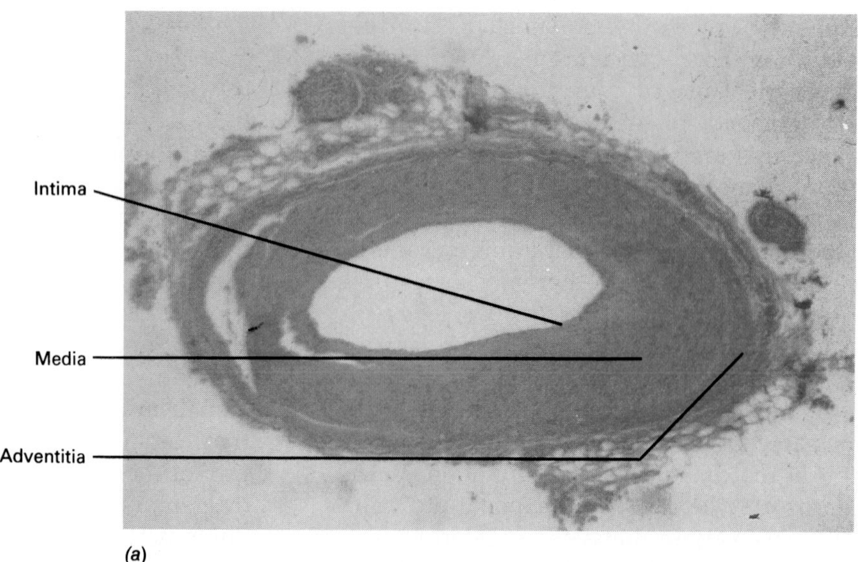

(a)

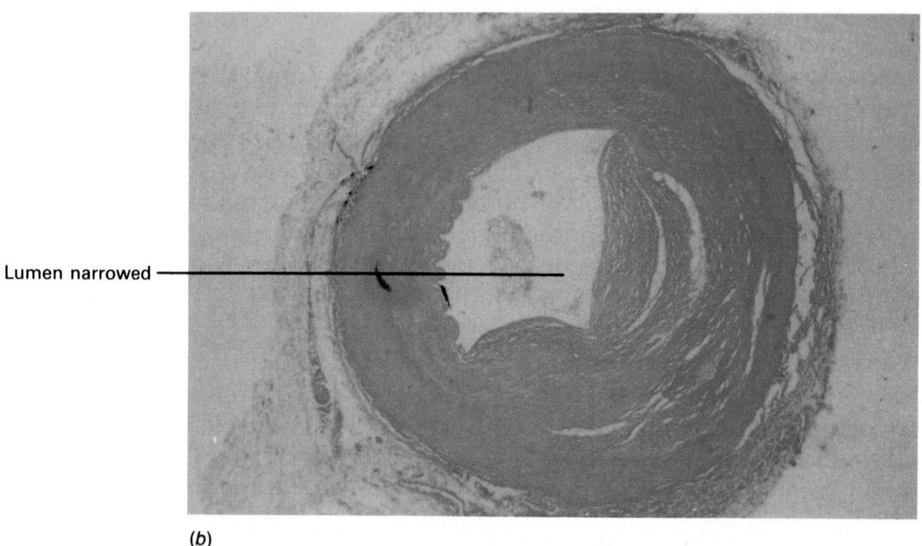

(b)

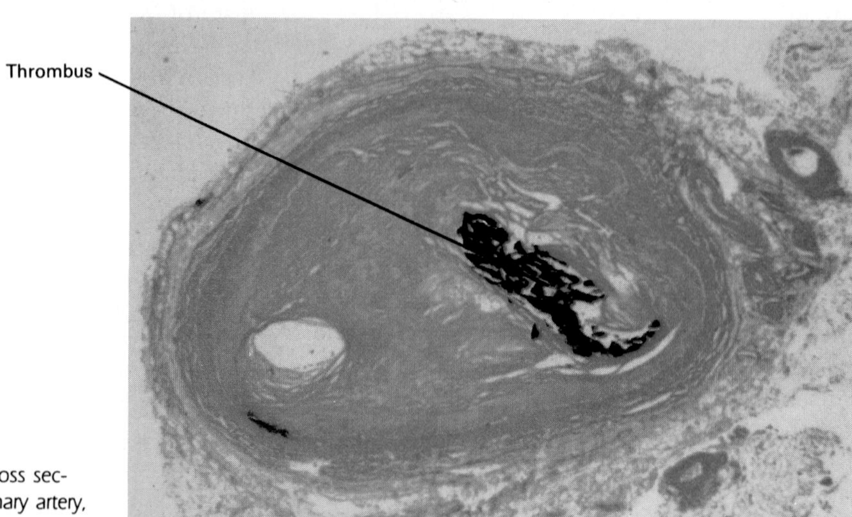

(c)

FIGURE 21-39

Progression of arteriosclerosis. Cross sections through (a) a normal coronary artery, (b) a coronary artery showing severe atherosclerosis, and (c) one with total occlusion.

blood supply to a local area. Atherosclerosis of the coronary arteries is the most common cause of ischemic heart disease. As coronary arteries become increasingly occluded, normal blood supply to the heart is reduced. When the disease progresses very slowly, collateral blood vessels may develop, allowing blood to bypass some of the clogged vessels. This improves circulation to the affected tissue somewhat. Unfortunately, the development of collateral vessels cannot indefinitely keep pace with the progress of the disease. Eventually the blood supply to the heart muscle is so reduced that clinical syndromes develop. Two of the most common are angina pectoris and myocardial infarction. See Focus on Bypass Surgery.

ANGINA PECTORIS IS A SYMPTOM OF CARDIAC ISCHEMIA

In a healthy person at rest the coronary arteries deliver more blood to the heart muscle than is needed. Therefore, blood supply can be diminished somewhat before metabolism of the cardiac muscle is affected. When individuals have even moderate amounts of atheromatous plaque in their coronary arteries, they may not exhibit symptoms of cardiovascular disease under resting conditions. However, the increased demands of physical exercise or emotional stress may require a greater blood supply than the diseased coronary arteries can provide. In those situations the heart muscle is so ischemic that the patient may experience the severe chest pains known as **angina pectoris** (**an**-ji-nah **pek**-to-ris). It is thought that the ischemia causes the pain. In some cases spasms of the already narrowed coronary arteries are thought to cause episodes of angina.

The pain of angina is felt posterior to the sternum and often radiates to the left shoulder and arm. The pain is usually described as a heavy or tight sensation that may occur in spasms but not as a stabbing pain. Most attacks last for only about 2 or 3 minutes. Rest decreases the demand upon the heart and relieves the pain. Many patients who suffer from angina carry nitroglycerin pills with them for use during an attack. This drug reduces venous return to the heart by dilating veins. As a result, cardiac output and arterial blood pressure are decreased, the load on the heart is reduced, and oxygen demand lessens.

FOCUS ON . . . Bypass surgery

Coronary bypass surgery, also called myocardial revascularization, is now a common cardiac surgical procedure. This surgery is performed on patients suffering from ischemic heart disease in order to increase the flow of blood and thus the oxygen supply to regions of the myocardium that lie beyond an obstructed coronary artery. Usually the superficial great saphenous vein is removed from the leg of the patient while the thoracic cavity is being opened. Then one to five segments of vein are grafted to the aorta at one end and to coronary blood vessels beyond the occlusion at the other end. Blood can then flow through the grafted blood vessels to reach ischemic portions of the heart muscle. Such revascularization cannot reverse existing damage from infarctions, nor can it prevent continued atherosclerotic degeneration of coronary arteries, but it can bring nourishment to ischemic tissue and perhaps help prevent further damage.

Some grafts gradually become blocked owing to thickening of the intima of the vein. It is thought that this may be the result of subjecting a vein to the higher pressures borne by arteries. For this reason the internal thoracic (mammary) artery is sometimes used in bypass surgery. However, there are also disadvantages to this procedure.

Bypass surgery has been controversial because it does not prolong life in all patients. However, the operation can improve blood flow to the heart and the quality of life, and in many patients, it does prolong life. In some cases bypass surgery is being replaced by a newer procedure called percutaneous transluminal coronary angioplasty (PTCA). With this technique a balloon is threaded through a catheter into a blocked artery. It is then inflated and deflated several times. This action compresses plaques against the wall of the artery, unblocking the artery and increasing blood flow. The balloon is then removed. This procedure has been successful in about 65% of patients, but in about 20% of these patients, the arteries became blocked again within a few months. Compared to bypass surgery, PTCA is less costly, less drastic, and less risky. However, controlled studies are needed before valid conclusions can be made about this procedure.

Clinical highlight

Patients with angina may live for many years. However, angina is a symptom of a diseased heart, and even in patients who seem to be doing well there is a constant risk of sudden death or myocardial infarction.

MYOCARDIAL INFARCTION IS CARDIAC TISSUE DEATH

Myocardial infarction (MI) is the disastrous, often fatal, form of ischemic heart disease usually due to a sudden decrease in the coronary blood supply. The term myocardial infarction is used as a synonym for heart attack. MI is the leading cause of death and disability in the United States, and causes 20 to 25% of all deaths in atherosclerosis-prone societies. The American Heart Association (AHA) states that about 4100 Americans suffer heart attacks every day (or about 1.5 million each year).

Just what precipitates the sudden decrease in blood supply that causes MI is a matter of some debate. Until recently it was thought that MI was always the result of the thrombus formation in a diseased coronary artery. Thrombus formation could be initiated by platelets adhering to the roughened area of the artery wall. If the thrombus blocks a sizable branch of a coronary artery, blood flow to a portion of heart muscle is impeded or completely halted. This condition is referred to as a coronary occlusion. Not all patients who suffer MI have thrombus formation, however. It is now thought that in some patients an episode of ischemia triggers a fatal arrhythmia such as ventricular fibrillation.

Once a portion of the heart muscle is deprived of oxygen, it dies within a few minutes. The affected area is called an **infarct.** If the infarcted area is small, the heart may continue to function, and the cardiac muscle cells in the affected area are slowly replaced by scar tissue. Should a large portion of the cardiac muscle be deprived of its blood supply, death may occur within a few minutes. About 40 to 50% of those suffering from MI die of it; 25% of this group die within moments or hours of the onset of symptoms. Sudden cardiac death following MI may be caused by ventricular fibrillation or severe damage resulting in cardiac failure. Sometimes the heart stops beating completely, the condition referred to as *cardiac arrest.* Such a heart can often be restarted by swift medical attention, including external heart massage (see Chapter 20).

Another cause of death following MI is cardiac aneurysm (a ballooning out of the heart wall) or rupture of the infarcted area (Fig. 21-40). Following MI there is a weakening of the heart wall because the dead muscle cells are being replaced

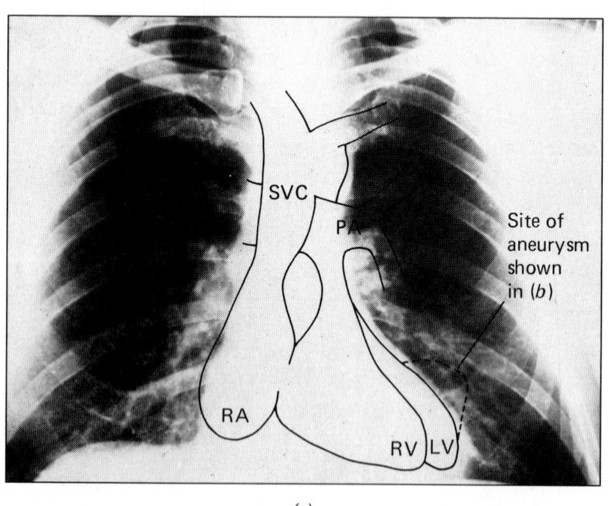

(a)

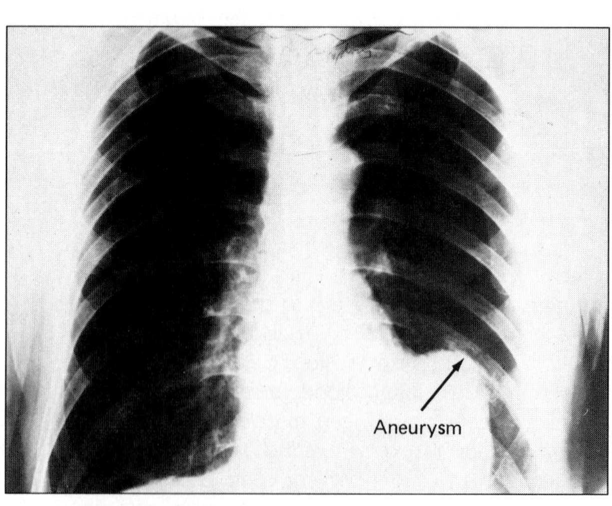

(b)

FIGURE 21-40

Comparison of a normal heart and one with a ventricular aneurysm. (a) X-ray of normal heart. The lines indicating the areas of the heart and the major vessels have been superimposed over the x-ray. RA, right atrium; RV, right ventricle; LV, left ventricle; PA, pulmonary artery; SVC, superior vena cava. (b) X-ray of heart with a ventricular aneurysm. (Courtesy of Dr. Dennis Pupello.)

by connective tissue, but the scar is not yet very strong. Any extra stress placed on the heart while it is healing may cause formation of an aneurysm or cause the wall to rupture so that blood pours into the pericardial cavity. Such accumulation of fluid in the pericardial cavity, called **cardiac tamponade,** prevents the heart from beating effectively and often leads to death.

Clinical highlight

Rapid diagnosis of MI is essential to effective treatment. Diagnosis is based upon clinical symptoms, changes in the ECG, and alterations in certain enzymes in the blood. Clinical symptoms may include severe constricting, crushing, or burning chest pain that often radiates to the left shoulder, arm, or jaw. Sweating, nausea, vomiting or breathlessness may accompany the pain. However, in about one-third of patients there are no symptoms, and the occurrence of MI is discovered by changes in the ECG. Among typical ECG changes are new Q waves and changes in the ST segment. Changes occur in enzymes present in the blood because cells damaged by ischemia leak cytoplasmic enzymes. An enzyme known as serum creatine phosphokinase (SCPK)-MB isoenzyme is found only in heart muscle. This enzyme can be identified in the serum within a few hours after an MI, and the quantity present is indicative of the amount of damage that has been done to the heart muscle. Other enzymes that increase in concentration in the blood following MI include lactic dehydrogenase (LDH) and serum glutamic oxalacetic transaminase (SGOT).

From this discussion of cardiovascular disease it should be clear that hypertension is a risk factor for atherosclerosis, and that atherosclerosis leads to a variety of complications including ischemic heart disease. Two clinical syndromes common in patients with ischemic heart disease are angina and myocardial infarction.

Aging of the cardiovascular system

As shown in Figure 21-38, the prevalence of high blood pressure increases with age. Some of the causes may be linked to diet, stress, and inactivity. Other possible causes include atherosclerosis and other forms of arteriosclerosis. The aorta and large arteries lose some of their distensibility with age, and venous valves may weaken, increasing the number of varicose veins. The cardiac muscle cells become somewhat smaller and weaker. Cardiac output tends to decline with age. Deaths attributed to coronary heart disease increase in the higher age brackets.

Development of the vascular system

Blood and blood vessels begin developing from the **mesoderm** of the embryo between the second and third weeks. The blood vessels form from **blood islands,** which are aggregations of **angioblasts** (**an**-je-o-blast), a type of mesenchymal cell. The spaces that appear within these blood islands become the lumens of the blood vessels. Angioblasts form the endothelial layer of the vessel, and other mesenchymal cells surround this layer and differentiate into the other tunics (Fig. 21-42).

As the primitive vessels grow, they fuse with other vessels and the developing heart to form an extensive vascular network through the embryo. Blood is initially produced by the endothelium of the vessels. The heart begins to pump by about week 4. At about the eighth week the bone marrow, liver, spleen, and lymph nodes are producing blood cells.

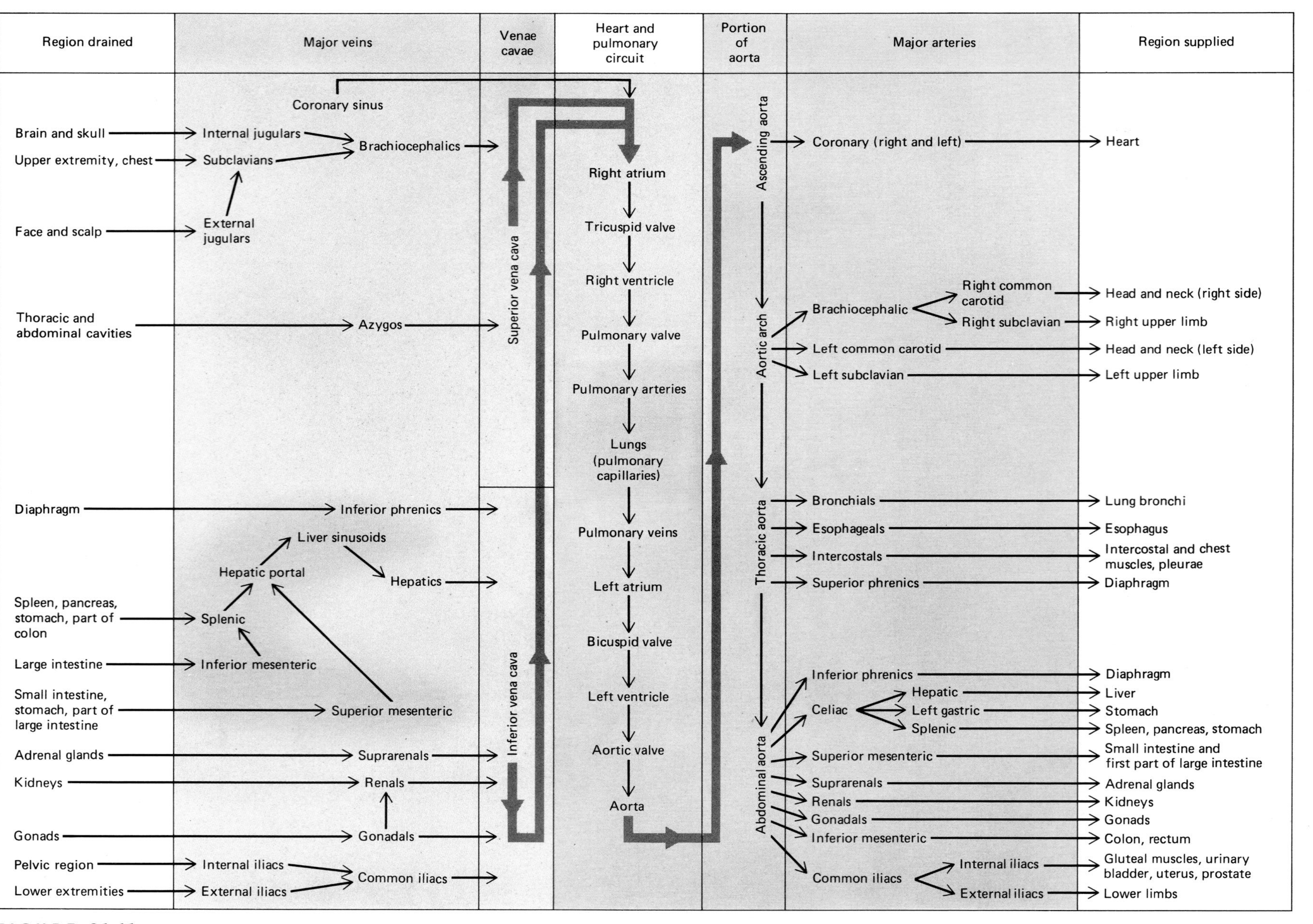

FIGURE 21-41

Summary of flow in major vessels and heart.

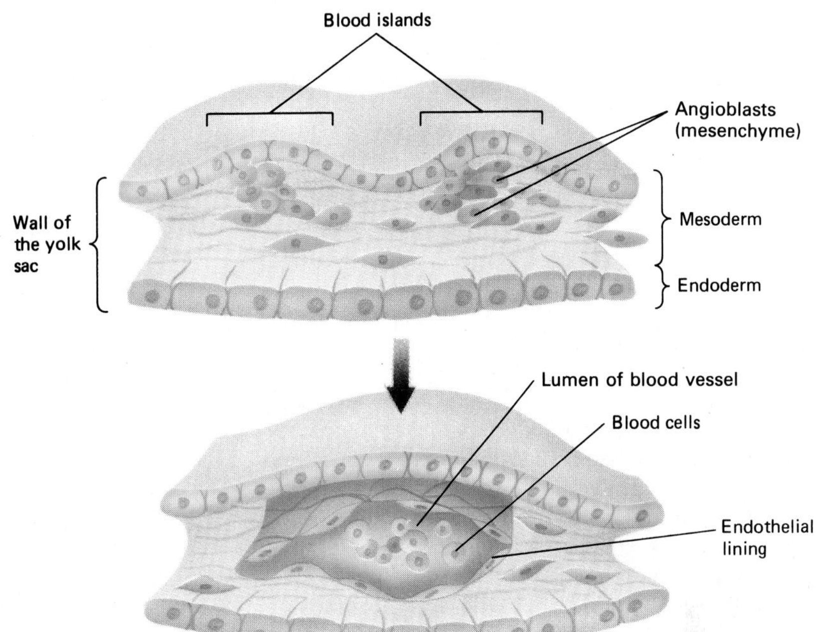

FIGURE 21-42

Development of the vascular system, showing the formation of blood vessels and blood cells.

Summary

I. The cardiovascular system is a closed circulatory system consisting of the heart and the various blood vessels.
   A. Arteries and arterioles take blood from the heart to the body tissues.
   B. Capillaries are the sites of various exchanges between the blood and the tissue cells.
   C. Venules and veins carry blood back to the heart.

II. The blood vessel wall consists of three layers:
   A. Tunica intima, the innermost layer that lines the blood vessel, consists of endothelium and some connective tissue. In capillaries the tunica intima makes up the entire wall.
   B. Tunica media, the middle layer, consists of smooth muscle and elastic connective tissue.
   C. Tunica adventitia, the outer layer, consists of fibrous connective tissue.

III. Blood leaving the heart flows through the following sequence of vessels:
   A. Artery. A thick-walled vessel carrying blood away from the heart and to the body tissues under relatively high pressure.
   B. Arteriole. A small artery that can constrict or dilate, thereby changing the flow of blood into a tissue and affecting blood pressure.
   C. Capillary. A microscopic vessel with a very thin wall through which materials can diffuse. Capillaries are the organs of exchange in the circulatory system, permitting oxygen and nutrients to pass from the blood into the tissues and wastes to pass from the cells into the blood. Continuous capillaries are less permeable than fenestrated capillaries.
   D. Venule. A small vein that receives blood from the capillaries.
   E. Vein. A thin-walled vessel carrying blood away from the body tissues and back to the heart under low pressure. Veins have valves that prevent a backflow of blood.

IV. Blood flow depends upon a pressure gradient and resistance.
   A. Blood flows from a higher pressure to a lower pressure.
   B. Blood flow is directly proportional to a pressure gradient (difference between the pressure at opposite ends of a vessel).
   C. Blood flow is inversely proportional to resistance. Resistance depends upon blood viscosity and the length and diameter of the vessel.

V. The blood is unevenly distributed within the vessels.
   A. At rest, the pulmonary circulation holds 9% of the blood, the heart 7%, and the systemic circuit 84%.
   B. Most of the blood at any given time is in the systemic veins (64%). Veins act as blood reservoirs.
   C. Capillaries have the greatest cross-sectional area for blood flow.
   D. The velocity of blood is inversely proportional to cross-sectional area. It is the greatest in the aorta and the lowest in the capillaries.
   E. Blood pressure is highest in the arteries and lowest in the veins. Much of the blood pressure is dissipated in the arterioles due to their high resistance.

VI. Blood pressure is the force exerted by the blood against the inner walls of the blood vessels. Blood pressure = blood flow × resistance.
   A. A small change in the radius of a blood vessel causes a big change in resistance and thus in blood pressure.
   B. The amount of blood pressure within the arteries as a whole is regulated mainly by the degree of vasoconstriction or vasodilation of the arterioles.
   C. Pulse is caused by the elastic expansion and recoil of arteries as they fill with blood.

VII. The regulation of blood pressure is mainly through the cardiovascular control centers (cardiac, vasomotor) in the medulla and the effects of chemicals and hormones.
   A. Stimulation of the vasomotor center of the medulla causes increased sympathetic output, which causes vasoconstriction.
   B. Higher brain centers (cerebral cortex, hypothalamus) send input to the cardiovascular centers.
   C. Baroreceptors in large arteries are sensitive to changes in blood pressure and send input to the cardiovascular centers.
   D. Chemoreceptors in the carotid and aortic bodies detect low oxygen levels and send input to the vasomotor center.
   E. Chemical vasodilators (kinins, ANP) cause vasodilation and lower blood pressure.
   F. Vasoconstrictors (Ep, NEp, ADH, angiotensins) cause vasoconstriction and raise blood pressure.
   G. Autoregulation within blood vessels and tissues can also cause local changes in blood pressure and blood flow.

VIII. Capillaries are sites of exchange between the blood and the tissue cells.
   A. Vasomotion causes blood flow through capillaries to be intermittent.

B. Oxygen and nutrients diffuse out of capillaries; carbon dioxide and wastes flow into capillaries.

C. Fluid moves out of (filtration) and into (absorption) the capillaries depending on the hydrostatic and osmotic pressure differences between the blood and the interstitial fluid.

D. Excess fluid that is filtered is removed from the interstitium by the lymph.

IX. Blood flows through veins under very low pressures, and several mechanisms (valves, skeletal muscle and respiratory pumps, and sympathetic innervation) help to return it to the heart.

X. Blood is pumped by the left ventricle into the systemic circulation, which brings blood rich in oxygen to all the tissues of the body. After circulating through the tissues, blood is conducted through veins back to the heart. Blood enters the right atrium and then passes into the right ventricle, which pumps it into the pulmonary circulation. In the lungs, carbon dioxide wastes diffuse out from the blood, and oxygen diffuses into the blood. Blood recharged with oxygen returns to the left atrium of the heart and is pumped by the left ventricle back into the systemic circulation.

XI. The aorta is the largest artery in the body.

A. The aorta receives blood from the left ventricle and gives off branches that deliver blood to all parts of the body.

B. The main divisions of the aorta are: ascending aorta, aortic arch, and descending aorta, the last of which can be subdivided into the thoracic and abdominal aorta.

C. The main branches of each division of the aorta are listed in Table 21-6.

XII. Two coronary arteries that branch from the ascending aorta bring blood to the wall of the heart. Blood circulates through a complex network of arteries and capillaries and then empties into the coronary veins. These join to form the coronary sinus, a large vein that empties into the right atrium.

XIII. Blood is conducted into the brain by the internal carotid arteries and the vertebral arteries. Branches of these arteries join to form the circle of Willis. From the brain capillaries, blood passes into venous sinuses in the dura mater and then into the internal jugular veins.

XIV. Blood from the digestive system drains into the hepatic portal vein, which conducts it to the liver. Within the liver, blood flows into an extensive network of sinusoids from which the liver removes excess nutrients. Blood from the hepatic sinusoids passes into hepatic veins, which empty into the inferior vena cava. This hepatic portal system is characterized by an extra set of exchange vessels (sinusoids), so that instead of conducting blood into another vein, the hepatic portal vein empties into a set of sinusoids.

XV. Major cardiovascular diseases include hypertension, atherosclerosis, and ischemic heart disease.

A. In essential hypertension the heart must pump against increased resistance; the left ventricle may increase in size and deteriorate in function. The increased blood pressure may damage blood vessels, leading to atherosclerosis, or may cause CVA or MI.

B. In atherosclerosis, atheromatous plaques develop within the arterial wall, eventually impeding the flow of blood. Atherosclerosis can lead to CVA, aneurysms, ischemic heart disease, or MI.

C. In ischemic heart disease the myocardium does not receive sufficient blood, usually because of atherosclerosis in the coronary arteries. Angina pectoris is a common symptom. Myocardial infarctions (heart attacks) may result from a sudden decrease in blood supply to the myocardium.

Post-test

1. Blood vessels that transport blood away from the heart and toward some organ or tissue are called ______________.
2. Materials are exchanged between blood and tissues through the thin walls of the ______________.
3. The left ventricle pumps blood into the ______________ circulation.
4. Blood from the right ventricle is pumped into the ______________ ______________.
5. The pulmonary vein carries ______________ (oxygenated or deoxygenated) blood.
6. The coronary arteries branch from the ______________ ______________.
7. In the lower abdominal cavity, the aorta divides to form the ______________ ______________ arteries.
8. Blood returning to the heart from the tissues above the level of the diaphragm drains into a large vein, the ______________ ______________ ______________.
9. The brachiocephalic artery branches from the ______________ ______________ and delivers blood to the right ______________ carotid artery and the right ______________ artery.

10. The coronary sinus drains blood from the ______________ veins and delivers it to the ______________ ______________.
11. An important arterial circuit at the base of the brain is the ______________.
12. Blood is delivered to the brain by the ______________ ______________ and the ______________ arteries.
13. Blood from the digestive tract passes from the superior mesenteric vein into the ______________, which takes it to the ______________.
14. Oxygenated blood is delivered to the liver by the ______________ ______________.
15. Blood from the kidneys passes into the ______________ veins, which deliver it to the ______________ ______________ ______________.
16. The force exerted by the blood against the inner walls of the blood vessels is called ______________ ______________.
17. Blood pressure is equal to blood flow times ______________.
18. A small change in the radius of a blood vessel causes a big change in resistance and ______________ ______________.
19. Arterial blood pressure is regulated mainly by the degree of vasoconstriction or vasodilation of the ______________.
20. The angiotensins are hormones that increase ______________ ______________.
21. Hypertension is a condition marked by ______________ ______________ ______________.
22. The term ischemic refers to inadequate ______________ ______________ to an area.

Match

____ 23. Greatest resistance to blood flow
____ 24. Lowest blood velocity
____ 25. Greatest amount of blood
____ 26. Largest luminal diameter
____ 27. Highest blood pressure
____ 28. Possesses valves
____ 29. Greatest cross-sectional area
____ 30. Receives blood from capillary
____ 31. Lowest blood pressure
____ 32. Greatest amount of smooth muscle
____ 33. Highest blood velocity
____ 34. Greatest permeability

a. artery
b. arteriole
c. capillary
d. venule
e. vein

Identify whether the following cause an increase or decrease in blood pressure.

____ 35. Blood loss
____ 36. Increased renin release
____ 37. Vasomotor center activation
____ 38. Decreased blood viscosity
____ 39. Decreased heart rate
____ 40. Arteriolar vasodilation
____ 41. Kinin release
____ 42. Arteriosclerosis
____ 43. Increased body temperature
____ 44. Low blood-oxygen
____ 45. Hemorrhage
____ 46. Baroreceptor activation
____ 47. Increased ANP release
____ 48. Increased ADH release

49. Label the following diagram.

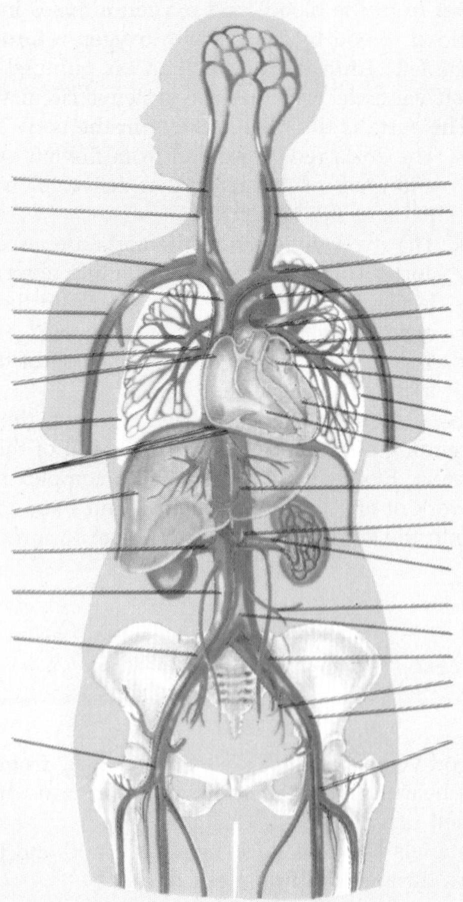

Review questions

1. Compare the wall of an artery with that of a capillary and a vein. Name and describe the layers in the wall of each.
2. Why is the ability of arterioles to dilate and constrict physiologically important?
3. Why do some veins have valves?
4. Why are capillaries sometimes referred to as the "functional structures" of the cardiovascular system?
5. Explain filtration and absorption of fluid at the capillary.
6. Why must blood pressure in the pulmonary circulation be lower than pressure in the systemic circulation?
7. How do the arterioles influence blood pressure? Explain.
8. How does blood manage to travel against gravity through veins in the legs on its way back to the heart?
9. Compare blood distribution, cross-sectional area, velocity, and pressure differences in the various types of blood vessels.
10. Explain how the baroreceptors and chemoreceptors help regulate blood pressure.
11. How do the angiotensins influence blood pressure? Aldosterone?
12. How do positive feedback mechanisms worsen progressive shock? Explain.
13. Name the divisions of the aorta and list the main arteries that branch from each division.
14. Trace a drop of blood from the inferior vena cava to the thoracic aorta by listing in sequence each blood vessel and each part of the heart through which it must pass.
15. What blood vessels bring blood to the brain? What is the significance of the circle of Willis?
16. Why does the heart, which is always full of blood, require a system of blood vessels to serve its wall? Trace the blood through the principal vessels that serve the heart.
17. Trace a drop of blood from the (a) left subclavian vein to the right coronary artery, (b) right atrium to the left renal vein, (c) inferior vena cava to the superior vena cava, (d) hepatic portal vein to the right common carotid artery.
18. Trace a drop of blood from the (a) coronary vein to a pulmonary capillary, (b) femoral vein to the brain, (c) kidney to the liver, (d) inferior vena cava to the arm, (e) heart to the celiac artery.
19. What is ischemic heart disease, and what are some of its consequences?
20. Describe the progression of atherosclerosis, list its risk factors, and relate this disease to various types of heart disease.
21. What is hypertension? Why is it often not treated?
22. Identify the numbered structures on the diagram on the previous page. See Figure 21-8.

Post-test answers

1. arteries **2.** capillaries **3.** systemic **4.** pulmonary trunk **5.** oxygenated **6.** ascending aorta **7.** common iliac **8.** superior vena cava **9.** aortic arch; common; subclavian **10.** coronary; right atrium **11.** circle of Willis **12.** internal carotid; vertebral **13.** hepatic portal vein; liver **14.** hepatic artery **15.** renal; inferior vena cava **16.** blood pressure **17.** resistance **18.** blood flow **19.** arterioles **20.** blood pressure **21.** high blood pressure **22.** blood supply **23.** b **24.** c **25.** e **26.** e **27.** a **28.** e **29.** c **30.** d **31.** e **32.** a **33.** a **34.** c **35.** decrease **36.** increase **37.** increase **38.** decrease **39.** decrease **40.** decrease **41.** decrease **42.** increase **43.** increase **44.** increase **45.** decrease **46.** decrease **47.** decrease **48.** increase **49.** See Fig. 21-8.

THE LYMPHATIC SYSTEM

CHAPTER OUTLINE

LEARNING OBJECTIVES

After you have studied this chapter you should be able to:

1 List three main functions of the lymphatic system.

2 Identify the main structures of the lymphatic system.

3 Trace a drop of lymph through the lymphatic circulation (e.g., from a lymph capillary in the thigh to the left subclavian vein.)

4 Contrast lymph nodules with lymph nodes.

5 Describe the structure and function of tonsils.

6 Relate the two main functions of lymph nodes to their structure.

7 Locate the major groups of lymph nodes in the body.

8 Relate the structure of the spleen to its function and explain why it is not considered a vital organ.

9 Locate the thymus and give its function.

10 Contrast differences in origin and composition between plasma, interstitial fluid, and lymph.

11 Summarize how the lymphatic system helps to regulate fluid balance.

12 Describe lymph formation and the mechanisms responsible for lymph flow.

13 Describe the consequences of disruption of lymph flow, and identify factors that might cause such disruption.

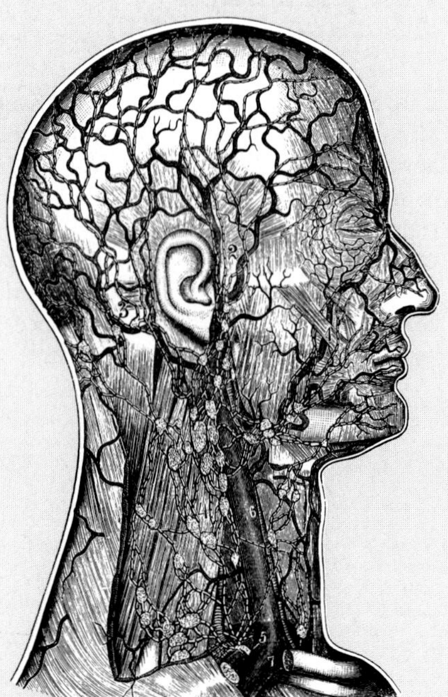

Lymphatic vessel. A valve is present in this section (approximately ×100). (Ed Reschke/Peter Arnold, Inc.)

22

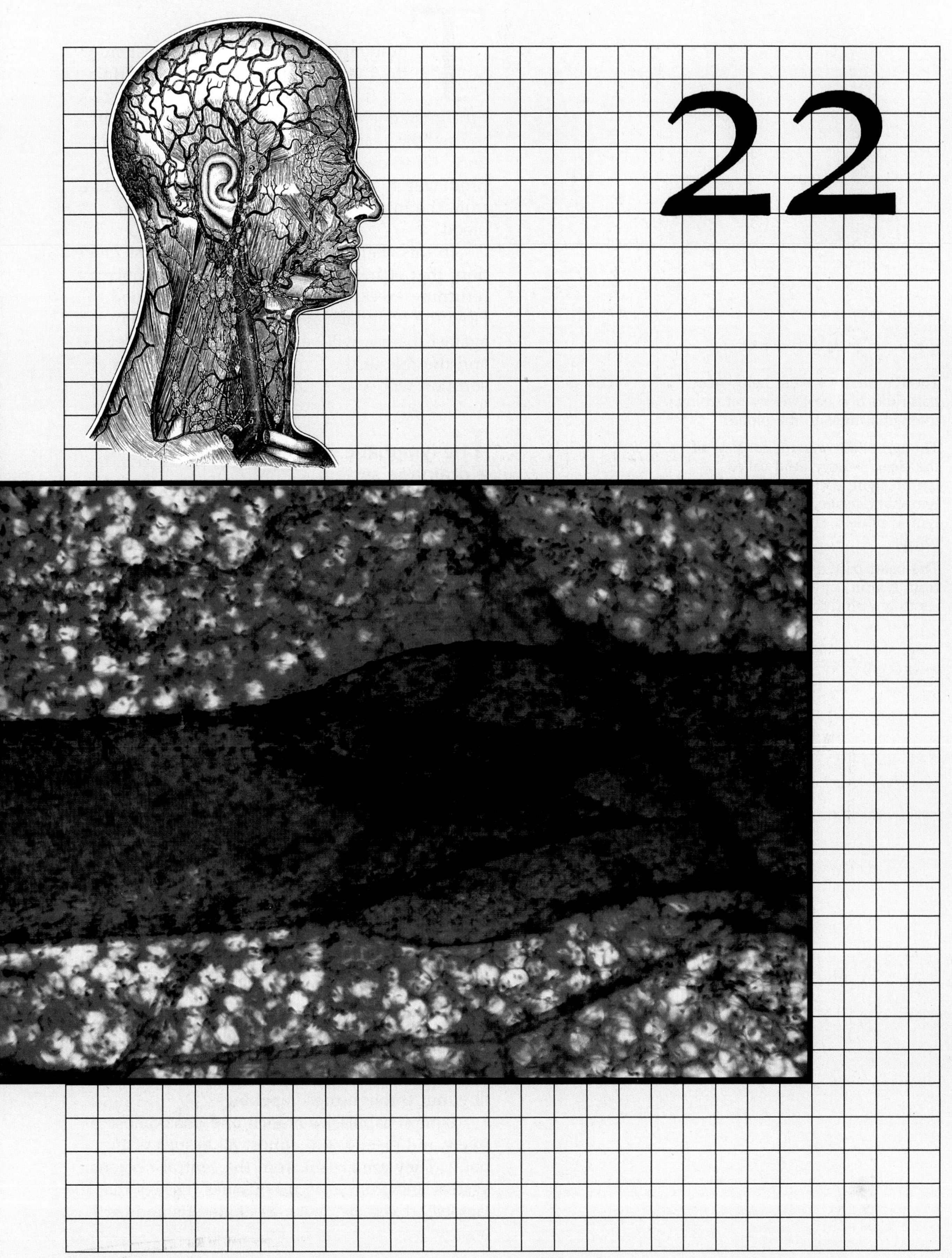

KEY CONCEPTS

The lymphatic system helps maintain fluid homeostasis by returning interstitial fluid to the blood.

The lymphatic system consists of the clear, watery fluid called lymph, lymphatic vessels, diffuse lymphatic tissue, lymph nodules, lymph nodes, thymus, spleen, and tonsils.

The basic pattern of lymph flow is from lymph capillaries to lymphatics to lymph ducts.

The **lymphatic system** is a subsystem of the circulatory system. Its three principal functions are: (1) to collect and return interstitial fluid, including plasma proteins, to the blood, and thus help maintain fluid balance, (2) to defend the body against disease by producing lymphocytes, and (3) to absorb lipids from the intestine and transport them to the blood.

In this chapter we will discuss the first function, that of helping to maintain fluid balance by returning excess interstitial fluid to the blood. How the lymphatic system defends the body against disease will be the subject of Chapter 23, and the role of the lymphatic system in lipid absorption will be described in Chapter 25.

The lymphatic circulation is a drainage system

The lymphatic system has neither a heart nor arteries. Its microscopic dead-end capillaries extend into most tissues, paralleling the blood capillaries (Fig. 22-1). The lymphatic circulation is a drainage system. Its job is to collect excess interstitial fluid and return it to the blood. Once interstitial fluid enters a lymph capillary, it is referred to as **lymph.**

The three main types of lymphatic vessels are lymph capillaries, lymphatics, and lymph ducts. **Lymph capillaries** are microscopic tubes located between cells. Lymph capillaries resemble blood capillaries somewhat, but differ in important ways. Whereas a blood capillary has an arterial and a venous end, a lymph capillary has no arterial end. Instead, each lymph capillary originates as a closed tube. Lymph capillaries also have a larger and more irregular lumen than blood capillaries and are more permeable.

The wall of a lymph capillary is constructed of endothelial cells that overlap one another. When fluid outside the capillary pushes against the overlapping cells, they swing slightly inward—like a swinging door that moves in only one direction. Fluid inside the capillary cannot flow out through these openings.

Lymph capillaries branch and anastomose freely and extend into almost all tissues of the body. They are absent from the central nervous system and from avascular tissues (tissues that lack blood vessels), such as epidermis and cartilage.

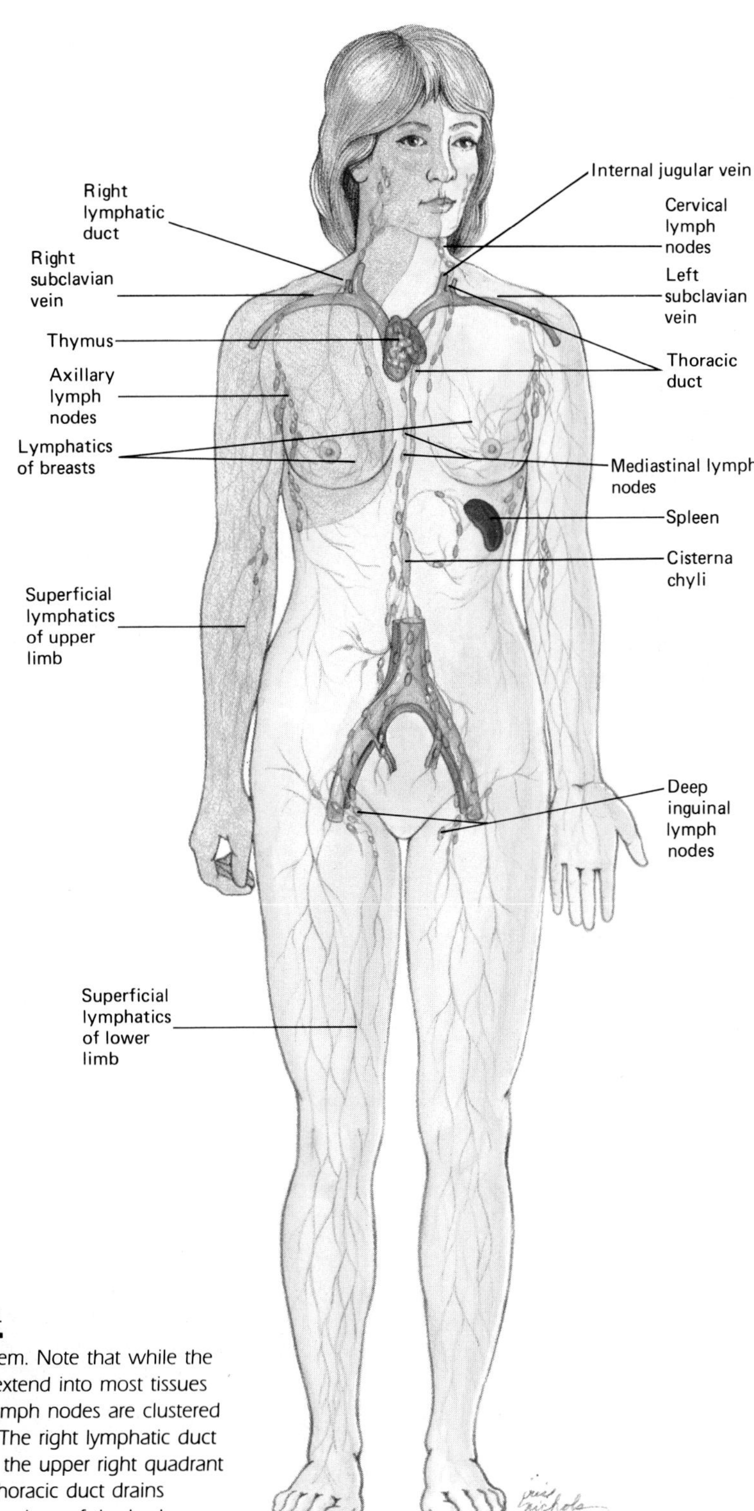

FIGURE 22-1

The lymphatic system. Note that while the lymphatic vessels extend into most tissues of the body, the lymph nodes are clustered in certain regions. The right lymphatic duct drains lymph from the upper right quadrant of the body. The thoracic duct drains lymph from other regions of the body.

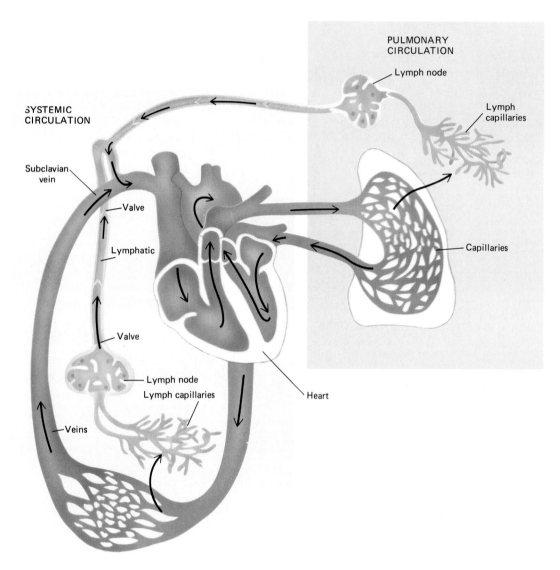

PULMONARY CIRCULATION
Lymph node
Lymph capillaries
Capillaries
SYSTEMIC CIRCULATION
Subclavian vein
Valve
Lymphatic
Valve
Lymph node
Lymph capillaries
Veins
Heart

FIGURE 22-2

Types of lymphatic vessels and pattern of lymph flow.

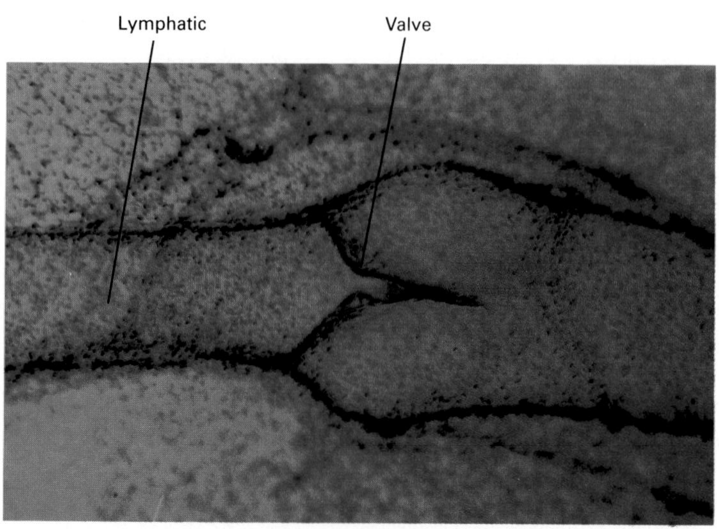

FIGURE 22-3

Photomicrograph of a lymphatic showing a valve. (John D. Cunningham/Visuals Unlimited.)

Lymph capillaries join to form larger vessels called **lymphatics,** or **lymph veins** (Figs. 22-2 and 22-3). Lymphatics resemble blood-conducting veins but have thinner walls and relatively larger lumens, and they have more valves. In the skin, lymphatics are located in subcutaneous tissue and follow the same paths as veins. In the viscera, lymphatics generally follow arteries and form plexuses (networks) around them.

At certain locations lymphatics enter **lymph nodes,** structures that consist of lymphatic tissue. As the lymph flows slowly through the lymph sinuses within the tissue of the lymph node, it is filtered. Macrophages remove bacteria and other foreign matter as well as debris.

Lymphatics leaving lymph nodes conduct lymph toward the shoulder region. Large lymphatics that drain groups of lymph nodes are called **lymph trunks.** Lymphatics from the lower portion of the body converge to form a dilated lymph vessel, the **cisterna chyli** (sis-**ter**-nah **kie**-lee), in the lumbar region of the abdominal cavity (Fig. 22-4). The cisterna chyli extends for about 6 centimeters just to the right of the abdominal aorta. At the level of the twelfth thoracic vertebra, the cisterna chyli narrows and becomes the **thoracic duct.**

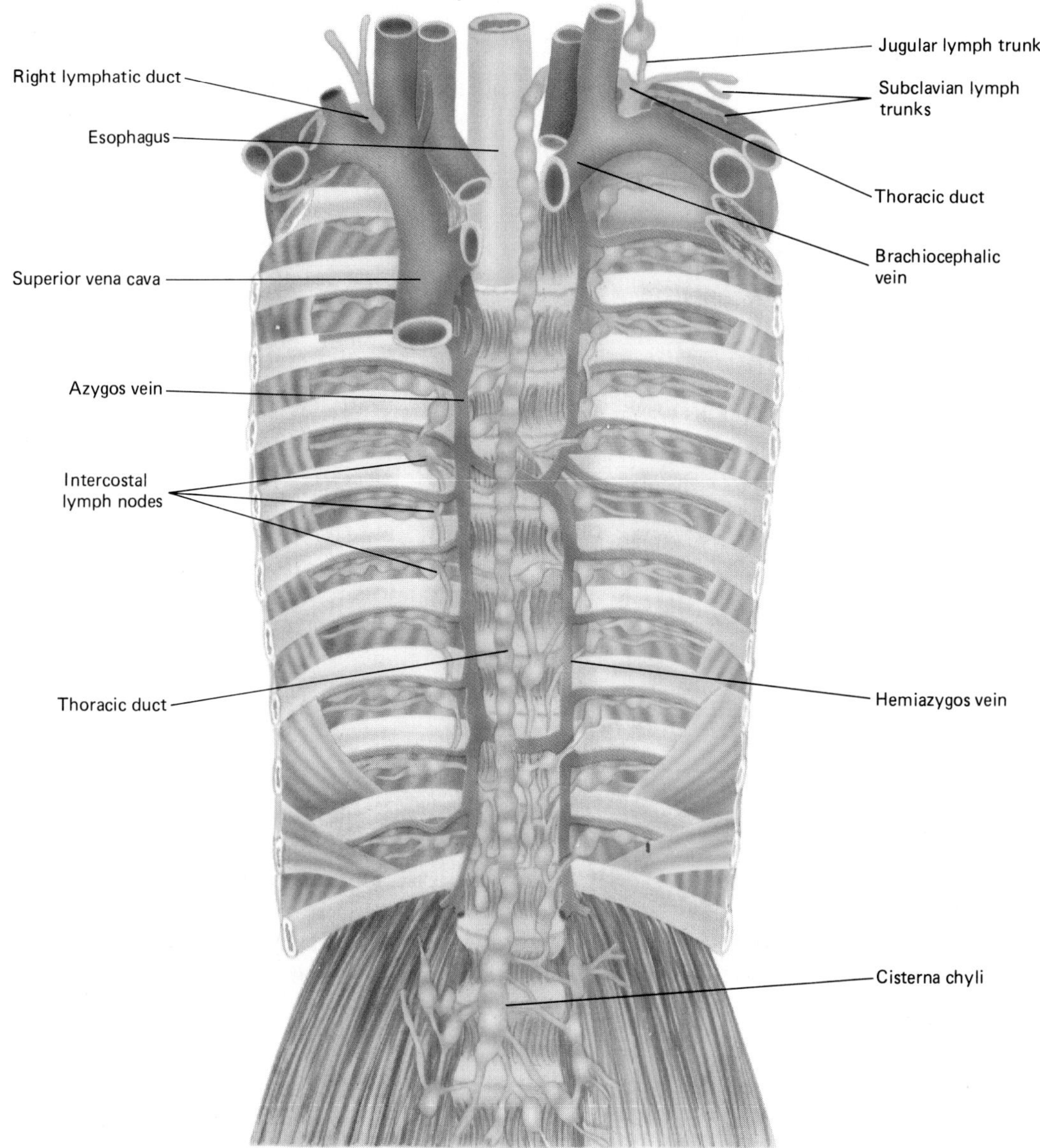

FIGURE 22-4

Magnified view of the cisterna chyli, thoracic duct, and right lymphatic duct.

Lymphatic vessels from all over the body, except the upper right quadrant, drain into the thoracic duct. This vessel delivers the lymph into the base of the left subclavian vein at the junction of the left subclavian and internal jugular veins. In this way lymph is continuously emptied into the blood where it mixes with the plasma. At the junction of the thoracic duct and the venous system, a valve prevents blood from flowing backward into the duct.

Only about 1 centimeter in length, the **right lymphatic duct** receives lymph from the lymphatic vessels in the upper right quadrant of the body (Fig. 22-1). The right lymphatic duct empties lymph into the base of the right subclavian vein (at the point where it unites with the internal jugular vein to form the brachiocephalic).

An example of the pattern of lymph circulation is:

Lymph capillaries ⟶ lymphatic ⟶ lymph node ⟶ lymphatic ⟶ cisterna chyli (drains lower portion of body) ⟶ thoracic duct

Clinical highlight

Lymphatic vessels and lymph nodes can be visualized by the process of **lymphangiography** (lim-*fan*-jee-**og**-rah-fee). A radiopaque (not transparent to x-rays) contrast material is injected into a lymphatic vessel. That vessel and lymphatic vessels emerging from it can then be visualized on x-ray film. X-rays are taken again 24 hours later to visualize the lymph nodes. Such an x-ray is called a **lymphangiogram** (see Fig. 22-11). Lymphangiograms are useful clinically in the diagnosis of neoplasms and certain other lymphatic disorders. They are also used to localize lymph nodes for radiation therapy or for surgical removal.

Lymphatic tissue may be organized as nodules or nodes

Lymphatic tissue is a type of connective tissue characterized by large numbers of lymphocytes. The stroma (framework) of lymphatic tissue is a network of reticular fibers. Connective tissue cells including fibroblasts and macrophages are present.

Lymphatic tissue is organized in different ways. **Diffuse lymphatic tissue** is widely distributed. Small amounts are present in almost every organ. It is also found in the lamina propria (thin layer of connective tissue underlying epithelial membranes) of the gastrointestinal (digestive) tract, respiratory tract, urinary tract, and reproductive tract.

Lymph tissue is also arranged in small aggregates called *nodules* and *nodes*. In addition, the spleen and thymus gland are considered lymphatic organs.

Lymph nodules are small masses of lymph tissue

Lymph nodules are small masses (up to a millimeter or so in diameter) of lymph tissue in which lymphocytes are produced. Lymph nodules are scattered throughout loose connective tissue, especially beneath moist epithelial membranes such as those that line the upper respiratory tract, intestine, and urinary tract. Lymph nodules appear to be strategically distributed to defend the body against disease organisms that penetrate the lining of passageways that communicate with the outside of the body.

A lymph nodule consists mainly of large numbers of lymphocytes enmeshed within reticular fibers (see chapter opening illustration and Fig. 22-5). Lymph nodules do not have vessels bringing lymph to them. The periphery of the nodule is not sharply defined. Some lymph nodules develop **germinal centers,** central areas filled with immature lymphocytes. Here new lymphocytes proliferate from stem cells that originate in the bone marrow. The lighter-staining germinal center is surrounded by a darker-staining region called the **cortex** (Fig. 22-6).

Most lymphatic nodules are small and solitary. However, some are found in large clusters. For example large aggregates of lymph nodules occur in the wall of the lower portion (ileum) of the small intestine. These large masses of lymph nodules are known as **Peyer's patches** (**pie**-erz) (Fig. 22-5).

Tonsils are also aggregates of lymph nodules. They are located strategically to defend against invading bacteria. The tonsils produce lymphocytes. They are located under the epithelial lining of the oral cavity and pharynx. The **lingual tonsils** are located at the base of the tongue. The single **pharyngeal tonsil** is located in the posterior wall of the nasal portion of the pharynx above the soft palate. When enlarged (usually owing to infection or allergy), the pharyngeal tonsil is called the **adenoid.**

Most prominent are the paired **palatine tonsils** on each side of the pharynx (throat). These oval masses of lymphatic tissue are thickenings in the mucous membrane of the throat. The stratified squamous epithelium of the throat that overlies the tonsils dips down to form 10 to 20 pits, or **crypts,** in each tonsil. Bacteria often accumulate in these crypts and may invade the lymphatic tissue of the tonsil. This may cause an increase in the mass of the tonsil. Sometimes bacterial invasion of the tonsils becomes a chronic problem, and the tonsils are surgically removed by the well-known procedure called *tonsillectomy.* After about age 7, the lymphatic tissue of the tonsils typically begins to shrink in size.

Lymph nodes filter lymph and produce lymphocytes

Lymph nodes, sometimes called lymph glands, are masses of lymph tissue surrounded by a connective tissue **capsule.** Their two main functions are (1) to filter the lymph and (2) to produce lymphocytes. Although their structure is generally similar, lymph nodes can be differentiated from lymph nodules by the presence of the connective tissue capsule and by the lymph vessels that deliver lymph to them.

Lymph nodes are distributed along the main lymphatic routes. As illustrated in Figure 22-1, they are most numerous in the axillary and groin regions, and many are located in the thorax and abdomen.

Many lymph nodes are shaped like lima beans (Fig. 22-6). Their size varies from 1 millimeter to 3 centimeters in diameter. On one side of the node there is an indentation called the **hilus.** The connective tissue capsule sends extensions, called **trabeculae,** into the node. The trabeculae divide the lymph node into sections and provide support for the node and the blood vessels that serve it.

The outer portion of the lymph node is the **cortex,** and the inner region is the **medulla.** The cortex is made up of lymph nodules containing germinal centers where lymphocytes are produced. The lymphocytes, macrophages, and other cells of the lymph nodes are loosely enmeshed in a network of reticular fibers. In the medulla, this tissue is arranged in strands called **medullary cords.** Extending through the tissue of the cortex and between the cords are large, irregular channels, the **lymph sinuses.**

The circulation of lymph through a node involves three types of lymph vessels—afferent lymphatics, lymph sinuses, and efferent lymphatics. As an **afferent lymphatic** approaches a node, it divides into several branches that enter the node at several points on its convex surface.

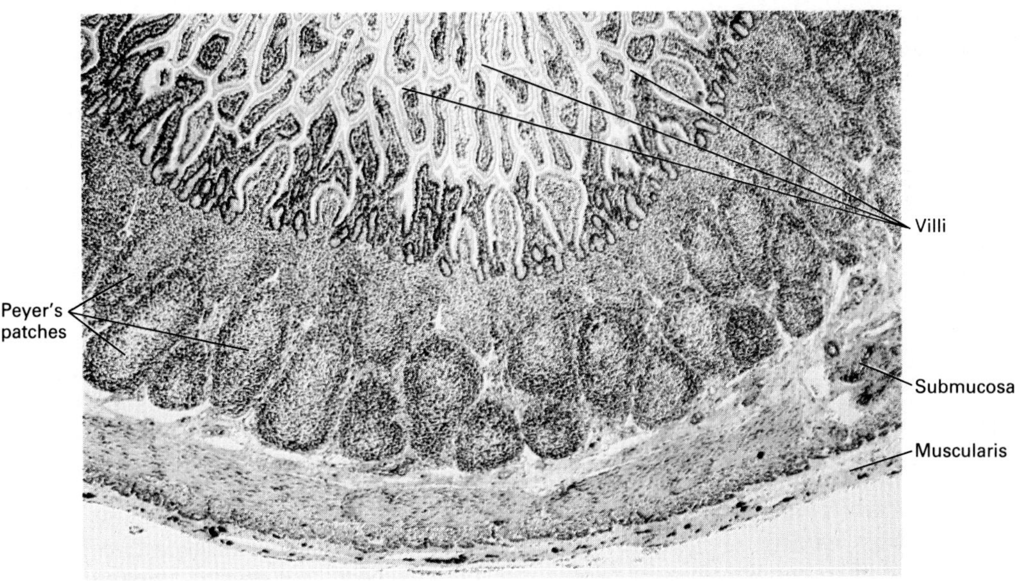

FIGURE 22-5
Photomicrograph of a section of the intestinal wall showing Peyer's patches, aggregates of lymph nodules. (Biophoto Associates/Photo Researchers.)

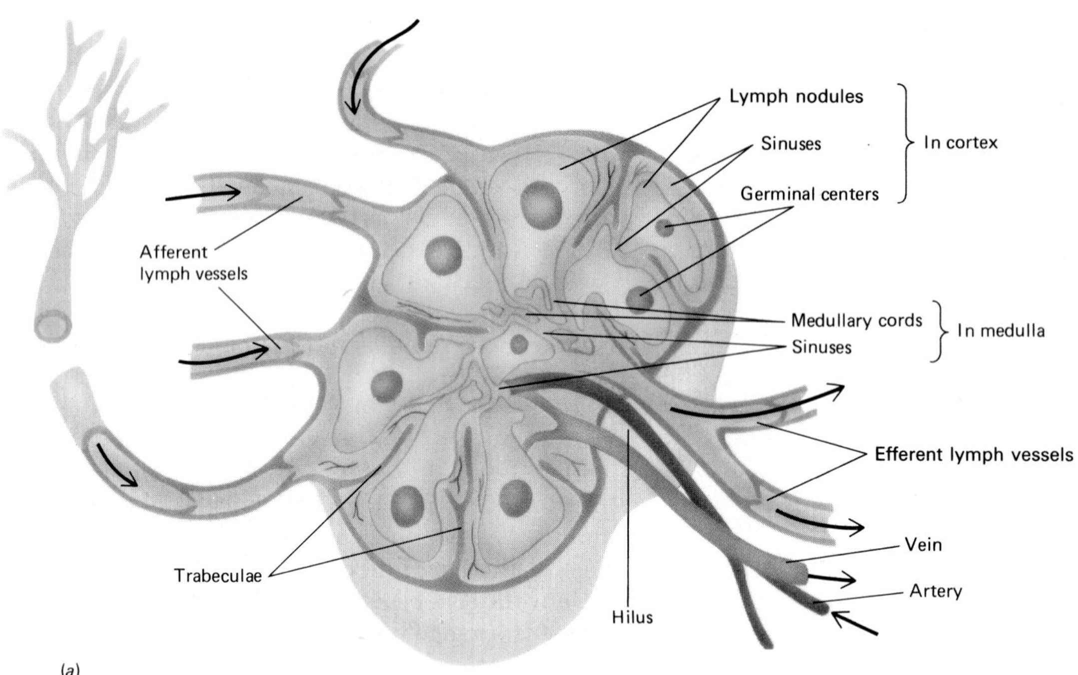

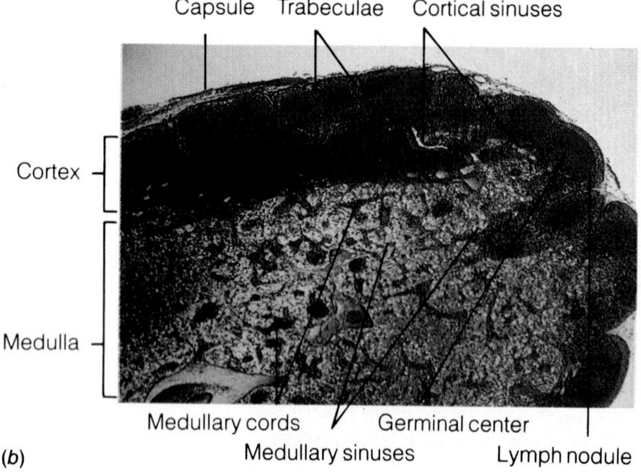

FIGURE 22-6

(*a*) Structure of a lymph node. The hilus is the indented region through which vessels enter and leave the lymph node. (*b*) Photomicrograph of a human lymph node (approximately ×80). (Ed Reschke/Peter Arnold, Inc.)

Valves within the afferent vessels near their entrance to the node prevent backflow of lymph. The afferent vessels open into a complex of lymph sinuses within the node.

As the lymph slowly percolates through these sinuses, it is filtered by resident phagocytes. Lymphocytes are added to the lymph as it flows through the sinuses, so that lymph leaving a node contains more lymphocytes than when it entered. Eventually many of these lymphocytes are carried with the lymph into the blood, where they help maintain the population of circulating leukocytes. From the lymph sinuses, lymph flows into **efferent lymphatics** that leave the node at its hilus. These vessels are also equipped with valves. In summary the pattern of lymph flow through a lymph node is:

Afferent lymphatic ⟶
lymph sinuses ⟶ efferent lymphatic

A lymph node must also have a blood supply. A small artery enters the node at the hilus and branches into a network of capillaries within the node. Blood leaves the node through small venules.

Clinical highlight

By filtering and phagocytizing bacteria from the lymph, the lymph nodes help prevent the spread of infection. When bacteria are present, lymph nodes may increase in size and become tender. You may have experienced the swollen cervical lymph nodes that often accompany a sore throat. An infection in almost any part of the body may result in swelling and tenderness of the lymph nodes that drain that area.

Major groups of lymph nodes are located along lymphatics

Lymph nodes usually occur in clusters or chains along lymphatics. Some groups of lymph nodes are superficial, others deep. The distribution of lymph nodes is important clinically because when they become enlarged and painful, they may help pinpoint the site of an infection. Also, cancer cells from a primary tumor are often transported in the lymph and spread to other parts of the body by this route. Secondary tumors then develop in new locations. For this reason the lymphatics and lymph nodes that drain the region of a primary tumor are often removed during cancer surgery.

Lymph nodes of the head and neck drain into deep cervical lymph nodes

All of the lymph vessels of the head and neck drain into the **deep cervical** group of lymph nodes (Fig. 22-7). These form a chain that extends along the internal jugular vein from the base of the skull to the clavicle. Most of them are deep to the sternocleidomastoid muscle.

Before passing through nodes of the deep cervical group, lymph may pass through one of several other groups of nodes in the head and neck. Among these are the *occipital nodes* that drain the occipital region of the scalp and upper neck. (These nodes become enlarged in German measles.) The *retroauricular nodes* lie on the mastoid process behind the ear and drain the scalp and skin of the ear. The *parotid nodes* are embedded in the tissue of and near the parotid salivary gland.

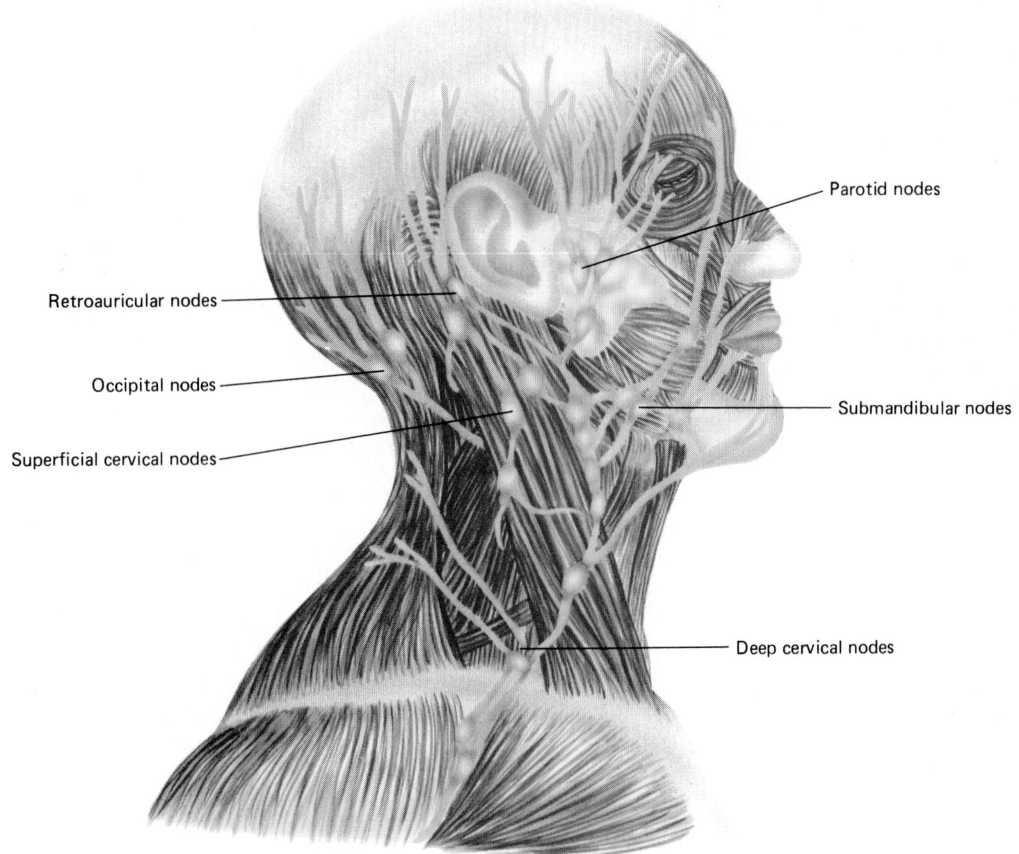

FIGURE 22-7

Principal lymph nodes of the head and neck.

They drain the scalp, cheek, part of the ear, and part of the nasal cavity. About six *submandibular nodes* lie on the surface of each submandibular salivary gland and along the inferior border of the lower jaw. They drain the chin, cheeks, nose, upper lip, gums, and tongue. The *superficial cervical nodes* are located beside the external jugular vein on the upper portion of the sternocleidomastoid. They drain part of the ear and lower part of the parotid region.

Lymph nodes drain the lymphatic vessels of the limbs

All of the lymph vessels of the upper limb drain into the **axillary lymph nodes** in the axilla (Fig. 22-8). Lymph may first pass through one of the *supratrochlear nodes* in the elbow region.

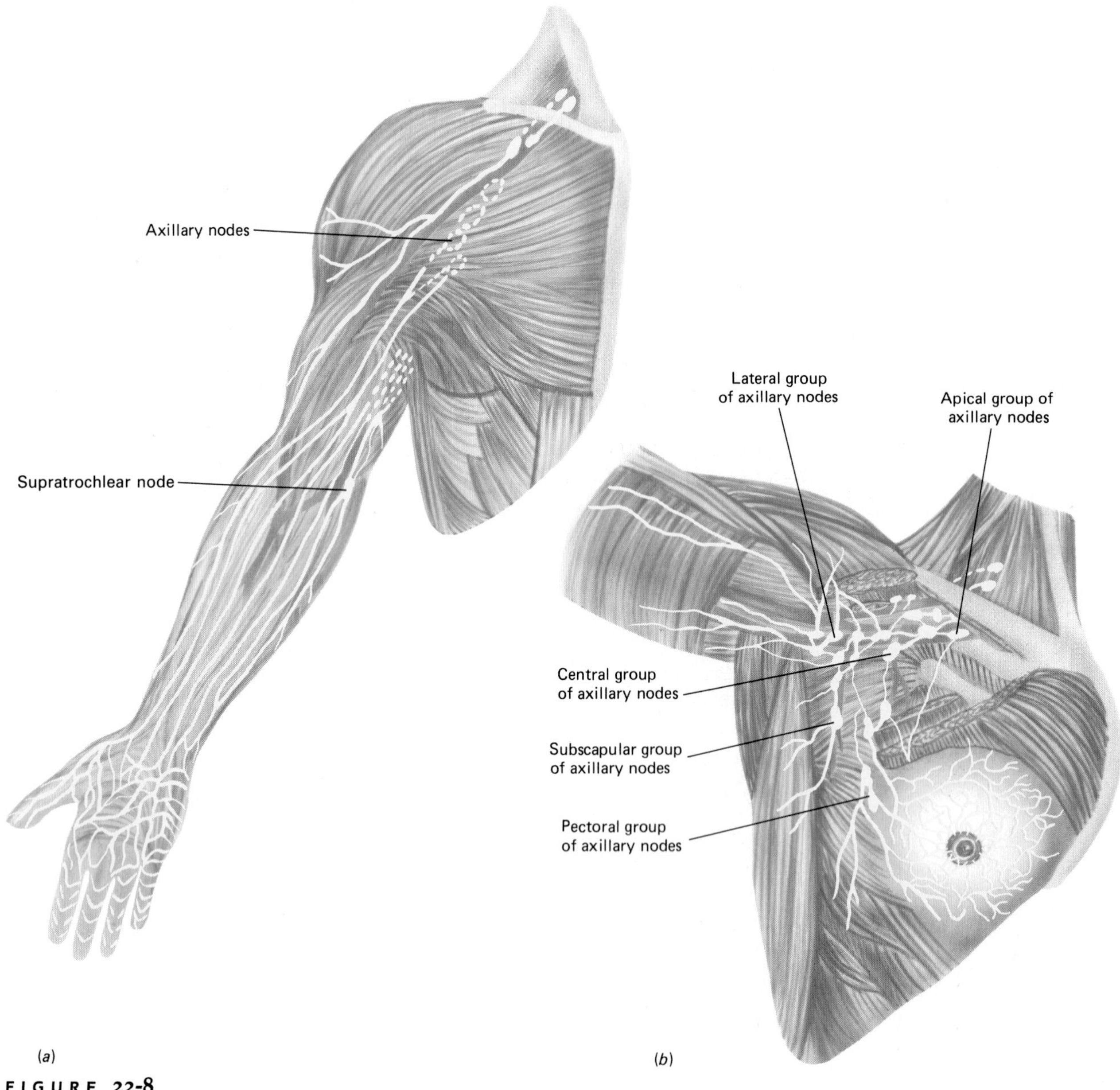

FIGURE 22-8

(*a*) Principal lymph nodes of the upper limb. (*b*) The lymph vessels of the breast also drain into the axillary lymph nodes.

Clinical highlight

An infection in the hand may cause swelling of the supratrochlear nodes. If it spreads upward, it may involve the axillary nodes. Sometimes in a serious infection red streaks extend along the entire arm following the lymphatics. (Although this condition is properly called **lymphangitis,** it is popularly referred to as "blood poisoning.")

The axillary lymph nodes are very important clinically because they receive most of the lymphatic drainage from the breast. In breast cancer these nodes often become infected with malignant cells. Should this occur a radical mastectomy may be performed. This surgical procedure involves not only removal of the breast but also its blood and lymph supply, the associated lymph nodes, and the underlying pectoral muscles.

In the lower limb the lymph nodes are located at the knee and groin (Fig. 22-9). The **popliteal nodes** at the knee (in the popliteal fossa) drain the foot and leg. Efferent lymphatics from them pass into the **inguinal lymph nodes** in the groin. The inguinal nodes consist of a superficial and a deep group. These nodes also receive lymph from the adjacent perineal and abdominal regions. The inguinal nodes ultimately drain into the thoracic duct.

Lymph nodes drain the abdomen and pelvis

Lymph from the pelvic and abdominal wall and viscera is returned to the bloodstream primarily via the thoracic duct. Lymph vessels accompany the corresponding arteries. Among the major groups of nodes that drain the body wall are the *external iliac nodes*, the *common iliac nodes*, the *internal iliac nodes*, and the *lumbar lymph nodes* (Figs. 22-10 and 22-11). Among the visceral groups are the *celiac*, *superior mesenteric*, and *inferior mesenteric* lymph nodes (Fig. 22-12).

There are more than 100 lymph nodes in the mesenteries (membranes anchoring parts of the intestine to the body wall) that receive lymph returning from the intestinal wall. Enlargement of these nodes occurs in many intestinal diseases including typhoid fever and cancer of this region. The enlarged nodes can often be felt through the wall of the abdomen.

Lymph nodes drain the thorax

Lymphatics from the deep tissues of the thoracic walls drain into three sets of lymph nodes—the *parasternal*, *intercostal*, and *diaphragmatic* lymph nodes. Lymph from the thoracic viscera drains into the *brachiocephalic*, *posterior mediastinal*, or *tracheobronchial* group of lymph nodes. Nodes of the tracheobronchial group often contain dark parti-

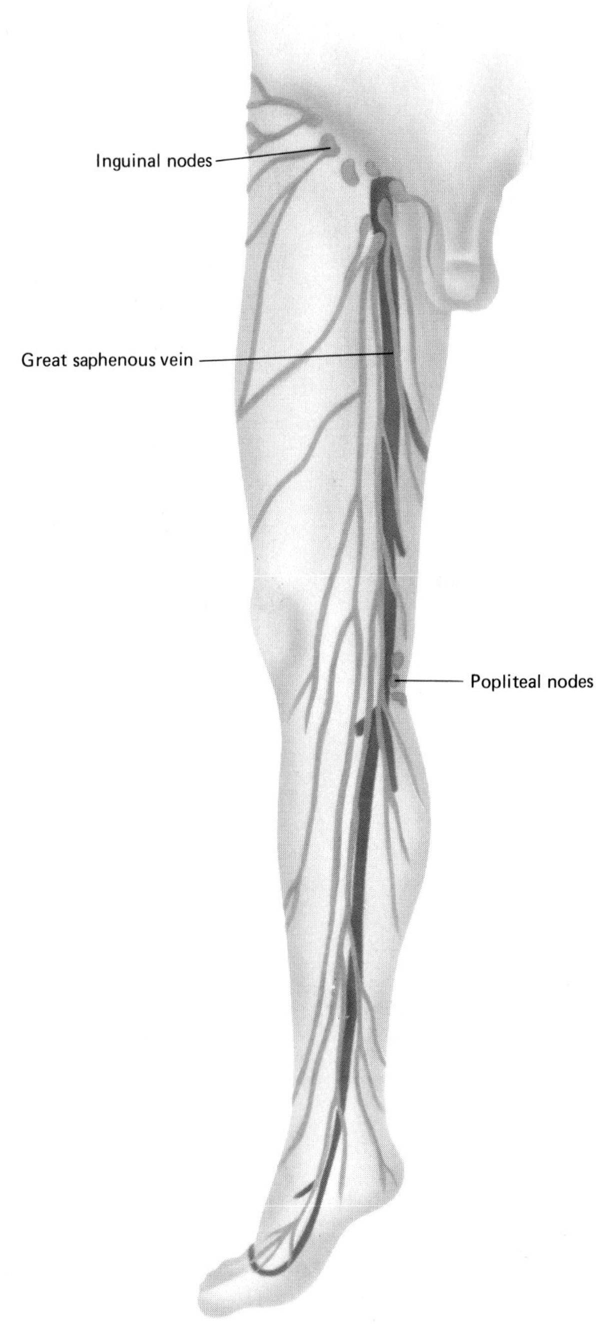

FIGURE 22-9

Principal lymph nodes of the lower limb.

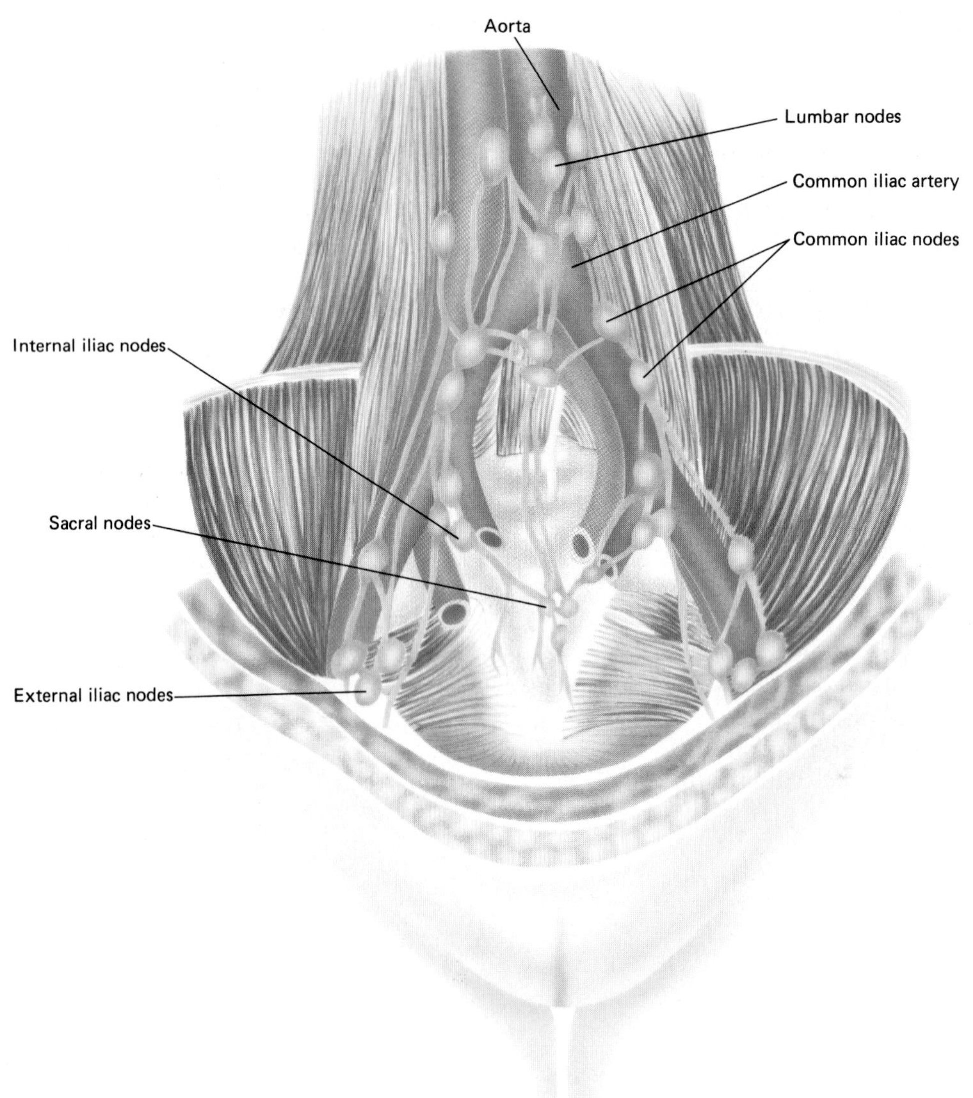

FIGURE 22-10

Principal lymph nodes of the pelvis.

cles of dust and dirt inhaled by those who live in urban areas or who work in occupations or industries where dust is endemic.

The spleen is the largest lymphatic organ

The **spleen** is the largest organ of the lymphatic system, measuring about 12 centimeters (5 in.) in length (Fig. 22-13). It lies in the abdominal cavity, posterior and lateral to the stomach and protected by the left ninth, tenth, and eleventh ribs. Because it holds a great deal of blood, the spleen has a distinctive rich purple color.

The spleen is structurally adapted for filtering blood

Structurally, the spleen is somewhat similar to a giant lymph node except that it is adapted to filter blood rather than lymph. The supporting tissue (stroma) of the spleen includes its connective tissue capsule and trabeculae, which extend in from the hilus like a branching tree.

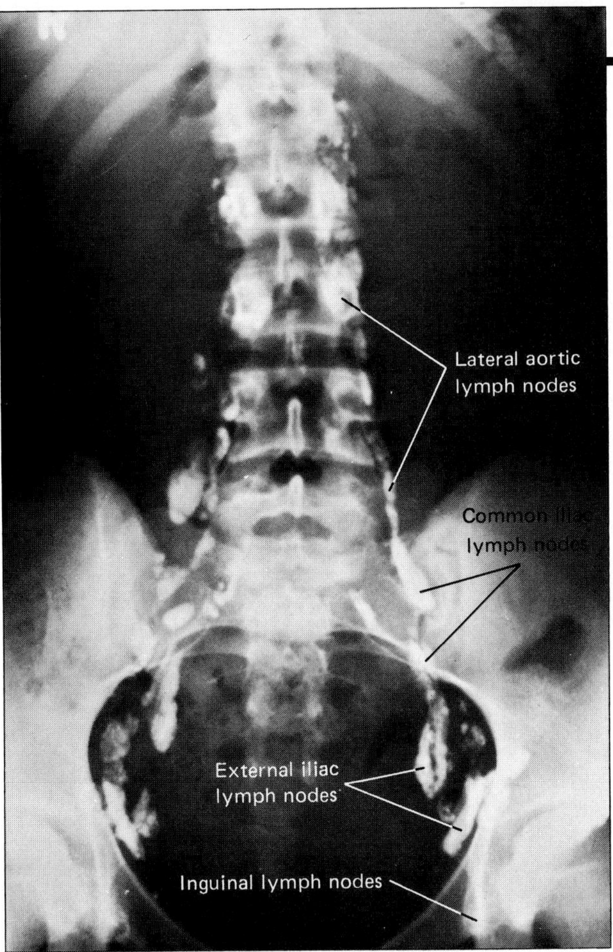

FIGURE 22-11

Lymphangiogram of normal pelvic and inguinal lymph nodes. (Courtesy of Professor Jon N. Ehringer.)

The parenchyma (specialized functional tissue) of the spleen consists of two kinds of splenic pulp—red and white (Fig. 22-14). The framework of the pulp consists of a network of reticular fibers. **White pulp** is made up of dense masses of white blood cells, mainly lymphocytes, arranged into lymph nodules. **Red pulp** consists of a network of reticular fibers filled with large blood sinuses. The sinuses are separated from one another by "cords" of pulp tissue containing large numbers of macrophages, lymphocytes, and other cells. Macrophages within the red pulp remove bacteria, worn-out blood cells and platelets, and debris from the circulation.

Blood vessels and nerves enter and leave the spleen through the *hilus*. As it approaches the spleen, the large **splenic artery** divides into several branches before entering the hilus. After bringing blood to the white pulp, arterial branches enter the adjacent red pulp. There blood courses through a complex of leaky blood sinuses, where it is filtered by the macrophages. Blood eventually enters small veins that merge to form the **splenic vein.** The splenic vein delivers blood to the hepatic portal vein.

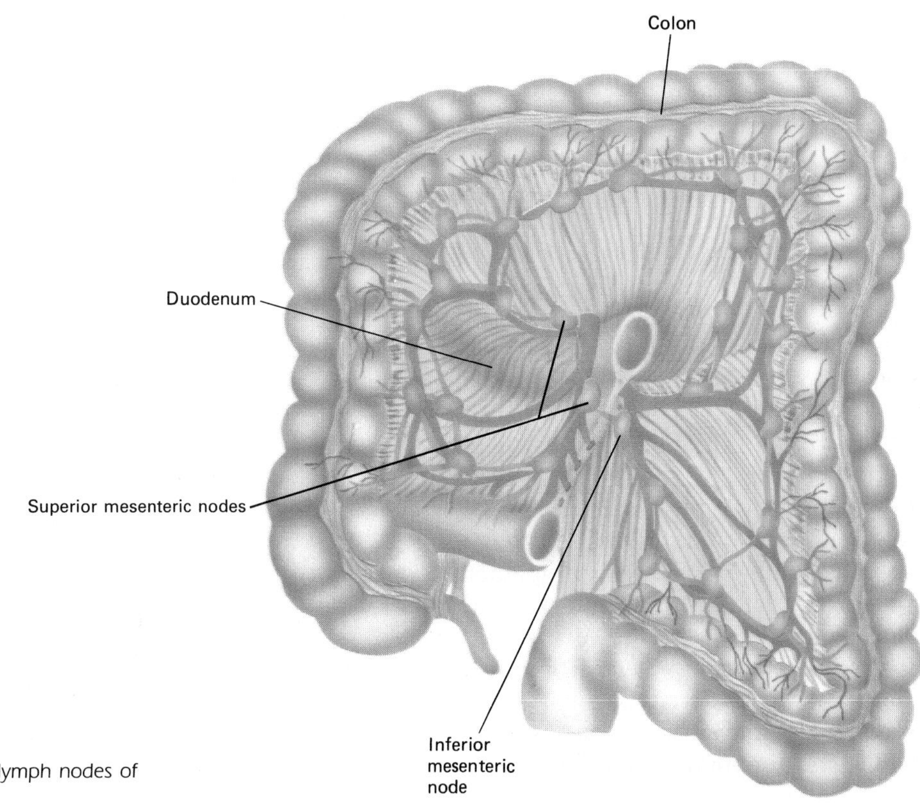

FIGURE 22-12

Some important visceral lymph nodes of the abdomen.

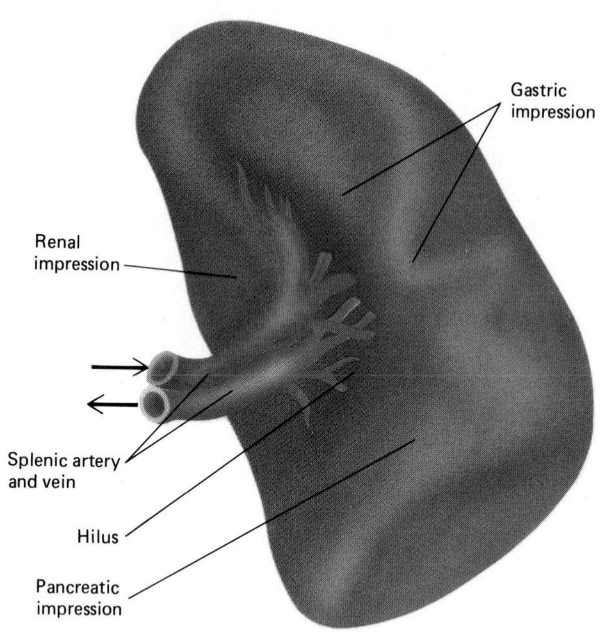

FIGURE 22-13

Visceral surface of the spleen.

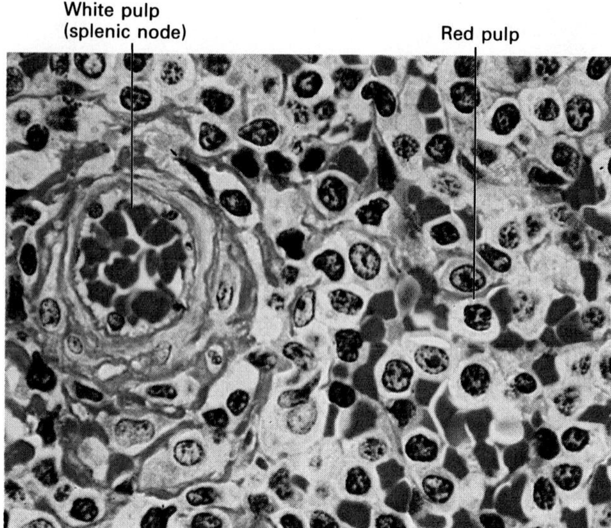

FIGURE 22-14

Photograph of a section through the spleen showing red and white pulp. (C. CNRI/Phototake-NYC.)

The spleen defends the body against disease

One of the main functions of the spleen is to bring blood into contact with lymphocytes. As blood flows slowly through the spleen, any disease organisms within it are likely to come into contact with *lymphocytes* in the spleen tissue. This contact activates the lymphocytes, which can then attack the foreign invaders. (This process will be discussed in more detail in Chapter 23, which deals with immune function.)

As blood flows through the spleen, *macrophages* remove worn-out red and white blood cells and platelets. These macrophages produce the pigment bilirubin from the breakdown of hemoglobin and release it into the blood plasma. Bilirubin is removed from the blood by the liver and kidneys and is excreted in the bile and to a lesser extent in the urine.

Because a great deal of blood circulates through the spleen, this organ serves as a kind of reservoir for blood. Epinephrine and sympathetic nerve discharge stimulate the spleen to contract, releasing much of its blood into the circulation. This function is important especially during hemorrhage, but it is not considered essential in humans. (The reservoir function of the spleen is considered especially important in dogs and other carnivores.) The spleen appears to store platelets in humans, and a large percentage of the body's platelets are normally found there.

Clinical highlight

Although the spleen performs many important functions, it is not vital to life. Fortunately so, for of all the abdominal organs, the spleen is the one most easily and most frequently injured. A severe blow or crushing injury to the upper abdomen or lower left chest may fracture the ribs that protect the spleen and cause rupture of the spleen itself. When the spleen is ruptured, extensive, sometimes massive hemorrhage occurs. This condition is usually treated by prompt surgical removal of the spleen (splenectomy) to prevent death due to loss of blood and shock. (When surgery—either splenectomy or occasionally surgical repair—is not performed on an injured spleen, the mortality rate is about 90%.) When the spleen is surgically removed, some of its functions are taken over by the bone marrow and liver; other functions are simply absent, and the body manages without them.

The thymus gland plays a key role in immune function

The **thymus gland** is a pinkish-gray lymphatic organ located in the superior mediastinum. It lies anterior to the great blood vessels as they emerge from the heart and posterior to the sternum (Fig. 22-15). During fetal life and childhood, the thy-

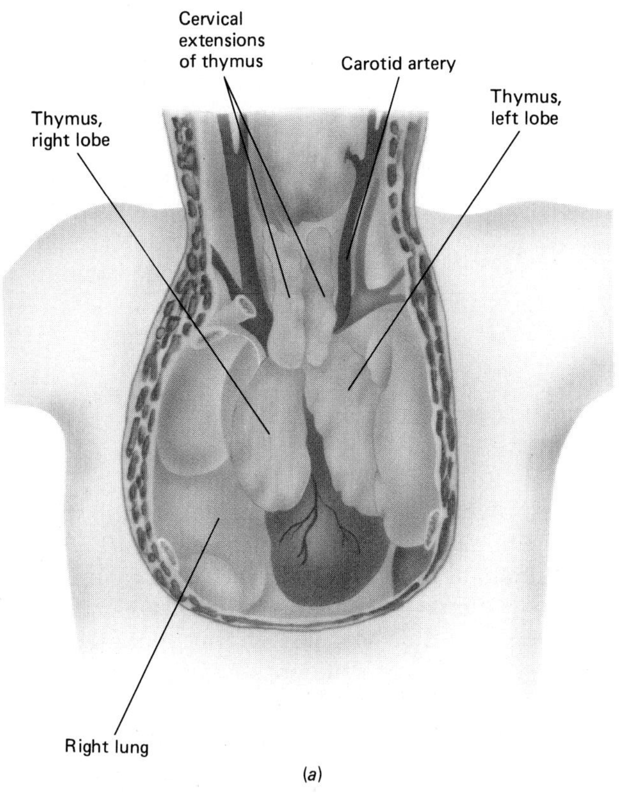

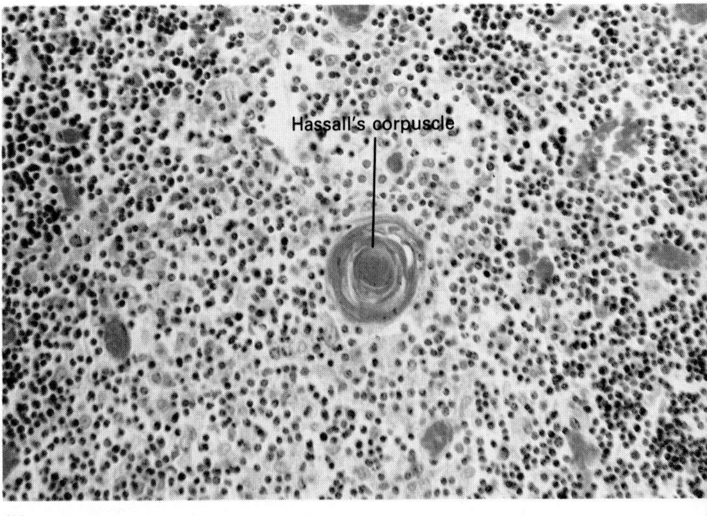

(b)

FIGURE 22-15

The thymus gland. (*a*) External view of the thymus of a newborn baby. (*b*) Photomicrograph of thymus tissue showing Hassall's corpuscles. (Cunningham/Visuals Unlimited.)

mus gland is quite large. It reaches its largest size at puberty and then begins to involute, becoming smaller with age.

The thymus consists of two **lobes** that in turn are divided into numerous **lobules.** Each lobule has an outer **cortex** and an inner **medulla.** Lymphocytes are heavily concentrated within the cortex. Small groups of epithelial cells known as **Hassall's corpuscles** are seen in the medulla (Fig. 22-15*b*). Their function is unknown.

Until recently the function of the thymus was a mystery. Although it is still not completely understood, the thymus is now known to play a key role in immunity. Stem cells from the bone marrow and liver migrate to the thymus before birth. Within the thymus they multiply and differentiate, producing a type of lymphocyte known as a **T lymphocyte.** (The T indicates its origin in the thymus.) Although the mechanism is not known, the thymus somehow "instructs" T lymphocytes to distinguish between "self" and "nonself." The T lymphocytes then take up residence in other lymph tissues of the body. Processing by the thymus permits T lymphocytes to respond effectively to disease-causing organisms that invade the body. The thymus also produces several hormones, including one called *thymosin.* The role of the thymus in immunity will be discussed in more detail in the next chapter.

The lymphatic system plays an important role in fluid homeostasis

Besides maintaining an overall fluid volume, the body must regulate the fluid equilibrium between its various compartments. Most of the fluid in the body is found within the cells themselves, the **intracellular compartment.** The remaining *extracellular fluid* is distributed mainly as plasma, lymph, and interstitial fluid. The lymphatic system plays an important role in maintaining fluid balance between the blood and the interstitial fluid.

Interstitial fluid is produced from blood plasma

As mentioned previously, blood is under high enough pressure as it enters a capillary network that some plasma is forced out through pores in the capillary wall. Once it has left the blood, this fluid is called **interstitial fluid,** or **tissue fluid**

(Fig. 22-16). Interstitial fluid resembles plasma but contains no red blood cells or platelets and only a few white blood cells. Its protein content is only about 25% that of plasma because many proteins, like platelets and blood cells, are too large to pass easily through the capillary wall. Interstitial fluid also contains oxygen, glucose, amino acids, and other nutrients that diffuse into it from the plasma. We may think of interstitial fluid as a rich sea of needed materials that bathes the cells of the tissues.

The main force moving the plasma out of the blood is the hydrostatic pressure of the blood, the pressure exerted by the blood on the capillary wall. At the venous ends of the capillaries, the hydrostatic pressure is much lower. Here the most significant force is the osmotic pressure of the blood, which draws fluid back into the capillaries. As a result, some of the interstitial fluid moves back into the blood (Fig. 22-16). Other forces are also involved. The entire topic of fluid balance will be discussed more extensively in Chapter 28.

Although interstitial fluid does tend to move back into the blood at the venous end of a capillary network, there are two potential problems: (1) The net inward force at the venous end of the capillary network is not as great as the net outward force at the arterial end. For this reason not as much fluid is returned to the circulation as escaped. (2) Protein does not return effectively into the venous capillaries but instead tends to accumulate within the interstitial fluid. These potential problems are extremely significant. If not for the activity of the lymphatic system, the fluid balance of the body would be seriously deranged within a few hours and death would occur within about 24 hours.

Lymph forms from interstitial fluid

The lymphatic system makes a vital contribution to fluid homeostasis by collecting about 10% of the interstitial fluid and the protein that accumulates in it. Once it enters the lymph capillaries, the interstitial fluid is called lymph. Note that we have assigned three different names to a fluid with a common origin. The portion of the *plasma* that escapes through the capillary walls and enters the tissues is called *interstitial fluid*. The interstitial fluid that enters the lymph vessels is called *lymph*. The appropriate name is determined by

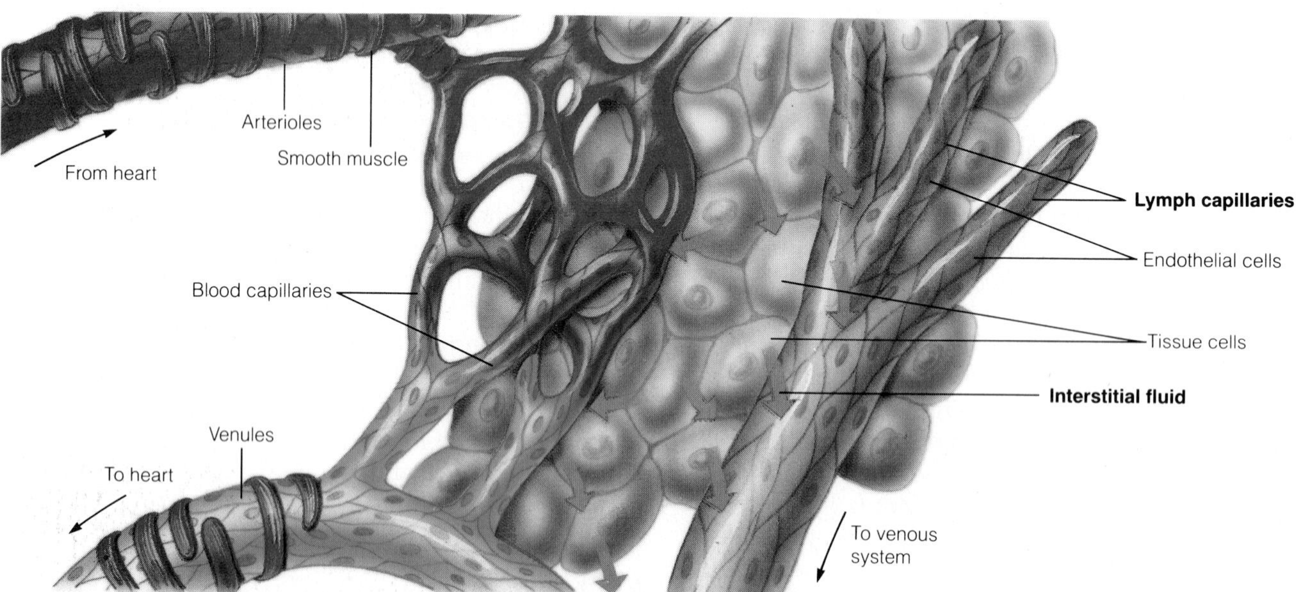

FIGURE 22-16

Formation of interstitial fluid and lymph. Interstitial fluid forms when plasma is forced out of capillaries at the arterial end of a capillary network. Most of the fluid reenters the capillaries at the venous end of the network. Excess interstitial fluid containing protein enters lymph capillaries and is eventually returned to the blood by the lymphatic system.

the location of the fluid, and of course the composition of each of these fluids varies somewhat.

You may be wondering how the lymph actually forms—that is, what makes excess interstitial fluid enter the blind capillaries of the lymphatic system? Several factors facilitate this process. As protein concentration increases in the interstitial fluid, its osmotic pressure increases correspondingly. This slows the passage of fluid into the venous capillaries while increasing the volume of interstitial fluid. With increased volume comes increased pressure. This increased pressure forces the interstitial fluid, including the protein, into the lymphatic capillaries.

Movement of interstitial fluid into the lymph capillaries is facilitated by the construction of the walls of these capillaries. The endothelial cells that make up the wall are each anchored to connective tissue but are not cemented together (Fig. 22-17). Instead, the cells overlap slightly and can be pushed inward when fluid presses against them. This mechanism works somewhat like a swinging door that opens only inward. As the volume of fluid increases within the lymph capillary, the cell door is pushed closed. As protein is removed from the interstitial fluid its osmotic pressure decreases, and the cycle begins anew.

Lymph flows from the first segment of the capillary, past a tiny valve, into the second segment. The now empty end of the capillary has a lower pressure than the surrounding interstitial fluid. As a result, it exerts a suction force, pulling more interstitial fluid into the lymph capillary.

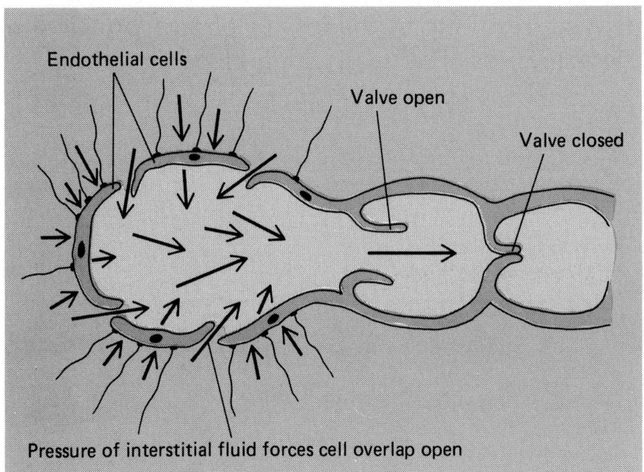

FIGURE 22-17

Formation of lymph. Interstitial fluid enters the blind ends of lymph capillaries between the endothelial cells of the capillary wall. Once inside the lymph vessel it is called lymph. Note the valves that present backflow of the lymph.

Lymph flow depends on compression of lymphatic vessels

Without a heart to pump it through the lymph vessels, what makes lymph flow? When muscles contract, the lymph vessels are compressed. This forces lymph through the vessel. Respiratory movements also promote lymph flow by creating pressure differences. When arteries pulsate or when anything compresses body tissues, lymphatic vessels are compressed and lymph flow is enhanced. Numerous valves within the lymph vessels ensure that lymph does not flow backward. Any forward progress is maintained. Some physiologists think that lymph is also pushed along by a pumping action of the wall of the lymph vessels themselves. As a segment of the vessel becomes stretched with lymph, smooth muscle in its wall contracts, pushing the fluid past the next valve in the next segment.

The rate of lymph flow in no way compares to that of blood flow. Only about 120 milliliters of lymph pass into the blood circulation each hour. Lymph flow is a vital but exceedingly slow process.

Disruption of lymph flow leads to edema

Any obstruction of the lymphatic vessels can lead to **edema,** excessive accumulation of interstitial fluid. Such obstruction can result from injury, inflammation, surgery, or parasitic infection.

Clinical highlight

When a breast is removed (mastectomy) because of cancer, lymph nodes in the axillary region may be surgically excised in an effort to prevent the spread of cancer cells. The patient's arm may swell tremendously as a result of the disrupted lymph circulation. However, new lymph vessels develop within a few months and the swelling slowly subsides.

Filariasis is a parasitic infection that affects the lymph system. It is caused by a larval nematode transmitted to humans by mosquitoes. The adult worms take up residence in the lymphatics, blocking lymph drainage. Interstitial fluid then accumulates, causing swelling in the body part involved. In persons who have suffered from this disease for long periods, legs and other body parts may swell to enormous proportions. Because affected legs resemble the huge limbs of an elephant, this disease is sometimes referred to as elephantiasis (Fig. 22-18).

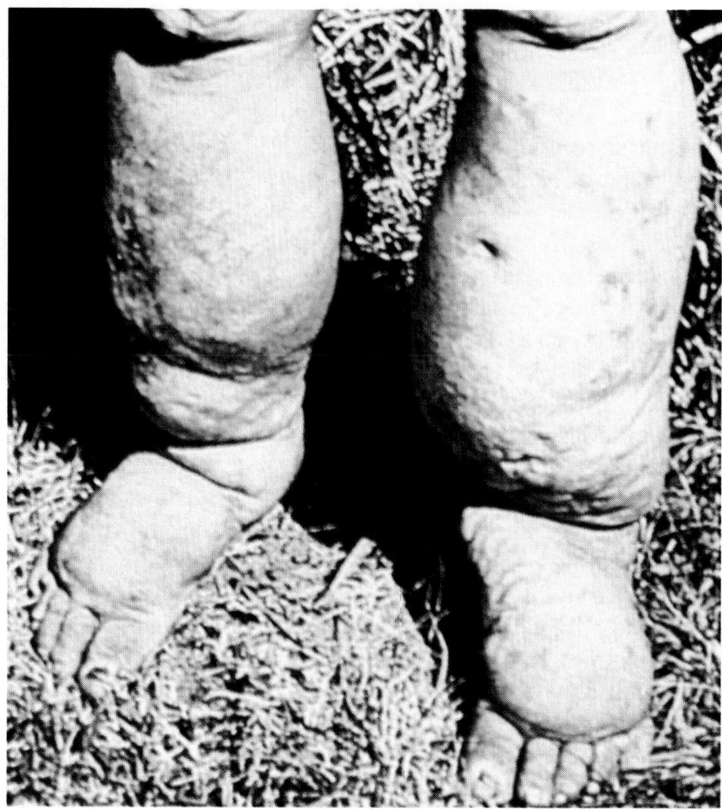

FIGURE 22-18

Lymphatic drainage is blocked in the limbs of this individual due to a parasitic infection known as filariasis. The condition characterized by such swollen limbs is elephantiasis. (Science VU—Fred Marsik/Visuals Unlimited.)

It is important to understand that lymphatic obstruction is not the only cause of edema. In fact, cardiac failure is the most important cause of systemic (widespread) edema. When the heart does not pump effectively, blood dams up in the venous system, causing the capillary pressure to rise. In turn, this increases the volume of the interstitial fluid, resulting in edema. Left-side heart failure or mitral valve disorder causes pulmonary edema. In this extremely dangerous condition, fluid may enter the air sacs of the lungs, causing rapid death by suffocation. Edema can also result from allergic reactions, venous obstruction, severe protein malnutrition (resulting in insufficient amounts of plasma proteins to maintain osmotic pressure in the blood), liver disease (resulting in reduced manufacture of plasma proteins), kidney disease (resulting in the loss of plasma proteins in the urine), or abnormally high blood pressure.

Summary

I. The lymphatic system is a subsystem of the circulatory system.
   A. It returns excess interstitial fluid to the blood, defends the body against disease organisms, and absorbs lipids from the intestine.
   B. The lymphatic system consists of lymph, lymphatic vessels, diffuse lymph tissue, lymph nodules and nodes, thymus, spleen, and tonsils.

II. Three main types of lymphatic vessels are lymph capillaries, lymphatics, and lymph ducts.

III. The basic pattern of lymph flow is from the lymph capillaries to the lymphatics to the lymph ducts.
   A. Lymphatics from the lower portion of the body converge to form the cisterna chyli, which empties into the thoracic duct.
      1. The thoracic duct receives lymph from all of the lymphatics except those that drain the upper right quadrant of the body.
      2. The thoracic duct empties into the base of the left subclavian vein.
   B. Lymphatics from the upper right quadrant of the body deliver lymph to the right lymphatic duct, which empties into the base of the right subclavian vein.
   C. An afferent lymphatic delivers lymph to a lymph node. From the afferent lymphatic, lymph flows through lymph sinuses in the node and then leaves the node through an efferent lymphatic.

IV. Lymph nodules are small masses of lymph tissue that produce lymphocytes.
   A. Lymph nodules are scattered throughout connective tissue, especially within the walls of passageways opening to the outside of the body.
   B. Aggregates of lymph nodules form Peyer's patches in the wall of the small intestine (ileum) and the tonsils in the throat region.

V. Lymph nodes are masses of lymph tissue surrounded by connective tissue capsules.
   A. The cortex (outer region) consists of lymph nodules containing germinal centers where lymphocytes are produced; the inner medulla contains medullary cords.
   B. Lymph nodes filter lymph and produce lymphocytes.
   C. They are distributed along the main lymphatic routes and are clustered especially in the axilla, groin, neck, thorax, and abdomen.

VI. The spleen filters blood and serves as a reservoir for blood. Disease-causing organisms in the blood come into contact with lymphocytes within the spleen tissue, activating lymphocytes.

VII. The thymus plays a key role in immunity by producing and "instructing" T lymphocytes and by producing hormones such as thymosin.

VIII. The lymphatic system plays an important role in fluid homeostasis.
   A. Interstitial fluid forms when plasma is forced out of capillaries.
   B. Although most interstitial fluid returns to the blood directly at the venous ends of capillaries, a small amount of excess fluid accumulates.
   C. The excess interstitial fluid (which contains protein) enters the lymph capillaries and is then called lymph.
   D. Mechanisms that contribute to lymph flow include muscle contraction, respiratory movements, arterial pulse, and the presence of valves within lymph vessels.

Post-test

1. Three functions of the lymphatic system are ______________, ______________, and ______________.
2. A drop of lymph is passing through the cisterna chyli. It will next pass into the ______________ ______________.
3. A drop of lymph in the right lymphatic duct will next pass into the ______________ ______________.
4. Tonsils are masses of ______________ ______________.
5. Two main functions of lymph nodes are to ______________ and ______________.
6. Vessels that conduct lymph into a lymph node are called ______________ ______________.
7. The spleen filters ______________.
8. The white pulp of the spleen consists of dense masses of ______________.
9. Bacteria are removed from blood circulating through the spleen by cells called ______________.
10. The ______________ is a lymphatic organ that plays a key role in immunity.

11. When plasma is forced out of the capillaries and into the tissues, it is called ______________ ______________.
12. Excess interstitial fluid is returned to the blood by the ______________ ______________.
13. When interstitial fluid enters a lymph capillary, it is called ______________.
14. Lymph vessels are equipped with ______________ that prevent backflow.
15. The effect of muscle contraction on lymph flow is to ______________ ______________.
16. Obstruction of lymph flow can lead to ______________.

Match the lymph node with the region of the body drained

____ **17.** Axillary nodes		a. Abdominal body wall
____ **18.** Submandibular nodes		b. Foot and leg
____ **19.** Lumbar nodes		c. Arm
____ **20.** Intercostal nodes		d. Thoracic wall
____ **21.** Deep cervical nodes		e. Nose, tongue
____ **22.** Popliteal nodes		f. Lymph vessels of head and neck

23. Label the diagram on the opposite page.

Review questions

1. In what ways does the lymphatic system function to maintain homeostasis?
2. What are the functions of lymph nodes? How are lymph nodes structurally adapted to perform these functions?
3. Contrast lymph nodules and lymph nodes.
4. What is the function of the spleen? How is the spleen structurally adapted to perform its function?
5. What is the relationship between plasma, interstitial fluid, and lymph?
6. What mechanisms contribute to lymph formation? To lymph flow?
7. What are some factors that could interfere with lymph flow? What are the consequences of such disruption? How does edema represent a threat to homeostasis?
8. Trace a drop of lymph from the right arm to the blood.
9. Trace a drop of lymph from the foot to the blood.

Post-test answers

1. Returns excess interstitial fluid to the blood, defends body against disease-causing organisms, absorbs lipids from intestine. **2.** thoracic duct **3.** right subclavian vein **4.** lymph nodules **5.** filter lymph, produce lymphocytes **6.** afferent lymphatics **7.** blood **8.** lymphocytes **9.** macrophages **10.** thymus **11.** interstitial fluid **12.** lymphatic system **13.** lymph **14.** valves **15.** speed flow **16.** edema **17.** c (d) **18.** e **19.** a **20.** d **21.** f **22.** b **23.** See Figure 22-1.

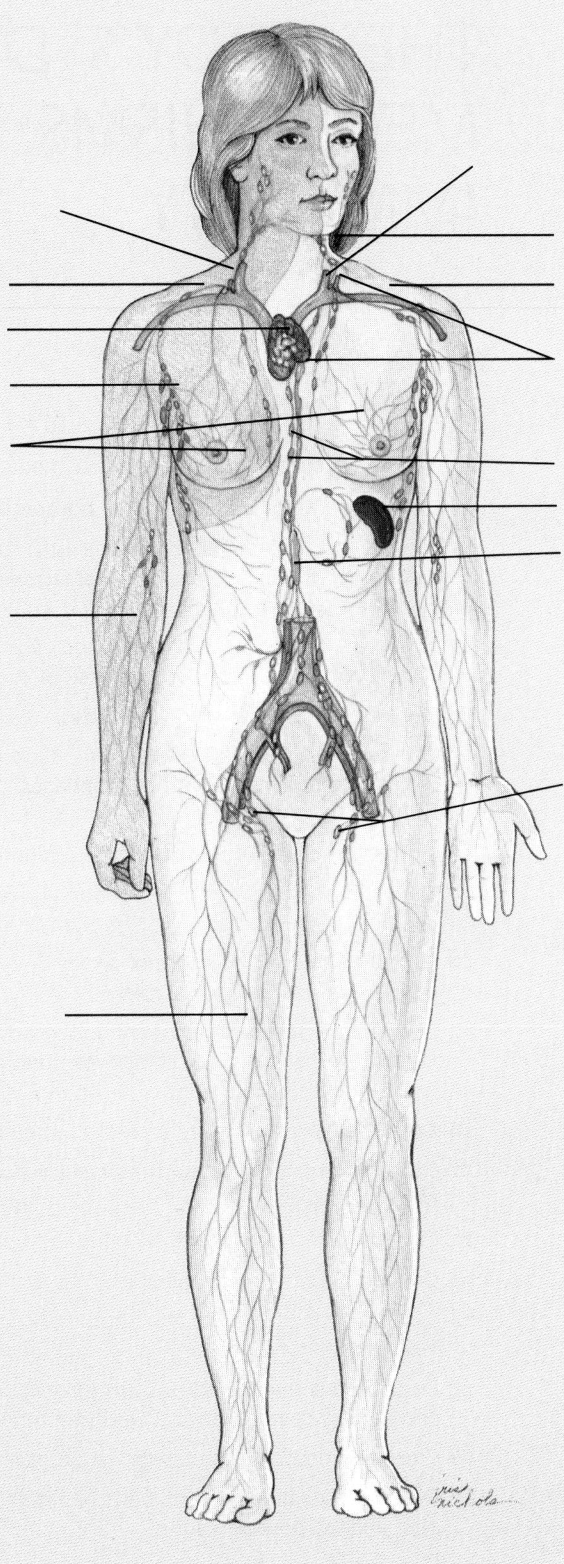

THE BODY'S DEFENSE MECHANISMS: IMMUNITY

CHAPTER OUTLINE

- I. **Self and nonself**
- II. **Nonspecific defense mechanisms**
  - A. Interferon
  - B. Inflammation
  - C. Phagocytosis
- III. **Specific defense mechanisms**
  - A. Cells important in immune responses
    - 1. T cells
    - 2. B cells
    - 3. Macrophages
  - B. Thymus
  - C. Major histocompatibility complex
  - D. Antibody-mediated immunity
    - □ Focus on AIDS
    - 1. Nature of antibodies
    - 2. Classes of antibodies
    - 3. Antigen-antibody binding
    - 4. Recognition of antigens
  - E. Cell-mediated immunity
  - F. Primary and secondary responses
  - G. Active immunity
  - H. Passive immunity
  - I. Body defenses against cancer
  - J. Rejection of transplanted tissue
  - K. Immunologically privileged sites
  - L. Induced immunological tolerance
  - M. Autoimmune disease
  - N. Allergic reactions

LEARNING OBJECTIVES

After you have studied this chapter you should be able to:

1 Distinguish between specific and nonspecific defense mechanisms.

2 Identify nonspecific defense mechanisms such as those provided by the skin, acid in the stomach, respiratory passageways, and interferon and explain how they protect against infection.

3 Relate the physiological changes and clinical symptoms associated with inflammation to its role in the defense of the body.

4 Describe the process of phagocytosis.

5 Contrast T and B lymphocytes with respect to life cycle and function, and identify other cells, such as macrophages, that function in immune responses.

6 Describe the role of the thymus in immune mechanisms.

7 Define the terms antigen and antibody, and describe how antigens stimulate immune responses.

8 Describe the basic structure of an antibody, and list the five classes of antibodies and their biological roles.

9 Describe the mechanisms of antibody-mediated immunity, including the effects of antigen-antibody complexes upon pathogens; include a discussion of the complement system.

10 Explain antibody diversity according to current theory.

11 Describe the mechanisms of cell-mediated immunity, including development of memory cells.

12 Contrast a secondary with a primary immune response.

13 Contrast active and passive immunity, giving examples of each.

14 Summarize the theory of immunosurveillance, and describe how the body destroys cancer cells.

15 Describe the immunological basis of graft rejection, and explain how the effects of graft rejection can be minimized.

16 Cite situations in which foreign tissue may be accepted by the body.

17 Describe the immunological basis of autoimmune diseases, give two examples, and list possible causes.

18 Explain the immunological basis of allergy, and briefly describe the events that occur during (a) a hayfever response and (b) systemic anaphylaxis.

A macrophage (grey) extends a pseudopod toward an invading *E. coli* bacterium (green) that is already multiplying. (Lennart Nilsson/©Boehringer Ingelheim International GmbH, from *The Incredible Machine*, p. 171.)

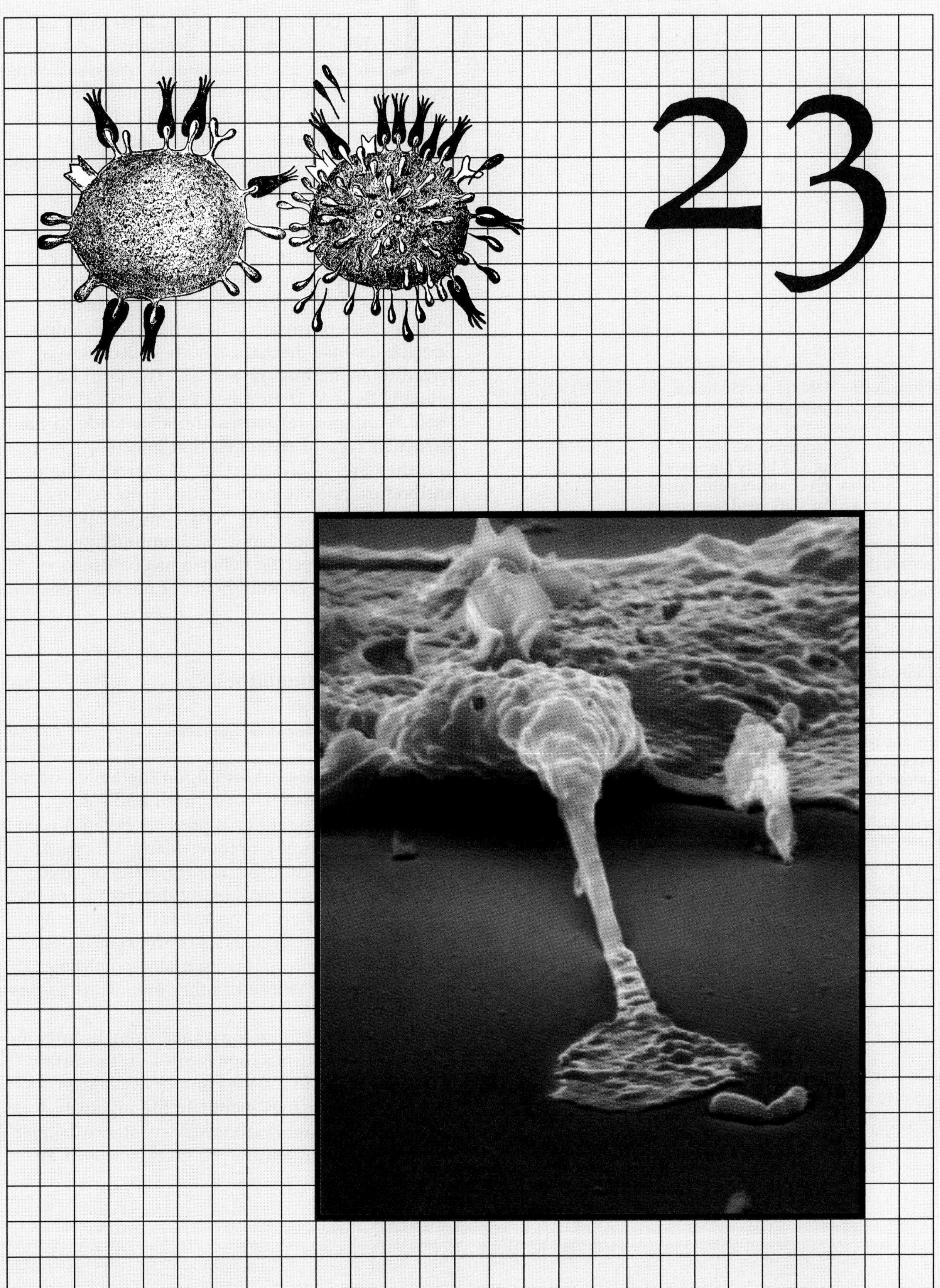
23

KEY CONCEPTS

Nonspecific defense mechanisms are aimed at preventing entrance of foreign agents and destroying those that manage to penetrate the defenses. Among the body's nonspecific defense mechanisms are barriers such as the skin, acid secretions in the stomach, phagocytosis, inflammatory response, and release of interferon.

Specific defense mechanisms are immune responses; these responses depend on the body's ability to produce cells and antibodies specifically tailored to attack particular antigens that gain entrance to the body.

In antibody-mediated immunity, specific B lymphocytes are activated when exposed to specific antigens. They differentiate and secrete specific antibodies that chemically attack the antigens.

In cell-mediated immunity, specific T lymphocytes are activated when exposed to specific antigens. These lymphocytes multiply and differentiate, producing cells that attack the antigen.

The body has a remarkable defense capability that provides protection against foreign agents, including disease-causing organisms, or **pathogens.** Defense mechanisms can be nonspecific or highly specific. **Nonspecific defense mechanisms** are directed against foreign agents in general, whereas **specific defense mechanisms** are directed against particular pathogens or toxins.

Nonspecific defense mechanisms deter a variety of pathogens, by preventing their entrance into the body or by destroying them quickly if they succeed in penetrating the body's barriers. Phagocytosis of invading bacteria is an example. Specific defense mechanisms are collectively referred to as immune responses. The term **immune** is derived from a Latin word meaning "safe." Immune responses are tailor-made to the particular type of pathogen that infects the body, and they are highly effective. The production of **antibodies,** specific proteins that help destroy pathogens, is one of the body's most important specific defense mechanisms. **Immunology,** the study of these specific defense mechanisms, is one of the most exciting fields of medical research today.

The body distinguishes self from nonself

Immune responses depend upon the ability of the body to distinguish between itself and foreign matter. Such recognition is possible because each of us is biochemically unique. Many cell types have surface macromolecules (proteins or large carbohydrates) that are slightly different from the surface macromolecules on the cells of other species or even other organisms of the same species. An organism "knows" its own macromolecules and "recognizes" those of other organisms as foreign.

A single bacterium may have from 10 to more than 1000 distinct macromolecules on its surface. When a bacterium invades another organism, these macromolecules stimulate the organism to launch an immune response. A substance capable of stimulating an immune response is called an **antigen** (**an**-tih-jen).

Nonspecific defense mechanisms operate rapidly

The body's outer covering is the first line of defense against pathogens. The **skin** is more than just a mechanical barrier. Millions of harmless microorganisms, the normal flora, populate the skin. These microorganisms live in harmony with their host, and their presence appears to inhibit the multiplication of potentially harmful microorganisms that happen to land on the skin. Such resident microorganisms compete successfully with invaders for essential nutrients and may maintain a pH best suited for their needs. Other nonspecific defenses of the skin include sweat and sebum, which contain chemicals that destroy certain kinds of bacteria.

Microorganisms that enter with food are usually destroyed by the acid secretions and enzymes of the **stomach** (Fig. 23-1). Pathogens that enter the body with inhaled air may be filtered out by hairs in the **nose** or trapped in the sticky mucous lining of the **respiratory passageways.** Once trapped, they may be destroyed by phagocytes.

Should pathogens invade the tissues, other nonspecific defense mechanisms are activated. Among these nonspecific defense mechanisms are interferon release, inflammation, and phagocytosis.

Interferons inhibit viral infection

When infected by viruses or other intracellular parasites (some types of bacteria, fungi, and protozoa), certain types of cells respond by secreting proteins called **interferons** (in-ter-**feer**-ons). This group of proteins stimulates other cells to produce antiviral proteins, which prevent the cell from manufacturing macromolecules required by the virus. The virus particles produced in cells exposed to interferon are less effective at infecting cells. Interferons also stimulate **natural killer (NK) cells.** NK cells recognize body cells that

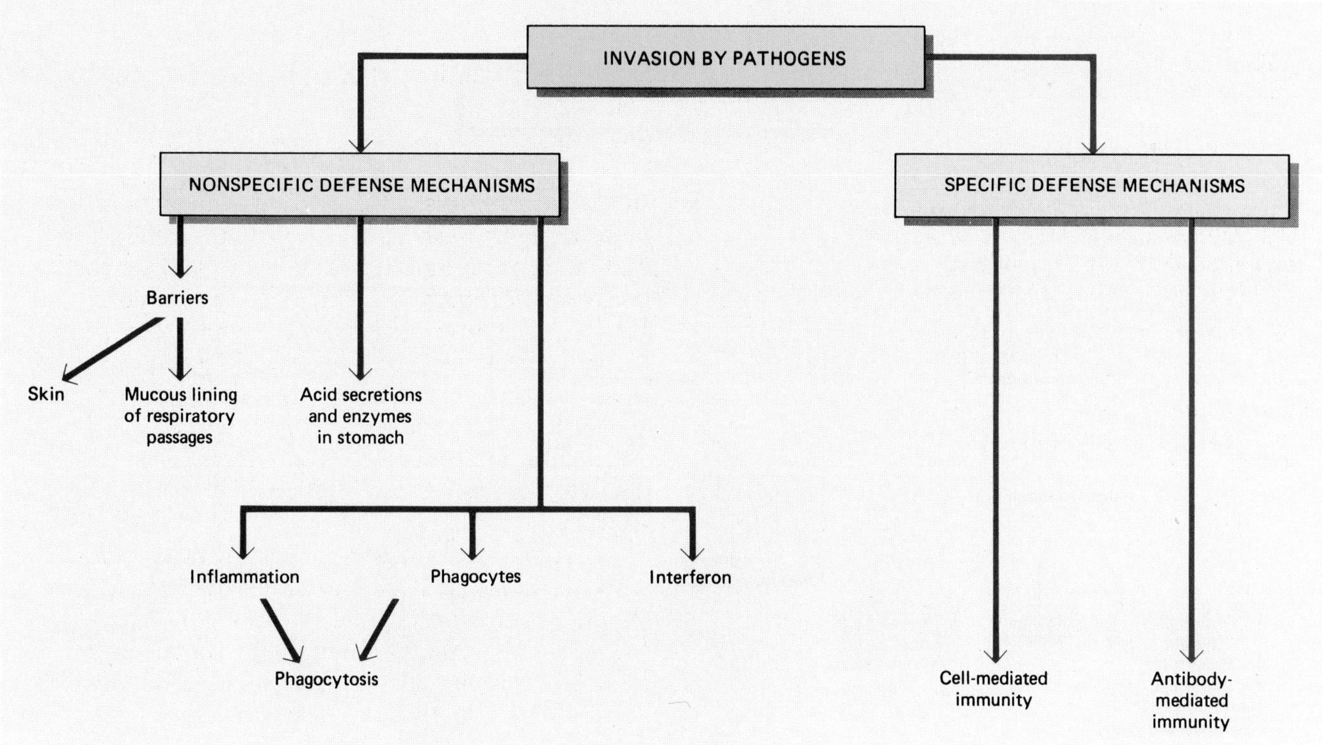

FIGURE 23-1

Summary of nonspecific and specific defense mechanisms. Nonspecific mechanisms prevent entrance of a great many pathogens and act rapidly to destroy those that manage to cross the barriers. Specific defense mechanisms take longer to mobilize but are highly effective in destroying invaders.

have been altered by viruses and quickly destroy them.

Drug companies have invested millions of dollars trying to develop an inexpensive, effective method of producing human interferon. Success has been achieved by using recombinant DNA techniques. Research has established that interferon is useful in treating some viral infections, and recent studies suggest that it might be helpful in treating certain forms of cancer.

Inflammation helps fight infection

When pathogens invade tissues, they trigger an **inflammatory response** (Fig. 23-2). Blood vessels in the affected area dilate, increasing blood flow to the infected region. The increased blood flow makes the skin look red and feel warm. Capillaries in the inflamed area become more permeable, allowing more fluid to leave the circulation and enter the tissues. As the volume of interstitial fluid increases, **edema** (swelling) occurs. The edema (and also certain substances released by the injured cells) is responsible for the pain that is characteristic of inflammation. Thus, the clinical characteristics of inflammation are *redness, heat, edema,* and *pain.*

The increased blood flow that occurs during inflammation brings great numbers of phagocytic cells (first neutrophils and, later, monocytes; see Chapter 19) to the infected area. The increased permeability of the blood vessels allows needed gamma globulins, which serve as antibodies, to leave the circulation and enter the tissues. As fluid leaves the circulation, it also brings with it needed oxygen and nutrients.

Although inflammation is often a local response, sometimes the entire body is involved. Fever is a common clinical symptom of widespread inflammatory response. A peptide called **interleukin 1,** released by macrophages, somehow resets the body's thermostat in the hypothalamus. Prostaglandins are also involved in this resetting process. Fever interferes with viral activity and decreases circulating levels of iron. When microorganisms have difficulty obtaining needed iron supplies, they are at a metabolic disadvantage.

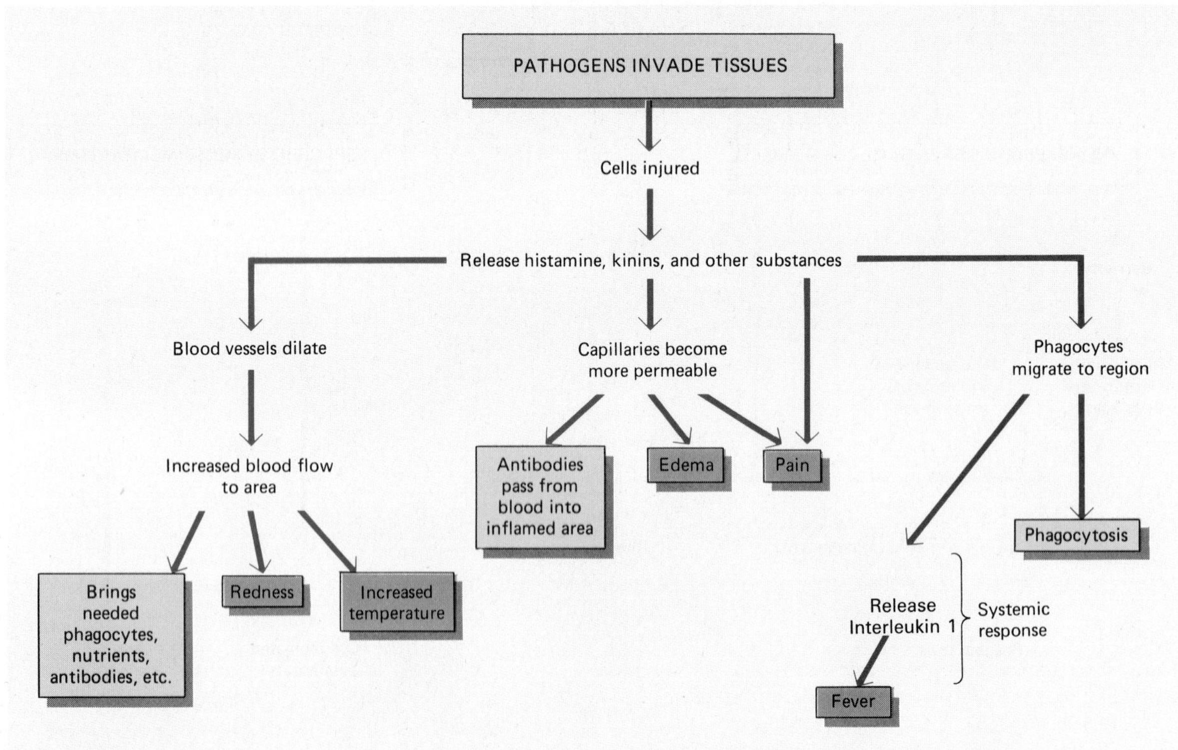

FIGURE 23-2

Inflammation is a mechanism by which protective immune mechanisms can be localized at a region where infection occurs. It is a vital process that permits phagocytic cells, antibodies, and other needed compounds to enter the tissue where microbial invasion is taking place.

Invading bacteria are destroyed by phagocytosis

One of the main functions of inflammation appears to be increased phagocytosis. Recall that a phagocyte ingests a bacterium or other invading organism by flowing around it and engulfing it (Fig. 23-3). As it ingests the organism, the phagocyte wraps it within membrane pinched off from the plasma membrane. The vesicle containing the bacterium is called a **phagosome** (**fag**-oh-sowm).

One or more lysosomes adhere to the phagosome membrane and fuse with it. Under a microscope the lysosomes look like granules, but when they fuse with the phagosome the granules seem to disappear. For this reason, the process is referred to as *degranulation*. The lysosome releases potent digestive enzymes onto the captured bacte-

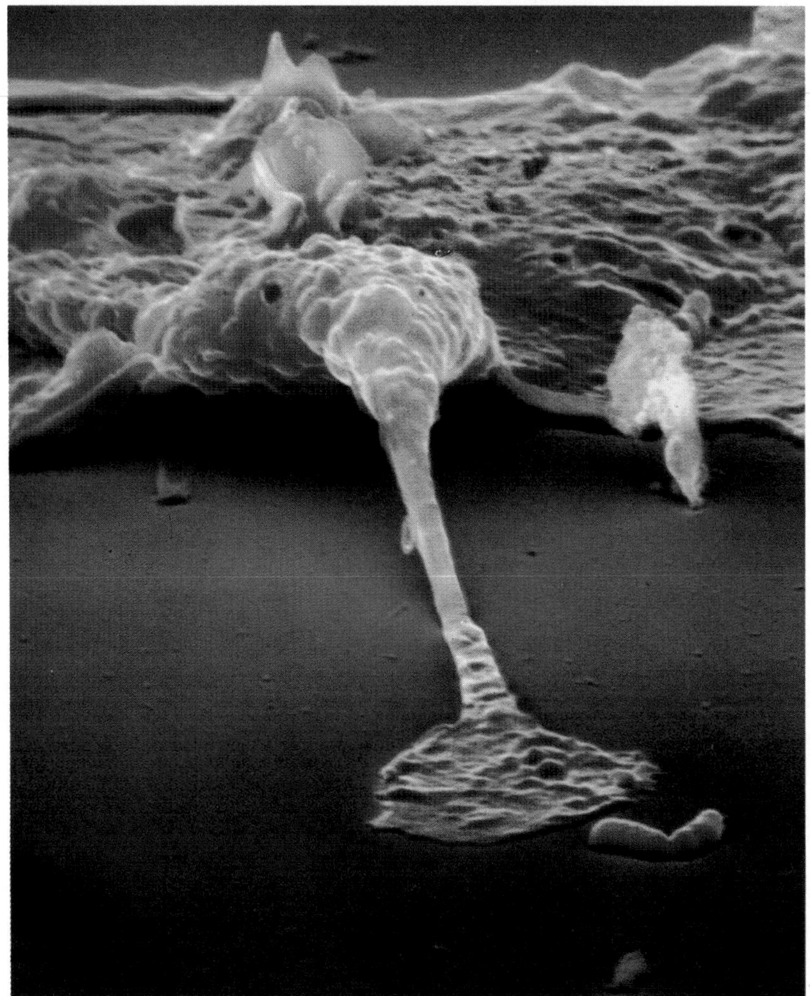

(*a*)

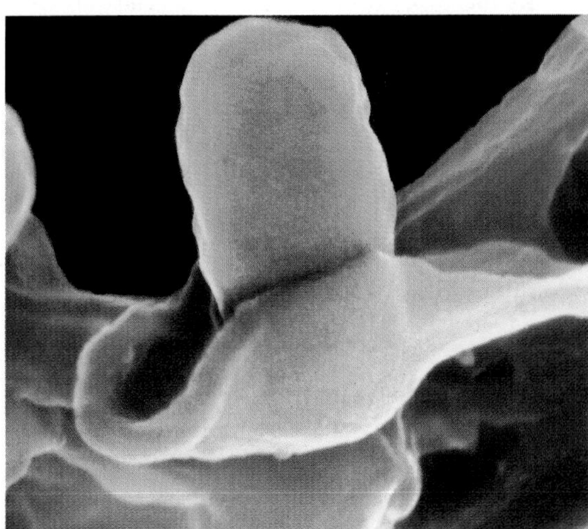

(*b*)

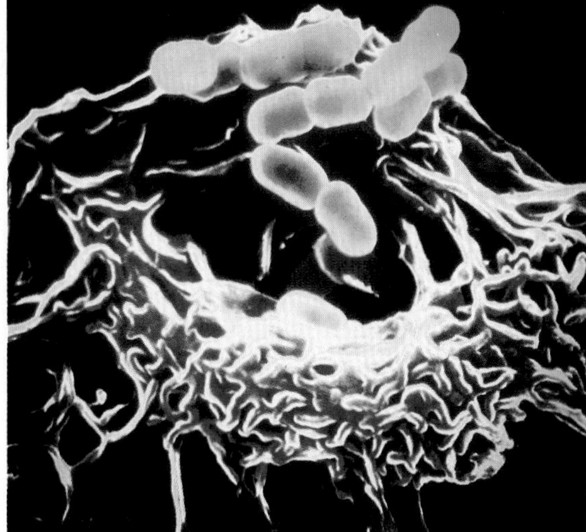

(*c*)

FIGURE 23-3

The macrophage is an incredibly efficient warrior. (*a*) A macrophage (gray) extends a pseudopod toward an invading *E. coli* bacterium (green) that is already multiplying. (Lennart Nilsson/© Boehringer Ingelheim International GmbH, from *The Incredible Machine*, p. 170.) (*b*) The bacterium is trapped within the engulfing pseudopod. (Lennart Nilsson/© Boehringer Ingelheim International GmbH, from *The Incredible Machine*, p. 171.) (*c*) The macrophage sucks the trapped bacteria in along with its own plasma membrane. The macrophage's plasma membrane will seal over the bacteria, and powerful lysosomal enzymes will destroy them. (Nilsson/Boehringer.)

rium, and the phagosome membrane releases hydrogen peroxide onto the invader. These substances destroy the bacterium and break down its macromolecules to small, harmless compounds that can be released or even utilized by the phagocyte.

After a neutrophil phagocytizes 20 or so bacteria, it becomes inactivated (perhaps by leaking lysosomal enzymes) and dies. A macrophage can phagocytize about 100 bacteria during its lifespan. Can bacteria counteract the body's attack? Certain bacteria are able to release enzymes that destroy the membranes of the lysosomes. The powerful lysosomal enzymes then spill out into the cytoplasm and may destroy the phagocyte. Other bacteria, such as those that cause tuberculosis, possess cell walls or capsules that resist the action of lysosomal enzymes.

Some macrophages wander through the tissue phagocytizing foreign matter and bacteria (Fig. 23-3); when appropriate, they release antiviral agents. Others stay in one place and destroy bacteria that pass by. For example, air sacs in the lungs contain large numbers of tissue macrophages that destroy foreign matter entering with inhaled air.

Specific defense mechanisms include cell- and antibody-mediated immunity

Nonspecific defense mechanisms destroy pathogens and prevent the spread of infection while specific defense mechanisms are being mobilized. Several days are required to activate specific immune responses, but once in gear, these mechanisms are extremely effective. There are two main types of specific immunity: **cell-mediated immunity,** in which lymphocytes attack the invading pathogen directly, and **antibody-mediated immunity,** in which lymphocytes produce specific antibodies designed to destroy the pathogen.

Several types of cells are important in immune responses

As discussed in Chapter 19, several types of mononuclear blood cells can be distinguished with the light microscope. The larger mononuclear cells (10 to 18 micrometers in diameter) containing a kidney-shaped nucleus and some light granules are monocytes. Recall that monocytes develop into macrophages, large phagocytic cells that engulf and destroy bacteria and other invaders (Table 23-1).

TABLE 23-1

Cells Important in Immune responses

Type of cell	Function
Macrophage	Phagocytosis; processes antigens, displays them on its cell surface, and presents them to antigen-sensitive lymphocytes; secretes a variety of substances that regulate immune responses including interleukin 1, which stimulates immune responses; secretes plasminogen activator, which stimulates T cells; secretes interferon and prostaglandins that tend to inhibit immune responses
T cells	When stimulated by antigen, divide, giving rise to clone of identical cells; some differentiate, becoming cytotoxic T cells, others become helper T cells or memory T cells
Cytotoxic T cells	Recognize cells bearing antigens and destroy these foreign cells by secreting perforins and lymphotoxins that lyse the cell; secrete a variety of lymphokines that attract macrophages, activate macrophages, and activate other lymphocytes
Helper T cells	Secrete interleukin 2, which stimulates cytotoxic T cells to respond; secrete B-cell growth factor and B-cell stimulatory factor that promote growth of B cells
Suppressor T cells	Suppress the response of other cells to antigens
Memory T cells	Remain in lymph nodes for many years after an infection; should the same pathogen enter the body again, these cells produce new clones of T cells, permitting a rapid response
B cells	When stimulated by antigen, divide to form clones of identical cells; some differentiate into plasma (antibody-producing) cells and others become memory B cells
Memory B cells	Continue to produce small amounts of antibody for years after an infection; should the same pathogen enter the body again, these cells multiply, producing new clones of plasma cells; this results in a rapid, enhanced antibody response
Natural killer cells (NK cells)	Important in destroying cells infected by virus and cancer cells

The small (6 to 10 micrometers in diameter) mononuclear blood cells are lymphocytes, the main warriors in specific immune responses. The trillion or so lymphocytes are stationed strategically in the lymphatic tissue throughout the body. The agranular mononuclear lymphocytes with a high ratio of nuclear volume to cytoplasmic volume are **T lymphocytes,** referred to as **T cells,** and **B lymphocytes,** or **B cells.** One population of mononuclear cells has some granules as well as a relatively low nuclear to cytoplasmic ratio. These are called large granular lymphocytes (LGL). The LGLs include the *NK cell* mentioned earlier, which is important in killing virally infected cells and cancer cells.

T CELLS ARE RESPONSIBLE FOR CELLULAR IMMUNITY

Like macrophages and B cells, T cells originate from stem cells in the bone marrow (Fig. 23-4). On their way to the lymph tissues, the future T cells stop off in the thymus gland for processing. The T in T lymphocytes stands for thymus-derived; somehow the thymus gland influences the differentiation of T lymphocytes so that they become capable of immunological response.

Stem cells in bone marrow ⟶ T cells ⟶ processed in thymus ⟶ migrate to lymph tissues ⟶ cellular immunity

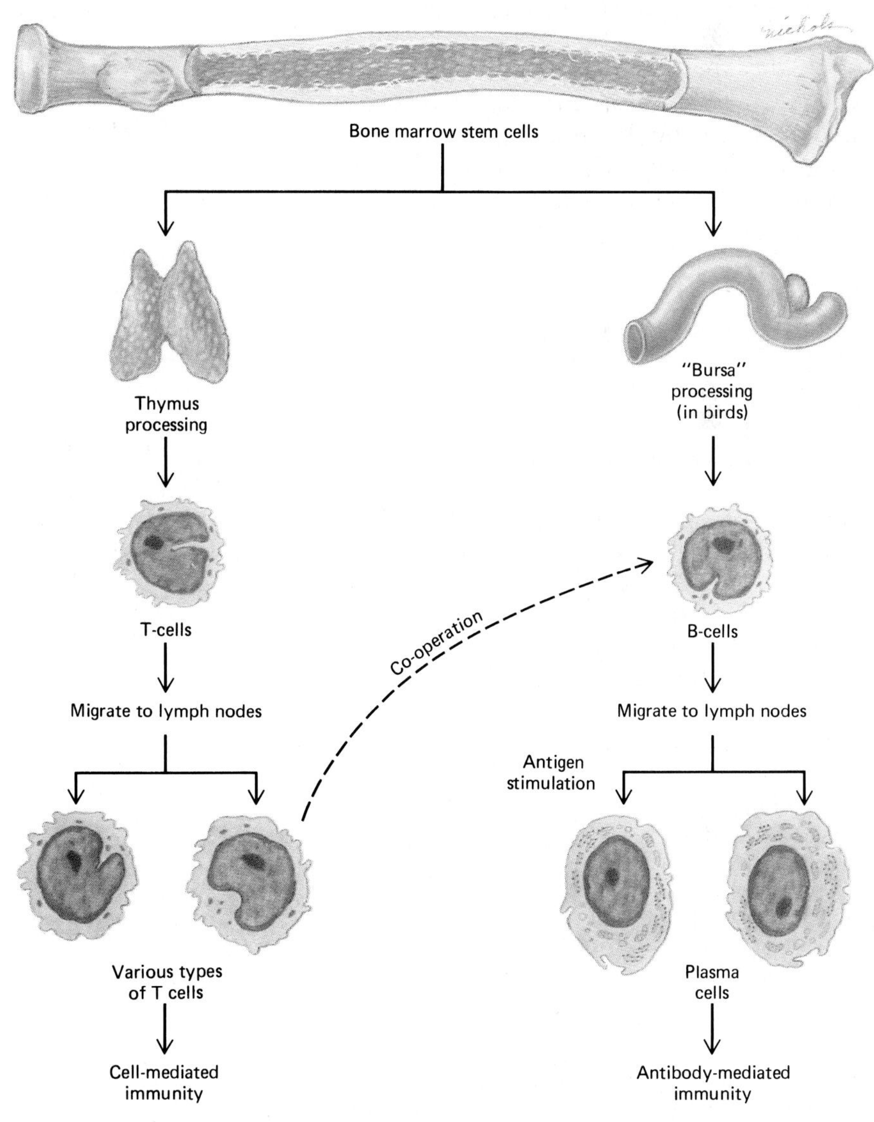

FIGURE 23-4

Origin and functions of T and B lymphocytes.

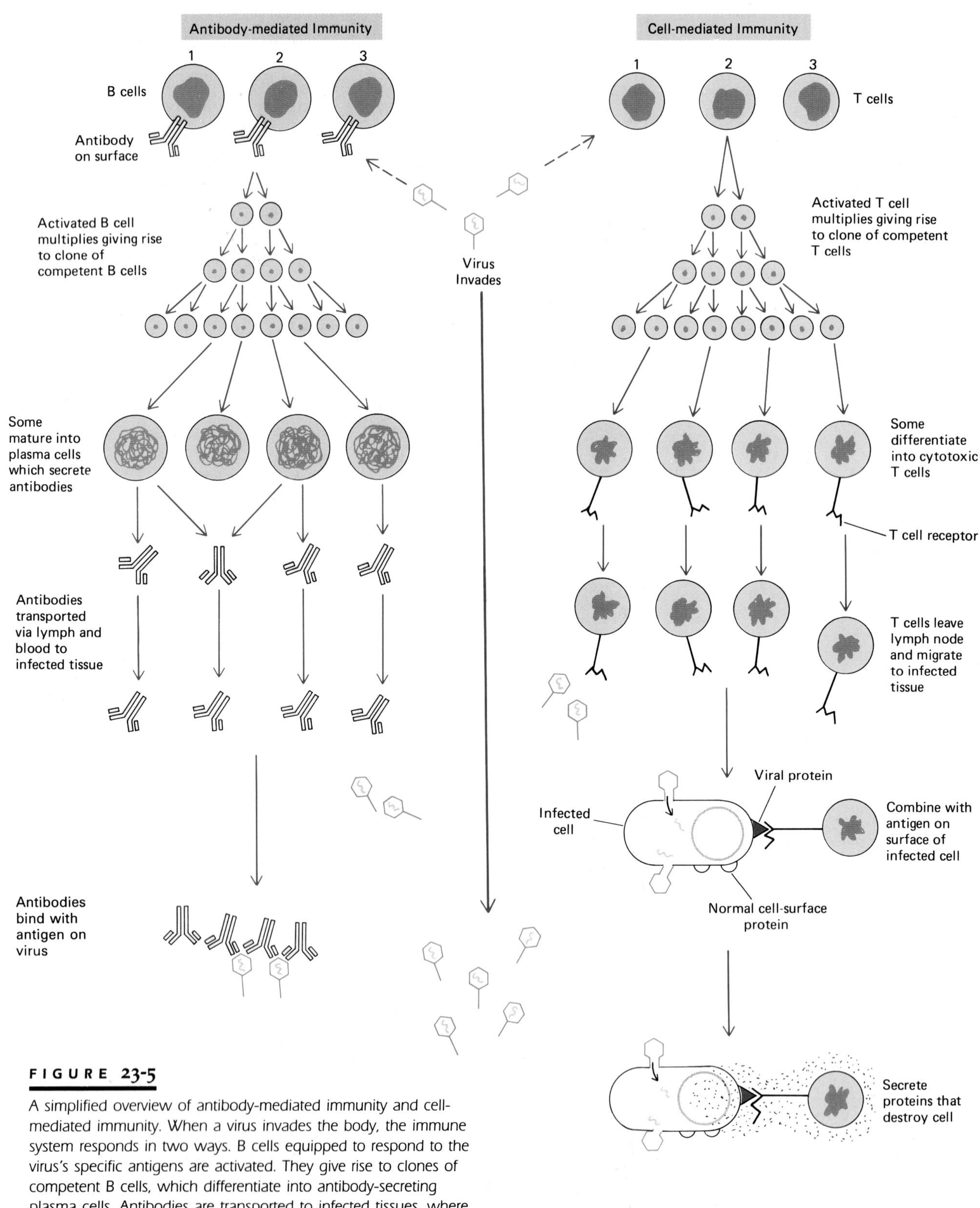

FIGURE 23-5

A simplified overview of antibody-mediated immunity and cell-mediated immunity. When a virus invades the body, the immune system responds in two ways. B cells equipped to respond to the virus's specific antigens are activated. They give rise to clones of competent B cells, which differentiate into antibody-secreting plasma cells. Antibodies are transported to infected tissues, where they bind with antigen on the virus. T cells competent to respond to the specific antigens are also activated and give rise to clones of T cells. Cytotoxic T cells leave the lymph nodes and migrate to infected tissues, where they combine with antigen on the surface of infected cells. The T cells secrete proteins that destroy the infected cells.

T lymphocytes are responsible for cellular immunity (Fig. 23-5). On their cell surfaces, T cells have antigen-binding molecules referred to as **T-cell receptors.** There are millions of different kinds of T cells, each with specific types of T-cell receptors. Each kind of T cell is capable of recognizing a specific foreign antigen. Three main types, or **subsets,** of T cells have been identified:

1. **Cytotoxic T cells,** sometimes called killer T cells, recognize cells with foreign antigens on their surfaces and destroy these cells.
2. **Helper T cells** assist other types of T cells, as well as B cells, in responding to antigens.
3. **Suppressor T cells** inhibit the activity of helper T cells and cytotoxic T cells.

B CELLS ARE RESPONSIBLE FOR ANTIBODY-MEDIATED IMMUNITY

In birds, B cells are processed in the bursa of Fabricius, a lymphatic organ. (The B in B cells refers to bursa-derived.) Other vertebrates do not have this kind of bursa, however, and an equivalent organ has not yet been identified. Nevertheless, mammals have a distinct, functional B lymphocyte system. It is thought that these B cells may be processed as they form in the fetal liver or bone marrow.

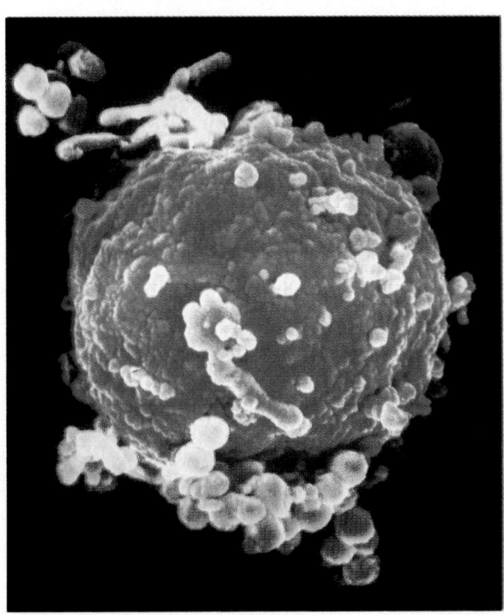

FIGURE 23-6

B cells are lymphocytes that are responsible for antibody-mediated immunity. In this scanning electron micrograph, a B cell (artificially colored red) is covered with bacteria (green). (Nilsson/Boehringer.)

As with T cells, millions of B cells are produced, each with a different antigen-binding specificity. When a B cell comes into contact with the specific type of antigen to which it is targeted, it divides rapidly to form a clone of identical cells (Figs. 23-5 and 23-6). These B cells develop into **plasma cells.** Plasma cells are the cells that produce antibodies and release them into the circulation. An adaptation for this function is their extensive, highly developed rough endoplasmic reticulum. (Recall that proteins are synthesized along the rough ER.)

Although T and B lymphocytes have different functions and life histories, they are similar in appearance when viewed with a light microscope. More sophisticated techniques such as fluorescence microscopy, however, have shown that the B and T cells can be differentiated by their unique cell-surface macromolecules. They also tend to locate in (or "home" to) separate regions of the spleen, lymph nodes, and other lymph tissues.

Clinical highlight

Certain diseases provide additional evidence for the existence of separate T and B lymphocyte systems. In children born without a thymus, a condition known as DiGeorge's syndrome, normal B cell functioning develops, but there are no functional T cells. Conversely, in the disease Bruton's agammaglobulinemia, the victim has normal T cell immunity but deficient B cell function. Patients with this disease have frequent bacterial infections, but are fairly resistant to viral and fungal invasion.

MACROPHAGES PLAY A CENTRAL ROLE IN IMMUNE RESPONSES

When a macrophage ingests a pathogen, it displays a few molecules of the antigen on its cell surface. This displayed antigen is necessary to stimulate antigen-sensitive white blood cells. Macrophages also secrete substances that promote and help regulate immune responses. When macrophages are stimulated by bacteria, they secrete interleukin 1, which helps activate B cells and helper T cells. Interleukin 1 also promotes a general response to injury; this substance causes fever, mobilizes neutrophils, and activates a variety of other mechanisms that defend the body against the invasion. Macrophages also secrete prostaglandins, which induce suppressor T cell activity and suppress immune response in other ways.

The thymus is an endocrine gland

The **thymus gland** (**thy**-mus) has at least two functions. First, in some unknown way this organ confers immunological competence upon T cells. Within the thymus these cells develop the ability to differentiate into cells that can distinguish self from nonself and respond to specific antigens. This "instruction" within the thymus is thought to take place just before birth and during the first few months of postnatal life. When the thymus is removed from an experimental animal before this processing takes place, the animal is not able to develop cellular immunity. If the thymus is removed after that time, cellular immunity is not seriously impaired.

The second function of the thymus is that of an endocrine gland. It secretes several hormones, including one known as **thymosin** (**thy**-mow-sin). Although not much is known about these hormones, thymosin is thought to affect T cells after they leave the thymus, stimulating them to complete their differentiation and to become immunologically active. Thymosin has been used clinically in patients who have poorly developed thymus glands. This hormone is also being tested as a modifier of biological response in patients with certain types of cancer; by stimulating cellular immunity in such patients, it may help to prevent the spread of the disease.

The major histocompatibility complex is distinct in each individual

The ability of the immune system to distinguish self from nonself depends largely on a group of protein markers (antigens) known as the **major histocompatibility complex (MHC).** These markers are present on the surface of every cell and are slightly different in each individual. The genes that code for these proteins are found linked together on one chromosome (chromosome 6 in humans).

In humans the MHC is called the **HLA (human leukocyte antigen) group.** HLA is determined by five different genes. Tissues from the same individual or from identical twins have the same HLA genes and thus identical HLA antigens.

On the basis of tissue distribution and structure, the MHC is divided into three groups of genes and the antigens for which these genes code. **Class I antigens** are found on all nucleated cells in the body, and are especially concentrated on the membranes of B cells, T cells, and macrophages. Class I antigens are important in distinguishing between self and nonself.

Class II antigens have a more limited distribution. These antigens are found on B cells, T cells, some macrophages, and, in small quantities, on some epithelial cells. Class II antigens regulate the interactions among T cells, B cells, and antigen-presenting cells. **Class III antigens** include components of a group of blood proteins known as complement (discussed in a later section).

Antibody-mediated immunity is chemical warfare

Antibody-mediated immunity, also called humoral immunity, is carried out by B cells. The antibody-mediated immune system (AMI) is interdependent with the cell-mediated immune system (CMI). Although the AMI is responsible for antibody production and the CMI responds primarily to foreign cells and viruses, there are important interactions and dual control between the two systems. The presence of antibody modulates the function of T cells and macrophages, and in turn, these cells are necessary for the AMI to produce certain types of antibodies. Furthermore, characteristics of the invading antigen and of the individual organism (e.g., age and genetic parameters) help determine the specifics of the response. In order to explain the basics of this sophisticated system, we will focus on the general actions, ignoring some of the secondary effects.

When bacteria enter the body, macrophages engulf some of them. The macrophage destroys the bacterial cell, but a few molecules of bacterial antigen are delivered to the surface of the macrophage and displayed. Thus, the macrophage is an *antigen-presenting cell* that displays bacterial antigens as well as its own surface proteins.

Antibodies on the surface of B cells serve as receptors. Only *competent* B cells—the variety of B cell with a matching receptor—can bind with a particular antigen presented by the macrophage. When a macrophage displaying antigen contacts a helper T cell, a complex interaction occurs. One result of this interaction is that the macrophage secretes **interleukins** (also referred to as monokines). Interleukin 1 (IL-1) activates helper T cells (and also acts on the hypothalamus, causing fever).

Activated helper T cells detect B cells that have bound to antigen on the macrophage, and bind to the same antigen. However, a T cell does not recognize an antigen that is presented alone; the antigen must be presented to the T cell as part of a complex with a molecule that the T cell recognizes as self. In humans this self-molecule is HLA. The helper T cell binds to both the antigen and the HLA attached to the macrophage. Then, the activated helper T cell secretes a group of interleukins that activate competent B cells. (These interleukins are also referred to as lymphokines because they are substances secreted by lymphocytes.)

Once activated, or sensitized, B cells increase in size. Then they divide by mitosis, each giving rise to a sizable clone of identical cells (Fig. 23-7). Some of these B cells mature into plasma cells that produce antibody. The antibody manufactured is of the same type as the cell's receptors. Unlike T cells, most plasma cells do not leave the lymph nodes. Only the antibodies they secrete pass out of the lymph tissues and make their way via the lymph and blood to the infected area. Thus, we can think of antibody-mediated immunity as chemical warfare in which the antibodies are the chemical weapons deployed throughout the body. (See Focus on AIDS.)

Pathogen invades body ⟶ competent B cell binds with antigen presented by macrophage ⟶ activated B cell ⟶ clone of competent B cells ⟶ plasma cells ⟶ antibody

Some activated B cells do not differentiate into plasma cells, but instead become **memory cells** that continue to produce small amounts of antibody long after an infection has been overcome. This antibody circulates as part of the gamma globulin fraction of the plasma and is an important component of the body's arsenal of chemical weapons. Should the same pathogen enter the body again, this circulating antibody is immediately present to destroy it. At the same time memory cells quickly divide to produce new clones of the appropriate plasma cells.

ANTIBODIES ARE PROTEINS

Antibodies are highly specific proteins called **immunoglobulins,** abbreviated **Ig,** that are produced in response to specific antigens. A main function of an antibody is to bind to an antigen. How does an antibody "recognize" a particular antigen? In a protein antigen there are sequences of amino acids that make up an **antigenic determinant.** These amino acids give part of the antigen molecule a specific configuration that can be recognized by an antibody or cell receptor.

However, the mechanism is even more complicated. Usually, an antigen has five to ten antigenic determinants on its surface. Some have 200 or even more. These antigenic determinants may differ from one another, so that several different kinds of antibodies can combine with a single complex antigen. **Multivalent antigens** have the same determinant repeated several times. An example of a multivalent antigen is a virus that has multiple copies of a single protein on its outer surface.

Some substances found in dust and certain drugs are too small to be antigenic; yet they do stimulate immune responses. These substances, called **haptens,** become antigenic by attaching to the surface of a protein.

An antibody molecule has two main functions. Its *binding domains* combine with the antigen. Its *effector domains* then activate processes that destroy the antigen with which it binds. For example, an effector domain may stimulate phagocytosis.

A typical immunoglobulin consists of four polypeptide chains: two identical long chains, called **heavy chains,** and two identical short chains, called **light chains** (Fig. 23-8). Each light chain is made up of approximately 214 amino acids, and each heavy chain of more than 400. The polypeptide chains are held together and their configurations are stabilized by disulfide (—S—S—) linkages and by noncovalent bonds.

Each chain has a constant region, a junctional region, and a variable region. In the *constant region,* or *C region,* the amino acid sequence is constant from one type of immunoglobulin to another. The C region may be thought of as the handle portion of a door key. The amino acid sequence of the *junctional region,* or *J region,* is somewhat variable. The *variable region,* or *V region,* has a highly variable amino acid sequence. The variable region of the immunoglobulin protrudes from the B cell, while the constant region anchors the molecule to the plasma membrane.

The V region is the part of the key that is unique for a specific antigen (the lock). At its variable regions the antibody assumes a specific three-dimensional shape that enables it to combine with a specific antigen. When they meet, antigen and antibody fit together somewhat like a lock and key and must fit in just the right way

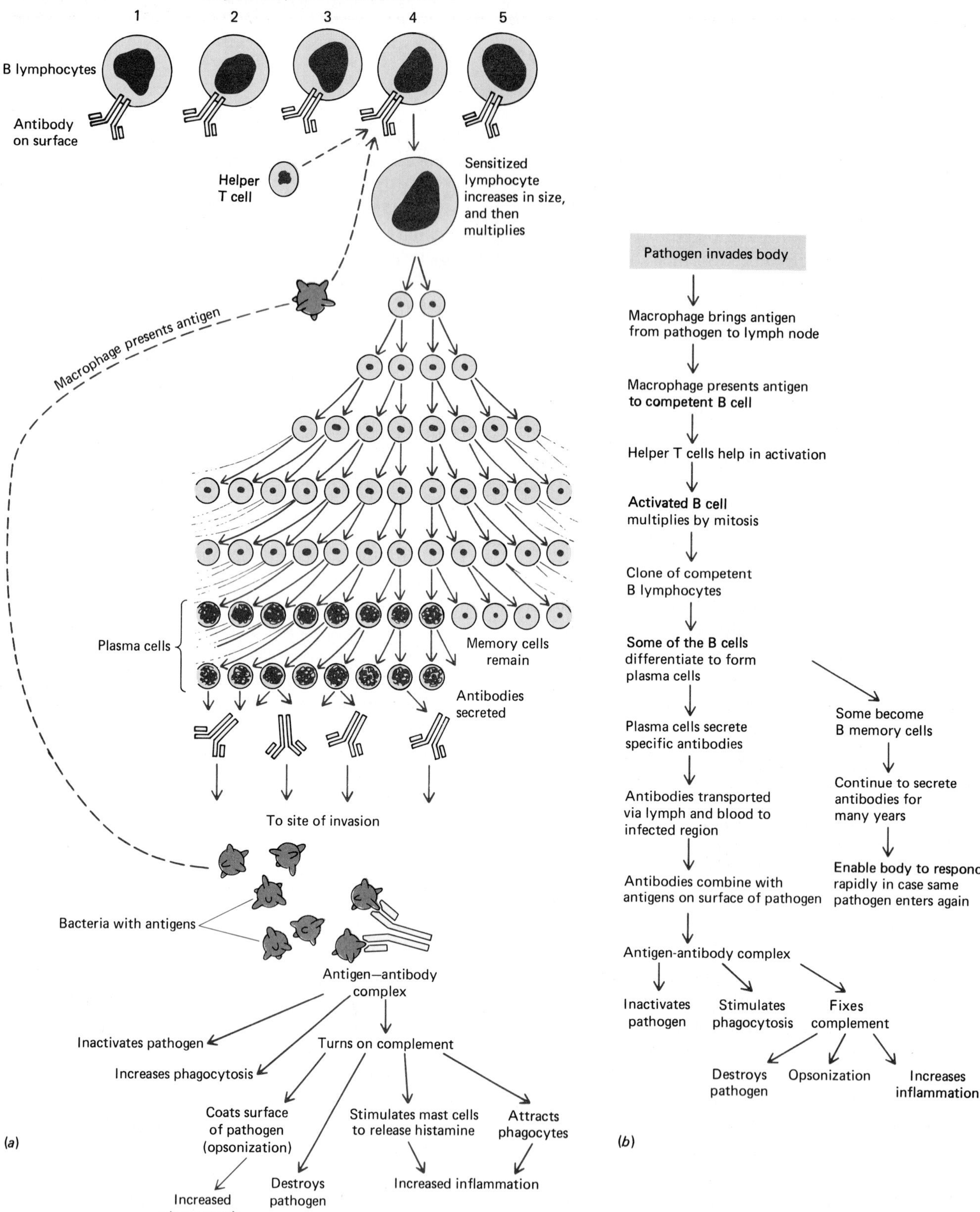
Only the competent B cell is sensitized
1
2
3
4
5
B lymphocytes
Antibody on surface
Helper T cell
Sensitized lymphocyte increases in size, and then multiplies
Macrophage presents antigen
Plasma cells
Memory cells remain
Antibodies secreted
To site of invasion
Bacteria with antigens
Antigen–antibody complex
Inactivates pathogen
Increases phagocytosis
Turns on complement
Coats surface of pathogen (opsonization)
Stimulates mast cells to release histamine
Attracts phagocytes
Increased phagocytosis
Destroys pathogen
Increased inflammation
(a)
Pathogen invades body
Macrophage brings antigen from pathogen to lymph node
Macrophage presents antigen to competent B cell
Helper T cells help in activation
Activated B cell multiplies by mitosis
Clone of competent B lymphocytes
Some of the B cells differentiate to form plasma cells
Plasma cells secrete specific antibodies
Antibodies transported via lymph and blood to infected region
Antibodies combine with antigens on surface of pathogen
Antigen-antibody complex
Inactivates pathogen
Stimulates phagocytosis
Fixes complement
Destroys pathogen
Opsonization
Increases inflammation
Some become B memory cells
Continue to secrete antibodies for many years
Enable body to respond rapidly in case same pathogen enters again
(b)

FIGURE 23-7

Antibody-mediated immunity. When a macrophage presents an antigen to a competent B cell, and a helper T cell releases appropriate interleukins, the B cell becomes sensitized. Once activated in this way, the competent B lymphocyte multiplies, producing a large clone of cells. Many of these differentiate and become plasma cells, which secrete antibodies. The plasma cells remain in the lymph tissues, but the antibodies are transported to the site of infection by the blood or lymph. Antigen-antibody complexes form, directly inactivating some pathogens and also turning on the complement system. Some of the B lymphocytes become memory cells that persist and continue to secrete small amounts of antibody for years after the infection is over.

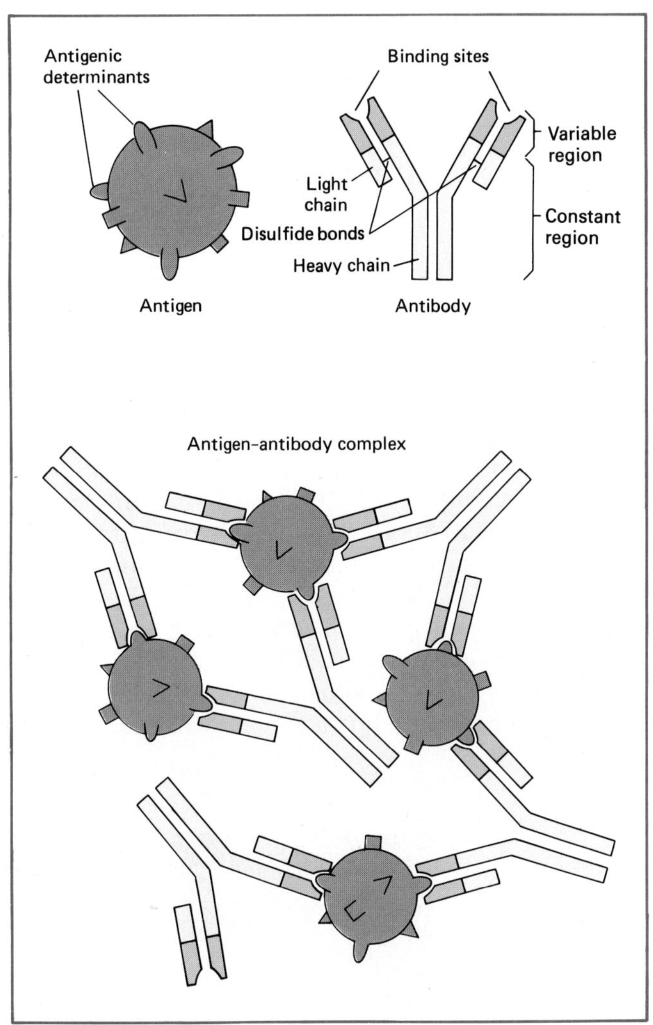

FIGURE 23-8

Antigen, antibody, and antigen-antibody complex. The antibody molecule is composed of two light chains and two heavy chains, joined together by disulfide bonds. The constant (C) and variable (V) regions of the chains are indicated.

for the antibody to be effective (Fig. 23-9). However, the fit is not as precise as with an enzyme and its substrate. A given antigen can bind with different strengths, or **affinities,** to different antibodies. In the course of an immune response, stronger (higher-affinity) antibodies are generated.

A typical antibody is a Y-shaped molecule that contains two binding sites (Fig. 23-8). Thus, the antibody can combine with two antigen molecules. This permits formation of **antigen-antibody complexes.**

THERE ARE FIVE CLASSES OF ANTIBODIES

Immunoglobulins (antibodies) are grouped in five classes according to their structure. At the constant end, the heavy chains of an antibody have amino acid sequences characteristic of the particular antibody class. Using the abbreviation Ig for immunoglobulin, the classes are designated IgG, IgM, IgA, IgD, and IgE. The classes of antibodies have different functions determined by their C regions.

In humans about 75% of the antibodies in the blood belong to the **IgG** group; these are part of the gamma globulin fraction of the plasma but are also found in other body fluids. IgG contributes to immunity against many blood-borne pathogens, including bacteria, viruses, and some fungi.

IgG, along with the **IgM** antibodies, stimulates macrophages and activates the complement system (discussed in the following section). IgM is highly effective against microorganisms such as viruses that have multivalent antigens. IgM also functions as the antibody characterizing blood type.

IgA is the principal immunoglobulin found in body secretions, such as mucous secretions of the nose, respiratory passageways, digestive tract, and tears, saliva, and vaginal secretions. IgA is thought to be important in protecting the body from infections by inhaled or ingested pathogens.

The function of the **IgD** type of immunoglobulin is not known. **IgE,** the mediator of allergic responses, is discussed in a later section.

THE BINDING OF ANTIGEN AND ANTIBODY ACTIVATES SEVERAL DEFENSE MECHANISMS

Antibodies identify a pathogen as foreign by combining with an antigen on its surface. Often several antibodies combine with several such antigens, creating a mass of clumped antigen-antibody complex (Fig. 23-8). The combination of antigen and antibody activates several defense mechanisms:

1. The antigen-antibody complex may inactivate the pathogen or its toxin. For example, when an antibody attaches to the surface of a virus, the virus may lose its ability to attach to a host cell.

2. The antigen-antibody complex stimulates phagocytosis of the pathogen by macrophages and neutrophils.

3. Antibodies of the IgG and IgM groups work mainly through the **complement system.** This system consists of about 11 proteins present in plasma and other body fluids. Normally, complement proteins are inactive, but an antigen-antibody complex stimulates a series of reactions that activates the system. The antibody is said to "fix" complement. Proteins of the complement system then work to destroy pathogens. Some complement proteins digest portions of the pathogen. Others coat the pathogens, a process called **opsonization.** This seems to make the pathogens "tastier" so that the macrophages and neutrophils rush to phagocytize them. Complement proteins also increase the extent of inflammation.

Complement proteins are not specific. They act against any antigen, provided they are activated. Antibodies identify the pathogen very specifically; then complement proteins *complement* that action by destroying the pathogens.

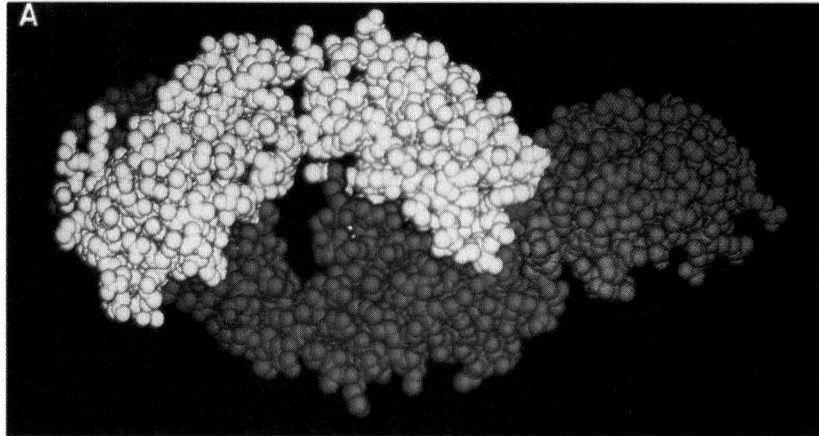

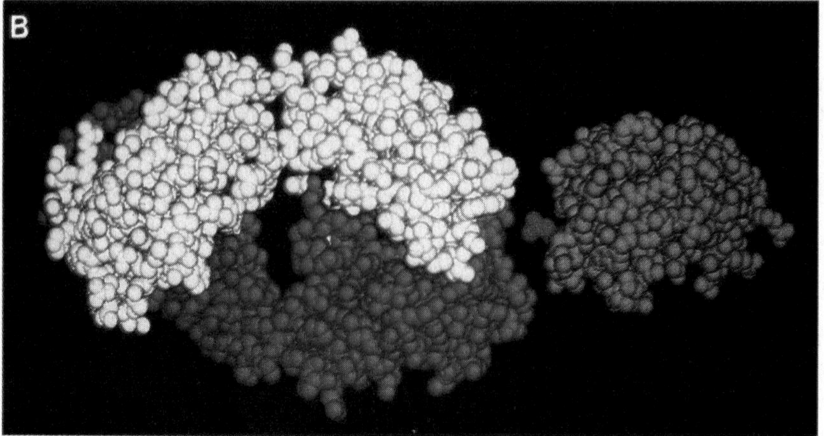

FIGURE 23-9

An antigen-antibody complex. The antigen lysozyme is shown in green. The heavy chain of the antibody is shown in blue, the light chain in yellow. (*a*) The antigenic determinant, shown in red, fits into a groove in the antibody molecule. (*b*) The antigen-antibody complex has been pulled apart. Note how they fit each other.

The complement system can be activated in the absence of antigen-antibody complex by way of the **properdin pathway.** This pathway depends on a protein, factor I, that circulates in the blood. Factor I recognizes repetitive sugar structures such as polyglucose that occur in bacteria and viruses but not in mammals. Factor I interacts with the surface of a virus or bacterium, and this interaction activates complement proteins. Another circulating protein, **properdin,** stabilizes the factor I complex that activates the complement system.

THE IMMUNE SYSTEM RECOGNIZES MILLIONS OF ANTIGENS

Remarkably, the immune system is able to recognize every possible antigen, even those that have never before been encountered during the evolution of the species. One of the most puzzling problems in immunology has been accounting for this tremendous diversity of antibodies. The immune system has the potential to produce millions of different antibodies, each programmed to respond to a different antigenic determinant. Two principal theories explaining this diversity have been debated.

The *germ line theory* proposed that we are born with a different gene for the production of every possible antibody variable region. One criticism of this theory has been that we have only about a million genes, and only a small number of these could be devoted to coding antibodies. Thus, we do not have sufficient numbers of genes to account for the millions of different antibodies.

The *somatic mutation theory* held that we inherit only a few types of genes for making antibody variable regions and that mutations occur within the DNA of the lymphocytes, producing thousands of lymphocytes with slightly different variable regions. Each somatically generated V (variable) region gene could combine with a C (constant) region gene to form the immunoglobulin molecule. Thus, each variety of lymphocyte would be programmed to produce certain specific antibodies. These mutations might occur in the thymus or bursa equivalent.

Recent research indicates that the correct explanation is probably a combination of these theories. The ability to make many different antibodies is inherited, but this diversity is probably increased by mutation as well as by recombination of genes. However, how can we hypothesize somatic development of diversity at one end of the molecule (V region) and maintenance of constant amino acid chains at the other (C region)? In 1965 Dreyer and Bennett proposed that two genes, not one, code for a single immunoglobulin chain.

More recent recombinant DNA techniques clearly describe the genes for immunoglobulin production. Several V region genes code for any V region. These genes have spaces between them as well as additional genes for joining V regions to C regions. These spacers and joining sequences increase the chance for recombination of genes. This process occurs in the production of both light and heavy chains. Then, the two chains associate to form the completed antibody.

Thus, immunoglobulin diversity results from multiple germ-line V genes, recombinational events, and to a lesser extent somatic mutations. The result to the individual is the existence of thousands of V regions that can bind to most foreign matter.

Cell-mediated immunity provides the body's infantry

The T cells and monocyte/macrophage system are responsible for cell-mediated immunity. These cellular warriors make up the body's infantry. They are especially effective in attacking viruses, fungi, and the types of bacteria that live within host cells. How do the T cells know which cells to attack? Once a pathogen invades a body cell, the host cell's macromolecules may be altered. The immune system then regards that cell as foreign, and T cells destroy it. Cytotoxic T cells also destroy cancer cells, and, unfortunately, the cells of transplanted organs.

As in antibody-mediated immunity, activated helper T cells are necessary for a response. Recall that T cells have receptors on their surfaces capable of reacting with antigens on the surfaces of invading cells or altered host cells. As with B cells, only the variety of lymphocyte able to react to the specific antigen presented—that is, the competent lymphocyte—becomes sensitized. However, as discussed earlier, a T cell cannot recognize an antigen if it is presented alone. The antigen must be presented to the T cell as part of a complex with HLA that the T cell recognizes as "self."

(text continued on p. 809)

FOCUS ON . . . AIDS

First recognized in 1981, **acquired immune deficiency syndrome (AIDS)** is a deadly disease that is spreading through the population at an alarming rate. More than 70,000 cases of AIDS have been reported in the United States, and the U.S. Public Health Service estimates that about 365,000 individuals will have had AIDS by 1992. Worldwide, at least 5 million people were infected by the AIDS virus by 1989; and a million new cases of AIDS are expected within the next five years.

AIDS results from infection with a retrovirus identified as **human immunodeficiency virus (HIV)**. (A retrovirus is a virus composed of RNA that uses its RNA as a template to make DNA with the help of an enzyme called reverse transcriptase.) The virus rapidly infects helper T cells, resulting in irreversible defects in immunity. Recall that helper T cells stimulate the proliferation of B and T cells, stimulate macrophages, and perform other functions that enhance the immune response. When the helper T cell population is depressed, the ability to resist infection is severely impaired. AIDS victims die within several months to about 5 years from rare forms of cancer, pneumonia, and other opportunistic infections that pose little threat to individuals with fully functioning immune systems.

About 90% of AIDS patients develop a neuropsychological disorder known as AIDS dementia complex, which results from direct infection of the central nervous system by the retrovirus. AIDS dementia complex is characterized by progressive cognitive, motor, and behavioral dysfunction that typically ends in coma and death.

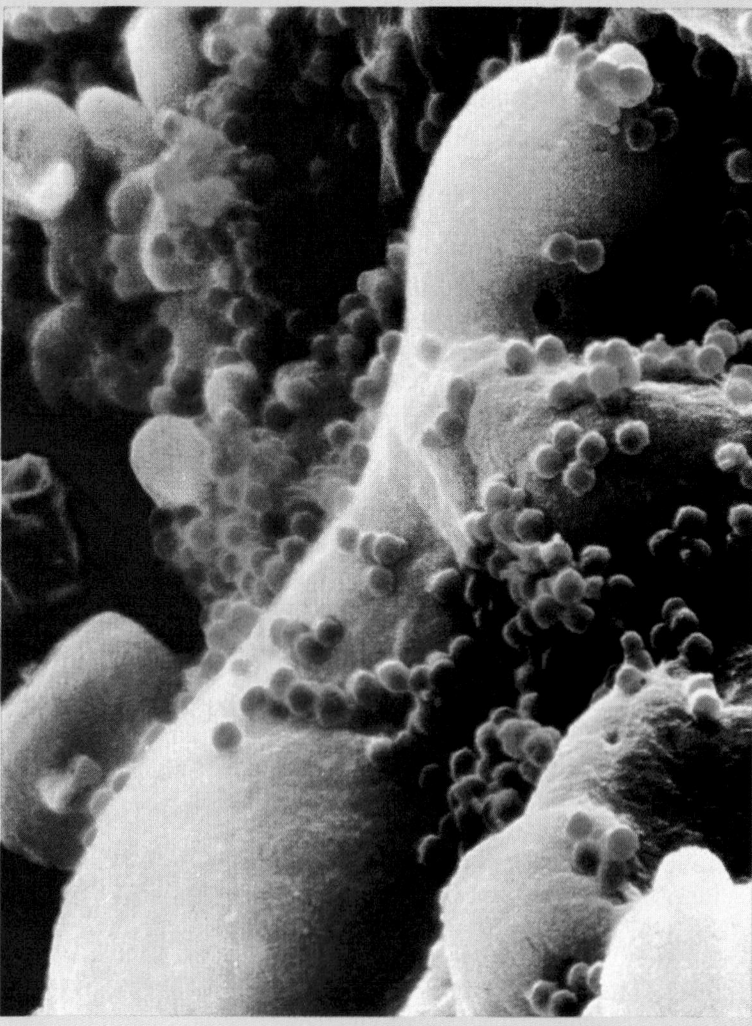

HIV virus particles (blue) that cause AIDS attack a helper T cell. HIV seriously impairs the immune system by rapidly destroying helper T cells.

Current evidence indicates that AIDS is transmitted mainly by semen during sexual intercourse with an infected person or by direct exposure to infected blood or blood products. Those most at risk are homosexual and bisexual men (72% of cases) and intravenous drug users (20%). Individuals such as hemophiliacs who require frequent blood transfusions are also at risk, as are infants born to mothers with AIDS and women who have sexual relations with bisexual men.

Effective blood-screening procedures have been developed to safeguard blood bank supplies, so that risk of infection from blood transfusion has been greatly reduced. Use of condoms during sexual intercourse provides some protection against the virus. AIDS is not spread by casual contact. People do not contract the disease by hugging, kissing, sharing a drink, or using the same bathroom facilities. Close friends and family members who live with AIDS patients are not more likely to get the disease.

It is estimated that more than 2 million persons in the United States have antibody to HIV (i.e., they are HIV positive) but have no symptoms of the disease. Possibly, not everyone exposed to HIV actually contracts the disease. AIDS may be an opportunistic infection that causes disease in individuals with inadequate immune function. Susceptibility to HIV may depend on a combination of genetic, environmental, and psychosocial factors. The latter include personality variables and coping styles that influence susceptibility to environmental stressors.

Many persons exposed to HIV develop the **AIDS related complex (ARC);** its symptoms include night sweats, fever, swollen lymph glands, and weight loss. Patients with ARC may eventually develop AIDS, but the extent of that risk is not yet known.

Research laboratories throughout the world are searching for drugs that will successfully combat the AIDS virus. Because this virus often infects

(box continued on p. 808)

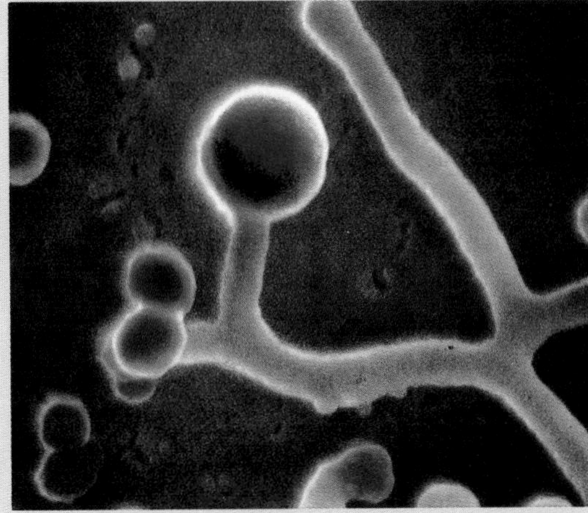

HIV virus particles budding from the ends of branched microvilli. Magnification about ×400,000.

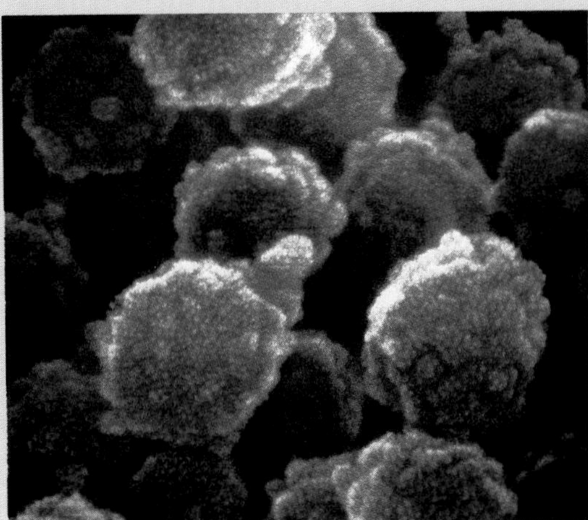

HIV virus particles at extremely high magnification (about ×1,200,000). The surfaces are grainy and the outlines slightly blurred because the preparation was coated with coarse-grained heavy-metal salt (palladium).

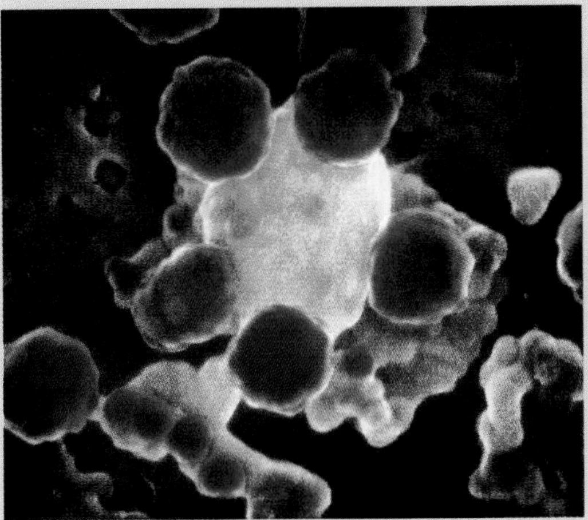

An even higher magnification of virus particles budding from a "bleb" (a cytoplasmic extension broader than a microvillus). Note the pentagonal symmetry often evident in other biological branching and flowering structures.

FOCUS ON . . . AIDS (*continued*)

the central nervous system, an effective drug must cross the blood-brain barrier. The drug AZT (azidothymidine), which has been approved by the FDA, blocks HIV replication. AZT blocks the action of reverse transcriptase, the enzyme needed by the retrovirus for incorporation into the host cell's DNA. Recent evidence suggests that AZT prolongs the onset of AIDS symptoms. Unfortunately, the virus has developed strains that are resistant to AZT. As other drugs effective against HIV are developed and approved, combination treatment may help slow the development of drug-resistant strains of the virus.

Vaccination is the most effective, simplest way of preventing a disease, and developing a vaccine against HIV has been a most pressing challenge for virologists. Unfortunately, research directed at developing a vaccine against HIV has not yet been successful because the retrovirus mutates rapidly, giving rise to many viral strains. Further slowing progress is the absence of an animal model for AIDS and the ethical and practical difficulties associated with finding human volunteers in whom to test the vaccine. For these reasons Surgeon General C. Everett Koop has warned the public that a vaccine against HIV is not likely to be available before the twenty-first century.

While immunologists work to develop a successful vaccine and effective drugs to treat patients with AIDS, massive educational programs are being developed that aim at slowing the spread of AIDS. Spreading the word that having multiple sexual partners increases the risk for AIDS and teaching sexually active individuals the importance of "safe" sex may help to slow the epidemic. Some have suggested that public health facilities offer free condoms to those who are sexually active and free sterile hypodermic needles to those addicted to drugs. The cost of these measures would be far less than the cost of medical care for increasing numbers of AIDS patients and the toll in human suffering.

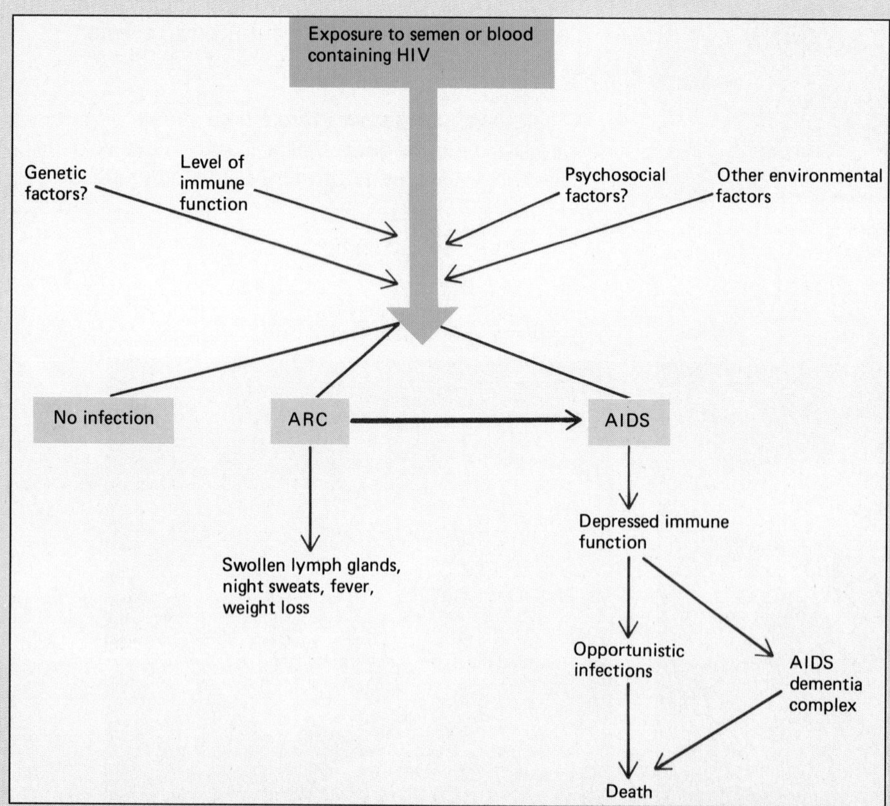

Exposure to semen or blood that contains HIV can lead to AIDS related complex (ARC) or to AIDS. Many factors apparently determine whether a person exposed to AIDS virus will contract the disease. Some individuals do not suffer infection. However, the risk increases with multiple exposures.

Once stimulated, T cells increase in size, proliferate, and give rise to a sizable clone of cytotoxic T cells and memory cells (Fig. 23-10). Cytotoxic T cells are the main soldiers in the cellular infantry; they leave the lymph nodes and make their way to the infected area. These killer cells can destroy a target cell within seconds after contact. Then, the T cell disengages itself from its victim cell and seeks out a new target cell.

Pathogen invades body ⟶ competent T cell activated by specific antigen ⟶ clone of competent T cells ⟶ cytotoxic T cells ⟶ migrate to area of infection ⟶ proteins that destroy pathogens

After a cytotoxic T cell combines with antigen on the surface of the target cell, it secretes a powerful group of proteins known as *perforins*. The T cell releases granules containing these cytotoxic proteins at the site of cell contact, producing le-

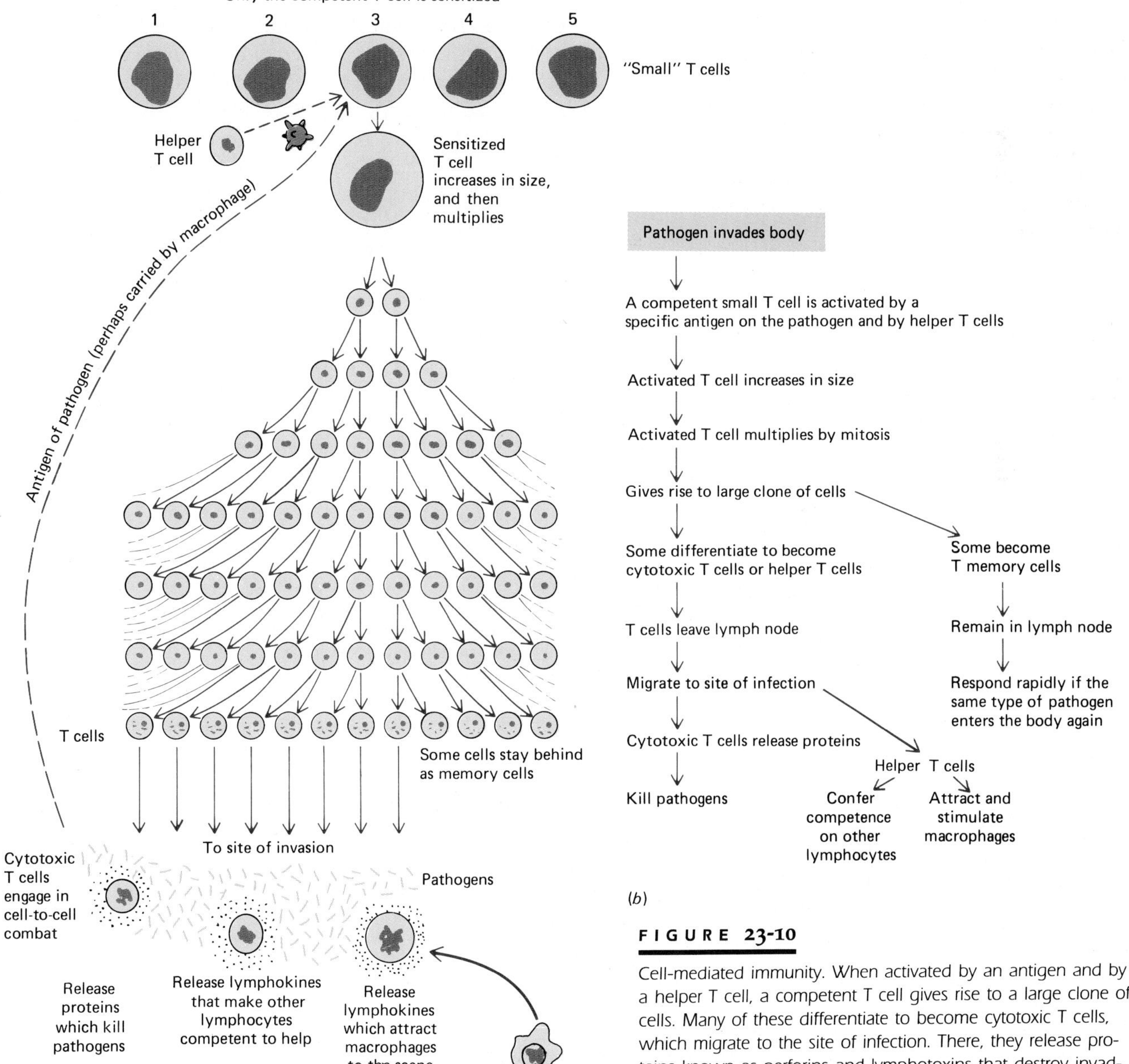

FIGURE 23-10

Cell-mediated immunity. When activated by an antigen and by a helper T cell, a competent T cell gives rise to a large clone of cells. Many of these differentiate to become cytotoxic T cells, which migrate to the site of infection. There, they release proteins known as perforins and lymphotoxins that destroy invading pathogens.

sions in the target cell and rapid lysis. Under some conditions, cytotoxic T cells release soluble proteins called *lymphotoxins,* which are especially toxic for cancer cells.

T cells and macrophages at the site of infection secrete interleukins, interferons, and a variety of other substances that help regulate immune function. Some interleukins confer competence upon other lymphocytes in the area, increasing the ranks of cytotoxic T cells. Other interleukins enhance the inflammatory reaction, attracting great numbers of macrophages to the site of infection. Interleukins and gamma interferon stimulate macrophages, making them more active and effective at destroying pathogens.

Suppressor T cells are stimulated by antigen. These cells help regulate both T cells and B cells. Suppressor T cells multiply more slowly than cytotoxic T cells, so more than a week generally elapses before they suppress an immune response.

Primary responses are slower than secondary responses

The first exposure to an antigen stimulates a **primary response.** Injection of an antigen into an immunocompetent animal causes specific antibodies to appear in the blood plasma in 3 to 14 days. After injection of the antigen there is a brief latent period, during which the antigen is recognized and appropriate lymphocytes begin to form clones. Then there is a logarithmic phase, during which the antibody concentration rises logarithmically for several days until it reaches a peak (Fig. 23-11). IgM is the principal antibody synthesized. Finally, there is a decline phase, during which the antibody concentration decreases to a very low level.

A second injection of the same antigen, even years later, evokes a **secondary response** (Fig. 23-11). Because memory cells bearing a living record of the encounter with the antigen persist throughout an individual's life, the secondary response is generally much more rapid than the primary response, with a shorter latent period. The amount of antigen necessary to evoke a secondary response is much less than that needed for a primary response. More antibodies are produced than in a primary response, and the decline phase is slower. In a secondary response the predominant antibody is IgG. The affinity, or strength of fit, of the antibody also increases following secondary exposure.

The body's ability to launch a rapid, effective response during a second encounter with an antigen explains why we do not usually suffer from the same disease several times. Most persons get measles or chicken pox only once. When exposed a second time, the immune system destroys the pathogens before they have time to establish

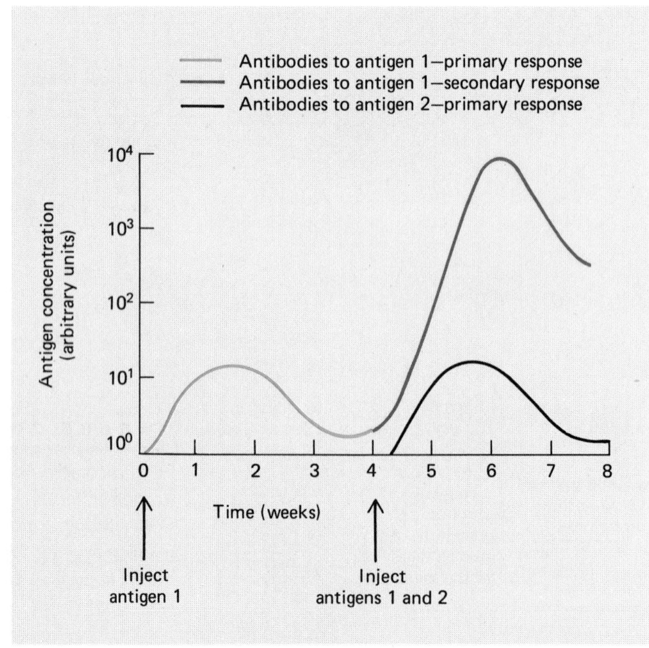

FIGURE 23-11

Primary and secondary responses of antibody formation to successive doses of antigens. Antigen 1 was injected at day 0, and the immune response was assessed by measuring antibody levels to the antigen. At week 4, the primary response had subsided. Antigen 1 was injected again along with a new protein, antigen 2. Note that the secondary response to antigen 1 was greater and more rapid than the primary response. A primary response was made to the newly encountered antigen 2.

themselves and cause symptoms of the disease. Booster shots of vaccine are given in order to elicit a secondary response, reinforcing the immunological memory of the disease-producing antigens.

You may wonder, then, how a person can get flu or a cold more than once. Unfortunately, there are many varieties of these diseases, each caused by a virus with slightly different antigens. For example, more than 100 different viruses cause the common cold, and new varieties of "cold" and flu virus evolve continuously by mutation (a survival mechanism for them), which may result in changes in their surface antigens. Even a slight change may prevent recognition by memory cells. Because the immune system is so specific, each different antigen is treated by the body as a new immunological challenge.

Active immunity develops after exposure to antigens

We have been considering **active immunity**, immunity developed following exposure to antigens. After you have had measles as a young child, for example, you develop immunity that protects you from contracting measles again. Active immunity can be *naturally* or *artificially* induced (Table 23-2). If someone with measles sneezes near you and you contract the disease, you naturally develop active immunity. Active immunity can also be artificially induced by **immunization**, that is, by injection of a vaccine. In this case, the body launches an immune response against the antigens contained in the measles vaccine and develops memory cells, so that future encounters with the same pathogen will be dealt with swiftly.

Effective vaccines can be prepared in a number of ways. A *virus may be attenuated* (weakened) by successive passage through cells of nonhuman hosts. In the process, mutations occur that adapt the pathogen to the nonhuman host, so that it can no longer cause disease in humans. This is how polio vaccine, smallpox vaccine, and measles vaccine are produced. Whooping cough and typhoid fever vaccines are made from *killed pathogens* that still have the necessary antigens to stimulate an immune response. Tetanus and botulism vaccines are made from toxins secreted by the respective pathogens. The *toxin is altered* so that it can no longer destroy tissues, but its antigens are still intact. When any of these vaccines is introduced into the body, the immune system actively develops clones, produces antibodies, and develops memory cells.

Passive immunity is borrowed immunity

In **passive immunity**, an individual is given antibodies actively produced by another organism. The serum or gamma globulin containing these antibodies can be obtained from humans or animals. Animal serum is less desirable because non-

TABLE 23-2

Active and passive immunity

Type of immunity	When developed	Development of memory cells	Duration of immunity
Active			
Naturally induced	Pathogens enter the body through natural encounter (e.g., person with measles sneezes on you)	Yes	Many years
Artificially induced	After immunization	Yes	Many years
Passive			
Naturally induced	After transfer of antibodies from mother to developing baby	No	Few months
Artificially induced	After injection with gamma globulin	No	Few months

human proteins can themselves act as antigens, stimulating an immune response that may result in a clinical illness termed *serum sickness*.

Passive immunity is borrowed immunity, and its effects are not lasting. It is used to boost the body's defense temporarily against a particular disease. For example, during the Vietnam War, in areas where hepatitis was widespread, soldiers were injected with gamma globulin containing antibodies to the hepatitis pathogen. Such injections of gamma globulin offer protection for only a few months. Because the body has not actively launched an immune response, it has no memory cells and cannot produce antibodies to the pathogen. Once the injected antibodies wear out, the immunity disappears.

Pregnant women confer natural passive immunity upon their developing babies by manufacturing antibodies for them. These maternal antibodies, of the IgG class, pass through the placenta (the organ of exchange between mother and developing child) and provide the fetus and newborn infant with a defense system until its own immune system matures. Babies who are breast-fed continue to receive immunoglobulins, particularly IgA, in their milk. These immunoglobulins provide considerable immunity to the pathogens responsible for gastrointestinal infection, and perhaps to other pathogens as well.

The body defends itself against cancer

Some immunologists think that a few normal cells are transformed into cancer cells every day in each of us in response to viruses, hormones, radiation, or carcinogens in the environment. Because they are abnormal cells, some of their surface proteins are different from those of normal body cells. Such proteins act as antigens, stimulating an immune response. According to the **theory of immune surveillance**, the body's immune system destroys these abnormal cells whenever they arise. Only when these mechanisms fail do the abnormal cells divide rapidly, resulting in cancer.

Every component of the immune system helps defend against cancer cells. Tumor cells exhibit abnormal surface antigens that induce both cellular and antibody-mediated responses. T cells produce interleukins, which attract macrophages and NK cells and activate them. The T cells also produce interferons, which have an antitumor effect. The macrophages themselves produce factors, including TNF (tumor necrosis factor), that inhibit tumor growth.

Cytotoxic T cells, macrophages, and natural killer cells attack cancer cells (Fig. 23-12). Natural killer cells are capable of killing tumor cells or virally infected cells upon first exposure to the foreign antigen. Patients with advanced cancer are thought to have lower natural killer cell activity than normal persons.

What prevents killer T cells, macrophages, and natural killer cells from effectively destroying cancer cells in some persons? The immune system cells may fail to recognize the cancer cells as foreign, or they may recognize them but be unable to destroy them. Sometimes the presence of cancer cells stimulates B cells to produce IgG antibodies that combine with antigens on the surfaces of the cancer cells. These **blocking antibodies** may block the T cells so that they are unable to adhere to the surface of the cancer cells and destroy them. For some unknown reason, the blocking antibodies are not able to activate the complement system that would destroy the cancer cells. Interestingly, the presence of antibodies in this case is harmful.

An exciting approach in cancer research involves the production of **monoclonal antibodies**. In this procedure, mice are injected with antigens from human cancer cells. After the mice have produced antibodies to the cancer cells, their spleens are removed and cells containing the antibodies are extracted from this tissue. These cells are fused with cancer cells from other mice. Because of the apparently unlimited ability of cancer cells to divide, these fused hybrid cells will continue to divide indefinitely. Researchers select hybrid cells that are manufacturing the specific antibodies needed, and then clone them in a separate cell culture. Cells of this clone produce large amounts of the specific antibodies needed—hence the name monoclonal antibodies.

Monoclonal antibodies can be injected into the very same cancer patients whose cancer cells were used to stimulate their production. Such antibodies are highly specific for destroying the cancer cells. (Monoclonal antibodies specific for a single antigenic determinant can now be produced.) In trial studies such antibodies are being tagged with toxic drugs that are then delivered specifically to the cancer cells.

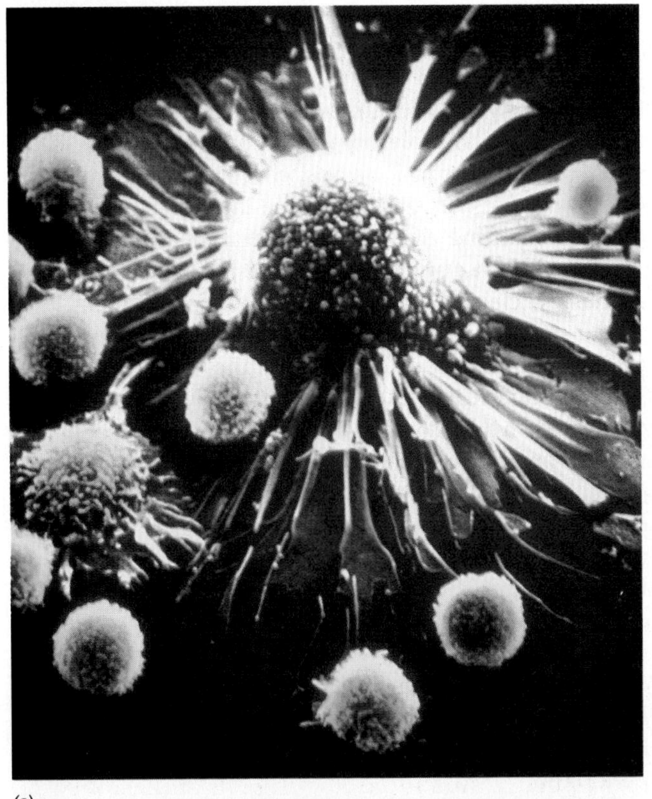

(a)

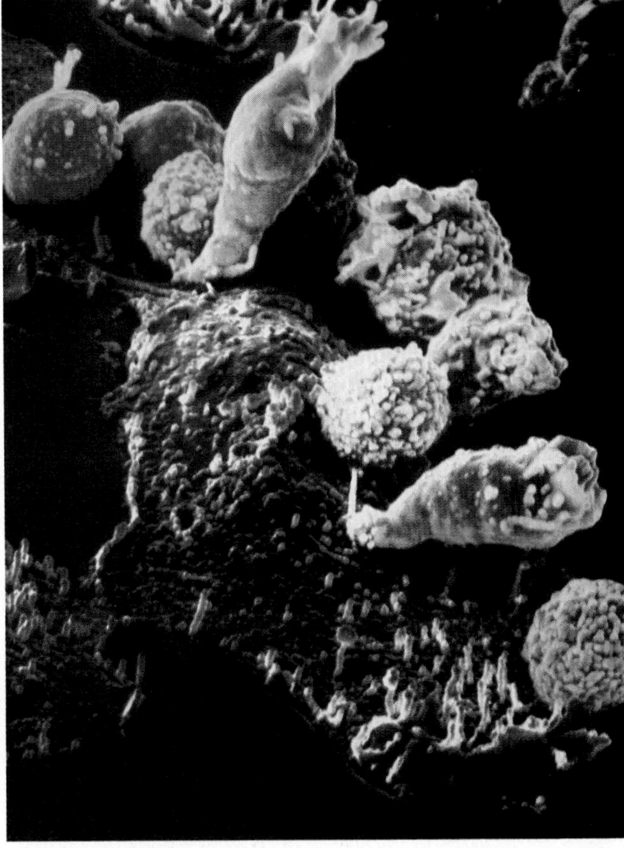

(b)

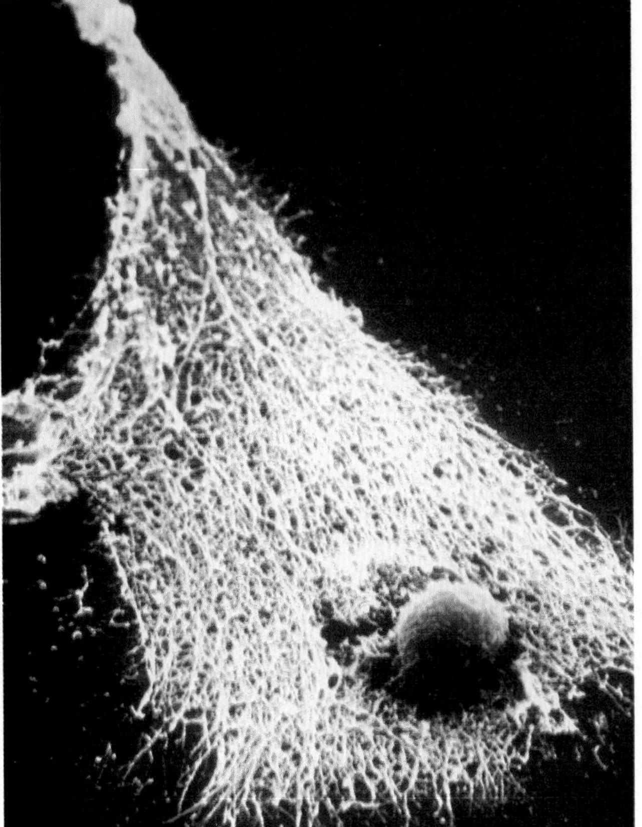

(c)

FIGURE 23-12

Cytotoxic T cells defend the body against cancer cells. (*a*) An army of cytotoxic T cells surround a large cancer cell. The T cells recognize the cancer cell as nonself because it displays altered antigens on its surface. (Nilsson/Boehringer.) (*b*) Some of the cytotoxic T cells elongate as they chemically attack the cancer cell, breaking down its plasma membrane. (*c*) The cancer cell has been destroyed; only a collapsed fibrous cytoskeleton remains.

The body rejects transplanted tissue

Skin can be successfully transplanted from one part of the body to another. However, when skin is taken from one individual and grafted onto the body of another, the skin graft is rejected and it sloughs off. Why?

Recall that tissues from the same individual or from identical twins have identical HLA alleles and thus the same HLA antigens. Because its HLA antigens are the same, the tissue is not rejected. Such tissues are *compatible*. Tissue transplanted from one location to another in the same individual is called an **autograft**.

Because there are several possible varieties (multiple alleles) of each of the HLA genes, it is difficult to find identical matches among strangers. If a tissue or organ is taken from a donor and transplanted to the body of an unrelated host, several of the HLA antigens are likely to be different. Such a graft made between members of the same species but of different genetic makeup is called a **homograft**. The host's immune system regards the graft as foreign and launches an effective immune response called **graft rejection**. T lymphocytes attack the transplanted tissue and can destroy it within a few days (Fig. 23–13).

Before transplants are performed, tissues from the patient and from potential donors must be typed and matched as well as possible. *Cell typing* is somewhat similar to blood typing but is more complex. The first obstacle is obtaining the typing sera. For ABO blood typing the sera are readily attainable because type A individuals naturally have anti-B antibodies, type B individuals have anti-A antibodies, and type O individuals have anti-A and anti-B antibodies.

In contrast, in order to obtain antibodies directed to antigens of the MHC, an individual must be actively immunized to the foreign proteins. Since some of these antigens are found on all nucleated cells, multiparous females (women who have experienced multiple births) inadvertently become immunized to the histocompatibility antigens of their offspring. Patients undergoing multiple blood transfusions also produce antibodies to the MHC. The antibodies from these serum sources are purified and the specific antibodies generated are used to type tissue. Since tissue typing has worldwide importance in the distribution of transplantable organs, internationally sponsored organizations and conferences help immunologists "speak the same language" in terms of naming a given antiserum or antigen.

Recall that antigens of the MHC are described as class I, class II, or class III. Class I antigens, found on all nucleated cells, serve as histocompatibility antigens or transplantation antigens. They are identified by the serological means just described. MHC class II antigens are found mainly on B cells, macrophages, and (in humans) on activated T cells. For an organ transplant these differences are significant. If a donor organ is only slightly different from a recipient in its class I antigens but the class II antigens are markedly different, a major immune response to the organ is likely to occur. Conversely, if a donor organ is only slightly different from a recipient in its class I antigens, but the class II antigens are closely matched, only a weak rejection response will be generated.

Serological typing of class II antigens is more difficult than typing class I antigens. Identification is often made by an in vitro lymphocyte proliferation test, which takes about 5 days. Therefore, the results of a tissue match may not be known until after the organ has been transplanted. The information is still useful, however, because it gives the physician an idea of how serious the graft rejection may be and how to treat it. If all five of the HLA group of antigens are matched, the graft has about a 95% chance of surviving the first year.

Unfortunately, not many persons are lucky enough to have an identical twin to supply spare parts, so perfect matches are difficult to find. Furthermore, some parts such as the heart cannot be spared. Most organs to be transplanted, therefore, are removed from unrelated donors, often from patients who have just died.

To try to prevent graft rejection in less compatible matches, drugs and x-rays are used to destroy T lymphocytes. These methods do not kill only T lymphocytes, however; all types of lymphocytes are indiscriminately destroyed. Unfortunately, lymphocyte destruction suppresses not only graft rejection but other immune responses as well, so that many transplant patients succumb to pneumonia or other infections. In *immunosuppressed* patients there is also an increased incidence of certain types of tumor growths.

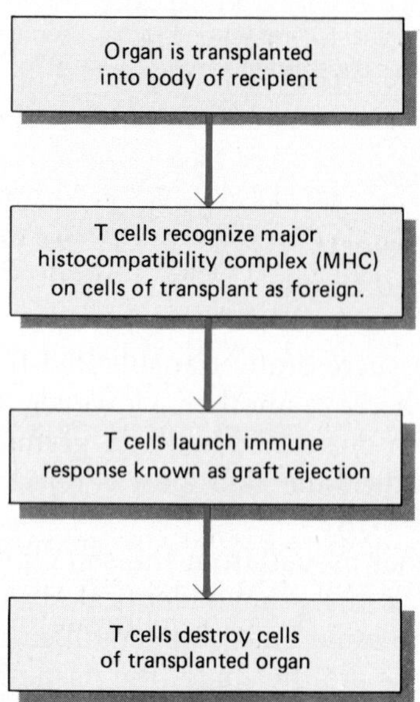

FIGURE 23-13

Graft rejection.

Cyclosporin A, an antibiotic extracted from fungi, prevents activated T cells from dividing but has little effect on B cells. Thus, the graft is not rejected and the patient can still resist infection. Virtually all organ graft recipients today are treated with cyclosporin A because of its significant effect on organ graft survival.

The body has a few immunologically privileged sites

There are a few **immunologically privileged** locations in the body in which foreign tissues will be accepted by a host. The *brain* is one such area. The *cornea* is another. Corneal transplants are highly successful because the cornea has almost no blood or lymphatic vessels associated with it and so is out of reach of most lymphocytes. Furthermore, antigens in the corneal graft probably would not find their way into the circulatory system, and so would not stimulate an immune response. The *uterus* is also thought to be an immunologically privileged site. There the human fetus is able to develop its own biochemical identity in safety.

Immunological tolerance can be induced

Immunological tolerance refers to a specific nonresponsiveness to an antigen. The immune system is a highly regulated machine which produces strong immune responses that allow us to fight infection, protect us against cancer, and confound the transplant physician. Remarkably, this system is selectively tolerant of our own individual tissues and cells.

Tolerance can be generated to specific antigens experimentally by eliminating either the T cell or B cell component of the immune response. Because most antigens have multiple antigenic determinants, it is best to choose simple antigens in these experiments. Stimulating immature cells by low concentrations of antigen can abort the development of either the T cell or the B cell. The absolute absence of a specific T or B cell would result in a specific nonresponsiveness.

Another way to generate tolerance is by stimulating suppressor T cells. This can be done with certain antigens, using strictly defined immunization protocols. Then, when the animal comes into contact with the antigen, the suppressor T cells prevent an immune reaction.

Immunological tolerance to foreign tissue can also be induced experimentally. Mice of a specific genetic strain, say strain A, are genetically similar, almost like identical twins, and so are tolerant to tissue transplanted among their group. However, a mouse from strain A differs genetically from a mouse of another strain, say strain B, and normally rejects tissue transplanted from a strain B donor.

If embryonic cells from a mouse of strain A are infused into a newborn mouse of strain B, the strain B mouse will develop immunological tolerance. The mouse will develop normally, but will not reject tissue transplants from a strain A mouse. By exposing the strain B mouse to the antigens from strain A before it develops immunological competence to produce a specific immune response to them, the development of that ability is delayed. If the antigens are present continuously, the ability to respond to them will be postponed indefinitely. However, this same animal will respond quite normally to the presence of other antigens, will form antibodies to them, and will reject grafts from other strains of mice.

Immunological tolerance can be induced in this manner only in fetal or neonatal animals. If the thymus gland of a newborn animal is removed, the animal's lymph nodes remain small and the animal is deficient in cellular immunity. An animal treated in this way will accept tissue grafts from other animals that differ from it genetically.

In autoimmune disease the body reacts against its own tissues

Sometimes self-tolerance appears to break down and the body reacts immunologically against its own tissues, causing an **autoimmune disease**. Some of the diseases that result from such failures in self-tolerance are rheumatoid arthritis, multiple sclerosis, Graves' disease, myasthenia gravis, systemic lupus erythematosus (SLE), insulin-dependent diabetes (Type I), and perhaps infectious mononucleosis.

Myasthenia gravis is an autoimmune disease in which function at the neuromuscular junctions is impaired. Affected persons (more than 15,000 in the United States) experience muscle weakness and are easily fatigued. Gradually, victims lose muscle control. Sometimes respiratory muscles are affected to a life-threatening extent. Most myasthenia gravis patients have a circulating antibody that combines with acetylcholine receptors in the motor end plates. This interaction blocks the receptors and can damage or even destroy them.

What causes the production of abnormal antibodies in myasthenia gravis and in other autoimmune diseases? No one really knows. Some investigators have suggested genetic predisposition, perhaps involving HLA types; others speculate that prior damage to the tissue is involved. Some studies suggest that a viral infection in the involved tissue previously stimulated the body to manufacture antibodies against the infected cells. Then, after the virus has been destroyed, the body continues to manufacture harmful antibodies capable of attacking the body cells—even though they are no longer infected. A combination of these factors may be responsible.

Allergic reactions are maladaptive immune responses

The immune system normally functions to defend the body against pathogens and to preserve homeostasis, but sometimes the system malfunctions. **Allergy** is a state of altered immune response that is harmful to the body. Allergic persons have a tendency to manufacture antibodies against mild antigens, called **allergens**, that do not stimulate a response in nonallergic individuals. In many kinds of allergic reactions, distinctive IgE immunoglobulins called *reagins* are produced. About 15% of the population of the United States are plagued by an allergic disorder such as allergic asthma or hayfever. There appears to be an inherited tendency to these disorders.

Let us examine a common allergic reaction—a **hayfever** response to ragweed pollen (Fig. 23-14). When an allergic person inhales the microscopic pollen, allergens stimulate the release of IgE from sensitized plasma cells in the nasal passages. The IgE attaches to receptors on the membrane of mast cells, large connective tissue cells filled with distinctive granules. Each mast cell has thousands of receptors to which the IgE may attach. Each IgE molecule attaches to a mast cell receptor by its C region end, leaving the V region end of the immunoglobulin free to combine with the ragweed pollen allergen.

When the allergen combines with IgE antibody, the mast cell rapidly releases its granules (Fig. 23-15). When exposed to extracellular fluid,

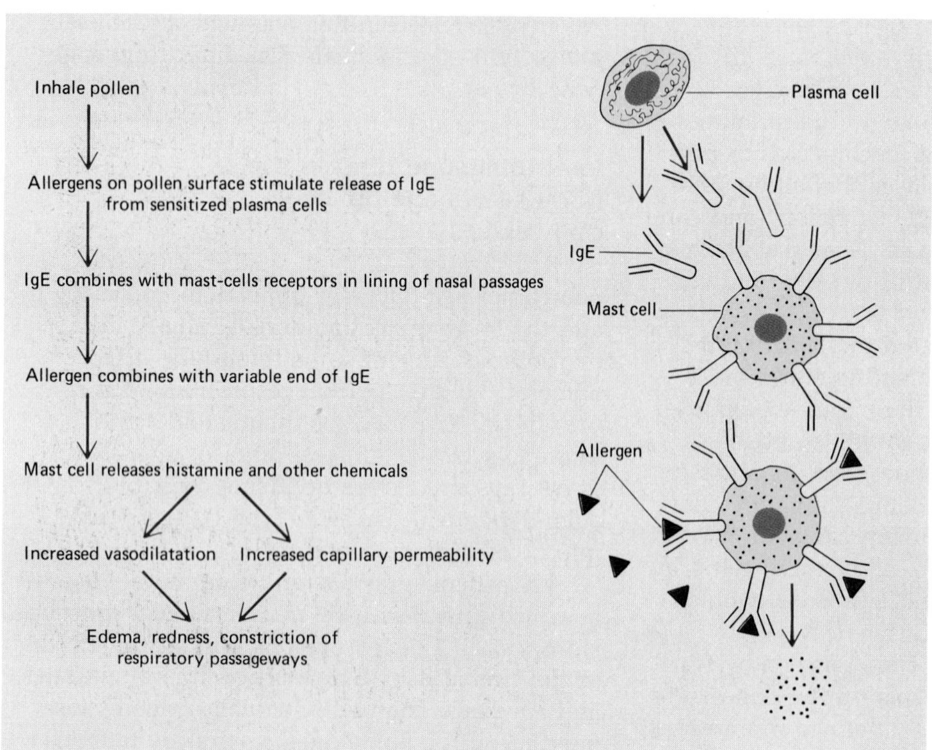

FIGURE 23-14

A common type of allergic response.

the granules release histamine, serotonin, and other chemicals that cause inflammation. These substances produce dilation of blood vessels and increased capillary permeability, leading to edema and redness. Such physiological responses cause the victims' nasal passages to become swollen and irritated. Their noses run, they sneeze, their eyes water, and they feel generally uncomfortable.

Allergens on pollen $\xrightarrow{\text{stimulate}}$ sensitized plasma cells ⟶ IgE ⟶ IgE combines with mast cell receptors ⟶ mast cell releases granules ⟶ histamine and other chemicals ⟶ inflammation

In **allergic asthma**, an allergen-IgE response occurs in the bronchioles of the lungs. Mast cells release SRS-A (slow-reacting substance of anaphylaxis), which causes smooth muscle to constrict. The airways in the lungs sometimes constrict for several hours, making breathing difficult.

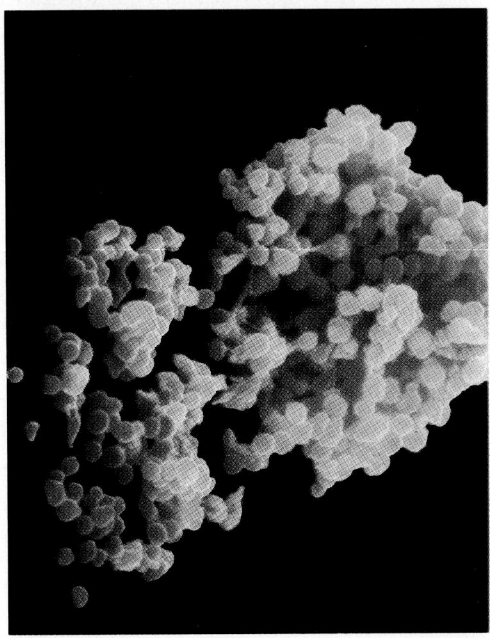

FIGURE 23-15

When an allergen combines with IgE bound to a mast-cell receptor, the mast cell explodes, releasing granules filled with histamine and other chemicals that cause the symptoms of an allergic response. (Lennart Nilsson/© Boehringer Ingelheim International GmbH, from *The Incredible Machine*, p. 211.)

Certain foods or drugs act as allergens in some persons, causing a reaction in the walls of the gastrointestinal tract that leads to discomfort and diarrhea. The allergen may be absorbed and cause mast cells to release granules elsewhere in the body. When the allergen-IgE reaction takes place in the skin, the histamine released by mast cells causes the swollen red welts known as **hives**.

Systemic anaphylaxis is a dangerous kind of allergic reaction that can occur when a person develops an allergy to a specific drug such as penicillin, or to compounds present in the venom injected by a stinging insect. Within minutes after the substance enters the body, a widespread allergic reaction takes place. Large amounts of histamine are released into the circulation, causing extreme vasodilation and permeability. So much plasma may be lost from the blood that circulatory shock and death can occur within a few minutes.

The symptoms of allergic reactions are often treated with **antihistamines**, drugs that block the effects of histamine. These drugs compete for the same receptor sites on cells targeted by histamine. When the antihistamine combines with the receptor, it prevents the histamine from combining and thus prevents its harmful effects. Antihistamines are useful clinically in relieving the symptoms of hives and hayfever. They are not completely effective, however, because mast cells release substances other than histamine that cause allergic symptoms.

In serious allergic disorders patients are sometimes given **desensitization therapy**. Very small amounts of the very antigen to which they are allergic are either injected or administered in the form of drops daily over a period of months or years. This stimulates production of IgG antibodies against the antigen. When the patient encounters the allergen, the IgG immunoglobulins combine with the allergen, blocking its receptors so that the IgE cannot combine with it. In this way a less harmful immune response is substituted for the allergic reaction. Desensitizing injections of the antigen are also thought to stimulate suppressor T cell activity.

Summary

I. Immune responses depend upon the ability of an organism to distinguish between self and nonself.

II. The body can launch both nonspecific and specific responses.
   - A. Nonspecific defense mechanisms that prevent entrance of pathogens include the skin, acid secretions in the stomach, and the mucous lining of the respiratory passageways.
   - B. Should pathogens succeed in breaking through the first line of defense, other nonspecific defense mechanisms are activated to destroy the invading pathogens.
     1. When pathogens invade tissues, they trigger an inflammatory response, which brings needed phagocytic cells and antibodies to the infected area.
     2. Neutrophils and macrophages phagocytize and destroy bacteria.

III. Specific immune responses include antibody-mediated immunity and cell-mediated immunity. Both T cells and B cells respond to antigens.
   - A. In antibody-mediated immunity, competent B cells are activated when specific antigens are presented by a macrophage and when exposed to interleukins secreted by helper T cells.
     1. B cells multiply, giving rise to clones of cells.
     2. Some B cells differentiate to become plasma cells, which secrete specific antibodies. Others become memory cells that continue to produce antibodies.
   - B. Antibodies are highly specific proteins; they are also called immunoglobulins. They are produced in response to specific antigens. Antibodies are grouped in five classes according to their structure.
   - C. Antibody combines with a specific antigen to form an antigen-antibody complex, which may inactivate the pathogen, stimulate phagocytosis, or activate the complement system. The complement system increases the inflammatory response and phagocytosis; some complement proteins digest portions of the pathogen.
   - D. In cell-mediated immunity, specific T cells are activated by the presence of specific antigens and by helper T cells; these activated T cells multiply, giving rise to a clone of cells.
     1. Some T cells differentiate to become cytotoxic T cells, which migrate to the site of infection and chemically destroy pathogens.
     2. Some sensitized T cells remain in the lymph nodes as memory cells; others become helper T cells or suppressor T cells.
   - E. Second exposure to an antigen evokes a secondary immune response, which is more rapid and more intense than the primary response.
   - F. Active immunity develops as a result of exposure to antigens; it may occur naturally or may be artificially induced by immunization.
   - G. Passive immunity is temporary. It develops when an individual receives antibodies produced by another person or animal.
   - H. According to the theory of immune surveillance, the immune system destroys abnormal cells whenever they arise; diseases such as cancer develop when this immune mechanism fails to operate effectively.
   - I. Transplanted tissues possess protein markers known as major histocompatibility complex that stimulate graft rejection, an immune response (launched mainly by T cells) that destroys the transplant.
   - J. Immunological tolerance to foreign tissues can be induced experimentally under certain conditions.
   - K. In autoimmune diseases the body reacts immunologically against its own tissues.
   - L. In an allergic response, an allergen can stimulate production of IgE antibody, which combines with the receptors on mast cells; the mast cells then release histamine and other substances, causing inflammation and other symptoms of allergy.

Post-test

1. An antigen is a substance capable of stimulating a(n) ______________ ______________.
2. Specific proteins produced in response to specific antigens are called ______________.
3. When infected by viruses, some cells respond by producing proteins called ______________.
4. The clinical characteristics of inflammation are ______________, ______________, ______________, and ______________.
5. T lymphocytes are thought to originate in the ______________ ______________; they are processed in the ______________; and then proliferate in the ______________ tissues.

6. Lymphokines are released by ______________.
7. When the body is invaded by the same pathogen a second time, the immune response can be launched more rapidly owing to the presence of ______________ cells.
8. The cells that produce antibodies are ______________ cells.
9. An antigenic determinant gives the antigen molecule a specific configuration that can be "recognized" by an ______________.
10. The ______________ confers immunological competence upon T cells.
11. The complement system is activated when an ______________ complex is formed.
12. In opsonization, complement proteins coat ______________.
13. Although artificially induced, immunization is a form of ______________ immunity.
14. An individual injected with antibodies produced by another organism is receiving ______________ immunity.
15. In humans the major histocompatibility complex is called the ______________ group.
16. An autograft consists of tissue transplanted from ______________.
17. In graft rejection the host launches an effective ______________ ______________ against ______________ tissue.
18. Cornea transplants are highly successful because the cornea is an immunologically ______________ site.
19. An ______________ is a mild antigen that does not stimulate a response in an individual who is not ______________.
20. In a typical allergic reaction, mast cells secrete ______________ and other compounds that cause ______________.

Review questions

1. How does the body distinguish between self and nonself?
2. Contrast specific and nonspecific defense mechanisms. Which type confronts invading pathogens immediately? How do the two systems work together?
3. How does inflammation help to restore homeostasis?
4. Explain two specific ways in which cell-mediated and antibody-mediated immune responses are similar, and three ways in which they are different.
5. Describe three ways in which antibodies work to destroy pathogens.
6. John is immunized against measles. Jack contracts measles from a playmate in nursery school before his mother gets around to having him immunized. Compare the immune responses in the two children. Five years later, John and Jack are playing together when Judy, who is coming down with measles, sneezes on both of them. Compare the immune responses in Jack and in John.
7. Why is passive immunity temporary?
8. What is immunological tolerance?
9. What is graft rejection? What is the immunological basis for it?
10. List the immunological events that take place in a common type of allergic reaction such as hayfever.
11. Explain the theory of immune surveillance. What happens when immune surveillance fails?
12. What is an autoimmune disease? Give two examples.
13. What public policy decisions would you recommend that might help slow the spread of AIDS?

Post-test answers

1. immune response 2. antibodies (immunoglobulins) 3. interferons 4. redness, heat, swelling (edema), pain 5. bone marrow; thymus; lymphatic 6. lymphocytes 7. memory 8. plasma (differentiated B cells) 9. antibody 10. thymus 11. antigen-antibody 12. pathogens 13. active 14. passive 15. HLA 16. one location to another in the same organism 17. immune response; transplanted 18. privileged 19. allergen; allergic 20. histamine; inflammation

OBTAINING OXYGEN AND NUTRIENTS AND MAINTAINING BODILY FLUIDS

The cells of the body require certain raw materials to perform the multitude of functions necessary to stay alive. The body utilizes specific areas of exchange with the external environment to procure these raw materials. Oxygen is obtained from the external environment through gas exchange within the respiratory system. After first being broken down, nutrients are exchanged through the digestive system. The body cells use these substances to build new body components and to produce energy for cellular activities. The digestive system eliminates substances that are not broken down and exchanged.

As the cells utilize (or metabolize) raw materials, they give off waste products, including carbon dioxide. If these wastes were allowed to accumulate within the cells or in their immediate surroundings, they would reach toxic or detrimental levels. Cell membranes and proteins would lose their integrity, and osmotic stress would cause the cells to cease functioning. The circulatory system transports the metabolic wastes from the tissue cells to other exchange surfaces for disposal. The kidneys filter waste substances from the blood and excrete them via the urinary system. The respiratory system eliminates carbon dioxide from the body.

Cellular activities alter the composition of their surrounding medium. Water and ions shift from inside the cells to outside the cells and vice versa. The respiratory system, digestive system, and most importantly, the urinary system supply exchange surfaces with the external environment that enable imbalances in water, electrolyte, and pH levels to be corrected. The nervous system and the endocrine system provide important controls over these exchange processes.

In this section we will study how the body obtains and utilizes oxygen and nutrients. We will also learn how it disposes of waste materials and how it regulates its internal environment to ensure homeostasis.

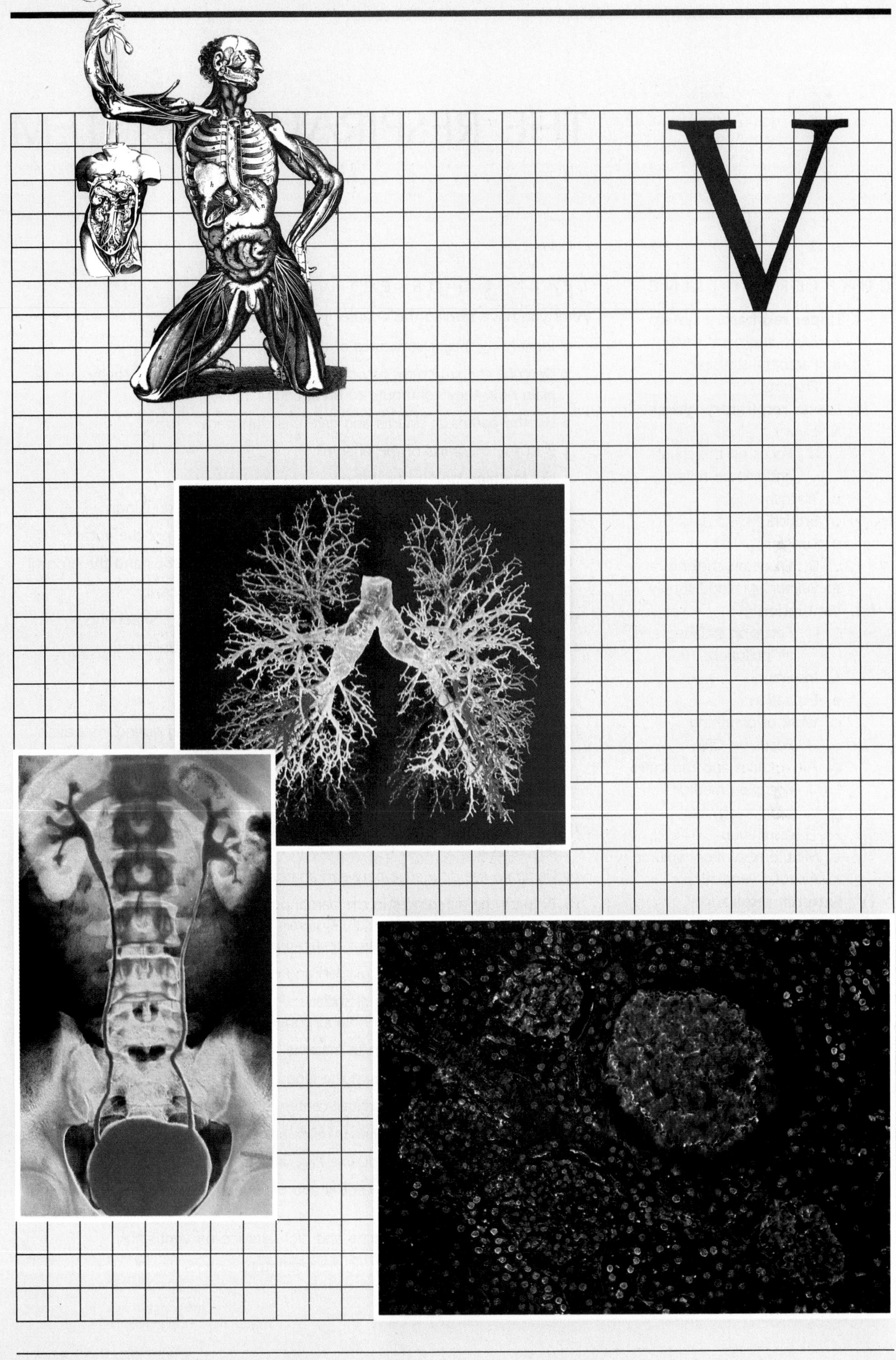

V

THE RESPIRATORY SYSTEM

CHAPTER OUTLINE

I. Upper respiratory system
- A. Nose and nasal cavity
- B. Paranasal sinuses
- C. Pharynx

II. Lower respiratory system
- A. Larynx
  - □ Focus on the cough and sneeze reflexes
- B. Trachea
- C. Bronchi
- D. Lungs
  - □ Focus on choking
- E. Pulmonary blood supply

III. Ventilation
- □ Focus on smoking and air pollution
- A. Inspiration
- B. Expiration
- C. Work of breathing
  - □ Focus on CPR
- D. Air volumes and capacities
  - □ Focus on medical terminology of respiration
- E. Minute respiratory volume
- F. Alveolar ventilation

IV. External respiration

V. Internal respiration

VI. Gas transport
- □ Focus on respiratory disorders
- A. Oxygen transport
- B. Oxyhemoglobin dissociation
- C. Carbon dioxide transport

VII. Control of respiration
- A. Local factors
- B. Medullary controls
- C. Pontile controls
- D. Hering-Breuer reflex
- E. Cortical input
- F. Chemical controls
- G. Effects of exercise
- H. Effects of high altitude

VIII. Aging of respiratory system

IX. Embryology

LEARNING OBJECTIVES

After you have studied this chapter you should be able to:

1 Identify the major structures of the respiratory system.

2 Describe the structures associated with the nose and nasal cavity and explain how they contribute to breathing.

3 List the paranasal sinuses and give their functions.

4 Describe the parts of the pharynx.

5 List the nine laryngeal cartilages.

6 Explain the function of the epiglottis when eating or drinking.

7 Compare differences in pitch based on the functioning of the vocal folds.

8 Compare the anatomical differences between the trachea and the bronchi.

9 Describe the positioning of the lungs in the thoracic cavity.

10 Define a bronchopulmonary segment and describe its components.

11 Explain the relation of the alveoli to the pulmonary capillaries.

12 Relate Dalton's law of partial pressures to respiration.

13 Relate Boyle's law to ventilation of the lungs.

14 Explain the physiological sequence of events occurring during inspiration and expiration.

15 Compare the secretion of surfactant to the work of breathing and lung compliance.

16 Define the basic pulmonary volumes and capacities and compare their average values.

17 Compare the difference between anatomical and physiological dead space.

18 Analyze the differences in the partial pressures of the respiratory gases in the alveoli, pulmonary vessels, systemic vessels, and tissue cells, and relate these to external and internal respiration.

19 Compare the transport of oxygen and carbon dioxide.

20 Define an oxyhemoglobin dissociation curve and explain how changes in pH, P_{CO_2}, temperature, and diphosphoglyceric acid (DPG) shift the curve.

21 Compare fetal hemoglobin to maternal hemoglobin.

22 Explain how local controls in the lungs provide for efficient gas exchange.

23 Describe the respiratory control centers of the brain.

24 Explain how the Hering-Breuer reflex protects the lungs.

25 Explain how the level of plasma P_{CO_2} affects ventilation.

26 Compare the roles of the central and peripheral chemoreceptors in the control of ventilation.

27 Explain the effects of exercise and high altitude on ventilation.

28 Define the major disorders of the respiratory system.

Resin cast of the bronchial passages from lungs. (Science Photo Library/Photo Researchers, Inc.)

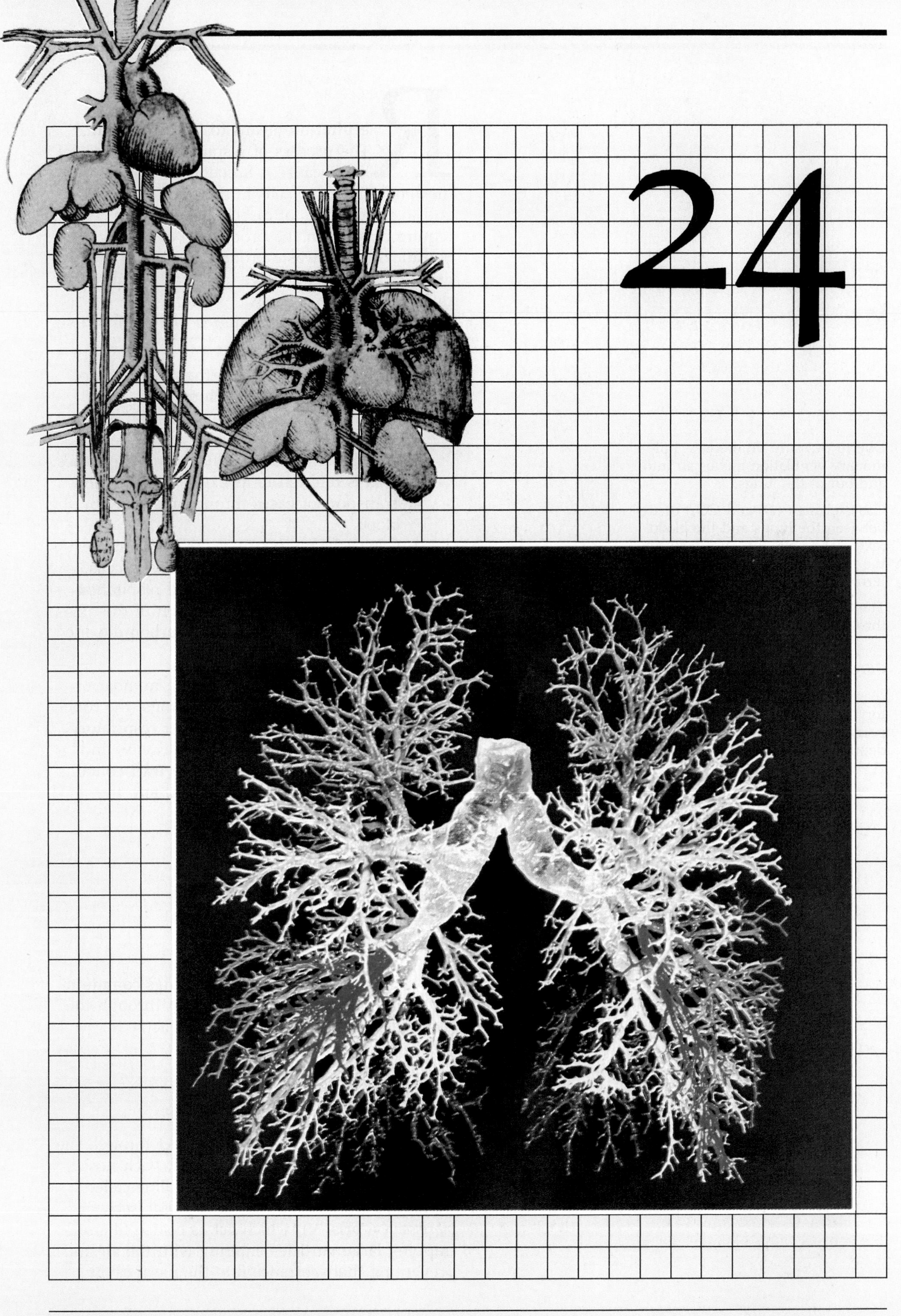

24

KEY CONCEPTS

Due to pressure differences, pulmonary ventilation moves air into and out of the lungs.

Gas exchange (O_2 and CO_2) occurs between the lungs and the blood (external respiration) and between the blood and the tissue cells (internal respiration).

The blood transports O_2 and CO_2 throughout the body.

Tissue cells use O_2 and release CO_2.

Many factors influence the respiratory centers of the medulla and pons, thereby affecting the rate and depth of breathing.

Respiration means to "breathe again." The process of respiration is critical to life because it functions to supply all metabolically active cells in the body with oxygen and to rid the cells of carbon dioxide. The cells require oxygen for the production of energy. Carbon dioxide is a waste product of cellular metabolism, and if it accumulates in the cells and tissue fluids, it leads to acidosis.

The process of respiration is divided into five stages:

1. Pulmonary ventilation (the movement of air into and out of the lungs).
2. Gas exchange (oxygen and carbon dioxide) between the respiratory units of the lungs and the blood of the pulmonary capillaries. This is referred to as external respiration.
3. Transport of gases through the body by the blood.
4. Gas exchange between the blood in the systemic capillaries and the tissue cells. This is referred to as internal respiration.
5. Cellular respiration (utilization of the oxygen and the production of carbon dioxide by the cells).

The respiratory system consists of a number of respiratory passageways and the lungs, the functional respiratory organs. The **upper respiratory tract** is made up of the nose, nasal cavity, and the pharynx. The **lower respiratory tract** contains the larynx, the trachea, the bronchi, and the lungs. See Figure 24-1.

The upper respiratory tract contains the nose, nasal cavity, and pharynx

The air entering and leaving the lungs communicates with the external environment through the passages of the upper respiratory tract.

The nose and nasal cavity contain a mucous membrane

Air enters the upper respiratory tract through the **nostrils,** or **external nares** (**na**-reez). Each nostril leads into a cavity lateral to the midline called a **vestibule.** The vestibule contains *nasal hairs,* or *vibrissae* (vi-**bris**-ee), which act as coarse filters, trapping large particles entering with the air and preventing their entrance into the nasal cavity.

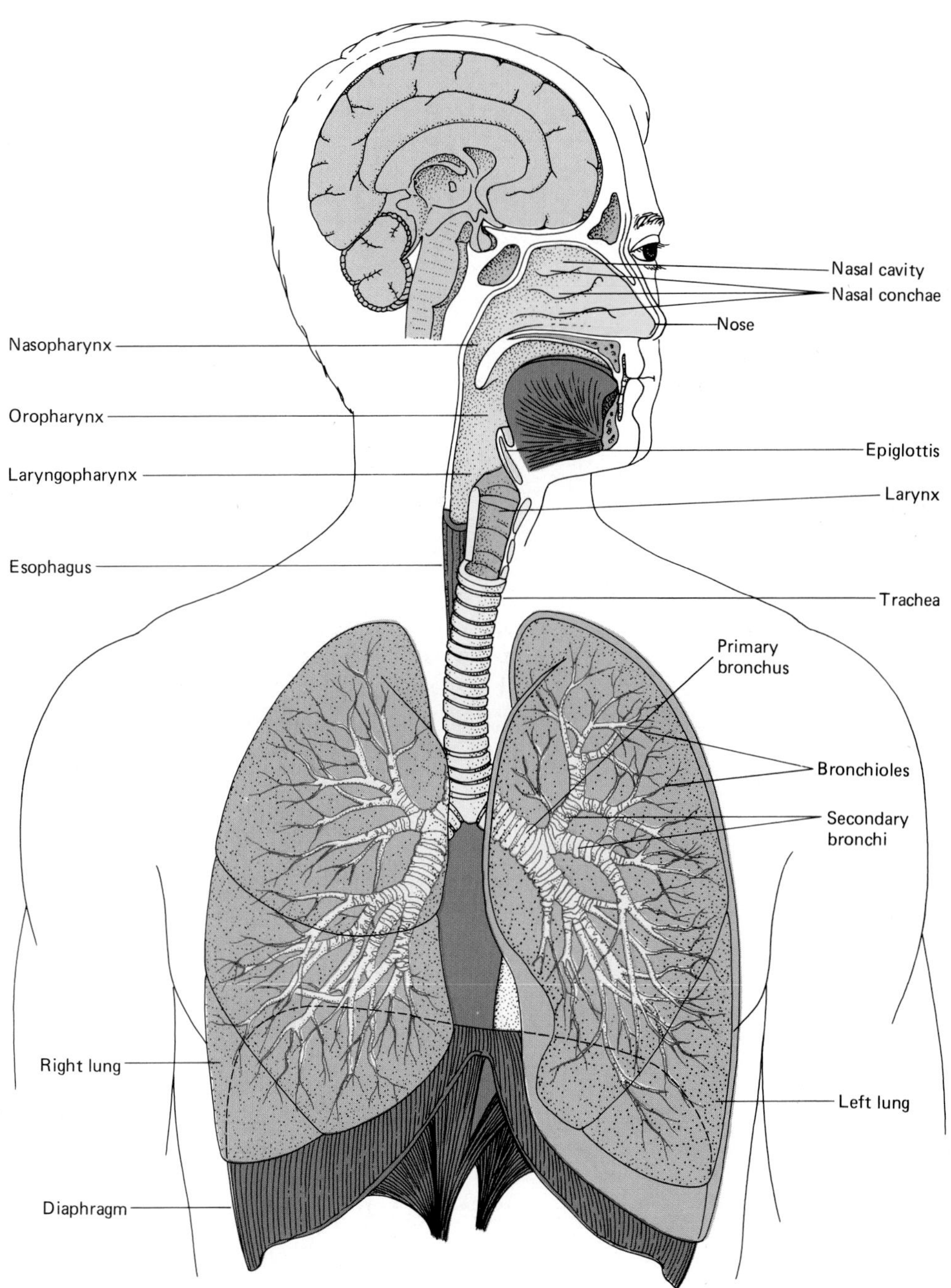

FIGURE 24-1

Anatomy of the human respiratory system.

The nasal bones form the bridge of the nose; the remainder of its pyramidal framework is composed of cartilage and connective tissue. The nasal cartilages are the septal, lateral nasal, greater alar, and lesser alar (Fig. 24-2). The *lateral nasal, greater alar,* and *lesser alar cartilages* form the shape of the external nose.

The internal **septal cartilage** joins the nasal bones superiorly, the perpendicular plate of the ethmoid posteriorly, and the vomer and maxillae inferiorly to form the **nasal septum.** The nasal septum divides the **nasal cavity** into a right and left chamber. The roof of the nasal cavity is the cribriform plate of the ethmoid. The lateral walls

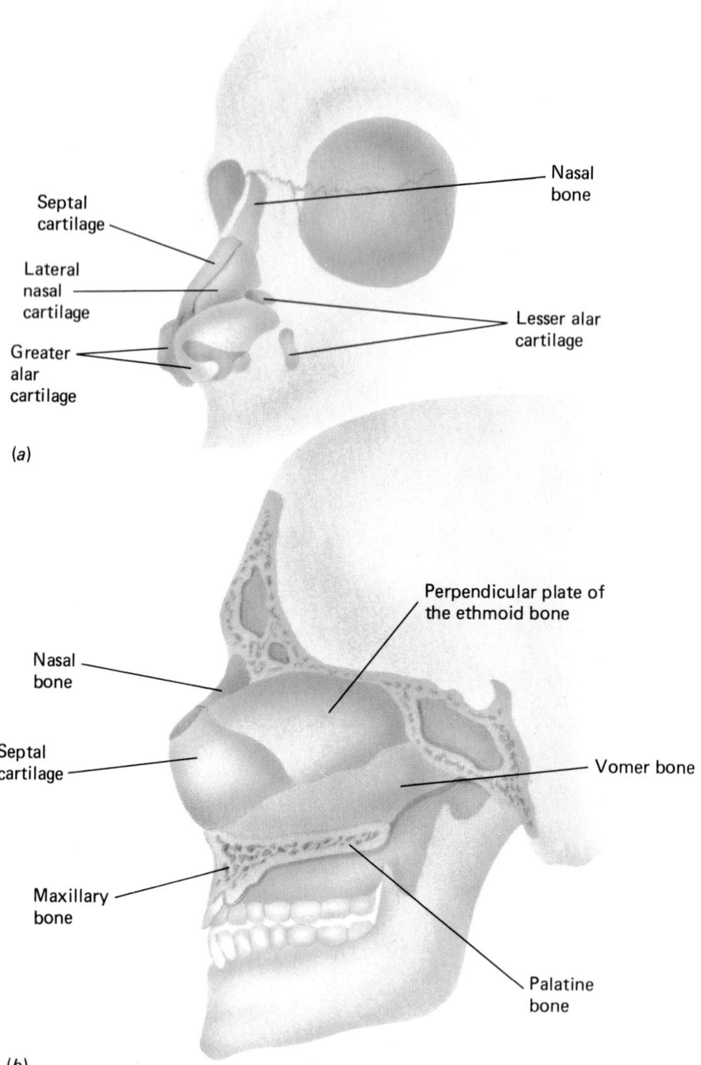

FIGURE 24-2

(*a*) Nasal cartilages. (*b*) Nasal septum (midsagittal section).

of the cavity are formed by the **nasal conchae** (superior and middle) of the ethmoid bone. The inferior conchae are separate and distinct from the ethmoid. Between the conchae are grooved passageways called **meatuses** (Fig. 24-3). The three pairs of conchae and their meatuses serve to increase surface area.

The nasal cavity is lined by a **nasal mucous membrane.** This membrane is composed of pseudostratified ciliated columnar epithelium containing numerous goblet cells that secrete mucus. The part of the membrane associated with the cribriform plate is modified for olfaction reception. (Refer to Chapter 17.) The nasal mucous membrane of the nasal conchae and meatuses is highly vascularized. The mucus and associated capillaries function to warm and humidify incoming air. The mucus also traps foreign particles, and the cilia of the mucous membrane help to move the mucus and trapped particles down into the pharynx. The floor of the nasal cavity is formed by the hard and soft palates. The posterior part of the nasal cavity opens through the **internal nares** into the **nasopharynx.**

Clinical highlight

Rhinitis is an inflammation of the mucous membrane of the nose. It may be caused by infection or by irritants. It may be acute or chronic. The swelling of the nasal mucous membrane results in a copious mucus discharge. Nose breathing becomes difficult. Sinusitis is common. Sneezing and watery eyes are also common symptoms.

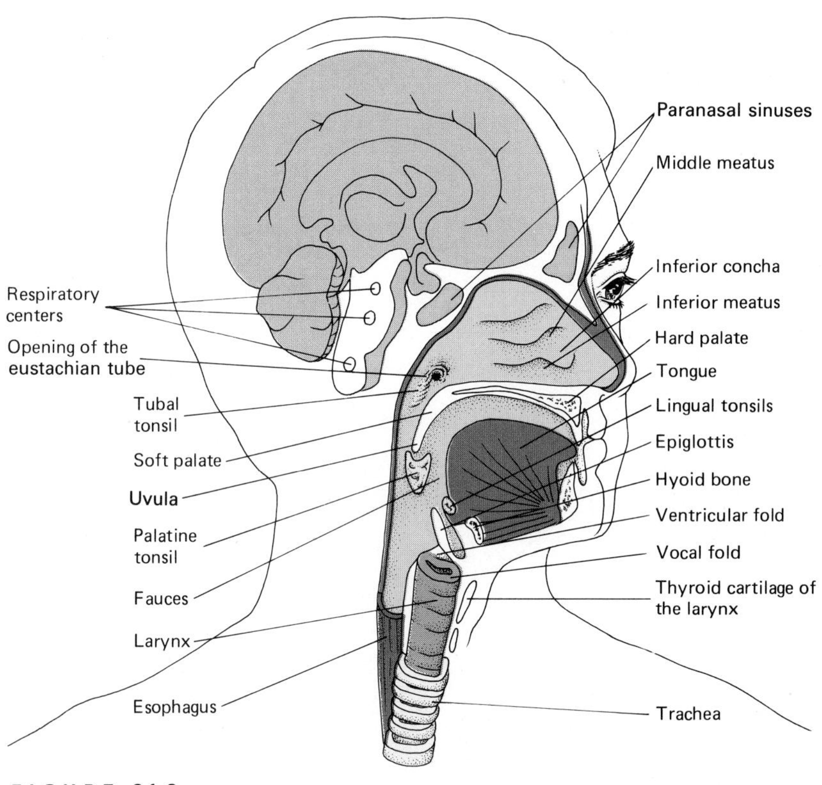

FIGURE 24-3

Internal anatomy of upper respiratory tract (sagittal section).

Paranasal sinuses open into the nasal cavity

Associated with the nasal cavity are ducts leading from air cavities called the **paranasal sinuses.** The four pairs of paranasal sinuses are named from the bones in which they lie—**frontal sinuses, ethmoid sinuses, sphenoid sinuses,** and **maxillary sinuses** (Fig. 24-4). The paranasal sinuses are lined by the nasal mucous membrane, which helps to warm and humidify air. The paranasal sinuses also lighten the weight of the skull and modify sounds by acting as resonating chambers.

Clinical highlight

Sinusitis is an inflammation of the paranasal sinuses resulting in an increase in mucus secretion. It may be caused by an infection or by irritants. Often the inflammation blocks passageways and increases pressure on the sinus walls. This results in symptoms such as headache, fever, discomfort, dizziness, pain, and difficulty in breathing.

The pharynx consists of the nasopharynx, oropharynx, and laryngopharynx

The funnel-shaped **pharynx** (**far**-inks) extends from the nasal cavity to the larynx and measures about 13 centimeters (5 in.) in length. Commonly called the throat, it is divided into three sections: the nasopharynx, the oropharynx, and the laryngopharynx. The **nasopharynx** is the most superior section and receives air from the nasal cavity via the internal nares. The nasopharynx is lined with pseudostratified ciliated columnar epithelium. The orifices of the two **eustachian (auditory) tubes** open into the nasopharynx. The **pharyngeal tonsils** (adenoids) are located on the posterior wall of the nasopharynx.

The **oropharynx** serves both respiration and digestion. It receives air from the nasopharynx and it receives food from the oral cavity by way of the **fauces** (**faw**-seez). The oropharynx is lined with a stratified squamous epithelium. A pair of **palatine tonsils** are located posterolaterally and a

FIGURE 24-4

The paranasal sinuses.

pair of **lingual tonsils** are located at the base of the tongue. These tonsils are the lymphoid areas of the oropharynx (Fig. 24-3).

Clinical highlight

Tonsilitis is an inflammation of the palatine tonsils. The removal of the palatine tonsils is called a tonsillectomy. The removal of the pharyngeal tonsils is called an adenoidectomy.

The **laryngopharynx** is the most inferior part of the pharynx. The laryngopharynx is lined with stratified squamous epithelium. It is continuous with the larynx anteriorly and the esophagus posteriorly. Thus it serves in both respiration and digestion.

The lower respiratory tract contains the larynx, trachea, bronchi, and lungs.

The larynx (voicebox), trachea (windpipe), and bronchi allow for airflow into and out of the lungs.

The larynx is the voicebox

The **larynx** (**lar**-inks) is the most superior structure of the lower respiratory tract. It is located anterior to the fourth through sixth cervical vertebrae. The upper esophagus is immediately posterior to the larynx. The laryngopharynx opens to the larynx via the glottis. At its inferior end, the larynx opens into the trachea.

The larynx contains nine laryngeal cartilages, muscle, and connective tissue. The nine **laryngeal** cartilages consist of one epiglottic, one thyroid, and one cricoid cartilage and two arytenoid, two cuneiform, and two corniculate cartilages (Fig. 24-5).

The **epiglottis** is a large leaf-shaped cartilage that extends into the laryngopharynx. It usually remains erect when breathing. When eating, the larynx moves up and the epiglottis closes over its superior opening, the **glottis.** This prevents food and drink from entering the lower respiratory tract. If something other than air enters the larynx, it stimulates a *cough reflex.* See Focus on The Cough and Sneeze Reflexes.

The **thyroid cartilage** is the largest of the laryngeal cartilages. It is formed by two plates of cartilage that fuse anteriorly but not posteriorly. In males, testosterone causes the thyroid cartilage

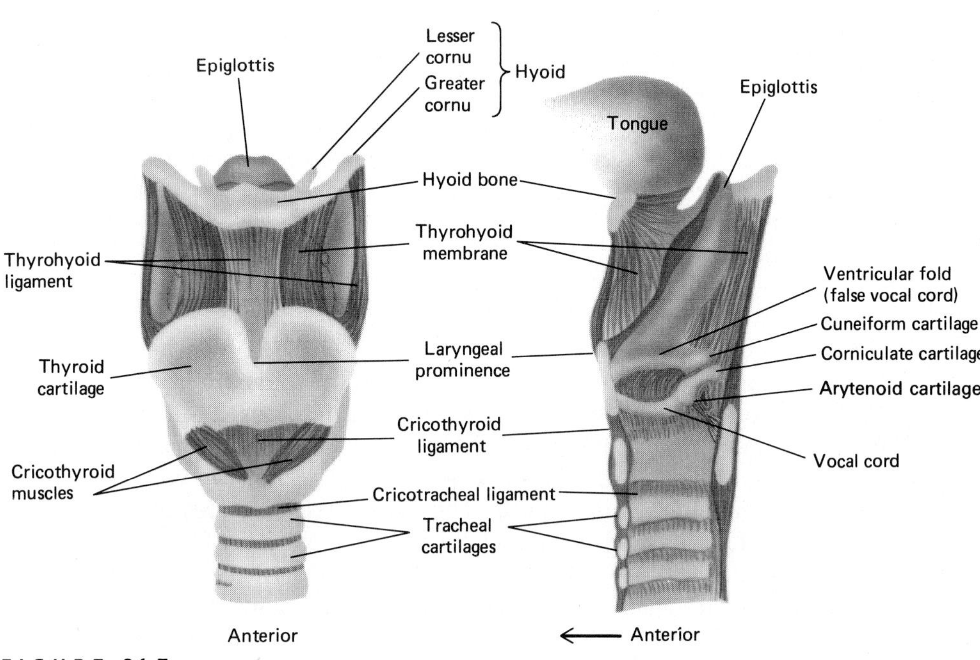

FIGURE 24-5

(*a*) Anterior anatomy of the larynx. (*b*) Internal anatomy of the larynx (sagittal section).

to enlarge, and it is referred to as the *Adam's apple*. Below the thyroid cartilage is located the **cricoid cartilage,** which connects to the trachea.

Of the paired laryngeal cartilages, the **arytenoid** (*ar*-e-**tee**-noid) **cartilages** are the largest. The arytenoid cartilages are pyramidal in shape and are attached to the superior-posterior margin of the cricoid. They are connected to the posterior ends of the vocal folds and help to move them in sound production. The small, paired **cuneiform** (kyou-**nee**-i-form) and **corniculate cartilages** are attached to the arytenoid cartilages. The cuneiform cartilages attach the arytenoid cartilages to the epiglottis.

FOCUS ON . . . The cough and sneeze reflexes

The larynx, trachea, and bronchi are very sensitive to light touch, and any irritation initiates the **cough reflex.** In addition, terminal bronchioles and alveoli are very sensitive to harmful chemical stimuli. The tactile and chemoreceptors respond to an irritation by stimulating afferent neurons which travel through the vagus nerves (CN X) to the respiratory center of the medulla. The medulla activates the sequence of events for the cough response.

Air is inspired into the lungs. The epiglottis then closes the glottis. The vocal cords shut to trap the air in the lungs. Next, expiratory muscles, including the abdominal muscles and the internal intercostals, contract forcefully. This greatly increases intra-alveolar pressure.

The epiglottis and the vocal cords suddenly open and the air within the lungs is forcefully expired. The powerful compression of the lungs also causes a partial collapse of the noncartilaginous parts of the bronchi and trachea so that the air passes out through bronchial and tracheal slits. The expulsion of air is so forceful that the velocity of the air expired may reach 100 miles per hour! This blast of air usually carries any foreign matter out with it.

The **sneeze reflex** is similar to the cough reflex except that it involves the nasal passageways. An irritation of the nasal passages causes receptors to stimulate afferent neurons traveling through the trigeminal nerve (CN V) to the respiratory center of the medulla. The medulla brings about a similar sequence of events as in the cough reflex. In addition, the uvula is also depressed so that the nasal passageways are open. The blast of air is carried through these passages as well as the mouth. This helps to remove any foreign matter from the nose.

The superior parts of the laryngeal mucous membrane consist of stratified squamous epithelium. The rest of the larynx is lined with a pseudostratified ciliated columnar epithelium. At the superior end of the larynx, the mucous membrane forms two pairs of horizontal folds. The superior folds are called the **ventricular folds (false vocal cords).** These false vocal cords do not function in sound production but keep the larynx closed during swallowing. The inferior folds are called the **vocal folds (true vocal cords)** (Fig. 24-6). The opening between the vocal folds is the **rima glottidis.** The true vocal cords function in sound production, giving the larynx the name "voice box."

Within the vocal folds are bands of ligaments that stretch to the thyroid, cricoid, and arytenoid cartilages. *Intrinsic skeletal muscles* are able to change the tension of these ligaments and also change the diameter of the rima glottidis. Entering air causes the vocal folds to vibrate and produce sounds.

Clinical highlight

Laryngitis is an inflammation of the mucous membrane of the larynx. It affects voice and breathing. Infection and irritants are often responsible for the condition. The inflammation and swelling of the vocal folds causes diminished vibrations, resulting in a deepening and a hoarseness of the voice. Sometimes the voice is completely lost for a time. Chronic laryngitis may produce granulations and thickening of the vocal folds resulting in a permanent deepening of the voice. Smokers often experience chronic laryngitis.

The tighter the vocal folds are pulled by the actions of the intrinsic muscles, the higher the pitch of the sounds. Lower-pitched sounds are produced when the tension of the vocal folds is decreased. The vocal folds in males tend to be longer and thicker than those in females and result in a deeper voice. Muscles associated with the pharynx, tongue, lips, and cheeks help to modify the sounds. The resonating effects of the nasal cavity, paranasal sinuses, oral cavity, and

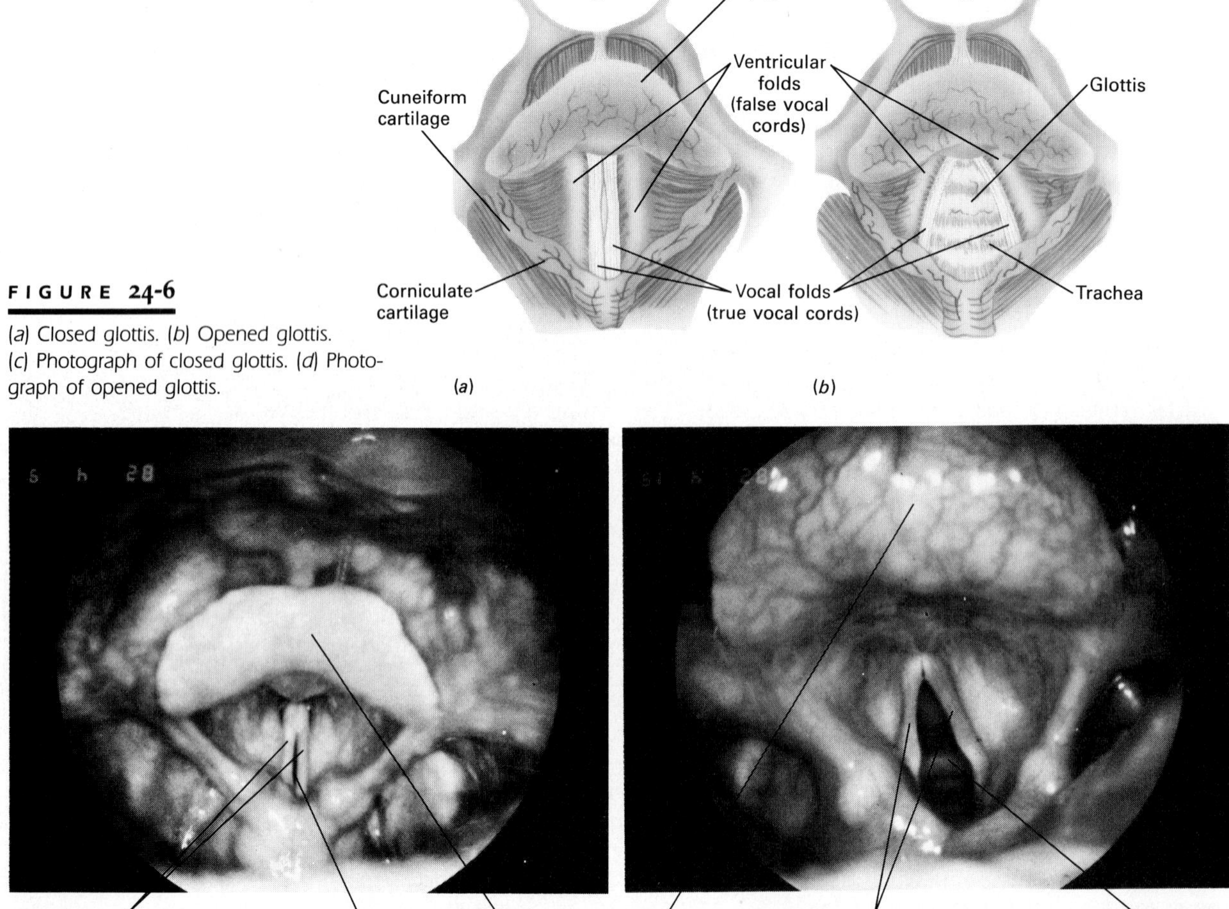

FIGURE 24-6
(*a*) Closed glottis. (*b*) Opened glottis. (*c*) Photograph of closed glottis. (*d*) Photograph of opened glottis.

pharynx also modify the sounds. See Focus on Choking, p. 835.

The trachea is the windpipe

The trachea (**tray**-kee-ah), commonly called the windpipe, is a thin-walled tube joining the larynx to the primary bronchi, tubes leading to the lungs. The trachea is about 11 centimeters (4 in.) in length and about 2.5 centimeters (1 in.) in diameter and lies anterior to the esophagus. It consists of C-shaped hyaline cartilages, the *tracheal cartilages,* which open posteriorly (Fig. 24-5). Smooth muscle and elastic connective tissue connect the open ends of the cartilage. The gaps allow the esophagus room to expand into the trachea when swallowing. The cartilage provides the necessary rigidity to keep the trachea open for breathing.

The mucous membrane lining the trachea consists of pseudostratified, ciliated columnar epithelium containing numerous goblet cells (Fig. 24-7). It is often called the *mucociliary escalator* because cilia beat in an upward direction, moving foreign substances trapped in the mucus away from the lungs and toward the laryngopharynx, where they are swallowed.

Near the level of the fifth thoracic vertebra, the trachea bifurcates into two smaller tubes, the primary bronchi. The last tracheal cartilage is modified for this bifurcation and is called the **carina** (kah-**rye**-na). See Figure 24-8.

Bronchi take air to and from the lungs

At the sternal angle and posterior to the aortic arch, the carina gives way to the **right** and **left primary bronchi** with the right one being shorter, wider, and descending more steeply than the left. The primary bronchi are extrapulmonary; they are bronchi located outside of the lungs. The walls of the primary bronchi are similar in composition to the trachea except that they have smaller diameters. Each primary bronchus divides into smaller **secondary bronchi** which lead into discrete com-

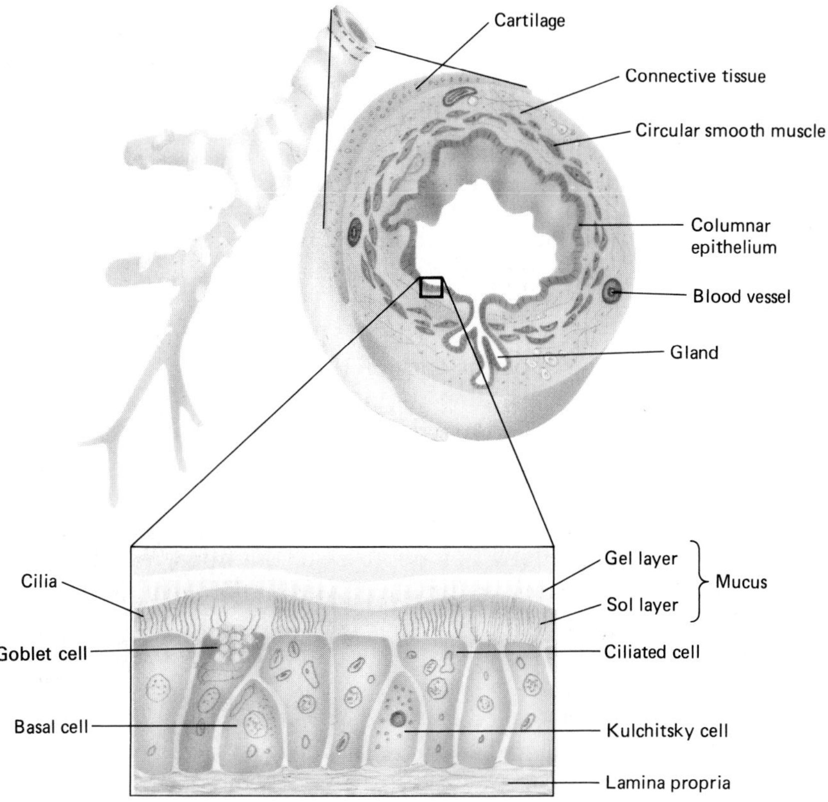

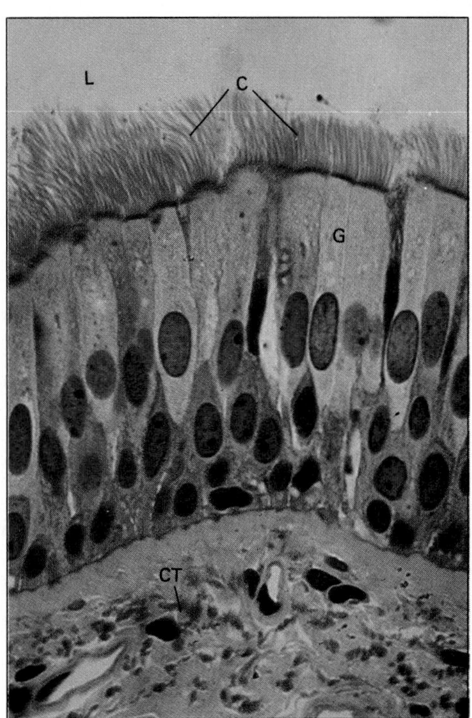

FIGURE 24-7

(*a*) Diagram of tracheal epithelium. (*b*) Photograph of tracheal epithelium (×600). L: lumen; C: cilia; G: goblet cell; CT: Connective tissue.

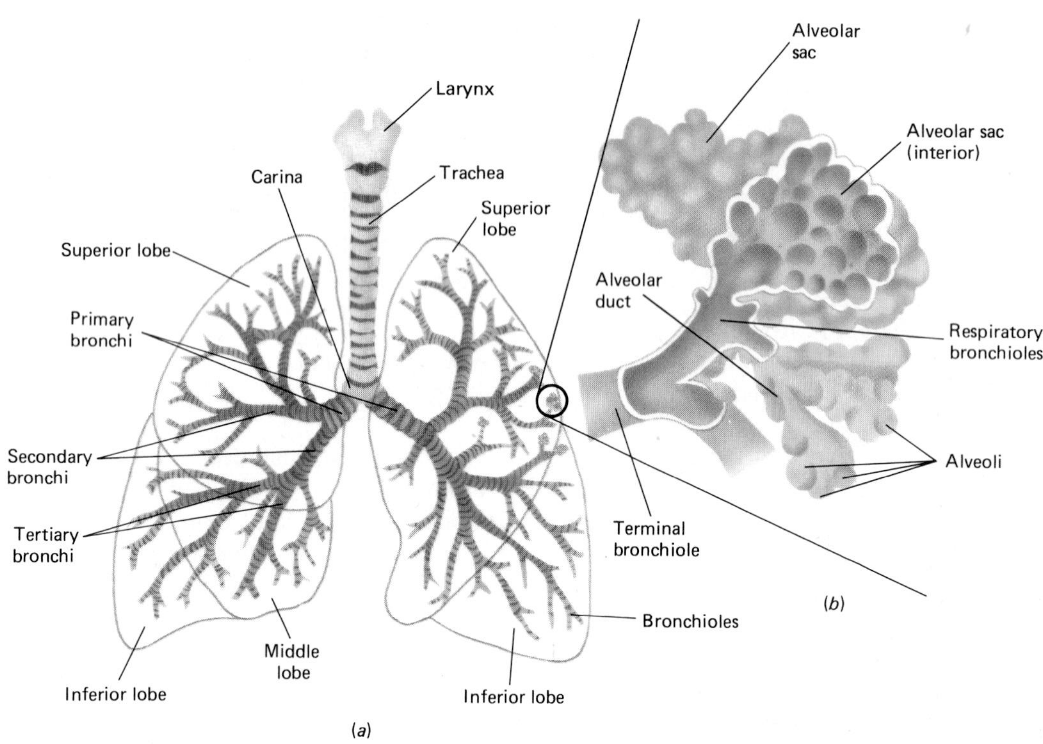

FIGURE 24-8

(a) Anatomy of the bronchial tree. (b) Bronchioles and alveoli.

partments, the lobes, of the lungs. Secondary bronchi within the lobes of the lungs branch into many **tertiary bronchi** (Fig. 24-8). The bronchial cartilage undergoes a series of changes as the tubes become smaller: from the incomplete rings of the primary bronchi to complete plates surrounding the bronchi to small, incomplete rings. The tertiary bronchi branch into many very small bronchi called **bronchioles.** The bronchioles lack cartilage but are completely surrounded by smooth muscle. This smooth muscle is important in regulating the airway resistance of the bronchioles. The bronchioles subdivide into many **terminal bronchioles** which contain simple cuboidal epithelium. The extensive branching into smaller and smaller tubes gives the bronchi and its branches a tree-like appearance; thus they are called the **bronchial tree** (Fig. 24-8).

The lungs are the functional organs of the respiratory system

There are two **lungs** within the thorax, a right lung and a left lung (Fig. 24-9). They are separated medially by the mediastinum. The mediastinum contains the heart and associated blood vessels, esophagus, thymus gland, and sections of the trachea and bronchi. Each lung is cone-shaped and is surrounded by a double membrane called the **pleura.** The superior surface of each lung forms a pointed **apex.** The broad inferior surface is the **base** of the lung. The base is concave and rests on the diaphragm. The right lung consists of three lobes, the superior, middle, and inferior lobes. The left lung consists of two lobes, the superior and inferior lobes.

Each lung contains an **oblique fissure** dividing the lungs into superior and inferior lobes. The right lung also contains a **horizontal fissure** partially subdividing the superior lobe and forming the middle lobe. Along the mediastinal border of each lung is a depression, the **hilus,** which is the junction of the lungs with the bronchi, pulmonary vessels, nerves, and lymphatics. The hilus marks the **root** of the lung. The mediastinal border of the left lung contains a concavity for the heart called the **cardiac notch.** The part of the lungs associating with the ribs is referred to as the **costal surface.**

The **pleura** encloses and protects the lungs. The outer membrane of the pleura is the **parietal pleura** which is attached to the inner thoracic

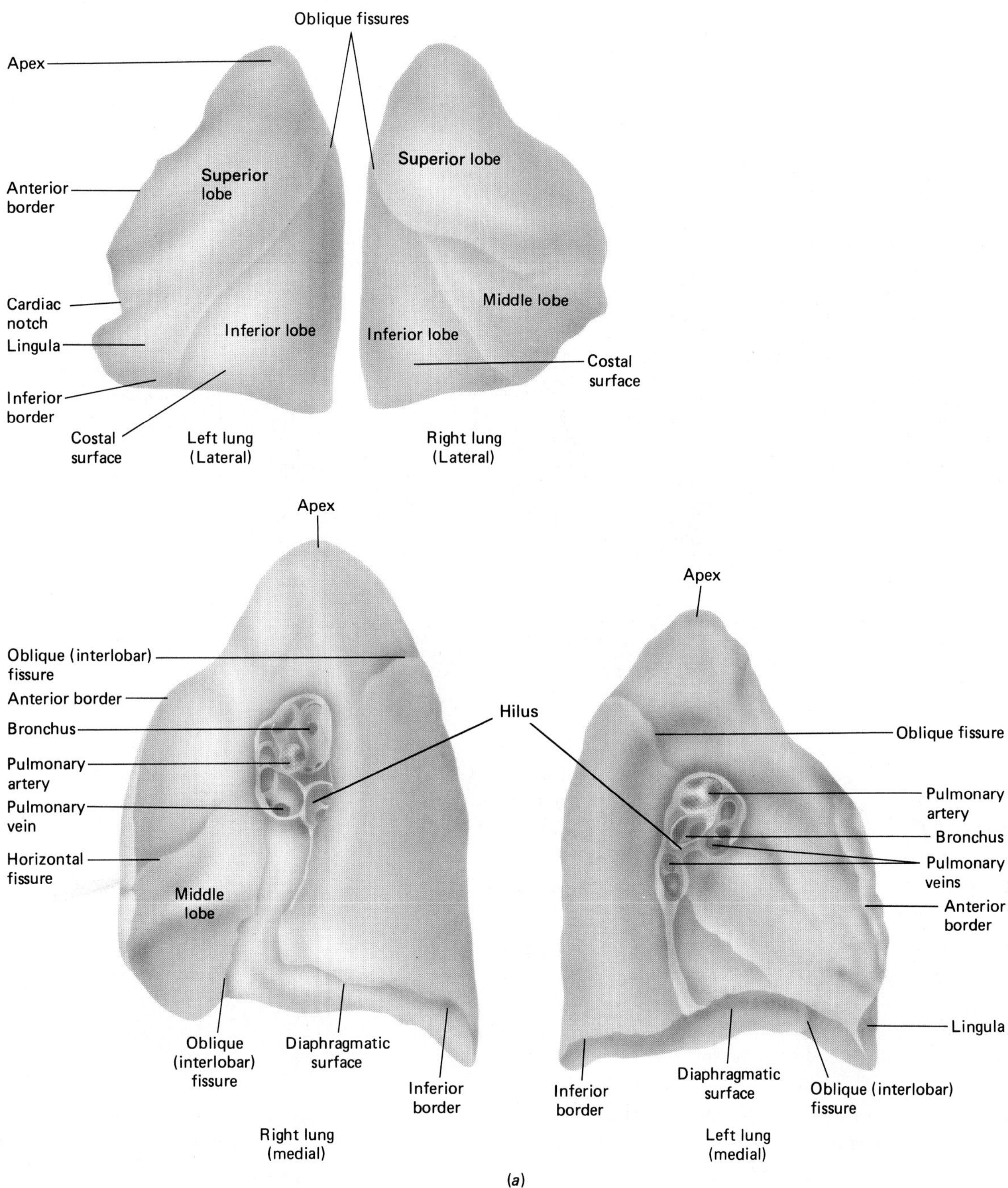

FIGURE 24-9

(a) TOP: Lateral view of lungs showing lobes and external surfaces. BOTTOM: Medial view of lungs showing hilus and associated blood vessels and bronchi.

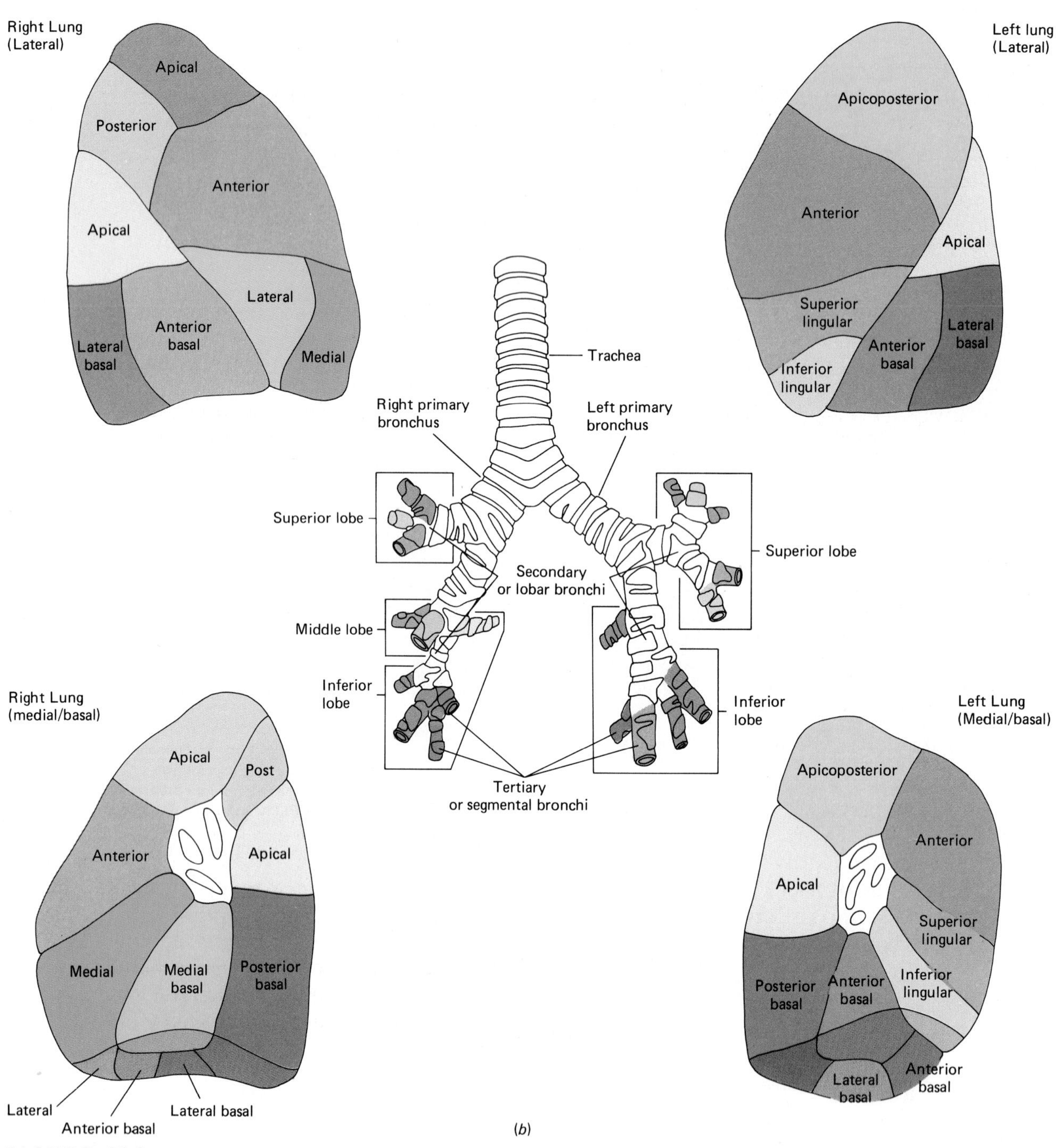

FIGURE 24-9

(*b*) The bronchopulmonary segments of the right and left lungs.

FOCUS ON . . . Choking

Choking kills an estimated 8000 to 10,000 people per year in the United States. Many of these have long suffered from some degree of paralysis or other malfunction of the muscles involved in swallowing, often without consciously realizing it. Swallowing is a very complex process in which the mouth, pharynx, esophagus, and vocal cords must be coordinated with great precision. Functional muscular disorders of this mechanism can originate in a variety of ways—as birth defects, for example, or from brain tumors or vascular accidents involving the swallowing center of the medulla.

Choking is more likely to occur in restaurants, where social interactions and unfamiliar surroundings are likely to distract one's attention from swallowing and where alcohol is more likely to be taken with the meal. A large number of choking victims have a substantial blood alcohol content upon autopsy, which suggests the possibility that in them a marginally effective swallowing reflex has been further and fatally compromised by the effects of alcohol on the brain.

Anyone who begins to choke and gasp during a meal should be asked if he or she can speak. If not, the person is probably suffering a laryngeal obstruction rather than a coronary heart attack. As a first step, deliver a strong blow to the victim's back with the open hand. If this fails, stand behind the victim, bring your arms around his waist, and clasp your hands just above his beltline. Your thumbs should be facing inward against his body. Then squeeze abruptly and strongly in an upward direction. In most instances the residual air in the lungs will pop the obstruction out like a cork from a bottle. This is called the **Heimlich maneuver.** It can also be performed in a horizontal position. If the Heimlich maneuver must be performed in the horizontal position, place the victim face up. Kneel astride his hips and with one of your hands on top of the other, place the heel of the bottom hand on the abdomen slightly above the navel but below the rib cage. Press into the victim's abdomen with a quick upward thrust. This may be repeated if necessary. If there is no response within 15 to 20 secs, it may be necessary to start cardiopulmonary resuscitation (CPR).

wall. The inner membrane of the pleura is the **visceral pleura** which covers the lungs. The potential space between these two pleural membranes is called the **pleural cavity,** and it is filled with **pleural fluid** secreted by the pleurae. The pleural fluid acts to lubricate and reduce the friction between the two pleural membranes during breathing.

Clinical highlight

Pleurisy is an inflammation of the pleura. It may be caused by infection or injury. Symptoms include coughing, shallow breathing, fever, chills, and pain. Many times pleurisy is a complication of another pulmonary disease.

The primary bronchus leading to the right lung divides into three secondary bronchi, the superior, middle, and inferior secondary bronchi. The left primary bronchus bifurcates into superior and inferior secondary bronchi. These five secondary bronchi supply the five lobes of the lungs. Within each lobe, the secondary bronchi branch into the tertiary bronchi which supply an area called the **bronchopulmonary segments** (Fig. 24-9*b*). These segments are surrounded by connective tissue. This arrangement makes surgical removal of a single bronchopulmonary segment feasible.

The bronchopulmonary segments are further subdivided into small compartments called **lobules.** Each lobule contains a terminal bronchiole and its pulmonary subdivisions, an arteriole, a venule, a lymphatic vessel, all surrounded by elastic connective tissue. Within the lobules, the terminal bronchioles divide into **respiratory bronchioles,** which branch into several **alveolar ducts** (Fig. 24-7*b*).

Clinical highlight

Bronchitis is an inflammation of the bronchial tree. Bronchitis may be due to a bacterial infection or to pulmonary irritants. Increased mucus secretion results in repeated coughing to clear the airways. Acute bronchitis is commonly encountered in children and the elderly. Symptoms include coughing, fever, chest pain, and malaise. Chronic bronchitis affects mainly middle-aged and elderly people. Symptoms include constant coughing, shortness of breath, and sputum expectoration. The irritated respiratory system is also at a higher risk of infection. Smoker's cough is usually chronic bronchitis.

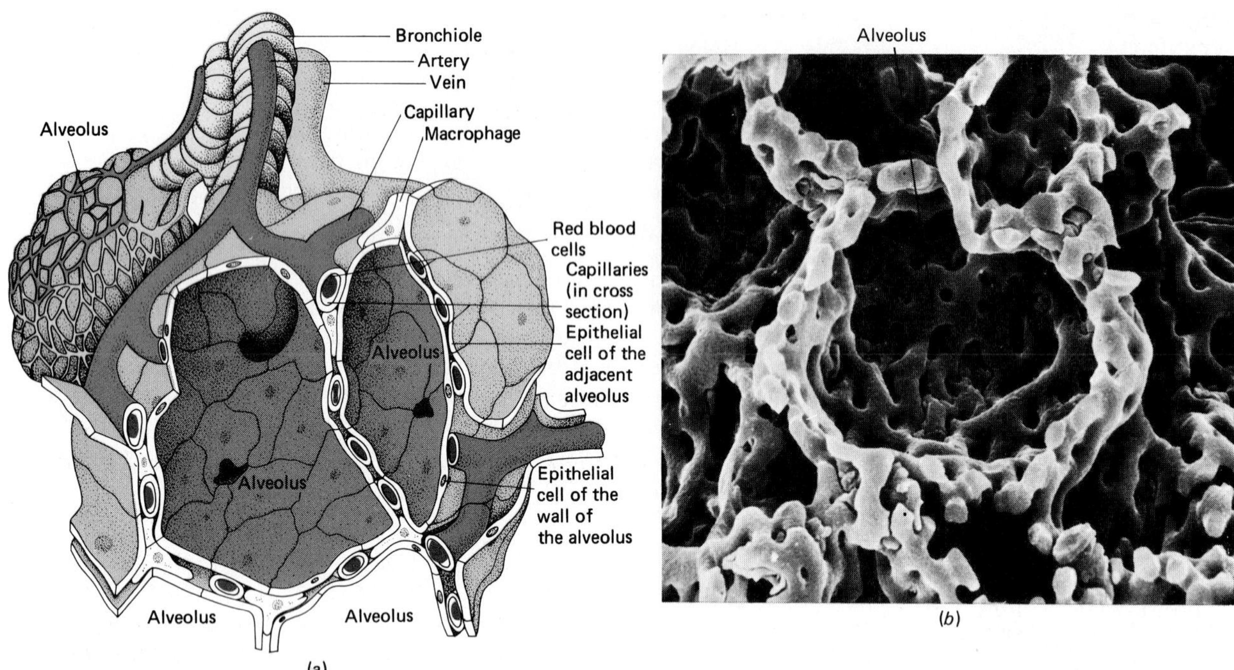

FIGURE 24-10

(*a*) Anatomy of the alveolus. (*b*) Pulmonary capillary network surrounding part of an alveolar sac (scanning electron micrograph, ×850). (From Kessell, R. G., and Kardon, R. H.: Tissues and Organs, *A Text-Atlas of Scanning Electron Microscopy.* San Francisco, W. H. Freeman Co., 1979.)

The alveolar ducts contain numerous outpocketings called **alveoli.** An alveolus is the unit of structure and function in external respiration (Fig. 24-10*a*,*b*). Some alveoli open into a common chamber called an **alveolar sac.** The alveolar wall is a single cell-layer thick and contains squamous **pulmonary epithelium** and occasional **septal cells.** Septal cells produce **pulmonary surfactant** (sur-**fak**-tant) which reduces surface tension of the fluids lining the alveoli. There are also *macrophages* (*dust cells*) present that remove dust particles and other substances (Fig. 24-10*a*).

The alveolar epithelium, the alveolar basement membrane, the pulmonary capillary basement membrane, and the endothelium of the capillary wall together form the **respiratory membrane** (Fig. 24-11). This membrane is extremely thin, measuring only 0.5 micrometer thick. The capillary network of the alveolar wall is more extensive than any other in the body. The estimated 300 million alveoli of the lungs provide an internal respiratory surface area of 70 square meters (753 ft^2).

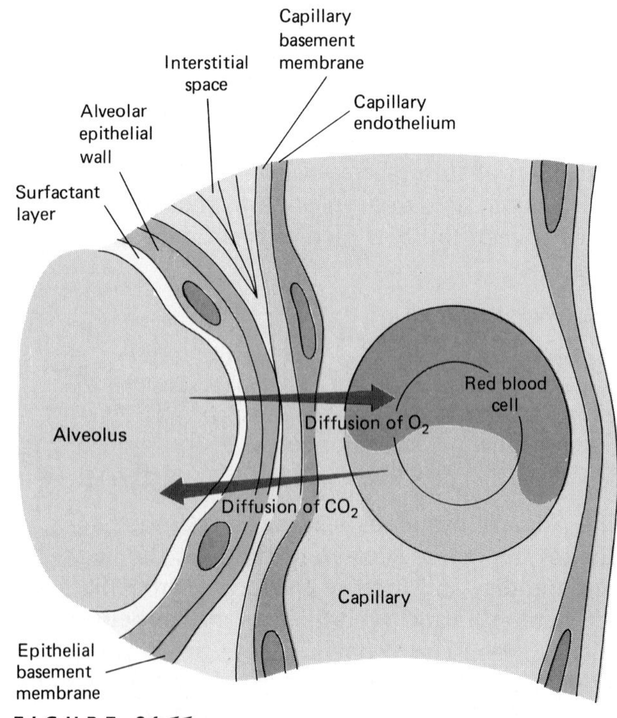

FIGURE 24-11

Anatomy of the respiratory membrane.

Clinical highlight

Emphysema is a condition in which the alveoli remain filled with air during expiration due to a loss of elasticity. Alveoli become damaged and merge into progressively larger air pockets. Gas exchange becomes diminished. The lungs become less elastic and, as a result, become permanently inflated. Much more work is expended in breathing. As the disease progresses, more scar tissue and air pockets form. Death is common. Emphysema is usually the result of a chronic irritation such as that caused by cigarette smoke. See Focus on Smoking and Air Pollution.

The pulmonary blood supply transports blood between the heart and the lungs

The **pulmonary trunk** divides into the **right** and **left pulmonary arteries,** directing oxygen-poor blood to the lungs. **Bronchial arteries** from the descending aorta take oxygen-rich blood to the bronchi and the nonrespiratory tissues of the lung. The **pulmonary capillaries** mark the place of gas exchange between the blood within the capillaries and the air in the alveoli. Two **pulmonary veins** from each lung take oxygen-rich blood to the left atrium of the heart.

Ventilation moves air into and out of the lungs

Ventilation is the movement of air into and out of the lungs. It consists of two stages: inspiration and expiration. **Inspiration (inhalation)** is the movement of air from the external environment into the lungs. **Expiration (exhalation)** is the movement of air from the lungs to the external environment. Ventilation depends upon pressure differences between the air of the external environment (atmospheric air) and the air within the lungs (alveolar air). See Figure 24-12 and Focus on CPR (p. 842).

The **atmospheric air pressure,** or barometric pressure, is the pressure exerted by the air upon the surface of the earth. At sea level, it is equivalent to the pressure required to raise a column of mercury (Hg) 760 millimeters high. Therefore, atmospheric pressure at sea level is equal to 760 mmHg.

The presence of the pleural fluid between the parietal and visceral layers of the pleural membrane exerts a pressure called the **intrapleural pressure.** Intrapleural pressure is normally below atmospheric pressure, or subatmospheric (756 mmHg). This is due to the differing rates of development of the thoracic wall and the lungs.

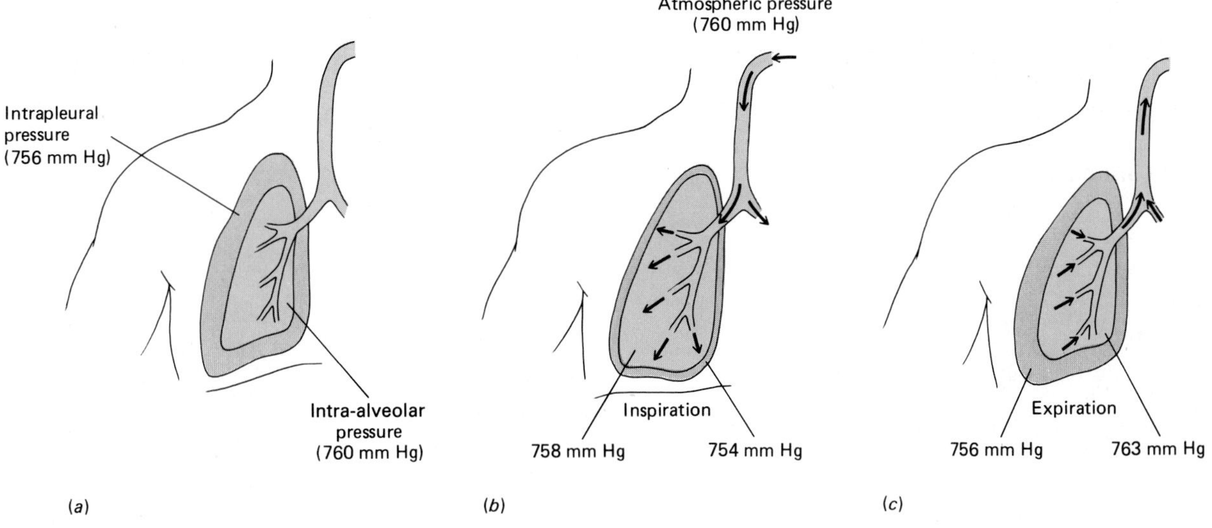

FIGURE 24-12

Pressure differences in pulmonary ventilation. *(a)* Lungs and pleural cavity prior to inspiration. *(b)* Inspiration. *(c)* Expiration.

FOCUS ON . . . Smoking and air pollution

The bronchogenic (originating in the bronchioles) form of lung cancer is apparently caused largely by cigarette smoking and is almost unknown among nonsmokers. To be sure, other factors make some contribution, but among responsible students of the problem there is no real controversy.

Smoking also increases one's susceptibility to most other respiratory diseases as well as to high blood pressure, stroke, heart disease, and even cancers of the bladder, kidney, mouth, larynx, and esophagus. The most striking health consequences of smoking are, however, lung cancer and COPD (chronic obstructive pulmonary disease—e.g., chronic bronchitis and emphysema).

Each puff of smoke destroys a small amount of ciliary epithelium in the bronchioles, which leads in turn to the accumulation of mucus in the bronchioles that causes what is called "smoker's cough." At the same time the smooth muscle of the bronchioles becomes hypertrophied, new mucus glands form and pour out their secretions into already overloaded passages, and the alveoli eventually collapse (see figure). The alkaloid **nicotine** in cigarette smoke also paralyzes cilia and interferes with the action of lung macrophages.

Nicotine has many effects on the body. It can reach the brain within 8 seconds after inhaling cigarette smoke. Here it initially stimulates the cerebral cortex, which can cause changes in behavior and mental activity. However, as its concentration decreases in the blood, it can cause withdrawal symptoms including nervousness, jitters, and even depression. Nicotine, by stimulating the adrenals which release epinephrine, increases heart rate and blood pressure. It also causes a peripheral vasoconstriction, decreasing peripheral temperature, especially in the hands and feet. Nicotine decreases the volume of urine formed by the kidneys. It affects the digestive system by dulling the taste buds, decreasing stomach contractions, and irritating the lining of the stomach (thus increasing the risk of peptic ulcers).

There is reason to think that smokers become addicted to nicotine. Little else seems to explain the persistence of smoking behavior even in those who seem strongly motivated to give it up. This has led to the attempt to develop *high* nicotine cigarettes, on the principle that a higher nicotine intake per cigarette should help to reduce the total number smoked and therefore the intake of tars believed to be responsible for inducing pulmonary cancer.

Cigarette smoke contains a complex mixture of hydrocarbons, carbon dioxide, carbon monoxide, particulate matter, cyanide, and even radioactive materials derived from the fertilizer used to grow the tobacco plant. Although the so-called "tar" fraction of tobacco smoke is probably the most dangerous, even low-tar and low-nicotine cigarettes cannot be considered safe. Tobacco smoke is a threat not only to smokers themselves but also to those around them, because it can seriously pollute the air that they also must breathe. Even the unborn infant is affected. Compared to nonsmoking mothers, smoking mothers have twice the number of stillbirths, spontaneous abortions, and infant deaths. They have 2–3 times the number of premature babies, and the babies of smoking mothers weigh about 6 ounces less at birth.

Air pollution itself constitutes a physiologically similar problem. Although almost anything can be a source of harmful impurities in the air, much air pollution tends to fall into the category of photochemical smog or sulfur oxide-particulate (SOP) smog. Most air pollution originates from transportation sources, especially automobiles. The automobile releases carbon monoxide and nitrogen oxide as combustion products. Additionally, gasoline evaporates from fuel tanks and crankcases, and some escapes unburned in exhaust gases. These interact in the pres-

In a newborn, the walls of the thorax (lined by parietal pleura) expand faster than the lungs (lined by visceral pleura). The cohesion of water molecules in the pleural cavity and their adhesion to the pleural layers force the lungs to expand with the thorax. The force of elastic fibers of the lungs resists this expansion but doesn't break the fluid bond. This creates a suction effect that causes the intrapleural pressure to drop below atmospheric pressure.

Changes in volume and pressure in the thorax and in the lungs demonstrate the inverse relationship between the volume of a gas and the pressure it exerts in a closed container. This relationship, called **Boyle's law,** states that with temperature constant, the pressure of a gas varies inversely with the volume of the gas. As the volume increases, the pressure decreases. Because the pressure results from the bombardment of gas molecules against the walls of the container, by increasing the volume of the container the number of bombardments, or the pressure, decreases.

ence of sunlight to produce ozone and a number of complex organic compounds, some of which are known to be carcinogenic and occur in cigarette smoke also. This medley is **photochemical smog. SOP smog** results mainly from combustion of sulfur-containing fossil fuels, especially from combustion occurring in power generation. Especially damaging components of SOP smog are carbon and cinder particles, nitrogen oxides, and sulfur oxides, particularly sulfur dioxide (see figure). The chronic effects of continuous air pollution are probably much the same as the effects of smoking.

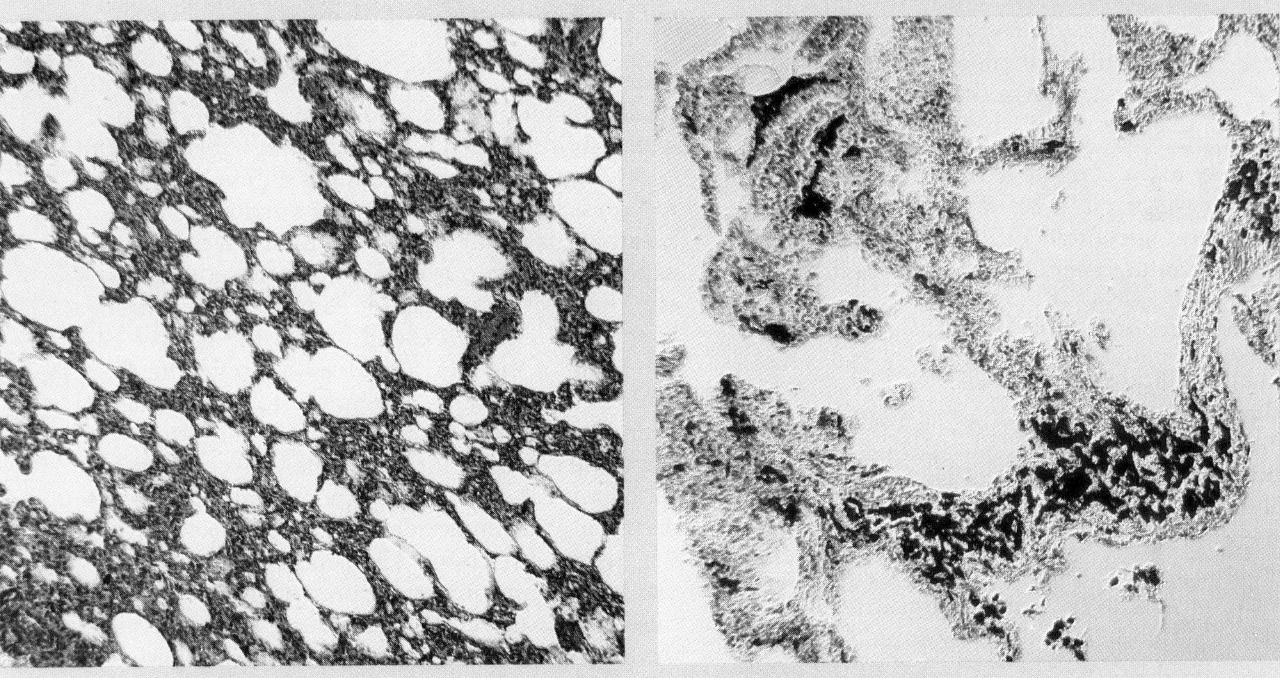

Lung tissue. *(a)* Normal lung tissue. *(b)* Lung tissue with accumulated carbon particles. Despite the body's defenses, when we inhale smoky, polluted air, especially over a long period of time, dirt particles do enter the lung tissue and remain lodged there. (Alfred Pasieka/Taurus Photos, Inc.)

If the volume of a container of gas is doubled, the pressure of the gas is halved.

Inspiration moves air into the lungs

Inspiration is initiated by the contraction of the diaphragm and the external intercostal muscles (Fig. 24-13). The diaphragm is a skeletal muscle separating the thorax from the abdomen. When the diaphragm contracts, its dome lowers, expanding the vertical dimension of the thoracic cavity. The external intercostal muscles are located between the ribs. When the external intercostals contract, they move the ribs up and out, increasing the horizontal dimension of the thoracic cavity. The contraction of these inspiratory muscles at the onset of inspiration causes the volume of the thorax to increase. This causes a drop in the intrapleural pressure from 756 mmHg to 754 mmHg. This drop in intrapleural pressure acts as a vacuum sucking the walls of the lungs outward.

As the lungs expand, the intra-alveolar pressure decreases from 760 mmHg to 758 mmHg due to the increased volume of the lungs. This creates a pressure gradient between the intra-alveolar pressure (758 mmHg) and the atmospheric pressure (760 mmHg). Air moves from a higher pressure to a lower pressure, or into the lungs (Fig. 24-12*b*). Air continues to move into the lungs until the intra-alveolar pressure once again equals the atmospheric pressure. Because the contraction of the inspiratory muscles requires energy in the form of ATP, inspiration is an active process.

Diaphragm and external intercostals contract ⟶ ↑ volume of thoracic cavity ⟶ ↓ Intrapleural pressure ⟶ lungs expand ⟶ ↑ lung volume ⟶ ↓ intra-alveolar pressure ⟶ air moves into lungs

Forced inspirations are able to expand the thoracic cavity to an even larger extent and increase the volume of inspired air. Forced inspirations also involve the contraction of the sternocleidomastoid, serratus anterior, and the scaleni muscles (Fig. 24-13*a*).

Expiration moves air out of the lungs

Expiration is the movement of air from the lungs to the external environment. Expiration is a passive process resulting from the relaxation of the inspiratory muscles (Fig. 24-13). The relaxation of the diaphragm moves its dome upward due to pressure exerted by abdominal viscera (especially the liver) from below. The relaxation of the external intercostals moves the rib cage down and in. This decreases the vertical and horizontal dimensions of the thoracic cavity. With a decrease in thoracic volume, the intrapleural pressure increases from 754 mmHg to 756 mmHg. This causes the lungs to recoil, decreasing their volume. The decreased lung volume increases intra-alveolar pressure to 763 mmHg. Now intra-alveolar pressure (763 mmHg) is greater than atmospheric pressure (760 mmHg) and air moves from the lungs through the respiratory tract and out of the body (Fig. 24-12*c*). This expiration of air continues until the intra-alveolar pressure becomes equal to the atmospheric pressure at 760 mmHg.

Inspiratory muscles relax ⟶ ↓ thoracic volume ⟶ ↑ intrapleural pressure ⟶ lungs recoil ⟶ ↓ lung volume ⟶ ↑ intra-alveolar pressure ⟶ air moves out of lungs

Forced expirations as occur during exercise are able to reduce the thoracic cavity even more, producing larger volumes of expelled air. Forced expirations are active; that is, they usually involve contractions of the abdominal muscles and internal intercostal muscles (Fig. 24-13*a*).

The work of breathing is reduced by surfactant

The amount of work the muscles must perform during inspiration depends upon the stretchability of the thorax and the lungs and upon the amount of resistance the air encounters within the respiratory passageways. At rest, the amount of work in breathing is about 1 to 2% of the total energy expended. Even during heavy exercise, the energy needed for ventilation is only about 3 to 5% of the total energy expenditure of the body.

Some of the work involved in stretching the thorax and the lungs is required to stretch elastic connective tissue. More work is required to overcome the cohesive force of water molecules associated with the respiratory membrane. The forces between water molecules create a surface tension that resists stretching. The septal cells of the alveolar epithelium produce a phospholipid mixture, **pulmonary surfactant,** that intersperses between the water molecules and reduces their cohesive force. This action markedly lowers the surface tension of the water, keeps the alveoli from collapsing, and reduces the energy needed to stretch the lungs.

The flow of air from the atmosphere into the lungs depends upon the pressure gradient between the atmosphere and the lungs and the resistance of the airways. The relationship is expressed as follows:

$$\text{Flow} = \frac{\text{pressure gradient}}{\text{resistance}}$$

The major factor affecting airway resistance is the diameter of the passageways. The larger the diameter of the airway, the less resistance to air flow. Normally, the airway resistance is negligible. Therefore, a large volume of air can move with only a small pressure difference. During a normal inspiration, the pressure gradient is only

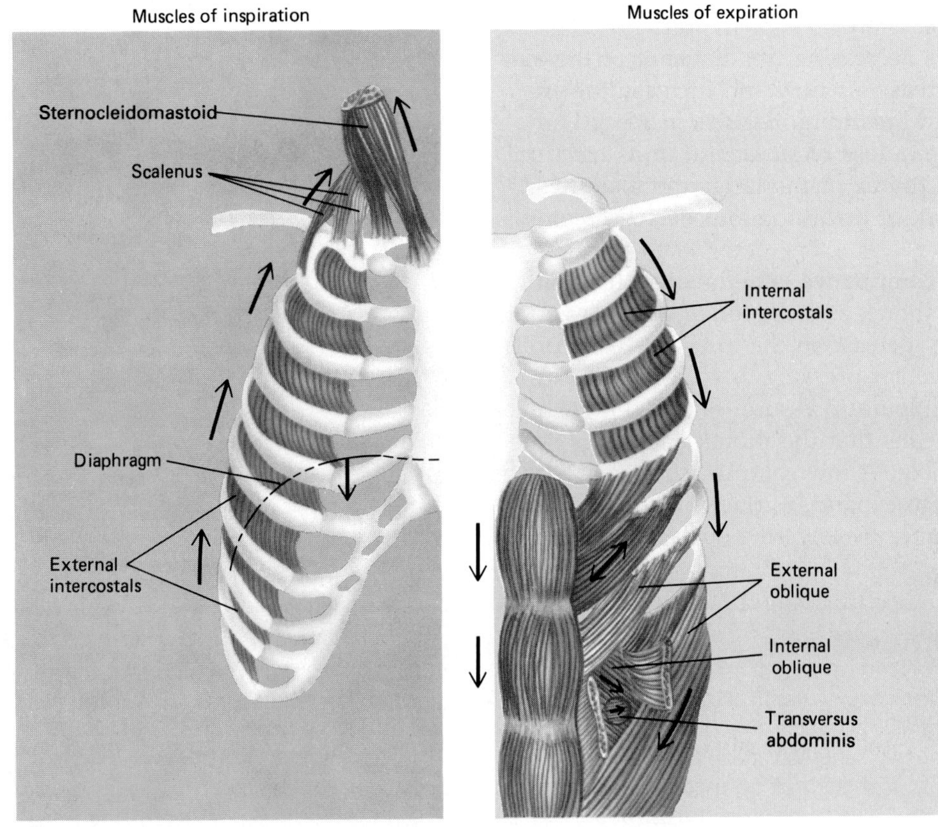

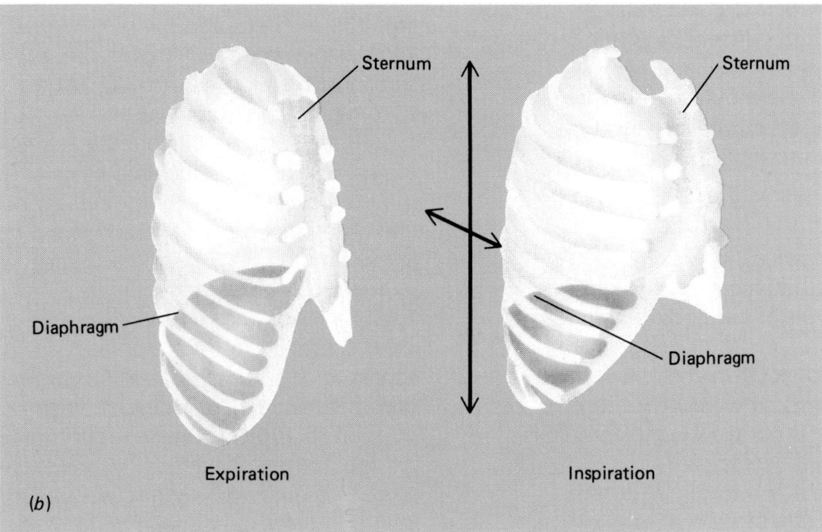

FIGURE 24-13

Respiratory muscles. (*a*) Inspiratory muscles and their actions (left), and expiratory muscles and their actions (right). (*b*) Changes in the size of the thoracic cavity during expiration and inspiration.

about 1–2 mmHg. This is enough of a difference to move about 500 milliliters of air into the lungs. (See the section on pulmonary air volumes for additional discussion.)

Any factor decreasing the diameter of the airways will decrease air flow and increase the energy needed in breathing. Besides increased airway resistance, a loss of surfactant or a structural change in the thorax or the lungs can also increase the work of breathing and decrease compliance.

The term **compliance** is defined as the distensibility of the thorax and the lungs. It is measured as the volume increase in the lungs for each unit increase in alveolar pressure or for each unit decrease in intrapleural pressure (Fig. 24-14). A high compliance means that the thorax and lungs are easily expandible. A low compliance means that they are hard to expand. Surfactant serves to increase compliance by lowering surface tension.

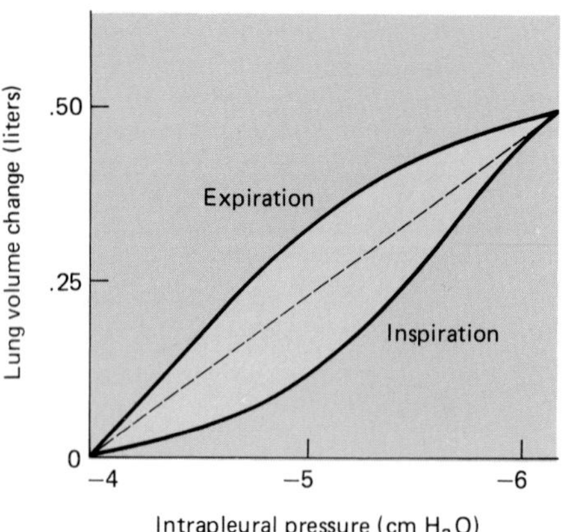

FIGURE 24-14

Compliance graph of a normal ventilation cycle of the lungs.

FOCUS ON . . . CPR

Cardiopulmonary resuscitation, or **CPR,** is a method for aiding victims of accidents or heart attacks who have suffered cardiac arrest and respiratory arrest. It should not be used if the victim has a pulse or is able to breathe. It must be started immediately, because irreversible brain damage may occur within about 3 minutes of respiratory arrest. Here are its ABCs:

Airway. Clear airway by extending victim's neck. This is sometimes sufficient to permit breathing to begin again.
Breathing. Use mouth-to-mouth resuscitation.
Circulation. Attempt to restore circulation by using external cardiac compression.

The procedure for CPR may be summarized as follows.

I. Establish unresponsiveness of victim.

II. Procedure for mouth-to-mouth resuscitation:
1. Place victim on his or her back on firm surface.
2. Clear throat and mouth and tilt head back so that chin points outward. Make sure that the tongue is not blocking airway. Pull tongue forward if necessary.
3. Pinch nostrils shut and forcefully exhale into victim's mouth. Be careful, especially in children, not to overinflate the lungs.
4. Remove your mouth and listen for air rushing out of the lungs.
5. Repeat about 12 times per minute. Do not interrupt for more than 5 seconds.

III. Procedure for external cardiac compression:
1. Place heel of hand on lower third of breastbone. Keep your fingertips lifted off the chest. (In infants, two fingers should be used for cardiac compression; in children, use only the heel of the hand.)
2. Place heel of the other hand at a right angle to and on top of the first hand.
3. Apply firm pressure downward so that the breastbone moves about 4 to 5 cm (1.6 to 2 in.) toward the spine. Downward pressure must be about 5.4 to 9 kg (12 to 20 lb) with adults (less with children). Excessive pressure can fracture the sternum or ribs, resulting in punctured lungs or a lacerated liver. This rhythmic pressure can often keep blood moving through the heart and great vessels of the thoracic cavity in sufficient quantities to sustain life.
4. Relax hands between compressions to allow chest to expand.
5. Repeat at the rate of at least 60 compressions per minute. (For infants or young children, 80 to 100 compressions per minute are appropriate.) If there is only one rescuer, 15 compressions should be applied, then two breaths, in a ratio of 15:2. If there are two rescuers, the ratio should be 5:1.

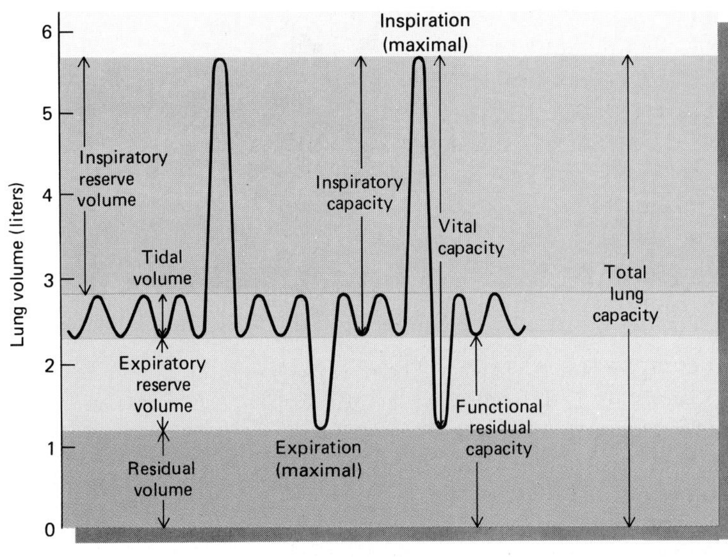

FIGURE 24-15

Spirogram showing pulmonary volumes and capacities.

Pulmonary air volumes and capacities are measured by a respirometer

The amount of air a person inspires and expires and the rate of ventilation are important clinical measurements that can be used to identify many pulmonary malfunctions. (See Focus on Medical Terminology of Respiration.) The instrument used to measure pulmonary dynamics is called a **respirometer** or **spirometer,** and its recording chart is called a **spirogram.**

During a normal inspiration, a person inspires about 500 milliliters of air. The person normally expires the same amount of air. This volume of air inspired (or expired) during normal breathing at rest is called the **tidal volume.** The amount of air that can be inspired above and beyond the normal tidal volume is called the **inspiratory reserve volume.** It averages about 3000 milliliters. The amount of air that can be expired beyond a normal tidal expiration is called the **expiratory reserve volume.** It normally is about 1200 milliliters. No matter how hard you try to exhale, there is always an amount of air remaining in the lungs. This 1200 milliliters of air remaining in the lungs is called the **residual volume.** The residual volume helps to keep the lungs from collapsing.

The sum of two or more pulmonary volumes is called a **pulmonary capacity.** The **inspiratory capacity** is the sum of the tidal volume and the inspiratory reserve volume. It is the total inspiratory potential of the lungs and averages about 3500 milliliters. The **expiratory capacity** is the sum of the tidal volume and the expiratory reserve volume. This 1700-milliliter capacity measures a total expiratory effort. The **functional residual capacity** is the sum of the expiratory reserve volume and the residual volume. It averages 2400 milliliters and is the volume of air normally within the lungs following a normal expiration. The **vital capacity** is the largest amount of air that can be ventilated. It spans from a maximal inspiratory effort to a maximal expiratory effort. The vital capacity is the sum of the tidal volume, the inspiratory reserve volume, and the expiratory reserve volume. It usually measures about 4700 milliliters. The **total lung capacity** is the sum of all the volumes of air that can exist at one time in the lungs. It is the sum of the tidal volume,

FOCUS ON . . . Medical terminology of respiration

Apnea—Cessation of breathing.
Bradypnea—Abnormally slow breathing.
Cheyne-Stokes breathing—An abnormal breathing pattern of alternating periods of hyperpnea and apnea, often a sign of impending death.
Dyspnea—Difficulty in breathing.
Eupnea—Normal breathing.
Hyperpnea—Abnormally rapid and deep breathing.
Orthopnea—Inability to breathe in a horizontal position.
Tachypnea—Rapid breathing, usually shallow.

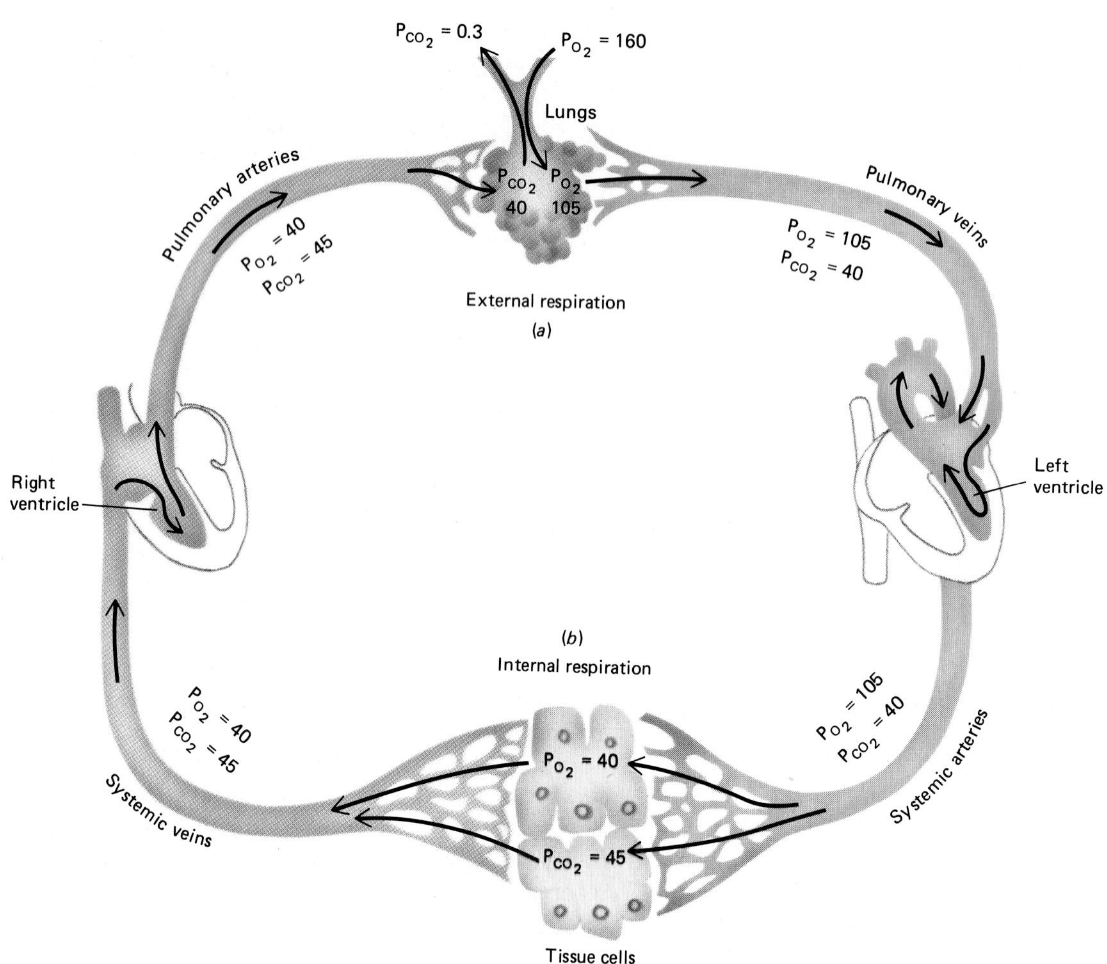

FIGURE 24-16

The partial pressures of gases involved in circulation and external respiration (*a*) and internal respiration (*b*). Values of pressures are in mmHg.

inspiratory reserve volume, expiratory reserve volume, and residual volume. It equals about 5900 milliliters. See Figure 24-15 for a summary of pulmonary volumes and capacities.

Not all of the air inspired reaches the alveoli and participates in gas exchange. Air remaining in the airways does not undergo gas exchange. Therefore the volume of the airways is referred to as the **anatomical dead space.** An average dead-space volume is about 150 milliliters.

For cases in which blood flow is not matched with air flow, some of the alveoli may not receive blood. Thus a certain amount of air is available for gas exchange but is not functionally used. The volume of the alveoli in such a condition is called the **physiologic dead space.** In a healthy person, the physiologic dead space of the lungs is about equal to the anatomical dead space of the passageways, or about 150 milliliters.

Clinical highlight

A number of conditions including vomiting, swallowing, and gagging interrupt ventilation and close the glottis, preventing substances from entering the lower respiratory tract. Besides coughing and sneezing (See Focus on the Cough Reflex and the Sneeze Reflex), there are other nonventilatory movements that interrupt normal air flow through the respiratory tract. Most of these modified movements are reflexes.

Hiccups result from spasms of the diaphragm that cause an inspiration that closes the glottis and produces the characteristic sound. **Yawning** involves a deep inspiration that occurs through a widely opened mouth. It is often accompanied by drowsiness. Although the specific cause and function of yawning are uncertain, it does result in an opening of alveoli and may help to prevent atelectasis (collapsed lung) and it does increase venous return. **Crying** is an inspiration followed by repeated short expirations with the glottis remaining open and the vocal cords vibrating. Characteristic facial expressions usually denote a negative emotional state. **Laughing** is similar in process to crying but it has a different rhythm of movements. Facial expressions usually denote a positive emotional state.

Minute respiratory volume is the total air entering the respiratory tract in one minute

The total amount of air that flows into the respiratory tract in one minute is called the **minute respiratory volume (MRV).** The MRV is equal to the breathing rate per minute times the tidal volume. Using average values for breathing rate (12 breaths/min) and tidal volume (500 ml), a normal MRV would equal 6000 milliliters per minute.

Alveolar ventilation measures the effective lung ventilation

Alveolar ventilation measures the amount of incoming air that actually enters the alveoli each minute and is not part of the anatomical dead space. Therefore, the alveolar ventilation is a measurement of the physiologically effective ventilation of the lungs because it measures the amount of incoming air that can undergo gas exchange with the pulmonary capillaries. The formula for calculating alveolar ventilation is:

Alveolar ventilation = breathing rate × (tidal volume − physiological dead space)

By using average values for breathing rate (12 breaths/min), tidal volume (500 ml), and physiological dead space (150 ml), a normal alveolar ventilation is about 4200 milliliters per minute. (See Focus on Respiratory Disorders.)

External respiration involves gas exchange between the blood and the lungs

Dalton's law states that each gas in a mixture of gases in a container will exert its own pressure on the sides of the container as if there were no other gases present. The pressure exerted by each gas in a mixture is called the **partial pressure** (designated by a capital P) of that particular gas. Each gas in a mixture of gases will diffuse along its own gradient, from a greater partial pressure to a lesser partial pressure, regardless of the direction of diffusion of any other gas in the mixture. The total pressure exerted by the entire mixture is the sum of all the partial pressures of the individual gases in the mixture. Atmospheric pressure is equal to the sum of all the gases in the atmosphere. The major gases in the atmosphere are nitrogen, oxygen, carbon dioxide, and water vapor.

$$\begin{aligned}\text{Atmospheric pressure} \\ &= P_{N_2} + P_{O_2} + P_{CO_2} + P_{H_2O} \\ &= 760 \text{ mmHg}\end{aligned}$$

The partial pressure of any one of these gases is equal to the percent of that gas in the atmosphere multiplied by the atmospheric pressure. Atmospheric air consists of 21% oxygen and 0.04% carbon dioxide.

$$\begin{aligned}\text{Atmospheric } P_{O_2} \\ &= \text{atmospheric pressure} \times 21\% \\ &= 760 \text{ mmHg} \times 21\% \\ &= 159.6 \text{ mmHg}\end{aligned}$$

$$\begin{aligned}\text{atmospheric } P_{CO_2} \\ &= \text{atmospheric pressure} \times 0.04\% \\ &= 760 \text{ mmHg} \times 0.04\% \\ &= 0.3 \text{ mmHg}\end{aligned}$$

External respiration is the gas exchange taking place between the air in the alveoli and the blood in the pulmonary capillaries (Fig. 24-16*a* and Table 24-1). Efficient gas exchange by diffusion is enhanced by the extensive network of capillaries that carry red blood cells single file under a very low pressure and velocity. The amount of gas exchanged across the respiratory membrane involves a diffusion of gases based on their partial

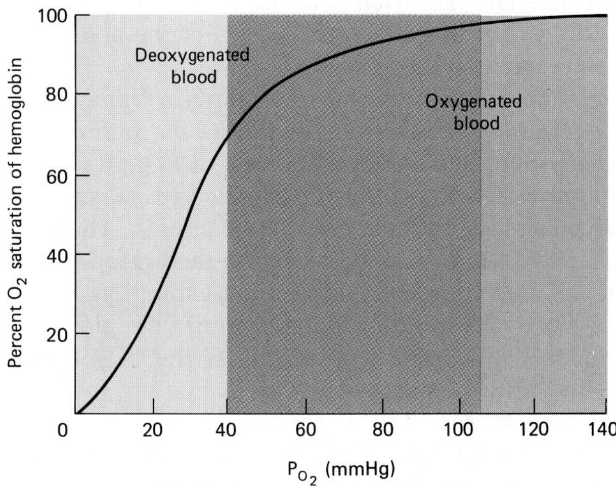

FIGURE 24-17

A normal oxyhemoglobin dissociation curve.

TABLE 24-1

Partial pressures (in mmHg) of respiratory gases

Gas	Atmospheric air (sea level)	Inspired air	Expired air	Alveolar air	Arterial blood	Tissue cells	Venous blood
P_{O_2}	160	152	120	105	105	40	40
P_{CO_2}	0.3	0.3	32	40	40	45	45

pressures and their solubility in water. This relationship **(Henry's law)** states that the amount of a gas that will dissolve in a liquid, with temperature remaining constant, is directly proportional to the partial pressure of the gas and its solubility coefficient. The solubility coefficient is a measure of the degree of affinity of the gas for the liquid. The solubility coefficient of oxygen is low at a value of 0.024 and that of carbon dioxide is high, 0.57. The diffusion of a gas in a liquid is its movement from a high pressure to a lower pressure.

Blood entering the pulmonary capillaries is relatively deoxygenated with a low partial pressure of oxygen (P_{O_2}) and a high partial pressure of carbon dioxide (P_{CO_2}). Newly inspired air in the alveoli has a higher P_{O_2} than that in the blood, whereas its P_{CO_2} is lower than the blood P_{CO_2}.

The P_{O_2} of inspired air is 160 mmHg and the P_{CO_2} of inspired air is 0.3 mmHg. The P_{O_2} of alveolar air is about 105 mmHg. The P_{O_2} of the blood entering the pulmonary capillaries is 40 mmHg. By diffusion, O_2 enters the capillaries from the alveoli. This diffusion continues until the P_{O_2} of the plasma becomes equal to that of the alveoli (105 mmHg).

The P_{CO_2} of alveolar air is about 40 mmHg, and the P_{CO_2} of the blood entering the pulmonary capillaries is 45 mmHg. CO_2 will diffuse from the blood into the alveoli until the blood P_{CO_2} and the alveolar P_{CO_2} become equal at 40 mmHg. The CO_2 that diffuses from the blood into the alveoli is eliminated from the body during expiration. The O_2 that diffuses from the alveoli into the blood is replenished during inspiration. As the CO_2 mixes with air in the airways during expiration, it becomes diluted. The P_{CO_2} of expired air is about 32 mmHg. During expiration, O_2 also mixes with dead-space air so that the P_{O_2} of expired air is 120 mmHg.

Internal respiration is gas exchange between the blood and the tissue cells

Internal respiration is the gas exchange taking place between the plasma of the systemic capillaries and the tissue cells (Fig. 24-16*b* and Table 24-1). The P_{O_2} of arterial blood is 105 mmHg and the P_{CO_2} of arterial blood is 40 mmHg. The P_{O_2} of tissue cells averages about 40 mmHg, and the P_{CO_2} in the tissue cells is about 45 mmHg. During cellular metabolism, O_2 is being used and CO_2 is being produced. In passing through the systemic capillaries, gases diffuse down their pressure gradients between the blood and the tissue cells.

O_2 diffuses from the capillary blood through the interstitial fluid into the tissue cells until the P_{O_2} of the blood reaches 40 mmHg. CO_2 diffuses from the cells through the interstitial fluid into the blood until the P_{CO_2} of the blood rises to 45 mmHg. The blood leaving the tissue capillaries (venous blood) is lower in O_2 and higher in CO_2 than the arterial blood that entered the capillaries. This venous blood returns to the heart, enters the pulmonary circulation, and undergoes external respiration with the alveoli.

Gas transport is the movement of O_2 and CO_2 through the blood

The oxygen added to the blood at the lungs is of no use to the tissue cells until it is distributed to them. The carbon dioxide released by the cells also needs to be transported to the lungs to be expelled. Mechanisms exist in the blood that ensure efficient gas transport.

The transport of oxygen involves hemoglobin

The blood carries O_2 and CO_2 throughout the body and thus plays a crucial role in external and internal respiration. The solubility of O_2 in the blood is so low that only a small amount of O_2 is dissolved in the plasma. There are only 3 milliliters of dissolved O_2 in 1 liter of arterial blood. Yet 1 liter of arterial blood contains a total of 197 milliliters of O_2. More than 98% of the O_2 (194 ml) is bound to the hemoglobin of red blood cells. Hemoglobin is found within red blood cells instead of being free in the plasma. Within the red blood cells the hemoglobin does not appreciably change the osmotic pressure of the plasma and also does not increase its viscosity.

Hemoglobin bound to O_2 is called **oxyhemoglobin.** Each hemoglobin molecule has four subunits, each containing a heme group and a protein group. The heme contains an iron atom that can combine with a molecule of O_2. A hemoglobin molecule is capable of carrying four molecules of O_2. In this state, oxyhemoglobin is referred to as being *fully saturated* (with O_2). The oxygenation of one of the four heme groups greatly accelerates the oxygenation of the others. This **heme-heme effect** increases the rate and efficiency of O_2 uptake at the respiratory membrane.

The principal factor determining the amount of O_2 that will combine with hemoglobin is the P_{O_2}. The extent to which hemoglobin becomes saturated with O_2 is represented by an oxyhemoglobin dissociation curve (Fig. 24-17). The sigmoid (S-shaped) nature of the curve is due to the heme-heme effect.

From the graph, note that when P_{O_2} levels are low, hemoglobin is only partially saturated with O_2 and is called *reduced hemoglobin*. The reduced hemoglobin has less affinity for the O_2 and gives it up more easily. At a high P_{O_2}, the hemoglobin shows a greater affinity for O_2 and becomes saturated.

During internal respiration, the P_{O_2} of the tissue cells under normal conditions is about 40 mmHg. At this P_{O_2}, the affinity for O_2 is lower, and hemoglobin gives up O_2 at the systemic capillaries. The P_{O_2} of the alveoli is high, and the hemoglobin of the pulmonary capillaries has a high affinity for O_2 and picks up large amounts of O_2 during external respiration.

Note that from 60 to 100 mmHg, the curve shows a plateau, with hemoglobin saturation being about 90%. So even if the P_{O_2} of inspired air decreases to 60 mmHg, the hemoglobin would still become about 90% saturated with O_2. This is important when considering the effects of high altitude or pulmonary diseases that can decrease alveolar P_{O_2}. At a P_{O_2} of 40 mmHg, the hemoglobin is still about 75% saturated. Therefore, at rest, venous blood leaving the tissues still contains high amounts of O_2. During exercise, the P_{O_2} of the tissue cells may decrease rapidly, approaching a P_{O_2} below 20 mmHg. The steep slope of the curve (P_{O_2} of 40 to 0 mmHg) shows the great extent to which hemoglobin will unload O_2.

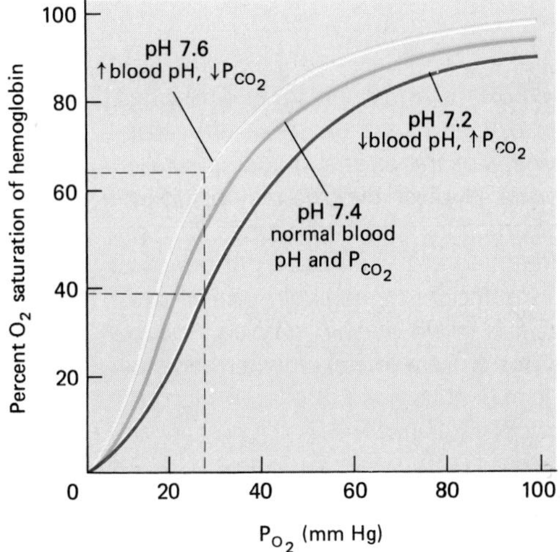

FIGURE 24-18

Shifts in the oxyhemoglobin dissociation curve resulting from changes in pH and P_{CO_2}. Note from the dotted lines that a shift of the curve to the right means there is less saturation at any given P_{O_2}. A shift to the left shows more saturation at any given P_{O_2}.

Metabolic factors can affect the oxyhemoglobin dissociation curve

A number of metabolic factors influence the affinity of hemoglobin to oxygen. Tissue acidity, P_{CO_2}, temperature, and diphosphoglyceric acid (DPG) can cause shifts in the oxyhemoglobin dissociation curve. Increases in each of these factors shifts the dissociation curve to the right. The shift to the right means that at any given P_{O_2} the hemoglobin is less saturated with oxygen. Increases in tissue alkalinity, decreased P_{CO_2}, and decreased temperature cause a shift in the oxyhemoglobin dissociation curve to the left. A shift to the left means that at any given P_{O_2} the hemoglobin is more saturated with oxygen.

FOCUS ON . . . Respiratory disorders

Asthma (*asthma,* panting). Asthma is a respiratory condition in which air flow becomes obstructed due to bronchoconstriction, increased mucus secretion, and inflammation. The smooth muscle of small bronchi and bronchioles spasm. Breathing is difficult and wheezing is present. The majority of asthma attacks are allergic reactions to substances in the air or in food.

Atelectasis (*ateles,* incomplete; *ektasis,* dilation). Atelectasis is a partially or completely collapsed lung. The primary cause is obstruction of the bronchus serving the affected part of the lung. Symptoms include pain, dyspnea, cyanosis, fever, a drop in blood pressure, and shock.

Bronchogenic carcinoma (lung cancer) (*broncho,* bronchial tree; *genic,* produced from; *carcin,* cancer; *oma,* tumor). Lung cancer is often initiated by irritants to the bronchi. Increased mucus secretion and inactivity of the cilia allow irritants to enter the lungs. Alveolar tissue is destroyed and emphysema follows. The lower respiratory tract is now ripe for invasion by squamous cancer cells. As the cells spread, more and more obstruction occurs. Metastasis to other body areas also occurs. Metastasis of other tissue cancers can infect the lungs. Heavy cigarette smokers are more than 20 times more likely to develop lung cancer than nonsmokers.

Carbon monoxide poisoning Carbon monoxide is a colorless, odorless gas. It is found in exhaust fumes of vehicles and in cigarette smoke. The affinity of hemoglobin for carbon monoxide is more than 200 times that of oxygen. When carbon monoxide is inhaled, it readily displaces the oxygen on hemoglobin, leading to a condition of hypoxia. Death from carbon monoxide poisoning results from asphyxia. Symptoms include dizziness, headache, weakness, shortness of breath, nausea, and unconsciousness. Treatment involves the administration of hyperbaric oxygen.

Common cold (coryza) The common cold is viral in origin. Several viruses can cause colds, with rhinoviruses being one of the major ones. The mucous membrane of the upper respiratory tract becomes inflamed, producing a watery mucus. Nasal congestion, sneezing, headaches, and coughing are common symptoms. Bacterial infection can accompany a cold, leading to other symptoms such as fever and ear infections. Antiviral sprays containing a type of interferon have been introduced with mixed reviews.

Chronic obstructive pulmonary disease (COPD) COPD is a functional category of pulmonary disorders that are indicative of a persistent obstruction of air flow through the bronchi. Asthma, bronchitis, and emphysema are often collectively referred to as COPD because they obstruct these airways. COPD is the major chronic pulmonary disorder in terms of U.S. morbidity rates, with heavy cigarette smoking being a significant factor.

Cyanosis (*kyanosis,* blue coloring). Cyanosis is a bluish discoloration of the mucous membranes and the skin due to high amounts of reduced hemoglobin in the blood. Reduced hemoglobin is lacking in oxygen and is a purplish red in color.

Decompression sickness (bends) Decompression sickness occurs as the result of nitrogen bubbles forming in the blood. These bubbles can block vessels and result in muscle and joint pain. Nitrogen dissolved in the blood can escape through the alveoli if a diver ascends slowly. With rapid ascension, nitrogen comes out of solution before reaching the lungs and bubbles form in the blood.

Hypoxia Hypoxia is a term meaning diminished availability of oxygen to the tissues. If the cause is due to a low P_{O_2} of the arterial blood, it is called *hypoxic hypoxia.* Hypoxic hypoxia may result from an airway obstruction, fluid in the lungs, or a response to breathing at high altitudes. If the cause is due to an insufficient hemoglobin concentration of the blood, it is called *anemic hypoxia.* Anemic hypoxia may result from anemia, hemorrhage, or binding-site competitors such as carbon monoxide. In *histotoxic hypoxia,* the cause is an inability of the tissue cells to utilize oxygen properly. If the blood is unable to deliver oxygen to the tissue cells at a rate sufficient to meet their needs, the resulting hypoxia is called *stagnant hypoxia.* Common causes are heart failure and circulatory shock.

Influenza (flu) (*influentia,* flowing in). Influenza is an acute virus infection usually entering the body through the respiratory tract. Symptoms include fever, chills, headache, sore throat, and muscular aches. Vaccines are available to protect against certain types of flu.

Pneumonia (*pneumon,* spirit, breath; *ia,* condition of). Pneumonia is an acute infection of the alveoli caused by a variety of microbes. One of the major agents is the bacterium *Streptococcus pneumoniae.* Alveolar edema occurs in this disease, which reduces the effective respiratory area. Less oxygen diffuses through the alveoli and the blood may become hypoxic.

Pneumothorax (*pneumon,* breath; *thorax,* thorax, chest). Pneumothorax is the condition in which the pleural cavity becomes filled with air or gas. The result is the collapse of the lung on the affected side. Pneumothorax may be caused by a perforation of the thoracic wall or it may be the result of a pulmonary disease.

Pulmonary edema (*pleumon,* lung; *ede,* swelling). Pulmonary edema is an accumulation of interstitial fluid in the alveoli. Increased pulmonary capillary pressure or permeability can result in edema. Common symptoms include dyspnea, wheezing, restlessness, and tachypnea.

Pulmonary embolism Pulmonary embolism is a condition in which an abnormal mass is lodged within the lung, causing an obstruction to pulmonary circulation. The embolus is commonly a blood clot from the pelvis or leg. This results in a decreased functioning of the area supplied by the blocked vessel. A large pulmonary embolus can result in sudden death. Symptoms include chest pain, tachycardia, cough, blood in sputum, and rapid, shallow breathing. Many conditions serve as risk factors for pulmonary embolism, including body trauma, immobilization, and malignancies. Anticoagulants and clot-dissolving enzymes are used in treatment.

Respiratory distress syndrome (RDS) of the newborn RDS is also called *hyaline membrane disease.* It is usually the result of insufficient surfactant. When the infant breathes, the surface tension of the alveoli remains very high and the alveoli collapse during expiration. Symptoms include difficulty in breathing, and death may follow. The alveoli become filled with a fluid high in proteins resembling a hyaline membrane. Intervention includes positive end-expiratory pressure (PEEP) and addition of surfactant.

Sudden infant distress syndrome (SIDS) SIDS, or crib death, is the leading cause of death in infants from 1 week to 1 year old. Although the exact cause is unknown, several possible reasons have been postulated, including viral or bacterial infection, malfunction of the respiratory center, hypoxia, overheating, and allergic responses.

Tracheitis (*trach,* trachea; *itis,* inflammation). Tracheitis is an inflammation of the trachea.

Tracheostomy (*trach,* trachea; *ostomy,* the cutting of an artificial opening). Tracheostomy is a surgical opening of the trachea through the neck with the insertion of a tube to facilitate ventilation and the passage of secretions.

Tuberculosis (*tuberculum,* tuber, swelling). Tuberculosis is a lung infection caused by the bacterium *Mycobacterium tuberculosis.* Tuberculosis is contagious and can be deadly. The bacterium destroys lung tissue, which is replaced by scar tissue. Gas exchange becomes diminished. Antibiotics are effective in treating the disease. Patients also should get plenty of rest.

Effect of pH and P_{CO_2} on hemoglobin With increases in hydrogen ion concentration, the affinity of hemoglobin for oxygen decreases and the oxyhemoglobin dissociation curve shifts to the right (Fig. 24-18). Hydrogen ions bind to hemoglobin, altering its chemical structure in such a way that less oxygen can be bound. This is known as the **Bohr effect.**

Increases in P_{CO_2} have a similar effect on the affinity of hemoglobin to oxygen. Higher amounts of CO_2 can shift the following reaction to the right:

$$CO_2 + H_2O \rightleftarrows H_2CO_3 \rightleftarrows H^+ + HCO_3^-$$

Carbonic anhydrase, located within the red blood cells, catalyzes the reaction. Hydrogen ions formed from the dissociation of carbonic acid (H_2CO_3) lower the pH. The hydrogen ions bind to hemoglobin, decreasing its affinity for oxygen. The tissue cells are able to receive more O_2 as a result.

Effect of temperature on hemoglobin Increases in temperature lower the affinity of hemoglobin for oxygen and also shift the dissociation curve to the right. Decreases in temperature shift the curve to the left (Fig. 24-19).

The acidity, P_{CO_2}, and temperature within a cell increase with increased metabolic activity of the cell. A higher cellular metabolism also increases the amount of oxygen required by the cell. By decreasing the affinity of hemoglobin to oxygen, these factors serve to allow more oxygen to be released by the hemoglobin; thereby, more oxygen is made available to the cells.

Effect of DPG on hemoglobin Whenever the oxygen supply to the tissues decreases, red blood cells produce **2,3-diphosphoglyceric acid** (dye-*fos*-foe-gli-**seer**-ik) **(DPG).** DPG reversibly binds to hemoglobin, altering its structure and decreasing the affinity of hemoglobin for oxygen. The hemoglobin releases oxygen more readily to the cells that need it.

Fetal hemoglobin Fetal hemoglobin is structurally distinct from adult hemoglobin. The fetal hemoglobin has a higher affinity for oxygen than does adult hemoglobin. Its dissociation curve is to the left of the mother's (see Fig. 24-20). Fetal blood has 50% more hemoglobin per unit of blood than adult hemoglobin and circulates faster due to a higher heart rate. The P_{O_2} of maternal blood flowing into the placenta is about 40 mmHg. The P_{O_2} of fetal blood entering the placenta is 20 mmHg and its hemoglobin is 58% saturated with O_2. In the placenta, oxygen readily leaves the maternal hemoglobin and binds to the fetal hemoglobin. The maternal hemoglobin leaving the placenta has a percent oxygen saturation of under 60%, whereas fetal hemoglobin is more than 80% saturated with O_2.

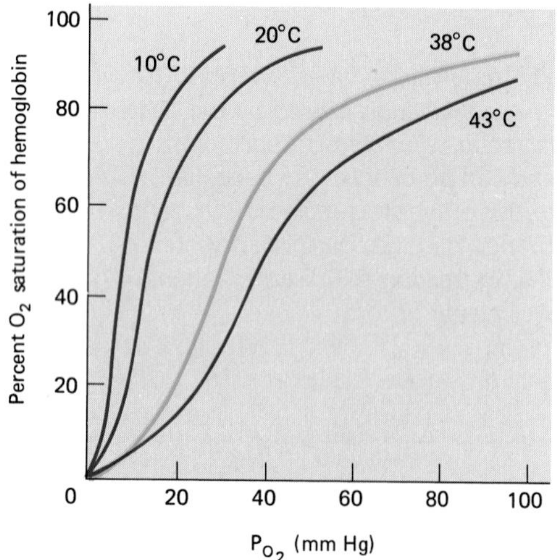

FIGURE 24-19

Shifts in the oxyhemoglobin dissociation curve associated with changes in temperature.

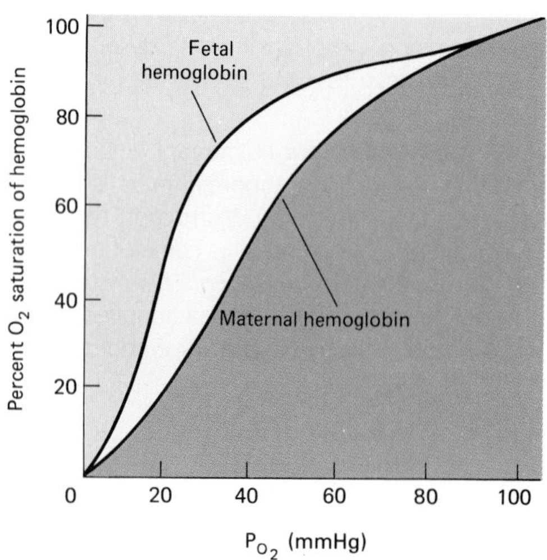

FIGURE 24-20

A comparison of the oxyhemoglobin dissociation curves of fetal and maternal hemoglobin.

Carbon dioxide are transported dissolved, as carbaminohemoglobin, or as bicarbonate

Carbon dioxide produced by the tissue cells is transported by the blood to the pulmonary capillaries where it diffuses into the alveoli and is expired from the body (Fig. 24-21). Only about 4 milliliters of carbon dioxide are transported in each 100 milliliters of blood. The transport of carbon dioxide by the blood is in three basic forms: dissolved carbon dioxide, carbaminohemoglobin (kar-*bam*-ih-no-*he*-moe-**glow**-bin), and bicarbonate. The smallest percent (7%) of carbon dioxide transported by the blood is **dissolved** in the plasma.

About 23% of the carbon dioxide is transported attached to hemoglobin, with a small amount attaching to plasma proteins. Carbon dioxide reacts with reduced hemoglobin to form **carbaminohemoglobin.** The carbon dioxide forms a loose reversible bond with the globin (protein) part of the hemoglobin molecule. The reduced hemoglobin has a higher affinity for carbon dioxide than fully saturated oxyhemoglobin. At the site of the systemic capillaries, hemoglobin releases oxygen, which raises its affinity for carbon dioxide. At the pulmonary capillaries, as oxygen combines to the hemoglobin, its affinity to carbon dioxide decreases and it releases the carbon dioxide that diffuses into the alveoli.

The highest percent of carbon dioxide (70%) transported by the blood is in the form of **bicarbonate.** As carbon dioxide enters the blood from the tissue interstitium it diffuses into the red blood cells. Here it reacts with water to form carbonic acid. Carbonic anhydrase, an enzyme within the red blood cells, catalyzes this reaction some 5000-fold. The carbonic acid dissociates into H^+ ions and bicarbonate (HCO_3^-) ions. The H^+ ions bind to hemoglobin. The bicarbonate ions diffuse from the red blood cells into the plasma in exchange for Cl^- ions. This is referred to as the **chloride shift.** Once in the red blood cells, the Cl^- ions combine with K^+ ions. The HCO_3^- ions in the plasma combine with Na^+ ions. When the

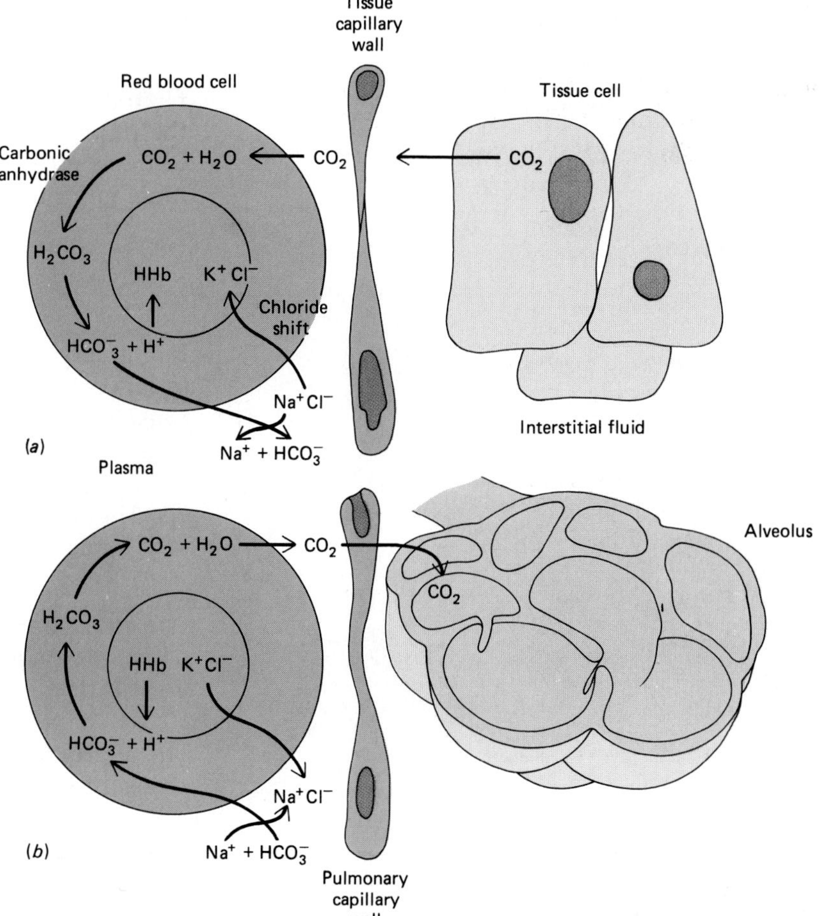

FIGURE 24-21

Carbon dioxide transport. (*a*) Internal respiration. (*b*) External respiration.

sodium bicarbonate ($NaHCO_3$) reaches the pulmonary capillaries, it dissociates into Na^+ and HCO_3^- ions, with the HCO_3^- entering the red blood cells. Meanwhile, H^+ ions are released from hemoglobin and combine with the HCO_3^- ions to form H_2CO_3. The H_2CO_3 dissociates into CO_2 and H_2O. The CO_2 diffuses into the alveoli.

Control of respiration involves intrinsic and extrinsic factors

Intrinsic, or local, factors within the lungs serve to promote efficient gas exchange. Areas of the brain function to coordinate ventilations and to compensate for changes in the P_{CO_2}, P_{O_2}, and H^+ ion levels of the blood.

Local factors in the lungs promote efficient gas exchange

Local factors within the lungs help to promote efficient gas exchange in the more than 300 million alveoli there. The smooth muscles of the bronchioles are sensitive to changes in CO_2. The smooth muscle of the pulmonary arterioles leading into the pulmonary capillaries is sensitive to changes in O_2 and H^+ ions. The local effects of O_2 and H^+ ions on pulmonary arterioles are opposite to their effects on systemic arterioles.

Increases in CO_2 cause bronchiolar smooth muscle to relax. This results in a bronchodilation, or an increase in the diameter of the bronchioles. More CO_2 can be expired out of the body. Low levels of CO_2 cause a bronchoconstriction (Fig. 24-22*a*).

$\uparrow CO_2 \longrightarrow$ relaxation of bronchiolar smooth muscle $\longrightarrow$ bronchodilation $\longrightarrow \uparrow CO_2$ expired

$\downarrow CO_2 \longrightarrow$ contraction of bronchiolar smooth muscle $\longrightarrow$ bronchoconstriction $\longrightarrow \downarrow CO_2$ expired

When levels of O_2 are low in some alveoli, the smooth muscle of pulmonary arterioles contracts. This causes a vasoconstriction of the arterioles and less blood flows to these alveoli. In this way, blood is shunted away from alveoli with low amounts of oxygen and toward those alveoli with high amounts of O_2.

$\downarrow$ Alveolar $O_2 \longrightarrow$ contraction of arteriolar smooth muscle $\longrightarrow$ vasoconstriction $\longrightarrow$ blood shunted away from these alveoli

High amounts of O_2 result in a vasodilation of the pulmonary arterioles. With more blood going to those areas of the lungs with more oxygen, a more efficient gas exchange occurs (Fig. 24-22*b*).

$\uparrow$ Alveolar $O_2 \longrightarrow$ relaxation of arteriolar smooth muscle $\longrightarrow$ vasodilation $\longrightarrow \uparrow$ blood flow to these alveoli

Pulmonary arterioles are also sensitive to changes in local H^+ ion concentrations. Increased H^+ ions cause an arteriolar vasoconstriction. Decreased H^+ ions cause an arteriolar vasodilation. Changes in H^+ ion levels reflect mainly changes in P_{CO_2} levels. Higher P_{CO_2} levels increase the concentration of H^+ ions.

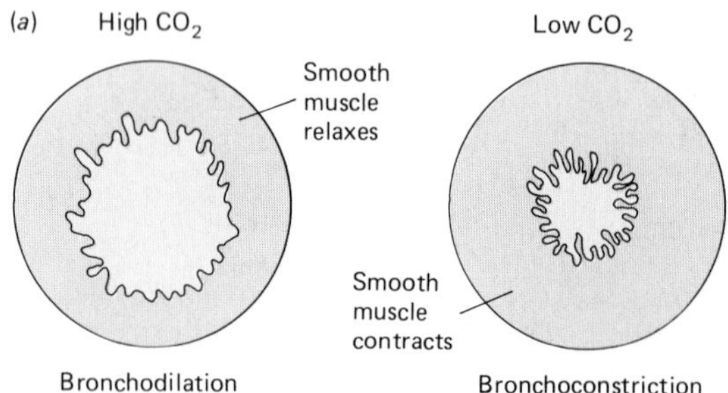

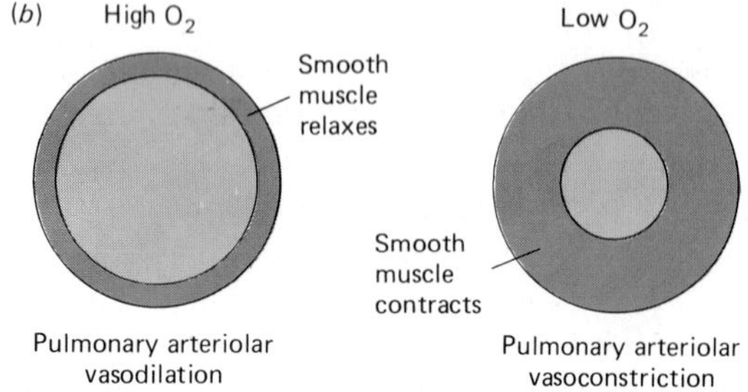

FIGURE 24-22

Local controls of external respiration.

The medulla contains the rhythmicity area controlling ventilation

The alternation of the inspiratory and expiratory stages of ventilation depends upon a cyclical stimulation of the inspiratory muscles. This stimulation originates from the respiratory centers of the brain located in the medulla and the pons (Fig.

24-23). Within the medulla are located the rhythmicity areas. The **medullary rhythmicity area** is composed of inspiratory neurons and expiratory neurons.

Impulses from **medullary inspiratory neurons** affect the inspiratory muscles, causing them to contract. Impulses to the diaphragm travel through the phrenic nerves, those to the external intercostals travel in intercostal nerves. After inspiration, the medullary inspiratory neurons cease firing. This causes the inspiratory muscles to relax and expiration to proceed. The inspiratory area of the respiratory center is believed to be autorhythmic. Thus it functions as the pacemaker of respiration. The medullary inspiratory neurons are active for about 2 seconds and then inactive for about 3 seconds. This provides for the cyclical alternation of inspiration and expiration.

The medullary inspiratory area is a diverse integrating center in that it receives input from many sources, including higher brain centers and the pons. The central chemoreceptors of the chemosensitive area of the medulla send impulses to the inspiratory area. The peripheral chemoreceptors and baroreceptors of the carotid and aortic bodies send afferent impulses through the glossopharyngeal (CN IX) and vagus (CN X) cranial nerves. The stretch receptors of the lungs send information to the inspiratory area.

There are also **expiratory neurons** within the respiratory center of the medulla. The expiratory neurons are believed to be inactive during normal quiet respiration. Normal expiration is a passive process brought about by a relaxation of the inspiratory muscles. With increased ventilation, the inspiratory area of the medulla activates the expiratory area. The expiratory neurons send impulses to the expiratory muscles (internal intercostals and abdominal muscles), causing them to contract. The expiratory area of the medulla receives input from the inspiratory area. This input is inhibitory.

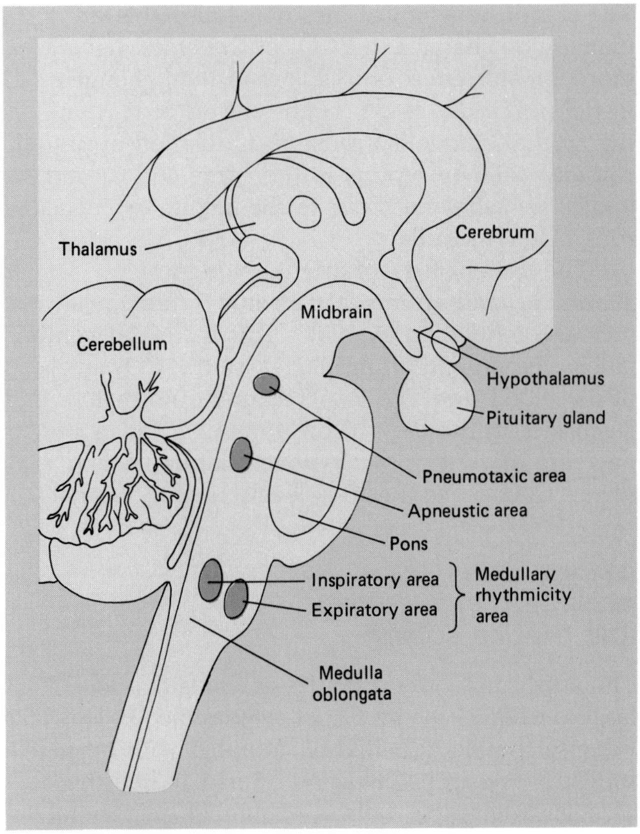

FIGURE 24-23

The respiratory center of the brain.

Pontile controls help coordinate inspiration and expiration

Respiratory centers in the pons (the pontile controls) help to control the transition from inspiration to expiration. The **pneumotaxic center** (*new*-moe-**tax**-ic) of the upper pons continuously sends inhibitory impulses to the medullary inspiratory area and the apneustic center of the pons. These impulses limit the time span of inspiration. This prevents an overinflation of the lungs. The **apneustic center** (ap-**new**-stik) of the lower pons sends stimulatory impulses to the medullary inspiratory area that act to extend the time span of inspiration. This gasping type of breathing is called apneustic breathing. The pneumotaxic center normally overrides the apneustic center.

The Hering–Breuer reflex prevents overinflation and overdeflation

Stretch receptors of the lungs provide an important protective mechanism (**Hering-Breuer reflex**), preventing the lungs from becoming overfilled or overdeflated. The activation of the stretch receptors by overdistension of the lungs activates these stretch receptors. The stretch receptors cause increased firing of vagal afferent neurons which serve to inhibit the medullary inspiratory center and the apneustic center of the pons. This facilitates expiration. The expiration of air from the lungs in turn ends the stimulation of the stretch receptors.

> ↑ Lung distension ⟶ ↑ firing of stretch receptors ⟶ ↑ vagal afferent stimulation ⟶ ↓ medullary inspiratory activity ⟶ expiration

A deflation reflex operates at the end of a forced expiration, preventing overdeflation. Here the decreased firing of the stretch receptors causes a stimulation of the medullary inspiratory center, which facilitates inspiration.

Cortical input to the medulla can alter ventilation

The cerebral cortex sends impulses to the respiratory center of the medulla. This provides a limited voluntary control of breathing. We are able to voluntarily interrupt the cyclical rhythm of respirations, especially in affording protection for the lungs. We are not able to hold our breaths for a very long period of time due to the effect of increased levels of P_{CO_2} on the inspiratory center of the medulla.

Chemical levels of the blood have a profound effect on ventilation

Ventilation supplies the body with O_2 and eliminates CO_2 from the body. The primary purpose of respiration is to regulate the levels of CO_2, H^+ ions, and O_2 in the body. The levels of these chemicals in the body fluids have a profound effect on ventilation.

Increases in **carbon dioxide** and **hydrogen ions** in the arterial blood have a direct excitatory effect on the respiratory center of the brain. This causes a marked increase in ventilation. More CO_2 is eliminated from the blood, and H^+ ions also decrease because the decreased CO_2 in the blood results in less carbonic acid formation. **Oxygen** has a less dramatic indirect effect on ventilation.

Chemoreceptors sensitive to changes in P_{O_2} and P_{CO_2} levels in the arterial blood are found in the aortic and carotid bodies. The *aortic bodies* are found at the aortic arch, and the *carotid bodies* are located at the bifurcations of the common carotid arteries. These receptors send input via afferent neurons to the respiratory centers, causing enhanced ventilation.

CARBON DIOXIDE AND HYDROGEN IONS AFFECT THE CHEMOSENSITIVE AREA OF THE MEDULLA

When the P_{CO_2} levels of arterial blood increase, ventilation increases. When H^+ ion levels of the arterial blood increase, ventilation increases, but not as much as with CO_2 increases. The proposed mechanism for both is a direct effect of H^+ ions on the chemosensitive area of the respiratory center.

The **chemosensitive area** has direct neuronal input to the inspiratory neurons of the respiratory center. The chemosensitive area is in the medulla. Although this area is very sensitive to changes in CO_2 levels in the blood, the mechanism for its activation is through H^+ ions. H^+ ions do not easily pass through the blood-brain barrier (choroid plexus), whereas CO_2 does. When the CO_2 enters the cerebrospinal fluid of the medulla, it reacts with H_2O to form carbonic acid (H_2CO_3). The H_2CO_3 dissociates into bicarbonate ions (HCO_3^-) and H^+ ions. The cerebrospinal fluid lacks buffers, and even a small change in H^+ ion concentration can have a dramatic effect on respiration via the chemosensitive area (Fig. 24-24). The response is almost instantaneous. This explains why changes in PCO_2 of the blood have a much greater effect on respiration than changes in the pH of the blood. Higher levels of P_{CO_2} in the arterial blood also cause a stimulation of **peripheral chemoreceptors** in the aortic and carotid bodies, which send input to the inspiratory neurons of the medulla.

The normal P_{CO_2} of arterial blood is 40 mmHg, and an increase of only 5 mmHg can increase ventilation by 100%. This increased ventilation, **hyperventilation,** decreases the CO_2 levels of the blood until the P_{CO_2} returns to normal. Decreases in the P_{CO_2} below 40 mmHg cause a decrease in ventilation, **hypoventilation,** which serves to increase the P_{CO_2} levels back to normal.

OXYGEN LEVELS ARE MONITORED BY THE AORTIC AND CAROTID BODIES

The aortic and carotid bodies are sensitive to large decreases in the P_{O_2} of arterial blood. This is because the blood is highly saturated with oxygen until the P_{O_2} drops below 60 mmHg. When the alveolar arterial P_{O_2} falls to 40 mmHg, peripheral chemoreceptors are stimulated and help to bring

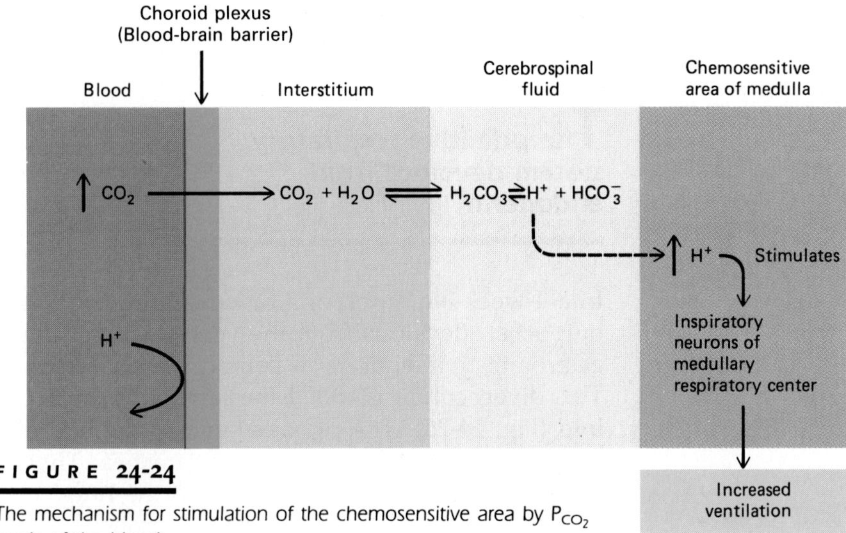

FIGURE 24-24

The mechanism for stimulation of the chemosensitive area by P_{CO_2} levels of the blood.

about a 1.5-fold increase in alveolar ventilation. This is not a dramatic increase when compared to an 11-fold increase in ventilation when arterial P_{CO_2} increases.

Exercise increases ventilation

Heavy exercise can cause O_2 utilization and CO_2 production to increase some 20-fold. Alveolar ventilation increases proportionately before leveling off, and there is very little change in arterial P_{CO_2}, P_{O_2}, and pH. Therefore, these chemical levels cannot alone account for the high ventilation during exercise.

The exact mechanisms for the enhanced ventilation are still not completely understood, but it is believed that many inputs are involved. One possible input is to the respiratory center from higher brain centers. As the higher brain centers send impulses to voluntary skeletal muscles during exercise, it is believed that impulses are also sent by collateral neurons to the medullary inspiratory area to stimulate ventilation. Another factor is that the body movements associated with exercise may increase ventilation by a stimulation of the respiratory center via input from joint proprioceptors. The increased temperature associated with prolonged exercise also is believed to enhance ventilation.

Long-term effects of high altitude include increased oxygen-carrying capacity of the blood

As altitude increases, the atmospheric pressure decreases, and so does the P_{O_2} of inspired air. At the top of Mt. Everest, the atmospheric pressure is only 245 mmHg and the P_{O_2} of inspired air is only about 50 mmHg. To compensate for a lower P_{O_2} in the alveoli, alveolar ventilation and cardiac output increase immediately. This is mediated by the aortic and carotid bodies.

If the person remains at the high altitude, other factors become important in the acclimatization. The oxyhemoglobin dissociation curve shifts to the right due to increased amounts of DPG. The hemoglobin content of the blood increases. The blood can now hold more oxygen. Diffusion at the alveoli is facilitated. Myoglobin levels of the skeletal muscles increase. The number of red blood cells in the blood increases (secondary polycythemia) if the person remains at a high altitude for a period of months. The number and size of functional capillaries also increase. Cellular levels of mitochondria and oxidative enzymes increase.

Clinical highlight

High-altitude sickness (acute mountain sickness) afflicts many people who ascend rapidly to high altitudes. Lower P_{O_2} levels of inspired air produce hypoxia (low oxygen) in the body. Symptoms include dizziness, shortness of breath, and nausea. A small number of people become acutely sick. Cerebral arterioles may dilate, causing cerebral edema. Some pulmonary arterioles constrict, which increases pulmonary capillary pressure in others. This can result in pulmonary edema.

Aging of the respiratory system results in less elasticity

The respiratory tract, the lungs, and the thoracic wall become less elastic with increasing age. A diminished lung capacity follows. The ciliary action of the respiratory tract decreases, as does the macrophage activity within the lungs. These factors increase the risk for pulmonary infections and disorders. Lung diseases also affect the integrity of the cardiovascular system. In *cor pulmonale,* the right ventricle of the heart hypertrophies (enlarges) in response to a pulmonary disorder.

The primitive respiratory system develops from endoderm

In a 4-week-old embryo, a diverticulum, or outpocket, develops from the ventral side of the gastrointestinal endoderm behind the pharynx. This diverticulum is called the **laryngotracheal bud** (Fig. 24-25). The proximal end of the bud differentiates into the larynx and the trachea. The distal end of the bud bifurcates into the **lung buds** which initially give rise to the bronchi. These lung buds continue to branch to form bronchioles. At their closed terminal ends, the bronchioles dilate, becoming the alveoli. The alveoli appear after the sixth month of gestation. Mesodermal cells become associated with the primitive respiratory system providing the pleura, smooth muscle, cartilage, and elastic tissue.

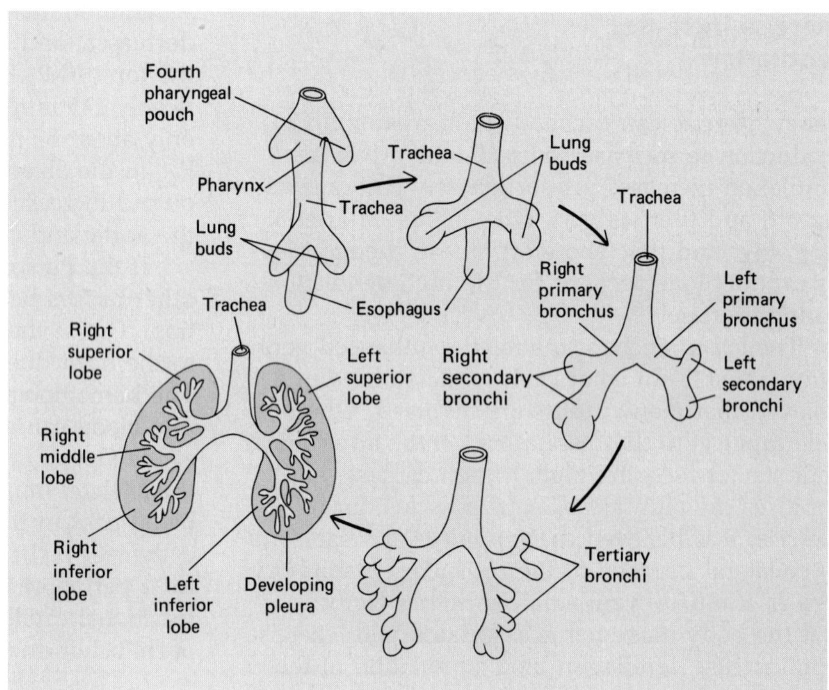

FIGURE 24-25

Embryology of the lower respiratory system.

Summary

I. The respiratory system consists of a number of respiratory passageways and the lungs, the functional respiratory organs.
   A. The upper respiratory tract is made up of the nose, nasal cavity, and the pharynx.
   B. The lower respiratory system contains the larynx, trachea, bronchi, and the lungs.

II. Ventilation is defined as the movement of air into and out of the lungs. It includes inspiration and expiration.
   A. Inspiration is the movement of air into the lungs due to the contraction of the respiratory muscles and changes in the pressures of the thorax.
   B. Expiration is the movement of air out of the lungs and is due to the relaxation of the respiratory muscles and changes in the pressures of the thorax.
   C. Pulmonary surfactant decreases the work of breathing by increasing lung compliance.
   D. Pulmonary volumes and capacities are important clinical measurements in evaluating breathing abnormalities.

III. External respiration is the gas exchange between the air in the alveoli and the blood in the pulmonary capillaries.
   A. O_2 diffuses from the alveoli to the pulmonary capillaries.
   B. CO_2 diffuses from the blood in the pulmonary capillaries into the alveoli.

IV. Internal respiration is the gas exchange between the blood of the systemic capillaries and the tissue cells.
   A. O_2 diffuses from the systemic capillaries into the tissue cells.
   B. CO_2 diffuses from the tissue cells into the systemic capillaries.

V. The respiratory gases are transported by the blood in different forms.
   A. O_2 is transported dissolved in the blood (2%) and bound to hemoglobin (98%).
   B. Metabolic factors affect the binding of oxygen to hemoglobin. These factors include pH, P_{CO_2}, temperature, and amounts of DPG.
   C. Fetal hemoglobin has a higher affinity for oxygen than does maternal hemoglobin.
   D. CO_2 is transported in the blood in three forms: dissolved (7%), bound to hemoglobin (23%), and as bicarbonate (70%).

VI. Respiration is controlled by intrinsic and extrinsic factors.
   A. Local controls of efficient gas exchange involve the effect of CO_2 levels on the bronchioles and O_2 levels on the pulmonary arterioles.
   B. The respiratory centers of the brain are located in the medulla and the pons.
   C. The chemosensitive area of the medulla is very sensitive to plasma P_{CO_2} levels. The mechanism for its activation is through H^+ ions.

Post-test

1. During inspiration, which one of the following decreases:
   a. Thoracic volume
   b. Atmospheric pressure
   c. Intrapleural pressure
   d. Rate of O_2 diffusion into pulmonary capillaries
   e. None of these
2. Which one of the following is not a part of a vital (lung) capacity:
   a. Tidal volume
   b. Expiratory reserve volume
   c. Residual volume
   d. Inspiratory reserve volume
   e. None of these
3. An increased level of DPG causes which one of the following:
   a. Less affinity of hemoglobin for O_2
   b. Shift of the oxyhemoglobin dissociation curve to the left
   c. Greater affinity of hemoglobin for O_2
   d. The Bohr effect
   e. None of these
4. High levels of alveolar P_{O_2} result in:
   a. Bronchoconstriction
   b. Pulmonary arteriolar vasodilation
   c. Bronchodilation
   d. Pulmonary arteriolar vasoconstriction
   e. None of these
5. Arterial blood normally has a P_{O_2} level of about:
   a. 152 mmHg
   b. 40 mmHg
   c. 45 mmHg
   d. 760 mmHg
   e. None of these
6. Anatomical dead space is about 150 ml. The volume of the physiological dead space is:
   a. 150 ml
   b. 1 ml

c. 350 ml
d. 500 ml
e. None of these

7. A normal minute-respiratory volume (MRV) would be about:
a. 0.20 liters/min
b. 1.5 liters/min
c. 6.0 liters/min
d. 25.0 liters/min
e. None of these

8. Increased P_{CO_2} causes all of the following except:
a. Hyperventilation
b. Heme-heme effect
c. Decreased hemoglobin affinity for O_2
d. Bronchodilation
e. None of these

9. All of the following increase the work of breathing except:
a. Decreased surfactant
b. Emphysema
c. Increased compliance
d. Increased surface tension at respiratory membrane
e. None of these

10. An individual at rest uses how much energy in ventilating the lungs?
a. 20 to 25%
b. 10 to 15%
c. 3 to 5%
d. 1 to 2%
e. 5 to 10%

11. Choose the incorrect association:
a. Hypoxia: decreased DPG
b. Heme-heme effect: sigmoid-shaped oxyhemoglobin dissociation curve
c. Fetal hemoglobin: higher affinity for O_2 than maternal hemoglobin
d. Increased hydrogen ions: Bohr effect

12. Choose the incorrect association:
a. Inspiration: P_{O_2} alveolar < P_{O_2} atmospheric
b. Inspiration: increased stroke volume
c. Inspiration: increasing pleural pressure
d. Inspiration: contraction of diaphragm and external intercostals

13. Choose the incorrect association:
a. Tissue cells: $P_{CO_2} > 45$ mmHg
b. Venous blood: $P_{CO_2} = 45$ mmHg
c. Arterial blood: $P_{CO_2} = 40$ mmHg
d. Alveoli: $P_{CO_2} = 45$ mmHg

Indicate whether the following would increase, decrease, or remain the same given the subsequent condition.

____ 14. Intrapleural pressure: during inspiration.
____ 15. Alveolar ventilation: during exercise.
____ 16. Atmospheric pressure: during inspiration.
____ 17. Percent hemoglobin saturation with oxygen at any P_{O_2}: during increased cellular metabolism.
____ 18. Percent hemoglobin saturation at any P_{O_2}: in fetus.
____ 19. Hemoglobin concentration in blood: long term at high altitude.
____ 20. Rate of lung stretch-receptor firing: during inspiration.
____ 21. Residual volume: during a maximal expiratory effort.
____ 22. Concentration of H^+ in cerebrospinal fluid: exercise.
____ 23. Lung compliance: destruction of lung tissue.
____ 24. Plasma P_{CO_2}: during breath holding.
____ 25. Total lung capacity: during exercise.
____ 26. Minute respiratory volume: during exercise.
____ 27. Work of breathing: decreased surfactant.
____ 28. Intrapleural pressure: increased thoracic volume.
____ 29. Diameter of bronchioles: decreased P_{CO_2}.
____ 30. Intra-alveolar pressure: before air moves in during inspiration.
____ 31. Percent hemoglobin saturation with O_2 at any given P_{O_2} compared to normal: increased DPG.

Review questions

1. Trace air flow from the nostril to the alveoli. Include all structures in the proper order.
2. Describe the structures of the external and internal nose.
3. Explain how incoming air is warmed and humidified.
4. Explain the physiological significance of nasal hairs, mucus, and ciliary action within the respiratory tract.
5. Explain how the larynx functions in respiration and voice production.
6. Compare the structure of the trachea and the bronchi.
7. What structures make up a bronchial tree? Bronchopulmonary segment? Respiratory membrane?
8. Define partial pressure. Contrast the partial pressures of oxygen and carbon dioxide in ventilation, external respiration, and internal respiration.
9. Compare normal inspiration and expiration to forced inspiration and expiration.
10. Define the basic pulmonary volumes and capacities. How are MRV and alveolar ventilation determined?

11. How are Boyle's law, Dalton's law, and Henry's law applied to the respiratory system?
12. Explain the transport of the respiratory gases. What is the chloride shift?
13. Explain the effects of pH, P_{CO_2}, temperature, and DPG on the oxyhemoglobin dissociation curve.
14. Explain the physiological mechanism of the chemosensitive area of the medulla in effecting respiration.
15. Compare the various inputs to the respiratory control centers of the brain.
16. How does aging affect the respiratory system?
17. Describe the embryology of the respiratory system.
18. Review the common respiratory disorders in terms of underlying causes and symptoms.
19. Label the numbered structures on the following diagram. (See Fig. 24-1.)

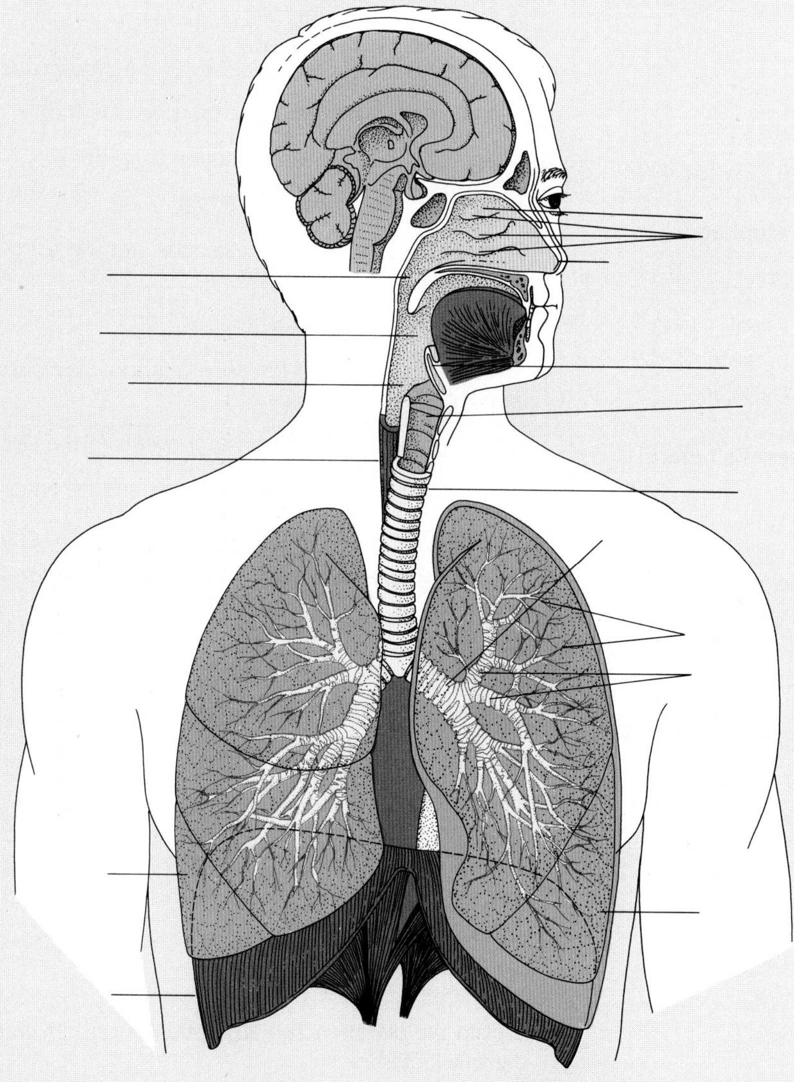

Post-test answers

1. c 2. c 3. a 4. b 5. e 6. a 7. c 8. b 9. c 10. d 11. a 12. c 13. d 14. decreases 15. increases 16. remains the same 17. decreases 18. increases 19. increases 20. increases 21. remains the same 22. increases 23. decreases 24. increases 25. remains the same 26. increases 27. increases 28. decreases 29. decreases 30. decreases 31. decreases

THE DIGESTIVE SYSTEM

CHAPTER OUTLINE

I. **Wall of the digestive tract**
II. **Peritoneum**
III. **Mouth**
  A. Tongue
  B. Teeth
  C. Salivary glands
    □ Focus on enzymes and digestion
IV. **Pharynx and esophagus**
V. **Stomach**
  A. Peristalsis
  B. The gastric glands
  C. Regulation of gastric motility and secretion
  D. Absorption
VI. **Accessory digestive organs**
  A. Pancreas
  B. Liver
  C. Gallbladder
VII. **Small intestine**
  A. Motility
  B. Secretions
VIII. **Digestion in the small intestine**
  A. Carbohydrates
  B. Proteins
  C. Fats
  D. Nucleic acids
IX. **Absorption in the small intestine**
  A. Monosaccharides
  B. Amino acids
  C. Fatty acids and monoglycerides
  D. Vitamins
  E. Water and electrolytes
X. **Large intestine**
  A. Transport of fecal material
  B. Absorption of vitamins and fluid
    □ Focus on disorders of the digestive system
XI. **Regulation by the hypothalamus**
XII. **Aging**
XIII. **Embryology**

LEARNING OBJECTIVES

After you have studied this chapter you should be able to:

1 Identify the parts of the digestive system, including accessory structures.

2 Describe the functional processes of the digestive system.

3 Describe the layers (tunics) of the digestive tract.

4 Discuss the position of the peritoneal membranes.

5 Identify the boundaries of the oral cavity.

6 Describe the structure of the tongue and the teeth and explain their role in digestion.

7 Define diphyodont and heterodont.

8 Identify the location of the salivary glands and discuss their role in digestion.

9 List the physiological sequence of events in the salivation reflex.

10 Describe the anatomy of the pharynx and esophagus.

11 List the physiological sequence of events in the deglutition reflex.

12 Define peristalsis and explain its importance to digestion.

13 Describe the external and internal anatomy of the stomach.

14 Discuss the function of each type of gastric secretory cell.

15 Describe gastric motility and secretion and their roles in digestion.

16 Discuss the anatomy of the pancreas, liver, and gallbladder.

17 Trace bile flow and blood flow through the liver.

18 List the major functions of the liver.

19 Trace the duct system from the accessory organs to the duodenum.

20 Describe the external and internal structure of the small intestine.

21 Describe the motility of the small intestine.

22 Explain the digestion and absorption of carbohydrates, proteins, and fats in the small intestine.

23 Explain the absorption of vitamins, water, and electrolytes in the small intestine.

24 Discuss the regulation of pancreatic and hepatic secretions to the duodenum.

25 Explain how the food-intake centers of the brain work.

26 Describe the external and internal structure of the large intestine.

27 Discuss the motility, the defecation reflex, and absorption in the large intestine.

28 Describe the major disorders of the digestive system.

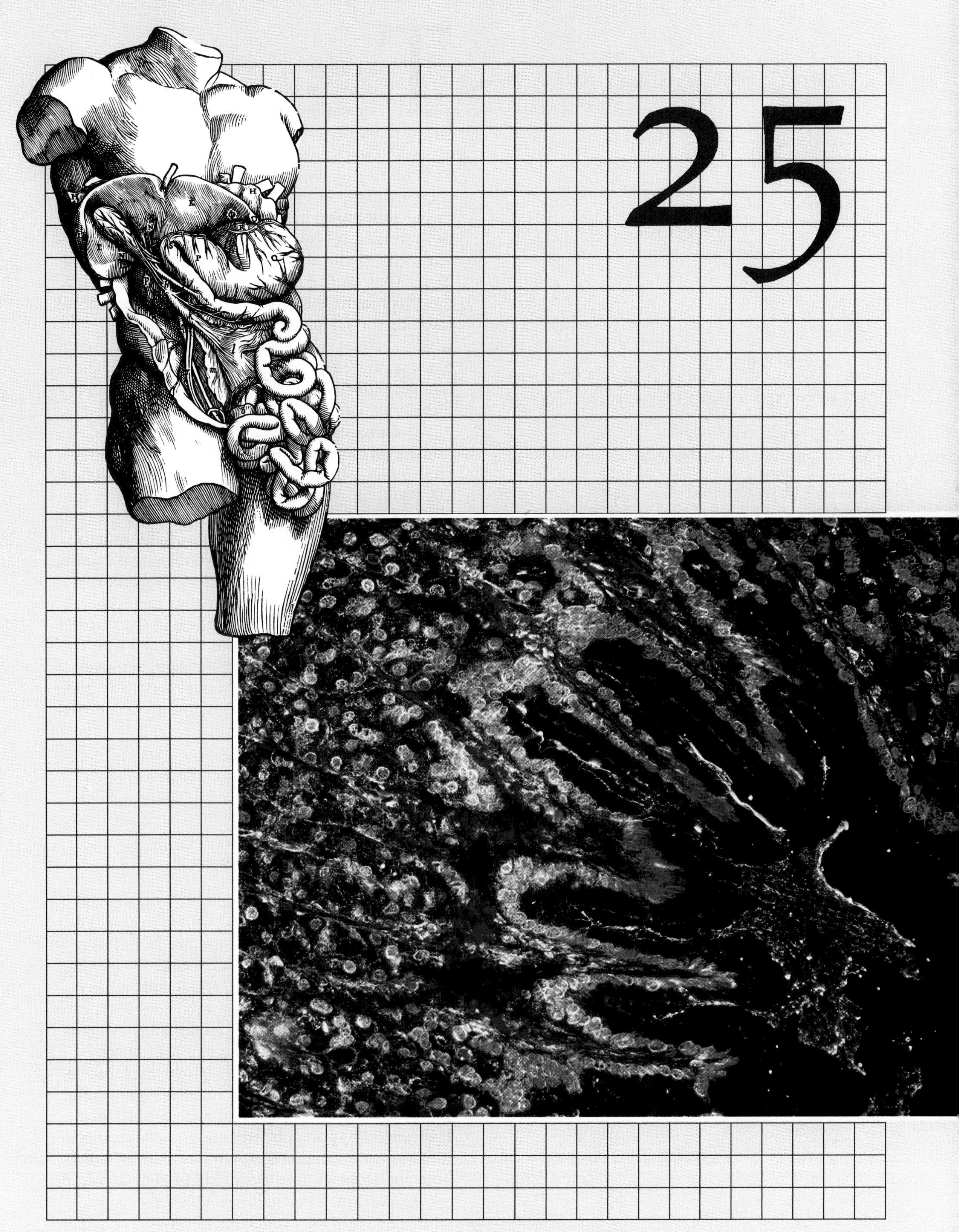

25

KEY CONCEPTS

The digestive tract is highly compartmentalized with each section containing specialized structures.

Ingested nutrients are mechanically and chemically digested to smaller molecules that are absorbed into the body.

Most digestion and absorption occurs in the small intestine, which receives input from the pancreas, liver, and gallbladder.

Food intake is regulated by centers in the hypothalamus. Digestive processes are coordinated by local, neural, and hormonal mechanisms.

The **digestive system** is made up of the digestive tract and accessory digestive structures. The digestive tract, also referred to as the **alimentary canal,** has the mouth as its anterior (proximal) opening and the anus as its posterior (distal) opening, with specialized compartments in between that have specific roles in the processing of food. These compartments include the oral cavity, pharynx, esophagus, stomach, small intestine, and large intestine (Fig. 25-1). That part of the digestive tract lying below the diaphragm is often called the **gastrointestinal tract,** or the **GI tract.** A mucous membrane, which secretes a protective mucus, covers the entire digestive tract internally. The accessory digestive structures include the tongue, teeth, salivary glands, pancreas, liver, and gall bladder.

The digestive system is responsible for a number of processes that result in the uptake of food molecules into the body. **Ingestion** involves the taking of food into the body. **Motility** is the movement of food through the digestive tract. **Secretion** adds substances (enzymes, bile, mucus, electrolytes) to the lumen of the digestive tract to enhance digestion and absorption. **Digestion** is the breakdown of food into smaller molecules (building block forms). **Absorption** is the transfer of digested nutrients from the GI lumen into the body proper. **Elimination** (defecation) removes indigestible substances and wastes from the body. All of these processes are regulated by local, neural, and/or hormonal mechanisms.

Four tunics form the wall of most of the digestive tract

Structurally, the wall of the digestive tract consists of four layers, or tunics. Moving from the inside to the outside, the tunics are as follows: mucosa, submucosa, muscularis, and serosa (Fig. 25-2). Above the diaphragm, the fourth tunic is referred to as the adventitia.

The **mucosa,** or mucous membrane, contains three layers. The *epithelial layer* of the mucosa functions in protecting the digestive tract and in secreting various substances into its lumen. It is also important in absorbing digested nutrients. The mucosal epithelium superior to the stomach is made up of stratified squamous cells whereas from the stomach on, it consists of simple columnar epithelium. The *lamina propria* consists of

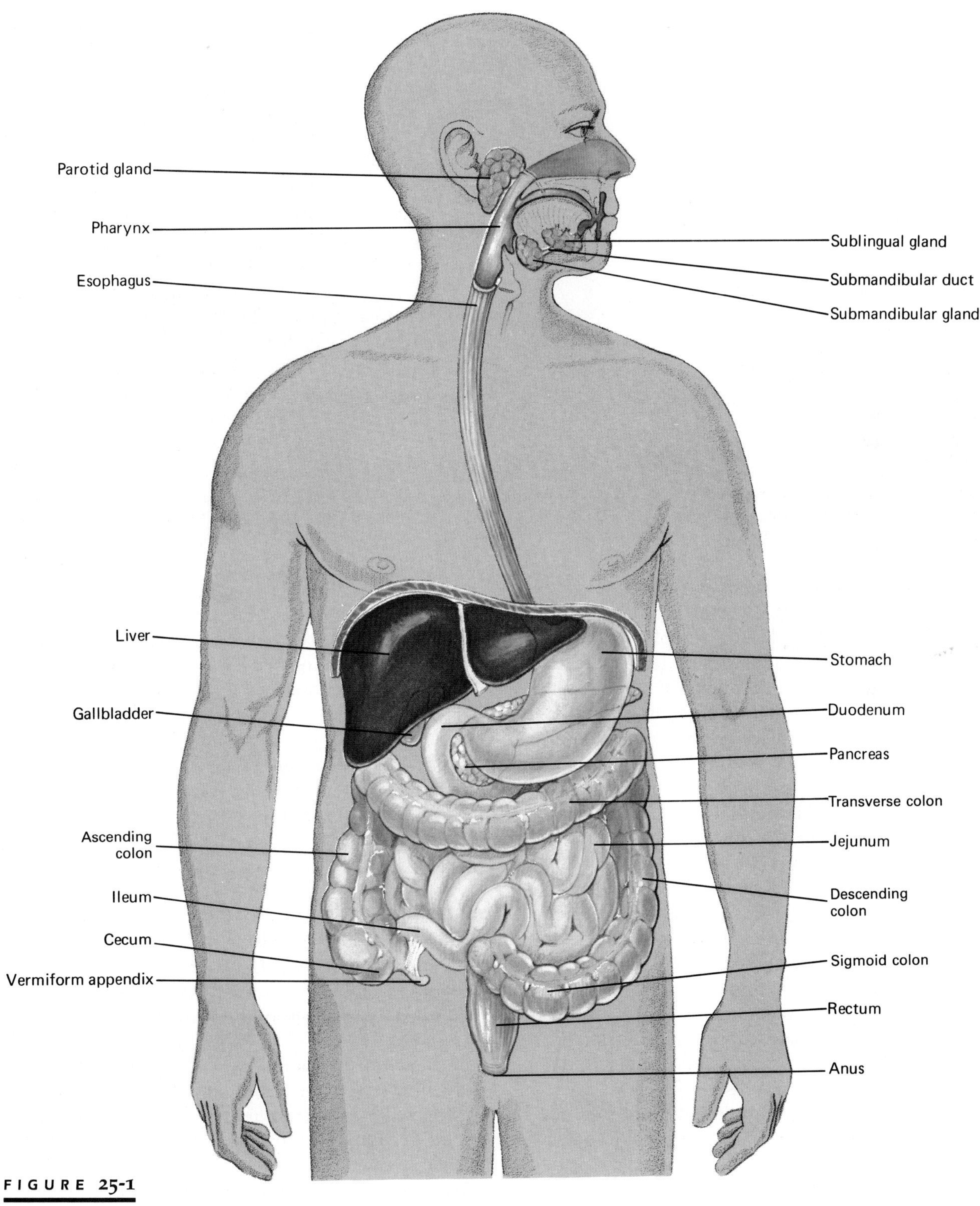

FIGURE 25-1

Anatomy of the digestive system.

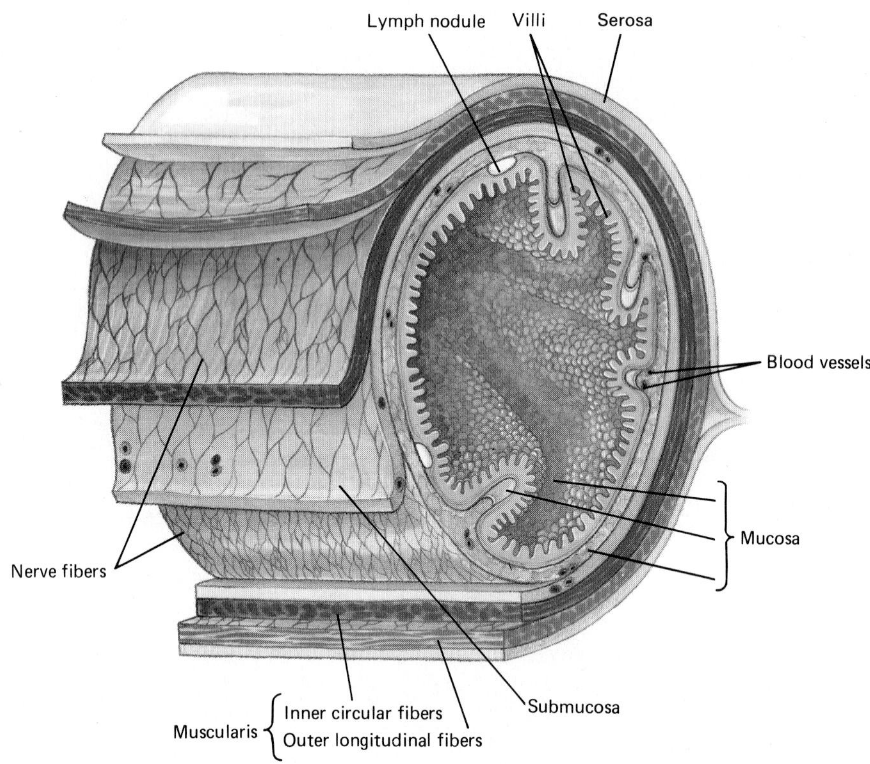

FIGURE 25-2

Cross section through the wall of the small intestine, illustrating the mucosa, submucosa, muscularis, and serosa.

loose connective tissue containing many blood and lymph vessels as well as lymph nodules that protect the body against ingested bacteria. The *muscularis mucosae* is a thin layer of smooth muscle that contracts to produce folds in the mucosa, thereby increasing surface area for digestion and absorption.

Deep to the mucosa is the **submucosa,** containing connective tissue that binds the mucosa to the muscularis layer. Glands in the submucosa connect with the lumen of the digestive tract. This layer also contains blood vessels and the **submucosal plexus (plexus of Meissner),** a network of autonomic nerves that control the secretions of the digestive tract.

The third layer of the digestive tract is the **muscularis,** which functions in motility and in the regulation of food flow through the digestive tract. In the mouth, pharynx, and upper third of the esophagus, it is composed of skeletal muscle important to the voluntary initiation of swallowing. In the rest of the digestive tract, the muscularis contains smooth muscle arranged as an innermost layer of *circular muscle* and an outermost layer of *longitudinal muscle.* Located between these two layers is the **myenteric plexus (plexus of Auerbach),** a system of autonomic nerves mediating the contraction of both muscularis layers. At points along the circular smooth muscle layer, there are thickenings called *sphincters* which help to regulate food flow.

The outermost connective tissue layer of the upper digestive tract is the **adventitia.** Below the diaphragm, this layer is called the **serosa** and also contains squamous epithelial cells. The epithelium of the serosa forms a serous membrane called the *visceral peritoneum.*

The peritoneum lines the abdominal cavity and holds the abdominal organs in place

The **visceral peritoneum** (*per*-ih-toe-**nee**-um), which covers some of the abdominal organs, is connected by folds and is continuous with the **parietal peritoneum** that lines the abdominal and pelvic cavities (Fig. 25-3). These two membranes are separated by a potential space called the **peri-**

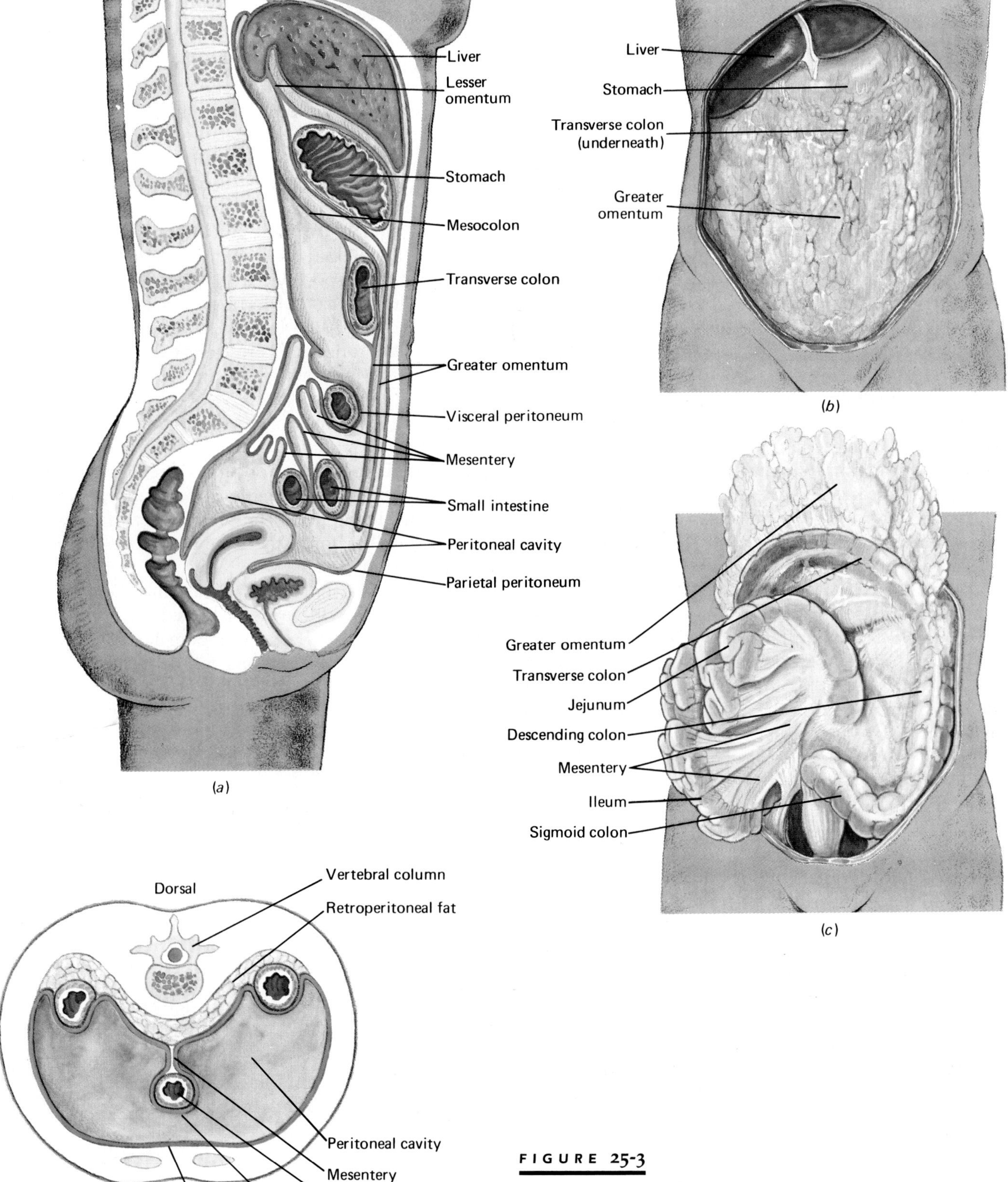

FIGURE 25-3

Cross section through abdomen showing relationship of visceral and parietal peritoneum and mesentery. (*a*) Sagittal view. (*b*) Frontal view. (*c*) Frontal view with folds of peritoneum, transverse colon, and greater omentum raised. (*d*) Cross-sectional view.

toneal cavity which contains a small amount of serous fluid. An inflammation of the peritoneum, called *peritonitis,* can be serious because infection may spread to adjoining organs. In certain disorders, such as cirrhosis, fluid may accumulate within the peritoneal cavity, causing a condition referred to as *ascites* (ah-**sie**-teez).

The peritoneum contains folds through which the viscera course, helping to anchor them to each other and to the abdominal wall. The folds of the peritoneum also support the blood vessels and nerves supplying the viscera. The **falciform ligament** (**fall**-si-form) is a fold that attaches the liver to the diaphragm and the anterior abdominal wall. Another fold, the **lesser omentum,** suspends the stomach and the first portion of the duodenum from the liver. A large fold, the **mesentery** (of the small intestine), extends from the parietal peritoneum and attaches to much of the small intestine. The mesentery anchors the small intestine to the posterior abdominal wall.

The **greater omentum** is the large fold that hangs down over the intestines and interconnects the stomach, duodenum, and large intestine. Because of its content of adipose tissue it is sometimes referred to as the "fatty apron." The greater omentum also contains lymph nodes which help to fight infection and prevent its spread to the peritoneum. The **transverse mesocolon** is a fold of the peritoneum that attaches a portion of the large intestine to the posterior abdominal wall.

The mouth is a cavity receiving food

The **mouth (oral cavity)** or buccal cavity opens anteriorly via the lips and posteriorly into the oropharynx. The oral cavity contains the tongue, the gums, and the teeth and receives the ducts of buccal glands and the salivary glands. The space between the teeth and the lips or cheeks is called the **vestibule.** The roof of the mouth consists of an anterior **hard palate** and a posterior **soft palate.** The hard palate is formed by the maxillary and palatine bones. The soft palate separates the oral cavity from the nasopharynx. The **uvula** (**you**-view-lah) is the posterior part of the soft palate. See Figures 25-4 and 25-5.

The tongue positions food and contains the taste buds

The **tongue** is a thick musculofibrous structure, covered by a mucous membrane and attached to the floor of the oral cavity by a midline fold of the mucous membrane called the **lingual frenulum** (**ling**-gwal **fren**-you-lum) (Fig. 25-5). Skeletal muscle of the tongue consists of both **extrinsic** and **intrinsic** muscle. The extrinsic muscles of the tongue originate from the hyoid bone, the mandible, and the styloid process of the temporal bone, and they are responsible for moving the tongue around the oral cavity. Intrinsic muscles originate and insert within the tongue and they change the shape of the tongue. These two sets of muscles also function in moving food in the oral cavity, in swallowing, and in speech.

The mucous membrane of the dorsum (top) of the tongue is modified by many small projections called **papillae,** which appear as three types: the filiform papillae, the fungiform papillae, and the circumvallate papillae. The fungiform and circumvallate papillae house the **taste buds.** See Figure 17-10 (Sense Organs).

The food is sensed (tasted) by the chemoreceptors located within the taste buds on the dorsum of the tongue. Refer to Figure 17-10*c* for the sites of the various chemoreceptors on the tongue. In order for the proper sensing of the food to occur, the food must be in solution.

The teeth mechanically break food down

The **teeth** extend into the oral cavity from **alveoli** (sockets lined by **periodontal membrane**) of the alveolar processes of the maxilla and the mandible. The gums, or **gingiva** (jin-**jih**-vah), that cover the alveolar processes are composed of stratified squamous epithelium and dense, fibrous connective tissue. The two major parts of a tooth are the part above the gum line, called the **crown,** and the part below the gum line, called the **root.** The root or roots of the tooth fit into the alveoli of the jaw bones. At the gum line, there is a slight constriction of the tooth referred to as the **neck** of the tooth.

Most of the tooth consists of hard, calcified **dentin.** On the crown it is covered by a protective layer of **enamel.** Enamel is principally calcium phosphate and calcium carbonate and it is harder than the dentin. The dentin of the root is covered by the **cementum,** a bonelike substance that helps to anchor the tooth to the periodontal ligament of the alveoli in the jaw bones. Connective tissue called **pulp** fills the pulp cavity within the crown of the tooth. The pulp cavity also contains the blood vessels, nerves, and lymphatics of the tooth. Extensions of the pulp cavity, called the **root canals** (Fig. 25-6), run through the roots to end at the **apical foramina**.

Humans are *diphyodonts* (**dih**-fee-oh-*donts*) in that they have two sets of teeth during their lifetimes. The first set of teeth is called the primary set, or **deciduous dentition** (dee-**sid**-you-us) (or the baby teeth or milk teeth). They begin to emerge at about 6 months of age and continue to appear until all 20 are present by about 2 ½ years of age. The second set of teeth is called the secondary set, or **permanent dentition.** The permanent dentition begins to replace the deciduous set at about 6 years of age and continues to adulthood. There are a total of 32 teeth in the permanent dentition.

Humans are also *heterodonts* in that their teeth differ in shape and have different functions. The permanent dentition consists of four different types of teeth: the incisors, the canines (cuspids), the premolars (bicuspids), and the molars. The **incisors,** which are located closest to the midline, are used mainly for cutting. The **canines** are used for tearing food. The **premolars** function in crushing and grinding, as do the **molars.**

The teeth in the oral cavity can be divided into four quadrants by separating the teeth of the upper and lower jaws at the midline. This divides the teeth into upper right and left quadrants and lower right and left quadrants. Each quadrant of

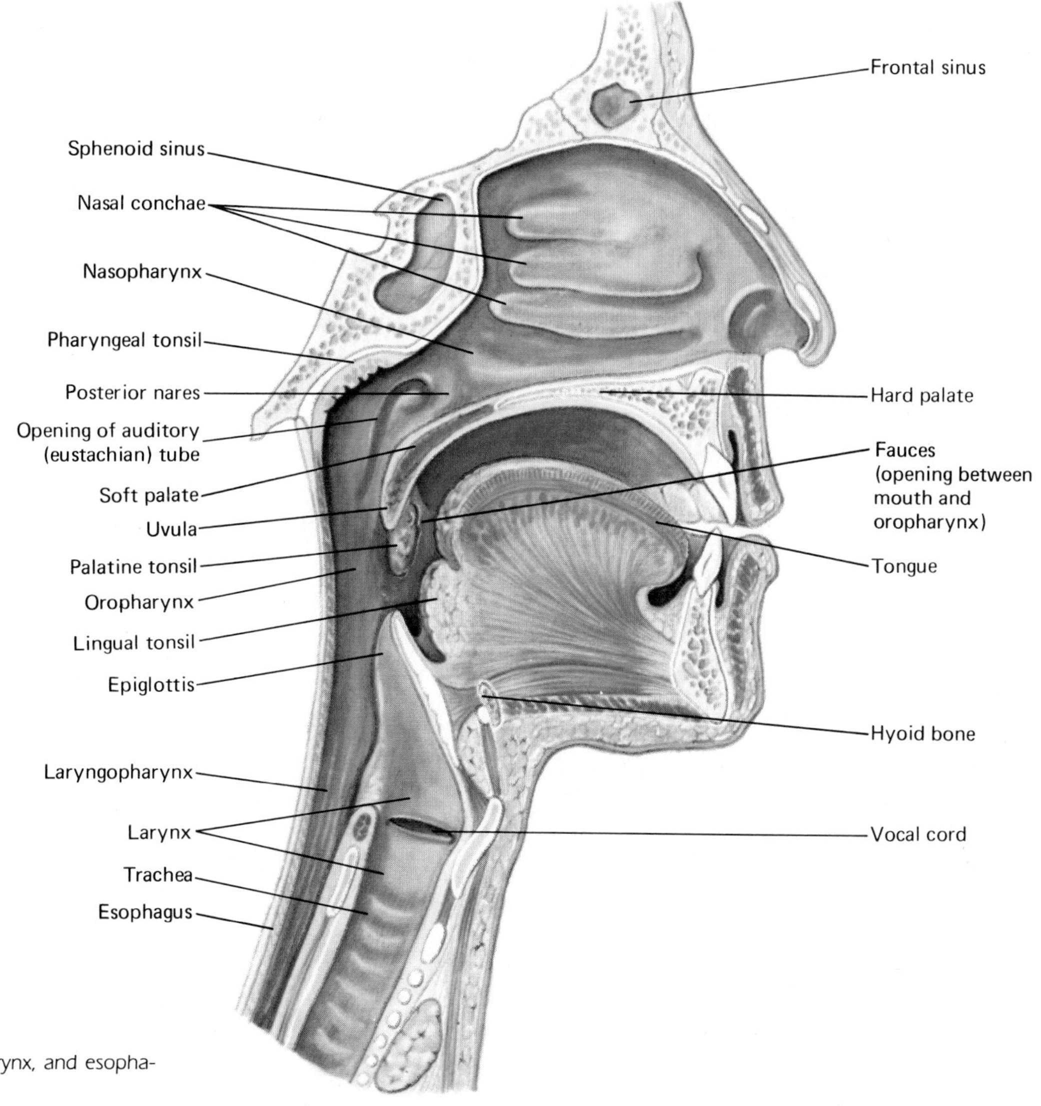

FIGURE 25-4

Anatomy of mouth, pharynx, and esophagus (sagittal section).

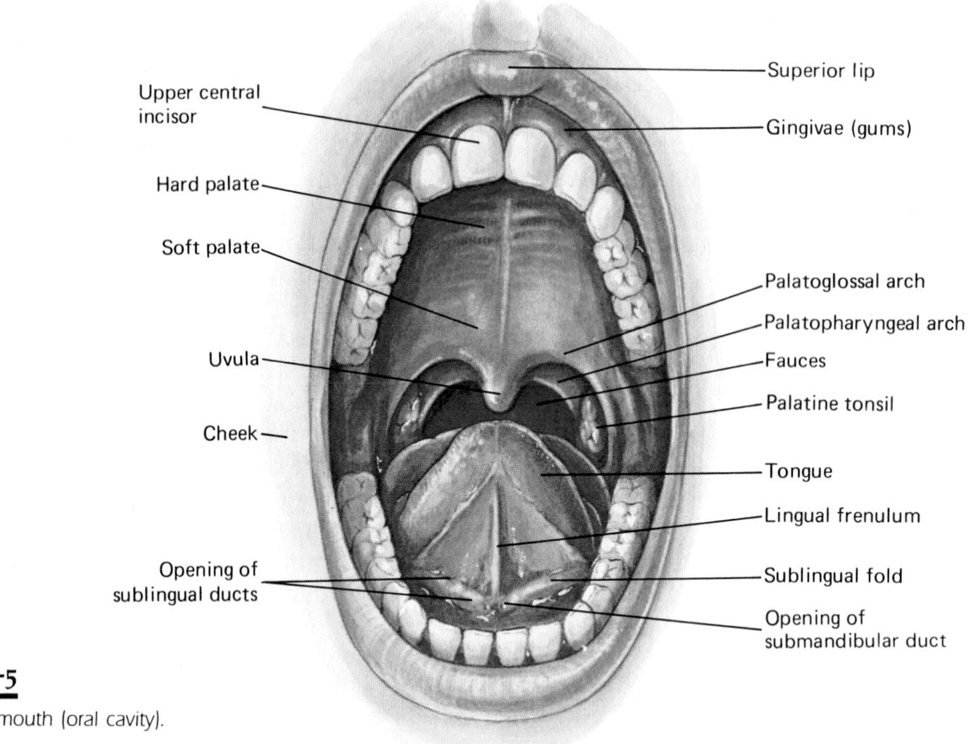

FIGURE 25-5

Anatomy of the mouth (oral cavity).

the adult permanent dentition contains eight teeth. Beginning at the midline and moving posterolaterally, each quadrant consists of 1 central incisor, 1 lateral incisor, 1 canine, 1 first premolar, 1 second premolar, 1 first molar, 1 second molar, and 1 third molar (wisdom tooth). See Figure 25-7*a*. If the jaws are too small, the third molars may not have enough room to erupt through the gums, remaining embedded within the alveolar bone. These embedded molars are said to be *impacted*, and they can be removed if too much pressure and pain ensues (Fig. 25-7*b*).

The adult permanent dentition can be represented in a human *dental formula* as follows:

$$\frac{2\ 1\ 2\ 3}{2\ 1\ 2\ 3} \times 2 = 32$$

The numerator 2123 designates the eight teeth in one quadrant of the upper jaw—2 incisors, 1 canine, 2 premolars, and 3 molars. Multiplying these eight teeth by 2 gives the sixteen teeth associated with the upper jaw. The same is done for the denominator (Fig. 25-7).

Once food enters the mouth, a number of events occur to prepare the food for digestion. The teeth break the food down into smaller and smaller pieces. This chewing, or **mastication** (mas-tih-**kay**-shun), of the food allows it to be swallowed more easily. Mastication also increases the surface area of food for mixing with saliva and for digestion that will occur later in the digestive tract. The tongue, lips, and cheeks assist the teeth in positioning the food within the oral cavity. This mechanical action of mixing the food with the saliva produces a softened **bolus** of food ready for swallowing.

Salivary glands secrete saliva

Three pairs of **salivary glands** supply **saliva** via ducts that open into the oral cavity (Fig. 25-8). The saliva from the salivary glands helps to moisten and dissolve the food. Numerous **buccal glands** (**buk**-al) within the mucous membrane also secrete small amounts of saliva.

The **parotid glands** (pah-**rot**-id), the largest of the salivary glands, are located inferior and anterior to the ears and superficial to the masseter muscles. Each parotid gland communicates with the oral cavity near the second upper molar teeth via *Stensen's duct*.

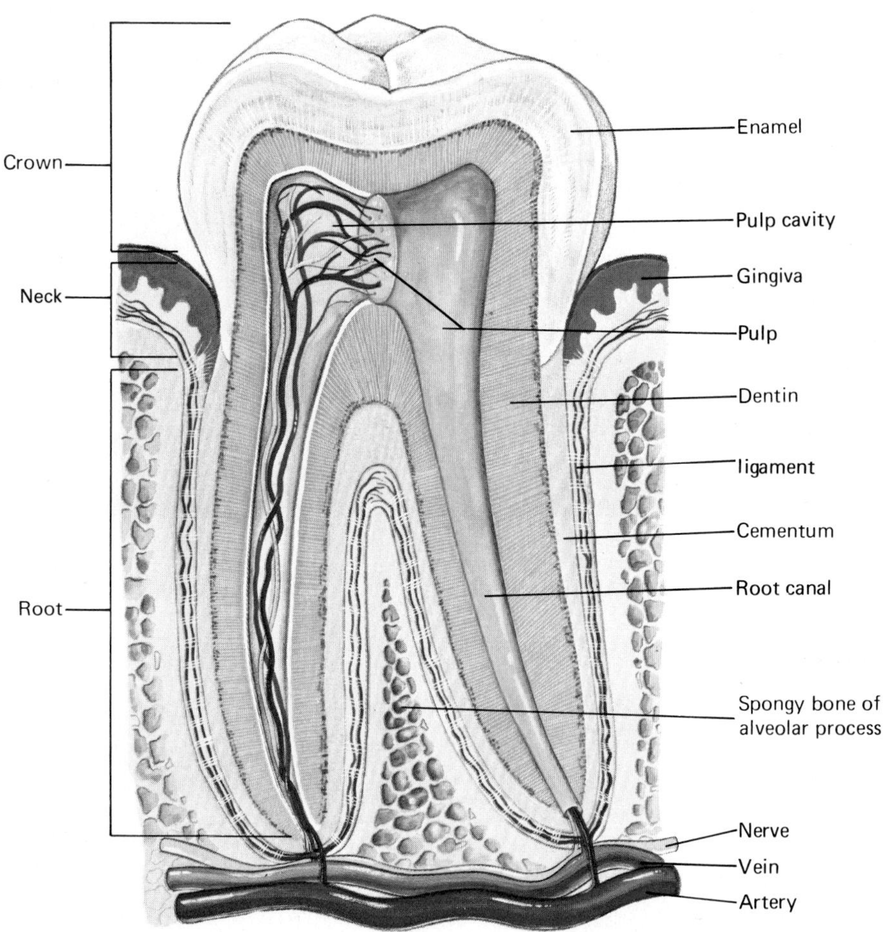

FIGURE 25-6

Anatomy of a tooth (molar).

The **submandibular glands** (sub-man-**dib**-you-lar) are located near the base of the tongue and medial to the angle of the mandible. Their ducts are called *Wharton's ducts* and empty at the frenulum of the tongue behind the lower central incisors.

The **sublingual glands** (sub-**ling**-gwal) are the smallest of the salivary glands and are found under the tongue within the mucous membrane. The sublingual glands empty into the oral cavity at its floor by way of several small ducts called *Rivinus's ducts*.

The average volume of saliva produced is about 1 to 1.5 liters per day and is normally composed of about 99% water and 1% solutes. The parotid glands produce a serous solution that contains water and the enzyme **salivary amylase** (ptyalin). The submandibular glands secrete both a serous solution and a mucus solution. The sublingual glands secrete primarily mucins, which are proteins that mix with water to become mucus. The solutes contain mucins, salivary amylase, lysozyme, urea and uric acid, and inorganic salts. Some of the inorganic salts (bicarbonates and phosphates) serve to buffer the contents of the oral cavity and keep it close to the pH optimum for salivary amylase. The lysozyme helps to kill bacteria. (See Focus on Enzymes and Digestion.)

Salivary amylase begins the digestion of carbohydrates. It splits starch molecules into smaller fragments called *dextrins*. Starch contains thousands of glucose molecules; dextrins contain several glucose molecules. Salivary amylase has a wide functional pH range but its optimum is pH 6.9.

$$\text{Starch} \xrightarrow{\text{salivary amylase}} \text{dextrins}$$

The secretion of saliva is a reflex response. The presence of food in the mouth stimulates tactile and taste receptors. These receptors activate affer-

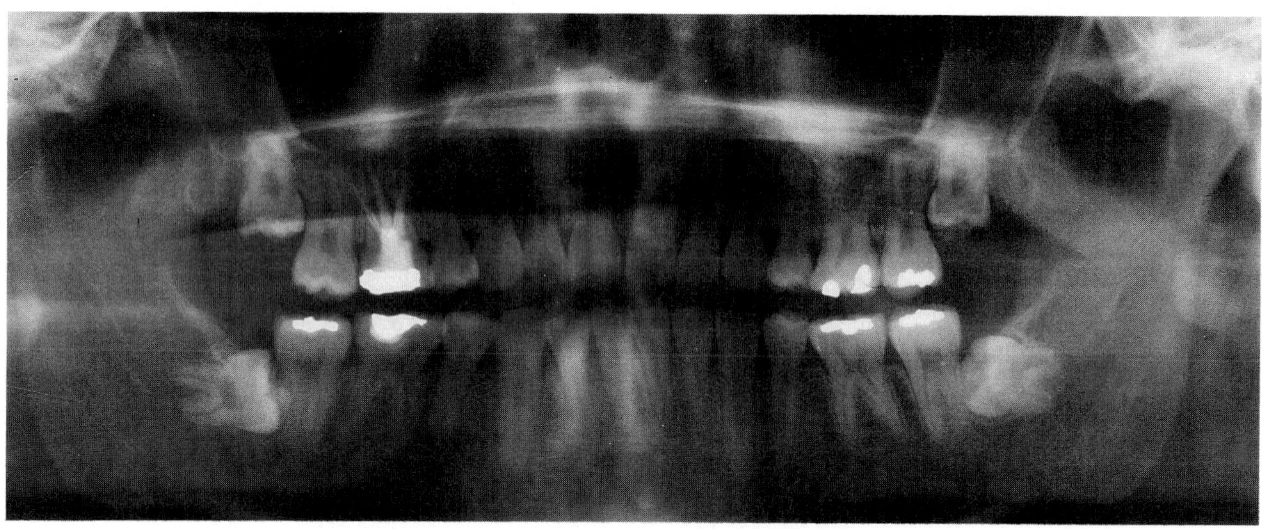

(a)

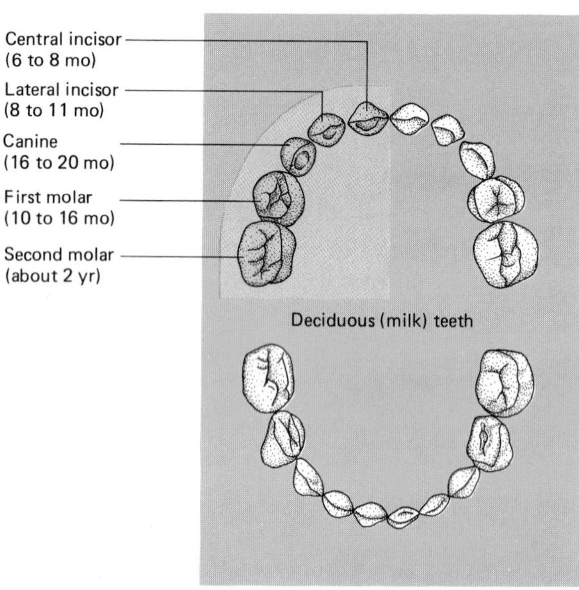

(b)

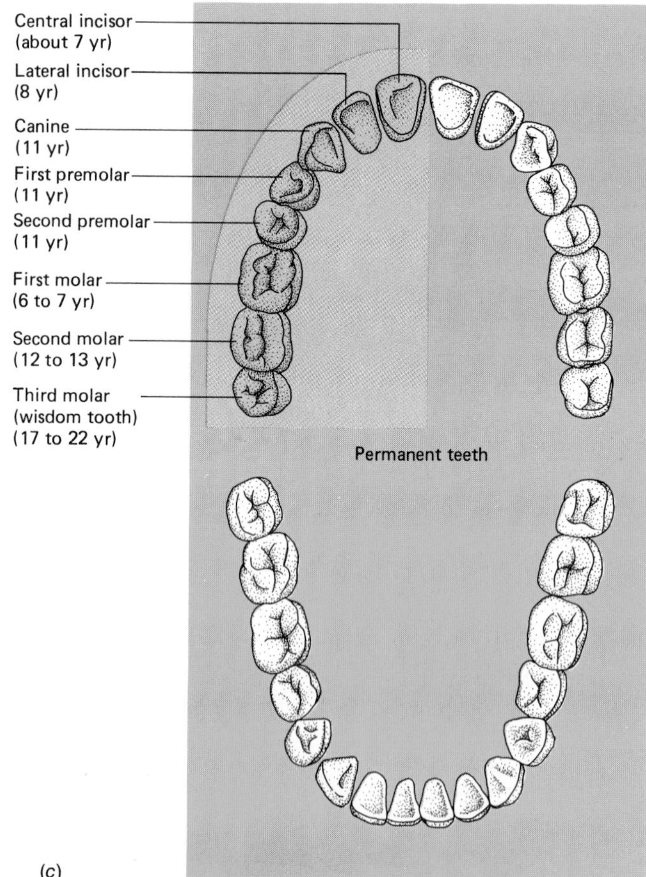

(c)

FIGURE 25-7

Human diphyodont dentition. (*a*) Panoramic radiograph illustrating the teeth of the upper and lower jaw. Notice the two impacted wisdom teeth in the lower jaw. Are you able to identify the maxillary sinus, angle of the mandible, and region of the temporomandibular joint? (Courtesy of Anthony Farole, D.M.D., Department of Oral and Maxillofacial Surgery, Thomas Jefferson University Hospital.) (*b*) Deciduous dentition. (*c*) Permanent dentition. Approximate time of eruption is shown in parentheses.

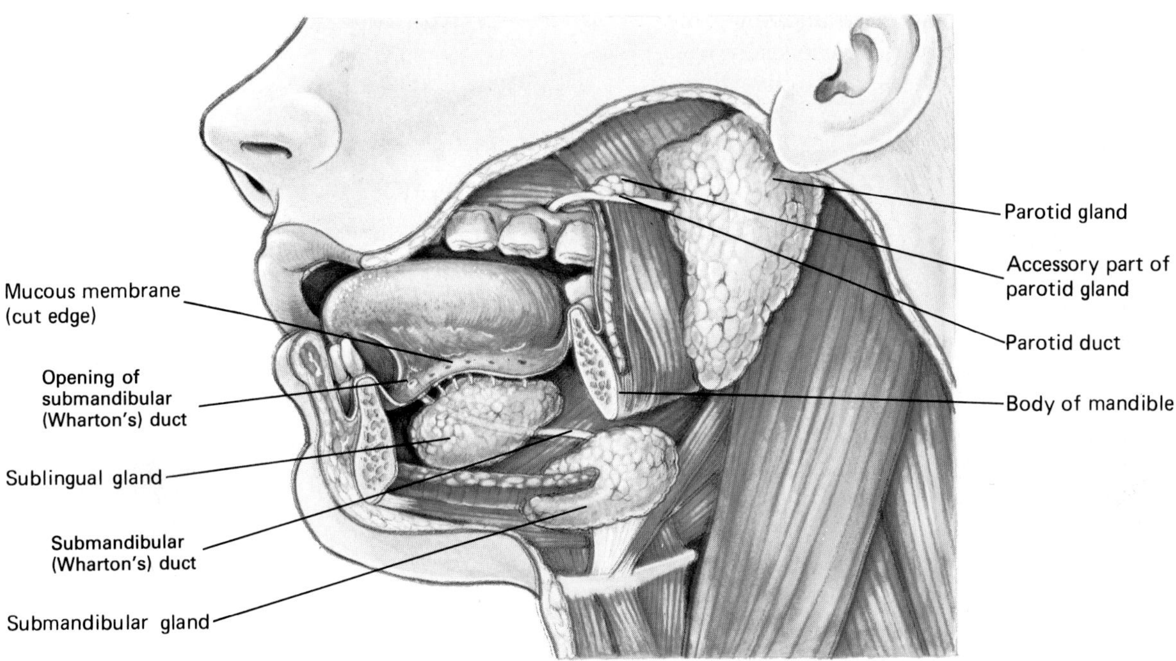

FIGURE 25-8

The salivary glands. Part of the mandible has been removed to show the submandibular and sublingual glands.

ent neurons which travel to the **salivation center** (salivatory nuclei) located between the medulla and the pons. Parasympathetic neurons running from the salivation center to the salivary glands increase their rate of firing and bring about an increase in the rate of saliva secretion by the salivary glands. Sympathetic nerves can decrease salivation.

Food in mouth ⟶ ↑ tactile and taste receptor stimulation ⟶ ↑ firing of afferent neurons ⟶ ↑ stimulation of salivation center ⟶ ↑ firing of parasympathetic neurons ⟶ ↑ secretion of saliva

Higher brain centers can also elicit saliva release through olfaction, vision, hearing, and even

FOCUS ON . . . Enzymes and digestion

Enzymes are proteins that act as organic catalysts enhancing the rate of chemical reactions without themselves being altered in the process. Since enzymes are proteins, they are temperature- and pH-sensitive, having an optimal temperature and pH range. They are inactive outside of this pH range. Enzymes act on a specific type of substrate and catalyze chemical reactions in both directions.

The hydrolytic enzymes are used to break down complex nutrients into their simpler building blocks. **Hydrolysis** (*hydro* = water, *lysis* = break apart) is the breaking down of a substance into smaller units by the addition of water.

The major nutrients cannot be absorbed and utilized by the body without being digested to their simpler building blocks. Carbohydrates are digested by amylases to monosaccharides; glucose is the major monosaccharide used in the body. Fats (lipids) are digested by lipases to fatty acids and glycerol, and proteins are digested by proteases to amino acids.

$$\text{Carbohydrates} \xrightarrow{\text{Amylases}} \text{monosaccharides}$$

$$\text{Fats} \xrightarrow{\text{Lipases}} \text{fatty acids and glycerol}$$

$$\text{Proteins} \xrightarrow{\text{Proteases}} \text{amino acids}$$

thought. Reflexes from the stomach and small intestine can also increase salivation, especially in response to irritating substances in the digestive tract.

The pharynx and esophagus transport food from the mouth to the stomach

When food is swallowed, it leaves the oral cavity and enters into the **oropharynx** (throat) and then into the **laryngopharynx.** The pharynx (**fair**-inks) serves as a passageway for both the digestive system and the respiratory system. The soft palate of the roof of the mouth closes off the nasopharynx during swallowing; the epiglottis closes off the lower respiratory tract. (See Fig. 25-4.)

The **esophagus** (ee-**sof**-a-gus) is a muscular tube about 25 centimeters (10 in.) long that directs the food from the pharynx to the stomach. It is usually collapsed upon itself unless food or drink is passing through it. The esophagus lies inferior to the laryngopharynx and posterior to the trachea. It passes through the mediastinum, through the diaphragm at the level of the tenth thoracic vertebrae via the *esophageal hiatus*, and joins the superior part of the stomach through the *cardiac sphincter*. The muscularis of the upper third of the esophagus contains skeletal muscle, the middle third is a mixture of skeletal and smooth muscle, and the lower third contains smooth muscle. (See Figs. 25-4 and 25-9.)

Oral cavity ⟶ oropharynx ⟶ laryngopharynx ⟶ esophagus ⟶ cardiac sphincter ⟶ stomach

Deglutition (*deg*-loo-**tish**-un), or **swallowing,** is the movement of the bolus of food from the oral cavity to the stomach. It involves the oral cavity, pharynx, and esophagus. Swallowing involves three stages: the voluntary stage, the pharyngeal stage, and the esophageal stage (Fig. 25-9).

The **voluntary stage** of deglutition involves the pushing of the bolus into the oropharynx by the tongue. From this point on, swallowing is primarily involuntary.

The **pharyngeal stage** is initiated by the entrance of the bolus into the oropharynx. This

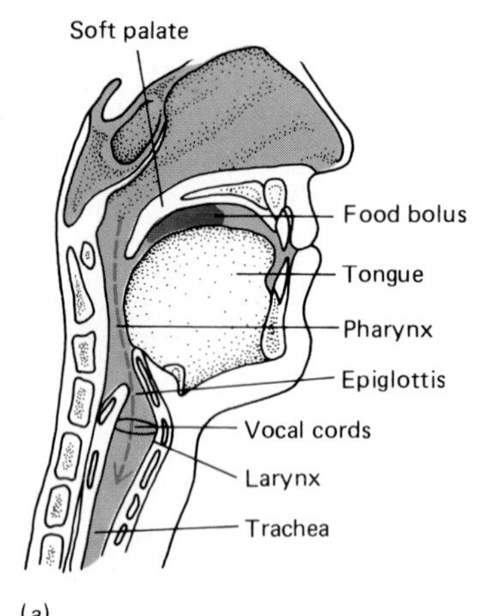

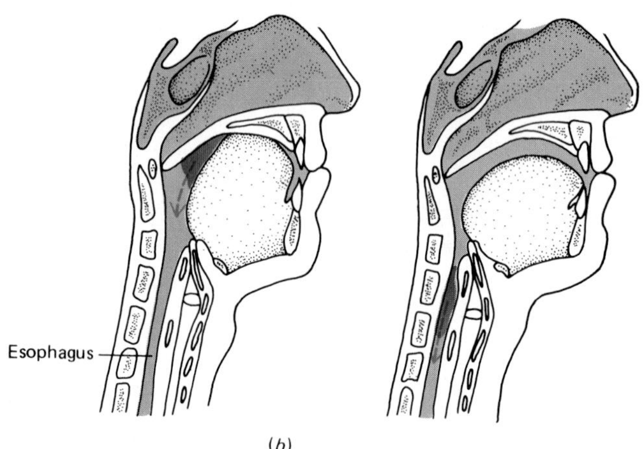

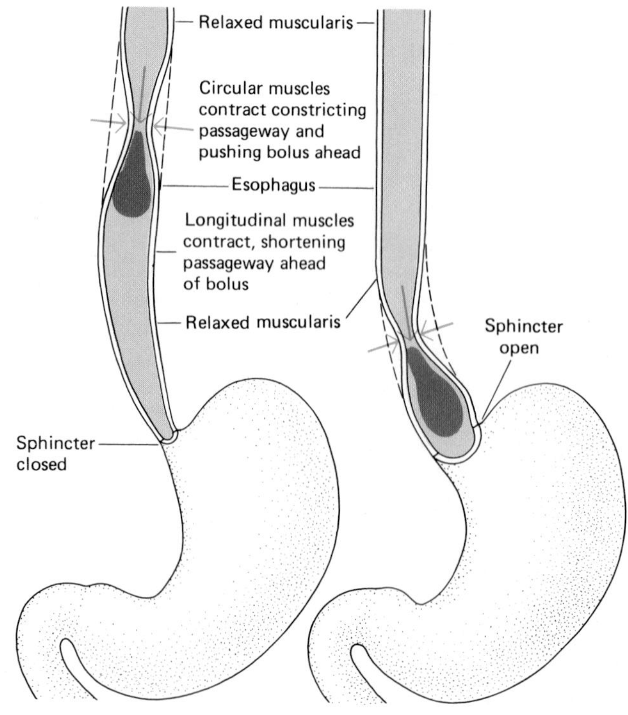

FIGURE 25-9

Deglutition. (*a*) Bolus in oral cavity. (*b*) Pharyngeal stage of swallowing. (*c*) Esophageal stage of swallowing showing peristalsis.

stage of swallowing is almost entirely a reflex response. Various receptors in this area bring about a stimulation of the **deglutition center** between the medulla and the pons to cause muscular contractions of the pharynx. The soft palate closes off the nasopharynx. The vocal cords of the larynx are moved upward and anteriorly, causing the epiglottis to close over the glottis of the larynx. This action prevents the bolus from entering the lower respiratory tract. This movement also widens the space available for the esophagus to stretch during swallowing. Pharyngeal muscles also produce **peristaltic contractions** (waves of muscle contractions) which help to propel the food down the pharynx and into the esophagus, all in about 1 to 2 seconds.

The last stage in swallowing, the **esophageal stage,** begins with the entrance of the bolus into the upper esophagus and takes about 4 to 8 seconds. Reflexes conveyed by the vagus nerve and the myenteric nerves produce peristaltic contractions in skeletal and smooth muscles. The peristaltic contractions propel the bolus down the esophagus and into the stomach, with mucus, secreted by the esophageal mucosa, serving to lubricate the bolus. Gravity is also important in moving the bolus down the esophagus. The cardiac sphincter relaxes during swallowing, as does the muscularis of the stomach. This facilitates the movement of the bolus into the stomach.

In the stomach, food mixes with gastric juices

The **stomach** is a muscular organ located in the upper left quadrant of the abdomen. See Window on the Human Body, View 3. It is typically J-shaped when empty. The concave medial border of the stomach is called the **lesser curvature.** The convex lateral border of the stomach is the **greater curvature.** The esophageal opening to the stomach is called the **cardiac orifice.** The entrance of the stomach to the small intestine is via the **pyloric sphincter** (pie-**lor**-ik). Food enters the stomach at its **cardiac end.** The part of the stomach projecting above the cardiac orifice is the **fundus.** The main section of the stomach is the **body.** The body tapers inferiorly to form the **antrum,** which leads to the **pyloric end** of the stomach (Fig. 25-10). When the stomach is empty, its mucosa and submucosa exist as large longitudinal folds called the **rugae** (**roo**-jee).

The muscularis layer of the gastric wall has an additional muscle layer located between the circular layer and the submucosa. This muscle layer runs obliquely and allows the stomach to contract in many directions and with extra force, permitting a thorough churning of the food with the gastric juices.

Peristalsis is the major type of motility in the stomach

Food remains in the stomach about 3 to 4 hours. Within minutes after the bolus enters the stomach, peristaltic contractions begin mixing it with the gastric juices. Peristalsis is the major contractile activity occurring in the stomach (Fig. 25-11). This mixing results in a churned semiliquid known as the **chyme** (kyme). With time, the peristaltic waves grow in intensity and slightly in frequency, moving from the body of the stomach to the pyloric end. The pyloric sphincter is usually slightly opened and only a small amount of the chyme enters the duodenum. Most of the chyme is forced back into the body of the stomach and further mixing occurs.

Cells of the gastric glands secrete the gastric juices

The gastric mucosa contains many **gastric glands** (**gas**-trik) which empty to the gastric lumen by way of the gastric pits. These gastric glands contain a number of specialized secretory cells: mucus-secreting cells, parietal (oxyntic) cells, zymogenic (chief) cells, and enteroendocrine cells. The **mucus-secreting cells** produce mucus. The **parietal cells** release hydrochloric acid (HCl) and intrinsic factor. The **zymogenic cells** produce gastric lipase and an inactive enzyme precursor, *pepsinogen* (Fig. 25-12). The **enteroendocrine** cells secrete the hormone *gastrin* (Table 25-1). Collectively the secretions of the gastric glands entering the lumen make up the gastric juices.

The gastric juices contain a high concentration of *HCl* from the parietal cells and some *digestive enzymes* from the zymogenic cells. The HCl causes the gastric lumen to have a very acidic pH of about 2. This acidity functions in disintegrating many cellular substances of the food. It breaks intermolecular bonds and dissolves plasma membranes, kills bacteria entering with the ingested food, and converts pepsinogen into its active form, **pepsin.**

(text continued on p. 876)

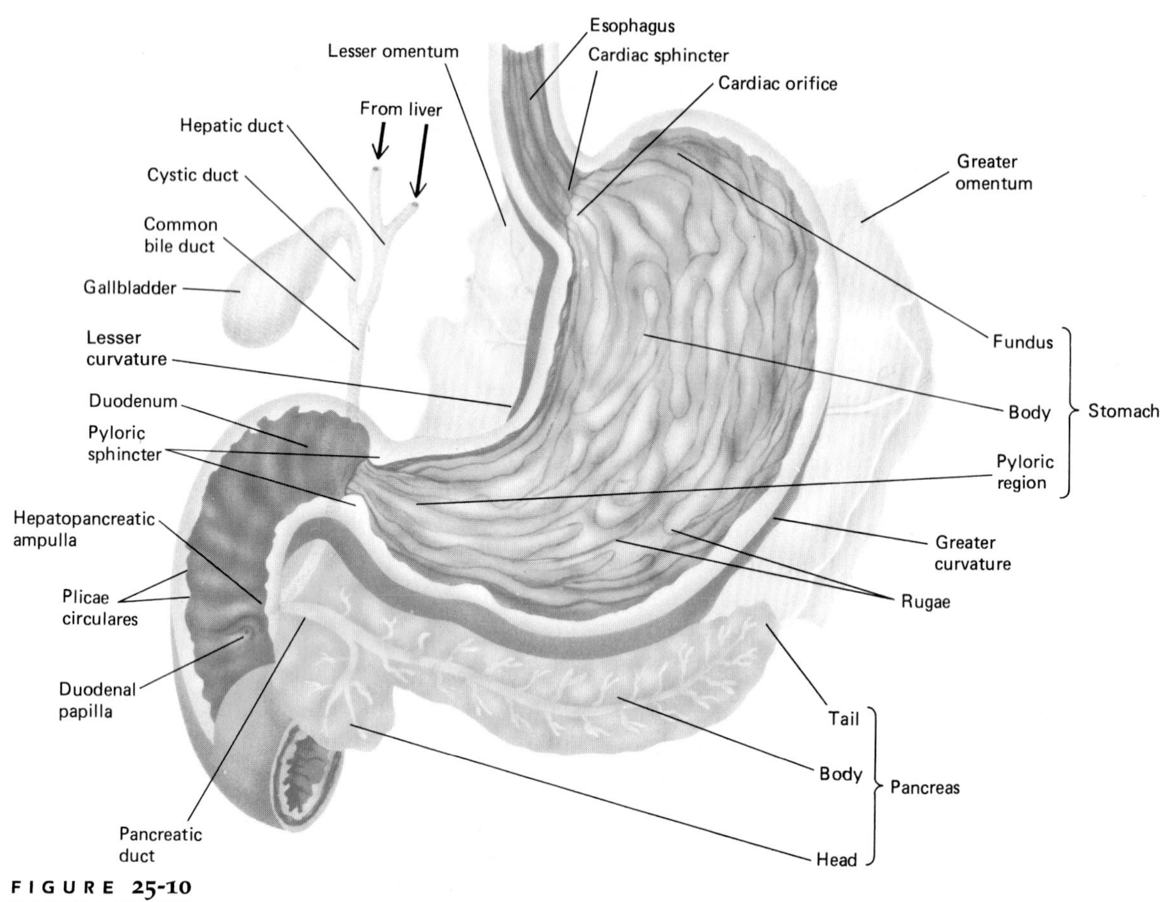

FIGURE 25-10

External and internal anatomy of the stomach and duodenum (frontal section).

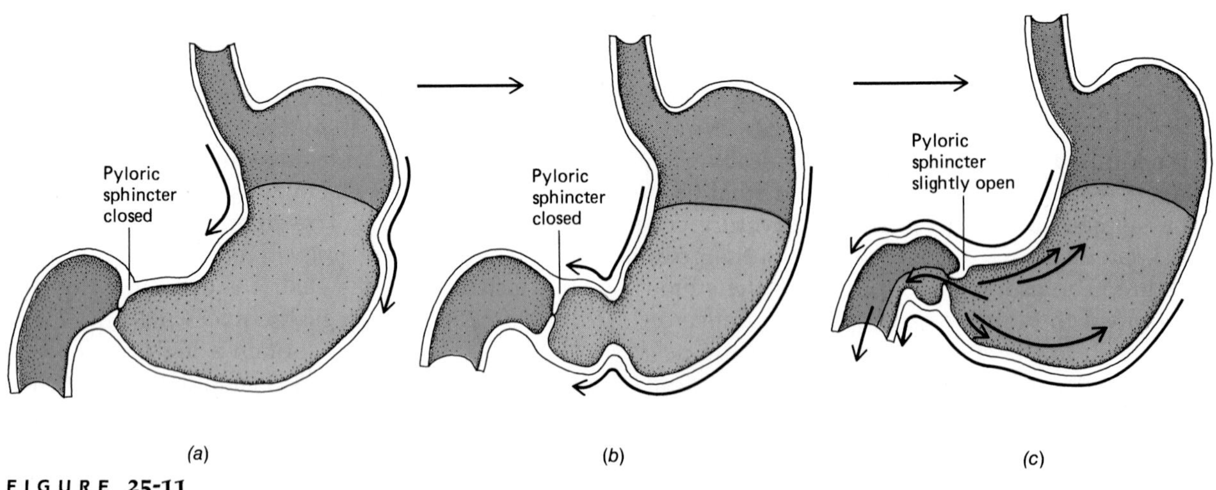

FIGURE 25-11

Peristalsis in the stomach. (*a*) Peristaltic waves move toward pyloric end of stomach. Pyloric sphincter is closed. Chyme is churned. (*b*) Peristaltic waves are the strongest at the pylorus. (*c*) "Pyloric pump" moves some chyme into duodenum. Most of the chyme stays in the stomach for further mixing.

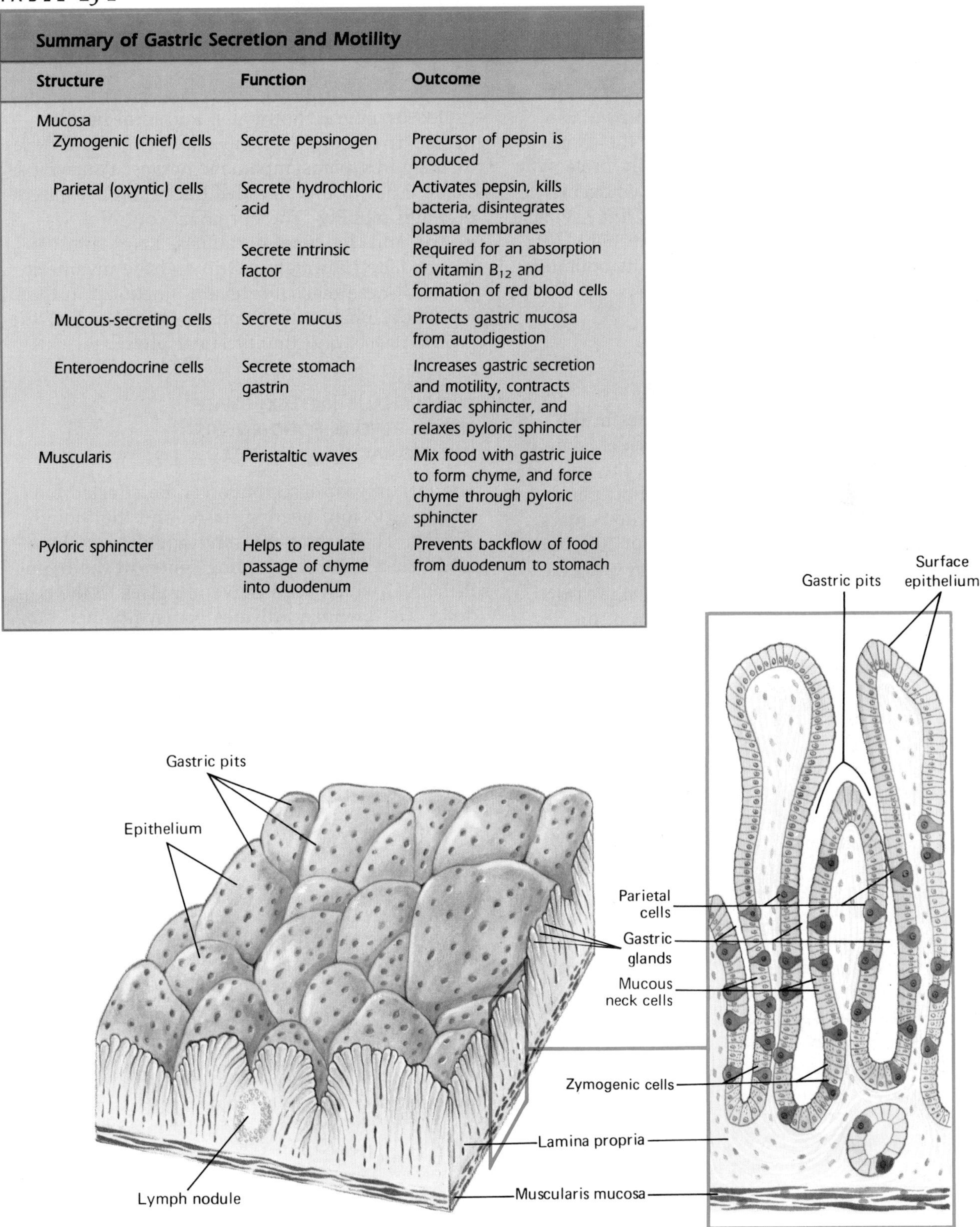

TABLE 25-1

Summary of Gastric Secretion and Motility

Structure	Function	Outcome
Mucosa		
Zymogenic (chief) cells	Secrete pepsinogen	Precursor of pepsin is produced
Parietal (oxyntic) cells	Secrete hydrochloric acid	Activates pepsin, kills bacteria, disintegrates plasma membranes
	Secrete intrinsic factor	Required for an absorption of vitamin B_{12} and formation of red blood cells
Mucous-secreting cells	Secrete mucus	Protects gastric mucosa from autodigestion
Enteroendocrine cells	Secrete stomach gastrin	Increases gastric secretion and motility, contracts cardiac sphincter, and relaxes pyloric sphincter
Muscularis	Peristaltic waves	Mix food with gastric juice to form chyme, and force chyme through pyloric sphincter
Pyloric sphincter	Helps to regulate passage of chyme into duodenum	Prevents backflow of food from duodenum to stomach

FIGURE 25-12

Anatomy of the gastric mucosa and gastric glands.

Pepsin, which has an optimum pH of about 2, begins the breakdown of proteins, the major digestive activity occurring in the stomach. This enzyme splits certain amino acid bonds and, thereby, breaks proteins into smaller peptide fragments called *proteoses* and *peptones*. Pepsin also digests collagen, which is present in the connective tissues of meat. Pepsin is the only proteolytic enzyme capable of this action. The zymogenic cells also produce the enzyme *gastric lipase*, which can split butterfat molecules found in milk. However, it has only a limited role since its optimum pH is about 5 to 6.

$$\text{Pepsinogen} \xrightarrow{\text{HCl}} \text{pepsin}$$

$$\text{Proteins} \xrightarrow{\text{pepsin}} \text{proteoses and peptones}$$

Limited digestion of starches continues in the stomach by the action of *salivary amylase*. Some of the salivary amylase may stay within the bolus of food and away from the HCl for a short period of time. Once salivary amylase comes into contact with HCl, it is inactivated. Only about 30% of the starch has been reduced to maltose by the time the food enters the small intestine. One reason for this is that the acidic environment of the stomach inactivates the salivary amylase. Another reason is that generally the enzyme does not remain a sufficient time in the mouth to digest large amounts of starch before it enters the stomach.

The acidity and the proteolytic activity of the gastric juices are very high. Yet the stomach does not digest itself **(autodigest).** There are several mechanisms protecting the stomach from autodigestion. The mucus-secreting cells produce an alkaline mucus that shields the gastric mucosa and locally neutralizes the acidity. The mucosal epithelial cells are very tightly bound to each other, preventing leakage of gastric juice into intercellular spaces. These cells are also replaced every 3 days, substituting healthy cells for any damaged ones. About half a million of these cells are shed and replaced every minute! Another protective feature is that the enzymes of the zymogenic cells are produced as zymogens (inactive enzyme precursors). They are activated in the presence of HCl in the gastric lumen, which prevents them from working on the mucosa.

Gastric motility and secretion are regulated by nerves and hormones

The secretion of gastric juices and gastrin is controlled by neural, hormonal, and local mechanisms. The neural pathways are generally reflexes mediated by parasympathetic nerves. Parasympathetic input to the digestive tract stimulates secretion and motility. The hormonal control is via gastrin and duodenal hormones. Local controls are mediated through gastrin and the myenteric plexus. These mechanisms are functional in three regulatory phases: the cephalic (reflex) phase, the gastric phase, and the intestinal phase.

THE CEPHALIC (REFLEX) PHASE BEGINS BEFORE FOOD ENTERS THE STOMACH

The rate of gastric secretion can be affected by olfaction, vision, hearing, taste, and the thought of food. These receptors send impulses to the cerebral cortex and the feeding center in the hypothalamus, which send nerve impulses to the medulla. The medulla activates parasympathetic stimulation to the gastric glands via the vagus nerve (CN X). Therefore, the rate of gastric secretions can increase even before the food enters the stomach.

> Cranial senses + thought ⟶ ↑ afferent input to hypothalamic feeding center and input to medulla ⟶ ↑ parasympathetic stimulation to gastric glands ⟶ ↑ rate of gastric secretion

FOOD IN THE STOMACH STIMULATES THE GASTRIC PHASE

The actual presence of food in the stomach stimulates gastric secretions. The food causes distension of the gastric wall, which stimulates stretch receptors that initiate a reflex pathway via the vagus nerve. Afferent nerves stimulate the medulla to enhance parasympathetic vagal input to the gastric glands, increasing the rate of gastric secretion.

> Food in stomach ⟶ ↑ stretch receptor stimulation ⟶ ↑ firing of vagal afferent neurons ⟶ ↑ medullary stimulation ⟶ ↑ vagal parasympathetic stimulation ⟶ ↑ gastric secretion

Local responses are also initiated. The presence of protein fragments, alcohol, and caffeine can directly stimulate a release of **gastrin.** Gastrin travels via the bloodstream to the gastric glands where it stimulates the release of gastric juice (Table 25-2). Besides increasing the secretion of gastric juice, gastrin also increases gastric motility. High levels of HCl in the stomach inhibit the release of gastrin.

> Protein fragments, etc. $\longrightarrow \uparrow$ gastrin release $\longrightarrow \uparrow$ gastric gland secretion $\longrightarrow \uparrow$ HCl in gastric lumen

The amount of hydrochloric acid secreted during a meal is directly proportional to the amount of protein in the meal. This is true for two reasons: (1) Proteins in the stomach buffer hydrogen ions. This allows more HCl to be secreted without appreciably lowering the pH. (2) More proteins in the stomach mean more protein digestion products. The protein digestion products stimulate the release of gastrin which will cause an increase in HCl secretion.

DISTENSION OF THE DUODENUM AND PRESENCE OF PROTEIN INITIATE THE INTESTINAL PHASE

Distension of the duodenum (the first part of the small intestine) and the presence of protein fragments in the duodenum are believed to trigger the release of enteric (from small intestine) gastrin, which can increase the rate of gastric secretion.

TABLE 25-2

Major hormones of the GI tract

Hormone	Origin	Stimulus	Targets	Actions
Stomach gastrin	Mucosa of pylorus	Protein digestion products in stomach	Stomach	Stimulates secretion of gastric juice
			Cardiac sphincter	Constriction
			Pyloric sphincter	Relaxation and opening
			Ileocecal sphincter (valve)	Relaxation and opening
Enteric gastrin	Mucosa of small intestine	Protein digestion products in small intestine	Stomach	Stimulates secretion of gastric juice
			Cardiac sphincter	Constriction
			Pyloric sphincter	Relaxation and opening
			Ileocecal sphincter (valve)	Relaxation and opening
Secretin	Intestinal mucosa	Acid, fats, protein digestion products, irritants, hypotonic and hypertonic fluids in small intestine	Stomach	Inhibits gastric secretion
			Pancreas	Stimulates secretion of pancreatic juice high in bicarbonate
			Liver	Stimulates bile secretion by hepatic cells
			Intestine	Stimulates secretion of intestinal juice
			GI tract	Decreases motility
Cholecystokinin (CCK)	Intestinal mucosa	Acid, fats, protein digestion products, irritants, hypotonic and hypertonic fluids in small intestine	Stomach	Inhibits gastric secretion
			Pancreas	Stimulates secretion of pancreatic juice high in enzymes
			Gallbladder	Contraction of gallbladder and ejection of bile
			Sphincter of Oddi	Relaxation and opening
			Small intestine	Stimulates secretion of intestinal juice
			GI tract	Decreases motility
Gastric inhibiting peptide (GIP)	Intestinal mucosa	Acid, fats, protein digestion products, irritants, hypotonic and hypertonic fluids in small intestine	Stomach	Inhibits secretion of gastric juice
			GI tract	Decreases motility

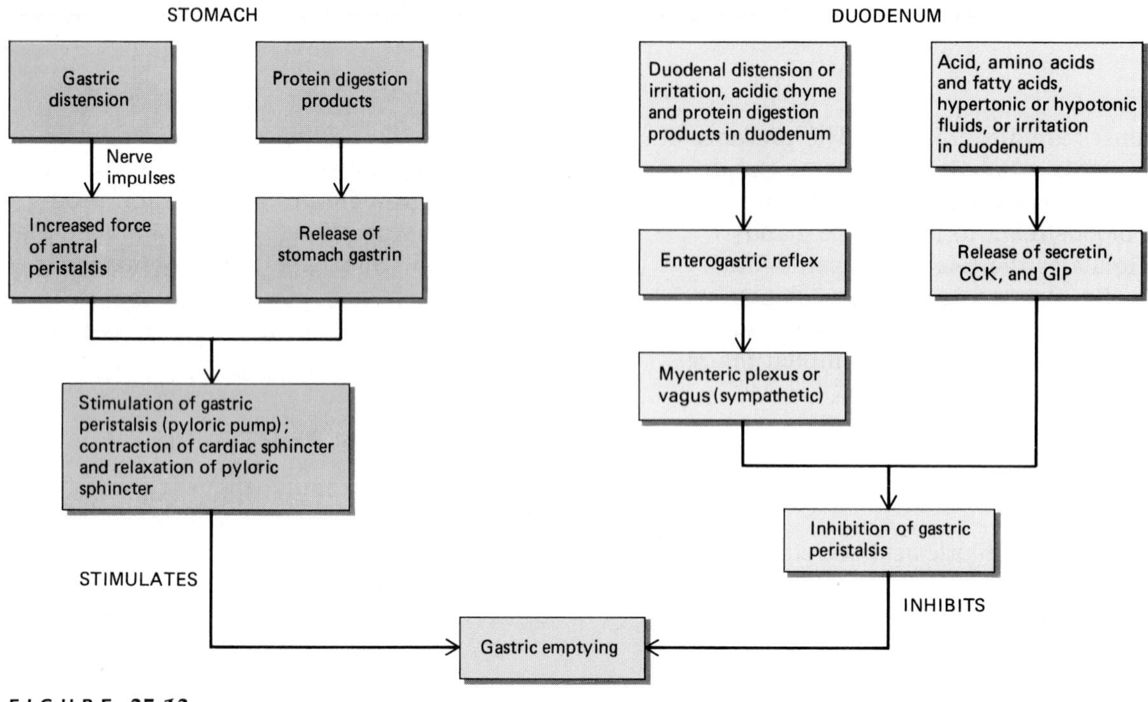

FIGURE 25-13

Factors determining the rate of gastric emptying.

Gastrin also causes the contraction of the cardiac sphincter, the relaxation of the pyloric sphincter, and an increased motility of the stomach. These facilitate **gastric emptying.** The other major stimulus to gastric emptying is the distension of the stomach, which is mediated by nerve impulses to cause an increased force of peristaltic contractions of the antrum of the stomach. This increased antral peristalsis is referred to as the *pyloric pump* because it propels chyme through the pyloric end of the stomach and into the duodenum. See Figure 25-13.

CHYME IN THE DUODENUM INHIBITS GASTRIC SECRETION AND MOTILITY

The presence of chyme in the duodenum initiates an **enterogastric reflex** which inhibits gastric secretion and motility. This allows more time for duodenal digestion and absorption to occur. The major stimuli for this inhibition include distension, irritants, high levels of acid, and protein digestion products in the duodenum. This reflex inhibition can go through the intrinsic nerve plexuses or be mediated through the vagus nerve and the medulla.

Duodenal distension, etc. ⟶ ↑ vagal afferent input ⟶ ↑ medullary stimulation ⟶ ↑ sympathetic stimulation ⟶ ↓ gastric secretion and motility

The chemical composition of the duodenal chyme also causes the release of several intestinal hormones that inhibit gastric secretion and gastric motility. These intestinal hormones include **secretin, cholecystokinin** (*koo*-le-*sis*-toe-**ky**-nin; **CCK**), and **gastric inhibiting peptide (GIP)** (Table 25-2). The stimuli for the release of these hormones are a very acidic chyme, the presence of amino acids and fatty acids in the duodenum, protein digestion products, irritating substances, and hypertonic or hypotonic chyme. Secretin and cholecystokinin have additional regulatory functions in the digestive system.

Acidic chyme, etc. in duodenum ⟶ ↑ duodenal hormone release ⟶ hormones travel through bloodstream to stomach ⟶ ↓ gastric secretion and motility

Absorption by the stomach is limited

The stomach lacks the expanded absorptive surfaces contained in the small intestine. It also has tight junctions between mucosal cells. Therefore, the gastric mucosa is a very poor absorptive part of the digestive tract. The only substances absorbed by the stomach, in small amounts, are a few highly fat-soluble substances including alcohol and aspirin.

Accessory digestive organs send secretions to the small intestine

The pancreas and the liver are very important in the digestion and absorption of nutrients. They function as exocrine glands in digestion by sending their secretions through ducts to the duodenum.

Pancreatic juice contains bicarbonates and digestive enzymes

The **pancreas** is an elongated retroperitoneal (located posterior to the parietal peritoneum) gland measuring about 15 centimeters long, 4 centimeters wide, and 2 centimeters thick. See Figure 25-14*a* and Window on the Human Body, View 5. Its **head** is associated with the C-shaped curve of the duodenum on the right side of the abdomen. Its **body** runs inferior to the stomach to its **tail** near the spleen on the left side. The pancreas is both

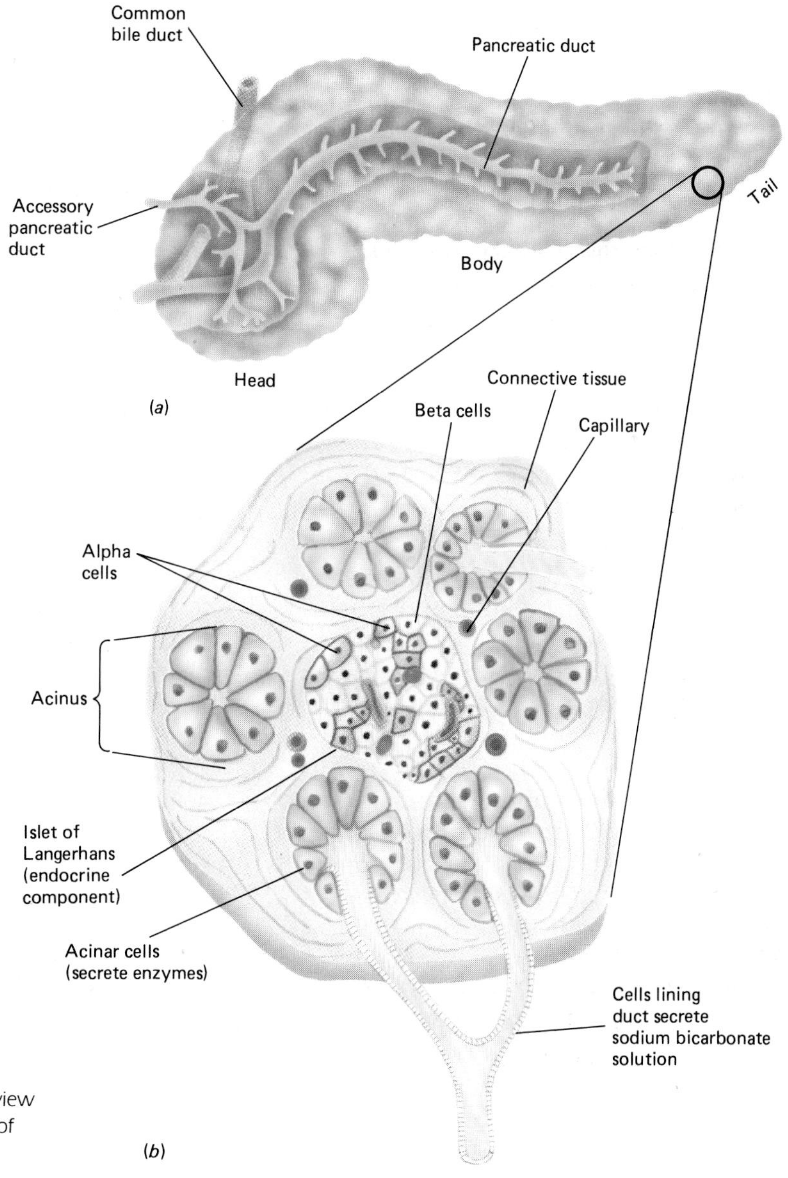

FIGURE 25-14

Anatomy of the pancreas. (*a*) External view with ducts exposed. (*b*) Secretory cells of pancreas.

an exocrine gland and an endocrine gland. As an endocrine gland, its islets of Langerhans produce the hormones insulin and glucagon. As an exocrine gland, it produces pancreatic juice which is rich in bicarbonates and digestive enzymes.

The exocrine glands of the pancreas make up about 99% of the pancreatic cells. These glands consist of **acinar cells** (**as**-ih-nar), which are arranged as **acini** (**as**-ih-nee) resembling small grape clusters and which secrete the zymogenic forms (proenzymes) of digestive enzymes. The ducts leading from the acini consist of **duct cells** which secrete a sodium bicarbonate solution (Fig. 25-14b).

The ducts leading from the exocrine glands converge and eventually join two major ducts of the pancreas. The largest of these runs the length of the pancreas and is called the **pancreatic duct (duct of Wirsung).** It usually joins the common bile duct to form the **hepatopancreatic ampulla** (*hep*-ah-toe-**pan**-kree-ah-tik) or the **ampulla of Vater.** A smaller **accessory pancreatic duct (duct of Santorini)** passes from the head of the pancreas to enter the duodenum superiorly to the ampulla. The accessory duct may be absent in some individuals.

Acini ⟶ exocrine ducts ⟶ pancreatic duct ⟶ ampulla of Vater

The liver produces bile

The **liver** is the largest gland of the body, weighing about 1500 grams (3 lb). It is located in the upper right quadrant of the abdomen under the diaphragm and is composed of **right** and **left lobes** separated by the **falciform ligament.** The right lobe is at least six times larger than the left lobe and has an inferior **quadrate lobe** and posterior **caudate lobe** associated with it (Fig. 25-15).

Each liver lobe is divided into many functional units called **lobules.** The lobules contain several plates of hepatic cells radiating out from a **central vein.** The hepatic cells secrete bile into small canals called **bile canaliculi** (kan-ah-**lik**-yoo-lie), which drain into **bile ducts** running between the lobules (Fig. 25-16). These bile ducts converge to form the **right** and **left hepatic ducts,** which join to become the **common hepatic duct.** This structure joins the *cystic duct* from the gallbladder to form the **common bile duct** (Figs. 25-15 and 25-17) which, along with the pancreatic duct, enters the duodenum through the ampulla of Vater.

Bile canaliculi ⟶ bile ducts ⟶ right and left hepatic ducts ⟶ common hepatic duct ⟶ common bile duct ⟶ ampulla of Vater ⟶ duodenum

Between the plates of hepatic cells are blood-filled spaces called **sinusoids.** The sinusoids are formed by branches of the hepatic artery and the hepatic portal vein and are the equivalent of hepatic capillaries. The hepatic artery contributes blood high in oxygen, and the hepatic portal vein carries blood rich in absorbed nutrients from the intestines. These substances can readily leave the blood and enter the hepatic cells (Fig. 25-16). Associated with the sinusoids are phagocytic **Kupffer cells (stellate reticuloendothelial cells).** The Kupffer cells remove bacteria, other foreign matter, and worn-out blood cells. The sinusoids empty into the central veins, which in turn empty into three larger **hepatic veins,** which drain into the inferior vena cava.

Blood in hepatic artery and hepatic portal vein ⟶ sinusoids ⟶ central veins ⟶ hepatic veins ⟶ inferior vena cava

Besides producing bile, the liver has other functions, including the following:

1. The liver removes excess nutrients from the blood. It can convert excess monosaccharides to glycogen or fat. It can convert excess amino acids into fatty acids and urea.
2. It functions in maintaining blood glucose levels by converting glycogen, fat, and proteins into glucose. This process is called glyconeogenesis.
3. It synthesizes plasma proteins and blood-clotting proteins.
4. It stores iron, copper, and certain vitamins (A, D, E, K, B_{12}).
5. It detoxifies harmful substances present in the blood. It can detoxify alcohol and some poisons. It converts nitrogenous wastes such as ammonia into urea, a less toxic form.
6. It phagocytizes bacteria and worn-out blood cells.
7. It plays a role in the activation of vitamin D.

(*text continued on p. 884*)

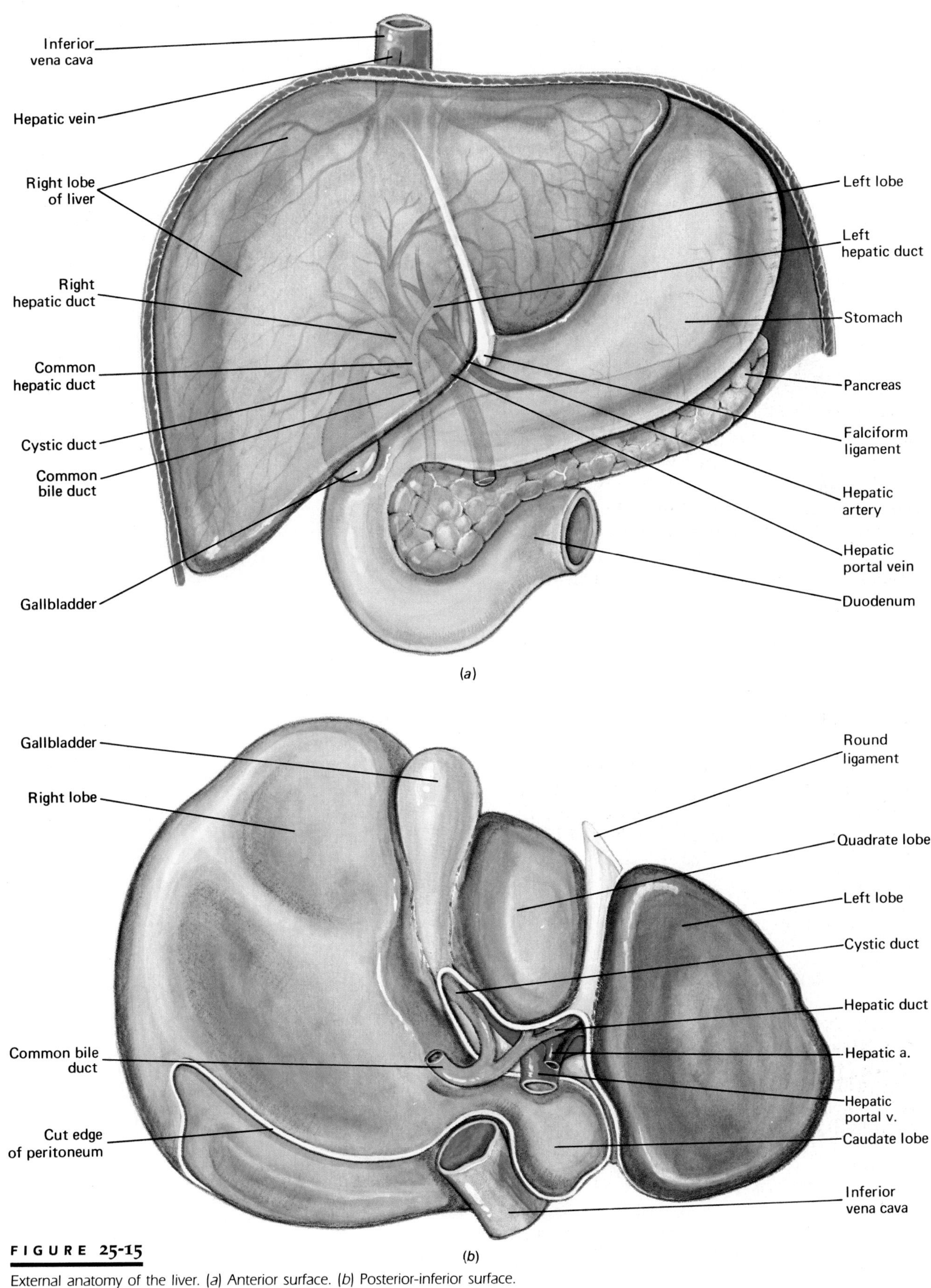

FIGURE 25-15

External anatomy of the liver. (*a*) Anterior surface. (*b*) Posterior-inferior surface.

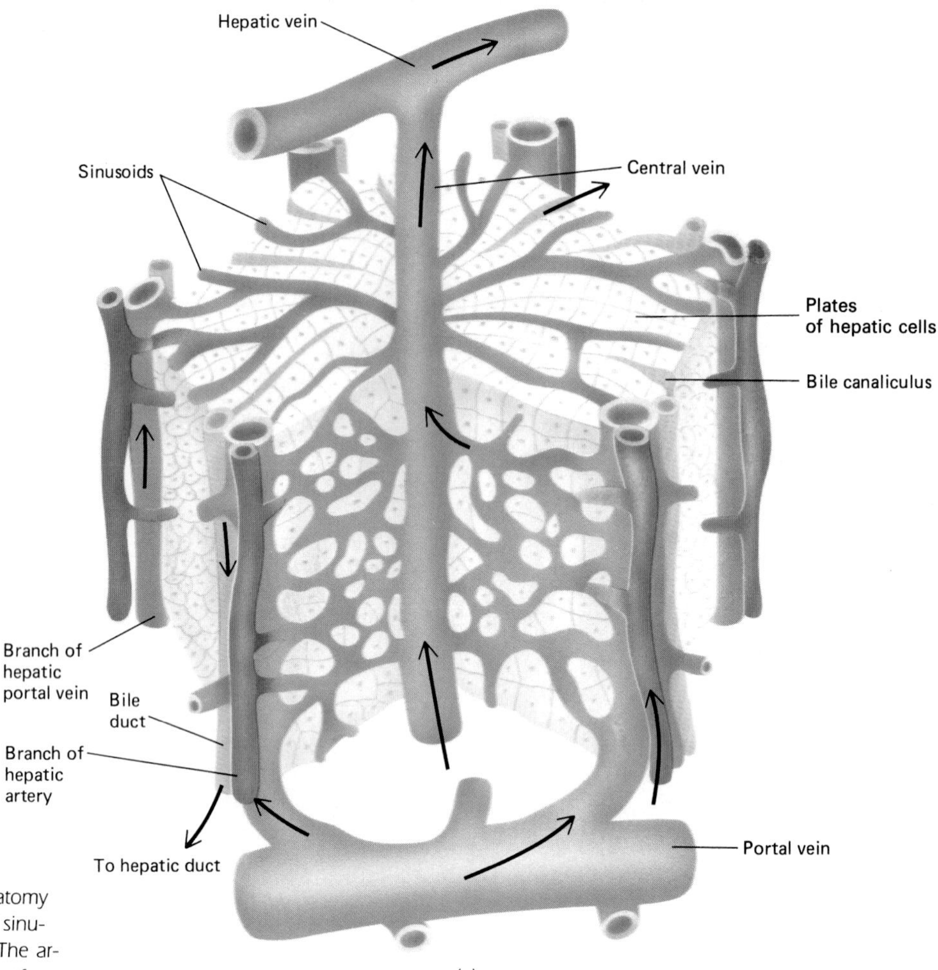

FIGURE 25-16

Internal anatomy of the liver. (*a*) Anatomy of a liver lobule. (*b*) Enlargement of sinusoids and associated blood vessels. The arrows show the direction of the flow of blood and bile.

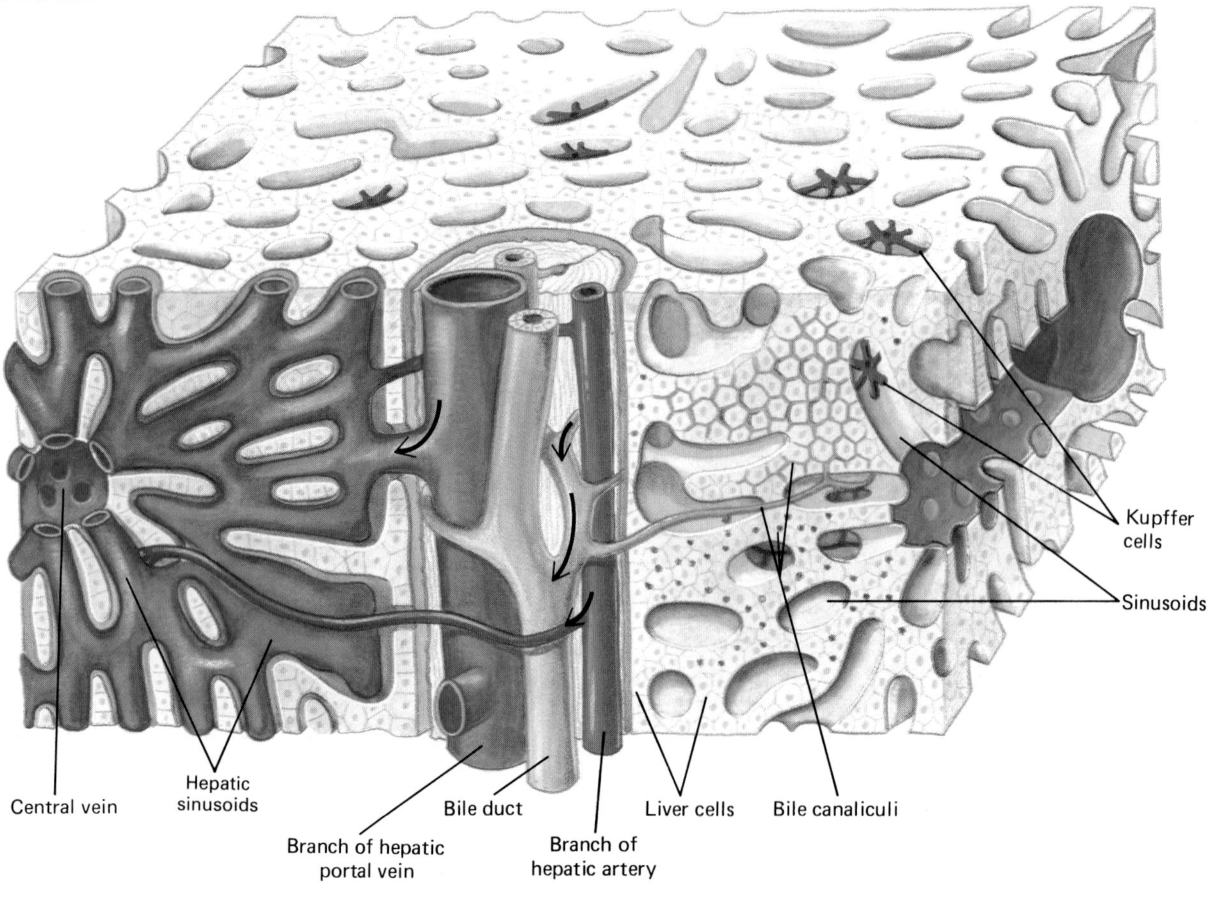

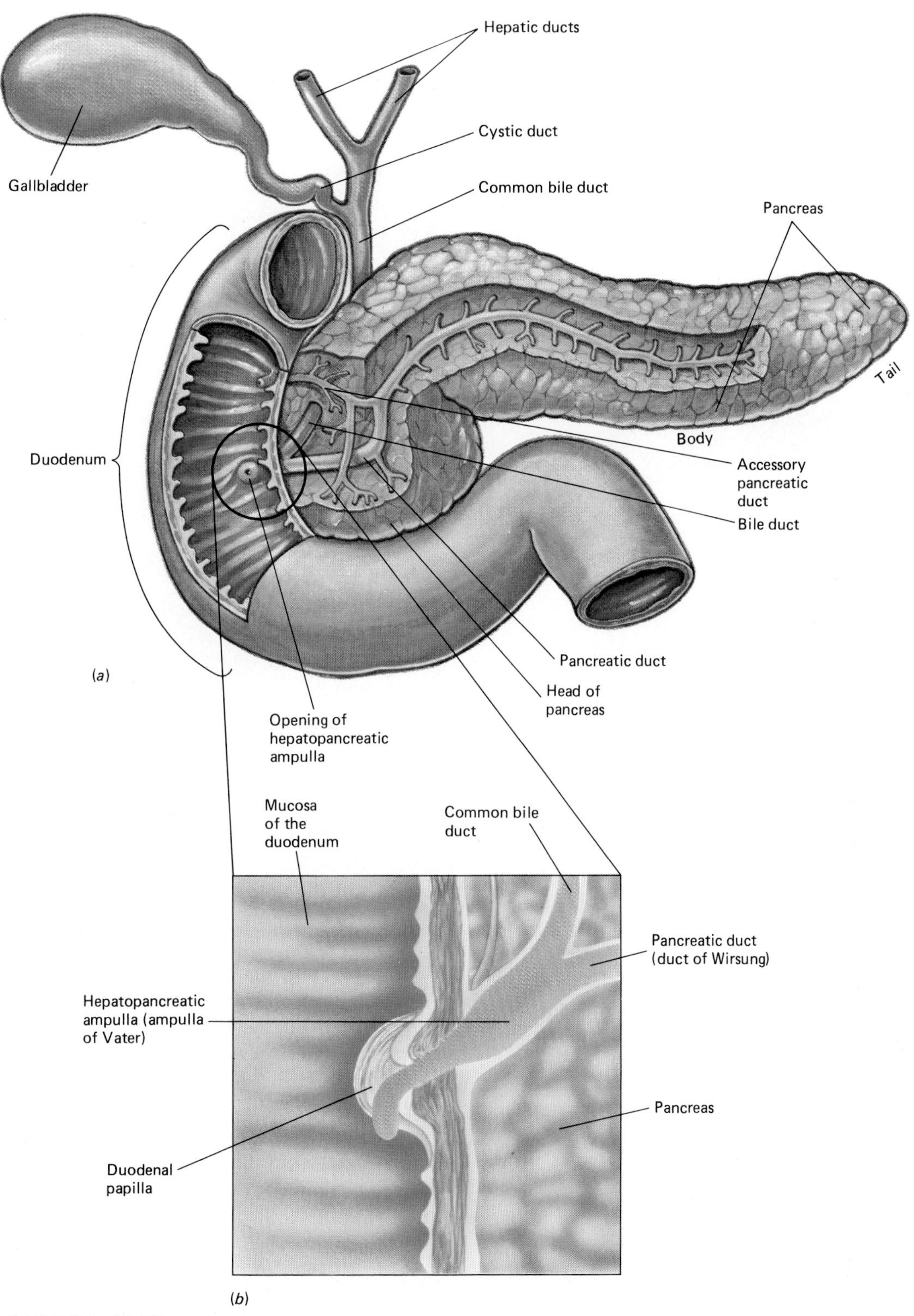

FIGURE 25-17

Anatomy of the gallbladder and bile ducts. (*a*) Longitudinal section showing internal duodenum. (*b*) Enlargement of ampulla of Vater (hepatopancreatic ampulla).

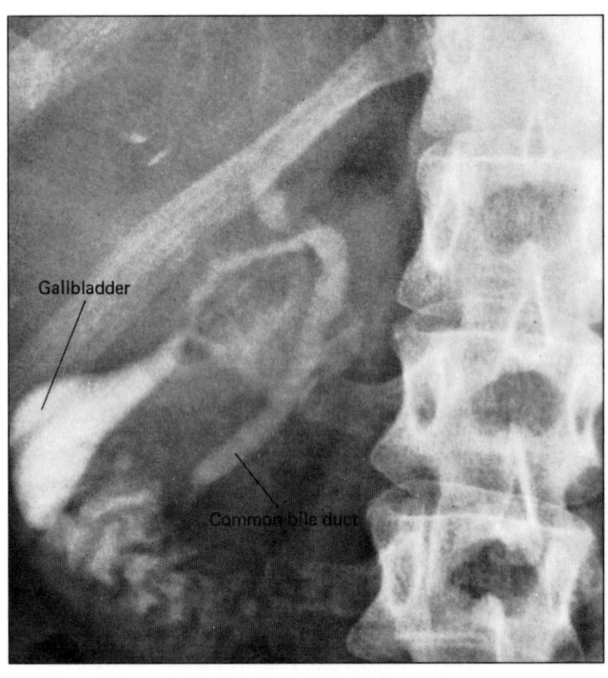

(a)

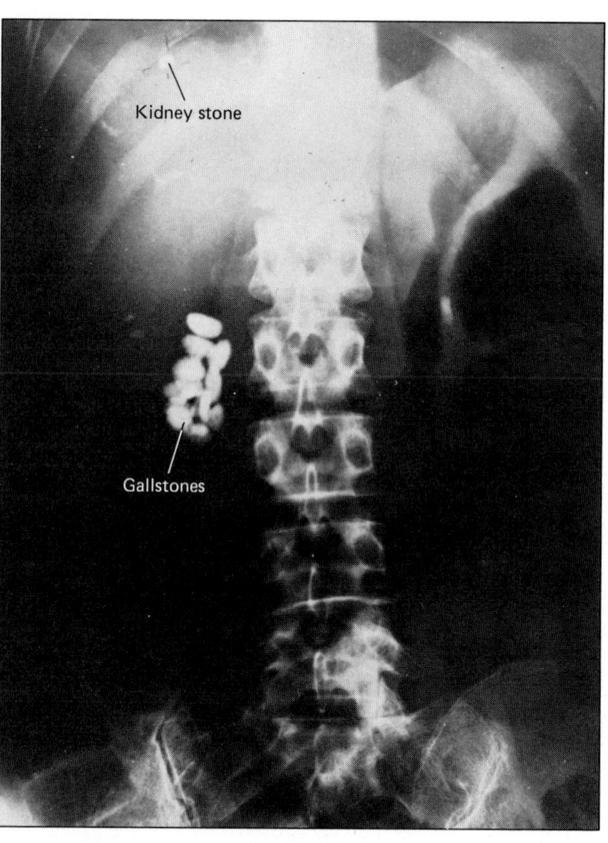

(b)

FIGURE 25-18

(a) X-ray showing gallbladder and common bile duct. (b) X-ray showing calcified gallstones in gallbladder. Also note kidney stone.

The gallbladder stores bile

The **gallbladder** is a small pear-shaped sac located on the inferior (visceral) side of the liver. When the small intestine is empty, a sphincter at the ampulla of Vater, called the **sphincter of Oddi,** closes, and bile backs up through the common bile duct and then into the gallbladder by way of the cystic duct. The gallbladder stores and concentrates the bile and releases it upon hormonal stimulation from the small intestine (Figs. 25-17, p. 883, and 25-18).

Gallbladder ⟶ cystic duct ⟶ common bile duct ⟶ sphincter of Oddi ⟶ duodenum

The small intestine has a large surface area

The **small intestine** starts at the pyloric sphincter and coils through the central and lower abdomen until ending at the **ileocecal** (il-ee-oh-**se**-kal) **sphincter** (valve), which directs undigested food into the large intestine. The small intestine is the part of the digestive tract in which most digestion and absorption takes place. It is about 5 to 6 meters (17 ft) in length and about 4 centimeters (1.5 in.) in diameter.

The **duodenum** (doo-oh-**dee**-num), which makes up about the first 22 centimeters of the small intestine, receives ducts from the liver and pancreas at an elevated area called the *ampulla of Vater*. Except for its first portion, it is retroperitoneal. The **jejunum** (jeh-**joo**-num) makes up the next 2 meters of the small intestine. The distal part of the small intestine is the **ileum** (ill-**ee**-um) and makes up the remaining 3½ meters. The ileum ends at the ileocecal sphincter. Associated with the ileum are lymphatic nodules. When these nodules are located in aggregates, they are referred to as *Peyer's patches*.

Stomach ⟶ pyloric sphincter ⟶ duodenum ⟶ jejunum ⟶ ileum ⟶ ileocecal sphincter ⟶ large intestine

The mucosa of the small intestine contains permanent circular folds called the **plicae circulares** (**ply**-key **sir**-kyoo-lar-es) (Fig. 25-19). Extending from the mucosa are millions of small finger-like

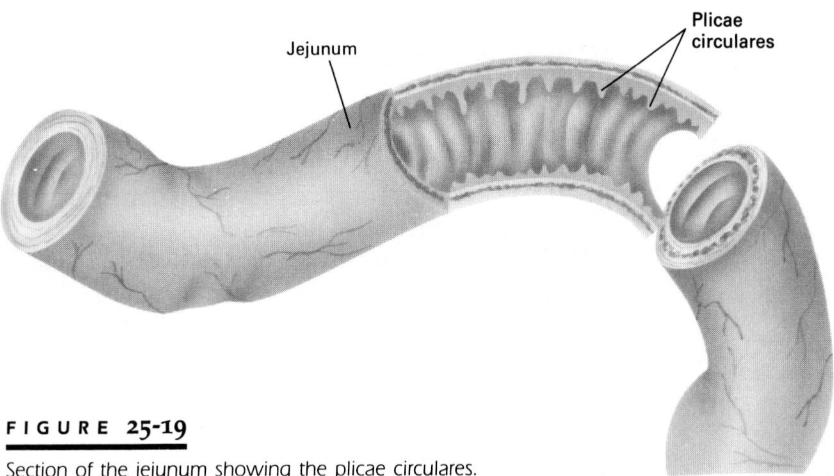

FIGURE 25-19

Section of the jejunum showing the plicae circulares.

projections, the **villi** (**vil**-ee), that give the mucosa a velvety appearance. The villi contain microscopic projections, the **microvilli,** extending from their epithelial cells. The microvilli form a *brush border* on which many of the digestive enzymes function. The plicae circulares, villi, and microvilli serve to greatly increase the surface area of the small intestine (600 times) for digestion and absorption. This surface area of the small intestine is equivalent to the surface area of a singles tennis court! The plicae circulares also enhance absorption by forcing the food to move in a spiral fashion instead of in a straight line.

Segmentation is the primary type of motility in the small intestine

The major contractile activity of the small intestine is called **segmentation.** Distension of the small intestine with chyme initiates a series of concentric contractions of the circular smooth muscle of the muscularis. These contractions form segments. When the smooth muscle relaxes, another set of contractions begins at a point between the previous contractions (Fig. 25-20). The contractions divide the chyme as often as 12 times per minute. Segmentation functions in a thorough mixing of the chyme with the digestive solutions present in the small intestine.

Peristalsis is also present in the small intestine, although it is weaker than in the esophagus and stomach. Peristalsis is propulsive, that is, it moves the chyme along the intestine, but it does this slowly, at a rate averaging about 1 centimeter per minute. Hence, food remains in the small intestine for 3 to 5 hours.

Stimulation by the submucosal plexus also causes contractions of the muscularis mucosa of the small intestine. These contractions form mucosal folds which increase surface area and the rate of absorption. Contractions of the villi milk the villi, enabling the lymph of the **lacteals** (**lak**-tee-als; intestinal lymph vessels in villi) to flow into the lymphatic system. The contractions also allow the villi to contact new areas of the chyme.

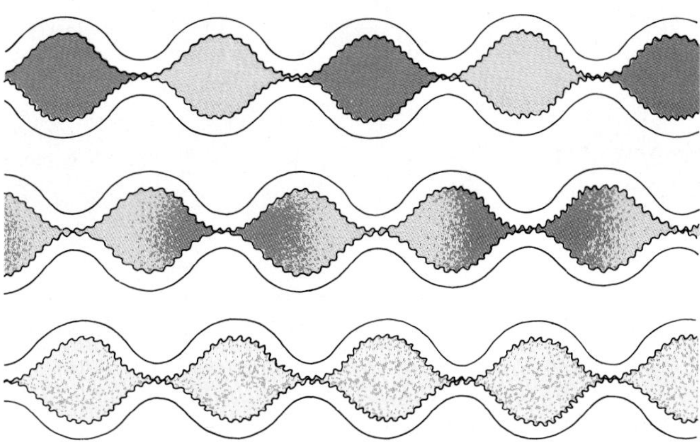

FIGURE 25-20

The mixing action of segmentation in the small intestine.

Secretions in the small intestine come from many sources

Most digestion occurs within the small intestine. The various secretions important in completing digestion come from the small intestine, pancreas, liver, and gallbladder.

THE SMALL INTESTINE PROVIDES SEVERAL SECRETIONS

The walls of the small intestine contribute a number of secretions to the digestive process: intestinal juices, mucus, and enzymes. Each *villus* of the intestinal wall consists of a single layer of absorptive epithelial cells surrounding a core that contains an arteriole, a capillary network, a venule, and a lymphatic vessel called a lacteal (Fig. 25-21). Digestive substances are absorbed through

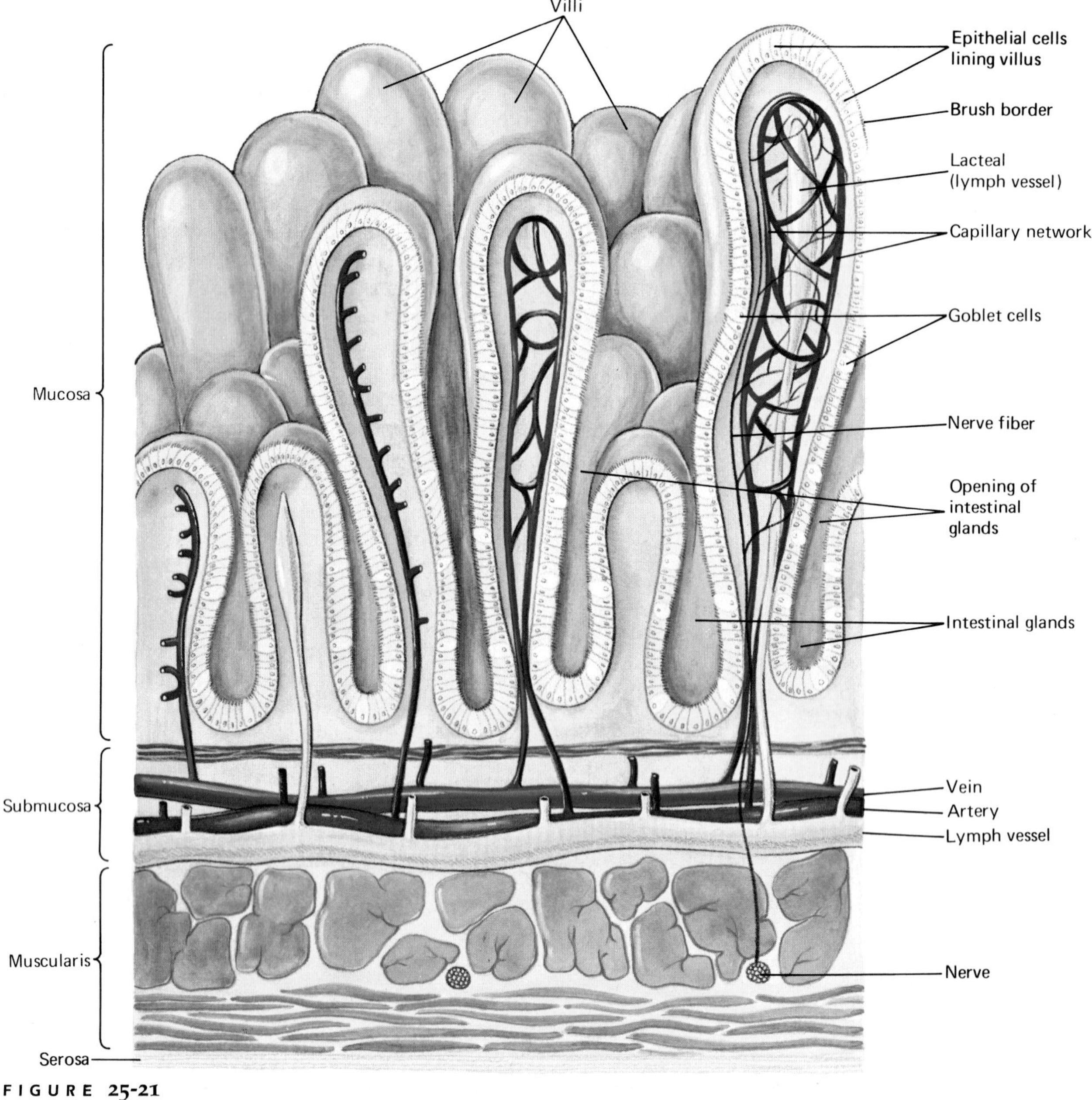

FIGURE 25-21

Anatomy of villi (cross section).

the intestinal epithelial cells and pass into intestinal capillaries or the lacteal.

At the bases of the villi, the mucosa contains the **intestinal glands (crypts of Lieberkuhn),** which secrete 2 to 3 liters of *intestinal juice* per day. This solution, almost pure interstitial fluid, functions as the medium for digestion and absorption. It is almost immediately reabsorbed by the villi. The rate of secretion of intestinal juice is regulated by local reflexes initiated by distension, irritation, and intestinal hormones (secretin, CCK, GIP).

Within the submucosa of the duodenum are mucous glands called **Brunner's glands** (duodenal glands or submucosal glands) which secrete an alkaline *mucus,* protecting the mucosa from the acidic chyme and enzymes (Fig. 25-22). *Goblet cells,* special types of mucosal epithelial cells, also secrete mucus (Fig. 25-21). Stimuli for the release of mucus include distension, irritation, vagal stimulation, and input from intestinal hormones.

The epithelial cells of the villi are constantly disintegrating and releasing digestive *enzymes* into the intestinal lumen. **Maltase, sucrase,** and **lactase** split disaccharides into monosaccharides. **Intestinal lipase** helps to digest fats. **Aminopeptidase** and **dipeptidases** help in protein digestion. Many of these enzymes stay in contact with the brush border of the microvilli.

PANCREATIC JUICE IS SECRETED BY THE PANCREAS

Pancreatic juice is secreted by the pancreas and travels to the duodenum by way of the pancreatic duct. Pancreatic juice, secreted at a rate of about 1400 milliliters per day, contains a high concentration of sodium bicarbonate and enzymes. The **sodium bicarbonate** functions to neutralize the acidic chyme in the duodenum, bringing the duodenal contents up to approximately pH 7 to 8, in which range most of the digestive enzymes operating in the small intestine are functional. This rise in pH also stops the action of pepsin.

Digestive enzymes secreted include **pancreatic amylase,** a carbohydrate-digesting enzyme. **Pancreatic lipase** digests fats. **Trypsin, chymotrypsin,** and **carboxypeptidase** digest proteins. **Ribonuclease** and **deoxyribonuclease** break down nucleic acids.

The proteolytic (protein-lysing) enzymes are produced by the acinar cells of the pancreas in the inactive forms of trypsinogen, chymotrypsinogen, and procarboxypeptidase. This prevents the autodigestion of the pancreas. The pancreas also produces **trypsin inhibitor,** which prevents the activation of trypsin in the pancreas and pancreatic duct.

When the inactive proteolytic enzymes from the pancreas enter the duodenum, they become activated. Trypsinogen is converted to trypsin by an enzyme produced by the intestinal mucosa called **enterokinase.**

$$\text{Trypsinogen} \xrightarrow{\text{enterokinase}} \text{trypsin}$$

In turn, trypsin activates chymotrypsin and carboxypeptidase.

$$\text{Chymotrypsinogen} \xrightarrow{\text{trypsin}} \text{chymotrypsin}$$

$$\text{Procarboxypeptidase} \xrightarrow{\text{trypsin}} \text{carboxypeptidase}$$

The release of pancreatic juice is controlled by both neural and hormonal mechanisms: Parasympathetic nerves can cause an increase in the secretion of pancreatic juice. **Secretin** from the duodenal mucosa enhances secretion of bicarbonates. **Cholecystokinin** (CCK) from the duodenal mucosa increases secretion of digestive enzymes. The major stimuli for secretin release are acids in the duodenum, including HCl, amino acids, and fatty acids. The major stimuli for cholecystokinin release are protein digestion products and fatty acids (Table 25-2).

Acids in duodenum ⟶ ↑ secretin release from duodenum ⟶ ↑ bicarbonate secretion of pancreas

Protein digestion products ⟶ ↑ cholecystokinin release from duodenum ⟶ ↑ enzyme secretion of pancreas

LIVER AND GALLBLADDER PROVIDE BILE

Bile is secreted by the liver at a rate of about 800 to 1000 milliliters per day and stored in the gallbladder. This rate can be increased by vagal stimulation, secretin, and high levels of bile salts in the blood. Bile is not an enzyme, rather it is primarily made up of **bile salts** and **bile pigments** along with some cholesterol, lecithin, and electrolytes. It is the bile salts that are important digestively. Bile salts emulsify fats in the small intestine. *Emulsification* (ee-mul-sih-fih-**kay**-shun) is the breaking down of large fat droplets into many smaller fat droplets. This action increases the surface area of fats, which greatly speeds up their digestion. Bile salts also play an important role in the absorption of fat digestion products.

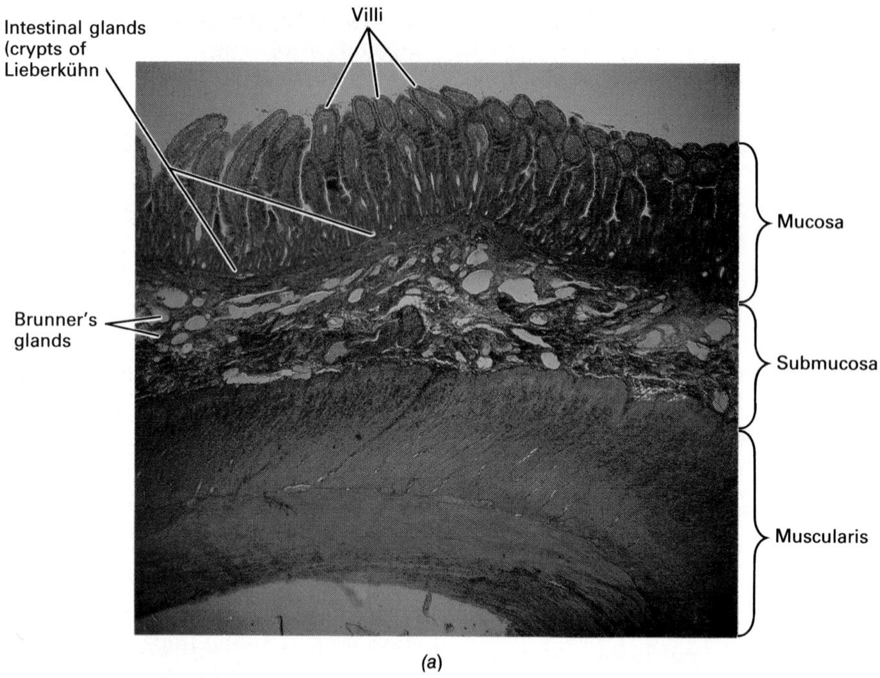

(a)

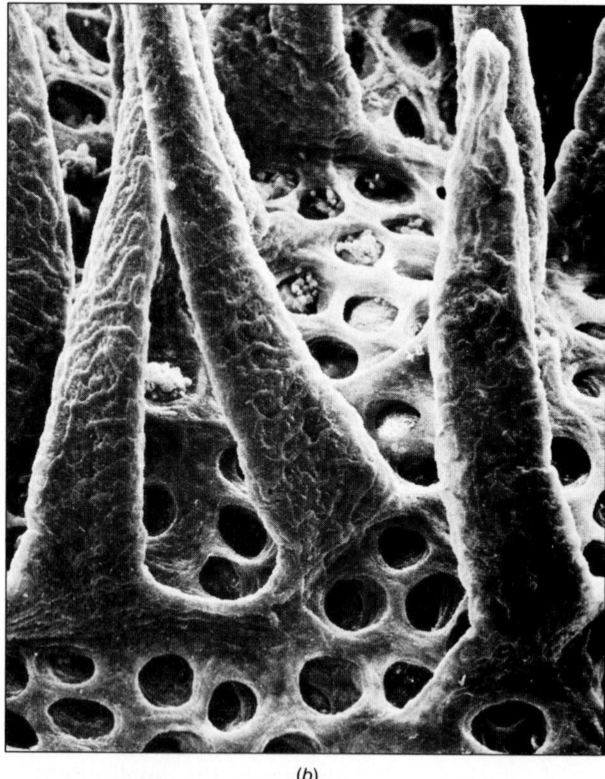

(b)

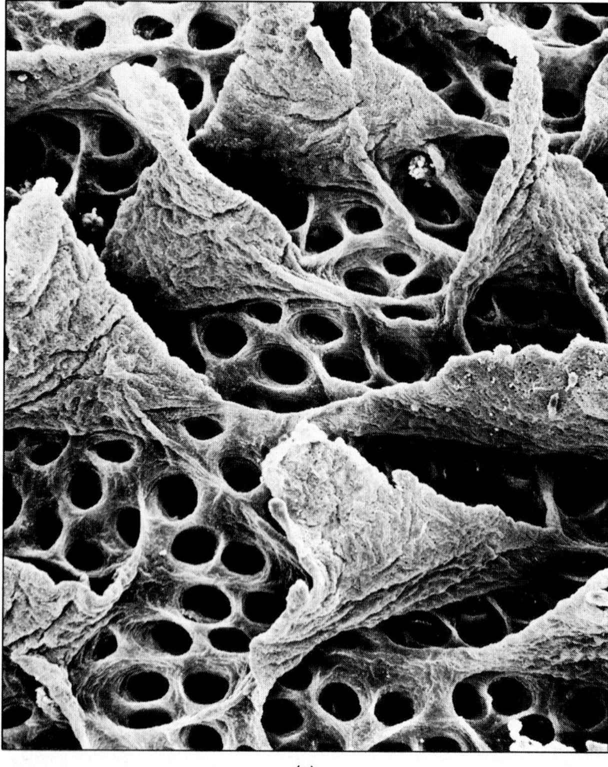

(c)

FIGURE 25-22

(*a*) Photomicrograph of a portion of the wall of the duodenum. (Roland Birke/Peter Arnold, Inc.) (*b*, *c*) Scanning electron micrographs of two differently shaped villi from the duodenum of a mouse. The holes are the openings into the intestinal glands. The ratio of glands to villi is higher in the mouse than in the human intestine. (*b*) Finger-like villi (approx. ×180). (*c*) Leaf-shaped villi (approx. ×180). Both types are found in the human intestine. (From Partridge, B. T., and Simpson, L. O.: Micron, vol. 11. New York, Pergamon Press, 1980.)

Cholecystokinin produces a contraction of the walls of the gallbladder, causing it to empty. CCK also results in a relaxation of the sphincter of Oddi (Table 25-2).

> Fats in duodenum ⟶ ↑ cholecystokinin release ⟶ ↑ contraction of gallbladder ⟶ ↑ bile flow into duodenum

Most digestion occurs in the small intestine

Most carbohydrate, protein, and fat digestion occurs in the small intestine.

Carbohydrate digestion continues in the small intestine

The end products of carbohydrate digestion are monosaccharides. **Salivary amylase** began the digestion of starches in the oral cavity. Some dextrins were formed (Fig. 25-23). The carbohydrates entering the small intestine consist of dextrins, maltose, starch, and sucrose. A small amount of lactose (milk sugar) may also be present.

Pancreatic amylase digests the rest of the starch and dextrins into maltose.

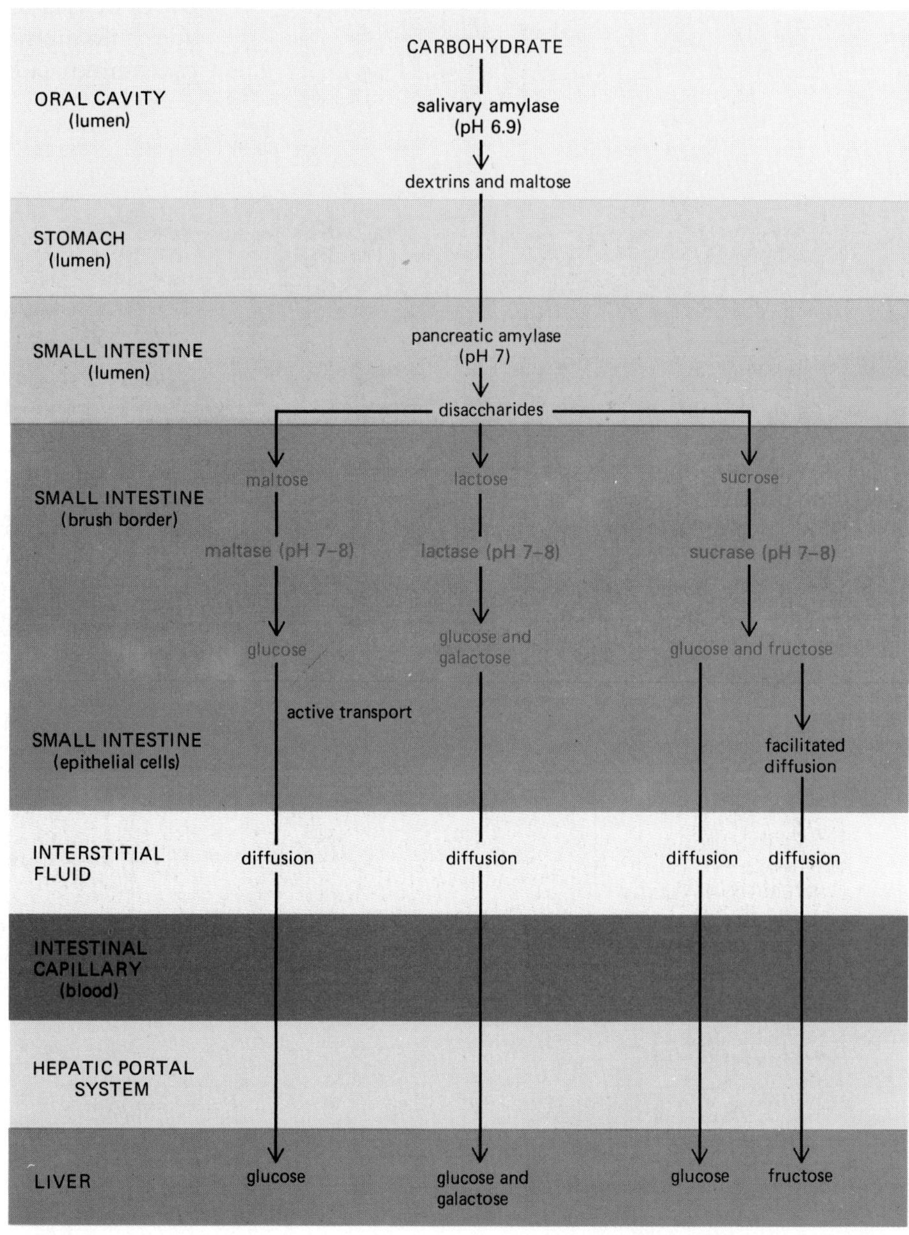

FIGURE 25-23

Carbohydrate digestion and absorption.

$$\text{Starch and dextrins} \xrightarrow{\text{pancreatic amylase}} \text{maltose}$$

Maltose and sucrose are disaccharides. Maltose is broken down by **maltase** into two glucose molecules. Sucrose is digested by **sucrase** into the monosaccharides glucose and fructose. Lactose is broken down by **lactase** into glucose and galactose. The enzymes breaking down the disaccharides into monosaccharides are byproducts of intestinal mucosal cell disintegration. Most of these enzymes are located at the brush border of the villi. For a summary, see Figure 25-23, p. 889.

$$\text{Maltose} \xrightarrow{\text{maltase}} \text{glucose} + \text{glucose}$$

$$\text{Sucrose} \xrightarrow{\text{sucrase}} \text{glucose} + \text{fructose}$$

$$\text{Lactose} \xrightarrow{\text{lactase}} \text{glucose} + \text{galactose}$$

Proteins are digested to amino acids

The end products of protein digestion are amino acids. Protein digestion begins in the stomach with **pepsin.** Pepsin breaks proteins down into smaller peptide fragments called proteoses and peptones. Within the small intestine, **trypsin** and **chymotrypsin** complete the breakdown of proteins into proteoses and peptones. Other enzymes are then able to break peptide bonds between different amino acids on these protein fragments. **Carboxypeptidase** splits off the terminal amino acid from these peptide fragments at their free carboxyl end. **Aminopeptidase** splits off the terminal amino acid from the free amine end. **Dipeptidases** break down the remaining dipeptides into amino acids. A dipeptide consists of two amino acids joined by a peptide bond. Ami-

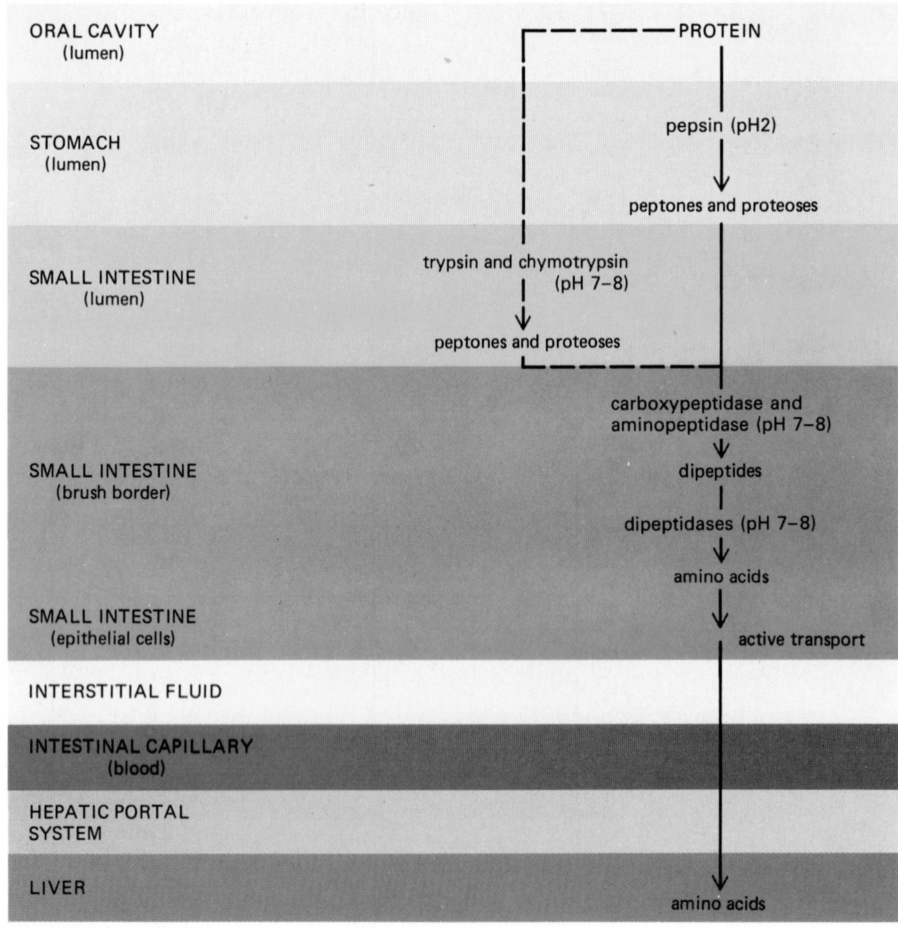

FIGURE 25-24

Protein digestion and absorption.

nopeptidase and the dipeptidases are associated with the brush border of the villi. A summary is given in Figure 25-24.

$$\text{Proteins} \xrightarrow{\text{chymotrypsin, trypsin, pepsin}} \text{proteoses and peptones}$$

$$\text{Proteoses and peptones} \xrightarrow{\text{carboxypeptidase, aminopeptidase}} \text{dipeptides}$$

$$\text{Dipeptides} \xrightarrow{\text{dipeptidases}} \text{amino acids}$$

Fats are broken down into fatty acids and monoglycerides

The end products of fat digestion are fatty acids and monoglycerides. Very little, if any, fat digestion has occurred before the fat enters the small intestine. In the duodenum, **bile salts** begin to emulsify fats into small fat droplets. This increases surface area for the action of **pancreatic lipase.** Pancreatic lipase is the major enzyme digesting fats. It breaks the fat droplets into fatty acids and monoglycerides. Most of the ingested fat is in the form of triglycerides. A triglyceride has a glycerol backbone with three fatty acids attached to it. Lipase splits off two of the fatty acids. The glycerol with the remaining fatty acid is called a monoglyceride. See Figure 25-25.

$$\text{Large fat droplets} \xrightarrow{\text{bile salts}} \text{small fat droplets}$$

$$\text{Small fat droplets} \xrightarrow{\text{pancreatic lipase}} \text{fatty acids + monoglycerides}$$

Nucleic acids become pentoses and nitrogen bases

Nucleic acids are digested by **ribonuclease** and **deoxyribonuclease** into pentoses (5-carbon monosaccharides) and nitrogen bases. The enzymes are produced in the pancreas and function in the intestinal lumen.

$$\text{Nucleic acids} \xrightarrow{\text{ribonuclease, deoxyribonuclease}} \text{pentoses + nitrogen bases}$$

See Table 25-3 for a summary of digestive agents.

Most absorption occurs in the small intestine

Any substance located within the lumen of the digestive tract technically is not part of the body proper. The substance still communicates directly with the external environment through the mouth and the anus. It is not until the substance is absorbed that it becomes part of the body proper.

Monosaccharides are absorbed in the small intestine

Most monosaccharides are absorbed in the duodenum and upper jejunum. **Glucose** and **galactose** are actively absorbed and their absorption is linked to a *sodium transport* system. The carrier protein for their absorption is located in the brush border of the villi. **Fructose** is absorbed by *facilitated diffusion.* Once these monosaccharides are absorbed into the epithelial cells of the villi, they leave the cells by facilitated diffusion and enter the intestinal capillaries of the villi. These capillaries are part of the hepatic portal system, which takes the monosaccharides to the liver (Fig. 25-23).

Amino acids are absorbed in the small intestine

By the end of the jejunum, most amino acids are actively absorbed and are believed to use the same *sodium transport system* as glucose. This system is located within the brush border of the villi. After being absorbed into the epithelial cells of the villi, the amino acids probably move into the intestinal capillaries by facilitated diffusion. The amino acids are taken to the liver by the hepatic portal system (Fig. 25-24). Newborns are able to absorb entire proteins for a few days after birth.

Fatty acids and monoglycerides are absorbed in the small intestine

Fat absorption occurs primarily in the duodenum and jejunum and is completed in the ileum. In the absence of bile salts, only 50 to 60% of fat is absorbed. Most of the bile salts are reabsorbed at

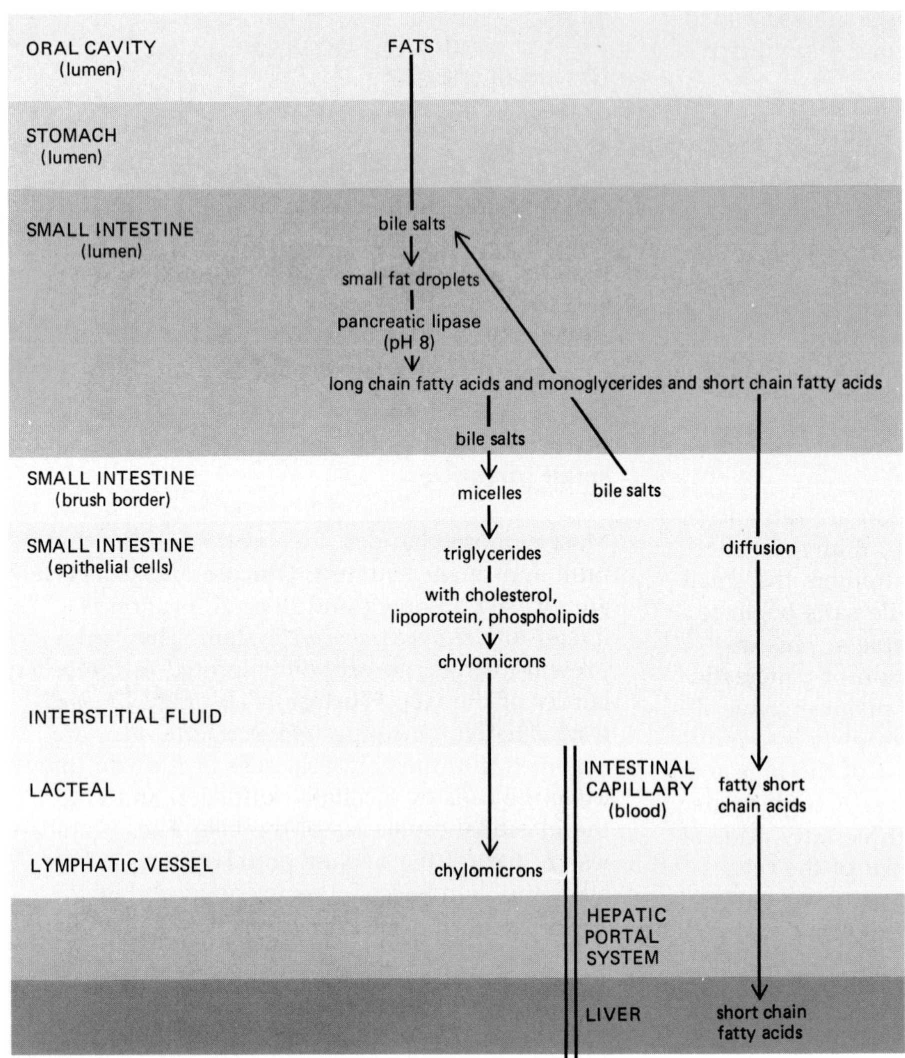

FIGURE 25-25

Fat digestion and absorption.

the ileum and taken back to the liver via the hepatic portal system.

Small quantities of very small fatty acids are able to directly enter the intestinal capillaries of the villi. However, the majority of fatty acids are long chained and are absorbed quite differently. Within the intestinal lumen, bile salts form aggregates called **micelles (my-selz)** that are water soluble. Fatty acids and monoglycerides are aggregated into the centers of the micelles. The micelles transport the fatty acids and monoglycerides to the brush borders. From here, the fatty acids and monoglycerides diffuse into the epithelial cells of the villi. The micelles continue their ferrying function in the intestinal lumen.

Within the epithelial cells, the fatty acids and monoglycerides are resynthesized into **triglycerides.** The triglycerides combine with cholesterol, lipoprotein, and phospholipids to form globules called **chylomicrons** (**ky**-low-my-krons). The chylomicrons leave the epithelial cells and enter into the lacteal of the villus. Lymphatic vessels carry the chylomicrons to the venous blood of the left subclavian vein via the thoracic duct (Fig. 25-25).

Vitamins are absorbed in the small intestine

The **fat-soluble vitamins (A, D, E, K)** affiliate with the micelles and are absorbed through the brush border. Most **water-soluble vitamins (C, B complex)** are absorbed by passive diffusion. **Vitamin B_{12}** has a more complex mechanism for ab-

TABLE 25-3

Summary of digestive agents

Agent (active form)	Optimum pH	Source	Substrate	Result
Oral cavity				
Salivary amylase	6.9	Parotid glands and submandibular glands	Carbohydrates	Dextrins and maltose
Mucus		Submandibular and sublingual glands	Food	Moistening and lubrication
Stomach				
Pepsin	2.0	Zymogenic cells	Proteins	Proteoses and peptones
Hydrochloric acid (HCl)		Parietal cells	Pepsinogen molecular bonds	Pepsin
Mucus		Mucus-secreting cells	Food and gastric mucosa	Protection
Liver				
Bile salts		Hepatic cells	Fats	Emulsification
Pancreas				
Pancreatic amylase	7.1	Acinar cells	Dextrins	Disaccharides
Pancreatic lipase	8.0	Acinar cells	Emulsified fats	Fatty acids and monoglycerides
Trypsin	8.0	Acinar cells	Proteins	Proteoses and peptones
Chymotrypsin	8.0	Acinar cells	Proteins	Proteoses and peptones
Carboxypeptidase	8.0	Acinar cells	Proteoses and peptones	Dipeptides and amino acids
Sodium bicarbonate		Duct cells	Acidic chyme	Neutralizes acidity
Small intestine				
Maltase	8.0	Intestinal mucosa	Maltose	Glucose
Sucrase	8.0	Intestinal mucosa	Sucrose	Glucose and lactose
Lactase	8.0	Intestinal mucosa	Lactose	Glucose and galactose
Aminopeptidase	8.0	Intestinal mucosa	Proteoses and peptones	Amino acids
Dipeptidase	8.0	Intestinal mucosa	Dipeptides	Amino acids
Ribonuclease	8.0	Intestinal mucosa	RNA	Pentoses and nitrogen bases
Deoxyribonuclease	8.0	Intestinal mucosa	DNA	Pentoses and nitrogen bases
Enterokinase	6.9	Intestinal mucosa	Trypsinogen	Trypsin (active)
Mucus		Brunner's glands and goblet cells	Intestinal mucosa	Protection
Intestinal juice		Intestinal glands	Chyme	Medium for digestion and absorption

sorption. Within the stomach, vitamin B_{12} combines with **intrinsic factor,** which is produced by the parietal cells. It is only in this combination that the vitamin can be actively absorbed by the ileum of the small intestine. It is one of the largest substances absorbed by the GI tract.

Water and electrolytes are absorbed in the small intestine

Fluid enters the small intestine as ingested liquids (about 1.5 liters per day) and as GI tract secretions (about 7.5 liters per day). Of this 9 liters of fluid entering the small intestine each day, nearly 8.5 liters of it is absorbed before leaving the small intestine. Most of the water absorbed in the small intestine is by osmosis through the epithelial cells of the villi and into the intestinal capillaries. Osmosis can occur across the epithelial cells in both directions. As electrolytes and digested nutrients are absorbed, water follows. This maintains an osmotic balance between the intestinal lumen and the blood.

Sodium can diffuse into and out of the epithelial cells. It is also actively transported into the epithelial cells for removal from the small intestine. Bicarbonate ions are actively absorbed in the duodenum and jejunum in the form of CO_2. This occurs when hydrogen ions are secreted into the intestinal lumen. Chloride ions follow the sodium and are absorbed passively in the duodenum and jejunum. Chloride ions can also be actively absorbed in the ileum in exchange for bicarbonate ions. This provides a buffer for acidic products of bacterial metabolism in the large intestine.

Potassium, magnesium, iron, phosphate, and calcium ions are actively absorbed. Calcium absorption is regulated by parathyroid hormone and vitamin D. Parathyroid hormone activates vitamin D in the kidneys, and the activated vitamin D increases the absorption of calcium.

The large intestine eliminates undigested food

The **large intestine** runs from the ileocecal sphincter (valve) to the anus, measuring about 1.5 meters (5 ft) in length and about 6.5 centimeters (2.5 in.) in diameter (Fig. 25-26). This diameter is larger than the diameter of the small intestine, hence, the name large intestine. The large intestine is made up of the cecum, colon, rectum, and anal canal. The large intestine functions in finishing absorption, forming and storing the feces, and eliminating the feces from the body. See Window on the Human Body, Views 3–5.

The first part of the large intestine is the **cecum** (**see**-kum). The cecum is a pouch located in the lower right quadrant of the abdomen. Extending from the cecum is a coiled tube about 8 centimeters (3 in.) in length called the **vermiform appendix.** The walls of the appendix contain many lymphatic nodules.

The next part of the large intestine is the **colon** (**koe**-lon), which is divided into the ascending colon, transverse colon, descending colon, and sigmoid colon. The ascending and descending colons are retroperitoneal. The **ascending colon** is the section of the colon located superior to the cecum on the right side of the abdomen. It stops at the lower border of the liver and then turns toward the left side of the body. This angle, or turn, is referred to as the **right colic** (**koe**-lik), or **hepatic, flexure.** From the right colic flexure, the colon continues across the upper abdomen as the **transverse colon.** At the left side, in the area of the spleen, the colon curves downward at the **left colic,** or **splenic, flexure** and becomes the **descending colon.** The descending colon courses downward on the left side of the abdomen until reaching the left iliac crest. At the iliac crest, the colon makes an S-shaped curve medially as the **sigmoid colon.** The sigmoid colon is located in the lower left quadrant of the abdomen. It leads into the rectum. The sigmoid colon has its own mesentery, the **sigmoid mesocolon.**

The short **rectum** makes up the last 12 centimeters or so of the digestive tract. Its final 4 centimeters are called the **anal canal.** The mucous membrane of the anal canal is arranged in vertical folds called **anal columns.** The opening of the anal canal to the exterior is the **anus.** Preceding the anus is an **internal anal sphincter** made up of smooth muscle (involuntary) and an **external anal sphincter** (voluntary) made up of skeletal muscle (Fig. 25-27).

Ileocecal sphincter ⟶ cecum ⟶ ascending colon ⟶ transverse colon ⟶ descending colon ⟶ sigmoid colon ⟶ rectum ⟶ anal canal ⟶ anal sphincters ⟶ anus

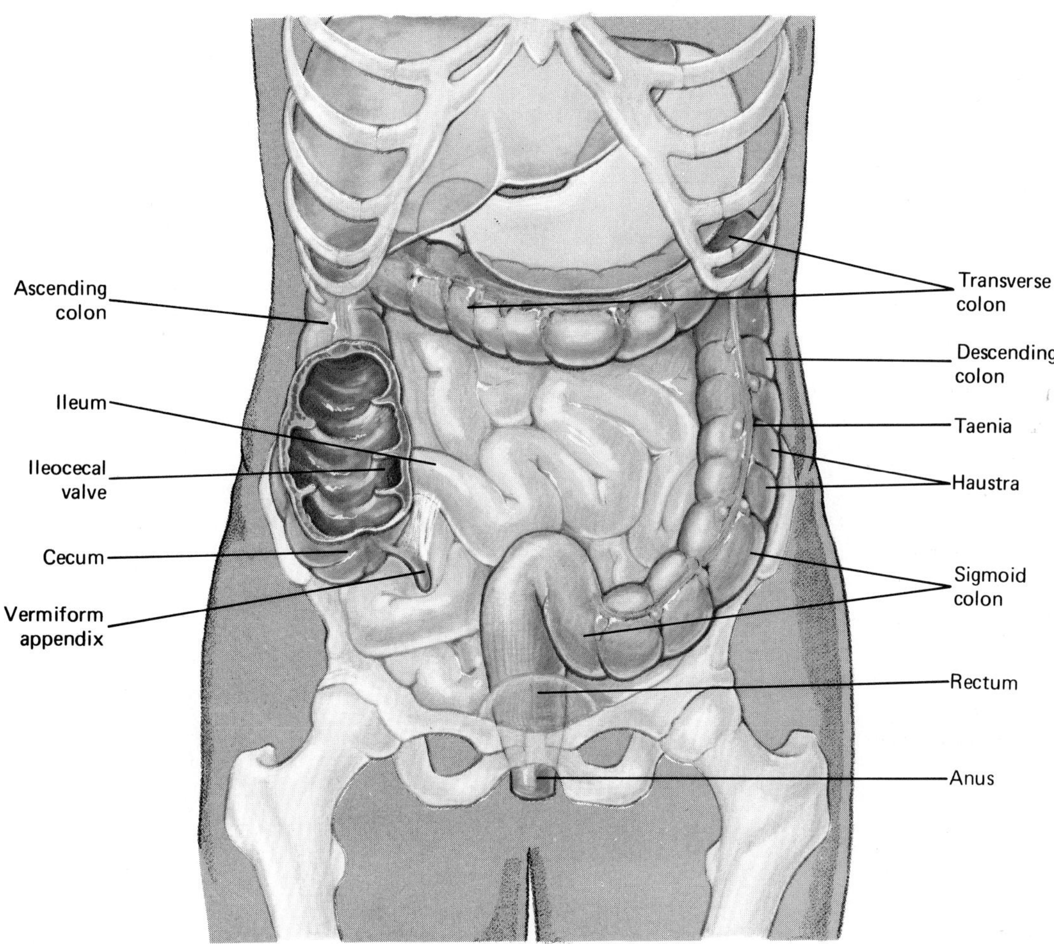

FIGURE 25-26

Anatomy of the large intestine, showing the ileocecal valve.

Mass movement rapidly transports fecal material through the large intestine

No enzymes are secreted by the large intestine. The mucosa of the large intestine consists primarily of simple columnar epithelium and numerous goblet cells. These are located within long intestinal glands. Villi are absent. Mucus is secreted by the goblet cells. The rate of mucus secretion is stimulated by distension, local reflexes, and parasympathetic input. The mucus serves in protection and in holding fecal matter together. The mucus also contains high levels of sodium bicarbonate, which neutralizes the acidity of bacterial metabolism.

The large intestine is also capable of secreting large amounts of water and electrolytes whenever it becomes severely irritated.

Material remains in the large intestine for as long as 24 hours. The motility of the large intestine is normally sluggish and similar to that of the small intestine in that there are mixing contractions and propulsive contractions. Combined with segmentation-like contractions are contractions of the three longitudinal muscle bands, the **taeniae coli** (**tee**-nee-ee **koe**-lye). The result is the formation of baglike pouches called **haustra** (**haw**-strah) (Fig. 25-26). Haustra are continually formed and re-formed in an analward direction, exposing the fecal material to the mucosa.

Peristalsis similar to that in the small intestine is almost nonexistent in the large intestine. The haustral contractions provide a slow movement analward, taking as much as 8 to 15 hours to move the chyme from the ileocecal sphincter (valve) to the transverse colon. Beyond this point, the propulsive movement of the colon is by "mass movement."

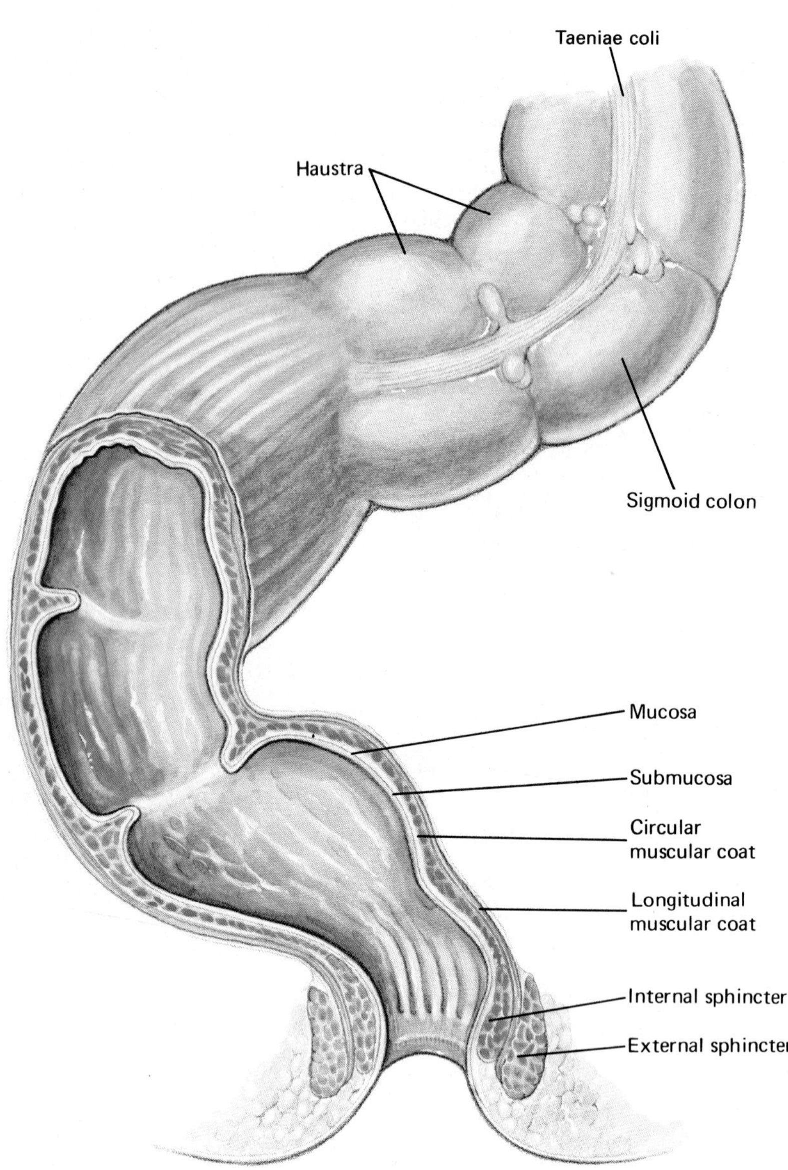

FIGURE 25-27

The rectum and anus. Note the internal and external anal sphincters.

Mass movement, or mass peristalsis, occurs when a part of the colon, most often the transverse colon, constricts and strong contractile waves move over large parts of the remaining colon. This forces the fecal material to move en masse through the colon and into the rectum. A single mass movement takes about 30 seconds and is followed by another one a few minutes later. A series of mass movements may take about 10 to 30 minutes and occur about 3 or 4 times daily, generally during and immediately after a meal. Distension of the stomach and duodenum reflexly causes the mass movement of the colon. These reflexes are called the **gastrocolic** (gas-tro-**ko**-lik) and **duodenocolic reflexes,** respectively.

When the fecal material reaches the rectum, it initiates a desire for **defecation** (deh-fih-**kay**-shun). By this time much of the water has been absorbed, and the feces (**fee**-seez) are solid in composition. Feces generally contain about 75% water by weight. The solid portion of the feces consists of about 30% bacteria, along with cellulose, cellular debris, salts, and bile pigments. The major bile pigment excreted by the large intestine is **bilirubin** (bil-ee-**roo**-bin). Bilirubin is a breakdown product of aging red blood cells. It is secreted by the liver as part of the bile. Bacteria in the large intestine convert bilirubin to *urobilin* and *stercobilin*. These derivatives of bilirubin are responsible for giving the feces their characteristic brown color.

Normally the rectum is devoid of feces due to the sharp angle of the union of the sigmoid colon with the rectum. Feces in the rectum initiate a **defecation reflex,** which moves the feces out of the lower colon and rectum. The distension causes stretch receptors to stimulate the myenteric plexus and afferent nerves to the sacral spinal cord. Peristaltic contractions resulting from the input of the myenteric plexus are relatively weak. Parasympathetic nerves from the spinal cord cause strong peristaltic contractions or mass movement of the descending colon, sigmoid colon, rectum, and anus. The peristalsis also causes a relaxation of the internal anal sphincter. If the external anal sphincter is voluntarily relaxed, defecation occurs. If the external anal sphincter is not relaxed, the feces are stored in the colon until the next mass movement occurs. Infants lack control of the external anal sphincter, and defecation automatically occurs in response to the defecation reflex.

Distension of rectum ⟶ ↑ firing of stretch receptors ⟶ ↑ afferent impulses ⟶ stimulation of sacral spinal cord ⟶ ↑ parasympathetic impulses ⟶ strong peristaltic contractions of lower large intestine ⟶ relaxation of internal anal sphincter ⟶ voluntary relaxation of external anal sphincter ⟶ defecation

Vitamins and fluid are absorbed in the large intestine

Any digestion in the large intestine is due to the action of bacteria. Most absorption takes place in the proximal parts of the large intestine, with the distal parts serving mainly for storage. Bacterial metabolism results in the formation of certain waste products such as nitrogen, carbon dioxide, hydrogen, methane, and hydrogen sulfide. This mixture of gases is referred to as **flatus** (gas). Other bacterial products contribute to the odor of the feces, including indoles, skatole, and mercaptans. The bacteria also synthesize several vitamins, including vitamin K and some of the B-complex vitamins. These vitamins are absorbed by the large intestine.

The large intestine normally absorbs most of the water that enters it. Of the 9 liters of fluid entering the intestines per day, the small intestine absorbs about 8 to 8.5 liters and the large intestine absorbs from 0.5 to 1 liter. About 100 milliliters of fluid is eliminated in the feces. The large intestine also actively absorbs sodium and chloride. The osmotic gradient that is produced causes the absorption of the water. Bicarbonates are secreted by the large intestine to neutralize acids produced by the bacteria. See Focus on Disorders of the Digestive System.

Centers in the hypothalamus regulate food intake

The two major centers for regulating food intake are found in the hypothalamus of the brain. One center, the **feeding (hunger) center,** is located in the lateral nuclei of the hypothalamus. Stimulation of the feeding center causes animals to start eating. The other center is the **satiety center,** located in the ventromedial nuclei of the hypothalamus. When the satiety center is stimulated, even starved animals refuse to eat.

It is believed that the feeding center is always active and the satiety center inhibits it under certain conditions. Glucose levels in the blood have an effect on food intake. The *glucostatic theory* states that when blood glucose levels are low, appetite increases. When glucose levels are high, the satiety center inhibits the feeding center and appetite decreases. When glucose levels are low, the feeding center is released from inhibition and appetite increases. Low blood levels of *amino acids* also can stimulate the feeding center. It is also believed that *fatty acids* in the blood can stimulate the satiety center which inhibits the feeding center. High *body temperature* has been found to depress appetite. The *distension* of the stomach and the duodenum causes a reflex inhibition of the feeding center and stimulation of the satiety center.

The autonomic center is very important in regulating digestive motility and secretion. The parasympathetic nerves stimulate the digestive tract and thus increase motility and secretion. The sympathetic nerves of the autonomic nervous system inhibit the digestive tract and thus decrease motility and secretion.

(*text continued on p. 900*)

FOCUS ON . . . Disorders of the digestive system

Oral Cavity

Cheilitis (kih-**lie**-tis). Cheilitis is an inflammation of the lips.

Dental caries. Dental caries is tooth decay, which occurs due to bacterial action on the enamel and dentin of the teeth. As the demineralization of the tooth progresses, a cavity is formed. Carbohydrates seem to accelerate tooth decay mainly because bacteria use these substances and release acids as metabolic waste products. The acids demineralize the enamel. Dental plaque is a composite of bacteria, dextran, and other debris that adheres to the surface of the teeth. Dextran is a product of sucrose metabolism. Prevention of caries includes brushing, flossing, irrigation, fluoride treatments, and dental sealing.

Gingivitis (jin-jih-**vie**-tis). Gingivitis is an inflammation of the gums or gingiva.

Glossitis. Glossitis is an inflammation of the tongue.

Mumps. Mumps is a viral disease that affects the parotid salivary glands. Swelling of the parotid(s) may last for over a week. The disease in the child is very mild but may be severe in the adult, causing complications of the pancreas, gonads, and central nervous system.

Periodontal disease. Periodontal disease is a term used to denote a number of conditions involving the teeth, gums, periodontal ligament, and alveolar bone. Periodontal disease usually results from poor hygiene, irritation, and infection. One symptom of this condition is gingival bleeding.

Pyorrhea alveolaris (pie-oh-**ree**-ah). Pyorrhea alveolaris is a peridontal disease in which the gums bleed, pus forms, and the soft tissue associated with the teeth becomes inflamed. If pyorrhea progresses, the soft tissue may deteriorate, the teeth may loosen, and the gums recede.

Tonsillitis. Tonsillitis is an inflammation of the tonsils. The hypertrophy of the tonsils may be due to an infection. Other symptoms include sore throat, fever, and weakness.

Esophagus

Achalasia. Achalasia is a failure of the smooth muscle of the GI tract to relax. It most frequently occurs in the lower esophagus.

Aphagia. Aphagia is an inability to swallow.

Dysphagia. Dysphagia is difficulty in swallowing.

Esophagitis. Esophagitis is an inflammation of the esophagus.

Hiatal hernia. Hiatal hernia occurs when there is a weakening in the diaphragm that allows a portion of the abdomen to protrude into the thorax. If gastric juices from the stomach enter the esophagus through the hernia, heartburn may occur due to an inflammation of the esophageal mucosa. Dysphagia, ulceration, and hemorrhage may also occur.

Stomach

Gastrectomy. Gastrectomy is the removal of part or all of the stomach.

Gastritis. Gastritis is an inflammation of the stomach.

Gastroenteritis. Gastroenteritis is a condition in which the mucosa of the stomach and intestines become inflamed. Gastroenteritis may occur as the result of psychosomatic, allergic, or infectious factors.

Nausea. Nausea is a feeling of discomfort in the stomach region, which is accompanied by a desire to vomit.

Peptic ulcers. Peptic ulcers may be either gastric or duodenal. A peptic ulcer is an open sore or lesion of the inner wall of the GI tract. Peptic ulcers are caused by the exposure of the GI wall to gastric juices (especially HCl and pepsin). Psychosomatic factors, irritating foods, and drugs may accelerate ulcer formation.

Pyloric stenosis. Pyloric stenosis is a congenital condition in which the pyloric muscle increases in size, causing an obstruction and impeding gastric emptying. Vomiting is an initial symptom.

Vomiting. Vomiting is a protective reflex of the body in which harmful substances are eliminated from the stomach or upper small intestine through the mouth. The center for vomiting is located in the medulla of the brain.

Small intestine

Crohn's disease. Crohn's disease is a condition of an inflamed intestine, most frequently occurring in the ileum.

Enteritis. Enteritis is an inflammation of the intestine. Irritants, infection, and stress may bring it about. Symptoms include abdominal pain, nausea, vomiting, and diarrhea.

Food poisoning. Food poisoning is commonly caused from ingesting a pathogenic bacterium or bacterial toxin. A common cause of food poisoning is *Salmonella* bacteria. **Botulism** is the most severe type of food poisoning. It is caused by neurotoxins of the bacterium *Clostridium botulinum.*

Lactose intolerance. Lactose intolerance is a condition in which lactase is not produced by the mucosa of the small intestine. Lactose is the major carbohydrate found in milk. The undigested lactose prevents water absorption in the small intestine. In the large intestine, bacteria break down the lactose but in doing so produce a large amount of gas. Osmolarity of the colon increases and water absorption decreases, resulting in diarrhea. Symptoms include diarrhea, cramps, flatus, and bloating.

Large intestine

Appendicitis. Appendicitis is an inflammation of the vermiform appendix. The condition may be serious if the appendix ruptures and releases bacteria into the sterile peritoneal fluids, leading to peritonitis. Symptoms include nausea, abdominal pain (especially in the lower right quadrant), and fever.

Colitis. Colitis is an inflammation of the colon. Symptoms include colic spasms, cramps, and constipation. Diarrhea may occur as the condition progresses. Causes include stress and irritants.

Constipation. Constipation is a condition in which the fecal material moves too slowly through the large intestine and too much water is absorbed. This results in hard, dry feces which may cause defecation to be difficult and painful. Constipation may be caused by stress, inactivity, and not enough fiber (roughage) in the diet.

Colostomy (koe-**loss**-toe-me). Colostomy is an artificial opening in the abdomen used to eliminate fecal material and to act as a substitute for the rectum and anus. A colostomy may be necessary after the removal of the rectum or sometimes in cases of ulcerative colitis. A person can readily learn to live with a colostomy and live a normal, active life.

Diarrhea. Diarrhea is a condition in which the fecal material moves too quickly through the large intestine and too little water is absorbed. The feces are very watery and defecation may be frequent. Diarrhea may result from stress, irritants, allergies, and infections.

Diverticulitis (*die*-ver-tik-you-**ly**-tis). Diverticulitis is an inflammation of diverticula, small blind pouches in the colon. Symptoms include colic spasms and cramp-like pain.

Dysentery (**dis**-in-ter-ee). Dysentery is an infection of the lower intestinal tract caused by a number of microorganisms. Symptoms include diarrhea and cramps. A major problem is dehydration.

Hemorrhoids. Hemorrhoids are weakened veins within the lining of the anal canal. These veins can become enlarged and cause pain, itching, discomfort, and bleeding.

Peritonitis. Peritonitis is an acute inflammation of the peritoneum. If bacteria are released into the peritoneal cavity, they readily attack the peritoneal cells for food. This results in an acute infection which can be life-threatening.

Ulcerative colitis. Ulcerative colitis is a condition in which the colon is inflamed due to the presence of ulcers. Symptoms include diarrhea and blood and mucus in the feces.

Accessory structures

Cholecystitis (koe-leh-sis-**ty**-tis). Cholecystitis is an inflammation of the gallbladder. The major cause is gallstones. Symptoms include indigestion, pain, fever, and other digestive disorders.

Cirrhosis (sih-**ro**-sis). Cirrhosis is a chronic liver disease in which hepatic cells become displaced by scar tissue. The liver progressively decreases its functions. Alcoholism is a major contributor to cirrhosis.

Cystic fibrosis. Cystic fibrosis is a hereditary disease of the pancreas which is marked by an accumulation of excessively thick mucus and abnormal secretions of sweat and saliva. Besides the pancreas, it affects the lungs, the liver, and digestive tract.

Gallstones (cholelithiasis, biliary calculi). Gallstones form in the gallbladder and are made up mainly of cholesterol and bile pigments. Gallstones can block the duct system leading to the duodenum. Symptoms include pain, fatty stools, gray or white stools, and jaundice.

Hepatitis. Hepatitis is an inflammation of the liver caused by viruses, drugs, and chemicals. Liver hypertrophy develops and functioning is impaired. Hepatitis A (infectious hepatitis) is caused by hepatitis A virus spread mainly by fecal contamination. Hepatitis B (serum hepatitis) is caused by hepatitis B virus spread mainly by contaminated body fluids. It may last a lifetime. Non-A, non-B hepatitis is not traced directly to the A or B virus. It is more similar to hepatitis B in that it is usually spread through the blood.

Jaundice. Jaundice is a yellowness of the skin and the eyes caused by a backup of bile pigments (especially bilirubin) into the blood. It is mainly symptomatic of diseases of the gallbladder and the liver.

Pancreatitis. Pancreatitis is an inflammation of the pancreas often caused by autodigestion. Complications include the activation of pancreatic enzymes within the pancreas and pancreatic duct and a marked decrease of these enzymes reaching the duodenum.

Regulatory (psychological)

Anorexia nervosa. Anorexia nervosa is associated with a lack of appetite and eating. Progressive starvation occurs. The condition is more frequent in young, single females and may be an abnormal response to a poor self-image or inability to accept adult roles. Emaciation may lead to death.

Bulimia (binge-purge syndrome). Bulimia is a condition of uncontrollable overeating usually followed by forced vomiting and overdoses of laxatives. Inability to cope with being overweight, depression, and stress are common causes. Bulimia can cause complications in the body resulting from electrolyte imbalances.

Motility and secretions decline as the digestive system ages

With age, there is a decline in secretion and motility of the digestive tract. Enzymatic and hormonal regulatory feedback declines, and therefore digestive and absorptive efficiency decreases. Muscle tone of the GI tract and its supporting structures decreases. Hiatal hernias occur more frequently, and constipation and hemorrhoids are more common.

Because receptor sensitivity declines, taste decreases. The incidence of pyorrhea and oral irritations increases. Disorders of the digestive tract and of the accessory organs increase. All of these changes can interfere with adequate nutrition as the individual ages.

The digestive system develops from a primitive gut

The internal lining of the embryo consists of **endoderm.** Two weeks after fertilization, endodermal cells form a cavity called the **primitive gut** that is continuous with the yolk sac. **Splanchnic mesoderm** (**splank**-nik) aligns with the primitive gut, forming an outer layer with the endoderm. The *endodermal layer* differentiates into the inner epithelium and the glands of the GI tract. The *mesodermal layer* differentiates into the smooth muscle and connective tissue of the GI tract.

By the beginning of the fourth week, the primitive gut has elongated into three sections: a foregut, a midgut, and a hindgut. See Figure 25-28. The **foregut** gives rise to the pharynx, esophagus, stomach, and part of the duodenum. The **midgut** becomes the rest of the small intestine

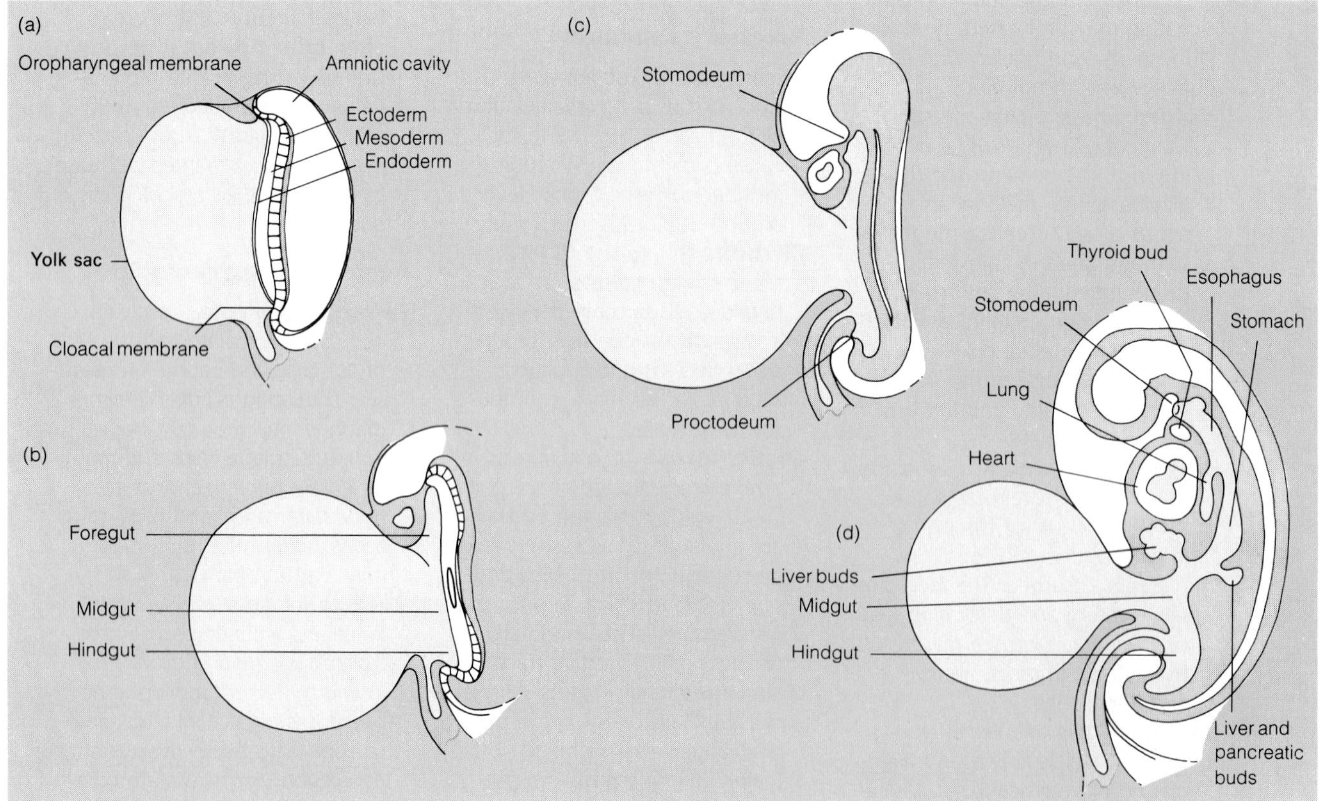

FIGURE 25-28

Embryology of the digestive system.

and the proximal part of the large intestine including most of the transverse colon. The **hindgut** differentiates into the rest of the large intestine.

Sometime after the fifth week, the yolk sac separates from the midgut area. An ectodermal depression forms in the area of the foregut called the **stomodeum.** This will differentiate into the oral cavity. A distal ectodermal depression forms in the area of the hindgut called the **proctodeum.** The proctodeum becomes the anus. With development, the membranes separating the ectodermal and endodermal areas break to form a continuous tube open to the external environment through the mouth and anus. The accessory glands (salivary glands, liver, gallbladder, and pancreas) develop as buds of the foregut, retaining their connection to it via ducts.

Summary

- I. The digestive system is made up of the digestive tract and accessory digestive structures.
  - A. The digestive tract includes the oral cavity, pharynx, esophagus, stomach, small intestine, and large intestine.
  - B. The accessory digestive structures include the tongue, teeth, salivary glands, pancreas, liver, and gallbladder.
- II. The wall of the digestive tract from the esophagus to the anus consists of four layers, or tunics: mucosa, submucosa, muscularis, and serosa. The mucosa is the innermost tunic, and the serosa is the outermost tunic.
  - A. The GI mucosa has three layers: epithelial layer, lamina propria, and muscularis mucosae.
  - B. There are nerve networks within the GI tunics.
    - 1. In the submucosa is the submucosal plexus, which helps control the secretions of the GI tract.
    - 2. Between the circular and longitudinal muscle layers of the muscularis is the myenteric plexus, which helps control the motility of the GI tract.
- III. The peritoneum lines the abdominal cavity and holds abdominal organs in place.
  - A. The parietal peritoneum lines the abdominal and pelvic cavities.
  - B. The visceral peritoneum covers some of the abdominal organs.
  - C. An inflammation of the peritoneum is called peritonitis.
  - D. Extensions of the peritoneum include the falciform ligament, the lesser omentum, the mesentery, the greater omentum, and the mesocolon.
- IV. The oral cavity receives and begins processing food; it contains the tongue, gums, teeth, and the ducts of the buccal and salivary glands.
  - A. The tongue positions food and contains the taste buds.
    - 1. The tongue forms the floor of the oral cavity and is made up of skeletal muscle and a mucous membrane.
    - 2. The extrinsic muscles of the tongue move the tongue around in the oral cavity; the intrinsic muscles change the shape of the tongue.
    - 3. The dorsum of the tongue contains small projections called papillae. The taste buds are found within these papillae and they sense ingested food.
  - B. The teeth function in the mechanical breakdown of large food substances.
    - 1. The teeth are attached to the alveolar processes of the maxilla and the mandible.
    - 2. The gums (gingiva) cover the alveolar processes.
    - 3. A tooth consists of a crown and a root separated by a neck.
    - 4. The outer covering of the crown is the enamel, and the outer covering of the root is the cementum.
    - 5. Inside the enamel and the cementum is the dentin.
    - 6. The pulp cavity contains the blood vessels, lymph vessels, and nerves of the tooth.
    - 7. Humans are diphyodonts; that is, they have both a deciduous dentition and a permanent dentition.
    - 8. Humans are heterodonts; that is, they have several kinds of teeth: incisors, canines, premolars, and molars.
  - C. The salivary glands secrete saliva upon parasympathetic stimulation.
    - 1. There are three pairs of salivary glands: the parotids, the submandibulars, and the sublinguals.
    - 2. Saliva contains the enzyme salivary amylase, which begins the digestion of carbohydrates.
- V. The pharynx and esophagus transport food from the mouth to the stomach.
  - A. The oropharynx and the laryngopharynx function in both digestion and respiration.
  - B. The esophagus connects the pharynx to the stomach, and consists of both skeletal and smooth muscle.
  - C. Deglutition, or swallowing, moves a bolus of food from the mouth through the pharynx and esophagus and into the stomach.
  - D. The deglutition center is located in the medulla.
  - E. Peristalsis moves the bolus through the esophagus and into the stomach.
- VI. The stomach, located in the upper left quadrant of the abdomen, consists of a cardiac portion, fundus, body, antrum, and a pylorus.
  - A. The longitudinal folds of the mucosa of the stomach are called rugae.
  - B. The mucosa of the stomach contains secretory cells: mucous-secreting cells, parietal cells, zymogenic cells, and enteroendocrine cells.
  - C. The major motility of the stomach is by peristalsis. The food is churned with gastric juices into a liquid called chyme.
  - D. HCl, secreted by the parietal cells, brings the stomach contents to a pH of about 2. HCl kills

bacteria, disintegrates plasma membranes, and activates gastric enzymes.

- E. The major enzyme secreted by the stomach is pepsin. Pepsin is produced by zymogenic cells in the inactive form pepsinogen. Pepsin begins the digestion of proteins.
- F. The cephalic phase of gastric secretion is initiated by olfaction, vision, hearing, taste, and thought.
- G. In the gastric phase, the presence of food in the stomach activates gastric secretions. Gastrin release is stimulated by the presence of protein fragments, alcohol, and caffeine in the stomach.
- H. Gastrin stimulates the secretion of gastric juice.
- I. The intestinal phase of gastric secretion involves the release of enteric gastrin.
- J. Enteric gastrin and gastric distension stimulate gastric emptying.
- K. The enterogastric reflex inhibits gastric secretion and motility.
- L. Intestinal hormones (secretin, cholecystokinin, and gastric-inhibiting peptide) decrease gastric motility and secretion.
- M. Alcohol and aspirin can be absorbed by the stomach.

VII. The pancreas, the liver, and the gallbladder are the accessory digestive organs that send secretions to the small intestine.

- A. The pancreas is made up of a head, body, and a tail.
    1. The pancreas has both endocrine and exocrine functions.
    2. The exocrine glands of the pancreas consist of acinar cells, which produce pancreatic juice containing bicarbonates and digestive enzymes.
    3. The main pancreatic duct joins the common bile duct to form the hepatopancreatic ampulla, or the ampulla of Vater.
- B. The liver, the largest gland of the body, is made up of a right lobe, left lobe, quadrate lobe, and caudate lobe.
    1. Hepatic cells secrete bile into bile canaliculi, which drain into bile ducts.
    2. The bile ducts join to form the right and left hepatic ducts, which join to form the common hepatic duct.
    3. The common hepatic duct joins the cystic duct from the gallbladder to become the common bile duct.
    4. The blood from branches of the hepatic artery and hepatic portal vein mix in the hepatic sinusoids.
    5. The liver has many functions, including the processing of absorbed nutrients.
- C. The gallbladder, located on the inferior side of the liver, stores and concentrates bile.

VIII. The small intestine is made up of the duodenum, jejunum, and ileum.

- A. The entrance to the small intestine is by way of the pyloric sphincter, and its exit is the ileocecal sphincter (valve).
- B. The small intestine contains plicae circulares, villi, and microvilli, which greatly increase the surface area for digestion and absorption of foods.
- C. Secretions in the small intestine come from many sources.
    1. Brunner's glands and goblet cells secrete mucus, which protects the intestinal mucosa.
    2. Intestinal glands secrete intestinal juice, which provides the fluid medium for absorption to take place.
    3. Intestinal epithelial cells supply several enzymes for digestion, including maltase, sucrase, lactase, intestinal lipase, aminopeptidase, and dipeptidase.
    4. Pancreatic juice contains sodium bicarbonate and several pancreatic enzymes. The pancreatic enzymes include pancreatic amylase, pancreatic lipase, trypsin, chymotrypsin, carboxypeptidase, ribonuclease, and deoxyribonuclease.
    5. The proteolytic enzymes supplied by the pancreas are produced in zymogenic form. Trypsinogen is activated by the intestinal enzyme enterokinase in the small intestine.
    6. Secretin controls the rate of bicarbonate secretion in the pancreas. Secretin is stimulated by the presence of acids in the duodenum. Cholecystokinin controls the rate of enzyme secretion in the pancreas. Cholecystokinin is stimulated by the presence of protein digestion products and fatty acids in the duodenum.
    7. Bile salts and bile pigments are produced by the liver. Bile salts emulsify fats in the small intestine. Cholecystokinin causes contraction of the gallbladder.

IX. Most digestion occurs in the small intestine.

- A. The major motility of the small intestine is from segmentation, which causes a thorough mixing of the chyme with the digestive solutions of the small intestine.
- B. In carbohydrate digestion pancreatic amylase breaks down starch and dextrins into maltose. Maltase breaks down maltose into two molecules of glucose. Sucrase breaks sucrose down into glucose and fructose. Lactase breaks down lactose into glucose and galactose.
- C. In protein digestion, trypsin and chymotrypsin break down proteins into proteoses and peptones. Carboxypeptidase and aminopeptidase continue this digestion to form dipeptides.

Dipeptidases break down dipeptides into amino acids.

D. In fat digestion bile salts emulsify fats into small fat droplets. Pancreatic lipase breaks the fat droplets down into fatty acids and monoglycerides.

E. Nucleic acids are broken down into pentoses and nitrogen bases by ribonuclease and deoxyribonuclease.

X. Most absorption occurs in the small intestine.

A. Monosaccharides and amino acids are absorbed into the blood of the intestinal capillaries in the villi.

B. Fatty acids and monoglycerides are aggregated into micelles by bile salts. The micelles transport the fatty acids and monoglycerides to the brush border of the microvilli. Within the epithelial cells, triglycerides are resynthesized and join with cholesterol, lipoprotein, and phospholipids to form chylomicrons. These enter the lacteal and flow through the lymph.

C. Vitamin B_{12} must combine with intrinsic factor from the stomach in order to be absorbed.

D. Most water is absorbed by the small intestine.

XI. The large intestine eliminates undigested food.

A. The large intestine consists of the cecum, ascending colon, transverse colon, descending colon, sigmoid colon, rectum, anal canal, and anus.

B. The longitudinal layer of the muscularis of the large intestine exists as three flat bands called the taeniae coli, which form haustra when they contract.

C. Mass movement, a kind of peristalsis, moves fecal material through the large intestine and into the rectum.

D. Intestinal glands and goblet cells secrete mucus for protection and to hold the feces together.

E. The defecation reflex involves parasympathetic stimulation of the muscularis of the colon and rectum and a relaxation of the internal anal sphincter.

F. The large intestine usually absorbs most of the water that enters it.

XII. Centers in the hypothalamus regulate food intake.

A. The hypothalamus contains a feeding center and a satiety center. These centers control hunger and "fullness," respectively.

B. A number of factors affect appetite, including the blood glucose levels, blood amino acid and fatty acid levels, body temperature, and the volume of food in the stomach and duodenum.

XIII. Disorders can arise in any portion of the digestive system.

A. In the oral cavity, infection and poor hygiene can cause tooth decay (caries), gingivitis, and periodontal disease.

B. In the esophagus, hiatal hernia occurs when there is a weakening in the diaphragm that allows a portion of an abdominal organ to protrude into the thorax.

C. A peptic ulcer is an open sore of the inner wall of the stomach or the duodenum. It is believed that psychosomatic factors can accelerate ulcer formation.

D. Vomiting is a protective reflex in which harmful substances are removed from the stomach and upper small intestine.

E. Enteritis is an inflammation of the intestine.

F. Food poisoning may result from the ingestion of a pathogenic bacterium or toxin. Botulism is the most severe type of food poisoning.

G. Appendicitis is an inflammation of the appendix. If the appendix ruptures, it may release bacteria into the abdominal cavity. The bacteria attack the peritoneum, causing peritonitis.

H. Colitis is an inflammation of the colon. Stress is a contributing factor in many cases.

I. Constipation is a condition in which the fecal material moves too slowly through the large intestine and too much water is absorbed. The feces are hard and dry, and defecation may be difficult and painful.

J. Diarrhea is a condition in which the fecal material moves too quickly through the large intestine and too little water is absorbed. The feces are watery, and defecation may be frequent.

K. Hemorrhoids are weakened veins within the lining of the anal canal. They become enlarged and cause pain.

L. Pancreatitis is an inflammation of the pancreas often caused by its autodigestion.

M. Hepatitis is an inflammation of the liver caused by viruses, drugs, and chemicals. There are different types of hepatitis.

N. Gallstones form in the gallbladder and may obstruct the bile ducts. Symptoms include pain, fatty stools, gray or white stools, and jaundice.

O. There are also regulatory disorders such as anorexia nervosa, which is associated with a lack of appetite and eating, and bulimia, a condition of uncontrollable overeating usually followed by self-induced vomiting and overdoses of laxatives.

Post-test

1. The inner lining of the wall of the digestive tract is the ______________.
2. The myenteric plexus controls much of the ______________ of the digestive tract.
3. Inferior to the diaphragm, the adventitia is called the ______________.
4. Rhythmic waves of contraction that push food along through the digestive tract are referred to as ______________.
5. The double fold of peritoneum that hangs down over the intestine like an apron is called the ______________ ______________.
6. The normal maximum number of teeth in the adult mouth is ______________.
7. The portion of a tooth above the gum is the ______________; the part below the gum is the ______________.
8. Each tooth is composed mainly of ______________, which in the crown region is covered by ______________.
9. The largest of the salivary glands are the ______________ ______________.
10. Salivary amylase hydrolyzes ______________.
11. The folds of the mucosa and submucosa of the stomach are called ______________.
12. The parietal cells of the stomach produce ______________ and ______________, whereas the zymogenic cells produce ______________.
13. The three divisions of the small intestines are the ______________, ______________, and ______________.
14. The circular folds, the ______________ ______________, and the ______________ all increase surface area of the small intestine.
15. Trypsin and chymotrypsin are produced by the ______________.
16. Bile is stored in the ______________.
17. Bilirubin is a bile ______________.
18. Gastrin is released by the ______________ ______________ and stimulates the ______________ ______________.
19. The hormone ______________ stimulates the gallbladder to release bile.
20. Pancreatic lipase hydrolyzes ______________ to ______________ and ______________.
21. The end products of protein digestion are ______________ ______________.
22. From the small intestine, chylomicrons enter the ______________.
23. Enterokinase functions to:
    a. Break down lipids
    b. Inhibit gastrin
    c. Stimulate HCl secretion
    d. Activate trypsinogen
    e. None of these
24. Select the incorrect association:
    a. Maltose ⟶ glucose and glucose
    b. Lactose ⟶ galactose and glucose
    c. Sucrose ⟶ glucose and fructose
    d. Lactose ⟶ galactose and fructose
25. Select the incorrect association:
    a. Disaccharides ⟶ dextrins
    b. Dipeptides ⟶ amino acids
    c. Carbohydrates ⟶ dextrins
    d. Proteins ⟶ peptones and proteoses
    e. Micelles ⟶ triglycerides
26. Select the incorrect association:
    a. Zymogenic cells ⟶ enzymes
    b. Brunner's glands ⟶ mucus
    c. Parietal cells ⟶ mucus
    d. Crypts of Lieberkuhn ⟶ extracellular fluid
    e. Sublingual glands ⟶ mucus
27. Select the incorrect association:
    a. Acid ⟶ increased secretin
    b. Carbohydrate ⟶ increased secretin
    c. Peptides ⟶ increased CCK
    d. Intestinal distension ⟶ increased CCK
    e. Gastrin ⟶ increased acid
28. The acinar cells of the pancreas are responsible for the secretion of:
    a. Enzymes
    b. Glucagon
    c. Bicarbonate solutions
    d. Insulin
    e. None of these
29. Label the following diagram.

Review questions

1. Name the structures of the digestive tract and the accessory digestive structures.
2. List the tunics of the GI tract from the innermost to the outermost.
3. What are the layers of the GI mucosa?
4. Where are the nerve plexuses of the GI tract located, and what are their functions?
5. Describe the layers of the peritoneum and some of their extensions.
6. List the internal boundaries of the oral cavity.
7. What are the functions of the two types of tongue muscles?
8. Where are the taste buds located?

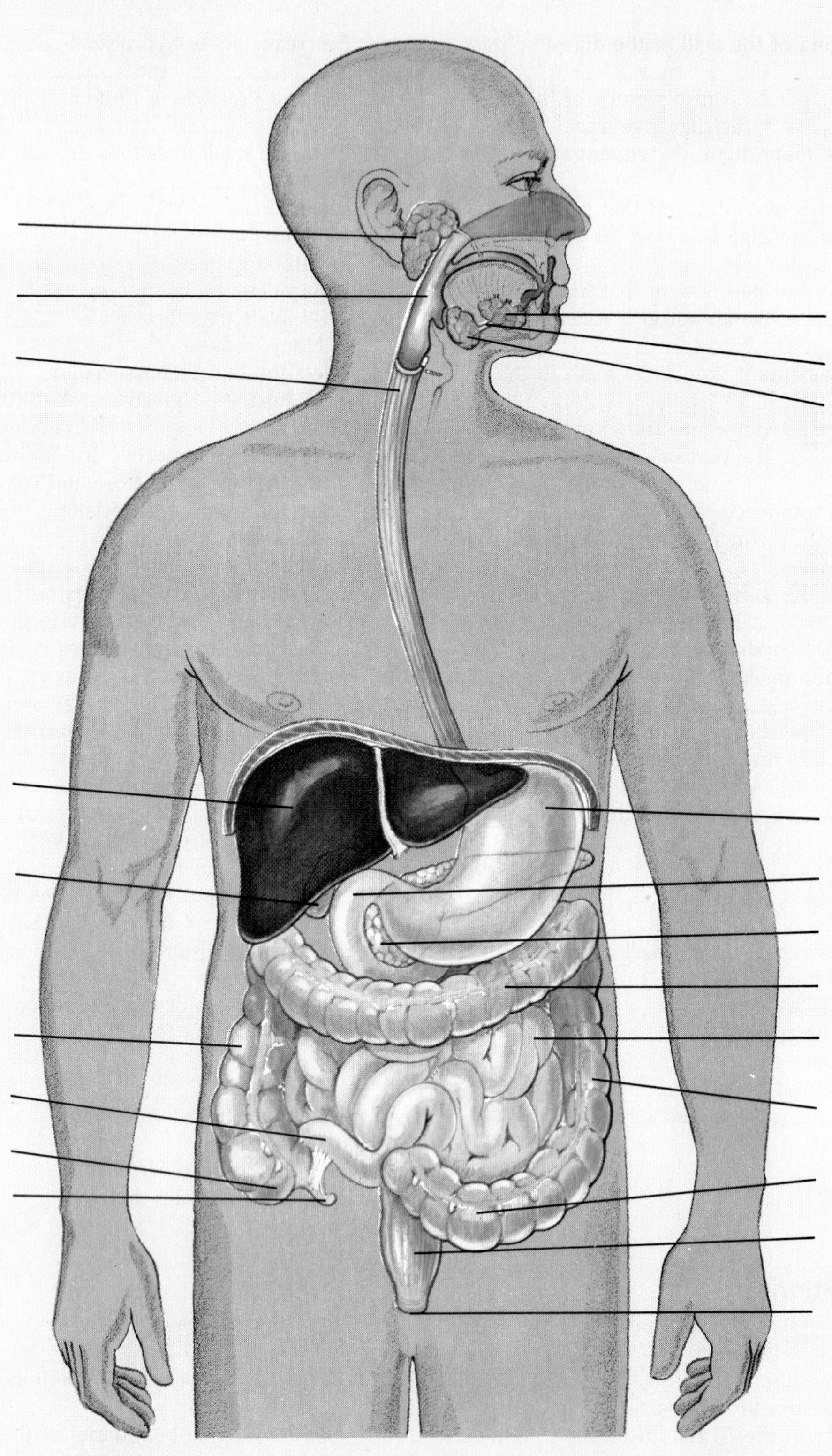

9. Describe the structure of a tooth and its association with the jaw bones.
10. What are the two sets of human dentition and the dental formulas of each?
11. Name the types of salivary glands and their ducts.
12. What is the optimum pH of salivary amylase?
13. Why does salivary amylase break down only about 30% of ingested starch?
14. Describe the salivation reflex.
15. Describe the phases of deglutition.
16. What are the types of secretory cells of the stomach and what does each type secrete?
17. List the functions of HCl in the stomach.
18. Why doesn't the stomach digest itself?
19. Explain how the cephalic, gastric, and intestinal phases of gastric secretion can account for an increased secretion of gastric juices.
20. Explain how the duodenum can inhibit gastric emptying.
21. Trace the flow of pancreatic juice from the pancreas to the duodenum.
22. Trace the flow of bile from the bile canaliculi of the liver to the duodenum.
23. How does bile get into the gallbladder to be stored?
24. Name the parts of the small intestine.
25. Describe the structure of a villus.
26. Where does intestinal juice come from?
27. How does the pancreas enhance digestion in the small intestine?
28. Why doesn't the pancreas digest itself?
29. What factors control pancreatic secretion?
30. List the functions of the liver.
31. Explain segmentation in the small intestine.
32. Discuss the role of bile in the digestion and absorption of fats.
33. Describe the digestion of carbohydrates, proteins, and fats in the small intestine.
34. Describe the absorption of foods in the small intestine.
35. List the parts of the large intestine.
36. Describe the composition of flatus and feces.
37. Describe defecation.
38. Trace a marble from the mouth to the anus, including all structures transversed.
39. Identify the quadrants of the abdomen in which the following are located: stomach, liver, cecum, sigmoid colon, gallbladder, appendix, duodenum.
40. Where are the feeding and satiety centers located? What are some factors that affect them?

Post-test answers

1. mucosa **2.** motility **3.** serosa **4.** peristalsis **5.** greater omentum **6.** 32 **7.** crown; root **8.** dentin; enamel **9.** parotid glands **10.** carbohydrates **11.** rugae **12.** hydrochloric acid, intrinsic factor; enzymes **13.** duodenum, jejunum, ileum **14.** plicae circulares; villi **15.** pancreas **16.** gallbladder **17.** pigment **18.** enteroendocrine cells; parietal cells + zymogenic cells (gastric glands) **19.** cholecystokinin **20.** fats; fatty acids + glycerol **21.** amino acids **22.** lymph **23.** d **24.** d **25.** a **26.** c **27.** b **28.** a **29.** See Fig. 25-1.

NUTRITION, METABOLISM, AND THERMOREGULATION

CHAPTER OUTLINE

- I. **Nutrients**
  - A. Importance of water
  - B. Metabolism
    - 1. Anabolism
    - 2. Catabolism
- II. **Carbohydrates**
  - A. Catabolism
    - □ Focus on ATP
    - 1. Glycolysis
    - □ Focus on glycolytic reactions
    - 2. Krebs cycle
    - □ Focus on the Krebs cycle reactions
    - 3. Electron transport system
    - 4. Anaerobic metabolism
    - 5. Regulation of cellular respiration
  - B. Anabolism
- III. **Lipids**
  - A. Catabolism
  - B. Anabolism
- IV. **Proteins**
  - □ Focus on vegetarian diets
  - A. Catabolism
  - B. Anabolism
- V. **Minerals**
- VI. **Vitamins**
- VII. **Metabolic states**
  - A. Absorptive state
  - B. Postabsorptive state
    - 1. Sources of blood glucose
    - 2. Glucose sparing
- VIII. **Nutritional balance**
  - A. Food intake
  - B. Basal metabolic rate
    - 1. Factors affecting BMR
    - 2. Total BMR
- IX. **Nutritional imbalance**
  - A. Starvation
  - B. Obesity
    - 1. Causes
    - 2. Cures
- X. **Thermoregulation**
  - A. Body temperature
  - B. Heat loss
  - C. Heat gain

LEARNING OBJECTIVES

After you have studied this chapter you should be able to:

1 Define nutrient and list the functions of nutrients.

2 Define metabolism and compare anabolism and catabolism.

3 Compare the types and sources of carbohydrates.

4 Analyze glycolysis, the Krebs cycle, and the electron transport system in terms of energy yield, substrates, and cellular location.

5 Compare aerobic and anaerobic respiration.

6 Compare the types and sources of lipids.

7 Explain the catabolism and anabolism of lipids.

8 Compare the types and sources of protein.

9 Explain the catabolism and anabolism of protein.

10 Explain the functions of minerals, and analyze the role of specific minerals in the body.

11 Differentiate between fat- and water-soluble vitamins, and list the major characteristics of each vitamin.

12 Contrast the absorptive state with the postabsorptive state.

13 Define basal metabolic rate and list factors that affect it.

14 Explain the physiological factors involved in starvation and obesity.

15 Define body temperature, and explain how the body loses and gains heat.

16 List the physiological sequence of events responsible for fever generation.

False-color transmission electron micrograph of liver cell (×2000). (CNRI/Science Photo Library/Photo Researchers, Inc.)

26

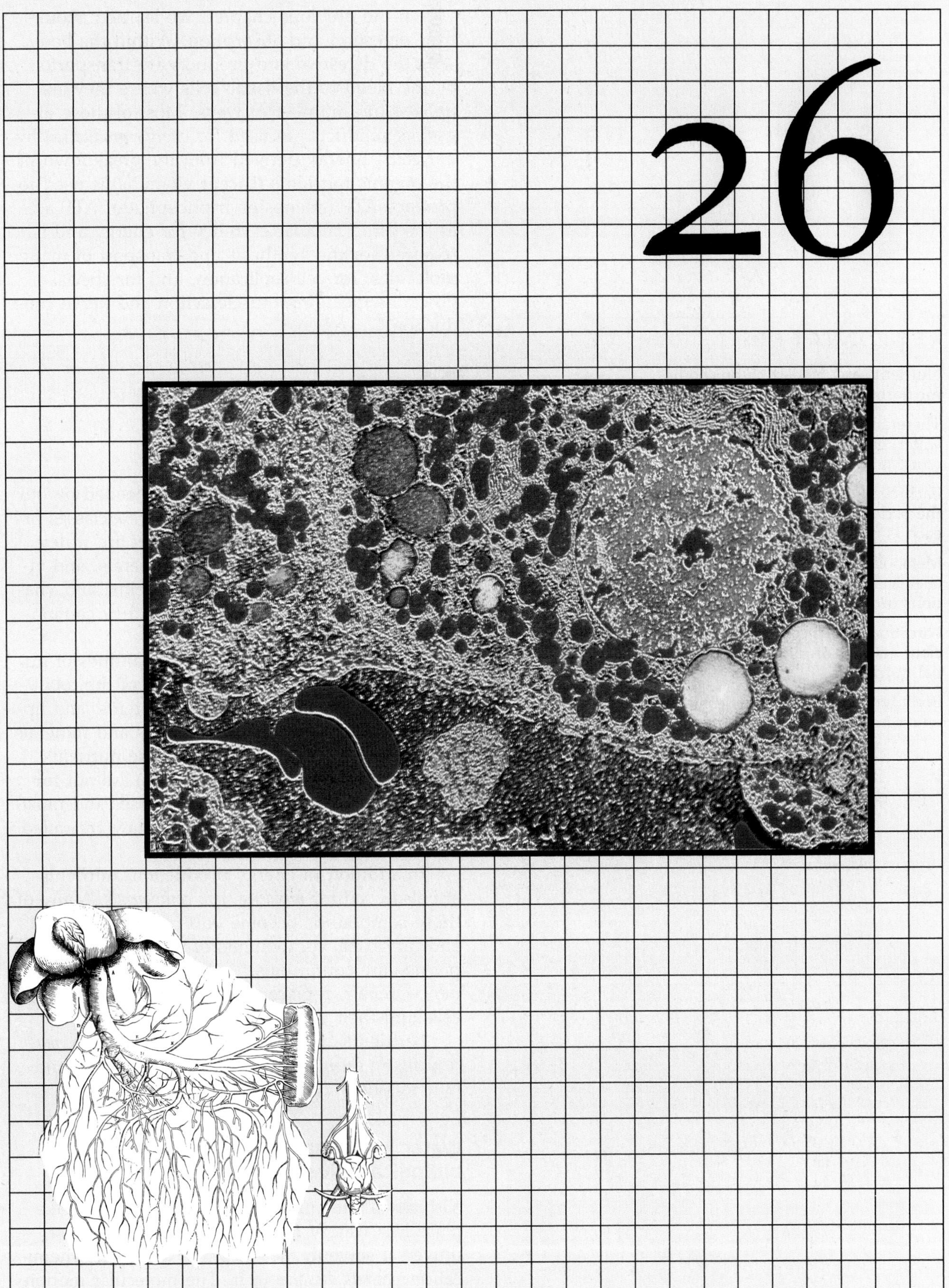

KEY CONCEPTS

Nutrients are needed by our bodies for normal functioning.

There are six classes of nutrients: water, carbohydrates, lipids, proteins, minerals, and vitamins.

Each class of nutrients is used by the body in different ways, and each is needed in varying amounts.

Metabolism is the total of all the chemical and energy transformations occurring in the body.

Nutritional balance requires a sufficient amount of calories and essential nutrients.

Body temperature remains constant when heat gain equals heat loss.

In the previous chapter, we learned about digestion and absorption. Within the body, the digestive end-products are transported by the blood to the tissue cells where they are utilized in a number of ways. Most of these digestive products are used for *energy production* by our cells. Energy derived from the breakdown of the organic nutrients (except vitamins) is used to produce ATP (adenosine triphosphate). ATP acts as the direct cellular currency for energy and is required for the synthesis and transport of many molecules, for cell replication, and for special functions including muscle action and nerve conduction.

Nutrients are required for normal body functioning

Nutrients are chemical substances needed by our bodies for normal functioning. The six classes of nutrients required in a balanced diet are water, carbohydrates, lipids, proteins, minerals, and vitamins. Carbohydrates, lipids, proteins, and vitamins are organic nutrients because they contain carbon.

Various foods offer different quantities of nutrients. Water makes up about 60% of the total food we ingest. Carbohydrates, proteins, and lipids are next in abundance. Vitamins and minerals are required in small amounts. Some nutrients (certain amino acids and fatty acids) are not furnished by our own synthetic processes and must be supplied in the diet. Therefore they are called **essential nutrients.**

In addition to energy production, nutrients are also used for *building new compounds.* Many of these compounds become parts of the structural and functional components of the body. Compounds are continuously needed for the maintenance, repair, replacement, and replication of cells and their components.

Nutrients also can function as necessary *participants in chemical reactions.* Many vitamins and minerals have roles in metabolic activities.

Water is the major biological solvent

Virtually all chemical reactions in the body take place in a watery medium. Water is an almost universal **solvent,** meaning that almost all chemical *compounds dissolve* in it. The molecular motion of the dissolved molecules (which is much greater than that of solid substances) permits them to contact one another and interact. In many metabolic reactions, water serves as an active ingredient. Digestion, for example, takes place by a series of hydrolytic reactions in which water must be chemically added to the breakdown products.

Water is also used to *transport materials* within cells and from one place in the body to another. Blood plasma (which is more than 90% water) transports nutrients, gases, hormones, nitrogenous wastes, and other substances. Urine and sweat (both more than 95% water) carry wastes from the body.

Water has the capacity to *absorb* considerable amounts of *heat* without rapidly changing its own temperature. Because of this property, water helps maintain the constant temperature of the body. In addition, when water evaporates from the skin as sweat and from the lungs as water vapor, it rids the body of excess heat.

When organic nutrients are used for energy production, their degradation also releases heat. Nutritionists measure the energy value of food in heat units called **kilocalories (kcal,** or **Cal** with a capital C). It is defined as the amount of heat required to raise the temperature of a kilogram of water at 1 atmosphere (760 mmHg) from 14.5°C to 15.5°C. The calorie unit (spelled with a lowercase c) used by chemists is 1000 times smaller.

Metabolism is all of the chemical and energy transformations of the body

Molecules are continuously synthesized, used, and then degraded. Cells proliferate, function, die, and are replaced by new cells. The term **metabolism** (meh-**tab**-oh-lizm) refers to all of these chemical and energy transformations that take place in the body. Chemical reactions either require energy or release energy. Thus metabolism can be divided into two broad phases: *anabolism* and *catabolism.*

ANABOLISM INVOLVES SYNTHETIC PROCESSES

Anabolism (a-**nab**-oh-lizm) is the building, or synthetic, aspect of metabolism. Through anabolic reactions simple compounds are converted into larger and more complex compounds. Amino acids are assembled into proteins, fats are transformed into phospholipids used to build plasma membranes, and nucleotides are joined to synthesize nucleic acids. Hormones are produced from simpler raw materials, and hundreds of glucose molecules are polymerized to synthesize glycogen. The building of more complex compounds requires a continuous input of energy. Where does the energy required for anabolic activities come from?

CATABOLISM INVOLVES DEGRADATIVE PROCESSES

The energy for anabolic activities comes from the degradation of complex energy-containing nutrients into their simplest components. As these are "burned," or oxidized, energy stored within their chemical bonds is released. This breaking-down aspect of metabolism is known as **catabolism** (ka-**tab**-oh-lizm). An important example that will be discussed in this chapter is the catabolism of glucose. As glucose is slowly degraded to carbon dioxide and water, energy is released and packaged temporarily within ATP. As needed, the ATP is catabolized, and the energy is made available for anabolic activities and other forms of cellular work. As we study the different groups of nutrients in this chapter, we will make frequent reference to anabolic and catabolic processes.

Polysaccharides, disaccharides, and monosaccharides are the main carbohydrates needed by the body

Types and sources **Carbohydrates** are ingested mainly as *polysaccharides* or as smaller *monosaccharides* and *disaccharides.* The major **polysaccharides** (complex carbohydrates) in foods are starch, cellulose, and glycogen. *Starch* is the form in which plant cells store glucose. *Cellulose* is the material that makes up plant cell walls. Even though humans do not have the enzymes needed to digest cellulose, it is an important source of dietary fiber, providing bulk needed for proper motility of the intestines. Foods rich in starches and cellulose include grains and vegetables. These tend to be the least expensive foods, and for this reason the proportion of carbohydrates in a family's diet may reflect economic status. Very poor people often subsist on diets that are almost exclusively carbohydrates, while more affluent persons enjoy more expensive protein-rich foods such as meat and dairy products.

The **monosaccharides** (especially glucose, fructose, and galactose) and **disaccharides** we ingest are sugars (simple carbohydrates). Sucrose (cane or beet sugar) and lactose (milk sugar) are common disaccharides that we consume. When a molecule of sucrose is digested, it yields one molecule of glucose and one molecule of fructose. Each molecule of lactose is digested into one molecule of glucose and one of galactose. Foods high in sugar include fruits, cane and beet sugar, honey, and milk.

Daily requirement Although the minimum daily requirement of carbohydrate is unknown, it is recommended that 100 grams be consumed daily to avoid excessive protein breakdown and fat utilization. Americans usually ingest about 200 to 300 grams of carbohydrate every day, which accounts for about 50% of the adult diet. Because 1 gram of carbohydrate yields about 4 kilocalories, 300 grams per day would account for 1200 kilocalories per day in caloric intake.

Americans currently have caloric intakes comprised of 24% sugar and 22% complex carbohydrates. Government reports recommend a decrease in the consumption of sugars to 10% and an increase of complex carbohydrates to 48%.

Absorption Most of the carbohydrates ingested into the body are digested to monosaccharides that can be absorbed. The primary monosaccharide absorbed into the body is glucose, and any fructose and galactose absorbed is converted into glucose by the liver. Therefore, the metabolism of carbohydrates is essentially that of glucose.

Role in body Glucose serves as the major fuel for all our cells. Its catabolism releases energy that is stored as ATP. Some cells (brain and red blood cells) are obligatory glucose utilizers; that is, they require it to meet their energy needs. Other body cells can use fats as a source of energy if glucose is unavailable. Carbohydrates are also needed in the body as a source of the 5-carbon sugars ribose and deoxyribose used in the synthesis of RNA and DNA. Lactose is produced by mammary glands during lactation.

Carbohydrate (glucose) catabolism provides energy

The cells of the body are dependent upon a continuous supply of energy. Glucose is the principal fuel used in **cellular respiration,** the complex series of chemical reactions by which the cell breaks down glucose to carbon dioxide and water in order to obtain the energy trapped within its chemical bonds. A summary equation for cellular respiration follows:

$$\underset{\text{Glucose}}{C_6H_{12}O_6} + \underset{\text{Oxygen}}{6\,O_2} \longrightarrow \underset{\text{Carbon dioxide}}{6\,CO_2} + \underset{\text{Water}}{6\,H_2O} + \underset{\text{ATP}}{\text{energy}} + \text{heat}$$

The energy is packaged within a remarkable chemical compound called adenosine triphosphate (ATP) (Fig. 26-1). For each glucose molecule oxi-

AMP (adenosine *mono*phosphate) is the same as adenosine ~ P

ADP (adenosine *di*phosphate) is the same as AMP ~ P

ATP (adenosine *tri*phosphate) is the same as AMP ~ P ~ P or ADP ~ P

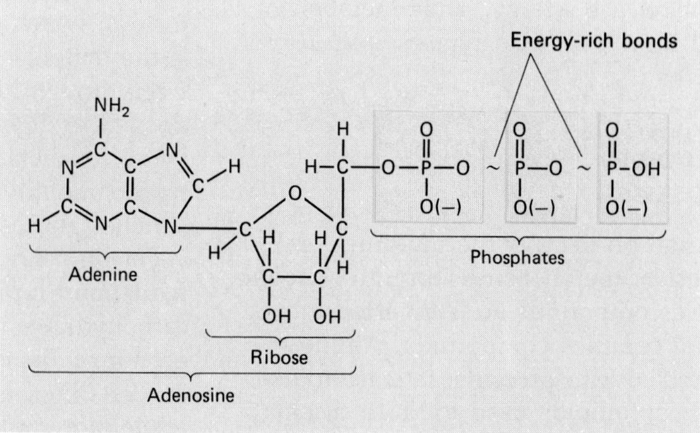

FIGURE 26-1

Chemical structure of ATP.

FOCUS ON . . . ATP

In Figure 26-1 we can see that ATP consists of three main parts: (1) a nitrogen-containing (N-containing) base called adenine, which also occurs in DNA and RNA; (2) a pentose sugar called ribose; and (3) three inorganic phosphate groups identifiable as phosphorus atoms (P) surrounded by oxygen atoms (O). The phosphate groups are attached to the end of the molecule in a series, rather like three passenger cars behind a locomotive. The chemical bonds attaching the last two phosphates also resemble those of a train in that they are readily attached and detached. When the third phosphate is removed, the remaining molecule is called **adenosine diphosphate,** or simply **ADP.** When two phosphate groups are removed, the molecule that remains is **adenosine monophosphate (AMP).** Conversely, when a phosphate is attached to AMP it becomes ADP, and when a phosphate is added to ADP, ATP is formed. These reactions are readily reversible.

$$AMP + P_i + \text{energy} \rightleftharpoons ADP$$

$$ADP + P_i + \text{energy} \rightleftharpoons ATP$$

As the equations indicate, energy is required to add a phosphate to either the AMP or the ADP molecule. Because energy can neither be created nor destroyed, it is released or transferred to another molecule when the phosphate is detached. Thus ATP is an important link between *exergonic* (*ek*-ser-**gon**-ik), or energy-releasing, reactions and *endergonic* (*en*-der-**gon**-ik), or energy-requiring, reactions. Most catabolic reactions are exergonic, whereas most anabolic reactions are endergonic. At the top of Figure 26-1, the wavy lines indicating the attachment of the phosphates represent energy-rich bonds. (Usually, inorganic phosphate is designated P_i.)

Energy released from exergonic reactions is packaged in ATP molecules for use in endergonic reactions (box figure). This energy may be used to produce fats or glycogen, molecules stockpiled for long-term energy storage. The cell contains a pool of ADP, ATP, and phosphate in a state of dynamic equilibrium. Large quantities of ATP cannot be stockpiled in the cell. In fact, recent studies suggest that a bacterial cell has no more than a 1-second supply of ATP. Thus ATP molecules are used almost as quickly as they are produced. Every second, thousands of ATPs are made from ADP and phosphate, and an equal number are broken down, yielding their energy to whichever life processes may require them. Thus ADP and phosphate are ceaselessly recycled, shuttling back and forth in a blur of energy between respiration and consumption.

ATP can be considered the energy currency of the cell. Just as your energy is stored symbolically in the money you make by working, so the energy of respiration is stored as ATP. Moreover, just as you dare not make less money than you spend, so too the cell must avoid energy bankruptcy—that would mean its death. Finally, just as you do not generally keep what you make very long, so too

(*continued*)

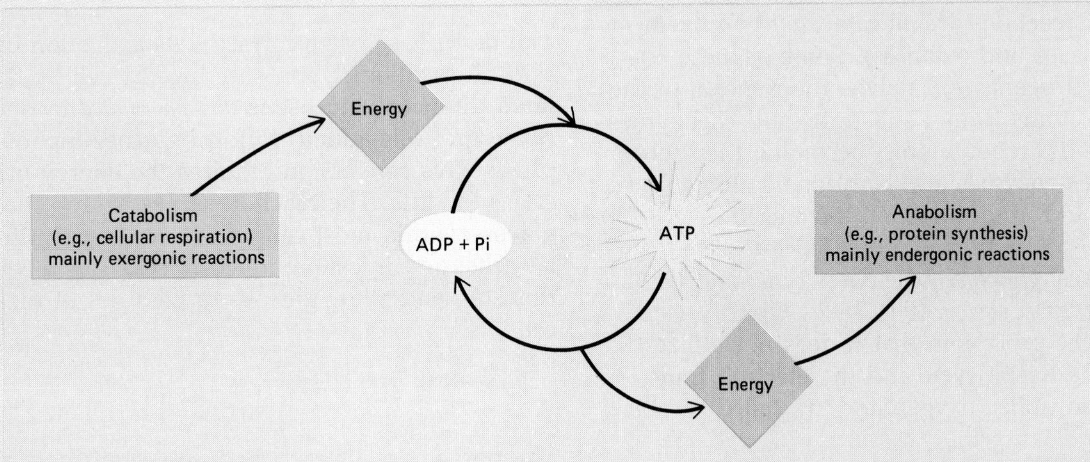

ATP: Link between anabolic and catabolic metabolism.

FOCUS ON . . . ATP (*continued*)

the cell is continuously spending its ATP.

A great deal of ATP is manufactured in the mitochondria by oxidative phosphorylation. **Oxidative phosphorylation** is a series of redox reactions in the mitochondrial membrane used to synthesize ATP. ATP can also be produced at the substrate (metabolic intermediate) level. This type of ATP formation is called **substrate-level phosphorylation** because the ATP is produced by transferring a phosphate group from substrate to ADP. Imagine a substance, which we will call "substrate," that is chemically combined with phosphate to form substrate-phosphate. With the help of an enzyme, this compound can donate its phosphate to ADP. In accepting the phosphate, ADP becomes ATP.

$$\text{Substrate-phosphate} + \text{ADP} \xrightarrow{\text{Enzyme}} \text{substrate} + \text{ATP}$$

Why does the phosphate leave the original substrate compound and join ADP? Chemical reactions tend to proceed from higher to lower total energy. Thus, because there is more total energy in the substrate-phosphate than in ATP, the reaction proceeds toward the production of ATP. Only a few compounds in the cell meet these requirements, however, so not much ATP is made in this way. Still, muscle cells make considerable use of this method of ATP production.

dized, as many as 38 molecules of ATP can be produced. For each gram of glucose oxidized, as much as 4.1 kilocalories are generated. See Focus on ATP.

The term **oxidation** means removal of electrons from atoms or, in the case of organic molecules, removal of hydrogen atoms (dehydrogenation). An opposite reaction, **reduction,** adds electrons or hydrogen atoms to a molecule. Both reactions are coupled within body cells, so that when a substance is oxidized, another one is reduced. Hence, they are referred to as *redox reactions.* When a substance undergoes oxidation, it loses energy, and when a substance undergoes reduction, it gains energy.

Redox reactions are all catalyzed by enzymes (hydrogenases and oxidases). Some of these enzymes (hydrogenases) catalyze the removal of the hydrogen atoms from a substrate, and coenzymes accept the hydrogen atoms, becoming themselves reduced. Coenzymes also can donate atoms to a substrate and, in doing so, are oxidized.

Cellular respiration can be divided into three main phases: *glycolysis,* the *Krebs cycle,* and the *electron transport system* (Fig. 26-2). **Glycolysis** is an anaerobic process in that it does not utilize oxygen; the **Krebs cycle** and the **electron transport system** utilize oxygen and are called aerobic pathways.

GLYCOLYSIS BREAKS GLUCOSE DOWN TO PYRUVIC ACID

Glycolysis (gly-**kol**-i-sis) encompasses the first ten reversible reactions in cellular respiration. In glycolysis a molecule of glucose is split and partially degraded to form two molecules of pyruvic acid (pyruvate), a 3-carbon compound. During this series of degradation reactions, each regulated by a specific enzyme, there is a net gain of two ATP molecules. Glycolysis can be summarized as follows:

$$\underset{\text{6 carbons}}{\text{Glucose}} \longrightarrow \underset{\text{3 carbons each}}{\text{2 pyruvic acid}} + 2\ \text{ATP} + 4\ \text{hydrogen}$$

The first phase of glycolysis is its activation by phosphorylation. Upon entering the cell by facilitated diffusion, glucose is *phosphorylated* (a phosphate group is added) to form glucose-6-phosphate. This conversion requires the energy of one ATP molecule. The reaction serves to trap the glucose within most cells. (Liver cells, renal tubular cells, and intestinal mucosal cells can reverse this step and allow glucose to pass out of the cells.)

$$\text{Glucose} + \text{ATP} \longrightarrow \text{glucose-6-phosphate} + \text{ADP}$$

The phosphorylation to glucose-6-phosphate also reduces the concentration of glucose in the cytoplasm, which serves to maintain a diffusion gradient for the entry of more glucose.

Glucose-6-phosphate is converted into fructose-6-phosphate, which is phosphorylated again to form fructose-1,6-diphosphate. The second phosphorylation uses up another ATP molecule.

The next phase in the oxidation of glucose is the cleavage of the fructose-1,6-diphosphate molecule into two 3-carbon compounds that are isomers:[1] glyceraldehyde-3-phosphate (PGAL) and dihydroxyacetone phosphate.

[1] Isomers are different chemical compounds that have the same molecular formula.

In the third phase of glycolysis, two hydrogen atoms are removed from the two 3-carbon compounds (thereby oxidizing them), and certain other atoms are rearranged so that each PGAL molecule is transformed into a molecule of pyruvic acid. During these last reactions enough chemical energy is obtained from the fuel molecule to produce four ATP molecules.

$$2\ \text{PGAL} + 4\ \text{ADP} + 4\ P_i \longrightarrow 2\ \text{pyruvic acid} + 4\ \text{H} + 4\ \text{ATP}$$

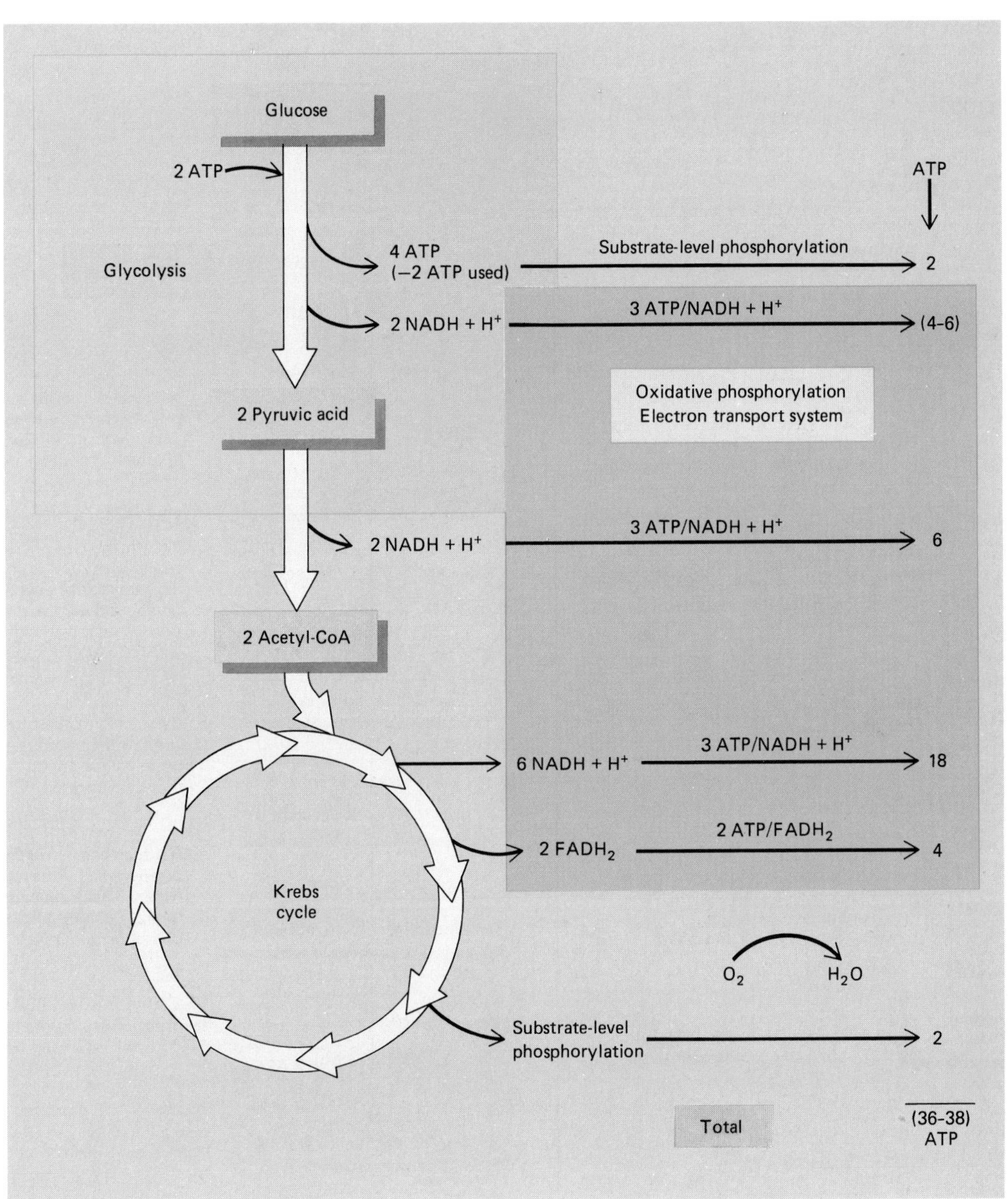

FIGURE 26-2

Summary of the energy yield of a molecule of glucose during aerobic oxidation. Note that 4 ATP molecules are produced by substrate-level phosphorylation and 34 (or 32) ATP molecules are produced by oxidative phosphorylation.

In the first phase of glycolysis, two molecules of ATP are consumed, and in the third phase, four ATP molecules are produced. Thus, glycolysis yields a direct net energy profit of two ATP molecules by substrate-level phosphorylation.

The hydrogen atoms[1] removed from each PGAL are in an "energized" state and immediately combine with the hydrogen-carrier coenzyme, NAD (nicotinamide adenine dinucleotide).

$$\underset{\text{Oxidized NAD}}{NAD^+} + 2\,H \longrightarrow \underset{\text{Reduced NAD}}{NADH + H^+}$$

The fate of these hydrogen atoms will be discussed in the sections dealing with the electron transport system and anaerobic metabolism.

The reactions of glycolysis take place in the cytoplasm. Necessary ingredients such as ADP, NAD, and phosphates float freely in the cytoplasm and are used as needed. A more detailed

[1] More precisely, the electrons from both hydrogens and one proton are transferred to the NAD. The other proton is liberated into the surrounding medium.

FOCUS ON . . . Glycolytic reactions

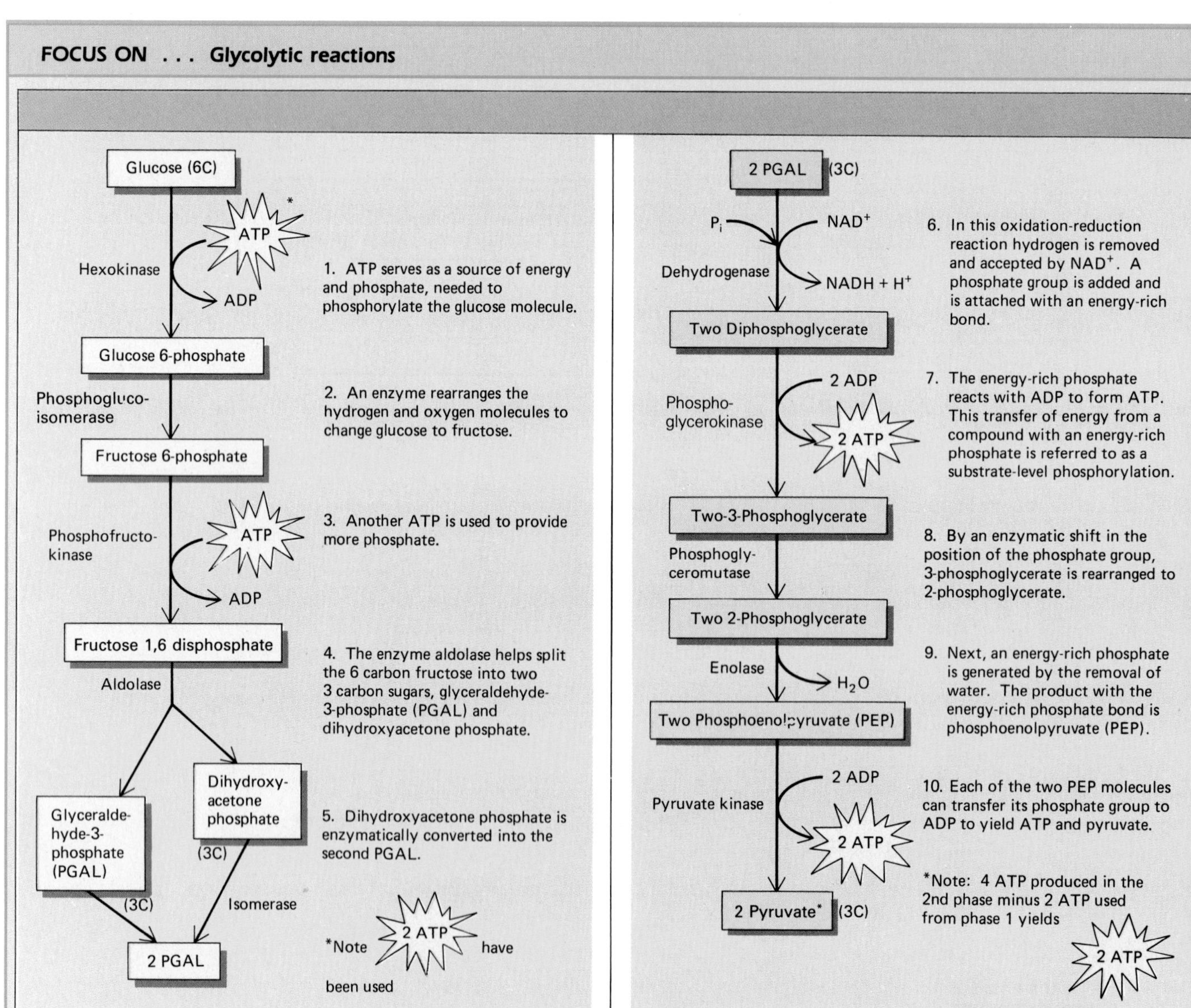

description of glycolysis is given in Focus on Glycolytic Reactions.

THE KREBS CYCLE DELIVERS HYDROGEN ATOMS TO NAD

The **Krebs cycle** (also known as the citric acid cycle and the tricarboxylic acid, or TCA, cycle) is the principal series of reactions that removes hydrogen atoms from fuel molecules and delivers them to NAD for further processing via the electron transport system. The reactions of the Krebs cycle are summarized below. (For more details of the individual steps, see Focus on the Krebs Cycle Reactions.)

Before the Krebs cycle actually begins, an important preliminary reaction takes place. Each 3-carbon molecule of pyruvic acid is degraded by the removal of hydrogen atoms and a carbon-oxygen segment. The carbon-oxygen segment is removed as carbon dioxide, which eventually finds its way to the lungs and is exhaled. This is accomplished during a very complex reaction in which pyruvic acid combines with a substance

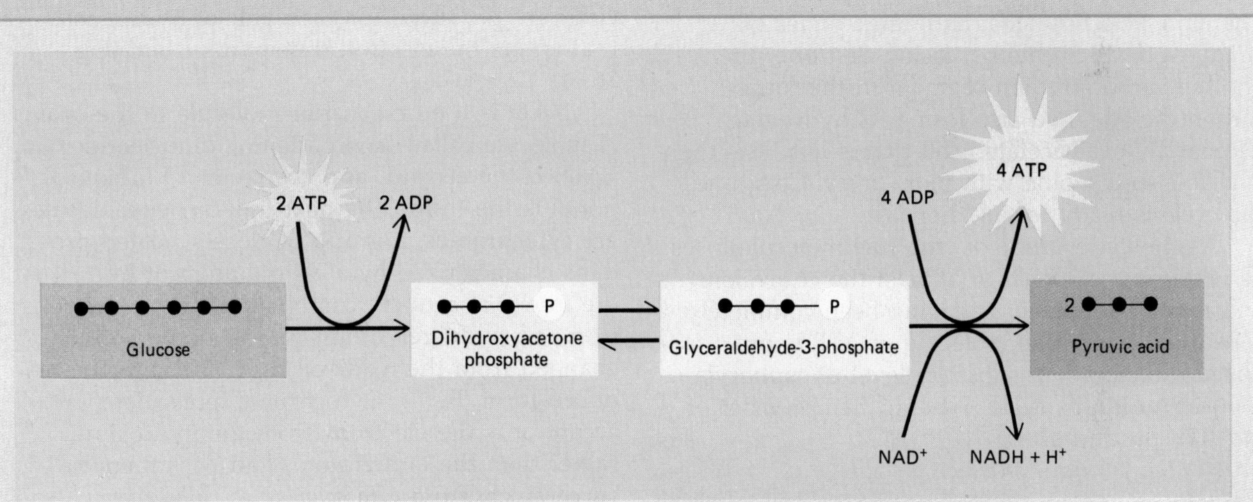

*Pyruvic acid and many other compounds in glycolysis and the Kreb's cycle exist as ions at the pH found in the cell. Thus, pyruvic acid is often referred to as pyruvate to indicate the ionic form.

called **coenzyme A (CoA)** and forms a 2-carbon fuel compound, the acetyl part of the acetyl-CoA. Coenzyme A is manufactured in the cell from one of the B vitamins, pantothenic acid.

$$2 \text{ Pyruvic acid} + 2 \text{ CoA} + 2 \text{ NAD}^+ \longrightarrow 2 \text{ acetyl-CoA} + 2 \text{ NADH} + 2 \text{ H} + 2 \text{ CO}_2$$

The 6-carbon atoms from the original glucose fuel molecule may now be accounted for as follows: four of the carbons are located in the two acetyl-CoA molecules, and the other two have been released as carbon dioxide.

Acetyl-CoA enters the Krebs cycle by combining with oxaloacetate (oxaloacetic acid), a 4-carbon compound already present in the mitochondrion, to form citrate (citric acid), a 6-carbon compound.

$$\underset{\text{4 carbons}}{\text{Oxaloacetate}} + \underset{\text{2 carbons}}{\text{acetyl-CoA}} \longrightarrow \underset{\text{6 carbons}}{\text{citrate}}$$

The citric acid now goes through a series of chemical transformations, losing first one, then another carbon-oxygen segment in the form of carbon dioxide, and also losing its hydrogens. Ultimately, oxaloacetate is all that is left. It is then available to combine with more acetyl-CoA, and the cycle is ready for another turn.

As the cycle proceeds, the fuel molecule loses its remaining carbons, or at least the equivalent, and may be regarded as having been completely consumed. Only one molecule of ATP is produced directly (by a substrate-level phosphorylation) in the Krebs cycle. Where, then, is most of the ATP produced?

THE ELECTRON TRANSPORT SYSTEM GENERATES ATP IN A SERIES OF REDOX REACTIONS

Now we turn our attention to the fate of all the hydrogen atoms removed from the fuel molecule during glycolysis, acetyl-CoA formation, and the functioning of the Krebs cycle. These hydrogens are transferred to hydrogen-acceptor coenzymes (NAD, FAD) which are linked to an electron transport system in the mitochondrial membrane. The **electron transport system** is a chain of several hydrogen-electron-carrier molecules that pass hydrogen atoms (or in some cases just their electrons) from one carrier molecule to the next in a specific, orderly sequence. Each carrier molecule is *reduced* (gains electrons) as it picks up the hydrogen, then *oxidized* (loses electrons) as it passes the hydrogen on. An estimated three ATP molecules are produced for each pair of hydrogens that enters the electron transport system (Fig. 26-3).

NAD is the first carrier molecule in the chain. A molecule called flavin adenine dinucleotide, or **FAD,** is the second, and coenzyme Q (ubiquinone) is the third. The next five carrier molecules are **cytochromes,** a group of closely related proteins characterized by a central atom of iron. It is the iron that actually combines with the electrons from the hydrogen atoms and in doing so is changed from the oxidized form (Fe^{3+}) to the reduced form (Fe^{2+}). Cytochrome molecules (Cyt) accept only the electrons from the hydrogen, rather than the entire atom, and pass them on successively from *cytochrome b* to *cytochrome* C_1 to

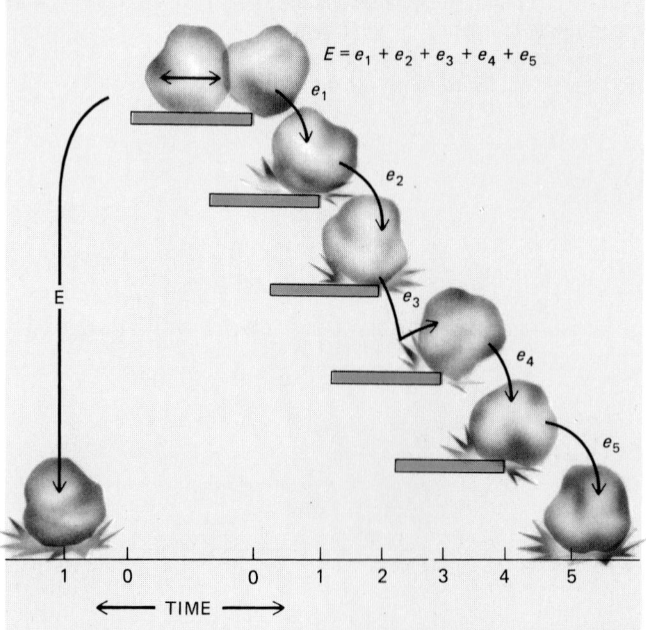

FIGURE 26-3

The electron transport system. Energy (E) is released in a controlled step-by-step manner. The final electron (and hydrogen) acceptor is molecular oxygen, so water is produced as a product of these reactions. For each pair of hydrogen molecules that enter this pathway, three molecules of ATP can be produced.

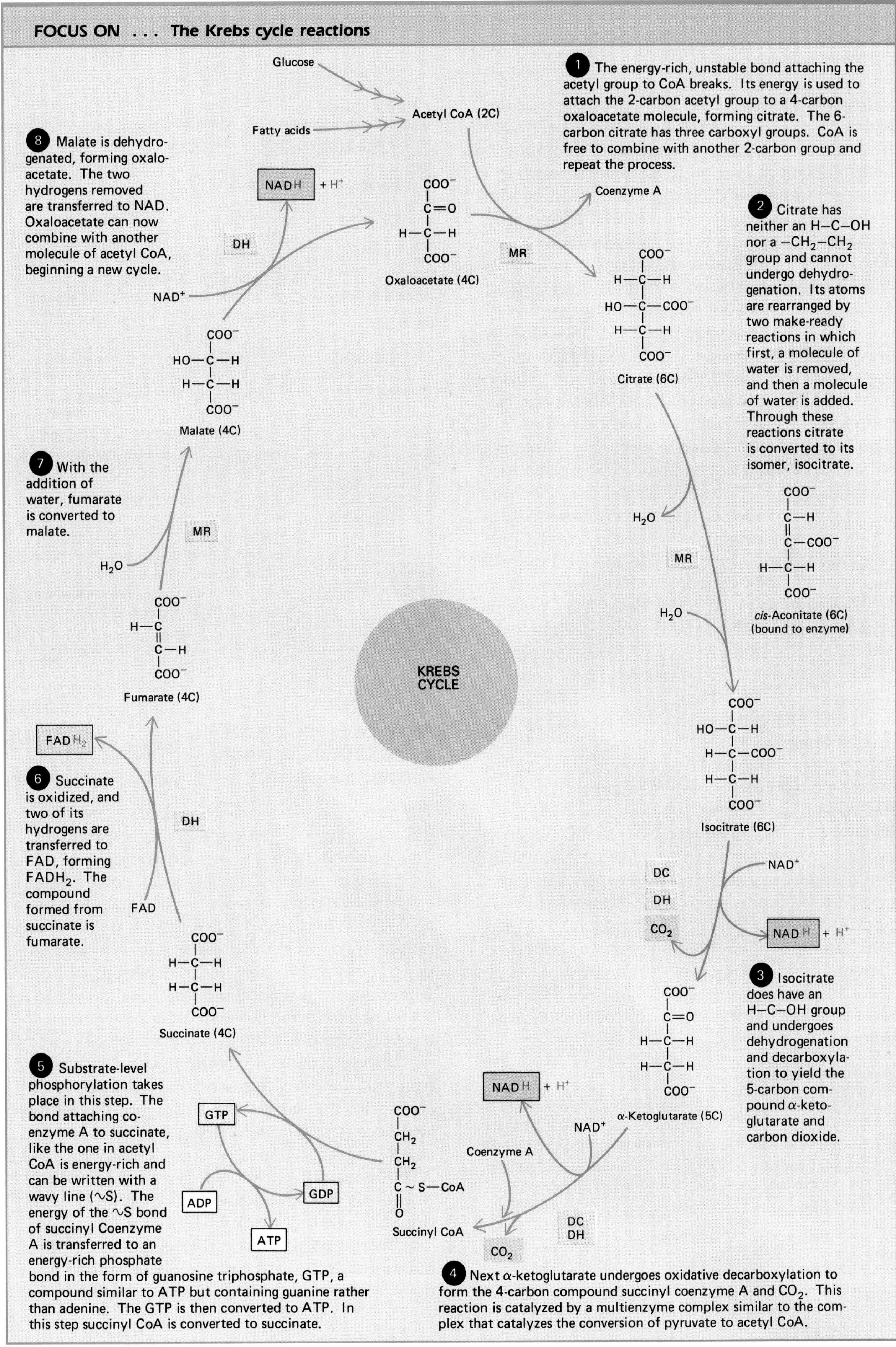
FOCUS ON . . . The Krebs cycle reactions
Glucose
Fatty acids
Acetyl CoA (2C)
1 The energy-rich, unstable bond attaching the acetyl group to CoA breaks. Its energy is used to attach the 2-carbon acetyl group to a 4-carbon oxaloacetate molecule, forming citrate. The 6-carbon citrate has three carboxyl groups. CoA is free to combine with another 2-carbon group and repeat the process.
Coenzyme A
MR
Citrate (6C)
2 Citrate has neither an H–C–OH nor a $-CH_2-CH_2$ group and cannot undergo dehydrogenation. Its atoms are rearranged by two make-ready reactions in which first, a molecule of water is removed, and then a molecule of water is added. Through these reactions citrate is converted to its isomer, isocitrate.
H_2O
MR
H_2O
cis-Aconitate (6C) (bound to enzyme)
Isocitrate (6C)
NAD^+
DC
DH
CO_2
NADH + H^+
3 Isocitrate does have an H–C–OH group and undergoes dehydrogenation and decarboxylation to yield the 5-carbon compound α-ketoglutarate and carbon dioxide.
α-Ketoglutarate (5C)
NADH + H^+
NAD^+
Coenzyme A
DC
DH
CO_2
Succinyl CoA
4 Next α-ketoglutarate undergoes oxidative decarboxylation to form the 4-carbon compound succinyl coenzyme A and CO_2. This reaction is catalyzed by a multienzyme complex similar to the complex that catalyzes the conversion of pyruvate to acetyl CoA.
GTP
GDP
ADP
ATP
5 Substrate-level phosphorylation takes place in this step. The bond attaching coenzyme A to succinate, like the one in acetyl CoA is energy-rich and can be written with a wavy line (~S). The energy of the ~S bond of succinyl Coenzyme A is transferred to an energy-rich phosphate bond in the form of guanosine triphosphate, GTP, a compound similar to ATP but containing guanine rather than adenine. The GTP is then converted to ATP. In this step succinyl CoA is converted to succinate.
Succinate (4C)
FAD
$FADH_2$
DH
6 Succinate is oxidized, and two of its hydrogens are transferred to FAD, forming $FADH_2$. The compound formed from succinate is fumarate.
Fumarate (4C)
H_2O
MR
7 With the addition of water, fumarate is converted to malate.
Malate (4C)
NAD^+
DH
NADH + H^+
Oxaloacetate (4C)
8 Malate is dehydrogenated, forming oxaloacetate. The two hydrogens removed are transferred to NAD. Oxaloacetate can now combine with another molecule of acetyl CoA, beginning a new cycle.
KREBS CYCLE

cytochrome c to *cytochrome a* to *cytochrome* a_3. See Figure 26-3. When the electrons are separated from the rest of the hydrogen, the remaining hydrogen ion (a proton) is temporarily set free in the surrounding medium. Hence, the energy liberated from fuel molecules is stored temporarily between the membranes of the mitochondria in the form of hydrogen protons. Using some of the energy freed by electron transport, these protons set up an electrochemical gradient across the inner mitochondrial membrane that provides energy for ATP synthesis. This is referred to as **chemiosmosis** because it links chemical and transport processes. The process of chemiosmosis can be compared to water that is backed up behind a dam being used to generate electricity. Protons backed up behind a membrane can be used to generate ATP. Cytochrome a_3, the last cytochrome in the chain, passes on the two electrons (which simultaneously reunite with their hydrogen protons) to molecular oxygen. The chemical union of the hydrogen and oxygen produces water.

Reduced NAD generates three ATPs per molecule, whereas reduced FAD generates only two. This is because the FAD coenzyme is the second hydrogen acceptor of the electron chain and is at a lower energy level than NAD. One ATP has already been liberated when NAD passes two hydrogen atoms to FAD.

Oxygen is the final hydrogen acceptor in the electron transport system. This is the vital role of the oxygen we breathe. What happens when the body is deprived of oxygen? When no oxygen is available to accept the hydrogen, the entire system becomes blocked, and no further ATP molecules can be produced by way of the electron transport system. Most cells of complex organisms cannot live long without oxygen, because the amount of energy they can produce in its absence is insufficient to sustain life. See Table 26-1 for a summary of the phases of cellular respiration.

Clinical highlight

Lack of oxygen is not the only factor that may interfere with the electron transport system. Some poisons such as cyanide inhibit the normal activity of the cytochrome system. Cyanide combines electrons tightly with one of the cytochrome molecules so that they cannot be passed on to the next member in the chain.

TABLE 26-1

Summary of cellular respiration

Phase	Summary
Glycolysis	Series of about ten reactions during which glucose is degraded to pyruvic acid. Maximum net profit of two ATPs by substrate-level phosphorylation. Hydrogen atoms released. These reactions can proceed anaerobically in the cytoplasm of the cell.
Krebs cycle	Series of about ten reactions in which the fuel molecule (part of acetyl coenzyme A) is degraded to hydrogens and carbon dioxide. Hydrogen electrons passed to NAD and FAD. 2 ATPs produced by substrate-level phosphorylation. Aerobic; in mitochondrion
Electron transport system	Chain of several hydrogen-electron carrier molecules. Hydrogen atoms (or their electrons) are passed along the chain. For each pair of hydrogens that enters the chain an estimated maximum of three ATPs are made. Total maximum yield 34 ATPs. Aerobic; in mitochondrion

ANAEROBIC METABOLISM YIELDS LESS ENERGY THAN AEROBIC METABOLISM

The preceding discussion has focused mainly upon **aerobic** (oxygen-dependent) **respiration.** The term *respiration* denotes an energy-generating process that utilizes coupled redox reactions and electron transport. Oxygen is the final electron acceptor. When sufficient oxygen is not available, muscle cells can shift to **anaerobic** (non-oxygen-dependent) **respiration** for brief periods of time. Under anaerobic conditions, the final acceptor is an inorganic molecule other than oxygen and the electron transport system is not involved.

During glycolysis, the hydrogens cleaved from the fuel molecule are accepted by pyruvic acid. With the addition of hydrogen, the pyruvic acid becomes lactic acid (Fig. 26-4). This lactic acid fermentation does not provide any additional ATP for the cell but it does permit reduced NAD to pass its hydrogens to other acceptor molecules, thus regenerating oxidized NAD for glycolysis. You should recall from earlier chapters that the buildup of lactic acid contributes to muscle fatigue. Lactic acid acidifies the blood, causing an increase in respiration and panting. It is as though by exercising vigorously an oxygen debt is incurred that must be repaid after the exertion is over. Some oxygen is used to oxidize a portion of the lactic acid. The rest of the lactic acid is changed back to pyruvic acid and then to glucose in the liver.

Anaerobic metabolism depends upon the substrate-level reactions of glycolysis that can proceed in the absence of oxygen. However, because a net profit of only two ATP molecules is gained from each molecule of glucose (representing only 5% of the total energy in the molecule), anaerobic metabolism requires a large fuel supply. By rapidly breaking down many fuel molecules, a cell can compensate somewhat for the small amount of energy that is gained from each. An anaerobic cell must therefore consume up to 20 times as much fuel as an aerobic cell to perform the same amount of work. For this reason skeletal muscle cells, which often respire anaerobically for shorter periods of time, store large quantities of glucose in the form of glycogen.

Using aerobic methods, up to 55% of the energy in a glucose molecule can be captured—a respectable amount. Thus it is not surprising that more than 90% of ATP formed in most cells is produced by the more efficient aerobic respiration. All usable energy is extracted from the glucose with a net maximum profit of about 38 ATP molecules per molecule of glucose.[1] Table 26-2 compares the number of ATP molecules generated from anaerobic and aerobic metabolism.

REGULATION OF CELLULAR RESPIRATION DEPENDS ON THE AMOUNTS OF ADP AND P_i

Cellular respiration requires a steady supply of nutrient fuel molecules and oxygen. Under normal conditions these materials are adequately provided and do not affect the rate of respiration. Instead, cellular respiration is regulated by the amount of ADP and phosphate available. As ATP is manufactured, the pool of ADP and phosphate diminishes and respiration slows. Then, as ATP is utilized for cellular activities, ADP and phosphate are released and become available for packaging energy once more. Thus cellular respiration adjusts to a more rapid pace. In this way the rate of

[1]This occurs in procaryotic cells. In eucaryotic cells, the actual yield of ATPs per molecule of glucose is 36 and not 38 because two of the reduced NADs made in glycolysis are converted to reduced FADs in the cytoplasm before transport to the mitochondrion.

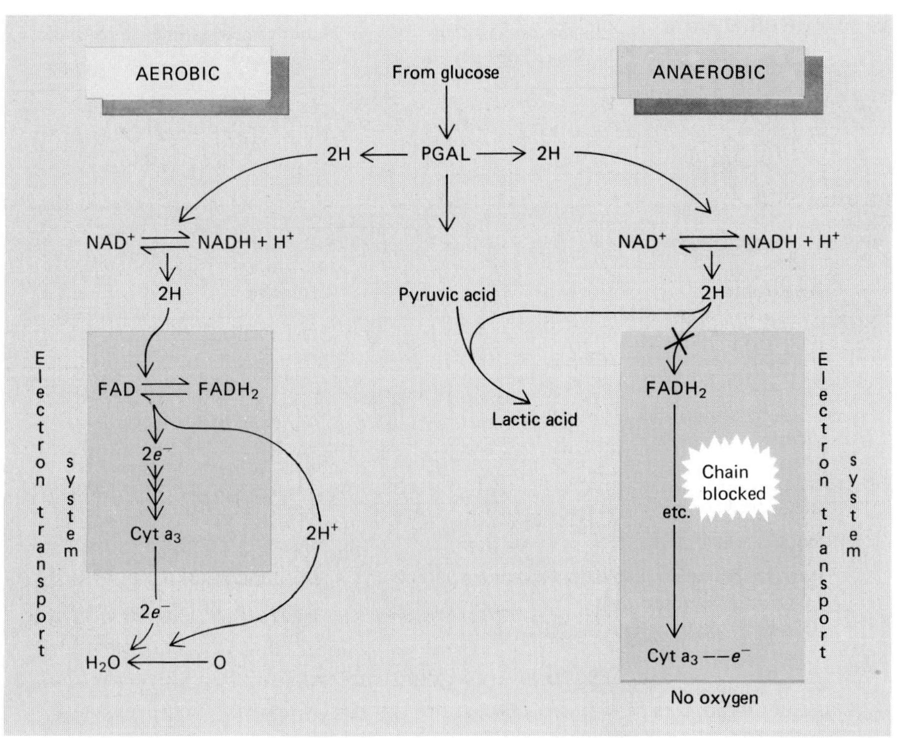

FIGURE 26-4

Comparison of anaerobic with aerobic pathways.

cellular respiration is self-regulated and can meet the immediate needs of the cell for energy.

Although the reactions of glycolysis take place in the cytoplasm, those of the Krebs cycle and the electron transport system occur within the mitochondria. The outer membrane of the mitochondria engages in active transport and regulates materials that enter. Most respiratory enzymes are associated with the mitochondrial inner membrane, as are the compounds of the cytochrome oxidase system. These enzymes must be exactly located with respect to one another so that molecules, electrons, and hydrogen may be passed from one to another in the sequenced reactions of cellular respiration. They are probably held in their positions by the physical constraint of the inner mitochondrial membrane, with which they are associated. No assembly line yet built can match the mitochondria for speed and efficiency.

Carbohydrate anabolism includes glycogenesis

Even though most of the glucose is catabolized to supply energy, some undergoes anabolic reactions involving glycogen synthesis and the conversion of some amino acids and glycerol into glucose molecules. The 5-carbon sugars ribose and deoxyribose are used in the synthesis of RNA and DNA, and lactose, milk sugar, is produced by the mammary glands during lactation.

The process of combining molecules of glucose into the long-chained glycogen molecule is called **glycogenesis** (*gly*-koe-**jen**-e-sis). The glucose is first converted into glucose-6-phosphate, then glucose-1-phosphate, then uridine diphosphate glucose, which is added to the glycogen. **Glycogenolysis** (*gly*-koe-je-**nol**-i-sis), the breakdown of glycogen into glucose, and **gluconeogenesis** (*gloo*-koe-*nee*-oh-**jen**-e-sis), the formation of "new" glucose from amino acids and glycerol, will be discussed in more detail under the section on the metabolic states. See Figure 26-5.

Lipids include fats, phospholipids, and steroids

Types and sources About 98% of lipids in the diet are ingested in the form of triglycerides[1] (also called triacylglycerols and neutral fats). Phospholipids and steroids are other types of lipids.[2] The triglycerides may be **saturated,** that

[1] You should recall from Chapter 2 that a triglyceride is a glycerol molecule chemically combined with three fatty acids. A monoglyceride consists of one fatty acid linked to a glycerol molecule, and a diglyceride consists of two fatty acids linked to a glycerol molecule.

[2] Phospholipids have a glycerol backbone attached to one or two fatty acids and also bonded to a phosphate group. Refer to Chapter 2. Steroids are quite different in structure from fats in that their backbone contains carbon atoms arranged in four connected rings; three rings have 6 carbons, and the fourth has 5 carbons.

TABLE 26-2

Comparison of anaerobic and aerobic metabolism

	Anaerobic	Aerobic
Maximum ATP profit		
From glycolysis	2 ATP	2 ATP (oxygen not required)
By way of electron transport system:		
4 H from glycolysis		6 (or 4) ATP
4 H from pyruvic acid		6 ATP
16 H from Krebs cycle		24 ATP
Maximum total ATP profit	2 ATP	38 (or 36) ATP
Final H acceptor	Pyruvic acid	O_2
End products	Pyruvic acid when respiration continues aerobically Lactic acid in muscle cells Alcohol in yeast, certain bacteria	CO_2 and H_2O

Note: The hydrogen input and hydrogen output are not balanced because water provides extra hydrogen atoms, which enter into the reactions. Also note that one ATP produced with each turn of the Krebs cycle is actually produced at the substrate level, not by way of the electron transport system.

is, fully loaded with hydrogens; **mono-unsaturated,** containing one double bond in the carbon chain of a fatty acid (thus, two more hydrogen atoms can be added); or **polyunsaturated,** containing two or more double bonds (thus, four or more hydrogen atoms can be added). See Figure 26-6.

As a rule, animal foods are rich in both saturated fats and cholesterol, and plant foods contain unsaturated fats (with the exception of palm and coconut oils which are high in saturated fats) and no cholesterol. Commonly used polyunsaturated vegetable oils are corn, soya, cottonseed, and safflower oils. Olive and peanut oils contain large amounts of monounsaturated fats. Butter contains mainly saturated fats: about 66% saturated fat, 31% monounsaturated, and only 3% polyunsaturated. Soybean oil contains only about 15% saturated fat, 25% monounsaturated, and 60% polyunsaturated fat. Safflower oil has an even greater percentage of polyunsaturated fat—about 75%.

Fatty acids are an essential part of all fats. The body is able to synthesize most fatty acids. However, two fatty acids, *linoleic acid* and *linolenic acid,* cannot be synthesized by the human body yet are essential to health. Therefore, they are known as **essential fatty acids.** Deficiencies of linoleic acid are rare because it is the most common polyunsaturated fatty acid found in foods.

Daily requirement Lipids account for about 40% of the kilocalories in the average American or Canadian diet. In poorer countries this percentage falls to less than 10% because most lipid-rich foods—meats, eggs, and dairy products—are relatively expensive.

The American Heart Association (AHA) recommends that fats be limited to 30% or less of the total caloric intake, with saturated fats kept at 10% or less of the total fat consumption. The AHA also recommends that the daily cholesterol intake be under 250 milligrams (about the amount in a single egg yolk), in contrast to American

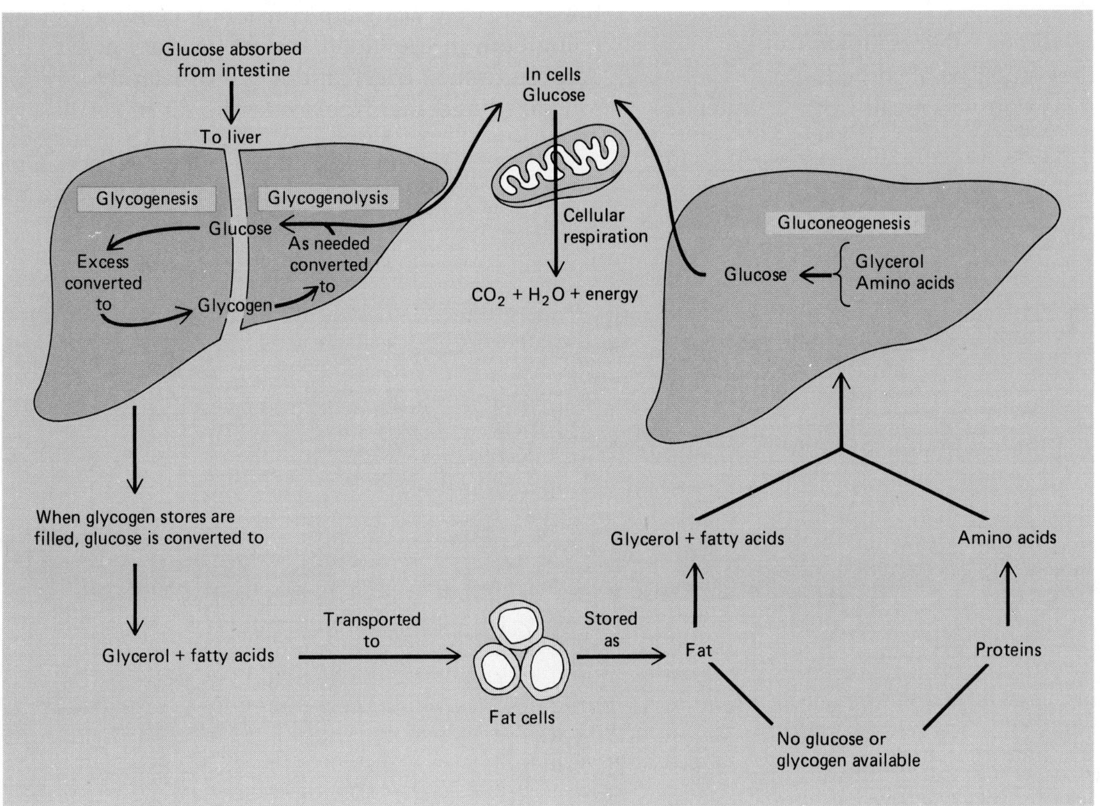

FIGURE 26-5

The fate of glucose in the body.

diets, which provide an average of 700 milligrams of cholesterol each day. Besides egg yolks, butter and meats are high in cholesterol.

Lipids have been the focus of much research because of the role they may play in developing atherosclerosis, a progressive disease in which the arteries become occluded with fatty material. As was discussed in Chapter 21, atherosclerosis leads to circulatory impairment and heart disease. A diet high in saturated fats and cholesterol increases the chances of developing atherosclerosis. Although cholesterol is synthesized daily in the liver even when the diet is very low in lipids, a diet high in saturated fats causes blood-cholesterol levels to increase as much as 25% above that. Ingestion of large amounts of cholesterol-rich foods also increases blood-cholesterol levels.

On the other hand, ingestion of polyunsaturated fats tends to decrease blood-cholesterol levels, thus affording some protection against the development of atherosclerosis. For these reasons many people now use vegetable oils and polyunsaturated margarines instead of butter and lard, skim or 1% milk instead of whole milk, and ice milk instead of ice cream.

Absorption and storage Before lipids can be metabolized they must be absorbed. Chylomicrons (as you will recall from Chapter 25) are tiny particles composed principally of fat. They are formed in the epithelial cells of the small intestine and absorbed into the lacteals of the villi. In the lymph circulation, chylomicrons are transported to the thoracic duct and eventually are emptied into the blood. As the blood courses through adipose tissues, most of the chylomicrons are removed rapidly from the blood by fat cells, so that within a few minutes after fat absorption the contents of the chylomicrons have been stored as fat. The stored fat is then mobilized from adipose tissue as needed. Triglycerides are hydrolyzed within the fat cells, and free fatty acids are sent into the blood, where they are transported in chemical combination with plasma globulins (proteins) such as albumin. About half of the fat is stored in subcutaneous tissues with the remaining adipose tissue being found associated with the kidneys, omenta, genitals, muscles, eyes, heart, and folds of the large intestine.

The turnover rate of free fatty acids in the blood is extremely rapid, but despite that, the body maintains a level of about 15 milligrams per 100 milliliters of free fatty acids in the blood at all times. This represents a steady-state equilibrium, however; fatty acids are constantly coming and going both in the blood and in the very active adipose tissue. Triglycerides are constantly mobilized and then replaced. The fat molecules

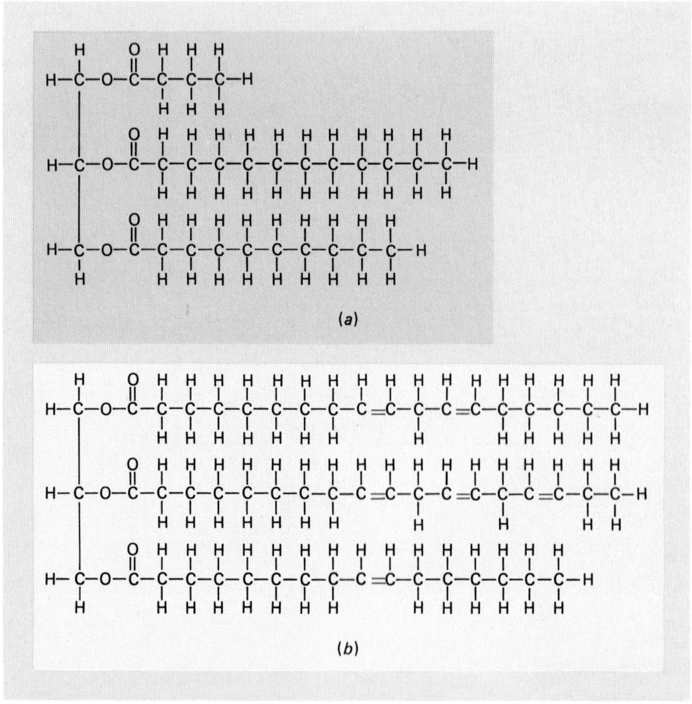

(a)

(b)

FIGURE 26-6

Comparison of a saturated with an unsaturated fat molecule. *(a)* A triglyceride containing three saturated fatty acids. *(b)* A triglyceride containing three unsaturated fatty acids. Note the double bonds.

you have stored in your fat cells today are not the same ones that were there last week, although the total amount is probably much the same!

Because chylomicrons contain both lipids and proteins, they are said to be composed of **lipoproteins.** The liver produces at least three other types of small lipoproteins, which, like chylomicrons, are a form in which lipids, especially cholesterol and phospholipids, are transported in the blood. One type of lipoprotein, called **low-density lipoprotein (LDL),** contains mainly cholesterol. A high plasma concentration of this lipoprotein is associated with the development of atherosclerosis.

Role in body Fats provide an important function in storing kilocalories; each gram of triglyceride contains more than twice as many kilocalories (9 kcal) as a gram of carbohydrate or protein. They also function in protection of some organs (kidneys and eyes are examples), insulation, and the storage of vitamins A, D, E, and K. Lipids are integral components of plasma membranes and the myelin sheaths surrounding many nerves. Prostaglandins, local hormones, are a kind of lipid. Cholesterol is used to produce important functional molecules including bile salts and steroid hormones.

Lipid catabolism provides energy

Body fat represents an important fuel reserve. When completely degraded in cellular respiration, a molecule of a 6-carbon fatty acid can generate up to 44 molecules of ATP (compared to 38 for glucose, which also has six carbons). Most cells can utilize fatty acids as fuel almost interchangeably with glucose. In fact, between meals most cells shift their energy metabolism so that fat is oxidized instead of glucose. In this way glucose is reserved for nerve cells, which are not able to utilize lipids as fuel under ordinary circumstances.

When the blood-glucose level falls, fat cells digest fat molecules with a hydrolytic enzyme, degrading them to glycerol and fatty acids. The fatty acids are extruded from the fat cell and allowed to float off in the bloodstream, bound for some other cellular destination (Fig. 26-7). Some

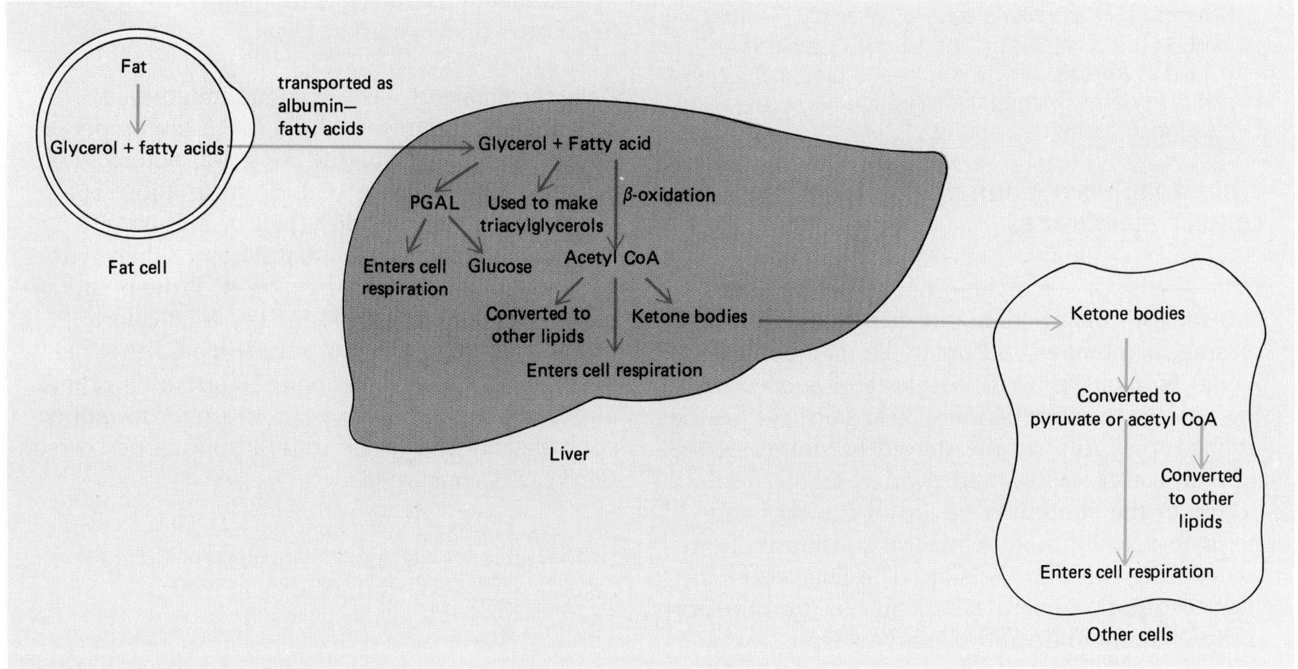

FIGURE 26-7

Overview of lipid metabolism.

glycerol is released into the plasma and catabolized by other cells, but apparently the fat cell catabolizes most of the glycerol. In either case, phosphate is added to glycerol, converting it to glyceraldehyde-3-phosphate or one of its daughter compounds. These intermediary fuel molecules then enter glycolysis at appropriate points, are degraded to pyruvic acid, and pass through the Krebs cycle.

Before fatty acids can be utilized as fuel they must be broken down into smaller compounds. Most of this initial degradation, you will recall, takes place in liver cells. Fatty acids are split by a complex chemical process called **beta (β-) oxidation,** in which they combine with coenzyme A. The fatty acid is chopped into progressively smaller segments, each time releasing a molecule of acetyl coenzyme A. In the mitochondria, acetyl-CoA enters the Krebs cycle and is oxidized as fuel. Liver cells oxidize some of the coenzyme A that they produce, but some must be dispatched to other cells. In order for acetyl-CoA to diffuse freely out of the liver cells and be transported in the blood, it is converted to one of three types of **ketone bodies** (acetone, acetoacetic acid, or β-hydroxybutyric acid).

Clinical highlight

Normally, the level of ketone bodies in the blood is about 3 milligrams per 100 milliliter. However, in certain abnormal conditions, such as starvation or diabetes mellitus, fat metabolism must be tremendously increased. Ketone bodies are then produced so rapidly that they reach an excessive level in the blood, a condition known as **ketosis.** Ketosis can lead to disruption of normal pH balance, making the blood too acidic and even resulting in death.

Lipid anabolism maintains cellular membranes

Cells use lipids for making needed compounds and for the construction and maintenance of their plasma membranes and organelle membranes. About 80% of the body's cholesterol is used by the liver in the production of bile salts; the rest is utilized to synthesize the steroid hormones of the adrenal cortex, testes, and ovaries. Cholesterol occurs in the stratum corneum of the skin and helps to prevent many chemical substances from penetrating through the skin. The liver also synthesizes lipoproteins that function in the transport of lipid compounds and thromboplastin that is used in clot formation. Phospholipids are used in the production of the myelin sheath that covers neurons.

Proteins consist of amino acids

Types and sources Protein consumption is often an index of a country's (or an individual's) economic status, because high-quality protein is the most expensive and least widely available of all nutrients. Protein poverty is one of the world's most pressing health problems; millions of human beings suffer from poor health and disease and even die as a consequence of protein malnutrition.

Of the 20 amino acids important in nutrition, the body is able to make several by rearranging the atoms of certain organic acids. Eight of the amino acids cannot by synthesized by the body cells at all, or at least not in sufficient quantity to meet the body's needs. These, which must be provided in the diet, are called the **essential amino acids.**[1]

Not all proteins contain the same kinds or quantities of amino acids, and many proteins lack some of the essential amino acids. **High-quality proteins,** or **complete proteins,** contain all the essential amino acids and are found in milk, eggs, meat, and fish. **Incomplete proteins** occur in beans and nuts; they lack one or more of the esssential amino acids. Most plant proteins are deficient in one or more of the essential amino acids, usually lysine, tryptophan, or threonine. See Focus on Vegetarian Diets.

Daily requirements The recommended daily amount of protein for adults is 0.8 grams per kilogram of body weight. For a 140-pound person, this would be equivalent to about 56 grams of protein per day (half of a Quarter Pounder!). Americans consume more than twice the amount of protein they need. Protein should make up about 12 to 15% of the total caloric intake each day. It has been estimated that the average American eats about 300 pounds of meat and dairy products per year. In underdeveloped countries an average of only 2 pounds per person per year is consumed.

[1]The essential amino acids include phenylalanine, valine, tryptophan, threonine, lysine, leucine, isoleucine, and methionine.

FOCUS ON . . . Vegetarian diets

Because most of the world's population depends almost exclusively upon plant foods for proteins and other nutrients, let us examine the vegetarian diet in more detail. Besides being deficient in some of the essential amino acids, plant foods have a lower percentage of protein than animal foods. Meat contains about 25% protein; the new high-yield grains contain 5 to 13%; and legumes contain about 8%. Another problem is that plant protein is less digestible than animal protein. Because humans cannot digest the cellulose cell walls surrounding all plant cells, much of the protein encased within the cells passes through the digestive tract as part of the bulk.

Another consideration with the vegetarian diet is that the body has no mechanism for storing amino acids. Cells cannot make anything comparable to glycogen, and the body has no protein depot in the sense that fat is stored in adipose tissue. One might almost say that, to be useful, all the essential amino acids must be ingested in the same meal. For example, even though corn and beans complement each other to provide the essential amino acids, if corn is eaten for lunch and beans for dinner, the body will not have all the essential amino acids at the same time and thus will not be able to manufacture needed proteins.

Does this mean, then, that vegetarian diets are always unhealthy? Not at all. With a variety of plant foods and some knowledge of nutrition one can plan a vegetarian diet that will provide all the needed amino acids. The main task is to select foods that complement one another. For example, if beans and corn or beans and rice are eaten together in the appropriate proportions, they will provide the required essential amino acids. When dairy products are available, they should be eaten together with the plant foods. For example, when cereal is eaten with milk, the meal has a much greater nutritional value. Macaroni and cheese is another example.

Soybeans, peanuts, and other legumes have more than twice the protein content of the cereal grains. Unfortunately, yields per acre are much lower than yields per acre of cereal grains. Also, most legumes are used as livestock feed rather than for human consumption. In fact, in the United States 91% of the cereal, legume, and other vegetable protein suitable for human use is fed to livestock. This represents a tremendous and serious loss of protein available to humans—for every 5 kilograms (11 lb) of vegetable and fish protein fed to livestock in addition to their forage intake, only 1 kilogram (2.2 lb) of animal protein is produced. Meat is expensive economically because it is expensive ecologically. As the human population continues to expand, more and more of us will have to turn to vegetarian diets.

Most humans depend upon cereal grains as their staple food, usually rice, wheat, or corn. None of these foods provides an adequate proportion of total amino acids or distribution of essential amino acids, especially not for growing children. In some underdeveloped countries starchy crops such as sweet potatoes or cassava are the principal food. The total protein content of these foods is less than 2%, far below minimum needs.

Of all the required nutrients, essential amino acids are the ones most often lacking in the diet. Millions suffer from poor health and lowered resistance to disease because of protein deficiency. In children, physical and mental development may be retarded when the essential building blocks of cells are not provided in the diet. Common childhood diseases such as measles, whooping cough, and chickenpox are often fatal in the malnourished. In underdeveloped countries the death rate from measles, for example, may be more than 300 times greater than it is in North America.

When a pregnant woman subsists on a diet lacking sufficient protein, the development of her fetus is jeopardized. Perhaps the greatest toll taken is upon the brain. A study of the brains of babies who died of malnutrition showed that some had developed only 40% of the normal number of brain cells. Brain development is most critical before birth and during the first 2 years of life. A child deprived of needed nutrients during that time may never make up the lost growth and development. Even moderate protein malnutrition manifests itself in clumsiness, reduced manual skills, retarded language development, and lower intelligence.

Severe protein malnutrition results in the condition known as **kwashiorkor.** The term, an African word that means "first-second," refers to the situation in which a first child is displaced from its mother's breast when a younger sibling is born. The older child is then placed on a diet of starchy cereal or cassava that is deficient in protein. Growth becomes stunted, muscles are wasted, edema develops (as displayed by a swollen belly), apathy and anemia ensue, and metabolism is impaired (Fig. 26-8). Without essential amino acids the digestive enzymes themselves cannot be manufactured, and eventually what little protein is ingested cannot be digested. Dehydration and diarrhea develop, often leading to death.

Absorption Ingested proteins are degraded in the digestive tract to their molecular units, amino acids, which are then absorbed into the blood and travel to the body cells. They enter the cell by active transport, under stimulation of growth hormone and insulin, to be utilized in making the types of proteins needed.

Role in body Why are proteins critical as nutrients? They are absolutely essential as building blocks of cells. Indeed, 75% of body solids consist of protein. Amino acids are used in making the proteins for new cells and cellular parts (Fig. 26-9). In muscle cells they are fashioned into myosin and actin, the proteins needed in muscle contraction. The liver uses amino acids to synthesize plasma proteins. They are used by the red blood cells to make hemoglobin. Antibodies and most hormones and enzymes are proteins in nature. Proteins are important in maintaining osmotic balances in the fluid compartments of the body.

The importance of amino acids as components of enzymes should be clearly understood. Almost every step in cellular respiration requires the participation of at least one enzyme. The transformation of pyruvic acid to acetyl coenzyme A, for example, requires the interaction of no less than four enzymes that together comprise a multienzyme complex that is almost large and elaborate enough to warrant status as an organelle. It is largely by producing proteins that the genetic machinery of the cell controls every detail of the cell's life processes.

Protein catabolism yields amino acids

As cells wear out, their proteins are extracted and broken down into amino acids, which can serve in the construction of new proteins. Some amino

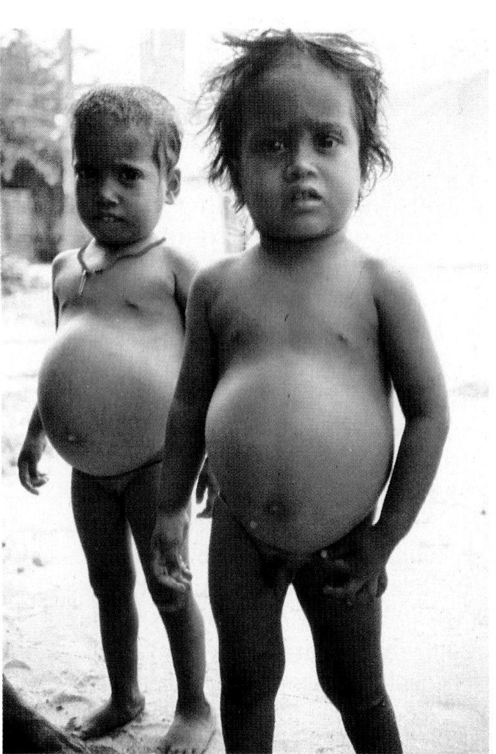

FIGURE 26-8

Children suffering from kwashiorkor, a disease caused by severe protein deficiency. Note the characteristic swollen belly, which results from fluid imbalance. (Food and Agriculture Organization of the United Nations.)

acids are utilized for energy, but only after being converted into a carbohydrate compound such as pyruvic acid, ketoglutaric acid, or other intermediates of the Krebs cycle.

Clinical highlight

Phenylketonuria (*fen*-il-*kee*-to-**nyou**-ree-a), or **PKU**, is a genetic defect of metabolism in which the enzyme responsible for the conversion of phenylalanine to tyrosine is lacking. Tyrosine is able to enter the Krebs cycle; phenylalanine is not. The accumulation of phenylalanine becomes toxic to the developing brain and leads to mental retardation and other abnormalities. A test of an infant's urine is used to detect the disorder, which can be treated by restricting phenylalanine in the child's diet.

Although small pools of amino acids accumulate in the cytoplasm of all cells, there is no mechanism for storing large quantities. Excess amino acids are removed from the blood by the liver cells and **deaminated** (de-**am**-i-nay-ted); that is, the amine group is removed from each amino acid.

$$R^1\text{—}\overset{\displaystyle NH_2}{\underset{\displaystyle H}{\overset{|}{\underset{|}{C}}}}\text{—}COOH + H_2O + NAD^+ \longrightarrow$$

$$R\text{—}\overset{\displaystyle O}{\overset{\|}{C}}\text{—}COOH + NH_3 + NADH + H^+$$

As they are cleaved from the amino acid, the amine groups are converted into ammonia. But ammonia is toxic and is quickly converted to urea.

$$H_2N\text{—}\overset{\displaystyle O}{\overset{\|}{C}}\text{—}NH_2$$

The urea then passes into the blood and is excreted by the kidneys. After deamination the remaining portion

$$R\text{—}\overset{\displaystyle O}{\overset{\|}{C}}\text{—}COOH$$

of the amino acid (now called a keto acid) may be converted into carbohydrate or lipid and either used as fuel or stored as fat. Excess amino acids are not stored as protein but are converted into fat or glycogen.

The amount of nitrogen in the urine reflects the amount of amino acid (and protein) breakdown. When the amount of nitrogen in the diet and the amount excreted in the urine of an adult are the same, the person is said to be in **nitrogen balance.** During starvation and certain hormone disorders, large amounts of protein are degraded, and the body excretes more nitrogen then it takes in, a state of *negative nitrogen balance.* When a child is growing or when an individual is recovering from an illness, intake of protein normally exceeds nitrogen excretion and the body is said to be in *positive nitrogen balance.*

[1] R stands for the rest of the compound, the remaining atoms of any amino acid.

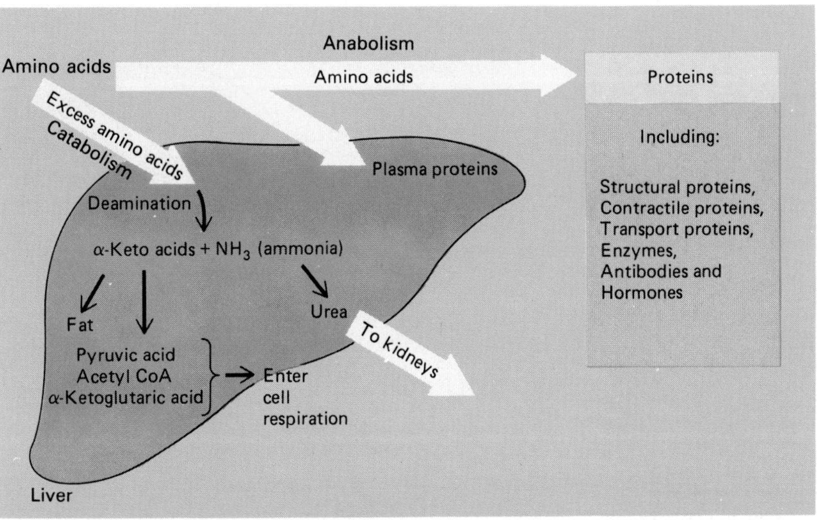

FIGURE 26-9

Overview of protein metabolism.

Protein anabolism builds structural and functional proteins

Whereas glucose and fatty acids are used mainly in catabolism, amino acids are utilized mainly in the anabolic (building) processes of the body (Fig. 26-9). Cells use amino acids to produce new proteins. The site of protein synthesis in the cells is the ribosomes, which are directed by DNA via RNA. Much of protein production is regulated by hormones such as thyroxine, insulin, growth hormone, and sex hormones.

The anabolism of amino acids provides the body with all structural proteins and most of its functional molecules as well. Excluding water, over half of the body consists of protein. Besides functioning as enzymes, hormones, and antibodies, proteins make up the myofibrils of muscle, most of the hemoglobin molecule, and many cellular and body structural components. They serve as the foundation for our bones, muscles, blood, hair, and fingernails.

Figure 26-10 summarizes the relationship between protein, lipid, and carbohydrate metabolism, and Table 26-3 summarizes the utilization of nutrients by the body. Note in the figure that carbohydrates, lipids, and proteins are able to utilize the Krebs cycle. Also, excess protein and carbohydrate, that not used in anabolism or for energy, is converted to fat and stored as such.

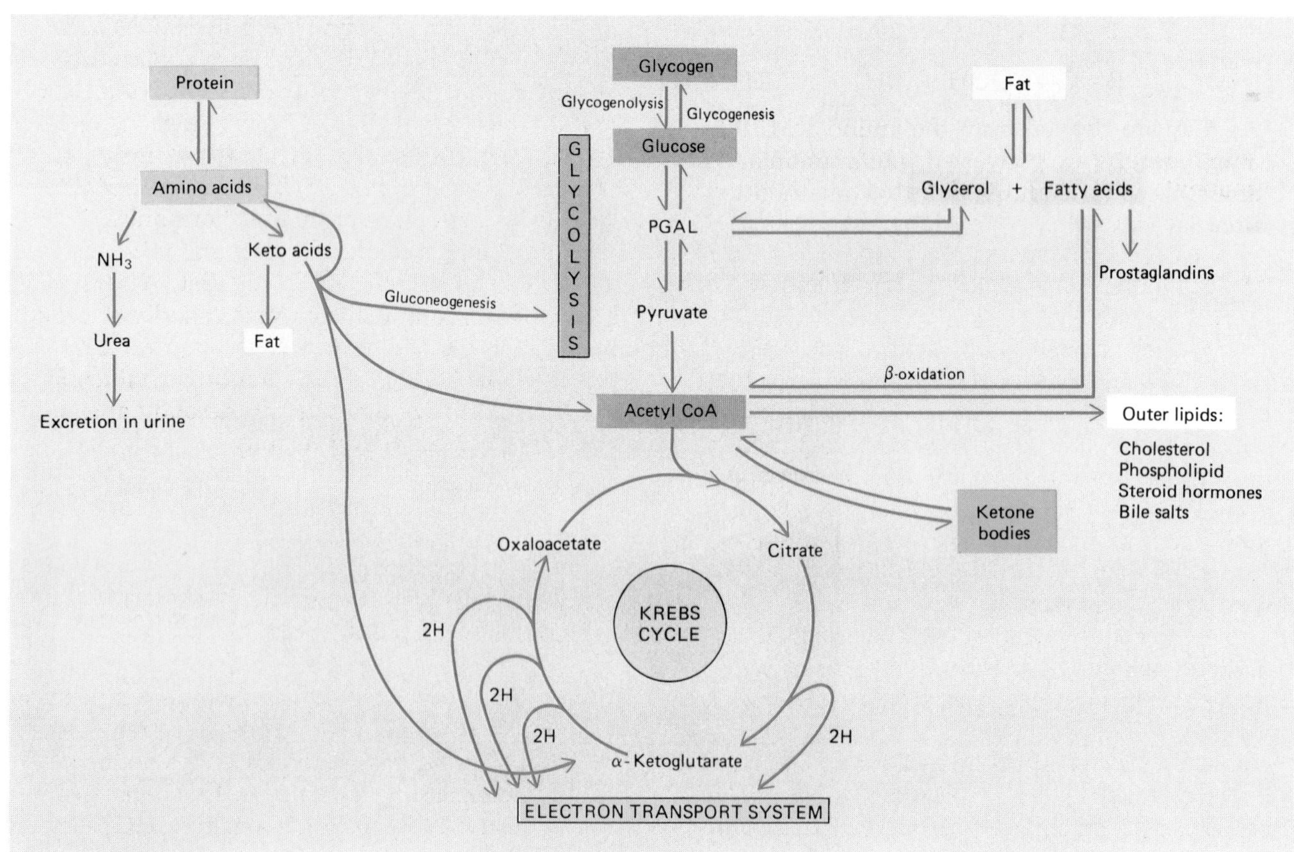

FIGURE 26-10

Overview of the integrated metabolism of carbohydrates, fats, and proteins.

TABLE 26-3

Utilization of nutrients		
Nutrient	**Principal uses in body**	**Fate of excess**
Carbohydrates		
Mainly glucose	Fuel for cellular respiration; degraded to carbon dioxide and water with production of ATP	Stored as glycogen (glycogenesis); after glycogen stores are filled, excess is converted to fat and stored in adipose tissue
Fats		
Fatty acids	Synthesis of cell membranes; converted to acetyl coenzyme A and used as fuel for cellular respiration	Stored as fat in adipose tissue
Glycerol	Used to make triglycerides; converted to PGAL (and glucose) for use as fuel	Stored as fat in adipose tissue
Proteins		
Amino acids	Synthesis of proteins (enzymes, structural proteins, hemoglobin, etc.); after deamination, keto acid portion may be used as fuel	Deaminated in liver; amine group converted to urea and excreted in urine, keto acid portion is used as fuel or stored as fat

Minerals are inorganic nutrients

Carbon, oxygen, hydrogen, and nitrogen make up about 96% of the weight of the body; the remaining 4% consists of inorganic minerals. Calcium and phosphorus make up about 75% of the mineral content of the body, with most located in bone and teeth.

Minerals are naturally occurring chemical elements that serve as inorganic nutrients and are ingested as salts dissolved in food or water. They are usually designated as major or trace minerals on the sole basis of their amounts in the body. **Major minerals** are found in amounts greater than 5 grams; **trace minerals** occur in the body in amounts less than 5 grams and are required in very small quantities.

A salt content of about 0.9% is needed to maintain an appropriate fluid balance in the body. As salts are lost from the body in sweat, urine, water vapor, and feces, they must be replaced by dietary intake. Sodium and chloride are major electrolytes, helping to maintain osmotic balances and contributing to the excitability of neurons and muscle cells. Sodium and phosphorus are important in acid-base buffering. Some minerals are needed to activate metabolic reactions. Others are essential components of important body chemicals including enzymes, coenzymes, and functional proteins. For example, iron is needed as a component of hemoglobin and iodine as an ingredient of thyroid hormones.

Iron, calcium, and iodine are the minerals most likely to be deficient in the diet. A deficiency of only a few micrograms of iodine needed each day can cause serious consequences to health. Table 26-4 lists some important minerals in order of relative amounts in the body and gives their functions in the body.

Vitamins are organic compounds acting as physiological regulators

Vitamins are organic compounds required in trace amounts in the diet. Vitamins serve as regulators in many physiological reactions in the body. Many, especially the B vitamins, function as coenzymes (also called cofactors). Vitamin deficiency

TABLE 26-4

Some important minerals and their functions		
Mineral	**Functions**	**Comments**
Major minerals		
Calcium	Component of bone and teeth; essential for normal blood clotting; needed for normal muscle and nerve function	Good sources are milk and other dairy products, green leafy vegetables; bones serve as calcium reservoir
Phosphorus	As calcium phosphate it is an important structural component of bone; essential in energy transfer and storage (component of ATP) and in many other metabolic processes; component of DNA and RNA	Performs more functions than any other mineral; antacids can impair phosphorus absorption
Potassium	Principal positive ion within cells; influences muscle contraction and nerve excitability	Occurs in many foods
Sulfur	Component of many proteins (e.g., insulin) and therefore essential for normal metabolic activity	Found in high-protein foods such as meat, fish, legumes, and nuts
Sodium	Principal positive ion (cation) in interstitial fluid; important in fluid balance; essential for conduction of nerve impulses	Occurs naturally in foods; sodium chloride (table salt) is added as seasoning; too much is ingested in the average American diet; excessive amounts may lead to high blood pressure
Chlorine	Principal negative ion (anion) of interstitial fluid; important in fluid balance and in acid-base balance	Occurs naturally in foods; is ingested as sodium chloride
Trace minerals		
Magnesium	Appropriate balance between magnesium and calcium ions needed for normal muscle and nerve function; component of many coenzymes; some evidence links magnesium deficiency in soft water with heart deaths	Occurs in many foods
Iron	Component of hemoglobin, myoglobin, important respiratory enzymes (cytochromes), and other enzymes essential to oxygen transport and cellular respiration	Mineral most likely to be deficient in diet; good sources are meat (especially liver), nuts, egg yolk, and legumes; deficiency results in anemia
Manganese	Necessary to activate arginase, an enzyme essential for urea formation; activates many other enzymes, including ATPase and cholinesterase	Poorly absorbed from intestine, found in whole-grain cereals, egg yolks, and green vegetables
Copper	Component of enzyme needed for melanin synthesis and of many other enzymes; essential for hemoglobin synthesis	Sources are liver, eggs, fish, whole wheat flour, beans
Iodine	Component of thyroid hormones (hormones that stimulate metabolic rate)	Found in seafoods, iodized salt, and vegetables grown in iodine-rich soils; deficiency results in goiter (abnormal enlargement of thyroid gland)
Fluorine	Component of bones and teeth; makes teeth resistant to decay	In areas where it does not occur naturally, fluorine may be added to municipal water supplies (fluoridation); excess causes tooth mottling
Cobalt	Component of vitamin B_{12}, and therefore essential for red blood cell production	Best sources are meat and dairy products; strict vegetarians may become deficient in this mineral
Zinc	Component of at least 70 enzymes, including carbonic anhydrase; also a component of some peptidases and thus important in protein digestion; may be important in wound healing	Occurs in many foods
Chromium	Enhances production and effect of insulin	Found in brewer's yeast, meat, poultry, whole grains, and cheese
Selenium	Component of some enzymes; antioxidant	Occurs in fish, cereals, meat, garlic

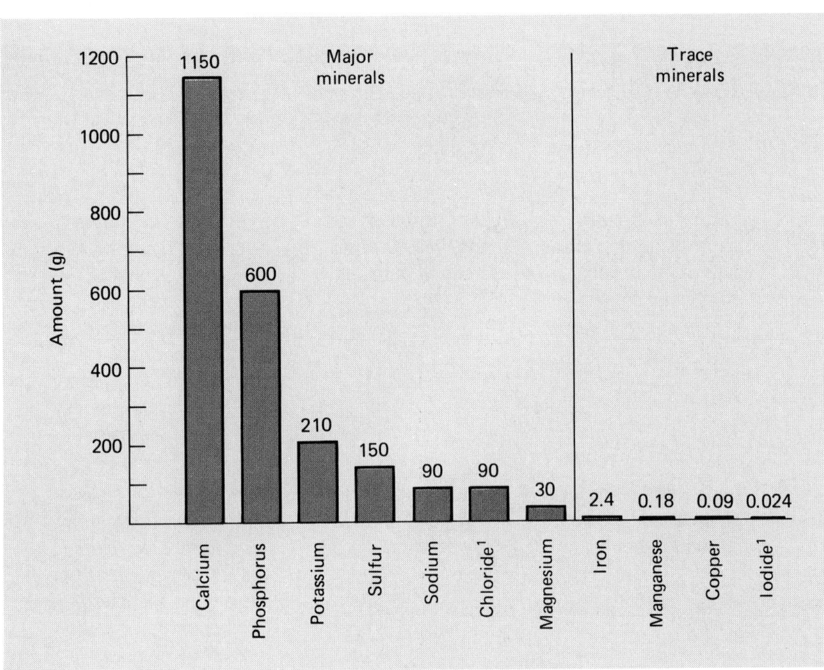

Minerals present in a 60-kg person. Chlorine and iodine appear as ions (chloride and iodide) in the body. (From Hamilton, Eva, et. al., *Nutrition: Concepts and Controversies,* 4th ed., St. Paul, West Publishing Co., 1988.)

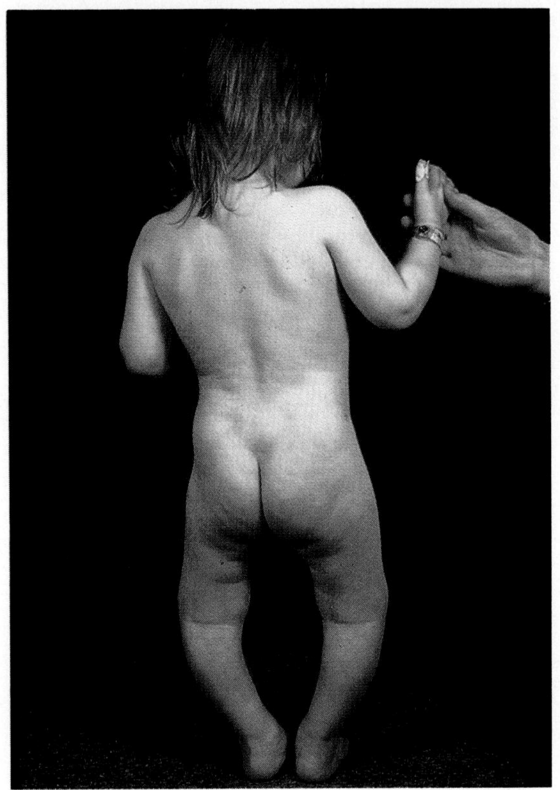

FIGURE 26-11

A child with rickets. A deficiency of vitamin D decreases the body's ability to absorb and use calcium and phosphorus and produces soft, malformed bones. These are most clearly evident in the ribs and in wrists and ankles. Note the bowed legs. (Biophoto Associates.)

produces clinical symptoms and predictable metabolic disorders (Fig. 26-11).

Vitamins are classified into two groups, fat-soluble and water-soluble. Vitamins A, D, E, and K are the **fat-soluble vitamins** and are absorbed with other lipids in the micelles. These vitamins can be stored in body cells where they may accumulate.

The **water-soluble vitamins** include vitamin C and the B-complex vitamins. These vitamins are absorbed along with water. (Vitamin B_{12} needs to first combine with intrinsic factor before being absorbed.) Water-soluble vitamins are not stored to any great extent in the body and excesses are excreted in the urine.

No single natural food contains all the vitamins. It is necessary for most vitamins to be ingested. However, several vitamins can be produced by the body. Vitamin K can by synthesized by bacteria within the large intestine and absorbed from there. Vitamin D can be produced by ultraviolet stimulation of cholesterol-like compounds in the skin. Vitamin A can be made from the provitamin (vitamin precursor) carotene.

Table 26-5 gives the recommended daily allowance, sources, and actions of vitamins and the effects of various vitamin deficiencies.

TABLE 26-5

The vitamins

Vitamins and U.S. RDA*	Actions	Effect of deficiency	Sources	Comments
Fat soluble				
A 5000 IU†	Component of retinal pigments essential for normal vision; essential for normal growth and integrity of epithelial tissue; promotes normal growth of bones and teeth by regulating activity of osteoblasts and osteoclasts	Failure of growth; night blindness; atrophy of epithelium; epithelium subject to infection; scaly skin	Liver, fish-liver oils, egg, yellow and green vegetables	Can be formed from provitamin carotene (a yellow or red pigment); sometimes called anti-infection vitamin because it helps maintain epithelial membranes; excessive amounts harmful
D 400 IU	Promotes calcium absorption from digestive tract; essential to normal growth and maintenance of bone	Bone deformities; rickets in children; osteomalacia in adults	Liver, fish-liver oils, egg yolk, fortified milk, butter, margarine	Two types: D_2 (calciferol), a synthetic form; D_3, formed by action of ultraviolet rays from sun upon a cholesterol compound in the skin; excessive amounts harmful
E 30 IU	Inhibits oxidation of unsaturated fatty acids and vitamin A that help form cell and organelle membranes; precise biochemical role not known	Increased catabolism of unsaturated fatty acids, so that not enough are available for maintenance of plasma membranes and other membranous organelles; prevents normal growth	Oils made from cereal seeds, liver, eggs, fish	
K (80 mg for male; 65 mg for female)	Essential for blood clotting	Prolonged blood-clotting time	Normally supplied by intestinal bacteria; green leafy vegetables	Antibiotics may kill bacteria; then supplements needed in surgical patients
Water soluble				
C (ascorbic acid) 60 mg	Needed for collagen synthesis and for other intercellular substances; formation of bone matrix and tooth dentin, intercellular cement; needed for metabolism of several amino acids; may help body withstand injury from burns and bacterial toxins	Scurvy (wounds heal very slowly and scars become weak and split open, capillaries become fragile, bone does not grow or heal properly)	Citrus fruits, strawberries, tomatoes	Possible role in preventing common cold or in the development of acquired immunity? Very excessive dose is harmful
B Complex				
Thiamine (B_1) 1.5 mg	Acts as coenzyme in many different enzyme systems; important in carbohydrate and amino acid metabolism	Beriberi (weakened heart muscle, enlarged right side of heart, nervous system and digestive tract disorders)	Liver, yeast, cereals, meat, green leafy vegetables	Deficiency common in alcoholics
Riboflavin 1.7 mg	Used to make coenzymes (FAD) essential in cellular respiration	Dermatitis, inflammation and cracking at corners of mouth; mental depression	Liver, cheese, milk, eggs, green leafy vegetables	

TABLE 26-5

(continued)

Vitamins and U.S. RDA*	Actions	Effect of deficiency	Sources	Comments
Water soluble				
Niacin (nicotinic acid) 20 mg	Component of important coenzymes (NAD and NADP) essential to cellular respiration	Pellagra (dermatitis, diarrhea, mental symptoms, muscular weakness, fatigue)	Liver, meat, fish, cereals, legumes, whole grain and enriched breads	
Pyridoxine (B_6) 2 mg	Coenzyme needed for amino acid synthesis and protein metabolism	Dermatitis; digestive tract disturbances; convulsions	Liver, meat, cereals, legumes	1.6 mg RDA for female
Pantothenic acid 10 mg	Constitutent of coenzyme A (a compound important in cellular metabolism)	Deficiency is extremely rare	Widespread in foods	
Folate 0.2 mg	Coenzyme needed for nucleic acid synthesis and for maturation of red blood cells	A type of anemia	Produced by intestinal bacteria; liver, cereals, dark green, leafy vegetables	0.18 mg RDA for female
Biotin 0.3 mg	Coenzyme needed for cellular metabolism	Deficiency unknown	Produced by intestinal bacteria; liver, chocolate, egg yolk	
B_{12} 2 mg	Coenzyme important in nucleic acid metabolism	Pernicious anemia	Liver, meat, fish	Contains cobalt; intrinsic factor secreted by gastric mucosa needed for absorption of B_{12}

*RDA is the recommended dietary allowance, established by the Food and Nutrition Board of the National Research Council (1989 report), to maintain good nutrition for healthy persons.

†International Unit: the amount that produces a specified biologic effect and is internationally accepted as a measure of the activity of the substance.

Clinical highlight

Controversy rages over the issue of vitamin supplements. Many nutritionists feel that a balanced diet provides all the vitamins needed. Others argue that even when people try to eat a balanced diet, they must depend on fruit and vegetables that are not freshly picked and upon processed foods that may not supply adequate amounts of vitamins. Still others believe that large amounts of specific vitamins are beneficial. You may be familiar with assertions that vitamin C helps prevent the common cold, and that vitamin E protects against vascular disease.

In 1989, the National Research Council, in its study titled "Diet and Health: Implications for Reducing Chronic Disease Risk," stated that a good health recommendation is to "avoid taking dietary supplements in excess of the RDA (recommended daily allowance) in any one day." A daily dose of multiple vitamins with 100% of the RDA "is not known to be harmful or beneficial." However, the report also said that vitamin-mineral supplements not only have no known health benefits, but their use may be detrimental to health.

Claims have been made that vitamins C, E, and A may help protect against certain types of cancer. The truth is that there is still a great deal not known about the actions of vitamins. Much more research is needed before their complex biochemical roles will be understood. *Meanwhile, moderation is recommended.*

Hypervitaminosis is a condition resulting from ingestion of excessive amounts of any vitamin. Hypervitaminosis of vitamin A or D is being seen with increasing frequency. Because vitamins A and D are fat-soluble, they are not easily excreted in the urine. Instead, they tend to accumulate in fatty tissues of the body (mainly in the liver), where they can build up to harmful levels. Hypervitaminosis A results in loss of hair and skin disorders. Hypervitaminosis D results in weakness, fatigue, loss of weight, and other symptoms. Even vitamin C in excessive amounts can be harmful, especially in children. Massive doses can cause kidney damage and intestinal disturbances.

Metabolic states vary in their energy sources

The direct sources of energy for the cells of the body may vary during the course of metabolism. Two different metabolic states exist, the absorptive state and the postabsorptive state.

The **absorptive state** (Fig. 26-12) is the time during which digestion end-products of nutrients are being absorbed into the blood and the lymph from the GI tract. A person is typically in the absorptive state for a 4-hour period during and after a meal. The **postabsorptive (fasting) state** (Fig. 26-13) is the period during which no digestion end-products are being absorbed and the body

(text continued on p. 938)

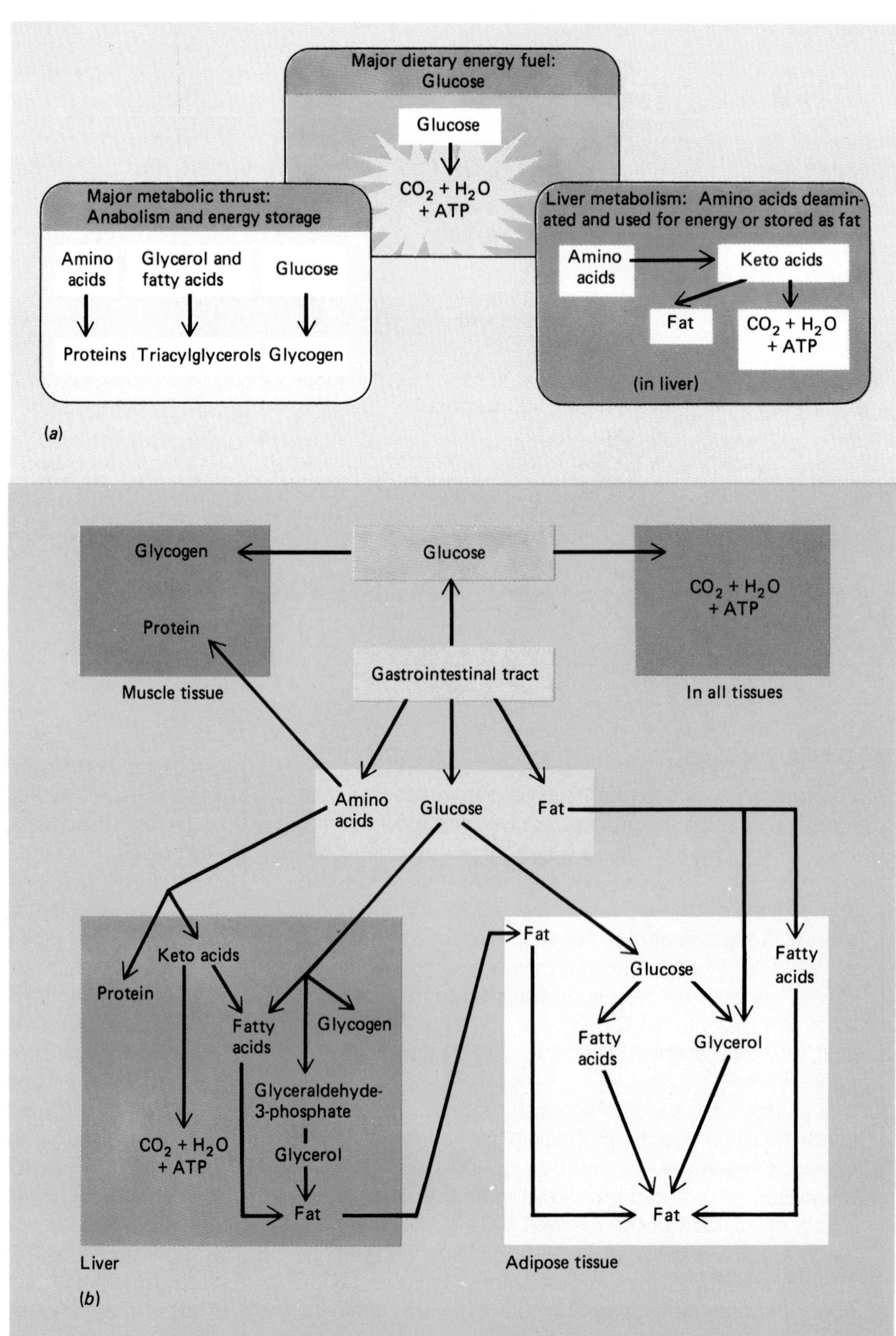

FIGURE 26-12

Summary of the absorptive state. Some amino acids are used by tissue cells for protein synthesis, and fats are the major energy fuel of liver cells, muscle, and adipose tissue.

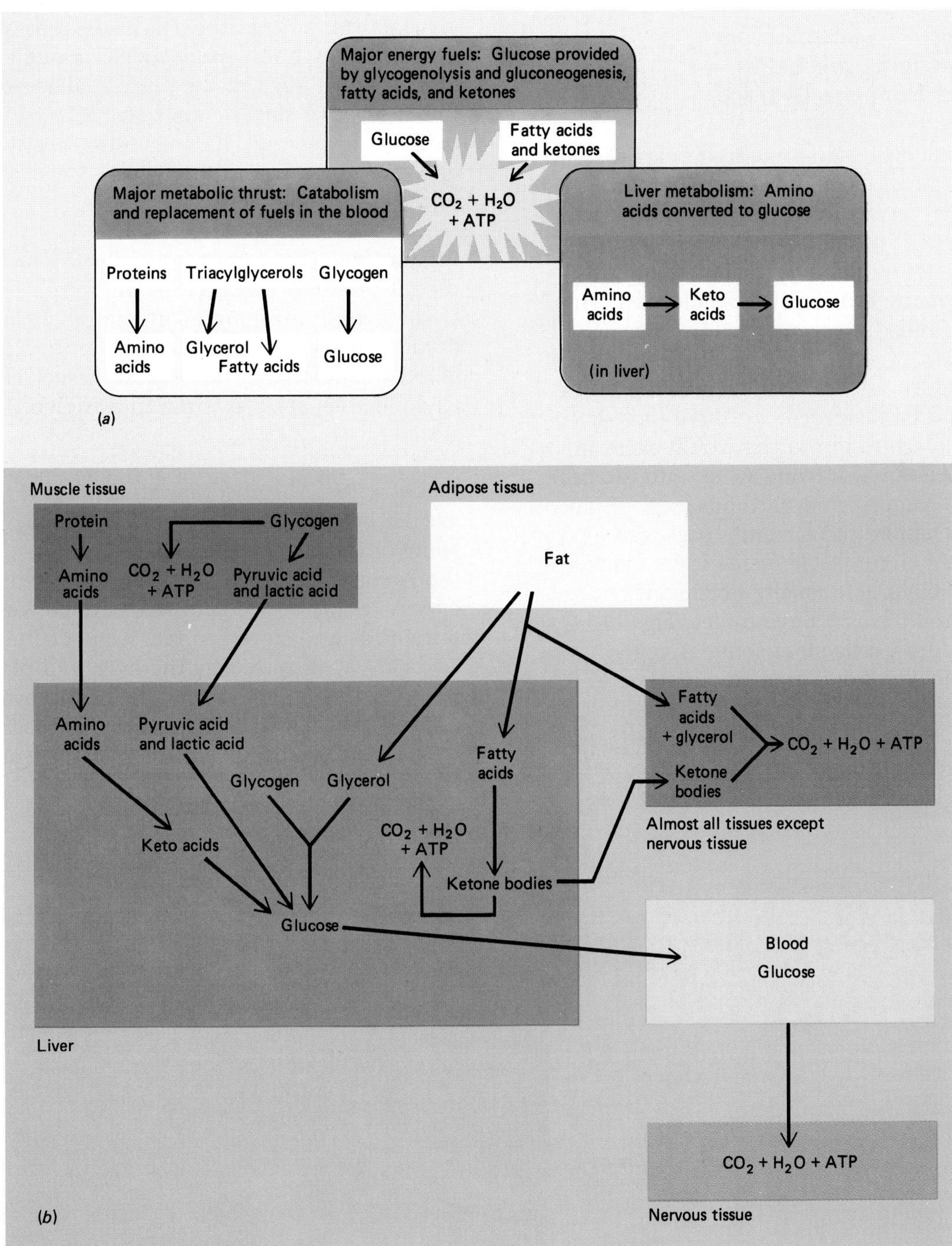

FIGURE 26-13

Summary of the postabsorptive (fasting) state.

must rely on stored sources of energy. For the person eating three basic meals each day, the postabsorptive state would occur in the late morning and afternoon and during the night.

The absorptive state occurs when nutrients are being absorbed from the GI tract

Monosaccharides All monosaccharides that are absorbed travel through the hepatic portal system to the liver. In the liver, fructose and galactose are converted into glucose. A portion of the glucose entering the liver cells is chemically joined to many other glucose molecules. This process is called **glycogenesis** (meaning "production of glycogen"). If left as individual glucose molecules, the osmotic balance of the cells would be disturbed, for thousands of small, soluble molecules in the cell would exert an osmotic pressure, drawing water into the cell. However, hundreds, even thousands, of glucose molecules can be conveniently packaged as glycogen, a large, stable, osmotically inactive molecule. Glycogen usually precipitates out of solution and forms little granules (Fig. 26-14). Although most cells store some glycogen, liver cells are able to store large amounts, up to 8% of their weight.

When glycogen stores become filled, the liver cells convert glucose into fat. The glycogen formed in the liver is stored there but the majority of formed fat leaves the liver and travels through the blood to adipose tissue where it is stored. Some of the plasma glucose is picked up directly by adipose tissue and converted into fat; and skeletal muscle can transform glucose into glycogen for storage there. Muscle cells store substantial amounts of glycogen, about 1% of their weight. Most of the glucose absorbed during the absorptive state enters body cells and is oxidized for energy. Its entry into cells is enhanced by a rise in the levels of insulin released into the blood.

Triglycerides The lymph picks up the majority of the fat products absorbed in the form of chylomicrons. Although some fat anabolism does occur in body cells, most fat that enters the bloodstream is taken to adipose tissue. Here the chylomicrons are converted into triglycerides and stored.

Amino acids Absorbed amino acids enter the liver via the hepatic portal system. The liver converts some of them into **keto acids,** which can enter the Krebs cycle of liver cells and be used for energy. Some of the keto acids are converted into fatty acids and stored as fat. Some of the amino acids are synthesized by the liver into plasma proteins. Many amino acids leave the liver and enter body cells, especially skeletal muscle cells, where they are used in protein anabolism.

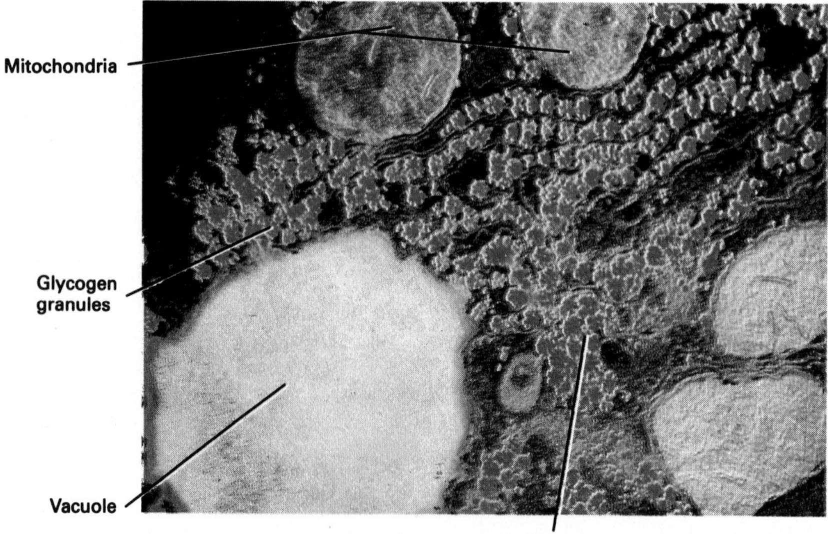

FIGURE 26-14

False-color transmission electron micrograph showing glycogen granules stored in the cytoplasm of a liver cell. Note the extensive smooth endoplasmic reticulum (approximately ×9000). (CNRI/Science Photo Library/Photo Researchers, Inc.)

Postabsorptive state is a period of fasting

Since nutrients are not being absorbed during the postabsorptive state, the body must rely on its own energy reserves to maintain blood-glucose levels within the normal range of 90 to 100 milligrams per 100 milliliters of blood. This is crucial because the brain relies on glucose as its sole energy source. The mechanisms utilized to achieve this involve the activation and formation of glucose from storage areas, a reduction in glucose oxidation by most body cells, and a switch to fat utilization for cellular energy.

SOURCES OF BLOOD GLUCOSE INCLUDE THE LIVER, SKELETAL MUSCLE, AND ADIPOSE TISSUE

Glycogenolysis by liver The glucose needed to maintain the proper blood-glucose levels comes from a number of sources. The first to contribute is the liver. Liver glycogen stores are mobilized, providing glucose through a process called **glycogenolysis** (meaning "the breaking down of glycogen"), and the glucose units are released into the blood. Chemically, glycogenolysis is not the reverse of the reactions used to make glycogen. Instead, each glucose molecule is split off from the glycogen by a phosphorylation process (phosphate is added to the glucose) requiring an enzyme called **phosphorylase.** The total amount of glycogen stored in the liver (100 g) is sufficient to maintain the blood-glucose level for several hours.

Glycogenolysis by skeletal muscle Other tissues, especially the skeletal muscle, indirectly supply glucose by glycogenolysis. Skeletal muscle has glycogen stores comparable to those of the liver. The muscle cells lack the enzymes required to convert glycogen into glucose, but they can partially break down glycogen into pyruvic acid (or, anaerobically, into lactic acid) and release it into the blood. Liver cells then pick up these substrates and transform pyruvic acid into glucose molecules.

Gluconeogenesis from fat When glycogen stores run out, liver and adipose cells break down triglycerides (a process called **lipolysis**) and the liver cells use the resulting glycerol to produce glucose. This process is appropriately called **gluconeogenesis** ("production of new glucose").

Gluconeogenesis from protein Cellular proteins can be utilized to produce glucose but only during prolonged fasting when glycogen and fat stores are near depletion. Skeletal muscle proteins are broken down into amino acids which are converted into glucose by liver cells (gluconeogenesis). In a fast of several weeks, kidney cells also contribute to gluconeogenesis from amino acids.

GLUCOSE SPARING CONSERVES GLUCOSE FOR THE BRAIN

As the postabsorptive state progresses, the brain continues to use glucose as its energy source but practically all other organs switch to fat utilization, thereby sparing glucose for the brain. Lipolysis in adipose tissue results in more fatty acids circulating in the blood. These fatty acids enter tissue cells, other than the brain, and are oxidized for energy. The liver forms ketone bodies from the fatty acids, which, in turn, can function as an energy source by body cells.

Nutritional balance involves sufficient calories and essential nutrients

Nutritional balance involves more than the intake of sufficient calories; adequate amounts of essential nutrients are also required. Caloric and nutrient amounts are dependent upon many factors.

Regulation of food intake occurs in the hypothalamus

People tend to eat when they feel hungry and stop when they feel satisfied, or "full." Habit also influences our patterns of eating; for example, we may be in the habit of eating three meals each day. Then, when we miss a meal, hunger contractions and psychological factors cause us to feel uncomfortable. People may also eat (or fail to eat adequately) because of such psychological factors as boredom, anxiety, or depression.

Food intake is also regulated metabolically. In the lateral hypothalamus of the brain, there is an **appetite center** (or feeding center) that motivates an organism to find food and eat it. A **satiety center** in the ventromedial portion of the hypothalamus then acts to inhibit the appetite center and thus to halt eating behavior. When the appetite center is damaged in an experimental animal, the animal will stop eating completely and eventually starve to death. Destruction of the satiety center causes an experimental animal to overeat and consequently to become extremely obese.

The hypothalamic centers are regulated by the level of nutrients in the body, especially the level of glucose. When the cells of the satiety center have too little glucose, they decrease their inhibitory action over the appetite center. The appetite center is then activated, and the individual seeks food. Other nutrients (amino acids, glycerol, fatty acids) also affect eating behavior, but glucose is thought to be the most important.

Other factors also affect the appetite center. For example, the appetite center is inhibited when the stomach and duodenum are distended with food. The hormone cholecystokinin (CCK) may also influence appetite regulation. It has been shown that there is much less CCK in the hypothalamus of obese mice than in nonobese mice. Other hormones such as insulin are thought to influence feeding behavior. Body temperature is also believed to play a role.

Basal metabolic rates are measured under rest

You will recall that metabolism refers to all the chemical reactions that take place in the body. **Metabolic rate** is measured as the amount of energy (heat) liberated by the body during metabolism. Metabolic rate is expressed either in kilocalories of heat energy expended per hour per day or as a percentage above or below a standard nor mal level. Almost all the energy expended by the body is ultimately converted to heat.

The **basal metabolic rate (BMR)** is the body's basic cost of metabolic living, the rate of energy use in the body during **basal conditions.** Under basal conditions a person is lying still but awake, has not eaten any food for at least 12 hours, and is in a comfortably warm environment. In other words, BMR is the amount of energy utilized under resting conditions.

BMR is measured by direct and indirect **calorimetry.** In **direct calorimetry** the heat released by a person in an enclosed chamber causes a rise in the temperature of water circulating around the chamber. The increased temperature of the water is directly proportional to the BMR.

A respirometer is used in determining BMR through **indirect calorimetry** by measuring the amount of oxygen consumed over a given time. It is known that for every liter of oxygen utilized by the body, about 4.8 kilocalories are liberated. Thus the amount of oxygen consumed in, say, 1 hour is multiplied by 4.8 to give the number of kilocalories liberated per hour. If your oxygen consumption is 0.25 liters per minute (15 liters/hr), then your BMR would be about 72 kilocalories per hour. This figure can be divided by the body surface area in square meters to give the kilocalories per square meter per hour.

Body surface area is even more critical than weight and height in measuring BMR because it determines the rate of heat loss that the BMR must compensate for. Consider two people with the same weight; the taller (thinner) one will have a higher body surface area and a higher BMR. Standardized charts (see Fig. 26-15) can be used to estimate body surface area. For example, a person weighing 70 kilograms (154 lb) and being 175 centimeters (5 ft 9 in.) tall has a body surface area of about 1.86 square meters and, therefore, a BMR of 38.7 kilocalories per square meter per hour. An individual with a metabolic rate 10% above normal is said to have a BMR of +10; one with a BMR 20% below normal has a −20 BMR.

MANY FACTORS AFFECT THE BMR

1. **Age.** As one grows older, the BMR decreases, due mainly to less lean body mass. A child has a BMR almost twice as great as an elderly person.
2. **Growth.** Growth also is a factor in increasing BMR. Children and pregnant women have higher BMRs.
3. **Height.** Tall, thin people tend to have higher BMRs.
4. **Sex.** Females have lower BMRs than men except during pregnancy and lactation.
5. **Body temperature.** A rise in body temperature increases the BMR.
6. **Stress.** Stress, through hormones and the sympathetic nerves, increases the BMR. Sleep decreases the BMR.
7. **Exercise.** Increased exercise increases the BMR.
8. **Food intake.** Food ingestion increases the BMR, especially proteins.
9. **Environmental temperature.** Changes in environmental temperature increase the BMR. Increased energy expenditure is needed to gain or lose heat in order to maintain a constant body temperature.

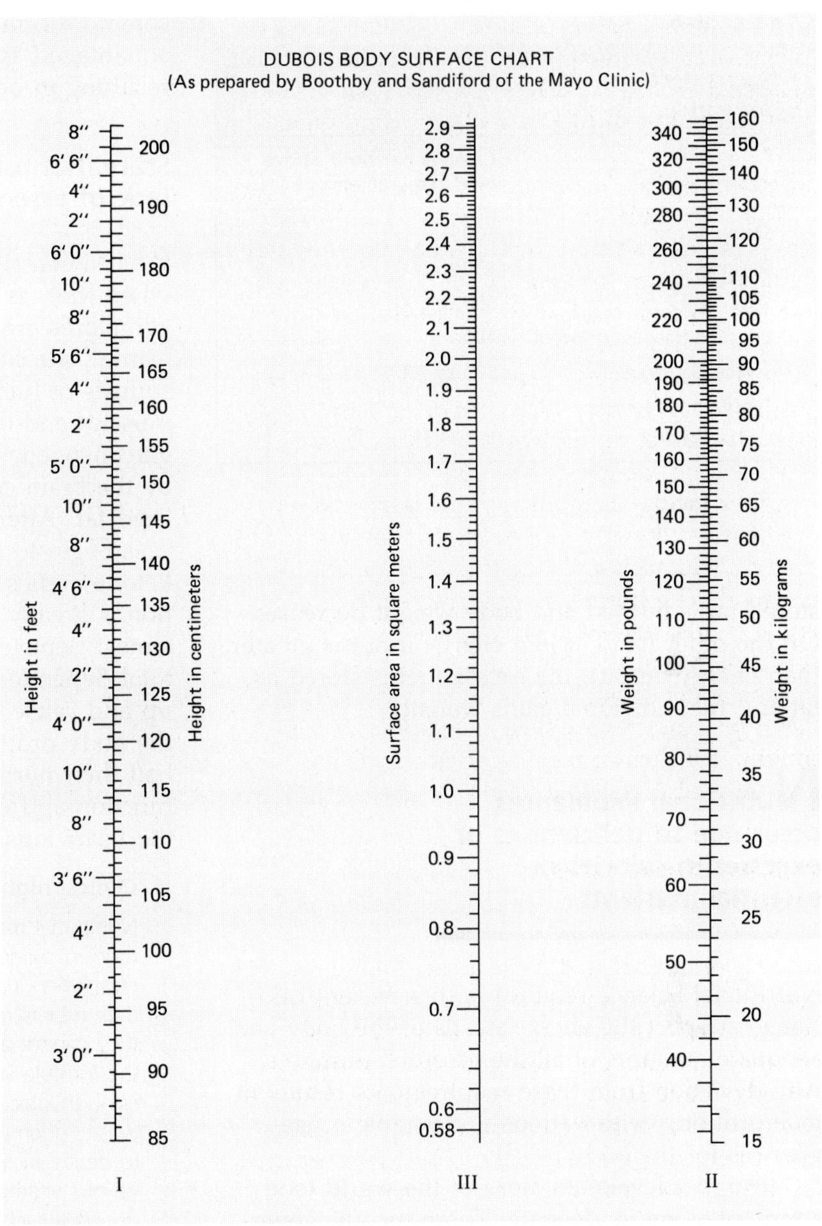

FIGURE 26-15

Determination of surface area. Extend a ruler from your height to your weight. The intersect with scale III gives your surface area.

10. **Fasting.** Fasting and starvation decrease the BMR.

11. **Malnutrition.** Malnutrition decreases the BMR.

12. **Hormones.** Increases in BMR occur with increases in norepinephrine, epinephrine, thyroxine, growth hormone, and testosterone.

TOTAL METABOLIC RATE EQUALS THE BMR PLUS ENERGY UTILIZED FOR ACTIVITIES

An individual's **total metabolic rate** is the sum of the BMR *and* the energy used to carry on all his or her daily activities. Obviously a laborer or someone who engages in a daily exercise program would have a greater total metabolic rate than one who sits behind a desk all day. Table 26-6 gives the amounts of energy expended per hour for several different types of activities.

An average-sized man who does not engage in any exercise program and who sits at a desk all day expends about 2000 kilocalories daily. If he ingests 2000 kilocalories in the food he eats each day, he will be in a state of energy balance; that is, his energy input will equal his energy output. This is an extremely important concept, for when energy (calories) input equals energy output, body weight remains constant. When energy output is greater than energy input,

TABLE 26-6

Approximate energy expenditure for various activities

Activity	Calories per hour above BMR requirements
Sitting at rest	100
Walking	130 to 200
Jogging	500 to 800
Bicycling (moderate speed)	400
Swimming (moderate)	500 to 700
Typewriting rapidly	140

stored fat is burned and body weight decreases. On the other hand, when energy input is greater than energy output, the excess fuel is stored as fat and the individual gains weight.

Nutritional imbalances occur due to deficiencies or excesses in calories or essential nutrients

Nutritional balance requires both sufficient calories to support the energy needs of the body and adequate amounts of all the essential nutrients. Any deviation from these requirements results in malnutrition,[1] with various undesirable consequences for the body.

In underdeveloped areas of the world food supply is often inadequate. There, people generally suffer from both inadequate caloric intake and from specific nutrient deficiencies. Such overall dietary insufficiency leads to malnutrition and starvation. The nutrients most likely to be lacking in the diet of both underdeveloped and economically developed societies are proteins, vitamins, and minerals such as iron and calcium.

In economically prosperous countries poor health is often associated with eating too much of the wrong foods. Cardiovascular disease and certain forms of cancer have been linked to diet. A common form of malnutrition in economically advantaged societies is excessive calorie intake resulting in obesity.

Starvation occurs due to a lack of essential nutrients

What metabolic changes take place in the body when there is a lack of all kinds of food? Glycogen stores are depleted within a few hours after eating. The cells then turn to protein and fat as sources of fuel. At first, protein is mobilized from muscles and other cells and converted to fuel by gluconeogenesis. The glucose formed is utilized by the brain cells. The rest of the cells use mobilized fat. After 4 or 5 days of fasting, the brain cells begin to activate enzymes needed to utilize ketone bodies for fuel. The rate of protein depletion is greatly decreased until the fat stores are almost depleted. During the periods of almost total dependence upon fats, ketone bodies build up and cause **ketosis.** After several weeks, when the body proteins have been depleted to about half their normal level, the body is unable to function and death occurs, often from failure of the heart muscle.

Clinical highlight

Nutritional **marasmus** is a form of starvation most common in children under 1 year of age. Sometimes it occurs when impoverished women decide to bottle-feed their infants rather than to breast-feed them. Because they cannot afford to buy sufficient formula, they dilute the formula with water; the infant then does not receive enough kilocalories. Growth slows, muscles begin to waste, anemia ensues, and the child then slowly starves to death. In marasmus and kwashiorkor, symptoms of various vitamin deficiencies also occur, because the diets generally lack adequate amounts of these nutrients too.

Obesity results from excess body fat

A person who has an excessive accumulation of body fat and who is more than 20% overweight is **obese.** (An athlete with well-developed muscles may be overweight without being obese.) Obesity is a serious form of malnutrition and has become an important public health problem in affluent societies. About 20% of adult Americans are overweight enough to affect their health and longevity.

[1]The term **malnutrition** does not just mean undernourished, as many people think, but indicates unbalanced or defective nutrition. (The prefix **mal** literally means "bad.")

Clinical highlight

An overweight person places an extra burden on his heart, since it has to work harder to pump blood through the excess adipose tissues. Obese persons are also more likely to have atherosclerosis, hypertension, hernia, and gallbladder disease. They also present greater surgical risks. According to insurance statistics, men who are 20% or more overweight have a 43% greater risk of dying from heart disease, a 53% greater risk of dying from cerebral hemorrhage, and more than a 150% greater chance of dying from diabetes.

THE MAJOR CAUSES OF OBESITY ARE OVEREATING AND INACTIVITY

People gain weight when they take in more kilocalories in food than they expend in daily activity. In other words,

Energy (kcal) input > energy output

Overeating is the only way to become obese. (Although water retention does increase body weight, it does not affect fat storage; water excess can be diminished faster and more easily than fat excess.) It has been estimated that for every 9.3 kilocalories of excess food taken into the body, 1 gram of fat is stored. (An excess of about 140 kilocalories per day for a month will result in gaining 1 pound.) A person who has gained weight will maintain that weight even if food intake is reduced so that energy intake and output are balanced. The only way to lose weight is to shift the energy balance so that output is greater than input.

A 16-year-old athlete requires a much larger food intake to support growth and physical activity than he or she does 10 years later as a sedentary accountant. Those who continue eating at the same level even after their activities have become less strenuous (requiring less energy) are destined to become overweight.

Most overweight people overeat because of a combination of *poor eating habits* and *psychological factors*. For many of them eating is a means of reducing anxiety and of self-nurturing. *Childhood obesity* may be a contributing factor to adult obesity. It has been found that fat cells proliferate in lean children during the first 2 years of life, remain constant until age 10, then multiply again from age 10 to 16. In obese children, fat cells proliferate almost continuously from birth to about age 16. Once adulthood is reached there is no further increase in the total number of fat cells in the body. Babies and children who are overfed (usually because of the notion that fat babies are cute) develop up to five times the normal number of fat cells and will have to struggle much harder against obesity than lean children for the rest of their lives.

The reason for this seems to be that fat cells are like tiny balloons that can be inflated with fat (see Fig. 4-7). They can expand to about 50% over their normal size as fat accumulates within. Then, as fat is mobilized, they shrink (or deflate) accordingly. If you were an overweight child, you have thousands of extra fat cells just waiting to fill with fat. Some investigators think that persons with excessive numbers of fat cells have a higher setting of the regulatory centers in the hypothalamus. In other words, they can eat more before the satiety center signals them to stop. It has been suggested that persons who live rather sedentary lives, expending little energy in exercise or labor, have feeding and satiety centers that do not operate properly.

Hormonal problems are the cause of only a small number of cases of obesity, and even these are the result of a positive energy balance. As more is learned about metabolism, it is likely that factors that encourage obesity will be uncovered. For example, it has been suggested that some people may have more *efficient digestive tracts* than others. Food may be more efficiently processed in them, resulting in absorption of a larger percentage of nutrients and consequently a larger actual kilocalorie absorption. Those who process food less efficiently waste more nutrients but can afford to eat more because a lower percentage of kilocalories is actually absorbed. Despite these possible individual differences, however, one can control weight by adjusting food intake to meet energy needs.

CURES INCLUDE MORE EXERCISE AND FEWER CALORIES

The only cure for obesity is to shift energy relationships so that energy intake is less than energy output. The body then must draw on its fat stores for the "missing" kilocalories, and as the fat is mobilized and "burned," body weight will decrease. This is best accomplished by a combination of increased exercise (i.e., energy expenditure) and decreased total kilocalorie intake.

Most nutritionists agree that the best reducing diet by far is a well-balanced diet, having a normal proportion of fats, carbohydrates, and proteins. In other words, eat everything but in smaller quantities.

Clinical highlight

Many people have become rich by promoting imaginative reducing diets, books, slenderizing devices, and formulas that appeal to millions of overweight individuals looking for an easy way to shed excess poundage. These gimmicks are of only psychological value; they may encourage the overweight individual to reduce food consumption. However, they often have drawbacks that can damage one's health and in a few cases may even cause death.

For example, high-protein diets tax the kidneys, which must excrete excessive amounts of urea, and may cause permanent kidney damage. The excess keto acids are converted to fat and stored, and the shift to fat catabolism tends to raise ketone body and triglyceride levels in the blood to unhealthy proportions. There is no truth to the claims that you can eat all you want of one particular type of nutrient (e.g., protein), for as you know, an excess of protein or carbohydrate is promptly converted to fat and stored.

Yet another disadvantage of many popular reducing diets is that they cannot be maintained for long periods of time. After a few weeks the dieter slips back into old eating habits and may rapidly regain the weight lost.

Dieters should also be wary of slenderizing devices and diets that depend upon reduction of fluid or salt intake. Whatever weight loss is achieved is the result of dehydration rather than metabolism of fat. Such loss may be unhealthy and is rapidly regained when water is replaced.

Thermoregulation maintains a stable body temperature

A stable body temperature is the result of heat-loss and heat-gain mechanisms operating in the body.

Body temperature determines the rate of many bodily activities

A stable body temperature (36.1°C to 37.8°C) is crucial for the optimal performance of enzymatic and regulatory activities. A rise of only 1°C increases the rate of chemical reactions by 10%. As heat is released by the cells from the metabolism of nutrients, some must be removed or our internal body temperature would continue to rise until, at about 41°C (106°F), we would start to have convulsions, and at 43°C (109.4°F) death would be imminent. At rest, the body tissues contributing most to heat generation are the liver, heart, brain, and endocrine glands. At rest, the inactive skeletal muscle is responsible for about 20 to 30% of the body heat but during strenuous exercise the heat produced by skeletal muscle may be 40 times that from the rest of the body.

Heat loss is through radiation, conduction, convection, and evaporation

When there is an increase in body temperature, sensory input to the hypothalamus causes an activation of the **heat-loss center** and an inhibition of the **heat-promoting center.** This increases parasympathetic output and decreases sympathetic output. The decreased sympathetic output causes a vasodilation of peripheral blood vessels and a decrease in metabolic rate.

$\uparrow$ Body temperature $\longrightarrow$ $\uparrow$ heat-loss center activation $\longrightarrow$ $\downarrow$ sympathetic output $\longrightarrow$ $\uparrow$ vasodilation + $\downarrow$ metabolic rate

Most of the heat loss of the body occurs through the skin by radiation, conduction, convection, and evaporation. **Radiation** transfers heat by infrared waves from a warmer object to a colder one without the objects being in contact. At normal room temperature, most (60%) of heat loss is by radiation. We can also gain heat by radiation from a warmer object such as the sun.

Conduction causes heat loss by transferring heat from a warmer object to a colder one in physical contact with it. Conduction accounts for about 3% of our heat loss. About 15% of heat loss is through **convection,** which transfers heat by way of the movement of a liquid or gas to a colder area. Cool air contacting our bodies is warmed by conduction and then rises by convection currents only to be replaced by cooler air molecules.

The process of **evaporation** removes heat by transforming a liquid to a gas (vapor). As water absorbs heat, it gains energy and may become water vapor. Water is able to absorb a large amount of heat—1 gram of water at 30°C needs about 0.58 kilocalorie to evaporate. About 22% of heat loss is through evaporation under normal conditions but, under extreme conditions, more than 30 times the basal level of heat produced can be removed utilizing perspiration.

Clinical highlight

If humidity is high along with temperature, evaporation becomes difficult and **heat stroke (sunstroke)** may occur. Perspiration declines and the skin becomes dry and hot as the body temperature soars. Brain damage may result if emergency treatment (immersion in cool water and fluid and electrolyte intake) is not enacted.

Heat gain involves sympathetic nerves, muscle activation, and hormones

If body temperature should decrease, the heat-promoting center of the hypothalamus is activated and the heat-loss center is inhibited. The heat-promoting center increases sympathetic stimulation and also sends input to centers causing increased muscle tone and release of TSH-releasing hormone.

Vasoconstriction Increases in sympathetic output cause a vasoconstriction in the periphery. Blood is shunted away from the skin and to the internal organs. This has the effect of decreasing the loss of heat and raising the temperature of the internal organs.

Heat-promoting center activation ⟶ ↑ Sympathetic output ⟶ ↑ peripheral vasoconstriction ⟶ ↓ blood flow to skin ⟶ ↓ heat loss

Adrenal medulla The increased sympathetic output also increases the secretion of epinephrine (Ep) and norepinephrine (NEp) by the adrenal medulla. These hormones increase cellular metabolism, which causes more heat to be generated in a process called **chemical thermogenesis.**

Heat-promoting center activation ⟶ ↑ sympathetic output ⟶ ↑ Ep and NEp secretion ⟶ ↑ cellular metabolism ⟶ ↑ heat production

Shivering The activation of the heat-promoting center sends stimulatory input to other areas of the brain that increase muscle tone. The increased muscle tone may cause an activation of stretch receptors in antagonistic muscles causing involuntary shivering. Shivering results in a large amount of heat being produced and helps to increase body temperature.

Heat-promoting center activation ⟶ ↑ stimulation of brain areas controlling muscle tone ⟶ ↑ muscle tone ⟶ ↑ stretch reflexes in antagonistic muscles ⟶ ↑ shivering ⟶ ↑ heat production

Thyroxine Colder environmental temperatures cause the hypothalamus to secrete more thyrotropic hormone releasing factor (TRF). The TRF activates the anterior pituitary to release more thyrotropic hormone, which results in more thyroxine being released from the thyroid gland. Thyroxine increases cellular metabolism, which increases heat production and serves to elevate body temperature.

Colder temperatures ⟶ ↑ thyrotropic hormone releasing factor ⟶ ↑ thyrotropic hormone release ⟶ ↑ thyroxine ⟶ ↑ cellular metabolism ⟶ ↑ heat production

FEVER INVOLVES THE ACTION OF PYROGENS

Clinical highlight

Fever is an abnormally high body temperature (above 37.2°C, or 99°F). It is most commonly caused by an infection by bacteria (or bacterial toxins) and viruses, but may also occur due to other conditions such as a widespread inflammation or congestive heart failure. An agent with the potential of producing fever is called a **pyrogen** (**pie**-row-jen).

The mechanism for fever production involves the entry of **exogenous** (ex-**ah**-jen-us) (originating from outside of the body) **pyrogens** into the body. These pyrogens activate monocytes and macrophages to secrete small proteins called **endogenous pyrogens** (en-**dah**-jen-us). Pyrogens such as interleukin I reset the thermostat of the hypothalamus to a higher temperature. Prostaglandins are also involved in this process. The utilization of antipyretic agents (aspirin and acetaminophen) usually stops prostaglandin synthesis and, thereby, reduces body temperature.

In response to the thermostat being set higher, *chills* may occur as heat-promoting mechanisms (including shivering) are set in motion but the skin is still cold. When the body temperature reaches the temperature of the thermostat, the chills cease. Once the thermostat is reset to normal (37°C, or 98.6°F), then heat-losing mechanisms bring about a lowering of the body temperature. Vasodilation and sweating cause the skin to warm and become moist during the *crisis* stage of the fever.

Even though high fevers are dangerous, fever is a protective mechanism believed to kill or inhibit the spread of invading microbes. The increased temperature causes increased heart rate, which causes increased circulation of white blood cells. Increased temperature also increases metabolism, which may speed repair mechanisms.

Summary

I. Nutrients are chemical substances needed by our bodies for normal functioning and include water, carbohydrates, lipids, proteins, minerals, and vitamins.
   A. Nutrients that are required in the diet because our bodies are unable to synthesize them are called essential nutrients.
   B. Nutrients are used in the body to produce energy, build new compounds, and assist in chemical reactions.
   C. Water provides a medium for chemical reactions, assists in some reactions, transports substances, and helps maintain fluid and temperature balances in the body.
   D. Nutritionists measure the energy value of food in heat units called kilocalories.

II. Metabolism is the sum of all the chemical and energy transformations that take place in the body.
   A. Anabolism is the synthetic aspect of metabolism, such as making proteins.
   B. Catabolism is the breaking-down aspect of metabolism, such as oxidizing nutrients to yield energy.

III. Carbohydrates are ingested mainly as polysaccharides, disaccharides, and monosaccharides. Glucose is the major monosaccharide used by the body, and carbohydrate metabolism is essentially that of glucose metabolism. Glucose is used as fuel in cellular respiration in the body cells.
   A. When oxygen is present, glucose is completely degraded to water and carbon dioxide with the release of energy packaged in ATP.
   B. ATP serves as a link between anabolic and catabolic metabolism. It is formed endergonically and broken down exergonically in such a way that energy can be transferred by phosphorylation and dephosphorylation.
   C. Cellular respiration is divided into three phases: glycolysis, the Krebs cycle, and the electron transport system. In glycolysis, a molecule of glucose is degraded to two molecules of pyruvic acid with a net profit of two ATP molecules. In the Krebs cycle, the fuel molecule (acetyl-CoA) is completely degraded to hydrogen atoms and carbon dioxide. In the electron transport system, the hydrogens removed from glycolysis and the Krebs cycle are passed along a chain of coenzymes. Energy is liberated and packaged as ATP. The final electron acceptor molecule is oxygen.
   D. A maximum of 38 ATP molecules can be made from aerobic respiration of one molecule of glucose. In anaerobic respiration only two ATP molecules can be made from a molecule of glucose.

IV. Lipids are ingested mainly in the form of triglycerides, which are classified as saturated, monounsaturated, and polyunsaturated. Saturated fats have been implicated in heart disease. Fat is stored primarily in adipose tissue. When blood-glucose levels fall, fat is mobilized for use as fuel.
   A. Glycerol can be converted to glyceraldehyde-3-phosphate and used as fuel.
   B. Fatty acids are degraded via β-oxidation to molecules of acetyl-CoA, which can be used as fuel or to make needed lipids. They can also be converted to ketone bodies for transport to other cells.

V. Proteins contain different quantities of amino acids, and some proteins lack some of the essential amino acids. Amino acids are utilized primarily in anabolic metabolism.
   A. Amino acids are used to make structural proteins and functional proteins such as enzymes and hemoglobin.
   B. Excess amino acids are deaminated in the liver, and the remaining keto acid is converted to carbohydrate fuel or to lipid for storage as fat.
   C. When the amount of nitrogen entering the body daily in amino acids equals that excreted from amino acid deamination, the body is in nitrogen balance.

VI. Minerals are inorganic nutrients required by the body. They include iron (a component of hemoglobin and some enzymes); iodine (a component of thyroid hormones); calcium and phosphorus (components of bone and teeth, essential for many body activities); and sodium and chlorine (needed for maintaining appropriate fluid balance). See Table 26-4.

VII. Vitamins are classfied as fat-soluble (A, D, E, K) and water-soluble (C, B complex). See Table 26-5.

VIII. During the absorptive state, digestion end-products are absorbed into the blood and the lymph.
   A. Excess glucose (that beyond energy requirements of the body) is converted to glycogen (glycogenesis) in the liver and may also be converted to fat.
   B. Most absorbed fat is stored in adipose tissue. Excess protein is converted into keto acids by the liver and stored as fat.

IX. During the postabsorptive state, the body relies on its own energy reserves to maintain glucose levels.
   A. The glucose used to maintain blood levels comes from the breakdown of glycogen (glycogenolysis) by the liver and skeletal muscle,

and the formation of new glucose (gluconeogenesis) by the liver from glycerol and amino acids.

B. During this fasting state, the brain continues to utilize glucose but practically all other organs switch to fat utilization in order to spare glucose for the brain (glucose sparing).

X. Basal metabolic rate (BMR) is the amount of energy utilized by the body under resting conditions. Total metabolic rate is the sum of the BMR and the energy needed to carry on one's daily activities.

XI. Body weight remains constant when energy input equals energy output.

A. When energy input exceeds output, the excess is stored as fat, and body weight increases.

B. When energy input is less than energy output, the body draws on its fuel reserves (fat), and body weight decreases.

XII. A stable body temperature is crucial for the optimal performance of enzymatic and regulatory activities.

A. An increase in body temperature activates parasympathetic output and inhibits sympathetic output via the heat-loss center of the hypothalamus. The resulting peripheral vasodilation stimulates heat loss by radiation, conduction, convection, and evaporation. These serve to decrease body temperature.

B. A decrease in body temperature stimulates sympathetic output (vasoconstriction and Ep and NEp release) via the heat-promoting center of the hypothalamus and also sends input causing increased muscle tone (shivering) and thyroxine release. These serve to increase body temperature.

C. Fever production involves pyrogens causing a release of prostaglandins, which reset the hypothalamic thermostat to a higher temperature.

Post-test

1. Synthesizing DNA or proteins is an example of the phase of metabolism called ____________.
2. Nutrients that are necessary to the diet are called ____________ ____________.
3. Starch is an example of the type of carbohydrate called ____________.
4. Most digestible carbohydrates are absorbed in the form of ____________.
5. The breakdown of glucose to pyruvic acid in cells is called ____________.
6. During the Krebs cycle a molecule of acetyl-CoA is degraded to hydrogen and ____________ ____________.
7. Production of glycogen from glucose is called ____________.
8. The type of fat implicated in heart disease is ____________ ____________.
9. In β-oxidation fatty acids are degraded to molecules of ____________.
10. Steroid hormones can be synthesized from ____________.
11. High-quality (complete) proteins contain a nutritional balance of essential ____________ ____________.
12. Kwashiorkor is a form of severe ____________ malnutrition.
13. Amino acids utilized for energy must first be converted to a ____________ ____________.
14. Inorganic nutrients ingested in the form of salts dissolved in food or water are called ____________.
15. Organic compounds required in trace amounts that usually function as coenzymes are called ____________.
16. Total metabolic rate is the sum of ____________ and ____________.

Match

____ 17.	Needed for hemoglobin synthesis	a. vitamin A
____ 18.	Needed for blood clotting and normal nerve function	b. vitamin D
____ 19.	Makes tooth enamel resistant to decay	c. vitamin K
____ 20.	Deficiency results in rickets	d. calcium
____ 21.	Component of coenzyme NAD	e. fluorine
____ 22.	Vitamin essential for blood clotting	f. iron
____ 23.	Deficiency may cause blindness	g. niacin
____ 24.	Needed for collagen synthesis; deficiency causes scurvy	h. vitamin C

Multiple choice

25. During the postabsorptive state blood-glucose concentrations are maintained in order to:
    a. Put color in your cheeks
    b. Prevent the liver from storing glycogen
    c. Maintain the brain
    d. Produce pyruvic acid in the muscles
    e. None of the above

26. The quantity of heat required to raise the temperature of a kilogram of water from 14.5°C to 15.5°C is a:
    a. Kilocalorie
    b. BMR
    c. β-oxidation
    d. Deamination
    e. None of the above
27. Select the incorrect association:
    a. Fat ⟶ 9 kcal/g
    b. Carbohydrate ⟶ 9 kcal/g
    c. Protein ⟶ 4 kcal/g
    d. 1000 grams = 1 kilogram
    e. 1 kcal = 1000 cal
28. The conversion of glycogen to glucose is called:
    a. Lipolysis
    b. Glycogenolysis
    c. Gluconeogenesis
    d. Glycogenesis
    e. None of the above
29. Which one of the following processes generates the most ATP?
    a. Anaerobic respiration
    b. Krebs cycle
    c. Electron transport system
    d. Glycolysis
    e. Glycogenesis
30. Which one of the following organic nutrients cannot be broken down and used for energy?
    a. Vitamin
    b. Protein
    c. Fat
    d. Carbohydrate
    e. None of the above
31. Which one of the following occurs in the cytoplasm of cells?
    a. Krebs cycle
    b. Glycolysis
    c. Electron transport system
    d. None of the above
32. Which one of the following does not help in heat generation?
    a. Vasoconstriction
    b. Shivering
    c. Increased thyroxine release
    d. Evaporation
    e. None of the above

Review questions

1. List the general classes of nutrients, and explain why each is required.
2. Distinguish between anabolism and catabolism, and give examples of each.
3. Gives the consequences of deficiencies of each of the following: iron, vitamin A, vitamin D, essential amino acids.
4. Define glycogenesis, glycogenolysis, gluconeogenesis, and lipolysis. Describe each process, and explain when it is used.
5. Compare the three main phases of cellular respiration, and explain where each reactant and product originates.
6. Give the function and significance of ATP.
7. Summarize the major phases of glycolysis.
8. What happens to a fuel molecule during the Krebs cycle?
9. Describe and explain the significance of the electron transport system.
10. Draw a diagram to summarize the fate of carbohydrates in the body. Do the same for amino acids and for lipids.
11. What happens to excess glucose? Excess amino acids?
12. Distinguish between saturated and unsaturated fats.
13. What is β-oxidation?
14. Explain how amino acids and fats can feed into the reaction of cellular respiration so that they can be degraded to produce energy.
15. Define (a) basal metabolic rate and (b) total metabolic rate.
16. Write an equation reflecting energy relationships for maintaining body weight; for losing weight.
17. Summarize metabolic changes that take place during starvation.
18. Explain why it is so important to maintain body temperature within narrow limits.
19. Give the physiological sequence of events used in the body to (a) lose heat, (b) gain heat, (c) produce fever.

Post-test answers

1. anabolism **2.** essential nutrients
3. polysaccharide **4.** monosaccharides
5. glycolysis **6.** carbon dioxide **7.** glycogenesis
8. saturated fat **9.** acetyl CoA
10. cholesterol **11.** amino acids **12.** protein
13. carbohydrate compounds **14.** minerals
15. vitamins **16.** BMR, energy used in activities
17. f **18.** d **19.** e **20.** b **21.** g **22.** c
23. a **24.** h **25.** c **26.** a **27.** b **28.** b
29. c **30.** a **31.** b **32.** d

THE URINARY SYSTEM

CHAPTER OUTLINE

LEARNING OBJECTIVES

After you have studied this chapter you should be able to:

1 Identify the major structures of the urinary system.

2 Describe the external and internal anatomy of the kidneys.

3 Define nephron, renal corpuscle, and renal tubule.

4 Describe the glomerular filtration barrier and explain how it functions.

5 Describe the juxtaglomerular apparatus.

6 Trace renal blood flow.

7 Describe the forces involved in glomerular filtration and explain how they operate.

8 Define tubular reabsorption and secretion.

9 Explain how the countercurrent multiplier system of the kidney accounts for a dilute urine.

10 Explain the role of antidiuretic hormone in determining urine volume.

11 Explain the role of the vasa recta in the countercurrent system.

12 Define plasma clearance.

13 Explain how the plasma clearance of inulin is used to measure the glomerular filtration rate.

14 List the major physical and chemical characteristics of urine.

15 Describe the anatomy and physiology of the ureters.

16 Describe the anatomy and physiology of the urinary bladder.

17 Discuss the micturition reflex and explain the voluntary role in voiding.

18 Describe and compare the male and female urethra.

19 Explain the embryology of the urinary system.

20 Describe the major disorders of the urinary system.

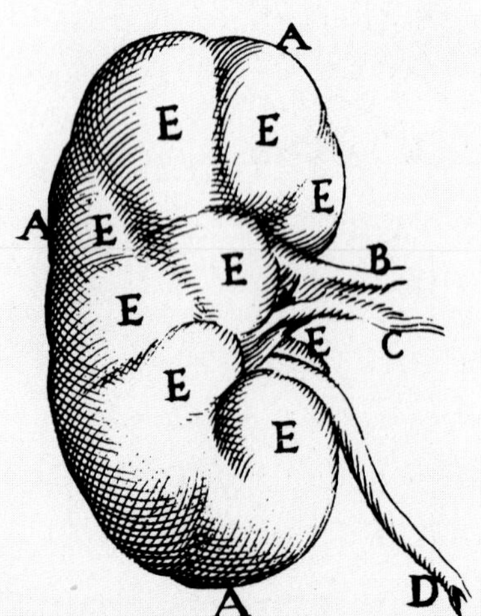

Glomeruli of nephrons in a human kidney (dark field, ×250). (Manfred Kage/Peter Arnold, Inc.)

27

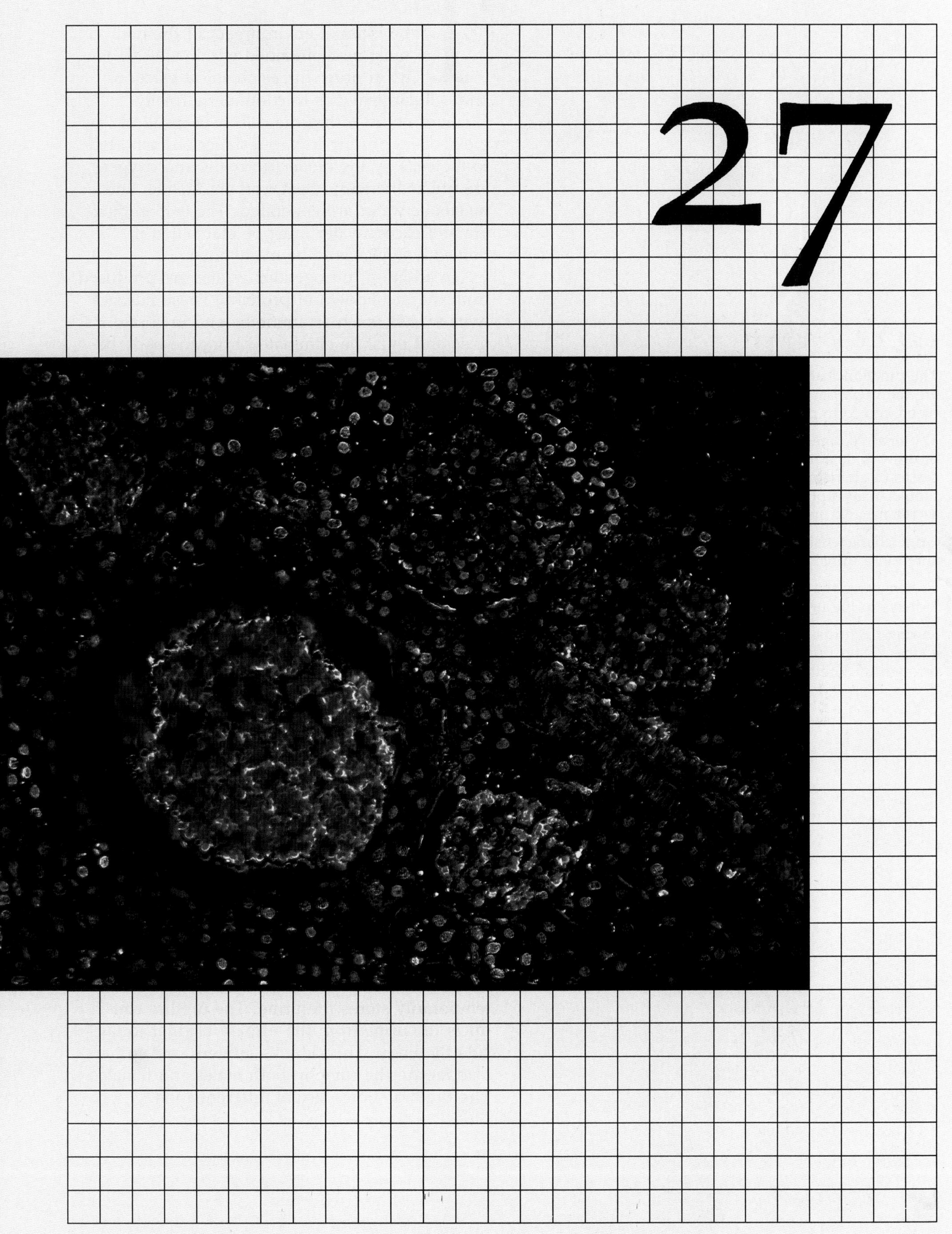

KEY CONCEPTS

The functional units of the kidneys are the nephrons, which filter the blood and form the urine.

The final volume and composition of urine is determined by the processes of glomerular filtration, renal tubular reabsorption, renal tubular secretion, and urine concentration.

Urine characteristics can be measured in a urinalysis.

Ureters carry the urine from the kidneys to the urinary bladder.

During micturition, the bladder contracts and urine is expelled through the urethra.

The internal environment of the body must be maintained within specific limits in order for its chemical reactions and cellular activities to continue normally. Changes occur within the cells as a result of the metabolism of nutrients. Substances transported to the cells by the blood (nutrients and oxygen) are utilized; energy, heat, carbon dioxide, and metabolic water are generated. The carbon dioxide and excess water must be eliminated if homeodynamics is to be maintained.

In addition, nitrogenous wastes are produced from the breakdown of proteins. These nitrogenous wastes (such as ammonia and urea) are toxic and must be eliminated from the body before they can accumulate and adversely affect metabolic activities. Many essential solutes may also accumulate in the body fluids, creating imbalances that may disrupt normal functioning. These must be eliminated as well. Toxic substances entering the body through the digestive tract must also be excreted. Most of these wastes, excess substances, and toxic substances are eliminated from the blood plasma by the kidneys and excreted from the body by the urinary system.

The major function of the **urinary system** is to maintain the homeodynamics of the body by regulating the volume and composition of the body fluids. The urinary system consists of kidneys, urinary bladder, ureters, and urethra (Fig. 27-1, Table 27-1, and Window on the Human Body, View 6).

The two kidneys are the actual organs of excretion—they produce the urine. The volume and composition of the urine is related to the capacity of the kidneys to eliminate wastes and control fluid, electrolyte, and acid-base balances in the body. The kidneys help regulate renal blood pressure by secreting renin. The kidneys produce renal erythropoietic factor, which stimulates red blood cell formation, and they also serve as an intermediate step in the activation of vitamin D.

The ureters transport the urine from the kidneys to the urinary bladder. The urinary bladder temporarily stores the urine. The urethra conducts the urine from the urinary bladder to outside the body. The kidneys, ureters, and urinary bladder are the same in both males and females. The urethra shows sexual differentiation.

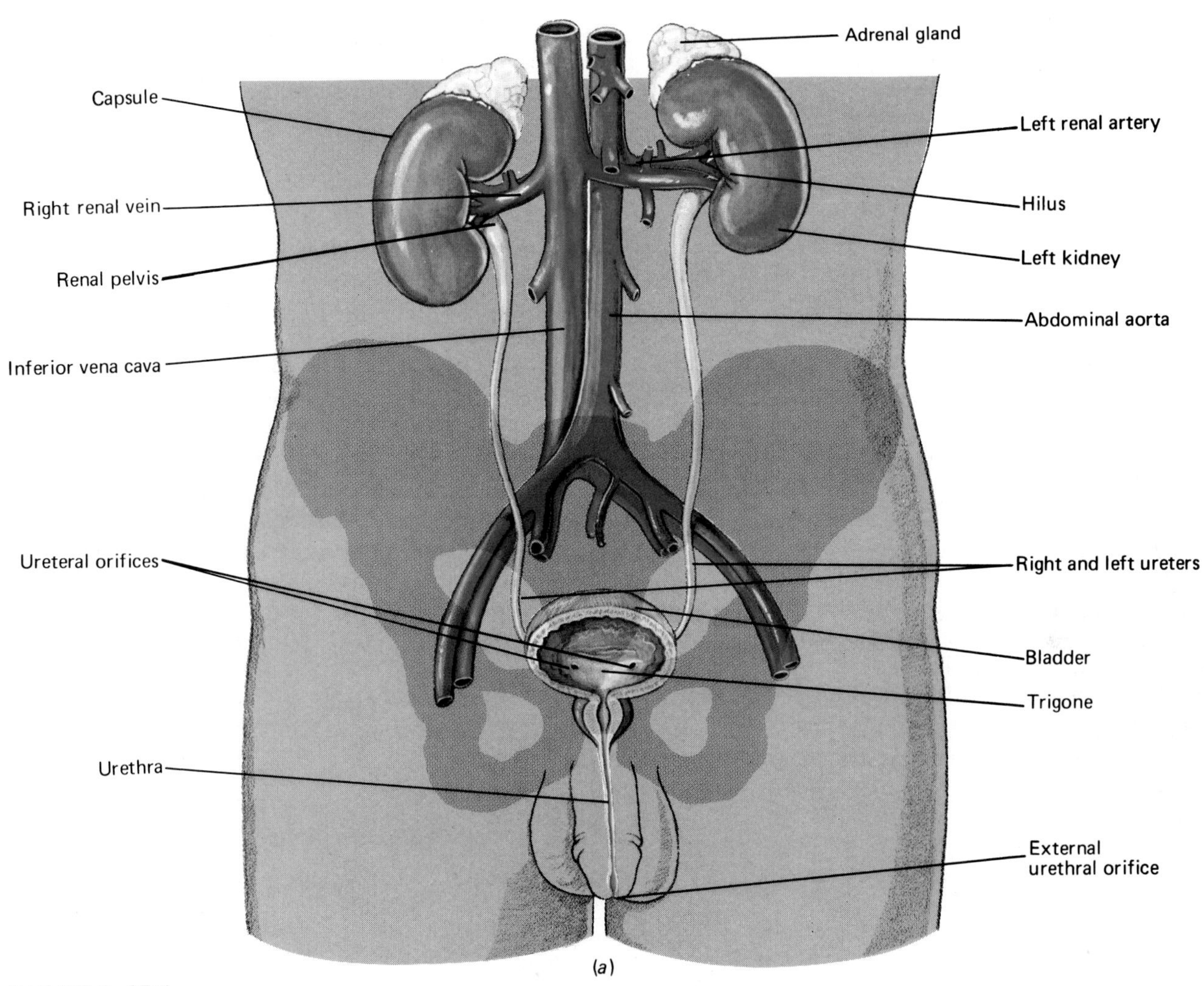

FIGURE 27-1

Structures of the urinary system.

TABLE 27-1

Characteristics of the urinary system

Structure	Number	Shape	Length	Width	Other
Kidney	2	Bean	11 cm (4.5 in.)	6 cm (2.5 in.)	Reddish-brown, about 5 oz each, retroperitoneal
Ureter	2	Tubular	28 cm (11 in.)		Retroperitoneal
Urinary bladder	1	Ovoid sac	13 cm (approx. 5 in.)	3 in.	Antoperitoneal
Urethra:		Tubular			
in female	1		4 cm (1½ in.)	Diameter ¼ in.	Serves only in excretion
in male	1		20 cm (approx. 8 in.)	¼ in.	Serves both in excretion and reproduction

The kidneys are retroperitoneal

The two **kidneys** (Fig. 27-1) are located posteriorly on either side of the vertebral column, between the twelfth thoracic vertebra and the third lumbar vertebra. The right kidney is generally positioned lower than the left one due to the large amount of space taken up by the liver on the right side. Both kidneys are **retroperitoneal** (*reh*-tro-*pare*-ih-tow-**nee**-al), that is, they lie posterior to the peritoneum of the abdomen. The adrenal glands are associated with the superior surface of the kidneys and are also retroperitoneal, as are the ureters.

The kidneys are about the size of a fist. They are about 11 centimeters (4.5 in.) long, 6 centimeters (2.5 in.) wide, and 2.5 centimeters (1 in.) thick. They weigh about 5 ounces each and are a reddish-brown color. See Table 27-1.

Each bean-shaped kidney has two borders—a concave medial border and a convex lateral border. The medial border faces the vertebrae and has an indentation called the **hilus.** This is the point at which the *ureter* leaves the kidney and the blood vessels, lymph vessels, and nerves communicate with the kidney. The *renal vein* leaves the kidney anteriorly at the hilus. The ureter leaves posteriorly at the hilus, and the *renal artery* enters the kidney at the hilus between the renal vein and the ureter. Internally, the hilus opens into a space called the **renal sinus.** The renal sinus contains the *renal pelvis* and the *renal vessels* (Fig. 27-2).

Each kidney is covered by three tissue layers. The innermost tissue layer is a fibrous **renal capsule,** which directly surrounds the kidney. The middle layer is referred to as the **adipose capsule.** This layer of fat helps to cushion the kidney. The outermost tissue layer of the kidney is a double layer of fascia called the **renal fascia.** The renal fascia covers both the kidney and the adipose capsule and serves to anchor the kidney to surrounding structures. Besides the protection afforded by these renal tissue layers, the kidneys are also partially protected by the floating ribs, pararenal fat, and the abdominal musculature.

Clinical highlight

Renal ptosis, or floating kidney, is a condition in which the kidneys drop to an abnormally low position. A complication of this floating kidney is that the ureters may become kinked. Very thin people are susceptible to ptosis because there may not be enough fat to hold the kidneys in their normal position.

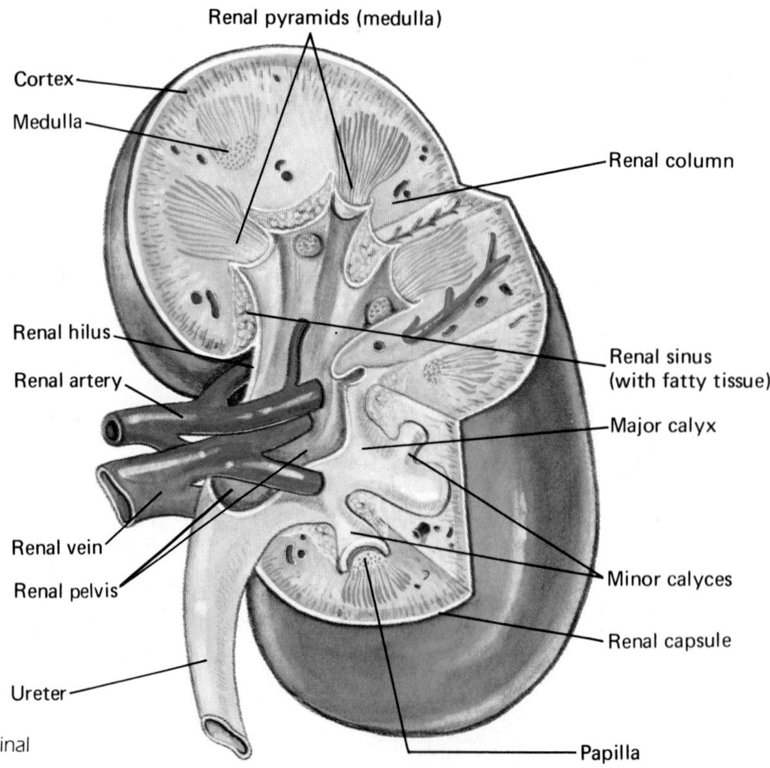

FIGURE 27-2

Internal anatomy of a kidney (longitudinal view).

There are two major regions of the kidney. The reddish outer region, the **cortex,** lies deep to the renal capsule. The reddish-brown **medulla** makes up the inner region and contains between 5 and 18 triangular structures called the **renal pyramids.** Each pyramid contains a wide base at its cortical end and an apex at its internal end. The apices are called **renal papillae** (pa-**pil**-lee). The pyramids are separated by continuations of the cortex called **renal columns.** The interlobar renal blood vessels course through the renal columns.

The renal papillae of the pyramids project into a small tube called a **minor calyx** (**kay**-liks). Several of these minor calyces converge to form the **major calyces** (**kay**-li-seez). The major calyces join to form a large cavity called the **renal pelvis.**

Urine travels along collecting tubules of the renal pyramids and passes through pores of the renal papillae into the minor calyces. From the minor calyces, the urine next flows into the major calyces, which conduct the urine into the renal pelvis. Urine from the renal pelvis then passes into the ureter.

Collecting tubule ⟶ renal papillae ⟶ minor calyx ⟶ major calyx ⟶ renal pelvis ⟶ ureter

The nephrons are the functional units of the kidney

The functional units of the kidneys are the **nephrons** (**nef**-rons). There are more than 1 million nephrons in each kidney. Two types of nephrons are located in the kidneys. There are **juxtamedullary nephrons,** which extend deep into the medulla, and there are **cortical nephrons,** which only occasionally penetrate into the medulla (Fig. 27-3).

Each nephron consists of a **renal corpuscle** (**kor**-pus-sul) and a **renal tubule.** The renal corpuscle is made up of a network of capillaries, the **glomerulus** (glo-**mare**-you-lus), and a double-layered cup of the renal tubule called the **glomerular capsule,** or **Bowman's capsule.** Both parts of the renal corpuscle are located in the cortex of the kidney.

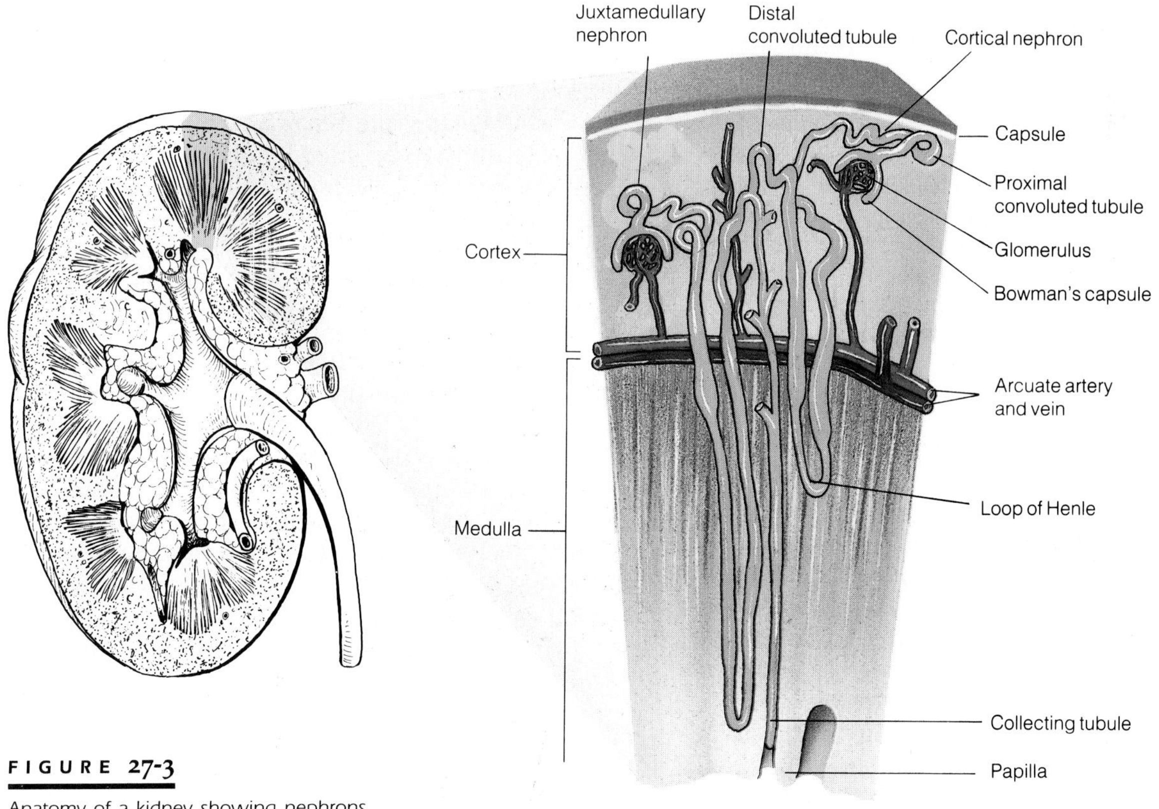

FIGURE 27-3

Anatomy of a kidney showing nephrons (longitudinal view).

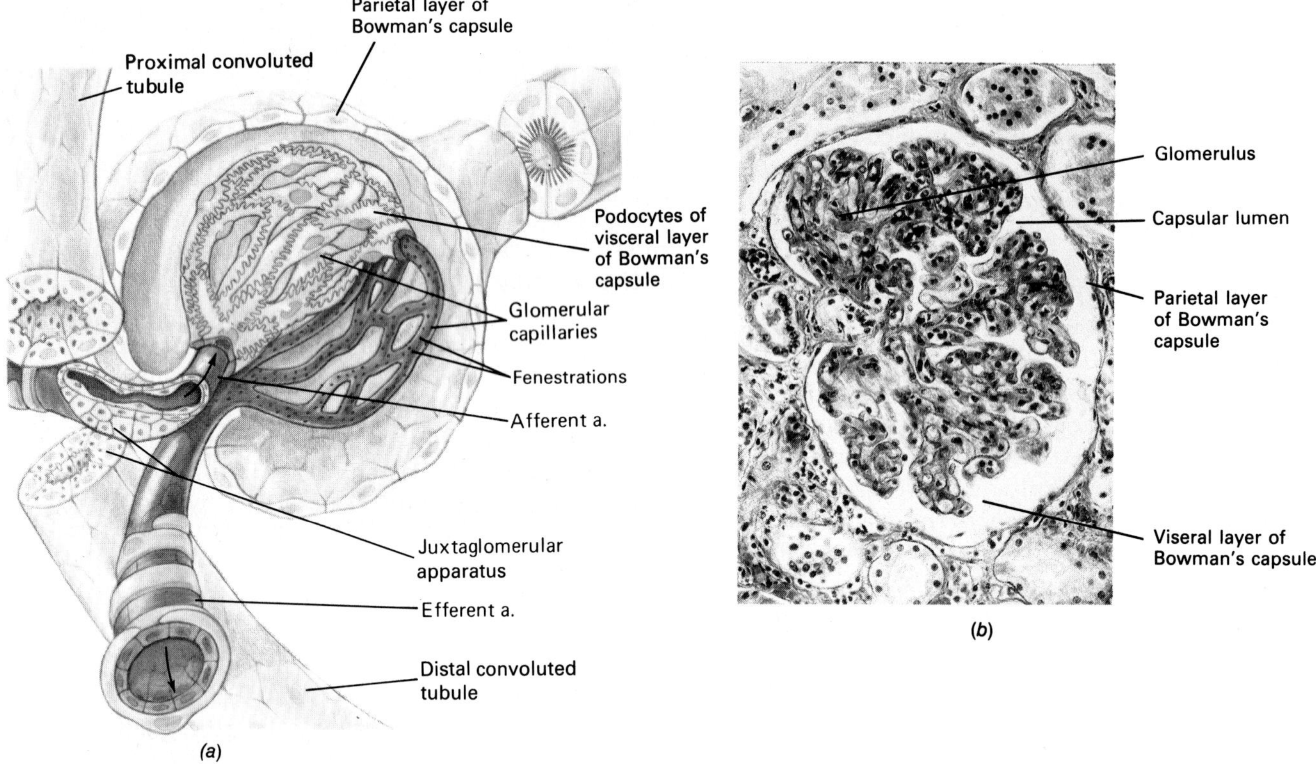

FIGURE 27-4

Anatomy of a renal corpuscle illustrated schematically (*a*) and in a photomicrograph (*b*). (Manfred Kage/Peter Arnold, Inc.)

Clinical highlight

Glomerulonephritis, or Bright's disease, is an inflammation of the kidneys involving the glomeruli. It is frequently associated with streptococcal infections, especially of the throat. The glomeruli become inflamed as a result of immune products entering the kidneys. This inflammation of the glomeruli causes them to become highly permeable and to leak proteins and blood cells into the filtrate. Damage to the glomeruli may result, leading to chronic renal disease.

The outer layer of Bowman's capsule is called the *parietal layer*. The inner layer of Bowman's capsule is called the *visceral layer* and contains special epithelial cells called **podocytes** (**pod**-oh-sites). See Figure 27-4.

The podocytes send out processes that adhere to the glomerular capillaries. Several processes radiate from the central body of each podocyte. These primary processes continue to branch to form secondary and tertiary processes. The tertiary processes are called **foot processes,** or **pedicles** (**ped**-i-kuls). Adjacent pedicles create small clefts between them called **filtration slits,** or **slit pores.** Thin **slit membranes** from the adjacent pedicles cover the slit pores (Fig. 27-5).

Many substances (including water and solutes) in the blood pass through the renal corpuscle and enter into the renal tubule. In order to do so, these substances must be filtered through a series of barriers collectively called the **filtration barrier.** The filtration barrier separates the blood of the glomerulus from the lumen of Bowman's capsule (Fig. 27-6). It consists of the following parts (in the order of filtration of a substance):

1. **Glomerular capillary endothelium.** The wall of the capillary is made up of a single layer of squamous cells which possess many small pores, or **fenestrations,** between them. The term *fenestrated endothelium* is often used to indicate that this endothelium has a large number of these pores. The pores have diameters ranging from 50 to 100 nanometers. They restrict the movement of blood cells[1] and most large molecules.

2. **Glomerular basement membrane (basal lamina).** This membrane has a glycoprotein ma-

[1]Red blood cells average about 8 micrometers in diameter, which is more than 800 times larger than the diameters of these pores.

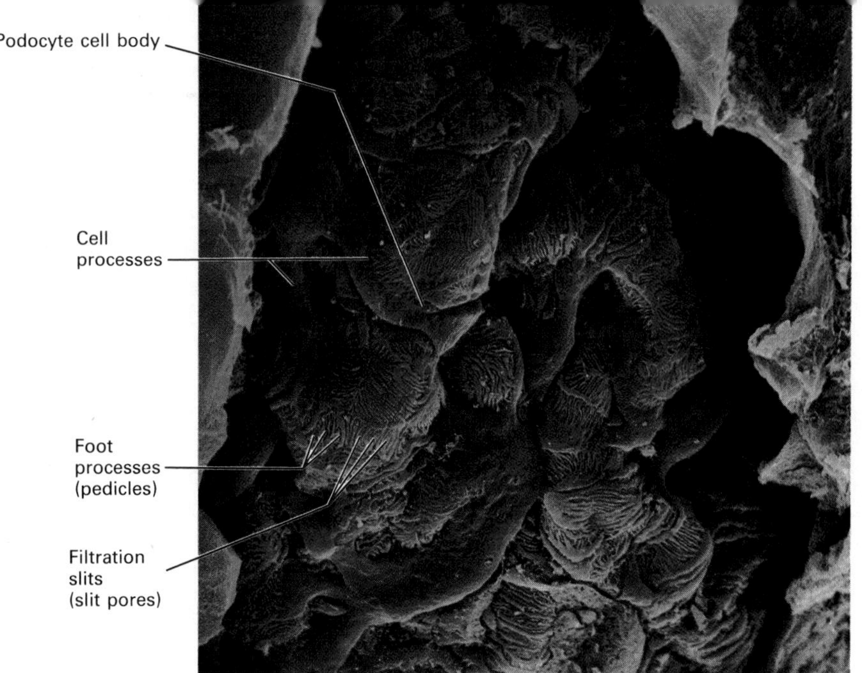

FIGURE 27-5

Scanning electron micrograph of podocytes (×600). (Manfred Kage/Peter Arnold, Inc.)

FIGURE 27-6

Filtration barrier of the kidney.

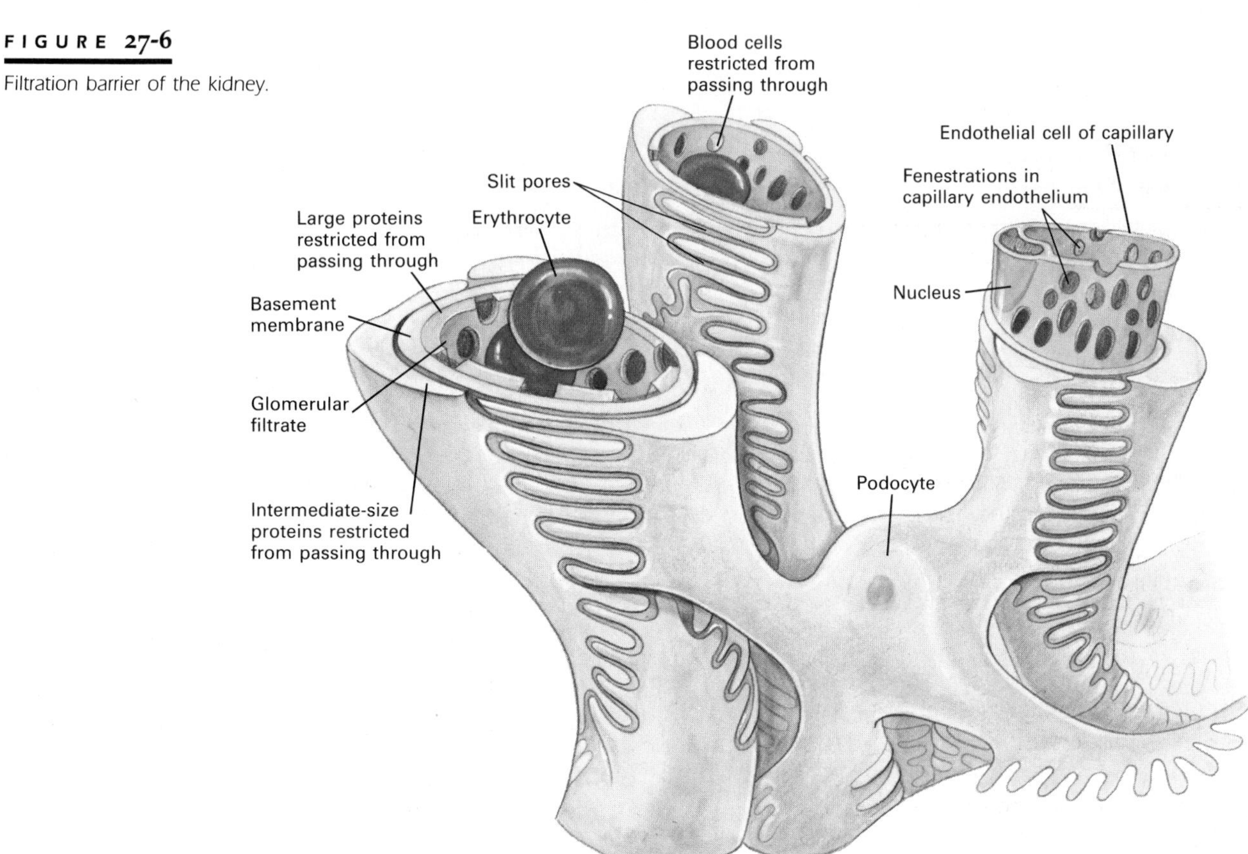

trix without pores and serves to allow the passage of molecules smaller than most plasma proteins.

3. **Visceral layer of Bowman's capsule.** Substances must pass through a thin slit membrane of the podocyte before entering the slit pores and passing into the lumen of Bowman's capsule.

Filterable substance in plasma ⟶
glomerular endothelium ⟶
glomerular basement membrane ⟶
visceral layer of Bowman's capsule ⟶
filtrate in lumen of Bowman's capsule

The renal tubule part of the nephron consists of a proximal convoluted tubule, a loop of Henle, and a distal convoluted tubule (Fig. 27-7). The **proximal convoluted tubule** is located in the cortex; it is the coiled part of the renal tubule lying nearest to the renal corpuscle. Its wall consists of a single-celled layer of cuboidal epithelium. These cuboidal cells possess microvilli which form a brush border that greatly increases the surface area for renal reabsorption and secretion.

Extending from the proximal convoluted tubule is the **descending limb of the loop of Henle.** The descending limb in juxtamedullary nephrons penetrates deeply into the pyramids of the medulla. The walls of the descending limb are thin and are composed of squamous cells. After a U-shaped loop, the renal tubule ascends toward the cortex via the **ascending limb of the loop of Henle.** The walls of the ascending limb are thicker than in the descending limb and contain mainly cuboidal cells.

Within the cortex, the renal tubule once again becomes coiled and is referred to as the **distal convoluted tubule.** The wall of the distal convoluted tubule is one cell-layer thick and contains cuboidal cells. Several distal convoluted tubules

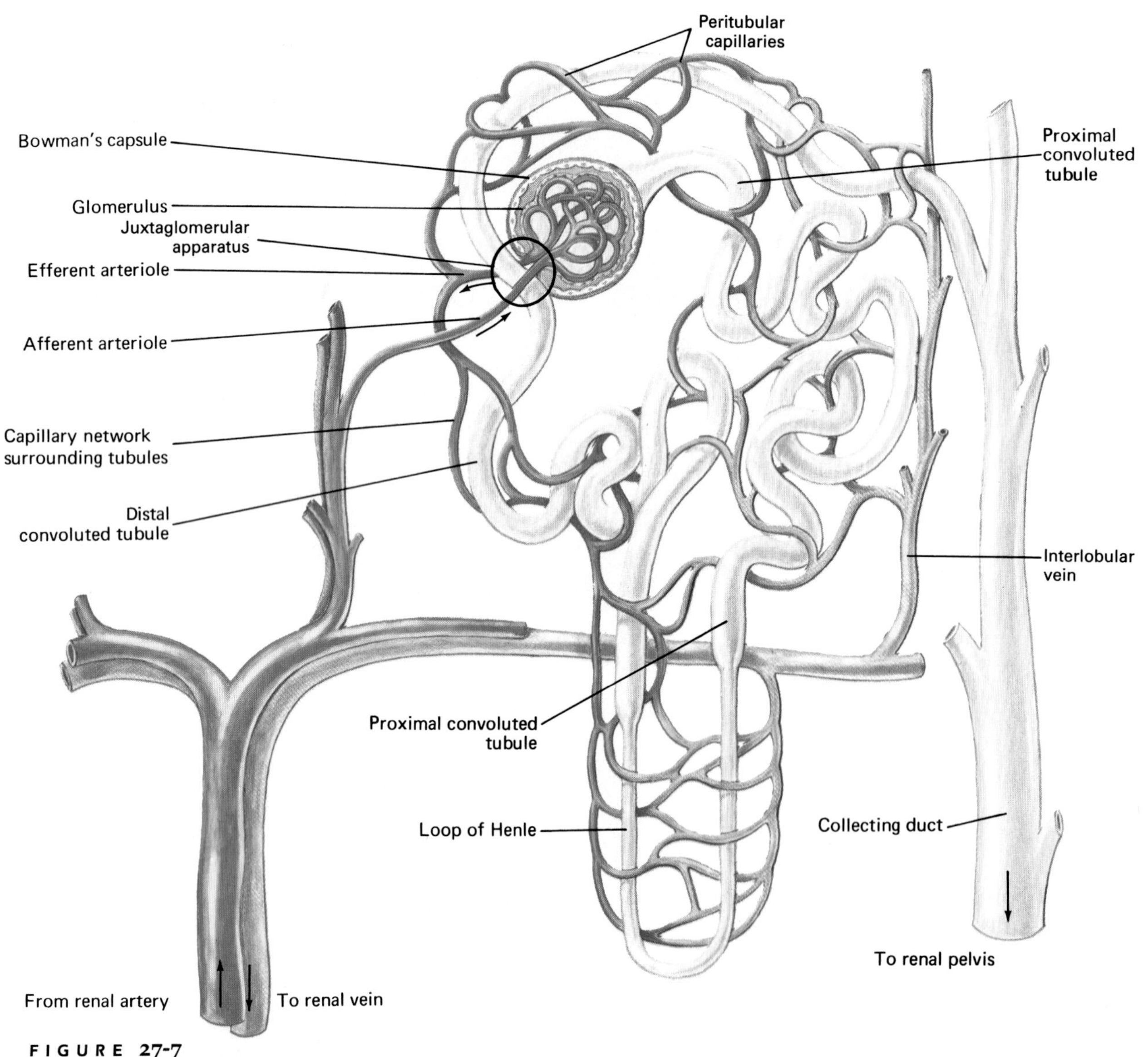

FIGURE 27-7

Anatomy of a juxtaglomerular nephron with associated blood vessels.

drain into a straight **collecting tubule.** The collecting tubules pass through the pyramids and open onto the papillae, which drain into the calyces.

> Filtrate in Bowman's capsule ⟶ proximal convoluted tubule ⟶ descending limb ⟶ loop of Henle ⟶ ascending limb ⟶ distal convoluted tubule ⟶ urine in collecting tubule

The distal convoluted tubule comes into close proximity to the afferent arteriole, the vessel that delivers blood to the glomerulus. This contact forms the **juxtaglomerular apparatus,** which secretes the enzyme **renin.** Renin is important in raising renal blood pressure, as will be discussed later in the chapter. The cuboidal cells of the tubule are narrower here and are called the **macula densa.** The smooth muscle cells of the arteriole also become modified and are referred to as the **juxtaglomerular (JG) cells** (Fig. 27-8).

A large part of the cardiac output goes to the kidneys

Even though the kidneys constitute less than 0.5% of the weight of the body, they receive about 25% of the total cardiac output. This demonstrates the importance of the nephrons in waste removal and fluid and electrolyte regulation.

Blood enters the kidneys through the **renal arteries.** In the area of the hilus, each renal artery divides into several **interlobar arteries,** which pass through the renal columns between the renal pyramids.

At the base of the pyramids, the interlobar arteries form arches over the bases of the pyramids and these are called the **arcuate arteries.** These arteries give off small branches, the **interlobular arteries,** which course through the cortex to give rise to several **afferent arterioles.** These arterioles have larger diameters than most sys-

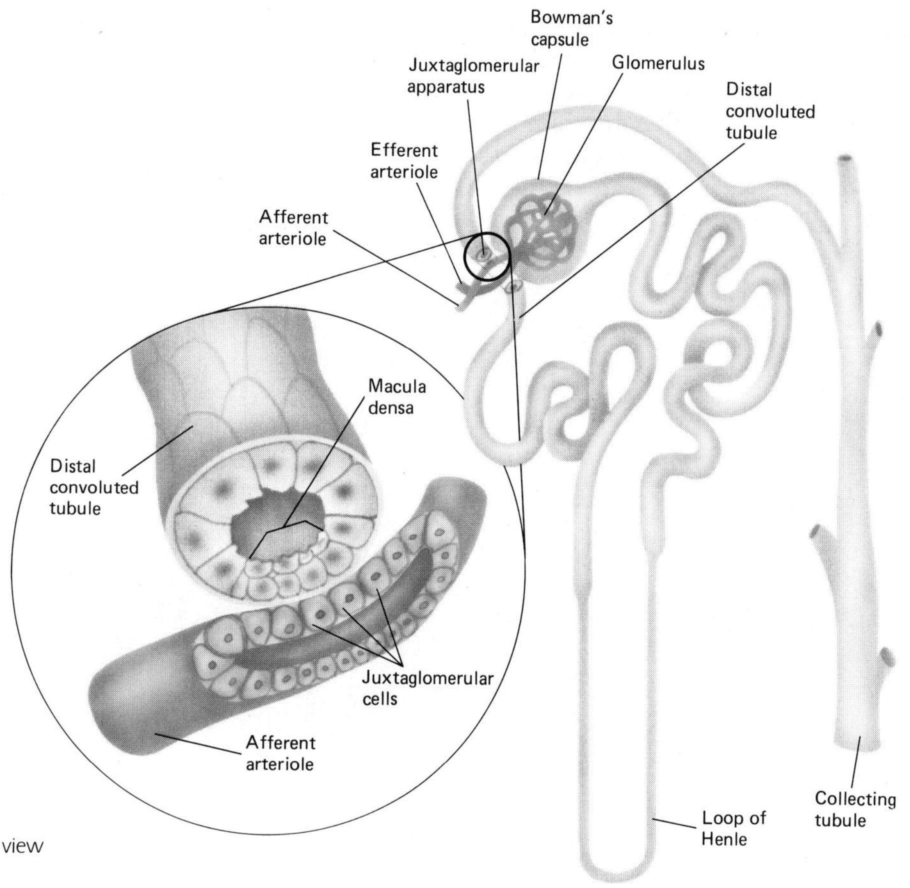

FIGURE 27-8

Juxtaglomerular apparatus, external view and cross section.

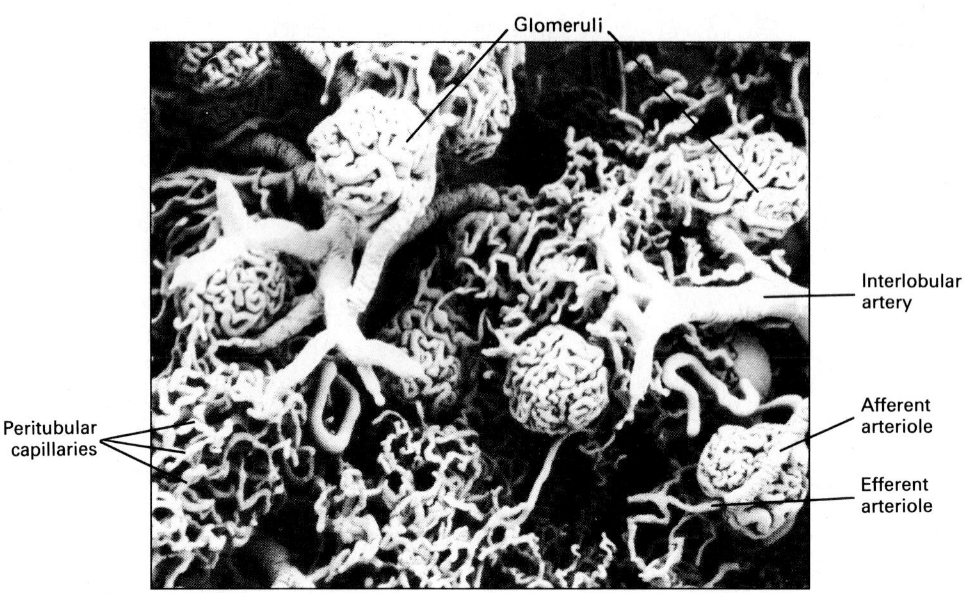

FIGURE 27-9

Low-power scanning electron micrograph of glomeruli and associated blood vessels. (CNRI/Science Photo Library/Photo Researchers, Inc.)

temic arterioles. The afferent arterioles form the capillary networks of the **glomerulus** (Fig. 27-9). It is here that some of the plasma and solutes are filtered into the lumen of Bowman's capsule.

The glomerular capillaries join to form an **efferent arteriole** whose diameter is less than that of the afferent arteriole. The efferent arteriole branches into a network of capillaries surrounding the proximal and distal convoluted tubules and are called **peritubular capillaries.** In juxtamedullary nephrons, long loops of thin-walled vessels called the **vasa recta** also pass into the medulla. The vasa recta are an extension of the efferent arteriole and run parallel to the loops of Henle and the collecting tubules. The vasa recta play a role in the concentration of the urine.

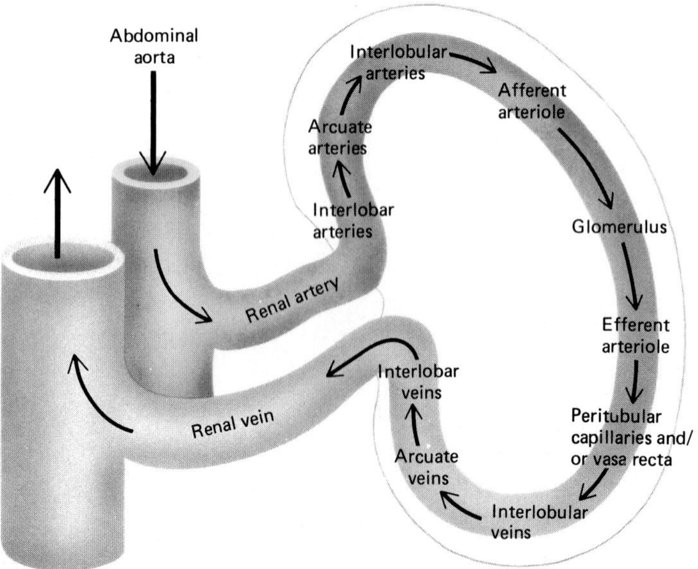

FIGURE 27-10

Schematic of renal circulation flow.

The peritubular capillaries and the vasa recta drain into **interlobular veins,** which course through the cortex to join the **arcuate veins** at the rim of the medulla. From the arcuate veins, the blood enters into the **interlobar veins** running through the renal columns. These veins join to form a single **renal vein** which exits the kidney and takes the blood to the inferior vena cava (Fig. 27-10).

Renal artery ⟶ interlobar artery ⟶ arcuate artery ⟶ interlobular artery ⟶ afferent arteriole ⟶ glomerulus ⟶ efferent arteriole ⟶ peritubular capillaries ⟶ interlobular vein ⟶ arcuate vein ⟶ interlobar vein ⟶ renal vein

Renal blood flow provides an exception to normal blood circulation, which proceeds from arteriole to capillary to venule. Blood from the glomerular capillaries does not flow into a venule but into the efferent arteriole. Therefore, the efferent arterioles in the kidney connect two capillary beds—the glomerulus and the peritubular capillaries. With blood entering and leaving the glomerulus through arterioles, a precise regulation over glomerular blood pressure exists. This occurs because the smooth muscle of arterioles can contract and relax due to different stimuli, especially sympathetic nerve stimulation. This results in a vasoconstriction or vasodilation that is able to keep glomerular blood pressure relatively stable even if dramatic changes are occurring elsewhere in the body.

The kidneys filter the blood and form the urine

The major processes determining the final volume and composition of urine are: glomerular filtration, renal tubular reabsorption, renal tubular secretion, and urine concentration.

Glomerular filtration moves substances from the blood into Bowman's capsule

Glomerular filtration is the movement of substances by bulk flow from the blood within the glomerulus into the lumen of Bowman's capsule. About 20% of the renal blood plasma is filtered. The composite of substances filtered into Bowman's capsule is called the **glomerular filtrate.** The glomerular filtrate is similar in composition to the blood plasma except that it is virtually free of proteins. This is due to the impermeability of the filtration barrier to larger molecules.

HYDROSTATIC AND OSMOTIC FORCES DETERMINE GLOMERULAR FILTRATION

The major forces contributing to glomerular filtration are hydrostatic forces and osmotic forces. **Hydrostatic forces** result from the pressure exerted by water in a closed system. **Osmotic forces** result from the effect of solutes on the movement of water. Refer to Chapter 21 for a detailed discussion of these forces.

The primary hydrostatic force operating within the glomerulus is the **glomerular capillary hydrostatic pressure.** This pressure is considerably higher in the glomerulus than in other systemic capillaries because there is less arteriolar resistance in the kidneys. The renal afferent arterioles have larger diameters than systemic arterioles and offer less resistance to blood flow. Another anatomical factor contributing to the high glomerular capillary hydrostatic pressure is that the diameter of the efferent arteriole is less than that of the afferent arteriole. Hence, more blood flows into the glomerulus than leaves it and this maintains a higher hydrostatic pressure within it. The glomerular capillary hydrostatic pressure averages about 60 mmHg and favors filtration from the glomerulus into Bowman's capsule.

Because the lumen of Bowman's capsule contains fluid, this fluid resists the movement of more fluid into the capsule. This hydrostatic force is called the **Bowman's capsule hydrostatic pressure** (about 20 mmHg) and it opposes filtration. The presence of proteins within the plasma of the glomerulus also creates an osmotic pressure that opposes filtration because, by osmosis, water will move in the direction of a higher concentration of solute. The force resulting from this osmotic pull of the plasma proteins is the oncotic (colloid) osmotic pressure. This **plasma oncotic osmotic pressure** of 30 mmHg combines with the Bowman's capsule hydrostatic pressure of 20 mmHg to offer a combined force of 50 mmHg opposing filtration (Fig. 27-11).

Subtracting the total force opposing filtration (50 mmHg) from the glomerular capillary pressure (60 mmHg) gives a **net filtration pressure,** or the **effective filtration pressure** (P_{eff}) of 10 mmHg

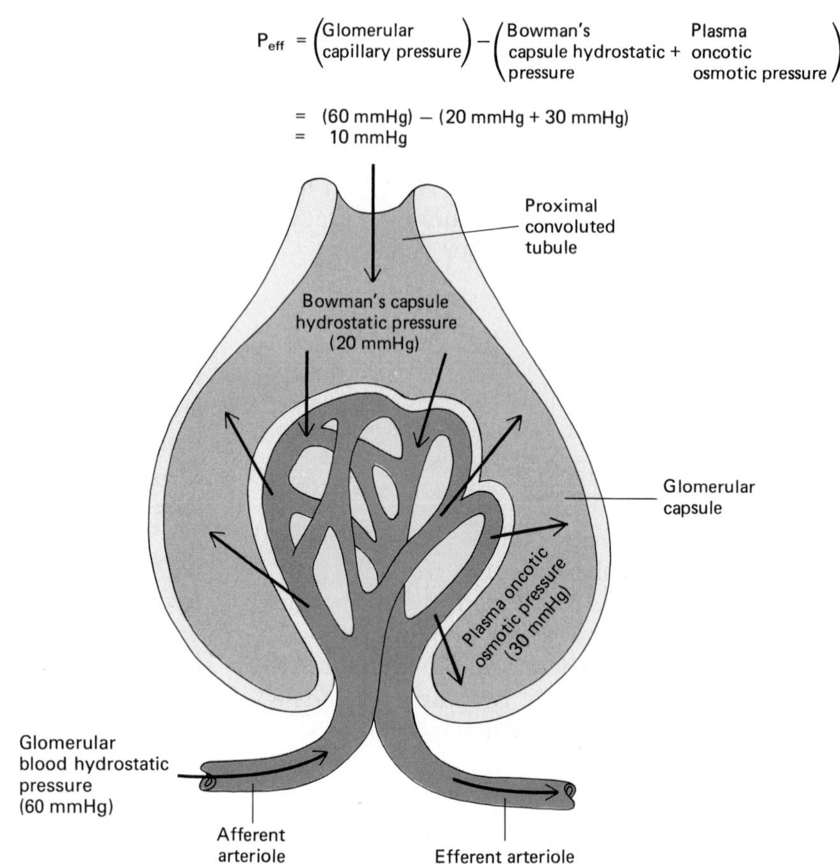

FIGURE 27-11

Forces involved in net (effective) filtration pressure (P_{eff}).

(Fig. 27-11). The net filtration pressure determines the **glomerular filtration rate (GFR),** or the rate at which water and small solutes flow from the glomerular capillaries into Bowman's capsule. A normal GFR is 125 milliliters per minute, or about 180 liters per day. This is equivalent to about 45 gallons per day. Of this amount, about 99% of the fluid is reabsorbed from the renal tubules into the peritubular capillaries. Because so much of the fluid is reclaimed by the body, the average urine output is only 1% of the GFR, or 1 to 2 liters of urine per day.

Changes in the osmotic or hydrostatic pressure can alter the P_{eff} and, therefore, the GFR. Decreases in plasma osmotic pressure result from *hypoproteinemia* (low protein levels in the blood). Because the plasma oncotic osmotic pressure under this condition is lower than normal, the net force opposing filtration is less and the P_{eff} increases. In the renal disease *glomerulonephritis,* there is an increased permeability of glomerular capillaries which allows plasma proteins to pass out of the blood and into the filtrate. This decreases the plasma oncotic osmotic pressure and produces an oncotic osmotic pressure in Bowman's capsule which favors filtration and increases the P_{eff}.

Increases in Bowman's capsule hydrostatic pressure can occur from an obstruction in the renal tubule or in the urinary tract. This causes the net pressure opposing filtration to increase and results in a reduction of the P_{eff} and the GFR.

Changes in the general blood pressure also affect the GFR. A drop in the arterial blood pressure, as would occur in severe hemorrhage, decreases the glomerular capillary hydrostatic pressure and reduces the P_{eff} and the GFR. If the glomerular capillary hydrostatic pressure becomes equal to the net pressure opposing filtration (50 mmHg), then no filtration results and renal suppression with low urine output follows.

THE REGULATION OF GLOMERULAR FILTRATION IS BY INTRINSIC AND EXTRINSIC MECHANISMS

Under normal conditions, the kidney utilizes intrinsic (autoregulatory) controls to regulate the glomerular blood pressure. This renal autoregulation operates by altering the diameters of the afferent and efferent arterioles associated with each nephron.

When vascular smooth muscle is stretched, as with an increase in blood pressure, it tends to contract. Hence, when arterial blood pressure increases, the renal afferent arterioles automatically constrict and, thereby, minimize an increase in glomerular capillary hydrostatic pressure. This serves to maintain a normal GFR.

Other autoregulatory mechanisms are found in the juxtaglomerular apparatus. The macula densa cells of the renal tubule directly promote vasodilation of the afferent arteriole when arterial blood pressure falls. This allows more blood to flow into the kidneys and increases the glomerular capillary hydrostatic pressure and the GFR. They can also cause a vasoconstriction of the afferent arterioles under conditions of high GFR.

The macula densa cells also stimulate the JG cells to release **renin.** Another factor affecting renin release is renal arterial blood pressure. When renal arterial blood pressure decreases, there is less stretching of the smooth muscle of the afferent arterioles and this triggers the JG cells to release renin.

↓ Arterial blood pressure ⟶ ↓ renal blood pressure ⟶ ↓ vascular smooth muscle stretching in afferent arteriole ⟶ ↑ renin release

Renin causes the conversion of a plasma protein, **angiotensinogen,** into its active form. Angiotensinogen is produced by the liver. **Angiotensin I,** the active form, travels through the blood to capillary beds where it is converted to **angiotensin II.** Angiotensin II is the most potent vasoconstrictor of the body and also is a profound stimulator of aldosterone secretion by the zona glomerulosa cells of the adrenal cortex.

↑ Renin ⟶ ↑ angiotensin I ⟶ ↑ angiotensin II ⟶ ↑ vasoconstriction + ↑ aldosterone release

The increased aldosterone causes an increase in the reabsorption of sodium (and to a lesser extent magnesium) by the distal convoluted and collecting tubules of the kidneys. Water, especially when antidiuretic hormone (ADH) is present, will passively follow the sodium. The increase in water reabsorption will raise the blood pressure back to normal.

↓ Blood pressure ⟶ ↑ renin → → → ↑ aldosterone ⟶ ↑ Na^+ (and H_2O) reabsorption ⟶ ↑ blood pressure

If blood pressure in the body increases, the stretching of the smooth muscle of the afferent arterioles inhibits renin release by the JG cells. This causes a decrease in angiotensin II, which means less vasoconstriction occurs, and it also means less aldosterone is secreted by the adrenals. The decreased aldosterone means that less sodium is reabsorbed by the kidneys and more sodium is excreted. Water will follow the excreted sodium. The increased water loss will serve to lower the blood volume and, in conjunction with less vasoconstriction, lowers the blood pressure back to normal (Fig. 27-12).

↑ Blood pressure ⟶ ↓ renin → → → ↓ aldosterone ⟶ ↓ vasoconstriction + ↓ Na^+ (and H_2O) reabsorption ⟶ ↓ blood pressure

Extrinsic control via sympathetic nerves regulates the GFR under conditions of stress. Large increases in sympathetic stimulation under extreme stress and increased epinephrine release by the adrenal medulla cause a vasoconstriction of renal afferent arterioles. Blood is shunted from the kidneys to the heart, skeletal muscle, and brain. The decreased renal blood flow decreases the GFR. Increased sympathetic output also stimulates the JG cells to release renin.

Extreme stress ⟶ ↑ sympathetic stimulation ⟶ ↑ renal vasoconstriction + ↑ renin release

The vasoconstriction lowers the glomerular capillary hydrostatic pressure and reduces the GFR. The renin brings about an increase in the arterial blood pressure, but the glomerular hydrostatic pressure does not rise because of the strong vasoconstriction of the afferent arteriole.

Under less intense sympathetic stimulation, vasoconstriction of the efferent arterioles also takes place and along with a similar effect on the afferent arterioles, the GFR decreases to a lesser extent.

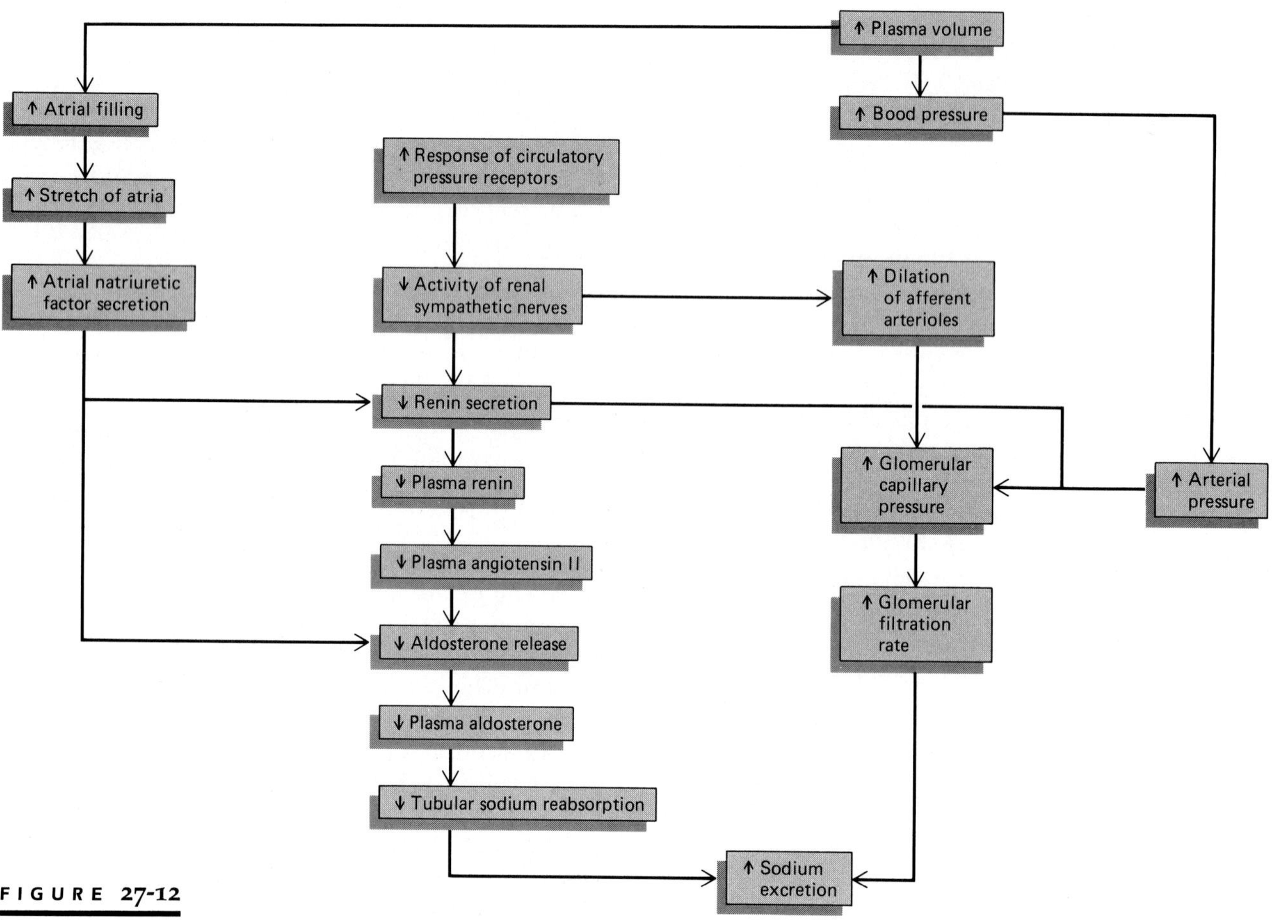

FIGURE 27-12

Renin-angiotensin-aldosterone pathway showing the effect of a plasma volume increase on renal sodium excretion. The atrial natriuretic factor is discussed in Chapter 28.

Tubular reabsorption moves substances out of the renal tubule and into the blood

Renal tubular reabsorption is the movement of a substance out of the renal tubule and into the peritubular capillaries. Many substances that are filtered are wholly or partially reabsorbed. Many solutes are reabsorbed to the extent that they are needed by the body. The reabsorption of water and certain solutes is under the influence of hormones. Most solutes have an upper limit on their rate of reabsorption **(maximum tubular capacity, T_m)** beyond which they can no longer be reabsorbed and remain in the tubule.

Renal reabsorption is enhanced by certain anatomical adaptations. The narrow diameter of the efferent arteriole presents much resistance to blood flow. Therefore, the pressure in the peritubular capillaries is low, which favors reabsorption by providing a low hydrostatic pressure in the peritubular capillaries. The extensive network of the peritubular capillaries around the renal tubule provides a large surface area of contact between the two. The peritubular capillaries are very porous, which increases permeability for the reabsorption of fluid. The proximal convoluted tubular cells contain microvilli forming a brush border, which enhances the contact of the cells with the filtrate and, thereby, increases reabsorption of solutes.

Tubular reabsorption occurs as the result of diffusion and active and passive transport. The transport of substances out of the renal tubule and into the peritubular capillaries often involves carrier molecules.

Tubular reabsorption can be active or passive. Active tubular reabsorption of a substance out of the renal tubule requires energy. Glucose, amino acids, and vitamins are **actively reabsorbed,** as are sodium, calcium, potassium, phosphate, and

TABLE 27-2

Reabsorption of common substances in filtrate

Substance	Percent Reabsorption	Site of reabsorption	Active or passive transport
Bicarbonate (HCO_3^-)	100	Proximal convoluted tubule	Passive
Chloride (Cl^-)		Loop of Henle	Active, passive
Glucose	100	Proximal convoluted tubule	Active
Potassium (K^+)	85	Proximal convoluted tubule	Active
Small proteins and amino acids	100	Proximal convoluted tubule (proteins enter by pinocytosis)	Active
Sodium (Na^+)	95	Entire renal tubule	Active, passive
Urea	50	Proximal convoluted tubule, collecting tubule	Passive
Water	99	Proximal convoluted tubule (obligatory, 80%), distal convoluted tubule and collecting tubule (facultative, 20%)	Passive
Calcium	99	Proximal convoluted tubule	Active
Phosphate	80	Proximal convoluted tubule	Active

urate ions (Table 27-2). Normally 100% of the glucose that is filtered is reabosrbed and, therefore, no glucose should be found in the urine.

About 95% of the filtered sodium is actively transported out of the proximal convoluted tubule. Sodium diffuses from the lumen of the tubule through the brush border and into the tubular cells, where it is actively transported into the interstitial fluid before entering the peritubular capillaries. The proximal convoluted tubule is always permeable to water, and most water reabsorption (80%) takes place by osmosis linked to sodium reabsorption here. This is called **obligatory reabsorption** of water. Glucose and amino acid reabsorption, although utilizing different carrier molecules, are connected to sodium reabsorption. It is the sodium-dependent ATPase pump that transports Na^+ and facilitates glucose and amino acid entry into the tubular cells.

Chloride and bicarbonate ions, which are negatively charged, follow an electrochemical gradient produced by sodium reabsorption and enter the peritubular capillaries by **passive diffusion.** A number of substances such as urea, many drugs, and pollutants are passively reabsorbed. These substances generally follow water as it is reabsorbed and are subject to the degree to which the renal tubules are permeable to them (Table 27-2).

Tubular secretion moves substances from the peritubular capillaries into the renal tubule

Renal tubular secretion is the movement of a substance out of the peritubular capillaries and into the renal tubule. Hydrogen and potassium ions, urea, creatinine, and ammonia are common substances that are secreted. Secretion may be either active or passive and is often regulated by hormones. Substances not filtered at the renal tubule may enter the tubule in this way.

Hydrogen ions are actively secreted into the renal tubule. The secretion of hydrogen ions is important in pH regulation. Potassium ions are passively secreted. This is under the control of aldosterone—aldosterone stimulates Na^+ reabsorption, which occurs through a Na^+-K^+ pump coupled to K^+ secretion. Penicillin and other foreign chemicals are also secreted into the renal tubule from the blood.

Secretion not only rids the body of undesirable and excessive substances, it also plays an important role in regulating plasma pH. When plasma pH levels decrease, more H^+ ions are actively secreted by the tubular cells and more bicarbonate (HCO_3^-) and K^+ ions are reabsorbed.

This causes an increase in plasma pH and an acidification of the urine, which rids the body of the excesses in acid. If plasma pH rises, more Cl^- is reabsorbed and HCO_3^- is excreted, bringing the plasma pH back down to its normal range. pH regulation is discussed in detail in Chapter 28.

The kidneys use three major mechanisms to return the pH to normal: the tubular secretion of hydrogen ions and the reabsorption of bicarbonate, a phosphate buffer system, and the ammonia buffer system.

The H^+ ions in the tubular lumen combine with HCO_3^- in the filtrate to form H_2CO_3. The H_2CO_3 is catalyzed by carbonic anhydrase to form CO_2 and H_2O. The CO_2 enters the tubular cells and combines with H_2O to form H_2CO_3. This reaction also is catalyzed by carbonic anhydrase. In the proximal tubular cell, the H_2CO_3 dissociates into H^+ ions and HCO_3^- ions. The hydrogen ions are actively transported into the tubular lumen in exchange for sodium ions. The sodium and the bicarbonate are reabsorbed into the peritubular capillary (Fig. 27-13).

Whenever the hydrogen ion concentration of the body increases, the secretion of hydrogen ions into the renal tubules from the peritubular capillaries increases over the rate of bicarbonate filtration into the tubule. Hydrogen ions that do not combine with bicarbonate are excreted in the urine. The hydrogen ions that do combine with bicarbonate result in bicarbonate and sodium reabsorption. As more bicarbonate is reabsorbed, more hydrogen ions can be buffered, which will serve to lower the hydrogen ion concentration of the body back to normal (Fig. 27-13).

If hydrogen ion concentrations in the body drop, less hydrogen is secreted into the renal tubules relative to the amount of bicarbonate entering with the filtrate. Excess bicarbonate is lost in the urine, which lowers its concentration in the body. This diminished buffering capacity causes a rise in the hydrogen ion concentration back to normal levels.

Secreted hydrogen ions are also buffered in the filtrate. In this way, more hydrogen ions can be excreted than if they remained free in solution. Phosphate compounds (HPO_4^{2-}) and ammonia (NH_3) can bind hydrogen ions and prevent dramatic drops in pH (Figs. 27-14 and 27-15). The HPO_4^{2-} combines with H^+ ions to form H_2PO_4, which usually combines with sodium to form NaH_2PO_4. Therefore, the hydrogen ions are excreted as a weakly acidic phosphate salt. Ammonia is produced in the distal tubular cells from the breakdown of amino acids, especially glutamic

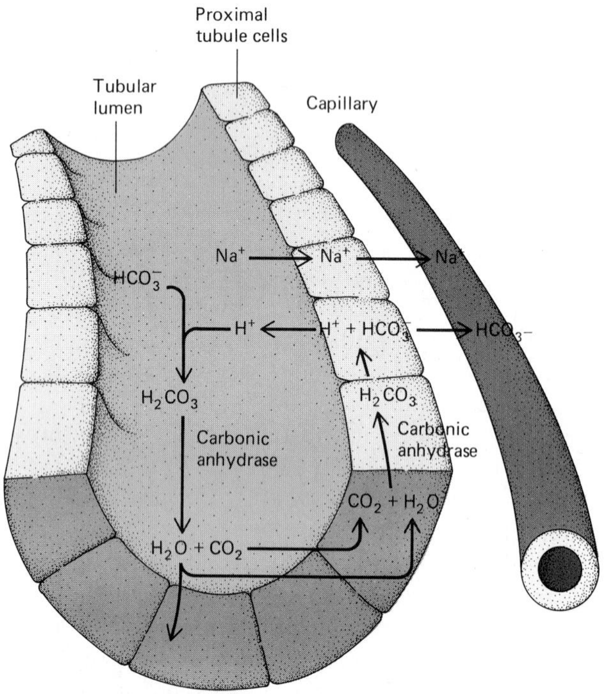

FIGURE 27-13

H^+ ion secretion and bicarbonate (HCO_3^-) reabsorption by the proximal convoluted tubule.

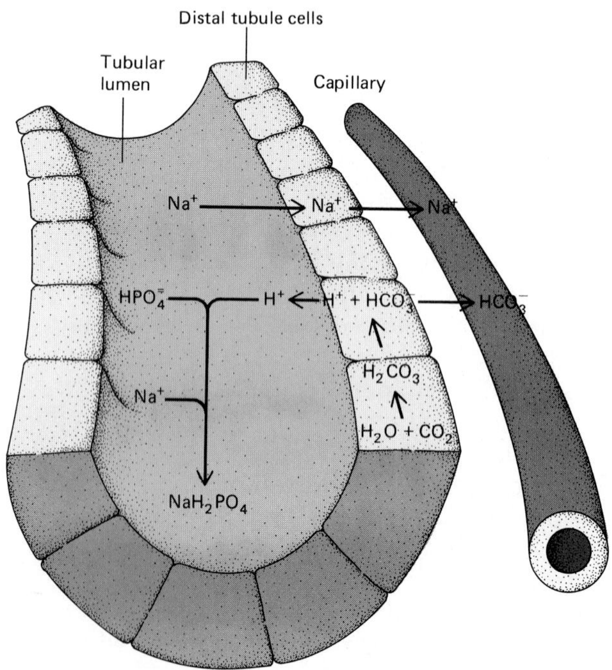

FIGURE 27-14

The renal phosphate buffer system.

acid. The ammonia diffuses into the tubular lumen and combines with hydrogen ions to form ammonium ions (NH_4^+). The NH_4^+ combines usually with Cl^- to form NH_4Cl, which is only slightly acidic and does not lower the pH.

Clinical highlight

Kidney stones, or **renal calculi,** are primarily made up of uric acid and calcium compounds such as calcium oxalate and calcium phosphate. Kidney stones may form and remain in the renal pelvis or may pass into the ureter. A kidney stone in the ureter distends the wall of the ureter and causes great pain. If a kidney stone becomes lodged in the ureter, it can obstruct urine flow and result in ulcerations of the urinary tract. A person is at a higher risk for developing kidney stones if suffering from hyperparathyroidism, vitamin A deficiency, or renal disease.

Kidney stones can be removed or dispersed by several techniques. Conventional surgery can be used for the removal of stones. In a noninvasive technique called extracorporeal shock wave lithotripsy (ESWL), the patient is placed in a water bath, and ultrasound waves are administered to shatter the stones. Stone fragments are expelled in the urine. In percutaneous ultrasonic lithotripsy (PUL), a surgeon inserts a scope tube into the kidney from the back, locates stones, disperses them by ultrasound waves, and then removes the fragments by suction.

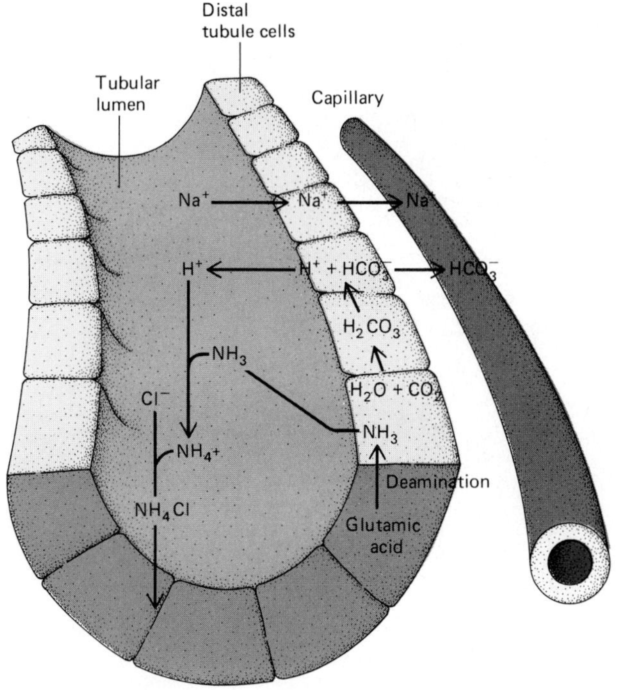

FIGURE 27-15

The renal ammonia buffer system.

Urine is concentrated as it travels through the renal and collecting tubules

The glomerular filtrate in the lumen of Bowman's capsule undergoes changes as it travels through the renal tubule to become urine.

The countercurrent multiplier maintains an osmotic gradient

In a **countercurrent flow,** fluid moves down one tube parallel to fluid moving up another tube. An example of a countercurrent system is the "heat exchanger" that exists between arteries and veins that run parallel to each other in the limbs. Heat is transferred from the warmer arteries to the cooler veins. This concentrates the heat in the body and minimizes heat loss in the limbs. In the kidneys, a countercurrent exchange occurs involving Na^+ ions, forming a concentration gradient in the medulla.

The medullary osmotic gradient set up in the interstitial fluid (interstitium) is the result of ion movements associated with the limbs of the loop of Henle of juxtamedullary nephrons, the collecting tubules, and the vasa recta. This osmotic gradient ranges from about 300 milliosmoles[1] (mOsm) per liter at the cortex to 1200 milliosmoles per liter at the tips of the pyramids. The high medullary osmolarity draws water from the collecting tubule into the interstitium and, depending upon ADH levels, enables the kidneys to vary urine volume.

Descending limb. The filtrate moving down the descending limb of the loop of Henle becomes more concentrated. As the filtrate moves from the proximal convoluted tubule into the descending limb, it is iso-osmotic with the interstitium. As it flows down the descending limb, it becomes associated with a progressively higher interstitial osmolarity. The descending limb is impermeable to sodium chloride and urea but permeable to water, and water moves out of the tubule and into the hyperosmotic interstitium.

[1] A milliosmol is one-thousandth of an osmol. An osmol is equal to a gram molecular weight of a substance divided by the number of ions or particles into which the substance dissociates when put into a liter of solution.

With the removal of water from the tubule, the filtrate osmolarity in the descending limb increases and approximates that of the interstitial fluid. By the time the filtrate reaches the tip of the medulla, it is about 1200 milliosmoles per liter or iso-osmotic to the interstitium. The filtrate osmolarity is due mainly to sodium chloride retained in the descending tubule, whereas that of the interstitium is due to a combination of sodium chloride and urea. Therefore, the concentration of sodium chloride in the filtrate of the lower part of the descending limb is actually higher than its concentration in the adjacent interstitium (Fig. 27-16).

Ascending limb. The filtrate moving through the ascending limb becomes more dilute. As the filtrate rounds the tip of the loop, the thin part of the ascending limb is impermeable to water, freely permeable to sodium chloride, and poorly permeable to urea. Sodium and chloride leave the tubule and enter the interstitium, and some urea leaves the interstitium and enters the tubule. The filtrate now enters the thick ascending limb, which actively transports chloride ions out of the tubule and into the interstitium. Sodium ions follow the chloride ions by passive diffusion, but water does not follow the sodium because the thick ascending limb is impermeable to water. The movement of the solutes out of the ascending limb dilutes the filtrate while maintaining the high osmotic gradient of the interstitium. Some of the NaCl moving out of the ascending limb enters the descending limb through the interstitium, thereby causing the NaCl concentration to multiply its effect as it repeats the cycle.

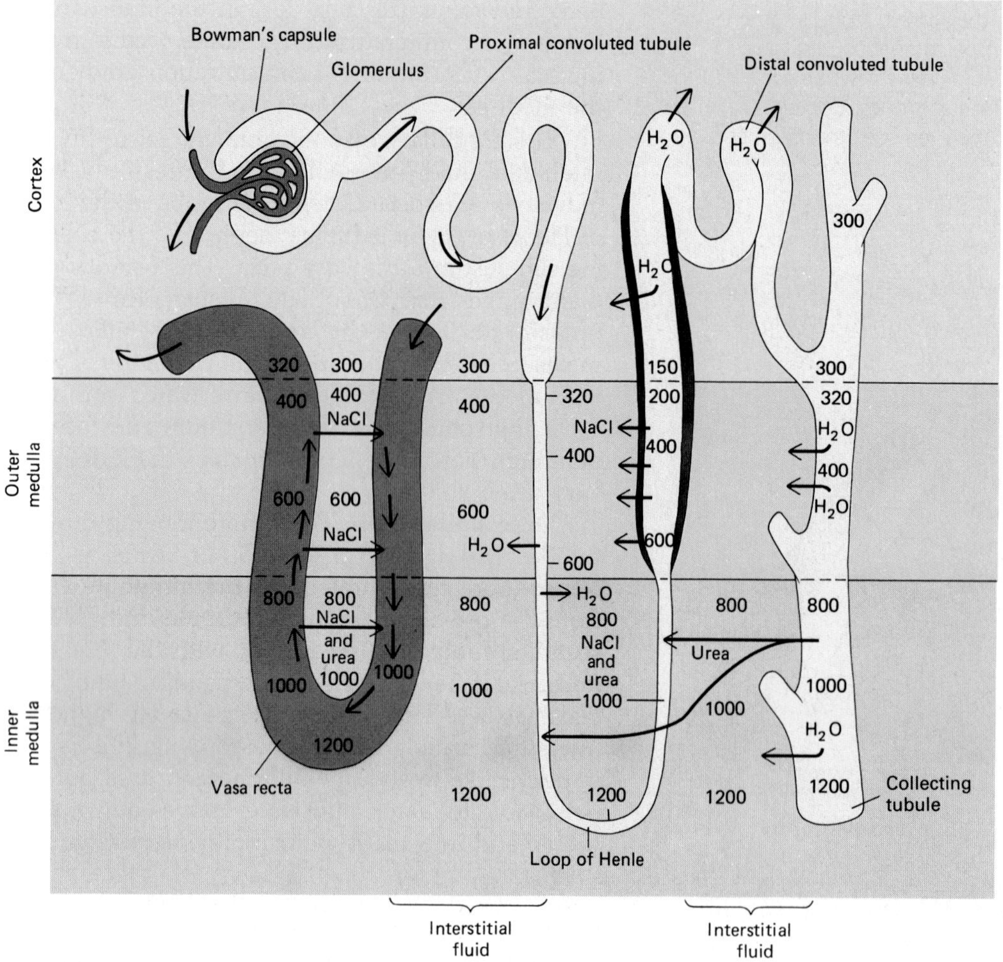

FIGURE 27-16

Counter current mechanism and urine concentration. Concentrations are in milliosmols. Bold lines depict water impermeability.

Distal convoluted tubule and collecting tubule. The diluted filtrate entering the distal convoluted tubule is hypo-osmotic. Sodium and chloride reabsorption continues throughout the distal convoluted tubule. So the filtrate leaving the distal convoluted tubule is more dilute and hypo-osmotic. It enters the collecting tubule, which courses down the medulla, encountering the increasingly higher osmotic gradient.

Besides furnishing nutrients to the medulla, the **vasa recta** is also important to the integrity of the osmotic gradient of the medulla. The role of the vasa recta in the countercurrent mechanism is based on its own countercurrent exchange and the slow movement of blood through it. The vasa recta runs parallel to the loop of Henle and the collecting tubule and has a descending and ascending portion. Blood in the descending vasa recta is flowing in the direction opposite the flow of blood in the ascending branch. The blood entering the initial section of the descending vasa recta has an osmolarity of about 300 milliosmoles per liter. As the descending vasa recta passes down the medulla, water leaves by osmosis and solutes diffuse from the concentrated interstitium into the vasa recta. As the ascending vasa recta courses toward the cortex, solutes leave by diffusion and water moves in by osmosis. (Remember that plasma proteins do not leave the blood but contribute to the osmotic pressure that pulls the water back into the ascending part of the vasa recta.) Therefore, as solutes are recirculated in the medulla, water bypasses it.

This recycling of solutes helps to maintain the osmotic gradient of the interstitium. The slow movement of the blood in the vasa recta ensures that only small amounts of solutes will be removed so as not to disrupt the existing osmotic gradient. Therefore, the countercurrent exchange of the vasa recta serves both to carry away the water reabsorbed from the descending limb of the loop of Henle and the collecting tubules and to prevent a buildup of solutes (Fig. 27-16).

Antidiuretic hormone increases water permeability in the kidneys

When the filtrate reaches the distal convoluted tubule and the collecting tubule, the final urine concentration and volume are regulated by **antidiuretic hormone (ADH).** This is accomplished by the separation of water reabsorption from solute reabsorption.

Water permeability in the distal convoluted tubules and collecting tubules of the kidneys is under the control of ADH. ADH is produced by the supraoptic nuclei of the hypothalamus and stored in the posterior pituitary, from which it is released. ADH functions to regulate water balance in the body and, because of this, it helps to control blood pressure and extracellular osmolarity. Osmolarity is a term used to define the osmotic activity of solutes.

In the absence of ADH, water permeability in the renal collecting tubules is low. Sodium reabsorption proceeds normally but water is not able to follow. This results in a high volume of dilute urine (Fig. 27-17). In the presence of ADH, water permeability is high and water reabsorption can keep pace with sodium reabsorption. The final urine is low in volume and concentrated in solutes.

↓ ADH ⟶ ↓ tubular water permeability ⟶ ↑ urine volume

↑ ADH ⟶ ↑ tubular water permeability ⟶ ↓ urine volume

ADH does not follow an all-or-none law, but shows a graded response. The more ADH present in the kidneys, the greater the tubular permeability of the collecting tubules and the greater the amount of water reabsorbed. This permits a fine degree of control over water balance in the body. This control also helps to regulate blood pressure. (It is thought that the ADH functions via a c-AMP mechanism to increase the size of the tubular pores.)

The ADH-producing cells of the hypothalamus receive input from baroreceptors in the body, especially those located in the left atrium. These baroreceptors monitor blood pressure. When blood pressure increases, the baroreceptors increase the firing of afferent neurons to the hypothalamus, which serves to inhibit the secretion of ADH. In the absence of ADH, the collecting tubules reabsorb less water and more water is excreted. This helps to lower the blood pressure back to normal.

↑ Blood pressure ⟶ ↑ baroreceptor input to hypothalamus ⟶ ↓ ADH release ⟶ ↑ urine volume ⟶ ↓ blood pressure

If blood pressure falls, the baroreceptors cause a decreased firing of impulses by the afferent neurons to the hypothalamus. This stimulates the

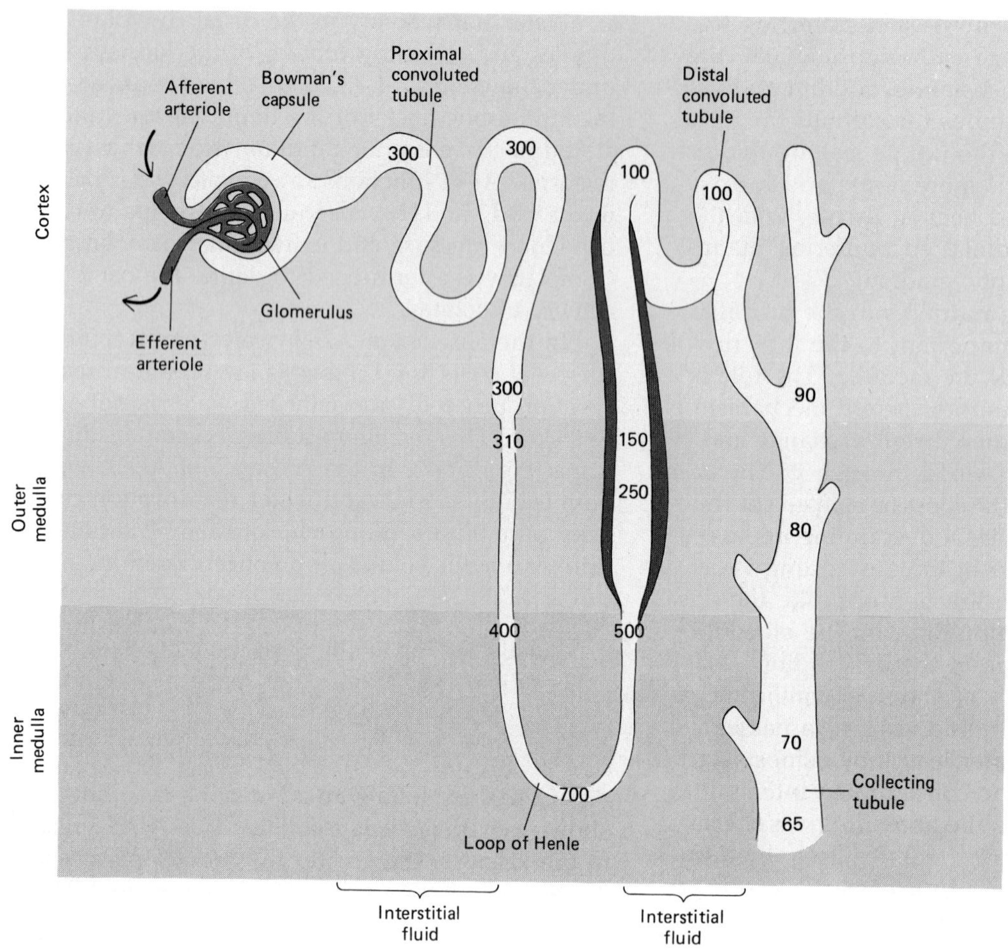

FIGURE 27-17

Counter current mechanism and urine dilution. Concentrations are in milliosmols. Bold lines depict water impermeability when ADH is absent.

ADH-producing cells to release more ADH. With more ADH present in the kidneys, the collecting tubules reabsorb more water and excrete less water. This water conservation helps to raise the blood pressure back to normal.

> ↓ Blood pressure ⟶ ↓ baroreceptor input to hypothalamus ⟶ ↑ ADH release ⟶ ↓ urine volume ⟶ ↑ blood pressure

The ADH mechanism also regulates extracellular osmolarity. The ADH-producing cells act as *osmoreceptors* (cells very sensitive to changes in extracellular osmolarity). Whenever there are pure fluid gains or deficits in the body, these cells respond to the change in extracellular osmolarity. Under the condition of pure water gains, the osmolarity of the interstitium decreases. This causes more water to enter the ADH-producing cells by osmosis. As the cells increase in volume (swell), they inhibit ADH secretion. This means that less water will be reabsorbed by the kidneys and more water will be excreted. With more water excreted, the osmolarity of the interstitium rises back to normal.

> Pure water gain ⟶ ↓ extracellular osmolarity ⟶ ↓ ADH release ⟶ ↑ urine volume ⟶ ↑ extracellular osmolarity

When water is lost from the body, the extracellular osmolarity increases. This will cause water to leave the ADH-producing cells and they will shrink. This stimulates ADH release and, thereby, water reabsorption by the kidneys. With more water retained, the osmolarity decreases to normal levels. This mechanism demonstrates the importance of the kidneys in the regulation of water and osmolarity balances in the body. It also shows the fine control that ADH exerts over water conservation and excretion by the kidneys. Alcohol inhibits the release of ADH and therefore results in a large urine volume output.

Water loss $\longrightarrow \uparrow$ extracellular osmolarity $\longrightarrow \uparrow$ ADH release $\longrightarrow \downarrow$ urine volume $\longrightarrow \downarrow$ extracellular osmolarity

The countercurrent multiplier of urea concentrates the urine

Urea concentration within the tubule increases as more water leaves due to ADH presence. Because the collecting tubule is permeable to urea at its lower end, more urea leaves by diffusion, further contributing to the high osmolarity of the interstitium in the inner medulla. This causes the removal of water from the filtrate of the descending limb, which also concentrates the filtrate concentration of NaCl in the descending limb (Fig. 27-16). Some urea can enter the thin ascending limb of the loop of Henle and form a **countercurrent multiplier** of urea with the collecting tubule. The recycling of urea in the lower medulla is crucial in maintaining the hyperosmotic gradient found in the medulla. This high osmolarity, in turn, draws more water out of the collecting tubules under ADH influence and thereby contributes to the formation of a concentrated urine.

Clinical highlight

Plasma clearance is defined as the rate at which a substance is eliminated (cleared) from the plasma by the kidneys. The clearance rates of substances are important diagnostically and are used to determine the renal plasma flow and the GFR. Table 27-3 gives the clearance rates of various substances. The plasma clearance of substance *b* can be calculated by using the following formula:

$$\text{Plasma clearance of } b \text{ (ml/min)} = \frac{\text{rate of urine formation (ml/min)} \times \text{concentration of } b \text{ in urine}}{\text{concentration of } b \text{ in plasma}}$$

The clearance of inulin is used to measure the GFR. Inulin is a nontoxic carbohydrate derived from dahlia tubers. It is freely filtered by the kidney but is neither reabsorbed nor secreted. A measurement of GFR would begin with an injection of inulin into the plasma and a determination of the plasma concentration of inulin. The bladder is immediately voided. A urine sample is taken after a measured period of time. The rate of urine formation is calculated and the concentration of inulin in the urine sample is measured. When the rate of urine formation is multiplied by the concentration of inulin in the urine, the excretion rate of inulin is determined. Using the formula for plasma clearance, the plasma clearance of inulin can be calculated.

As an example, we will inject inulin into a person's blood until the inulin plasma concentration is 0.2 milligrams per milliliter. The person voids, and after 1 hour the person voids again but with the urine being collected. The volume of urine in this 1-hour sample turns out to be 66 milliliters. Therefore, the rate of urine formation in this example is 66 milliliters of urine in 1 hour, or 1.1 milliliters per minute. The concentration of the

TABLE 27-3

Relative concentrations of substances in the glomerular filtrate and in the urine

	Glomerular filtrate (*125 ml/min*)		Urine (*1 ml/min*)		Conc. urine/ conc. plasma (*plasma clearance per min*)
	Quantity/min	Concentration	Quantity/min	Concentration	
Na^+	17.7 mEq	142 mEq/L	0.128 mEq	128 mEq/L	0.9
K^+	0.63	5	0.06	60	12
Ca^{++}	0.5	4	0.0048	4.8	1.2
Cl^-	12.9	103	0.134	134	1.3
HCO_3^-	3.5	28	0.014	14	0.5
$H_2PO_4^-$	0.25	2	0.05	50	25
Glucose	125 mg	100 mg/dl	0 mg	0 mg/dl	0.0
Urea	33	26	18.2	1820	70
Uric acid	3.8	3	0.42	42	14
Creatinine	1.4	1.1	1.96	196	140
Inulin	—	—	—	—	125

Adapted from Guyton, Arthur C., *Textbook of Medical Physiology*, 7th ed., 1986. (Courtesy W. B. Saunders Co., Philadelphia.)

inulin in this urine sample is measured to be 22.7 milligrams per milliliter. By using the formula for plasma clearance, we obtain a plasma clearance for inulin of 7500 milliliters in 1 hour, or 125 milliliters per minute (180 liters/day). This plasma clearance rate for inulin is the same as the GFR. This is because the amount of inulin appearing in the urine must be equal to the amount of inulin filtered during the same time period. None of the inulin is lost in reabsorption or is added through secretion.

Urine characteristics can be measured by a urinalysis

Since Hippocrates, the content of urine has been considered to have diagnostic significance in evaluating the health of a person. The determination of the physical, chemical, and microscopic characteristics of the urine is called **urinalysis.** Table 27-4 contains the major diagnostic parameters identified in a routine urinalysis.

The final urine composition depends upon the amount of glomerular filtrate and the amount of reabsorption and secretion occurring in the renal tubules. Urine output ranges from 1 to 2 liters per day. About 95% of the urine is water. The other 5% is made up mainly of inorganic and organic solutes. NaCl is the major inorganic solute and urea is the major organic solute found in the urine.

The volume of urine is altered by a number of factors affecting blood pressure and ADH secretion. As we have already seen, the JG cells are sensitive to changes in blood pressure and increase renin release when renal blood pressure declines. This activates the renin-angiotensin-aldosterone pathway. The resultant increase in angiotensin II causes vasoconstriction, which increases blood pressure and increases aldosterone

TABLE 27-4

Urinalysis

Characteristic	Normal range in urine	Comments
Color	Yellow or amber	Darker if more concentrated; chemicals may change color
Odor	Aromatic	Ammonia smell upon standing
pH	4.6–8.0 (average = 6.0)	Varies with diet
Specific gravity	1.001–1.035	Inversely related to volume (specific gravity of H_2O = 1.000)
Turbidity	Transparent	Clouds upon standing
Volume	1–2 Liters/day	Depends upon diet, blood pressure, osmolarity, temperature, emotional state
Substances normally not found in urine (or in trace amounts)	**Clinical term for presence in urine**	**Possible pathology (if present)**
Albumin	Albuminuria	Renal disease
Bilirubin	Bilirubinuria	Hepatic disease
Casts (usually cellular materials)		Infection
Erythrocytes	Hematuria	Renal disease
Glucose	Glycosuria	Diabetes mellitus
Ketones	Acetonuria	Diabetes mellitus, fasting
Leukocytes	Pyuria	Urinary tract infection
Microbes	Pyuria	Infection
Protein	Proteinuria	Renal disease
Urobilinogen	Urobilinuria	Hepatic disease

secretion. The aldosterone increases Na^+ and water reabsorption. Therefore, decreases in blood pressure result in a decreased urine volume, because more water is being reabsorbed.

Stress and strong emotions, by increasing sympathetic output, can increase blood pressure, which increases the glomerular capillary hydrostatic pressure, increases the GFR, and increases urine volume. However, intense sympathetic stimulation decreases the GFR due to vasoconstriction of the afferent arteriole.

Other factors act on the osmoreceptors of the hypothalamus to influence ADH secretion. Increases in external temperature, metabolism, and physical activity tend to increase body temperature and activate mechanisms for heat loss, including perspiration. Perspiration is enhanced by a peripheral vasodilation. As fluid is lost, the hypothalamic osmoreceptors are stimulated to secrete more ADH, which causes an increased facultative water reabsorption by the kidneys. Along with the peripheral vasodilation, there is an internal visceral vasoconstriction, which reduces renal blood pressure and lowers the GFR. The urine volume, therefore, is lowered by both mechanisms.

Plasma constituents, especially water and solutes, can also influence the volume of urine. Plasma sodium concentrations affect aldosterone secretion. A decrease in the concentration of plasma Na^+ stimulates aldosterone release, which increases Na^+ reabsorption in the kidneys and also increases obligatory water reabsorption. This results in a reduction of urine volume.

Changes in fluid gain or loss also alter urine volume by changing extracellular osmolarity and affecting the osmoreceptors of the hypothalamus as previously discussed. Fluid gains that decrease extracellular osmolarity decrease ADH secretion and increase urine volume (**water diuresis** [die-you-**ree**-sis]), whereas increases in extracellular osmolarity stimulate ADH secretion and reduce urine volume. However, if the renal tubules contain large amounts of unreabsorbed solutes, these solutes exert an osmotic pull of water into the tubule and urine volume is increased **(osmotic diuresis).**

Chemical diuretics inhibit facultative water reabsorption and thus increase urine volume. Some act directly on the renal and collecting tubules while others inhibit ADH release.

Ureters carry urine from the kidneys to the urinary bladder

The two **ureters** (you-**ree**-ters) are continuations of the renal pelvis of each kidney. These tubes conduct the urine formed by the kidneys to the urinary bladder. The ureters are retroperitoneal and measure about 28 centimeters (11 in.) in length and 6 millimeters (0.25 in.) in diameter. They enter the urinary bladder at its posterior inferior surface. There are no sphincters regulating the flow of urine into the bladder. When pressure increases in the bladder, the walls of the bladder compress the ureters as they pass obliquely through the bladder wall, preventing a backflow of urine into the kidneys.

The walls of the ureters consist of three layers. The innermost layer is the **mucosa.** The mucosal epithelium is transitional, allowing stretching without tearing. It secretes mucus to protect the ureter from the acidic urine. The middle layer, the **muscularis,** contains inner longitudinal and outer circular smooth muscle fibers. The outermost layer is made up of fibrous and areolar **connective tissue** and **adipose tissue.** The smooth muscle fibers typically contract to form peristaltic waves which propel the urine. Gravity and hydrostatic pressure also contribute to the movement of urine through the ureters. Urine enters the bladder from the ureters in spurts.

If the ureter should become blocked, nociceptors cause a sympathetic reflex back to the kidney, producing a vasoconstriction of the afferent arterioles, which serves to decrease urine output. This **ureterorenal reflex** prevents excessive urine flow into the renal pelvis supplying the obstructed ureter.

The urinary bladder stores and expels the urine

The **urinary bladder** is a hollow organ located at the floor of the pelvis just posterior to the pubic symphysis. The bladder is held in position by folds of the peritoneum. It is located anterior to the rectum in a male and anterior to the uterus in a female. The bladder functions to temporarily store urine and help in its expulsion.

The wall of the urinary bladder has four layers. The innermost layer is the **mucosa** which is a mucous membrane. The mucus that is secreted protects the bladder from the urine. The mucosa contains transitional epithelium, which is able to stretch, and also contains folds (rugae), which increase its potential for stretching. Not only does the transitional epithelium safeguard against tearing, it also increases the distensibility of the bladder for the storage of wastes. The next layer is the **submucosa** which contains connective tissue. The third layer consists of smooth muscle called the **detrusor muscle.** The detrusor muscle is made up of two longitudinal muscle layers separated by a circular muscle layer. The outermost layer of the bladder is the **serosa,** which is formed by the peritoneum and covers only the superior part of the bladder.

The entrance of the two ureters marks the *base* of the bladder. The *apex* is where the urethra leaves the bladder. These openings form the parameters of a triangular area called the **trigone** (**try**-gohn). The trigone of the urinary bladder is directed anteriorly and is smooth, lacking the folds present in the superior part of the bladder (Fig. 27-18). It is firmly anchored to the pelvic floor, which prevents a distortion of the ureter openings into the bladder.

Near the opening to the urethra, the circular layer of the detrusor muscle forms an **internal urethral sphincter.** Just below this sphincter is an **external urethral sphincter** consisting of skeletal muscle.

Clinical highlight

Cystitis is an inflammation of the urinary bladder. It often is accompanied by dysuria (difficult or painful urination) and hematuria (blood in urine). Cystitis may result from a bacterial infection, mechanical trauma, or chemical injury.

When the content of the bladder rises to more than about 300 milliliters of urine, a reflex is initiated that serves to expel the urine from the bladder. The act of expulsion of urine from the bladder is called **micturition** (*mik*-tyou-**rish**-un), or urination.

(a)

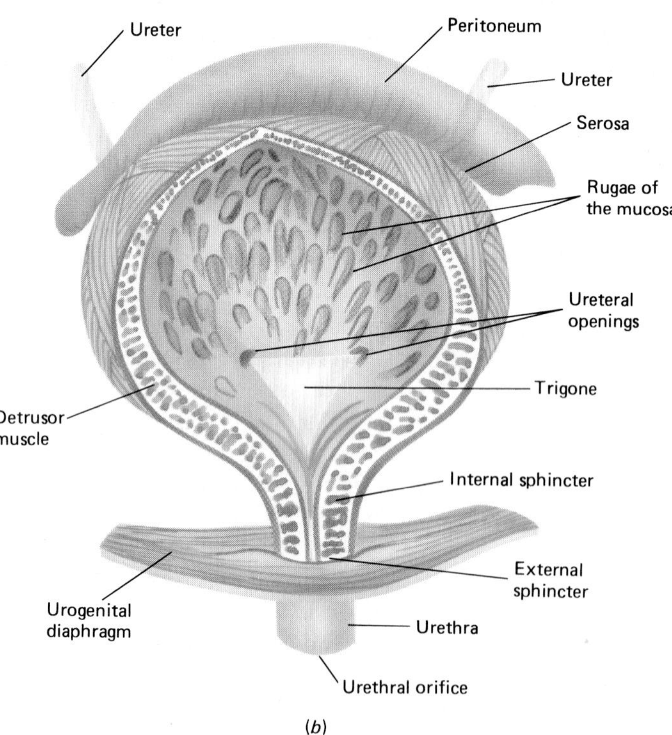

(b)

FIGURE 27-18

Urinary bladder. (*a*) Scanning electron micrograph of the mucosa of the urinary bladder illustrating the transitional epithelium and folds resulting from contraction of the underlying smooth muscle. As urine accumulates in the bladder, the folds stretch out. (From Kessel, R. G., and Kardon, R. H.: *Tissues and Organs: A Text-Atlas of Scanning Electron Microscopy.* San Francisco, W. H. Freeman, 1979). (*b*) Internal anatomy of urinary bladder and female urethra.

The stimulus for this **micturition reflex** is the stretching of the bladder wall by the volume of urine. Stretch receptors in the wall of the bladder signal afferent neurons which take the information to the sacral spinal cord. These impulses are integrated in such a way that they give rise to a conscious desire to urinate. They also stimulate parasympathetic neurons, which carry the impulses from the spinal cord to the bladder. These impulses cause a contraction of the detrusor muscle and a relaxation of the internal sphincter. The cerebrum of the brain sends impulses to the external sphincter that cause it to relax. As the detrusor muscle contracts, the pressure within the bladder increases, forcing the urine out of the bladder through the opened sphincters and into the urethra.

↑ Volume of bladder ⟶ ↑ stretch receptor input to sacral spinal cord ⟶
↑ parasympathetic input to bladder ⟶
↑ contraction of detrusor muscle ⟶
↑ urine expulsion

Cerebral control of the external sphincter can also cause a voluntary expulsion or retention of urine. In an infant, micturition is solely a spinal reflex because the motor neurons to the external sphincter have not yet fully developed. Therefore, an infant under 2 years old urinates whenever the bladder becomes sufficiently full to initiate the micturition reflex. When the voluntary neuronal circuit to the external sphincter develops, it can serve to inhibit the spinal reflex. With practice, a person exercises more and more control over urination until the voluntary act is the one that initiates the spinal reflex.

The urethra is different in the male and female

The **urethra** (you-**ree**-thruh) is a muscular tube that leaves the urinary bladder at its inferior surface. Its inner wall is made up of a mucous membrane. The urethra carries the urine from the bladder to the exterior surface of the body.

The walls of the female urethra consist of three layers: an inner **mucosa;** a middle **spongy layer,** thick and elastic, containing an extensive network of veins; and an outer **muscular layer** consisting of circular smooth muscle.

The urethral wall in the male has an inner mucosa and an outer submucous layer possessing connective tissue that attaches the urethra to surrounding structures.

The urethra shows sexual differences. In the female, the urethra is short (about 4 centimeters, or 1.5 in.) and is embedded in the anterior wall of the vagina. The external opening of the urethra, the **urinary meatus,** or **external urethral orifice,** is located between the clitoris and the vaginal orifice (Fig. 27-19*a*). The female urethra functions only in the excretion of urine.

The male urethra is about five times longer (20 centimeters, or about 8 in.) than its female counterpart. It is made up of three parts: the **prostatic urethra,** the **membranous urethra,** and the **spongy urethra.** These parts are named in accordance with the area in which they are located. The prostatic urethra runs through the prostate gland, and it receives the ejaculatory ducts of the reproductive system. Hence, the male urethra functions in both the excretion of urine and the transport of sperm, but not simultaneously. The membranous urethra is the part passing through the urogenital diaphragm. The spongy urethra passes through the penis and is surrounded by erectile tissue. The male urethra reaches the exterior of the body at the opening of the tip of the glans penis called the **external urethral orifice** (Fig. 27-19*b*).

Clinical highlight

Prostatic hypertrophy, an enlargement of the prostate gland in males, can compress the urethra and result in dysuria and a backup of urine into the kidneys. The GFR may decrease, interfering with renal regulation of body fluids.

Aging of the urinary system results in decreased renal function

Renal function decreases with age. Incontinence and urinary tract infections increase with age. The occurrence of kidney stones and renal inflammations increases. Elderly people also experience more dysuria (painful or difficult urination) and polyuria (copious urination). In elderly men, complications of the prostate gland are much more frequent, with prostate cancer being a major problem.

See Focus on Disorders of the Urinary System, p. 979.

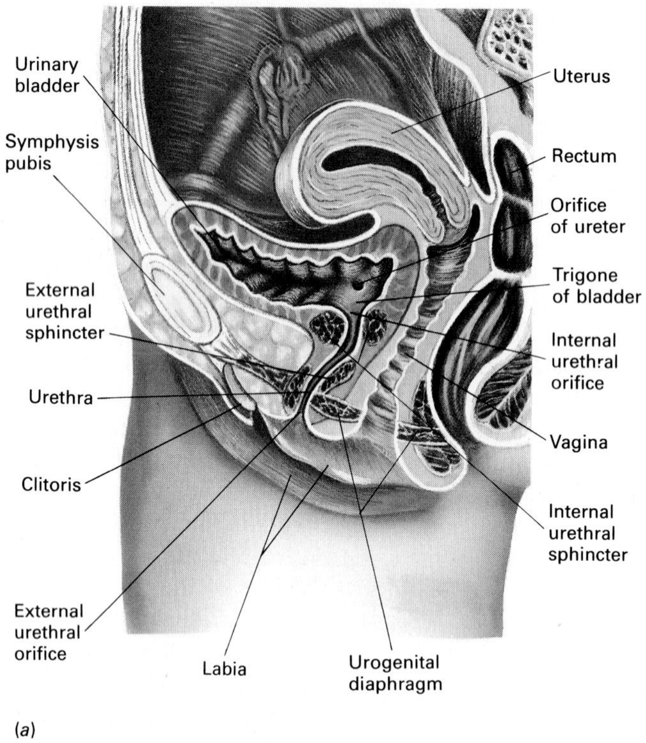
Urinary bladder
Symphysis pubis
External urethral sphincter
Urethra
Clitoris
External urethral orifice
Labia
Urogenital diaphragm
Uterus
Rectum
Orifice of ureter
Trigone of bladder
Internal urethral orifice
Vagina
Internal urethral sphincter
(a)

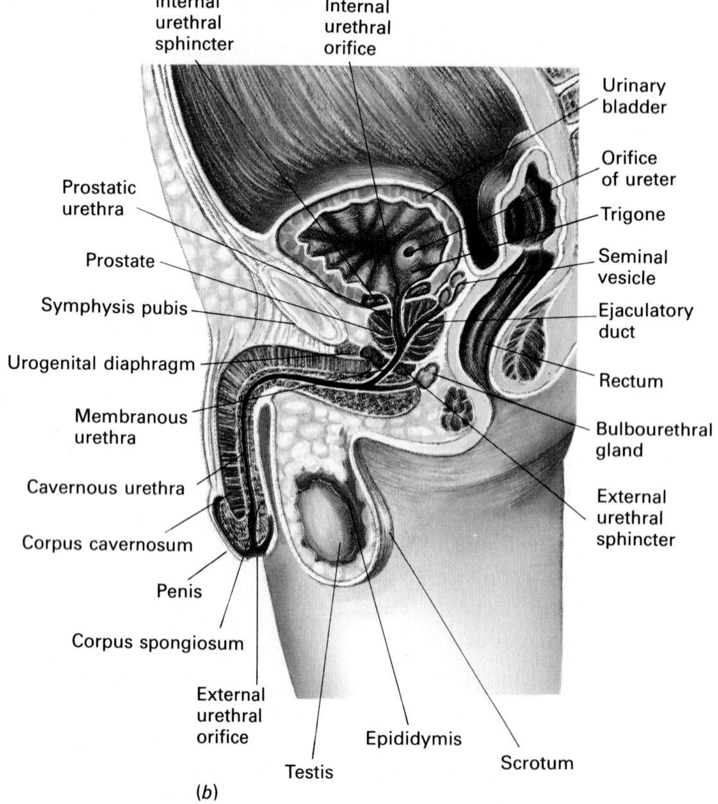
Internal urethral sphincter
Internal urethral orifice
Urinary bladder
Orifice of ureter
Trigone
Seminal vesicle
Ejaculatory duct
Rectum
Bulbourethral gland
External urethral sphincter
Prostatic urethra
Prostate
Symphysis pubis
Urogenital diaphragm
Membranous urethra
Cavernous urethra
Corpus cavernosum
Penis
Corpus spongiosum
External urethral orifice
Testis
Epididymis
Scrotum
(b)

FIGURE 27-19

Anatomy of urethra. (*a*) Female. (*b*) Male (sagittal section).

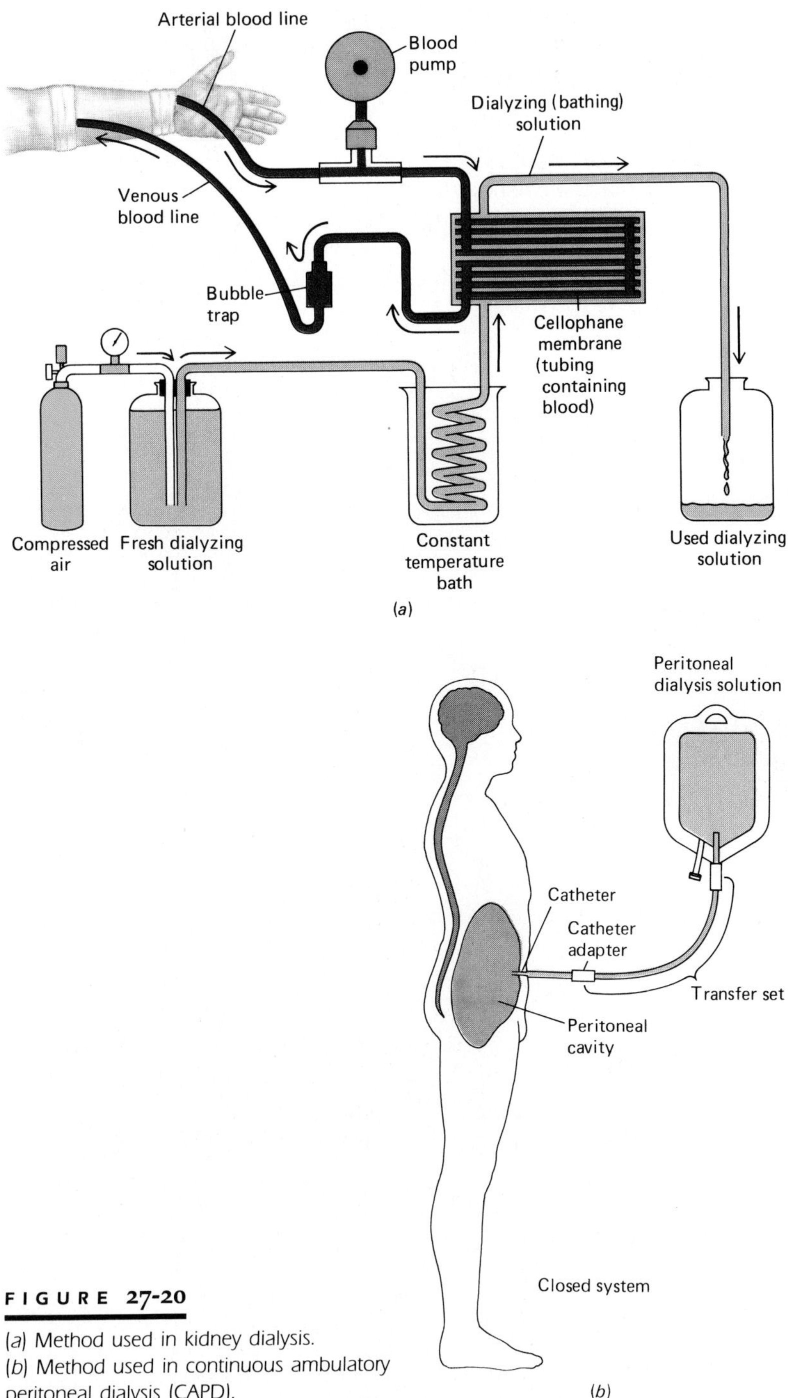

FIGURE 27-20

(*a*) Method used in kidney dialysis.
(*b*) Method used in continuous ambulatory peritoneal dialysis (CAPD).

Clinical highlight

Chronic renal infections, physical and chemical damage, and circulatory problems may lead to the inability of the kidneys to adequately filter the blood. In order to maintain homeodynamics, the blood can be filtered artificially by **hemodialysis** (*he*-mo-dye-**al**-i-sis). As the blood is circulated outside of the body, hemodialysis removes certain substances based on differences in diffusion rates through a semipermeable membrane.

A common hemodialysis apparatus is the kidney machine. See Figure 27-20a. Blood from the patient's radial artery is pumped through tubes to a dialysis chamber containing a membrane of cellulose acetate that is permeable to substances such as nitrogenous wastes and potassium but not to blood cells and proteins. Outside of the membrane tube, a dialyzing (bathing) solution exists that does not contain the permeable substances and that is constantly being washed. It has an electrolyte concentration equal to that of normal plasma. As the blood moves through the membrane tube, substances diffuse back and forth between the blood and the dialyzing solution.

Excess electrolytes and wastes move out of the blood and into the dialyzing solution and are removed. Needed substances are returned to the blood, and nutrients (glucose) can also be added to the dialyzing solution and diffuse into the blood. Therefore, the kidney machine operates as an artificial nephron.

Artificial renal dialysis is a time-consuming process because a large amount of the patient's blood must be passed through the machine at a slow rate to guarantee effective processing.

New portable devices such as the continuous ambulatory peritoneal dialysis (CAPD) make the process of

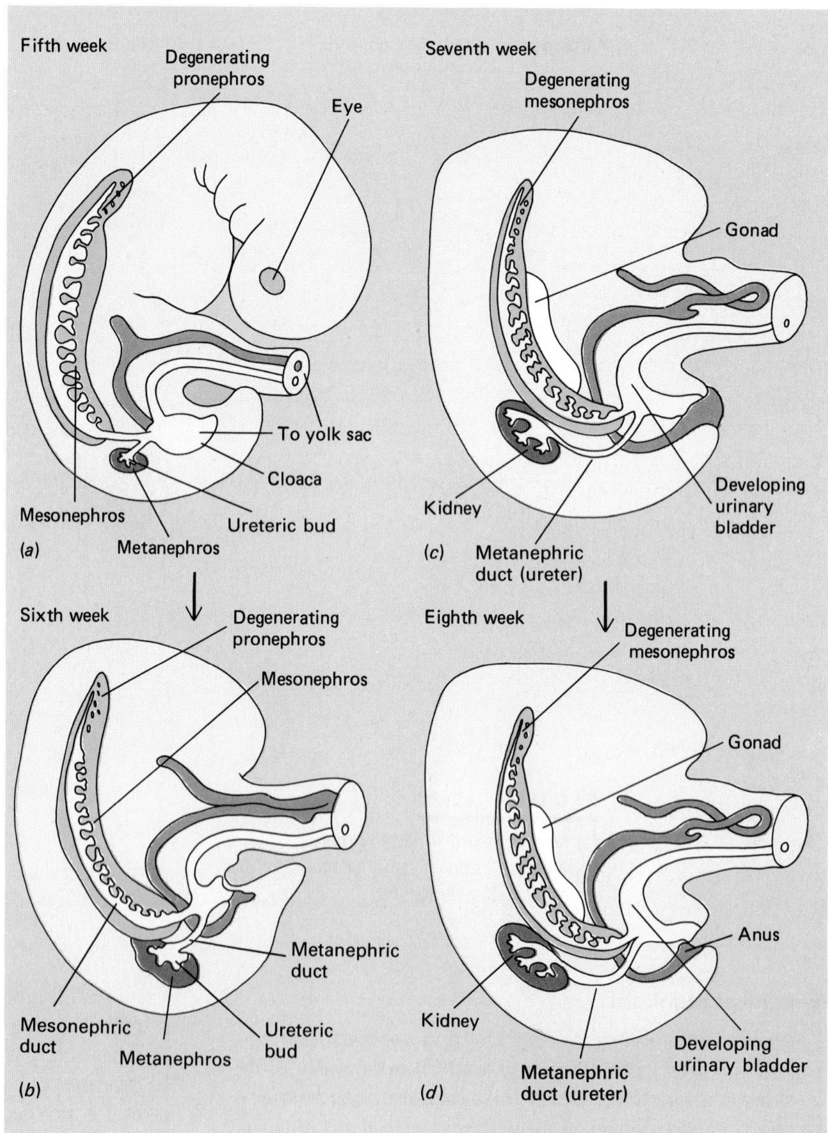

FIGURE 27-21

Embryology of the urinary system.

dialysis less time-consuming and more convenient. See Figure 27-20b. The CAPD uses the peritoneum as the dialyzing membrane. From an external container, the dialyzing fluid enters the peritoneal cavity through a catheter. Gravity is used to control the rate of fluid entry, by raising or lowering the container. After remaining in the peritoneal cavity for a controlled time period, the dialyzing fluid is drained back into the container and discarded.

Embryology of the urinary system includes three stages of kidney development

The kidneys develop from mesodermal tissue located on either side of the somites. This mesoderm is called the **intermediate mesoderm** and it begins to differentiate at about the third week of gestation. The kidneys form in three distinct stages: the pronephros, the mesonephros, and the metanephros. Development begins from the superior end of the intermediate mesoderm and proceeds to the inferior end (Fig. 27-21).

The first stage of kidney development is the **pronephros** (pro-**nef**-ros). The pronephros never becomes functional in humans. Its **pronephric duct** leads to the cloaca. The pronephros starts to degenerate during the fourth week and is completely gone by about the sixth week of development. The pronephric ducts remain and become part of the second stage, the mesonephros.

The **mesonephros** (mez-o-**nef**-ros) begins developing as the pronephros degenerates. It develops from the intermediate mesoderm located below the pronephric tissue. As the mesonephros develops, its tubules join the pronephric duct which becomes the **mesonephric duct** (mez-o-**nef**-rik). The mesonephros begins to degenerate during the sixth week starting at its superior end. The most inferior part of the mesonephros is all that remains by the eighth week. It is thought that the mesonephros never functions in humans.

The third and last stage in kidney development is the **metanephros** (met-ah-**nef**-ros). The metanephros is the functional kidney in humans. The metanephros starts out as an outgrowth, the **ureteric bud** (you-reh-**ter**-ik), from the distal end of the mesonephric duct. The ureteric bud is covered by intermediate mesoderm. The end of the ureteric bud expands as it grows cranially to the final position near the upper lumbar vertebrae.

FOCUS ON . . . Disorders of the urinary system

Diabetes insipidus (*diabetes* = overflow, *insipidus* = tasteless). Diabetes insipidus is a dysfunction of the posterior pituitary in which insufficient ADH is released. Polyuria and thirst are manifestations of the condition due to the inability to retain fluids.

Gout. Gout is a hereditary disease caused by an excess of uric acid in the blood. The kidneys do not excrete uric acid as fast as it is being produced and it accumulates in the body. The excess uric acid crystallizes in the joints and in the kidneys and can be very painful. The big toe is a common site of a gout attack.

Incontinence. Incontinence is the lack of voluntary control over urination. It is normal for infants below 2 years old. In adults, it is caused by a number of conditions, including unconsciousness and stress.

Nephrosis (*nephr* = kidney; neh-**froe**-sis). Nephrosis is a condition in which the glomeruli are highly permeable and allow large amounts of proteins to be excreted. Edema results especially in the ankles, feet, abdomen, and eyes.

Polycystic disease (*poly* = many, *cyst* = sac). Polycystic disease is an inherited condition in which the kidneys contain numerous cysts and holes. These cysts progress in size and cause renal hypertrophy and uremia.

Pyelitis (*pyel* = renal pelvis, *itis* = inflammation; *pie*-eh-**lie**-tis). Pyelitis is an inflammation of the renal pelvis and calyces.

Pyelonephritis (*pyel* = renal pelvis, *nephr* = kidney, *itis* = inflammation; *pie*-eh-low-neh-**fry**-tis). Pyelonephritis is an inflammation of the kidney, involving the pelvis and the nephrons. It is usually associated with a bacterial infection somewhere else in the body.

Renal failure. Renal failure is a term used to describe a decrease in glomerular filtration. It can be either acute or chronic. **Acute renal failure** (ARF) is a sudden cessation or near cessation of kidney function. Oliguria and anuria are manifestations of ARF. ARF may result from decreased cardiac output, decreased blood volume, kidney stone obstruction, or tubular necrosis. **Chronic renal failure** (CRF) is a progressive condition of decreased glomerular filtration. It usually is a complication of a renal disease.

Retention. Retention is the failure to void urine.

Stricture. Stricture is a narrowing of the lumen of a tube such as the ureters and the urethra.

Urethritis (*urethr* = urethra, *itis* = inflammation). Urethritis is an inflammation of the urethra. It is often caused by bacterial infection or highly acidic urine.

The unexpanded part of the bud is called the **metanephric duct** (met-ah-**nef**-rik). The expanded end of the ureteric bud develops into the collecting tubules, calyces, and the renal pelvis. The metanephric duct becomes the ureter. The intermediate mesoderm surrounding the bud develops into the nephrons.

With development, the cloaca divides into a urogenital area and a digestive tract area (rectum). The urogenital area is called the **urogenital sinus.** The urinary bladder and the urethra develop from the urogenital sinus.

Summary

I. The urinary system maintains the homeodynamics of the body by regulating the volume and composition of the body fluids.

II. The two bean-shaped kidneys are retroperitoneal organs about the size of a fist.

III. The kidneys are covered by three tissue layers: renal capsule, adipose capsule, and a renal fascia.

IV. The kidneys are made up of two major regions: an outer cortex and an inner medulla.

V. The nephron is the unit of structure and function of the kidney, and it consists of a renal corpuscle and a renal tubule.
   - A. The renal corpuscle of a nephron contains a glomerulus and a Bowman's capsule. The renal corpuscle is located in the cortex of the kidney.
   - B. The filtration barrier of the renal corpuscle is made up of a glomerular capillary endothelium, a glomerular basement membrane, and the visceral layer of Bowman's capsule.
   - C. The renal tubule of a nephron is made up of a proximal convoluted tubule, a loop of Henle, and a distal convoluted tubule.

VI. The renal arteries and renal veins take blood into and out of the kidneys. An afferent arteriole delivers blood to the glomerulus. The blood from the glomerulus leaves through an efferent arteriole which takes the blood into the peritubular capillaries.

VII. Urine is formed by the processes of filtration, reabsorption, and secretion.
   - A. Glomerular filtration is the movement of substances by bulk flow from the blood within the glomerulus into the lumen of Bowman's capsule.
   - B. The two major forces involved in filtration are hydrostatic forces and osmotic forces. There is normally a net filtration pressure moving substances from the glomerular blood into the lumen of Bowman's capsule.
   - C. Reabsorption is the movement of a substance from the renal tubule into the peritubular capillaries. Reabsorption can be either active or passive.
   - D. Secretion is the movement of a substance from the blood within the peritubular capillaries into the renal tubule. Secretion may be either active or passive.

VIII. The countercurrent multiplier of the kidney maintains an osmotic gradient in the medulla of the kidney important in concentrating the urine.
   - A. Antidiuretic hormone (ADH) causes renal tubular reabsorption of water, which results in a concentrated urine of low volume. In the absence of ADH, there is a dilute copious urine.
   - B. Urea undergoes a countercurrent mechanism that helps to concentrate the urine.

IX. Urine characteristics can be measured by a urinalysis.
   - A. Of the 1 to 2 liters of urine excreted per day, 95% is water and the other 5% is primarily made up of solutes. The main inorganic solute excreted is NaCl, and the main organic solute excreted is urea.
   - B. The volume of the urine can be altered by factors affecting blood pressure and ADH secretion.

X. The ureters are retroperitoneal and are made up of three layers: mucosa, muscularis, and connective tissue.

XI. The ureters take urine from the renal pelvis of the kidneys to the urinary bladder. Peristalsis is the major force moving the urine through the ureters.

XII. The urinary bladder is made up of four layers: mucosa, submucosa, muscularis (detrusor muscle), and a serosa.
   - A. The urinary bladder stores urine and helps in its expulsion.
   - B. The expulsion of urine from the urinary bladder is called micturition. Micturition is a reflex stimulated by the volume of urine in the bladder.

XIII. The urethra carries the urine from the urinary bladder to the exterior. The male urethra is longer than the female urethra and also functions in conducting semen.

XIV. Renal function decreases with age.

XV. The kidneys develop from intermediate mesoderm in three stages: pronephros, mesonephros, and metanephros. The functional kidney in the human is the metanephros.

Post-test

1. The kidneys are located behind the peritoneum of the abdomen and, therefore, are ______.
2. Blood leaves the kidneys in the ______ ______.
3. The innermost tissue layer surrounding a kidney is called the ______.
4. The outer region of a kidney is the ______; the inner region of a kidney is the ______.
5. The major calyces form a large cavity called the ______ ______.
6. The functional units of the kidneys are the ______.
7. The ______ and Bowman's capsule make up a renal corpuscle.
8. Podocytes belong to the ______ layer of Bowman's capsule.
9. The filtration barrier consists of the ______ ______ ______, ______ ______ ______, and the ______ ______ ______.
10. The renal tubule of a nephron consists of the ______ ______, ______ ______, and ______.
11. From the nephron, urine passes into the ______ tubule.
12. The specialized cells of the renal tubule that are located in the juxtaglomerular apparatus are the ______ ______.
13. The rate at which water and small solutes flow from the glomerulus into Bowman's capsule is the ______ ______ ______.
14. A potent vasoconstrictor that also stimulates aldosterone release is ______.
15. ______ is the movement of a substance out of the renal tubule and into the peritubular capillaries; ______ is the movement of a substance from the peritubular capillaries into the renal tubule.
16. ______ reabsorption of water is linked to sodium reabsorption.
17. The thin ______ ______ part of the loop of Henle is impermeable to water, freely permeable to sodium chloride, and poorly permeable to urea.
18. ADH increases the permeability of the collecting tubules for ______.
19. The ______ carry the urine from the kidneys to the urinary bladder.
20. The act of expulsion of urine from the bladder is called urination or ______.

Indicate whether the following show proportional or inversely proportional relationships, or are independent, by marking a *P* for proportional, an *I* for inversely proportional, and an *N* for independent.

____ 21. Volume versus specific gravity.
____ 22. Sodium excretion versus aldosterone levels.
____ 23. GFR versus blood pressure.
____ 24. Aldosterone versus plasma renin secretion.
____ 25. Extracellular osmolarity versus volume of ADH-secreting cells.
____ 26. Plasma glucose level versus maximal tubular capacity for glucose.
____ 27. Alcohol ingestion versus water reabsorption.
____ 28. ADH secretion versus body fluid volume.
____ 29. Extracellular osmolarity versus body fluid volume.
____ 30. Urine volume versus ADH secretion.
____ 31. Osmols of solute versus osmotic pressure.
____ 32. GFR versus plasma oncotic pressure.

A pure water gain to the body would increase (↑), decrease (↓), or not affect (=) the following:

____ 33. Blood plasma volume.
____ 34. ADH secretion.
____ 35. Aldosterone secretion.
____ 36. Urine volume.
____ 37. Renal tubular Na^+.
____ 38. Volume of ADH-producing cells.
____ 39. Atrial baroreceptor firing.
____ 40. GFR.
____ 41. Water reabsorption.
____ 42. Renin secretion.
____ 43. Glomerular blood pressure.
____ 44. Extracellular osmolarity.
____ 45. Angiotensinogen production.
____ 46. Collecting tubular water permeability.
____ 47. Maximal tubular capacity for glucose.

Review questions

1. Why is the right kidney usually lower in position than the left one?
2. What are the three tissue layers surrounding the kidneys and what is their function?
3. List the structures involved in the flow of urine from the collecting tubules to the ureters.
4. What are the differences between a juxtamedullary nephron and a cortical nephron?
5. List the components of a renal corpuscle.
6. List the components of a renal tubule.
7. Define a podocyte and a pedicle.
8. List the barriers in the filtration membrane.
9. Describe the make-up of a juxtaglomerular apparatus and explain its function.
10. Trace filtrate flow through a nephron.
11. Trace renal blood flow through the kidneys.
12. Define glomerular filtration.
13. List all the forces involved in determining the net filtration pressure.
14. Define renal reabsorption and list some substances that are actively and passively reabsorbed.
15. Define renal secretion and list some substances secreted by the kidneys.
16. Describe the countercurrent mechanism of the kidneys.
17. Explain the function of the countercurrent multiplier of the kidneys.
18. Explain the role of ADH in determining the concentration and volume of urine.
19. What is the role of the vasa recta?
20. Define plasma clearance of the kidney.
21. Why is inulin used to determine GFR?
22. Define urine. List the major constituents of the urine.
23. What are the major parameters measured in a urinalysis?
24. Explain why urine does not usually flow back into the kidneys from the urinary bladder.
25. Describe the micturition reflex.
26. What are the major differences between the male and female urethra?
27. Define: glomerulonephritis, gout, incontinence, nephrosis, ptosis, pyelonephritis, renal failure, and urethritis.

Post-test answers

1. retroperitoneal **2.** renal veins **3.** renal capsule **4.** cortex; medulla **5.** renal pelvis **6.** nephrons **7.** glomerulus **8.** visceral **9.** glomerular capillary endothelium, glomerular basement membrane, visceral layer of Bowman's capsule **10.** proximal convoluted tubule, loop of Henle, distal convoluted tubule **11.** collecting **12.** macula densa **13.** glomerular filtration rate (GFR) **14.** angiotensin II

15. reabsorption; secretion **16.** obligatory **17.** ascending limb **18.** water **19.** ureters **20.** micturition **21.** I **22.** I **23.** P **24.** P **25.** I **26.** N **27.** I **28.** P **29.** I **30.** I **31.** P **32.** I **33.** ↑ **34.** ↓ **35.** ↓ **36.** ↑ **37.** ↓ **38.** ↑ **39.** ↑ **40.** ↑ **41.** ↓ **42.** ↓ **43.** ↑ **44.** ↓ **45.** = **46.** ↓ **47.** =

FLUID, ELECTROLYTE, AND ACID–BASE BALANCE

CHAPTER OUTLINE

I. Properties and content of water in the body
- A. Fluid compartments
- B. Water balance
  - 1. Role of ADH
  - 2. Thirst
    - □ Focus on fluid imbalance

II. Electrolytes
- A. Sodium balance
- B. Potassium balance
- C. Calcium and phosphate balance
- D. Magnesium balance
- E. Chloride balance
  - □ Focus on electrolyte imbalance

III. pH balance
- A. Importance of pH regulation
- B. Mechanisms of pH regulation
  - 1. Chemical buffers
  - 2. Respiratory system
  - 3. Kidneys
    - □ Focus on acid-base imbalance

LEARNING OBJECTIVES

After you have studied this chapter you should be able to:

1 List the functions of water in the body.

2 List the sources of water input and water output of the body.

3 Explain how the thirst mechanism works.

4 List and compare the major fluid compartments of the body.

5 Compare electrolyte differences in the major compartments.

6 Describe the bodily mechanisms regulating water balance.

7 Describe the mechanisms regulating sodium balances in the body.

8 Explain the relationship between sodium reabsorption and blood pressure.

9 Describe potassium regulation in the body.

10 Describe calcium and phosphate regulation in the body.

11 Describe magnesium and chloride regulation in the body.

12 Define electrolyte imbalances in the body.

13 Define pH and list the normal pH range of the blood.

14 Explain how each of the chemical buffer systems helps to regulate pH.

15 Describe how hemoglobin acts as a buffer.

16 Explain the role of the respiratory system in the regulation of pH.

17 Define the major renal mechanisms involved in pH regulation.

18 Define edema, dehydration, and overhydration; describe possible causes and effects.

19 Describe the causes and effects of respiratory acidosis and alkalosis.

20 Describe the causes and effects of metabolic acidosis and alkalosis.

False-color x-ray showing the ureters (red tubes) connecting the kidneys (green) to the urinary bladder (red). (CNRI/Science Photo Library/Photo Researchers, Inc.)

28

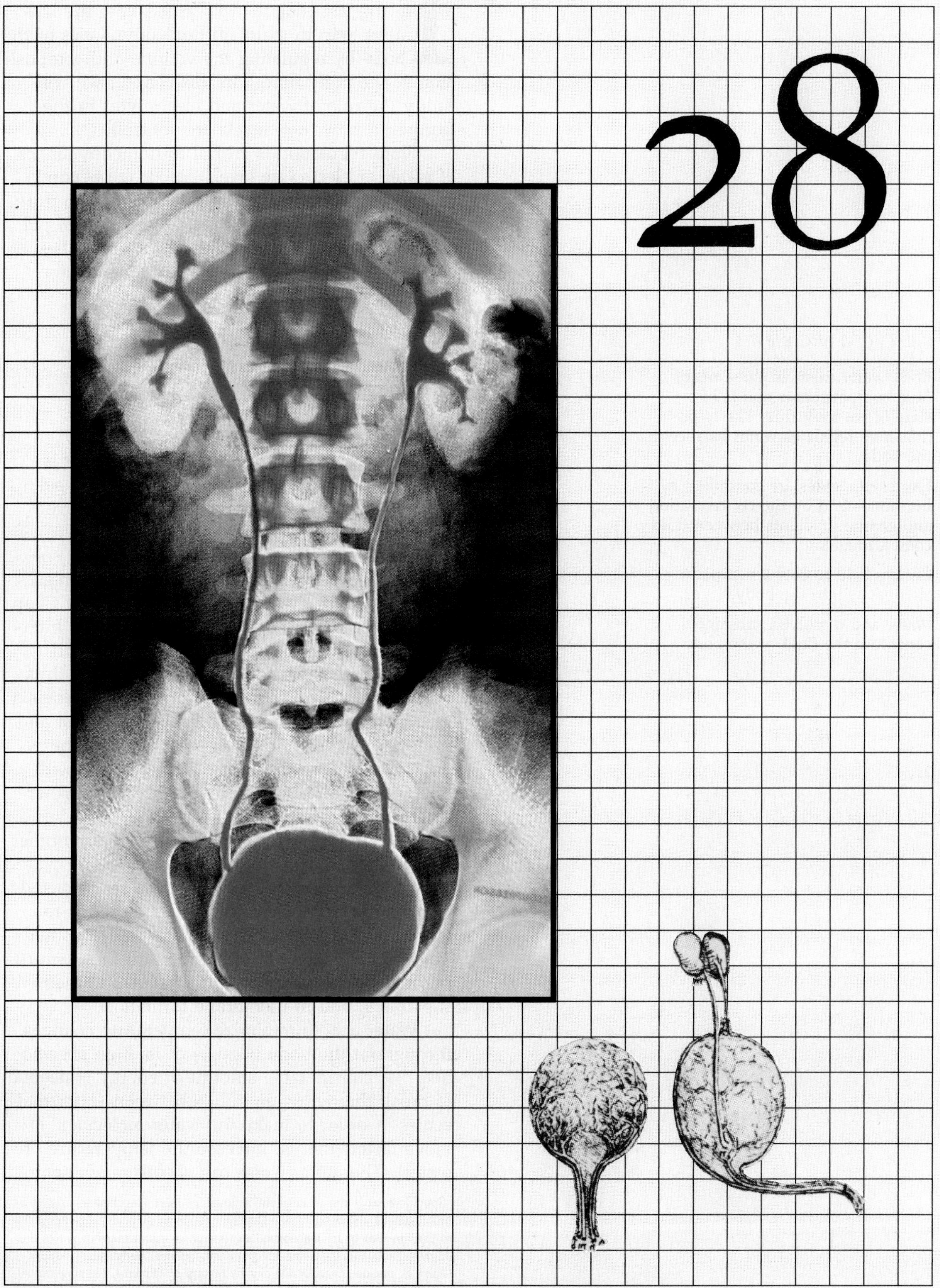

KEY CONCEPTS

Body water exists in three major fluid compartments and is in a state of constant flux. The hypothalamus regulates water balance in the body.

Electrolyte levels are controlled by hormones and by the concentration and charge gradients between fluid compartments.

Buffers help to counteract pH changes within the body.

Water and dissolved substances constitute the fluid of the body.

In the last chapter we learned how the kidneys help to maintain homeodynamics of the body by regulating the volume and composition of the body fluids. In this chapter we will study the role of water and electrolytes in the body and how their levels are controlled.

Fluid regulation is critical to homeodynamics. If water or electrolyte levels rise or fall beyond normal limits, many bodily functions fail to proceed at their normal rates. The regulation of pH is also crucial for normal body functioning because small changes in pH can produce major changes in metabolism.

Water is the universal biological solvent

Water is a constituent of all living things. It is often referred to as the universal biological solvent. Only liquid ammonia is able to dissolve more substances than water.

The importance of water as a biological solvent is due to its polar asymmetry and its high affinity for other water molecules. (Refer to Chapter 2.) As a polar molecule, water is highly interactive with other polar molecules and acts to compete with them for hydrogen bonding, thus weakening their electrostatic forces. This allows a greater number of polar molecules to coexist and undergo reactions; in a nonpolar solvent, these polar molecules would form strong bonds with one another and thus be unavailable for further reaction.

The affinity of water molecules for each other is very high. When nonpolar molecules are placed in water, the polar water molecules are attracted to other water molecules. This action tends to leave the nonpolar molecules clustered together. This clustering property is important in structuring macromolecules, binding enzymes to their substrates, and in membrane formation.

Water acts to minimize temperature changes throughout the body because of its high specific heat.[1] A considerable amount of energy is needed to break the hydrogen bonds between water molecules in order to make the water molecules move faster (that is, increase the temperature of water). Therefore, water can absorb much heat

[1]Specific heat is the ratio of the amount of heat absorbed in raising a unit mass of a substance one degree Celsius at a specified temperature to the amount of heat absorbed in raising an equal mass of water one degree Celsius at the same temperature. (Miller, Benjamin F., and Claire B. Keane. *Encyclopedia and Dictionary of Medicine, Nursing and Allied Health,* 4th ed. W.B. Saunders, Phila., 1987.)

without rapidly changing its own temperature. This property contributes to the thermally stable internal environment needed for chemical reactions to occur.

The adult human body consists of about 60% water by weight, depending upon age and the amount of body fat. The water content of the tissues of the body varies. Adipose tissue (fat) has the lowest percent of water; the skeleton has the second lowest water content. Skeletal muscle, skin, and the blood are among the tissues that have the highest content of water in the body. See Table 28-1.

Infants have a higher percent of water than adults—as much as 77%. The total water content of the body decreases most dramatically during the first 10 years and continues to decline through old age, at which time it may be only 45% of the total body weight. Men tend to have higher percentages of water (about 65%) than women (about 55%) mainly because of their increased muscle mass and lower amount of subcutaneous fat. Fat has less water content than any other body tissue. This also accounts for a lower than normal water percent of the body weight in obese people.

The water in the body has many important functions. It is the medium in which all of the chemical reactions in the body take place. Because many compounds dissociate into ions when in water, water is crucial in regulating chemical and electrical distributions in the cells. Water is important in transporting substances (such as nutrients and hormones) between fluid compartments and the cells, and it transports oxygen from the lungs to all the cells of the body. Water carries carbon dioxide from the cells to the lungs. It dilutes toxic substances and metabolic wastes and transports them to the liver and kidneys. It also functions in distributing heat throughout the body.

The water in the body is in a continual state of flux. Water shifts between the fluid compartments of the body, and thus a change in the water content of one compartment may affect the other compartments as well. Besides the exchange of water between these compartments, water is constantly being added to and lost from the body. Water input normally equals water output. This is critical in maintaining a balance of water between the compartments and in the functioning of many bodily reactions. About 90% of the water is added to the body through the gastrointestinal tract by the food and fluid ingested. The remaining 10%, called *metabolic water*, is added by various catabolic reactions in the body's cells. Water is lost mainly through the gastrointestinal tract (feces), the lungs (water vapor), the skin (diffu-

TABLE 28-1

Distribution of water and percentage of body weight in various tissues of 70-kg man*

Tissue	% of water	% of body weight	Liters of water per 70 kg
Skin	72	18	9.07
Muscle	75.6	41.7	22.10
Skeleton	22	15.9	2.45
Brain	74.8	2.0	1.05
Liver	68.3	2.3	1.03
Heart	79.2	0.5	0.28
Lungs	79.0	0.7	0.39
Kidneys	82.7	0.4	0.25
Spleen	75.8	0.2	0.10
Blood	83.0	8.0	4.65
Intestine	74.5	1.8	0.94
Adipose tissue	10	±10.0	0.70

*From Skelton, H.: Arch. Int. Med. 40:140, 1927.

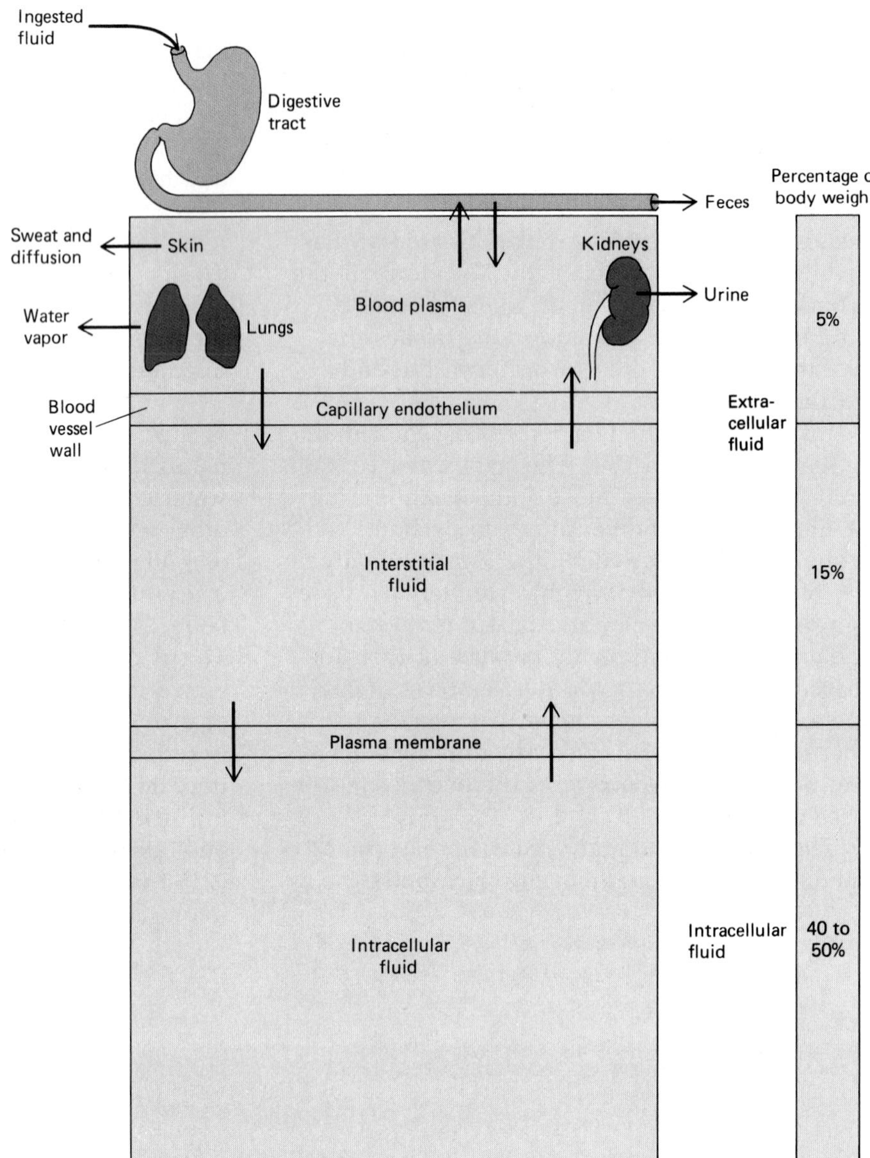

FIGURE 28-1

Major fluid compartments of the body.

TABLE 28-2

Daily fluid gain and loss

Fluid gain		Fluid loss	
Ingested			
Fluid	1700 ml	Kidneys	1650 ml
Food	750 ml	Skin	500 ml
Metabolic	200 ml	Lungs	350 ml
		GI tract	150 ml
Total fluid gain	2650 ml	Total fluid loss	2650 ml

Total fluid gain = Total fluid loss (normal)

sion and sweat), and the kidneys (urine) (Fig. 28-1 and Table 28-2). The amount of water lost in the urine is under hormonal control.

Body water exists in three major fluid compartments

Water and dissolved substances make up the **body fluid,** which totals about 40 liters. The three major fluid compartments of the body are the blood plasma, the interstitial fluid, and the intracellular fluid (Fig. 28-1 and Table 28-3). The blood plasma and the interstitial fluid together make up

TABLE 28-3

Total body water volume (40 liters, 60% of body weight)			
	Volume (liters)	% of body weight	% of total body water
Extracellular fluid (ECF)	15	20	37.5
Blood plasma	3	5	7.5
Interstitial fluid	12	15	30
Intracellular fluid (ICF)	25	40	62.5

most of the **extracellular fluid (ECF).** As the term implies, this fluid is located outside of the cells. Besides the blood plasma and the interstitial fluid, the extracellular fluid also includes the cerebrospinal fluid, synovial fluid, and fluid within the digestive tract, urinary tract, lymphatics, and compartments of the eye.

The **blood plasma** is the part of the body fluid that resides in the blood. It constitutes about 5% of the body weight and about 20% of the ECF. **Interstitial fluid,** or **interstitium,** is the fluid that surrounds the body's cells. The interstitial fluid compartment makes up about 15% of the body weight and about 80% of the ECF.

The walls of the blood vessels form the barrier between the plasma fluid and the interstitial fluid. The capillary wall is a single cell-layer thick and is generally permeable to water and small solutes but not to larger molecules such as proteins. Thus the blood plasma contains a higher concentration of proteins and large molecules than the interstitial fluid. Because water and small solutes (especially electrolytes) can freely be exchanged between the blood and the interstitium, water and electrolyte regulation of the blood by the kidneys also acts to regulate these substances in the interstitial fluid.

Fluid exchange between the blood and the interstitium depends mainly upon the hydrostatic and osmotic forces of both fluid compartments (Fig. 28-2). These forces were fully discussed in Chapter 21. The forces favoring the movement of water from the blood into the interstitial fluid include the capillary hydrostatic pressure (CHP), the interstitial fluid osmotic pressure (IFOP), and the negative interstitial fluid hydrostatic pressure (IFHP). The forces favoring the movement of water from the interstitial fluid into the blood constitute the capillary osmotic pressure (COP).

More water moves out of the capillary at its arteriolar end than moves in at its venular end. The excess fluid and proteins entering the interstitial compartment are taken up by the lymph vessels and eventually returned to the plasma (Fig. 28-2). Hence, the lymphatics serve as a connector system between the interstitial fluid and the plasma.

The **intracellular fluid** makes up about 40% of the body weight and about 62.5% of the total body water content. The intracellular fluid compartment is separated from the interstitial fluid by

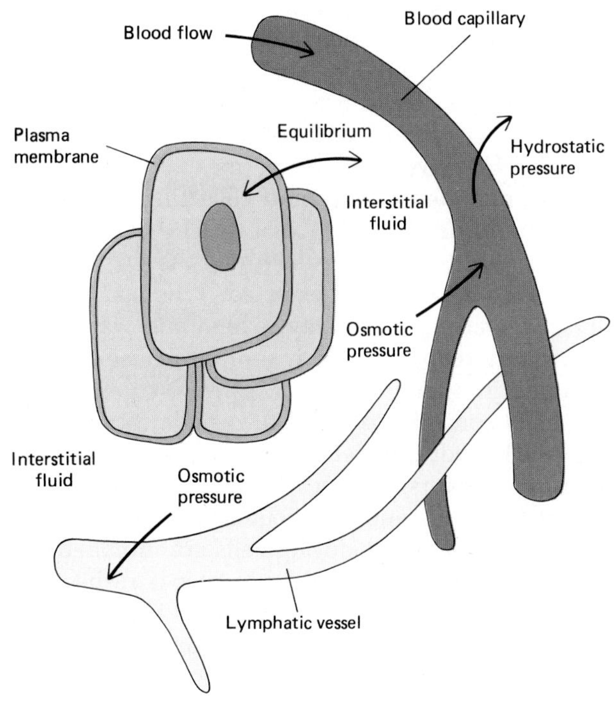

FIGURE 28-2

Fluid exchange between the fluid compartments results from differences in hydrostatic and osmotic pressure.

the plasma membrane of the body cells. This barrier allows the cells to maintain quite a different internal environment of substances than the interstitium. The plasma membrane prevents proteins and large molecules from freely diffusing from the cells. This results in a higher protein concentration within the cells than in the interstitium. The plasma membrane also contains special ion pumps and carriers which maintain electrolyte and metabolite concentrations within the cell. Generally, water movement is substantial in both directions, but most ion movement is restricted and involves active transport. Nutrients and O_2 move passively into the cell while wastes, including CO_2, move out of the cell.

Water balance centers are located in the hypothalamus

Mechanisms for the regulation of body fluid volume and extracellular osmolarity are coordinated by centers in the hypothalamus. The hypothalamus also receives input from the digestive tract for its regulation of thirst.

ADH REGULATES BODY FLUID VOLUME AND EXTRACELLULAR OSMOLARITY

The regulation of body fluid volume and extracellular osmolarity is under the control of **antidiuretic hormone (ADH),** which is produced in the hypothalamus. The mechanisms were fully discussed in Chapter 27 and will only be highlighted here. ADH increases water permeability in the distal convoluted tubules and collecting tubules of the kidneys. In the absence of ADH, water permeability in these tubules is low. Less water is reabsorbed and more is excreted. When ADH is present, water permeability is high and water reabsorption keeps pace with sodium reabsorption, resulting in a low volume of urine.

ADH controls extracellular osmolarity, and the ADH-producing cells in the hypothalamus act as osmoreceptors. Whenever there is an increase in water volume and extracellular osmolarity decreases, the ADH-producing cells are inhibited. Less ADH is secreted and less water is reabsorbed; thus more water is excreted. This reduces the total fluid volume in the body and returns extracellular osmolarity to normal.

> ↑ Water volume in body ⟶ ↓ extracellular osmolarity ⟶ ↓ ADH release ⟶ ↓ water reabsorption by kidneys ⟶ ↓ body fluid volume ⟶ ↑ extracellular osmolarity

When water is lost from the body or when extracellular osmolarity increases, the ADH-producing cells secrete larger amounts of ADH, which increases water reabsorption, increasing body fluid volume and decreasing extracellular osmolarity.

> ↓ Water volume in body ⟶ ↑ extracellular osmolarity ⟶ ↑ ADH release ⟶ ↑ water reabsorption by kidneys ⟶ ↑ body fluid volume ⟶ ↓ extracellular osmolarity

THE HYPOTHALAMIC THIRST CENTER ALSO CONTAINS OSMORECEPTORS

Although water intake varies considerably in people and is subject to habit and social mores, it does average about 2450 milliliters daily. The conscious desire for water, which we call **thirst,** is the major regulator of water intake. The thirst center is located in the hypothalamus. Even though the mechanism for thirst is not fully understood, it is believed that osmoreceptors in the thirst center respond to changes in extracellular osmolarity. When water is added to the body and the osmolarity decreases, the osmoreceptors are inhibited. Impulses are transmitted to higher brain centers and the sensation of thirst ceases.

> ↑ Plasma volume ⟶ ↓ extracellular osmolarity ⟶ thirst center osmoreceptor inhibition ⟶ input to higher brain centers ⟶ ↓ thirst sensation

Thirst can cease even before the water is absorbed into the extracellular fluid. It takes up to 1 hour before ingested water is absorbed and distributed to the fluid compartments. How does a person know what amount of fluid to drink to maintain extracellular osmolarity and not create an electrolyte imbalance? A temporary relief of thirst occurs due to mechanisms initiated within the digestive tract.

Initially a moistening of the mucosa of the mouth and pharynx does quench thirst, but more importantly, stretch receptors in the GI tract are stimulated by water intake and send sensory messages to the hypothalamus to inhibit the thirst center. The temporary relief of thirst that results actually takes place before much water has been absorbed from the intestines.

↑ Water intake ⟶ ↑ GI tract distension ⟶ ↑ stretch receptor stimulation ⟶ ↑ sensory input to thirst center ⟶ inhibition of thirst center ⟶ input to higher brain centers ⟶ ↓ thirst sensation

When extracellular osmolarity increases, the thirst center osmoreceptors are stimulated and a sensation of thirst occurs. See Figure 28-3. This is also enhanced by a dry mouth and pharynx. The dryness occurs because increased extracellular osmolarity acts to decrease saliva secretion so the plasma can retain more fluid.

↑ Extracellular osmolarity ⟶ ↓ saliva secretion ⟶ ↑ dryness of mouth ⟶ ↑ thirst sensation

A decreased blood volume also causes baroreceptor activation, which may provide sensory stimulation to the thirst center. In addition, a decrease in blood volume activates the renin-angiotensin-aldosterone pathway. The increases in angiotensin II stimulate brain areas that signal the thirst center, resulting in an increased thirst sensation.

See Focus on Fluid Imbalance.

FOCUS ON . . . Fluid imbalance

Edema is a condition in which there is an excess of fluid within the interstitial compartment. This excess fluid leads to tissue swelling (see figure). Edema may result when high blood pressure causes the hydrostatic pressure of the blood to increase to such an extent as to force more water out of the capillaries and into the interstitium. Edema is common when there is a lymphatic blockage, with decreased fluid and protein being returned to the venous blood. Inflammation, especially in the kidneys, may result in edema by causing an increased capillary permeability and protein leakage into the interstitium. The increased oncotic pressure of the interstitium that results will pull water into the interstitial fluid and cause swelling.

Dehydration is a condition of body fluid depletion. It may result from a variety of conditions. In *hypertonic dehydration,* water is lost from the body at a higher rate than are electrolytes. This causes blood pressure to fall and the blood to become more viscous, possibly leading to heart failure. Hypertonic dehydration may result from severe diarrhea or vomiting, excessive sweating, and burns. In *isotonic dehydration* there is no noticeable decrease in electrolyte concentration with the fluid loss. Isotonic dehydration may also occur from excessive vomiting or diarrhea, burns, surgical removal of fluid, or hemorrhage. *Hypotonic dehydration* occurs when both fluid and electrolyte levels become depressed. Any input of pure water during a dehydrated state will cause a lowering of the concentration of electrolytes. Vomiting of gastric contents and persistent nausea with an inability to drink can lead to hypotonic dehydration.

Overhydration and extreme overhydration, called **water intoxication,** result when the water concentration of the intracellular compartment increases. The most common cause of these conditions is a loss of sodium from the interstitial fluid. This sodium loss decreases the osmotic pressure of the interstitial fluid and more water moves into the cells. Excessive sweating and severe vomiting and diarrhea can lead to overhydration. Overhydration can lead to neurological dysfunctions and circulatory shock.

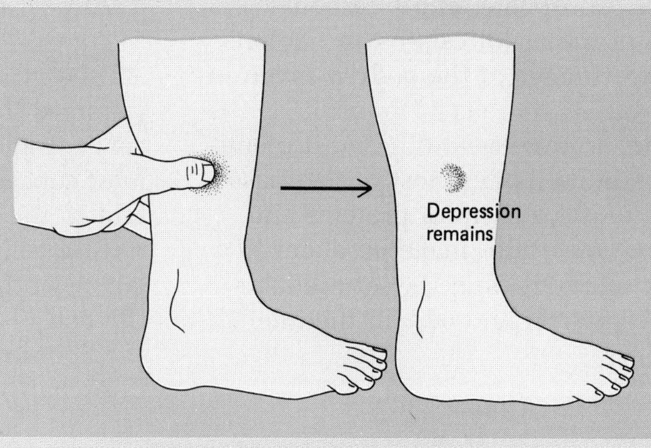

Test for edema. After compressing thumb on calf for a few seconds, if a depression remains upon removal of thumb it indicates fluid retention in the tissues. Thus edema is present.

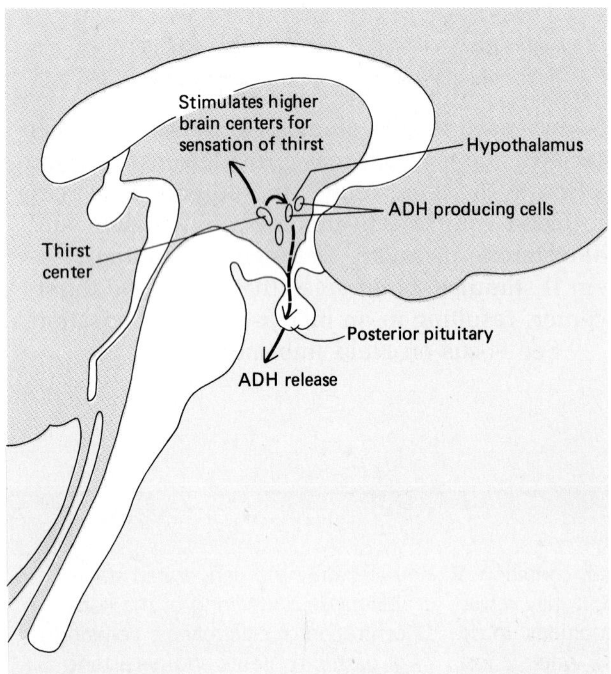

FIGURE 28-3

Thirst center of hypothalamus. Increase in extracellular osmolarity (or decreases in extracellular volume) stimulate the osmoreceptors of the thirst center. The thirst center then signals higher brain centers resulting in a sensation of thirst. The thirst center also stimulates ADH-producing cells.

Electrolytes form ions in solution

An **electrolyte** is a chemical that dissociates into ions in solution and can conduct an electric current. The ions are either positively charged **(cations)** or negatively charged **(anions).** The major electrolytes of the body are sodium, potassium, calcium, chloride, phosphate, and bicarbonate. The distribution of the major cations and anions in the fluid compartments of the body is given in Figure 28-4.

Although the electrolytes are the most plentiful of the solutes in the body, most of the mass of dissolved solute is made up of proteins and lipids. These large molecules make up about 97% of the dissolved solute mass in the intracellular fluid, 90% in the plasma, and 60% in the interstitial fluid.

Sodium balance involves aldosterone

Sodium is the major cation of the blood plasma and the interstitium, making up about 90% of the total extracellular cation concentration. It has an extracellular concentration 14 times that of its intracellular concentration (Fig. 28-4). It plays a crucial role in water and electrolyte balance and the excitability of neurons and muscle cells. Sodium levels of the body are closely regulated by the kidneys.

Sodium is freely filtered at the glomerulus, and usually most of the filtered sodium is actively reabsorbed by the proximal convoluted tubules. Sodium excretion is directly influenced by the changes in the glomerular filtration rate (GFR). The major factors controlling the GFR are the glomerular blood pressure and sympathetic nerve stimulation of the renal afferent arterioles.

The adrenal cortex produces a hormone that helps to regulate sodium reabsorption of the distal convoluted and collecting tubules of the kidneys. This hormone, **aldosterone,** increases sodium reabsorption by these renal tubules. Aldosterone secretion is controlled by a complex mechanism called *the renin-angiotensin-aldosterone pathway*. (Refer to Chapter 27 and Figure 27-12.) Aldosterone, in conjunction with ADH, helps to regulate fluid output from the body. When both are present, more water is reabsorbed along with the sodium.

An increased blood pressure causes the release of **atrial natriuretic factor** from the atria of the heart. This hormone inhibits renin and aldosterone release and stimulates renal excretion of sodium. These events enhance water loss and help return the blood pressure to normal.

Potassium balance also involves aldosterone

As shown in Figure 28-4, potassium is the major cation of the intracellular fluid; its intracellular concentration is 28 times greater than its extracellular concentration. Potassium is extremely important to the functioning of excitable cells (neurons, muscle cells, receptors), in intracellular fluid regulation, and in pH regulation. Potassium input into the body is usually equal to potassium output.

Sodium reabsorption by aldosterone is usually in exchange for potassium or hydrogen ions.

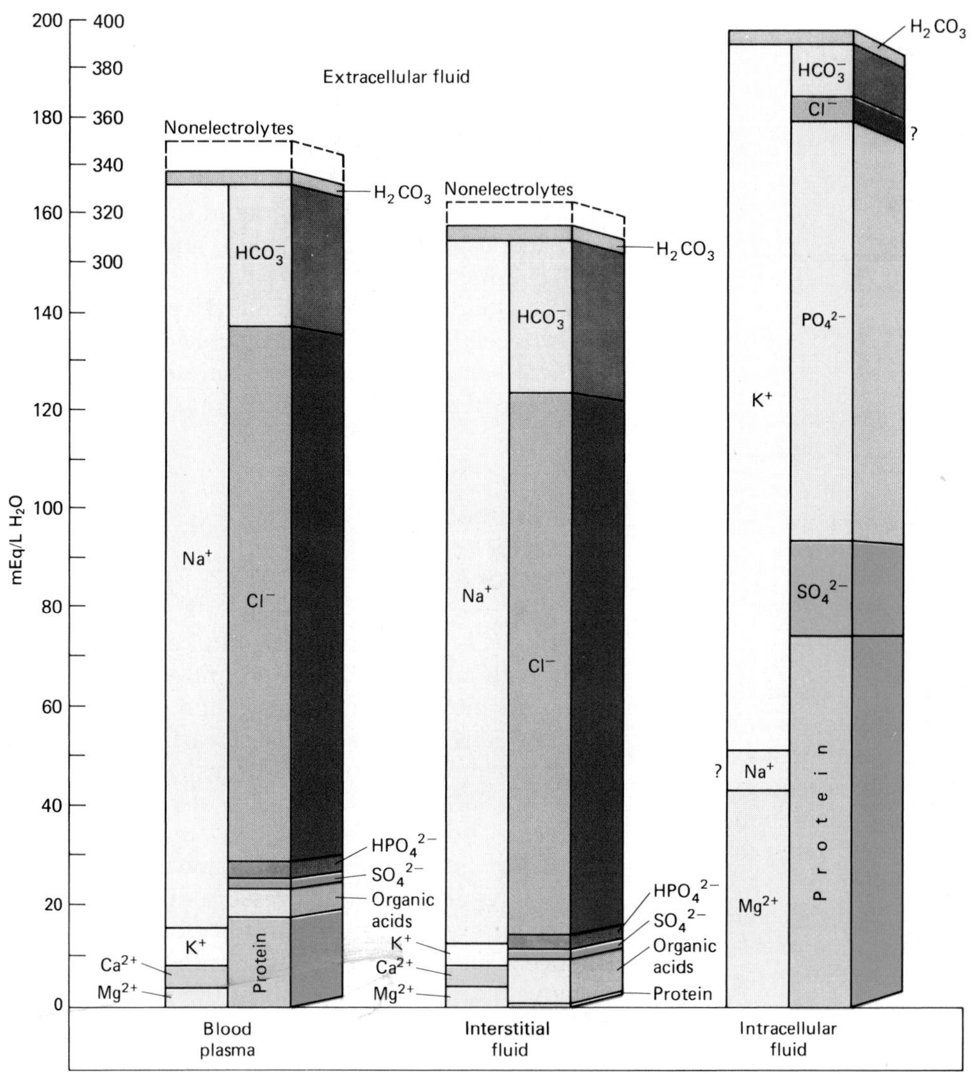

FIGURE 28-4

Solutes in the fluid compartments. The left side of the scale gives amounts of individual solutes. The right side of the scale gives the sum of cations and anions.

Therefore, an increase in aldosterone release will increase sodium reabsorption and also increase potassium (and hydrogen) excretion.

When the potassium levels of the extracellular fluid increase, more potassium will be filtered and less will be actively reabsorbed. Potassium is able to be both reabsorbed and secreted by the kidneys, so the amount of potassium excreted will also depend on an increased amount of it being secreted into the renal tubules. Another factor influencing potassium balance in the body is aldosterone. High levels of potassium in the interstitium also stimulate the release of aldosterone. Aldosterone not only increases sodium reabsorption by the kidneys, it also stimulates potassium secretion and excretion. See Figure 28-5 and Chapters 18 and 27.

Calcium and phosphate balance involves parathyroid hormone and calcitonin

Calcium is found mainly in the extracellular compartments, whereas phosphate is the most abundant intracellular anion (see Fig. 28-4). Calcium and phosphate are important to the integrity of the skeletal system and the teeth. Calcium is also

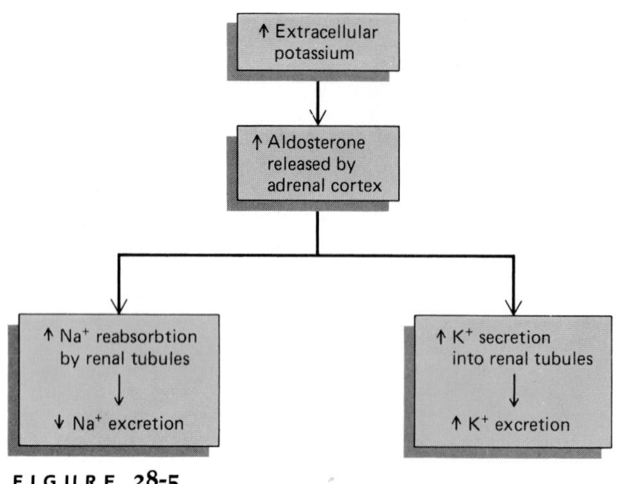

FIGURE 28-5

The effect of aldosterone on sodium reabsorption and potassium excretion.

important in synaptic transmission, blood clotting, and muscle contraction. Low levels of calcium in the body cause an increased excitability in nerves and muscles. Phosphate is required in the synthesis of nucleic acids and high-energy compounds. It also is an important buffer in red blood cells and in the renal tubules.

When the levels of calcium in the plasma become too low, the parathyroid glands release **parathyroid hormone.** (Refer to Chapter 18.) This hormone causes an increase in calcium and phosphate levels in the extracellular fluid by releasing calcium and phosphate from the bones and teeth. Parathyroid hormone also decreases renal calcium excretion.

↓ Calcium in plasma ⟶ ↑ parathyroid hormone ⟶ ↑ calcium in plasma

When the calcium levels of the blood become too high, the thyroid gland releases the hormone **calcitonin,** which lowers the calcium concentration of the plasma. Calcitonin inhibits the release of calcium and phosphate by the bones and the absorption of calcium from the gastrointestinal tract. It also increases the amount of calcium excreted from the kidneys.

↑ Calcium in plasma ⟶ ↑ calcitonin ⟶ ↓ calcium in plasma

Magnesium balance involves aldosterone

Most magnesium (Mg^{2+}) is found in the intracellular fluid and in bone (Fig. 28-4). Within cells Mg^{2+} functions in the Na-K pump and as an enzymatic cofactor. It plays a role in muscle contraction, action potential conduction, and bone and teeth production.

Aldosterone controls Mg^{2+} concentrations in the extracellular fluid. Low Mg^{2+} levels result in an increased aldosterone secretion, and the aldosterone increases Mg^{2+} reabsorption by the kidneys.

Chloride balance is indirectly regulated by aldosterone

Chloride (Cl^-) is the most plentiful extracellular anion with an extracellular concentration 26 times that of its intracellular concentration (Fig. 28-4). Chloride ions are able to diffuse easily across plasma membranes and their transport is closely linked to Na^+ movement, which also explains the indirect role of aldosterone in Cl^- regulation. When Na^+ is reabsorbed, Cl^- follows passively. It helps to regulate osmotic pressure differences between fluid compartments and is essential in pH balance. The chloride shift within the blood helps to move bicarbonate ions out of the red blood cells and into the plasma for transport. In the gastric mucosa, Cl^- and H^+ combine to form hydrochloric acid.

See Focus on Electrolyte Imbalance.

The pH balance utilizes buffer systems

pH is a measurement of the hydrogen concentration of a solution. Lower pH values indicate a higher hydrogen concentration, or a higher acidity. Higher pH values indicate a lower hydrogen ion concentration, or a higher alkalinity. An alkaline solution is also referred to as a basic solution. Therefore, hydrogen ion balance is often referred to as pH balance, or acid-base balance. (Refer to Chapter 2 for a discussion of acids, bases, and pH.)

FOCUS ON . . . Electrolyte imbalance

Ion	Condition caused by excess	Typical cause	Effects	Treatment
Na^+	Hypernatremia	Hyperaldosteronism, hypertonic dehydration, excessive salt intake	Mental impairment, coma, probably hypertension	Adrenalectomy, administration of water, dialysis (depending on cause)
K^+	Hyperkalemia	Hypoaldosteronism, loss of K^+ from damaged cells	Cardiac arrhythmia, skeletal muscle paralysis	Administration of aldosterone, administration of insulin (causes K^+ to enter body cells), dialysis, administration of ion-exchange resin orally or rectally
Ca^{2+}	Hypercalcemia	Hyperparathyroidism	Kidney stones; muscular weakness	Parathyroidectomy
Mg^{2+}	Hypermagnesemia	Aldosterone deficiency, ingestion of large amounts of Mg^{2+}-containing antacids	Central nervous system depression, respiratory depression, hypotension, possible coma	Administration of aldosterone
Cl^-	Hyperchloremia	Fluid deficit compensated for by water (and Cl^-) reabsorption	Metabolic acidosis, rapid respirations, stupor, loss of consciousness	Treatment usually corresponds to that for metabolic acidosis

Ion	Condition caused by deficiency	Typical cause	Effects	Treatment
Na^+	Hyponatremia	Hypoaldosteronism, hypotonic dehydration, blood pH disturbance	Muscular weakness, stupor	Administration of Na^+; administration of aldosterone
K^+	Hypokalemia	Hyperaldosteronism, diuretic use	K^+ leaves cells and is replaced by Na^+, with disturbances of action potential. Ascending skeletal muscle paralysis, cardiac arrhythmia	Adrenalectomy, administration of K^+
Ca^{2+}	Hypocalcemia	Dietary deficiency, hypoparathyroidism	Muscular cramps, convulsive tetany	Administration of Ca^{2+}, administration of parathyroid hormone
Mg^{2+}	Hypomagnesemia	Alcoholism, severe malnutrition, loss of contents of intestines	Neuromuscular hyperirritability, tremor, tetany, possible convulsions, cardiac arrhythmias	Administration of Mg^{2+}
Cl^-	Hypochloremia	Severe vomiting, hypokalemia, dehydration, some diuretics	Metabolic alkalosis, muscle spasms, reduced respiratory rate, possible coma	Administration of Cl^-

Regulation of pH is critically important to health

Hydrogen ion regulation in the fluid compartments of the body is of critical importance to health. Even a slight change in hydrogen ion concentration can result in a marked alteration in the rate of chemical reactions. Changes in hydrogen ion concentration can also affect the distribution of ions such as sodium, potassium, and calcium. It also can affect the structure and function of proteins.

The normal pH of the arterial blood is 7.4, whereas that of the venous blood is 7.35. The lower pH of the venous blood is due to the higher concentration of carbon dioxide in venous blood. When the pH changes in the arterial blood, two conditions may result—acidosis or alkalosis. **Acidosis** is a condition occurring when the hydrogen ion concentration of the arterial blood increases and, therefore, the pH decreases. **Alkalosis** is the condition occurring when the hydrogen ion concentration in the arterial blood decreases and the pH increases.

$\uparrow$ Hydrogen ions $\longrightarrow$ $\downarrow$ pH (acidosis)

$\downarrow$ Hydrogen ions $\longrightarrow$ $\uparrow$ pH (alkalosis)

Sources of hydrogen ions in the body include H_2CO_3 (from CO_2 combining with H_2O), H_2SO_4 (a byproduct in the breakdown of proteins), H_3PO_4 (a byproduct of protein and phospholipid metabolism), ketone bodies from fat metabolism, and lactic acid (a product formed in skeletal muscle during exercise). See Figure 28-6.

Mechanisms for pH regulation include chemical buffers, the lungs, and the kidneys

About half of all the acid formed or introduced into the body is neutralized by the ingestion of alkaline foods. The remaining acid is neutralized by three major mechanisms of the body: chemical buffers, the respiratory system, and the kidneys. **Chemical buffers** have an instantaneous effect on pH changes. They are very effective in minimizing pH changes but do not entirely eliminate the change. Within cells, chemical buffers generally take about 2 to 4 hours to minimize changes in pH. The **respiratory system** minimizes pH changes; the effects occur within minutes. **Renal regulation** of pH is able to completely return the pH to normal and requires from hours to several days.

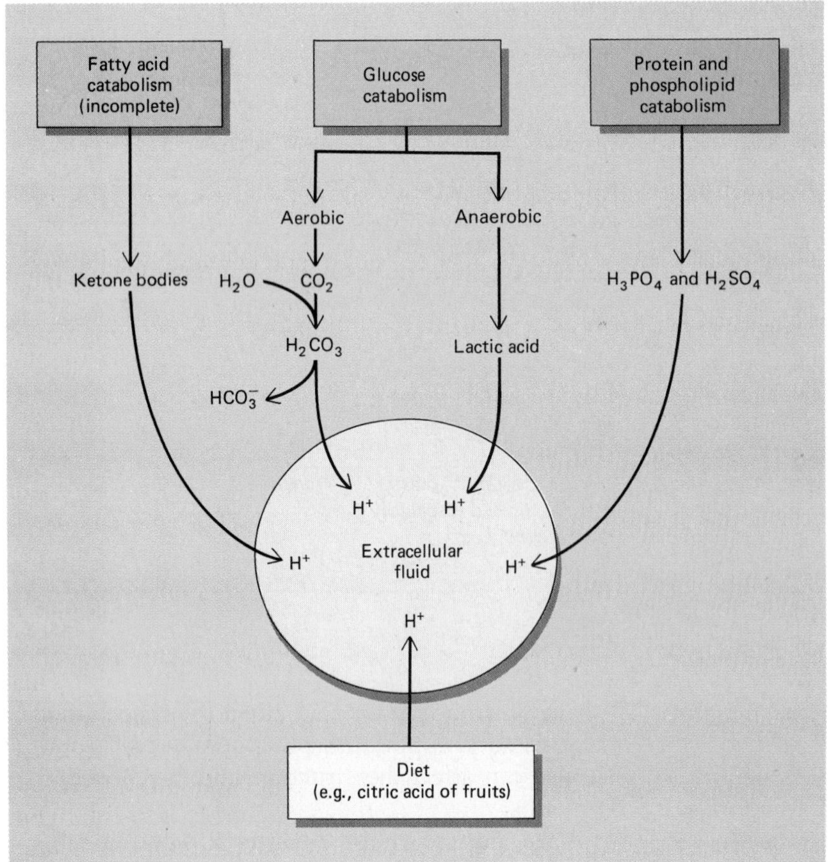

FIGURE 28-6

Major sources of hydrogen ions in the body.

CHEMICAL BUFFERS MINIMIZE pH CHANGES

A **buffer** is a solution of two or more chemical compounds that is capable of preventing a marked change in hydrogen ion concentration when either an acid or a base is added. (Refer to Chapter 2.) The major chemical buffering systems of the body are the bicarbonate buffer system, the protein buffer system, and the phosphate buffer system. See Figure 28-7. In the **bicarbonate buffer system,** the two chemical compounds preventing a marked change in hydrogen ion concentration are carbonic acid (H_2CO_3) and sodium bicarbonate ($NaHCO_3$). If a strong acid is added, it reacts with $NaHCO_3$ to produce a weak acid (H_2CO_3). Using the addition of hydrochloric acid (HCl) as an example, the following reaction takes place:

$$HCl + NaHCO_3 \longrightarrow H_2CO_3 + NaCl$$

This conversion of the strong acid to a weak acid serves to minimize pH changes because the carbonic acid (H_2CO_3) dissociates to a far lesser degree than hydrochloric acid and contributes far fewer hydrogen ions to the solution.

If a strong alkaline solution is added, it reacts with H_2CO_3 to produce a weak base. Using the addition of sodium hydroxide (NaOH) as the example, the following reaction occurs:

$$NaOH + H_2CO_3 \longrightarrow NaHCO_3 + H_2O$$

This reaction results in a weaker base, which minimizes any rise in pH.

The **protein buffer system** is the most plentiful buffering system in the blood and tissue cells. Proteins are able to take hydrogen ions out of solution and bind them to their structure, thereby decreasing the hydrogen ion concentration of the solution and minimizing pH changes. Proteins are made up of amino acids containing at least one carboxyl group (COOH) and one amine group (NH_2). This makes proteins capable of buffering both acids and bases.

The carboxyl group of the amino acid can dissociate and act like an acid:

$$\begin{array}{c} \quad\;\; R \\ \quad\;\; | \\ NH_2\text{—}C\text{—}COO^- + H^+ \\ \quad\;\; | \\ \quad\;\; H \end{array}$$

In this ionized form, the hydrogen (H^+) ions can attract hydroxyl (OH^-) ions to form water. This reduces the pH when excessive OH^- ions are present.

The amine group (NH_2) can bind with a hydrogen ion and act as a base:

$$\begin{array}{c} \quad\quad R \\ \quad\quad | \\ COOH\text{—}C\text{—}NH_3^+ \\ \quad\quad | \\ \quad\quad H \end{array}$$

This can increase the pH when excessive H^+ ions are present.

The proteins within cells can also bind hydrogen to minimize its effect within the cells. Hemoglobin is a type of intracellular chemical buffer. Carbon dioxide in the blood enters into the red blood cells. The concentration of carbon dioxide is a major contributor to the hydrogen ion concentration in the blood. Within the blood the carbon dioxide undergoes a reaction with water to form carbonic acid, which can dissociate into hydrogen ions and bicarbonate ions. The reaction is as follows:

$$CO_2 + H_2O \rightleftharpoons H_2CO_3 \rightleftharpoons H^+ + HCO_3^-$$

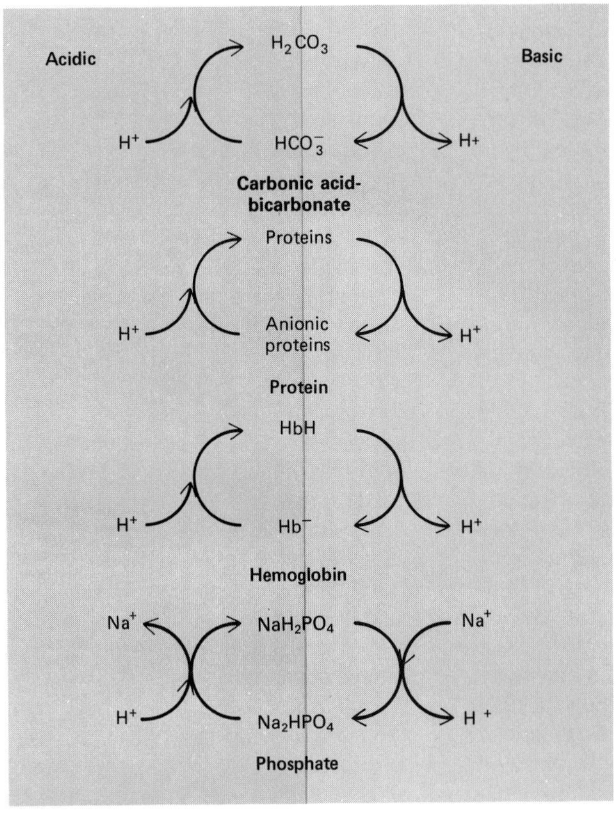

FIGURE 28-7

The major chemical buffers in the body.

When the concentration of CO_2 increases in the blood, this reaction shifts to the right and the concentration of hydrogen ions increases. A high concentration of carbonic anhydrase in the red blood cells catalyzes the conversion of carbon dioxide to carbonic acid by the addition of water. Bicarbonate resulting from the dissociation of carbonic acid passes into the plasma and is carried in this way.

The hydrogen ions formed are buffered by the hemoglobin. When oxyhemoglobin releases oxygen, the reduced hemoglobin possesses a net negative charge that can bind hydrogen ions.

The **phosphate buffer system** allows a buffering similar to that of the bicarbonate buffer system. Sodium dihydrogen phosphate (NaH_2PO_4) acts as a weak acid to buffer strong bases. Sodium monohydrogen phosphate (Na_2HPO_4) acts as a weak base to buffer strong acids. In the kidneys, secreted hydrogen ions combine with Na_2HPO_4 (weak base) to form NaH_2PO_4 (weak acid), which is excreted in the urine.

THE RESPIRATORY SYSTEM ACTS AS A BUFFER BY CHANGING THE RATE OF VENTILATION

Changing the rate of ventilation of air into and out of the lungs can also change the carbon dioxide concentration of the blood. In the reaction

$$CO_2 + H_2O \rightleftharpoons H_2CO_3 \rightleftharpoons H^+ + HCO_3^-$$

the more CO_2 in the blood, the more carbonic acid is formed and the more H^+ ions are formed. Whenever the CO_2 levels of the blood decrease, the reaction shifts to the left and fewer H^+ ions are present. By the removal of CO_2 from the lungs, changes in the dissociation of H_2CO_3 can

FOCUS ON . . . Acid–base imbalance

The normal pH of the blood ranges from 7.45 to 7.35. When the pH of the blood falls below 7.35, the condition of acidosis exists. When the pH of the blood rises above 7.45, alkalosis exists. The states of acidosis and alkalosis may be defined by the conditions causing them. Acidosis may result from a respiratory cause (respiratory acidosis) or a metabolic cause (metabolic acidosis). Alkalosis may result from a respiratory cause (respiratory alkalosis) or a metabolic cause (metabolic alkalosis).

The primary cause of **respiratory acidosis** is hypoventilation. Decreased ventilations allow for a build-up of carbon dioxide (CO_2) in the blood. With the increased CO_2, there is an increase in carbonic acid and in hydrogen ions. The increased hydrogen ions lower the pH. Hypoventilation may occur due to respiratory diseases such as emphysema, bronchitis, and pulmonary edema. The treatment of respiratory acidosis involves increasing the expiration of carbon dioxide.

The primary cause of **respiratory alkalosis** is hyperventilation. Increased ventilations result in a decrease of CO_2 in the blood. The decreased CO_2 leads to a decrease in hydrogen ions and the pH increases. Hyperventilation may occur due to a stimulation of the medullary respiratory centers by such factors as high altitude, stress, and aspirin overdose. Treatment of respiratory alkalosis involves increasing the carbon dioxide concentration in the blood.

Metabolic acidosis is caused by either an increase in acidic metabolites in the body or a decrease in the acid-buffering capacity. Ketosis, common in diabetes mellitus, and intense exercise both increase the level of metabolic acids. This can lower the pH. Renal failure, diarrhea, and vomiting duodenal contents can also cause metabolic acidosis by lowering the acid-buffering capacity of the body especially by the loss of bicarbonate ions. Metabolic acidosis causes a depression of neural transmission, which leads to a depression of the central nervous system. The person suffering from metabolic acidosis may experience hyperventilation, erratic muscular coordination, disorientation, and coma. Treatments include the administration of sodium bicarbonate and the correction of the underlying cause.

Metabolic alkalosis is caused by a decrease in acids from the body or an excess of alkaline chemicals. This may result from the vomiting of gastric juices or a $NaHCO_3$ injection. Both bring about an increase in pH. Metabolic alkalosis stimulates neural transmission and overexcites the central nervous system. Some symptoms of metabolic alkalosis include hypoventilation, overreaction to normal stimuli, tetany, confusion, and convulsions. Possible treatments include the administration of chlorides and the correction of the underlying cause.

be minimized. High CO_2 levels in the blood result in more hydrogen ions formed. Hydrogen ions stimulate the respiratory centers of the medulla of the brain. Ventilation increases, and more CO_2 is exhaled, which lowers the hydrogen ion concentration.

$\uparrow$ Plasma $CO_2 \longrightarrow \uparrow H^+$ ions $\longrightarrow \uparrow$ medullary respiratory center stimulation $\longrightarrow$ $\uparrow$ ventilation $\longrightarrow \uparrow CO_2$ expelled $\longrightarrow \downarrow H^+$ ions

Low CO_2 levels in the blood result in fewer hydrogen ions. The resultant rise in pH causes the respiratory centers of the medulla to decrease ventilation, which will cause an increase in CO_2 in the blood and a rise in hydrogen ion concentration (lower pH).

$\downarrow$ Plasma $CO_2 \longrightarrow \downarrow H^+$ ions $\longrightarrow \downarrow$ medullary respiratory center stimulation $\longrightarrow$ $\downarrow$ ventilation $\longrightarrow \downarrow CO_2$ expelled $\longrightarrow \uparrow H^+$ ions

RENAL REGULATION RETURNS pH TO NORMAL

The kidneys eliminate excess acids and bases and return pH to normal. Hydrogen ions are secreted into the tubular cells from the blood and enter the tubular lumen, causing bicarbonate reabsorption. The H^+ ions in the lumen are buffered and expelled as H_2O (bicarbonate reabsorption), NaH_2PO_4 (phosphate buffer system), and NH_4Cl (ammonia buffer system). These renal pH buffer systems are discussed in detail in Chapter 27.

See Focus on Acid–Base Imbalance.

Summary

I. Water is the universal biological solvent.
   A. Water is a polar molecule with a high specific heat.
   B. The adult human body is about 60% water.
   C. Water is added to the body by food and fluid ingestion and by water formed in cellular metabolism.
   D. Water is lost by the body through the GI tract (feces), the lungs (water vapor), the skin (diffusion and sweat), and the kidneys (urine).

II. The three major fluid compartments of the body are blood plasma, interstitial fluid, and intracellular fluid.
   A. The blood plasma and interstitial fluid are extracellular fluids. Extracellular fluid makes up about one-third of the body fluid.
   B. Intracellular fluid is the fluid located within the cells of the body and it makes up about two-thirds of the body fluid.

III. ADH functions to regulate water balance in the body.
   A. ADH is produced in the hypothalamus and released by the posterior pituitary. The cells producing ADH are in the supraoptic nuclei of the hypothalamus.
   B. The supraoptic nuclei receive input from baroreceptors in the body. Baroreceptors monitor blood pressure.
   C. The thirst center is located in the hypothalamus.

IV. The major electrolytes of the body are sodium, potassium, calcium, phosphate, magnesium, and chloride.
   A. Sodium levels of the blood are regulated by a renin-angiotensin-aldosterone mechanism.
   B. Potassium levels are controlled by aldosterone.
   C. Calcium and phosphate levels are regulated by parathyroid hormone and calcitonin.
   D. Magnesium levels are regulated by aldosterone.
   E. Chloride levels are indirectly regulated by aldosterone because Cl^- generally follows Na^+.

V. pH is a measurement of the hydrogen ion concentration of a solution. Low pH values represent a high hydrogen ion concentration; high pH values represent a low hydrogen ion concentration.
   A. The normal pH of the arterial blood is 7.4. The normal pH of venous blood is 7.35.
   B. Acidosis occurs when hydrogen ions increase and pH decreases. Alkalosis occurs when hydrogen ions decrease and pH increases.

VI. The major mechanisms for regulating pH changes in the body are chemical buffers, the respiratory system, and the kidneys.
   A. Chemical buffers minimize pH changes; they include the bicarbonate buffer system, the protein buffer system, and the phosphate buffer system.
   B. Within red blood cells, hemoglobin can bind hydrogen ions and thereby buffer pH changes.
   C. Increases in ventilation reduce hydrogen ion concentrations and raise pH. Decreases in ventilation raise hydrogen ion concentrations and lower pH.
   D. The kidneys regulate pH through the tubular secretion of hydrogen ions and the reabsorption of bicarbonate, a phosphate buffer system, and an ammonia buffer system.

Post-test

1. Water minimizes temperature changes due to its high ______ ______.
2. Among body tissues with the lowest percent of water by weight is ______; the body tissues with the highest water content are ______ and ______.
3. Women have a lower percentage of water than men because they usually have more ______ ______ and less ______.
4. The fluid located outside the tissue cells is called ______ fluid; the fluid within the cells is called the ______ fluid.
5. The thirst center is located in the ______.
6. A temporary quenching of thirst before water is absorbed into the body occurs mainly due to the wetting of the ______ and ______ and input from the stretching of the walls of the ______.
7. The major cation of the extracellular fluid is ______; the major anion of the extracellular fluid is ______.
8. The major cation of the intracellular fluid is ______; the major anion of the intracellular fluid is ______.
9. Sodium levels are regulated mainly by the adrenocortical hormone ______.

10. An increase in Na^+ reabsorption by aldosterone also increases the ______ of potassium by the kidneys.
11. The ______ hormone increases calcium concentrations in the blood.
12. The hormone ______ decreases calcium concentrations in the blood.
13. ______ is a condition of increased pH; ______ is a condition of decreased pH.
14. The ______ buffers instantaneously minimize pH changes in the body.
15. The ______ buffering system is the most plentiful one in the blood and tissue cells.
16. The respiratory system acts as a buffer by changing the rate of ______.
17. The kidneys secrete H^+ ions, which are buffered by the ______ buffer system and the ______ buffer system.

Review questions

1. Explain why water is an excellent solvent.
2. How is water gained and lost by the body?
3. What are the fluid compartments of the body and what percent of the total fluid of the body do they contain?
4. Describe the thirst mechanism.
5. List the major cations and anions in each of the fluid compartments.
6. How does ADH regulate water balance in the body?
7. Give the mechanism involved in the regulation of extracellular osmolarity.
8. Describe the regulation of sodium, potassium, calcium, phosphate, magnesium, and chloride in the body.
9. List the mechanisms of the body used to regulate pH changes.
10. Describe the chemical buffers of the body.
11. Describe how hemoglobin buffers pH changes.
12. Describe how the lungs help to minimize pH changes.
13. List the renal mechanisms for regulating pH changes.
14. Define edema, dehydration, and overhydration.
15. Define respiratory acidosis and alkalosis. Define metabolic acidosis and alkalosis. How does respiratory acidosis (alkalosis) differ from metabolic acidosis (alkalosis)?

Post-test answers

1. specific heat 2. fat (adipose tissue); skeletal muscle, skin 3. subcutaneous fat; muscle 4. extracellular; intracellular 5. hypothalamus 6. mouth, pharynx; GI tract 7. sodium; chloride 8. potassium; phosphate 9. aldosterone 10. excretion 11. parathyroid 12. calcitonin 13. Alkalosis; acidosis 14. chemical 15. protein 16. ventilation 17. phosphate, ammonia

PERPETUATING THE HUMAN SPECIES

Each body system actively works to maintain homeostasis. The reproductive system is not always homeostatic on the level of an individual organism, as anyone who has been pregnant will probably acknowledge. In fact, during pregnancy, the other systems must serve the reproductive system, compensating for the imbalances caused by reproduction. On the species level, however, the reproductive system is homeostatic: Without reproduction our overpopulated earth would be free of human life before the year 2100.

In this unit we will discuss the processes by which the human species is perpetuated. In Chapter 29 we will describe the male and female reproductive systems and their hormonal regulation. We will also discuss contraception, abortion, and sexually transmitted disease. Chapter 30 will focus on development of the human embryo and the human life cycle. Finally, in Chapter 31 we will present a brief overview of human inheritance.

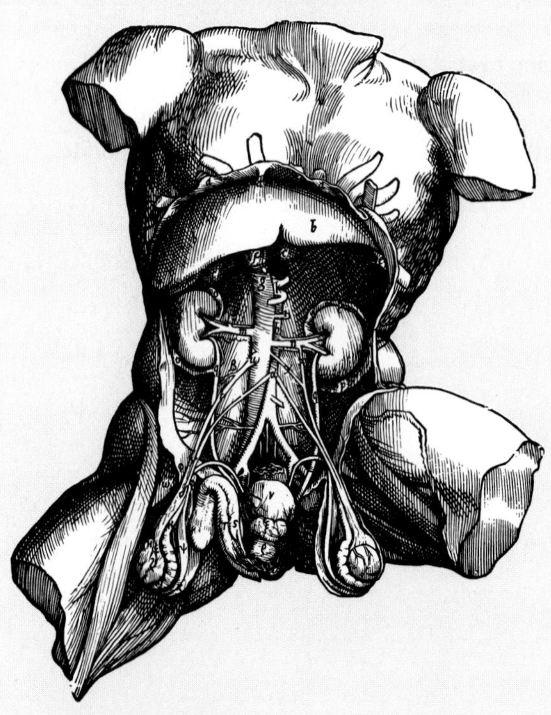

VI

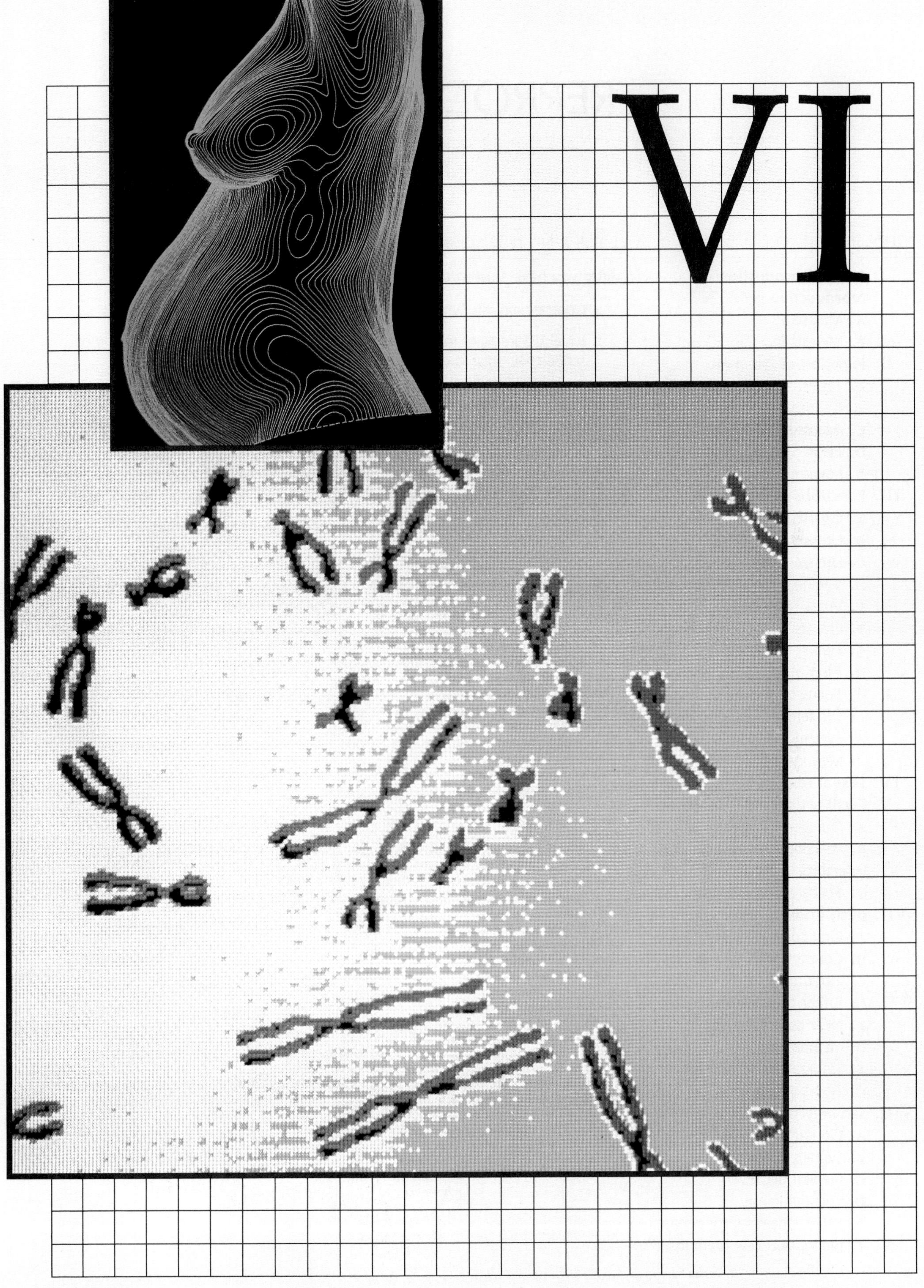

REPRODUCTION

CHAPTER OUTLINE

- **I. Meiosis: production of reproductive cells**
  - A. Meiosis I
  - B. Meiosis II
- **II. Function of the male**
  - A. Testes: sperm production
  - B. Conducting tubes
  - C. Accessory glands
  - D. Penis
  - E. Male hormones
- **III. Functions of the female**
  - A. Ovaries
  - B. Uterine tubes
  - C. Uterus
  - D. Vagina
  - E. Vulva
  - F. Breasts
  - G. Female hormones
  - H. Menstrual cycle
  - □ Focus on some disorders of the female reproductive system
  - I. Menopause
- **IV. Sexual response**
- **V. Fertilization**
  - A. Numbers of sperm required
  - B. Reactions in the ovum
- **VI. Infertility**
  - □ Focus on novel origins
- **VII. Birth Control methods**
  - A. Oral contraceptives
  - B. Contraceptive sponge
  - C. Intrauterine devices (IUDs)
  - D. Other common methods
  - E. New contraceptive methods
  - F. Sterilization
  - G. Abortion
- **VIII. Sexually transmitted disease**
  - A. Gonorrhea
  - B. Syphilis
  - C. Genital herpes
  - D. Trichomoniasis
  - E. Pelvic inflammatory disease
  - F. Nongonococcal urethritis

LEARNING OBJECTIVES

After you have studied this chapter you should be able to:

1 Contrast meiosis with mitosis, giving the essential features of meiosis.

2 Label diagrams of internal and external male reproductive organs and describe their structure and functions.

3 Trace the development of a sperm cell from spermatogonium to maturity.

4 Draw and label a diagram of a mature sperm cell; give functions of its unique structures (e.g., acrosome and tail).

5 Trace the passage of sperm from the seminiferous tubules through the conducting tubes, describing changes that may occur along the way.

6 Describe the composition of semen and relate to male sterility.

7 Compare the physiological bases for erection and ejaculation.

8 Summarize the actions of the male gonadotropic hormones and of testosterone, and describe how they are regulated.

9 Label diagrams of internal and external female reproductive organs and describe their structure and functions.

10 Trace the development of an ovum in time and space from oogonium through fertilization.

11 Trace the development of a corpus luteum and give its function.

12 List the hormones that affect breast development and lactation, and cite their specific functions.

13 Describe the principal events of the menstrual cycle, correlating pituitary, hypothalamic, ovarian, and uterine responses and interactions.

14 List the principal actions of the gonadotropic and ovarian hormones, and diagram feedback mechanisms involved in their regulation.

15 Relate physiological changes in the female to hormonal changes during menopause.

16 Describe the physiological changes taking place during sexual response; compare male and female responses.

17 Describe the process of fertilization and identify the time of the menstrual cycle at which sexual intercourse is most likely to result in conception.

18 Compare the mode of action of the methods of birth control, and describe their advantages and disadvantages.

19 Identify the causative agent and describe the course of common sexually transmitted diseases, including gonorrhea, syphilis, genital herpes, trichomoniasis, and pelvic inflammatory disease.

A body contour map of a woman who is 36 weeks pregnant. (Robin Williams/Photo Researchers, Inc.)

29

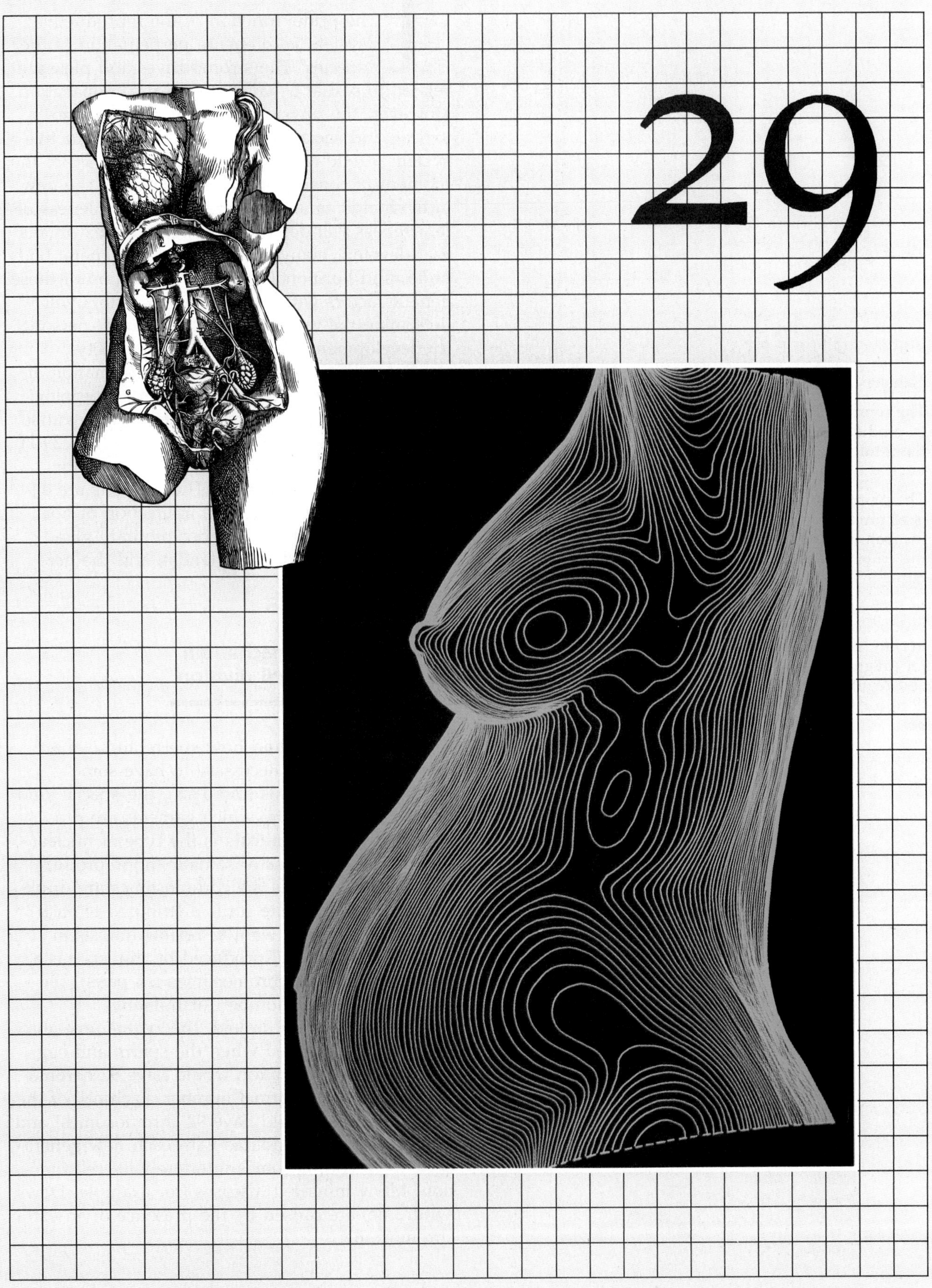

KEY CONCEPTS

Gametes are produced by meiosis.

The reproductive role of the male is to produce sperm cells and deliver them into the female reproductive tract.

The reproductive role of the female is to produce ova, receive sperm, incubate and nourish the developing embryo, and nourish the newborn.

In both sexes, hormones regulate production of gametes. In females, hormones also prepare the body for pregnancy, maintain pregnancy, and regulate lactation (milk production) for nourishment of the newborn.

The prime function of the reproductive system is to ensure perpetuation of the species. The strong drives and pleasure related to sexual behavior do ensure propagation. However, the physical, physiological, psychological, and social influences of the reproductive system extend far beyond that function. From the moment of conception, when the sex of the new individual is genetically specified, its maleness or femaleness will determine the type of sex organs that develop, many characteristics of general body build, and hormonal makeup. Interaction of these genetic factors with environmental factors will determine the way the person is reared, personality development, and even roles in society.

Reproductive processes include formation of **gametes** (**gam**-etes; eggs and sperm), physiological preparation for pregnancy, sexual intercourse, **fertilization** (union of sperm and egg) (Fig. 29-1), pregnancy, and **lactation** (producing milk for nourishment of the infant). These events are exquisitely orchestrated by the interaction of hormones secreted by the anterior pituitary gland, the **gonads** (**go**-nads; sex glands), and the nervous system.

Meiosis is the mechanism of reproductive cell division

In order to understand how sperm and ova are manufactured, it is necessary to have some knowledge of **meiosis** (my-**o**-sis), the special kind of nuclear division by which gametes are produced. Recall that **mitosis** is the type of nuclear division characteristic of somatic (nonreproductive) cells. In mitosis the chromosomes are duplicated, and a complete set is distributed to each new cell. (You may want to review mitosis in Chapter 3.) Each cell produced by mitosis has a complete set of 46 chromosomes (23 pairs), the **diploid** (**dip**-loyd) number for humans.

If gametes were diploid, the **zygote** (**zye**-goat; fertilized egg) formed when the sperm and egg fused during fertilization would have 92 chromosomes, twice the normal number. Each cell of the new individual would have 92 chromosomes, and the number would double with each new generation. Extra chromosomes interfere with cell function. Many inherited diseases (for example, Down syndrome) are caused by the presence of an extra chromosome.

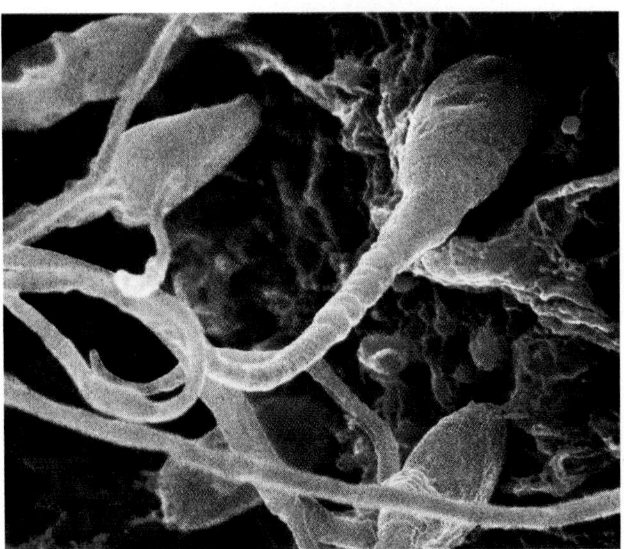

FIGURE 29-1

Human sperm fertilizing ovum. (Lennart Nilsson, from *The Incredible Machine,* p. 22; National Geographic Society.)

Fortunately, meiosis neatly solves the dilemma by producing **haploid** (**hap**-loyd) gametes, cells that contain only 23 *unpaired* chromosomes. During fertilization the sperm contributes one set of 23 chromosomes and the egg another set of 23. Thus the zygote receives half its chromosomes from each parent, and the normal diploid number is restored. The 23 **paternal chromosomes** (those inherited from one's father) can be paired with the 23 **maternal chromosomes** (the ones contributed by the mother). The corresponding members of each set are identical in size and shape and bear genes governing the same traits. Such a corresponding chromosome pair is referred to as a **homologous pair.**

One pair of chromosomes is known as the **sex chromosomes.** The two sex chromosomes are similar in shape in the female but do not match in the male. In the female the sex chromosomes consist of two **X chromosomes,** whereas in the male the sex chromosomes consist of one X chromosome and one **Y chromosome.** The Y chromosome is much shorter than the X and bears genes that determine masculinity. Figure 31-1 shows the X and Y chromosomes; Figure 31-15 shows what can happen if meiosis fails to produce haploid gametes.

Meiosis is compared and contrasted with mitosis in Figure 29-2. In meiosis there are two successive nuclear divisions so that each primary sex cell gives rise to four daughter cells. A more detailed view of meiosis is shown in Figure 29-3.

Meiosis I is reduction division

Meiosis I, the first nuclear division, is known as **reduction division.** The chromosomes are replicated during the interphase before reduction division. Then, during **prophase I** the members of each homologous pair of chromosomes come together in a process known as **synapsis** (sih-**nap**-sis). (In mitosis homologous chromosomes do not pair.) Each chromosome is in the duplicated condition consisting of two chromatids, so that a synapsed pair actually consists of four chromatids. Appropriately, it is called a **tetrad.** Synapsis provides the opportunity for homologous pairs to exchange genes, a mechanism called **crossing-over.** This exchange of genes greatly enhances the prospects for variety among offspring of sexual partners. Variety among members of a species increases the probability that some individuals will be able to adapt to changing environmental conditions. Thus, variety helps ensure survival of the species.

During **metaphase I,** the chromosomes line up along the equator of the cell. As in mitosis a spindle forms, and microtubules of the spindle attach the centromeres to opposite poles of the cell. During **anaphase I** homologous chromosomes separate, and one from each pair moves randomly into each new cell. **Telophase I** and cytokinesis are similar to the corresponding steps in mitosis. Each new cell is haploid; it contains a total of 23 chromosomes (one of each pair).

Although it is possible that one cell could receive a complete set of 23 maternal chromosomes and the other a complete set of 23 paternal chromosomes, it is highly unlikely. More probably, each gamete will receive some chromosomes donated by each parent, so that the daughter cell will contain a genetic combination from both parents. The possible number of combinations for distributing the 23 pairs of chromosomes is so great that every gamete has a different complement of genes, and individuals have different characteristics.

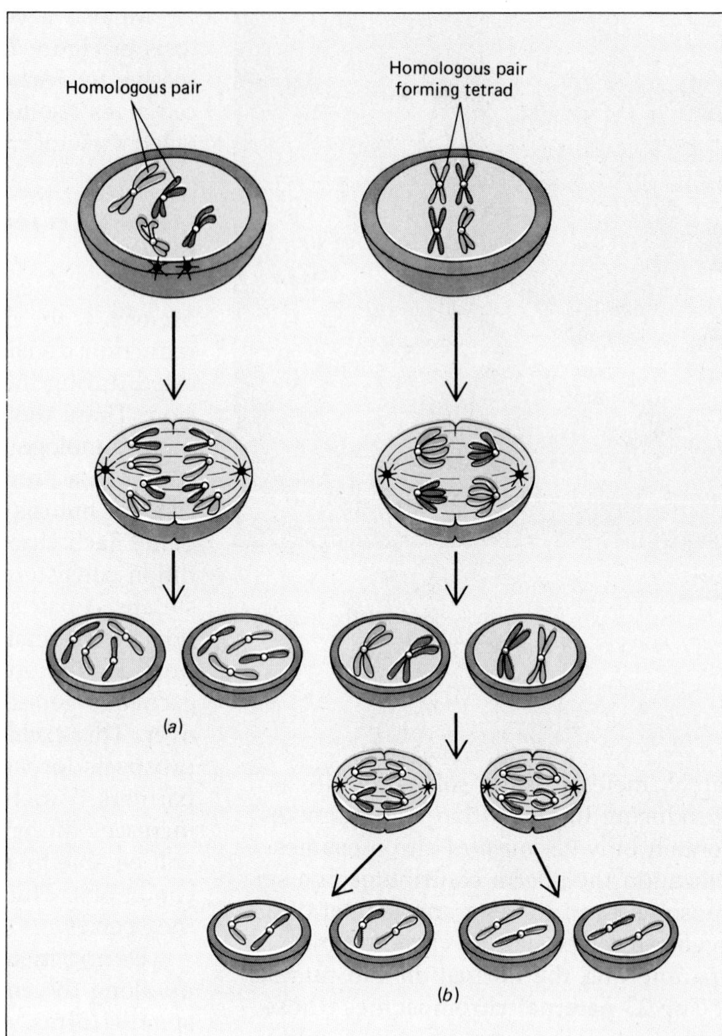

FIGURE 29-2

Meiosis compared with mitosis. *(a)* Mitosis. Note that each new cell has an identical set of four chromosomes (two pairs). *(b)* Meiosis. Two divisions take place, giving rise to four new (daughter) cells. Each daughter cell has only two chromosomes, one of each pair. The chromosomes shown in blue originally came from one parent; those shown in pink came from the other parent.

Meiosis II permits the chromatids to separate

No further chromosome duplication occurs between meiotic divisions. **Meiosis II** simply permits the chromatids to separate. As in mitosis, the chromosomes, each consisting of two chromatids, line up along the equator of the cell. Then, the chromatids of each chromosome separate. Telophase II and cytokinesis occur, resulting in a total of four haploid cells from each primary sex cell.

The reproductive function of the male is to produce sperm and to deliver them into the female

The specific reproductive responsibility of the male is to produce sperm cells and to deliver them into the female reproductive tract. When a sperm combines with an egg, it contributes half the genetic endowment of the offspring and determines its sex. Male reproductive structures include the testes and scrotum, conducting tubes that lead from the testes to the outside of the body, accessory glands, and the penis (Fig. 29-4).

Centrioles

Chromatin Nucleolus

Interphase I

Interphase preceding meiosis; DNA replicates.

Prophase I

Homologous chromosomes come together forming tetrads; crossing-over and genetic recombination occur.

Metaphase I

Note orientation of homologous chromosomes.

Anaphase I

Homologous chromosomess separate, and one of each pair moves to opposite ends of the cell. Note that the chromatids remain attached at their centromeres.

Telophase I

One of each pair of homologous chromosomes is at each end of cell. Note that the chromosome number will be haploid when the cells divide.

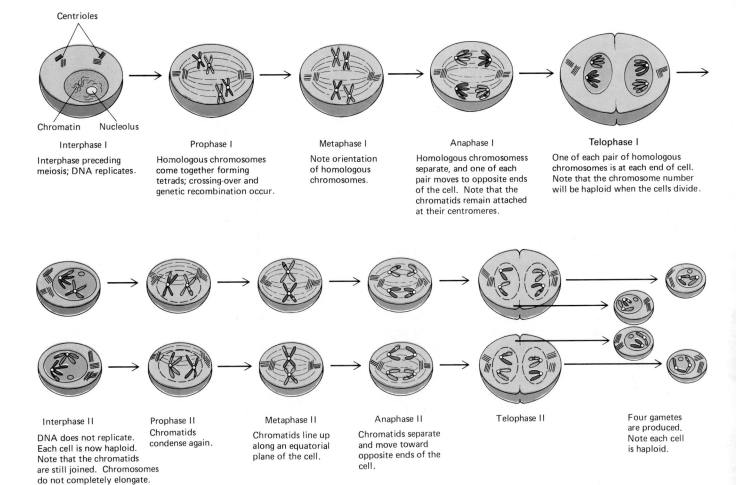

Interphase II

DNA does not replicate. Each cell is now haploid. Note that the chromatids are still joined. Chromosomes do not completely elongate.

Prophase II

Chromatids condense again.

Metaphase II

Chromatids line up along an equatorial plane of the cell.

Anaphase II

Chromatids separate and move toward opposite ends of the cell.

Telophase II

Four gametes are produced. Note each cell is haploid.

FIGURE 29-3

The stages of meiosis. Only four chromosomes are shown in the diploid cell.

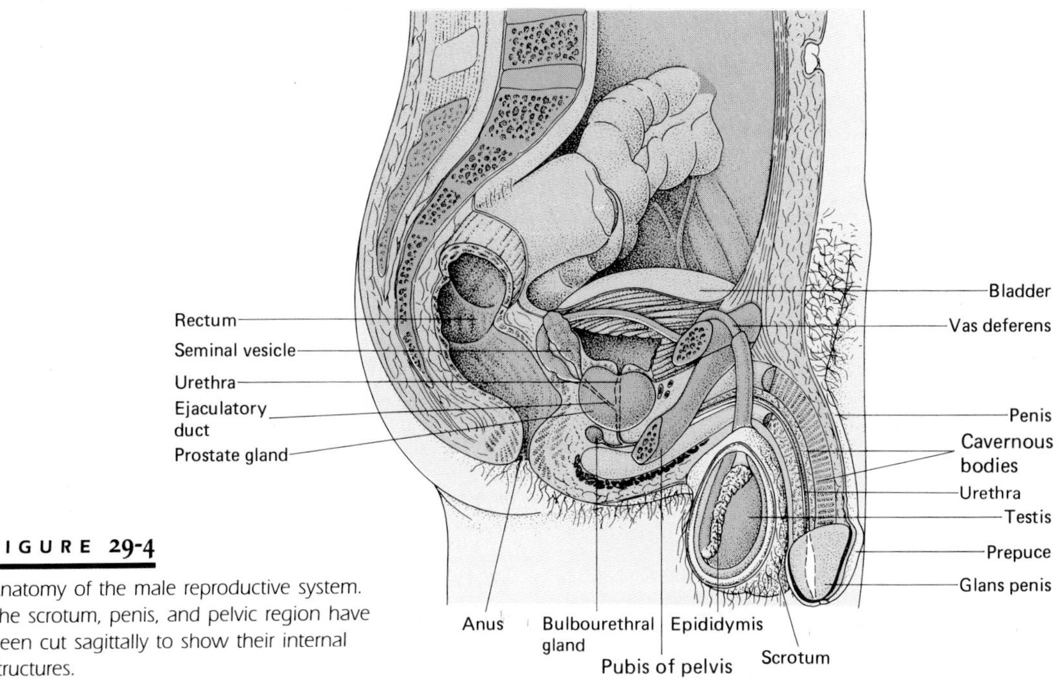

FIGURE 29-4

Anatomy of the male reproductive system. The scrotum, penis, and pelvic region have been cut sagittally to show their internal structures.

Production of sperm takes place in the testes

Sperm production begins at **puberty** (**pew**-ber-tee), the period of sexual maturation, and continues into old age. Millions of sperm cells are manufactured each day within the paired male gonads, the testes.

THE TESTES ARE THE MALE GONADS

Each **testis** (**tes**-tis) is one of a pair of male reproductive glands, or gonads. It is oval in shape, about 4 to 5 centimeters (1.6 to 2 in.) long, and covered by a thick white capsule of connective tissue, the **tunica albuginea** (**too**-nik-ah *al*-bew-**jin**-ee-ah) (white tunic) (Fig. 29-5). At the posterior border of each testis, the sheath thickens and extends into the interior substance of the gland to form an incomplete partition. The thickened part of the sheath and the partition constitute the **mediastinum** (*me*-de-ah-**sti**-num) of the testis. Extensions of the partition, called **septa,** radiate outward to form incomplete walls that partially separate the testis into about 250 cone-shaped lobules. Within these lobules lie the tiny coiled **seminiferous tubules** (*sem*-ih-**nif**-er-us), the sperm-cell factories. In the hilus area, the seminiferous tubules are uncoiled and form a complex network called the **rete testis** (**ree**-tee).

About 1000 seminiferous tubules can be found in each testis. If uncoiled and placed end to end, these threadlike microscopic tubules would span almost one-third of a mile! In an adult male these structures produce millions of sperm cells each day.

SPERMATOGENESIS IS THE MECHANISM BY WHICH SPERM CELLS ARE PRODUCED

The process of sperm cell production, called **spermatogenesis** (*sper*-mah-toe-**jen**-eh-sis), requires about 74 days. Sperm develop from stem cells called **spermatogonia** (*sper*-mah-toe-**go**-nee-ah), found next to the basement membrane of the seminiferous tubules (Fig. 29-6). These cells multiply by mitosis, ensuring that a large population of spermatogonia is maintained. About half the spermatogonia produced differentiate slightly to become **primary spermatocytes.** These cells then undergo *meiosis*.

Before dividing, each primary spermatocyte enlarges. In prophase I, 46 chromosomes (each consisting of two chromatids) are present. Homologous pairs of chromosomes line up along the equatorial plane of the cell during synapsis. Crossing over takes place, the meiotic spindle forms, and the chromosome pairs separate into opposite ends of the cell. The cell divides, pro-

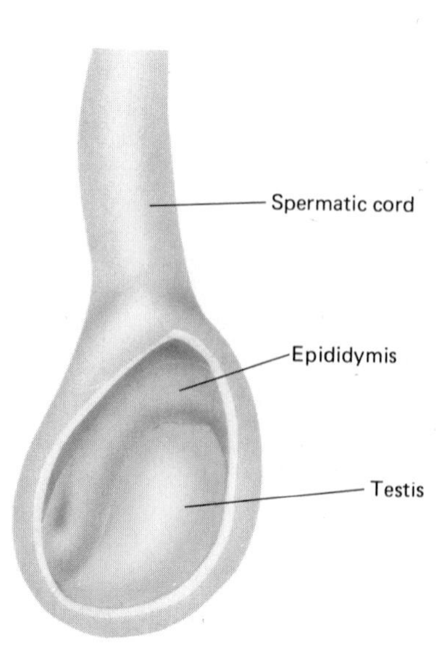

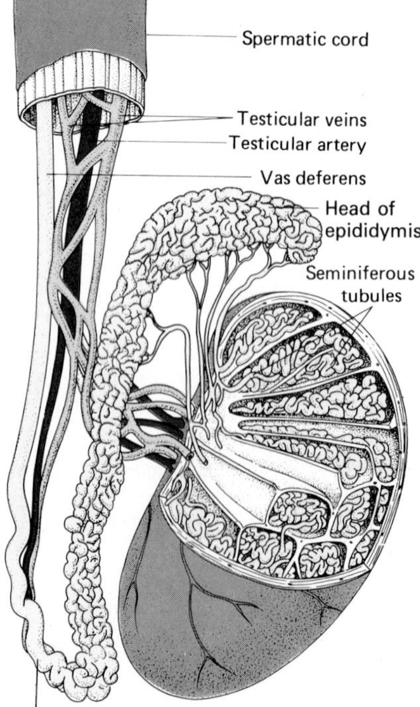

FIGURE 29-5

Structure of the testis, epididymis, and spermatic cord. (*a*) External view of the testis inside the scrotum. (*b*) The testis is shown in sagittal section to illustrate the arrangement of the seminiferous tubules.

ducing two **secondary spermatocytes.** Each is haploid, having only one member of each chromosome pair; the chromosomes are still in the form of chromatids.

During meiosis II, the chromatids separate. The four cells produced are **spermatids.** Each spermatid contains 23 chromosomes and is haploid. During the final stage of spermatogenesis, known as **spermiogenesis** (*sper*-me-oh-**gen**-eh-sis), the spermatids undergo differentiation to become mature sperm cells, or **spermatozoa** (*sper*-mah-toe-**zo**-ah).

Spermatogonium ⟶ primary spermatocyte ⟶ two secondary spermatocytes ⟶ four spermatids (haploid) ⟶ four spermatozoa (haploid)

All of the spermatogenic cells undergo division and differentiate, surrounded by and interspersed between supporting cells called **Sertoli**

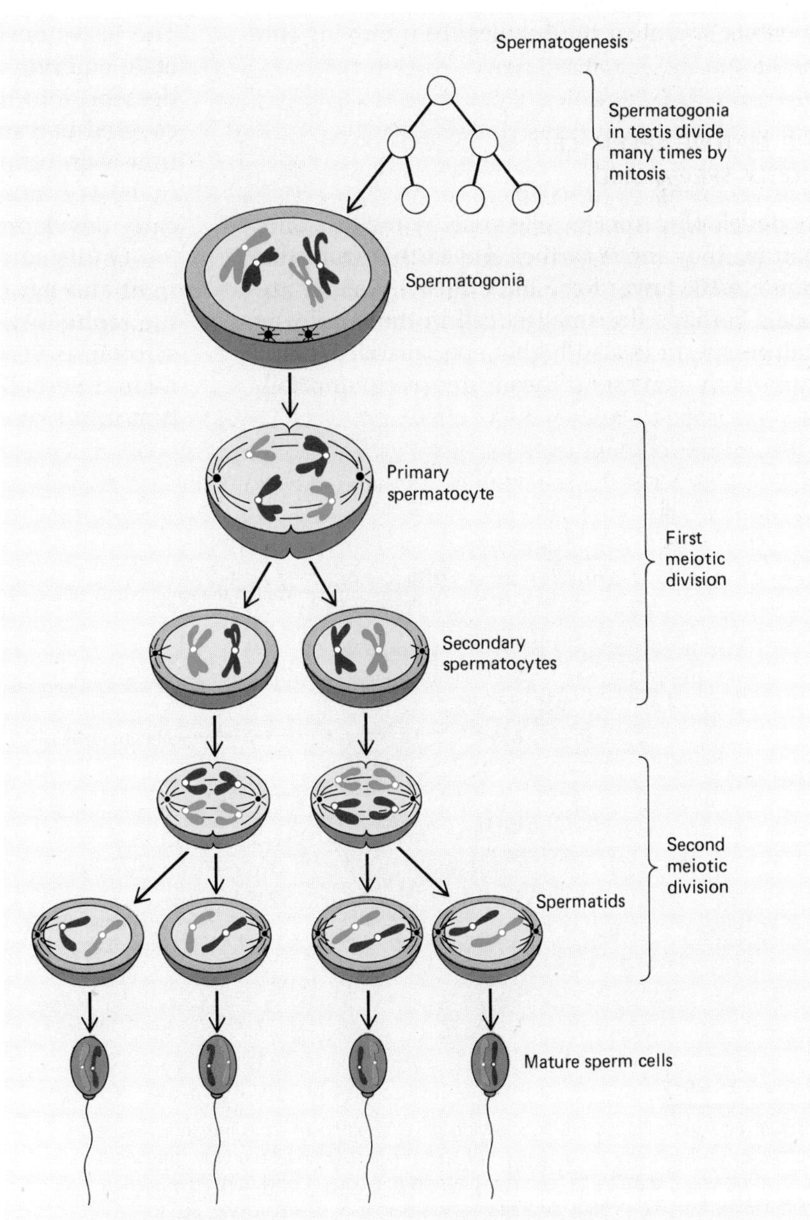

FIGURE 29-6

Spermatogenesis. The primary spermatocyte divides by meiosis, giving rise to two secondary spermatocytes and then four spermatids. The spermatids differentiate (become specialized), forming mature sperm cells.

cells (Ser-**toe**-lee) (Fig. 29-7). These large cells extending from the wall of the tubules to the lumen provide nourishment, support, and protection for the developing sperm cells. Sertoli cells secrete a fluid rich in nutrients, enzymes, proteins, and certain ions such as potassium and bicarbonate. One protein component of the fluid is the hormone *inhibin,* which is transported by the blood to the pituitary gland. As we will discuss in a later section, inhibin regulates secretion of the follicle-stimulating hormone (FSH).

At their bases Sertoli cells are joined by tight junctions. They form a **blood-testes barrier** which prevents entrance of harmful substances into the seminiferous tubule. This blood-testes barrier also prevents sperm in the tubules from moving into the blood.

THE MATURE SPERM CELL IS HIGHLY SPECIALIZED

As developing sperm cells arise by meiosis and mature, they move farther and farther from the tubule wall, toward the lumen (cavity of the tubule). Perhaps the smallest cell in the body, the mature sperm is also highly specialized. Its elongated body consists of head, midpiece, and tail. The head contains the nucleus and, at its front tip, an **acrosome** (**ak**-row-sowm) formed from the Golgi body (Fig. 29-8). Enzymes within the acrosome aid in fertilization by dissolving the intercellular materials surrounding the egg at the point of sperm entry. Mitochondria are concentrated in the **midpiece** of the sperm. By carrying on aerobic respiration, they provide the energy needed for locomotion. The **tail,** a flagellum, consists of filaments that slide across one another to produce the whiplike movements that propel the sperm.

THE SCROTUM MAINTAINS SPERM AT A LOW TEMPERATURE

The testes develop in the abdominal cavity of the male embryo. About 2 months before birth they descend into the **scrotum** (**skrow**-tum), a skin-covered bag suspended from the groin. The scrotum is an outpocketing of the abdomen and its cavity is continuous with the pelvic cavity during early development.

On its surface the scrotum is divided into right and left halves by a ridge of tissue called the **raphe** (**ray**-fee). The brownish skin of the scrotum is very thin and is often thrown into folds. Internally the scrotum is divided by a septum into two cavities, one for each testis.

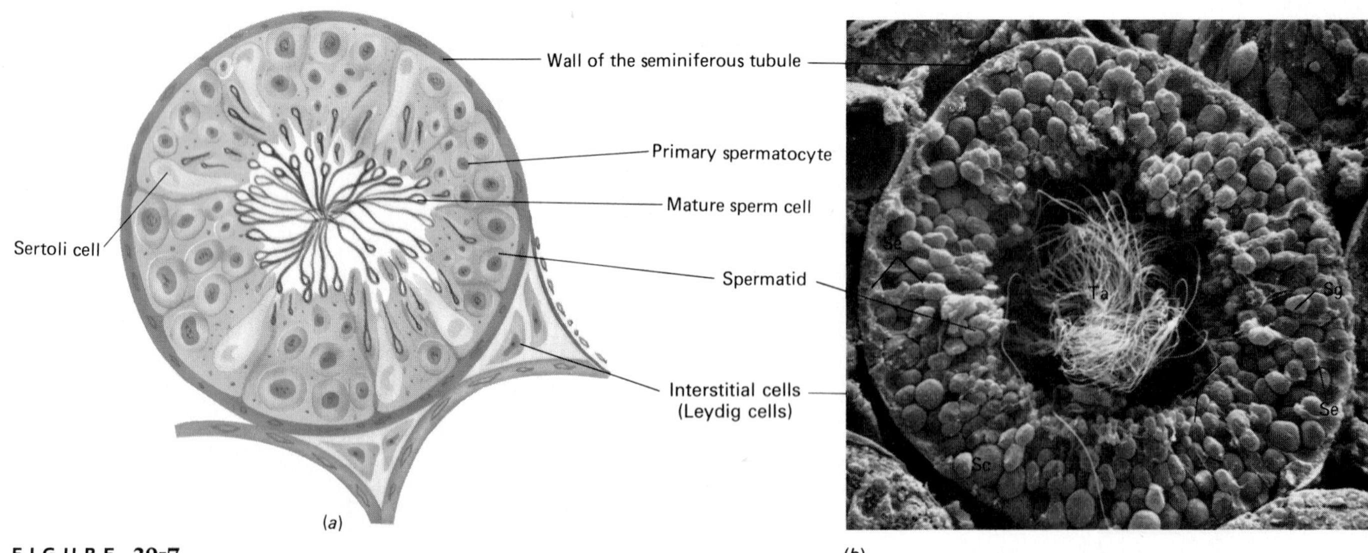

FIGURE 29-7

Structure of a seminiferous tubule showing developing sperm cells in various stages of spermatogenesis. (*a*) Identify the sequence of sperm cell differentiation. Note the Sertoli cells and the interstitial cells. (*b*) A scanning electron micrograph of a transverse section through a seminiferous tubule (×580). Se, Sertoli cell; Sc, primary spermatocyte; Sg, spermatogonium. (Courtesy of Richard G. Kessel and Randy H. Kardon, *Tissues and Organs: A Text-Atlas of Scanning Electron Microscopy,* W. H. Freeman and Company, San Francisco, 1979.)

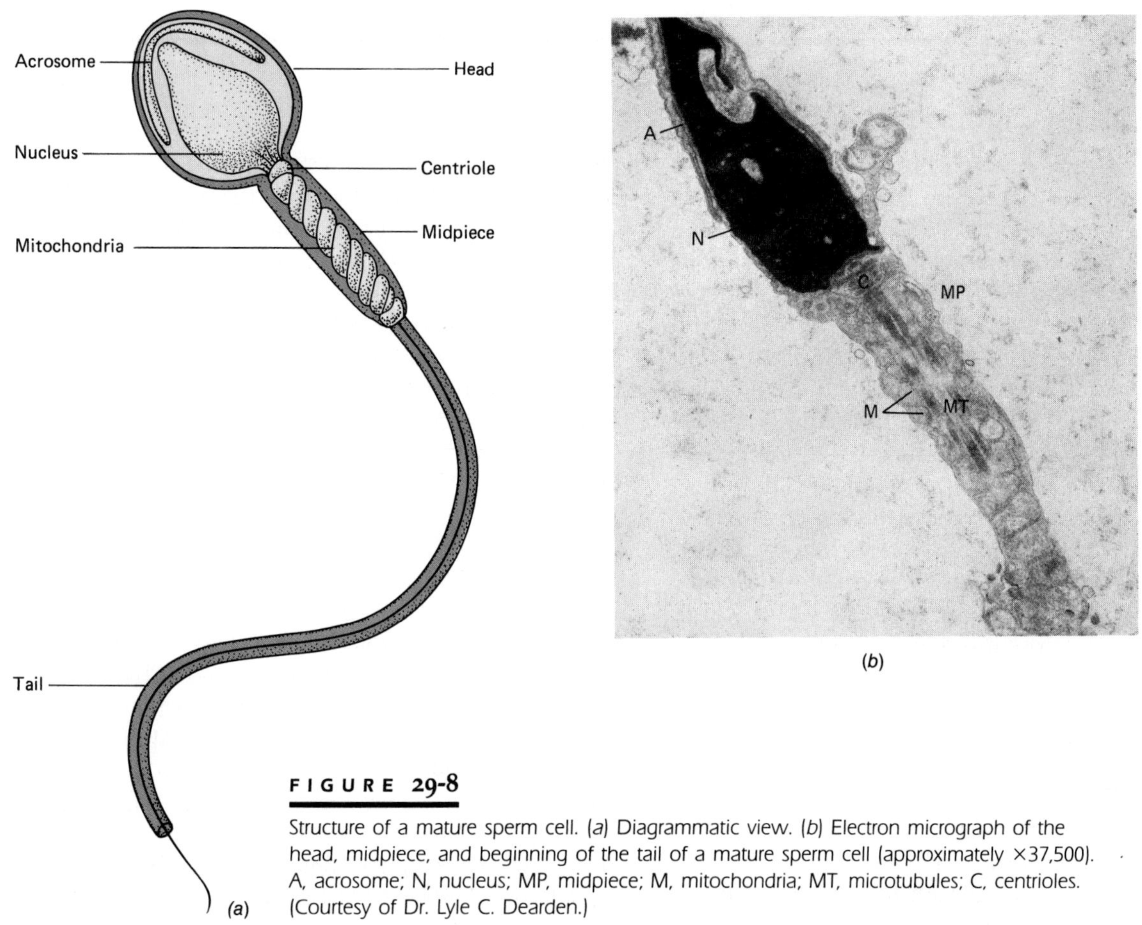

FIGURE 29-8

Structure of a mature sperm cell. (*a*) Diagrammatic view. (*b*) Electron micrograph of the head, midpiece, and beginning of the tail of a mature sperm cell (approximately ×37,500). A, acrosome; N, nucleus; MP, midpiece; M, mitochondria; MT, microtubules; C, centrioles. (Courtesy of Dr. Lyle C. Dearden.)

As the testes descend before birth, they move through the **inguinal canals** (**ing**-gwih-nal), the passageways connecting the scrotal and abdominal cavities. The testes pull their arteries, veins, nerves, and conducting tubes after them. These structures, encased by the cremaster muscle and by layers of fascia, constitute the **spermatic cord** (Fig. 29-9).

Clinical highlight

The inguinal region remains a weak place in the abdominal wall and therefore a common site of hernia in the male. Straining the abdominal muscles by lifting a very heavy object may result in a tear, through which a loop of intestine can bulge into the scrotum; this condition is called an **inguinal hernia.**

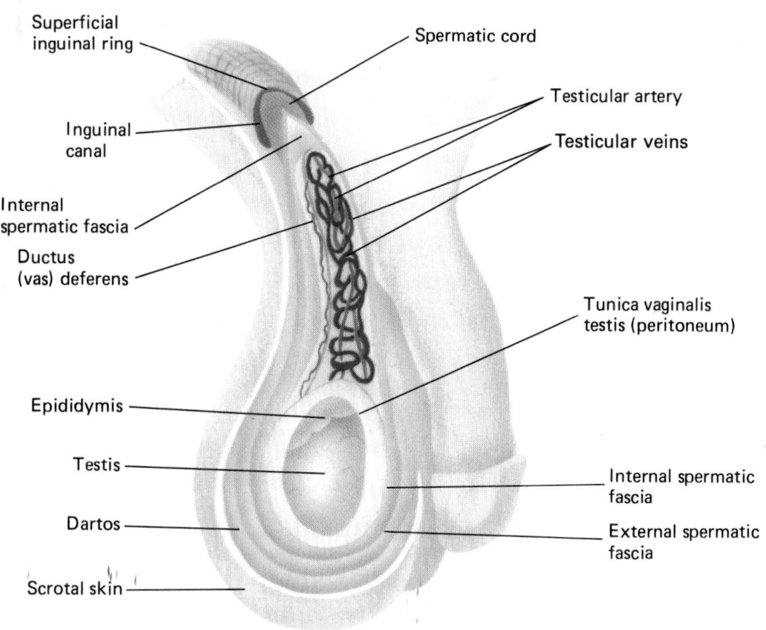

FIGURE 29-9

Spermatic cord and inguinal canal.

Sperm cells are not able to develop at body temperature and the scrotum serves as a cooling unit, maintaining them at about 2°C below body temperature. An abundance of sweat glands in the wall of the scrotum helps to maintain the cool temperature. Another factor helping to maintain a desirable temperature is the scrotal skin, which is thin and contains little insulating fat.

In hot weather involuntary **dartos muscles** (**dar**-tos) in the scrotal wall relax, positioning the testes away from the body and allowing the sperm to remain cool. In cold weather the dartos muscles and cremasteric muscles of the spermatic cord contract, drawing the testes up close to the abdominal wall, where they are kept warm. Contraction of the dartos muscle causes the skin of the scrotum to wrinkle.

Clinical highlight

If the testes fail to descend into the scrotum, viable sperm cells are not produced. This condition, termed **cryptorchism** (krip-**tor**-kizm), can sometimes be corrected by treatment with gonadotropic hormones which stimulate descent. Frequently, however, surgery is required. If cryptorchism is not treated, the seminiferous tubules eventually degenerate, and the male becomes **sterile,** that is, unable to father offspring. Secretion of male hormone is not affected, however, so masculinity is not altered.

The conducting tubes transport sperm

A series of conducting tubes transport sperm from the testes to the outside of the body. After sperm are produced, they pass from the convoluted seminiferous tubules to straight tubules. Then, sperm pass through a network of passageways, the rete testis, in the mediastinum.

THE EPIDIDYMIS IS THE SITE OF SPERM MATURATION

The rete testis leads into 12 to 20 small tubules, the **efferent ducts** that exit from the testis. The efferent ducts pass into the epididymis and eventually empty into a single, large tube, the **duct of the epididymis** (*ep*-ih-**did**-ih-mus), or ductus epididymis.

The **epididymis** (plural, epididymides) is an elongated structure that lies along the posterolateral side of the testis. The epididymis is divided into a head, body, and tail (Fig. 29-5). The large, superior, head of the epididymis consists of the efferent ducts. The body of the epididymis is formed by the convoluted duct of the epididymis. This duct is very long—more than 6 meters (20 ft)—and so must be highly coiled to fit into the epididymis, which is only about 3.8 centimeters (1.5 in.) in length. The thin wall of the ductus epididymis is lined with pseudostratified columnar epithelium and contains smooth muscle. As it emerges in the tail of the epididymis, the ductus epididymis is continuous with the vas deferens.

Seminiferous tubules ⟶ rete testis ⟶ efferent ducts ⟶ epididymis ⟶ vas deferens

The epididymis and the first portion of the vas deferens are storage areas for sperm cells. The epididymis stores sperm for up to 4 weeks. After that time, they are reabsorbed. The duct of the epididymis plays a role in sperm maturation. Sperm taken from the seminiferous tubules are not very motile and cannot fertilize an egg, but after they have been in the epididymis for at least 18 hours, they mature and become viable. During ejaculation, peristaltic contractions of the smooth muscle of the duct of the epididymis propel the mature sperm toward the urethra.

THE VAS DEFERENS CONDUCTS SPERM FROM THE EPIDIDYMIS TO THE EJACULATORY DUCT

Each epididymis continues as a straight tube known as the **vas deferens** (**def**-eh-rens; plural, vasa deferentia), or sperm duct. (The vas deferens is also known as the ductus deferens, or seminal duct.) The vas deferens passes from the scrotum through the inguinal canal as part of the spermatic cord. After entering the pelvic cavity, the vas deferens loops over the side and down the posterior surface of the urinary bladder (Figs. 29-4, 29-10). Pseudostratified epithelium lines the vas deferens.

Within the passageways of the vas deferens, sperm are stored and retain their fertility for several months. During ejaculation a coat of three layers of muscle contained in the wall of the vas deferens propels the sperm towards the urethra.

SPERM ARE CONDUCTED THROUGH THE EJACULATORY DUCT AND URETHRA

The vas deferens is joined by the duct from the seminal vesicles (see below) to become the **ejaculatory duct.** This very short duct passes through the prostate gland and then opens into the pros-

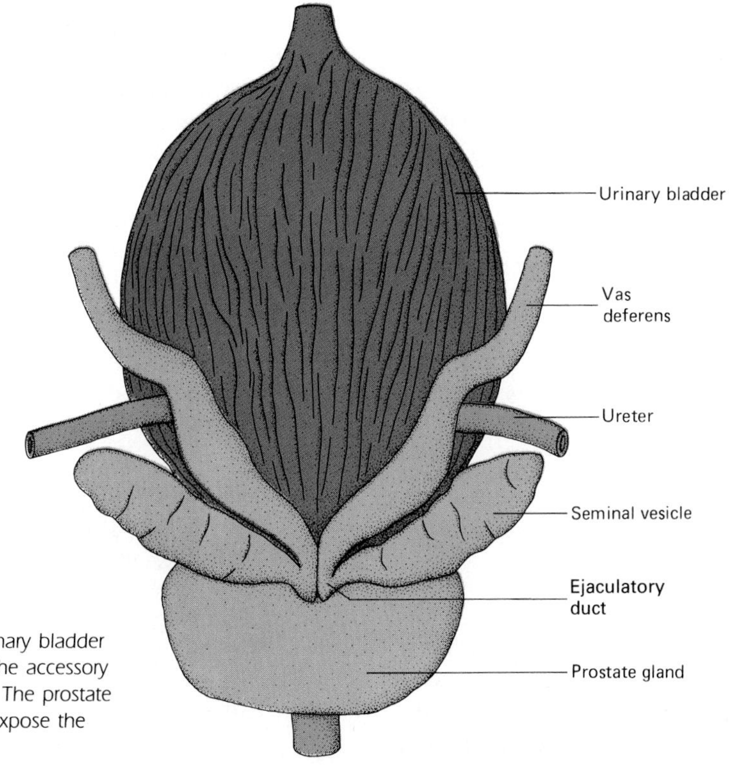

FIGURE 29-10

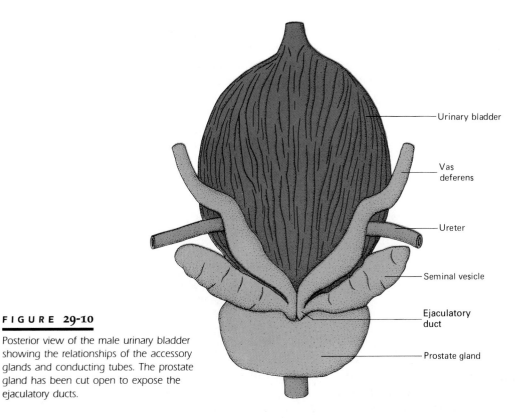

Posterior view of the male urinary bladder showing the relationships of the accessory glands and conducting tubes. The prostate gland has been cut open to expose the ejaculatory ducts.

tatic portion of the urethra. The urethra passes through the penis as the spongy urethra and opens to the outside of the body. The testes, epididymides, vas deferentia, and ejaculatory ducts are *paired;* only the urethra is a single tube.

Vas deferens ⟶ ejaculatory duct ⟶ urethra ⟶ opens to outside of body

The accessory glands produce the fluid portion of semen

Semen (**see**-mun) is a thick, whitish fluid consisting of sperm cells suspended in secretions from the seminal vesicles, the prostate gland, and the bulbourethral glands. These glands continuously secrete small amounts of fluid, producing larger quantities during sexual stimulation.

THE SEMINAL VESICLES PRODUCE MOST OF THE SEMEN

The paired **seminal vesicles** are saclike glands that empty into the vasa deferentia. Secretions of the seminal vesicles account for about 60% of the semen volume.

The mucus-like fluid secreted by the seminal vesicles contains the sugar fructose plus other nutrients that nourish and provide fuel for the sperm cells. Prostaglandins in the seminal vesicle fluid stimulate contractions of the uterus in the female; these contractions help move sperm through the female reproductive tract.

THE PROSTATE GLAND CONTRIBUTES TO SPERM MOTILITY

The single **prostate gland** (**pros**-tate) measures about 4 centimeters at its base and surrounds the urethra as the urethra emerges from the bladder. It contributes about 20% of the semen volume, producing a thick, milky, alkaline secretion that is important in neutralizing the mild acidity of other fluids contributed to the semen. This change in pH contributes to sperm motility.

Clinical highlight

In older men the prostate gland often enlarges and exerts pressure on the urethra, making urination difficult. When necessary, a portion or all of the prostate can be removed surgically, often with no adverse effect on sexual performance.

Cancer is another common affliction of this gland, accounting for a significant number of malignancies in men over age 50. Generally, prostatic cancer grows slowly and is confined to the gland. Growth in more virulent forms is related to testosterone levels. Progress of the disease may be slowed by hormone control therapy or by removing the testes.

THE BULBOURETHRAL GLANDS NEUTRALIZE THE ACIDITY OF THE URETHRA

The **bulbourethral glands** (*bul*-bow-u-**ree**-thral), also called **Cowper's glands,** are about the size and shape of two peas, one on each side of the urethra. Their ducts open into the urethra. Upon sexual arousal they release a few drops of clear, alkaline pre-ejaculatory fluid. This fluid neutralizes the acidity of the urethra in preparation for ejaculation, and also lubricates the penis.

SEMEN IS COMPOSED OF SPERM CELLS SUSPENDED IN SECRETIONS

About 3 to 5 milliliters (5 ml = about one teaspoon) of semen (seminal fluid) is ejaculated during sexual orgasm. Semen consists of about 300 million sperm cells (about 100 million per milliliter) suspended in the secretions of the seminal vesicles, prostate, bulbourethral glands, and small glands in the wall of the ducts. Sperm cells are so tiny that they account for very little (less than 1%) of the semen volume. With repeated ejaculation during a short period of time, the sperm count and the semen volume decrease. Men with fewer than 20 million sperm per milliliter of semen usually are sterile (see section on Infertility).

The penis deposits spermatozoa into the vagina

The **penis** is an erectile copulatory organ designed to deliver sperm into the female reproductive tract during sexual intercourse. It consists of a long **shaft** that enlarges to form an expanded tip, the **glans penis** (Figs. 29-4 and 29-11). Part of the loose-fitting skin of the penis folds down and covers the proximal portion of the glans, forming a cuff called the **prepuce** (**pree**-pyous), or **fore-**

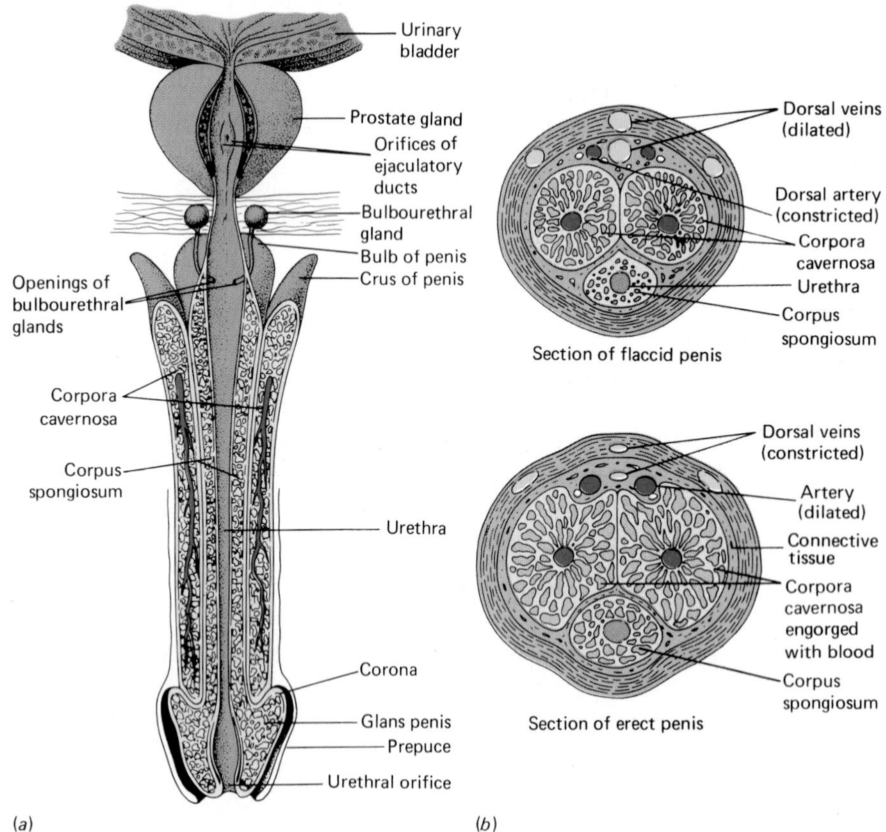

FIGURE 29-11

Internal structure of the penis. (*a*) Longitudinal section through prostate gland and penis. (*b*) Cross section through flaccid and erect penis. Note that the erectile tissues of the corpora cavernosa and corpus spongiosum are engorged with blood in the erect penis.

skin. This cuff of skin can be removed in a procedure known as **circumcision.**

Clinical highlight

Although the pros and cons of circumcision are a matter of some debate, this simple surgical procedure is routinely performed on male infants in many hospitals. (Circumcision is also performed as a religious ritual by Jews and Moslems.) One medical argument in favor of circumcision is that uncircumcised males are more likely to develop infections of the penis. This may occur because oil glands beneath the foreskin and along the rim of the glans secrete a material known as **smegma,** which, if permitted to accumulate, may irritate the glans and lead to infection.

Numerous sensory nerves in the glans make this structure the most sensitive part of the penis, especially about its rim, or **corona,** and **frenulum,** a ventral fold of skin connecting the glans with the foreskin. (The frenulum is not removed during circumcision.)

Under the skin, the penis consists of three parallel cylinders of erectile tissue, each enclosed by coats of fibrous connective tissue. The erectile tissue of these cylinders consists of large venous sinusoids. Two of the cylinders, the cavernous bodies, or **corpora cavernosa** (**kore**-pore-ah *kav*-er-**no**-sah), are paired (Fig. 29-11). Ventral to them lies the **corpus cavernosum urethrae,** also called the **corpus spongiosum** (**kor**-pus *spon*-jee-**oh**-sum), or spongy body, through which the urethra passes. The distal end of the corpus spongiosum enlarges, forming the glans penis.

The average penis is about 9 centimeters long when flaccid (relaxed) and 16 to 19 centimeters when erect. Its size and shape are not related to race, body build, virility, or a man's ability to give or receive sexual pleasure. Smaller penises tend to become proportionately larger when erect, so the size of erect penises varies less than that of flaccid ones. Penis size does not change as a consequence of frequent use.

VASOCONGESTION OF THE ERECTILE TISSUE RESULTS IN ERECTION OF THE PENIS

Penile **erection** is the first response to sexual stimulation and is essential for effective sexual intercourse. Erection is a reflex action that can be initiated directly by tactile stimulation of the penis, thighs, or groin region. Erotic thoughts can also trigger this reflex, for the brain is linked to the reflex center in the lumbar region of the spinal cord. Erection can also be triggered by visual, sound, taste, and smell stimuli. Most often, a combination of stimuli is involved.

Once the erection center is stimulated, parasympathetic nerves (nervi erigentes) convey impulses to the arteries of the penis, causing them to dilate. Blood rushes into the sinusoids of the corpora cavernosa. As the erectile tissue fills with blood it swells, compressing veins that conduct blood away from the penis. Thus, much more blood enters the penis than can leave, causing the erectile tissue to become engorged with blood and making the penis longer, larger in circumference, and firm. The process is reversed when sympathetic impulses result in constriction of the arteries.

↑ Stimulation of erection center ⟶ ↑ parasympathetic nerve impulses ⟶ arteries of penis dilate ⟶ ↑ blood in erectile tissue ⟶ compresses veins in penis ⟶ erectile tissue filled with blood ⟶ penis erect

Erection can occur in less than 10 seconds, but the time required varies with the individual and according to the situation. Younger men are generally capable of more rapid response. The extent of the erection may also vary. Chronic inability to sustain an erection is termed **erectile dysfunction** (sometimes referred to as impotence). Erectile dysfunction is often caused by psychological factors such as anxiety about adequate sexual performance.

SEMEN IS EXPELLED FROM THE PENIS DURING EJACULATION

Ejaculation is the discharge of semen from the penis. Like erection, ejaculation is a reflex action. When the level of sexual excitement reaches a peak, sympathetic nerves from the lumbar region of the spinal cord induce the prostate, seminal vesicles, and vasa deferentia to pour their contents into the urethra. This process, called **emission,** gives the male the feeling that ejaculation must occur imminently. Peristaltic contractions of the ducts and contractions of the muscles surrounding the root of the penis (where it connects to the pelvic floor) result in ejaculation.

Male hormones regulate male sexuality and reproduction

Between the seminiferous tubules in the testes are small islands of **interstitial cells,** sometimes called **Leydig cells** (**li**-dig) (Fig. 29-7). These cells produce **androgens,** the male hormones. Although several different androgens are produced by the testes and also by the adrenal cortex, the principal one, **testosterone,** is by far the most potent and most abundant. It is a 19-carbon steroid, synthesized from cholesterol or acetyl coenzyme A in the testes.

Small amounts of female hormones, **estrogens,** are also present in the male (about 20% of the amount present in the nonpregnant female). Some estrogens are produced by the prostate, seminal vesicles, and adrenal cortex, and some may be produced from testosterone in other parts of the body.

MASCULINITY IS ESTABLISHED IN THE EMBRYO

Until the sixth week of embryonic development the sexual structures of male and female appear identical. Differentiation into male or female after that time depends upon the presence or absence of the Y chromosome and its male-determining genes. The Y chromosome is thought to contain a gene that codes for a protein known as **histocompatibility-Y antigen,** or **H-Y antigen.** This antigen is found on the surfaces of male cells. Current evidence suggests that H-Y antigen binds to H-Y receptors in the undifferentiated embryonic gonad and induces gonadal cells to differentiate as testes.

Testosterone produced by the fetal testes stimulates the descent of the testes into the scrotum before birth. After birth the interstitial cells in the testes become difficult to distinguish microscopically until puberty, and the gonads remain quiescent throughout childhood.

TABLE 29-1

Principal male reproductive hormones and their actions

Endocrine gland and hormone	Principal site of action	Principal actions
Hypothalamus		
Gonadotropin releasing hormone (GnRH)	Anterior pituitary	Stimulates release of the gonadotropins (FSH and LH)
Anterior pituitary		
Follicle-stimulating hormone (FSH)	Testes	Stimulates development of seminiferous tubules; stimulates spermatogenesis; stimulates Sertoli cells
Luteinizing hormone (LH) (also called interstitial cell–stimulating hormone or ICSH)	Testes	Stimulates interstitial cells to secrete testosterone; promotes spermatogenesis
Testes		
Testosterone	General	*Before birth:* stimulates development of primary sex organs and descent of testes into scrotum *At puberty:* responsible for growth spurt; stimulates development of reproductive structures; stimulates development of secondary sex characteristics (male body build, growth of beard, pubic and axillary hair, deep voice) *In adult:* responsible for maintaining secondary sex characteristics; stimulates spermatogenesis
Inhibin	Anterior pituitary	Inhibits release of FSH

TESTOSTERONE SECRETION IS REGULATED BY GONADOTROPIC HORMONES

At about age 10 years, the hypothalamus begins to mature with regard to its function of regulating sex hormones. During childhood the hypothalamus is apparently extremely sensitive to even minute amounts of testosterone and is inhibited by its presence. Then, at about age 10, it becomes less sensitive and begins secreting **gonadotropin-releasing hormone** (GnRH), which stimulates the anterior pituitary to secrete the gonadotropic hormones, **follicle-stimulating hormone (FSH)** and **luteinizing hormone (LH)** (see Table 29-1). The release of FSH and LH is regulated by the hypothalamus (Fig. 29-12).

FSH stimulates development of the seminiferous tubules and promotes spermatogenesis. In addition, FSH stimulates the Sertoli cells. LH also promotes spermatogenesis, but its main function is to stimulate the interstitial cells to secrete testosterone (Fig. 29-13). Increased testosterone influences spermatogenesis.

A negative feedback system exists between LH and testosterone. When the concentration of testosterone in the blood reaches a certain level, it inhibits the hypothalamus so that less GnRH is released. Less GnRH results in less LH secretion by the pituitary, and the testosterone level is decreased. This system maintains a steady level of testosterone.

$$\uparrow \text{Testosterone} \xrightarrow{\text{inhibits}} \text{hypothalamus} \longrightarrow$$
$$\downarrow \text{GnRH} \xrightarrow{\text{inhibits}} \text{anterior pituitary} \longrightarrow$$
$$\downarrow \text{LH} \longrightarrow \downarrow \text{testosterone}$$

The hormone **inhibin** produced by the Sertoli cells inhibits FSH release by the anterior pituitary gland. Inhibin is released when sufficient sperm cells have been produced by spermatogenesis. It is not known whether this hormone acts directly on the hypothalamus, inhibiting release of GnRH.

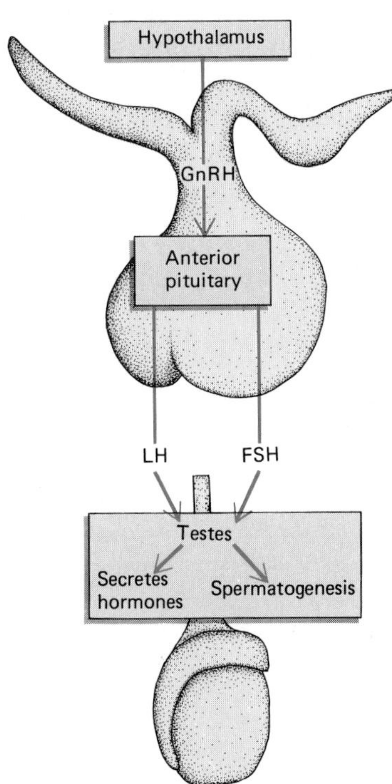

FIGURE 29-12

Relationship among the hypothalamus, anterior pituitary gland, and testes.

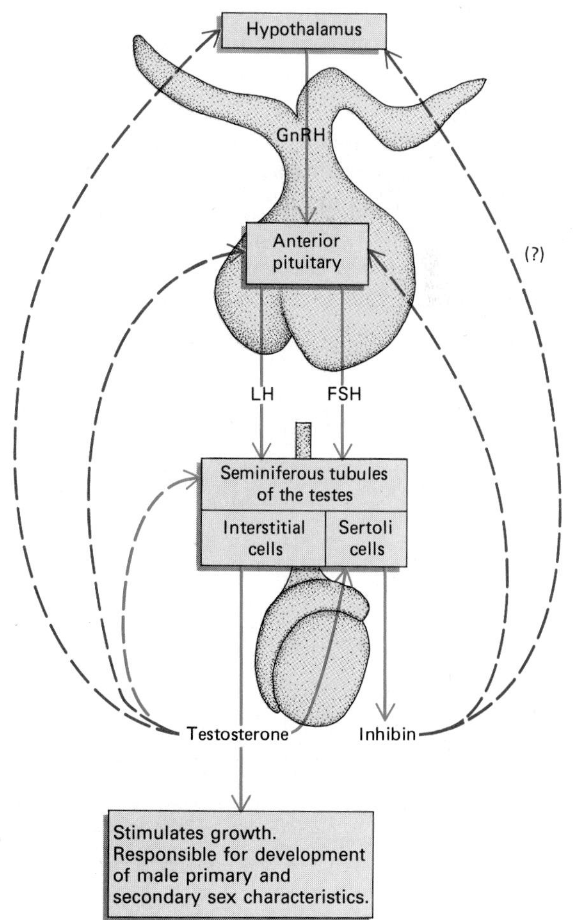

FIGURE 29-13

Reproductive hormone relationships in the male. Note the feedback loops within the hypothalamic-pituitary-testis system.

TESTOSTERONE PROMOTES GROWTH AND IS RESPONSIBLE FOR DEVELOPMENT OF SEXUAL CHARACTERISTICS

One of the main actions of testosterone is to promote growth. As large quantities of testosterone begin to circulate in the blood at the time of puberty (about age 13 years), boys experience an adolescent growth spurt. After a few years, however, testosterone affects the epiphyses of the bones, causing them to fuse to the diaphyses and thereby permanently halting growth by eliminating the metaphyses. Testosterone stimulates growth by increasing the synthesis of proteins and decreasing protein breakdown. Thus it has an anabolic effect on proteins. This hormone also increases the basal metabolic rate by about 5 to 10%.

Testosterone is responsible for the development of adult primary sexual structures. The penis, scrotum, and testes increase in size, and the scrotum may become pigmented. Internal genital structures enlarge and become active. Testosterone is apparently essential for spermatogenesis to occur.

Testosterone is also responsible for all the secondary sexual characteristics that develop at puberty. The beard begins to grow, and pubic and axillary hair appear. Vocal cords increase in length and thickness, causing the voice to deepen, and muscle development is stimulated. Testosterone stimulates the rate of secretion of the sebaceous glands in the skin, predisposing the adolescent to acne.

Clinical highlight

When a male is **castrated,** that is, his testes are removed, testosterone levels decrease sharply and he becomes a **eunuch.** If the testes are removed before puberty, the sex organs remain childlike, and the individual does not develop secondary sexual characteristics. Such eunuchs are often slightly taller than normal men because their epiphyses remain open, and although growth is slowed, it continues beyond the normal age of puberty.

If castration occurs after puberty, a gradual loss of some of the secondary sex characteristics occurs. Sex drive is reduced, but sexual activity may continue to some extent. In fact, artificial administration of testosterone can preserve masculinity and sexuality.

The reproductive functions of the female include ova production and incubation of the embryo

The female reproductive system is designed to produce **ova** (eggs), to accept the penis and the sperm released from it during sexual intercourse, to house and nourish the embryo during its prenatal development, and to nourish the infant.

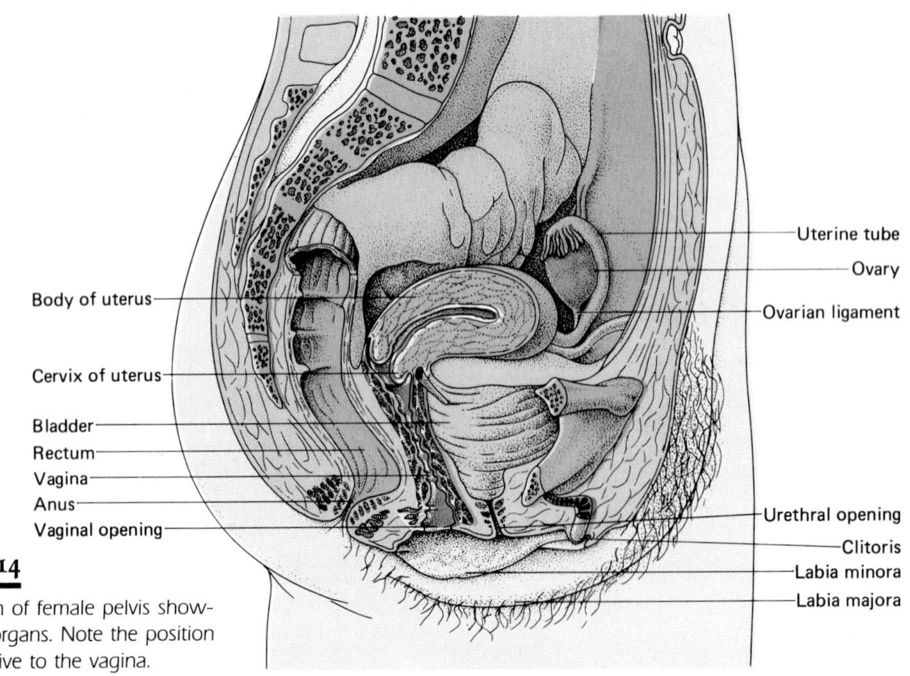

FIGURE 29-14

Midsagittal section of female pelvis showing reproductive organs. Note the position of the uterus relative to the vagina.

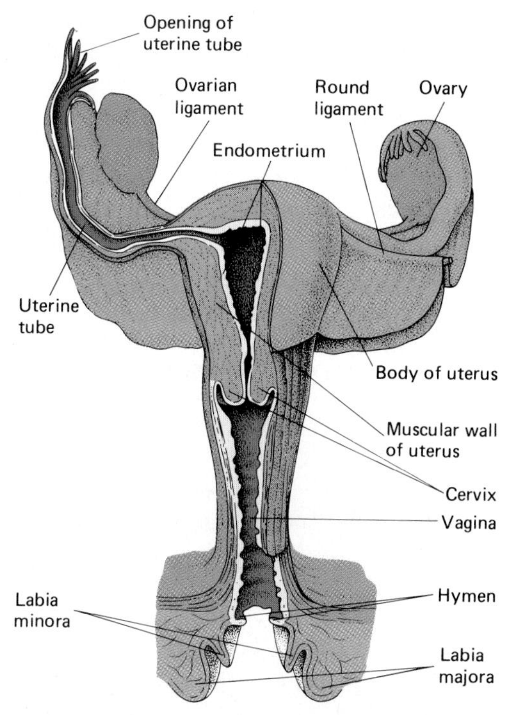

FIGURE 29-15

Anterior view of female reproductive system. Some structures have been cut open to expose the internal structure.

Because it must perform all these diverse functions, the physiology of the female reproductive system is more complex than that of the male. Much of its activity centers about the **menstrual cycle,** the monthly preparation for possible pregnancy.

Principal organs of the female reproductive system (Figs. 29-14 and 29-15) are the ovaries, which produce ova and female hormones; the uterine tubes, where fertilization takes place; the uterus, which is the incubator for the developing child; the vagina, which receives the penis and serves as a birth canal; the vulva, the external genital structures; and the breasts, which produce milk.

The ovaries produce ova and hormones

The paired **ovaries,** the female gonads, produce ova and the female sex hormones, **estrogen** and **progesterone.** About the size and shape of large almonds, the ovaries are located close to the lateral walls of the pelvic cavity (Fig. 29-14). The ovaries are held in position by several connective tissue ligaments (Fig. 29-16). The anterior wall of

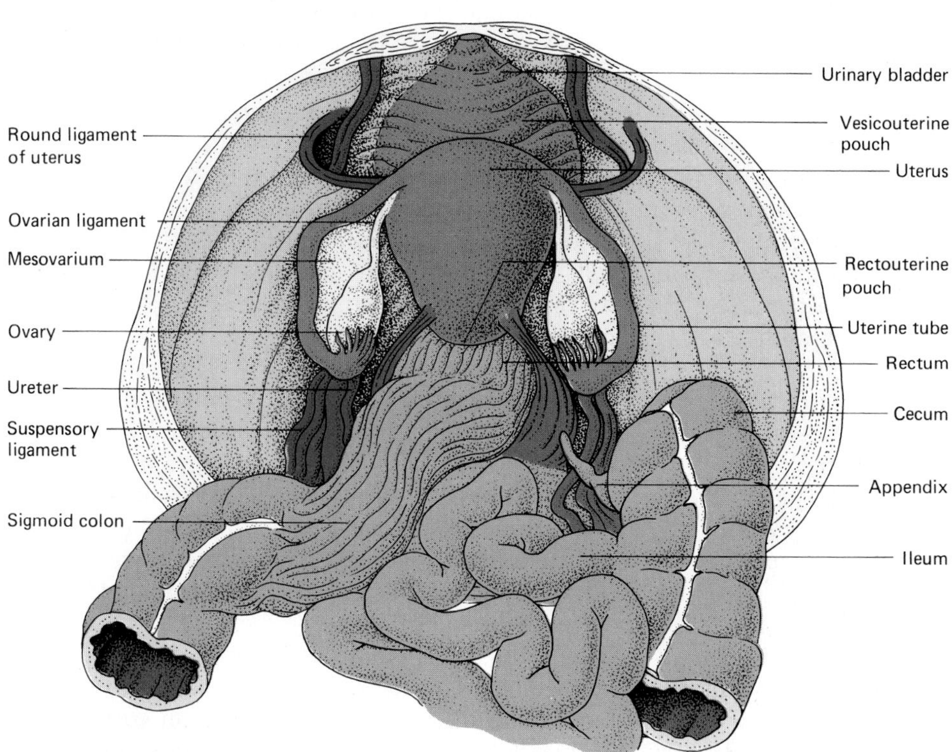

FIGURE 29-16

View of female pelvis showing ovarian and uterine ligaments.

each ovary is attached to the broad ligament of the uterus (part of the parietal peritoneum) by a fold of peritoneum called the **mesovarium** (mes-o-**vare**-e-um). Blood vessels and nerves pass through the mesovarium to and from the hilus (an indented region) of the ovary. The **ovarian ligament** anchors the medial end of the ovary to the uterus. A fold of peritoneum, the **suspensory ligament,** anchors the ovary to the pelvic wall.

The ovary is covered with a single layer of cuboidal epithelium. Just beneath is a layer of dense fibrous connective tissue called the **tunica albuginea.** The tunica albuginea is the outer portion of the **cortex.** The rest of the cortex consists of connective tissue containing a high proportion of cells. This connective tissue is called the **stroma** and contains ova in various stages of maturation. The innermost portion of the ovary, its **medulla,** is made up of loose connective tissue containing many blood and lymph vessels and nerves.

OVA DEVELOP BY MEIOSIS DURING OOGENESIS

Before birth hundreds of thousands of **oogonia** (*o*-o-**go**-ne-ah), cells that give rise to ova, are present in the ovaries. The oogonia are diploid cells which reproduce by mitosis during prenatal development. (Note that oogonia are analogous to spermatogonia in the male.) Each oogonium is surrounded by a cluster of **granulosa cells.** Together the developing ovum and its granulosa cells constitute a **follicle.** Eventually, the oogonia in the follicles lose their ability to carry on mitosis. The female's entire lifetime complement of gametes is established during embryonic development; no new oogonia arise after birth. Development of the oogonium to an eventual mature **ovum** (egg) is called **oogenesis** (*o*-o-**gen**-eh-sis). Oogenesis is illustrated in Figure 29-17.

During the third month of prenatal development the oogonia increase in size to become **primary oocytes.** By the time of birth, the primary oocytes are in the prophase of the first meiotic division (reduction division). At this stage they enter a resting phase that lasts throughout childhood and into adult life.

With the onset of puberty, at about age 12 or 13 years, a few follicles develop each month in response to FSH secreted by the anterior pituitary gland. As the follicle grows, the primary oocyte completes its first meiotic division, producing two haploid cells that are markedly disproportionate in size. The smaller one, called the **first polar body,** may later divide, producing two polar bodies. Both of these eventually disintegrate. The larger cell, the **secondary oocyte,** may continue to develop.

During the process of **ovulation,** the secondary oocyte is ejected through the wall of the ovary and finds its way into the uterine (Fallopian) tube. *If* fertilization occurs, the oocyte undergoes the second meiotic division. Meiosis II produces two disproportionately sized haploid cells. The larger cell, the **ootid,** matures into the **ovum.** The smaller cell is the **second polar body.**

Oogonium ⟶ primary oocyte ⟶ secondary oocyte (+polar body) (both haploid) ⟶ ootid (+polar body) (both haploid) ⟶ ovum (haploid)

In summary, each oogonium undergoes meiosis and gives rise to four cells—three haploid polar bodies and one haploid ovum. The polar bodies disintegrate, leaving one functional haploid ovum. In contrast, recall that each primary spermatocyte gives rise to four functional spermatozoa.

A FEW FOLLICLES DEVELOP EACH MONTH

Normally only one follicle matures each month. Several others develop for about a week, then deteriorate, becoming **atretic follicles** (ah-**tret**-ik; deteriorated follicles). As an oocyte develops, it becomes separated from its surrounding granulosa cells by a thick membrane, the **zona pellucida** (**zo**-nah pel-**loo**-sih-dah) (Fig. 29-18). The zona pellucida consists of mucopolysaccharides secreted by the granulosa cells. Like the Sertoli cells in the testes, the granulosa cells form a barrier around the developing gametes. This barrier prevents harmful substances such as proteins and drugs from reaching the oocyte. The granulosa cells also secrete estrogens. The follicle itself grows by proliferation of its cells and by growth of the stroma that comes to surround it. This surrounding stroma differs somewhat from the general stroma of the ovary and is called the **theca.** As the follicle develops, granulosa cells secrete fluid that collects in a space, or **antrum,** created between them.

As the follicle matures it moves closer to the surface of the ovary, eventually coming to resemble a fluid-filled blister on the ovarian surface. Mature follicles are known as **graafian follicles** (**graf**-ee-an).

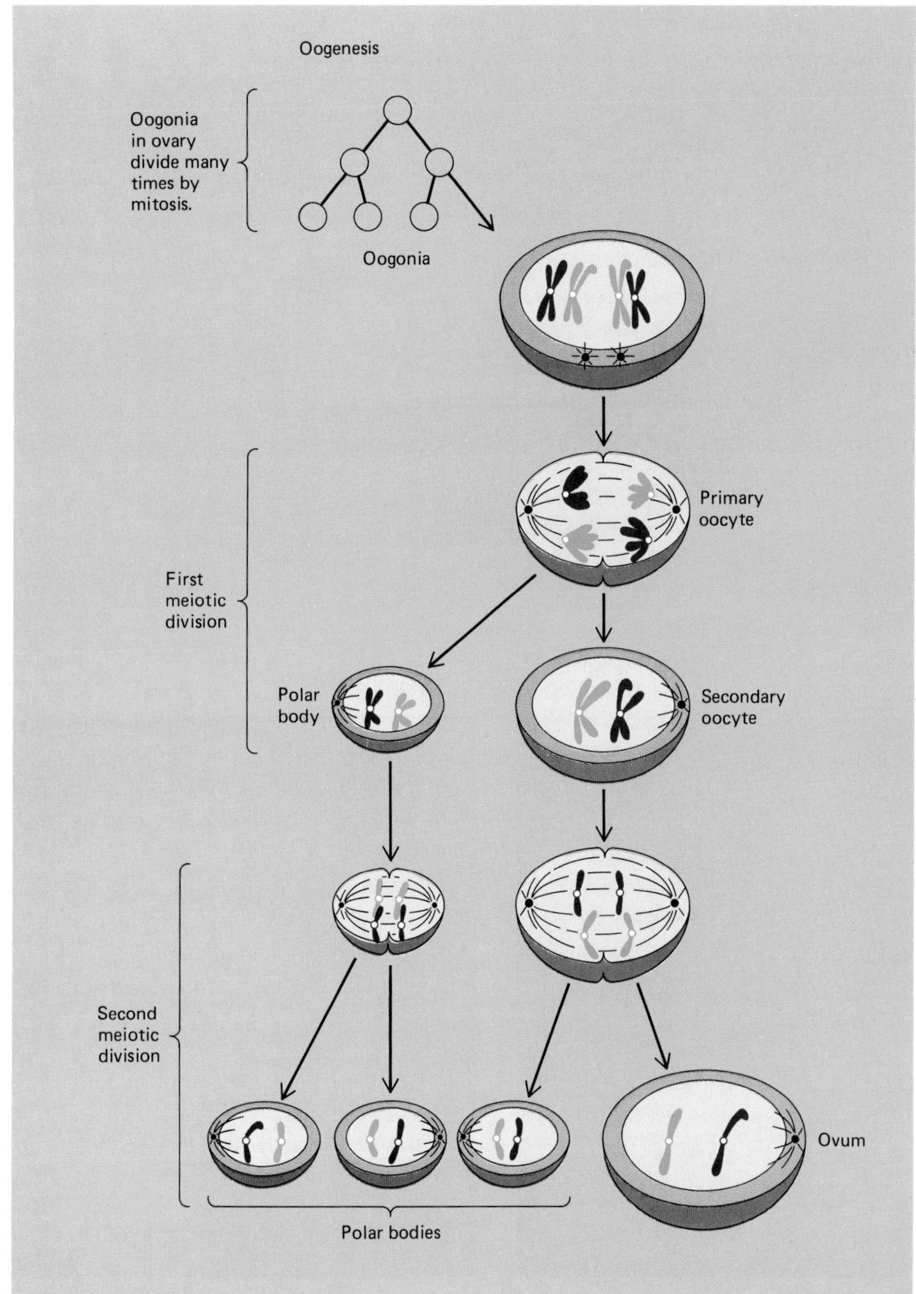

FIGURE 29-17

Oogenesis. In the male, meiosis results in four functional sperm cells, but in the female only one functional ovum is produced. The other three cells produced are polar bodies that degenerate.

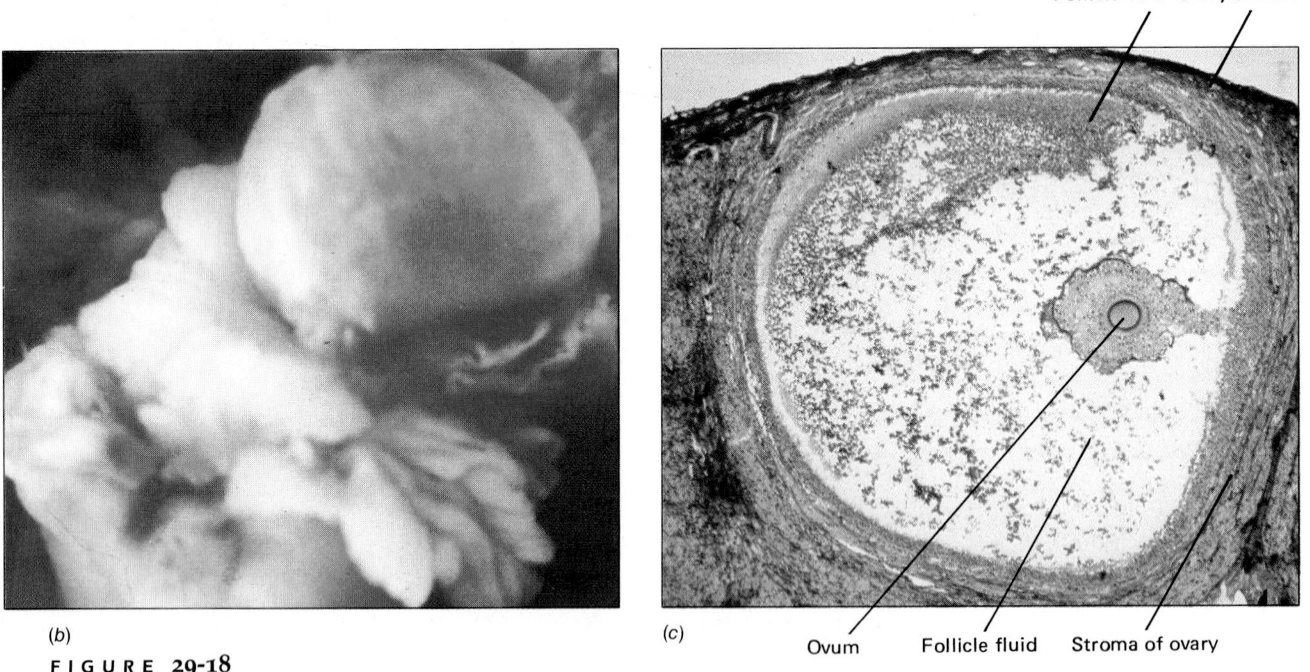

(b) (c)

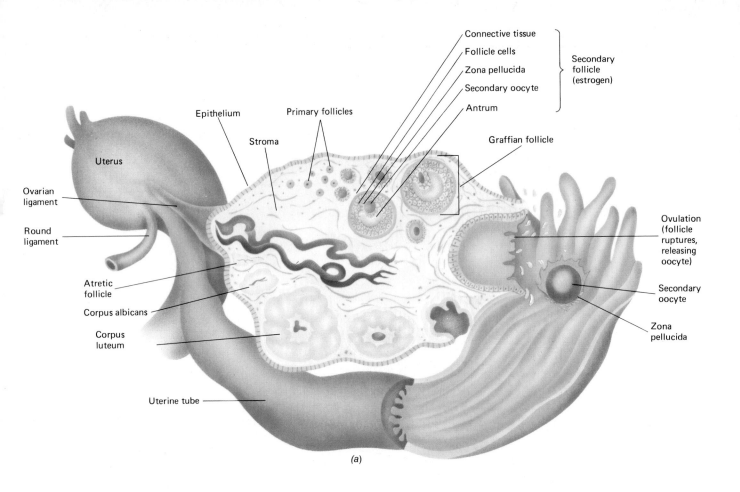

FIGURE 29-18

(*a*) Microscopic structure of the ovary. Follicles in various stages of development may be seen scattered throughout the ovary. (*b*) The mature follicle forms just under the surface of the ovary, producing a tightly stretched fluid-filled blister (shown here from the outside) that will eventually burst, releasing the ovum and the follicle cells surrounding it. The remaining follicle cells then form the corpus luteum. (*c*) This stained microscope slide shows the ovum surrounded by a layer of follicle cells that will be released along with it. These follicle cells become the corona radiata, a layer that acts as a barrier to sperm cells and may help to ensure that the egg is fertilized by only one of the many sperm that crowd around it. (*b*, Petit Format/Photo Researchers, Inc., *c*, Biophoto Associates/Photo Researchers, Inc.)

OVULATION IS THE RELEASE OF THE OVUM FROM THE OVARY

In response to FSH and LH from the anterior pituitary gland, the single mature follicle ruptures after about 2 weeks of development. During **ovulation,** the secondary oocyte is ejected through the wall of the ovary and into the pelvic cavity. Other details of ovulation are discussed in a later section.

THE RUPTURED FOLLICLE DEVELOPS INTO THE CORPUS LUTEUM

Following ovulation the ruptured follicle fills with blood. Granulosa and theca cells then proliferate, replacing clotted blood with yellowish **luteal cells,** which are rich in lipid. LH is responsible for transforming the ruptured follicle into the corpus luteum.

The **corpus luteum** (**kor**-pus **loo**-te-um) is a small mass of endocrine tissue that develops from the follicle after ovulation has occurred. It functions as a temporary endocrine gland, secreting progesterone and estrogen, which helps prepare the uterus for possible pregnancy. Should pregnancy occur, the corpus luteum remains active for several months. If not, it begins to degenerate after about 10 days, remaining in the ovary as a white scar called a **corpus albicans.**

Fertilization takes place in the uterine tubes

At ovulation the secondary oocyte is released into the pelvic cavity. The free end of the **uterine tube,** also called the **fallopian tube** or **oviduct,** is strategically located and designed so that the ovum enters it almost immediately (Fig. 29-18).

Each uterine tube is about 12 centimeters long. Its free end, the **infundibulum,** is shaped like a funnel and has long, finger-like projections called **fimbriae.** The inner lining of the uterine tube consists of a ciliated mucous membrane thrown into longitudinal folds. Beneath this, the wall of the tube is composed of a double layer of smooth muscle. Its thick outer layer is a peritoneal serosa.

The current created by the beating of the cilia and the movements of the fimbriae help to draw the ovum into the uterine tube. Some sort of chemical attraction may also exist. There have been cases in which women who have only a single ovary on one side of the body and a single uterine tube on the opposite side (because of a birth defect or surgery) have become pregnant.

Once inside the uterine tube, the secondary oocyte is moved through the infundibulum to the **ampulla,** the longest part of the tube. Then the oocyte passes through the **isthmus,** the short, narrow portion near the uterus, and finally through the **intramural** passageway into the uterus.

Ovary ⟶ pelvic cavity ⟶ uterine tube (infundibulum ⟶ ampulla ⟶ isthmus ⟶ intramural passageway) ⟶ uterus

The ovum is not capable of independent locomotion. Peristaltic contractions of the muscular wall and the action of the cilia move the ovum toward the uterus.

Fertilization, if it occurs, takes place in the upper third of the uterine tube, and the zygote, or fertilized egg, begins its development as it is moved along toward the uterus. If fertilization does not occur, the ovum degenerates in the uterine tube.

Because the uterine tubes open into the peritoneal cavity, microorganisms that enter through the vagina can pose serious clinical problems. This route of infection has led to many deaths from abortions performed under nonsterile conditions and may also be involved in the spread of some sexually transmitted infections, especially gonorrhea.

Clinical highlight

Inflammation of the uterine tubes, called **salpingitis,** is most often caused by gonorrheal infection. The scarring that sometimes results may partially constrict the tube, resulting in sterility because passage of the ovum is blocked. Sometimes partial tubal constriction results in **tubal pregnancy,** in which the embryo begins to develop in the wall of the uterine tube because it cannot progress to the uterus. Such pregnancies must be diagnosed early so that the tube can be surgically removed before it ruptures, endangering the life of the mother. Uterine tubes are not adapted to bear the burden of a developing embryo. Tubal pregnancies are the most common type of **ectopic pregnancy,** a pregnancy in which the embryo begins to develop outside the uterus.

The uterus incubates the developing embryo

Each month during a woman's reproductive life, the **uterus** prepares for possible pregnancy. Should pregnancy occur, the uterus serves as the incubator for the developing embryo. The tiny embryo implants itself in the wall of the uterus and develops there as a parasite until it is able to live independently. When that time comes, the uterine wall contracts powerfully and rhythmically (the process of labor), expelling the new baby from the mother's body. Each month, if pregnancy does not occur, the inner lining of the uterus sloughs off and is discarded. This process is called **menstruation** (*men*-stroo-**ay**-shun).

THE UTERUS IS A HOLLOW STRUCTURE POSITIONED IN THE PELVIC CAVITY

The uterus, or **womb,** is a single hollow organ shaped somewhat like a pear. In the nonpregnant condition it is about the size of a small fist [about 7.5 centimeters (3 in.) in length and 5 centimeters (2 in.) in width at its widest region]. The uterus lies in the bottom of the pelvic cavity, anterior to the rectum and posterior to the urinary bladder.

Seven ligaments, which are tough, thick, peritoneal folds, anchor the uterus in the pelvic cavity. The **broad ligament** is a double fold of parietal peritoneum that attaches the uterus to the pelvic wall. Uterine blood vessels and nerves pass through the broad ligament. The **round ligaments** are cords of fibrous connective tissue extending between the layers of the broad ligament (Fig. 29-16). They extend from the upper portion of the uterus just below the uterine tubes to the external genital structures known as the labia majora. Other ligaments include the two *uterosacral ligaments,* which attach the uterus to the sacrum; the *posterior ligament,* which attaches the uterus to the rectum; and the *anterior ligament,* which attaches the uterus to the posterior surface of the bladder.

The main portion of the uterus is its **corpus,** or **body.** Above the level of the entrance of the uterine tubes, the rounded portion of the uterus is the **fundus.** The lower narrow portion is the **cervix.** Part of the cervix projects into the vagina (Fig. 29-15).

The cavity of the body of the uterus is called the **uterine cavity,** and the narrower cavity of the cervix is called the **cervical canal.** The junction of the uterine cavity with the cervical canal is the **internal os.** At its lower end the cervical canal is constricted, forming the **external os,** which opens into the vagina.

Uterine cavity ⟶ internal os ⟶ cervical canal ⟶ external os ⟶ vagina

Normally the uterus is flexed between its corpus and cervix, so that it forms almost a right angle with the vagina. The corpus lies over the superior surface of the bladder, pointing in an anterior and slightly superior direction. This anterior tipping is called **anteflexion.** Posterior tipping of the uterus is an abnormal condition called **retroflection.**

THE ENDOMETRIUM OF THE UTERUS CHANGES THROUGHOUT THE MENSTRUAL CYCLE

The wall of the body and fundus of the uterus consists of three layers: endometrium, myometrium, and serosa. The **serosa** is a peritoneal membrane consisting of a single layer of mesothelial cells supported by a thin layer of loose connective tissue. Laterally the serosa is continuous with the broad ligament on each side. Anteriorly it is reflected (bent back) over the urinary bladder, forming the shallow **vesicouterine pouch** behind this organ. Posteriorly the serosa is similarly reflected over the rectum, forming the deep **rectouterine pouch** (or pouch of Douglas) (Fig. 29-16). This pouch is the lowest region in the pelvic cavity.

The middle layer of the uterine wall is the thick **myometrium,** which consists of three poorly defined layers of smooth muscle. The smooth muscle fibers are somewhat scattered through connective tissue. In each layer the muscle fibers are arranged in a different direction.

Lining the uterus is a mucous membrane, the **endometrium.** The thin, deep layer of the endometrium, its **basilar layer,** is continuous with the myometrium. Its thick superficial layer is called the **functional layer.** From the columnar epithelium of the functional layer, uterine glands extend downward through the endometrium (Fig. 29-19).

Just as the ovary develops a new ovum each month, the uterus is also cyclic in its activity. Each month, in response to estrogen and progesterone from the ovary, the endometrium prepares for possible pregnancy. Its functional layer becomes thick, vascular, and secretory. If pregnancy does not occur, most of the functional layer sloughs off during menstruation (Fig. 29-25). These changes will be described in more detail in the discussion of the menstrual cycle.

Clinical highlight

Cancer of the cervix is one of the most common types of cancer in women; it accounts for about 13,000 deaths per year in the United States alone. About 50% of cases of cervical cancer are now detected at very early stages when cures are most likely. Detection is aided by the routine Papanicolaou test (Pap smear), in which a few cells are scraped from the cervix during a regular gynecological examination and studied microscopically. Cells are ranked in one of five classes: class I, normal; class II, probably normal (slightly atypical); class III, doubtful (atypical cells may indicate possible cancer); class IV, probable cancer; class V, cancer. About 95% of cervical cancer cases are squamous cell carcinomas, which arise in the squamous epithelium.

Although the cause of cervical cancer is not known, studies indicate that there is a higher incidence in women who begin having sexual intercourse at an early age, have many sexual partners, or have frequent intercourse. Incidence is lowest in nuns and in women whose sexual partners were circumcised at an early age. It has been suggested that infection with herpes simplex virus type 2 may play a role in cervical cancer.

The vagina functions in intercourse, menstruation, and birth

The **vagina** functions as the sexual organ that receives the penis during sexual intercourse. During menstruation, the vagina serves as an exit through which the discarded endometrium is discharged. The vagina also functions as the lower part of the birth canal.

Located anterior to the rectum and posterior to the urethra and urinary bladder, the vagina is an elastic muscular tube capable of considerable distension. It extends from the cervix to its orifice (opening) into the vestibule outside (Fig. 29-20). The vagina surrounds the end of the cervix. The recesses formed between the vaginal wall and cervix are called **fornices** (singular, **fornix**). The posterior fornix is larger than the ventral and two lateral fornices.

The vagina is normally collapsed so that its anterior and posterior walls touch each other, and the lumen appears in cross section as no more than a slit. Two longitudinal ridges run along anterior and posterior walls, and there are numerous transverse folds called **rugae** (**roo**-jee). During intercourse when the penis is inserted into the vagina or during childbirth when the baby's head emerges into the vagina, the rugae straighten out, greatly enlarging the vagina.

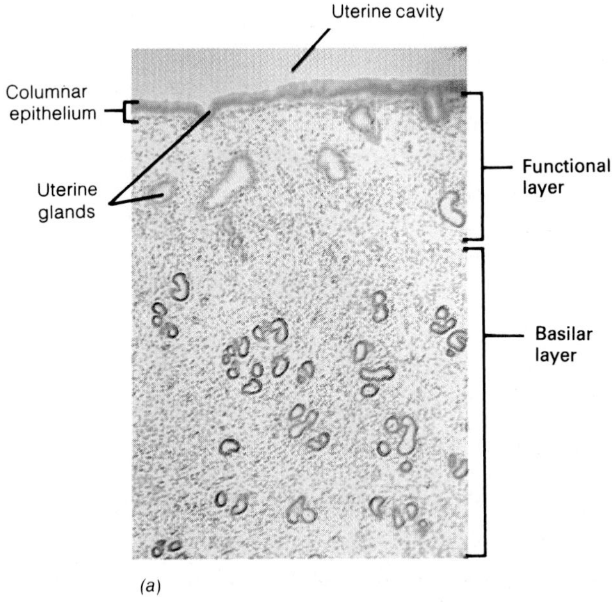

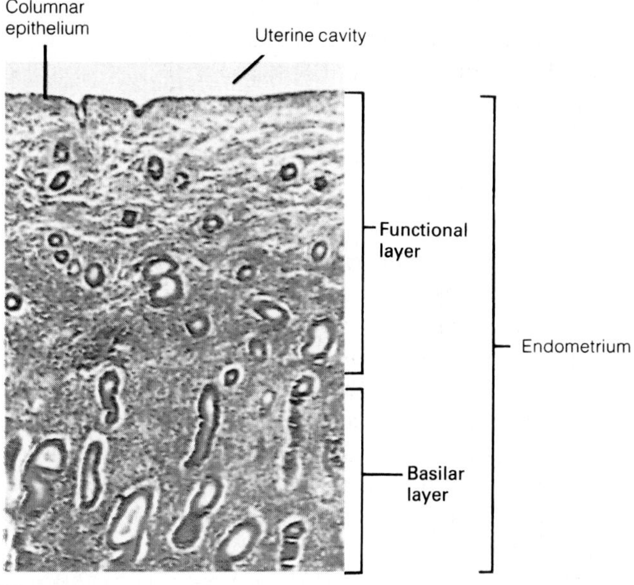

FIGURE 29-19

The endometrium of the uterine wall. (*a*) Photomicrograph of a section of the uterine wall during the early part of the menstrual cycle. Because the functional layer and the basilar layer are defined more on the basis of function than structure, the dividing line between them is only approximate. (*b*) Photomicrograph of a section of the uterine wall later in the menstrual cycle, after ovulation. Note the increased development of the functional layer. (*a*, Ed Reschke/ Peter Arnold, Inc., *b*, Biophoto Associates/Photo Researchers, Inc.)

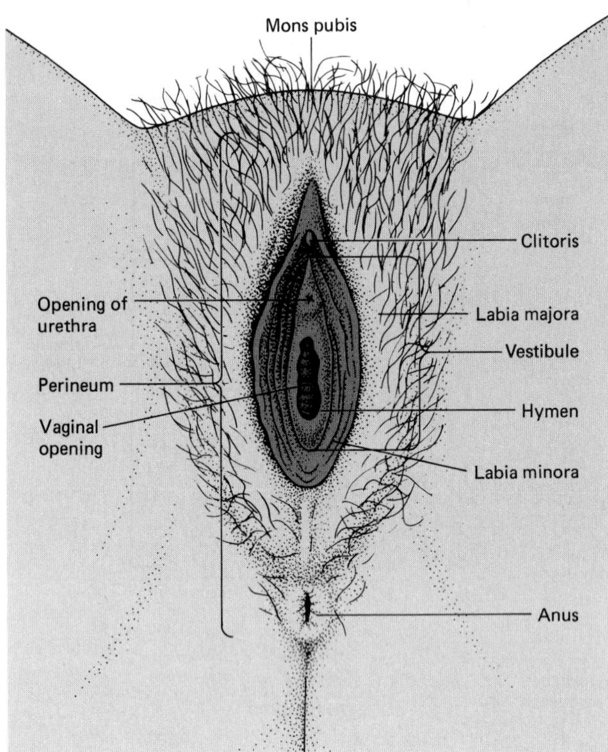

FIGURE 29-20

Vulva.

A mucous membrane consisting of stratified squamous epithelium resting upon connective tissue lines the vagina. The vaginal wall is lubricated by fluids of two origins. Although the vaginal wall contains no glands, during sexual excitement its numerous small blood vessels become engorged with blood, and fluid filters out through the epithelium. Mucus secreted by the cervix contributes to the lubrication of the vagina. Additionally, secretions from the greater vestibular glands (see next section) provide lubrication.

A thin ring of mucous membrane, the **hymen** (sometimes popularly referred to as the maidenhead), partially blocks the entrance to the vagina. Through the ages the hymen has been heralded as the symbol of virginity because it is often ruptured during a woman's first coitus (sexual intercourse). All the attention focused on the hymen is not merited, however, since it is not necessarily a reliable indicator of virginity. In some women the hymen is elastic and may persist despite coitus. And in many cases it ruptures during strenuous physical exercise in childhood or as a result of inserting tampons to absorb the menstrual flow.

Clinical highlight

An **imperforate hymen,** one that completely blocks the vaginal orifice, occurs rarely. It must be surgically perforated before puberty so that the menstrual flow can be discharged to the exterior of the body.

The external female genitalia are the vulva

The term **vulva,** or **pudendum,** refers to the external female genital structures. They include the mons pubis, labia majora, labia minora, clitoris, and vestibule of the vagina (Fig. 29-20). The **mons pubis** is a mound of fatty tissue that covers the pubic symphysis. At puberty it becomes covered by coarse pubic hair. Its many touch receptors make the mons pubis a highly sensitive organ.

The paired **labia majora** (meaning large lips) are folds of skin that pass from the mons pubis to the region behind the vaginal opening. Normally the labia majora meet in the midline, providing protection for the genital structures beneath. After puberty the outer epidermis of the lips is pigmented and covered with coarse hair. Sensory receptors are abundant. Two thin folds of skin, the **labia minora** (small lips), are located just within the labia majora. Anteriorly they merge to form the prepuce of the clitoris.

The **clitoris** is a small body of erectile tissue, homologous to the male glans penis. It consists of two columns of erectile tissue called corpora cavernosa. The clitoris projects from the anterior end of the vulva at the anterior junction of the labia minora. Although it is about 2 centimeters long and 0.5 centimeter in diameter, most of the clitoris is not visible because it is embedded in the tissues of the vulva. It is almost covered by a fold of flesh, its prepuce, which is formed by the merging labial tissue. The exposed portion of the clitoris is its **glans.** A receptor of sexual stimuli, the clitoris is the main focus of sexual sensation in the female. During sexual excitement its erectile tissue becomes engorged with blood.

The space enclosed by the labia minora is the **vestibule.** Two openings are apparent in the vestibule, the urethral orifice anteriorly and the vaginal orifice posteriorly.

Two small **Bartholin's glands,** also called greater vestibular glands, open on each side of the vaginal orifice. These glands secrete mucus. A group of smaller glands, the **lesser vestibular** (or Skene's) **glands,** open into the vestibule near the urethral orifice and also secrete mucus. The vestibular glands help provide lubrication during sex-

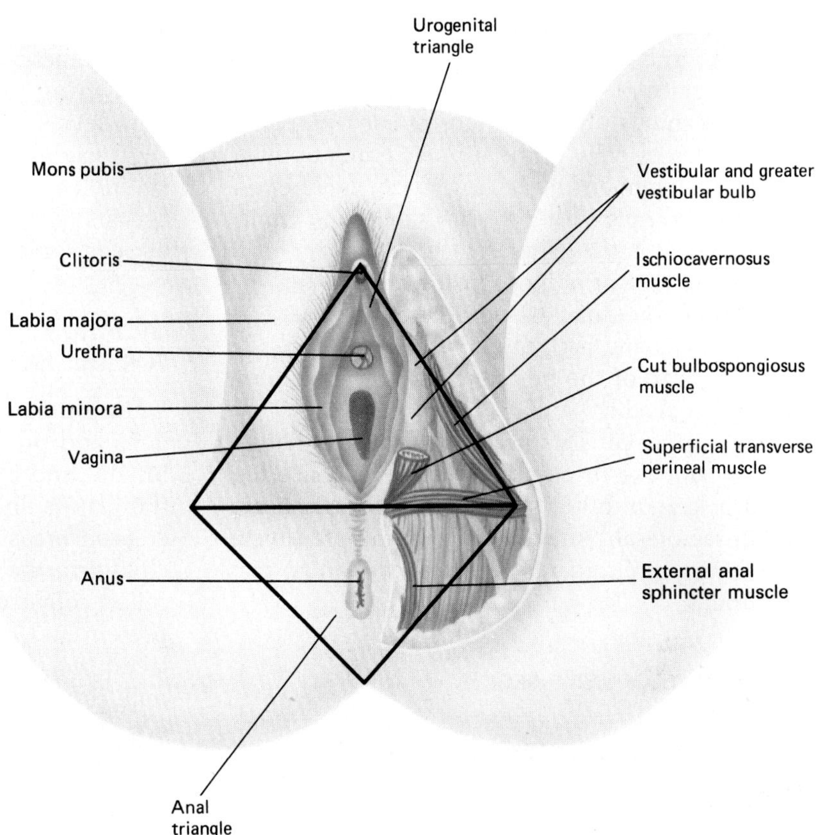

FIGURE 29-21

The perineum in the female.

ual intercourse. These glands are vulnerable to infection, especially from the bacteria that cause gonorrhea.

Two elongated masses of erectile tissue, the **bulbs of the vestibule,** are located beneath the surface on each side of the vaginal opening. In both male and female the diamond-shaped region between the pubic arch and the anus is the **perineum.** In the female the region between the vagina and anus is called the **clinical** (gynecological) **perineum** (Fig. 29-21).

The breasts contain the mammary glands

Lactation (milk production) is the function of the **mammary glands** located within the breasts. The breasts overlie the pectoralis muscles and are attached to them by fasciae. Fibrous bands of tissue called **ligaments of Cooper** firmly connect the breasts to the skin.

Each breast is composed of 15 to 20 lobes of glandular tissue, further subdivided into lobules. The lobules consist of connective tissue in which gland cells are embedded. The secretory cells are arranged in little grapelike clusters called **alveoli** (Fig. 29-22). Ducts from each cluster unite to form

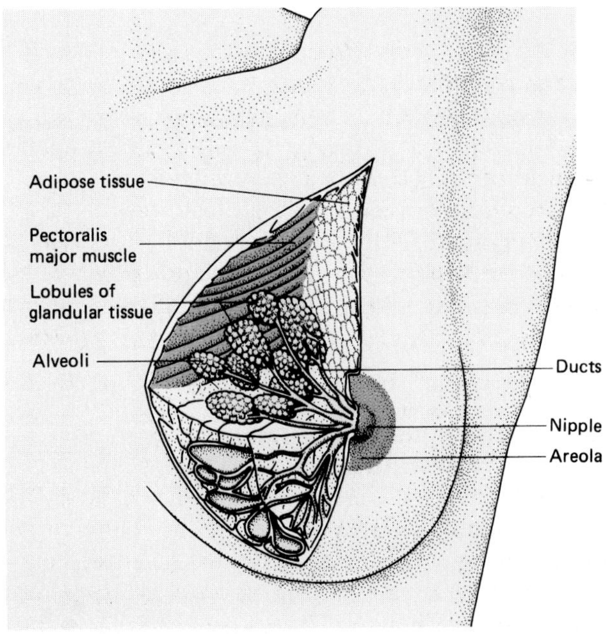

FIGURE 29-22

The mature female breast.

a single duct from each lobe. These main ducts enlarge slightly into **ampullae** just before opening on the surface of the nipple. Thus, there are 15 to 20 tiny openings on the surface of each nipple. (Some types of baby bottle nipples emulate this natural arrangement by having many small openings in the nipple rather than a single one, as in old-fashioned bottle nipples.)

The amount of adipose tissue around the lobes of the glandular tissue determines the size of the breasts and accounts for their soft consistency. The size of the breasts does not affect their capacity to produce milk.

The nipple consists of smooth muscle that can contract to make the nipple erect in response to sexual or certain other stimuli. In the pinkish **areola** (ah-**ree**-oh-lah) surrounding the nipple several rudimentary milk glands (the areolar glands) may be found.

BREAST DEVELOPMENT BEGINS AT PUBERTY

In childhood the breasts contain only rudimentary ducts (Fig. 29-23). At puberty, estrogens and progesterone, in the presence of growth hormone and prolactin, stimulate development of the glands and ducts and the deposition of fatty tissue characteristic of the adult breast.

During the latter part of each menstrual cycle high levels of circulating progesterone stimulate the secretory cells in the breast. Progesterone also promotes water retention, and as a result the breasts tend to swell slightly, become tender, and appear somewhat larger.

LACTATION PROVIDES NUTRIENTS FOR THE INFANT

During pregnancy high concentrations of estrogens and progesterone produced by the corpus luteum and by the placenta (Chapter 30) stimulate the glands and ducts to develop, resulting in increased breast size. For the first few days after childbirth the mammary glands produce a fluid called **colostrum** (kow-**los**-trum), which contains protein and lactose but little fat. After birth, prolactin secreted by the anterior pituitary stimulates milk production, and by the third day after delivery, milk itself is produced.

When the infant suckles at the breast, a reflex action results in release of prolactin and oxytocin from the pituitary gland. Oxytocin causes contrac-

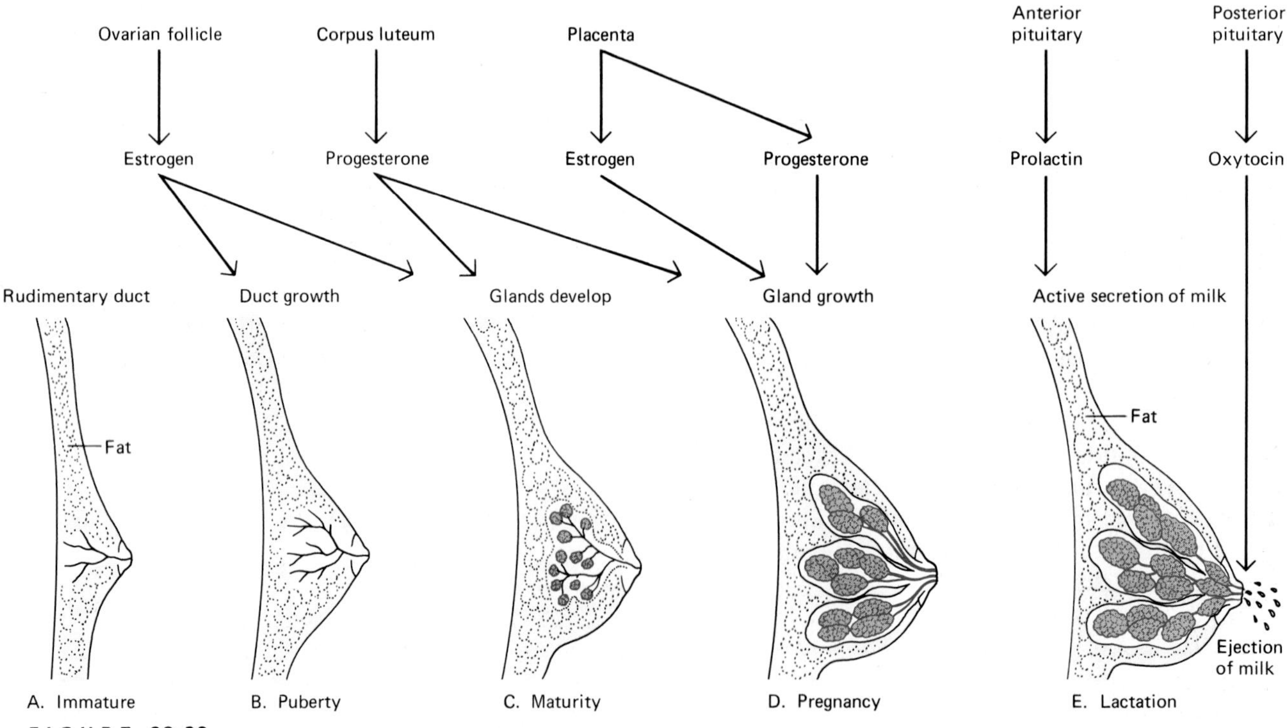

FIGURE 29-23

Development of the female breast.

tion of myoepithelial cells in the alveolar ducts, leading to release of milk from the breasts.

Breast-feeding a baby offers many advantages, including promoting a close bond between the mother and child. Breast milk is tailored to the nutritional needs of a human infant, whereas in sensitive infants, cow's milk is more likely to produce allergies to dairy products. Furthermore, breast-fed babies receive antibodies from the colostrum and from breast milk that are thought to play a protective role, resulting in a lower incidence of infant diarrhea and even of respiratory infection during the second 6 months of life. Breast-feeding also helps the uterus to recover from childbirth because oxytocin stimulates it to contract to nonpregnant size.

Clinical highlight

Breast cancer is the most common type of cancer among women. Breast cancer incidence has increased in recent years and now strikes about 1 in every 10 women; it is the leading cause of cancer deaths in women. About 50% of breast cancers begin in the upper outer quadrant of the breast (Fig. 29-22). As a malignant tumor grows, it may adhere to the deep fascia of the chest wall. Sometimes it extends to the skin, causing dimpling. Eventually the cancer spreads to the lymphatic system, often to the axillary nodes or the nodes along the internal thoracic (mammary) artery. About two-thirds of breast cancers have metastasized (spread) to the lymph nodes by the time the cancer is first diagnosed.

Mastectomy (mas-**tek**-tow-me; surgical removal of the breast) and **radiation treatment** are common methods of treating breast cancer. **Chemotherapy** is especially useful in preventing metastasis, especially in premenopausal patients. A recent development in cancer treatment is the use of **biological response modifiers** such as interferons, interleukins, and monoclonal antibodies.

About one-third of breast cancers are estrogen-dependent; that is, their growth depends upon circulating estrogens. Removing the ovaries in patients with these tumors relieves the symptoms and may cause the disease to regress for months or even years. When diagnosis and treatment begin early, 80% of patients survive for 5 years and 62% for 10 years or longer. Untreated patients have only a 20% 5-year survival rate.

Because early detection of these cancers greatly increases the chances of cure and survival, campaigns have been launched to educate women on the importance of self-examination. **Mammography** (mah-**mog**-rah-fee), a soft-tissue radiological study of the breast, is a technique helpful in detecting very small lesions that might not be identified by palpation. Lesions show on an x-ray plate as areas of increased density. In **xeromammography,** the x-ray image is produced on paper rather than on film. This method requires less radiation and provides excellent detail. (See the mammogram in Figure 29-24.) Other techniques that are proving helpful in early detection are **ultrasonic** studies (in which high-frequency sound waves bounced off the body indicate the presence of neoplasms) and thermography. **Thermography** records temperature differences on the skin surface that reflect differences in vascularity of underlying tissues. (Cancers produce increased vascularity because they stimulate growth of new blood vessels required to sustain them.) Breast thermography has a high rate of false positives (up to 25%) and so is being replaced by ultrasonography and low-dose mammography.

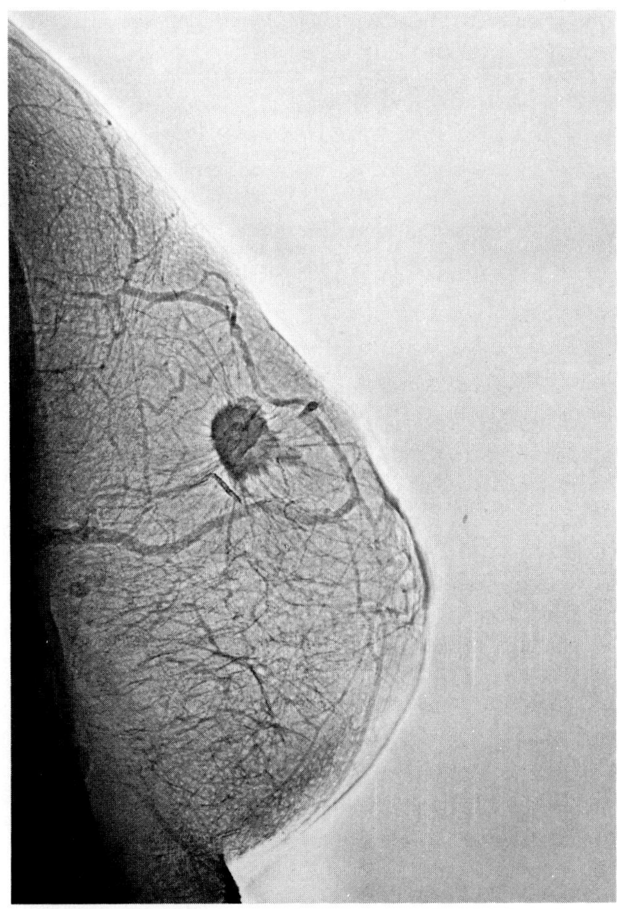

FIGURE 29-24

Mammogram showing breast cancer. Note extensive vascularization.

Hormones regulate female sexuality and reproduction

Table 29-2 lists both the gonadotropic and ovarian female reproductive hormones. The hypothalamus secretes gonadotropin-releasing hormone (GnRH), which stimulates the release of the gonadotropic hormones FSH and LH from the anterior pituitary

TABLE 29-2

Principal female reproductive hormones

Endocrine gland and hormone	Principal target tissue	Principal actions
Hypothalamus		
Gonadotropin releasing hormone (GnRH)	Anterior pituitary	Stimulates release of FSH and LH
Anterior pituitary		
Follicle-stimulating hormone (FSH)	Ovary	Stimulates development of follicles; with LH, stimulates secretion of estrogens and ovulation
Luteinizing hormone (LH)	Ovary	Stimulates final development of follicle; stimulates ovulation; stimulates development of corpus luteum
Prolactin	Breasts	Stimulates milk production (after breast has been prepared by estrogens and progesterone)
Posterior pituitary		
Oxytocin	Breasts	Stimulates release of milk into ducts
	Uterus	Stimulates contraction
Ovary		
Estrogens	General	Growth of body and sex organs at puberty; development of secondary sex characteristics (breast development, broadening of pelvis, distribution of fat and muscle)
	Reproductive structures	Maturation; monthly preparation of the endometrium for pregnancy; makes cervical mucus thinner and more alkaline
Progesterone	Uterus	Completes preparation of and maintains endometrium for pregnancy
	Breasts	Stimulates development of lobules and alveoli of mammary glands

gland (Fig. 29-25). FSH stimulates development of follicles in the ovary and the secretion of estrogens by the follicles. LH stimulates final maturation of follicles, production of estrogens and progesterone, and ovulation. LH is also responsible for the development of the corpus luteum from the ruptured follicle.

Estrogens is a general term that has been used here to refer collectively to a group of closely related 18-carbon steroid hormones. Only three of these hormones—*estrone*, *estriol*, and β-estradiol—are present in significant amounts. β-estradiol is the most potent and is considered the major estrogen.

Estrogens are secreted by the theca cells of the follicles, by the corpus luteum, and by the placenta during pregnancy. Minute amounts are secreted by the adrenal cortex. Estrogens are synthesized in the body from androgens.

Like testosterone in the male, estrogens are responsible for the growth of sex organs at puberty and for the development of secondary sex characteristics—initiation of breast development, broadening of the pelvis, and characteristic distribution of fat and muscle. Actual growth of pubic hair is thought to be stimulated by androgens secreted by the adrenal glands, but estrogens apparently influence the pattern of pubic hair growth.

During the menstrual cycle, estrogens enhance the growth of follicles, stimulate growth of the endometrium, increase peristaltic movements of the uterine tubes, and make the cervical mucus thinner and more alkaline. The more alkaline pH is favorable to sperm survival.

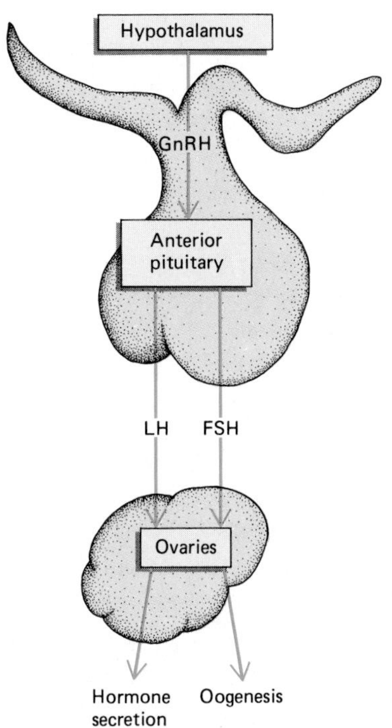

FIGURE 29-25

Relationship among the hypothalamus, anterior pituitary gland, and ovaries.

Progesterone (pro-**jes**-ter-own) is a 21-carbon steroid secreted by the corpus luteum and by the placenta during pregnancy. It is a precursor of both androgens and estrogens. One of its most important actions is to stimulate the endometrium to complete its preparation for pregnancy. Under its influence, glands of the endometrium secrete nutrients for the early embryo.

Progesterone inhibits contractions of the uterus and uterine tubes so that the embryo will not be expelled prematurely. It also stimulates characteristic cyclic changes in the lining of the vagina and cervix and promotes further development of the mammary glands. Progesterone is responsible for the slight rise in body temperature during the second half of the menstrual cycle.

It should be clear that both males and females have the same sex hormones. What is important is the difference in concentration. Testosterone circulates in the blood of adult women but at only about one-fifth the amount in adult males. The actions of the androgens in the female are not completely understood. They may contribute, along with estrogens, to the growth spurt at puberty and to the closure of the epiphyses.

The menstrual cycle prepares the body for pregnancy

As a girl approaches puberty the anterior pituitary gland secretes the gonadotropic hormones FSH and LH, which signal the ovaries to begin functioning. Interaction of FSH and LH with estrogens and progesterone from the ovaries regulates the menstrual cycle, which runs its course every month from puberty until menopause, the end of a woman's reproductive life. The menstrual cycle stimulates production of an ovum each month and prepares the uterus for pregnancy.

Although there is wide variation, a "typical" menstrual cycle is 28 days long. However, the menstrual cycle may be thrown off by stress, excessive physical exercise, or change in diet.

The first day of menstruation marks the first day of the cycle. Ovulation occurs about 14 days before the next cycle begins; in a 28-day cycle this would correspond to about the fourteenth day (Fig. 29-26).

MENSTRUATION IS THE FIRST PHASE OF THE MENSTRUAL CYCLE

Low levels of estrogen and progesterone result in menstruation, which lasts for about the first 5 days of the menstrual cycle. During menstruation the thickened endometrium of the uterus is gradually sloughed off. Total blood loss is about 35 milliliters (1 fl oz), but an additional 35 ml of fluids from the uterine glands is also discharged. Menstrual blood normally does not clot because of the presence of an anticoagulant released by the endometrium. During this phase of the menstrual cycle, FSH is the principal hormone released by the pituitary gland. It stimulates a group of follicles to develop in the ovary.

THE PREOVULATORY PHASE IS THE SECOND PHASE OF THE MENSTRUAL CYCLE

During the **preovulatory phase** (also called the proliferative or estrogen phase) of the menstrual cycle, FSH and LH stimulate the follicles developing in the ovary to produce estrogens. The estrogens stimulate growth of the endometrium once again. Its blood vessels and glands begin to develop anew. As the estogen level rises, the ante-

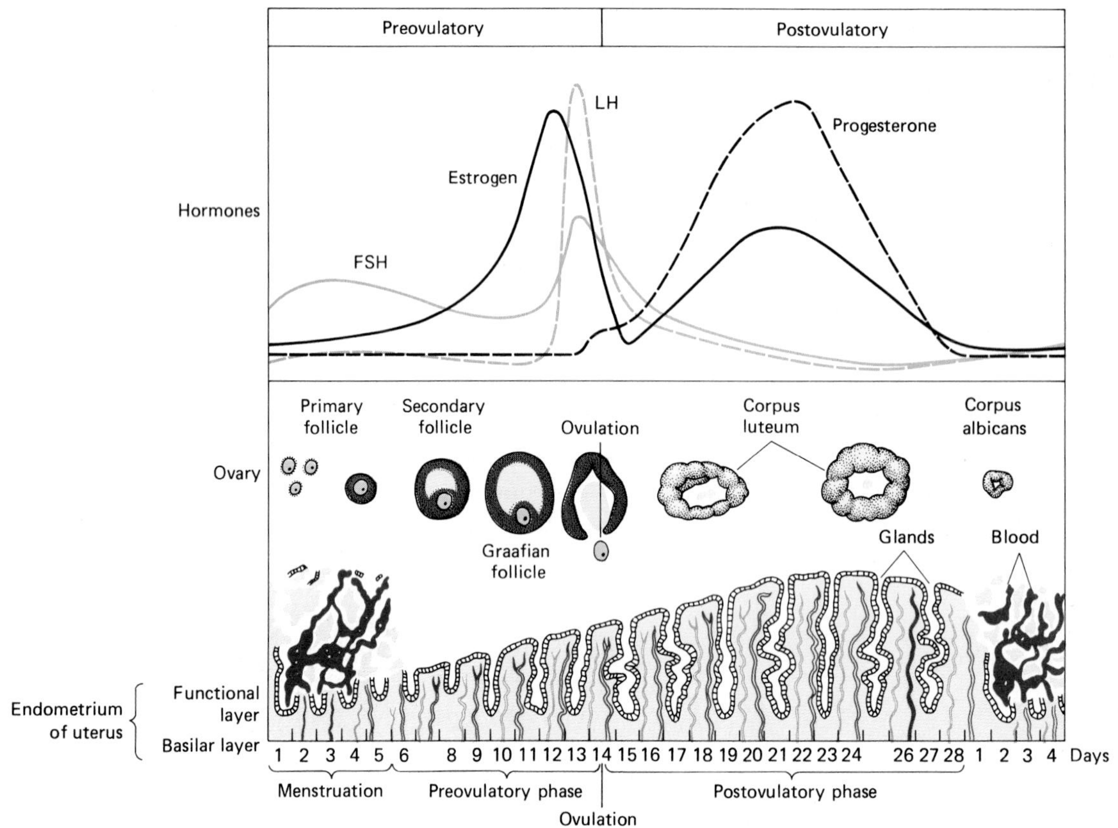

FIGURE 29-26

The menstrual cycle. The events that take place within the pituitary, ovary, and uterus are precisely synchronized. When fertilization does not occur, the cycle repeats itself about every 28 days.

rior pituitary increases its secretion of LH. The rise in LH stimulates the granulosa cells of the follicle to secrete progesterone (Fig. 29-27). The rise in LH also stimulates the theca cells to secrete testosterone and another androgen. These androgens diffuse into the granulosa cells of the follicle and serve as precursors for estrogen production.

↑ FSH and ↑ LH ⟶ growth of follicles
⟶ ↑ estrogens ⟶ growth of endometrium

↑ Estrogen ⟶ anterior pituitary ⟶
↑ LH ⟶ follicle ⟶ ↑ progesterone ⟶
growth of endometrium

At midcycle the large amounts of estrogens secreted from the follicles inhibit GnRH production by the hypothalamus (Fig. 29-26). As a result the anterior pituitary slows its release of FSH. Note that this is a negative feedback cycle.

↑ Estrogens - - → hypothalamus ⟶ ↓ GnRH
- - → anterior pituitary ⟶ ↓ FSH

The rise in estrogen secretion has a different effect on the anterior pituitary. The estrogen *stimulates* the anterior pituitary to secrete a surge of LH. This stimulating effect is a positive feedback mechanism. The surge of LH is necessary for the final maturation of the follicle and for ovulation to occur.

↑Estrogens ⟶ anterior pituitary ⟶
↑ LH ⟶ final maturation of follicle and ovulation

THE POSTOVULATORY PHASE IS THE THIRD PHASE OF THE MENSTRUAL CYCLE

After ovulation the **postovulatory phase** (also called the secretory, or luteal, phase) begins. LH stimulates development of the corpus luteum, which releases progesterone as well as estrogens. These hormones stimulate continued thickening of the endometrium (Fig. 29-28). Progesterone

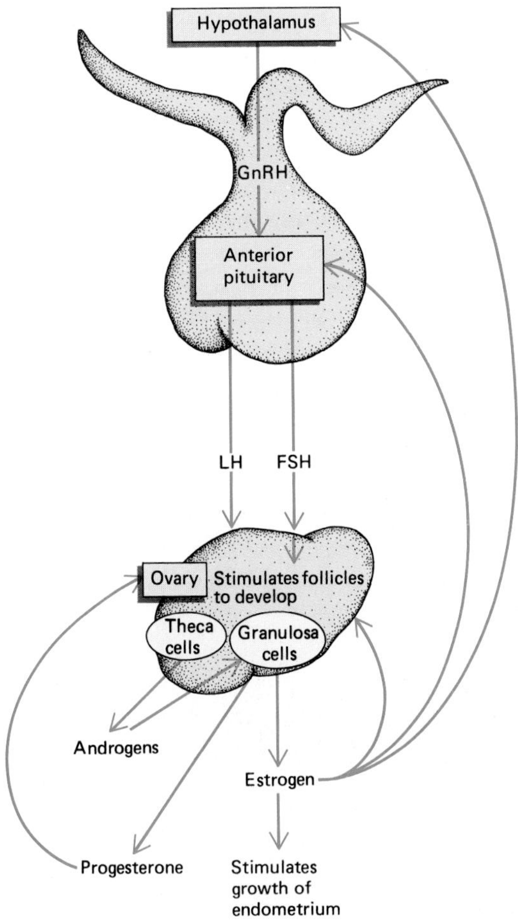

FIGURE 29-27

Hormonal interactions during the preovulatory phase.

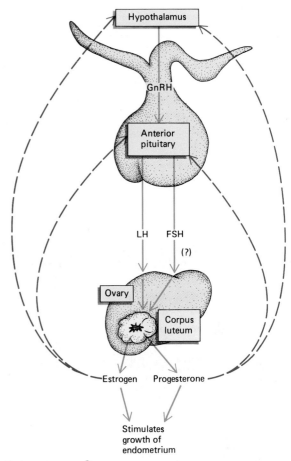

Hypothalamus
GnRH
Anterior pituitary
LH
FSH
(?)
Ovary
Corpus luteum
Estrogen
Progesterone
Stimulates growth of endometrium

FIGURE 29-28

Hormonal interactions during the postovulatory phase.

especially affects the small glands in the endometrium, stimulating them to secrete a fluid rich in nutrients.

Should fertilization occur, this nutritive fluid nourishes the early embryo when it arrives in the uterus on about the fourth day of development. On about the seventh day after fertilization, the embryo begins to implant itself in the thick endometrium of the uterus (Fig. 29-29). The placenta begins to develop and secretes a hormone called **human chorionic gonadotropin (HCG),** which signals the corpus luteum to continue to function.

Fertilization ⟶ placenta develops ⟶ ↑ HCG ⟶ maintains corpus luteum

If pregnancy does not occur, the high concentrations of estrogens and progesterone from the corpus luteum inhibit GnRH and LH secretion. As a result, the corpus luteum begins to degenerate, and progesterone and estrogen concentration in the blood fall markedly. Spiral arteries in the uterine wall constrict, and the part of the endometrium they supply becomes ischemic (oxygen-deprived). Menstruation begins once again as cells begin to die and damaged arteries rupture and bleed. Prostaglandins liberated in the endometrium are thought to help stimulate the sloughing off of the endometrial tissue. See Focus on Some Disorders of the Female Reproductive System.

No fertilization: ↑ estrogens and progesterone --→ hypothalamus and anterior pituitary ⟶ ↓ GnRH and ↓ LH ⟶ corpus luteum degenerates ⟶ ↓ estrogen and ↓ progesterone ⟶ menstruation

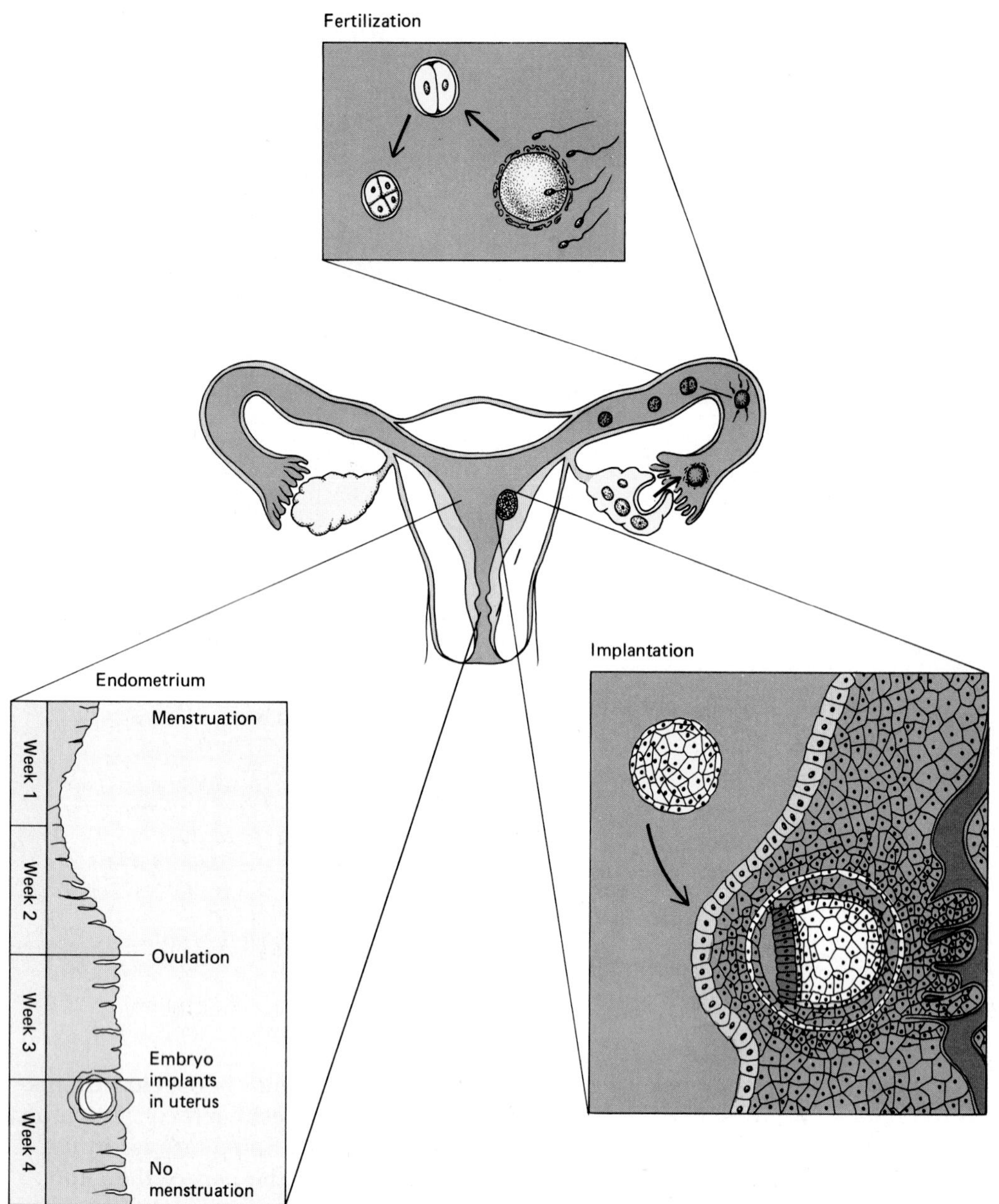

FIGURE 29-29

The menstrual cycle is interrupted when pregnancy occurs. The corpus luteum does not degenerate, and menstruation does not take place. The endometrium remains very thick, providing the embryo with an ideal environment for development.

PINPOINTING OVULATION IS HELPFUL IN FACILITATING CONCEPTION OR CONTRACEPTION

When a couple attempts to conceive a child, it is helpful to know just when ovulation takes place. This information is equally important for those who practice the rhythm method of birth control. Several indicators of ovulation have been identified, but unfortunately none is completely reliable. One method for pinpointing the time of ovulation depends upon changes in body temperature. About the time of ovulation, body temperature first dips, then rises about 0.3°C (0.5°F) above average body temperature. It remains elevated until just before menstruation; if pregnancy occurs, the elevation continues.

Sometimes ovulation is accompanied by pelvic discomfort referred to as "middle pain" **(mittelschmerz).** Another indicator of ovulation is the

FOCUS ON . . . Some disorders of the female reproductive system

Amenorrhea	Absence of menstruation. Indicates failure of the hypothalamic-pituitary-ovarian interaction to produce the cyclic changes in the endometrium of the uterus essential to menstruation. Amenorrhea may be a sign of any of a large number of disorders involving several organ systems. **Primary amenorrhea** is the absence of menarche (first menstruation) by age 16. **Secondary amenorrhea** is the absence of menstruation for 3 months in a woman who has experienced menstruation. A common cause of amenorrhea is chronic anovulation (ovulation does not occur). Failure to ovulate can be linked to malnutrition, including the malnutrition that occurs in the psychologic disorder anorexia nervosa. Anovulation can also be associated with rigorous exercise. Other causes involve disorders of the pituitary gland, ovaries, adrenal, or thyroid gland.
Abnormal uterine bleeding	May be associated with prolonged menstruation, excessive amount of menstruation, too frequent menstruation, intermenstrual bleeding, or postmenopausal bleeding. In about 75% of patients there is a functional abnormality of the hypothalamic-pituitary-ovarian interaction. Such dysfunctional bleeding is most common during the early reproductive years. In about 25% of patients with abnormal uterine bleeding there is an organic cause such as a neoplasm of the reproductive tract. Fibroid tumors, for example, are a common cause.
Dysmenorrhea	Painful menstruation. **Primary dysmenorrhea** is cyclic pain associated with menstruation that is not caused by neoplasms that affect the reproductive cycle. The pain is thought to result from uterine contractions and ischemia. Prostaglandins produced in excessive amount by the uterus may be the cause of these uterine contractions. This common condition usually appears during adolescence and decreases with age and following pregnancy. **Secondary dysmenorrhea** is painful menstruation caused by neoplasms such as endometriosis (see below).
Endometriosis	The presence of endometrial tissue in abnormal locations, that is, outside the uterus. Found in 25 to 50% of infertile women. Intra-abdominal endometriosis is thought to be due to retrograde flow of menstrual tissue through the uterine tubes. Endometriosis at distant sites such as the lung may result from transport of fragments of endometrial tissue by the blood or lymph. Symptoms include premenstrual pain or unusual pain during menstruation. Treatment is controversial and may consist of medically suppressing the ovaries so that the activity of the abnormal endometrial tissue will be inhibited.
Toxic shock syndrome	A disorder characterized by sudden onset, high fever, headache, vomiting, skin rash, and confusion. The condition can rapidly progress to severe shock. Although first described in children and sometimes diagnosed in males, toxic shock syndrome is most common in women age 13 to 52. It is almost always linked with the use of vaginal tampons to absorb the menstrual flow. Almost all patients have been found to have an infection with a virally infected strain of the bacterium *Staphylococcus aureus*. The virus apparently is responsible for the production by the bacterium of toxic shock toxin. Women most at risk apparently have preexisting colonies of *S. aureus* in their vaginas and also use tampons. During the past few years manufacturers of tampons have been increasing the absorptive properties of tampons. Treatment generally involves immediate hospitalization, treatment of symptoms, and antibiotic therapy.

quality of the cervical mucus. As ovulation approaches, the cervical mucus becomes abundant and creamy rather than sticky. At ovulation, discharge becomes elastic, wet, and slippery like the consistency of raw egg white. When spread on a slide, it dries in a fernlike pattern. Women using the rhythm method of contraception may predict ovulation about 24 hours after the last day of abundant, slippery discharge. It can be assumed that a woman's fertile period has ended 4 days after the last day of abundant, slippery discharge. However, discharge charting should not be used alone to determine safe days for intercourse. During ovulation the cervical mucus is very rich in glucose. This can be measured with a fertility kit available at pharmacies. Another method of pinpointing ovulation involves a simple test that detects the midcycle surge of LH.

Menopause is marked by the degeneration of the ovaries

At about age 45 to 52 years the ovaries become less responsive to gonadotropic hormones, and the amount of estrogens and progesterone secreted diminishes. Perhaps there are not enough follicles left to develop and secrete hormones. The ovaries then begin to degenerate, and the menstrual cycle becomes irregular and eventually halts. A sensation of heat ("hot flashes") sometimes occurs, probably because of the effect of decreased estrogen on the temperature-regulating center in the hypothalamus. Estrogen deficiency may also contribute to headaches and to feelings of depression experienced by some women. The vaginal lining thins, and the breasts and vulva begin to atrophy.

Despite these physical changes, menopause does not usually affect a woman's interest in sex or her sexual performance. When missing hormones are replaced clinically, many of the symptoms of menopause are alleviated.

Sexual response is a physiological cycle

Sexual stimulation results in two basic physiological responses: (1) **vasocongestion,** increased blood flow to certain areas, and (2) **myotonia,** increased muscle tension. During vasocongestion, blood flow is increased to the genital structures and to certain other tissues such as the breasts, skin, and earlobes. These structures become engorged with blood; the penis and clitoris become tumescent (swollen). Myotonia affects both smooth and skeletal muscle. Limb muscles become more irritable, and there is an increase in rhythmic movement, both voluntary and involuntary.

Sexual response involves four phases: sexual desire, excitement, orgasm, and resolution. The desire to have sexual activity may be motivated by thinking about sexual activity or by sexual contact. Anticipating sexual activity can lead to sexual excitement.

As an individual becomes psychologically and physically stimulated, he or she experiences a sense of sexual pleasure. The excitement phase involves vasocongestion and increased muscle tension. In order for the penis to enter the vagina and function in intercourse, it must be erect; penile erection is the first male response to sexual excitement. During the excitement phase the testes increase in size and become elevated because of shortening of the spermatic cords.

In the female, vaginal lubrication is the first response to effective sexual stimulation. Lubricating fluid is produced in the vaginal wall as a result of vasocongestion (glands are not present in the vagina). The amount of lubricating fluid produced, however, varies at different times of the menstrual cycle. During the excitement phase, the vagina lengthens and expands in preparation for receiving the penis; the clitoris and breasts become vasocongested, and the nipples become erect.

If erotic stimulation continues, sexual excitement heightens. Vasocongestion and muscle tension increase markedly. In the female the inner two-thirds of the vagina continues to expand and lengthen. The walls of the outer one-third of the vagina become greatly vasocongested so that the vaginal entrance becomes somewhat constricted. In this narrowed state the outer one-third of the vagina is referred to as the orgasmic platform. In the male the penis increases in circumference. In both sexes, blood pressure increases and heart rate and breathing are accelerated.

During sexual intercourse the penis is moved back and forth in the vagina by movements known as pelvic thrusts. The vaginal walls and vulva become engorged with blood, narrowing the passageway somewhat, so that friction between the penis and the vagina and clitoris is increased. Physical and psychological sensations resulting from this friction and from the entire intimate experience between the partners leads to **orgasm,** the physical and psychological climax of sexual excitement. Though lasting only a few seconds, orgasm is the achievement of maximum sexual tension and its release. In both sexes heart rate and respiration more than double, and blood pressure rises to a peak. Orgasm is a reflex action. When sufficient stimulation has been received by the genital structures and transmitted to a reflex center in the spinal cord, orgasm occurs as a muscular response.

In the male, orgasm is marked by a sensation that ejaculation of the semen is inevitable, followed by emission of the semen. Contractions of the vas deferens propel sperm into the ejaculatory ducts. The accessory glands contract, adding their secretions; then contractions of the ejaculatory ducts, urethra, and certain muscles of the pelvic floor eject the semen from the penis. Muscle contractions continue rhythmically at 0.8-second intervals. After the first several contractions their intensity decreases, and they become less regular and less frequent.

In the female, stimulation of the clitoris heightens sexual excitement that leads to orgasm. Sexual climax is marked by rhythmic contractions of the orgasmic platform, starting at 0.8-second intervals and recurring 5 to 12 times. (One of the muscles involved is the pubococcygeus muscle, which controls flow of urine as well as constriction of the vagina.) After the first three to six contractions the intensity of the contractions decreases, and the time interval between them increases. The uterus and anal sphincter may also contract.

Orgasm is followed by the **resolution phase,** a state of well-being during which relaxation and **detumescence** (subsiding of swelling) restore the body to its normal state. In most adult males there is a **refractory period** during which they are not able to respond again physiologically to sexual stimuli. Duration of the refractory period varies in different individuals and also in different situations. Women are able to repeat the cycle, reaching orgasm again from any point in the resolution phase if appropriately stimulated.

Fertilization occurs when sperm meets ovum

During vaginal intercourse, sperm are released in the vicinity of the cervix, but during most of the menstrual cycle the female reproductive tract is a hostile environment for sperm. The acidic nature of the vagina is spermicidal (meaning that it kills sperm), and the thick plug of mucus blocking the cervix presents a formidable barrier. As the time of ovulation approaches, however, this situation begins to change. The vagina becomes slightly alkaline, and the cervical mucus thins, permitting sperm to pass into the uterus.

When conditions are favorable, sperm begin to arrive at the site of fertilization in the upper uterine tube within 30 to 60 minutes after ejaculation. Since sperm are able to propel themselves with a velocity of only about 4 millimeters per minute, they could not make so long a journey so quickly under their own power. There is some evidence that contractions of the uterus and uterine tubes (perhaps stimulated by prostaglandins in the semen) transport the sperm. The sperms' own motility may be most important in permitting them to actually approach and fertilize the ovum.

Large numbers of sperm are required for fertilization

If only one sperm actually fertilizes the ovum, why are millions required? Sperm movement is undirected, so that many die or lose their way. Only about 2000 succeed in reaching the "correct" upper uterine tube; many probably traverse the "wrong" tube. (Remember that generally only one ovum is released each month, and it moves into the uterine tube nearest the ovary that produced it.)

Large numbers of sperm are only necessary to penetrate the follicle cells surrounding the ovum and the jelly-like zona pellucida covering the ovum (Fig. 29-30). Each sperm releases small amounts of hydrolytic enzymes from its acrosome. These enzymes help to break down the cement-like substance holding together the layer of follicle cells and the zona pellucida surrounding the ovum. The acrosomal enzymes may also play a role in helping the sperm pass through the cervical mucous plug.

Only one sperm fertilizes the ovum

As soon as one sperm penetrates the zona pellucida and enters the ovum, a series of reactions occurs that prevents other sperm from entering the ovum. As the fertilizing sperm enters the ovum, it usually loses its tail. Sperm entry stimulates the ovum to complete its second meiotic division. Then the haploid nuclei of the sperm and ovum (called **pronuclei)** become one, completing the process of fertilization. The zygote formed contains the diploid number of chromosomes and begins to develop into a new human being. The process of fertilization and the subsequent establishment of pregnancy are referred to as **conception.**

After ejaculation, sperm remain viable for only about 48 hours. The ovum remains fertile for about 24 hours after ovulation. Thus there are only about 3 or 4 days during each menstrual cycle (perhaps days 12 to 15 in a regular cycle) when sexual intercourse is likely to result in fertilization.

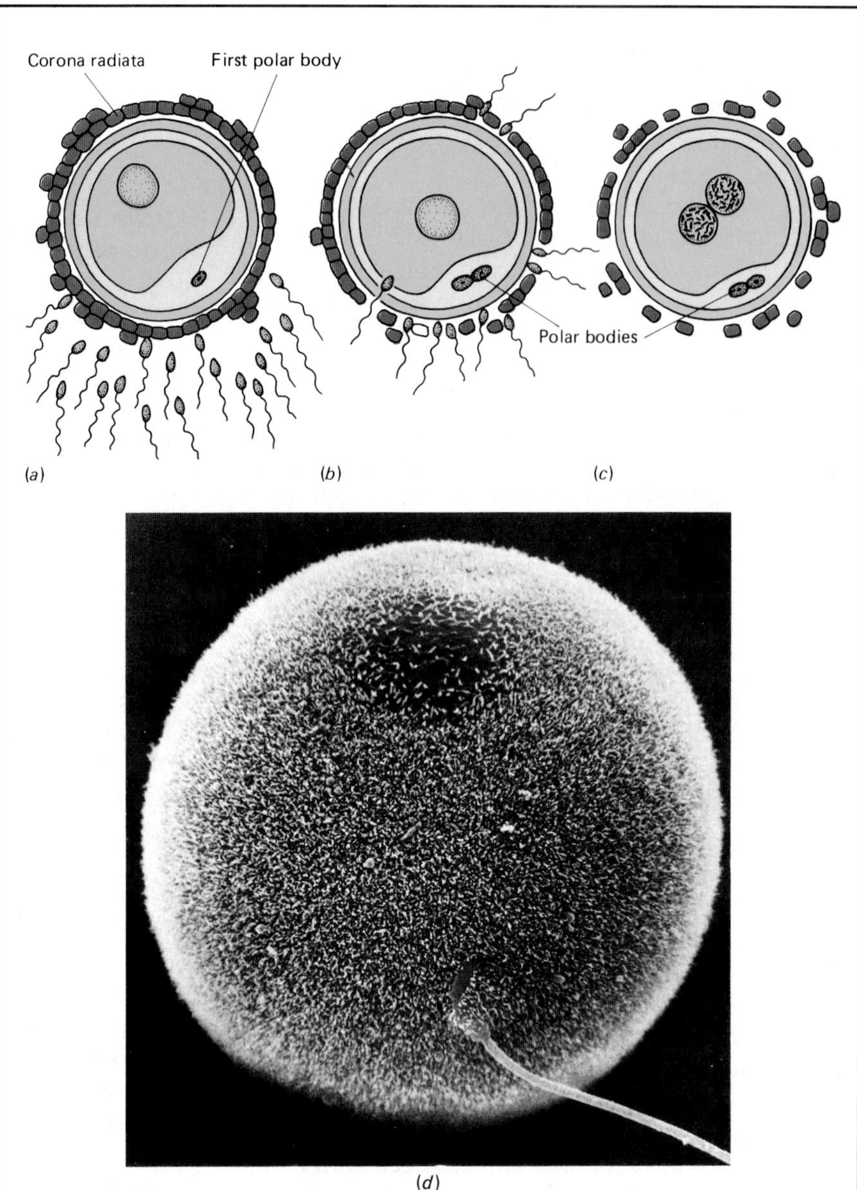

FIGURE 29-30

Fertilization. (*a*) Each sperm is thought to release a small amount of enzyme that disperses the follicle cells surrounding the ovum. (*b*) After a sperm cell enters the ovum, the ovum completes its second meiotic division, producing an ovum and a polar body. (*c*) Pronuclei of sperm and ovum combine, producing a zygote with 46 chromosomes. (*d*) A scanning electron micrograph of a sperm cell fertilizing a hamster ovum. (David M. Phillips, The Population Council.)

Infertility is the inability to conceive

Infertility is the inability of a couple to conceive after not using birth control methods for at least one year. About 15% of married couples in the United States are affected by infertility. Approximately 30% of cases involve both male and female factors.

A major cause of male infertility is **sterility,** lack of sperm production. Men with fewer than 20 million sperm per milliliter of semen are usually considered to be sterile. When a couple's attempts to produce a child are unsuccessful, a sperm count and analysis may be performed in a clinical laboratory. Sometimes semen is found to contain large numbers of abnormal sperm, or occasionally no sperm at all. In about one-fourth of the cases of mumps in adult males, the testes become inflamed; in some of these cases the spermatogonia die, resulting in permanent sterility.

Low sperm counts have been linked to chronic marijuana use, alcohol abuse, and cigarette smoking, and studies show that men who smoke tobacco are more likely than nonsmokers to produce abnormal sperm. Exposure to chemicals such as DDT and PCBs may also result in low sperm count and sterility.

FOCUS ON . . . Novel origins

About 10,000 children born each year are products of **artificial insemination.** Usually this procedure is sought when the male partner of a couple desiring a child is sterile or carries a genetic defect. Although the sperm donor remains anonymous to the couple involved, his genetic qualifications are screened by physicians.

In vitro fertilization is a technique by which an ovum is removed from a woman's ovary, fertilized in a test tube, and then reimplanted in her uterus. Such a procedure may be attempted if a woman's fallopian tubes are blocked or if they have been surgically removed. With the help of this technique a healthy baby was born in England in 1978 to a couple who had tried unsuccessfully for several years to have a child. Since that time, thousands of children have been conceived within laboratory glassware.

Another novel procedure is **host mothering.** In this procedure, a tiny embryo is removed from its natural mother and implanted into a female substitute. The foster mother can support the developing embryo either until birth or temporarily until it is implanted again into the original mother or into another host. This technique has already proved useful to animal breeders. For example, embryos from prize sheep can be temporarily implanted into rabbits for easy shipping by air, and then reimplanted into a foster mother sheep, perhaps of inferior quality. Host mothering also has the advantage of allowing an animal of superior quality to produce more offspring than would be naturally possible. In one recent series of experiments mouse embryos were frozen for up to 8 days and then successfully transplanted into host mothers. Host mothering may someday be popular with women who can produce embryos but are unable to carry them to term.

Someday society may have to deal with cloning (not yet a reality in the case of humans). In this process the nucleus would be removed from an ovum and replaced with the nucleus of a cell from a person who wished to produce a human copy of himself. Theoretically, any cell nucleus could be used, even a white blood cell nucleus. The fertilized ovum would then be placed into a human uterus for incubation; the resulting baby would be an identical, though younger, twin to the individual whose nucleus was used.

One cause of female infertility is scarring of the uterine tubes. Inflammation of the uterine tubes, frequently caused by gonorrhea (see section on Sexually Transmitted Diseases), may result in scarring, which blocks the tubes so that the ovum can no longer pass to the uterus. Scarring may also block passage of sperm to the region of the uterine tube where fertilization takes place. Sometimes partial constriction of the uterine tube results in tubal pregnancy, in which the embryo begins to develop in the wall of the uterine tube because it cannot progress to the uterus.

Women with blocked uterine tubes usually can produce ova and can incubate an embryo. However, they need clinical assistance in getting the ovum from the ovary to the uterus. The ovum can be removed from the ovary, fertilized with the husband's sperm in laboratory glassware (in vitro fertilization), and then placed in the woman's uterus, where it may develop normally (see Focus on Novel Origins).

Birth control methods allow individuals to choose

More than 3 million unplanned pregnancies occur each year in the U.S. Any method for deliberately separating sexual intercourse from the production of a baby may be considered a form of **birth control. Contraception** (literally "against conception") is specifically the prevention of conception. Highly effective contraceptive methods are now available (Fig. 29-31 and Table 29-3), but all have side effects, inconveniences, or other disadvantages. A completely ideal contraceptive has not yet been developed. More than 1 million women become pregnant each year even though they use some form of contraception. According to a 1989 study by the Alan Guttmacher Institute, birth control methods fail more frequently than indicated by the failure rates reported in Table 29-3 (which are based on earlier studies).

TABLE 29-3

Birth control methods

Method	Failure rate*	Mode of action	Advantages	Disadvantages
Oral contraceptives	0.3; 5	Prevents ovulation; may also affect endometrium and cervical mucus and prevent implantation	Highly effective; sexual freedom; regular menstrual cycle	Minor discomfort in some women; possible thromboembolism; hypertension, heart disease in some users; possible increased risk of infertility; should not be used by women who smoke
Intrauterine device (IUD)	1; 5	Not known; probably stimulates inflammatory response	Provides continuous protection; highly effective	Cramps; increased menstrual flow; spontaneous expulsion; prescribed less frequently due to increased risk of pelvic inflammatory disease and infertility; no longer manufactured in United States
Spermicides (sponges, foams, jellies, creams)	3; 20	Chemically kill sperm	No side effects (?); vaginal sponges are effective in vagina for up to 24 hours after insertion. Sponges also act as physical barriers to sperm cells.	Some evidence linking spermicides to birth defects
Contraceptive diaphragm (with jelly)**	3; 14	Diaphragm mechanically blocks entrance to cervix; jelly is spermicidal	No side effects	Must be prescribed (and fitted) by physician; must be inserted prior to coitus and left in place for several hours after intercourse
Condom	2.6; 10	Mechanical; prevents sperm from entering vagina	No side effects; some protection against STD, including AIDS	Interruption of foreplay to fit; slightly decreased sensation for male; could break
Rhythm†	13; 21	Abstinence during fertile period	No side effects (?)	Not very reliable
Douche	40	Flushes semen from vagina	No side effects	Not reliable; sperm beyond reach of douche in seconds
Withdrawal (coitus interruptus)	9; 22	Male withdraws penis from vagina prior to ejaculation	No side effects	Not reliable; contrary to powerful drives present when an orgasm is approached. Sperm present in fluid secretion before ejaculation may be sufficient for conception
Sterilization				
Tubal ligation	0.04	Prevents ovum from leaving uterine tube	Most reliable method	Usually not reversible
Vasectomy	0.15	Prevents sperm from leaving scrotum	Most reliable method	Usually not reversible
Chance (no contraception)	About 90			

*The lower figure is the failure rate of the method; the higher figure is the rate of method failure plus failure of the user to utilize the method correctly. Based on number of failures per 100 women who use the method per year in the United States.

**Failure rate is lower when used together with spermicidal foam.

†There are several variations of the rhythm method. For those who use the calendar method alone, the failure rate is about 35. However, by taking the body temperature daily and keeping careful records (temperature rises after ovulation), the failure rate can be reduced. Also, by keeping a daily record of the type of vaginal secretion, changes in cervical mucus can be noted and used to determine time of ovulation. This type of rhythm contraception is also slightly more effective. When women use the temperature or mucus method and have intercourse *only* more than 48 hours *after* ovulation, the failure rate can be reduced to about 7.

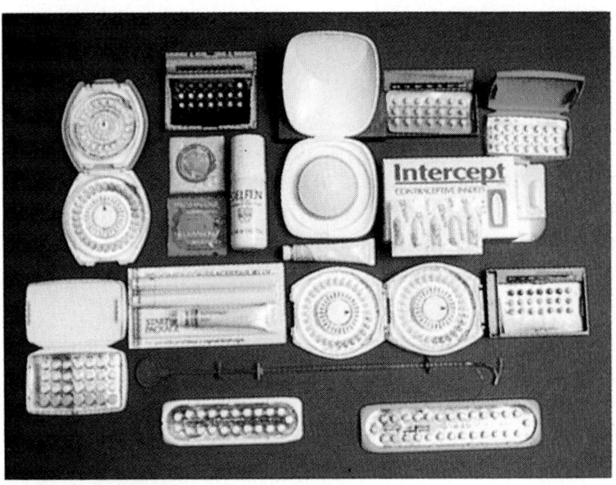

FIGURE 29-31

A variety of available contraceptive devices. (Ray Ellis/Photo Researchers, Inc.)

Oral contraceptives are hormones taken to prevent pregnancy

More than eight million women in the United States alone use oral contraceptives, and worldwide the figure is estimated at more than 80 million. The most common preparations are composed of a combination of progestin (synthetic progesterone) and synthetic estrogen. (Natural hormones are destroyed by the liver almost immediately, but the synthetic ones resist destruction.) When taken correctly, these pills are about 99% effective in preventing pregnancy. Beginning on day 5 of the menstrual cycle, a woman takes one pill each day for 20 days. She then stops taking the pill, and about 3 days later menstruation begins.

Most oral contraceptives prevent pregnancy by preventing follicle maturation and ovulation. By maintaining critical concentrations of ovarian hormones in the blood, these substances inhibit the release of both FSH and LH from the pituitary. The pituitary, of course, has no way of "knowing" that the hormones are synthetic rather than the product of a fully functioning ovary. The pituitary functions as though the woman is already pregnant.

Oral contraceptives that utilize very low doses of hormones probably do not prevent ovulation. They are thought to accelerate passage of the embryo (should there be one) through the uterine tube so that it arrives in the uterus too soon to implant itself. They also affect the endometrium so that it is not appropriately prepared for reception of an embryo. And finally, they apparently cause the cervical mucus to become viscous so that it presents a barrier to sperm penetration.

THE CHIEF ADVANTAGE OF ORAL CONTRACEPTIVES IS THEIR HIGH RATE OF EFFECTIVENESS

The pill provides the best contraceptive protection among temporary birth control methods. Many women enjoy the sexual freedom that oral contraceptives afford, because no special preparations must be made for birth control prior to each act of sexual intercourse. Another advantage is that because of their precise hormonal control they maintain a highly regular menstrual cycle.

DISADVANTAGES OF ORAL CONTRACEPTIVES INCLUDE SIDE EFFECTS FROM HORMONAL CHANGES

Some women experience minor discomfort when they first begin to use these contraceptives. Some gain weight, and about 29% experience a harmless darkening of facial skin pigment known as **chloasma.** The metabolism of certain vitamins may be interrupted. One common side effect is depression, which is caused by vitamin B_6 deficiency. This side effect may be corrected by increasing the amount of green, leafy vegetables in the diet. Certain antibiotics interfere with the effectiveness of oral contraceptives and necessitate the use of some other birth control method.

A serious side effect is thromboembolic disease, in which blood clots develop within the blood vessels and may lead to death. Statistically, however, the risk is small; contraceptive pills result in death in only about 4 per 100,000 users. This compares favorably with the death rate of about 9 per 100,000 pregnancies (Table 29-4).

A direct relationship between the estrogen component of the pill and hypertension has also been demonstrated in about 18% of users. The estrogen hormone has been shown to alter the chemistry involved in blood clotting. Also, blood lipid levels may be altered. Because of the complications associated with circulation, it has been suggested that women over age 35, smokers, and diabetics should not take the pill. Studies suggest that use of the combined pill protects users from ovarian and uterine cancer probably because of the progestin.

TABLE 29-4

Deaths in the United States from pregnancy and childbirth and from various birth control methods

	Death rate per 100,000 women who experience process or procedure
Pregnancy and childbirth	9
Oral contraceptive	4
IUD	0.5
Legal abortions	
First trimester	1.9
After first trimester	12.5
Illegal abortion performed by medically untrained individuals	about 100

The sponge is both a barrier method and a chemical method of contraception

The contraceptive sponge is made of polyurethane and soaked in nonoxynol-9 spermicide. It is a convenient form of contraception because it is available without a prescription. Another advantage is that once inserted in the vagina, intercourse is protected for up to 24 hours.

Any time an object is in the vagina for an extended period of time, the risk of toxic shock syndrome is increased. Therefore, the sponge, like the diaphragm and the tampon, poses the risk of toxic shock syndrome. To decrease this risk, the sponge should not be used during the menstrual cycle when the menstrual blood supports bacterial growth.

Use of intrauterine devices (IUDs) has been controversial

The IUD is a small plastic loop or coil that must be inserted into the uterus by a medical professional. Once in place, it can be left in the uterus indefinitely or until the woman wishes to conceive. Some types of IUDs are about 99% effective. Their mode of action is not well understood. One explanation is that the IUD sets up a minor local inflammation in the uterus, attracting macrophages. Breakdown products of these macrophages are toxic to sperm cells (and to the embryo should fertilization occur). Increased levels of immunoglobulin in IUD users support the idea that an immunological mechanism is involved. Some IUDs (copper T and copper 7) contain copper, which is thought to dissolve slowly in the uterine secretions, interfering with both migration of sperm and implantation of the embryo. Because they cause changes in the epithelium, their safety has been questioned.

Women who suffer no side effects extol the IUD as being an excellent contraceptive because once inserted it provides continuous protection. There is no need to remember to take a pill each day or to do anything specific before coitus.

Some women, especially nulliparous women (those who have never borne children), experience pain when the IUD is inserted. Others suffer side effects such as cramps, bleeding, or increased menstrual flow. During the first year after insertion, about 20% of IUD users either have them removed for these reasons or find that they have been spontaneously expelled.

Other common methods include the condom and diaphragm

Other common contraceptive methods are listed and compared in Table 29-3. The contraceptive diaphragm (Fig. 29-32) and the condom are enjoying a revival in popularity. The **contraceptive diaphragm** mechanically blocks the passage of sperm from the vagina into the cervix. It is covered with spermicidal jelly or cream and may be inserted just prior to intercourse. The spermicide chemically destroys sperm.

The **condom** is also a mechanical method of birth control. The only male contraceptive device in the United States, the condom contains the semen so that sperm cannot enter the female tract. The latex condom is the only contraceptive that provides some protection against AIDS and other sexually transmitted diseases.

New contraceptive methods are being studied

At present the main focus of contraception research is on making hormonal contraceptives safer and more convenient. Currently available hormonal contraceptives are taken by mouth, but new methods for introducing long-acting hormones into the body are being tested. One is a silicone rod that can be inserted under the skin in the buttock or forearm. The rod is impregnated with a hormone that is then released gradually over a period of months. Another is a vaginal ring that is inserted like a contraceptive diaphragm and slowly releases synthetic progesterone.

Prostaglandin tampons may eventually be developed that will prevent implantation of an embryo by causing uterine contractions. Or perhaps a woman will insert one each month just before she expects menstruation to occur. If by chance she were pregnant, the prostaglandin would stimulate a mini-abortion. Research continues on prostaglandin contraceptives; so far they have caused unpleasant side effects such as nausea.

Short of sterilization, the only method of contraception available to men is the condom. Recent attempts to suppress sperm production by interfering with FSH secretion have not been successful; sperm production occurred despite the absence of FSH. Research continues on the effects of suppressing releasing hormones. Gossypol, a yellow pigment in cottonseed oil, has been studied since a 1978 Chinese investigation claimed that it was 99% effective in preventing pregnancy. Gossypol apparently inhibits an enzyme essential for sperm development. Unfortunately, some men taking gossypol suffer side effects such as low blood pressure and potassium loss.

Sterilization renders an individual incapable of parenting offspring

Short of total abstinence, the only foolproof method of contraception is sterilization. Currently, sterilization is the most popular contraceptive method for couples in which the woman is over age 30. About 75% of sterilization operations are currently performed on men.

MALE STERILIZATION IS PERFORMED BY VASECTOMY

An estimated one million **vasectomies** (vah-**sek**-toe-mees) are performed each year in the United States. After injection of a local anesthetic, a small incision is made on each side of the scrotum. Next, each vas deferens is separated from the other structures of the spermatic cord and then cut. Its ends are tied or clipped so that they cannot grow back together (Fig. 29-33a).

Because testosterone secretion and transport are not affected, a vasectomy does not affect masculinity. Sperm continue to be produced, though at a much slower rate, and are destroyed by macrophages in the testes. No change in the amount of semen ejaculated is noticed because sperm account for very little of the semen volume.

In a study of more than 1000 men who had vasectomies, 99% said that they had no regrets, and 73% claimed an increase in sexual pleasure, probably because anxiety about pregnancy was

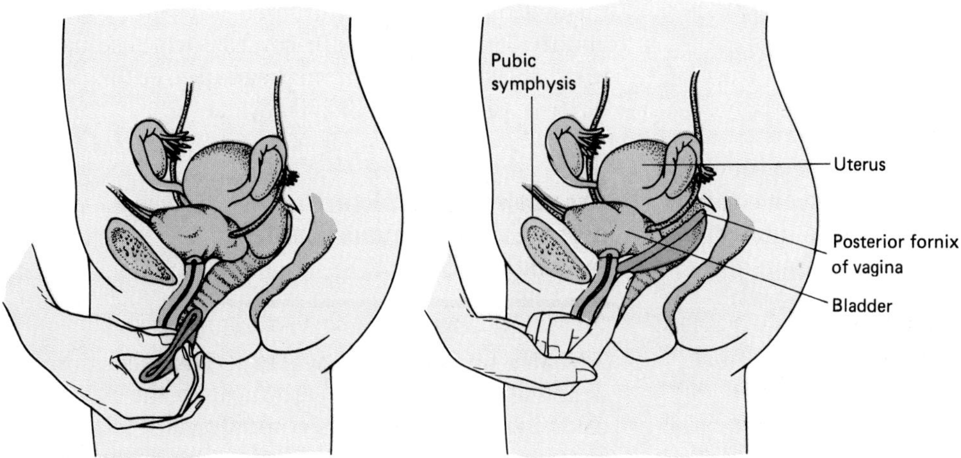

FIGURE 29-32

Insertion of a contraceptive diaphragm.

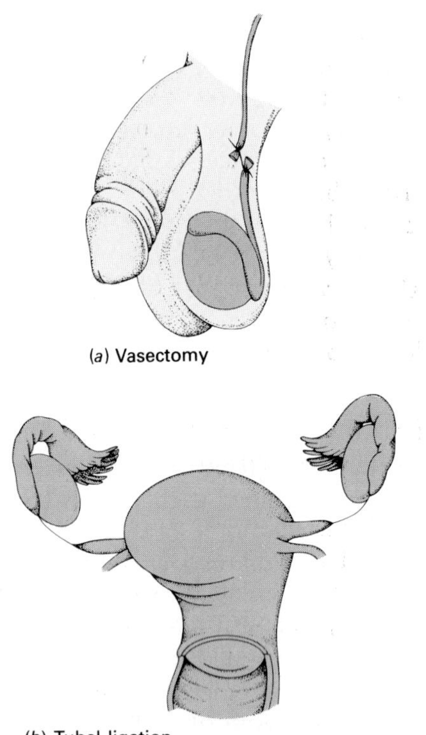

FIGURE 29-33

Sterilization. (*a*) In vasectomy the vas deferens on each side is cut and tied. (*b*) In tubal ligation each uterine tube is cut and tied so that ovum and sperm can no longer meet.

erased. By surgically reuniting the ends of the vasa deferentia, surgeons can successfully reverse sterilization in about 50% of attempts made. Apparently, some sterilized men eventually develop antibodies against their own sperm, making the sperm nonviable.

FEMALE STERILIZATION IS PERFORMED BY TUBAL LIGATION

Several techniques are in current use for preventing transport of ova. Most of them involve **tubal ligation,** cutting and tying the uterine tubes (Fig. 29-33b). Although this can be done through the vagina, it is usually performed through an abdominal incision and requires general anesthesia. Female sterilization carries with it an estimated risk of 25 deaths per 100,000 procedures performed, whereas there is almost no risk of death in vasectomy. New techniques are being developed that would make tubal ligation a simpler, safer procedure and also improve chances of reversing it. As in the male, hormone balance and sexual performance are not affected.

Abortion is the premature termination of pregnancy

More than one million abortions are performed each year in the United States, and an estimated 40 million worldwide. Actually there are three kinds of abortions. **Spontaneous abortions** (popularly known as miscarriages) occur without intervention and often are nature's way of destroying a defective embryo. **Therapeutic abortions** are performed in order to preserve the health of the mother or when there is reason to believe that the embryo is grossly abnormal. The third type of abortion—the kind performed as a means of birth control—is the most controversial. A 1989 decision of the U.S. Supreme Court returned the right to regulate abortions to the states. This decision has inspired heated debate, and the future of therapeutic and contraceptive abortion remains unclear at this time.

Most first-trimester abortions (those done in the first 3 months of pregnancy) and some later ones are performed using a suction method. After the cervix is dilated, a suction aspirator is inserted into the uterus and the fetus and other products of conception are evacuated. In pregnancies more than twelve weeks, the method most commonly used is dilation and evacuation ("D & E"). The cervix is dilated, forceps are used to remove the fetus, and suction is used to aspirate the endometrium.

When abortion is performed during the first trimester by skilled medical personnel, the mortality rate is about 1.9 per 100,000. After the first trimester this rate rises to 12.5 per 100,000 (Table 29-4). The death rate from illegal abortions performed by medically untrained individuals is about 100 per 100,000. In contrast to these figures, the death rate from pregnancy and childbirth is about 9 per 100,000.

Sexually transmitted diseases are communicable by sexual contact

Sexually transmitted diseases (STD), also called **venereal diseases (VD),** are, next to the common cold, the most prevalent communicable diseases in the world. The World Health Organization has estimated that more than 250 million people are infected each year with gonorrhea and more than

50 million with syphilis. AIDS, described by former President Reagan as "Public Enemy Number One," is discussed in Chapter 23 in the Focus on AIDS. Some common sexually transmitted diseases are discussed in the following sections.

Gonorrhea is a common communicable disease

More than 2 million patients with **gonorrhea** are treated each year in the United States, making it the most prevalent communicable disease except for the common cold. One reason for its frequency is that there are many strains of the causative organism. Although individuals may develop immunity to one strain after infection, they can be reinfected whenever they are exposed to another strain.

Gonorrhea is caused by a bacterium, *Neisseria gonorrhoeae.* Infection most often results from direct sexual contact, but recent evidence indicates that it may sometimes (probably quite rarely) be transmitted indirectly by contact with towels or toilet seats bearing the infective bacteria.

From 2 to 31 days after exposure, the bacteria produce endotoxin (antigens), which may cause redness and swelling at the site of infection. In the male the infection usually begins in the urethra. Symptoms include frequent urination accompanied by a severe burning sensation, and a profuse discharge from the penis. Infection may spread to the prostate, seminal vesicles, and epididymides. Abscesses may develop in the epididymides, causing extensive destruction leading to sterility.

In about 60% of infected women no symptoms occur, so that treatment is sought only after the woman learns that a sexual partner is infected. The urethra, Bartholin's glands, Skene's glands, and cervix provide the most favorable environments for development of the bacteria. The stratified squamous epithelium of the vulva and adult vagina are highly resistant.

If untreated, the infection may spread to the uterine tubes and cause gonococcal salpingitis. This type of infection tends to heal leaving dense scar tissue, which may effectively close the lumen of the uterine tubes and result in sterility. In both sexes, untreated gonorrhea may spread to other parts of the body, including heart valves, meninges, and joints. Joint involvement causes a type of arthritis.

Diagnostic criteria include clinical symptoms and positive identification of *N. gonorrhoeae* bacteria in cultures of body secretions. Penicillin is the drug of choice, but other antibiotics, such as tetracyclines, have been used effectively also. Strains of gonorrhea bacteria that produce penicillin-resistant enzymes have been known since about 1976, and the tetracycline spectinomycin has been used as a backup drug since that time. Recently, however, a strain of gonorrhea resistant to both of these drugs has been reported.

Syphilis is a serious disease caused by a spirochete

Although not as common as gonorrhea, **syphilis** is a more serious disease, causing death in 5 to 10% of those infected. It is caused by a slender, corkscrew-shaped spirochete, *Treponema pallidum,* and is contracted almost exclusively by direct sexual contact. *Treponema pallidum* enters the body through a tiny break in the skin or mucous membrane. Within 24 hours it invades the lymph or circulatory system and spreads throughout the body.

The course of the disease may be divided into four stages: primary, secondary, latent, and advanced. The primary stage begins about 3 weeks after infection (although the time may vary considerably) with the appearance of a **primary chancre** (**shang**-ker), a small, painless ulcer at the site of infection, usually the penis in the male or the vulva, vagina, or cervix in the female (Fig. 29-34). The primary chancre is highly infectious, and sexual contact at this time will almost certainly transmit the disease to an uninfected partner. In many cases the chancre goes unnoticed and spontaneously heals within about a month.

About 2 months after initial infection the secondary stage occurs, sometimes marked by an influenza-like syndrome accompanied by a mild rash. Sometimes anular (circular) scaling lesions develop. Mucous membranes of the mouth and genital structures may exhibit lesions containing large populations of spirochetes. The secondary stage is the most highly contagious because the many lesions literally teem with spirochetes.

If untreated, the disease enters a long latent (hidden) stage, which may last for 20 years or longer. Although there may be no obvious symptoms at this time, the spirochetes invade various organs of the body.

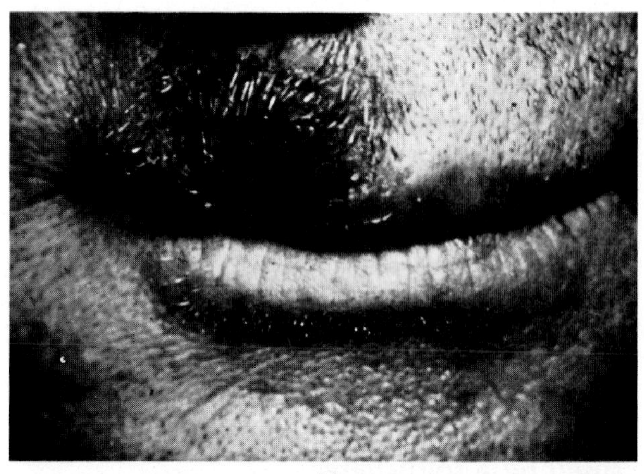

(a)

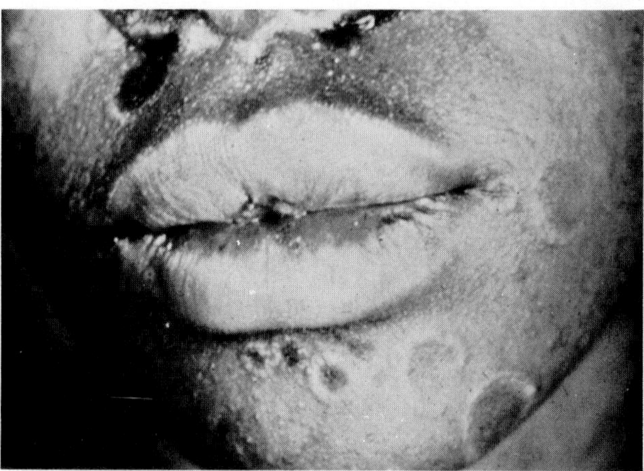

(b)

FIGURE 29-34

Clinical symptoms of syphilis. (a) Primary syphilitic chancre. This is usually the first symptom of syphilis. (U.S. Department of Health, Education, and Welfare, Center for Disease Control, Atlanta, Georgia) (b) Lesions of secondary syphilis. (Courtesy of Dr. Wilfred D. Little.)

About one-third of untreated patients recover spontaneously. Another third retain the disease in the latent form. The remaining third develop lesions, usually in the cardiovascular system, less frequently in the central nervous system or elsewhere. Lesions known as **gummas** are characteristic of advanced syphilis; they occur mainly in skin, liver, bone, and spleen. Involvement of the cardiovascular system is the principal cause of death from syphilis.

In the early primary stage, syphilis can be diagnosed by dark-field examination, which involves identifying the spirochete (using microscopic techniques) in serum collected from a lesion. Within 2 weeks after the appearance of the primary chancre, blood tests may be utilized for diagnoses. One of the most common tests in current use is the VDRL (Venereal Disease Research Laboratory) serological test, which is based on the presence of an antibody-like substance, **reagin,** which appears in the blood in response to the infection.

As with gonorrhea, penicillin is the drug of choice. When treated in its early stages, syphilis can be completely cured. Late syphilis is more difficult to cure, and lesions may have already caused permanent damage to various organs.

Genital herpes is caused by a virus

Genital herpes is an increasingly common disease caused by herpes simplex virus type 2. (This should not be confused with the herpes simplex type 1 virus, which causes ordinary cold sores.) Symptoms usually appear within a week after infection. First infections are often very mild, however, and may even go unnoticed. When they occur, symptoms take the form of tiny, painful blisters on the genital structures. The blisters may break down into ulcers. Fever, enlarged lymph nodes, and other influenza-like symptoms may appear. The ulcers usually heal within a few days or weeks.

In some patients the disease leaves permanently; in others it recurs periodically for many years. It is thought that the virus may be harbored in the dorsal root ganglia, which receive sensory fibers from the reproductive structures.

There is no cure for genital herpes. Pain medications are often prescribed, and sulfa drugs are used to treat secondary bacterial infections that may develop. Because a link has been shown between genital herpes and cervical cancer, women with this disease should have annual Pap smears.

Trichomoniasis is caused by a protozoan

Trichomoniasis is a common infection of the genital tract caused by the flagellate protozoan *Trichomonas vaginalis*. It can easily be transmitted by dirty toilet seats and towels as well as sexual contact. This disease affects about 20% of women during their reproductive years. Symptoms include vaginal itch and vaginal discharge in women. Males may not have symptoms.

Pelvic inflammatory disease is a common cause of sterility in women

Pelvic inflammatory disease (PID) is an infection of the cervix, uterus, uterine tubes, or ovaries. It results most commonly from infection transmitted by intercourse but also from abortion procedures performed under unsanitary conditions. Patients with IUDs are especially susceptible. PID, now the most common sexually transmitted disease in the United States, is often caused by chlamydial infections (a type of bacterial infection). PID may now be the most common cause of sterility in women, since it leaves women sterile in more than 15% of cases.

Nongonococcal urethritis is an inflammation of the urethra

Nongonococcal urethritis (NGU), also known as nonspecific urethritis, is an inflammation of the urethra that is not caused by the bacterium *Neisseria gonorrhoeae.* NGU is frequently caused by *Chlamydia* bacteria and responds to treatment with tetracycline. Symptoms of this disease include swelling and narrowing of the urethra so that urination becomes difficult, burning pain accompanying urination, and sometimes a pus-containing discharge.

Summary

I. The reproductive function of the male is to produce sperm cells and to deliver them into the female reproductive tract.
  A. Sperm are produced in the seminiferous tubules of the testes.
    1. Primary spermatocytes undergo meiosis, each giving rise to four spermatids.
    2. A spermatid undergoes differentiation to become a mature sperm cell complete with flagellum for locomotion.
  B. From the seminiferous tubules in the testes, sperm pass into an epididymis where they complete maturation and may be stored. From the epididymis they enter the vas deferens for further storage. During ejaculation, sperm pass into the ejaculatory duct and then into the urethra, which extends through the penis.
  C. Most of the volume of the semen is produced by the seminal vesicles and the prostate gland. The bulbourethral glands produce a few drops of alkaline fluid prior to ejaculation.
  D. The penis consists of three columns of erectile tissue. When the large venous sinusoids of this tissue become engorged with blood, the penis becomes erect.
  E. The anterior pituitary gland releases the gonadotropic hormones FSH and LH. The release of FSH and LH is regulated by GnRH from the hypothalamus.
    1. FSH stimulates development of the seminiferous tubules and may promote spermatogenesis.
    2. LH stimulates the interstitial cells to release testosterone.
  F. Testosterone is responsible for the development of reproductive structures and the development and maintenance of secondary sex characteristics associated with masculinity.

II. The reproductive role of the female includes production of ova, reception of sperm, incubation and nourishment of the developing embryo, and lactation.
  A. Ova develop in the ovaries as part of follicles.
    1. After puberty a few follicles begin to develop each month when stimulated by FSH.
    2. At ovulation the ovum (a secondary oocyte) is ejected into the pelvic cavity. It then passes into the uterine tube, where it is either fertilized or deteriorates.
  B. If fertilized, the ovum begins to develop, and the tiny embryo passes into the uterus, which serves as its incubator.
  C. The vagina is the lower part of the birth canal. It also receives the penis during sexual intercourse and serves as an outlet for menstrual discharge.
  D. The term vulva refers to the external female genital structures.
  E. The mammary glands within the breasts function in lactation. Each breast consists of 15 to 20 lobes of glandular tissue surrounded by adipose tissue.
  F. The first day of menstrual bleeding marks the first day of the menstrual cycle.
    1. In a "typical" 28-day cycle, ovulation occurs on about the fourteenth day.
    2. Events of the menstrual cycle are coordinated by the interaction of gonadotropic and ovarian hormones.
      a. FSH stimulates follicle growth during the preovulatory phase of the cycle.
      b. Estrogens released from the developing follicles stimulate the endometrium to thicken.
      c. LH released from the pituitary stimulates ovulation and the development of the corpus luteum.
      d. The corpus luteum secretes progesterone during the postovulatory phase of the cycle. Progesterone stimulates the glands in the endometrium to secrete a nutritive fluid.
      e. If fertilization does not occur, the corpus luteum degenerates, estrogen and progesterone levels fall, and the endometrium begins to slough off again (menstruation).
  G. Estrogens are responsible for the development and maintenance of secondary sex characteristics; estrogens and progesterone prepare the endometrium each month for possible pregnancy.

III. The cycle of sexual response includes arousal, excitement phase, orgasm, and resolution. Vasocongestion and increased muscle tension are two basic physiologic responses to sexual stimulation.

IV. Fertilization restores the diploid chromosome number, determines the sex of the offspring, and triggers development.

V. Although an ideal contraceptive has not yet been developed, effective methods of birth control are available.
  A. Oral contraceptives work hormonally, inhibiting the production of FSH and LH so that ovulation does not occur.
  B. The IUD sets up a local inflammation in the uterus, causing the embryo to be destroyed by macrophages.
  C. Sterilization is accomplished by vasectomy in the male and by tubal ligation in the female.

VI. Gonorrhea, syphilis, and genital herpes are three serious and common varieties of STD.

Post-test

1. Sperm cells are produced in the ______________ tubules of the ______________.
2. Each primary spermatocyte gives rise by meiosis to ______________ spermatids.
3. Crossing-over occurs during the first prophase of ______________.
4. The passageways connecting the scrotal and abdominal cavities are the ______________ ______________.
5. From the epididymis, sperm pass into the ______________.
6. Most of the semen is produced by the ______________ ______________.
7. The corpora cavernosa are columns of ______________ tissue found in the ______________.
8. The interstitial cells of the testes produce ______________.
9. The term castration refers to the removal of the ______________.
10. The two ovarian hormones are ______________ and ______________.

Match

___ **11.** Place where ova are produced		**a.** vulva
___ **12.** Site of fertilization		**b.** uterine tube
___ **13.** Part of uterus that projects into vagina		**c.** ovary
___ **14.** Attach uterus to pelvic wall		**d.** broad ligaments
___ **15.** External female genital structures		**e.** cervix

16. Ejection of the ovum from the follicle and out of the ovary is called ______________.
17. Progesterone levels are high during the ______________ phase of the menstrual cycle.
18. The corpus luteum secretes estrogen and ______________.
19. The mucous membrane lining the uterus is the ______________.
20. Menstrual bleeding marks day ______________ of the menstrual cycle.
21. Vasectomy is a common form of male ______________.
22. ______________ ______________ disease is a sexually transmitted disease that may now be the most common cause of sterility in women.

Review questions

1. How does meiosis differ from mitosis? What is the main significance of meiosis?
2. Draw a mature sperm cell and label its parts.
3. Trace a sperm cell from its origin as a stem cell through the steps of spermatogenesis.
4. Trace the path traveled by a mature sperm cell from the testis to its release from the body during ejaculation.
5. Explain the physiology of erection of the penis.
6. What are the actions of testosterone?
7. What are the actions of FSH and LH in the male?
8. What is (a) sterility, (b) infertility, (c) erectile dysfunction?
9. Trace the development of the ovum from its origin to fertilization.
10. What is the function of the corpus luteum? How does it develop?
11. Draw a diagram of the internal female reproductive structures and label them.
12. Why is it important that ovarian and uterine cycles be precisely synchronized? How is this synchronization regulated?
13. What are the actions of FSH and LH in the female?
14. What are the actions of estrogen and progesterone?
15. What are the advantages of breast-feeding an infant?
16. What is puberty? What is menopause?
17. Which contraceptive methods are the most effective?
18. What is the mode of action of oral contraceptives? Of the contraceptive diaphragm?
19. What are the physiological consequences of vasectomy?
20. How is the sex of the offspring determined?
21. What are the symptoms of syphilis? Of gonorrhea? How are these diseases treated?

Post-test answers

1. seminiferous; testes **2.** four **3.** meiosis **4.** inguinal canals **5.** vas deferens **6.** seminal vesicles **7.** erectile; penis **8.** testosterone **9.** testes **10.** estradiol (estrogens), progesterone

11. c **12.** b **13.** e **14.** d **15.** a **16.** ovulation **17.** postovulatory **18.** progesterone **19.** endometrium **20.** one **21.** sterilization **22.** Pelvic inflammatory

DEVELOPMENT

CHAPTER OUTLINE

I. **Morphogenesis and cellular differentiation**
 □ Focus on multiple births

II. **Implantation**

III. **The fetal membranes**
 A. Amnion
 B. Placenta

IV. **Prenatal development**
 A. First trimester
 B. Second and third trimesters

V. **Parturition**

VI. **Adaptation to extrauterine life**
 A. Fetal circulation
 B. Changes in the circulation at birth

VII. **The embryo and adverse environmental influences**

VIII. **Life as a continuous cycle**

IX. **The aging process**
 A. Effects of aging on bodily systems
 B. Mystery of the aging process

LEARNING OBJECTIVES

After you have studied this chapter you should be able to:

1 Discuss growth, morphogenesis, and cellular differentiation as basic processes in the development of the human organism.

2 Describe the development of the embryo during the first week of gestation.

3 Describe the process of implantation.

4 Discuss the development of the fetal membranes and placenta.

5 Identify structures that develop from each primary germ layer.

6 Discuss the changes that occur in the conceptus during the later embryonic and fetal periods.

7 Describe each stage of labor.

8 Discuss three fetal shunts and the changes that occur in the circulatory system of the newborn at birth.

9 Describe the stage of prenatal life that is most susceptible to the effects of adverse environmental influences.

10 Discuss the stages of the human life cycle.

11 Discuss what occurs in the aging process.

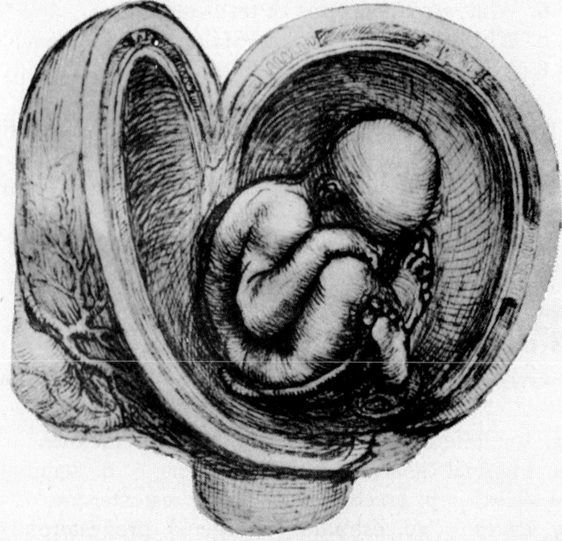

False-color x-ray of a woman who is 8 months pregnant. The head of the fetus rests in the lower pelvic area; its spine and ribs are to the right of the mother's spine. (CNRI/Science Photo Library/Photo Researchers, Inc.)

30

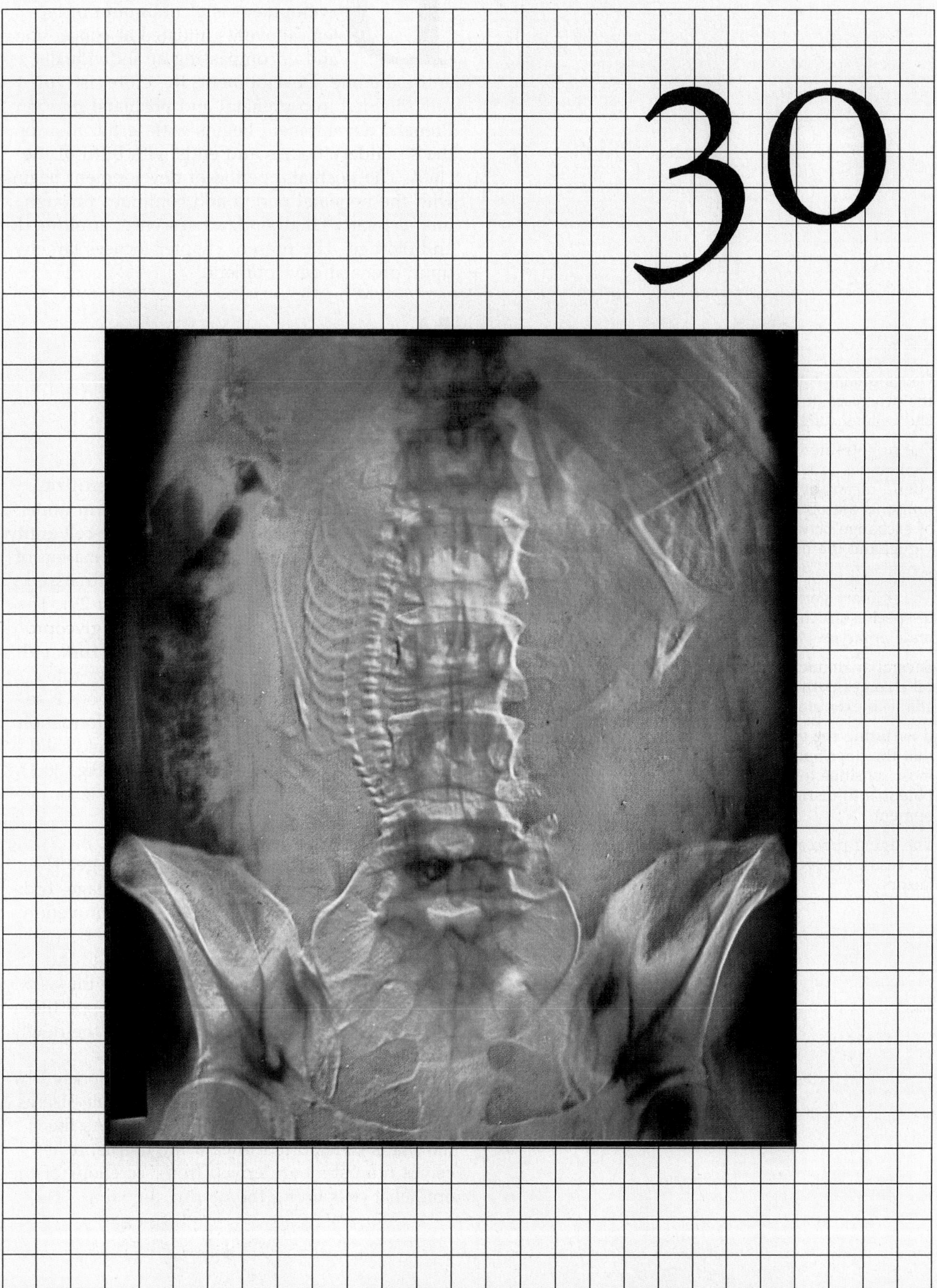

KEY CONCEPTS

Development is predicated upon the processes of morphogenesis and cellular differentiation.

During intrauterine life, the fetal membranes provide protection and offer a means by which oxygen and nutrients are obtained. The organ of exchange between the new individual and the mother is the placenta.

The primary germ layers give rise to specific structures in all vertebrate embryos.

Several anatomical and physiological changes permit the newborn to adapt to extrauterine life.

It is during the embryonic period that the developing individual is most sensitive to factors having the potential to disrupt normal development.

The aging process is thought to be the result of several contributing factors.

Development is a continuum of biological events initiated at conception and encompassing an individual's entire lifetime. Development, therefore, is typically divided into **prenatal** and **postnatal** periods. Prenatal development begins with fertilization of the secondary oocyte and ends with birth of the child. The postnatal period of development begins with the neonatal period and continues through infancy, early childhood, adolescence, adulthood, and old age. The present chapter focuses largely upon prenatal development.

Morphogenesis and cellular differentiation are the primary events of prenatal development

Early prenatal development begins at **fertilization,** when a secondary oocyte and sperm unite within the uterine tube to form a single-cell entity called a **zygote** (**zy**-goat) (Fig. 30-1). Formation of eggs and sperm, or **gametogenesis,** is discussed in the chapter on reproduction (Chapter 29). The surface of the zygote is covered with a glycoprotein-rich membranous layer termed the **zona pellucida** (**zone**-ah pe-**loo**-se-dah). As the zygote passes along the uterine tube, it undergoes a series of mitotic divisions, leading to the formation of 12 to 16 small cells arranged in a single solid mass termed a **morula** (**more**-you-lah) (Fig. 30-1). The morula remains surrounded by the zona pellucida.

Collectively, the mitotic divisions of the zygote are known as the process of **cleavage.** The first division, resulting in the two-cell stage, ordinarily requires about 24 hours for its completion. Each newly formed cell continues to divide rapidly, and the original cytoplasmic mass of the zygote is partitioned among the cells of the morula. Such divisions also result in the partitioning of messenger RNA into the cells of the newly formed morula.

Because the divisions are not accompanied by cell growth, the morula remains the same size as the zygote from which it was derived. As the morula is transported toward the uterus, it receives nourishment derived from secretions of the epithelial cells lining the uterine tube (Fig. 30-2).

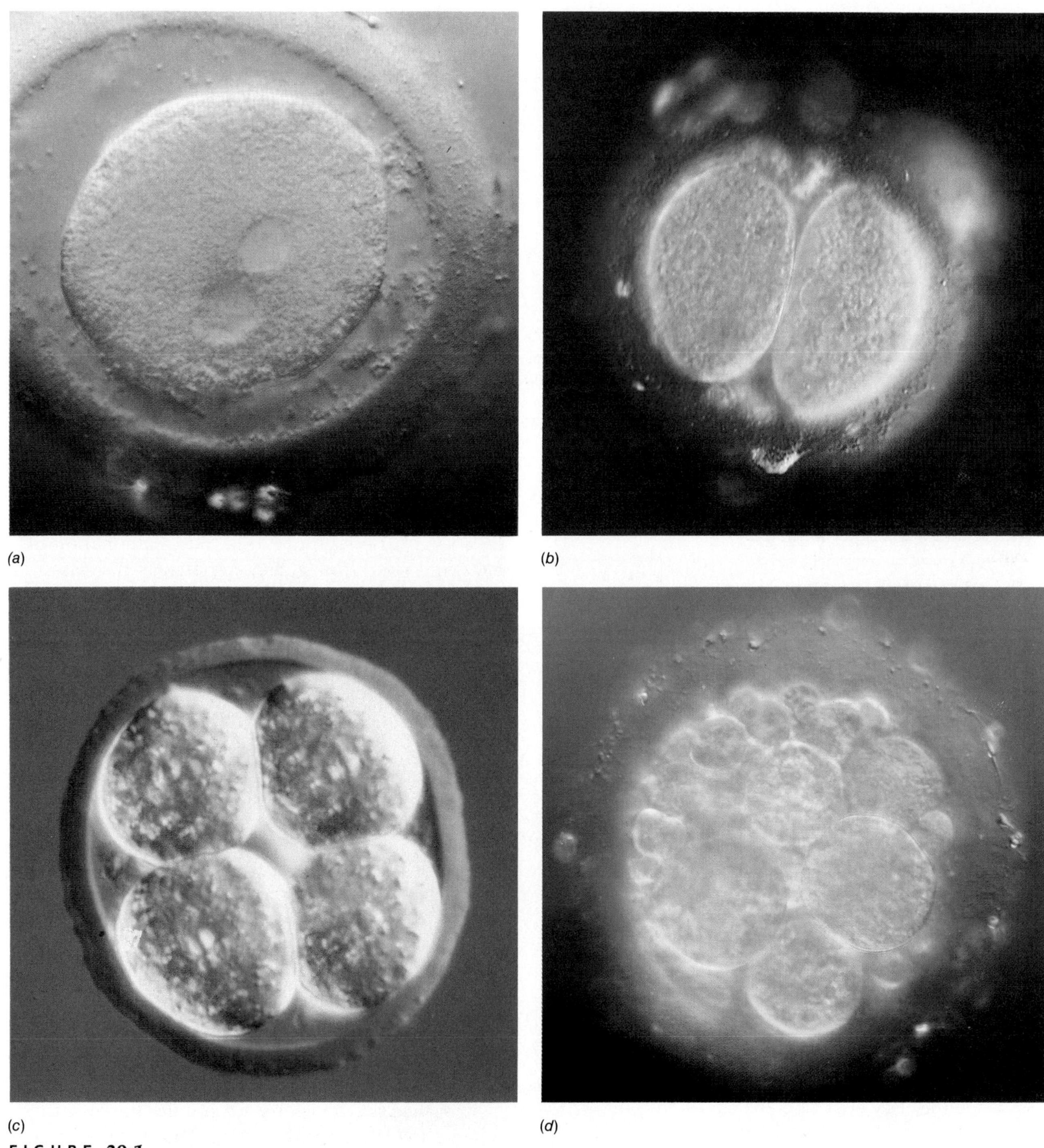

(a) (b) (c) (d)

FIGURE 30-1

Early human development (approximately ×250). (*a*) Human zygote. This single cell contains the genetic instructions for producing a complete human being. (*b*) Two-cell stage. (*c*) Eight-cell stage. (*d*) Cleavage continues, giving rise to a cluster of cells termed the morula. (Lennart Nilsson, from *Being Born;* pp. 14, 15, 17.)

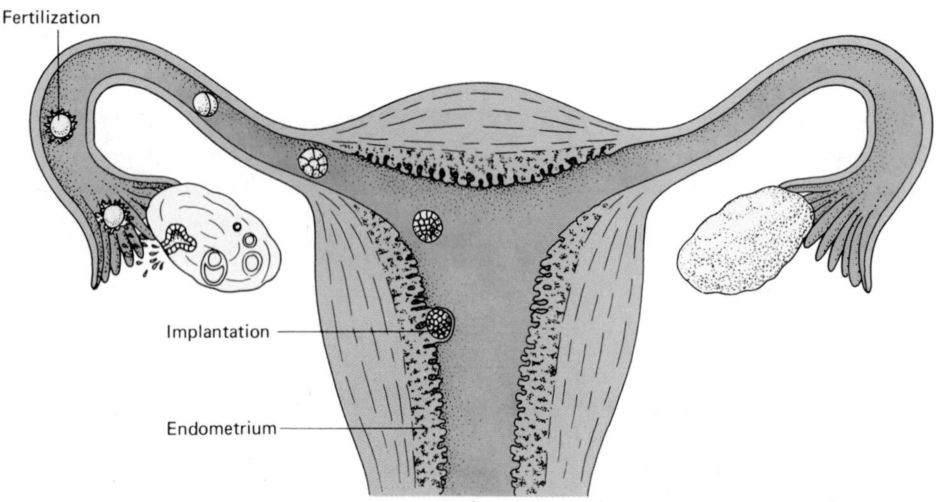

FIGURE 30-2

Passage of the human embryo through the uterine tube to the uterus. Once fertilization occurs, cleavage divisions continue throughout this journey.

FOCUS ON . . . Multiple births

Several different events may be involved in the formation of twins. Occasionally the inner cell mass subdivides to form two separate groups of cells. Each group may have the potential to develop into a complete human. Because the cells of each group possess identical genes, they lead to the formation of **identical twins.** The two groups may, although rarely, separate incompletely and give rise to **conjoined** (Siamese) **twins.** If two ova are released during ovulation and each is fertilized, **fraternal twins** result. Each egg is being fertilized by a separate sperm. Thus, fraternal twins each possess a unique genetic composition and are therefore not identical. They may even be of the opposite sex. Identical and fraternal twins may occur in a multiple birth involving more than two newborns.

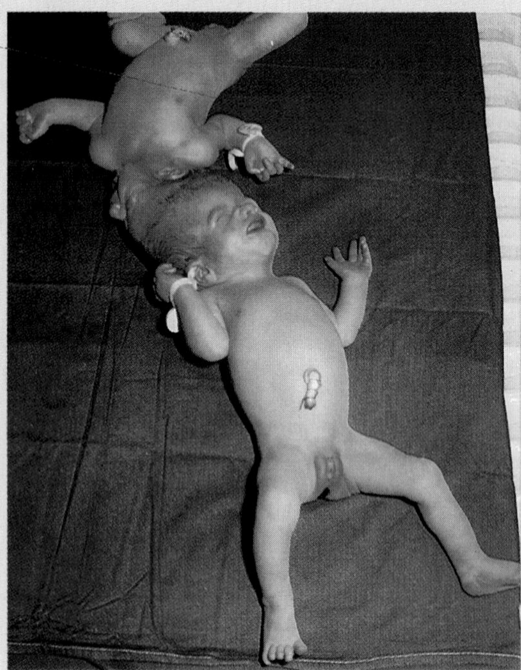

Conjoined or Siamese twins joined at the head. (Biophoto Associates.)

The morula enters the uterine cavity approximately 3 days subsequent to fertilization. A fluid-filled cavity develops within the morula, and the morula is converted into a structure called a **blastocyst** (Fig. 30-3). The cells of the blastocyst are arranged into a peripheral layer called the **trophoblast** (**trof**-oh-blast) and an inner group known as the **inner cell mass** (Fig. 30-3). It is these latter cells that ultimately give rise to the **embryo** (See Focus on Multiple Births). The trophoblastic cells participate in formation of the **placenta** and the **chorion.**

Once the blastocyst is formed, it floats free within the uterine cavity for approximately 48 hours. At this time the zona pellucida, covering the surface of the blastocyst, breaks down and disappears. The blastocyst is now ready for attachment to the uterine lining. This is followed by implantation of the blastocyst within the wall of the uterus.

During and subsequent to implantation, cells of the inner cell mass continue to divide. The embryo grows as a result of this cellular proliferation, but much more is required for the ultimate formation of a new human being. The individual cells must **differentiate** and give rise to a multitude of cell types. This process of cellular differentiation begins early in development and leads to the development of cell types specialized to contract, respond, transmit messages, secrete,

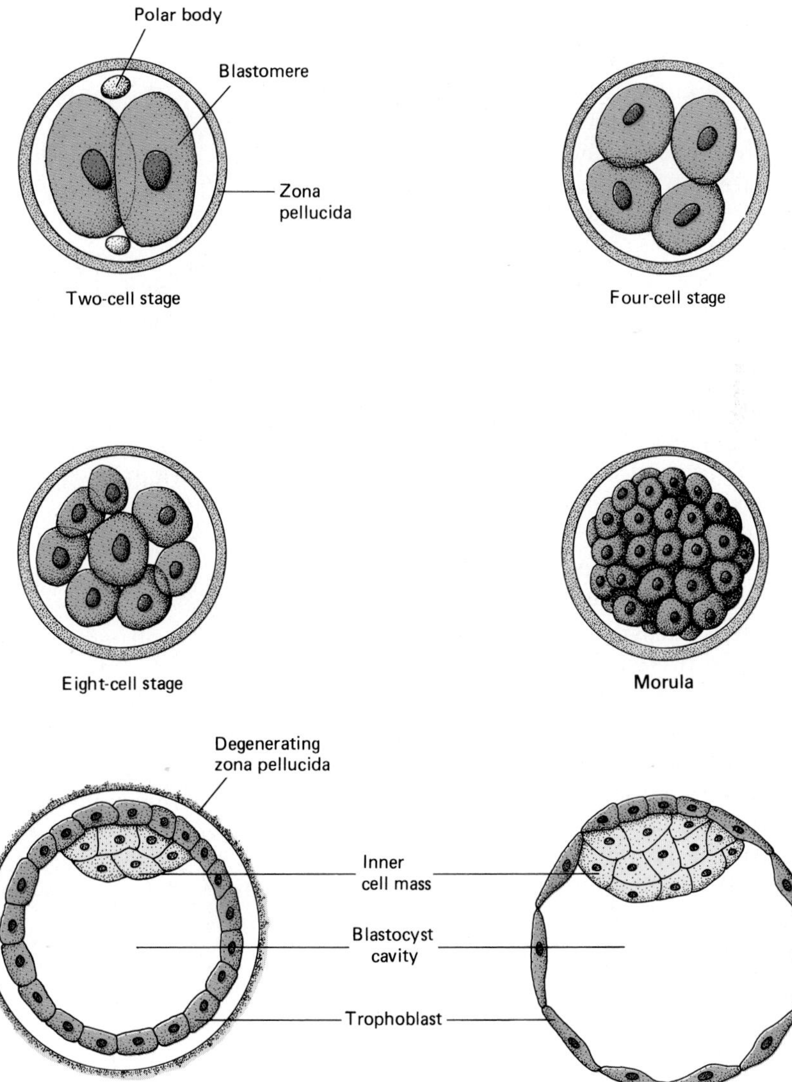

FIGURE 30-3

Cleavage of the zygote and formation of the blastocyst. The polar bodies are nonfunctional and degenerate. The morula is established at the 12- to 16-cell stage. The blastocyst is formed when there are approximately 50 to 60 cells present. The zona pellucida has disappeared by the late blastocyst stage.

and perform hundreds of additional functions. More than 200 distinct cell types, each specialized biochemically and structurally to perform specific tasks, originate as a result of cellular differentiation.

Growth and differentiation alone, however, are still not enough. The proliferating cells must be able to arrange themselves in a precise manner such that the body acquires its characteristic shape and the individual organs develop normally and on schedule. This process of movement and rearrangement of the embryonic cells is called **morphogenesis** (*more*-foe-**jen**-ih-sis).

Implantation involves tissues of the embryo and of the uterine wall

Near the end of the sixth day after fertilization and during the seventh, the trophoblast cells of the embryo differentiate and form two distinct cell populations. These are termed the **syncytiotrophoblast** (sin-*sit*-ee-oh-**troe**-foe-blast) and the **cytotrophoblast** (*sigh*-toe-**troe**-foe-blast) (Figs. 30-4 and 30-5). Cells of the syncytiotrophoblast produce and release lytic enzymes that actively erode the adjacent wall and vessels of the uterus. The cytotrophoblast contains many mitotically active cells which subsequently migrate into the syncytiotrophoblast as it continues to expand. The cytotrophoblast eventually surrounds the entire trophoblast and is responsible for attaching the chorionic sac to the endometrial tissue of the mother's uterus.

Ultimately, isolated spaces, or **lacunae,** develop within the syncytiotrophoblast, and these become filled with maternal blood (Fig. 30-6). Nutrients present in the maternal blood are now available to the developing embryo.

By the tenth day the embryo lies entirely embedded within the uterine wall. The opening through which it entered is covered initially by a blood clot and later (day 12) by regenerated uterine epithelium (Fig. 30-6). The site at which implantation typically occurs is near the middle part of the body of the uterus. Implantations on the posterior wall at this level are somewhat more frequent than those occurring on the anterior wall of the uterus. All further development occurs within the uterine wall.

Clinical highlight

In certain instances implantation takes place outside the cavity of the uterus. These are referred to as **ectopic** (eck-**top**-ik) **implantations.** The most common form of ectopic implantation occurs within the uterine tube and is clinically known as an **ectopic tubal pregnancy.** As the developing embryo continues to enlarge within the restricted confines of the uterine tube, the pregnant woman experiences intense pain. Rupture of the uterine tube, subsequent hemorrhage, and death of the embryo typically occur within the first 8 weeks of pregnancy should the condition go undiagnosed. Severe hemorrhage in these instances is of grave clinical concern and may threaten the life of the woman involved.

Fetal membranes serve important functions in the developing embryo and fetus

The human, as well as all terrestrial vertebrates, possesses four distinct fetal membranes. These are the yolk sac, chorion, allantois, and amnion. The individual membranes are not really part of the embryo proper and are discarded at birth. Collectively, the fetal membranes function to protect the developing embryo and fetus, provide it with a means for obtaining oxygen and nutrients, and remove metabolic waste products.

Although the human ovum does not contain any yolk, a **primary** and **secondary yolk sac** are formed during early embryonic development. Initially, cells derived from the cytotrophoblast come to line the original blastocyst cavity. The cavity at this time is referred to as the primary yolk sac (Fig. 30-7, p. 1062) and its lining cells are continuous with those on the inferior aspect of the inner cell mass.

The amnion, which is discussed in more detail below, lies above the inner cell mass (Fig. 30-8, p. 1062). Additional trophoblast cells form a layer of loosely arranged cells, the **extraembryonic mesoderm,** which surrounds the amnion and primary yolk sac (Fig. 30-7). A cavity ultimately develops within this extraembryonic mesoderm and is called the **extraembryonic coelom** (**see**-lom). The primary yolk sac begins to decrease in size as the extraembryonic coelom is being formed. A second yolk sac then develops within the cavity of the primary yolk sac and represents an actual outpocketing of the developing gut of the em-

(*text continued on p. 1062*)

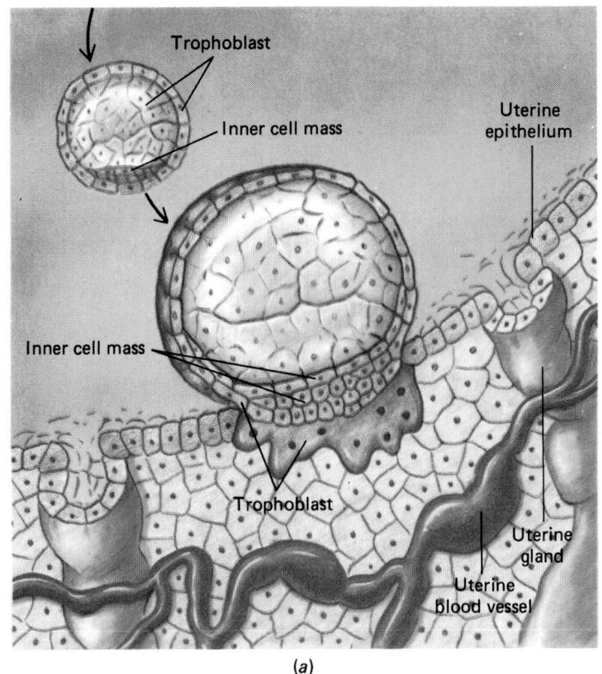

(a)

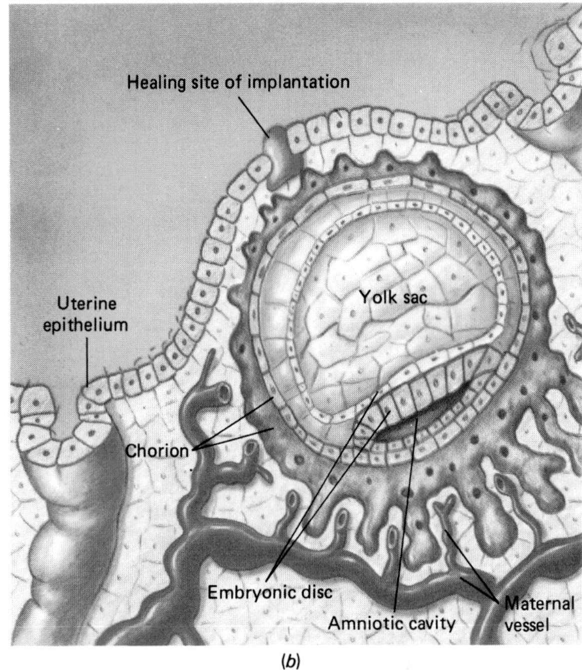

(b)

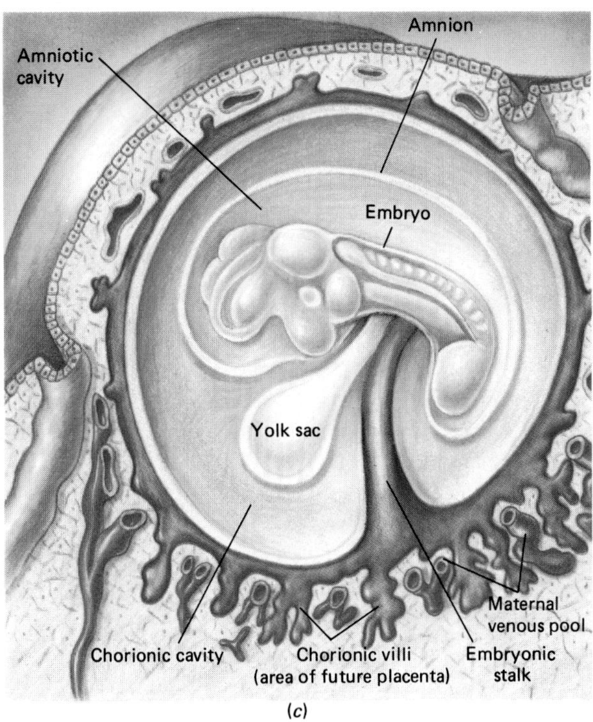

(c)

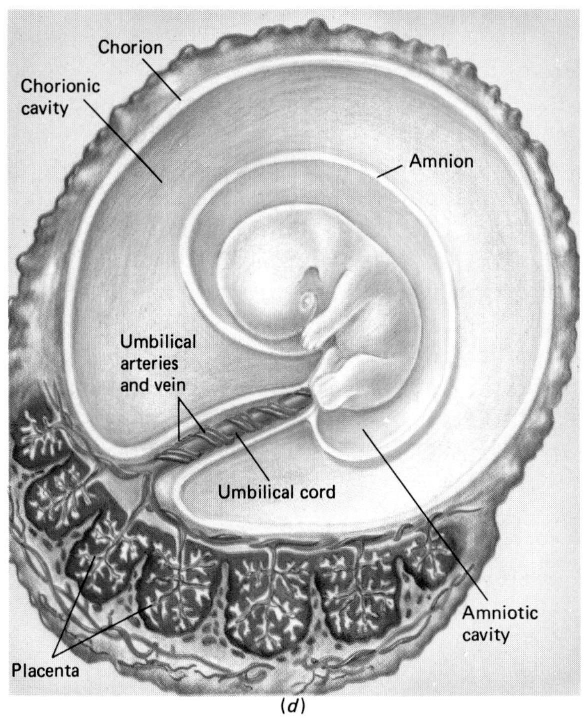

(d)

FIGURE 30-4

Development of the fetal membranes and placenta. (*a*) At about 7 days after fertilization, the blastocyst drifts to the site of implantation within the uterus. The cells of the trophoblast proliferate and invade the endometrium. (*b*) About 10 days after fertilization, the chorion has formed from the trophoblast. The inner cell mass has differentiated into the two-layered embryonic disc, from which the embryo will develop. Extensions of the upper endodermal layer form the wall of the developing yolk sac. Extensions of the lower epidermal layer give rise to the developing amnion. (*c*) By 25 days, intimate relationships have been successfully established between the embryo and the maternal uterine blood vessels. Oxygen and nutrients from the maternal blood are now satisfying the embryo's needs. Note the specialized region of the chorion that is soon to contribute to the placenta. The embryonic stalk will become the umbilical cord. (*d*) At about 45 days, the embryo and its membranes together are about the size of a ping-pong ball, and the mother may still be unaware of her pregnancy. The amnion surrounds the embryo, which is now cushioned by the amniotic fluid. The yolk sac has been incorporated into the umbilical cord. Blood circulation has been established through the umbilical cord to the placenta.

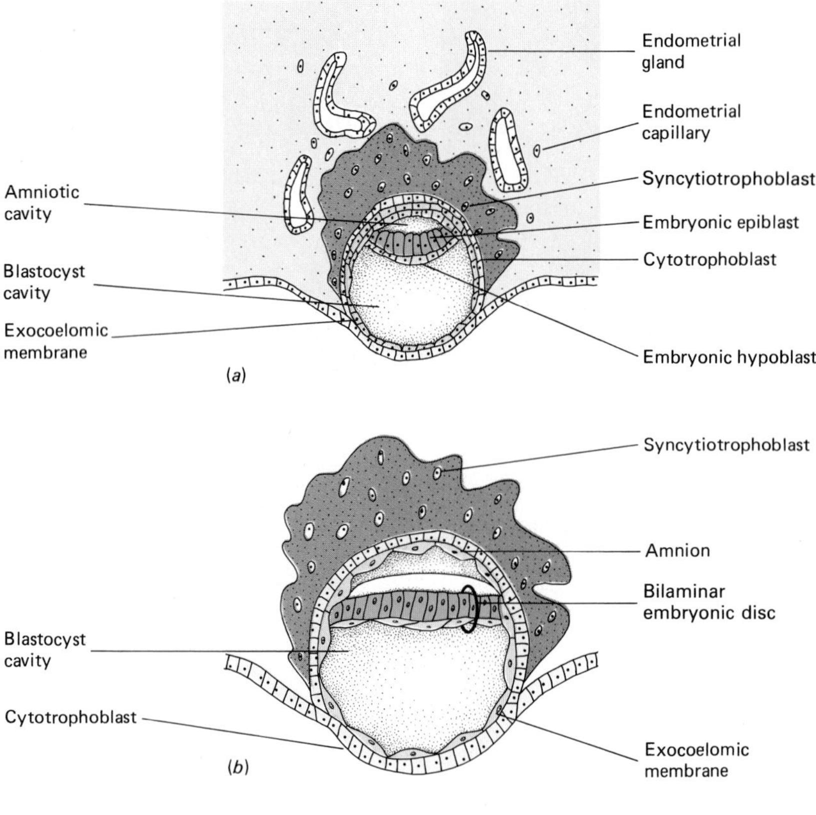

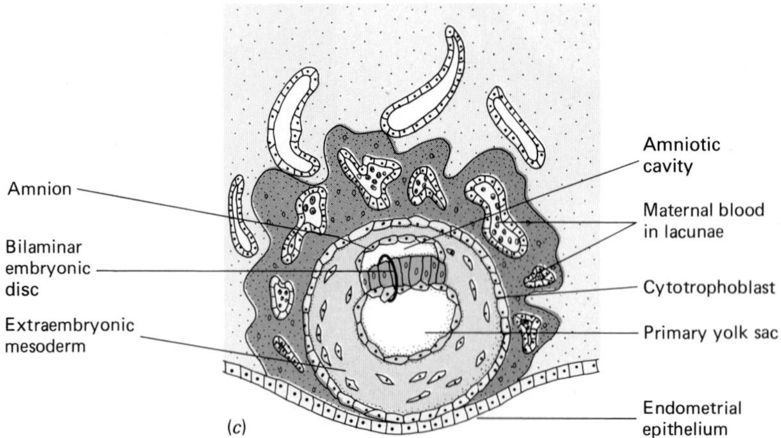

FIGURE 30-5

Implantation of the blastocyst into the uterine lining (endometrium). (*a*) Partial implantation at about eight days. (*b*) Later blastocyst showing larger amniotic cavity and very extensive syncytiotrophoblast layer. (*c*) Implanted blastocyst at nine days. Notice the primary yolk sac.

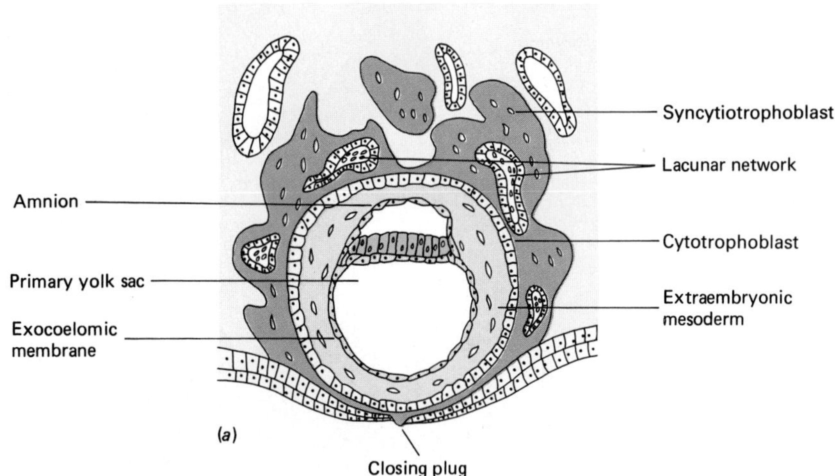

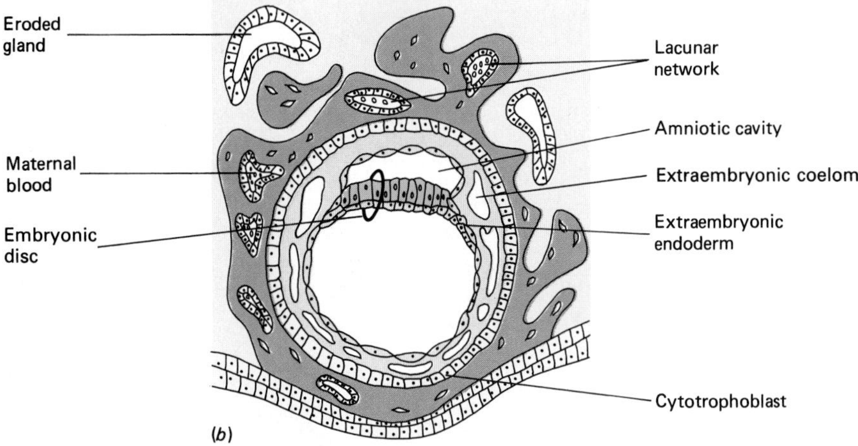

FIGURE 30-6

Implanted blastocysts at (*a*) 10 days and (*b*) 12 days. Note the lacunae filled with maternal blood. The extraembryonic coelom is also starting to form.

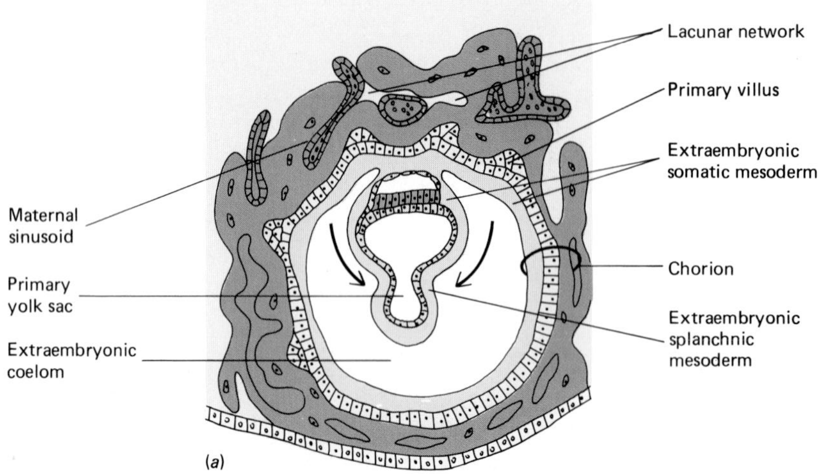

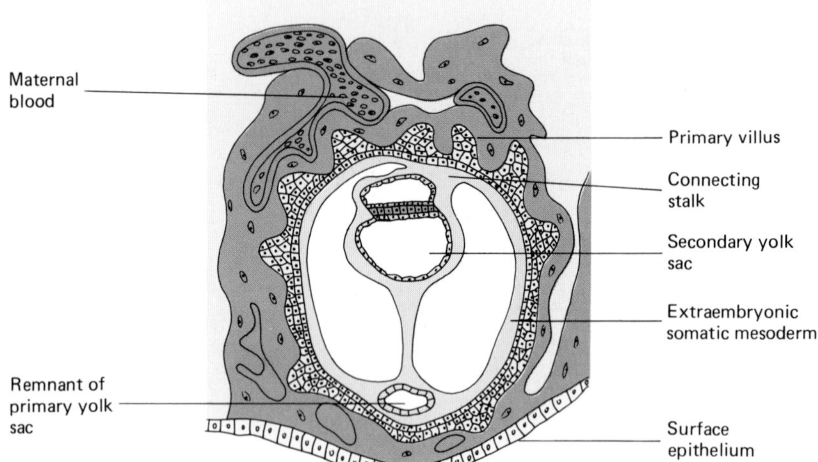

FIGURE 30-7

Implanted embryos at (*a*) 13 days and (*b*) 14 days. In (*a*) notice the formation of the primary chorionic villi and the pinching off of the primary yolk sac. The secondary yolk sac is illustrated in (*b*).

bryo. The cells that line this secondary yolk sac are derived from the inferior surface of the embryonic disc (Fig. 30-7). The walls of the secondary yolk sac function as a temporary center for the formation of blood cells. Notice that the formation of the extraembryonic coelom effectively splits the extraembryonic mesoderm into two distinct layers (Fig. 30-7). That which lines the trophoblast and also covers the amnion is termed the **extraembryonic somatic mesoderm.** The resulting mesodermal layer that covers the yolk sac is called the **extraembryonic splanchnic mesoderm** (Fig. 30-7).

Together the trophoblast and the extraembryonic somatic mesoderm represent the **chorion** (**koe**-ree-on) (Fig. 30-7). Notice (Fig. 30-7) that the embryo, together with its yolk sac and amnion, lines the **chorionic cavity** and is attached to the chorion by a *connecting stalk.*

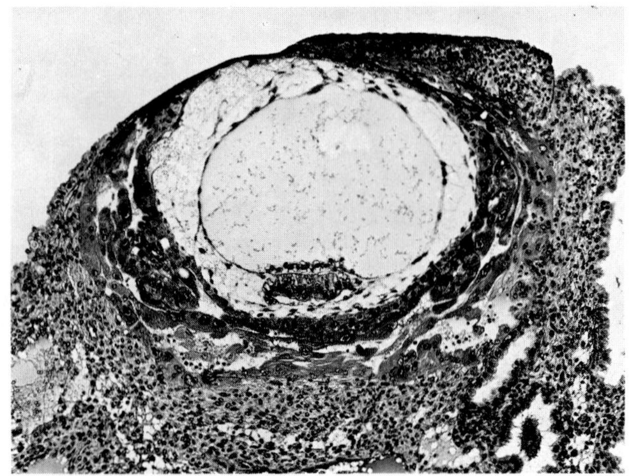

FIGURE 30-8

Photomicrograph of implanted blastocyst at 12 days after fertilization. (Courtesy of Carnegie Institution of Washington.)

The **allantois** (uh-**lan**-toe-iss) forms as an outpocketing from the posterior aspect of the secondary yolk sac. Although it is associated with the development of the urinary bladder, and its blood supply does contribute to the formation of the umbilical vessels, the allantois, like the yolk sac, is thought to be a vestigial structure in the human embryo.

The amnion keeps the embryo moist and protects it from physical injury

A series of small spaces begins to form above the inner cell mass at about the same time the trophoblast differentiates into its two layers. These spaces have united by the eighth day after fertilization and now form what is termed the **amniotic cavity** (Fig. 30-9). The cells that come to line the inner surface of the amniotic cavity form the **amnion** and are most likely derived from cells of the cytotrophoblast.

The amnion ultimately expands, and its fluid-filled cavity surrounds the entire embryo (Fig. 30-9). The clear amniotic fluid bathes the developing embryo and provides it with its own private swimming pool. In addition to keeping the embryo moist, the amniotic fluid functions as an effective shock absorber, protecting the embryo from mechanical insults. During the latter part of gestation, the fetus may swallow amniotic fluid from time to time. Eventually the swallowed fluid is passed on to the maternal blood for processing and excretion by the mother's kidneys.

The placenta is the organ of exchange between the fetus and the mother

As the **placenta** develops, some of its tissues are derived from the embryonic chorion while others take their origin from the maternal endometrium. The placenta has several important functional roles, among which are (1) *respiration,* (2) *nutrition,* (3) *excretion,* (4) *protection,* and (5) *production of hormones.*

Even after implantation occurs, the chorion continues its rapid growth. Its cells invade the adjacent endometrium and begin to form structures known as **chorionic villi** (Figs. 30-7 and 30-9). These villi ultimately become vascularized as the embryonic circulatory system becomes established. Cells of the invading chorion release lytic enzymes that destroy nearby endometrial tissue, including many small blood vessels. As this occurs, pools of maternal blood begin to bathe the chorionic villi. Initially the entire surface of the chorion is covered with villi. With time, however, many of the villi degenerate and only those associated with the maternal portion of the placenta

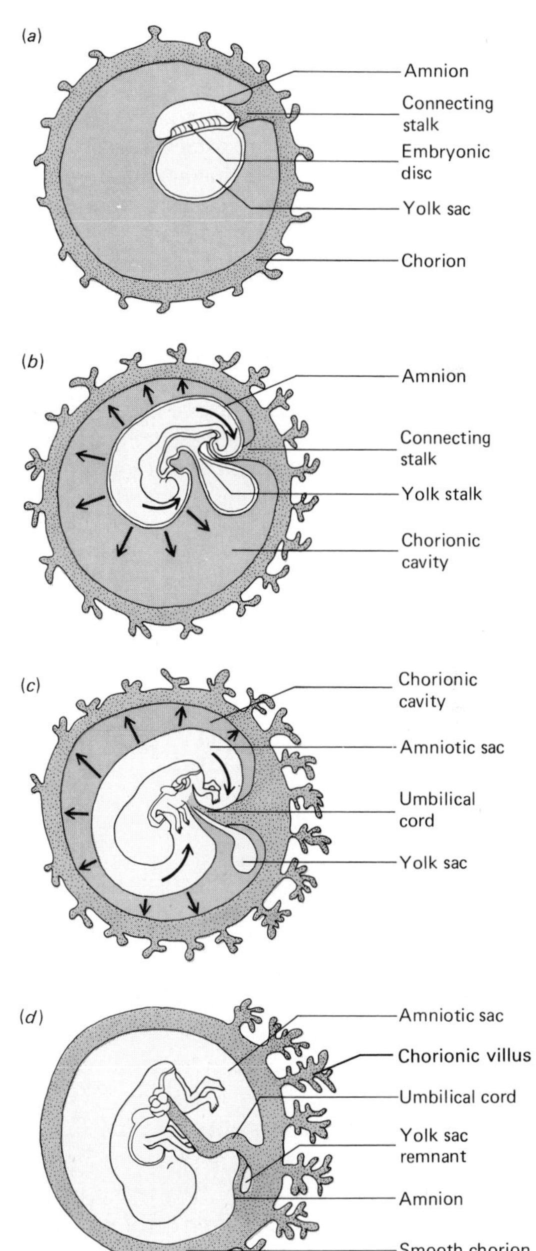

FIGURE 30-9

Illustration of how the amnion comes to cover the developing embryo and umbilical cord. Notice that a portion of the yolk sac is actually incorporated into the developing gut. (*a*) Approximately 21 days; (*b*) approximately 28 days; (*c*) approximately 70 days; (*d*) approximately 140 days.

(*decidua basalis*) remain. Thus, the placenta actually consists of the villous portion of the chorion together with the endometrial tissues of the mother. The latter lie between the villi and contain maternal capillaries and small pools of maternal blood.

Clinical highlight

The procedure of **amniocentesis** (**am**-nee-oh-sen-*tee*-sis) has been used extensively for the identification of fetal genetic abnormalities. Desquamated (shed into the amniotic fluid) fetal fibroblasts are obtained from a sample of the amniotic fluid and cultured for later genetic and biochemical analysis. The procedure cannot be performed until approximately the sixteenth week of gestation, and the time required for culturing of the cells varies from 5 days to 2 weeks. The patient must realistically wait 2 or 3 weeks for her clinical report.

The method of **chorionic villus sampling,** on the other hand, is typically performed between the ninth and eleventh weeks of gestation. Using ultrasound to guide a catheter to the sampling location, 10 to 25 milligrams of chorionic villus tissue is obtained by suction into a syringe containing sterile tissue culture medium (Fig. 30-10). The chorionic villi represent the functional units of the fetal component of the placenta. The amount of tissue obtained in this manner is sufficient to perform direct biochemical, DNA, and chromosomal studies without the necessity for tissue culture (Fig. 30-11).

In contrast to the time required for amniocentesis, the clinician is able to arrive at a diagnosis within hours following the tissue sampling. The risks to the mother and fetus during chorionic villus sampling are minimal and comparable to those associated with amniocentesis. Many clinicians think the procedure of chorionic villus sampling provides a safe and accurate approach to fetal genetic diagnosis during the first trimester of development.

As development proceeds, an **umbilical cord** forms within the region of the connecting stalk. The umbilical cord connects the embryo with the placenta (Fig. 30-9). Two **umbilical arteries** pass through the umbilical cord and anastomose with a complex network of capillaries developing within the chorionic villi. A single **umbilical vein,** also passing through the umbilical cord, functions to convey blood from the chorionic villi to the developing embryo and fetus.

Although the structural arrangement of the placenta is such that it brings the maternal and fetal blood into close proximity, the two circulatory systems are completely separate from one another. Oxygen and nutrients pass from the maternal blood through the placental tissue and enter the embryo's blood via diffusion. These materials are in turn transported to the tissues of the embryo and fetus along the umbilical vein.

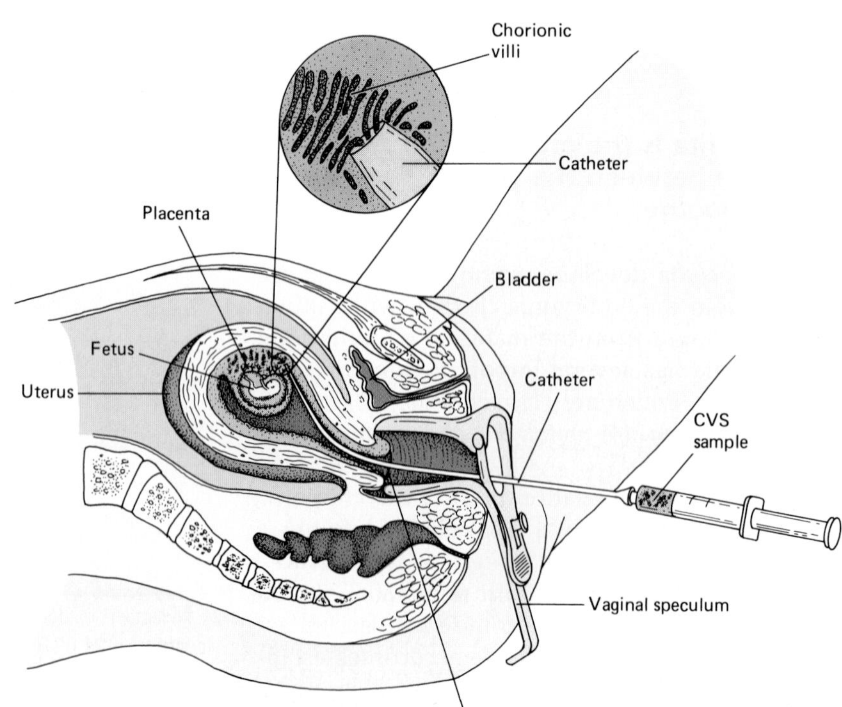

FIGURE 30-10

Method for obtaining the tissue sample during chorionic villus sampling. The catheter is guided to the sampling site using ultrasonography. The syringe attached to the catheter is used to aspirate 10 to 25 mg of chorionic tissue. (After L. Jackson, 1985.)

Metabolic waste products are conveyed from the developing organism to the maternal circulation via the paired umbilical arteries. These waste products are destined for excretion by the maternal kidneys.

Tissues of the placenta are responsible for the production of several hormones. Cells of the trophoblast, for example, begin to secrete **human chorionic gonadotropin (HCG)** immediately after the embryo begins to implant itself in the uterine wall. It is this hormone which signals the corpus luteum that pregnancy has in fact begun. In response to HCG, the corpus luteum increases in size and releases large quantities of progesterone and estrogen, which in turn stimulate continued development of the endometrium and placenta. In the absence of HCG the corpus luteum would degenerate, as in the nonpregnant menstrual cycle, and the embryo would be aborted and subsequently flushed out with the menstrual flow. It may be that the woman might not have even known that she had been pregnant. Should the corpus luteum stop functioning prior to the eleventh week of pregnancy, the embryo would be

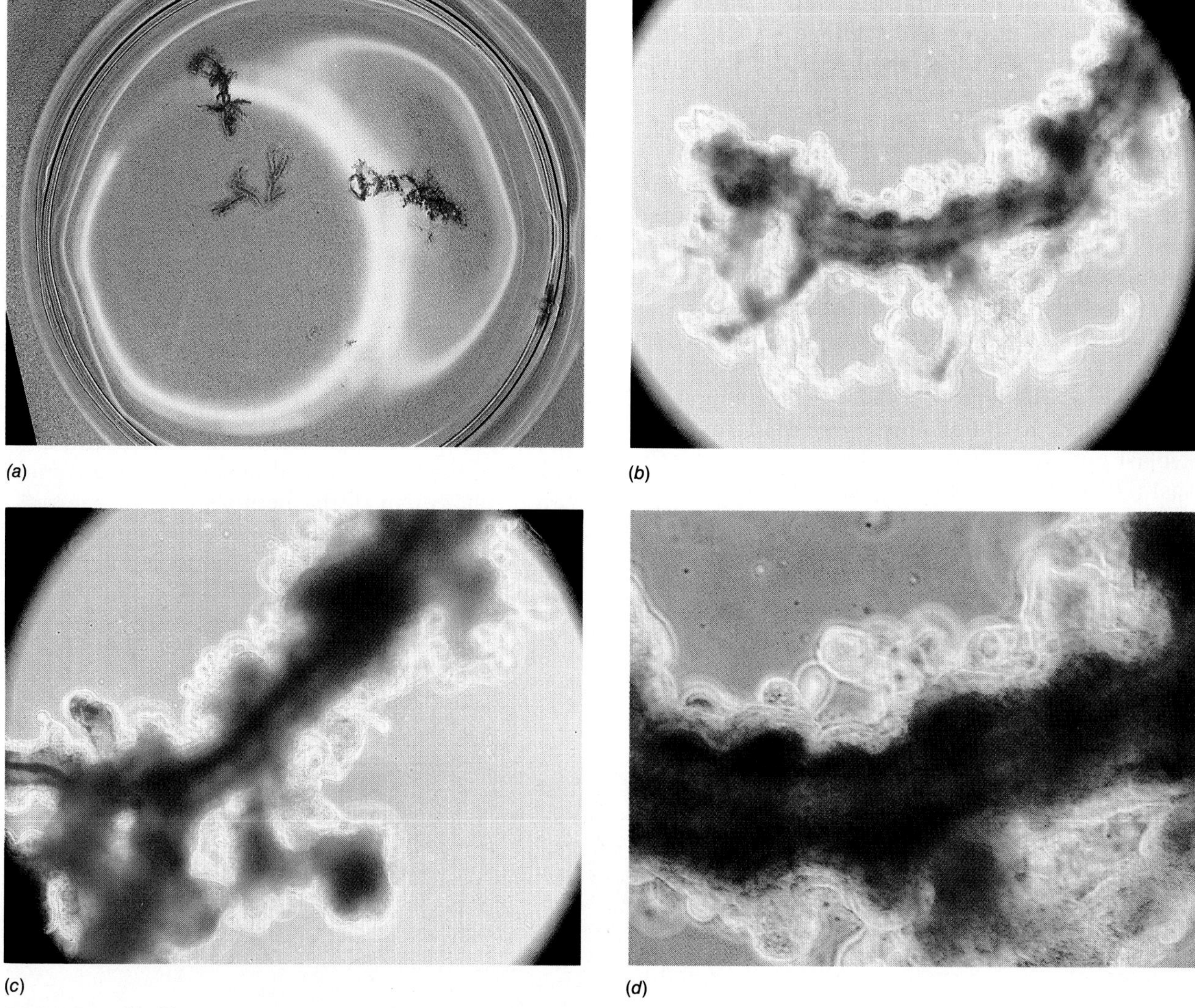

FIGURE 30-11

Chorionic villi. (*a*) Freshly sampled villi as seen with the naked eye. Note their branched appearance. (*b*) Low-magnification view showing fetal capillaries within individual villi. (*c*) Note the mesenchymal core with capillaries, cytotrophoblast, and syncytiotrophoblast. Note how the surface of the villus is characterized by numerous small buds. (*d*) Individual bud seen at high magnification. (Laird Jackson, M.D., Jefferson Medical College of Thomas Jefferson University.)

spontaneously aborted. Subsequent to the eleventh week the placenta itself produces sufficient quantities of progesterone and estrogen to maintain the pregnancy.

Prenatal development can be divided into the embryonic and fetal periods

Development of the fetal membranes and placenta is accompanied by significant changes within the inner cell mass which will ultimately give rise to the entire embryo. By the end of the second week of pregnancy these cells have arranged themselves into a **bilaminar embryonic disc** (Fig. 30-6). Those cells of the embryonic disc which form the floor of the amnionic cavity constitute the **epiblast** (ectoderm), and the layer below them is designated as the **hypoblast** (endoderm).

During the third week of gestation this bilaminar embryonic disc is converted into a **trilaminar embryonic disc** by means of a process termed **gastrulation** (*gas*-troo-**lay**-shun). Gastrulation involves the detachment of some cells of the epiblast which then migrate to a position between the epiblast (ectoderm) and underlying hypoblast (endoderm). The layer formed by these migrating cells is called the **intraembryonic mesoderm.** The epiblast gives rise to the **ectoderm,** and the hypoblast develops into the **endoderm.**

Ectoderm, endoderm, and mesoderm are known as the three primary **germ layers,** or embryonic tissue layers. Each of these will ultimately give rise to specific structures in all vertebrate embryos as indicated in Table 30-1.

Once the primary germ layers are formed, development continues in a precisely ordered sequence of events. This temporal sequence is so ordered that it is possible to predict with startling precision which structures will begin to develop and function on a particular day of gestation. By the end of the eighth week of pregnancy all the organ systems of the conceptus (embryo plus the extraembryonic membranes) are present; this stage marks the end of the **embryonic period.** During the remainder of its intrauterine life the new individual is referred to as a **fetus,** and this portion of the gestational period is termed the **fetal period.**

The first trimester of pregnancy includes the embryonic period and the beginning of the fetal period

As the embryo enters the third week of development, a cylindrical rod of cells grows forward along the length of the embryonic disc, forming a structure termed the **notochord** (Fig. 30-12). This important structure induces the adjacent ectoderm to thicken and subsequently form what is known as the **neural plate.** This plate of cells is converted into the **neural tube** by the end of the fourth week. It is from the neural tube that the central nervous system will develop. Concurrent with development of the neural tube, the mesodermal germ layer is partitioned into segments that will ultimately give rise to muscles, dermis, and skeletal structures.

TABLE 30-1

Fate of the germ layers

Inner cell mass of blastocyst	Ectoderm	Nervous system Outer layer of skin (epidermis) and its associated structures (nails, hair, etc.) Pituitary gland
	Mesoderm	Skeleton (bone and cartilage) Muscles Circulatory system Excretory system Reproductive system Inner layer of skin (dermis) Outer layers of digestive tube
	Endoderm	Lining of digestive tube and of structures which develop from it, such as respiratory system

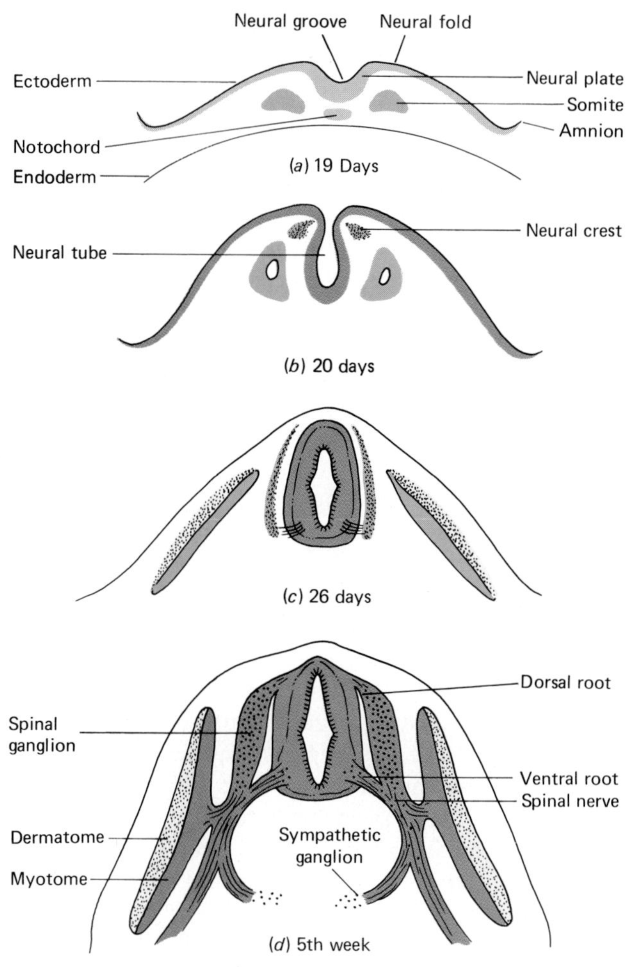

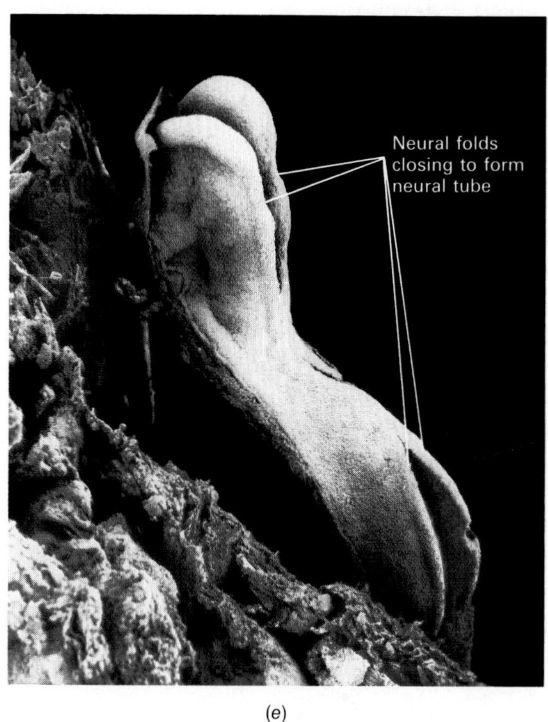

(e)

FIGURE 30-12

Development of the nervous system. Cross sections through the embryo at various stages of development. (*a*) Approximately 19 days. The neural plate is surrounded by neural folds so that it now forms a shallow groove. (*b*) Approximately 20 days. The neural folds approach one another to form the neural tube. The neural crest cells will give rise to dorsal root ganglia, sympathetic ganglia, Schwann cells, chromaffin cells of the adrenal medulla, odontoblasts, and cartilage cells of the facial region. (*c*) Approximately 26 days. The neural tube has now formed and will give rise to the brain at the anterior end and the spinal cord at the posterior end of the embryo. (*d*) During the second month spinal nerves begin to develop. (Note also the developing dermatomes and myotomes). (*e*) The human embryo at 20 days of development. The neural folds are prominent at this stage. (Lennart Nilsson © Boehringer Ingelheim International GmbH, from *The Incredible Machine,* p. 25.)

Focus your attention on Figure 30-13a, which is representative of an embryo toward the end of the first month of development. The embryo at this time weighs approximately 0.02 grams and is about 5 millimeters (0.2 in.) in length from crown to rump. Although the embryo is still quite small, it is roughly 10,000 times as heavy as the zygote from which it developed.

Because the cephalic portion of the embryo develops at a significantly faster rate during the early portion of gestation, the head at this time is disproportionately large compared to the remainder of the embryo. The prosencephalon, mesencephalon, and rhombencephalon, which represent the embryonic divisions of the brain, have differentiated by the end of the fourth week. The eyes, ears, and olfactory organs have also begun to develop by this time. The limb buds that give rise to the upper and lower limbs have just initiated their development, and the embryonic heart beats about 60 times per minute.

Notice also the presence of the **branchial (pharyngeal) arches** in the pharyngeal region at the end of the fourth week (Fig. 30-13a). These arches are separated from each other on the surface of the embryo by the **pharyngeal grooves.** Interior to each branchial groove lies a **pharyngeal pouch.** Gills develop along the pharyngeal arches in fish and in certain amphibians; in humans and other terrestrial vertebrates these structures become modified to form organs more appropriate for terrestrial existence. As an example of such modification, the tissue separating the first pharyngeal groove and the internal pharyngeal pouch gives rise to the eardrum. The groove itself develops into the external auditory meatus, and the first pharyngeal pouch gives rise to the eustachian tube connecting the pharynx with the middle ear cavity. The lung buds also arise from the pharyngeal region of the foregut at the level of the fourth pharyngeal pouch and are initially represented as a tube of endodermal cells.

The digestive system and its associated glands also begin to form during the first month of gestation. The liver, pancreas, and gall bladder are evident as outgrowths (evaginations) of the primitive gut tube. The thyroid gland develops from the floor of the pharyngeal gut and migrates caudally in the embryo.

As the embryo enters the second month of gestation the existing organs continue their development. The face has begun to assume a human appearance by the seventh week (Fig. 30-13b). The embryo has a prominent nose, upper and lower lips, eyelids, cheeks, and even ears, although the latter are situated in the neck region

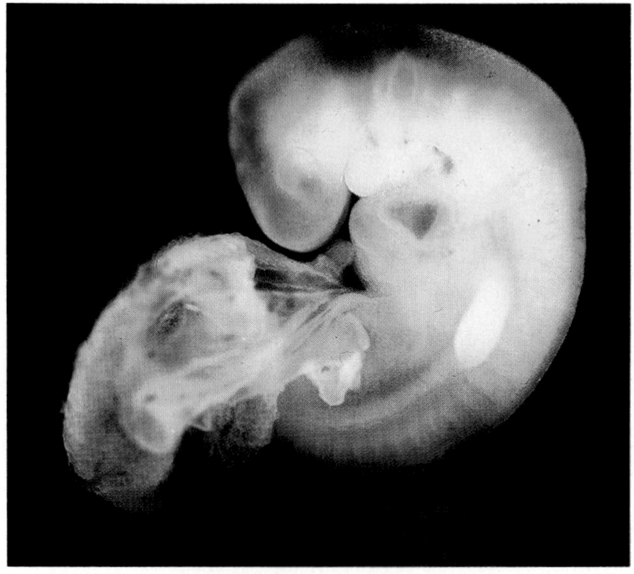

(a)

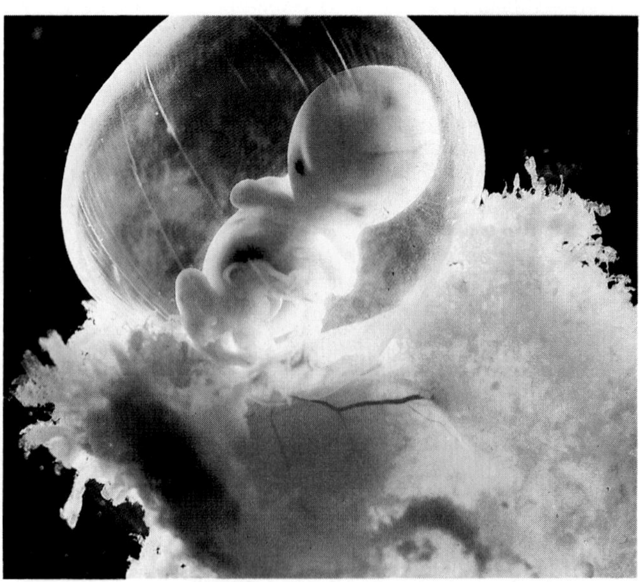

(b)

FIGURE 30-13

(*a*) Photograph of human embryo at 29 days. (*b*) Embryo in the seventh week of development, surrounded by its intact amnion and other fetal membranes. (*a* and *b*; Lennart Nilsson, from *A Child Is Born,* Dell Publishing Co., Inc., 1977.)

at this time. The developing limb buds have further differentiated, and rudiments of fingers and toes are clearly evident. The tissue between the prospective digits undergoes a process of "programmed cell death" and thus the individual digits are established. A prominent tail, which appeared during the fifth week of development, has not kept pace with the rapid growth of the rest of the body, and by the end of the second month it has become inconspicuous. By this time the embryo weighs approximately 1 gram (0.04 oz) and measures roughly 30 millimeters (1.2 in.) in length.

Internally the embryonic liver has become quite large and the tubular small intestine has formed a series of coils. Major blood vessels assume their final positions, and the heart acquires its final shape. Muscular tissue continues to differentiate and the embryo is capable of limited movements. The brain has established connections with other organs and has begun to send impulses to initiate the regulation of their function. In this regard, a few simple reflexes are evident by the end of the second month.

Although sex determination cannot be made externally at this time, rudiments of external genital structures are visible. Internally, however, the testes or ovaries can be recognized. It is important to realize that by the end of the eighth week the rudiments of all the future organs have developed. The end of the second month also marks the termination of the **embryonic period** and the beginning of the **fetal period.**

The fetus takes on a distinctly human appearance during the third month of gestation (Fig. 30-14). By the end of the twelfth week it measures nearly 56 millimeters (2.2 in.) in length and weighs approximately 14 grams (0.5 oz). The sex of the individual is evident by this time as the external genitalia have undergone further differentiation. Eyes and ears have approached their final position. The notochord has largely degenerated and some bones are evident. Remnants of the notochord remain in the form of the intervertebral discs located between adjacent vertebrae. Studies indicate that the fetus performs breathing movements as it pumps amniotic fluid in and out of its developing lungs. Sucking movements have also been observed toward the end of the third month.

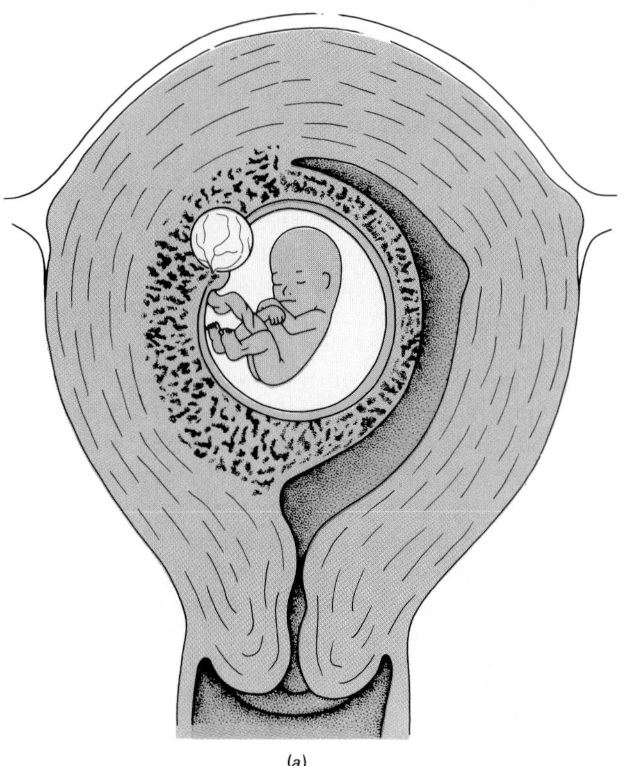

(*a*)

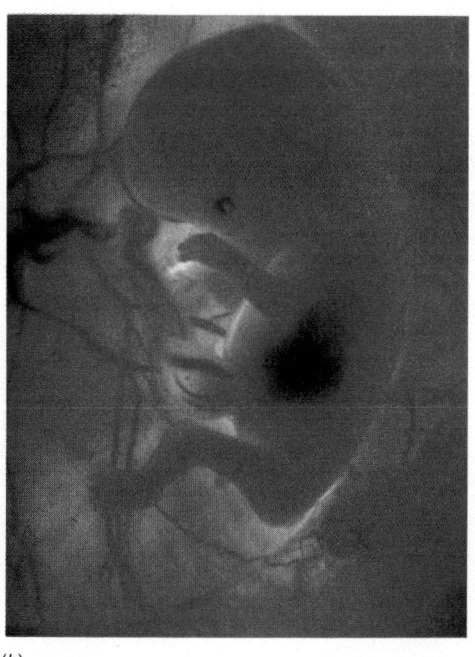

(*b*)

FIGURE 30-14

The embryo at ten weeks of development. (*a*) Position of the embryo within the uterine wall. (*b*) Photograph of the human embryo at ten weeks. (Nestle/Petit Format/Photo Researchers, Inc.)

Rapid growth and continued differentiation characterize the second and third trimesters of gestation

By 16 weeks the fetus measures a little more than 5 inches in length (Fig. 30-15). This length doubles during the ensuing 4 weeks so that by 5 months the fetus is approximately 250 millimeters (10 in.) long and typically weighs slightly more than a pound. The fetus usually doubles in length between 5 months and birth. The heart rate of the fetus, as heard with a stethoscope, measures about 150 beats per minute at 5 months. As the fetus moves freely within the amniotic cavity, it is usually during the fifth month that the expectant mother first becomes aware of fetal movements **(quickening).**

Probably because the skin of the fetus grows at a faster rate than the underlying connective tissue, the former has assumed a wrinkled appearance by the beginning of the sixth month. Were birth to occur at this stage, the fetus would be able to move, cry, and attempt to breathe. Its brain, however, has not developed sufficiently to sustain vital functions such as rhythmic breathing and regulation of body temperature. Thus, in most instances the newborn at this age is not capable of extrauterine life and nearly always dies.

The presence of a downy hair, or **lanugo** (la-**new**-go), is evident during the seventh month of gestation. Typically the lanugo is shed prior to birth, but in certain instances this may not occur until a few days after delivery. The cerebrum grows rapidly and its convolutions become highly differentiated. Grasping and sucking reflexes are apparent and the fetus may actually suck its thumb. Rapid growth occurs during the final months of intrauterine life and the skin becomes less wrinkled as a layer of fat is deposited within the subcutaneous tissue. Hair begins to grow on the fetal head and a creamlike protective substance, the **vernix,** covers the skin. A full-term baby typically measures about 52 centimeters (20 in.) in length and weighs approximately 3000 grams (7 lb) (Table 30-2).

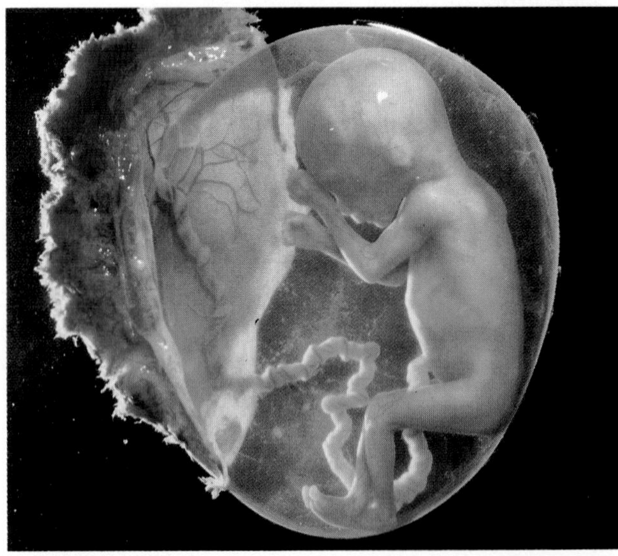

FIGURE 30-15

Photograph of the developing human at 16 weeks. At this stage the fetus measures a little more than 5 inches in length. (Lennart Nilsson, from *A Child Is Born,* Dell Publishing Co., Inc., 1977.)

Parturition is the process by which the baby is expelled from the uterus

The time required for full development of the baby is usually 266 days from the occurrence of fertilization. Near the end of gestation the fetus typically assumes an upside-down position such that its head will enter the birth canal first. The process by which the baby is expelled from the uterus is called **parturition** (par-too-**rish**-un).

The uterus periodically undergoes rhythmic contractions during pregnancy; however, at the end these become quite strong and occur with increasing frequency and intensity. These later contractions form part of the process referred to as **labor.** Several factors combine to initiate labor. The uterus becomes fully distended and its tissue highly irritable as the fetus outgrows its home. Reflex contractions of the uterus occur as the fetal head exerts pressure on the uterine cervix, stretching it. These events initiate a positive feedback cycle, leading to increased contractions.

Stretching of the uterine cervix results in the release of **oxytocin** (*ok*-see-**toe**-sin) from cells of the posterior pituitary. Oxytocin stimulates additional contractions of the uterus and initiates another positive feedback cycle. Increased irritability of the uterine tissue is also thought to result from elevated levels of estrogen (compared to progesterone) during the latter stages of pregnancy. Estrogen is known to markedly increase uterine contractility, whereas progesterone inhibits this process.

TABLE 30-2

Some important development events

Time from fertilization	Event
24 hours	Embryo reaches two-cell stage.
3d day	Morula reaches uterus.
7th day	Blastocyst begins to implant.
2.5 weeks	Notochord and neural plate are formed; tissue that will give rise to heart is differentiating; blood cells are forming in yolk sac and chorion.
3.5 weeks	Neural tube forming; primordial eye and ear visible; pharyngeal pouches forming; liver bud differentiating; respiratory system and thyroid gland just beginning to develop; heart tubes fuse, bend, and begin to beat; blood vessels laid down.
4 weeks	Limb buds appear; three primary vesicles of brain formed.
2d month	Muscles differentiating; embryo capable of movement. Gonad distinguishable as testis or ovary. Bones begin to ossify. Cerebral cortex differentiating. Principal blood vessels assume final positions.
3d month	Sex can be determined by external inspection. Notochord degenerates. Lymph glands develop.
4th month	Face begins to look human. Lobes of cerebrum differentiate. Eye, ear, and nose look more "normal."
Third trimester	Lanugo appears, then later is shed. Neurons start to become myelinated. Tremendous growth of body.
266 days	Birth.

The expectant mother becomes aware of increasingly stronger uterine contractions during the **first stage** of labor. Initially these occur about every 30 minutes or so. Ultimately they become much more intense, rhythmic, and frequent. Late in labor they occur as often as every minute (or less). As each contraction begins, the woman experiences a sensation which begins in the lower-back region and subsequently extends around the anterior abdominal wall. It is not uncommon for the amnion to rupture during this stage of labor; it is popularly referred to as the "breaking of the bag of waters." When this occurs, the amniotic fluid gushes forth through the vagina.

As the first stage of labor progresses, the uterine cervix becomes **dilated** to approximately 10 centimeter (4 in.) and **effaced,** that is, it loses its normal shape and flattens such that it cannot be distinguished from the body of the uterus. The dilatation and effacement prepare the uterine cervix for passage of the fetal head during delivery. The first stage of labor is the longest, frequently lasting 8 to 24 hours during the first pregnancy (Fig. 30-16).

The passage of the baby through the vaginal canal and its subsequent delivery characterize the **second stage** of labor. This is illustrated in Figure 30-16. The second stage begins when the cervix is fully dilated. The mother usually helps push the baby through the vaginal canal by increasing her intra-abdominal pressure through contraction of her abdominal muscles. The baby's head typically rotates as it passes along the vaginal canal in order to facilitate delivery to the outside world.

Clinical highlight

In certain instances, just prior to birth, the physician may elect to perform a surgical procedure called an **episiotomy** (eh-*piz*-ee-**ah**-toe-me). This is a surgical incision in the perineal region extending from the vagina toward the anus. Episiotomy facilitates expulsion of the baby and prevents uneven tearing of the maternal tissue. The incision is sutured closed following delivery and typically heals within a few weeks.

Once the baby's head has emerged from the vagina, only a few additional contractions are required to remove the entire body into the physi-

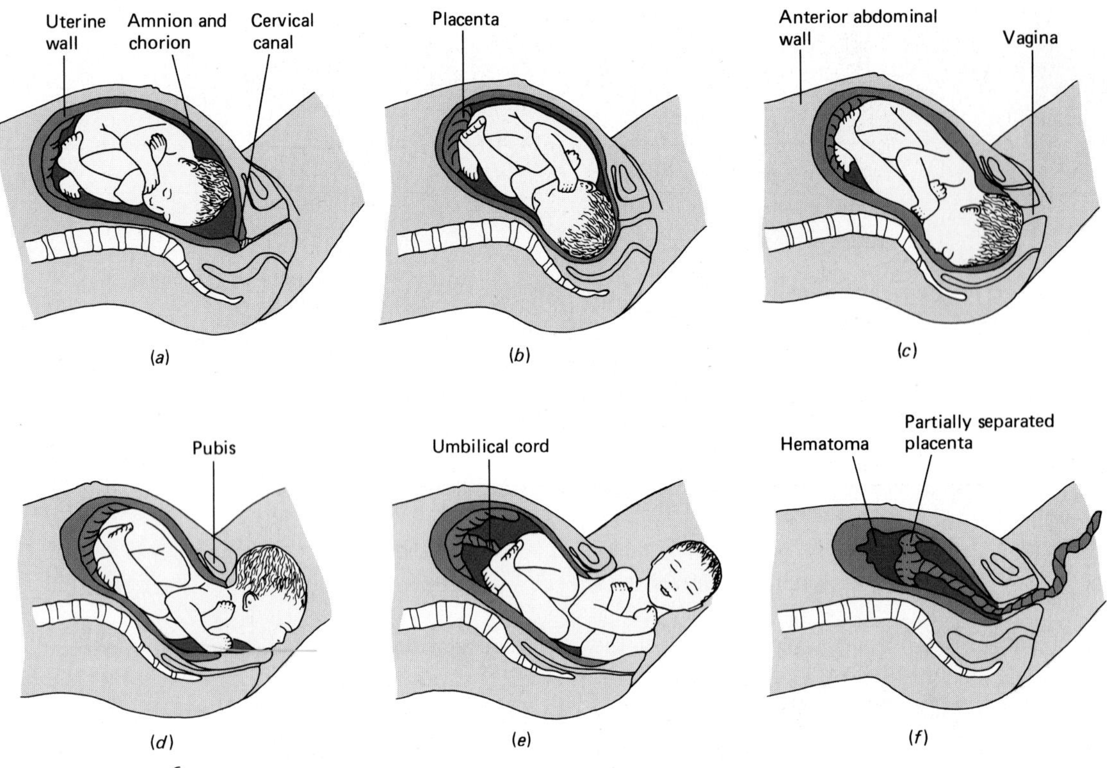

FIGURE 30-16

The birth process. (*a* and *b*) The cervix dilates during the first stage of labor. (*c* through *e*) The fetus passes through the cervix and vagina during the second stage of labor. During the third stage of labor, the uterus contracts, and the placenta folds upon itself and detaches from the uterine wall. Bleeding that results from torn blood vessels causes a large hematoma to form.

cian's waiting hands (Fig. 30-17). At this time the baby is still connected to the placenta via the umbilical cord. The cord is usually attached near the central portion of the placenta and varies in length from 30 to 90 centimeters. Its diameter measures about 1 to 2 centimeters. Immediately after the baby has been delivered, most physicians clamp and cut the umbilical cord. The second stage of labor, during a first pregnancy, typically lasts for approximately 50 minutes. This time usually decreases in subsequent pregnancies.

Once the baby is delivered, the **third stage** of labor begins (Fig. 30-16). This stage is also referred to as the **placental stage** and ends when the placenta and fetal membranes are delivered. This final stage of labor typically lasts for about 10 minutes. The uterus continues to contract following delivery of the baby, and a large blood clot forms in the uterine wall as the placenta separates from it. As the placenta is expelled from the vagina, excessive bleeding from the uterus is prevented by means of its persistent contractions. At birth the placenta usually weighs about 500 to 600 grams and has a disc-shaped configuration. It measures approximately 15 to 20 centimeters in diameter and is nearly 2 to 3 centimeters in thickness. Once delivered, the placenta together with the umbilical cord and fetal membranes is called the **afterbirth.** The physician examines these structures for abnormalities and then typically discards them. Abnormal findings may yield information regarding the possible causes of fetal death, neonatal illness, growth retardation, or placental dysfunction.

Several changes permit the baby to adapt to extrauterine life

While living its intrauterine life, the fetus functions much like a parasite, extracting from its mother all the necessary oxygen and nutrients for growth and development. All are obtained at the expense of the mother's own homeostasis. If the

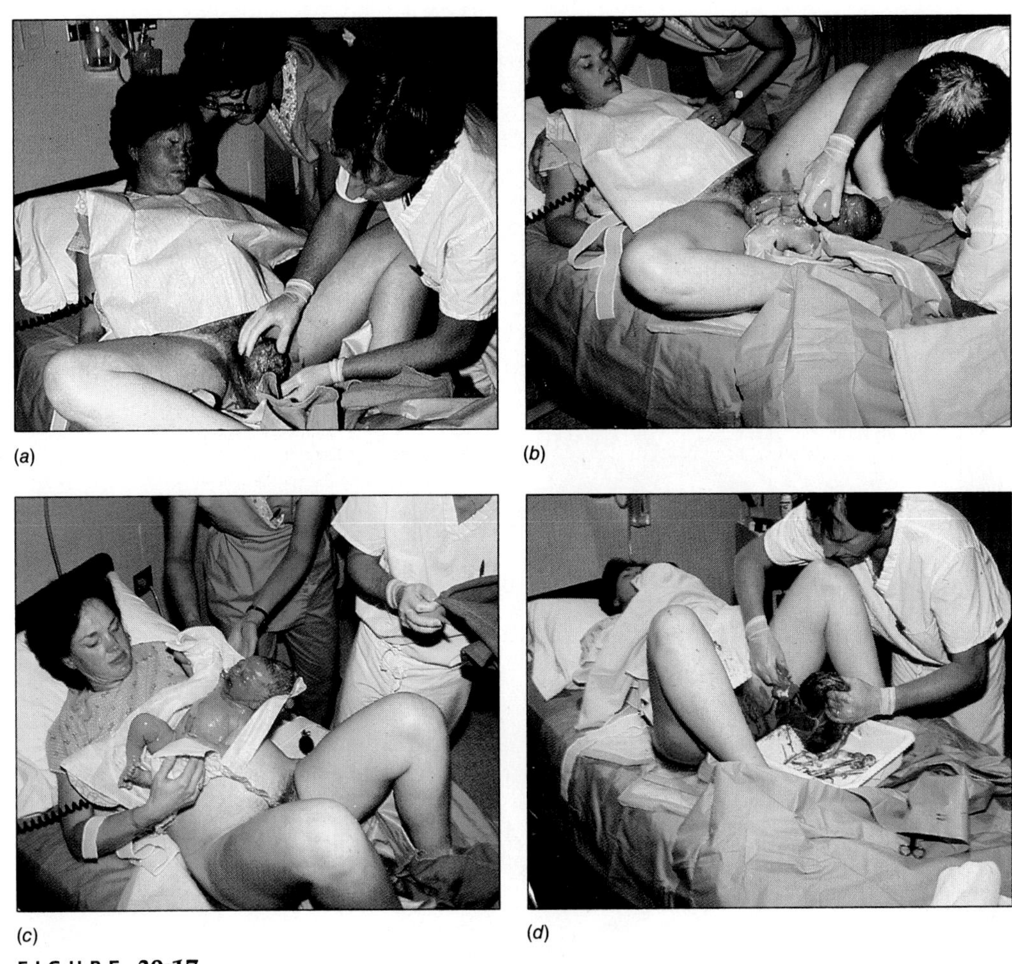

(a) (b) (c) (d)

FIGURE 30-17

Birth of a baby. In about 95% of all human births, the baby descends through the cervix and vagina in the head-down position. (*a*) The baby's head appears. (*b*) When the head fully appears, the physician or midwife can gently grasp it and guide the infant's emergence into the outside world. (*c*) The baby, still attached to the placenta by its umbilical cord, is presented to its mother. (*d*) During the third stage of labor the placenta is delivered. (Courtesy of Dan Atchison.)

mother's dietary calcium intake is insufficient, for example, calcium will be removed from her bones in order to supply the needs of the rapidly growing skeletal system of the fetus. Once delivered, the newborn must immediately begin to carry on independently its own physiological activities.

Ordinarily, the **neonate** (newborn infant) initiates its own rhythmic breathing within seconds following delivery and cries within a half a minute or so. If the mother has received anesthetics during labor, the fetus may also exhibit effects of exposure to such agents. Respiratory function and other activities may be depressed in such instances. In some cases, breathing may not begin for several minutes. This is one of the principal reasons for the current trend toward natural childbirth, a practice in which as little medication as possible is utilized.

The intrauterine environment requires a special kind of circulation

Fetal circulation (Fig. 30-18) exhibits three important characteristics resulting from its parasitic and aquatic existence:

1. Blood must be circulated to and from the placenta through the umbilical vessels. When returning from the placenta to the right atrium,

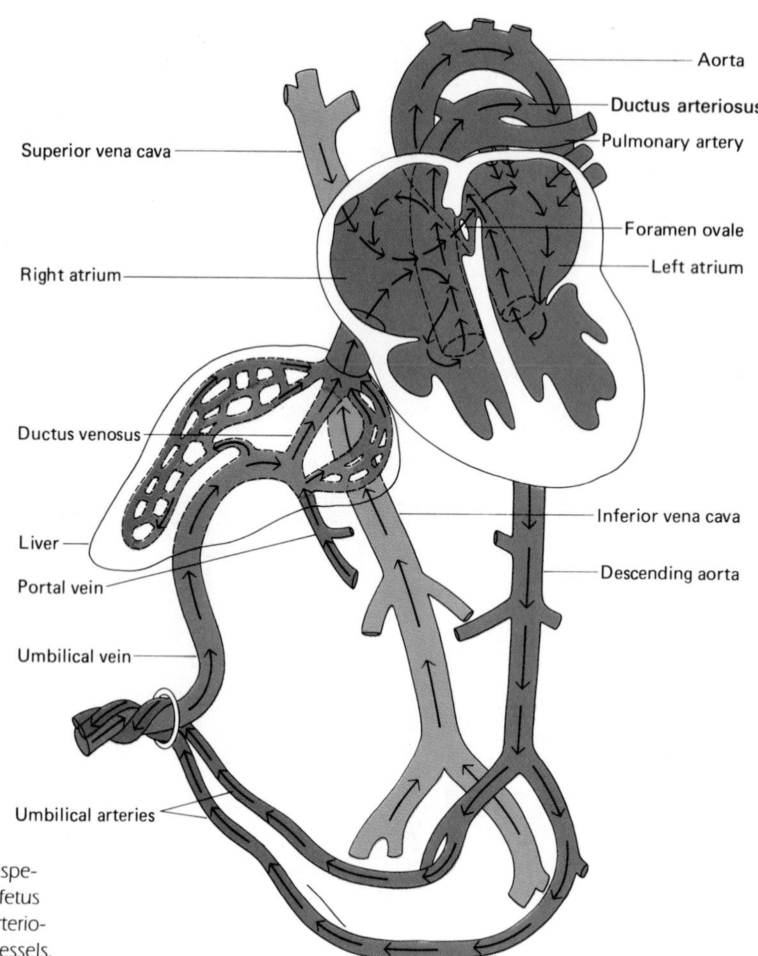

FIGURE 30-18

The fetal circulation. The structures especially designed for the needs of the fetus include the foramen ovale, ductus arteriosus, ductus venosus, and umbilical vessels.

much of the blood courses through the liver sinusoids of the fetus. However, there exists a fetal shunt, the **ductus venosus,** by means of which some of the blood is distributed directly to the inferior vena cava.

2. Because the lungs do not function as respiratory structures during prenatal life, an extensive pulmonary circulation is not necessary. The maternal lungs, in fact, perform oxygen and carbon dioxide exchange for the fetus. Thus, a second fetal shunt, the **foramen ovale,** exists between the two atria. This is an opening in the interatrial wall through which some of the blood entering the right atrium from the inferior vena cava is diverted into the left atrium and thence into the systemic circulation.

3. Some blood is pumped from the right atrium into the right ventricle and then into the pulmonary artery. The greater proportion of this, however, is diverted by a third fetal shunt, the **ductus arteriosus,** into the descending aorta and bypasses the pulmonary circulation. Once in the descending aorta, the blood is carried toward the placenta through the umbilical arteries.

Three circulatory changes facilitate adaptation to extrauterine life

Circulatory changes occurring at birth (Fig. 30-19) include the following:

1. The umbilical arteries collapse and close abruptly, resulting in cessation of blood flow to the placenta. This is followed by contraction and closure of the ductus venosus within 3 hours after birth. Now blood from the portal vein, which used this former shunt, passes directly to the liver sinusoids.

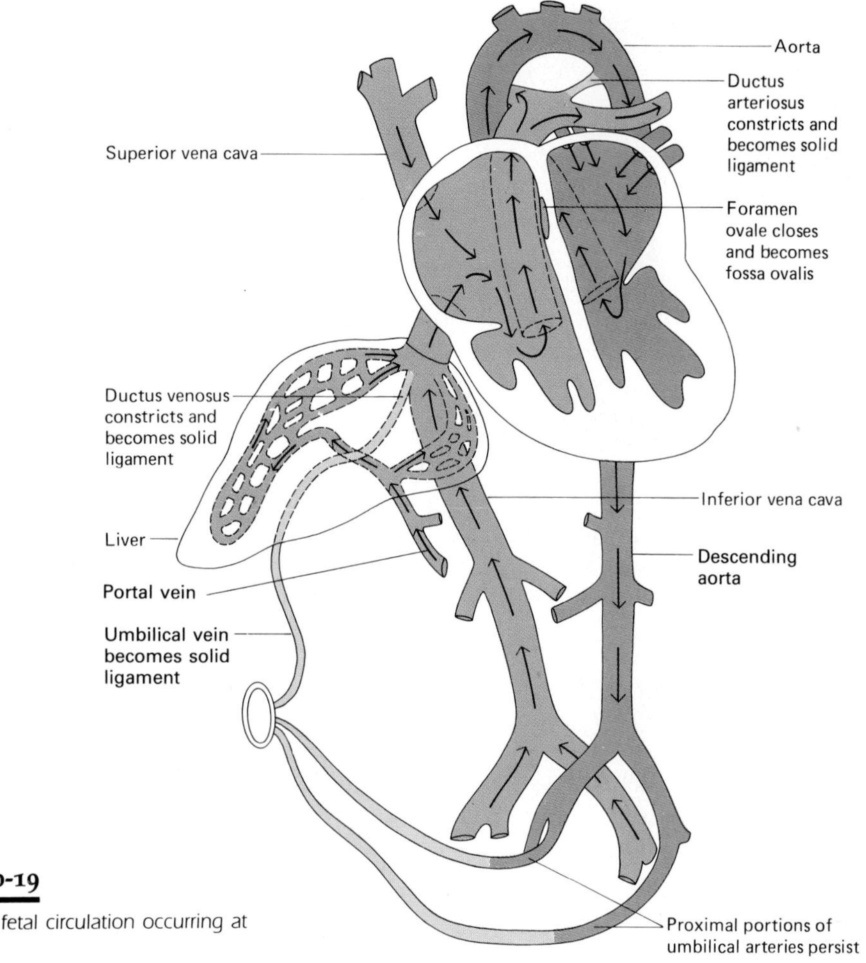

FIGURE 30-19

Changes in the fetal circulation occurring at birth.

2. Changes in blood pressure occur due to the closure of the placental circulation and an opening of the pulmonary circulation. As a result, there is a reversal of blood flow through the foramen ovale, and a small tissue flap is pressed into place, covering the opening and completing the interatrial wall. Ordinarily this tissue flap grows firmly in place within the first 3 months after birth.

3. The wall of the ductus arteriosus constricts reflexly, and circulation through this fetal shunt completely ceases within a few days following birth. By the end of the second postnatal month fibrous tissue has occluded the lumen of the ductus arteriosus, and only a ligamentous structure, the **ligamentum arteriosum,** remains. Examine these circulatory changes in Figures 30-18 and 30-19.

The embryo and fetus are affected by adverse environmental influences

Each year nearly 200,000 babies (7% of all live births) are born with a clinically significant defect. These birth defects may be the result of environmental influences, genetic factors, or a combination of the two (Table 30-3). Our current discussion focuses on environmental influences.

Previously it was thought that the placenta constituted an impervious barrier, preventing all deleterious substances in the mother from reaching the developing individual. Scientists now are of the opinion that most, if not all, chemicals and drugs ingested by the mother, hormones, and even certain viruses may cross the placenta and place the developing individual at risk. Typically,

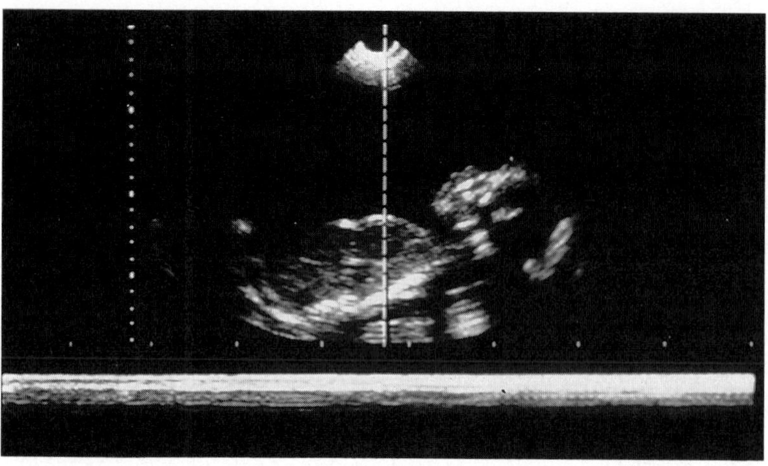

FIGURE 30-20

Sonogram of a fetus. The fetus has been visualized using the process of ultrasonography. Such photographs are valuable to the physician in diagnosing multiple births and birth defects. (© Siemens-Lutheran Hospital/Peter Arnold, Inc.)

these potentially harmful agents must achieve a specific concentration before they result in damage to the embryo or fetus. It is no longer a question of whether or not an agent will cross the placenta, but rather whether or not it reaches the tissues of the unborn in a harmful concentration. The concentration within the tissues of the developing individual is dependent on several factors. Included among these are maternal homeostatic mechanisms, fetal metabolic capabilities, and placental metabolic functions.

Moreover, it is well established that during the first 8 weeks of gestation (embryonic period) the embryo is most susceptible to developmentally toxic influences. Even within this time frame the individual organ systems are differentially vulnerable. Typically these critical periods occur early in the development of a given organ or structure, when any interference with cell migration or cell division alters the attainment of normal size or shape, resulting in a permanent malformation. Since this period of maximal susceptibility occurs at such an early stage of development, it is possible that the mother may not even realize that she is pregnant. Recent experimental findings also support the notion that the fetal stage of development (beyond the first 8 weeks) is not totally immune to harmful environmental influences. However, defects occurring at this stage of development tend to be reflected as functional deficits rather than alterations in morphology.

Clinical highlight

The ingestion of alcohol during pregnancy has recently been documented as leading to a condition affecting the newborn called the **fetal alcohol syndrome.** Retrospective studies indicate that nearly 1 out of every 1000 newborns are afflicted with this condition. Typically the intrauterine growth of the individual is retarded. At birth the individual exhibits numerous head and facial abnormalities, and frequently there are cardiac and limb defects as well. Additional developmental abnormalities seen later in the postnatal period include various degrees of mental retardation and behavioral disorders.

Currently there are several clinical approaches aimed at permitting the physician to diagnose, in utero, defects of the developing individual. Two of these, *chorionic villus sampling*, and amniocentesis, were discussed earlier in the present chapter. **Ultrasonography** (Fig. 30-20) is an additional procedure that has been developed for this purpose. This technique is used to visualize structures of the body by recording the reflection of ultrasonic waves. In some instances great scientific strides have been made in the diagnosis of genetic disorders in utero. Should it be determined that the embryo will develop into a grossly malformed baby, some women may elect to clini-

TABLE 30-3

Environmental influences on the human embryo

Factor	Example and effect	Comment
Nutrition	Severe protein malnutrition doubles the risk of birth defects, Fewer brain cells are produced, and learning ability may be permanently affected.	Growth rate is mainly determined by rate of net protein synthesis by embryo's cells.
Excessive amounts of vitamins	Vitamin D is essential, but excessive amounts may result in a form of mental retardation. Too much vitamin A and K may also be harmful.	Vitamin supplements are normally prescribed for pregnant women, but some women mistakenly reason that if one vitamin pill is beneficial, four or five might be even better.
Drugs	Many drugs affect the development of the fetus. Even aspirin has been shown to inhibit growth of human fetal cells (especially kidney cells) cultured in the laboratory. It may also inhibit prostaglandins, which are concentrated in growing tissue.	Common prescription drugs are generally taken in amounts based on the body weight of the mother, which may be hundreds or thousands of times too much for the tiny embryo.
Alcohol	When a woman drinks heavily during pregnancy, the baby may be born with fetal alcohol syndrome, that is, deformed and mentally and physically retarded. Low birth weight and structural abnormalities have been associated with as little as two drinks a day. It is thought that some cases of hyperactivity and learning disabilities may be caused by alcohol intake of the pregnant mother.	Fetal alcohol syndrome is thought to be one of the leading causes of mental retardation in the United States.
Heroin	Maternal heroin use is associated with a high mortality rate and high prematurity rate.	Infants that survive are born addicted to the drug and must be treated for weeks or months.
Cocaine	Maternal cocaine use is associated with physical and mental retardation in offspring. Some cocaine babies are premature and immediately exhibit signs of damage. Many have low birth weights, small heads, cardiac defects, and additional medical problems.	The rising number of cocaine babies is a problem of increasing clinical concern. In one study, nearly 10% of the babies delivered during a 30-day period in a large metropolitan hospital tested positive for cocaine.
Methadone	Methadone use by mother results in addiction also.	
Thalidomide	Thalidomide, marketed as a mild sedative, was responsible for more than 7000 grossly deformed babies born in the late 1950s in 20 different countries. Principal defect was **phocomelia,** a condition in which babies are born with extremely short limbs, often with no fingers or toes.	Interferes with cellular metabolism, most hazardous when taken during the fourth to sixth weeks, when limbs are developing.
Cigarette smoking	Cigarette smoking reduces the amount of oxygen available to the fetus because both maternal and fetal hemoglobin are combined with carbon monoxide. May slow growth and can cause subtle forms of damage. (In extreme form carbon monoxide poisoning causes gross defects such as hydrocephaly.)	Mothers who smoke deliver babies with lower than average birth weights. They also have a higher incidence of spontaneous abortions, stillbirths, and neonatal deaths. Studies also indicate a possible link between maternal smoking and slower intellectual development in the offspring.
Pathogens	Rubella (German measles) virus crosses the placenta and infects the embryo; interferes with normal metabolism and cell movements. Causes a syndrome that involves blinding cataracts, deafness, heart malformations, and mental retardation. The risk is greatest (about 50%) when a pregnant woman contracts rubella during the first month of pregnancy; it declines with each succeeding month.	A rubella epidemic in the United States in 1963–65 caused about 20,000 fetal deaths and 30,000 infants born with gross defects.
	Syphilis is transmitted to the fetus in about 40% of infected women. Fetus may die or be born with defects and congenital syphilis.	Pregnant women are routinely tested for syphilis during prenatal examinations.
Ionizing radiation	When mother is subjected to x rays or other forms of radiation during pregnancy, infant has higher risk of birth defects and leukemia.	Radiation was one of the earliest teratogens to be recognized.

cally terminate (abort) the pregnancy. However, in the minds of many individuals, exercising or even considering such an option raises serious ethical questions as yet unresolved in today's society.

The life cycle begins at conception and terminates at death

The human life cycle is divided into several stages for descriptive purposes. Life begins at conception and passes through a series of identifiable stages (Table 30-4) until death occurs. Up to this point we have focused on the development of the embryo and fetus, the birth process, and the postnatal adaptation of the neonate. Typically the **neonatal period** is considered as extending from birth to the end of the first month of extrauterine life. The period of **infancy** follows the neonatal period and lasts until the infant is able to assume an erect posture (i.e., walk). This usually occurs sometime between 10 and 14 months of age, although considerable variation exists in this regard. Certain physicians consider the infancy period to encompass the first 2 years of life. **Childhood** continues as a rapid period of growth and development, and extends from infancy until **adolescence.**

The period of adolescence is one marked by profound physical, physiological, and psychological development. It is during this time that an individual experiences the changes resulting in reproductive maturity. It is also a time for making the adjustments that permit the individual to assume the responsibilities associated with adulthood. **Young adulthood** follows adolescence and ends at about the age of 40, when the individual becomes a **middle-aged adult.** Middle-aged adulthood extends between the ages of 40 and 65. **Old age** begins after the age of 65 and continues until death.

Aging is a part of life's continuum

The process of aging incorporates all of the functional and structural alterations that occur in the body with the passage of time. Eventually these changes lead to various forms of functional impairment and ultimately to death. There is a progressive decrease in the body's homeostatic ability to respond to various forms of stress as aging proceeds. In the event that all of the current major causes of death were to be eliminated, the actual length of the human life would most probably not increase greatly beyond existing limits.

No bodily system escapes the effects of the aging process

Many morphological and functional changes occur with advancing age. Muscular strength reaches its peak between the ages of 20 and 30 years, and after that there is a progressive decline that seems to accelerate as we get older. The aging process of skeletal muscle tissue involves biochemical alterations in muscle fibers as well as a reduction in the number of fibers. These changes are also accompanied by alterations in neuromuscular junctions. Simultaneously, the density of long bones decreases and pathological changes in joints develop.

As seen earlier, the cardiac output in a young adult can increase up to seven times during rigorous exercise. However, as one ages, the heart also loses its ability to respond to this degree, and this in turn imparts specific limitations on the amount of physical exercise that the aged individual can perform. Alterations in respiratory function also ensue as aging progresses. In the young adult the blood can take up approximately 3 liters per minute of oxygen from the lungs. This capability is reduced to about one-half as the individual approaches 75 years of age. (It is recognized, however, that regular exercise may delay or even reverse some of these changes.) Furthermore, the metabolic rate of a young individual, relative to his or her size, is approximately double that of an aged person.

Renal function also declines with advancing age. The number of functioning nephrons decreases and this is accompanied by a progressive decline in the glomerular filtration rate, tubular excretion and absorption rates, and renal blood flow. The aged individual is able to maintain body temperature, blood-sugar levels, and an acceptable acid–base balance under basal conditions. In times of stress, however, these homeostatic mechanisms tend to fail more easily than in earlier years.

TABLE 30-4

Stages in the human life cycle

	Time period	Characteristics
Embryo	Conception to end of eighth week of prenatal development	Development proceeds from single-celled zygote to an embryo that is about 30 mm long, weighs 1 g, and has the rudiments of all its organs.
Fetus	Beginning of ninth week of prenatal development to birth	Period of rapid growth, morphogenesis, and cellular differentiation, changing the tiny parasitic embryo to a physiologically independent organism.
Neonate	Birth to 4 weeks of age	Neonate must make vital physiological adjustments to independent life. For example, it must now process its own food, excrete its wastes, obtain oxygen, and make circulatory changes appropriate to its new mode of life.
Infant	End of fourth week to 2 years of age. (Sometimes ability to walk is considered the end of infancy.)	Rapid growth; deciduous teeth begin to erupt; nervous system develops (myelinization), making coordinated activities possible; language skills begin to develop.
Child	Two years to puberty	Rapid growth; deciduous teeth erupt, are slowly shed, and replaced by permanent teeth; development of muscular coordination; development of language skills and other intellectual abilities.
Adolescent	Puberty (approximately age 11–14) to adult	Growth spurt; primary and secondary sexual characteristics develop; development of motor skills; development of intellectual abilities; psychological changes as adolescent prepares to assume adult responsibilities.
Young adult	End of adolescence (approximately age 20) to about age 40	Peak of physical development reached; individual assumes adult responsibilities that may include marriage, fulfilling reproductive potential, and establishing a career. After age 30 physiological changes associated with aging begin.
Middle-aged adult	Age 40 to about age 65	Physiological aging continues through this period, leading to menopause in women and physical changes associated with aging in both sexes (e.g., graying hair, decline in athletic abilities, skin wrinkling). This is a period of adjustment for many as they begin to face their own mortality.
Old adult	Age 65 to death	Period of senescence (old age). Physiological aging continues; homeostatic return to steady state is more difficult when the body is challenged by stress. Death often results from failure of the cardiovascular or immune system.

With advancing age the immune system also becomes less competent. The results of recent studies permit the suggestion that suppressor T cells progressively increase in numbers and activity as one ages. As a result, the individual becomes less effective in his or her capability to respond to various diseases.

Aging is likewise associated with a variety of psychological problems. Typically there is a loss of occupation. This represents not only a loss of income, but more importantly the loss of a meaningful activity in life. Aging is more often than not accompanied by a loss of friends and family. The separation from children, as the years go by, can become painful. Finally, the changes in one's physical appearance and the decline of health serve as reminders that the end of the life cycle is drawing near.

The mechanism of aging remains a mystery

Several theories have been proposed to explain the aging process. It is most probable that no one theory incorporates all of the essential elements. The real answer most likely includes factors from all the existing theories.

The **loss of proliferative capacity** theory is predicated on the notion that a cell lineage (a cell and its descendants) can only divide a finite number of times. For example, when normal human fibroblasts are cultured, they can divide 50 times (i.e., they give rise to 50 generations of cells before they die). Although one can vary the experimental conditions, the number of divisions seems to be "fixed," as though the cells have an inherent, genetically programmed "biological clock" that marks the number of mitoses. Such cells can be made "immortal" only if they are chemically or virally transformed into cancer cells.

The **cellular wear and tear** theory represents another explanation for the aging process. Its proponents claim that throughout life, cells suffer the progressive effects of injury from such things as ionizing radiation and ingested chemicals, as well as from mechanical and thermal insults. The physiological imbalances that result lead ultimately to aging and death.

Ionizing radiation is believed to penetrate the body's cells and produce free radicals (intermediate substances possessing at least one free electron). Subsequently the free radicals may strike lipid molecules, causing them to release a hydrogen atom and initiate the peroxidation of polyunsaturated lipids. The resulting nonfunctional peroxide molecules lead to a particular type of cellular damage to which the mitochondria and endoplasmic reticulum are particularly susceptible. Cellular respiration may cease, and this is followed by death of the cell. The effects of aging gradually appear as progressively greater numbers of cells are affected in this manner. The cells are thought to literally "burn out."

Considerable evidence exists to support the notion that vitamin E is a potent antioxidant and thus protects lipids from excessive oxidation. The effects of vitamin E appear to be enhanced by the presence of vitamin C and, according to the wear and tear theory, may play some role in retarding the aging process.

Thus far we have addressed several anatomical and functional alterations that occur with advancing age. Some changes may be the result of simple wear and tear, and others may have links with genetic timetables associated with DNA. According to some **genetic theories** of aging, genes may be preprogrammed to initiate age-related changes. A variation on this theme holds that a program could be encoded within brain cells that would account for growth, development, aging, and death, in other words, "programmed cell death" on the organismic level. Because there is substantial evidence that such a process exists in regions of the body, it is not unreasonable to consider that it may apply more broadly. It is not difficult to imagine the dispatching of hormonal and neural messages destined to signal various body parts to initiate such changes.

Clinical highlight

In humans there is an inherited condition called **progeria** that provides a clinical model for studies on aging. Children with progeria develop normally until about the age of one year and then begin to exhibit numerous signs of premature aging. Such individuals typically die at 10 to 15 years of age from heart disease related to atherosclerosis.

Additional theories suggest that mutations accumulate throughout life, resulting in the production of defective proteins. It is believed that the defective proteins are not able to effectively carry out normal physiological processes, resulting in a progressive deterioration of cellular function and ultimately death.

Although the precise mechanisms involved in the aging process are not fully understood, it is a fact of life that the risk of death increases nearly geometrically with age. A meaningful understanding of the specific cause or causes of aging requires a great deal more study and experimentation. The answer lies somewhere along the continuum of the life cycle, possibly in the form of a question not yet proposed. Maybe the reader will ultimately unravel the pieces to this most intriguing puzzle.

Summary

I. There are three basic developmental process that enter into the formation of a new individual: growth, morphogenesis, and cellular differentiation.

II. The zygote goes through a series of cleavage divisions, becomes a morula and then a blastocyst.
  - A. A blastocyst consists of the trophoblast and an inner cell mass.
  - B. The trophoblast enzymatically erodes the endometrial tissue, and the blastocyst implants itself within the uterine wall.

III. Fetal membranes provide protection and offer a means by which oxygen and nutrients are obtained.
  - A. The amnion surrounds the embryo, keeping it moist and protecting it from mechanical injury.
  - B. The chorion gives rise to the fetal portion of the placenta, which acts as the organ of exchange between the mother and the developing individual.
    1. The placenta provides a means for the developing individual to obtain oxygen and nutrients.
    2. Metabolic waste products are removed by the placenta.
    3. Hormones are produced by placental tissues.

IV. The process of development involves a sequence of predictable biological events.
  - A. Cells of the early embryo differentiate to form the three primary germ layers: ectoderm, mesoderm, and endoderm.
  - B. The primordia of all organs are formed during the first 8 weeks of prenatal development.
  - C. Limb buds arise during the second month of gestation. The testes and ovaries also begin to differentiate at this time.
  - D. The embryo becomes recognizably human during the third month of gestation.
  - E. The third trimester is characterized by rapid growth. The brain and other organs continue to develop in preparation for extrauterine life.

V. The process of parturition occurs approximately 266 days following fertilization. Labor is divided into three stages:
  - A. First stage—rhythmic uterine contractions, dilatation of the uterine cervix, and cervical effacement.
  - B. Second stage—passage of the fetus through the vaginal canal, terminating in delivery of the newborn.
  - C. Third stage—delivery of the placenta.

VI. The neonate must rapidly adjust to extrauterine life.
  - A. Blood is diverted from the nonfunctioning lungs in the fetus. The placenta serves as an organ of exchange between the fetal and maternal circulations.
  - B. At birth, circulation through the placenta ceases abruptly, the foramen ovale closes, separating the two atria, and the ductus arteriosus closes so that blood now reaches the pulmonary circulation. The ductus venosus also closes and the portal vein carries blood directly to the hepatic sinusoids.

VII. A variety of environmental factors can influence the development of the embryo and fetus.

VIII. The human life cycle is typically divided into a series of stages: embryo, fetus, neonate, infant, child, adolescent, young adult, middle-aged adult, and old adult.

IX. A progressive decline in the body's homeostatic capabilities marks the aging process.

Post-test

1. The mitotic divisions that the zygote goes through are referred to as ______________.
2. Cells of the developing embryo specialize biochemically and structurally through a process called ______________.
3. The process by which cells arrange themselves in specific patterns and shapes is ______________.
4. The morula rearranges itself to form a hollow ball of cells called a ______________.
5. The process by which the embryo embeds itself in the uterine wall is called ______________.
6. The cells of the blastocyst that ultimately give rise to the embryo proper are called the ______________ ______________ ______________.
7. The fluid-filled sac that surrounds the developing embryo is called the ______________.

8. The organ of exchange between the mother and the developing individual is called the ______________.
9. Cells of the inner cell mass give rise to three primary germ layers, the ______________, ______________, and ______________.
10. The ______________ ______________ system arises from the neural tube.
11. The developing individual is called a ______________ following the second month of gestation.
12. Late in development, the body of the fetus is covered by a downy hair called ______________.
13. Passage of the fetus through the vaginal canal and subsequent delivery is termed ______________.
14. The ______________ is delivered during the third stage of labor.
15. The fetal shunt between the two atria is known as the foramen ______________.
16. The ductus arteriosus is a fetal shunt connecting the pulmonary artery with the ______________ ______________.
17. The newborn infant is termed a ______________.
18. The period of development between ______________ and ______________ ______________ is called adolescence.
19. Structural and functional changes that occur in the body with the passage of time, leading ultimately to physical disability and death, are referred to as the ______________ process.
20. Prenatal development is most susceptible to environmental insult in the ______________ period.
21. The trophoblast differentiates into the ______________ and the ______________.
22. A surgical incision performed during childbirth and extending from the vagina toward the anus is called an ______________.
23. The ______________ is the creamlike protective substance covering the skin of the fetus during the latter months of pregnancy.
24. The hormone produced by the placenta that signals the corpus luteum that pregnancy has begun is called ______________ ______________ ______________.
25. Four fetal membranes possessed by all terrestrial vertebrates are the ______________, ______________, ______________, and ______________.

Review questions

1. Describe the development of the new individual from the zygote stage to the blastocyst. Utilize diagrams to illustrate your description.
2. What are the functions of the fetal membranes?
3. What is meant by implantation, and how does it occur?
4. Discuss the three stages of labor. During which stage is the placenta delivered?
5. Discuss three fetal circulatory shunts. What happens to them at birth?
6. When is the developing individual most vulnerable to potentially harmful environmental influences?
7. Discuss the stages of the human life cycle.
8. Discuss the major theories of the aging process. What are some of the physical, physiological, and psychological changes that develop as part of aging?
9. What is meant by dilatation and effacement of the uterine cervix?
10. Discuss the advantages of chorionic villus sampling versus amniocentesis in regard to prenatal diagnosis.
11. What are some of the conditions that lead to multiple births?

Post-test answers

1. cleavage **2.** differentiation **3.** morphogenesis **4.** blastula **5.** implantation **6.** inner cell mass **7.** amnion **8.** placenta **9.** ectoderm, endoderm, mesoderm **10.** central nervous **11.** fetus **12.** lanugo **13.** parturition **14.** placenta **15.** ovale **16.** aortic arch **17.** neonate **18.** childhood; young adulthood **19.** aging **20.** embryonic **21.** placenta, chorion **22.** episiotomy **23.** vernix **24.** human chorionic gonadotropin (HCG) **25.** yolk sac, chorion, allantois, amnion.

INHERITANCE

CHAPTER OUTLINE

LEARNING OBJECTIVES

After you have studied this chapter you should be able to:

1 Describe or diagram the basic chemical structure of a nucleic acid strand, distinguish between DNA and the varieties of RNA, and summarize the basic nature of the genetic code.

2 Describe the general sequence of information transfer from DNA to finished protein.

3 Explain the origin of mutations by nucleotide miscopying and relate this to the relationships between DNA, RNA, and protein synthesis.

4 Define the basic terms relating to genetic inheritance, such as gene, chromosome, homologous, alleles, dominant, recessive, genotype, phenotype, codominant, homozygous, and heterozygous.

5 Relate the inheritance of genetic traits to the behavior of chromosomes in meiosis.

6 Summarize the concepts of homologous chromosomes and allelic genes.

7 Distinguish between homozygous and heterozygous genotypes. Relate genotype to phenotype in terms of dominance.

8 Describe the inheritance of the Rh and ABO factors.

9 Summarize the characteristics of the chromosomal disorders described in this chapter.

10 Summarize the characteristics of three genetic diseases described in this chapter.

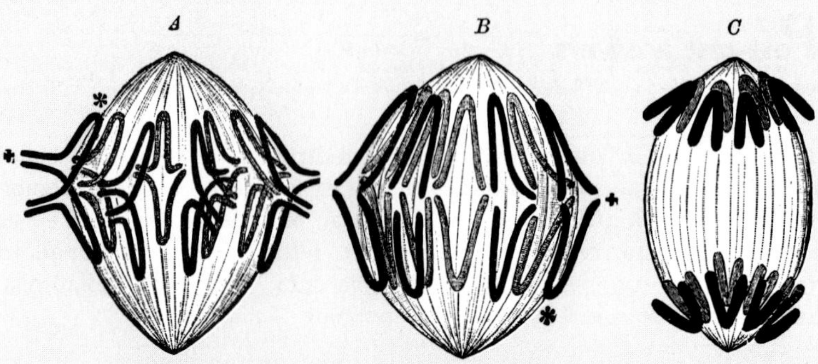

Human chromosomes. (Alfred Pasieka/Taurus Photos, NYC.)

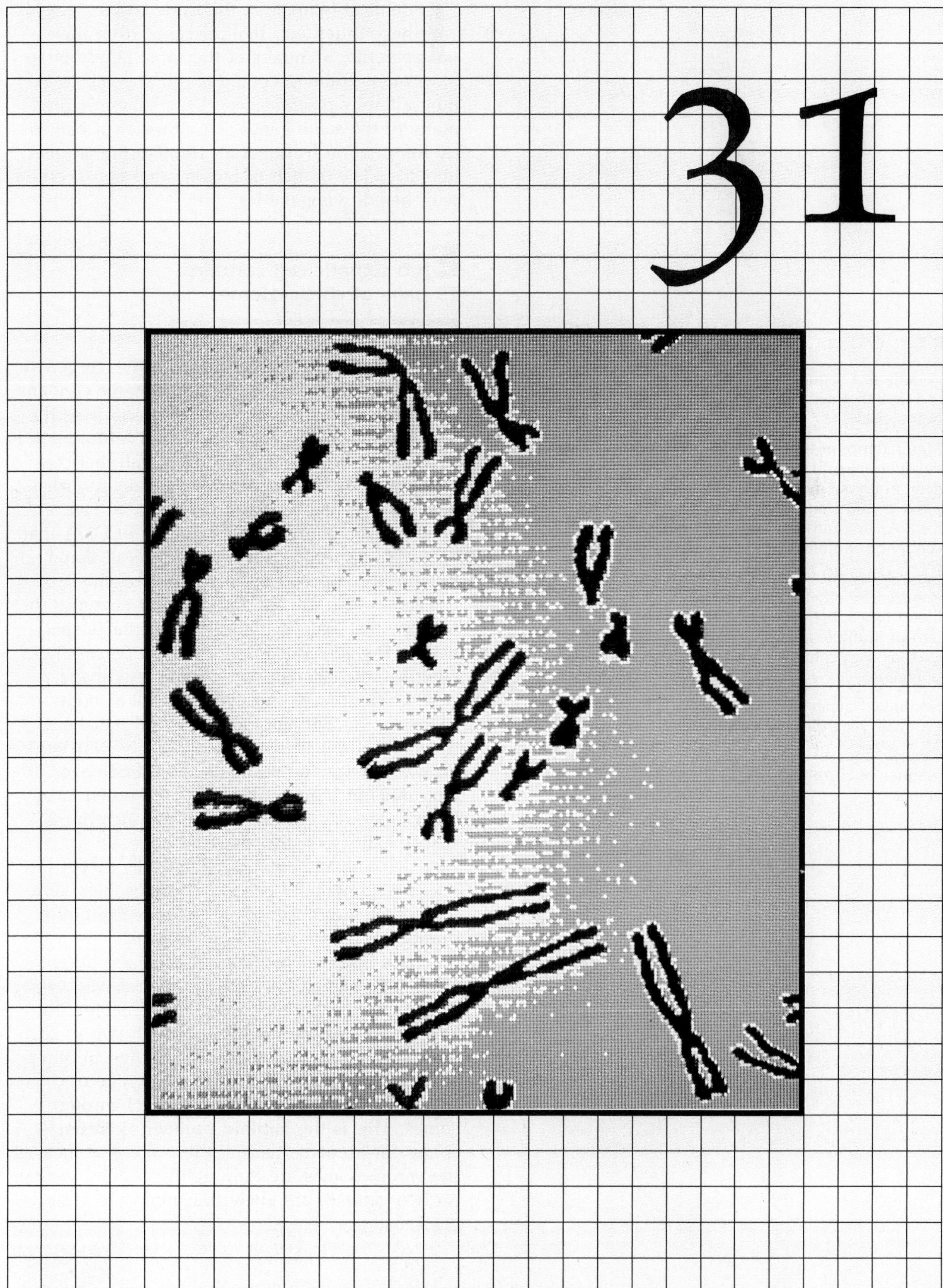
31

KEY CONCEPTS

A gene is a sequence of nucleotides in DNA that codes for a specific polypeptide.

Manufacture of a polypeptide involves transcription, in which the code is transferred from DNA to mRNA, and translation of the mRNA code into the appropriate sequence of amino acids.

Some traits are inherited by simple dominance; others, such as ABO blood types, are inherited by a system of multiple alleles; still others such as skin color are governed by polygenes.

Sex-linked genes are expressed in the male regardless of dominance.

Genetic diseases result from abnormalities of chromosomes or specific genes.

Identical twins look the same because they have inherited identical genes from their parents. Members of the same family often have many traits in common and are said to exhibit a family resemblance. They have inherited many of the same genes. The transfer of biological information from parent to offspring is called **heredity.** The branch of biology that is concerned with heredity is **genetics.**

Each somatic cell contains 23 pairs of chromosomes

Chromosomes are tiny packages in which genetic information is stored. Each chromosome contains thousands of **genes,** and each gene contains the information for a specific trait. That information is in the form of a chemical code. Recall that the chemical compound that codes genetic information is **DNA** (deoxyribonucleic acid). In fact, a gene may be defined as a sequence of DNA that codes for a specific polypeptide. (Recall that a protein is composed of polypeptide chains.)

Genes code for the hundreds of enzymes that regulate metabolic activities. The proteins specified by the genes determine what a person looks like (including height, body build and shape, color of skin, hair, and eyes) as well as body chemistry (including blood type and metabolic function). They also specify at least a framework for intelligence and many aspects of behavior. Hundreds of human disorders are known to be inherited, and genes are thought to determine susceptibility to many diseases.

Each human **somatic** cell (all cells except the sex cells) contain 23 pairs of chromosomes, or a total of 46 chromosomes. This is the **diploid** number of chromosomes for humans.

Only the **gametes** (the sex cells) are different. Recall that gametes are formed by a special type of cell division known as **meiosis** (Chapter 29). During meiosis the members of each pair of chromosomes are separated and distributed to different cells. Each gamete contains only one of each pair of chromosomes, or a total of 23 chromosomes. This is the **haploid** number of chromosomes for humans. During the process of meiosis the chromosomes are thoroughly shuffled so that no two gametes are likely to contain the same chromosomes.

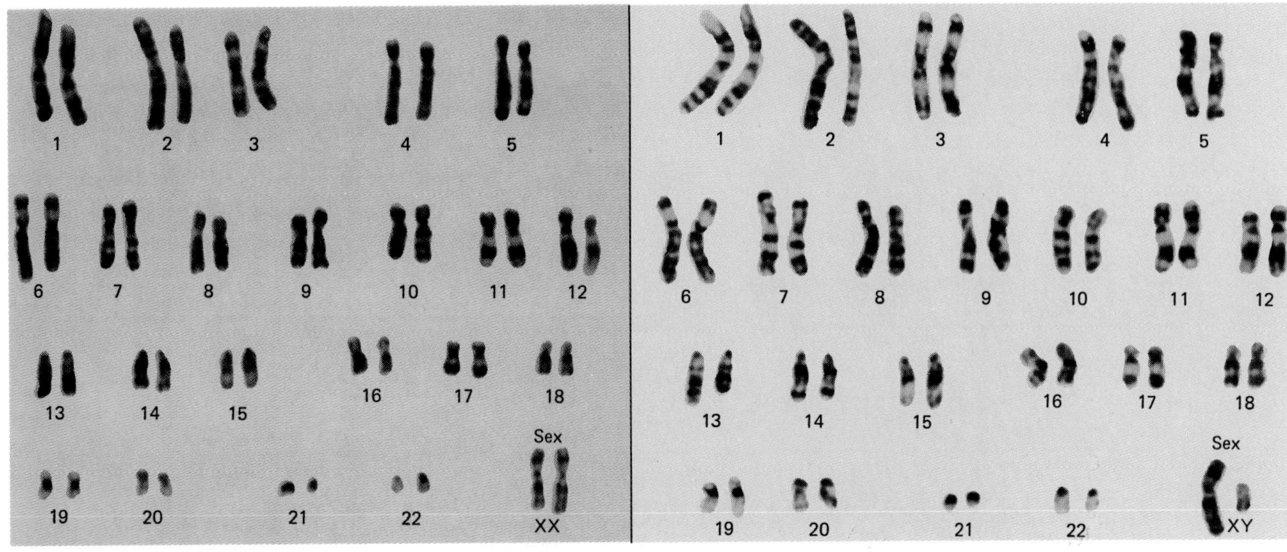

(*a*) Female karyotype

(*b*) Male karyotype

FIGURE 31-1

Karyotypes, photomicrographs showing the chromosome composition, of (*a*) a normal human female and (*b*) a normal male. Homologous chromosomes have been placed side by side. Note the sex chromosomes—XX in the female and XY in the male.

One of each pair of chromosomes is inherited from the father and the other from the mother. When sperm and egg unite in fertilization, they form a single cell, the zygote, which then contains 46 chromosomes. Before the zygote divides to form the first two cells of the embryo, the chromosomes are duplicated, and then during mitosis a complete set of chromosomes is distributed to each end of the cell. When cell division occurs, each new cell has an identical set of 46 chromosomes. This process is repeated over and over so that each of the billions of somatic cells of the completed human being contains an identical set of 46 chromosomes (Fig. 31-1).

Biological information is written in the genetic code

To understand inheritance it is important to have a knowledge of the basic hereditary substance, DNA. Recall from Chapter 2 that DNA is a nucleic acid contained in the nucleus of every cell. Although the cell nucleus is microscopic, the amount of information contained in it is astonishingly large. This information is coded in the very long molecules of DNA. If the cell nucleus were the size of a basketball, the strands of DNA contained in it would stretch from New York to Washington. The library of information contained in DNA enables the nucleus of a single cell to specify instructions for the formation, structure, and function of an entire, immensely complex organism such as the human body.

A single strand of DNA is composed of *base* units projecting at approximately right angles from a backbone of alternating *sugar* and *phosphate* units. Each unit consisting of one sugar, one phosphate group, and one base is called a **nucleotide.** The sugar is the pentose **deoxyribose.** The four nitrogen-containing bases of DNA are **adenine (A), thymine (T), guanine (G),** and **cytosine (C).**

The bases occur in groups of three, called **triplets,** or **codons** (**koe**-dons). Each triplet specifies a particular amino acid. The sequence in which these bases occur registers the genetic code. Thus the sequence ACG/TCC/ATC/CGA bears a different set of instructions than the sequence TGG/AAC/TAG/TCC.

DNA forms a double helix

DNA exists in nature in the form of two strands (Fig. 31-2). The ladder-like double strands of DNA are attached to each other by means of hydrogen bonds between their bases and are twisted into a spiral or, more correctly, a helix,

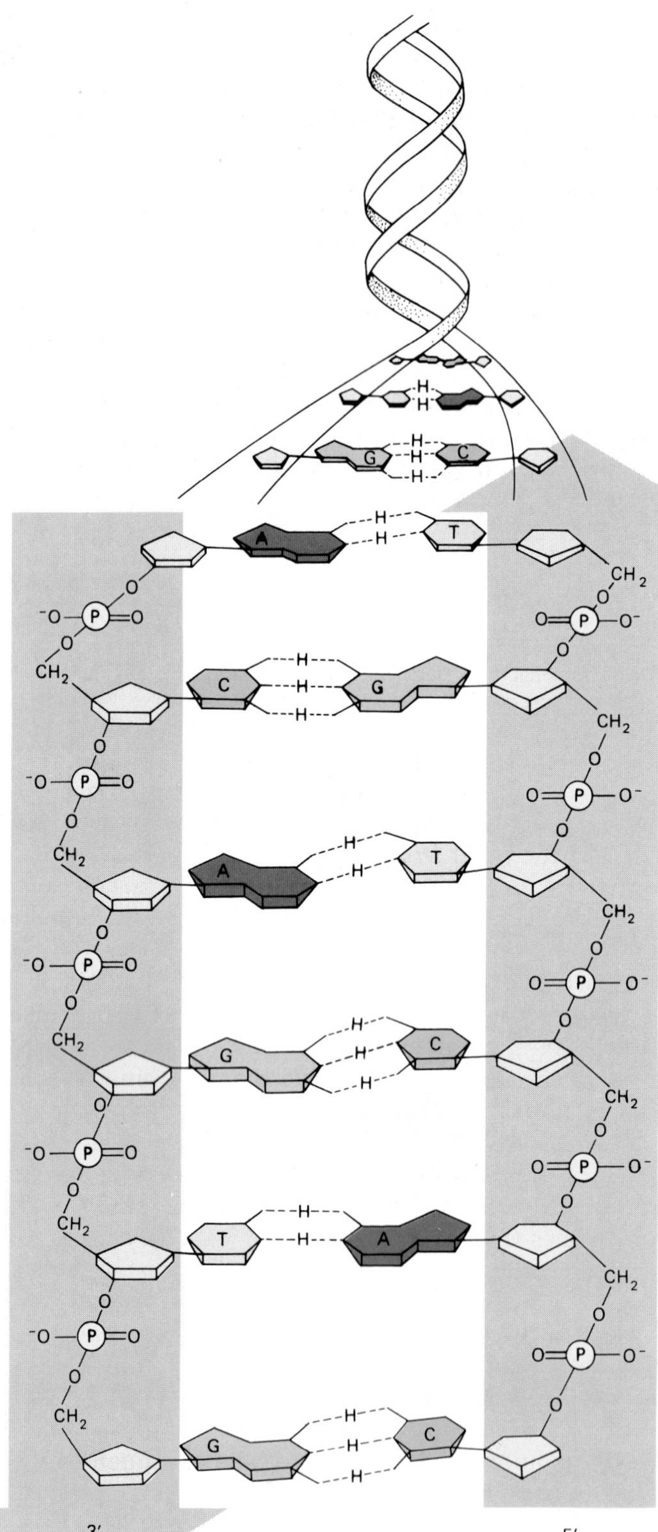

FIGURE 31-2

Structure of DNA. The DNA molecule consists of subunits called nucleotides. Each nucleotide consists of a phosphate group (labeled P); deoxyribose, a sugar (shown in green); and a nitrogen base (shown in red or blue). The four types of bases found in DNA are adenine (A), thymine (T), cytosine (C), and guanine (G). The sequence of these bases spells out the genetic code. A sequence of several hundred nucleotides make up a gene and codes for a specific polypeptide.

somewhat like a spiral staircase. Protein is also associated with the helix in a characteristic and regular pattern.

The most important point to remember concerning the strands of the DNA helix is that if you know the sequence of the bases on one of the two DNA strands, you can predict the base sequence of the other. This is because the adenine on one strand will pair only with thymine on the other strand, and cytosine will pair only with guanine. No other pairing relationship is normally possible. The genetically active strand is called the **coding,** or **plus, strand** of DNA. The plus strand sequence of AAT/CGT/TTG/CGT would be reflected in its mate, the **minus strand,** by the sequence TTA/GCA/AAC/GCA. The minus strand is the complement of the plus strand.

DNA is replicated before mitosis

Each strand of DNA duplicates, or **replicates,** itself before mitosis (Chapter 3). Thus, just prior to mitosis, the two strands separate (Figs. 31-3 and 31-4), and under the control of the proper enzymes, each builds a complement of itself. This process, called **semiconservative replication,** results in two identical double strands of DNA. After replication, mitosis and cell division can proceed.

Transcription is the synthesis of RNA from a DNA template

The manufacture of a polypeptide involves two complex processes: transcription and translation. In **transcription** a segment of DNA (a gene) is copied in the form of a **messenger RNA (mRNA)** molecule. The mRNA then contains the information that specifies the amino acid sequence of a polypeptide chain. DNA begins to make a protein by uncoiling the portion of the DNA double strand that is responsible for that particular protein. The plus and the minus strands then separate, and a complement to the plus strand forms. That complement is made from RNA components.

RNA is similar to DNA in many ways, but it is always a much shorter molecule, and it consists of only one strand per molecule. Recall from Chapter 2 that chemically RNA differs from DNA in two respects: it has a different sugar, called ribose, in its backbone, and it has the base uracil in place of thymine. Uracil behaves, however, like thymine. For instance, if the plus strand of DNA had the sequence AAT/CGT/TTG/CGT, the corresponding minus RNA strand would have the sequence UUA/GCA/AAC/GCA. Genetic information is coded in mRNA in sets of three bases, called **codons.** Each codon specifies one amino acid.

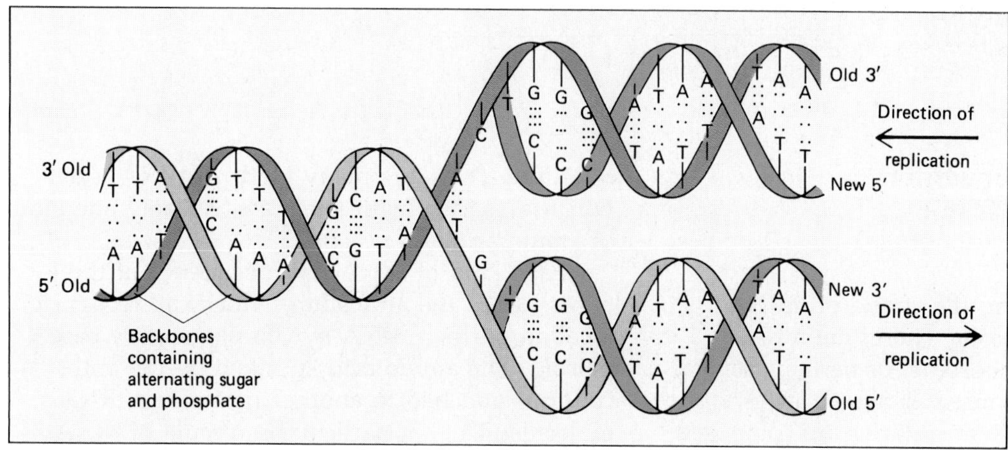

FIGURE 31-3

Mechanism of the replication of DNA. The two ends of each strand of this helix are labeled 3′ and 5′ so as to establish the direction of replication. The two strands are shown separating; both are being copied. Replication proceeds in the same direction (3′ to 5′) on both strands.

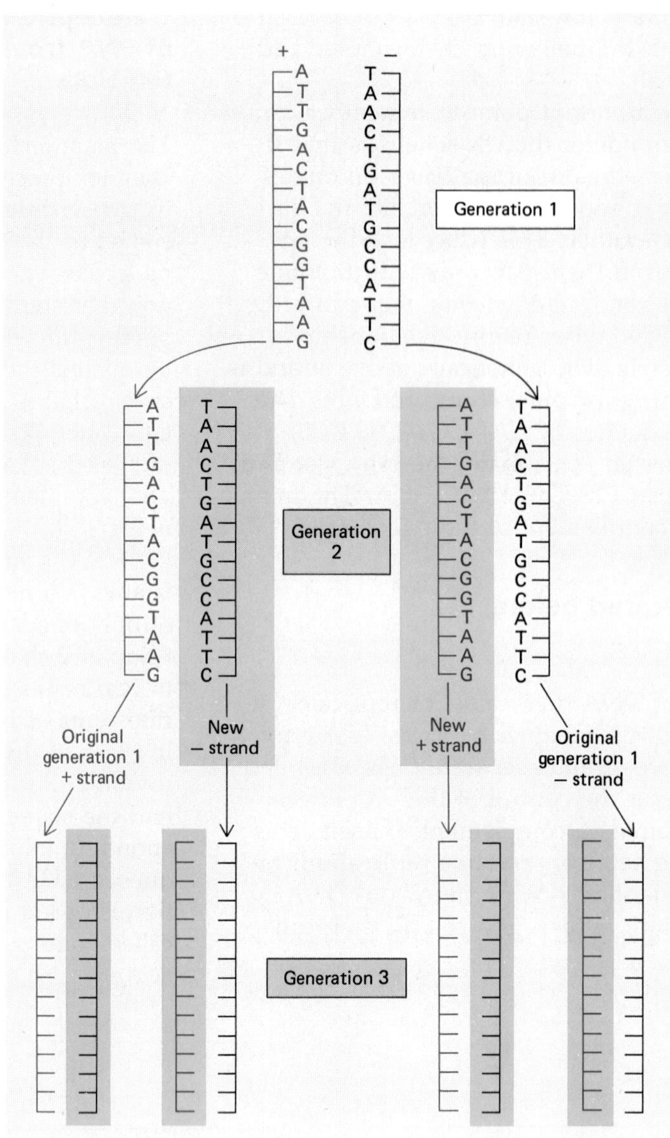

FIGURE 31-4

Semiconservative DNA replication. The relationship between the plus and minus strands of DNA is something like that between a photographic positive print and its negative.

Translation is the conversion of information in mRNA into a polypeptide

Following transcription, the strand of mRNA passes into the cytoplasm. There, the mRNA strand encounters a ribosome, or perhaps several of them. Ribosomes consist of two particles, one large and one small. Both particles are composed of **ribosomal RNA** and globular protein. Physical interaction between the ribosome and the mRNA strand is necessary for the production of a protein. Another essential component of this process is yet another kind of RNA called **transfer RNA,** or **tRNA.** There are many kinds of tRNA, each of which associates with and transfers only one kind of amino acid.

Each kind of tRNA has a sequence of three bases, called the **anticodon,** which can recognize a codon on the mRNA by complementary base pairing. The amino acid specified by the anticodon is attached to another part of the tRNA molecule. Thus, a particular molecule of tRNA, carrying its own distinctive kind of amino acid, will attach itself to the mRNA strand only at the codon whose three bases are complementary to the anticodon of the tRNA molecule. For exam-

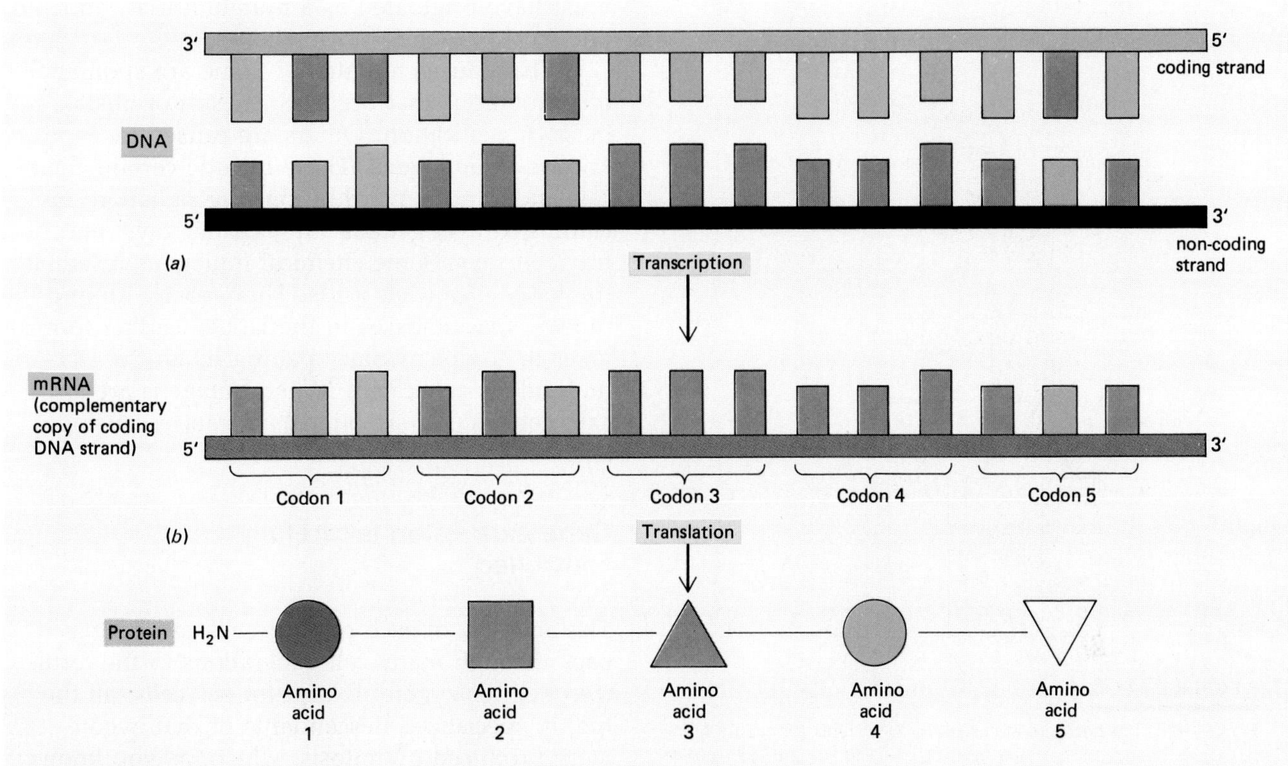

FIGURE 31-5

Protein synthesis involves (*a*) transcription, or mRNA synthesis, and (*b*) translation, or polypeptide synthesis. In transcription, the DNA strands separate in one region and a strand of mRNA is produced. The mRNA leaves the nucleus and becomes associated with ribosomes. Genetic information in mRNA is composed of sets of three bases called codons, each of which specifies one amino acid. Messenger RNA codons are translated consecutively, specifying the sequence of amino acids in the polypeptide chain. The amino acids are delivered to the mRNA by tRNA molecules.

ple, the tRNA carrying tyrosine will attach itself to the mRNA strand only over a codon that specifies tyrosine. The amino acids carried by tRNA molecules are then polymerized (joined together) into the proper sequence for the protein specified by the gene (Fig. 35-5).

In summary, the base sequence (codons) of the mRNA strand dictates the type of tRNA molecules (based on codon-anticodon interaction) that deliver amino acids to the ribosome. Thus, ultimately the base sequence of mRNA determines the type and sequence of amino acid units that will be joined at the ribosome into some distinctive protein such as albumin. This final step, in which the information encoded in the mRNA is converted into a sequence of amino acids to produce a polypeptide chain, is called **translation.**

Errors sometimes occur in DNA

What would happen if by some accident one of the bases of a DNA strand were changed to some other one? First, this error would be transmitted to all strands of DNA that were replicated from the one in which it originally occurred (Fig. 31-6). Thus all the descendants of that particular cell would share its genetic error. Second, the error would lead to a corresponding defect in the complementary strand of mRNA and ultimately to a wrong amino acid in a protein (Fig. 31-6). If the error resulted in what is known as a "nonsense" sequence of bases, that is, a codon that has no amino acid equivalent, the protein would suffer a break at that point and perhaps be only a fraction

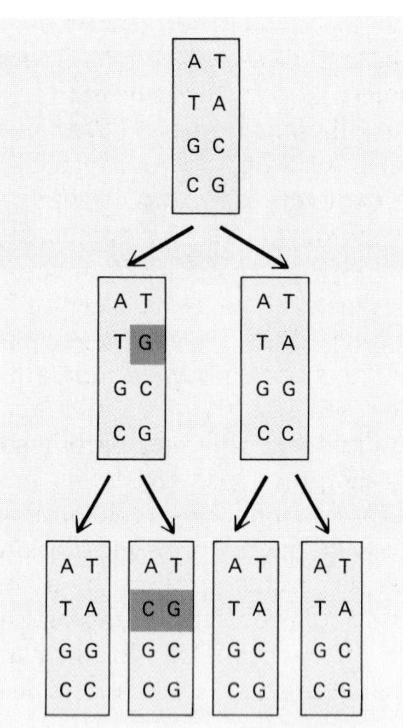

FIGURE 31-6

How a mutation becomes stabilized by DNA replication. A guanine base has replaced an adenine base. This could occur by an error in DNA replication. When the DNA molecule is replicated again, one of the strands gives rise to a molecule that is exactly like the original parent strand. The other, mutated, strand gives rise to a molecule with a new combination of bases that will be perpetuated generation after generation.

of its normal length. If the sequence had an amino acid equivalent, the protein might be little affected or considerably damaged, depending upon the exact nature of the change

Sickle-cell anemia (Chapter 19) probably originated in much this way, as did perhaps the incompetent enzyme of albinism and many other genetic diseases. Such an abrupt change in the genetic information of a cell is called a **mutation.** If it occurs in a sex cell or one of the precursors of a sex cell, a mutation can be passed on from parent to offspring. Mutations are important in the survival of species because they provide variety among members of a species. When environmental conditions change, at least some individuals may be able to adapt.

It is unlikely that a single random genetic change will improve any organism, just as it is unlikely that the random removal of a transistor or silicon chip will improve a computer. Each of the genetic diseases discussed later in this chapter must have originated as a mutation that rendered one or more genes incompetent.

What causes mutations? Some are spontaneous mutations that occur as a result of mistakes in DNA replication. Others are caused by agents known as **mutagens.** These include certain chemicals and various types of ionizing radiation, including x-rays, gamma rays, cosmic rays, and ultraviolet rays. Some chemical mutagens resemble the bases of nucleic acids. They react with and modify specific bases in the DNA, leading to mistakes in complementary pairing when the DNA molecule is replicated. Many mutagens are also **carcinogens** (kar-**sin**-o-jens), or cancer-causing agents.

Gene expression is carefully controlled

The ancestry of each of your cells can be traced back through many cell generations to the fertilized egg, or zygote. Except for sex cells, all the highly specialized descendants of that zygote were produced by mitosis, which, as you know, ensures that all daughter cells have exactly the same DNA. That fact would seem to indicate that all these different cells share the same genetic information and that in this regard they are identical cells.

Yet obviously all the body's cells are not identical. How can this be? Although the various differentiated cells of an organism probably have the same genetic information, different parts of that information are *expressed* in different tissues. Whatever information is inappropriate—and that must be a vast fund—is **repressed,** not only in each cell but also in the descendants of that cell. In the case of a differentiated cell that actively divides such as, for example, an epithelial cell, the very suppression of much of its heredity has become hereditary.

Some cells express some of the information they contain only at certain times. For example, the cells of the thyroid gland secrete thyroid hormones only when stimulated to do so by thyroid-stimulating hormone released into the blood from the pituitary gland. Apparently some of its genes function only when the cell is stimulated in a certain way.

Genes behave according to certain rules

Recall that a complete set of chromosomes is inherited from each parent. Thus, there is a set of maternal chromosomes inherited from the mother and a set of paternal chromosomes inherited from the father. The two members of a pair are said to be **homologous** (hoe-**mol**-uh-gus).

Homologous chromosomes contain genes governing the same traits. The gene for any particular trait occupies a specific location, or **locus,** on a specific chromosome. Members of a pair of chromosomes have genes for similar traits arranged in similar order. For example, suppose that one chromosome of a pair contains a gene specifying eye color. In that case, the other chromosome of the pair will also contain a gene at the same locus specifying eye color. Two genes that govern the same trait are referred to as **alleles** (Fig. 31-7).

Gregor Mendel, considered the father of genetics, worked out some basic rules of inheritance. According to Mendel's **principle of segregation,** during meiosis the alleles for each locus separate, or segregate, from each other when the homologous chromosomes separate. When the gametes form, each will contain one and only one allele for each locus.

Mendel's **principle of independent assortment** holds that during meiosis, each pair of alleles separate independently of the pairs of alleles located on other pairs of homologous chromosomes. Alleles of different loci therefore assort randomly into the gametes. Genes that are located near one another on the same chromosome are **linked** and do not undergo independent assortment.

Gender is determined by the sperm cell

Inheritance of gender provides a good example of separation of chromosomes during meiosis, sorting into different gametes, and then recombination of chromosomes during fertilization. Of the 23 pairs of chromosomes, 22 pairs are matched. For example, the two chromosomes of pair 1 are alike (see Fig. 31-1).

The 22 pairs of matched chromosomes are called **autosomes** (**aw**-toe-sohms). One pair of chromosomes, the **sex chromosomes,** are alike in females but different in males. Every normal female has two X chromosomes in each of her body cells, whereas every normal male has one X chromosome and one smaller Y chromosome. As a result every egg cell contains an X chromosome, but every sperm cell contains *either* an X *or* a Y chromosome. During spermatogenesis, when the homologous chromosomes separate during meiosis, one sex chromosome is distributed to one gamete and the other sex chromosome is distributed to the other gamete.

Gender of the offspring is determined by the sperm cell at the moment of fertilization (Fig. 31-8). If the egg cell is fertilized by a sperm cell containing an X chromosome, the offspring will be a female. If the egg is fertilized by a Y-bearing sperm cell, the offspring will be a male.

A monohybrid cross illustrates basic principles

Some basic genetic terminology and principles of inheritance can be illustrated by examples of a **monohybrid cross**—a cross between two individuals that differ with respect to the alleles they carry for a single locus.

Individuals with the disorder **albinism** (**al**-bih-nizm) are unable to make the pigment melanin, which is responsible for much of the color of skin, hair, and eyes. Due to a genetic mutation, an albino cannot produce an enzyme necessary to produce melanin.

Let us say that the recipe for producing the enzyme needed to synthesize melanin is encoded in a gene which we will represent with the upper case letter *A*. We can indicate the abnormal (mutated) version of this gene with the lower case letter *a*. In a normally pigmented person with no history of albinism both members of the pair of chromosomes that code for this enzyme will contain a normal gene, *A*.

In a person who is a genetic carrier for albinism, one chromosome will carry a normal gene and the homologous chromosome will carry the abnormal gene. An albino will have two mutated genes, *aa*. Thus, every individual has one of the following genetic makeups, or **genotypes** (**jee**-no-types): *AA*, *Aa*, or *aa*. The term **phenotype** (**fee**-no-type) refers to how the genes are expressed. A

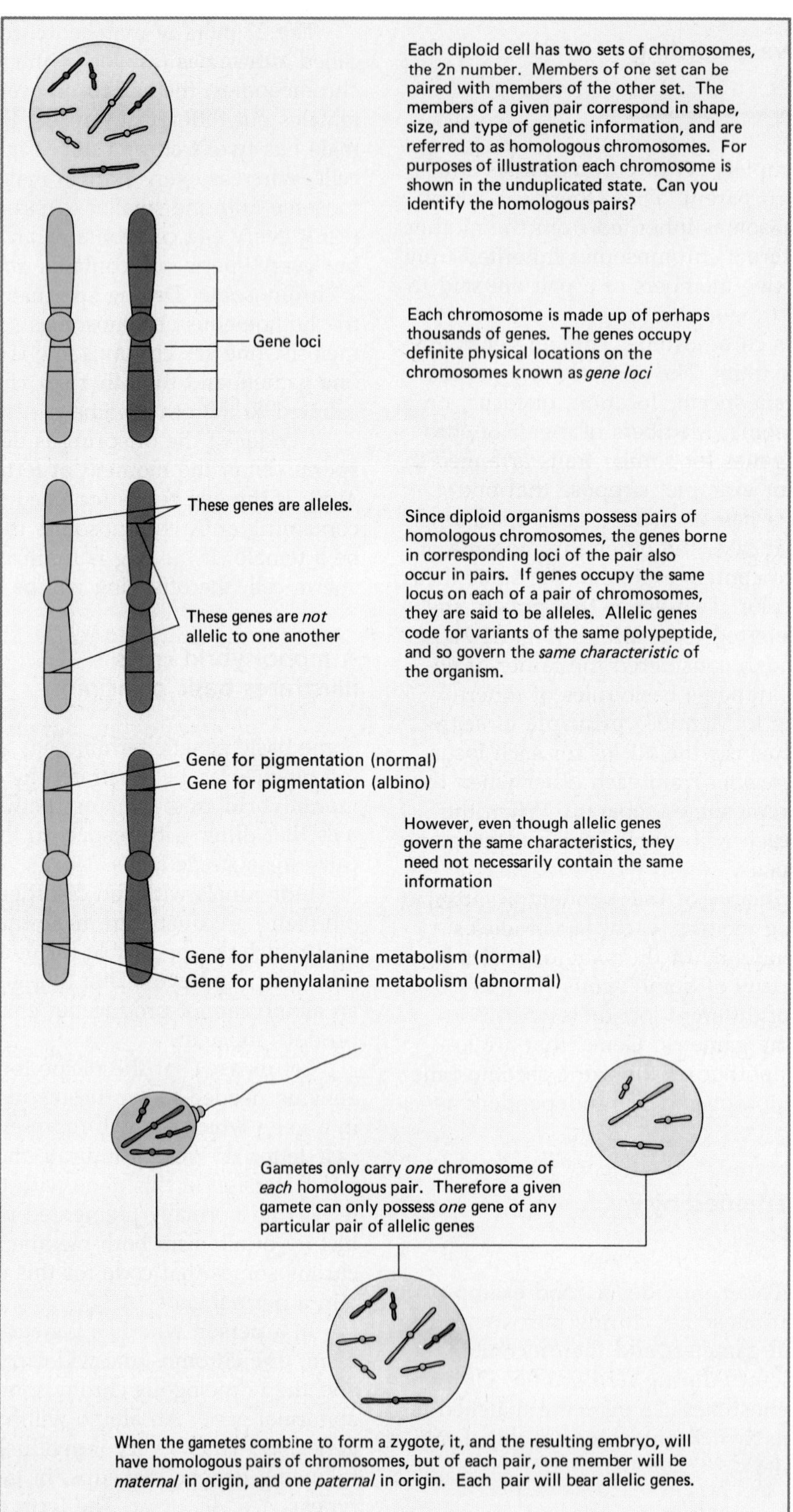

Each diploid cell has two sets of chromosomes, the 2n number. Members of one set can be paired with members of the other set. The members of a given pair correspond in shape, size, and type of genetic information, and are referred to as homologous chromosomes. For purposes of illustration each chromosome is shown in the unduplicated state. Can you identify the homologous pairs?
Gene loci
Each chromosome is made up of perhaps thousands of genes. The genes occupy definite physical locations on the chromosomes known as *gene loci*
These genes are alleles.
These genes are *not* allelic to one another
Since diploid organisms possess pairs of homologous chromosomes, the genes borne in corresponding loci of the pair also occur in pairs. If genes occupy the same locus on each of a pair of chromosomes, they are said to be alleles. Allelic genes code for variants of the same polypeptide, and so govern the *same characteristic* of the organism.
Gene for pigmentation (normal)
Gene for pigmentation (albino)
However, even though allelic genes govern the same characteristics, they need not necessarily contain the same information
Gene for phenylalanine metabolism (normal)
Gene for phenylalanine metabolism (abnormal)
Gametes only carry *one* chromosome of *each* homologous pair. Therefore a given gamete can only possess *one* gene of any particular pair of allelic genes
When the gametes combine to form a zygote, it, and the resulting embryo, will have homologous pairs of chromosomes, but of each pair, one member will be *maternal* in origin, and one *paternal* in origin. Each pair will bear allelic genes.

FIGURE 31-7

Genes that govern the same trait occupy the same locus on each of a pair of homologous chromosomes. Such gene pairs are called alleles.

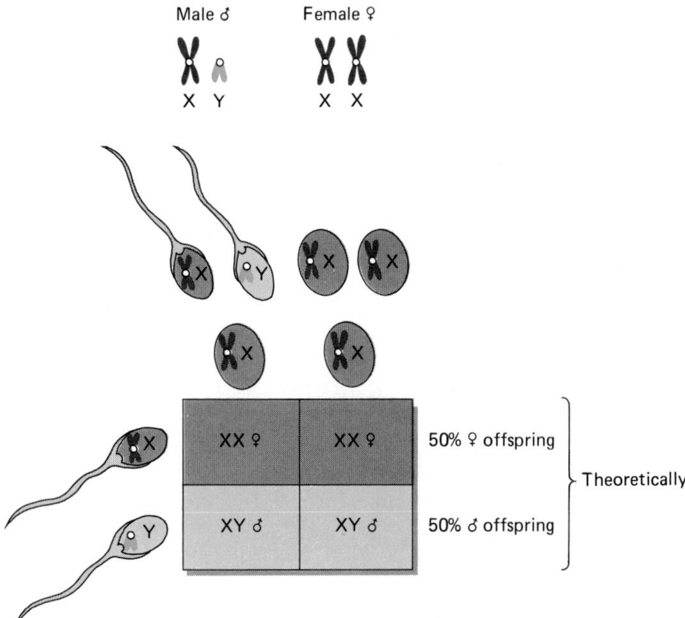

FIGURE 31-8

The inheritance of gender. Sex is determined by the sperm at the moment of fertilization. When the egg is fertilized by an X-bearing sperm, the offspring will be a female. When the egg is fertilized by a Y-bearing sperm, the offspring will be a male.

person with two normal allelic genes for melanin production *(AA)* has a different genotype than a carrier for albinism *(Aa)*, but both have a normal phenotype for pigmentation.

When the alleles for a particular trait are the same, for example *AA* or *aa*, the individual is described as having a **homozygous** (*hoe*-mow-**zy**-gus) genotype for the trait. When the alleles are different, for example *Aa*, the individual has a **heterozygous** (*het*-er-oh-**zy**-gus) genotype for that trait.

Consider what would happen if an albino man were to have a child with a normally pigmented woman. As a result of meiosis the sex cells contain only one chromosome from each homologous pair. The albino male's sperm, then, will each contain one *a* gene (Fig. 31-9). The female's ova will each contain one *A* gene. When a baby is conceived, it receives an *a* gene from its father and an *A* gene from its mother. The child is therefore heterozygous *(Aa)*. Luckily, the *A* allele produces enough of the needed enzyme for normal coloration; by inspection one could not determine that the baby also possesses a mutated gene for albinism. Sensitive chemical tests, however, might well disclose that the baby has much less than the normal amount of the enzyme.

In analyzing the probable combinations of genes, special charts called **Punnett squares** can be constructed (Fig. 31-9b). The genetic contribution of one parent can be indicated across the top, and the genetic contribution of the other parent can be indicated along the left side of the chart. The squares are then filled with the resulting zygote combinations so that the letters in each square represent the genotype of one genetic type of offspring.

In albinism, as in most genetic disorders, the normal gene is the **dominant gene.** When present, it dominates over the abnormal gene. The abnormal gene is a **recessive gene.** It is expressed only when homozygous; that is, a person must have two abnormal genes, *aa*, for melanin production to be albino.

Let us consider what happens when two individuals heterozygous for albinism have a child (Fig. 31-9b). During meiosis, the woman's homologous chromosomes separate. The ovum she releases each month has a 50% chance of carrying the normal *A* allele and a 50% chance of carrying the abnormal *a* allele. Likewise, 50% of the husband's sperm will have the *A*, and 50% will have the *a* allele.

It is useful to calculate the probability of genetic events. In the example just presented, there is a 1-in-4 chance for the offspring to be albino, *aa*; a 2-in-4 or 1:2, probability of being a carrier, *Aa*; and a 1-in-4 probability that the genotype will be *AA*. Drawing and studying a pedigree is some-

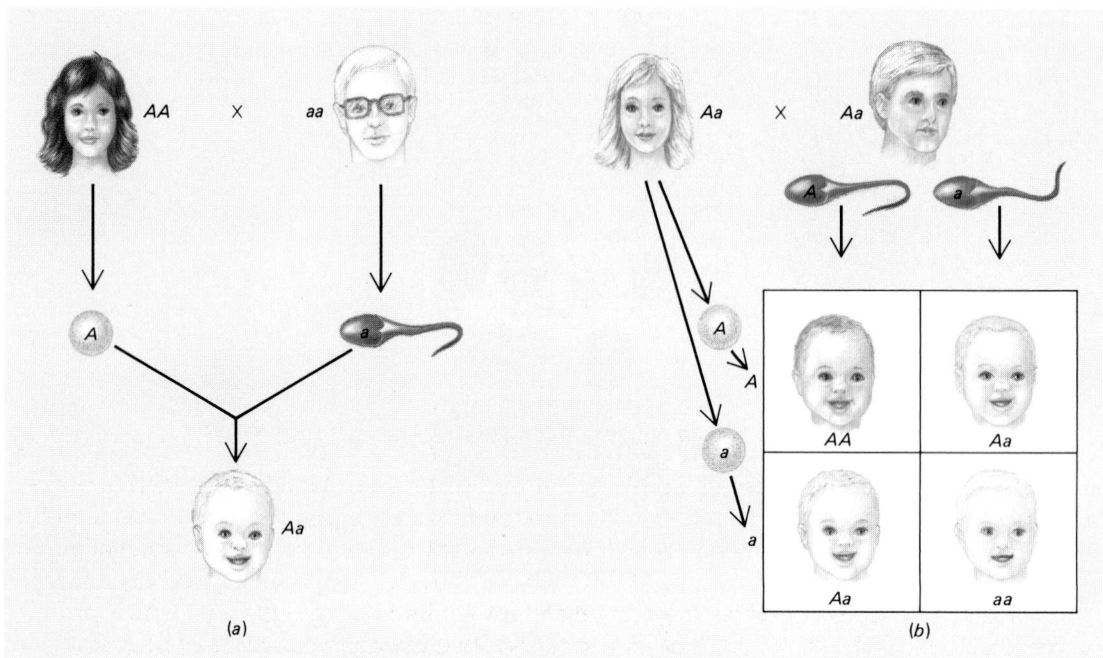

FIGURE 31-9

Examples of monohybrid crosses. Normal skin color is dominant over albinism. (*a*) The cross between a homozygous normal and an albino parent produces offspring with a normal phenotype. However, note that the offspring is a genetic carrier for albinism. (*b*) Example of a heterozygous cross. The offspring of two heterozygous parents can have one of three possible genetic combinations. There is a 1-in-4 chance that the offspring will be homozygous normal; a 2-in-4, or 1:2, probability of having a normal phenotype but being a carrier for albinism; and a 1-in-4 probability that the child will be an albino. The appearance of the albino trait in the child demonstrates the existence of the abnormal gene in the apparently normal parents.

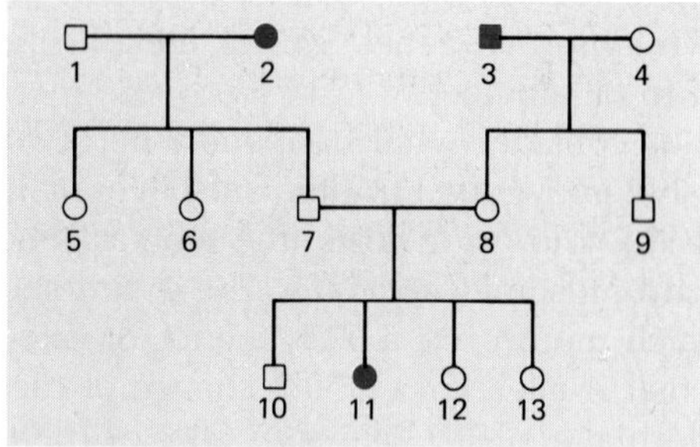

FIGURE 31-10

A pedigree for a family with albinism, which is inherited as an autosomal recessive trait. Males are indicated by squares and females by circles. Individuals showing the trait being studied are indicated by color symbols. Relationships are indicated by connecting lines. All members of the same generation are placed on the same row. Thus, 11 is an albino girl whose paternal grandmother, 2, and maternal grandfather, 3, are albinos. All of her other relatives shown are phenotypically normal. What would the pattern be if albinism were a dominant trait?

times useful in understanding the pattern of inheritance of a trait (Fig. 31-10).

Many genes are not clearly dominant or recessive. They may be **codominant,** in which case both are fully expressed. This is true in the inheritance of human blood types (to be discussed in the next section). Alleles may also be **incompletely dominant,** in which case the phenotype tends to be a compromise. The expression and interaction of genes can be quite complex. For example, a single gene may have multiple effects.

Inheritance of blood types is governed by multiple alleles

When there are more than two forms of a particular gene that can occupy one given chromosomal location, or locus, these forms are called **multiple alleles.** These alleles can occur with varying frequency within a population, but a single individual can have only two alleles at a time (one on each member of a homologous pair of chromosomes). Three alleles are known for the ABO se-

TABLE 31-1

ABO blood types				
Phenotype	**Genotype**	**Antigens, Cells**	**Antibodies in Plasma**	**Notes**
A	*AA, AO*	A	Anti-B	Dominant
B	*BB, BO*	B	Anti-A	Dominant
AB	*AB*	A and B	None	Codominant
O	*OO*	None	Anti-A and B	Recessive

ries, which by their interaction can produce blood types A, B, AB, and O, depending upon the exact combination of genes in an individual's particular allelic pair. (A normal person can possess no more than two of the ABO alleles.) Tables 19-1 and 31-1 gives some basic facts about the antibodies and antigens of the ABO series, and several examples of crosses involving these blood types can be found in Figure 31-11.

Type O gene is recessive to all other genes, and A and B exhibit codominance with respect to each other. Thus two genotypes (*AA* or *AO*) can give rise to type *A*, and two (*BB* or *BO*) to type *B*. AB and O each have only one possible genotype (*AB* or *OO*, respectively) (Fig. 31-11).

	A	*B*
A	*AA*	*AB*
A	*AA*	*AB*

	A	*B*
A	*AA*	*AB*
O	*AO*	*BO*

	A	*B*
A	*AA*	*AB*
B	*AB*	*BB*

	A	*A*
B	*AB*	*AB*
B	*AB*	*AB*

	A	*O*
B	*AB*	*BO*
B	*AB*	*BO*

	A	*O*
A	*AA*	*AO*
B	*AB*	*BO*

	A	*O*
B	*AB*	*BO*
O	*AO*	*OO*

FIGURE 31-11

Some representative crosses showing the inheritance of the ABO blood type. Note that there are three alleles.

In the Rh series of blood types there are several codominant varieties, but all may be thought of as producing either a positive or a negative phenotype. For our purposes we will lump the several alleles into two groups—*R*, which produces positive phenotypes, and *r*, which produces negative ones. *R* is dominant. Thus a person with Rh-positive blood has the genotype *RR* or *Rr*. A person with the negative phenotype can only be *rr*. A person with Rh-positive blood has antigens (most importantly antigen D) associated with the blood-cell plasma membranes and, as you might expect, no anti-Rh antibodies in the plasma (Fig. 31-12).

An Rh-negative person possesses no Rh antigens and has no anti-Rh antibodies in the plasma, either. That is, none are present naturally. But if an Rh-negative individual were to receive a transfusion of Rh-positive blood, he or she would quickly develop anti-Rh antibodies, which would then hemolyze the cells of the next transfusion of Rh-positive blood. The first such transfusion would, however, be relatively harmless. Recall that an Rh-negative woman can become sensitized to Rh-positive blood through pregnancy with an Rh-positive fetus.

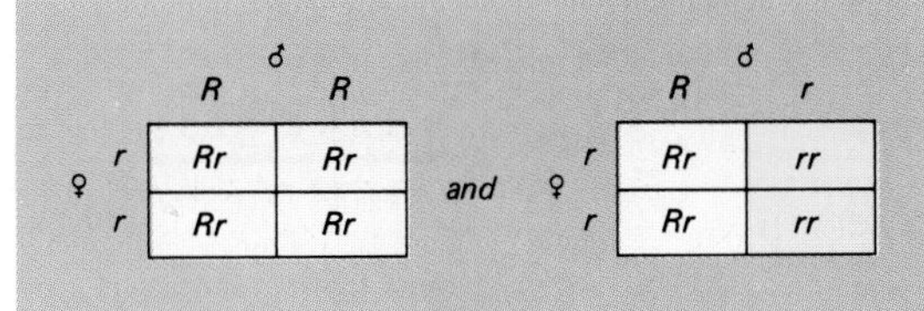

FIGURE 31-12

Representative crosses showing the inheritance of Rh blood type.

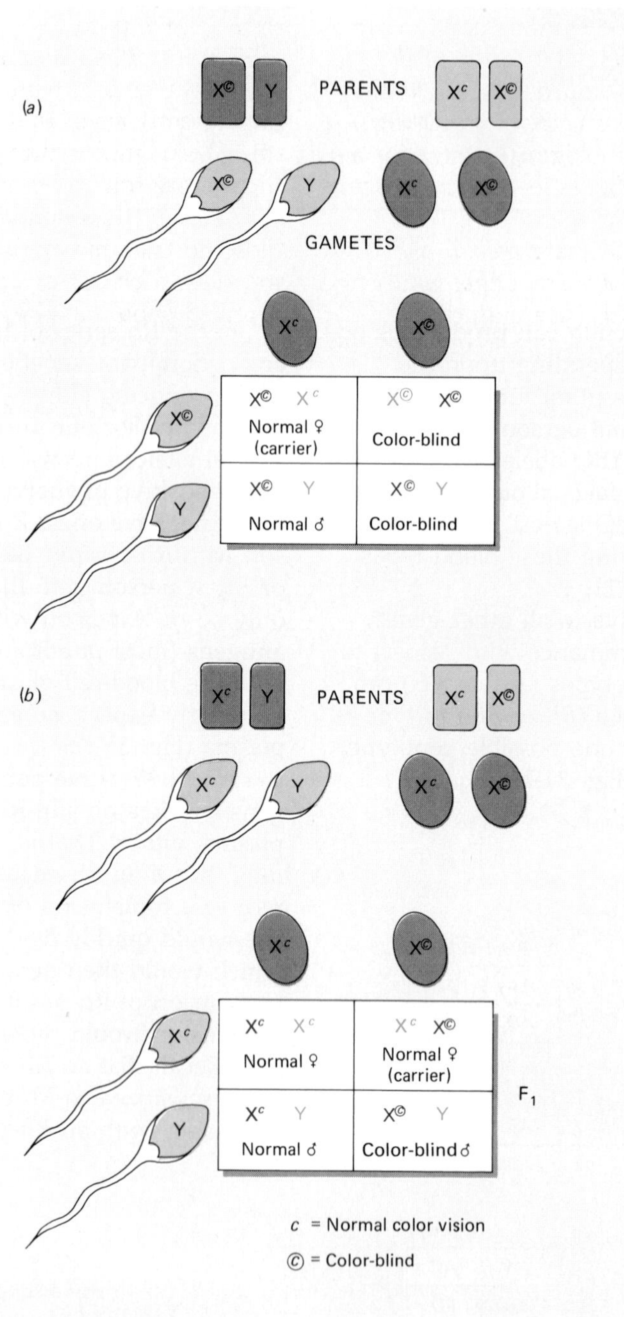

FIGURE 31-13

X-linkage. Two crosses showing the inheritance of color blindness, an X-linked recessive trait. Note that the Y chromosome does not carry a gene for color vision.

A male receives all of his X-linked genes from his mother

Human beings have 44 autosomes and two sex chromosomes. As explained earlier, the sex chromosomes are alike in females but different in males. Although the Y chromosome pairs with the X chromosome in meiosis, the Y and X chromosomes are not truly homologous, except for a short segment that may exist solely for purposes of meiosis. The Y chromosome contains only a few genes, mainly those for maleness. However, the X chromosome contains many genes that govern traits in both sexes. This means that certain genes found on the X chromosome have no corresponding alleles on the Y chromosome. In the male, therefore, any allele that lies on the nonhomologous portion of the X chromosome will be expressed, regardless of whether it is dominant or recessive in the XX female. Because **X-linked** genes are especially important in medicine, it is the X chromosome that is meant when the term *sex linkage* is used.

Because the large majority of X-linked genes are recessive, in a female they must be present on both X chromosomes to be expressed. One practical consequence is that although females may carry these traits, the traits usually find expression only in their sons. A boy receives his X chromosome from his mother, never from his father. In order to be expressed in a female, a recessive X-linked gene must be inherited from both parents. A color-blind girl, to take an example, must have a color-blind father and a mother who is at least heterozygous for color blindness (Fig. 31-13).

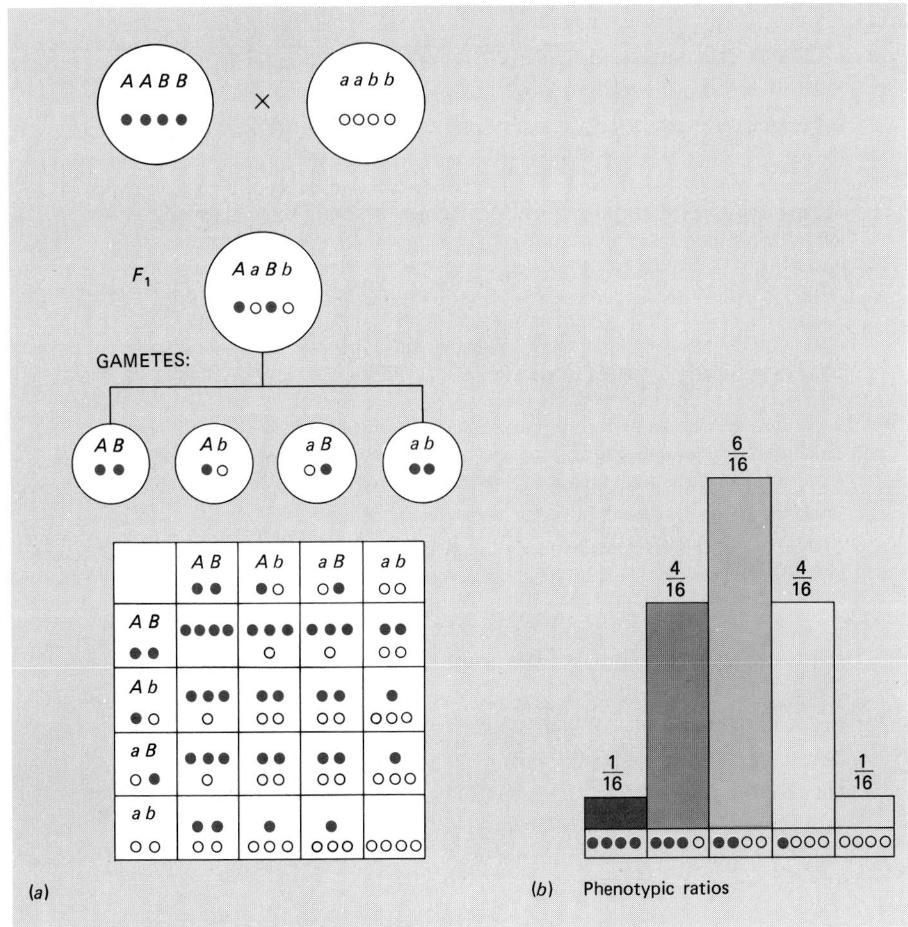

	AB ●●	Ab ●○	aB ○●	ab ○○
AB ●●	●●●●	●●● ○	●●● ○	●● ○○
Ab ●○	●●● ○	●● ○○	●● ○○	● ○○○
aB ○●	●●● ○	●● ○○	●● ○○	● ○○○
ab ○○	●● ○○	● ○○○	● ○○○	○○○○

FIGURE 31-14

A simplified model to illustrate polygenic inheritance of skin color in humans. Only two pairs of genes at two loci are shown. The alleles coding for dark skin are shown as capitals, but they are not dominant. Instead they act in an additive fashion.

Such a combination is unusual, to say the least. Yet a color-blind boy need only have a mother who is heterozygous for the trait. His father can be normal both phenotypically and genetically.

Some traits are governed by polygenes

Skin color, height, and intelligence are traits that are governed by **polygenes;** the trait is produced by the combined effects of several genes each consisting of a pair of alleles. Polygenic inheritance is characterized by continuous variation in phenotypes. Human skin color appears to be influenced by at least four pairs of alleles, which we will call A, B, C, and D. A person who is very dark would be AABBCCDD. An extremely blond person, almost albino in appearance, would be aabbccdd. Intermediate shades (such as most of us possess) would be signified by a mixture of these. An olive-complexioned brunette, for example, might be AaBbccdd or (equally probably) might be aaBbccDd. Darkness of skin coloration is related to the number of capital-letter (dominant) genes in the genotype. The offspring of two persons of intermediate skin color (Fig. 31-14, p. 1099) will have skin ranging from light to dark (Fig. 31-14).

TABLE 31-2

Some chromosome abnormalities

Karyotype	Common name	Clinical description
Trisomy 13		Multiple defects, with death by age 1 to 3 months
Trisomy 15		Multiple defects, with death by age 1 to 3 months
Trisomy 18		Ear deformities, heart defects, spasticity, and other damage; death by age 1 year
Trisomy 21	Down syndrome	Overall frequency is about 1 in 700 live births. True trisomy is usually found among children of older (age 40+) mothers, but translocation resulting in the equivalent of trisomy may occur in children of younger women. A similar, though less marked, influence is exerted by the age of the father. Trisomy 21 is characterized by an epicanthic skin fold (i.e., a fold of skin above the eye) which, although not the same as that in the Mongolian race, produces an Oriental appearance—hence the former name *mongolism* for this syndrome; varying degrees of mental retardation (usually an IQ of 70 or below), although more intelligent exceptions are known; and short stature, protruding furrowed tongue, transverse palmar crease, and cardiac deformities, all of which are common. Patients usually die by age 30 to 35 years. 50% die by age 3 or 4 years. Affected persons are unusually susceptible to respiratory infections, leukemia, and Alzheimer's disease. Females are fertile, if they live to sexual maturity; if able to reproduce, they produce Down syndrome in 50% of their offspring.
Trisomy 22		Similar to Down syndrome, but with more skeletal deformities
XO	Turner syndrome (gonadal dysgenesis)	Short stature, webbed neck, sometimes slight mental retardation; ovaries degenerate in late embryonic life, leading to rudimentary sexual characteristics; gender is female
XXY	Klinefelter syndrome	Male with slowly degenerating testes, enlarged breasts
XYY		Unusually tall male with heavy acne; some tendency to mild mental retardation
XXX		Despite triploid X chromosomes, usually fertile, fairly normal females
Short 5 (deletion of short arm of chromosome 5)	Cri-du-chat syndrome	Microcephaly, severe mental retardation; in infancy, cry resembles that of a cat; defective chromosome is heterozygous
Deletion of one arm of chromosome 21	Philadelphia chromosome	Chronic granulocytic leukemia

FOCUS ON . . . Genetic counseling

Couples who have had one abnormal child or who have a familial history of hereditary disease may seek genetic counseling. Genetic clinics offering such counseling are available in most metropolitan centers. Modern enzyme analysis and other sophisticated chemical techniques can now be used to detect many recessive genetic diseases in the heterozygous state. Carriers of many genetic diseases can be identified by analyzing blood samples. Screening programs have been set up in more than 50 major cities for Tay-Sachs disease, a degenerative neurological disease that causes death in early childhood.

When both parents are known to be carriers for a genetic disease, the fetus can be evaluated early in development. Amniocentesis is used to remove samples of amniotic fluid. Then embryonic cells found in the fluid can be analyzed.

Some genetic diseases are now treatable. In **phenylketonuria (PKU)** an enzyme needed to metabolize a common amino acid (phenylalanine) is lacking. When untreated, a very high percentage of children with PKU become mentally retarded. When treated with a special diet (low in phenylalanine), mental retardation is prevented. In many states all babies are routinely screened during the first days of life for this genetic disease.

Chromosome abnormalities can result in disease

Occasionally something goes wrong and a pair of chromosomes fail to separate during meiosis. Or sometimes a part of a chromosome may break off and attach to another chromosome. Having three (instead of two) of one kind of chromosome is called a **trisomy** (**try**-sow-mee). A trisomy can result in serious imbalance of body chemistry (because the extra genes may be causing production of extra proteins) (Table 31-2). Trisomies of most chromosome pairs are lethal and result in spontaneous abortion.

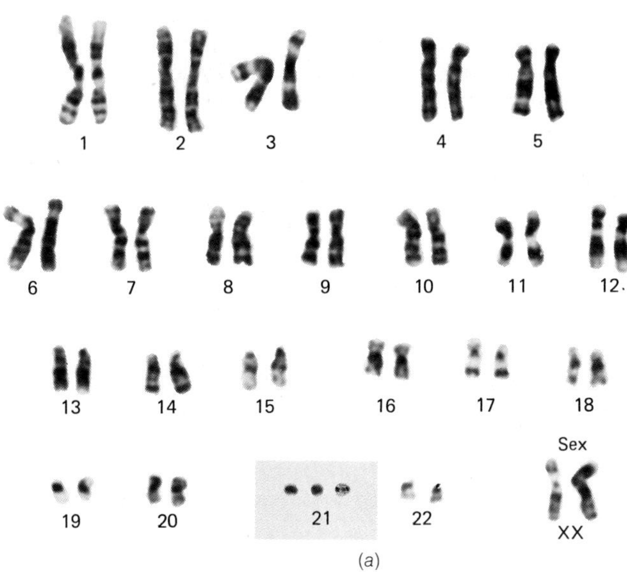

(a)

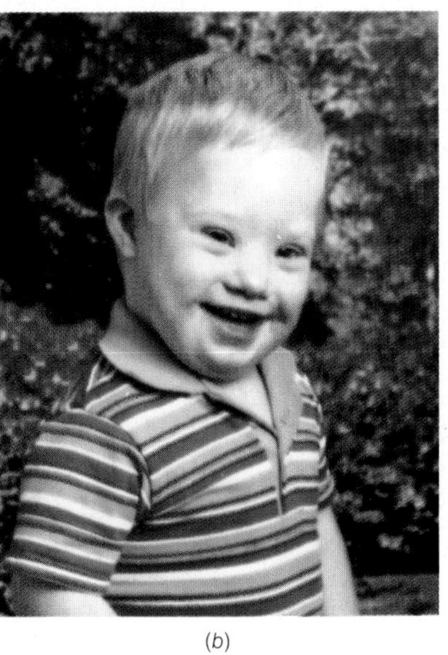

(b)

FIGURE 31-15

Down syndrome, a disease usually associated with trisomy of the twenty-first chromosome. (a) A karyotype of a child with Down syndrome. Note the extra chromosome #21. (b) A 2-year-old boy with Down syndrome. (Courtesy of Mr. and Mrs. Beny Peretz)

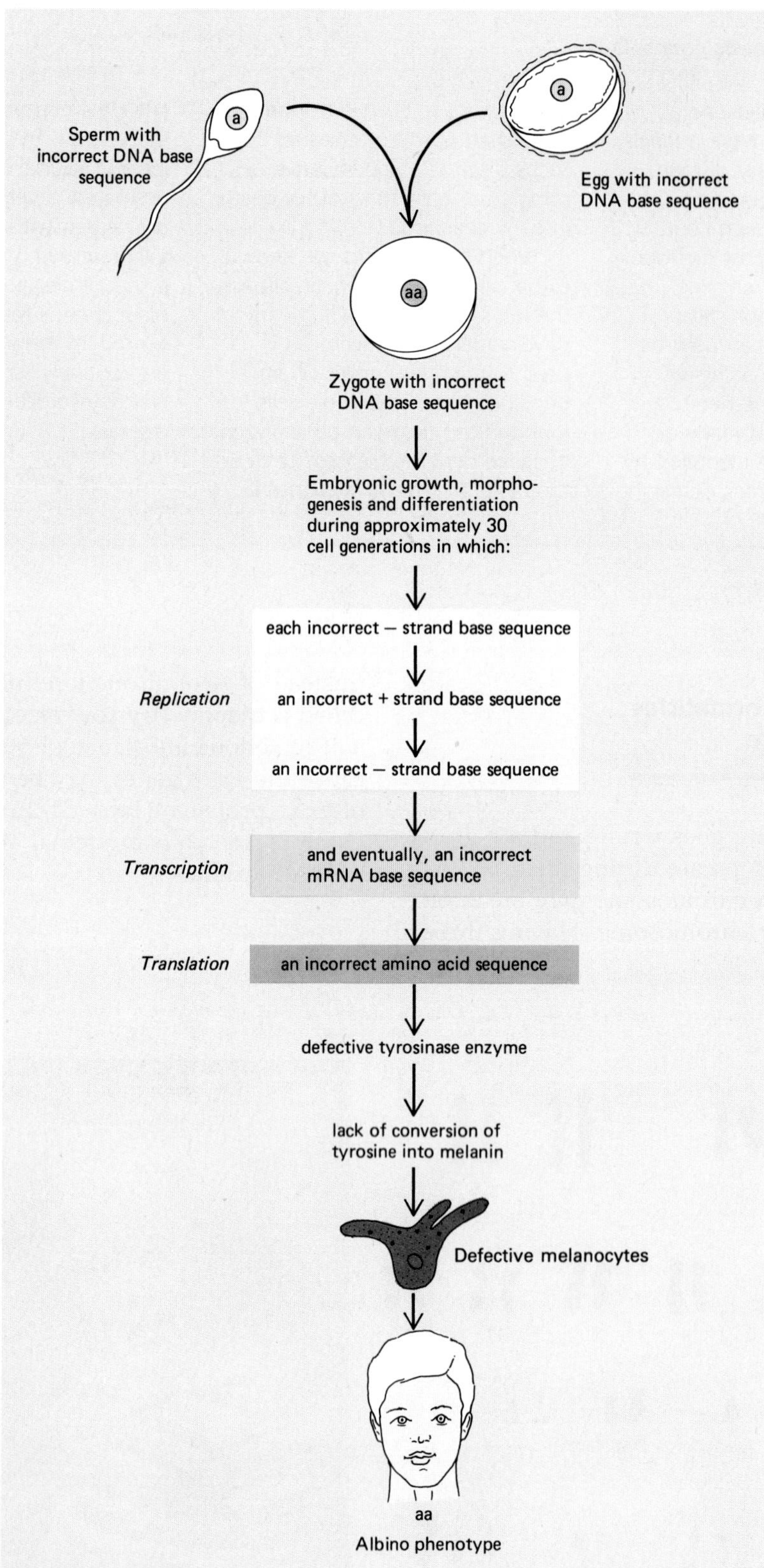

FIGURE 31-16

How an error in DNA base sequence produces genetic disease.

Trisomy of the twenty-first chromosome results in Down syndrome, a disorder characterized by profound mental retardation, short stature, an epicanthic skin fold (a vertical fold of skin on either side of the nose), cardiac defects, and other deformities (Fig. 31-15, p. 1101). The frequency of Down syndrome is about 1 in 700 live births, and the disorder is most common in the offspring of older women.

Mutations can result in disease

Genetic diseases result from mutations (Fig. 31-16). Among the disorders linked to mutations are sickle-cell anemia, hemophilia (bleeder's disease) cystic fibrosis, Tay-Sachs disease, and phenylketonuria (PKU) (Table 31-3). See Focus on Genetic Counseling, p. 1101.

TABLE 31-3

Some important genetic disorders

Name of disorder	Mode of inheritance	Clinical description	Treatment, if any	Comments
Alkaptonuria	Autosomal recessive	Pigmentation of cartilage and fibrous tissue, with eventual development of arthritis; presence of homogentisic acid causes urine to darken when it stands	Arthritis may be treated	Deficiency of enzyme homogentisic acid dehydrogenase
Childhood pseudohypertrophic muscular dystrophy	X-linked recessive	Begins in the first 3 years of life. Muscles swell, then undergo fatty degeneration. Progressive muscular deterioration leads to confinement, then to death in the early 20s	Symptomatic	Also known as Duchenne-type muscular dystrophy; extremely rare in females, but heterozygotes sometimes exhibit minor muscle function defects
Cystic fibrosis	Autosomal recessive	High level of sweat electrolytes, pulmonary disease, cirrhosis of the liver, pancreatic malfunction, and, especially, nonsecretion of digestive enzymes. No spermatogenesis in males, but females sometimes reproduce. Life expectancy is 12–16 years, with some affected persons living into their 30s or 40s. Commonest in persons of Northern European extraction	Symptomatic, with emphasis on digestive enzyme replacement and control of respiratory infections	Kills more children than diabetes, rheumatic fever, and poliomyelitis combined; exists in different degrees of severity; thick mucus interferes with lung clearance
Gangliosidosis (e.g., Tay-Sachs disease)	Autosomal recessive	Several types exist. One, Tay-Sachs disease, results from the deficiency of hexosaminidase A. All variants involve the abnormal accumulation of sphingolipids, ordinarily released from nerve and other cells by the action of whatever enzyme is		Tay-Sachs disease is especially prevalent among Jews of Eastern European ancestry

(table continued on p. 1104)

TABLE 31-3 *(continued)*

Some important genetic disorders				
Name of disorder	**Mode of inheritance**	**Clinical description**	**Treatment, if any**	**Comments**
		deficient. Evidently several different enzymes are required. In most cases blindness, paralysis, and death occur in first few years of life		
Hemoglobinopathic disease (e.g., sickle-cell anemia)	Group of autosomal recessive or incompletely dominant traits	Abnormalities of red blood cells caused by the presence of certain inappropriate amino acids at crucial locations in the hemoglobin molecule. In sickle-cell anemia, for instance, one of the beta-chain amino acids is the "wrong" one, resulting in decreased solubility of hemoglobin molecules in low-oxygen environments such as tissue capillaries. This causes extreme shape distortions such as sickling, which in turn leads to premature destruction of the cell	Varies with type of disease. Some (e.g., hereditary methemoglobinemia) may require no treatment; some cannot be treated at all. Sickle-cell anemia can be treated to some degree	These traits are similar and related but not allelic. Microcytic anemia is commonest in Mediterranean populations, sickle-cell anemia in some black populations. In heterozygotes, sickle-cell anemia offers some protection against malaria
Hemophilia	X-linked recessive	Chronic bleeding, including bleeding into joints, with resultant arthritis; more than one variety of hemophilia exists	Treated with clotting factors	Even heterozygotes have some clotting factor deficiencies
Lesch-Nyhan syndrome	X-linked recessive	Slowly developing paralysis accompanied by mental deficiency and self-mutilation, with patients persistently biting themselves. Gout usually develops because of deficiency of the enzyme involved in purine metabolism. The heterozygous condition is detectable (see comments)	Gout may be treated. Neurological symptoms are not treatable, and early death is inevitable	Deficiency of a specific enzyme is to blame. Half the cells of the female carrier are enzyme-deficient. If her hair follicles are biopsied and studied, they will be found to be enzyme-negative, enzyme-positive, or mixed, but not all of them will contain the enzyme, which they normally would
Phenylketonuria (PKU)	Autosomal recessive	Deficiency of liver phenylalanine hydroxylase leads to a chain of events beginning with excessive phenylalanine in the blood. This causes a depression in the levels of other amino acids, leading in turn to excessively light coloration and mental deficiency	A low-phenylalanine diet minimizes symptoms. Most states have extensive PKU screening programs in which newborns are tested for excessive blood phenylalanine, or for presence of metabolic products in the urine	Since melanin is synthesized from tyrosine, tyrosine deficiency caused by phenylalanine hydroxylase deficiency results in light coloring of skin and hair

(table continued on p. 1105)

TABLE 31-3 *(continued)*

Some important genetic disorders

Name of disorder	Mode of inheritance	Clinical description	Treatment, if any	Comments
Red-green color-blindness				
Deutan variety	X-linked recessive	Patient can distinguish only 5 to 25 hues, as against the normal ability to see 150 +. Though visual acuity is normal, the "green" cone pigment is deficient. Subjectively, all colors are perceived as hues of blue and yellow		Actually a series of alleles of differing degrees of severity, with the more normal dominant over the more deficient varieties. In both protan and deutan forms, heterozygous females show some color vision defects
Protan variety	X-linked recessive, not allelic to deutan	Similar to deutan variety, but here the "red" cone pigment is missing. NOTE: Other defects of color vision associated with cone deficiencies also exist. Most of these are X-linked		
Tyrosinase-negative oculocutaneous albinism (T − albinism)	Autosomal recessive	Absence of pigmentation due to functional absence of tyrosinase; visual acuity 20/200 or less; marked susceptibility to skin cancer	Avoidance of sunlight	Somewhat more common among blacks than whites
Tyrosinase-positive oculocutaneous albinism (T + albinism)	Autosomal recessive	Reduction of pigmentation due to malabsorption of tyrosine by body cells. If heavy pigmentation is genetically specified, some pigmentation will survive, though in some cases phenotype is virtually identical with T −. Pigmentation and visual acuity improve with age		Highest incidence in American Indians, less in blacks, least in whites. Heterozygous T + /T − persons appear normal

Summary

I. DNA is a long molecule that assumes the shape of a double helix. Its backbone consists of alternating deoxyribose-phosphate units, and from this axis protrude the bases adenine (A), cytosine (C), thymine (T), and guanine (G). The two complementary strands pair via the bases. A pairs with T, C with G.
   A. In replication the strands of DNA separate, and each builds a complement of itself. This is semiconservative replication.
   B. In transcription the plus strand of DNA builds an RNA complement of itself.
   C. The mRNA then moves into the cytoplasm of the cell, where it encounters ribosomes. Using tRNA, the ribosomes are able to build proteins whose sequence of amino acids is specified by the mRNA. The conversion of information encoded in mRNA into a sequence of amino acids forming a polypeptide is called translation.
   D. A mutation is a sudden, permanent change in a gene. It may result from some change in the base sequence of a nucleic acid, especially DNA. This change may result in the inactivity, effective absence, or other defect in the protein product of the affected gene or genes.
   E. Although all body cells are presumed to share the same heredity, they differ greatly from one another in shape and function. This occurs because genes inappropriate for any specific type of cell are repressed.

II. Much of the science of genetics can be reduced to a series of basic rules describing the behavior of genes and their interactions. They are:
   A. The basic unit of heredity is the gene.
   B. Fundamentally, a gene acts by directing the production of a polypeptide, and ultimately a protein.
   C. Characteristics of these proteins determine the traits of an organism.
   D. Chromosomes are composed of genes.
   E. The behavior of genes can be accounted for by the behavior of chromosomes.
   F. Most cells possess both chromosomes of a given pair; that is, they are diploid. Gametes, however, are haploid; that is, each gamete possesses only one member of each chromosome pair.
   G. The production of any protein is governed by two genes present in all body cells. These genes are alleles.
   H. Allelic genes are carried on homologous chromosomes. Both allelic genes and homologous chromosomes are paired.
   I. One member of each homologous pair of chromosomes is maternal in origin; the other is paternal in origin.
   J. Members of a gene pair may be alike (homozygous) or unlike (heterozygous).
   K. When members of a gene pair are unlike, the traits they govern may in some cases be determined by one of them, if it is clearly dominant, and in other cases by both of them. A gene that is expressed only when it is homozygous is said to be recessive.
   L. Normally no offspring can receive more or less than one representative of a homologous pair of chromosomes from each parent.
   M. The member of a pair of chromosomes or its contained genes that a gamete receives is entirely random.
   N. The particular combination of maternal and paternal chromosomes received by an offspring is therefore also random.
   O. The inheritance of a particular chromosome has no influence on the inheritance of any other chromosome not homologous to it.
   P. The inheritance of a particular gene has no influence on the inheritance of any other gene borne on a nonhomologous chromosome.
   Q. The X chromosome is exceptional in that it has no homologous chromosome in the male. A defective gene located on one X chromosome will not be expressed in the female unless it is dominant but will be expressed in the male regardless of dominance.

III. Three alleles are known to govern inheritance of ABO blood type. These alleles produce antigens A, B, or no antigen. *A* and *B* are mutually codominant, so that the ABO blood phenotypes include A, B, AB, and O. The independent Rh series of blood types may be divided into positive and negative phenotypes.

IV. Chromosome abnormalities result in a number of disorders such as trisomy 21 (Down syndrome) and Klinefelter syndrome (XXY).

V. Abnormal alleles of a number of genes are responsible for many inherited diseases such as PKU, sickle-cell anemia, and cystic fibrosis. Most human genetic diseases that show a simple inheritance pattern are transmitted as autosomal recessive traits.

Post-test

1. The genetic information of the cell is stored primarily in the ______________ of the nucleus.
2. DNA consists of a backbone of deoxyribose, a 5-carbon sugar, and ______________.
3. The bases of DNA are ______________, ______________, ______________, and ______________. The genetic code is based on the ______________ of these bases.
4. Mutations are genetic ______________ involving incorrect ______________ ______________ in DNA.

Match

____ 5. Gene
____ 6. Heterozygous
____ 7. Phenotype
____ 8. Alleles

a. corresponding genes on homologous chromosomes
b. identical alleles at same locus
c. physical expression of genotype
d. different alleles at same locus
e. unit of hereditary information

9. Because meiosis separates ______________ chromosomes, a ______________ can usually possess only ______________ gene of an ______________ pair.
10. If an albino marries a phenotypically normal person, any normally pigmented offspring will be ______________ (homozygous/heterozygous) for albinism; albinism is a ______________ trait.
11. Type A blood can be produced by ______________ genotype(s), type AB by ______________ genotype(s), and type O by ______________ genotype(s). (Write numbers in the spaces.)
12. The ABO blood type is inherited by a system of ______________ alleles.

Match

____ 13. Profoundly to moderately retarded, protruding tongue, eyefold present.
____ 14. Thick respiratory and other secretions; recurrent respiratory infections.
____ 15. Abnormal hemoglobin causes distorted red blood cells
____ 16. Excessively tall, sterile male individuals

a. cystic fibrosis
b. XO
c. XXY
d. trisomy 21
e. sickle-cell anemia

Review questions

1. If a strand of DNA has the base sequence ATT/GCG/AAG for part of its length, what is the corresponding sequence of its complement?
2. Why must DNA replication take place before the chromosomes are distributed in mitosis?
3. What is the function of a ribosome?
4. What are mutations? Are they desirable? What factors produce them?
5. Why can one receive only one member of a homologous pair of chromosomes from each parent?
6. What are alleles?
7. What is meant by the terms homozygous and heterozygous?
8. Define dominant, recessive, codominant, incompletely dominant.
9. What are polygenes? Give an example.
10. What usually makes a gene dominant? Why are most genetic defects recessive?
11. What chromosome bears sex-linked traits?
12. What are the benefits of genetic screening?
13. Give two examples of chromosome abnormalities that cause disorders.

Post-test answers

1. DNA 2. phosphate 3. adenine, thymine, guanine, cytosine; sequence 4. misinformation (or a similar answer); base sequence(s) 5. e 6. d 7. c 8. a 9. homologous; gamete; one; allelic 10. heterozygous; recessive 11. two; one, one 12. multiple 13. d 14. a 15. e 16. c

FUNDAMENTALS OF EXERCISE PHYSIOLOGY

CHAPTER OUTLINE

LEARNING OBJECTIVES

After you have studied this chapter you should be able to:

1 Discuss the mechanisms by which the respiratory and cardiovascular systems function to maintain homeostasis during exercise.

2 Compare and contrast the energy requirements of muscle tissue at rest and during exercise.

3 Discuss those factors that influence oxygen consumption during exercise.

4 Compare and contrast repayment of the oxygen debt incurred during light to moderate versus strenuous exercise.

5 Discuss minute respiratory volume and its regulation during exercise.

6 Discuss factors influencing alveolar gas diffusion during exercise.

7 Compare and contrast the flow rate and distribution of blood to various organs while at rest and during exercise.

8 Discuss the effects of blood flow on thermoregulation during exercise.

9 Discuss the effects of exercise on cardiac output, stroke volume, and heart rate.

10 Compare the secretory levels of several hormones in response to exercise of varying intensity.

11 Discuss the effects of exercise on various cell populations of the immune system.

12 Discuss the pros and cons of using synthetic anabolic steroids to increase athletic performance.

13 Discuss the pros and cons of red blood cell packing and bicarbonate loading as they relate to athletic performance.

14 Discuss a potential danger of analgesic medications as they relate to competitive sports.

False-color thermogram of a professional athlete in action. (Nelson/Peter Arnold, Inc.)

32

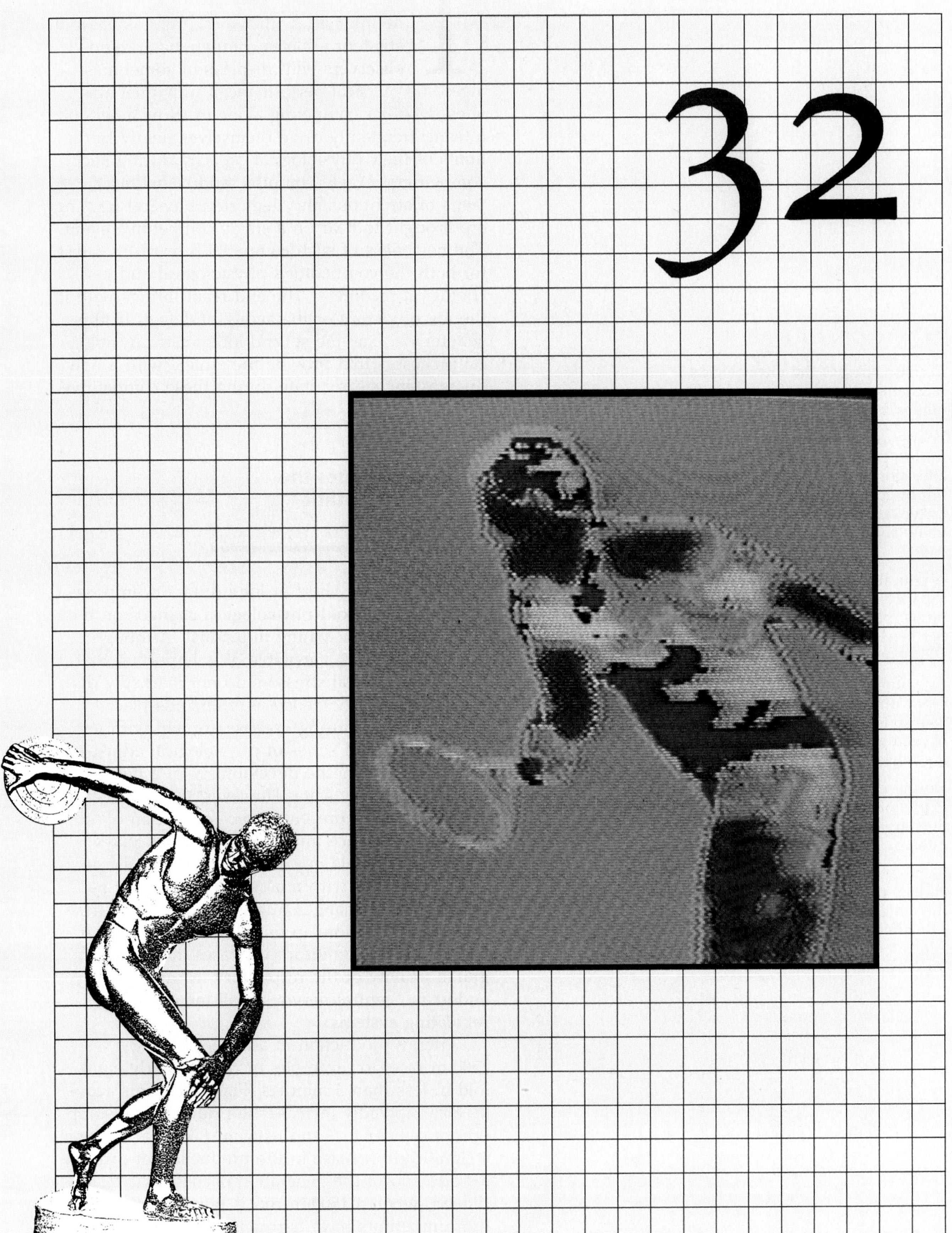

KEY CONCEPTS

Exercise stresses the physiological mechanisms responsible for maintaining homeostasis.

Energy requirements of muscle during exercise are met not only by alteration in its own metabolism, but by integrated activity of the cardiovascular, respiratory, nervous, and endocrine systems as well.

A critical factor in an individual's capacity to perform extended, vigorous, physical exercise is his or her level of maximal oxygen consumption or $\dot{V}O_2max$.

Alterations in cardiovascular physiology during exercise are in response to increased demands for oxygen and nutrients by contracting muscles.

During exercise, a cardiac output in excess of 14 liters per minute is due largely to an increasing heart rate.

Some methods used to increase athletic performance often subject the athlete to a number of adverse side effects.

The intensity with which professional and amateur athletes compete has provided observers with displays of sometimes awesome physical performance. Individual athletes, whether competing alone or as members of a team, frequently drive themselves nearly to the limits of their physiological capacity during such competition. Weeks, months, and sometimes years of strenuous and dedicated physical training are brought to bear on a single competitive event. The fierceness of such competition provides a test for both the competitor's physiological and psychological readiness. The end result brings with it the joy of victory or the agony of defeat. In this chapter we examine several integrated physiological processes that provide the athlete with a new homeostatic steady state during these competitive events.

Exercise stresses the body's homeostatic mechanisms

Exercise, be it of short or long duration, imposes a variety of marked physiological changes on the body of the participating individual. Although these changes are inevitable, it is important that such physiological stressors do not markedly disturb the body's homeostasis. Demands placed upon the body during exercise are met with a well-orchestrated series of physiological adjustments, leading to the development of a new and temporary steady state. However, the new steady state does not represent a true restoration of homeostasis. Since muscular contraction plays such a central role in exercise, the metabolic processes associated with muscular contraction undergo marked changes during this activity. These metabolic alterations in muscle tissue are also accompanied by significant increases in the integrated activity of the respiratory, cardiovascular, endocrine, central nervous, and temperature-regulating systems.

Energy production in a runner during a 1500-m race, for example, increases nearly eightfold in less than 3 minutes (Fig. 32-1). This activity also markedly increases the runner's consumption of cellular fuel and oxygen. Likewise, there is a significant increase in the production of carbon dioxide and in the generation of metabolic heat. Indeed, when a 1500-m run is finished, most of the competitors have narrowly approached their

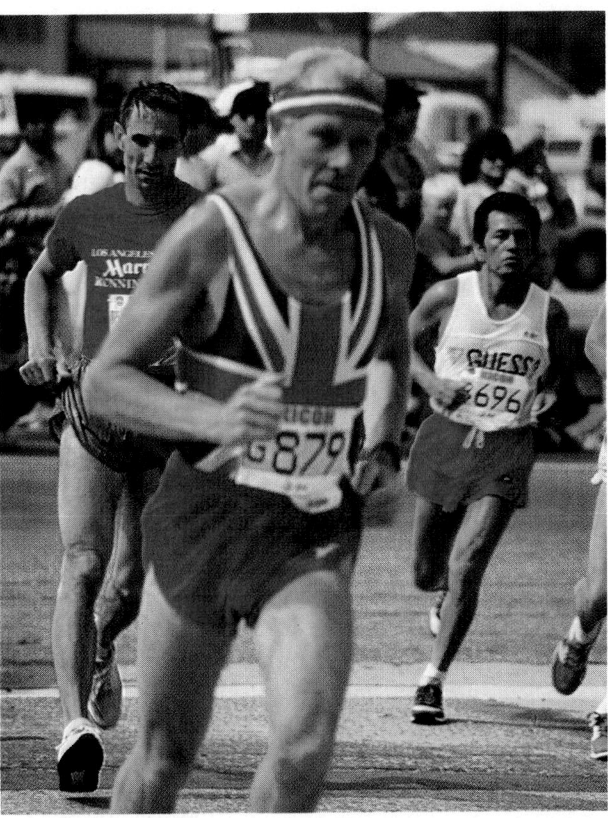

FIGURE 32-1

Energy production by these athletes will have increased nearly eight fold in the first 3 minutes of this 1500-meter race. (McCarten/PhotoEdit.)

physiological limits. So closely are these limits approached, in fact, that merely running a few more meters would place their bodies on the verge of physiological collapse. Let us now examine just how the body makes these physiological adjustments in order to meet the stressful demands of exercise.

The energy requirements of muscle are markedly altered during exercise

In Chapter 10 we discussed the importance of factors influencing muscle strength, power, and endurance. Muscle cells, like all other cells, require energy, and the high-energy phosphate bonds of **adenosine triphosphate (ATP)** provide such a source. However, the amount of ATP in muscle is only sufficient to provide energy for strenuous muscular activity lasting a few seconds (5 or 6 sec at best). Thus, it is this small amount of stored ATP that is utilized for energy during the initial stage of either vigorous or light exercise (Fig. 32-2).

Muscle cells also contain **creatine phosphate (CP),** a high-energy compound capable of providing phosphate groups to reconstitute ATP from adenosine diphosphate (ADP) and adenosine monophosphate (AMP). In fact, the amount of CP in muscle tissue exceeds that of ATP by two- or three-fold. Storage of energy within muscle tissue occurs in the form of CP. Creatine phosphate, by reconstituting ATP from ADP and AMP, provides energy for maximal physical activity for an additional 5 to 9 seconds over that derived from the ATP originally present. Creatine phosphate, like the ATP already present in muscle prior to exercise, is also utilized during the early stages of physical activity (Fig. 32-2).

Metabolism of glucose, fatty acids, and amino acids also provides a source of ATP for muscle contraction. Glucose is converted to pyruvic acid during an anaerobic process termed **glycolysis** (Chapter 26). Then, if sufficient oxygen is available, additional ATP will be generated aerobically via the Krebs cycle and the electron transport sys-

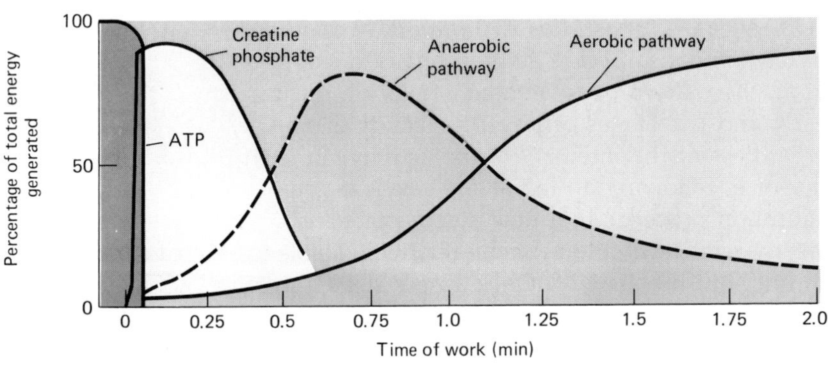

FIGURE 32-2

During the early stages of light to vigorous exercise, energy is obtained primarily from initial stores of ATP and creatine phosphate metabolism. Notice the predominance of the aerobic pathway as exercise progresses.

tem. With prolonged light exercise the aerobic pathway, although not nearly as rapid as the anaerobic pathway, serves as the principal energy source (Fig. 32-2).

The pathway for glucose metabolism changes markedly when too little oxygen is available. In this instance, only two molecules of ATP are produced for each molecule of glucose that is broken down. Pyruvic acid is then converted to lactic acid through the addition of hydrogen atoms. The anerobic pathway of energy metabolism is much less efficient in terms of ATP production compared to the aerobic pathway and requires significantly more substrate to accomplish a similar amount of work. Thus, it will support light to vigorous physical activity for little more than 30 seconds and reaches its peak activity at this time (Fig. 32-2). Most of the energy generated during strenuous physical activity is derived aerobically; however, some is generated anaerobically. It is during anaerobic metabolism that lactic acid accumulates and fatigue and muscle cramps often occur.

Several factors influence oxygen consumption during exercise

Muscular contraction during all types of physical activity is accompanied by increased oxygen consumption. Depending upon the specific type of exercise and the degree of training of the individual athlete, the increase may vary from three- to twenty-fold above the level observed under resting conditions. Oxygen consumption is a measure of the rate of oxygen utilization by the body's tissues during exercise. The rate at which the cardiovascular system delivers oxygen to the muscles during exercise is a limiting factor with regard to oxygen consumption. An additional factor influencing oxygen consumption during physical activity is the oxygen diffusion capacity of the lungs.

Figure 32-3 illustrates two important aspects of oxygen consumption as they relate to exercise. First, the pattern of oxygen consumption during early and late stages of physical activity is similar, regardless of the intensity of the activity. In each instance, following an initial rise, oxygen consumption proceeds to a new **steady-state** (or **steady-rate**) **level** and remains relatively stable throughout the activity. Once a new steady-state level has been reached, accumulation of lactic acid tends to be minimal. This is not to imply that once a new steady state is reached the individual can continue to perform at that level indefinitely. Rather, factors such as fluid loss, electrolyte depletion, and adequate fuel reserves typically become limiting features as exercise continues.

A second aspect of oxygen consumption, its new steady-state level, also increases as the intensity of exercise increases. With increasing intensity there is a demand for additional energy required to perform the activity. This requirement imparts a further load on an individual's capacity for aerobic energy metabolism. Ultimately, a limit in the steady-state level of oxygen consumption will be reached and will not change despite additional increases in physical activity. This level, termed **maximal oxygen consumption** or **$\dot{V}O_2$max,** represents a critical factor in one's capacity to perform extended vigorous physical activity. Increasing physical activity once the $\dot{V}O_2$max has been attained leads to an increased accumulation of lactic acid and the onset of fatigue. Figure 32-4 illustrates the effect of increasing physical activity on oxygen consumption and lactic acid accumulation.

Maximal oxygen consumption is also influenced by one's age and sex. Levels of $\dot{V}O_2$max rise markedly until we enter our late teens or early twenties and remain relatively constant until about age 25. Thereafter the level of $\dot{V}O_2$max declines steadily in both males and females. The fact that females exhibit lower $\dot{V}O_2$max levels in

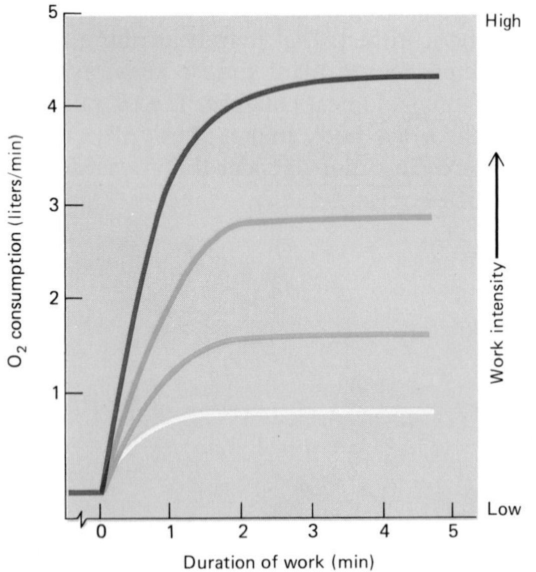

FIGURE 32-3

Relationship between oxygen consumption and exercise of increasing intensity versus time. Notice the similar pattern for all intensity levels shown.

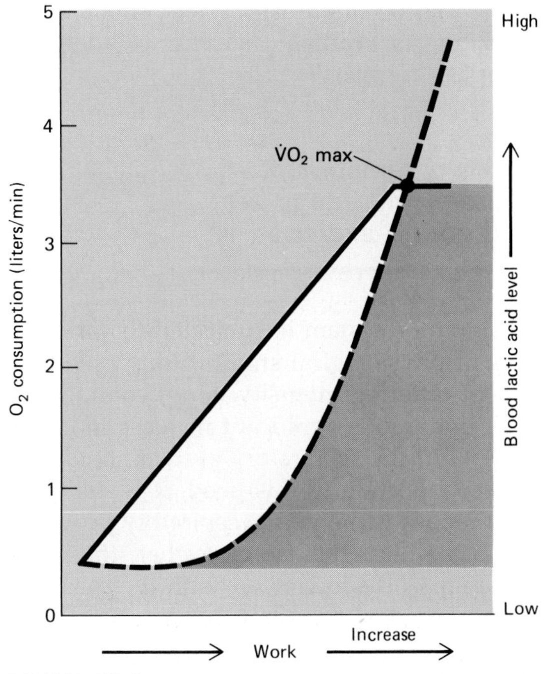

FIGURE 32-4

Relationship between oxygen consumption, blood lactic acid accumulation, and increasing work. Notice the plateau in oxygen consumption at the $\dot{V}O_2$max.

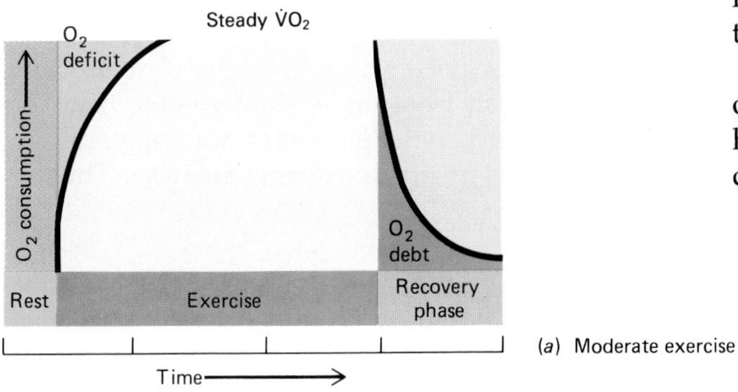

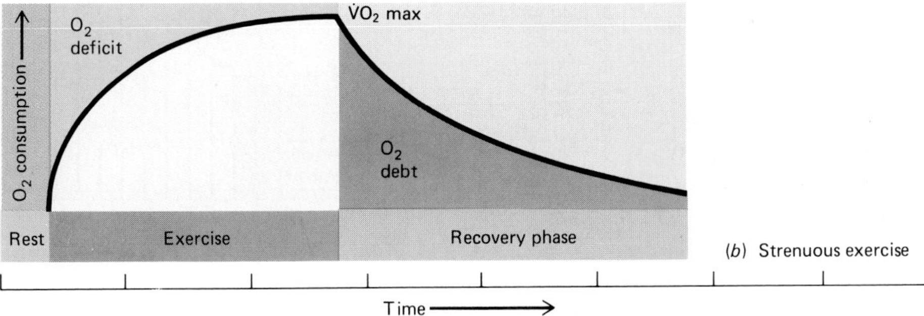

FIGURE 32-5

Relationship between oxygen consumption during (a) moderate and (b) strenuous exercise, and during the recovery phase following each level of intensity.

general is most likely related to their overall lower body mass.

The everyday level of physical activity also influences $\dot{V}O_2$max. Simply changing from a sedentary to a more active lifestyle, walking and swimming for example, can often retard the declining $\dot{V}O_2$max that ensues with advancing age. Employment of a graded regimen of increasing physical activity over a period of several weeks is sufficient to appreciably elevate one's $\dot{V}O_2$max. Increased cardiac output is thought to be chiefly responsible for the increased $\dot{V}O_2$max observed with physical training.

Physical exercise requires repayment of the oxygen debt

Active participation in light, moderate, or strenuous physical activity requires an almost immediate increase in oxygen consumption. When the activity is terminated, the amount of oxygen utilized that is in excess of the person's resting level is called the **oxygen debt.** In light exercise a new steady-state level is reached early on, and once the activity is halted, the recovery period is minimal. This is because the oxygen debt is small to begin with, and the oxygen consumed during the recovery phase is likewise small. Hence, return to the resting state requires very little time.

Figure 32-5 illustrates oxygen consumption as observed during and subsequent to moderate and heavy physical activity. In terms of the oxygen debt, the major difference between moderate and heavy exercise is that during the latter, the level of anaerobic energy metabolism is markedly elevated over that of the aerobic pathway, and this results in the accumulation of lactic acid. Moderate exercise is characterized by predominantly aerobic energy metabolism. As such, nearly 50% of the oxygen debt incurred will be paid back within approximately 30 seconds, whereas the remainder requires several additional minutes.

Collectively, the time required for repayment of the oxygen debt following moderate exercise is called the **fast component** of the recovery phase. During the fast component of recovery, oxygen is utilized to replenish bodily oxygen stores and reestablish resting levels of ATP and CP. Since little if any lactic acid has accumulated, this phase of recovery is also termed the **alactic,** or **alactic acid, oxygen debt** (without accumulation of lactic acid).

During heavy physical exercise, lactic acid accumulates markedly and body temperature rises significantly. In this instance, the amount of oxygen utilized during the recovery phase is often in excess of that utilized during the strenuous activity itself. Thus, the recovery phase and repayment of the oxygen debt require much more time. As with recovery from moderate exercise, there is also a fast component that lasts for several minutes. A second or **slow component** also exists when recovering from strenuous exercise. Several hours, or even a day, may be required to fully repay the incurred oxygen debt. Since lactic acid has accumulated, this phase of recovery is also known as the **lactic acid oxygen debt.** During this phase of recovery, the accumulated lactic acid must be disposed of. A portion of the lactic acid is converted to glucose in the liver and then transported to muscle tissue for storage. The remaining lactic acid is converted to pyruvic acid and further metabolized.

Thorough knowledge of repayment of the oxygen debt that occurs during the recovery phase is a primary consideration in athletic performance. Such knowledge has an impact on training regimens and on performance during competition. Recovery is rapid following short spurts of strenuous activity or during short periods of steady-state aerobic exercise, as little if any lactic acid accumulates. Athletes may soon perform competitively following a relatively short rest without suffering the effects of fatigue.

Aerobic exercise when continued for longer intervals is accompanied by lactic acid accumulation, and recovery requires significantly more time. In competition, if the athlete is pushed to his or her physiological limit for extended intervals, rest that occurs during brief periods of the competition, for example, may not be adequate for complete recovery.

Various parameters of respiratory physiology are altered during exercise

The respiratory system is subjected to various degrees of physiological stress during physical activity of differing intensity. Since contracting muscles undergo a significant increase in oxygen consumption, the respiratory system adjusts to help meet a portion of this need. It is also worth noting that adjustments in respiratory function cannot accomplish this alone. Rather, the respiratory system works in concert with the cardiovascular and nervous systems to achieve this goal.

Minute respiratory volume varies as a function of the intensity of exercise

Ordinarily, the resting level of **minute respiratory volume (MRV)** is on the order of 5 or 6 liters of air per minute. As the rate and depth of breathing increase, the MRV also increases. The number of breaths experienced per minute during strenuous physical activity may exceed 55, compared to 12 while at rest. In terms of tidal volume (see Chapter 24), it is not uncommon for values to reach 2.0 liters or greater during exercise. Thus,

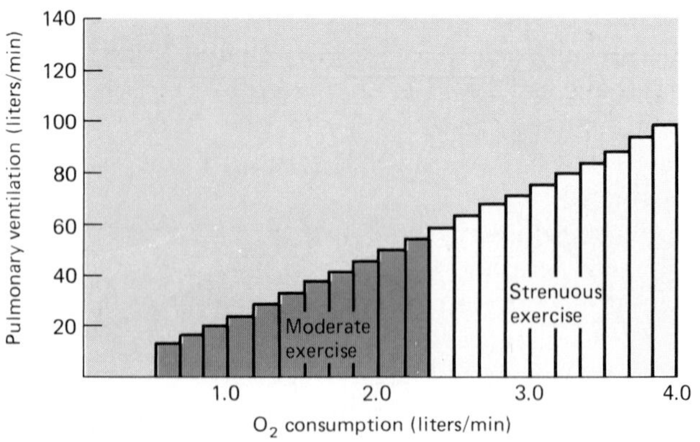

FIGURE 32-6

Relationship between pulmonary ventilation and oxygen consumption during moderate and strenuous exercise.

as a consequence of strenuous physical activity the MRV may actually exceed 150 liters per minute. The relationship of total MRV to oxygen consumption at various intensities of physical activity is illustrated in Figure 32-6.

MRV is regulated by various mechanisms during physical activity

MRV at rest is characterized by an intrinsic rhythm brought about by integration of activities in the CNS, peripheral chemoreceptors, and pulmonary stretch receptors. Many of these same activities function in meeting the respiratory needs of the body during physical activity. The specific mechanisms responsible for the increased MRV observed during exercise are not completely understood at the present time. These regulatory mechanisms do, however, provide the body with the means for maintaining circulating blood gases at or near normal concentrations.

Even as an athlete approaches and settles into the starting block and prepares for an 800-meter sprint, the runner's MRV increases markedly. This initial increase has an obvious psychological component and most likely results from accelerated CNS stimulatory activity. As the runner begins and continues the race, his or her level of MRV increases even further until a steady-state level is attained. This additional increase is most likely related to the activities of additional neuronal elements as well as metabolic changes acting on the CNS via the circulatory system. Although increased carbon dioxide and hydrogen ion levels, together with decreased levels of oxygen, occur to a limited extent during moderate exercise, it is not until one undertakes strenuous and sustained physical activity that such factors may have a marked effect on MRV. Moreover, their changes are so small that even then their role in regulation of MRV is questionable (see Chapter 24).

Increased activity of pulmonary stretch receptors and peripheral joint receptors, in addition to increased body temperature, have been proposed as mechanisms responsible for increasing MRV during moderate to heavy exercise (see Chapter 24). Furthermore, some researchers think that CNS respiratory centers become especially sensitive (up-regulated) with regard to minor alterations in P_{CO_2} levels during physical activity. Considerably more research is needed to clearly delineate the specific mechanism(s) involved in the regulation of MRV during various levels of physical activity.

Alveolar diffusion increases during physical activity

The rate of alveolar diffusion for O_2 and CO_2 increases during physical activity. Furthermore, an increase in tidal volume (deeper breathing) allows for a more effective alveolar diffusion than that achieved merely by an increased breathing rate. During exercise the diffusion capacity of oxygen may rise approximately 3.5-fold. However, this increase in oxygen diffusion capacity is not so much the result of an adjustment in respiratory physiology as it is the consequence of an increased pulmonary blood flow. Increase in pulmonary blood flow permits maximal perfusion of the pulmonary capillary bed and, as such, serves to markedly increase the surface area available for gaseous exchange of CO_2 and O_2.

Changes in the rate and distribution of blood flow occur during exercise

Exercise has a profound influence on the rate and distribution of blood flow to the body's organs (see Chapter 21). The demand for a markedly increased oxygen supply by contracting muscles is met by greatly enhanced blood flow to these organs. The rate of blood flow to the muscles during strenuous physical activity may be multiplied 15 to 20 times over that observed during the resting state. This increase helps meet the increased demand for oxygen as well as the increased need for removal of CO_2 and additional metabolic byproducts generated during physical activity.

The increased flow of blood to the muscles during exercise is accompanied by an altered rate of blood flow to some of the other organs. Although the rate of blood flow to the brain remains nearly constant during strenuous physical activity, that to the organs of the gastrointestinal tract and to the kidneys is markedly reduced. Blood flow in the coronary circulation itself may reach levels approaching one liter per minute during heavy exercise, representing nearly a four-fold increase over the resting state value.

Redistribution of blood flow during exercise helps regulate body temperature

During the beginning stages of exercise, prior to a marked elevation of body temperature, blood flow to the skin is diminished. With continued physical activity and increasing body temperature, the blood flow rate to the skin also increases in an attempt to dissipate the heat generated during the activity. Normally the body temperature during exercise will reach a new steady-state level after increasing 3°C or 4°C. Thermoregulation will now function around this new steady-state level unless extremes in environmental temperature and humidity are encountered during the activity.

Prolonged strenuous activity with profuse sweating on a hot day often leads to relatively less blood flow to the skin. This represents an example of the body's attempt to maintain adequate cardiac output even as plasma volume decreases. However, this is done at the expense of thermoregulation. An increase of 5°C over the resting body temperature can lead to symptoms of heat stroke (see Chapter 26) and even death if the body is not cooled sufficiently.

Increase in body temperature is a precisely regulated response of the body to increasing physical activity. Such an increase during exercise occurs regardless of the environmental temperature. Although body temperature increases as the intensity of exercise increases, the variation observed between individuals in this regard is most likely due to how close each one is to their maximal capacity for that particular physical activity. In fact, there is nearly a linear relationship between the increase in body temperature and the percent of maximum oxygen consumption experienced by individuals during physical activity of increasing intensity.

Cardiac function is altered during exercise

Heart function undergoes several important changes as a result of increasing physical activity. Cardiac output, stroke volume, and heart rate all increase during exercise. These changes are largely in response to the increased demands for oxygen and nutrients by the contracting muscles.

Cardiac output increases during exercise

Cardiac output, or the volume of blood pumped by one ventricle during one minute, varies as a function of physical activity and degree of physical training experienced by a given individual. A normal individual with no athletic training typically has a resting cardiac output of approximately 5.04 liters per minute, whereas that for the trained athlete may be 5.25 liters per minute. During strenuous exercise the cardiac output in the untrained person may increase to 21.5 liters per minute. The trained athlete, however, may experience cardiac output levels in excess of 30 liters per minute. The increase in cardiac output during strenuous physical activity by the trained athlete is markedly greater than that of the untrained individual.

Prolonged athletic training often leads to enlargement (hypertrophy) of the heart. The thickness of the heart walls and the size of its chambers are typically increased as it undergoes enlargement. This leads to an increase in stroke volume in addition to an increase in the strength of cardiac muscle contraction. As such, the heart becomes much more efficient in its pumping capacity.

As seen in Chapter 20, the venous return to the heart also influences cardiac output. This is important because increasing physical activity normally results in an increased venous-return volume. The increased venous return leads to an increased stroke volume and subsequently to an increased cardiac output. This relationship between venous return and stroke volume is linear up to a level of nearly 14 liters per minute. Increased sympathetic stimulation and force of contraction contribute to increased cardiac output exceeding 14 liters per minute.

Stroke volume and heart rate increase during exercise

Stroke volume and heart rate are directly related to cardiac output (see Chapter 20). In athletes and nonathletes, stroke volume and heart rate vary to different degrees with increasing levels of physical activity. Although the heart rate for the trained athlete is lower than that of the untrained individual at rest and during strenuous physical activity, his or her stroke volume is markedly greater. Thus, as the intensity of exercise increases, the stroke volume and heart rate increase until cardiac output approaches 14 liters per minute. At this point the stroke volume reaches a plateau level, and, as indicated above, additional increase in cardiac output is largely due to a further increase in heart rate. Therefore as individuals approach their limit of strenuous physical activity, the percentage increase in heart rate over that in the resting state greatly exceeds the percentage increase in stroke volume.

Environmental conditions also influence stroke volume during light to moderate physical activity. For example, exercise during extremely hot temperatures is usually accompanied by a reduction in stroke volume. The precise mechanism for the reduction in stroke volume under such conditions is unknown. It is compensated for, however, by an increase in heart rate.

Exercise influences the activity of the endocrine system

The secretion of several hormones increases with increasing intensity of exercise. Growth hormone (GH), TSH, prolactin, ADH (vasopressin), and the endorphins are all released from the pituitary gland in increasing amounts during exercise. Strenuous physical activity also results in increased secretion of corticosterone and aldosterone from the adrenal cortex and epinephrine from the adrenal medulla. Secretion of norepinephrine from the adrenal medulla and thyroxine and triiodothyronine from the thyroid gland all increase with increasing levels of physical activity. Additional hormones whose secretions are elevated with increasing intensity of exercise include insulin, glucagon, estrogen, progesterone, testosterone, and renin.

During exercise the increased secretion of GH is thought to benefit the growth of muscle, bone, and connective tissue structures. The catecholamines, epinephrine, and norepinephrine, are released from the adrenal medulla in response to increased sympathetic stimulation before and during exercise. Catecholamines influence cardiovascular function during exercise and also regulate nutrient levels by inducing lipolysis (fat mobilization) and glycogenolysis.

Prolactin secretion increases during exercise, but to a lesser degree than GH. Increased secretion of prolactin may have an inhibitory effect upon the ovaries. As such, females undertaking excessive exercise training frequently experience a **delay in the onset of menstruation,** and increased incidence of **amenorrhea** (ah-*men*-oh-**ree**-uh), as well as an increased incidence of **oligomenorrhea** (*ohl*-i-goh-*men*-oh-**ree**-uh). Females developing amenorrhea experience an absence of the menstrual flow, while those with oligomenorrhea have markedly diminished menstrual flows.

During exercise the kidneys secrete an increased amount of renin, which in turn is responsible for increased secretion of angiotensins. Angiotensins act upon the adrenal cortex to increase the secretion of aldosterone. Aldosterone levels during strenuous physical activity may exceed resting levels by 5 or 6 times.

Increased secretion of cortisol during exercise results in stimulation of protein catabolism. The free amino acids, in response to the increased levels of cortisol, are conveyed to the liver for participation in glucose synthesis. Blood glucose and insulin levels decrease as exercise increases in duration and intensity. As insulin levels continue to decrease during prolonged physical activity, the contracting muscles begin to extract more energy from fatty acid metabolism.

The effect of exercise on the immune system is controversial

Professional athletes, amateur athletes, and even individuals who actively participate in a routine regimen of physical activity such as jogging, swimming, or bicycling seem to experience a lower incidence of infectious diseases. It is not unreasonable to assume that a link exists between exercise and the functional status of the immune system. However, studies designed to explore this possibility are not abundant and the findings reported are often inconclusive.

It is known, for example, that strenuous physical activity of short duration often leads to a condition called **lymphocytosis** (*lim*-foe-sigh-**toe**-sis), a transitory increase in the number of circulating lymphocytes. A disproportionate increase in the number of B cells has been observed relative to the T cell population. However, whether these same cells exhibit elevated levels of immunocompetence in vivo is presently unclear. Studies undertaken to examine natural-killer (NK) cell levels and activity following short-term exercise are also inconclusive. A regimen of chronic physical training does not appear to have an effect on the numbers of macrophages, T cells, B cells, or their various subpopulations. Following competition, marathon runners may exhibit increased levels of cortisol as well as increased numbers of NK cells and neutrophils. Again, these reported changes are of a transitory nature.

The relationship between anabolic steroids and athletic performance is controversial

Significant evidence has accumulated indicating markedly increased use of anabolic steroids by professional and amateur athletes alike. Some athletes and trainers believe that using such agents promotes body growth and muscular development, thereby increasing athletic performance. However, the precise value of such agents as related to athletic performance is open to controversy. In the case of many compounds, adequate research is not currently available regarding their effect(s) during training and competition. Moreover, the use of such compounds has not been demonstrated conclusively to markedly increase aerobic athletic performance.

Synthetic derivatives of the male hormone testosterone are among the anabolic steroids used most widely by athletes today. These derivatives are typically classified as drugs since they are not synthesized by the body. In addition to increasing anabolic activity, they all promote varying degrees of androgenic activity, especially when administered in high doses. Females may experience menstrual irregularities and enlargement of the clitoris while taking synthetic anabolic steroids. Males may experience enlargement of the breasts, **gynecomastia** (*jin*-eh-koe-**mas**-tee-uh), since synthetic anabolic steroids, like naturally occurring androgens, may be converted to estrogens.

Naturally occurring androgens are rapidly metabolized by the liver. Synthetic derivatives that are more slowly metabolized or are released at a slow rate from sites of injection have been formulated. Moreover, some of these synthetic compounds are thought to possess significantly more anabolic than androgenic or masculinizing properties.

Clinically, synthetic anabolic steroids have several applications. Included among these are their uses in testosterone deficiency, states of protein depletion, anemia, osteoporosis, arthritis, and carcinoma of the breast.

The synthetic anabolic steroid most frequently utilized by athletes today is **methandrostenolone** (meth-*an*-droe-**sten**-oh-lone), one of the 17 alpha-alkylated derivatives of testosterone (Fig. 32-7). Compare the structure of methadrostenolone with that of testosterone (Fig. 32-8). This particular anabolic steroid may be taken orally since it is not rapidly metabolized by the liver. Furthermore, its capacity for binding to plasma proteins is markedly less than that of testosterone. The latter feature may enhance the biological activity of this synthetic compound. In general, orally administered synthetic anabolic steroids have relatively short half-lives and usually require daily doses.

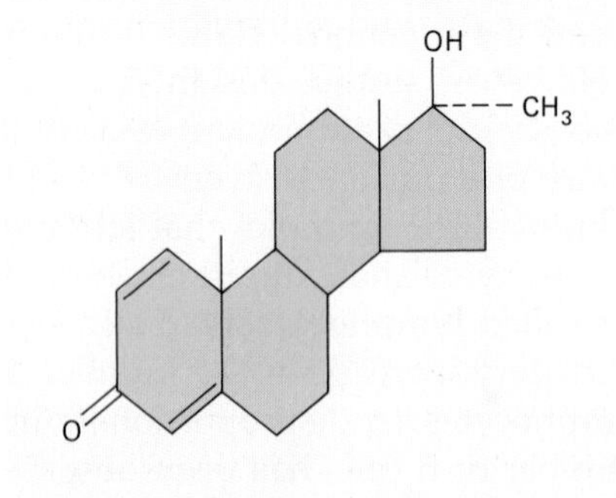

Methandrostenolone

FIGURE 32-7

Structural formula of methandrostenolone. This compound is a 17 alpha-alkylated derivative of testosterone. Compare with Figures 32-8 and 32-9.

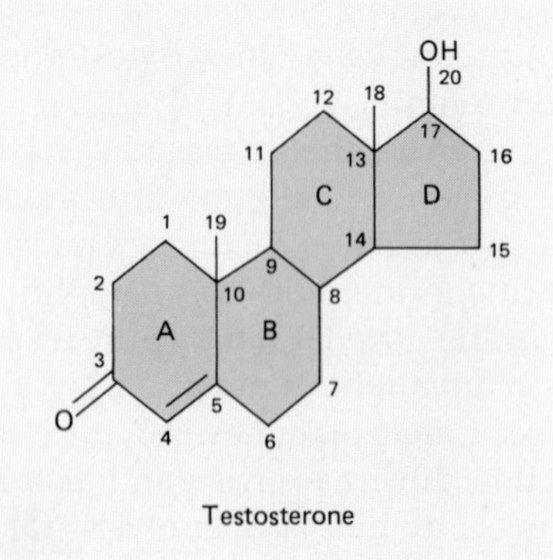

FIGURE 32-8

Structural formula of testosterone. Note the lettering of the rings and the numbering of the carbon atoms. Compare with Figures 32-7 and 32-9.

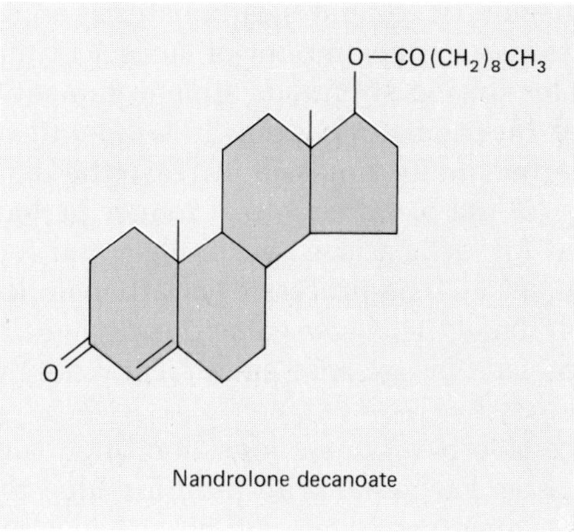

FIGURE 32-9

Structural formula of nandrolone decanoate. This compound is a 17 beta-esterified derivative of testosterone. Compare with Figures 32-7 and 32-8.

The structure of another widely used anabolic steroid, **nandrolone decanoate** (**nan**-droe-lone deck-uh-**no**-ate), is shown in Figure 32-9. This compound is an example of a synthetic group called the 17 beta-esterified testosterone derivatives. In general, these synthetic compounds are administered by intramuscular injection and are released slowly from such sites. Once released, the derivative requires hydrolysis in the liver or plasma in order to acquire the ability to bind to androgen receptors of target cells and exert its biological effect. The side effects associated with use of the 17 beta-esterified compounds appear to be less severe than those with the 17 alpha-alkylated group. The latter derivatives are reported to be highly toxic to the liver.

Anabolic steroids are abused by some athletes

The actions of synthetic anabolic steroids are multiple and accompanied by a variety of side effects. Even though their use is purported to increase muscular mass, strength, and overall physical performance, the abuse of these compounds carries with it profound risks for the individual. During intense athletic training, a combination of orally and intramuscularly administered synthetic anabolic steroids is typically used. In addition to the assumed physiological effects of such a regimen, a psychological effect also persists in some athletes.

Certain athletes develop low ratios of high-density lipoproteins to cholesterol with chronic anabolic steroid use. The long-term use of synthetic anabolic steroids has recently been linked to an increased incidence of atherosclerosis and coronary heart disease. In addition to the toxic effects on the liver mentioned earlier, the extended use of synthetic anabolic steroids may also lead to infertility in both male and female athletes. The use of anabolic steroids by athletes during adolescence may result in premature closure of epiphyseal plates, leading to reduced stature.

Although synthetic anabolic steroids have proven clinical applications, their use (and possible abuse) by professional and amateur athletes requires much more rigorous investigation. Until the specific physiological benefits and adverse long-term effects can be more thoroughly evaluated, it would be prudent to avoid the routine use of these compounds as an attempt to improve athletic performance.

Additional measures have been utilized by athletes to gain a competitive edge

The demand for excellence in competitive sports is a stimulus of such magnitude that it drives many athletes and trainers alike to employ nearly any approach that brings them nearer to victory. The use and abuse of anabolic steroids in this regard has been discussed. Additional measures have been developed and utilized with the same goal in mind. Red blood cell packing (blood doping), growth hormone administration, bicarbonate loading, and use of various analgesic agents are a few examples of many such approaches.

The collection, storage, and subsequent reinfusion of an athlete's red blood cells is a process called **red blood cell packing** or **blood doping.** It was designed with the notion that one can increase the number of red blood cells per unit volume of blood available for oxygen transport. Once the red blood cells are removed, the hematocrit and blood hemoglobin remain low for a period of approximately six weeks. A reduction in these values may in fact impede the training process. Furthermore, the number of red blood cells and the time of their reinfusion must be precisely calculated. Studies show that maximum blood hemoglobin and hematocrit levels are achieved about one week after infusion. It should be noted that red blood cell packing can increase the oxygen content in arterial blood, but whether this directly influences aerobic athletic performance is not clear. This would certainly be the case if the amount of oxygen delivered to the contracting muscles is not the limiting step in oxidative metabolism. Athletic training at high altitudes leads to a naturally occurring form of red blood cell packing or **polycythemia** (*pol*-ee-sigh-**thee**-me-uh).

Red blood cell packing has one major drawback worthy of consideration: There is always the risk that increased blood viscosity, due to a significantly increased hematocrit, will impede venous return, reduce cardiac output, and result in possible tissue damage. Furthermore, the long-term effects of routine red blood cell packing have not been studied adequately.

Some athletes receive small doses of **growth hormone (GH)** during training in attempts to increase their muscle mass. This results from the anabolic effects of GH. Whether GH also enhances athletic performance in terms of endurance or strength has not been conclusively demonstrated. The half-life of GH in the blood is of short duration. Therefore, in order to increase muscle mass it must be used routinely for long periods in preparation for major competitive events.

There are several undesirable complications of GH use since this hormone exerts its effects on nearly every tissue of the body. Following closure of the epiphyseal plates, chronic use of GH may lead to a condition called **acromegaly** (*ack*-row-**meg**-uh-lee). Although many organs of the body are affected, alterations in skeletal structure and various soft tissues predominate. The hands and feet enlarge dramatically together with development of characteristic facial features including an enlarged mandible and tongue. Additional abnormalities occur in the joints and the skin. Enlargement of the heart, liver, spleen, pancreas, and kidneys may occur as well. A variety of hormone imbalances have also been reported with long-term GH administration.

Ingestion of sodium bicarbonate, in an attempt to reduce the amount of lactic acid that accumulates during strenuous athletic competition, is called **bicarbonate loading.** It is thought that the bicarbonate loading will increase the buffering capacity of the blood such that longer periods are required for lactic acid to accumulate and for fatigue to set in. The process of bicarbonate loading probably has little if any value during light to moderate aerobic exercise since lactic acid levels remain low.

Excessive bicarbonate ingestion often leads to diarrhea, and together with fluid loss due to sweating, may precipitate a fluid and electrolyte imbalance. Long-term bicarbonate ingestion can result in alkalosis with subsequent alteration in respiratory, cardiac, and neuromuscular function.

A multitude of pharmaceutical agents have been developed whose sole purpose for use in the athletic arena is to reduce or eliminate the feeling of pain. All athletes experience pain at one time or another and to varying degrees depending upon the severity of the injury and the individual concerned. The body itself produces several types of endogenous opioids during stressful conditions. These are released into the blood and bind to various opioid receptors that, in turn, modulate a pain-reducing, or **analgesic** (an-al-**jee**-zick), effect. The synthesis and release of endogenous opioids is thought to be responsible for the "runner's high" often experienced by marathoners.

Several narcotic analgesics such as morphine, codeine, demerol, and levorphanol have been used by athletes to alleviate pain resulting from injury. In addition, many aspirin-like compounds have been employed for a similar purpose. Although the analgesic agents may alleviate the pain so that the athlete may compete, they do not remove the cause of the pain. The long-term effects of competing with serious injuries are just now beginning to be documented. In these instances it might be safe to say that the ultimate price of victory is not immediately apparent.

Summary

I. Exercise stresses the homeostatic mechanisms of the body.

II. Muscular contraction plays a central role in exercise, and its metabolism is altered markedly during such activity.
   A. Adenosine triphosphate and creatinine phosphate together provide sufficient energy for only 10 to 15 seconds of maximal physical activity.
   B. Aerobic metabolism is the primary energy pathway during prolonged light exercise.
   C. Anaerobic energy metabolism will support light to vigorous exercise for approximately 30 seconds.
   D. During strenuous physical activity, the major source of energy metabolism is derived from the aerobic pathway.

III. Oxygen consumption increases during exercise.
   A. Blood flow to contracting muscles is a limiting factor in terms of oxygen consumption.
   B. The pattern of oxygen consumption during the early and late stages of exercise is similar and not dependent upon the intensity of the exercise.
   C. The new steady-state level of oxygen consumption increases with exercise of increasing intensity.
   D. Once $\dot{V}O_2max$ is attained, further increases in physical activity lead to lactic acid accumulation and the onset of fatigue.
      1. $\dot{V}O_2max$ levels are affected by the age and sex of an individual.
      2. A physically active lifestyle may often retard the decline of $\dot{V}O_2max$ that accompanies advancing age.

IV. Subsequent to physical activity, the amount of oxygen used in excess of an individual's resting level is called the oxygen debt.
   A. Repayment of the oxygen debt consists of fast and slow components.
   B. Understanding repayment of the oxygen debt is important for athletic training and competition.

V. Several parameters of respiratory physiology are altered during exercise.
   A. Minute respiratory volume increases as the rate and depth of breathing increase during exercise.
   B. Several mechanisms are most likely responsible for regulation of minute respiratory volume during exercise.
   C. Increased alveolar diffusion during exercise is related to an increased blood flow rate through the pulmonary capillary bed.

VI. Exercise influences the flow rate and distribution of blood to the body's organs.
   A. Blood flow to the skin varies with the stage and intensity of the physical activity.
   B. Heat stroke or death may follow a rise in body temperature of greater than 5°C.

VII. Changes in cardiac function during exercise reflect the increased demands for oxygen and nutrients by contracting muscles.
   A. During exercise, the increase in cardiac output by the trained athlete is much greater than that of an untrained individual.
   B. During exercise, stroke volume plateaus at approximately 14 liters per minute. Further increase in cardiac output is largely due to increasing heart rate.

VIII. The secretion of various hormones is elevated with increasing intensity of exercise.
   A. Catecholamines influence cardiovascular function and nutrient levels during exercise.
   B. Female athletes participating in strenuous training programs may experience amenorrhea, oligomenorrhea, or even a delay in the onset of menstruation.

IX. Exercise may influence the number of specific cell types belonging to the immune system.
   A. Such changes in cell numbers are transitory in nature.
   B. Exercise has not been shown to directly influence one's resistance to disease.

X. The most widely used synthetic anabolic steroids are derivatives of the male hormone testosterone.
   A. Anabolic steroids have not been documented to significantly enhance aerobic athletic performance.
   B. Side effects of the 17 beta-esterified derivatives of testosterone appear less severe than those of the 17 alpha-alkylated derivatives.

XI. Abuse of synthetic anabolic steroids by athletes is a problem of increasing concern.
   A. Chronic use of synthetic anabolic steroids may be related to atherosclerosis and coronary heart disease.
   B. Liver toxicity and infertility may also result from chronic use of synthetic anabolic steroids.

XII. Red blood cell packing, bicarbonate loading, and the use of analgesics are examples of approaches taken to give athletes a competitive edge.

Post-test

1. A series of physiological adjustments occurs during exercise and leads to the development of a new homeostatic ______________ state.
2. The ATP present in muscle tissue prior to exercise will provide energy to support strenuous physical activity for about ______________ or ______________ seconds.
3. In addition to the energy derived from ATP, energy from ______________ ______________ is also utilized during the early phase of exercise.
4. The ______________ pathway of energy metabolism serves as the chief source of energy during extended light exercise.
5. Most of the energy generated during strenuous physical activity is obtained from the ______________ pathway.
6. The accumulation of ______________ ______________ precedes the onset of fatigue and muscle cramps often experienced with prolonged physical activity.
7. The steady-state level of oxygen consumption beyond which no further increase occurs even with increased physical activity is called the ______________ ______________ ______________.
8. The fast component of recovery from an oxygen debt is also called the ______________ debt.
9. The lactic acid oxygen debt is also called the ______________ component of the recovery phase.
10. Minute respiratory volume may exceed ______________ liters of air per minute during strenuous physical activity.
11. The increase in alveolar diffusion during exercise is due in part to a markedly increased ______________ blood flow.
12. Decide whether there is an increase or decrease in the following:
    (a) heart rate during exercise
    (b) blood flow to muscles during exercise
    (c) blood flow to skin during the early phase of exercise prior to an increased body temperature
    (d) cardiac output during moderate exercise
    (e) heart rate once cardiac output exceeds 14 liters per minute and exercise intensity continues to increase
    (f) lipolysis following catecholamine release during exercise
    (g) prolactin secretion during exercise
    (h) blood glucose with prolonged exercise
    (i) hematocrit immediately following red blood cell packing
    (j) blood viscosity immediately following red blood cell packing
    (k) time required for lactic acid accumulation following bicarbonate loading
13. An increased secretion of ______________ in females during strenuous exercise may have an inhibitory effect on the ovaries, which could lead to a condition called amenorrhea.
14. Enlargement of the breasts in males is called ______________ and may result from the fact that synthetic anabolic steroids may be converted to ______________ by the body.
15. Chronic use of GH following closure of the epiphyseal plates may lead to a condition called ______________ in which the hands and feet are enlarged and the individual possesses characteristic facial features.
16. Prolonged athletic training often leads to ______________ (enlargement) of the heart.

Review questions

1. Discuss the metabolic changes in muscle tissue energy metabolism during exercise.
2. Discuss the factors regulating cardiac output before and after a value of 14 liters per minute is reached.
3. Discuss the factors that influence alveolar diffusion during exercise.
4. Describe the effects of exercise upon the immune system. Do the alterations observed demonstrate an increased resistance to disease?
5. Discuss the adverse side effects of chronic use of synthetic anabolic steroids as an attempt to improve athletic performance.
6. Discuss the mechanisms that are thought to regulate the MRV during exercise.
7. Compare and contrast the fast and slow components of the oxygen debt during the recovery phase of exercise.
8. Describe the adjustments in various systems of the body that occur in order to meet the increased demand for oxygen and nutrients by muscle during strenuous exercise.
9. Discuss the effects of age, gender, and lifestyle on one's $\dot{V}O_2$max.
10. Discuss the alterations in blood flow rate and distribution to various organs of the body during exercise.

Post-test answers

1. steady **2.** five; six **3.** creatine phosphate
4. aerobic **5.** aerobic **6.** lactic acid
7. maximum oxygen consumption **8.** alactic
9. slow **10.** 150 **11.** pulmonary
12. (a) increase (b) increase (c) decrease (d) increase (e) increase (f) increase (g) increase (h) decrease (i) increase (j) increase (k) increase **13.** prolactin
14. gynecomastia; estrogens **15.** acromegaly
16. hypertrophy

APPENDIX **A:**

DISSECTING TERMS

Your task of mastering new terms will be greatly simplified if you learn to dissect each new word. Many terms can be divided into a prefix, the part of the word that precedes the main root, the word root itself, and often a suffix, a word ending that may add to or modify the meaning of the root. As you progress in your study of anatomy and physiology, you will learn to recognize the more common prefixes, word roots, and suffixes. Such recognition will help you analyze new terms so that you can determine their meaning, and will also help you remember them.

Prefixes

a-, ab- from, away, apart (*ab*duct, lead away, move away from the midline of the body)
a-, an- un-, -less, lack, not (*a*symmetrical, not symmetrical)
ad- (also **af-, ag-, an-, ap-**) to, toward (*ad*duct, move toward the midline of the body)
ambi- both sides (*ambi*dextrous, able to use either hand)
andro- male (*andro*gen, male hormone)
ante- forward, before (*ante*flexion, bending forward)
anti- against (*anti*coagulant, a substance that prevents coagulation of blood)
bi- two (*bi*ceps, a muscle with two heads of origin)
bio- life (*bio*logy, the study of life)
brady- slow (*brady*cardia, abnormally slow heart beat)
circum-, circ- around (*circum*cision, a cutting around)
co-, con- with, together (*con*genital, existing with or before birth)
contra- against (*contra*ception, against conception)
crypt- hidden (*crypt*orchidism, undescended or hidden testes)
cyt- cell (*cyt*ology, the study of cells)
di- two (*di*saccharide, a compound made of two sugar molecules chemically combined)
dis- (also **di-** or **dif-**) apart, un-, not (*dis*sect, cut apart)
dys- painful, difficult (*dys*pnea, difficult breathing)
ecto- outside (*ecto*derm, outer embryonic tissue layer)
end-, endo- within, inner (*endo*plasmic reticulum, a network of membranes found within the cytoplasm)
epi- on, upon (*epi*dermis, upon the dermis)
eu- good, well (*eu*phoria, a sense of well-being)
ex-, e-, ef- out from, out of (*ex*tension, a straightening out)
extra- outside, beyond (*extra*embryonic membrane, a membrane such as the amnion that protects the embryo)
hemi- half (cerebral *hemi*sphere, lateral half of the cerebrum)
hetero- other, different (*hetero*geneous, made of different substances)
homo-, hom- same (*homo*logous, corresponding in structure)
hyper- excessive, above normal (*hyper*secretion, excessive secretion)
hypo- under, below, deficient (*hypo*dermic, below the skin; *hypo*thyroidism, insufficiency of thyroid hormones)

in-, im- not (*im*balance, condition in which there is no balance)
inter- between, among (*inter*stitial, situated between parts)
intra- within (*intra*cellular, within the cell)
iso- equal, like (*iso*tonic, equal strength)
macro- large (*macro*molecule, large molecule)
mal- bad, abnormal (*mal*nutrition, poor nutrition)
mega- large, great (*mega*karyocyte, giant cell of bone marrow)
meso- middle (*meso*derm, middle embryonic tissue layer)
meta- after, beyond (*meta*phase, the stage of mitosis after prophase)
micro- small (*micro*scope, instrument for viewing small objects)
mono- one (*mono*cyte, a type of white blood cell)
neo- (*neo*natal, newborn during the first 4 weeks after birth)
oligo- small, deficient (*olig*uria, abnormally small volume of urine)
oo- egg (*oo*cyte, developing egg cell)
para- near, beside, beyond (*para*central, near the center)
peri- around (*peri*cardial membrane, membrane that surrounds the heart)
poly- multiple, complex (*poly*saccharide, a carbohydrate composed of many simple sugars)
post- after, behind (*post*natal, after birth)
pre- before (*pre*natal, before birth)
pseudo- false (*pseudo*pod, a temporary extension of a cell, i.e., "false foot.")
retro- backward (*retro*peritoneal, located behind the peritoneum)
semi- half (*semi*lunar, half-moon)
sub- under (*sub*cutaneous tissue, tissue immediately under the skin)
super-, supra- above (*supra*renal, above the kidney)
syn- with, together (*syn*drome, a group of symptoms that occur together and characterize a disease)
trans- across, beyond (*trans*port, carry across)

Suffixes

-able, -ible able (vi*able*, able to live)
-ac pertaining to (cardi*ac*, pertaining to the heart)
-ad used in anatomy to form adverbs of direction (cephal*ad*, toward the head)
-asis, -asia, -esis condition or state of (hemost*asis*, stopping of bleeding)
-cide kill, destroy (bio*cide*, substance that kills living things)
-ectomy surgical removal (append*ectomy*, surgical removal of the appendix)
-emia condition of blood (an*emia*, without enough blood)
-gen something produced or generated or something that produces or generates (patho*gen*, something that can cause disease)
-gram record, write (electrocardio*gram*, a record of the electrical activity of the heart)
-graph record, write (electrocardio*graph*, an instrument for recording the electrical activity of the heart)
-itis inflammation of (appendic*itis*, inflammation of the appendix)
-logy study or science of (physio*logy*, study of the function of the body)
-oid like, in the form of (thyr*oid*, in the form of a shield)
-oma tumor (carcin*oma*, a malignant tumor)
-osis indicates disease (psych*osis*, a mental disease)
-ous, -ose full of (poison*ous*, full of poison)
-scope instrument for viewing or observing (micro*scope*, instrument for viewing small objects)
-stomy refers to a surgical procedure in which an artificial opening is made (colo*stomy*, surgical formation of an artificial anus)
-tomy cutting or section (appendec*tomy*, cutting out the appendix)
-uria refers to urine (poly*uria*, excessive production of urine)

Some common word roots

aden gland, glandular (*aden*osis, a glandular disease)
alg pain (neur*alg*ia, nerve pain)
arthr joint (*arthr*itis, inflammation of the joints)
bi, bio life (*bi*ology, study of life)
blast a formative cell, germ layer (osteo*blast*, cell that gives rise to bone cells)
brachi arm (*brachi*al artery, blood vessel that supplies the arm)
bronch branch of the trachea (*bronch*itis, inflammation of the bronchi)
bry grow, swell (em*bry*o, an organism in the early stages of development)
carcin cancer (*carcin*ogenic, cancer-producing)
cardi heart (*cardi*ac, pertaining to the heart)
cephal head (*cephal*ad, toward the head)
cerebr brain (*cerebr*al, pertaining to the brain)
cervic, cervix neck (*cervic*al, pertaining to the neck)
chol bile (*chol*ecystogram, an x-ray of the gallbladder)
chondr cartilage (*chondr*ocyte, a cartilage cell)
chrom color (*chromo*some, deeply staining body in nucleus)
cran skull (*cran*ial, pertaining to the skull)
cyt cell (*cyt*ology, study of the cells)
derm skin (*derm*atology, study of the skin)
duct, duc lead (*duct*, passageway)
ecol dwelling, house (*ecol*ogy, the study of organisms in relation to their environment)
enter intestine (*enter*itis, inflammation of the intestine)
evol to unroll (*evol*ution, descent of complex organisms from simpler ancestors)

gastr stomach (*gastr*itis, inflammation of the stomach)
gen generate, produce (*gen*e, a hereditary factor)
glyc, glyco sweet, sugar (*glyco*gen, storage form of glucose)
gon semen, seed (*gon*ad, an organ producing gametes)
hem, em blood (*hem*atology, the study of blood)
hepat, hepar liver (*hepat*itis, inflammation of the liver)
hist tissue (*hist*ology, study of tissues)
hom, homeo same, unchanging, steady (*homeo*stasis, reaching a steady state)
hydr water (*hydr*olysis, a breakdown reaction involving water)
leuk white (*leuk*ocyte, white blood cell)
macro large (*macro*phage, large janitor cell)
mamm breast (*mamm*ary glands, the glands that produce milk to nourish the young)
micro small (*micro*scope, instrument for viewing small objects)
morph form (*morph*ogenesis, development of body form)
my, mys muscle (*my*ocardium, muscle layer of the heart)
nephr kidney (*nephr*on, microscopic unit of the kidney)
neur, nerv nerve (*neur*algia, pain associated with nerve)
neutr neither one nor the other (*neutr*on, a subatomic particle that is neither positively nor negatively charged)
occiput back part of the head (*occipit*al, back region of the head)
ost, oss bone (*ost*eology, study of bones)
path disease (*path*ologist, one who studies disease processes)
ped child (*ped*iatrics, branch of medicine specializing in children)
ped, pod foot (bi*ped*, organism with two feet)
phag eat (*phag*ocytosis, process by which certain cells ingest particles and foreign matter)
phil love (hydro*phil*ic, a substance that attracts water)
proct anus (*proct*oscope, instrument for examining rectum and anal canal)
psych mind (*psych*ology, study of the mind)
scler hard (athero*scler*osis, hardening of the arterial wall)
som body (chromo*som*e, deeply staining body in the nucleus)
stas, stat stand (*stas*is, condition in which blood stands, as opposed to flowing)
thromb clot (*thromb*us, a clot within a blood vessel)
ur urea, urine (*ur*ologist, a physician specializing in the urinary tract)
visc pertaining to an internal organ or body cavity (*visc*era, internal organs)

APPENDIX **B:**

ABBREVIATIONS

The biological and medical sciences employ a great many abbreviations, and with good reason. Many technical terms in these sciences are both long and difficult to pronounce. Yet it can be difficult for beginners, when confronted with something like NADPH or COPD, to understand the reference. Here are some of the common abbreviations employed in anatomy and physiology for your ready reference.

ACTH The pituitary hormone, **A**dreno**C**ortico **T**ropic **H**ormone, that governs the production of adrenal cortical hormones, by the adrenal cortex.

ADH The pituitary hormone, **A**nti**D**iuretic **H**ormone, also called arginine vasopressin, that governs the reabsorption of water by the kidney, and thus the amount of urine that is produced. ADH is antidiuretic: The more ADH present, the less urine produced.

ADP **A**denosine **D**i**P**hosphate. A form of the almost universal energy transfer substance of the cell, ATP, in its "discharged" state. Even ADP, however, contains some transferable energy that is employed in certain biochemical reactions.

AIDS **A**cquired **I**mmune **D**eficiency **S**yndrome. Caused by a virus, AIDS is an "acquired" condition, distinguishable from hereditary defects of the immune system with which the sufferer may have been born.

AMP **A**denosine **M**ono**P**hosphate. The basic "stem" of the energy transfer substance ATP, AMP contains no readily transferable energy.

ANS **A**utonomic **N**ervous **S**ystem.

ATP **A**denosine **T**ri**P**hosphate. The almost universal energy transfer substance of the cell. Typically, ATP donates its terminal phosphate group to some substance, along with much of the energy formerly contained in the bond that held it to the remainder of the ATP molecule. ADP is left over, and in due course, is recycled.

ATPase An enzyme or protein that breaks down ATP, usually producing ADP. Most ATPases perform some function such as active transport or contraction which utilizes the energy that is discharged in the breakdown of ATP. One important class of ATPase, The F_0-F_1 and CF_0-cF_1 complexes of the mitochondria and chloroplasts, operate in reverse. These actually *produce* ATP, using the energy of a proton gradient to add the terminal phosphate to the ATP molecule.

AV node **A**trio-**V**entricular node. A mass of tissue located near the junction of the heart atria and ventricles that is responsible for the coordination of the contraction of the ventricles with that of the atria.

B lymphocyte The lymphocyte responsible for the production of antibody-mediated immunity. Originally named for the bursa of Fabricius, a structure in which these cells mature in birds.

BMR **B**asal **M**etabolic **R**ate. The rate of energy production, indirectly measured by the rate of consumption. Called "basal" because it is the basic metabolic cost of living apart from any special exertion.

cAMP **C**yclic **A**denosine **M**ono**P**hosphate. Most commonly, a "second messenger" substance produced within the cell in response to a hormone. It is made from ATP.

CNS Central Nervous System.

COPD Chronic Obstructive Pulmonary Disease.

CP Creatine Phosphate. An important energy storage substance in vertebrate muscle.

DNA Deoxyribonucleic Acid. The fundamental substance in which hereditary information is stored.

DPN Synonym for **NAD**, below.

FAD (also **FADH,** etc.) Flavine Adenine Dinucleotide. A hydrogen acceptor and donor involved in cellular metabolism and in photosynthesis.

FSH Follicle Stimulating Hormone. A hormone secreted by the anterior pituitary that was originally discovered in female mammals, though it also occurs in males. Stimulates the growth of the ovarian follicles.

GABA Gamma Amino Butyric Acid. A neurotransmitter that acts as an inhibitor in the brain and spinal cord.

GH Growth Hormone, otherwise known as somatotropin.

GTP Guanosine TriPhosphate. An energy-rich compound sometimes used by cells in place of ATP.

Hb Hemoglobin.

HCG Human Chorionic Gonadotropin. A peptide hormone produced by the embryo that helps to maintain pregnancy. Similar hormones occur in other mammals, but they are known simply as CG.

HDL High-Density Lipoprotein. Blood particle of relatively high density that transports fats.

HLA Human Leukocyte Antigen. A major complex of antigens found on human body cells that governs graft compatibility, which is governed by specific genes, the HLA genes.

Ig Immunoglobin, as in IgA, IgG, IgM.

LDH Lactic DeHydrogenase enzyme.

LH Luteinizing Hormone. Although this anterior pituitary hormone also occurs and functions in males, it was discovered in females and named for its action in them, namely, to convert an ovarian follicle into a progesterone-secreting corpus luteum.

MAO Monoamine Oxidase. An enzyme that destroys epinephrine-like neurotransmitter substances.

MHC Major Histocompatibility Complex. Group of genes governing the tissue antigens, which in turn determine graft compatibility in humans.

mRNA Messenger Ribonucleic Acid. A form of RNA (see below) that carries the genetic message from DNA to the cytoplasm, where it is translated into peptides or proteins.

MSH Melanocyte Stimulating Hormone. An anterior pituitary hormone that darkens the skin by stepping up the activity of melanocytes.

NAD (also **NADP, NADH,** etc.) Nicotine Adenine Dinucleotide. A series of cellular coenzymes widely utilized by cells as a hydrogen acceptor or donor in a variety of metabolic reactions and in photosynthesis. NAD is also called DPN; NADP is also called TPN.

PNS Peripheral Nervous System.

RAS Reticular Activating System. The system of the brain important in maintaining a conscious state.

RBC Red Blood Cell, erythrocyte.

RNA RiboNucleic Acid. Nucleic acid responsible for the expression of genetic information. There are three known varieties: mRNA, tRNA, and rRNA.

rRNA Ribosomal Ribonucleic Acid. RNA that forms part of the structure of the ribosome.

SA node Sino-Atrial Node of the heart; responsible for the initiation and timing of the heartbeat.

SEM Scanning Electron Microscope.

STD Sexually Transmitted Disease.

T lymphocyte Lymphocyte with a wide variety of functions, primarily concerned with cell-mediated immunity. Named "T" for the fact that these cells mature in the thymus gland.

tRNA Transfer Ribonucleic Acid. A variety of RNA responsible for carrying (transfering) amino acids to the ribosomal protein construction site.

TSH Thyroid Stimulating Hormone.

WBC White Blood Cell, leukocyte.

GLOSSARY*

A

abatement (a-**bait**-ment) A decrease in the severity of a condition such as pain, symptoms, or a disorder.
abdomen (**ab**-doe-men) The region of the body between the diaphragm and the pelvis.
abdominal cavity (ab-**dom**-ih-nal) The superior part of the abdominopelvic cavity containing the liver, gallbladder, spleen, stomach, pancreas, small intestine, and part of the large intestine.
abdominopelvic cavity (ab-*dom*-ih-no-**pel**-vic) The lower part of the ventral body cavity below the thoracic cavity.
abduction (ab-**duk**-shun) A movement whereby a body part is drawn away from the main body axis or the axis of a limb.
ABO blood types A system of categorizing blood based on the presence or absence of specific surface antigens.
abortion (ah-**bor**-shun) Expulsion of an embryo or fetus before it is capable of surviving.
abscess (**ab**-sess) A localized accumulation of pus within a cavity.
absorption (ab-**sorp**-shun) The passage of material into or through a cell or tissue, as in the movement of digested nutrients from the GI tracts into the blood or lymph.
absorptive state Time during which digested nutrients are being absorbed into the bloodstream, or the lymph from the GI tract.
accessory duct A pancreatic duct emptying into the duodenum near the ampulla of Vater. This duct is also known as the duct of Santorini.
accommodation (a-*kom*-o-**day**-shun) An adjustment of the lens of the eye for vision at various distances.
acetabulum (*as*-e-**tab**-you-lum) The cup-shaped cavity of the lateral side of the hip bone that articulates with the head of the femur.
acetylcholine (*as*-ee-til-**koe**-leen) A neurotransmitter released by cholinergic nerves as in those stimulating skeletal muscle contraction.
Achilles' tendon (ah-**kil**-eez) The tendon of the gastrocnemius and soleus muscle that inserts upon the calcaneus (heel) bone.
acid (**as**-id) A proton donor or compound that dissociates in solution to produce hydrogen ions and some type of anion.
acidosis (*as*-i-**doe**-sis) An abnormal state resulting from the accumulation of acid, or loss of base from, the body, often produced by respiratory system malfunction. In acidosis the blood pH falls below 7.35.
acini (**as**-ih-nee) The smallest lobules in a compound gland. The acini of the pancreas produce digestive enzymes.
acne (**ak**-nee) A disorder of the skin caused by an inflammation of the sebaceous glands. It usually begins at puberty.
acoustic (a-**koos**-tik) Pertaining to the sense of hearing or sound production.
acquired immune deficiency syndrome (AIDS) A disease caused by the HIV virus in which a deficiency develops in helper T cells. Symptoms include fever, night sweats, sore throat, coughing, enlarged lymph nodes, body aches, fatigue, and weight loss. No cure is presently known.
acromegaly (*ak*-roe-**meg**-ah-lee) A condition resulting from a hypersecretion of growth hormone in the adult. It is characterized by enlarged bones in the extremities and face along with the enlargement of other tissues.
acrosome (**ak**-roe-sowm) An anterior cap of the head of a spermatozoan which contains lytic enzymes allowing for penetration into the ovum.
actin (**ak**-tin) A contractile protein of the thin filaments within a muscle cell.
action potential The depolarization that spreads along the neuronal surface. It is also called a nerve impulse.
active immunity An acquired immunity resulting from the production of antibodies in response to a natural exposure to antigens.
active transport The movement of substances through cell membranes against concentration gradients. Active transport requires energy expenditure.
acuity (a-**kyou**-i-tee) The ability to distinguish between two points in space; a sharpness of vision.
acupuncture (**ak**-you-*punk*-chur) Inserting needles into specific parts of the body for the relief of pain or the removal of fluids. It is based on ancient Chinese practices.
acute (a-**kyout**) Having a short and relatively severe course; not chronic.

*Many definitions and pronunciations taken from Miller, Benjamin, and Keane, Claire B., Encyclopedia and Dictionary of Medicine, Nursing and Allied Health, 4th ed., Philadelphia, W.B. Saunders, 1987.

Adam's apple The thyroid cartilage of the larynx. In males, it is pronounced due to enlargement caused by testosterone.
adaptation (*ad*-ap-**tay**-shun) Decline in the response of a receptor subjected to repeated or prolonged stimulation. Adjustment of the pupil to variations in illumination entering eye.
Addison's disease (**add**-i-sonz) Hypofunction of adrenal cortex in which lowered secretions of glucocorticoids and mineralocorticoids cause symptoms including muscular weakness, weight loss, low blood pressure, dehydration, hyperpigmentation, and mental lethargy.
adduction (ad-**duk**-shun) A movement whereby a body part is drawn toward the main body axis or the axis of a limb.
adenohypophysis (*ad*-e-no-high-**pof**-i-sis) The anterior part of the hypophysis or pituitary gland.
adenoids (**ad**-e-noydz) Glandular tissue in the nasopharynx, also known as the pharyngeal tonsils.
adenosine triphosphate (ATP) (a-**den**-oh-seen try-**fos**-fate) The energy currency of the cell. A chemical compound used to transfer energy from those biochemical reactions that yield energy to those that require it.
adenylate cyclase (ah-**den**-ih-late **sye**-klaze) The enzyme converting ATP to cyclic-AMP.
adipocyte (**ad**-i-poe-site) Fat cell.
adipose tissue A type of connective tissue characterized by the presence of many fat cells.
adrenal cortex (ah-**dree**-nal **kore**-tekz) The outer part of the adrenal gland. It has three zones, each producing different hormones.
adrenal glands (ah-**dree**-nal) The two glands located superior to the kidneys. They are also known as the suprarenal glands.
adrenal medulla (ah-**dree**-nal meh-**dul**-ah) The inner part of the adrenal gland that secretes catecholamines (epinephrine and norepinephrine) in response to sympathetic stimulation.
adrenergic fiber (*ad*-ren-**er**-jik) A neuron releasing epinephrine or norepinephrine as a neurotransmitter.
adrenocorticotropic hormone (ACTH) (ad-*ree*-no-kore-ti-kow-**trope**-ik) A hormone produced and released by the anterior pituitary that causes the production and release of hormones of the adrenal cortex.
adventitia (*ad*-ven-**tish**-eah) The outermost layer or covering of an organ or structure.
aerobic (air-**oh**-bik) Requiring molecular oxygen.
afferent (**af**-er-ent) Movement toward a structure.
afferent arteriole (**af**-er-ent ar-**tee**-ree-ole) The blood vessel within the kidney that carries blood to the glomerulus.
afferent neuron A nerve cell that carries information toward the central nervous system. It is also called a sensory neuron.
afterbirth The separated placenta and membranes expelled from the uterus after childbirth.
agglutination (a-*glue*-tin-**nay**-shun) The aggregation of particles into masses or clumps especially used in reference to microbes and blood cells.
agglutinin (a-**glue**-ti-nin) A substance in the blood plasma with which an agglutinogen reacts. It is also known as an isoantibody.
agglutinogen (*ag*-lou-**tin**-oh-gen) A substance that acts as an antigen stimulating the production of agglutinin. These proteins determine the ABO blood type of an individual.
agnosia (ag-**no**-zee-ah) The inability to recognize familiar sensory impressions.
albinism (**al**-bi-nizm) A hereditary inability to form pigment, resulting in abnormally light coloration of skin, eyes, and hair.
albumin (al-**byou**-min) A class of protein found in animal tissues. The smallest and most abundant of the plasma proteins, it is important in plasma osmoregulation.
albuminuria (al-*byou*-min-**your**-ea) The presence of albumin in urine.
aldosterone (al-**dos**-ter-own) The principal mineralocorticoid of the adrenal cortex. It increases sodium reabsorption in the kidneys. It also enhances water reabsorption and potassium excretion.
alimentary canal (*al*-ih-**men**-tah-ree) The digestive tract.
alkali (**al**-kuh-lie) A substance which, when dissolved in water, produces a pH greater than 7. Also known as a base.
alkaline (**al**-kuh-line) A solution containing more hydroxyl ions than hydrogen ions resulting in a pH greater than 7.
alkalosis (*al*-kuh-**low**-sis) An abnormal state resulting from the accumulation of base in, or loss of acid from, the body; often produced by respiratory system malfunction. In alkalosis the blood pH rises above 7.45.
allantois (a-**lan**-toe-is) One of the extraembryonic membranes; a ventral outgrowth of the embryo between the chorion and the amnion.
allergen (**al**-er-jen) An antigen that produces a hypersensitivity reaction.
allergic (a-**ler**-jik) A sensitivity to an allergen.
allergy (**al**-ur-jee) A state of altered immunological reactivity or hypersensitivity.
All-or-none law The phenomenon by which a stimulus produces maximal response or no response at all. If the stimulus is subthreshold, no response occurs. If the stimulus is threshold or greater, a maximal response occurs.
allosteric (*al*-o-**steer**-ik) Referring to an alteration of one site on a protein molecule that affects the function of another site, or otherwise alters the functional configuration of the protein molecule.
alpha cell (**al**-fah) Endocrine cells of the islets of Langerhans of the pancreas that produce the hormone glucagon.
alpha receptor A receptor located on visceral effectors which generally lead to excitation when stimulated by sympathetic postganglionic fibers.
altitude sickness A disorder resulting from a decreased alveolar P_{O_2} when one is increasing altitude. Symptoms include shortness of breath, dizziness, and nausea.
alveolar gland (al-**vee**-oh-lar) A type of gland characterized by a small hollow sac.
alveolar duct The extension of a bronchiole that leads into the lobules of alveoli.
alveolar macrophage (al-**vee**-oh-lar **mak**-roe-fayj) Phagocytic cells in the alveolar walls of the lungs. It is also called a dust cell.
alveolus (al-**vee**-oh-lus) A small hollow sac. The air sacs of the lungs functioning in gas exchange with the blood. The milk-secreting sacs of a mammary gland.
Alzheimer's disease (**altz**-high-merz) Irreversible neurological disorder; senile dementia characterized by intellectual deterioration and changes in personality and alertness.
amenorrhea (a-*men*-oh-**ree**-ah) An absence of menstruation.
amino acid An organic acid possessing both an amine (NH_2) and carboxyl group (COOH). Amino acids are the basic units of proteins.
amnesia (am-**nee**-zee-ah) An impairment or loss of memory.
amniocentesis (*am*-nee-oh-sen-**tee**-sis) A perforation of the amniotic sac by inserting a needle transabdominally in order to obtain a sample of amniotic fluid.
amnion (**am**-nee-on) An extraembryonic membrane that forms a fluid-filled sac for the protection of the developing embryo.
amphiarthrosis (*am*-fee-ar-**throw**-sis) Joint showing slight movement

because of an elastic substance that joins the bone surfaces, as exists between vertebrae.

ampulla (am-**pool**-la) A flasklike expansion of a tubular structure.

ampulla of Vater The hepatopancreatic ampulla or the raised part of the duodenum where the common bile duct and principal pancreatic duct enter.

anabolism (a-**nab**-o-*lizm*) The synthesizing or building-up part of metabolism in which small molecules combine to form larger ones.

anaerobic (*an*-air-**oh**-bik) Processes not requiring molecules of oxygen.

anal canal The terminal end of the rectum.

analgesia (*an*-al-**jee**-zee-ah) Absence of pain sensation.

anaphase (**an**-ah-faze) Third stage of mitosis in which the chromatids of each chromosome separate at their centromeres and move to opposite poles.

anaphylaxis (*an*-ah-fih-**lak**-sis) An unusual or exaggerated allergic reaction.

anastomosis (ah-*nas*-toe-**moe**-sis) The union or communication of blood vessels, nerves, or lymphatics.

anatomical position (*an*-ah-**tom**-ih-kal) The positioning of the body for descriptive purposes in which the body stands erect, facing the viewer, with upper limbs at sides and palms facing anteriorly.

anatomy (a-**nat**-o-mee) The study of the structures of the body and their relationships.

androgen (**an**-drow-jen) A substance, such as testosterone, stimulating or producing male characteristics.

anemia (ah-**nee**-mee-ah) A deficiency of hemoglobin or number of red blood cells.

anesthesia (*an*-es-**thee**-zee-ah) A loss of sensation or feeling especially with respect to pain.

aneurysm (**an**-you-rizm) An enlargement or sac along a blood vessel or in the heart caused by a weakening of the wall.

angina pectoris (an-**jie**-nah **pek**-toe-ris) Acute pain in the chest caused by a decrease in the blood supply to the heart.

angiography (*an*-jee-**og**-rah-fee) X-ray examination of blood vessels in the body after injection of a radiopaque substance.

angiotensins (*an*-jee-o-**ten**-sins) Two compounds found in blood which stimulate the secretion of aldosterone by the adrenal cortex. Angiotensin I is produced by the action of renin on angiotensinogen. Angiotensin I is converted to angiotensin II by a converting enzyme. Angiotensin II is one of the most potent vasoconstrictors known.

anion (**an**-eye-on) A negatively charged ion such as Cl^-.

ankyloglossia (*ang*-ki-low-**gloss**-ee-ah) Restriction of movements of the tongue because of an abnormally short frenulum; tongue-tied.

anopsia (an-**op**-see-ah) A defect in vision.

anorexia nervosa (*an*-o-**rek**-see-ah ner-**voe**-sah) Loss of appetite and abnormal eating patterns that are psychologically based; an eating disorder.

anosmia (an-**oz**-mee-ah) The loss of olfaction.

anoxia (ah-**nok**-see-ah) A deficiency or lack of oxygen.

antagonist (an-**tag**-o-nist) A muscle opposing the action of another muscle, its agonist.

antepartum (*an*-tee-**par**-tum) Occurring before childbirth.

anterior (an-**tee**-ree-or) Located in front of or nearer to the front of the body. In a biped, anterior is also ventral or at the belly-side.

anterior root The ventral root of a spinal nerve carrying motor fibers.

antibiotic (*an*-ti-bye-**ot**-ik) A chemical substance produced by a microbe that inhibits growth or kills other microorganisms.

antibody (**an**-ti-*bod*-ee) A protein compound that is produced by plasma cells in response to a specific antigen. The antibody renders the antigen harmless. It is also called an immunoglobulin.

antidiuretic (*an*-ti-die-you-**ret**-ik) A substance that decreases or inhibits the formation of urine.

antidiuretic hormone (ADH) A hormone produced in the paraventricular nuclei of the hypothalamus and stored in the posterior pituitary. ADH increases the permeability of water in the kidneys which increases water reabsorption. It also causes arteriolar vasoconstriction.

antigen (**an**-tih-jen) A substance foreign to the body that causes the production of antibodies when introduced into the body.

antihistamine (*an*-ti-**his**-tah-min) A drug blocking the effects of histamine.

anuria (ah-**noo**-ree-ah) The suppression of urine formation by the kidneys; a urine output of less than 50 ml per day.

anus (**ay**-nus) The distal end and outlet of the digestive tract.

aorta (ay-**or**-tah) The largest and main systemic artery of the body. It arises from the left ventricle and branches to distribute blood to all parts of the body.

aortic arch (ay-**or**-tik) The most superior section of the aorta, located between the ascending aorta and the descending aorta. In the human it gives off three branches. It is also called the arch of the aorta.

aortic body Chemoreceptive area near the aortic arch that monitors levels of oxygen, carbon dioxide, and hydrogen ions in the blood.

aphasia (ah-**fay**-zee-ah) A loss or defect in the ability to express oneself by speech, writing, or signs, or loss of verbal comprehension.

apnea (ap-**nee**-ah) A temporary interruption of breathing.

apneustic area (ap-**noo**-stik) The part of the respiratory center located in the pons that sends stimulatory impulses to the medullary inspiratory area, prolonging inspiration and inhibiting expiration.

aponeurosis (*ap*-o-noo-**roe**-sis) A sheet of tendinous connective tissue that connects muscle to other muscle or to bone.

appendicitis (ah-*pen*-dih-**sye**-tis) An inflammation of the vermiform appendix.

appositional growth (*ap*-o-**zish**-o-nal) Process in which cartilage increases in width as a new cartilage is produced on the sides of a cartilage model by the proliferation and differentiation of cells within the surrounding perichondrium.

aqueous humor (**ak**-wee-us **hyou**-mor) A serous fluid within the anterior cavity of the eye.

arachnoid membrane (ah-**rak**-noyd) The middle meninx of the central nervous system located between the dura mater and the pia mater.

arbor vitae (**ar**-bor **vee**-tee) The treelike appearance of the cerebellar tracts as seen in a midsagittal section. The term literally means "tree of life."

areola (ah-**ree**-o-lah) The dark pigmented area surrounding the nipple of the mammary gland. It also refers to a small space in a tissue.

arm The region of the upper limb between the shoulder and the elbow.

arrector pili (a-**rek**-tor **pi**-lee) The smooth muscle associated with hairs whose contraction causes the hair to assume a more vertical position. The contraction of the arrector pili results in "goose bumps."

arrythmia (ah-**ryth**-mee-ah) Any variation in the normal rhythm of the heart beat.

arteriogram (ar-**teer**-ee-o-*gram*) A roentgenogram of an artery.

arteriole (ar-**tee**-ree-ole) A small artery that carries blood to capillaries. Vasoconstriction and vasodilation of arterioles help regulate blood pressure and blood distribution to the tissues.

artery (**ar**-ter-ee) A thick-walled blood vessel that carries blood away from the heart under relatively high pressure.

arthritis (ar-**thrye**-tis) The inflammation of a joint.

arthrology (ar-**throl**-o-jee) The study of joints.

arthroscopy (ar-**thros**-ko-pee) A surgical procedure in which an arthroscope is placed through a small incision into a joint (usually the knee) to repair damaged cartilage.

articular cartilage (ar-**tik**-you-lar **kar**-ti-lij) Hyaline cartilage that is attached to articular bone surfaces.

articulation (ar-*tik*-you-**lay**-shun) A joint.

arytenoid cartilages (*ar*-ih-**tee**-noyd) Small paired cartilages of the larynx.

ascending colon (**koe**-lon) The part of the large intestine that extends from the cecum upward to the lower border of the liver. The ascending colon is on the right side of the abdomen. At the right colic (hepatic) flexure the ascending colon becomes the transverse colon.

ascites (as-**sye**-teez) The presence of serous fluid in the peritoneal cavity.

aseptic (ah-**sep**-tik) Free from septic matter or infectious material.

asphyxia (as-**fix**-ee-ah) A condition of oxygen deficiency in the blood or increased levels of carbon dioxide in the blood.

association area Cortical area of cerebrum having sensory and motor fibers connected to other cortical areas. The association area is involved with higher mental and emotional processes.

association neuron A nerve cell located entirely within the central nervous system which transmits information between sensory and motor neurons. It is also called an interneuron or internuncial neuron.

asthma (**az**-muh) A disease characterized by airway constriction, often leading to difficult breathing or dyspnea.

astigmatism (ah-**stig**-mah-tizm) A defect of vision resulting from irregularity in the curvature of the cornea or lens.

astrocyte (**as**-troe-site) A star-shaped type of glial cell that structurally supports the neurons of the central nervous system and attaches them to blood vessels.

ataxia (ah-**tak**-see-ah) Partial or complete loss of voluntary muscular coordination.

atelectasis (*at*-ee-**lek**-tah-sis) A collapsed or airless condition of the lungs or a part of a lung.

atherosclerosis (*ath*-er-o-skleh-**roe**-sis) A progressive disease in which smooth muscle cells and lipid deposits accumulate in the inner lining of arteries leading to decreased arterial luminal diameters and impairment of circulation.

atom The smallest particle of an element with the chemical properties of that element. An atom has a nucleus and electrons.

atomic number The number of protons in the nucleus of an atom.

atomic weight The total number of the neutrons and protons in an atom.

atrial fibrillation (**ay**-tree-al fib-ri-**lay**-shun) An abnormal rhythm of atrial contractions resulting in diminished atrial pumping.

atrial flutter Cardiac arrhythmia due to rapid contractions of the atria (200–320 per minute).

atrioventricular bundle (*ay*-tree-o-ven-**trik**-you-lar) The part of the conduction system of the heart that passes from the atrioventricular node down the interventricular septum and branches to supply the ventricles. It is also called the bundle of His.

atrioventricular node The part of the cardiac conduction system within the right atrium near the opening of the coronary sinus.

atrioventricular valve A valve between each atrium and its ventricle that prevents a backflow of blood.

atrium (**ay**-tree-um) A superior chamber of the heart that receives blood from veins.

auditory ossicle (aw-di-*toe*-ree **os**-sih-kul) One of the three bones of the middle ear.

auditory tube The tube connecting the middle ear cavity with the nasopharynx. It is also called the eustachian tube.

auricle (**or**-i-kul) A small, muscular pouch of the atria of the heart. The pinna or flap of the outer ear.

autoimmune disease A disease in which the body produces antibodies against its own cells or tissues.

autolysis (aw-**tol**-i-sis) An internal destruction of a cell by its digestive enzymes occurring spontaneously during cell death or certain pathologies.

autonomic ganglion (*aw*-toe-**nom**-ik **gang**-lee-on) A collection of cell bodies of either the sympathetic or parasympathetic nervous systems located outside of the central nervous system.

autonomic nervous system The portion of the peripheral nervous system that controls the visceral functions of the body by innervating smooth muscle, cardiac muscle, or glands.

autoregulation (*aw*-toe-*reg*-you-**lay**-shun) Local control of blood flow to a particular region in response to that region's metabolic needs.

autosome (**aw**-toe-sowm) A chromosome other than the sex (X and Y) chromosomes.

avitaminosis (ah-*vie*-tah-min-**oh**-sis) A vitamin deficiency in the diet.

axilla (ak-**sil**-ah) The armpit area of the shoulder region of the body.

axon (**ak**-son) The long, tubular extension of a neuron that transmits nerve impulses away from the cell body.

axonal terminal The end branches of the axon.

B

Babinski sign (bah-**bin**-skee) A reflex action causing extension of the great toe as a result of stimulation of sole of the foot. This is normal up to about 18 months, but beyond this age it may be indicative of abnormalities of the motor pathways from the cerebral cortex.

back The dorsal part of the trunk of the body.

Bainbridge reflex (**bane**-bridge) An increase in heart rate due to increased distension or pressure of the right atrium.

ball-and-socket joint The type of synovial joint in which the rounded head of one bone moves within a fossa or cup-shaped depression of another.

baroreceptor (*bar*-oh-re-**sep**-tor) Receptor found within certain blood vessels that are stimulated by changes in blood pressure.

basal ganglia (**bay**-sal **gang**-lee-ah) The cerebral nuclei located deep within the white matter of the cerebrum that play an important role in movement.

basal metabolic rate (BMR) The rate of metabolism measured under standard or basal conditions.

base A substance which when dissolved in water produces a pH greater than 7. Most bases yield hydroxyl ions (OH) when dissolved in water. A base is also referred to as an alkali.

basement membrane An extracellular layer of cells made up of a basal lamina and a reticular lamina.

basilar membrane (**bas**-ih-lar) A membrane located in the cochlea of the inner ear that contains the organ of Corti. The basilar membrane separates the cochlear duct from the scala tympani.

basophil (**bay**-so-fil) A type of white blood cell (leukocyte), stained by basic dyes, that is involved in allergic and inflammatory reactions.

B cell A type of white blood cell responsible for antibody-mediated immunity. When stimulated, B cells differentiate to become plasma cells that produce antibodies. B cells are also called B lymphocytes.

belly The bulge in the middle of spindle-shaped muscle. The abdomen.

benign (be-**nine**) Refers to a tumor that is not malignant.

beta cell (**bay**-tah) A cell in the islets of Langerhans of the pancreas producing insulin.

beta receptor A receptor on visceral effectors innervated by postganglionic fibers of the sympathetic nervous system.

bicuspid valve (bye-**kus**-pid) The left atrioventricular valve separating the left atrium from the left ventricle. It is also known as the mitral valve.

bilateral (bye-**lat**-er-al) Referring to the two sides of the body.

bile (byl) The greenish fluid secreted by the liver containing bile salts and bile pigments. Bile salts emulsify fats in the small intestine.

biliary calculi (**bil**-ee-a-ree **cal**-kyou-lee) Gallstones resulting from the crystallization of cholesterol found in bile.

bilirubin (*bil*-ee-**roo**-bin) A red bile pigment coloring the feces their characteristic brown color. Bilirubin is produced by the breakdown of hemoglobin in the liver.

biliverdin (*bil*-ee-**ver**-din) A green bile pigment from hemoglobin breakdown in the liver that is sometimes converted to bilirubin.

biofeedback Input from visceral tissues to the central nervous system; important in maintaining homeostasis.

bipolar neuron Neurons having one dendrite and one axon extending from their cell bodies.

bladder A membranous sac. Examples are the urinary bladder and the gallbladder.

blastocoel (**blas**-toe-seal) The cavity within a blastocyst that is filled with fluid.

blastocyst (**blas**-toe-sist) The blastula stage in the early development of the human embryo which consists of a hollow ball of cells from which a small cluster, the inner cell mass, projects into the central cavity.

blastula (**blas**-tyou-lah) A spherical structure formed by cleavage of a fertilized ovum that consists of a single cell layer surrounding a fluid-filled cavity.

blepharism (**blef**-ah-rizm) Eyelid spasms causing continuous blinking.

blind spot The area of the retina in which the optic nerve ends and which lacks photoreceptors.

blood The fluid circulating within the heart and blood vessels and which provides the main transport of substances throughout the body.

blood-brain barrier The barrier separating the blood from the brain which prevents many substances from entering the cerebrospinal fluid from the blood.

blood island Areas of mesenchyme in the mesoderm that give rise to blood vessels.

blood pressure The force exerted upon the walls of the blood vessels by the blood. A blood pressure measurement is a measure of pressure during ventricular contraction and ventricular relaxation.

blood reservoir The holding of large amounts of blood in systemic veins which can be quickly distributed to areas of need.

blood vessel A tube transporting blood in a circulatory system. The major blood vessels are the arteries, capillaries, and veins.

body cavity A space of the body containing organs.

bolus (**boe**-lus) A rounded mass of food that has been moistened for swallowing.

bone A hard type of connective tissue containing calcium salts which makes up most of the skeletal system.

bony labyrinth Cavities within the temporal bone forming the chambers of the inner ear.

Bowman's capsule The expanded cuplike end of proximal nephron surrounding the glomerulus.

bradycardia (*brad*-i-**kar**-dee-ah) A slow heart rate of less than 60 beats per minute.

brain Nervous tissue in the cranial cavity that with the spinal cord makes up the central nervous system.

brain stem The elongated part of the brain located superior to the spinal cord that contains the medulla, pons, and midbrain.

Broca's area (**broe**-kaz) A part of the premotor area of the cerebrum involved with directing the formation of words.

bronchiole (**brong**-kee-ol) A small branch of a tertiary bronchus whose terminal branches (respiratory bronchioles) divide into alveolar ducts.

bronchitis (brong-**kye**-tis) An inflammation of the bronchi.

bronchopulmonary segment (*brong*-koe-**pul**-moe-*ner*-ee) A branch of a secondary bronchus to one of the lungs and all the lung tissue it supplies.

Brunner's gland The special mucous glands of the submucosa of the duodenum. It is also called the duodenal gland.

buccal (**buk**-al) Pertaining to the mouth or the cheek area.

buffer (**buf**-er) A substance that minimizes changes in pH.

bulbourethral gland (*bul*-boe-you-**ree**-thral) One of two glands located inferior to the prostate gland of the male, secreting an alkaline solution into the urethra during sexual excitation. It is also called Cowper's gland.

bulimia (boo-**lim**-ee-ah) An eating disorder characterized by eating binges followed by self-induced vomiting or overdoses of laxatives.

bundle of His Cardiac conduction tissue connecting the atria and the ventricles. It is also called the atrioventricular bundle.

burn Injury to tissues as a result of heat, chemicals, electricity, or ultraviolet radiation.

bursa (**bur**-sah) A small sac lined with synovial membrane and filled with fluid interposed between nearby body parts that move in relation to each other.

bursitis (bur-**sye**-tis) An inflammation of the bursa.

buttocks (**but**-okz) A pair of prominences of the lower back formed by the gluteal muscles.

C

calcaneus (kal-**kay**-nee-us) The heel bone.

calcitonin (*kal*-sih-**toe**-nin) A thyroid hormone that lowers calcium and phosphate levels in the blood by stimulating calcium absorption by bone and inhibiting the breakdown of bone.

calculus (**kal**-kyou-lus) A stone of crystalline mass formed within the kidney, urinary bladder, or gallbladder.

callus (**kal**-lus) New growth of incompletely organized tissue surrounding the healing break of a bone.

calorie (**kal**-o-ree) A unit of heat that is used in the study of metabolism and is defined as the amount of heat required to raise the temperature of 1 kilogram of water 1 degree Celsius.

calyx (**kayl**-ikz) A process of the renal pelvis of the kidney. *Plural,* calyces.
canaliculus (*kan*-ah-**lik**-you-lus) A very narrow tubular channel or passage, as in those of bone that connect the lacunae. *Plural,* canaliculi.
canal of Schlemm The venous sinus of the sclera of the eye.
cancellous Spongy or latticelike, as in cancellous bone.
cancer (**kan**-ser) A malignant tumor in which cells multiply uncontrollably and invasively, infiltrating adjacent tissues and often spreading to other parts of the body. Also called carcinoma.
canine (**kay**-nine) The tooth between the incisors and the premolars of each quadrant of human dentition.
capillary (**kap**-ih-lar-ee) The smallest blood vessel that permits exchanges to take place between the blood and body tissues.
carbohydrate (*kar*-boe-**hye**-drayt) An organic compound (e.g., sugar or starch) composed of carbon, hydrogen, and oxygen in which the numbers of hydrogen and oxygen atoms are in approximately 2:1 proportion.
carbon monoxide poisoning Hypoxia resulting from the displacement of oxygen from hemoglobin as carbon monoxide takes its place.
carboxypeptidase (kar-*bok*-se-**pep**-tih-daze) A digestive enzyme that breaks the peptide bond of a terminal amino acid with a free carboxyl group.
carcinogen (kar-**sin**-o-jen) A substance that causes cancer or accelerates its development.
cardiac (**kar**-dee-ak) Pertaining to the heart.
cardiac cycle The sequence of events occurring during one complete heartbeat.
cardiac muscle One of three types of muscle. Cardiac muscle is located within the heart.
cardiac output The volume of blood pumped by one ventricle in one minute. Cardiac output averages about 5.2 l/min at rest.
cardiac reserve The greatest percentage of increase in cardiac output over normal.
cardiac tamponade (**kar**-dee-ak *tam*-pon-**aid**) A compression of the heart due to fluid within the pericardial cavity.
cardiology (kar-dee-**ol**-o-jee) The study of the heart and its pathology.
cardiopulmonary resuscitation (CPR) A technique used to restore breathing and heartbeat to a person apparently dying or unconscious.
carotid body (kah-**rot**-id) Chemoreceptors lying in the bifurcation of the left and right carotid arteries that monitor blood oxygen, carbon dioxide, and hydrogen ion levels.
carotid sinus A dilated area of the internal carotid artery near the bifurcation of the common carotid artery, containing pressoreceptors that monitor blood pressure.
carpus (**kar**-pus) The wrist or the collective name for the eight carpal bones.
cartilage (**kar**-tih-lij) A specialized fibrous connective tissue that forms most of the temporary skeleton of the embryo. It also serves as the skeletal tissue for certain regions of the body such as the external ear and the tip of the nose.
cartilaginous joint (*kar*-tih-**laj**-i-nus) An amphiarthrosis or joint cushioned by cartilage between two bones, providing for little or no movement.
castration (kas-**tray**-shun) Surgical removal of the gonads, especially the testes.
catabolism (kah-**tab**-o-lizm) The breaking-down phase of metabolism in which complex substances are broken down into simpler compounds with the release of energy.
catecholamine (*kat*-e-**kole**-ah-*mean*) A class of chemical compounds that includes the transmitter substances epinephrine, norepinephrine, and dopamine.
cation A positively charged ion.
cauda equina (**kaw**-dah ee-**kwy**-nah) A collection of roots of spinal nerves at the inferior spinal canal that resemble a horse's tail.
caudate nucleus (**kaw**-dayt) One pair of the basal ganglia.
cecum The blind sac which marks the first part of the large intestine.
cell The basic structural and functional unit of the body, consisting of a complex of organelles bounded by a cellular membrane, and usually microscopic in size.
cell body The part of a neuron, containing the nucleus, where most of the materials needed by the neuron are produced.
cell-mediated immunity The immunologic process whereby specially sensitized lymphocytes or T cells combine with antigens and destroy them. Also called cellular immunity.
cementum (se-**men**-tum) A bonelike substance forming the outer layer of the root of a tooth which attaches the root to the jaw bones.
central canal (1) The circular canal running the length of the spinal cord and located within the gray commissure. (2) The center channel of an osteon carrying blood vessels, lymphatic vessels, and nerves. The central canal of bone is also referred to as the haversian canal.
central fovea (**foe**-vee-ah) A depression of the retina within the center of the macula lutea containing only cones and providing the clearest vision.
central nervous system (CNS) The subdivision of the nervous system containing the brain and the spinal cord.
centriole (**sen**-tree-ole) One of a pair of organelles composed of microtubules that function in mitosis.
centromere (**sen**-troe-meer) A specialized region of a chromosome that unites chromatids and serves as a point of anchorage for spindle fibers in mitosis.
centrosome (**sen**-troe-sowm) A dense specialized part of condensed cytoplasm near the nucleus which contains the centrioles.
cephalic (se-**fal**-ik) Pertaining to, or directionally close to, the head.
cerebellar peduncle (*ser*-eh-**bel**-ar pe-**dung**-kul) Nerve fiber bundle connecting the cerebellum to the brain stem.
cerebellum (*ser*-eh-**bel**-um) The deeply convoluted subdivision of the brain lying beneath the cerebrum which is concerned with the coordination of muscular movements. It is part of the metencephalon.
cerebral aqueduct (**ser**-eh-bral **ak**-we-dukt) The channel running through the midbrain which connects the third and fourth ventricles. It is also called the aqueduct of Sylvius.
cerebral cortex The outer part of the cerebrum, composed of gray matter and consisting mainly of nerve cell bodies.
cerebral palsy (**pal**-zee) Nonprogressive motor disorders caused by perinatal damage to the motor areas of the brain.
cerebral peduncle One of a pair of large bundles of neurons connecting the cerebrum to the brainstem.
cerebrospinal fluid (CSF) (se-*ree*-broe-**spy**-nal) A clear fluid that circulates within the cavities of the central nervous system and within the subarachnoid space.
cerebrovascular accident (CVA) (se-*ree*-broe-**vas**-kyou-lar) Disorders of the blood vessels supplying the brain that result in damage to neural tissues of the brain. Also called a stroke.
cerebrum (se-**ree**-brum) The largest subdivision of the brain containing centers for learning, volun-

tary movement, and the interpretation of sensation.

ceruminous gland (se-**roo**-mih-nus) A type of sudiferous gland located in the external auditory meatus and secreting ear wax (cerumen).

cervical (**ser**-vih-kul) Pertaining to the neck or cervix.

cervical plexus (**plek**-sus) A network of the branches of anterior rami of cervical nerves C1–C4 which mainly supplies neck structures.

cervix (**ser**-viks) Neck or a constricted area of an organ, as in the cervix of the uterus.

chemotaxis (*kee*-moe-**tak**-sis) The attraction to a chemical stimulus, as in that of phagocytes to microbes.

chiasma (kye-**az**-mah) An X-shaped crossing, as in the optic chiasma formed by the crossing of the optic nerves.

chief cells The zymogenic cells of the stomach that produce the digestive enzyme precursor, pepsinogen.

chloride shift The diffusion of chloride ions from the plasma into red blood cells and the diffusion of bicarbonate ions from the red blood cells into the plasma.

cholecystectomy (*koe*-lee-sis-**tek**-toe-mee) The removal of the gallbladder.

cholesterol (koe-**les**-te-rol) The steroid alcohol found in animal fats that is a component of cell membranes and is used in the production of steroid hormones and bile salts.

cholinergic fiber (*koe*-lin-**er**-jik) A neuron releasing acetylcholine as its transmitter substance.

cholinesterase (*koe*-lin-**es**-ter-ayz) An enzyme breaking down acetylcholine.

chondrocyte (**kon**-droe-site) A mature cartilage cell.

chordae tendineae (**kor**-dee **ten**-di-nee) Cords connecting the cardiac papillary muscles with the atrioventricular valves.

chorion (**koe**-ree-on) The outermost membrane surrounding the fetus which forms the fetal portion of the placenta.

choroid (**koe**-royd) The black vascular coat of the eye between the sclera and the retina.

choroid plexus Specialized capillary network projecting from the pia mater into the ventricles of the brain, forming cerebrospinal fluid.

chromaffin cell (kroe-**maf**-in) Cells with an affinity for chromium salts such as those found in the adrenal medulla.

chromatid (**kroe**-mah-tid) One of a pair of sister chromosomes resulting from the replication of the parent chromosome and attached at the centromere until separation during anaphase.

chromatin (**kroe**-mah-tin) Darkly stained granular material which represents the loosely coiled, extended chromosomes during interphase.

chromosome (**kroe**-moe-sowm) One of 46 discrete rod-shaped bodies in the nucleus of a cell undergoing mitosis which contains genes composed of DNA.

chronic (**kron**-ik) Of a long duration or recurring frequently, as in a chronic disease.

chylomicron (*kie*-loe-**my**-kron) Aggregates of triglycerides, cholesterol, and phospholipids surrounded by protein that are absorbed from intestinal cells into the lacteal of a villus.

chyme (kime) The semifluid mixture of partially digested food and gastric juices.

cilia (**sil**-ee-uh) Threadlike cellular organelles that project from the surface of some cells and which by their movement can propel a stream of fluid.

ciliary body (**sil**-ee-*ar*-ee) Ring-shaped part of the vascular tunic of the eye that contains the ciliary muscle employed to change the focus of the lens. It divides the anterior from the posterior chamber.

ciliary muscle Smooth muscle of the ciliary body of the eye which functions in visual accommodation.

circle of Willis A circular anastomosis at the base of the brain.

circumcision (*ser*-kum-**sizh**-un) Removal of the prepuce (foreskin) of the penis.

circumduction (*ser*-kum-**duk**-shun) The movement of a limb in such a manner that its distal part describes a circle.

circumvallate papillae (*ser*-kum-**val**-ayt pa-**pil**-ah) Broad projections of the tongue found along its V-shaped posterior boundary.

cirrhosis (si-**roe**-sis) A chronic liver disease in which there is progressive scarring following death of groups of hepatic cells.

cisterna chyli (sis-**ter**-nah **kye**-lee) A dilated lymphatic vessel in the lumbar region of the abdominal cavity which gives rise to the thoracic duct.

cleavage The series of mitoses early in development between the zygote stage and the blastocyst.

climax The time of greatest intensity, as in sexual response or the course of a disease.

clitoris (**kli**-to-ris) A small erectile organ located at the top of the vulva which serves as the center of sexual sensation in the female. It is homologous to the male penis.

clot A semisolid mass. A blood clot results from a cascade of biochemical reactions ending in the conversion of fibrinogen into fibrin.

coccygeal plexus Branches of the anterior rami of the fourth and fifth sacral nerves and the coccygeal nerve that form a network supplying the skin in the coccygeal region.

coccyx (**kok**-six) The bone formed by the fusion of the four coccygeal vertebrae at the inferior end of the vertebral column.

cochlea (**koke**-lee-ah) The spirally shaped portion of the temporal bone which houses the membranous labyrinth employed in the sense of hearing.

coenzyme A small, nonprotein molecule which is essential for an enzyme to operate.

coitus (**koe**-i-tus) The act of copulation or sexual intercourse in which the penis is inserted into the vagina.

collagen (**kol**-a-jen) A fibrous protein found in collagen fibers that is the principal support of many connective tissues.

collateral circulation The alternate passageway for the blood in an anastomosis.

colloid A mixture in which there is suspended material of large molecular size.

colon The part of the large intestine consisting of the ascending, transverse, descending, and sigmoid sections.

color blindness An abnormal perception of one or more colors due to the absence of one or more of the photopigments in the cones.

colostomy (koe-**los**-toe-mee) Surgery in which part of the colon is attached to the abdominal wall, providing an outlet for the feces.

colostrum (koe-**los**-trum) A fluid produced by the mammary glands during the first few days after childbirth which contains protein and lactose but little fat.

coma (**koe**-mah) A profound unconsciousness from which the patient is unable to be aroused.

commissure (**kom**-i-shyour) A joining site between corresponding parts as in the eyelids or lips.

common bile duct The duct formed by the union of the common hepatic duct with the cystic duct which takes bile to the duodenum via the ampulla of Vater.

compact bone Dense skeletal tissue that has no interlacing spaces within it but has tightly joined layers, or lamellae.

complement A sequence of proteins in plasma and other body fluids activated by an antigen-antibody complex, functioning in destroying invading pathogens.
compliance The ease of distensibility of the lungs and thoracic wall when expanding.
compound In chemistry, a substance composed of two or more chemically united elements in definite proportion.
conception The process of fertilization and the subsequent establishment of pregnancy.
concha (**kong**-kah) Skull bones with a shell-like shape.
concussion (kon-**kush**-un) A violent injury or shock to the brain that may result in a temporary loss of consciousness.
condyle (**kon**-dial) A rounded projection on a bone.
cone The photoreceptors of the retina of the eye involved in color vision.
congenital (kon-**jen**-i-tal) Refers to a condition existing before or at birth.
congestive heart failure A condition in which the heart cannot meet the oxygen demands of the body.
conjunctiva (*kon*-junk-**tye**-vah) The membrane covering the eyeball and eyelids.
conjunctival sac The sac enclosing the anterior part of the eyeball that is lined with the conjunctival membrane.
conjunctivitis (kon-*junk*-tih-**vye**-tis) An inflammation of the conjunctiva.
connective tissue A diverse group of tissues that support and protect the organs of the body and hold body parts together; characterized by a large proportion of intercellular substance through which its cells are scattered.
constipation (*kon*-stih-**pay**-shun) The condition resulting from an abnormally slow movement of fecal material through the large intestine in which more water than usual is reabsorbed and the feces are hard and dry.
contraception (*kon*-trah-**sep**-shun) Prevention of conception; the prevention, by mechanical, chemical, or other means, of conception despite coitus.
contractility (*kon*-trak-**til**-ih-tee) The ability of muscle to contract or shorten.
contralateral (*kon*-trah-**lat**-er-al) Referring to the opposite side of the body or a body part.
convergence (kon-**ver**-jens) (1) Termination of a number of presynaptic neurons on one postsynaptic neuron. (2) The coordinated movement of both eyeballs medially to direct each toward a common point of fixation in order to form a single image.
convulsion (kon-**vul**-shun) A tetanic, involuntary contraction of a group of muscles that is often violent.
cornea (**kor**-nee-ah) The transparent anterior portion of the outer covering of the eyeball.
coronal plane (koe-**roe**-nal) A plane running vertical to the ground and dividing the body into anterior and posterior parts. Also called a frontal plane.
corona radiata The inner layer of follicular cells surrounding the ovum.
coronary (**kor**-o-na-ree) Pertaining to the heart.
coronary artery disease A disorder in which the cardiac muscle receives an inadequate amount of blood due to a disruption of its blood supply.
coronary sinus A large vein on the posterior side of the heart that drains smaller coronary veins and empties into the right atrium.
corpora cavernosa (**kor**-por-ah ka-ver-**noe**-sah) Two areas of erectile tissue, contributing to the body of the penis or clitoris.
corpora quadrigemina (**kor**-por-ah *kwad*-ri-**jem**-in-ah) The four bodies of the dorsal region of the mesencephalon (midbrain) involved with visual and auditory reflexes.
cor pulmonale (kor pul-mone-**ale**) A hypertrophy of the right ventricle due to disorders causing hypertension in the pulmonary circuit.
corpus albicans (**kor**-pus **al**-bi-kanz) A white scar in the ovary caused by the degeneration of the corpus luteum.
corpus callosum (kal-**loe**-sum) The largest cerebral commissure that connects the neocortex of the cerebral hemispheres.
corpus luteum (**loo**-tee-um) The yellow endocrine body that develops from the ruptured follicle after ovulation and which secretes progesterone and estrogen.
corpus spongiosum (spon-**jee**-o-sum) The spongy body or erectile tissue through which the spongy urethra of the penis passes.
corpus striatum (stry-**ay**-tum) A subcortical mass containing the white matter of the internal capsule and the caudate and lentiform nuclei of the basal ganglia; located anterior and lateral to the thalamus.
cortex (**kor**-teks) The outer portion of an organ, as in the adrenal cortex or outer part of the cerebrum.
cortisol (**kor**-ti-sol) Principal glucocorticoid secreted by the adrenal cortex.
costal cartilage (**kos**-tal **kar**-ti-lij) The hyaline cartilage forming the articulation of the first ten ribs to the sternum or each other.
covalent bond A chemical bond between atoms in which each atom contributes electrons which are shared by both.
Cowper's gland *See* Bulbourethral gland.
cranial nerves The 12 pairs of nerves emerging from the brain that transmit information directly between certain sensory receptors and the brain and between the brain and certain effectors.
craniosacral outflow (*kray*-nee-oh-**say**-kral) The preganglionic fibers of the parasympathetic nervous system which have their cell bodies either in the brainstem or the sacral spinal cord.
cranium (**kray**-nee-um) The bones of the skull case, including the frontal, parietal, temporal, occipital, ethmoid, and sphenoid bones.
creatine phosphate An intermediate energy-transfer compound occurring mainly in muscles.
cretinism (**kree**-tin-izm) A condition in which a person is dwarfed and mentally retarded due to severe deficiency of thyroid hormones during childhood.
crista (**kris**-tah) A fold of the inner membrane of the mitochondrion.
crypt of Lieberkuhn (**lee**-ber-keen) The intestinal gland opening at the muscosal surface of the small intestine and secreting digestive enzymes.
cupula (**kup**-you-lah) A gelatinous mass covering the hair cells of the crista in the inner ear.
Cushing's syndrome A condition caused by abnormally large amounts of glucocorticoids; characterized by edema, an abnormal deposition of fat to the face and trunk, and an increased susceptibility to infection.
cutaneous (kyou-**tay**-nee-us) Referring to the skin.
cyanosis (*sye*-ah-**no**-sis) A bluish or purple discoloration of the skin and mucous membranes caused by abnormally high amounts of reduced (oxygen deficient) hemoglobin in the blood.
cyclic adenosine-3,5-monophosphate (cyclic AMP) A substance that acts as a second messenger in many hormonal mechanisms.
cystic duct (**sis**-tik) The duct carrying bile from the gallbladder to the common bile duct.
cystitis (sis-**tye**-tis) An inflammation of the urinary bladder.
cytochrome (**sye**-toe-krowm) An iron-containing protein that is able to undergo reduction and oxidation.

cytokinesis (*sye*-toe-kih-**nee**-sis) The division of the cytoplasm.
cytology (sye-**tol**-o-jee) The study of cells.
cytoplasm (**sye**-toe-plazm) The protoplasm or living substance of a cell other than its nucleus.

D

dead space Those parts of the respiratory tract that hold air but do not function in gas exchange.
deafness Partial or complete inability to hear.
deamination The removal of an amino group from an amino acid.
decibel (**des**-i-bel) A unit of measurement of sound intensity.
deciduous teeth (dee-**sid**-you-us) The primary teeth or the first set of human dentition. Also called the milk or baby teeth.
decompression sickness A condition resulting from undergoing a reduction in environmental pressure so quickly that nitrogen in the blood comes out of solution and bubbles, forming air emboli which occlude blood vessels. The symptoms include joint pain and neurological imbalances. Also called bends or caisson disease.
decubitus ulcer (dee-**kyou**-bi-tus) The destruction of tissue due to a continuous deficiency of blood flow to tissues overlying a hard structure, such as bone, and compressed against a hard object, such as a bed or cast. Also known as bedsore and pressure sore.
deep Toward the interior or away from the periphery of the body.
deep fascia The connective tissue sheet surrounding a muscle and serving to hold it in place.
defecation (def-e-**kay**-shun) Elimination of waste material from the digestive tract by way of the anus.
defibrillation (dee-*fib*-rih-**lay**-shun) Stimulating with a strong electrical current in order to stop ventricular fibrillation.
deglutition (deg-lue-**tish**-un) The process of swallowing.
dehydration (*dee*-hi-**dray**-shun) The condition due to excessive water loss from the body or its parts.
dehydration synthesis A chemical reaction that proceeds with the chemical removal of water.
delta cell An endocrine cell of the pancreas producing somatostatin.
dendrite (**den**-dryt) A short branch of a neuron that receives nerve impulses and conducts them to the cell body.
dental caries (**ka**-reez) Tooth decay or a gradual demineralization of the layers of the tooth.
dentin (**den**-tin) The osseous layer forming the body of the tooth which lies under the enamel and cementum and encloses the pulp.
deoxyribonucleic acid (DNA) (dee-*ok*-see-*ri*-boe-nyoo-**klee**-ik) A nucleic acid forming a double helix made up of nucleotides containing deoxyribose, a phosphate group, and one of four bases (cytosine, guanine, adenine, or thymine).
depolarization (dee-*poe*-lar-i-**zay**-shun) Decreasing the electrical voltage across a plasma membrane or neutralizing its polarity.
dermis (**der**-mis) The thick layer of skin composed of irregular dense connective tissue that is located beneath the epidermis.
descending colon The section of the large intestine located between the left colic flexure and sigmoid colon.
desmosome A type of cell junction characterized by a disc-shaped structure formed by a dense network of microfilaments extending out from the cytoplasm of adjacent cells.
detrusor muscle (de-**troo**-ser) A muscle of several layers located in the walls of the urinary bladder.
dextrin (**dek**-strin) A small polysaccharide containing several glucose molecules.
diabetes insipidus (*dye*-ah-**bee**-teez in-**sip**-i-dus) A disease resulting from insufficiency of antidiuretic hormone (ADH) and characterized by the production of large volumes of urine.
diabetes mellitus (**mel**-ih-tus) A disease resulting from insulin deficiency in which there is an excessive amount of glucose in the blood and an excessive volume of urine is produced.
dialysis (dye-**al**-ih-sis) The diffusion of solutes through a selectively permeable membrane, resulting in separation of solutes.
diapedesis (*dye*-ah-peh-**dee**-sis) An outward movement of white blood cells through blood vessel walls.
diaphragm (**dye**-ah-fram) The muscle separating the thoracic cavity from the abdominal cavity. It functions in breathing.
diaphysis (dye-**af**-ih-sis) The shaft of a long bone.
diarrhea (*dye*-ah-**ree**-ah) The condition resulting from a faster than normal movement of fecal material through the large intestine with less water than normal being absorbed. Elimination is frequent and the feces are very watery.
diarthroses (*dye*-ar-**throe**-seez) Joint articulations in which the bones are freely movable. Also called synovial joints.
diastole (dye-**as**-toe-lee) The time during the cardiac cycle in which the ventricles are relaxing.
diencephalon (*dye*-en-**sef**-a-lon) The part of the prosencephalon (forebrain) of the brain that primarily consists of the thalamus and the hypothalamus.
diffusion (dif-**you**-zhun) The net movement of solvent or solute molecules from a higher concentration to a lower concentration, resulting in the tendency of a molecular mixture to attain a uniform composition throughout.
digestion (di-**jes**-chun) The process of mechanical or chemical breaking-down of food into molecules small enough to be absorbed.
digestive system The digestive tract and the accessory digestive structures.
diploid number (**dip**-loyd) The full number of chromosomes normal for each body cell. In humans the diploid number is 46.
diplopia (di-**ploe**-pee-ah) State of double vision.
distal (**dis**-tal) Farther from the midline or point of attachment to the trunk.
diuretic (dye-you-**ret**-ik) A substance that inhibits the reabsorption of water and thus increases urine output.
divergence (di-**ver**-jens) Having the axonal terminals of one presynaptic neuron end on several postsynaptic neurons.
diverticulitis (*dye*-ver-tik-you-**lye**-tis) Inflammation of diverticula of the colon.
diverticulum (*dye*-ver-**tik**-you-lum) A pouch or sac in the wall of an organ or a passageway, as seen in the colon.
dominant gene A gene that is expressed when present in a heterozygous state.
dorsiflexion (*dor*-si-**flek**-shun) The flexion of the foot.
Down's syndrome A congenital disorder, involving an extra copy of chromosome 21, characterized by some degree of mental retardation and some physical malformations.
duct of Santorini *See* Accessory duct.
duct of Wirsung The major pancreatic duct that joins the common bile duct and delivers pancreatic juice into the duodenum through the ampulla of Vater. It is also called the pancreatic duct.
ductus arteriosus (**duk**-tus ar-*tee*-ree-**o**-sus) A fetal bypass vessel connecting the pulmonary artery to the aorta.

ductus deferens (**def**-er-ens) The tube transporting sperm from the epididymis to the ejaculatory duct. It is also known as the vas deferens or seminal duct.
ductus epididymis (*ep*-ih-**did**-ih-mis) The coiled tube within the epididymis in which the spermatozoa mature.
ductus venosus (ve-**no**-sus) The liver bypass vessel of the fetus.
duodenal gland (*doo*-o-**dee**-nal) *See* Brunner's gland.
duodenum (*doo*-o-**dee**-num) The first portion of the small intestine.
dura mater (**dyoo**-ra **may**-ter) The outer meninx of the central nervous system.
dynamic equilibrium Balance of the body, especially the head, in response to sudden actions such as acceleration, deceleration, and rotation.
dyslexia (dis-**lek**-see-ah) An inability or difficulty in reading, spelling, and writing words.
dysmenorrhea (*dis*-men-o-**ree**-ah) A painful menstruation.
dyspnea (**disp**-nee-ah) Diffucult or labored breathing.

E

ectoderm The outermost germ layer, which gives rise to the nervous system and skin epidermis.
ectopic (ek-**top**-ik) Other than in the normal location.
eczema (**ek**-ze-mah) A skin rash or superficial inflammation of the epidermis.
edema (e-**dee**-mah) An abnormal accumulation of fluid in the tissues.
effector A muscle or gland that contracts or secretes in direct response to nerve stimulation.
efferent (**ef**-er-ent) Carrying or conducting away from a structure.
efferent arteriole The blood vessel taking blood from the glomerulus to the peritubular capillary.
efferent duct One of a series of tubes carrying sperm from the rete testis to the epididymis.
efferent neuron A neuron carrying nerve impulses away from the central nervous system and toward an effector. It is also called a motor neuron.
ejaculation (e-*jak*-yoo-**lay**-shun) The reflex expulsion of semen from the penis.
ejaculatory duct (e-**jak**-yoo-lah-*toe*-ree) The tube transporting sperm from the vas deferens to the prostatic urethra.
electrocardiogram (ECG or EKG) (e-*lek*-troe-**kar**-dee-o-gram) A graphic recording of the electrical changes occurring during the cardiac cycle.
electroencephalogram (EEG) (e-*lek*-troe-en-**sef**-ah-loe-gram) A graphic recording of the electrical changes associated with the activity of the cerebral cortex.
electrolyte (ee-**lek**-troe-lite) A compound that dissociates into ions when dissolved in water.
electron A negatively charged subatomic particle located at some distance from the atomic nucleus.
electron transport system A series of chemical reactions during which hydrogens or their electrons are passed from one acceptor molecule to another, with the release of energy.
element Any one of the more than 100 pure chemical substances which in combination make up chemical compounds.
elimination The ejection of waste products, especially undigested food remnants from the digestive tract.
embolism (**em**-boe-lizm) The occlusion of a blood vessel by foreign matter, causing various syndromes.
embolus (**em**-boe-lus) A circulating fragment of foreign matter in the blood, such as a blood clot, foreign object, cancer cell, or tissue.
embryo (**em**-bree-o) The developing human organism until the end of the second month.
embryology (*em*-bree-**ol**-o-jee) The study of the development from the fertilized egg to the termination of the eighth week.
emesis (**em**-e-sis) Vomiting.
emmetropia (*em*-eh-**troe**-pee-ah) In vision, the normal or ideal optical condition.
emphysema (*em*-fih-**see**-mah) A disease in which air accumulates in the respiratory passageways, due to decreased alveolar elasticity.
emulsification (ee-*mul*-si-fi-**kay**-shun) The breaking down of large fat droplets into smaller ones.
enamel (e-**nam**-el) The osseous outer covering of the crown of the tooth.
end-diastolic volume (EDV) (*dye*-ah-**stol**-ik) The volume of blood flowing into a ventricle during diastole.
endocardium (en-doe-**kar**-dee-um) The inner layer of the heart wall, consisting of an endothelial lining resting upon connective tissue.
endochondral ossification (*en*-doe-**kon**-dral *os*-ih-fi-**kay**-shun) Cartilage replacement by bone. It is also referred to as intracartilaginous ossification.
endocrine gland (**en**-doe-krin) A ductless gland that secretes hormones.
endocrinology (*en*-doe-kri-**nol**-o-jee) The study of the endocrine glands and their hormones.
endocytosis (*en*-doe-sye-**toe**-sis) The process in which a cell encloses large molecules or particles into its structure by surrounding the substance with a part of the plasma membrane.
endoderm The innermost germ layer that gives rise to the GI tract, respiratory tract, and the urinary bladder and urethra.
endogenous (en-**doj**-e-nus) Produced within the body or due to internal causes.
endolymph (**en**-doe-*lymf*) The fluid of the membranous labyrinth of the ear.
endometrium (*en*-doe-**mee**-tree-um) The inner mucous membrane lining of the uterus.
endomysium (*en*-doe-**meez**-ee-um) The connective tissue covering each muscle cell.
endoneurium (*en*-doe-**nyoo**-ree-um) The connective tissue covering a neuron.
endoplasmic reticulum (*en*-doe-**plaz**-mik re-**tik**-yoo-lum) An intracellular system of membranes continuous with the plasma membrane and functioning in transporting material through the cell, storage, synthesis, and packaging.
endorphin (en-**dor**-fin) A peptide in the central nervous system that affects pain perception and other aspects of behavior.
endosteum (en-**dos**-tee-um) The thin layer of connective tissue lining the marrow cavity of a bone.
endothelium (*en*-doe-**thee**-lee-um) The simple epithelial tissue that lines the cavities of the heart and of the blood and lymphatic vessels.
end-systolic volume (ESV) (sis-**to**-lik) The volume of blood that remains in the ventricle after systole.
enkephalin (en-**kef**-ah-lin) A peptide of the nervous system that affects pain perception.
enteroendocrine cell (*en*-ter-o-**en**-doe-krin) A stomach cell producing the hormone gastric gastrin.
enterogastric reflex (*en*-teh-roe-**gas**-trik) An inhibitory reflex decreasing gastric secretion in response to food in the small intestine.
enuresis (*en*-yoo-**ree**-sis) The involuntary expulsion of urine after the age of three.
enzyme (**en**-zime) An organic catalyst, usually a protein, that promotes or regulates a biochemical reaction.
eosinophil (*ee*-o-**sin**-o-fil) A type of white blood cell with a granular cytoplasm.

ependyma (eh-**pen**-dih-mah) Glial cells lining the ventricles of the brain and helping in cerebrospinal fluid flow.

epidermis (*ep*-i-**derm**-is) The outermost layer of the skin including dead cells of the stratum corneum and the living sublayers of cells that give rise to them.

epididymis (*ep*-i-**did**-i-mis) A coiled tube that receives sperm from the testes and conveys it to the vas deferens.

epidural space (*ep*-ih-**doo**-ral) Space between the wall of the vertebral canal and the dura mater surrounding the spinal cord; contains venous plexus and loose connective tissue.

epiglottis (*ep*-ih-**glot**-is) Cartilage guarding the superior opening into the larynx.

epilepsy (**ep**-ih-*lep*-see) Neurological condition in which the affected individual suffers periodically from short sensory, motor, or psychological disturbances.

epimysium (*ep*-ih-**miz**-ee-um) The fibrous connective tissue which envelops muscles.

epinephrine (*ep*-ih-**nef**-rin) Hormone secreted by the adrenal medulla. Its actions are similar to those produced by stimulation of the sympathetic nervous system. Also known as adrenaline.

epineurium (*ep*-ih-**nyoo**-ree-um) Outermost connective tissue covering that surrounds a peripheral nerve.

epiphyseal plate (*ep*-ih-**feez**-eal) Cartilage plate separating the epiphysis from the diaphysis in growing long bones.

epiphysis (eh-**pif**-ih-sis) One end of a long bone. The two epiphyses are connected by the shaft or diaphysis.

episiotomy (eh-*peez*-ee-**ot**-oe-me) Surgical incision in the perineal region that facilitates expulsion of the baby during delivery.

epistaxis (*ep*-ih-**stax**-sis) Nosebleed; hemorrhage from rupture of vessels in the nasal mucous membrane.

epithelial tissue (*ep*-ih-**thee**-lee-uhl) Tissue of which glands and the external layer of the skin are formed. This tissue also lines the hollow organs, blood vessels, and the orifices leading to the surface of the body. Epithelial tissue is classified according to the number of cell layers present and the shape of the superficial cells.

epitheliitis (*ep*-ih-*thee*-lee-**eye**-tis) Inflammation of epithelium.

eponychium (*ep*-oh-**nik**-ee-um) The narrow portion of the stratum corneum located at the proximal part of the nail extending from the border of the nail wall. Also termed the cuticle.

erection (ee-**rek**-shun) Engorgement of the spongy erectile tissue of the penis or clitoris, resulting in enlargement and stiffening of the organ.

erythema (*er*-ih-**thee**-muh) Redness of the skin, typically resulting from engorgement of the underlying capillaries.

erythrocyte (eh-**rith**-roe-site) A red blood cell.

erythrocythemia (eh-*rith*-roe-sigh-**thee**-me-ah) An increased number of erythrocytes in the blood.

erythropenia (eh-*rith*-roe-**pee**-nee-ah) Decrease in the number of erythrocytes.

erythropoiesis (eh-*rith*-roe-poy-**ee**-sis) The formation of red blood cells or erythrocytes.

erythropoietin (eh-*rith*-roe-**poy**-ih-tin) Hormone that stimulates erythropoiesis or red blood cell formation. Formed from a protein in the blood plasma.

esophagus (eh-**sof**-ah-gus) A portion of the digestive tract, consisting of a hollow muscular tube that interconnects the pharynx and the stomach.

essential amino acids Amino acids that cannot be synthesized by the body in appropriate amounts and therefore need to be acquired through one's diet. There are ten essential amino acids.

estradiol (*es*-trah-**die**-ol) Most potent of the naturally occurring estrogens in humans.

estrogens (**es**-trow-jens) Female sex hormones produced by the ovaries. Function in the development and maintenance of the female reproductive organs as well as secondary sex characteristics. Estrogens also play roles in protein anabolism and in fluid and electrolyte balance. Also produced by the testes in the male.

ethmoid air cells (**eth**-moid) Air cells located within the substance of the ethmoid bone and comprising one group of the paranasal sinuses.

eumenorrhea (*yoo*-men-oh-**ree**-ah) A normal menstruation.

euphoria (yoo-**foe**-ree-ah) Abnormal or exaggerated sense of well being.

eustachian tube (yoo-**stay**-key-an) Tube connecting the middle ear with the pharynx. Also called the auditory tube.

euthanasia (*yoo*-thah-**na**-zhe-ah) The deliberate termination of a life in a painless manner so as to end suffering, as in the case of an incurable disease. Also called mercy killing.

evagination (eh-*vaj*-ih-**nay**-shun) An outpocketing of a layer or portion of a structure.

eversion (eh-**ver**-zhun) Elevation of the lateral border of the foot such that the sole of the foot is directed laterally.

excitability The property of muscle tissue to receive and respond to stimuli. The property of neurons to respond to a stimulus and convert it to an electrochemical impulse.

excitatory postsynaptic potential (EPSP) A localized decrease in negative potential on the postsynaptic membrane that follows stimulation by a presynaptic terminal.

excretion (eks-**kree**-shun) Elimination of waste products from individual cells, tissues, or the body as a whole.

exocrine gland (**ek**-so-krin) A type of gland that secretes its products by way of ducts that open onto lining or covering epithelium. Such ducts may open onto any free surface. Opposite of endocrine.

exocytosis (*eks*-oh-sigh-**toe**-sis) Cellular release of products too large to pass directly through the plasma membrane. Products are incorporated into membranous vesicles which in turn fuse with the plasma membrane as they are released from the cell.

exogenous (eks-**oj**-en-us) Having an origin outside of the body.

expiration (*eks*-pih-ray-shun) The process of moving air from the lungs into the atmosphere. Also called exhalation.

expiratory capacity The sum of the tidal volume and the expiratory reserve volume.

expiratory neurons Neurons located within the respiratory center of the medulla oblongata. They are thought to be inactive during normal quiet respiration.

expiratory reserve volume The amount of air that can be expired beyond a normal tidal expiration. Normally this is approximately 1200 milliliters.

extension An angular form of movement resulting in an increase in the angle between adjoining bones; the opposite of flexion.

external auditory canal or meatus (me-**ay**-tus) Passageway composed of cartilage and bone and leading from the exterior to the eardrum or tympanic membrane.

external ear Outer portion of the ear composed of the pinna, external auditory canal, and eardrum or tympanic membrane.

external respiration Exchange of respiratory gases that occurs between the lungs and the blood.

exteroceptor (*eks*-ter-oh-**sep**-tor) Receptor specialized for receiving stimuli from the external environment.

extracellular (*eks*-trah-**sell**-yoo-lar) Outside of a cell.
extracellular fluid (ECF) Fluid, such as plasma and interstitial fluid, that is located outside of the body's cells.
extraembryonic coelom (**see**-lom) Cavity that ultimately develops within the extraembryonic mesoderm.
extraembryonic mesoderm Layer of loosely arranged cells derived from the trophoblast; surrounds the amnion and primary yolk sac.
extravasation (eks-*trav*-ah-**say**-shun) Movement of fluid such as blood, serum, or lymph, from a vessel into the surrounding tissues.
extrinsic (eks-**trin**-sik) Having an external origin, arising from outside of the body.
exudate (**eks**-yoo-date) Fluid that issues forth from a wound, for example, and which may be composed of cellular debris, serum, and pus.
eyeball The ball-shaped part or globe of the eye.
eyebrow Ridge of skin located along the superior orbital margin and characterized by the presence of numerous hairs.
eyelids The two movable tissue folds protecting the anterior aspect of the eyeball.

F

face Anterior region of the head.
facet (**fas**-et) Small planar surface on a bone serving as an articular surface for another bone.
facilitated diffusion Utilization of a carrier substance in the transport of a nonlipid-soluble substance across a selectively permeable membrane.
facilitation (fah-*sil*-ih-**tay**-shun) Partial depolarization of the plasma membrane of a neuron brought about by subliminal stimulation. A subsequent subliminal stimulus can then bring about depolarization to the threshold level, thereby initiating a nerve impulse.
falciform ligament (**fal**-sih-form) A sickle-shaped fold of parietal peritoneum extending between the umbilicus and the two lobes of the liver. Contains the remnant of the umbilical vein in its free edge.
fallopian tube (fal-**low**-pee-an) Also called uterine tube. Passageway through which either the zygote or secondary oocyte reaches the uterine cavity.
falx cerebelli (falks *ser*-eh-**bell**-eye) Triangular projection of the dura mater between the two hemispheres of the cerebellum in the posterior cranial fossa.
falx cerebri (falks **ser**-ee-brye) Fold of dura mater projecting downward into the fissure between the two cerebral hemispheres. Contains the superior sagittal venous sinus.
familial hypercholesterolemia (*hi*-per-ko-*les*-ter-ol-**ee**-me-ah) Inherited condition in which excess cholesterol occurs typically in the form of LDL.
fascia (**fash**-ee-ah) Fibrous tissue forming the investing layer for muscles and various organs of the body.
fascicle (**fas**-ih-kul) A small grouping of nerve or muscle fibers surrounded by a connective tissue envelope.
fat Adipose tissue. Normally existing as a liquid at body temperature. Composed of fatty acids esterified to a glycerol backbone.
febrile (**feb**-rile) Pertaining to a fever or characterized by the presence of a fever.
feces (**fee**-seez) Bodily waste excreted from the anus.
feedback Mechanism by which a form of output is utilized as input in order to exert some degree of control over a specific process. Classified as positive and negative feedback. Such mechanisms are used by most of the body's systems in an attempt to maintain homeostasis.
fenestrated (**fen**-es-*tray*-ted) Characterized by the presence of one or more openings.
ferritin (**fer**-ih-tin) One of the principal forms in which iron is stored in the body, particularly in the liver.
fertility (fer-**till**-ih-tee) Having the capability to conceive or to induce conception.
fertilization Union of a secondary oocyte and sperm to form a single-cell entity called a zygote.
fetal alcohol syndrome A condition affecting the newborn that results from the ingestion of alcohol during pregnancy. Occurs in nearly 1 of every 1000 newborns and is characterized by growth retardation, head and facial abnormalities, cardiac and limb defects, mental retardation, and behavioral disorders.
fetal circulation Cardiovascular system of the fetus. Includes the placenta and specialized vascular shunts, such as the ductus arteriosus, ductus venosus, and foramen ovale, for diverting blood in the developing individual.
fetus (**fee**-tus) During intrauterine life, the term applied to the new individual starting at the end of the embryonic period; that is, at the end of the eighth week of gestation.
fever (**fee**-vur) Condition in which the body temperature is elevated above normal. Normal body temperature is 37°C or 98.6°F.
fibrillation (fih-brih-**lay**-shun) Contraction of cardiac muscle at an extremely high rate and in an uncoordinated fashion. Little or no blood is actually pumped by the heart.
fibrin (**fye**-brin) The protein formed by the action of thrombin on fibrinogen during normal clotting of blood.
fibrinogen (fye-**brin**-oh-jin) Plasma protein converted to fibrin when acted upon by thrombin. Also called Factor I.
fibroblast (**fye**-bro-blast) A large cell common to connective tissue that produces the fibers of the connective tissue.
fibrocartilage A specific type of cartilage containing numerous collagen fibers in its amorphous matrix. Its characteristics are intermediate between those of hyaline cartilage and dense ordinary connective tissue.
fibrocystic breast disease Development of benign cysts within the breast. Most common disease of the breast, occurring in nearly 20% of postmenopausal women.
fibrocyte (fye-**brow**-site) Fibroblast that has undergone maturational processes to the point where it no longer produces the fibers of the connective tissue matrix.
fibrosis (**fye**-bro-sis) Abnormal condition or development of fibrous connective tissue.
fibrous joint A type of joint that permits little or no movement. Examples include sutures, gomphoses, and syndesmoses.
fibrous skeleton of heart Connective tissue network separating the atrial syncytium from the ventricular syncytium. Provides attachment for cardiac muscle and lends support to the AV valves.
filiform papillae (**fil**-ih-form pa-**pil**-ee) Threadlike structures located on the surface of the anterior two-thirds of the tongue. They do not contain taste buds.
filtration (fil-**tray**-shun) Movement of a liquid through a membrane that serves as a filter.
filum terminale (**fye**-lum ter-mih-**nah**-lee) Fibrous connective tissue covering of the spinal cord lying within the vertebral canal and extending from the level of the conus medullaris to the coccyx.

fimbriae (**fim**-bree-ee) Finger-like extensions of the infundibulum of the uterine tube.

finger Any one of the five digits of the hand.

fissure (**fish**-yoor) Structure characterized as a groove or slit between two adjacent structures. Fissures may be either normal or abnormal in their occurrence. For example, the longitudinal fissure partially separates the two cerebral hemispheres.

fistula (**fiss**-chew-lah) An abnormal passageway that occurs between two cavities or between an organ cavity and the external surface of the body.

fixator (**fick**-say-tor) A muscle that by its action tends to fix a body part in position or to limit its range of motion.

flaccid paralysis (flak-sid) Complete loss of muscle tone in affected muscles following a severe spinal cord injury.

flagellum (fla-**jel**-um) A whiplike cellular organelle utilized in movement, e.g., by sperm cells.

flatfoot Condition in which one or more of the arches of the foot have weakened and become flat. Also called pes planus.

flatulence (**flat**-yoo-lence) Presence of an excessive amount of gas within the stomach and/or intestines.

flexion An angular form of movement that reduces the angle between the adjoining bones.

fluoroscope (**floor**-oh-skope) Instrument utilizing x-rays for internal observation of the body.

follicle-stimulating hormone (FSH) Hormone that is secreted by the anterior lobe of the pituitary gland. Its action stimulates development of the ovarian follicles in the female and spermatogenesis in the male. It also stimulates the ovarian follicles to produce and secrete estrogens.

fontanelle (fon-tah-**nell**) A gap or interval between adjacent bones that is typically covered by membranous tissue until the bones have completed their growth. Examples include the anterior and posterior fontanelles of the fetal skull.

foot The most distal portion of the lower limb.

foramen (foe-**ray**-men) A perforation or opening, especially within a bone. Examples include the foramen rotundum, the foramen spinosum, and the infraorbital foramen. Plural is foramina.

foramen ovale (o-**va**-lee) Opening between the right and left atria of the fetal heart. Serves as a fetal shunt to bypass the nonfunctioning fetal lungs; normally closes at birth.

forearm (**four**-arm) The region of the upper limb located between the elbow proximally and the wrist distally.

foreskin The prepuce of the penis, which is removed during the process of circumcision.

fornix (**four**-niks) Circumferential recess of the uterine cervix where it projects into the vaginal cavity; an association tract of the brain interconnecting the mammillary bodies and the hippocampus; an arched or folded structure.

fossa (**foes**-ah) A depression or hollow located below the surface level of a structure or part of structure. For example, the fossa ovalis of the heart and the subscapular fossa. Plural is fossae.

fossa ovalis (oh-**val**-us) Depression on interatrial wall of the right atrium, representing the location of the foramen ovale in the fetus.

fourth ventricle (**ven**-trih-kul) Broad, shallow cavity of the hindbrain which extends inferiorly to the medulla and superiorly to the cerebral aqueduct of the midbrain.

fovea centralis (**foe**-vee-ah) The location of the sharpest photopic vision within the retina. Situated in the center of the macula lutea.

fracture (**frack**-chur) Clinical term for a broken bone. Fractures may be classified as complete, incomplete, simple, compound, comminuted, or pathologic.

fraternal twins Offspring resulting from the release and fertilization of two separate ova at conception.

frontal plane Plane of section directed perpendicular to the midsagittal plane of the body and dividing the body into anterior and posterior parts. Also called a coronal plane or section.

functional residual volume Collective term for the sum of the residual and expiratory reserve volumes. Ordinarily this volume is approximately 2400 ml.

fundus (**fun**-dus) In a hollow organ, or viscus, that part which is located farthest from its opening or exit. Examples include the fundus of the stomach and the fundus of the uterus.

fungiform papillae (**fun**-jeh-form pa-**pil**-ee) Mushroom-shaped structures seen as red dots on the upper surface of the tongue. The majority of these structures are characterized by the presence of taste buds.

funiculus (fuh-**nik**-yoo-lus) Generalized term for a cordlike structure; one of the columns of white matter located within the spinal cord and consisting of ascending and descending tracts.

fusiform (**few**-zih-form) Convergent arrangement of muscle fibers giving rise to a muscle with a round or spindle-like shape.

G

gallbladder Small, pouchlike organ located on the visceral aspect of the liver. It serves to store bile. The cystic duct conveys bile to and from this organ.

gallstone A stonelike formation, usually composed of cholesterol, that develops in the gallbladder or bile duct.

gamete (**gam**-eet) A sperm or ovum.

gametogenesis (*gam*-ee-toe-**jen**-ih-sis) Biological process responsible for the formation of the eggs and sperm.

gamma globulins A group of plasma proteins that serve as antibodies or substances providing immunity against disease.

ganglion (**gang**-lee-on) A group of nerve-cell bodies usually located outside of the central nervous system.

gangliosidoses (*gang*-lee-oh-sigh-**doe**-seez) A family of genetic disorders involving the abnormal intracellular accumulation of sphingolipids. An example is Tay-Sachs disease resulting from a deficiency of the enzyme hexosaminidase A.

gap junctions Specialized cell junctions as seen, for example, in smooth muscle cells. These offer little resistance to impulses traveling between cells. Also called nexuses.

gastric glands (**gas**-trik) Tiny glands located within the wall of the stomach that secrete gastric juice.

gastric inhibitory peptide (GIP) Hormone secreted by the mucosa of the duodenum inhibiting motor activity of the stomach. Its action slows stomach emptying when the duodenum is filled with chyme.

gastrin Hormone released by the stomach mucosa in response to stretching or the presence of substances such as caffeine and partially digested proteins. Its action stimulates the release of gastric juice from the gastric glands.

gastritis (gas-**try**-tis) Infammation of the stomach.

gastrointestinal tract That portion of the digestive tract located inferior to the diaphragm. Also called the GI tract.

gastrulation (*gas-troo*-**lay**-shun) Process by which the two-layered embryonic disc is converted to a three-layered disc. This conversion occurs during the third week of intrauterine development.

gene That portion of a chromosome that contains the biological information for a specific trait. The gene represents the biological unit of heredity.

genetics (jeh-**net**-iks) The branch of biology that is concerned with the study of heredity.

genital herpes Increasingly common infectious disorder of the genital structures caused by herpes simplex virus type 1. Initially tiny painful blisters appear and may be replaced by ulcers at a later time. There is no cure for genital herpes and in some patients it recurs periodically for many years.

genitalia (*jen*-ih-**tal**-ee-ah) The reproductive organs of the male and female.

genotype (**jen**-oh-type) The genetic constitution of an individual.

geriatrics (*jer*-ee-**at**-riks) Specialty in medicine that focuses on the medical and social problems of the aged.

germinal center Centrally located mass of immature lymphocytes within a lymph nodule. It is here that new lymphocytes proliferate from stem cells that originate in the bone marrow.

germ layers Primary embryonic tissue layers composed of the ectoderm, mesoderm, and endoderm.

gigantism Clinical condition occurring when the anterior pituitary secretes excessive amounts of growth hormone during childhood.

gingiva (**jin**-jih-vah) The mucosal lining of the alveolar processes. Also called the gums.

gingivitis (*jin*-jih-**vye**-tis) Inflammation of the gingivae or gums.

ginglymus joint (**jin**-glih-mus) A type of synovial joint; also known as a hinge joint. An example is the ankle or talocrural joint.

gland A cell, tissue, or organ that discharges a substance used by or eliminated from the body.

glaucoma (glaw-**koe**-mah) One of several diseases produced by excessive intraocular pressure.

glial cells Non-neuronal cellular elements of nervous tissue. They provide physical and functional support to adjacent neurons.

gliding joint Type of synovial joint in which the participating bones possess rather flat surfaces for the purpose of articulation. Examples include the intermetatarsal joints. Also referred to as a plane joint.

globulin A class of proteins; one of the plasma protein fractions.

glomerulonephritis (glo-*mer*-yoo-low-neh-**fry**-tis) Inflammation of the glomeruler capillary loops.

glomerulus (glo-**mer**-yoo-lus) The tuft of capillaries located within Bowman's capsule of the kidney tubule. Also applies to any spherical mass of blood vessels or nerves.

glossitis (glos-**sigh**-tis) Inflammation of the tongue.

glottis (**glot**-iss) The two vocal folds located immediately superior to the vocal cords.

glucagon (**gloo**-kuh-gon) Hormone released by the islets of Langerhans of the pancreas. Its action elevates the level of blood sugar.

glucocorticoid hormones (*gloo*-koe-**kor**-tih-koyd) Class of hormones secreted by the adrenal cortex that affects glucose metabolism; the principal glucocorticoid is called cortisol.

gluconeogenesis (*gloo*-koe-*nee*-oh-**jen**-ih-sis) Formation of glucose by the liver from noncarbohydrate precursors.

glucose (**gloo**-kose) Monosaccharide occurring in blood plasma; it serves as the principal cellular fuel of the body.

glucosuria (*gloo*-koe-**soo**-ree-uh) Condition characterized by the presence of glucose in the urine.

glycogen (**gly**-ko-jen) Polysaccharide carbohydrate resembling starch occurring in many tissues, particularly the liver and skeletal muscles.

glycogenesis (*gly*-koe-**jen**-ih-sis) The process of synthesizing glycogen from glucose.

glycogenolysis (*gly*-koe-jeh-**nol**-ih-sis) The process of breaking down glycogen to liberate glucose.

glycolysis (gly-**kol**-ih-sis) Process of conversion of carbohydrate (usually glucose) to pyruvic acid or lactic acid with release of energy.

glycoprotein (*gly*-koe-**pro**-teen) A member of a class of conjugated proteins composed of protein with an attached carbohydrate group.

glycosaminoglycans (*gly*-ko-sah-me-no-**gly**-kans) Macromolecules present within the ground substance of bone and cartilage. Examples include hyaluronic acid, chondroitin sulfate, and keratin sulfate.

goiter Any abnormal enlargement of the thyroid gland. Such a condition may be associated with either hyposecretion or hypersecretion of thyroid hormone. Endemic goiter is caused by dietary iodine deficiency.

Golgi complex (**goal**-jee) A specialized cellular organelle composed of a set of cytoplasmic membranes associated with cellular secretion and the production of lysosomes. Also called Golgi apparatus.

Golgi tendon organ Sensory receptor that responds to the stretching of a tendon by initiating an inhibitory signal called the inverse stretch reflex, and which results in relaxation of the muscle.

gomphosis (gom-**foe**-sis) A specific type of fibrous joint such as that occurring between a tooth and either the maxilla or mandible.

gonad (**go**-nad) Generalized term for ovary or testis; an organ that produces gametes.

gonadotropic hormone (*gon*-ad-oh-**trow**-pik) Hormone involved in the regulation of gonadal function.

gonorrhea (*gon*-oh-**ree**-ah) Sexually transmitted infectious disease characterized by painful expulsion of the urine, pus discharge, and inflammation of the urogenital mucosa. The causative organism is the bacterium Neisseria gonorrhoeae.

gout (gowt) A hereditary disease, most frequently affecting men, in which the blood uric acid level is abnormally elevated. Crystalline sodium urate is deposited in various connective tissues and articular cartilages; gout may lead to chronic arthritis.

graafian follicle A mature ovarian follicle. Normally only one follicle matures each month in the human female. Those in which the maturation process is terminated early deteriorate and are known as atretic follicles.

graft rejection An effective immune response launched against a graft when the host's immune system regards the graft as being foreign.

granulosa cells (*gran*-yoo-**low**-sah) Cluster of cells that surround each oogonia. Collectively the ovum and its granulosa cells constitute a follicle.

Graves' disease A condition of hyperthyroidism in which the thyroid gland increases in both size and activity. It is thought to be an autoimmune disorder. The autoantibodies exhibit a function similar to that of TSH, i.e., they bind to the TSH receptors and produce long-acting stimulation of the thyroid gland.

gray matter Those portions of the central nervous system consisting of large masses of cell bodies, dendrites of association and efferent neurons, and unmyelinated axons.

gray ramus communicans (**ray**-mus ko-**myoo**-nih-kans) Short nerve trunk connecting the sympathetic chain with a spinal nerve. The ramus contains fibers of postganglionic sympathetic neurons.

greater omentum (oh-**men**-tum) Large double fold of peritoneum attached to the duodenum, the greater curvature of the stomach, and a portion of the large intestine. It contains large deposits of adipose and lymphatic tissue.

greater vestibular glands (ves-**tib**-yoo-lar) Mucus-secreting glands that open onto each side of the vaginal orifice. Their secretion helps provide lubrication during sexual intercourse. They are especially vulnerable to infections. Also called Bartholin's glands.

groin (groyn) Depression located at the junction of the anterior aspect of the thigh with the trunk. Also called the inguinal region.

growth hormone An anterior pituitary hormone that stimulates body growth. Also called somatotropin.

guanine One of the four nitrogen-containing bases of DNA.

gustatory (**gus**-tah-*toe*-ree) Of or pertaining to the sense of taste.

gynecology (*guy*-neh-**kol**-eh-jee) Medical specialty focusing on the study and treatment of diseases of the reproductive system in the female.

gynecomastia (*jin*-eh-koe-**mas**-tee-ah) Abnormal and excessive development of the mammary glands in the male. A functional status may even be achieved.

gyrus (**jye**-rus) A single convolution of the cerebral cortex. Plural is gyri.

H

hair One of the fine, threadlike appendages of the skin. Hair is typically located on the entire surface of the body excepting the palms of the hands and soles of the feet.

hair follicle (**fol**-ih-kul) An epithelial ingrowth of the epidermis that moves down into the dermis and surrounds the hair.

hamstrings Group of posterior thigh muscles consisting of the biceps femoris, semitendinosus, and semimembranosus.

hand The most distal region of the upper limb.

haploid (**hap**-loyd) Chromosome number characteristic of the gametes; half the diploid number of chromosomes.

haptens (**hap**-tens) Substances found in dust and certain drugs that stimulate immune responses yet are too small to be antigenic. They become antigenic by attaching to the surface of proteins.

hard palate (**pal**-at) The more anterior portion of the roof of the mouth, which is formed by the fusion of portions of the maxillae and palatine bones.

haustra (**haw**-struh) Sacculations of the colon due to the fact that the longitudinal muscle is shorter than the overall length of the colon. This gives rise to a series of pouchlike sacculations.

haversian system Lamellar bone deposited in concentric rings around a centrally located blood vessel. The system has a general spindle-shaped configuration and is also called an osteon.

heart block Myocardial infarction involving a portion of the heart's conduction system; ventricles may contract independently. May be classified as bundle branch, incomplete, first-degree, second-degree, or third-degree.

heart failure A condition in which a diseased heart is unable to pump all of the blood returned to it. A common disorder that can be the result of untreated hypertension.

heart murmur Abnormal heart sound resulting from turbulent blood flow of sufficient magnitude to make vibrations occur.

heart rate The number of times the heart beats in one minute; normally this is about 72 beats per minute in the adult.

heart sounds Characteristic sounds of the heartbeat typically heard with the assistance of a stethoscope. Specific sounds result from closure of specific valves.

heatstroke Failure of the body to effectively rid itself of excess heat. It may be the result of strenuous physical activity in very hot and humid weather. Sweating is reduced and the body temperature is elevated above normal.

heavy chains The two identical long chains of a typical immunoglobulin molecule; usually consisting of more than 400 amino acids each.

Heimlich maneuver Emergency maneuver in which a choking victim is grasped and squeezed in such a manner that residual air in the lungs is forcefully driven outward to help dislodge the obstructing object. The maneuver may be performed in either the standing or supine position. Also called the abdominal thrust maneuver.

helicotrema (*hel*-ih-ko-**tree**-mah) Tiny, short canal connecting the scalae at the apex of the cochlea.

helix (**hee**-licks) Any spiral, but in biochemistry, usually one that does not vary in diameter.

helper T cells Differentiated T lymphocytes that play a role in the stimulation of B lymphocytes.

hematocrit (hee-**mat**-o-krit) Percentage of red blood cells present in the total blood volume. The determination of this value is a routine clinical blood test.

hematoma (*hem*-ah-**toe**-mah) Swelling or tumor filled with blood.

hematopoiesis (*hem*-ah-toe-poy-**ee**-sis) The formation of blood cells in the red bone marrow.

hematuria (*hem*-ah-**too**-ree-ah) The presence of blood in the urine.

heme group That portion of the hemoglobin molecule containing iron.

hemiplegia (*hem*-ih-**plee**-jee-uh) Paralysis involving the upper and lower limbs and trunk on one side of the body only.

hemizygous genes (*hem*-ih-**zigh**-gus) Having only one of a pair of genes influencing the determination of a specific trait.

hemocytoblast (*hee*-moh-**sigh**-tow-blast) Colony-forming units or stem cells of the bone marrow that multiply and give rise to several types of committed stem cells; each gives rise to one specific type of blood cell.

hemodynamics (*hee*-moh-die-**nam**-iks) Study of the mechanisms responsible for and influencing the circulation of blood through the vessels.

hemoglobin (*hee*-moh-**glo**-bin) The respiratory pigment of red blood cells that has the property of taking up oxygen or releasing it.

hemoglobin S The abnormal hemoglobin found in patients with sickle-cell anemia. When exposed to low concentrations of oxygen, hemoglobin S forms intermolecular cross links and subsequent crystals that deform the red blood cell.

hemolysis (he-**mol**-ih-sis) The destruction of red blood cells and the resultant escape of hemoglobin.

hemolytic anemia (*hee*-moh-**lit**-ik ah-**nee**-mee-ah) A deficiency of hemoglobin typically caused by an increased destruction of red blood cells.

hemolytic disease of the newborn A condition of hemolytic anemia in the newborn in which the child's red blood cells are destroyed by maternal antibodies; antibodies formed in response to Rh incompatibility. Also called erythroblastosis fetalis.

hemophilia (*hee*-moh-**fil**-ee-ah) Disease in which one of the clotting factors is absent due to a genetic mutation. In 83% of all hemophiliacs factor VIII is missing.

hemorrhage (**hem**-or-ij) Escape of blood from the blood vessels; typically referring to excessive bleeding.
hemorrhoids (**hem**-oh-royds) Varicose dilatations of the veins in the anal region. Hemorrhoids typically develop when venous pressure is constantly elevated.
hemostasis (*hee*-moh-**stay**-sis) The arrest of bleeding. This may be accomplished by physiological processes or by surgical means.
heparin (**hep**-ah-rin) A mucopolysaccharide acid, abundant in the lungs and liver. Heparin inhibits the clotting process.
hepatic (he-**pat**-ik) Of or pertaining to the liver.
hepatic portal system System of veins returning blood from the digestive tract to the liver where a second set of exchange vessels (capillaries or sinusoids) is present.
hepatitis (*hep*-ah-**tie**-tis) Inflammation of the liver. May be viral in origin or due to exposure to certain drugs or chemicals.
heredity (heh-**red**-ih-tee) The transfer of biological information from parent to offspring.
hernia (**her**-nee-ah) Protrusion of a portion of an organ or tissue through an abnormal opening; for example, an inguinal hernia or a hiatal hernia.
herniated disc (**her**-nee-*ay*-ted) A ruptured intervertebral disc in which the nucleus pulposus extends through the annulus fibrosus into the vertebral canal. Referred to by laymen as a slipped disc.
herpes, genital *See* Genital herpes
heterozygous (het-er-oh-**zy**-gus) A condition of genotype in which the alleles for a particular trait are different.
hilus of kidney (**high**-lus) Region on the concave border of the kidney where the ureter and blood vessels are attached.
hippocampus (*hip*-oh-**kam**-pus) An important functional component of the limbic system of the CNS.
histamine (**hiss**-tah-meen) A substance released from a variety of cells in response to injury. Histamine produces vasodilation, bronchiolar constriction, and increased permeability of the blood vessels.
histiocyte (**his**-tee-oh-*site*) A sessile or fixed macrophage that is typically stretched out along collagen fibers of connective tissue.
histology (hiss-**tol**-oh-jee) The study of tissues.
holocrine gland (**hole**-oh-krin) Specific type of gland, such as a sebaceous gland, in which the secretory product consists not only of the excretory product, but of the cell itself.
homeostasis (*ho*-mee-oh-**stay**-sis) The automatic tendency to maintain a relatively constant internal environment within the body. Also called homeodynamics.
homograft (**hoe**-moe-graft) A tissue or organ graft made between members of the same species but having different genetic composition.
homologous chromosomes (hoe-**mole**-o-gus) Pair of chromosomes in which one is inherited from the mother and one from the father.
homozygous (*hoe*-moh-**zy**-gus) A condition of genotype when the alleles for a particular trait are the same.
horizontal plane Anatomical plane that parallels the ground. It divides the body into inferior and superior portions. Also called a transverse plane.
hormone (**hoar**-moan) Chemical messenger that helps regulate the activity of other tissues and organs. Secreted by endocrine or ductless glands.
human chorionic gonadotropin (HCG) (*ko*-ree-**on**-ik *gon*-ah-do-**trow**-pin) Hormone secreted by cells of the trophoblast that signals the corpus luteum that pregnancy has begun.
human immunodeficiency virus (HIV) A retrovirus responsible for the deadly disease called acquired immune deficiency syndrome (AIDS). The virus rapidly infects helper T cells, resulting in irreversible defects in immunity.
human leukocyte antigen (HLA) group Term applied to the major histocompatibility complex in humans.
hyaline (**high**-ah-line) Clear, glassy, apparently without structure. Hyaline cartilage is a clear cartilage, without large fibers, which occurs in synovial joints.
hydrocephalus (high-droe-**sef**-ah-lus) Abnormal enlargement of the head due to the accumulation of excessive amounts of fluid within the cranium. May be due to either blockage of CSF circulation or to an abnormally increased production of the same. Also known as "water on the head."
hydrogen bond (**high**-droe-jen) A very weak chemical bond formed between an already bonded hydrogen atom and a negatively charged atom such as oxygen or nitrogen.
hydrolysis (high-**drol**-ih-sis) A chemical reaction involving water in which a large molecule is usually broken down into smaller products with the addition of water.
hydrophilic (*high*-droe-**fil**-ik) Attracted to water.
hydrophobic (*high*-droe-**fo**-bik) Repelled by water.
hydrostatic pressure (*high*-droe-**stat**-ik) A liquid pressure head.
hymen (**high**-men) A fold of membrane that either partially or completely covers the external opening of the vagina.
hypercalcemia (*high*-pur-kal-**see**-mee-ah) An excessive amount of calcium in the blood.
hypercapnia (*high*-pur-**kap**-nee-uh) Abnormal concentration of carbon dioxide in the blood.
hyperchloremia (*high*-pur-klo-**ree**-me-ah) An excessive amount of chloride in the blood.
hyperextension (*high*-pur-ek-**sten**-shun) Movement of a joint past its normal limit of extension. Hyperextension of the cervical spine is known as a "whiplash" injury.
hyperglycemia (*high*-pur-gly-**see**-me-ah) A condition in which the blood-sugar level is elevated.
hyperkalemia (*high*-pur-kah-**lee**-me-ah) An excessive amount of potassium in the blood; typically the result of defective excretion by the kidneys.
hypernatremia (*high*-pur-nah-**tree**-me-ah) An excessive amount of sodium in the blood.
hyperplasia (*high*-pur-**play**-zee-ah) Abnormal increase in the size of an organ or part due to an increase in the number of normal cells.
hyperpolarization (*high*-pur-*po*-lar-eye-**zay**-shun) An increase in the negativity across the plasma membrane such that the potential for firing is reduced.
hypertension (*high*-pur-**ten**-shun) Elevated blood pressure.
hyperthermia (*high*-pur-**ther**-mee-ah) Elevation of body temperature.
hypertonic (*high*-pur-**ton**-ik) Having an osmotic pressure or solute concentration greater than that of some other solution which is taken as a standard.
hypertrophy (high-**per**-trow-fee) Excessive enlargement of an existing cell. The term is also applied to an abnormal enlargement of a tissue in the absence of cell division.
hyperventilation (*high*-pur-*ven*-tih-**lay**-shun) Abnormally rapid, deep breathing.
hypervitaminosis (*high*-pur-*vie*-tah-mih-**noh**-sis) A condition brought about by taking in an excess of one or more vitamins.
hypoblast (**high**-poe-blast) Cells of the embryonic disc that will ultimately give rise to endodermally derived structures.
hypocalcemia (*high*-poe-kal-**see**-mee-ah) Reduction in the blood-calcium level to below normal.
hypoglycemia (*high*-poe-gly-**see**-mee-ah) Reduction in the blood-glucose level to below normal.

hypokalemia (*high*-poe-kah-**lee**-mee-ah) Reduction in the blood-potassium level to below normal.

hyponatremia (*high*-poe-nah-**tree**-me-ah) Reduction in the blood-sodium level to below normal.

hypophysis (high-**pof**-ih-sis) The pituitary gland.

hypothalamopituitary portal system (*high*-poe-**thah**-lam-oh-pih-**too**-ih-tear-ee) Important system of blood vessels that connect the hypothalamus with the anterior portion of the pituitary gland.

hypothalamus (*high*-poe-**thal**-ah-mus) A portion of the brain that functions in the regulation of the pituitary gland, the autonomic nervous system, emotional responses, body temperature, water balance, and appetite; located inferior to the thalamus.

hypothermia (*high*-poe-**ther**-mee-ah) The lowering of body temperature.

hypothyroidism (*high*-poe-**thigh**-royd-izm) A condition of deficient thyroid gland activity. Characterized by a decreased thyroid gland activity, resulting in a decreased basal metabolic rate, lethargy, and increased sensitivity to cold temperatures. If untreated the condition may develop into myxedema.

hypotonic (high-poe-**ton**-ik) Referring to a solution whose osmotic pressure or solute content is less than that of some standard of comparison.

hypoxia (high-**pock**-see-ah) Oxygen deficiency.

hysterectomy (*his*-teh-**reck**-toe-mee) Surgical removal of a portion or all of the uterus, either through the abdominal wall or the vagina.

I

identical twins Twins resulting from the division of the inner cell mass into two separate groups of cells possessing identical genes.

ileum (**il**-ee-um) The terminal portion of the small intestine extending from the jejunum to the cecum.

immune (ih-**mewn**) **response** Any reaction designed to defend the body against pathogens or other foreign substances.

immunity (ih-**mew**-nih-tee) The ability to resist and overcome infection or disease; nonsusceptibility to the pathogenic effects of foreign microorganisms or to the toxic effect of antigenic substances.

immunization (*im*-yoo-nih-**zay**-shun) The process of inducing active immunity by the injection of a vaccine.

immunoglobulins (*im*-yoo-no-**glob**-yoo-lins) Antibodies produced by plasma cells in response to antigenic stimulation. The five classes of immunoglobulin include IgG, IgA, IgM, IgD, and IgE.

immunology (*im*-yoo-**nol**-oh-jee) The study of the body's specific defense mechanisms.

immunosuppression Inhibition of the body's ability to mount an effective immune response. Immunosuppression may be due to certain drugs or exposure to ionizing radiation.

implantation (*im*-plan-**tay**-shun) Attachment, penetration, and embedding of the blastocyst within the uterine wall, occurring seven or eight days following fertilization.

impotence (**im**-poe-tence) Chronic inability to sustain an erection; often caused by psychological factors. It may also be the result of motor nerve paralysis or spinal cord lesions.

incontinence (in-**kon**-tih-nence) A condition in which the individual is no longer able to retain urine or feces due to a loss of sphincter control.

infancy (**in**-fan-see) That period of postnatal development extending from the end of the neonatal period to the time when the individual is able to assume an erect posture. Some physicians consider the period of infancy to encompass the first two years of life.

infarct (**in**-farkt) A localized area of dead tissue caused by an inadequate blood supply and the resulting oxygen deprivation.

infectious arthritis (ar-**thry**-tis) Inflammation of a joint, usually resulting from the direct invasion of the joint by an infectious organism.

inferior (in-**fe**-ree-or) Anatomic directional term describing a structure located below, or directed downward, as compared to another structure or part.

inferior vena cava Large vein returning blood to the right atrium from the abdominopelvic structures and the lower limbs.

infertility Condition in which the individual is unable to conceive or to cause conception. Also referred to as being sterile.

inflammation (*in*-flah-**may**-shun) The response of the body tissues to injury or infection, characterized clinically by heat, swelling, redness, and pain, and physiologically by increased vasodilation and capillary permeability.

infundibulum (*in*-fun-**dib**-yoo-lum) A funnel-shaped passage as in the infundibulum of the uterine tube. Also used to designate the stalk of tissue connecting the hypothalamus with the pituitary gland.

ingestion (in-**jes**-chun) The process of eating; taking substances into the mouth and swallowing them.

inguinal canal (**ing**-gwih-nal) One of the two passageways that serve to connect the scrotal and abdominal cavities. The testes descend into the scrotum by way of the inguinal canals.

inhalation *See* Inspiration

inhibitory postsynaptic potential Hyperpolarization of the postsynaptic membrane that results in an elevation of the membrane potential. Brings the neuron farther away from its firing potential.

inner cell mass The inner group of cells of the blastocyst that will ultimately give rise to the embryo.

inner ear Portion of the ear within the temporal bone consisting of the osseous labyrinth, the membranous labyrinth, and the cochlea.

insertion (in-**sir**-shun) The more movable point of attachment of muscle to bone; contrasts with the origin or less movable point of attachment of muscle to bone.

insomnia (in-**som**-nee-uh) A condition in which one has difficulty in falling asleep and may awake several times during the night.

inspiration (*in*-spih-**ray**-shun) The drawing of air into the lungs.

insula (**in**-soo-lah) A portion of the cerebral cortex also called the central lobe or island of Reil. Its connections are not well understood although it is thought to be involved in both autonomic and somatic activities.

insulin (**in**-suh-lin) A hormone released by the islets of Langerhans of the pancreas that facilitates diffusion of glucose into cells.

integration (*in*-teh-**gray**-shun) The process of sorting and interpreting neural impulses in order to determine an appropriate response.

integument (in-**teg**-yoo-ment) A covering, especially the skin.

integumentary system A body system consisting of the skin, its glands, nails, and hair.

interatrial septum (*in*-ter-**a**-tree-uhl) Wall located between the right and left atria of the heart. In fetal life the septum is perforated by the foramen ovale.

intercalated discs (in-**ter**-kah-lay-ted) Specialized cell junctions between individual cardiac muscle fibers; offer little resistance to passage of action potential between the two cells. Seen as dense bands between cardiac muscle cells in histologic preparations.

intercellular Between the cells of a structure.

interferons (*in*-ter-**feer**-ons) Proteins secreted by certain cells when the body is invaded by viruses or other intracellular parasites. This group of proteins stimulates other cells to produce antiviral proteins.

interleukins (*in*-ter-**loo**-kins) Peptides produced by various cells of the body's immune system. These substances play important regulatory roles in the body's defense mechanisms.

internal respiration Exchange of the respiratory gases that occurs between the blood and the cells of the body.

interneuron An association neuron; one that links sensory and motor neurons within the central nervous system.

internodal fiber bundles Specialized cardiac muscle fibers responsible for conducting the action potential to the atrioventricular (AV) node.

interoceptor (*in*-ter-o-**sep**-tor) A sensory receptor that transmits information from the viscera to the central nervous system.

interphase (**in**-ter-faze) The period in the life of a cell in which there is no mitotic division.

interpubic disc (*in*-ter-**pew**-bik) Fibrocartilaginous disc intervening between the two pubic bones at the pubic symphysis.

interstitial (*in*-ter-**stish**-al) Located between parts or cells.

interstitial bone growth Growth in length of the cartilage bone model without removal of the pre-existing matrix.

interstitial cells Cells located in groups between the seminiferous tubules in the testes; produce the male hormone, testosterone. Also called the interstitial cells of Leydig.

interstitial fluid Fluid located between cells or body parts; tissue fluid.

interventricular septum (*in*-ter-ven-**trik**-yoo-lar) That portion of the heart wall located between the two ventricles.

intervertebral disc (*in*-ter-**ver**-teh-brahl) Fibrocartilaginous disc located between two adjacent vertebral bodies.

intervertebral foramen Passageway formed by two adjacent vertebrae through which the spinal nerves exit the vertebral canal.

intracellular (*in*-trah-**sell**-yoo-lar) Located within the cell, as in the case of intracellular fluid.

intraembryonic mesoderm Layer of cells located between the ectoderm and the endoderm. It is formed by cells of the epiblast that detach and migrate between the epiblast and hypoblast.

intramembranous bone formation One type of bone formation in which a primitive connective tissue precedes bone development. As in endochondral bone formation, the connective tissue is replaced by bone itself.

intrauterine device (IUD) (*in*-trah-**yoo**-ter-in) Contraceptive device consisting of a small plastic (or metal) loop or coil that must be inserted into the uterus by a physician.

intrinsic factor (in-**trin**-sik) Substance secreted by the parietal cells on the upper portions of the gastric glands and which is required for adequate intestinal absorption of vitamin B_{12}.

intrinsic pathway of blood clotting One of the reaction pathways leading to the formation of prothrombin activator, which is initiated by a clotting factor present in the blood itself.

in utero (**yoo**-tur-oh) Pertaining to within the uterus.

invagination (in-*vaj*-ih-**nay**-shun) The ingrowth or infolding of one part within another.

inverse stretch reflex The inhibitory response initiated by a Golgi tendon organ during stretching of a muscle and its tendon; results in relaxation of the muscle.

inversion (in-**ver**-zhun) Elevation of the medial border of the foot such that the sole or plantar aspect is directed medially.

in vitro (**vee**-trow) In an artificial environment, as when cells are grown in culture dishes.

in vivo (**vee**-vo) Within the body.

ion (**eye**-on) A charged atom or group of atoms. (The electric charge results from gain or loss of electrons.)

ionic bond Type of bond formed when one atom donates an electron to another atom. Also called an electrovalent bond.

ionization (*eye*-on-eye-**zay**-shun) The dissociation of a substance (acid, base, salt) in solution into ions.

ipsilateral (*ip*-sih-**lat**-er-al) Pertaining to the same side of the body.

iris (**eye**-ris) The visible, colored, circular disc of the eye which functions to control the amount of light entering the eye.

ischemia (is-**kee**-me-ah) Deficiency of blood to a body part due to functional constriction or actual obstruction of a blood vessel.

ischemic heart disease Heart disease resulting from coronary artery insufficiency; may be of an acute or chronic nature.

ischiorectal fossa (*is*-kee-oh-**rek**-tal) Potential space located lateral to the anus and between the urogenital diaphragm anteriorly and the gluteus maximus posteriorly; largely occupied by adipose tissue and dense connective tissue strands.

ischium (**is**-kee-um) The dorsal and inferior portion of the hip bone.

islets of Langerhans (**eye**-lits of **Lahng**-er-hanz) The endocrine portion of the pancreas; alpha cells of the islets release glucagon while beta cells secrete insulin. These hormones regulate the blood-sugar level.

isomer (**eye**-so-mer) One of two or more chemical compounds having the same proportional chemical formula, but in which the component atoms are arranged differently.

isometric (*eye*-so-**met**-rik) Maintaining the same measure or length. In muscle physiology, a contraction that produces no change in the length of the muscle.

isotonic (*eye*-so-**ton**-ik) (1) A solution having the same solute concentration or osmotic pressure as some other solution to which it is being compared. Also a solution in which body cells can be immersed without a net flow of water across the semipermeable plasma membrane. (2) A form of muscle contraction in which the length but not the tension of the muscle changes.

isotope (**eye**-so-tope) An alternate form of an element with a different number of neutrons in its atomic nucleus, but with the same number of protons and electrons.

isthmus (**is**-mus) The narrow connection between two larger cavities or parts.

J

jaundice (**jawn**-dis) Condition resulting when bilirubin cannot be eliminated from the body. The skin and mucous membranes of the body take on a yellowish appearance.

jejunitis (*je*-joo-**nye**-tis) Inflammation of the jejunum.

jejunum (jeh-**joo**-num) The middle portion of the small intestine located between the duodenum and the ileum.

jerk Sudden reflex or involuntary movement such as the knee jerk produced by tapping on the patellar tendon.

joint The site of junction or union between two or more bones of the skeleton. Also called an articulation.

juxtaglomerular cells (*juks*-tah-glo-**mer**-yoo-lar) A cuff of specialized cells located around the afferent arteriole of the glomerulus.

K

karyotype (**kar**-ee-oh-type) The specific chromosomal characteristics of an individual, that is, their chromosomal constitution.

keloid (**key**-loyd) An elevated, irregular, enlarging scar due to the production of excessive amounts of collagen in the dermis during connective tissue repair.

keratin (**ker**-ah-tin) An insoluble protein found in epidermis, hair, nails, and other horny tissues.

keratinocyte (keh-**rat**-ih-no-site) Epidermal cells that function in the synthesis of keratin.

ketone bodies (**key**-tone) Compounds such as acetone, beta hydroxybutyric acid, and acetoacetic acid that are produced during fat metabolism.

ketonuria (*key*-toe-**noo**-ree-ah) Presence of ketone bodies in the urine, as in diabetes mellitus.

ketosis (kee-**tow**-sis) Abnormal condition marked by an elevated concentration of ketone bodies in the body fluids and tissues; a complication of diabetes mellitus and of starvation.

kidney (**kid**-nee) One of two organs of the urinary system responsible for the production of urine. Function in the regulation of fluid volume and composition. Located in a retroperitoneal position on the posterior abdominal wall in the lumbar region.

kidney, horseshoe A congenital malformation in which the two kidneys have fused as one organ.

kidney stone A crystalline calculus composed typically of calcium phosphate, uric acid, and calcium oxalate. Formation may occur in a variety of locations within the urinary system.

kilocalorie (**kil**-oh-*kal*-oh-ree) Quantity of heat required to elevate the temperature of 1 kg of water 1°C; also the unit of measurement of the basal metabolic rate.

kinesiologist (ki-*nee*-see-**ol**-oh-jist) One who specializes in the study of movement of body parts.

kinesiology (ki-*nee*-see-**ol**-oh-jee) Study focusing on the movement of body parts.

kinins (**kye**-nins) Small polypeptides that are derived from alpha-globulins in the plasma and which stimulate vasodilation. These substances are thought to play important roles in circulation regulation. Bradykinin is an example.

knuckle (**nuk**-ul) Dorsal aspect of any phalangeal joint of the hand, especially the metacarpophalangeal joints.

Krebs cycle An aerobic series of respiratory chemical reactions that produce energy in the typical cell; during this cycle, acetate becomes oxidized to carbon dioxide and water with the release of energy. Also called the citric acid cycle.

Kupffer cells Phagocytic cells that line the sinusoids of the liver. They form part of the reticuloendothelial system.

kwashiorkor (kwash-ee-**or**-kor) Condition caused by severe protein deficiency in which there occurs growth retardation, edema, alterations in the skin and hair, and changes in the liver.

kyphosis (kigh-**foe**-sis) Abnormal convex angular curvature of the thoracic spine in an anteroposterior plane.

L

labia (**lay**-bee-ah) The liplike borders of the vulva.

labor Strong contractions of the uterus that occur with increasing frequency and intensity during the latter part of pregnancy. Labor is divided into three distinct stages.

labyrinth (**lab**-ih-rinth) The system of intercommunicating canals and cavities that make up the inner ear.

lacrimal duct (**lak**-rih-mal) The duct connecting the conjunctival sac with the nasal cavity through which tears drain. Also called the nasolacrimal duct.

lacrimal gland (**lak**-rih-mal) Gland responsible for the production of tears and located in the superolateral region of the orbit.

lacrimal sac (**lak**-rih-mal) The upper expanded region of the lacrimal duct located near the inferomedial aspect of the orbit; receives tears elaborated by the lacrimal gland.

lactase (**lak**-tase) Enzyme capable of splitting the disaccharide lactose into its constituent monosaccharide. Found in epithelial cells lining the small intestine.

lactation (lak-**tay**-shun) The production or release of milk from the breast. Also the period during which the child is nourished from the breast.

lacteal (**lak**-tee-al) One of the many lymphatic vessels in the intestinal villi that absorb fat; so called because during absorption they appear white and milky from the absorbed fat.

lactic acid (**lak**-tik) Compound generated from glycogen during anaerobic energy metabolism. Its accumulation in muscle produces the sensation of fatigue, and oxygen is required for its elimination.

lactose (**lak**-tose) A disaccharide composed of one molecule of glucose and one molecule of galactose.

lacunae (la-**koo**-nee) (1) Small, isolated spaces, each containing an osteoblast. (2) Also used to describe spaces that develop within the syncytiotrophoblast and become filled with maternal blood.

lambdoidal suture (lam-**doy**-dal) The joint or line of articulation between the parietal bones and occipital bone of the skull.

lamellar bone (lah-**mel**-are) Mature bone in which the collagen fibers are arranged in distinct concentric rings called lamellae. This type of bone ultimately replaces woven bone.

lamina (**lahm**-ih-nah) A thin sheet of tissue, such as bone; used to denote the posterolateral sides of the neural arch of the vertebra that connect the neural spine with the transverse processes.

lamina propria (**lahm**-ih-nah **pro**-pree-ah) Loose connective tissue layer of a mucous membrane located immediately below the epithelium and basement membrane.

lanugo (la-**new**-go) Downy hair evident on the developing individual during the seventh month of gestation.

laryngopharynx (lah-*ring*-oh-**far**-inks) One of three divisions of the musculofibrous tube called the pharynx.

laryngotracheal bud (lah-*ring*-oh-**tray**-kee-al) An evagination of the endoderm of the embryonic foregut that will give rise to the respiratory system.

larynx (**lar**-inks) The organ at the superior end of the trachea that contains the vocal cords, located between the pharynx and trachea.

lateral (**lat**-er-al) Positional term designating a location away from the midline of the body or one of its organs or parts.

leg That portion of the lower limb located between the knee and the ankle.

lens Originally derived from the embryonic skin, this transparent structure is responsible for focusing images upon the retina. Differential focusing of near and far objects is related to the lens's ability to alter its shape.

Lesch-Nyhan syndrome An X-linked recessive disorder characterized by slowly developing paralysis, mental deficiency, and self-mutilation, caused by the deficiency of a specific enzyme.

lesion (**lee**-zhun) Any local damage to tissue or loss of function of a part; may be the result of injury or disease.

lesser omentum (oh-**men**-tum) The peritoneal fold connecting the liver with the lesser curvature of the stomach and the initial portion of the duodenum. The free edge of this fold contains the common bile duct, the hepatic portal vein, and the hepatic artery.

lesser vestibular glands (ves-**tib**-yoo-lar) Mucus-producing glands whose ducts open into the female vestibule near the external urethral orifice.

leukemia (loo-**key**-mee-ah) A form of cancer in which any one of the kinds of white blood cells proliferates wildly in the bone marrow; may be either of an acute or chronic nature.

leukocyte (**loo**-ko-site) A white blood cell.

leukocytosis (*loo*-ko-sigh-**toe**-sis) An elevated white blood cell count greater than 10,000 per cubic millimeter. Quite common in acute infections.

leukopenia (*loo*-ko-**pee**-nee-ah) Decreased white blood cell count, usually indicative of a reduction in the number of circulating neutrophils. Viral infections typically yield a depressed white blood cell count.

lever (**lev**-ur) A mechanical arrangement of a rigid bar rotating around a fixed point called a fulcrum.

ligament (**lig**-ah-ment) Strong, tensile, connective tissue cord, or band, that unites bones.

light chains The two identical short chains of a typical immunoglobulin molecule. Usually consisting of approximately 214 amino acids each.

lingual frenulum (**ling**-gwal **fren**-yoo-lum) A fold of mucous membrane in the midline of the inferior surface of the tongue that attaches it to the floor of the mouth.

lipid Any of a group of organic compounds that are insoluble in water but soluble in fat solvents such as alcohol; they serve as a storage form of fuel and an important constituent of cellular membranes.

lipogenesis (*lipe*-oh-**jen**-eh-sis) The production of lipids from precursors such as glucose and amino acids.

lipoma (lye-**poe**-mah) Typically a benign tumor of fatty tissue.

lobe A well-defined portion of any organ, especially of the brain, lungs, and glands.

lordosis (lor-**doe**-sis) Condition in which the concavity of the lumbar curve of the vertebral column is exaggerated.

low-density lipoprotein (LDL) One of a class of compounds that contain lipid and protein and are characterized by their density as determined by ultracentrifugation. Low-density lipoproteins are composed of relatively little triglyceride and a very high percentage of cholesterol.

lumen (**loo**-men) The space within a tubelike structure such as a blood or lymphatic vessel or intestine.

lunula (**loo**-noo-la) The crescent-shaped white region located at the base of a fingernail or toenail.

luteinizing hormone (LH) (**loo**-tee-in-*eye*-zing) Hormone secreted by the anterior lobe of the pituitary gland. Serves to stimulate ovulation and progesterone secretion by the corpus luteum. Helps prepare the mammary glands for milk secretion. In males, LH stimulates the testes to secrete testosterone.

lymph (limf) The fluid within the lymphatic vessels that is collected from the interstitial fluid and ultimately returned to the circulatory system.

lymphangiography (lim-*fan*-jee-**og**-rah-fee) Clinical procedure used to visualize lymphatic vessels with x-rays following their filling with a radiopaque substance.

lymphatic (lim-**fat**-ik) Of or pertaining to lymph. Also one of several large lymph vessels that unite to form the right and left lymphatic ducts.

lymph node A mass of lymphatic tissue surrounded by a connective tissue capsule; filters lymph and produces lymphocytes.

lymph nodules Small masses of lymphatic tissue without a connective tissue capsule. Found scattered throughout loose connective tissue, especially beneath moist epithelial membranes, and produce lymphocytes.

lymphocyte (**lim**-foe-site) A small mononuclear white blood cell. This class of cells includes the T and B lymphocytes, large agranular lymphocytes, and natural killer (NK) cells.

lymphokines (**lim**-foe-kines) Another term for the peptides known as the interleukins.

lymphoma (lim-**foe**-mah) General term used to designate any neoplastic disorder of lymphatic tissue.

lymphostasis (lim-**fose**-tay-sis) The stoppage of lymph flow.

lymphotoxins (*lim*-foe-**tox**-ins) Soluble proteins released by cytotoxic T cells under certain conditions and which are especially toxic for cancer cells.

lysosome (**lye**-so-sowm) A cytoplasmic organelle containing lytic enzymes and surrounded by a membrane.

lysozyme (**lye**-so-zyme) A crystalline, antibacterial enzyme present in saliva, tears, and additional animal fluids.

M

macrophage (**mak**-roe-faje) A large phagocytic cell capable of ingesting and digesting bacteria and cellular debris.

macula lutea (**mak**-yoo-la **loo**-tee-ah) The yellowish spot located in the center of the fovea centralis of the retina.

magnetic resonance imaging (MRI) Modern diagnostic technique used to examine tissues of the body by monitoring the behavior of hydrogen atoms in a magnetic field.

major histocompatibility complex (MHC) Group of protein markers present on the surface of all of an organism's cells. The immune system utilizes these markers to distinguish between self and nonself.

malignant (muh-**lig**-nant) Typically pertaining to those neoplastic diseases which cause death; especially tumors that metastasize or spread.

maltase (**mawl**-tase) A dissacharide-splitting enzyme.

maltose (**mawl**-tose) A dissacharide sugar, produced when starch is hydrolyzed by amylase.

mammary gland (**mam**-er-ee) An organ of the female that produces and secretes milk, providing nutrition for the young; it develops as a modified sweat gland.

mammography (mam-**og**-rah-fee) A soft-tissue radiological study of the breast.

manubrium (mah-**noo**-bree-um) Superior portion of the sternum.

mast cell A specialized type of cell present in connective tissue, it contains histamine and is important in allergic reactions.

mastectomy (mas-**tek**-toe-me) Surgical removal of breast tissue.

mastication (*mas*-tih-**kay**-shun) The act of chewing.

mastitis (mas-**tie**-tis) Inflammation of the mammary gland or breast.

mastocytosis (*mas*-toy-sigh-**toe**-sis) A condition in which greatly elevated numbers of mast cells accumulate in the tissues of the body.

mastoiditis (*mas*-toe-**die**-tis) Inflammation of the mucous membrane lining of the mastoid air cells of the temporal bone.

meatus (mee-**ay**-tus) A passageway or opening.

medial (**me**-dee-al) Directional term meaning nearer to the midline of the body or structure.

median plane A vertical plane situated at a right angle to a frontal or coronal plane and dividing the body into right and left halves.

mediastinum (*mee*-dee-as-**tie**-num) Region between the lungs that holds several organs.

medulla (meh-**dull**-ah) The inner portion of an organ such as the kidney, suprarenal gland, or thymus.

medulla oblongata (*ob*-lon-**ga**-tah) The most inferior aspect of the brain stem which connects the brain with the spinal cord.

meiosis (mi-**oh**-sis) Reduction division; the special type of cell division by which gametes are produced, involving the reduction of chromosomes to the haploid number.

melanin (**mel**-ah-nin) A group of dark pigments produced by certain cells (melanocytes) in the epidermis of the skin.

membrane bones Bones of the body that develop by intramembranous formation, for example, the parietal bones of the cranium.

memory B cells Activated B cells that do not differentiate into plasma cells. They continue to produce small quantities of antibody long after an infection has been overcome.

meninges (meh-**nin**-jeez) The three membranes that envelop the brain and spinal cord: the dura mater, arachnoid, and pia mater.

meniscus (meh-**nis**-kus) Articular disc found in certain types of synovial joints and consisting almost entirely of fibrocartilage.

menopause (**men**-oh-pawz) The period during which menstruation ceases in the human female, usually at about age 50.

menstrual cycle (**men**-stroo-al) Series of physiological changes resulting in preparation of the uterine lining for the reception of a fertilized ovum. Occurs on approximately a monthly basis in the nonpregnant female.

menstruation (*men*-stroo-**ay**-shun) The monthly discharge of blood and degenerated uterine lining in the human female; marks the initiation of each menstrual cycle.

merocrine gland (**mer**-oh-krine) A type of gland cell that remains intact during the production and elaboration of its secretory product.

mesenchyme (**mes**-eng-kime) Embryonic connective tissue.

mesentery (**mez**-en-terr-ee) A fold attaching various organs to the body wall, especially the peritoneum connecting the intestine to the posterior abdominal wall.

mesocolon (*mez*-oh-**ko**-lon) A fold of peritoneum connecting a portion of the colon to the posterior abdominal wall.

mesoderm (**mez**-oh-derm) One of the three primary embryonic germ layers; gives rise to bone, cartilage, muscles, blood vessels, outer layers of the digestive tube, the dermis of the skin, and portions of the reproductive and excretory systems.

mesothelium (*mez*-oh-**thee**-lee-um) Simple squamous epithelium lining the pleural and peritoneal cavities of the body.

messenger RNA Transcribed segment of DNA containing the information specifying the amino acid sequence of a polypeptide chain.

metabolism (meh-**tab**-oh-liz-um) Collective term for all of the chemical processes that take place within the body.

metaphase (**met**-ah-faze) Stage of mitosis characterized by pairs of chromatids lining up along the length of the equatorial plate.

metaphysis (meh-**taf**-ih-sis) Region of growing long bone where the epiphyseal plate blends with the diaphysis, typically characterized by the presence of columns of cancellous bone.

metarterioles (*met*-are-**tee**-ree-ohls) Vessels that connect arterioles and venules after traversing a capillary network.

metastasis (meh-**tas**-tah-sis) The transfer of a disease such as cancer from one organ or part to another not directly connected to it.

metatarsus (*met*-ah-**tar**-sus) The group of five bones of the lower limb located between the tarsal bones and the phalanges.

methemoglobin (met-*hee*-mow-**glow**-bin) The ferric form of hemoglobin in which it is incapable of transporting oxygen.

microfilaments Tiny rodlike structures with contractile properties that make up part of the internal skeleton of the cell.

microglia (my-**krog**-lee-ah) Glial cells of the CNS having phagocytic properties. Also referred to as brain macrophages.

microtubules (*my*-krow-**too**-bewls) Hollow, cytoplasmic cylinders, composed mainly of tubulin protein, which comprise such organelles as flagella and centrioles, and serve as a skeletal component of the cell.

microvilli (*my*-krow-**vill**-ee) Minute projections of the plasma membrane which increase the surface area of the cell; present mainly in cells concerned with absorption and secretion such as those lining the intestine or kidney tubules.

micturition (*mik*-tu-**rish**-un) Urination; the passage of urine from the urinary bladder.

midbrain That portion of the brain that is situated between the pons and the diencephalon. Also referred to as the mesencephalon.

midsagittal plane Vertical plane, situated perpendicular to a coronal or frontal plane, which serves to divide the body into equal right and left halves.

mineralocorticoids (*min*-er-al-oh-**kor**-tih-koyds) A class of hormones produced by the adrenal cortex that regulates mineral metabolism and, indirectly, fluid balance. The principal mineralocorticoid is called aldosterone.

mitochondria (*my*-tow-**kon**-dree-ah) Cellular organelles that are the site of most cellular respiration; sometimes they are referred to as the power plants of the cell.

mitosis (my-**tow**-sis) Division of the cell nucleus resulting in the distribution of a complete set of chromosomes to each end of the cell. Cytokinesis (actual division of the cell itself) usually occurs during the telophase stage of mitosis, giving rise to two daughter cells.

mitral stenosis (**my**-tral) Thickening and narrowing of the mitral valve that impedes blood flow from the left atrium into the left ventricle.

mitral valve Alternate term for the right atrioventricular or bicuspid valve.

mitral valve insufficiency Incomplete closure of the cusps of the mitral or bicuspid valve. Blood regurgitates into the left atrium as the left ventricle contracts.

molecule (**mol**-eh-kewl) A chemical combination of two or more atoms which form a specific chemical substance; also the smallest quantity into which a chemical compound can be divided and still maintain its characteristic properties.

mongolism (**mon**-go-lizm) Former name for the genetic disorder known as trisomy 21 or Down syndrome.

monoclonal antibody Specific antibody produced in vitro by hybrid cell clones. Such clones are formed through the fusion of activated B cells with cancer cells.

monocyte (**mon**-oh-site) A white blood cell; a large phagocytic nongranular leukocyte that enters the tissues and differentiates into a macrophage.

monoglyceride (*mon*-oh-**gliss**-er-ide) A fat that contains only one fatty acid per molecule.

monohybrid cross (*mon*-oh-**high**-brid) A cross between two individuals that differ with respect to the alleles they carry for a single locus.

monosaccharide (*mon*-oh-**sak**-ah-ride) A simple sugar; one that cannot be degraded by hydrolysis to a simpler sugar.

morphogenesis (*more*-foe-**jen**-ih-sis) Process of movement and rearrangement of embryonic cells such that the body acquires its characteristic shape and the organs develop normally on schedule.

morula (**more**-you-lah) The single solid mass of 12 to 16 small cells resulting from division of the zygote as the latter passes along the uterine tube.

mucosa (mew-**ko**-sah) A mucous membrane, for example, the lining of the gastrointestinal tract.

mucus (**mew**-kus) A sticky secretion produced by certain glandular cells (e.g., goblet cells), especially in the lining of the gastrointestinal and respiratory tracts. It serves to lubricate body parts and trap particles of dirt or additional contaminants. The adjectival form is spelled as mucous.

multiaxial joint Type of joint in which three axes of movement, together with all intermediate movements, are permitted.

multivalent antigen An antigen which has the same antigenic determinant repeated several times. For example, a virus that has multiple copies of a single protein on its outer surface.

mumps A contagious viral disease occurring primarily in children, characterized by inflammation and enlargement of the parotid glands. It is accompanied by high fever and severe pain during swallowing.

muscarinic receptor (*mus*-ka-**rhin**-ik) Specific type of cholinergic receptor originally found to be activated by muscarine, a poison found in toadstools. These receptors are present in all receptor cells innervated by postganglionic parasympathetic neurons and also in those stimulated by postganglionic sympathetic neurons that release acetylcholine.

muscle (**mus**-ul) An organ that produces movement by contraction.

muscle tissue A tissue composed of cells specialized for contraction; three main types are skeletal, smooth, and cardiac.

muscle tone The incomplete but sustained contraction of a portion of a skeletal muscle caused by the activation of stretch receptors.

mutagen Certain chemicals and forms of ionizing radiation that produce mutations in the genetic information contained in the DNA molecule.

mutation A change in one of the bases of a DNA strand, resulting in an alteration of the genetic information.

musculi pectinati (**mus**-que-lie **peck**-tin-ah-*tee*) Small muscular bundles located in the wall of the auricles associated with the right and left atria.

myelin (**my**-eh-lin) The white fatty substance forming a sheath around certain nerve fibers which are then called myelinated fibers.

myenteric nerve plexus (*my*-en-**ter**-ik) Meshwork of nerve fibers from the sympathetic and parasympathetic divisions of the autonomic nervous system that is located in the muscularis portion of the small intestine. Also referred to as the plexus of Auerbach.

myocardial infarct (*my*-oh-**kar**-dee-al) Necrosis of the myocardium supplied by a branch of a coronary artery when the vessel is suddenly occluded.

myocardial ischemia (is-**kee**-me-ah) Inadequate blood supply to the myocardium. May be due to narrowing or stenosis of the coronary arteries as a result of atherosclerosis.

myocardium (*my*-oh-**kar**-dee-um) Cardiac muscle fibers forming the greatest mass of the heart wall. Fibers are intricately branched and interwoven and their rhythmical contraction is responsible for pumping of the blood.

myofibril (*my*-oh-**fye**-bril) Any threadlike organelle found in the cytoplasm of striated and cardiac muscle that is responsible for contraction.

myofilament (*my*-oh-**fil**-ah-ment) One of the filaments making up the myofibril; the structural unit of muscle proteins in a muscle cell.

myoglobin (*my*-oh-**glow**-bin) The form of hemoglobin that is present in muscle cells.

myology (my-**ol**-oh-jee) The study of muscles.

myolysis (my-**ol**-ih-sis) The degeneration or disintegration of muscle tissue.

myoneural cleft (*my*-oh-**new**-ral) The space, corresponding to a synaptic cleft, between a motor neuron ending and a muscle cell.

myopathy (my-**op**-ah-thee) Any disease of muscle tissue.

myopia (my-**oh**-pee-ah) A refractive error of vision in which only nearby objects can be brought into focus.

myosin (**my**-oh-sin) A protein which, together with actin, is responsible for muscle contraction.

myositis (*mi*-oh-**sigh**-tis) Inflammation of a skeletal muscle.

myotome (**my**-oh-tome) That portion of the somite mesoderm in the embryo that gives rise to skeletal muscle.

myotonia (*my*-oh-**toe**-nee-ah) A condition characterized by tonic spasms or temporary rigidity of muscle.

myxedema (*mik*-seh-**dee**-mah) A condition arising from untreated hypothyroidism. Patients exhibit generalized edema and elevated cholesterol levels leading to atherosclerosis.

N

nail The hard cutaneous plate situated on the dorsal aspect of the distal region of each digit of the hand or foot.

narcotic (nar-**kot**-ik) A substance that induces a state of insensibility or stupor.

nares (**nay**-reez) The external openings of the nose; also referred to as the nostrils.

nasolacrimal duct (*nay*-zoh-**lak**-rih-mal) Passageway lined by mucous membrane and extending from the lacrimal sac to the nasal cavity; route by which tears make their way to the nasal cavity.

nasopharynx (*nay*-zo-**far**-inks) One of three divisions of the musculofibrous tube called the pharynx.

natural killer (NK) cells Specific cells of the body's immune system that recognize and kill body cells that have been altered by viruses. NK cells are stimulated by interferons.

nausea (**naw**-zee-ah) An unpleasant sensation, often referred to the region of the upper abdomen and frequently culminating in vomiting.

necrosis (neh-**krow**-sis) Death of tissue.

neonate Term applied to the newborn infant.

neoplasm (**nee**-oh-plazm) A tumor; new and abnormal growth of cells or tissues.

nephritis (neh-**fry**-tis) Inflammation of the kidney; may be of an acute or chronic nature.

nephron (**nef**-ron) The functional and microscopic anatomical unit of the kidney.

nerve (nerv) A large bundle of axons (or dendrites) wrapped in connective tissue, which conveys impulses between the central nervous system and some other part of the body.

neuralgia (new-**rhal**-jee-ah) Pain that extends along the course of one or more nerves.

neural plate Plate of cells formed by induction from the notochord during the third week of development.

neural tube Formed from the neural plate during the fourth week of embryonic development. This structure will give rise to the central nervous system.

neurohypophysis (*new*-row-high-**pawf**-ih-sis) The posterior lobe of the pituitary gland.

neurology (new-**rhol**-oh-jee) A medical specialty that focuses on the study of normal and disease states of the nervous system.

neuroma (new-**row**-mah) A tumor composed largely of nerve cell bodies or nerve fibers.

neuron (**new**-ron) A nerve cell; an impulse-conducting cell of the nervous system which typically consists of a cell body, dendrites, and an axon.

neutron (**new**-tron) A neutrally charged subatomic particle present in the atomic nucleus.

neutrophil (**new**-tro-fil) A type of granular leukocyte.

nitrogen narcosis (nar-**ko**-sis) Condition resembling alcoholic intoxication that may lead to irrational, life-threatening behavior. Result of nitrogen gas being driven into the blood and tissues by increased pressure as occurs when diving down into the ocean depths.

norepinephrine (*nor*-ep-ih-**nef**-rin) A neurotransmitter substance. Also a hormone produced by the adrenal medulla.

normoblast (**nor**-moe-blast) A nucleated precursor in the series giving rise to red blood cells.

notochord (**no**-toe-kord) Cylindrical rod of cells that grows forward along the length of the embryo during the third week. It induces the adjacent ectoderm to form the neural plate.

nucleic acids (new-**klee**-ik) DNA or RNA; a very large compound composed of carbon, oxygen, hydrogen, nitrogen, and phosphorus arranged in molecular subunits called nucleotides. Nucleic acid codes information specifying the structure and function of the organism.

nucleolus (new-**klee**-oh-lus) Sphere-like organelle located within the nucleus and containing DNA, RNA, and protein; is not surrounded by a membrane; plays role in the synthesis and storage of ribosomal RNA.

nucleotide (**new**-klee-oh-tide) A unit of the backbone of DNA consisting of the sugar deoxyribose, one phosphate group, and one nitrogen-containing base, either adenine, thymine, guanine, or cytosine.

nucleus (**new**-klee-us) (1) The core of an atom which contains the protons and neutrons. (2) A cellular organelle containing DNA and serving as the control center of the cell. (3) A mass of nerve cell bodies in the central nervous system concerned with a particular function.

nutrients (**new**-tree-ents) The chemical substances present in food that are utilized by the body as components for synthesizing needed materials and for fuel.

nutrition (new-**trish**-un) The utilization of food by an organism; nourishment.

nystagmus (nis-**tag**-mus) The rapid, involuntary movement of the eyeballs in a horizontal, vertical, or rotary direction. The movement is extremely rhythmic in nature.

O

obesity (oh-**bees**-ih-tee) The condition of being extremely overweight.

occlusion (o-**klew**-zhun) Closing or the state of closure, as in bringing the teeth of the upper and lower jaws together.

olfaction (ohl-**fak**-shun) The sense of smell; smelling.

olfactory tract (ohl-**fak**-toe-ree) Axonal tract projecting from the olfactory bulb to the olfactory region of the cerebral cortex.

oliguria (ohl-ih-**goo**-ree-ah) Excretion of a small amount of urine in relation to fluid intake.

oncogene (**ong**-koh-jeen) A gene possessing the capacity to transform a normal cell into one that is neoplastic or cancerous.

oncologist (ong-**kol**-oh-jist) One who specializes in the treatment and study of tumors.

oncology (ong-**kol**-oh-jee) The study of tumors.

oncotic pressure (ong-**kot**-ik) The osmotic pressure exerted by colloids in a solution; in microcirculatory dynamics it operates to counterbalance capillary blood pressure.

oocyte (**oh**-oh-site) A developing egg cell in either the primary or secondary stage.

opposition Type of movement unique to the thumb. This movement is a combination of rotation and adduction.

optic (**op**-tik) Of or pertaining to the eye or vision.

optimum (**op**-ti-mum) Most favorable; optimum conditions are the most favorable conditions under which a particular function can occur.

oral contraceptive An orally administered hormonal compound that prevents ovulation in the female. Also referred to as "the pill."

orbit (**or**-bit) The bony chamber that houses the eye and which exhibits a shape similar to a truncated pyramid.

organ (**or**-gan) A differentiated part of the body made up of tissues and adapted to perform a specific function or group of functions.

organelle One of many specialized parts of an individual cell. Examples include mitochondria, Golgi apparatus, nucleus, and the plasma membrane.

organ of Corti The cochlear organ that contains the special sensory receptors for hearing.

orgasm (**or**-gazm) The culmination of sexual excitement including ejaculation for the male and involuntary contraction of the perineal muscles in both sexes. Incorporates a host of sensory and cardiovascular responses as well.

orifice (**or**-ih-fis) The entrance or outlet of any body cavity.

origin (**or**-ih-jin) The more fixed end of attachment of a muscle to a bone; the end opposite the insertion.

oropharynx (*or*-oh-**far**-inks) The part of the pharynx between the soft palate and the upper edge of the epiglottis.

osmosis (oz-**mow**-sis) The passage of water molecules through a selectively permeable membrane from a region of higher water concentration to one of lower concentration.

osmotic pressure The pressure necessary to stop the flow of water across a selectively permeable membrane; depends on the relative concentrations of the two solutions on either side of the membrane.

osseous (**os**-ee-us) Bony.

ossicle (**os**-ih-kul) A small bone, especially one of the three bones of the middle ear (malleus, incus, stapes).

ossification (*os*-ih-fih-**kay**-shun) Formation of bone; also called osteogenesis.

osteoblast (**os**-tee-oh-*blast*) A cell that produces bone.

osteoclast (**os**-tee-oh-*klast*) A large, multinuclear cell that resorbs, or breaks down, bone.

osteocyte (**os**-tee-oh-*site*) An osteoblast that has become embedded within the bone matrix and occupies a lacuna.

osteogenic layer (*os*-tee-oh-**jen**-ik) The inner layer of the periosteum that contains cells that form new bone during growth and repair.

osteomalacia (*os*-tee-oh-mah-**lay**-she-ah) A disorder in which the bones become soft as a result of impaired mineralization; caused by vitamin D deficiency in adults.

osteomyelitis (*os*-tee-oh-my-eh-**lie**-tis) Inflammation of bone due to infection.

osteon (**os**-tee-on) The basic unit of structure of compact bone consisting of concentric rings of lamellae arranged around a central (haversian) canal. Also called a haversian system.

osteoporosis (*os*-tee-oh-poe-**row**-sis) A disease in which there is a severe reduction in bone mass; most common bone disease.

otic (**oh**-tik) Pertaining to the ear.

otitis media (oh-**tie**-tus **me**-dee-ah) Inflammation of the middle ear, occurring most often in young children.

otolith (**oh**-toe-lith) A granule of calcium carbonate embedded in the otolithic membrane that helps maintain static equilibrium.

oval window of ear Opening between the middle and inner ear on which the footplate of the stapes rests.

ovarian ligament The cord of connective tissue that attaches the ovary to the uterus.

ovary (**oh**-var-ee) The female gonad; produces ova and sex hormones, principally estrogens and progesterone.

ovulation (*oh*-vu-**lay**-shun) The discharge of the ovum (actually a secondary oocyte) from the mature (graafian) follicle into the pelvic cavity.

ovum (**oh**-vum) Egg cell; the female gamete.

oxidation (oks-ih-**day**-shun) The removal of electrons, or loss of hydrogen, from a compound. The oxidation of glucose is called cellular respiration.

oxygen debt The amount of oxygen needed to oxidize the lactic acid produced during exercise.

oxyhemoglobin (*ok*-see-**he**-mow-glow-bin) Hemoglobin combined with oxygen; the form in which oxygen is transported in the body.

oxyphil cell (**ok**-sih-fil) A cell in the parathyroid gland that secretes parathyroid hormone (PTH).

oxytocin (*ok*-see-**toe**-sin) A hormone produced by the hypothalamus and released by the posterior lobe of the pituitary gland; stimulates contraction of uterus and release of milk from lactating breast.

P

pacinian corpuscle Encapsulated, onion-shaped tactile receptor that responds to heavy pressure and vibration.

Paget's disease A disease in which normal bone is replaced by inadequately mineralized tissue. Also called osteitis deformans.

palate (**pal**-at) The roof of the mouth; the horizontal partition separating the oral and nasal cavities.

palpate (**pal**-pate) To examine by feeling with the hand.

pancreas (**pan**-kree-as) A large, elongated gland located behind the stomach, between the spleen and duodenum. Composed of both exocrine tissue (secretes pancreatic juice) and endocrine tissue (secretes insulin and glucagon).

pancreatic duct A single tube that joins the common bile duct, forming a single duct that passes into the wall of the duodenum at the hepatopancreatic ampulla. (Formerly known as the duct of Wirsung.)

Papanicolaou test (smear) (*pap*-a-*nik*-oh-**lay**-oo) A test for the diagnosis of premalignant and malignant conditions of the female reproductive tract (and certain other organs). Cells gently scraped from the organ are stained and then studied under a microscope. Also called Pap smear.

papilla (pa-**pil**-ah) A small, nipple-like mound, for example, the papilla at the base of each hair follicle.

paralysis (pah-**ral**-ih-sis) Loss or impairment of motor function in a part, usually due to a lesion of nervous or muscular structures.

paranasal sinuses (*par*-ah-**nay**-zal) Mucus-lined air cavities in bones of the skull, communicating with the nasal cavity.

paraplegia (*par*-ah-**plee**-jee-ah) Paralysis of both lower limbs, and in some cases, the lower part of the body.

parasympathetic division (*par*-ah-*sim*-pah-**thet**-ik) One of the two subdivisions of the autonomic nervous system; the craniosacral portion of the autonomic nervous system. Its general effect is to conserve and restore energy in the body.

parathyroid glands (*par*-ah-**thy**-royd) Small endocrine glands located within the connective tissue surrounding the thyroid gland; they secrete parathyroid hormone.

parathyroid hormone (PTH) A hormone secreted by the parathyroid glands that regulates calcium and phosphate concentrations in the blood.

parenchyma (pah-**reng**-kih-mah) The functional tissue of an organ, as distinguished from its supportive connective tissue (stroma).

parietal (pa-**rye**-eh-tal) (1) Pertaining to the walls of an organ or cavity. (2) Pertaining to the parietal bone of the skull.

Parkinson's disease A slowly progressive disease in which structures of the extrapyramidal system degenerate, resulting in decreased production of dopamine; characterized by tremor of resting muscles, muscle weakness, and slowing of voluntary movements.

parotid glands (pah-**rot**-id) The largest of the three main pairs of salivary glands, located on either side of the face, just inferior and anterior to the ears.

parturition (*par*-too-**rish**-un) The process of giving birth to a child; delivery of a baby.

patellar reflex (pah-**tell**-ar) Involuntary contraction of the quadriceps muscle and jerky extension of the leg when the patellar ligament is sharply tapped.

pathogen (**path**-o-jen) Any disease-producing organism or agent.

pathogenesis (*path*-o-**jen**-eh-sis) The cellular events and other mechanisms occurring in the development of disease.

pectoral (**pek**-to-ral) Pertaining to the chest or breast.

pedicle (**ped**-ih-kul) One of the paired parts of the vertebral arch that connects a transverse process to the vertebral body.

pelvic cavity (**pel**-vik) Inferior portion of the abdominopelvic cavity; contains the urinary bladder, sigmoid colon, rectum, and internal female and male reproductive structures.

pelvis (**pel**-vis) Any basinlike structure, for example, the basinlike structure formed by the hip bones, the sacrum, and the coccyx.

penis (**pee**-nis) The external male organ that functions in urination and in copulation.

pepsin (**pep**-sin) A protein-digesting enzyme that is the main digestive component of gastric juice.

peptic ulcer (**pep**-tik) An ulceration (open sore) of the mucous membrane of the esophagus, stomach, or duodenum, caused by the action of the acid gastric juice.

peptide (**pep**-tide) A compound composed of two or more amino acids; peptides form the constituent parts of proteins.

pericardial cavity (*per*-ih-**kar**-dee-al) Potential space between the visceral and parietal layers of the serous pericardium.

pericardium (*per*-ih-**kar**-dee-um) The loose-fitting sac enclosing the heart, composed of an outer fibrous layer and an inner serous layer.

perichondrium (*per*-ih-**kon**-dree-um) The membrane that covers cartilage; composed of fibrous connective tissue.

perilymph (**per**-ih-limf) The fluid contained between the bony and membranous labyrinths of the inner ear.

perimysium (*per*-ih-**mis**-ee-um) Connective tissue that surrounds the fascicles (bundles) of skeletal muscle fibers.

perineum (*per*-ih-**nee**-um) The diamond-shaped region bounded by the coccyx, symphysis pubis, and ischial tuberosities.

perineurium (*per*-ih-**nyoo**-ree-um) Connective tissue wrapping around each bundle of nerve fibers (fascicle) in a peripheral nerve.

periodontal membrane (*per*-ee-oh-**don**-tal) The periosteum lining the sockets for the teeth in the alveolar processes of the mandible and maxilla.

periosteum (*per*-ee-**os**-tee-um) The connective tissue membrane covering bones; possesses bone-forming potential.

peripheral (peh-**rif**-er-al) Located on the outer part of a structure or on a surface of the body.

peripheral nervous system (PNS) That portion of the nervous system consisting of the receptors, the nerves that link receptors with the central nervous system (CNS), and the nerves that link the CNS with the effectors.

peripheral resistance The impedance to blood flow due to friction between the blood and the blood vessel walls; affected by viscosity of the blood and diameter and length of the blood vessels.

peristalsis (*per*-ih-**stal**-sis) Waves of muscle contractions along the wall of a tube such as the digestive tract.

peritoneum (*per*-ih-tow-**nee**-um) The largest serous membrane of the body; lines the walls of the abdominal and pelvic cavities (parietal peritoneum) and covers the contained viscera (visceral peritoneum).

peritonitis (*per*-ih-tow-**nie**-tis) Inflammation of the peritoneum.

perspiration Sweat; the salty fluid, consisting mainly of water, excreted by the sweat glands in the skin.

Peyer's patches (**pie**-erz) Oval, whitish patches of closely packed lymph follicles in wall of small intestine.

pH A symbol of the measure of the acidity or alkalinity of a solution. The pH scale extends from 0 to 14, with 7 being neutral; values lower than 7 indicate increasing acidity, and values higher than 7 indicate increasing alkalinity.

phagocytosis (*fag*-oh-sigh-**toe**-sis) Engulfing and ingestion of microorganisms, other cells, or foreign particles by cells.

phalanx (**fay**-lanks) The bone of a toe or finger. Plural, phalanges (fay-**lan**-jeez).

phantom pain Pain felt as if it were arising in an amputated limb or organ.

pharynx (**far**-inks) The throat; a tube that begins at the internal nares and extends part way down the neck, communicating with the mouth and opening into the esophagus posteriorly and into the larynx anteriorly.

phenotype (**fee**-no-type) The visible expression of the genotype; physical or other characteristics which are produced by genes and influenced by the interaction between genes and environmental factors.

phenylketonuria (PKU) (*fen*-il-kee-tow-**noo**-ree-ah) A genetic disease in which the amino acid phenylalanine is not metabolized properly.

photoreceptor (*fo*-tow-re-**sep**-tor) A neural receptor sensitive to light.

physiology (*fiz*-ee-**ol**-oh-jee) Science that deals with the functions of the living organism and its parts.

pia mater (**pee**-ah **may**-ter) The inner of the three meninges (membranes) covering the brain and spinal cord.

pineal gland (**pin**-ee-al) The cone-shaped gland attached by a stalk to the posterior wall of the third ventricle of the cerebrum.

pinna (**pin**-ah) The projecting part of the external ear composed of elastic cartilage and covered with skin.

pinocytosis (*pin*-o-sigh-**toe**-sis) A type of ingestion by cells in which extracellular fluid and its contents are taken into the cell; it involves invaginations by the plasma membrane and formation of vesicles (sacs) at the cell surface.

pituitary gland (pih-**too**-ih-*terr*-ee) An endocrine gland attached by a stalk to the hypothalamus of the brain; secretes a variety of hormones influencing a wide range of physiologic processes. Sometimes called the master gland. Also called the hypophysis.

placenta (plah-**sen**-tah) The organ of exchange between mother and developing fetus.

plasma (**plaz**-muh) The fluid portion of blood consisting of a pale yellowish fluid containing proteins, salts, and other substances.

plasma cell A differentiated, functioning B lymphocyte; produces antibodies.

plasma membrane Cell membrane; outer, limiting membrane of the cell that separates the cell from its external environment.

platelet (**plate**-let) A blood platelet or thrombocyte; a cell fragment suspended in the plasma that functions in blood clotting.

platelet plug Aggregation of platelets at the damaged wall of a blood vessel forming a temporary patch that prevents blood loss.

pleura (**ploor**-ah) The serous membrane that surrounds the lungs (visceral pleura) and lines the walls of the thoracic cavity (parietal pleura).

pleural cavity Potential space between the visceral and parietal pleura.

plexus (**plex**-us) A network of veins or nerves.

plicae circulares (**ply**-kee **ser**-kyoo-lar-es) Deep, transverse folds in the wall of the small intestine that increase the surface area for absorption.

polar body The smaller, nonfunctional cell that results from the unequal division of cytoplasm during the meiotic divisions of the oocyte.

polycythemia (*pol*-ee-sie-**thee**-me-ah) An increase in the number of red blood cells in the blood.

polysaccharides (*pol*-ee-**sak**-uh-rides) Carbohydrates consisting of three or more, usually many, sugar units chemically combined to form a large molecule.

polyunsaturated fat A fat that contains two or more double bonds between its carbon atoms. Most vegetable oils are polyunsaturated.

polyuria (*pol*-ee-**yoo**-ree-ah) Excessive excretion of urine.

pons (ponz) That part of the brainstem that forms a bridge between the medulla and the midbrain, anterior to the cerebellum; connects various other parts of the brain.

positron emission tomography (PET) A nuclear medicine imaging technique similar to computed tomography (CT), which produces a cross-sectional image of the distribution of radioactivity in a slice through the subject a few centimeters thick.

posterior (pos-**teer**-ee-or) Toward or at the back of the body; dorsal.

postganglionic neuron (*post*-gang-glee-**on**-ik) Neuron located distal to a ganglion. The second efferent neuron in an autonomic pathway.

postsynaptic neuron (*post*-sin-**ap**-tik) A neuron that transmits action potentials away from a synapse.

precentral gyrus The gyrus just anterior to the central sulcus that contains the primary motor area.

preganglionic neuron (*pre*-gang-glee-**on**-ik) Neuron located proximal to a ganglion. The first efferent neuron in an autonomic pathway; synapses with a postganglionic neuron.

pregnancy The condition of having a developing embryo or fetus in the body.

premenstrual syndrome (PMS) Physical and emotional symptoms experienced by some women during the postovulatory phase of the menstrual cycle.

prepuce (**pre**-pyoos) The loose-fitting skin covering the glans of the penis or clitoris. Also referred to as the foreskin.

presbyopia (*pres*-be-**oh**-pee-ah) Loss of the power of accommodation of the lens of the eye which occurs with aging; usually results in hyperopia, or farsightedness.

presynaptic neuron (*pre*-sin-**ap**-tik) A neuron that transmits action potentials toward a synapse.

prevertebral ganglion (pre-**vert**-eh-bral) A mass of cell bodies of postganglionic sympathetic neurons located close to blood vessels. Also called collateral ganglion.

primary motor area A region within the precentral gyrus of the frontal lobe of the cerebrum that controls skeletal muscles. Also called the motor cortex.

progesterone (pro-**jes**-ter-own) A steroid sex hormone secreted by the corpus luteum (in the ovary) and by the placenta; stimulates thickening of the endometrium of the uterus and helps prepare the mammary glands for milk secretion.

prolactin (pro-**lak**-tin) A hormone secreted by the anterior lobe of the pituitary gland that stimulates lactation (milk production). Also called lactogenic hormone.

prolapse (**pro**-laps) The downward displacement, or falling down, of a part or organ.

proliferation (pro-*lif*-er-**a**-shun) Multiplication of new parts, especially cells.

pronation (pro-**nay**-shun) The act of assuming the prone (lying face-downward) position. Applied to the hand, the turning of the palm of the hand downward (posteriorly).

prophase (**pro**-faze) The first stage of cell replication in either mitosis or meiosis.

proprioceptors (*pro*-pre-oh-**sep**-tors) Mechanoreceptors located within the skeletal muscles, tendons, joints, and inner ear that send sensory information to the brain allowing us to know the location of one body part in relation to another, the degree of joint flexibility, the degree of muscle contraction and tendon stress, and head and body position during movement.

prostaglandins (PG) (*pros*-tah-**glan**-dins) A group of fatty acids released by many different tissues that affect the action of certain hormones and have a wide range of physiologic effects.

prostate gland (**pros**-tate) A gland in the male that surrounds the neck of the bladder and the urethra and secretes an alkaline fluid that is a component of semen.

protein (**pro**-teen) A complex organic compound composed of chemically linked amino acid subunits; contains carbon, hydrogen, oxygen, nitrogen, and sulfur.

prothrombin (pro-**throm**-bin) An inactive protein synthesized by the liver, present in the plasma, and converted to thrombin during blood clotting.

proximal (**prok**-sih-mal) Nearer to the center of the body or to the point of attachment or origin.

pseudostratified epithelium (*soo*-dow-**strat**-ih-fide) Refers to an epithelial tissue that appears to be stratified (layered) but is not.

ptosis (**tow**-sis) Prolapse or drooping of an organ or part.

puberty (**pyoo**-ber-tee) The period during which the secondary sex characteristics begin to develop and the individual becomes capable of sexual reproduction. Girls usually reach puberty between ages 11 and 13, and boys between 13 and 15.

pudendum (poo-**den**-dum) The female external reproductive structures. Also called vulva.

pulmonary (**pul**-mow-*ner*-ee) Pertaining to the lungs.

pulmonary circulation The circuit of blood flow between the heart and lungs. The flow of oxygen-poor blood from the right ventricle to the lungs where it is oxygenated and the return of the oxygen-rich blood from the lungs to the left atrium.

pulp cavity A cavity within the tooth filled with pulp, a connective tissue containing blood vessels, nerves, and lymphatics.

pulse The rhythmic expansion and recoil of the elastic arteries each time the left ventricle pumps blood into the aorta. The pulse rate corresponds to the heart rate.

pupil The opening in the center of the iris through which light enters the eye.

Purkinje fibers (per-**kin**-jee) Modified cardiac muscle fibers concerned with conducting impulses through the heart.

pus The liquid product of inflammation that contains white blood cells and debris of dead cells.

P wave The wave of an electrocardiogram that records atrial depolarization.

pyloric sphincter (pie-**lor**-ik) A thick ring of muscle that serves as a gate, closing the opening of the stomach into the duodenum.

pyramid (**pir**-a-mid) A pointed or cone-shaped structure. (1) Pyramids of the medulla oblongata are two prominent bulges of white matter on the ventral side of the medulla containing descending fibers of the pyramidal tracts which pass from the cerebrum to the spinal cord. (2) Renal pyramids are conical masses that make up the medulla of the kidney.

pyramidal tracts (pih-**ram**-i-dal) Groups of descending tracts arising in the cerebral cortex, crossing in the pyramids of the medulla, and extending into the spinal cord; provide for control of skilled voluntary movement.

Q

QRS wave The wave of an electrocardiogram that records ventricular depolarization.

quadriplegia (*kwod*-rih-**plee**-jee-ah) Paralysis of all four limbs.

R

ramus (**ray**-mus) A general term for a branch of a nerve, artery, or vein.

rapid eye movement (REM) sleep A stage of sleep characterized by rapid movement of the eyes and a brain wave pattern similar to that of an awake individual.

receptor (re-**sep**-tor) (1) A sensory structure that responds to specific stimuli such as light, sound, touch, pressure, or change in position. (2) A specific chemical grouping (usually a protein) on a cell surface that may combine with a specific chemical such as a neurotransmitter or hormone.

receptor-mediated endocytosis A selective process by which cells take in large molecules or particles.

recessive trait In genetics, refers to a trait that is expressed only when it is homozygous.

reciprocal innervation The process by which neural impulses stimulate contraction of one muscle while they simultaneously inhibit contraction of antagonistic muscles.

rectum (**rek**-tum) The distal portion of the large intestine, extending from the sigmoid colon to the anus.

red nucleus An oval mass in the midbrain where neurons conveying impulses regarding muscle tone and posture from the cerebellum and motor areas of the cerebrum synapse with neurons of the rubrospinal tract (an extrapyramidal pathway).

reduction The addition of electrons or hydrogen to a molecule.

referred pain Pain that is felt at a different location than where it originates.

reflex (**re**-flex) A predictable, automatic sequence of stimulus-response usually involving a reflex arc (pathway) consisting of at least three neurons: a sensory neuron, an association neuron, and a motor neuron.

refraction (re-**frak**-shun) The bending of light as it passes from one medium to another of different density.

refractory period (re-**frak**-to-ree) The time period during which a neuron cannot respond to a stimulus that is usually sufficient to result in an action potential.

renal (**ree**-nul) Pertaining to the kidney.

renal pelvis The funnel-shaped expansion of the upper end of the ureter into which the renal calices open.

renin (**reh**-nin) A proteolytic enzyme synthesized by the juxtaglomerular cells of the kidney; it plays a role in the regulation of blood pressure by catalyzing the conversion of angiotensinogen to angiotensin I.

residual volume The approximately 1200 ml of air that remains in the lungs after a maximal expiration.

respiration (*res*-pih-**ray**-shun) The exchange of oxygen and carbon dioxide between the atmosphere and the body cells, including inspiration and expiration, diffusion of gases between the alveoli and blood, transport of oxygen and carbon dioxide, and cellular respiration.

respiratory membrane A thin membrane composed of an alveolar wall and the wall of a pulmonary capillary.

resting potential The membrane potential of an inactive neuron; the inside of the cell is negative relative to the outside.

resuscitation (re-*sus*-ih-**tay**-shun) Restoration of life or consciousness of one who is apparently dead, or who has stopped breathing.

rete testis (**ree**-tee) The network of channels formed in the testes by the seminiferous tubules.

reticular activating system (RAS) (reh-**tik**-yoo-lur) An action system of the brain responsible for the overall extent of CNS activity including wakefulness, attentiveness, and sleep; the system of neurons of the reticular formation that project to higher centers.

reticulocyte (reh-**tik**-u-low-*site*) An immature red blood cell.

retina (**ret**-ih-na) The inner coat of the eyeball; composed of light-sensitive neurons including the rods and cones.

retinal (**ret**-ih-nal) A compound that combines with opsins in the retinal cones to form the pigments responsible for color vision.

retroperitoneal (*reh*-trow-*per*-ih-tow-**nee**-al) External to the peritoneal lining of the abdominal cavity; behind the peritoneum.

Rh system A system of blood types with at least eight different kinds of Rh antigens, each referred to as an Rh factor.

rhodopsin (row-**dop**-sin) A photosensitive pigment in the retinal rods. Also called visual purple.

ribonucleic acid (RNA) Functions mainly in the expression of the cell's genetic information. It is a single-stranded nucleic acid whose pentose sugar is ribose and whose bases are adenine, uracil, guanine, and cytosine. (Varieties are messenger RNA, transfer RNA, ribosomal RNA.)

ribosome (**rye**-bo-sowm) Organelle containing RNA that may be attached to the ER and that functions in protein synthesis.

rickets (**rik**-ets) A condition affecting children in which vitamin D deficiency leads to altered calcium metabolism and disturbance of ossification of bone; bones become soft and deformed.

right lymphatic duct A lymphatic vessel that drains lymph from the upper right side of the body and empties it into the right subclavian vein.

rods Photoreceptors in the retina that are stimulated by low light intensities. There are more than 100 million rods in each eye.

roentgenogram (**rent**-gen-oh-*gram*) An x-ray; a film produced by taking pictures of internal structures by passage of x-rays through the body.

root canal The narrow extension of the pulp cavity that lies within the root of a tooth.

rotation The process of turning around an axis. Moving a bone around its own axis.

round ligament A fibrous band of connective tissue attached to the uterus near the uterine tube, passing through the abdominal wall to end in the labia majora; helps maintain the anteflexed position of the uterus.

rugae (**roo**-jee) Folds in the mucosa of an organ such as the stomach or vagina.

S

saccule (**sak**-yool) One of two sacs in the membranous labyrinth within the vestibule of the inner ear; the saccule is connected to the other sac, the utricle, by the endolymphatic duct.

sacral plexus (**say**-kral) The network formed by the anterior branches of spinal nerves L4 through S3.

saddle joint A synovial joint in which the articular surfaces of both bones are saddle shaped.

sagittal plane (**sadj**-ih-tul) A section or plane through the body that divides the body into right and left parts. The term may also be applied to an organ or other body part.

saliva The enzyme-containing secretion of the salivary glands.

salivary amylase (**sal**-ih-ver-ee **am**-ih-lase) An enzyme in saliva that initiates the digestion of starch, mainly in the mouth.

salivary glands Glands that secrete saliva into the mouth. The major ones are the paired parotid, submaxillary, and sublingual glands.

salpingitis (*sal*-pin-**jie**-tis) (1) Inflammation of the uterine tube. (2) Inflammation of the eustachian tube.

saltatory conduction (**sal**-tah-*tow*-ree) Transmission of an action potential (nerve impulse) along a myelinated nerve fiber; the action potential appears to leap from one node of Ranvier to the next where the nerve fiber is exposed.

sarcolemma (*sar*-koe-**lem**-ma) The plasma membrane of a muscle cell, especially of a skeletal muscle cell.

sarcoma (sar-**koe**-ma) A tumor, often highly malignant, composed of cells derived from connective tissue. Sarcomas usually develop rapidly and metastasize through the lymph circulation.

sarcomere (**sar**-koe-mere) The contractile unit of a muscle cell extending from one Z band to the next along the length of the myofibril.

sarcoplasm (**sar**-koe-plazm) The cytoplasm of a muscle cell.

sarcoplasmic reticulum (*sar*-koe-**plaz**-mik re-**tik**-yoo-lum) The system of membranous vesicles of a muscle fiber which releases calcium during contraction; corresponds to endoplasmic reticulum of other cell types.

saturated fat A fat that contains no double bonds between any of its carbon atoms; each carbon is bonded to the maximum number of hydrogen atoms. Saturated fat is found in animal foods such as meat, milk, dairy products, and eggs.

scala tympani (**skay**-lah **tim**-pan-ee) The lower chamber of the bony cochlea; filled with perilymph.

scala vestibuli (**skay**-lah ves-**tib**-yoo-lee) The upper chamber of the bony cochlea; filled with perilymph.

Schwann cell (shvon) A type of glial cell found in the peripheral nervous system that forms the myelin sheath and cellular sheath of a nerve fiber by wrapping itself around the fiber.

sciatica (sie-**at**-ih-kah) Pain along the course of the sciatic nerve; felt along the posterior of the thigh and extending down the inside of the leg.

sclera (**skleh**-rah) The tough, white outer coat of the eyeball; continuous anteriorly with the cornea and posteriorly with the covering of the optic nerve.

scoliosis (*scow*-lee-**oh**-sis) An abnormal lateral curvature of the spine from the normal straight vertical line.

scotopsin (skow-**top**-sin) The protein in the rods of the retina that combines with 11-cis-retinal to form rhodopsin.

scrotum (**skrow**-tum) A skin-covered pouch that contains the testes and their accessory structures.

sebaceous gland (see-**bay**-shus) An exocrine gland in the dermis of the skin that secretes sebum, an oily material that lubricates the skin surface; its duct opens into a hair follicle. Also called oil gland.

sebum (**see**-bum) The oily secretion of the sebaceous glands.

secondary sex characteristics Characteristic male or female features (not directly involved in sexual reproduction) that develop at puberty in response to sex hormones such as shape of body, muscle development, pubic hair, and pitch of voice.

secretion (se-**kree**-shun) (1) The process by which a cell releases a specific product. (2) Any substance produced by secretion, for example, saliva produced by the cells of the salivary glands.

sella turcica (**sel**-ah **tur**-sih-kah) The depression on the upper surface of the sphenoid bone that houses the pituitary gland.

semen (**see**-men) Fluid discharged at ejaculation in the male, consisting of sperm and the secretions of the seminal vesicles, prostate gland, and bulbourethral glands. Also called seminal fluid.

semicircular canals The three channels located in the bony labyrinth of the inner ear which contain receptors for dynamic equilibrium.

semicircular ducts The three extensions of the membranous labyrinth of the inner ear that are located within the bony semicircular canals. Contain the cristae that function in dynamic equilibrium.

semilunar valve (*sem*-ee-**loo**-nar) A valve between each ventricle and the great artery into which it pumps blood; consists of flaps shaped like half-moons.

seminal vesicles (**sem**-ih-nul **ves**-ih-kuls) Glands that secrete a major portion of the semen into the ejaculatory ducts.

seminiferous tubules (*sem*-ih-**nif**-ur-us) The tubules within the testes where sperm cells are produced.

sensation A feeling; awareness of sensory input.

sensory areas of cerebrum Areas in the cerebrum that receive and interpret information from the sense receptors.

septum (**sep**-tum) A wall dividing a body cavity.

serosa (ser-**oh**-sah) Any serous membrane. Serous membranes line the pleural, pericardial, and peritoneal cavities.

serum (**see**-rum) The clear portion of blood that remains after the solid components (cells and platelets) have been separated out.

sesamoid bone (**ses**-ah-moyd) A small bone that typically occurs in a tendon subject to stress or pressure; it does not form a joint directly.

sex chromosomes The X and Y chromosomes. Females have two X chromosomes, whereas males have one X and one Y chromosome.

sexually transmitted disease (STD) A disease spread by sexual contact. Also called venereal disease.

sigmoid colon (**sig**-moyd **koe**-lon) The distal S-shaped part of the colon from the level of the iliac crest to the rectum.

sinoatrial (SA) node (*sigh*-no-**ay**-tree-al) Pacemaker of the heart; a mass of cardiac muscle specialized for conduction, located in the posterior wall of the right atrium near the opening of the superior vena cava.

sinus (**sigh**-nus) A cavity or channel such as the air cavities in the cranial bones (paranasal sinuses) or dilated channels for venous blood.

sinusoids (**sigh**-nuh-soyds) Tiny blood vessels (slightly larger than capillaries) found in certain organs such as the liver and spleen.

skeletal muscle An organ specialized for contraction, composed of striated (striped) muscle fibers (cells), surrounded and supported by connective tissue; stimulated by somatic efferent (motor) neurons.

skin The outer covering of the body; consists of two main layers, epidermis and dermis; the largest organ of the body. The skin and its associated structures, such as hair and sweat glands, make up the integumentary system.

skull The bony framework of the head consisting of the cranium and facial skeleton.

small intestine The region of the digestive tract that extends from the stomach to the large intestine; it is a long, coiled tube consisting of the duodenum, jejunum, and ileum.

smooth muscle A tissue specialized for contraction, composed of smooth (non-striated) muscle fibers (cells) located in the walls of hollow organs such as the intestine or uterus; innervated by a visceral efferent neuron.

sodium-potassium pump An active transport system located in the plasma membrane that uses the energy from ATP to transport sodium out of the cell and potassium into the cell; functions to maintain the concentrations of these ions at homeostatic levels.

soft palate (**pal**-at) The posterior portion of the roof of the mouth; a muscular partition lined with mucous membrane that extends from the palatine bones to the uvula.

solute (**sol**-yoot) The substance that is dissolved in a liquid (solvent) to form a solution.

solution A liquid (solvent) in which is dissolved one or more substances (solutes).

solvent (**sol**-vent) A liquid that dissolves another substance (solute) to form a solution without chemical change in either.

somatic nervous system (so-**mat**-ik) The part of the peripheral nervous system that keeps the body in adjustment with the external environment; includes the sensory receptors on the body surface and within the muscles, the nerves that link them with the central nervous system (CNS), and the efferent nerves that link the CNS with the skeletal muscles.

somesthetic (*sow*-mes-**thet**-ik) Pertaining to sensations and sensory structures of the body.

somatomedins (*so*-mah-tow-**me**-dins) A group of peptides found in many tissues, including the liver, that mediate the effect of growth hormone on cartilage.

spasm A sudden, involuntary contraction of a muscle or group of muscles.

sperm cell Male gamete (sex cell) that combines with an ovum in sexual reproduction to produce a new individual. Also called spermatozoan.

spermatic cord (sper-**mat**-ik) The male reproductive structure extending from the abdominal inguinal ring to the testis; includes the vas deferens, testicular artery, veins, nerves, cremaster muscle, and connective tissue.

spermatid (**sper**-mah-tid) A cell produced by meiotic division of a secondary spermatocyte; it develops into a mature sperm cell.

spermatocytes (spur-**mat**-oh-sites) Cells formed during spermatogenesis that give rise to spermatids and, ultimately, to mature sperm cells.

spermatogenesis (*spur*-mah-tow-**jen**-eh-sis) The development of mature sperm cells from spermatogonia. The process involves meiosis.

spermatozoa (*spur*-mah-tow-**zow**-ah) Mature sperm cells.

spermicide (**spur**-muh-side) An agent that kills sperm cells.

sphincter (**sfink**-ter) A circular muscle that constricts a passageway or orifice.

sphygmomanometer (*sfig*-mow-mah-**nom**-eh-ter) An instrument for measuring arterial blood pressure.

spinal cord (**spy**-nal) The part of the central nervous system located in the vertebral canal and extending from the foramen magnum to the upper part of the lumbar region.

spinal ganglion Dorsal root ganglion; consists of the cell bodies of sensory neurons and is located along the dorsal root just before it joins the spinal cord.

spinal nerve Any of the 31 pairs of nerves that arise from the spinal cord and pass out between the vertebrae.

spinal shock A period of several days to several weeks following transection of the spinal cord, during which there is a loss of reflex activity.

spleen The largest organ of the lymphatic system, located in the upper part of the abdominal cavity on the left side; filters blood and provides the opportunity for lymphocyte activation.

sprain Wrenching or twisting of a joint with partial rupture of its ligaments.

sputum (**spoo**-tum) Mucous secretion from the respiratory passageways that is ejected through the mouth.

squamous epithelium (**skway**-mus) Epithelium consisting of flat, scalelike cells.

Starling's law of the heart The greater the volume of blood returned to the heart by the veins, the greater the volume of blood pumped by the heart, within physiological limits.

stasis (**stay**-sis) A slowing or stoppage of flow, as of blood or other body fluid.

static equilibrium Gravitational balance; the orientation of the body relative to the ground; involves posture and positioning of the head and body.

stenosis (steh-**no**-sis) Narrowing or contraction of a body passage or opening.

stereognosis (*ster*-ee-og-**no**-sis) The sense by which the form (size, shape, texture) of objects is perceived.

sterile (**ster**-il) (1) Not fertile; not producing young. (2) Aseptic; free from living microorganisms.

sterilization (*ster*-il-ih-**zay**-shun) The process of rendering an individual incapable of producing offspring, for example, vasectomy.

stimulus Any change in the environment that produces a response in a receptor or irritable tissue.

stomach (**stum**-ak) The curved, muscular, saclike part of the digestive tract between the esophagus and the small intestine; occupies the abdominal cavity just below the diaphragm.

stratum (**stray**-tum) Plural, strata. A sheetlike mass of tissue of fairly uniform thickness; used to designate distinct sublayers making up various tissues or organs, for example, the strata of the skin.

stressor Any factor that disturbs homeostasis, producing stress.

stroke volume The volume of blood pumped by one ventricle during one contraction.

stroma (**strow**-mah) The tissue forming the framework, ground substance, or matrix of an organ, as opposed to the functioning part, or parenchyma.

subarachnoid space (*sub*-ah-**rak**-noyd) The space between the arachnoid and pia mater through which cerebrospinal fluid circulates.

subcutaneous (*sub*-kyoo-**tay**-nee-us) Beneath the skin.

subcutaneous layer The layer of loose connective tissue and adipose tissue beneath the skin.

subdural space (sub-**doo**-ral) The space between the dura mater and arachnoid.

sublingual glands (sub-**ling**-gwal) The paired salivary glands located in the floor of the mouth under the tongue.

submandibular glands (*sub*-man-**dib**-yoo-lar) The paired salivary glands located in the posterior region of the floor of the mouth posterior to the sublingual glands.

submucosa (*sub*-myoo-**koe**-sah) A layer of connective tissue located beneath a mucous membrane, as in the digestive tract.

substrate (**sub**-strate) Any substance upon which an enzyme acts.

sulcus (**sul**-kus) A groove or furrow; a linear depression as is found between the gyri of the brain.

summation (sum-**may**-shun) The addition of excitatory postsynaptic potentials; may be temporal or spatial.

superficial (*soo*-per-**fish**-al) Located on or near the body surface.

superior (sue-**peer**-ee-ur) Higher; refers to structures nearer the head than the feet.

superior vena cava (**vee**-nah **kay**-vah) Large vein that receives blood from parts of the body superior to the heart and returns it to the right atrium.

supination (*soo*-pih-**nay**-shun) The act of assuming the supine position, that is, lying on the back. Applied to the hand, the act of turning the palm upward.

surfactant (ser-**fak**-tant) A phospholipid substance secreted by the lungs that decreases surface tension of pulmonary fluids and thus contributes to the elastic properties of lung tissues.

suspensory ligament (of ovary) (sus-**pen**-sow-ree) A fold of peritoneum that extends laterally from the surface of the ovary to the wall of the pelvis.

suture (**soo**-cher) The fibrous joint between adjoining bones in the skull.

sweat (swet) Perspiration; the salty fluid, consisting mainly of water, excreted by the sweat glands in the skin.

sympathetic division (*sim*-pah-**thet**-ik) The thoracolumbar portion of the autonomic nervous system; its general effect is to mobilize energy, especially during stress situations; prepares body for fight-or-flight response.

sympathomimetic (*sim*-pah-thow-my-**met**-ik) Adrenergic; producing effects resembling those produced by the sympathetic nervous system.

symphysis (**sim**-fih-sis) A relatively immovable type of joint in which the two joining bones are firmly united by a plate of fibrocartilage.

symphysis pubis (**pyoo**-bis) A slightly movable cartilaginous joint between the pubic bones.

symptom (**simp**-tum) Any indication of disease perceived by the patient.

synapse (**sin**-aps) Junction between two neurons or between a neuron and an effector.

synaptic cleft (sin-**ap**-tik) The narrow gap that separates the axon terminal of one neuron from another neuron or from a muscle fiber. Neurotransmitter diffuses across the cleft to affect the postsynaptic cell.

synaptic knobs Tiny enlargements in the axon terminal that synthesize neurotransmitter and store it in synaptic vesicles.

synaptic vesicle Membrane-enclosed sac containing neurotransmitter; found in the synaptic knobs of axons.

synarthrosis (*sin*-are-**throw**-sis) An immovable joint; a joint in which the bones are tightly united by fibrous tissue.

synchondrosis (*sin*-kon-**drow**-sis) A type of cartilaginous joint in which the cartilage is usually converted to bone before adulthood.

syndesmosis (*sin*-des-**mow**-sis) A joint in which the bones are united by dense fibrous connective tissue.

syndrome (**sin**-drome) A combination of symptoms that occur together forming a pattern characteristic of a particular disorder.

synergist (**sin**-er-jist) An agent that acts with or enhances the action of another; a muscle that helps the prime mover by reducing undesired movement.

synostosis (*sin*-os-**tow**-sis) Joint in which the dense fibrous connective tissue that unites bones at a suture has been replaced by bone, resulting in a complete fusion of the two bones.

synovial fluid (sih-**no**-vee-al) The transparent, viscous fluid secreted by the synovial membrane and found in joint cavities, bursae, and tendon sheaths.

synovial joint A fully movable or diarthrotic joint in which a synovial cavity is present between the two articulating bones.

syphilis (**sif**-ih-lis) A sexually transmitted disease caused by the spiral-shaped (spirochete) bacterium *Treponema pallidum.*

systemic (sis-**tem**-ik) Affecting the body as a whole.

systemic circulation The circuit of blood vessels through which oxygen-rich blood flows from the left ventricle through the aorta to all of the organs of the body and oxygen-poor blood returns to the right atrium.

systole (**sis**-toe-lee) The phase of contraction of the heart during which blood is forced into the aorta and pulmonary artery.

systolic blood pressure (sis-**tol**-ik) The force exerted by the blood on arterial walls during ventricular contraction; about 120 mmHg under normal conditions for a young adult.

T

tachycardia (*tak*-ih-**kar**-dee-ah) An abnormally rapid heart rate, usually defined as more than 100 beats per minute.

tactile (**tak**-tile) Pertaining to the sense of touch.

taenia coli (**tee**-nee-ee **koe**-lye) Three longitudinal bands of smooth muscle extending the length of the large intestine.

target cell A cell whose activity is affected by a particular hormone.

tarsus (**tar**-sus) The seven bones that make up the ankle.

Tay-Sachs disease A genetic disease inherited as an autosomal recessive trait; the inborn error of metabolism is a deficiency of an enzyme that results in accumulation of a ganglioside (a type of lipid) in the brain.

T cell A T lymphocyte; a lymphocyte responsible for cell-mediated immunity. Subtypes include cytotoxic, memory, helper, and suppressor T cells.

tectorial membrane (tek-**toe**-ree-al) A flexible, gelatinous membrane that extends from the spiral lamina and projects over the organ of Corti.

telophase (**tel**-oh-faze) The last of the four stages of mitosis and of the two divisions of meiosis; the cytoplasm usually divides during telophase, giving rise to two daughter cells.

tendinitis (*ten*-din-**i**-tis) Inflammation of tendons and tendon-muscle attachments; frequently associated with calcium deposits and may also involve the bursa around the tendon, causing bursitis.

tendon (**ten**-don) A cord of strong white fibrous tissue that connects a muscle to a bone.

tentorium (ten-**tow**-ree-um) A structure resembling a tent or covering.

teratogen (**ter**-ah-two-jen) A drug or other agent that causes physical defects in the developing embryo.

testis (**tes**-tis) The male gonad; either of the paired glands located in the scrotum which produce sperm and the male sex hormone testosterone. Also called testicle. Plural, testes.

testosterone (tes-**tos**-teh-rone) The principal male sex hormone (androgen); produced by the interstitial cells in the testes; stimulates development of the male reproductive organs and secondary sex characteristics.

tetanus (**tet**-ah-nus) A fatal disease caused by the tetanus bacillus (*Clostridium tetani*) and characterized by muscle spasms and convulsions.

tetany (**tet**-ah-nee) (1) Steady contraction of a muscle without distinct twitching; continuous topic spasm of a muscle. (2) A syndrome characterized by muscle twitchings, cramps, and convulsions; due to abnormal calcium metabolism.

thalamus (**thal**-uh-mus) A large oval structure composed of gray matter covered by a thin layer of white matter and located at the base of the cerebrum. The thalamus serves as a main relay center transmitting information between the spinal cord and the cerebrum.

thalassemia (*thal*-ah-**see**-me-ah) A group of inherited hemolytic anemias characterized by decreased synthesis of one or more hemoglobin polypeptide chains.

therapy (**ther**-ah-pee) The treatment of a disease or disorder.

thermoreceptor (*ther*-mow-ree-**sep**-tor) A receptor that detects changes in temperature.

thigh The part of the lower limb between the hip and the knee.

third ventricle (**ven**-trih-kul) The cavity between the lateral ventricles and between the right and left halves of the thalamus.

thoracic cavity (thow-**ras**-ik) The superior part of the ventral body cavity; contains the two pleural cavities, pericardial cavity, and mediastinum.

thoracic duct A lymphatic vessel that receives lymph from the cisterna chyli and empties it into the left subclavian vein.

thoracolumbar outflow (*thow*-ra-koe-**lum**-bar) The fibers of the sympathetic preganglionic neurons that emerge from the thoracic and lumbar regions of the spinal cord.

thorax (**thow**-rax) The chest.

thrombin (**throm**-bin) An enzyme formed by the activation of prothrombin, which catalyzes the conversion of fibrinogen to fibrin.

thrombocyte (**throm**-bow-site) A fragment of cytoplasm enclosed in plasma membrane that plays a role in blood clotting; found in the circulation. Also called platelet.

thromboplastin (*throm*-bow-**plas**-tin) A complex of several phospholipids and a proteolytic enzyme released from damaged tissue; important in the clotting process.

thrombosis (throm-**bow**-sis) Formation or presence of a clot in an unbroken blood vessel or heart chamber.

thrombus (**throm**-bus) A blood clot formed within a blood vessel or within the heart.

thymus gland (**thy**-mus) A gland located in the upper mediastinum beneath the sternum which reaches its maximum development during puberty, and plays a role in immunologic function throughout life.

thyroglobulin (*thy*-row-**glob**-yoo-lin) An iodine-containing glycoprotein, occuring in the colloid of the follicles of the thyroid gland; the iodized tyrosine components of thyroglobulin form the active thyroid hormones.

thyroid cartilage (**thy**-royd **kar**-tih-lij) The shield-shaped cartilage of the larynx; it produces the prominence on the neck called the Adam's apple.

thyroid gland An endocrine gland located in the front and sides of the neck just below the thyroid cartilage; its hormones are essential for normal growth and metabolism.

thyroid-stimulating-hormone (TSH) A tropic hormone secreted by the anterior lobe of the pituitary gland that stimulates the synthesis and secretion of hormones produced by the thyroid gland.

thyroxine (T_4) (thy-**rok**-sin) One of the hormones secreted by the thyroid gland; essential for normal growth and metabolism.

tidal volume The volume of air inspired or expired during normal breathing at rest.

tinnitus (tie-**nie**-tus) A ringing, buzzing, or roaring noise in the ears.

tissue (**tiss**-you) A group of closely associated similar cells that work together to carry out specific functions.

tongue A large muscular organ on the floor of the mouth that functions in chewing, swallowing, and speech.

tonsil (**ton**-sil) Aggregate of lymph nodules embedded in the mucous membrane in the throat region. The tonsils are located strategically to deal with pathogens that enter through the mouth or nose.

total lung capacity The sum of all volumes of air that can exist at one time in the lungs; about 5900 ml.

toxic (**tok**-sik) Poisonous; pertaining to poison.

toxic shock syndrome A severe illness characterized by high fever of sudden onset, vomiting, diarrhea, and muscle pain, followed by hypotension, and in severe cases, shock and death. It occurs almost exclusively in menstruating women using tampons.

trabecula (trah-**bek**-you-lah) (1) A supporting structure. (2) Anastomosing bony spicules of cancellous bone which form a meshwork of intercommunicating spaces that are filled with bone marrow.

trachea (**tray**-kee-ah) The air passageway extending from the larynx to the main bronchi. Also called windpipe.

tract A bundle of nerve fibers in the central nervous system.

transcription (tran-**skrip**-shun) The synthesis of messenger RNA using a DNA template; the first step in the transfer of genetic information from DNA to protein.

translation The synthesis of a polypeptide using messenger RNA as a template.

transmission (trans-**mish**-un) Conduction of an action potential (neural impulse) along a neuron or from one neuron to another.

transverse colon (trans-**verse koe**-lon) The portion of the large intestine extending across the abdomen from the ascending to the descending colon.

transverse fissure (**fish**-er) The cleft that separates the cerebrum from the cerebellum.

trauma (**traw**-mah) A wound or injury, especially damage caused by external force.

tricuspid valve (try-**kus**-pid) The valve consisting of three flaps that guards the opening between the right atrium and right ventricle.

trigone (**try**-goan) A triangular area at the base of the urinary bladder.

triiodothyronine (T_3) (*try*-i-o-dow-**thy**-row-nene) One of the thyroid hormones; essential for normal growth and metabolism.

triplet In genetics, a sequence of three nucleic acid bases in DNA that serves as the basic unit of genetic information, usually signifying the identity and position of an amino acid unit in a protein.

tropic hormone (**trow**-pik) A hormone that helps to regulate another endocrine gland, for example, thyroid-stimulating hormone released by the pituitary regulates the thyroid gland.

trunk (1) The main part of the body to which the head and limbs are attached. (2) A large structure, such as a nerve or blood vessel, from which smaller branches arise, or which is formed by small branches.

tubal ligation (lie-**gay**-shun) A sterilization procedure during which the uterine tubes are tied and cut.

tubular reabsorption The movement of a substance out of the renal tubule and into the peritubular capillaries.

tubular secretion The movement of a substance out of the peritubular capillaries and into the renal tubule.

tumor (**too**-mor) Neoplasm; a new growth of tissue in which cell multiplication is uncontrolled and progressive.

tunica albuginea (**too**-nih-kah *al*-byoo-**jin**-ee-ah) A dense white fibrous connective tissue sheath enclosing an organ such as the testis.

tunica externa (ex-**ter**-nah) The outer coat of an artery or vein. Also called tunica adventitia.

tunica interna (in-**ter**-nah) The inner layer of an artery or vein consisting of endothelium and an underlying layer of connective tissue rich in elastic fibers. Also called tunica intima.

tunica media The middle layer of an artery or vein consisting of elastic connective tissue and circular smooth muscle cells.

T wave The wave of an electrocardiogram that records ventricular repolarization.

twitch Rapid, brief, jerky contraction of a muscle in response to a single stimulus.

tympanic membrane (tim-**pan**-ik) Thin, semitransparent membrane that stretches across the ear canal, separating the outer ear from the middle ear.

U

ulcer (**ul**-ser) An open lesion, or excavation, of a tissue produced by the sloughing of inflamed, dying tissue.

umbilical cord (um-**bil**-ih-kal) The long, ropelike structure that connects the fetus and placenta; contains the umbilical arteries and vein.

uremia (yoo-**ree**-me-ah) An excess in the blood of urea and other nitrogenous wastes, generally resulting from kidney malfunction. A sign of renal failure.

ureter (**you**-ree-ter) One of the paired tubes that conducts urine from the kidneys to the bladder.

urethra (you-**ree**-thruh) A muscular tube that conducts urine from the bladder to the exterior surface of the body.

urinalysis (*u*-rih-**nal**-ih-sis) Examination of the physical, chemical, and microscopic characteristics of urine used as an aid in the diagnosis of disease.

urinary bladder A muscular sac in the anterior floor of the pelvic cavity that serves as a storage sac for urine.

urine (**u**-rin) The fluid containing water, waste products, salts, and traces of other substances that is produced by the kidneys.

uterine tube (**you**-tur-in) One of the paired tubes attached to each end of the uterus; site of fertilization. Also called fallopian tube or oviduct.

uterus (**you**-tur-us) The womb; the organ that houses the embryo and fetus during development.

utricle (**u**-trih-kul) The larger of the two divisions of the membranous labyrinth of the inner ear.

uvula (**u**-vue-lah) A fleshy mass of tissue, especially the structure extending from the soft palate.

V

vacuole (**vac**-you-ole) A cavity enclosed by membrane and located in the cytoplasm.

vagina (vah-**jye**-nuh) The elastic, muscular tube extending from the cervix to the vestibule; receives the penis during sexual intercourse and serves as the birth canal.

vagus nerve (**vay**-gus) The tenth cranial nerve; each vagus nerve emerges from the medulla and innervates thoracic and abdominal organs; the main nerve of the parasympathetic system.

varicose veins (**var**-ih-kose) Swollen, distended veins usually located in the subcutaneous tissues of the leg.

vasa vasorum (**vay**-sah vah-**sow**-rum) The small blood vessels supplying nutrients to the walls of larger blood vessels.

vascular (**vas**-kyoo-lar) Pertaining to or containing many blood vessels.

vas deferens (**def**-ur-enz) One of the paired ducts that conveys semen from the epididymis to the ejaculatory duct.

vasectomy (vah-**sek**-tow-me) A sterilization procedure in which a portion of each vas deferens is removed.

vasoconstriction (*vas*-o-kon-**strik**-shun) The narrowing of blood vessels; refers especially to the narrowing of the arterioles.

vasodilation (*vas*-o-die-**lay**-shun) The widening of blood vessels; refers especially to the widening of arterioles.

vasopressin (*vas*-o-**pres**-in) Antidiuretic hormone (ADH); a hormone secreted by the hypothalamus and stored in the posterior lobe of the pituitary gland.

vein (vane) A vessel that conducts blood from tissues back to the heart.

vena cava (**vee**-nah **kay**-vah) The superior or inferior vein that opens into the right atrium returning oxygen-poor blood to the heart.

ventral (**ven**-tral) Pertaining to the abdomen or anterior (front side) of the body; opposite of dorsal.

ventricle (**ven**-tri-kul) A small cavity or chamber, such as one of the cavities of the brain or heart.

venule (**ven**-yule) A small vein that collects blood from capillaries and delivers it to a larger vein.

vermiform appendix (**ver**-mih-form) A small appendage attached to the cecum.

vertebral canal (**ver**-teh-bral) The canal formed by the series of vertebral foramina together, containing the spinal cord.

vertebral column The spine; the rigid structure in the midline of the back, composed of the vertebrae.

vesicle (**ves**-ih-kul) A small sac containing fluid.

vestibular membrane (ves-**tib**-you-lar) The membrane that separates the cochlear duct from the scala vestibuli.

vestibule (**ves**-tih-byool) A small space or region at the beginning of a canal, for example, the vagina opens into a vestibule.

villus (**vil**-us) A small vascular projection from the free surface of a membrane, for example, intestinal villi project from the surface of the small intestine.

viscera (**vis**-ur-uh) The organs located within the body cavities.

visceral (**vis**-er-al) Pertaining to the organs or to the covering of an organ.

visceral effector (ee-**fek**-tor) Cardiac muscle, smooth muscle, and glands.

visceral peritoneum The inner layer of the serous membrane that covers the abdominal viscera.

viscosity (vis-**kos**-ih-tee) Resistance to flow; related to how sticky a substance is.

vital capacity The largest amount of air that can be ventilated; spans from a maximal inspiratory effort to a maximal expiratory effort; usually measures about 4700 ml.

vitamin (**vie**-tah-min) An organic compound essential in the diet in small amounts; acts as a coenzyme in metabolic reactions and is essential for normal growth and health.

vitreous humor (**vit**-ree-us **hyoo**-mor) A clear, jelly-like fluid that fills the posterior cavity of the eye lying between the lens and retina.

vocal cords The folds of mucous membranes in the larynx that vibrate to make vocal sounds during speaking. The inferior folds are called true vocal cords or vocal folds.

Volkmann's canals (**folk**-mahnz) Tiny passageways communicating with haversian canals; for passage of blood vessels through bone.

vomiting Forcible ejection of contents of stomach through the mouth.

vulva (**vul**-vah) The external genital organs in the female. Also called pudendum.

W

white blood cells (WBC) Leukocytes.

white matter Nervous tissue composed mainly of myelinated nerve fibers; makes up the conducting portion of the brain and spinal cord.

white ramus communicans (ko-**myoo**-nih-kans) The part of a preganglionic sympathetic nerve fiber that branches away from the ventral ramus of a spinal nerve and enters the nearest sympathetic chain ganglion.

wormian bone (**wer**-me-an) A small bone located within a suture of some cranial bones. Also called sutural bone.

wound A bodily injury caused by physical means, with disruption of the normal continuity of structures.

X

xiphoid (**zif**-oid) Sword-shaped. The xiphoid process is the inferior end of the sternum.

Y

yolk sac An extraembryonic membrane that extends from the developing gut. Its walls serve as a temporary center for development of blood cells.

Z

zona fasciculata (**zow**-nah fah-*sik*-you-**lay**-tah) The thick middle layer of the adrenal cortex that secretes glucocorticoid hormones.

zona glomerulosa (glow-*mer*-you-**low**-sah) The outer layer of the adrenal cortex that secretes mineralocorticoid hormones.

zona pellucida (peh-**loo**-sih-da) The transparent, noncellular layer that surrounds an ovum.

zona reticularis (reh-*tik*-you-**lar**-is) The inner layer of the adrenal cortex that secretes sex hormones, mainly androgens.

zygote (**zye**-goat) Fertilized ovum; the cell resulting from the fusion of male and female gametes.

zymogen (**zye**-mow-gen) An inactive precursor that is converted into an active enzyme by the action of an acid or another enzyme or by other means; a proenzyme.

INDEX*

A

*Boldface page numbers indicate pages on which the index term is defined; "il" following the page number indicates an illustration, "t" a table, and "f" a focus box. Individual muscles and blood vessels can be found in tables in Chapters 11 and 21.

B

C

E

F

G

H

I

J

K

L

M

N

P

R

T

U

V

Z